Atomic Numbers and Atomic Masses of the Elements

Based on $^{12}_{6}C$. Numbers in parentheses are the mass numbers of the most stable isotopes of radioactive elements

Element	Symbol	Atomic Number	Atomic Mass	Element	Symbol	Atomic Number	Atomic Mass
Actinium	Ac	89	(227)	Meitnerium	Mt	109	(276)
Aluminum	Al	13	26.98	Mendelevium	Md	101	(258)
Americium	Am	95	(243)	Mercury	Hg	80	200.59
Antimony	Sb	51	121.76	Molybdenum	Mo	42	95.94
Argon	Ar	18	39.95	Neodymium	Nd	60	144.24
Arsenic	As	33	74.92	Neon	Ne	10	20.18
Astatine	At	85	(210)	Neptunium	Np	93	(237)
Barium	Ba	56	137.33	Nickel	Ni	28	58.69
Berkelium	Bk	97	(247)	Niobium	Nb	41	92.91
Beryllium	Be	4	9.01	Nitrogen	N	7	14.01
Bismuth	Bi	83	208.98	Nobelium	No	102	(259)
Bohrium	Bh	107	(264)	Osmium	Os	76	190.23
Boron	B	5	10.81	Oxygen	O	8	16.00
Bromine	Br	35	79.90	Palladium	Pd	46	106.42
Cadmium	Cd	48	112.41	Phosphorus	P	15	30.97
Calcium	Ca	20	40.08	Platinum	Pt	78	195.08
Californium	Cf	98	(251)	Plutonium	Pu	94	(244)
Carbon	C	6	12.01	Polonium	Po	84	(209)
Cerium	Ce	58	140.12	Potassium	K	19	39.10
Cesium	Cs	55	132.91	Praseodymium	Pr	59	140.91
Chlorine	Cl	17	35.45	Promethium	Pm	61	(145)
Chromium	Cr	24	52.00	Protactinium	Pa	91	(231)
Cobalt	Co	27	58.93	Radium	Ra	88	(226)
Copernicium	Cn	112	(285)	Radon	Rn	86	(222)
Copper	Cu	29	63.55	Rhenium	Re	75	186.21
Curium	Cm	96	(247)	Rhodium	Rh	45	102.91
Darmstadtium	Ds	110	(271)	Roentgenium	Rg	111	(280)
Dubnium	Db	105	(262)	Rubidium	Rb	37	85.47
Dysprosium	Dy	66	162.50	Ruthenium	Ru	44	101.07
Einsteinium	Es	99	(252)	Rutherfordium	Rf	104	(263)
Erbium	Er	68	167.26	Samarium	Sm	62	150.36
Europium	Eu	63	151.96	Scandium	Sc	21	44.96
Fermium	Fm	100	(257)	Seaborgium	Sg	106	(266)
Fluorine	F	9	19.00	Selenium	Se	34	78.96
Francium	Fr	87	(223)	Silicon	Si	14	28.09
Gadolinium	Gd	64	157.25	Silver	Ag	47	107.87
Gallium	Ga	31	69.72	Sodium	Na	11	22.99
Germanium	Ge	32	72.64	Strontium	Sr	38	87.62
Gold	Au	79	196.97	Sulfur	S	16	32.07
Hafnium	Hf	72	178.49	Tantalum	Ta	73	180.95
Hassium	Hs	108	(277)	Technetium	Tc	43	(98)
Helium	He	2	4.00	Tellurium	Te	52	127.60
Holmium	Ho	67	164.93	Terbium	Tb	65	158.93
Hydrogen	H	1	1.01	Thallium	Tl	81	204.38
Indium	In	49	114.82	Thorium	Th	90	(232)
Iodine	I	53	126.90	Thulium	Tm	69	168.93
Iridium	Ir	77	192.22	Tin	Sn	50	118.71
Iron	Fe	26	55.85	Titanium	Ti	22	47.87
Krypton	Kr	36	83.80	Tungsten	W	74	183.84
Lanthanum	La	57	138.91	Uranium	U	92	(238)
Lawrencium	Lr	103	(262)	Vanadium	V	23	50.94
Lead	Pb	82	207.19	Xenon	Xe	54	131.29
Lithium	Li	3	6.94	Ytterbium	Yb	70	173.04
Lutetium	Lu	71	174.97	Yttrium	Y	39	88.91
Magnesium	Mg	12	24.31	Zinc	Zn	30	65.41
Manganese	Mn	25	54.94	Zirconium	Zr	40	91.22

General, Organic, and Biological Chemistry

Chem 2A/2B

Sierra College

H. Stephen Stoker

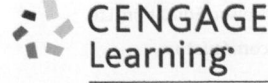
CENGAGE
Learning·

Australia • Brazil • Japan • Korea • Mexico • Singapore • Spain • United Kingdom • United States

CENGAGE
Learning

General, Organic, and Biological Chemistry: Chem 2A/2B, Sierra College

General, Organic, and Biological Chemistry, 7th Edition
H. Stephen Stoker

© 2016, 2013 Cengage Learning. All rights reserved.

Introduction to Microbiology: A Case-History Study Approach, 3rd Edition
John L. Ingraham | Catherine A. Ingraham

© 2004 Cengage Learning. All rights reserved.

Human Physiology: From Cells to Systems, 9th Edition
Lauralee Sherwood

© 2016 Cengage Learning. All rights reserved.

Introductory Chemistry: A Foundation, 8th Edition
Steven S. Zumdahl | Donald J. DeCoste

© 2015 Cengage Learning. All rights reserved.

Chemistry for Today: General, Organic, and Biochemistry, 8th Edition - See
Spencer L. Seager | Michael R. Slabaugh

© 2014 Cengage Learning. All rights reserved.

For product information and technology assistance, contact us at
Cengage Learning Customer & Sales Support, 1-800-354-9706

For permission to use material from this text or product,
submit all requests online at **cengage.com/permissions**
Further permissions questions can be emailed to
permissionrequest@cengage.com

This book contains select works from existing Cengage Learning resources and was produced by Cengage Learning Custom Solutions for collegiate use. As such, those adopting and/or contributing to this work are responsible for editorial content accuracy, continuity and completeness.

Compilation © 2016 Cengage Learning

ISBN: 978-1-337-05931-2

WCN: 01-100-101

Cengage Learning
20 Channel Center Street
Boston, MA 02210
USA

Cengage Learning is a leading provider of customized learning solutions with office locations around the globe, including Singapore, the United Kingdom, Australia, Mexico, Brazil, and Japan. Locate your local office at:
www.international.cengage.com/region.

Cengage Learning products are represented in Canada by Nelson Education, Ltd.

For your lifelong learning solutions, visit **www.cengage.com/custom.**

Visit our corporate website at **www.cengage.com.**

Printed at CLDPC, USA, 05-18

Brief Contents

Contents

PART II ORGANIC CHEMISTRY

PART III BIOLOGICAL CHEMISTRY

Preface

The positive responses of instructors and students who used the previous six editions of this text have been gratifying—and have led to the new seventh edition that you hold in your hands. This new edition represents a renewed commitment to the goals I initially set when writing the first edition. These goals have not changed with the passage of time. My initial and still ongoing goals are to write a text in which:

- The needs are simultaneously met for the many students in the fields of nursing, allied health, biological sciences, agricultural sciences, food sciences, and public health who are required to take such a course.
- The development of chemical topics always starts out at ground level. The students who will use this text often have little or no background in chemistry and hence approach the course with a good deal of trepidation. This "ground level" approach addresses this situation.
- The amount and level of mathematics is purposefully restricted. Clearly, some chemical principles cannot be divorced entirely from mathematics and, when this is the case, appropriate mathematical coverage is included.
- The early chapters focus on fundamental chemical principles, and the later chapters—built on these principles—develop the concepts and applications central to the fields of organic chemistry and biochemistry.

New Features Added to the Seventh Edition

Two new features are present in this seventh edition of the text. They are: (1) Section Quick Quizzes, and (2) Section Learning Focus Statements.

Section Quick Quizzes: Each section in each chapter of the text now ends with a "Section Quick Quiz." Depending on the section length and the number of concepts covered, the quick quiz consists of two to six multiple choice questions which highlight the key terms and concepts covered in the section that a student should be aware of after the initial reading of the text section. Answers to the quick quiz questions are given immediately following the set of questions. The word "quick" in the phrase "quick quiz" is significant. The questions are designed to generate immediate answers. In most cases a time of no more than a minute is sufficient to complete the quiz.

Two important purposes for this new quick quiz feature are: (1) to serve as a guide to the most important terms and concepts found in the section under study, and (2) to serve as an important review system for a student when he or she is studying for an upcoming class exam on the subject matter under study.

Learning Focus Statements: Learning focus statements are now found at the beginning of each section in each chapter of the text. These statements provide the student with insights into the focus of the section in terms of topics covered and the needed learning outcomes associated with these topics.

Important Continuing Features in the Seventh Edition

Focus on Biochemistry Most students taking this course have a greater interest in the biochemistry portion of the course than the preceding two parts. But biochemistry, of course, cannot be understood without a knowledge of the fundamentals of organic chemistry, and understanding organic chemistry in turn depends on knowing the key concepts of general chemistry. Thus, in writing this text, I essentially started from the back and worked forward. I began by determining what topics would be considered in the biochemistry chapters and then tailored the organic and then general sections to support that presentation. Users of the previous editions confirm that this approach ensures an efficient but thorough coverage of the principles needed to understand biochemistry.

Art Program See the story of general, organic, and biological chemistry come alive on each page! In addition to the narrative, the art and photography program helps tell a very important story—the story of ourselves and the world around us. Chemistry is everywhere! An integrated talking label system in the art and photography program gives key figures a "voice" and helps students learn more effectively.

Emphasis on Visual Support I believe strongly in visual reinforcement of key concepts in a textbook; thus this book uses art and photos wherever possible to teach key concepts. Artwork is used to make connections and highlight what is important for the student to know. Reaction equations use color to emphasize the portions of a molecule that undergo change. Colors are likewise assigned to things like valence shells and classes of compounds to help students follow trends. Computer-generated, three-dimensional molecular models accompany many discussions in the organic and biochemistry sections of the text. Color photographs show applications of chemistry to help make concepts real and more readily remembered. The following example is representative of the art program.

- Carbon
- Nitrogen
- Hydrogen
- Oxygen
- Side group

a Arrangement of protein backbone with no detail shown.

b Backbone arrangement with hydrogen-bonding interactions shown.

c Backbone atomic detail shown, as well as hydrogen-bonding interactions.

d Top view of an α helix showing that amino acid side chains (R groups) point away from the long axis of the helix.

Chemistry at a Glance Visual summaries called *Chemistry at a Glance* pull together material from several sections of a chapter to help students see the larger picture. Representative of such features are those entitled

- Relationships involving the Mole Concept (Section 6-7)
- Factors that increase Chemical Reaction Rates (Section 9-6)
- Properties of Alkanes and Cycloalkanes (Section 12-17)

- Types of Glycosidic Linkages for Disaccharides and Polysaccharides (Section 18-17)
- Types of Lipids in Terms of How They Function (Section 19-14)
- Summary of the Reactions of the Citric Acid Cycle (Section 23-7)

Given the popularity of the *Chemistry at a Glance* summaries in the previous editions, several new ones have been added and several existing ones have been revised. New and revised *Chemistry at a Glance* topics include:

- Types of Unsaturated Hydrocarbon (Section 13-16)
- Summary of Chemical Reactions Involving Alcohols (Section 14-9)
- Summary of Chemical Reactions Involving Carboxylic Acids (Section 16-7)
- Constitution Isomers and Stereoisomers (Section 18-6)
- Interrelationships Among Carbohydrate, Lipid, and Protein Metabolism (Section 26-8)

Chemical Connections   In every chapter *Chemical Connection* boxes emphasize the relevancy of chemical topics under consideration. They focus on issues relevant to a student's own life in terms of health issues, societal issues, and environmental issues. Representative of issues selected for *Chemical Connection* coverage are the following:

- Fresh Water, Seawater, Hard Water, and Soft Water (Section 4-8)
- The Chemical Sense of Smell (Section 5-8)
- Stratospheric Ozone: An Equilibrium Situation (Section 9-8)
- Red Wine and Resveratrol (Section 14-14)
- The Fatty Content of Tree Nuts and Peanuts (Section 19-4)

New topics selected for *Chemical Connection* emphasis in this edition are:

- Electrons in Excited States (Section 3-7)
- Edible Fiber and Health (Section 18-17)
- The Circadian Clock: Clock Genes (Section 22-9)
- EPO: Red Blood Cells, Mutations, and Athletic Performance (Section 22-13)
- Adenosine Phosphates and Muscle Relaxation/Contraction (Section 23-3)
- Phytochemicals: Compounds with Color and Antioxidant Properties (Section 23-11)

Updated *Chemical Connection* boxes include

- Elemental Composition of the Human Body (Section 1-7)
- Combustion Reactions: Carbon Dioxide and Global Warming (Section 9-1)
- Human Body Temperature and Chemical Reaction Rates (Section 9-6)
- Electrolytes and Body Fluids (Section 10-15)
- Caffeine: A Widely Used Central Nervous System Stimulant (Section 17-9)
- Lactose Intolerance or Lactase Persistence (Section 18-13)
- Trans Fatty Acid Content of Foods (Section 19-6)
- Enzymes, Prescription Medications and the "Grapefruit Effect" (Section 21-11)

Commitment to Student Learning   In addition to the study help *Chemistry at a Glance* offers, the text is built on a strong foundation of learning aids designed to help students master the course material.

- **Problem-solving pedagogy.** Because problem solving is often difficult for students in this course to master, I have taken special care to provide support to help students build their skills. Within the chapters, worked-out *Examples* follow the explanation of many concepts. These examples walk students through the thought processes involved in problem solving, carefully outlining all of the steps involved.

Diversity of Worked-out Examples   *Worked-out examples* are a standard feature in the general chemistry portion of all textbooks for this market. This relates primarily to the mathematical nature of many general chemistry topics. In most texts, fewer worked-out examples appear in the organic chemistry chapters, and still fewer (almost none) are found in the biochemistry portion due to decreased dependence of the topical matter on mathematical concepts. Such is not the case in this textbook. All chapters in the latter portions of the text contain numerous worked-out examples. Several additional worked-out examples have been added to this new edition. Newly added worked-out examples include the following topics:

- Classifying Matter as a Pure Substance or a Mixture (Section 1-3)
- Classifying Substances as Elements or Compounds (Section 1-7)
- Distinguishing Between Chemical Symbols and Chemical Formulas (Section 1-8)
- Diagramming Coordinate Covalent Bond Formation Using Lewis Structures (Section 5-2)
- Using Delta Notation to Specify the Direction of Bond Polarity (Section 5-6)
- Using Electronegativity Difference to Predict Chemical Bond Type (Section 5-7)
- Using Clinical Laboratory Concentration Units (Section 8-7)
- Converting an Ion Concentration from moles/L to mEq/L (Section 10-13)
- Identifying Components of a Nucleotide (Section 22-1)
- **Margin notes.** Liberally distributed throughout the text, *margin notes* provide tips for remembering and distinguishing between concepts, highlight links across chapters, and describe interesting historical background information.
- **Defined terms.** All definitions are highlighted in the text when they are first presented, using boldface and italic type. Each defined term appears as a complete sentence; students are never forced to deduce a definition from context. In addition, the definitions of all terms appear in the combined *Index/Glossary* found at the end of the text. A major emphasis in this new edition has been "refinements" of the defined terms. All defined terms were reexamined to see if they could be stated with greater clarity. The result was a "rewording" of many defined terms.
- **Concepts to Remember review.** A concise review of key concepts presented in each chapter appears at the end of the chapter, placed just before the end-of-chapter problems. This is a helpful aid for students as they prepare for exams.
- **End-of-chapter problems.** An extensive set of end-of-chapter problems complements the worked-out examples within the chapters. These end-of-chapter problems are organized by topic and paired, with each pair testing similar material. The answer to the odd-numbered member of the pair is given at the back of the book are two problem-set features:

  Problems denoted with a ▲ involve concepts found not only in the section under consideration but also concepts found in one or more earlier sections of the chapter.

Over 1000 of the 3284 total end-of-chapter problems are new to this edition of the text. This total number of end-of-chapter problems significantly exceeds that of most other texts.

Content Changes   Coverage of a number of topics has been expanded in this edition. The two driving forces in expanded coverage considerations were (1) the requests of users and reviewers of the previous editions and (2) my desire to incorporate new research findings, particularly in the area of biochemistry, into the text. Topics with expanded coverage include:

- Clinical Laboratory Concentration Units (Section 8-5)
- Concentration Units for Isotopic Solutions (Section 8-10)
- Equivalents and Milliequivalents of Electrolytes (Section 10-15)
- Charge Balance in Electrolytic Solutions (Section 10-15)

- Preparation of Alkenes (Section 13-9)
- Functional Group Isomerism (Section 14-7)
- Alcohol Condensation Reactions (Section 14-9)
- Carboxylic Acid Decarboxylation Reactions (Section 16-9)
- OxyContin Formulations (Section 17-12)
- Medical Uses of Enzymes (Section 21-11)
- Fat-Soluble Vitamins (Section 21-15)
- The Human Transcriptome (Section 22-9)
- Mutations (Section 22-13)
- Transamination Reactions (Section 26-3)
- Proteins and the Element Sulfur (Section 26-8)

Supporting Materials

Please visit http://www.cengage.com/chemistry/stoker/gob7E for information about the student and instructor resources for this text.

Acknowledgments

The publication of a book such as this requires the efforts of many more people than merely the author. Special thanks to the Editorial and Production Team at Cengage: Alyssa White, my Content Developer; Maureen Rosener, my Product Manager, Teresa Trego, my Senior Content Product Manager; I would also like to thank Katy Gabel, my Senior Project Manager at Lumina Datamatics, Inc., and my Photo Researcher, Abbey Stebing at Lumina Datamatics, Inc.

I also appreciate the time and expertise of my reviewers, who read my manuscript and provided many helpful comments.

Special thanks to my accuracy reviewers:

David Shinn, *United States Merchant Marine Academy*

Jordan Fantini; *Denison University*

Reviewers of the 7th edition:

Marcia Gillette, *Indiana University—Kokomo*
Michael Keck, *Keuka College*
Jared Mays, *Augustana College*
Michael Muhitch, *Rochester College*
Jennifer Powers, *Kennesaw State University*
Meredith Ward, *Elmira College*

Reviewers of the 6th edition:

Maryfran Barber, *Wayne State University*
Keri Clemens, *Sierra College*
John Haseltine, *Kennesaw State University*
Maria Longas, *Purdue University*
Jennifer Powers, *Kennesaw State University*
Heather Sklenicka, *Rochester Community and Technical College/Science*
Angie Spencer, *Greenville Technical College*
David Tramontozzi, *Macomb CC/Science*

Reviewers of the 5th edition:

Jennifer Adamski, *Old Dominion University*

M. Reza Asdjodi, *University of Wisconsin—Eau Claire*

Irene Gerow, *East Carolina University*

Ernest Kho, *University of Hawaii at Hilo*

Larry L. Land, *University of Florida*

Michael Myers, *California State University—Long Beach*

H. A. Peoples, *Las Positas College*

Shashi Rishi, *Greenville Technical College*

Steven M. Socol, *McHenry County College*

Basic Concepts About Matter

1

Numerous physical and chemical changes in matter occur during a volcanic eruption.

© Karen Grigoryan/Shutterstock.com

In this chapter, the question "What exactly is chemistry about?" is addressed. In addition, common terminology associated with the field of chemistry is considered. Much of this terminology is introduced in the context of the ways in which matter is classified. Like all other sciences, chemistry has its own specific language. It is necessary to restrict the meanings of some words so that all chemists (and those who study chemistry) can understand a given description of a chemical phenomenon in the same way.

1-1 Chemistry: The Study of Matter

LEARNING FOCUS

Define the term *matter*; indicate whether or not various entities are considered to be matter.

Chemistry *is the field of study concerned with the characteristics, composition, and transformations of matter.* What is matter? **Matter** *is anything that has mass and occupies space.* The term *mass* refers to the amount of matter present in a sample. ◀

Matter includes all naturally occurring things—both living and nonliving—that can be seen (such as plants, soil, and rocks), as well as things

▶ *The* mass *of a sample of matter is a measure of the amount of matter present in the sample.*

| 1

that cannot be seen (such as air and bacteria). Matter also includes materials that do not occur naturally, that is, synthetic materials that are produced in a laboratory or industrial setting using, directly or indirectly, naturally occurring starting materials. Various forms of energy such as heat, light, and electricity are not considered to be matter. However, chemists must be concerned with energy as well as with matter because nearly all changes that matter undergoes involve the release or absorption of energy. ◀

▶ *The universe is composed entirely of matter and energy.*

The scope of chemistry is extremely broad, and it touches every aspect of our lives. An iron gate rusting, a chocolate cake baking, the production in a laboratory of an antibiotic or a plastic composite, the diagnosis and treatment of a heart attack, the propulsion of a jet airliner, and the digesting of food all fall within the realm of chemistry. The key to understanding such diverse processes is understanding the fundamental nature of matter, which is what is now considered.

Section 1-1 Quick Quiz

1. Which of the following is a characteristic of all types of matter?
   a. naturally occurring
   b. visible to the naked eye
   c. has mass
   d. no correct response
2. Which of the following is classified as matter?
   a. heat energy
   b. a scientific theory
   c. chocolate milk
   d. no correct response
3. Which of the following processes <u>does not</u> fall within the realm of chemistry?
   a. detonation of an explosive
   b. cooking of a hamburger patty
   c. production of a blood pressure medication
   d. no correct response

Answers: 1. c; 2. c; 3. d

1-2 Physical States of Matter

LEARNING FOCUS
Characterize each of the three states of matter in terms of the definiteness or indefiniteness of its shape and volume.

Three physical states exist for matter: solid, liquid, and gas. The classification of a given matter sample in terms of physical state is based on whether its shape and volume are definite or indefinite. ◀

▶ *The volume of a sample of matter is a measure of the amount of space occupied by the sample.*

Solid *is the physical state characterized by a definite shape and a definite volume.* A dollar coin has the same shape and volume whether it is placed in a large container or on a table top (Figure 1-1a). For solids in powdered or granulated forms, such as sugar or salt, a quantity of the solid takes the shape of the portion of the container it occupies, but each individual particle has a definite shape and definite volume. **Liquid** *is the physical state characterized by an indefinite shape and a definite volume.* A liquid always takes the shape of its container to the extent that it fills the container (Figure 1-1b). **Gas** *is the physical state characterized by an indefinite shape and an indefinite volume.* A gas always completely fills its container, adopting both the container's volume and its shape (Figure 1-1c).

The state of matter observed for a particular substance depends on its temperature, the surrounding pressure, and the strength of the forces holding its structural particles together. At the temperatures and pressures normally encountered on Earth, water is one of the few substances found in all three physical states: solid ice, liquid

A solid has a definite shape and a definite volume.

A liquid has an indefinite shape—it takes the shape of its container—and a definite volume.

A gas has an indefinite shape and an indefinite volume—it assumes the shape and volume of its container.

Figure 1-1 A comparison of the volume and shape characteristics of solids, liquids, and gases.

© Cengage Learning

water, and gaseous steam (Figure 1-2). Under laboratory conditions, states other than those commonly observed can be attained for almost all substances. Oxygen, which is nearly always thought of as a gas, becomes a liquid at $-183°C$ and a solid at $-218°C$. The metal iron is a gas at extremely high temperatures (above 3000°C).

Section 1-2 Quick Quiz

1. Which of the following is a characteristic of both liquids and gases?
   a. definite shape
   b. definite volume
   c. indefinite shape
   d. no correct response
2. The characterization "completely fills its container" describes the
   a. solid state
   b. liquid state
   c. gaseous state
   d. no correct response
3. The characterization "indefinite shape, definite volume" applies to
   a. a solid
   b. a liquid
   c. both a solid and a liquid
   d. no correct response

Answers: 1. c; 2. c; 3. b

1-3 Properties of Matter

LEARNING FOCUS

Classify a given property of a substance as a *physical property* or a *chemical property*.

Various kinds of matter are distinguished from each other by their properties. A **property** *is a distinguishing characteristic of a substance that is used in its identification and description.* Each substance has a unique set of properties that distinguishes it from all other substances. Properties of matter are of two general types: physical and chemical.

A **physical property** *is a characteristic of a substance that can be observed without changing the basic identity of the substance.* Common physical properties include color, physical state (solid, liquid, or gas), melting point, boiling point, and hardness. ◄

▶ *Physical properties are properties associated with a substance's physical existence. They can be determined without reference to any other substance, and determining them causes no change in the identity of the substance.*

Figure 1-2 Water can be found in the solid, liquid, and vapor (gaseous) forms simultaneously, as shown here at Yellowstone National Park.

FRILET Patrick / Hemis / Alamy

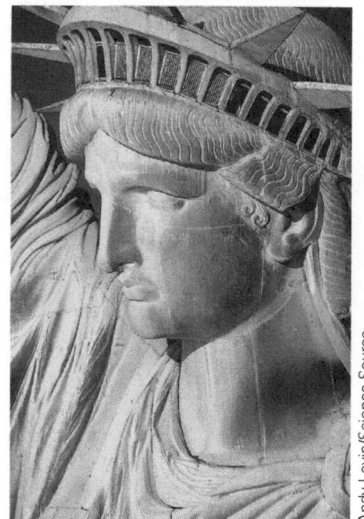

Andy Levin/Science Source

Figure 1-3 The green color of the Statue of Liberty results from the reaction of the copper skin of the statue with the components of air. That copper will react with the components of air is a chemical property of copper.

▶ *Chemical properties describe the ability of a substance to form new substances, either by reaction with other substances or by decomposition.*

During the process of determining a physical property, the physical appearance of a substance may change, but the substance's identity does not. For example, it is impossible to measure the melting point of a solid without changing the solid into a liquid. Although the liquid's appearance is much different from that of the solid, the substance is still the same; its chemical identity has not changed. Hence, melting point is a physical property.

A **chemical property** *is a characteristic of a substance that describes the way the substance undergoes or resists change to form a new substance.* For example, copper objects turn green when exposed to moist air for long periods of time (Figure 1-3); this is a chemical property of copper. The green coating formed on the copper is a new substance that results from the copper's reaction with oxygen, carbon dioxide, and water present in air. The properties of this new substance (the green coating) are very different from those of metallic copper. On the other hand, gold objects resist change when exposed to air for long periods of time. The lack of reactivity of gold with air is a chemical property of gold.

Most often, the changes associated with chemical properties result from the interaction (reaction) of a substance with one or more other substances. However, the presence of a second substance is not an absolute requirement. Sometimes the presence of energy (usually heat or light) can trigger the change known as *decomposition*. That hydrogen peroxide, in the presence of either heat or light, decomposes into the substances water and oxygen is a chemical property of hydrogen peroxide. ◀

When chemical properties are specified, conditions such as temperature and pressure are usually given because they influence the interactions between substances. For example, the gases oxygen and hydrogen do not react with each other at room temperature, but they react explosively at a temperature of several hundred degrees.

EXAMPLE 1-1

Classifying Properties as Physical or Chemical

Classify each of the following properties of selected metals as a *physical* property or a *chemical* property.

a. Iron metal rusts in an atmosphere of moist air.
b. Mercury metal is a liquid at room temperature.
c. Nickel metal dissolves in acid to produce a light green solution.
d. Potassium metal has a melting point of 63°C.

Solution

a. *Chemical property*. The interaction of iron metal with moist air produces a new substance (rust).

b. *Physical property*. Visually determining the physical state of a substance does not produce a new substance.

c. *Chemical property*. A change in color indicates the formation of a new substance.

d. *Physical property*. Measuring the melting point of a substance does not change the substance's composition.

The focus on relevancy feature Chemical Connections 1-A—Carbon Monoxide: A Substance with Both "Good" and "Bad" Properties—discusses the important concept that a decision about the significance or usefulness of a substance should not be made solely on the basis of just one or two of its many chemical or physical properties. The discussion there focuses on both the "bad" and "good" properties possessed by the gas carbon monoxide.

CHEMICAL CONNECTIONS 1-A

Carbon Monoxide: A Substance with Both "Good" and "Bad" Properties

Possession of a "bad" property, such as toxicity or a strong noxious odor, does not mean that a chemical substance has nothing to contribute to the betterment of human society. The gas carbon monoxide is an important example of this concept.

It is common knowledge that carbon monoxide is toxic to humans and at higher concentrations can cause death. This gas, which can be present in significant concentrations in both automobile exhaust and cigarette smoke, impairs human health by reducing the oxygen-carrying capacity of the blood. It does this by interacting with the hemoglobin in red blood cells in a way that prevents the hemoglobin from distributing oxygen throughout the body. Someone who dies from carbon monoxide poisoning actually dies from lack of oxygen. (Additional information about the human health effects of the air pollutant carbon monoxide is found in Chemical Connections 6-A) Because of its toxicity, many people automatically label carbon monoxide a "bad substance," a substance that is not wanted and not needed.

The fact that carbon monoxide is colorless, odorless, and tasteless is very significant. Because of these properties, carbon monoxide gives no warning of its initial presence. Several other common air pollutants are more toxic than carbon monoxide. However, they have properties that warn of their presence and hence are not considered as "dangerous" as carbon monoxide.

Despite its toxicity, carbon monoxide plays an important role in the maintenance of the high standard of living we now enjoy. Its contribution lies in the field of iron metallurgy and the production of steel. The isolation of iron from iron ores, necessary for the production of steel, involves a series of high-temperature reactions, carried out in a blast furnace, in which the iron content of molten iron ores reacts with carbon monoxide. These reactions release the iron from its ores. The carbon monoxide needed in steel-making is obtained by reacting coke (a product derived by heating coal to a high temperature without air being present) with oxygen.

The industrial consumption of the metal iron, both in the United States and worldwide, is approximately 10 times greater than that of all other metals combined. Steel production accounts for nearly all of this demand for iron. Without steel, our standard of living would drop dramatically, and carbon monoxide is necessary for the production of steel.

Carbon monoxide is needed to produce molten iron from iron ore in a blast furnace.

© Huyangshu/Shutterstock.com

Is carbon monoxide a "good" or a "bad" chemical substance? The answer to this question depends on the context in which the carbon monoxide is encountered. In terms of air pollution, it is a "bad" substance. In terms of steel-making, it is a "good" substance. A similar "good–bad" dichotomy exists for almost every chemical substance.

Section 1-3 Quick Quiz

1. Which of the following statements about various substances describes a *physical property* of the substance?
   a. Copper metal can be drawn into thin wires.
   b. Gold metal does not tarnish in air.
   c. Hydrogen peroxide decomposes in the presence of light.
   d. no correct response
2. Which of the following statement about various substances describes a *chemical property* of the substance?
   a. Silver metal will not dissolve in hydrochloric acid.
   b. Beryllium metal has a silvery-gray color.
   c. Water (ice) melts at 32°F.
   d. no correct response
3. In which of the following pairs of properties are both *physical* properties?
   a. low density, flammable
   b. reacts with oxygen, does not react with iodine
   c. very brittle, very toxic
   d. no correct response

Answers: 1. a; 2. a; 3. d

1-4   Changes in Matter

LEARNING FOCUS

Classify a given change that occurs in matter as a *physical change* or a *chemical change*.

Changes in matter are common and familiar occurrences. Changes take place when food is digested, paper is burned, and a pencil is sharpened. Like properties of matter, changes in matter are classified into two categories: physical and chemical.

A **physical change** *is a process in which a substance changes its physical appearance but not its chemical composition.* A new substance is never formed as a result of a physical change. ◄

A change in physical state is the most common type of physical change. Melting, freezing, evaporation, and condensation are all changes of state. In any of these processes, the composition of the substance undergoing change remains the same even though its physical state and appearance change. The melting of ice does not produce a new substance; the substance is water both before and after the change. Similarly, the steam produced from boiling water is still water.

A **chemical change** *is a process in which a substance undergoes a change in chemical composition.* Chemical changes always involve conversion of the material or materials under consideration into one or more new substances, each of which has properties and a composition distinctly different from those of the original materials. Consider, for example, the rusting of iron objects left exposed to moist air (Figure 1-4). The reddish-brown substance (the rust) that forms is a new substance with chemical properties that are obviously different from those of the original iron.

► *Physical changes need not involve a change of state. Pulverizing an aspirin tablet into a powder and cutting a piece of adhesive tape into small pieces are physical changes that involve only the solid state.*

Figure 1-4 As a result of chemical change, bright steel girders become rusty when exposed to moist air.

EXAMPLE 1-2

Correct Use of the Terms *Physical* and *Chemical* in Describing Changes

Complete each of the following statements about changes in matter by placing the word *physical* or *chemical* in the blank.

a. The fashioning of a piece of wood into a round table leg involves a _____ change.
b. The vigorous reaction of potassium metal with water to produce hydrogen gas is a _____ change.
c. Straightening a bent piece of iron with a hammer is an example of a _____ change.
d. The ignition and burning of a match involve a _____ change.

Solution

a. *Physical.* The table leg is still wood. No new substances have been formed.
b. *Chemical.* A new substance, hydrogen, is produced.
c. *Physical.* The piece of iron is still a piece of iron.
d. *Chemical.* New gaseous substances, as well as heat and light, are produced as the match burns.

Chemists study the nature of changes in matter to learn how to bring about favorable changes and prevent undesirable ones. The control of chemical change has been a major factor in attaining the modern standard of living now enjoyed by most people in the developed world. The many plastics, synthetic fibers, and prescription drugs now in common use are produced using controlled chemical change.

Chemistry at a Glance—Use of the Terms *Physical* and *Chemical*—reviews the ways in which the terms *physical* and *chemical* are used to describe the properties of substances and the changes that substances undergo. Note that the term *physical*, used as a modifier, always conveys the idea that the composition (chemical identity) of a substance did not change, and that the term *chemical*, used as a modifier, always conveys the idea that the composition of a substance did change.

Section 1-4 Quick Quiz

1. Which of the following processes <u>is not</u> a *physical* change?
   a. crushing ice cubes to make ice chips
   b. melting ice cubes to produce liquid water
   c. freezing liquid water to produce ice cubes
   d. no correct response
2. Which of the following processes is an example of *chemical* change?
   a. grating a piece of cheese
   b. burning a piece of wood
   c. pulverizing a hard sugar cube
   d. no correct response
3. Which of the following is <u>always</u> a characteristic of *chemical* change?
   a. heat is produced
   b. light is emitted
   c. one or more new substances are produced
   d. no correct answer

Answers: 1. d; 2. b; 3. c

1-5 Pure Substances and Mixtures

LEARNING FOCUS

Know the major differences among the matter classifications *pure substance, heterogeneous mixture,* and *homogeneous mixture.*

In addition to its classification by physical state (Section 1-2), matter can also be classified in terms of its chemical composition as a pure substance or as a mixture. A **pure substance** *is a single kind of matter that cannot be separated into other kinds of matter by any physical means.* All samples of a pure substance contain only that substance and nothing else. Pure water is water and nothing else. Pure sucrose (table sugar) contains only that substance and nothing else. ◀

A pure substance always has a definite and constant composition. This invariant composition dictates that the properties of a pure substance are always the same under a given set of conditions. Collectively, these definite and constant physical and chemical properties constitute the means by which we identify the pure substance.

A **mixture** *is a physical combination of two or more pure substances in which each substance retains its own chemical identity.* Components of a mixture retain their

▶ Substance *is a general term used to denote any variety of matter. Pure substance is a specific term that is applied to matter that contains only a single substance. All samples of a pure substance, no matter what their source, have the same properties under the same conditions.*

CHEMISTRY AT A GLANCE   Use of the Terms *Physical* and *Chemical*

PHYSICAL

This term conveys the idea that the composition (chemical identity) of a substance DOES NOT CHANGE.

Physical Properties

Properties observable without changing composition

- Color and shape
- Solid, liquid, or gas
- Boiling point, melting point

Physical Changes

Changes observable without changing composition

- Change in physical state (melting, boiling, freezing, etc.)
- Change in state of subdivision with no change in physical state (pulverizing a solid)

CHEMICAL

This term conveys the idea that the composition (chemical identity) of a substance DOES CHANGE.

Chemical Properties

Properties that describe how a substance changes (or resists change) to form a new substance

- Flammability (or non-flammability)
- Decomposition at a high temperature (or lack of decomposition)
- Reaction with chlorine (or lack of reaction with chlorine)

Chemical Changes

Changes in which one or more new substances are formed

- Decomposition
- Reaction with another substance

identity because they are physically mixed rather than chemically combined. Consider a mixture of small rock salt crystals and ordinary sand. Mixing these two substances changes neither the salt nor the sand in any way. The larger, colorless salt particles are easily distinguished from the smaller, light-gray sand granules.

One characteristic of any mixture is that its components can be separated by using physical means. In our salt–sand mixture, the larger salt crystals could be—though very tediously—"picked out" from the sand. A somewhat easier separation method would be to dissolve the salt in water, which would leave the undissolved sand behind. The salt could then be recovered by evaporation of the water. Figure 1-5a shows a mixture of potassium dichromate (orange crystals) and iron filings. A magnet can be used to separate the components of this mixture (Figure 1-5b).

Another characteristic of a mixture is variable composition. Numerous different salt–sand mixtures, with compositions ranging from a slightly salty sand mixture to a slightly sandy salt mixture, could be made by varying the amounts of the two components. ◄

▶ *Most naturally occurring samples of matter are mixtures. Gold and diamond are two of the few naturally occurring pure substances. Despite their scarcity in nature, numerous pure substances exist. They are obtained from natural mixtures by using various types of separation techniques or are synthesized in the laboratory from naturally occurring materials.*

Figure 1-5 Physical separation of the two components of a mixture using the magnetic properties of one of the mixture components.

A magnet (on the left) and a mixture consisting of potassium dichromate (the orange crystals) and iron filings.

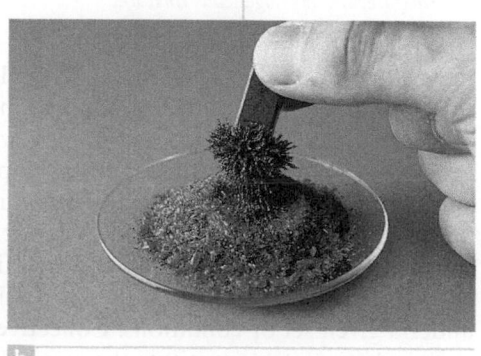

The magnet can be used to separate the iron filings from the potassium dichromate.

a

b

(a) James Scherer © Cengage Learning;
(b) © Cengage Learning

Mixtures are subclassified as heterogeneous or homogeneous. This subclassification is based on visual recognition of the mixture's components. A **heterogeneous mixture** *is a mixture that contains visibly different phases (parts), each of which has different properties.* A nonuniform appearance is a characteristic of all heterogeneous mixtures. Examples include chocolate chip cookies and blueberry muffins. Naturally occurring heterogeneous mixtures include rocks, soils, and wood.

A **homogeneous mixture** *is a mixture that contains only one visibly distinct phase (part), which has uniform properties throughout.* The components present in a homogeneous mixture cannot be visually distinguished. A sugar–water mixture in which all of the sugar has dissolved has an appearance similar to that of pure water. Air is a homogeneous mixture of gases; motor oil and gasoline are multicomponent homogeneous mixtures of liquids; and metal alloys such as 14-karat gold (a mixture of copper and gold) are examples of homogeneous mixtures of solids. The homogeneity present in solid-state metallic alloys is achieved by mixing the metals while they are in the molten state. ◄

Figure 1-6 summarizes key concepts presented in this section about various classifications of matter.

▶ *All human body fluids, such as urine, blood, or sweat are mixtures of many substances. Since their components cannot be visually distinguished from each other, they are* homogeneous *mixtures.*

EXAMPLE 1-3

Classifying Matter as a Pure Substance or a Mixture

Classify each of the following as a *heterogeneous mixture*, a *homogeneous mixture*, or a *pure substance*. Assume that each sample has been well stirred.

a. a "pinch" of table salt, one quart of water
b. a "pinch" of ground black pepper, one quart of water
c. one substance present, one phase present
d. two substances present, same properties throughout

Solution

a. Two substances present means *mixture*; since table salt is soluble in water only one phase is present, a characteristic of a *homogeneous mixture*.
b. Two substances present means *mixture*; since black pepper is insoluble in water two phases are present (solid and liquid), a characteristic of a *heterogeneous mixture*.
c. One substance present means *pure substance* rather than mixture; a mixture requires the presence of two substances. The presence of two phases does not cause the classification to change from pure substance to mixture. An example of a "one substance, two phase" situation is ice cubes in water. Water (a pure substance) is present in two states (solid and liquid).
d. This *mixture* (two substances present) is a *homogeneous mixture* as the same properties throughout denotes homogeneity.

Figure 1-6 Matter falls into two basic classes: pure substances and mixtures. Mixtures, in turn, may be homogeneous or heterogeneous.

1-6 Elements and Compounds

LEARNING FOCUS

Know the major differences between the matter classifications *element* and *compound* and between the matter classifications *mixture* and *compound*.

Chemists have isolated and characterized an estimated 9 million pure substances. A very small number of these pure substances, 118 to be exact, are different from all of the others. They are elements. All of the rest, the remaining millions, are compounds. What distinguishes an element from a compound?

An **element** *is a pure substance that cannot be broken down into simpler pure substances by chemical means such as a chemical reaction, an electric current, heat, or a beam of light.* The metals gold, silver, and copper are all elements. ◀

A **compound** *is a pure substance that can be broken down into two or more simpler pure substances by chemical means.* Water is a compound. By means of an electric current, water can be broken down into the gases hydrogen and oxygen, both of which are elements. ◀ The ultimate breakdown products for any compound are elements (Figure 1-7). A compound's properties are always different from those of

▶ *The definition for the term* element *that is given here will do for now. After considering the concept of atomic number (Section 3-2), a more precise definition will be given.*

▶ *Both elements and compounds are pure substances.*

Figure 1-7 A pure substance can be either an element or a compound.

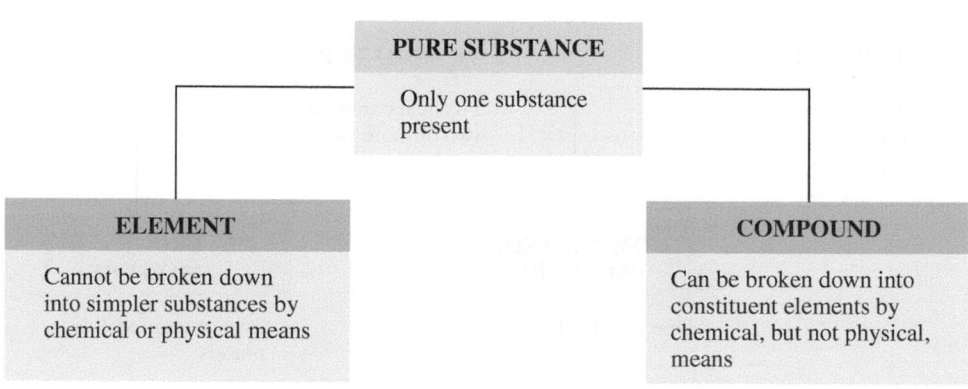

PURE SUBSTANCE

Only one substance present

ELEMENT

Cannot be broken down into simpler substances by chemical or physical means

COMPOUND

Can be broken down into constituent elements by chemical, but not physical, means its component elements, because the elements are chemically rather than physically combined in the compound.

Even though two or more elements are obtained from decomposition of compounds, compounds are not mixtures. Why is this so? Substances can be combined either physically or chemically. Physical combination of substances produces a mixture. Chemical combination of substances produces a compound, a substance in which the combining entities are *bound* together. No such binding occurs during physical combination. Example 1-4, which involves two comparisons involving locks and their keys, nicely illustrates the difference between compounds and mixtures. ◄

Chemistry at a Glance—Classes of Matter—summarizes concepts presented thus far about the subdivisions of matter called pure substances, elements, compounds, and mixtures.

► *Every known compound is made up of some combination of two or more of the 118 known elements. In any given compound, the elements are combined chemically in fixed proportions by mass.*

EXAMPLE 1-4

The "Composition" Difference Between a Mixture and a Compound

Consider two boxes with the following contents: the first contains 10 locks and 10 keys that fit the locks; the second contains 10 locks with each lock's key inserted into the cylinder. Which box has contents that would be an analogy for a mixture, and which box has contents that would be an analogy for a compound?

Solution

The box containing the locks with their keys inserted in the cylinder represents a compound. Two objects withdrawn from this box will always be the same; each will be a lock with its associated key. Each item in the box has the same "composition."

The box containing separated locks and keys represents a mixture. Two objects withdrawn from this box need not be the same; results could be two locks, two keys, or a lock and a key. All items in the box do not have the same "composition."

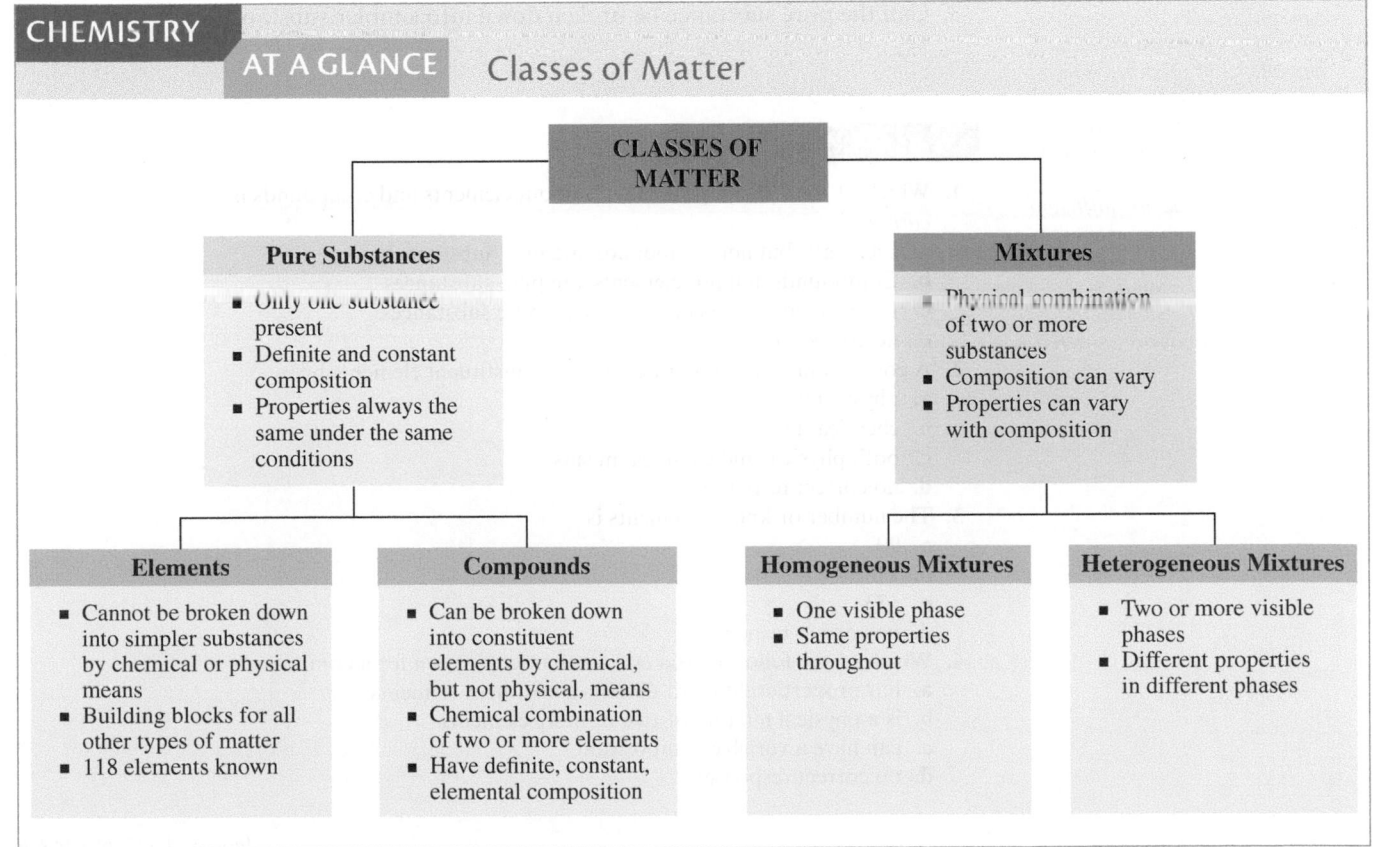

CHEMISTRY AT A GLANCE Classes of Matter

CLASSES OF MATTER

Pure Substances
- Only one substance present
- Definite and constant composition
- Properties always the same under the same conditions

Mixtures
- Physical combination of two or more substances
- Composition can vary
- Properties can vary with composition

Elements
- Cannot be broken down into simpler substances by chemical or physical means
- Building blocks for all other types of matter
- 118 elements known

Compounds
- Can be broken down into constituent elements by chemical, but not physical, means
- Chemical combination of two or more elements
- Have definite, constant, elemental composition

Homogeneous Mixtures
- One visible phase
- Same properties throughout

Heterogeneous Mixtures
- Two or more visible phases
- Different properties in different phases

Figure 1-8 Questions used in classifying matter into various categories.

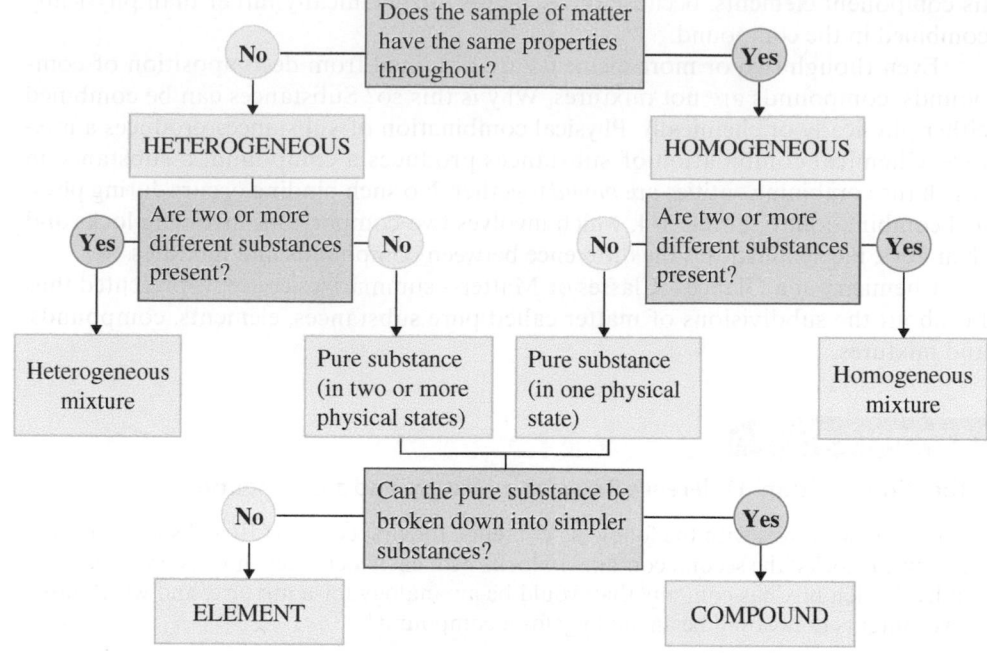

Figure 1-8 summarizes the thought processes a chemist goes through in classifying a sample of matter as a heterogeneous mixture, a homogeneous mixture, an element, or a compound. ◄ This figure is based on the following three questions about a sample of matter:

1. Does the sample of matter have the same properties throughout?
2. Are two or more different substances present?
3. Can the pure substance be broken down into simpler substances?

▶ *There are three major distinctions between compounds and mixtures.*

1. *Compounds have properties distinctly different from those of the substances that combined to form the compound. The components of mixtures retain their individual properties.*
2. *Compounds have a definite composition. Mixtures have a variable composition.*
3. *Physical methods are sufficient to separate the components of a mixture. The components of a compound cannot be separated by physical methods; chemical methods are required.*

Section 1-6 Quick Quiz

1. Which of the following statements about elements and compounds is *correct*?
   a. Elements, but not compounds, are pure substances.
   b. Compounds, but not elements, are pure substances.
   c. Both elements and compounds are pure substances.
   d. no correct response
2. A compound can be separated into its constituent elements by
   a. physical means
   b. chemical means
   c. both physical and chemical means
   d. no correct response
3. The number of known elements is
   a. 90
   b. 118
   c. 133
   d. no correct response
4. Which of the following is a *correct* characterization for a compound?
   a. has properties different than its constituent elements
   b. is a physical mixture of two or more elements
   c. can have a variable composition
   d. no correct response

Answers: 1. c; 2. b; 3. b; 4. a

1-7 Discovery and Abundance of the Elements

LEARNING FOCUS

Know important generalizations concerning the discovery of and the abundances of the elements.

The discovery and isolation of the 118 known elements, the building blocks for all matter, have taken place over a period of several centuries. Most of the discoveries have occurred since 1700, with the 1800s being the most active period. ◀

Eighty-eight of the 118 elements occur naturally, and 30 have been synthesized in the laboratory by bombarding samples of naturally occurring elements with small particles. Figure 1-9 shows samples of selected naturally occurring elements. The synthetic (laboratory-produced) elements are all unstable (radioactive) and usually revert quickly back to naturally occurring elements (see Section 11-5). ◀

The naturally occurring elements are not evenly distributed on Earth and in the universe. What is startling is the nonuniformity of the distribution. A small number of elements account for the majority of elemental particles (atoms). (An atom is the smallest particle of an element that can exist; see Section 1-9.)

Studies of the radiation emitted by stars enable scientists to estimate the elemental composition of the universe (Figure 1-10a). Results indicate that two elements, hydrogen and helium, are absolutely dominant. All other elements are mere "impurities" when their abundances are compared with those of these two dominant elements. In this big picture, in which the Earth is but a tiny microdot, 91% of all elemental particles (atoms) are hydrogen, and nearly all of the remaining 9% are helium.

Narrowing considerations to the chemical world of humans—Earth's crust (its waters, atmosphere, and outer solid surface)—a different perspective emerges. Again, two elements dominate, but this time they are oxygen and silicon. Figure 1-10b provides information on elemental abundances for Earth's crust. The numbers given are atom percents—that is, the percentage of total atoms that are of a given type. Note that the eight elements listed (the only elements with atom percents greater than 1%) account for more than 98% of total atoms in Earth's crust. Note also the dominance of oxygen and silicon; these two elements account for 80% of the atoms that make up the chemical world of humans.

The focus on relevancy feature Chemical Connections 1-B—Elemental Composition of the Human Body—considers the elemental composition of the human body, which differs markedly from that of the Earth's crust, and also considers the major reason for this difference.

▶ *A student who attended a university in the year 1700 would have been taught that 13 elements existed. In 1750 he or she would have learned about 16 elements, in 1800 about 34, in 1850 about 59, in 1900 about 82, in 1950 about 98, and in 2000 about 113. Today's total of 118 elements was reached in the year 2010.*

▶ *Any increase in the number of known elements from 118 will result from the production of additional synthetic elements. Current chemical theory strongly suggests that all naturally occurring elements have been identified. The isolation of the last of the known naturally occurring elements, rhenium, occurred in 1925.*

a Sulfur b Arsenic c Iodine
d Magnesium e Bismuth f Mercury

Figure 1-9 Outward physical appearance of six naturally occurring elements.

CHEMICAL CONNECTIONS 1-B

Elemental Composition of the Human Body

What are the most abundant element(s) or substances in the human body? There are several ways for answering this question. Three common methods for specifying human body composition are (1) mass percent composition by element, (2) atom percent composition by element, and (3) mass percent composition by nutrient type. Human body composition obviously varies from individual to individual. The numbers used in the ensuing discussion are averages obtained from a wide range of data.

In terms of elemental mass composition data oxygen is the dominant element (61%), with carbon (23%) and hydrogen (10%) being second and third. Thus, three elements constitute 94% of total body mass (see accompanying graph a).

Most of the oxygen and hydrogen present in the body is present in the form of water, a substance that contains hydrogen and oxygen. An adult human body averages 53% water by mass, varying substantially with age, sex, and body fat content. Subtracting out water's contribution to total body mass, carbon is the dominant element in that which remains (see accompanying graph b). The dramatic

Thus, the answer to the question "What is the most abundant element in the human body?" is dependent on frame of reference: Graph a says it is oxygen, graph b says it is carbon, and graph c says it is hydrogen.

Hydrogen, carbon, and nitrogen are all much more abundant in the human body than in the Earth's crust (Figure 1-10b) and oxygen is less abundant. This results from living systems *selectively* taking up matter from their external environment rather than simply accumulating matter representative of their surroundings. Food intake constitutes the primary selective intake process.

In food science, nutritionists classify the components of food and drink taken into the human body into six categories: (1) water, (2) carbohydrates, (3) fats, (4) proteins, (5) minerals, and (6) vitamins. The first four of these "food groups" are needed by the body in large amounts and the latter two in much smaller amounts. Independent of the amount needed, all six groups are absolutely necessary for the proper functioning of the human body. Human body composition specified in terms of mass percent "food group" present is as follows.

a HUMAN BODY MASS PERCENT COMPOSITION BY ELEMENT

b HUMAN BODY MASS PERCENT COMPOSITION BY ELEMENT (after removal of water)

c HUMAN BODY ATOM PERCENT COMPOSITION BY ELEMENT

drop of oxygen mass percent stems from water being 89% oxygen by mass and only 11% hydrogen.

Atom mass percent composition data for the human body differs markedly from mass percent data. Mass percent data take into account that some atoms are heavier than other atoms; for example, oxygen atoms are 16 times heavier than hydrogen atoms. Taking into account only the number of atoms present, disregarding mass difference, puts hydrogen at the top of the list of elements present with oxygen a distant second (see accompanying graph c). In terms of atoms, four elements (hydrogen, oxygen, carbon, and nitrogen) are the source of 99% of the atoms in the human body.

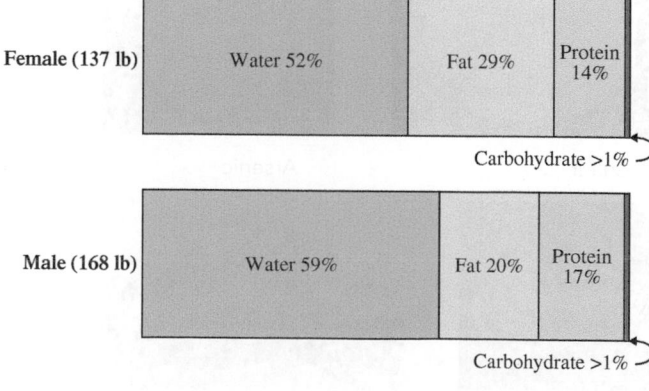

Representative mass composition of human body

Figure 1-10 Abundance of elements (in atom percent) in the universe (a) and in Earth's crust (b).

a UNIVERSE

b EARTH'S CRUST

Section 1-7 Quick Quiz

1. Which of the following statements concerning the known elements is correct?
   a. All known elements are naturally occurring substances.
   b. The discovery of the last of the known elements occurred in 1885.
   c. Synthetic (laboratory-produced) elements that do not occur in nature exist.
   d. no correct response

2. The most abundant element in the universe as a whole and in the Earth's crust is, respectively.
   a. hydrogen and iron
   b. hydrogen and oxygen
   c. oxygen and iron
   d. no correct response

3. Which of the following statements concerning atom percent elemental abundances in the Earth's crust is *incorrect*?
   a. One element accounts for over one-half of all atoms.
   b. Two elements account for over three-fourths of all atoms.
   c. There is a wide variance in elemental abundance.
   d. no correct response

4. The two most abundant elements in the Earth's crust are
   a. oxygen and hydrogen
   b. hydrogen and silicon
   c. nitrogen and oxygen
   d. no correct response

Answers: 1. c; 2. b; 3. d; 4. d

1-8 Names and Chemical Symbols of the Elements

LEARNING FOCUS

For the most common elements, given the name of the element write its chemical symbol, or given its chemical symbol write its name.

Each element has a unique name that, in most cases, was selected by its discoverer. A wide variety of rationales for choosing a name have been applied. Some elements bear geographical names: germanium is named after the native country of its German discoverer, and the elements francium and polonium are named after France and Poland. The elements mercury, uranium, and neptunium are all named for planets. Helium gets its name from the Greek word *helios*, for "sun," because it was first observed spectroscopically in the sun's corona during an eclipse. Some elements carry names that reflect specific properties of the element or of the compounds that contain it. Chlorine's name is derived from the Greek *chloros*, denoting "greenish-yellow," the color of chlorine gas. Iridium gets its name from the Greek *iris*, meaning "rainbow"; this alludes to the varying colors of the compounds from which it was isolated.

Abbreviations called chemical symbols also exist for the names of the elements. A **chemical symbol** *is a one- or two-letter designation for an element derived from the element's name.* These chemical symbols are used more frequently than the elements' names. Chemical symbols can be written more quickly than the names, and they occupy less space. A list of the known elements and their chemical symbols is given in Table 1-1. The chemical symbols and names of the more frequently encountered elements are shown in red in this table. ◄

▶ *Learning the chemical symbols of the more common elements is an important key to success in studying chemistry. Knowledge of chemical symbols is essential for writing chemical formulas (Section 1-10) and chemical equations (Section 6-6).*

▶ Table 1-1 **The Chemical Symbols for the Elements**

The names and symbols of the more frequently encountered elements are shown in red.

Ac	actinium	Ga	gallium	Pm	promethium
Ag	silver*	Gd	gadolinium	Po	polonium
Al	aluminum	Ge	germanium	Pr	praseodymium
Am	americium	H	hydrogen	Pt	platinum
Ar	argon	He	helium	Pu	plutonium
As	arsenic	Hf	hafnium	Ra	radium
At	astatine	Hg	mercury*	Rb	rubidium
Au	gold*	Ho	holmium	Re	rhenium
B	boron	Hs	hassium	Rf	rutherfordium
Ba	barium	I	iodine	Rg	roentgenium
Be	beryllium	In	indium	Rh	rhodium
Bh	bohrium	Ir	iridium	Rn	radon
Bi	bismuth	K	potassium*	Ru	ruthenium
Bk	berkelium	Kr	krypton	S	sulfur
Br	bromine	La	lanthanum	Sb	antimony*
C	carbon	Li	lithium	Sc	scandium
Ca	calcium	Lr	lawrencium	Se	selenium
Cd	cadmium	Lu	lutetium	Sg	seaborgium
Ce	cerium	Lv	livermorium	Si	silicon
Cf	californium	Md	mendelevium	Sm	samarium
Cl	chlorine	Mg	magnesium	Sn	tin*
Cm	curium	Mn	manganese	Sr	strontium
Cn	copernicium	Mo	molybdenum	Ta	tantalum
Co	cobalt	Mt	meitnerium	Tb	terbium
Cr	chromium	N	nitrogen	Tc	technetium
Cs	cesium	Na	sodium*	Te	tellurium
Cu	copper*	Nb	niobium	Th	thorium
Db	dubnium	Nd	neodymium	Ti	titanium
Ds	darmstadtium	Ne	neon	Tl	thallium
Dy	dysprosium	Ni	nickel	Tm	thulium
Er	erbium	No	nobelium	U	uranium
Es	einsteinium	Np	neptunium	V	vanadium
Eu	europium	O	oxygen	W	tungsten*
F	fluorine	Os	osmium	Xe	xenon
Fe	iron*	P	phosphorus	Y	yttrium
Fl	flerovium	Pa	protactinium	Yb	ytterbium
Fm	fermium	Pb	lead*	Zn	zinc
Fr	francium	Pd	palladium	Zr	zirconium

Only 114 elements are listed in this table. The remaining four elements, discovered (synthesized) between 2004 and 2010, are yet to be named.

*These elements have symbols that were derived from non-English names.

Note that the first letter of a chemical symbol is always capitalized and the second is not. Two-letter chemical symbols are often, but not always, the first two letters of the element's name.

Eleven elements have chemical symbols that bear no relationship to the element's English-language name. In ten of these cases, the symbol is derived from the Latin name of the element; in the case of the element tungsten, its German name is the symbol's source. Most of these elements have been known for hundreds of years and date back to the time when Latin was the language of scientists. Elements whose chemical symbols are derived from non-English names are marked with an asterisk in Table 1-1.

EXAMPLE 1-5

Writing Correct Names for Elements

Each of the following names for elements is misspelled. What is the correct spelling for each element?

a. zink   **b.** sulfer   **c.** clorine   **d.** phosphorous

Solution

The correct spellings for these elements can be found in Table 1-1.

a. Zinc is spelled with a *c* rather than a *k*.
b. Sulfur ends in -ur rather than -er.
c. Chlorine has an *h* in it.
d. Phosphorous ends in -us rather than -ous.

EXAMPLE 1-6

Writing Correct Chemical Symbols for Elements

What is wrong with each of the following attempts to write correct chemical symbols for elements.

a. CU for copper   **b.** si for silicon   **c.** Ca for carbon   **d.** H e for helium

Solution

The correct symbols for these elements can be found in Table 1-1. Three of the four symbols are wrong because they violate chemical symbol "punctuation rules."

a. The second letter in a chemical symbol is never capitalized; Cu
b. The first letter in a chemical symbol is always capitalized; Si
c. The chemical symbol for carbon is a one-letter symbol; C
d. In two-letter chemical symbols there is never a space between the two letters; He

Section 1-8 Quick Quiz

1. The correct chemical symbol for the element beryllium, which contains the first two letters of the elements name, is
   a. be
   b. Be
   c. BE
   d. no correct response
2. The elements oxygen, hydrogen, carbon, and nitrogen have the chemical symbols
   a. O, H, Ca, Ni
   b. Ox, H, C, Ni
   c. O, H, C, N
   d. no correct response
   It is assumed that Table 1-1 is available for answering the following two questions.

(continued)

3. In which of the following listings of elements do each of the elements have a two-letter chemical symbol?
a. tin, sulfur, zinc
b. potassium, fluorine, phosphorus
c. lead, aluminum, iodine
d. no correct response

4. In which of the following listing of elements do each of the elements have a chemical symbol which starts with a letter different from the first letter of the element's English name?
a. silver, gold, mercury
b. copper, helium, neon
c. silicon, barium, sodium
d. no correct answer

Answers: 1. b; 2. c; 3. d; 4. a

1-9 ▍ Atoms and Molecules

LEARNING FOCUS

Distinguish between the terms *atom* and *molecule* and be familiar with the molecular classifications *diatomic*, *triatomic*, and so forth and *heteroatomic* and *homoatomic*.

Figure 1-11 254 million atoms arranged in a straight line would extend a distance of approximately 1 inch.

Consider the process of subdividing a sample of the element gold (or any other element) into smaller and smaller pieces. It seems reasonable that eventually a "smallest possible piece" of gold would be reached that could not be divided further and still be the element gold. This smallest possible unit of gold is called a gold atom. An **atom** *is the smallest particle of an element that can exist and still have the properties of the element.*

A sample of any element is composed of atoms of a single type, those of that element. In contrast, a compound must have two or more types of atoms present, because by definition at least two elements must be present (Section 1-6).

No one has ever seen or ever will see an atom with the naked eye; atoms are simply too small for such observation. However, sophisticated electron microscopes, with magnification factors in the millions, have made it possible to photograph "images" of individual atoms.

Atoms are incredibly small particles. Atomic dimensions, although not directly measurable, can be calculated from measurements made on large-size samples of elements. The diameter of an atom is approximately four-billionths of an inch. If atoms of such diameter were arranged in a straight line, it would take 254 million of them to extend a distance of 1 inch (Figure 1-11).

Free atoms are rarely encountered in nature. Instead, under normal conditions of temperature and pressure, atoms are almost always found together in aggregates or clusters ranging in size from two atoms to numbers too large to count. When the group or cluster of atoms is relatively small and bound together tightly, the resulting entity is called a molecule. ◀ A **molecule** *is a group of two or more atoms that functions as a unit because the atoms are tightly bound together.* This resultant "package" of atoms behaves in many ways as a single, distinct particle would. ◀

A **diatomic molecule** *is a molecule that contains two atoms.* It is the simplest type of molecule that can exist. Next in complexity are triatomic molecules. A **triatomic molecule** *is a molecule that contains three atoms.* Continuing on numerically, we have *tetraatomic* molecules, *pentatomic* molecules, and so on.

The atoms present in a molecule may all be of the same kind, or two or more kinds may be present. On the basis of this observation, molecules are classified into two categories: *homoatomic* and *heteroatomic*. A **homoatomic molecule** *is a molecule in which all atoms present are of the same kind.* A substance containing homoatomic

▶ *The Latin word* mole *means "a mass." The word* molecule *denotes "a little mass."*

▶ *Reasons for the tendency of atoms to assemble into molecules and information on the binding forces involved are considered in Chapter 4.*

CHLORINE MOLECULE

b **PHOSPHORUS MOLECULE**

c **SULFUR MOLECULE**

Figure 1-12 Molecular structure of (a) chlorine molecule, (b) phosphorus molecule, and (c) sulfur molecule.

molecules must be an element. The fact that homoatomic molecules exist indicates that *individual* atoms are not always the preferred structural unit for an element. The gaseous elements hydrogen, oxygen, nitrogen, and chlorine exist in the form of diatomic molecules. There are four atoms present in a gaseous phosphorus molecule and eight atoms present in a gaseous sulfur molecule (Figure 1-12).

A **heteroatomic molecule** *is a molecule in which two or more kinds of atoms are present.* Substances that contain heteroatomic molecules must be compounds because the presence of two or more kinds of atoms reflects the presence of two or more kinds of elements. The number of atoms present in the heteroatomic molecules associated with compounds varies over a wide range. A water molecule contains 3 atoms: 2 hydrogen atoms and 1 oxygen atom. A sucrose (table sugar) molecule is much larger: 45 atoms are present, of which 12 are carbon atoms, 22 are hydrogen atoms, and 11 are oxygen atoms. Figure 1-13 shows general models for four simple types of heteroatomic molecules. Comparison of parts (c) and (d) of this figure shows that molecules with the same number of atoms need not have the same arrangement of atoms. ◄

A molecule is the smallest particle of a compound capable of a stable independent existence. Continued subdivision of a quantity of table sugar to yield smaller and smaller amounts would ultimately lead to the isolation of one single "unit" of table sugar: a molecule of table sugar. This table sugar molecule can not be broken down any further and still exhibit the physical and chemical properties of table sugar. The table sugar molecule could be broken down further by chemical (not physical) means to produce atoms, but if that occurred, we would no longer have table sugar. The *molecule* is the limit of *physical* subdivision. The *atom* is the limit of *chemical* subdivision.

► *The concept that heteroatomic molecules are the building blocks for* all *compounds will have to be modified when certain solids, called ionic solids, are considered in Section 4-8.*

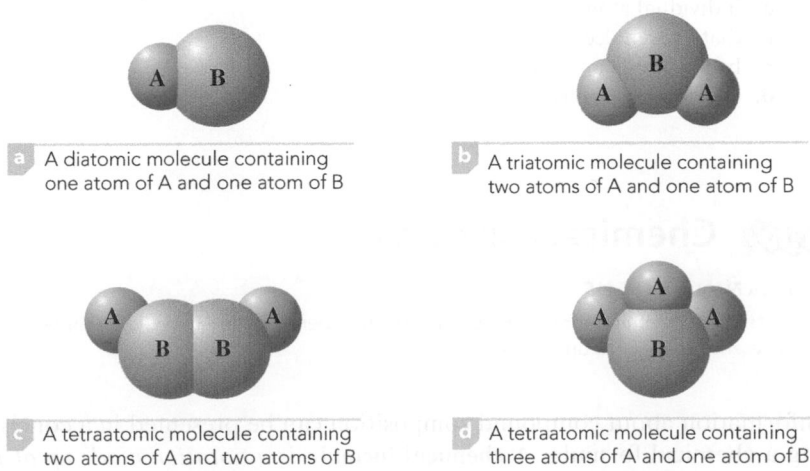

a A diatomic molecule containing one atom of A and one atom of B

b A triatomic molecule containing two atoms of A and one atom of B

c A tetraatomic molecule containing two atoms of A and two atoms of B

d A tetraatomic molecule containing three atoms of A and one atom of B

Figure 1-13 Depictions of various simple heteroatomic molecules using models. Spheres of different sizes and colors represent different kinds of atoms.

EXAMPLE 1-7

Classifying Substances as Elements or Compounds Based on Molecular Makeup

Assign each of the following molecular descriptions for a pure substance to the categories (1) must be an element, (2) must be a compound, or (3) could be an element or a compound.

a. molecules are all diatomic
b. molecules are all heteroatomic
c. molecules contain two kinds of atoms
d. molecules are all identical

Solution

a. Could be an element or compound; diatomic homoatomic molecules are possible for an element and diatomic heteroatomic molecules are possible for a compound.
b. Must be a compound; heteroatomic molecules are present only in compounds; elements have homoatomic molecules.
c. Must be a compound; elements have homoatomic molecules (one kind of atom) and compounds have heteroatomic molecules (two or more kinds of atoms).
d. Could be an element or compound; both elements and compounds are pure substances and pure substances contain only one kind of molecule. If two kinds of molecules were present, it would be a mixture rather than a pure substance.

Section 1-9 Quick Quiz

1. Which of the following characterizations is <u>not</u> compatible with the term *triatomic molecule*?
   a. all atoms can be different
   b. all atoms can be the same
   c. two kinds of atoms must be present
   d. no correct response
2. Which of the following types of molecules is an impossibility?
   a. triatomic molecule containing three elements
   b. heteroatomic molecule containing four elements
   c. homoatomic molecule containing two elements
   d. no correct response
3. The molecules present in a compound must be
   a. heteroatomic
   b. triatomic
   c. diatomic
   d. no correct response
4. Which of the following structural terms is <u>not</u> compatible with the matter classification *element*?
   a. individual atoms
   b. diatomic molecules
   c. homoatomic molecules
   d. no correct response

Answers: 1. c; 2. c; 3. a; 4. d

1-10 ## Chemical Formulas

LEARNING FOCUS
Interpret a chemical formula in terms of the number of elements and the number of atoms present in a formula unit of a substance.

Information about compound composition can be presented in a concise way by using a chemical formula. A **chemical formula** *is a notation made up of the chemical symbols of the elements present in a compound and numerical subscripts (located to the* *right of each chemical symbol) that indicate the number of atoms of each element present in a molecule of the compound.*

The chemical formula for the compound aspirin is $C_9H_8O_4$. This chemical formula conveys the information that an aspirin molecule contains three different elements—carbon (C), hydrogen (H), and oxygen (O)—and 21 atoms—9 carbon atoms, 8 hydrogen atoms, and 4 oxygen atoms.

When only one atom of a particular element is present in a molecule of a compound, that element's symbol is written without a numerical subscript in the formula for the compound. The formula for rubbing alcohol, C_3H_8O, reflects this practice for the element oxygen.

In order to write formulas correctly, one must follow the capitalization rules for elemental symbols (Section 1-8). Making the error of capitalizing the second letter of an element's symbol can dramatically alter the meaning of a chemical formula. The formulas $CoCl_2$ and $COCl_2$ illustrate this point; the symbol Co stands for the element cobalt, whereas CO stands for one atom of carbon and one atom of oxygen.

Sometimes chemical formulas contain parentheses; an example is $Al_2(SO_4)_3$. The interpretation of this formula is straightforward; in a formula unit, 2 aluminum (Al) atoms and 3 SO_4 groups are present. The subscript following the parentheses always indicates the number of units in the formula of the polyatomic entity inside the parentheses. In terms of atoms, the formula $Al_2(SO_4)_3$ denotes 2 aluminum (Al) atoms, $3 \times 1 = 3$ sulfur (S) atoms, and $3 \times 4 = 12$ oxygen (O) atoms. Example 1-9 contains further comments about chemical formulas that contain parentheses. ◄

▶ *Further information about the use of parentheses in chemical formulas (when and why) will be presented in Section 4-11. The important concern now is being able to interpret chemical formulas that contain parentheses in terms of total atoms present.*

EXAMPLE 1-8

Distinguishing Between Chemical Symbols and Chemical Formulas

Indicate whether each of the following notations is the chemical symbol for an element or a chemical formula for a compound.

a. CO **b.** Co **c.** O_3 **d.** SO_3

Solution

a. Chemical formula for a compound: The presence of two capital letters in this notation indicated that two elements are present—C (carbon) and O (oxygen). Compounds contain two or more elements.

b. Chemical symbol for an element: Only one capital letter is present, meaning the notation is a two-letter symbol for an element. The element cobalt has the chemical symbol Co.

c. Chemical symbol for an element: Again, only one capital letter is present, meaning the notation is that for an element, the element oxygen. The subscript 3 conveys the information that the oxygen atoms present are in the form of triatomic molecules.

d. Chemical formula for a compound: Sulfur (S) and oxygen (O) are present and molecules of this compound are tetraatomic, containing one S atom and three O atoms.

EXAMPLE 1-9

Interpreting Chemical Formulas in Terms of Atoms and Elements Present

For each of the following chemical formulas, determine how many atoms of each element are present in one molecule of the compound.

a. HCN—hydrogen cyanide, a poisonous gas
b. $C_{18}H_{21}NO_3$—codeine, a pain-killing drug
c. $Ca_{10}(PO_4)_6(OH)_2$—hydroxyapatite, present in tooth enamel

(continued)

Solution

a. One atom each of the elements hydrogen, carbon, and nitrogen is present. Remember that the subscript 1 is implied when no subscript is written.

b. This formula indicates that 18 carbon atoms, 21 hydrogen atoms, 1 nitrogen atom, and 3 oxygen atoms are present in one molecule of the compound.

c. There are 10 calcium atoms. The amounts of phosphorus, hydrogen, and oxygen are affected by the subscripts outside the parentheses. There are 6 phosphorus atoms and 2 hydrogen atoms present. Oxygen atoms are present in two locations in the formula. There are a total of 26 oxygen atoms: 24 from the PO_4 subunits (6×4) and 2 from the OH subunits (2×1).

Section 1-10 Quick Quiz

1. For which of the following chemical formulas are there seven atoms present per molecule?
   a. H_2SO_4
   b. NaSCN
   c. $AgCO_3$
   d. no correct response

2. Which of the following chemical formulas fits the description "number of elements present and number of atoms present are the same?"
   a. $HClO_2$
   b. $C_2H_2Cl_2$
   c. H_2O_2
   d. no correct response

3. Which of the following pairings of chemical formulas and "molecular descriptions" is *incorrect*?
   a. HCN and triatomic
   b. SO_2 and heteroatomic
   c. CO_2 and diatomic
   d. no correct response

4. What is the numerical value for the subscript x in the chemical formula H_xPO_4 given that molecules of the compound contain 8 atoms?
   a. one
   b. two
   c. three
   d. no correct response

5. Consider the chemical formulas $CoCl_2$ and $COCl_2$. It is true that they
   a. contain the same number of elements
   b. are identical in meaning
   c. contain different numbers of atoms
   d. no correct response

6. The total number of atoms present in a formula unit of $Al_2(SO_4)_3$ is
   a. 15
   b. 16
   c. 17
   d. no correct response

Answers: 1. a; 2. d; 3. c; 4. c; 5. c; 6. c

Concepts to Remember

Chemistry. Chemistry is the field of study that is concerned with the characteristics, composition, and transformations of matter (Section 1-1).

Matter. Matter, the substances of the physical universe, is anything that has mass and occupies space. Matter exists in three physical states: solid, liquid, and gas (Section 1-2).

Properties of matter. Properties, the distinguishing characteristics of a substance that are used in its identification and description, are of two types: physical and chemical. Physical properties are properties that can be observed without changing a substance into another substance. Chemical properties are properties that matter exhibits as it undergoes or resists changes in chemical composition. The failure of a substance to undergo change in the presence of another substance is considered a chemical property (Section 1-3).

Changes in matter. Changes that can occur in matter are classified into two types: physical and chemical. A physical change is a process that does not alter the basic nature (chemical composition) of the substance under consideration. No new substances are ever formed as a result of a physical change. A chemical change is a process that involves a change in the basic nature (chemical composition) of the substance. Such changes always involve conversion of the material or materials under consideration into one or more new substances that have properties and a composition distinctly different from those of the original materials (Section 1-4).

Pure substances and mixtures. All specimens of matter are either pure substances or mixtures. A pure substance is a form of matter that has a definite and constant composition. A mixture is a physical combination of two or more pure substances in which the pure substances retain their identity (Section 1-5).

Types of mixtures. Mixtures can be classified as heterogeneous or homogeneous on the basis of the visual recognition of the components present. A heterogeneous mixture contains visibly different parts or phases, each of which has different properties. A homogeneous mixture contains only one phase, which has uniform properties throughout (Section 1-5).

Types of pure substances. A pure substance can be classified as either an element or a compound on the basis of whether it can be broken down into two or more simpler substances by chemical means. Elements cannot be broken down into simpler substances. Compounds yield two or more simpler substances when broken down. There are 118 pure substances that qualify as elements. There are millions of compounds (Section 1-6).

Chemical symbols. Chemical symbols are a shorthand notation for the names of the elements. Most consist of two letters; a few involve a single letter. The first letter of a chemical symbol is always capitalized, and the second letter is always lowercase (Section 1-8).

Atoms and molecules. An atom is the smallest particle of an element that can exist and still have the properties of the element. Free isolated atoms are rarely encountered in nature. Instead, atoms are almost always found together in aggregates or clusters. A molecule is a group of two or more atoms that functions as a unit because the atoms are tightly bound together (Section 1-9).

Types of molecules. Molecules are of two types: homoatomic and heteroatomic. Homoatomic molecules are molecules in which all atoms present are of the same kind. A pure substance containing homoatomic molecules is an element. Heteroatomic molecules are molecules in which two or more different kinds of atoms are present. Pure substances that contain heteroatomic molecules must be compounds (Section 1-9).

Chemical formulas. Chemical formulas are used to specify compound composition in a concise manner. They consist of the symbols of the elements present in the compound and numerical subscripts (located to the right of each symbol) that indicate the number of atoms of each element present in a molecule of the compound (Section 1-10).

Exercises and Problems

Exercises and problems are arranged in matched pairs with the two members of a pair addressing the same concept(s). The answer to the odd-numbered member of a pair is given at the back of the book. Problems denoted with a ▲ involve concepts found not only in the section under consideration but also concepts found in one or more earlier sections of the chapter.

Chemistry: The Study of Matter (Section 1-1)

1-1 What are the two general characteristics that all types of matter possess?

1-2 What are the three aspects of matter that are of particular interest to chemists?

1-3 Classify each of the following as matter or energy (nonmatter).
- a. Air
- b. Pizza
- c. Sound
- d. Gold

1-4 Classify each of the following as matter or energy (nonmatter).
- a. Silver
- b. Cake
- c. Heat
- d. Water

Physical States of Matter (Section 1-2)

1-5 What physical characteristic distinguishes
- a. liquids from solids
- b. gases from liquids

1-6 What physical characteristic is the same for
- a. liquids and solids
- b. gases and liquids

1-7 Indicate whether each of the following substances does or does not take the shape of its container and also whether it has a definite volume.
- a. Copper wire
- b. Oxygen gas
- c. Granulated sugar
- d. Liquid water

1-8 Indicate whether each of the following substances does or does not take the shape of its container and also whether it has an indefinite volume.
- a. Aluminum powder
- b. Carbon dioxide gas
- c. Clean air
- d. Gasoline

Properties of Matter (Section 1-3)

1-9 Classify each of the following properties of the metal magnesium as a physical property or a chemical property.
- a. Solid at room temperature
- b. Ignites upon heating in air
- c. Hydrogen gas is produced when it is dissolved in acids
- d. Has a density of 1.738 g/cm^3 at 20°C

1-10 Classify each of the following properties of the metal magnesium as a physical property or a chemical property.
- a. Silvery-white in color
- b. Does not react with cold water
- c. Melts at 651°C
- d. Finely divided form burns in oxygen with a dazzling white flame

1-11 Indicate whether each of the following statements describes a physical or a chemical property.
a. Silver salts discolor the skin by reacting with skin protein.
b. Hemoglobin molecules have a red color.
c. Beryllium metal vapor is extremely toxic to humans.
d. Aspirin tablets can be pulverized with a hammer.

1-12 Indicate whether each of the following statements describes a physical or a chemical property.
a. Diamonds are very hard substances.
b. Gold metal does not react with nitric acid.
c. Lithium metal is light enough to float on water.
d. Mercury is a liquid at room temperature.

1-13 Classify each of the following observations about the behavior of a substance as a physical property or chemical property of the substance.
a. does not react with oxygen at 50°C
b. reacts explosively with oxygen at 425°C
c. does not melt when heated to 100°C
d. melts at temperatures that exceed 250°C

1-14 Classify each of the following observations about the behavior of a substance as a physical property or chemical property of the substance.
a. does not tarnish when exposed to dry air at 25°C
b. does tarnish when exposed to moist air at 25°C
c. is a liquid at 75°C
d. is a solid at 15°C

Changes in Matter (Section 1-4)

1-15 Classify each of the following changes as physical or chemical.
a. Crushing a dry leaf
b. Hammering a metal into a thin sheet
c. Burning your chemistry textbook
d. Slicing a ham

1-16 Classify each of the following changes as physical or chemical.
a. Evaporation of water from a lake
b. "Scabbing over" of a skin cut
c. Cutting a string into two pieces
d. Melting of some candle wax

1-17 Classify each of the following changes as physical or chemical.
a. A newspaper is shredded.
b. Molten candle wax solidifies in a mold.
c. A container of unrefrigerated milk sours.
d. Fingernails are trimmed.

1-18 Classify each of the following changes as physical or chemical.
a. A newspaper page turns yellow over time.
b. A rubber band breaks.
c. A firecracker explodes.
d. Dry ice "disappears" over time.

1-19 Correctly complete each of the following sentences by placing the word *chemical* or *physical* in the blank.
a. The freezing over of a pond's surface is a _____ process.
b. The crushing of ice to make ice chips is a _____ procedure.

c. The destruction of a newspaper by burning it is a _____ process.
d. Pulverizing a hard sugar cube using a mallet is a _____ procedure.

1-20 Correctly complete each of the following sentences by placing the word *chemical* or *physical* in the blank.
a. Bending glass tubing using a hot flame is a _____ technique.
b. The grating of a piece of cheese is a _____ procedure.
c. The heating of a blue powdered material to produce a white glassy substance and a gas is a _____ process.
d. Wool is spun into yarn using _____ means.

▲1-21 Classify each of the following as (1) a physical property, (2) a physical change, (3) a chemical property, or (4) a chemical change.
a. the process of burning a piece of newspaper
b. the fact that metallic copper reacts with chlorine gas
c. the process of melting ice
d. the fact that metallic gold is a solid at room temperature

▲1-22 Classify each of the following as (1) a physical property, (2) a physical change, (3) a chemical property, or (4) a chemical change.
a. the process of decomposing hydrogen peroxide
b. the fact that a block of ice can be chipped into smaller pieces
c. the process of evaporating a liquid
d. the fact that water freezes at 32°F

Pure Substances and Mixtures (Section 1-5)

1-23 Classify each of the following statements as true or false.
a. All heterogeneous mixtures must contain three or more substances.
b. Pure substances cannot have a variable composition.
c. Substances maintain their identity in a heterogeneous mixture but not in a homogeneous mixture.
d. Pure substances are seldom encountered in the "everyday" world.

1-24 Classify each of the following statements as true or false.
a. All homogeneous mixtures must contain at least two substances.
b. Heterogeneous mixtures, but not homogeneous mixtures, can have a variable composition.
c. Pure substances cannot be separated into other kinds of matter by physical means.
d. The number of known pure substances is less than 100,000.

1-25 Assign each of the following descriptions of matter to one of the following categories: *heterogeneous mixture*, *homogeneous mixture*, or *pure substance*.
a. Two substances present, two phases present
b. Two substances present, one phase present
c. One substance present, two phases present
d. Three substances present, three phases present

1-26 Assign each of the following descriptions of matter to one of the following categories: *heterogeneous mixture*, *homogeneous mixture*, or *pure substance*.
a. Three substances present, one phase present
b. One substance present, three phases present

c. One substance present, one phase present

d. Two substances present, three phases present

1-27 Classify each of the following as a *heterogeneous mixture*, *homogeneous mixture*, or a *pure substance*. Also indicate how many phases are present, assuming all components are present in the same container.

a. Water and dissolved salt

b. Water and sand

c. Water, ice, and oil

d. Water, dissolved sugar, and undissolved sugar

1-28 Classify each of the following as a *heterogeneous mixture*, *homogeneous mixture*, or a *pure substance*. Also indicate how many phases are present, assuming all components are present in the same container.

a. Water and dissolved sugar

b. Water and oil

c. Water, wax, and pieces of copper metal

d. Water, dissolved salt, and dissolved sugar

Elements and Compounds (Section 1-6)

1-29 From the information given, classify each of the pure substances A through D as elements or compounds, or indicate that no such classification is possible because of insufficient information.

a. Analysis with an elaborate instrument indicates that substance A contains two elements.

b. Substance B decomposes upon heating.

c. Heating substance C to 1000°C causes no change in it.

d. Heating substance D to 500°C causes it to change from a solid to a liquid.

1-30 From the information given, classify each of the pure substances A through D as elements or compounds, or indicate that no such classification is possible because of insufficient information.

a. Substance A cannot be broken down into simpler substances by chemical means.

b. Substance B cannot be broken down into simpler substances by physical means.

c. Substance C readily dissolves in water.

d. Substance D readily reacts with the element chlorine.

1-31 From the information given in the following equations, classify each of the pure substances A through G as elements or compounds, or indicate that no such classification is possible because of insufficient information.

a. $A + B \rightarrow C$ b. $D \rightarrow E + F + G$

1-32 From the information given in the following equations, classify each of the pure substances A through G as elements or compounds, or indicate that no such classification is possible because of insufficient information.

a. $A \rightarrow B + C$ b. $D + E \rightarrow F + G$

1-33 Indicate whether each of the following statements is true or false.

a. Both elements and compounds are pure substances.

b. A compound results from the physical combination of two or more elements.

c. In order for matter to be heterogeneous, at least two compounds must be present.

d. Compounds, but not elements, can have a variable composition.

1-34 Indicate whether each of the following statements is true or false.

a. Compounds can be separated into their constituent elements by chemical means.

b. Elements can be separated into their constituent compounds by physical means.

c. A compound must contain at least two elements.

d. A compound is a physical mixture of different elements.

1-35 Consider two boxes with the following contents: the first contains 30 bolts and 30 nuts that fit the bolts; the second contains the same number of nuts and bolts with the difference that each bolt has the nut screwed on it. Which box has contents that would be an analogy for a mixture, and which box has contents that would be an analogy for a compound?

1-36 Consider two boxes with the following contents: the first box contains 10 blue paper clips and 10 red paper clips; the second contains the same number of each color of paper clip with the difference that each blue paper clip is interlocked with a red paper clip. Which box has contents that would be an analogy for a mixture, and which box has contents that would be an analogy for a compound?

▲**1-37** Assign each of the following descriptions of matter to one of the following categories: *element*, *compound*, or *mixture*.

a. One substance present, three elements present

b. Two substances present, one phase present

c. One substance present, one phase present, substance cannot be decomposed using chemical means

d. Two elements present, composition is variable

▲**1-38** Assign each of the following descriptions of matter to one of the following categories: *element*, *compound*, or *mixture*.

a. One substance present, two elements present

b. Two substances present, two phases present

c. One substance present, one phase present, substance can be decomposed using chemical means

d. Three elements present, composition is definite and constant

▲**1-39** Indicate whether each of the following samples of matter is a *heterogeneous mixture*, a *homogeneous mixture*, a *compound*, or an *element*.

a. a blue-colored, single-phase liquid that when boiled away (evaporated) leaves behind a solid residue

b. a "cloudy" liquid that separates into two layers upon standing overnight

c. a nonuniform, white crystalline substance, part of which dissolves in alcohol and part of which does not dissolve in alcohol

d. a colorless gas that cannot be separated into simpler substances using physical means and that reacts with the metal magnesium to produce both a magnesium–oxygen compound and a magnesium–nitrogen compound

▲**1-40** Indicate whether each of the following samples of matter is a *heterogeneous mixture*, a *homogeneous mixture*, a *compound*, or an *element*.

a. a colorless gas, only part of which reacts with hot iron

b. a uniform red liquid with a boiling point of 60°C that cannot be broken down into simpler substances using chemical means

c. a yellow solid, all of which melts at a temperature of 45°C to produce a liquid that decomposes upon further heating

d. a single-phase liquid that completely evaporates without decomposition when heated to produce a gas that can be separated into simpler components using physical means

▲1-41 Indicate whether each of the following characterizations of the elements copper and sulfur is true or false.
a. A mixture containing copper and sulfur can have a variable composition.
b. In a mixture of copper and sulfur, the two elements maintain their individual properties.
c. In a compound containing copper and sulfur, physical methods can be used to separate the substances present.
d. In a compound containing copper and sulfur, the two elements are chemically combined rather than physically combined.

▲1-42 Indicate whether each of the following characterizations of the elements copper and sulfur is true or false.
a. A compound containing copper and sulfur can have a variable composition.
b. In a compound of copper and sulfur, the two elements maintain their individual properties.
c. In a mixture containing copper and sulfur, physical methods can be used to separate the substances present.
d. In a mixture containing copper and sulfur, the two elements are chemically combined rather than physically combined.

Discovery and Abundance of the Elements (Section 1-7)

1-43 Indicate whether each of the following statements about elements is true or false.
a. Elements that do not occur in nature have been produced in a laboratory setting.
b. At present, 108 elements are known.
c. Current chemical theory suggests there are more naturally occurring elements yet to be discovered.
d. More laboratory-produced elements exist than naturally occurring elements.

1-44 Indicate whether each of the following statements about elements is true or false.
a. The majority of the known elements have been discovered since 1990.
b. New naturally occurring elements have been identified within the past 10 years.
c. More than 25 laboratory-produced elements are known.
d. All laboratory-produced elements are unstable.

1-45 Indicate whether each of the following statements about elemental abundances is true or false.
a. Silicon is the second-most abundant element in Earth's crust.
b. Hydrogen is the most abundant element in the universe but not in Earth's crust.
c. Oxygen and hydrogen are the two most abundant elements in the universe.
d. One element accounts for more than one-half of the atoms in Earth's crust.

1-46 Indicate whether each of the following statements about elemental abundances is true or false.
a. Hydrogen is the most abundant element in both Earth's crust and the universe.
b. Oxygen and silicon are the two most abundant elements in the universe.
c. Helium is the second-most abundant element in Earth's crust.
d. Two elements account for more than three-fourths of the atoms in Earth's crust.

1-47 With the help of Figure 1-10, indicate whether the first listed element in each of the given pairs of elements is more abundant or less abundant in Earth's crust, in terms of atom percent, than the second listed element.
a. Silicon and aluminum
b. Calcium and hydrogen
c. Iron and oxygen
d. Sodium and potassium

1-48 With the help of Figure 1-10, indicate whether the first listed element in each of the given pairs of elements is more abundant or less abundant in Earth's crust, in terms of atom percent, than the second listed element.
a. Oxygen and hydrogen
b. Iron and aluminum
c. Calcium and magnesium
d. Copper and sodium

Names and Chemical Symbols of the Elements (Section 1-8)

1-49 Give the name of the element denoted by each of the following chemical symbols.
a. N   b. Ni   c. Pb   d. Sn

1-50 Give the name of the element denoted by each of the following chemical symbols.
a. Li   b. He   c. F   d. Zn

1-51 Give the chemical symbol for each of the following elements.
a. Aluminum   b. Neon
c. Hydrogen   d. Uranium

1-52 Give the chemical symbol for each of the following elements.
a. Mercury   b. Chlorine
c. Gold   d. Beryllium

1-53 Write the chemical symbol for each member of the following pairs of elements.
a. Sodium and sulfur
b. Magnesium and manganese
c. Calcium and cadmium
d. Arsenic and argon

1-54 Write the chemical symbol for each member of the following pairs of elements.
a. Copper and cobalt
b. Potassium and phosphorus
c. Iron and iodine
d. Silicon and silver

1-55 In which of the following sequences of elements do all the elements have two-letter symbols?
a. Magnesium, nitrogen, phosphorus
b. Bromine, iron, calcium

c. Aluminum, copper, chlorine

d. Boron, barium, beryllium

1-56 In which of the following sequences of elements do all the elements have symbols that start with a letter that is *not* the first letter of the element's English name?

a. Silver, gold, mercury

b. Copper, helium, neon

c. Cobalt, chromium, sodium

d. Potassium, iron, lead

Atoms and Molecules (Section 1-9)

1-57 Classify the substances represented by the following models as *homoatomic* or *heteroatomic* molecules.

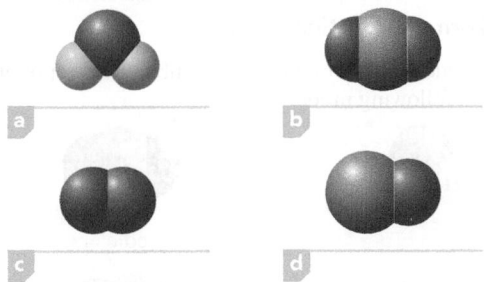

1-58 Classify the substances represented by the following models as *homoatomic* or *heteroatomic* molecules.

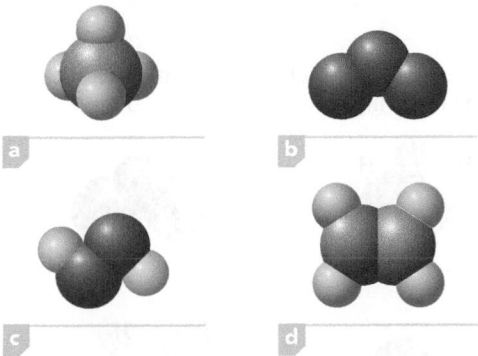

1-59 Classify the substances represented by the models in Problem 1-57 as to the number of atoms present per molecule, that is, as *diatomic, triatomic, tetraatomic*, etc.

1-60 Classify the substances represented by the models in Problem 1-58 as to the number of atoms present per molecule, that is, as *diatomic, triatomic, tetraatomic*, etc.

1-61 Classify the substances represented by the models in Problem 1-57 as to the type of pure substance, that is, as *element* or *compound*.

1-62 Classify the substances represented by the models in Problem 1-58 as to the type of pure substance, that is, as *element* or *compound*.

1-63 Assign each of the following molecular descriptions for a *pure substance* to the categories (1) must be an element, (2) must be a compound, or (3) could be an element or a compound.

a. Molecules are triatomic.

b. Molecules contain only one kind of atom.

c. Molecules are heteroatomic.

d. Molecules are both homoatomic and diatomic.

1-64 Assign each of the following molecular descriptions for a *pure substance* to the categories (1) must be an element, (2) must be a compound, or (3) could be an element or a compound.

a. Molecules contain three kinds of atoms.

b. Molecules are homoatomic.

c. Molecules are tetraatomic.

d. Molecules are both heteroatomic and triatomic.

1-65 Indicate whether each of the following statements is true or false. If a statement is false, change it to make it true. (Such a rewriting should involve more than merely converting the statement to the negative of itself.)

a. The atom is the limit of chemical subdivision for both elements and compounds.

b. Triatomic molecules must contain at least two kinds of atoms.

c. A molecule of a compound must be heteroatomic.

d. Only heteroatomic molecules may contain three or more atoms.

1-66 Indicate whether each of the following statements is true or false. If a statement is false, change it to make it true. (Such a rewriting should involve more than merely converting the statement to the negative of itself.)

a. A molecule of an element may be homoatomic or heteroatomic, depending on which element is involved.

b. The limit of chemical subdivision for a compound is a molecule.

c. Heteroatomic molecules do not maintain the properties of their constituent elements.

d. Only one kind of atom may be present in a homoatomic molecule.

▲**1-67** In the following diagrams, the different colored spheres represent atoms of different elements.

I II III IV

Select the diagram or diagrams that represent each of the listed situations. (Note that there may be more than one correct answer for a given situation and that answers may be used more than once or not at all.)

a. Which diagram(s) represent(s) a compound whose molecules are triatomic?

b. Which diagram(s) represent(s) a mixture of two compounds?

c. Which diagram(s) represent(s) a mixture that contains two different types of diatomic molecules?

d. Which diagram(s) represent(s) a pure substance?

▲1-68 In the following diagrams, different colored spheres represent atoms of different elements.

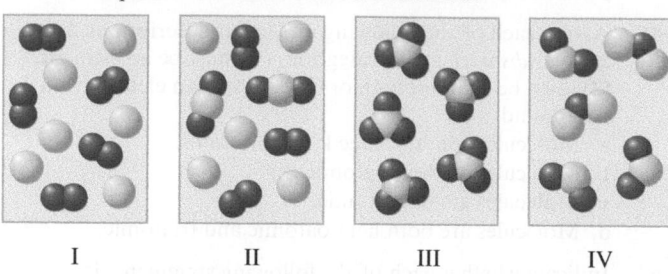

I   II   III   IV

Select the diagram or diagrams that represent each of the listed situations. (Note that there may be more than one correct answer for a given situation and that answers may be used more than once or not at all.)

a. Which diagram(s) represent(s) a compound whose molecules are tetraatomic?
b. Which diagram(s) represent(s) a mixture of two substances?
c. Which diagram(s) represent(s) a mixture of two elements?
d. Which diagram(s) represent(s) a pure substance?

▲1-69 Assign each of the following descriptions of matter to one of the following categories: *element, compound,* or *mixture.*

a. one substance present, one phase present, one kind of homoatomic molecule present
b. two substances present, two phases present, all molecules present are heteroatomic
c. one phase present, two kinds of homoatomic molecules are present
d. triatomic, homoatomic, and diatomic heteroatomic molecules are present

▲1-70 Assign each of the following descriptions of matter to one of the following categories: *element, compound,* or *mixture*

a. two substances present, one phase present, all molecules present are heteroatomic
b. one substance present, two phases present, one kind of heteroatomic molecule present
c. one phase present; all molecules are triatomic, heteroatomic, and identical
d. diatomic, homoatomic, and triatomic heteroatomic molecules are present

▲1-71 In the following diagram, the different colored spheres represent atoms of different elements. Four changes, denoted by the four numbered arrows, are shown.

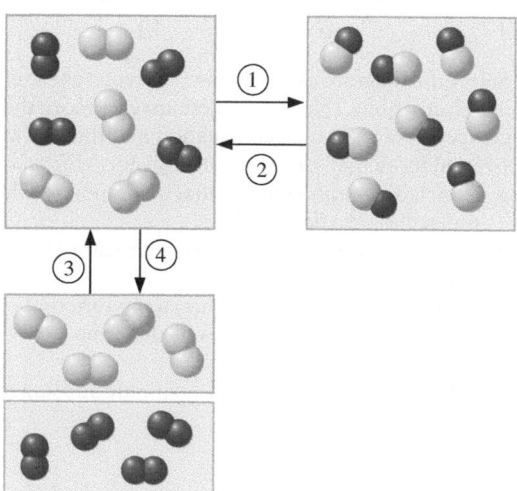

Select the change, by listing the arrow number, that represents each of the listed situations. (Note that there may be more than one correct answer for a given situation and that answers may be used more than once or not at all.)

a. Which change(s) is a (are) physical change(s)?
b. Which change(s) is a (are) change(s) in which two elements combine to form a compound?

▲1-72 Using the diagrams given in Problem 1-71, select the change, by listing the arrow number, that represents each of the following situations.

a. Which change(s) is a (are) chemical change(s)?
b. Which change(s) is a (are) change(s) in which a compound is decomposed into its constituent elements?

Chemical Formulas (Section 1-10)

1-73 Write chemical formulas for the substances represented by the following models.

1-74 Write chemical formulas for the substances represented by the following models.

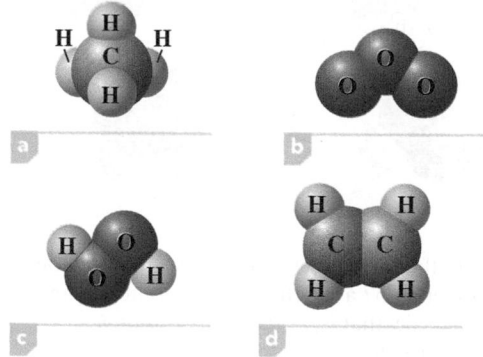

1-75 Indicate whether each of the following chemical notations is the chemical symbol for an element or a chemical formula for a compound and also indicate how many atoms are present in one formula unit of the substance.

a. Li_2CO_3 b. $LiClO_3$
c. No   d. NO

1-76 Indicate whether each of the following chemical notations is the chemical symbol for an element or a chemical formula for a compound and also indicate how many atoms are present in one formula unit of the substance.

a. Hf   b. HF
c. $CoCl_2$ d. $COCl_2$

1-77 Write chemical formulas for compounds in which the following numbers of atoms are present in a molecule of the compound.

a. Table sugar: 12 C atoms, 22 H atoms, and 11 O atoms
b. Caffeine: 8 C atoms, 10 H atoms, 4 O atoms, and 2 N atoms

1-78 Write chemical formulas for compounds in which the following numbers of atoms are present in a molecule of the compound.
a. Vitamin C: 6 C atoms, 8 H atoms, and 6 O atoms
b. Nicotine: 10 C atoms, 14 H atoms, and 2 N atoms

1-79 Write all possible chemical formulas for a substance that are consistent with the description "contains the hypothetical elements X and Z and has molecules that are pentatomic."

1-80 Write all possible chemical formulas for a substance that are consistent with the description "contains the hypothetical elements A and Z and has molecules that are hexatomic."

▲**1-81** Write a chemical formula for each of the following substances based on the information given about a molecule of the substance.
a. A molecule of hydrogen cyanide is triatomic and contains the elements hydrogen, carbon, and nitrogen.
b. A molecule of sulfuric acid is heptaatomic and contains two atoms of hydrogen, one atom of sulfur, and the element oxygen.

▲**1-82** Write a chemical formula for each of the following substances based on the information given about a molecule of the substance.
a. A molecule of nitrous oxide contains twice as many atoms of nitrogen as of oxygen and is triatomic.
b. A molecule of nitric acid is pentaatomic and contains three atoms of oxygen and the elements hydrogen and nitrogen.

▲**1-83** In each of the following pairs of chemical formulas, indicate whether the first chemical formula listed denotes *more total atoms, the same number of total atoms,* or *fewer total atoms* than the second chemical formula listed.
a. HN_3 and NH_3
b. $CaSO_4$ and $Mg(OH)_2$
c. $NaClO_3$ and $Be(CN)_2$
d. $Be_3(PO_4)_2$ and $Mg(C_2H_3O_2)_2$

▲**1-84** In each of the following pairs of chemical formulas, indicate whether the first listed chemical formula denotes *more total atoms, the same number of total atoms,* or *fewer total atoms* than the second listed chemical formula.
a. NO_2 and N_2O
b. $Cu(SO_4)_2$ and $CuSO_4$
c. $KSCN$ and $NaBrO_2$
d. $Al(C_2H_3O_2)_3$ and $Ba(H_2PO_4)_2$

▲**1-85** On the basis of the given information, determine the numerical value of the subscript x in each of the following chemical formulas.
a. BaS_2O_x; formula unit contains 6 atoms
b. $Al_2(SO_x)_3$; formula unit contains 17 atoms
c. SO_xCl_2; formula unit contains 5 atoms
d. $C_xH_{2x}Cl_x$; formula unit contains 8 atoms

▲**1-86** On the basis of the information given, determine the numerical value of the subscript x in each of the following chemical formulas.
a. $NaNO_x$; formula unit contains 5 atoms
b. $Ba(CO_x)_2$; formula unit contains 9 atoms
c. $C_xH_5Cl_x$; formula unit contains 11 atoms
d. $H_xS_xO_{4x}$; formula unit contains 12 atoms

▲**1-87** A mixture contains the following five pure substances: N_2, N_2H_4, NH_3, CH_4, and CH_3Cl.
a. How many different kinds of molecules that contain four or fewer atoms are present in the mixture?
b. How many different kinds of atoms are present in the mixture?
c. How many total atoms are present in a mixture sample containing five molecules of each component?
d. How many total hydrogen atoms are present in a mixture sample containing four molecules of each component?

▲**1-88** A mixture contains the following five pure substances: Cl_2, C_2Cl_6, H_2CO_3, H_2SO_4, and HCl.
a. How many different kinds of diatomic molecules are present in the mixture?
b. How many different kinds of atoms are present in the mixture?
c. How many total atoms are in a mixture sample containing four molecules of each component?
d. How many total carbon atoms are present in a mixture sample containing three molecules of each component?

Measurements in Chemistry

Measurements can never be exact; there is always some degree of uncertainty.

© iStockphoto.com/stevecoleimages

It would be extremely difficult for a carpenter to build cabinets without being able to use tools such as hammers, saws, drills, tape measures, rulers, straight edges, and T-squares. They are the tools of a carpenter's trade. Chemists also have "tools of the trade." The tool they use most is called *measurement*. Understanding measurement is indispensable in the study of chemistry. Questions such as "How much … ?," "How long … ?," and "How many … ?" simply cannot be answered without resorting to measurements. This chapter considers those concepts needed to deal properly with measurement. Much of the material in the chapter is mathematical. This is necessary; measurements require the use of numbers.

2-1 Measurement Systems

LEARNING FOCUS

Understand why scientists prefer to use metric system units rather than English system units when making measurements.

Measurements are made on a routine basis. For example, measurements are involved in following a recipe for making brownies, in determining our height and weight, and in fueling a car with gasoline. **Measurement** *is the determination of the dimensions, capacity, quantity, or extent of something.* In chemical laboratories, the most common types of measurements are those of mass, volume, length, time, temperature, pressure, and concentration.

Two systems of measurement are in use in the United States: (1) the English system of units and (2) the metric system of units. ◀ Common measurements of commerce, such as those used in a grocery store, are made in the *English system*. The units of this system include the inch, foot, pound, quart, and gallon. The *metric system* is used in scientific work. The units of this system include the gram, meter, and liter.

The United States is in the process of voluntary conversion to the metric system for measurements of commerce. Metric system units now appear on numerous consumer products. Soft drinks now come in 1-, 2-, and 3-liter containers. Road signs in some states display distances in both miles and kilometers (Figure 2-1). Canned and packaged goods such as cereals and mixes on grocery store shelves now have the masses of their contents listed in grams as well as in pounds and ounces.

The rate at which voluntary conversion is proceeding is "slow," with economic considerations being a major damping factor. The cost of "retooling" in most manufacturing industries is very high, almost prohibitive in many situations at present.

The preference that scientists have for metric system use is not related to measurement precision. Measurements made using the English system can be just as precise as those made in the metric system. The "superiority" of the metric system stems from the interrelationships between units of the same type (volume, length, etc.). Metric unit interrelationships are less complicated than English unit interrelationships because the metric system is a decimal unit system. In the metric system, conversion from one unit size to another can be accomplished simply by moving the decimal point to the right or left an appropriate number of places. Thus, the metric system is simply more convenient to use.

▶ *The word* metric *is derived from the Greek word* metron, *which means "measure."*

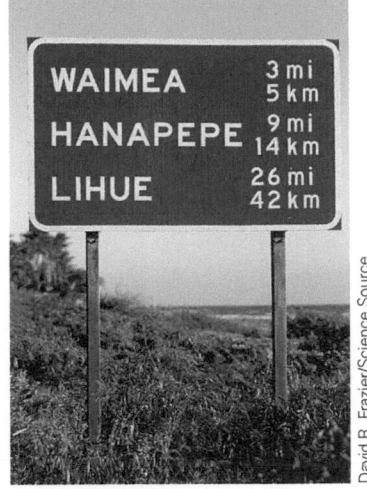

David R. Frazier/Science Source

Figure 2-1 Metric system units are becoming increasingly evident on highway signs.

Section 2-1 Quick Quiz

1. In the United States the switch from English system use to metric system use is
   a. proceeding rapidly
   b. proceeding slowly
   c. prohibited by law
   d. no correct response
2. Preference by scientists for metric system unit use is because
   a. more precise measurements result from their use
   b. metric unit interrelationships are mathematically simpler
   c. metric unit names are easier to spell
   d. no correct response

Answers: 1. b; 2. b

2-2 Metric System Units

LEARNING FOCUS

Recognize metric system units by name and abbreviation; know the numerical meaning associated with common metric system prefixes.

In the metric system, there is one base unit (unprefixed unit) for each type of measurement (length, mass, volume, etc.). The names of fractional parts of the base unit and multiples of the base unit are constructed by adding prefixes to the base unit. These prefixes indicate the size of the unit relative to the base unit. Table 2-1 lists common metric system prefixes, along with their symbols or abbreviations and mathematical meanings. The prefixes in red are the ones most frequently used.

▶ Table 2-1   **Common Metric System Prefixes with Their Symbols and Mathematical Meanings**

	Prefix*	Symbol	Mathematical Meaning†
Multiples	giga-	G	1,000,000,000 (10^9, billion)
	mega-	M	1,000,000 (10^6, million)
	kilo-	k	1000 (10^3, thousand)
Fractional Parts	deci-	d	0.1 (10^{-1}, one-tenth)
	centi-	c	0.01 (10^{-2}, one-hundredth)
	milli-	m	0.001 (10^{-3}, one-thousandth)
	micro-	μ (Greek mu)	0.000001 (10^{-6}, one-millionth)
	nano-	n	0.000000001 (10^{-9}, one-billionth)
	pico-	p	0.000000000001 (10^{-12}, one-trillionth)

*Other prefixes also are available but are less commonly used.
†The power-of-10 notation for denoting numbers is considered in Section 2-6.

The meaning of a metric system prefix is independent of the base unit it modifies and always remains constant. For example, the prefix *kilo-* always means 1000; a *kilo*second is 1000 seconds, a *kilo*watt is 1000 watts, and a *kilo*calorie is 1000 calories. Similarly, the prefix *nano-* always means one-billionth; a *nano*meter is one-billionth of a meter, a *nano*gram is one-billionth of a gram, and a *nano*liter is one-billionth of a liter. ◀

▶ *The modern version of the metric system is called the International System, or SI (the abbreviation is taken from the French name,* le Système International*).*

▶ *The use of numerical prefixes should not be new to you. Consider the use of the prefix* tri- *in the words* tri*angle,* tri*cycle,* tri*o, tri*nity, *and* tri*ple. Each of these words conveys the idea of three of something. The metric system prefixes are used in the same way.*

EXAMPLE 2-1

Recognizing the Mathematical Meanings of Metric System Prefixes

Using Table 2-1, write the name of the metric system prefix associated with the listed power of 10 or the power of 10 associated with the listed metric system prefix. ◀

a. nano-   **b.** micro-   **c.** deci-   **d.** 10^3 **e.** 10^6 **f.** 10^9

Solution

a. The prefix nano- denotes 10^{-9} (one-billionth).
b. The prefix micro- denotes 10^{-6} (one-millionth).
c. The prefix deci- denotes 10^{-1} (one-tenth).
d. 10^3 (one thousand) is denoted by the prefix *kilo-*.
e. 10^6 (one million) is denoted by the prefix *mega-*.
f. 10^9 (one billion) is denoted by the prefix *giga-*.

Metric Length Units

The **meter** (m) *is the base* (unprefixed) *unit of length in the metric system*. It is about the same size as the English yard; 1 meter equals 1.09 yards (Figure 2-2a). The prefixes listed in Table 2-1 enable us to derive other units of length from the meter. The kilometer (km) is 1000 times larger than the meter; the centimeter (cm) and millimeter (mm) are, respectively, one-hundredth and one-thousandth of a meter. Most laboratory length measurements are made in centimeters rather than meters because of the meter's relatively large size. ◀

Metric Mass Units

▶ Length *is measured by determining the distance between two points.*

The **gram** (g) *is the base* (unprefixed) *unit of mass in the metric system*. It is a very small unit compared with the English ounce and pound (Figure 2-2b). It takes approximately 28 grams to equal 1 ounce and nearly 454 grams to equal 1 pound. Both grams and milligrams (mg) are commonly used in the laboratory, where the kilogram (kg) is generally too large.

LENGTH	MASS	VOLUME
■ A meter is slightly larger than a yard.	■ A gram is a small unit compared to a pound.	■ A liter is slightly larger than a quart.
■ 1 meter = 1.09 yards.	■ 1 gram = 1/454 pound.	■ 1 liter = 1.06 quarts.
■ A baseball bat is about 1 meter long.	■ Two pennies, five paper-clips, and a marble have masses of about 5, 2, and 5 grams, respectively.	■ Most beverages are now sold by the liter rather than by the quart.
a	b	c

Figure 2-2 Comparisons of the base metric system units of length (meter), mass (gram), and volume (liter) with common objects.

(a) © tatnix/Shutterstock.com; (b) © Cengage Learning; (c) © Rachel Epstein/Photo Edit

The terms *mass* and *weight* are often used interchangeably in measurement discussions; technically, however, they have different meanings. ◄ **Mass** *is a measure of the total quantity of matter in an object.* **Weight** *is a measure of the force exerted on an object by gravitational forces.*

The mass of a substance is a constant; the weight of an object varies with the object's geographical location. For example, matter weighs less at the equator than it would at the North Pole because the pull of gravity is less at the equator. Because Earth is not a perfect sphere, but bulges at the equator, the magnitude of gravitational attraction is less at the equator. An object would weigh less on the moon than on Earth because of the smaller size of the moon and the correspondingly lower gravitational attraction. Quantitatively, a 22.0-lb mass weighing 22.0 lb at Earth's North Pole would weigh 21.9 lb at Earth's equator and only 3.7 lb on the moon. In outer space, an astronaut may be weightless but never massless. In fact, he or she has the same mass in space as on Earth.

► Mass *is measured by determining the amount of matter in an object.*

Metric Volume Units

The **liter** (L) *is the base* (unprefixed) *unit of volume in the metric system.* The abbreviation for liter is a capital L rather than a lowercase l because a lowercase l is easily confused with the number 1. A liter is a volume equal to that occupied by a cube that is 10 centimeters on each side. Because the volume of a cube is calculated by multiplying length times width times height (which are all the same for a cube), we have

$$1 \text{ liter} = \text{volume of a cube with 10 cm edges}$$
$$= 10 \text{ cm} \times 10 \text{ cm} \times 10 \text{ cm}$$
$$= 1000 \text{ cm}^3$$

A liter is also equal to 1000 milliliters; the prefix *milli-* means one-thousandth. Therefore,

$$1000 \text{ mL} = 1000 \text{ cm}^3$$

Dividing both sides of this equation by 1000 shows that

$$1 \text{ mL} = 1 \text{ cm}^3$$

Consequently, the units milliliter and cubic centimeter are the same. In practice, mL is used for volumes of liquids and gases, and cm^3 for volumes of solids. Figure 2-3 shows the relationship between 1 mL (1 cm^3) and its parent unit, the liter, in terms of cubic measurements. ◄

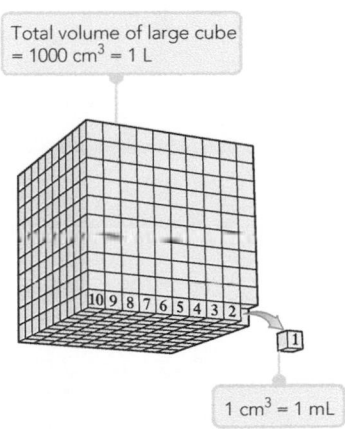

Total volume of large cube = 1000 cm^3 = 1 L

1 cm^3 = 1 mL

Figure 2-3 A cube 10 cm on a side has a volume of 1000 cm^3, which is equal to 1 L. A cube 1 cm on a side has a volume of 1 cm^3, which is equal to 1 mL.

► Volume *is measured by determining the amount of space that a three-dimensional object occupies. Changing the shape of an object, such as kneaded bread dough, does not change its volume.*

► *Another abbreviation for the unit cubic centimeter, used in medical situations, is cc.*

$$1 \ cm^3 = 1 \ cc$$

In terms of milliliters, a teaspoon of liquid is 5 mL (4.93) and a tablespoon of liquid is 15 mL (14.8)

A liter and a quart have approximately the same volume; 1 liter equals 1.06 quarts (Figure 2-2c). The milliliter and deciliter (dL) are commonly used in the laboratory. Deciliter units are routinely encountered in clinical laboratory reports detailing the composition of body fluids (Figure 2-4). A deciliter is equal to 100 mL (0.100 L). ◄

CLINICAL LABORATORY REPORT

PATIENT NAME: Healthy, I.M.   DATE: 1/23/14   1/23/14   1/25/14

SEX: M   AGE: 37   LAB NO: 05169

Your Doctor
Anywhere, U.S.A

SSN: 000-00-0000   ID: 032136

TEST NAME	RESULT	UNITS	NORMAL REFERENCE RANGE
Chem-Screen Profile			
Calcium	9.70	mg/dL	9.00–10.40
Phosphate (As Phosphorus)	3.00	mg/dL	2.20–4.30
Bun	16.00	mg/dL	9.00–23.0
Creatinine	1.30	mg/dL	0.80–1.30
Bun/Creat Ratio	12.31		12–20
Uric Acid	7.50	mg/dL	3.60–8.30
Glucose	114.00	mg/dL	65.0–130
Total Protein	7.90	g/dL	6.50–8.00
Albumin	5.10	g/dL	3.90–4.90
Globulin	2.80	g/dL	2.10–3.50
Alb/Glob Ratio	1.82		1.20–2.20
Total Bilirubin	0.55	mg/dL	0.30–1.40
Direct Bilirubin	0.18	mg/dL	0.04–0.20
Cholesterol	203.00	mg/dL	140–233
Cholesterol Percentile	50	Percentile	1–74
HDL Cholesterol	71	mg/dL	
Chol./HDL Cholesterol	*(01)-2.77		
Triglycerides	148.00	mg/dL	50.0–200

(01) THE RESULT OBTAINED FOR THE CHOLESTEROL/HDL CHOLESTEROL RATIO FOR THIS PATIENT'S SAMPLE IS ASSOCIATED WITH THE LOWEST CORONARY HEART DISEASE (CHD) RISK.

Figure 2-4 The use of the concentration unit milligrams per deciliter (mg/dL) is common in clinical laboratory reports dealing with the composition of human body fluids.

Section 2-2 Quick Quiz

1. In which of the following pairings of metric system prefixes and powers of 10 is the pairing *incorrect*?
   a. kilo- and 10^3
   b. micro- and 10^{-6}
   c. deci- and 10^{-2}
   d. no correct response
2. In which of the following sequences are the metric system prefixes listed in order of decreasing size?
   a. centi-, milli-
   b. mega-, giga-
   c. nano-, micro-
   d. no correct response
3. Which of the following is a correct pairing of concepts?
   a. gram, metric unit of mass
   b. liter, metric unit of length
   c. meter, metric unit of volume
   d. no correct response

4. A meter denotes about the same length as the English system unit
   a. yard
   b. foot
   c. inch
   d. no correct response
5. One cubic centimeter is equal to one
   a. milliliter
   b. deciliter
   c. liter
   d. no correct response
6. The milliliter equivalent for a liquid volume of one teaspoon is
   a. 2 mL
   b. 5 mL
   c. 25 mL
   d. no correct response
7. Which comparison of the gram and pound mass units is correct?
   a. The gram is a much smaller unit than the pound.
   b. The gram and pound units are about the same size.
   c. The gram is a much larger unit than the pound.
   d. no correct response

Answers: 1. c; 2. a; 3. a; 4. a; 5. a; 6. b; 7. a

2-3 Exact and Inexact Numbers

LEARNING FOCUS
Classify a number as being *exact* or *inexact* on the basis of the context of its use.

In scientific work, numbers are grouped in two categories: *exact numbers* and *inexact numbers*. An **exact number** *is a number whose value has no uncertainty associated with it—that is, it is known exactly*. Exact numbers occur in definitions (for example, there are exactly 12 objects in a dozen, not 12.01 or 12.02); in counting (for example, there can be 7 people in a room, but never 6.99 or 7.03); and in simple fractions (for example, 1/3, 3/5, and 5/9).

An **inexact number** *is a number whose value has a degree of uncertainty associated with it*. Inexact numbers result any time a measurement is made. It is impossible to make an *exact* measurement; some uncertainty will always be present. Flaws in measuring device construction, improper calibration of an instrument, and the skills (or lack of skills) possessed by a person using a measuring device all contribute to error (uncertainty). Section 2-4 considers further the origins of the uncertainty associated with measurements and also the methods used to "keep track" of such uncertainty. ◄

▶ *All measurements have some degree of uncertainty associated with them. Thus, the numerical value associated with a measurement is always an inexact number.*

Section 2-3 Quick Quiz

1. Which of the following will always involve an *inexact* number?
   a. a definition containing a numerical value
   b. a measurement containing a numerical value
   c. a numerical value obtained by counting
   d. no correct response
2. Which of the following statements contains an *exact* number?
   a. The thickness of a sheet of paper is 0.0045 inch.
   b. The size of a sheet of paper is 8.5 × 11 inches.
   c. The number of sheets of paper in a ream is 500.
   d. no correct response

Answers: 1. b; 2. c

2-4 Uncertainty in Measurement and Significant Figures

LEARNING FOCUS

Know the rule that governs the number of digits recorded in a measurement; be able to determine the number of significant figures in a given measurement.

As noted in the previous section, because of the limitations of the measuring device and the limited observational powers of the individual making the measurement, every measurement carries a degree of uncertainty or error. Even when very elaborate measuring devices are used, some degree of uncertainty is always present.

Origin of Measurement Uncertainty

To illustrate how measurement uncertainty arises, consider how two different rulers, shown in Figure 2-5, are used to measure a given length. Using ruler A, it is known with certainty that the length of the object is between 3 and 4 centimeters. The actual length is closer to 4 centimeters and is estimated to be 3.7 centimeters. Ruler B has more subdivisions on its scale than ruler A. It is marked off in tenths of a centimeter instead of in centimeters. Using ruler B, it is known that the length of the object is between 3.7 and 3.8 centimeters and is estimated to be 3.74 centimeters.

Note how both length measurements (taken with ruler A and ruler B) contain some digits (all those except the last one) that are exactly known and one digit (the last one) that is estimated. It is this last digit, the estimated one, that produces uncertainty in a measurement. Note also that the uncertainty in the second length measurement is less than that in the first one—an uncertainty in the hundredths place compared with an uncertainty in the tenths place. The second measurement is more *precise* than the first one; that is, it has less uncertainty than the first measurement.

Only one estimated digit is ever recorded as part of a measurement. It would be incorrect for a scientist to report that the length of the object in Figure 2-5 is 3.745 centimeters as read by using ruler B. The value 3.745 contains two estimated digits, the 4 and the 5, and indicates a measurement with less uncertainty than what is actually obtainable with that particular measuring device. Again, only one estimated digit is ever recorded as part of a measurement.

Measurements obtained using instrumentation that displays data electronically still have uncertainty associated with them. The last digit in any digital measurement is considered to be an estimated digit.

Because measurements are never exact, two types of information must be conveyed whenever a numerical value for a measurement is recorded: (1) the magnitude of the measurement and (2) the uncertainty of the measurement. The magnitude is indicated by the digit values. Uncertainty is indicated by the number of significant figures recorded. **Significant figures** *are the digits in a measurement that are known with certainty plus one digit that is estimated.* To summarize, in equation form,

> Number of significant figures = all certain digits + one estimated digit

Guidelines for Determining Significant Figures

Recognizing the number of significant figures in a measured quantity is easy for measurements that someone personally makes, because the type of instrument used and its limitations are known to that person. However, when someone else makes the measurement, such information is often not available. In such cases, a set of guidelines

Read as —| 3.7 cm |

Ruler A

Read as —| 3.74 cm |

Ruler B

Figure 2-5 The scale on a measuring device determines the magnitude of the uncertainty for the recorded measurement. Measurements made with ruler A will have greater uncertainty than those made with ruler B.

exists for determining the number of significant figures in a measured quantity. These guidelines are:

1. In any measurement, all nonzero digits are significant. ◄
2. *Zeros* may or may not be significant because zeros can be used in two ways: (1) to position a decimal point and (2) to indicate a measured value. Zeros that perform the first function are not significant, and zeros that perform the second function are significant. When zeros are present in a measured number, the following rules are used:

   a. *Leading zeros,* those at the beginning of a number, are never significant.

   0.0141 has three significant figures.

   0.0000000048 has two significant figures.

   b. *Confined zeros,* those between nonzero digits, are always significant.

   3.063 has four significant figures.

   0.001004 has four significant figures.

   c. *Trailing zeros,* those at the end of a number, are significant if a decimal point is present in the number.

   56.00 has four significant figures.

   0.05050 has four significant figures.

   d. *Trailing zeros,* those at the end of a number, are not significant if the number lacks an explicitly shown decimal point.

   59,000,000 has two significant figures.

   6010 has three significant figures.

▶ *The term* significant figures *is often verbalized in shortened form as "sig figs."*

It is important to remember what is "significant" about significant figures. The number of significant figures in a measurement conveys information about the uncertainty associated with the measurement. The "location" of the last significant digit in the numerical value of a measurement specifies the measurement's uncertainty: Is this last significant digit located in the hundredths, tenths, ones, or tens position, and so forth? Consider the following measurement values (with the last significant digit "boxed" for emphasis):

4620.0 (five significant figures) has an uncertainty of tenths.
4620 (three significant figures) has an uncertainty in the tens place.
462,000 (three significant figures) has an uncertainty in the thousands place.

Chemistry at a Glance—Significant Figures—reviews the rules that govern which digits in a measurement are significant.

EXAMPLE 2-2

Determining the Number of Significant Figures in a Measurement and the Uncertainty Associated with the Measurement

For each of the following measurements, give the number of significant figures present and the uncertainty associated with the measurement.

a. 5623.00   **b.** 0.0031   **c.** 97,200   **d.** 637

Solution

a. Six significant figures are present because trailing zeros are significant when a decimal point is present. The uncertainty is in the hundredths place (±0.01), the location of the last significant digit.
b. Two significant figures are present because leading zeros are never significant. The uncertainty is in the ten-thousandths place (±0.0001), the location of the last significant digit.
c. Three significant figures are present because the trailing zeros are not significant (no explicit decimal point is shown). The uncertainty is in the hundreds place (±100).
d. Three significant figures are present, and the uncertainty is in the ones place (±1).

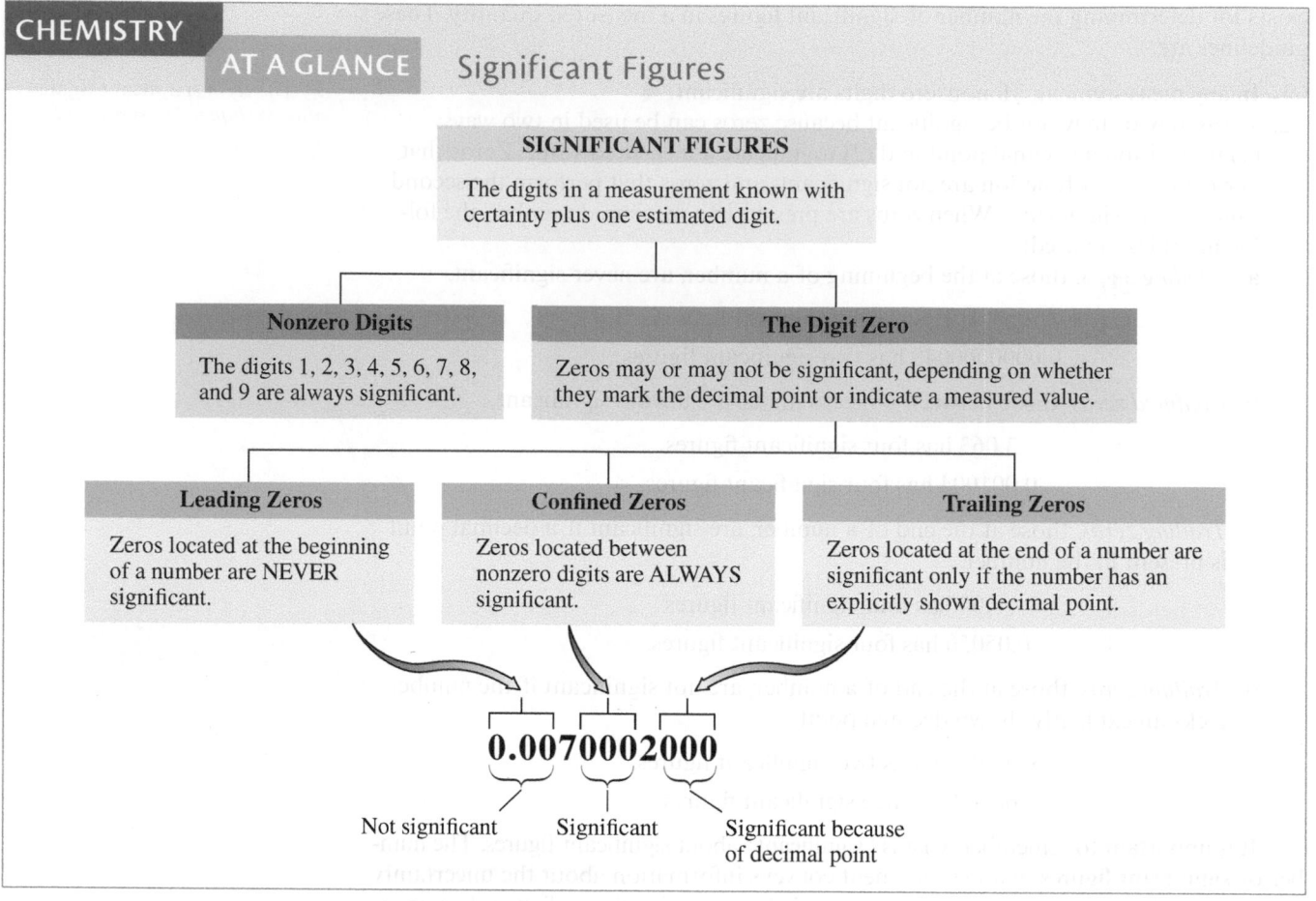

Section 2-4 Quick Quiz

1. To what decimal position should a measurement be recorded if the smallest markings on the measurement scale are tenths of a millimeter?
   a. to the closest millimeter
   b. to tenths of a millimeter
   c. to hundredths of a millimeter
   d. no correct response
2. Which of the following statements about the "significance" of zeros in recorded measurements is *incorrect*?
   a. leading zeros are never significant
   b. confined zeros are always significant
   c. trailing zeros are never significant
   d. no correct response
3. How many significant figures are present in the measurement 0.0330?
   a. two
   b. three
   c. four
   d. no correct response
4. How many significant figures are present in the measurement 32.00?
   a. two
   b. three
   c. four
   d. no correct response
5. The estimated digit in the measurement 65,430 seconds is
   a. the zero
   b. the three
   c. the four
   d. no correct response

6. The uncertainty in the measurement 56.00 seconds is plus/minus what value?
   a. one
   b. one-tenth
   c. one-hundredth
   d. no correct response

Answers: 1. c; 2. c; 3. b; 4. c; 5. b; 6. c

2-5 Significant Figures and Mathematical Operations

LEARNING FOCUS

Be able to round numbers obtained by mathematical computation to the correct number of significant figures.

When measurements are added, subtracted, multiplied, or divided, consideration must be given to the number of significant figures in the computed result. Mathematical operations should not increase (or decrease) the uncertainty of experimental measurements.

Hand-held electronic calculators generally "complicate" uncertainty considerations because they are not programmed to take significant figures into account. Consequently, the digital readouts display more digits than are warranted (Figure 2-6). It is a mistake to record these extra digits, because they are not significant figures and hence are meaningless.

Rounding Off Numbers

When calculator answers contain too many digits, it is necessary to delete (drop) the nonsignificant digits, a process that is called rounding off. **Rounding off** *is the process of deleting unwanted (nonsignificant) digits from calculated numbers.* There are two rules for rounding off numbers.

1. *If the first digit to be deleted is 4 or less, simply drop it and all the following digits.* For example, the number 3.724567 becomes 3.72 when rounded to three significant figures.
2. *If the first digit to be deleted is 5 or greater, that digit and all that follow are dropped, and the last retained digit is increased by one.* The number 5.00673 becomes 5.01 when rounded to three significant figures.

These rounding rules must be modified slightly when digits to the left of the decimal point are to be dropped. To maintain the inferred position of the decimal point in such situations, zeros must replace all the dropped digits that are to the left of the inferred decimal point. Parts (c) and (d) of Example 2-3 illustrate this point.

Figure 2-6 The digital readout on an electronic calculator usually shows more digits than are warranted. Calculators are not programmed to account for significant figures.

© Cengage Learning

EXAMPLE 2-3

Rounding Numbers to a Specified Number of Significant Figures

Round off each of the following numbers to two significant figures.

a. 25.7   **b.** 0.4327   **c.** 432,117   **d.** 13,500

Solution

a. Rule 2 applies. The last retained digit (the 5) is increased in value by one unit.

25.7 becomes 26

b. Rule 1 applies. The last retained digit (the 3) remains the same, and all digits that follow it are simply dropped.

0.4327 becomes 0.43

(continued)

c. Since the first digit to be dropped is a 2, rule 1 applies

432,117 becomes 430,000

Note that to maintain the position of the inferred decimal point, zeros must replace all of the dropped digits. This will always be the case when digits to the left of the inferred decimal place are dropped.

d. This is a rule 2 situation because the first digit to be dropped is a 5. The 3 is rounded up to a 4 and zeros take the place of all digits to the left of the inferred decimal place that are dropped.

13,500 becomes 14,000

Operational Rules

Significant-figure considerations in mathematical operations that involve measured numbers are governed by two rules, one for multiplication and division and one for addition and subtraction.

1. *In multiplication and division, the number of significant figures in the answer is the same as the number of significant figures in the measurement that contains the fewest significant figures.* For example,

Four significant figures   Three significant figures

$$6.038 \times 2.57 = 15.51766 \quad \text{(calculator answer)}$$
$$= 15.5 \quad \text{(correct answer)}$$

Three significant figures

The calculator answer is rounded to three significant figures because the measurement with the fewest significant figures (2.57) contains only three significant figures.

2. *In addition and subtraction, the answer has no more digits to the right of the decimal point than are found in the measurement with the fewest digits to the right of the decimal point.* For example,

$$
\begin{array}{l}
9.333 \quad \leftarrow \text{Uncertain digit (thousandths)} \\
+1.4 \quad \leftarrow \text{Uncertain digit (tenths)} \\
\hline
10.733 \quad \text{(calculator answer)} \\
10.7 \quad \text{(correct answer)}
\end{array}
$$

Uncertain digit (tenths)

The calculator answer is rounded to the tenths place because the uncertainty in the number 1.4 is in the tenths place.

Note the contrast between the rule for multiplication and division and the rule for addition and subtraction. In multiplication and division, significant figures are counted; in addition and subtraction, decimal places are counted. It is possible to gain or lose significant figures during addition or subtraction, but *never* during multiplication or division. In our previous sample addition problem, one of the input numbers (1.4) has two significant figures, and the correct answer (10.7) has three significant figures. This is allowable in addition (and subtraction) because we are counting decimal places, not significant figures. ◀

▶ *Concisely stated, the significant-figure operational rules are*

× *or* ÷ : *Keep smallest number of significant figures in answer.*

+ *or* − : *Keep smallest number of decimal places in answer.*

EXAMPLE 2-4

Expressing Answers to the Proper Number of Significant Figures

Perform the following computations, expressing your answers to the proper number of significant figures.

a. 6.7321×0.0021 **b.** $\dfrac{16{,}340}{23.42}$ **c.** 6.000×4.000

d. $8.3 + 1.2 + 1.7$ **e.** $3.07 \times (17.6 - 13.73)$

Solution

a. The calculator answer to this problem is

$$6.7321 \times 0.0021 = 0.01413741$$

The input number with the least number of significant figures is 0.0021.

$$6.7321 \times 0.0021$$

Five significant figures   Two significant figures

Thus the calculator answer must be rounded to two significant figures.

0.01413741   becomes   0.014
Calculator answer   Correct answer

b. The calculator answer to this problem is

$$\frac{16{,}340}{23.42} = 697.69427$$

Both input numbers contain four significant figures. Thus the correct answer will also contain four significant figures.

697.69427   becomes   697.7
Calculator answer   Correct answer

c. The calculator answer to this problem is

$$6.000 \times 4.000 = 24$$

Both input numbers contain four significant figures. Thus the correct answer must also contain four significant figures, and

24   becomes   24.00
(calculator answer)   (correct answer)

Note here how the calculator answer had too few significant figures. Most calculators cut off zeros after the decimal point even if those zeros are significant. Using too few significant figures in an answer is just as wrong as using too many.

d. The calculator answer to this problem is

$$8.3 + 1.2 + 1.7 = 11.2$$

All three input numbers have uncertainty in the tenths place. Thus the last retained digit in the correct answer will be that of tenths. (In this particular problem, the calculator answer and the correct answer are the same, a situation that does not occur very often.) ◄

e. This problem involves the use of both multiplication and subtraction significant-figure rules. The subtraction is done first.

$$17.6 - 13.73 = 3.87 \quad \text{(calculator answer)}$$
$$= 3.9 \quad \text{(correct answer)}$$

This answer must be rounded to tenths because the input number 17.6 involves only tenths. The multiplication is then done.

$$3.07 \times 3.9 = 11.973 \quad \text{(calculator answer)}$$
$$= 12 \quad \text{(correct answer)}$$

The number 3.9 limits the answer to two significant figures.

▶ *Calculators are not programmed to take significant figures into account, which means that students must always adjust their calculator answer to the correct number of significant figures. Sometimes this involves deleting a number of digits through rounding, and other times it involves adding zeros to increase the number of significant figures.*

Some numbers used in computations may be *exact numbers* rather than measured numbers. Because exact numbers (Section 2-3) have no uncertainty associated with them, they possess an unlimited number of significant figures. Therefore, such numbers never limit the number of significant figures in a computational answer.

Section 2-5 Quick Quiz

1. In which of the following cases is the given number correctly rounded to three significant figures?
   a. 0.01136 becomes 0.0113
   b. 32.57 becomes 32.6
   c. 1.2001 becomes 1.21
   d. no correct response
2. When rounded to three significant figures, the number 43,267 becomes
   a. 433
   b. 43,267
   c. 43,300
   d. no correct answer
3. The calculator answer obtained by multiplying the measurements 53.534 and 5.00 is 267.67. This answer
   a. is correct as written
   b. should be rounded to 267.7
   c. should be rounded to 268
   d. no correct response
4. The calculator answer obtained by adding the measurements 8.1, 2.19, and 3.123 is 13.413. The answer
   a. is correct as written
   b. should be rounded to two significant figures
   c. should be rounded to 13.4
   d. no correct response

Answers: 1. b; 2. c; 3. c; 4. c

2-6 Scientific Notation

LEARNING FOCUS

Be able to convert numbers from decimal notation to scientific notation and vice versa; be able to perform mathematical operations using scientific notation numbers; be able to specify the number of significant figures present and uncertainty for scientific notation numbers.

Up to this point in the chapter, all numbers have been expressed in decimal notation, the everyday method for expressing numbers. Such notation becomes cumbersome for very large and very small numbers (which occur frequently in scientific work). For example, in one drop of blood, which is 92% water by mass, there are approximately

$$1,600,000,000,000,000,000,000 \text{ molecules}$$

of water, each of which has a mass of

$$0.000000000000000000000030 \text{ gram}$$

Recording such large and small numbers is not only time consuming but also open to error; often, too many or too few zeros are recorded. Also, it is impossible to multiply or divide such numbers with most calculators because they can't accept that many digits. (Most calculators accept either 8 or 10 digits.)

A method called *scientific notation* exists for expressing in compact form multidigit numbers that involve many zeros. ◄ **Scientific notation** *is a numerical system in which numbers are expressed in the form $A \times 10^n$, where A is a number with a single nonzero digit to the left of the decimal place and n is a whole number. The number A is*

► *Scientific notation is also called exponential notation.*

called the *coefficient*. The number 10^n is called the *exponential term*. The coefficient is always multiplied by the exponential term.

The two previously cited numbers that deal with molecules of water are expressed in scientific notation as

$$1.6 \times 10^{21} \text{ molecules}$$

and

$$3.0 \times 10^{-23} \text{ gram}$$

Obviously, scientific notation is a much more concise way of expressing numbers. Such scientific notation is compatible with most calculators.

Converting from Decimal to Scientific Notation

The procedure for converting a number from decimal notation to scientific notation has two parts.

1. *The decimal point in the decimal number is moved to the position behind (to the right of) the first nonzero digit.*
2. *The exponent for the exponential term is equal to the number of places the decimal point has been moved.* The exponent is positive if the original decimal number is 10 or greater and is negative if the original decimal number is less than 1. For numbers between 1 and 10, the exponent is zero.

The following two examples illustrate the use of these procedures:

$$93{,}000{,}000 = 9.3 \times 10^7$$

Decimal point is
moved 7 places

$$0.0000037 = 3.7 \times 10^{-6}$$

Decimal point is
moved 6 places

Significant Figures and Scientific Notation

How do significant-figure considerations affect scientific notation? The answer is simple. *Only significant figures become part of the coefficient.* ◀ The numbers 63, 63.0, and 63.00, which respectively have two, three, and four significant figures, when converted to scientific notation become, respectively,

▶ *The decimal and scientific notation forms of a number always contain the same number of significant figures.*

$$6.3 \times 10^1 \qquad \text{(two significant figures)}$$
$$6.30 \times 10^1 \qquad \text{(three significant figures)}$$
$$6.300 \times 10^1 \qquad \text{(four significant figures)}$$

Multiplication and Division in Scientific Notation

Multiplication and division of numbers expressed in scientific notation are common procedures. For these two types of operations, the coefficients, which are decimal numbers, are combined in the usual way. The rules for handling the exponential terms are

1. To multiply exponential terms, *add* the exponents.
2. To divide exponential terms, *subtract* the exponents.

EXAMPLE 2-5

Multiplication and Division in Scientific Notation

Carry out the following mathematical operations involving numbers that are expressed in scientific notation.

a. $(2.33 \times 10^3) \times (1.55 \times 10^4)$ **b.** $\dfrac{8.42 \times 10^6}{3.02 \times 10^4}$

Solution

a. Multiplying the two coefficients gives

$$2.33 \times 1.55 = 3.6115 \quad \text{(calculator answer)}$$
$$= 3.61 \quad \text{(correct answer)}$$

Remember that the coefficient obtained by multiplication can have only three significant figures in this case, the same number as in both input numbers for the multiplication.

Multiplication of the two powers of 10 to give the exponential term requires that the exponents be added.

$$10^3 \times 10^4 = 10^{3+4} = 10^7$$

Combining the new coefficient with the new exponential term gives the answer.

$$3.61 \times 10^7$$

b. Performing the indicated division of the coefficients gives

$$\frac{8.42}{3.02} = 2.7880794 \quad \text{(calculator answer)}$$
$$= 2.79 \quad \text{(correct answer)}$$

Because both input numbers have three significant figures, the answer also has three significant figures.

The division of exponential terms requires that the exponents be subtracted.

$$\frac{10^6}{10^4} = 10^{(+6)-(+4)} = 10^2$$

Combining the new coefficient and the new exponential term gives

$$2.79 \times 10^2$$

Calculators and Scientific Notation

Entering a number written in scientific notation directly into a calculator requires use of the $\boxed{\text{EE}}$ or $\boxed{\text{EXP}}$ function key. The coefficient is entered first, then the $\boxed{\text{EE}}$ (or $\boxed{\text{EXP}}$) function key is pressed and the value of the power of 10 (but not its sign) is entered. (The $\boxed{\text{EE}}$ function key already includes ($\times 10$), so 10 itself is not entered into the calculator.) If the power of 10 is negative, the $\boxed{\text{+/-}}$ key is pressed (not the key for subtraction).

Thus, the sequence of operations for entering the number 7.2×10^5 into a calculator is

$$7.2 \; \boxed{\text{EE}} \; 5$$

and the digital readout appears as

$$7.2 \; 05 \quad \text{or} \quad 7.2^{05} \quad \text{or} \quad 7.2 \; \text{E}05$$

The number 6.78×10^{-8} is entered into a calculator using the operational sequence

$$6.78 \; \boxed{\text{EE}} \; 8 \; \boxed{\text{+/-}}$$

and the digital readout appears as

$$6.78-08 \quad \text{or} \quad 6.78^{-08} \quad \text{or} \quad 6.78\,E-08$$

Uncertainty and Scientific Notation

The uncertainty associated with a measurement whose value is expressed in scientific notation cannot be obtained directly from the coefficient in the scientific notation. The coefficient decimal point location is not the true location for the decimal point. The value of the exponent in the exponential term must be taken into account in determining the uncertainty.

The uncertainty associated with a scientific notation number is obtained by determining the uncertainty associated with the coefficient and then multiplying this value by the exponential term. For the number 3.72×10^{-3}, we have

$$\underset{\substack{\text{Uncertainty} \\ \text{in coefficient}}}{10^{-2}} \quad \underset{}{\times} \quad \underset{\substack{\text{Exponential} \\ \text{term}}}{10^{-3}} \quad \underset{}{=} \quad \underset{\substack{\text{Uncertainty} \\ \text{in number}}}{10^{-5}}$$

That the uncertainty is, indeed, 1×10^{-5} can be readily seen by rewriting the number in decimal notation.

$$3.72 \times 10^{-3} = 0.00372$$

The uncertainty for the decimal number is in the hundred-thousandths place (10^{-5}).

Section 2-6 Quick Quiz

1. The number 273.00, when expressed in scientific notation, becomes
   a. 2.73×10^2
   b. 2.73×10^{-2}
   c. 2.7300×10^2
   d. no correct response
2. The number 0.000123, when expressed in scientific notation, becomes
   a. 1.23×10^{-3}
   b. 1.23×10^{-4}
   c. 1.23×10^{-6}
   d. no correct response
3. The number 3.20×10^{-2}, when expressed in decimal notation, becomes
   a. 0.0032
   b. 0.00320
   c. 32.0
   d. no correct response
4. The number of significant figures in the measurement 3.20×10^3 is
   a. two
   b. three
   c. four
   d. no correct response
5. The uncertainty in the measurement 3.22×10^4 is
   a. 10^{-2}
   b. 10^2
   c. 10^4
   d. no correct response
6. The correct answer for the multiplication $(2.0 \times 10^2) \times (3.00 \times 10^1)$ is
   a. 6×10^3
   b. 6.0×10^1
   c. 6.0×10^3
   d. no correct response

Answers: 1. c; 2. b; 3. d; 4. b; 5. b; 6. c

2-7   Conversion Factors

LEARNING FOCUS

Understand how conversion factors are obtained from both defined and measured unit relationships.

With both the English unit and metric unit systems in common use in the United States, measurements must often be changed from one system to their equivalent in the other system. The mathematical tool used to accomplish this task is a general method of problem solving called *dimensional analysis*. Central to the use of dimensional analysis is the concept of conversion factors. A **conversion factor** *is a ratio that specifies how one unit of measurement is related to another unit of measurement.*

Conversion factors are derived from equations (equalities) that relate units. Consider the quantities "1 minute" and "60 seconds," both of which describe the same amount of time. We may write an equation describing this fact.

$$1 \text{ min} = 60 \text{ sec}$$

This fixed relationship is the basis for the construction of a pair of conversion factors that relate seconds and minutes.

$$\frac{1 \text{ min}}{60 \text{ sec}} \quad \text{and} \quad \frac{60 \text{ sec}}{1 \text{ min}} \qquad \text{These two quantities are the same}$$

Note that conversion factors always come in pairs, one member of the pair being the reciprocal of the other. Also note that the numerator and the denominator of a conversion factor always describe the same amount of whatever is being considered. One minute and 60 seconds denote the same amount of time.

Conversion Factors Within a System of Units

Most students are familiar with and have memorized numerous conversion factors within the English system of measurement (English-to-English conversion factors). Some of these factors, with only one member of a conversion factor pair being listed, are

$$\frac{12 \text{ in.}}{1 \text{ ft}} \quad \frac{3 \text{ ft}}{1 \text{ yd}} \quad \frac{4 \text{ qt}}{1 \text{ gal}} \quad \frac{16 \text{ oz}}{1 \text{ lb}}$$

▶ *In order to avoid confusion with the word in, the abbreviation for inches, in., includes a period. This is the only unit abbreviation in which a period appears.*

Such conversion factors contain an unlimited number of significant figures because the numbers within them arise from definitions. ◀

Metric-to-metric conversion factors are similar to English-to-English conversion factors in that they arise from definitions. Individual conversion factors are derived from the meanings of the metric system prefixes (Section 2-2). For example, the set of conversion factors involving kilometer and meter come from the equality

$$1 \text{ kilometer} = 10^3 \text{ meters}$$

and those relating microgram and gram come from the equality

$$1 \text{ microgram} = 10^{-6} \text{ gram}$$

The two pairs of conversion factors are

$$\frac{10^3 \text{ m}}{1 \text{ km}} \quad \text{and} \quad \frac{1 \text{ km}}{10^3 \text{ m}} \qquad \frac{1 \text{ } \mu\text{g}}{10^{-6} \text{ g}} \quad \text{and} \quad \frac{10^{-6} \text{ g}}{1 \text{ } \mu\text{g}}$$

▶ *In order to obtain metric-to-metric conversion factors, you need to know the meaning of the metric system prefixes in terms of powers of 10 (Table 2-1).*

Note that the numerical equivalent of the prefix is always associated with the base (unprefixed) unit in a metric-to-metric conversion factor. ◀

The number 1 always goes with the *prefixed* unit. ⟶

$$\frac{1 \text{ mL}}{10^{-3} \text{ L}}$$

The power of 10 always ↗ goes with the *unprefixed* unit.

Conversion Factors Between Systems of Units

Conversion factors that relate metric units to English units and vice versa are not defined quantities because they involve two different systems of measurement. The numbers associated with these conversion factors must be determined experimentally (Figure 2-7). Table 2-2 lists commonly encountered relationships between metric system and English system units. These few conversion factors are sufficient to solve most problems encountered.

Metric-to-English conversion factors can be specified to differing numbers of significant figures. For example,

$$1.00 \text{ lb} = 454 \text{ g}$$

$$1.000 \text{ lb} = 453.6 \text{ g}$$

$$1.0000 \text{ lb} = 453.59 \text{ g}$$

In a problem-solving context, which "version" of a conversion factor is used depends on how many significant figures there are in the other numbers of the problem. Conversion factors should never limit the number of significant figures in the answer to a problem. The conversion factors in Table 2-2 are given to three significant figures, which is sufficient for the applications we will make of them.

Chemistry at a Glance—Conversion Factors—summarizes the concepts discussed in this section about conversion factors.

Figure 2-7 It is experimentally determined that 1 inch equals 2.54 centimeters, or 1 centimeter equals 0.394 inch.

▶ **Table 2-2 Equalities and Conversion Factors That Relate the English and Metric Systems of Measurement**

	Metric to English	English to Metric
Length		
1.00 inch = 2.54 centimeters	$\dfrac{1.00 \text{ in.}}{2.54 \text{ cm}}$	$\dfrac{2.54 \text{ cm}}{1.00 \text{ in.}}$
1.00 meter = 39.4 inches	$\dfrac{39.4 \text{ in.}}{1.00 \text{ m}}$	$\dfrac{1.00 \text{ m}}{39.4 \text{ in.}}$
1.00 kilometer = 0.621 mile	$\dfrac{0.621 \text{ mi}}{1.00 \text{ km}}$	$\dfrac{1.00 \text{ km}}{0.621 \text{ mi}}$
Mass		
1.00 pound = 454 grams	$\dfrac{1.00 \text{ lb}}{454 \text{ g}}$	$\dfrac{454 \text{ g}}{1.00 \text{ lb}}$
1.00 kilogram = 2.20 pounds	$\dfrac{2.20 \text{ lb}}{1.00 \text{ kg}}$	$\dfrac{1.00 \text{ kg}}{2.20 \text{ lb}}$
1.00 ounce = 28.3 grams	$\dfrac{1.00 \text{ oz}}{28.3 \text{ g}}$	$\dfrac{28.3 \text{ g}}{1.00 \text{ oz}}$
Volume		
1.00 quart = 0.946 liter	$\dfrac{1.00 \text{ qt}}{0.946 \text{ L}}$	$\dfrac{0.946 \text{ L}}{1.00 \text{ qt}}$
1.00 liter = 0.265 gallon	$\dfrac{0.265 \text{ gal}}{1.00 \text{ L}}$	$\dfrac{1.00 \text{ L}}{0.265 \text{ gal}}$
1.00 milliliter = 0.0338 fluid ounce	$\dfrac{0.0338 \text{ fl oz}}{1.00 \text{ mL}}$	$\dfrac{1.00 \text{ mL}}{0.0338 \text{ fl oz}}$

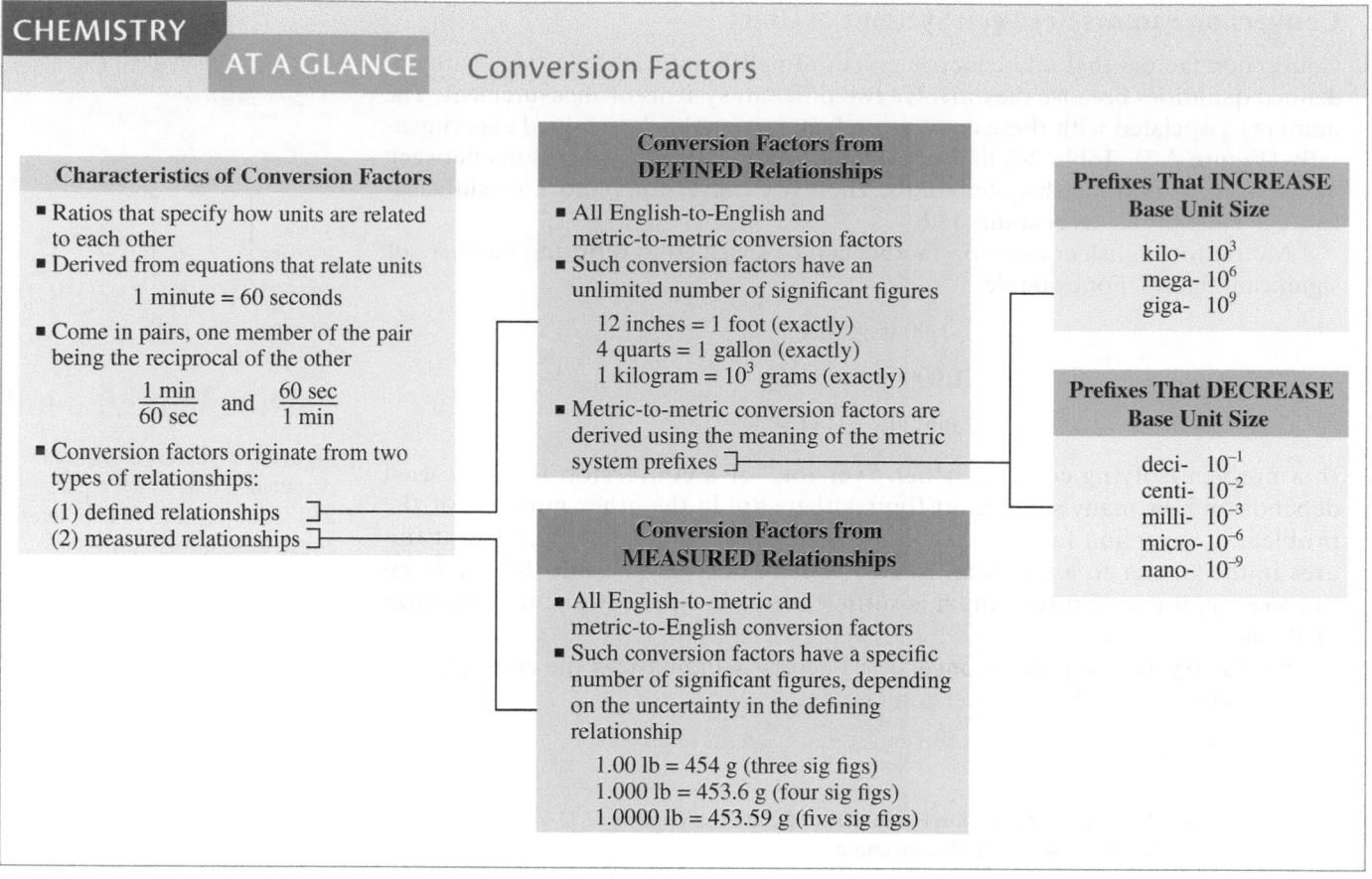

CHEMISTRY AT A GLANCE   Conversion Factors

Characteristics of Conversion Factors

- Ratios that specify how units are related to each other
- Derived from equations that relate units
    1 minute = 60 seconds
- Come in pairs, one member of the pair being the reciprocal of the other
    $\dfrac{1 \text{ min}}{60 \text{ sec}}$ and $\dfrac{60 \text{ sec}}{1 \text{ min}}$
- Conversion factors originate from two types of relationships:
    (1) defined relationships
    (2) measured relationships

Conversion Factors from DEFINED Relationships

- All English-to-English and metric-to-metric conversion factors
- Such conversion factors have an unlimited number of significant figures
    12 inches = 1 foot (exactly)
    4 quarts = 1 gallon (exactly)
    1 kilogram = 10^3 grams (exactly)
- Metric-to-metric conversion factors are derived using the meaning of the metric system prefixes

Conversion Factors from MEASURED Relationships

- All English-to-metric and metric-to-English conversion factors
- Such conversion factors have a specific number of significant figures, depending on the uncertainty in the defining relationship
    1.00 lb = 454 g (three sig figs)
    1.000 lb = 453.6 g (four sig figs)
    1.0000 lb = 453.59 g (five sig figs)

Prefixes That INCREASE Base Unit Size

kilo- 10^3
mega- 10^6
giga- 10^9

Prefixes That DECREASE Base Unit Size

deci- 10^{-1}
centi- 10^{-2}
milli- 10^{-3}
micro- 10^{-6}
nano- 10^{-9}

1. Which of the following conversion factor types is not definition-based?
   a. English–English
   b. metric–metric
   c. metric–English
   d. no correct response
2. How many conversion factors can be derived from the equality 24 hours = 1 day?
   a. two
   b. three
   c. four
   d. no correct response
3. Which of the following is an <u>incorrect</u> conversion factor?
   a. 3 ft/1 yd
   b. 36 in./1 yd
   c. 12 ft/1 mile
   d. no correct response
4. Which of the following is a <u>correct</u> conversion factor?
   a. 1 m/10^3 km
   b. 1 mm/10^{-3} m
   c. 1 m/10^{-2} cm
   d. no correct response

Answers: 1. c; 2. a; 3. c; 4. b

2-8 Dimensional Analysis

LEARNING FOCUS

Set up and work unit system conversion problems using the dimensional analysis method of problem solving.

Dimensional analysis *is a general problem-solving method in which the units associated with numbers are used as a guide in setting up calculations.* In this method, units are treated in the same way as numbers; that is, they can be multiplied, divided, or canceled. For example, just as

$$5 \times 5 = 5^2 \qquad \text{(5 squared)}$$

we have

$$cm \times cm = cm^2 \qquad \text{(cm squared)}$$

Also, just as the 3's cancel in the expression

$$\frac{\cancel{3} \times 5 \times 7}{\cancel{3} \times 2}$$

the centimeters cancel in the expression

$$\frac{\cancel{(cm)} \times (in.)}{\cancel{(cm)}}$$

"Like units" found in the numerator and denominator of a fraction will always cancel, just as like numbers do.

The following steps show how to set up a problem using dimensional analysis.

Step 1: *Identify the known or given quantity (both numerical value and units) and the units of the new quantity to be determined.*

This information will always be found in the statement of the problem. Write an equation with the given quantity on the left and the units of the desired quantity on the right.

Step 2: *Multiply the given quantity by one or more conversion factors in such a manner that the unwanted (original) units are canceled, leaving only the desired units.*

The general format for the multiplication is

(information given) $\times$ (conversion factors) = (information sought)

The number of conversion factors used depends on the individual problem.

Step 3: *Perform the mathematical operations indicated by the conversion factor setup.*

When performing the calculation, double-check to make sure all units except the desired set have canceled.

EXAMPLE 2-6

Unit Conversions Within the Metric System

A standard aspirin tablet contains 324 mg of aspirin. How many grams of aspirin are in a standard aspirin tablet?

Solution

Step 1: The given quantity is 324 mg, the mass of aspirin in the tablet. The unit of the desired quantity is grams.

$$324 \text{ mg} = ? \text{ g}$$

(continued)

Step 2: Only one conversion factor will be needed to convert from milligrams to grams, one that relates milligrams to grams. The two forms of this conversion factor are

$$\frac{1 \text{ mg}}{10^{-3} \text{ g}} \quad \text{and} \quad \frac{10^{-3} \text{ g}}{1 \text{ mg}}$$

The second factor is the one needed because it allows for cancellation of the milligram units, leaving grams as the new units.

$$324 \text{ mg} \times \left(\frac{10^{-3} \text{ g}}{1 \text{ mg}}\right) = ? \text{ g}$$

These units cancel each other.

Step 3: Combining numerical terms as indicated generates the final answer.

$$\left(324 \times \frac{10^{-3}}{1}\right) \text{ g} = 0.324 \text{ g}$$

Number from first factor

Numbers from second factor

The answer is given to three significant figures because the given quantity in the problem, 324 mg, has three significant figures. The conversion factor used arises from a definition and thus does not limit significant figures in any way.

EXAMPLE 2-7

Unit Conversions Between the Metric and English System

Capillaries, the microscopic vessels that carry blood from small arteries to small veins, are on the average only 1 mm long. What is the average length of a capillary in inches?

Solution

Step 1: The given quantity is 1 mm, and the unit of the desired quantity is inches.

$$1 \text{ mm} = ? \text{ in.}$$

Step 2: The conversion factor needed for a one-step solution, millimeters to inches, is not given in Table 2-2. However, a related conversion factor, meters to inches, is given. Therefore, we first convert millimeters to meters and then use the meters-to-inches conversion factor in Table 2-2.

$$\text{mm} \longrightarrow \text{m} \longrightarrow \text{in.}$$

The correct conversion factor setup is

These units cancel each other.

$$1 \text{ mm} \times \left(\frac{10^{-3} \text{ m}}{1 \text{ mm}}\right) \times \left(\frac{39.4 \text{ in.}}{1.00 \text{ m}}\right) = ? \text{ in.}$$

These units cancel each other.

All of the units except for inches cancel, which is what is needed. The information for the first conversion factor was obtained from the meaning of the prefix *milli-*.

This setup illustrates the fact that sometimes the given units must be changed to intermediate units before common conversion factors, such as those found in Table 2-2, are applicable.

Step 3: Collecting the numerical factors and performing the indicated math gives

$$\left(\frac{1 \times 10^{-3} \times 39.4}{1 \times 1.00}\right) \text{in.} = 0.0394 \text{ in.} \quad \text{(calculator answer)}$$

$$= 0.04 \text{ in.} \quad \text{(correct answer)}$$

The calculator answer must be rounded to one significant figure because 1 mm, the given quantity, contains only one significant figure.

Section 2-8 Quick Quiz

1. Which of the following conversion factors is needed to solve the problem "3.25 kg = ? g" using dimensional analysis?
   a. $1 \text{ kg}/10^3 \text{ g}$
   b. $10^3 \text{ g}/1 \text{ kg}$
   c. $1 \text{ mg}/10^{-3} \text{ g}$
   d. no correct response
2. Which of the following conversion factors is needed to solve the problem "1 hour = ? seconds" using dimensional analysis and the unit pathway "hours to minutes to seconds?"
   a. 1 hr/60 min
   b. 60 min/1hr
   c. 1 min/60 sec
   d. no correct response

Answers: 1. b; 2. b

2-9 Density

LEARNING FOCUS

Be able to calculate density given mass and volume; be able to use density as a conversion factor in mass/volume calculations.

Density *is the ratio of the mass of an object to the volume occupied by that object.* ◀

$$\text{Density} = \frac{\text{mass}}{\text{volume}}$$

▶ *Density is a physical property specific to a given substance or mixture under fixed conditions.*

People often speak of a substance as being heavier or lighter than another substance. What they actually mean is that the two substances have different densities; a specific volume of one substance is heavier or lighter than the same volume of the second substance. Equal masses of substances with different densities occupy different volumes; the contrast in volume is often very striking (Figure 2-8).

A correct density expression includes a number, a mass unit, and a volume unit. Although any mass and volume units can be used, densities are generally expressed in grams per cubic centimeter (g/cm³) for solids, grams per milliliter (g/mL) for liquids, and grams per liter (g/L) for gases. Table 2-3 gives density values for a number of substances. Note that temperature must be specified with density values because substances expand and contract with changes in temperature. For the same reason, the pressure of gases is also given with their density values. Example 2-8 illustrates how the known mass and known volume of a sample of a substance can be used to calculate its density.

© Cengage Learning

Figure 2-8 Both of these items have a mass of 23 grams, but they have very different volumes; therefore, their densities are different as well.

Table 2-3 **Densities of Selected Substances**

Solids (25°C)			
gold	19.3 g/cm³	table salt	2.16 g/cm³
lead	11.3 g/cm³	bone	1.7–2.0 g/cm³
copper	8.93 g/cm³	table sugar	1.59 g/cm³
aluminum	2.70 g/cm³	wood (pine)	0.30–0.50 g/cm³
Liquids (25°C)			
mercury	13.55 g/mL	water	0.997 g/mL
milk	1.028–1.035 g/mL	olive oil	0.92 g/mL
blood plasma	1.027 g/mL	ethyl alcohol	0.79 g/mL
urine	1.003–1.030 g/mL	gasoline	0.56 g/mL
Gases (25°C and 1 atmosphere pressure)			
chlorine	3.17 g/L	nitrogen	1.25 g/L
carbon dioxide	1.96 g/L	methane	0.66 g/L
oxygen	1.42 g/L	helium	0.16 g/L
air (dry)	1.29 g/L	hydrogen	0.08 g/L

© Cengage Learning

Figure 2-9 The penny is less dense than the mercury it floats on.

An object placed in a liquid either floats on the liquid's surface, sinks to the bottom of the liquid, or remains at some intermediate position in which it has been placed in the liquid (neither floating nor sinking), depending on how its density compares to that of the liquid. A floating object has a density that is less than that of the liquid (Figure 2-9), a sinking object has a density that is greater than that of the liquid, and a stationary object (neither floats nor sinks) has a density that is the same as that of the liquid.

The focus on relevancy feature Chemical Connections 2-A—Body Density and Percent Body Fat—considers how the density difference between fat cells and water is used as the basis for the hydrostatic weighing procedure for determining a person's percent body fat. ◄

▶ *Bone density is an important health parameter for older people. As a person ages, bone density decreases making bones more brittle and more subject to fracture. Determination of bone density does not actually involve measurement of bone density. Instead, X-rays are used to determine the mineral content of bones, which correlates well with actual bone density.*

EXAMPLE 2-8

Calculating Density Given a Mass and a Volume

A student determines that the mass of a 20.0-mL sample of olive oil is 18.4 g. What is the density of the olive oil in grams per milliliter?

Solution

To calculate density, we substitute the given mass and volume values into the defining formula for density.

$$\text{Density} = \frac{\text{mass}}{\text{volume}} = \frac{18.4 \text{ g}}{20.0 \text{ mL}} = 0.92 \frac{\text{g}}{\text{mL}} \quad \text{(calculator answer)}$$

$$= 0.920 \frac{\text{g}}{\text{mL}} \quad \text{(correct answer)}$$

Because both input numbers contain three significant figures, the density is specified to three significant figures.

CHEMICAL CONNECTIONS 2-A

Body Density and Percent Body Fat

More than half the adult population of the United States is overweight. But what does "overweight" mean? In years past, people were considered overweight if they weighed more for their height than called for in standard height/mass charts. Such charts are now considered outdated. Today, it is realized that body composition is more important than total body mass. The proportion of fat to total body mass—that is, the percent of body fat—is the key to defining *overweight*. A very muscular person, for example, can be overweight according to height/mass charts although he or she has very little body fat. Some athletes fall into this category. Body composition ratings, tied to percent body fat, are listed here.

Body Composition Rating	Percent Body Fat	
	Men	**Women***
excellent	less than 13	less than 18
good	13–17	18–22
average	18–21	23–26
fair	22–30	27–35
poor	greater than 30	greater than 35

* Women are genetically predisposed to maintain a higher percentage of body fat.

The percentage of fat in a person's body can be determined by hydrostatic (underwater) weighing. Fat cells, unlike most other human body cells and fluids, are less dense than water. Consequently, a person with a high percentage of body fat is more buoyed up by water than a lean person. The hydrostatic-weighing technique for determining body fat is based on this difference in density. A person is first weighed in air and then weighed again submerged in water. The difference between these two masses (with a correction for

Permission from Jeffrey L. Gage (photographer) and Michael L. Pollack, Ph.D., Center for Exercise Science, University of Florida

Weighing a person underwater can be used to determine the person's percent body fat.

residual air in the lungs and for the temperature of the water) is used to calculate body density. The higher the density of the body, the lower the percent of body fat. Sample values relating body density and percent body fat are given here.

Body Density (g/mL)	Percent Body Fat
1.070	12.22
1.062	15.25
1.052	19.29
1.036	25.35
1.027	29.39

Density as a Conversion Factor

Density can be used as a conversion factor that relates the volume of a substance to its mass. This use of density enables us to calculate the volume of a substance if we know its mass. Conversely, the mass can be calculated if the volume is known. ◀

Density conversion factors, like all other conversion factors, have two reciprocal forms. For a density of 1.03 g/mL, the two conversion factor forms are

$$\frac{1.03\ \text{g}}{1\ \text{mL}} \quad \text{and} \quad \frac{1\ \text{mL}}{1.03\ \text{g}}$$

Note that the number 1 always goes in front of a "naked" unit in a conversion factor; that is, a density given as 5.2 g/mL means 5.2 grams per 1 mL.

▶ *Density may be used as a conversion factor to convert from mass to volume or vice versa.*

EXAMPLE 2-9

Converting from Mass to Volume by Using Density as a Conversion Factor

Blood plasma has a density of 1.027 g/mL at 25°C. What volume, in milliliters, does 125 g of plasma occupy?

Solution

Step 1:   The given quantity is 125 g of blood plasma. The units of the desired quantity are milliliters. Thus the starting point is

$$125 \text{ g} = ? \text{ mL}$$

Step 2:   The conversion from grams to milliliters can be accomplished in one step because the given density, used as a conversion factor, directly relates grams to milliliters. Of the two conversion factor forms

$$\frac{1.027 \text{ g}}{1 \text{ mL}} \quad \text{and} \quad \frac{1 \text{ mL}}{1.027 \text{ g}}$$

the latter is used because it allows for cancellation of gram units, leaving milliliters.

$$125 \text{ g} \times \left(\frac{1 \text{ mL}}{1.027 \text{ g}}\right) = ? \text{ mL}$$

Step 3:   Doing the necessary arithmetic gives us our answer:

$$\left(\frac{125 \times 1}{1.027}\right) \text{ mL} = 121.71372 \text{ mL} \quad \text{(calculator answer)}$$
$$= 122 \text{ mL} \quad \text{(correct answer)}$$

Even though the given density contained four significant figures, the correct answer is limited to three significant figures. This is because the other given number, the mass of blood plasma, had only three significant figures.

Section 2-9 Quick Quiz

1. The density of an object is the ratio of its
   a. length to volume
   b. length to mass
   c. mass to volume
   d. no correct response
2. What is the density, in g/mL, of an object with a mass of 25 g and a volume of 5.0 mL?
   a. 125 g/mL
   b. 30 g/mL
   c. 5.0 g/mL
   d. no correct response
3. What is the volume, in milliliters, of 30.0 g of liquid if its density is 2.00 g/mL?
   a. 60.0 mL
   b. 15.0 mL
   c. 1.25 mL
   d. no correct response
4. What is the mass, in grams, of 30.0 mL of liquid if its density is 2.00 g/mL?
   a. 60.0 g
   b. 15.0 g
   c. 1.25 g
   d. no correct response

Answers: 1. c; 2. c; 3. b; 4. a

2-10   Temperature Scales

LEARNING FOCUS

Know the relationships that exist among the Fahrenheit, Celsius, and Kelvin temperature scales; be able to convert a temperature reading on one scale to that on another scale.

Heat is a form of energy. Heat energy flows from objects of higher temperature to objects of lower temperature. Thus, **temperature** *is an indicator of the tendency of heat energy to be transferred from one object to another.*

Temperature is measured using a *thermometer*, a narrow tube containing a liquid that expands when heated. The higher the temperature, the farther the liquid column will rise in the narrow tube. Graduations on the tube indicate the height of the liquid column in terms of defined units, most often called *degrees*. ◄

Three different temperature scales are in common use: Celsius, Kelvin, and Fahrenheit (Figure 2-10). Both the Celsius and the Kelvin scales are part of the metric measurement system; the Fahrenheit scale belongs to the English measurement system. Degrees of different size and different reference points are what produce the various temperature scales.

The *Celsius scale* is the scale most commonly encountered in scientific work. The normal boiling and freezing points of water serve as reference points on this scale, the former having a value of 100° and the latter 0°. Thus there are 100 "degree intervals" between the two reference points. ◄

The *Kelvin scale*, a close relative of the Celsius scale, is divided into *kelvins (K)* instead of degrees. The kelvin is the same size unit as the Celsius degree. There are 100 kelvins between the freezing and boiling points of water, just as there are 100 Celsius degrees between these same reference points. The assignment of different numerical values to the reference points causes the two scales to differ numerically. On the Kelvin scale, the boiling point of water is 373 K and the freezing point of water is 273 K. The choice of these reference-point values makes all temperatures on the Kelvin scale positive values. ◄

The *Fahrenheit scale* has a smaller degree size than the other two temperature scales. On this scale, there are 180 degrees between the freezing and boiling points of water in contrast to 100 degrees on the other two scales. Thus the Celsius (and Kelvin) degree size is almost two times ($\frac{9}{5}$) larger than the Fahrenheit degree size. Reference points on the Fahrenheit scale are 32° for the freezing point of water and 212° for the normal boiling point of water. ◄

Besides the boiling and freezing points for water, a third reference point is shown in Figure 2-10 for each of the temperature scales—normal human body temperature. The focus on relevancy feature Chemical Connections 2-B—Normal Human Body Temperature—explores the topic of "normal" body temperature and the fact that there is considerable variance in its value, with diverse conditions affecting what the value turns out to be.

▶ *When a low temperature object, such as an ice cube, is held in a bare hand a feeling of "coldness" develops. In actuality, heat is flowing from the hand to the low temperature object.*

▶ *On the Celsius scale*
   Thirty is hot,
   Twenty is pleasing;
   Ten is quite cool,
   And zero is freezing.

▶ *Zero on the Kelvin scale is known as* absolute zero. *It corresponds to the lowest temperature allowed by nature. How fast particles (molecules) move depends on temperature. The colder it gets, the more slowly they move. At absolute zero, movement stops. Scientists in laboratories have been able to attain temperatures as low as 0.0001 K, but a temperature of 0 K is impossible.*

▶ *In the United States, the Fahrenheit scale is usually used in weather reporting and in specifying human body temperature.*

Conversions Between Temperature Scales

Because the size of the degree is the same, the relationship between the Kelvin and Celsius scales is very simple. No conversion factors are needed; all that is required is

Figure 2-10 The relationships among the Celsius, Kelvin, and Fahrenheit temperature scales are determined by the degree sizes and the reference point values. The reference point values are not drawn to scale.

Normal Human Body Temperature

Studies show that "normal" human body temperature varies from individual to individual. For oral temperature measurements, this individual variance spans the range from 96°F to 101°F.

Furthermore, individual body temperatures vary with exercise and with the temperature of the surroundings. When excessive heat is produced in the body by strenuous exercise, oral temperature can rise as high as 103°F. On the other hand, when the body is exposed to cold, oral temperature can fall to values considerably below 96°F. A rapid fall in temperature of 2°F to 3°F produces uncontrollable shivering.

Each individual also has a characteristic pattern of temperature variation during the day, with differences of as much as 1°F to 3°F between high and low points. Body temperature is typically lowest in the very early morning, after several hours of sleep, when one is inactive and not digesting food. During the day, body temperature rises to a peak and begins to fall again. "Morning people"—people who are most productive early in the day—have a body temperature peak at midmorning or midday. "Night people"—people who feel as though they are just getting started as evening approaches and who work best late at night—have a body temperature peak in the evening.

What, then, is the average (normal) human body temperature? Reference books list the value 98.6°F (37.0°C) as the answer to this question. The source for this value is a study involving more than 1 million human body temperature readings that was published in 1868, more than 140 years ago.

A 1992 study, published in the *Journal of the American Medical Association*, questions the validity of this average value (98.6°F). This new study notes that the 1868 study was carried out using thermometers that were more difficult to get accurate readings from than modern thermometers. The 1992 study is based on oral temperature readings obtained using electronic thermometers. Findings of this new study include the following:

1. The range of temperatures was 96.0°F to 100.8°F.
2. The mean (average) temperature was 98.2°F (36.8°C).
3. At 6 A.M., the temperature 98.9°F is the upper limit of the normal temperature range.
4. In late afternoon (4 P.M.), the temperature 99.9°F is the upper limit of the normal temperature range.
5. Women have a slightly higher average temperature than men (98.4°F versus 98.1°F).
6. Over the temperature range 96°F to 101°F, there is an average increase in heart rate of 2.44 beats per minute for each 1°F rise in temperature.

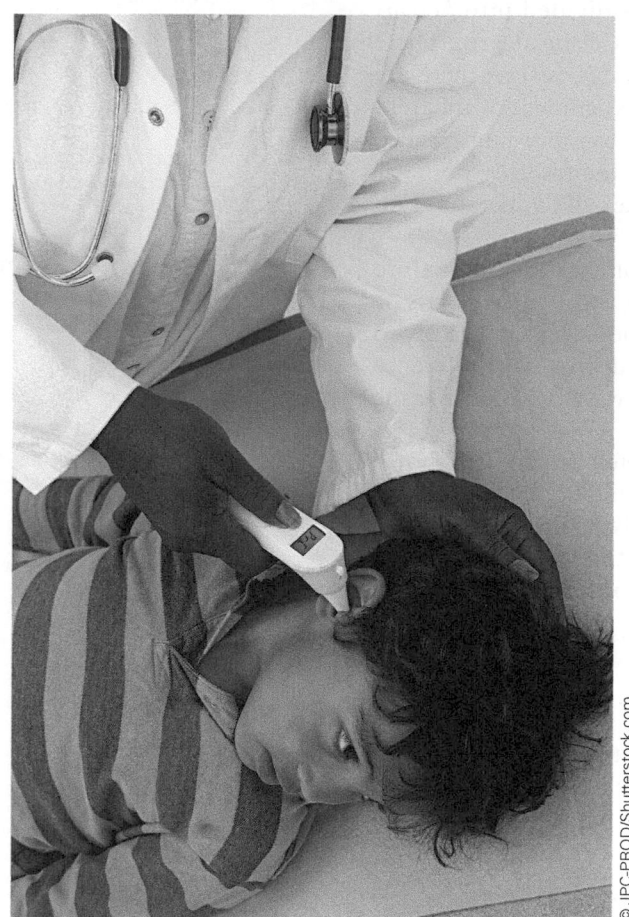

© JPC-PROD/Shutterstock.com

Normal body temperature falls in the range of 96°F to 101°F.

an adjustment for the differing numerical scale values. The adjustment factor is 273, the number of degrees by which the two scales are offset from one another.

$$K = °C + 273$$
$$°C = K - 273$$

The relationship between the Fahrenheit and Celsius scales can also be stated in an equation format.

$$°F = \frac{9}{5}(°C) + 32 \qquad \text{or} \qquad °C = \frac{5}{9}(°F - 32)$$

EXAMPLE 2-10

Converting from One Temperature Scale to Another

The body temperature of a person with a high fever is found to be 104°F. What is this temperature equivalent to on the following scales?

a. Celsius scale   **b.** Kelvin scale

Solution

a. The value 104 for °F is substituted into the equation

$$°C = \frac{5}{9}(°F - 32)$$

Solving for °C gives

$$°C = \frac{5}{9}(104 - 32) = \frac{5}{9}(72) = 40°$$

b. Using the answer from part **a** and the equation

$$K = °C + 273$$

the Kelvin temperature is 313 K,

$$K = 40 + 273 = 313$$

Temperature Readings and Significant Figures

Standard operating procedure in reading a thermometer is to estimate the temperature to the closest degree, giving a degree reading having an uncertainty in the "ones place." This means that Celsius or Fahrenheit temperatures of 10°, 20°, 30°, and so forth, are considered to have two significant figures even though no decimal point is explicitly shown after the zero. A temperature reading of 100°C or 100°F is considered to possess three significant figures.

Section 2-10 Quick Quiz

1. The freezing point of water is
   a. 0°F
   b. 0 K
   c. 0°C
   d. no correct response
2. A Kelvin scale temperature reading is converted to a Celsius scale reading by
   a. adding 100
   b. adding 273
   c. subtracting 273
   d. no correct response
3. Which of the following statements concerning major temperature scales is <u>incorrect</u>?
   a. Kelvin scale temperatures can never be negative.
   b. The addition of 100 to a Fahrenheit reading converts it to a Celsius temperature.
   c. Water boils at 212° on the Fahrenheit scale.
   d. no correct response
4. Which of the following scale comparisons among the major temperature scales is correct?
   a. A Kelvin unit is larger than a Celsius degree.
   b. A Fahrenheit degree and a Celsius degree are equal in size.
   c. A Kelvin unit is smaller than a Fahrenheit degree.
   d. no correct response

Answers: 1. c; 2. c; 3. b; 4. d

Concepts to Remember

The metric system. The metric system, the measurement system preferred by scientists, is a decimal system in which larger and smaller units of a quantity are related by factors of 10. Prefixes are used to designate relationships between the base unit and larger or smaller units of a quantity. Units in the metric system include the gram (mass), liter (volume), and meter (length) (Section 2-2).

Exact and inexact numbers. Numbers are of two kinds: exact and inexact. An exact number has a value that has no uncertainty associated with it. Exact numbers occur in definitions, in counting, and in simple fractions. An inexact number has a value that has a degree of uncertainty associated with it. Inexact numbers are generated any time a measurement is made (Section 2-3).

Significant figures. Significant figures in a measurement are those digits that are certain, plus a last digit that has been estimated. The maximum number of significant figures possible in a measurement is determined by the design of the measuring device (Section 2-4).

Calculations and significant figures. Calculations should never increase (or decrease) the precision of experimental measurements. In multiplication and division, the number of significant figures in the answer is the same as that in the measurement containing the fewest significant figures. In addition and subtraction, the answer has no more digits to the right of the decimal point than are found in the measurement with the fewest digits to the right of the decimal point (Section 2-5).

Scientific notation. Scientific notation is a system for writing decimal numbers in a more compact form that greatly simplifies the mathematical operations of multiplication and division. In this system, numbers are expressed as the product of a number between 1 and 10 and 10 raised to a power (Section 2-6).

Conversion factors. A conversion factor is a ratio that specifies how one unit of measurement is related to another. These factors are derived from equations (equalities) that relate units, and they always come in reciprocal pairs (Section 2-7).

Dimensional analysis. Dimensional analysis is a general problem-solving method in which the units associated with numbers are used as a guide in setting up calculations. A given quantity is multiplied by one or more conversion factors in such a manner that the unwanted (original) units are canceled, leaving only the desired units (Section 2-8).

Density. Density is the ratio of the mass of an object to the volume of the object. A correct density expression includes a number, a mass unit, and a volume unit (Section 2-9).

Temperature scales. The three major temperature scales are the Celsius, Kelvin, and Fahrenheit scales. The size of the degree for the Celsius and Kelvin scales is the same; they differ only in the numerical values assigned to the reference points. The Fahrenheit scale has a smaller degree size than the other two temperature scales (Section 2-10).

Exercises and Problems

Exercises and problems are arranged in matched pairs with the two members of a pair addressing the same concept(s). The answer to the odd-numbered member of a pair is given at the back of the book. Problems denoted with a ▲ involve concepts found not only in the section under consideration but also concepts found in one or more earlier sections of the chapter.

Measurement Systems (Section 2-1)

2-1 What is the main reason scientists prefer to use the metric system of measurement rather than the English system of measurement?

2-2 List the more common types of measurements made in chemical laboratories.

Metric System Units (Section 2-2)

2-3 Complete the following table by filling in the "blanks" in each row with the name of the metric system prefix, its abbreviation, and/or the power of 10 to which it is equivalent. The first row has been completed as an example.

	Metric Prefix	Abbreviation for Prefix	Mathematical Meaning of Prefix
	milli-	m	10^{-3}
a.		G	
b.	nano-		
c.			10^{6}
d.		μ	

2-4 Complete the following table by filling in the "blanks" in each row with the name of the metric system prefix, its abbreviation, and/or the power of 10 to which it is equivalent. The first row has been completed as an example.

	Metric Prefix	Abbreviation for Prefix	Mathematical Meaning of Prefix
	centi-	c	10^{-2}
a.		k	
b.	mega-		
c.			10^{-12}
d.	deci-		

2-5 Complete the following table by filling in the "blanks" in each row with the name of the metric unit, the property being measured (mass, length, volume), and/or the abbreviation for the metric unit. The first row has been completed as an example.

	Metric Unit	Property Being Measured	Abbreviation for Metric Unit
	microliter	volume	μL
a.			kg
b.	megameter		
c.			ng
d.	milliliter		

2-6 Complete the following table by filling in the "blanks" in each row with the name of the metric unit, the property being measured (mass, length, volume), and/or the abbreviation for the metric unit. The first row has been completed as an example.

	Metric Unit	Property Being Measured	Abbreviation for Metric Unit
	gigagram	mass	Gg
a.			cm
b.	deciliter		
c.			pm
d.	kilogram		

2-7 Arrange each of the following from smallest to largest.
a. Milligram, centigram, nanogram
b. Gigameter, megameter, kilometer
c. Microliter, deciliter, picoliter
d. Milligram, kilogram, microgram

2-8 Arrange each of the following from smallest to largest.
a. Milliliter, gigaliter, microliter
b. Centigram, megagram, decigram
c. Micrometer, picometer, kilometer
d. Nanoliter, milliliter, centiliter

2-9 Which of the two given units is the more logical unit for expressing each of the following measurements?
a. thickness of a chemistry textbook (centimeter or meter)
b. mass of a cantaloupe seed (kilogram or milligram)
c. capacity of a car's gasoline tank (milliliter or liter)
d. length of a man's tie (decimeter or micrometer)

2-10 Which of the two given units is the more logical unit for expressing each of the following measurements?
a. length of an ant's body (centimeter or micrometer)
b. width of a football field (meter or kilometer)
c. volume of glass of milk (megaliter or milliliter)
d. mass of an elephant (gram or kilogram)

Exact and Inexact Numbers (Section 2-3)

2-11 A person is told that there are 60 minutes in an hour and also that a section of fence is 60 feet long. What is the difference relative to uncertainty between the value of 60 in these two pieces of information?

2-12 A person is told that there are 27 people in attendance at a meeting and also that the speed of a bicyclist is 27 miles per hour. What is the difference relative to uncertainty between the value of 27 in these two pieces of information?

2-13 Indicate whether the number in each of the following statements is an *exact* or an *inexact* number.
a. A classroom contains 32 chairs.
b. There are 60 seconds in a minute.
c. A bowl of cherries weighs 3.2 pounds.
d. A newspaper article contains 323 words.

2-14 Indicate whether the number in each of the following statements is an *exact* or an *inexact* number.
a. A classroom contains 63 students.
b. The car is traveling at a speed of 56 miles per hour.
c. The temperature on the back porch is −3°F.
d. There are 3 feet in a yard.

2-15 Indicate whether each of the following quantities would involve an *exact* number or an *inexact* number.
a. The length of a swimming pool
b. The number of gummi bears in a bag
c. The number of quarts in a gallon
d. The surface area of a living room rug

2-16 Indicate whether each of the following quantities would involve an *exact* number or an *inexact* number.
a. The number of pages in a chemistry textbook
b. The number of teeth in a bear's mouth
c. The distance from Earth to the sun
d. The temperature of a heated oven

Uncertainty in Measurement (Section 2-4)

2-17 Identify the estimated digit in each of the following measurements?
a. 234   b. 234.0
c. 0.234   d. 0.00234

2-18 Identify the estimated digit in each of the following measurements?
a. 317   b. 317.0
c. 3.170   d. 0.0317

2-19 What is the magnitude of the uncertainty (± 10, ± 0.01, etc.) associated with each of the measurements in Problem 2-17?

2-20 What is the magnitude of the uncertainty (± 10, ± 0.01, etc.) associated with each of the measurements in Problem 2-18?

2-21 Indicate to what decimal position readings should be recorded (nearest 0.1, 0.01, etc.) for measurements made with the following devices.
a. A thermometer with a smallest scale marking of 1°C
b. A graduated cylinder with a smallest scale marking of 0.1 mL
c. A volumetric device with a smallest scale marking of 10 mL
d. A ruler with a smallest scale marking of 1 mm

2-22 Indicate to what decimal position readings should be recorded (nearest 0.1, 0.01, etc.) for measurements made with the following devices.
a. A ruler with a smallest scale marking of 1 cm
b. A device for measuring angles with a smallest scale marking of 1°
c. A thermometer with a smallest scale marking of 0.1°F
d. A graduated cylinder with a smallest scale marking of 10 mL

2-23 Consider the following rulers as instruments for the measurement of length.

What would the uncertainty be in measurements made using the following?
a. Ruler 1   b. Ruler 4

2-24 Using the rulers given in Problem 2-23, what would the uncertainty be in measurements made using the following?
a. Ruler 2   b. Ruler 3

2-25 Using the rulers given in Problem 2-23, what is the length of the paper clip shown by the side of the following?
a. Ruler 2   b. Ruler 3

2-26 Using the rulers given in Problem 2-23, what is the length of the paper clip shown by the side of the following?
a. Ruler 1   b. Ruler 4

2-27 With which of the rulers in Problem 2-23 was each of the following measurements made, assuming that you cannot use a ruler multiple times in making the measurement? (It is possible that there may be more than one correct answer.)
a. 20.4 cm   b. 2.3 cm   c. 3.74 cm   d. 32 cm

2-28 With which of the rulers in Problem 2-23 was each of the following measurements made, assuming that you cannot use a ruler multiple times in making the measurement? (It is possible that there may be more than one correct answer.)
a. 3.2 cm   b. 3.22 cm   c. 22 cm   d. 3 cm

Significant Figures and Measurement (Section 2-4)

2-29 Determine the number of significant figures in each of the following measured values.
a. 0.444
b. 0.00444
c. 0.04040
d. 0.00004

2-30 Determine the number of significant figures in each of the following measured values.
a. 0.372
b. 0.0372
c. 0.37202
d. 0.37200

2-31 Determine the number of significant figures in each of the following measured values.
a. 275.00
b. 27,500
c. 6,720,000
d. 6,720,100

2-32 Determine the number of significant figures in each of the following measured values.
a. 303.00
b. 30,300
c. 5,703,000
d. 570,002

2-33 In which of the following pairs of numbers do both members of the pair contain the same number of significant figures?
a. 11.01 and 11.00
b. 2002 and 2020
c. 0.000066 and 660,000
d. 0.05700 and 0.05070

2-34 In which of the following pairs of numbers do both members of the pair contain the same number of significant figures?
a. 345,000 and 340,500
b. 2302 and 2320
c. 0.6600 and 0.66
d. 936 and 936,000

▲**2-35** In the pairs of numbers of Problem 2-33, tell whether both members of the pair have the same uncertainty.

▲**2-36** In the pairs of numbers of Problem 2-34, tell whether both members of the pair have the same uncertainty.

▲**2-37** Complete the following table by filling in the blanks in each row with numerical values that are consistent with the number given in the first column. The first row is completed as an example.

	Measured Number	Number of Significant Figures	Estimated Digit in Measurement	Magnitude of Uncertainty
	53.71	4	the 1	±0.01
a.	5371			
b.	0.41			
c.	3200			
d.	5050			

▲**2-38** Complete the following table by filling in the blanks in each row with numerical values that are consistent with the number given in the first column. The first row is completed as an example.

	Measured Number	Number of Significant Figures	Estimated Digit in Measurement	Magnitude of Uncertainty
	3.25	3	the 5	±0.01
a.	0.030			
b.	2100			
c.	7005			
d.	1.23			

▲**2-39** The number of people watching a parade was estimated by police to be 50,000. What is the high and low estimate for the number of people watching the parade if it is assumed that this estimate has each of the following uncertainties?
a. 10,000   b. 1000   c. 100   d. 10

▲**2-40** The number of people present at an outdoor rock concert was estimated by police to be 40,000. What is the high and low estimate for the number of people present at the concert if it is assumed that this estimate has each of the following uncertainties?
a. 10,000   b. 1000   c. 100   d. 10

Significant Figures and Mathematical Operations (Section 2-5)

2-41 Round off each of the following numbers to the number of significant figures indicated in parentheses.
a. 0.350763 (four)
b. 13.43 (three)
c. 22.4555 (two)
d. 0.030303 (three)

2-42 Round off each of the following numbers to the number of significant figures indicated in parentheses.
a. 340.272 (four)
b. 133.133 (three)
c. 0.04470 (two)
d. 0.35726 (three)

2-43 Round off (or add zeros) to each of the following measured values to give a value that contains three significant figures.
a. 3567   b. 323,200
c. 18   d. 2,345,346

2-44 Round off (or add zeros) to each of the following measured values to give a value that contains three significant figures.
a. 1234   b. 25,730
c. 7.2   d. 3,666,432

2-45 Complete the following table by filling in the blanks in each row with numerical values obtained by rounding the given values to the specified number of significant figures (sig figs). The first row is completed as an example.

Measured Value	4 sig fig Value for Measurement	2 sig fig Value for Measurement
2.3547	2.355	2.4
a. 1.8828		
b. 24,233		
c. 0.51181		
d. 7.4500		

2-46 Complete the following table by filling in the blanks in each row with numerical values obtained by rounding the given values to the specified number of significant figures (sig figs). The first row is completed as an example.

Measured Value	4 sig fig Value for Measurement	2 sig fig Value for Measurement
0.12772	0.1277	0.13
a. 0.53731		
b. 34.406		
c. 25,549		
d. 7.1009		

2-47 Without actually solving, indicate the number of significant figures that should be present in the answers to the following multiplication and division problems.
a. $10.300 \times 0.30 \times 0.300$
b. $3300 \times 3330 \times 333.0$
c. $\dfrac{6.0}{33.0}$
d. $\dfrac{6.000}{33}$

2-48 Without actually solving, indicate the number of significant figures that should be present in the answers to the following multiplication and division problems.
a. $3.00 \times 0.0003 \times 30.00$
b. $0.3 \times 0.30 \times 3.0$
c. $\dfrac{6.00}{33,000}$
d. $\dfrac{6.00000}{3}$

2-49 Carry out the following multiplications and divisions, expressing your answer to the correct number of significant figures. Assume that all numbers are measured numbers.
a. $2.0000 \times 2.00 \times 0.0020$
b. 4.1567×0.00345
c. $0.0037 \times 3700 \times 1.001$
d. $\dfrac{6.00}{33.0}$
e. $\dfrac{530,000}{465.300}$
f. $\dfrac{4670 \times 3.00}{2.450}$

2-50 Carry out the following multiplications and divisions, expressing your answer to the correct number of significant figures. Assume that all numbers are measured numbers.
a. $2.000 \times 0.200 \times 0.20$
b. 3.6750×0.04503
c. $0.0030 \times 0.400 \times 4.00$
d. $\dfrac{6.0000}{33.00}$
e. $\dfrac{45,000}{1.2345}$
f. $\dfrac{3.00 \times 6.53}{13.567}$

2-51 Carry out the following additions and subtractions, expressing your answer to the correct number of significant figures. Assume that all numbers are measured numbers.
a. $12 + 23 + 127$
b. $3.111 + 3.11 + 3.1$
c. $1237.6 + 23 + 0.12$
d. $43.65 - 23.7$

2-52 Carry out the following additions and subtractions, expressing your answer to the correct number of significant figures. Assume that all numbers are measured numbers.
a. $237 + 37.0 + 7.0$
b. $4.000 + 4.002 + 4.20$
c. $235.45 + 37 + 36.4$
d. $3.111 - 2.07$

▲**2-53** What is the uncertainty in the measured value 12.37050 after it is rounded to the following number of significant figures?
a. 6   b. 4
c. 3   d. 2

▲**2-54** What is the uncertainty in the measured value 87.20030 after it is rounded to the following number of significant figures?
a. 6   b. 5
c. 4   d. 2

Scientific Notation (Section 2-6)

2-55 For each of the following numbers, will the exponent be positive, negative, or zero when the number is expressed in scientific notation?
a. 0.0123   b. 375,000
c. 0.100   d. 68.75

2-56 For each of the following numbers, will the exponent be positive, negative, or zero when the number is expressed in scientific notation?
a. 50.031
b. 650,010
c. 0.1030
d. 735

2-57 For each of the numbers in Problem 2-55, specify the number of places the decimal point has to be moved in order to express the number in scientific notation.

2-58 For each of the numbers in Problem 2-56, specify the number of places the decimal point has to be moved in order to express the number in scientific notation.

2-59 For each of the numbers in Problem 2-55, how many significant figures should be present in the scientific notation form of the number?

2-60 For each of the numbers in Problem 2-56, how many significant figures should be present in the scientific notation form of the number?

2-61 Express the following measured values in scientific notation to the correct number of significant figures.
a. 120.7   b. 0.0034
c. 231.00   d. 23,100

2-62 Express the following measured values in scientific notation to the correct number of significant figures.
a. 37.22   b. 0.00102
c. 34.000   d. 234,000

2-63 Change each of the following measured values from scientific notation to decimal notation.
a. 2.34×10^2
b. 2.3400×10^2
c. 2.34×10^{-3}
d. 2.3400×10^{-3}

2-64 Change each of the following measured values from scientific notation to decimal notation.
a. 3.721×10^3
b. 3.7210×10^2
c. 6.76×10^{-2}
d. 6.7600×10^{-2}

2-65 Carry out the following multiplications and divisions, expressing your answer in scientific notation to the correct number of significant figures.
a. $(3.20 \times 10^7) \times (1.720 \times 10^5)$
b. $(1.00 \times 10^3) \times (5.00 \times 10^3) \times (3.0 \times 10^{-3})$
c. $\dfrac{3.0 \times 10^{-5}}{1.5 \times 10^2}$
d. $\dfrac{(2.2 \times 10^6) \times (2.3 \times 10^{-6})}{(1.2 \times 10^{-3}) \times (3.5 \times 10^{-3})}$

2-66 Carry out the following multiplications and divisions, expressing your answer in scientific notation to the correct number of significant figures.
a. $(4.0 \times 10^4) \times (1.32 \times 10^8)$
b. $(3.200 \times 10^7) \times (1.10 \times 10^{-2}) \times (2.3 \times 10^{-7})$
c. $\dfrac{6.0 \times 10^{-5}}{3.0 \times 10^3}$
d. $\dfrac{(3.2 \times 10^2) \times (3.31 \times 10^6)}{(4.00 \times 10^{-3}) \times (2.0 \times 10^6)}$

2-67 What is the uncertainty, in terms of a power of 10, associated with each of the following measured values?
a. 3.60×10^4
b. 3.60×10^6
c. 3.6×10^5
d. 3.6×10^{-3}

2-68 What is the uncertainty, in terms of a power of 10, associated with each of the following measured values?
a. 4.30×10^{-2}
b. 4.300×10^{-1}
c. 4.3×10^3
d. 4.300×10^5

▲**2-69** Write each of the following numbers in scientific notation to the number of significant figures indicated in parentheses.
a. 0.00300300 (three)
b. 936,000 (two)
c. 23.5003 (three)
d. 450,000,001 (six)

▲**2-70** Write each of the following numbers in scientific notation to the number of significant figures indicated in parentheses.
a. 0.303030 (four)
b. 15.0670 (three)
c. 3,263,300 (three)
d. 32,000,071 (four)

Conversion Factors (Section 2-7)

2-71 Give the two forms of the conversion factor that relate each of the following pairs of units.
a. Days and hours
b. Decades and centuries
c. Feet and yards
d. Quarts and gallons

2-72 Give the two forms of the conversion factor that relate each of the following pairs of units.
a. Days and weeks
b. Years and centuries
c. Inches and feet
d. Pints and quarts

2-73 Give the two forms of the conversion factor that relate each of the following pairs of units.
a. kL and L
b. mg and g
c. m and cm
d. μsec and sec

2-74 Give the two forms of the conversion factor that relate each of the following pairs of units.
a. ng and g
b. dL and L
c. m and Mm
d. psec and sec

2-75 Indicate whether each of the following equations relating units would generate an *exact* set of conversion factors or an *inexact* set of conversion factors relative to significant figures.
a. 1 dozen = 12 objects
b. 1 kilogram = 2.20 pounds
c. 1 minute = 60 seconds
d. 1 millimeter = 10^{-3} meter

2-76 Indicate whether each of the following equations relating units would generate an *exact* set of conversion factors or an *inexact* set of conversion factors relative to significant figures.
a. 1 gallon = 16 cups
b. 1 week = 7 days
c. 1 pint = 0.4732 liter
d. 1 mile = 5280 feet

Dimensional Analysis (Section 2-8)

2-77 Using dimensional analysis, convert each of the following measurements to meters.
a. 1.6×10^3 dm
b. 24 nm
c. 0.003 km
d. 3.0×10^8 mm

2-78 Using dimensional analysis, convert each of the following measurements to meters.
a. 2.7×10^3 mm
b. 24 μm
c. 0.003 pm
d. 4.0×10^5 cm

2-79 The human stomach produces approximately 2500 mL of gastric juice per day. What is the volume, in liters, of gastric juice produced?

2-80 A typical loss of water through sweating for a human is 450 mL per day. What is the volume, in liters, of sweat produced per day?

2-81 The mass of premature babies is customarily determined in grams. If a premature baby weighs 1550 g, what is its mass in pounds?

2-82 The smallest bone in the human body, which is in the ear, has a mass of 0.0030 g. What is the mass of this bone in pounds?

2-83 What volume of water, in gallons, would be required to fill a 25-mL container?

2-84 What volume of gasoline, in milliliters, would be required to fill a 17.0-gal gasoline tank?

2-85 An individual weighs 83.2 kg and is 1.92 m tall. What are the person's equivalent measurements in pounds and feet?

2-86 An individual weighs 135 lb and is 5 ft 4 in. tall. What are the person's equivalent measurements in kilograms and meters?

▲**2-87** When each of the following measurements of length is converted to inches, using a conversion factor obtained from the equality 1 foot = 12 inches, how many significant figures should the answer have?
a. 4.3 ft
b. 3.09 ft
c. 0.33030 ft
d. 5.12310 ft

▲**2-88** When each of the following measurements of mass is converted to tons, using a conversion factor obtained from the equality 1 ton = 2000 pounds, how many significant figures should the answer have?
a. 6.4 lb
b. 3.2091 lb
c. 0.400040 lb
d. 423,000 lb

▲**2-89** When each of the following measurements of volume is converted to liters, using a conversion factor obtained from the relationship 1 quart = 0.9463 liter, how many significant figures should the answer have?
a. 4.3 qt
b. 3.09 qt
c. 0.33030 qt
d. 5.12310 qt

▲**2-90** When each of the following measurements of mass is converted to grams, using a conversion factor obtained from the relationship 1 pound = 453.6 grams, how many significant figures should the answer have?
a. 6.4 lb
b. 3.2091 lb
c. 0.400040 lb
d. 423,000 lb

Density (Section 2-9)

2-91 A sample of mercury is found to have a mass of 524.5 g and to have a volume of 38.72 cm³. What is its density in grams per cubic centimeter?

2-92 A sample of sand is found to have a mass of 12.0 g and to have a volume of 2.69 cm³. What is its density in grams per cubic centimeter?

2-93 Acetone, the solvent in nail polish remover, has a density of 0.791 g/mL. What is the volume, in milliliters, of 20.0 g of acetone?

2-94 Silver metal has a density of 10.40 g/cm³. What is the volume, in cubic centimeters, of a 100.0-g bar of silver metal?

2-95 The density of homogenized milk is 1.03 g/mL. How much does 1 cup (236 mL) of homogenized milk weigh in grams?

2-96 Nickel metal has a density of 8.90 g/cm³. How much does 15 cm³ of nickel metal weigh in grams?

2-97 Water has a density of 1.0 g/cm³ at room temperature. State whether each of the following will sink or float when placed in water.
a. Paraffin wax (density = 0.90 g/cm³)
b. Limestone (density = 2.8 g/cm³)

2-98 Air has a density of 1.29 g/L at room temperature. State whether each of the following will rise or sink in air.
a. Helium gas (density = 0.18 g/L)
b. Argon gas (density = 1.78 g/L)

▲**2-99** A one-gram sample of a powdery white solid is found to have a volume of two cubic centimeters. Calculate the solid's density using the following uncertainty specifications, and express your answers in scientific notation.
a. 1.0 g and 2.0 cm³
b. 1.000 g and 2.00 cm³
c. 1.0000 g and 2.0000 cm³
d. 1.000 g and 2.0000 cm³

▲**2-100** A two-gram sample of a red-colored liquid is found to have a volume of four cubic centimeters. Calculate the liquid's density using the following uncertainty

specifications, and express your answers in scientific notation.
  a. 2.00 g and 4.000 cm³
  b. 2.000 g and 4.0 cm³
  c. 2.0000 g and 4.000 cm³
  d. 2.000 g and 4.0000 cm³

▲2-101 Calculate the volume, in *milliliters*, for each of the following 75.0-g masses of substances.
  a. 75.0 g of gasoline (density = 0.56 g/mL)
  b. 75.0 g of sodium metal (density = 0.93 g/cm³)
  c. 75.0 g of ammonia gas (density = 0.759 g/L)
  d. 75.0 g of mercury (density = 13.6 g/mL)

▲2-102 Calculate the volume, in *milliliters*, for each of the following 66.0-g masses of substances.
  a. 66.0 g of blood plasma (density = 1.027 g/mL)
  b. 66.0 g of dry air (density = 1.29 g/L)
  c. 66.0 g of lead metal (density = 11.3 g/cm³)
  d. 66.0 g of milk (density = 1.03 g/mL)

Temperature Scales (Section 2-10)

2-103 An oven for baking pizza operates at approximately 525°F. What is this temperature in degrees Celsius?

2-104 A comfortable temperature for bathtub water is 95°F. What temperature is this in degrees Celsius?

2-105 Mercury freezes at −38.9°C. What is the coldest temperature, in degrees Fahrenheit, that can be measured using a mercury thermometer?

2-106 The body temperature for a hypothermia victim is found to have dropped to 29.1°C. What is this temperature in degrees Fahrenheit?

2-107 Which is the higher temperature, −10°C or 10°F?

2-108 Which is the higher temperature, −15°C or 4°F?

Chapter 2 Appendix:

Section 2.11 HEAT ENERGY AND SPECIFIC HEAT from General, Organic, and Biological Chemistry, Fifth Edition, H. Stephen Stoker

EXAMPLE 2.10

Converting from One Temperature Scale to Another

Body temperature for a person with a high fever is found to be 104°F. To what is this temperature equivalent on the following scales?

a. Celsius scale   **b.** Kelvin scale

Solution

a. We substitute 104 for °F in the equation

$$°C = \frac{5}{9} (°F - 32)$$

Then solving for °C gives

$$°C = \frac{5}{9} (104 - 32) = \frac{5}{9} (72) = 40°$$

b. Using the answer from part **a** and the equation

$$K = °C + 273$$

we get, by substitution,

$$K = 40 + 273 = 313$$

Practice Exercise 2.10

In the human body, heat stroke occurs at a temperature of 41°C. To what is this temperature equivalent on the following scales?

a. Fahrenheit scale   **b.** Kelvin scale

Answers: a. 106°F; **b.** 314 K

TABLE 2.4
Specific Heats of Selected Common Substances

Substance	Specific Heat (cal/g · °C)*
water, liquid	1.00
ethyl alcohol	0.58
olive oil	0.47
wood	0.42
aluminum	0.21
glass	0.12
silver	0.057
gold	0.031

*The unit notation cal/g · °C means calories per gram per degree Celsius.

In discussions involving nutrition, the energy content of foods, and dietary tables, the term *Calorie* (spelled with a capital C) is used. The dietetic Calorie is actually 1 kilocalorie (1000 calories). The statement that an oatmeal raisin cookie contains 60 Calories means that 60 kcal (60,000 cal) of energy is released when the cookie is metabolized (undergoes chemical change) within the body.

Temperature Readings and Significant Figures

Standard operating procedure in reading a thermometer is to estimate the temperature to the closest degree, giving a degree reading having an uncertainty in the "ones place." This means that Celsius or Fahrenheit temperatures of 10°, 20°, 30°, etc., are considered to have two significant figures even though no decimal point is explicitly shown after the zero. A temperature reading of 100°C or 100°F is considered to possess three significant figures.

2.11 HEAT ENERGY AND SPECIFIC HEAT

The form of energy most often required for or released by chemical reactions and physical changes is *heat energy*. A commonly used unit for the measurement of heat energy is the calorie. A **calorie** (cal) *is the amount of heat energy needed to raise the temperature of 1 gram of water by 1 degree Celsius.* For large amounts of heat energy, the measurement is usually expressed in kilocalories.

$$1 \text{ kilocalorie} = 1000 \text{ calories}$$

Another unit for heat energy that is used with increasing frequency is the joule (J). The relationship between the joule (which rhymes with *pool*) and the calorie is

$$1 \text{ calorie} = 4.184 \text{ joules}$$

Heat energy values in calories can be converted to joules by using the conversion factor

$$\frac{4.184 \text{ J}}{1 \text{ cal}}$$

Specific heat *is the quantity of heat energy, in calories, necessary to raise the temperature of 1 gram of a substance by 1 degree Celsius.* Specific heats for a number of substances in various states are given in Table 2.4.

Normal Human Body Temperature

Studies show that "normal" human body temperature varies from individual to individual. For oral temperature measurements, this individual variance spans the range from 96°F to 101°F.

Furthermore, individual body temperatures vary with exercise and with the temperature of the surroundings. When excessive heat is produced in the body by strenuous exercise, oral temperature can rise as high as 103°F. On the other hand, when the body is exposed to cold, oral temperature can fall to values considerably below 96°F. A rapid fall in temperature of 2°F to 3°F produces uncontrollable shivering.

Each individual also has a characteristic pattern of temperature variation during the day, with differences of as much as 1°F to 3°F between high and low points. Body temperature is typically lowest in the very early morning, after several hours of sleep, when one is inactive and not digesting food. During the day, body temperature rises to a peak and begins to fall again. "Morning people"—people who are most productive early in the day—have a body temperature peak at midmorning or midday. "Night people"—people who feel as though they are just getting started as evening approaches and who work best late at night—have a body temperature peak in the evening.

What, then, is the average (normal) human body temperature? Reference books list the value 98.6°F (37.0°C) as the answer to this question. The source for this value is a study involving over 1 million human body temperature readings that was published in 1868, over 140 years ago.

A 1992 study, published in the *Journal of the American Medical Association,* questions the validity of this average value (98.6°F). This new study notes that the 1868 study was carried out using thermometers that were more difficult to get accurate readings from than modern thermometers. The 1992 study is based on oral temperature readings obtained using electronic thermometers. Findings of this new study include the following:

1. The range of temperatures was 96.0°F to 100.8°F.
2. The mean (average) temperature was 98.2°F (36.8°C).
3. At 6 A.M., the temperature 98.9°F is the upper limit of the normal temperature range.
4. In late afternoon (4 P.M.), the temperature 99.9°F is the upper limit of the normal temperature range.
5. Women have a slightly higher average temperature than men (98.4°F versus 98.1°F).
6. Over the temperature range 96°F to 101°F, there is an average increase in heart rate of 2.44 beats per minute for each 1°F rise in temperature.

As a result of this study, future reference books will probably use 98.2°F rather than 98.6°F as the value for average (normal) human body temperature.

The higher the specific heat of a substance, the less its temperature will change as it absorbs a given amount of heat. Water has a relatively high specific heat; it is thus a very effective coolant. The moderate climates of geographical areas near large bodies of water—the Hawaiian Islands, for example—are related to the ability of water to absorb large amounts of heat without undergoing drastic temperature changes. Desert areas (obviously lacking in water) experience low- and high-temperature extremes.

> Water has the highest specific heat of all common substances.

Specific heat is an important quantity because it can be used to calculate the number of calories required to heat a known mass of a substance from one temperature to another. It can also be used to calculate how much the temperature of a substance increases when it absorbs a known number of calories of heat. The equation used for such calculations is

> The property of specific heat varies *slightly* with temperature and pressure. We will ignore such variations in this text.

$$\text{Heat absorbed} = \text{specific heat} \times \text{mass} \times \text{temperature change}$$

If any three of the four quantities in this equation are known, the fourth quantity can be calculated. If the units for specific heat are cal/g · °C, the units for mass are grams, and the units for temperature change are °C; then the heat absorbed has units of calories.

● **EXAMPLE 2.11**

Calculating the Amount of Heat Released as the Result of a Temperature Decrease

▶ If a hot-water bottle contains 1200 g of water at 65°C, how much heat, in calories, will it have supplied to a person's "aching back" by the time it has cooled to 37°C (assuming all of the heat energy goes into the person's back)?

Solution

We will substitute known quantities into the equation

Heat released = specific heat × mass × temperature change

Table 2.4 shows that the specific heat of liquid water is 1.00 cal/g · °C. The mass of the water is given as 1200 g. The temperature change in going from 65°C to 37°C is 28°C. Substituting these values into the preceding equation gives

$$\text{Heat released} = \left(\frac{1.00 \text{ cal}}{g \cdot °C} \right) \times (1200 \, g) \times (28 °C)$$

$$= 33{,}600 \text{ cal} \qquad \text{(calculator answer)}$$

$$= 34{,}000 \text{ cal} \qquad \text{(correct answer)}$$

The given quantity of 1200 g and the temperature difference of 28°C, both of which have only two significant figures, limit the answer to two significant figures.

Practice Exercise 2.11

How much heat energy, in calories, must be absorbed by 125.0 g of water to raise its temperature by 12°C?

Answer: 1500 cal

C ONCEPTS TO REMEMBER

The metric system. The metric system, the measurement system preferred by scientists, is a decimal system in which larger and smaller units of a quantity are related by factors of 10. Prefixes are used to designate relationships between the basic unit and larger or smaller units of a quantity. Units in the metric system include the gram (mass), liter (volume), and meter (length) (Section 2.2).

Exact and inexact numbers. Numbers are of two kinds: exact and inexact. An exact number has a value that has no uncertainty associated with it. Exact numbers occur in definitions, in counting, and in simple fractions. An inexact number has a value that has a degree of uncertainty associated with it. Inexact numbers are generated any time a measurement is made (Section 2.3).

Significant figures. Significant figures in a measurement are those digits that are certain, plus a last digit that has been estimated. The maximum number of significant figures possible in a measurement is determined by the design of the measuring device (Section 2.4).

Calculations and significant figures. Calculations should never increase (or decrease) the precision of experimental measurements. In multiplication and division, the number of significant figures in the answer is the same as that in the measurement containing the fewest significant figures. In addition and subtraction, the answer has no more digits to the right of the decimal point than are found in the measurement with the fewest digits to the right of the decimal point (Section 2.5).

Scientific notation. Scientific notation is a system for writing decimal numbers in a more compact form that greatly simplifies the mathematical operations of multiplication and division. In this system,

numbers are expressed as the product of a number between 1 and 10 and 10 raised to a power (Section 2.6).

Conversion factors. A conversion factor is a ratio that specifies how one unit of measurement is related to another. They are derived from equations (equalities) that relate units and they always come in reciprocal pairs (Section 2.7).

Dimensional analysis. Dimensional analysis is a general problem-solving method in which the units associated with numbers are used as a guide in setting up calculations. A given quantity is multiplied by one or more conversion factors in such a manner that the unwanted (original) units are canceled, leaving only the desired units (Section 2.8).

Density. Density is the ratio of the mass of an object to the volume occupied by that object. A correct density expression includes a number, a mass unit, and a volume unit (Section 2.9).

Temperature scales. The three major temperature scales are the Celsius, Kelvin, and Fahrenheit scales. The size of the degree for the Celsius and Kelvin scales is the same; they differ only in the numerical values assigned to the reference points. The Fahrenheit scale has a smaller degree size than the other two temperature scales (Section 2.10).

Heat energy and specific heat. The most commonly used units of measurement for heat energy are the calorie and the joule. A calorie is the amount of heat energy needed to raise the temperature of 1 gram of water by 1 degree Celsius. A calorie is equivalent to 4.184 joules. The specific heat of a substance is the quantity of heat energy, in calories, that is necessary to raise the temperature of 1 gram of the substance by 1 degree Celsius (Section 2.11).

Atomic Structure and the Periodic Table

3

© Novastock/PhotoEdit

Music consists of a series of tones that build octave after octave. Similarly, elements have properties that recur period after period.

Until late in the nineteenth century (1880s), scientists considered atoms (Section 1-9) to be solid, indivisible spheres without any internal structure. Today, this model of the atom is known to be incorrect. Evidence from a variety of sources indicates that atoms themselves have substructure; that is, they are made up of small particles called *subatomic particles*. In this chapter, consideration is given to the characteristics of such subatomic particles, how they arrange themselves in an atom, and the relationship between an atom's subatomic makeup and its chemical identity.

3-1 Internal Structure of an Atom

LEARNING FOCUS

Be able to specify electric charge, relative mass, and location within an atom for each of the three major types of subatomic particles.

Atoms possess internal structure; that is, they are made up of even smaller particles, which are called subatomic particles. A **subatomic particle** *is a very small particle that is a building block for atoms.* Three types of subatomic

Table 3-1   **Charge and Mass Characteristics of Electrons, Protons, and Neutrons**

	Electron	Proton	Neutron
Charge	-1	$+1$	0
Actual mass (g)	9.109×10^{-28}	1.673×10^{-24}	1.675×10^{-24}
Relative mass (based on the electron being 1 unit)	1	1837	1839

particles are found within atoms: electrons, protons, and neutrons. Information concerning the key properties of electrical charge and relative mass for the three types of subatomic particles is found in Table 3-1. An **electron** *is a subatomic particle that possesses a negative (−) electrical charge.* It is the smallest, in terms of mass, of the three types of subatomic particles. A **proton** *is a subatomic particle that possesses a positive (+) electrical charge.* Protons and electrons carry the *same amount* of charge; the charges, however, are opposite (positive versus negative). A **neutron** *is a subatomic particle that has no charge associated with it; that is, it is neutral.* Both protons and neutrons are massive particles compared to electrons; they are almost 2000 times heavier. ◀

Arrangement of Subatomic Particles Within an Atom

▶ *Atoms of all 118 elements contain the same three types of subatomic particles. Different elements differ only in the numbers of the various subatomic particles they contain.*

The arrangement of subatomic particles within an atom is not haphazard. *All* protons and *all* neutrons present are found at the center of an atom in a very tiny volume called the *nucleus* (Figure 3-1). The **nucleus** *is the small, dense, positively charged center of an atom.* A nucleus is always positively charged because it contains positively charged protons. Because the nucleus houses the heavy subatomic particles (protons and neutrons), almost all (more than 99.9%) of the mass of an atom is concentrated in its nucleus. The small size of the nucleus, coupled with its large amount of mass, causes nuclear material to be extremely dense. ◀

▶ *The radius of a nucleus is approximately 10,000 times smaller than the radius of an entire atom.*

The outer (extranuclear) region of an atom contains all of the electrons. In this region, which accounts for most of the volume of an atom, the electrons move rapidly about the nucleus. The electrons are attracted to the positively charged protons of the nucleus by the forces that exist between particles of opposite charge. The motion of the electrons in the extranuclear region determines the volume (size) of the atom in the same way that the blade of a fan determines a volume by its circular motion. The volume occupied by the electrons is sometimes referred to as the *electron cloud.* Because electrons are negatively charged, the electron cloud is also negatively charged. Figure 3-1 contrasts the nuclear and extranuclear regions of an atom. The attractive force between the nucleus (positively charged) and the electrons (negatively charged) keeps the electrons within the extranuclear region of the atom. By analogy, the attractive force of gravity keeps the planets in their positions about the sun.

Closely resembling the term *nucleus* is the term *nucleon.* A **nucleon** *is any subatomic particle found in the nucleus of an atom.* Thus both protons and neutrons are nucleons, and the nucleus can be regarded as containing a collection of nucleons (protons and neutrons).

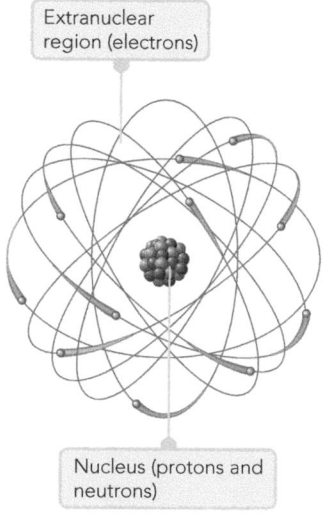

Figure 3-1 The protons and neutrons of an atom are found in the central nuclear region, or nucleus, and the electrons are found in an electron cloud outside the nucleus. Note that this figure is not drawn to scale; the correct scale would be comparable to a penny (the nucleus) in the center of a baseball field (the atom).

Charge Neutrality of an Atom

An atom as a whole is electrically neutral; that is, it has no *net* electrical charge. For this to be the case, the same number of positive and negative charges must be present in the atom. Equal numbers of positive and negative charges give a *net* electrical charge of zero. Thus equal numbers of protons and electrons are present in an atom.

> Number of protons = number of electrons

Size Relationships Within an Atom

The following imaginary example is helpful in gaining a correct perspective about the size relationship between a nucleus and an atom as a whole. Imagine enlarging (magnifying) the nucleus until it is the size of a baseball (about 2.9 inches in diameter). If the nucleus were this large, the whole atom would have a diameter of approximately 2.5 miles. The electrons would still be smaller than the periods used to end sentences in this text, and they would move about at random within that 2.5-mile region.

The concentration of nearly all of the mass of an atom in the nucleus can also be illustrated by using an imaginary example. If a coin the same size as a copper penny contained copper nuclei (copper atoms stripped of their electrons) rather than copper atoms (which are mostly empty space), the coin would weigh 190,000,000 tons! Nuclei are indeed very dense matter.

Despite the existence of subatomic particles, atoms are still considered to be the fundamental building blocks for all types of matter. Subatomic particles do not lead an independent existence for any appreciable length of time; they gain stability by joining together to form atoms.

Section 3-1 Quick Quiz

1. Which of the following statements concerning the three types of subatomic particles is correct?
   a. All types carry electrical charge.
   b. One of the three types carries electrical charge.
   c. None of the three types carry electrical charge.
   d. no correct response
2. Which of the following statements concerning a *neutron* is correct?
   a. Its mass is slightly less than that of a proton.
   b. It carries a positive charge of one unit.
   c. It carries a positive charge of two units.
   d. no correct response
3. How many electrons are required to equal the mass of one proton?
   a. 1
   b. 23
   c. about 1800
   d. no correct response
4. Which of the following statements concerning an atom's *nucleus* is correct?
   a. It contains all protons and all electrons.
   b. It is always positively charged.
   c. It accounts for most of the total volume of an atom.
   d. no correct response
5. Atoms as a whole are neutral because
   a. The numbers of neutrons exceeds that of protons or electrons.
   b. Charged subatomic particles lose their charge once they become part of an atom.
   c. Equal numbers of protons and electrons are present.
   d. no correct response

Answers: 1. d; 2. d; 3. c; 4. b; 5. c

3-2 Atomic Number and Mass Number

LEARNING FOCUS
Define the terms *atomic number* and *mass number*; given these two numbers, be able to determine the number of protons, neutrons, and electrons present in an atom.

An **atomic number** *is the number of protons in the nucleus of an atom.* Because an atom has the same number of electrons as protons (Section 3-1), the atomic number also specifies the number of electrons present. ◄

▶ *Atomic number and mass number are always whole numbers because they are obtained by counting whole objects (protons, neutrons, and electrons).*

Atomic number = number of protons = number of electrons

The symbol Z is used as a general designation for atomic number.

A **mass number** *is the sum of the number of protons and the number of neutrons in the nucleus of an atom.* Thus the mass number gives the number of subatomic particles present in the nucleus.

$$\text{Mass number} = \text{number of protons} + \text{number of neutrons}$$

The mass of an atom is almost totally accounted for by the protons and neutrons present—hence the term *mass number.* The symbol A is used as a general designation for mass number.

The number and identity of subatomic particles present in an atom can be calculated from its atomic and mass numbers in the following manner.

$$\text{Number of protons} = \text{atomic number} = Z$$

$$\text{Number of electrons} = \text{atomic number} = Z$$

$$\text{Number of neutrons} = \text{mass number} - \text{atomic number} = A - Z$$

Note that neutron count is obtained by subtracting atomic number from mass number. ◄

▶ *The sum of the mass number and the atomic number for an atom $(A + Z)$ corresponds to the total number of subatomic particles present in the atom (protons, neutrons, and electrons).*

EXAMPLE 3-1

Determining the Subatomic Particle Makeup of an Atom Given Its Atomic Number and Mass Number

An atom has an atomic number of 5 and a mass number of 11.

a. Determine the number of protons present.
b. Determine the number of neutrons present.
c. Determine the number of electrons present.

Solution

a. There are 5 protons because the atomic number is always equal to the number of protons present.
b. There are 6 neutrons because the number of neutrons is always obtained by subtracting the atomic number from the mass number $(11 - 5 = 6)$.

$$\underbrace{(\text{Protons} + \text{neutrons})}_{\text{Mass number}} - \underbrace{\text{protons}}_{\substack{\text{Atomic} \\ \text{number}}} = \text{neutrons}$$

A pictorial representation of this calculation is

Nucleus contains 11 particles (mass number)

5 protons are present (atomic number)   6 additional particles present are neutrons

c. There are 5 electrons because the number of protons and the number of electrons are always the same in an atom.

An alphabetical list of the 118 known elements, with their atomic numbers as well as other information, is found on the inside front cover of this text. Checking the atomic number column in this tabulation shows an entry for each of the numbers in the sequence 1 through 118. Scientists interpret this continuous atomic number sequence as evidence that there are no "missing elements" yet to be discovered in nature. The naturally occurring element with the highest atomic number is element 92 (uranium). Elements 93 through 118 are all laboratory produced (Section 1-7).

The mass and atomic numbers of a given atom are often specified using the notation

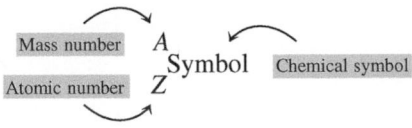

In this notation, often called *complete chemical symbol notation,* the atomic number is placed as a subscript in front of the chemical symbol and the mass number is placed as a superscript in front of the chemical symbol. Examples of such notations for actual atoms include

$$^{19}_{9}F \qquad ^{23}_{11}Na \qquad ^{197}_{79}Au$$

The first of these notations specifies a fluorine atom that has an atomic number of 9 and a mass number of 19.

Electrons and Chemical Properties

The chemical properties of an atom, which are the basis for its identification, are determined by the number and arrangement of the electrons about the nucleus. When two atoms interact, the outer part (electrons) of one interacts with the outer part (electrons) of the other. The small nuclear centers never come in contact with each other in a chemical reaction. The number of electrons about a nucleus may be considered to be determined by the number of protons in the nucleus; charge balance requires an equal number of the two (Section 3-1). Hence the number of protons (which is the atomic number) characterizes an atom. All atoms with the same atomic number have the same chemical properties and are atoms of the same element.

In Section 1-6, an element was defined as a pure substance that cannot be broken down into simpler substances by ordinary chemical means. Although this is a good historical definition of an element, a more rigorous definition can now be given by using the concept of atomic number. An **element** *is a pure substance in which all atoms present have the same atomic number.*

Section 3-2 Quick Quiz

1. The atomic number for an atom containing 10 neutrons and 8 protons is
   a. 8
   b. 10
   c. 18
   d. no correct response
2. An atom that has an atomic number of 11 and a mass number of 23 contains how many neutrons?
   a. 11
   b. 12
   c. 23
   d. no correct response
3. How many electrons are present in an atom of $^{31}_{15}P$?
   a. 15
   b. 16
   c. 31
   d. no correct response

(continued)

4. The identity of an atom is determined by the number of
   a. protons in the nucleus
   b. neutrons in the nucleus
   c. subatomic particles in the nucleus
   d. no correct response
5. Which of the following statements is correct for $^{27}_{14}Si$?
   a. contains more protons than neutrons
   b. contains more electrons than protons
   c. contains an equal number of protons and neutrons
   d. no correct response

Answers: 1. a; 2. b; 3. a; 4. a; 5. a

3-3   Isotopes and Atomic Masses

LEARNING FOCUS

Be able to define the term *isotope*; write the complete chemical symbol for a given isotope; calculate the atomic mass for an element from isotopic masses and percent abundances.

Charge neutrality (Section 3-1) requires the presence in an atom of an equal number of protons and electrons. However, because neutrons have no electrical charge, their numbers in atoms do not have to be the same as the number of protons or electrons. Most atoms contain more neutrons than either protons or electrons.

Studies of atoms of various elements also show that the number of neutrons present in atoms of an element is not constant; it varies over a small range. This means that not all atoms of an element have to be identical. They must have the same number of protons and electrons, but they can differ in the number of neutrons.

Isotopes

▶ *The word* isotope *comes from the Greek* iso, *meaning "equal," and* topos, *meaning "place." Isotopes occupy an equal place (location) in listings of elements because all isotopes of an element have the same atomic number.*

Atoms of an element that differ in neutron count are called isotopes. **Isotopes** *are atoms of an element that have the same number of protons and the same number of electrons but different numbers of neutrons.* Different isotopes always have the same atomic number and different mass numbers. ◀

Isotopes of an element have the same chemical properties, but their physical properties are often slightly different. Isotopes of an element have the same chemical properties because they have the same number of electrons. They have slightly different physical properties because they have different numbers of neutrons and therefore different masses.

▶ *There are a few elements for which all naturally occurring atoms have the same number of neutrons—that is, for which all atoms are identical. They include the elements Be, F, Na, Al, P, and Au.*

Most elements found in nature exist in isotopic forms, with the number of naturally occurring isotopes ranging from 2 to 10. For example, all silicon atoms have 14 protons and 14 electrons. Most silicon atoms also contain 14 neutrons. However, some silicon atoms contain 15 neutrons and others contain 16 neutrons. Thus three different kinds of silicon atoms exist. ◀

When it is necessary to distinguish between isotopes of an element, complete chemical symbol notation (Section 3-2) is used. The three silicon isotopes are designated, respectively, as

$$^{28}_{14}Si, \qquad ^{29}_{14}Si, \qquad \text{and} \qquad ^{30}_{14}Si$$

▶ *A mass number, in contrast to an atomic number, lacks uniqueness. Atoms of different elements can have the same mass number. For example, carbon-14 and nitrogen-14 have the same mass numbers. Atoms of different elements, however, cannot have the same atomic number.*

Names for isotopes include the mass number. $^{28}_{14}Si$ is called silicon-28, and $^{29}_{14}Si$ is called silicon-29. The atomic number is not included in the name because it is the same for all isotopes of an element. ◀

The various isotopes of a given element are of varying abundance; usually one isotope is predominant. Silicon is typical of this situation. The percentage abundances for its three isotopes are 92.21% ($^{28}_{14}Si$), 4.70% ($^{29}_{14}Si$), and 3.09% ($^{30}_{14}Si$).

Percentage abundances are number percentages (numbers of atoms) rather than mass percentages. A sample of 10,000 silicon atoms contains 9221 $^{28}_{14}$Si atoms, 470 $^{29}_{14}$Si atoms, and 309 $^{30}_{14}$Si atoms.

There are 286 isotopes that occur naturally. More than 2000 additional isotopes have been synthesized in the laboratory via nuclear rather than chemical reactions (Section 11-5). All these synthetic isotopes are unstable (radioactive). Despite their instability, many are used in chemical research, as well as in medicine.

EXAMPLE 3-2

Determining the Subatomic Particle Characteristics of an Atom Given Its Complete Chemical Symbol

Determine the following for an atom whose complete chemical symbol is $^{26}_{12}$Mg.

a. The total number of subatomic particles present in the atom
b. The total number of subatomic particles present in the nucleus of the atom
c. The total number of nucleons present in the atom
d. The total charge (including sign) associated with the nucleus of the atom

Solution

a. The mass number gives the combined number of protons and neutrons present. The atomic number gives the number of electrons present. Adding these two numbers together gives the total number of subatomic particles present. There are 38 subatomic particles present (26 + 12 = 38).

b. The nucleus contains all protons and all neutrons. The mass number (protons + neutrons) thus gives the total number of subatomic particles present in the nucleus of an atom. There are 26 subatomic particles present in the nucleus.

c. A nucleon is any subatomic particle present in the nucleus. Thus, both protons and neutrons are nucleons. There are 26 such particles present in the nucleus. Parts **b** and **c** of this example are thus asking the same thing using different terminology.

d. The charge associated with a nucleus originates from the protons present. It will always be positive because protons are positively charged particles. The atomic number, 12, indicates that 12 protons are present. Thus, the nuclear charge is +12.

Atomic Masses

The existence of isotopes means that atoms of an element can have several different masses. For example, silicon atoms can have any one of three masses because there are three silicon isotopes. Which of these three silicon isotopic masses is used in situations in which the mass of the element silicon needs to be specified? The answer is none of them. Instead a *weighted-average mass* that takes into account the existence of isotopes and their relative abundances is used. ◀

The *weighted-average mass* of the isotopes of an element is known as the element's atomic mass. An **atomic mass** *is the calculated average mass for the isotopes of an element, expressed on a scale where* $^{12}_{6}$C *serves as the reference point.* Information needed to calculate an atomic mass are the masses of the various isotopes on the $^{12}_{6}$C reference scale and the percentage abundance of each isotope. ◀

The $^{12}_{6}$C reference scale mentioned in the definition of *atomic mass* is a scale scientists have set up for comparing the masses of atoms. On this scale, the mass of a $^{12}_{6}$C atom is defined to be exactly 12 atomic mass units (amu). The masses of all other atoms are then determined relative to that of $^{12}_{6}$C. For example, if an atom is twice as heavy as $^{12}_{6}$C, its mass is 24 amu, and if an atom weighs half as much as an atom of $^{12}_{6}$C, its mass is 6 amu.

Example 3-3 shows how an atomic mass is calculated using the amu ($^{12}_{6}$C) scale, the percentage abundances of isotopes, and the number of isotopes of an element.

▶ *An analogy involving isotopes and identical twins may be helpful: Identical twins need not weigh the same, even though they have identical "gene packages." Likewise, isotopes, even though they have different masses, have the same number of protons.*

▶ *The terms* atomic mass *and* atomic weight *are often used interchangeably.* Atomic mass, *however, is the correct term.*

EXAMPLE 3-3

Calculation of an Element's Atomic Mass

Naturally occurring chlorine exists in two isotopic forms, $^{35}_{17}Cl$ and $^{37}_{17}Cl$. The relative mass of $^{35}_{17}Cl$ is 34.97 amu, and its abundance is 75.53%; the relative mass of $^{37}_{17}Cl$ is 36.97 amu, and its abundance is 24.47%. What is the atomic mass of chlorine?

Solution

An element's atomic mass is calculated by multiplying the relative mass of each isotope by its fractional abundance and then totaling the products. The fractional abundance for an isotope is its percentage abundance converted to decimal form (divided by 100). ◀

▶ *When calculating an atomic mass using isotope data, the amu masses of the isotopes are used rather than the mass numbers of the isotopes.*

$$^{35}_{17}Cl: \quad \left(\frac{75.53}{100}\right) \times 34.97 \text{ amu} = (0.7553) \times 34.97 \text{ amu} = 26.41 \text{ amu}$$

$$^{37}_{17}Cl: \quad \left(\frac{24.47}{100}\right) \times 36.97 \text{ amu} = (0.2447) \times 36.97 \text{ amu} = 9.047 \text{ amu}$$

$$\text{Atomic mass of Cl} = (26.41 + 9.047) \text{ amu}$$
$$= 35.46 \text{ amu}$$

This calculation involved an element containing just two isotopes. A similar calculation for an element having three isotopes would be carried out the same way, but it would have three terms in the final sum; an element possessing four isotopes would have four terms in the final sum.

The alphabetical list of the known elements printed inside the front cover of this text gives the calculated atomic mass for each of the elements; this information is provided in the last column of numbers. Table 3-2 gives isotopic data for the elements with atomic numbers 1 through 12.

Chemistry at a Glance—Atomic Structure—summarizes the important concepts about atoms that have been presented in Sections 3-1 through 3-3.

▶ Table 3-2 **Isotopic Data for Elements with Atomic Numbers 1 Through 12**

Information given for each isotope includes mass number, isotopic mass in terms of amu, and percentage abundance.

1 HYDROGEN	**2** HELIUM	**3** LITHIUM
^1_1H 1.008 amu 99.985% ^2_1H 2.014 amu 0.015% ^3_1H 3.016 amu trace	^3_2He 3.016 amu trace ^4_2He 4.003 amu 100%	^6_3Li 6.015 amu 7.42% ^7_3Li 7.016 amu 92.58%
4 BERYLLIUM	**5** BORON	**6** CARBON
^9_4Be 9.012 amu 100%	$^{10}_5B$ 10.013 amu 19.6% $^{11}_5B$ 11.009 amu 80.4%	$^{12}_6C$ 12.000 amu 98.89% $^{13}_6C$ 13.003 amu 1.11% $^{14}_6C$ 14.003 amu trace
7 NITROGEN	**8** OXYGEN	**9** FLUORINE
$^{14}_7N$ 14.003 amu 99.63% $^{15}_7N$ 15.000 amu 0.37%	$^{16}_8O$ 15.995 amu 99.759% $^{17}_8O$ 16.999 amu 0.037% $^{18}_8O$ 17.999 amu 0.204%	$^{19}_9F$ 18.998 amu 100%
10 NEON	**11** SODIUM	**12** MAGNESIUM
$^{20}_{10}Ne$ 19.992 amu 90.92% $^{21}_{10}Ne$ 20.994 amu 0.26% $^{22}_{10}Ne$ 21.991 amu 8.82%	$^{23}_{11}Na$ 22.990 amu 100%	$^{24}_{12}Mg$ 23.985 amu 78.70% $^{25}_{12}Mg$ 24.986 amu 10.13% $^{26}_{12}Mg$ 25.983 amu 11.17%

AT A GLANCE Atomic Structure

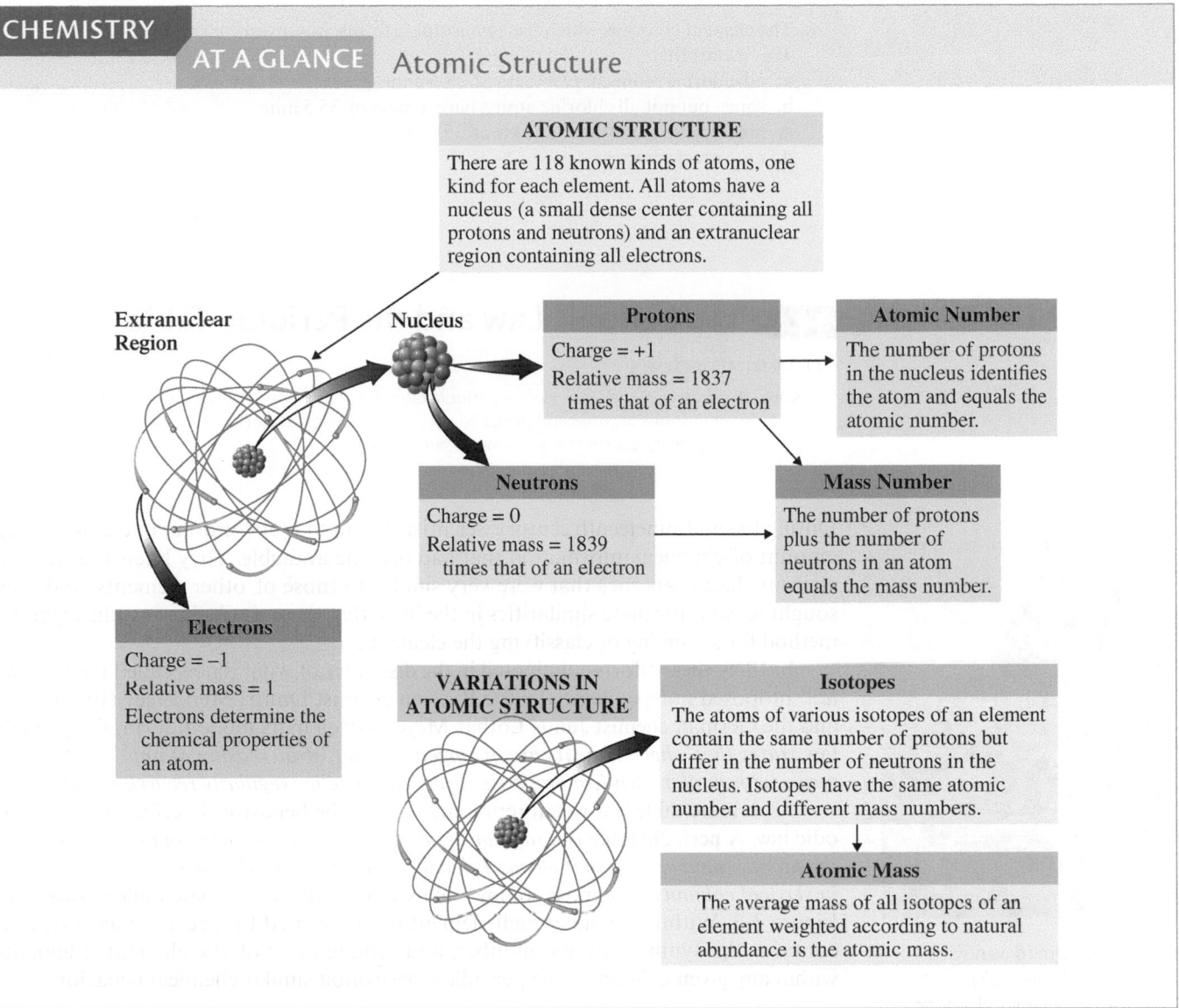

ATOMIC STRUCTURE

There are 118 known kinds of atoms, one kind for each element. All atoms have a nucleus (a small dense center containing all protons and neutrons) and an extranuclear region containing all electrons.

Extranuclear Region

Nucleus

Protons

Charge = +1
Relative mass = 1837 times that of an electron

Atomic Number

The number of protons in the nucleus identifies the atom and equals the atomic number.

Neutrons

Charge = 0
Relative mass = 1839 times that of an electron

Mass Number

The number of protons plus the number of neutrons in an atom equals the mass number.

Electrons

Charge = −1
Relative mass = 1
Electrons determine the chemical properties of an atom.

VARIATIONS IN ATOMIC STRUCTURE

Isotopes

The atoms of various isotopes of an element contain the same number of protons but differ in the number of neutrons in the nucleus. Isotopes have the same atomic number and different mass numbers.

Atomic Mass

The average mass of all isotopes of an element weighted according to natural abundance is the atomic mass.

Section 3-3 Quick Quiz

1. Isotopes of an element always have the
   a. same mass number and different atomic numbers
   b. same atomic number and different mass numbers
   c. different atomic numbers and different mass numbers
   d. no correct response
2. Isotopes of an element always have the
   a. same number of protons and same number of neutrons
   b. same number of protons and different numbers of neutrons
   c. same number of neutrons and different numbers of protons
   d. no correct response
3. What is the atomic mass of a hypothetical element that exists in two isotopic forms that have masses of 8.00 amu and 10.00 amu, respectively, and percent abundances of 80.00% and 20.00%, respectively?
   a. 8.40 amu
   b. 9.00 amu
   c. 9.20 amu
   d. no correct response

(continued)

4. The element chlorine, which has two isotopic forms, has an atomic mass of 35.5 amu. This means that
   a. all chlorine atoms have a mass of 35.5 amu
   b. some, but not all chlorine atoms have a mass of 35.5 amu
   c. no chlorine atoms have a mass of 35.5 amu
   d. no correct response

Answers: 1. b; 2. b; 3. a; 4. c

3-4 The Periodic Law and the Periodic Table

LEARNING FOCUS

Know the organizational basis for the periodic table; be able to specify periodic table location for an element in terms of *group* and *period*; know periodic table locations for elements known as *alkali metals*, *alkaline earth metals*, *halogens*, and *noble gases*.

Figure 3-2 Dmitri Ivanovich Mendeleev (1834–1907). Mendeleev constructed a periodic table as part of his effort to systematize chemistry. He received many international honors for his work, but his reception at home in czarist Russia was mixed. Element 101 carries his name.

Edgar Fahs Smith Collection, University of Pennsylvania Library

During the mid-nineteenth century, scientists began to look for order in the increasing amount of chemical information that had become available. They knew that certain elements had properties that were very similar to those of other elements, and they sought reasons for these similarities in the hope that these similarities would suggest a method for arranging or classifying the elements.

In 1869, these efforts culminated in the discovery of what is now called the *periodic law,* proposed independently by the Russian chemist Dmitri Mendeleev (Figure 3-2) and the German chemist Julius Lothar Meyer. Given in its modern form, the **periodic law** *states that when elements are arranged in order of increasing atomic number, elements with similar chemical properties occur at periodic (regularly recurring) intervals.*

A periodic table is a visual representation of the behavior described by the periodic law. A **periodic table** *is a tabular arrangement of the elements in order of increasing atomic number such that elements having similar chemical properties are positioned in vertical columns.* The most commonly used form of the periodic table is shown in Figure 3-3. Within the table, each element is represented by a rectangular box that contains the symbol, atomic number, and atomic mass of the element. Elements within any given column of the periodic table exhibit similar chemical behavior.

Groups and Periods of Elements

The location of an element within the periodic table is specified by giving its period number and group number.

A **period** *is a horizontal row of elements in the periodic table.* For identification purposes, the periods are numbered sequentially with Arabic numbers, starting at the top of the periodic table. In Figure 3-3, period numbers are found on the left side of the table. The elements Na, Mg, Al, Si, P, S, Cl, and Ar are all members of Period 3, the third row of elements. Period 4 is the fourth row of elements, and so on. There are only two elements in Period 1, H and He.

A **group** *is a vertical column of elements in the periodic table.* Two notations are used to designate individual periodic-table groups. In the first notation, which has been in use for many years, groups are designated by using Roman numerals and the letters A and B. In the second notation, which an international scientific commission recommended several years ago, the Arabic numbers 1 through 18 are used. Note that in Figure 3-3 both group notations are given at the top of each group. The elements with atomic numbers 8, 16, 34, 52, and 84 (O, S, Se, Te, and Po) constitute Group VIA (old notation) or Group 16 (new notation). ◄

Four groups of elements also have common (non-numerical) names. On the extreme left side of the periodic table are found the *alkali metals* (Li, Na, K, Rb, Cs, Fr) and the *alkaline earth metals* (Be, Mg, Ca, Sr, Ba, Ra). **Alkali metal** *is a general name for any element in Group IA of the periodic table, excluding hydrogen.* The alkali metals

▶ *The number of protons and electrons present in atoms of an element can easily be determined using the information present on a periodic table. However, no information concerning neutrons is available from a periodic table; mass numbers are not part of the information given because they are not unique to an element.*

Figure 3-3 The periodic table of the elements is a graphical way to show relationships among the elements. Elements with similar chemical properties fall in the same vertical column.

are soft, shiny metals that readily react with water. **Alkaline earth metal** *is a general name for any element in Group IIA of the periodic table.* The alkaline earth metals are also soft, shiny metals, but they are only moderately reactive toward water. On the extreme right of the periodic table are found the *halogens* (F, Cl, Br, I, At) and the *noble gases* (He, Ne, Ar, Kr, Xe, Rn). **Halogen** *is a general name for any element in Group VIIA of the periodic table.* The halogens are reactive elements that are gases at room temperature or become such at temperatures slightly above room temperature. **Noble gas** *is a general name for any element in Group VIIIA of the periodic table.* Noble gases are unreactive gases that undergo few, if any, chemical reactions.

The location of any element in the periodic table is specified by giving its group number and its period number. The element gold, with an atomic number of 79, belongs to Group IB (or 11) and is in Period 6. The element nitrogen, with an atomic number of 7, belongs to Group VA (or 15) and is in Period 2. ◀

▶ *The elements within a given periodic-table group show numerous similarities in properties, the degree of similarity varying from group to group. In no case are the group members "clones" of one another. Each element has some individual characteristics not found in other elements of the group. By analogy, the members of a human family often bear many resemblances to each other, but each member also has some (and often much) individuality.*

EXAMPLE 3-4

Identifying Groups, Periods, and Specially Named Families of Elements

What is the chemical symbol of the element that fits each of the following descriptions based on periodic table location?

a. Located in both Period 3 and Group IVA
b. The Period 4 noble gas
c. The Period 2 alkaline earth metal
d. The Period 3 halogen

(continued)

Solution

a. Period 3 is the third row of elements, and Group IVA is the fifth column from the right side of the periodic table. The element that has this row–column (period–group) location is Si (silicon).

b. The noble gases are the elements of Group VIIIA (the right-most column in the periodic table). The Period 4 (fourth row) noble gas is Kr (krypton).

c. The alkaline earth metals are the elements of Group IIA (the second column from the left side of the periodic table). The Period 2 (second row) alkaline earth metal is Be (beryllium).

d. The halogens are the elements of Group VIIA (the second column from the right side of the periodic table). The Period 3 (third row) halogen is Cl (chlorine).

The Shape of the Periodic Table

Within the periodic table of Figure 3-3, the practice of arranging the elements according to increasing atomic number is violated in Groups IIIB and IVB. Element 72 follows element 57, and element 104 follows element 89. The missing elements, elements 58 through 71 and 90 through 103 are located in two rows at the bottom of the periodic table. Technically, the elements at the bottom of the table should be included in the body of the table, as shown in the top portion of Figure 3-4. However, in order to have a more compact table, they are placed at the bottom of the table as shown in the lower portion of Figure 3-4. ◄

▶ *When the phrase "the first ten elements" is used, it means the first 10 elements in the periodic table, the elements with atomic numbers 1 through 10.*

Figure 3-4 The "long" version and "space-saving" standard version of the periodic table.

1. Based on periodic table location, which pair of elements would be expected to have similar chemical properties?

    a. $_3$Li and $_4$Be

    b. $_6$C and $_7$N

    c. $_8$O and $_{16}$S

    d. no correct response

2. A standard periodic table arranges the elements in order of
   a. year of discovery
   b. increasing atomic number
   c. increasing reactivity with oxygen
   d. no correct response
3. Which of the following elements is located in both Period 3 and Group IIIA?
   a. $_6$C
   b. $_{13}$Al
   c. $_{31}$Ga
   d. no correct response
4. Which of the following pieces of information about an element is not found on a standard periodic table?
   a. chemical symbol
   b. atomic number
   c. mass number
   d. no correct response
5. The elements known as *halogens* and *alkali metals* are found, respectively, in which groups in the periodic table?
   a. IA and IIA
   b. VIA and IIA
   c. VIIA and IA
   d. no correct response

Answers: 1. c; 2. b; 3. b; 4. c; 5. c

3-5 Metals and Nonmetals

LEARNING FOCUS

Distinguish metals from nonmetals based on general physical properties; classify an element as metal or nonmetal based on periodic table location.

It was noted in the previous section that the Group IA and Group IIA elements are known, respectively, as the alkali metals and the alkaline earth metals. Both of these designations contain the word *metal*. What is a metal?

On the basis of selected physical properties, elements are classified into the categories metal and nonmetal. A **metal** *is an element that has the characteristic properties of luster, thermal conductivity, electrical conductivity, and malleability.* With the exception of mercury, all metals are solids at room temperature (25°C). Metals are good conductors of heat and electricity. Most metals are ductile (can be drawn into wires) and malleable (can be rolled into sheets). Most metals have high luster (shine), high density, and high melting points. Among the more familiar metals are the elements iron, aluminum, copper, silver, gold, lead, tin, and zinc (Figure 3-5a).

A **nonmetal** *is an element characterized by the absence of the properties of luster, thermal conductivity, electrical conductivity, and malleability.* Many of the nonmetals, such as hydrogen, oxygen, nitrogen, and the noble gases, are gases. The only nonmetal that is a liquid at room temperature is bromine. Solid nonmetals include carbon, iodine, sulfur, and phosphorus (Figure 3-5b). In general, the nonmetals have lower densities and lower melting points than metals. Table 3-3 contrasts selected physical properties of metals and nonmetals. ◄

Periodic Table Locations for Metals and Nonmetals

The majority of the elements are metals. Only 23 elements are nonmetals. It is not necessary to memorize which elements are nonmetals and which are metals; this information is obtainable from a periodic table (Figure 3-6). The steplike heavy line that runs through the right third of the periodic table separates the metals on the left from the nonmetals on the right. Note also that the element hydrogen is a nonmetal.

The fact that the vast majority of elements are metals in no way indicates that metals are more important than nonmetals. Most nonmetals are relatively common

▶ Metals *generally are malleable, ductile, and lustrous and are good thermal and electrical conductors.* Nonmetals *tend to lack these properties. In many ways, the general properties of metals and nonmetals are opposites.*

Figure 3-5 Physical characteristics of selected metals and nonmetals.

© Cengage Learning

a Some familiar metals (clockwise, starting on left) are aluminum, lead, tin, and zinc.

b Some familiar nonmetals are sulfur (yellow), phosphorus (dark red), and bromine (reddish-brown liquid).

Table 3-3 **Selected Physical Properties of Metals and Nonmetals**

Metals	Nonmetals
1. High electrical conductivity that decreases with increasing temperature	1. Poor electrical conductivity (except carbon in the form of graphite)
2. High thermal conductivity	2. Good heat insulators (except carbon in the form of diamond)
3. Metallic gray or silver luster*	3. No metallic luster
4. Almost all are solids†	4. Solids, liquids, or gases
5. Malleable (can be hammered into sheets)	5. Brittle in solid state
6. Ductile (can be drawn into wires)	6. Nonductile

*Except copper and gold.
†Except mercury; cesium and gallium melt on a hot summer day (85°F) or when held in a person's hand.

Figure 3-6 This portion of the periodic table shows the dividing line between metals and nonmetals. All elements that are not shown are metals.

							VIIIA
1 H		Group					2 He
		IIA	IIIA	IVA	VA	VIIA	
			5 B	6 C	7 N	8 O	9 F	10 Ne

Metal
Nonmetal

	13 Al	14 Si	15 P	16 S	17 Cl	18 Ar
30 Zn	31 Ga	32 Ge	33 As	34 Se	35 Br	36 Kr
48 Cd	49 In	50 Sn	51 Sb	52 Te	53 I	54 Xe
80 Hg	81 Tl	82 Pb	83 Bi	84 Po	85 At	86 Rn
112 Cn	113 —	114 Fl	115 —	116 Lv	117	118

and are found in many important compounds. For example, water (H_2O) is a compound involving two nonmetals.

An analysis of the abundance of the elements in Earth's crust (Figure 1-10) in terms of metals and nonmetals shows that the two most abundant elements, which account for 80.2% of all atoms, are nonmetals—oxygen and silicon. The four most abundant elements in the human body (see Chemical Connections 1-B), which comprise more than 99% of all atoms in the body, are nonmetals—hydrogen, oxygen, carbon, and nitrogen. Besides these four "abundant" nonmetals, a number of other elements are needed by the body in *smaller* amounts. These elements, which must be obtained from food sources, are called *dietary minerals*. Several of the dietary minerals are metals rather than nonmetals. The focus on relevancy feature Chemical Connections 3-A—Dietary Minerals and the Human Body—considers the topic of metals and nonmetals needed by the body in small rather than large amounts.

Section 3-5 Quick Quiz

1. Which of the following is a general characteristic of most metals?
   a. low thermal conductivity
   b. nonductile
   c. malleable
   d. no correct response
2. Which of the following statements about metallic and nonmetallic elements is correct?
   a. The vast majority of elements are metals.
   b. The vast majority of elements are nonmetals.
   c. Approximately the same number of metallic and nonmetallic elements exist.
   d. no correct response
3. Which of the following elements is a nonmetal?
   a. $_{19}K$
   b. $_{31}Ga$
   c. $_{34}Se$
   d. no correct response
4. Which of the following elements is a metal?
   a. $_7N$
   b. $_{33}As$
   c. $_{51}Sb$
   d. no correct response

Answers: 1. c; 2. a; 3. c; 4. c

3-6 Electron Arrangements Within Atoms

LEARNING FOCUS

Understand how the concepts of *electron shell, electron subshell,* and *electron orbital* are used in describing electron arrangement within an atom.

As electrons move about an atom's nucleus, they are restricted to specific regions within the extranuclear portion of the atom. Such restrictions are determined by the amount of energy the electrons possess. Furthermore, electron energies are limited to certain values, and a specific "behavior" is associated with each allowed energy value.

The space in which electrons move rapidly about a nucleus is divided into subspaces called *shells, subshells,* and *orbitals.*

Electron Shells

Electrons within an atom are grouped into main energy levels called electron shells. An **electron shell** *is a region of space about a nucleus that contains electrons that have approximately the same energy and that spend most of their time approximately the same distance from the nucleus.*

Electron shells are numbered 1, 2, 3, and so on, outward from the nucleus. Electron energy increases as the distance of the electron shell from the nucleus increases. An electron in shell 1 has the minimum amount of energy that an electron can have. ◀

The maximum number of electrons that an electron shell can accommodate varies; the higher the shell number (*n*), the more electrons that can be present.

▶ *Electrons that occupy the first electron shell are closer to the nucleus and have a lower energy than electrons in the second electron shell.*

Dietary Minerals and the Human Body

Four elements—hydrogen, oxygen, carbon, and nitrogen—supply 99% of the atoms in the human body, as was discussed in Chemical Connections 1-B. These four "dominant" elements, often called the *building block elements,* are all nonmetals. Given that most of the atoms in the human body have nonmetallic properties, docs this mean that metals, which constitute the majority of the elements (Section 3-5), are unimportant in the proper functioning of the human body? The answer is a definite no.

Another group of elements essential to proper human body function, which includes several metals, are the *dietary minerals,* elements needed in small amounts that must be obtained from food. There are the *major minerals* and the *trace minerals,* with the former being required in larger amounts than the latter.

The major minerals, seven in number, include four metals and three nonmetals. The four metals, all located on the left side of the periodic table, are sodium, potassium, magnesium, and calcium. The three nonmetals, all Period 3 nonmetals, are phosphorus, sulfur, and chlorine. The relative amounts of the major minerals present in a human body are given in the top part of the accompanying graph. Note that these minerals are not present in the body in elemental form, but rather as constituents of compounds; for example, sodium is not present as sodium metal but as the compound sodium chloride (table salt).

Trace minerals are needed in much smaller quantities than the major minerals. The least abundant major mineral is more than ten times more abundant than the most abundant trace mineral, as shown in the bottom part of the accompanying graph. This graph shows only the six most abundant trace minerals, four of which are metals. Other trace minerals that are metals include cobalt, molybdenum, and chromium. One of the purposes of many dietary supplements of the multivitamin type is to ensure that adequate amounts of trace minerals are part of a person's dietary intake (see accompanying dietary supplement label). The biological importance of iron, the most abundant of the trace minerals, is considered in a Chemical Connections feature later in this chapter.

As knowledge concerning the biological functions of trace minerals increases as the result of research endeavors, the way doctors and nutritionists think about diet and health changes. For example, it is now known that a

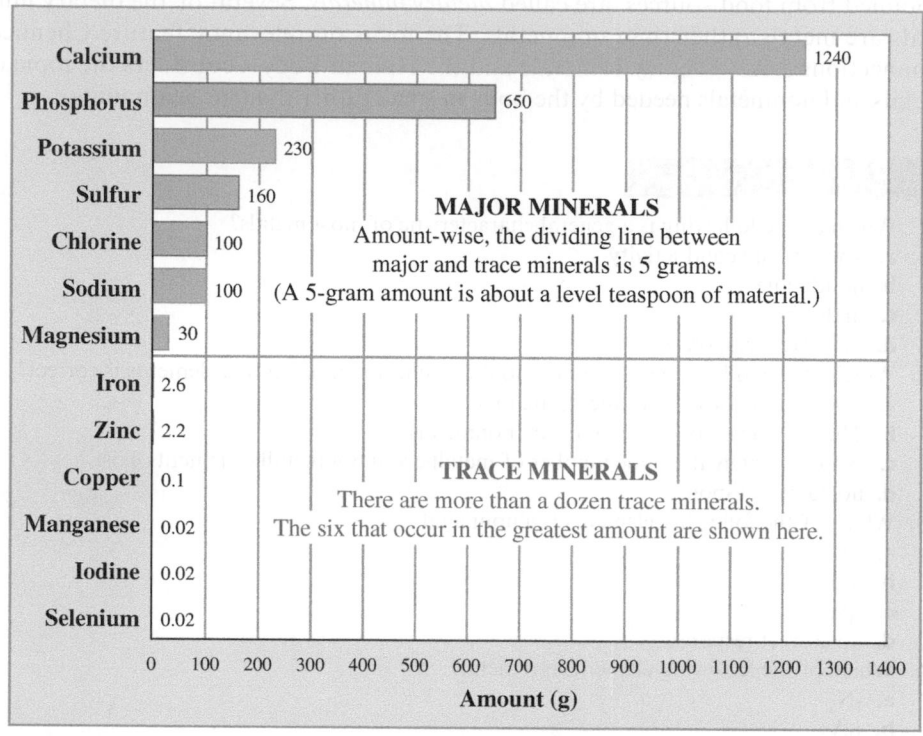

MAJOR MINERALS
Amount-wise, the dividing line between major and trace minerals is 5 grams.
(A 5-gram amount is about a level teaspoon of material.)

TRACE MINERALS
There are more than a dozen trace minerals.
The six that occur in the greatest amount are shown here.

Amounts of minerals found in a 65-kilogram (143-pound) human body. (Metals are shown in green, and nonmetals are shown in orange.)

Dietary supplements of the multivitamin type supply small amounts of numerous compounds that contain metallic elements.

combined supplement of manganese, copper, and zinc, in combination with calcium, improves bone health to a greater degree than a calcium supplement alone. Likewise, trace amounts of copper are needed for the proper absorption and mobilization of iron in the body.

In higher-energy shells, the electrons are farther from the nucleus, and a greater volume of space is available for them; hence more electrons can be accommodated. (Conceptually, electron shells may be considered to be nested one inside another, somewhat like the layers of flavors inside a jawbreaker or similar type of candy.)

The lowest-energy shell ($n = 1$) accommodates a maximum of two electrons. In the second, third, and fourth shells, 8, 18, and 32 electrons, respectively, are allowed. The relationship among these numbers is given by the formula $2n^2$, where n is the shell number. For example, when $n = 4$, the quantity $2n^2 = 2(4)^2 = 32$.

Electron Subshells

Within each electron shell, electrons are further grouped into energy sublevels called electron subshells. An **electron subshell** *is a region of space within an electron shell that contains electrons that have the same energy.* We can draw an analogy between the relationship of shells and subshells and the physical layout of a high-rise apartment complex. The shells are analogous to the floors of the apartment complex, and the subshells are the counterparts of the various apartments on each floor.

The number of subshells within a shell is the same as the shell number. Shell 1 contains one subshell, shell 2 contains two subshells, shell 3 contains three subshells, and so on.

Subshells within a shell differ in size (that is, the maximum number of electrons they can accommodate) and energy. The higher the energy of the contained electrons, the larger the subshell.

Subshell size (type) is designated using the letters *s*, *p*, *d*, and *f*. Listed in this order, these letters denote subshells of increasing energy and size. ◀ The lowest-energy subshell within a shell is always the *s* subshell, the next highest is the *p* subshell, then the *d* subshell, and finally the *f* subshell. An *s* subshell can accommodate 2 electrons, a *p* subshell 6 electrons, a *d* subshell 10 electrons, and an *f* subshell 14 electrons.

Both a number and a letter are used in identifying subshells. The number gives the shell within which the subshell is located, and the letter gives the type of subshell. Shell 1 has only one subshell—the 1*s*. Shell 2 has two subshells—the 2*s* and 2*p*. Shell 3 has three subshells—the 3*s*, 3*p*, and 3*d*, and so on. Figure 3-7 summarizes the relationships between electron shells and electron subshells for the first four shells.

▶ *The letters used to label the different types of subshells come from old spectroscopic terminology associated with the lines in the spectrum of the element hydrogen. These lines were denoted as sharp, principal, diffuse, and fundamental. Relationships exist between such lines and the arrangement of electrons in an atom.*

Figure 3-7 The number of subshells within a shell is equal to the shell number, as shown here for the first four shells. Each individual subshell is denoted with both a number (its shell) and a letter (the type of subshell it is in).

The four subshell types (*s*, *p*, *d*, and *f*) are sufficient when dealing with shells of higher number than shell 4 because in such shells any additional subshells present are not needed to accommodate electrons. For example, in shell 5 there are five subshell types (5*s*, 5*p*, 5*d*, 5*f*, and a fifth one that is never used). The reason why some subshells are not needed involves consideration of the order of filling of subshells with electrons, which is the topic of Section 3-7.

Electron Orbitals

▶ *An electron orbital is also often called an atomic orbital.*

Electron subshells have within them a certain, definite number of locations (regions of space), called electron orbitals, where electrons may be found. ◀ In our apartment complex analogy, if shells are the counterparts of floor levels and subshells are the apartments, then electron orbitals are the rooms of the apartments. An **electron orbital** *is a region of space within an electron subshell where an electron with a specific energy is most likely to be found.*

An electron orbital, independent of all other considerations, can accommodate a maximum of two electrons. Thus an *s* subshell (2 electrons) contains one orbital, a *p* subshell (6 electrons) contains three orbitals, a *d* subshell (10 electrons) contains five orbitals, and an *f* subshell (14 electrons) contains seven orbitals.

Orbitals have distinct shapes that are related to the type of subshell in which they are found. Note that it is not the shape of an electron, but rather the shape of the region in which the electron is found that is being considered. An orbital in an *s* subshell, which is called an *s* orbital, has a spherical shape (Figure 3-8a). Orbitals found in *p* subshells—*p* orbitals—have shapes similar to the "figure 8" of an ice skater (Figure 3-8b). More complex shapes involving four and eight lobes, respectively, are associated with *d* and *f* orbitals (Figures 3-8c and 3-8d). Some *d* and *f* orbitals have shapes related to, but not identical to, those shown in Figure 3-8.

Orbitals within the same subshell, which have the same shape, differ mainly in orientation. For example, the three 2*p* orbitals extend out from the nucleus at 90° angles to one another (along the *x*, *y*, and *z* axes in a Cartesian coordinate system), as is shown in Figure 3-9. Chemistry at a Glance—Shell–Subshell–Orbital Interrelationships—shows key interrelationships among electron shells, electron subshells, and electron orbitals.

Figure 3-8 An *s* orbital has a spherical shape, a *p* orbital has two lobes, a *d* orbital has four lobes, and an *f* orbital has eight lobes. The *f* orbital is shown within a cube to illustrate that its lobes are directed toward the corners of a cube. Some *d* and *f* orbitals have shapes related to, but not identical to, those shown.

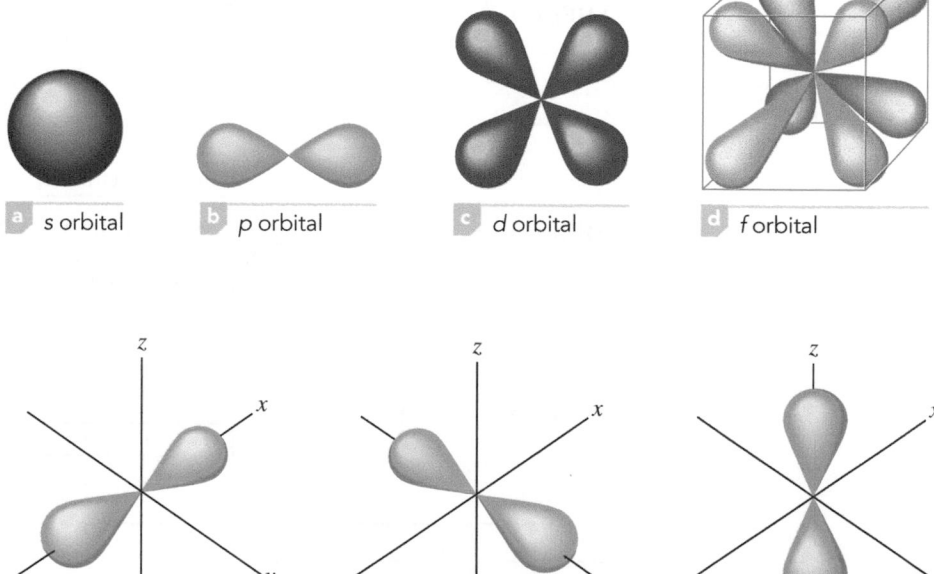

| a | *s* orbital | b | *p* orbital | c | *d* orbital | d | *f* orbital |

Figure 3-9 Orbitals within a subshell differ mainly in orientation. For example, the three *p* orbitals within a *p* subshell lie along the *x*, *y*, and *z* axes of a Cartesian coordinate system.

CHEMISTRY
AT A GLANCE Shell–Subshell–Orbital Interrelationships

IMPORTANT NUMERICAL RELATIONSHIPS

- Subshells within a shell = shell number
- Orbitals within a subshell depend on shell type:
  1 for s 3 for p 5 for d 7 for f
- Electrons within an orbital = 2

Beginning with shell 5, not all subshells are needed to accommodate electrons. Those needed are

Electron Spin

Experimental studies indicate that as an electron "moves about" within an orbital, it spins on its own axis in either a clockwise or a counterclockwise direction. Furthermore, when two electrons are present in an orbital, they always have opposite spins; that is, one is spinning clockwise and the other counterclockwise. This situation of opposite spins is energetically the most favorable state for two electrons in the same orbital. The concept of electron spin is considered in further detail in Section 3-7.

Section 3-6 Quick Quiz

1. The maximum number of electrons that an *electron shell* can accommodate
   a. is two
   b. is ten
   c. varies, depending on shell number
   d. no correct response
2. The maximum number of *electron subshells* within an *electron shell*
   a. is three
   b. is five
   c. varies, depending on the shell number
   d. no correct response
3. The maximum number of electrons that an *electron orbital* can accommodate
   a. is two
   b. is six
   c. varies, depending on the type of orbital
   d. no correct response

(continued)

4. The shape of a $1s$ orbital is
   a. circular
   b. spherical
   c. figure eight shape
   d. no correct response
5. In which of the following pairs of electron subshells does the first listed subshell have a higher energy than the second listed subshell?
   a. $2s$, $2p$
   b. $2s$, $3s$
   c. $3d$, $2p$
   d. no correct response
6. How many electrons can a $3d$ *subshell* accommodate?
   a. 2
   b. 6
   c. 10
   d. no correct response
7. How many electrons can a $3d$ *orbital* accommodate?
   a. 2
   b. 6
   c. 10
   d. no correct response

Answers: 1. c; 2. c; 3. a; 4. b; 5. c; 6. c; 7. a

3-7 Electron Configurations and Orbital Diagrams

LEARNING FOCUS

Be able to write an electron configuration (subshell occupancy) as well as an orbital diagram (orbital occupancy) for atoms of a given element.

Electron shells, subshells, and orbitals describe "permissible" locations for electrons—that is, where electrons *can* be found. The *actual* locations of the electrons in specific atoms will now be considered.

There are many orbitals about the nucleus of an atom. Electrons do not occupy these orbitals in a random, haphazard fashion; a very predictable pattern exists for electron orbital occupancy. There are three rules, all quite simple, for assigning electrons to various shells, subshells, and orbitals.

1. *Electron subshells are filled in the order of increasing energy.*
2. *Electrons occupy the orbitals of a subshell such that each orbital acquires one electron before any orbital acquires a second electron.* All electrons in such singly occupied orbitals must have the same spin.
3. *No more than two electrons may exist in a given orbital—and then only if they have opposite spins.*

Subshell Energy Order

The ordering of electron subshells in terms of increasing energy, which is experimentally determined, is more complex than might be expected. This is because the energies of subshells in different shells often "overlap," as shown in Figure 3-10. This diagram shows, for example, that the $4s$ subshell has lower energy than the $3d$ subshell.

A useful mnemonic (memory) device for remembering subshell filling order, which incorporates "overlap" situations such as those in Figure 3-10, is given in Figure 3-11. This diagram, which lists all subshells needed to specify the electron arrangements for all 118 elements, is constructed by locating all s subshells in column 1, all p subshells in column 2, and so on. Subshells that belong to the same shell are found in the same row. The order of subshell filling is given by following the diagonal arrows, starting at the top. The $1s$ subshell fills first. The second arrow points to (goes through) the $2s$

Figure 3-10 The order of filling of various electron subshells is shown on the right-hand side of this diagram. Above the $3p$ subshell, subshells of different shells "overlap."

subshell, which fills next. The third arrow points to both the $2p$ and the $3s$ subshells. The $2p$ fills first, followed by the $3s$. When a single arrow points to more than one subshell, the proper filling sequence is determined by starting at the tail of the arrow and moving toward the head of the arrow.

Writing Electron Configurations and Orbital Diagrams

An **electron configuration** *is a statement of how many electrons an atom has in each of its electron subshells.* Because subshells group electrons according to energy, electron configurations indicate how many electrons of various energies an atom has.

Electron configurations are not written out in words; rather, a shorthand system with symbols is used. Subshells containing electrons, listed in the order of increasing energy, are designated by using number–letter combinations ($1s$, $2s$, and $2p$). A superscript following each subshell designation indicates the number of electrons in that subshell. The electron configuration for nitrogen in this shorthand notation is

$$1s^2 2s^2 2p^3$$

Thus a nitrogen atom has an electron arrangement of two electrons in the $1s$ subshell, two electrons in the $2s$ subshell, and three electrons in the $2p$ subshell.

An **orbital diagram** *is a notation that shows how many electrons an atom has in each of its occupied electron orbitals.* Note that electron configurations deal with *subshell* occupancy and that orbital diagrams deal with *orbital* occupancy. ◄ The orbital diagram for the element nitrogen is

$$\begin{array}{ccc} 1s & 2s & 2p \\ \boxed{\uparrow\downarrow} & \boxed{\uparrow\downarrow} & \boxed{\uparrow}\,\boxed{\uparrow}\,\boxed{\uparrow} \end{array}$$

This diagram indicates that both the $1s$ and the $2s$ orbitals are filled, each containing two electrons of opposite spin. In addition, each of the three $2p$ orbitals contains one electron. Electron spin is denoted by the direction (up or down) in which an arrow points. For two electrons of opposite spin, which is the case in a fully occupied orbital, one arrow must point up and the other down. Electron configurations and orbital diagrams for the first few elements (elements 1 through 11) will now be systematically considered.

Hydrogen (atomic number = 1) has only one electron, which goes into the $1s$ subshell; this subshell has the lowest energy of all subshells. Hydrogen's electron configuration is written as $1s^1$, and its orbital diagram is

$$\text{H:} \quad \begin{array}{c} 1s \\ \boxed{\uparrow} \end{array}$$

Helium (atomic number = 2) has two electrons, both of which occupy the $1s$ subshell. (Remember, an s subshell contains one orbital, and an orbital can accommodate two electrons.) Helium's electron configuration is $1s^2$, and its orbital diagram is

$$\text{He:} \quad \begin{array}{c} 1s \\ \boxed{\uparrow\downarrow} \end{array}$$

The two electrons present are of opposite spin.

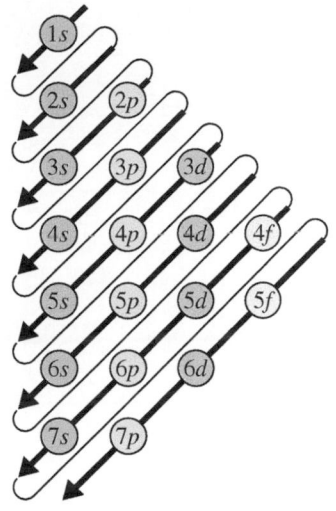

Figure 3-11 The order for filling electron subshells with electrons follows the order given by the arrows in this diagram. Start with the arrow at the top of the diagram and work toward the bottom of the diagram, moving from the bottom of one arrow to the top of the next-lower arrow.

▶ *All electrons in a given subshell have the same energy because all orbitals within a subshell have the same energy.*

An electron configuration *specifies* subshell *occupancy for electrons, and an* orbital diagram *specifies* orbital *occupancy for electrons.*

Lithium (atomic number = 3) has three electrons, and the third electron cannot enter the 1s subshell because its maximum capacity is two electrons. (All s subshells are completely filled with two electrons.) The third electron is placed in the next-highest-energy subshell, the 2s. The electron configuration for lithium is $1s^2 2s^1$, and its orbital diagram is

1s   2s

Li: [↑↓] [↑]

For *beryllium* (atomic number = 4), the additional electron is placed in the 2s subshell, which is now completely filled, giving beryllium the electron configuration $1s^2 2s^2$. The orbital diagram for beryllium is

1s   2s

Be: [↑↓] [↑↓]

For *boron* (atomic number = 5), the 2p subshell, which is the subshell of next highest energy (Figures 3-10 and 3-11), becomes occupied for the first time. Boron's electron configuration is $1s^2 2s^2 2p^1$, and its orbital diagram is

1s   2s   2p

B: [↑↓] [↑↓] [↑ | |]

The 2p subshell contains three orbitals of equal energy. It does not matter which of the 2p orbitals is occupied because they are of equivalent energy.

With the next element, *carbon* (atomic number = 6), a new situation arises. The sixth electron must go into a 2p orbital. However, does this new electron go into the 2p orbital that already has one electron or into one of the others? Rule 2 at the start of this section covers this situation. Electrons will occupy equal-energy orbitals singly to the maximum extent possible before any orbital acquires a second electron. Thus, for carbon, we have the electron configuration $1s^2 2s^2 2p^2$ and the orbital diagram is

1s   2s   2p

C: [↑↓] [↑↓] [↑ | ↑ |]

Atoms of carbon, as shown in this orbital diagram, possess two *unpaired* electrons.

A p subshell can accommodate six electrons because there are three orbitals within it. The 2p subshell can thus accommodate the additional electrons found in the elements with atomic numbers 7 through 10: *nitrogen* (N), *oxygen* (O), *fluorine* (F), and *neon* (Ne). The electron configurations and orbital diagrams for these elements are

▶ *The symbols 1s², 2s², and 2p³ are read as "one s two," "two s two," and "two p three," not as "one s squared," "two s squared," and "two p cubed."*

The sum of the superscripts in an electron configuration equals the total number of electrons present and hence must equal the atomic number of the element.

			1s	2s	2p
N:	$1s^2 2s^2 2p^3$	N:	[↑↓]	[↑↓]	[↑	↑	↑]
O:	$1s^2 2s^2 2p^4$	O:	[↑↓]	[↑↓]	[↑↓	↑	↑]
F:	$1s^2 2s^2 2p^5$	F:	[↑↓]	[↑↓]	[↑↓	↑↓	↑]
Ne:	$1s^2 2s^2 2p^6$	Ne:	[↑↓]	[↑↓]	[↑↓	↑↓	↑↓]

Atoms of the elements nitrogen, oxygen, fluorine, and neon contain, respectively, three, two, one, and zero unpaired electrons. ◀

With sodium (atomic number = 11), the $3s$ subshell acquires an electron for the first time. Sodium's electron configuration is

$$1s^2 2s^2 2p^6 3s^1$$

Note the pattern that is developing in the electron configurations that have been written so far. Each element has an electron configuration that is the same as the one just before it except for the addition of one electron.

Electron configurations for other elements are obtained by simply extending the principles that have just been illustrated. A subshell of lower energy is always filled before electrons are added to the next highest subshell; this continues until the correct number of electrons have been accommodated.

For a few elements in the middle of the periodic table, the actual distribution of electrons within subshells differs slightly from that obtained by using the procedures outlined in this section. These exceptions are caused by very small energy differences between some subshells and are not important in the uses that are made of electron configurations in this text.

EXAMPLE 3-5

Writing an Electron Configuration

Write the electron configurations for the following elements.

a. Strontium (atomic number = 38)
b. Lead (atomic number = 82)

Solution

a. The number of electrons in a strontium atom is 38. Remember that the atomic number gives the number of electrons (Section 3-2). Subshells are filled, in order of increasing energy, until 38 electrons have been accommodated.

The $1s$, $2s$, and $2p$ subshells fill first, accommodating a total of 10 electrons among them.

$$1s^2 2s^2 2p^6 \ldots$$

Next, according to Figures 3-10 and 3-11, the $3s$ subshell fills and then the $3p$ subshell.

$$1s^2 2s^2 2p^6 \overline{\left(3s^2 3p^6\right)} \ldots$$

At this point, 18 electrons have been accommodated. To get the desired number of 38 electrons, 20 more electrons are still needed.

The $4s$ subshell fills next, followed by the $3d$ subshell, giving a total of 30 electrons at this point.

$$1s^2 2s^2 2p^6 3s^2 3p^6 \overline{\left(4s^2 3d^{10}\right)} \ldots$$

Note that the maximum electron population for d subshells is 10 electrons.

Eight more electrons are needed, which are added to the next two higher subshells, the $4p$ and the $5s$. The $4p$ subshell can accommodate 6 electrons, and the $5s$ can accommodate 2 electrons.

$$1s^2 2s^2 2p^6 3s^2 3p^6 4s^2 3d^{10} \overline{\left(4p^6 5s^2\right)}$$

To double-check that we have the correct number of electrons, 38, the superscripts in our final electron configuration are added together.

$$2 + 2 + 6 + 2 + 6 + 2 + 10 + 6 + 2 = 38$$

The sum of the superscripts in any electron configuration should add up to the atomic number if the configuration is for a neutral atom.

b. To write this configuration, the same procedures are followed as in part **a**, remembering that the maximum electron subshell populations are $s = 2$, $p = 6$, $d = 10$, and $f = 14$.

Lead, with an atomic number of 82, contains 82 electrons, which are added to subshells in the following order. (The line of numbers beneath the electron

(continued)

configuration is a running total of added electrons and is obtained by adding the superscripts up to that point. Adding of electrons stops when 82 electrons are present.)

$$1s^2 2s^2 2p^6 3s^2 3p^6 4s^2 3d^{10} 4p^6 5s^2 4d^{10} 5p^6 6s^2 4f^{14} 5d^{10} 6p^2$$

2 4 10 12 18 20 30 36 38 48 54 56 70 80 82

Running total of electrons added

Note in this electron configuration that the $6p$ subshell contains only 2 electrons, even though it can hold a maximum of 6. Only 2 electrons are added to this subshell because that is sufficient to give 82 total electrons. If the subshell had been completely filled, 86 total electrons would be present, which is too many.

The focus on relevancy feature Chemical Connections 3-B—Electrons in Excited States—extends this section's discussion of electron configurations by considering the distinction between electronic *ground states* and electronic *excited states* and then noting several important situations where electron excited states are important.

Section 3-7 Quick Quiz

1. An electron configuration is a statement of how many electrons an atom has in each of its
   a. electron shells
   b. electron subshells
   c. electron orbitals
   d. no correct response

2. How many electrons are present in atoms of the element whose electron configuration is $1s^2 2s^2 2p^6 3s^1$?
   a. four
   b. eight
   c. eleven
   d. no correct response

3. The correct electron configuration for atoms of oxygen (element #8) is
   a. $1s^2 2s^2 3s^2 4s^2$
   b. $1s^2 1p^6 2s^2$
   c. $1s^2 2s^2 2p^4$
   d. no correct response

4. Which of the following statements is consistent with the electron configuration $1s^2 2s^2 2p^3$?
   a. There are 3 electrons in the $2p$ orbital.
   b. There are 3 electrons in the $2p$ subshell.
   c. There are 3 electrons in the $2p$ shell.
   d. no correct response

5. How many different orbitals contain electrons in atoms with the electron configuration $1s^2 2s^2 2p^2$?
   a. three
   b. four
   c. six
   d. no correct response

6. How many *unpaired* electrons are presents in the orbital diagram for an atom whose electron configuration is $1s^2 2s^2 2p^4$?
   a. none
   b. two
   c. four
   d. no correct response

Answers: 1. b; 2. c; 3. c; 4. b; 5. b; 6. b

Electrons in Excited States

When an atom has its electrons positioned in the lowest-energy orbitals available, it is said to be in its electronic *ground state*. An atom's ground state is the normal (most-stable) electronic state for an atom.

It is possible to elevate electrons in atoms to higher-energy unoccupied orbitals by subjecting the atoms to a beam of light, an electrical discharge, or an influx of heat energy. With electrons in higher, normally unoccupied orbitals, the atom is said to be in an electronic *excited state*. An excited state is an unstable state that has a short life span. Quickly, the excited electrons return to their previous positions (the ground state). Accompanying the transition from the excited state to the ground state is a release of energy. Often this release of energy is in the form of visible light; it can also be in the form of ultraviolet light.

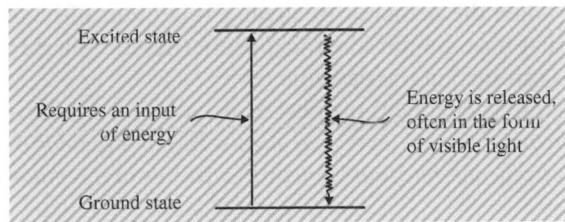

The principle of electron excitation through energy absorption has numerous useful applications including the following:

1. *"Neon" Advertising Signs.* In such signs, gaseous atoms present are excited by an electric discharge to higher-energy states; return of the electrons to the ground state releases visible radiation. The color of the visible radiation depends on the identity of the gas present. Neon gas produces an orange-red light, argon gas a blue-purple light, and krypton gas a white light.
2. *Fireworks.* Metal atoms excited by heat are responsible for the color of fireworks. Strontium (red color), barium (green color), copper (blue color), and aluminum (white color) are some of the metals involved. The metals are present in the form of metal-containing compounds rather than as pure metals.
3. *Compact Fluorescent Light Bulbs.* For energy conservation reasons, compact fluorescent light bulbs (CFLBs) have replaced the standard incandescent light bulb in almost all lighting applications. Electricity costs are cut by up to 70% using CFLBs. The mechanism for light generation in a CFLB involves electron excitation. Structurally a CFLB contains two electrodes and is filled with a gaseous mixture of argon and mercury. Turning the light switch on causes electrons to move between the electrodes. Many of these moving electrons collide with mercury atoms causing electron excitation within the mercury atoms. As the higher-energy excited electrons fall back to their lower-energy original levels energy is released in the form of ultraviolet (not visible) light. The

ultraviolet light interacts with a phosphor coating on the inside walls of the bulb; visible light is produced as the result of fluorescence.

The different colors of fireworks result when heat excites the electrons of different kinds of metal atoms present.

Electronic excited states for mercury atoms play a role in the operation of a compact fluorescent light bulb.

3-8   The Electronic Basis for the Periodic Law and the Periodic Table

LEARNING FOCUS

Be able to relate the periodic law and the shape of the periodic table to electron configurations for atoms of the elements.

For many years, there was no explanation available for either the periodic law or why the periodic table has the shape that it has. It is now known that the theoretical basis for both the periodic law and the periodic table is found in electronic theory. When two atoms interact, it is their electrons that interact (Section 3-2). Thus the number and arrangement of electrons determine how an atom reacts with other atoms—that is, what its chemical properties are. The properties of the elements repeat themselves in a periodic manner because the arrangement of electrons about the nucleus of an atom follows a periodic pattern, as was shown in Section 3-7.

Electron Configurations and the Periodic Law

The periodic law (Section 3-4) points out that the properties of the elements repeat themselves in a regular manner when the elements are arranged in order of increasing atomic number. The elements that have similar chemical properties are placed under one another in vertical columns (groups) in the periodic table.

Groups of elements have similar chemical properties because of similarities in their electron configuration. *Chemical properties repeat themselves in a regular manner among the elements because electron configurations repeat themselves in a regular manner among the elements.*

This correlation between similar chemical properties and similar electron configurations can be illustrated by looking at the electron configurations of two groups of elements known to have similar chemical properties.

The elements lithium, sodium, potassium, and rubidium are all members of Group IA of the periodic table. The electron configurations for these elements are

$$_3\text{Li:} \quad 1s^2 \overparen{2s^1}$$
$$_{11}\text{Na:} \quad 1s^2 2s^2 2p^6 \overparen{3s^1}$$
$$_{19}\text{K:} \quad 1s^2 2s^2 2p^6 3s^2 3p^6 \overparen{4s^1}$$
$$_{37}\text{Rb:} \quad 1s^2 2s^2 2p^6 3s^2 3p^6 4s^2 3d^{10} 4p^6 \overparen{5s^1}$$

Note that each of these elements has one electron in its outermost shell. (The outermost shell is the shell with the highest number.) This similarity in outer-shell electron arrangements causes these elements to have similar chemical properties. In general, elements with similar outer-shell electron configurations have similar chemical properties. ◀

Another group of elements known to have similar chemical properties includes fluorine, chlorine, bromine, and iodine of Group VIIA of the periodic table. The electron configurations for these four elements are

$$_9\text{F:} \quad 1s^2 \overparen{2s^2 2p^5}$$
$$_{17}\text{Cl:} \quad 1s^2 2s^2 2p^6 \overparen{3s^2 3p^5}$$
$$_{35}\text{Br:} \quad 1s^2 2s^2 2p^6 3s^2 3p^6 \overparen{4s^2} 3d^{10} \overparen{4p^5}$$
$$_{53}\text{I:} \quad 1s^2 2s^2 2p^6 3s^2 3p^6 4s^2 \, 3d^{10} 4p^6 \overparen{5s^2} 4d^{10} \overparen{5p^5}$$

▶ *The electron arrangement in the outermost shell is the same for elements in the same group. This is why elements in the same group have similar chemical properties.*

Once again, similarities in electron configuration are readily apparent. This time, the repeating pattern involves an outermost *s* and *p* subshell containing a combined total of seven electrons (shown in color). Remember that for Br and I, shell numbers 4 and 5 designate, respectively, electrons in the outermost shells.

Electron Configurations and the Periodic Table

One of the strongest pieces of supporting evidence for the assignment of electrons to shells, subshells, and orbitals is the periodic table itself. The basic shape and structure of this table, which were determined many years before electrons were even discovered, are consistent with and can be explained by electron configurations. Indeed, the specific location of an element in the periodic table can be used to obtain information about its electron configuration.

As the first step in linking electron configurations to the periodic table, the general shape of the periodic table in terms of columns of elements is considered. As shown in Figure 3-12, on the extreme left of the table, there are 2 columns of elements; in the center there is a region containing 10 columns of elements; to the right there is a block of 6 columns of elements; and in the two rows at the bottom of the table, there are 14 columns of elements.

The number of columns of elements in the various regions of the periodic table—2, 6, 10, and 14—is the same as the maximum number of electrons that the various types of subshells can accommodate. This is a very significant observation as will be shown shortly; the number matchup is no coincidence. The various columnar regions of the periodic table are called the *s* area (2 columns), the *p* area (6 columns), the *d* area (10 columns), and the *f* area (14 columns), as shown in Figure 3-12.

The concept of *distinguishing electrons* is the key to obtaining electron configuration information from the periodic table. A **distinguishing electron** *is the last electron added to the electron configuration for an element when electron subshells are filled in order of increasing energy.* This last electron is the one that causes an element's electron configuration to differ from that of the element immediately preceding it in the periodic table.

For all elements located in the *s* area of the periodic table, the distinguishing electron is always found in an *s* subshell. All *p* area elements have distinguishing electrons in *p* subshells. Similarly, elements in the *d* and *f* areas of the periodic table have distinguishing electrons located in *d* and *f* subshells, respectively. Thus the area location of an element in the periodic table can be used to determine the type of subshell that contains the distinguishing electron. Note that the element helium belongs to the *s* rather than the *p* area of the periodic table, even though its periodic table position is on the right-hand side. (The reason for this placement of helium will be explained in Section 4-3.)

Figure 3-12 Electron configurations and the positions of elements in the periodic table. The periodic table can be divided into four areas that are 2, 6, 10, and 14 columns wide. The four areas contain elements whose distinguishing electron is located, respectively, in *s*, *p*, *d*, and *f* subshells. The extent of filling of the subshell that contains an element's distinguishing electron can be determined from the element's position in the periodic table.

The extent to which the subshell containing an element's distinguishing electron is filled can also be determined from the element's position in the periodic table. All elements in the first column of a specific area contain only one electron in the subshell; all elements in the second column contain two electrons in the subshell; and so on. Thus all elements in the first column of the p area (Group IIIA) have an electron configuration ending in p^1. Elements in the second column of the p area (Group IVA) have electron configurations ending in p^2; and so on. Similar relationships hold in other areas of the table, as shown in Figure 3-12.

Section 3-8 Quick Quiz

1. Which pair of elements would be expected to have similarities in chemical properties?
   a. $_3$Li and $_4$Be
   b. $_9$F and $_{10}$Ne
   c. $_{12}$Mg and $_{20}$Ca
   d. no correct response
2. Which pair of electron configurations represent elements in the same periodic table group?
   a. $1s^2 2s^1$ and $1s^2 2s^2$
   b. $1s^2 2s^2 2p^1$ and $1s^2 2s^2 2p^6 3s^1$
   c. $1s^2 2s^2$ and $1s^2 2s^2 2p^6 3s^2$
   d. no correct response
3. Which of the following elements is located in the d area of the periodic table?
   a. $_{20}$Ca
   b. $_{26}$Fe
   c. $_{33}$As
   d. no correct response
4. Which of the following elements is located in the p^4 column of the periodic table?
   a. $_{15}$P
   b. $_{34}$Se
   c. $_{53}$I
   d. no correct response

Answers: 1. c; 2. c; 3. b; 4. b

3-9 Classification of the Elements

LEARNING FOCUS

Be able to classify an element, based on its periodic table position, as a *noble-gas element, representative element, transition element,* or *inner transition element.*

The elements can be classified in several ways. The two most common classification systems are

1. A system based on selected physical properties of the elements, in which they are described as metals or nonmetals. This classification scheme was discussed in Section 3-5.
2. A system based on the electron configurations of the elements, in which elements are described as *noble-gas, representative, transition,* or *inner transition elements.*

The classification scheme based on electron configurations of the elements is depicted in Figure 3-13.

A **noble-gas element** *is an element located in the far right column of the periodic table.* These elements are all gases at room temperature, and they have little tendency to form chemical compounds. With one exception, the distinguishing electron for a noble gas completes the p subshell; therefore, noble gases have electron configurations ending in p^6. The exception is helium, in which the distinguishing electron completes the first shell—a shell that has only two electrons. Helium's electron configuration is $1s^2$. ◀

▶ *The electron configurations of the noble gases will be an important focal point when chemical bonding theory in Chapters 4 and 5 is considered.*

Figure 3-13 A classification scheme for the elements based on their electron configurations. Representative elements occupy the s area and most of the p area shown in Figure 3-12. The noble-gas elements occupy the last column of the p area. The transition elements are found in the d area, and the inner transition elements are found in the f area.

A **representative element** *is an element located in the* s *area or the first five columns of the* p *area of the periodic table.* The distinguishing electron in these elements partially or completely fills an *s* subshell or partially fills a *p* subshell. Some representative elements are nonmetals, whereas others are metals. The four most abundant elements in the human body—hydrogen, oxygen, carbon, and nitrogen—are nonmetallic representative elements.

A **transition element** *is an element located in the* d *area of the periodic table.* Each has its distinguishing electron in a *d* subshell. All of the transition elements are metals. The most abundant transition element in the human body is iron. The focus on relevancy feature Chemical Connections 3-C—Iron: The Most Abundant Transition Element in the Human Body—considers several aspects of the biochemical role of iron in the human body.

An **inner transition element** *is an element located in the* f *area of the periodic table.* Each has its distinguishing electron in an *f* subshell. All of the inner transition elements are metals. Many of them are laboratory-produced elements rather than naturally occurring elements (Section 11-5).

Chemistry at a Glance—Element Classification Schemes and the Periodic Table—contrasts the three element classification schemes that have been considered so far in this chapter: by physical properties (Section 3-5), by electronic properties (Section 3-9), and by non-numerical periodic table group names (Section 3-4).

(continued)

3. Which of the following in an *incorrect* pairing of concepts?
  a. transition element—*d* area of periodic table
  b. representative element—some are metals and some are nonmetals
  c. noble-gas element—electron configuration ends in p^5 or p^6
  d. no correct response

Answers: 1. d; 2. c; 3. c

CHEMICAL CONNECTIONS 3-C

Iron: The Most Abundant Transition Element in the Human Body

Small amounts of nine transition metals are necessary for the proper functioning of the human body. They include all of the Period 4 transition metals except scandium and titanium plus the Period 5 transition metal molybdenum, as shown in the following transition metal-portion of the periodic table.

Transition Metals

Period 4		V	Cr	Mn	Fe	Co	Ni	Cu	Zn
Period 5			Mo						
Period 6									

Iron is the most abundant, from a biochemical standpoint, of these transition metals; zinc is the second most abundant.

Most of the body's iron is found as a component of the proteins hemoglobin and myoglobin, where it functions in the transport and storage of oxygen. Hemoglobin is the oxygen carrier in red blood cells, and myoglobin stores oxygen in muscle cells. Iron-deficient blood has less oxygen-carrying capacity and often cannot completely meet the body's energy needs. Energy deficiency—tiredness and apathy—is one of the symptoms of iron deficiency.

Iron deficiency is a worldwide problem. Millions of people are unknowingly deficient. Even in the United States and Canada, about 20% of women and 3% of men have this problem; some 8% of women and 1% of men are anemic, experiencing fatigue, weakness, apathy, and headaches.

Inadequate intake of iron, either from malnutrition or from high consumption of the wrong foods, is the usual cause of iron deficiency. In the Western world, the cause is often displacement of iron-rich foods by foods high in sugar and fat.

About 80% of the iron in the body is in the blood, so iron losses are greatest whenever blood is lost. Blood loss from menstruation makes a woman's need for iron nearly twice as great as a man's. Also, women usually consume less food than men do. These two factors—lower intake and higher loss—cause iron deficiency to be likelier in women than in men. The iron RDA (recommended dietary allowance) is 8 mg per day for adult males and older women. For women of childbearing age, the RDA is 18 mg. This amount is necessary to replace menstrual loss and to provide the extra iron needed during pregnancy.

Iron deficiency may also be caused by poor absorption of ingested iron. A normal, healthy person absorbs about 2%–10% of the iron in vegetables and about 10%–30% in meats. About 40% of the iron in meat, fish, and poultry is bound to molecules of heme, the iron-containing part of hemoglobin and myoglobin. Heme iron is much more readily absorbed (23%) than nonheme iron (2%–10%). (See the accompanying charts.)

Cooking utensils can enhance the amount of iron delivered by the diet. The iron content of 100 g of spaghetti sauce simmered in a glass dish is 3 mg, but it is 87 mg when the sauce is cooked in an unenameled iron skillet. Even in the short time it takes to scramble eggs, their iron content can be tripled by cooking them in an iron pan.

CHEMISTRY

AT A GLANCE   Element Classification Schemes and the Periodic Table

CLASSIFICATION BY PHYSICAL PROPERTIES

| Nonmetals | • No metallic luster
• Poor electrical conductivity
• Good heat insulators
• Brittle and nonmalleable |
| Metals | • Metallic gray or silver luster
• High electrical and thermal conductivity
• Malleable and ductile |

CLASSIFICATION BY ELECTRONIC PROPERTIES

Representative elements	• Found in s area and first five columns of the p area • Some are metals, some nonmetals
Noble-gas elements	• Found in last column of p area plus He (s area) • All are nonmetals
Transition elements	• Found in d area • All are metals
Inner transition elements	• Found in f area • All are metals

PERIODIC TABLE GROUPS WITH SPECIAL NAMES

Alkali metals	• Group IA elements (except for H, a nonmetal) • Electron configurations end in s^1
Alkaline earth metals	• Group IIA elements • Electron configurations end in s^2
Halogens	• Group VIIA elements • Electron configurations end in p^5
Noble gases	• Group VIIIA elements • Electron configurations end in p^6, except for He, which ends in s^2

Concepts to Remember

Subatomic particles. Subatomic particles, the very small building blocks from which atoms are made, are of three major types: electrons, protons, and neutrons. Electrons are negatively charged, protons are positively charged, and neutrons have no charge. All neutrons and protons are found at the center of the atom in the nucleus. The electrons occupy the region about the nucleus. Protons and neutrons have much larger masses than electrons (Section 3-1).

Atomic number and mass number. Each atom has a characteristic atomic number and mass number. The atomic number is equal to the number of protons in the nucleus of the atom. The mass number is equal to the total number of protons and neutrons in the nucleus (Section 3-2).

Isotopes. Isotopes are atoms that have the same number of protons and electrons but have different numbers of neutrons.

The isotopes of an element always have the same atomic number and different mass numbers. Isotopes of an element have the same chemical properties (Section 3-3).

Atomic mass. The atomic mass of an element is a calculated average mass. It depends on the percentage abundances and masses of the naturally occurring isotopes of the element (Section 3-3).

Periodic law and periodic table. The periodic law states that when elements are arranged in order of increasing atomic number, elements with similar chemical properties occur at periodic (regularly recurring) intervals. The periodic table is a graphical representation of the behavior described by the periodic law. In a modern periodic table, vertical columns contain elements with similar chemical properties. A group in the periodic table is a vertical column of elements. A period in the periodic table is a horizontal row of elements (Section 3-4).

Metals and nonmetals. Metals exhibit luster, thermal conductivity, electrical conductivity, and malleability. Nonmetals are characterized by the absence of the properties associated with metals. The majority of the elements are metals. The steplike heavy line that runs through the right third of the periodic table separates the metals on the left from the nonmetals on the right (Section 3-5).

Electron shell. An electron shell contains electrons that have approximately the same energy and spend most of their time approximately the same distance from the nucleus (Section 3-6).

Electron subshell. An electron subshell contains electrons that all have the same energy. The number of subshells in a particular shell is equal to the shell number. Each subshell can hold a specific maximum number of electrons. These values are 2, 6, 10, and 14 for s, p, d, and f subshells, respectively (Section 3-6).

Electron orbital. An electron orbital is a region of space about a nucleus where an electron with a specific energy is most likely to be found. Each subshell consists of one or more orbitals. For s, p, d, and f subshells there are 1, 3, 5, and 7 orbitals, respectively. No more than two electrons may occupy any orbital (Section 3-6).

Electron configuration. An electron configuration is a statement of how many electrons an atom has in each of its subshells. The principle that electrons normally occupy the lowest-energy subshell available is used to write electron configurations (Section 3-7).

Orbital diagram. An orbital diagram is a notation that shows how many electrons an atom has in each of its orbitals. Electrons occupy the orbitals of a subshell such that each orbital within the subshell acquires one electron before any orbital acquires a second electron. All electrons in such singly occupied orbitals must have the same spin (Section 3-7).

Electron configurations and the periodic law. Chemical properties repeat themselves in a regular manner among the elements because electron configurations repeat themselves in a regular manner among the elements (Section 3-8).

Electron configurations and the periodic table. The groups of the periodic table consist of elements with similar electron configurations. Thus the location of an element in the periodic table can be used to obtain information about its electron configuration (Section 3-8).

Classification system for the elements. On the basis of electron configuration, elements can be classified into four categories: noble gases (far right column of the periodic table); representative elements (s and p areas of the periodic table, with the exception of the noble gases); transition elements (d area of the periodic table); and inner transition elements (f area of the periodic table) (Section 3-9).

Exercises and Problems

Exercises and problems are arranged in matched pairs with the two members of a pair addressing the same concept(s). The answer to the odd-numbered member of a pair is given at the back of the book. Problems denoted with a ▲ involve concepts found not only in the section under consideration but also concepts found in one or more earlier sections of the chapter.

Internal Structure of an Atom (Section 3-1)

3-1 Indicate which subatomic particle (proton, neutron, or electron) correctly matches each of the following phrases. More than one particle can be used as an answer.
  a. Possesses a negative charge
  b. Has no charge
  c. Has a mass slightly less than that of a neutron
  d. Has a charge equal to, but opposite in sign from, that of an electron

3-2 Indicate which subatomic particle (proton, neutron, or electron) correctly matches each of the following phrases. More than one particle can be used as an answer.
  a. Is not found in the nucleus
  b. Has a positive charge
  c. Can be called a nucleon
  d. Has a relative mass of 1837 if the relative mass of an electron is 1

3-3 Indicate whether each of the following statements about the nucleus of an atom is true or false.
  a. The nucleus of an atom is neutral.
  b. The nucleus of an atom contains only neutrons.
  c. The number of nucleons present in the nucleus is equal to the number of electrons present outside the nucleus.
  d. The nucleus accounts for almost all the mass of an atom.

3-4 Indicate whether each of the following statements about the nucleus of an atom is true or false.
  a. The nucleus of an atom contains all of the "heavy" subatomic particles.
  b. The nucleus of an atom accounts for almost all of the volume of the atom.
  c. The nucleus of an atom has an extremely low density compared to that of the atom as a whole.
  d. The nucleus of an atom can be positively or negatively charged, depending on the identity of the atom.

Atomic Number and Mass Number (Section 3-2)

3-5 How many protons, neutrons, and electrons are present in atoms with the following characteristics?
  a. atomic number = 7, mass number = 15
  b. atomic number = 20, mass number = 40
  c. $Z = 11$, $A = 23$
  d. $Z = 35$, $A = 79$

3-6 How many protons, neutrons, and electrons are present in atoms with the following characteristics?
  a. atomic number = 8, mass number = 18
  b. atomic number = 19, mass number = 39
  c. $Z = 18$, $A = 40$
  d. $Z = 24$, $A = 52$

3-7 How many protons, neutrons, and electrons are present in atoms with the following characteristics?
  a. $^{118}_{50}Sn$ b. $^{195}_{78}Pt$
  c. $^{72}_{31}Ga$ d. $^{26}_{12}Mg$

3-8 How many protons, neutrons, and electrons are present in atoms with the following characteristics?
  a. $^{58}_{26}Fe$ b. $^{10}_{4}Be$
  c. $^{197}_{79}Au$ d. $^{208}_{82}Pb$

3-9 What is the atomic number for atoms composed of the following sets of subatomic particles?
a. 5 protons, 5 electrons, and 6 neutrons
b. 7 electrons, 8 neutrons, and 7 protons
c. 13 protons, 14 neutrons, and 13 electrons
d. 28 neutrons, 20 electrons, and 20 protons

3-10 What is the atomic number for atoms composed of the following sets of subatomic particles?
a. 4 protons, 4 electrons, and 5 neutrons
b. 8 electrons, 8 neutrons, and 8 protons
c. 15 protons, 16 neutrons, and 15 electrons
d. 22 neutrons, 18 electrons, and 18 protons

3-11 What is the mass number for each of the atoms in Problem 3-9?

3-12 What is the mass number for each of the atoms is Problem 3-10?

3-13 What is the total number of nucleons present for each of the atoms is Problem 3-9?

3-14 What is the total number of nucleons present for each of the atoms in Problem 3-10?

3-15 What is the total number of charged subatomic particles present for each of the atoms in Problem 3-9?

3-16 What is the total number of charged subatomic particles present for each of the atoms in Problem 3-10?

3-17 What is the total charge (including sign) associated with the nucleus for each of the atoms in Problem 3-9?

3-18 What is the total charge (including sign) associated with the nucleus for each of the atoms in Problem 3-10?

3-19 Complete the following table by filling in the blanks in each row. The first row has been completed as an example.

Symbol	Atomic Number	Mass Number	Number of Protons	Number of Neutrons
$^{37}_{17}Cl$	17	37	17	20
a.		232		138
b. $^{32}_{16}S$				
c.		56	26	
d.	20	40		

3-20 Complete the following table by filling in the blanks in each row. The first row has been completed as an example.

Symbol	Atomic Number	Mass Number	Number of Protons	Number of Neutrons
$^{3}_{2}He$	2	3	2	1
a.	28	60		
b.	18			17
c.		90	38	
d. $^{235}_{92}U$				

3-21 An atom with an number of 11 contains 36 subatomic particles. How many of these subatomic particles have each of the following characteristics?
a. carry a charge
b. carry no charge
c. found in the nucleus
d. not found in the nucleus

3-22 An atom with an atomic number of 17 contains 52 subatomic particles. How many of these subatomic particles have each of the following characteristics?
a. carry a charge
b. carry no charge
c. found in the nucleus
d. not found in the nucleus

3-23 Determine the following information for an atom whose complete chemical symbol is $^{23}_{11}Na$.
a. The total number of subatomic particles present
b. The total number of subatomic particles present in the nucleus of the atom
c. The total number of nucleons present
d. The total charge (including sign) associated with the nucleus of the atom

3-24 Determine the following information for an atom whose complete chemical symbol is $^{37}_{17}Cl$.
a. The total number of subatomic particles present
b. The total number of subatomic particles present in the nucleus of the atom
c. The total number of nucleons present
d. The total charge (including sign) associated with the nucleus of the atom

3-25 Characterize each of the following pairs of atoms as containing (1) the same number of neutrons, (2) the same number of protons, (3) the same number of nucleons, or (4) the same total number of subatomic particles.
a. $^{13}_{7}C$ and $^{13}_{6}N$
b. $^{37}_{17}Cl$ and $^{36}_{18}Ar$
c. $^{35}_{17}Cl$ and $^{37}_{17}Cl$
d. $^{18}_{8}O$ and $^{19}_{9}F$

3-26 Characterize each of the following pairs of atoms as containing (1) the same number of neutrons, (2) the same number of protons, (3) the same number of nucleons, or (4) the same total number of subatomic particles.
a. $^{40}_{18}Ar$ and $^{40}_{20}Ca$
b. $^{14}_{7}N$ and $^{15}_{7}N$
c. $^{14}_{6}C$ and $^{15}_{7}N$
d. $^{38}_{18}Ar$ and $^{39}_{19}K$

Isotopes and Atomic Masses (Section 3-3)

3-27 The atomic number of the element carbon (C) is 6. Write the complete chemical symbols for each of the following carbon isotopes: carbon-12, carbon-13, and carbon-14.

3-28 The atomic number of the element sulfur (S) is 16. Write the complete chemical symbols for each of the following sulfur isotopes: sulfur-32, sulfur-33, sulfur-34, and sulfur-36.

3-29 The following are selected properties of the most abundant isotope of a particular element. Which of these properties would also be the same for the second-most-abundant isotope of the element?
a. Mass number is 70
b. 31 electrons are present
c. Isotopic mass is 69.92 amu
d. Isotope reacts with chlorine to give a green compound

3-30 The following are selected properties of the most abundant isotope of a particular element. Which of these properties would also be the same for the second-most-abundant isotope of the element?
a. Atomic number is 31
b. Does not react with the element gold
c. 40 neutrons are present
d. Density is 1.03 g/mL

3-31 Calculate the atomic mass of each of the following elements using the given data for the percentage abundance and mass of each isotope.
a. Lithium: 7.42% ^{6}Li (6.01 amu) and 92.58% ^{7}Li (7.02 amu)
b. Magnesium: 78.99% ^{24}Mg (23.99 amu), 10.00% ^{25}Mg (24.99 amu), and 11.01% ^{26}Mg (25.98 amu)

3-32 Calculate the atomic mass of each of the following elements using the given data for the percentage abundance and mass of each isotope.
a. Silver: 51.82% ^{107}Ag (106.9 amu) and 48.18% ^{109}Ag (108.9 amu)
b. Silicon: 92.21% ^{28}Si (27.98 amu), 4.70% ^{29}Si (28.98 amu), and 3.09% ^{30}Si (29.97 amu)

3-33 The element copper (Cu) has an atomic mass of 63.55 amu and has two naturally occurring isotopic forms. Based on this information, indicate whether each of the following statements is true or false?
a. All Cu atoms have a mass of 63.55 amu.
b. Some Cu atoms have a mass of 63.55 amu.
c. Some Cu atoms have a mass less than 63.55 amu.
d. Some Cu atoms have a mass greater than 63.55 amu.

3-34 The element lithium (Li) has an atomic mass of 6.94 amu and has two naturally occurring isotopic forms. Based on this information, indicate whether each of the following statements is true or false?
a. All Li atoms have a mass of 6.94 amu.
b. Some Li atoms have a mass of 6.94 amu.
c. Some Li atoms have a mass of less than 6.94 amu.
d. Some Li atoms have a mass of greater than 6.94 amu.

▲3-35 Using the information given in the following table, indicate whether each of the following pairs of atoms are isotopes.

	Protons	Neutrons	Electrons
Atom A	9	10	9
Atom B	10	9	10
Atom C	10	10	10
Atom D	9	9	9

a. Atom A and atom B
b. Atom A and atom C
c. Atom A and atom D

▲3-36 Using the information given in the table in Problem 3-35 indicate whether each of the following pairs of atoms are isotopes.
a. Atom B and atom C
b. Atom B and atom D
c. Atom C and atom D

▲3-37 Indicate whether each of the following statements about sodium isotopes is true or false.
a. $^{23}_{11}$Na has one more electron than $^{24}_{11}$Na.
b. $^{23}_{11}$Na and $^{24}_{11}$Na contain the same number of neutrons.
c. $^{23}_{11}$Na has one less subatomic particle than $^{24}_{11}$Na.
d. $^{23}_{11}$Na and $^{24}_{11}$Na have the same atomic number.

▲3-38 Indicate whether each of the following statements about magnesium isotopes is true or false.
a. $^{24}_{12}$Mg has one more proton than $^{25}_{12}$Mg.
b. $^{24}_{12}$Mg and $^{25}_{12}$Mg contain the same number of subatomic particles.
c. $^{24}_{12}$Mg has one less neutron than $^{25}_{12}$Mg.
d. $^{24}_{12}$Mg and $^{25}_{12}$Mg have different mass numbers.

▲3-39 Indicate whether each of the following numbers are the same or different for two isotopes of an element.
a. number of protons
b. number of nucleons
c. atomic number
d. $A + Z$

▲3-40 Indicate whether each of the following numbers are the same or different for two isotopes of an element.
a. number of electrons
b. number of neutrons
c. mass number
d. $A - Z$

▲3-41 Write the complete chemical symbol (^A_ZE) for the isotope of chromium with the following individual characteristics.
a. 30 more neutrons than protons
b. Two fewer subatomic particles than $^{52}_{24}$Cr
c. The same number of neutrons as $^{55}_{25}$Mn
d. The same number of subatomic particles as $^{60}_{29}$Cu

▲3-42 Write the complete chemical symbol (^A_ZE) for the isotope of copper with the following individual characteristics.
a. 32 more neutrons than protons
b. Two more subatomic particles than $^{66}_{30}$Zn
c. The same number of neutrons as $^{58}_{28}$Ni
d. The same number of nucleons as $^{60}_{30}$Zn

The Periodic Law and the Periodic Table (Section 3-4)

3-43 Specify the location of each of the following elements in the periodic table by giving its period number and Roman numeral group number.
a. $_4$Be   b. $_{15}$P
c. $_{19}$K   d. $_{53}$I

3-44 Specify the location of each of the following elements in the periodic table by giving its period number and Roman numeral group number.
a. $_6$C   b. $_{13}$Al
c. $_{20}$Ca   d. $_{50}$Sn

3-45 Using the periodic table, determine the following.
a. The atomic number of the element carbon
b. The atomic mass of the element silicon
c. The atomic number of the element with an atomic mass of 88.91 amu
d. The atomic mass of the element located in Period 2 and Group IIA

3-46 Using the periodic table, determine the following.
a. The atomic number of the element magnesium
b. The atomic mass of the element nitrogen
c. The atomic mass of the element with an atomic number of 10
d. The atomic number of the element located in Group IIIA and Period 3

3-47 Based on periodic table position, select the two elements in each set of elements that would be expected to have similar chemical properties.
a. $_{19}K, _{29}Cu, _{37}Rb, _{41}Nb$
b. $_{13}Al, _{14}Si, _{15}P, _{33}As$
c. $_{9}F, _{40}Zr, _{50}Sn, _{53}I$
d. $_{11}Na, _{12}Mg, _{54}Xe, _{55}Cs$

3-48 Based on periodic table position, select the two elements in each set of elements that would be expected to have similar chemical properties.
a. $_{11}Na, _{14}Si, _{23}V, _{55}Cs$
b. $_{13}Al, _{19}K, _{32}Ge, _{50}Sn$
c. $_{37}Rb, _{38}Sr, _{54}Xe, _{56}Ba$
d. $_{2}He, _{6}C, _{8}O, _{10}Ne$

3-49 Identify the Period 2 element that fits each of the following descriptions.
a. a halogen
b. an alkaline earth metal
c. an alkali metal
d. a noble gas

3-50 Identify the Period 3 element that fits each of the following descriptions.
a. a noble gas
b. a halogen
c. an alkali metal
d. an alkaline earth metal

3-51 How many elements exist with an atomic number less than 40 that are
a. Halogens
b. Noble gases
c. Alkali metals
d. Alkaline earth metals

3-52 How many elements exist with an atomic number greater than 20 that are
a. Halogens
b. Noble gases
c. Alkali metals
d. Alkaline earth metals

3-53 Determine the following for the "highlighted" elements in the given periodic table. (Specify your answer by giving the "color" of the element.)

a. Which of the highlighted elements is a halogen?
b. Which of the highlighted elements is an alkaline earth metal?
c. Which of the highlighted elements is in Group IIA?
d. Which of the highlighted elements is in Period 3?

3-54 Determine the following for the "highlighted" elements in the periodic table given in Problem 3-53. (Specify your answer by giving the "color" of the element.)
a. Which of the highlighted elements is an alkali metal?
b. Which of the highlighted elements is a noble gas?
c. Which of the highlighted elements is in Group VIIA?
d. Which of the highlighted elements is in Period 2?

▲3-55 With the help of the periodic table, write complete chemical symbols ($_{Z}^{A}E$) for atoms with the following characteristics.
a. In Period 2 and Group IIA and has 4 more neutrons than protons
b. In Period 4 and Group VIIIA and has a mass number of 132
c. In Period 2 and Group VIA and has an equal number of the two kinds of nucleons
d. In Period 4 and Group IIA and has an equal number of all three kinds of subatomic particles

▲3-56 With the help of the periodic table, write complete chemical symbols ($_{Z}^{A}E$) for atoms with the following characteristics.
a. In Period 4 and Group IA and has one more neutron than protons
b. In Period 2 and Group VIIIA and has a relative mass of 21.991 amu
c. In Period 5 and Group IVA and contains 170 subatomic particles
d. In Period 2 and Group IIA and contains 9 nucleons

Metals and Nonmetals (Section 3-5)

3-57 In which of the following pairs of elements are both members metals?
a. $_{17}Cl$ and $_{35}Br$ b. $_{13}Al$ and $_{14}Si$
c. $_{29}Cu$ and $_{42}Mo$ d. $_{30}Zn$ and $_{83}Bi$

3-58 In which of the following pairs of elements are both members metals?
a. $_{7}N$ and $_{34}Se$ b. $_{16}S$ and $_{48}Cd$
c. $_{3}Li$ and $_{26}Fe$ d. $_{50}Sn$ and $_{53}I$

3-59 Identify the nonmetal in each of the following sets of elements.
a. S, Na, K   b. Cu, Li, P
c. Be, I, Ca   d. Fe, Cl, Ga

3-60 Identify the nonmetal in each of the following sets of elements.
a. Al, H, Mg   b. C, Sn, Sb
c. Ti, V, F   d. Sr, Se, Sm

3-61 Classify each of the following general physical properties as a property of metallic elements or of nonmetallic elements.
a. Ductile
b. Low electrical conductivity
c. High thermal conductivity
d. Good heat insulator

3-62 Classify each of the following general physical properties as a property of metallic elements or of nonmetallic elements.
a. Nonmalleable
b. High luster
c. Low thermal conductivity
d. Brittle

3-63 Determine the following for the "highlighted" elements in the given periodic table.

a. Is the element highlighted in red a metal or nonmetal?
b. Is the element highlighted in green a metal or nonmetal?
c. Is the element highlighted in yellow a good or poor conductor of electricity?
d. Is the element highlighted in blue a good or poor conductor of heat?

3-64 Determine the following, using the periodic table given in Problem 3-63.
a. Is the element highlighted in yellow a metal or nonmetal?
b. Is the element highlighted in blue a metal or nonmetal?
c. Is the element highlighted in red a good or poor conductor of electricity?
d. Is the element highlighted in green a good or poor conductor of heat?

▲**3-65** Which of the six elements nitrogen, beryllium, argon, aluminum, silver, and gold is (are) described by the following characteristics?
a. Period number and Roman numeral group number are numerically equal
b. Readily conducts electricity
c. Has an atomic mass greater than its atomic number
d. Nuclear charge is greater than +20

▲**3-66** Which of the six elements carbon, chlorine, phosphorus, calcium, copper, and bromine is (are) described by the following characteristics?
a. Located in Period 3 of the periodic table
b. Belongs to the halogen family of elements
c. Readily conducts heat
d. Nuclear charge is less than +16

Electron Arrangements Within Atoms (Section 3-6)

3-67 Identify the electron shell to which each of the following electron subshells belongs.
a. 2s
b. 4s
c. 3d
d. 5p

3-68 Identify the electron shell to which each of the following electron subshells belongs.
a. 3p
b. 4p
c. 6s
d. 4d

3-69 How many electrons can be accommodated in each of the electron subshells listed in Problem 3-67?

3-70 How many electrons can be accommodated in each of the electron subshells listed in Problem 3-68?

3-71 How many electrons can be accommodated in an electron orbital of each of the following types?
a. 2s
b. 2p
c. 3s
d. 3d

3-72 How many electrons can be accommodated in an electron orbital of each of the following types?
a. 3p
b. 4p
c. 4s
d. 4d

3-73 How many electron orbitals are there of each of the subshell types listed in Problem 3-67?

3-74 How many electron orbitals are there of each of the subshell types listed in Problem 3-68?

3-75 Indicate whether each of the following statements is true or false.
a. An orbital has a definite size and shape, which are related to the energy of the electrons it could contain.
b. All the orbitals in a subshell have the same energy.
c. All subshells accommodate the same number of electrons.
d. A 2p subshell and a 3p subshell contain the same number of orbitals.

3-76 Indicate whether each of the following statements is true or false.
a. All the subshells in a shell have the same energy.
b. An s orbital has a shape that resembles a four-leaf clover.
c. The third shell can accommodate a maximum of 18 electrons.
d. All orbitals accommodate the same number of electrons.

Electron Configurations and Orbital Diagrams (Section 3-7)

3-77 Write complete electron configurations for atoms of each of the following elements.
a. $_6$C
b. $_{11}$Na
c. $_{16}$S
d. $_{18}$Ar

3-78 Write complete electron configurations for atoms of each of the following elements.
a. $_{10}$Ne
b. $_{13}$Al
c. $_{19}$K
d. $_{22}$Ti

3-79 On the basis of the total number of electrons present, identify the elements whose electron configurations are
a. $1s^2 2s^2 2p^4$
b. $1s^2 2s^2 2p^6$
c. $1s^2 2s^2 2p^6 3s^2 3p^1$
d. $1s^2 2s^2 2p^6 3s^2 3p^6 4s^2$

3-80 On the basis of the total number of electrons present, identify the elements whose electron configurations are
a. $1s^2 2s^2 2p^2$
b. $1s^2 2s^2 2p^6 3s^1$
c. $1s^2 2s^2 2p^6 3s^2 3p^5$
d. $1s^2 2s^2 2p^6 3s^2 3p^6 4s^2 3d^{10} 4p^3$

3-81 Write *complete* electron configurations for atoms whose electron configurations *end* as follows.
    a. $3p^5$ b. $4d^7$
    c. $4s^2$ d. $3d^1$

3-82 Write *complete* electron configurations for atoms whose electron configurations *end* as follows.
    a. $4p^2$ b. $3d^{10}$
    c. $5s^1$ d. $4p^6$

3-83 Draw the orbital diagram associated with each of the following electron configurations.
    a. $1s^2 2s^2 2p^2$
    b. $1s^2 2s^2 2p^6 3s^2$
    c. $1s^2 2s^2 2p^6 3s^2 3p^3$
    d. $1s^2 2s^2 2p^6 3s^2 3p^6 4s^2 3d^7$

3-84 Draw the orbital diagram associated with each of the following electron configurations.
    a. $1s^2 2s^2 2p^5$
    b. $1s^2 2s^2 2p^6 3s^1$
    c. $1s^2 2s^2 2p^6 3s^2 3p^1$
    d. $1s^2 2s^2 2p^6 3s^2 3p^6 4s^2 3d^6$

3-85 How many unpaired electrons are present in each of the electron configurations in Problem 3-83?

3-86 How many unpaired electrons are present in each of the electron configuration in Problem 3-84?

▲3-87 The electron configuration of the isotope ^{16}O is $1s^2 2s^2 2p^4$. What is the electron configuration of the isotope ^{18}O?

▲3-88 The electron configuration of the isotope ^{24}Mg is $1s^2 2s^2 2p^6 3s^2$. What is the electron configuration of the isotope ^{25}Mg?

▲3-89 Write electron configurations for the following elements.
    a. The Group IIIA element in the same period as $_4$Be
    b. The Period 3 element in the same group as $_5$B
    c. The lowest-atomic-numbered *metal* in Group IIA
    d. The two Period 3 elements that have no unpaired electrons

▲3-90 Write electrons configurations for the following elements.
    a. The Group VIIA element in the same period as $_{12}$Mg
    b. The Period 2 element in the same group as $_{50}$Sn
    c. The lowest-atomic-numbered *nonmetal* in Period 3
    d. The two Period 2 elements that contain two unpaired electrons

Electron Configurations and the Periodic Table (Section 3-8)

3-91 Indicate whether the elements represented by the given pairs of electron configurations have similar chemical properties.
    a. $1s^2 2s^1$ and $1s^2 2s^2$
    b. $1s^2 2s^2 2p^6$ and $1s^2 2s^2 2p^6 3s^2 3p^6$
    c. $1s^2 2s^2 2p^3$ and $1s^2 2s^2 2p^6 3s^2 3p^6 4s^2 3d^3$
    d. $1s^2 2s^2 2p^6 3s^2 3p^4$ and $1s^2 2s^2 2p^6 3s^2 3p^6 4s^2 3d^{10} 4p^4$

3-92 Indicate whether the elements represented by the given pairs of electron configurations have similar chemical properties.
    a. $1s^2 2s^2 2p^4$ and $1s^2 2s^2 2p^5$
    b. $1s^2 2s^2$ and $1s^2 2s^2 2p^2$

    c. $1s^2 2s^1$ and $1s^2 2s^2 2p^6 3s^2 3p^6 4s^1$
    d. $1s^2 2s^2 2p^6$ and $1s^2 2s^2 2p^6 3s^2 3p^6 4s^2 3d^6$

3-93 Specify the location of each of the following elements in the periodic table in terms of *s* area, *p* area, *d* area, or *f* area.
    a. Magnesium   b. Copper
    c. Bromine   d. Iron

3-94 Specify the location of each of the following elements in the periodic table in terms of *s* area, *p* area, *d* area, or *f* area.
    a. Aluminum   b. Potassium
    c. Sulfur   d. Gold

3-95 For each of the following elements, specify the extent to which the subshell containing the distinguishing electron is filled (s^2, p^3, p^5, d^4, etc.).
    a. $_{13}$Al   b. $_{23}$V
    c. $_{20}$Ca   d. $_{36}$Kr

3-96 For each of the following elements, specify the extent to which the subshell containing the distinguishing electron is filled (s^2, p^3, p^5, d^4, etc.).
    a. $_{10}$Ne   b. $_{19}$K
    c. $_{33}$As   d. $_{30}$Zn

3-97 Determine the following for the "highlighted" elements in the given periodic table.

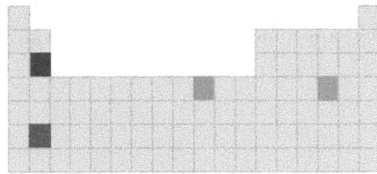

    a. Is the element highlighted in red in the *s* area or *p* area of the periodic table?
    b. Is the element highlighted in green in the *d* area or *p* area of the periodic table?
    c. Is the element highlighted in yellow a p^2 or a p^4 element?
    d. Is the element highlighted in blue a d^2 or an s^2 element?

3-98 Determine the following, using the periodic table given in Problem 3-97.
    a. Is the element highlighted in yellow in the *p* area or *d* area of the periodic table?
    b. Is the element highlighted in blue in the *s* area or *d* area of the periodic table?
    c. Is the element highlighted in red an s^2 or a d^2 element?
    d. Is the element highlighted in green a d^6 or a d^8 element?

Classification of the Elements (Section 3-9)

3-99 Classify each of the following elements as a noble gas, representative element, transition element, or inner transition element.
    a. $_{15}$P   b. $_{18}$Ar
    c. $_{79}$Au   d. $_{92}$U

3-100 Classify each of the following elements as a noble gas, representative element, transition element, or inner transition element.
    a. $_1$H   b. $_{44}$Ru
    c. $_{51}$Sb   d. $_{86}$Rn

3-101 Determine the following for the "highlighted" elements in the given periodic table.

a. How many of the highlighted elements are representative elements?
b. How many of the highlighted elements are noble gases?
c. How many of the highlighted elements are nonmetallic representative elements?
d. How many of the highlighted elements are metals?

3-102 Determine the following for the "highlighted" elements in the periodic table given in Problem 3-101.
a. How many of the highlighted elements are inner transition elements?
b. How many of the highlighted elements are transition elements?
c. How many of the highlighted elements are metallic representative elements?
d. How many of the highlighted elements are nonmetals?

▲3-103 Classify the element with each of the following electron configurations as a representative element, transition element, noble gas, or inner transition element.
a. $1s^2 2s^2 2p^6$
b. $1s^2 2s^2 2p^6 3s^2 3p^4$
c. $1s^2 2s^2 2p^6 3s^2 3p^6 4s^2 3d^1$
d. $1s^2 2s^2 2p^6 3s^2 3p^6 4s^2$

▲3-104 Classify the element with each of the following electron configurations as a representative element, transition element, noble gas, or inner transition element.
a. $1s^2 2s^2 2p^6 3s^1$
b. $1s^2 2s^2 2p^6 3s^2 3p^6$
c. $1s^2 2s^2 2p^6 3s^2 3p^6 4s^2 3d^7$
d. $1s^2 2s^2 2p^6 3s^2 3p^6 4s^2 3d^{10} 4p^5$

Chemical Bonding: The Ionic Bond Model

MS Davidson/Science Source

Magnification of crystals of sodium chloride (table salt), one of the most commonly encountered ionic compounds. Color has been added to the image by computer.

Atoms are seldom encountered in the "free state," that is, singly and separately. Instead, under normal conditions of temperature and pressure, atoms are almost always found associated together in aggregates or clusters ranging in size from two atoms to numbers too large to count.

In this chapter, an explanation for why atoms tend to join together in larger units is considered, as well as the nature of the binding forces (chemical bonds) that hold the atoms together in these larger units. Both the tendency and the capacity of an atom to be associated with other atoms are directly related to an atom's electron configuration (Section 3-7).

4-1 Chemical Bonds

LEARNING FOCUS

Define the term *chemical bond* and using electron behavior concepts distinguish between the *ionic* and *covalent* bonding models.

Chemical compounds are conveniently divided into two broad classes called *ionic compounds* and *molecular compounds*. Ionic and molecular compounds can be distinguished from each other on the basis of general physical properties. Ionic compounds tend to have high melting points (500°C–2000°C) and are good conductors of electricity when they are in a molten (liquid) state or in solution. Molecular compounds, on the other hand, generally have much lower melting points and tend to be gases, liquids, or low melting-point solids. They do not conduct electricity in the molten state. Ionic compounds, unlike molecular compounds, do not have molecules as their basic structural unit. Instead, an extended array of positively and negatively charged particles called *ions* is present (Section 4-8).

Some combinations of elements produce ionic compounds, whereas other combinations of elements form molecular compounds. What determines whether the interaction of two elements produces ions (an ionic compound) or molecules (a molecular compound)? The answer to this question involves the concept of *chemical bonds*. A **chemical bond** *is the attractive force that holds two atoms together in a more complex unit.* Chemical bonds form as a result of interactions between electrons found in the combining atoms. Thus the nature of chemical bonds is closely linked to electron configurations (Section 3-7). ◄

▶ *Another designation for* molecular compound *is* covalent compound. *The two designations are used interchangeably. The modifier* molecular *draws attention to the basic structural unit present (the molecule), and the modifier* covalent *focuses on the mode of bond formation (electron sharing).*

Corresponding to the two broad categories of chemical compounds are two types of chemical attractive forces (chemical bonds): ionic bonds and covalent bonds. An **ionic bond** *is a chemical bond formed through the transfer of one or more electrons from one atom or group of atoms to another atom or group of atoms.* As its name suggests, the ionic bond model (electron transfer) is used in describing the attractive forces in ionic compounds. An **ionic compound** *is a compound in which ionic bonds are present.*

A **covalent bond** *is a chemical bond formed through the sharing of one or more pairs of electrons between two atoms.* The covalent bond model (electron sharing) is used in describing the attractions between atoms in molecular compounds. A **molecular compound** *is a compound in which covalent bonds are present.*

Even before considering the details of these two bond models, it is important to emphasize that the concepts of ionic and covalent bonds are actually "convenience concepts." Most bonds are not 100% ionic or 100% covalent. Instead, most bonds have some degree of both ionic and covalent characteristics—that is, some degree of both the transfer and the sharing of electrons. However, it is easiest to understand these intermediate bonds (the real bonds) by relating them to the pure or ideal bond types called ionic and covalent. ◄

▶ Purely *ionic bonds involve a complete transfer of electrons from one atom to another.* Purely *covalent bonds involve equal sharing of electrons. Experimentally, it is found that most actual bonds have some degree of both ionic and covalent characteristics. The exceptions are bonds between identical atoms; here, the bonding is purely covalent.*

Two concepts fundamental to understanding both the ionic and the covalent bonding models are

1. Not all electrons in an atom participate in bonding. Those that do are called *valence electrons.*
2. Certain arrangements of electrons are more stable than others, as is explained by the *octet rule.*

Section 4-2 addresses the concept of valence electrons, and Section 4-3 discusses the octet rule.

Section 4-1 Quick Quiz

1. The concept of *electron transfer* is closely associated with
   a. the ionic bond model
   b. the covalent bond model
   c. both the ionic and covalent bond models
   d. no correct response
2. The concept of *electron sharing* is closely associated with
   a. the ionic bond model
   b. the covalent bond model
   c. both the ionic and covalent bond models
   d. no correct response
3. Which of the following is a general characteristic of most ionic compounds?
   a. relatively low melting points
   b. generally gases at room temperature
   c. good electrical conductors in the molten state
   d. no correct response

Answers: 1. a; 2. b; 3. c

4-2 Valence Electrons and Lewis Symbols

LEARNING FOCUS

For atoms of representative elements, be able to determine the number of valence electrons present based on the element's electron configuration or periodic table position; given valence electron information, be able to write a Lewis symbol for an element.

Certain electrons called *valence* electrons are particularly important in determining the bonding characteristics of a given atom. A **valence electron** *is an electron in the outermost electron shell of a representative element or noble-gas element.* Note the restriction in this definition; it applies only to representative elements and noble-gas elements. For such elements, valence electrons are always found in either s or p subshells. (More complicated valence-electron definitions for transition and inner transition elements will not be considered in this text; for these elements, the presence of incompletely filled d or f subshells is a complicating factor.) ◄

The number of valence electrons in an atom of a representative element can be determined from the atom's electron configuration, as is illustrated in Example 4-1.

Scientists have developed a shorthand system for designating the number of valence electrons present in atoms of an element. This system involves the use of Lewis symbols. A **Lewis symbol** *is the chemical symbol of an element surrounded by dots equal in number to the number of valence electrons present in atoms of the element.* Figure 4-1 gives the Lewis symbols for the first 20 elements, all of which are representative elements or noble gases. Lewis symbols, named in honor of the American chemist Gilbert Newton Lewis (Figure 4-2), who first introduced them, are also frequently called *electron-dot structures.* ◄

► The term valence *is derived from the Latin word* valentia, *which means "capacity" (to form bonds).*

► *In a Lewis symbol, the chemical symbol represents the nucleus and all of the nonvalence electrons. The valence electrons are then shown as "dots."*

Figure 4-1 Lewis symbols for selected representative and noble-gas elements.

EXAMPLE 4-1

Determining the Number of Valence Electrons in an Atom

Determine the number of valence electrons in atoms of each of the following elements.

a. $_{12}Mg$ **b.** $_{14}Si$ **c.** $_{33}As$

Solution

a. Atoms of the element magnesium have two valence electrons, as can be seen by examining magnesium's electron configuration.

Number of valence electrons

$$1s^2 2s^2 2p^6 \, 3 \, s^{2}$$

Highest value of the electron shell number

The highest value of the electron shell number is $n = 3$. Only two electrons are found in shell 3, the two electrons in the $3s$ subshell.

(continued)

b. Atoms of the element silicon have four valence electrons.

$$1s^22s^22p^6\underset{\uparrow}{\textcircled{3}}s\textcircled{2}\underset{\uparrow}{\textcircled{3}}p\textcircled{2}$$

Number of valence electrons — indicated by circled ② marks

Highest value of the electron shell number — indicated by circled ③ marks

Electrons in two different subshells can simultaneously be valence electrons. The highest shell number is 3, and both the 3s and the 3p subshells belong to this shell. Hence all of the electrons in both of these subshells are valence electrons.

c. Atoms of the element arsenic have five valence electrons.

$$1s^22s^22p^63s^23p^6\underset{\uparrow}{\textcircled{4}}s\textcircled{2}3d^{10}\underset{\uparrow}{\textcircled{4}}p\textcircled{3}$$

Number of valence electrons

Highest value of the electron shell number

The 3d electrons are not counted as valence electrons because the 3d subshell is in shell 3, and this shell does not have the maximum n value. Shell 4 is the outermost shell and has the maximum n value.

Figure 4-2 Gilbert Newton Lewis (1875–1946), one of the foremost chemists of the twentieth century, made significant contributions in other areas of chemistry besides his pioneering work in describing chemical bonding. He formulated a generalized theory for describing acids and bases and was the first to isolate deuterium (heavy hydrogen).

Edgar Fahs Smith Collection, University of Pennsylvania Library

The general practice in writing Lewis symbols is to place the first four "dots" separately on the four sides of the chemical symbol and then begin pairing the dots as further dots are added. It makes no difference on which side of the symbol the process of adding dots begins. The following notations for the Lewis symbol of the element calcium are all equivalent.

$$\dot{\mathrm{Ca}}\cdot \qquad \mathrm{Ca}\cdot \qquad \cdot\dot{\mathrm{Ca}} \qquad \cdot\mathrm{Ca}\cdot$$

Three important generalizations about valence electrons can be drawn from a study of the Lewis symbols shown in Figure 4-1.

1. *Representative elements in the same group of the periodic table have the same number of valence electrons.* This should not be surprising. Elements in the same group in the periodic table have similar chemical properties as a result of their similar outer-shell electron configurations (Section 3-8). The electrons in the outermost shell are the valence electrons.
2. *The number of valence electrons for representative elements is the same as the Roman numeral periodic-table group number.* For example, the Lewis symbols for oxygen and sulfur, which are both members of Group VIA, have six dots. Similarly, the Lewis symbols for hydrogen, lithium, sodium, and potassium, which are all members of Group IA, have one dot.
3. *The maximum number of valence electrons for any element is eight.* Only the noble gases (Section 3-9), beginning with neon, have the maximum number of eight electrons. Helium, which has only two valence electrons, is the exception in the noble-gas family. Obviously, an element with a total of two electrons cannot have eight valence electrons. Although electron shells with n greater than 2 are capable of holding more than eight electrons, they do so only when they are no longer the outermost shell and thus are not the valence shell. For example, arsenic has 18 electrons in its third shell; however, shell 4 is the valence shell for arsenic.

EXAMPLE 4-2

Writing Lewis Symbols for Elements

Write Lewis symbols for the following elements.

a. O, S, and Se   **b.** B, C, and N

Solution

a. These elements are all Group VIA elements and thus possess six valence electrons. (The number of valence electrons and the periodic-table group number will always match for representative elements.) The Lewis symbols, which all have six "dots," are

$$\cdot \ddot{\underset{\cdot \cdot}{O}} : \quad \cdot \ddot{\underset{\cdot}{S}} : \quad \cdot \ddot{\underset{\cdot}{Se}} :$$

b. These elements are sequential elements in Period 2 of the periodic table; B is in Group IIIA (three valence electrons), C is in Group IVA (four valence electrons), and N is in Group VA (five valence electrons). The Lewis symbols for these elements are

$$\cdot \dot{B} \cdot \quad \cdot \dot{C} \cdot \quad : \dot{N} \cdot$$

Section 4-2 Quick Quiz

1. How many valence electrons are present in an atom with the electron configuration $1s^2 2s^2 2p^6 3s^1$?
   a. one
   b. three
   c. seven
   d. no correct response
2. How many valence electrons are present in an atom with the electron configuration $1s^2 2s^2 2p^6 3s^2 3p^5$?
   a. two
   b. five
   c. seven
   d. no correct response
3. How many valence electrons are present in atoms of Li, a Group IA element?
   a. one
   b. two
   c. three
   d. no correct response
4. How many "dots" are present in the Lewis symbol for the element oxygen, a Group VIA element?
   a. two
   b. four
   c. six
   d. no correct response
5. Which of the following elements would have the same number of valence electrons as $_7N$?
   a. $_6C$
   b. $_8O$
   c. $_{15}P$
   d. no correct response

Answers: 1. a; 2. c; 3. a; 4. c; 5. c

4-3 The Octet Rule

LEARNING FOCUS

State the octet rule and understand the basis for the rule.

A key concept in elementary bonding theory is that certain arrangements of valence electrons are more stable than others. The term *stable* as used here refers to the idea that a system, which in this case is an arrangement of electrons, does not easily undergo spontaneous change.

The valence electron configurations of the noble gases (helium, neon, argon, krypton, xenon, and radon) are considered the *most stable of all valence electron configurations.* All of the noble gases except helium possess eight valence electrons, which is the maximum number possible. Helium's valence electron configuration is $1s^2$. All of the other noble gases possess ns^2np^6 valence electron configurations, where n has the maximum value found in the atom.

He: $1s^2$

Ne: $1s^2 2s^2 2p^6$

Ar: $1s^2 2s^2 2p^6 3s^2 3p^6$

Kr: $1s^2 2s^2 2p^6 3s^2 3p^6 4s^2 3d^{10} 4p^6$

Xe: $1s^2 2s^2 2p^6 3s^2 3p^6 4s^2 3d^{10} 4p^6 5s^2 4d^{10} 5p^6$

Rn: $1s^2 2s^2 2p^6 3s^2 3p^6 4s^2 3d^{10} 4p^6 5s^2 4d^{10} 5p^6 6s^2 4f^{14} 5d^{10} 6p^6$

Except for helium, all the noble-gas valence electron configurations have the outermost s and p subshells *completely filled.* ◀

▶ *The outermost electron shell of an atom is also called the valence electron shell.*

The conclusion that an ns^2np^6 configuration ($1s^2$ for helium) is the most stable of all valence electron configurations is based on the chemical properties of the noble gases. The noble gases are the *most unreactive* of all the elements. They are the only elemental gases found in nature in the form of individual uncombined atoms. There are no known compounds of helium and neon, and only a few compounds of argon, krypton, xenon, and radon are known. The noble gases have little or no tendency to form bonds to other atoms.

Atoms of many elements that lack the very stable noble-gas valence electron configuration tend to acquire it through chemical reactions that result in compound formation. This observation is known as the **octet rule**: *In forming compounds, atoms of elements lose, gain, or share electrons in such a way as to produce a noble-gas electron configuration for each of the atoms involved.* ◀

▶ *Some compounds exist whose formulation is not consistent with the octet rule, but the vast majority of simple compounds have formulas that are consistent with its precepts.*

Section 4-3 Quick Quiz

1. The most stable of all valence electron configurations is that of the
   a. element carbon
   b. element oxygen
   c. noble gases
   d. no correct response
2. Which of the following is a very stable valence electron configuration?
   a. ns^2np^2
   b. ns^2np^4
   c. ns^2np^6
   d. no correct response
3. The *octet rule* relates to the number 8 because
   a. Atoms undergo chemical reaction only if 8 valence electrons are present.
   b. All electron subshells can hold 8 electrons.
   c. Atoms, during compound formation, frequently obtain 8 valence electrons.
   d. no correct response

Answers: 1. c; 2. c; 3. c

4-4 The Ionic Bond Model

LEARNING FOCUS

Define the term *ion*, understand the notation used to denote ions, and be able to write chemical symbols for ions.

The governing concept for the ionic bond model is electron transfer between two or more atoms. In this electron transfer process between atoms, the electrons lost by one or more atoms become the electrons gained by one or more other atoms. This electron transfer converts the atoms involved into charged particles called *ions*. ◄ An **ion** *is an atom (or group of atoms) that is electrically charged as a result of the loss or gain of electrons.* An atom is neutral when the number of protons (positive charges) is equal to the number of electrons (negative charges). Loss or gain of electrons destroys this proton–electron balance; the number of electrons no longer equals the number of protons (which has not changed).

▶ *The word* ion *is pronounced "eye-on."*

If an atom *gains* one or more electrons, it becomes a *negatively* charged ion; excess negative charge is present because electrons outnumber protons. If an atom *loses* one or more electrons, it becomes a *positively* charged ion; more protons are present than electrons. There is excess positive charge (Figure 4-3). Note that the excess positive charge associated with a positive ion is never caused by proton gain but always by electron loss. If the number of protons remains constant and the number of electrons decreases, the result is net positive charge. The number of protons, which determines the identity of an element, never changes during ion formation. ◄

The charge on an ion depends on the number of electrons that are lost or gained. Loss of one, two, or three electrons gives ions with 1+, 2+, or 3+ charges, respectively. A gain of one, two, or three electrons gives ions with 1−, 2−, or 3− charges, respectively. (Ions that have lost or gained more than three electrons are very seldom encountered.) ◄

▶ *An atom's nucleus* never *changes during the process of ion formation. The number of neutrons and protons remains constant.*

▶ *A loss of electrons by an atom always produces a positive ion. A gain of electrons by an atom always produces a negative ion.*

The notation for charges on ions is a superscript placed to the right of the chemical symbol. Some examples of ion symbols are

Positive ions: $Na^+, K^+, Ca^{2+}, Mg^{2+}, Al^{3+}$

Negative ions: $Cl^-, Br^-, O^{2-}, S^{2-}, N^{3-}$

Figure 4-3 Loss of an electron from a sodium atom leaves it with one more proton than electrons, so it has a net electrical charge of 1+. When chlorine gains an electron, it has one more electron than protons, so it has a net electrical charge of 1−.

Note that a single plus or minus sign is used to denote a charge of 1, instead of using the notation $^{1+}$ or $^{1-}$. Also note that in multicharged ions, the number precedes the charge sign; that is, the notation for a charge of plus two is $^{2+}$ rather than $^{+2}$.

EXAMPLE 4-3

Writing Chemical Symbols for Ions

Give the chemical symbol for each of the following ions.

a. The ion formed when a sodium atom loses one electron
b. The ion formed when a phosphorus atom gains three electrons

Solution

a. The atomic number of sodium is 11. Thus, sodium atoms have 11 protons and 11 electrons. The sodium ion produced by the loss of one electron contains 11 protons and 10 electrons. The negative charge of the 10 electrons "cancels" the positive charge on 10 of the 11 protons, leaving one "uncanceled" positive charge. Therefore, the sodium ion has a charge of 1+ and is denoted using the symbol Na^+. Pictorially, this proton–electron charge situation can be shown in this manner:

b. The atomic number of phosphorus is 15. Thus 15 protons and 15 electrons are present in a neutral phosphorus atom. A gain of 3 electrons raises the electron count to 18.

$$\begin{array}{l} 15 \text{ protons} = 15 + \text{charges} \\ \underline{18 \text{ electrons} = 18 - \text{charges}} \\ \text{Net charge} = 3- \end{array}$$

The chemical symbol for the ion is P^{3-}.

The chemical properties of a particle (atom or ion) depend on the particle's electron arrangement. Because an ion has a different electron configuration (fewer or more electrons) from the atom from which it was formed, it has different chemical properties as well. For example, the drug many people call lithium, which is used to treat mental illness (such as manic-depressive symptoms), does not involve lithium (Li, the element) but, rather, lithium ions (Li^+). The element lithium, if ingested, would be poisonous and possibly fatal. The lithium ion, ingested in the form of lithium carbonate, has entirely different effects on the human body.

Section 4-4 Quick Quiz

1. In terms of subatomic particles, a Ca^{2+} ion contains
   a. more electrons than protons
   b. more protons than electrons
   c. the same number of electrons and protons
   d. no correct response
2. Which of the following is the correct symbol for an atom of X that has gained three electrons?
   a. X^{3+}
   b. X^{3-}
   c. $3X^-$
   d. no correct response

3. An Al^{3+} ion is an Al atom that has
   a. lost three electrons
   b. gained three electrons
   c. lost three protons
   d. no correct response
4. Ion formation through loss of electrons
   a. always produces a negative ion
   b. always produces a positive ion
   c. can produce a negative or positive ion depending on element identity
   d. no correct response

Answers: 1. b; 2. b; 3. a; 4. b

4-5 The Sign and Magnitude of Ionic Charge

LEARNING FOCUS

Based on octet rule use, determine the sign and magnitude of the ionic charge for simple representative element ions; determine whether two ions or an atom and an ion are isoelectronic species.

The octet rule provides a very simple and straightforward explanation for the charge magnitude associated with ions of the representative elements. *Atoms tend to gain or lose electrons until they have obtained an electron configuration that is the same as that of a noble gas.* The element sodium has the electron configuration

$$1s^2 2s^2 2p^6 3s^1$$

One valence electron is present. Sodium can attain a noble-gas electron configuration by losing this valence electron (to give it the electron configuration of neon) or by gaining seven electrons (to give it the electron configuration of argon).

Na $(1s^2 2s^2 2p^6 3s^1)$
  $\xrightarrow{\text{Loss of 1 e}^-}$ Na$^+$ $(1s^2 2s^2 2p^6)$
    Electron configuration of neon
  $\xrightarrow{\text{Gain of 7 e}^-}$ Na^{7-} $(1s^2 2s^2 2p^6 3s^2 3p^6)$
    Electron configuration of argon

The electron loss or gain that involves the fewest electrons will always be the more favorable process from an energy standpoint and will be the process that occurs. Thus for sodium the loss of one electron to form the Na$^+$ ion is the process that occurs.

The element chlorine has the electron configuration

$$1s^2 2s^2 2p^6 3s^2 3p^5$$

Seven valence electrons are present. Chlorine can attain a noble-gas electron configuration by losing seven electrons (to give it the electron configuration of neon) or by gaining one electron (to give it the electron configuration of argon). The latter occurs for the reason previously cited.

Cl $(1s^2 2s^2 2p^6 3s^2 3p^5)$
  $\xrightarrow{\text{Loss of 7 e}^-}$ Cl^{7+} $(1s^2 2s^2 2p^6)$
    Electron configuration of neon
  $\xrightarrow{\text{Gain of 1 e}^-}$ Cl$^-$ $(1s^2 2s^2 2p^6 3s^2 3p^6)$
    Electron configuration of argon

The concepts just used in determining the electron-loss-electron-gain behavior of sodium and chlorine atoms can be generalized to give the following useful guidelines about electron loss and electron gain by atoms of various elements.

▶ *The positive charge on metal ions from Groups IA, IIA, and IIIA has a magnitude equal to the metal's periodic-table group number.*

1. Metal atoms containing one, two, or three valence electrons (the metals in Groups IA, IIA, and IIIA of the periodic table) tend to lose electrons to acquire a noble-gas electron configuration. The noble gas involved is the one preceding the metal in the periodic table. ◀
   Group IA metals form 1^+ ions.
   Group IIA metals form 2^+ ions.
   Group IIIA metals form 3^+ ions.

2. Nonmetal atoms containing five, six, or seven valence electrons (the nonmetals in Groups VA, VIA, and VIIA of the periodic table) tend to gain electrons to acquire a noble-gas electron configuration. The noble gas involved is the one following the nonmetal in the periodic table. ◀
   Group VIIA nonmetals form 1^- ions.
   Group VIA nonmetals form 2^- ions.
   Group VA nonmetals form 3^- ions.

▶ *Nonmetals from Groups VA, VIA, and VIIA form negative ions whose charge is equal to the group number minus 8. For example, S, in Group VIA, forms S^{2-} ions $(6 - 8 = -2)$.*

3. Elements in Group IVA occupy unique positions relative to the noble gases. They would have to gain or lose four electrons to attain a noble-gas structure. Theoretically, ions with charges of $4+$ or $4-$ could be formed by carbon, but in most cases the bonding that results is more adequately described by the covalent bond model discussed in Chapter 5.

Isoelectronic Species

Ions with electron configurations that are the same as that of a noble gas are said to be *isoelectronic* with the noble gas. **Isoelectronic species** *are an atom and an ion, or two ions, that have the same number and configuration of electrons.* An atom and an ion or two ions may be isoelectronic. The following is a list of ions that are isoelectronic with the element Ne; all, like Ne, have the electron configuration $1s^2 2s^2 2p^6$.

$$N^{3-} \quad O^{2-} \quad F^- \quad Na^+ \quad Mg^{2+} \quad Al^{3+}$$

It should be emphasized that an ion that is isoelectronic with a noble gas does not have the properties of the noble gas. It has not been converted into the noble gas. The number of protons in the nucleus of the isoelectronic ion is different from that in the noble gas. This point is emphasized by the comparison in Table 4-1 between Mg^{2+} ion and Ne, the noble gas with which Mg^{2+} is isoelectronic.

▶ Table 4-1 **Comparison of the Characteristics of the Isoelectronic Species Ne and Mg^{2+}**

	Ne Atom	Mg^{2+} Ion
Atomic number	10	12
Protons (in the nucleus)	10	12
Electrons (around the nucleus)	10	10
Charge	0	2+

Section 4-5 Quick Quiz

1. An atom with a $1s^2 2s^2 2p^4$ electron configuration would most likely form a
   a. $4-$ ion
   b. $6+$ ion
   c. $2-$ ion
   d. no correct answer

2. An atom with one valence electron would most likely form a
   a. 1+ ion
   b. 1− ion
   c. 7+ ion
   d. no correct answer
3. Magnesium (Group IIA) and Fluorine (Group VIIA) would, respectively, be expected to form ions with charges of
   a. 2+ and 1−
   b. 1+ and 2−
   c. 2+ and 7+
   d. no correct response
4. Two ions that are isoelectronic would have the same
   a. nuclear charge
   b. ionic charge
   c. electron configuration
   d. no correct response
5. The ion O^{2-} is isoelectronic with a
   a. N atom
   b. F atom
   c. Ne atom
   d. no correct response

Answers: 1. c; 2. a; 3. a; 4. c; 5. c

4-6 Lewis Structures for Ionic Compounds

LEARNING FOCUS
Use Lewis structures to describe the bonding in simple ionic compounds.

Ion formation through the loss or gain of electrons by atoms is not an isolated, singular process. In reality, electron loss and electron gain are always partner processes; if one occurs, the other also occurs. Ion formation requires the presence of two elements: a metal that can donate electrons and a nonmetal that can accept electrons. The electrons lost by the metal are the same ones gained by the nonmetal. The positive and negative ions simultaneously formed from such *electron transfer* attract one another. The result is the formation of an ionic compound. ◄

Lewis structures are helpful in visualizing the formation of simple ionic compounds. A **Lewis structure** *is a combination of Lewis symbols that represents either the transfer or the sharing of electrons in chemical bonds.* Lewis *symbols* involve individual elements. Lewis *structures* involve compounds. The reaction between the element sodium (with one valence electron) and chlorine (with seven valence electrons) is represented as follows with a Lewis structure:

$$\text{Na} \overset{\frown}{+}\, \ddot{\underset{\cdot\cdot}{\text{Cl}}}: \longrightarrow [\text{Na}]^+ \left[:\ddot{\underset{\cdot\cdot}{\text{Cl}}}:\right]^- \longrightarrow \text{NaCl}$$

► *No atom can lose electrons unless another atom is available to accept them.*

By losing its one valence electron the sodium atom achieves an octet of electrons. The loss of this electron by sodium empties its valence shell. The next inner shell, which contains eight electrons, becomes the valence shell. By adding one valence electron to the seven that it already possesses, the chlorine atom also achieves an octet of electrons. The two resulting ions (Na^+ and Cl^-) both have noble gas electron configurations; the octet rule (Section 4-3) has been satisfied.

When sodium, which has one valence electron, combines with oxygen, which has six valence electrons, two sodium atoms are required to meet the "electron needs" of one oxygen atom.

$$\begin{array}{c}
\text{Na} \cdot \\
\\
+ \;:\!\ddot{\text{O}}: \\
\\
\text{Na} \cdot
\end{array} \longrightarrow \begin{array}{c}
[\text{Na}]^+ \\
\\
\left[:\ddot{\underset{\cdot\cdot}{\text{O}}}:\right]^{2-} \\
\\
[\text{Na}]^+
\end{array} \longrightarrow \text{Na}_2\text{O}$$

The resulting three ions, all of which have eight valence electrons, combine to give a compound with the chemical formula Na_2O.

An opposite situation to that in Na_2O occurs in the reaction between calcium, which has two valence electrons, and chlorine, which has seven valence electrons. Here, two chlorine atoms are necessary to accommodate electrons transferred from one calcium atom because a chlorine atom can accept only one electron. (It has seven valence electrons and needs only one more.)

$$Ca \left\{ \begin{array}{c} \overset{..}{\underset{..}{Cl}}: \\ \\ \overset{..}{\underset{..}{Cl}}: \end{array} \right. \longrightarrow [Ca]^{2+} \begin{array}{c} \left[:\overset{..}{\underset{..}{Cl}}: \right]^{-} \\ \left[:\overset{..}{\underset{..}{Cl}}: \right]^{-} \end{array} \longrightarrow CaCl_2$$

An important generalization that can be drawn from the preceding Lewis structures depicting ionic compound formation is that the number of electrons that atoms of an element lose or gain is not dependent on the number of electrons that atoms of the other element lose or gain. Rather, the number of electrons lost or gained depends on the electron configurations of the elements themselves.

EXAMPLE 4-4

Using Lewis Structures to Depict Ionic Compound Formation

Show the formation of the following ionic compounds using Lewis structures.

a. Na_3N **b.** MgO   **c.** Al_2S_3

Solution

a. Sodium (a Group IA element) has one valence electron, which it would "like" to lose. Nitrogen (a Group VA element) has five valence electrons and would thus "like" to acquire three more. Three sodium atoms are needed to supply enough electrons for one nitrogen atom.

$$\begin{array}{c} Na \cdot \\ Na \cdot \\ Na \cdot \end{array} \!\! N: \longrightarrow \begin{array}{c} [Na]^{+} \\ [Na]^{+} \\ [Na]^{+} \end{array} \left[:\overset{..}{\underset{..}{N}}: \right]^{3-} \longrightarrow Na_3N$$

b. Magnesium (a Group IIA element) has two valence electrons, and oxygen (a Group VIA element) has six valence electrons. The transfer of the two magnesium valence electrons to an oxygen atom results in each atom having a noble-gas electron configuration. Thus these two elements combine in a 1-to-1 ratio.

$$Mg + \overset{..}{\underset{..}{O}}: \longrightarrow [Mg]^{2+} \left[:\overset{..}{\underset{..}{O}}: \right]^{2-} \longrightarrow MgO$$

c. Aluminum (a Group IIIA element) has three valence electrons, all of which need to be lost through electron transfer. Sulfur (a Group VIA element) has six valence electrons and thus needs to acquire two more. Three sulfur atoms are needed to accommodate the electrons given up by two aluminum atoms.

$$\begin{array}{c} Al \cdot \\ \\ Al \cdot \end{array} \begin{array}{c} \overset{..}{S}: \\ \overset{..}{S}: \\ \overset{..}{\underset{..}{S}}: \end{array} \longrightarrow \begin{array}{c} [Al]^{3+} \\ [Al]^{3+} \end{array} \begin{array}{c} \left[:\overset{..}{\underset{..}{S}}: \right]^{2-} \\ \left[:\overset{..}{\underset{..}{S}}: \right]^{2-} \\ \left[:\overset{..}{\underset{..}{S}}: \right]^{2-} \end{array} \longrightarrow Al_2S_3$$

1. In forming the ionic compound K_2O from K (1 valence electron) and O (6 valence electrons), how many electrons does each oxygen atom acquire via electron transfer?
   a. one
   b. two
   c. three
   d. no correct response
2. In forming an ionic compound from Ca (2 valence electrons) and S (6 valence electrons), how many calcium atoms are needed to meet the "electron needs" of one S atom?
   a. one
   b. two
   c. three
   d. no correct response
3. When magnesium (2 valence electrons) combines with chlorine (7 valence electrons) the resulting ionic compound has the chemical formula
   a. $MgCl$
   b. Mg_2Cl
   c. $MgCl_2$
   d. no correct response

Answers: 1. b; 2. a; 3. c

4-7 Chemical Formulas for Ionic Compounds

LEARNING FOCUS

Write the chemical formula for an ionic compound given the identity and charge on the ions present.

Electron loss always equals electron gain in an electron transfer process. Consequently, ionic compounds are always neutral; no net charge is present. The total positive charge present on the ions that have lost electrons always is exactly counterbalanced by the total negative charge on the ions that have gained electrons. Thus *the ratio in which positive and negative ions combine is the ratio that achieves charge neutrality for the resulting compound.* This generalization can be used instead of Lewis structures to determine ionic compound formulas. Ions are combined in the ratio that causes the positive and negative charges to add to zero.

The correct combining ratio when K^+ ions and S^{2-} ions combine is two to one. Two K^+ ions (each of 1+ charge) are required to counterbalance the charge on a single S^{2-} ion,

$$2(K^+): \quad (2 \text{ ions}) \times (\text{charge of } 1+) = 2+$$
$$\underline{S^{2-}: \quad (1 \text{ ion}) \ \times (\text{charge of } 2-) = 2-}$$
$$\text{Net charge} = 0$$

The formula of the compound formed is thus K_2S.

There are three rules to remember when writing chemical formulas for ionic compounds.

1. The symbol for the positive ions is always written first.
2. The charges on the ions that are present are *not* shown in the formula. Ionic charges must be known to determine the formula; however, the charges are not explicitly shown in the formula.
3. The numbers in the formula (the subscripts) give the combining ratio for the ions.

EXAMPLE 4-5

Using Ionic Charges to Determine the Chemical Formula of an Ionic Compound

Determine the chemical formula for the compound that is formed when each of the following pairs of ions interact.

a. Na^+ and P^{3-} **b.** Be^{2+} and P^{3-}

Solution

a. The Na^+ and P^{3-} ions combine in a 3-to-1 ratio because this combination causes the charges to add to zero. Three Na^+ ions give 3 units of positive charge. One P^{3-} ion results in 3 units of negative charge. Thus the chemical formula for the compound is Na_3P.

b. The numbers in the charges for these ions are 2 and 3. The lowest common multiple of 2 and 3 is 6 ($2 \times 3 = 6$). Thus we need 6 units of positive charge and 6 units of negative charge. Three Be^{2+} ions are needed to give the 6 units of positive charge, and two P^{3-} ions are needed to give the 6 units of negative charge. The combining ratio of ions is three to two, and the chemical formula is Be_3P_2.

    The strategy of finding the lowest common multiple of the numbers in the charges of the ions always works, and it is a faster process than that of drawing the Lewis structures.

Section 4-7 Quick Quiz

1. What is the chemical formula of the ionic compound formed when Ca^{2+} ions and F^- ions combine?
   a. CaF
   b. Ca_2F
   c. CaF_2
   d. no correct response
2. What is the chemical formula of the ionic compound formed when Al^{3+} ions and S^{2-} ions combine?
   a. Al_2S_3
   b. Al_3S_2
   c. Al_3S
   d. no correct response
3. Given that Z^{2-} ions are present in the ionic compound X_2Z, what is the charge on the X ions present?
   a. 1+
   b. 2+
   c. 3+
   d. no correct response
4. The correct chemical formula for an ionic compound that contains Z^{2-} ions and X^{2+} ions is
   a. ZX
   b. XZ
   c. Z_2X_2
   d. no correct response

Answers: 1. c; 2. a; 3. a; 4. b

4-8   The Structure of Ionic Compounds

LEARNING FOCUS

Understand the structural characteristics of ionic compounds including the concept of a *formula unit*.

An ionic compound in the solid state consists of positive and negative ions arranged in such a way that each ion is surrounded by nearest neighbors of the opposite charge.

Figure 4-4 (a, b) A two-dimensional cross-section and a three-dimensional view of sodium chloride (NaCl), an ionic solid. Both views show an alternating array of positive and negative ions.

Any given ion is bonded by electrostatic (positive–negative) attractions to all the other ions of opposite charge immediately surrounding it. Figure 4-4 shows a two-dimensional cross-section and a three-dimensional view of the arrangement of ions in the ionic compound sodium chloride (NaCl). Note in these structural representations that no given ion has a single partner. A given sodium ion has six immediate neighbors (chloride ions) that are equidistant from it. A given chloride ion in turn has six immediate sodium ion neighbors.

The alternating array of positive and negative ions present in an ionic compound means that discrete molecules do not exist in such compounds. Therefore, the chemical formulas of ionic compounds cannot represent the composition of molecules of these substances. Instead, such chemical formulas represent the simplest combining ratio for the ions present. The chemical formula for sodium chloride, NaCl, indicates that sodium and chloride ions are present in a 1-to-1 ratio in this compound. Chemists use the term *formula unit*, rather than *molecule*, to refer to the smallest unit of an ionic compound. A **formula unit** *is the smallest whole-number repeating ratio of ions present in an ionic compound that results in charge neutrality.* A formula unit is "hypothetical" because it does not exist as a separate entity; it is only "a part" of the extended array of ions that constitute an ionic solid (Figure 4-5). ◄

Although the chemical formulas for ionic compounds represent only ratios, they are used in equations and chemical calculations in the same way as are the chemical formulas for molecular species. Remember, however, that they cannot be interpreted as indicating that molecules exist for these substances; they merely represent the simplest ratio of ions present.

The ions present in an ionic solid adopt an arrangement that maximizes attractions between ions of opposite charge and minimizes repulsions between ions of like charge. The specific arrangement that is adopted depends on ion sizes and on the ratio between positive and negative ions. Arrangements are usually very symmetrical and result in crystalline solids—that is, solids with highly regular shapes. Crystalline solids usually have flat surfaces or faces that make definite angles with one another, as is shown in Figure 4-6.

▶ *In Section 1-9, the molecule was described as the smallest unit of a pure substance that is capable of a stable, independent existence. Ionic compounds, with their formula units, are exceptions to this generalization.*

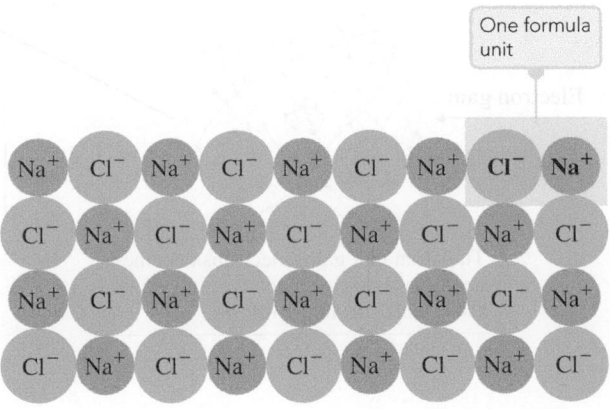

Figure 4-5 Cross-section of the structure of the ionic solid NaCl. No molecule can be distinguished in this structure. Instead, a basic *formula unit* is present that is repeated indefinitely.

Figure 4-6 Ionic compounds usually have crystalline forms in the solid state, such as those associated with (a) fluorite and (b) ruby.

© Marvin Dembinsky Photo Associates/Alamy

Peter Arnold/Alamy

a Fluorite

b Ruby

Chemistry at a Glance—Ionic Bonds and Ionic Compounds—reviews the general concepts we have considered so far about ionic compounds.

Many ionic solids are soluble in water. The dissolving process breaks up the solid's highly ordered array of positive and negative ions, freeing them up to move about, independent of each other, in the aqueous solution (Section 8-3). Such "freed" ions play an important role in most aqueous-based solutions. Ions obtained from dissolved ionic compounds are present in all of the Earth's water resources, both seawater and fresh water. The focus on relevancy feature Chemical Connections 4-A—Fresh Water, Seawater, Hard Water, and Soft Water: A Matter of Ions—considers the types of ions present in the Earth's waters.

CHEMISTRY AT A GLANCE   Ionic Bonds and Ionic Compounds

An ionic bond is the force of attraction between oppositely charged particles. Ionic bonds form between atoms of dissimilar elements (metals and nonmetals).

Atom

Ionic bonds form when one atom (or group of atoms) loses electrons and another atom (or group of atoms) gains electrons.

Atom

Electron loss

Electron transfer

Electron gain

The atom that loses electrons becomes positively charged because it now has more protons than electrons.

Positive ion

Negative ion

Positive and negative ions attract each other

The atom that gains electrons becomes negatively charged because it now has more electrons than protons.

Ionic compound

Negative ion   Positive ion

Ionic compounds consist of highly ordered arrays of positive and negative ions. They do not contain discrete molecules.

CHEMICAL CONNECTIONS 4-A

Fresh Water, Seawater, Hard Water, and Soft Water: A Matter of Ions

Water is the most abundant compound on the face of Earth. We encounter it everywhere we go: as water vapor in the air; as a liquid in rivers, lakes, and oceans; and as a solid (ice and snow) both on land and in the oceans.

It is estimated that 97.5% of the Earth's water is found in the oceans. Such water is commonly referred to as seawater (or salt water). The remaining 2.5% of Earth's water is fresh water, which consists of three components. Solid-state fresh water (1.72%) is found in ice caps, snowpack, and glaciers. Ground water (0.77%) is found in large underground natural aquifers. Surface fresh water (0.01%) is found in lakes, streams, reservoirs, soil, and the atmosphere. The following diagram depicts quantitatively the various categories of water present on and in the Earth. Note the "smallness" of the amount of surface fresh water that is available for use by humans.

The dominant ions in fresh water and seawater are not the same. In seawater, Na^+ ion is the dominant positive ion and Cl^- ion is the dominant negative ion. This contrasts with fresh water, in which Ca^{2+} and Mg^{2+} ions are the most abundant positive ions and HCO_3^- (a polyatomic ion; Section 4-10) is the most abundant negative ion.

When fresh water is purified for drinking purposes, suspended particles, disease-causing agents, and objectionable odors are removed. Dissolved ions are not removed. At the concentrations at which they are normally present in fresh water, dissolved ions are not harmful to health. Indeed, some of the taste of water is caused by the ions present; water without any ions present would taste "unpleasant" to most people.

Hard water is water that contains Ca^{2+}, Mg^{2+}, and Fe^{2+} ions. The presence of these ions does not affect the drinkability of water, but it does affect other uses for the water.

TOTAL WATER (mass %)

Seawater 97.5%

Fresh water 2.5%

FRESH WATER (mass %)

Solid state water 68.8%

Surface water 0.4%

Ground water 30.8%

All water as it occurs in nature is impure in a chemical sense. The impurities present include suspended matter, microbiological organisms, dissolved gases, and dissolved *ionic compounds*. When dissolved in water, ionic compounds release their constituent ions, which are then free to move about in the water. For example, rock salt (NaCl) dissolves in water to produce Na^+ and Cl^- ions.

The major distinction between *fresh water* and *seawater* (salt water) is the number and identity of the dissolved ions present in the water. On a relative scale, where the total number of dissolved ions in fresh water is assigned a value of 1, seawater has a value of approximately 500; that is, seawater has a concentration of dissolved ions 500 times greater than that of fresh water.

The hard-water ions form insoluble compounds with soap (producing scum) and lead to the production of deposits of scale in steam boilers, tea kettles, and hot-water pipes.

The most popular method for obtaining *soft water* from hard water involves the process of "ion exchange." In this process, the offending hard-water ions are exchanged for Na^+ ions. Sodium ions do not form insoluble soap compounds or scale. People with high blood pressure or kidney problems are often advised to avoid drinking soft water because of its high sodium content.

Human body fluids, including blood and cellular fluids, also contain dissolved ionic compounds. Information concerning the ions present in these fluids is presented in Chapter 10 in the feature box Chemical Connections 10-E.

Section 4-8 Quick Quiz

1. The structure of an ionic compound, in the solid state, involves which of the following?
  a. individual molecules in which positive and negative ions are present
  b. a nonmolecular random arrangement of positive and negative ions
  c. a nonmolecular highly ordered arrangement of positive and negative ions
  d. no correct response

(continued)

2. Which of the following is a correct description of the structure of the ionic compound NaCl?

a. Alternating layers of Na^+ and Cl^- ions are present.

b. Individual molecules containing Na^+ and Cl^- ions are present.

c. Each ion present is surrounded by six ions of opposite charge.

d. no correct response

Answers: 1. c; 2. c

4-9 Recognizing and Naming Binary Ionic Compounds

LEARNING FOCUS

Based on chemical formula be able to recognize whether a binary compound is ionic or not; be able to name a binary ionic compound given its chemical formula or vice versa.

The term *binary* means "two." A **binary compound** *is a compound in which only two elements are present.* The compounds NaCl, CO_2, NH_3, and P_4O_{10} are all binary compounds. Any number of atoms of the two elements may be present in a molecule or formula unit of a binary compound, but only two elements may be present. A **binary ionic compound** *is an ionic compound in which one element present is a metal and the other element present is a nonmetal.* The metal is always present as the positive ion, and the nonmetal is always present as the negative ion. The joint presence of a metal and a nonmetal in a binary compound is the "recognition key" that the compound is an ionic compound.

EXAMPLE 4-6

Recognizing a Binary Ionic Compound on the Basis of Its Chemical Formula

Which of the following binary compounds would be expected to be an ionic compound?

a. Al_2S_3 **b.** H_2O **c.** KF   **d.** NH_3

Solution

a. Ionic; a metal (Al) and a nonmetal (S) are present.

b. Not ionic; two nonmetals are present.

c. Ionic; a metal (K) and a nonmetal (F) are present.

d. Not ionic; two nonmetals are present.

The two compounds that are not ionic are *molecular* compounds (Section 4-1). Chapter 5 includes an extended discussion of molecular compounds. In general, molecular compounds contain just nonmetals.

Binary ionic compounds are named using the following rule: *The full name of the metallic element is given first, followed by a separate word containing the stem of the nonmetallic element name and the suffix* -ide. Thus, in order to name the compound NaF, start with the name of the metal (sodium), follow it with the stem of the name of the nonmetal (fluor-), and then add the suffix *-ide.* The name becomes *sodium fluoride.*

The stem of the name of the nonmetal is the name of the nonmetal with its ending chopped off. Table 4-2 gives the stem part of the name for each of the most common nonmetallic elements. The name of the metal ion is always exactly the same as the name of the metal itself; the metal's name is never shortened. Example 4-7 illustrates the use of the rule for naming binary ionic compounds.

▶ Table 4-2 **Names of Selected Common Nonmetallic Ions**

Element	Stem	Name of Ion	Formula of Ion
bromine	brom-	bromide	Br^-
carbon	carb-	carbide	C^{4-}
chlorine	chlor-	chloride	Cl^-
fluorine	fluor-	fluoride	F^-
hydrogen	hydr-	hydride	H^-
iodine	iod-	iodide	I^-
nitrogen	nitr-	nitride	N^{3-}
oxygen	ox-	oxide	O^{2-}
phosphorus	phosph-	phosphide	P^{3-}
sulfur	sulf-	sulfide	S^{2-}

EXAMPLE 4-7

Naming Binary Ionic Compounds

Name the following binary ionic compounds.

a. MgO   **b.** Al_2S_3 **c.** K_3N **d.** $CaCl_2$

Solution

The general pattern for naming binary ionic compounds is

Name of metal + stem of name of nonmetal + -ide

a. The metal is magnesium and the nonmetal is oxygen. Thus the compound's name is *magnesium oxide.*

b. The metal is aluminum and the nonmetal is sulfur; the compound's name is *aluminum sulfide.* Note that no mention is made of the subscripts present in the formula—the 2 and the 3. The name of an ionic compound never contains any reference to formula subscript numbers. There is only one ratio in which aluminum and sulfur atoms combine. Thus just telling the names of the elements present in the compound is adequate nomenclature.

c. Potassium (K) and nitrogen (N) are present in the compound, and its name is *potassium nitride.*

d. The compound's name is *calcium chloride.*

Thus far in our discussion of ionic compounds, it has been assumed that the only behavior allowable for an element is that predicted by the octet rule. This is a good assumption for nonmetals and for most representative element metals. However, for most transition and inner transition metals (the majority of all metals; Section 3-9) a less predictable behavior occurs because these metals are able to form more than one type of ion. For example, iron can form either Fe^{2+} ions or Fe^{3+} ions depending on chemical circumstances. Similarly, copper can form either Cu^+ ions or Cu^{2+} ions.

When naming compounds that contain metals with variable ionic charges, the charge on the metal ion must be incorporated into the name. This is done by using Roman numerals. For example, the chlorides of Fe^{2+} and Fe^{3+} ($FeCl_2$ and $FeCl_3$, respectively) are named iron(II) chloride and iron(III) chloride (Figure 4-7). Likewise, CuO is named copper(II) oxide. The charge on the nonmetal ion present (which does not vary) can be used to calculate the charge on the metal ion if the latter is unknown. For example, determination of the charge on the copper ion present in CuO is based on the fact that the oxide ion carries a 2− charge (oxygen is in Group VIA). This means the copper ion must have a 2+ charge to counterbalance the 2− charge; the total charge must always add to zero.

Copper (II) Oxide

Copper (I) Oxide

Iron (II) Chloride

Iron (III) Chloride

© Cengage Learning

Figure 4-7 Copper(II) oxide (CuO) is black, whereas copper(I) oxide (Cu_2O) is reddish brown. Iron(II) chloride ($FeCl_2$) is green, whereas iron(III) chloride ($FeCl_3$) is bright yellow.

EXAMPLE 4-8

Using Roman Numerals in the Naming of Binary Ionic Compounds

Name the following binary ionic compounds, each of which contains a metal whose ionic charge can vary.

a. AuCl   **b.** Fe_2O_3

Solution

For ionic compounds containing a variable-charge metal, the magnitude of the charge on the metal ion must be indicated in the name of the compound by using a Roman numeral. ◄

▶ *All the inner transition elements (f area of the periodic table), most of the transition elements (d area), and a few representative metals (p area) exhibit variable ionic charge behavior.*

a. To calculate the metal ion charge, use the fact that total ionic charge (both positive and negative) must add to zero.

$$(\text{gold charge}) + (\text{chlorine charge}) = 0$$

The chloride ion has a $1-$ charge (Section 4-5). Therefore,

$$(\text{gold charge}) + (1-) = 0$$

Thus,

$$\text{gold charge} = 1+$$

Therefore, the gold ion present is Au^+, and the name of the compound is *gold(I) chloride*.

b. For charge balance in this compound, we have the equation

$$2(\text{iron charge}) + 3(\text{oxygen charge}) = 0$$

Note that the number of each kind of ion present (2 and 3 in this case) must be taken into account in the charge balance equation. Oxide ions carry a $2-$ charge (Section 4-5). Therefore,

$$2(\text{iron charge}) + 3(2-) = 0$$
$$2(\text{iron charge}) = 6+$$
$$\text{Iron charge} = 3+$$

It is the charge on a single iron atom $(3+)$ and not the total positive charge $(6+)$ that is indicated in the name of the compound by using a Roman numeral. The compound is named *iron(III) oxide* because Fe^{3+} ions are present. As is the case for all ionic compounds, the name does not contain any reference to the numerical subscripts in the compound's formula. ◄

▶ *An older method for indicating the charge on metal ions uses the suffixes -ic and -ous rather than the Roman numeral system. It is mentioned here because it is still sometimes encountered. In this system, when a metal has two common ionic charges, the suffix -ous is used for the ion of lower charge and the suffix -ic for the ion of higher charge. The metal's Latin name is also used. In this older system, iron(II) ion is called ferrous ion, and iron(III) ion is called ferric ion.*

Knowledge about which metals exhibit variable ionic charge and which have a fixed ionic charge is a prerequisite for determining when to use Roman numerals in binary ionic compound names. There are many more of the former (variable-charge; Roman numeral required) than the latter (fixed-charge; no Roman numeral required). The identity of the fixed metal charges (the short list) is given in Figure 4-8; any metal not on the short list exhibits variable-charge behavior. Ionic compounds that contain fixed-charge metals are the only ones without Roman numerals in their names.

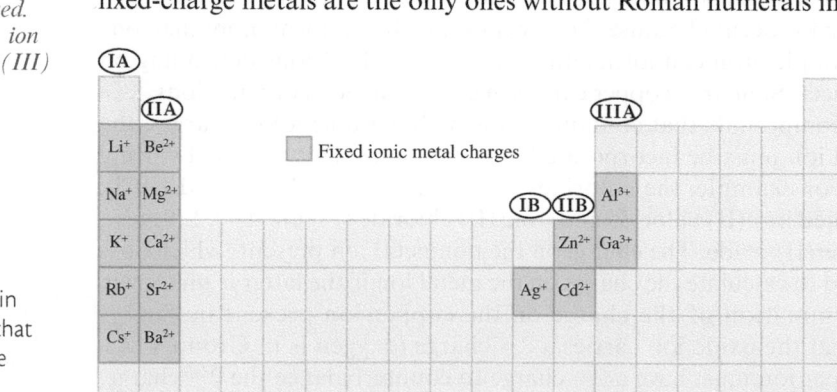

Figure 4-8 A periodic table in which the metallic elements that exhibit a fixed ionic charge are highlighted.

EXAMPLE 4-9

Determining the Chemical Formula of an Ionic Compound Given Its Name

Determine chemical formulas of the following binary ionic compounds.

a. magnesium fluoride   **b.** tin(IV) oxide

Solution

Ionic charges are determined first, and then the chemical formula is obtained by combining the ions in the ratio that causes the ionic charges present to add to zero.

a. The elements magnesium and fluorine are present. Magnesium, a Group IIA element (2 valence electrons), forms a 2+ ion (Mg^{2+}). Fluorine, a Group VIIA element (7 valence electrons), forms a 1− ion ($F^−$). Combining the ions in a 1-to-2 ratio causes the total charge to add to zero. The chemical formula is MgF_2.

b. The elements tin and oxygen are present. The Roman numeral present in the compound's name indicates that tin is present as a 4+ ion (Sn^{4+}). Oxygen, a Group VIA element (6 valence electrons), forms a 2− ion ($O^{2−}$). The correct combining ratio for the total charge to add to zero is a 1-to-2 ratio, producing the chemical formula SnO_2.

For most metals where variable ionic charge behavior occurs, one of the two or more ions that are possible is more stable than the others and is the preferred ionic state. Such is not the case for the element iron. Here, both the Fe^{2+} and Fe^{3+} ions are readily formed and it is relatively easy to convert back and forth between the two ionic states. The interconversion between the Fe^{2+} state and the Fe^{3+} state, or vice versa, is an important biochemical process. These changes, which involve the loss or gain of one electron, are a key component of the series of reactions called the electron transport chain (Section 23-8), a reaction series through which biochemical energy production occurs. To a lesser extent, electron transfer involving Cu^+ and Cu^{2+} ions is also a part of the electron transport chain process.

Section 4-9 Quick Quiz

1. Which of the following is a characteristic of binary ionic compounds?
   a. Two different metals are present.
   b. Two different nonmetals are present.
   c. Both a metal and a nonmetal are present.
   d. no correct response
2. Which of the following is a binary ionic compound?
   a. SO_3
   b. CO_2
   c. C_2H_6
   d. no correct response
3. The correct name for the binary ionic compound NaF is
   a. sodium fluorine
   b. sodium fluoride
   c. sodium fluorate
   d. no correct response
4. Which of the following binary ionic compounds is paired with an incorrect name?
   a. CaS—calcium sulfide
   b. K_2O—dipotassium oxide
   c. AlN—aluminum nitride
   d. no correct response
5. Which of the following is a variable charge metal?
   a. Zn
   b. Ag
   c. K
   d. no correct response

(continued)

6. Which of the following binary ionic compounds has a name that includes a Roman numeral?
   a. Na_2O
   b. Fe_2O_3
   c. $MgCl_2$
   d. no correct response
7. The correct name for the binary ionic compound Cu_2S is
   a. copper sulfide
   b. copper(I) sulfide
   c. copper(II) sulfide
   d. no correct response
8. What is the chemical formula for the compound tin(II) oxide?
   a. SnO
   b. SnO_2
   c. Sn_2O
   d. no correct response

Answers: 1. c; 2. d; 3. b; 4. b; 5. d; 6. b; 7. b; 8. a

4-10 Polyatomic Ions

LEARNING FOCUS
Be familiar with the names and chemical formulas of commonly occurring polyatomic ions.

There are two categories of ions: monatomic and polyatomic. A **monatomic ion** *is an ion formed from a single atom through loss or gain of electrons.* All of the ions we have discussed so far have been monatomic (Cl^-, Na^+, Ca^{2+}, N^{3-}, and so on).

A **polyatomic ion** *is an ion formed from a group of atoms (held together by covalent bonds) through loss or gain of electrons.* An example of a polyatomic ion is the sulfate ion, SO_4^{2-}. This ion contains four oxygen atoms and one sulfur atom, and the whole group of five atoms has acquired a 2− charge. The whole sulfate group is the ion rather than any one atom within the group. Covalent bonding, discussed in Chapter 5, holds the sulfur and oxygen atoms together. ◄

There are numerous ionic compounds in which the positive or negative ion (sometimes both) is polyatomic. Polyatomic ions are very stable and generally maintain their identity during chemical reactions.

Note that polyatomic ions are not molecules. They never occur alone as molecules do. Instead, they are always found associated with ions of opposite charge. Polyatomic ions are *charged pieces* of compounds, not compounds. Ionic compounds require the presence of both positive and negative ions and are neutral overall.

Hundreds of different polyatomic ions exist. The names and chemical formulas for 12 of these ions, all very important in terms of their occurrence in biochemical systems, are given in Table 4-3. Familiarity with these polyatomic ions, in terms of name and chemical formula recognition, is necessary; they will be encountered frequently in later chapters of the textbook.

The following generalizations concerning the names and chemical formulas of the Table 4-3 ions emerge from consideration of formula interrelationships that exist among the listed ions.

1. Most, but not all, of these ions carry a negative charge, which can vary from 1− to 3−. There are, however, two positive polyatomic ions in the group: H_3O^+ (hydronium) and NH_4^+ (ammonium).
2. Most, but not all, of these ions contain oxygen atoms. There are, however, two ions that do not: CN^- (cyanide) and NH_4^+ (ammonium).
3. Most, but not all, of the negative ions have names that end in *-ate*. There are, however, two exceptions: hydroxide (OH^-) and cyanide (CN^-).

▶ *A polyatomic ion is an ion (either positively or negatively charged) that contains more than one atom.*

Table 4-3 **Formulas and Names of Some Common Polyatomic Ions** ◀

Key Element Present	Formula	Name of Ion
nitrogen	NO_3^-	nitrate
	NH_4^+	ammonium
sulfur	SO_4^{2-}	sulfate
	HSO_4^-	hydrogen sulfate or bisulfate
phosphorus	PO_4^{3-}	phosphate
	HPO_4^{2-}	hydrogen phosphate
	$H_2PO_4^-$	dihydrogen phosphate
carbon	CO_3^{2-}	carbonate
	HCO_3^-	hydrogen carbonate or bicarbonate
	CN^-	cyanide
hydrogen	H_3O^+	hydronium
	OH^-	hydroxide

▶ *Learning the names of the common polyatomic ions is a memorization project. There is no shortcut. The charges and formulas for the various polyatomic ions cannot be easily related to the periodic table (as was the case for many of the monatomic ions).*

The prefix bi- in polyatomic ion names means hydrogen *rather than the number* two.

4. Two positive ions have names that end in -*ium*: hydronium (H_3O^+) and ammonium (NH_4^+).
5. A number of pairs of ions exist wherein one member of the pair differs from the other by having a hydrogen atom present, as in CO_3^{2-} (carbonate) and HCO_3^- (hydrogen carbonate or bicarbonate). In such pairs, the charge on the ion that contains hydrogen is always 1 less than that on the other ion.

The focus on relevancy feature Chemical Connections 4-B—Tooth Enamel: A Combination of Monatomic and Polyatomic Ions—considers particulars about the structure of tooth enamel, a substance that contains the polyatomic ions phosphate (PO_4^{3-}) and hydroxide (OH^-) as well as monatomic calcium ions (Ca^{2+}).

Section 4-10 Quick Quiz

1. Which of the following chemical formulas is that of a polyatomic ion?
   a. Cl^-
   b. OH^-
   c. S^{2-}
   d. no correct response
2. Which of the following statements about polyatomic ions is correct?
   a. All must contain oxygen.
   b. All must carry a negative charge.
   c. All have names that end in -*ide*.
   d. no correct response
3. The nitrate, sulfate, and phosphate ions have, respectively, the chemical formulas
   a. NO_4^-, SO_4^{2-}, and PO_4^{3-}
   b. NO_3^-, SO_3^{2-}, and PO_3^{3-}
   c. NO_3^-, SO_4^{2-}, and PO_4^{3-}
   d. no correct response
4. The hydronium, ammonium, and hydroxide ions have, respectively, the chemical formulas
   a. H_3O^+, NH_4^+, and OH^+
   b. H_3O^-, NH_4^-, and OH^-
   c. H_3O^+, NH_4^+, and OH^-
   d. no correct response

Answers: 1. b; 2. d; 3. c; 4. c

CHEMICAL CONNECTIONS 4-B

Tooth Enamel: A Combination of Monatomic and Polyatomic Ions

The hard outer covering of a tooth, its enamel, is made up of a three-dimensional network of calcium ions (Ca^{2+}), phosphate ions (PO_4^{3-}), and hydroxide ions (OH^-) arranged in a regular pattern. The formula for this material is $Ca_{10}(PO_4)_6(OH)_2$, and its name is hydroxyapatite. Fibrous protein is dispersed in the spaces between the ions. (See the accompanying figure.)

Hydroxyapatite continually dissolves and reforms within the mouth. Tooth enamel is continually dissolving to a slight extent, to give a water solution in saliva of Ca^{2+}, PO_4^{3-}, and OH^- ions. This process is called *demineralization*. At the same time, however, the ions in the saliva solution are recombining to deposit enamel back on the teeth. This process is called *mineralization*. As long as demineralization and mineralization occur at equal rates, no net loss of tooth enamel occurs.

$$Ca_{10}(PO_4)_6(OH)_2 \underset{\text{mineralization}}{\overset{\text{demineralization}}{\rightleftharpoons}} 10Ca^{2+} + 6PO_4^{3-} + 2OH^-$$

Tooth decay results when chemical factors within the mouth cause the rate of demineralization to exceed the rate of mineralization. The acidic H^+ ion is the chemical species that most often causes the demineralization process to dominate. The continuation of this process over an extended period of time results in the formation of pits or cavities in tooth enamel. Eventually, the pits break through the enamel, allowing bacteria to enter the tooth structure and cause decay.

When fluoride ion (F^-) exchanges with hydroxide ion in the hydroxyapatite structure, tooth enamel is strengthened.

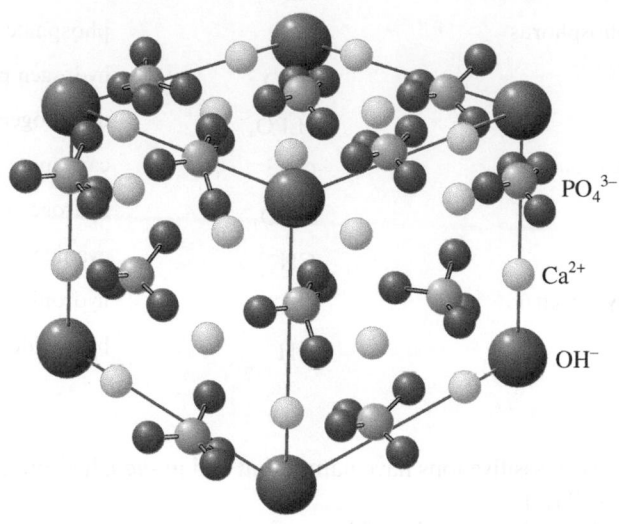

$$Ca_{10}(PO_4)_6(OH)_2 + 2\,F^- \longrightarrow Ca_{10}(PO_4)_6F_2 + 2\,OH^-$$

Hydroxyapatite   Fluoroapatite

This replacement of hydroxide by fluoride in the apatite crystal produces an enamel that is less soluble in acidic medium—hence the effectiveness of fluoride mouthwashes and fluoride-containing toothpastes.

4-11 Chemical Formulas and Names for Ionic Compounds Containing Polyatomic Ions

LEARNING FOCUS

Using standard nomenclature rules, determine the name of a polyatomic-ion-containing compound given its chemical formula or vice versa.

Chemical formulas for ionic compounds that contain polyatomic ions are determined in the same way as those for ionic compounds that contain monatomic ions (Section 4-7). The positive and negative charges present must add to zero.

Two conventions not encountered previously in chemical formula writing often arise when writing chemical formulas containing polyatomic ions.

1. When more than one polyatomic ion of a given kind is required in a chemical formula, the polyatomic ion is enclosed in parentheses, and a subscript, placed outside the parentheses, is used to indicate the number of polyatomic ions needed. An example is $Fe(OH)_3$.

2. So that the identity of polyatomic ions is preserved, the same elemental symbol may be used more than once in a chemical formula. An example is the formula NH_4NO_3, where the chemical symbol for nitrogen (N) appears in two locations because both the NH_4^+ and NO_3^- ions contain N.

Example 4-10 illustrates the use of both of these new conventions.

EXAMPLE 4-10

Writing Chemical Formulas for Ionic Compounds Containing Polyatomic Ions

Determine the chemical formulas for the ionic compounds that contain these pairs of ions.

a. Na^+ and SO_4^{2-} **b.** Mg^{2+} and NO_3^- **c.** NH_4^+ and CN^-

Solution

a. In order to equalize the total positive and negative charge, two sodium ions are needed (1+ charge) for each sulfate ion (2− charge). The presence of two Na^+ ions is indicated using the subscript 2 following the symbol of the ion. The chemical formula of the compound is Na_2SO_4. The convention that the positive ion is always written first in a chemical formula still holds when polyatomic ions are present.

b. Two nitrate ions (1− charge) are required to balance the charge on one magnesium ion (2+ charge). Because more than one polyatomic ion is needed, the chemical formula contains parentheses: $Mg(NO_3)_2$. The subscript 2 outside the parentheses indicates two of what is inside the parentheses. If parentheses were not used, the chemical formula would appear to be $MgNO_{32}$, which is not intended and conveys false information.

c. In this compound, both ions are polyatomic, which is a perfectly legitimate situation. Because the ions have equal but opposite charges, they combine in a 1-to-1 ratio. Thus the chemical formula is NH_4CN. No parentheses are necessary because we need only one polyatomic ion of each type in a formula unit. The appearance of the symbol for the element nitrogen (N) at two locations in the chemical formula could be prevented by combining the two nitrogens, resulting in N_2H_4C. But the chemical formula N_2H_4C does not indicate that NH_4^+ and CN^- ions are present. Thus, when writing chemical formulas that contain polyatomic ions, always maintain the identities of these ions, even if it means having the same elemental symbol at more than one location in the formula.

The names of ionic compounds containing polyatomic ions are derived in a manner similar to that for binary ionic compounds (Section 4-9). The rule for naming binary ionic compounds is as follows: Give the name of the metallic element first (including, when needed, a Roman numeral indicating ion charge), and then give a separate word containing the stem of the nonmetallic name and the suffix -*ide*. Modification of this binary naming rule to accommodate polyatomic ions is as follows:

1. If a positive polyatomic ion is present, its name is substituted for that of the metal.
2. If a negative polyatomic ion is present, its name is substituted for that of the nonmetal stem name and the "ide" suffix.
3. If both positive and negative polyatomic ions are present, dual name-substitution occurs, and the resulting name includes just the names of the polyatomic ions.

EXAMPLE 4-11

Naming Ionic Compounds in Which Polyatomic Ions Are Present

Name the following compounds, which contain one or more polyatomic ions.

a. $Ca_3(PO_4)_2$ **b.** $Fe_2(SO_4)_3$ **c.** $(NH_4)_2CO_3$

Solution

a. The positive ion present is the calcium ion (Ca^{2+}). A Roman numeral is not needed to specify the charge on a Ca^{2+} ion because calcium is a fixed-charge metal (Figure 4-8). The negative ion is the polyatomic phosphate ion (PO_4^{3-}). The name

(continued)

of the compound is *calcium phosphate*. As in naming binary ionic compounds, subscripts in the formula are not incorporated into the name.

b. The positive ion present is iron(III). The negative ion is the polyatomic sulfate ion (SO_4^{2-}). The name of the compound is *iron(III) sulfate*. The determination that iron is present as iron(III) involves the following calculation dealing with charge balance:

$$2(\text{iron charge}) + 3(\text{sulfate charge}) = 0$$

The sulfate charge is 2− (Table 4-3). Therefore,

$$2(\text{iron charge}) + 3(2-) = 0$$
$$2(\text{iron charge}) = 6+$$
$$\text{Iron charge} = 3+$$

c. Both the positive and the negative ions in this compound are polyatomic—the ammonium ion (NH_4^+) and the carbonate ion (CO_3^{2-}). The name of the compound is simply the combination of the names of the two polyatomic ions: *ammonium carbonate*.

Chemistry at a Glance—Nomenclature of Ionic Compounds—summarizes the "thought processes" involved in naming ionic compounds, both those with monatomic ions and those with polyatomic ions.

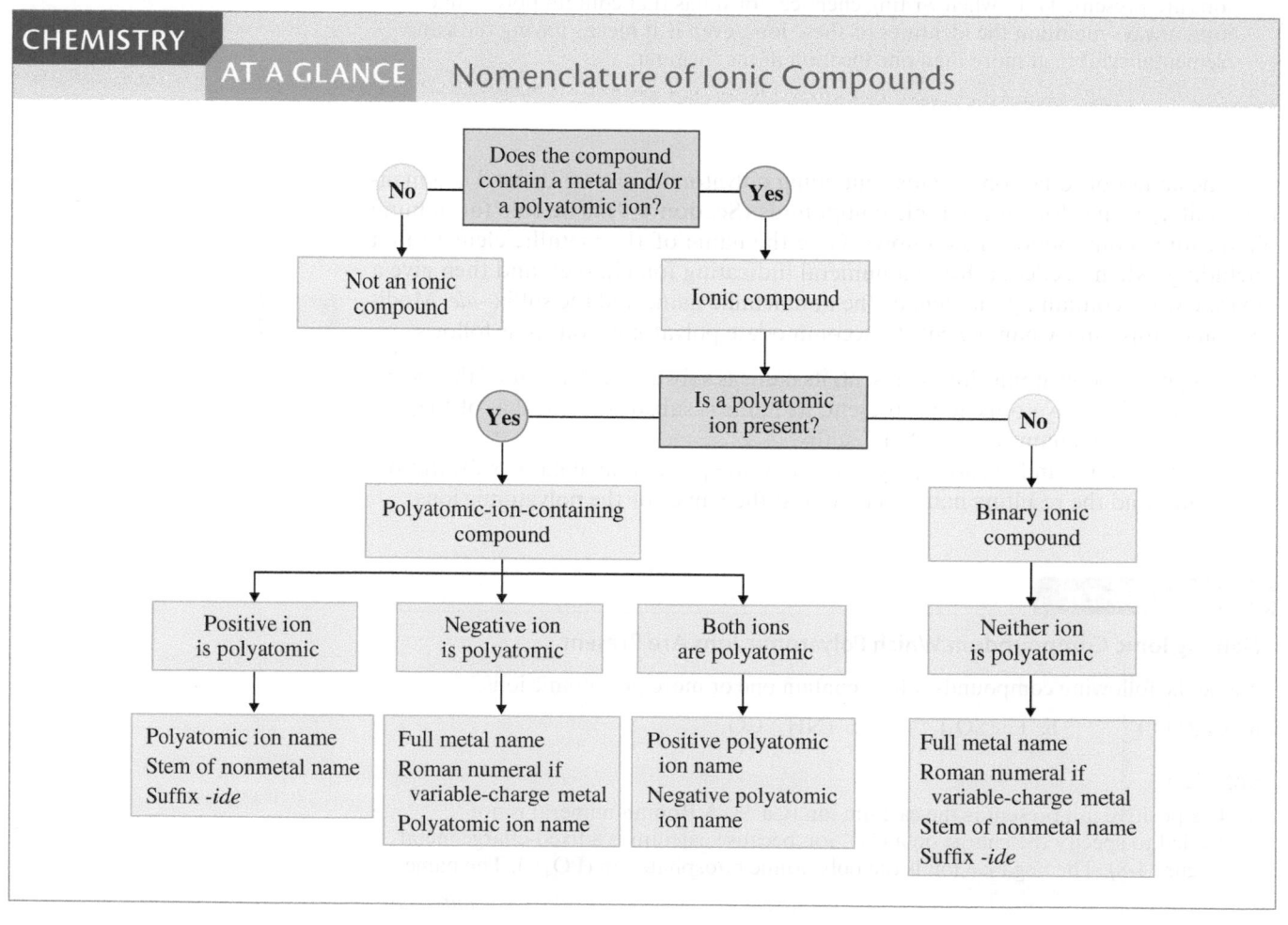

CHEMISTRY AT A GLANCE   Nomenclature of Ionic Compounds

1. What is the chemical formula for a compound that contains K^+ ions and PO_4^{3-} ions?
   a. KPO_4
   b. K_2PO_4
   c. K_3PO_4
   d. no correct response
2. What is the chemical formula for a compound that contains Al^{3+} ions and OH^- ions?
   a. $AlOH$
   b. $AlOH_3$
   c. $Al(OH)_3$
   d. no correct response
3. The compound $Mg(SCN)_2$ contains Mg^{2+} ions and polyatomic thiocyanate ions. What charge does the thiocyanate ion carry?
   a. $1+$
   b. $1-$
   c. $2-$
   d. no correct response
4. What is the name for the compound Na_2CO_3?
   a. disodium carbon trioxide
   b. disodium carbonate
   c. sodium carbonate
   d. no correct response
5. What is the name for the compound $(NH_4)_2S$?
   a. ammonium sulfate
   b. ammonium sulfide
   c. hydronium sulfide
   d. no correct response
6. What is the chemical formula for the compound copper(II) nitrate?
   a. $CuNO_3$
   b. $Cu(NO_3)_2$
   c. $Cu(CN)_2$
   d. no correct response

Answers: 1. c; 2. c; 3. b; 4. c; 5. b; 6. b

Concepts to Remember

Chemical bonds. Chemical bonds are the attractive forces that hold atoms together in more complex units. Chemical bonds result from the transfer of valence electrons between atoms (ionic bond) or from the sharing of electrons between atoms (covalent bond) (Section 4-1).

Valence electrons. Valence electrons for representative elements are the electrons in the outermost electron shell, which is the shell with the highest shell number. These electrons are particularly important in determining the bonding characteristics of a given atom (Section 4-2).

Octet rule. In compound formation, atoms of representative elements lose, gain, or share electrons in such a way that their electron configurations become identical to those of the noble gas nearest them in the periodic table (Section 4-3).

Ionic compounds. Ionic compounds commonly involve a metal atom and a nonmetal atom. Metal atoms lose one or more electrons, producing positive ions. Nonmetal atoms acquire the electrons lost by the metal atoms, producing negative ions. The oppositely charged ions attract one another, creating ionic bonds (Section 4-4).

Charge magnitude for ions. Metal atoms containing one, two, or three valence electrons tend to lose such electrons, producing

ions of $1+$, $2+$, or $3+$ charge, respectively. Nonmetal atoms containing five, six, or seven valence electrons tend to gain electrons, producing ions of $3-$, $2-$, or $1-$ charge, respectively (Section 4-5).

Chemical formulas for ionic compounds. The ratio in which positive and negative ions combine is the ratio that causes the total amount of positive and negative charges to add up to zero (Section 4-7).

Structure of ionic compounds. Ionic solids consist of positive and negative ions arranged in such a way that each ion is surrounded by ions of the opposite charge (Section 4-8).

Binary ionic compound nomenclature. Binary ionic compounds are named by giving the full name of the metallic element first, followed by a separate word containing the stem of the nonmetallic element name and the suffix *-ide*. A Roman numeral specifying ionic charge is appended to the name of the metallic element if it is a metal that exhibits variable ionic charge (Section 4-9).

Polyatomic ions. A polyatomic ion is a group of covalently bonded atoms that has acquired a charge through the loss or gain of electrons. Polyatomic ions are very stable entities that generally maintain their identity during chemical reactions (Section 4-10).

Exercises and Problems

Exercises and problems are arranged in matched pairs with the two members of a pair addressing the same concept(s). The answer to the odd-numbered member of a pair is given at the back of the book. Problems denoted with a ▲ involve concepts found not only in the section under consideration but also concepts found in one or more earlier sections of the chapter.

Types of Chemical Bonds (Section 4-1)

4-1   Contrast the two general types of chemical *bonds* in terms of the mechanism by which they form.

4-2   Contrast the two general types of chemical *compounds* in terms of their general physical properties.

Valence Electrons (Section 4-2)

4-3   How many valence electrons do atoms with the following electron configurations have?
a. $1s^2 2s^2$
b. $1s^2 2s^2 2p^6 3s^2$
c. $1s^2 2s^2 2p^6 3s^2 3p^1$
d. $1s^2 2s^2 2p^6 3s^2 3p^6 4s^2 3d^{10} 4p^2$

4-4   How many valence electrons do atoms with the following electron configurations have?
a. $1s^2 2s^2 2p^6$
b. $1s^2 2s^2 2p^6 3s^2 3p^1$
c. $1s^2 2s^2 2p^6 3s^1$
d. $1s^2 2s^2 2p^6 3s^2 3p^6 4s^2 3d^{10} 4p^5$

4-5   Give the Roman numeral periodic-table group number for and the number of valence electrons present in each of the following representative elements.
a. $_7N$
b. $_{11}Na$
c. $_{16}S$
d. $_{19}K$

4-6   Give the Roman numeral periodic-table group number for and the number of valence electrons present in each of the following representative elements.
a. $_8O$
b. $_{13}Al$
c. $_{17}Cl$
d. $_{35}Br$

4-7   Write the complete electron configuration for each of the following representative elements.
a. Period 2 element with four valence electrons
b. Period 2 element with seven valence electrons
c. Period 3 element with two valence electrons
d. Period 3 element with five valence electrons

4-8   Write the complete electron configuration for each of the following representative elements.
a. Period 2 element with one valence electron
b. Period 2 element with six valence electrons
c. Period 3 element with seven valence electrons
d. Period 3 element with three valence electrons

4-9   For each of the following pairs of representative elements, indicate whether the first listed element has (1) more valence electrons, (2) fewer valence electrons, or (3) the same number of valence electrons compared to the second listed element.
a. Mg, Na   b. P, As   c. O, N   d. Si, Cl

4-10   For each of the following pairs of representative elements, indicate whether the first listed element has (1) more valence electrons, (2) fewer valence electrons, or (3) the same number of valence electrons compared to the second listed element.
a. K, Ca   b. O, S   c. B, N   d. Be, P

4-11   How many of the highlighted elements in the following periodic table have the valence electron characteristics listed below?

a. Five valence electrons are present.
b. One valence electron is present.
c. Seven valence electrons are present.
d. Two valence electrons are present.

4-12   How many of the highlighted elements in the periodic table in Problem 4-11 have the valence electron characteristics listed below?
a. Eight valence electrons are present.
b. Three valence electrons are present.
c. Six valence electrons are present.
d. Four valence electrons are present.

Lewis Symbols for Atoms (Section 4-2)

4-13   Draw Lewis symbols for atoms of each of the elements in the following sets of elements.
a. $_{15}P$, $_{16}S$, and $_{17}Cl$
b. $_{11}Na$, $_{19}K$, and $_{37}Rb$

4-14   Draw Lewis symbols for atoms of each of the elements in the following sets of elements.
a. $_{17}Cl$, $_{35}Br$ and $_{53}I$
b. $_7N$, $_8O$, and $_9F$

4-15   Each of the following Lewis symbols represents a Period 2 element. Determine each element's identity.
a. X·
b. :X:
c. X·
d. ·X·

4-16   Each of the following Lewis symbols represents a Period 3 element. Determine each element's identity.
a. ·X·
b. ·X·
c. ·X:
d. :X:

▲4-17   Draw Lewis symbols for elements with the following electron configurations.
a. $1s^2 2s^2$
b. $1s^2 2s^2 2p^6 3s^2$
c. $1s^2 2s^2 2p^6 3s^2 3p^4$
d. $1s^2 2s^2 2p^6 3s^2 3p^6 4s^2 3d^{10} 4p^2$

▲4-18   Draw Lewis symbols for elements with the following electron configurations.
a. $1s^2 2s^2 2p^1$
b. $1s^2 2s^2 2p^6 3s^2 3p^1$
c. $1s^2 2s^2 2p^6 3s^2 3p^3$
d. $1s^2 2s^2 2p^6 3s^2 3p^6 4s^2 3d^{10} 4p^5$

The Octet Rule (Section 4-3)

4-19   What is the chemical property of the noble gases that leads to the conclusion that they possess extremely stable electron arrangements?

4-20   What is the maximum number of valence electrons that a representative element/noble gas can possess, and which group of elements possesses this maximum number of valence electrons?

4-21   What does the octet rule indicate happens to elements that lack a noble-gas electron configuration?

4-22 Which noble gas is an exception to the rule that noble-gas elements possess eight valence electrons?

Notation for Ions (Section 4-4)

4-23 Give the chemical symbol for each of the following ions.
a. An oxygen atom that has gained two electrons
b. A magnesium atom that has lost two electrons
c. A fluorine atom that has gained one electron
d. An aluminum atom that has lost three electrons

4-24 Give the chemical symbol for each of the following ions.
a. A chlorine atom that has gained one electron
b. A sulfur atom that has gained two electrons
c. A potassium atom that has lost one electron
d. A beryllium atom that has lost two electrons

4-25 What would be the chemical symbol for an ion with each of the following numbers of protons and electrons?
a. 20 protons and 18 electrons
b. 8 protons and 10 electrons
c. 7 protons and 10 electrons
d. 4 protons and 2 electrons

4-26 What would be the chemical symbol for an ion with each of the following numbers of protons and electrons?
a. 15 protons and 18 electrons
b. 17 protons and 18 electrons
c. 12 protons and 10 electrons
d. 19 protons and 18 electrons

4-27 Fill in the blanks in each line in the following table. The first line is already completed as an example.

	Ion	Number of Protons	Number of Electrons	Electrons Lost/Gained
	Na^+	11p	10e	1e lost
a.			10e	3e gained
b.	Mg^{2+}			
c.		9p		1e gained
d.		3p	2e	

4-28 Fill in the blanks in each line in the following table. The first line is already completed as an example.

	Ion	Number of Protons	Number of Electrons	Electrons Lost/Gained
	O^{2-}	8p	10e	2e gained
a.		13p	10e	
b.	Ca^{2+}			
c.		16p		2e gained
d.			$18e^-$	1e lost

4-29 Fill in the blanks in each line of the following table. The first line is already completed as an example.

	Chemical Symbol	Ion Formed	Number of Electrons in Ion	Number of Protons in Ion
	Ca	Ca^{2+}	18	20
a.	Be		2	
b.			54	53
c.		Al^{3+}	10	
d.		S^{2-}		

4-30 Fill in the blanks in each line of the following table. The first line is already completed as an example.

	Chemical Symbol	Ion Formed	Number of Electrons in Ion	Number of Protons in Ion
	Mg	Mg^{2+}	10	12
a.	K		18	
b.			36	34
c.		P^{3-}		15
d.		O^{2-}		

4-31 Identify element **X** by giving its chemical symbol, based on the following information about an ion that it forms.
a. Forms a X^{2+} ion containing 10 electrons
b. Forms a X^{2+} ion containing 18 electrons
c. Forms a X^{3-} ion containing 18 electrons
d. Forms a X^- ion containing 10 electrons

4-32 Identify element **X** by giving its chemical symbol, based on the following information about an ion that it forms.
a. Forms a X^{2-} ion containing 10 electrons
b. Forms a X^{2-} ion containing 18 electrons
c. Forms a X^{3+} ion containing 10 electrons
d. Forms a X^+ ion containing 10 electrons

4-33 What would be the most likely chemical symbol for the Period 2 ion with each of the following characteristics?
a. Two more protons than electrons
b. Two fewer protons than electrons
c. Three more protons than electrons
d. Four fewer protons than electrons

4-34 What would be the most likely chemical symbol for the Period 2 ion with each of the following characteristics?
a. One more proton than electrons
b. One fewer proton than electrons
c. Three fewer protons than electrons
d. Four more protons than electrons

▲**4-35** Draw Lewis symbols for the following ions.
a. P^{3-}　　b. N^{3-}　　c. C^{4-}　　d. F^-

▲**4-36** Draw Lewis symbols for the following ions.
a. O^{2-}　　b. S^{2-}　　c. Si^{4-}　　d. Cl^-

Ionic Charge Sign and Magnitude (Section 4-5)

4-37 What is the charge on the monatomic ion formed by each of the following elements?
a. $_{12}Mg$　　b. $_7N$　　c. $_{19}K$　　d. $_9F$

4-38 What is the charge on the monatomic ion formed by each of the following elements?
a. $_3Li$　　b. $_{15}P$　　c. $_{16}S$　　d. $_{13}Al$

4-39 Indicate the number of electrons lost or gained when each of the following atoms forms an ion.
a. $_4Be$　　b. $_{35}Br$　　c. $_{38}Sr$　　d. $_{34}Se$

4-40 Indicate the number of electrons lost or gained when each of the following atoms forms an ion.
a. $_{37}Rb$　　b. $_{53}I$　　c. $_8O$　　d. $_{11}Na$

4-41 Which noble gas has an electron configuration identical to that of each of the following ions?
a. O^{2-}　　b. P^{3-}　　c. Ca^{2+}　　d. K^+

4-42 Which noble gas has an electron configuration identical to that of each of the following ions?
a. F^- b. Al^{3+} c. Si^{4+} d. C^{4-}

4-43 Which noble gas is isoelectronic with each of the ions in Problem 4-41?

4-44 Which noble gas is isoelectronic with each of the ions in Problem 4-42?

4-45 Indicate whether or not each of the following pairs of atoms/ions are isoelectronic.
a. Ca^{2+} and Ar b. Mg^{2+} and F^-
c. Ar and Kr d. O^{2-} and N^{3-}

4-46 Indicate whether or not each of the following pairs of atoms/ions are isoelectronic.
a. K^+ and Ar b. Al^{3+} and Cl^-
c. S and Cl^- d. Na^+ and Mg^{2+}

4-47 How many of the "highlighted" elements in the following periodic table will form ions with each of the listed characteristics?

a. forms a positively charged ion
b. forms an ion through loss of electron(s)
c. forms an ion that has a charge magnitude of 2
d. forms an ion that involves gain of two or more electrons

4-48 How many of the "highlighted" elements in the periodic table of Problem 4-47 will form ions with each of the listed characteristics?
a. forms a negatively charged ion
b. forms an ion through gain of electron(s)
c. forms an ion that has a charge magnitude of 1
d. forms an ion that involves loss of two or more electrons

4-49 Write the electron configuration of the following.
a. An aluminum atom
b. An aluminum ion

4-50 Write the electron configuration of the following.
a. An oxygen atom
b. An oxygen ion

▲**4-51** How many valence electrons are present in each of the following ions?
a. N^{3-} b. P^{3-} c. Al^{3+} d. Li^+

▲**4-52** How many valence electrons are present in each of the following ions?
a. O^{2-} b. S^{2-} c. Mg^{2+} d. Be^{2+}

Lewis Structures for Ionic Compounds (Section 4-6)

4-53 Using Lewis structures, show how ionic compounds are formed by atoms of
a. Be and O b. Mg and S
c. K and N d. F and Ca

4-54 Using Lewis structures, show how ionic compounds are formed by atoms of
a. Na and F b. Li and S
c. Be and S d. P and K

4-55 The following Lewis symbols for ions have the charges omitted. Determine the number of extra electrons that each structure contains, and give the proper charge for each ion.
a. $\left[: \overset{..}{\underset{..}{S}} : \right]$ b. $\left[: \overset{..}{\underset{..}{F}} : \right]$ c. $\left[: \overset{..}{\underset{..}{N}} : \right]$ d. $\left[: \overset{..}{\underset{..}{Se}} : \right]$

4-56 The following Lewis symbols for ions have the charges omitted. Determine the number of extra electrons that each structure contains, and give the proper charge for each ion.
a. $\left[: \overset{..}{\underset{..}{P}} : \right]$ b. $\left[: \overset{..}{\underset{..}{O}} : \right]$ c. $\left[: \overset{..}{\underset{..}{Br}} : \right]$ d. $\left[: \overset{..}{\underset{..}{I}} : \right]$

Chemical Formulas for Ionic Compounds (Section 4-7)

4-57 Write the chemical formula for an ionic compound formed from the following ions.
a. Na^+ and S^{2-} b. Ca^{2+} and I^-
c. Li^+ and N^{3-} d. Al^{3+} and Br^-

4-58 Write the chemical formula for an ionic compound formed from the following ions.
a. Li^+ and O^{2-} b. Al^{3+} and N^{3-}
c. K^+ and Cl^- d. Mg^{2+} and I^-

4-59 Fill in the blanks to complete the following table of chemical formulas for ionic compounds. For each compound, the positive ion present is listed on the left side of the table and the negative ion present is listed at the top. The first line of the table is already completed as an example.

		F^-	O^{2-}	N^{3-}	C^{4-}
	Na^+	NaF	Na_2O	Na_3N	Na_4C
a.	Ca^{2+}				
b.	Al^{3+}				
c.	Ag^+				
d.	Zn^{2+}				

4-60 Fill in the blanks to complete the following table of chemical formulas for ionic compounds. For each compound, the negative ion present is listed on the left side of the table and the positive ion present is listed at the top. The first line of the table is already completed as an example.

		Na^+	Mg^{2+}	Al^{3+}	Si^{4+}
	Cl^-	NaCl	$MgCl_2$	$AlCl_3$	$SiCl_4$
a.	Br^-				
b.	S^{2-}				
c.	P^{3-}				
d.	N^{3-}				

▲**4-61** The component elements for four binary ionic compounds are shown with different colors on the following periodic table.

What is the likely chemical formula for the following?
a. Red compound b. Blue compound
c. Yellow compound d. Green compound

▲4-62 The component elements for four binary ionic compounds are shown with different colors on the following periodic table.

What is the likely chemical formula for the following?
a. Red compound   b. Blue compound
c. Yellow compound   d. Green compound

▲4-63 Write the complete chemical formula (symbol and charge) for the positive ion present in each of the following ionic compounds.
a. KCl   b. CaS   c. MgF_2 d. Al_2S_3

▲4-64 Write the complete chemical formula (symbol and charge) for the negative ion present in each of the following ionic compounds.
a. MgO   b. AlN   c. Na_2S d. Ba_3P_2

▲4-65 Write the chemical formula for the ionic compound that would form from the elements X and Z if
a. X has two valence electrons and Z has seven valence electrons
b. X has one valence electron and Z has six valence electrons
c. X has three valence electrons and Z has five valence electrons
d. X has six valence electrons and Z has two valence electrons

▲4-66 Write the chemical formula for the ionic compound that would form from the elements X and Z if
a. X has three valence electrons and Z has seven valence electrons
b. X has one valence electron and Z has five valence electrons
c. X has two valence electrons and Z has six valence electrons
d. X has five valence electrons and Z has one valence electron

▲4-67 What is the chemical formula of the ionic compound produced through interaction of each of the following pairs of elements?
a. Li and Cl   b. Mg and F
c. Ca and S   d. K and N

▲4-68 What is the chemical formula of the ionic compound produced through interaction of each of the following pairs of elements?
a. Li and S   b. Mg and N
c. Ca and Cl   d. K and F

▲4-69 A representative element (X) forms an ion with a 2− charge. What is the
a. Roman numeral group number for element X
b. Lewis symbol for element X
c. number of valence electrons possessed by X
d. the chemical formula of the compound formed between X and the Ca^{2+} ion

▲4-70 A representative element (Z) forms an ion with a 2+ charge. What is the

a. Roman numeral group number for element Z
b. Lewis symbol for element Z
c. number of valence electrons possessed by Z
d. the chemical formula of the compound formed between Z and the N^{3-} ion

▲4-71 The following questions pertain to the ionic compound K_2S.
a. Which element loses electrons and how many electrons are lost per atom?
b. Which element gains electrons and how many electrons are gained per atom?
c. What is the identity and charge on the positive ions present?
d. What is the identity and charge on the negative ions present?

▲4-72 The following questions pertain to the ionic compound $CaCl_2$.
a. Which element loses electrons and how many electrons are lost per atom?
b. Which element gains electrons and how many electrons are gained per atom?
c. What is the identity and charge on the positive ions present?
d. What is the identity and charge on the negative ions present?

Structure of Ionic Compounds (Section 4-8)

4-73 Describe the general structure of a solid-state ionic compound.

4-74 Explain why ionic compounds do not contain individual molecules.

4-75 What is a *formula unit* of an ionic compound?

4-76 In general terms, how many *formula units* are present in a crystal of an ionic compound?

▲4-77 The known and stable compound OF_2 is incorrectly characterized as being an ionic compound containing O^{2-} and F^- ions. Explain why this is not possible even though both O^{2-} and F^- ions exist.

▲4-78 The known and stable compound N_2O_3 is incorrectly characterized as being an ionic compound containing N^{3-} and O^{2-} ions. Explain why this is not possible even though both N^{3-} and O^{2-} ions exist.

Recognizing and Naming Binary Ionic Compounds (Section 4-9)

4-79 Which of the following binary compounds would be expected to be an ionic compound?
a. Al_2O_3 b. H_2O_2 c. K_2S d. N_2H_4

4-80 Which of the following binary compounds would be expected to be an ionic compound?
a. Cu_2O b. CO   c. NaBr   d. Be_3P_2

4-81 Name the following binary ionic compounds, each of which contains a fixed-charge metal.
a. KI   b. BeO   c. AlF_3 d. Na_3P

4-82 Name the following binary ionic compounds, each of which contains a fixed-charge metal.
a. $CaCl_2$ b. Ca_2C c. Be_3N_2 d. K_2S

4-83 Calculate the charge on the metal ion in the following binary ionic compounds, each of which contains a variable-charge metal.
a. Au_2O b. NiO   c. SnO_2 d. SnO

4-84 Calculate the charge on the metal ion in the following binary ionic compounds, each of which contains a variable-charge metal.
  a. Fe_2O_3 b. FeO   c. $SnCl_4$ d. Cu_2S

4-85 Name each of the compounds in Problem 4-83.

4-86 Name each of the compounds in Problem 4-84.

4-87 The correct name for CaO is calcium oxide but the correct name for CuO is not copper oxide. Why is the latter name incorrect?

4-88 The correct name for ZnS is zinc sulfide but the correct name for FeS is not iron sulfide. Why is the latter name incorrect?

4-89 Name each of the following binary ionic compounds.
  a. AuCl   b. KCl   c. AgCl   d. $CuCl_2$

4-90 Name each of the following binary ionic compounds.
  a. NiO   b. FeN   c. AlN   d. BeO

4-91 Name each compound in the following pairs of binary ionic compounds.
  a. PbO and PbO_2 b. $MgCl_2$ and $FeCl_2$
  c. Na_2O and MgO   d. Cu_2S and CuS

4-92 Name each compound in the following pairs of binary ionic compounds.
  a. LiCl and Li_2S b. CuCl and $CuCl_2$
  c. AgCl and AuCl   d. FeO and Fe_2O_3

4-93 Write chemical formulas for the following binary ionic compounds.
  a. Potassium bromide   b. Silver oxide
  c. Beryllium fluoride   d. Barium phosphide

4-94 Write chemical formulas for the following binary ionic compounds.
  a. Gallium nitride   b. Zinc chloride
  c. Magnesium sulfide   d. Aluminum nitride

4-95 Write chemical formulas for the following binary ionic compounds.
  a. Cobalt(II) sulfide   b. Cobalt(III) sulfide
  c. Tin(IV) iodide   d. Lead(II) nitride

4-96 Write chemical formulas for the following binary ionic compounds.
  a. Iron(III) oxide   b. Iron(II) oxide
  c. Nickel(III) sulfide   d. Copper(I) bromide

▲4-97 Answer the following questions about an ionic compound formed from the ions Mg^{2+} and N^{3-}.
  a. What is the name of the compound?
  b. What is the chemical formula of the compound?
  c. How many ions are present in one formula unit of the compound?
  d. How many electrons are transferred per formula unit of compound?

▲4-98 Answer the following questions about an ionic compound formed from the ions Al^{3+} and O^{2-}.
  a. What is the name of the compound?
  b. What is the chemical formula of the compound?
  c. How many ions are present in one formula unit of the compound?
  d. How many electrons are transferred per formula unit of compound?

▲4-99 Fill in the blanks in each line of the following table that involves the representative elements X and Y. The first line is already completed as an example.

	Period Number	Electron-Dot Symbols	Formula of Compound	Name of Compound
	2	$\dot{X}\cdot$ and $:\ddot{Y}\cdot$	BeO	Beryllium oxide
a.	3	$X\cdot$ and $:\ddot{Y}\cdot$		
b.	4	$X\cdot$ and $:\ddot{Y}\cdot$		
c.	2	$\dot{X}\cdot$ and $:\ddot{Y}\cdot$		
d.	3	$\cdot\dot{X}\cdot$ and $\cdot\dot{Y}\cdot$		

▲4-100 Fill in the blanks in each line of the following table that involves the representative elements X and Y. The first line is already completed as an example.

	Period Number	Electron-Dot Symbols	Formula of Compound	Name of Compound
	3	$\dot{X}\cdot$ and $:\dot{Y}\cdot$	MgS	Magnesium sulfide
a.	2	$X\cdot$ and $\cdot\ddot{Y}\cdot$		
b.	4	$\dot{X}\cdot$ and $:\dot{Y}\cdot$		
c.	4	$X\cdot$ and $:\dot{Y}\cdot$		
d.	3	$\cdot\dot{X}\cdot$ and $:\ddot{Y}\cdot$		

Chemical Formulas and Names for Polyatomic Ions (Section 4-10)

4-101 What is the charge associated with each of the following Table 4-3 polyatomic ions?
  a. sulfate   b. nitrate
  c. phosphate   d. carbonate

4-102 What is the charge associated with each of the following Table 4-3 polyatomic ions?
  a. hydronium   b. cyanide
  c. hydroxide   d. ammonium

4-103 How many oxygen atoms are present in each of the following Table 4-3 polyatomic ions?
  a. hydronium   b. cyanide
  c. hydroxide   d. ammonium

4-104 How many oxygen atoms are present in each of the following Table 4-3 polyatomic ions?
  a. sulfate   b. nitrate
  c. phosphate   d. carbonate

4-105 What is the name of each of the following Table 4-3 polyatomic ions?
  a. HCO_3^- b. $H_2PO_4^-$
  c. H_3O^+ d. NH_4^+

4-106 What is the name of each of the following Table 4-3 polyatomic ions?
  a. HPO_4^{2-} b. HSO_4^-
  c. OH^- d. CN^-

Chemical Formulas and Names for Compounds Containing Polyatomic Ions (Section 4-11)

4-107 Write chemical formulas for the compounds formed between the following positive and negative ions.
  a. Na^+ and OH^- b. Fe^{3+} and HSO_4^-
  c. Ba^{2+} and NO_3^- d. Al^{3+} and CO_3^{2-}

4-108 Write chemical formulas for the compounds formed between the following positive and negative ions.
a. K^+ and CN^- b. NH_4^+ and SO_4^{2-}
c. Co^{2+} and $H_2PO_4^-$ d. Ca^{2+} and PO_4^{3-}

4-109 Fill in the blanks to complete the following table of chemical formulas for polyatomic-ion-containing ionic compounds. For each compound, the positive ion present is listed on the left side of the table and the negative ion present is listed at the top. The first line of the table is already completed as an example.

		CN^-	NO_3^-	HCO_3^-	SO_4^{2-}
	Na^+	NaCN	$NaNO_3$	$NaHCO_3$	Na_2SO_4
a.	Al^{3+}				
b.	Ag^+				
c.	Ca^{2+}				
d.	NH_4^+				

4-110 Fill in the blanks to complete the following table of chemical formulas for polyatomic-ion-containing ionic compounds. For each compound, the positive ion present is listed on the left side of the table and the negative ion present is listed at the top. The first line of the table is already completed as an example.

		OH^-	PO_4^{3-}	CO_3^{2-}	HSO_4^-
	Li^+	LiOH	Li_3PO_4	Li_2CO_3	$LiHSO_4$
a.	Cu^{2+}				
b.	Ba^{2+}				
c.	Fe^{3+}				
d.	NH_4^+				

4-111 How many ions are present per formula unit in each of the following polyatomic-ion-containing compounds?
a. $LiHCO_3$ b. $BeCO_3$
c. $Al_2(SO_4)_3$ d. NH_4NO_3

4-112 How many ions are present per formula unit in each of the following polyatomic-ion-containing compounds?
a. KH_2PO_4 b. Li_2SO_4
c. $Fe(NO_3)_3$ d. NH_4CN

4-113 Name the following compounds, all of which contain polyatomic ions and fixed-charge metals.
a. $MgCO_3$ b. $ZnSO_4$
c. $Be(NO_3)_2$ d. Ag_3PO_4

4-114 Name the following compounds, all of which contain polyatomic ions and fixed-charge metals.
a. $LiOH$ b. $Al(CN)_3$
c. $BaSO_4$ d. $NaNO_3$

4-115 Name the following compounds, all of which contain polyatomic ions and variable-charge metals.
a. $Fe(OH)_2$ b. $CuCO_3$
c. $AuCN$ d. $Mn_3(PO_4)_2$

4-116 Name the following compounds, all of which contain polyatomic ions and variable-charge metals.
a. $Fe(NO_3)_3$ b. $Co_2(CO_3)_3$
c. Cu_3PO_4 d. $Pb(SO_4)_2$

4-117 Write formulas for the following compounds, all of which contain polyatomic ions.
a. Potassium bicarbonate   b. Gold(III) sulfate
c. Silver nitrate   d. Copper(II) phosphate

4-118 Write formulas for the following compounds, all of which contain polyatomic ions.
a. Aluminum nitrate   b. Iron(III) sulfate
c. Calcium cyanide   d. Lead(IV) hydroxide

▲4-119 Write chemical formulas for the following compounds.
a. Sodium sulfide
b. Sodium sulfate
c. Sodium carbonate
d. Sodium hydrogen carbonate

▲4-120 Write chemical formulas for the following compounds.
a. Potassium nitrate   b. Potassium nitride
c. Potassium cyanide   d. Potassium hydroxide

▲4-121 Answer the following questions about the ionic compound formed from the ions Al^{3+} and CO_3^{2-}.
a. What is the name of the compound?
b. What is the chemical formula of the compound?
c. How many polyatomic ions are present in one formula unit of the compound?
d. How many monatomic ions are present in one formula unit of the compound?

▲4-122 Answer the following questions about the ionic compound formed from the ions Ca^{2+} and PO_4^{3-}.
a. What is the name of the compound?
b. What is the chemical formula of the compound?
c. How many polyatomic ions are present in one formula unit of the compound?
d. How many monatomic ions are present in one formula unit of the compound?

▲4-123 Fill in the blanks to complete the following table of information about selected ionic compounds. The first line of the table is already completed as an example.

	Formula of Positive Ion	Formula of Negative Ion	Chemical Formula	Compound Name
	Mg^{2+}	OH^-	$Mg(OH)_2$	Magnesium hydroxide
a.			$BaBr_2$	
b.	Zn^{2+}	NO_3^-		
c.				Iron(III) carbonate
d.			PbO_2	

▲4-124 Fill in the blanks to complete the following table of information about selected ionic compounds. The first line of the table is already completed as an example.

	Formula of Positive Ion	Formula of Negative Ion	Chemical Formula	Compound Name
	K^+	I^-	KI	Potassium iodide
a.			Cu_2SO_4	
b.				Lithium nitride
c.	Al^{3+}	S^{2-}		
d.			$Co_3(PO_4)_2$	

Chemical Bonding: The Covalent Bond Model

5

Anneclaire Le Royer/E+/Getty Images

The pleasant odor of flowers is produced by a mixture of volatile molecular compounds emitted from the flower blooms. Such molecular compounds contain covalent bonds.

The forces that hold atoms in compounds together as a unit are of two general types: (1) ionic bonds (which involve electron transfer) and (2) covalent bonds (which involve electron sharing). The ionic bond model was considered in Chapter 4. The covalent bond model is the subject of this chapter.

5-1 The Covalent Bond Model

LEARNING FOCUS
List major differences between the covalent bond model and the ionic bond model.

A listing of several key differences between ionic and covalent bonding and their resultant ionic and molecular compounds is the starting point for consideration of the topic of covalent bonding.

1. Ionic bonds form between atoms of dissimilar elements (a metal and a nonmetal). Covalent bond formation occurs between *similar* or even *identical* atoms. Most often, two nonmetals are involved.
2. Electron transfer is the mechanism by which ionic bond formation occurs. Covalent bond formation involves *electron sharing*.

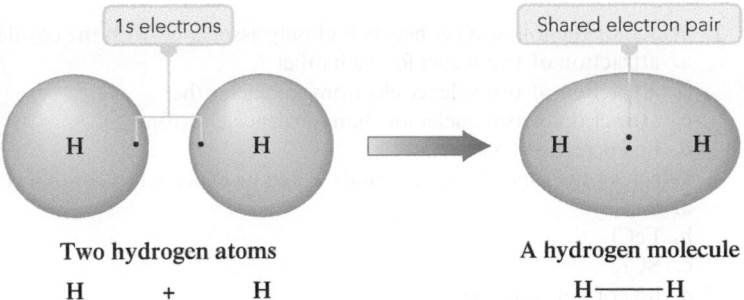

Figure 5-1 Electron sharing can occur only when electron orbitals from two different atoms overlap.

3. Ionic compounds do not contain discrete molecules. Instead, such compounds consist of an extended array of alternating positive and negative ions. In covalently bonded compounds, the basic structural unit is a molecule. Indeed, such compounds are called molecular compounds.

4. All ionic compounds are solids at room temperature. Molecular compounds may be solids (glucose), liquids (water), or gases (carbon dioxide) at room temperature.

5. An ionic solid, if soluble in water, forms an aqueous solution that conducts electricity. The electrical conductance is related to the presence of ions (charged particles) in the solution. A molecular compound, if soluble in water, usually produces a nonconducting aqueous solution.

A **covalent bond** *is a chemical bond resulting from two nuclei attracting the same shared electrons.* Consideration of the hydrogen molecule (H_2), the simplest of all molecules, provides initial insights into the nature of the covalent bond and its formation. When two hydrogen atoms, each with a single electron, are brought together, the orbitals that contain the valence electrons *overlap* to create an orbital common to both atoms. This overlapping is shown in Figure 5-1. The two electrons, one from each H atom, now move throughout this new orbital and are said to be *shared* by the two nuclei. ◄

Once two orbitals overlap, the most favorable location for the shared electrons is the area directly between the two nuclei. Here the two electrons can simultaneously interact with (be attracted to) both nuclei, a situation that produces increased stability. This concept of increased stability can be explained by using an analogy. Consider the nuclei of the two hydrogen atoms in H_2 to be "old potbellied stoves" and the two electrons to be running around each of the stoves trying to keep warm. When the two nuclei are together (an H_2 molecule), the electrons have two sources of heat. In particular, in the region between the nuclei (the overlap region), the electrons can keep both "front and back" warm at the same time. This is a better situation than when each electron has only one "stove" (nucleus) as a source of heat.

In terms of Lewis notation, this sharing of electrons by the two hydrogen atoms is diagrammed as follows:

Shared electron pair

$$H \; H \longrightarrow H \!:\! H$$

The two shared electrons do double duty, helping each hydrogen atom achieve a helium noble-gas configuration.

► *Among the millions of compounds that are known, those that have covalent bonds are dominant. Almost all compounds encountered in the fields of organic chemistry and biochemistry contain covalent bonds.*

Section 5-1 Quick Quiz

1. Covalent bond formation most often involves electron sharing between
   a. two nonmetal atoms
   b. a metal atom and a nonmetal atom
   c. a metal atom and a noble-gas atom
   d. no correct response

(continued)

2. Which of the following concepts is closely associated with the covalent bond model?
   a. attraction of two nuclei for each other
   b. attraction of two valence electrons for each other
   c. attraction of two nuclei for shared valence electrons
   d. no correct response
3. Which of the following compounds would be expected to contain covalent bonds?
   a. $CuCl_2$
   b. $FeCl_2$
   c. SCl_2
   d. no correct response
4. Which of the following compounds has molecules as its basic structural unit?
   a. FeO
   b. Al_2O_3
   c. SO_3
   d. no correct response

Answers: 1. a; 2. c; 3. c; 4. c

5-2 Lewis Structures for Molecular Compounds

LEARNING FOCUS

Write Lewis structures to describe the bonding in simple molecular compounds; interpret a Lewis structure in terms of numbers of bonding and nonbonding electrons present.

Lewis structures are useful in visualizing the electron sharing associated with covalent bond formation, just as they were useful in visualizing the electron transfer associated with ionic bond formation (Section 4-6).

A consideration of the formation of selected simple covalent compounds containing the element fluorine, based on Lewis structure use, shows how such structures portray the electron sharing concept associated with covalent bond formation. Fluorine, located in Group VIIA of the periodic table, has seven valence electrons. Its Lewis symbol is

$$\cdot \ddot{\underset{\cdot\cdot}{F}} :$$

Fluorine needs only one electron to achieve the octet of electrons that enables it to have a noble-gas electron configuration. When fluorine bonds to other nonmetals, the octet of electrons is completed by means of electron sharing. The molecules HF, F_2, and BrF, whose Lewis structures follow, are representative of this situation.

$$H \underset{\curvearrowright}{} \ddot{\underset{\cdot\cdot}{F}} : \longrightarrow H : \ddot{\underset{\cdot\cdot}{F}} :$$
$$: \ddot{\underset{\cdot\cdot}{F}} \underset{\curvearrowright}{} \ddot{\underset{\cdot\cdot}{F}} : \longrightarrow : \ddot{\underset{\cdot\cdot}{F}} : \ddot{\underset{\cdot\cdot}{F}} :$$
$$: \ddot{\underset{\cdot\cdot}{Br}} \underset{\curvearrowright}{} \ddot{\underset{\cdot\cdot}{F}} : \longrightarrow : \ddot{\underset{\cdot\cdot}{Br}} : \ddot{\underset{\cdot\cdot}{F}} :$$

The HF and BrF molecules illustrate the point that the two atoms involved in a covalent bond need not be identical (as is the case with H_2 and F_2).

A common practice in writing Lewis structures for covalently bonded molecules is to represent the *shared* electron pairs with dashes. Using this notation, the H_2, HF, F_2, and BrF molecules are written as

$$H—H \qquad H—\ddot{\underset{\cdot\cdot}{F}} : \qquad : \ddot{\underset{\cdot\cdot}{F}}—\ddot{\underset{\cdot\cdot}{F}} : \qquad : \ddot{\underset{\cdot\cdot}{Br}}—\ddot{\underset{\cdot\cdot}{F}} :$$

The atoms in covalently bonded molecules often possess both *bonding* and *nonbonding* electrons. **Bonding electrons** *are pairs of valence electrons that are shared between atoms in a covalent bond.* Each of the fluorine atoms in the molecules HF, F_2, and BrF possesses one pair of bonding electrons. **Nonbonding electrons** *are pairs of valence electrons on an atom that are not involved in electron sharing.* Each of the fluorine atoms in HF, F_2, and BrF possesses three pairs of nonbonding electrons, as does the bromine atom in BrF. ◄

▶ *Nonbonding electron pairs are often also referred to as* unshared electron pairs *or* lone electron pairs *(or simply* lone pairs*).*

In Section 5-8, it will be shown that nonbonding electrons play an important role in determining the shape (geometry) of molecules when three or more atoms are present.

Bonding electrons

Nonbonding electrons

H : H   H : F :   : F : F :   : Br : F :

Bonding electrons (black)
Nonbonding electrons (blue)

The preceding four examples of Lewis structures involved diatomic molecules, the simplest type of molecule. The "thinking pattern" used to draw these diatomic Lewis structures easily extends to triatomic and larger molecules. Consider the molecules H_2O, NH_3, and CH_4, molecules in which two, three, and four hydrogen atoms are attached, respectively, to the O, N, and C atoms. The hydrogen content of these molecules is correlated directly with the fact that oxygen, nitrogen, and carbon have six, five, and four valence electrons, respectively, and therefore need to gain two, three, and four electrons, respectively, through electron sharing in order for the octet rule to be obeyed. The electron-sharing patterns and Lewis structures for these three molecules are as follows:

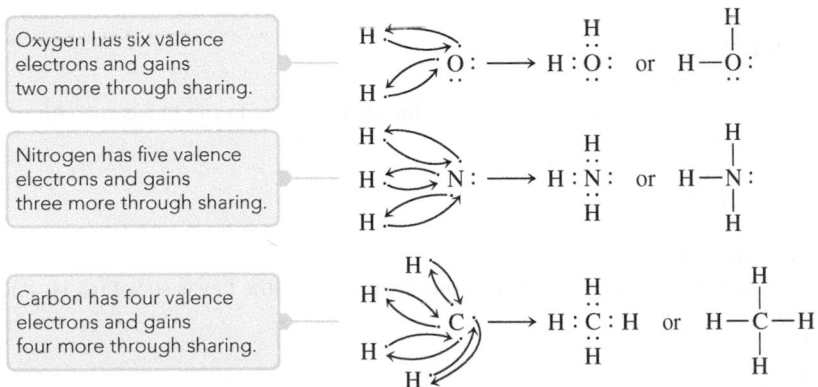

Thus, just as the octet rule was useful in determining the ratio of ions in ionic compounds (Section 4-6), it can be used to predict chemical formulas for molecular compounds. Figure 5-2 and Example 5-1 illustrate further the use of the octet rule to determine chemical formulas for molecular compounds.

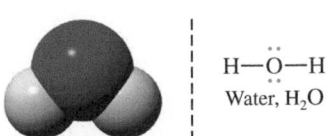

H—O—H
Water, H_2O

a O, with six valence electrons, forms two covalent bonds.

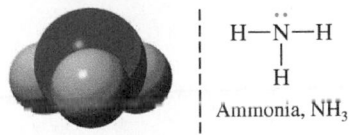

H—N—H
|
H
Ammonia, NH_3

b N, with five valence electrons, forms three covalent bonds.

H
|
H—C—H
|
H
Methane, CH_4

c C, with four valence electrons, forms four covalent bonds.

Figure 5-2 The number of covalent bonds formed by a nonmetallic element is directly correlated with the number of electrons it must share in order to obtain an octet of electrons.

EXAMPLE 5-1

Using the Octet Rule to Predict the Formulas of Simple Molecular Compounds

Draw Lewis structures for the simplest binary compounds that can be formed from the following pairs of nonmetals.

a. Nitrogen and iodine   **b.** Sulfur and hydrogen

Solution

a. Nitrogen is in Group VA of the periodic table and has five valence electrons. It will need to form three covalent bonds to achieve an octet of electrons. Iodine, in Group VIIA of the periodic table, has seven valence electrons and will need to form only one covalent bond in order to have an octet of electrons. Therefore, three

(continued)

iodine atoms will be needed to meet the needs of one nitrogen atom. The Lewis structure for this molecule is

Each atom in NI_3 has an octet of electrons; these octets are circled in color in the following diagram.

b. Sulfur has six valence electrons, and hydrogen has one valence electron. Thus sulfur will form two covalent bonds ($6 + 2 = 8$), and hydrogen will form one covalent bond ($1 + 1 = 2$). Remember that for hydrogen, an "octet" is two electrons; the noble gas that hydrogen mimics is helium, which has only two valence electrons.

$$H\!:\!\ddot{S}\!: \longrightarrow H\!:\!\ddot{S}\!: \longrightarrow H\!-\!\ddot{S}\!:$$
$$H \qquad\qquad H \qquad\qquad H$$

Section 5-2 Quick Quiz

1. Which of the following characterizations for the bond line in the Lewis structure H— F: is *incorrect?*
   a. it represents two shared electrons
   b. it represents a covalent bond
   c. it represents an octet of electrons
   d. no correct response
2. How many nonbonding valence electrons are present in the Lewis structure H— F̈:?
   a. 3
   b. 6
   c. 8
   d. no correct response
3. How many hydrogen atoms (1 valence electron) would be expected to bond to a phosphorus atom (5 valence electrons) during covalent compound formation?
   a. 1
   b. 3
   c. 5
   d. no correct response
4. Both Cl and F atoms contain seven valence electrons. The expected chemical formula for the simplest covalent compound formed between these two elements is
   a. ClF_7
   b. Cl_2F
   c. ClF
   d. no correct response
5. In covalent bond formation the two atoms sharing electrons
   a. must be identical
   b. must be different
   c. can be the same or different
   d. no correct response
6. In a completed Lewis structure for a molecular compound all atoms
   a. must have an octet of electrons
   b. except hydrogen must have an octet of electrons
   c. except hydrogen and oxygen must have an octet of electrons
   d. no correct response

Answers: 1. c; 2. b; 3. b; 4. c; 5. c; 6. b

5-3 Single, Double, and Triple Covalent Bonds

LEARNING FOCUS

Understand how single, double, and triple covalent bonds differ; be able to recognize such bond types in Lewis structures.

A **single covalent bond** *is a covalent bond in which two atoms share one pair of electrons.* All of the bonds in all of the molecules considered in the previous section were *single* covalent bonds.

Single covalent bonds are not adequate to explain covalent bonding in all molecules. Sometimes two atoms must share two or three pairs of electrons in order to provide a complete octet of electrons for each atom involved in the bonding. Such bonds are called *double* covalent bonds and *triple* covalent bonds, respectively. A **double covalent bond** *is a covalent bond in which two atoms share two pairs of electrons.* A double covalent bond between two atoms is approximately twice as strong as a single covalent bond between the same two atoms; that is, it takes approximately twice as much energy to break the double bond as it does the single bond. A **triple covalent bond** *is a covalent bond in which two atoms share three pairs of electrons.* A triple covalent bond is approximately three times as strong as a single covalent bond between the same two atoms. The term *multiple covalent bond* is a designation that applies to both double and triple covalent bonds.

One of the simplest molecules possessing a multiple covalent bond is the N_2 molecule, which has a triple covalent bond. A nitrogen atom has five valence electrons and needs three additional electrons to complete its octet.

$$\cdot \ddot{N} \cdot$$

In order to acquire a noble-gas electron configuration, each nitrogen atom must share three of its electrons with the other nitrogen atom.

$$:N \overset{\curvearrowright}{\underset{\curvearrowright}{\longrightarrow}} \overset{\curvearrowleft}{\underset{\curvearrowleft}{\longleftarrow}} \cdot N: \longrightarrow :N:::N: \quad \text{or} \quad :N\equiv N:$$

Note that all three shared electron pairs are placed in the area between the two nitrogen atoms in the Lewis structure. Just as one line is used to denote a single covalent bond, three lines are used to denote a triple covalent bond. ◄

When "counting" electrons in a Lewis structure to make sure that all atoms in the molecule have achieved their octet of electrons, *all* electrons in a double or triple bond are considered to belong to *both* of the atoms involved in that bond. The "counting" for the N_2 molecule would be

$$\big(:N(::)N:\big)$$

Eight electrons   Eight electrons

▶ *A single line (dash) is used to denote a single covalent bond, two lines to denote a double covalent bond, and three lines to denote a triple covalent bond.*

Each of the circles around a nitrogen atom contains eight valence electrons. Circles are never drawn to include just some of the electrons in a double or triple bond.

A slightly more complicated molecule containing a triple covalent bond is the molecule C_2H_2 (acetylene). A carbon–carbon triple covalent bond is present, as well as two carbon–hydrogen single bonds. The arrangement of valence electrons in C_2H_2 is as follows:

$$H \overset{\curvearrowright}{C} \cdot \overset{\curvearrowright}{\underset{\curvearrowright}{\longrightarrow}} \overset{\curvearrowleft}{\underset{\curvearrowleft}{\longleftarrow}} \cdot C \overset{\curvearrowleft}{H} \longrightarrow H:C:::C:H \quad \text{or} \quad H-C\equiv C-H$$

The two atoms in a triple covalent bond are commonly the same element. However, they do not have to be. The molecule HCN (hydrogen cyanide) contains a heteroatomic triple covalent bond.

$$H:C:::N: \quad \text{or} \quad H-C\equiv N:$$

A common molecule that contains a double covalent bond is CO_2 (carbon dioxide). In fact, there are two carbon–oxygen double covalent bonds present in CO_2.

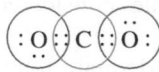

Note for the CO_2 Lewis structure how the circles are drawn for the octet of electrons about each of the atoms.

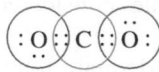

Section 5-3 Quick Quiz

1. The number of electrons present in a triple covalent bond is
   a. 2
   b. 3
   c. 6
   d. no correct response
2. The number of single, double, and triple covalent bonds present, respectively, in a molecule whose Lewis structure is H:Ö:Ö:H is
   a. 1, 2, and 0
   b. 1, 0, and 2
   c. 3, 0 and 0
   d. no correct response
3. The number of single, double, and triple covalent bonds present, respectively, in a molecule whose Lewis structure is H:C:::N: is
   a. 1, 1, and 0
   b. 1, 0, and 1
   c. 0, 1 and 1
   d. no correct response
4. The term *multiple covalent bond* applies to
   a. both single and double bonds
   b. both double and triple bonds
   c. single, double, and triple bonds
   d. no correct response
5. Single and double covalent bonds
   a. have about the same strength
   b. cannot be present in the same molecule
   c. both involve sharing of two electron pairs
   d. no correct response

Answers: 1. c; 2. c; 3. b; 4. b; 5. d

5-4 Valence Electrons and Number of Covalent Bonds Formed

LEARNING FOCUS

Describe the octet rule-based normal bonding behavior for the elements oxygen, nitrogen, and carbon.

Not all elements can form double or triple covalent bonds. There must be at least two vacancies in an atom's valence electron shell prior to bond formation if it is to participate in a double bond, and at least three vacancies are necessary for triple-bond formation. This requirement eliminates Group VIIA elements (fluorine, chlorine, bromine, iodine) and hydrogen from participating in such bonds. The Group VIIA elements have seven valence electrons and one vacancy, and hydrogen has one valence electron and one vacancy. All covalent bonds formed by these elements are single covalent bonds.

Double bonding becomes possible for elements that need two electrons to complete their octet, and triple bonding becomes possible when three or more electrons are needed to complete an octet. Note that the word *possible* was used twice in the previous sentence. Multiple bonding does not have to occur when an element has two, three, or four vacancies in its octet; single covalent bonds can be formed instead. When more than one behavior is possible, the "bonding behavior" of an element is determined by the element or elements to which it is bonded.

The possible "bonding behaviors" for O (six valence electrons, two octet vacancies), N (five valence electrons, three octet vacancies), and C (four valence electrons, four octet vacancies) are as follows.

To complete its octet by electron sharing, an oxygen atom can form either two single bonds or one double bond.

$$:\overset{\displaystyle |}{\underset{\displaystyle \cdot\cdot}{O}}- \qquad :\overset{}{\underset{\displaystyle \cdot\cdot}{O}}=$$

Two single bonds   One double bond

Nitrogen is a very versatile element with respect to bonding. It can form single, double, or triple covalent bonds as dictated by the other atoms present in a molecule.

$$-\overset{\displaystyle \cdot\cdot}{\underset{\displaystyle |}{N}}- \qquad -\overset{\displaystyle \cdot\cdot}{N}= \qquad :N\equiv$$

Three single bonds   One single and   One triple bond
                        one double bond

Note that the nitrogen atom forms three bonds in each of these bonding situations. A double bond counts as two bonds, a triple bond as three. Because nitrogen has only five valence electrons, it must form three covalent bonds to complete its octet. ◄

Carbon is an even more versatile element than nitrogen with respect to variety of types of bonding, as illustrated by the following possibilities. In each case, carbon forms four bonds.

$$-\overset{\displaystyle |}{\underset{\displaystyle |}{C}}- \qquad -\overset{\displaystyle |}{C}= \qquad =C= \qquad -C\equiv$$

Four single bonds   Two single bonds and   Two double bonds   One single bond and
                     one double bond   one triple bond

► *There is a strong tendency for atoms of nonmetallic elements to form a specific number of covalent bonds. The number of bonds formed is equal to the number of electrons the nonmetallic atom must share to obtain an octet of electrons.*

Section 5-4 Quick Quiz

1. During covalent bond formation, there is a strong tendency for atoms of nitrogen to form
   a. one covalent bond
   b. two covalent bonds
   c. three covalent bonds
   d. no correct response
2. Carbon atoms normally form four covalent bonds. This is indicative of the presence of how many vacancies in the valence electron shell of carbon atoms?
   a. two
   b. four
   c. eight
   d. no correct response
3. Which of the following is not a normal bonding behavior for oxygen atoms (six valence electrons)?
   a. formation of two single bonds
   b. formation of one double bond
   c. formation of two double bonds
   d. no correct response

Answers: 1. c; 2. b; 3. c

5-5   Coordinate Covalent Bonds

LEARNING FOCUS

Distinguish between a coordinate covalent bond and a regular covalent bond; know the effect that coordinate covalent bond formation has on the normal bonding patterns for nonmetallic elements.

A special case of electron sharing exists in which one atom participating in a covalent bond supplies two electrons to the bond and the other atom supplies zero electrons to the bond. This can occur when one atom, the donor, has a nonbonding pair of electrons and the other atom, the acceptor, has two vacancies in its valence electron shell. Bonds of this type are called *coordinate covalent bonds*. A **coordinate covalent bond** *is a covalent bond in which both electrons in a shared pair of electrons come from one of the two atoms in the bond.*

> ▶ An "ordinary" covalent bond can be thought of as a "Dutch-treat" bond; each atom "pays" its part of the bill. A coordinate covalent bond can be thought of as a "you-treat" bond; one atom pays the whole bill.

The molecule HOClO (HClO$_2$) is an example of a coordinate-covalent-bond-containing molecule. Its formation can be envisioned as resulting from the addition of an oxygen atom, which has six valence electrons, to a HOCl molecule. ◀

$$H-\overset{..}{\underset{..}{O}}-\overset{..}{\underset{..}{Cl}}: \ + \ \overset{..}{\underset{..}{O}}:$$

Combining these two entities together produces the HOClO molecule through coordinate covalent bond formation that involves the Cl atom of HOCl and the new O atom, as is shown in the following Lewis structure diagram:

$$H-\overset{..}{\underset{..}{O}}-\overset{..}{\underset{..}{Cl}}: + \overset{..}{\underset{..}{O}}: \quad \text{produces} \quad H-\overset{..}{\underset{..}{O}}-\overset{..}{\underset{..}{Cl}}:\overset{..}{\underset{..}{O}}:$$

coordinate covalent bond

both electrons in this bond come from the Cl atom

The oxygen atom, with two vacancies in its valence electron shell and needing two electrons to achieve an octet of electrons, uses a nonbonding pair of electrons on the Cl atom to meet its "electron needs." The Cl atom still has its existent octet of electrons. Thus, coordinate covalent bonding enables an atom that has two vacancies in its valence electron shell to share a pair of nonbonding electrons on another atom.

> ▶ Once a coordinate covalent bond forms, it is indistinguishable from other covalent bonds in a molecule.

Once a coordinate covalent bond is formed, there is no way to distinguish it from any of the other covalent bonds in a molecule; all electrons are identical regardless of their source. ◀ The main use of the concept of coordinate covalency is to help rationalize the existence of certain molecules and polyatomic ions whose electron-bonding arrangement would otherwise present problems. Figure 5-3 contrasts the formation of a "regular" covalent bond with that of a coordinate covalent bond.

Figure 5-3 (a) A "regular" covalent single bond is the result of overlap of two half-filled orbitals. (b) A coordinate covalent single bond is the result of overlap of a filled and a vacant orbital.

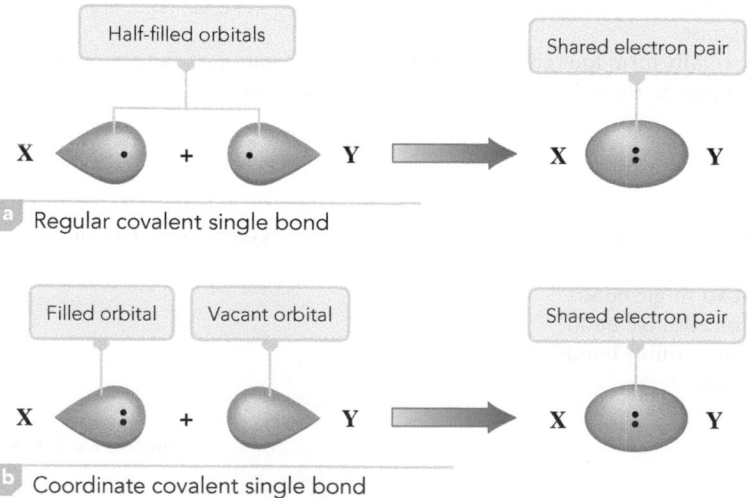

a Regular covalent single bond

b Coordinate covalent single bond

An atom participating in a coordinate covalent bond deviates from the common bonding pattern (Section 5-4) expected for that type of atom. For example, oxygen normally forms two bonds; yet in the HOClO molecule just discussed, the terminal O atom has only one bond. Group VIIA elements, of which Cl is one, normally form one bond yet in HOClO the Cl atom forms two bonds. This deviation from normal bonding patterns for O and Cl results from their participation in the coordinate covalent bond. The O atom forms one less bond than normal because it did not donate any electrons to the bond and the Cl atom forms one more bond than normal because it donates two electrons rather than one electron to the bond.

EXAMPLE 5-2

Diagramming Coordinate Covalent Bond Formation Using Lewis Structures

Show the formation of the molecule $HOClO_2$ from the molecule HOClO and an O atom using the given Lewis structures and then identify the location of the coordinate covalent bond in HOClO.

$$H—\ddot{O}—\ddot{Cl}—\ddot{O}: \quad \text{and} \quad H—\ddot{O}—\ddot{Cl}—\ddot{O}:$$
$$\underset{:\ddot{O}:}{|}$$

Solution

The combining of the Lewis structures of HOClO and atomic O to produce $HOClO_2$ is depicted in this manner:

$$H—\ddot{O}—\ddot{Cl}—\ddot{O}: \; + \; \ddot{O}: \quad \text{produces} \quad H—\ddot{O}—\ddot{Cl}—\ddot{O}:$$
$$\underset{:\ddot{O}:}{|}$$

newly formed coordinate covalent bond

The Cl—O bond at the bottom in the $HOClO_2$ Lewis structure is the newly formed coordinate covalent bond. Both electrons in this bond are supplied by the Cl atom.

There are actually two coordinate covalent bonds in the newly formed $HOClO_2$ molecule because HOClO itself contains a coordinate covalent bond as was discussed earlier in this section when its formation was considered. The fact that the Cl atom in $HOClO_2$ participates in three bonds, when normal is one bond, is indicative of the presence of two coordinate covalent bonds.

Section 5-5 Quick Quiz

1. Which of the following is an incorrect statement about coordinate covalent bonds?
   a. Both atoms involved in the bond contribute an equal number of electrons to the bond.
   b. Both electrons of a shared electron pair come from the same atom.
   c. Once formed, they are indistinguishable from other covalent bonds.
   d. no correct response
2. For the molecule $:N≡N—\ddot{O}:$, the concept of a coordinate covalent bond is needed to explain the bonding between
   a. the two N atoms
   b. the N and O atoms
   c. atoms in both bonds
   d. no correct response
3. In which of the following molecules is a coordinate covalent bond present?
   a. $:\ddot{Cl}—\ddot{Cl}:$
   b. $:N≡N:$
   c. $H—\ddot{Br}:$
   d. no correct response

Answers: 1. a; 2. b; 3. d

5-6 Systematic Procedures for Drawing Lewis Structures

LEARNING FOCUS

Using systematic procedures, draw Lewis structures for molecules given the arrangement of atoms within the molecules.

A systematic stepwise procedure exists for distributing electrons as bonding and nonbonding electron pairs in a Lewis structure. This systematic approach is particularly useful in situations where a molecule contains one or more multiple bonds (Section 5-3) and when coordinate covalency (Section 5-5) is present in a molecule.

This systematic approach for drawing a Lewis structure is illustrated as follows using the molecule SO_2, a molecule in which two oxygen atoms are bonded to a central sulfur atom (Figure 5-4).

Step 1: *Calculate the total number of valence electrons available in the molecule by adding together the valence electron counts for all atoms in the molecule.* The periodic table is a useful guide for determining this number.

An SO_2 molecule has 18 valence electrons available for bonding. Sulfur (Group VIA) has 6 valence electrons, and each oxygen (also Group VIA) has 6 valence electrons. The total number is therefore $6 + 2(6) = 18$.

Step 2: *Write the chemical symbols of the atoms in the molecule in the order in which they are bonded to one another, and then place a single covalent bond, involving two electrons, between each pair of bonded atoms.* For SO_2, the S atom is the central atom, and the structure becomes

O:S:O

Figure 5-4 The sulfur dioxide (SO_2) molecule. A computer-generated model.

Determining which atom is the *central atom*—that is, which atom has the most other atoms bonded to it—is the key to determining the arrangement of atoms in a molecule or polyatomic ion. Most other atoms present will be bonded to the central atom. For common binary molecular compounds, the molecular formula is often helpful in determining the identity of the central atom. The central atom is the atom that appears only once in the formula; for example, S is the central atom in SO_3, O is the central atom in H_2O, and P is the central atom in PF_3. In molecular compounds containing hydrogen, oxygen, and an additional element, that additional element is the central atom; for example, N is the central atom in HNO_3, and S is the central atom in H_2SO_4. In compounds of this type, the oxygen atoms are bonded to the central atom, and the hydrogen atoms are bonded to the oxygens. Carbon is the central atom in nearly all carbon-containing compounds. Neither hydrogen nor fluorine is ever the central atom.

Step 3: *Add nonbonding electron pairs to the structure such that each atom bonded to the central atom has an octet of electrons. Remember that for hydrogen, an "octet" is only two electrons.*

For SO_2, addition of the nonbonding electrons gives

:Ö:S:Ö:

At this point, 16 of the 18 available electrons have been used.

Step 4: *Place any remaining electrons on the central atom of the structure.*

Placing the two remaining electrons on the S atom gives

:Ö:S̈:Ö:

Step 5: *If there are not enough electrons to give the central atom an octet, then use one or more pairs of nonbonding electrons on the atoms bonded to the central atom to form double or triple bonds.*

The S atom has only six electrons. Thus a nonbonding electron pair from an O atom is used to form a sulfur–oxygen double bond.

$$:\ddot{O}:\ddot{S}:\underset{\curvearrowright}{\ddot{O}}: \longrightarrow :\ddot{O}:\ddot{S}::\ddot{O}:$$

This structure now obeys the octet rule.

Step 6: *Count the total number of electrons in the completed Lewis structure to make sure it is equal to the total number of valence electrons available for bonding, as calculated in Step 1.* This step serves as a "double-check" on the correctness of the Lewis structure.

For SO_2, there are 18 valence electrons in the Lewis structure of Step 5, the same number calculated in Step 1.

EXAMPLE 5-3

Drawing a Lewis Structure Using Systematic Procedures

Draw Lewis structures for the following molecules.

a. PF_3, a molecule in which P is the central atom and all F atoms are bonded to it (see Figure 5-5).
b. HCN, a molecule in which C is the central atom (see Figure 5-6).

Solution

a. Step 1: Phosphorus (Group VA) has 5 valence electrons, and each of the fluorine atoms (Group VIIA) has 7 valence electrons. The total electron count is $5 + 3(7) = 26$.

Step 2: Drawing the molecular skeleton with single covalent bonds (2 electrons) placed between all bonded atoms gives

$$F:P:F$$
$$\overset{\ \ }{F}$$

Step 3: Adding nonbonding electrons to the structure to complete the octets of all atoms bonded to the central atom gives

$$:\ddot{F}:P:\ddot{F}:$$
$$:\ddot{F}:$$

At this point, 24 of the 26 available electrons have been used.

Step 4: The central P atom has only 6 electrons; it needs 2 more. The 2 remaining available electrons are placed on the P atom, completing its octet. All atoms now have an octet of electrons.

$$:\ddot{F}:\ddot{P}:\ddot{F}:$$
$$:\ddot{F}:$$

Step 5: This step is not needed; the central atom already has an octet of electrons.

Step 6: There are 26 electrons in the Lewis structure, the same number of electrons we calculated in Step 1.

b. Step 1: Hydrogen (Group IA) has 1 valence electron, carbon (Group IVA) has 4 valence electrons, and nitrogen (Group VA) has 5 valence electrons. The total number of electrons is 10.

Step 2: Drawing the molecular skeleton with single covalent bonds between bonded atoms gives

$$H:C:N$$

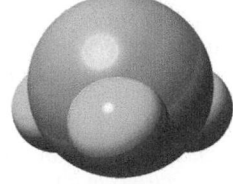

Figure 5-5 A computer-generated model of the phosphorus trifluoride (PF_3) molecule.

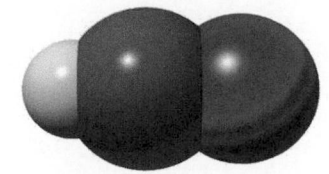

Figure 5-6 A computer-generated model of the hydrogen cyanide (HCN) molecule.

(continued)

Step 3: Adding nonbonding electron pairs to the structure such that the atoms bonded to the central atom have "octets" gives

$$H : C : \ddot{N} :$$

Remember that hydrogen needs only 2 electrons.

Step 4: The structure in Step 3 has 10 valence electrons, the total number available. Thus there are no additional electrons available to place on the carbon atom to give it an octet of electrons.

Step 5: To give the central carbon atom its octet, 2 nonbonding electron pairs on the nitrogen atom are used to form a carbon–nitrogen triple bond.

$$H : C : \ddot{N} : \longrightarrow H : C ::: N :$$

Step 6: The Lewis structure has 10 electrons, as calculated in Step 1.

The systematic approach to writing Lewis structures illustrated in this section generates correct Lewis structures for most compounds containing the commonly encountered elements carbon, nitrogen, oxygen, and the halogens (Section 3-4). There are, however, a few compounds that violate the "rules" just considered. The focus on relevancy feature Chemical Connections 5-A—Nitric Oxide: A Molecule Whose Bonding Does Not Follow "The Rules"—discusses one such "rule-violating" compound—nitric oxide (NO), an extremely important compound in both an environmental and biochemical context. ◄

▶ *Systematic procedures for drawing Lewis structures do not differentiate between regular covalent bonds and coordinate covalent bonds. This is fine since these two types of bonds are indistinguishable once they are formed. Electrons in bonds do not have labels on them that tell which atom they came from.*

Section 5-6 Quick Quiz

1. In Lewis structures depicting covalent bonding, an "octet" of electrons for atoms of H means
   a. 2 electrons
   b. 4 electrons
   c. 8 electrons
   d. no correct response
2. The Lewis structure for a N_2 molecule contains a triple covalent bond, and a total of 10 valence electrons. How many nonbonding electrons are present in the Lewis structure for this molecule?
   a. 2 electrons
   b. 4 electrons
   c. 8 electrons
   d. no correct response
3. The Lewis structure for a H_2S molecule contains eight valence electrons, four of which are nonbonding. How many single and double bonds are present, respectively in this molecule?
   a. two and zero
   b. one and one
   c. zero and two
   d. no correct response
4. Carbon has four valence electrons and H has one valence electron. The Lewis structure for the CH_4 molecule contains how many nonbonding electrons?
   a. 2 electrons
   b. 4 electrons
   c. 8 electrons
   d. no correct response
5. Nitrogen has five valence electrons and Cl has seven valence electrons. The Lewis structure for the molecule NCl_3 contains
   a. three single bonds
   b. two single bonds and one double bond
   c. three double bonds
   d. no correct response

Answers: 1. a; 2. b; 3. a; 4. d; 5. a

CHEMICAL CONNECTIONS 5-A

Nitric Oxide: A Molecule Whose Bonding Does Not Follow "The Rules"

The bonding in most, *but not all,* simple molecules is easily explained using the systematic procedures for drawing Lewis structures described in Section 5-6. The molecule NO (nitric oxide) is an example of a simple molecule whose bonding does not conform to the standard rules for bonding. The presence of an odd number of valence electrons (11) in nitric oxide (5 from nitrogen and 6 from oxygen) makes it impossible to write a Lewis structure in which all electrons are paired as required by the octet rule. Thus an unpaired electron is present in the Lewis structure of NO.

Unpaired electron $:\!\overset{\frown}{N}\!\!=\!\!\overset{..}{\underset{..}{O}}:$

Despite the "nonconforming" nature of the bonding in nitric oxide, it is an important naturally occurring compound found both within the Earth's atmosphere and within the human body. A reactive, colorless, odorless, nonflammable gas, it is generated in low concentrations by numerous natural and human-caused processes, as well as by several physiological processes within humans and animals.

Natural processes releasing NO to the environment include (1) lightning passing through air, which causes the nitrogen and oxygen in air to react (to a slight extent) with each other to produce NO and (2) emissions from soil as the result of the action of soil bacteria. The major human-caused sources are automobile engines and power-plant operations. In these contexts, the high operational temperatures reached cause the nitrogen and oxygen in air to become reactive toward each other. A burning cigarette is also a source of NO gas.

The composition of air is 78% nitrogen and 21% oxygen, with small amounts of other gases also present. At ambient temperatures and pressures, the nitrogen and oxygen of air are unreactive toward each other. At the high temperatures reached in an operating internal combustion engine, a slight reaction between nitrogen and oxygen occurs, producing small amounts of NO gas. It is impossible to prevent this reaction from occurring at high temperatures. All that can be done is instigate control measures after the NO has been produced. One of the major purposes for mandated catalytic converters on cars is to minimize NO emissions. Much of the NO passing through the converter is changed back into the nitrogen and oxygen from which it was formed; nitrogen and oxygen then enter the air rather than NO (see accompanying photo).

Despite rigorous control efforts, small amounts of NO still enter the environment from the sources previously mentioned. Such NO is considered to be a major air pollutant. The environmental effects of NO are well documented, with it serving as a precursor for the formation of both photochemical smog and acid rain (Section 10-9).

In 1987, researchers, much to their surprise, discovered that NO is naturally present in the human body. It is

Determining that automobile catalytic converter systems are properly functioning is the basis for automobile emission testing requirements. NO emission levels are among the measurements taken in such testing.

generated within the body from reactions involving amino acids (Section 20-2). The biochemical role of this internally generated NO is that of a chemical messenger; it was the first known example of a chemical messenger within the body that is a gas. More information concerning biochemical NO is presented in Chemical Connections 26-A—The Chemical Composition of Urine.

Lightning causes small amounts of the nitrogen and oxygen in air to react with each other producing nitric oxide (NO).

5-7   Bonding in Compounds with Polyatomic Ions Present

LEARNING FOCUS

Using systematic procedures, draw Lewis structures for polyatomic ions given the arrangement of atoms within the ions; understand the relative roles of ionic and covalent bonding in polyatomic-ion-containing compounds.

Ionic compounds containing polyatomic ions (Section 4-10) present an interesting combination of both ionic and covalent bonds: covalent bonding *within* the polyatomic ion and ionic bonding *between* it and ions of opposite charge.

Polyatomic ion Lewis structures, which show the covalent bonding within such ions, are drawn using the same procedures as for molecular compounds (Section 5-6), with the accommodation that the total number of electrons used in the structure must be adjusted (increased or decreased) to take into account ion charge. The number of electrons is increased in the case of negatively charged ions and decreased in the case of positively charged ions. ◄

In the Lewis structure for an *ionic compound* that contains a polyatomic ion, the positive and negative ions are treated separately to show that they are individual ions not linked by covalent bonds. The Lewis structure of potassium sulfate, K_2SO_4, is written as

► *It is often erroneously assumed that the charge associated with a polyatomic ion is assigned to a particular atom within the ion. Polyatomic ion charge is not localized on a particular atom, but rather is associated with the ion as a whole.*

When writing the Lewis structure of an ion (monatomic or polyatomic), it is customary to use brackets and to show ionic charge outside the brackets.

$$[K]^+ \begin{bmatrix} \ddot{\text{O}}: \\ :\ddot{\text{O}}-\text{S}-\ddot{\text{O}}: \\ :\ddot{\text{O}}: \end{bmatrix}^{2-} [K]^+ \quad \text{and not as} \quad \text{K}-\ddot{\text{O}}-\text{S}-\ddot{\text{O}}-\text{K}$$

Correct structure   Incorrect structure

EXAMPLE 5-4

Drawing Lewis Structures for Polyatomic Ions

Draw a Lewis structure for SO_4^{2-}, a polyatomic ion in which S is the central atom and all O atoms are bonded to the S atom (see Figure 5-7).

Solution

Step 1: Both S and O are Group VIA elements. Thus each of the atoms has 6 valence electrons. Two extra electrons are also present, which accounts for the 2− charge on the ion. The total electron count is $6 + 4(6) + 2 = 32$.

Step 2: Drawing the molecular skeleton with single covalent bonds between bonded atoms gives

$$\begin{bmatrix} \text{O} \\ \text{O}:\text{S}:\text{O} \\ \text{O} \end{bmatrix}^{2-}$$

Step 3: Adding nonbonding electron pairs to give each oxygen atom an octet of electrons yields

$$\begin{bmatrix} :\ddot{\text{O}}: \\ :\ddot{\text{O}}:\text{S}:\ddot{\text{O}}: \\ :\ddot{\text{O}}: \end{bmatrix}^{2-}$$

Step 4: The Step 3 structure has 32 electrons, the total number available. No more electrons can be added to the structure, and, indeed, none need to be added because the central S atom has an octet of electrons. There is no need to proceed to Step 5.

Figure 5-7 A computer-generated model of the sulfate ion (SO_4^{2-}).

1. The bonding *within* a polyatomic ion is
   a. ionic
   b. covalent
   c. a combination of ionic and covalent
   d. no correct response
2. Both ionic and covalent bonding are present in which of the following chemical species?
   a. SO_4^{2-} ion
   b. H_2SO_4
   c. Na_2SO_4
   d. no correct response
3. Given that P has five valence electrons and O has six valence electrons, how many total valence electrons are present in the Lewis structure for the PO_4^{3-} ion?
   a. 11 electrons
   b. 29 electrons
   c. 32 electrons
   d. no correct response

Answers: 1. b; 2. c; 3. c

5-8 Molecular Geometry

LEARNING FOCUS

Given a Lewis structure for a molecule, determine its molecular geometry using VSEPR theory.

Lewis structures show the numbers and types of bonds present in molecules. They do not, however, convey any information about molecular geometry—that is, molecular shape. **Molecular geometry** *is a description of the three-dimensional arrangement of atoms within a molecule.* Indeed, Lewis structures falsely imply that all molecules have flat, two-dimensional shapes. This is not the case, as can be seen from the previously presented computer-generated models for the molecules SO_2 and PF_3. (Figures 5-4 and 5-5).

Molecular geometry is an important factor in determining the physical and chemical properties of a substance. Dramatic relationships between geometry and properties are often observed in research associated with the development of prescription drugs. A small change in overall molecular geometry, caused by the addition or removal of atoms, can enhance drug effectiveness and/or decrease drug side effects. Studies also show that the human senses of taste and smell depend in part on the geometries of molecules.

For molecules that contain only a few atoms, molecular geometry can be predicted by using the information present in a molecule's Lewis structure and a process called valence shell electron pair repulsion (VSEPR) theory. **VSEPR theory** *is a set of procedures for predicting the molecular geometry of a molecule using the information contained in the molecule's Lewis structure.*

The central concept of VSEPR theory is that electron pairs in the valence shell of an atom adopt an arrangement in space that minimizes the repulsions between the like-charged (all negative) electron pairs. The specific arrangement adopted by the electron pairs depends on the number of electron pairs present. The electron pair arrangements about a *central atom* in the cases of two, three, and four electron pairs are as follows:

1. Two electron pairs, to be as far apart as possible from one another, are found on opposite sides of a nucleus—that is, at 180° angles to one another (Figure 5-8a). Such an electron pair arrangement is said to be *linear*.
2. Three electron pairs are as far apart as possible when they are found at the corners of an equilateral triangle. In such an arrangement, they are separated by 120° angles, giving a *trigonal planar* arrangement of electron pairs (Figure 5-8b).

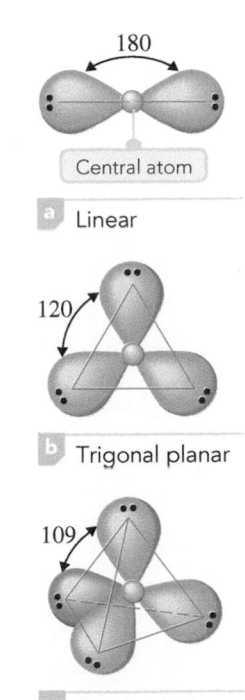

180
Central atom
a Linear

120
b Trigonal planar

109
c Tetrahedral

Figure 5-8 Arrangements of valence electron pairs about a central atom that minimize repulsions between the pairs.

3. A *tetrahedral* arrangement of electron pairs minimizes repulsions among four sets of electron pairs (Figure 5-8c). A tetrahedron is a four-sided solid in which all four sides are identical equilateral triangles. The angle between any two electron pairs is 109°. ◄

▶ *The preferred arrangement of a given number of valence electron pairs about a central atom is the arrangement that minimizes repulsions between electron pairs.*

▶ *The acronym VSEPR is pronounced "vesper."*

Electron Groups

Before using VSEPR theory to predict molecular geometry, an expansion of the concept of an "electron pair" to that of an "electron group" is needed. ◄ This will enable VSEPR theory to be extended to molecules in which double and triple bonds are present. A **VSEPR electron group** *is a collection of valence electrons present in a localized region about the central atom in a molecule.* A VSEPR electron group may contain two electrons (a single covalent bond), four electrons (a double covalent bond), or six electrons (a triple covalent bond). VSEPR electron groups that contain four and six electrons repel other VSEPR electron groups in the same way electron pairs do. The four electrons in a double bond or the six electrons in a triple bond are localized in the region between two bonded atoms in a manner similar to the two electrons of a single bond.

The operational rules associated with the use of VSEPR theory are as follows.

1. Draw a Lewis structure for the molecule, and identify the specific atom for which geometrical information is desired. (This atom will usually be the central atom in the molecule.)
2. Determine the number of VSEPR electron groups present about the central atom. The following conventions govern this determination:
   a. No distinction is made between bonding and nonbonding electron groups. Both are counted.
   b. Single, double, and triple bonds are all counted equally as "one electron group" because each takes up only one region of space about a central atom.
3. Predict the VSEPR electron group arrangement about the atom by assuming that the electron groups orient themselves in a manner that minimizes repulsions (see Figure 5-8).

Molecules with Two VSEPR Electron Groups

All molecules with two VSEPR electron groups are *linear.* Two common molecules with two VSEPR electron groups are carbon dioxide (CO_2) and hydrogen cyanide (HCN), whose Lewis structures are

$$\ddot{\text{O}}=\text{C}=\ddot{\text{O}}: \qquad \text{H}-\text{C}\equiv\text{N}:$$

In CO_2, the central carbon atom's two VSEPR electron groups are the two double bonds. In HCN, the central carbon atom's two VSEPR electron groups are a single bond and a triple bond. In both molecules, the VSEPR electron groups arrange themselves on opposite sides of the carbon atom, which produces a linear molecule.

Molecules with Three VSEPR Electron Groups

Molecules with three VSEPR electron groups have two possible molecular structures: *trigonal planar* and *angular.* The former occurs when all three VSEPR electron groups are bonding and the latter when one of the three VSEPR electron groups is nonbonding. The molecules H_2CO (formaldehyde) and SO_2 (sulfur dioxide) illustrate these two possibilities. Their Lewis structures are

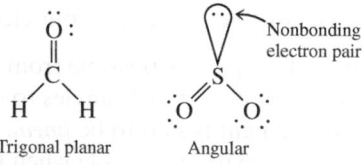

In both molecules, the VSEPR electron groups are found at the corners of an equilateral triangle.

The shape of the SO_2 molecule is described as *angular* rather than *trigonal planar,* because molecular geometry describes only *atom positions.* Although the positions of nonbonding electron groups are not taken into account in describing molecular geometry, this does not mean that nonbonding electron groups are unimportant in molecular geometry determinations; indeed, in the case of SO_2, it is the presence of the nonbonding electron group that makes the molecule angular rather than linear. ◄

Molecules with Four VSEPR Electron Groups

Molecules with four VSEPR electron groups have three possible molecular geometries: *tetrahedral* (no nonbonding electron groups present), *trigonal pyramidal* (one nonbonding electron group present), and *angular* (two nonbonding electron groups present). The molecules CH_4 (methane), NH_3 (ammonia), and H_2O (water) illustrate this sequence of molecular geometries. ◄

▶ *VSEPR electron group arrangement and molecular geometry are not the same when a central atom possesses nonbonding electron pairs. The word used to describe the molecular geometry in such cases does not include the positions of the nonbonding electron groups.*

▶ *"Dotted line" and "wedge" bonds can be used to indicate the directionality of bonds, as shown below.*

		Nonbonding electron group		Nonbonding electron groups

Tetrahedral   Trigonal pyramidal   Angular

Bond behind page	H	Bonds in the plane of the page

Bond in front of page

In all three molecules, the VSEPR electron groups arrange themselves at the corners of a tetrahedron. Again, note that the word used to describe the geometry of the molecule does not take into account the positioning of nonbonding electron groups.

Molecules with More Than One Central Atom

The molecular shape of molecules that contain more than one central atom can be obtained by considering each central atom separately and then combining the results. Let us apply this principle to the molecules C_2H_2 (acetylene), H_2O_2 (hydrogen peroxide), and HN_3 (hydrogen azide), all of which have a four-atom "chain" structure. Their Lewis structures and VSEPR electron group counts are as follows:

Acetylene   Hydrogen peroxide   Hydrogen azide

H—C≡C—H   H—O—O—H   H—N=N=N:

2 VSEPR electron groups	2 VSEPR electron groups	4 VSEPR electron groups	4 VSEPR electron groups	3 VSEPR electron groups	2 VSEPR electron groups
Linear C center	Linear C center	Angular O center	Angular O center	Angular N center	Linear N center

These three molecules thus have, respectively, zero bends, two bends, and one bend in their four-atom chain.

H—C≡C—H   O—O   N=N=N:

Zero bends in the chain	Two bends in the chain	One bend in the chain

Computer-generated three-dimensional models for these three molecules are given in Figure 5-9.

Chemistry at a Glance—The Geometry of Molecules—summarizes the key concepts involved in using VSEPR theory to predict molecular geometry.

For many years, scientists believed that molecular shape was the key factor that determined whether a substance possessed an odor. The shape of an odoriferous molecule was thought to be complementary to that of a receptor site on olfactory nerve endings within the nose. This explanation for odor is now considered to be an

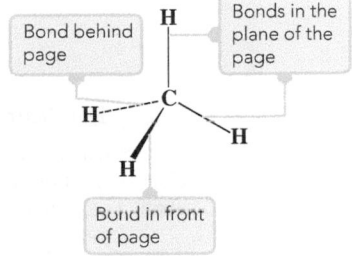

a The acetylene (C_2H_2) molecule.

b The hydrogen peroxide (H_2O_2) molecule.

c The hydrogen azide (HN_3) molecule.

Figure 5-9 Computer-generated models of (a) C_2H_2, (b) H_2O_2, and (c) HN_3.

oversimplification of what occurs within the nose as odor is perceived. The focus on relevancy feature Chemical Connections 5-B—The Chemical Sense of Smell—considers how scientific thought about odor has been modified in recent years.

CHEMISTRY
AT A GLANCE   The Geometry of Molecules

PREDICTING MOLECULAR GEOMETRY USING VSEPR THEORY

Operational rules
1. Draw a Lewis structure for the molecule.
2. Count the number of VSEPR electron groups about the central atom in the Lewis structure.
3. Assign a geometry based on minimizing repulsions between electron groups.

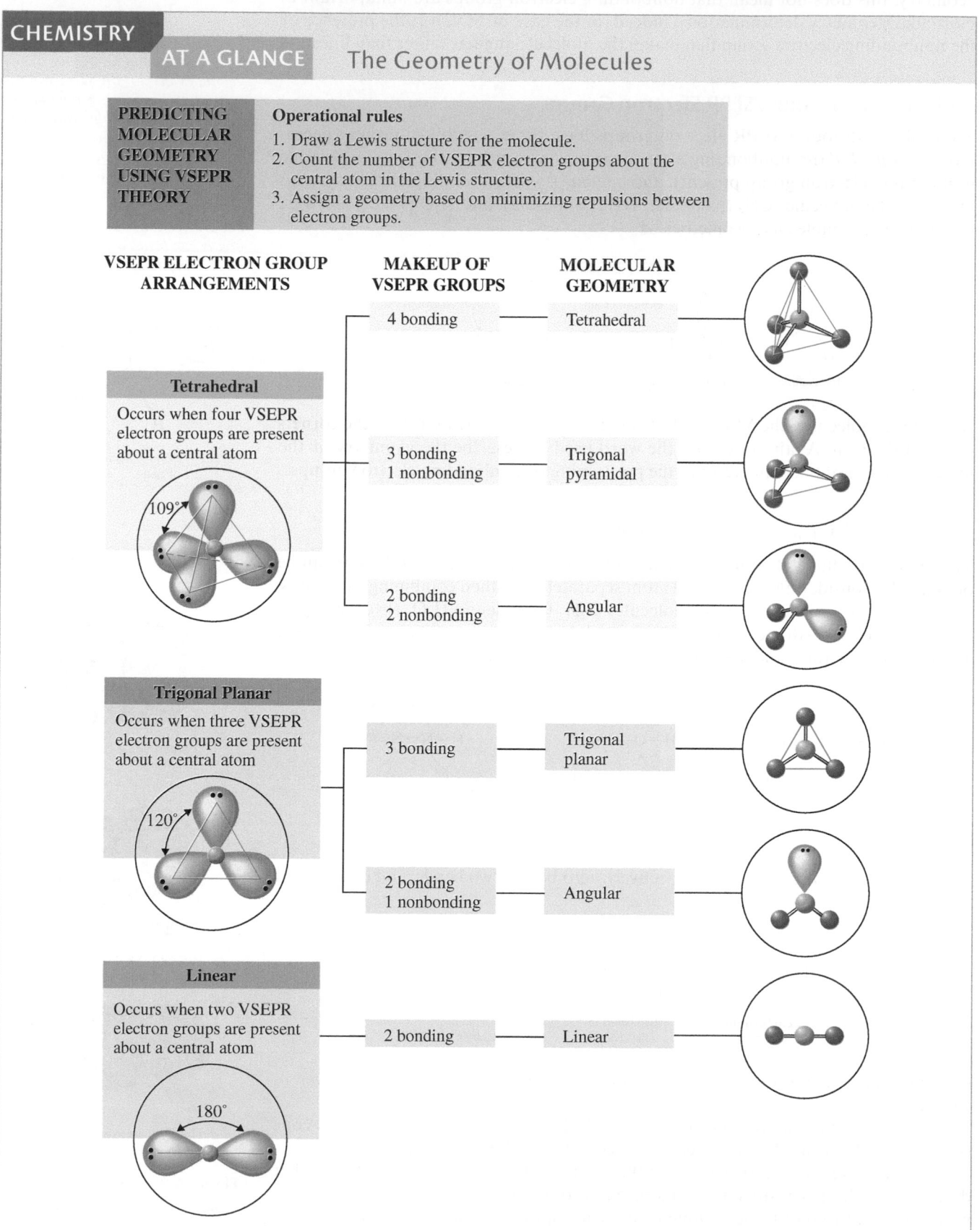

VSEPR ELECTRON GROUP ARRANGEMENTS | **MAKEUP OF VSEPR GROUPS** | **MOLECULAR GEOMETRY**

4 bonding	Tetrahedral

Tetrahedral
Occurs when four VSEPR electron groups are present about a central atom

109°

3 bonding 1 nonbonding	Trigonal pyramidal
2 bonding 2 nonbonding	Angular

Trigonal Planar
Occurs when three VSEPR electron groups are present about a central atom

120°

3 bonding	Trigonal planar
2 bonding 1 nonbonding	Angular

Linear
Occurs when two VSEPR electron groups are present about a central atom

180°

2 bonding	Linear

The Chemical Sense of Smell

Whether a chemical substance has an odor depends on whether it can excite (activate) olfactory receptor protein (ORP) sites in the nose. Factors that determine whether such excitation occurs include:

1. *Molecular volatility*. Odorant substances must be either gases or easily vaporized liquids or solids at room temperature; otherwise, the molecules of such substances would never reach the nose.
2. *Molecular solubility*. ORP sites in the nose are covered with *mucus,* an aqueous solution containing dissolved proteins and carbohydrates. Odorant molecules must, therefore, be somewhat water soluble in order to dissolve in the mucus. When a person has a cold, his or her sense of smell is diminished because odorant molecules cannot reach the ORPs as easily due to nasal congestion associated with the cold.
3. *Molecular geometry and polarity*. To interact with a given ORP, an incoming odorant must have a polarity and molecular shape that is compatible with the ORP.

The best known, but now seldom used, theory for explaining the sense of smell at a molecular level, first proposed in 1946, suggests that odor detection is related to an odorant having a molecular shape complementary to that of an activation site on an ORP (see the accompanying diagram).

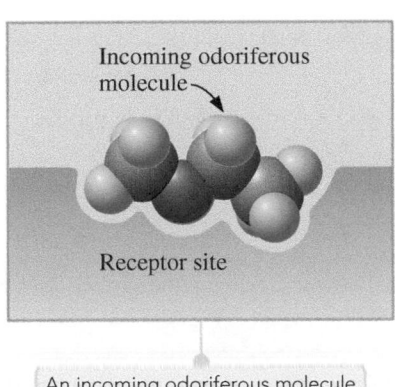

Incoming odoriferous molecule

Receptor site

An incoming odoriferous molecule must have a shape complementary to that of the receptor site.

This theory further suggests that every known odor can be made from a combination of seven primary odors (see the accompanying table) in much the same way that all colors can be made from the three primary colors of red, yellow, and blue. Associated with each of the primary odors is a particular molecular polarity and/or molecular geometry requirement.

Another aspect of this theory suggests that two substances with similar molecular shapes that fit the same receptor site should produce the same odor. This is true in many, but not all, cases. If different parts of a large molecule fit different receptor sites, the combined interactions should produce a "mixed" odor, different from any of the primary odors. Such is the case in many, but not all, situations.

Primary Odor	Familiar Substance with This Odor	Molecular Characteristics
ethereal	dry-cleaning fluid	rodlike shape
peppermint	mint candy	wedgelike shape
musk	some perfumes	disclike shape
camphoraceous	moth balls	spherical shape
floral	rose	disc with tail (kite) shape
pungent*	vinegar	negative polarity interaction
putrid*	skunk odor	positive polarity interaction

*These odors are less specific than are the other five odors, which indicates that they involve different interactions.

More recent research suggests that this "shape-odor theory" is too simplistic and is not valid in most respects. Odor perception is now known to be a much more complex process than that of an odorant interacting with a single receptor. Instead, incoming odorants are now thought to activate many receptors.

It is estimated that there are about 340 ORPs in humans, with these ORPs having the following characteristics.

1. Each ORP can recognize a limited number of odorants.
2. Each odorant can be detected by several different ORPs.
3. Different odorants are detected by different combinations (mixes) of ORPs.
4. Most odors are composed of multiple odorant molecules, and each odorant molecule activates several ORPs.

It is the mix of ORPs activated by an odorant that is of prime importance. Nerve impulses are sent from such a mix to the area of the brain responsible for smell. It is the pattern of signals arriving in the brain that constitute the "smell" of a molecule.

This activation of a mix of ORPs by a given odorant explains why humans can recognize 10,000 or more different odors despite having only about 340 ORPs. A small change in the structure of an odorant can generate a different "smell" because of the different mix of ORPs activated. Even a concentration change can alter the mix of activated ORPs.

The importance of odor detection should not be underestimated. Loss of the sense of smell is a serious handicap for both humans and animals. Without smell, warning signals such as smoke from a fire might not be detected. Some young animals use their sense of smell to find the teats of their mother and obtain milk. Adult animals observe and interpret their environment largely on the basis of smell. The enhanced capabilities that dogs have for smell, compared to humans, relates to the size of the area where ORPs are found; this area is approximately 40 times larger in dogs than in humans.

Section 5-8 Quick Quiz

1. In VSEPR theory, the geometric arrangement that minimizes repulsions among three valence electron pairs on a central atom is
   a. tetrahedral
   b. trigonal pyramid
   c. trigonal planar
   d. no correct response

2. In VSEPR theory, an angular molecular geometry is associated with molecules in which the central atom has
   a. three bonding groups and one nonbonding group
   b. two bonding groups and two nonbonding groups
   c. two bonding groups and zero nonbonding group
   d. no correct response

3. The molecular geometry associated with three bonding groups and one nonbonding group about a central atom is
   a. linear
   b. angular
   c. trigonal planar
   d. no correct response

4. Which of the following is not a possible molecular geometry for molecules that have four electron groups about a central atom?
   a. tetrahedral
   b. trigonal pyramidal
   c. trigonal planar
   d. no correct response

5. Which of the following molecules would have a linear geometry?
   a. H—Ö—H
   b. :Ö=C=Ö:
   c. :N=S—F̈:
   d. no correct response

Answers: 1. c; 2. b; 3. d; 4. c; 5. b

Figure 5-10 Linus Carl Pauling (1901–1994). Pauling received the Nobel Prize in chemistry in 1954 for his work on the nature of the chemical bond. In 1962, he received the Nobel Peace Prize in recognition of his efforts to end nuclear weapons testing.

5-9 Electronegativity

LEARNING FOCUS

Define the term *electronegativity*; know the relationship between the magnitude of an element's electronegativity and its periodic table location.

The ionic and covalent bonding models seem to represent two very distinct forms of bonding. Actually, the two models are closely related; they are the extremes of a broad continuum of bonding patterns. The close relationship between the two bonding models becomes apparent when the concepts of *electronegativity* (discussed in this section) and *bond polarity* (discussed in the next section) are considered.

The electronegativity concept has its origins in the fact that the nuclei of various elements have differing abilities to attract shared electrons (in a bond) to themselves. Some elements are better electron attractors than other elements. **Electronegativity** *is a measure of the relative attraction that an atom has for the shared electrons in a bond.*

Linus Pauling (Figure 5-10), whose contributions to chemical bonding theory earned him a Nobel Prize in chemistry, was the first chemist to develop a *numerical* scale of electronegativity. Figure 5-11 gives Pauling electronegativity values for the more frequently encountered representative elements. The higher the electronegativity value for an element, the greater the attraction of atoms of that element for the shared electrons in bonds. The element fluorine, whose Pauling electronegativity value is 4.0, is the most electronegative of all elements; that is, it possesses the greatest electron-attracting ability for electrons in a bond.

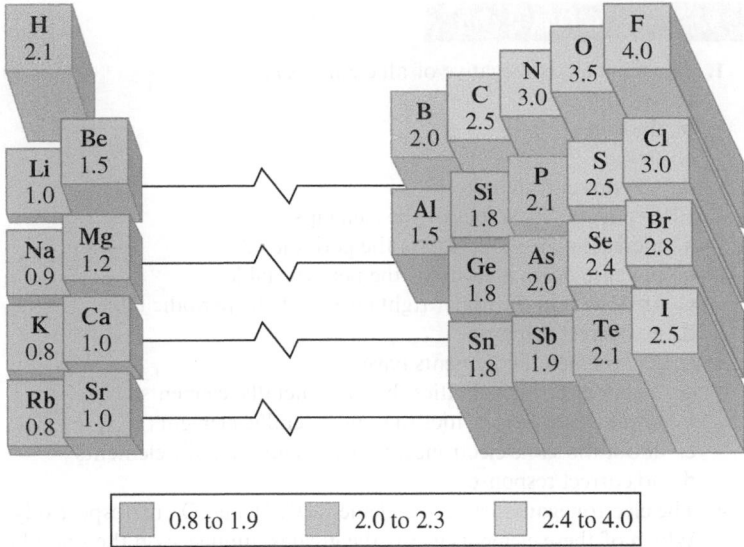

Figure 5-11 Abbreviated periodic table showing Pauling electronegativity values for selected representative elements.

As Figure 5-11 shows, electronegativity values increase from left to right across periods and from bottom to top within groups of the periodic table. These two trends result in nonmetals generally having higher electronegativities than metals. This fact is consistent with the generalization (Section 4-5) that metals tend to lose electrons and nonmetals tend to gain electrons when an ionic bond is formed. Metals (low electronegativities, poor electron attractors) give up electrons to nonmetals (high electronegativities, good electron attractors).

Note that the electronegativity of an element is not a directly measurable quantity. Rather, electronegativity values are calculated from bond energy information and other related experimental data. Values differ from element to element because of differences in atom size, nuclear charge, and number of inner-shell (nonvalence) electrons.

EXAMPLE 5-5

Predicting Electronegativity Relationships Using General Periodic Table Trends

Predict which member of each of the following pairs of elements has the greater electronegativity value based on periodic table electronegativity relationships.

a. Cl or Br   **b.** C or O   **c.** Li or K   **d.** Al or N

Solution

a. Cl and Br are in the same periodic table group, with Cl being above Br. Therefore Cl is the more electronegative element, as electronegativity decreases going down a group.

b. C and O are in the same periodic table period, with O being farther to the right. Therefore O has the greater electronegativity, as electronegativity increases going across a period.

c. Li and K are in the same group, with Li being two positions above K. Therefore Li is the more electronegative element, as electronegativity decreases going down a group.

d. Al is in Period 3, and N is in Period 2. The element P can be used as a "link" between the two elements. It is in the same period as Al and the same group as N. The periodic table period trend predicts that P is more electronegative than Al, and the periodic table group trend predicts that N is more electronegative than P. Therefore, N is more electronegative than Al.

Section 5-9 Quick Quiz

1. The most electronegative of all elements is
   a. sodium
   b. fluorine
   c. oxygen
   d. no correct response
2. Electronegativity values of the elements
   a. increase across a period in the periodic table
   b. increase down a group of the periodic table
   c. are lowest in the upper right corner of the periodic table
   d. no correct response
3. In general metallic elements have
   a. higher electronegativities than nonmetallic elements
   b. lower electronegativities than nonmetallic elements
   c. about the same electronegativities as nonmetallic elements
   d. no correct response
4. The electronegativities of the elements C, N, and O are, respectively, 2.5, 3.0, and 3.5. Which of these elements exerts the greatest influence on the shared electrons in a covalent bond.
   a. carbon
   b. oxygen
   c. nitrogen and oxygen exert about the same effect
   d. no correct response

Answers: 1. b; 2. a; 3. b; 4. b

5-10 Bond Polarity

LEARNING FOCUS

Use electronegativity values to classify a bond as *nonpolar covalent, polar covalent,* or *ionic* and to determine the bond polarity in terms of partial positive and partial negative charges.

The valence electrons present in a covalent chemical bond may be shared *equally* or shared *unequally* between the two atoms participating in the bond. **Bond polarity** *is a measure of the degree of inequality in the sharing of electrons between two atoms in a chemical bond.*

When two atoms of equal electronegativity share one or more pairs of electrons, each atom exerts the same attraction for the electrons, which results in the electrons being *equally* shared. This type of bond is called a nonpolar covalent bond. A **nonpolar covalent bond** *is a covalent bond in which there is equal sharing of electrons between two atoms.*

When the two atoms involved in a covalent bond have different electronegativities, the electron-sharing situation is more complex. The atom that has the higher electronegativity attracts the electrons more strongly than the other atom, which results in an *unequal* sharing of electrons. This type of covalent bond is called a polar covalent bond. A **polar covalent bond** *is a covalent bond in which there is unequal sharing of electrons between two atoms.* Figure 5-12 pictorially contrasts a nonpolar covalent bond and a polar covalent bond using the molecules H_2 and HCl.

The significance of unequal sharing of electrons in a polar covalent bond is that it creates fractional positive and negative charges on atoms. Although both atoms involved in a polar covalent bond are initially uncharged, the unequal sharing means that the electrons spend more time near the more electronegative atom of the bond (producing a fractional negative charge) and less time near the less electronegative atom of the bond (producing a fractional positive charge). The presence of such fractional charges on atoms within a molecule often significantly affects molecular properties (see Section 5-11).

Figure 5-12 The symmetrical distribution of electron density in a nonpolar covalent bond contrasted with the unsymmetrical distribution of electron density in a polar covalent bond.

In the nonpolar covalent bond present in H_2 (H—H), there is a symmetrical distribution of electron density between the two atoms; that is, equal sharing of electrons occurs.

In the polar covalent bond present in HCl (H—Cl), electron density is displaced toward the Cl atom because of its greater electronegativity; that is, unequal sharing of electrons occurs.

Bond Polarity and Fractional Charges

The fractional charges associated with atoms involved in a polar covalent bond are always values less than 1 because complete electron transfer does not occur. Complete electron transfer, which produces an ionic bond, would produce charges of 1+ and 1−. A notation that involves the lowercase Greek letter delta (δ) is used to denote fractional charge. The symbol δ^-, meaning "fractional negative charge," is placed above the more electronegative atom of the bond, and the symbol δ^+, meaning "fractional positive charge," is placed above the less electronegative atom of the bond. ◄

With delta notation, the direction of polarity of the bond in hydrogen chloride (HCl) is depicted as

$$\overset{\delta^+}{H}\!-\!\overset{\delta^-}{\underset{..}{\overset{..}{Cl}}}\!:$$

Chlorine is the more electronegative of the two elements; it dominates the electron-sharing process and draws the shared electrons closer to itself. Hence the chlorine end of the bond has the δ^- designation (the more electronegative element always has the δ^- designation).

The direction of polarity of a polar covalent bond can also be designated by using an arrow whose tail has a perpendicular line through it.

$$\longmapsto$$

The head of the arrow is positioned above the more electronegative element, and the tail is positioned above the less electronegative element. Using this arrow notation, the polar bond associated with the HCl molecule is denoted as

$$\overset{\longmapsto}{H}\!-\!\overset{..}{\underset{..}{Cl}}\!:$$

An extension of the reasoning used in characterizing the covalent bond in the HCl molecule as polar leads to the generalization that most chemical bonds are not 100% covalent (equal sharing) or 100% ionic (no sharing). Instead, most bonds are somewhere in between (unequal sharing).

▶ *The δ^+ and δ^- symbols are pronounced "delta plus" and "delta minus." Whatever the magnitude of δ^+, it must be the same as that of δ^- because the sum of δ^+ and δ^- must be zero.*

The notation δ^+ means an atom is "electron deficient"; that is, it has a partial positive charge. The notation δ^- means an atom is "electron rich"; that is, it has a partial negative charge. The partial charges result from the unequal sharing of the electrons involved in a bond.

EXAMPLE 5-6

Using Delta Notation to Specify the Direction of Bond Polarity

For the following polar covalent bonds, specify the direction of bond polarity using delta notation.

a. oxygen–sulfur bond　　**b.** phosphorus–fluorine bond

(continued)

Solution

a. Oxygen has an electronegativity of 3.0 and that of sulfur is 2.5 (Figure 5-11). Thus, oxygen has the greater electron attracting ability for the shared electrons in the bond and these electrons will move toward the oxygen atom. The movement (unequal sharing of electrons) produces a fractional negative charge on the O atom (the more electronegative atom) and a fractional positive charge on the S atom (the less electronegative atom). Using delta notation, this situation is diagrammed in the following manner:

$$\overset{\delta^-}{\text{O}}\!-\!\overset{\delta^+}{\text{S}}$$

b. Analyzing this bonding situation in a manner similar to that done in part **a**, it is found that the electronegativity of F (4.0) exceeds that of P (2.1). The unequal sharing that results from the electronegativity difference causes the more electronegative F atom to have a fractional negative charge and the less electronegative P atom to have a fractional positive charge. The delta notation for this bond is

$$\overset{\delta^+}{\text{P}}\!-\!\overset{\delta^-}{\text{F}}$$

Bond Classification Based on Electronegativity Difference

The numerical value of the electronegativity difference between two bonded atoms gives an approximate measure of the polarity of the bond. The greater the numerical difference, the greater the inequality of electron sharing and the greater the polarity of the bond. As the polarity of the bond increases, the bond is increasingly ionic.

The existence of *bond polarity* means that there is no natural boundary between ionic and covalent bonding. Most bonds are a mixture of pure ionic and pure covalent bonds; that is, unequal sharing of electrons occurs. Most bonds have both ionic and covalent character. Nevertheless, it is still convenient to use the terms *ionic* and *covalent* in describing chemical bonds, based on the following arbitrary but useful (though not infallible) guidelines, which relate to electronegativity difference between bonded atoms.

1. Bonds that involve atoms with the same or very similar electronegativities are called *nonpolar covalent bonds.* "Similar" here means an electronegativity difference of 0.4 or less.

   Technically, the only purely nonpolar covalent bonds are those between identical atoms. However, bonds with a small electronegativity difference behave very similarly to purely nonpolar covalent bonds.
2. Bonds with an electronegativity difference greater that 0.4 but less than 1.5 are called *polar covalent bonds.*
3. Bonds with an electronegativity difference greater than 2.0 are called *ionic bonds.*
4. Bonds with an electronegativity difference between 1.5 and 2.0 are considered *ionic* if the bond involves a metal and a nonmetal, and *polar covalent* if the bond involves two nonmetals. In the 1.5–2.0 range of electronegativity difference, some compounds exhibit characteristics associated with ionic compounds and others exhibit characteristics associated with molecular compounds (see Sections 4-1 and 5-1). This rule helps in dealing with this "borderline" area.

Figure 5-13 summarizes diagrammatically the concepts associated with the "bond polarity rules" just considered.

Chemistry at a Glance—Covalent Bonds and Molecular Compounds— summarizes that which has been covered so far in this chapter about chemical bonds.

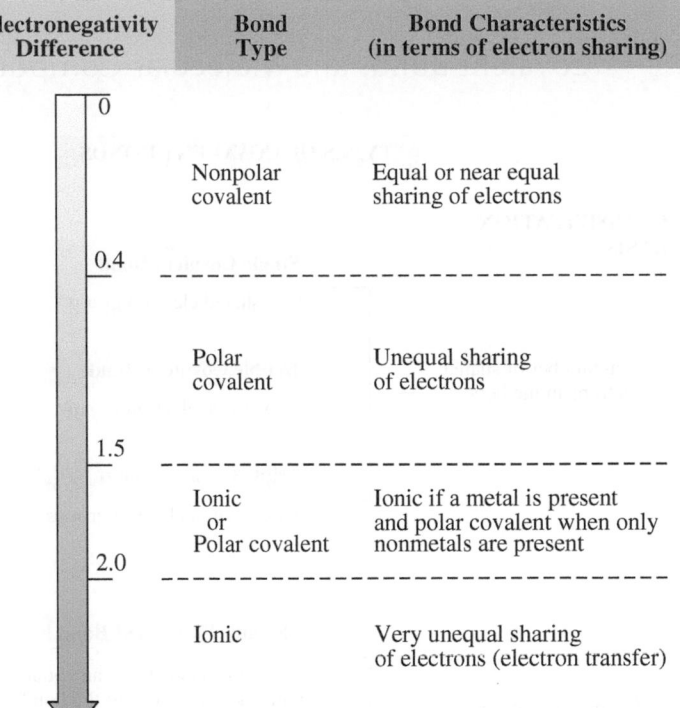

Electronegativity Difference	Bond Type	Bond Characteristics (in terms of electron sharing)
0		
	Nonpolar covalent	Equal or near equal sharing of electrons
0.4		
	Polar covalent	Unequal sharing of electrons
1.5		
	Ionic or Polar covalent	Ionic if a metal is present and polar covalent when only nonmetals are present
2.0		
	Ionic	Very unequal sharing of electrons (electron transfer)

Figure 5-13 Chemical bond type classification based on electronegativity difference.

EXAMPLE 5-7

Using Electronegativity Difference to Predict Chemical Bond Type

Classify each of the following chemical bonds as *nonpolar covalent, polar covalent,* or *ionic.*

a. Ca—O   **b.** N—P   **c.** B—H   **d.** F—I

Solution

a. From Figure 5-11, the electronegativity of Ca is 1.0 and that of O is 3.5. The electronegativity difference is

$$3.5 - 1.0 = 2.5$$

Rule 3 of the bond classification rules applies in this situation. It indicates that bonds where the electronegativity difference is greater than 2.0 are considered to be *ionic*.

b. From Figure 5-11, the electronegativity of N is 3.0 and that of P is 2.1. The electronegativity difference is

$$3.0 - 2.1 = 0.9$$

Rule 2 of the bond classification rules indicates that bonds where the electronegativity difference is greater than 0.4 but less than 1.5 are considered to be *polar covalent* bonds.

c. Similarly, the electronegativity difference between B (2.0) and H (2.1) is 0.1. Rule 1 of the bond type rules indicates that bonds with an electronegativity difference of 0.4 or less are considered to be *nonpolar covalent.*

d. The electronegativity of F is 4.0 and that of I is 2.5. A electronegativity difference of 1.5 is covered by Rule 4 of the bond type rules. For differences in the range 1.5 to 2.0 some bonds are considered to be ionic and others to be polar covalent. If the bond involves a metal and nonmetal, the ionic classification is used and if the bond involves two nonmetals the polar covalent classification is used. The latter situation applies to a F—I bond, as both of these elements are nonmetals. Thus the bond classification is *polar covalent.*

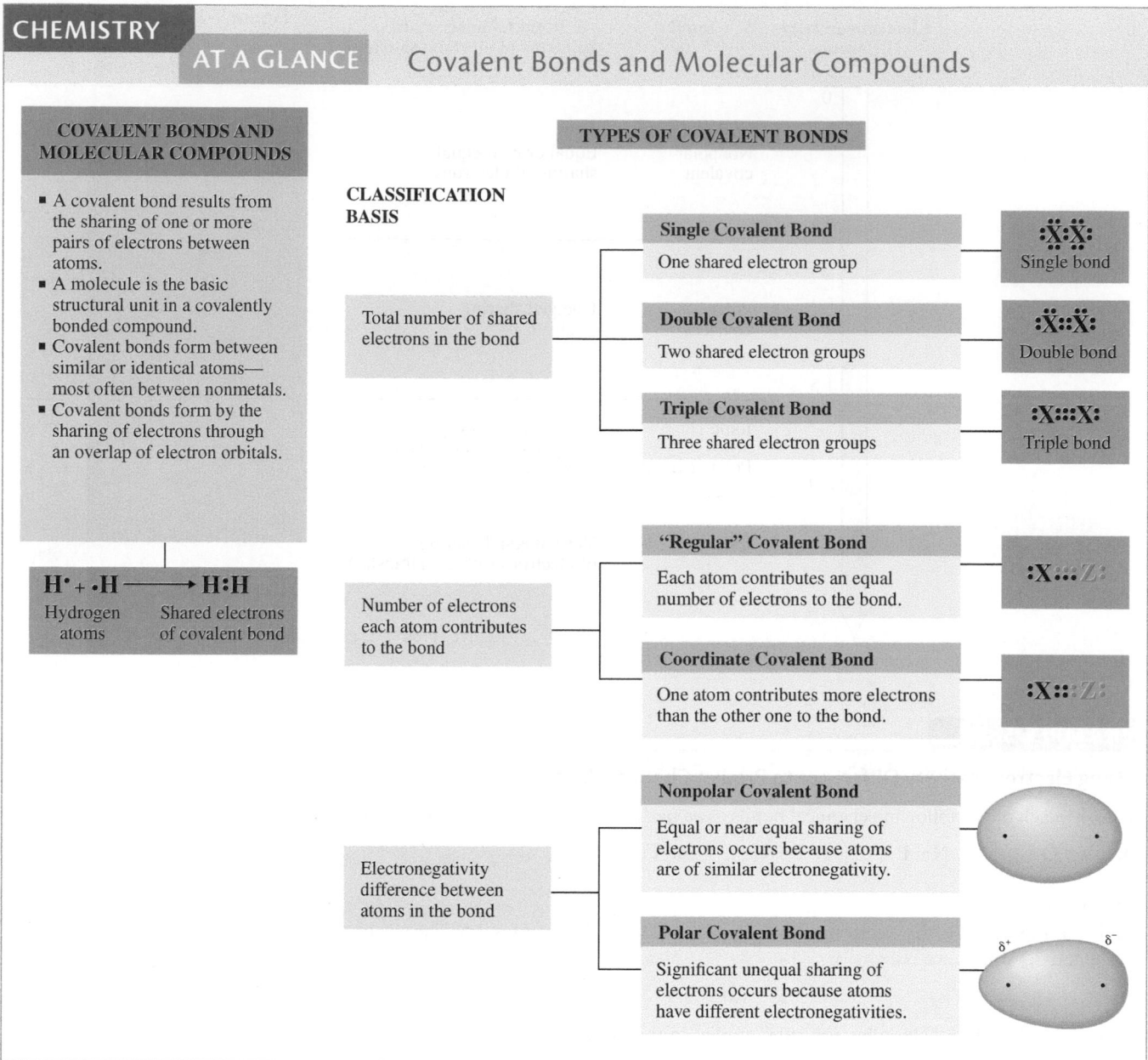

CHEMISTRY
AT A GLANCE Covalent Bonds and Molecular Compounds

COVALENT BONDS AND MOLECULAR COMPOUNDS

- A covalent bond results from the sharing of one or more pairs of electrons between atoms.
- A molecule is the basic structural unit in a covalently bonded compound.
- Covalent bonds form between similar or identical atoms— most often between nonmetals.
- Covalent bonds form by the sharing of electrons through an overlap of electron orbitals.

H· + ·H ⟶ H:H
Hydrogen atoms / Shared electrons of covalent bond

TYPES OF COVALENT BONDS

CLASSIFICATION BASIS

Total number of shared electrons in the bond

Single Covalent Bond
One shared electron group
:X:X:
Single bond

Double Covalent Bond
Two shared electron groups
:X::X:
Double bond

Triple Covalent Bond
Three shared electron groups
:X:::X:
Triple bond

Number of electrons each atom contributes to the bond

"Regular" Covalent Bond
Each atom contributes an equal number of electrons to the bond.
:X:::Z:

Coordinate Covalent Bond
One atom contributes more electrons than the other one to the bond.
:X::Z:

Electronegativity difference between atoms in the bond

Nonpolar Covalent Bond
Equal or near equal sharing of electrons occurs because atoms are of similar electronegativity.

Polar Covalent Bond
Significant unequal sharing of electrons occurs because atoms have different electronegativities.
δ^+ δ^-

Section 5-10 Quick Quiz

1. The concept of electronegativity can be used to determine
   a. the number of electrons present in a bond
   b. whether a bond is coordinate covalent or not
   c. the relative attraction of an atom for shared electrons in a bond
   d. no correct response
2. A chemical bond for which the electronegativity difference between atoms is 1.2 is classified as a(n)
   a. ionic bond
   b. polar covalent bond
   c. nonpolar covalent bond
   d. no correct response

3. The degree of inequality in electron sharing for a nonpolar covalent bond is
   a. very small or zero
   b. very large
   c. moderately large to very large
   d. no correct response
4. As the difference in electronegativity between two bonded atoms decreases the bond becomes more
   a. ionic
   b. covalent
   c. polar
   d. no correct response
5. In a polar covalent bond the atom of greater electronegativity bears a
   a. fractional positive charge
   b. fractional negative charge
   c. full positive charge
   d. no correct response
6. In a polar covalent bond the notation called a "delta plus symbol" is assigned to
   a. all atoms with electronegativity greater than 1.5
   b. the atom with the largest electronegativity
   c. the atom with the smallest electronegativity
   d. no correct response

Answers: 1. c; 2. b; 3. a; 4. b; 5. b; 6. c

5-11 Molecular Polarity

LEARNING FOCUS
Given its molecular geometry, predict whether a molecule is polar or nonpolar.

Molecules, as well as bonds (Section 5-10), can have polarity. **Molecular polarity** *is a measure of the degree of inequality in the attraction of bonding electrons to various locations within a molecule.* In terms of electron attraction, if one part of a molecule is favored over other parts, then the molecule is *polar.* A **polar molecule** *is a molecule in which there is an unsymmetrical distribution of electronic charge.* In a polar molecule, bonding electrons are more attracted to one part of the molecule than to other parts. A **nonpolar molecule** *is a molecule in which there is a symmetrical distribution of electron charge.* Attraction for bonding electrons is the same in all parts of a *nonpolar* molecule. Molecular polarity depends on two factors: (1) bond polarities and (2) molecular geometry (Section 5-8). In molecules that are symmetrical, the effects of polar bonds may cancel each other, resulting in the molecule as a whole having no polarity. ◀

▶ *A prerequisite for determining molecular polarity is a knowledge of molecular geometry.*

Determining the molecular polarity of a diatomic molecule is simple because only one bond is present. If that bond is nonpolar, then the molecule is nonpolar; if the bond is polar, then the molecule is polar.

Determining molecular polarity for triatomic molecules is more complicated. Two different molecular geometries are possible: linear and angular. In addition, the symmetrical nature of the molecule must be considered. The following discussion of the polarities of three specific triatomic molecules—CO_2, H_2O, and HCN—shows the interplay between molecular geometry and molecular symmetry in determining molecular polarity.

In the linear CO_2 molecule, both bonds are polar (oxygen is more electronegative than carbon). Despite the presence of these polar bonds, CO_2 molecules are *nonpolar.* The effects of the two polar bonds are canceled as a result of the oxygen atoms being arranged symmetrically around the carbon atom. ◀ The shift of electronic charge toward one oxygen atom is exactly compensated for by the shift of electronic charge

▶ *Molecules in which all bonds are polar can be nonpolar if the bonds are so oriented in space that the polarity effects cancel each other.*

toward the other oxygen atom. Thus one end of the molecule is not negatively charged relative to the other end (a requirement for polarity), and the molecule is nonpolar. This cancellation of individual bond polarities, with crossed arrows used to denote the polarities, is diagrammed as follows:

$$\overset{\longleftarrow+\;\;\longmapsto}{O=C=O}$$

The nonlinear (angular) triatomic H_2O molecule is polar. The bond polarities associated with the two hydrogen–oxygen bonds do not cancel one another because of the nonlinearity of the molecule.

$$\underset{H\qquad H}{\overset{O}{\diagup\;\diagdown}}$$

As a result of their orientation, both bonds contribute to an accumulation of negative charge on the oxygen atom. The two bond polarities are equal in magnitude but are not opposite in direction.

It is tempting to make the generalization that linear triatomic molecules are nonpolar and angular triatomic molecules are nonpolar based on the preceding discussion of CO_2 and H_2O polarities. This generalization is not valid. The linear molecule HCN, which is polar, invalidates this statement. Both bond polarities contribute to nitrogen's acquiring a partial negative charge relative to hydrogen in HCN.

$$\overset{\longmapsto\;\;\longmapsto}{H-C\equiv N}$$

(The two polarity arrows point in the same direction because nitrogen is more electronegative than carbon, and carbon is more electronegative than hydrogen.)

Molecules that contain four and five atoms commonly have trigonal planar and tetrahedral geometries, respectively. Such molecules in which all of the atoms attached to the central atom are identical, such as SO_3 (trigonal planar) and CH_4 (tetrahedral), are *nonpolar*. The individual bond polarities cancel as a result of the highly symmetrical arrangement of atoms around the central atom.

If two or more kinds of atoms are attached to the central atom in a trigonal planar or tetrahedral molecule, the molecule is polar. The high degree of symmetry required for cancellation of the individual bond polarities is no longer present. For example, if one of the hydrogen atoms in CH_4 (a nonpolar molecule) is replaced by a chlorine atom, then a polar molecule results, even though the resulting CH_3Cl is still a tetrahedral molecule. A carbon–chlorine bond has a greater polarity than a carbon–hydrogen bond; chlorine has an electronegativity of 3.0, and hydrogen has an electronegativity of only 2.1. Figure 5-14 contrasts the polar CH_3Cl and nonpolar CH_4 molecules. Note that the direction of polarity of the carbon–chlorine bond is opposite that of the carbon–hydrogen bonds.

Figure 5-14 The polarity of a molecule depends not only on its molecular geometry but also on whether the atoms attached to the central atom are all alike or of differing identity.

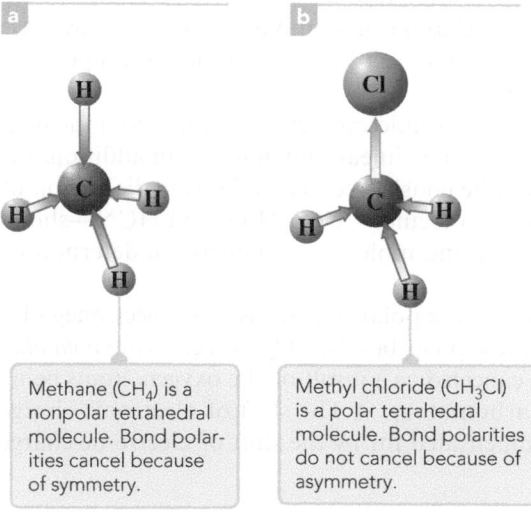

Methane (CH_4) is a nonpolar tetrahedral molecule. Bond polarities cancel because of symmetry.

Methyl chloride (CH_3Cl) is a polar tetrahedral molecule. Bond polarities do not cancel because of asymmetry.

EXAMPLE 5-8

Predicting the Polarity of Molecules Given Their Molecular Geometry

Predict the polarity of each of the following molecules.

a. PF_3 (trigonal pyramidal)   **b.** SCl_2 (angular)

c. $SiBr_4$ (tetrahedral)   **d.** C_2Cl_2 (linear)

Solution

Knowledge of a molecule's geometry, which is given for each molecule in this example, is a prerequisite for predicting molecular polarity.

a. Noncancellation of the individual bond polarities in the trigonal pyramidal PF_3 molecule results in it being a *polar* molecule.

The bond polarity arrows all point toward fluorine atoms because fluorine is more electronegative than phosphorus.

b. For the bent SCl_2 molecule, the shift in electron density in the polar sulfur–chlorine bonds will be toward the chlorine atoms because chlorine is more electronegative than sulfur. The SCl_2 molecule as a whole is *polar* because of the noncancellation of the individual sulfur–chlorine bond polarities.

c. The $SiBr_4$ molecule is a tetrahedral molecule, and all four atoms attached to the central atom (Si) are the same. This, and the highly symmetrical nature of a tetrahedral geometry (all bond angles are the same), means that the Si—Br bond polarities cancel each other and the molecule as a whole is *nonpolar*.

d. The carbon–carbon bond is nonpolar. The two carbon–chlorine bonds are polar and are "equal but opposite" in terms of effect; that is, they cancel. The C_2Cl_2 molecule as a whole is thus *nonpolar*.

Section 5-11 Quick Quiz

1. In a polar molecule there is
   a. an unsymmetrical distribution of electronic charge
   b. a symmetrical distribution of electronic charge
   c. an equal attraction for bonding electrons in all parts of the molecule
   d. no correct response

2. Molecules containing polar covalent bonds
   a. are always polar
   b. can be polar or nonpolar depending on molecular geometry
   c. cannot be nonpolar
   d. no correct response

(continued)

3. Which of the following diatomic molecules is polar?
 a. H_2
 b. F_2
 c. N_2
 d. no correct response
4. Which of the following molecules, all of which are linear, is nonpolar?
 a. carbon dioxide (OCO)
 b. hydrogen cyanide (HCN)
 c. dinitrogen monoxide (NNO)
 d. no correct response
5. Based on the given molecular geometry, which of the following molecules is nonpolar?
 a. NF_3 (trigonal pyramidal)
 b. CH_4 (tetrahedral)
 c. H_2S (angular)
 d. no correct response

Answers: 1. a; 2. b; 3. d; 4. a; 5. b

5-12 Recognizing and Naming Binary Molecular Compounds

LEARNING FOCUS

Name a binary molecular compound given its chemical formula or vice versa.

A **binary molecular compound** *is a molecular compound in which only two nonmetallic elements are present.* The names of binary molecular compounds are derived by using a rule very similar to that used for naming binary ionic compounds (Section 4-9). However, one major difference exists. Names for binary molecular compounds usually contain numerical prefixes that give the number of each type of atom present in addition to the names of the elements present. This is in direct contrast to binary ionic compound nomenclature, where formula subscripts are never mentioned in the names.

The rule used when constructing the name of a binary molecular compound is: *The full name of the nonmetal of lower electronegativity is given first, followed by a separate word containing the stem of the name of the more electronegative nonmetal and the suffix -ide. Numerical prefixes, giving numbers of atoms, precede the names of both nonmetals.* ◀

▶ *Numerical prefixes are used in naming binary molecular compounds. They are never used, however, in naming binary ionic compounds.*

Prefixes are necessary because several different compounds exist for most pairs of nonmetals. For example, the following nitrogen–oxygen compounds exist: NO, NO_2, N_2O, N_2O_3, N_2O_4, and N_2O_5. Such diverse behavior between two elements is related to the fact that single, double, and triple covalent bonds exist. Prefix use is required to give each compound a distinct name. Representative of such prefix use is the name *dinitrogen pentoxide* for the compound N_2O_5 and the name *dinitrogen trioxide* for the compound N_2O_3.

In using the numerical prefixes, the prefix *mono-* is treated in a way different from the other prefixes. It is never used to modify the name of the first element in the compound's name, but is used to modify the name of the second element in the compound's name. Thus, the name of the compound CO is carbon monoxide rather than monocarbon monoxide, and the name of the compound CO_2 is carbon dioxide rather than monocarbon dioxide.

Table 5-1 gives the standard numerical prefixes for the numbers 1 through 10, as well as an example of each prefix used in the name of a binary molecular compound. Example 5-9 gives further examples of the use of numerical prefixes in the context of binary molecular compound nomenclature.

▶ *In Section 10-3, it will be explained that placing hydrogen first in a formula indicates that the compound behaves as an acid in aqueous solution.*

There is one standard exception to the use of numerical prefixes when naming binary molecular compounds. Compounds in which hydrogen is the first listed element in the formula are named without numerical prefixes. Thus the compounds H_2S and HCl are hydrogen sulfide and hydrogen chloride, respectively. ◀

▶ Table 5-1 **Numerical Prefixes for the Numbers 1 Through 10**

Number	Numerical Prefix	Example of Prefix Use*	
1	mono-	CO	carbon monoxide
2	di-	O_2F_2	dioxygen difluoride
3	tri-	PCl_3	phosphorus trichloride
4	tetra-	N_2O_4	dinitrogen tetroxide
5	penta-	ClF_5	chlorine pentafluoride
6	hexa-	I_2F_6	diiodine hexafluoride
7	hepta-	IF_7	iodine heptafluoride
8	octa-	P_4O_8	tetraphosphorus octoxide
9	nona-	P_4S_9	tetraphosphorus nonasulfide
10	deca-	P_4Se_{10}	tetraphosphorus decaselenide

* When the prefix ends in "a" or "o" and the element name begins with "a" or "o," the final vowel of the prefix is usually dropped for ease of pronunciation. For example, "monoxide" is used instead of "monooxide," and "hexoxide" is used instead of "hexaoxide."

A few binary molecular compounds have names that are completely unrelated to the naming rules just discussed. They have common names that were coined prior to the development of systematic rules. At one time, in the early history of chemistry, all compounds had common names. With the advent of systematic nomenclature, most common names were discontinued. A few, however, have persisted and are now officially accepted. The most "famous" example is the compound H_2O, which has the systematic name *hydrogen oxide*, a name that is never used. The compound H_2O is *water,* a name that will never change. Table 5-2 lists other compounds for which common names are used in preference to systematic names.

▶ Table 5-2 **Selected Binary Molecular Compounds That Have Common Names**

Compound Formula	Accepted Common Name
H_2O	water
H_2O_2	hydrogen peroxide
NH_3	ammonia
N_2H_4	hydrazine
CH_4	methane
C_2H_6	ethane
N_2O	nitrous oxide
NO	nitric oxide

EXAMPLE 5-9

Naming Binary Molecular Compounds ◀

Name the following binary molecular compounds.

a. S_2Cl_2 **b.** CS_2 **c.** P_4O_{10} **d.** HBr

Solution

The names of each of these compounds will consist of two words. These words will have the following general formats:

$$\text{First word: } (\text{prefix}) + \left(\begin{array}{c}\text{full name of least}\\\text{electronegative nonmetal}\end{array}\right)$$

$$\text{Second word: } (\text{prefix}) + \left(\begin{array}{c}\text{stem of name of more}\\\text{electronegative nonmetal}\end{array}\right) + (\text{ide})$$

a. The elements present are sulfur and chlorine. The two portions of the name (including prefixes) are *disulfur* and *dichloride,* which are combined to give the name *disulfur dichloride.*

b. When only one atom of the first nonmetal is present, it is customary to omit the initial prefix *mono-.* Thus the name of this compound is *carbon disulfide.*

c. The prefix for four atoms is *tetra-* and for ten atoms is *deca-.* This compound has the name *tetraphosphorus decoxide.*

d. Binary molecular compounds in which hydrogen is the first listed element in the chemical formula are always named without any prefix use. The name of this compound is *hydrogen bromide.*

▶ *Classification of a compound as ionic or molecular determines which set of nomenclature rules is used. For* nomenclature purposes, *binary compounds in which a metal and a nonmetal are present are considered ionic, and binary compounds that contain two nonmetals are considered covalent. Electronegativity differences are* not *used in classifying a compound as ionic or molecular for nomenclature purposes.*

Section 5-12 Quick Quiz

1. Which of the following compounds is a binary molecular compound?
   a. HCN
   b. NaCl
   c. CO_2
   d. no correct response

2. Names for binary molecular compounds, except for a few common names, always
   a. end with the suffix -ide
   b. contain two numerical prefixes
   c. contain one numerical prefix
   d. no correct response

3. In which of the following situations is an incorrect numerical prefix present in the compound's name?
   a. N_2O_3—dinitrogen trioxide
   b. NO_2—nitrogen dioxide
   c. N_2O_5—dinitrogen tetroxide
   d. no correct response

4. Which of the following is the correct name for the compound CO?
   a. monocarbon monoxide
   b. carbon monoxide
   c. carbon oxide
   d. no correct response

5. Which of the following is the correct name for the compound HF?
   a. monohydrogen monofluoride
   b. hydrogen monofluoride
   c. hydrogen fluoride
   d. no correct response

6. Which of the following binary molecular compounds is paired with an incorrect common name?
   a. NO—nitric oxide
   b. NH_3—hydrazine
   c. H_2O_2—hydrogen peroxide
   d. no correct response

Answers: 1. c; 2. a; 3. c; 4. b; 5. c; 6. b

Concepts to Remember

Molecular compounds. Molecular compounds usually involve two or more nonmetals. The covalent bonds within molecular compounds involve electron sharing between atoms. The covalent bond results from the common attraction of the two nuclei for the shared electrons (Section 5-1).

Bonding and nonbonding electron pairs. Bonding electrons are pairs of valence electrons that are shared between atoms in a covalent bond. Nonbonding electrons are pairs of valence electrons about an atom that are not involved in electron sharing (Section 5-2).

Types of covalent bonds. One shared pair of electrons constitutes a single covalent bond. Two or three pairs of electrons may be shared between atoms to give double and triple covalent bonds. Most often, both atoms of the bond contribute an equal number of electrons to the bond. In a few cases, however, both electrons of a shared pair come from the same atom; this is a coordinate covalent bond (Sections 5-3 and 5-5).

Number of covalent bonds formed. There is a strong tendency for nonmetals to form a particular number of covalent bonds. The number of valence electrons the nonmetal has and the number of covalent bonds it forms give a sum of 8 (Section 5-4).

Molecular geometry. Molecular geometry describes the way atoms in a molecule are arranged in space relative to one another. VSEPR theory is a set of procedures used to predict molecular geometry from a compound's Lewis structure. VSEPR theory is based on the concept that valence shell electron groups about an atom (bonding or nonbonding) orient themselves as far away from one another as possible (to minimize repulsions) (Section 5-8).

Electronegativity. Electronegativity is a measure of the relative attraction that an atom has for the shared electrons in a bond. Electronegativity values are useful in predicting the type of bond that forms (ionic or covalent) (Section 5-9).

Bond polarity. When atoms of like electronegativity participate in a bond, the bonding electrons are equally shared and the bond is nonpolar. When atoms of differing electronegativity participate in a bond, the bonding electrons are unequally shared and the bond is polar. In a polar bond, the more electronegative atom dominates the sharing process. The greater the electronegativity difference between two bonded atoms, the greater the polarity of the bond (Section 5-10).

Molecular polarity. Molecules as a whole can have polarity. If individual bond polarities do not cancel because of the symmetrical nature of a molecule, then the molecule as a whole is polar (Section 5-11).

Binary molecular compound nomenclature. Names for binary molecular compounds usually contain numerical prefixes that give the number of each type of atom present per molecule in addition to the names of the elements (Section 5-12).

Exercises and problems are arranged in matched pairs with the two members of a pair addressing the same concept(s). The answer to the odd-numbered member of a pair is given at the back of the book. Problems denoted with a ▲ involve concepts found not only in the section under consideration but also concepts found in one or more earlier sections of the chapter.

The Covalent Bond Model (Section 5-1)

5-1 Contrast the types of elements involved in ionic and covalent bonds.

5-2 Contrast the mechanisms by which ionic and covalent bonds form.

5-3 Contrast the basic structural unit in ionic and molecular compounds.

5-4 Contrast the general physical state at room temperature and room pressure for ionic and molecular compounds.

5-5 Indicate whether or not covalent bond formation is likely between each of the following pairs of atoms.
a. two N atoms
b. a H atom and a F atom
c. two Cl atoms
d. a Cu atom and an O atom

5-6 Indicate whether or not covalent bond formation is likely between each of the following pairs of atoms.
a. two F atoms
b. a H atom and a S atom
c. two O atoms
d. an Al atom and a N atom

Lewis Structures for Molecular Compounds (Section 5-2)

5-7 Draw Lewis structures to illustrate the covalent bonding in the following diatomic molecules.
a. Cl_2
b. HCl
c. BrCl
d. ClF

5-8 Draw Lewis structures to illustrate the covalent bonding in the following diatomic molecules.
a. Br_2
b. HBr
c. BrF
d. IBr

5-9 How many nonbonding electron pairs are present in each of the following Lewis structures?

a. $:\ddot{F}:\ddot{S}:\ddot{F}:$

b. $H:\ddot{O}:\ddot{O}:H$

c. $H:\overset{H}{\underset{H}{\overset{..}{C}}}:H$

d. $:\ddot{Cl}:\overset{H}{\underset{H}{C}}:\ddot{Cl}:$

5-10 How many nonbonding electron pairs are present in each of the following Lewis structures?

a. $H:\ddot{O}:\ddot{Cl}:$

b. $:\ddot{Cl}:\ddot{O}:\ddot{Cl}:$

c. $H:\overset{..}{\underset{H}{N}}:H$

d. $H:\ddot{N}:\overset{H}{\underset{H}{\ddot{N}}}:H$

5-11 The component elements for four binary molecular compounds are shown with different colors on the following periodic table.

What is the chemical formula for the simplest compound likely to be formed in each case?
a. Red compound
b. Blue compound
c. Yellow compound
d. Green compound

5-12 The component elements for four binary molecular compounds are shown with different colors on the following periodic table.

What is the chemical formula for the simplest compound likely to be formed in each case?
a. Blue compound
b. Green compound
c. Yellow compound
d. Red compound

Single, Double, and Triple Covalent Bonds (Section 5-3)

5-13 Specify the number of single, double, and triple covalent bonds present in molecules represented by the following Lewis structures.

a. $:N:::N:$

b. $H:\ddot{O}:\ddot{O}:H$

c. $H:\overset{..}{\underset{:\ddot{O}:}{C}}:H$

d. $H:\overset{..}{C}::\overset{..}{C}:H$ with H H below

5-14 Specify the number of single, double, and triple covalent bonds present in molecules represented by the following Lewis structures.

a. $:C:::O:$

b. $H:\ddot{N}:\overset{H}{\underset{H}{\ddot{N}}}:H$

c. $:\ddot{O}:\overset{..}{\underset{:\ddot{O}:}{S}}:\ddot{O}:$

d. $H:C:::C:H$

5-15 Convert each of the Lewis structures in Problem 5-13 into the form in which lines are used to denote shared electron pairs. Include nonbonding electron pairs in the rewritten structures.

5-16 Convert each of the Lewis structures in Problem 5-14 into the form in which lines are used to denote shared electron pairs. Include nonbonding electron pairs in the rewritten structures.

Valence Electrons and Number of Covalent Bonds Formed (Section 5-4)

5-17 Indicate whether each of the following is or is not a normally expected bonding pattern for the element shown.

a. $-\ddot{O}-$
b. $:N\equiv$
c. $:\ddot{C}=$
d. $:\ddot{O}=$

5-18 Indicate whether each of the following is or is not a normally expected bonding pattern for the element shown.

a. $-\ddot{N}=$
b. $:O\equiv$
c. $-C\equiv$
d. $=C=$

5-19 Identify the Period 2 nonmetal that would normally be expected to exhibit each of the following bonding capabilities.
a. Forms three single bonds
b. Forms two double bonds
c. Forms one single bond and one double bond
d. Forms two single bonds and one double bond

5-20 Identify the Period 3 nonmetal that would normally be expected to exhibit each of the following bonding capabilities.
a. Forms one triple bond
b. Forms one single bond and one triple bond
c. Forms four single bonds
d. Forms one double bond

5-21 How many valence electrons do atoms possess that exhibit each of the covalent bonding behaviors described in Problem 5-19?

5-22 How many valence electrons do atoms possess that exhibit each of the covalent bonding behaviors described in Problem 5-20?

Coordinate Covalent Bonds (Section 5-5)

5-23 What aspect of the following Lewis structure indicates that the concept of coordinate covalency is needed to explain the bonding in the molecule?

$$:C:::O:$$

5-24 What aspect of the following Lewis structure indicates that the concept of coordinate covalency is needed to explain the bonding in the molecule?

$$:N:::N:\ddot{O}:$$

5-25 Identify the coordinate covalent bond(s) present, if any, in each of the following molecules by listing the two atoms involved in the bond. Name the atom on the left or the bottom in the bond first.

a. $:N\equiv N-\ddot{O}:$ b. $H-\ddot{O}-\ddot{F}:$

c. $:\ddot{O}-\ddot{Cl}-\ddot{O}-H$ d. $:\ddot{O}-\ddot{Br}-\ddot{O}-H$
$\qquad\qquad\qquad\qquad\qquad |$
$\qquad\qquad\qquad\qquad\quad :\ddot{O}:$

5-26 Identify the coordinate covalent bond(s) present, if any, in each of the following molecules by listing the two atoms involved in the bond. Name the atom on the left or the bottom in the bond first.

a. $:\ddot{S}=\ddot{S}-\ddot{O}:$ b. $H-\ddot{O}-\ddot{Br}:$

c. $:\ddot{O}-\ddot{I}-\ddot{O}-H$ d. $:\ddot{O}-\ddot{Cl}-\ddot{O}-H$
$\qquad\qquad\qquad\qquad\qquad |$
$\qquad\qquad\qquad\qquad\quad :\ddot{O}:$

Drawing Lewis Structures (Section 5-6)

5-27 Without actually drawing the Lewis structure, determine how many valence electrons are available for covalent bonding in each of the following molecules.
a. CBr_4 b. SF_2 c. PH_3 d. OF_2

5-28 Without actually drawing the Lewis structure, determine how many valence electrons are available for covalent bonding in each of the following molecules.
a. SiH_4 b. NCl_3 c. H_2S d. Cl_2O

5-29 Without actually drawing the Lewis structure, determine how many "electron dots" should be present in the Lewis structure of each of the molecules in Problem 5-27.

5-30 Without actually drawing the Lewis structure, determine how many "electron dots" should be present in the Lewis structure of each of the molecules in Problem 5-28.

5-31 Draw the Lewis structure for each of the molecules in Problem 5-27.

5-32 Draw the Lewis structure for each of the molecules in Problem 5-28.

5-33 Draw Lewis structures to illustrate the bonding in the following molecules. In each case, there will be at least one multiple bond present in a molecule.
a. C_3H_4: A central carbon atom has two other carbon atoms bonded to it. Each of the noncentral carbon atoms also has two hydrogen atoms bonded to it.
b. N_2F_2: The two nitrogen atoms are bonded to one another, and each nitrogen atom also has a fluorine atom bonded to it.
c. C_2H_3N: The two carbon atoms are bonded to each other. One of the carbon atoms has a nitrogen atom bonded to it, and the other carbon atom has three hydrogen atoms bonded to it.
d. C_3H_4: A central carbon atom has two other carbon atoms bonded to it. One of the noncentral carbon atoms also has one hydrogen atom bonded to it, and the other one has three hydrogen atoms bonded to it.

5-34 Draw Lewis structures to illustrate the bonding in the following molecules. In each case, there will be at least one multiple bond present in a molecule.
a. $COCl_2$: Both chlorine atoms and the oxygen atom are bonded to the carbon atom.
b. $C_2H_2Br_2$: The two carbon atoms are bonded to one another. Each carbon atom also has a bromine atom and a hydrogen atom bonded to it.
c. C_2N_2: The two carbon atoms are bonded to one another, and each carbon atom also has a nitrogen bonded to it.
d. CH_2N_2: A central carbon atom has both nitrogen atoms bonded to it. Both hydrogen atoms are bonded to one of the two nitrogen atoms.

Lewis Structures for Polyatomic Ions (Section 5-7)

5-35 How many "electron dots" should appear in the Lewis structures for each of the following polyatomic ions?
a. ClO^- b. ClO_2^- c. S_2^{2-} d. NH_4^+

5-36 How many "electron dots" should appear in the Lewis structures for each of the following polyatomic ions?
a. PO_3^{3-} b. PO_4^{3-} c. H_3O^+ d. BrO_4^-

5-37 Draw Lewis structures for the following polyatomic ions.
a. OH^- b. BeH_4^{2-} c. $AlCl_4^-$ d. NO_3^-

5-38 Draw Lewis structures for the following polyatomic ions.
a. CN^- b. PF_4^+ c. BH_4^- d. ClO_3^-

5-39 Draw Lewis structures for the following compounds that contain polyatomic ions.
a. $NaCN$ b. K_3PO_4

5-40 Draw Lewis structures for the following compounds that contain polyatomic ions.
a. KOH b. NH_4Br

▲5-41 Draw Lewis structures for the following molecules or polyatomic ions.
a. SO_3 b. SO_3^{2-}

▲5-42 Draw Lewis structures for the following molecules or polyatomic ions.
a. NH_3 b. NH_4^+

▲5-43 In which of the following pairs of diatomic species do both members of the pair have bonds of the same multiplicity (single, double, triple)?
a. HCl and HI   b. S_2 and Cl_2
c. CO and NO^+ d. OH^- and HS^-

▲5-44 In which of the following pairs of diatomic species do both members of the pair have bonds of the same multiplicity (single, double, triple)?
a. N_2 and F_2 b. CO and CN^-
c. HBr and ClF   d. O_2 and O_2^{2-}

Molecular Geometry (VSEPR Theory) (Section 5-8)

5-45 What is the molecular geometry associated with each of the following VSEPR electron groups?
a. 4 bonding groups and 0 nonbonding groups
b. 2 bonding groups and 2 nonbonding groups
c. 3 bonding groups and 0 nonbonding groups

5-46 What is the molecular geometry associated with each of the following VSEPR electron groups?
a. 3 bonding groups and 1 nonbonding group
b. 2 bonding groups and 1 nonbonding group
c. 2 bonding groups and 0 nonbonding groups

5-47 Specify the molecular geometry of each of the following molecules using the terms *linear*, *angular*, *trigonal pyramidal*, and *tetrahedral*.

a

b

c

d

5-48 Specify the molecular geometry of each of the following molecules using the terms *linear*, *angular*, *trigonal pyramidal*, and *tetrahedral*.

a

b

c

d

5-49 Using VSEPR theory, predict whether each of the following triatomic molecules is linear or angular (bent).
a. H : S̈ : H   b. H : Ö : Cl̈:
c. :Ö : : Ö : Ö: d. : N̈ : : N̈ : Ö:

5-50 Using VSEPR theory, predict whether each of the following triatomic molecules is linear or angular (bent).
a. H:C:::N: b. : N̈ : : S̈ : F̈ :
c. : F̈ : S̈ : F̈ :   d. :Cl̈ : Ö : Cl̈:

5-51 Using VSEPR theory, predict the molecular geometry of the following molecules.
a. : F̈ : N̈ : F̈ :   b. :Cl̈ : C : Cl̈:
   : F̈ :   : Ö :
c. :Ö: d. H
:Cl̈ : P : Cl̈:   :Cl̈ : C : Cl̈:
:Cl̈:   :Cl̈:

5-52 Using VSEPR theory, predict the molecular geometry of the following molecules.
a. H : P̈ : H   b. :Cl̈ : C : : Ö :
   :Cl̈:   H
c. H   d. : F̈ :
:Cl̈ : C : Cl̈:   H : Si : H
H   :Cl̈:

5-53 Using VSEPR theory, predict the molecular geometry of the following molecules.
a. H : C : : C : H   b. H
   H   H   H : C : Ö : H
                          H

5-54 Using VSEPR theory, predict the molecular geometry of the following molecules.
a. : Ö :   b. H Ö :
:Ö : : N : Ö : H   H : C : C : H
                          H

▲5-55 Using VSEPR theory, predict the molecular geometry of the following molecules.
a. NCl_3 b. $SiCl_4$
c. H_2Se d. SBr_2

▲5-56 Using VSEPR theory, predict the molecular geometry of the following molecules.
a. HOBr   b. H_2Te
c. NBr_3 d. SiF_4

▲5-57 Specify both the VSEPR electron group geometry about the central atom and the molecular geometry for each of the following molecules or polyatomic ions.
a. SiH_4 b. NH_2^-
c. ClNO   d. CO_3^{2-}

▲5-58 Specify both the VSEPR electron group geometry about the central atom and the molecular geometry for each of the following molecules or polyatomic ions.
a. CH_4 b. PH_4^+
c. PH_3 d. NO_3^-

Electronegativity (Section 5-9)

5-59 Indicate whether or not each of the statements relating to electronegativity values of the "highlighted" elements in the following periodic table are true or false. Use periodic table trends rather than actual electronegativity values in determining answers for the statements.

a. Element 1 has a higher electronegativity value than element 2.

b. Element 4 has a higher electronegativity value than element 5.

c. Element 3 has a higher electronegativity value than element 8.

d. Element 7 has a higher electronegativity value than element 6.

5-60 Indicate whether or not each of the statements relating to electronegativity values of the "highlighted" elements in the periodic table in Problem 5-59 are true or false. Use periodic table trends rather than actual electronegativity values in determining answers for the statements.

a. Element 2 has a higher electronegativity value than element 4.

b. Element 5 has a higher electronegativity value than element 6.

c. Element 7 has a higher electronegativity value than element 8.

d. Element 3 has a higher electronegativity value than element 1.

5-61 Using a periodic table, but not a table of electronegativity values, arrange each of the following sets of atoms in order of increasing electronegativity.

a. Na, Al, P, Mg   b. Cl, Br, I, F

c. S, P, O, Al   d. Ca, Mg, O, C

5-62 Using a periodic table, but not a table of electronegativity values, arrange each of the following sets of atoms in order of increasing electronegativity.

a. Be, N, O, B   b. Li, C, B, K

c. S, Te, Cl, Se   d. S, Mg, K, Ca

5-63 Use the information in Figure 5-11 as a basis for answering the following questions.

a. Which elements have electronegativity values that exceed that of the element carbon?

b. Which elements have electronegativity values of less than 1.0?

c. What are the four most electronegative elements listed in Figure 5-11?

d. By what constant amount do the electronegativity values for sequential Period 2 elements differ?

5-64 Use the information in Figure 5-11 as a basis for answering the following questions.

a. Which elements have electronegativity values that exceed that of the element sulfur?

b. What are the three least electronegative elements listed in Figure 5-11?

c. Which three elements in Figure 5-11 have an electronegativity of 2.5?

d. How does the electronegativity of the element hydrogen compare to that of the Period 2 elements?

Bond Polarity (Section 5-10)

5-65 Place δ^+ above the atom that is relatively positive and δ^- above the atom that is relatively negative in each of the following bonds. Try to answer this question without referring to Figure 5-11.

a. B—N   b. Cl—F

c. N—C   d. F—O

5-66 Place δ^+ above the atom that is relatively positive and δ^- above the atom that is relatively negative in each of the following bonds. Try to answer this question without referring to Figure 5-11.

a. Cl—Br   b. Al—S

c. Br—S   d. O—N

5-67 Rank the following bonds in order of increasing polarity.

a. H—Cl, H—O, H—Br   b. O—F, P—O, Al—O

c. H—Cl, Br—Br, B—N d. P—N, S—O, Br—F

5-68 Rank the following bonds in order of increasing polarity.

a. H—Br, H—Cl, H—S   b. N—O, Be—N, N—F

c. N—P, P—P, P—S   d. B—Si, Br—I, C—H

5-69 Classify each of the following bonds as nonpolar covalent, polar covalent, or ionic on the basis of electronegativity differences.

a. C—O   b. Na—Cl

c. C—I   d. Ca—S

5-70 Classify each of the following bonds as nonpolar covalent, polar covalent, or ionic on the basis of electronegativity differences.

a. Cl—F   b. P—H

c. C—H   d. Ca—O

5-71 Classify the bond formed between a carbon atom and an atom of each of the following elements as (1) nonpolar covalent, (2) polar covalent, or (3) ionic.

a. Nitrogen   b. Oxygen

c. Hydrogen   d. Iodine

5-72 Classify the bond formed between a nitrogen atom and an atom of each of the following elements as (1) nonpolar covalent, (2) polar covalent, or (3) ionic.

a. Hydrogen   b. Carbon

c. Sulfur   d. Chlorine

▲**5-73** Fill in the blanks in each line of the following table that involves characteristics of various bonds between nonmetals. The first line is already completed as an example.

	Bond Identity	More Electronegative Atom	Atom with Negative Partial Charge (δ^-)	Bond Type
	N—P	N	N	polar covalent
a.	Se—P			
b.	O—P			
c.	Br—P			
d.	F—P			

▲5-74 Fill in the blanks in each line of the following table that involves characteristics of various bonds between nonmetals. The first line is already completed as an example.

Bond Identity	More Electronegative Atom	Atom with Negative Partial Charge (δ^-)	Bond Type
C—H	C	C	nonpolar covalent
a. S—H			
b. O—H			
c. As—H			
d. F—H			

▲5-75 Four hypothetical elements, A, B, C, and D, have electronegativities A = 3.8, B = 3.3, C = 2.8, and D = 1.3. These elements form the compounds BA, DA, DB, and CA. Arrange the compounds in order of
a. Increasing ionic bond character
b. Decreasing covalent bond character

▲5-76 Four hypothetical elements, A, B, C, and D, have electronegativities A = 3.4, B = 3.1, C = 2.5, end D = 1.7. These elements form the compounds CB, DC, DA, and BA. Arrange the compounds in order of
a. Increasing ionic bond character
b. Decreasing covalent bond character

Molecular Polarity (Section 5-11)

5-77 Indicate whether each of the following hypothetical triatomic molecules is polar or nonpolar. Assume that A, X, and Y have different electronegativities.
a. a linear X—A—X molecule
b. a linear X—X—A molecule
c. an angular A—X—Y molecule
d. an angular X—A—Y molecule

5-78 Indicate whether each of the following hypothetical triatomic molecules is polar or nonpolar. Assume that A, X, and Y have different electronegativities.
a. a linear X—A—Y molecule
b. a linear A—Y—A molecule
c. an angular X—A—X molecule
d. an angular X—X—X molecule

5-79 Indicate whether each of the following triatomic molecules is polar or nonpolar. The molecular geometry is given in parentheses.
a. CS_2 (linear with C in the center position)
b. H_2Se (angular with Se in the center position)
c. FNO (angular with N in the center position)
d. N_2O (linear with N in the center position)

5-80 Indicate whether each of the following triatomic molecules is polar or nonpolar. The molecular geometry is given in parentheses.
a. ONBr (angular with N in the center position)
b. OF_2 (angular with O in the center position)
c. SO_2 (angular with S in the center position)
d. H_2S (angular with S in the center position)

5-81 Indicate whether each of the following molecules is polar or nonpolar. The molecular geometry is given in parentheses.
a. NF_3 (trigonal pyramidal with N at the apex)
b. NF_2Cl (trigonal pyramidal with N at the apex)
c. CS_2 (linear with C in the center position)
d. $CHCl_3$ (tetrahedral with C in the center position)

5-82 Indicate whether each of the following molecules is polar or nonpolar. The molecular geometry is given in parentheses.
a. PH_2Cl (trigonal pyramidal with P at the apex)
b. SO_3 (trigonal planar with S in the center position)
c. CH_2Cl_2 (tetrahedral with C in the center position)
d. CCl_4 (tetrahedral with C in the center position)

5-83 Classify each of the following molecules as (1) polar, (2) nonpolar, or (3) polarity cannot be determined because of insufficient information.
a. A molecule in which all bonds are polar
b. A molecule with two bonds, one that is polar and one that is nonpolar

5-84 Classify each of the following molecules as (1) polar, (2) nonpolar, or (3) polarity cannot be determined because of insufficient information.
a. A molecule in which all bonds are nonpolar
b. A molecule with two bonds, both of which are polar

▲5-85 Indicate which molecule in each of the following pairs of molecules has the greatest molecular polarity.
a. BrCl and BrI
b. CO_2 and SO_2
c. SO_3 and NH_3
d. CH_4 and CH_3Cl (C is the central atom)

▲5-86 Indicate which molecule in each of the following pairs of molecules has the greatest molecular polarity.
a. H_2S and H_2O
b. CO_2 and CO
c. HCN and SO_3
d. SiH_4 and SiH_2Cl_2 (Si is the central atom)

▲5-87 Successive substitution of F atoms for H atoms in the molecule CH_4 produces the molecules CH_3F, CH_2F_2, CHF_3, and CF_4.
a. Draw Lewis structures for each of the five molecules.
b. Using VSEPR theory, predict the geometry of each of the five molecules.
c. Specify the polarity (polar or nonpolar) for each of the five molecules.

▲5-88 Successive substitution of F atoms for H atoms in the molecule NH_3 produces the molecules NH_2F, NHF_2, and NF_3.
a. Draw Lewis structures for each of the four molecules.
b. Using VSEPR theory, predict the geometry of each of the four molecules.
c. Specify the polarity (polar or nonpolar) for each of the four molecules.

Recognizing and Naming Binary Molecular Compounds (Section 5-12)

5-89 Indicate whether or not each of the following compounds is a binary molecular compound?
a. NaCl   b. $AlCl_3$ c. CCl_4 d. Cl_2O

5-90 Indicate whether or not each of the following compounds is a binary molecular compound?
a. BeO   b. NO_2 c. SO_3 d. Na_2O

5-91 Name the following binary molecular compounds?
a. N_2F_4 b. CCl_4 c. OF_2 d. CO

5-92 Name the following binary molecular compounds?
a. SF_4 b. CO_2 c. P_4O_6 d. N_2O_5

5-93 How many numerical prefixes are present in the names of the following binary molecular compounds?
a. NO_2 b. H_2S c. HI   d. N_2O_3

5-94 How many numerical prefixes are present in the names of the following binary molecular compounds?
a. SO_2 b. N_2O_2 c. H_2Se d. HBr

5-95 Name the following binary molecular compounds, all of which have common names?
a. H_2O_2 b. NO   c. CH_4 d. NH_3

5-96 Name the following binary molecular compounds, all of which have common names?
a. C_2H_6 b. N_2O c. N_2H_4 d. H_2O

5-97 Each of the following diagrams depicts a collection of sulfur–oxygen molecules, where the yellow atoms are sulfur and the red atoms are oxygen.

I   II   III   IV

Which diagram depicts the following?
a. Sulfur dioxide molecules
b. Disulfur monoxide molecules
c. A mixture of sulfur dioxide and disulfur monoxide molecules
d. A mixture of sulfur dioxide and sulfur trioxide molecules

5-98 Each of the following diagrams depicts a collection of nitrogen–oxygen molecules, where the blue atoms are nitrogen and the red atoms are oxygen.

I   II   III   IV

Which diagram depicts the following?
a. Dinitrogen monoxide molecules
b. Nitrogen monoxide molecules
c. A mixture of nitrogen dioxide and dinitrogen monoxide molecules
d. A mixture of dinitrogen monoxide, nitrogen dioxide, and nitrogen monoxide molecules

5-99 Write chemical formulas for the following binary molecular compounds.
a. Iodine monochloride   b. Dinitrogen dioxide
c. Nitrogen trichloride   d. Hydrogen bromide

5-100 Write chemical formulas for the following binary molecular compounds.
a. Bromine monochloride   b. Tetrasulfur dinitride
c. Sulfur trioxide   d. Dioxygen difluoride

5-101 Write chemical formulas for the following binary molecular compounds.
a. Hydrogen peroxide   b. Methane
c. Ammonia   d. Nitric oxide

5-102 Write chemical formulas for the following binary molecular compounds.
a. Ethane   b. Water
c. Hydrazine   d. Nitrous oxide

5-103 The compound whose molecules contain one atom of C and one atom of O is named carbon monoxide rather than oxygen monocarbide. Why is this the case?

5-104 The compound whose molecules contain one atom of C and two atoms of O is named carbon dioxide rather that dioxygen monocarbide. Why is this the case?

▲**5-105** The correct name for the compound Na_2CO_3 is not disodium monocarbon trioxide. Explain why this name is incorrect.

▲**5-106** The correct name for the compound K_2SO_4 is not dipotassium monosulfur tetroxide. Explain why this name is incorrect.

▲**5-107** Which of the compounds N_2O_3, KCl, HF, CH_4, and CO_2 have names that
a. end in the suffix -ide?
b. contain two numerical prefixes?
c. contain the prefix mono-?
d. do not contain numerical prefixes?

▲**5-108** Which of the compounds NH_3, Na_2O, H_2S, N_2H_4, and CO have names that
a. end in the suffix -ide?
b. contain two numerical prefixes?
c. contain the prefix mono-?
d. do not contain numerical prefixes?

Chemical Calculations: Formula Masses, Moles, and Chemical Equations

6

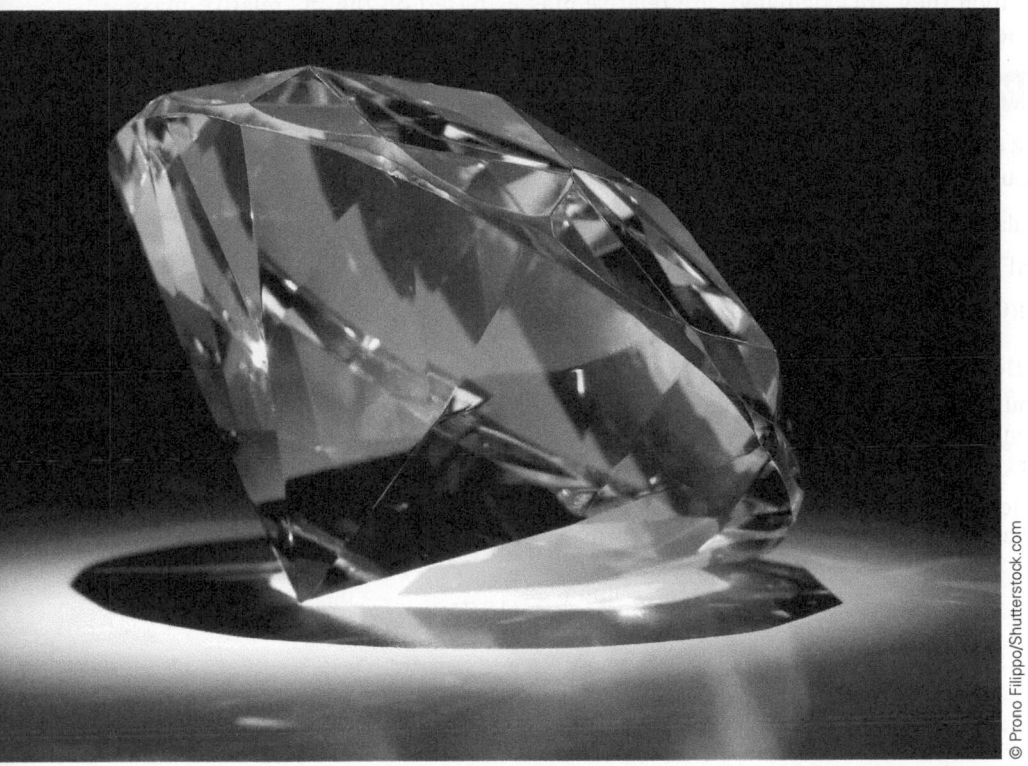

© Prono Filippo/Shutterstock.com

A half-carat diamond contains approximately 5 × 10²¹ carbon atoms. In this chapter, how to calculate the number of atoms in a particular amount of substance is considered.

In this chapter "chemical arithmetic," the quantitative relationships between elements and compounds, is discussed. Anyone who deals with chemical processes needs to understand at least the simpler aspects of this topic. All chemical processes, regardless of where they occur—in the human body, at a steel mill, on top of the kitchen stove, or in a clinical laboratory setting—are governed by the same mathematical rules.

Central to the topic of "chemical arithmetic" are chemical formulas and chemical equations. There is more to chemical formula use than simply using such formulas to describe the composition of a compound in terms of atoms and elements (Section 1-10). The topic of chemical equations is considered in this chapter for the first time. How chemical equations are used to represent that which occurs in a chemical reaction is discussed. The chemist's counting unit, the mole, is introduced and its use in chemical calculations presented.

6-1 Formula Masses

LEARNING FOCUS

Calculate the formula mass of a substance given its chemical formula and a listing of atomic masses.

Our entry point into the realm of "chemical arithmetic" is a discussion of the quantity called formula mass. A **formula mass** *is the sum of the atomic masses of all the atoms represented in the chemical formula of a substance.* Formula masses, like the atomic masses from which they are calculated, are relative masses based on the $^{12}_{6}C$ relative-mass scale (Section 3-3). Example 6-1 illustrates how formula masses are calculated. ◄

▶ *Many chemists use the term* molecular mass *interchangeably with* formula mass *when dealing with substances that contain discrete molecules. It is incorrect, however, to use the term* molecular mass *when dealing with ionic compounds because such compounds do not have molecules as their basic structural unit (Section 4-8).*

EXAMPLE 6-1

Using a Compound's Chemical Formula and Atomic Masses to Calculate Its Formula Mass

Calculate the formula mass of each of the following substances.

a. SnF_2 (tin(II) fluoride, a toothpaste additive)

b. $Al(OH)_3$ (aluminum hydroxide, a water purification chemical)

Solution

Formula masses are obtained simply by adding the atomic masses of the constituent elements, counting each atomic mass as many times as the symbol for the element occurs in the chemical formula.

a. A formula unit of SnF_2 contains three atoms: one atom of Sn and two atoms of F. The formula mass, the collective mass of these three atoms, is calculated as follows:

$$1 \text{ atom Sn} \times \left(\frac{118.71 \text{ amu}}{1 \text{ atom Sn}} \right) = 118.71 \text{ amu}$$

$$2 \text{ atoms F} \times \left(\frac{19.00 \text{ amu}}{1 \text{ atom F}} \right) = \underline{38.00 \text{ amu}}$$

$$\text{Formula mass} = 156.71 \text{ amu}$$

The conversion factors used in this calculation were derived from the atomic masses listed on the inside front cover of the text. The use of these conversion factors is governed by the rules previously presented in Section 2-7.

Conversion factors are usually not explicitly shown in a formula mass calculation, as they are in the preceding calculation; the calculation is simplified as follows:

$$\begin{array}{ll} \text{Sn:} & 1 \times 118.71 \text{ amu} = 118.71 \text{ amu} \\ \text{F:} & 2 \times 19.00 \text{ amu} = \underline{38.00 \text{ amu}} \\ & \text{Formula mass} = 156.71 \text{ amu} \end{array}$$

b. The chemical formula for this compound contains parentheses. Improper interpretation of parentheses (see Section 4-11) is a common error made by students doing formula mass calculations. In the formula $Al(OH)_3$, the subscript 3 outside the parentheses affects both of the symbols inside the parentheses. Thus we have

$$\begin{array}{ll} \text{Al:} & 1 \times 26.98 \text{ amu} = 26.98 \text{ amu} \\ \text{O:} & 3 \times 16.00 \text{ amu} = 48.00 \text{ amu} \\ \text{H:} & 3 \times 1.01 \text{ amu} = \underline{3.03 \text{ amu}} \\ & \text{Formula mass} = 78.01 \text{ amu} \end{array}$$

In this text, atomic masses will always be rounded to the hundredths place before use in a calculation, as was done in this example. A benefit of this operational rule is that the same atomic mass is always encountered for a given element, and the atomic masses for the common elements become familiar quantities.

Section 6-1 Quick Quiz

1. The formula mass for a compound is calculated by summing which of the following numbers for all atoms in a formula unit of the compound?
   a. atomic number
   b. mass number
   c. nuclear charge
   d. no correct response
2. The atomic mass of C is 12.01 amu and that of O is 16.00 amu. The formula mass for the compound CO_2 is:
   a. 28.01 amu
   b. 44.01 amu
   c. 56.02 amu
   d. no correct response
3. The atomic mass of H is 1.01 amu and that of N is 14.01 amu. What is the value of x in the chemical formula NH_x given that the formula mass of this compound is 17.04 amu?
   a. 2
   b. 3
   c. 4
   d. no correct response

Answers: 1. d; 2. b; 3. b

 Mass

b Amount

Figure 6-1 Oranges may be bought in units of mass (4-lb bag) or units of amount (three oranges).

6-2 The Mole: A Counting Unit for Chemists

LEARNING FOCUS

Know the value for the counting unit called a mole; be able to calculate the number of particles (atoms or molecules) in a given number of moles of a chemical substance.

The quantity of material in a sample of a substance can be specified either in terms of units of *mass* or in terms of units of *amount*. Mass is specified in terms of units such as grams, kilograms, and pounds. The amount of a substance is specified by indicating the number of objects present—3, 17, or 437, for instance.

Both mass units and amount units are routinely used on a daily basis. For example, at a grocery store, oranges may be bought on a mass basis (4-lb bag or 10-lb bag) or an amount basis (three oranges or eight oranges), as is shown in Figure 6-1. In chemistry, as in everyday life, both mass and amount methods of specifying quantity are used. In laboratory work, practicality dictates working with quantities of known mass (Figure 6-2). Counting out a given number of atoms for a laboratory experiment is impossible because atoms are too small to be seen.

When performing chemical calculations after laboratory measurements have been made, it is often useful and even necessary to think of the quantities of substances present in terms of numbers of atoms or molecules instead of mass. When this is done, very large numbers are always encountered. Any macroscopic-sized sample of a chemical substance contains many trillions of atoms or molecules. ◄

In order to cope with this large-number problem, chemists have found it convenient to use a special unit when counting atoms and molecules. Specialized counting units are used in many areas—for example, a *dozen* eggs or a *ream* (500 sheets) of paper (Figure 6-3).

The chemist's counting unit is the *mole*. What is unusual about the mole is its magnitude. A **mole** is 6.02×10^{23} *objects*. The extremely large size of the mole unit is necessitated by the extremely small size of atoms and molecules. To the chemist, *one mole* always means 6.02×10^{23} objects, just as *one dozen* always means 12 objects. Two moles of objects is two times 6.02×10^{23} objects, and five moles of objects is five times 6.02×10^{23} objects.

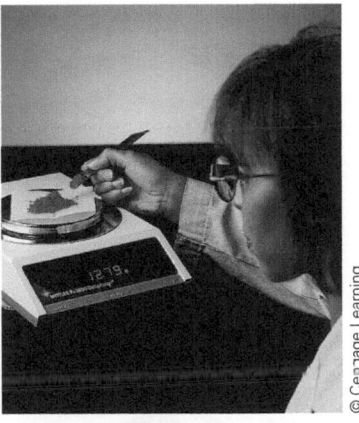

Figure 6-2 A basic process in chemical laboratory work is determining the mass of a substance.

▶ *How large is the number 6.02×10^{23}? It would take a modern computer that can count 100 million times a second 190 million years to count 6.02×10^{23} times. If each of the 6 billion people on Earth were made a millionaire (receiving 1 million dollar bills), we would still need 100 million other worlds, each inhabited with the same number of millionaires, in order to have 6.02×10^{23} dollar bills in circulation.*

a A dozen

b A pair

c Two reams

Figure 6-3 Everyday counting units—a dozen, a pair, and two reams.

Avogadro's number *is the name given to the numerical value* 6.02×10^{23}. This designation honors Amedeo Avogadro (Figure 6-4), an Italian physicist whose pioneering work on gases later proved valuable in determining the number of particles present in given volumes of substances. When solving problems dealing with the number of objects (atoms or molecules) present in a given number of moles of a substance, Avogadro's number becomes part of the conversion factor used to relate the number of objects present to the number of moles present. ◄

From the definition

$$1 \text{ mole} = 6.02 \times 10^{23} \text{ objects}$$

two conversion factors can be derived:

$$\frac{6.02 \times 10^{23} \text{ objects}}{1 \text{ mole}} \quad \text{and} \quad \frac{1 \text{ mole}}{6.02 \times 10^{23} \text{ objects}}$$

Example 6-2 illustrates the use of these conversion factors in solving problems.

▶ *Why the number* 6.02×10^{23}, *rather than some other number, was chosen as the counting unit of chemists is discussed in Section 6-3. A more formal definition of the mole will also be presented in that section.*

EXAMPLE 6-2

Calculating the Number of Objects in a Molar Quantity

How many objects are there in each of the following quantities?

a. 0.23 mole of aspirin molecules   **b.** 1.6 moles of oxygen atoms

Solution

Dimensional analysis (Section 2-8) will be used to solve both parts of this problem. The two parts are similar in that a certain number of moles of substance is the given quantity and the number of objects present in the given molar amount is to be calculated. Avogadro's number, used in conversion factor form, is needed to solve each of these mole-to-particles problems.

$$\boxed{\begin{array}{c} \text{Moles of} \\ \text{Substance} \end{array}} \xrightarrow[\text{involving Avogadro's number}]{\text{Conversion factor}} \boxed{\begin{array}{c} \text{Particles of} \\ \text{Substance} \end{array}}$$

a. The objects of concern are molecules of aspirin. The given quantity is 0.23 mole of aspirin molecules, and the desired quantity is the number of aspirin molecules.

$$0.23 \text{ mole aspirin molecules} = ? \text{ aspirin molecules}$$

Applying dimensional analysis here involves the use of a single conversion factor, one that relates moles and molecules.

$$0.23 \text{ mole aspirin molecules} \times \left(\frac{6.02 \times 10^{23} \text{ aspirin molecules}}{1 \text{ mole aspirin molecules}} \right)$$
$$= 1.4 \times 10^{23} \text{ aspirin molecules}$$

Figure 6-4 Amedeo Avogadro (1776–1856) was the first scientist to distinguish between atoms and molecules. His name is associated with the number 6.02×10^{23}, the number of particles (atoms or molecules) in a mole.

b. This problem deals with atoms instead of molecules. This change in type of particle does not change the way the problem is worked. A conversion factor involving Avogadro's number will again be needed.

The given quantity is 1.6 moles of oxygen atoms, and the desired quantity is the actual number of oxygen atoms present.

$$1.6 \text{ moles oxygen atoms} = ? \text{ oxygen atoms}$$

The setup is

$$1.6 \; \cancel{\text{moles oxygen atoms}} \times \left(\frac{6.02 \times 10^{23} \text{ oxygen atoms}}{1 \; \cancel{\text{mole oxygen atoms}}} \right)$$
$$= 9.6 \times 10^{23} \text{ oxygen atoms}$$

Section 6-2 Quick Quiz

1. The numerical value for Avogadro's number is
   a. 6.02×10^{21}
   b. 6.02×10^{24}
   c. 6.02×10^{26}
   d. no correct response
2. The number of atoms present in 1 mole of P atoms is
   a. 6.02×10^{21}
   b. 6.02×10^{23}
   c. 6.02×10^{25}
   d. no correct response
3. One mole of S atoms contains twice as many atoms as
   a. one mole of O atoms
   b. one-half mole of O atoms
   c. one-eighth mole of O atoms
   d. no correct response
4. The number of molecules present in 1.50 moles of CO_2 is
   a. Avogadro's number
   b. 1.50 times Avogadro's number
   c. Avogadro's number divided by 1.50
   d. no correct response

Answers: 1. d; 2. b; 3. b; 4. b

6-3 The Mass of a Mole

LEARNING FOCUS

Calculate the mass, in grams, of a given number of moles of a substance given its chemical formula or vice versa.

How much does a mole weigh? Uncertainty about the answer to this question is quickly removed by first considering a similar but more familiar question: "How much does a dozen weigh?" The response is now immediate: "A dozen what?" The mass of a dozen identical objects obviously depends on the identity of the object. For example, the mass of a dozen elephants is greater than the mass of a dozen peanuts. The mass of a mole, like the mass of a dozen, depends on the identity of the object. Thus the mass of a mole, or *molar mass,* is not a set number; it varies and is different for each chemical substance (see Figure 6-5). This is in direct contrast to the *molar number,* Avogadro's number, which is the same for all chemical substances.

The **molar mass** *is the mass, in grams, of a substance that is numerically equal to the substance's formula mass.* For example, the formula mass (atomic mass) of the element sodium is 22.99 amu; therefore, 1 mole of sodium weighs 22.99 g. In Example 6-1, it was calculated that the formula mass of tin(II) fluoride is 156.71 amu; therefore, 1 mole of tin(II) fluoride weighs 156.71 g. Thus the actual mass, in grams, of 1 mole of any substance can be obtained by calculating its formula

Figure 6-5 The mass of a mole is not a set number of grams; it depends on the substance. For the substances shown, the mass of 1 mole (clockwise from sulfur, the yellow solid) is as follows: sulfur, 32.07 g; zinc, 65.38 g; carbon, 12.01 g; magnesium, 24.31 g; lead, 207.2 g; silicon, 28.09 g; copper, 63.55 g; and, in the center, mercury, 200.59 g.

mass (atomic mass for elements) and appending to it the unit of grams. When atomic masses are added to obtain the formula mass of a compound (in amus), the mass of 1 mole of compound (in grams) is simultaneously obtained.

It is not a coincidence that the molar mass of a substance, in grams, and its formula mass or atomic mass, in amu, match numerically. The value selected for Avogadro's number is the one that validates this relationship; only for this unique value is the relationship valid. Figure 6-6 shows the relationship between atomic mass values and molar mass values for selected elements in their atomic forms. The numerical match between molar mass and atomic or formula mass makes calculating the mass of any given number of moles of a substance a very simple procedure. When solving problems of this type, the numerical value of the molar mass becomes part of the conversion factor used to convert from moles to grams. ◀

▶ *The mass value below each symbol in the periodic table is both an atomic mass in atomic mass units and a molar mass in grams. For example, the mass of one nitrogen atom is 14.01 amu, and the mass of 1 mole of nitrogen atoms is 14.01 g.*

For example, for the compound CO_2, which has a formula mass of 44.01 amu, we can write the equality

$$44.01 \text{ g } CO_2 = 1 \text{ mole } CO_2$$

From this statement (equality), two conversion factors can be written:

$$\frac{44.01 \text{ g } CO_2}{1 \text{ mole } CO_2} \quad \text{and} \quad \frac{1 \text{ mole } CO_2}{44.01 \text{ g } CO_2}$$

Example 6-3 illustrates the use of gram-to-mole conversion factors like these in solving problems.

Figure 6-6 The relationship between periodic table atomic mass values and molar mass values for selected elements in their atomic forms.

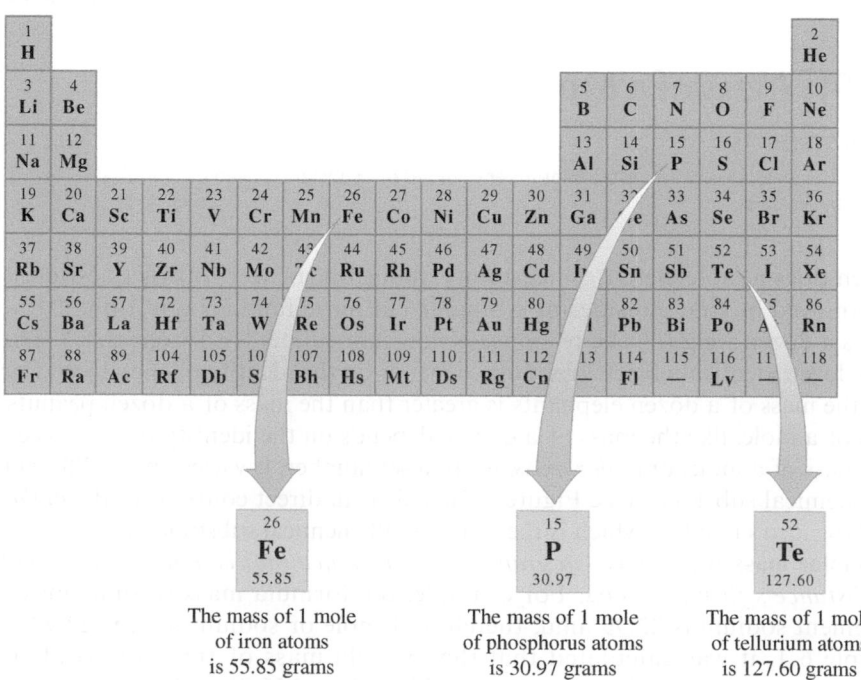

EXAMPLE 6-3

Calculating the Mass of a Molar Quantity of Compound

Acetaminophen, the pain-killing ingredient in Tylenol formulations, has the formula $C_8H_9O_2N$. Calculate the mass, in grams, of a 0.30-mole sample of this pain reliever.

Solution

The relationship between molar mass and formula mass is used to generate the conversion factor needed in the setup of this problem. ◄

$$\boxed{\text{Moles of Substance}} \xrightarrow[\text{involving molar mass}]{\text{Conversion factor}} \boxed{\text{Grams of Substance}}$$

The given quantity is 0.30 mole of $C_8H_9O_2N$, and the desired quantity is grams of this same substance.

$$0.30 \text{ mole } C_8H_9O_2N = ? \text{ grams } C_8H_9O_2N$$

The calculated formula mass of $C_8H_9O_2N$ is 151.18 amu. Thus,

$$151.18 \text{ grams } C_8H_9O_2N = 1 \text{ mole } C_8H_9O_2N$$

With this relationship in the form of a conversion factor, the setup for the problem becomes

$$0.30 \text{ mole } C_8H_9O_2N \times \left(\frac{151.18 \text{ g } C_8H_9O_2N}{1 \text{ mole } C_8H_9O_2N} \right) = 45 \text{ g } C_8H_9O_2N$$

▶ *Molar masses are conversion factors between grams and moles for any substance. Because the periodic table is the usual source of the atomic masses needed to calculate molar masses, the periodic table can be considered to be a useful source of conversion factors.*

The molar mass of an *element* is unique. No two natural elements have the same molar mass. The molar mass of a *compound* lacks uniqueness. More than one compound can have the same molar mass. For example, the compounds carbon dioxide (CO_2), nitrous oxide (N_2O), and propane (C_3H_8) all have a three-significant-figure molar mass of 44.0 g. Despite having like molar masses, these compounds have very different chemical properties. Chemical properties are related to electron arrangements of atoms (Section 3-6) and to the bonding that results when the atoms interact in compound formation. Molar mass is a physical rather than a chemical property of a substance. ◄

The atomic mass unit (amu) and the grams (g) unit are related to one another through Avogadro's number. That this is the case can be deduced from the following equalities:

$$\text{Atomic mass of N} = \text{mass of 1 N atom} = 14.01 \text{ amu}$$
$$\text{Molar mass of N} = \text{mass of } 6.02 \times 10^{23} \text{ N atoms} = 14.01 \text{ g}$$

Because the second equality involves 6.02×10^{23} times as many atoms as the first equality and the masses come out numerically equal, the gram unit must be 6.02×10^{23} times larger than the amu unit. ◄

$$6.02 \times 10^{23} \text{ amu} = 1.00 \text{ g}$$

In Section 6-2 the mole was defined simply as

$$1 \text{ mole} = 6.02 \times 10^{23} \text{ objects}$$

Although this statement conveys correct information (the value of Avogadro's number to three significant figures is 6.02×10^{23}), it is not the officially accepted definition for the mole. The official definition, which is based on mass, is as follows: The **mole** *is the amount of a substance that contains as many elementary particles (atoms, molecules, or formula units) as there are atoms in exactly 12 grams of $^{12}_{6}C$.* The value of Avogadro's number is an experimentally determined quantity (the number of atoms in exactly 12 g of $^{12}_{6}C$ atoms) rather than a defined quantity. Its value is not even mentioned in the preceding definition. The most up-to-date experimental value for Avogadro's number is $6.02214179 \times 10^{23}$, which is consistent with the previous definition (Section 6-2).

▶ *Although the mass of an atom and the mass of a mole of the same atom have identical numerical values the masses differ in units. The mass of an atom is specified in* atomic mass units *(an extremely small unit) and the molar mass is specified in* grams *(a relatively large unit).*

▶ *The numerical relationship between the amu unit and the grams unit is*

$$6.02 \times 10^{23} \text{ amu} = 1.00 \text{ g}$$

or

$$1 \text{ amu} = 1.66 \times 10^{-24} \text{ g}$$

This second equality is obtained from the first by dividing each side of the first equality by 6.02×10^{23}.

6-4 Chemical Formulas and the Mole Concept

LEARNING FOCUS

Interpret the subscripts in a chemical formula in terms of the number of moles of the various elements present in a given molar amount of the substance.

A chemical formula has two meanings or interpretations: a microscopic-level interpretation and a macroscopic-level interpretation. At a microscopic level, a chemical formula indicates the number of atoms of each element present in one molecule or formula unit of a substance (Section 1-10). *The numerical subscripts in a chemical formula give the number of atoms of the various elements present in 1 formula unit of the substance.* The formula N_2O_4, interpreted at the microscopic level, conveys the information that two atoms of nitrogen and four atoms of oxygen are present in one molecule of N_2O_4 (Figure 6-7).

Now that the mole concept has been introduced, a macroscopic interpretation of chemical formulas is possible. At a macroscopic level, a chemical formula indicates the number of moles of atoms of each element present in one mole of a substance. *The numerical subscripts in a chemical formula give the number of moles of atoms of the various elements present in 1 mole of the substance.* The designation *macroscopic* is given to this molar interpretation because moles are laboratory-sized quantities of atoms. The formula N_2O_4, interpreted at the macroscopic level, conveys the information that 2 moles of nitrogen atoms and 4 moles of oxygen atoms are present in 1 mole of N_2O_4 molecules. Thus the subscripts in a formula always carry a dual meaning: atoms at the microscopic level and moles of atoms at the macroscopic level.

Figure 6-8 illustrates diagrammatically the molar interpretation of chemical formula subscripts for the more complex molecule $C_{13}H_{18}O_2$ (ibuprofen), a molecule containing 3 elements and 33 atoms.

Figure 6-7 A computer-generated model of the molecular structure of the compound N_2O_4.

Figure 6-8 Interpretation of the subscripts in the chemical formula of the substance ibuprofen ($C_{13}H_{18}O_2$) in terms of molar amounts of atoms present.

When it is necessary to know the number of moles of a particular element *within* a compound, the subscript of that element's symbol in the chemical formula becomes part of the conversion factor used to convert from moles of compound to moles of element *within* the compound. ◀ Using N_2O_4 as our chemical formula, we can write the following conversion factors:

For N: $\dfrac{2 \text{ moles N atoms}}{1 \text{ mole } N_2O_4 \text{ molecules}}$ or $\dfrac{1 \text{ mole } N_2O_4 \text{ molecules}}{2 \text{ moles N atoms}}$

For O: $\dfrac{4 \text{ moles O atoms}}{1 \text{ mole } N_2O_4 \text{ molecules}}$ or $\dfrac{1 \text{ mole } N_2O_4 \text{ molecules}}{4 \text{ moles O atoms}}$

Example 6-4 illustrates the use of this type of conversion factor in problem solving.

▶ *The molar (macroscopic-level) interpretation of a chemical formula is used in calculations where information about a particular element within a compound is needed.*

Conversion factors that relate a component of a substance to the substance as a whole are dependent on the formula of the substance. By analogy, the relationship of body parts of an animal to the animal as a whole is dependent on the animal's identity. For example, in 1 mole of elephants there would be 4 moles of elephant legs, 2 moles of elephant ears, 1 mole of elephant tails, and 1 mole of elephant trunks.

EXAMPLE 6-4

Calculating Molar Quantities of Compound Components

Lactic acid, the substance that builds up in muscles and causes them to hurt when they are worked hard, has the formula $C_3H_6O_3$. How many moles of carbon atoms, hydrogen atoms, and oxygen atoms are present in a 1.2-mole sample of lactic acid?

Solution

One mole of $C_3H_6O_3$ contains 3 moles of carbon atoms, 6 moles of hydrogen atoms, and 3 moles of oxygen atoms. Consistent with this statement are the following conversion factors:

$$\left(\frac{3 \text{ moles C atoms}}{1 \text{ mole } C_3H_6O_3}\right) \left(\frac{6 \text{ moles H atoms}}{1 \text{ mole } C_3H_6O_3}\right) \left(\frac{3 \text{ moles O atoms}}{1 \text{ mole } C_3H_6O_3}\right)$$

Using the first conversion factor, the moles of carbon atoms present are calculated as follows:

$$1.2 \text{ moles } C_3H_6O_3 \times \left(\frac{3 \text{ moles C atoms}}{1 \text{ mole } C_3H_6O_3}\right) = 3.6 \text{ moles C atoms}$$

Similarly, from the second and third conversion factors, the moles of hydrogen and oxygen atoms present are calculated as follows:

$$1.2 \text{ moles } C_3H_6O_3 \times \left(\frac{6 \text{ moles H atoms}}{1 \text{ mole } C_3H_6O_3}\right) = 7.2 \text{ moles H atoms}$$

$$1.2 \text{ moles } C_3H_6O_3 \times \left(\frac{3 \text{ moles O atoms}}{1 \text{ mole } C_3H_6O_3}\right) = 3.6 \text{ moles O atoms}$$

Section 6-4 Quick Quiz

1. How many moles of H atoms are present in one mole of H_3PO_4 molecules?
   a. 1 mole
   b. 2 moles
   c. 3 moles
   d. no correct response
2. Which of the following samples contains 4.0 moles of O atoms?
   a. 1.0 mole SO_2
   b. 2.0 moles SO_2
   c. 1.0 mole SO_3
   d. no correct response
3. The total number of moles of atoms present in 4.00 moles of CO_2 is
   a. 3.00 moles
   b. 8.00 moles
   c. 12.0 moles
   d. no correct response
4. Which of the following is the needed conversion factor to convert from moles of N_2H_4 to moles of N?
   a. 1 mole N_2H_4/1 mole N
   b. 1 mole N_2H_4/2 moles N
   c. 2 moles N/1 mole N_2H_4
   d. no correct response

Answers: 1. c; 2. b; 3. c; 4. c

6-5 The Mole and Chemical Calculations

LEARNING FOCUS

When given information (moles, grams, particles) about a particular substance be able to calculate additional information (moles, grams, particles) about the same substance or about a component of the substance.

In this section, concepts about moles presented in previous sections are combined to produce a general approach to problem solving that is applicable to a variety of chemical situations. In Section 6-2, the concept that *Avogadro's number* provides a relationship between the number of particles of a substance and the number of moles of that same substance was introduced.

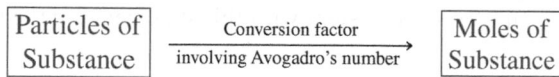

In Section 6-3, the concept that *molar mass* provides a relationship between the number of grams of a substance and the number of moles of that substance was introduced.

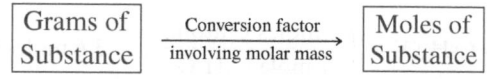

In Section 6-4, the concept that the *molar interpretation of chemical formula subscripts* provides a relationship between the number of moles of a substance and the number of moles of its components was introduced.

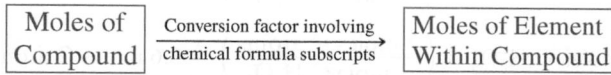

The preceding three concepts can be combined into a single diagram that is very useful in problem solving. This diagram, Figure 6-9, can be viewed as a road map

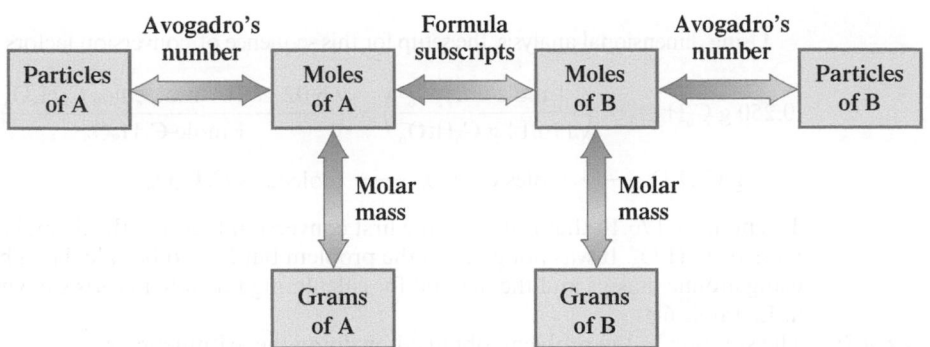

Figure 6-9 In solving chemical-formula-based problems, the only "transitions" allowed are those between quantities (boxes) connected by arrows. Associated with each arrow is the concept on which the required conversion factor is based.

from which conversion factor sequences (pathways) may be obtained. It gives all the relationships needed for solving two general types of problems:

1. Calculations where information (moles, particles, or grams) is given about a particular substance, and additional information (moles, particles, or grams) is needed concerning the same substance.
2. Calculations where information (moles, particles, or grams) is given about a particular substance, and information is needed concerning a *component* of that same substance.

For the first type of problem, only the left side of Figure 6-9 (the "A" boxes) is needed. For problems of the second type, both sides of the diagram (both "A" and "B" boxes) are used.

The thinking pattern needed to use Figure 6-9 is very simple.

1. Determine which box in the diagram represents the *given* quantity in the problem.
2. Locate the box that represents the *desired* quantity.
3. Follow the indicated pathway that takes you from the given quantity to the desired quantity. This involves simply following the arrows. There will always be only one pathway possible for the needed transition.

Examples 6-5 and 6-6 illustrate two of the types of problems that can be solved by using the relationships shown in Figure 6-9.

EXAMPLE 6-5

Calculating the Number of Particles in a Given Mass of Compound

Vitamin C has the formula $C_6H_8O_6$. Calculate the number of vitamin C molecules present in a 0.250-g tablet of pure vitamin C.

Solution

Solving this problem by using the three steps of dimensional analysis (Section 2-8) and Figure 6-9 proceeds in the following manner:

Step 1: The given quantity is 0.250 g of $C_6H_8O_6$, and the desired quantity is molecules of $C_6H_8O_6$.

$$0.250 \text{ g } C_6H_8O_6 = ? \text{ molecules } C_6H_8O_6$$

In terms of Figure 6-9, this is a "grams of A" to "particles of A" problem. We are given grams of a substance, A, and desire to find molecules (particles) of that same substance.

Step 2: Figure 6-9 gives the pathway needed to solve this problem. "Grams of A" are converted to "moles of A," which are then converted to "particles of A." The arrows between the boxes along our path give the type of conversion factor needed for each step.

$$\boxed{\text{Grams of A}} \xrightarrow[\text{mass}]{\text{Molar}} \boxed{\text{Moles of A}} \xrightarrow[\text{number}]{\text{Avogadro's}} \boxed{\text{Particles of A}}$$

(continued)

Using dimensional analysis, the setup for this sequence of conversion factors is

$$0.250 \text{ g } \cancel{C_6H_8O_6} \times \left(\frac{1 \text{ mole } \cancel{C_6H_8O_6}}{176.14 \text{ g } \cancel{C_6H_8O_6}} \right) \times \left(\frac{6.02 \times 10^{23} \text{ molecules } C_6H_8O_6}{1 \text{ mole } \cancel{C_6H_8O_6}} \right)$$

$$\text{g } C_6H_8O_6 \longrightarrow \text{moles } C_6H_8O_6 \longrightarrow \text{molecules } C_6H_8O_6$$

The number 176.14 that is used in the first conversion factor is the formula mass of $C_6H_8O_6$. It was not given in the problem but had to be calculated by using atomic masses and the method for calculating formula masses shown in Example 6-1.

Step 3: The solution to the problem, obtained by doing the arithmetic, is

$$\frac{0.250 \times 1 \times 6.02 \times 10^{23}}{176.14 \times 1} \text{ molecules } C_6H_8O_6$$

$$= 8.54 \times 10^{20} \text{ molecules } C_6H_8O_6$$

EXAMPLE 6-6

Calculating the Mass of an Element Present in a Given Mass of Compound

How many grams of nitrogen are present in a 0.10-g sample of caffeine, the stimulant in coffee and tea? The formula of caffeine is $C_8H_{10}N_4O_2$.

Solution

Step 1: There is an important difference between this problem and the preceding one; here we are dealing with not one but *two* substances, caffeine and nitrogen. The given quantity is grams of caffeine (substance A), and the needed quantity is grams of nitrogen (substance B). This is a "grams of A" to "grams of B" problem.

$$0.10 \text{ g } C_8H_{10}N_4O_2 = ? \text{ g N}$$

Step 2: The appropriate set of conversions for a "grams of A" to "grams of B" problem, from Figure 6-9, is

$$\boxed{\text{Grams of A}} \xrightarrow[\text{mass}]{\text{Molar}} \boxed{\text{Moles of A}} \xrightarrow[\text{subscripts}]{\text{Formula}} \boxed{\text{Moles of B}} \xrightarrow[\text{mass}]{\text{Molar}} \boxed{\text{Grams of B}}$$

The conversion factor setup is

$$0.10 \text{ g } \cancel{C_8H_{10}N_4O_2} \times \left(\frac{1 \text{ mole } \cancel{C_8H_{10}N_4O_2}}{194.22 \text{ g } \cancel{C_8H_{10}N_4O_2}} \right) \times \left(\frac{4 \text{ moles N}}{1 \text{ mole } \cancel{C_8H_{10}N_4O_2}} \right) \times \left(\frac{14.01 \text{ g N}}{1 \text{ mole N}} \right)$$

The number 194.22 that is used in the first conversion factor is the formula mass for caffeine. The conversion from "moles of A" to "moles of B" (the second conversion factor) is made by using the information contained in the formula $C_8H_{10}N_4O_2$. One mole of caffeine contains 4 moles of nitrogen. The number 14.01 in the final conversion factor is the molar mass of nitrogen.

Step 3: Collecting the numbers from the various conversion factors and doing the arithmetic give us our answer.

$$\left(\frac{0.10 \times 1 \times 4 \times 14.01}{194.22 \times 1 \times 1} \right) \text{ g N} = 0.029 \text{ g N}$$

Section 6-5 Quick Quiz

1. The problem "How many molecules of H_2O are present in 25.4 g of H_2O?" is characterized as a
   a. "particles of A" to "grams of A" problem
   b. "grams of A" to "moles of A" problem
   c. "grams of A" to "particles of A" problem
   d. no correct response

2. The pathway for solving a "grams of A" to "grams of B" problem using conversion factors is
   a. grams A to moles A to grams B
   b. moles A to moles B to grams A to grams B
   c. grams A to moles A to moles B to grams B
   d. no correct response

3. How many conversion factors are needed in solving a "particles of A" to "grams of A" problem?
   a. one
   b. two
   c. three
   d. no correct response

4. Which of the following is the correct conversion factor setup for the problem "How many atoms are present in 10.0 g of S?"

   a. $10.0 \text{ g S} \times \left(\dfrac{6.02 \times 10^{23} \text{ atoms S}}{1.00 \text{ g S}} \right)$

   b. $10.0 \text{ g S} \times \left(\dfrac{1 \text{ mole S}}{32.07 \text{ g S}} \right) \times \left(\dfrac{1 \text{ atom S}}{6.02 \times 10^{23} \text{ moles S}} \right)$

   c. $10.0 \text{ g S} \times \left(\dfrac{1 \text{ mole S}}{32.07 \text{ g S}} \right) \times \left(\dfrac{6.02 \times 10^{23} \text{ atoms S}}{1 \text{ mole S}} \right)$

   d. no correct response

Answers: 1. c; 2. c; 3. b; 4. c

6-6 Writing and Balancing Chemical Equations

LEARNING FOCUS

Understand the conventions used in writing chemical equations; balance a chemical equation given the chemical formulas of all reactants and all products.

A **chemical equation** *is a written statement that uses chemical symbols and chemical formulas instead of words to describe the changes that occur in a chemical reaction.* The following example shows the contrast between a word description of a chemical reaction and a chemical equation for the same reaction.

Word description: Calcium sulfide reacts with water to produce calcium oxide and hydrogen sulfide.

Chemical equation: $CaS + H_2O \longrightarrow CaO + H_2S$

In the same way that chemical symbols are considered the *letters* of chemical language, and chemical formulas are considered the *words* of the language, chemical equations can be considered the *sentences* of chemical language.

The substances present at the start of a chemical reaction are called *reactants*. A **reactant** *is a starting material in a chemical reaction that undergoes change in the chemical reaction.* As a chemical reaction proceeds, reactants are consumed (used up) and new materials with new chemical properties, called *products,* are produced. A **product** *is a substance produced as a result of the chemical reaction.*

Conventions Used in Writing Chemical Equations

Four conventions are used to write chemical equations. ◄

1. *The correct formulas of the **reactants** are always written on the **left** side of the equation.*

   $\boxed{CaS} + \boxed{H_2O} \longrightarrow CaO + H_2S$

2. *The correct formulas of the **products** are always written on the **right** side of the equation.*

   $CaS + H_2O \longrightarrow \boxed{CaO} + \boxed{H_2S}$

► *In a chemical equation, the* reactants *are always written on the left side of the equation, and the* products *are always written on the right side of the equation.*

3. *The reactants and products are separated by an arrow pointing toward the products.*

$$CaS + H_2O \Longrightarrow CaO + H_2S$$

This arrow means "to produce."

4. *Plus signs are used to separate different reactants or different products.*

$$CaS \oplus H_2O \longrightarrow CaO \oplus H_2S$$

Plus signs on the reactant side of the equation mean "reacts with," and plus signs on the product side mean "and."

A *valid* chemical equation must satisfy two conditions:

1. *It must be consistent with experimental facts.* Only the reactants and products that are actually involved in a reaction are shown in an equation. An accurate formula must be used for each of these substances. Elements in solid and liquid states are represented in equations by the chemical symbol for the element. Elements that are gases at room temperature are represented by the molecular formula denoting the form in which they actually occur in nature. The following monoatomic, diatomic, and tetraatomic elemental gases are known. ◀

▶ *The diatomic elemental gases are the elements whose names end in -gen (hydrogen, oxygen, and nitrogen) or -ine (fluorine, chlorine, bromine, and iodine).*

Monoatomic:	He, Ne, Ar, Kr, Xe
Diatomic:	H_2, O_2, N_2, F_2, Cl_2, Br_2 (vapor), I_2 (vapor)
Tetraatomic:	P_4 (vapor), As_4 (vapor)*

2. *There must be the same number of atoms of each kind on both sides of the chemical equation.* Chemical equations that satisfy this condition are said to be balanced. A **balanced chemical equation** *is a chemical equation that has the same number of atoms of each element involved in a chemical reaction on each side of the equation.* Because the conventions previously listed for writing equations do not guarantee that an equation will be balanced, procedures for balancing equations are now considered.

Guidelines for Balancing Chemical Equations

An unbalanced chemical equation is brought into balance by adding *coefficients* to the equation to adjust the number of reactant or product molecules present. An **equation coefficient** *is a number that is placed to the left of the chemical formula of a substance in a chemical equation that changes the amount, but not the identity, of the substance.* In the notation $2H_2O$, the 2 on the left is a coefficient; $2H_2O$ means two molecules of H_2O, and $3H_2O$ means three molecules of H_2O. Thus equation coefficients tell how many molecules or formula units of a given substance are present. ◀

▶ *The coefficients of a balanced equation represent numbers of molecules or formula units of various species involved in the chemical reaction.*

The following is a balanced chemical equation, with the coefficients shown in color.

$$4NH_3 + 3O_2 \longrightarrow 2N_2 + 6H_2O$$

This balanced equation indicates that four NH_3 molecules react with three O_2 molecules to produce two N_2 molecules and six H_2O molecules.

A coefficient of 1 in a balanced equation is not explicitly written; it is considered to be understood. Both Na_2SO_4 and Na_2S have "understood coefficients" of 1 in the following balanced equation:

$$Na_2SO_4 + 2C \longrightarrow Na_2S + 2CO_2$$

An equation coefficient placed in front of a formula applies to the whole formula. By contrast, subscripts, which are also present in formulas, affect only parts of a formula.

Coefficient (affects both H and O)
$$2H_2O$$
Subscript (affects only H)

---

*The four elements listed as vapors are not gases at room temperature but vaporize at slightly higher temperatures. The resultant vapors contain molecules with the formulas indicated.

The preceding notation denotes two molecules of H_2O; it also denotes a total of four H atoms and two O atoms.

The mechanics involved in determining the coefficients needed to balance a chemical equation are as follows.

Suppose we want to balance the chemical equation

$$FeI_2 + Cl_2 \longrightarrow FeCl_3 + I_2$$

Step 1: *Examine the equation and pick one element to balance first.* It is often convenient to start with the compound that contains the greatest number of atoms, whether a reactant or a product, and focus on the element in that compound that has the greatest number of atoms. Using this guideline, we select $FeCl_3$ and the element chlorine within it.

Note that there are three chlorine atoms on the right side of the equation and two atoms of chlorine on the left (in Cl_2). For the chlorine atoms to balance, six will be needed on each side; 6 is the lowest number that both 3 and 2 will divide into evenly. In order to obtain six atoms of chlorine on each side of the equation, the coefficient 3 is placed in front of Cl_2 and the coefficient 2 in front of $FeCl_3$. ◀

$$FeI_2 + ③Cl_2 \longrightarrow ②FeCl_3 + I_2$$

There are now six chlorine atoms on each side of the equation.

$$3Cl_2: \quad 3 \times 2 = 6$$

$$2FeCl_3: \quad 2 \times 3 = 6$$

Step 2: *Next a second element is picked to balance.* Iron will be balanced next. The number of iron atoms on the right side has already been set at 2 by the coefficient previously placed in front of $FeCl_3$. Two iron atoms are needed on the reactant side of the equation instead of the one iron atom now present. This is accomplished by placing the coefficient 2 in front of FeI_2.

$$②FeI_2 + 3Cl_2 \longrightarrow 2FeCl_3 + I_2$$

It is always wise to pick, as the second element to balance, one whose amount is already set on one side of the equation by a previously determined coefficient. If we had chosen iodine as the second element to balance instead of iron, a problem would have been encountered. Because the coefficient for neither FeI_2 nor I_2 had been determined, there would be no guidelines for deciding on the amount of iodine needed.

Step 3: *Next pick a third element to balance.* Only one element is left to balance—iodine. The number of iodine atoms on the left side of the equation is already set at four ($2FeI_2$). In order to obtain four iodine atoms on the right side of the equation, we place the coefficient 2 in front of I_2.

$$2FeI_2 + 3Cl_2 \longrightarrow 2FeCl_3 + ②I_2$$

The addition of the coefficient 2 in front of I_2 completes the balancing process; all the coefficients have been determined.

Step 4: *As a final check on the correctness of the balancing procedure, count atoms on each side of the equation.* The following table can be constructed from the balanced equation.

$$2FeI_2 + 3Cl_2 \longrightarrow 2FeCl_3 + 2I_2$$

Atom	Left Side	Right Side
Fe	$2 \times 1 = 2$	$2 \times 1 = 2$
I	$2 \times 2 = 4$	$2 \times 2 = 4$
Cl	$3 \times 2 = 6$	$2 \times 3 = 6$

▶ *In balancing a chemical equation, formula subscripts are* never changed. *Chemical formulas must always be used in the form in which they are given.* The only thing to be done is add coefficients.

Figure 6-10 When 16.90 g of the compound CaS (left photo) is decomposed into its constituent elements, the Ca and S produced (right photo) have an identical mass of 16.90 g. Because atoms are neither created nor destroyed in a chemical reaction, the masses of reactants and products in a chemical reaction are always equal.

 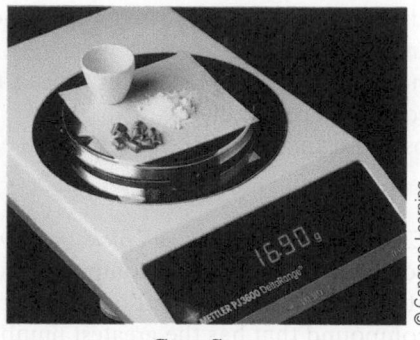

$$CaS \longrightarrow Ca + S$$

Atoms are neither created nor destroyed in a chemical reaction. The production of new substances in a chemical reaction results from the rearrangement of the existent groupings of atoms into new groupings. Because only rearrangement occurs, the products always contain the same number of atoms of each kind as do the reactants. This generalization is often referred to as the *law of conservation of mass*. The mass of the reactants and the mass of the products are the same, because both contain exactly the same number of atoms of each kind present (Figure 6-10).

In Example 6-7, the balancing of another chemical equation is carried out.

EXAMPLE 6-7

Balancing a Chemical Equation

Balance the following chemical equation:

$$C_2H_6O + O_2 \longrightarrow CO_2 + H_2O$$

Solution

The element oxygen appears in four different places in this chemical equation. This means the balancing process should not begin with the element oxygen. Always start the balancing process with an element that appears only once on both the reactant and product sides of the equation.

Step 1: *Balancing of H atoms.* There are six H atoms on the left and two H atoms on the right. Placing the coefficient 1 in front of C_2H_6O and the coefficient 3 in front of H_2O balances the H atoms at six on each side.

$$1C_2H_6O + O_2 \longrightarrow CO_2 + 3H_2O$$

Step 2: *Balancing of C atoms.* An effect of balancing the H atoms at six (Step 1) is the setting of the C atoms on the left side at two. Placing the coefficient 2 in front of CO_2 causes the carbon atoms to balance at two on each side of the chemical equation.

$$1C_2H_6O + O_2 \longrightarrow 2CO_2 + 3H_2O$$

Step 3: *Balancing of O atoms.* The oxygen content of the right side of the chemical equation is set at seven atoms: four oxygen atoms from $2CO_2$ and three oxygen atoms from $3H_2O$. To obtain seven oxygen atoms on the left side of the chemical equation, we place the coefficient 3 in front of O_2; $3O_2$ gives six oxygen atoms, and there is an additional O in $1C_2H_6O$. The element oxygen is present in all four formulas in the chemical equation.

$$1C_2H_6O + 3O_2 \longrightarrow 2CO_2 + 3H_2O$$

Step 4: *Final check.* The equation is balanced. There are two carbon atoms, six hydrogen atoms, and seven oxygen atoms on each side of the chemical equation.

$$C_2H_6O + 3O_2 \longrightarrow 2CO_2 + 3H_2O$$

Some additional comments and guidelines concerning chemical equations in general, and the process of balancing in particular, are given here.

1. The coefficients in a balanced chemical equation are always the *smallest set of whole numbers* that will balance the equation. This is mentioned because more than one set of coefficients will balance a chemical equation. Consider the following three equations:

$$2H_2 + O_2 \longrightarrow 2H_2O$$
$$4H_2 + 2O_2 \longrightarrow 4H_2O$$
$$8H_2 + 4O_2 \longrightarrow 8H_2O$$

All three of these chemical equations are mathematically correct; there are equal numbers of hydrogen and oxygen atoms on both sides of the equation. However, the first equation is considered the correct form because the coefficients used there are the smallest set of whole numbers that will balance the equation. The coefficients in the second equation are two times those in the first equation, and the third equation has coefficients that are four times those of the first equation.

2. After learning how to balance chemical equations, students sometimes get the mistaken idea that they ought to be able to write down the products for a chemical reaction when given the identity of the reactants. This is not the case. More chemical knowledge is needed before such a task may be carried out. The procedures just presented are adequate to balance simple chemical equations when given *all* of the reactant chemical formulas and *all* of the product chemical formulas.

3. It is often useful to know the physical state of the substances involved in a chemical reaction. Physical state is specified by using the symbols (*s*) for solid, (*l*) for liquid, (*g*) for gas, and (*aq*) for aqueous solution (a substance dissolved in water). Two examples of such symbol use in chemical equations are

$$2Fe_2O_3(s) + 3C(s) \longrightarrow 4Fe(s) + 3CO_2(g)$$
$$2HNO_3(aq) + 3H_2S(aq) \longrightarrow 2NO(g) + 3S(s) + 4H_2O(l)$$

Section 6-6 Quick Quiz

1. When the chemical equation Na + S $\longrightarrow$ Na$_2$S is correctly balanced, the proper sequence of coefficients is
   a. 1,2,2
   b. 2,1,2
   c. 2,1,2
   d. no correct response
2. When the chemical equation Al + O$_2$ $\longrightarrow$ Al$_2$O$_3$ is correctly balanced, which of the following expressions appears in it?
   a. 3 Al
   b. 3 O$_2$
   c. 3 Al$_2$O$_3$
   d. no correct response
3. A balanced chemical equation contains the expression 2 FeCl$_3$. How many atoms does this expression represent?
   a. two
   b. four
   c. eight
   d. no correct response

(continued)

4. Which of the following elemental gases is <u>not</u> written as a diatomic molecule in a chemical equation?
   a. hydrogen
   b. nitrogen
   c. helium
   d. no correct response
5. Which of the following statements is true for all balanced chemical equations?
   a. The sum of the coefficients on each side of the equation must be equal.
   b. The sum of the formula subscripts on each side of the equation must be equal.
   c. The total number of atoms on each side of the equation must be equal.
   d. no correct response

Answers: 1. d; 2. b; 3. c; 4. c; 5. c

6-7 Chemical Equations and the Mole Concept

LEARNING FOCUS

Interpret the coefficients in a balanced chemical equation in terms of molar amounts of substances.

The coefficients in a balanced chemical equation, like the subscripts in a chemical formula (Section 6-4), have two levels of interpretation—a microscopic level of meaning and a macroscopic level of meaning. The microscopic level of interpretation, which was used in the previous two sections, is: *The coefficients in a balanced chemical equation give the numerical relationships among formula units consumed or produced in the chemical reaction.* Interpreted at the microscopic level, the chemical equation

$$N_2 + 3H_2 \longrightarrow 2NH_3$$

conveys the information that one molecule of N_2 reacts with three molecules of H_2 to produce two molecules of NH_3.

At the macroscopic level of interpretation, chemical equations are used to relate mole-sized quantities of reactants and products to each other. At this level, *the coefficients in a balanced chemical equation give the fixed molar ratios between substances consumed or produced in the chemical reaction.* Interpreted at the macroscopic level, the chemical equation

$$N_2 + 3H_2 \longrightarrow 2NH_3$$

conveys the information that 1 mole of N_2 reacts with 3 moles of H_2 to produce 2 moles of NH_3.

The coefficients in a balanced chemical equation can be used to generate mole-based conversion factors to be used in solving problems. Several pairs of conversion factors are obtainable from a single balanced chemical equation. ◀ Consider the following balanced chemical equation:

▶ *Conversion factors that relate two different substances to one another are valid only for systems governed by the chemical equation from which they were obtained.*

$$4Fe + 3O_2 \longrightarrow 2Fe_2O_3$$

Three mole-to-mole relationships are obtainable from this chemical equation:

4 moles of Fe produce 2 moles of Fe_2O_3.

3 moles of O_2 produce 2 moles of Fe_2O_3.

4 moles of Fe react with 3 moles of O_2.

From each of these macroscopic-level relationships, two conversion factors can be written. The conversion factors for the first relationship are

$$\left(\frac{4 \text{ moles Fe}}{2 \text{ moles Fe}_2\text{O}_3} \right) \text{ and } \left(\frac{2 \text{ moles Fe}_2\text{O}_3}{4 \text{ moles Fe}} \right)$$

All balanced chemical equations are the source of numerous conversion factors. The more reactants and products there are in the chemical equation, the greater the number of derivable conversion factors. The next section details how conversion factors such as those in the preceding illustration are used in solving problems.

An additional concept about chemical equation writing that is important to know is that a given set of reactants can react to produce different products depending on reaction conditions such as temperature, pressure, presence of a catalyst (Section 9-6), and the molar ratio in which the reactants are present. For example, the gas ammonia (NH_3) reacts with oxygen (O_2) in two different ways depending on reaction conditions.

$$4NH_3(g) + 3\,O_2 \longrightarrow 2N_2(g) + 6H_2O(g)$$
$$4NH_3(g) + 5\,O_2(g) \longrightarrow 4NO(g) + 6H_2O(g)$$

Another example of two reactants reacting in different molar ratios is the reaction between the fuel methane (CH_4) and O_2 gas. The product is either carbon dioxide or carbon monoxide depending on the amount of O_2 gas available for the reaction.

$$CH_4(g) + 2\,O_2(g) \longrightarrow CO_2(g) + 2H_2O(g)$$
$$2CH_4(g) + 3\,O_2(g) \longrightarrow 2CO(g) + 4H_2O(g)$$

The focus on relevancy feature Chemical Connections 6-A—Carbon Monoxide Air Pollution: A Case of Incomplete Combustion—explores further the significance of the molar CH_4/O_2 reactant ratio in the production of carbon monoxide as an air pollutant.

Chemistry at a Glance—Relationships Involving the Mole Concept—summarizes the various concepts that have been presented so far in this chapter about the mole, that is, how the mole concept relates to Avogadro's number (Section 6-2), molar mass (Section 6-3), chemical formulas (Section 6-4), and chemical equations (Section 6-7).

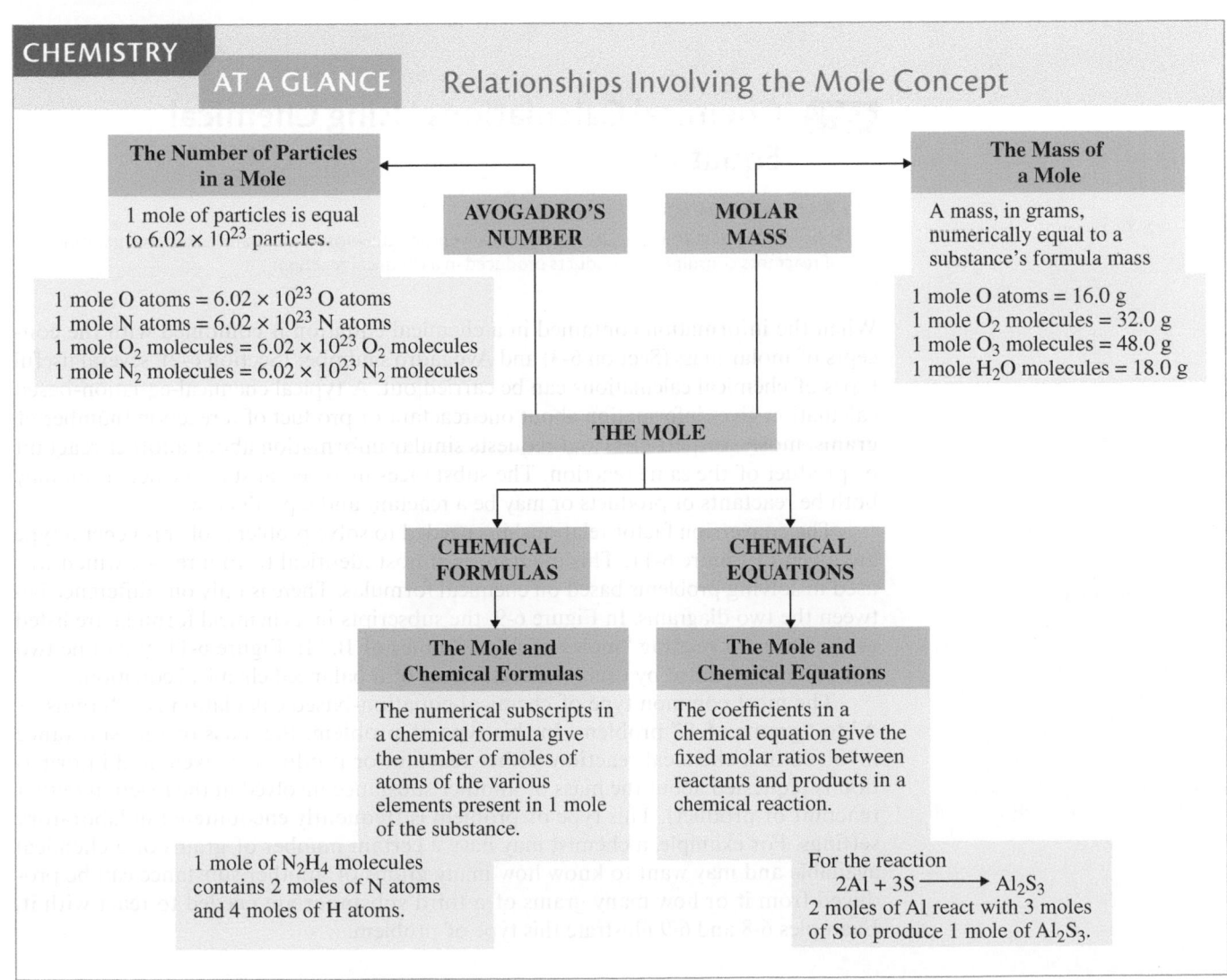

CHEMISTRY AT A GLANCE Relationships Involving the Mole Concept

The Number of Particles in a Mole

1 mole of particles is equal to 6.02×10^{23} particles.

1 mole O atoms = 6.02×10^{23} O atoms
1 mole N atoms = 6.02×10^{23} N atoms
1 mole O_2 molecules = 6.02×10^{23} O_2 molecules
1 mole N_2 molecules = 6.02×10^{23} N_2 molecules

AVOGADRO'S NUMBER

MOLAR MASS

The Mass of a Mole

A mass, in grams, numerically equal to a substance's formula mass

1 mole O atoms = 16.0 g
1 mole O_2 molecules = 32.0 g
1 mole O_3 molecules = 48.0 g
1 mole H_2O molecules = 18.0 g

THE MOLE

CHEMICAL FORMULAS

CHEMICAL EQUATIONS

The Mole and Chemical Formulas

The numerical subscripts in a chemical formula give the number of moles of atoms of the various elements present in 1 mole of the substance.

1 mole of N_2H_4 molecules contains 2 moles of N atoms and 4 moles of H atoms.

The Mole and Chemical Equations

The coefficients in a chemical equation give the fixed molar ratios between reactants and products in a chemical reaction.

For the reaction
$$2Al + 3S \longrightarrow Al_2S_3$$
2 moles of Al react with 3 moles of S to produce 1 mole of Al_2S_3.

Section 6-7 Quick Quiz

1. Which of the following statements is consistent with the information found in the chemical equation $N_2 + 3H_2 \longrightarrow 2NH_3$?
   a. 1 mole of NH_3 is produced when 1 mole of N_2 reacts
   b. 3 moles of H_2 are needed to produce 1 mole of NH_3
   c. N_2 and H_2 react in a 1-to-3 molar ratio
   d. no correct response
2. How many moles of Al are needed to produce 6.0 moles of Al_2S_3 via the chemical reaction $2Al + 3S \longrightarrow Al_2S_3$?
   a. 2.0 moles
   b. 6.0 moles
   c. 12.0 moles
   d. no correct response
3. How many moles of CO_2 are formed at the same time 2.0 moles of H_2O are formed in the chemical reaction $CH_4 + 2O_2 \longrightarrow CO_2 + 2H_2O$?
   a. 2.0 moles
   b. 3.0 moles
   c. 4.0 moles
   d. no correct response
4. Which of the following conversion factors is <u>not</u> consistent with the chemical equation $4NH_3 + 5O_2 \longrightarrow 4NO + 6H_2O$?
   a. 5 moles O_2/4 moles NH_3
   b. 4 moles NO/6 moles H_2O
   c. 4 moles NH_3/4 moles H_2O
   d. no correct response

Answers: 1. c; 2. c; 3. d; 4. c

6-8 Chemical Calculations Using Chemical Equations

LEARNING FOCUS

Use a balanced chemical equation and other appropriate information to calculate the quantities of reactants consumed or products produced in a chemical reaction.

When the information contained in a chemical equation is combined with the concepts of molar mass (Section 6-3) and Avogadro's number (Section 6-2), several useful types of chemical calculations can be carried out. A typical chemical-equation-based calculation gives information about one reactant or product of a reaction (number of grams, moles, or particles) and requests similar information about another reactant or product of the same reaction. The substances involved in such a calculation may both be reactants or products or may be a reactant and a product. ◀

▶ *The quantitative study of the relationships among reactants and products in a chemical reaction is called* chemical stoichiometry. *The word* stoichiometry, *pronounced stoy-key-om-eh-tree, is derived from the Greek* stoicheion *("element") and* metron *("measure"). The stoichiometry of a chemical reaction always involves the* molar relationships *between reactants and products and thus is given by the coefficients in the balanced equation for the chemical reaction.*

The conversion factor relationships needed to solve problems of this general type are given in Figure 6-11. This diagram is almost identical to Figure 6-9, which was used in solving problems based on chemical formulas. There is only one difference between the two diagrams. In Figure 6-9, the subscripts in a chemical formula are listed as the basis for relating "moles of A" to "moles of B." In Figure 6-11, the same two quantities are related by using the coefficients of a balanced chemical equation.

The most common type of chemical-equation-based calculation is a "grams of A" to "grams of B" problem. In this type of problem, the mass of one substance involved in a chemical reaction (either reactant or product) is given, and information is requested about the mass of another substance involved in the reaction (either reactant or product). This type of problem is frequently encountered in laboratory settings. For example, a chemist may have a certain number of grams of a chemical available and may want to know how many grams of another substance can be produced from it or how many grams of a third substance are needed to react with it. Examples 6-8 and 6-9 illustrate this type of problem.

Carbon Monoxide Air Pollution: A Case of Incomplete Combustion

Experimental conditions—such as temperature, pressure, and the relative amounts of different reactants present—are often key factors in determining the products of a chemical reaction. Under one set of experimental conditions two reactants may produce a certain set of products, and under a different set of experimental conditions these same two reactants may produce another set of products. Such is the case when methane gas (CH_4) reacts with oxygen gas from the air.

When methane is burned in an excess of oxygen, the products are carbon dioxide and water.

$$CH_4(g) + 2O_2(g) \longrightarrow CO_2(g) + 2H_2O(g)$$

These same two reactants, with less oxygen present, undergo combustion to produce carbon monoxide and water.

$$2CH_4(g) + 3O_2(g) \longrightarrow 2CO(g) + 4H_2O(g)$$

The difference between the two reactions is the molar combining ratio for the two reactants: 1 to 2 (twice as many moles of oxygen) in the first case and 2 to 3 (1.5 times as many moles of oxygen) in the second case.

Methane gas, the reactant in both of the preceding reactions, is the major component present in the natural gas used in home heating during the winter season. Natural gas furnaces are designed to operate under conditions that favor the first reaction and at the same time minimize the second reaction. With a properly operating gas furnace, the products of combustion are, thus, predominately CO_2 and H_2O (with a small amount of CO), all of which leave the home through an external venting system. However, if the gas burners are out of adjustment (improper oxygen/fuel ratio) or the venting system becomes obstructed, CO levels within the home can build up to levels that are toxic to humans.

Within the human body, inhaled CO reacts with the hemoglobin (Hb) present in red blood cells to form the substance carboxyhemoglobin (COHb). Such COHb formation reduces the ability of hemoglobin to transport oxygen from the lungs to the tissues of the body.

The important factor concerning the effect of CO on the human body is the amount of COHb present in the blood. The higher the percentage of COHb present, the more serious the effect, as indicated in the following table:

Health Effects of COHb Blood Levels

COHb Blood Level (%)	Demonstrated Effects
Less than 1.0	No apparent effect.
1.0 to 2.0	Some evidence of effect on behavioral performance.
2.0 to 5.0	Central nervous system effects. Impairment of time-interval discrimination, visual acuity, brightness discrimination, and certain other psychomotor functions.
Greater than 5.0	Cardiac and pulmonary functional changes.
10.0 to 80.0	Headache, fatigue, drowsiness, coma, respiratory failure, death.

The CO concentration of inhaled air determines COHb levels in the blood. A CO concentration of 10 ppm (parts per million) is required to produce a blood COHb level of 2.0%. A 10-ppm CO concentration is seldom encountered in ambient air, even in locations with high air-pollution levels. The normally encountered range for air CO concentrations is from 3 to 4 ppm in urban areas with large numbers of automobiles and coal-burning industrial complexes to about 0.1 ppm in rural environments.

Cigarette smoking is a form of individualized CO air pollution. Cigarette smoke contains a CO concentration greater than 20,000 ppm, the result of the oxygen-deficient conditions (smoldering) under which the cigarette burns. During inhalation, this high CO concentration is diluted to a level of about 400–500 ppm. This "diluted" CO concentration is still sufficiently high to produce elevated COHb levels in the blood of smokers, as shown in the following table:

Blood COHb Levels of Smokers

Category of Smoker	Blood Level of COHb (%)
Never smoked	1.3
Ex-smoker	1.4
Light cigarette smoker	3.8
Moderate cigarette smoker	5.9
Heavy cigarette smoker	6.9

Indoor CO air pollution caused by cigarette smoking is significant enough that most states have banned smoking in public gathering areas ranging from airports to restaurants. Studies indicate that nonsmokers present for an extended time in areas where smoking occurs have elevated levels of COHb. The elevated levels are not as high, however, as those of the smokers themselves.

Figure 6-11 In solving chemical-equation-based problems, the only "transitions" allowed are those between quantities (boxes) connected by arrows. Associated with each arrow is the concept on which the required conversion factor is based.

EXAMPLE 6-8

Calculating the Mass of a Product in a Chemical Reaction

The human body converts the glucose, $C_6H_{12}O_6$, contained in foods to carbon dioxide, CO_2, and water, H_2O. The net chemical equation for the chemical reaction is

$$C_6H_{12}O_6 + 6O_2 \longrightarrow 6CO_2 + 6H_2O$$

Assume a person eats a candy bar containing 14.2 g (1/2 oz) of glucose. How many grams of water will the body produce from the ingested glucose, assuming all of the glucose undergoes reaction?

Solution

Step 1: The given quantity is 14.2 g of glucose. The desired quantity is grams of water.

$$14.2 \text{ g } C_6H_{12}O_6 = ? \text{ g } H_2O$$

In terms of Figure 6-11, this is a "grams of A" to "grams of B" problem.

Step 2: Using Figure 6-11 as a road map, the pathway for this problem becomes

$$\boxed{\text{Grams of A}} \xrightarrow{\substack{\text{Molar} \\ \text{mass}}} \boxed{\text{Moles of A}} \xrightarrow{\substack{\text{Equation} \\ \text{coefficients}}} \boxed{\text{Moles of B}} \xrightarrow{\substack{\text{Molar} \\ \text{mass}}} \boxed{\text{Grams of B}}$$

The mathematical setup for this problem is

$$14.2 \text{ g } C_6H_{12}O_6 \times \left(\frac{1 \text{ mole } C_6H_{12}O_6}{180.18 \text{ g } C_6H_{12}O_6}\right) \times \left(\frac{6 \text{ moles } H_2O}{1 \text{ mole } C_6H_{12}O_6}\right) \times \left(\frac{18.02 \text{ g } H_2O}{1 \text{ mole } H_2O}\right)$$

$$\text{g } C_6H_{12}O_6 \longrightarrow \text{moles } C_6H_{12}O_6 \longrightarrow \text{moles } H_2O \longrightarrow \text{g } H_2O$$

The 180.18 g in the first conversion factor is the molar mass of glucose, the 6 and 1 in the second conversion factor are the coefficients, respectively, of H_2O and $C_6H_{12}O_6$ in the balanced chemical equation, and the 18.02 g in the third conversion factor is the molar mass of H_2O.

Step 3: The solution to the problem, obtained by doing the arithmetic after all the numerical factors have been collected, is

$$\left(\frac{14.2 \times 1 \times 6 \times 18.02}{180.18 \times 1 \times 1}\right) \text{ g } H_2O = 8.52 \text{ g } H_2O$$

EXAMPLE 6-9

Calculating the Mass of a Reactant Taking Part in a Chemical Reaction

The active ingredient in many commercial antacids is magnesium hydroxide, $Mg(OH)_2$, which reacts with stomach acid (HCl) to produce magnesium chloride ($MgCl_2$) and water. The equation for the reaction is

$$Mg(OH)_2 + 2HCl \longrightarrow MgCl_2 + 2H_2O$$

How many grams of $Mg(OH)_2$ are needed to react with 0.30 g of HCl?

Solution

Step 1: This problem, like Example 6-8, is a "grams of A" to "grams of B" problem. It differs from the previous problem in that both the given and the desired quantities involve reactants.

$$0.30 \text{ g HCl} \longrightarrow \text{? g Mg(OH)}_2$$

Step 2: The pathway used to solve it will be the same as in Example 6-8.

$$\boxed{\text{Grams of A}} \xrightarrow[\text{mass}]{\text{Molar}} \boxed{\text{Moles of A}} \xrightarrow[\text{coefficients}]{\text{Equation}} \boxed{\text{Moles of B}} \xrightarrow[\text{mass}]{\text{Molar}} \boxed{\text{Grams of B}}$$

The dimensional-analysis setup is

$$0.30 \text{ g HCl} \times \left(\frac{1 \text{ mole HCl}}{36.46 \text{ g HCl}}\right) \times \left(\frac{1 \text{ mole Mg(OH)}_2}{2 \text{ moles HCl}}\right) \times \left(\frac{58.33 \text{ g Mg(OH)}_2}{1 \text{ mole Mg(OH)}_2}\right)$$

$$\text{g HCl} \longrightarrow \text{moles HCl} \longrightarrow \text{moles Mg(OH)}_2 \longrightarrow \text{g Mg(OH)}_2$$

The balanced chemical equation for the reaction is used as the bridge that enables us to go from HCl to $Mg(OH)_2$. The numbers in the second conversion factor are coefficients from this equation.

Step 3: The solution obtained by combining all of the numbers in the manner indicated in the setup is

$$\left(\frac{0.30 \times 1 \times 1 \times 58.33}{36.46 \times 2 \times 1}\right) \text{ g Mg(OH)}_2 = 0.24 \text{ g Mg(OH)}_2$$

To put our answer in perspective, note that a common brand of antacid tablets contains 0.10 g of $Mg(OH)_2$.

"Grams of A" to "grams of B" problems (Examples 6-8 and 6-9) are not the only type of problem for which the coefficients in a balanced equation can be used to relate the quantities of two substances. As a further example of the use of equation coefficients in problem solving, consider Example 6-10 (a "particles of A" to "moles of B" problem).

EXAMPLE 6-10

Calculating the Amount of a Substance Taking Part in a Chemical Reaction

Automotive airbags inflate when sodium azide, NaN_3, rapidly decomposes to its constituent elements. The equation for the chemical reaction is

$$2NaN_3(s) \longrightarrow 2Na(s) + 3N_2(g)$$

The gaseous N_2 so generated inflates the airbag (Figure 6-12). How many moles of NaN_3 would have to decompose in order to generate 253 million (2.53×10^8) molecules of N_2?

Solution

Although a calculation of this type does not have a lot of practical significance, it does test the depth of understanding of the problem-solving relationships discussed in this section of the text.

Step 1: The given quantity is 2.53×10^8 molecules of N_2, and the desired quantity is moles of NaN_3.

$$2.53 \times 10^8 \text{ molecules N}_2 = \text{? moles NaN}_3$$

In terms of Figure 6-11, this is a "particles of A" to "moles of B" problem.

Step 2: Using Figure 6-11 as a road map, we determine that the pathway for this problem is

$$\boxed{\text{Particles of A}} \xrightarrow[\text{number}]{\text{Avogadro's}} \boxed{\text{Moles of A}} \xrightarrow[\text{coefficients}]{\text{Equation}} \boxed{\text{Moles of B}}$$

(continued)

Figure 6-12 Testing apparatus for measuring the effects of airbag deployment.

Courtesy Daimler Chrysler Corporation

The mathematical setup is

$$2.53 \times 10^8 \text{ molecules } N_2 \times \left(\frac{1 \text{ mole } N_2}{6.02 \times 10^{23} \text{ molecules } N_2} \right) \times \left(\frac{2 \text{ moles } NaN_3}{3 \text{ moles } N_2} \right)$$

Avogadro's number is present in the first conversion factor. The 2 and 3 in the second conversion factor are the coefficients, respectively, of NaN_3 and N_2 in the balanced chemical equation.

Step 3: The solution to the problem, obtained by doing the arithmetic after all the numerical factors have been collected, is

$$\left(\frac{2.53 \times 10^8 \times 1 \times 2}{6.02 \times 10^{23} \times 3} \right) \text{ mole } NaN_3 = 2.80 \times 10^{-16} \text{ mole } NaN_3$$

CHEMICAL CONNECTIONS 6-B

Chemical Reactions on an Industrial Scale: Sulfuric Acid

The industrial production of chemical substances is a multibillion dollar enterprise in the United States. About 50 of the many thousands of compounds produced industrially in the United States are produced in amounts exceeding 1 billion pounds per year.

The number-one chemical in the United States, in terms of production amount, is sulfuric acid (H_2SO_4), with an annual production of 70 billion pounds. Its production amount is almost twice that of any other chemical. So important is sulfuric acid production in the United States (and the world) that some economists use sulfuric acid production as a measure of a nation's industrial strength.

Why is so much sulfuric acid produced in the United States? What are its uses? What are its properties? Where is it encountered in everyday life?

Pure sulfuric acid is a colorless, corrosive, oily liquid. It is usually marketed as a concentrated (96% by mass) aqueous solution. People rarely have direct contact with this strong acid because it is seldom part of finished consumer products. The closest encounter most people have with the acid (other than in a chemical laboratory) is involvement with automobile batteries. The acid in a standard automobile battery is a 38%-by-mass aqueous solution of sulfuric acid. However, less than 1% of annual sulfuric acid production ends up in car batteries.

Approximately two-thirds of sulfuric acid production is used in the manufacture of chemical fertilizers. These fertilizer compounds are an absolute necessity if the food needs of an ever-increasing population are to be met. The connection between sulfuric acid and fertilizer revolves around the element phosphorus, which is necessary for plant growth. The starting material for phosphate fertilizer production is phosphate rock, a highly insoluble material containing calcium phosphate, $Ca_3(PO_4)_2$. The treatment of phosphate rock with H_2SO_4 results in the formation of phosphoric acid, H_3PO_4.

$$Ca_3(PO_4)_2 + 3H_2SO_4 \longrightarrow 3CaSO_4 + 2H_3PO_4$$

The phosphoric acid so produced is then used to produce soluble phosphate compounds that plants can use as a source of phosphorus. The major phosphoric acid fertilizer derivative is ammonium hydrogen phosphate [$(NH_4)_2HPO_4$].

The source of phosphorus for ammonium phosphate fertilizer is phosphate rock.

The raw materials needed to produce sulfuric acid are simple: sulfur, air, and water. In the first step of production, elemental sulfur is burned to give sulfur dioxide gas.

$$S + O_2 \longrightarrow SO_2$$

Some SO_2 is also obtainable as a by-product of metallurgical operations associated with zinc and copper production. Next, the SO_2 gas is combined with additional O_2 (air) to produce sulfur trioxide gas.

$$2SO_2 + O_2 \longrightarrow 2SO_3$$

The SO_3 is then dissolved in water, which yields sulfuric acid as the product.

$$SO_3 + H_2O \longrightarrow H_2SO_4$$

Reactions similar to the last two steps in commercial H_2SO_4 production can also occur naturally in the atmosphere. The H_2SO_4 so produced is a major contributor to the phenomenon called acid rain (see Chemical Connections 10-B—pH Values for Acid Rain).

The example calculations carried out in this section can be considered to be "laboratory-based" calculations. Chemical substance amounts were always specified in grams, the commonly used laboratory unit for mass. These gram-sized laboratory amounts are very small, almost "infinitesimal," when compared with industrial production figures for various "high-volume" chemicals. The focus on relevancy feature Chemical Connections 6-B—Chemical Reactions on an Industrial Scale: Sulfuric Acid—considers industrial-scale chemical production in the context of sulfuric acid production; the chemical industry in the United States produces more sulfuric acid than any other substance.

Section 6-8 Quick Quiz

1. The problem "How many grams of O_2 are needed to produce 2.00 moles of H_2O via the chemical reaction $2H_2 + O_2 \longrightarrow 2H_2O$?" is characterized as a
   a. "moles of A" to "grams of A" problem
   b. "grams of A" to "moles of B" problem
   c. "moles of A" to "grams of B" problem
   d. no correct response
2. The pathway for solving a "grams of A" to "moles of B" problem using conversion factors is
   a. grams A to moles A to moles B
   b. moles A to moles B to grams A to grams B
   c. grams A to moles A to moles B to grams B
   d. no correct response
3. How many conversion factors are needed in solving a "particles of A" to "grams of B" problem?
   a. one
   b. two
   c. three
   d. no correct response
4. Which of the following is the correct conversion factor setup for the problem "How many grams of H_2O can be produced from 3.2 moles of O_2 and an excess of H_2S via the chemical reaction $2H_2S + 3O_2 \longrightarrow 2H_2O + 2SO_2$?"

   a. $3.2 \text{ moles } O_2 \times \left(\dfrac{32.00 \text{ g } O_2}{1 \text{ mole } O_2}\right) \times \left(\dfrac{18.02 \text{ g } H_2O}{32.00 \text{ g } O_2}\right)$

   b. $3.2 \text{ moles } O_2 \times \left(\dfrac{2 \text{ moles } H_2O}{3 \text{ moles } O_2}\right) \times \left(\dfrac{18.02 \text{ g } H_2O}{1 \text{ mole } H_2O}\right)$

   c. $3.2 \text{ moles } O_2 \times \left(\dfrac{32.00 \text{ g } O_2}{1 \text{ mole } O_2}\right) \times \left(\dfrac{2 \text{ moles } H_2O}{3 \text{ moles } O_2}\right)$

   d. no correct response

Answers: 1. c; 2. a; 3. c; 4. b

6-9 Yields: Theoretical, Actual, and Percent

LEARNING FOCUS

Be able to distinguish from each other the concepts of theoretical yield, actual yield, and percent yield.

Calculating the amount of product that is produced in a chemical reaction from given amounts of reactants, as was illustrated in Example 6-8 in the last section, provides the *theoretical yield* of the product. A **theoretical yield** is *the maximum amount of a product that can be obtained from given amounts of reactants in a chemical reaction if no losses or inefficiencies of any kind occur.*

It is almost always the case that the amount of product actually obtained from a chemical reaction is less than that predicted by calculation; that is, the amount of product obtained is less than the *theoretical yield*.

There are two reasons why this is so.

1. Some product is almost always lost in the mechanical process of isolating the product, such as in transferring materials from one container to another.

2. Often, unwanted side reactions occur because of factors such as impurities present; for example, the glassware used in the lab may not be perfectly clean. These side reactions consume small amounts of reactants, which decreases the amount of desired product formed.

The net effect of these "imperfections" is that the actual quantity of desired product obtained, that is, the *actual yield*, is less, sometimes far less, than the theoretically calculated amount. An **actual yield** *is the amount of product actually obtained from a chemical reaction*. Actual yield of product cannot be calculated; it must be measured.

Product loss is specified in terms of *percent yield*. The **percent yield** *is the ratio of the actual (measured) yield of a product in a chemical reaction to the theoretical (calculated) yield multiplied by 100 (to give percent)*. The mathematical equation for percent yield is

$$\text{percent yield} = \frac{\text{actual yield}}{\text{theoretical yield}} \times 100$$

If the theoretical yield of a product for a reaction is 22.3 grams and the actual yield is only 20.4 grams, the percent yield is 91.5%.

$$\text{percent yield} = \frac{20.4 \text{ g}}{22.3 \text{ g}} \times 100 = 91.5\%$$

Note that percent yield cannot exceed 100%; you cannot obtain a yield greater than that which is theoretically possible.

EXAMPLE 6-11

Calculating the Percent Yield of Product in a Chemical Reaction

When 12.3 g of CO react with O_2 according to the chemical equation

$$2CO + O_2 \longrightarrow 2CO_2$$

18.0 g of CO_2 are obtained. What is the percent yield of CO_2 for this reaction?

Solution

To calculate a percent yield, both the actual yield and the theoretical yield must be known. The actual yield, 18.0 g of CO_2, was given in the problem statement. The theoretical yield is not given; it can, however, be calculated in the manner previously illustrated in Example 6-8.

Step 1: The given quantity is 12.3 g of CO, and the desired quantity is grams of CO_2.

$$12.3 \text{ g CO} = ? \text{ g CO}_2$$

In terms of Figure 6-11, this is a "grams of A" to "grams of B" problem.

Step 2: Using Figure 6-11 as a road map, the pathway for the problem becomes

$$\boxed{\text{Grams of A}} \xrightarrow[\text{mass}]{\text{Molar}} \boxed{\text{Moles of A}} \xrightarrow[\text{coefficients}]{\text{Equation}} \boxed{\text{Moles of B}} \xrightarrow[\text{mass}]{\text{Molar}} \boxed{\text{Grams of B}}$$

The dimensional-analysis setup is

$$12.3 \text{ g CO} \times \frac{1 \text{ mole CO}}{28.01 \text{ g CO}} \times \frac{2 \text{ moles CO}_2}{2 \text{ moles CO}} \times \frac{44.01 \text{ g CO}_2}{1 \text{ mole CO}_2}$$

Step 3: The theoretical yield is obtained by doing the arithmetic after all the numerical factors have been collected.

$$\left(\frac{12.3 \times 1 \times 2 \times 44.01}{28.01 \times 2 \times 1} \right) \text{g CO}_2 = 19.3 \text{ g CO}_2$$

With the theoretical yield now known and the actual yield given in the problem statement, the percent yield can be calculated.

$$\text{actual yield} = \frac{18.0 \text{ g}}{19.3 \text{ g}} \times 100 = 93.3\%$$

1. The maximum amount of product that can be obtained from given amounts of reactants in a chemical reaction is designated as the
   a. theoretical yield
   b. actual yield
   c. percent yield
   d. no correct response
2. Which of the following is a quantity that can be measured but that cannot be calculated from other measurements?
   a. theoretical yield
   b. actual yield
   c. percent yield
   d. no correct response
3. Which of the following percent yield values is based on measurements obtained using incorrect experimental data?
   a. 93.5%
   b. 98.7%
   c. 102.0%
   d. no correct response
4. The percent yield of product for a chemical reaction where the theoretical yield and actual yield are, respectively, 5.0 g and 4.0 g is
   a. 1.0 g
   b. 80%
   c. 125%
   d. no correct response

Answers: 1. a; 2. b; 3. c; 4. b

Concepts to Remember

Formula mass. The formula mass of a substance is the sum of the atomic masses of the atoms in its chemical formula (Section 6-1).

The mole concept. The mole is the chemist's counting unit. One mole of any substance—element or compound—consists of 6.02×10^{23} formula units of the substance. Avogadro's number is the name given to the numerical value 6.02×10^{23} (Section 6-2).

Molar mass. The molar mass of a substance is the mass in grams that is numerically equal to the substance's formula mass. Molar mass is not a set number; it varies and is usually different for each chemical substance (Section 6-3).

The mole and chemical formulas. The numerical subscripts in a chemical formula give the number of moles of atoms of the various elements present in 1 mole of the substance (Section 6-4).

Chemical equation. A chemical equation is a written statement that uses symbols and formulas instead of words to represent how reactants undergo transformation into products in a chemical reaction (Section 6-6).

Balanced chemical equation. A balanced chemical equation has the same number of atoms of each element involved in the reaction on each side of the equation. An unbalanced chemical equation is brought into balance through the use of equation coefficients. An equation coefficient is a number that is placed to the left of the formula of a substance in a chemical equation that changes the amount, but not the identity, of the substance (Section 6-6).

The mole and chemical equations. The equation coefficients in a balanced chemical equation give the molar ratios between substances consumed or produced in the chemical reaction described by the equation (Section 6-7).

Chemical calculations using chemical equations. When information is given about one reactant or product in a chemical reaction (number of grams, moles, or particles), similar information concerning another reactant or product in the same reaction can be calculated based on the molar relationships specified by the coefficients in the balanced equation for the chemical reaction (Section 6-8).

Theoretical yield, actual yield, and percent yield. In chemical reactions, the amount of a given product (obtained) from the reaction, the actual yield, is less than that which is theoretically possible. The percent yield compares the actual and theoretical yields (Section 6-9).

Exercises and Problems

The members of each pair of problems test similar material. Answers to odd-numbered problems are given at the back of the book. Problems denoted with a ▲ are multi-concept problems that test concepts found not only in the section under consideration, but also concepts found in one or more earlier sections of the chapter.

Formula Masses (Section 6-1)

6-1 Calculate, to two decimal places, the formula mass of each of the following substances. Obtain the needed atomic masses from the inside front cover of the text.
   a. $C_{12}H_{22}O_{11}$ (sucrose, table sugar)
   b. C_7H_{16} (heptane, a component of gasoline)
   c. $C_7H_5NO_3S$ (saccharin, an artificial sweetener)
   d. $(NH_4)_2SO_4$ (ammonium sulfate, a lawn fertilizer)

6-2 Calculate, to two decimal places, the formula mass of each of the following substances. Obtain the needed atomic masses from the inside front cover of the text.
   a. $C_{20}H_{30}O$ (vitamin A)
   b. $C_{14}H_9Cl_5$ (DDT, formerly used as an insecticide)
   c. $C_8H_{10}N_4O_2$ (caffeine, a central nervous system stimulant)
   d. $Ca(NO_3)_2$ (calcium nitrate, gives fireworks their red color)

6-3 The compound 1-propanethiol, which is the eye irritant released when fresh onions are chopped up, has the chemical formula C_3H_yS and a formula mass of 76.18 amu. What number does y stand for in the chemical formula of the compound?

6-4 A compound associated with the odor of garlic on a person's breath has the chemical formula C_yH_8S and a formula mass of 88.19 amu. What number does y stand for in the chemical formula of the compound?

The Mole as a Counting Unit (Section 6-2)

6-5 Indicate the number of objects present in each of the following molar quantities.
   a. Number of apples in 1.00 mole of apples
   b. Number of elephants in 1.00 mole of elephants
   c. Number of atoms in 1.00 mole of Zn atoms
   d. Number of molecules in 1.00 mole of CO_2 molecules

6-6 Indicate the number of objects present in each of the following molar quantities.
   a. Number of oranges in 1.00 mole of oranges
   b. Number of camels in 1.00 mole of camels
   c. Number of atoms in 1.00 mole of Cu atoms
   d. Number of molecules in 1.00 mole of CO molecules

6-7 A sample is found to contain 0.500 mole of a chemical substance.
   a. How many atoms are present if the substance is the element Cu?
   b. How many atoms are present if the substance is the element Na?
   c. How many molecules are present if the substance is the compound CO_2?
   d. How many molecules are present if the substance is the compound SiF_4?

6-8 A sample is found to contain 0.800 mole of a chemical substance.
   a. How many atoms are present if the substance is the element Al?
   b. How many atoms are present if the substance is the element Ca?
   c. How many molecules are present if the substance is the compound NO_2?
   d. How many molecules are present if the substance is the compound NF_3?

6-9 Select the quantity that contains the greater number of atoms in each of the following pairs of substances.
   a. 0.100 mole C atoms or 0.200 mole Al atoms
   b. Avogadro's number of C atoms or 0.750 mole Al atoms
   c. 6.02×10^{23} C atoms or 1.50 moles Al atoms
   d. 6.50×10^{23} C atoms or Avogadro's number of Al atoms

6-10 Select the quantity that contains the greater number of atoms in each of the following pairs of substances.
   a. 0.100 mole N atoms or 0.300 mole P atoms
   b. 6.18×10^{23} N atoms or Avogadro's number of P atoms
   c. Avogadro's number of N atoms or 1.20 moles of P atoms
   d. 6.18×10^{23} N atoms or 2.00 moles P atoms

Molar Mass (Section 6-3)

6-11 What is the mass, in grams, of 1.000 mole of each of the following substances?
   a. Ca (calcium)
   b. Ag (silver)
   c. NO (nitric oxide)
   d. HNO_3 (nitric acid)

6-12 What is the mass, in grams, of 1.000 mole of each of the following substances?
   a. S (sulfur)
   b. Mg (magnesium)
   c. NH_3 (ammonia)
   d. H_2SO_4 (sulfuric acid)

6-13 How much, in grams, does each of the following quantities of matter weigh?
   a. 2.00 moles of C atoms
   b. 3.00 moles of CO molecules
   c. 5.00 moles of F atoms
   d. 5.00 moles of F_2 molecules

6-14 How much, in grams, does each of the following quantities of matter weigh?
   a. 3.00 moles of P atoms
   b. 2.00 moles of SO_2 molecules
   c. 5.00 moles of Cl atoms
   d. 5.00 moles of Cl_2 molecules

6-15 How many moles of specified particles are present in a sample of each of the following substances if each sample weighs 5.00 g?
   a. CO molecules
   b. CO_2 molecules

c. B_4H_{10} molecules
d. U atoms

6-16 How many moles of specified particles are present in a sample of each of the following substances if each sample weighs 7.00 g?
a. N_2O molecules
b. NO_2 molecules
c. P_4O_{10} molecules
d. V atoms

▲**6-17** What is the formula mass of a compound whose molar mass is 44.01 g?

▲**6-18** What is the formula mass of a compound whose molar mass is 28.01 g?

▲**6-19** The mass of 7.00 moles of a compound is determined to be 140.07 g. What is the formula mass of the compound?

▲**6-20** The mass of 5.00 moles of a compound is determined to be 308.05 g. What is the formula mass of the compound?

Chemical Formulas and the Mole Concept (Section 6-4)

6-21 How many moles of oxygen atoms are present in 2.00-mole samples of each of the following compounds?
a. H_2SO_3
b. $H_2S_2O_7$
c. $SOCl_2$
d. SO_2Cl_2

6-22 How many moles of nitrogen atoms are present in 3.00-mole samples of each of the following compounds?
a. S_2N_2
b. S_4N_4
c. NSF
d. $N_4S_4Cl_4$

6-23 How many *total moles* of atoms are present in each of the samples in Problem 6-21?

6-24 How many *total moles* of atoms are present in each of the samples in Problem 6-22?

6-25 Write the six mole-to-mole conversion factors that can be derived from each of the following chemical formulas.
a. H_2SO_4
b. $POCl_3$

6-26 Write the six mole-to-mole conversion factors that can be derived from each of the following chemical formulas.
a. HNO_3
b. $C_2H_4Br_2$

6-27 Based on the chemical formula H_3PO_4, write the conversion factor that would be needed to do each of the following one-step conversions.
a. Moles of H_3PO_4 to moles of H atoms
b. Moles of H_3PO_4 to moles of O atoms
c. Moles of H_3PO_4 to total moles of atoms
d. Moles of P atoms to moles of O atoms

6-28 Based on the chemical formula H_2CO_3, write the conversion factor that would be needed to do each of the following one-step conversions.
a. Moles of H_2CO_3 to moles of C atoms
b. Moles of H_2CO_3 to moles of H atoms
c. Moles of H_2CO_3 to total moles of atoms
d. Moles of H atoms to moles of O atoms

Calculations Based on Chemical Formulas (Section 6-5)

6-29 Determine the number of atoms present in 20.0 g samples of each of the following elements?
a. Be
b. Ar
c. Cr
d. Sn

6-30 Determine the number of atoms present in 30.0 g samples of each of the following elements?
a. B
b. Kr
c. Fe
d. Pb

6-31 Determine the mass, in grams, of each of the following quantities of substance.
a. 6.02×10^{23} copper atoms
b. 3.01×10^{23} copper atoms
c. 557 copper atoms
d. 1 copper atom

6-32 Determine the mass, in grams, of each of the following quantities of substance.
a. 6.02×10^{23} silver atoms
b. 3.01×10^{23} silver atoms
c. 1.00×10^6 silver atoms
d. 1 silver atom

6-33 Determine the number of moles of substance present in each of the following quantities.
a. 10.0 g He
b. 10.0 g N_2O
c. 4.0×10^{10} atoms P
d. 4.0×10^{10} atoms Be

6-34 Determine the number of moles of substance present in each of the following quantities.
a. 25.0 g N
b. 25.0 g Li
c. 8.50×10^{15} atoms S
d. 8.50×10^{15} atoms Cl

6-35 Determine the number of atoms of sulfur present in each of the following quantities.
a. 10.0 g H_2SO_4
b. 20.0 g SO_3
c. 30.0 g Al_2S_3
d. 2.00 moles S_2O

6-36 Determine the number of atoms of nitrogen present in each of the following quantities.
a. 10.0 g N_2H_4
b. 20.0 g HN_3
c. 30.0 g $LiNO_3$
d. 4.00 moles N_2O_5

6-37 Determine the number of grams of sulfur present in each of the following quantities.
a. 3.01×10^{23} S_2O molecules
b. 3 S_4N_4 molecules
c. 2.00 moles SO_2 molecules
d. 4.50 moles S_8 molecules

6-38 Determine the number of grams of oxygen present in each of the following quantities.
a. 4.50×10^{22} SO_3 molecules
b. 7 P_4O_{10} molecules
c. 3.00 moles H_2SO_4 molecules
d. 1.50 moles O_3 molecules

▲**6-39** Select the quantity that contains the greater number of atoms in each of the following pairs of substance amounts. Make your selection using the periodic table, but without performing an actual calculation.
a. 1.00 mole of S or 1.00 mole of S_8
b. 28.00 g of Al or 1.00 mole of Al
c. 28.09 g of Si or 30.09 g of Mg
d. 2.00 g of Na or 6.02×10^{23} atoms of He

▲**6-40** Select the quantity that contains the greater number of atoms in each of the following pairs of substance amounts. Make your selection using the periodic table, but without performing an actual calculation.
a. 2.00 moles of Ne or 6.02×10^{23} atoms of Ar
b. 10.00 g of O_2 or 10.00 g of N_2
c. 1.00 mole of Cu or 1.01 mole of Ni
d. 26.98 g of Al or 6.02×10^{22} atoms of Al

▲**6-41** A compound has a molar mass of 34.02 g. What is its chemical formula if hydrogen and oxygen are present in the compound in a 1-to-1 molar ratio?

▲**6-42** A compound has a molar mass of 32.06 g. What is its chemical formula if nitrogen and hydrogen are present in the compound in a 1-to-2 molar ratio?

Writing and Balancing Chemical Equations
(Section 6-6)

6-43 Indicate whether each of the following chemical equations is balanced.
a. $SO_3 + H_2O \rightarrow H_2SO_4$
b. $CuO + H_2 \rightarrow Cu + H_2O$
c. $CS_2 + O_2 \rightarrow CO_2 + SO_2$
d. $AgNO_3 + KCl \rightarrow KNO_3 + AgCl$

6-44 Indicate whether each of the following chemical equations is balanced.
a. $H_2 + O_2 \rightarrow H_2O$
b. $NO + O_2 \rightarrow NO_2$
c. $C + O_2 \rightarrow CO_2$
d. $HNO_3 + NaOH \rightarrow NaNO_3 + H_2O$

6-45 How many *total atoms* does each of the following expressions, extracted from balanced chemical equations, represent?
a. $2SO_3$
b. $4N_2H_4$
c. $3H_3PO_4$
d. $6Al(OH)_3$

6-46 How many *total atoms* does each of the following expressions, extracted from balanced chemical equations, represent?
a. $2POCl_3$
b. $3H_2O_2$
c. $6HClO_3$
d. $Al_2(SO_4)_3$

6-47 How many oxygen atoms are present on the reactant side and on the product side of each of the following balanced chemical equations?
a. $Cs_2O + H_2O \rightarrow 2CsOH$
b. $K_2SO_4 + BaCl_2 \rightarrow BaSO_4 + 2KCl$
c. $2C_4H_{10} + 13O_2 \rightarrow 8CO_2 + 10H_2O$
d. $4NO_2 + 2H_2O + O_2 \rightarrow 4HNO_3$

6-48 How many oxygen atoms are present on the reactant side and on the product side of each of the following balanced chemical equations?
a. $4Al + 3O_2 \rightarrow 2Al_2O_3$
b. $2Na_3PO_4 + 3BaCl_2 \rightarrow Ba_3(PO_4)_2 + 6NaCl$
c. $2C_3H_6 + 9O_2 \rightarrow 6CO_2 + 6H_2O$
d. $3Cu + 8HNO_3 \rightarrow 3Cu(NO_3)_2 + 2NO + 4H_2O$

6-49 Balance the following chemical equations.
a. $Na + H_2O \rightarrow NaOH + H_2$
b. $Na + ZnSO_4 \rightarrow Na_2SO_4 + Zn$
c. $NaBr + Cl_2 \rightarrow NaCl + Br_2$
d. $ZnS + O_2 \rightarrow ZnO + SO_2$

6-50 Balance the following chemical equations.
a. $H_2S + O_2 \rightarrow SO_2 + H_2O$
b. $Ni + HCl \rightarrow NiCl_2 + H_2$
c. $IBr + NH_3 \rightarrow NH_4Br + NI_3$
d. $C_2H_6 + O_2 \rightarrow CO_2 + H_2O$

6-51 Balance the following chemical equations.
a. $CH_4 + O_2 \rightarrow CO_2 + H_2O$
b. $C_6H_6 + O_2 \rightarrow CO_2 + H_2O$
c. $C_4H_8O_2 + O_2 \rightarrow CO_2 + H_2O$
d. $C_5H_{10}O + O_2 \rightarrow CO_2 + H_2O$

6-52 Balance the following chemical equations.
a. $C_2H_4 + O_2 \rightarrow CO_2 + H_2O$
b. $C_6H_{12} + O_2 \rightarrow CO_2 + H_2O$
c. $C_3H_6O + O_2 \rightarrow CO_2 + H_2O$
d. $C_5H_{10}O_2 + O_2 \rightarrow CO_2 + H_2O$

6-53 After the following chemical equation was balanced, the name of one of the reactants was substituted for its formula.

$$2 \text{ butyne} + 11O_2 \longrightarrow 8CO_2 + 6H_2O$$

Using only the information found within the chemical equation, determine the molecular formula of butyne.

6-54 After the following chemical equation was balanced, the name of one of the reactants was substituted for its formula.

$$\text{propane} + 5O_2 \longrightarrow 3CO_2 + 4H_2O$$

Using only the information found within the chemical equation, determine the molecular formula of propane.

6-55 The following diagrams represent the reaction of A_2 (red spheres) with B_2 (blue spheres) to give specific products. Write a balanced equation for each reaction based on the information in the diagram.

Reactants   Products

a

Reactants   Products

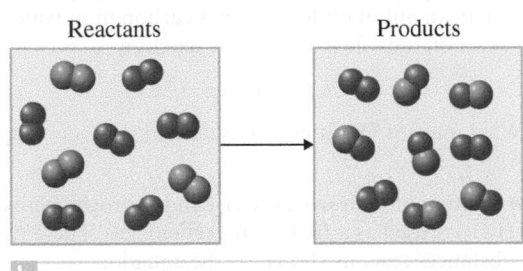

b

6-56 The following diagrams represent the reaction of A_2 (red spheres) with B_2 (blue spheres) to give specific products. Write a balanced equation for each reaction based on the information in the diagram.

Reactants   Products

a

Reactants   Products

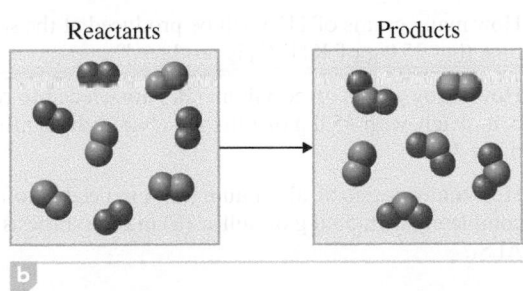

b

6-57 Diagram I represents the reactant mixture for a chemical reaction. Select from diagrams II through IV the product mixture that is consistent with both diagram I and the concepts associated with a balanced chemical equation.

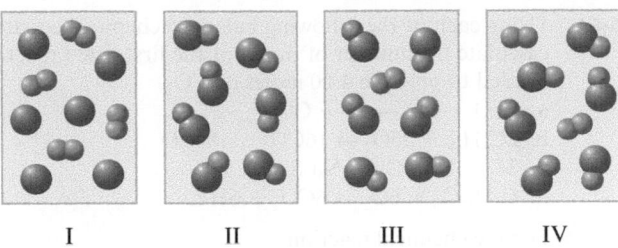

I   II   III   IV

6-58 Diagram I represents the reactant mixture for a chemical reaction. Select from diagrams II through IV the product mixture that is consistent with both diagram I and the concepts associated with a balanced chemical equation.

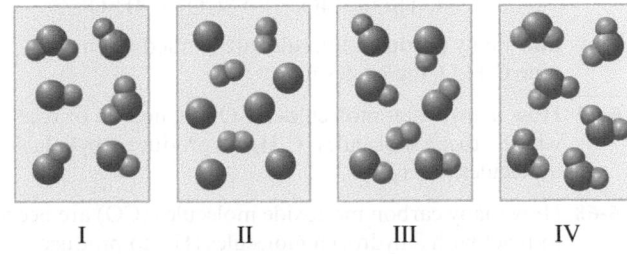

I   II   III   IV

Chemical Equations and the Mole Concept (Section 6-7)

6-59 Write the six mole-to-mole conversion factors that can be derived from the balanced chemical equation

$$2NH_3 \longrightarrow 3H_2 + N_2$$

6-60 Write the six mole-to-mole conversion factors that can be derived from the balanced chemical equation

$$2H_2O_2 \longrightarrow 2H_2O + O_2$$

6-61 For the chemical reaction

$$Sb_2S_3 + 6HCl \longrightarrow 2SbCl_3 + 3H_2S$$

write the conversion factor that would be needed to do each of the following one-step conversions.
a. Moles of $SbCl_3$ to moles of H_2S
b. Moles of Sb_2S_3 to moles of HCl
c. Moles of H_2S to moles of HCl
d. Moles of Sb_2S_3 to moles of $SbCl_3$

6-62 For the chemical reaction

$$UF_6 + 2H_2O \longrightarrow UO_2F_2 + 4HF$$

write the conversion factor that would be needed to do each of the following one-step conversions.
a. Moles of UF_6 to moles of HF
b. Moles of UO_2F_2 to moles of H_2O
c. Moles of HF to moles of UO_2F_2
d. Moles of H_2O to moles of UF_6

6-63 Using each of the following balanced chemical equations, calculate the number of moles of the first listed reactant needed to produce 5.00 moles of CO_2.
a. $C_7H_{16} + 11O_2 \rightarrow 7CO_2 + 8H_2O$
b. $CS_2 + O_2 \rightarrow 2SO_2 + CO_2$
c. $Fe_3O_4 + CO \rightarrow 3FeO + CO_2$
d. $2HCl + CaCO_3 \rightarrow CaCl_2 + CO_2 + H_2O$

6-64 Using each of the following balanced chemical equations, calculate the number of moles of the first listed reactant needed to produce 4.00 moles of CO_2.
a. $FeO + CO \rightarrow Fe + CO_2$
b. $2C_8H_{18} + 25O_2 \rightarrow 16CO_2 + 18H_2O$
c. $2C + Na_2SO_4 \rightarrow Na_2S + 2CO_2$
d. $C_6H_{12}O_6 + 6O_2 \rightarrow 6CO_2 + 6H_2O$

▲**6-65** For the chemical reaction

$$C_6H_{12}O_6 + 6O_2 \longrightarrow 6CO_2 + 6H_2O$$

how many product molecules are formed when seven $C_6H_{12}O_6$ molecules react?

▲**6-66** For the chemical reaction

$$C_3H_8O_2 + 4O_2 \longrightarrow 3CO_2 + 4H_2O$$

how many product molecules are formed when nine $C_3H_8O_2$ molecules react?

▲**6-67** How many water molecules (H_2O) are needed to react with 8 ethene molecules (C_2H_4) to produce ethyl alcohol molecules (C_2H_5OH)?

▲**6-68** How many carbon monoxide molecules (CO) are needed to react with 8 hydrogen molecules (H_2) to produce methyl alcohol molecules (CH_3OH)?

▲**6-69** The following diagram represents the high-temperature reaction between CH_4 and O_2.

Reactants   Products

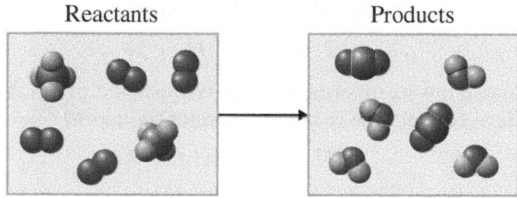

Use this diagram to answer the following questions.
a. What are the chemical formulas of the products?
b. How many moles of each product can be obtained if 6.0 moles of CH_4 react?

▲**6-70** The following diagram represents the high-temperature reaction between CH_4 and H_2O.

Reactants   Products

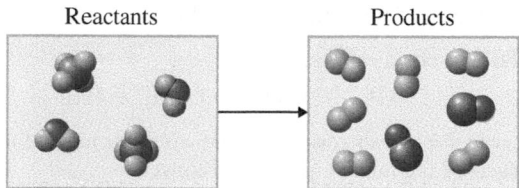

Use this diagram to answer the following questions.
a. What are the chemical formulas of the products?
b. How many moles of each product can be obtained if 6.0 moles of CH_4 react?

▲**6-71** How many moles of beryllium (Be) are needed to completely react with 10.0 moles of N_2 in the synthesis of the compound Be_3N_2?

▲**6-72** How many moles of magnesium (Mg) are needed to completely react with 8.0 moles of O_2 in the synthesis of the compound MgO?

Calculations Based on Chemical Equations (Section 6-8)

6-73 The principal constituent of natural gas is methane, which burns in air according to the reaction

$$CH_4 + 2O_2 \longrightarrow CO_2 + 2H_2O$$

How many grams of O_2 are needed to produce 3.50 g of CO_2?

6-74 Tungsten (W) metal, which is used to make incandescent bulb filaments, is produced by the reaction

$$WO_3 + 3H_2 \longrightarrow 3H_2O + W$$

How many grams of H_2 are needed to produce 1.00 g of W?

6-75 The catalytic converter that is standard equipment on American automobiles converts carbon monoxide (CO) to carbon dioxide (CO_2) by the reaction

$$2CO + O_2 \longrightarrow 2CO_2$$

What mass of O_2, in grams, is needed to react completely with 25.0 g of CO?

6-76 A mixture of hydrazine (N_2H_4) and hydrogen peroxide (H_2O_2) is used as a fuel for rocket engines. These two substances react as shown by the equation

$$N_2H_4 + 2H_2O_2 \longrightarrow N_2 + 4H_2O$$

What mass of N_2H_4, in grams, is needed to react completely with 35.0 g of H_2O_2?

6-77 Both water and sulfur dioxide are products from the reaction of sulfuric acid (H_2SO_4) with copper metal, as shown by the equation

$$2H_2SO_4 + Cu \longrightarrow SO_2 + 2H_2O + CuSO_4$$

How many grams of H_2O will be produced at the same time that 10.0 g of SO_2 is produced?

6-78 Potassium thiosulfate ($K_2S_2O_3$) is used to remove any excess chlorine from fibers and fabrics that have been bleached with that gas. The reaction is

$$K_2S_2O_3 + 4Cl_2 + 5H_2O \longrightarrow 2KHSO_4 + 8HCl$$

How many grams of HCl will be produced at the same time that 25.0 g of $KHSO_4$ is produced?

▲**6-79** How many grams of beryllium (Be) are needed to react completely with 45.0 g of nitrogen (N_2) in the synthesis of Be_3N_2?

▲**6-80** How many grams of aluminum (Al) are needed to react completely with 55.0 g of sulfur (S) in the synthesis of Al_2S_3?

Yields: Theoretical, Actual, and Percent (Section 6-9)

6-81 The theoretical yield of product for a particular reaction is 32.03 g. A very meticulous student obtained 31.87 g of product after carrying out this reaction. What is the percent yield that this student obtained?

6-82 The theoretical yield of product for a particular reaction is 64.55 g. A very careless student obtained only 19.21 g of product after carrying out this reaction. What is the percent yield that this student obtained?

6-83 In an experiment designed to produce sulfur dioxide by the chemical reaction

$$2S + O_2 \longrightarrow 2SO_2$$

9.75 g of SO_2 was obtained out of a possible 11.2 g of SO_2.
a. What is the theoretical yield of SO_2?
b. What is the actual yield of SO_2?
c. What is the percent yield of SO_2?

6-84 In an experiment designed to produce calcium oxide by the chemical reaction

$$2Ca + O_2 \longrightarrow 2CaO$$

177.2 g of CaO was obtained out of a possible 203.9 g of CaO.
a. What is the theoretical yield of CaO?
b. What is the actual yield of CaO?
c. What is the percent yield of CaO?

6-85 If 125.5 g of Ca_3N_2 were produced from 29.0 g of N_2 and an excess of Ca according to the reaction

$$3Ca + N_2 \longrightarrow Ca_3N_2$$

what was the percent yield of Ca_3N_2?

6-86 If 64.15 g of HCl were produced from 2.07 g of H_2 and an excess of Cl_2 according to the reaction

$$H_2 + Cl_2 \longrightarrow 2HCl$$

what was the percent yield of HCl?

Chapter 6 Appendix:

Section 5.10 The Limiting Reactant from Seager/Slabaugh Chemistry for Today: General, Organic, and Biochemistry, 6th Edition.

Sections 8.6 – 8.9 Percent Composition of Compounds, Formulas of Compounds, Calculation of Empirical Formulas and Calculation of Molecular Formulas from Zumdahl/DeCoste Introductory Chemistry: A Foundation, 8th Edition

Thus, the pathway involves three calculations, which can be done individually or combined. We will show the solution in combined form.

The steps in the factor-unit method are as follows:

Step 1. 8.42 g CO_2

Step 2. 8.42 g CO_2 $=$ g O_2

Step 3. 8.42 g $\cancel{CO_2} \times \dfrac{1 \text{ mol } \cancel{CO_2}}{44.0 \text{ g } \cancel{CO_2}} \times \dfrac{2 \text{ mol } \cancel{O_2}}{1 \text{ mol } \cancel{CO_2}} \times \dfrac{32.0 \text{ g } O_2}{1 \text{ mol } \cancel{O_2}} =$ g O_2

Step 4. $(8.42)\left(\dfrac{1}{44.0}\right)\left(\dfrac{2}{1}\right)\left(\dfrac{32.0 \text{ g } O_2}{1}\right) = 12.2$ g O_2

■ **Learning Check 5.7** The following reaction equation is balanced:

$$N_2(g) + 3H_2(g) \rightarrow 2NH_3(g)$$

a. Write two factors that could be used in factor-unit calculations involving the pathway

$$\text{mol } H_2 \rightarrow \text{mol } NH_3$$

b. Calculate the mol NH_3 that would be produced if 2.11 mol H_2 was reacted with excess N_2.
c. Calculate the g N_2 required to react with 9.47 g H_2.

5.10 The Limiting Reactant

◤ **LEARNING OBJECTIVE**

7. Use the mole concept to do calculations based on the limiting-reactant principle.

Nearly everyone is familiar with two characteristics of automobiles. They stop running when they run out of gasoline, and they stop running when the air intake to the engine becomes clogged. Most people also know that gasoline and air are mixed, and the mixture is burned inside the automobile engine. However, the combustion reaction occurs only as long as both reactants, gasoline and air, are present. The reaction (and engine) stops when gasoline is absent, despite the presence of ample amounts of air. On the other hand, the reaction stops when air is absent, even though plenty of gasoline is available.

The behavior of the auto engine illustrates the **limiting-reactant principle** that a chemical reaction will take place only as long as all necessary reactants are present. The reaction will stop when one of the reactants, the **limiting reactant,** is used up. According to this principle, the amount of product formed depends on the amount of limiting reactant present because the reaction will stop (and no more product will form) when the limiting reactant is used up. This is represented in ■ Figure 5.12 for the reaction $F_2(g) + H_2(g) \rightarrow 2HF(g)$.

limiting-reactant principle
The maximum amount of product possible from a reaction is determined by the amount of reactant present in the least amount, based on its reaction coefficient and molecular weight.

limiting reactant
The reactant present in a reaction in the least amount, based on its reaction coefficients and molecular weight. It is the reactant that determines the maximum amount of product that can be formed.

H_2 $+$ F_2 ⟶ Mixture of reactants ⟶ HF + unreacted H_2

■ **FIGURE 5.12** The limiting reactant is used up in a reaction.

CHEMISTRY AROUND US 5.2   Air Bag Chemistry

Air bags installed in automobiles have proven to be effective, yet somewhat controversial, safety devices. According to the National Transportation Safety Administration, air bags have saved an estimated 1100 lives and prevented many more serious injuries from automobile accidents. This effectiveness is tempered by the fact that air bags have caused the deaths of a number of small children and infants. Short adults have also died as a result of being hit in the face rather than the chest by an expanding air bag. For this reason, it is now generally recommended that infants, small children, and short adults not occupy the front passenger seat. Also, most newer model automobiles are equipped with a switch that allows the air bag to be deactivated.

An air bag is essentially a nylon fabric bag that fills very rapidly with a gas when a collision occurs. Inflated air bags cushion and protect the driver and front-seat passenger. The gas that inflates an air bag is nitrogen, N_2, that is produced in a gas generator by a redox reaction of a toxic, explosive material called sodium azide, NaN_3. When a collision occurs, an electrical impulse triggers the rapid decomposition of the sodium azide according to the following equation:

$$2NaN_3(s) \rightarrow 2Na(g) + 3N_2(g)$$

The sodium vapor produced by this reaction would be very hazardous to the occupants of the automobile, but potassium nitrate, KNO_3, also included in the gas-generating mixture, reacts with the sodium vapor to produce potassium oxide, K_2O, sodium oxide, Na_2O, and some additional nitrogen gas. The equation for the reaction is

$$10Na(g) + 2KNO_3(s) \rightarrow K_2O(s) + 5Na_2O(s) + N_2(g)$$

The potassium oxide and sodium oxide are also hazardous materials; they are both basic oxides that react with water to form very caustic potassium hydroxide and sodium hydrox-

ide, respectively. However, silicon dioxide, SiO_2, a third substance included in the gas-generating mixture of chemicals, is an acidic oxide that reacts with the basic potassium and sodium oxides, neutralizes their caustic characteristics, and converts them into a safe silicate-glass powder.

Thus, we see that from a chemical standpoint, the products of an air bag inflation are rendered safe by a series of carefully designed reactions. However, most air bags are never inflated, which means that old cars sent to scrap yards still contain a small amount of very toxic and explosive sodium azide. This is a recycling or disposal problem that is yet to be resolved.

Air bags: Protection provided by chemical reactions.

▼ EXAMPLE 5.8

A mixture containing 20.0 g CH_4 and 100 g O_2 is ignited and burns according to Equation 5.27, which is repeated here: $CH_4(g) + 2O_2(g) \rightarrow CO_2(g) + 2H_2O(\ell)$. What substances will be found in the mixture after the reaction stops?

Solution

The task is to identify the limiting reactant. It will be completely used up, and the other reactant will be found mixed with the products (CO_2 and H_2O) after the reaction stops. A simple way to identify the limiting reactant is to find out which reactant will give the least amount of products. To do this, two problems must be solved, one in which the known quantity is 20.0 g CH_4 and one in which the known quantity is 100.0 g O_2. In each case, the theoretical amount of CO_2 produced is calculated, although the same information would be obtained by solving for the amount of water produced.

$$(20.0 \text{ g } CH_4)\left(\frac{1 \text{ mol } CH_4}{16.0 \text{ g } CH_4}\right)\left(\frac{1 \text{ mol } CO_2}{1 \text{ mol } CH_4}\right)\left(\frac{44.0 \text{ g } CO_2}{1 \text{ mol } CO_2}\right) = 55.0 \text{ g } CO_2$$

$$(100 \text{ g } O_2)\left(\frac{1 \text{ mol } O_2}{32.0 \text{ g } O_2}\right)\left(\frac{1 \text{ mol } CO_2}{2 \text{ mol } O_2}\right)\left(\frac{44.0 \text{ g } CO_2}{1 \text{ mol } CO_2}\right) = 68.8 \text{ g } CO_2$$

Since the 20.0 g CH_4 produces the smaller amount of CO_2, CH_4 is the limiting reactant. Therefore, the final mixture will contain the products CO_2 and H_2O and the leftover O_2.

CENGAGENOW™ Go to Coached Problems to practice identifying **limiting reactants.**

EXAMPLE 5.9

The reaction shown in Figure 5.8 was carried out by a student who wanted to produce some silver metal. The equation for the reaction is

$$Cu(s) + 2AgNO_3(aq) \rightarrow 2Ag(s) + Cu(NO_3)_2(aq)$$

The student dissolved 17.0 g of $AgNO_3$ in distilled water, then added 8.50 g of copper metal, Cu, to the resulting solution. What mass of silver metal, Ag, was produced?

Solution

The limiting reactant must be identified because it will determine the amount of silver produced. To find the limiting reactant, we calculate the theoretical amount of silver produced by each reactant. The reactant that will produce the smallest mass of silver is the limiting reactant, and the mass of silver calculated for it is the amount produced by the reaction.

$$17.0 \text{ g AgNO}_3 \left(\frac{1 \text{ mol AgNO}_3}{170 \text{ g AgNO}_3} \right) \left(\frac{2 \text{ mol Ag}}{2 \text{ mol AgNO}_3} \right) \left(\frac{108 \text{ g Ag}}{1 \text{ mol Ag}} \right) = 10.8 \text{ g Ag}$$

$$8.50 \text{ g Cu} \left(\frac{1 \text{ mol Cu}}{63.6 \text{ g Cu}} \right) \left(\frac{2 \text{ mol Ag}}{1 \text{ mol Cu}} \right) \left(\frac{108 \text{ Ag}}{1 \text{ mol Ag}} \right) = 28.9 \text{ g Ag}$$

We see that the $AgNO_3$ is the limiting reactant, and it will produce 10.8 g of Ag.

■ **Learning Check 5.8** Refer to the reaction used for Learning Check 5.7. Assume that 2.00 mol H_2 and 15.5 g N_2 are reacted. What is the maximum mass of ammonia (NH_3) that can be produced? Which reactant is the limiting reactant?

5.11 Reaction Yields

LEARNING OBJECTIVE

8. Use the mole concept to do percentage-yield calculations.

In Sections 5.9 and 5.10, calculations were done to determine how much product could be obtained from the reaction of specified amounts of reactants. In many instances, the amount determined by such calculations would be greater than the amount produced by reacting the specified reactants in a laboratory. Does this mean matter is destroyed when reactions are actually done in the laboratory? No, this would violate the law of conservation of matter, a fundamental law of nature. Less product might be obtained because some of the reactants form compounds other than the desired product. Such reactions are called **side reactions.** Carbon dioxide gas, CO_2, is produced when carbon-containing fuels burn in an ample supply of oxygen. However, a side reaction produces toxic carbon monoxide gas, CO, when the oxygen supply is limited.

Another cause of less product than expected might be poor laboratory technique resulting in such things as losses when materials are transferred from one container to another. Whatever the cause, the mass of product obtained in an experiment is called the *actual yield,* and the mass calculated according to the methods of Sections

CENGAGENOW™ Go to Coached Problems to calculate a **theoretical yield.**

side reactions
Reactions that do not give the desired product of a reaction.

| 8-6 | # Percent Composition of Compounds |

OBJECTIVE

To learn to find the mass percent of an element in a given compound.

So far we have discussed the composition of compounds in terms of the numbers of constituent atoms. It is often useful to know a compound's composition in terms of the *masses* of its elements. We can obtain this information from the formula of the compound by comparing the mass of each element present in 1 mole of the compound to the total mass of 1 mole of the compound. The mass fraction for each element is calculated as follows:

Math skill builder

$$\text{Percent} = \frac{\text{Part}}{\text{Whole}} \times 100\%$$

$$\text{Mass fraction for a given element} = \frac{\text{mass of the element present in 1 mole of compound}}{\text{mass of 1 mole of compound}}$$

The mass fraction is converted to *mass percent* by multiplying by 100%.

We will illustrate this concept using the compound ethanol, an alcohol obtained by fermenting the sugar in grapes, corn, and other fruits and grains. Ethanol is often added to gasoline as an octane enhancer to form a fuel called gasohol. The added ethanol has the effect of increasing the octane of the gasoline and also lowering the carbon monoxide in automobile exhaust.

The formula for ethanol is written C_2H_5OH, although you might expect it to be written simply as C_2H_6O.

Note from its formula that each molecule of ethanol contains two carbon atoms, six hydrogen atoms, and one oxygen atom. This means that each mole of ethanol contains 2 moles of carbon atoms, 6 moles of hydrogen atoms, and 1 mole of oxygen atoms. We calculate the mass of each element present and the molar mass for ethanol as follows:

$$\text{Mass of C} = 2 \text{ mol} \times 12.01 \frac{\text{g}}{\text{mol}} = 24.02 \text{ g}$$

$$\text{Mass of H} = 6 \text{ mol} \times 1.008 \frac{\text{g}}{\text{mol}} = 6.048 \text{ g}$$

$$\text{Mass of O} = 1 \text{ mol} \times 16.00 \frac{\text{g}}{\text{mol}} = 16.00 \text{ g}$$

$$\text{Mass of 1 mol } C_2H_5OH = 46.07 \text{ g} = \text{molar mass}$$

The **mass percent** (sometimes called the weight percent) of carbon in ethanol can be computed by comparing the mass of carbon in 1 mole of ethanol with the total mass of 1 mole of ethanol and multiplying the result by 100%.

$$\text{Mass percent of C} = \frac{\text{mass of C in 1 mol } C_2H_5OH}{\text{mass of 1 mol } C_2H_5OH} \times 100\%$$

$$= \frac{24.02 \text{ g}}{46.07 \text{ g}} \times 100\% = 52.14\%$$

That is, ethanol contains 52.14% by mass of carbon. The mass percents of hydrogen and oxygen in ethanol are obtained in a similar manner.

$$\text{Mass percent of H} = \frac{\text{mass of H in 1 mol } C_2H_5OH}{\text{mass of 1 mol } C_2H_5OH} \times 100\%$$

$$= \frac{6.048 \text{ g}}{46.07 \text{ g}} \times 100\% = 13.13\%$$

Math skill builder

Sometimes, because of rounding-off effects, the sum of the mass percents in a compound is not exactly 100%.

$$\text{Mass percent of O} = \frac{\text{mass of O in 1 mol } C_2H_5OH}{\text{mass of 1 mol } C_2H_5OH} \times 100\%$$

$$= \frac{16.00 \text{ g}}{46.07 \text{ g}} \times 100\% = 34.73\%$$

The mass percents of all the elements in a compound add up to 100%, although rounding-off effects may produce a small deviation. Adding up the percentages is a good way to check the calculations. In this case, the sum of the mass percents is $52.14\% + 13.13\% + 34.73\% = 100.00\%$.

Interactive Example 8.9

Calculating Mass Percent

Carvone is a substance that occurs in two forms, both of which have the same molecular formula ($C_{10}H_{14}O$) and molar mass. One type of carvone gives caraway seeds their characteristic smell; the other is responsible for the smell of spearmint oil. Compute the mass percent of each element in carvone.

SOLUTION

Where Are We Going?

We want to determine the mass percent of each element in carvone.

What Do We Know?

- The formula for carvone is $C_{10}H_{14}O$.
- We know the atomic masses of carbon (12.01 g/mol), hydrogen (1.008 g/mol), and oxygen (16.00 g/mol).
- The mass of isopentyl acetate is 1×10^{-6} g.
- There are 6.022×10^{23} molecules in 1 mole.

What Do We Need To Know?

- The mass of each element (we'll use 1 mole of carvone)
- Molar mass of carvone

How Do We Get There?

Because the formula for carvone is $C_{10}H_{14}O$, the masses of the various elements in 1 mole of carvone are

$$\text{Mass of C in 1 mol} = 10 \text{ mol} \times 12.01 \frac{g}{\text{mol}} = 120.1 \text{ g}$$

$$\text{Mass of H in 1 mol} = 14 \text{ mol} \times 1.008 \frac{g}{\text{mol}} = 14.11 \text{ g}$$

$$\text{Mass of O in 1 mol} = 1 \text{ mol} \times 16.00 \frac{g}{\text{mol}} = 16.00 \text{ g}$$

$$\text{Mass of 1 mol } C_{10}H_{14}O = 150.21 \text{ g}$$
$$\text{Molar mass} = 150.2 \text{ g}$$

(rounding to the correct number of significant figures)

Math skill builder

The 120.1 limits the sum to one decimal place.

Next we find the fraction of the total mass contributed by each element and convert it to a percentage.

$$\text{Mass percent of C} = \frac{120.1 \text{ g C}}{150.2 \text{ g } C_{10}H_{14}O} \times 100\% = 79.96\%$$

$$\text{Mass percent of H} = \frac{14.11 \text{ g H}}{150.2 \text{ g } C_{10}H_{14}O} \times 100\% = 9.394\%$$

$$\text{Mass percent of O} = \frac{16.00 \text{ g O}}{150.2 \text{ g } C_{10}H_{14}O} \times 100\% = 10.65\%$$

REALITY CHECK Add the individual mass percent values—they should total 100% within a small range due to rounding off. In this case, the percentages add up to 100.00%.

Exercise 8.7 Penicillin, an important antibiotic (antibacterial agent), was discovered accidentally by the Scottish bacteriologist Alexander Fleming in 1928, although he was never able to isolate it as a pure compound. This and similar antibiotics have saved millions of lives that would otherwise have been lost to infections. Penicillin, like many of the molecules produced by living systems, is a large molecule containing many atoms. One type of penicillin, penicillin F, has the formula $C_{14}H_{20}N_2SO_4$. Compute the mass percent of each element in this compound.

See Problems 8.45 through 8.50. ∎

8-7 Formulas of Compounds

OBJECTIVE   To understand the meaning of empirical formulas of compounds.

Assume that you have mixed two solutions, and a solid product (a precipitate) forms. How can you find out what the solid is? What is its formula? There are several possible approaches you can take to answering these questions. For example, we saw in Chapter 7 that we can usually predict the identity of a precipitate formed when two solutions are mixed in a reaction of this type if we know some facts about the solubilities of ionic compounds.

However, although an experienced chemist can often predict the product expected in a chemical reaction, the only sure way to identify the product is to perform experiments. Usually we compare the physical properties of the product to the properties of known compounds.

Sometimes a chemical reaction gives a product that has never been obtained before. In such a case, a chemist determines what compound has been formed by determining which elements are present and how much of each. These data can be used to obtain the formula of the compound. In Section 8-6 we used the formula of the compound to determine the mass of each element present in a mole of the compound. To obtain the formula of an unknown compound, we do the opposite. That is, we use the measured masses of the elements present to determine the formula.

Recall that the formula of a compound represents the relative numbers of the various types of atoms present. For example, the molecular formula CO_2 tells us that for each carbon atom there are two oxygen atoms in each molecule of carbon dioxide. So to determine the formula of a substance we need to count the atoms. As we have seen in this chapter, we can do this by weighing. Suppose we know that a compound contains only the elements carbon, hydrogen, and oxygen, and we weigh out a 0.2015-g sample for analysis. Using methods we will not discuss here, we find that this 0.2015-g sample of compound contains 0.0806 g of carbon, 0.01353 g of hydrogen, and 0.1074 g of oxygen. We have just learned how to convert these masses to numbers of atoms by using the atomic mass of each element. We begin by converting to moles.

Carbon

$$0.0806 \; \cancel{g \; C} \times \frac{1 \; mol \; C \; atoms}{12.01 \; \cancel{g \; C}} = 0.00671 \; mol \; C \; atoms$$

Hydrogen

$$0.01353 \; \cancel{g \; H} \times \frac{1 \; mol \; H \; atoms}{1.008 \; \cancel{g \; H}} = 0.01342 \; mol \; H \; atoms$$

Oxygen

$$0.1074 \text{ g O} \times \frac{1 \text{ mol O atoms}}{16.00 \text{ g O}} = 0.006713 \text{ mol O atoms}$$

Let's review what we have established. We now know that 0.2015 g of the compound contains 0.00671 mole of C atoms, 0.01342 mole of H atoms, and 0.006713 mole of O atoms. Because 1 mole is 6.022×10^{23}, these quantities can be converted to actual numbers of atoms.

Carbon

$$0.00671 \text{ mol C atoms} \frac{6.022 \times 10^{23} \text{ C atoms}}{1 \text{ mol C atoms}} = 4.04 \times 10^{21} \text{ C atoms}$$

Hydrogen

$$0.01342 \text{ mol H atoms} \frac{6.022 \times 10^{23} \text{ H atoms}}{1 \text{ mol H atoms}} = 8.08 \times 10^{21} \text{ H atoms}$$

Oxygen

$$0.006713 \text{ mol O atoms} \frac{6.022 \times 10^{23} \text{ O atoms}}{1 \text{ mol O atoms}} = 4.043 \times 10^{21} \text{ O atoms}$$

These are the numbers of the various types of atoms *in 0.2015 g of compound*. What do these numbers tell us about the formula of the compound? Note the following:

1. The compound contains the same number of C and O atoms.

2. There are twice as many H atoms as C atoms or O atoms.

We can represent this information by the formula CH_2O, which expresses the *relative* numbers of C, H, and O atoms present. Is this the true formula for the compound? In other words, is the compound made up of CH_2O molecules? It may be. However, it might also be made up of $C_2H_4O_2$ molecules, $C_3H_6O_3$ molecules, $C_4H_8O_4$ molecules, $C_5H_{10}O_5$ molecules, $C_6H_{12}O_6$ molecules, and so on. Note that each of these molecules has the required 1:2:1 ratio of carbon to hydrogen to oxygen atoms (the ratio shown by experiment to be present in the compound).

When we break a compound down into its separate elements and "count" the atoms present, we learn only the ratio of atoms—we get only the *relative* numbers of atoms. The formula of a compound that expresses the smallest whole-number ratio of the atoms present is called the **empirical formula** or *simplest formula*. A compound that contains the molecules $C_4H_8O_4$ has the same empirical formula as a compound that contains $C_6H_{12}O_6$ molecules. The empirical formula for both is CH_2O. The actual formula of a compound—the one that gives the composition of the molecules that are present—is called the **molecular formula.** The sugar called glucose is made of molecules with the molecular formula $C_6H_{12}O_6$ (Fig. 8.4). Note from the molecular formula for glucose that the empirical formula is CH_2O. We can represent the molecular formula as a multiple (by 6) of the empirical formula:

$$C_6H_{12}O_6 = (CH_2O)_6$$

Figure 8.4 ▶ The glucose molecule. The molecular formula is $C_6H_{12}O_6$, as can be verified by counting the atoms. The empirical formula for glucose is CH_2O.

In the next section, we will explore in more detail how to calculate the empirical formula for a compound from the relative masses of the elements present. As we will see in Sections 8-8 and 8-9, we must know the molar mass of a compound to determine its molecular formula.

Interactive Example 8.10

Determining Empirical Formulas

In each case below, the molecular formula for a compound is given. Determine the empirical formula for each compound.

a. C_6H_6. This is the molecular formula for benzene, a liquid commonly used in industry as a starting material for many important products.

b. $C_{12}H_4Cl_4O_2$. This is the molecular formula for a substance commonly called dioxin, a powerful poison that sometimes occurs as a by-product in the production of other chemicals.

c. $C_6H_{16}N_2$. This is the molecular formula for one of the reactants used to produce nylon.

SOLUTION

a. $C_6H_6 = (CH)_6$; CH is the empirical formula. Each subscript in the empirical formula is multiplied by 6 to obtain the molecular formula.

b. $C_{12}H_4Cl_4O_2$; $C_{12}H_4Cl_4O_2 = (C_6H_2Cl_2O)_2$; $C_6H_2Cl_2O$ is the empirical formula. Each subscript in the empirical formula is multiplied by 2 to obtain the molecular formula.

c. $C_6H_{16}N_2 = (C_3H_8N)_2$; C_3H_8N is the empirical formula. Each subscript in the empirical formula is multiplied by 2 to obtain the molecular formula. ∎

8-8 Calculation of Empirical Formulas

OBJECTIVE   **To learn to calculate empirical formulas.**

As we said in the previous section, one of the most important things we can learn about a new compound is its chemical formula. To calculate the empirical formula of a compound, we first determine the relative masses of the various elements that are present.

One way to do this is to measure the masses of elements that react to form the compound. For example, suppose we weigh out 0.2636 g of pure nickel metal into a crucible and heat this metal in the air so that the nickel can react with oxygen to form a nickel oxide compound. After the sample has cooled, we weigh it again and find its mass to be 0.3354 g. The gain in mass is due to the oxygen that reacts with the nickel to form the oxide. Therefore, the mass of oxygen present in the compound is the total mass of the product minus the mass of the nickel:

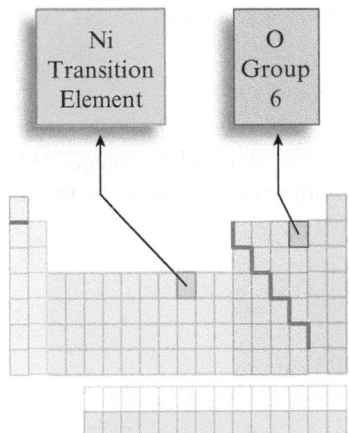

Total mass of nickel oxide	−	Mass of nickel originally present	=	Mass of oxygen that reacted with the nickel
0.3354 g		0.2636 g		0.0718 g

Note that the mass of nickel present in the compound is the nickel metal originally weighed out. So we know that the nickel oxide contains 0.2636 g of nickel and 0.0718 g of oxygen. What is the empirical formula of this compound?

To answer this question we must convert the masses to numbers of atoms, using atomic masses:

Four significant figures allowed.

$$0.2636 \; \text{g Ni} \times \frac{1 \; \text{mol Ni atoms}}{58.69 \; \text{g Ni}} = 0.004491 \; \text{mol Ni atoms}$$

Three significant figures allowed.

$$0.0718 \; \text{g O} \times \frac{1 \; \text{mol O atoms}}{16.00 \; \text{g O}} = 0.00449 \; \text{mol O atoms}$$

These mole quantities represent numbers of atoms (remember that a mole of atoms is 6.022×10^{23} atoms). It is clear from the moles of atoms that the compound contains an equal number of Ni and O atoms, so the formula is NiO. This is the *empirical formula;* it expresses the smallest whole-number (integer) ratio of atoms:

$$\frac{0.004491 \text{ mol Ni atoms}}{0.00449 \text{ mol O atoms}} = \frac{1 \text{ Ni}}{1 \text{ O}}$$

That is, this compound contains equal numbers of nickel atoms and oxygen atoms. We say the ratio of nickel atoms to oxygen atoms is 1:1 (1 to 1).

Interactive Example 8.11

Calculating Empirical Formulas

An oxide of aluminum is formed by the reaction of 4.151 g of aluminum with 3.692 g of oxygen. Calculate the empirical formula for this compound.

SOLUTION

Where Are We Going?

We want to determine the empirical formula for the aluminum oxide, Al_xO_y. That is, we want to solve for x and y.

What Do We Know?

- The compound contains 4.151 g of aluminum and 3.692 g of oxygen.
- We know the atomic masses of aluminum (26.98 g/mol), and oxygen (16.00 g/mol).

What Do We Need To Know?

- x and y represent moles of atoms in 1 mole of the compound, so we need to determine the relative number of moles of Al and O.

How Do We Get There?

We need to know the relative numbers of each type of atom to write the formula, so we must convert these masses to moles of atoms to get the empirical formula. We carry out the conversion by using the atomic masses of the elements.

$$4.151 \text{ g Al} \times \frac{1 \text{ mol Al}}{26.98 \text{ g Al}} = 0.1539 \text{ mol Al atoms}$$

$$3.692 \text{ g O} \times \frac{1 \text{ mol O}}{16.00 \text{ g O}} = 0.2308 \text{ mol O atoms}$$

Because chemical formulas use only whole numbers, we next find the integer (whole-number) ratio of the atoms. To do this we start by dividing both numbers by the smallest of the two. This converts the smallest number to 1.

$$\frac{0.1539 \text{ mol Al}}{0.1539} = 1.000 \text{ mol Al atoms}$$

$$\frac{0.2308 \text{ mol O}}{0.1539} = 1.500 \text{ mol O atoms}$$

Note that dividing both numbers of moles of atoms by the *same* number does not change the *relative* numbers of oxygen and aluminum atoms. That is,

$$\frac{0.2308 \text{ mol O}}{0.1539 \text{ mol Al}} = \frac{1.500 \text{ mol O}}{1.000 \text{ mol Al}}$$

Thus we know that the compound contains 1.500 moles of O atoms for every 1.000 mole of Al atoms, or, in terms of individual atoms, we could say that the compound contains

We might express these data as:

$$Al_{1.000\ mol}O_{1.500\ mol}$$

or

$$Al_{2.000\ mol}O_{3.000\ mol}$$

or

$$Al_2O_3$$

1.500 O atoms for every 1.000 Al atom. However, because only *whole* atoms combine to form compounds, we must find a set of *whole numbers* to express the empirical formula. When we multiply both 1.000 and 1.500 by 2, we get the integers we need.

$$1.500\ O \times 2 = 3.000 = 3\ O\ atoms$$

$$1.000\ Al \times 2 = 2.000 = 2\ Al\ atoms$$

Therefore, this compound contains two Al atoms for every three O atoms, and the empirical formula is Al_2O_3. Note that the *ratio* of atoms in this compound is given by each of the following fractions:

$$\frac{0.2308\ O}{0.1539\ Al} = \frac{1.500\ O}{1.000\ Al} = \frac{\frac{3}{2}O}{1\ Al} = \frac{3\ O}{2\ Al}$$

The smallest whole-number ratio corresponds to the subscripts of the empirical formula, Al_2O_3.

REALITY CHECK The values for x and y are whole numbers. ∎

Sometimes the relative numbers of moles you get when you calculate an empirical formula will turn out to be nonintegers, as was the case in Example 8.11. When this happens, you must convert to the appropriate whole numbers. This is done by multiplying all the numbers by the same small integer, which can be found by trial and error. The multiplier needed is almost always between 1 and 6. We will now summarize what we have learned about calculating empirical formulas.

Steps for Determining the Empirical Formula of a Compound

Step 1 Obtain the mass of each element present (in grams).

Step 2 Determine the number of moles of each type of atom present.

Step 3 Divide the number of moles of each element by the smallest number of moles to convert the smallest number to 1. If all of the numbers so obtained are integers (whole numbers), these are the subscripts in the empirical formula. If one or more of these numbers are not integers, go on to step 4.

Step 4 Multiply the numbers you derived in step 3 by the smallest integer that will convert all of them to whole numbers. This set of whole numbers represents the subscripts in the empirical formula.

Interactive Example 8.12

Calculating Empirical Formulas for Binary Compounds

When a 0.3546-g sample of vanadium metal is heated in air, it reacts with oxygen to achieve a final mass of 0.6330 g. Calculate the empirical formula of this vanadium oxide.

SOLUTION   **Where Are We Going?**

We want to determine the empirical formula for the vanadium oxide, V_xO_y. That is, we want to solve for x and y.

What Do We Know?

- The compound contains 0.3546 g of vanadium and has a total mass of 0.6330 g.
- We know the atomic masses of vanadium (50.94 g/mol) and oxygen (16.00 g/mol).

What Do We Need To Know?

- We need to know the mass of oxygen in the sample.
- x and y represent moles of atoms in 1 mole of the compound, so we need to determine the relative number of moles of V and O.

How Do We Get There?

Step 1 All the vanadium that was originally present will be found in the final compound, so we can calculate the mass of oxygen that reacted by taking the following difference:

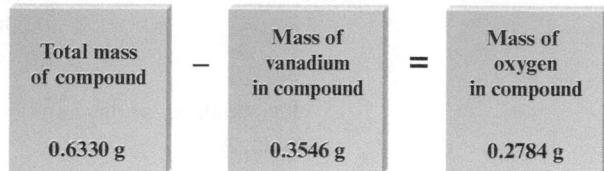

Total mass of compound	−	Mass of vanadium in compound	=	Mass of oxygen in compound
0.6330 g		0.3546 g		0.2784 g

Step 2 Using the atomic masses (50.94 for V and 16.00 for O), we obtain

$$0.3546 \ \text{g V} \times \frac{1 \ \text{mol V atoms}}{50.94 \ \text{g V}} = 0.006961 \ \text{mol V atoms}$$

$$0.2784 \ \text{g O} \times \frac{1 \ \text{mol O atoms}}{16.00 \ \text{g O}} = 0.01740 \ \text{mol O atoms}$$

Step 3 Then we divide both numbers of moles by the smaller, 0.006961.

$$\frac{0.006961 \ \text{mol V atoms}}{0.006961} = 1.000 \ \text{mol V atoms}$$

$$\frac{0.01740 \ \text{mol O atoms}}{0.006961} = 2.500 \ \text{mol O atoms}$$

Because one of these numbers (2.500) is not an integer, we go on to step 4.

Math skill builder

$V_{1.000}O_{2.500}$ becomes V_2O_5.

Step 4 We note that $2 \times 2.500 = 5.000$ and $2 \times 1.000 = 2.000$, so we multiply both numbers by 2 to get integers.

$$2 \times 1.000 \ \text{V} = 2.000 \ \text{V} = 2 \ \text{V}$$

$$2 \times 2.500 \ \text{O} = 5.000 \ \text{O} = 5 \ \text{O}$$

This compound contains 2 V atoms for every 5 O atoms, and the empirical formula is V_2O_5.

REALITY CHECK The values for x and y are whole numbers.

SELF CHECK

Exercise 8.8 In a lab experiment it was observed that 0.6884 g of lead combines with 0.2356 g of chlorine to form a binary compound. Calculate the empirical formula of this compound.

See Problems 8.61, 8.63, 8.65, and 8.66. ■

The same procedures we have used for binary compounds also apply to compounds containing three or more elements, as Example 8.13 illustrates.

Interactive Example 8.13

Calculating Empirical Formulas for Compounds Containing Three or More Elements

A sample of lead arsenate, an insecticide used against the potato beetle, contains 1.3813 g of lead, 0.00672 g of hydrogen, 0.4995 g of arsenic, and 0.4267 g of oxygen. Calculate the empirical formula for lead arsenate.

SOLUTION   **Where Are We Going?**

We want to determine the empirical formula for lead arsenate, $Pb_aH_bAs_cO_d$. That is, we want to solve for a, b, c, and d.

What Do We Know?

- The compound contains 1.3813 g of Pb, 0.00672 g of H, 0.4995 g of As, and 0.4267 g of O.
- We know the atomic masses of lead (207.2 g/mol), hydrogen (1.008 g/mol), arsenic (74.92 g/mol), and oxygen (16.00 g/mol).

What Do We Need To Know?

- a, b, c, and d represent moles of atoms in 1 mole of the compound, so we need to determine the relative number of moles of Pb, H, As, and O.

How Do We Get There?

Step 1 The compound contains 1.3813 g Pb, 0.00672 g H, 0.4995 g As, and 0.4267 g O.

Step 2 We use the atomic masses of the elements present to calculate the moles of each.

$$1.3813 \text{ g Pb} \times \frac{1 \text{ mol Pb}}{207.2 \text{ g Pb}} = 0.006667 \text{ mol Pb}$$

$$0.00672 \text{ g H} \times \frac{1 \text{ mol H}}{1.008 \text{ g H}} = 0.00667 \text{ mol H}$$

$$0.4995 \text{ g As} \times \frac{1 \text{ mol As}}{74.92 \text{ g As}} = 0.006667 \text{ mol As}$$

$$0.4267 \text{ g O} \times \frac{1 \text{ mol O}}{16.00 \text{ g O}} = 0.02667 \text{ mol O}$$

Step 3 Now we divide by the smallest number of moles.

$$\frac{0.006667 \text{ mol Pb}}{0.006667} = 1.000 \text{ mol Pb}$$

$$\frac{0.00667 \text{ mol H}}{0.006667} = 1.00 \text{ mol H}$$

$$\frac{0.006667 \text{ mol As}}{0.006667} = 1.000 \text{ mol As}$$

$$\frac{0.02667 \text{ mol O}}{0.006667} = 4.000 \text{ mol O}$$

The numbers of moles are all whole numbers, so the empirical formula is $PbHAsO_4$.

REALITY CHECK The values for a, b, c, and d are whole numbers.

SELF CHECK   **Exercise 8.9** Sevin, the commercial name for an insecticide used to protect crops such as cotton, vegetables, and fruit, is made from carbamic acid. A chemist analyzing a sample of carbamic acid finds 0.8007 g of carbon, 0.9333 g of nitrogen, 0.2016 g of hydrogen, and 2.133 g of oxygen. Determine the empirical formula for carbamic acid.

See Problems 8.57 and 8.59. ∎

When a compound is analyzed to determine the relative amounts of the elements present, the results are usually given in terms of percentages by masses of the various elements. In Section 8-6 we learned to calculate the percent composition of a com-

Math skill builder

Percent by mass for a given element means the grams of that element in 100 g of the compound.

pound from its formula. Now we will do the opposite. Given the percent composition, we will calculate the empirical formula.

To understand this procedure, you must understand the meaning of *percent*. Remember that percent means parts of a given component per 100 parts of the total mixture. For example, if a given compound is 15% carbon (by mass), the compound contains 15 g of carbon per 100 g of compound.

Calculation of the empirical formula of a compound when one is given its percent composition is illustrated in Example 8.14.

Interactive Example 8.14

Calculating Empirical Formulas from Percent Composition

Cisplatin, the common name for a platinum compound that is used to treat cancerous tumors, has the composition (mass percent) 65.02% platinum, 9.34% nitrogen, 2.02% hydrogen, and 23.63% chlorine. Calculate the empirical formula for cisplatin.

SOLUTION

Where Are We Going?

We want to determine the empirical formula for cisplatin, $Pt_aN_bH_cCl_d$. That is, we want to solve for *a, b, c,* and *d.*

What Do We Know?

- The compound has the composition (mass percent) 65.02% Pt, 9.34% N, 2.02% H, and 23.63% Cl.
- We know the atomic masses of platinum (195.1 g/mol), nitrogen (14.01 g/mol), hydrogen (1.008 g/mol), and chlorine (35.45 g/mol).

What Do We Need To Know?

- *a, b, c,* and *d* represent moles of atoms in 1 mole of the compound, so we need to determine the relative number of moles of Pt, N, H, and Cl.
- We have mass percent data, and to get to the number of moles we need to know the mass of each element (g) in the sample.

How Do We Get There?

Step 1 Determine how many grams of each element are present in 100 g of compound. Cisplatin is 65.02% platinum (by mass), which means there is 65.02 g of platinum (Pt) per 100.00 g of compound. Similarly, a 100.00-g sample of cisplatin contains 9.34 g of nitrogen (N), 2.02 g of hydrogen (H), and 26.63 g of chlorine (Cl).

If we have a 100.00-g sample of cisplatin, we have 65.02 g Pt, 9.34 g N, 2.02 g H, and 23.63 g Cl.

Step 2 Determine the number of moles of each type of atom. We use the atomic masses to calculate moles.

$$65.02 \text{ g Pt} \times \frac{1 \text{ mol Pt}}{195.1 \text{ g Pt}} = 0.3333 \text{ mol Pt}$$

$$9.34 \text{ g N} \times \frac{1 \text{ mol N}}{14.01 \text{ g N}} = 0.667 \text{ mol N}$$

$$2.02 \text{ g H} \times \frac{1 \text{ mol H}}{1.008 \text{ g H}} = 2.00 \text{ mol H}$$

$$23.63 \text{ g Cl} \times \frac{1 \text{ mol Cl}}{35.45 \text{ g Cl}} = 0.6666 \text{ mol Cl}$$

Step 3 Divide through by the smallest number of moles.

$$\frac{0.3333 \text{ mol Pt}}{0.3333} = 1.000 \text{ mol Pt}$$

$$\frac{0.667 \text{ mol N}}{0.3333} = 2.00 \text{ mol N}$$

$$\frac{2.00 \text{ mol H}}{0.3333} = 6.01 \text{ mol H}$$

$$\frac{0.6666 \text{ mol Cl}}{0.3333} = 2.000 \text{ mol Cl}$$

The empirical formula for cisplatin is $PtN_2H_6Cl_2$. Note that the number for hydrogen is slightly greater than 6 because of rounding-off effects.

REALITY CHECK The values for *a, b, c,* and *d* are whole numbers.

Critical Thinking

One part of the problem-solving strategy for empirical formula determination is to base the calculation on 100 g of compound. What if you chose a mass other than 100 g? Would this work? What if you chose to base the calculation on 100 moles of compound? Would this work?

SELF CHECK

Exercise 8.10 The most common form of nylon (Nylon-6) is 63.68% carbon, 12.38% nitrogen, 9.80% hydrogen, and 14.14% oxygen. Calculate the empirical formula for Nylon-6.

See Problems 8.67 through 8.74. ∎

Note from Example 8.14 that once the percentages are converted to masses, this example is the same as earlier examples in which the masses were given directly.

8-9 Calculation of Molecular Formulas

OBJECTIVE

To learn to calculate the molecular formula of a compound, given its empirical formula and molar mass.

If we know the composition of a compound in terms of the masses (or mass percentages) of the elements present, we can calculate the empirical formula but not the molecular formula. For reasons that will become clear as we consider Example 8.15, to obtain the molecular formula we must know the molar mass. In this section we will consider compounds where both the percent composition and the molar mass are known.

Interactive Example 8.15

Calculating Molecular Formulas

A white powder is analyzed and found to have an empirical formula of P_2O_5. The compound has a molar mass of 283.88 g. What is the compound's molecular formula?

SOLUTION

Where Are We Going?

We want to determine the molecular formula (P_xO_y) for a compound. That is, we want to solve for *x* and *y*.

What Do We Know?

- The empirical formula of the compound is P_2O_5.
- The molar mass of the compound is 283.88 g/mol.
- We know the atomic masses of phosphorus (30.97 g/mol) and oxygen (16.00 g/mol).
- The molecular formula contains a whole number of empirical formula units. So, the molecular formula will be $P_{2x}O_{5y}$.

What Do We Need To Know?

- We need to know the empirical formula mass.

How Do We Get There?

To obtain the molecular formula, we must compare the empirical formula mass to the molar mass. The empirical formula mass for P_2O_5 is the mass of 1 mole of P_2O_5 units.

Atomic
mass of P

2 mol P: 2 × 30.97 g =   61.94 g
5 mol O: 5 × 16.00 g =   80.00 g
                        141.94 g   Mass of 1 mole of P_2O_5 units

Atomic
mass of O

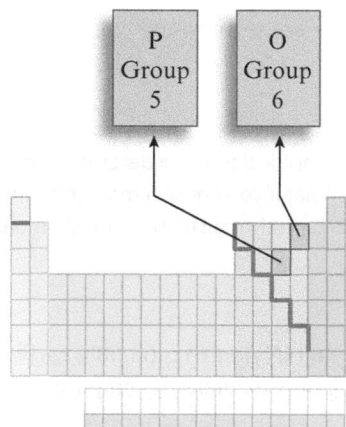

P Group 5   O Group 6

Recall that the molecular formula contains a whole number of empirical formula units. That is,

$$\text{Molecular formula} = (\text{empirical formula})_n$$

where n is a small whole number. Now, because

$$\text{Molecular formula} = n \times \text{empirical formula}$$

then

$$\text{Molar mass} = n \times \text{empirical formula mass}$$

Solving for n gives

$$n = \frac{\text{molar mass}}{\text{empirical formula mass}}$$

Thus, to determine the molecular formula, we first divide the molar mass by the empirical formula mass. This tells us how many empirical formula masses there are in one molar mass.

$$\frac{\text{Molar mass}}{\text{Empirical formula mass}} = \frac{283.88 \text{ g}}{141.94 \text{ g}} = 2$$

This result means that $n = 2$ for this compound, so the molecular formula consists of two empirical formula units, and the molecular formula is $(P_2O_5)_2$, or P_4O_{10}. The structure of this interesting compound is shown in Fig. 8.5.

REALITY CHECK The values for x and y are whole numbers. Also, the ratio of P:O in the molecular formula (4:10) is 2:5.

= P
= O

Figure 8.5 ▶ The structure of P_4O_{10} as a "ball-and-stick" model. This compound has a great affinity for water and is often used as a desiccant, or drying agent.

Exercise 8.11 A compound used as an additive for gasoline to help prevent engine knock shows the following percent composition:

$$71.65\% \text{ Cl} \qquad 24.27\% \text{ C} \qquad 4.07\% \text{ H}$$

The molar mass is known to be 98.96 g. Determine the empirical formula and the molecular formula for this compound.

See Problems 8.81 and 8.82. ∎

It is important to realize that the molecular formula is always an integer multiple of the empirical formula. For example, the sugar glucose (Fig. 8.4) has the empirical formula CH_2O and the molecular formula $C_6H_{12}O_6$. In this case there are six empirical formula units in each glucose molecule:

$$(CH_2O)_6 = C_6H_{12}O_6$$

In general, we can represent the molecular formula in terms of the empirical formula as follows:

$$(\text{Empirical formula})_n = \text{molecular formula}$$

where n is an integer. If $n = 1$, the molecular formula is the same as the empirical formula. For example, for carbon dioxide the empirical formula (CO_2) and the molecular formula (CO_2) are the same, so $n = 1$. On the other hand, for tetraphosphorus decoxide the empirical formula is P_2O_5 and the molecular formula is $P_4O_{10} = (P_2O_5)_2$. In this case $n = 2$.

Gases, Liquids, and Solids

7

During a volcanic eruption, many interconversions occur among the three states of matter. Products of the eruption include gaseous substances, liquid (molten) substances, and solid substances.

In Chapters 3, 4, and 5, the structure of matter from a submicroscopic point of view—in terms of molecules, atoms, protons, neutrons, and electrons—was considered. In this chapter, the macroscopic characteristics of matter as represented by the physical states of matter—solid, liquid, and gas—is the topic for discussion.

7-1 The Kinetic Molecular Theory of Matter

LEARNING FOCUS

Be familiar with the five core concepts associated with the kinetic molecular theory of matter; be able to describe the roles that kinetic energy and potential energy play in determining the physical state of a system.

Solids, liquids, and gases (Section 1-2) are easily distinguished by using four common physical properties of matter: (1) volume and shape, (2) density, (3) compressibility, and (4) thermal expansion. The property of density was discussed in Section 2-9. **Compressibility** *is a measure of the change in volume of a sample of matter resulting from a pressure change.* **Thermal expansion** *is a measure of the change in volume of a sample of matter resulting from a temperature change.* These distinguishing characteristics are compared in

▶ **Table 7-1 Distinguishing Properties of Solids, Liquids, and Gases**

Property	Solid State	Liquid State	Gaseous State
volume and shape	definite volume and definite shape	definite volume and indefinite shape; takes the shape of its container to the extent that it is filled	indefinite volume and indefinite shape; takes the volume and shape of the container that it completely fills
density	high	high, but usually lower than corresponding solid	low
compressibility	small	small, but usually greater than corresponding solid	large
thermal expansion	very small: about 0.01% per °C	small: about 0.10% per °C	moderate: about 0.30% per °C

Table 7-1 for the three states of matter. The physical characteristics of the solid, liquid, and gaseous states listed in Table 7-1 can be explained by kinetic molecular theory, which is one of the fundamental theories of chemistry. The **kinetic molecular theory of matter** *is a set of five statements used to explain the physical behavior of the three states of matter (solids, liquids, and gases).* The basic idea of this theory is that the particles (atoms, molecules, or ions) present in a substance, independent of the physical state of the substance, are always in motion. ◄

The five statements of the kinetic molecular theory of matter are:

Statement 1: *Matter is ultimately composed of tiny particles (atoms, molecules, or ions) that have definite and characteristic sizes that do not change.*

Statement 2: *The particles are in constant random motion and therefore possess kinetic energy.*

Kinetic energy *is energy that matter possesses because of particle motion.* An object that is in motion has the ability to transfer its kinetic energy to another object upon collision with that object.

Statement 3: *The particles interact with one another through attractions and repulsions and therefore possess potential energy.* ◄

Potential energy *is stored energy that matter possesses as a result of its position, condition, and/or composition* (Figure 7-1). The potential energy of greatest importance when considering the differences among the three states of matter is that which originates from electrostatic interactions among particles. An **electrostatic interaction** *is an attraction or repulsion that occurs between charged particles.* Particles of opposite charge (one positive and the other negative) attract one another, and particles of like charge (both positive or both negative) repel one another. Further use of the term *potential energy* in this text will mean potential energy of electrostatic origin.

Statement 4: *The kinetic energy (velocity) of the particles increases as the temperature is increased.*

The *average* kinetic energy (velocity) of all particles in a system depends on the temperature; kinetic energy increases as temperature increases.

Statement 5: *The particles in a system transfer energy to each other through elastic collisions.*

In an elastic collision, the total kinetic energy remains constant; no kinetic energy is lost. The difference between an *elastic* and an *inelastic* collision is illustrated by comparing the collision of two hard steel spheres with the collision of two masses of putty. The collision of spheres approximates an elastic collision (the spheres bounce off one another and continue moving, as in Figure 7-2); the putty collision has none of these characteristics (the masses "glob" together with no resulting movement). ◄

▶ *The word* kinetic *comes from the Greek* kinesis, *which means "movement." The kinetic molecular theory deals with the movement of particles.*

▶ *For gases, the attractions between particles (statement 3) are minimal and as a first approximation are considered to be zero (see Section 7-2).*

Figure 7-1 The water in the lake behind the dam has potential energy as a result of its position. When the water flows over the dam, its potential energy becomes kinetic energy that can be used to turn the turbines of a hydroelectric plant.

▶ *Two consequences of the elasticity of particle collisions (statement 5) are that (1) the energy of any given particle is continually changing and (2) particle energies for a system are not all the same; a range of particle energies is always encountered.*

Figure 7-2 Upon release, the steel ball on the left transmits its kinetic energy through a series of elastic collisions to the ball on the right.

The differences among the solid, liquid, and gaseous states of matter can be explained by the relative magnitudes of kinetic energy and potential energy (in this case, electrostatic attractions) associated with the physical state. Kinetic energy can be considered a *disruptive force* that tends to make the particles of a system increasingly independent of one another. This is because the particles tend to move away from one another as a result of the energy of motion. Potential energy of attraction can be considered a *cohesive force* that tends to cause order and stability among the particles of a system.

How much kinetic energy a chemical system has depends on its temperature. Kinetic energy increases as temperature increases (statement 4 of the kinetic molecular theory of matter). Thus the higher the temperature, the greater the magnitude of disruptive influences within a chemical system. Potential energy magnitude, or cohesive force magnitude, is essentially independent of temperature. The fact that one of the types of forces depends on temperature (disruptive forces) and the other does not (cohesive forces) causes temperature to be the factor that determines in which of the three physical states a given sample of matter is found. The critical role that temperature plays in determining physical state is further considered in Section 7-2.

Section 7-1 Quick Quiz

1. Which of the following statements is <u>not</u> consistent with the kinetic molecular theory of matter?
   a. Matter is composed of particles that are in constant motion.
   b. Particles in a system cannot transfer energy to each other.
   c. Particle interactions involve electrostatic attractions and repulsions.
   d. no correct response
2. The kinetic energy of a particle
   a. is a constant that never changes
   b. increases with increasing temperature
   c. does not depend on temperature
   d. no correct response
3. In which of the following groupings of terms are the three terms closely related?
   a. potential energy, repulsive forces, disruptive forces
   b. kinetic energy, electrostatic forces, cohesive forces
   c. potential energy, attractive forces, cohesive forces
   d. no correct response

Answers: 1. b; 2. b; 3. c

7-2 Kinetic Molecular Theory and Physical States

LEARNING FOCUS

Use kinetic molecular theory concepts to explain the differing physical characteristics of the solid, liquid, and gaseous states.

A **solid** *is the physical state characterized by a dominance of potential energy (cohesive forces) over kinetic energy (disruptive forces).* The particles in a solid are drawn close together in a regular pattern by the strong cohesive forces present (Figure 7-3a). Each particle occupies a fixed position, about which it vibrates because of disruptive kinetic energy. With this model, the characteristic properties of solids (Table 7-1) can be explained as follows:

1. *Definite volume and definite shape.* The strong, cohesive forces hold the particles in essentially fixed positions, resulting in definite volume and definite shape.
2. *High density.* The constituent particles of solids are located as close together as possible (touching each other). Therefore, a given volume contains large numbers of particles, resulting in a high density.

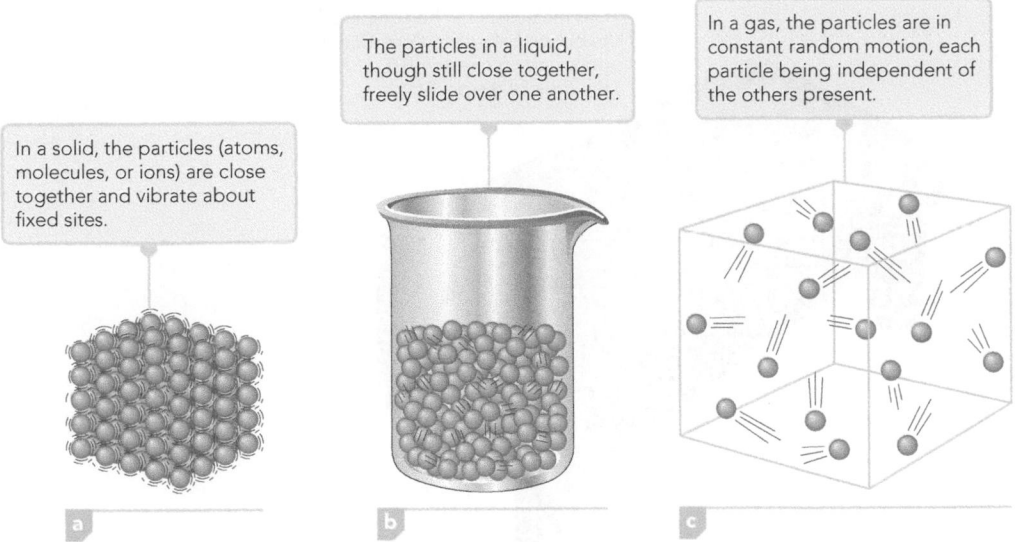

In a solid, the particles (atoms, molecules, or ions) are close together and vibrate about fixed sites.

The particles in a liquid, though still close together, freely slide over one another.

In a gas, the particles are in constant random motion, each particle being independent of the others present.

Figure 7-3 Distance between particles and particle movement visually contrasted for the three physical states of matter.

3. *Small compressibility.* Because there is very little space between particles, increased pressure cannot push the particles any closer together; therefore, it has little effect on the solid's volume.
4. *Very small thermal expansion.* An increased temperature increases the kinetic energy (disruptive forces), thereby causing more vibrational motion of the particles. Each particle occupies a slightly larger volume, and the result is a slight expansion of the solid. The strong, cohesive forces prevent this effect from becoming very large.

A **liquid** *is the physical state characterized by potential energy (cohesive forces) and kinetic energy (disruptive forces) of about the same magnitude.* The liquid state consists of particles that are randomly packed but relatively near one another (Figure 7-3b). The molecules are in constant, random motion; they slide freely over one another but do not move with enough energy to separate. The fact that the particles freely slide over each other indicates the influence of disruptive forces; however, the fact that the particles do not separate indicates fairly strong cohesive forces. With this model, the characteristic properties of liquids (Table 7-1) can be explained as follows:

1. *Definite volume and indefinite shape.* The attractive forces are strong enough to restrict particles to movement within a definite volume. They are not strong enough, however, to prevent the particles from moving over each other in a random manner that is limited only by the container walls. Thus liquids have no definite shape except that they maintain a horizontal upper surface in containers that are not completely filled.
2. *High density.* The particles in a liquid are not widely separated; they are still touching one another. Therefore, there will be a large number of particles in a given volume—a high density.
3. *Small compressibility.* Because the particles in a liquid are still touching each other, there is very little empty space. Therefore, an increase in pressure cannot squeeze the particles much closer together.
4. *Small thermal expansion.* Most of the particle movement in a liquid is vibrational because a particle can move only a short distance before colliding with a neighbor. The increased particle velocity that accompanies a temperature increase results only in increased vibrational amplitudes. The net effect is an increase in the effective volume a particle occupies, which causes a slight volume increase in the liquid.

Figure 7-4 Collision characteristics for molecules in the gaseous states are similar to those for moving billiard balls on a pool table.

Gas molecules can be compared to billiard balls in random motion, bouncing off one another and off the sides of the pool table.

A **gas** *is the physical state characterized by a complete dominance of kinetic energy (disruptive forces) over potential energy (cohesive forces).* Attractive forces among particles are very weak and, as a first approximation, are considered to be zero. As a result, the particles of a gas move essentially independently of one another in a totally random manner (Figure 7-3c). Under ordinary pressure, the particles are relatively far apart, except when they collide with one another. In between collisions with one another or with the container walls, gas particles travel in straight lines (Figure 7-4).

The kinetic molecular theory explanation of the properties of gases parallels that described previously for solids and liquids.

1. *Indefinite volume and indefinite shape.* The attractive (cohesive) forces between particles have been overcome by high kinetic energy, and the particles are free to travel in all directions. Therefore, gas particles completely fill their container, and the shape of the gas is that of the container.
2. *Low density.* The particles of a gas are widely separated. There are relatively few particles in a given volume (compared with liquids and solids), which means little mass per volume (a low density).
3. *Large compressibility.* Particles in a gas are widely separated; essentially, a gas is mostly empty space. When pressure is applied, the particles are easily pushed closer together, decreasing the amount of empty space and the volume of the gas (Figure 7-5).
4. *Moderate thermal expansion.* An increase in temperature means an increase in particle velocity. The increased kinetic energy of the particles enables them to push back whatever barrier is confining them into a given volume, and the volume increases. Note that the size of the particles is not changed during expansion or compression of gases, solids, or liquids; they merely move either farther apart or closer together. It is the space between the particles that changes.

The focus on relevancy feature Chemical Connections 7-A—The Importance of Gas Densities—discusses a number of common phenomena that occur because of the large density difference between the gaseous state (low density) and the solid and liquid states (high density).

Chemistry at a Glance—Kinetic Molecular Theory and the States of Matter—connects key parameters associated with the three states of matter with kinetic molecular theory concepts relating to these parameters.

Gas at low pressure

Gas at higher pressure

Figure 7-5 When a gas is compressed, the amount of empty space in the container is decreased. The size of the molecules does not change; they simply move closer together.

Section 7-2 Quick Quiz

1. The phrases "definite volume" and "indefinite shape" apply collectively to the
   a. solid state of matter
   b. liquid state of matter
   c. both the liquid and gaseous states of matter
   d. no correct response
2. In the liquid state, disruptive forces are
   a. roughly of the same magnitude as cohesive forces
   b. very weak compared to cohesive forces
   c. dominant over cohesive forces
   d. no correct response
3. The phrases "particles close together and held in fixed positions" and "completely fills the container" apply, respectively, to
   a. liquids and solids
   b. solids and gases
   c. gases and liquids
   d. no correct response

Answers: 1. b; 2. a; 3. b

CHEMISTRY AT A GLANCE — Kinetic Molecular Theory and the States of Matter

Solid	Liquid	Gas
Shape and Volume		
Definite Shape Definite Volume	Indefinite Shape, that of its container Definite Volume	Indefinite Shape, that of its container Indefinite Volume, that of its container
Arrangement of Particles		
Fixed arrangement of particles that are very close together	Random arrangement of particles that are very close together	Random arrangement of particles that are far apart
Interactions Among Particles		
Very strong	Very strong, but less than that of corresponding solid	Very weak (almost zero)
Relative Importance of Kinetic Energy		
Kinetic energy is less than potential energy	Kinetic energy and potential energy are of about the same magnitude	Kinetic energy dominates over potential energy

CHEMICAL CONNECTIONS 7-A

The Importance of Gas Densities

The density difference between liquid water and steam is the cause for popcorn popping when it is heated to a high temperature.

In the gaseous state, particles are approximately 10 times farther apart than in the solid or liquid state at a given temperature and pressure. Consequently, gases have densities much lower than those of solids and liquids. The fact that gases have low densities is a major factor in explaining many commonly encountered phenomena.

Popcorn pops because of the difference in density between liquid and gaseous water (1.0 g/mL versus 0.001 g/mL). As the corn kernels are heated, water within the kernels is converted into steam. The steam's volume, approximately 1000 times greater than that of the water from which it was generated, causes the kernels of corn to "blow up."

Changes in density that occur as a solid is converted to gases via a chemical reaction are the basis for the operation of automobile air bags and the effects of explosives. Automobile air bags are designed to inflate rapidly (in a

fraction of a second) in the event of a crash and then to deflate immediately. Their activation involves mechanical shock causing a steel ball to compress a spring that electronically ignites a detonator cap, which in turn causes solid sodium azide (NaN_3) to decompose. The decomposition reaction is

$$2NaN_3(s) \longrightarrow 2Na(l) + 3N_2(g)$$

The nitrogen gas so generated inflates the air bag. A small amount of NaN_3 (high density) will generate more than 50 L of N_2 gas at 25°C. Because the air bag is porous, it goes limp quickly as the generated N_2 gas escapes.

Millions of hours of hard manual labor are saved annually by the use of industrial explosives in quarrying rock, constructing tunnels, and mining coal and metal ores. The active ingredient in dynamite, a heavily used industrial explosive, is nitroglycerin, whose destructive power comes from the generation of large volumes of gases at high temperatures. The reaction is

$$4C_3H_5O_3(NO_2)_3(s) \longrightarrow$$
Nitroglycerin
$$12CO_2(g) + 10H_2O(g) + 6N_2(g) + O_2(g)$$

At the temperature of the explosion, about 5000°C, there is an approximately 20,000-fold increase in volume as the result of density changes. No wonder such explosives can blow materials to pieces!

The density difference associated with temperature change is the basis for the operation of hot-air balloons. Hot air, which is less dense than cold air, rises.

Weather balloons and blimps are filled with helium, a gas less dense than air. Thus, such objects rise in air.

Water vapor is less dense than air. Thus, moist air is less dense than dry air. Decreasing barometric pressure (from lower-density moist air) is an indication that a storm front is approaching.

7-3 Gas Law Variables

LEARNING FOCUS

List the units commonly used for each of the following gas law variables: amount, pressure, temperature, and volume.

The behavior of a gas can be described reasonably well by *simple* quantitative relationships called *gas laws*. A **gas law** *is a generalization that describes in mathematical terms the relationships among the amount, pressure, temperature, and volume of a gas.*

Gas laws involve four variables: amount, pressure, temperature, and volume. Three of these four variables (amount, volume, and temperature) have been previously discussed (Sections 6-2, 2-2, and 2-10, respectively). Amount is usually specified in terms of *moles* of gas present. The units *liter* and *milliliter* are generally used in specifying gas volume. Only one of the three temperature scales discussed in Section 2-10, the *Kelvin scale,* can be used in gas law calculations if the results are to be valid. Pressure, the fourth gas law variable, has not been previously considered in this text. The remainder of this section addresses concepts about pressure needed for understanding gas laws.

Pressure *is the force applied per unit area on an object—that is, the total force on a surface divided by the area of that surface.* The mathematical equation for pressure is

$$\text{pressure} = \frac{\text{force}}{\text{area}}$$

For a gas, the force that creates pressure is that which is exerted by the gas molecules or atoms as they constantly collide with the walls of their container. Barometers, manometers, and gauges are the instruments most commonly used to measure gas pressures.

The air that surrounds Earth exerts pressure on every object it touches. A **barometer** *is a device used to measure atmospheric pressure.* The essential components of a simple barometer are shown in Figure 7-6. Atmospheric pressure is expressed in terms of the height of the barometer's mercury column, usually *in millimeters of mercury* (mm Hg). Another name for millimeters of mercury is *torr,* used in honor of Evangelista Torricelli (1608–1647), the Italian physicist who invented the barometer. ◄

$$1 \text{ mm Hg} = 1 \text{ torr}$$

Atmospheric pressure varies with the weather and the altitude. It averages about 760 mm Hg at sea level, and it decreases by approximately 25 mm Hg for every 1000-ft increase in altitude. The pressure unit *atmosphere* (atm) is defined in terms of this average pressure at sea level. By definition,

$$1 \text{ atm} = 760 \text{ mm Hg} = 760 \text{ torr}$$

Another commonly used pressure unit is *pounds per square inch* (psi or lb/in²). One atmosphere is equal to 14.7 psi.

$$1 \text{ atm} = 14.7 \text{ psi}$$

Pressure Readings and Significant Figures

Standard procedure in obtaining pressures that are based on the height of a column of mercury (barometric readings) is to estimate the column height to the closest millimeter. Thus such pressure readings have an uncertainty in the "ones place," that is, to the closest millimeter of mercury. The preceding operational procedure means that millimeter of mercury pressure readings such as 750, 730, and 650 are considered to have three significant figures even though no decimal point is explicitly shown after the zero (Section 2-4). Likewise, a pressure reading of 700 mm Hg or 600 mm Hg is considered to possess three significant figures.

▶ *"Millimeters of mercury" is the pressure unit most often encountered in clinical work in allied health fields. For example, oxygen and carbon dioxide pressures in respiration are almost always specified in millimeters of mercury.*

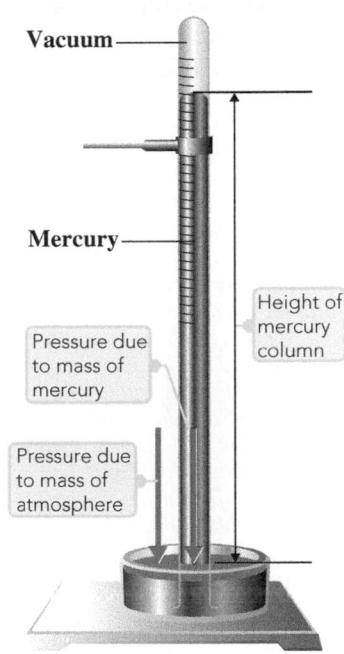

Figure 7-6 The essential components of a mercury barometer are a graduated glass tube, a glass dish, and liquid mercury.

Figure 7-7 Robert Boyle (1627–1691), like most men of the seventeenth century who devoted themselves to science, was self-taught. It was through his efforts that the true value of experimental investigation was first recognized.

▶ *Blood pressure is measured with the aid of an apparatus known as a sphygmomanometer, which is essentially a barometer tube connected to an inflatable cuff by a hollow tube. A typical blood pressure is 120/80; this ratio means a systolic pressure of 120 mm Hg above atmospheric pressure and a diastolic pressure of 80 mm Hg above atmospheric pressure. (See Chemical Connections 7-B—Blood Pressure and the Sodium Ion/Potassium Ion Ratio—for further information about blood pressure.)*

7-4 Boyle's Law: A Pressure–Volume Relationship

LEARNING FOCUS

State Boyle's law in words and as a mathematical equation; know how to use the law in problem-solving situations to which it applies.

Of the several relationships that exist among gas law variables, the first to be discovered relates gas pressure to gas volume. It was formulated more than 350 years ago, in 1662, by the British chemist and physicist Robert Boyle (Figure 7-7). **Boyle's law** states that *the volume of a fixed amount of a gas is inversely proportional to the pressure applied to the gas if the temperature is kept constant.* This means that if the pressure on the gas increases, the volume decreases proportionally; conversely, if the pressure decreases, the volume increases. Doubling the pressure cuts the volume in half; tripling the pressure reduces the volume to one-third its original value; quadrupling the pressure reduces the volume to one-fourth its original value; and so on. Figure 7-8 illustrates Boyle's law.

The mathematical equation for Boyle's law is

$$P_1 \times V_1 = P_2 \times V_2$$

where P_1 and V_1 are the pressure and volume of a gas at an initial set of conditions, and P_2 and V_2 are the pressure and volume of the same sample of gas under a new set of conditions, with the temperature and amount of gas remaining constant. ◀

100 mm Hg
8 L

200 mm Hg
4 L

400 mm Hg
2 L

Pressure and volume

Figure 7-8 Data illustrating the inverse proportionality associated with Boyle's law.

EXAMPLE 7-1

Using Boyle's Law to Calculate the New Volume of a Gas

A sample of O_2 gas occupies a volume of 1.50 L at a pressure of 735 mm Hg and a temperature of 25°C. What volume will it occupy, in liters, if the pressure is increased to 770 mm Hg with no change in temperature?

Solution

A suggested first step in working gas law problems that involve two sets of conditions is to analyze the given data in terms of initial and final conditions.

$$P_1 = 735 \text{ mm Hg} \qquad P_2 = 770 \text{ mm Hg}$$
$$V_1 = 1.50 \text{ L} \qquad V_2 = ? \text{ L}$$

Three of the four variables in the Boyle's law equation—P_1, V_1, and P_2—are known, so the fourth variable—V_2—can be calculated. The Boyle's law equation is algebraically rearranged to isolate V_2 (the quantity to be calculated) on one side of the equation. This is accomplished by dividing both sides of the Boyle's law equation by P_2.

$$P_1V_1 = P_2V_2 \quad \text{(Boyle's law)}$$

$$\frac{P_1V_1}{P_2} = \frac{P_2V_2}{P_2} \quad \begin{array}{l}\text{(Divide each side}\\ \text{of the equation by } P_2.)\end{array}$$

$$V_2 = V_1 \times \frac{P_1}{P_2}$$

Substituting the given data into the rearranged equation and doing the arithmetic give

$$V_2 = 1.50 \text{ L} \times \left(\frac{735 \text{ mm Hg}}{770 \text{ mm Hg}}\right) = 1.43 \text{ L}$$

Boyle's law is consistent with kinetic molecular theory. The pressure that a gas exerts results from collisions of the gas molecules with the sides of the container. If the volume of a container holding a specific number of gas molecules is increased, the total wall area of the container will also increase, and the number of collisions in a given area (the pressure) will decrease because of the greater wall area. Conversely, if the volume of the container is decreased, the wall area will be smaller and there will be more collisions within a given wall area. Figure 7-9 illustrates this concept.

Filling a medical syringe with a liquid demonstrates Boyle's law. As the plunger is drawn out of the syringe (Figure 7-10), the increase in volume inside the syringe chamber results in decreased pressure there. The liquid, which is at atmospheric pressure, flows into this reduced-pressure area. This liquid is then expelled from the chamber by pushing the plunger back in. This ejection of the liquid does not involve Boyle's law; a liquid is incompressible, and mechanical force pushes it out. ◀

▶ *Boyle's law explains the process of breathing. Breathing in occurs when the diaphragm flattens out (contracts). This contraction causes the volume of the thoracic cavity to increase and the pressure within the cavity to drop (Boyle's law) below atmospheric pressure. Air flows into the lungs and expands them, because the pressure is greater outside the lungs than within them. Breathing out occurs when the diaphragm relaxes (moves up), decreasing the volume of the thoracic cavity and increasing the pressure (Boyle's law) within the cavity to a value greater than the external pressure. Air flows out of the lungs. The air flow direction is always from a high-pressure region to a low-pressure region.*

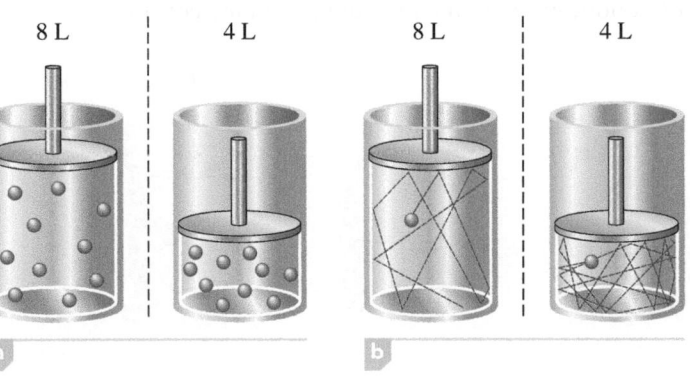

8 L   4 L   8 L   4 L

a   b

Figure 7-9 When the volume of a gas at constant temperature decreases by half (a), the average number of times a molecule hits the container walls is doubled (b).

---

1. In calculations based on Boyle's law, which two of the gas law variables are held constant?
   a. P and n
   b. V and T
   c. P and V
   d. no correct response
2. Boyle's law involves which of the following?
   a. a direct proportion
   b. an inverse proportion
   c. a constant volume
   d. no correct response
3. Based on Boyle's law, if the pressure on 30.0 mL of a gas is changed from 1.00 atm to 2.00 atm the new volume, in mL, will be
   a. 15.0 mL
   b. 32.0 mL
   c. 60.0 mL
   d. no correct response

Figure 7-10 Filling a syringe with a liquid is an application of Boyle's law.

Answers: 1. d; 2. b; 3. a

Figure 7-11 Jacques Charles (1746–1823), a French physicist, in the process of working with hot-air balloons, made the observations that ultimately led to the formulation of what is now known as Charles's law.

Figure 7-12 Data illustrating the direct proportionality associated with Charles's law.

Edgar Fahs Smith Collection, University of Pennsylvania Library

7-5 Charles's Law: A Temperature–Volume Relationship

LEARNING FOCUS

State Charles's law in words and as a mathematical equation; know how to use this law in problem-solving situations to which it applies.

The relationship between the temperature and the volume of a gas at constant pressure is called *Charles's law* after the French scientist Jacques Charles (Figure 7-11). This law was discovered in 1787, more than 100 years after the discovery of Boyle's law. **Charles's law** states that *the volume of a fixed amount of gas is directly proportional to its Kelvin temperature if the pressure is kept constant* (Figure 7-12). Whenever a *direct* proportion exists between two quantities, one increases when the other increases and one decreases when the other decreases. The direct-proportion relationship of Charles's law means that if the temperature increases, the volume will also increase and that if the temperature decreases, the volume will also decrease.

A balloon filled with air illustrates Charles's law. If the balloon is placed near a heat source, such as a light bulb that has been on for some time, the heat will cause the balloon to increase visibly in size (volume). Putting the same balloon in the refrigerator will cause it to shrink.

Charles's law, stated mathematically, is

$$\frac{V_1}{T_1} = \frac{V_2}{T_2}$$

where V_1 is the volume of a gas at a given pressure, T_1 is the Kelvin temperature of the gas, and V_2 and T_2 are the volume and Kelvin temperature of the gas under a new set of conditions, with the pressure remaining constant.

100 K
2 L

200 K
4 L

400 K
8 L

Temperature and volume

EXAMPLE 7-2

Using Charles's Law to Calculate the New Volume of a Gas

A sample of the gaseous anesthetic cyclopropane, with a volume of 425 mL at a temperature of 27°C, is cooled at constant pressure to 20°C. What is the new volume, in milliliters, of the sample?

Solution

First, we will analyze the data in terms of initial and final conditions.

$$V_1 = 425 \text{ mL} \qquad\qquad V_2 = ? \text{ mL}$$
$$T_1 = 27°C + 273 = 300 \text{ K} \qquad T_2 = 20°C + 273 = 293 \text{ K}$$

Note that both of the given temperatures have been converted to Kelvin scale readings. This change is accomplished by simply adding 273 to the Celsius scale value (Section 2-10).

Three of the four variables in the Charles's law equation are known, so the fourth variable, V_2, can be calculated. The Charles's law equation is algebraically rearranged to isolate V_2 (the quantity desired) by multiplying each side of the equation by T_2. ◄

▶ *When using the mathematical form of Charles's law, the temperatures used* must be *Kelvin scale temperatures.*

$$\frac{V_1}{T_1} = \frac{V_2}{T_2} \qquad \text{(Charles's law)}$$

$$\frac{V_1 T_2}{T_1} = \frac{V_2 \cancel{T_2}}{\cancel{T_2}} \qquad \text{(Multiply each side by } T_2.)$$

$$V_2 = V_1 \times \frac{T_2}{T_1}$$

Substituting the given data into the equation and doing the arithmetic give

$$V_2 = 425 \text{ mL} \times \left(\frac{293 \text{ K}}{300 \text{ K}}\right) = 415 \text{ mL}$$

Charles's law is consistent with kinetic molecular theory. When the temperature of a gas increases, the kinetic energy (velocity) of the gas molecules increases. The speedier particles hit the container walls harder. In order for the pressure of the gas to remain constant, the container volume must increase. This will result in fewer particles hitting a unit area of wall at a given instant. A similar argument applies when the temperature of a gas is lowered. This time the velocity of the molecules decreases, and the wall area (volume) must also decrease in order to increase the number of collisions in a given area in a given time. ◄

Charles's law is the principle used in the operation of a convection heater. When air comes in contact with the heating element, it expands (its density becomes less). The hot, less-dense air rises, causing continuous circulation of warm air. This same principle has ramifications in closed rooms that lack effective air circulation. The warmer and less-dense air stays near the top of the room. This is desirable in the summer but not in the winter.

In a similar manner, Charles's law offers an explanation for the wind currents (breezes) prevalent in many beach locations. Air above land heats up faster than air above water. As the temperature of the air above land increases, the density of this air decreases because the air occupies a larger volume (Charles's law). This less-dense air rises and the lower temperature air above the water moves inland, replacing the rising less-dense air and creating a "breeze."

▶ *Charles's law predicts that gas volume will become smaller and smaller as temperature is reduced, until eventually a temperature is reached at which gas volume becomes zero. This "zero-volume" temperature is calculated to be* $-273°C$ *and is known as* absolute zero *(see Section 2-10). Absolute zero is the basis for the Kelvin temperature scale. In reality, gas volume never vanishes. As temperature is lowered, at some point before absolute zero, the gas condenses to a liquid, at which point Charles's law is no longer valid,*

Section 7-5 Quick Quiz

1. Charles's law involves which of the following?
   a. an inverse proportion
   b. a constant volume
   c. a constant pressure
   d. no correct response
2. Based on Charles's law, which of the following temperature changes would decrease the volume of a sample of gas?
   a. 0°C to 10°C
   b. 300 K to 400 K
   c. 20°C to 10°C
   d. no correct response
3. Based on Charles's law, when the Kelvin temperature of a sample of gas is doubled the
   a. volume of the gas also doubles
   b. volume of the gas is cut in half
   c. pressure of the gas also doubles
   d. no correct response

Answers: 1. c; 2. c; 3. a

7-6 The Combined Gas Law

LEARNING FOCUS

State the combined gas law in words and as a mathematical equation; know how to use the law in problem solving.

Boyle's and Charles's laws can be mathematically combined to give a more versatile equation than either of the laws by themselves. The **combined gas law** states that *the product of the pressure and volume of a fixed amount of gas is directly proportional to its Kelvin temperature.* The mathematical equation for the combined gas law is

$$\frac{P_1 V_1}{T_1} = \frac{P_2 V_2}{T_2}$$

Using this equation, the change in pressure, temperature, or volume that is brought about by a change in the other two variables can be calculated. ◀

▶ *Any time a gas law contains temperature terms, as is the case for both Charles's law and the combined gas law, these temperatures must be specified on the Kelvin temperature scale.*

EXAMPLE 7-3

Using the Combined Gas Law to Calculate the New Volume of a Gas

A sample of O_2 gas occupies a volume of 1.62 L at 755 mm Hg pressure and a temperature of 0°C. What volume, in liters, will this gas sample occupy at 725 mm Hg pressure and 50°C?

Solution

First, we analyze the data in terms of initial and final conditions.

$$P_1 = 755 \text{ mm Hg} \qquad P_2 = 725 \text{ mm Hg}$$
$$V_1 = 1.62 \text{ L} \qquad V_2 = ? \text{ L}$$
$$T_1 = 0°C + 273 = 273 \text{ K} \qquad T_2 = 50°C + 273 = 323 \text{ K}$$

Five of the six variables in the combined gas law are known, so the sixth variable, V_2 in this case, can be calculated. Rearranging the combined gas law to isolate the variable V_2 on a side by itself gives

$$V_2 = \frac{V_1 P_1 T_2}{P_2 T_1}$$

Substituting numerical values into this "version" of the combined gas law gives

$$V_2 = 1.62 \text{ L} \times \frac{755 \text{ mm Hg}}{725 \text{ mm Hg}} \times \frac{323 \text{ K}}{273 \text{ K}} = 2.00 \text{ L}$$

Section 7-6 Quick Quiz

1. How many of the four gas law variables (P, V, n, T) are held constant when using the combined gas law?
   a. one
   b. two
   c. three
   d. no correct response
2. The variables in the combined gas law are
   a. P, V, and T
   b. P and T
   c. n and V
   d. no correct response
3. If both the pressure and Kelvin temperature of a fixed quantity of gas are doubled, the volume of the gas
   a. is doubled
   b. is halved
   c. does not change
   d. no correct response

Answers: 1. a; 2. a; 3. c

The Ideal Gas Law

LEARNING FOCUS

Be able to write the mathematical equation for the ideal gas law; know how to use the law in problem-solving situations.

The three gas laws so far considered in this chapter are used to describe gaseous systems where change occurs. Two sets of conditions, with one unknown variable, is the common feature of the systems they describe. It is also useful to have a gas law that describes a gaseous system where no changes in condition occur. Such a law exists and is known as the *ideal gas law*. The **ideal gas law** *gives the relationships among the four variables temperature, pressure, volume, and molar amount for a gaseous substance at a given set of conditions.*

Mathematically, the ideal gas law has the form

$$PV = nRT$$

In this equation, pressure, temperature, and volume are defined in the same manner as in the gas laws that have already been discussed. The symbol n stands for the *number of moles* of gas present in the sample. The symbol R represents the *ideal gas constant,* the proportionality constant that makes the equation valid.

The value of the ideal gas constant (R) varies with the units chosen for pressure and volume. With pressure in atmospheres and volume in liters, R has the value

$$R = \frac{PV}{nT} = 0.0821 \frac{\text{atm} \cdot \text{L}}{\text{mole} \cdot \text{K}}$$

The value of R is the same for all gases under normally encountered conditions of temperature, pressure, and volume.

If three of the four variables in the ideal gas law equation are known, then the fourth can be calculated using the equation. Example 7-4 illustrates the use of the ideal gas law.

EXAMPLE 7-4

Using the Ideal Gas Law to Calculate the Volume of a Gas

The colorless, odorless, tasteless gas carbon monoxide, CO, is a by-product of incomplete combustion of any material that contains the element carbon. Calculate the volume, in liters, occupied by 1.52 moles of this gas at 0.992 atm pressure and a temperature of 65°C.

Solution

This problem deals with only one set of conditions, so the ideal gas equation is applicable. Three of the four variables in the ideal gas equation (P, n, and T) are given, and the fourth (V) is to be calculated.

$$P = 0.992 \text{ atm} \qquad n = 1.52 \text{ moles}$$
$$V = ? \text{ L} \qquad T = 65°C = 338 \text{ K}$$

Rearranging the ideal gas equation to isolate V on the left side of the equation gives

$$V = \frac{nRT}{P}$$

Because the pressure is given in atmospheres and the volume unit is liters, the R value 0.0821 is valid. Substituting known numerical values into the equation gives

$$V = \frac{(1.52 \text{ moles}) \times \left(0.0821 \dfrac{\text{atm} \cdot \text{L}}{\text{mole} \cdot \text{K}}\right)(338 \text{ K})}{0.992 \text{ atm}}$$

Note that all the parts of the ideal gas constant unit cancel except for one, the volume part. Doing the arithmetic yields the volume of CO.

$$V = \left(\frac{1.52 \times 0.0821 \times 338}{0.992}\right) \text{L} = 42.5 \text{ L}$$

Section 7-7 Quick Quiz

1. Which of the following is a correct equation for the ideal gas law?
   a. $PT = nRV$
   b. $PV = nRT$
   c. $PV = \dfrac{n}{RT}$
   d. no correct response

2. The variable n in the ideal gas law equation stands for
   a. number of atoms
   b. number of moles
   c. number of grams
   d. no correct response

3. The units for the ideal gas law constant when it has the numerical value 0.0821 are
   a. (atm)(mole)/(L)(K)
   b. (L)(K)/(atm)(mole)
   c. (atm)(L)/(mole)(K)
   d. no correct response

4. Which of the following is the correct mathematical setup for the problem "What volume, in liters, does 1.00 mole of a gas occupy at 27°C and 1.00 atm pressure"?
   a. (1 mole)(R)(27°C)/(1.00 atm)
   b. (1 mole)(R)(300 K)/(1.00 atm)
   c. (1 mole)(1.00 atm)/(R)(300 K)
   d. no correct response

Answers: 1. b; 2. b; 3. c; 4. b

7-8   Dalton's Law of Partial Pressures

LEARNING FOCUS

Given appropriate information, be able to calculate partial pressures for the components of a gaseous mixture using Dalton's law of partial pressures.

In a mixture of gases that do not react with one another, each type of molecule moves around in the container as though the other kinds were not there. This type of behavior is possible because a gas is mostly empty space, and attractions between molecules in the gaseous state are negligible at most temperatures and pressures. Each gas in the mixture occupies the entire volume of the container; that is, it distributes itself uniformly throughout the container. The molecules of each type strike the walls of the container as frequently and with the same energy as though they were the only gas in the mixture. Consequently, the pressure exerted by each gas in a mixture is the same as it would be if the gas were alone in the same container under the same conditions.

The English scientist John Dalton (Figure 7-13) was the first to notice the independent behavior of gases in mixtures. In 1803, he published a summary statement concerning this behavior that is now known as Dalton's law of partial pressures. **Dalton's law of partial pressures** states that *the total pressure exerted by a mixture of gases is the sum of the partial pressures of the individual gases present.* A **partial pressure** *is the pressure that a gas in a mixture of gases would exert if it were present alone under the same conditions.*

Expressed mathematically, Dalton's law states that

$$P_{\text{Total}} = P_1 + P_2 + P_3 + \cdots$$

where P_{Total} is the total pressure of a gaseous mixture and P_1, P_2, P_3, and so on are the partial pressures of the individual gaseous components of the mixture. ◀

As an illustration of Dalton's law, consider the four identical gas containers shown in Figure 7-14. Suppose known amounts of three different gases (represented by A, B, and C) are placed in three of the containers (one gas per container), and the pressure exerted by each gas is measured. Then all three of the gas samples are moved into the fourth container, and the pressure exerted by the resulting mixture of gases is

Figure 7-13 John Dalton (1766–1844) throughout his life had a particular interest in the study of weather. From "weather," he turned his attention to the nature of the atmosphere and then to the study of gases in general.

▶ *A sample of clean air is the most common example of a mixture of gases that do not react with one another.*

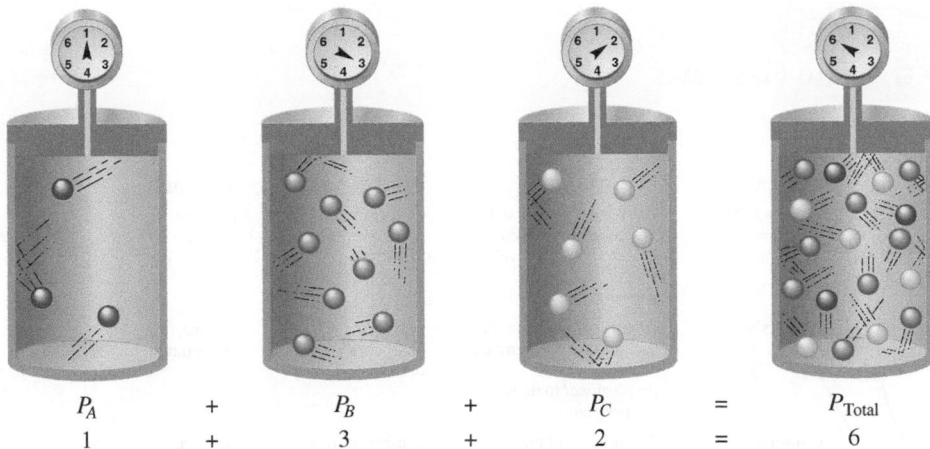

Figure 7-14 A set of four identical containers can be used to illustrate Dalton's law of partial pressures. The pressure in the fourth container (the mixture of gases) is equal to the sum of the pressures in the first three containers (the individual gases).

$$P_A \quad + \quad P_B \quad + \quad P_C \quad = \quad P_{\text{Total}}$$
$$1 \quad + \quad 3 \quad + \quad 2 \quad = \quad 6$$

measured. In accordance with Dalton's law of partial pressures, the mixture pressure will be found to be equal to the sum of the three individual gas pressures; that is,

$$P_{\text{Total}} = P_A + P_B + P_C$$

Using the actual gauge pressure values given in Figure 7-14, it is found that

$$P_{\text{Total}} = 1 + 3 + 2 = 6$$

EXAMPLE 7-5

Using Dalton's Law to Calculate a Partial Pressure

The total pressure exerted by a mixture of the three gases nitrogen, oxygen, and water vapor is 742 mm Hg. The partial pressures of the nitrogen and oxygen in the sample are 581 mm Hg and 143 mm Hg, respectively. What is the partial pressure of the water vapor present in the mixture?

Solution

Dalton's law says that

$$P_{\text{Total}} = P_{N_2} + P_{O_2} + P_{H_2O}$$

The known values for variables in this equation are

$$P_{\text{Total}} = 742 \text{ mm Hg}$$
$$P_{N_2} = 581 \text{ mm Hg}$$
$$P_{O_2} = 143 \text{ mm Hg}$$

Rearranging Dalton's law to isolate P_{H_2O} on the left side of the equation gives

$$P_{H_2O} = P_{\text{Total}} - P_{N_2} - P_{O_2}$$

Substituting the known numerical values into this equation and doing the arithmetic give

$$P_{H_2O} = 742 \text{ mm Hg} - 581 \text{ mm Hg} - 143 \text{ mm Hg} = 18 \text{ mm Hg}$$

Dalton's law of partial pressures is important when considering events that involve the air of the Earth's atmosphere, as air is a mixture of numerous gases. At higher altitudes, the total pressure of air decreases, as do the partial pressures of the individual components of air. An individual going from sea level to a higher altitude usually experiences some tiredness because his or her body is not functioning as efficiently at the higher altitude. At higher elevation, the red blood cells absorb a smaller amount of oxygen because the oxygen partial pressure at the higher altitude is lower. A person's body acclimates itself to the higher altitude after a period of time as additional red blood cells are produced by the body. ◄

Chemistry at a Glance—The Gas Laws—summarizes key concepts about the gas laws we have considered in this chapter.

▶ *In going to higher altitudes, the composition of the Earth's atmosphere does not change even though the total atmospheric pressure does change (decreases). Decreasing atmospheric pressure evokes a corresponding decrease in the partial pressure of each component of the Earth's atmosphere.*

CHEMISTRY AT A GLANCE   The Gas Laws

GAS LAW	SYNOPSIS	CONSTANTS	VARIABLES
Boyle's Law $P_1V_1 = P_2V_2$	At constant temperature, the volume of a fixed amount of gas is *inversely proportional* to the pressure applied to it.	temperature, number of moles of gas	pressure, volume
Charles's Law $\dfrac{V_1}{T_1} = \dfrac{V_2}{T_2}$	At constant pressure, the volume of a fixed amount of gas is *directly proportional* to its Kelvin temperature.	pressure, number of moles of gas	volume, temperature
Combined Gas Law $\dfrac{P_1V_1}{T_1} = \dfrac{P_2V_2}{T_2}$	The product of the pressure and the volume of a fixed amount of gas is *directly proportional* to its Kelvin temperature.	number of moles of gas	pressure, temperature, volume
Ideal Gas Law $PV = nRT$	Relates volume, pressure, temperature, and molar amount of a gas under one set of conditions. If three of the four variables are known, the fourth can be calculated from the equation.	$R = 0.0821 \dfrac{\text{L} \cdot \text{atm}}{\text{mole} \cdot \text{K}}$	pressure, volume, temperature, number of moles
Dalton's Law $P_{\text{Total}} = P_1 + P_2 + P_3$	The total pressure exerted by a sample that consists of a mixture of gases is equal to the sum of the partial pressures of the individual gases.		

Boyle's Law
Doubling the pressure halves the volume.
Constants: temperature, number of moles of gas

Charles's Law
Doubling the Kelvin temperature doubles the volume.
Constants: pressure, number of moles of gas

Dalton's Law	P_1	+	P_2	+	P_3	=	P_{Total}
	1	+	3	+	2	=	6

---

1. The partial pressure of helium gas in a gaseous mixture of helium and hydrogen is
   a. the pressure that the helium would exert in the absence of hydrogen.
   b. equal to the total pressure times the hydrogen's partial pressure.
   c. equal to the total pressure times the helium's partial pressure.
   d. no correct response.

2. In a three-component gaseous mixture the partial pressure of component A is 0.3 atm and the total pressure is 0.9 atm. What is the sum of the partial pressures of components B and C?
   a. 0.9 atm + 0.3 atm
   b. 0.9 atm − 0.3 atm
   c. 0.9 atm − 0.6 atm
   d. no correct response

3. In a three-component gaseous mixture the partial pressure of component A is 0.3 atm, the total pressure is 0.9 atm, and equal numbers of molecules of components B and C are present. What is the partial pressure of component B.
   a. 1.2 atm
   b. 0.6 atm
   c. 0.3 atm
   d. no correct response

Answers: 1. a; 2. b; 3. c

7-9 Changes of State

LEARNING FOCUS

Know the terms used to describe the various changes of state; be able to characterize a particular change of state as exothermic or endothermic.

A **change of state** *is a process in which a substance is transformed from one physical state to another physical state.* Changes of state are usually accomplished by heating or cooling a substance. Pressure change is also a factor in some systems. Changes of state are examples of physical changes—that is, changes in which chemical composition remains constant. No new substances are ever formed as a result of a change of state. ◀

There are six possible changes of state. Figure 7-15 identifies each of these changes and gives the terminology used to describe them. Four of the six terms used in describing state changes are familiar: freezing, melting, evaporation, and condensation. The other two terms—sublimation and deposition—are not so common. *Sublimation* is the direct change from the solid to the gaseous state; *deposition* is the reverse of this, the direct change from the gaseous to the solid state (Figure 7-16).

▶ *Although the processes of sublimation and deposition are not common, they are encountered in everyday life. Dry ice sublimes, as do mothballs placed in a clothing storage area. It is because of sublimation that ice cubes left in a freezer get smaller as time passes. Ice or snow forming in clouds (from water vapor) during the winter season is an example of deposition.*

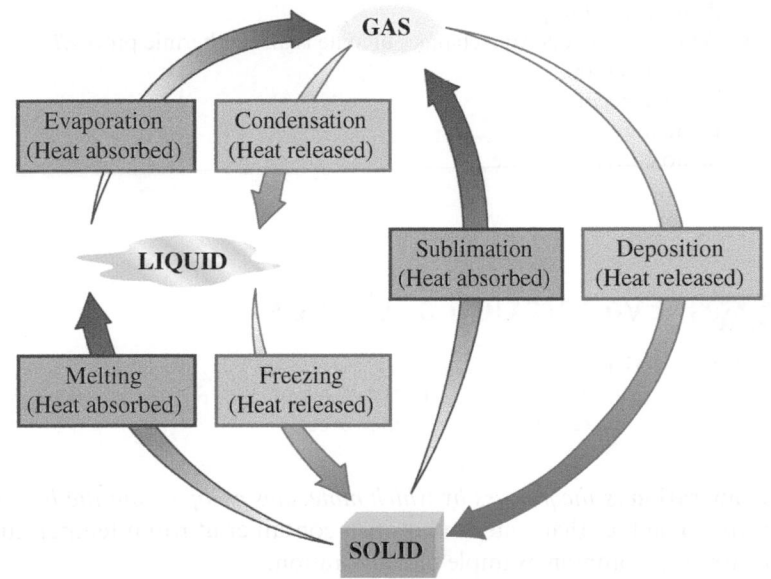

Figure 7-15 There are six changes of state possible for substances. The three endothermic changes, which require the input of heat, are melting, evaporation, and sublimation. The three exothermic changes, which release heat, are freezing, condensation, and deposition.

The beaker contains iodine crystals, I_2; a dish of ice rests on top of the beaker.

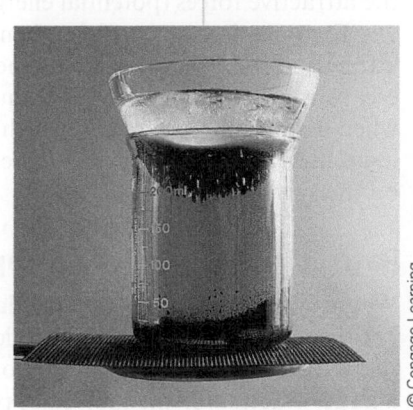

Iodine has an appreciable vapor pressure even below its melting point (114°C), thus, when heated carefully, the solid sublimes without melting. The vapor deposits crystals on the cool underside of the dish, the process of deposition.

Figure 7-16 Sublimation and deposition of iodine.

Changes of state are classified into two categories based on whether heat (thermal energy) is given up or absorbed during the change process. An **endothermic change of state** *is a change of state in which heat energy is absorbed.* The endothermic changes of state are melting, sublimation, and evaporation. An **exothermic change of state** *is a change of state in which heat energy is given off.* Exothermic changes of state are the reverse of endothermic changes of state; they are freezing, condensation, and deposition.

Section 7-9 Quick Quiz

1. The total number of possible changes of state is
   a. 3
   b. 4
   c. 5
   d. no correct answer
2. For which of the following changes of state is the final state that of solid?
   a. sublimation
   b. condensation
   c. melting
   d. no correct response
3. Which of the following changes of state is an exothermic process?
   a. sublimation
   b. condensation
   c. melting
   d. no correct response

Answers: 1. d; 2. d; 3. b

7-10 Evaporation of Liquids

LEARNING FOCUS

Explain, at the molecular level, what happens during the process of evaporation; list the factors that affect the rate at which evaporation occurs.

Evaporation *is the process by which molecules escape from the liquid phase to the gas phase.* The fact that water in an open container at room temperature slowly "disappears" is a common example of evaporation.

Evaporation can be explained using kinetic molecular theory. Statement 4 of this theory (Section 7-1) indicates that not all the molecules in a liquid (or solid or gas) possess the same kinetic energy. At any given instant, some molecules will have above-average kinetic energies and others will have below-average kinetic energies as a result of collisions between molecules. A given molecule's energy constantly changes as a result of collisions with neighboring molecules. When molecules that happen to be considerably above average in kinetic energy at a given moment are on the liquid surface and are moving in a favorable direction relative to the surface, they can overcome the attractive forces (potential energy) holding them in the liquid and escape. ◄

Evaporation is a surface phenomenon. Surface molecules are subject to fewer attractive forces because they are not completely surrounded by other molecules; thus escape is much more probable. Liquid surface area is an important factor to consider when determining the rate at which evaporation occurs. Increased surface area results in an increased evaporation rate because a greater fraction of the total molecules are on the surface.

▶ *For a liquid to evaporate, its molecules must gain enough kinetic energy to overcome the attractive forces among them.*

Rate of Evaporation and Temperature

Water evaporates faster from a glass of hot water than from a glass of cold water, because a certain minimum kinetic energy is required for molecules to escape from the attractions of neighboring molecules. As the temperature of a liquid increases, a larger fraction of the molecules present acquire this minimum kinetic energy. Consequently, the rate of evaporation always increases as liquid temperature increases.

The escape of high-energy molecules from a liquid during evaporation affects the liquid in two ways: The amount of liquid decreases, and the liquid temperature is lowered. The lower temperature reflects the loss of the most energetic molecules. (Analogously, when all the tall people are removed from a classroom of students, the average height of the remaining students decreases.) A lower average kinetic energy corresponds to a lower temperature (statement 4 of the kinetic molecular theory); hence a cooling effect is produced. ◄

The molecules that escape from an evaporating liquid are often collectively referred to as vapor, rather than gas. A **vapor** *is a gas that exists at a temperature and pressure at which it ordinarily would be thought of as a liquid or solid.* For example, at room temperature and atmospheric pressure, the normal state for water is the liquid state. Molecules that escape (evaporate) from liquid water at these conditions are frequently called *water vapor.*

▶ *Evaporative cooling helps maintain human body temperature at a constant level. Humans perspire in hot weather, and evaporation of the perspiration cools their skin. The cooling effect of evaporation is quite noticeable when one first comes out of an outdoor swimming pool on a hot, breezy day.*

Section 7-10 Quick Quiz

1. Which of the following statements about the molecules that enter the vapor state during an evaporation process is *incorrect*?
   a. They occupied positions on the surface of the liquid.
   b. They possessed above average kinetic energy.
   c. They overcame attractive forces with other molecules.
   d. no correct answer
2. The rate at which a liquid evaporates does not depend on which of the following factors?
   a. liquid surface area
   b. amount of liquid present
   c. temperature of liquid
   d. no correct response
3. During the process of evaporation from an insulated container the temperature of remaining liquid
   a. always increases
   b. always decreases
   c. sometimes remains constant
   d. no correct response

Answers: 1. d; 2. b; 3. b

7-11 Vapor Pressure of Liquids

LEARNING FOCUS

Be able to explain the concept of an equilibrium state; know the relationship between vapor pressure and an equilibrium state; know the factors that determine vapor pressure magnitude.

The evaporative behavior of a liquid in a closed container is quite different from its behavior in an open container. Some liquid evaporation occurs in a closed container; this is indicated by a drop in liquid level. However, unlike the liquid level in an open-container system, the liquid level in a closed-container system eventually ceases to drop (becomes constant).

Kinetic molecular theory explains these observations in the following way. The molecules that evaporate in a closed container do not leave the system as they do in an open container. They find themselves confined in a fixed space immediately above the liquid (see Figure 7-17a). These trapped vapor molecules undergo many random collisions with the container walls, other vapor molecules, and the liquid surface. Molecules that collide with the liquid surface are recaptured by the liquid. Thus two processes, evaporation (escape) and condensation (recapture), take place in a closed container (see Figure 7-17b).

For a short time, the rate of evaporation in a closed container exceeds the rate of condensation, and the liquid level drops. However, as more of the liquid evaporates, the number of vapor molecules increases; the chance of their recapture through striking the liquid surface also increases. Eventually, the rate of condensation becomes equal to the rate of evaporation, and the liquid level stops dropping (Figure 7-17c).

Figure 7-17 In the evaporation of a liquid in a closed container (a), the liquid level drops for a time (b) and then becomes constant (ceases to drop) (c). At that point, a state of physical equilibrium has been reached in which the rate of evaporation equals the rate of condensation.

Constant liquid level

▶ *Remember that for a system at physical equilibrium, change at the molecular level is still occurring even though it cannot be visually observed.*

At this point, the number of molecules that escape in a given time is the same as the number recaptured; a steady-state situation has been reached. The amounts of liquid and vapor in the container do not change, even though both evaporation and condensation are still occurring.

This steady-state situation, which will continue as long as the temperature of the system remains constant, is an example of physical equilibrium. **Physical equilibrium** *is a state in which two opposing physical processes take place at the same rate.* For systems in a state of physical equilibrium, no net macroscopic changes can be detected. However, the system is dynamic; the forward and reverse processes are occurring at equal rates. ◀

When there is a liquid–vapor equilibrium in a closed container, the vapor in the fixed space immediately above the liquid exerts a constant pressure on both the liquid surface and the walls of the container. This pressure is called the *vapor pressure* of the liquid. **Vapor pressure** *is the pressure exerted by a vapor above a liquid when the liquid and vapor are in physical equilibrium with each other.*

The magnitude of a vapor pressure depends on the nature and temperature of the liquid. Liquids that have strong attractive forces between molecules have lower vapor pressures than liquids that have weak attractive forces between molecules. Substances that have high *vapor pressures* (weak attractive forces) evaporate readily—that is, they are *volatile.* A **volatile substance** *is a substance that readily evaporates at room temperature because of a high vapor pressure.* Gasoline is a substance whose components are very volatile.

The vapor pressure of all liquids increases with temperature because an increase in temperature results in more molecules having the minimum kinetic energy required for evaporation. Table 7-2 shows the variation in vapor pressure, as temperature increases, of water.

▶ Table 7-2   **Vapor Pressure of Water at Various Temperatures**

Temperature (°C)	Vapor Pressure (mm Hg)	Temperature (°C)	Vapor Pressure (mm Hg)
0	4.6	50	92.5
10	9.2	60	149.4
20	17.5	70	233.7
25*	23.8	80	355.1
30	31.8	90	525.8
37†	37.1	100	760.0
40	55.3		

* Room temperature.
† Body temperature.

In a manner similar to gases, liquids also exert a pressure on the walls of their container. Thus blood exerts a pressure on the walls of the body's blood vessels as it moves through the body. Such pressure, generated by a contracting heart, is necessary to move the blood to all parts of the body. The pressure that blood exerts within blood vessels is an important indicator of health. If the pressure is too low, dizziness from a shortage of oxygen-carrying blood to the brain can result. If it is too high, the risk of kidney damage, stroke, and heart failure increases. The focus on relevancy feature Chemical Connections 7-B—Blood Pressure and the Sodium Ion/Potassium Ion Ratio—contains further information on the subject of blood pressure.

CHEMICAL CONNECTIONS 7-B

Blood Pressure and the Sodium Ion/Potassium Ion Ratio

Blood pressure readings are reported as a ratio of two numbers, such as 120/80. Such numbers represent pressures in terms of the height of a column of mercury (in millimeters) that the pressure can support. The higher of the two numbers in a blood pressure reading (the systolic pressure) represents pressure when the heart contracts, pushing blood into the arteries. The smaller number (the diastolic pressure) represents pressure when the heart is "resting" between contractions. Normal range systolic values are 100−120 mm Hg for young adults and 115−135 mm Hg for older adults. The corresponding normal diastolic ranges are 60−80 mm Hg and 75−85 mm Hg, respectively.

High blood pressure, or hypertension, occurs in an estimated one-third of the U.S. population. While high blood pressure by itself doesn't make a person feel sick, it is the most common risk factor for heart disease. And heart disease is the leading cause of death in the United States. Hypertension forces the heart to work too hard, and it damages blood vessels.

Besides taking medication, factors known to help reduce high blood pressure include increasing physical activity, losing weight, decreasing the consumption of alcohol, and limiting the intake of sodium.

The major dietary source of sodium is sodium chloride (NaCl, table salt), the world's most common food additive. Most people find its taste innately appealing. Salt use tends to enhance other flavors, probably by suppressing the bitter flavors. In general, processed foods contain the most sodium chloride, and unprocessed foods, such as fresh fruits and vegetables, contain the least. Studies on the sodium content of foods show that as much as 75% of it is added during processing and manufacturing, 15% comes from salt added during cooking and at the table, and only 10% is naturally present in the food.

The presence of sodium in body fluids, in the form of Na^+ ion, is a major factor in determining blood volume, which in turn is directly related to blood pressure. The greater the blood volume, the greater the blood pressure. When blood sodium levels increase through dietary intake of sodium, the body's natural response is generation of a "thirst signal" prompting a person to drink water until the sodium-to-water ratio is restored to the normal range.

Recent research indicates that sodium's relationship to hypertension is more complex than originally thought.

More important than total sodium intake is the dietary sodium/potassium (Na^+ ion/K^+ ion) ratio. Potassium causes the kidneys to excrete excess sodium from the body, reducing the need for additional water to lower the sodium/water ratio.

Ideally, the dietary sodium/potassium ratio should be about 0.6, meaning significantly more potassium is needed than sodium. The sodium/potassium ratio in a typical American diet is about 1.1.

Increasing dietary potassium and at the same time decreasing dietary sodium has a positive effect on reducing hypertension. The following two tables list low sodium ion/high potassium ion foods (desirable) and high sodium ion/low potassium ion foods (undesirable).

Low Sodium Ion/High Potassium Ion Foods (Desirable)

Food Category	Examples
Fruit and fruit juices	Pineapple, grapefruit, pears, strawberries, watermelon, raisins, bananas, apricots, oranges
Low-sodium cereals	Oatmeal (unsalted), shredded wheat
Nuts (unsalted)	Hazelnuts, macadamia nuts, almonds, peanuts, cashews, coconut
Vegetables	Summer squash, zucchini, eggplant, cucumber, onions, lettuce, green beans, broccoli
Beans (dry, cooked)	Great Northern beans, lentils, lima beans, red kidney beans

High Sodium Ion/Low Potassium Ion Foods (Undesirable)

Food Category	Examples
Fats	Butter, margarine, salad dressings
Soups	Onion, mushroom, chicken noodle, tomato, split pea
Breakfast cereals	Many varieties; consult the label for specific nutritional information
Breads	Most varieties
Processed meats	Most varieties
Cheese	Most varieties

1. Which of the following statements *correctly* describes a liquid–vapor state of equilibrium?
   a. The amounts of liquid and vapor do not change.
   b. The process of evaporation has ceased.
   c. The process of condensation has ceased.
   d. no correct response
2. For a system at physical equilibrium, change at the molecular level
   a. has ceased
   b. is occurring but cannot be observed
   c. is occurring and can be observed
   d. no correct response
3. Vapor pressure is the pressure exerted by a vapor above a liquid when
   a. equal amounts of vapor and liquid are present
   b. rates of evaporation and condensation are equal
   c. when 90% of the liquid has evaporated
   d. no correct response
4. Which of the following is *not* a factor in determining the magnitude of the vapor pressure of a liquid?
   a. the temperature of the liquid
   b. the size of the liquid container
   c. the strength of intermolecular forces with the liquid
   d. no correct response
5. A volatile substance is a substance that
   a. readily evaporates
   b. readily condenses
   c. cannot exist in the vapor state
   d. no correct response
6. What effect will decreasing the temperature of a liquid by 15°C have on the rate at which the liquid evaporates?
   a. increase the rate
   b. decrease the rate
   c. will not change the rate
   d. no correct response

Answers: 1. a; 2. b; 3. b; 4. b; 5. a; 6. b

7-12 Boiling and Boiling Point

LEARNING FOCUS

Be able to describe the process of boiling from a molecular viewpoint; distinguish between the terms *boiling point* and *normal boiling point*; know the general relationship between boiling point and external pressure.

Figure 7-18 Bubbles of vapor form within a liquid when the temperature of the liquid reaches the liquid's boiling point.

In order for a molecule to escape from the liquid state, it usually must be on the surface of the liquid. **Boiling** *is a form of evaporation where conversion from the liquid state to the vapor state occurs within the body of the liquid through bubble formation.* This phenomenon begins to occur when the vapor pressure of a liquid, which steadily increases as the liquid is heated, reaches a value equal to that of the prevailing external pressure on the liquid; for liquids in open containers, this value is atmospheric pressure. When these two pressures become equal, bubbles of vapor form around any speck of dust or around any irregularity associated with the container surface (Figure 7-18). These vapor bubbles quickly rise to the surface and escape because they are less dense than the liquid itself. The liquid is said to be boiling.

A **boiling point** *is the temperature at which the vapor pressure of a liquid becomes equal to the external (atmospheric) pressure exerted on the liquid.* Because the atmospheric pressure fluctuates from day to day, the boiling point of a liquid does also. Thus, in order for us to compare the boiling points of different liquids, the external pressure must be the same. The boiling point of a liquid that is most often used for comparison and tabulation purposes is called the *normal* boiling point. A **normal boiling point** *is the temperature at which a liquid boils under a pressure of 760 mm Hg.*

Conditions That Affect Boiling Point

At any given location, the changes in the boiling point of a liquid caused by *natural* variations in atmospheric pressure seldom exceed a few degrees; in the case of water, the maximum is about 2°C. However, variations in boiling points *between* locations at different elevations can be quite striking, as shown in Table 7-3.

The boiling point of a liquid can be increased by increasing the external pressure. This principle is used in the operation of a pressure cooker. Foods cook faster in pressure cookers because the elevated pressure causes water to boil above 100°C. An increase in temperature of only 10°C will cause food to cook in approximately half the normal time (Figure 7-19). Table 7-4 gives the boiling temperatures reached by water under several household pressure cooker conditions. Hospitals use this same principle to sterilize instruments and laundry in autoclaves, where sufficiently high temperatures are reached to destroy bacteria.

Liquids that have high normal boiling points or that undergo undesirable chemical reactions at elevated temperatures can be made to boil at low temperatures by reducing the external pressure. This principle is used in the preparation of numerous food products, including frozen fruit juice concentrates. Some of the water in a fruit juice is boiled away at a reduced pressure, thus concentrating the juice without heating it to a high temperature (which spoils the taste of the juice and reduces its nutritional value).

Figure 7-19 The converse of the pressure cooker "phenomenon" is that food cooks more slowly at reduced pressures. The pressure reduction associated with higher altitudes, and the accompanying reduction in boiling points of liquids, mean that food cooked over a campfire in the mountains requires longer cooking times.

> Table 7-3 **Boiling Point of Water at Various Locations That Differ in Elevation**

Location	Feet Above Sea Level	Atmospheric Pressure (mm Hg)	Boiling Point (°C)
Top of Mt. Everest, Tibet	29,028	240	70
Top of Mt. McKinley, Alaska	20,320	340	79
Leadville, Colorado	10,150	430	89
Salt Lake City, Utah	4,390	650	96
Madison, Wisconsin	900	730	99
New York City, New York	10	760	100
Death Valley, California	−282	770	100.4

> Table 7-4 **Boiling Point of Water at Various Pressure Cooker Settings When Atmospheric Pressure is 1 Atmosphere**

Pressure Cooker Setting (additional pressure beyond atmospheric, lb/in.^{2})	Internal Pressure in Cooker (atm)	Boiling Point of Water (°C)
5	1.34	108
10	1.68	116
15	2.02	121

Section 7-12 Quick Quiz

1. The boiling point of a liquid is the temperature at which
   a. liquid–vapor equilibrium is reached
   b. vapor pressure and external pressure become equal
   c. the substance begins to evaporate
   d. no correct response
2. Liquids boil at lower temperatures at higher elevations because the
   a. intermolecular forces are weaker
   b. intermolecular forces are stronger
   c. atmospheric pressure increases
   d. no correct response

(continued)

3. The *normal* boiling point of a liquid is reached when the
    a. temperature of the liquid becomes equal to the external pressure
    b. vapor pressure of the liquid becomes equal to the external pressure
    c. vapor pressure of the liquid becomes equal to 760 mm Hg
    d. no correct response

Answers: 1. b; 2. d; 3. c

7-13 Intermolecular Forces in Liquids

LEARNING FOCUS

Distinguish among the three main types of intermolecular forces; understand how the physical properties of water are affected by hydrogen bonding.

Boiling points vary greatly among substances. The boiling points of some substances are well below 0°C; for example, oxygen has a boiling point of −183°C. Numerous other substances do not boil until the temperature is much higher. An explanation of this variation in boiling points involves a consideration of the nature of the intermolecular forces that must be overcome in order for molecules to escape from the liquid state into the vapor state. An **intermolecular force** *is an attractive force that acts between a molecule and another molecule.*

Intermolecular forces are similar in one way to the previously discussed *intramolecular* forces (forces *within* molecules) that are involved in covalent bonding (Sections 5-3 and 5-4): they are electrostatic in origin; that is, they involve positive–negative interactions. A major difference between inter- and intramolecular forces is their strength. Intermolecular forces are weak compared to intramolecular forces (true chemical bonds). Generally, their strength is less than one-tenth that of a single covalent bond. However, intermolecular forces are strong enough to influence the behavior of liquids, and they often do so in very dramatic ways.

There are three main types of intermolecular forces: dipole–dipole interactions, hydrogen bonds, and London forces.

Dipole–Dipole Interactions

A **dipole–dipole interaction** *is an intermolecular force that occurs between polar molecules.* A polar molecule (Section 5-10) has a negative end and a positive end; that is, it has a *dipole* (two poles resulting from opposite charges being separated from one another). As a consequence, the positive end of one molecule attracts the negative end of another molecule, and vice versa. This attraction constitutes a dipole–dipole interaction. The greater the polarity of the molecules, the greater the strength of the dipole–dipole interactions. And the greater the strength of the dipole–dipole interactions, the higher the boiling point of the liquid. Figure 7-20 shows the many dipole–dipole interactions that are possible for a random arrangement of polar chlorine monofluoride (ClF) molecules.

Hydrogen Bonds

Unusually strong dipole–dipole interactions are observed among hydrogen-containing molecules in which hydrogen is covalently bonded to a highly electronegative element of small atomic size (fluorine, oxygen, and nitrogen). Two factors account for the extra strength of these dipole–dipole interactions. ◀

1. The highly electronegative element to which hydrogen is covalently bonded attracts the bonding electrons to such a degree that the hydrogen atom is left with a significant δ^+ charge.

$$\overset{\delta^+\ \ \delta^-}{\text{H—F}} \qquad \overset{\delta^+\ \ \delta^-}{\text{H—O}} \qquad \overset{\delta^+\ \ \delta^-}{\text{H—N}}$$

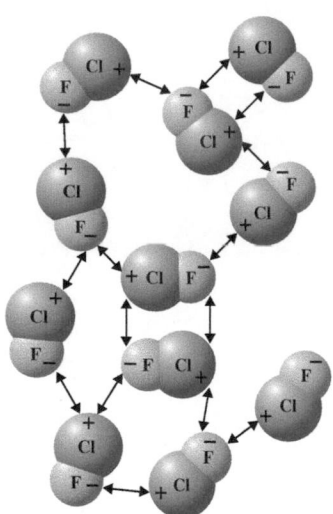

Figure 7-20 There are many dipole–dipole interactions possible between randomly arranged ClF molecules. In each interaction, the positive end of one molecule is attracted to the negative end of a neighboring molecule.

▶ *The use of the word* bond *in the term* hydrogen bond *is misleading in that a hydrogen bond is not a true chemical bond (covalent bond). Rather than involving electron sharing, it is simply an attractive force between positive and negative charge centers. Hydrogen bonds are much weaker than "regular" chemical bonds.*

Indeed, the hydrogen atom is essentially a "bare" nucleus because it has no electrons besides the one attracted to the electronegative element—a unique property of hydrogen.

2. The small size of the "bare" hydrogen nucleus allows it to approach closely, and be strongly attracted to, a lone pair of electrons on the electronegative atom of another molecule.

Dipole–dipole interactions of this type are given a special name, hydrogen bonds. A **hydrogen bond** *is an extra-strong dipole–dipole interaction between a hydrogen atom covalently bonded to a small, very electronegative atom (F, O, or N) and a lone pair of electrons on another small, very electronegative atom (F, O, or N) associated with another nearby molecule.* ◀

Water (H_2O) is the most commonly encountered substance wherein hydrogen bonding is significant. Figure 7-21 depicts the process of hydrogen bonding among water molecules. Note that the oxygen atom in water can participate in two hydrogen bonds—one involving each of its nonbonding electron pairs.

The two molecules that participate in a hydrogen bond need not be identical. Hydrogen bond formation is possible whenever two molecules, the same or different, have the following characteristics:

1. One molecule has a hydrogen atom attached by a covalent bond to an atom of nitrogen, oxygen, or fluorine. ◀
2. The other molecule has a nitrogen, oxygen, or fluorine atom present that possesses one or more nonbonding electron pairs.

Figure 7-22 shows several examples of hydrogen bonding between nonidentical simple molecules.

▶ *The three elements that have significant hydrogen-bonding ability are fluorine, oxygen, and nitrogen. They are all very electronegative elements of small atomic size. Chlorine has the same electronegativity as nitrogen, but its larger atomic size causes it to have little hydrogen-bonding ability.*

▶ *A series of dots is used to represent a hydrogen bond, as in the notation*

$$—X—H \cdots Y—$$

X and Y represent small, highly electronegative elements (fluorine, oxygen, or nitrogen).

Figure 7-21 Depiction of hydrogen bonding among water molecules. The dotted lines are the hydrogen bonds.

Hydrogen fluoride–hydrogen fluoride	**Ammonia–ammonia**
Hydrogen fluoride–water	**Ammonia–water**
Water–hydrogen fluoride	**Water–ammonia**

Figure 7-22 Diagrams of hydrogen bonding involving selected simple molecules. The solid lines represent covalent bonds; the dotted lines represent hydrogen bonds.

EXAMPLE 7-6

Predicting Whether Hydrogen Bonding Will Occur Between Molecules

Indicate whether hydrogen bonding should occur between two molecules of each of the following substances.

a. Ethyl amine

$$
\begin{array}{ccccc}
& H & H & H & \\
& | & | & | & \\
H\!-\!&C&\!-\!C&\!-\!N&\!-\!H \\
& | & | & \ddots & \\
& H & H & &
\end{array}
$$

b. Methyl alcohol

$$
\begin{array}{ccc}
& H & \\
& | & \\
H\!-\!&C&\!-\!\underset{\cdot\cdot}{O}\!-\!H \\
& | & \\
& H &
\end{array}
$$

c. Diethyl ether

$$
\begin{array}{ccccccc}
& H & H & & H & H & \\
& | & | & & | & | & \\
H\!-\!&C&\!-\!C&\!-\!\underset{\cdot\cdot}{O}\!-\!&C&\!-\!C&\!-\!H \\
& | & | & & | & | & \\
& H & H & & H & H &
\end{array}
$$

Solution

a. Hydrogen bonding should occur because we have an N—H bond and a nitrogen atom with a nonbonding electron pair.
b. Hydrogen bonding should occur because we have an O—H bond and an oxygen atom with nonbonding electron pairs.
c. Hydrogen bonding should not occur. We have an oxygen atom with nonbonding electron pairs, but no N—H, O—H, or F—H bond is present. ◄

▶ *Hydrogen bonding plays an important role in many biochemical systems because biomolecules contain many oxygen and nitrogen atoms that can participate in hydrogen bonding. This type of bonding is particularly important in determining the structural characteristics and functionality of proteins (Chapter 20) and nucleic acids (Chapter 22).*

▶ *Liquids in which strong hydrogen bonding effects are present have higher boiling points than those in which weak hydrogen bonding or no hydrogen bonding occurs.*

The vapor pressures (Section 7-11) of liquids that have significant hydrogen bonding are much lower than those of similar liquids wherein little or no hydrogen bonding occurs. This is because the presence of hydrogen bonds makes it more difficult for molecules to escape from the condensed state; additional energy is needed to overcome the hydrogen bonds. For this reason, boiling points are much higher for liquids in which hydrogen bonding occurs. The effect that hydrogen bonding has on boiling point can be seen by comparing water's boiling point with those of other hydrogen compounds of Group VIA elements—H_2S, H_2Se, and H_2Te (Figure 7-23). Water is the only compound in this series where significant hydrogen bonding occurs. ◄

Besides dramatically increasing the boiling point of water, hydrogen bonding also affects water's density. The density of water has an "abnormal" temperature-dependence pattern near its freezing point because of hydrogen bonding effects. This unusual density pattern and its ramifications are discussed in the focus on relevancy feature Chemical Connections 7-C—Hydrogen Bonding and the Density of Water.

Figure 7-23 If there were no hydrogen bonding between water molecules, the boiling point of water would be approximately −80°C; this value is obtained by extrapolation (extension of the line connecting the three heavier compounds). Because of hydrogen bonding, the actual boiling point of water, 100°C, is nearly 200°C higher than predicted. Indeed, in the absence of hydrogen bonding, water would be a gas at room temperature, and life as known on Earth would not be possible.

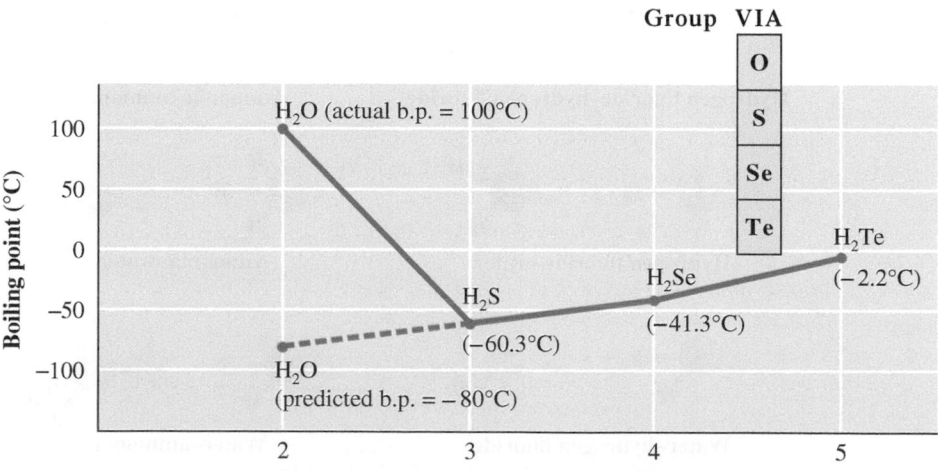

Hydrogen Bonding and the Density of Water

The density pattern that liquid water exhibits as its temperature is lowered is different from that of nearly all other liquids. For most liquids, density increases with decreasing temperature and reaches a maximum for the liquid at its freezing point. Water's maximum density is reached at a temperature of 4°C rather than at its freezing point (see the accompanying graph).

This "abnormality"—that water at its freezing point is less dense than water at slightly higher temperatures—is a consequence of hydrogen bonding between water molecules. Furthermore, at 0°C, solid water (ice) is significantly less dense than liquid water (0.9170 g/mL versus 0.9999 g/mL) because of hydrogen bonding.

Hydrogen bonds can form only between water molecules that are positioned at certain angles to each other. These angles are dictated by the location of the nonbonding pairs of electrons of water's oxygen atom. The net result is that when water molecules are hydrogen bonded, they are farther apart than when they are not hydrogen bonded.

The accompanying diagram shows the hydrogen-bonding pattern that is characteristic of ice.

When natural bodies of water are gradually cooled as winter approaches, the surface water eventually reaches a temperature of 4°C, the temperature of water's highest density. Such water "sinks" to the bottom. Over time, this process results in a stratification (layering) that creates temperature zones. The "heaviest" water, at 4°C, is on the bottom; "lighter" water of lower temperatures comes next, with ice at the surface. The fact that ice is less dense than liquid water explains why lakes freeze from top to bottom, a phenomenon that allows aquatic life to continue to exist for extended periods of time in bodies of water that are frozen over.

Because ice is less dense than water, ice floats in liquid water; also, liquid water expands upon freezing. Such expansion is why antifreeze is used in car radiators in the winter in cold climates. During the winter season, the weathering of rocks and concrete and the formation of potholes in streets are hastened by the expansion of freezing water in cracks.

London Forces

The third type of intermolecular force, and the weakest, is the London force, named after the German physicist Fritz London (1900–1954), who first postulated its existence. A **London force** *is a weak temporary intermolecular force that occurs between an atom or molecule (polar or nonpolar) and another atom or molecule (polar or nonpolar).* The origin of London forces is more difficult to visualize than that of dipole–dipole interactions.

London forces result from momentary (temporary) uneven electron distributions in molecules. Most of the time, the electrons in a molecule can be considered to have a predictable distribution determined by their energies and the electronegativities of the atoms present. However, there is a small statistical chance (probability) that the electrons will deviate from their normal pattern. For example, in the case of a nonpolar diatomic molecule, more electron density may temporarily be located on one side of the molecule than on the other. This condition causes the molecule to become polar for an instant. The negative side of this *instantaneously* polar molecule tends to repel electrons of adjoining molecules and causes these molecules also to become polar (*induced polarity*). The original polar molecule and all of the molecules with induced polarity are then attracted to one another. This happens many, many times per second throughout the liquid, resulting in a net attractive force. Figure 7-24 depicts the situation that prevails when London forces exist.

As an analogy for London forces, consider what happens when a bucket filled with water is moved. The water will "slosh" from side to side. This is similar to the movement of electrons. The "sloshing" from side to side is instantaneous; a given "slosh" quickly disappears. "Uneven" electron distribution is likewise a temporary situation. ◀

The strength of London forces depends on the ease with which an electron distribution in a molecule can be distorted (polarized) by the polarity present in another molecule. In large molecules, the outermost electrons are necessarily located farther from the nucleus than are the outermost electrons in small molecules. The farther electrons are from the nucleus, the weaker the attractive forces that act on them, the more freedom they have, and the more susceptible they are to polarization. This leads to the observation that for *related* molecules, boiling points increase with molecular mass, which usually parallels size. This trend is reflected in the boiling points given in Table 7-5 for two series of related substances: the noble gases and the halogens (Group VIIA).

Chemistry at a Glance—Intermolecular Forces in Liquids—provides a summary of what was discussed about intermolecular forces in liquids.

▶ *The boiling points of substances with similar molar masses increase in this order: nonpolar molecules < polar molecules with no hydrogen bonding < polar molecules with hydrogen bonding.*

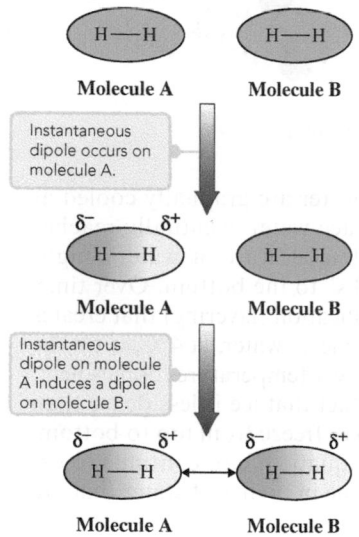

Figure 7-24 Nonpolar molecules such as H₂ can develop instantaneous dipoles and induced dipoles. The attractions between such dipoles, even though they are transitory, create London forces.

▶ Table 7-5 **Boiling Point Trends for Related Series of Nonpolar Molecules: (a) Noble Gases, (b) Halogens**

(a) Noble Gases (Group VIIIA Elements)			(b) Halogens (Group VIIA Elements)		
Substance	Molecular Mass (amu)	Boiling Point (°C)	Substance	Molecular Mass (amu)	Boiling Point (°C)
He	4.0	−269	F₂	38.0	−187
Ne	20.2	−246	Cl₂	70.9	−35
Ar	39.9	−186	Br₂	159.8	+59
Kr	83.8	−153			
Xe	131.3	−107			
Rn	222.0	−62			

4. Hydrogen bonds are extra strong
   a. chemical bonds
   b. dipole–dipole interactions
   c. London forces
   d. no correct response
5. Liquids in which hydrogen bonding is present have
   a. elevated vapor pressures
   b. elevated boiling points
   c. higher than normal formula masses
   d. no correct response
6. How many hydrogen bonds can form between a single water molecule and other water molecules?
   a. two
   b. three
   c. four
   d. no correct response

Answers: 1. d; 2. a; 3. c; 4. b; 5. b; 6. c

CHEMISTRY AT A GLANCE — Intermolecular Forces in Liquids

INTERMOLECULAR FORCES
- Electrostatic forces that act BETWEEN a molecule and other molecules
- Weaker than chemical bonds (intramolecular forces)
- Strength is generally less than one-tenth that of a single covalent bond
- The greater the strength the higher the boiling point

Dipole–Dipole Interactions
- Occur between POLAR molecules
- The positive end of one molecule attracts the negative end of another molecule
- Strength depends on the extent of molecular polarity

London Forces
- Occur between ALL molecules
- Only type of intermolecular force present between NONPOLAR molecules
- Instantaneous dipole–dipole interactions caused by momentary uneven electron distributions in molecules
- Weakest type of intermolecular force, but important because of their sheer numbers

Hydrogen Bonds
- Extra-strong dipole–dipole interactions
- Require the presence of hydrogen covalently bonded to a small, very electronegative atom (F, O, or N)
- Interaction is between the H atom and a lone pair of electrons on another small electronegative atom (F, O, or N)

Concepts to Remember

Kinetic molecular theory. The kinetic molecular theory of matter is a set of five statements that explain the physical behavior of the three states of matter (solids, liquids, and gases). The basic idea of this theory is that the particles (atoms, molecules, or ions) present in a substance are in constant motion and are attracted or repelled by each other (Section 7-1).

The solid state. A solid is characterized by a dominance of potential energy (cohesive forces) over kinetic energy (disruptive forces). As a result, the particles of solids are held in a rigid three-dimensional arrangement in which the particle kinetic energy is manifest as vibrational movement of particles (Section 7-2).

The liquid state. A liquid is characterized by neither potential energy (cohesive forces) nor kinetic energy (disruptive forces) being dominant. As a result, particles of liquids are randomly arranged but are relatively close to each other and are in constant random motion, sliding freely over each other but without enough kinetic energy to become separated (Section 7-2).

The gaseous state. A gas is characterized by a complete dominance of kinetic energy (disruptive forces) over potential energy (cohesive forces). As a result, particles move randomly, essentially independently of each other. Under ordinary pressure, the particles of a gas are separated from each other by relatively large distances, except when they collide (Section 7-2).

Gas laws. Gas laws are generalizations that describe, in mathematical terms, the relationships among the amount, pressure, temperature, and volume of a specific quantity of gas. When these relationships are used, it is necessary to express the temperature on the Kelvin scale. Pressure is usually expressed in atm, mm Hg, or torr units (Section 7-3).

Boyle's law. Boyle's law, the pressure–volume law, states that the volume of a fixed amount of a gas is inversely proportional to the pressure applied to the gas if the temperature is kept constant. This means that when the pressure on the gas increases, the volume decreases proportionally; conversely, when the volume decreases, the pressure increases (Section 7-4).

Charles's law. Charles's law, the volume–temperature law, states that the volume of a fixed amount of gas is directly proportional to its Kelvin temperature if the pressure is kept constant. This means that when the temperature increases, the volume also increases and that when the temperature decreases, the volume also decreases (Section 7-5).

The combined gas law. The combined gas law is an expression obtained by mathematically combining Boyle's and Charles's laws. A change in pressure, temperature, or volume that is brought about by changes in the other two variables can be calculated using this law (Section 7-6).

Ideal gas law. The ideal gas law has the form $PV = nRT$, where R is the ideal gas constant (0.0821 atm · L/mole · K). With this equation, any one of the characteristic gas properties (P, V, T, or n) can be calculated, given the other three (Section 7-7).

Dalton's law of partial pressures. Dalton's law of partial pressures states that the total pressure exerted by a mixture of gases is the sum of the partial pressures of the individual gases. A partial pressure is the pressure that a gas in a mixture would exert if it were present alone under the same conditions (Section 7-8).

Changes of state. Most matter can be changed from one physical state to another by heating, cooling, or changing pressure. The state changes that release heat are called exothermic (condensation, deposition, and freezing), and those that absorb heat are called endothermic (melting, evaporation, and sublimation) (Section 7-9).

Vapor pressure. The pressure exerted by vapor in physical equilibrium with its liquid is the vapor pressure of the liquid. Vapor pressure increases as liquid temperature increases (Section 7-11).

Boiling and boiling point. Boiling is a form of evaporation in which bubbles of vapor form within the liquid and rise to the surface. The boiling point of a liquid is the temperature at which the vapor pressure of the liquid becomes equal to the external (atmospheric) pressure exerted on the liquid. The boiling point of a liquid increases or decreases as the prevailing atmospheric pressure increases or decreases (Section 7-12).

Intermolecular forces. Intermolecular forces are forces that act between a molecule and another molecule. The three principal types of intermolecular forces in liquids are dipole–dipole interactions, hydrogen bonds, and London forces (Section 7-13).

Hydrogen bonds. A hydrogen bond is an extra-strong dipole–dipole interaction between a hydrogen atom covalently bonded to a very electronegative atom (F, O, or N) and a lone pair of electrons on another small, very electronegative atom (F, O, or N) associated with another nearby molecule (Section 7-13).

Exercises and Problems

Exercises and problems are arranged in matched pairs, with the two members of a pair addressing the same concept(s). The answer to the odd-numbered member of a pair is given at the back of the book. Problems denoted with a ▲ involve concepts found not only in the section under consideration but also concepts found in one or more earlier sections of the chapter.

Kinetic Molecular Theory of Matter (Section 7-1)

7-1 Indicate whether each of the following statements about the physical states of matter is true or false.
   a. The term "definite volume" applies to both solids and liquids.
   b. Thermal expansion for a liquid is generally greater than that of the corresponding solid.
   c. The compressibility of a gas is generally less than that of the corresponding liquid.
   d. The density of a solid is about the same as that of the corresponding gas.

7-2 Indicate whether each of the following statements about the physical states of matter is true or false.
   a. The term "indefinite shape" applies to both liquids and gases.
   b. Thermal expansion for a gas is generally less than that of the corresponding liquid.
   c. The compressibility of a liquid is generally greater than that of the corresponding solid.
   d. The density of a liquid is about the same as that of the corresponding gas.

7-3 Using kinetic molecular theory concepts, answer the following questions.
  a. What type of energy is related to cohesive forces?
  b. What effect does temperature have on the magnitude of disruptive forces?
  c. What is the general effect of cohesive forces on a system of particles?
  d. What type of potential energy is particularly important when considering the physical states of matter?

7-4 Using kinetic molecular theory concepts, answer the following questions.
  a. What type of energy is related to disruptive forces?
  b. What effect does temperature have on the magnitude of cohesive forces?
  c. What is the general effect of disruptive forces on a system of particles?
  d. How do molecules transfer energy from one to another?

Kinetic Molecular Theory and Physical States (Section 7-2)

7-5 Indicate the state of matter to which each of the following characterizations applies. There may be more than one correct answer for some characterizations.
  a. Disruptive forces and cohesive forces are of about the same magnitude.
  b. Disruptive forces are significantly less than cohesive forces.
  c. Kinetic energy dominates over potential energy.
  d. Kinetic energy is significantly less than potential energy.

7-6 Indicate the state of matter to which each of the following characterizations applies. There may be more than one correct answer for some characterizations.
  a. Disruptive forces are significantly greater than cohesive forces.
  b. Cohesive forces are significantly less than disruptive forces.
  c. Potential energy dominates over kinetic energy.
  d. Kinetic energy and potential energy are of about the same magnitude.

7-7 Indicate whether each of the following characterizations describes a gas, a liquid, or a solid. More than one answer may be correct for some characterizations.
  a. On a relative scale, density is described as high rather than low.
  b. On a relative scale, thermal expansion is described as very small rather than small.
  c. In general, the interactions between particles are very weak (almost zero).
  d. In general, particles are far apart in a random arrangement.

7-8 Indicate whether each of the following characterizations describes a gas, a liquid, or a solid. More than one answer may be correct for some characterizations.
  a. On a relative scale, compressibility is described as large rather than small.
  b. On a relative scale, thermal expansion is described as moderate rather than small.
  c. In general, particles are held together in a rigid structural arrangement.
  d. In general, particles are very close together in a random arrangement.

Gas Law Variables (Section 7-3)

7-9 Identify the gas law variable with which each of the following measurements is associated.
  a. 7.4 moles   b. 3.70 L
  c. 173 mm Hg   d. 32.3 K

7-10 Identify the gas law variable with which each of the following measurements is associated.
  a. 343 K   b. 6.7 mL
  c. 673 torr   d. 0.23 mole

7-11 Specify each of the following pressure values in atmosphere pressure units.
  a. 555 mm Hg   b. 32.0 psi
  c. 675 torr   d. 75.2 mm Hg

7-12 Specify each of the following pressures values in millimeter of Hg pressure units.
  a. 625 torr   b. 1.25 atm
  c. 4.40 psi   d. 0.622 atm

7-13 Based on logic, how many significant figures are there in each of the following pressure measurements?
  a. 678 torr   b. 680 torr
  c. 699 torr   d. 700 torr

7-14 Based on logic, how many significant figures are there in each of the following pressure measurements?
  a. 598 torr   b. 600 torr
  c. 609 torr   d. 610 torr

7-15 Specify each of the following pressure values in atmosphere pressure units.
  a. 678 torr   b. 680 torr
  c. 690 torr   d. 700 torr

7-16 Specify each of the following pressure values in atmosphere pressure units.
  a. 489 torr   b. 490 torr
  c. 500 torr   d. 510 torr

Boyle's Law (Section 7-4)

7-17 At constant temperature, a sample of 6.0 L of O_2 at 3.0 atm pressure is compressed until the volume decreases to 2.5 L. What is the new pressure, in atmospheres?

7-18 At constant temperature, a sample of 6.0 L of N_2 at 2.0 atm pressure is allowed to expand until the volume reaches 9.5 L. What is the new pressure, in atmospheres?

7-19 A sample of ammonia (NH_3), a colorless gas with a pungent odor, occupies a volume of 3.00 L at a pressure of 655 mm Hg and a temperature of 25°C. What volume, in liters, will this NH_3 sample occupy at the same temperature if the pressure is increased to 725 mm Hg?

7-20 A sample of nitrogen dioxide (NO_2), a toxic gas with a reddish-brown color, occupies a volume of 4.00 L at a pressure of 725 mm Hg and a temperature of 35°C. What volume, in liters, will this NO_2 sample occupy at the same temperature if the pressure is decreased to 125 mm Hg?

7-21 All entries in the following table involve pressure–volume data for a sample of a gas under conditions of constant temperature and constant moles of gas. Each row in the table is a separate set of data. Based on Boyle's law, fill in the blank in each row in the table. The first row in the table is already completed as an example.

	P_1	V_1	P_2	V_2
	4.00 atm	4.00 L	8.00 atm	2.00 L
a.	3.00 atm	2.00 L		3.00 L
b.	1.00 atm		3.00 atm	2.00 L
c.	2.00 atm	2.00 L	4.00 atm	
d.		1.00 L	4.00 atm	2.00 L

7-22 All entries in the following table involve pressure–volume data for a sample of a gas under conditions of constant temperature and constant moles of gas. Each row in the table is a separate set of data. Based on Boyle's law, fill in the blank in each row in the table. The first row in the table is already completed as an example.

	P_1	V_1	P_2	V_2
	8.00 atm	2.00 L	4.00 atm	4.00 L
a.	2.00 atm	4.00 L	4.00 atm	
b.		3.00 L	3.00 atm	2.00 L
c.	4.00 atm		6.00 atm	1.00 L
d.	1.00 atm	5.00 L		2.00 L

7-23 Diagram I depicts a gas, in a cylinder of variable volume, at the conditions specified in the diagram. Which of the diagrams II through IV depicts the result of doubling the pressure at constant temperature and constant number of moles of gas?

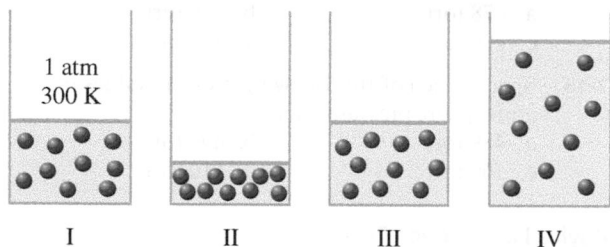

1 atm
300 K

I   II   III   IV

7-24 Using the diagrams given in Problem 7-23, which of the diagrams II through IV correctly depicts the result of halving the pressure at constant temperature and constant number of moles for the gas in diagram I?

Charles's Law (Section 7-5)

7-25 At atmospheric pressure, a sample of H_2 gas has a volume of 2.73 L at 27°C. What volume, in liters, will the H_2 gas occupy if the temperature is increased to 127°C and the pressure is held constant?

7-26 At atmospheric pressure, a sample of O_2 gas has a volume of 55 mL at 27°C. What volume, in milliliters, will the O_2 gas occupy if the temperature is decreased to 0°C and the pressure is held constant?

7-27 A sample of N_2 gas occupies a volume of 375 mL at 25°C and a pressure of 2.0 atm. Determine the temperature, in degrees Celsius, at which the volume of the gas would be 525 mL at the same pressure.

7-28 A sample of Ar gas occupies a volume of 1.2 L at 125°C and a pressure of 1.0 atm. Determine the temperature, in degrees Celsius, at which the volume of the gas would be 1.0 L at the same pressure.

7-29 All entries in the following table involve temperature–volume data for a sample of a gas under conditions of constant pressure and constant moles of gas. Each row in the table is a separate set of data. Based on Charles's law, fill in the blank in each row of the table. The first row in the table is already completed as an example.

	V_1	T_1	V_2	T_2
	1.00 L	27°C	1.33 L	127°C
a.		100°C	1.00 L	110°C
b.	1.25 L	127°C	1.50 L	
c.	2.50 L		4.00 L	367°C
d.	3.33 L	149°C		49°C

7-30 All entries in the following table involve temperature–volume data for a sample of a gas under conditions of constant pressure and constant moles of gas. Each row in the table is a separate set of data. Based on Charles's law, fill in the blank in each row in the table. The first row in the table is already completed as an example.

	V_1	T_1	V_2	T_2
	2.00 L	27°C	4.00 L	327°C
a.	3.30 L	165°C		265°C
b.	7.90 L	270°C	4.45 L	
c.		227°C	4.50 L	535°C
d.	4.21 L		4.35 L	45°C

7-31 Diagram I depicts a gas, in a cylinder of variable volume, at the conditions specified in the diagram. Which of the diagrams II through IV depicts the results of decreasing the Kelvin temperature by a factor of 2 at constant pressure and constant number of moles of gas?

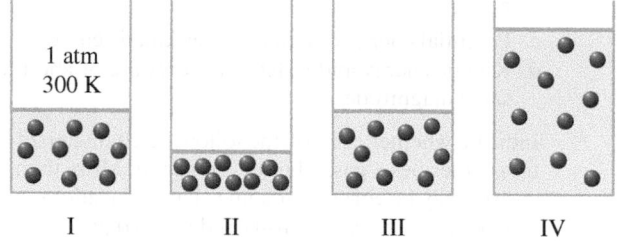

1 atm
300 K

I   II   III   IV

7-32 Using the diagrams given in Problem 7-31, which of the diagrams II through IV correctly depicts the result of increasing the Kelvin temperature by a factor of 2 at constant pressure and constant number of moles for the gas in diagram I?

Combined Gas Law (Section 7-6)

7-33 Rearrange the standard form of the combined gas law equation such that
a. the variable P_1 is by itself on the left side of the equation
b. the variable V_2 is by itself on the left side of the equation

7-34 Rearrange the standard form of the combined gas law equation such that
a. the variable V_1 is by itself on the left side of the equation
b. the variable P_2 is by itself on the left side of the equation

7-35 A sample of carbon dioxide (CO_2) gas has a volume of 15.2 L at a pressure of 1.35 atm and a temperature of 33°C. Determine the following for this gas sample.
 a. Volume, in liters, at $T = 35°C$ and $P = 3.50$ atm
 b. Pressure, in atmospheres, at $T = 42°C$ and $V = 10.0$ L
 c. Temperature, in degrees Celsius, at $P = 7.00$ atm and $V = 0.973$ L
 d. Volume, in milliliters, at $T = 97°C$ and $P = 6.70$ atm

7-36 A sample of carbon monoxide (CO) gas has a volume of 7.31 L at a pressure of 735 mm Hg and a temperature of 45°C. Determine the following for this gas sample.
 a. Pressure, in millimeters of mercury, at $T = 357°C$ and $V = 13.5$ L
 b. Temperature, in degrees Celsius, at $P = 1275$ mm Hg and $V = 0.800$ L
 c. Volume, in liters, at $T = 45°C$ and $P = 325$ mm Hg
 d. Pressure, in atmospheres, at $T = 325°C$ and $V = 2.31$ L

7-37 Diagram I depicts a gas, in a cylinder of variable volume, at conditions given in the diagram. Which of the diagrams II through IV correctly depicts the result of doubling the pressure and doubling the Kelvin temperature of the gas while keeping the number of moles of gas constant?

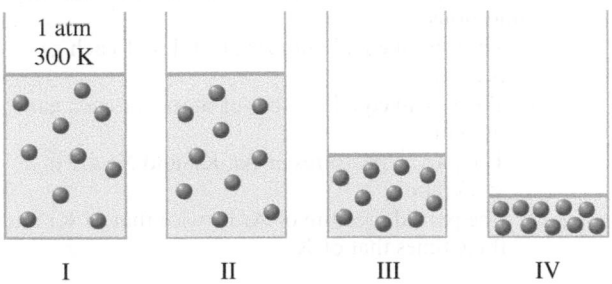

7-38 Using the diagrams given in Problem 7-37, which of the diagrams II through IV correctly depicts the result of doubling the pressure and halving the Kelvin temperature of the gas while keeping the number of moles of the gas in diagram I constant?

7-39 A sample of NO_2 gas in a 575-mL container at a pressure of 1.25 atm and a temperature of 125°C is transferred to a new container with a volume of 825 mL.
 a. What is the new pressure, in atmospheres, if there is no change in temperature?
 b. What is the new pressure, in atmospheres, if the temperature increases by 20°C?

7-40 A sample of CO_2 gas in a 475-mL container at a pressure of 3.25 atm and a temperature of 145°C is transferred to a new container with a volume of 725 mL.
 a. What is the new temperature, in degrees Celsius, if there is no change in pressure?
 b. What is the new temperature, in degrees Celsius, if the pressure increases by 0.75 atm?

▲**7-41** Match each of the listed restrictions on variables to the following gas laws: *Boyle's law, Charles's law,* and *the combined gas law.* More than one answer may be correct in a given situation.
 a. The number of moles is constant.
 b. The temperature is constant.

▲**7-42** Match each of the listed restrictions on variables to the following gas laws: *Boyle's law, Charles's law,* and *the combined gas law.* More than one answer may be correct in a given situation.
 a. The pressure is constant.
 b. The number of moles and the temperature are constant.

▲**7-43** To which of the simpler gas laws does the combined gas law revert when the pressure is held constant?

▲**7-44** To which of the simpler gas laws does the combined gas law revert when the temperature is held constant?

Ideal Gas Law (Section 7-7)

7-45 All entries in the following table involve pressure–volume–temperature–amount data for a sample of a gas. Each row in the table is a separate set of data. Using the ideal gas law, fill in the blank in each row of the table. The first row in the table is already completed as an example.

	P	*V*	*n*	*T*
	24.6 atm	1.00 L	1.00 mole	27°C
a.		2.00 L	2.00 mole	127°C
b.	6.00 atm		4.00 mole	−73°C
c.	3.75 atm	3.75 L		100°C
d.	1.22 atm	2.00 L	0.500 mole	

7-46 All entries in the following table involve pressure–volume–temperature–amount data for a sample of a gas. Each row in the table is a separate set of data. Based on the ideal gas law, fill in the blank in each row in the table. The first row in the table is already completed as an example.

	P	*V*	*n*	*T*
	10.9 atm	3.00 L	1.00 mole	127°C
a.	22.4 atm		3.00 mole	27°C
b.		8.00 L	2.00 mole	73°C
c.	2.50 atm	2.50 L		−173°C
d.	5.00 atm	10.0 L	2.00 mole	

7-47 What is the temperature, in degrees Celsius, of 5.23 moles of helium (He) gas confined to a volume of 5.23 L at a pressure of 5.23 atm?

7-48 What is the temperature, in degrees Celsius, of 1.50 moles of neon (Ne) gas confined to a volume of 2.50 L at a pressure of 1.00 atm?

7-49 Calculate the volume, in liters, of 0.100 mole of O_2 gas at 0°C and 2.00 atm pressure.

7-50 Calculate the pressure, in atmospheres, of 0.100 mole of O_2 gas in a 2.00-L container at a temperature of 75°C.

7-51 Determine the following for a 0.250-mole sample of CO_2 gas.
 a. Volume, in liters, at 27°C and 1.50 atm
 b. Pressure, in atmospheres, at 35°C in a 2.00-L container
 c. Temperature, in degrees Celsius, at 1.20 atm pressure in a 3.00-L container
 d. Volume, in milliliters, at 125°C and 0.500 atm pressure

7-52   Determine the following for a 0.500-mole sample of CO gas.
   a. Pressure, in atmospheres, at 35°C in a 1.00-L container
   b. Temperature, in degrees Celsius, at 5.00 atm pressure in a 5.00-L container
   c. Volume, in liters, at 127°C and 3.00 atm
   d. Pressure, in millimeters of mercury, at 25°C in a 2.00-L container

7-53   What is the pressure, in atmospheres, inside a 4.00-L container that contains the following amounts of O_2 gas at 40°C?
   a. 0.72 mole   b. 4.5 moles
   c. 0.72 g   d. 4.5 g

7-54   What is the pressure, in atmospheres, inside a 2.00-L container that contains the following amounts of N_2 gas at 50°C?
   a. 0.50 mole   b. 2.3 moles
   c. 0.35 g   d. 3.7 g

▲**7-55**   What is the value of the ideal gas constant R if the pressure is specified in torr rather than atmospheres?

▲**7-56**   What is the value of the ideal gas constant R if the volume is specified in milliliters rather than liters?

Dalton's Law of Partial Pressures (Section 7-8)

7-57   The total pressure exerted by a mixture of O_2, N_2, and He gases is 1.50 atm. What is the partial pressure, in atmospheres, of the O_2, given that the partial pressures of the N_2 and He are 0.75 and 0.33 atm, respectively?

7-58   The total pressure exerted by a mixture of He, Ne, and Ar gases is 2.00 atm. What is the partial pressure, in atmospheres, of Ne, given that the partial pressures of the other gases are both 0.25 atm?

7-59   A gas mixture contains O_2, N_2, and Ar at partial pressures of 125, 175, and 225 mm Hg, respectively. If CO_2 gas is added to the mixture until the total pressure reaches 623 mm Hg, what is the partial pressure, in millimeters of mercury, of CO_2?

7-60   A gas mixture contains He, Ne, and H_2S at partial pressures of 125, 175, and 225 mm Hg, respectively. If all of the H_2S is removed from the mixture, what will be the partial pressure, in millimeters of mercury, of Ne?

7-61   The following diagram depicts a gaseous mixture of neon (red spheres), argon (black spheres), and krypton (yellow spheres).

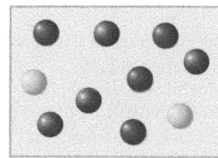

If the total pressure in the container is 6.0 atm, what is the partial pressure, in atm, of the following?
   a. Neon   b. Argon   c. Krypton

7-62   The following diagram depicts a gaseous mixture of O_2 (red spheres), N_2 (blue spheres), and Cl_2 (yellow spheres).

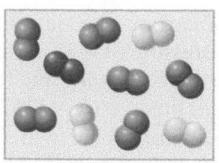

Assuming that the gases do not react with each other, what is the total pressure, in atm, in the container if the partial pressure of the O_2 gas is 2.0 atm?

7-63   A gaseous mixture containing He, Ne, and Ar exerts a pressure of 3.00 atm. What is the partial pressure of each gas present in the mixture under the following conditions?
   a. There is an equal number of moles of each gas present.
   b. There is an equal number of atoms of each gas present.
   c. The partial pressures of He, Ne, and Ar are in a 3:2:1 ratio.
   d. The partial pressure of He is one-half that of Ne and one-third that of Ar.

7-64   A gaseous mixture containing Ar, Kr, and Xe exerts a pressure of 6.00 atm. What is the partial pressure of each gas present in the mixture under the following conditions?
   a. There is an equal number of moles of each gas present.
   b. There is an equal number of atoms of each gas present.
   c. The partial pressures of Ar, Kr, and Xe are in a 2:1:3 ratio.
   d. The partial pressure of Ar is twice that of Kr and three times that of Xe.

Changes of State (Section 7-9)

7-65   Indicate whether or not both members of each of the following pairs of physical state changes have the same thermicity (both exothermic or both endothermic).
   a. evaporation and freezing
   b. melting and deposition
   c. freezing and condensation
   d. sublimation and evaporation

7-66   Indicate whether or not both members of each of the following pairs of physical state changes have the same thermicity (both exothermic or both endothermic).
   a. sublimation and condensation
   b. freezing and deposition
   c. melting and evaporation
   d. deposition and condensation

7-67   Indicate whether or not both members of each of the pairs of physical state changes in Problem 7-65 have the same final state (solid, liquid, gas).

7-68   Indicate whether or not both members of each of the pairs of physical state changes in Problem 7-66 have the same final state (solid, liquid, gas).

7-69   Indicate whether or not the members of each of the pairs of physical state changes in Problem 7-65 are opposite physical processes.

7-70 Indicate whether or not the members of each of the pairs of physical state changes in Problem 7-66 are opposite physical processes.

▲7-71 A 1.00-mole sample of dry ice (solid CO_2) is placed in a flexible, sealed container and allowed to sublime. After complete sublimation, what will be the container volume, in liters, at 23°C and 0.983 atm pressure?

▲7-72 A 1.00-mole sample of naphthalene (mothballs) is placed in a flexible, sealed container and allowed to sublime. After complete sublimation, what will be the container volume, in liters, at 33°C and 1.183 atm pressure?

Evaporation of Liquids (Section 7-10)

7-73 What are the two ways in which the escape of high-energy molecules from the surface of a liquid during the process of evaporation affects the liquid?

7-74 What are the two general requirements that must be met before a molecule can escape from the surface of a liquid during the evaporation process?

7-75 How does an increase in the temperature of a liquid affect the rate of evaporation of the liquid?

7-76 How does an increase in the surface area of a liquid affect the rate of evaporation of the liquid?

7-77 Identical amounts of liquids A and B are placed in identical open containers on a tabletop. Liquid B evaporates at a faster rate than liquid A even though both liquids are at the same temperature. Explain why this could be so.

7-78 Two identical-volume samples of the same liquid are placed in open cylindrical containers of different diameters on a table top. The liquid in one container evaporates faster than the liquid in the other container even though both liquids are at the same temperature. Explain why this could be so.

Vapor Pressure of Liquids (Section 7-11)

7-79 Indicate whether or not each of the following statements about a physical equilibrium state is true or false.
a. For systems in a state of physical equilibrium, two opposite processes take place at equal rates.
b. A liquid–vapor equilibrium situation is an example of a physical equilibrium state.

7-80 Indicate whether or not each of the following statements about a physical equilibrium state is true or false.
a. For systems in a state of physical equilibrium, no net macroscopic changes can be detected.
b. For a liquid–vapor equilibrium situation, the two opposite processes occurring are evaporation and condensation.

7-81 What is the relationship between the temperature of a liquid and the vapor pressure of that liquid?

7-82 What is the relationship between the strength of the attractive forces in a liquid and the liquid's vapor pressure?

7-83 What term is used to describe a substance that readily evaporates at room temperature because of a high vapor pressure?

7-84 What term is used to describe gaseous molecules of a substance at a temperature and pressure at which it is ordinarily thought of as being a liquid or solid?

Boiling and Boiling Point (Section 7-12)

7-85 Indicate whether each of the following statements concerning boiling or boiling point is true or false.
a. The process of boiling is a form of evaporation.
b. The boiling point of a liquid heated in an open container is determined by atmospheric pressure.
c. The normal boiling point of a liquid is the temperature at which it boils when the liquid is at sea level.
d. At a pressure of 760 mm Hg, all liquids boil at the same temperature.

7-86 Indicate whether each of the following statements concerning boiling and boiling point is true or false.
a. A liquid can be made to boil at temperatures higher than its normal boiling point.
b. A liquid can be made to boil at temperatures lower than its normal boiling point.
c. In a boiling liquid, vapor formation occurs within the body of the liquid.
d. To compare the boiling points of two different liquids, the external pressure should be the same.

7-87 What is the relationship between external pressure and the boiling point of a liquid?

7-88 What is the relationship between location (elevation) and the boiling point of a liquid?

7-89 Indicate whether or not a liquid will boil under each of the following "pressure situations."
a. Vapor pressure and atmospheric pressure are equal.
b. Vapor pressure = 635 torr, and atmospheric pressure = 735 torr.

7-90 Indicate whether or not a liquid will boil under each of the following "pressure situations."
a. Vapor pressure is greater than atmospheric pressure.
b. Vapor pressure = 735 torr, and atmospheric pressure = 765 torr.

Intermolecular Forces in Liquids (Section 7-13)

7-91 Indicate whether or not each of the following statements about intermolecular forces is true or false.
a. Hydrogen bonds are extra strong London forces.
b. A London force is a very weak permanent dipole–dipole interaction.
c. The strength of dipole–dipole interactions increases as molecular polarity increases.
d. All molecules with H atoms can participate in hydrogen bonding.

7-92 Indicate whether or not each of the following statements about intermolecular forces is true or false.
a. The two molecules that participate in a hydrogen bond must be identical.
b. London forces are the only intermolecular forces between nonpolar molecules.
c. One of the atoms participating in a hydrogen bond must possess a nonbonding pair of electrons.
d. Both molecules participating in a dipole–dipole interaction must be polar molecules.

7-93 In liquids, what is the relationship between boiling point and the strength of intermolecular forces?

7-94 In liquids, what is the relationship between vapor pressure magnitude and the strength of intermolecular forces?

7-95 For liquid-state samples of the following diatomic molecules, indicate the type or types of intermolecular forces (dipole–dipole interactions, hydrogen bonding, London forces) present. There may be more than one correct answer in a given situation.
a. H_2
b. HF
c. CO
d. F_2

7-96 For liquid-state samples of the following diatomic molecules, indicate the type or types of intermolecular forces (dipole–dipole interactions, hydrogen bonding, London forces) present. There may be more than one correct answer in a given situation.
a. O_2
b. HCl
c. Cl_2
d. BrCl

7-97 For liquid-state samples of each of the molecules in Problem 7-95, identify the dominant type of intermolecular force present in the liquid.

7-98 For liquid-state samples of each of the molecules in Problem 7-96, identify the dominant type of intermolecular force present in the liquid.

7-99 In which of the following substances, in the pure liquid state, would hydrogen bonding occur?

a.
$$H-\overset{\overset{\displaystyle H}{|}}{C}-\overset{..}{\underset{..}{O}}-\overset{\overset{\displaystyle H}{|}}{C}-H$$
(with H below each C)

b.
$$H-\overset{\overset{\displaystyle H}{|}}{C}-\overset{..}{N}-H$$
(with H below C and N)

c.
$$H-\overset{\overset{\displaystyle H}{|}}{C}-\overset{\overset{\displaystyle H}{|}}{C}-\overset{\overset{\displaystyle H}{|}}{C}-\overset{..}{\underset{..}{O}}-H$$

d. $H-\overset{..}{\underset{..}{I}}:$

7-100 In which of the following substances, in the pure liquid state, would hydrogen bonding occur?

a.
$$H-\overset{\overset{\displaystyle H}{|}}{C}-\overset{\overset{\displaystyle H}{|}}{C}-H$$

b.
$$Cl-\overset{..}{\underset{\overset{\displaystyle |}{H}}{N}}-H$$

c.
$$H-\overset{..}{\underset{\overset{\displaystyle |}{H}}{N}}-\overset{..}{\underset{\overset{\displaystyle |}{H}}{N}}-H$$

d.
$$H-\overset{\overset{\displaystyle H}{|}}{C}-\overset{..}{\underset{..}{\overset{\overset{\displaystyle O}{||}}{C}}}-H$$

7-101 How many hydrogen bonds can form between a single water molecule and other water molecules?

7-102 How many hydrogen bonds can form between a single ammonia molecule (NH_3) and other ammonia molecules?

7-103 The following molecule can form two types of hydrogen bonds with a water molecule.

$$H-\overset{..}{\underset{..}{O}}-\overset{..}{\underset{..}{O}}-H$$

Draw representations for the two types of hydrogen bonds that can form.

7-104 The following molecule can form two types of hydrogen bonds with a water molecule.

$$H-\overset{..}{\underset{\overset{\displaystyle |}{H}}{N}}-H$$

Draw representations for the two types of hydrogen bonds than can form.

7-105 In each of the following pairs of substances, indicate which member of the pair would be expected to have the higher boiling point.
a. Cl_2 or Br_2
b. H_2O and H_2S
c. O_2 and CO
d. HCl and HF

7-106 In each of the following pairs of substances, indicate which member of the pair would be expected to have the higher boiling point.
a. He or Ne
b. H_2 and HCl
c. ClF and HF
d. CO and N_2

Chapter 7 Appendix:

Section 13.10 Gas Stoichiometry from Zumdahl/DeCoste Introductory Chemistry:
   A Foundation, 8th Edition

The Chemistry of Air Bags

The inclusion of air bags in modern automobiles has led to a significant reduction in the number of injuries as a result of car crashes. Air bags are stored in the steering wheel and dashboard of all cars, and many autos now have additional air bags that protect the occupant's knees, head, and shoulders. In fact, some auto manufacturers now include air bags in the seat belts. Also, because deployment of an air bag can severely injure a child, all cars now have "smart" air bags that deploy with an inflation force that is proportional to the seat occupant's weight.

The term "air bag" is really a misnomer because air is not involved in the inflation process. Rather, an air bag inflates rapidly (in about 30 ms) due to the explosive production of N_2 gas. Originally, sodium azide, which decomposes to produce N_2,

$$2NaN_3(s) \rightarrow 2Na(s) + 3N_2(g)$$

was used, but it has now been replaced by less toxic materials.

The sensing devices that trigger the air bags must react very rapidly. For example, consider a car hitting a concrete bridge abutment. When this happens, an internal accelerometer sends a message to the control module that a collision possibly is occurring. The microprocessor then analyzes the measured deceleration from several accelerometers and door pressure sensors and decides whether air bag deployment is appropriate. All this happens within 8 to 40 ms of the initial impact.

Because an air bag must provide the appropriate cushioning effect, the bag begins to vent even as it is being filled. In fact, the maximum pressure in the bag is 5 pounds per square inch (psi), even in the middle of a collision event. Air bags represent a case where an explosive chemical reaction saves lives rather than the reverse.

Inflated air bags.

13-10 Gas Stoichiometry

OBJECTIVES
- To understand the molar volume of an ideal gas.
- To learn the definition of STP.
- To use these concepts and the ideal gas equation.

We have seen repeatedly in this chapter just how useful the ideal gas equation is. For example, if we know the pressure, volume, and temperature for a given sample of gas, we can calculate the number of moles present: $n = PV/RT$. This fact makes it possible to do stoichiometric calculations for reactions involving gases. We will illustrate this process in Example 13.15.

Interactive Example 13.15

Gas Stoichiometry: Calculating Volume

Calculate the volume of oxygen gas produced at 1.00 atm and 25 °C by the complete decomposition of 10.5 g of potassium chlorate. The balanced equation for the reaction is

$$2KClO_3(s) \rightarrow 2KCl(s) + 3O_2(g)$$

SOLUTION   **Where Are We Going?**

We want to determine the volume of oxygen gas collected by the decomposition of $KClO_3$.

What Do We Know?

- We know the temperature and pressure of oxygen gas.
- We know the mass of $KClO_3$.
- The balanced equation: $2KClO_3(s) \rightarrow 2KCl(s) + 3O_2(g)$.
- Ideal gas law: $PV = nRT$.

What Information Do We Need?

- $R = 0.08206$ L atm/mol K.
- We need the number of moles of oxygen gas.
- Molar mass of $KClO_3$.

How Do We Get There?

This is a stoichiometry problem very much like the type we considered in Chapter 9. The only difference is that in this case, we want to calculate the volume of a gaseous product rather than the number of grams. To do so, we can use the relationship between moles and volume given by the ideal gas law.

We'll summarize the steps required to do this problem in the following schematic:

Math skill builder

$$\frac{10.5}{122.6} = 0.085644$$

$0.085644 \Rightarrow 0.0856$

Round off

$0.0856 = 8.56 \times 10^{-2}$

Step 1   To find the moles of $KClO_3$ in 10.5 g, we use the molar mass of $KClO_3$ (122.6 g).

$$10.5 \text{ g } KClO_3 \times \frac{1 \text{ mol } KClO_3}{122.6 \text{ g } KClO_3} = 8.56 \times 10^{-2} \text{ mol } KClO_3$$

Step 2   To find the moles of O_2 produced, we use the mole ratio of O_2 to $KClO_3$ derived from the balanced equation.

$$8.56 \times 10^{-2} \text{ mol } KClO_3 \times \frac{3 \text{ mol } O_2}{2 \text{ mol } KClO_3} = 1.28 \times 10^{-1} \text{ mol } O_2$$

Step 3   To find the volume of oxygen produced, we use the ideal gas law $PV = nRT$, where

$$P = 1.00 \text{ atm}$$
$$V = ?$$
$$n = 1.28 \times 10^{-1} \text{ mol, the moles of } O_2 \text{ we calculated}$$
$$R = 0.08206 \text{ L atm/K mol}$$
$$T = 25 \,°C = 25 + 273 = 298 \text{ K}$$

Solving the ideal gas law for V gives

$$V = \frac{nRT}{P} = \frac{(1.28 \times 10^{-1} \text{ mol}) \left(0.08206 \dfrac{\text{L atm}}{\text{K mol}} \right) (298 \text{ K})}{1.00 \text{ atm}} = 3.13 \text{ L}$$

Thus 3.13 L of O_2 will be produced.

SELF CHECK

Exercise 13.11 Calculate the volume of hydrogen produced at 1.50 atm and 19 °C by the reaction of 26.5 g of zinc with excess hydrochloric acid according to the balanced equation

$$Zn(s) + 2HCl(aq) \rightarrow ZnCl_2(aq) + H_2(g)$$

See Problems 13.85 through 13.92. ∎

In dealing with the stoichiometry of reactions involving gases, it is useful to define the volume occupied by 1 mole of a gas under certain specified conditions. For 1 mole of an ideal gas at 0 °C (273 K) and 1 atm, the volume of the gas given by the ideal gas law is

$$V = \frac{nRT}{P} = \frac{(1.00 \ \text{mol})(0.08206 \ \text{L atm/K mol})(273 \ \text{K})}{1.00 \ \text{atm}} = 22.4 \ \text{L}$$

This volume of 22.4 L is called the **molar volume** of an ideal gas.

The conditions 0 °C and 1 atm are called **standard temperature and pressure (STP)**. Properties of gases are often given under these conditions. Remember, the molar volume of an ideal gas is 22.4 L *at STP*. That is, 22.4 L contains 1 mole of an ideal gas at STP.

Critical Thinking

What if STP was defined as normal room temperature (22 °C) and 1 atm? How would this affect the molar volume of an ideal gas? Include an explanation and a number.

Interactive Example 13.16

Gas Stoichiometry: Calculations Involving Gases at STP

A sample of nitrogen gas has a volume of 1.75 L at STP. How many moles of N_2 are present?

SOLUTION

Where Are We Going?

We want to determine the number of moles of nitrogen gas.

What Do We Know?

- The nitrogen gas has a volume of 1.75 L at STP.

What Information Do We Need?

- STP = 1.00 atm, 0 °C.
- At STP, 1 mole of an ideal gas occupies a volume of 22.4 L.

How Do We Get There?

We could solve this problem by using the ideal gas equation, but we can take a shortcut by using the molar volume of an ideal gas at STP. Because 1 mole of an ideal gas at STP has a volume of 22.4 L, a 1.75-L sample of N_2 at STP contains considerably less than 1 mole. We can find how many moles by using the equivalence statement

$$1.000 \ \text{mol} = 22.4 \ \text{L (STP)}$$

which leads to the conversion factor we need:

$$1.75 \ \text{L} \ N_2 \times \frac{1.000 \ \text{mol} \ N_2}{22.4 \ \text{L} \ N_2} = 7.81 \times 10^{-2} \ \text{mol} \ N_2$$

Exercise 13.12 Ammonia is commonly used as a fertilizer to provide a source of nitrogen for plants. A sample of $NH_3(g)$ occupies a volume of 5.00 L at 25 °C and 15.0 atm. What volume will this sample occupy at STP?

See Problems 13.95 through 13.98. ∎

Standard conditions (STP) and molar volume are also useful in carrying out stoichiometric calculations on reactions involving gases, as shown in Example 13.17.

Interactive Example 13.17

Gas Stoichiometry: Reactions Involving Gases at STP

Quicklime, CaO, is produced by heating calcium carbonate, $CaCO_3$. Calculate the volume of CO_2 produced at STP from the decomposition of 152 g of $CaCO_3$ according to the reaction

$$CaCO_3(s) \rightarrow CaO(s) + CO_2(g)$$

SOLUTION

Where Are We Going?

We want to determine the volume of carbon dioxide produced from 152 g of $CaCO_3$.

What Do We Know?

- We know the temperature and pressure of carbon dioxide gas (STP).
- We know the mass of $CaCO_3$.
- The balanced equation: $CaCO_3(s) \rightarrow CaO(s) + CO_2(g)$.

What Information Do We Need?

- STP = 1.00 atm, 0 °C.
- At STP, 1 mole of an ideal gas occupies a volume of 22.4 L.
- We need the number of moles of carbon dioxide gas.
- Molar mass of $CaCO_3$.

How Do We Get There?

The strategy for solving this problem is summarized by the following schematic:

Step 1 Using the molar mass of $CaCO_3$ (100.1 g/mol), we calculate the number of moles of $CaCO_3$.

$$152 \text{ g CaCO}_3 \times \frac{1 \text{ mol CaCO}_3}{100.1 \text{ g CaCO}_3} = 1.52 \text{ mol CaCO}_3$$

Step 2 Each mole of $CaCO_3$ produces 1 mole of CO_2, so 1.52 moles of CO_2 will be formed.

Step 3 We can convert the moles of CO_2 to volume by using the molar volume of an ideal gas, because the conditions are STP.

$$1.52 \text{ mol CO}_2 \times \frac{22.4 \text{ L CO}_2}{1 \text{ mol CO}_2} = 34.1 \text{ L CO}_2$$

Thus the decomposition of 152 g of $CaCO_3$ produces 34.1 L of CO_2 at STP. ∎

Note that the final step in Example 13.17 involves calculating the volume of gas from the number of moles. Because the conditions were specified as STP, we were able to use the molar volume of a gas at STP. If the conditions of a problem are different from STP, we must use the ideal gas law to compute the volume, as we did in Section 13-5.

Solutions

© Sergiy Kuzmin/Shutterstock.com

Ocean water is a solution in which many different substances are dissolved.

S olutions are common in nature, and they represent an abundant form of matter. Solutions carry nutrients to the cells of our bodies and carry away waste products. The ocean is a solution of water, sodium chloride, and many other substances (even gold). A large percentage of all chemical reactions take place in solution, including most of those discussed in later chapters in this text.

8-1 Characteristics of Solutions

LEARNING FOCUS
Know the defining characteristics for a solution; know the meaning of the terms *solute* and *solvent*.

All samples of matter are either *pure substances* or *mixtures* (Section 1-5). Pure substances are of two types: *elements* and *compounds*. Mixtures are of two types: *homogeneous* (uniform properties throughout) and *heterogeneous* (different properties in different regions). ◄

Where do solutions fit in this classification scheme? The term *solution* is an alternative way of saying *homogeneous mixture*. **A solution** *is a homogeneous mixture of two or more substances with each substance retaining its own chemical identity.*

▶ *"All solutions are mixtures" is a valid statement. However, the reverse statement, "All mixtures are solutions," is not valid. Only those mixtures that are* homogeneous *are solutions.*

203

Figure 8-1 The colored crystals are the solute, and the clear liquid is the solvent. Stirring produces the solution.

It is often convenient to call one component of a solution the solvent and other components that are present solutes (see Figure 8-1). A **solvent** *is the component of a solution that is present in the greatest amount.* A solvent can be thought of as the medium in which the other substances present are dissolved. A **solute** *is a component of a solution that is present in a lesser amount relative to that of the solvent.* More than one solute can be present in the same solution. For example, both sugar and salt (two solutes) can be dissolved in a container of water (solvent) to give salty sugar water.

In most situations encountered in this chapter, the focus will be on the solute(s) present in a solution rather than on the solvent. The solutes are the active ingredients in the solution. They are the substances that undergo reaction when solutions are mixed.

The general properties of a solution (homogeneous mixture) were outlined in Section 1-5. These properties, restated using the concepts of solvent and solute, are as follows:

▶ *Generally, solutions are transparent; that is, you can see through them. A synonym for* transparent *is* clear. *Clear solutions may be colorless or colored. A solution of potassium dichromate is a clear yellow-orange solution.*

1. A solution contains two or more components: a solvent (the substance present in the greatest amount) and one or more solutes. ◀
2. A solution has a variable composition; that is, the ratio of solute to solvent may be varied.
3. The properties of a solution change as the ratio of solute to solvent is changed.
4. The dissolved solutes are present as individual particles (molecules, atoms, or ions). Intermingling of components at the particle level is a requirement for homogeneity.
5. The solutes remain uniformly distributed throughout the solution and will not settle out with time. Every part of a solution has exactly the same properties and composition as every other part.
6. The solute(s) generally can be separated from the solvent by physical means such as evaporation.

Solutions used in laboratories and clinical settings are most often liquids, and the solvent is nearly always water. However, gaseous solutions (dry air), solid solutions (metal alloys—Figure 8-2), and liquid solutions in which water is not the solvent (gasoline, for example) are also possible and are relatively common.

Figure 8-2 Jewelry often involves solid solutions in which one metal has been dissolved in another metal.

Section 8-1 Quick Quiz

1. In a solution containing 15 mL of water and 25 mL of isopropyl alcohol
   a. the water is the solvent
   b. the alcohol is the solute
   c. both the water and alcohol are considered to be solvents
   d. no correct response
2. Which of the following in not a general property of solutions.
   a. They are homogeneous mixtures.
   b. They have a variable composition.
   c. Solutes remain uniformly distributed throughout the solution.
   d. no correct response

3. Which of the following statements about solutions is *incorrect*?
  a. Solutions in which both solute and solvent are in the solid state are not possible.
  b. Solutions readily separate into solute and solvent if left undisturbed for 24 hours.
  c. Solutions can contain more than one solute.
  d. no correct response

Answers: 1. d; 2. d; 3. b

8-2 Solubility

LEARNING FOCUS

Know the general factors that affect solute solubility; know the meaning of the terms *saturated, unsaturated, supersaturated, dilute, concentrated, aqueous,* and *nonaqueous* when they are applied to a solution.

In addition to *solvent* and *solute*, several other terms are used to describe characteristics of solutions. **Solubility** *is the maximum amount of solute that will dissolve in a given amount of solvent under a given set of conditions.* Many factors affect the numerical value of a solute's solubility in a given solvent, including the nature of the solvent itself, the temperature, and, in some cases, the pressure and presence of other solutes. Solubility is commonly expressed as grams of solute per 100 grams of solvent.

Effect of Temperature on Solubility

Most solids become more soluble in water with increasing temperature. The data in Table 8-1 illustrate this temperature–solubility pattern. Here, the solubilities of selected ionic solids in water are given at three different temperatures.

In contrast to the solubilities of solids, gas solubilities in water decrease with increasing temperature. For example, both N_2 and O_2, the major components of air, are less soluble in hot water than in cold water. The focus on relevancy feature Chemical Connections 8-A—Factors Affecting Gas Solubility—considers several everyday applications relating to the topic of *temperature change* and gas solubility, as well as the effects of *pressure change* on gas solubility.

Effect of Pressure on Solubility

Pressure has little effect on the solubility of solids and liquids in water. However, it has a major effect on the solubility of gases in water. The pressure–solubility relationship for gases was first formalized by the English chemist William Henry (1775–1836) and is now known as *Henry's law.* **Henry's law** states that *the amount of gas that will dissolve in a liquid at a given temperature is directly proportional to the partial pressure of the gas above the liquid.* In other words, as the pressure of a gas above a liquid increases, the solubility of the gas increases; conversely, as the pressure of the gas decreases, its solubility decreases. ◄ The focus on relevancy feature Chemical

▶ *Respiratory therapy procedures take advantage of the fact that increased pressure increases the solubility of a gas. Patients with lung problems who are unable to get sufficient oxygen from air are given an oxygen-enriched mixture of gases to breathe. The larger oxygen partial pressure in the enriched mixture translates into increased oxygen uptake in the patient's lungs.*

▶ Table 8-1 **Solubilities of Various Compounds in Water at 0°C, 50°C, and 100°C**

Solute	Solubility (g solute/100 g H_2O)		
	0°C	50°C	100°C
lead(II) bromide ($PbBr_2$)	0.455	1.94	4.75
silver sulfate (Ag_2SO_4)	0.573	1.08	1.41
copper(II) sulfate ($CuSO_4$)	14.3	33.3	75.4
sodium chloride (NaCl)	35.7	37.0	39.8
silver nitrate ($AgNO_3$)	122	455	952
cesium chloride (CsCl)	161.4	218.5	270.5

Factors Affecting Gas Solubility

Both temperature and pressure affect the solubility of a gas in water. The effects are opposite. Increased temperature decreases gas solubility, and increased pressure increases gas solubility. The following table quantifies such effects for carbon dioxide (CO_2), a gas often encountered dissolved in water.

Solubility of CO_2 (g/100 mL water)

Temperature Effect (at 1 atm pressure)		Pressure Effect (at 0°C)	
0°C	0.348	1 atm	0.348
20°C	0.176	2 atm	0.696
40°C	0.097	3 atm	1.044
60°C	0.058		

The effect of temperature on gas solubility has important environmental consequences because of the use of water from rivers and lakes for industrial cooling. Water used for cooling and then returned to its source at higher than ambient temperatures contains less oxygen and is less dense than when it was diverted. This lower-density "oxygen-deficient" water tends to "float" on colder water

Carbon dioxide escaping from an opened bottle of a carbonated beverage.

below, which blocks normal oxygen adsorption processes. This makes it more difficult for fish and other aquatic forms to obtain the oxygen they need to sustain life. This overall situation is known as *thermal pollution*.

Thermal pollution is sometimes unrelated to human activities. On hot summer days, the temperature of shallow water sometimes reaches the point where dissolved oxygen levels are insufficient to support some life. Under these conditions, suffocated fish may be found on the surface.

A flat taste is often associated with boiled water. This is due in part to the removal of dissolved gases during the boiling process. The removal of dissolved carbon dioxide particularly affects the taste.

The effect of pressure on gas solubility is observed every time a can or bottle of carbonated beverage is opened. The fizzing that occurs results from the escape of gaseous CO_2. The atmospheric pressure associated with an open container is much lower than the pressure used in the bottling process.

Pressure is a factor in the solubility of gases in the bloodstream. In hospitals, persons who are having difficulty obtaining oxygen are given supplementary oxygen. The result is an oxygen pressure greater than that in air. Hyperbaric medical procedures involve the use of pure oxygen. Oxygen pressure is sufficient to cause it to dissolve directly into the bloodstream, bypassing the body's normal mechanism for oxygen uptake (hemoglobin). Treatment of carbon monoxide poisoning is a situation where hyperbaric procedures are often needed.

Deep-sea divers can experience solubility-pressure problems. For every 30 feet that divers descend, the pressure increases by 1 atm. As a result, the air they breathe (particularly the N_2 component) dissolves to a greater extent in the blood. If a diver returns to the surface too quickly after a deep dive, the dissolved gases form bubbles in the blood (in the same way CO_2 does in a freshly opened can of carbonated beverage). This bubble formation may interfere with nerve impulse transmission and restrict blood flow. This painful condition, known as the *bends*, can cause paralysis or death.

Divers can avoid the bends by returning to the surface slowly and by using a helium–oxygen gas mixture instead of air in their breathing apparatus. Helium is less soluble in blood than N_2 and, because of its small atomic size, can escape from body tissues. Nitrogen must be removed via normal respiration.

Connections 8-A—Factors Affecting Gas Solubility—considers several applications of the dependency of gas solubility on pressure.

Saturated, Supersaturated, and Unsaturated Solutions

▶ *When the amount of dissolved solute in a solution corresponds to the solute's solubility in the solvent, the solution formed is a saturated solution.*

A **saturated solution** *is a solution that contains the maximum amount of solute that can be dissolved under the conditions at which the solution exists.* A saturated solution containing excess undissolved solute is an equilibrium situation where an amount of undissolved solute is continuously dissolving while an equal amount of dissolved solute is continuously crystallizing. ◀

Consider the process of adding table sugar (sucrose) to a container of water. Initially, the added sugar dissolves as the solution is stirred. Finally, as more sugar is added, a point is reached where no amount of stirring will cause the added sugar to dissolve. The last-added sugar remains as a solid on the bottom of the container; the solution is saturated. Although it appears to the eye that nothing is happening once the saturation point is reached, this is not the case on the molecular level. Solid sugar from the bottom of the container is continuously dissolving in the water, and an equal amount of sugar is coming out of solution. Accordingly, the net number of sugar molecules in the liquid remains the same. The equilibrium situation in the saturated solution is somewhat similar to the evaporation of a liquid in a closed container (Section 7-10). Figure 8-3 illustrates the dynamic equilibrium process occurring in a saturated solution that contains undissolved excess solute.

Sometimes it is possible to exceed the maximum solubility of a compound, producing a *supersaturated* solution. A **supersaturated solution** *is an unstable solution that temporarily contains more dissolved solute than that present in a saturated solution.* An indirect rather than a direct procedure is needed to prepare a supersaturated solution; it involves the slow cooling, without agitation of any kind, of a high-temperature saturated solution in which no excess solid solute is present. Even though solute solubility decreases as the temperature is reduced, the excess solute often remains in solution. A supersaturated solution is an unstable situation; with time, excess solute will crystallize out, and the solution will revert to a saturated solution. A supersaturated solution will produce crystals rapidly, often in a dramatic manner, if it is slightly disturbed or if it is "seeded" with a tiny crystal of solute.

An **unsaturated solution** *is a solution that contains less than the maximum amount of solute that can be dissolved under the conditions at which the solution exists.* Most commonly encountered solutions fall into this category.

The terms *concentrated* and *dilute* are also used to convey qualitative information about the degree of saturation of a solution. A **concentrated solution** *is a solution that contains a large amount of solute relative to the amount that could dissolve.* A concentrated solution does not have to be a saturated solution (see Figure 8-4). A **dilute solution** *is a solution that contains a small amount of solute relative to the amount that could dissolve.*

Aqueous and Nonaqueous Solutions

Another set of solution terms involves the modifiers *aqueous* and *nonaqueous*. An **aqueous solution** *is a solution in which water is the solvent.* The presence of water is not a prerequisite for a solution, however. A **nonaqueous solution** *is a solution in which a substance other than water is the solvent.* Alcohol-based solutions are often encountered in a medical setting. ◀

Figure 8-3 In a saturated solution, the dissolved solute is in dynamic equilibrium with the undissolved solute. Solute enters and leaves the solution at the same rate.

Figure 8-4 Both solutions contain the same amount of solute. A concentrated solution (left) contains a relatively large amount of solute compared with the amount that could dissolve. A dilute solution (right) contains a relatively small amount of solute compared with the amount that could dissolve.

▶ *When the term solution is used, it is generally assumed that "aqueous solution" is meant, unless the context makes it clear that the solvent is not water.*

© Cengage Learning

Section 8-2 Quick Quiz

1. Which of the following statements concerning a *saturated* solution is *incorrect*?
   a. undissolved solute must be present
   b. undissolved solute may or may not be present
   c. undissolved solute, if present, is in equilibrium with dissolved solvent
   d. no correct response
2. In general, the solubilities of gaseous solutes in water
   a. increase with increasing temperature
   b. increase with increasing pressure
   c. are independent of temperature and pressure changes
   d. no correct response
3. If addition of a small crystal of NaCl to an NaCl solution causes additional crystals to form then the original solution was
   a. unsaturated
   b. supersaturated
   c. saturated
   d. no correct response

Answers: 1. a; 2. b; 3. b

8-3 ## 8-3 Solution Formation

LEARNING FOCUS

Describe the solution process, at a particle level, as an ionic solute dissolves in water; be familiar with the factors that affect the rate of solution formation.

In a solution, solute particles are uniformly dispersed throughout the solvent. Considering what is happening, at a molecular level, in a solution gives insights into how this uniformity is achieved.

In order for a solute to dissolve in a solvent, two types of interparticle attractions must be overcome: (1) attractions between solute particles (solute–solute attractions) and (2) attractions between solvent particles (solvent–solvent attractions). Only when these attractions are overcome can particles in both pure solute and pure solvent separate from one another and begin to intermingle. A new type of interaction, which does not exist prior to solution formation, arises as a result of the mixing of solute and solvent. This new interaction is the attraction between solute and solvent particles (solute–solvent attractions). These attractions are the primary driving force for solution formation.

An important type of solution process is one in which an ionic solid dissolves in water. Figure 8-5 diagrammatically details what is happening at the molecular level when sodium chloride, a typical ionic solid, dissolves in water. The polar water molecules become oriented in such a way that the negative oxygen portion points toward positive sodium ions and the positive hydrogen portions point toward negative chloride ions. As the polar water molecules begin to surround ions on the crystal surface, they exert sufficient attraction to cause these ions to break away from the crystal surface. After leaving the crystal, an ion retains its surrounding group of water molecules; it has become a *hydrated ion*. As each hydrated ion leaves the surface, other ions are exposed to the water, and the crystal is picked apart ion by ion. Once in solution, the hydrated ions are uniformly distributed either by stirring or by random collisions with other water molecules or hydrated ions. ◄

▶ *The fact that water molecules are polar is very important in the dissolving of an ionic solid in water.*

The random motion of solute ions in solutions causes them to collide with one another, with solvent molecules, and occasionally with the surface of any undissolved solute. Ions undergoing the latter type of collision occasionally stick to the solid surface and thus leave the solution. When the number of ions in solution is low, the chances for collision with the undissolved solute are low. However, as the number of ions in solution increases, so do the chances for collisions, and more ions are recaptured by the undissolved solute. Eventually, the number of ions in solution reaches a level where ions return to the undissolved solute at the same rate at which other ions leave. At this point, the solution is saturated, and the equilibrium process discussed in the previous section is in operation.

Figure 8-5 When an ionic solid, such as sodium chloride, dissolves in water, the water molecules *hydrate* the ions. The positive ions are bound to the water molecules by their attraction for the fractional negative charge on the water's oxygen atom, and the negative ions are bound to the water molecules by their attraction for the fractional positive charge on the water's hydrogen atoms.

Water molecule

Positive ion

Negative ion

Ionic compound

Hydrated ions

Key:
= H
= O

Factors Affecting the Rate of Solution Formation

The rate at which a solution forms is governed by how rapidly the solute particles are distributed throughout the solvent. Three factors that affect the rate of solution formation are the following:

1. *The state of subdivision of the solute.* A crushed aspirin tablet will dissolve in water more rapidly than a whole aspirin tablet. The more compact whole aspirin tablet has less surface area, and thus fewer solvent molecules can interact with it at a given time.
2. *The degree of agitation during solution preparation.* Stirring solution components disperses the solute particles more rapidly, increasing the possibilities for solute–solvent interactions. Hence the rate of solution formation is increased.
3. *The temperature of the solution components.* Solution formation occurs more rapidly as the temperature is increased. At a higher temperature, both solute and solvent molecules move more rapidly (Section 7-1), so more interactions between them occur within a given time period.

Section 8-3 Quick Quiz

1. When an ionic solute dissolves in water, the water molecules *hydrate*
   a. positive ions but not negative ions
   b. negative ions but not positive ions
   c. both positive ions and negative ions
   d. no correct response
2. Which of the following does <u>not</u> affect the *rate* at which a solute dissolves in a solvent?
   a. state of subdivision of the solute
   b. temperature of the solvent
   c. stirring during the dissolving process
   d. no correct response
3. Solution formation occurs more rapidly at higher temperatures because molecules of
   a. solute, but not solvent, move more rapidly
   b. solvent, but not solute, move more rapidly
   c. both solute and solvent move more rapidly
   d. no correct response

Answers: 1. c; 2. d; 3. c

8-4 Solubility Rules

LEARNING FOCUS

Know the basis for the solubility rule "like dissolves like"; be able to apply solubility guidelines for common ionic solutes in water.

Several generalized rules exist for qualitatively predicting solute solubilities. These rules are based on polarity considerations—specifically, on the magnitude of the difference between the polarity of the solute and solvent. In general, it is found that the greater the difference in solute–solvent polarity, the less soluble is the solute. This means that *substances of like polarity tend to be more soluble in each other than substances that differ in polarity.* This conclusion is often expressed as the simple phrase *"like dissolves like."* Polar substances, in general, are good solvents for other polar substances but not for nonpolar substances (Figure 8-6). Similarly, nonpolar substances exhibit greater solubility in nonpolar solvents than in polar solvents.

The generalization "like dissolves like" is a useful tool for predicting solubility behavior in many, but not all, solute–solvent situations. Results that agree with this generalization are nearly always obtained in the cases of gas-in-liquid and liquid-in-liquid solutions and for solid-in-liquid solutions in which the solute is not an ionic compound. For example, NH_3 gas (a polar gas) is much more soluble in H_2O (a polar liquid) than is O_2 gas (a nonpolar gas).

Figure 8-6 Oil spills can be contained to some extent by using trawlers and a boom apparatus because oil and water, having different polarities, are relatively insoluble in each other. The oil, which is of lower density, floats on top of the water.

▶ *All ionic compounds, even the most insoluble ones, dissolve to a slight extent in water. Thus the "insoluble" designation for an ionic compound really means ionic compounds that have very limited solubility in water. Generally, the term* insoluble *is used when the solubility is less than 1 gram per liter of solution.*

In the common case of solid-in-liquid solutions in which the solute is an ionic compound, the rule "like dissolves like" is not adequate. Their polar nature would suggest that all ionic compounds are soluble in a polar solvent such as water, but this is not the case. The failure of the generalization for ionic compounds is related to the complexity of the factors involved in determining the magnitude of the solute–solute (ion–ion) and solvent–solute (solvent–ion) interactions. Among other things, both the charge and the size of the ions in the solute must be considered. Changes in these factors affect both types of interactions, but not to the same extent.

Some guidelines concerning the solubility of ionic compounds in water, which should be used in place of "like dissolves like," are given in Table 8-2.

Water's solvent properties differ from those of other commonly encountered liquid solvents in a very important way. The molecular polarity of water (Section 5-11) is sufficient to overcome the ion–ion attractions within many ionic compounds; hence many such compounds (Table 8-2) are soluble in water. Polar molecular compounds also dissolve readily in water. This ability to dissolve numerous ionic compounds as well as polar molecular compounds makes water an ideal solvent for human body solutions such as blood. Blood, as an aqueous solution, must carry ions (Na^+ ions, K^+ ions, HCO_3^- ions, etc.) and molecular substances (glucose, amino acids, etc.). Because nonpolar molecular substances, such as fats and cholesterol, have limited solubility in water, their presence in the blood requires the presence of "protein carriers" to which they are attached; such protein carrier molecules, called lipoproteins, are considered in Section 20-19. ◀

▶ Table 8-2 **Solubility Guidelines for Ionic Compounds in Water**

Soluble Compounds	Important Exceptions
Compounds containing the following ions are soluble with exceptions as noted.	
Group IA (Li^+, Na^+, K^+, etc.)	none
ammonium (NH_4^+)	none
acetate ($C_2H_3O_2^-$)	none
nitrate (NO_3^-)	none
chloride (Cl^-), bromide (Br^-), and iodide (I^-)	Ag^+, Pb^{2+}, Hg_2^{2+}
sulfate (SO_4^{2-})	Ca^{2+}, Sr^{2+}, Ba^{2+}, Ag^+, Pb^{2+}

Insoluble Compounds	Important Exceptions
Compounds containing the following ions are insoluble with exceptions as noted.	
carbonate (CO_3^{2-})	NH_4^+, group IA ions
phosphate (PO_4^{3-})	NH_4^+, group IA ions
sulfide (S^{2-})	NH_4^+, group IA ions, Ca^{2+}, Sr^{2+}, Ba^{2+}
hydroxide (OH^-)	group IA ions, Ca^{2+}, Sr^{2+}, Ba^{2+}

EXAMPLE 8-1

Predicting Solute Solubility Using Solubility Rules

Predict the solubility of each of the following solutes in the solvent indicated. Information from Table 8-2 is needed in some cases.

a. Methane (a nonpolar gas) in water
b. Ethyl alcohol (a polar liquid) in chloroform (a polar liquid)
c. AgCl (an ionic solid) in water
d. Na_2SO_4 (an ionic solid) in water
e. $AgNO_3$ (an ionic solid) in water

David Woodfall/The Image Bank/Getty Images

Solution

a. Insoluble. They are of unlike polarity because water is polar.

b. Soluble. Both substances are polar, so they should be relatively soluble in one another—like dissolves like.

c. Insoluble. Table 8-2 indicates that all chlorides except those of silver, lead, and mercury(I) are soluble. AgCl is one of the exceptions.

d. Soluble. Table 8-2 indicates that all ionic sodium-containing compounds are soluble.

e. Soluble. Table 8-2 indicates that all compounds containing the nitrate ion (NO_3^-) are soluble.

The focus on relevancy feature Chemical Connections 8-B—Solubility of Vitamins—considers further the topic of polarity and solubility as it relates to the important biochemical substances called *vitamins*.

CHEMICAL CONNECTIONS 8-B

Solubility of Vitamins

Polarity plays an important role in the solubility of many substances in the fluids and tissues of the human body. Consider vitamin solubilities. The 13 known vitamins fall naturally into two classes: fat soluble and water soluble. The fat-soluble vitamins are A, D, E, and K. Water-soluble vitamins are vitamin C and the eight B vitamins (thiamin, riboflavin, niacin, vitamin B_6, folate, vitamin B_{12}, pantothenic acid, and biotin). Water-soluble vitamins have polar molecular structures, as does water. By contrast, fat-soluble vitamins have nonpolar molecular structures that are compatible with the nonpolar nature of fats.

Vitamin C is water soluble. Because of this, vitamin C is not stored in the body and must be ingested in our daily diet. Unused vitamin C is eliminated rapidly from the body via bodily fluids. Vitamin A, however, is fat soluble. It can be, and is, stored by the body in fat tissue for later use. If vitamin A is consumed in excess quantities (from excessive vitamin supplements), illness can result. Because of its limited water solubility, vitamin A cannot be rapidly eliminated from the body by bodily fluids.

The water-soluble vitamins can be easily leached out of foods as they are prepared. As a rule of thumb, foods should be eaten every day that are rich in water-soluble vitamins. Taking megadose vitamin supplements of water-soluble vitamins is seldom effective. The extra amounts of these vitamins are usually picked up by the extracellular fluids, carried away by blood, and excreted in the urine. As one person aptly noted, "If you take supplements of water-soluble vitamins, you may have the most expensive urine in town."

Many vegetables, including asparagus, are good B vitamin sources, although cooking them in water can leach out much of their B vitamin content.

© Tatiana Belova/Shutterstock.com

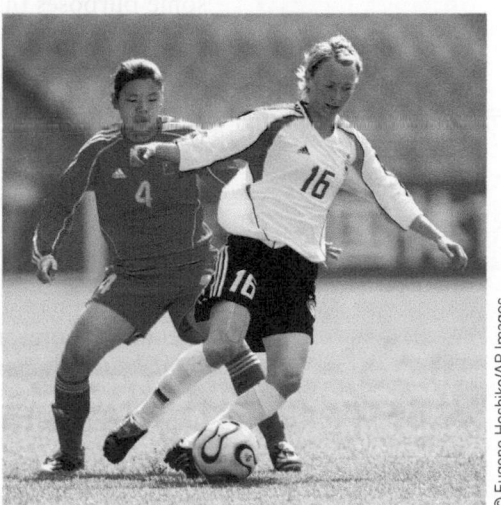

© Eugene Hoshiko/AP Images

Vitamin E, which is soluble in fatty tissue because of its nonpolar structure, helps to protect the lungs against air pollutants, especially when a person is breathing rapidly during strenuous exercise.

Section 8-4 Quick Quiz

1. The word "like" in the solubility rule "like dissolves like" refers to
   a. like polarity
   b. like physical state
   c. like boiling point
   d. no correct response
2. The rule "like dissolves like" is not adequate when predicting solubility in water when the solute is a(n)
   a. nonpolar gas
   b. polar liquid
   c. ionic solid
   d. no correct response
3. For which of the following types of ionic compounds are most examples insoluble in water?
   a. nitrates
   b. phosphates
   c. acetates
   d. no correct response
4. Chlorides, bromides, and iodides are soluble in water except for those of
   a. silver, lead, and mercury
   b. lithium, sodium, and potassium
   c. ammonium, magnesium, and calcium
   d. no correct response

Answers: 1. a; 2. c; 3. b; 4. a

8-5 Percent Concentration Units

LEARNING FOCUS

Be able to calculate solution concentration in the units *percent by mass, percent by volume,* and *mass–volume percent;* be able to use these concentrations units as conversion factors in problem solving.

Because solutions are mixtures (Section 8-1), they have a variable composition. Specifying what the composition of a solution is involves specifying solute concentrations. A **concentration** *is the amount of solute present in a specified amount of solution.* Many methods of expressing concentration exist, and certain methods are better suited for some purposes than others. In this section the percent concentration unit is considered and in the following section the molarity concentration unit is discussed.

Percent Concentration

Percent concentration may be indicated in three different ways.

1. Percent by mass (or mass–mass percent)
2. Percent by volume (or volume–volume percent)
3. Mass–volume percent

Percent by mass (or mass–mass percent) is the percentage unit most often used in chemical laboratories. **Percent by mass** *is the mass of solute in a solution divided by the total mass of solution, multiplied by 100 (to put the value in terms of percentage).*

$$\text{Percent by mass} = \frac{\text{mass of solute}}{\text{mass of solution}} \times 100$$

The solute and solution masses must be measured in the same unit, which is usually grams. The mass of the solution is equal to the mass of the solute plus the mass of the solvent. ◀

$$\text{Mass of solution} = \text{mass of solute} + \text{mass of solvent}$$

A solution whose mass percent concentration is 5.0% would contain 5.0 g of solute per 100.0 g of solution (5.0 g of solute and 95.0 g of solvent). Thus percent by mass directly gives the number of grams of solute in 100 g of solution. The percent-by-mass concentration unit is often abbreviated as %(m/m).

▶ *The concentration of butterfat in milk is expressed in terms of percent by mass. When you buy 1% milk, you are buying milk that contains 1 g of butterfat per 100 g of milk.*

EXAMPLE 8-2

Calculating the Percent-by-Mass Concentration of a Solution

What is the percent-by-mass, %(m/m), concentration of sucrose (table sugar) in a solution made by dissolving 7.6 g of sucrose in 83.4 g of water?

Solution

Both the mass of solute and the mass of solvent are known. Substituting these values into the percent-by-mass equation

$$\%(m/m) = \frac{\text{mass of solute}}{\text{mass of solution}} \times 100$$

gives

$$\%(m/m) = \frac{7.6 \text{ g sucrose}}{7.6 \text{ g sucrose} + 83.4 \text{ g water}} \times 100$$

Remember that the denominator of the preceding equation (mass of solution) is the combined mass of the solute and the solvent.

Doing the mathematics gives

$$\%(m/m) = \frac{7.6 \text{ g}}{91.0 \text{ g}} \times 100 = 8.4\%$$

The second type of percentage unit, percent by volume (or volume–volume percent), which is abbreviated %(v/v), is used as a concentration unit in situations where the solute and solvent are both liquids or both gases. In these cases, it is more convenient to measure volumes than masses. **Percent by volume** *is the volume of solute in a solution divided by the total volume of solution, multiplied by 100.*

$$\text{Percent by volume} = \frac{\text{volume of solute}}{\text{volume of solution}} \times 100$$

Solute and solution volumes must always be expressed in the same units when percent by volume units are used.

When the numerical value of a concentration is expressed as a percent by volume, it directly gives the number of milliliters of solute in 100 mL of solution. Thus a 100-mL sample of a 5.0%(v/v) alcohol-in-water solution contains 5.0 mL of alcohol dissolved in enough water to give 100 mL of solution. Note that such a 5.0%(v/v) solution could not be made by adding 5 mL of alcohol to 95 mL of water, because the volumes of different liquids are not usually additive. ◄ Differences in the way molecules are packed, as well as differences in distances between molecules, almost always result in the volume of the solution being less than the sum of the volumes of solute and solvent (Figure 8-7). For example, the final volume resulting from the addition of

▶ *The proof system for specifying the alcoholic content of beverages is twice the percent by volume. Hence 40 proof is 20%(v/v) alcohol; 100 proof is 50%(v/v) alcohol.*

© Cengage Learning

Figure 8-7 When volumes of two different liquids are combined, the volumes are not additive. This process is somewhat analogous to pouring marbles and golf balls together. The marbles can fill in the spaces between the golf balls. This results in the "mixed" volume being less than the sum of the "premixed" volumes.

Figure 8-8 Identical volumetric flasks are filled to the 50.0-mL mark with ethanol and with water. When the two liquids are poured into a 100-mL volumetric flask, the volume is seen to be less than the expected 100.0 mL; it is only 96.5 mL.

© Cengage Learning

50.0 mL of ethyl alcohol to 50.0 mL of water is 96.5 mL of solution (see Figure 8-8). Working problems involving percent by volume entails using the same procedures as those used for problems involving percent by mass.

EXAMPLE 8-3

Calculating the Percent-by-Volume Concentration of a Solution

A 125-mL sample of a mouthwash contains 12 mL of ethyl alcohol. What is the percent-by-volume concentration of ethyl alcohol in the mouthwash?

Solution

Both the volume of solute and the volume of solution are known. Substitution of these values into the defining equation for percent by volume gives

$$\%(v/v) = \frac{\text{volume solute}}{\text{volume solution}} \times 100$$

$$= \frac{12 \text{ mL}}{125 \text{ mL}} \times 100 = 9.6\%(v/v)$$

The third type of percentage unit in common use is mass–volume percent; it is abbreviated %(m/v). This unit, which is often encountered in clinical and hospital settings, is particularly convenient to use in situations involving a solid solute, which is easily weighed, and a liquid solvent. Solutions of drugs for internal and external use, intravenous and intramuscular injectables, and reagent solutions for testing are usually labeled in mass–volume percent.

Mass–volume percent *is the mass of solute in a solution (in grams) divided by the total volume of solution (in milliliters), multiplied by 100.*

$$\text{Mass–volume percent} = \frac{\text{mass of solute (g)}}{\text{volume of solution (mL)}} \times 100$$

Note that in the definition of mass–volume percent, specific mass and volume units are given. This is necessary because the units do not cancel, as was the case with mass percent and volume percent. ◀

▶ *For dilute aqueous solutions, where the density is close to 1.00 g/mL, %(m/m) and %(m/v) are almost the same because mass in grams of the solution equals the volume in milliliters of the solution.*

Mass–volume percent indicates the number of grams of solute dissolved in each 100 mL of solution. Thus a 2.3%(m/v) solution of any solute contains 2.3 g of solute in each 100 mL of solution, and a 5.4%(m/v) solution contains 5.4 g of solute in each 100 mL of solution.

EXAMPLE 8-4

Calculating the Mass–Volume Percent Concentration of a Solution

A solution is prepared by dissolving 10.0 grams of glucose in enough water to give 325 mL of solution.
What is the mass–volume percent concentration of glucose in the solution?

Solution

Both the mass of solute (in grams) and the volume of solution (in milliliters) are known. Substituting these values into the defining equation for mass–volume percent gives

$$\%(m/v) = \frac{\text{mass solute (g)}}{\text{volume solution (mL)}} \times 100$$

$$= \frac{10.0 \text{ g solute}}{325 \text{ mL solution}} \times 100 = 3.08\%(m/v)$$

Using Percent Concentrations as Conversion Factors

It is often necessary to prepare solutions of a specific percent concentration. Such a preparation requires knowledge about the amount of solute needed and/or the final volume of solution. These quantities are easily calculated using percent concentration as a conversion factor. Table 8-3 shows the relationship between the definitions for the three types of percent concentrations and the conversion factors that can be derived from them. Examples 8-5 and 8-6 illustrate how these definition-derived conversion factors are used in a problem-solving context. ◄

▶ *When a percent concentration is given without specifying which of the three types of percent concentration it is (not a desirable situation), it is assumed to mean percent by mass. Thus a 5% NaCl solution is assumed to be a 5%(m/m) NaCl solution.*

▶ Table 8-3 **Conversion Factors Obtained from Percent Concentration Units**

Percent Concentration	Meaning in Words	Conversion Factors	
15%(m/m) NaCl solution	There are 15 g of NaCl in 100 g of solution.	$\dfrac{15 \text{ g NaCl}}{100 \text{ g solution}}$ and	$\dfrac{100 \text{ g solution}}{15 \text{ g NaCl}}$
6%(v/v) methanol solution	There are 6 mL of methanol in 100 mL of solution.	$\dfrac{6 \text{ mL methanol}}{100 \text{ mL solution}}$ and	$\dfrac{100 \text{ mL solution}}{6 \text{ mL methanol}}$
25%(m/v) sucrose solution	There are 25 g of sucrose in 100 mL of solution.	$\dfrac{25 \text{ g sucrose}}{100 \text{ mL solution}}$ and	$\dfrac{100 \text{ mL solution}}{25 \text{ g sucrose}}$

EXAMPLE 8-5

Calculating the Mass of Solute Needed to Produce a Solution of a Given Percent-by-Mass Concentration

How many grams of sucrose must be added to 375 g of water to prepare a 2.75%(m/m) solution of sucrose?

Solution

Usually, when a solution concentration is given as part of a problem statement, the concentration information is used in the form of a conversion factor when the problem is solved. That will be the case in this problem.

The given quantity is 375 g of H_2O (grams of solvent), and the desired quantity is grams of sucrose (grams of solute).

$$375 \text{ g } H_2O = ? \text{ g sucrose}$$

The conversion factor relating these two quantities (solvent and solute) is obtained from the given concentration. In a 2.75%-by-mass sucrose solution, there are 2.75 g of sucrose for every 97.25 g of water.

$$100.00 \text{ g solution} - 2.75 \text{ g sucrose} = 97.25 \text{ g } H_2O$$

(continued)

The relationship between grams of solute and grams of solvent (2.75 to 97.25) produces the needed conversion factor.

$$\frac{2.75 \text{ g sucrose}}{97.25 \text{ g H}_2\text{O}}$$

The problem is set up and solved, using dimensional analysis, as follows:

$$375 \text{ g H}_2\text{O} \times \left(\frac{2.75 \text{ g sucrose}}{97.25 \text{ g H}_2\text{O}}\right) = 10.6 \text{ g sucrose}$$

EXAMPLE 8-6

Calculating the Mass of Solute Needed to Produce a Solution of a Given Mass–Volume Percent Concentration

Normal saline solution that is used to dissolve drugs for intravenous use is 0.92%(m/v) NaCl in water. How many grams of NaCl are required to prepare 35.0 mL of normal saline solution?

Solution

The given quantity is 35.0 mL of solution, and the desired quantity is grams of NaCl.

$$35.0 \text{ mL solution} = ? \text{ g NaCl}$$

The given concentration, 0.92%(m/v), which means 0.92 g of NaCl per 100 mL of solution, is used as a conversion factor to go from milliliters of solution to grams of NaCl. The setup for the conversion is

$$35.0 \text{ mL solution} \times \left(\frac{0.92 \text{ g NaCl}}{100 \text{ mL solution}}\right)$$

Doing the arithmetic after canceling the units gives

$$\left(\frac{35.0 \times 0.92}{100}\right) \text{ g NaCl} = 0.32 \text{ g NaCl}$$

Clinical Laboratory Concentration Units

Most solutes present in human blood, as well as in other body fluids, are present in low concentrations. For example, a typical concentration of free iron in the blood is 0.0000085 g/100 mL. Concentration values such as this one are inconvenient to work with because of the numerous zeros present. This "zero inconvenience" is avoided by using modified percent (m/v) concentration units in which the mass of the solute is expressed in milligrams (10^{-3} g) or micrograms (10^{-6} g) and the volume is specified in deciliters (10^{-1} L). Thus, the units encountered in blood analysis reports and other similar reports are often

$$\text{mg/dL} \quad \text{or} \quad \mu\text{g/dL}$$

An illustration of such mass per deciliter unit use in a clinical laboratory report is found in Chapter 2 (Figure 2-4).

Modified percent (m/v) units use the deciliter volume unit. A volume of one deciliter is equivalent to a volume of 100 milliliters as shown by the following equations:

$$1 \text{ deciliter} = 10^{-1} \text{ liter} = 100 \text{ milliliters}$$

Thus, a solute concentration of 1 g/dL is equivalent to a 1%(m/v) concentration

$$1 \text{ g/dL} = 1 \text{ g}/100 \text{ mL} = 1\%(\text{m/v})$$

EXAMPLE 8-7

Using Clinical Laboratory Concentration Units

What is the mass–volume percent glucose concentration in blood plasma if the glucose concentration is known to be 92 mg/dL?

Solution

The given quantity is 92 mg glucose/1 dL solution and the desired quantity is g glucose/100 mL solution

$$92 \text{ mg glucose/1 dL solution} = ? \text{ g glucose/100 mL solution}$$

The conversion factors needed for effecting this unit change are

$$\frac{10^{-3} \text{ g glucose}}{1 \text{ mg glucose}} \quad \text{and} \quad \frac{1 \text{ dL solution}}{100 \text{ mL solution}}$$

The dimensional-analysis setup for the unit change is

$$\frac{92 \text{ mg glucose}}{1 \text{ dL solution}} \times \frac{10^{-3} \text{ g glucose}}{1 \text{ mg glucose}} \times \frac{1 \text{ dL solution}}{100 \text{ mL solution}}$$

$$= 0.092 \text{ g glucose/100 mL solution}$$

$$= 0.092\%(\text{m/v}) \text{ glucose}$$

Note that the number 100 in the 100 mL found in the denominator of the second conversion factor is not used in obtaining the numerical answer because the definition for mass–volume percent is g solute/100 mL solution. This 100 is part of the definition for the concentration unit.

Section 8-5 Quick Quiz

1. The percent-by-mass concentration of a solution containing 5.0 g of NaCl in 500.0 g of solution is
   a. 1.0%(m/m)
   b. 5.0%(m/m)
   c. 10.0%(m/m)
   d. no correct response
2. The defining equation for percent-by-volume concentration is
   a. (volume solute + volume solution) × 100
   b. (volume solute × volume solution) × 100
   c. (volume solute/volume solution) × 100
3. A 2.0%(m/v) NaCl solution contains 2.0 g of NaCl per
   a. 100.0 g solution
   b. 100.0 mL solution
   c. 1000 g solution
   d. no correct response
4. The number of grams of NaCl present in 10.0 g of a 1.00 %(m/m) NaCl solution is
   a. 0.100 g
   b. 1.00 g
   c. 10.0 g
   d. no correct response
5. The percent concentration unit most often encountered in a hospital (medical) setting is
   a. percent by mass
   b. percent by volume
   c. mass–volume percent
   d. no correct response
6. The dL volume unit is equivalent to
   a. 10 mL
   b. 100 mL
   c. 10 L
   d. no correct response

Answers: 1. a; 2. c; 3. b; 4. a; 5. c; 6. b

8-6 Molarity Concentration Unit

LEARNING FOCUS

Be able to calculate solution concentration in terms of molarity; be able to use molarity as a conversion factor in problem solving.

Molarity *is the moles of solute in a solution divided by the liters of solution.* The mathematical equation for molarity is

$$\text{Molarity (M)} = \frac{\text{moles of solute}}{\text{liters of solution}}$$

Note that the abbreviation for molarity is a capital M. A solution containing 1 mole of KBr in 1 L of solution has a molarity of 1 and is said to be a 1 M (1 *molar*) solution.

The molarity concentration unit is often used in laboratories where chemical reactions are being studied. Because chemical reactions occur between molecules and atoms, use of the mole—a unit that counts particles—is desirable. Equal volumes of two solutions of the same molarity contain the same number of solute molecules.

In order to find the molarity of a solution, the solution volume in liters and the number of moles of solute present are needed. An alternative to knowing the number of moles of solute is knowing the number of grams of solute present and the solute's formula mass. The number of moles can be calculated by using these two quantities (Section 6-4).

EXAMPLE 8-8

▶ *In molarity calculations, the chemical identity of the solute must be known. Changing grams of solute to moles of solute requires a molar mass value; such is obtained using the chemical formula of the solute. By contrast, when calculating percent concentration, chemical identity of the solute is not needed; all that is needed is the grams or volume of solute present. Moles are not involved in this type of calculation.*

Calculating the Molarity of a Solution ◀

Determine the molarities of the following solutions.

a. 4.35 moles of $KMnO_4$ are dissolved in enough water to give 750 mL of solution.
b. 20.0 g of NaOH are dissolved in enough water to give 1.50 L of solution.

Solution

a. The number of moles of solute is given in the problem statement.

$$\text{Moles of solute } (KMnO_4) = 4.35 \text{ moles}$$

The volume of the solution is also given in the problem statement, but not in the right units. Molarity requires liters for the volume units, and milliliters of solution are given. Making the unit change yields

$$750 \text{ mL} \times \left(\frac{10^{-3} \text{ L}}{1 \text{ mL}}\right) = 0.750 \text{ L}$$

The molarity of the solution is obtained by substituting the known quantities into the equation

$$M = \frac{\text{moles of solute}}{\text{liters of solution}}$$

which gives

$$M = \frac{4.35 \text{ moles } KMnO_4}{0.750 \text{ L solution}} = 5.80 \frac{\text{moles } KMnO_4}{\text{L solution}}$$

Note that the units for molarity are always moles per liter.

b. The amount of solute is given in grams rather than moles. This is a common situation since amount is routinely determined in a laboratory setting by weighing using a balance. The moles of solute must be calculated from the given grams of solute (NaOH) using the solute's molar mass, which is 40.00 g/mole (calculated from atomic masses).

$$20.0 \text{ g NaOH} \times \left(\frac{1 \text{ mole NaOH}}{40.00 \text{ g NaOH}}\right) = 0.500 \text{ mole NaOH}$$

The given volume of solution, 1.50 L, has the correct units for molarity (liters) and thus can be directly used without change.

Substituting the known quantities into the defining equation for molarity gives

$$M = \frac{0.500 \text{ mole NaOH}}{1.50 \text{ L solution}} = 0.333 \frac{\text{mole NaOH}}{\text{L solution}}$$

Using Molarity as a Conversion Factor

The mass of solute present in a known volume of solution is an easily calculable quantity if the molarity of the solution is known. When such a calculation is carried out, molarity serves as a conversion factor that relates liters of solution to moles of solute. In a similar manner, the volume of solution needed to supply a given amount of solute can be calculated by using the solution's molarity as a conversion factor. Examples 8-9 and 8-10 show, respectively, these uses of molarity as a conversion factor. ◄

▶ *In preparing 100 mL of a solution of a specific molarity, enough solvent is added to a weighed amount of solute to give a* final *volume of 100 mL. The weighed solute is not added to a* starting *volume of 100 mL; this would produce a final volume greater than 100 mL because the solute volume increases the total volume.*

EXAMPLE 8-9

Calculating the Amount of Solute Present in a Given Amount of Solution

How many grams of sucrose (table sugar, $C_{12}H_{22}O_{11}$) are present in 185 mL of a 2.50 M sucrose solution?

Solution

The given quantity is 185 mL of solution, and the desired quantity is grams of $C_{12}H_{22}O_{11}$.

$$185 \text{ mL of solution} = ? \text{ g } C_{12}H_{22}O_{11}$$

The pathway used to solve this problem is

$$\text{mL solution} \longrightarrow \text{L solution} \longrightarrow \text{moles } C_{12}H_{22}O_{11} \longrightarrow \text{g } C_{12}H_{22}O_{11}$$

The given molarity (2.50 M) serves as the conversion factor for the second unit change; the formula mass of sucrose (which is not given and must be calculated) is used to accomplish the third unit change.

The dimensional-analysis setup for this pathway is

$$185 \text{ mL solution} \times \left(\frac{10^{-3} \text{ L solution}}{1 \text{ mL solution}}\right) \times \left(\frac{2.50 \text{ moles } C_{12}H_{22}O_{11}}{1 \text{ L solution}}\right)$$

$$\times \left(\frac{342.34 \text{ g } C_{12}H_{22}O_{11}}{1 \text{ mole } C_{12}H_{22}O_{11}}\right)$$

Canceling the units and doing the arithmetic, shows that

$$\left(\frac{185 \times 10^{-3} \times 2.50 \times 342.34}{1 \times 1 \times 1}\right) \text{ g } C_{12}H_{22}O_{11} = 158 \text{ g } C_{12}H_{22}O_{11}$$

EXAMPLE 8-10

Calculating the Amount of Solution Needed to Supply a Given Amount of Solute

A typical dose of iron(II) sulfate ($FeSO_4$) used in the treatment of iron-deficiency anemia is 0.35 g. How many milliliters of a 0.10 M iron(II) sulfate solution would be needed to supply this dose?

Solution

The given quantity is 0.35 g of $FeSO_4$; the desired quantity is milliliters of $FeSO_4$ solution.

$$0.35 \text{ g } FeSO_4 = ? \text{ mL } FeSO_4 \text{ solution}$$

(continued)

The pathway used to solve this problem is

$$g\ FeSO_4 \longrightarrow moles\ FeSO_4 \longrightarrow L\ FeSO_4\ solution \longrightarrow mL\ FeSO_4\ solution$$

The first unit conversion is accomplished by using the formula mass of $FeSO_4$ (which must be calculated) as a conversion factor. The second unit conversion involves the use of the given molarity as a conversion factor.

$$0.35\ g\ FeSO_4 \times \left(\frac{1\ mole\ FeSO_4}{151.92\ g\ FeSO_4}\right) \times \left(\frac{1\ L\ solution}{0.10\ mole\ FeSO_4}\right) \times \left(\frac{1\ mL\ solution}{10^{-3}\ L\ solution}\right)$$

Canceling units and doing the arithmetic, shows that

$$\left(\frac{0.35 \times 1 \times 1 \times 1}{151.92 \times 0.10 \times 10^{-3}}\right)\ mL\ solution = 23\ mL\ solution$$

The focus on relevancy feature Chemical Connections 8-C—Controlled-Release Drugs: Regulating Concentration, Rate, and Location of Release—discusses several methods used by pharmaceutical companies to control drug-concentration levels within the human body for orally taken medications.

Chemistry at a Glance—Specifying Solution Concentrations—reviews the ways in which solution concentrations are specified.

CHEMICAL CONNECTIONS 8-C

Controlled-Release Drugs: Regulating Concentration, Rate, and Location of Release

In the use of both prescription and over-the-counter drugs, body concentration levels of the drug are obviously of vital importance. All drugs have an optimum concentration range where they are most effective. Below this optimum concentration range, a drug is ineffective, and above it the drug may have adverse side effects. Hence, the much-repeated warning "Take as directed."

Ordinarily, in the administration of a drug, the body's concentration level of the drug rapidly increases toward the higher end of the effective concentration range and then gradually declines and falls below the effective limit. The period of effectiveness of the drug can be extended by using the drug in a controlled-release form. This causes the drug to be released in a regulated, continuous manner over a longer period of time. The accompanying graph contrasts "ordinary-release" and "controlled-release" modes of drug action.

The use of controlled-release medication began in the early 1960s with the introduction of the decongestant Contac. Contac's controlled-release mechanism, which is now found in many drugs and used by all drug manufacturers, involves drug particles encapsulated within a slowly dissolving coating that *varies in thickness* from particle to particle. Particles of the drug with a thinner coating dissolve fast. Those particles with a thicker coating dissolve more slowly, extending the period of drug release. The number of particles of various thicknesses, within a formulation, is predetermined by the manufacturer.

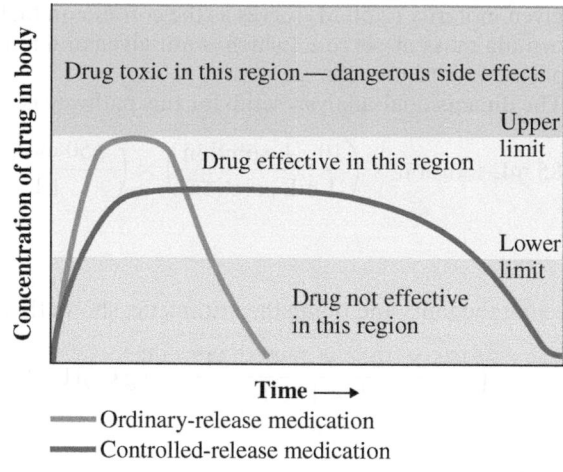

When drugs are taken orally, they first encounter the acidic environment of the stomach. Two problems can occur here: (1) The drug itself may damage the stomach lining or (2) the drug may be rendered inactive by the gastric acid present in the stomach. Controlled-release techniques are useful in overcoming these problems. Drug particle coatings are now available that are acid resistant; that is, they do not dissolve in acidic solution. Drugs with such coatings pass from the stomach into the small intestine in undissolved form. Within the nonacidic (basic) environment of the small intestine, the dissolving process then begins.

CHEMISTRY

AT A GLANCE Specifying Solution Concentrations

SOLVENT
The component of a solution present in the greatest quantity

SOLUTE
The component of a solution present in the least quantity

SOLUTION
A homogeneous mixture of two or more substances in which each substance retains its chemical identity

CONCENTRATION OF A SOLUTION
The amount of solute in a specified amount of solution

PERCENT BY MASS	PERCENT BY VOLUME	MASS–VOLUME PERCENT	MOLARITY
$\%(m/m)$ $= \dfrac{\text{mass of solute}}{\text{mass of solution}} \times 100$	$\%(v/v)$ $= \dfrac{\text{volume of solute}}{\text{volume of solution}} \times 100$	$\%(m/v)$ $= \dfrac{\text{mass of solute (g)}}{\text{volume of solution (mL)}} \times 100$	M $= \dfrac{\text{moles of solute}}{\text{liters of solution}}$
1%(m/m) milk	**70%(v/v)** rubbing alcohol	**0.9%(m/v)** physiological saline solution	**6.0 M** hydrochloric acid

© Felicia Martinez Photography/PhotoEdit

© Editorial Image, LLC/Alamy

© Phototake/Alamy

© Cengage Learning

Section 8-6 Quick Quiz

1. The defining equation for the molarity concentration unit is
   a. moles solute/mL solution
   b. moles solute/L solution
   c. grams solute/L solution
   d. no correct response
2. For which of the following solutions is the concentration 1.0 molar?
   a. 3.0 moles of solute in 1.5 L of solution
   b. 2.0 moles of solute in 500.0 mL solution
   c. 1.0 mole of solute in 100.0 mL solution
   d. no correct response
3. A 0.200 M solution of NaCl which contains 0.200 mole of NaCl would have a volume of
   a. 0.100 L
   b. 1.00 L
   c. 10.0 L
   d. no correct response

Answers: 1. b; 2. d; 3. b

Dilution

LEARNING FOCUS

Be able to calculate the new concentration of a solution prepared by diluting a solution of known concentration.

Figure 8-9 Frozen orange juice concentrate is diluted with water prior to drinking.

A common activity encountered when working with solutions is that of diluting a solution of known concentration (usually called a stock solution) to a lower concentration. **Dilution** *is the process in which more solvent is added to a solution in order to lower its concentration.* The same amount of solute is present, but it is now distributed in a larger amount of solvent (the original solvent plus the added solvent).

Often, a solution of a specific concentration is prepared by adding a predetermined volume of solvent to a specific volume of stock solution (Figure 8-9). A simple relationship exists between the volumes and concentrations of the diluted and stock solutions. This relationship is

$$\left(\begin{array}{c}\text{Concentration of}\\\text{stock solution}\end{array}\right) \times \left(\begin{array}{c}\text{volume of}\\\text{stock solution}\end{array}\right) = \left(\begin{array}{c}\text{concentration of}\\\text{diluted solution}\end{array}\right) \times \left(\begin{array}{c}\text{volume of}\\\text{diluted solution}\end{array}\right)$$

or

$$C_s \times V_s = C_d \times V_d$$

Use of this equation in a problem-solving context is shown in Example 8-11.

EXAMPLE 8-11

Calculating the Amount of Solvent That Must Be Added to a Stock Solution to Dilute It to a Specified Concentration

A nurse wants to prepare a 1.0%(m/v) silver nitrate solution from 24 mL of a 3.0%(m/v) stock solution of silver nitrate. How much water should be added to the 24 mL of stock solution?

Solution

The volume of water to be added will be equal to the difference between the final and initial volumes. The initial volume is known (24 mL). The final volume can be calculated by using the equation

$$C_s \times V_s = C_d \times V_d$$

Once the final volume is known, the difference between the two volumes can be obtained.

Substituting the known quantities into the dilution equation, which has been rearranged to isolate V_d on the left side, gives

$$V_d = \frac{C_s \times V_s}{C_d} = \frac{3.0\%\cancel{(m/v)} \times 24 \text{ mL}}{1.0\%\cancel{(m/v)}} = 72 \text{ mL}$$

The solvent added is

$$V_d - V_s = (72 - 24) \text{ mL} = 48 \text{ mL}$$

Section 8-7 Quick Quiz

1. When 60.0 mL of a 1.00 M solution is diluted by adding 30.0 mL of water, the amount of solute present
   a. increases
   b. decreases
   c. remains the same
   d. no correct response

2. If 200.0 mL of a 0.40 M NaCl solution is diluted with water to form 800.0 mL of solution, the molarity of the new solution is
   a. 0.10 M
   b. 0.20 M
   c. 0.80 M
   d. no correct response
3. If 100.0 mL of 8.0 M NaCl solution is diluted with water to form a 4.0 M solution, what is the volume, in mL, of the new solution?
   a. 400.0 mL
   b. 200.0 mL
   c. 50.0 mL
   d. no correct response

Answers: 1. c; 2. a; 3. b

8-8 Colloidal Dispersions and Suspensions

LEARNING FOCUS

On the basis of properties, identify a given mixture as a *solution*, a *colloidal dispersion*, or a *suspension*.

Colloidal dispersions are mixtures that have many properties similar to those of solutions, although they are not true solutions. In a broad sense, colloidal dispersions may be thought of as mixtures in which a material is *dispersed* rather than *dissolved*. A **colloidal dispersion** *is a homogeneous mixture that contains dispersed particles that are intermediate in size between those of a true solution and those of an ordinary heterogeneous mixture.* The terms *solute* and *solvent* are not used to indicate the components of a colloidal dispersion. Instead, the particles dispersed in a colloidal dispersion are called the *dispersed phase*, and the material in which they are dispersed is called the *dispersing medium.* ◀

Particles of the dispersed phase in a colloidal dispersion are so small that (1) they are not usually discernible by the naked eye, (2) they do not settle out under the influence of gravity, and (3) they cannot be filtered out using filter paper that has relatively large pores. In these respects, the dispersed phase behaves similarly to a solute in a solution.

However, the dispersed-phase particle size is sufficiently large to make the dispersion nonhomogeneous to light. When a beam of light is focused on a true solution, the path of the light through the solution cannot be detected (seen). However, a beam of light passing through a colloidal dispersion can be observed because the light is scattered by the dispersed phase (Figure 8-10). ◀ This scattered light can be seen. This phenomenon, first described by the Irish physicist John Tyndall (1820–1893), is called the *Tyndall effect.* The **Tyndall effect** *is the light-scattering phenomenon that causes the path of a beam of visible light through a colloidal dispersion to be observable.*

Many different biochemical colloidal dispersions occur within the human body. Foremost among them is blood, which has numerous components that are colloidal in size. Fat is transported in the blood and lymph systems as colloidal-sized particles.

▶ *Some chemists use the term* colloid *instead of colloidal dispersion.*

▶ *The fact that milk is a colloidal dispersion can be demonstrated using the experimental setup depicted in Figure 8-10. (For the best effect, the milk should be diluted with water just until it looks cloudy.)*

Figure 8-10 A beam of light travels through a true solution (the yellow liquid) without being scattered—that is, its path cannot be seen. This is not the case for a colloidal dispersion (the red liquid), where scattering of light by the dispersed phase makes the light pathway visible.

© Cengage Learning

▶ Table 8-4 **Property Comparison for Solutions, Colloidal Dispersions, and Suspensions**

Property	Solution	Colloidal Dispersion	Suspension
type of mixture	homogeneous	homogeneous	heterogeneous
type of particles	atoms, ions, and small molecules	groups of small particles or individual larger molecules	very large particles, which are often visible
effect of light	transparent	scatters light (Tyndall effect)	not transparent
settling properties	particles do not settle	particles do not settle	particles settle rapidly
filtration properties	particles cannot be filtered out	particles cannot be filtered out	particles can be filtered out

The diameters of the dispersed particles in a colloidal dispersion are in the range of 10^{-7} cm to 10^{-5} cm. This compares with diameters of less than 10^{-7} cm for particles such as ions, atoms, and molecules. Thus colloidal particles are up to 1000 times larger than those present in a true solution. The dispersed particles are usually aggregates of molecules, but this is not always the case. Some protein molecules are large enough to form colloidal dispersions that contain single molecules in suspension. ◀

▶ *Particle size for the dispersed phase in a colloidal dispersion is larger than that for solutes in a true solution.*

Colloidal dispersions that contain particles with diameters larger than 10^{-5} cm are usually not encountered. Suspended particles of this size usually settle out under the influence of gravity. For example, within a short period of time, the particles in a sample of stirred "muddy water" will settle to the bottom of a container, producing a clear liquid above the sediment. Stirred muddy water is an example of a *suspension* rather than a colloidal dispersion. A **suspension** *is a heterogeneous mixture that contains dispersed particles that are heavy enough that they settle out under the influence of gravity.* Most filters will remove the dispersed particles from a suspension, which is in direct contrast to the effect of filtration on a colloidal dispersion. Table 8-4 compares the properties of "true" solutions, colloidal dispersions, and suspensions. ◀

▶ *Several medications are intended to be used as suspensions. They always carry the instructions "shake well before using." Included among suspension medications are Kaopectate, calamine lotion, and milk of magnesia.*

Section 8-8 Quick Quiz

1. A colloidal dispersion differs from a true solution in that colloidal particles
   a. settle rapidly
   b. are large enough to be seen with the naked eye
   c. are large enough to be removed by most filters
   d. no correct response
2. For which of the following types of mixtures do the particles present scatter light?
   a. colloidal dispersion
   b. true solution
   c. suspension
   d. no correct response
3. Which of the following is a characteristic of a suspension?
   a. it is a homogeneous mixture
   b. filters remove most suspended particles
   c. appears transparent to a beam of light
   d. no correct response

Answers: 1. d; 2. a; 3. b

8-9 Colligative Properties of Solutions

LEARNING FOCUS

Understand the meaning of the term *colligative property*; know the molecular basis for the colligative properties *vapor-pressure lowering, boiling-point elevation,* and *freezing-point depression.*

Adding a solute to a pure solvent causes the solvent's physical properties to change. A special group of physical properties that change when a solute is added are called colligative properties. A **colligative property** *is a physical property of a solution* *that depends only on the number of solute particles (molecules or ions) present in a given quantity of solvent and not on their chemical identities.* Examples of colligative properties include vapor-pressure lowering, boiling-point elevation, freezing-point depression, and osmotic pressure. The first three of these colligative properties are discussed in this section. The fourth, osmotic pressure, will be considered in Section 8-10.

Of utmost importance in the preceding definition of a colligative property is the phrase "number of solute particles present." The number of solute particles present in a solution depends not only on the concentration of solute present but also on whether the solute breaks up (dissociates) into ions once it is in solution. Thus, two factors rather than one determine the number of particles present. Molecular (covalent) solutes do not break up to produce ions in solution. Soluble ionic compounds do dissociate into ions in solution. It is the total number of particles (ions or molecules) present in solution that determines the magnitude of a colligative property effect.

Consideration of three different solutes present in solutions of the same concentration illustrates the importance of this "total number" of particles concept. The solutes are glucose (a molecular solute), and NaCl and CaCl$_2$ (both soluble ionic solutes). The results of dissolving these solutes in water are:

1. 1 mole of glucose produces 1 mole of particles (molecules) since molecular solutes remain in molecular form in solution.
2. 1 mole of NaCl produces 2 moles of particles (ions) since soluble ionic solutes dissociate into ions. Two moles of ions are produced from one mole of NaCl.

$$NaCl \longrightarrow Na^+ + Cl^-$$

3. 1 mole of CaCl$_2$ produces 3 moles of particles (ions) when dissociation occurs.

$$CaCl_2 \longrightarrow Ca^{2+} + 2Cl^-$$

Thus, the effect of 1 mole of NaCl on colligative properties will be twice that of 1 mole of glucose; twice as many particles are present even though the molar amounts of solute are the same. The effect of 1 mole of CaCl$_2$ on colligative properties will be three times that of 1 mole of glucose on colligative properties.

Vapor-Pressure Lowering

Adding a nonvolatile solute to a solvent *lowers* the vapor pressure of the resulting solution below that of the pure solvent at the same temperature. (A nonvolatile solute is one that has a low vapor pressure and therefore a low tendency to vaporize; Section 7-11.) This lowering of vapor pressure is a direct consequence of some of the solute molecules or ions occupying positions on the surface of the liquid. Their presence decreases the probability of solvent molecules escaping; that is, the number of surface-occupying solvent molecules has been decreased. Figure 8-11 illustrates the decrease in surface concentration of solvent molecules when a solute is added. As the *number* of solute particles increases, the reduction in vapor pressure also increases; thus vapor pressure is a colligative property. What is important is not the identity of the solute molecules but the fact that they take up room on the surface of the liquid.

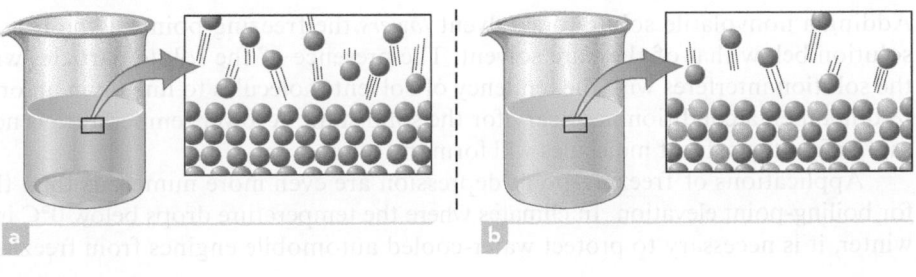

Figure 8-11 Close-ups of the surface of a liquid solvent (a) before and (b) after solute has been added. There are fewer solvent molecules on the surface of the liquid after solute has been added. This results in a decreased vapor pressure for the solution compared with pure solvent.

▶ *The boiling-point increase of 0.51°C applies only when two conditions are met: (1) 1 mole of solute particles (molecules or ions) are present and (2) 1 kilogram of water is present. If 2.0 kg of water and 1 mole of particles are present, the boiling-point increase would be one-half of 0.51°C because of the dilution factor associated with twice as much water. If 0.50 kg of water and 1 mole of particles are present, the boiling-point increase would be twice the 0.51°C value.*

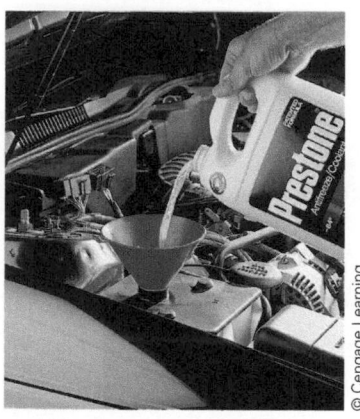

Figure 8-12 A water–antifreeze mixture has a higher boiling point and a lower freezing point than pure water.

© Cengage Learning

Boiling-Point Elevation

Adding a nonvolatile solute to a solvent *raises* the boiling point of the resulting solution above that of the pure solvent. This is logical when we remember that the vapor pressure of the solution is lower than that of the pure solvent and that the boiling point is dependent on vapor pressure (Section 7-12). A higher temperature will be needed to raise the depressed vapor pressure of the solution to atmospheric pressure; this is the condition required for boiling. ◀

A common application of the phenomenon of boiling-point elevation involves automobiles. The coolant ethylene glycol (a nonvolatile solute) is added to car radiators to prevent boilover in hot weather (Figure 8-12). The engine may not run any cooler, but the coolant–water mixture will not boil until it reaches a temperature well above the normal boiling point of water.

One mole of any molecular solute raises the boiling point of one kilogram of water by the same amount, which is 0.51°C. One mole of any ionic solute whose dissociation produces two ions per formula unit raises the boiling point of one kilogram of water by 1.02°C (2 × 0.51°C), and one mole of any ionic solute that dissociates to produce three ions per formula unit raises the boiling point of one kilogram of water by 1.53°C (3 × 0.51°C).

EXAMPLE 8-12

Calculating the Boiling Point of an Aqueous Solution

What is the boiling point of a solution that contains 0.25 mole of the ionic solute NaBr per one kilogram of water?

Solution

Formula units of NaBr will dissociate to produce 2 ions per formula unit.

$$NaBr \longrightarrow Na^+ + Br^-$$

Using this fact and the conversion factor

$$\frac{0.51°C}{1 \text{ mole of particles}}$$

the dimensional-analysis setup for the calculation of the boiling-point increase (elevation) caused by solute presence proceeds as follows:

$$0.25 \text{ mole NaBr} \times \frac{2 \text{ moles particles}}{1 \text{ mole NaBr}} \times \frac{0.51°C}{1 \text{ mole particles}}$$
$$= 0.26°C \text{ (boiling point increase)}$$

The boiling point of the solution is obtained by adding the boiling-point increase to the original boiling point value for water.

$$100.00°C + 0.26°C = 100.26°C$$

▶ *The freezing-point decrease of 1.86°C applies only when two conditions are met: (1) 1 mole of solute particles (molecules or ions) are present and (2) 1 kilogram of water is present. If 2.0 kg of water and 1 mole of particles are present, the freezing-point decrease would be one-half of 1.86°C because of the dilution factor associated with twice as much water. If 0.50 kg of water and 1 mole of particles are present, the freezing-point decrease would be twice the 1.86°C value.*

Freezing-Point Depression

Adding a nonvolatile solute to a solvent *lowers* the freezing point of the resulting solution below that of the pure solvent. The presence of the solute particles within the solution interferes with the tendency of solvent molecules to line up in an organized manner, a condition necessary for the solid state. A lower temperature is necessary before the solvent molecules will form the solid.

Applications of freezing-point depression are even more numerous than those for boiling-point elevation. In climates where the temperature drops below 0°C in the winter, it is necessary to protect water-cooled automobile engines from freezing. ◀

This is done by adding antifreeze (usually ethylene glycol) to the radiator. The addition of this nonvolatile material causes the vapor pressure and freezing point of the resulting solution to be much lower than those of pure water. Also in the winter, a salt, usually NaCl or $CaCl_2$, is spread on roads and sidewalks to melt ice or prevent it from forming. The salt dissolves in the water to form a solution that will not freeze until the temperature drops much lower than 0°C, the normal freezing point of water.

The effect of solute presence on the freezing point of water is more than three times greater than that on water's boiling point. One mole of solute particles lowers the freezing point of one kilogram of water by 1.86°C. The boiling-point elevation for water was only 0.51°C under similar circumstances.

EXAMPLE 8-13

Calculating the Freezing Point of an Aqueous Solution ◄

What is the freezing point of an aqueous solution that contains 3.00 moles of the ionic solute $CaCl_2$ (a deicing compound) per one kilogram of water?

Solution

A formula unit of $CaCl_2$ dissociates to produce three ions.

$$CaCl_2 \longrightarrow Ca^{2+} + 2Cl^-$$

Proceeding in a manner similar to that used in Example 8-12, the dimensional-analysis setup for the problem is

$$3.00 \text{ moles } CaCl_2 \times \frac{3 \text{ moles particles}}{1 \text{ mole } CaCl_2} \times \frac{1.86°C}{1 \text{ mole particles}}$$

$$= 16.7°C \text{ (freezing-point decrease)}$$

The freezing point of the solution is

$$0.0°C + (-16.7°C) = -16.7°C$$

▶ *In the making of homemade ice cream, the function of the rock salt added to the ice is to depress the freezing point of the ice–water mixture surrounding the ice cream mix sufficiently to allow the mix (which contains sugar and other solutes and thus has a freezing point below 0°C) to freeze.*

Section 8-9 Quick Quiz

1. Adding a nonvolatile solute to a pure solvent produces which of the following effects?
   a. vapor-pressure lowering
   b. freezing-point elevation
   c. boiling-point depression
   d. no correct response
2. The numerical value for a colligative property is dependent on the
   a. identity of the solute present
   b. number of solute particles present
   c. the boiling point of the solute present
   d. no correct response
3. What is the freezing point for a solution containing 1.00 mole of glucose (a nondissociating solute) dissolved in 1.00 kg water?
   a. +1.86°C
   b. −1.86°C
   c. −0.51°C
   d. no correct response
4. Which of the following solutions would have a lower freezing point than a solution containing 0.20 mole of glucose per kilogram of solvent?
   a. solution containing 0.10 mole of glucose per kilogram of solvent
   b. solution containing 0.10 mole of NaCl per kilogram of solvent
   c. solution containing 0.10 mole of $MgCl_2$ per kilogram of solvent
   d. no correct response

Answers: 1. a; 2. b; 3. b; 4. c

8-10 Osmosis and Osmotic Pressure

LEARNING FOCUS

Be able to describe the concepts of *osmosis, osmotic pressure,* and *osmolarity;* distinguish among the terms *hypotonic solution, hypertonic solution,* and *isotonic solution.*

The process of osmosis and the colligative property of osmotic pressure are extremely important phenomena when biochemical solutions are considered. These phenomena govern many of the processes important to a functioning human body.

Osmosis

▶ *The term* osmosis *comes from the Greek* osmos, *which means "push."*

▶ *An osmotic semipermeable membrane contains very small pores (holes)—too small to see— that are big enough to let small solvent molecules pass through but not big enough to let larger solute molecules pass through.*

▶ *A process called* reverse osmosis *is used in the desalination of seawater to make drinking water. Pressure greater than the osmotic pressure is applied on the salt water side of the membrane to force solvent water across the membrane from the salt water side to the "pure" water side.*

Osmosis *is the passage of a solvent through a semipermeable membrane separating a dilute solution (or pure solvent) from a more concentrated solution.* The simple apparatus shown in Figure 8-13a is helpful in explaining, at the molecular level, what actually occurs during the osmotic process. ◀ The apparatus consists of a tube containing a concentrated salt–water solution that has been immersed in a dilute salt–water solution. The immersed end of the tube is covered with a semipermeable membrane. A **semipermeable membrane** *is a membrane that allows certain types of molecules to pass through it but prohibits the passage of other types of molecules.* The selectivity of a semipermeable membrane is based on size differences of molecules. The particles that are allowed to pass through (usually just solvent molecules like water) are relatively small. ◀ Thus the membrane functions somewhat like a sieve. Using the experimental setup of Figure 8-13a, a net flow of solvent from the dilute to the concentrated solution can be observed over the course of time. This is indicated by a rise in the level of the solution in the tube and a drop in the level of the dilute solution, as shown in Figure 8-13b. ◀

What is actually happening on a molecular level as the process of osmosis occurs? Water is flowing in both directions through the membrane. However, the rate of flow into the concentrated solution is greater than the rate of flow in the other direction (Figure 8-14). Why? The presence of solute molecules diminishes the ability of water

At equilibrium, more dilute than before

Dilute salt solution

Semipermeable membrane

Concentrated salt solution

At equilibrium, more concentrated than before

a Osmosis, the flow of solvent through a semipermeable membrane from a dilute to a more concentrated solution, can be observed with this apparatus.

b The liquid level in the tube rises until equilibrium is reached. At equilibrium, the solvent molecules move back and forth across the membrane at equal rates.

Figure 8-13 Changing liquid levels associated with the osmotic flow of solvent through a semipermeable membrane is observable until an equilibrium condition is reached. At equilibrium, the flow rate of solvent in both directions across the membrane is the same.

Figure 8-14 Enlarged views of a semipermeable membrane separating (a) pure water and a salt–water solution, and (b) a dilute salt–water solution and a concentrated salt–water solution. In both cases, net water movement is from the area of lower solute concentration to the area of higher solute concentration.

molecules to cross the membrane. The solute molecules literally get in the way; they occupy some of the surface positions next to the membrane. Because there is a greater concentration of solute molecules on one side of the membrane than on the other, the flow rates differ. The flow rate is diminished to a greater extent on the side of the membrane where the greater concentration of solute is present.

The net transfer of solvent across the membrane continues until (1) the concentrations of solute particles on both sides of the membrane become equal or (2) the hydrostatic pressure on the concentrated side of the membrane (from the difference in liquid levels) becomes sufficient to counterbalance the greater escaping tendency of molecules from the dilute side. From this point on, there is an equal flow of solvent in both directions across the membrane, and the volume of liquid on each side of the membrane remains constant.

Osmotic Pressure

Osmotic pressure *is the pressure that must be applied to prevent the net flow of solvent through a semipermeable membrane from a solution of lower solute concentration to a solution of higher solute concentration.* In terms of Figure 8-13, osmotic pressure is the pressure required to prevent water from rising in the tube. Figure 8-15 shows how this pressure can be measured. The greater the concentration difference between the separated solutions, the greater the magnitude of the osmotic pressure.

Cell membranes in both plants and animals are semipermeable in nature. The selective passage of fluid materials through these membranes governs the balance of fluids in living systems (see Figure 8-16). Thus osmotic-type phenomena are of prime importance for life. The term "osmotic-type phenomena" is used instead of "osmosis" because the semipermeable membranes found in living cells usually permit the passage of small solute molecules (nutrients and waste products) in addition to solvent. The term *osmosis* implies the passage of solvent only. The substances prohibited from passing through the membrane in osmotic-type processes are colloidal-sized molecules and insoluble suspended materials.

It is because of an osmotic-type process that plants will die if they are watered with salt water. The salt solution outside the root membranes is more concentrated than the solution in the root, so water flows out of the roots; then the plant becomes dehydrated and dies. This same principle is the reason for not drinking excessive amounts of salt water if stranded on a raft in the middle of the ocean. When salt water is taken into the stomach, water flows out of the stomach wall membranes and into the stomach; then the tissues become dehydrated. Drinking seawater will cause greater thirst because the body will lose water rather than absorb it.

Figure 8-15 Osmotic pressure is the amount of pressure needed to prevent the solution in the tube from rising as a result of the process of osmosis.

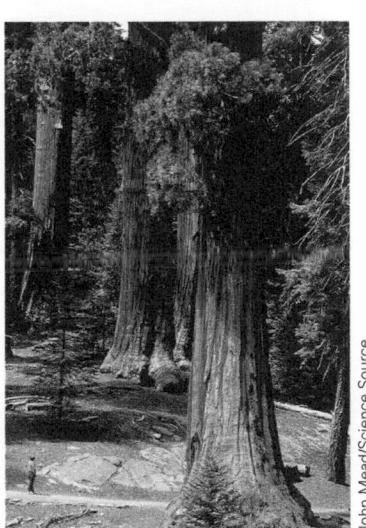

Figure 8-16 The dissolved substances in tree sap create a more concentrated solution than the surrounding ground water. Water enters membranes in the roots and rises in the tree, creating an osmotic pressure that can exceed 20 atm in extremely tall trees.

John Mead/Science Source

Osmolarity

The osmotic pressure of a solution, like a solution's freezing point and boiling point (Section 8-8), depends on the number of solute particles present. This in turn depends on the solute concentration and on whether the solute forms ions once it is in solution.

The concentration unit *osmolarity* is used to compare the osmotic pressures of solutions. **Osmolarity** *is the product of a solution's molarity and the number of particles produced per formula unit if the solute dissociates.* The equation for osmolarity is

$$\text{Osmolarity} = \text{molarity} \times i$$

where i is the number of particles produced from the dissociation of one formula unit of solute. ◄ The abbreviation for osmolarity is osmol.

▶ *Osmolarity is greater for ionic solutes than for molecular solutes (solutes that do not separate into ions, such as glucose and sucrose) if the molar concentrations of the solutions are equal, because ionic solutes dissociate to form more than 1 mole of particles per mole of compound.*

EXAMPLE 8-14

Calculating the Osmolarity of Various Solutions

What is the osmolarity of each of the following solutions?

a. 2 M NaCl   **b.** 2 M $CaCl_2$ **c.** 2 M glucose
d. 2 M in both NaCl and glucose
e. 2 M in NaCl and 1 M in glucose

Solution

The general equation for osmolarity will be applicable in each of the parts of the problem.

$$\text{Osmolarity} = \text{molarity} \times i$$

a. Two particles per dissociation are produced when NaCl dissociates in solution.

$$NaCl \longrightarrow Na^+ + Cl^-$$

The value of i is 2, and the osmolarity is twice the molarity.

$$\text{Osmolarity} = 2\text{ M} \times 2 = 4 \text{ osmol}$$

b. For $CaCl_2$, the value of i is 3, because three ions are produced from the dissociation of one $CaCl_2$ formula unit.

$$CaCl_2 \longrightarrow Ca^{2+} + 2Cl^-$$

The osmolarity will therefore be triple the molarity:

$$\text{Osmolarity} = 2\text{ M} \times 3 = 6 \text{ osmol}$$

c. Glucose is a nondissociating solute. Thus the value of i is 1, and the molarity and osmolarity will be the same—two molar and two osmolar. ◄

d. When two solutes are present, the collective effects of both solutes must be considered. For NaCl, $i = 2$; and for glucose, $i = 1$. The osmolarity is calculated as follows:

$$\text{Osmolarity} = \underbrace{2\text{ M} \times 2}_{\text{NaCl}} + \underbrace{2\text{ M} \times 1}_{\text{glucose}} = 6 \text{ osmol}$$

▶ *The molarity of a 5.0%(m/v) glucose solution is 0.31 M. The molarity of a 0.92%(m/v) NaCl solution is 0.16 M. Despite the differing molarities, these two solutions have the same osmotic pressure. The concept of osmolarity explains why these solutions of different concentration can exhibit the same osmotic pressure. For glucose* i = 1 *and for NaCl* i = 2.

e. This problem differs from the previous one in that the two solutes are not present in equal concentrations. This does not change the way the problem is worked. The i values are the same as before, and the osmolarity is

$$\text{Osmolarity} = \underbrace{2\text{ M} \times 2}_{\text{NaCl}} + \underbrace{1\text{ M} \times 1}_{\text{glucose}} = 5 \text{ osmol}$$

Solutions of equal osmolarity have equal osmotic pressures. If the osmolarity of one solution is three times that of another, then the osmotic pressure of the first solution is three times that of the second solution. A solution with high osmotic pressure will take up more water than a solution of lower osmotic pressure; thus more pressure must be applied to prevent osmosis.

Hypotonic, Hypertonic, and Isotonic Solutions

The terms *hypotonic solution*, *hypertonic solution*, and *isotonic solution* pertain to osmotic-type phenomena that occur in the human body. A consideration of what happens to red blood cells when they are placed in three different liquids is of help in understanding the differences in meaning of these three terms. The liquid media are distilled water, concentrated sodium chloride solution, and physiological saline solution.

When red blood cells are placed in pure water, they swell up (enlarge in size) and finally rupture (burst); this process is called *hemolysis* (Figure 8-17a). Hemolysis is caused by an increase in the amount of water entering the cells compared with the amount of water leaving the cells. This is the result of cellular fluid having a greater osmotic pressure than pure water.

When red blood cells are placed in a concentrated sodium chloride solution, a process opposite of hemolysis occurs. This time, water moves from the cells to the solution, causing the cells to shrivel (shrink in size); this process is called *crenation* (Figure 8-17b). Crenation occurs because the osmotic pressure of the concentrated salt solution surrounding the red cells is greater than that of the fluid within the cells. Water always moves in the direction of greater osmotic pressure. ◀

Finally, when red blood cells are placed in physiological saline solution, a 0.92%(m/v) sodium chloride solution, water flow is balanced and neither hemolysis nor crenation occurs (Figure 8-17c). The osmotic pressure of physiological saline solution is the same as that of red blood cell fluid. Thus, the rates of water flow into and out of the red blood cells are the same.

Formal definitions for the terms *hypotonic*, *hypertonic*, and *isotonic* are as follows. A **hypotonic solution** *is a solution with a lower osmotic pressure than that within cells.* The prefix *hypo-* means "under" or "less than normal." Distilled water is hypotonic with respect to red blood cell fluid, and these cells will hemolyze when placed in it (Figure 8-17a). A **hypertonic solution** *is a solution with a higher osmotic pressure than that within cells.* The prefix *hyper-* means "over" or "more than normal." Concentrated sodium chloride solution is hypertonic with respect to red blood cell fluid, and these cells undergo crenation when placed in it (Figure 8-17b). An **isotonic solution** *is a solution with an osmotic pressure that is equal to that within cells.* The prefix *iso-* means "equal." Red blood cell fluid, physiological saline solution, and 5.0%(m/v) glucose water are all isotonic with respect to one another. (Two solutions that have the same osmotic pressure are said to be isotonic.) The processes of replacing body fluids and supplying nutrients to the body intravenously require the use of isotonic solutions such as physiological saline and glucose water. If isotonic solutions were not used, the damaging effects of hemolysis or crenation would occur. ◀

▶ *The pickling of cucumbers and salt curing of meat are practical applications of the concept of crenation. A concentrated salt solution (brine) is used to draw water from the cells of the cucumber to produce a pickle. Salt on the surface of the meat preserves the meat by crenation of bacterial cells.*

▶ *The terminology "D5W," often heard in television shows involving doctors and paramedics, refers to a 5%(m/v) solution of glucose (also called dextrose [D]) in water (W).*

(a) Hemolysis occurs in pure water (a hypotonic solution).

(b) Crenation occurs in concentrated sodium chloride solution (a hypertonic solution).

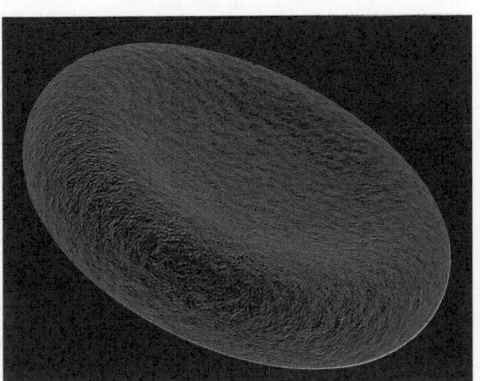

(c) Cells neither swell nor shrink in physiological saline solution (an isotonic solution).

(a, b) David M. Phillips/Science Source
(c) © istockphoto.com/Alllex

Figure 8-17 Effects of bathing red blood cells in various types of solutions.

▶ Table 8-5 **Characteristics of Hypotonic, Hypertonic, and Isotonic Solutions**

	Type of Solution		
	Hypotonic	Hypertonic	Isotonic
osmolarity relative to body fluids	less than	greater than	equal
osmotic pressure relative to body fluids	less than	greater than	equal
osmotic effect on cells	net flow of water into cells	net flow of water out of cells	equal water flow into and out of cells

▶ *The use of 5%(m/v) glucose solution for intravenous feeding has a shortcoming. A patient can accommodate only about 3 L of water in a day. Three liters of 5%(m/v) glucose water will supply only about 640 kcal of energy, an inadequate amount of energy. A resting patient requires about 1400 kcal per day.*

This problem is solved by using solutions that are about six times as concentrated as isotonic solutions. They are administered, through a tube, directly into a large blood vessel leading to the heart (the superior vena cava) rather than through a small vein in the arm or leg. The large volume of blood flowing through this vein quickly dilutes the solution to levels that do not upset the osmotic balance in body fluids. Using this technique, patients can be given up to 5000 kcal per day of nourishment.

It is sometimes necessary to introduce a hypotonic or hypertonic solution, under controlled conditions, into the body to correct an improper "water balance" in a patient. A hypotonic solution can be used to cause water to flow from the blood into surrounding tissue; blood pressure can be decreased in this manner. A hypertonic solution will cause the net transfer of water from tissues to blood; then the kidneys will remove the water. Some laxatives, such as Epsom salts, act by forming hypertonic solutions in the intestines. Table 8-5 summarizes the differences in meaning among the terms *hypotonic, hypertonic*, and *isotonic*. ◀

Concentration Units for Isotonic Solutions

A 5.0%(m/v) glucose solution and a 0.92%(m/v) sodium chloride solution are isotonic solutions for red blood cells, as has been previously noted. A 9.5%(m/v) lactose solution is another example of an isotonic solution for red blood cells. When isotonicity is denoted using mass–volume percent, as is the case here, various isotonic solutions have different concentrations (5.0%, 0.92%, 9.5%, etc.). This is because isotonicity depends on the total number of solute particles present in solution (a colligative property; Section 8-9) and mass–volume percent is not a direct measure of this parameter.

If the molarity concentration unit is used for expressing isotonic concentration a different "picture" emerges. Because molarity (moles) is a measure of the number of solute particles present, all solutions isotonic with red blood cells have the same concentration. A 5.0%(m/v) glucose solution is 0.28 molar, a 0.92%(m/v) sodium chloride solution produces a 0.28 molar solution of ions, and a 9.5%(m/v) lactose solution is also 0.28 molar.

A useful generalization about solutions isotonic with red blood cells is that all solutions whose *total* solute concentration, taking into account the formation of ions by some solutes, is 0.28 M are isotonic. Thus, not only are 0.28 M glucose and 0.28 M lactose solutions isotonic with red blood cells, but also isotonic is a solution that is 0.14 M in glucose and 0.14 M in lactose. For this latter situation, the sum of the two solute concentrations is 0.28 M. Another isotonic glucose–lactose solution is one that is 0.10 M in glucose and 0.18 M in lactose; again the sum of the molarities is 0.28.

In the human body, red blood cells are suspended in an aqueous solution called blood plasma. This plasma contains numerous solutes, the sum of whose molar concentrations is 0.28 M. Table 8-6 gives the various solutes present in blood plasma as well as their molar concentrations; the sum of the molar concentrations adds to 0.28 molar, taking into account the ionic nature of some solutes. Table 8-6 also gives, for comparison, the molar composition of the intracellular fluid. Note that the solutes are different than for blood plasma but that the sum of the concentrations again adds to 0.28 molar.

Chemistry at a Glance—Summary of Colligative Property Terminology— summarizes this chapter's discussion of colligative properties of solutions.

▶ **Table 8-6 Typical Molar Concentrations for Solutes Present in Blood Plasma and Cellular Solution**

Blood Plasma	
Solute Identity	**Solute Concentration**
Na^+ ion	0.12 M
Cl^- ion	0.10 M
HCO_3^- ion	0.02 M
Proteins	0.02 M
Additional solutes	0.02 M
Total solute concentration	0.28 M

Intercellular Fluid	
Solute Identity	**Solute Concentration**
K^+ ion	0.12 M
Proteins	0.07 M
HPO_4^{2-} ion	0.04 M
$H_2PO_4^-$ ion	0.03 M
Additional solutes	0.02 M
Total solute concentration	0.28 M

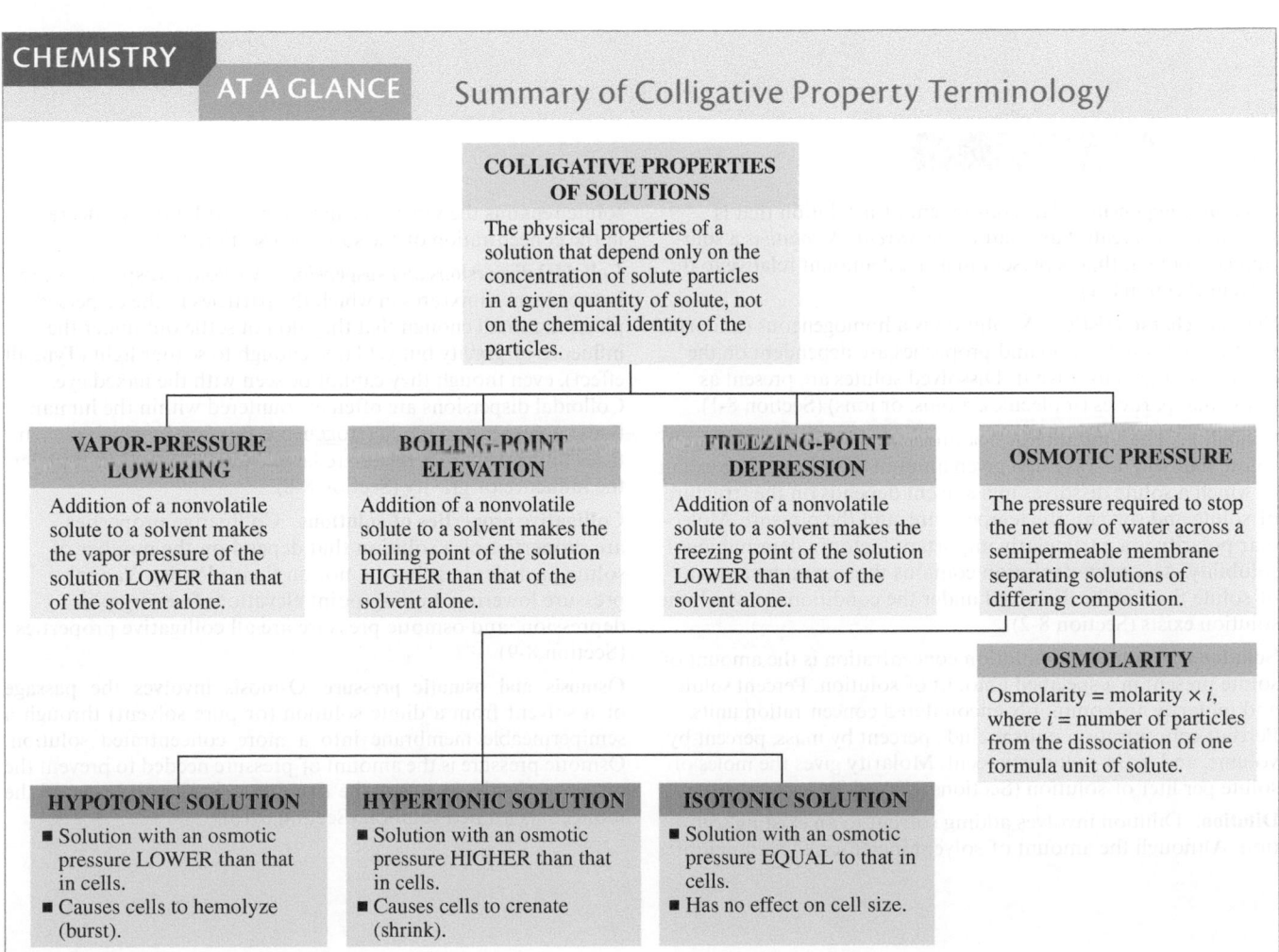

CHEMISTRY AT A GLANCE Summary of Colligative Property Terminology

COLLIGATIVE PROPERTIES OF SOLUTIONS

The physical properties of a solution that depend only on the concentration of solute particles in a given quantity of solute, not on the chemical identity of the particles.

VAPOR-PRESSURE LOWERING

Addition of a nonvolatile solute to a solvent makes the vapor pressure of the solution LOWER than that of the solvent alone.

BOILING-POINT ELEVATION

Addition of a nonvolatile solute to a solvent makes the boiling point of the solution HIGHER than that of the solvent alone.

FREEZING-POINT DEPRESSION

Addition of a nonvolatile solute to a solvent makes the freezing point of the solution LOWER than that of the solvent alone.

OSMOTIC PRESSURE

The pressure required to stop the net flow of water across a semipermeable membrane separating solutions of differing composition.

OSMOLARITY

Osmolarity = molarity × i, where i = number of particles from the dissociation of one formula unit of solute.

HYPOTONIC SOLUTION

■ Solution with an osmotic pressure LOWER than that in cells.
■ Causes cells to hemolyze (burst).

HYPERTONIC SOLUTION

■ Solution with an osmotic pressure HIGHER than that in cells.
■ Causes cells to crenate (shrink).

ISOTONIC SOLUTION

■ Solution with an osmotic pressure EQUAL to that in cells.
■ Has no effect on cell size.

Section 8-10 Quick Quiz

1. In the process of osmosis, solvent passes through a semipermeable membrane
   a. from a dilute solution to a more concentrated solution
   b. from a concentrated solution to a more dilute solution
   c. in only one direction
   d. no correct response
2. The osmolarity of a 0.40 molar NaCl solution is
   a. 0.20
   b. 0.40
   c. 0.80
   d. no correct response
3. When red blood cells are placed in a hypotonic solution
   a. hemolysis occurs
   b. crenation occurs
   c. cells shrink in size
   d. no correct response
4. Which of the following solutions is hypertonic with respect to red blood cells?
   a. 2.0%(m/v) glucose
   b. 4.0%(m/v) glucose
   c. 6.0%(m/v) glucose
   d. no correct response
5. Which of the following solutions is isotonic with respect to red blood cells?
   a. 0.20 M lactose
   b. 0.28 M lactose
   c. 0.35 M lactose
   d. no correct response

Answers: 1. a; 2. c; 3. a; 4. c; 5. b

Concepts to Remember

Solution components. The component of a solution that is present in the greatest amount is the *solvent*. A *solute* is a solution component that is present in a small amount relative to the solvent (Section 8-1).

Solution characteristics. A solution is a homogeneous (uniform) mixture. Its composition and properties are dependent on the ratio of solute(s) to solvent. Dissolved solutes are present as individual particles (molecules, atoms, or ions) (Section 8-1).

Solubility. The solubility of a solute is the maximum amount of solute that will dissolve in a given amount of solvent. The extent to which a solute dissolves in a solvent depends on the structure of solute and solvent, the temperature, and the pressure. Molecular polarity is a particularly important factor in determining solubility. A *saturated* solution contains the maximum amount of solute that can be dissolved under the conditions at which the solution exists (Section 8-2).

Solution concentration. Solution concentration is the amount of solute present in a specified amount of solution. Percent solute and molarity are commonly encountered concentration units. Percent concentration units include percent by mass, percent by volume, and mass–volume percent. Molarity gives the moles of solute per liter of solution (Sections 8-5 and 8-6).

Dilution. Dilution involves adding solvent to an existing solution. Although the amount of solvent increases, the amount of solute remains the same. The net effect of dilution is a decrease in the concentration of the solution (Section 8-7).

Colloidal dispersions and suspensions. Colloidal dispersions are homogeneous mixtures in which the particles in the dispersed phase are small enough that they do not settle out under the influence of gravity but yet large enough to scatter light (Tyndall effect), even though they cannot be seen with the naked eye. Colloidal dispersions are often encountered within the human body. A suspension is a heterogeneous mixture in which the particles in the dispersed phase are large enough to settle out under the influence of gravity (Section 8-8).

Colligative properties of solutions. Colligative properties are properties of a solution that depend on the number of solute particles in solution, not on their identity. Vapor-pressure lowering, boiling-point elevation, freezing-point depression, and osmotic pressure are all colligative properties (Section 8-9).

Osmosis and osmotic pressure. Osmosis involves the passage of a solvent from a dilute solution (or pure solvent) through a semipermeable membrane into a more concentrated solution. Osmotic pressure is the amount of pressure needed to prevent the net flow of solvent across the membrane in the direction of the more concentrated solution (Section 8-10).

Exercises and Problems

Exercises and problems are arranged in matched pairs with the two members of a pair addressing the same concept(s). The answer to the odd-numbered member of a pair is given at the back of the book. Problems denoted with a ▲ involve concepts found not only in the section under consideration but also concepts found in one or more earlier sections of the chapter.

Characteristics of Solutions (Section 8-1)

8-1 Indicate whether each of the following statements about the general properties of solutions is true or false.
a. A solution may contain more than one solute.
b. All solutions are homogeneous mixtures.
c. Every part of a solution has exactly the same properties as every other part.
d. The solutes present in a solution will "settle out" with time if the solution is left undisturbed.

8-2 Indicate whether each of the following statements about the general properties of solutions is true or false.
a. All solutions have a variable composition.
b. For solution formation to occur, the solute and solvent must chemically react with each other.
c. Solutes are present as individual particles (molecules, atoms, or ions) in a solution.
d. A general characteristic of all solutions is the liquid state.

8-3 Identify the *solute* and the *solvent* in solutions composed of the following:
a. 5.00 g of sodium chloride (table salt) and 50.0 g of water
b. 4.00 g of sucrose (table sugar) and 1000 g of water
c. 2.00 mL of water and 20.0 mL of ethyl alcohol
d. 60.0 mL of methyl alcohol and 20.0 mL of ethyl alcohol

8-4 Identify the *solute* and the *solvent* in solutions composed of the following:
a. 5.00 g of NaBr and 200.0 g of water
b. 50.0 g of $AgNO_3$ and 1000 g of water
c. 50.0 mL of water and 100.0 mL of methyl alcohol
d. 50.0 mL of isopropyl alcohol and 20.0 mL of ethyl alcohol

Solubility (Section 8-2)

8-5 For each of the following pairs of solutions, select the solution for which solute solubility is greatest.
a. Ammonia gas in water with P = 1 atm and T = 50°C
   Ammonia gas in water with P = 1 atm and T = 90°C
b. Carbon dioxide gas in water with P = 2 atm and T = 50°C
   Carbon dioxide gas in water with P = 1 atm and T = 50°C
c. Table salt in water with P = 1 atm and T = 60°C
   Table salt in water with P = 1 atm and T = 50°C
d. Table sugar in water with P = 2 atm and T = 40°C
   Table sugar in water with P = 1 atm and T = 70°C

8-6 For each of the following pairs of solutions, select the solution for which solute solubility is greatest.
a. Oxygen gas in water with P = 1 atm and T = 10°C
   Oxygen gas in water with P = 1 atm and T = 20°C

b. Nitrogen gas in water with P = 2 atm and T = 50°C
   Nitrogen gas in water with P = 1 atm and T = 70°C
c. Table salt in water with P = 1 atm and T = 40°C
   Table salt in water with P = 1 atm and T = 70°C
d. Table sugar in water with P = 3 atm and T = 30°C
   Table sugar in water with P = 1 atm and T = 80°C

8-7 Classify each of the following solutions as *saturated, unsaturated,* or *supersaturated* based on the following observations.
a. Agitation of the solution produces a large amount of solid crystals.
b. Heating the solution causes excess undissolved solute present to dissolve.
c. Excess undissolved solute is present at the bottom of the solution container.
d. The amount of solute dissolved is less than the maximum amount that could dissolve under the conditions at which the solution exists.

8-8 Classify each of the following solutions as *saturated, unsaturated,* or *supersaturated* based on the following observations made after adding a small piece of solid solute to the solution.
a. The added solute rapidly dissolves.
b. The added solute falls to the bottom of the container where it remains without any decrease in size.
c. The added solute falls to the bottom of the container where it decreases in size for several hours and thereafter its size remains constant.
d. The added solute causes the production of a large amount of solid white crystals.

8-9 A solution is made by dissolving 34.0 g of NaCl in 100 g of H_2O at 0°C. Based on the data in Table 8-1, should this solution be characterized as
a. saturated or unsaturated
b. dilute or concentrated

8-10 A solution is made by dissolving 0.455 g of $PbBr_2$ in 100 g of H_2O at 50°C. Based on the data in Table 8-1, should this solution be characterized as
a. saturated or unsaturated
b. dilute or concentrated

8-11 A compound has a solubility in water of 35 g/L at 0°C. If 25 g of this compound is added to 0.5 L of water at 0°C, is the resulting solution saturated or unsaturated?

8-12 A compound has a solubility in water of 40 g/L at 0°C. If 62 g of this compound is added to 1.5 L of water at 0°C, is the resulting solution saturated or unsaturated?

Solution Formation (Section 8-3)

8-13 Match each of the following statements about the dissolving of the ionic solid NaCl in water with the term *hydrated ion, hydrogen atom,* or *oxygen atom.*
a. A Na^+ ion surrounded with water molecules
b. A Cl^- ion surrounded with water molecules
c. The portion of a water molecule that is attracted to a Na^+ ion
d. The portion of a water molecule that is attracted to a Cl^- ion

8-14   Match each of the following statements about the dissolving of the ionic solid KBr in water with the term *hydrated ion, hydrogen atom,* or *oxygen atom.*
a. A K^+ ion surrounded with water molecules
b. A Br^- ion surrounded with water molecules
c. The portion of a water molecule that is attracted to a K^+ ion
d. The portion of a water molecule that is attracted to a Br^- ion

8-15   Indicate whether each of the following actions will *increase* or *decrease* the rate of dissolving of a sugar cube in water.
a. Cooling the sugar cube–water mixture
b. Stirring the sugar cube–water mixture
c. Breaking the sugar cube up into smaller "chunks"
d. Crushing the sugar cube to give a granulated form of sugar

8-16   Indicate whether each of the following actions will *increase* or *decrease* the rate of dissolving of table salt in water.
a. Heating the table salt–water mixture
b. Shaking the table salt–water mixture
c. Heating the table salt prior to adding it to the water
d. Heating the water prior to its receiving the table salt

Solubility Rules (Section 8-4)

8-17   Predict whether the following solutes are *very soluble* or *slightly soluble* in water.
a. O_2 (a nonpolar gas)
b. CH_3OH (a polar liquid)
c. CBr_4 (a nonpolar liquid)
d. AgCl (an ionic solid)

8-18   Predict whether the following solutes are *very soluble* or *slightly soluble* in water.
a. NH_3 (a polar gas)
b. N_2 (a nonpolar gas)
c. C_6H_6 (a nonpolar liquid)
d. Na_3PO_4 (an ionic solid)

8-19   Ethanol is a polar solvent and carbon tetrachloride is a nonpolar solvent. In which of these two solvents are each of the following solutes more likely to be soluble?
a. NaCl, ionic   b. Cooking oil, nonpolar
c. Sugar, polar   d. $LiNO_3$, ionic

8-20   Methanol is a polar solvent and heptane is a nonpolar solvent. In which of these two solvents are each of the following solutes more likely to be soluble?
a. KCl, ionic   b. Rubbing alcohol, polar
c. Gasoline, nonpolar   d. $NaNO_3$, ionic

8-21   Using Table 8-2, classify each of the following types of ionic compounds using the solubility categories *soluble, soluble with exceptions, insoluble,* or *insoluble with exceptions.*
a. chlorides   b. nitrates
c. carbonates   d. phosphates

8-22   Using Table 8-2, classify each of the following types of ionic compounds using the solubility categories *soluble, soluble with exceptions, insoluble,* or *insoluble with exceptions.*
a. bromides   b. sulfates
c. hydroxides   d. sulfides

8-23   Using Table 8-2, indicate whether each of the following ionic compounds is soluble or insoluble in water.
a. calcium nitrate   b. sodium phosphate
c. silver chloride   d. ammonium phosphate

8-24   Using Table 8-2, indicate whether each of the following ionic compounds is soluble or insoluble in water.
a. sodium sulfate   b. ammonium chloride
c. barium phosphate   d. zinc nitrate

8-25   Using Table 8-2, indicate whether each of the following ionic compounds is soluble or insoluble in water.
a. $CuSO_4$ b. $Cu(OH)_2$
c. $Cu(NO_3)_2$ d. $CuCl_2$

8-26   Using Table 8-2, indicate whether each of the following ionic compounds is soluble or insoluble in water.
a. $FeSO_4$ b. $FeCO_3$
c. $Fe(NO_3)_2$ d. $FeCl_2$

8-27   Indicate whether or not the two members of each of the following pairs of compounds have like solubility (both soluble or both insoluble).
a. NH_4Cl and NH_4Br b. KNO_3 and K_2SO_4
c. $CaCO_3$ and $Ca_3(PO_4)_2$ d. $Ni(OH)_2$ and $Ni_3(PO_4)_2$

8-28   Indicate whether or not the two members of each of the following pairs of compounds have like solubility (both soluble or both insoluble).
a. $NaNO_3$ and Na_3PO_4 b. $CuBr_2$ and CuI_2
c. $Pb(NO_3)_2$ and $PbCl_2$ d. $FeCO_3$ and FeS

8-29   A compound has a solubility in water of 250 mg/L at 25°C. Should this compound be characterized as a soluble or insoluble compound at 25°C?

8-30   A compound has a solubility in water of 750 mg/L at 25°C. Should this compound be characterized as a soluble or insoluble compound at 25°C?

Percent Concentration Units (Section 8-5)

8-31   The following diagrams show varying amounts of the same solute (the red spheres) in varying amounts of solution.

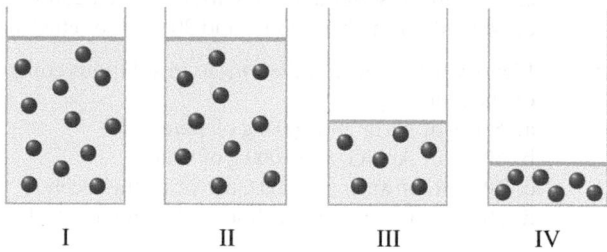

I   II   III   IV

a. In which of the diagrams is the solution concentration the largest?
b. In which two of the diagrams are the solution concentrations the same?

8-32   The following diagrams show varying amounts of the same solute (the red spheres) in varying amounts of solution.

I   II   III   IV

a. In which of the diagrams is the solution concentration the largest?
b. In which two of the diagrams are the solution concentrations the same?

8-33 Calculate the mass percent of solute in the following solutions.
a. 6.50 g of NaCl dissolved in 85.0 g of H_2O
b. 2.31 g of LiBr dissolved in 35.0 g of H_2O
c. 12.5 g of KNO_3 dissolved in 125 g of H_2O
d. 0.0032 g of NaOH dissolved in 1.2 g of H_2O

8-34 Calculate the mass percent of solute in the following solutions.
a. 2.13 g of $AgNO_3$ dissolved in 30.0 g of H_2O
b. 135 g of CsCl dissolved in 455 g of H_2O
c. 10.3 g of K_2SO_4 dissolved in 93.7 g of H_2O
d. 10.3 g of KBr dissolved in 125 g of H_2O

8-35 For each of the following aqueous NaCl solutions, the mass of solute and the mass of solvent present are given. Calculate the mass percent of NaCl present in each solution.
a. 10.0 g NaCl, 40.0 g H_2O
b. 5.00 g NaCl, 355 g H_2O
c. 20.0 g NaCl, 565.0 g H_2O
d. 520.0 mg NaCl, 2.00 g H_2O

8-36 For each of the following aqueous NaCl solutions, the mass of solute and the mass of solvent present are given. Calculate the mass percent of NaCl present in each solution.
a. 15.0 g NaCl, 27.0 g H_2O
b. 8.00 g NaCl, 433 g H_2O
c. 25.0 g NaCl, 137.0 g H_2O
d. 729 mg NaCl, 3.00 g H_2O

8-37 How many grams of glucose must be added to 275 g of water in order to prepare each of the following percent-by-mass concentrations of aqueous glucose solution?
a. 1.30%   b. 5.00%   c. 20.0%   d. 31.0%

8-38 How many grams of lactose must be added to 655 g of water in order to prepare each of the following percent-by-mass concentrations of aqueous lactose solution?
a. 0.50%   b. 2.00%   c. 10.0%   d. 25.0%

8-39 Calculate the mass, in grams, of K_2SO_4 needed to prepare 32.00 g of 2.000%(m/m) K_2SO_4 solution.

8-40 Calculate the mass, in grams, of KCl needed to prepare 200.0 g of 5.000%(m/m) KCl solution.

8-41 The concentration of bilirubin in a blood sample is found to be 0.55 mg/dL. Express this concentration in the following units:
a. mg/100 mL   b. g/100 mL
c. g/L   d. mass–volume percent

8-42 The concentration of cholesterol in a blood sample is found to be 203 mg/dL. Express this concentration in the following units:
a. mg/100 mL   b. g/100 mL
c. g/L   d. mass–volume percent

8-43 Calculate the volume percent of solute in each of the following solutions.
a. 20.0 mL of methyl alcohol in enough water to give 475 mL of solution
b. 4.00 mL of bromine in enough carbon tetrachloride to give 87.0 mL of solution

8-44 Calculate the volume percent of solute in each of the following solutions.
a. 60.0 mL of water in enough ethylene glycol to give 970.0 mL of solution
b. 455 mL of ethyl alcohol in enough water to give 1375 mL of solution

8-45 What is the percent by volume of isopropyl alcohol in an aqueous solution made by diluting 22 mL of pure isopropyl alcohol with water to give a volume of 125 mL of solution?

8-46 What is the percent by volume of acetone in an aqueous solution made by diluting 75 mL of pure acetone with water to give a volume of 785 mL of solution?

8-47 Calculate the mass–volume percent of $MgCl_2$ in each of the following solutions.
a. 5.0 g of $MgCl_2$ in enough water to give 250 mL of solution
b. 85 g of $MgCl_2$ in enough water to give 580 mL of solution

8-48 Calculate the mass–volume percent of $NaNO_3$ in each of the following solutions.
a. 1.00 g of $NaNO_3$ in enough water to give 75.0 mL of solution
b. 100.0 g of $NaNO_3$ in enough water to give 1250 mL of solution

8-49 How many grams of Na_2CO_3 are needed to prepare 25.0 mL of a 2.00%(m/v) Na_2CO_3 solution?

8-50 How many grams of $Na_2S_2O_3$ are needed to prepare 50.0 mL of a 5.00%(m/v) $Na_2S_2O_3$ solution?

8-51 How many grams of NaCl are present in 50.0 mL of a 7.50%(m/v) NaCl solution?

8-52 How many grams of glucose are present in 250.0 mL of a 10.0%(m/v) glucose solution?

Molarity Concentration Unit (Section 8-6)

8-53 For each of the following HCl solutions, the moles or grams of solute present and the total solution volume are given. Calculate the molarity of each solution.
a. 1.40 moles HCl, 1.45 L solution
b. 0.850 mole HCl, 0.867 L solution
c. 30.0 g HCl, 1.45 L solution
d. 30.0 g HCl, 875 mL solution

8-54 For each of the following KOH solutions, the moles or grams of solute present and the total solution volume are given. Calculate the molarity of each solution.
a. 1.20 moles KOH, 1.65 L solution
b. 0.650 mole KOH, 0.777 L solution
c. 10.0 g KOH, 1.15 L solution
d. 10.0 g KOH, 925 mL solution

8-55 For each of the following NaOH solutions, the volume of the solution and its molarity are given. Calculate the number of moles of NaOH present in each solution.
a. 1.35 L solution, 0.300 M
b. 0.800 L solution, 0.100 M
c. 875 mL solution, 0.600 M
d. 125 mL solution, 0.125 M

8-56 For each of the following HNO_3 solutions, the volume of the solution and its molarity are given. Calculate the number of moles of HNO_3 present in each solution.
a. 2.35 L solution, 0.500 M
b. 0.500 L solution, 0.200 M
c. 750 mL solution, 1.200 M
d. 225 mL solution, 0.225 M

8-57 Calculate the number of grams of NaOH needed to prepare each of the following amounts of solution.
a. 1.00 L of 1.00 M NaOH
b. 2.00 L of 2.00 M NaOH
c. 0.100 L of 0.50 M NaOH
d. 552 mL of 0.333 M NaOH

8-58 Calculate the number of grams of LiOH needed to prepare each of the following amounts of solution.
a. 1.00 L of 1.00 M LiOH
b. 2.00 L of 2.00 M LiOH
c. 0.100 L of 0.50 M LiOH
d. 552 mL of 0.333 M LiOH

8-59 How many liters of a 0.100 M solution can be prepared from 60.0 g of each of the following solutes?
a. $NaNO_3$ b. HNO_3
c. KOH   d. LiCl

8-60 How many liters of a 0.200 M solution can be prepared from 1.00 g of each of the following solutes?
a. Na_2SO_4 b. NaOH
c. NaCl   d. NH_3

▲**8-61** Calculate the molarity of a 10.0%(m/v) NaOH solution.

▲**8-62** Calculate the mass–volume percent concentration for a 6.0 M NaOH solution.

▲**8-63** After all of the water is evaporated from 10.0 mL of a CsCl solution, 3.75 g of solid CsCl remains. Calculate the original concentration of the CsCl solution in the following units.
a. mass–volume percent   b. molarity

▲**8-64** After all of the water is evaporated from 25.0 mL of a NaCl solution, 2.00 g of solid NaCl remains. Calculate the original concentration of the NaCl solution in the following units.
a. mass–volume percent   b. molarity

Dilution (Section 8-7)

8-65 What is the molarity of the solution prepared by diluting 25.0 mL of 0.220 M NaCl to each of the following final volumes?
a. 30.0 mL   b. 75.0 mL
c. 457 mL   d. 2.00 L

8-66 What is the molarity of the solution prepared by diluting 35.0 mL of 1.25 M $AgNO_3$ to each of the following final volumes?
a. 50.0 mL   b. 95.0 mL
c. 975 mL   d. 3.60 L

8-67 For each of the following solutions, how many milliliters of water should be added to yield a solution that has a concentration of 0.100 M?
a. 50.0 mL of 3.00 M NaCl
b. 2.00 mL of 1.00 M NaCl
c. 1.45 L of 6.00 M NaCl
d. 75.0 mL of 0.110 M NaCl

8-68 For each of the following solutions, how many milliliters of water should be added to yield a solution that has a concentration of 0.125 M?
a. 25.0 mL of 1.00 M $AgNO_3$
b. 5.00 mL of 10.0 M $AgNO_3$
c. 2.50 L of 2.50 M $AgNO_3$
d. 75.0 mL of 0.130 M $AgNO_3$

8-69 Determine the final concentration of each of the following solutions after 20.0 mL of water has been added.
a. 30.0 mL of 5.0 M NaCl solution
b. 30.0 mL of 5.0 M $AgNO_3$ solution

c. 30.0 mL of 7.5 M NaCl solution
d. 60.0 mL of 2.0 M NaCl solution

8-70 Determine the final concentration of each of the following solutions after 30.0 mL of water has been added.
a. 20.0 mL of 5.0 M NaCl solution
b. 20.0 mL of 5.0 M $AgNO_3$ solution
c. 20.0 mL of 0.50 M NaCl solution
d. 60.0 mL of 3.0 M NaCl solution

8-71 The following diagrams show various amounts of the same solute (the red spheres) in varying amounts of solution. If one-half of the solution in diagram I is withdrawn and then diluted by a factor of 4, which of the other diagrams (II–IV) represent the newly formed solution?

I   II   III   IV

8-72 The following diagrams show various amounts of the same solute (the red spheres) in varying amounts of solution. If one-half of the solution in diagram I is withdrawn and then diluted by a factor of 2, which of the other diagrams (II–IV) represent the newly formed solution?

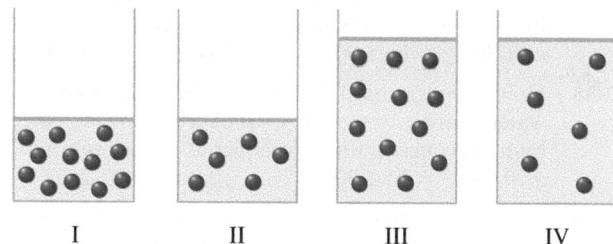

I   II   III   IV

8-73 What is the molarity of the solution prepared by concentrating, by evaporation of solvent, 2212 mL of 0.400 M K_2SO_4 solution to a volume of 853 mL?

8-74 What is the molarity of the solution prepared by concentrating, by evaporation of solvent, 755 mL of 0.200%(m/v) $NaNO_3$ to a volume of 715 mL?

▲**8-75** A solution of hydrogen peroxide (H_2O_2) in water with a volume of 70.0 mL is diluted by adding 50.0 mL of water. Calculate the solution's new concentration given the following original concentrations. (Addition of 50.0 mL of water is equivalent to adding 50.0 g of water since the density of water is 1.00 g/mL.)
a. 2.0%(m/v)   b. 2.0%(v/v)
c. 2.0%(m/m)   d. 2.0 M

▲**8-76** A solution of hydrogen peroxide (H_2O_2) in water with a volume of 50.0 mL is diluted by adding 70.0 mL of water. Calculate the solution's new concentration given the following original concentrations. (Addition of 70.0 mL of water is equivalent to adding 70.0 g of water since the density of water is 1.00 g/mL.)
a. 2.0%(m/v)   b. 2.0%(v/v)
c. 2.0%(m/m)   d. 2.0 M

Colloidal Dispersions and Suspensions (Section 8-8)

8-77 Indicate whether each of the following characterizations applies to a *true solution*, a *colloidal dispersion*, or a *suspension*. There may be more than one correct answer for a given characterization.
a. Dispersed phase can be trapped by filter paper.
b. Dispersed phase can often be seen with the naked eye.
c. Appearance is that of a homogeneous mixture.
d. Dispersed phase is transparent to light.

8-78 Indicate whether each of the following characterizations applies to a *true solution*, a *colloidal dispersion*, or a *suspension*. There may be more than one correct answer for a given characterization.
a. Dispersed phase cannot be trapped by filter paper.
b. Dispersed phase rapidly settles out under the influence of gravity.
c. Dispersed phase scatters light.
d. Dispersed phase contains very large particles.

8-79 Indicate whether each of the following statements about colloidal dispersions and suspensions is *true* or *false*.
a. The dispersed particles in a colloidal dispersion can be seen with the naked eye.
b. With time, the particles in a colloidal dispersion settle out under the influence of gravity.
c. Milk is an example of a suspension.
d. The dispersed phase in a suspension can be trapped by filter paper.

8-80 Indicate whether each of the following statements about colloidal dispersions and suspensions is *true* or *false*.
a. Blood is an example of a colloidal dispersion.
b. The dispersed particles in a colloidal dispersion are several times larger than those in a suspension.
c. A beam of light is scattered by the dispersed phase in a colloidal dispersion.
d. With time, the particles in a suspension settle out under the influence of gravity.

Colligative Properties of Solutions (Section 8-9)

8-81 Why is the vapor pressure of a solution that contains a nonvolatile solute always less than that of pure solvent?

8-82 How are the boiling point and freezing point of water affected by the addition of solute?

8-83 Why does seawater evaporate more slowly than fresh water at the same temperature?

8-84 How does the freezing point of seawater compare with that of fresh water?

8-85 Assume that you have identical volumes of two liquids; the first is pure water and the second is 0.1 M sucrose (table sugar) solution. Consider the following diagrams, where red is the pure water and blue is the sucrose solution.

I   II   III

Which one of these diagrams best represents the two liquids after they have stood uncovered for a few days and some evaporation of liquid has occurred?

8-86 Assume that you have identical volumes of two liquids; the first is 0.3 M glucose solution and the second is 0.1 M glucose solution. Based on the diagrams in Problem 8-85, where red is the 0.3 M glucose and blue is the 0.1 M glucose, which one of the diagrams best represents the two liquids after they have stood uncovered for a few days and some evaporation of liquid has occurred?

8-87 What is the boiling point of a solution that contains 1.00 kg of water and each of the following quantities of solute?
a. 3.00 moles of glucose (a molecular compound)
b. 3.00 moles of lactose (a molecular compound)
c. 3.00 moles of NaCl (an ionic compound)
d. 3.00 moles of Na_3PO_4 (an ionic compound)

8-88 What is the boiling point of a solution that contains 1.00 kg of water and each of the following quantities of solute?
a. 2.00 moles of sucrose (a molecular compound)
b. 2.00 moles of fructose (a molecular compound)
c. 2.00 moles of Na_2SO_4 (an ionic compound)
d. 2.00 moles of KCl (an ionic compound)

8-89 What is the freezing point of each of the solutions in Problem 8-87?

8-90 What is the freezing point of each of the solutions in Problem 8-88?

8-91 Which member of each of the following pairs of compounds has the higher boiling point?
a. 1.0 M glucose or 1.0 M NaCl
b. 1.0 M NaCl or 1.0 M Na_2SO_4
c. 1.0 M KBr or 2.0 M KBr
d. 2.0 M glucose or 1.0 M Na_2SO_4

8-92 Which member of each of the following pairs of compounds has the lower freezing point?
a. 3.0 M glucose or 1.0 M NaCl
b. 4.0 M NaCl or 1.0 M Na_2SO_4
c. 1.0 M $CaCl_2$ or 2.0 M $CaCl_2$
d. 2.0 M glucose or 0.50 M Na_2SO_4

8-93 What would be the freezing point of a solution formed by adding 1.0 mole of glucose (a molecular compound) to the following amounts of water?
a. 250 g (0.25 kg)
b. 500 g (0.500 kg)
c. 1000 g (1.000 kg)
d. 2000 g (2.000 kg)

8-94 What would be the boiling point of a solution formed by adding 1.0 mole of sucrose (a molecular compound) to the following amounts of water?
a. 250 g (0.25 kg)
b. 500 g (0.500 kg)
c. 1000 g (1.000 kg)
d. 2000 g (2.000 kg)

Osmosis and Osmotic Pressure (Section 8-10)

8-95 Indicate whether the osmotic pressure of a 0.1 M NaCl solution will be *less than, the same as,* or *greater than* that of each of the following solutions.
a. 0.1 M NaBr   b. 0.050 M $MgCl_2$
c. 0.1 M $MgCl_2$ d. 0.1 M glucose

8-96 Indicate whether the osmotic pressure of a 0.1 M $NaNO_3$ solution will be *less than, the same as,* or *greater than* that of each of the following solutions.

a. 0.1 M NaCl   b. 0.1 M KNO₃
c. 0.1 M Na₂SO₄   d. 0.1 M glucose

8-97 What is the ratio of the osmotic pressures of 0.30 M NaCl and 0.10 M CaCl₂?

8-98 What is the ratio of the osmotic pressures of 0.20 M NaCl and 0.30 M CaCl₂?

8-99 What is the osmolarity of each of the following solutions?
  a. 2.0 M KNO₃
  b. 2.0 M Na₂SO₄
  c. 2.0 M in both KNO₃ and NaCl
  d. 2.0 M in both KNO₃ and glucose

8-100 What is the osmolarity of each of the following solutions?
  a. 1.0 M KNO₃
  b. 1.0 M K₂SO₄
  c. 1.0 M in both KNO₃ and Na₂SO₄
  d. 1.0 M in both KNO₃ and glucose

8-101 Classify each of the following solutions as *hypotonic, isotonic,* or *hypertonic* relative to red blood cells?
  a. 0.92%(m/v) glucose solution
  b. 0.92%(m/v) NaCl solution
  c. 2.3%(m/v) glucose solution
  d. 5.0%(m/v) NaCl solution

8-102 Classify each of the following solutions as *hypotonic, isotonic,* or *hypertonic* relative to red blood cells?
  a. 0.80%(m/v) NaCl solution
  b. 1.20%(m/v) NaCl solution
  c. 5.0%(m/v) glucose solution
  d. 6.0%(m/v) glucose solution

8-103 Will red blood cells *swell, remain the same size,* or *shrink* when placed in each of the solutions in Problem 8-101?

8-104 Will red blood cells *swell, remain the same size,* or *shrink* when placed in each of the solutions in Problem 8-102?

8-105 Will red blood cells *crenate, hemolyze,* or *remain unaffected* when placed in each of the solutions in Problem 8-101?

8-106 Will red blood cells *crenate, hemolyze,* or *remain unaffected* when placed in each of the solutions in Problem 8-102?

8-107 Classify each of the following solutions as *hypotonic, isotonic,* or *hypertonic* relative to red blood cells?
  a. 0.28 M glucose
  b. 0.28 M in both glucose and sucrose
  c. 0.14 M in both glucose and sucrose
  d. 0.28 M NaCl

8-108 Classify each of the following solutions as *hypotonic, isotonic,* or *hypertonic* relative to red blood cells?
  a. 0.28 M lactose
  b. 0.28 M in both lactose and sucrose
  c. 0.14 M in both lactose and sucrose
  d. 0.28 M KCl

8-109 Will red blood cells *swell, remain the same size,* or *shrink* when placed in each of the solutions in Problem 8-107?

8-110 Will red blood cells *swell, remain the same size,* or *shrink* when placed in each of the solutions in Problem 8-108?

8-111 Will red blood cells *crenate, hemolyze,* or *remain unaffected* when placed in each of the solutions in Problem 8-107?

8-112 Will red blood cells *crenate, hemolyze,* or *remain unaffected* when placed in each of the solutions in Problem 8-108?

8-113 Consider two solutions, A and B, separated by an osmotic semipermeable membrane that allows only water to pass through, as shown in the following diagram.

Osmotic
membrane

Based on each of the following identities for solutions A and B, indicate whether the liquid level in compartment A, with time, will *increase, decrease,* or *not change.*
  a. A = 1.0 M NaCl solution and B = 2.0 M NaCl solution
  b. A = 5.0%(m/v) glucose solution and B = 4.0%(m/v) glucose solution
  c. A = 2.0 M KCl solution and B = 2.0 M KNO₃ solution
  d. A = 1.0 M glucose solution and B = 1.0 M NaCl solution

8-114 Consider two solutions, A and B, separated by an osmotic semipermeable membrane that allows only water to pass through, as shown in the diagram in Problem 8-113. Based on each of the following identities for solutions A and B, indicate whether the liquid level in compartment A, with time, will *increase, decrease,* or *not change.*
  a. A = 1.0 M glucose solution and B = 2.0 M glucose solution
  b. A = 5.0%(m/v) NaCl solution and B = 4.0%(m/v) NaCl solution
  c. A = 2.0 M Na₂SO₄ solution and B = 3.0 M KNO₃ solution
  d. A = 2.0 M glucose solution and B = 1.0 M NaCl solution

▲**8-115** At a given temperature, which of the two aqueous solutions 1.0 M glucose or 1.0 M NaCl has the higher
  a. vapor pressure   b. boiling point
  c. freezing point   d. osmotic pressure

▲**8-116** At a given temperature, which of the two aqueous solutions 1.0 M Na₂SO₄ or 1.0 M NaCl has the lower
  a. vapor pressure   b. boiling point
  c. freezing point   d. osmotic pressure

▲**8-117** Which of the following aqueous solutions would give rise to a greater osmotic pressure?
  a. 8.00 g of NaCl in 375 mL of solution or 4.00 g of NaBr in 155 mL of solution
  b. 7.00 g of NaCl in 775 mL of solution or 6.00 g of NaBr in 275 mL of solution

▲**8-118** Which of the following aqueous solutions would give rise to a greater osmotic pressure?
  a. 18.00 g of KCl in 375 mL of solution or 9.00 g of KF in 155 mL of solution
  b. 7.00 g of KCl in 625 mL of solution or 7.00 g of KF in 525 mL of solution

Chemical Reactions

A fireworks display involves numerous different chemical reactions occurring at the same time.

I n the previous two chapters, the properties of matter in various pure and mixed (solution) states were considered. Nearly all of the subject matter dealt with interactions and changes of a *physical* nature. In this chapter, the *chemical* changes that occur when various types of matter interact are considered.

First, five general types of chemical reactions are considered, and then important fundamentals common to all chemical changes are discussed. Of particular concern will be how fast chemical change occurs (chemical reaction rates) and the extent to which chemical change occurs (chemical equilibrium).

9-1 Types of Chemical Reactions

LEARNING FOCUS

Know the defining characteristic for a chemical reaction; be able to recognize the following chemical reaction types: combination, decomposition, displacement, exchange, and combustion.

A **chemical reaction** *is a process in which at least one new substance is produced as a result of chemical change.* An almost inconceivable number of chemical reactions are possible. The majority of chemical reactions (but not all) fall into five major categories: *combination* reactions, *decomposition* reactions, *displacement* reactions, *exchange* reactions, and *combustion* reactions.

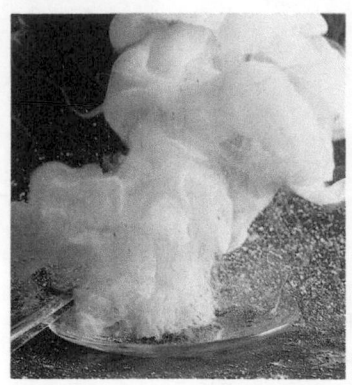

Figure 9-1 When a hot nail is stuck into a pile of zinc and sulfur, a fiery combination reaction occurs and zinc sulfide forms.

$$Zn + S \longrightarrow ZnS$$

▶ *In organic chemistry (Chapters 12–17), combination reactions are often called* addition reactions. *One reactant, usually a small molecule, is considered to be added to a larger reactant molecule to produce a single product.*

Combination Reactions

A **combination reaction** *is a chemical reaction in which a single product is produced from two (or more) reactants.* The general equation for a combination reaction involving two reactants is

$$X + Y \longrightarrow XY$$

In such a combination reaction, two substances join together to form a more complicated product (Figure 9-1). The reactants X and Y can be elements or compounds or an element and a compound. ◀ The product of the reaction (XY) is always a compound. Some representative combination reactions that have elements as the reactants are

$$Ca + S \longrightarrow CaS$$
$$N_2 + 3H_2 \longrightarrow 2NH_3$$
$$2Na + O_2 \longrightarrow Na_2O_2$$

Some examples of combination reactions in which compounds are involved as reactants are

$$SO_3 + H_2O \longrightarrow H_2SO_4$$
$$2NO + O_2 \longrightarrow 2NO_2$$
$$2NO_2 + H_2O_2 \longrightarrow 2HNO_3$$

Decomposition Reactions

A **decomposition reaction** *is a chemical reaction in which a single reactant is converted into two (or more) simpler substances (elements or compounds).* Thus a decomposition reaction is the opposite of a combination reaction. The general equation for a decomposition reaction in which there are two products is

$$XY \longrightarrow X + Y$$

Although the products may be elements or compounds, the reactant is *always* a compound.

At sufficiently high temperatures, all compounds can be broken down (decomposed) into their constituent elements. Examples of such reactions include

$$2CuO \longrightarrow 2Cu + O_2$$
$$2H_2O \longrightarrow 2H_2 + O_2$$

At lower temperatures, compound decomposition often produces other compounds as products.

$$CaCO_3 \longrightarrow CaO + CO_2$$
$$2KClO_3 \longrightarrow 2KCl + 3O_2$$
$$4HNO_3 \longrightarrow 4NO_2 + 2H_2O + O_2$$

Decomposition reactions are easy to recognize because they are the only type of reaction in which there is only one reactant. ◀

▶ *In organic chemistry, decomposition reactions are often called* elimination reactions. *In many reactions, including some metabolic reactions that occur in the human body, either H_2O or CO_2 is eliminated from a molecule (a decomposition).*

Displacement Reactions

A **displacement reaction** *is a chemical reaction in which an atom or molecule displaces an atom or group of atoms from a compound.* There are always two reactants and two products in a displacement reaction. The general equation for a displacement reaction is

$$X + YZ \longrightarrow Y + XZ$$

A common type of displacement reaction is one in which an element and a compound are reactants, and an element and a compound are products. Examples of this type of displacement reaction include

$$Fe + CuSO_4 \longrightarrow Cu + FeSO_4$$
$$Mg + Ni(NO_3)_2 \longrightarrow Ni + Mg(NO_3)_2$$
$$Cl_2 + NiI_2 \longrightarrow I_2 + NiCl_2$$
$$F_2 + 2NaCl \longrightarrow Cl_2 + 2NaF$$

The first two equations illustrate one metal displacing another metal from its compound. The latter two equations illustrate one nonmetal displacing another nonmetal from its compound. A more complicated example of a displacement reaction, in which all reactants and products are compounds, is

$$4PH_3 + Ni(CO)_4 \longrightarrow 4CO + Ni(PH_3)_4$$

Exchange Reactions

An **exchange reaction** *is a chemical reaction in which two substances exchange parts with one another and form two different substances.* The general equation for an exchange reaction is

$$AX + BY \longrightarrow AY + BX$$

Such reactions can be thought of as involving "partner switching." The AX and BY partnerships are disrupted, and new AY and BX partnerships are formed in their place. ◀

When the reactants in an exchange reaction are ionic compounds in solution, the parts exchanged are the positive and negative ions of the compounds present.

$$AgNO_3(aq) + NaCl(aq) \longrightarrow AgCl(s) + NaNO_3(aq)$$
$$2KI(aq) + Pb(NO_3)_2(aq) \longrightarrow 2KNO_3(aq) + PbI_2(s)$$

In most reactions of this type, one of the product compounds is in a different physical state (solid or gas) from that of the reactants (Figure 9-2). Insoluble solids formed from such a reaction are called *precipitates;* AgCl and PbI_2 are precipitates in the foregoing reactions.

Combustion Reactions

Combustion reactions are a most common type of chemical reaction. **A combustion reaction** *is a chemical reaction between a substance and oxygen (usually from air) that proceeds with the evolution of heat and light (usually from a flame).* Hydrocarbons— binary compounds of carbon and hydrogen (of which many exist)—are the most common type of compound that undergoes combustion. ◀ In hydrocarbon combustion, the carbon of the hydrocarbon combines with the oxygen of air to produce carbon dioxide (CO_2). The hydrogen of the hydrocarbon also interacts with the oxygen of air to give water (H_2O) as a product. The relative amounts of CO_2 and H_2O produced depend on the composition of the hydrocarbon.

$$2C_2H_2 + 5O_2 \longrightarrow 4CO_2 + 2H_2O$$
$$C_3H_8 + 5O_2 \longrightarrow 3CO_2 + 4H_2O$$
$$C_4H_8 + 6O_2 \longrightarrow 4CO_2 + 4H_2O$$

Major environmental concerns are associated with many combustion reactions in which CO_2 is a product. The combustion-generated CO_2, after entering the atmosphere, becomes a major contributor to the process called *global warming*. The focus on relevancy feature Chemical Connections 9-A—Combustion Reactions, Carbon Dioxide, and Global Warming—gives further details about atmospheric CO_2 levels and discusses the relationship between atmospheric CO_2 and the process called global warming.

© Cengage Learning

Figure 9-2 An exchange reaction involving solutions of potassium iodide and lead(II) nitrate (both colorless solutions) produces yellow, insoluble lead(II) iodide as one of the products.

$$2KI(aq) + Pb(NO_3)_2(aq) \longrightarrow$$
$$2KNO_3(aq) + PbI_2(s)$$

▶ *In organic chemistry, displacement and exchange reactions are often called* substitution *reactions. Substitution reactions of the exchange type are very frequently encountered.*

▶ *Hydrocarbon combustion reactions are the basis of an industrial society, making possible the burning of gasoline in cars, of natural gas in homes, and of coal in factories. Gasoline, natural gas, and coal all contain hydrocarbons. Unlike most other chemical reactions, hydrocarbon combustion reactions are carried out for the energy they produce rather than for the material products.*

Combustion Reactions, Carbon Dioxide, and Global Warming

Coal, petroleum, and natural gas, the fuels needed to run the majority of transportation vehicles and to generate most electrical power, are mixtures of carbon–hydrogen compounds. When such fuels are burned (combustion; Section 9-1), carbon dioxide is one of the combustion products. For example, equations for the combustion of methane (CH_4) and propane (C_3H_8) are

$$CH_4 + 2O_2 \longrightarrow CO_2 + 2H_2O$$
$$C_3H_8 + 5O_2 \longrightarrow 3CO_2 + 4H_2O$$

Almost all combustion-generated CO_2 enters the atmosphere. Significant amounts of this atmospheric CO_2 are absorbed into the oceans because of this compound's solubility in water, and plants also remove CO_2 from the atmosphere via the process of photosynthesis. However, these removal mechanisms are not sufficient to remove all the combustion-generated CO_2; it is being generated faster than it can be removed. Consequently, atmospheric concentrations of CO_2 are slowly increasing, as the following graph shows.

The concentration unit on the vertical axis is parts per million (ppm)—the number of molecules of CO_2 per million molecules present in air. Data for periods before 1958 were derived from analysis of air trapped in bubbles in glacial ice.

Increasing atmospheric CO_2 levels pose an environmental concern because within the atmosphere, CO_2 acts as a heat-trapping agent. During the day, Earth receives energy from the sun, mostly in the form of *visible light*. At night, as Earth cools, it re-radiates the energy it received during the day in the form of *infrared light* (heat energy). Carbon dioxide does not absorb visible light, but it has the ability to absorb infrared light. The CO_2 thus traps some of the heat energy re-radiated by the surface of the Earth as it cools, preventing this energy from escaping to outer space. Because this action is similar to that of glass in a greenhouse, CO_2 is called a *greenhouse gas*. The warming caused by CO_2 as it prevents heat loss from Earth is called the *greenhouse effect* or *global warming*.

Most, but not all, scientists conclude that the increasing presence of CO_2 (as well as other greenhouse gases) in the atmosphere is the major contributing cause for an observed small rise in the average temperature of Earth's surface. Because additional factors, such as periodic variations involving sun activity and absorption of heat by ocean waters, are also involved in determining climate change, absolute conclusions cannot, however, be drawn.

A 2013 study found that despite the small increase in Earth's surface temperature, the temperature of Earth's atmosphere has remained essentially constant since 2000 and that over 90% of the heat trapped by greenhouse gases has been diverted to Earth's oceans. Interestingly, the ocean warming is concentrated at a depth of about one-half mile beneath the surface.

Projected consequences of a significant increase in average Earth surface temperature include an increased melting of glacial ice and polar ice caps, with a consequential rise in ocean levels. A sea-level increase would significantly impact low-lying coastal areas, even to the extent of putting them underwater.

Additional greenhouse gases besides CO_2 enter the atmosphere on a continual basis in smaller amounts. They include methane (CH_4), nitrous oxide (N_2O), and fluorinated gases such as chlorofluorocarbons (CFCs). Total U.S. greenhouse gas emissions in 2010 are as follows:

Contributions of the other greenhouse gases to global warming are substantial, despite their lower concentrations, because they are all more effective absorbers of infrared radiation than CO_2. The effect of a given greenhouse gas on climate change (global warming) depends not only on concentration and ability to absorb infrared radiation but also on how long they stay in the atmosphere. The global warming potential of CH_4 is estimated to be 21 times that of CO_2 and that of N_2O to be 300 times that of CO_2. CFCs and related compounds have an even higher global warming potential. Further information about CFCs is given in the Chemical Connections feature—Chlorofluorocarbons and the Ozone Layer—in Chapter 12.

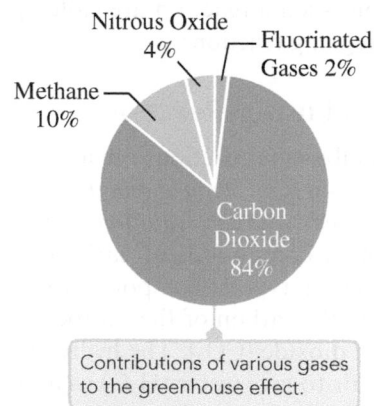

Contributions of various gases to the greenhouse effect.

U.S. Greenhouse Gas Emissions in 2010. Total Emissions in 2010 = 6822 Million Tons of CO_2 Equivalent.

Products other than CO_2 and H_2O can be produced in a combustion reaction, as is shown by the following combustion reaction equations.

$$CS_2 + 3O_2 \longrightarrow CO_2 + 2SO_2$$
$$2H_2S + 3O_2 \longrightarrow 2SO_2 + 2H_2O$$
$$4NH_3 + 5O_2 \longrightarrow 4NO + 6H_2O$$
$$2ZnS + 3O_2 \longrightarrow 2ZnO + 2SO_2$$

Combination reactions in which oxygen reacts with another element to form a single product are also combustion reactions. Two such reactions are

$$S + O_2 \longrightarrow SO_2$$
$$2Mg + O_2 \longrightarrow 2MgO$$

EXAMPLE 9-1

Classifying Chemical Reactions

Classify each of the following chemical reactions as a *combination, decomposition, displacement, exchange,* or *combustion* reaction.

a. $2KNO_3 \rightarrow 2KNO_2 + O_2$
b. $Zn + 2AgNO_3 \rightarrow Zn(NO_3)_2 + 2Ag$
c. $Ni(NO_3)_2 + 2NaOH \rightarrow Ni(OH)_2 + 2NaNO_3$
d. $3Mg + N_2 \rightarrow Mg_3N_2$

Solution

a. Decomposition. Two substances are produced from a single substance.
b. Displacement. An element and a compound are reactants, and an element and a compound are products.
c. Exchange. Two compounds exchange parts with each other; the nickel ion (Ni^{2+}) and sodium ion (Na^+) are "swapping partners."
d. Combination. Two substances combine to form a single substance.

Many, *but not all,* chemical reactions fall into one of the five categories discussed in this section. Even though this classification system is not all-inclusive, it is still very useful because of the many reactions it does help correlate. Chemistry at a Glance—Types of Chemical Reactions—summarizes pictorially reaction types that have been considered in this section.

Section 9-1 Quick Quiz

1. Which of the following general reaction types is characterized by there being a single reactant?
   a. combination
   b. decomposition
   c. exchange
   d. no correct response
2. Which of the following general equations is a representation for a displacement reaction?
   a. $X + Y \rightarrow XY$
   b. $XY \rightarrow X + Y$
   c. $AX + BY \rightarrow AY + BX$
   d. no correct response
3. Combustion reactions are always characterized by
   a. oxygen being one of the reactants
   b. water being one of the products
   c. both reactants being elements
   d. no correct response

Answers: 1. b; 2. d; 3. a

CHEMISTRY AT A GLANCE Types of Chemical Reactions

COMBINATION REACTION

$$2Al + 3I_2 \longrightarrow 2AlI_3$$

Aluminum reacts with iodine to form aluminum iodide.

DECOMPOSITION REACTION

$$2HgO \longrightarrow 2Hg + O_2$$

Mercury(II) oxide decomposes to form mercury and oxygen.

DISPLACEMENT REACTION

$$Zn + CuSO_4 \longrightarrow Cu + ZnSO_4$$

Zinc reacts with copper(II) sulfate to form copper and zinc sulfate.

EXCHANGE REACTION

$$AgNO_3 + NaCl \longrightarrow AgCl + NaNO_3$$

Silver nitrate reacts with sodium chloride to form silver chloride and sodium nitrate.

9-2 Redox and Nonredox Chemical Reactions

LEARNING FOCUS

Be able to assign oxidation numbers to the elements in a chemical formula; be able to determine whether or not a chemical reaction is a redox reaction using oxidation numbers.

▶ The term redox *is pronounced* "REE-docks."

Chemical reactions can also be classified, in terms of whether transfer of electrons occurs, as either oxidation–reduction (redox) or nonoxidation–reduction (nonredox) reactions. ▶ An **oxidation–reduction (redox) chemical reaction** *is a chemical reaction in which there is a transfer of electrons from one reactant to another reactant.* A **nonoxidation–reduction (nonredox) chemical reaction** *is a chemical reaction in which there is no transfer of electrons from one reactant to another reactant.*

A "bookkeeping system" known as oxidation numbers is used to identify whether electron transfer occurs in a chemical reaction. An **oxidation number** *is a number that represents the charge that an atom appears to have when the electrons in each bond it is participating in are assigned to the more electronegative of the two atoms involved in the bond.*

There are several rules for determining oxidation numbers.

1. *The oxidation number of an element in its elemental state is zero.* For example, the oxidation number of copper in Cu is zero, and the oxidation number of chlorine in Cl_2 is zero.

▶ Oxidation numbers *are also sometimes called* oxidation states.

2. *The oxidation number of a monatomic ion is equal to the charge on the ion.* For example, the Na^+ ion has an oxidation number of $+1$, and the S^{2-} ion has an oxidation number of -2. ◀

3. *The oxidation numbers of Groups IA and IIA metals in compounds are always +1 and +2, respectively.*
4. *The oxidation number of hydrogen is +1 in most hydrogen-containing compounds.*
5. *The oxidation number of oxygen is −2 in most oxygen-containing compounds.*
6. *In binary molecular compounds, the more electronegative element is assigned a negative oxidation number equal to its charge in binary ionic compounds. For example, in CCl_4 the element Cl is the more electronegative, and its oxidation number is −1 (the same as in the simple Cl^- ion).*
7. *For a compound, the sum of the individual oxidation numbers is equal to zero; for a polyatomic ion, the sum is equal to the charge on the ion.*

Example 9-2 illustrates the use of these rules.

EXAMPLE 9-2

Assigning Oxidation Numbers to Elements in a Compound or Polyatomic Ion

Assign an oxidation number to each element in the following compounds or polyatomic ions.

a. P_2O_5 **b.** $KMnO_4$ **c.** NO_3^-

Solution

a. The sum of the oxidation numbers of all the atoms present must add to zero (rule 7).

$$2(\text{oxid. no. P}) + 5(\text{oxid. no. O}) = 0$$

The oxidation number of oxygen is −2 (rule 5 or rule 6). By substituting this value into the previous equation, the oxidation number of phosphorus can be calculated.

$$2(\text{oxid. no. P}) + 5(-2) = 0$$
$$2(\text{oxid. no. P}) = +10$$
$$(\text{oxid. no. P}) = +5$$

Thus the oxidation numbers for the elements involved in this compound are

$$P = +5 \quad \text{and} \quad O = -2$$

Note that the oxidation number of phosphorus is not +10; that is the calculated charge associated with two phosphorus atoms. Oxidation number is always specified on a *per atom* basis.

b. The sum of the oxidation numbers of all the atoms present must add to zero (rule 7).

$$(\text{oxid. no. K}) + (\text{oxid. no. Mn}) + 4(\text{oxid. no. O}) = 0$$

The oxidation number of potassium, a Group IA element, is +1 (rule 3), and the oxidation number of oxygen is −2 (rule 5). Substituting these two values into the rule 7 equation enables us to calculate the oxidation number of manganese.

$$(+1) + (\text{oxid. no. Mn}) + 4(-2) = 0$$
$$(\text{oxid. no. Mn}) = 8 - 1 = +7$$

Thus the oxidation numbers for the elements involved in this compound are

$$K = +1 \quad Mn = +7 \quad \text{and} \quad O = -2$$

Note that all the oxidation numbers add to zero when it is taken into account that there are four oxygen atoms.

$$(+1) + (+7) + 4(-2) = 0$$

c. The species NO_3^- is a polyatomic ion rather than a neutral compound. Thus the second part of rule 7 applies: The oxidation numbers must add to −1, the charge on the ion.

$$(\text{oxid. no. N}) + 3(\text{oxid. no. O}) = -1$$

(continued)

The oxidation number of oxygen is -2 (rule 5). Substituting this value into the sum equation gives

$$(\text{oxid. no. N}) + 3(-2) = -1$$
$$(\text{oxid. no. N}) = -1 + 6 = +5$$

Thus the oxidation numbers for the elements involved in the polyatomic ion are

$$N = +5 \quad \text{and} \quad O = -2$$

Many elements display a range of oxidation numbers in their various compounds. For example, nitrogen exhibits oxidation numbers ranging from -3 to $+5$.

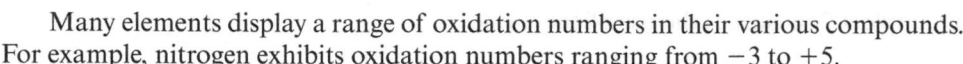

NH_3	N_2H_4	NH_2OH	N_2O	NO	N_2O_3	NO_2	HNO_3
-3	-2	-1	$+1$	$+2$	$+3$	$+4$	$+5$

As shown in this listing of nitrogen-containing compounds, the oxidation number of an atom is written *underneath* the symbol of that atom in the chemical formula. This convention is used to avoid confusion with the charge on an ion.

Assigning oxidation numbers to all elements in the substances involved in a chemical reaction and then looking for oxidation number changes is the basis for determining whether a chemical reaction is a redox reaction or a nonredox reaction. Changes in oxidation number are a requirement for a redox reaction. The reaction between calcium metal and chlorine gas (Figure 9-3) is a redox reaction.

Figure 9-3 The burning of calcium metal in chlorine is a redox reaction. The burning calcium emits a red-orange flame.

$$\underset{0}{\text{Ca}} + \underset{0}{\text{Cl}_2} \longrightarrow \underset{+2\ -1}{\text{CaCl}_2}$$

The oxidation number of Ca changes from zero to $+2$, and the oxidation number of Cl changes from zero to -1.

The decomposition of calcium carbonate is a nonredox reaction.

$$\underset{+2+4-2}{\text{CaCO}_3} \longrightarrow \underset{+2\ -2}{\text{CaO}} + \underset{+4\ -2}{\text{CO}_2}$$

It is a nonredox reaction because there are no changes in oxidation number.

EXAMPLE 9-3

Using Oxidation Numbers to Determine Whether a Chemical Reaction Is a Redox Reaction

By using oxidation numbers, determine whether the following reaction is a redox reaction or a nonredox reaction.

$$4NH_3 + 3O_2 \longrightarrow 2N_2 + 6H_2O$$

Solution

For the reactant NH_3, H has an oxidation number of $+1$ (rule 4) and N an oxidation number of -3 (rule 7). The other reactant, O_2, is an element and thus has an oxidation number of zero (rule 1). The product N_2 also has an oxidation number of zero because it is an element. In H_2O, the other product, H has an oxidation number of $+1$ (rule 4) and oxygen an oxidation number of -2 (rule 5).

The overall oxidation number analysis is

$$\underset{-3\ +1}{4NH_3} + \underset{0}{3O_2} \longrightarrow \underset{0}{2N_2} + \underset{+1\ -2}{6H_2O}$$

This reaction is a redox reaction because the oxidation numbers of both N and O change.

1. The proper assignment of oxidation numbers to the elements in the compound H_2SO_4 is
   a. +2 for H, +6 for S, −8 for O
   b. +1 for H, +6 for S, −2 for O
   c. +2 for H, +1 for S, −4 for O
   d. no correct response

2. The proper assignment of oxidation numbers to the elements in the polyatomic ion PO_4^{3-} is
   a. +8 for P, −8 for O
   b. +5 for P, −2 for O
   c. +5 for P, −8 for O
   d. no correct response

3. Which of the following chemical reactions is a *nonredox reaction*?
   a. $Ca + S \longrightarrow CaS$
   b. $SO_3 + H_2O \longrightarrow H_2SO_4$
   c. $2NO + O_2 \longrightarrow 2NO_2$
   d. no correct response

Answers: 1.b; 2. b; 3. b

9-3 Terminology Associated with Redox Processes

LEARNING FOCUS

Be able to distinguish among meanings for the four terms *oxidation, reduction, oxidizing agent,* and *reducing agent.*

Four key terms used in describing redox processes are *oxidation, reduction, oxidizing agent,* and *reducing agent.* The definitions for these terms are closely tied to the concepts of "electron transfer" and "oxidation number change"—concepts considered in Section 9-2. It is electron transfer that links all redox processes together. Change in oxidation number is a direct consequence of electron transfer.

In a redox reaction, one reactant undergoes oxidation, and another reactant undergoes reduction. **Oxidation** *is the process whereby a reactant in a chemical reaction loses one or more electrons.* **Reduction** *is the process whereby a reactant in a chemical reaction gains one or more electrons.*

Oxidation and reduction are complementary processes that always occur together. When electrons are lost by one species, they do not disappear: rather, they are always gained by another species. Thus electron transfer always involves both oxidation and reduction. ◀

Electron loss (oxidation) always leads to an increase in oxidation number. Conversely, electron gain (reduction) always leads to a decrease in oxidation number. These generalizations are consistent with the rules for monatomic ion formation (Section 4-5); electron loss produces positive ions (increase in oxidation number), and electron gain produces negative ions (decrease in oxidation number). Figure 9-4 summarizes the relationship between change in oxidation number and the processes of oxidation and reduction.

▶ *Oxidation involves the loss of electrons, and reduction involves the gain of electrons. Students often have trouble remembering which is which. Two helpful mnemonic devices follow.*

LEO *the lion says* GER

Loss of Electrons: Oxidation.
Gain of Electrons: Reduction.

OIL RIG

Oxidation Is Loss (of electrons).
Reduction Is Gain (of electrons).

Figure 9-4 An increase in oxidation number is associated with the process of oxidation, a decrease with the process of reduction.

Oxidizing Agents and Reducing Agents

There are two different ways of looking at the reactants in a redox reaction. First, the reactants can be viewed as being "acted on." From this perspective, one reactant is *oxidized* (the one that loses electrons), and one is *reduced* (the one that gains electrons). Second, the reactants can be looked on as "bringing about" the reaction. In this approach, the terms *oxidizing agent* and *reducing agent* are used. An **oxidizing agent** *is the reactant in a redox reaction that causes oxidation of another reactant by accepting electrons from it.* This acceptance of electrons means that the oxidizing agent itself is reduced. Similarly, a **reducing agent** *is the reactant in a redox reaction that causes reduction of another reactant by providing electrons for the other reactant to accept.* Thus the reducing agent and the substance oxidized are one and the same, as are the oxidizing agent and the substance reduced:

$$\text{Substance oxidized} = \text{reducing agent}$$
$$\text{Substance reduced} = \text{oxidizing agent}$$

Table 9-1 summarizes the redox terminology presented in this section in terms of electron transfer. ◀

▶ *The terms* oxidizing agent *and* reducing agent *sometimes cause confusion because the oxidizing agent is not oxidized (it is reduced) and the reducing agent is not reduced (it is oxidized). A simple analogy is that a travel agent is not the one who takes a trip; he or she is the one who plans (causes) the trip that is taken.*

▶ **Table 9-1 Summary of Redox Terminology in Terms of Electron Transfer**

Term	Electron Transfer
oxidation	loss of electron(s)
reduction	gain of electron(s)
oxidizing agent (substance reduced)	electron(s) gained
reducing agent (substance oxidized)	electron(s) lost

EXAMPLE 9-4

Identifying the Oxidizing Agent and Reducing Agent in a Redox Reaction

For the redox reaction

$$\text{FeO} + \text{CO} \longrightarrow \text{Fe} + \text{CO}_2$$

identify the following.

a. The substance oxidized
b. The substance reduced
c. The oxidizing agent
d. The reducing agent

Solution

Oxidation numbers are determined using the methods illustrated in Example 9-2.

$$\text{FeO} + \text{CO} \longrightarrow \text{Fe} + \text{CO}_2$$
$$\text{+2 −2} \quad \text{+2 −2} \qquad \text{0} \quad \text{+4 −2}$$

a. Oxidation involves an increase in oxidation number. The oxidation number of C has increased from +2 to +4. Therefore, the reactant that contains C, which is CO, is the substance that has been oxidized.
b. Reduction involves a decrease in oxidation number. The oxidation number of Fe has decreased from +2 to zero. Therefore, the reactant that contains Fe, which is FeO, is the substance that has been reduced.
c. The oxidizing agent and the substance reduced are always one and the same. Therefore, FeO is the oxidizing agent.
d. The reducing agent and the substance oxidized are always one and the same. Therefore, CO is the reducing agent.

1. Which of the following are characteristics of the process of oxidation?
   a. loss of one or more electrons and an oxidation number increase
   b. gain of one or more electrons and an oxidation number decrease
   c. loss of one or more electrons and an oxidation number decrease
   d. no correct response
2. The oxidizing agent in a redox reaction is itself
   a. reduced
   b. oxidized
   c. neither oxidized nor reduced
   d. no correct response
3. In a redox reaction the substance oxidized
   a. must be a reactant
   b. must be a product
   c. can be either a reactant or a product
   d. no correct response
4. Which substance is reduced in the following redox reaction?

$$CO + H_2O \longrightarrow CO_2 + H_2$$

   a. CO
   b. H_2O
   c. CO_2
   d. no correct response
5. Which substance is the reducing agent in the following redox reaction?

$$CO + H_2O \longrightarrow CO_2 + H_2$$

   a. H_2O
   b. CO_2
   c. H_2
   d. no correct response

Answers: 1. a; 2. a; 3. a; 4. b; 5. d

9-4 Collision Theory and Chemical Reactions

LEARNING FOCUS

Based on collision theory concepts, list the three requirements that must be met for a chemical reaction to take place.

What causes a chemical reaction, either redox or nonredox, to take place? A set of three generalizations, developed after the study of thousands of different reactions, helps answer this question. Collectively these generalizations are known as collision theory. **Collision theory** *is a set of statements that give the conditions necessary for a chemical reaction to occur.* Central to collision theory are the concepts of molecular collisions, activation energy, and collision orientation. The statements of collision theory are

1. *Molecular collisions.* Reactant particles must interact (that is, collide) with one another before any reaction can occur.
2. *Activation energy.* Colliding particles must possess a certain minimum total amount of energy, called the activation energy, if the collision is to be effective (that is, result in reaction).
3. *Collision orientation.* Colliding particles must come together in the proper orientation unless the particles involved are single atoms or small, symmetrical molecules.

These concepts are further considered in the context of a reaction between two particles (molecules or ions).

Molecular Collisions

For a reaction involving two reactants, collision theory assumes (statement 1) that the reactant molecules, ions, or atoms must come in contact (collide) with one another in order for any chemical change to occur. The validity of this statement is fairly obvious. Reactants cannot react if they are separated from each other.

Most reactions are carried out either in liquid solution or in the gaseous phase, wherein reacting particles are more free to move around, thus making it easier for the reactants to come in contact with one another. Reactions in which reactants are solids can and do occur; however, the conditions for molecular collisions are not as favorable as they are for liquids and gases. Reactions of solids usually take place only on the solid surface and thus include only a small fraction of the total particles present in the solid. As the reaction proceeds and products dissolve, diffuse, or fall from the surface, fresh solid is exposed. Thus the reaction eventually consumes all of the solid. The rusting of iron is an example of this type of process.

Activation Energy

Figure 9-5 Rubbing a match head against a rough surface provides the activation energy needed for the match to ignite.

The collisions between reactant particles do not always result in the formation of reaction products. Sometimes, reactant particles rebound unchanged from a collision. Statement 2 of collision theory indicates that in order for a reaction to occur, particles must collide with a certain minimum energy; that is, the kinetic energies of the colliding particles must add to a certain minimum value. **Activation energy** is *the minimum combined kinetic energy that colliding reactant particles must possess in order for their collision to result in a chemical reaction.* Every chemical reaction has a different activation energy. In a slow reaction, the activation energy is far above the average energy content of the reacting particles. Only those few particles with above-average energy undergo collisions that result in reaction; this is the reason for the overall slowness of the reaction.

It is sometimes possible to start a reaction by providing activation energy and then have the reaction continue on its own. Once the reaction is started, enough energy is released to activate other molecules and keep the reaction going. The striking of a kitchen match is an example of such a situation (Figure 9-5). Activation energy is initially provided by rubbing the match head against a rough surface; heat is generated by friction. Once the reaction is started, the match continues to burn.

Collision Orientation

Reaction rates are sometimes very slow because reactant molecules must be oriented in a certain way in order for collisions to lead successfully to products. For nonspherical molecules and nonspherical polyatomic ions, orientation relative to one another at the moment of collision is a factor that determines whether a collision produces a reaction.

▶ *Many reactions in the human body do not occur unless specialized proteins called* enzymes *(Chapter 21) are present. One of the functions of these enzymes is to hold reactant molecules in the orientation required for a reaction to occur.*

As an illustration of the importance of proper collision orientation, consider the chemical reaction between NO_2 and CO to produce NO and CO_2.

$$NO_2(g) + CO(g) \longrightarrow NO(g) + CO_2(g)$$

In this reaction, an O atom is transferred from an NO_2 molecule to a CO molecule. The collision orientation most favorable for this to occur is one that puts an O atom from NO_2 near a C atom from CO at the moment of collision. Such an orientation is shown in Figure 9-6 (top). Figure 9-6 (bottom) shows three undesirable NO_2-CO orientations, where the likelihood of successful reaction is very low. ◀

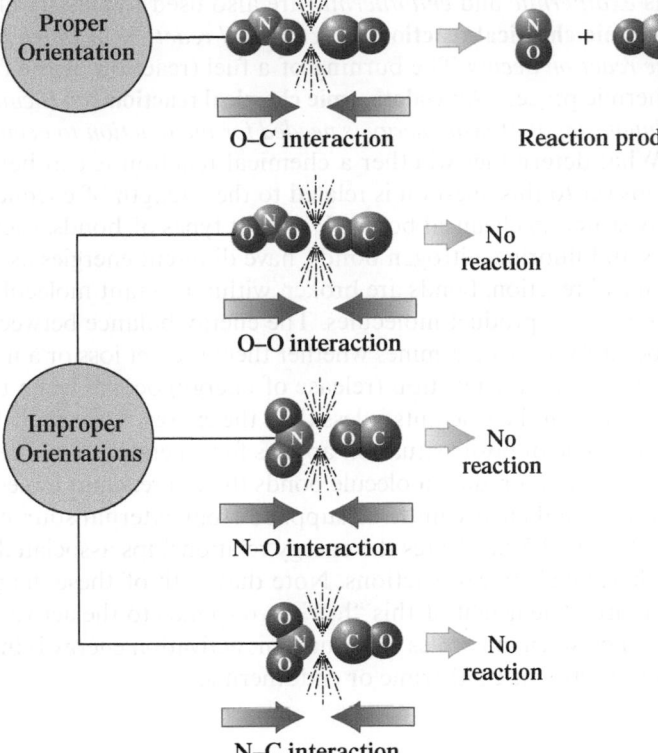

Figure 9-6 In the reaction of NO_2 with CO to produce NO and CO_2, the most favorable collision orientation is one that puts an O atom from NO_2 in close proximity to the C atom of CO.

O–C interaction   Reaction products

O–O interaction

N–O interaction

N–C interaction

Section 9-4 Quick Quiz

1. The three core concepts upon which collision theory is based are:
   a. activation energy, equal reactant concentrations, molecular collisions
   b. equal reactant concentrations, molecular collisions, collision orientation
   c. molecular collisions, collision orientation, activation energy
   d. no correct response
2. The minimum combined kinetic energy reactant molecules must possess in order for their collision to result in a chemical reaction is called the
   a. activation energy
   b. collision energy
   c. orientation energy
   d. no correct response
3. The rate at which a chemical reaction occurs decreases as the activation energy
   a. increases
   b. decreases
   c. approaches zero
   d. no correct response

Answers: 1. c; 2. a; 3. a

9-5 ## Exothermic and Endothermic Chemical Reactions

LEARNING FOCUS
Describe the differing characteristics of exothermic and endothermic reactions.

In Section 7-9, the terms *exothermic* and *endothermic* were used to classify changes of state. Melting, sublimation, and evaporation are endothermic changes of state, and freezing, condensation, and deposition are exothermic changes of state. The terms *exothermic* and *endothermic* are also used to classify chemical reactions. An **exothermic chemical reaction** *is a chemical reaction in which heat energy is released as the reaction occurs.* The burning of a fuel (reaction of the fuel with oxygen) is an exothermic process. An **endothermic chemical reaction** *is a chemical reaction in which a continuous input of heat energy is needed for the reaction to occur.*

What determines whether a chemical reaction is exothermic or endothermic? The answer to this question is related to the strength of chemical bonds—that is, the energy stored in chemical bonds. Different types of bonds, such as oxygen–hydrogen bonds and fluorine–nitrogen bonds, have different energies associated with them. In a chemical reaction, bonds are broken within reactant molecules, and new bonds are formed within product molecules. The energy balance between this bond-breaking and bond-forming determines whether there is a net loss or a net gain of energy.

An exothermic reaction (release of energy) occurs when the energy required to break bonds in the reactants is less than the energy released by bond formation in the products. The opposite situation applies for an endothermic reaction. There is more energy stored in product molecule bonds than in reactant molecule bonds. The necessary additional energy must be supplied from external sources as the reaction proceeds. Figure 9-7 illustrates the energy relationships associated with exothermic and endothermic chemical reactions. Note that both of these diagrams contain a "hill" or "hump." The height of this "hill" corresponds to the activation energy needed for reaction between molecules to occur. This activation energy is independent of whether a given reaction is exothermic or endothermic.

Figure 9-7 Energy diagrams showing the difference between an exothermic and an endothermic reaction.

Exothermic reaction

a In an exothermic reaction, the average energy of the reactants is higher than that of the products, indicating that energy has been released in the reaction.

Endothermic reaction

b In an endothermic reaction, the average energy of the reactants is less than that of the products, indicating that energy has been absorbed in the reaction.

Section 9-5 Quick Quiz

1. Heat energy production is a characteristic of
   a. all chemical reactions
   b. exothermic chemical reactions
   c. endothermic chemical reactions
   d. no correct response

2. For exothermic chemical reactions the average energy of the products is
   a. greater than that of the reactants
   b. less than that of the reactants
   c. greater than the activation energy for the reaction
   d. no correct response
3. For endothermic chemical reactions the energy needed to break reactant chemical bonds is
   a. greater than that released in product chemical bond formation
   b. less than that released in product chemical bond formation
   c. less than the activation energy for the reaction
   d. no correct response

Answers: 1. b; 2. b; 3. a

9-6 Factors That Influence Chemical Reaction Rates

LEARNING FOCUS

List four factors that affect chemical reaction rates and explain how each relates to the concepts embodied in collision theory.

A **chemical reaction rate** *is the rate at which reactants are consumed or products produced in a given time period in a chemical reaction.* Natural processes have a wide range of reaction rates (see Figure 9-8). In this section, four different factors that affect reaction rate are considered: (1) the physical nature of the reactants, (2) reactant concentrations, (3) reaction temperature, and (4) the presence of catalysts.

Physical Nature of Reactants

The physical nature of reactants includes not only the physical state of each reactant (solid, liquid, or gas) but also the particle size. In reactions where reactants are all in the same physical state, the reaction rate is generally faster between liquid-state

Figure 9-8 Natural processes occur at a wide range of reaction rates. A fire (a) is a much faster reaction than the ripening of fruit (b), which is much faster than the process of rusting (c), which is much faster than the process of aging (d).

reactants than between solid-state reactants and is fastest between gaseous-state reactants. Of the three states of matter, the gaseous state is the one where there is the most freedom of movement; hence collisions between reactants are the most frequent in this state.

In the solid state, reactions occur at the boundary surface between reactants. The reaction rate increases as the amount of boundary surface area increases. Subdividing a solid into smaller particles increases surface area and thus increases reaction rate. ◄

When the particle size of a solid is extremely small, reaction rates can be so fast that an explosion results. Although a lump of coal is difficult to ignite, the spontaneous ignition of coal dust is a real threat to underground coal-mining operations.

▶ For reactants in the solid state, reaction rate increases as subdivision of the solid increases.

Reactant Concentrations

An increase in the concentration of a reactant causes an increase in the rate of the reaction. Combustible substances burn much more rapidly in pure oxygen than in air (21% oxygen). A person with a respiratory problem such as pneumonia or emphysema is often given air enriched with oxygen because an increased partial pressure of oxygen facilitates the absorption of oxygen in the alveoli of the lungs and thus expedites all subsequent steps in respiration.

Increasing the concentration of a reactant means that there are more molecules of that reactant present in the reaction mixture; thus collisions between this reactant and other reactant particles are more likely. An analogy can be drawn to the game of billiards. The more billiard balls there are on the table, the greater the probability that a moving cue ball will strike one of them. Figure 9-9 numerically illustrates how increasing the concentration of one reactant increases the number of possible collisions between this reactant and another reactant. ◄

▶ Reaction rate increases as the concentration of the reactants increases.

When the concentration of reactants is increased, the actual quantitative change in reaction rate is determined by the specific reaction. The rate usually increases, but not to the same extent in all cases. Sometimes the rate doubles with a doubling of concentration, but not always.

Reaction Temperature

The effect of temperature on reaction rates can also be explained by using the molecular-collision concept. An increase in the temperature of a system results in an increase in the average kinetic energy of the reacting molecules. ◄ The increased molecular speed causes more collisions to take place in a given time. Because the average energy of the colliding molecules is greater, a larger fraction of the collisions will result in reaction from the point of view of activation energy. As a rule of thumb, chemists

▶ Reaction rate increases as the temperature of the reactants increases.

Figure 9-9 Increasing the concentration of a reactant increases the number of possible collisions between it and another reactant.

Number of Reactant Molecules	Collision Possibilities	Number of Possibilities
1 and 1		one
2 and 1		two
2 and 2		four

have found that for the temperature ranges normally encountered, the rate of a chemical reaction doubles for every 10°C increase in temperature.

The effect of increased or decreased temperature on chemical reaction rates is of critical importance when considering the chemical reactions that occur within the human body. When body temperature increases above the normal range, chemical reaction rates accelerate. More rapid breathing occurs and the heart must pump faster to supply, via the blood, the extra oxygen needed for the faster-occurring reactions. Above 41°C, the condition called *hyperthermia* occurs. **Hyperthermia** *is an uncontrolled increase in body temperature resulting from the body's inability to lose all of the extra internal heat energy generated by reactions occurring at an increased rate.*

Conversely, at temperatures below 36°C, the condition of *hypothermia* occurs. **Hypothermia** *is an uncontrolled decrease in body temperature resulting from the body's inability to generate enough internal heat energy to maintain normal body temperature and normal reaction rates.* All chemical reaction rates within the body decrease as the result of the lowered body temperature. The focus on relevancy feature Chemical Connections 9-B—Changes in Human Body Temperature and Chemical Reaction Rates—further explores the interconnection between body temperature and chemical reaction rates as it pertains to the proper functioning of the human body.

Presence of Catalysts

A **catalyst** *is a substance that increases a chemical reaction rate without being consumed in the chemical reaction.* Catalysts enhance reaction rates by providing alternative reaction pathways that have lower activation energies than the original, uncatalyzed pathway. This lowering of activation energy is diagrammatically shown in Figure 9-10. ◀

Catalysts exert their effects in varying ways. Some catalysts provide a lower-energy pathway by entering into a reaction and forming an "intermediate," which then reacts further to produce the desired products and regenerate the catalyst. The following equations, where C is the catalyst, illustrate this concept. ◀

> ▶ *Catalysts lower the activation energy for a reaction. Lowered activation energy increases the rate of a reaction.*

> ▶ *Catalysts are extremely important for the proper functioning of the human body and other biochemical systems. Enzymes, which are proteins, are the catalysts within the human body (Chapter 21). They cause many reactions to take place rapidly under mild conditions and at normal body temperature. Without these enzymes, the reactions would proceed very slowly and then only under harsher conditions.*

$$\text{Uncatalyzed reaction:} \quad X + Y \longrightarrow XY$$

$$\text{Catalyzed reaction:} \quad \textit{Step 1:} \quad X + C \longrightarrow XC$$

$$\textit{Step 2:} \quad XC + Y \longrightarrow XY + C$$

Solid catalysts often act by providing a surface to which reactant molecules are physically attracted and on which they are held with a particular orientation. These "held" reactants are sufficiently close to and favorably oriented toward one another so that the reaction takes place. The products of the reaction then leave the surface and make it available to catalyze other reactants.

Chemistry at a Glance—Factors That Increase Chemical Reaction Rates—summarizes the factors that increase reaction rates.

Figure 9-10 Catalysts lower the activation energy for chemical reactions. Reactions proceed more rapidly with the lowered activation energy.

Changes in Human Body Temperature and Chemical Reaction Rates

As is true for all chemical reactions, the rates for chemical reactions within the human body are temperature-dependent. Such rates increase when body temperature increases and decrease when body temperature decreases.

When a person has a fever, the rates for many chemical reactions in the body are higher (faster) than normal. The fever's effect translates into an increased pulse rate and increased breathing rate. For every 1°F increase in body temperature, body tissues require 6%–7% more oxygen because of increased reaction rates. The onset of a fever is one of the body's defense mechanisms against invading organisms such as bacteria. The increase in temperature speeds up reactions designed to kill the bacteria.

The body temperature of a patient with a fever typically maximizes in the 102°F–104°F range. A fever above 105°F signals the onset of a hyperthermic state (also often called heat stroke), with a temperature of 106°F (41°C) considered a life-threatening situation (see accompanying diagram). At this latter temperatures, the catalysts (enzymes; see Chapter 21) for many body reactions become deactivated. Such deactivation can lead to a total breakdown of body chemistry.

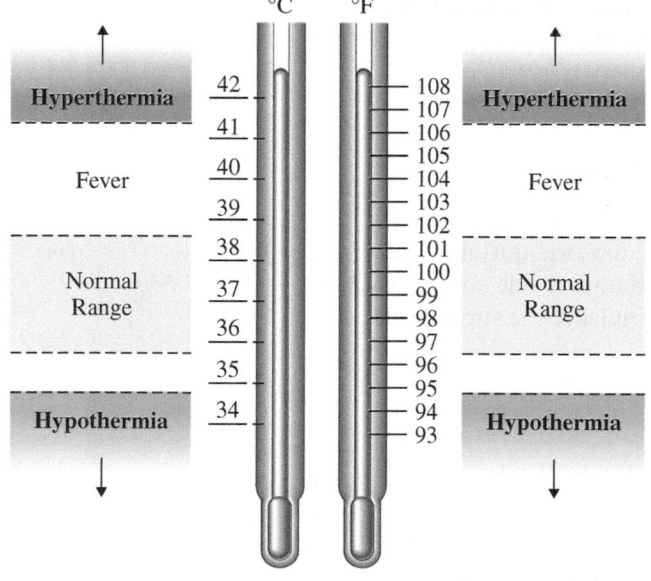

At elevated body temperatures, the increased internal heat energy production associated with increased reaction rates cannot be completely dissipated through normal heat-loss channels. Increased sweating occurs and its evaporation from the skin's surface causes some heat loss via evaporative cooling (Section 7-10). Dilation of blood vessels near the skin's surface also occurs. This allows more blood flow close to the skin, where contact with air removes additional heat. These mechanisms are not sufficient, however, to remove all of the heat buildup. With extreme hyperthermia, sweat production stops.

A number of cases of *exertional* hyperthermia (or heat stroke) are reported each year for athletes. On a very hot summer day, the body temperatures of football players (in preseason conditioning camps and practices) and marathon runners can increase to the 102°C–106°C range as the body's internal production of heat energy exceeds the body's ability to dissipate the heat. Such a situation can cause a person to collapse. Such collapse is survivable if it is quickly recognized as due to a heat stroke situation and the person's body is cooled (using cold water and ice) within 10 minutes of the collapse.

A decrease in body temperature slows down chemical reactions. Cells use less oxygen than they normally do. This knowledge is applied clinically in several medical situations using what is called *therapeutic* hypothermia. During open-heart surgery, a patient's body temperature is lowered to the 60°F–68°F range. At the lowered temperatures, the brain can function on a diminished oxygen supply for about an hour and not be affected.

A new, very promising form of therapeutic hypothermia treatment is now in use at high-level trauma centers for stabilizing unconscious patients in which cardiac arrest has occurred. Body cooling to about 91°F occurs (7 degrees below normal body temperature). With such treatment, patients who would otherwise be severely impaired by brain damage (if they survive) are often leaving the hospital with minimal impairment. To be effective, the cooling must be done within 30–60 minutes of the cardiac arrest; treatment can last for up to 24 hours. The body is then slowly rewarmed to a normal temperature.

In situations other than the highly controlled medical contexts just considered, lowered body temperature can be life-threatening. Hypothermic conditions begin when body temperature falls below 95°F (35°C), with the resulting slowdown in body chemistry affecting vital body processes such as heartbeat rate, which becomes irregular.

Exposure in extremely cold weather is often a cause of hypothermia. Uncontrolled shivering may be an outward sign of the onset of a hypothermic condition. This shivering is an attempt by the body to increase its temperature by using internal heat generated through muscular action. In the shivering process, not only skeletal muscles but also the tiny muscles attached to hair follicles contract. These latter involuntary muscle contractions cause "goose bumps." Contraction of blood vessels in the skin also occurs in an attempt to reduce heat loss. As body core temperature further drops, muscular rigidity begins (90°F–86°F). As this rigidity increases, a person no longer has the ability to help himself or herself. Unconsciousness then occurs.

CHEMISTRY AT A GLANCE — Factors That Increase Chemical Reaction Rates

FACTORS THAT INCREASE CHEMICAL REACTION RATES

Increase in State of Subdivision	Increase in Reactant Concentration	Increase in Temperature	Addition of a Catalyst
▪ Subdivision increases solid-state surface areas. ▪ Increased available surface area increases likelihood of reactant collisions.	▪ An increase in reactant concentration increases the number of reactant molecules. ▪ The likelihood of reactant collisions increases with more molecules available for collision. ▪ Increased numbers of reactant molecules increases the frequency of collisions.	▪ An increase in temperature increases molecular energies (molecular speeds). ▪ Reactant collisions occur more frequently. ▪ More reactant collisions meet the energy requirements for an effective collision.	▪ New reaction pathways are created that involve the catalyst. ▪ New reaction pathways created have lower activation energies. ▪ More reactant collisions meet the lowered activation energy requirements.

Section 9-6 Quick Quiz

1. Increasing the temperature at which a chemical reaction occurs will cause which of the following effects?
   a. increase the activation energy
   b. cause more reactant collisions to take place within a given time
   c. increase the energy of the system, thus decreasing the reaction rate
   d. no correct response

2. Which of the following changes will <u>decrease</u> the *reaction rate* for the chemical reaction

$$S(s) + O_2(g) \longrightarrow SO_2(g)$$

   a. increase the state of subdivision of the solid-state S
   b. increase the amount of O_2 present in the reaction mixture
   c. decrease the amount of S present in the reaction mixture
   d. no correct response

3. Catalysts are substances that
   a. increase the energy of reactant molecules
   b. lower the activation energy for a chemical reaction
   c. increase the rate at which reactant molecules collide with each other
   d. no correct response

Answers: 1. b; 2. c; 3. b

9-7 Chemical Equilibrium

LEARNING FOCUS

Define the term *chemical equilibrium* and know the conditions necessary for attainment of an equilibrium state.

In discussions of chemical reactions up to this point, it has been assumed that chemical reactions go to completion; that is, reactions continue until one or more of the reactants are used up. This assumption is valid as long as product concentrations are not allowed to build up in the reaction mixture. If one or more products are gases that can escape from the reaction mixture or insoluble solids that can be removed from the reaction mixture, no product buildup occurs.

When product buildup does occur, reactions do not go to completion. This is because product molecules begin to react with one another to re-form reactants. With time, a steady-state situation results wherein the rate of formation of products and the rate of re-formation of reactants are equal. At this point, the concentrations of all reactants and all products remain constant, and a state of *chemical equilibrium* is reached. **Chemical equilibrium** *is the state in which forward and reverse chemical reactions occur simultaneously at the same rate.* The concept of *equilibrium* has been encountered twice previously in this text—in Section 7-11 (vapor pressure) and Section 8-2 (saturated solutions). These previous encounters with equilibrium involved *physical* equilibrium rather than *chemical* equilibrium. In *physical* equilibrium, two opposing physical processes, such as evaporation and condensation, are occurring at the same rate. Chemical reactions do not occur in a *physical* equilibrium situation.

The conditions that exist in a system in a state of chemical equilibrium can best be seen by considering an actual chemical reaction. Suppose equal molar amounts of gaseous H_2 and I_2 are mixed together in a closed container and allowed to react to produce gaseous HI.

$$H_2 + I_2 \longrightarrow 2HI$$

Initially, no HI is present, so the only reaction that can occur is that between H_2 and I_2. However, as the HI concentration increases, some HI molecules collide with one another in a way that causes a reverse reaction to occur:

$$2HI \longrightarrow H_2 + I_2$$

The initially low concentration of HI makes this reverse reaction slow at first, but as the concentration of HI increases, the reaction rate also increases. At the same time that the reverse-reaction rate is increasing, the forward-reaction rate (production of HI) is decreasing as the reactants are used up. Eventually, the concentrations of H_2, I_2, and HI in the reaction mixture reach a level at which the rates of the forward and reverse reactions become equal. At this point, a state of chemical equilibrium has been reached. ◀

Figure 9-11a illustrates the behavior of reaction rates over time for both the forward and reverse reactions in the H_2-I_2-HI system. Figure 9-11b illustrates the important point that the reactant and product concentrations are usually not equal at the point at which equilibrium is reached.

 ▶ *A chemical reaction is in a state of chemical equilibrium when the rates of the forward and reverse reactions are equal. At this point, the concentrations of reactants and products no longer change.*

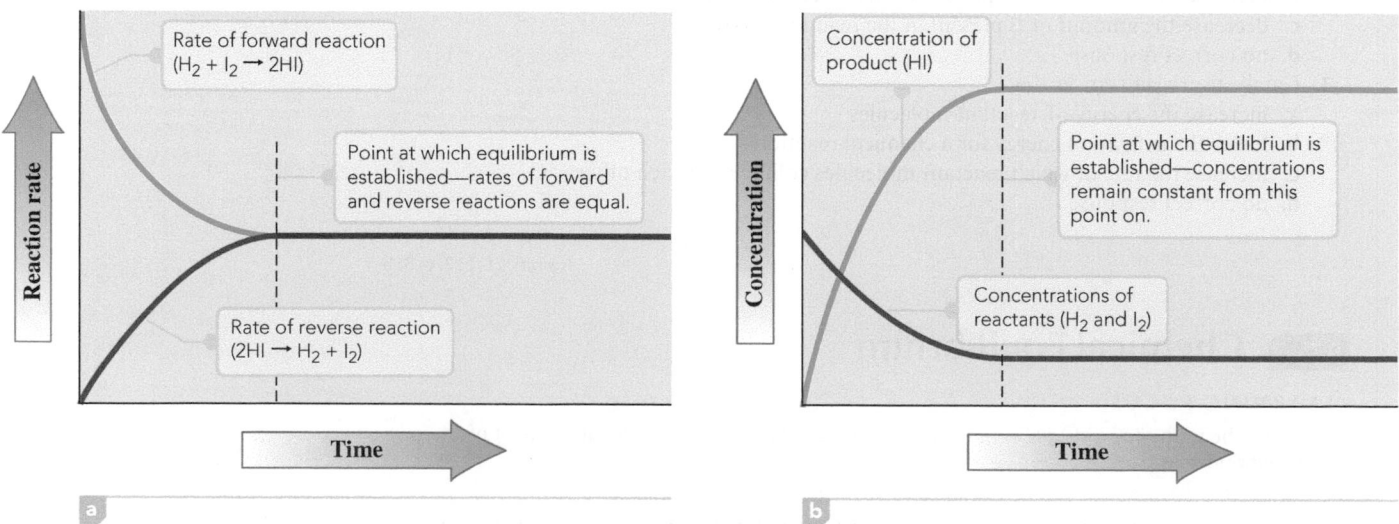

Figure 9-11 Graphs showing how reaction rates and reactant concentrations vary with time for the chemical system H_2-I_2-HI. (a) At equilibrium, rates of reaction are equal. (b) At equilibrium, concentrations of reactants remain constant but are not equal.

The equilibrium involving H_2, I_2, and HI could have been established just as easily by starting with pure HI and allowing it to change into H_2 and I_2 (the reverse reaction). The final position of equilibrium does not depend on the direction from which equilibrium is approached. ◄

It is normal procedure to represent an equilibrium by using a single equation and two half-headed arrows pointing in opposite directions. Thus the reaction between H_2 and I_2 at equilibrium is written as

$$H_2 + I_2 \rightleftharpoons 2HI$$

The half-headed arrows denote a chemical system at equilibrium.

The term *reversible* is often used to describe a reaction like the one just discussed. A **reversible chemical reaction** *is a chemical reaction in which the conversion of reactants to products (the forward reaction) and the conversion of products to reactants (the reverse reaction) occur simultaneously.* When the half-headed arrow notation is used in an equation, it means that a reaction is reversible. ◄

An important environmental equilibrium situation involving reversible reactions occurs in the upper atmosphere in what is called the "ozone layer." The focus on relevancy feature Chemical Connections 9-C—Stratospheric Ozone: An Equilibrium Situation—gives information about this equilibrium system, a system that involves two different molecular forms of the element oxygen, O_2 and O_3 (ozone).

▶ *At chemical equilibrium, forward and reverse reaction rates are equal. Reactant and product concentrations, although constant, do not have to be equal.*

▶ *Theoretically, all reactions are reversible (can go in either direction). Sometimes, the reverse reaction is so slight, however, that the reaction is described as having "gone to completion" because no detectable reactants remain.*

Section 9-7 Quick Quiz

1. Which of the following statements is correct for a system at chemical equilibrium?
   a. forward and reverse reaction rates are zero
   b. forward and reverse reaction rates are equal
   c. reverse reaction rate exceeds the forward reaction rate
   d. no correct response
2. Which of the following is not a characteristic of a chemical system in an equilibrium state?
   a. product molecules are reacting with each other
   b. reactant molecules are reacting with each other
   c. product molecules are reacting with reactant molecules
   d. no correct response
3. Which of the following is constantly changing for a system in a state of chemical equilibrium?
   a. reactant concentrations
   b. rate at which reactant molecules react
   c. actual reactant molecules present
   d. no correct response

Answers: 1. b; 2. c; 3. c

9-8 Equilibrium Constants

LEARNING FOCUS

For a given chemical reaction be able to write an *equilibrium constant expression* and then, given concentration data, be able to numerically evaluate the expression.

As noted in Section 9-7, the concentrations of reactants and products are constant (not changing) in a system at chemical equilibrium. This constancy allows us to describe the extent of reaction in a given equilibrium system by a single number called an equilibrium constant. An **equilibrium constant** *is a numerical value that characterizes the relationship between the concentrations of reactants and products in a system at chemical equilibrium.*

Stratospheric Ozone: An Equilibrium Situation

Ozone is oxygen that has undergone conversion from its normal diatomic form (O_2) to a triatomic form (O_3). The presence of ozone in the *lower atmosphere* is considered undesirable because its production contributes to air pollution; it is the major "active ingredient" in smog.

Los Angeles smog.

In the *upper atmosphere* (stratosphere), ozone is a naturally occurring species whose presence is not only desirable but absolutely essential to the well-being of humans on Earth. Stratospheric ozone screens out 95% to 99% of the ultraviolet radiation that comes from the sun. It is ultraviolet light that causes sunburn and that can be a causative factor in some types of skin cancer. The upper region of the stratosphere, where ozone concentrations are greatest, is often called the ozone layer. This ozone maximization occurs at altitudes of 25 to 30 miles (see the accompanying graph).

Within the ozone layer, ozone is continually being consumed and formed through the equilibrium process

$$3O_2(g) \rightleftharpoons 2O_3(g)$$

The source for ozone is thus diatomic oxygen. It is estimated that on any given day, 300 million tons of stratospheric ozone is formed and an equal amount destroyed in this equilibrium process.

Since the mid-1970s, scientists have observed a seasonal thinning (depletion) of ozone in the stratosphere above Antarctica (the South Pole region). This phenomenon, which is commonly called the *ozone hole*, occurs in September and October of each year, the beginning of the Antarctic spring. Up to 70% of the ozone above Antarctica is lost during these two months. (A similar, but smaller, manifestation of this same phenomenon also occurs in the North Pole region.)

Winter conditions in Antarctica include extreme cold (it is the coldest location on Earth) and total darkness. When sunlight appears in the spring, it triggers the chemical reactions that lead to ozone depletion. By the end of November, weather conditions are such that the ozone-depletion reactions stop. Then the ozone hole disappears as air from nonpolar areas flows into the polar region, replenishing the depleted ozone levels.

Chlorofluorocarbons (CFCs), synthetic compounds that have been developed primarily for use as refrigerants, are considered a causative factor for this ozone hole phenomenon. How their presence in the atmosphere contributes to this situation is considered in the Chemical Connections feature—Chlorofluorocarbons and the Ozone Layer—in Chapter 12.

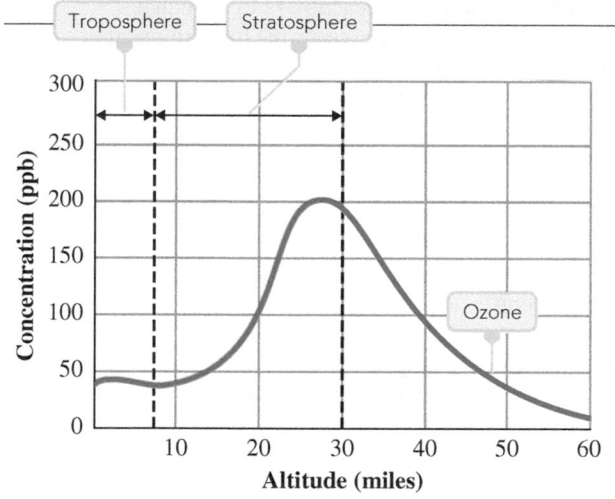

Atmospheric ozone concentration as a function of altitude.

An equilibrium constant is obtained by writing an *equilibrium constant expression* and then evaluating it numerically. For a hypothetical chemical reaction in which A and B are reactants, C and D are products, and w, x, y, and z are equation coefficients,

$$wA + xB \rightleftharpoons yC + zD$$

the equilibrium constant expression is

$$K_{eq} = \frac{[C]^y[D]^z}{[A]^w[B]^x}$$

Note the following points about this general equilibrium constant expression:

▶ *In equilibrium constants, square brackets mean that concentrations are expressed in molarity units.*

1. The square brackets refer to molar (moles/liter) concentrations. ◀
2. Product concentrations are always placed in the numerator of the equilibrium constant expression and they are multiplied together.

3. Reactant concentrations are always placed in the denominator of the equilibrium constant expression and they are multiplied together.
4. The coefficients in the balanced chemical equation for the equilibrium system determine the powers to which the concentrations are raised.
5. The abbreviation K_{eq} is used to denote an equilibrium constant.

An additional convention in writing equilibrium constant expressions, which is not apparent from the equilibrium constant definition, is that only *concentrations of gases and substances in solution* are written in an equilibrium constant expression. The reason for this convention is that other substances (pure solids and pure liquids) have constant concentrations. These constant concentrations are incorporated into the equilibrium constant itself. For example, pure water in the liquid state has a concentration of 55.5 moles/L. It does not matter whether 1, 50, or 750 mL of liquid water is present. The concentration will be the same. In the liquid state, pure water is pure water, and it has only one concentration. Similar reasoning applies to other pure liquids and pure solids. All such substances have constant concentrations. ◄

▶ *The concentrations of* pure liquids *and* pure solids, *which are constants, are never included in an equilibrium constant expression.*

The only information needed to write an equilibrium constant expression is a balanced chemical equation, which includes information about physical state. Using the preceding generalizations about equilibrium constant expressions, for the reaction

$$4NH_3(g) + 7O_2(g) \rightleftharpoons 4NO_2(g) + 6H_2O(g)$$

the equilibrium constant expression is written as

$$
\overset{\text{Coefficient of } NO_2 \searrow \qquad \swarrow \text{Coefficient of } H_2O}{K_{eq} = \frac{[NO_2]^4[H_2O]^6}{[NH_3]^4_\uparrow[O_2]^7_\uparrow}}
$$
Coefficient of NH_3 ———┘   └——— Coefficient of O_2

EXAMPLE 9-5

Writing the Equilibrium Constant Expression for a Chemical Reaction from the Chemical Equation for the Reaction

Write the equilibrium constant expression for each of the following reactions.

a. $I_2(g) + Cl_2(g) \rightleftharpoons 2ICl(g)$ **b.** $C(s) + H_2O(g) \rightleftharpoons CO(g) + H_2(g)$

Solution

a. All of the substances involved in this reaction are gases. Therefore, each reactant and product will appear in the equilibrium constant expression.

   The numerator of an equilibrium constant expression always contains product concentrations. There is only one product, ICl. Write its concentration in the numerator and square it, because the coefficient of ICl in the equation is 2.

$$[ICl]^2$$

Next, place the concentrations of the reactants in the denominator. Their powers will be an understood (not written) 1, because the coefficient of each reactant is 1.

$$K_{eq} = \frac{[ICl]^2}{[I_2][Cl_2]}$$

The equilibrium constant expression is now complete.

b. The reactant carbon (C) is a solid and thus will not appear in the equilibrium constant expression. Therefore,

$$K_{eq} = \frac{[CO][H_2]}{[H_2O]}$$

Note that all of the powers in this expression are 1 as a result of all the coefficients in the balanced equation being equal to unity.

If the concentrations of all reactants and products are known at equilibrium, the numerical value of the equilibrium constant can be calculated by using the equilibrium constant expression.

EXAMPLE 9-6

Calculating the Value of an Equilibrium Constant from Equilibrium Concentrations

Calculate the value of the equilibrium constant for the equilibrium system

$$2NO(g) \rightleftharpoons N_2(g) + O_2(g)$$

at 1000°C, given that the equilibrium concentrations are 0.0026 M for NO, 0.024 M for N_2, and 0.024 M for O_2.

Solution

First, write the equilibrium constant expression.

$$K_{eq} = \frac{[N_2][O_2]}{[NO]^2}$$

Next, substitute the equilibrium concentrations into the equilibrium constant expression and solve the equation.

$$K_{eq} = \frac{[0.024][0.024]}{[0.0026]^2}$$

$$K_{eq} = 85$$

In doing the mathematics, remember that the number 0.0026 must be squared.

Temperature Dependence of Equilibrium Constants

The value of K_{eq} for a reaction depends on the reaction temperature. If the temperature changes, the value of K_{eq} also changes, and thus differing amounts of reactants and products will be present. Note that the equilibrium constant calculated in Example 9-6 is for a temperature of 1000°C. The equilibrium constant for this reaction would have a different value at a lower or a higher temperature.

Does the value of an equilibrium constant increase or decrease when reaction temperature is increased? For reactions where the forward reaction is *exothermic*, the equilibrium constant *decreases* with increasing temperature. For reactions where the forward reaction is *endothermic*, the equilibrium constant *increases* with increasing temperature (Section 9-5).

Equilibrium Constant Values and Reaction Completeness

The magnitude of an equilibrium constant value conveys information about how far a reaction has proceeded toward completion. If the equilibrium constant value is large (10^3 or greater), the equilibrium system contains more products than reactants. Conversely, if the equilibrium constant value is small (10^{-3} or less), the equilibrium system contains more reactants than products. Table 9-2 further compares equilibrium constant values and the extent to which a chemical reaction has occurred.

Equilibrium position *is a qualitative indication of the relative amounts of reactants and products present when a chemical reaction reaches equilibrium.* As shown in the last column of Table 9-2, the terms *far to the right, to the right, neither to the right nor to the left, to the left,* and *far to the left* are used in describing equilibrium position. In equilibrium situations where the concentrations of products are greater than those of reactants, the equilibrium position is said to lie to the *right* because products are always listed on the right side of a chemical equation. Conversely, when reactants dominate at equilibrium, the equilibrium position lies to the *left*. The terminology *neither to the right nor to the left* indicates that significant amounts of both reactants and products are present in an equilibrium mixture.

▶ Table 9-2 **Equilibrium Constant Values and the Extent to Which a Chemical Reaction Has Taken Place**

Value of K_{eq}	Relative Amounts of Products and Reactants	Description of Equilibrium Position
very large (10^{30})	essentially all products	far to the right
large (10^{10})	more products than reactants	to the right
near unity (between 10^3 and 10^{-3})	significant amounts of both reactants and products	neither to the right nor to the left
small (10^{-10})	more reactants than products	to the left
very small (10^{-30})	essentially all reactants	far to the left

Equilibrium position can also be indicated by varying the length of the arrows in the half-headed arrow notation for a reversible reaction. The longer arrow indicates the direction of the predominant reaction. For example, the arrow notation in the equation

$$CO_2 + H_2O \rightleftharpoons H_2CO_3$$

indicates that the equilibrium position lies to the right.

Section 9-8 Quick Quiz

1. Which of the following is the correct equilibrium constant expression for the reaction

$$3C(g) \longrightarrow A(g) + 2B(g)$$

   a. [A][2B]/[3C]
   b. [3C]/[A][2B]
   c. [A][B]/[C]
   d. no correct response

2. Which of the following is the correct equilibrium constant expression for the reaction

$$2D(s) \longrightarrow 2E(s) + F(g)$$

   a. [E][F]/[D]
   b. [E]^2[F]/[D]^2
   c. [F]
   d. no correct response

3. A very small value for an equilibrium constant characterizes a chemical reaction where the equilibrium position lies
   a. far to the left
   b. far to the right
   c. neither to the right nor the left
   d. no correct response

Answers: 1. d; 2. c; 3. a

9-9 Altering Equilibrium Conditions: Le Châtelier's Principle

LEARNING FOCUS

Be able to use Le Châtelier's principle to predict the effect that concentration, temperature, and pressure changes will have on a system at chemical equilibrium.

A chemical system at equilibrium is very susceptible to disruption from outside forces. A change in temperature or a change in pressure can upset the balance within the equilibrium system. Changes in the concentrations of reactants or products also upset an equilibrium.

Disturbing an equilibrium has one of two results: Either the forward reaction speeds up (to produce more products), or the reverse reaction speeds up (to produce additional reactants). Over time, the forward and reverse reactions again become equal, and a new equilibrium, different from the previous one, is established. If more products have been produced as a result of the disruption, the equilibrium is said to have *shifted to the right*. Similarly, when disruption causes more reactants to form, the equilibrium has *shifted to the left*. ◀

An equilibrium system's response to disrupting influences can be predicted by using a principle introduced by the French chemist Henri Louis Le Châtelier (Figure 9-12). **Le Châtelier's principle** *states that if a stress (change of conditions) is applied to a system in equilibrium, the system will readjust (change the equilibrium position) in the direction that best reduces the stress imposed on the system.* This principle will be used to consider how four types of change affect equilibrium position. The changes are (1) concentration changes (2) temperature changes (3) pressure changes and (4) addition of catalysts.

Concentration Changes

Adding a reactant or product to, or removing it from, a reaction mixture at equilibrium always upsets the equilibrium. If an additional amount of any reactant or product has been *added* to the system, the stress is relieved by shifting the equilibrium in the direction that *consumes* (uses up) some of the added reactant or product. Conversely, if a reactant or product is *removed* from an equilibrium system, the equilibrium shifts in a direction that *produces* more of the substance that was removed.

The effect that concentration changes will have on the gaseous equilibrium

$$N_2(g) + 3H_2(g) \rightleftharpoons 2NH_3(g)$$

is now considered. Suppose some additional H_2 is added to the equilibrium mixture. The stress of "added H_2" causes the equilibrium to shift to the right; that is, the forward reaction rate increases in order to use up some of the additional H_2.

Stress: Too much H_2 $\qquad\qquad N_2(g) + 3H_2(g) \rightleftharpoons 2NH_3(g)$
Response: Use up some of the "added" H_2 $\qquad\qquad$ Shift to the right

$[N_2]$	$[H_2]$	$[NH_3]$
decreases	decreases	increases

As the H_2 reacts, the amount of N_2 also decreases (it reacts with the H_2) and the amount of NH_3 increases (it is formed as H_2 and N_2 react).

With time, the equilibrium shift to the right caused by the addition of H_2 will cease because a new equilibrium condition (not identical to the original one) has been reached. At this new equilibrium condition, most (but not all) of the added H_2 will have been converted to NH_3. Necessary accompaniments to this change are a decreased N_2 concentration (some of it reacted with the H_2) and an increased NH_3 concentration (produced from the N_2–H_2 reaction). Figure 9-13 quantifies the changes that occur in the N_2–H_2–NH_3 equilibrium system when it is upset by the addition of H_2 for a specific set of concentrations.

Consider again the reaction between N_2 and H_2 to form NH_3.

$$N_2(g) + 3H_2(g) \rightleftharpoons 2NH_3(g)$$

Le Châtelier's principle applies in the same way to removing a reactant or product from the equilibrium mixture as it does to adding a reactant or product at equilibrium. Suppose that at equilibrium some NH_3 is removed. The equilibrium position shifts to the right to replenish the NH_3.

Within the human body, numerous equilibrium situations exist that shift in response to a concentration change. ◀ Consider, for example, the equilibrium between glucose in the blood and stored glucose (glycogen) in the liver:

$$\text{Glucose in blood} \rightleftharpoons \text{stored glucose} + H_2O$$

Strenuous exercise or hard work causes blood glucose levels to decrease. The human body's response to this stress (not enough glucose in the blood) involves the liver converting glycogen into glucose. Conversely, when an excess of glucose is present in the blood (after a meal), the liver converts the excess glucose in the blood into its storage form (glycogen).

◀ *Products are written on the right side of a chemical equation. A shift to the right means more products are produced. Conversely, because reactants are written on the left side of an equation, a shift to the left means more reactants are produced.*

Figure 9-12 Henri Louis Le Châtelier (1850–1936), although most famous for the principle that bears his name, was amazingly diverse in his interests. He worked on metallurgical processes, cements, glasses, fuels, and explosives and was also noted for his skills in industrial management.

◀ *Thousands of chemical equilibria simultaneously exist in biochemical systems. Many of them are interrelated. When the concentration of one substance changes, many equilibria are affected.*

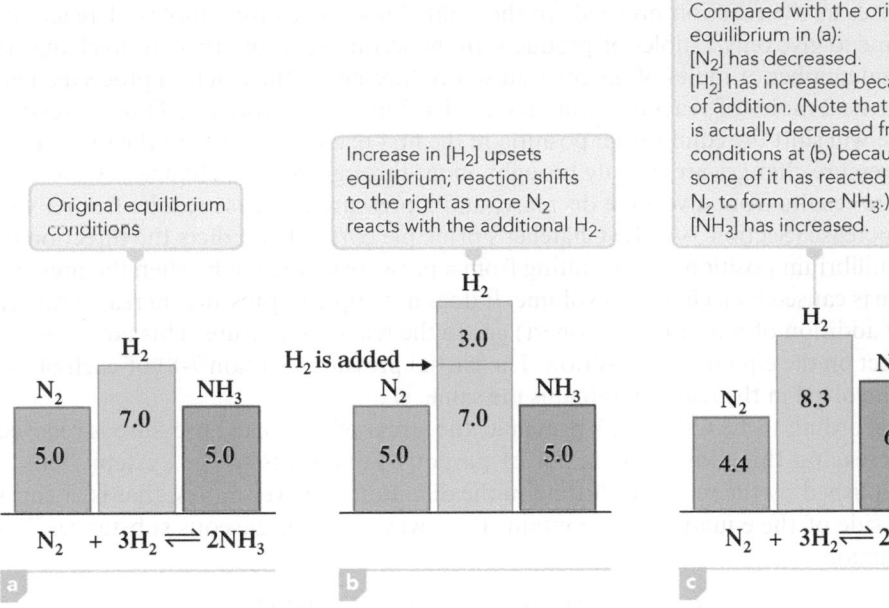

Original equilibrium conditions

Increase in [H$_2$] upsets equilibrium; reaction shifts to the right as more N$_2$ reacts with the additional H$_2$.

New equilibrium conditions. Compared with the original equilibrium in (a): [N$_2$] has decreased. [H$_2$] has increased because of addition. (Note that [H$_2$] is actually decreased from conditions at (b) because some of it has reacted with N$_2$ to form more NH$_3$.) [NH$_3$] has increased.

Figure 9-13 Concentration changes that result when H$_2$ is added to an equilibrium mixture involving the system

$$N_2(g) + 3H_2(g) \rightleftharpoons 2NH_3(g)$$

Temperature Changes

Le Châtelier's principle can be used to predict the influence of temperature changes on an equilibrium, provided whether the reaction is exothermic or endothermic is known. For *exothermic reactions*, heat can be treated as one of the *products;* for *endothermic reactions*, heat can be treated as one of the *reactants.*

Consider the exothermic reaction

$$H_2(g) + F_2(g) \rightleftharpoons 2HF(g) + \text{heat}$$

Heat is produced when the reaction proceeds to the right. Thus if heat is added to an exothermic system at equilibrium (by raising the temperature), the system will shift to the left in an attempt to decrease the amount of heat present. When equilibrium is reestablished, the concentrations of H$_2$ and F$_2$ will be higher, and the concentration of HF will have decreased. Lowering the temperature of an exothermic reaction mixture causes the reaction to shift to the right as the system acts to replace the lost heat (Figure 9-14).

The behavior, with temperature change, of an equilibrium system involving an endothermic reaction, such as

$$\text{Heat} + 2CO_2(g) \rightleftharpoons 2CO(g) + O_2(g)$$

is opposite that of an exothermic reaction because a shift to the left produces heat. Consequently, an increase in temperature will cause the equilibrium to shift to the right (to decrease the amount of heat present), and a decrease in temperature will produce a shift to the left (to generate more heat).

Pressure Changes

Pressure changes affect systems at equilibrium only when gases are involved—and then only in cases where the chemical reaction is such that a change in the total number of moles in the gaseous state occurs. This latter point can be illustrated by considering the following two gas-phase reactions:

$$\underbrace{2H_2(g) + O_2(g)}_{\text{3 moles of gas}} \longrightarrow \underbrace{2H_2O(g)}_{\text{2 moles of gas}}$$

$$\underbrace{H_2(g) + Cl_2(g)}_{\text{2 moles of gas}} \longrightarrow \underbrace{2HCl(g)}_{\text{2 moles of gas}}$$

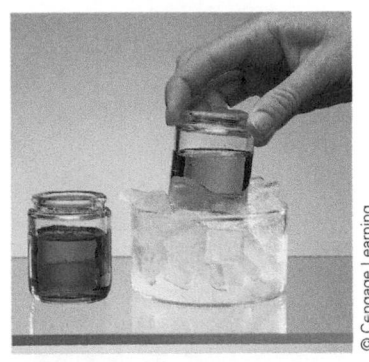

© Cengage Learning

Figure 9-14 Effect of temperature change on the equilibrium mixture

$$CoCl_4^{2-} + 6H_2O \rightleftharpoons$$
Blue
$$Co(H_2O)_6^{2+} + 4Cl^- + \text{heat}$$
Pink

At room temperature, the equilibrium mixture is blue from $CoCl_4^{2-}$. When cooled by the ice bath, the equilibrium mixture turns pink from $Co(H_2O)_6^{2+}$. The temperature decrease causes the equilibrium position to shift to the right.

In the first reaction, the total number of moles of gaseous reactants and products decreases as the reaction proceeds to the right. This is because 3 moles of reactants combine to give only 2 moles of products. In the second reaction, there is no change in the total number of moles of gaseous substances present as the reaction proceeds. This is because 2 moles of reactants combine to give 2 moles of products. Thus a pressure change will shift the equilibrium position in the first reaction but not in the second.

Pressure changes are usually brought about through volume changes. A pressure increase results from a volume decrease, and a pressure decrease results from a volume increase (Section 7-4). Le Châtelier's principle correctly predicts the direction of the equilibrium position shift resulting from a pressure change only when the pressure change is caused by a change in volume. It does not apply to pressure increases caused by the addition of a nonreactive (inert) gas to the reaction mixture. This addition has no effect on the equilibrium position. The partial pressure (Section 7-8) of each of the gases involved in the reaction remains the same. ◄

▶ *Increasing the pressure associated with an equilibrium system by adding an inert gas (a gas that is not a reactant or a product in the reaction) does not affect the position of the equilibrium.*

According to Le Châtelier's principle, the stress of increased pressure is relieved by decreasing the number of moles of gaseous substances in the system. This is accomplished by the reaction shifting in the direction of fewer moles; that is, it shifts to the side of the equation that contains the fewer moles of gaseous substances. For the reaction

$$2NO_2(g) + 7H_2(g) \rightleftharpoons 2NH_3(g) + 4H_2O(g)$$

an increase in pressure would shift the equilibrium position to the right because there are 9 moles of gaseous reactants and only 6 moles of gaseous products. On the other hand, the stress of decreased pressure causes an equilibrium system to produce more moles of gaseous substances.

EXAMPLE 9-7

Using Le Châtelier's Principle to Predict How Various Changes Affect an Equilibrium System

How will the gas-phase equilibrium

$$CH_4(g) + 2H_2S(g) + heat \rightleftharpoons CS_2(g) + 4H_2(g)$$

be affected by each of the following?

a. The removal of $H_2(g)$
b. The addition of $CS_2(g)$
c. An increase in the temperature
d. An increase in the volume of the container (a decrease in pressure)

Solution

a. The equilibrium will *shift to the right*, according to Le Châtelier's principle, in an attempt to replenish the H_2 that was removed.
b. The equilibrium will *shift to the left* in an attempt to use up the extra CS_2 that has been placed in the system.
c. Raising the temperature means that heat energy has been added. In an attempt to minimize the effect of this extra heat, the position of the equilibrium will *shift to the right*, the direction that consumes heat; heat is one of the reactants in an endothermic reaction.
d. The system will *shift to the right*, the direction that produces more moles of gaseous substances (an increase of pressure). In this way, the reaction produces 5 moles of gaseous products for every 3 moles of gaseous reactants consumed.

Addition of Catalysts

Catalysts cannot change the position of an equilibrium. A catalyst functions by lowering the activation energy for a reaction. It speeds up both the forward and the reverse reactions, so it has no net effect on the position of the equilibrium. However, the lowered activation energy allows equilibrium to be established more quickly than if the catalyst were absent.

Chemistry at a Glance—Le Châtelier's Principle and Altered Equilibrium Conditions—summarizes the behavior of an equilibrium system when "stressed" by concentration changes, temperature changes, or pressure changes.

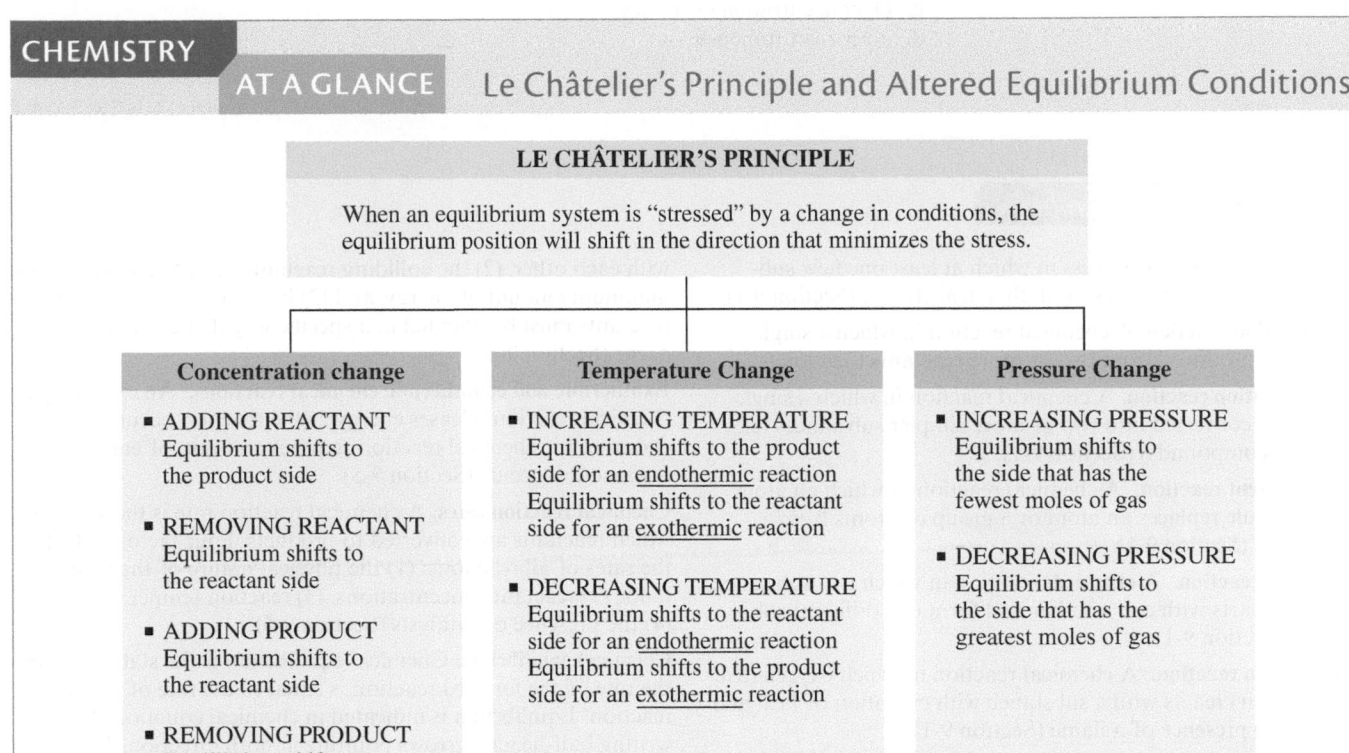

CHEMISTRY AT A GLANCE — Le Châtelier's Principle and Altered Equilibrium Conditions

LE CHÂTELIER'S PRINCIPLE

When an equilibrium system is "stressed" by a change in conditions, the equilibrium position will shift in the direction that minimizes the stress.

Concentration change

- ADDING REACTANT
  Equilibrium shifts to the product side

- REMOVING REACTANT
  Equilibrium shifts to the reactant side

- ADDING PRODUCT
  Equilibrium shifts to the reactant side

- REMOVING PRODUCT
  Equilibrium shifts to the product side

Temperature Change

- INCREASING TEMPERATURE
  Equilibrium shifts to the product side for an endothermic reaction
  Equilibrium shifts to the reactant side for an exothermic reaction

- DECREASING TEMPERATURE
  Equilibrium shifts to the reactant side for an endothermic reaction
  Equilibrium shifts to the product side for an exothermic reaction

Pressure Change

- INCREASING PRESSURE
  Equilibrium shifts to the side that has the fewest moles of gas

- DECREASING PRESSURE
  Equilibrium shifts to the side that has the greatest moles of gas

Section 9-9 Quick Quiz

1. Le Châtelier's principle states that if an equilibrium is disturbed
   a. the temperature of the system will always increase
   b. the system will shift such that equilibrium is reestablished
   c. the concentration of reactants will always decrease
   d. no correct response

2. Which of the following changes will shift the position of the equilibrium to the left for the chemical reaction

$$N_2(g) + 3H_2(g) \longrightarrow 2NH_3(g)$$

   a. decrease the concentration of NH_3
   b. increase the concentration of H_2
   c. decrease the concentration of N_2
   d. no correct response

3. Which of the following effects will occur if the temperature of the following equilibrium system is increased?

$$H_2(g) + F_2(g) \longrightarrow 2HF(g) + \text{heat}$$

   a. the equilibrium shifts to the right
   b. HF concentration increases
   c. H_2 and F_2 concentrations increase
   d. no correct response

(continued)

4. Which of the following effects will occur if the pressure on the following equilibrium system is decreased?

$$2NO_2(g) \longrightarrow N_2(g) + 2O_2(g)$$

a. NO_2 concentration increases
b. N_2 concentration remains the same
c. O_2 concentration decreases
d. no correct response

Answers: 1. b; 2. c; 3. c; 4. d

Concepts to Remember

Chemical reaction. A process in which at least one new substance is produced as a result of chemical change (Section 9-1).

Combination reaction. A chemical reaction in which a single product is produced from two or more reactants (Section 9-1).

Decomposition reaction. A chemical reaction in which a single reactant is converted into two or more simpler substances (elements or compounds) (Section 9-1).

Displacement reaction. A chemical reaction in which an atom or a molecule replaces an atom or a group of atoms from a compound (Section 9-1).

Exchange reaction. A chemical reaction in which two substances exchange parts with one another and form two different substances (Section 9-1).

Combustion reaction. A chemical reaction in which oxygen (usually from air) reacts with a substance with evolution of heat and usually the presence of a flame (Section 9-1).

Redox reaction. A chemical reaction in which there is a transfer of electrons from one reactant to another reactant (Section 9-2).

Nonredox reaction. A chemical reaction in which there is no transfer of electrons from one reactant to another reactant (Section 9-2).

Oxidation number. A number that represents the charge that an atom appears to have when the electrons in each bond it is participating in are assigned to the more electronegative of the two atoms involved in the bond. Oxidation numbers are used to identify the electron transfer that occurs in a redox reaction (Section 9-2).

Oxidation-reduction terminology. Oxidation is the loss of electrons; reduction is the gain of electrons. An oxidizing agent causes oxidation by accepting electrons from the other reactant. A reducing agent causes reduction by providing electrons for the other reactant to accept (Section 9-3).

Collision theory. Collision theory summarizes the conditions required for a chemical reaction to take place. The three basic tenets of collision theory are: (1) reactant molecules must collide with each other, (2) the colliding reactants must possess a certain minimum amount of energy, and (3) in some cases, colliding reactants must be oriented in a specific way if the reaction is to occur (Section 9-4).

Exothermic and endothermic chemical reactions. An exothermic chemical reaction releases energy as the reaction occurs. An endothermic chemical reaction requires an input of energy as the reaction occurs (Section 9-5).

Chemical reaction rates. A chemical reaction rate is the speed at which reactants are converted to products. Four factors affect the rates of all reactions: (1) the physical nature of the reactants, (2) reactant concentrations, (3) reaction temperature, and (4) the presence of catalysts (Section 9-6).

Chemical equilibrium. Chemical equilibrium is the state wherein the rate of the forward reaction is equal to the rate of the reverse reaction. Equilibrium is indicated in chemical equations by writing half-headed arrows pointing in both directions between reactants and products (Section 9-7).

Equilibrium constant. The equilibrium constant relates the concentrations of reactants and products at equilibrium. The value of an equilibrium constant is obtained by writing an equilibrium constant expression and then numerically evaluating it. Equilibrium constant expressions can be obtained from the balanced chemical equations for reactions (Section 9-8).

Equilibrium position. The relative amounts of reactants and products present in a system at equilibrium define the equilibrium position. The equilibrium position is toward the right when a large amount of product is present and is toward the left when a large amount of reactant is present (Section 9-8).

Le Châtelier's principle. Le Châtelier's principle states that when a stress (change of conditions) is applied to a system in equilibrium, the system will readjust (change the equilibrium position) in the direction that best reduces the stress imposed on it. Stresses that change an equilibrium position include (1) changes in amount of reactants and/or products, (2) changes in temperature, and (3) changes in pressure (Section 9-9).

Exercises and Problems

The members of each pair of problems test similar materials. Answers to odd-numbered problems are given at the back of the book. Problems denoted with a ▲ are multi-concept problems that test concepts found not only in the section under consideration but also concepts found in one or more earlier sections of the chapter.

Types of Chemical Reactions (Section 9-1)

9-1   What is the general chemical equation for each of the following types of chemical reactions?
  a. Displacement reaction
  b. Combination reaction

9-2 What is the general chemical equation for each of the following types of chemical reactions?
a. Exchange reaction   b. Decomposition reaction

9-3 Classify each of the following reactions as a combination, decomposition, displacement, exchange, or combustion reaction.
a. $3CuSO_4 + 2Al \rightarrow Al_2(SO_4)_3 + 3Cu$
b. $K_2CO_3 \rightarrow K_2O + CO_2$
c. $2AgNO_3 + K_2SO_4 \rightarrow Ag_2SO_4 + 2KNO_3$
d. $2P + 3H_2 \rightarrow 2PH_3$

9-4 Classify each of the following reactions as a combination, decomposition, displacement, exchange, or combustion reaction.
a. $2NaHCO_3 \rightarrow Na_2CO_3 + CO_2 + H_2O$
b. $2Ag_2CO_3 \rightarrow 4Ag + 2CO_2 + O_2$
c. $2C_2H_6 + 7O_2 \rightarrow 4CO_2 + 6H_2O$
d. $Mg + 2HCl \rightarrow MgCl_2 + H_2$

9-5 Write the chemical formulas for the products formed when each of the following hydrocarbons undergoes complete combustion.
a. CH_4 b. C_4H_{10} c. C_4H_6 d. C_6H_6

9-6 Write the chemical formulas for the products formed when each of the following hydrocarbons undergoes complete combustion.
a. C_2H_6 b. C_2H_4 c. C_7H_8 d. C_5H_{10}

9-7 Indicate whether or not each of the following chemical reactions represents a combustion reaction.
a. $4Fe + 3O_2 \rightarrow 2Fe_2O_3$
b. $C_2H_6O + 3O_2 \rightarrow 2CO_2 + 3H_2O$
c. $4NH_3 + 3O_2 \rightarrow 2N_2 + 6H_2O$
d. $C + CO_2 \rightarrow 2CO$

9-8 Indicate whether or not each of the following chemical reactions represents a combustion reaction.
a. $2CuS + 3O_2 \rightarrow 2CuO + 2SO_2$
b. $2Mg + O_2 \rightarrow 2MgO$
c. $H_2O + CO \rightarrow H_2 + CO_2$
d. $C_4H_{10}O + 6O_2 \rightarrow 4CO_2 + 5H_2O$

9-9 Indicate to which of the following types of reactions each of the statements listed applies: *combination, decomposition, displacement, exchange,* and *combustion.* More than one answer is possible for a given statement.
a. An element may be a reactant.
b. An element may be a product.
c. A compound may be a reactant.
d. A compound may be a product.

9-10 Indicate to which of the following types of reactions each of the statements listed applies: *combination, decomposition, displacement, exchange,* and *combustion.* More than one answer is possible for a given statement.
a. Two reactants are required.
b. Only one reactant is present.
c. Two products are present.
d. Only one product is present.

Redox and Nonredox Chemical Reactions (Section 9-2)

9-11 What is the oxidation number of S in each of the following molecules?
a. S_2 b. S_8 c. H_2S d. SO_3

9-12 What is the oxidation number of N in each of the following molecules?
a. N_2 b. NO_2 c. NO d. N_2O

9-13 Determine the oxidation number of the indicated element in each of the following ions.
a. Al in Al^{3+} b. S in S^{2-}
c. N in NO_3^- d. P in PO_4^{3-}

9-14 Determine the oxidation number of the indicated element in each of the following ions.
a. Mg in Mg^{2+} b. N in N^{3-}
c. Cl in ClO^- d. Cl in ClO_4^-

9-15 What is the oxidation number of chlorine in each of the following chlorine-containing compounds?
a. $NaClO$ b. $NaClO_3$
c. $HClO_4$ d. PCl_3

9-16 What is the oxidation number of carbon in each of the following carbon-containing compounds?
a. CO b. CO_2 c. CCl_4 d. Na_2CO_3

9-17 What is the oxidation number of each element present in the following compounds or ions?
a. SiF_4 b. H_2SO_4 c. Na_3PO_4 d. $Cr_2O_7^{2-}$

9-18 What is the oxidation number of each element present in the following compounds or ions?
a. NF_3 b. HNO_3 c. K_2SO_4 d. MnO_4^-

9-19 Classify each of the following reactions as a redox reaction or a nonredox reaction.
a. $2Cu + O_2 \rightarrow 2CuO$
b. $K_2O + H_2O \rightarrow 2KOH$
c. $2KClO_3 \rightarrow 2KCl + 3O_2$
d. $CH_4 + 2O_2 \rightarrow CO_2 + 2H_2O$

9-20 Classify each of the following reactions as a redox reaction or a nonredox reaction.
a. $2NO + O_2 \rightarrow 2NO_2$
b. $CO_2 + H_2O \rightarrow H_2CO_3$
c. $Zn + 2AgNO_3 \rightarrow Zn(NO_3)_2 + 2Ag$
d. $HNO_3 + NaOH \rightarrow NaNO_3 + H_2O$

▲**9-21** Classify each of the following reactions as (1) a redox reaction (2) a nonredox reaction or (3) "can't classify" because of insufficient information.
a. A combination reaction in which one reactant is an element
b. A decomposition reaction in which the products are all elements
c. A decomposition reaction in which one of the products is an element
d. A displacement reaction in which both of the reactants are compounds

▲**9-22** Classify each of the following reactions as (1) a redox reaction (2) a nonredox reaction or (3) "can't classify" because of insufficient information.
a. A combination reaction in which both reactants are elements
b. A combination reaction in which all reactants and products are compounds
c. A decomposition reaction in which all reactants and products are compounds
d. A combustion reaction in which CO_2 and H_2O are the products

▲9-23 Classify each of the following reactions using one selection from the choices *redox* and *nonredox* combined with one selection from the choices *combination, decomposition, displacement, exchange,* and *combustion.*
 a. $Zn + Cu(NO_3)_2 \rightarrow Zn(NO_3)_2 + Cu$
 b. $CH_4 + O_2 \rightarrow CO_2 + 2H_2O$
 c. $2CuO \rightarrow 2Cu + O_2$
 d. $NaCl + AgNO_3 \rightarrow AgCl + NaNO_3$

▲9-24 Classify each of the following reactions using one selection from the choices *redox* and *nonredox* combined with one selection from the choices *combination, decomposition, displacement, exchange,* and *combustion.*
 a. $HCl + NaOH \rightarrow NaCl + HOH$
 b. $H_2SO_4 \rightarrow SO_3 + H_2O$
 c. $C_3H_8 + 5O_2 \rightarrow 3CO_2 + 4H_2O$
 d. $Ca + Cl_2 \rightarrow CaCl_2$

Terminology Associated with Redox Processes (Section 9-3)

9-25 In each of the following changes is the reactant undergoing oxidation or reduction? (The given equation for the change is not a complete chemical equation.)
 a. $SO_2 \rightarrow SO_3$ b. $N_2O \rightarrow NO$
 c. $Cr^{3+} \rightarrow Cr^{2+}$ d. $S^{2-} \rightarrow S$

9-26 In each of the following changes is the reactant undergoing oxidation or reduction? (The given equation for the change is not a complete chemical equation.)
 a. $S \rightarrow SO_2$ b. $NO_2 \rightarrow NO$
 c. $Fe^{2+} \rightarrow Fe^{3+}$ d. $Mg^{2+} \rightarrow Mg$

9-27 Identify which substance is oxidized and which substance is reduced in each of the following redox reactions.
 a. $N_2 + 3H_2 \rightarrow 2NH_3$
 b. $Cl_2 + 2KI \rightarrow 2KCl + I_2$
 c. $Sb_2O_3 + 3Fe \rightarrow 2Sb + 3FeO$
 d. $3H_2SO_3 + 2HNO_3 \rightarrow 2NO + H_2O + 3H_2SO_4$

9-28 Identify which substance is oxidized and which substance is reduced in each of the following redox reactions.
 a. $2Al + 3Cl_2 \rightarrow 2AlCl_3$
 b. $Zn + CuCl_2 \rightarrow ZnCl_2 + Cu$
 c. $2NiS + 3O_2 \rightarrow 2NiO + 2SO_2$
 d. $3H_2S + 2HNO_3 \rightarrow 3S + 2NO + 4H_2O$

9-29 Identify which substance is the oxidizing agent and which substance is the reducing agent in each of the redox reactions of Problem 9-27.

9-30 Identify which substance is the oxidizing agent and which substance is the reducing agent in each of the redox reactions of Problem 9-28.

9-31 Indicate whether each of the following substances loses or gains electrons in a redox reaction.
 a. The oxidizing agent
 b. The reducing agent
 c. The substance undergoing oxidation
 d. The substance undergoing reduction

9-32 Indicate whether each of the following substances undergoes an oxidation number increase or decrease in a redox reaction.
 a. The oxidizing agent
 b. The reducing agent
 c. The substance undergoing oxidation
 d. The substance undergoing reduction

9-33 Indicate whether each of the following pairings of concepts is a correct or an incorrect pairing.
 a. reducing agent and gain of electrons
 b. substance oxidized and loss of electrons
 c. oxidizing agent and increase in oxidation number
 d. oxidizing agent and substance oxidized

9-34 Indicate whether each of the following pairings of concepts is a correct or an incorrect pairing.
 a. reducing agent and gain of electrons
 b. substance oxidized and increase in oxidation number
 c. oxidizing agent and gain of electrons
 d. reducing agent and substance reduced

Collision Theory and Chemical Reactions (Section 9-4)

9-35 What are the three central concepts associated with collision theory?

9-36 Why are most chemical reactions carried out either in liquid solution or in the gaseous phase?

9-37 What two factors determine whether a collision between two reactant molecules will result in a reaction?

9-38 What happens to the reactants in an ineffective molecular collision?

Exothermic and Endothermic Chemical Reactions (Section 9-5)

9-39 Which of the following reactions are endothermic, and which are exothermic?
 a. $C_2H_4 + 3O_2 \rightarrow 2CO_2 + 2H_2O + heat$
 b. $N_2 + 2O_2 + heat \rightarrow 2NO_2$
 c. $2H_2O + heat \rightarrow 2H_2 + O_2$
 d. $2KClO_3 \rightarrow 2KCl + 3O_2 + heat$

9-40 Which of the following reactions are endothermic, and which are exothermic?
 a. $CaCO_3 + heat \rightarrow CaO + CO_2$
 b. $N_2 + 3H_2 \rightarrow 2NH_3 + heat$
 c. $CO + 3H_2 + heat \rightarrow CH_4 + H_2O$
 d. $2N_2 + 6H_2O + heat \rightarrow 4NH_3 + 3O_2$

9-41 Should *heat* be added as a reactant or as a product to each of the following equations for chemical reactions based on the given thermicity for the reaction?
 a. $H_2 + Cl_2 \rightarrow 2HCl$ (exothermic)
 b. $4NO + 6H_2O \rightarrow 4NH_3 + 5O_2$ (endothermic)
 c. $2H_2O + 2Cl_2 \rightarrow 4HCl + O_2$ (endothermic)
 d. $2H_2O \rightarrow 2H_2 + O_2$ (exothermic)

9-42 Should *heat* be added as a reactant or as a product to each of the following equations for chemical reactions based on the given thermicity for the reaction?
 a. $2SO_2 + O_2 \rightarrow 2SO_3$ (exothermic)
 b. $N_2 + O_2 \rightarrow 2NO$ (endothermic)
 c. $CH_4 + 2O_2 \rightarrow CO_2 + 2H_2O$ (exothermic)
 d. $2H_2O + 2Cl_2 \rightarrow 4HCl + O_2$ (endothermic)

9-43 In a certain chemical reaction, the average energy of the products is lower than the average energy of the reactants.
 a. Is the chemical reaction exothermic or endothermic?
 b. Is energy released or absorbed in the chemical reaction?

9-44 Indicate whether each of the following is a characteristic of an endothermic or an exothermic chemical reaction.
a. There is more energy stored in product molecule bonds than in reactant molecule bonds.
b. The energy required to break bonds in the reactants is less than the energy released by bond formation in the products.

9-45 Sketch an energy diagram graph representing an exothermic reaction, and label the following.
a. Average energy of reactants
b. Average energy of products
c. Activation energy
d. Amount of energy liberated during the reaction

9-46 Sketch an energy diagram graph representing an endothermic reaction, and label the following.
a. Average energy of reactants
b. Average energy of products
c. Activation energy
d. Amount of energy absorbed during the reaction

Factors That Influence Chemical Reaction Rates (Section 9-6)

9-47 Using collision theory, indicate why each of the following factors influences the rate of a reaction.
a. Temperature of reactants
b. Presence of a catalyst

9-48 Using collision theory, indicate why each of the following factors influences the rate of a reaction.
a. Physical nature of reactants
b. Reactant concentrations

9-49 Substances burn more rapidly in pure oxygen than in air. Explain why.

9-50 Milk will sour in a couple of days when left at room temperature, yet it can remain unspoiled for two weeks when refrigerated. Explain why.

9-51 Will each of the changes listed increase or decrease the rate of the following chemical reaction?

$$2CO + O_2 \rightarrow 2CO_2$$

a. Adding some O_2 to the reaction mixture
b. Lowering the temperature of the reaction mixture
c. Adding a catalyst to the reaction mixture
d. Removing some CO from the reaction mixture

9-52 Will each of the changes listed increase or decrease the rate of the following chemical reaction?

$$N_2 + 3H_2 \rightarrow 2NH_3$$

a. Adding some N_2 to the reaction mixture
b. Raising the temperature of the reaction mixture
c. Removing a catalyst present in the reaction mixture
d. Removing some H_2 from the reaction mixture

9-53 For each of the changes listed will the rate of the following chemical reaction increase, decrease, or remain the same?

$$Cu(s) + H_2SO_4(aq) \rightarrow CuSO_4(aq) + H_2(g)$$

a. the concentration of H_2SO_4 is increased
b. the copper is ground into a powder
c. the mixture is stirred rapidly
d. the temperature of the solution is increased

9-54 For each of the changes listed will the rate of the following chemical reaction increase, decrease, or remain the same?

$$Fe(s) + 2HCl(aq) \rightarrow FeCl_2(aq) + H_2(g)$$

a. the concentration of HCl is decreased
b. the iron is ground into a powder
c. a catalyst is added to the reaction mixture
d. the temperature of the solution is decreased

9-55 Draw an energy diagram graph for an exothermic reaction where no catalyst is present. Then draw an energy diagram graph for the same reaction when a catalyst is present. Indicate the similarities and differences between the two diagrams.

9-56 Draw an energy diagram graph for an endothermic reaction where no catalyst is present. Then draw an energy diagram graph for the same reaction when a catalyst is present. Indicate the similarities and differences between the two diagrams.

▲**9-57** The characteristics of four reactions, each of which involves only two reactants, are given.

Reaction	Activation Energy	Temperature	Concentration of Reactants
1	low	low	1 mole/L of each
2	high	low	1 mole/L of each
3	low	high	1 mole/L of each
4	low	low	1 mole/L of first reactant and 4 moles/L of second reactant

For each of the following pairs of the preceding reactions, compare the reaction rates when the two reactants are first mixed by indicating which reaction is faster.

a. 1 and 2   b. 1 and 3   c. 1 and 4   d. 2 and 3

▲**9-58** The characteristics of four reactions, each of which involves only two reactants, are given.

Reaction	Activation Energy	Temperature	Concentration of Reactants
1	high	low	1 mole/L of each
2	high	high	1 mole/L of each
3	low	low	1 mole/L of first reactant and 4 moles/L of second reactant
4	low	low	4 moles/L of each

For each of the following pairs of the preceding reactions, compare the reaction rates when the two reactants are first mixed by indicating which reaction is faster.

a. 1 and 2   b. 1 and 3   c. 1 and 4   d. 3 and 4

Chemical Equilibrium (Section 9-7)

9-59 What condition must be met in order for a system to be in a state of chemical equilibrium?

9-60 What relationship exists between the rates of the forward and reverse reactions for a system in a state of chemical equilibrium?

9-61 What does the term *reversible reaction* mean?

9-62 What does the notation $\rightleftharpoons$ denote when it is used in a chemical equation?

9-63 Consider the following equilibrium system.

$$N_2(g) + O_2(g) \rightleftharpoons 2NO(g)$$

a. Write the chemical equation for the forward reaction.
b. Write the chemical equation for the reverse reaction.

9-64 Consider the following equilibrium system.

$$N_2(g) + 3H_2(g) \rightleftharpoons 2NH_3(g)$$

a. Write the chemical equation for the forward reaction.
b. Write the chemical equation for the reverse reaction.

9-65 Sketch a graph showing how the concentrations of the reactants and products of a typical reversible chemical reaction vary with time.

9-66 Sketch a graph showing how the rates of the forward and reverse reactions for a typical reversible chemical reaction vary with time.

9-67 The following series of diagrams represent the reaction $X \rightleftharpoons Y$ followed over a period of time. The X molecules are red and the Y molecules are green.

──────────── **Increasing time** ────────────▶

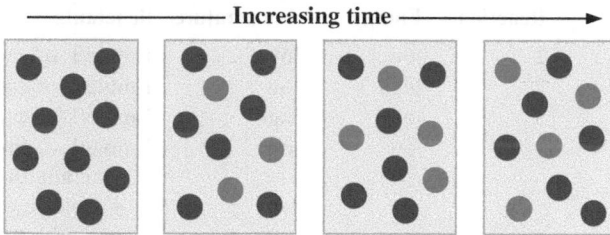

At the end of the time period depicted, has the reaction system reached equilibrium? Justify your answer with a one-sentence explanation.

9-68 The following series of diagrams represent the reaction $X \rightleftharpoons Y$ followed over a period of time. The X molecules are red and the Y molecules are green.

──────────── **Increasing time** ────────────▶

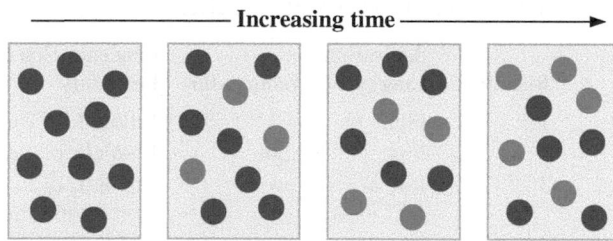

At the end of the time period depicted, has the reaction system reached equilibrium? Justify your answer with a one-sentence explanation.

9-69 For the reaction $A_2 + 2B \rightarrow 2AB$, diagram I depicts an initial reaction mixture, where A_2 molecules are red and B atoms are green. Which of the diagrams II through IV is a possible equilibrium state for the reaction system? There may be more than one correct answer.

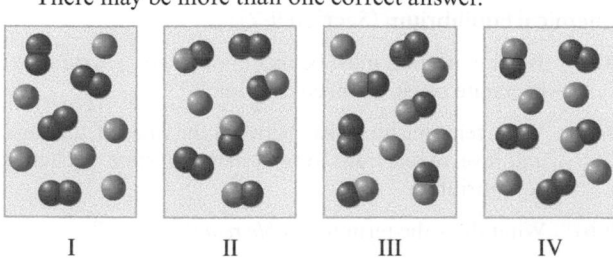

    I   II   III   IV

9-70 For the reaction $A_2 + B_2 \rightarrow 2AB$, diagram I depicts an initial reaction mixture, where A_2 molecules are red and B_2 molecules are green. Which of the diagrams II through IV is a possible equilibrium state for the reaction system? There may be more than one correct answer.

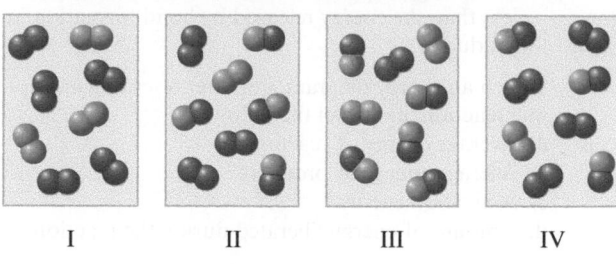

    I   II   III   IV

Equilibrium Constants (Section 9-8)

9-71 Write equilibrium constant expressions for the following generalized reactions.
a. $2X(g) + 3Y(g) \rightleftharpoons 2Z(g)$
b. $2X(g) + 3Y(s) \rightleftharpoons 2Z(g)$
c. $2X(s) + 3Y(s) \rightleftharpoons 2Z(g)$
d. $2X(g) + 3Y(g) \rightleftharpoons 2Z(s)$

9-72 Write equilibrium constant expressions for the following generalized reactions.
a. $3X(g) + 2Y(g) \rightleftharpoons Z(g)$
b. $3X(g) + 2Y(s) \rightleftharpoons Z(g)$
c. $3X(s) + 2Y(s) \rightleftharpoons Z(g)$
d. $3X(g) + 2Y(g) \rightleftharpoons Z(s)$

9-73 Write equilibrium constant expressions for the following reactions.
a. $2NOCl(g) \rightleftharpoons 2NO(g) + Cl_2(g)$
b. $4NH_3(g) + 5O_2(g) \rightleftharpoons 4NO(g) + 6H_2O(g)$
c. $Ca(s) + Cl_2(g) \rightleftharpoons CaCl_2(s)$
d. $AgNO_3(aq) + NaCl(aq) \rightleftharpoons AgCl(s) + NaNO_3(aq)$

9-74 Write equilibrium constant expressions for the following reactions.
a. $2SO_2(g) + O_2(g) \rightleftharpoons 2SO_3(g)$
b. $CS_2(g) + 4H_2(g) \rightleftharpoons CH_4(g) + 2H_2S(g)$
c. $PCl_5(s) \rightleftharpoons PCl_3(l) + Cl_2(g)$
d. $BaCl_2(aq) + Na_2SO_4(aq) \rightleftharpoons 2NaCl(aq) + BaSO_4(s)$

9-75 Calculate the value of the equilibrium constant for the reaction

$$N_2O_4(g) \rightleftharpoons 2NO_2(g)$$

if the concentrations of the species at equilibrium are $[N_2O_4] = 0.213$ and $[NO_2] = 0.0032$.

9-76 Calculate the value of the equilibrium constant for the reaction

$$N_2(g) + 2O_2(g) \rightleftharpoons 2NO_2(g)$$

if the concentrations of the species at equilibrium are $[N_2] = 0.0013$, $[O_2] = 0.0024$, and $[NO_2] = 0.00065$.

9-77 Use the given K_{eq} value and the terminology in Table 9-2 to describe the relative amounts of reactants and products present in each of the following equilibrium situations.
a. $H_2(g) + Br_2(g) \rightleftharpoons 2HBr(g)$ K_{eq} (25°C) $= 2.0 \times 10^9$
b. $2HCl(g) \rightleftharpoons H_2(g) + Cl_2(g)$ K_{eq} (25°C) $= 3.2 \times 10^{-34}$
c. $SO_2(g) + NO_2(g) \rightleftharpoons NO(g) + SO_3(g)$ K_{eq} (460°C) $= 85.0$
d. $COCl_2(g) \rightleftharpoons CO(g) + Cl_2(g)$ K_{eq}(395°C) $= 0.046$

9-78 Use the given K_{eq} value and the terminology in Table 9-2 to describe the relative amounts of reactants and products present in each of the following equilibrium situations.
a. $2NO(g) \rightleftharpoons N_2(g) + O_2(g)$ $K_{eq}(25°C) = 1 \times 10^{30}$
b. $N_2(g) + 3H_2(g) \rightleftharpoons 2NH_3(g)$ $K_{eq}(25°C) = 1 \times 10^9$
c. $PCl_5(g) \rightleftharpoons PCl_3(g) + Cl_2(g)$ $K_{eq}(127°C) = 1 \times 10^{-2}$
d. $2Na_2O(s) \rightleftharpoons 4Na(l) + O_2(g)$ $K_{eq}(427°C) = 1 \times 10^{-25}$

9-79 Write a balanced chemical equation for a totally gaseous equilibrium system that would lead to the following equilibrium constant expression.

$$K_{eq} = \frac{[N_2]^2[H_2O]^6}{[NH_3]^4[O_2]^3}$$

9-80 Write a balanced chemical equation for a totally gaseous equilibrium system that would lead to the following equilibrium constant expression.

$$K_{eq} = \frac{[CH_4][H_2S]^2}{[CS_2][H_2]^4}$$

9-81 The following four diagrams represent gaseous equilibrium mixtures for the reaction $A_2 + B_2 \rightarrow 2AB$ at four different temperatures. For which of the diagrams is the numerical value of the equilibrium constant the largest? (A atoms are red and B atoms are green in the various diagrams.)

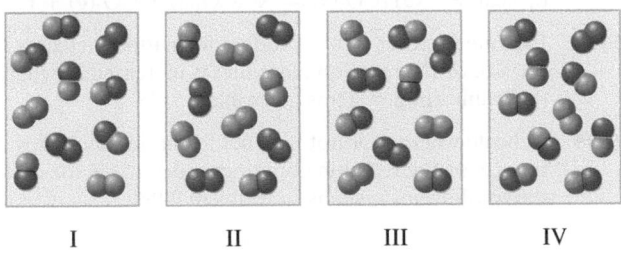

I II III IV

9-82 Based on the diagrams, chemical reaction, and reaction conditions depicted in Problem 9-81, for which of the diagrams is the numerical value of the equilibrium constant the smallest?

9-83 The following four diagrams represent gaseous reaction mixtures for the chemical reaction $A_2 + B_2 \rightarrow 2AB$. If the numerical value of the equilibrium constant for the reaction is 64, which of the diagrams represents the equilibrium mixture? (A atoms are red and B atoms are green in the various diagrams.)

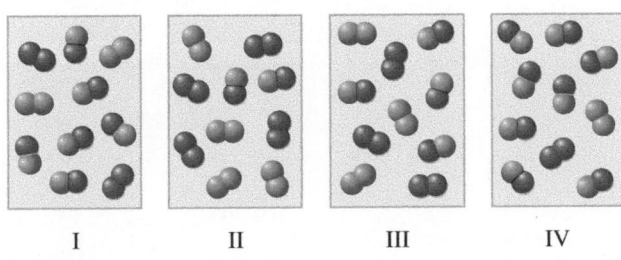

I II III IV

9-84 Based on the diagrams, chemical reaction, and reaction conditions depicted in Problem 9-83, which of the diagrams represents the equilibrium mixture if the numerical value of the equilibrium constant is 9.0?

9-85 Indicate whether or not each of the following changes would affect the *value* of a system's equilibrium constant.
a. Removal of a reactant from the equilibrium mixture
b. Decrease in the system's total pressure
c. Decrease in the system's temperature
d. Addition of a catalyst to the equilibrium mixture

9-86 Indicate whether or not each of the following changes would affect the *value* of a system's equilibrium constant.
a. Addition of a product to the equilibrium mixture
b. Increase in the system's total pressure
c. Increase in the system's temperature
d. Addition of both a reactant and a product to the equilibrium mixture

Le Châtelier's Principle (Section 9-9)

9-87 For the generalized chemical reaction

$$A(g) + B(g) \rightleftharpoons C(g) + D(g)$$

determine whether the concentration of A in an equilibrium mixture will (1) increase, (2) decrease, or (3) not change when each of the following changes is effected.
a. concentration of B is increased
b. concentration of C is decreased
c. concentration of D is increased
d. concentration of D is decreased

9-88 For the generalized chemical reaction

$$A(g) + B(g) \rightleftharpoons C(g) + D(g)$$

determine whether the concentration of D in an equilibrium mixture will (1) increase, (2) decrease, or (3) not change when each of the following changes is effected.
a. concentration of A is increased
b. concentration of B is decreased
c. concentration of C is increased
d. concentration of C is decreased

9-89 For the reaction

$$C_6H_6(g) + 3H_2(g) \rightleftharpoons C_6H_{12}(g) + \text{heat}$$

determine in what direction the equilibrium will be shifted by each of the following changes.
a. Increasing the concentration of C_6H_{12}
b. Decreasing the concentration of C_6H_6
c. Increasing the temperature
d. Decreasing the pressure by increasing the volume of the container

9-90 For the reaction

$$C_6H_6(g) + 3H_2(g) \rightleftharpoons C_6H_{12}(g) + \text{heat}$$

determine in what direction the equilibrium will be shifted by each of the following changes.
a. Decreasing the concentration of H_2
b. Increasing the concentration of C_6H_6
c. Decreasing the temperature
d. Increasing the pressure by decreasing the volume of the container

9-91 Consider the following chemical system at equilibrium.

$$CO(g) + H_2O(g) + \text{heat} \rightleftharpoons CO_2(g) + H_2(g)$$

For each of the following adjustments of conditions, indicate the effect (shifts left, shifts right, or no effect) on the position of equilibrium.
a. Refrigerating the equilibrium mixture
b. Adding a catalyst to the equilibrium mixture
c. Adding CO to the equilibrium mixture
d. Increasing the size of the reaction container

9-92 Consider the following chemical system at equilibrium.

$$CO(g) + H_2O(g) + heat \rightleftharpoons CO_2(g) + H_2(g)$$

For each of the following adjustments of conditions, indicate the effect (shifts left, shifts right, or no effect) on the position of equilibrium.
a. Heating the equilibrium mixture
b. Increasing the pressure on the equilibrium mixture by adding a nonreactive gas
c. Adding H_2 to the equilibrium mixture
d. Decreasing the size of the reaction container

9-93 The following two diagrams represent the composition of an equilibrium mixture for the reaction $A_2 + B_2 \rightarrow 2AB$ at two different temperatures. Based on the diagrams, is the chemical reaction endothermic or exothermic? Explain your answer using Le Châtelier's principle. (A atoms are red and B atoms are green in the diagrams.)

$T = 150°C$ $\qquad$ $T = 200°C$

9-94 The following two diagrams represent the composition of an equilibrium mixture for the reaction $A_2 + B_2 \rightarrow 2AB$ at two different temperatures. Based on the diagrams, is the chemical reaction endothermic or exothermic? Explain your answer using Le Châtelier's principle. (A atoms are red and B atoms are green in the diagrams.)

$T = 250°C$ $\qquad$ $T = 400°C$

9-95 Indicate whether or not product formation increases with increasing temperature in each of the following equilibrium systems.
a. $N_2(g) + 2O_2(g) + heat \rightleftharpoons 2NO_2(g)$
b. $heat + 2N_2(g) + 6H_2O(g) \rightleftharpoons 4NH_3(g) + 3O_2(g)$
c. $C_2H_4(g) + 3O_2(g) \rightleftharpoons 2CO_2(g) + 2H_2O(g) + heat$
d. $2KClO_3(s) + heat \rightleftharpoons 2KCl(s) + 3O_2(g)$

9-96 Indicate whether or not product formation increases with increasing temperature in each of the following equilibrium systems.
a. $heat + H_2(g) + I_2(g) \rightleftharpoons 2HI(g)$
b. $CO(g) + 2H_2(g) \rightleftharpoons CH_4O(g) + heat$
c. $4NH_3(g) + 5O_2(g) \rightleftharpoons heat + 4NO(g) + 6H_2O(g)$
d. $heat + 2NaHCO_3(s) \rightleftharpoons Na_2CO_3(s) + CO_2(g) + H_2O(g)$

9-97 Indicate whether or not product formation increases if the size of the reaction container is increased for each of the equilibrium systems in Problem 9-95.

9-98 Indicate whether or not product formation increases if the size of the reaction container is decreased for each of the equilibrium systems in Problem 9-96.

Acids, Bases, and Salts

10

Jose Antonio Santiso FernÁndez/Getty images

The tartness of a vinegar-based salad dressing is caused by the acetic acid present in the vinegar.

Acids, bases, and salts are among the most common and important compounds known. In the form of aqueous solutions, these compounds are key materials in both biochemical systems and the chemical industry. A major ingredient of gastric juice in the stomach is hydrochloric acid. Quantities of lactic acid are produced when the human body is subjected to strenuous exercise. The lye used in making homemade soap contains the base sodium hydroxide. Bases are ingredients in many stomach antacid formulations. The table salt used at the dinner table for seasoning food is only one of many hundreds of salts that exist.

10-1 Arrhenius Acid–Base Theory

LEARNING FOCUS

Be able to define what an acid and a base are using Arrhenius acid–base theory concepts; distinguish between the terms *ionization* and *dissociation*.

In 1884, the Swedish chemist Svante August Arrhenius (1859–1927) proposed that acids and bases be defined in terms of the chemical species they form when they dissolve in water. An **Arrhenius acid** *is a*

Figure 10-1 The difference between the aqueous solution processes of ionization (Arrhenius acids) and dissociation (Arrhenius bases).

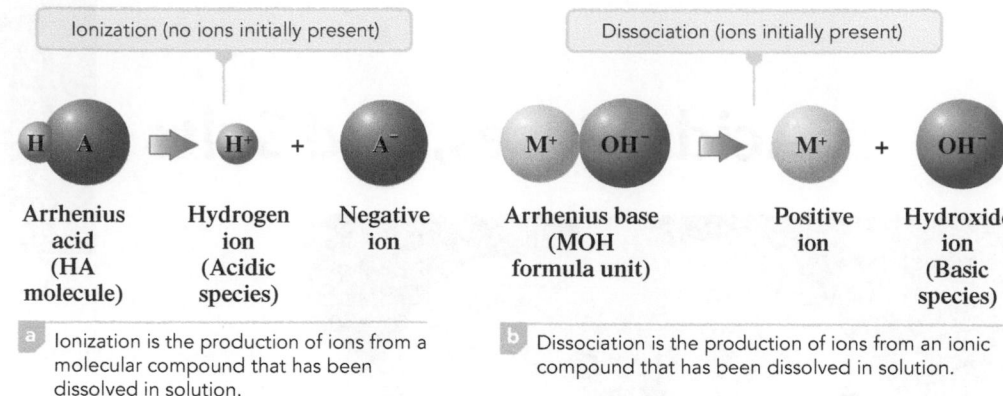

Ionization (no ions initially present)

| Arrhenius acid (HA molecule) | Hydrogen ion (Acidic species) | Negative ion |

Dissociation (ions initially present)

| Arrhenius base (MOH formula unit) | Positive ion | Hydroxide ion (Basic species) |

a Ionization is the production of ions from a molecular compound that has been dissolved in solution.

b Dissociation is the production of ions from an ionic compound that has been dissolved in solution.

hydrogen-containing compound that, in water, produces hydrogen ions (H^+ ions). The acidic species in Arrhenius theory is thus the hydrogen ion. An **Arrhenius base** *is a hydroxide-containing compound that, in water, produces hydroxide ions (OH^- ions).* The basic species in Arrhenius theory is thus the hydroxide ion. For this reason, Arrhenius bases are also called *hydroxide bases.*

Two common examples of Arrhenius acids are HNO_3 (nitric acid) and HCl (hydrochloric acid).

$$HNO_3(l) \xrightarrow{H_2O} H^+(aq) + NO_3^-(aq)$$

$$HCl(g) \xrightarrow{H_2O} H^+(aq) + Cl^-(aq)$$

When Arrhenius acids are in the pure state (not in solution), they are covalent compounds; that is, they do not contain H^+ ions. This ion is formed through an interaction between water and the acid when they are mixed. **Ionization** *is the process in which individual positive and negative ions are produced from a molecular compound that is dissolved in solution.*

Two common examples of Arrhenius bases are NaOH (sodium hydroxide) and KOH (potassium hydroxide).

$$NaOH(s) \xrightarrow{H_2O} Na^+(aq) + OH^-(aq)$$

$$KOH(s) \xrightarrow{H_2O} K^+(aq) + OH^-(aq)$$

In direct contrast to acids, Arrhenius bases are ionic compounds in the pure state. When these compounds dissolve in water, the ions separate to yield positive ions and OH^- ions. **Dissociation** *is the process in which individual positive and negative ions are released from an ionic compound that is dissolved in solution.* Figure 10-1 contrasts the processes of ionization (acids) and dissociation (bases).

Arrhenius acids have a sour taste, change blue litmus paper to red (Figure 10-2), and are corrosive to many materials. Arrhenius bases have a bitter taste, change red litmus paper to blue, and are slippery (soapy) to the touch. (The bases themselves are not slippery, but they react with the oils in the skin to form new slippery compounds.)

© Cengage Learning

Figure 10-2 Litmus is a vegetable dye obtained from certain lichens found principally in the Netherlands. Paper treated with this dye turns from blue to red in acids (left) and from red to blue in bases (right).

Section 10-1 Quick Quiz

1. In an Arrhenius acid–base theory context, the acidic species in an aqueous solution is the
   a. H^+ ion
   b. OH^- ion
   c. Cl^- ion
   d. no correct response

2. In an Arrhenius acid–base theory context, the compounds HCl, HNO₃, and NaOH, when dissolved in water, are, respectively, which of the following?
   a. acid, acid, base
   b. base, base, acid
   c. base, acid, base
   d. no correct response
3. Which of the following statements concerning Arrhenius bases is correct?
   a. In the pure state they are molecular compounds.
   b. The basic species is produced through the process of ionization.
   c. The basic species is produced through the process of dissociation.
   d. no correct response

Answers: 1. a; 2. a; 3. c

10-2 Brønsted–Lowry Acid–Base Theory

LEARNING FOCUS

Be able to define what an acid and a base are using Brønsted–Lowry acid–base theory concepts; be able to recognize the conjugate acid–base pairs present in a Brønsted–Lowry acid–base reaction; know the characteristics that define an amphiprotic substance.

Although it is widely used, Arrhenius acid–base theory has some shortcomings. It is restricted to aqueous solutions, and it does not explain why compounds like ammonia (NH₃), which do not contain hydroxide ion, produce a basic water solution.

In 1923, Johannes Nicolaus Brønsted (1879–1947), a Danish chemist, and Thomas Martin Lowry (1874–1936), a British chemist, independently and almost simultaneously proposed broadened definitions for acids and bases—definitions that applied in both aqueous and nonaqueous solutions and that also explained how some non-hydroxide-containing substances, when added to water, produce basic solutions.

A **Brønsted–Lowry acid** *is a substance that can donate a proton (H^+ ion) to some other substance.* A **Brønsted–Lowry base** *is a substance that can accept a proton (H^+ ion) from some other substance.* In short, a Brønsted–Lowry acid is a *proton donor* (or hydrogen ion donor), and a Brønsted–Lowry base is a *proton acceptor* (or hydrogen ion acceptor). The terms *proton* and *hydrogen ion* are used interchangeably in acid–base discussions. Remember that an H^+ ion is a hydrogen atom (proton plus electron) that has lost its electron; hence it is a proton.

Any chemical reaction involving a Brønsted–Lowry acid must also involve a Brønsted–Lowry base. Proton donation and proton acceptance are complementary processes that always occur together. For proton donation (from an acid) to occur, a proton acceptor (a base) must be present.

Brønsted–Lowry acid–base theory also includes the concept that hydrogen ions in an aqueous solution do not exist in the free state but, rather, react with water to form *hydronium ions* (H_3O^+). The attraction between a hydrogen ion and a polar water molecule is sufficiently strong to bond the hydrogen ion to the water molecule forming a hydronium ion. The bond between them is a coordinate covalent bond (Section 5-5) because both electrons are furnished by the oxygen atom.

When gaseous hydrogen chloride dissolves in water, it forms hydrochloric acid. This is a simple Brønsted–Lowry acid–base reaction. The chemical equation for this process is

$$H_2O(l) + HCl(g) \longrightarrow H_3O^+(aq) + Cl^-(aq)$$

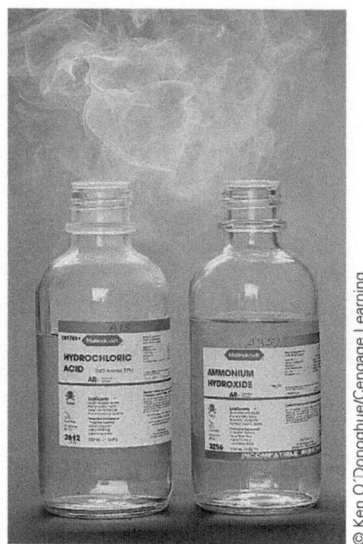

Figure 10-3 A white cloud of finely divided solid NH_4Cl is produced by the acid–base reaction that results when the colorless gases HCl and NH_3 mix. (The gases escaped from the concentrated solutions of HCl and NH_3.)

The hydrogen chloride behaves as an acid by donating a proton to a water molecule. Because the water molecule accepts the proton, to become H_3O^+, it is the base.

It is not necessary that a water molecule be one of the reactants in a Brønsted–Lowry acid–base reaction; the reaction does not have to take place in the liquid state. Brønsted–Lowry acid–base theory can be used to describe gas-phase reactions. The white solid haze that often covers glassware in a chemistry laboratory results from the gas-phase reaction between HCl and NH_3:

$$\underset{\substack{\text{Base:}\\ \text{H}^+ \text{ acceptor}}}{NH_3(g)} + \underset{\substack{\text{Acid:}\\ \text{H}^+ \text{ donor}}}{HCl(g)} \longrightarrow NH_4^+(g) + Cl^-(g)$$

This is a Brønsted–Lowry acid–base reaction because the HCl molecules donate protons to the NH_3, forming NH_4^+ and Cl^- ions. These ions instantaneously combine to form the white solid NH_4Cl (Figure 10-3).

All acids and bases included in Arrhenius theory are also acids and bases according to Brønsted–Lowry theory. However, the converse is not true; some substances that are not considered Arrhenius bases are Brønsted–Lowry bases.

Generalizations About Brønsted–Lowry Acids and Bases

An absolute structural requirement for a Brønsted–Lowry acid is the presence of a hydrogen atom. The generalized notation for a Brønsted–Lowry acid, which is HA, draws attention to this fact. The A in this notation (the rest of the acid's structure) can be a single atom (as in HCl or HF) or a group of atoms (as in HNO_3 or HCN).

Many Brønsted–Lowry acids are neutral molecules (as in the preceding examples). Neutrality (no net charge) is, however, not an absolute requirement. Brønsted–Lowry acids with a positive or negative charge also exist. Examples include the ions H_3O^+, HCO_3^-, and HPO_4^{2-}, all of which can function as proton donors. A Brønsted–Lowry acid may also contain more than one hydrogen atom. Examples include H_2SO_4, H_3PO_4, and $H_2PO_4^-$.

An absolute structural requirement for a Brønsted–Lowry base is the presence of a nonbonding pair (lone pair) of electrons. This is the site where the coordinate covalent bond forms when an incoming proton (from an acid) is accepted by the base. The generalized notation for a Brønsted–Lowry base is B:; the lone pair of electrons is explicitly shown. Each of the following species is capable of functioning as a Brønsted–Lowry base:

$$H\!-\!\overset{\displaystyle ..}{\underset{\displaystyle |}{N}}\!-\!H \qquad H\!-\!\overset{..}{\underset{..}{O}}\!-\!H \qquad \left[\,:\!\overset{..}{\underset{..}{F}}\!:\,\right]^- \qquad \left[\,:\!\overset{..}{\underset{..}{O}}\!-\!H\,\right]^-$$
$$\quad\;\; H$$

Common to all of these species is the presence of at least one lone pair of electrons. Note also, as shown in two of the preceding examples, that a Brønsted–Lowry base can carry a net charge, that is, be an ion. Note also that hydrogen atoms may be initially present in a Brønsted–Lowry base; it then accepts an additional hydrogen atom.

The proton transfer that occurs between a Brønsted–Lowry acid and Brønsted–Lowry base, using generalized notation, is

$$\underset{\text{Acid}}{HA} + \underset{\text{Base}}{B:} \longrightarrow A^- + \left[B{:}H\right]^+$$

Conjugate Acid–Base Pairs

For most Brønsted–Lowry acid–base reactions, 100% proton transfer does not occur. Instead, an equilibrium situation (Section 9-7) is reached in which a forward reaction and a reverse reaction occur at the same rate.

The equilibrium mixture for a Brønsted–Lowry acid–base reaction always has two acids and two bases present. Consider the acid–base reaction involving hydrogen fluoride and water:

$$HF(aq) + H_2O(l) \rightleftharpoons H_3O^+(aq) + F^-(aq)$$

For the forward reaction, the HF molecules donate protons to water molecules. Thus the HF is functioning as an acid, and the H_2O is functioning as a base.

$$HF(aq) + H_2O(l) \longrightarrow H_3O^+(aq) + F^-(aq)$$

Acid   Base

For the reverse reaction, the one going from right to left, a different picture emerges. Here, H_3O^+ is functioning as an acid (by donating a proton), and F^- behaves as a base (by accepting the proton).

$$H_3O^+(aq) + F^-(aq) \longrightarrow HF(aq) + H_2O(l)$$

Acid   Base

The two acids and two bases involved in a Brønsted–Lowry acid–base equilibrium mixture can be grouped into two conjugate acid–base pairs. ◀ A **conjugate acid–base pair** *is two chemical species, one an acid and one a base, that differ from each other through the loss or gain of a proton (H^+ ion).* The two conjugate acid–base pairs for the preceding reaction are (1) HF and F^- and (2) H_3O^+ and H_2O as is shown in the following diagram. ◀

▶ Conjugate *means "coupled" or "joined together" (as in a pair).*

▶ *Every Brønsted–Lowry acid has a conjugate base, and every Brønsted–Lowry base has a conjugate acid. In general terms, these relationships can be diagrammed as follows:*

The notation for specifying a conjugate acid–base pair, as shown in the preceding diagram, is "acid/base." With such notation, the two conjugate acid–base pairs present are HF/F^- and H_3O^+/H_2O. Brønsted–Lowry acid–base equations will always contain two conjugate acid–base pairs. One member of each pair is always a reactant and the other is always a product.

For any given conjugate acid–base pair

1. The *acid* in the acid–base pair always has one *more* H atom and one *fewer* negative charges than the base. Note this relationship for the HF/F^- conjugate acid–base pair.
2. The *base* in the acid–base pair always has one *fewer* H atom and one *more* negative charge than the acid. Note this relationship for the HF/F^- conjugate acid–base pair.

The acid in a conjugate acid–base pair is called the *conjugate acid* of the base, and the base in the conjugate acid–base pair is called the *conjugate base* of the acid. A **conjugate acid** *is the chemical species formed when a proton (H^+ ion) is added to a Brønsted–Lowry base.* The H_3O^+ ion is the conjugate acid of an H_2O molecule. A **conjugate base** *is the chemical species that remains when a proton (H^+ ion) is removed from a Brønsted–Lowry acid.* The H_2O molecule is the conjugate base of the H_3O^+ ion.

EXAMPLE 10-1

Determining the Formula of One Member of a Conjugate Acid–Base Pair When Given the Other Member

Write the chemical formula of each of the following.

a. The conjugate base of HSO_4^-
b. The conjugate acid of NO_3^-
c. The conjugate base of H_3PO_4
d. The conjugate acid of $HC_2O_4^-$

(continued)

Solution

a. A conjugate base can always be found by removing one H^+ from a given acid. Removing one H^+ (both the atom and the charge) from HSO_4^- leaves SO_4^{2-}. Thus SO_4^{2-} is the conjugate base of HSO_4^-.

b. A conjugate acid can always be found by adding one H^+ to a given base. Adding one H^+ (both the atom and the charge) to NO_3^- produces HNO_3. Thus HNO_3 is the conjugate acid of NO_3^-.

c. Proceeding as in part **a**, the removal of an H^+ ion from H_3PO_4 produces the $H_2PO_4^-$ ion. Thus $H_2PO_4^-$ is the conjugate base of H_3PO_4.

d. Proceeding as in part **b**, the addition of an H^+ ion to $HC_2O_4^-$ produces the $H_2C_2O_4$ molecule. Thus $H_2C_2O_4$ is the conjugate acid of $HC_2O_4^-$.

Amphiprotic Substances

▶ *The term* amphiprotic *is related to the Greek* amphoteres, *which means "partly one and partly the other." Just as an amphibian is an animal that lives partly on land and partly in the water, an amphiprotic substance is sometimes an acid and sometimes a base.*

Some molecules and ions are able to function as either Brønsted–Lowry acids or bases, depending on the kind of substance with which they react. Such molecules are said to be amphiprotic. ◀ An **amphiprotic substance** *is a substance that can either lose or accept a proton and thus can function as either a Brønsted–Lowry acid or a Brønsted–Lowry base.*

The absolute structural requirement for an amphiprotic substance is the presence of both a hydrogen atom and a lone pair of electrons. Water is the most common amphiprotic substance.

$$H—\overset{..}{\underset{..}{O}}—H$$

▶ *Other amphiprotic substances besides H_2O that are commonly encountered in biochemical settings include the negative ions HCO_3^-, $H_2PO_4^-$, and HPO_4^{2-}. These ions are formed when polyprotic acids (Section 10-3) lose the hydrogen atoms present in a stepwise fashion.*

Water functions as a base in the first of the following two reactions and as an acid in the second. ◀

$$\underset{\text{Acid}}{HNO_3(aq)} + \underset{\text{Base}}{H_2O(l)} \rightleftharpoons H_3O^+(aq) + NO_3^-(aq)$$

$$\underset{\text{Base}}{NH_3(aq)} + \underset{\text{Acid}}{H_2O(l)} \rightleftharpoons NH_4^+(aq) + OH^-(aq)$$

Chemistry at a Glance—Acid–Base Definitions—summarizes the terminology associated with defining what acids and bases are.

Section 10-2 Quick Quiz

1. A Brønsted–Lowry acid is a substance that can
   a. donate a proton to some other substance
   b. donate a pair of electrons to some other substance
   c. accept a proton from some other substance
   d. no correct response

2. For the chemical reaction $N_3^- + H_2O \longrightarrow HN_3 + OH^-$, the Brønsted–Lowry base is
   a. N_3^-
   b. H_2O
   c. HN_3
   d. no correct response

3. The chemical formula for the conjugate acid of ClO^- is
   a. $HClO^-$
   b. $HClO$
   c. Cl^-
   d. no correct response

4. Which of the following is a conjugate acid–base pair?
   a. H_2CO_3/CO_3^{2-}
   b. H_3PO_4/PO_4^{3-}
   c. HCN/CN^-
   d. no correct response

5. An amphiprotic substance is a substance that can function as
   a. a Brønsted–Lowry acid but not as a Brønsted–Lowry base
   b. a Brønsted–Lowry base but not as a Brønsted–Lowry acid
   c. both a Brønsted–Lowry acid and a Brønsted–Lowry base
   d. no correct response

Answers: 1. a; 2. a; 3. b; 4. c; 5. c

CHEMISTRY **AT A GLANCE** Acid–Base Definitions

10-3 Mono-, Di-, and Triprotic Acids

LEARNING FOCUS

Based on chemical formula, differentiate among mono-, di-, and triprotic acids; write chemical equations for the stepwise transfer of protons for di- and triprotic acids.

Acids can be classified according to the number of hydrogen ions they can transfer per molecule during an acid–base reaction. A **monoprotic acid** *is an acid that supplies one proton (H^+ ion) per molecule during an acid–base reaction.* Hydrochloric acid (HCl) and nitric acid (HNO_3) are both monoprotic acids.

A **diprotic acid** *is an acid that supplies two protons (H⁺ ions) per molecule during an acid–base reaction.* Carbonic acid (H_2CO_3) is a diprotic acid. The transfer of protons for a diprotic acid always occurs in steps. For H_2CO_3, the two steps are

$$H_2CO_3(aq) + H_2O(l) \rightleftharpoons H_3O^+(aq) + HCO_3^-(aq) \blacktriangleleft$$

$$HCO_3^-(aq) + H_2O(l) \rightleftharpoons H_3O^+(aq) + CO_3^{2-}(aq)$$

▶ *If the double arrows in the equation for a system at equilibrium are of unequal length, the longer arrow indicates the direction in which the equilibrium is displaced.*

$\rightleftharpoons$ *Equilibrium displaced toward reactants*

$\rightleftharpoons$ *Equilibrium displaced toward products*

A few triprotic acids exist. A **triprotic acid** *is an acid that supplies three protons (H⁺ ions) per molecule during an acid–base reaction.* Phosphoric acid, H_3PO_4, is the most common triprotic acid. The three proton-transfer steps for this acid are

$$H_3PO_4(aq) + H_2O(l) \rightleftharpoons H_3O^+(aq) + H_2PO_4^-(aq)$$

$$H_2PO_4^-(aq) + H_2O(l) \rightleftharpoons H_3O^+(aq) + HPO_4^{2-}(aq)$$

$$HPO_4^{2-}(aq) + H_2O(l) \rightleftharpoons H_3O^+(aq) + PO_4^{3-}(aq)$$

A **polyprotic acid** *is an acid that supplies two or more protons (H⁺ ions) during an acid–base reaction.* Both diprotic and triprotic acids are examples of polyprotic acids.

The number of hydrogen atoms present in one molecule of an acid *cannot* always be used to classify the acid as mono-, di-, or triprotic. For example, a molecule of acetic acid contains four hydrogen atoms, and yet it is a monoprotic acid. Only one of the hydrogen atoms in acetic acid is *acidic;* the other three hydrogen atoms are *nonacidic.* An **acidic hydrogen atom** *is a hydrogen atom in an acid molecule that can be transferred to a base in an acid–base reaction.*

Whether a hydrogen atom is acidic or nonacidic is related to its location in a molecule—that is, to which other atom it is bonded. From a structural viewpoint, the acidic behavior of acetic acid can be represented by the equation

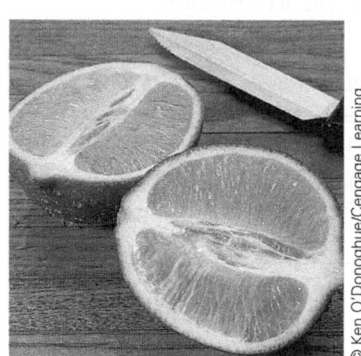

Note that one hydrogen atom is bonded to an oxygen atom and the other three hydrogen atoms are bonded to a carbon atom. The hydrogen atom bonded to the oxygen atom is the acidic hydrogen atom; the hydrogen atoms that are bonded to carbon atoms are too tightly held to be removed by reaction with water molecules. Water has very little effect on a carbon–hydrogen bond because that bond is only slightly polar. On the other hand, the hydrogen bonded to oxygen is involved in a very polar bond because of oxygen's large electronegativity (Section 5-9). Water, which is a polar molecule, readily attacks this bond.

Writing the formula for acetic acid as $HC_2H_3O_2$ instead of $C_2H_4O_2$ indicates that there are two different kinds of hydrogen atoms present. One of the hydrogen atoms is acidic, and the other three are not. When some hydrogen atoms are acidic and others are not, the acidic hydrogens are written first, thus separating them from the other hydrogen atoms in the formula. Citric acid, the principal acid in citrus fruits (Figure 10-4), is another example of an acid that contains both acidic and nonacidic hydrogens. Its formula, $H_3C_6H_5O_7$, indicates that three of the eight hydrogen atoms present in a molecule are acidic.

Figure 10-4 The sour taste of limes and other citrus fruit is due to the citric acid present in the fruit juice.

Section 10-3 Quick Quiz

1. Which of the following is not a polyprotic acid?
   a. HCN
   b. H_3PO_4
   c. H_2SO_4
   d. no correct response
2. For the triprotic acid H_3PO_4, the reactant in the second proton-transfer step is
   a. H_3PO_3
   b. H_2PO_4
   c. $H_2PO_4^-$
   d. no correct response

3. Which of the following acids contains the greatest number of acidic hydrogen atoms?
   a. H_2SO_4
   b. $HC_3H_3O_3$
   c. $HC_3H_5O_3$
   d. no correct response

Answers: 1. a; 2. c; 3. a

10-4 Strengths of Acids and Bases

LEARNING FOCUS

Know the basis for the classifications strong acid/weak acid and strong base/weak base. Know the chemical formulas for the common strong acids and the common strong bases.

Brønsted–Lowry acids vary in their ability to transfer protons and produce hydronium ions in aqueous solution. Acids can be classified as strong or weak on the basis of the extent to which proton transfer occurs in aqueous solution. A **strong acid** *is an acid that transfers 100%, or very nearly 100%, of its protons (H^+ ions) to water in an aqueous solution.* Thus if an acid is strong, nearly all of the acid molecules present give up protons to water. This extensive transfer of protons produces many hydronium ions (the acidic species) within the solution. A **weak acid** *is an acid that transfers only a small percentage of its protons (H^+ ions) to water in an aqueous solution.* The extent of proton transfer for weak acids is usually less than 5%.

The extent to which an acid undergoes ionization depends on the molecular structure of the acid; molecular polarity and the strength and polarity of individual bonds are particularly important factors in determining whether an acid is strong or weak. The vast majority of acids are weak rather than strong.

Only seven commonly encountered acids are strong. Their chemical formulas and names are given in Table 10-1. ◄

The difference between a strong acid and a weak acid can also be stated in terms of equilibrium position (Section 9-7). Consider the reaction wherein HA represents the acid and H_3O^+ and A^- are the products from the proton transfer to H_2O. For strong acids, the equilibrium lies far to the right (100% or almost 100%):

$$HA + H_2O \rightleftharpoons H_3O^+ + A^-$$

For weak acids, the equilibrium position lies far to the left:

$$HA + H_2O \rightleftharpoons H_3O^+ + A^-$$

Thus, in solutions of strong acids, the predominant species are H_3O^+ and A^-. In solutions of weak acids, the predominant species is HA; very little proton transfer has occurred. The differences between strong and weak acids, in terms of species present in solution, are illustrated in Figure 10-5.

Table 10-1 Commonly Encountered Strong Acids

HCl	hydrochloric acid
HBr	hydrobromic acid
HI	hydroiodic acid
HNO_3	nitric acid
$HClO_3$	chloric acid
$HClO_4$	perchloric acid
H_2SO_4	sulfuric acid

► *Learn the names and formulas of the seven commonly encountered strong acids, and then assume that all other acids you encounter are weak unless you are told otherwise.*

Figure 10-5 A comparison of the number of H_3O^+ ions (the acidic species) present in strong acid and weak acid solutions of the same concentration.

▶ **Table 10-2 Commonly Encountered Strong Hydroxide Bases**

Group IA Hydroxides	Group IIA Hydroxides
LiOH	—
NaOH	—
KOH	$Ca(OH)_2$
RbOH	$Sr(OH)_2$
CsOH	$Ba(OH)_2$

▶ *It is important not to confuse the terms* strong *and* weak *with the terms* concentrated *and* dilute. Strong *and* weak *apply to the extent of proton transfer, not to the concentration of acid or base.* Concentrated *and* dilute *are relative concentration terms. Stomach acid (gastric juice) is a dilute (not weak) solution of a strong acid (HCl); it is 5% by mass hydrochloric acid.*

Just as there are strong acids and weak acids, there are also strong bases and weak bases. As with acids, there are only a few strong bases. Strong bases are limited to the hydroxides of Groups IA and IIA listed in Table 10-2. Of the strong bases, only NaOH and KOH are commonly encountered in a chemical laboratory.

Only one of the many weak bases that exist is fairly common—aqueous ammonia. In a solution of ammonia gas (NH_3) in water, small amounts of OH^- ions are produced through the reaction of NH_3 molecules with water.

$$NH_3(g) + H_2O(l) \rightleftharpoons NH_4^+(aq) + OH^-(aq)$$

A solution of aqueous ammonia is sometimes erroneously called ammonium hydroxide. Aqueous ammonia is the preferred designation because most of the NH_3 present has not reacted with water; the equilibrium position lies far to the left. Only a few ammonium ions (NH_4^+) and hydroxide ions (OH^-) are present. ◀

Section 10-4 Quick Quiz

1. In which of the following pairs of acids are both members of the pair *strong* acids?
   a. H_2CO_3 and H_2SO_4
   b. HCl and HF
   c. HCl and HNO_3
   d. no correct response
2. In which of the following pairs of bases are both bases *weak* bases?
   a. NaOH and KOH
   b. $Ca(OH)_2$ and $Ba(OH)_2$
   c. LiOH and $Sr(OH)_2$
   d. no correct response
3. In an aqueous solution of a weak acid, HA, the concentration of A^- ion
   a. is greater than that of HA
   b. is equal to that of H^+
   c. is less than that of H^+
   d. no correct response

Answers: 1. c; 2. d; 3. b

10-5 Ionization Constants for Acids and Bases

LEARNING FOCUS

Be able to write the equilibrium constant expression for a weak acid or a weak base; know the relationships among acid strength, percent ionization, and K_a value for a given weak acid.

The strengths of various acids and bases can be quantified by use of ionization constants, which are forms of equilibrium constants (Section 9-8).

An **acid ionization constant** *is an equilibrium constant for the reaction of a weak acid with water.* For an acid with the general formula HA, the acid ionization constant is obtained by writing the equilibrium constant expression for the reaction ◀

$$HA(aq) + H_2O(I) \rightleftharpoons H_3O^+(aq) + A^-(aq)$$

▶ *HA is a frequently used general formula for a monoprotic acid. Similarly, H_2A denotes a diprotic acid.*

which is

$$K_a = \frac{[H_3O^+][A^-]}{[HA]}$$

The concentration of water is not included in the equilibrium constant expression because water is a pure liquid (Section 9-8). The symbol K_a is used to denote an acid ionization constant.

Table 10-3 gives K_a values and percent ionization values (which can be calculated from K_a values) for selected weak acids. Acid strength increases as the K_a value

▶ **Table 10-3 Ionization Constant Values (K_a) and Percent Ionization Values for 1.0 M Solutions, at 24°C, of Selected Weak Acids**

Name	Formula	K_a	Percent Ionization
phosphoric acid	H_3PO_4	7.5×10^{-3}	8.3
hydrofluoric acid	HF	6.8×10^{-4}	2.6
nitrous acid	HNO_2	4.5×10^{-4}	2.1
acetic acid	$HC_2H_3O_2$	1.8×10^{-5}	0.42
carbonic acid	H_2CO_3	4.3×10^{-7}	0.065
dihydrogen phosphate ion	$H_2PO_4^-$	6.2×10^{-8}	0.025
hydrocyanic acid	HCN	4.9×10^{-10}	0.0022
hydrogen carbonate ion	HCO_3^-	5.6×10^{-11}	0.00075
hydrogen phosphate ion	HPO_4^{2-}	4.2×10^{-13}	0.000065

▶ *Note the following relationships among acid strength, percent ionization, and K_a magnitude.*

- *Acid strength increases as percent ionization increases.*
- *Acid strength increases as the magnitude of K_a increases.*
- *Percent ionization increases as the magnitude of K_a increases.*

increases. The actual value of K_a for a given acid must be determined by experimentally measuring the concentrations of HA, H_3O^+, and A^- in the acid solution and then using these values to calculate K_a. Example 10-2 shows how an acid ionization constant value (K_a) can be calculated by using concentration (molarity) and percent ionization data for an acid. ◀

EXAMPLE 10-2

Calculating the Acid Ionization Constant for an Acid When Given Its Concentration and Percent Ionization ◀

A 0.0100 M solution of an acid, HA, is 15% ionized. Calculate the acid ionization constant for this acid.

Solution

To calculate K_a for the acid, the molar concentrations of H_3O^+, A^-, and HA in the aqueous solution are needed.

The concentration of H_3O^+ will be 15% of the original HA concentration. Thus the concentration of hydronium ion is

$$H_3O^+ = (0.15) \times (0.0100 \text{ M}) = 0.0015 \text{ M}$$

The ionization of a monoprotic acid produces hydronium ions and the conjugate base of the acid (A^- ions) in a 1-to-1 ratio. Thus the concentration of A^- will be the same as that of hydronium ion—that is, 0.0015 M.

The concentration of HA is equal to the original concentration diminished by that which ionized (15%, or 0.0015 M):

$$HA = 0.0100 \text{ M} - 0.0015 \text{ M} = 0.0085 \text{ M}$$

Substituting these values in the equilibrium expression gives

$$K_a = \frac{[H_3O^+][A^-]}{[HA]} = \frac{[0.0015][0.0015]}{[0.0085]} = 2.6 \times 10^{-4}$$

▶ *The acids HNO_3, $HClO_4$, $HClO_3$, and H_2SO_4 are strong acids. The acids HNO_2, $HClO_2$, $HClO$, H_2SO_3, H_2CO_3, and H_3PO_4 are weak acids. A "generalization" exists relative to this situation. For simple oxyacids (H, O, and one other nonmetal), if the number of oxygen atoms present exceeds the number of acidic hydrogen atoms present by two or more, the acid strength is strong. For oxyacids in which the oxygen–hydrogen difference is less than two, the acid strength is weak.*

In Section 10-3, it was noted that dissociation of a polyprotic acid occurs in a stepwise manner. In general, each successive step of proton transfer for a polyprotic acid occurs to a lesser extent than the previous step. For the dissociation series

$$H_2CO_3(aq) + H_2O(l) \rightleftharpoons H_3O^+(aq) + HCO_3^-(aq)$$

$$HCO_3^-(aq) + H_2O(l) \rightleftharpoons H_3O^+(aq) + CO_3^{2-}(aq)$$

the second proton is not as easily transferred as the first because it must be pulled away from a negatively charged ion, HCO_3^-. (Remember that particles with opposite charge attract one another.) Accordingly, HCO_3^- is a weaker acid than H_2CO_3. The K_a values for these two acids (Table 10-3) are 5.6×10^{-11} and 4.3×10^{-7}, respectively.

Base strength follows the same principle as acid strength. Here, however, a base ionization constant, K_b, is needed. A **base ionization constant** *is the equilibrium constant for the reaction of a weak base with water.* The general expression for K_b is

$$K_b = \frac{[BH^+][OH^-]}{[B]}$$

where the reaction is

$$B(aq) + H_2O(l) \rightleftharpoons BH^+(aq) + OH^-(aq)$$

For the reaction involving the weak base NH_3,

$$NH_3(aq) + H_2O(l) \rightleftharpoons NH_4^+(aq) + OH^-(aq)$$

the base ionization constant expression is

$$K_b = \frac{[NH_4^+][OH^-]}{[NH_3]}$$

The K_b value for NH_3, the only common weak base, is 1.8×10^{-5}.

Section 10-5 Quick Quiz

1. Acid ionization constants give information about
   a. the strength of an acid
   b. the number of nonacidic hydrogen atoms present in an acid molecule
   c. whether an acid is monoprotic or polyprotic
   d. no correct answer
2. The general expression for the acid ionization constant for a weak acid, HA, is
   a. $[HA][H^+]/[A^-]$
   b. $[HA]/[H^+][A^-]$
   c. $[H^+][A^-]/[HA]$
   d. no correct response
3. Which of the following is the strongest acid?
   a. HX, $K_a = 1.0 \times 10^{-3}$
   b. HY, $K_a = 1.0 \times 10^{-5}$
   c. HZ, $K_a = 1.0 \times 10^{-7}$
   d. all have the same strength
4. Acid A is weaker than acid B if, at equal concentrations,
   a. the percent ionization of A is less than that of B
   b. the K_a value for A is greater than that of B
   c. acid A contains more hydrogen atoms than B
   d. no correct response

Answers: 1. a; 2. c; 3. a; 4. a

10-6 Salts

LEARNING FOCUS

Know the general characteristics for salts; classify a substance as a salt based on its chemical formula.

To a nonscientist, the term *salt* denotes a white granular substance that is used as a seasoning for food. To the chemist, the term *salt* has a much broader meaning; sodium chloride (table salt) is only one of thousands of salts known to a chemist. A **salt** *is an ionic compound containing a metal or polyatomic ion as the positive ion and a nonmetal or polyatomic ion (except hydroxide) as the negative ion.* (Ionic compounds that contain hydroxide ion are bases rather than salts.)

Much information about salts has been presented in previous chapters, although the term *salt* was not explicitly used in these discussions. Formula writing and nomenclature for binary ionic compounds (salts) were covered in Sections 4-7 and 4-9. Many salts contain polyatomic ions such as nitrate and sulfate; these ions were discussed in Section 4-10. The solubility of ionic compounds (salts) in water was the topic of Section 8-4.

All common soluble salts are *completely* dissociated into ions in solution (Section 8-3). Even if a salt is only slightly soluble, the small amount that does dissolve completely dissociates. Thus the terms *weak* and *strong,* which are used to denote qualitatively the percent ionization/dissociation of acids and bases, are not applicable to salts. The terms *weak salt* and *strong salt* are not used.

Acids, bases, and salts are related in that a salt is one of the products that results from the chemical reaction of an acid with a hydroxide base. This particular type of reaction will be discussed in Section 10-7.

Section 10-6 Quick Quiz

1. Which of the following is an inappropriate designation for a salt?
   a. insoluble salt
   b. completely dissociated salt
   c. weak salt
   d. no correct response
2. Which of the following ions cannot be present in a salt?
   a. Na^+
   b. SO_4^{2-}
   c. OH^-
   d. no correct response
3. In which of the following pairs of substances are both members of the pair salts?
   a. NaCl and NaOH
   b. HBr and NaBr
   c. KNO_3 and KCN
   d. no correct response

Answers: 1. c; 2. c; 3. c

10-7 Acid–Base Neutralization Chemical Reactions

LEARNING FOCUS
Be able to write chemical equations for acid–base neutralization reactions.

When acids and hydroxide bases are mixed, they react with one another and their acidic and basic properties disappear; we say they have neutralized each other. An **acid–base neutralization reaction** *is the chemical reaction between an acid and a hydroxide base in which a salt and water are the products.* The neutralization process can be viewed as either an exchange reaction or a proton-transfer reaction.

From an *exchange viewpoint* (Section 9-1),

$$AX + BY \longrightarrow AY + BX$$

the equation for the HCl–KOH neutralization is

$$\underset{\text{Acid}}{HCl} + \underset{\text{Base}}{KOH} \longrightarrow \underset{\text{Water}}{HOH} + \underset{\text{Salt}}{KCl}$$

The salt that is formed contains the negative ion from the acid ionization and the positive ion from the base dissociation (Figure 10-6).

From a *proton-transfer viewpoint,* the formation of water results from the transfer of protons from H_3O^+ ions (the acidic species in aqueous solution) to OH^- ions (the basic species) (Figure 10-7).

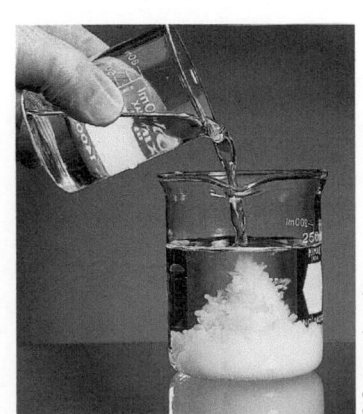

Figure 10-6 The acid–base reaction between sulfuric acid and barium hydroxide produces the insoluble salt barium sulfate.

© Cengage Learning

Figure 10-7 Formation of water by the transfer of protons from H_3O^+ ions to OH^- ions.

Hydronium ion		Hydroxide ion		Water		Water
H_3O^+	+	OH^-		H_2O	+	H_2O

Any time an acid is completely reacted with a base, neutralization occurs. It does not matter whether the acid and base are strong or weak. Sodium hydroxide (a strong base) and nitric acid (a strong acid) react as follows:

$$HNO_3 + NaOH \longrightarrow NaNO_3 + H_2O$$

The equation for the reaction of potassium hydroxide (a strong base) with hydrocyanic acid (a weak acid) is

$$HCN + KOH \longrightarrow KCN + H_2O$$

Note that in both reactions, the products are a salt ($NaNO_3$ in the first reaction and KCN in the second) and water.

One of the methods by which excess acidity in the stomach ("acid indigestion") can be combated involves acid–base neutralization with an antacid functioning as the base. The focus on relevancy feature Chemical Connections 10-A—Excessive Acidity Within the Stomach: Antacids and Acid Inhibitors—gives further information about reducing stomach acidity by using antacids, as well as about using acid inhibitors for the same purpose. The mechanism by which acid inhibitors work does not involve neutralization.

Balancing Acid–Base Neutralization Equations

In any acid–base neutralization reaction, the amounts of H^+ ion and OH^- ion that react are equal. These two ions always react in a 1-to-1 ratio to form water.

$$H^+ + OH^- \longrightarrow H_2O \text{ (HOH)}$$

This constant reaction ratio between the two ions enables us to balance chemical equations for neutralization reactions quickly.

Let us consider the neutralization reaction between H_2SO_4 and KOH.

$$H_2SO_4 + KOH \longrightarrow \text{salt} + H_2O$$

Because the acid H_2SO_4 is diprotic and the base KOH contains only one OH^- ion, we will need twice as many base molecules as acid molecules. Thus we place the coefficient 2 in front of the formula for KOH in the chemical equation; this gives two H^+ ions reacting with two OH^- ions to produce two H_2O molecules.

$$H_2SO_4 + 2KOH \longrightarrow \text{salt} + 2H_2O$$

The salt formed is K_2SO_4; there are two K^+ ions and one SO_4^{2-} ion on the left side of the equation, which combine to give the salt. The balanced equation is

$$H_2SO_4 + 2KOH \longrightarrow K_2SO_4 + 2H_2O$$

Section 10-7 Quick Quiz

1. Which of the following is always a product of an acid–base neutralization reaction?
   a. an acid
   b. a base
   c. a salt
   d. no correct response

2. Which of the following chemical equations is that for an acid–base neutralization reaction?
   a. $H_2SO_4 + Zn \longrightarrow ZnSO_4 + H_2$
   b. $HNO_3 + KOH \longrightarrow KNO_3 + H_2O$
   c. $AgNO_3 + NaCl \longrightarrow AgCl + NaNO_3$
   d. no correct response
3. For a complete neutralization reaction between 0.10 M $Ca(OH)_2$ and 0.10 M HNO_3, the base and the acid will react in which of the following molar ratios?
   a. 1-to-1
   b. 2-to-2
   c. 1-to-2
   d. no correct response

Answers: 1. c; 2. b; 3. c

CHEMICAL CONNECTIONS 10-A

Excessive Acidity Within the Stomach: Antacids and Acid Inhibitors

Gastric juice, an acidic digestive fluid secreted by glands in the mucous membrane that lines the stomach, is produced at the rate of 2–3 liters per day in an average adult. It contains hydrochloric acid (HCl), a substance necessary for the proper digestion of food, at a concentration of about 0.03 M.

Overeating and emotional factors can cause the stomach to produce too much HCl. This leads to hyperacidity, the condition often called "acid indigestion" or "heartburn." Ordinarily, the stomach and digestive tract are protected from the corrosive effect of excess stomach acid by the stomach's mucosal lining. Constant excess acid can, however, damage this lining to the extent that swelling, inflammation, and bleeding (symptoms of ulcers) occur.

There are two approaches to combating the problem of excess stomach acid: (1) removing the excess acid through neutralization and (2) decreasing the production of stomach acid. The first approach involves the use of *antacids,* and the second approach involves the use of *acid inhibitors.*

An *antacid* is an over-the-counter drug containing one or more basic substances that are capable of neutralizing the HCl present in gastric juice. Neutralizing agents present in selected brand-name antacids are shown in the accompanying table.

Magnesium hydroxide and aluminum hydroxide neutralize HCl to produce a salt and water as follows:

$$2HCl + Mg(OH)_2 \longrightarrow MgCl_2 + 2H_2O$$
$$3HCl + Al(OH)_3 \longrightarrow AlCl_3 + 3H_2O$$

Brand Name	Neutralizing Agent(s)
Alka-Seltzer	$NaHCO_3$
Bisodol	$NaHCO_3$
Di-Gel	$Mg(OH)_2, Al(OH)_3$
Gaviscon	$Al(OH)_3, NaHCO_3$
Gelusil	$Mg(OH)_2, Al(OH)_3$
Maalox	$Mg(OH)_2, Al(OH)_3$
Milk of magnesia	$Mg(OH)_2$
Mylanta	$Mg(OH)_2, Al(OH)_3$
Riopan	$AlMg(OH)_5$
Rolaids	$NaAl(OH)_2CO_3$
Tums	$CaCO_3$

Neutralization involving sodium bicarbonate and calcium carbonate produce the gas carbon dioxide in addition to a salt and water.

$$HCl + NaHCO_3 \longrightarrow NaCl + CO_2 + H_2O$$
$$2HCl + CaCO_3 \longrightarrow CaCl_2 + CO_2 + H_2O$$

The CO_2 released by these reactions increases the gas pressure in the stomach, causing a person to belch often.

Brand-name over-the-counter *acid inhibitors* include Pepcid, Tagamet, and Zantac. These substances inhibit gastric acid production by blocking the action of histamine, a gastric acid secretion regulator, at receptor sites in the gastric-acid-secreting cells of the stomach lining. The net effect is decreased amounts of gastric secretion in the stomach. This lowered acidity allows for healing of ulcerated tissue.

D.A. Weinstein/Custom Medical Stock Photo Custom Medical Stock Photo/Newscom

A large variety of over-the-counter antacid formulations are available for a consumer to select from.

10-8 Self-Ionization of Water

LEARNING FOCUS

Understand how the *ion product constant for water* is obtained; be able to calculate, in an aqueous solution, [H$^+$] given [OH$^-$] or vice versa; classify a solution as acidic, basic, or neutral given [H$^+$] or [OH$^-$].

Although water is usually thought of as a covalent substance, experiments show that an *extremely small* percentage of water molecules in pure water interact with one another to form ions, a process that is called *self-ionization* (Figure 10-8). This interaction can be thought of as the transfer of protons between water molecules (Brønsted–Lowry theory, Section 10-2):

$$H_2O + H_2O \rightleftharpoons H_3O^+ + OH^-$$

The net effect of this transfer is the formation of *equal amounts* of hydronium and hydroxide ion. Such behavior for water should not seem surprising; the fact that water is an amphiprotic substance (Section 10-2)—one that can either gain or lose protons—has already been discussed.

At any given time, the number of H$_3$O$^+$ and OH$^-$ ions present in a sample of pure water is always extremely small. At equilibrium and 24°C, the H$_3$O$^+$ and OH$^-$ concentrations are 1.00×10^{-7} M (0.000000100 M).

Ion Product Constant for Water

The constant concentration of H$_3$O$^+$ and OH$^-$ ions present in pure water at 24°C can be used to calculate a very useful number called the ion product constant for water. The **ion product constant for water** *is the numerical value* 1.00×10^{-14}, *obtained by multiplying together the molar concentrations of H$_3$O$^+$ ion and OH$^-$ ion present in pure water at 24°C.* The equation for the ion product constant for water is

$$\begin{aligned} \text{Ion product constant for water} &= [H_3O^+] \times [OH^-] \\ &= (1.00 \times 10^{-7}) \times (1.00 \times 10^{-7}) \\ &= 1.00 \times 10^{-14} \end{aligned}$$

▶ *The smallness of the amount of H$_3$O$^+$ ion present in water (1.00×10^{-7} M) is illustrated by this example: If once every second one molecule (or ion) were removed from a liter of water, examined, and then returned, an H$^+$ ion would be encountered once every 17.4 years.*

Remember that square brackets mean concentration in moles per liter (molarity). ◀

The ion product constant expression for water is valid not only in pure water but also in water with solutes present. At all times, the product of the hydronium ion and hydroxide ion molarities in an aqueous solution at 24°C must equal 1.00×10^{-14}. Thus if [H$_3$O$^+$] is increased by the addition of an acidic solute, then [OH$^-$] must decrease so that their product will still be 1.00×10^{-14}. Similarly, if additional OH$^-$ ions are added to the water, then [H$_3$O$^+$] must correspondingly decrease.

The concentration of either H$_3$O$^+$ ion or OH$^-$ ion present in an aqueous solution can be calculated, if the concentration of the other ion is known, by simply rearranging the ion product expression [H$_3$O$^+$] × [OH$^-$] = 1.00×10^{-14}.

$$[H_3O^+] = \frac{1.00 \times 10^{-14}}{[OH^-]} \quad \text{and} \quad [OH^-] = \frac{1.00 \times 10^{-14}}{[H_3O^+]}$$

Figure 10-8 Self-ionization of water through proton transfer between water molecules.

| Water | | Water | | Hydronium ion | | Hydroxide ion |
| H$_2$O | + | H$_2$O | | H$_3$O$^+$ | + | OH$^-$ |

EXAMPLE 10-3

Calculating the Hydroxide Ion Concentration in a Solution from a Given Hydronium Ion Concentration

Sufficient acidic solute is added to a quantity of water to produce a solution with $[H_3O^+] = 4.0 \times 10^{-3}$. What is the $[OH^-]$ in this solution?

Solution

$[OH^-]$ can be calculated by using the ion product expression for water, rearranged in the form

$$[OH^-] = \frac{1.00 \times 10^{-14}}{[H_3O^+]}$$

Substituting into this expression the known $[H_3O^+]$ and doing the arithmetic gives

$$[OH^-] = \frac{1.00 \times 10^{-14}}{4.0 \times 10^{-3}} = 2.5 \times 10^{-12}$$

The relationship between $[H_3O^+]$ and $[OH^-]$ is that of an inverse proportion; when one increases, the other decreases. If $[H_3O^+]$ increases by a factor of 10^2, then $[OH^-]$ decreases by the same factor, 10^2. A graphic portrayal of this increase–decrease relationship for $[H_3O^+]$ and $[OH^-]$ is given in Figure 10-9. ◀

▶ *Neither $[H_3O^+]$ nor $[OH^-]$ is ever zero in an aqueous solution.*

Acidic, Basic, and Neutral Solutions

Small amounts of both H_3O^+ ion and OH^- ion are present in all aqueous solutions. What, then, determines whether a given solution is acidic or basic? ◀ It is the relative amounts of these two ions present. An **acidic solution** *is an aqueous solution in which the concentration of H_3O^+ ion is higher than that of OH^- ion. A **basic solution** is an aqueous solution in which the concentration of the OH^- ion is higher than that of the H_3O^+ ion.* It is possible to have an aqueous solution that is neither acidic nor basic but is, rather, a neutral solution. A **neutral solution** *is an aqueous solution in which the concentrations of H_3O^+ ion and OH^- ion are equal.* Table 10-4 summarizes the relationships between $[H_3O^+]$ and $[OH^-]$ that have just been considered.

▶ *A basic solution is also often referred to as an* alkaline solution.

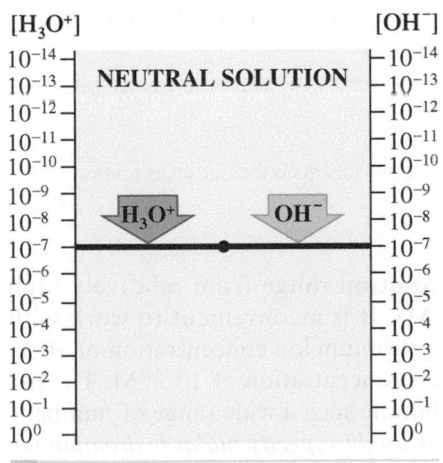

a In pure water, the concentration of hydronium ions, $[H_3O^+]$, and that of hydroxide ions, $[OH^-]$, are equal. Both are 1.00×10^{-7} M at 24°C.

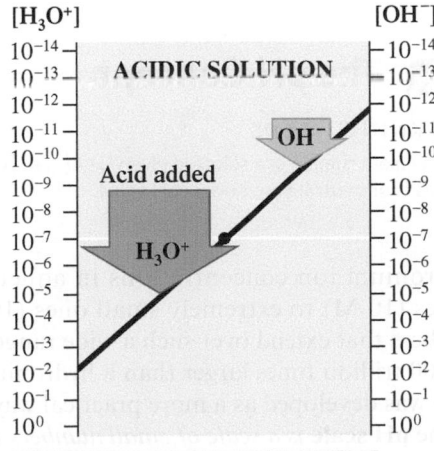

b If $[H_3O^+]$ is increased by a factor of 10^5 (from 10^{-7} M to 10^{-2} M), then $[OH^-]$ is decreased by a factor of 10^5 (from 10^{-7} M to 10^{-12} M).

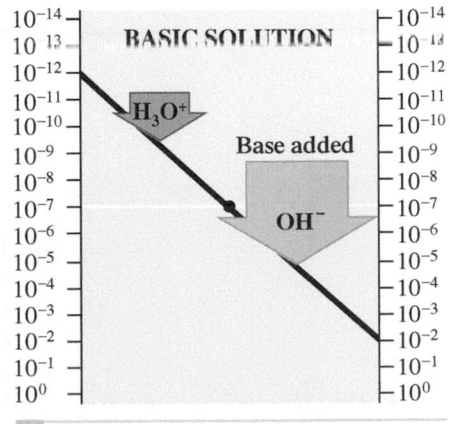

c If $[OH^-]$ is increased by a factor of 10^5 (from 10^{-7} M to 10^{-2} M), then $[H_3O^+]$ is decreased by a factor of 10^5 (from 10^{-7} M to 10^{-12} M).

Figure 10-9 The relationship between $[H_3O^+]$ and $[OH^-]$ in aqueous solution is an inverse proportion; when $[H_3O^+]$ is increased, $[OH^-]$ decreases, and vice versa.

▶ Table 10-4 **Relationship Between [H₃O⁺] and [OH⁻] in Neutral, Acidic, and Basic Solutions**

Type of Solution	Relationship Between $[H_3O^+]$ and $[OH^-]$
neutral solution	$[H_3O^+] = [OH^-] = 1.00 \times 10^{-7}$
acidic solution $[H_3O^+] > [OH^-]$	$[H_3O^+]$ is greater than 1.00×10^{-7} $[OH^-]$ is less than 1.00×10^{-7}
basic solution $[OH^-] > [H_3O^+]$	$[H_3O^+]$ is less than 1.00×10^{-7} $[OH^-]$ is greater than 1.00×10^{-7}

Section 10-8 Quick Quiz

1. At 24°C, the molar concentrations of H_3O^+ and OH^- ions in *pure* water are
   a. both zero
   b. both 1.00×10^{-7} M
   c. both 1.00×10^{-14} M
   d. no correct answer
2. At 24°C, the ion product constant for water has the value
   a. 1.00×10^{-7}
   b. 1.00×10^{-10}
   c. 1.00×10^{-13}
   d. no correct answer
3. What is the $[OH^-]$ in an aqueous solution in which $[H_3O^+]$ is 1.00×10^{-5}?
   a. 1.00×10^{-5}
   b. 1.00×10^{-7}
   c. 1.00×10^{-9}
   d. no correct response
4. Which of the following situations describes a basic aqueous solution?
   a. $[H_3O^+]$ is greater than $[OH^-]$
   b. $[H_3O^+]$ is equal to $[OH^-]$
   c. $[H_3O^+]$ is less than $[OH^-]$
   d. no correct response
5. What is the $[H_3O^+]$ in a neutral solution?
   a. zero
   b. equal to 1.00×10^{-5}
   c. greater than 1.00×10^{-7}
   d. no correct response

Answers: 1. b; 2. d; 3. c; 4. c; 5. d

10-9 The pH Concept

LEARNING FOCUS

Calculate the pH of a solution given $[H_3O^+]$ or $[OH^-]$; classify an aqueous solution as acidic, basic, or neutral based on its pH value.

Hydronium ion concentrations in aqueous solution range from relatively high values (10 M) to extremely small ones (10^{-14} M). It is inconvenient to work with numbers that extend over such a wide range; a hydronium ion concentration of 10 M is 1000 trillion times larger than a hydronium ion concentration of 10^{-14} M. The pH scale was developed as a more practical way to handle such a wide range of numbers.

▶ The **pH scale** *is a scale of small numbers that is used to specify molar hydronium ion concentration in an aqueous solution.*

The calculation of pH scale values involves the use of logarithms. The **pH** *is the negative logarithm of an aqueous solution's molar hydronium ion concentration.* Expressed mathematically, the definition of pH is

$$pH = -\log[H_3O^+]$$

(The letter *p*, as in pH, means "negative logarithm of.")

▶ *The pH scale is a compact method for representing solution acidity. The p in pH comes from the German word* potenz, *which means "power," as in "power of 10."*

Integral pH Values

For any hydronium ion concentration expressed in exponential notation in which the coefficient is 1.0, the pH is given directly by the negative of the exponent value of the power of 10:

$$[H_3O^+] = 1.0 \times 10^{-x}$$
$$pH = x$$

Thus, if the hydronium ion concentration is 1.0×10^{-9}, then the pH will be 9.00. This simple relationship between pH and hydronium ion concentration is valid only when the coefficient in the exponential notation expression for the hydronium ion concentration is 1.0. ◄

► *The rule for the number of significant figures in a logarithm is: The number of digits after the decimal place in a logarithm is equal to the number of significant figures in the original number.*

$$[H_3O^+] = \underline{6.3} \times 10^{-5}$$
Two significant figures

$$pH = \underline{4.20}$$
Two digits

EXAMPLE 10-4

Calculating the pH of a Solution When Given Its Hydronium Ion or Hydroxide Ion Concentration

Calculate the pH for each of the following solutions.

a. $[H_3O^+] = 1.0 \times 10^{-6}$ **b.** $[OH^-] = 1.0 \times 10^{-6}$

Solution

a. Because the coefficient in the exponential expression for the molar hydronium ion concentration is 1.0, the pH can be obtained from the relationships

$$[H_3O^+] = 1.0 \times 10^{-x}$$
$$pH = x$$

The power of 10 is −6 in this case, so the pH will be 6.00.
b. The given quantity involves hydroxide ion rather than hydronium ion. The hydronium ion concentration must be calculated first and then the pH is calculated

$$[H_3O^+] = \frac{1.00 \times 10^{-14}}{1.0 \times 10^{-6}} = 1.0 \times 10^{-8}$$

A solution with a hydronium ion concentration of 1.0×10^{-8} M will have a pH of 8.00.

Nonintegral pH Values

If the coefficient in the exponential expression for the molar hydronium ion concentration is *not* 1.0, then the pH will have a nonintegral value; that is, it will not be a whole number. For example, consider the following nonintegral pH values.

$$[H_3O^+] = 6.3 \times 10^{-5} \quad pH = 4.20$$
$$[H_3O^+] = 5.3 \times 10^{-5} \quad pH = 4.28$$
$$[H_3O^+] = 2.2 \times 10^{-4} \quad pH = 3.66$$

Use of nonintegral pH values allows narrow pH ranges to be easily defined. Figure 10-10 gives nonintegral pH ranges for selected fruits and vegetables as well as butter and eggs.

The easiest way to obtain nonintegral pH values such as these involves using an electronic calculator that allows for the input of exponential numbers and that has a base-10 logarithm key (LOG).

In using such an electronic calculator, logarithm values are obtained simply by pressing the LOG key after having entered the number whose log is desired. To obtain the pH value, the sign (plus or minus) of the logarithm value must be changed because of the negative sign in the defining equation for pH.

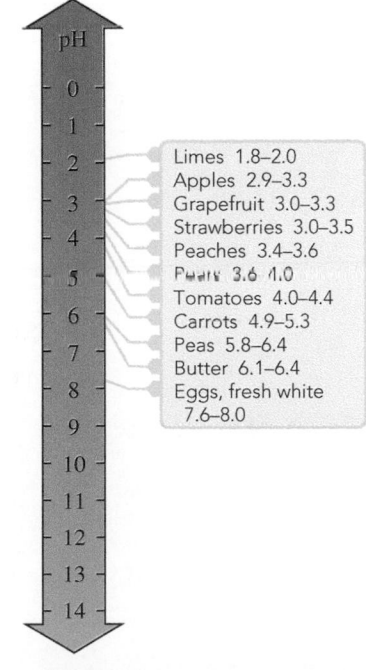

Figure 10-10 Most fruits and vegetables are acidic. A tart or sour taste is an indication that such is the case. Nonintegral pH values for selected foods are as shown here.

EXAMPLE 10-5

Calculating the pH of a Solution When Given Its Hydronium Ion Concentration

Calculate the pH for each of the following solutions.

a. $[H_3O^+] = 7.23 \times 10^{-8}$ b. $[H_3O^+] = 5.70 \times 10^{-3}$

Solution

a. Using an electronic calculator, first enter the number 7.23×10^{-8} into the calculator. Then use the **LOG** key to obtain the logarithm value, -7.1408617. Changing the sign of this number (because of the minus sign in the definition of pH) and adjusting for significant figures yields a pH value of 7.141.

b. Entering the number 5.70×10^{-3} into the calculator and then using the **LOG** key gives a logarithm value of -2.2441251. This value translates into a pH value, after rounding, of 2.244.

pH Values and Hydronium Ion Concentration

It is often necessary to calculate the hydronium ion concentration for a solution from its pH value. This type of calculation, which is the reverse of that illustrated in Examples 10-4 and 10-5, is shown in Example 10-6.

EXAMPLE 10-6

Calculating the Molar Hydronium Ion Concentration of a Solution from the Solution's pH

The pH of a solution is 6.80. What is the molar hydronium ion concentration for this solution?

Solution

From the defining equation for pH, we have

$$pH = -\log[H_3O^+] = 6.80$$

$$\log[H_3O^+] = -6.80$$

To find $[H_3O^+]$, we need to determine the *antilog* of -6.80.

How an antilog is obtained using a calculator depends on the type of calculator. Many calculators have an antilog function (sometimes labeled **INV log**) that performs this operation. If this key is present, then

1. Enter the number -6.80. Note that it is the *negative* of the pH that is entered into the calculator.
2. Press the **INV log** key (or an inverse key and then a log key). The result is the desired hydronium ion concentration.

$$\log[H_3O^+] = -6.80$$

$$\text{antilog}[H_3O^+] = 1.5848931 \times 10^{-7}$$

Rounded off, this value translates into a hydronium ion concentration of 1.6×10^{-7} M.

Some calculators use a 10^x key to perform the antilog operation. Use of this key is based on the mathematical identity

$$\text{antilog } x = 10^x$$

This means that

$$\text{antilog } -6.80 = 10^{-6.80}$$

If the 10^x key is present, then

1. Enter the number -6.80 (the negative of the pH).
2. Press the function key 10^x. The result is the desired hydronium ion concentration.

$$[H_3O^+] = 10^{-6.80} = 1.6 \times 10^{-7}$$

Interpreting pH Values

Identifying an aqueous solution as acidic, basic, or neutral based on pH value is a straightforward process. A **neutral solution** *is an aqueous solution whose pH is 7.0.* An **acidic solution** *is an aqueous solution whose pH is less than 7.0.* A **basic solution** *is an aqueous solution whose pH is greater than 7.0.* The relationships among $[H_3O^+]$, $[OH^-]$, and pH are summarized in Figure 10-11. Note the following trends from the information presented in this figure.

1. The higher the concentration of hydronium ion, the lower the pH value. Another statement of this same trend is that lowering the pH always corresponds to increasing the hydronium ion concentration.
2. A change of 1 unit in pH always corresponds to a tenfold change in hydronium ion concentration. For example,

$$\text{Difference of 1} \begin{cases} \text{pH} = 1.0, \text{ then } [H_3O^+] = 0.1 \text{ M} \\ \text{pH} = 2.0, \text{ then } [H_3O^+] = 0.01 \text{ M} \end{cases} \text{ tenfold difference}$$

pH Values for Human Body Tissues and Acid Rain

In a chemical laboratory, solutions of any pH value can be created. Such pH diversity is not found within the human body. Most human body fluids, except gastric juice, have pH values within one unit of neutrality, as is shown in Table 10-5. The wide variance in pH for urine (4.8–8.4) relates to whether the body needs to eliminate acids or bases from the blood. Such need in turn depends on an individual's recent dietary intake and exercise.

The effects that liquids of various pH have on living tissue, particularly mucous membranes, are shown in Table 10-6.

Acid rain is rainfall that has a significantly lower pH value than that of rain that falls in pristine locations unaffected by environmental pollution. ◀ The focus on relevancy feature Chemical Connections 10-B—pH Values for Acid Rain—discusses the extent of the pH change associated with acid rain, as well as the chemical reactions associated with acid rain formation.

Chemistry at a Glance—Acids and Acidic Solutions—summarizes what has been presented about acids and acidity.

Figure 10-11 Relationships among pH values, $[H_3O^+]$, and $[OH^-]$ at 24°C.

▶ Table 10-5 **The Normal pH Range of Selected Body Fluids**

Type of Fluid	pH Value
bile	6.8–7.0
blood plasma	7.3–7.5
gastric juices	1.0–3.0
milk	6.6–7.6
pancreatic fluid	7.8–8.0
saliva	6.5–7.5
spinal fluid	7.3–7.5
urine	4.8–8.4

▶ *Solutions of low pH are more acidic than solutions of high pH; conversely, solutions of high pH are more basic than solutions of low pH.*

▶ Table 10-6 **Effects of Liquids of Various pH on Living Tissue**

pH range	Common Substances Within pH Range	Effects on Living Tissue
less than 1	battery acid acid cleaning products	hazardous to all living tissue
1–2	gastric juice	irritating to skin can damage mucous membranes
2–5	citrus juices vinegar	generally nonhazardous can irritate mucous membranes
5–8	cola drinks coffee milk tap water intestinal fluids urine	nonhazardous to living tissue
8–11	seawater soap detergents	generally nonhazardous can irritate mucous membranes
11–13	household ammonia household bleach	irritating to skin can damage mucous membranes
greater than 13	oven cleaner drain cleaner	hazardous to all living tissues

pH Values for Acid Rain

Rainfall, even in a pristine environment, has always been and will always be acidic. This acidity results from the presence of carbon dioxide in the atmosphere, which dissolves in water to produce carbonic acid (H_2CO_3), a weak acid.

$$CO_2(g) + H_2O(l) \rightarrow H_2CO_3(aq)$$

This reaction produces rainwater with a pH of approximately 5.6–5.7.

Acid rain is a generic term used to describe rainfall (or snowfall) whose pH is lower than the naturally produced value of 5.6. Acid rain has been observed with increasing frequency in many areas of the world. Rainfall with pH values between 4.0 and 5.0 is now common, and occasionally rainfall with a pH as low as 2.0 is encountered. Within the United States, the lowest acid-rain pH values are encountered in the northeastern states (see the accompanying map). The maritime provinces of Canada have also been greatly affected.

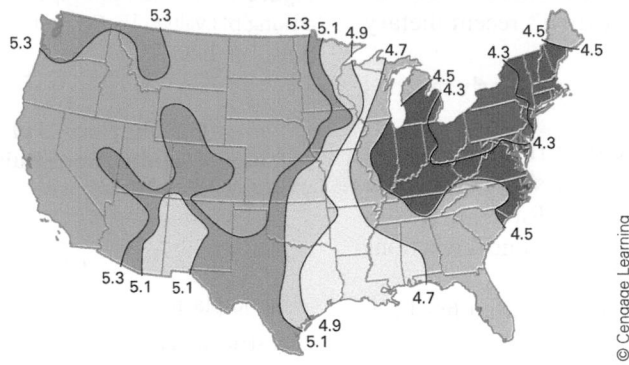

Average annual pH of precipitation in the United States.

Acid rain originates from the presence of sulfur oxides (SO_2 and SO_3) and, to a lesser extent, nitrogen oxides (NO and NO_2) in the atmosphere. After being discharged into the atmosphere, these pollutants can be converted into sulfuric acid (H_2SO_4) and nitric acid (HNO_3) through oxidation processes.

Simplified equations for the formation of these two acids are

$$H_2SO_4: \quad 2\,SO_2 + O_2 \longrightarrow 2\,SO_3$$
$$SO_3 + H_2O \longrightarrow H_2SO_4$$
$$HNO_3: \quad 2\,NO + O_2 \longrightarrow 2\,NO_2$$
$$3\,NO_2 + H_2O \longrightarrow 2\,HNO_3 + NO$$

The high solubility of sulfur oxides in water is a major factor contributing to atmospheric sulfuric acid production; SO_2 is approximately 70 times more soluble in water than CO_2 and 2600 times more soluble in water than O_2.

Small amounts of sulfur oxides and nitrogen oxides arise naturally from volcanic activity, lightning, and forest fires, but their major sources are human-related. The major source of sulfur oxide emissions is the combustion of coal associated with power plant operations. (The sulfur content of coal can be as high as 5% by mass.) Automobile exhaust is the major source of nitrogen oxides.

The most observable effect of acid rain is the corrosion of building materials. Sulfuric acid (acid rain) readily attacks carbonate-based building materials (limestone, marble); the calcium carbonate is slowly converted into calcium sulfate.

$$CaCO_3(s) + H_2SO_4(aq) \rightarrow CaSO_4(s) + CO_2(g) + H_2O(l)$$

The $CaSO_4$, which is more soluble than $CaCO_3$, is gradually eroded away. Many stone monuments show distinctly discernible erosion damage.

Erosion damage to an 1869 grave marker.

How does the acidity of acid rain compare to the acidity of other common acidic substances? A soft drink is 10 times as acidic as commonly encountered acid rain (pH = 4.5), vinegar is 15 times more acidic, lemon juice is 50 times more acidic, and automobile battery acid (sulfuric acid) is 3200 times more acidic.

CHEMISTRY AT A GLANCE

Acids and Acidic Solutions

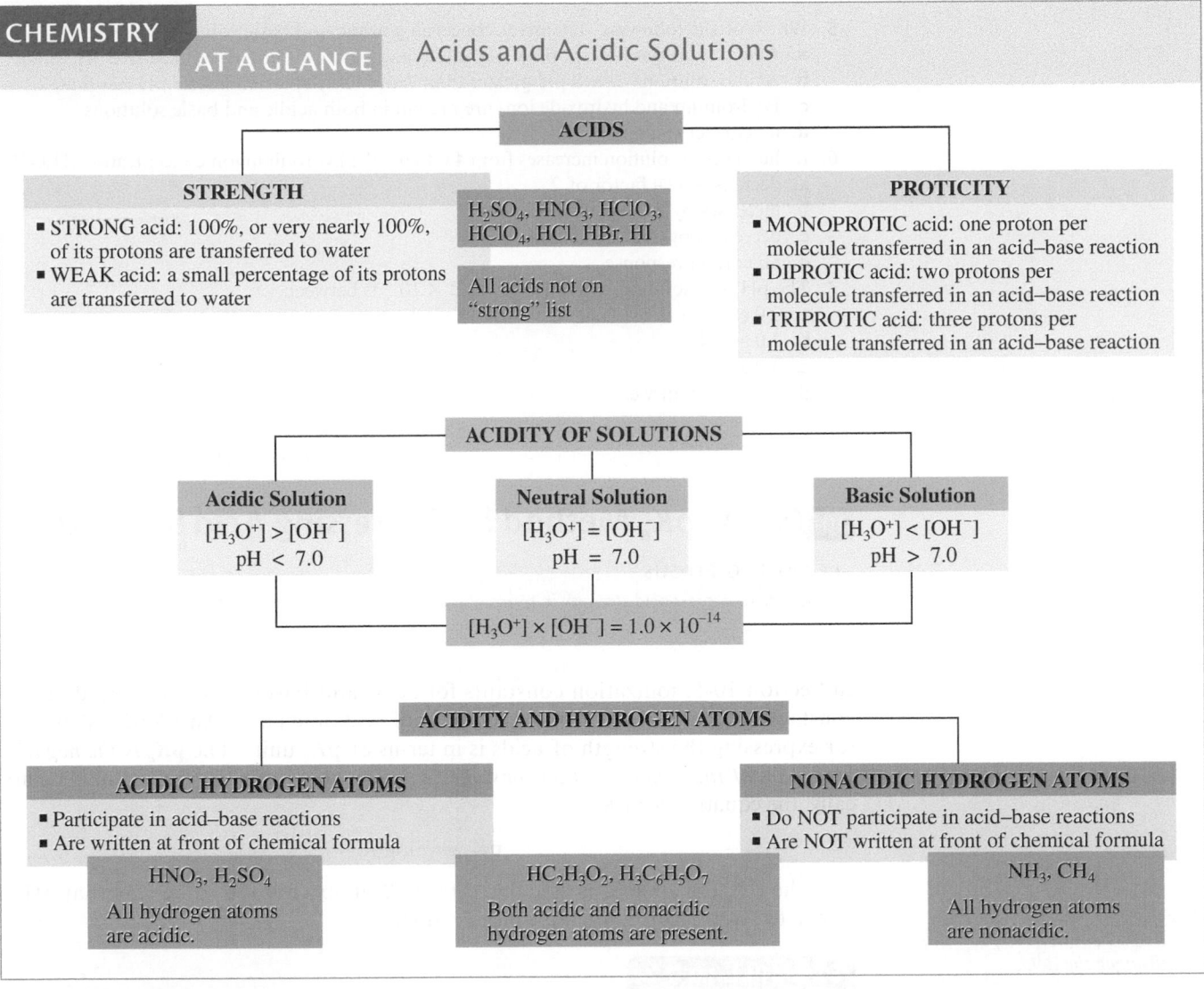

ACIDS

STRENGTH

- STRONG acid: 100%, or very nearly 100%, of its protons are transferred to water
- WEAK acid: a small percentage of its protons are transferred to water

H_2SO_4, HNO_3, $HClO_3$, $HClO_4$, HCl, HBr, HI

All acids not on "strong" list

PROTICITY

- MONOPROTIC acid: one proton per molecule transferred in an acid–base reaction
- DIPROTIC acid: two protons per molecule transferred in an acid–base reaction
- TRIPROTIC acid: three protons per molecule transferred in an acid–base reaction

ACIDITY OF SOLUTIONS

Acidic Solution
$[H_3O^+] > [OH^-]$
pH < 7.0

Neutral Solution
$[H_3O^+] = [OH^-]$
pH = 7.0

Basic Solution
$[H_3O^+] < [OH^-]$
pH > 7.0

$[H_3O^+] \times [OH^-] = 1.0 \times 10^{-14}$

ACIDITY AND HYDROGEN ATOMS

ACIDIC HYDROGEN ATOMS
- Participate in acid–base reactions
- Are written at front of chemical formula

HNO_3, H_2SO_4

All hydrogen atoms are acidic.

$HC_2H_3O_2$, $H_3C_6H_5O_7$

Both acidic and nonacidic hydrogen atoms are present.

NONACIDIC HYDROGEN ATOMS
- Do NOT participate in acid–base reactions
- Are NOT written at front of chemical formula

NH_3, CH_4

All hydrogen atoms are nonacidic.

Section 10-9 Quick Quiz

1. The pH for a solution with $[H_3O^+] = 1.0 \times 10^{-6}$ is
   a. 1.00
   b. 6.00
   c. −6.00
   d. no correct response
2. The pH for a solution with $[OH^-] = 1.0 \times 10^{-6}$ is
   a. 1.00
   b. 6.00
   c. 8.00
   d. no correct response
3. Which of the following does *not* describe an acidic solution at 24°C?
   a. the pH is less than 7.0
   b. the $[H_3O^+]$ is greater than the $[OH^-]$
   c. the $[H_3O^+]$ is 1.0×10^{-8}
   d. no correct response
4. A solution with a pH of 12.0 is
   a. weakly acid
   b. weakly basic
   c. strongly basic
   d. no correct response

(continued)

5. Which of the following statements concerning acidic and basic solutions is *correct*?
   a. Acidic solutions have positive pH values and basic solutions have negative pH values.
   b. Acidic solutions have a pH greater than 7 and basic solution have a pH less than 7.
   c. Hydronium and hydroxide ions are present in both acidic and basic solutions.
   d. no correct response
6. If the pH of a solution increases from 4.0 to 6.0 the hydronium ion concentration $[H_3O^+]$
   a. decreases by a factor of 2
   b. increases by a factor of 2
   c. decreases by a factor of 100
   d. no correct response
7. The pH of a solution with $[H_3O^+] = 2.2 \times 10^{-4}$ is between
   a. 2.0 and 3.0
   b. 3.0 and 4.0
   c. 4.0 and 5.0
   d. no correct answer

Answers: 1. b; 2. c; 3. c; 4. c; 5. c; 6. c; 7. b

10-10   The pK$_a$ Method for Expressing Acid Strength

LEARNING FOCUS

Be able to express acid strength in terms of pK$_a$ values.

In Section 10-5, ionization constants for acids and bases were introduced. These constants give an indication of the strengths of acids and bases. An additional method for expressing the strength of acids is in terms of pK$_a$ units. The **pK$_a$** *is the negative logarithm of the acid ionization constant (K$_a$) for a weak acid.* Expressed mathematically, the equation for pK$_a$ is

$$pK_a = -\log K_a$$

The pK$_a$ for an acid is calculated from K_a in exactly the same way that pH is calculated from hydronium ion concentration. ◄

▶ *Like pH, pK$_a$ is a positive number. The lower the pK$_a$ value, the stronger the acid.*

EXAMPLE 10-7

Calculating the pK$_a$ of an Acid from the Acid's K$_a$ Value

Determine the pK$_a$ for acetic acid, $HC_2H_3O_2$, given that K_a for this acid is 1.8×10^{-5}.

Solution

Because the K_a value is 1.8×10^{-5} and $pK_a = -\log K_a$,

$$pK_a = -\log(1.8 \times 10^{-5}) = 4.74$$

The logarithm value 4.74 was obtained using an electronic calculator, as explained in Example 10-5.

Section 10-10 Quick Quiz

1. The defining equation for the calculation of a pK$_a$ value is
   a. $pK_a = -\log[H^+]$
   b. $pK_a = \log K_a$
   c. $pK_a = -\log K_a$
   d. no correct response
2. The pK$_a$ for an acid whose K_a is 1.0×10^{-5} is
   a. 1.0
   b. 5.0
   c. −5.0
   d. no correct response

Answers: 1. c; 2. b

10-11 The pH of Aqueous Salt Solutions

LEARNING FOCUS

Be able to predict whether a salt will hydrolyze and if it does whether an acidic or basic solution is produced; be able to write chemical equations for salt hydrolysis reactions.

The addition of an acid to water produces an acidic solution. The addition of a base to water produces a basic solution. What type of solution is produced when a salt is added to water? Because salts are the products of acid–base neutralizations, a logical supposition would be that salts dissolve in water to produce neutral (pH = 7.0) solutions. Such is the case for a *few* salts. Aqueous solutions of *most* salts, however, are either acidic or basic rather than neutral. Why is this so?

When a salt is dissolved in water, it completely ionizes; that is, it completely breaks up into the ions of which it is composed (Section 8-3). For many salts, one or more of the ions so produced are reactive toward water. The ensuing reaction, which is called salt hydrolysis, causes the solution to have a non-neutral pH. ◄ A **salt hydrolysis reaction** *is the chemical reaction of a salt with water to produce hydronium ion or hydroxide ion or both.*

▶ *The term* hydrolysis *comes from the Greek* hydro, *which means "water," and* lysis, *which means "splitting."*

Types of Salt Hydrolysis

Not all salts hydrolyze. Which ones do and which ones do not? Of those salts that do hydrolyze, which produce acidic solutions and which produce basic solutions? The following guidelines, based on the neutralization "parentage" of a salt— that is, on the acid and base that produce the salt through neutralization—can be used to answer these questions.

1. The salt of a *strong acid* and a *strong base* does not hydrolyze, so the solution is neutral.
2. The salt of a *strong acid* and a *weak base* hydrolyzes to produce an acidic solution.
3. The salt of a *weak acid* and a *strong base* hydrolyzes to produce a basic solution.
4. The salt of a *weak acid* and a *weak base* hydrolyzes to produce a slightly acidic, neutral, or slightly basic solution, depending on the relative weaknesses of the acid and base.

These guidelines are summarized in Table 10-7.

The first prerequisite for using these guidelines is the ability to classify a salt into one of the four categories mentioned in the guidelines. This classification is accomplished by writing the neutralization equation (Section 10-7) that produces the salt and then specifying the strength (strong or weak) of the acid and base involved. The "parent" acid and base for the salt are identified by pairing the negative ion of the salt with H^+ (to form the acid) and pairing the positive ion of the salt with OH^- (to form the base). The following two equations illustrate the overall procedure.

Table 10-7 Neutralization "Parentage" of Salts and the Nature of the Aqueous Solutions They Form

Type of Salt	Nature of Aqueous Solution	Examples
strong acid–strong base	neutral	$NaCl$, KBr
strong acid–weak base	acidic	NH_4Cl, NH_4NO_3
weak acid–strong base	basic	$NaC_2H_3O_2$, K_2CO_3
weak acid–weak base	depends on the salt	$NH_4C_2H_3O_2$, NH_4NO_2

Knowing which acids and bases are strong and which are weak (Section 10-4) is a necessary part of the classification process. Once the salt has been so classified, the guideline that is appropriate for the situation is easily selected.

EXAMPLE 10-8

Predicting Whether a Salt's Aqueous Solution Will Be Acidic, Basic, or Neutral

Determine the acid–base "parentage" of each of the following salts, and then use this information to predict whether each salt's aqueous solution is acidic, basic, or neutral.

a. Sodium acetate, $NaC_2H_3O_2$ **b.** Ammonium chloride, NH_4Cl
c. Potassium chloride, KCl **d.** Ammonium fluoride, NH_4F

Solution

a. The ions present are Na^+ and $C_2H_3O_2^-$. The "parent" base of Na^+ is NaOH, a strong base. The "parent" acid of $C_2H_3O_2^-$ is $HC_2H_3O_2$, a weak acid. Thus the acid–base neutralization that produces this salt is

$$NaOH + HC_2H_3O_2 \longrightarrow H_2O + NaC_2H_3O_2$$
Strong base   Weak acid   Weak acid–strong base salt

The solution of a weak acid–strong base salt (guideline 3) produces a basic solution.

b. The ions present are NH_4^+ and Cl^-. The "parent" base of NH_4^+ is NH_3, a weak base. The "parent" acid of Cl^- is HCl, a strong acid. This "parentage" will produce a strong acid–weak base salt through neutralization. Such a salt gives an acidic solution upon hydrolysis (guideline 2).

c. The ions present are K^+ and Cl^-. The "parent" base is KOH (a strong base), and the "parent" acid is HCl (a strong acid). The salt produced from neutralization involving this acid–base pair will be a strong acid–strong base salt. Such salts do not hydrolyze. The aqueous solution is neutral (guideline 1).

d. The ions present are NH_4^+ and F^-. Both ions are of weak "parentage"; NH_3 is a weak base, and HF is a weak acid. Thus NH_4F is a weak acid–weak base salt. This is a guideline 4 situation. In this situation, the effect of hydrolysis on pH cannot be predicted unless the relative strengths of the weak acid and weak base (that is, which is the weaker of the two) are known. HF has a K_a of 6.8×10^{-4} (Table 10-3). NH_3 has a K_b of 1.8×10^{-5} (Section 10-5). Thus, NH_3 is the weaker of the two and will hydrolyze to the greater extent, causing the solution to be acidic.

Chemical Equations for Salt Hydrolysis Reactions

Salt hydrolysis reactions are Brønsted–Lowry acid–base (proton transfer) reactions (Section 10-2). Such reactions are of the following two general types.

1. *Basic hydrolysis:* The reaction of the *negative ion* from a salt with water to produce the ion's conjugate acid and hydroxide ion. ◀

▶ *The only negative ions that undergo hydrolysis are those of "weak-acid parentage." The driving force for the reaction is the formation of the weak-acid "parent."*

Conjugate acid–base pair

$$CN^- + H_2O \longrightarrow HCN + OH^-$$
Proton   Proton   Weak   Makes solution
acceptor   donor   acid   basic

Conjugate acid–base pair

$$F^- + H_2O \longrightarrow HF + OH^-$$
Proton   Proton   Weak   Makes solution
acceptor   donor   acid   basic

2. *Acidic hydrolysis:* The reaction of the *positive ion* from a salt with water to produce the ion's conjugate base and hydronium ion. The most common ion to undergo this type of reaction is the NH_4^+ ion. ◀

▶ *The only positive ions that undergo hydrolysis are those of "weak-base parentage." The driving force for the reaction is the formation of the weak-base "parent."*

Conjugate acid–base pair

$$NH_4^+ + H_2O \longrightarrow NH_3 + H_3O^+$$
Proton   Proton   Weak   Makes solution
donor   acceptor   base   acidic

▶ Table 10-8 **Approximate pH of Selected 0.1 M Aqueous Salt Solutions at 24°C**

Name of Salt	Formula of Salt	pH	Category of Salt
ammonium nitrate	NH_4NO_3	5.1	strong acid–weak base
ammonium nitrite	NH_4NO_2	6.3	weak acid–weak base
ammonium acetate	$NH_4C_2H_3O_2$	7.0	weak acid–weak base
sodium chloride	$NaCl$	7.0	strong acid–strong base
sodium fluoride	NaF	8.1	weak acid–strong base
sodium acetate	$NaC_2H_3O_2$	8.9	weak acid–strong base
ammonium cyanide	NH_4CN	9.3	weak acid–weak base
sodium cyanide	$NaCN$	11.1	weak acid–strong base

Hydrolysis reactions do not go 100% to completion. They occur only until equilibrium conditions are reached (Section 9-7). At the equilibrium point, solution pH change can be significant—differing from neutrality by two to four units. Table 10-8 shows the range of pH values encountered for selected 0.1 M aqueous salt solutions after hydrolysis has occurred.

Blood plasma has a slightly basic pH because of salt hydrolysis reactions. In the focus on relevancy feature Chemical Connections 10-C—Composition and Characteristics of Blood Plasma—consideration is given to the specific chemical reactions that contribute to blood plasma's pH having a value greater than 7.0.

Section 10-11 Quick Quiz

1. Which of the following salts contains an ion that undergoes hydrolysis in aqueous solution?
   a. NaCl
   b. $NaNO_3$
   c. Na_2SO_4
   d. no correct response
2. Aqueous solution hydrolysis for the salt NaF produces a(n)
   a. acidic solution
   b. basic solution
   c. neutral solution
   d. no correct response
3. Which of the following is the correct chemical equation for the aqueous solution hydrolysis of the CN^- ion?
   a. $CN^- + H_2O \longrightarrow HCN + OH^-$
   b. $CN^- + H^+ \longrightarrow HCN$
   c. $CN^- + H_3O^+ \longrightarrow HCN + H_2O$
   d. no correct response

Answers: 1. d; 2. b; 3. a

10-12 Buffers

LEARNING FOCUS

Be able to recognize pairs of substances that can function as an aqueous buffer system; be able to write chemical equations describing the buffering action of a conjugate acid–base pair.

A **buffer** *is an aqueous solution containing substances that prevent major changes in solution pH when small amounts of acid or base are added to it.* Buffers are used in a laboratory setting to maintain optimum pH conditions for chemical reactions. Many commercial products contain buffers, which are needed to maintain optimum pH conditions for product behavior. Examples include buffered aspirin (Bufferin) and pH-controlled hair shampoos. Most human body fluids are highly buffered. For example, a buffer system maintains blood's pH at a value close to 7.4, an optimum pH for oxygen transport.

CHEMICAL CONNECTIONS 10-C

Composition and Characteristics of Blood Plasma

Blood plasma is the liquid component of blood. It is obtained from whole blood through removal of the cellular portion of the blood (red blood cells, white blood cells, and platelets). This removal of cellular components is achieved by spinning a tube of whole blood in a centrifuge; the cellular components are drawn to the bottom of the tube by gravity and the plasma is then poured out of the tube.

In terms of chemical composition, blood plasma is mostly water (90% by volume). Dissolved in the water are ions from salts, proteins, glucose, antibodies, hormones, and carbon dioxide. Through the circulatory system, the blood plasma distributes these vital substances (as well as the cellular components) throughout the body. Red blood cells carry oxygen from the lungs, white blood cells fight infections, and platelets are involved in the blood-clotting process.

Separation of whole blood into its plasma and cellular components is accomplished using a centrifuge. The straw-colored liquid layer on top is the plasma.

Antonia Reeve/Science Source

The blood plasma component of whole blood is no less important than the cellular components of whole blood. Saying that the cellular components of blood are more important than the plasma portion is like saying that fish are more important than the water in which they swim.

The pH of blood plasma falls in the narrow range of 7.35–7.45; it is thus a slightly basic solution. The cause for this basicity is ion hydrolysis (Section 10-11). That this is the case becomes apparent when the identity of the ions present in blood plasma is considered.

The most abundant positive ion in blood plasma is the Na^+ ion, an ion associated with a strong base (NaOH). Thus it does not hydrolyze. The predominant negative ion present is Cl^-, an ion that comes from a strong acid (HCl). Thus it also does not hydrolyze. A solution containing just these two ions (Na^+ and Cl^-) is neutral due to the lack of a hydrolysis reaction.

The third most abundant ion in blood plasma (Chemical Connections 10-E—Electrolytes and Body Fluids) is the hydrogen carbonate ion (HCO_3^-), which comes from the weak acid H_2CO_3. This ion does hydrolyze in water, with hydroxide ion being a product of the hydrolysis.

$$HCO_3^- + H_2O \longrightarrow H_2CO_3 + \boxed{OH^-}$$

This hydrolysis reaction is the primary cause for blood plasma's basic pH value.

There is another hydrolyzable negative ion present, at lower concentrations than HCO_3^-, in blood plasma. It is the hydrogen phosphate ion, HPO_4^{2-}. This hydrolysis contributes, to a smaller extent, to the basicity of the plasma.

$$HPO_4^{2-} + H_2O \longrightarrow H_2PO_4^- + \boxed{OH^-}$$

The concentration of the HCO_3^- ion in blood plasma is 16 times greater than that of the HPO_4^{2-} ion.

Buffers contain two active chemical species: (1) a substance to react with and remove added base and (2) a substance to react with and remove added acid. Typically, a buffer system is composed of a weak acid *and* its conjugate base—that is, a conjugate acid–base pair (Section 10-2). Conjugate acid–base pairs that are commonly employed as buffers include $HC_2H_3O_2/C_2H_3O_2^-$, $H_2PO_4^-/HPO_4^{2-}$, and H_2CO_3/HCO_3^-. ◀

▶ *A less common type of buffer involves a weak base and its conjugate acid. We will not consider this type of buffer here.*

EXAMPLE 10-9

Recognizing Pairs of Chemical Substances That Can Function as a Buffer in Aqueous Solution

Predict whether each of the following pairs of substances could function as a buffer system in aqueous solution.

a. HCl and NaCl **b.** HCN and KCN
c. HCl and HCN **d.** NaCN and KCN

Solution

Buffer solutions contain either a weak acid and a salt of that weak acid or a weak base and a salt of that weak base.

a. No. An acid and the salt of that acid are present. However, the acid is a strong acid rather than a weak acid.
b. Yes. HCN is a weak acid, and KCN is a salt of that weak acid.
c. No. Both HCl and HCN are acids. No salt is present.
d. No. Both NaCN and KCN are salts. No weak acid is present.

As an illustration of buffer action, consider a buffer solution containing approximately equal concentrations of acetic acid (a weak acid) and sodium acetate (a salt of this weak acid). This solution resists pH change by the following mechanisms:

1. When a small amount of a strong acid such as HCl is added to the solution, the newly added H_3O^+ ions react with the acetate ions from the sodium acetate to give acetic acid.

$$H_3O^+ + C_2H_3O_2^- \longrightarrow HC_2H_3O_2 + H_2O$$

Most of the added H_3O^+ ions are tied up in acetic acid molecules, and the pH changes very little.

2. When a small amount of a strong base such as NaOH is added to the solution, the newly added OH^- ions react with the acetic acid (neutralization) to give acetate ions and water. ◀

$$OH^- + HC_2H_3O_2 \longrightarrow C_2H_3O_2^- + H_2O$$

Most of the added OH^- ions are converted to water, and the pH changes only slightly.

The reactions that are responsible for the buffering action in the acetic acid/acetate ion system can be summarized as follows:

$$C_2H_3O_2^- \overset{H_3O^+}{\underset{OH^-}{\rightleftharpoons}} HC_2H_3O_2$$

Note that one member of the buffer pair (acetate ion) removes excess H_3O^+ ion and that the other (acetic acid) removes excess OH^- ion. The buffering action always results in the active species being converted to its partner species.

▶ *To resist both increases and decreases in pH effectively, a weak-acid buffer must contain significant amounts of both the weak acid and its conjugate base. If a solution has a large amount of weak acid but very little conjugate base, it will be unable to consume much added acid. Consequently, the pH tends to drop significantly when acid is added. Conversely, a solution that contains a large amount of conjugate base but very little weak acid will provide very little protection against added base. Addition of just a little base will cause a big change in pH.*

EXAMPLE 10-10

Writing Equations for Reactions That Occur in a Buffered Solution

Write an equation for each of the following buffering actions.

a. The response of $H_2PO_4^-/HPO_4^{2-}$ buffer to the addition of H_3O^+ ions
b. The response of HCN/CN^- buffer to the addition of OH^- ions

Solution

a. The base in a conjugate acid–base pair is the species that responds to the addition of acid. (Recall, from Section 10-2, that the base in a conjugate acid–base pair always has one less hydrogen than the acid.) The base for this reaction is HPO_4^{2-}. The equation for the buffering action is

$$H_3O^+ + HPO_4^{2-} \longrightarrow H_2PO_4^- + H_2O$$

In the buffering response, the base is always converted into its conjugate acid.
b. The acid in a conjugate acid–base pair is the species that responds to the addition of base. The acid for this reaction is HCN. The equation for the buffering action is

$$HCN + OH^- \longrightarrow CN^- + H_2O$$

Water will always be one of the products of buffering action.

Figure 10-12 A comparison of pH changes in buffered and unbuffered solutions. When 0.01 mole of strong acid and 0.01 mole of strong base are added to 1.0 L of pure water and to 1.0 L of 0.1 M HPO_4^{2-} ion/0.1 M $H_2PO_4^{-}$ ion buffer, the pH of the water varies between 2.0 and 12.0, while the pH of the buffer stays in the narrow range of 7.1 to 7.3.

▶ *A common misconception about buffers is that a buffered solution is always a neutral (pH 7.0) solution. This is false. Laboratory-produced buffers of any desired pH can be made. A pH 7.4 buffer will hold the pH of the solution near pH 7.4, whereas a pH 9.3 buffer will tend to hold the pH of a solution near pH 9.3. The pH of a buffer is determined by the degree of weakness of the weak acid used and by the concentrations of the acid and its conjugate base.*

A false idea about buffers is that they will hold the pH of a solution *absolutely* constant. The addition of even small amounts of a strong acid or a strong base to any solution, buffered or not, will lead to a change in pH. The important concept is that the shift in pH will be minimized when an effective buffer is present (Figure 10-12). ◀

Buffer systems have their limits. If large amounts of H_3O^+ or OH^- are added to a buffer, the buffer capacity can be exceeded; then the buffer system is overwhelmed and the pH changes. For example, if large amounts of H_3O^+ were added to the acetate/acetic acid buffer previously discussed, the H_3O^+ ion would react with acetate ion until the acetate was depleted. Then the pH would begin to drop as free H_3O^+ ions accumulated in the solution.

Additional insights into the workings of buffer systems are obtained by considering buffer action within the framework of Le Châtelier's principle and an equilibrium system.

For an acetic acid/acetate ion buffer system the equilibrium equation involving the two buffer components is

$$HC_2H_3O_2(aq) + H_2O(l) \rightleftharpoons H_3O^+(aq) + C_2H_3O_2^-(aq)$$

This equilibrium system functions in accordance with *Le Châtelier's principle* (Section 9-9), which states that an equilibrium system, when stressed, will shift its position in such a way as to counteract the stress. Stresses for the buffer will be (1) addition of base (hydroxide ion) and (2) addition of acid (hydronium ion). Further details concerning these two stress situations are as follows.

Addition of base [OH^- ion] *to the buffer.* The addition of base causes the following changes to occur in the solution:

1. The added OH^- ion reacts with H_3O^+ ion, producing water (neutralization).
2. The neutralization reaction produces the stress of *not enough* H_3O^+ ion because H_3O^+ ion was consumed in the neutralization.
3. The equilibrium shifts to the right, in accordance with Le Châtelier's principle, to produce more H_3O^+ ion, which maintains the pH close to its original level.

Addition of acid [H_3O^+ ion] *to the buffer.* The addition of acid causes the following changes to occur in the solution:

1. The added H_3O^+ ion increases the overall amount of H_3O^+ ion present.
2. The stress on the system is *too much* H_3O^+ ion.
3. The equilibrium shifts to the left, in accordance with Le Châtelier's principle, consuming most of the excess H_3O^+ ion and resulting in a pH close to the original level.

The foremost buffering system in blood involves the hydrogen carbonate ion (HCO_3^-). The focus on relevancy feature Chemical Connections 10-D—Acidosis and Alkalosis—gives details about this buffering system, as well as about the conditions of *acidosis* and *alkalosis* that occur when this primary buffering system is "overwhelmed."

Chemistry at a Glance—Buffer Systems—reviews important concepts about buffer systems.

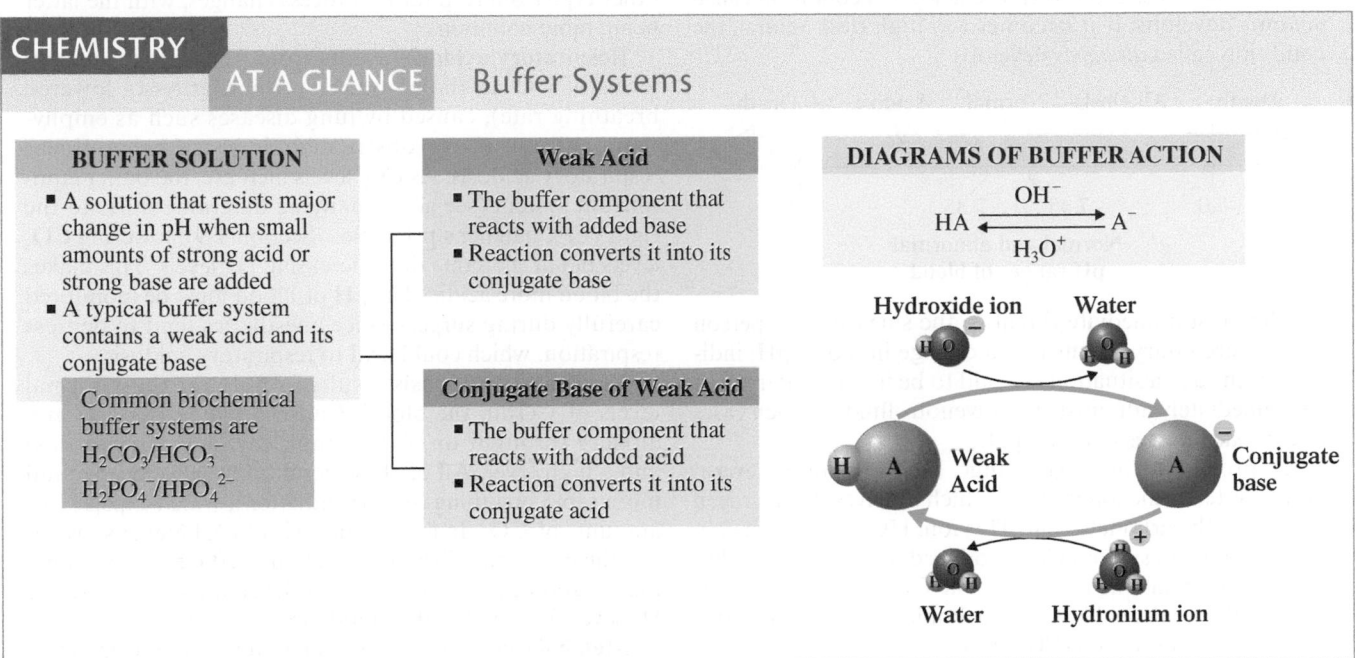

CHEMISTRY AT A GLANCE Buffer Systems

BUFFER SOLUTION

- A solution that resists major change in pH when small amounts of strong acid or strong base are added
- A typical buffer system contains a weak acid and its conjugate base

Common biochemical buffer systems are H_2CO_3/HCO_3^- $H_2PO_4^-/HPO_4^{2-}$

Weak Acid

- The buffer component that reacts with added base
- Reaction converts it into its conjugate base

Conjugate Base of Weak Acid

- The buffer component that reacts with added acid
- Reaction converts it into its conjugate acid

DIAGRAMS OF BUFFER ACTION

$$HA \underset{H_3O^+}{\overset{OH^-}{\rightleftarrows}} A^-$$

Hydroxide ion   Water

Weak Acid   Conjugate base

Water   Hydronium ion

Section 10-12 Quick Quiz

1. Which of the following combinations of substances would produce a buffer?
   a. a strong acid and a salt of the strong acid
   b. a weak acid and a salt of the weak acid
   c. a salt of a strong acid and a salt of a weak acid
   d. no correct response
2. Which of the following pairs of substance could function as a buffer in aqueous solution?
   a. HCl and HF
   b. H_2CO_3 and $NaHCO_3$
   c. Na_2CO_3 and $NaHCO_3$
   d. no correct response
3. After the addition of a small amount of acid, a solution that is buffered at a pH of 8.0 will have an approximate pH of
   a. 7.0
   b. 8.0
   c. 9.0
   d. no correct response
4. The chemical reaction that occurs when a HCN/CN^- buffer system responds to the addition of a small amount of acid is
   a. $HCN + H_2O \longrightarrow H_3O^+ + CN^-$
   b. $H_3O^+ + OH^- \longrightarrow 2\,H_2O$
   c. $CN^- + H_3O^+ \longrightarrow H_2O + HCN$
   d. no correct response

Answers: 1. b; 2. b; 3. b; 4. c

CHEMICAL CONNECTIONS 10-D

Acidosis and Alkalosis

In healthy individuals, the pH of blood falls within the narrow range of 7.35–7.45. Even small departures from this normal range can cause serious illness, and death can result from pH variations of only a few tenths of a unit. If the pH of blood becomes too low (more acidic), a condition called *acidosis* develops; if it becomes too high (less acidic), the condition called *alkalosis* develops.

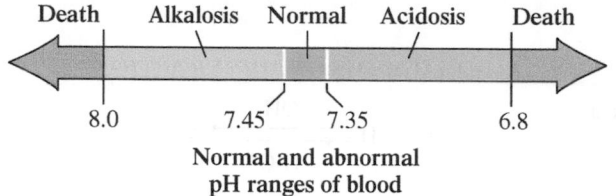

Normal and abnormal pH ranges of blood

The most immediate threat to the survival of a person with severe injury or burns is a change in blood pH; individuals in such a situation are said to be in *shock*. Paramedics immediately administer intravenous fluids in such cases to combat changes in blood pH.

To protect against pH change, blood contains several buffer systems, the foremost of which involves the hydrogen carbonate (bicarbonate) ion. This ion, HCO_3^-, is formed in a two-step process from CO_2 produced in the body as a by-product of metabolic reactions. The CO_2 dissolves in water to form the weak acid H_2CO_3 (carbonic acid), which in turn dissociates to produce HCO_3^- ion.

$$CO_2(g) + H_2O(l) \rightleftharpoons H_2CO_3(aq) \rightleftharpoons H^+(aq) + HCO_3^-(aq)$$

The concentration ratio of H_2CO_3 to HCO_3^- in the blood's H_2CO_3/HCO_3^- buffer system is approximately 1 to 10. Reactions that involve the kidneys help to maintain the HCO_3^- ion concentration at an appropriate level, and reactions that involve the lungs help maintain the H_2CO_3 concentration at its appropriate level.

Small amounts of excess acid that enter the blood react with the HCO_3^- ion component of the buffer system, and any excess base reacts with the H_2CO_3 component of the system.

$$H_3O^+ + HCO_3^- \longrightarrow H_2CO_3 + H_2O$$
$$OH^- + H_2CO_3 \longrightarrow HCO_3^- + H_2O$$

"Stressful" body conditions can overwhelm the blood's buffer system, resulting in acidosis or alkalosis situations. There are two general types of both acidosis and alkalosis—one type resulting from metabolic process changes and the other type from respiratory process changes, with the latter being more common.

Respiratory acidosis results from higher than normal levels of CO_2 in the blood. Hypoventilation (a lowered breathing rate), caused by lung diseases such as emphysema and asthma or obstructed air passages, produces respiratory acidosis. As CO_2 levels increase, the buffer equilibrium system (see accompanying diagram) shifts to the right (Le Châtelier's principle—Section 9-9), lowering CO_2 levels but at the same time increasing H^+ levels. This makes the blood more acidic. The pH of blood must be monitored carefully during surgery since anesthetics tend to depress respiration, which could lead to respiratory acidosis.

Respiratory alkalosis results from lower than normal levels of CO_2 in the blood. Causes include hysteria and anxiety (brought on, for example, by chemistry exams) and a high fever. All of these conditions cause deeper and more rapid breathing (hyperventilation), which expels large amounts of CO_2. In accordance with Le Châtelier's principle, the buffer equilibrium shifts to the left (see accompanying diagram), increasing the CO_2 level and decreasing the H^+ level. This makes the blood more basic.

Metabolic acidosis results from lower than normal levels of HCO_3^- ion in the blood. Causes include severe diabetes and severe diarrhea. Temporary metabolic acidosis occurs in all individuals after strenuous exercise; the exercise metabolically generates lactic acid in the muscles, which enters the bloodstream. The body's response to such stress is to shift the buffer equilibrium position to the right (see accompanying diagram), which produces more HCO_3^- and H^+.

Metabolic alkalosis results from higher than normal levels of HCO_3^- in the blood. This condition, less common than metabolic acidosis, can be caused by prolonged vomiting and is also a side effect of certain drugs that, like vomiting, change electrolyte concentrations of Na^+, K^+, and Cl^- ions in the blood (Section 10-14). To reduce the HCO_3^- concentration, the buffer equilibrium position shifts to the left (see accompanying diagram), which consumes both HCO_3^- and H^+ ion.

$$lungs \rightleftharpoons CO_2 + H_2O \rightleftharpoons H_2CO_3 \rightleftharpoons H^+ + HCO_3^- \rightleftharpoons kidneys$$

Condition	Cause	Equilibrium Position Shift	Effect		
Respiratory acidosis	High CO_2	to the right	CO_2 ↓		H^+ ↑
Respiratory alkalosis	Low CO_2	to the left	CO_2 ↑		H^+ ↓
Metabolic acidosis	Low HCO_3^-	to the right	HCO_3^- ↑		H^+ ↑
Metabolic alkalosis	High HCO_3^-	to the left	HCO_3^- ↓		H^+ ↓

10-13 The Henderson–Hasselbalch Equation

LEARNING FOCUS

Be able to use the Henderson–Hasselbalch equation to calculate the pH of a buffer.

Buffers may be prepared from any ratio of concentrations of a weak acid and the salt of its conjugate base. However, a buffer is most effective in counteracting pH change when the acid-to-conjugate-base molar concentration ratio is 1-to-1. If a buffer contains considerably more acid than the conjugate base, it is less efficient in handling an acid. Conversely, a buffer with considerably more of the conjugate base than the acid is less efficient in handling added base.

When the molar concentrations of an acid and its conjugate base are equal in a buffer solution, the solution's hydronium ion concentration is equal to the acid ionization constant of the weak acid—or, stated more concisely, the pH of the solution is equal to the pK_a of the weak acid. The mathematical basis for this equality is as follows:

For the weak acid,

$$K_a = \frac{[H_3O^+][A^-]}{[HA]}$$

If [HA] and [A$^-$] are equal, then they cancel from the equation, and the equation simplifies to

$$K_a = [H_3O^+]$$

Taking the negative logarithm of both sides of this equation gives

$$pK_a = pH$$

The relationship between pK_a and pH for buffer solutions in which the conjugate acid–base pair concentration ratio is something other than 1-to-1 is given by the equation

$$pH = pK_a + \log \frac{[A^-]}{[HA]}$$

This equation is called the *Henderson–Hasselbalch equation*. The Henderson–Hasselbalch equation indicates that if there is more A$^-$ than HA in a solution, the pH is higher than pK_a; and if there is more HA than A$^-$, the pH is lower than pK_a.

EXAMPLE 10-11

Calculating the pH of a Buffer Solution Using the Henderson–Hasselbalch Equation

What is the pH of a buffer solution that is 0.50 M in formic acid (HCHO$_2$) and 1.0 M in sodium formate (NaCHO$_2$)? The pK_a for formic acid is 3.74.

Solution

The concentrations for the buffering species are

$$HCHO_2 = 0.50 \text{ M} \qquad CHO_2^- = 1.0 \text{ M}$$

Substituting these values into the Henderson–Hasselbalch equation gives

$$pH = pK_a + \log \frac{[CHO_2^-]}{[HCHO_2]} = 3.74 + \log \frac{1.0}{0.50}$$

$$= 3.74 + \log 2.0 = 3.74 + 0.30$$

$$= 4.04$$

Section 10-13 Quick Quiz

1. Which of the following quantities is *not* present in the Henderson–Hasselbalch equation?
   a. pH
   b. pK_a
   c. $\log[[A^-]/[HA]]$
   d. no correct response
2. For a buffer where the acid and conjugate base are present in a 1-to-1 molar ratio, the Henderson–Hasselbalch equation simplifies to
   a. pH = pK_a
   b. pH = K_a
   c. pH = $-\log(pK_a)$
   d. no correct response

Answers: 1. d; 2. a

10-14 Electrolytes

LEARNING FOCUS

Know general substance types that are classified as strong electrolytes and as weak electrolytes; be able to classify a specific substance as a strong electrolyte, weak electrolyte, or nonelectrolyte.

▶ *The differences between the processes of* ionization *and* dissociation *were considered in Section 10-1.*

Figure 10-13 This simple device can be used to distinguish among strong electrolytes, weak electrolytes, and nonelectrolytes. The light bulb glows strongly for strong electrolytes (left), weakly for weak electrolytes (center), and not at all for nonelectrolytes (right).

Aqueous solutions in which ions are present are good conductors of electricity, and the greater the number of ions present, the better the solution conducts electricity. Acids, bases, and soluble salts all produce ions in solution; thus they all produce solutions that conduct electricity. All three types of compounds are said to be electrolytes. An **electrolyte** *is a substance whose aqueous solution conducts electricity.* The presence of ions (charged particles) explains the electrical conductivity.

Some substances, such as table sugar (sucrose), glucose, and isopropyl alcohol, do not produce ions in solution. These substances are called nonelectrolytes. A **nonelectrolyte** *is a substance whose aqueous solution does not conduct electricity.*

Electrolytes can be divided into two groups—strong electrolytes and weak electrolytes. A **strong electrolyte** *is a substance that completely (or almost completely) ionizes/dissociates into ions in aqueous solution.* Strong electrolytes produce strongly conducting solutions. All strong acids and strong bases and all soluble salts are strong electrolytes. A **weak electrolyte** *is a substance that incompletely ionizes/dissociates into ions in aqueous solution.* Weak electrolytes produce solutions that are intermediate between those containing strong electrolytes and those containing nonelectrolytes in their ability to conduct an electric current. Weak acids and weak bases constitute the weak electrolytes. ◀

Whether a substance is an electrolyte in solution can be determined by testing the ability of the solution to conduct an electric current. A device such as that shown in Figure 10-13 can be used to distinguish among strong electrolytes, weak electrolytes, and nonelectrolytes. If the medium between the electrodes (the solution) is a conductor of electricity, the light bulb glows. A strong glow indicates a strong electrolyte. A faint glow occurs for a weak electrolyte, and there is no glow for a nonelectrolyte.

1. Which of the following statements concerning electrolytes is *correct*?
   a. All strong acids are strong electrolytes.
   b. All salts are weak electrolytes.
   c. Some, but not all, molecular substances are strong electrolytes.
   d. no correct response
2. In which of the following pairs of compounds are both members of the pair *strong* electrolytes?
   a. NaOH and NaCl
   b. NH_3 and HCl
   c. NaCN and HCN
   d. no correct response
3. Which of the following statements concerning the conduction of electricity by an aqueous solution is correct?
   a. All electrolytes produce strongly conducting solutions.
   b. All nonelectrolytes produce weakly conducting solutions.
   c. All soluble salts produce weakly conducting solutions.
   d. no correct response

Answers: 1. a; 2. a; 3. d

10-15 Equivalents and Milliequivalents of Electrolytes

LEARNING FOCUS

Be able to express electrolyte ion concentrations in terms of equivalents and milliequivalents concentration units; be able to determine whether charge balance is present in a solution containing several different ions.

The solution that results from dissolving equal molar amounts of the soluble salts KNO_3 and NaCl in water contains four ions in equal concentrations; they are the K^+, Na^+, NO_3^-, and Cl^- ions (Section 10-14). An identical solution to this one could be made from dissolving the same molar amounts of the soluble salts $NaNO_3$ and KCl in water; again, the ions K^+, Na^+, NO_3^-, and Cl^- are present. In solutions such as these, trying to assign specific positive ions to specific anions, or to talk about specific ionic compounds being present, has lost meaning. The solution contains individual ions of four types; the "original partners" for the ions are no longer important. What is important is the identity of the ions present and the total number of each type of ion present.

A similar situation occurs in the human body. All body fluids are electrolyte solutions that contain several positive and negative ions. The ions present usually have more than one source. In discussing such mixtures of ions, the focus is on ion identity and amount of ion present, rather than on the compounds from which the ions were originally supplied.

Equivalent and Milliequivalent Concentration Units

For body fluids, as well as other electrolytic solutions, ion concentrations are most often specified in terms of equivalents per liter or milliequivalents per liter instead of in molarity units. Milliequivalents rather than equivalents is the preferred unit when dealing with body fluids because of the relatively low concentrations of ions present in body fluids.

What is an equivalent? An **Equivalent (Eq) of an ion** *is the molar amount of that ion needed to supply one mole of positive or negative charge.* Mathematically, this definition translates into the following relationships:

For ions with 1+ or 1− charge

$$1 \text{ mole} = 1 \text{ equivalent}$$

For ions with 2+ or 2− charge

$$1 \text{ mole} = 2 \text{ equivalents}$$

For ions with 3+ or 3− charge

$$1 \text{ mole} = 3 \text{ equivalents}$$

Thus,

$$1 \text{ mole } SO_4^{2-} \text{ ion} = 2 \text{ equivalents } SO_4^{2-} \text{ ion}$$
$$1 \text{ mole } Cl^- \text{ ion} = 1 \text{ equivalent } Cl^- \text{ ion}$$
$$1 \text{ mole } NH_4^+ \text{ ion} = 1 \text{ equivalent } NH_4^+ \text{ ion}$$
$$1 \text{ mole } PO_4^{3-} \text{ ion} = 3 \text{ equivalents } PO_4^{3-} \text{ ion}$$

Example 10-12 illustrates the process of converting from moles of ion to equivalents of ion in the context of dimensional analysis. Example 10-13 that follows involves changing from moles/liter (molarity) units to milliequivalents (mEq)/liter units.

EXAMPLE 10-12

Converting an Ion Amount from Moles to Equivalents

A solution contains 0.23 mole of sulfate ion (SO_4^{2-}). How many equivalents of SO_4^{2-} ion are present in the solution?

Solution

For ions with a charge of 2 (plus or minus) the mole–equivalent relationship is

$$1 \text{ mole of ion} = 2 \text{ equivalents of ion}$$

The dimensional-analysis setup for this problem, using this relationship in conversion factor form, is

$$0.23 \text{ mole } SO_4^{2-} \times \frac{2 \text{ Eq } SO_4^{2-}}{1 \text{ mole } SO_4^{2-}} = 0.46 \text{ Eq } SO_4^{2-}$$

Thus, the solution contains 0.46 Eq of SO_4^{2-} ion.

EXAMPLE 10-13

Converting an Ion Concentration from moles/L to mEq/L

A solution is 0.0030 M in PO_4^{3-} ion. What is this ion concentration in mEq/L?

Solution

The given quantity is 0.0030 moles/L of PO_4^{3-} and the desired quantity is mEq/L PO_4^{3-}. The pathway for solving the problem is

$$\boxed{\text{moles } PO_4^{3-}} \longrightarrow \boxed{\text{Eq } PO_4^{3-}} \longrightarrow \boxed{\text{mEq } PO_4^{3-}}$$

The dimensional-analysis setup for this sequence of unit changes is

$$\frac{0.0030 \text{ mole } PO_4^{3-}}{L} \times \frac{3 \text{ Eq } PO_4^{3-}}{1 \text{ mole } PO_4^{3-}} \times \frac{1 \text{ mEq } PO_4^{3-}}{10^{-3} \text{ Eq } PO_4^{3-}} = \frac{9.0 \text{ mEq } PO_4^{3-}}{L}$$

The first conversion factor in the setup comes from the mole–equivalent relationship for ions with a charge of 3, which is

$$1 \text{ mole} = 3 \text{ equivalents}$$

The second conversion factor comes from the relationship

$$1 \text{ milliequivalent} = 10^{-3} \text{ equivalents}$$

Charge Balance in Electrolytic Solutions

In electrolytic solutions a charge balance must exist among the ions present. Equal *amounts* of positive and negative charge must be present. This does not imply that equal *numbers* of positive and negative ions must be present, however, because all ions do not necessarily carry the same amount of charge.

That the charge-balance requirement is met in solutions that contain many types of ions, such as human body fluids, is easily shown when ion concentrations are expressed in mEq/L or Eq/L, units which take into account ion charge. Charge balance occurs when the *sum* of negative ion concentrations and the *sum* of positive ion concentrations are equal in mEq/L or Eq/L concentration units. Table 10-9 shows the charge balance that occurs in human blood plasma, a solution of electrolytes in which a number of different ions are present. Note, in Table 10-9 that the total mEq/L of positive ions (151 mEq/L) is the same as the total mEq/L of negative ions (151 mEq/L).

The focus on relevancy feature Chemical Connections 10-E—Electrolytes and Body Fluids—considers the three major types of body fluids—(blood plasma, interstitial fluid, and intracellular fluid)—in terms of the identity and amounts of electrolytes present in each type of fluid.

▶ Table 10-9 **Concentrations of Major Electrolytes in Blood Plasma***

Positive Ions		Negative Ions	
Ion Identity	**Concentration (mEq/L)**	**Ion Identity**	**Concentration (mEq/L)**
Na^+	138	Cl^-	108
K^+	5	HCO_3^-	26
Ca^{2+}	4	Proteins	10
Mg^{2+}	3	HPO_4^{2-}	4
Other	1	SO_4^{2-}	1
		Other	2
Total	151	Total	151

*Blood plasma composition is variable. The values given here fall within the normal range.

Section 10-15 Quick Quiz

1. How many equivalents of Ca^{2+} ion are present in a solution that contains 0.30 mole of Ca^{2+} ion?
   a. 0.15 Eq
   b. 0.30 Eq
   c. 0.60 Eq
   d. no correct response
2. Which of the following molar amounts of an ion is *not* equal to one equivalent of ion?
   a. 1.0 mole Cl^-
   b. 0.50 mole SO_4^{2-} ion
   c. 0.50 mole NH_4^+ ion
   d. no correct response
3. The charge-balance requirement for a solution of ions requires that
   a. equal numbers of positive and negative ions are present
   b. equal moles of positive and negative ions are present
   c. equal equivalents of positive and negative ions are present
   d. no correct response
4. Which of the following hypothetical solutions of ions is out-of-balance relative to ion charge?
   a. 1.0 mEq Na^+, 2.0 mEq Ca^{2+}, and 3.0 mEq Cl^-
   b. 2.0 mEq Mg^{2+}, 1.0 mEq Cl^-, and 1.0 mEq NO_3^-
   c. 2.0 mEq Na^+, 2.0 mEq K^+, and 2.0 mEq PO_4^{3-}
   d. no correct response

Answers: 1. c; 2. c; 3.c; 4. c

Electrolytes and Body Fluids

Structurally speaking, there are three types of body fluids: blood plasma, which is the liquid part of the blood; interstitial fluid, which is the fluid in tissues between and around cells; and intracellular fluids, which are the fluids within cells. For every kilogram of its mass, the body contains about 400 mL of intracellular fluid, 160 mL of interstitial fluid, and 40 mL of blood plasma.

Water is the main component of any type of body fluid. In addition, all body fluids contain electrolytes. It is the electrolytes present in body fluids that govern numerous body processes. The chemical makeup of the three types of body fluids, in terms of electrolytes (ions present), is shown in the accompanying figure.

Chemically, two of the body fluids (plasma and interstitial fluid) are almost identical. Intracellular fluid, on the other hand, shows striking differences. For example, K^+ is the dominant positive ion in intracellular fluid, and Na^+ dominates in the other two fluids. A similar situation occurs with negative ions. A different ion dominates in intracellular fluid (HPO_4^{2-}) than in the other two fluids (Cl^-).

The electrolytes present in body fluids (1) govern the movement of water between body fluid compartments and (2) maintain acid–base balance within the body fluids. Osmotic pressure, a major factor in controlling water movement, is directly related to electrolyte concentration gradients.

The fact that the presence of ions causes a solution to conduct electricity is of extreme biochemical significance. For example, messages to and from the brain are sent in the form of electrical signals. Ions in intracellular and interstitial fluids are often the carriers of these signals. The presence of electrolytes (ions) is essential to the proper functioning of the human body.

In a hospital setting, patients routinely receive fluids in an intravenous manner. The specific composition of the solutions used, all of which contain electrolytes, depends on the nutritional and fluid needs of the individual. If a patient's system is out of balance from an electrolyte perspective, the solution used is one designed to restore balance. The table below lists commonly used intravenous electrolyte solutions, the conditions they are used for, and the concentrations of the electrolytes present.

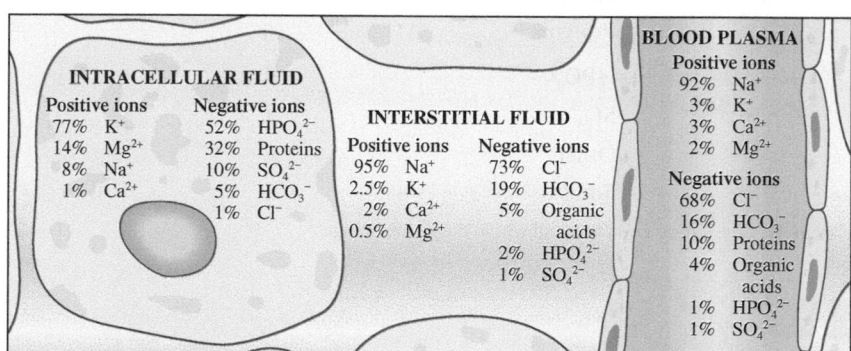

Commonly Used Intravenous Replacement Solutions

Condition Being Treated	Solution Used	Electrolytes (mEq/L)
replacement of fluid loss	sodium chloride (0.9%)	Cations: 154: [Na^+(154)] Anions: 154: [Cl^-(154)]
replacement of electrolytes in extracellular fluids	replacement solution (extracellular)	Cations: 158: [Na^+(140), K^+(10), Ca^{2+}(5), Mg^{2+}(3)] Anions: 158 [Cl^-(103), acetate$^-$(47), citrate^{3-}(8)]
replacement of fluids and electrolytes lost through dehydration	Ringer's solution	Cations: 155: [Na^+(147), K^+(4), Ca^{2+}(4)] Anions: 155: [Cl^-(155)]
maintenance of fluid and electrolyte levels	maintenance solution with 5% glucose	Cations: 75: [Na^+(40), K^+(35)] Anions: 75: [Cl^-(40), lactate$^-$(20), HPO_4^{2-} (15)]
treatment of malnutrition (low potassium levels)	potassium chloride with 5% glucose	Cations: 40: [K^+(40)] Anions: 40: [Cl^-(40)]

10-16 Acid–Base Titrations

LEARNING FOCUS

Be able to calculate the molarity of an acid or base using acid–base titration data.

The analysis of solutions to determine the concentration of acid or base present is performed regularly in many laboratories. Such activity is different from determining a solution's pH value. The pH of a solution gives information about the *concentration* of hydronium ions in solution. Only ionized molecules influence the pH value. The concentration of an acid or a base gives information about the *total number* of acid or base molecules present; both dissociated and undissociated molecules are counted. Thus acid or base concentration is a measure of total acidity or total basicity.

The procedure most frequently used to determine the concentration of an acid or a base solution is an acid–base titration. An **acid–base titration** *involves a neutralization reaction in which a measured volume of an acid or a base of known concentration is completely reacted with a measured volume of a base or an acid of unknown concentration.* Note that the chemical reaction that occurs in an acid–base titration is that of *neutralization* (Section 10-7).

How is the concentration of an acid solution determined by means of titration? First, a known volume of acid solution is placed into a beaker or flask. Then a solution of base of known concentration is slowly added to the beaker or flask by means of a buret (Figure 10-14). Base addition is continued until all of the acid has completely reacted with the base. The volume of base added to reach the "endpoint" is obtained from the markings on the buret. Knowing (1) the original volume of acid, (2) the concentration of the base, and (3) the volume of added base, the concentration of the acid can be calculated.

To complete a titration successfully, the point at which acid and base have completely reacted with each other must be detectable. Neither the acid nor the base gives any outward sign that the reaction is complete. Thus an indicator is always added to the reaction mixture (Figure 10-15). An **acid–base indicator** *is a compound that exhibits different colors in a solution depending on the pH of its solution.* Typically, an indicator is one color in basic solutions and another color in acidic solutions. An indicator is selected that changes color at a pH that corresponds as nearly as possible to the pH of the solution when the titration is complete. If the acid and base are both strong, the pH at that point is 7.0. However, because of hydrolysis (Section 10-11), the pH is not 7.0 if a weak acid or weak base is part of the titration system.

Figure 10-14 A schematic diagram showing the setup used for titration procedures.

  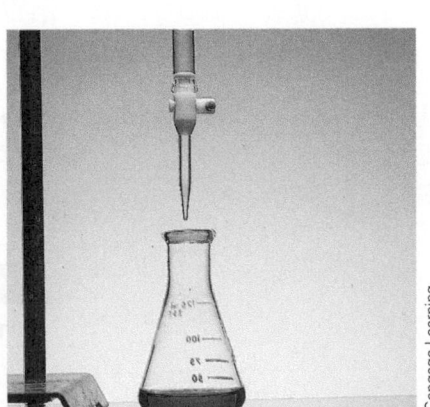

Figure 10-15 An acid–base titration using an indicator that is yellow in acidic solution and red in basic solution.

Titration of a weak acid by a strong base requires an indicator that changes color above pH 7.0 because the salt formed in the titration will hydrolyze to form a basic solution. Conversely, titration of a weak base by a strong acid requires an indicator that changes color below pH 7.0.

Example 10-14 shows how titration data are used to calculate the molarity of an acid solution of unknown concentration.

EXAMPLE 10-14

Calculating an Unknown Molarity from Acid–Base Titration Data

In a sulfuric acid (H_2SO_4)–sodium hydroxide (NaOH) acid–base titration, 17.3 mL of 0.126 M NaOH is needed to neutralize 25.0 mL of H_2SO_4 of unknown concentration. Find the molarity of the H_2SO_4 solution, given that the neutralization reaction that occurs is

$$H_2SO_4(aq) + 2NaOH(aq) \rightarrow Na_2SO_4(aq) + 2H_2O(l)$$

Solution

First, the number of moles of H_2SO_4 that reacted with the NaOH is calculated. The pathway for this calculation, using dimensional analysis (Section 6-8), is

$$\boxed{\text{mL of NaOH}} \longrightarrow \boxed{\text{L of NaOH}} \longrightarrow \boxed{\text{moles of NaOH}} \longrightarrow \boxed{\text{moles of } H_2SO_4}$$

The sequence of conversion factors that effects this series of unit changes is

$$17.3 \text{ mL NaOH} \times \left(\frac{10^{-3} \text{ L NaOH}}{1 \text{ mL NaOH}}\right) \times \left(\frac{0.126 \text{ mole NaOH}}{1 \text{ L NaOH}}\right) \times \left(\frac{1 \text{ mole } H_2SO_4}{2 \text{ moles NaOH}}\right)$$

The first conversion factor derives from the definition of a milliliter, the second conversion factor derives from the definition of molarity (Section 8-5), and the third conversion factor uses the coefficients in the balanced chemical equation for the titration reaction (Section 6-7).

The number of moles of H_2SO_4 that react is obtained by combining all the numbers in the dimensional-analysis setup in the manner indicated.

$$\left(\frac{17.3 \times 10^{-3} \times 0.126 \times 1}{1 \times 1 \times 2}\right) \text{ mole } H_2SO_4 = 0.00109 \text{ mole } H_2SO_4$$

Now that the number of moles of H_2SO_4 that reacted is known, the molarity of the H_2SO_4 solution can be calculated by using definition for molarity.

$$\text{Molarity } H_2SO_4 = \frac{\text{moles } H_2SO_4}{\text{L } H_2SO_4 \text{ solution}} = \frac{0.00109 \text{ mole}}{0.0250 \text{ L}}$$

$$= 0.0436 \frac{\text{mole}}{\text{L}}$$

Note that the units in the denominator of the molarity equation must be liters (0.0250) rather than milliliters (25.0).

Section 10-16 Quick Quiz

1. Determining the concentration of an acid using an acid–base titration involves completely reacting a measured volume of the acid with a measured volume of
   a. base of unknown concentration
   b. base of known concentration
   c. indicator of known concentration
   d. no correct response

2. Determining the concentration of an acid using an acid–base titration involves which of the following?

    a. reacting a strong acid with a weak base

    b. reacting a 1.0 M acid solution with a 1.0 M base solution

    c. carrying out an acid–base neutralization reaction

    d. no correct response

3. If 25.0 mL of 1.0 M NaOH is needed to completely react with 25.0 mL of a monoprotic acid in an acid–base titration, the molarity of the acid is

    a. equal to 1.0 M

    b. greater than 1.0 M

    c. less than 1.0 M

    d. no correct response

Answers: 1. b; 2. c; 3. a

Concepts to Remember

Arrhenius acid–base theory. An Arrhenius acid is a hydrogen-containing compound that, in water, produces hydrogen ions. An Arrhenius base is a hydroxide-containing compound that, in water, produces hydroxide ions (Section 10-1).

Brønsted–Lowry acid–base theory. A Brønsted–Lowry acid is any substance that can donate a proton (H^+) to some other substance. A Brønsted–Lowry base is any substance that can accept a proton from some other substance. Proton donation (from an acid) cannot occur unless an acceptor (a base) is present (Section 10-2).

Conjugate acids and bases. A conjugate acid–base pair consists of two species that differ by one proton. The conjugate base of an acid is the species that remains when the acid loses a proton. The conjugate acid of a base is the species formed when the base accepts a proton (Section 10-2).

Polyprotic acids. Polyprotic acids are acids that can transfer two or more hydrogen ions during an acid–base reaction (Section 10-3).

Strengths of acids and bases. Acids can be classified as strong or weak based on the extent to which proton transfer occurs in aqueous solution. A strong acid completely transfers its protons to water. A weak acid transfers only a small percentage of its protons to water (Section 10-4).

Acid ionization constant. The acid ionization constant quantitatively describes the degree of ionization of an acid. It is the equilibrium constant expression that corresponds to the ionization of the acid (Section 10-5).

Salts. Salts are ionic compounds containing a metal or polyatomic ion as the positive ion and a nonmetal or polyatomic ion (except hydroxide ion) as the negative ion. Ionic compounds containing hydroxide ion are bases rather than salts (Section 10-6).

Acid–base neutralization. Acid–base neutralization is the chemical reaction between an acid and a hydroxide base to form a salt and water (Section 10-7).

Self-ionization of water. In pure water, a small number of water molecules (1.0×10^{-7} mole/L) donate protons to other water molecules to produce small concentrations (1.0×10^{-7} mole/L) of hydronium and hydroxide ions (Section 10-8).

The pH scale. The pH scale is a scale of small numbers that is used to specify molar hydronium ion concentration in an aqueous solution. Mathematically, the pH is the negative logarithm of the molar hydronium ion concentration. Solutions with a pH lower than 7.0 are acidic, those with a pH higher than 7.0 are basic, and those with a pH equal to 7.0 are neutral (Section 10-9).

Hydrolysis of salts. Salt hydrolysis is a chemical reaction in which a salt interacts with water to produce an acidic or a basic solution. Only salts that contain the conjugate base of a weak acid and/or the conjugate acid of a weak base hydrolyze (Section 10-11).

Buffer solutions. A buffer solution is a solution that resists pH change when small amounts of acid or base are added to it. The resistance to pH change in most buffers is caused by the presence of a weak acid and a salt of its conjugate base (Section 10-12).

Electrolytes. An electrolyte is a substance that forms a solution in water that conducts electricity. Strong acids, strong bases, and soluble salts are strong electrolytes. Weak acids and weak bases are weak electrolytes (Section 10-14).

Equivalents and milliequivalents. Body fluids contain small amounts of many different electrolytes, whose concentrations are expressed in equivalents or milliequivalents per liter. An equivalent is the amount of an electrolyte that carries one mole of positive or negative charge (Section 10-15).

Acid–base titrations. An acid–base titration is a procedure in which an acid–base neutralization reaction is used to determine an unknown concentration. A measured volume of an acid or a base of known concentration is exactly reacted with a measured volume of a base or an acid of unknown concentration (Section 10-16).

Exercises and Problems

Exercises and problems are arranged in matched pairs with the two members of a pair addressing the same concept(s). The answer to the odd-numbered member of a pair is given at the back of the book. Problems denoted with a ▲ involve concepts found not only in the section under consideration but also concepts found in one or more earlier sections of the chapter.

Arrhenius Acid–Base Theory (Section 10-1)

10-1 In Arrhenius acid–base theory, what ion is responsible for the properties of

    a. acidic solutions

    b. basic solutions

10-2 What term is used to describe the formation of ions, in aqueous solution, from
a. a molecular compound
b. an ionic compound

10-3 Classify each of the following as a property of an Arrhenius acid or the property of an Arrhenius base.
a. Has a sour taste
b. Has a bitter taste

10-4 Classify each of the following as a property of an Arrhenius acid or the property of an Arrhenius base.
a. changes the color of blue litmus paper to red
b. changes the color of red litmus paper to blue

10-5 Write equations depicting the behavior of the following Arrhenius acids and bases in water.
a. HI (hydroiodic acid)
b. HClO (hypochlorous acid)
c. LiOH (lithium hydroxide)
d. CsOH (cesium hydroxide)

10-6 Write equations depicting the behavior of the following Arrhenius acids and bases in water.
a. HBr (hydrobromic acid)
b. HCN (hydrocyanic acid)
c. RbOH (rubidium hydroxide)
d. KOH (potassium hydroxide)

Brønsted–Lowry Acid–Base Theory (Section 10-2)

10-7 Indicate whether the first listed reactant in each of the following Brønsted–Lowry acid–base reactions is functioning as an acid or a base.
a. $HF + H_2O \rightarrow H_3O^+ + F^-$
b. $CN^- + H_2O \rightarrow HCN + OH^-$
c. $HCN + NO_2^- \rightarrow HNO_2 + CN^-$
d. $NH_3 + HNO_3 \rightarrow NH_4^+ + NO_3^-$

10-8 Indicate whether the first listed reactant in each of the following Brønsted–Lowry acid–base reactions is functioning as an acid or a base.
a. $F^- + H_2O \rightarrow HF + OH^-$
b. $HClO + H_2O \rightarrow H_3O^+ + ClO^-$
c. $H_3PO_4 + NH_3 \rightarrow NH_4^+ + H_2PO_4^-$
d. $HNO_2 + HS^- \rightarrow H_2S + NO_2^-$

10-9 Write chemical equations that show the indicated behavior in aqueous solution for each of the following chemical species.
a. HOCl behaves as a Brønsted–Lowry acid
b. NH_3 behaves as a Brønsted–Lowry base
c. $H_2PO_4^-$ behaves as a Brønsted–Lowry acid
d. CO_3^{2-} behaves as a Brønsted–Lowry base

10-10 Write chemical equations that show the indicated behavior in aqueous solution for each of the following chemical species.
a. $HC_2O_4^-$ behaves as a Brønsted–Lowry acid
b. F^- behaves as a Brønsted–Lowry base
c. H_2CO_3 behaves as a Brønsted–Lowry acid
d. NH_2^- behaves as a Brønsted–Lowry base

10-11 Indicate whether or not the two members of each of the following pairs of substances constitute a conjugate acid–base pair.
a. HCl and Cl^-
b. NH_4^+ and NH_3
c. H_2CO_3 and CO_3^{2-}
d. $H_2PO_4^-$ and HPO_4^{2-}

10-12 Indicate whether or not the two members of each of the following pairs of substances constitute a conjugate acid–base pair.
a. HN_3 and N_3^-
b. H_2SO_4 and SO_4^{2-}
c. NH_3 and NH_2^-
d. HCO_3^- and CO_3^{2-}

10-13 Write the formula of each of the following.
a. conjugate base of H_2SO_3
b. conjugate acid of CN^-
c. conjugate base of $HC_2O_4^-$
d. conjugate acid of HPO_4^{2-}

10-14 Write the formula of each of the following.
a. conjugate base of NH_4^+
b. conjugate acid of OH^-
c. conjugate base of H_2S
d. conjugate acid of NO_2^-

10-15 Identify the conjugate acid–base pairs associated with the following acid–base reaction.

$$HC_2H_3O_2 + H_2O \rightleftharpoons H_3O^+ + C_2H_3O_2^-$$

10-16 Identify the conjugate acid–base pairs associated with the following acid–base reaction.

$$HC_3H_5O_3 + H_2O \rightleftharpoons H_3O^+ + C_3H_5O_3^-$$

10-17 The ion HCO_3^- is an amphiprotic ion. Write the chemical equation to describe its behavior in aqueous solution when it functions as a
a. Brønsted–Lowry base
b. Brønsted–Lowry acid

10-18 The ion HPO_4^{2-} is an amphiprotic ion. Write the chemical equation to describe its behavior in aqueous solution when it functions as a
a. Brønsted–Lowry base
b. Brønsted–Lowry acid

Polyprotic Acids (Section 10-3)

10-19 Classify each of the following acids as monoprotic, diprotic, or triprotic.
a. $HClO_3$ (chloric acid)
b. $HC_3H_5O_4$ (glyceric acid)
c. $H_3C_6H_5O_7$ (citric acid)
d. H_3PO_4 (phosphoric acid)

10-20 Classify each of the following acids as monoprotic, diprotic, or triprotic.
a. H_2SO_4 (sulfuric acid)
b. $HC_2H_3O_2$ (acetic acid)
c. $H_2C_5H_6O_4$ (glutaric acid)
d. HCN (cyanic acid)

10-21 For each of the acids in Problem 10-19 indicate how many acidic hydrogen atoms and how many nonacidic hydrogen atoms are present.

10-22 For each of the acids in Problem 10-20 indicate how many acidic hydrogen atoms and how many nonacidic hydrogen atoms are present.

10-23 Write chemical equations showing the individual proton-transfer steps that occur in aqueous solution for each of the following acids.
 a. H_2CO_3 (carbonic acid)
 b. $H_2C_3H_2O_4$ (malonic acid)

10-24 Write chemical equations showing the individual proton-transfer steps that occur in aqueous solution for each of the following acids.
 a. $H_2C_2O_4$ (oxalic acid)
 b. $H_2C_4H_4O_6$ (tartaric acid)

10-25 The formula for lactic acid is preferably written as $HC_3H_5O_3$ rather than as $C_3H_6O_3$. Explain why.

10-26 The formula for tartaric acid is preferably written as $H_2C_4H_4O_6$ rather than as $C_4H_6O_6$. Explain why.

10-27 Pyruvic acid, which is produced in metabolic reactions, has the structure

$$
\begin{array}{c}
\quad H \quad O \quad O \\
\quad | \quad\ || \quad\ || \\
H-C-C-C-O-H \\
\quad | \\
\quad H
\end{array}
$$

Would you predict that this acid is a mono-, di-, tri-, or tetraprotic acid? Give your reasoning.

10-28 Oxaloacetic acid, which is produced in metabolic reactions, has the structure

$$
\begin{array}{c}
\quad\ O \quad O \quad H \quad O \\
\quad\ || \quad\ || \quad | \quad\ || \\
H-O-C-C-C-C-O-H \\
\quad\quad\quad\quad | \\
\quad\quad\quad\quad H
\end{array}
$$

Would you predict that this acid is a mono-, di-, tri-, or tetraprotic acid? Give your reasoning.

Strengths of Acids and Bases (Section 10-4)

10-29 Classify each of the acids in Problem 10-19 as a strong acid or a weak acid.

10-30 Classify each of the acids in Problem 10-20 as a strong acid or a weak acid.

10-31 For each of the following pairs of acids, indicate whether the first member of the pair is a stronger or weaker acid than the second member of the pair.
 a. HNO_3 and HNO_2
 b. HF and HBr
 c. H_2CO_3 and $HClO_3$
 d. HCN and HCl

10-32 For each of the following pairs of acids, indicate whether the first member of the pair is a stronger or weaker acid than the second member of the pair.
 a. $HClO_4$ and $HClO_2$
 b. H_2SO_3 and H_2SO_4
 c. H_3PO_4 and HI
 d. HClO and HCl

10-33 For each of the following pairings of acid and base indicate whether both the acid and the base are classified as strong?
 a. H_2SO_4 and KOH
 b. HCl and NaOH
 c. $HClO_4$ and $Sr(OH)_2$
 d. HF and $Ba(OH)_2$

10-34 For each of the following pairings of acid and base indicate whether both the acid and the base are classified as strong?
 a. HNO_3 and KOH
 b. H_3PO_4 and NaOH
 c. H_2CO_3 and $Ca(OH)_2$
 d. $HC_2H_3O_2$ and RbOH

10-35 The HCl in a 0.10 M HCl solution is 100% dissociated. What are the molar concentrations of HCl, H_3O^+, and Cl^- in the solution?

10-36 The HNO_3 in a 0.50 M HNO_3 solution is 100% dissociated. What are the molar concentrations of HNO_3, H_3O^+, and NO_3^- in the solution?

10-37 The following four diagrams represent aqueous solutions of four different acids with the general formula HA. Which of the four acids is the strongest acid?

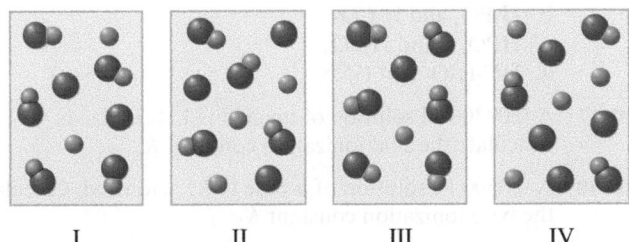

I   II   III   IV

10-38 Using the diagrams shown in Problem 10-37, which of the four acids is the weakest acid?

▲**10-39** Which of the terms *weak, strong, monoprotic, diprotic,* and *triprotic* characterize(s) each of the following acids? More than one term may apply in a given situation.
 a. H_3PO_4
 b. H_3PO_3
 c. HBr
 d. $HC_2H_3O_2$

▲**10-40** Which of the terms *weak, strong, monoprotic, diprotic,* and *triprotic* characterize(s) each of the following acids? More than one term may apply in a given situation.
 a. $HC_3H_3O_3$
 b. HCN
 c. H_2SO_4
 d. H_2SO_3

Ionization Constants for Acids and Bases (Section 10-5)

10-41 Write the acid ionization constant expression for the ionization of each of the following monoprotic acids.
a. HF (hydrofluoric acid)
b. $HC_2H_3O_2$ (acetic acid)

10-42 Write the acid ionization constant expression for the ionization of each of the following monoprotic acids.
a. HCN (hydrocyanic acid)
b. $HC_6H_7O_6$ (ascorbic acid)

10-43 Write the base ionization constant expression for the ionization of each of the following bases. In each case, the nitrogen atom accepts the proton.
a. NH_3 (ammonia)
b. $C_6H_5NH_2$ (aniline)

10-44 Write the base ionization constant expression for the ionization of each of the following bases. In each case, the nitrogen atom accepts the proton.
a. CH_3NH_2 (methylamine)
b. $C_2H_5NH_2$ (ethylamine)

10-45 Using the acid ionization constant information given in Table 10-3, indicate which acid is the stronger in each of the following acid pairs.
a. H_3PO_4 and HNO_2
b. HCN and HF
c. H_2CO_3 and HCO_3^-
d. HNO_2 and HCN

10-46 Using the acid ionization constant information given in Table 10-3, indicate which acid is the stronger in each of the following acid pairs.
a. H_3PO_4 and $H_2PO_4^-$
b. H_3PO_4 and H_2CO_3
c. HPO_4^{2-} and $H_2PO_4^-$
d. $HC_2H_3O_2$ and HCN

10-47 A 0.00300 M solution of an acid is 12% ionized. Calculate the acid ionization constant K_a.

10-48 A 0.0500 M solution of a base is 7.5% ionized. Calculate the base ionization constant K_b.

▲10-49 Is the monoprotic acid Y or the monoprotic acid Z the stronger acid in each of the following situations?
a. At equal concentrations, Y dissociates to a greater extent than Z in water.
b. K_a for Z is larger than K_a for Y.
c. The equilibrium position for the dissociation of Y lies farther to the right than that for Z.
d. Proton transfer to water occurs to a lesser extent for Z than for Y.

▲10-50 Is the monoprotic acid Y or the monoprotic acid Z the stronger acid in each of the following situations?
a. At equal concentrations, the percent ionization for Z is greater than that for Y.
b. K_a for Y is smaller than K_a for Z.
c. The equilibrium position for the dissociation of Z lies farther to the left than that for Y.
d. At equal concentrations and equal volumes, more hydronium ions are present in the Z solution than the Y solution.

Salts (Section 10-6)

10-51 Classify each of the following substances as an acid, a base, or a salt.
a. HBr
b. NaI
c. NH_4NO_3
d. $Ba(OH)_2$

10-52 Classify each of the following substances as an acid, a base, or a salt.
a. $AlPO_4$
b. KOH
c. HNO_3
d. $HC_2H_3O_2$

10-53 Indicate whether or not both members of each of the following pairs of substances are salts.
a. KCN and NaCN
b. HCl and LiCl
c. Na_2SO_4 and NaOH
d. $Al(NO_3)_3$ and $Ca(NO_3)_2$

10-54 Indicate whether or not both members of each of the following pairs of substances are salts.
a. LiOH and LiBr
b. NaClO and HClO
c. KF and K_2O
d. K_2S and K_2SO_4

10-55 Write a balanced equation for the dissociation into ions of each of the following soluble salts in aqueous solution.
a. $Ba(NO_3)_2$
b. Na_2SO_4
c. $CaBr_2$
d. K_2CO_3

10-56 Write a balanced equation for the dissociation into ions of each of the following soluble salts in aqueous solution.
a. CaS
b. $BeSO_4$
c. $MgCl_2$
d. $NaC_2H_3O_2$

Acid–Base Neutralization Reactions (Section 10-7)

10-57 Indicate whether each of the following reactions is an acid–base neutralization reaction.
a. $NaCl + AgNO_3 \longrightarrow AgCl + NaNO_3$
b. $HNO_3 + NaOH \longrightarrow NaNO_3 + H_2O$
c. $HBr + KOH \longrightarrow KBr + H_2O$
d. $H_2SO_4 + Pb(NO_3)_2 \longrightarrow PbSO_4 + 2HNO_3$

10-58 Indicate whether each of the following reactions is an acid–base neutralization reaction.
a. $H_2S + CuSO_4 \longrightarrow H_2SO_4 + CuS$
b. $HCN + LiOH \longrightarrow LiCN + H_2O$
c. $H_2SO_4 + Ba(OH)_2 \longrightarrow BaSO_4 + 2H_2O$
d. $Ni + 2HCl \longrightarrow NiCl_2 + H_2$

10-59 Without writing an equation, specify the molecular ratio in which each of the following acid–base pairs will react.
 a. HNO_3 and NaOH
 b. H_2SO_4 and NaOH
 c. H_2SO_4 and $Ba(OH)_2$
 d. HNO_3 and $Ba(OH)_2$

10-60 Without writing an equation, specify the molecular ratio in which each of the following acid base pairs will react.
 a. HCl and KOH
 b. H_2CO_3 and KOH
 c. HCl and $Ca(OH)_2$
 d. H_2CO_3 and $Ca(OH)_2$

10-61 Write a balanced chemical equation to represent each of the following acid–base neutralization reactions.
 a. HCl and NaOH
 b. HNO_3 and KOH
 c. H_2SO_4 and LiOH
 d. $Ba(OH)_2$ and H_3PO_4

10-62 Write a balanced chemical equation to represent each of the following acid–base neutralization reactions.
 a. HCl and LiOH
 b. HNO_3 and $Ba(OH)_2$
 c. H_2SO_4 and NaOH
 d. KOH and H_3PO_4

10-63 Write a balanced molecular equation for the preparation of each of the following salts, using an acid–base neutralization reaction.
 a. Li_2SO_4 (lithium sulfate)
 b. NaCl (sodium chloride)
 c. KNO_3 (potassium nitrate)
 d. $Ba_3(PO_4)_2$ (barium phosphate)

10-64 Write a balanced molecular equation for the preparation of each of the following salts, using an acid–base neutralization reaction.
 a. $LiNO_3$ (lithium nitrate)
 b. $BaCl_2$ (barium chloride)
 c. K_3PO_4 (potassium phosphate)
 d. Na_2SO_4 (sodium sulfate)

Hydronium Ion and Hydroxide Ion Concentrations (Section 10-8)

10-65 What is the molar hydronium ion concentration in aqueous solutions with the following hydroxide ion concentrations?
 a. 3.5×10^{-3} M
 b. 4.7×10^{-6} M
 c. 1.1×10^{-8} M
 d. 8.7×10^{-10} M

10-66 What is the molar hydronium ion concentration in aqueous solutions with the following hydroxide ion concentrations?
 a. 4.2×10^{-4} M
 b. 6.0×10^{-5} M
 c. 3.4×10^{-9} M
 d. 7.3×10^{-11} M

10-67 Indicate whether each of the solutions in Problem 10-65 is acidic, basic, or neutral.

10-68 Indicate whether each of the solutions in Problem 10-66 is acidic, basic, or neutral.

10-69 What is $[OH^-]$ in aqueous solutions with the following $[H_3O^+]$ concentrations?
 a. 5.5×10^{-2}
 b. 9.4×10^{-5}
 c. 2.3×10^{-7}
 d. 6.6×10^{-12}

10-70 What is $[OH^-]$ in aqueous solutions with the following $[H_3O^+]$ concentrations?
 a. 2.4×10^{-3}
 b. 7.5×10^{-6}
 c. 6.7×10^{-8}
 d. 5.0×10^{-10}

10-71 Indicate whether each of the solutions in Problem 10-69 is acidic, basic, or neutral.

10-72 Indicate whether each of the solutions in Problem 10-70 is acidic, basic, or neutral.

10-73 Selected information about five solutions, each at 24°C, is given in the following table. Fill in the blanks in each line in the table. The first line is already completed as an example.

	$[H_3O^+]$	$[OH^-]$	Acidic or Basic
	2.2×10^{-2}	4.5×10^{-13}	acidic
a.		3.3×10^{-3}	
b.	6.8×10^{-8}		
c.		7.2×10^{-8}	
d.	4.7×10^{-5}		

10-74 Selected information about five solutions, each at 24°C, is given in the following table. Fill in the blanks in each line in the table. The first line is already completed as an example.

	$[H_3O^+]$	$[OH^-]$	Acidic or Basic
	1.3×10^{-13}	7.7×10^{-2}	basic
a.	6.3×10^{-8}		
b.	4.2×10^{-6}		
c.		3.3×10^{-10}	
d.		3.3×10^{-5}	

pH Scale (Section 10-9)

10-75 Calculate the pH of solutions with the following hydronium ion concentrations.
 a. 1.00×10^{-5} M
 b. 1.00×10^{-8} M
 c. 4.75×10^{-6} M
 d. 8.88×10^{-8} M

10-76 Calculate the pH of solutions with the following hydronium ion concentrations.
a. 1.00×10^{-3} M
b. 1.00×10^{-9} M
c. 3.73×10^{-7} M
d. 7.77×10^{-11} M

10-77 Calculate the pH of solutions with the following hydroxide ion concentrations.
a. 1.00×10^{-4} M
b. 1.00×10^{-10} M
c. 1.11×10^{-3} M
d. 6.05×10^{-7} M

10-78 Calculate the pH of solutions with the following hydroxide ion concentrations.
a. 1.00×10^{-6} M
b. 1.00×10^{-12} M
c. 2.73×10^{-4} M
d. 9.13×10^{-8} M

10-79 What is the $[H_3O^+]$ value in solutions with each of the following pH values?
a. 5.00   b. 7.00
c. 3.45   d. 7.15

10-80 What is the $[H_3O^+]$ value in solutions with each of the following pH values?
a. 4.00   b. 6.00
c. 4.34   d. 8.22

10-81 What is the molar hydronium ion concentration in solutions with each of the following pH values?
a. 3.13   b. 3.25
c. 3.50   d. 3.75

10-82 What is the molar hydronium ion concentration in solutions with each of the following pH values?
a. 4.22   b. 4.25
c. 4.50   d. 4.75

10-83 Indicate whether each of the following samples is acidic, basic, or neutral.
a. milk, pH 6.4
b. seawater, pH 8.5
c. drinking water, pH 7.2
d. strawberry, pH 3.4

10-84 Indicate whether each of the following samples is acidic, basic, or neutral.
a. butter, pH 6.1
b. lemon juice, pH 2.2
c. peach, pH 3.5
d. milk of magnesia, pH 10.5

10-85 Selected information about five solutions, each at 24°C, is given in the following table. Fill in the blanks in each line in the table. The first line is already completed as an example.

	$[H_3O^+]$	$[OH^-]$	pH	Acidic or Basic
	6.2×10^{-8}	1.6×10^{-7}	7.21	basic
a.	7.2×10^{-10}			
b.			5.30	
c.		7.2×10^{-10}		
d.			8.23	

10-86 Selected information about five solutions, each at 24°C, is given in the following table. Fill in the blanks in each line in the table. The first line is already completed as an example.

	$[H_3O^+]$	$[OH^-]$	pH	Acidic or Basic
	1.9×10^{-9}	5.4×10^{-6}	8.73	basic
a.		7.2×10^{-5}		
b.	6.3×10^{-3}			
c.			2.00	
d.			12.00	

▲**10-87** Consider the following four solutions: (1) apple juice, pH 3.8, (2) pickle juice, pH 3.5, (3) carbonated beverage, pH 3.0, and (4) drinking water, pH 7.2.
a. Which solution has the highest $[H_3O^+]$?
b. Which solution has the highest $[OH^-]$?
c. List the solutions in order of increasing acidity.
d. List the solutions in order of decreasing basicity.

▲**10-88** Consider the following four biological solutions: (1) bile, pH 8.0, (2) blood, pH 7.4, (3) urine, pH 6.0, and (4) gastric juice, pH 1.6.
a. Which solution has the lowest $[H_3O^+]$?
b. Which solution has the lowest $[OH^-]$?
c. List the solutions in order of decreasing acidity.
d. List the solutions in order of increasing basicity.

▲**10-89** For each of the following pairs of solutions, indicate whether the first listed solution has a higher or lower pH than the second listed solution.
a. 1.0 M NaOH and 1.0 M HCl
b. 1.0 M HNO_3 and 0.10 M HNO_3
c. 0.10 M $HClO_4$ and 0.10 M HCN
d. $[H_3O^+] = 3.3 \times 10^{-3}$ and $[H_3O^+] = 9.3 \times 10^{-3}$

▲**10-90** For each of the following pairs of solutions, indicate whether the first listed solution has a higher or lower pH than the second listed solution.
a. 1.0 M HCl and 0.10 M HCl
b. 1.0 M NaOH and 1.0 M H_2CO_3
c. 0.10 M $HClO_3$ and 0.10 M HF
d. $[H_3O^+] = 7.3 \times 10^{-4}$ and $[H_3O^+] = 1.2 \times 10^{-4}$

pK_a Values (Section 10-10)

10-91 Calculate the pK_a value for each of the following acids.
a. Nitrous acid (HNO_2), $K_a = 4.5 \times 10^{-4}$
b. Carbonic acid (H_2CO_3), $K_a = 4.3 \times 10^{-7}$
c. Dihydrogen phosphate ion ($H_2PO_4^-$), $K_a = 6.2 \times 10^{-8}$
d. Sulfurous acid (H_2SO_3), $K_a = 1.5 \times 10^{-2}$

10-92 Calculate the pK_a value for each of the following acids.
a. Phosphoric acid (H_3PO_4), $K_a = 7.5 \times 10^{-3}$
b. Hydrofluoric acid (HF), $K_a = 6.8 \times 10^{-4}$
c. Hydrogen phosphate ion (HPO_4^{2-}), $K_a = 4.2 \times 10^{-13}$
d. Propanoic acid ($HC_3H_5O_2$), $K_a = 1.3 \times 10^{-5}$

10-93 Acid A has a pK_a value of 4.23, and acid B has a pK_a value of 3.97. Which of the two acids is stronger?

10-94 Acid A has a pK_a value of 5.71, and acid B has a pK_a value of 5.30. Which of the two acids is weaker?

10-95 If a weak acid has a pK_a value of 8.73, what is the value of K_a for the acid?

10-96 If a weak acid has a pK_a value of 7.21, what is the value of K_a for the acid?

Hydrolysis of Salts (Section 10-11)

10-97 Classify each of the following salts as a "strong acid–strong base salt," a "strong acid–weak base salt," a "weak acid–strong base salt," or a "weak acid–weak base salt."
a. $NaCl$
b. $KC_2H_3O_2$
c. NH_4Br
d. $Ba(NO_3)_2$

10-98 Classify each of the following salts as a "strong acid–strong base salt," a "strong acid–weak base salt," a "weak acid–strong base salt," or a "weak acid–weak base salt."
a. K_3PO_4
b. $NaNO_3$
c. KCl
d. $Na_2C_2O_4$

10-99 Identify the ion (or ions) present in each of the salts in Problem 10-97 that will undergo hydrolysis in aqueous solution.

10-100 Identify the ion (or ions) present in each of the salts in Problem 10-98 that will undergo hydrolysis in aqueous solution.

10-101 Predict whether solutions of each of the salts in Problem 10-97 will be acidic, basic, or neutral.

10-102 Predict whether solutions of each of the salts in Problem 10-98 will be acidic, basic, or neutral.

10-103 Both ions in the salt ammonium cyanide (NH_4CN) hydrolyze in aqueous solution. Explain why this hydrolysis produces a basic solution rather than an acidic solution.

10-104 Both ions in the salt ammonium acetate ($NH_4C_2H_3O_2$) hydrolyze in aqueous solution. Explain why this hydrolysis produces a neutral solution rather than an acidic or basic solution.

▲**10-105** Arrange the following 0.10 M aqueous solutions in order of increasing pH: HCl, NaCl, HCN, and NaCN.

▲**10-106** Arrange the following 0.10 M aqueous solutions in order of increasing pH: HF, NaF, HNO_3, and $NaNO_3$.

Buffers (Section 10-12)

10-107 Predict whether each of the following pairs of substances could function as a buffer system in aqueous solution.
a. HNO_3 and $NaNO_3$
b. HF and NaF
c. KCl and KCN
d. H_2CO_3 and $NaHCO_3$

10-108 Predict whether each of the following pairs of substances could function as a buffer system in aqueous solution.
a. HNO_3 and HCl
b. HNO_2 and KNO_2
c. $NaC_2H_3O_2$ and $KC_2H_3O_2$
d. $HC_2H_3O_2$ and $NaNO_3$

10-109 Identify the two "active species" in each of the following buffer systems.
a. HCN and KCN
b. H_3PO_4 and NaH_2PO_4
c. H_2CO_3 and $KHCO_3$
d. $NaHCO_3$ and K_2CO_3

10-110 Identify the two "active species" in each of the following buffer systems.
a. HF and LiF
b. Na_2HPO_4 and KH_2PO_4
c. K_2CO_3 and $KHCO_3$
d. $NaNO_2$ and HNO_2

10-111 Write an equation for each of the following buffering actions.
a. the response of a HF/F^- buffer to the addition of H_3O^+ ions
b. the response of a H_2CO_3/HCO_3^- buffer to the addition of OH^- ions
c. the response of a HCO_3^-/CO_3^{2-} buffer to the addition of H_3O^+ ions
d. the response of a $H_3PO_4/H_2PO_4^-$ buffer to the addition of OH^- ions

10-112 Write an equation for each of the following buffering actions.
a. the response of a HPO_4^{2-}/PO_4^{3-} buffer to the addition of OH^- ions
b. the response of a HF/F^- buffer to the addition of OH^- ions
c. the response of a HCN/CN^- buffer to the addition of H_3O^+ ions
d. the response of a $H_3PO_4/H_2PO_4^-$ buffer to the addition of H_3O^+ ions

10-113 For the buffer system HNO_2/NO_2^-, do the concentrations of HNO_2 and NO_2^- increase or decrease when a small amount of strong acid is added to the buffer?

10-114 For the buffer system HNO_2/NO_2^-, do the concentrations of HNO_2 and NO_2^- increase or decrease when a small amount of strong base is added to the buffer?

10-115 A buffer solution has a pH value of 8.2. Which value in the set of pH values

$$7.1 \quad 8.1 \quad 8.2 \quad 8.3 \quad 9.3$$

is the most likely value for the buffer solution pH after
a. a small amount of strong acid has been added?
b. a small amount of strong base has been added?

10-116 A buffer solution has a pH value of 9.8. Which value in the set of pH values

$$8.7 \quad 9.7 \quad 9.8 \quad 9.9 \quad 10.9$$

is the most likely value for the buffer solution pH after
a. a small amount of strong acid has been added?
b. a small amount of strong base has been added?

10-117 The following four diagrams represent aqueous solutions containing a weak acid (HA) and/or its conjugate base (A^-). Which of the four solutions is a buffer solution? There may be more than one correct answer.

I   II   III   IV

10-118 Using the diagrams shown in Problem 10-117, which of the solutions would have the greatest buffer capacity, that is, greatest protection against pH change, when the following occurs?
  a. A strong acid is added to the solution.
  b. A strong base is added to the solution.

▲**10-119** Identify the buffer system(s)—the conjugate acid–base pair(s)—present in a solution that contains equal molar amounts of the following:
  a. HCN, KCN, HClO, and $NaClO_2$
  b. H_2CO_3, Na_2CO_3, $NaNO_2$, and HNO_2

▲**10-120** Identify the buffer system(s)—the conjugate acid–base pair(s)—present in a solution that contains equal molar amounts of the following:
  a. HF, $KC_2H_3O_2$, $NaC_2H_3O_2$, and NaF
  b. HNO_3, NaOH, H_3PO_4, and NaH_2PO_4

▲**10-121** Which of the four species Cl^-, HPO_4^{2-}, CO_3^{2-}, and H_2SO_3 have the following properties?
  a. amphiprotic
  b. does not hydrolyze in water
  c. hydrolyzes in water to give a basic solution
  d. can function as a buffer system component

▲**10-122** Which of the four species F^-, NO_3^-, HCO_3^-, and H_3PO_4 have the following properties?
  a. amphiprotic
  b. does not hydrolyze in water
  c. hydrolyzes in water to give a basic solution
  d. can function as a buffer system component

The Henderson–Hasselbalch Equation (Section 10-13)

10-123 What is the pH of a buffer that is 0.230 M in a weak acid and 0.500 M in the acid's conjugate base? The pK_a for the acid is 6.72.

10-124 What is the pH of a buffer that is 0.250 M in a weak acid and 0.260 M in the acid's conjugate base? The pK_a for the acid is 5.53.

10-125 What is the pH of a buffer that is 0.150 M in a weak acid and 0.150 M in the acid's conjugate base? The acid's ionization constant is 6.8×10^{-6}.

10-126 What is the pH of a buffer that is 0.175 M in a weak acid and 0.200 M in the acid's conjugate base? The acid's ionization constant is 5.7×10^{-4}.

Electrolytes (Section 10-14)

10-127 Classify each of the following compounds as a strong electrolyte or a weak electrolyte.
  a. H_2CO_3
  b. KOH
  c. NaCl
  d. H_2SO_4

10-128 Classify each of the following compounds as a strong electrolyte or a weak electrolyte.
  a. H_3PO_4
  b. HNO_3
  c. KNO_3
  d. NaOH

10-129 Indicate whether solutions of each of the following substances contain ions, molecules, or both.
  a. acetic acid, a weak acid
  b. sucrose, a nonelectrolyte
  c. sodium sulfate, a soluble salt
  d. hydrofluoric acid, a weak electrolyte

10-130 Indicate whether solutions of each of the following substances contain ions, molecules, or both.
  a. hydrochloric acid, a strong acid
  b. sodium nitrate, a soluble salt
  c. potassium chloride, a strong electrolyte
  d. ethanol, a nonelectrolyte

10-131 How many ions, per formula unit, are produced when each of the following soluble salts (strong electrolytes) dissolves in water?
  a. NaCl   b. $Mg(NO_3)_2$
  c. K_2S d. NH_4CN

10-132 How many ions, per formula unit, are produced when each of the following soluble salts (strong electrolytes) dissolves in water?
  a. KNO_3 b. Na_2CO_3
  c. $MgCl_2$ d. K_3N

10-133 Write a balanced chemical equation for the dissociation in water of each of the salts listed in Problem 10-131.

10-134 Write a balanced chemical equation for the dissociation in water of each of the salts listed in Problem 10-132.

10-135 Four different substances of the generalized formula HA were dissolved in water, with the results shown in the diagrams. Which of the diagrams represents the substance that is the strongest electrolyte?

 I   II   III   IV

10-136 Which of the diagrams in Problem 10-135 represents the substance that is the weakest electrolyte?

Equivalents and Milliequivalents of Electrolytes (Section 10-15)

10-137 Indicate the number of equivalents in each of the following molar quantities of ions.
  a. 1 mole Na^+ b. 1 mole NO_3^-
  c. 1 mole Mg^{2+} d. 1 mole HCO_3^-

10-138 Indicate the number of equivalents in each of the following molar quantities of ions.
  a. 1 mole K^+
  b. 1 mole $H_2PO_4^-$
  c. 1 mole HPO_4^{2-}
  d. 1 mole Ca^{2+}

10-139 Indicate the number of equivalents in each of the following molar quantities of ions.
a. 2 moles K^+
b. 3 moles $H_2PO_4^-$
c. 2 moles HPO_4^{2-}
d. 7 moles Ca^{2+}

10-140 Indicate the number of equivalents in each of the following molar quantities of ions.
a. 4 moles Na^+
b. 2 moles NO_3^-
c. 3 moles Mg^{2+}
d. 5 moles HCO_3^-

10-141 A solution contains 48 mEq of Ca^{2+} ion. Based on this information,
a. how many Eq of Ca^{2+} ion are present?
b. how many moles of Ca^{2+} ion are present?

10-142 A solution contains 5.0 mEq of SO_4^{2-} ion. Based on this information,
a. how many Eq of SO_4^{2-} ion are present?
b. how many moles of SO_4^{2-} ion are present?

10-143 A solution is 0.0030 M in HPO_4^{2-} ion. What is this ion concentration in mEq/L?

10-144 A solution is 0.0030 M in $H_2PO_4^-$ ion. What is this ion concentration in mEq/L?

10-145 Based on charge-balance considerations, indicate whether it would be possible to prepare solutions with each of the following total compositions.
a. 75 mEq Na^+, 25 mEq K^+, 95 mEq Cl^-, and 5 mEq NO_3^-
b. 73 Eq K^+, 55 Eq Cl^-, and 25 Eq $C_2H_3O_2^-$
c. 750 mEq Na^+ and 0.750 Eq Cl^-
d. 0.025 mole Na^+, 0.025 mole Ca^{2+} and 0.075 mole Cl^-

10-146 Based on charge-balance considerations, indicate whether it would be possible to prepare solutions with each of the following total compositions.
a. 75 mEq Na^+, 35 mEq K^+, 95 mEq Cl^-, and 5 mEq NO_3^-
b. 73 Eq K^+, 55 Eq Cl^-, and 18 Eq $C_2H_3O_2^-$
c. 750 mEq Na^+ and 0.075 Eq Cl^-
d. 0.050 mole Na^+, 0.025 mole Ca^{2+} and 0.075 mole Cl^-

10-147 How many mEq of HCO_3^- are present in a solution that also contains 75 mEq of Na^+, 83 mEq K^+, 10 mEq Ca^{2+}, and 153 mEq Cl^-?

10-148 How many mEq of Ca^{2+} are present in a solution that also contains 75 mEq of Na^+, 83 mEq K^+, 35 mEq HCO_3^-, and 153 mEq Cl^-?

Titration Calculations (Section 10-16)

10-149 Determine the molarity of a NaOH solution when each of the following amounts of acid neutralizes 25.0 mL of the NaOH solution.
a. 5.00 mL of 0.250 M HNO_3
b. 20.00 mL of 0.500 M H_2SO_4
c. 23.76 mL of 1.00 M HCl
d. 10.00 mL of 0.100 M H_3PO_4

10-150 Determine the molarity of a KOH solution when each of the following amounts of acid neutralizes 25.0 mL of the KOH solution.
a. 5.00 mL of 0.500 M H_2SO_4
b. 20.00 mL of 0.250 M HNO_3
c. 13.07 mL of 0.100 M H_3PO_4
d. 10.00 mL of 1.00 M HCl

Nuclear Chemistry

National Institute of Mental Health/Photodisc/Getty Images

Associated with brain-scan technology is the use of small amounts of radioactive substances.

In this chapter, nuclear reactions, a class of reactions that are very different from chemical reactions, are considered. It is in the study of nuclear reactions that the terms *radioactivity, nuclear power plants, nuclear weapons,* and *nuclear medicine* are encountered. The electricity produced by a nuclear power plant is generated through the use of heat energy obtained from nuclear reactions. In modern medicine, nuclear reactions are used in the diagnosis and treatment of numerous diseases. Despite some controversy concerning the use of nuclear reactions in weapons and power plants, it is important to remember that a person's life is much more likely to be extended by nuclear medicine than to be taken by nuclear weapons.

11-1 Stable and Unstable Nuclides

LEARNING FOCUS

Be conversant with terminology and notation associated with nuclear instability and the major ramification of such instability.

A **nuclear reaction** *is a reaction in which changes occur in the nucleus of an atom.* Nuclear reactions are not considered to be ordinary chemical reactions. The governing principles for ordinary chemical reactions deal with the rearrangement of electrons; this rearrangement occurs as the result of electron transfer or electron sharing (Section 4-1). In nuclear reactions, it is nuclei rather than electron arrangements that undergo change.

In nuclear chemistry discussions, specific atoms are called *nuclides* rather than *isotopes*. The term *isotopes* refers to atoms of the same element that have different mass numbers (Section 3-3). The term *nuclide,* a much more general term, refers to atoms of either the same or different elements. A **nuclide** *is an atom with a specific atomic number and a specific mass number.* In practice, the designation *nuclides* is used to describe atoms of different elements and the designation *isotopes* is used to describe different types of atoms of the same element. The species $^{12}_{6}C$ and $^{16}_{8}O$ are *nuclides* of different elements, whereas the species $^{12}_{6}C$ and $^{13}_{6}C$ are *isotopes* of the same element.

To identify a nucleus or atom uniquely, both its atomic number and its mass number must be specified. Three different notation systems exist for doing this. Consider a nuclide of nitrogen that has seven protons and eight neutrons. This nuclide can be denoted as $^{15}_{7}N$ or nitrogen-15 or N-15. In the first notation, the superscript is the mass number and the subscript is the atomic number. In the second and third notations, the mass number is placed immediately after the name or chemical symbol of the element. All three types of notation will be used in this chapter. Note that all notations give the mass number.

Nuclides (atoms) may be divided into two types based on nuclear stability. Some nuclides have nuclei that are stable and others possess nuclei that are unstable. A **stable nuclide** *is a nuclide with a nucleus that does not readily undergo change.* Conversely, an **unstable nuclide** *is a nuclide with a nucleus that spontaneously undergoes change.* The spontaneous change that unstable nuclei undergo involves emission of radiation from the nucleus, a process by which the unstable nucleus can become more stable. The radiation emitted from unstable nuclei is called *radioactivity.* **Radioactivity** *is the radiation spontaneously emitted from an unstable nucleus.* Nuclides that possess unstable nuclei are said to be radioactive. A **radioactive nuclide** *is a nuclide with an unstable nucleus from which radiation is spontaneously emitted.* The term *radioactive nuclide* is often shortened to simply *radionuclide.* ◄

Naturally occurring radionuclides exist for 29 of the 88 elements that occur in nature (Section 1-7). Radionuclides are known for *all* 118 elements, however, even though they occur naturally for only the above-mentioned 29. This is because laboratory procedures have been developed by which scientists can convert nonradioactive nuclides (stable nucleus) into radioactive nuclides (unstable nucleus). Such procedures are considered in Section 11-5.

No simple rule exists for predicting whether a particular nuclide is radioactive. However, considering some observations about those nuclides that are *stable* is helpful in understanding why some nuclides are stable and others are not. Two generalizations are readily apparent from a study of the properties of naturally occurring stable nuclides.

▶ *In some textbooks, the term* radioactive isotope *is used in lieu of the term* radioactive nuclide. *The latter term will be used exclusively in this textbook.*

1. *There is a correlation between nuclear stability and the total number of nucleons found in a nucleus.* All nuclei with 84 or more protons are unstable. The largest stable nucleus known is that of $^{209}_{83}Bi$, a nucleus that contains 209 nucleons. It thus appears that there is a limit to the number of nucleons that can be packed into a stable nucleus.

2. *There is a correlation between nuclear stability and neutron-to-proton ratio in a nucleus.* The number of neutrons found in a stable nucleus increases as the number of protons increases. For elements of low atomic number, neutron-to-proton ratios are very close to 1. For heavier elements, stable nuclei have higher neutron-to-proton ratios, and the ratio reaches approximately 1.5 for the heaviest stable elements. These observations suggest that neutrons are at least partially responsible for the stability of a nucleus. It should be remembered that like charges repel each other and that most nuclei contain many protons (with identical positive charges) squeezed together into a very small volume. As the number of protons increases, the forces of repulsion between protons sharply increase. Therefore, a greater number of neutrons is necessary to counteract the increasing repulsions. Finally, at element 84, the repulsive forces become sufficiently great that the nuclei are unstable regardless of the number of neutrons present.

Section 11-1 Quick Quiz

1. The term *nuclide* is a term used to describe
   a. stable, but not unstable, atoms
   b. unstable, but not stable, atoms
   c. both stable and unstable atoms
   d. no correct response
2. The term *radioactive nuclide* designates an atom whose nucleus
   a. is unstable
   b. absorbs radiation
   c. contain 75 or more neutrons
   d. no correct response
3. In the notation *carbon-14*, the number 14 is
   a. the atomic number of the carbon atom
   b. the mass number of the carbon atom
   c. the number of neutrons in the nucleus of the carbon atom
   d. no correct response

Answers: 1. c; 2. a; 3. b

11-2 The Nature of Radioactive Emissions

LEARNING FOCUS

Be able to characterize the three types of natural radioactive emissions by name and by symbol.

Figure 11-1 Marie Curie, one of the pioneers in the study of radioactivity, is the first person to have been awarded two Nobel Prizes for scientific work. In 1903, she, her husband Pierre, and Henri Becquerel were corecipients of the Nobel Prize in physics. In 1911, she received the Nobel Prize in chemistry. In 1934, Marie, now respectfully called Madame Curie, died of leukemia caused by overexposure to radiation.

The fact that unstable nuclei spontaneously emit radiation was accidentally discovered by the French physicist and engineer Antoine Henri Becquerel (1852–1908) in 1896. While working on an experiment involving rocks that phosphoresce, Becquerel discovered that a particular uranium-containing rock gave off radiation. Soon other scientists, such as the French chemists Marie (1867–1934; Figure 11-1) and Pierre (1859–1906) Curie and the British chemist Ernest Rutherford (1871–1937), began their own investigations into this strange phenomenon—a phenomenon that Marie Curie named radioactivity.

The first information concerning the nature of the radiation emanating from naturally radioactive materials was obtained by Rutherford in 1898–1899. Using an apparatus similar to that shown in Figure 11-2, he found that if radiation from uranium is passed between electrically charged plates, it is split into three components. This finding indicates the presence of three different types of emissions from naturally radioactive materials. A closer analysis of Rutherford's experiment reveals that one radiation component is positively charged (it is attracted to the negative plate); a second component is negatively charged (it is attracted to the positive plate); and the third component carries no charge (it is unaffected by either charged plate). Rutherford chose to call the three radiation components alpha rays (α rays)—the positive component; beta rays (β rays)—the negative component; and gamma rays (γ rays)—the uncharged component. (Alpha, beta, and gamma are the first three letters of the Greek alphabet.) Rutherford's nomenclature system, with slight modification, is still in use today. Current terminology is alpha *particles* instead of alpha rays, beta *particles* instead of beta rays, and gamma rays (no change). Further research has shown that alpha and beta emissions have mass and hence are particles and that gamma emissions have no mass and hence are a form of energy.

The complete characterization of the three types of natural radioactive emissions required many years. Early work in the field was hampered by the fact that many of the details concerning atomic structure were not yet known. For example, the neutron was not discovered until 1932, 36 years after the discovery of radioactivity.

Figure 11-2 The effect of an electromagnetic field on alpha, beta, and gamma radiation. Alpha and beta particles are deflected in opposite directions, whereas gamma radiation is not affected.

In terms of modern-day scientific knowledge, Rutherford's three types of "radiation" are characterized as follows:

An **alpha particle** *is a particle in which two protons and two neutrons are present that is emitted by certain radioactive nuclei.* The notation used to represent an alpha particle is $^4_2\alpha$. The numerical subscript indicates that the charge on the particle is 2+ (from the two protons). The numerical superscript indicates a mass of 4 amu. Alpha particles are identical to the nuclei of helium-4 ($^4_2$He) atoms; because of this, an alternative designation for an alpha particle is $^4_2$He.

A **beta particle** *is a particle whose charge and mass are identical to those of an electron that is emitted by certain radioactive nuclei.* Beta particles are not extranuclear electrons; they are particles that have been produced inside the nucleus and then ejected. This formation process is discussed in Section 11-3. The symbol used to represent a beta particle is $^{\,0}_{-1}\beta$. The numerical subscript indicates that the charge on the beta particle is 1−; it is the same as that of an electron. The use of the superscript zero for the mass of a beta particle should not be interpreted as meaning that a beta particle has no mass but, rather, that the mass is very close to zero amu. The actual mass of a beta particle is 0.00055 amu.

A **gamma ray** *is a form of high-energy radiation without mass or charge that is emitted by certain radioactive nuclei.* Gamma rays are similar to X-rays except that gamma rays have higher energy. The symbol for gamma rays is $^0_0\gamma$.

1. Which of the following types of radioactive emissions has a charge and mass identical to that of an electron?
   a. alpha particle
   b. beta particle
   c. gamma radiation
   d. no correct response
2. Which of the following types of radioactive emissions has a subatomic particle composition of two protons and two neutrons?
   a. alpha particle
   b. beta particle
   c. gamma radiation
   d. no correct response
3. Which of the following types of radioactive emissions has a mass of 2 amu?
   a. alpha particle
   b. beta particle
   c. gamma radiation
   d. no correct response

Answers: 1. b; 2. a; 3. d

11-3 Equations for Radioactive Decay

LEARNING FOCUS

Be able to write balanced nuclear equations representing various alpha, beta, and gamma decay processes; understand what is meant by the terms *parent nuclide* and *daughter nuclide*.

Alpha, beta, and gamma emissions come from the nucleus of an atom. These spontaneous emissions alter nuclei; obviously, if a nucleus loses an alpha particle (two protons and two neutrons), it will not be the same as it was before the departure of the particle. In the case of alpha and beta emissions, the nuclear alteration causes the identity of atoms to change, forming a new element. Thus nuclear reactions differ dramatically from ordinary chemical reactions, where the identities of the elements are always maintained. **Radioactive decay** *is the process whereby a radionuclide is transformed into a nuclide of another element as a result of the emission of radiation from its nucleus.* The terms *parent nuclide* and *daughter nuclide* are often used in descriptions of radioactive decay processes. A **parent nuclide** *is the nuclide that undergoes decay in a radioactive decay process.* A **daughter nuclide** *is the nuclide that is produced in a radioactive decay process.*

Alpha Particle Decay

Alpha particle decay *is the radioactive decay process in which an alpha particle is emitted from an unstable nucleus.* It always results in the formation of a nuclide of a different element. The product nucleus has an atomic number that is 2 less than that of the original nucleus and a mass number that is 4 less than that of the original nucleus. A generalized nuclear equation for alpha particle decay is

$$\ce{^{A}_{Z}X} \longrightarrow \ce{^{4}_{2}\alpha} + \ce{^{A-4}_{Z-2}Y}$$

▶ *In a* chemical *reaction, element identity is maintained. Atoms are rearranged to form new substances involving the same elements. In a nuclear reaction, element identity is not maintained. An element changes into a different element.*

where X is the chemical symbol for the nucleus of the original element undergoing decay and Y is the chemical symbol of the nucleus formed as a result of the decay. ◀

Specific radioactive decay processes are represented using *nuclear equations*. A **nuclear equation** *is an equation in which the chemical symbols present represent atomic nuclei rather than atoms.* Both $\ce{^{211}_{83}Bi}$ and $\ce{^{238}_{92}U}$ are radionuclides that undergo alpha particle decay. The nuclear equations for these two decay processes are

$$\ce{^{211}_{83}Bi} \longrightarrow \ce{^{4}_{2}\alpha} + \ce{^{207}_{81}Tl}$$

$$\ce{^{238}_{92}U} \longrightarrow \ce{^{4}_{2}\alpha} + \ce{^{234}_{90}Th}$$

▶ *The symbols in nuclear equations stand for* nuclei *rather than atoms. Electrons are not considered when writing a nuclear equation.*

In the first equation, $\ce{^{211}_{83}Bi}$ is the parent nuclide and $\ce{^{207}_{81}Tl}$ the daughter nuclide; in the second equation, $\ce{^{238}_{92}U}$ is the parent nuclide and $\ce{^{234}_{90}Th}$ the daughter nuclide. ◀

Nuclear equations differ from ordinary chemical equations in three important ways:

1. The symbols in nuclear equations stand for nuclei rather than atoms. Thus the number of electrons present in an atom is not a consideration when writing a nuclear equation.
2. Mass numbers and atomic numbers (nuclear charge) are always specifically included in nuclear equations.
3. The elemental symbols on both sides of the equation frequently are not the same in nuclear equations.

▶ *The rules for balancing nuclear equations are*

1. The sum of the subscripts must be the same on both sides of the equation.
2. The sum of the superscripts must be the same on both sides of the equation.

The procedures for balancing nuclear equations are different from those used for ordinary chemical equations. A **balanced nuclear equation** *is a nuclear equation in which the sum of the subscripts (atomic numbers or particle charges) on both sides of the equation are equal, and the sum of the superscripts (mass numbers) on both sides of the equation are equal.* Both of the preceding nuclear equations are balanced. In the alpha decay of $\ce{^{211}_{83}Bi}$, the subscripts on both sides total 83, and the superscripts total 211. For the alpha decay of $\ce{^{238}_{92}U}$, the subscripts total 92 on both sides, and the superscripts total 238. ◀

Beta Particle Decay

Beta particle decay *is the radioactive decay process in which a beta particle is emitted from an unstable nucleus.* Beta particle decay, like alpha particle decay, always produces a nuclide of a different element. The mass number of the new nuclide is the same as that of the parent nuclide. However, the atomic number has increased by 1 unit. A generalized nuclear equation for beta particle decay is

$$_{Z}^{A}X \longrightarrow _{-1}^{0}\beta + _{Z+1}^{A}Y$$

Specific examples of beta particle decay are

$$_{4}^{10}Be \longrightarrow _{-1}^{0}\beta + _{5}^{10}B$$

$$_{90}^{234}Th \longrightarrow _{-1}^{0}\beta + _{91}^{234}Pa$$

Both of these nuclear equations are balanced; superscripts and subscripts add to the same sums on both sides of the equation. ◄

How can a nucleus, which contains only neutrons and protons, eject a negative particle (a beta particle) when such a particle is not present in the nucleus? Explained simply (it is not completely understood even today), a neutron in the nucleus is transformed into a proton and a beta particle is also produced as part of this interconversion process. Once produced, the beta particle is immediately ejected from the nucleus with a high velocity.

$$Neutron \longrightarrow proton + beta\ particle$$

$$_{0}^{1}n \longrightarrow _{1}^{1}p + _{-1}^{0}\beta$$

Note the symbols used to denote a neutron ($_{0}^{1}n$; no charge and a mass of 1 amu) and a proton ($_{1}^{1}p$; a 1+ charge and a mass of 1 amu).

▶ *Loss of a beta particle from an unstable nucleus results in (1) no change in the mass number (A), and (2) an increase of 1 unit in the atomic number (Z).*

Gamma Ray Emission

Gamma ray emission *is the radioactive decay process in which a gamma ray is emitted from an unstable nucleus.* For naturally occurring radionuclides, gamma ray emission always takes place in conjunction with an alpha or a beta decay process; it never occurs independently. These gamma rays are often not included in the nuclear equation because they do not affect the balancing of the equation or the identity of the daughter nuclide. ◄ This can be seen from the following two nuclear equations.

$$_{88}^{226}Ra \longrightarrow _{86}^{222}Rn + _{2}^{4}\alpha + _{0}^{0}\gamma$$

Balanced nuclear equation with gamma radiation included

$$_{88}^{226}Ra \longrightarrow _{86}^{222}Rn + _{2}^{4}\alpha$$

Balanced nuclear equation with gamma radiation omitted

The fact that gamma rays are often left out of balanced nuclear equations should not be interpreted to mean that such rays are not important in nuclear chemistry. On the contrary, gamma rays are more important than alpha and beta particles when the effects of external radiation exposure on living organisms are considered (Section 11-9). ◄

▶ *Gamma rays are to nuclear reactions what heat is to ordinary chemical reactions.*

▶ *Among* synthetically *produced radionuclides (Section 11-5), pure "gamma emitters," radionuclides that give off gamma rays but no alpha or beta particles, occur. These radionuclides are important in diagnostic nuclear medicine (Section 11-11). Pure "gamma emitters" are not found among naturally occurring radionuclides.*

EXAMPLE 11-1

Writing Balanced Nuclear Equations, Given the Parent Nuclide and Its Mode of Decay

Write a balanced nuclear equation for the decay of each of the following radioactive nuclides. The mode of decay is indicated in parentheses.

a. $_{31}^{70}Ga$ (beta emission)

b. $_{60}^{144}Nd$ (alpha emission)

c. $_{100}^{248}Fm$ (alpha emission)

d. $_{47}^{113}Ag$ (beta emission)

(continued)

Solution

In each case, the atomic and mass numbers of the daughter nucleus are obtained by writing the symbols of the parent nucleus and the particle emitted by the nucleus (alpha or beta). Then the equation is balanced.

a. Let X represent the daughter nuclide, the product of the radioactive decay. Then

$$^{70}_{31}\text{Ga} \longrightarrow ^{0}_{-1}\beta + \text{X}$$

The sum of the superscripts on both sides of the equation must be equal, so the superscript for X must be 70. In order for the sum of the subscripts on both sides of the equation to be equal, the subscript for X must be 32. Then $31 = (-1) + (32)$. As soon as the subscript for X is determined, the identity of X can be determined by looking at a periodic table and finding the element with that atomic number. The element with an atomic number of 32 is Ge (germanium). Therefore,

$$^{70}_{31}\text{Ga} \longrightarrow ^{0}_{-1}\beta + ^{70}_{32}\text{Ge}$$

b. Letting X represent the daughter nuclide, the equation for the alpha decay of $^{144}_{60}\text{Nd}$ is

$$^{144}_{60}\text{Nd} \longrightarrow ^{4}_{2}\alpha + \text{X}$$

This equation is balanced by making the superscripts on each side of the equation total 144 and the subscripts total 60.

$$^{144}_{60}\text{Nd} \longrightarrow ^{4}_{2}\alpha + ^{140}_{58}\text{Ce}$$

c. The equation to be balanced is

$$^{248}_{100}\text{Fm} \longrightarrow ^{4}_{2}\alpha + \text{X}$$

Balancing superscripts and subscripts, gives the equation

$$^{248}_{100}\text{Fm} \longrightarrow ^{4}_{2}\alpha + ^{244}_{98}\text{Cf}$$

In alpha emission, the atomic number of the daughter nuclide always decreases by 2, and the mass number of the daughter nuclide always decreases by 4.

d. The equation to be balanced is

$$^{113}_{47}\text{Ag} \longrightarrow ^{0}_{-1}\beta + \text{X}$$

In beta emission, the atomic number of the daughter nuclide always increases by 1, and the mass number does not change from that of the parent. This balancing procedure produces the result

$$^{113}_{47}\text{Ag} \longrightarrow ^{0}_{-1}\beta + ^{113}_{48}\text{Cd}$$

Section 11-3 Quick Quiz

1. Which of the following is *not* a balanced nuclear equation?
   a. $^{121}_{50}\text{Sn} \longrightarrow ^{0}_{-1}\beta + ^{121}_{51}\text{Sb}$
   b. $^{238}_{92}\text{U} \longrightarrow ^{4}_{2}\alpha + ^{232}_{90}\text{Th}$
   c. $^{10}_{4}\text{Be} \longrightarrow ^{10}_{5}\text{B} + ^{0}_{-1}\beta$
   d. no correct response
2. The beta decay of $^{234}_{90}\text{Th}$ produces a nuclide of which of the following elements?
   a. element 88
   b. element 89
   c. element 91
   d. no correct response
3. Which of the following is the daughter nuclide for the alpha decay of $^{212}_{84}\text{Po}$?
   a. $^{208}_{82}\text{Pb}$
   b. $^{216}_{82}\text{Pb}$
   c. $^{216}_{86}\text{Rn}$
   d. no correct response

4. The explanation for how a beta particle is produced in the nucleus of a radionuclide and then ejected involves the conversion (in a complex series of steps) of a
   a. proton to a neutron and a beta particle
   b. neutron to a proton and a beta particle
   c. beta particle to a proton and a neutron
   d. no correct response

Answers: 1. b; 2. c; 3. a; 4. b

11-4 Rate of Radioactive Decay

LEARNING FOCUS

Understand the concept of a half-life as it relates to radioactive decay; be able to determine the amount of radionuclide left after a given number of half-lives or vice versa.

Radioactive nuclides do not all decay at the same rate. Some decay very rapidly; others undergo disintegration at extremely low rates. This indicates that radionuclides are not all equally unstable. The greater the decay rate, the lower the stability of the nuclide.

The concept of *half-life* is used to express nuclear stability quantitatively. A **half-life** *($t_{1/2}$) is the time required for one-half of a given quantity of a radioactive substance to undergo decay.* For example, when a 4.00-g sample of a radionuclide with a half-life of 12 days undergoes decay, after one half-life (12 days) only 2.00 g of the sample (one-half of the original amount) will remain undecayed; the other half will have decayed into some other substance. Similarly, during the next half-life, one-half of the 2.00 g remaining will decay, leaving one-fourth of the original atoms (1.00 g) unchanged. After three half-lives, one-eighth (1/2 × 1/2 × 1/2) of the original sample will remain undecayed. Figure 11-3 illustrates the radioactive decay curve for a radionuclide. ◄

▶ *The greater the decay rate for a radionuclide, the shorter its half-life.*

Number of half-lives	Fraction of initial quantity remaining	Quantity remaining (mg)
0	1	80.0 (initial)
1	1/2	40.0
2	1/4	20.0
3	1/8	10.0
4	1/16	5.0

Figure 11-3 Decay of 80.0 mg of ^{131}I, which has a half-life of 8.0 days. After each half-life period, the quantity of material present at the beginning of the period is reduced by half.

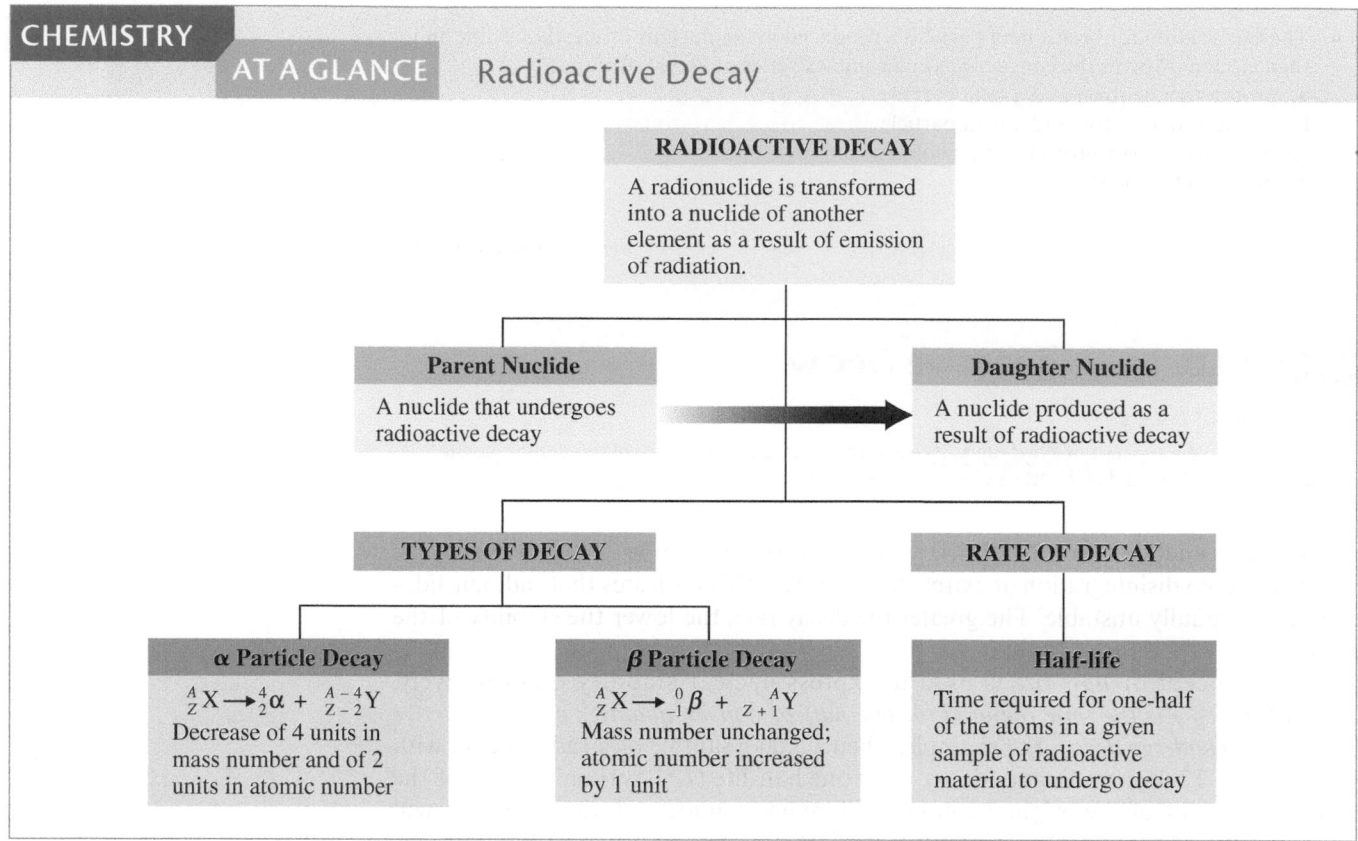

CHEMISTRY AT A GLANCE Radioactive Decay

RADIOACTIVE DECAY
A radionuclide is transformed into a nuclide of another element as a result of emission of radiation.

Parent Nuclide
A nuclide that undergoes radioactive decay

Daughter Nuclide
A nuclide produced as a result of radioactive decay

TYPES OF DECAY

α Particle Decay
$$_Z^A X \longrightarrow\ _2^4\alpha\ +\ _{Z-2}^{A-4}Y$$
Decrease of 4 units in mass number and of 2 units in atomic number

β Particle Decay
$$_Z^A X \longrightarrow\ _{-1}^0\beta\ +\ _{Z+1}^A Y$$
Mass number unchanged; atomic number increased by 1 unit

RATE OF DECAY

Half-life
Time required for one-half of the atoms in a given sample of radioactive material to undergo decay

▶ *Most radionuclides used in diagnostic medicine have short half-lives. This limits to a short time interval the exposure of the human body to radiation.*

▶ **Table 11-1 Range of Half-Lives Found for Naturally Occurring Radionuclides**

Element	Half-Life ($t_{1/2}$)
vanadium-50	6×10^{15} yr
platinum-190	6.9×10^{11} yr
uranium-238	4.5×10^9 yr
uranium-235	7.1×10^8 yr
thorium-230	7.5×10^4 yr
lead-210	22 yr
bismuth-214	19.7 min
polonium-212	3.0×10^{-7} sec

There is a wide range of half-lives for radionuclides. Half-lives as long as billions of years and as short as a fraction of a second have been determined (Table 11-1). ◀ Most naturally occurring radionuclides have long half-lives. However, some radionuclides with short half-lives are also found in nature. Naturally occurring mechanisms exist for the continual production of the short-lived species.

The decay rate (half-life) of a radionuclide is constant. It is independent of physical conditions such as temperature, pressure, and state of chemical combination. It depends only on the identity of the radionuclide. For example, radioactive sodium-24 decays at the same rate whether it is incorporated in NaCl, NaBr, Na_2SO_4, or $NaC_2H_3O_2$. If a nuclide is radioactive, nothing will stop it from decaying and nothing will increase or decrease its decay rate.

Calculations involving amounts of radioactive material decayed, amounts remaining undecayed, and time elapsed can be carried out by using the following equation:

$$\begin{pmatrix} \text{Amount of radionuclide} \\ \text{undecayed after } n \text{ half-lives} \end{pmatrix} = \begin{pmatrix} \text{original amount} \\ \text{of radionuclide} \end{pmatrix} \times \left(\frac{1}{2^n} \right)$$

Chemistry at a Glance—Radioactive Decay—summarizes important concepts about radioactive decay that have been considered so far in this chapter.

EXAMPLE 11-2

Using Half-Life to Calculate the Amount of Radioisotope That Remains Undecayed After a Certain Time

Iodine-131 is a radionuclide that is frequently used in nuclear medicine. Among other things, it is used to detect fluid buildup in the brain. The half-life of iodine-131 is 8.0 days. How much, in grams, of a 0.16-g sample of iodine-131 will remain undecayed after a period of 32 days?

Solution

First, determine the number of half-lives that have elapsed.

$$32 \ \cancel{\text{days}} \times \left(\frac{1 \ \text{half-life}}{8.0 \ \cancel{\text{days}}} \right) = 4 \ \text{half-lives}$$

Knowing the number of elapsed half-lives and the original amount of radioactive iodine present, the following equation can be used.

$$\left(\begin{matrix} \text{Amount of radionuclide} \\ \text{undecayed after } n \text{ half-lives} \end{matrix} \right) = \left(\begin{matrix} \text{original amount} \\ \text{of radionuclide} \end{matrix} \right) \times \left(\frac{1}{2^n} \right)$$

$$= 0.16 \ \text{g} \times \frac{1}{2^4} \quad \longleftarrow \ {}^{4 \ \text{half-lives}}$$

$$= 0.16 \text{g} \times \frac{1}{16} = 0.010 \text{g}$$

Constructing a tabular summary of the amount of sample remaining after each of the elapsed half-lives yields

Half-lives	0	1	2	3	4
Number of days	0	8	16	24	32
Amount remaining	0.16 g	0.080 g	0.040 g	0.020 g	0.010 g

EXAMPLE 11-3

Using Half-Life to Calculate the Time Needed to Reduce Radioactivity to a Specific Level

Strontium-90 is a nuclide found in radioactive fallout from nuclear weapon explosions. Its half-life is 28.0 years. How long, in years, will it take for 94% (15/16) of the strontium-90 atoms present in a sample of material to undergo decay?

Solution

If 15/16 of the sample has decayed, then 1/16 of the sample remains undecayed. In terms of $1/2^n$, 1/16 is equal to $1/2^4$; that is,

$$\frac{1}{2} \times \frac{1}{2} \times \frac{1}{2} \times \frac{1}{2} = \frac{1}{2^4} = \frac{1}{16}$$

Thus four half-lives have elapsed in reducing the amount of strontium-90 to 1/16 of its original amount.

The half-life of strontium-90 is 28 years, so the total time elapsed will be

$$4 \ \cancel{\text{half-lives}} \times \left(\frac{28.0 \ \text{years}}{1 \ \cancel{\text{half-life}}} \right) = 112 \ \text{years}$$

Section 11-4 Quick Quiz

1. The half-life of cobalt-60 is 5.2 years. This means that after 5.2 years a cobalt-60 sample
   a. has been changed into cobalt-30
   b. contains half as many cobalt-60 atoms as it did originally
   c. contains twice as many cobalt-60 atoms as it did originally
   d. no correct response
2. After three half-lives have elapsed, the amount of a radioactive sample which *has not* decayed is which of the following?
   a. 1/3 the original amount
   b. 1/8 the original amount
   c. 1/9 the original amount
   d. no correct response

(continued)

3. After four half-lives have elapsed, the amount of a radioactive sample that *has* decayed is which of the following?
   a. 1/4 the original amount
   b. 3/4 the original amount
   c. 1/16 the original amount
   d. no correct response
4. If 1.50 gram of a 2.00-gram sample of a radioactive substance undergoes decay in 60 minutes, then the half-life of the sample is
   a. 15 minutes
   b. 30 minutes
   c. 120 minutes
   d. no correct response
5. If the half-life of a 2.0-gram sample of a radionuclide is 14 hours, then the half-life of a 1.0 gram sample of the same radionuclide would be
   a. 7 hours
   b. 14 hours
   c. 28 hours
   d. no correct response

Answers: 1. b; 2. b; 3. d; 4. b; 5. b

11-5 Transmutation and Bombardment Reactions

LEARNING FOCUS

Understand the concept of a nuclear bombardment reaction and how laboratory-produced radionuclides are made using such reactions.

Radioactive decay, discussed in the previous two sections, is an example of a natural transmutation reaction. A **transmutation reaction** *is a nuclear reaction in which a nuclide of one element is changed into a nuclide of another element.* It is also possible to cause a transmutation reaction to occur in a laboratory setting by means of a bombardment reaction. A **bombardment reaction** *is a nuclear reaction brought about by bombarding stable nuclei with small particles traveling at very high speeds.* In bombardment reactions, there are always two reactants (the target nuclide and the small, high-energy bombarding particle) and also two products (the daughter nuclide and another small particle such as a neutron or proton).

The first successful bombardment reaction was carried out in 1919 by Ernest Rutherford (Figure 11-4) 25 years after the discovery of radioactive decay. The reaction involved bombarding nitrogen gas with alpha particles from a natural source (radium). In this process, a new stable nuclide was formed: oxygen-17. The nuclear equation for this initial bombardment reaction is

$$^{14}_{7}\text{N} + {}^{4}_{2}\alpha \longrightarrow {}^{17}_{8}\text{O} + {}^{1}_{1}\text{p}$$

Further research carried out by many investigators has shown that numerous nuclei undergo change under the stress of bombardment by small, high-energy particles. In most cases, the new nuclide that is produced is radioactive (unstable). Two examples of bombardment reactions carried out in laboratories in which the product nuclide is radioactive are

$$^{44}_{20}\text{Ca} + {}^{1}_{1}\text{p} \longrightarrow {}^{44}_{21}\text{Sc} + {}^{1}_{0}\text{n}$$

$$^{23}_{11}\text{Na} + {}^{2}_{1}\text{H} \longrightarrow {}^{21}_{10}\text{Ne} + {}^{4}_{2}\alpha$$

Radioactive nuclides produced by bombardment reactions obey the same laws as naturally occurring radionuclides. In many cases, the previously discussed alpha and beta modes of decay occur (Section 11-3).

Figure 11-4 Ernest Rutherford (1871–1937), the first person to carry out a bombardment reaction, was a "world-class" researcher. Earlier, he discovered that an atom has a nucleus (Section 3-1), and he was the discoverer of the alpha and beta radiation associated with radioactivity.

Bettmann/Fine Art/Corbis

Synthetic Elements

More than 2000 bombardment-produced radionuclides that do not occur naturally are now known. This number is seven times greater than the number of naturally occurring nuclides (Section 3-3). In this total is at least one radionuclide of every naturally occurring element. In addition, nuclides of 30 elements that do not occur in nature have been produced in small quantities as the result of bombardment reactions. Four of these "synthetic" elements, produced between 1937 and 1941, filled gaps in the periodic table for which no naturally occurring element had been found. These four elements are technetium (Tc, element 43), an element with numerous uses in nuclear medicine (Section 11-11); promethium (Pm, element 61); astatine (At, element 85); and francium (Fr, element 87). The remainder of the "synthetic" elements, elements 93 to 118, are called the *transuranium elements* because they occur immediately following uranium in the periodic table. (Uranium is the naturally occurring element with the highest atomic number.) All nuclides of all of the transuranium elements are radioactive. Table 11-2 gives information about the stability of the transuranium elements. Note the extremely short half-lives of the more recently produced elements. ◄

Most radioisotopes used in the field of medicine are "synthetic" radionuclides. For example, the synthetic radionuclides cobalt-60, yttrium-90, iodine-131, and

▶ *Production of the small, high-energy bombarding particles needed to effect a bombardment reaction requires use of a cyclotron or a linear accelerator (both very expensive pieces of equipment). Both use magnetic fields to accelerate charged particles to velocities at which the energy is sufficient to allow the particle to penetrate the nucleus and induce a nuclear reaction.*

All nuclides of all elements beyond bismuth (Z = 83) in the periodic table are radioactive.

▶ Table 11-2 **The Transuranium Elements**

Name	Symbol	Atomic Number	Mass Number of Most Stable Nuclide	Half-Life of Most Stable Nuclide	Discovery Year for First Isotope
neptunium	Np	93	237	2.14×10^6 yr	1940
plutonium	Pu	94	244	7.6×10^7 yr	1940
americium	Am	95	243	8.0×10^3 yr	1944
curium	Cm	96	247	1.6×10^7 yr	1944
berkelium	Bk	97	247	1400 yr	1950
californium	Cf	98	251	900 yr	1950
einsteinium	Es	99	252	472 days	1952
fermium	Fm	100	257	100 days	1953
mendelevium	Md	101	258	52 days	1955
nobelium	No	102	259	58 min	1958
lawrencium	Lr	103	262	3.6 hr	1961
rutherfordium	Rf	104	263	10 min	1969
dubnium	Db	105	262	34 sec	1970
seaborgium	Sg	106	266	21 sec	1974
bohrium	Bh	107	267	17 sec	1980
hassium	Hs	108	277	11 min	1984
meitnerium	Mt	109	276	0.72 sec	1982
darmstadtium	Ds	110	281	11.1 sec	1994
roentgenium	Rg	111	280	3.6 sec	1994
copernicium	Cn	112	285	34 sec	1996
element 113	—	113	284	0.48 sec	2004
flerovium	Fl	114	289	2.6 sec	1999
element 115	—	115	288	87 msec	2004
livermorium	Lv	116	293	61 msec	2006
element 117	—	117	294	78 msec	2010
element 118	—	118	294	0.89 msec	2006

Figure 11-5 The synthetic element americium (element 95) is a component of nearly all standard smoke detectors. Small amounts of Am-241, which has a half-life of 458 years, produce radiation that ionizes air within the detector, causing it to conduct electricity. The presence of smoke in the detector causes a drop in electrical conductivity, and the alarm sounds.

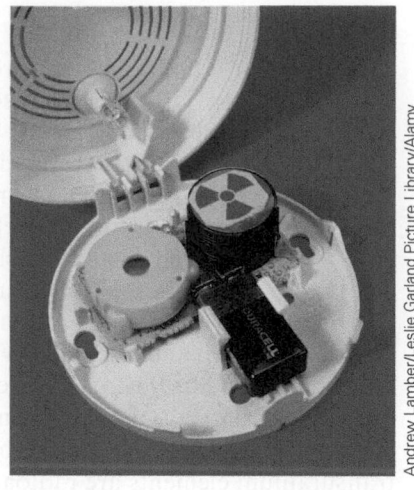

gold-198 are used in radiotherapy treatments for cancer. Section 11-11 provides more information about the medical uses for radionuclides. The synthetic element americium (element 95) is present in nearly all standard smoke detectors (see Figure 11-5).

Section 11-5 Quick Quiz

1. During a bombardment reaction the particles colliding with target nuclei are
   a. small and traveling very fast
   b. small and traveling slow
   c. large and traveling very fast
   d. no correct response
2. The bombardment reaction involving $^{23}_{11}\text{Na}$ and $^{2}_{1}\text{H}$ gives two products, one of which is $^{1}_{1}\text{H}$. The other product is

   a. $^{24}_{11}\text{Na}$

   b. $^{24}_{12}\text{Mg}$

   c. $^{25}_{12}\text{Mg}$

   d. no correct response
3. Element 118, the highest-atomic-numbered laboratory-produced element, has a half-life measured in
   a. hours
   b. minutes
   c. milliseconds
   d. no correct response
4. Which of the following statements about laboratory-produced (synthetic) radionuclides is *not* correct?
   a. Synthetic radionuclides outnumber naturally occurring nuclides by a 7-to-1 ratio.
   b. Synthetic radionuclides are now known for each of the naturally occurring elements.
   c. Almost all radionuclides used in nuclear medicine are synthetic radionuclides.
   d. no correct response

Answers: 1. a; 2. a; 3. c; 4. d

11-6 Radioactive Decay Series

LEARNING FOCUS
Be able to describe the concept of a radioactive decay series.

Radioactive nuclides with high atomic numbers attain nuclear stability through a series of decay steps. When such nuclides decay, they produce daughter nuclei that are also radioactive. These daughter nuclei in turn decay to a third radioactive product,

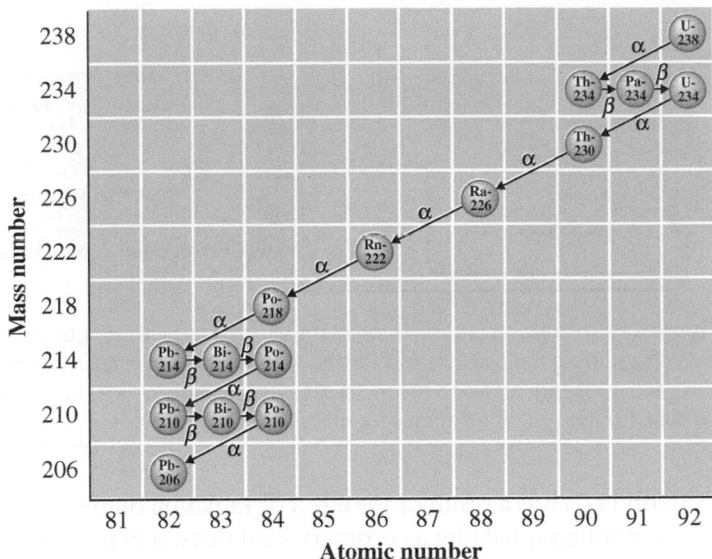

Figure 11-6 In the $^{238}_{92}$U decay series, each nuclide except $^{206}_{82}$Pb (the stable end product) is unstable; the successive transformations continue until this stable product is formed.

and so on. Eventually, a stable nucleus is produced. Such a sequence of decay products is called a radioactive decay series. A **radioactive decay series** *is a series of radioactive decay processes beginning with a long-lived radionuclide and ending with a stable nuclide of lower atomic number.*

Uranium-238, the most abundant isotope of uranium (99.2%), is the beginning nuclide for an important naturally occurring decay series. As shown in Figure 11-6, 14 steps are needed for uranium-238 to reach lead-206, its stable end product. Note from Figure 11-6 that both alpha and beta emissions are part of the decay sequence and that there is no simple pattern as to which is emitted when. ◀

In the uranium-238 decay series, all the intermediate products are solids except one. Radon-222 is a gas at normal temperatures and is therefore a very mobile species. Its presence has been detected in both aqueous and atmospheric environments. Exposure to radon-222 constitutes the major source of radiation exposure for the average American (Section 11-10).

▶ *In a decay series such as the one involving uranium-238, gamma rays are emitted at each step (even though they are not shown) in addition to the alpha or beta particle. Such gamma rays are very important in the effects of radiation exposure on health (Section 11-9).*

Section 11-6 Quick Quiz

1. In a radioactive decay series all daughter nuclides
   a. are radioactive
   b. are stable
   c. except the last one are radioactive
   d. no correct response
2. In the 14-step uranium-238 decay series
   a. all steps involve alpha decay
   b. all steps involve beta decay
   c. both alpha decay and beta decay steps occur
   d. no correct response

Answers: 1. c; 2. c

11-7 Detection of Radiation

LEARNING FOCUS

Be able to describe how radiation can be detected using film badges or Geiger counters.

Low levels of radiation cannot be detected by the physical senses. Radiation at these levels cannot be heard, felt, tasted, seen, or smelled. Despite this, numerous physical methods exist for its detection. Becquerel's initial discovery of radioactivity

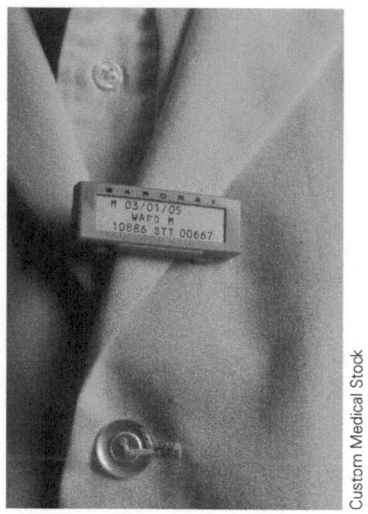

Figure 11-7 Film badges, such as the one worn by this technician, are used to determine a person's exposure to radiation.

Figure 11-8 Radiation passing through the window of a Geiger counter ionizes one or more gas atoms, producing positive ions and electrons. The electrons are attracted to the central wire, and the positive ions are drawn to the metal tube. This constitutes a pulse of electric current, which is amplified and displayed on a meter or other readout.

(Section 11-2) was a result of the effect of radiation on photographic plates. Radiation affects photographic film as ordinary light does; it exposes the film. Technicians and others who work around radiation usually wear film badges (Figure 11-7) to record the extent of their exposure to radiation. When the film from the badge is developed, the degree of darkening of the film negative indicates the extent of radiation exposure. Different filters are present in the badge, so various parts of the film register exposures to the different types of radiations (alpha, beta, gamma, and X-rays).

Radiation can also be detected by making use of the fact that it ionizes atoms and molecules (Section 11-8). The Geiger counter operates on this principle. The basic components of a Geiger counter are shown in Figure 11-8. The detection part of such a counter is a metal tube filled with a gas (usually argon). The tube has a thin-walled window made of a material that can be penetrated by alpha, beta, or gamma rays. In the center of the tube is a wire attached to the positive terminal of an electrical power source. The metal tube is attached to the negative terminal of the same source. Radiation entering the tube ionizes the gas, which allows a pulse of electricity to flow. This pulse of electricity is then amplified and displayed on a meter or some other type of readout display.

Section 11-7 Quick Quiz

1. Film badges, worn by technicians working with radiation, can detect
   a. both extent and type of radiation exposure
   b. extent, but not type, of radiation exposure
   c. type, but not extent, of radiation exposure
   d. no correct response
2. A Geiger counter operates on the principle that radiation
   a. darkens a photographic film
   b. can be detected by its odor
   c. ionizes atoms and molecules
   d. no correct response

Answers: 1. a; 2. c

11-8 Chemical Effects of Radiation

LEARNING FOCUS

Be able to contrast the characteristics of ionizing and nonionizing radiation; be familiar with the concepts of *ion pairs* and *free radicals*.

The very energetic radiations produced from radioactive decay travel outward from their nuclear sources into the material surrounding the radioactive source. There, they interact with the atoms and molecules of the material, which dissipates their excess energy.

Numerous interactions (collisions) between atoms or molecules and a "particle" of radiation are required before the energy of the radiation is reduced to the level of surrounding materials. At this point, the radiation is "harmless." The interactions that do occur between radiation and atoms or molecules will now be considered in closer detail.

It is the electrons of molecules that are most directly affected by radiation, whether that radiation is from a radioactive material or some other source. In general, two things can happen to an electron subjected to radiation: excitation or ionization. *Excitation* occurs when radiation, through energy release, excites an electron from an occupied orbital into an empty, higher-energy orbital. *Ionization* occurs when the radiation carries enough energy to remove an electron from an atom or molecule.

Based on its effects on electrons, radiation of various types is classified into the categories *nonionizing radiation* and *ionizing radiation*. **Nonionizing radiation** *is radiation with insufficient energy to remove an electron from an atom or molecule.* Radio waves, microwaves, infrared light, and visible light are forms of nonionizing radiation. The first three possess insufficient energy to excite electrons to higher energy states. Such radiation can, however, cause increased movement, vibration, and rotation of molecules with a resultant increase in the temperature of a material. Visible light, the fourth type of nonionizing radiation, possesses sufficient energy to excite electrons to higher energy states. Electrons that undergo such excitation return, with time, to their normal states.

Ionizing radiation *is radiation with sufficient energy to remove an electron from an atom or molecule.* Most radiation associated with radioactive decay processes is ionizing radiation. Cosmic rays, X-rays, and ultraviolet light are also forms of ionizing radiation. (Cosmic rays are energetic particles coming from interstellar space; they are made up primarily of protons, alpha particles, and beta particles.)

The result of the interaction of ionizing radiation with matter is *ion pair formation*. In ion pair formation, the incoming radiation transfers sufficient energy into a molecule to knock an electron out of it, converting the molecule into a positive ion (see Figure 11-9); that is, ionization occurs and an ion pair is formed. An **ion pair** *is the electron and positive ion that are produced during an interaction between an atom or molecule and ionizing radiation.* This ionization process is not the normal "voluntary" transfer of electrons that occurs during ionic compound formation (Section 4-6), but, rather, the involuntary, nonchemical removal of an electron from a molecule to form an ion. Many ion pairs are produced by a single "particle" of radiation because such a particle must undergo many collisions before its energy is reduced to the level of surrounding material. The electrons ejected from atoms or molecules during ion pair formation frequently have enough energy to bombard neighboring molecules and cause additional ionizations.

Free-radical formation, either directly or indirectly, usually accompanies ion pair formation. A **free radical** *is an atom, molecule, or ion that contains an unpaired electron.* The presence of the unpaired electron in a free radical usually causes it to be a very reactive species. (Recall from Section 5-2 that electrons normally occur in pairs in

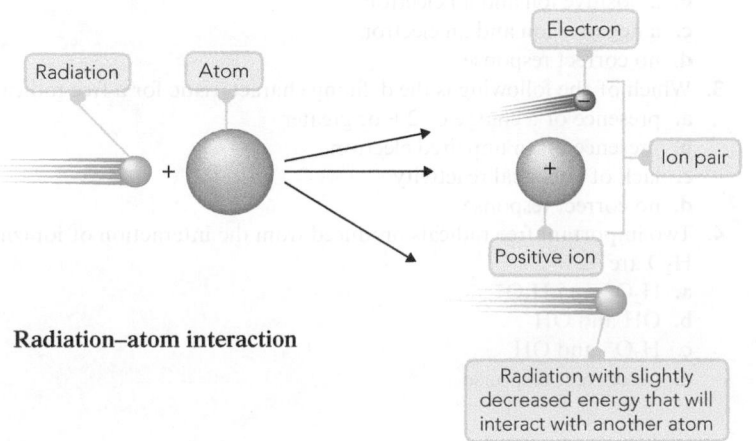

Radiation–atom interaction

Figure 11-9 Ion pair formation. When radiation interacts with an atom, electrons are often knocked away from the atom. The atoms that lose electrons become ions. An ion so produced and its "free electron" constitute an ion pair.

molecules.) Free radicals can rapidly react with other chemical species nearby, often precipitating a series of totally undesirable chemical reactions inside a living cell. Once formed, a free radical can combine with another free radical to form a molecule in which electrons are paired, or it can react with another molecule to produce a new free radical. The latter is a common occurrence. It is such production of new free radicals in a "chainlike" manner that causes major problems within a living cell. Such free-radical production is what makes the injury from radiation exposure far greater in magnitude than that expected merely on the basis of the energy of the incoming radiation.

Because water is the most abundant molecule in living organisms, the effects of ionizing radiation on water are of prime importance in assessing the effects of radiation exposure on health and life. The first step in the interaction of ionizing radiation with water is usually ion pair formation.

$$H_2O + radiation \longrightarrow \underbrace{H_2O^+ + e^-}_{Ion\ pair}$$

The H_2O^+ ion formed in this interaction should not be confused with the H_3O^+ ion produced when acids dissolve in water (Section 10-2). The H_2O^+ ion is a free radical and is extremely reactive; the H_3O^+ ion is not a free radical. The Lewis structure for the water free radical (H_2O^+) is

The highly reactive H_2O^+, a species not normally present in biochemical systems, can then react with another water molecule, causing further free-radical formation.

$$\underset{\substack{Free\\radical}}{H_2O^+} + H_2O \longrightarrow H_3O^+ + \underset{\substack{New\ free\\radical}}{OH}$$

The OH free radicals produced in this manner then interact with many different biomolecules to produce new free radicals, which in turn can react further. The result often devastatingly upsets cellular activity. ◀

▶ *Just as the water free radical (H_2O^+) is not to be confused with the acidic species H_3O^+, the hydroxyl free radical (OH) is not to be confused with the hydroxide ion (OH^-); the latter is the basic species in aqueous solution. The difference between these two species is one electron, as comparing their Lewis structures illustrates:*

Hydroxyl free   Hydroxide ion
radical

Section 11-8 Quick Quiz

1. Which of the following is *not* a form of ionizing radiation?
   a. ultraviolet rays
   b. gamma rays
   c. alpha particles
   d. no correct response
2. The two species present in an ion pair are
   a. a positive ion and a negative ion
   b. a positive ion and an electron
   c. a negative ion and an electron
   d. no correct response
3. Which of the following is the defining characteristic for a free radical?
   a. presence of a charge of 2+ or greater
   b. presence of an unpaired electron
   c. lack of chemical reactivity
   d. no correct response
4. Two important free radicals produced from the interaction of ionizing radiation with H_2O are
   a. H_2O^+ and H_3O^+
   b. OH and OH^-
   c. H_2O^+ and OH
   d. no correct response

Answers: 1. d; 2. b; 3. b; 4. c

11-9 Biochemical Effects of Radiation

LEARNING FOCUS

Contrast the biological effects of alpha, beta, and gamma radiation in terms of both penetrating ability and ion pair formation ability.

The three types of naturally occurring radioactive emissions—alpha particles, beta particles, and gamma rays—differ in their ability to penetrate matter and cause ionization. Consequently, the extent of the biochemical effects of radiation depends on the type of radiation involved.

Alpha Particle Effects

Alpha particles are the most massive and also the slowest particles involved in natural radioactive decay processes. Maximum alpha particle velocities are on the order of one-tenth of the speed of light. ◀ For a given alpha-emitting radionuclide, all alpha particles have the same energy; different alpha-emitting radionuclides, however, produce alpha particles of differing energies.

▶ *The speed of light, 3.0×10^8 m/sec (186,000 miles/sec), is the maximum limit of velocity. Objects cannot travel faster than the speed of light.*

Because of their "slowness," alpha particles have low penetrating power and cannot penetrate the body's outer layers of skin. The major damage from alpha radiation occurs when alpha-emitting radionuclides are ingested—for example, in contaminated food. There are no protective layers of skin within the body.

Beta Particle Effects

Unlike alpha particles, which are all emitted with the same discrete energy from a given radionuclide, beta particles emerge from a beta-emitting substance with a continuous range of energies up to a specific limit that is characteristic of the particular radionuclide. Maximum beta particle velocities are on the order of nine-tenths of the speed of light.

With their greater velocity, beta particles can penetrate much deeper than alpha particles and can cause severe skin burns if their source remains in contact with the skin for an appreciable time. Because of their much smaller size, they do not ionize molecules (Section 11-8) as readily as alpha particles do. An alpha particle is approximately 8000 times heavier than a beta particle. A typical alpha particle travels about 6 cm in air and produces 40,000 ion pairs, and a typical beta particle travels 1000 cm in air and produces about 2000 ion pairs. Internal exposure to beta radiation is as serious as internal alpha exposure.

Gamma Radiation Effects

Gamma radiation is released at a velocity equal to the speed of light. Gamma rays readily penetrate deeply into organs, bone, and tissue. ◀ Ion pair formation that occurs is very limited when compared to that for alpha and beta pairs.

▶ *X-rays and gamma rays are similar except that X-rays are of lower energy. X-rays used in diagnostic medicine have energies approximately 10% of that of gamma rays.*

Because of the great penetrating power of gamma rays, gamma radiation is used in more than 100 different diagnostic medical procedures (see Section 11-11) and also in the preservation of food. The focus on relevancy feature Chemical Connections 11-A—Preserving Food Through Food Irradiation—explores the topic of food irradiation using gamma radiation.

Comparisons of Effects of Various Types of Radiations

Figure 11-10 contrasts the abilities of alpha, beta, and gamma radiation to penetrate paper, aluminum foil, and a thin layer of a lead–concrete mixture.

Preserving Food Through Food Irradiation

In some parts of the world, spoilage of food can claim up to 50% of a year's harvest. This is not so in the United States and many other countries, where food preservation, which takes many forms, is routinely carried out. Accepted modes of food preservation include freezing, canning, refrigeration, the use of chemical additives (such as antioxidants and mold inhibitors), and packaging (to keep out pests).

Food irradiation with gamma rays from cobalt-60 or cesium-137 sources is a newer form of food preservation. It is used extensively in Europe but has been "slow to catch on" in the United States even though it has been endorsed by the World Health Organization, the American Medical Association, and the U.S. Food and Drug Administration.

Spoilage of food is a biochemical process that usually involves bacteria, molds, and yeasts. Gamma radiation either kills or retards the growth of such species, the effects being determined by the irradiation dosage. Treatment levels can be grouped into three general categories:

1. "Low"-dose irradiation is used to delay physiological processes, including the ripening of fresh fruits and the sprouting of vegetables (such as onions and potatoes), and to control insects and parasites in foods. For example, irradiated strawberries stay unspoiled for up to three weeks, compared with three to five days for untreated berries (see accompanying photo).
2. "Medium"-dose irradiation is used to reduce spoilage and pathogenic microorganisms, to improve technological properties of food (such as reduced cooking time for dehydrated vegetables), and to extend the shelf life of many foods. Salmonella and other food-borne pathogens in meat, fish, and poultry are reduced by "medium"-dose irradiation. Such irradiation kills the parasite in pork that results in trichinosis.
3. "High"-dose irradiation is used to sterilize meat, poultry, and seafood and to kill insects in spices and seasonings.

Irradiation does not make foods radioactive, just as an airport luggage scanner does not make luggage radioactive.

Nor does it cause harmful chemical changes. Some small loss of vitamin activity and nutrients may occur, but these losses are usually several orders of magnitude smaller than that which occurs with heat treatment (cooking). Scientists have repeatedly concluded from animal-feeding studies that there are no toxic effects associated with irradiated foods.

The Food and Drug Administration has approved irradiation of meat and poultry and allows its use for a variety of other foods, including spices and fresh fruits and vegetables. Federal rules require irradiated foods to be labeled as such to distinguish them from nonirradiated foods. Studies show that consumers are getting less "leery" of irradiated foods as more information becomes available about the safety of this technology. Irradiated foods usually cost slightly more than their conventional counterparts. The estimated increase is two to three cents a pound for fruits and vegetables and three to five cents a pound for meat and poultry products.

Irradiation increases the "shelf-life" of many types of foods, including strawberries.

Figure 11-10 Alpha, beta, and gamma radiation differ in penetrating ability.

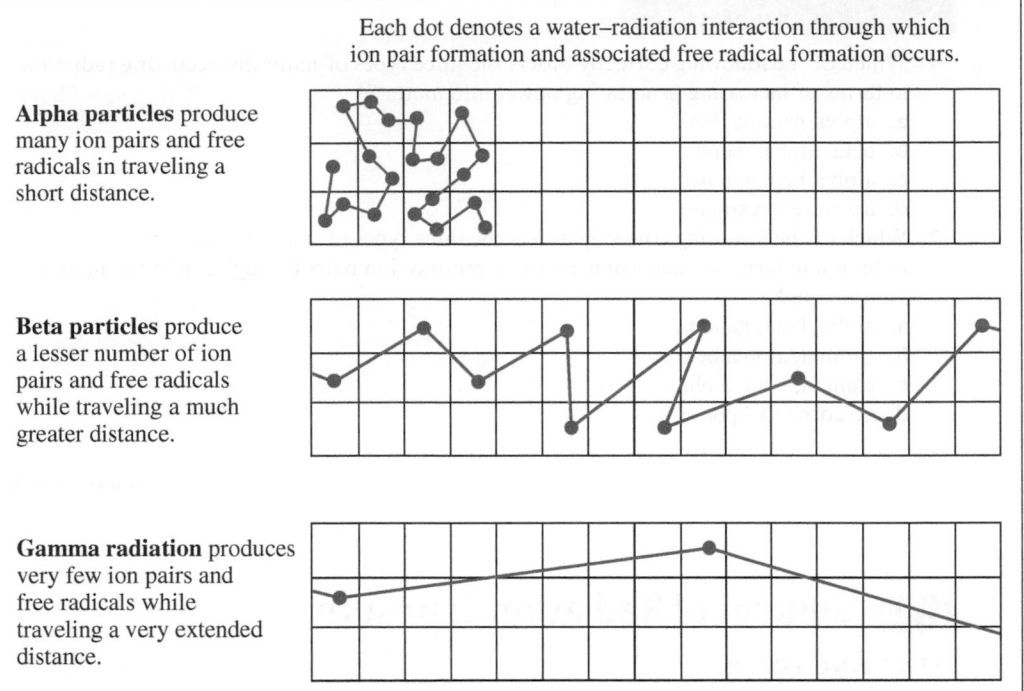

Each dot denotes a water–radiation interaction through which ion pair formation and associated free radical formation occurs.

Alpha particles produce many ion pairs and free radicals in traveling a short distance.

Beta particles produce a lesser number of ion pairs and free radicals while traveling a much greater distance.

Gamma radiation produces very few ion pairs and free radicals while traveling a very extended distance.

Figure 11-11 The extent of ion pair formation through radiation–water interactions in cells.

Figure 11-11 pictorially compares the abilities of the three types of radiation to cause ion pair formation in the context of interaction with water molecules within cells.

Short-Term Radiation Exposure

The *minimum* whole-body radiation dosage that can cause human health effects is unknown. However, the effects of larger doses have been studied (Table 11-3). Very serious damage or death can result from larger doses of ionizing radiation. Exposure to the radiation dosages necessary to cause the effects listed in Table 11-3 is, however, very unlikely.

▶ **Table 11-3 The Effects of Short-Term Whole-Body Radiation Exposure on Humans**

Dose (rems)*	Effects
0–25	No detectable clinical effects.
25–100	Slight short-term reduction in number of some blood cells; disabling sickness not common.
100–200	Nausea and fatigue, vomiting if dose is greater than 125 rems; longer-term reduction in number of some blood cells.
200–300	Nausea and vomiting first day of exposure; up to a 2-week latent period followed by appetite loss, general malaise, sore throat, pallor, diarrhea, and moderate emaciation. Recovery in about 3 months, unless complicated by infection or injury.
300–600	Nausea, vomiting, and diarrhea in first few hours. Up to a 1-week latent period followed by loss of appetite, fever, and general malaise in the second week, followed by hemorrhage, inflammation of mouth and throat, diarrhea, and emaciation. Some deaths in 2 to 6 weeks. Eventual death for 50% if exposure is above 450 rems; others recover in about 6 months.
600 or more	Nausea, vomiting, and diarrhea in first few hours. Rapid emaciation and death as early as second week. Eventual death of nearly 100%.

*A rem is the quantity of ionizing radiation that must be absorbed by a human to produce the same biological effect as 1 roentgen of high-penetration X-rays. A roentgen is the quantity of high-penetration X-rays that produces approximately 2×10^9 ion pairs per cubic centimeter of dry air at 0°C and 1 atm.

1. Which of the following correctly orders the three types of naturally occurring radiation in terms of increasing penetrating power into matter?
   a. alpha, gamma, beta
   b. beta, alpha, gamma
   c. alpha, beta gamma
   d. no correct response
2. Which of the following correctly orders the three types of naturally occurring radiation in terms of increasing ability to produce ion pairs through radiation–matter interactions?
   a. alpha, beta, gamma
   b. gamma, alpha, beta
   c. gamma, beta, alpha
   d. no correct response

Answers: 1. c; 2. c

11-10   Sources of Radiation Exposure

LEARNING FOCUS

Be familiar with the concept of *background radiation* and major sources for such; be familiar with radiation exposure sources related to human activities.

Low-level exposure to ionizing radiation is something constantly encountered. In fact, there is no way a person can totally avoid this low-level exposure because much of it results from naturally occurring environmental processes.

Radiation that comes from natural environmental sources is called *background radiation*. **Background radiation** *is radiation that comes from natural sources to which living organisms are exposed on a continuing basis.* Numerous sources for background radiation exist, including the following:

1. *Cosmic radiation*: Earth, and all things on it, are constantly bombarded by radiation from outer space. Some cosmic radiation, but not all of it, comes from the sun; sources outside the solar system also exist. ◀
2. *Rocks and minerals*: Trace to larger amounts of thorium and uranium minerals are present in almost all rocks and soil. Building materials, including brick and concrete, also contain small amounts of these substances. Consequently, such radiation exists in all types of buildings, including work environments, schools, and homes.
3. *Food and drink*: The main radioactive substance present in food and drink is potassium-40. Potassium-40 is a naturally occurring radioactive isotope of potassium (0.012% abundance; Section 3-3) and is therefore found in all potassium-containing foods. It is estimated that, on average, 30 mg of potassium-40 is present in a human body.
4. *Radon seepage in buildings*: Radon-222 exposure, which is an airborne exposure, is the greatest background radiation exposure source for most individuals. The focus on relevancy feature Chemical Connections 11-B—The Indoor Radon-222 Problem—considers in further detail several aspects of radon-222 exposure experienced by individuals living in the United States.

Figure 11-12 quantifies exposure amounts for various sources of background radiation and also gives data for radiation exposure arising from human activities, which include (1) medical X-rays, (2) nuclear medicine, (3) consumer products, and (4) miscellaneous sources, including occupational exposure, nuclear fallout from

▶ *Exposure to cosmic radiation increases with altitude. At higher elevations, there are fewer molecules present in the atmosphere and thus there are fewer molecules available to absorb incoming radiation. Passengers in an airplane receive increased exposure to cosmic radiation during the flight. People who live at an altitude of 5000 feet receive approximately twice the exposure to cosmic radiation as those who live at sea level.*

CHEMICAL CONNECTIONS 11-B

The Indoor Radon-222 Problem

More than 80% of the radiation exposure that an average American experiences comes from naturally occurring environmental processes. Foremost among these processes, both in terms of amount and seriousness of radiation exposure, is the generation of radon gas. Radon gas accounts for more than half the background radioactivity on Earth (Figure 11-12).

The element radon, located in Group VIIIA of the periodic table, is a member of the noble-gas family and thus is a very unreactive substance. Substances that are chemically unreactive are not ordinarily thought of as posing any health risks. However, radon's nuclear properties—its radioactivity—causes it to be a health risk. More than 20 isotopes of radon exist, all of which are radioactive. Radon-222, the radon isotope with the longest half-life (3.82 days), is the isotope of most concern relative to human exposure. Its source is uranium ores and minerals. Radon-222 is one of the intermediate decay products in the uranium-238 decay series (Figure 11-6).

Because uranium compounds are present in trace amounts in many types of rocks and soils, radon-222 (and its decay products) are found almost everywhere in our environment. What distinguishes radon-222 from other decay products in the uranium-238 decay series is the fact that it is a gas whereas other decay products are solids. In the gaseous state, radon-222 readily migrates from soil and rocks into the surrounding air and sometimes into water sources. Radon gas is sparingly soluble in water.

In outdoor situations, radon-222 gas is not considered a major health hazard because it dissipates into the air. However, indoor exposure to radon-222, where ventilation is restricted, is a serious hazard because the radon can be *directly* inhaled by those living or working in the indoor space. If a person inhales air containing radon and then exhales before the radon-222 undergoes radioactive decay, no harm is done. If, however, the radon-222 undergoes decay in the lungs, five solid-state decay products are generated in rapid sequence and can become attached to lung tissue. The first four solids are short-lived (see accompanying diagram), but the fifth, lead-210, has a half-life of 20.6 years and so can remain in the lungs for an extended period of time. Of importance is the radiation aspect of the decay scheme from radon-222 to lead-210. A rapid burst of radiation (two alpha particles, two beta particles, and then a third alpha particle) is produced, as shown in the accompanying diagram.

Additional radiation exposure related to radon-222 can *indirectly* occur by breathing air in which radon-222 decay has already occurred. The solid radioactive products from the radon-222 decay adhere to airborne dust and smoke, which are inhaled into the lungs and deposited in the respiratory tract where the solids undergo further alpha particle decay.

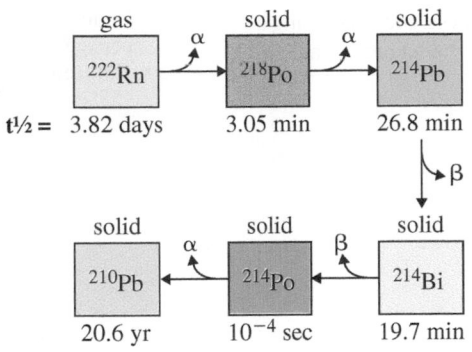

Serious radon-222 contamination of homes has been found to occur in several areas in the United States, where the natural uranium content of the soil is high. The radon-222 seeps into the homes through cracks in the cement foundation or through other openings and then accumulates in basements. Because of this problem, commercially available kits for testing radon in the home are now readily available in stores. As radon-222 awareness increases, an increasing number of home buyers ask for a determination of radon levels before buying a house.

Because of their alpha particle emissions, the decay products of radon-222 that accumulate in the lungs are able to irradiate tissue, damage cells, and possibly lead to lung cancer. The U.S. Environmental Protection Agency (EPA) estimates that 10% of all lung cancer deaths are related to radon-222 exposure. Radon-222 exposure is believed to be the leading cause of lung cancer among nonsmokers (30% of deaths).

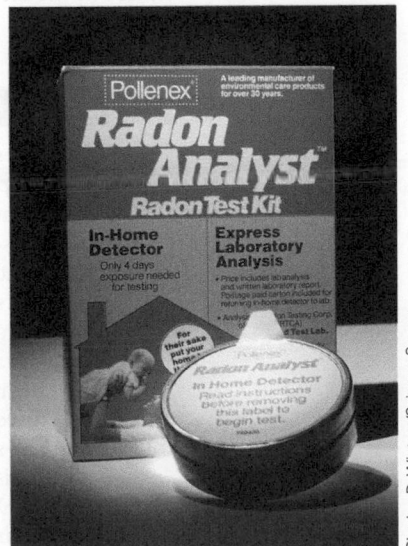

A commercially available kit to test for radon gas in the home.

Figure 11-12 Components of the estimated annual radiation exposure (in millirems) of an average American. Individual exposures vary widely, but most such radiation comes from natural sources, the largest single contributor being radon gas.

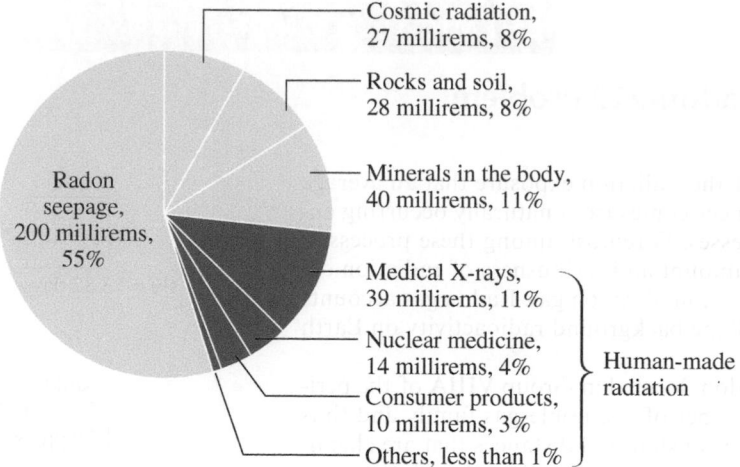

Cosmic radiation, 27 millirems, 8%

Rocks and soil, 28 millirems, 8%

Minerals in the body, 40 millirems, 11%

Medical X-rays, 39 millirems, 11%

Nuclear medicine, 14 millirems, 4%

Consumer products, 10 millirems, 3%

Others, less than 1%

Human-made radiation

Radon seepage, 200 millirems, 55%

weapons testing, and nuclear power plants. The estimates of per capita radiation exposure given in Figure 11-12 are averages for all Americans; the actual exposure of individuals varies according to where they live and work, their medical history, and other factors.

Comparing the values in Figure 11-12 with those of Table 11-3, taking into account that the units in the former are millirems and those in the latter are rems, shows that the current dosage levels received by the general population are very small compared with those known to cause serious radiation sickness.

With low-level radiation exposure, chromosome damage rather than cell death can occur. If the damaged genetic material repairs itself improperly, then new, abnormal cells are produced when the cells replicate.

Cells that reproduce at a rapid rate, such as those in bone marrow, lymph nodes, and embryonic tissue, are the most sensitive to radiation damage. The sensitivity of embryonic tissue to radiation damage is the reason why pregnant women need to be protected from radiation exposure. One of the first signs of overexposure to radiation is a drop in red blood count. This is a direct consequence of the sensitivity of bone marrow, the site of red blood cell formation, to radiation.

Section 11-10 Quick Quiz

1. The largest source of radiation exposure from all sources, for the average American, is
   a. nuclear power plant emissions
   b. dental and medical X-rays
   c. natural sources
   d. no correct response
2. The largest source of background radiation exposure, for the average American, is
   a. cosmic radiation
   b. rocks and minerals
   c. radon gas
   d. no correct response
3. The largest source of radiation exposure from human activities, for the average American, is
   a. medical X-rays
   b. nuclear imaging processes
   c. nuclear power plants
   d. no correct response

Answers: 1. c; 2. c; 3. a

11-11 Nuclear Medicine

LEARNING FOCUS

Be familiar with the basic principles behind the use of radionuclides in diagnostic and therapeutic nuclear medicine.

Nuclear medicine *is a field of medicine in which radionuclides are used for diagnostic and therapeutic purposes.* In diagnostic applications, technicians use small amounts of radionuclides whose progress through the body or localization in specific organs can be followed. Larger quantities of radionuclides are used in therapeutic applications. ◄

Diagnostic Uses for Radionuclides

The fundamental chemical principle behind the use of radionuclides in diagnostic medical work is the fact that a radioactive nuclide of an element has the same chemical properties as a nonradioactive nuclide of the element. Thus, body chemistry is not upset by the presence of a small amount of a radioactive substance whose nonradioactive form is already present in the body. ◄

The criteria used in selecting radionuclides for diagnostic procedures include the following:

1. At low concentrations (to minimize radiation damage), the radionuclide must be detectable by instrumentation placed outside the body. Nearly all diagnostic radionuclides are gamma emitters because the penetrating power of alpha and beta particles is too low.
2. The radionuclide must have a short half-life so that the intensity of the radiation is sufficiently great to be detected. A short half-life also limits the time period of radiation exposure.
3. The radionuclide must have a known mechanism for elimination from the body so that the material does not remain in the body indefinitely.
4. The chemical properties of the radionuclide must be such that it is compatible with normal body chemistry. It must be able to be selectively transmitted to the part or system of the body that is under study.

The following examples illustrate the diverse uses of radionuclides in procedures for diagnosis of disease or malfunction in the human body.

- *Location of Sites of Infection.* Abscesses and additional sites of infection can be located using gallium-67, a gamma ray emitter. The gallium-67 is incorporated into a compound that binds to white blood cells. The tagged white blood cells, as well as untagged white blood cells, migrate to sites of infection. The tagged white blood cells enable the infection site to be located because of the gamma ray emission that occurs from the gallium-67.
- *Diagnosis of Impaired Heart Muscle.* The radionuclide thallium-201 has been found to be effective in helping to diagnose heart disease. This radionuclide, when injected into the blood, is found to have a particular affinity for heart muscle. Only heart muscle tissue that receives a normal flow of blood will bond to the thallium-201. This leads to the detection of heart tissue that lacks sufficient blood because of narrowed arteries.
- *Location of Impaired Circulation.* Sodium-24 is used to follow the circulation of blood in the body. A small amount of this radionuclide is injected into the bloodstream in the form of a sodium chloride solution. The movement of the sodium-24 through the circulatory system is followed with radiation detection equipment. If it takes longer than normal for the radionuclide to show up at a particular spot in the body, this is an indication that the circulation is impaired at that spot.

▶ *An additional use for radionuclides in medicine, besides diagnostic and therapeutic uses, is as a source of power (see Section 11-12). Cardiac pacemakers powered by plutonium-238 can remain in a patient for longer periods than those powered by chemical batteries, and the additional surgery required to replace batteries is not needed.*

▶ *Radionuclides used in diagnostic nuclear medicine are often called* radioactive tracers. *Techniques in which radioactive tracers are used are called* nuclear imaging *procedures.*

Figure 11-13 Iodine-123 is the radionuclide involved in obtaining these thyroid gland scans. The scan on the left, which shows uniform iodine-123 uptake, is considered a normal scan. The scan on the right shows a thyroid gland in which the right lobe is not functioning properly.

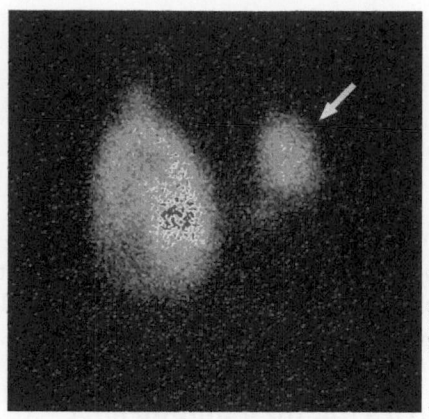

- *Assessment of Thyroid Activity.* Administering iodine-123, used in the form of a sodium iodide solution, gives information about the functioning of the thyroid gland. The radioactive iodide is absorbed by the thyroid at a rate related to the activity of the gland. If a hypothyroid condition exists, then the amount accumulated is less than normal; if a hyperthyroid condition exists, then a greater-than-average amount accumulates. Figure 11-13 shows the contrast between a normal and an abnormal thyroid scan.

- *Determination of Tumor Size and Shape.* The size and shape of organs, as well as the presence of tumors, can be determined in some situations by scanning the organ in which a radionuclide tends to concentrate. Iodine-131 and technetium-99m are used to generate thyroid and brain scans, respectively. In the brain, technetium-99m, in the form of a polyatomic ion (TcO_4^-), concentrates in brain tumors more than in normal brain tissue; this helps radiologists determine the presence, size, and location of brain tumors. The radionuclide technetium-99m is the most commonly used radionuclide in diagnostic medical work. Further information about its chemistry and how it is obtained is found in the focus on relevancy feature Chemical Connections 11-C—Technetium-99m: The "Workhorse" of Nuclear Medicine.

- *Assessment of Bile Duct Obstruction* The presence of gallstones in the gallbladder can be detected using ultrasound procedures or X-rays. However, gallstones that have moved into the bile duct, causing blockage there, cannot be detected using these methods. The presence of such blockage is a vital consideration in gallbladder surgery procedures.

  A new method for detecting bile duct obstruction, using technetium-99m, is now in use. Bound to an organic carrier molecule, injected technetium-99m rapidly moves to the liver where the organic molecule is metabolized. Metabolism products are carried in bile to the gallbladder. Stimulation of the gallbladder (by an additional injection) moves the bile to the bile duct (if it is open). Failure of the bile to enter the bile duct indicates an obstruction. The movement of the technetium-99m through the body is followed by monitoring the gamma ray emissions it produces.

Table 11-4 lists a number of radionuclides that are used in diagnostic procedures. The half-life of the radionuclide, the body locations wherein it concentrates, and its diagnostic function are also given.

Therapeutic Uses for Radionuclides

The objectives in therapeutic radionuclide use are entirely different from those for diagnostic procedures. The main objective in the therapeutic use of radionuclides is to *selectively destroy* abnormal (usually cancerous) cells. The radionuclide is often, but

Technetium-99m: The "Workhorse" of Nuclear Medicine

The designation "workhorse of nuclear medicine" is appropriate for the radionuclide technetium-99m (^{99m}Tc). Approximately 80%–85% of the 23–25 million doses of diagnostic radionuclides received by patients in the United States each year involve tissue-targeting agents in which ^{99m}Tc is present.

The *m* in the designation ^{99m}Tc, which stands for *metastable,* indicates that this radionuclide is in a higher energy state than normal (an excited state). In most cases, metastable states revert to their normal lower energy states (ground states) in a matter of seconds. Such is not the case for ^{99m}Tc. The half-life for the excited state is 6.0 hours (a very unusual occurrence). When transition to the ground state does occur, the excess energy associated with the metastable state is lost in the form of a gamma ray. The energy of this gamma ray is ideally suited for detection using imaging equipment.

$$^{99m}\text{Tc} \longrightarrow {}^{99}\text{Tc} + \text{gamma ray}$$

No alpha or beta radiation is produced during this transition; ^{99m}Tc is a pure gamma emitter.

The fact that both the *physical* half-life (6.0 hours) and the *biological* half-life (24 hours) of ^{99m}Tc are very short leads to a very fast clearing time for this radionuclide from the body after an imaging process. (A *biological* half-life relates to the time a radionuclide remains in the body.) Also, the short physical half-life is still long enough to allow for adequate preparation of the needed tissue-targeting agent that contains the ^{99m}Tc.

The source for ^{99m}Tc is ^{99}Mo. (Molybdenum is the element preceding technetium in the periodic table.) Nuclear reactors specifically designed for production of medical isotopes produce ^{99}Mo from the decay of neutron-bombarded ^{235}U (Section 11-12). The half-life of ^{99}Mo is 2.75 days.

Hospitals and clinics that have nuclear medicine facilities receive overnight shipments of ^{99}Mo in the form of the molybdate ion (MoO_4^{2-}) absorbed on an alumina (Al_2O_3) column. As the $^{99}MoO_4^{2-}$ decays, pertechnetate ion ($^{99m}TcO_4^{-}$) is produced.

$$^{99}\text{MoO}_4^{2-} \longrightarrow {}^{99m}\text{TcO}_4^{-} + {}_{-1}^{0}\beta$$

The TcO_4^{-} ion is separated from its MoO_4^{2-} source based on different affinities of the two ions for the alumina column. Because of its lesser negative charge, the TcO_4^{-} ion is held less tightly to the column than is MoO_4^{2-}. Pouring normal saline solution through the column elutes the soluble TcO_4^{-} ion. The 2.75-day half-life of the ^{99}Mo means that the ^{99}Mo cannot be stockpiled. Once received, it must be used almost immediately.

Technetium, element 43, is the lowest-atomic-numbered element that does not occur in nature. All isotopes are radioactive and all are laboratory produced. It is a transition metal (Section 3-9) with a number of stable oxidation states (Section 9-2), and this gives it a diversified chemistry. It has the ability to react with many different organic substances, creating many different tissue-targeting agents. Targeted systems of the human body include cardiac and gastric tissue, kidney, blood, bone, and brain. There are more than 100 different ways in which technetium-99m can be used in diagnostic nuclear medicine.

Preparation of an injectable technetium-99m sample using a generator (held in the clamp) that contains molybdenum-99 (produced in nuclear reactors).

Syringe apparatus used in injecting radioactive technetium-99 into the bloodstream of a patient.

▶ **Table 11-4 Selected Radionuclides Used in Diagnostic Procedures**

Nuclide	Half-Life	Part of Body Affected	Use in Diagnosis
barium-131	11.6 days	bone	detection of bone tumors
gallium-67	3.2 days	blood	detection of sites of infection
iodine-123	13 hours	thyroid	assessment of thyroid gland activity
iron-59	45 days	blood	evaluation of iron metabolism in blood
phosphorus-32	14.3 days	blood breast	blood studies assessment of breast carcinoma
potassium-42	12.4 hours	tissue	determination of intercellular spaces in fluids
sodium-24	15.0 hours	blood	detection of circulatory problems; assessment of peripheral vascular disease
technetium-99m*	6.0 hours	brain spleen thyroid lung gall bladder	detection of brain tumors, hemorrhages, or blood clots measurement of size and shape of spleen measurement of size and shape of thyroid location of blood clots bile duct obstruction
thallium-201	3.0 days	blood	assessment of normal flow of blood in heart muscle

*The form in which the technetium-99m is administered, such as a phosphate or a chloride, determines its target location; e.g., technetium-99m as a phosphate is adsorbed on the surface of bone.

▶ *Abnormal cells are more susceptible to radiation damage than normal cells because abnormal cells divide more frequently.*

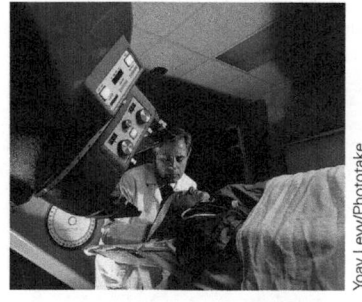

Yoav Levy/Phototake

Figure 11-14 Cobalt-60 is used as a source of gamma radiation in radiation therapy.

not always, placed within the body. Therapeutic radionuclides implanted in the body are usually alpha or beta emitters because an intense dose of radiation in a small localized area is needed. ◀

A commonly used implantation radionuclide that is effective in the localized treatment of tumors is yttrium-90, a beta emitter with a half-life of 64 hours. Yttrium-90 salts are implanted by inserting small, hollow needles into the tumor.

External, high-energy beams of gamma radiation are also extensively used in the treatment of certain cancers. Cobalt-60 is frequently used for this purpose; a beam of radiation is focused on the small area of the body where the tumor is located (Figure 11-14). This therapy usually causes some radiation sickness because normal cells are also affected, but to a lesser extent. The operating principle here is that abnormal cells are more susceptible to radiation damage than normal cells. Radiation sickness is the price paid for abnormal-cell destruction. Table 11-5 lists some radionuclides that are used in therapy.

▶ **Table 11-5 Some Radionuclides Used in Radiation Therapy**

Nuclide	Half-Life	Type of Emitter	Use in Therapy
cobalt-60	5.3 years	gamma	external source of radiation in treatment of cancer
iodine-131	8 days	beta, gamma	treatment of thyroid cancer
phosphorus-32	14.3 days	beta, gamma	treatment of some types of leukemia and widespread carcinomas
radium-226	1620 years	alpha, gamma	used in implantation cancer therapy
radon-222	3.8 days	alpha, gamma	used in treatment of uterine, cervical, oral, and bladder cancers
yttrium-90	64 hours	beta, gamma	implantation therapy

1. Which of the following is *not* a general property of radionuclides used is diagnostic medical procedures?
   a. must be detectable by instrumentation placed outside the body
   b. must have a known mechanism for elimination from the body
   c. must have a long half-life
   d. no correct response
2. The "most used" radionuclide in diagnostic medicine is
   a. technetium-99m
   b. sodium-24
   c. iodine-123
   d. no correct response
3. The implantation of a radionuclide in living tissue is a common procedure in
   a. therapeutic, but not diagnostic, medicine
   b. diagnostic, but not therapeutic, medicine
   c. both diagnostic and therapeutic medicine
   d. no correct response

Answers: 1. c; 2. a; 3. a

11-12 Nuclear Fission and Nuclear Fusion

LEARNING FOCUS

Describe the general characteristics of and importance of both *nuclear fission* reactions and *nuclear fusion* reactions.

Any treatment of the topic of nuclear chemistry would be incomplete without mentioning two additional types of nuclear reactions that are used as sources of energy: nuclear fission and nuclear fusion.

Fission Reactions

Nuclear fission *is a nuclear reaction in which a large nucleus (high atomic number) splits into two medium-sized nuclei with the release of several free neutrons and a large amount of energy.* The most important nucleus that undergoes fission is uranium-235. Bombardment of this nucleus with neutrons causes it to split into two fragments. Characteristics of the uranium-235 fission reaction include the following:

1. There is no unique way in which the uranium-235 nucleus splits. Thus many different, lighter elements are produced during uranium-235 fission reactions. The following are examples of the ways in which this fission process proceeds.

$$^{235}_{92}U + ^{1}_{0}n \begin{cases} ^{135}_{53}I + ^{97}_{39}Y + 4\,^{1}_{0}n \\ ^{139}_{56}Ba + ^{94}_{36}Kr + 3\,^{1}_{0}n \\ ^{131}_{50}Sn + ^{103}_{42}Mo + 2\,^{1}_{0}n \\ ^{139}_{54}Xe + ^{95}_{38}Sr + 2\,^{1}_{0}n \end{cases}$$

2. Very large amounts of energy, which are many times greater than that released by ordinary radioactive decay, are emitted during the fission process. It is this large release of energy that makes nuclear fission of uranium-235 the important process that it is. In general, the term *nuclear energy* is used to refer to the energy released during a nuclear fission process. An older term for this energy is *atomic energy.*
3. Neutrons, which are reactants in the fission process, are also produced as products. The number of neutrons produced per fission depends on the way in which the nucleus splits; it ranges from 2 to 4 (as can be seen from the foregoing fission equations). On the average, 2.4 neutrons are produced per fission. The significance of the neutrons that are produced is that they can cause the fission process to continue by colliding with further uranium-235 nuclei. Figure 11-15 shows the chain reaction that can occur once the fission process is started.

Figure 11-15 A fission chain reaction is caused by further reaction of the neutrons produced during fission.

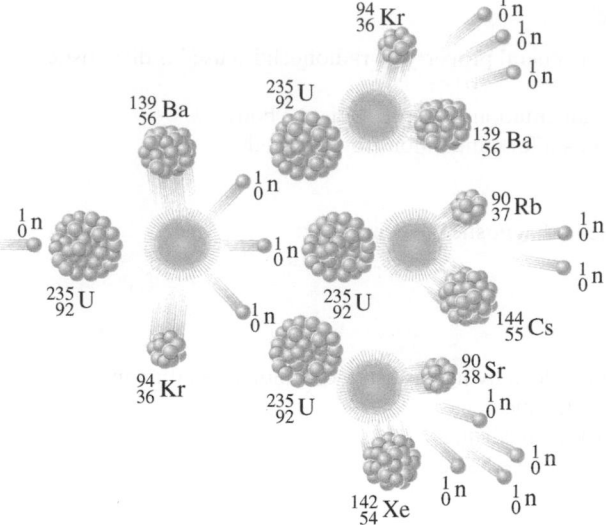

The process of nuclear fission—or "splitting the atom," as it is called in popularized science—can be carried out in both an uncontrolled and a controlled manner. The key to this control lies in what happens to the neutrons produced during fission. Do they react further, causing further fission, or do they escape into the surroundings? If the majority of produced neutrons react further (Figure 11-15), an uncontrolled nuclear reaction (an atomic bomb) results (see Figure 11-16). When only a few neutrons react further (on the average, one per fission), the fission reaction self-propagates in a controlled manner.

The process of *controlled* nuclear fission is the basis for the operation of nuclear power plants that are used to produce electricity (see Figure 11-17). The reaction is controlled with rods that absorb excess neutrons (so that they cannot cause unwanted fissions) and with moderating substances that decrease the speed of the neutrons. The energy produced during the fission process, which appears as heat, is used to operate steam-powered electricity-generating equipment.

Fusion Reactions

Another type of nuclear reaction, nuclear fusion, produces even more energy than nuclear fission. **Nuclear fusion** *is a nuclear reaction in which two small nuclei are collided together to produce a larger nucleus with the release of a large amount of energy.* This process is essentially the opposite of nuclear fission. In order for fusion to occur, a very high temperature (several hundred million degrees) is required.

Figure 11-16 Enormous amounts of energy are released in the explosion of a nuclear fission bomb.

Historical/Corbis

Figure 11-17 A nuclear power plant. The cooling towers at the Trojan nuclear power plant in Oregon dominates the landscape. The nuclear reactor is housed in the dome-shaped enclosure.

Nuclear fusion is the process by which the sun generates its energy (see Figure 11-18). Within the sun, hydrogen-1 nuclei are converted to helium-4 nuclei with the release of extraordinarily large amounts of energy. ◀

The use of nuclear fusion on Earth might seem impossible because of the high temperatures required. It has, however, been accomplished in a hydrogen bomb. In such a weapon, a *fission* bomb is used to achieve the high temperatures needed to start the following process:

$$\ce{^3_1H + ^2_1H \longrightarrow ^4_2He + ^1_0n}$$

The use of nuclear fusion as a *controlled* (peaceful) energy source is a very active area of current scientific research. "Harnessing" this type of nuclear reaction would have numerous advantages:

1. Unlike the by-products of fission reactions, the by-products of fusion reactions are stable (nonradioactive) nuclides. Thus the problem of storing radioactive wastes does not arise.
2. The major fuel under study for controlled fusion is $\ce{^2_1H}$ (called deuterium), a hydrogen isotope that can be readily extracted from ocean water (0.015% of all hydrogen atoms are $\ce{^2_1H}$). Just 0.005 km^3 of ocean water contains enough $\ce{^2_1H}$ to supply the United States with all the energy it needs for 1 year!

▶ *At the high temperature of fusion reactions, electrons completely separate from nuclei. Neutral atoms cannot exist. This high-temperature, gaslike mixture of nuclei and electrons is called a* plasma *and is considered by some scientists to represent a fourth state of matter.*

Figure 11-18 A close-up view of the sun. The process of nuclear fusion maintains the interior of the sun at a temperature of approximately 15 million degrees.

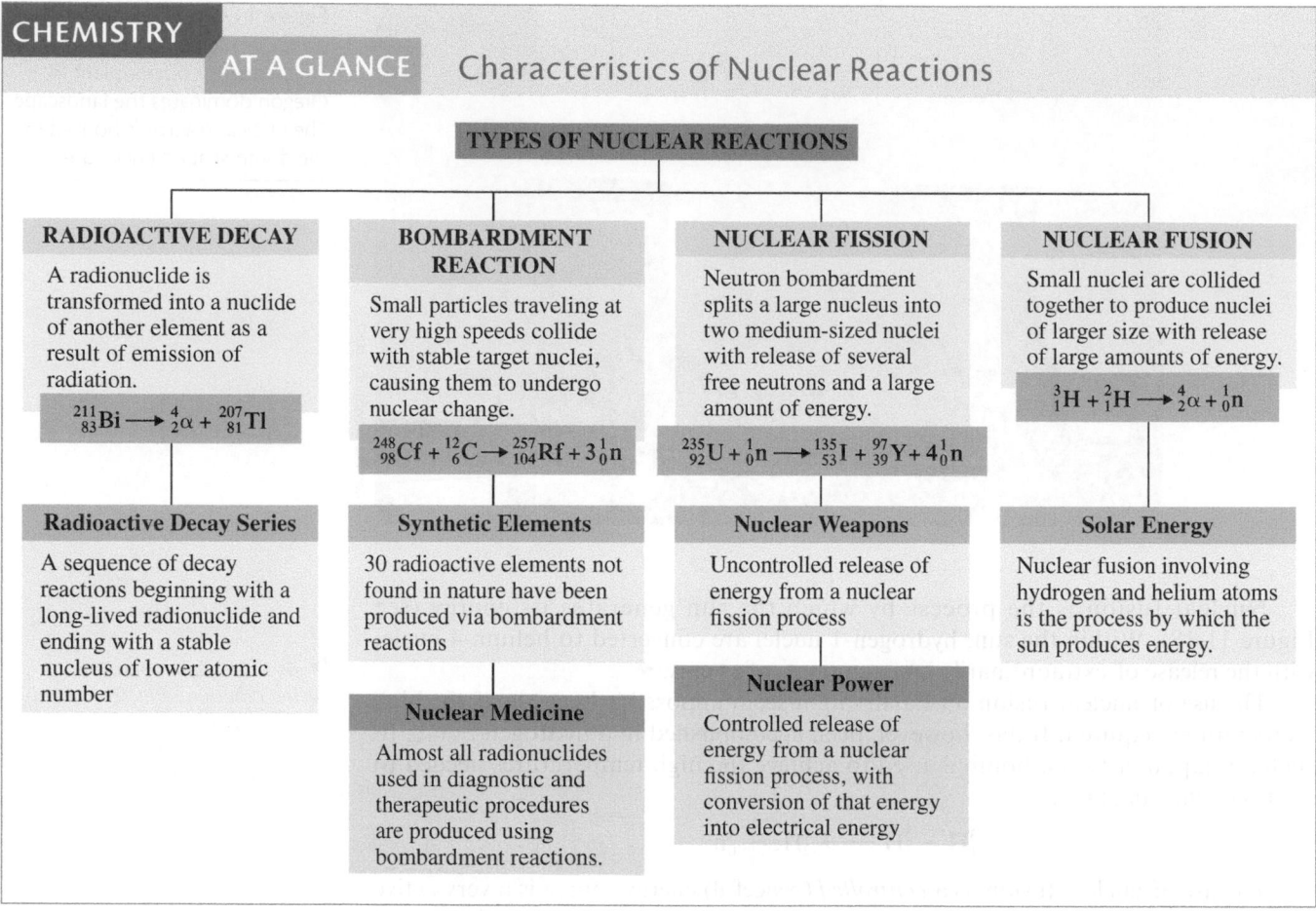

CHEMISTRY AT A GLANCE — Characteristics of Nuclear Reactions

TYPES OF NUCLEAR REACTIONS

RADIOACTIVE DECAY

A radionuclide is transformed into a nuclide of another element as a result of emission of radiation.

$$^{211}_{83}\text{Bi} \longrightarrow {}^{4}_{2}\alpha + {}^{207}_{81}\text{Tl}$$

Radioactive Decay Series

A sequence of decay reactions beginning with a long-lived radionuclide and ending with a stable nucleus of lower atomic number

BOMBARDMENT REACTION

Small particles traveling at very high speeds collide with stable target nuclei, causing them to undergo nuclear change.

$$^{248}_{98}\text{Cf} + {}^{12}_{6}\text{C} \longrightarrow {}^{257}_{104}\text{Rf} + 3{}^{1}_{0}\text{n}$$

Synthetic Elements

30 radioactive elements not found in nature have been produced via bombardment reactions

Nuclear Medicine

Almost all radionuclides used in diagnostic and therapeutic procedures are produced using bombardment reactions.

NUCLEAR FISSION

Neutron bombardment splits a large nucleus into two medium-sized nuclei with release of several free neutrons and a large amount of energy.

$$^{235}_{92}\text{U} + {}^{1}_{0}\text{n} \longrightarrow {}^{135}_{53}\text{I} + {}^{97}_{39}\text{Y} + 4{}^{1}_{0}\text{n}$$

Nuclear Weapons

Uncontrolled release of energy from a nuclear fission process

Nuclear Power

Controlled release of energy from a nuclear fission process, with conversion of that energy into electrical energy

NUCLEAR FUSION

Small nuclei are collided together to produce nuclei of larger size with release of large amounts of energy.

$$^{3}_{1}\text{H} + {}^{2}_{1}\text{H} \longrightarrow {}^{4}_{2}\alpha + {}^{1}_{0}\text{n}$$

Solar Energy

Nuclear fusion involving hydrogen and helium atoms is the process by which the sun produces energy.

However, difficult scientific and engineering problems still remain to be solved before controlled fusion is a reality.

Chemistry at a Glance—Characteristics of Nuclear Reactions—summarizes important concepts about the major types of nuclear reactions that have been considered in this chapter.

Section 11-12 Quick Quiz

1. Which of the following statements concerning nuclear *fission* is *incorrect*?
   a. Neutrons are both reactants and products in the fission process.
   b. Uranium-238 is the most important fissionable radionuclide.
   c. Two intermediate-sized nuclides are products in the fission process.
   d. no correct response
2. The reactants for a nuclear *fusion* process are nuclides whose mass, on a relative scale, would be classified as
   a. very low
   b. low intermediate
   c. high intermediate
   d. no correct response
3. Generation of electricity in a nuclear power plant involves
   a. both nuclear fission and nuclear fusion
   b. nuclear fission but not nuclear fusion
   c. nuclear fusion but not nuclear fission
   d. no correct response
4. Generation of energy within the sun involves
   a. both nuclear fission and nuclear fusion
   b. nuclear fission but not nuclear fusion
   c. nuclear fusion but not nuclear fission
   d. no correct response

Answers: 1. b; 2. a; 3. b; 4. c

11-13 Nuclear and Chemical Reactions Compared

LEARNING FOCUS
Contrast the major differences between nuclear reactions and ordinary chemical reactions.

As the discussions in this chapter have shown, nuclear chemistry is quite different from ordinary chemistry. Many of the laws of chemistry must be modified when nuclear reactions are considered. The major differences between nuclear reactions and ordinary chemical reactions are listed in Table 11-6. This table serves as a summary of many of the concepts presented in this chapter.

▶ **Table 11-6 Differences Between Nuclear and Chemical Reactions**

Chemical Reaction	Nuclear Reaction
1. Different isotopes of an element have identical chemical properties.	1. Different isotopes of an element have different nuclear properties.
2. The chemical reactivity of an element depends on the element's state of combination (free element, compound, etc.).	2. The nuclear reactivity of an element is independent of the state of chemical combination.
3. Elements retain their identity in chemical reactions.	3. Elements may be changed into other elements during nuclear reactions.
4. Energy changes that accompany chemical reactions are relatively small.	4. Energy changes that accompany nuclear reactions are a number of orders of magnitude larger than those in chemical reactions.
5. Reaction rates are influenced by temperature, pressure, catalysts, and reactant concentrations.	5. Reaction rates are independent of temperature, pressure, catalysts, and reactant concentrations.

Section 11-13 Quick Quiz

1. Different isotopes of an element have
   a. the same chemical properties but different nuclear properties
   b. the same nuclear properties but different chemical properties
   c. the same chemical properties and the same nuclear properties
   d. no correct response
2. Which of the following is an *incorrect* statement?
   a. Elements maintain their identity in chemical reactions but not in nuclear reactions.
   b. Energy changes in chemical reactions are small compared to those in nuclear reactions.
   c. Reaction rates in chemical reactions are temperature dependent but those in nuclear reactions are not.
   d. no correct response

Answers: 1. a; 2. d

Concepts to Remember

Radioactivity. Some atoms possess nuclei that are unstable. To achieve stability, these unstable nuclei spontaneously emit energy (radiation). Such atoms are said to be radioactive (Section 11-1).

Emissions from radioactive nuclei. The types of radiation emitted by naturally occurring radioactive nuclei are alpha, beta, and gamma. These radiations can be characterized by mass and charge values. Alpha particles carry a positive charge, beta particles carry a negative charge, and gamma radiation has no charge (Section 11-2).

Balanced nuclear equations. The procedures for balancing nuclear equations are different from those for balancing ordinary chemical equations. In nuclear equations, mass numbers and atomic numbers (rather than atoms) balance on both sides (Section 11-3).

Half-life. Every radionuclide decays at a characteristic rate given by its half-life. One half-life is the time required for half of any given quantity of a radioactive substance to undergo decay (Section 11-4).

Bombardment reactions. A bombardment reaction is a nuclear reaction in which small particles traveling at very high speeds are collided with stable nuclei; this causes these nuclei to undergo nuclear change (become unstable). More than 2000 synthetically produced radionuclides that do not occur naturally have been produced by using bombardment reactions (Section 11-5).

Radioactive decay series. The product of the radioactive decay of an unstable nuclide is a nuclide of another element, which may or may not be stable. If it is not stable, it will decay and produce still another nuclide. Further decay will continue until a stable nuclide is formed. Such a sequence of reactions is called a radioactive decay series (Section 11-6).

Detection of radiation. Radiation can be detected by making use of the fact that radiation ionizes atoms and molecules. The Geiger counter operates on this principle. Radiation also affects photographic film in the same way as ordinary light; the film is exposed. Hence film badges are used to record the extent of radiation exposure (Section 11-7).

Chemical effects of radiation. Radiation from radioactive decay is ionizing radiation—radiation with enough energy to remove an electron from an atom or molecule. Interaction of ionizing radiation with matter produces ion pairs, with many ion pairs being produced by a single "particle" of radiation. Free-radical formation usually accompanies ion pair formation. A free radical is a chemical species that contains an unpaired electron. Free radicals, very reactive species, rapidly interact with other chemical species nearby, causing many of the undesirable effects that, in living organisms, are associated with radiation exposure (Section 11-8).

Biochemical effects of radiation. The biochemical effects of radiation depend on the energy, ionizing ability, and penetrating ability of the radiation. Alpha particles exhibit the greatest ionizing effect, and gamma rays have the greatest penetrating ability (Section 11-9).

Sources of radiation exposure. Both natural and human-generated sources of low-level radiation exposure exist, with natural sources accounting for almost 80% of exposure (on the average). Current dosage levels received by the general population are very small compared with those known to cause serious radiation sickness (Section 11-10).

Nuclear medicine. Radionuclides are used in medicine for both diagnosis and therapy. The choice of radionuclide is dictated by the purpose as well as the target organ. Bombardment reactions are used to produce the nuclides used in medicine; such nuclides all have short half-lives (Section 11-11).

Nuclear fission. Nuclear fission occurs when fissionable nuclides are bombarded with neutrons. The nuclides split into two fragments of about the same size. Also, more neutrons and large amounts of energy are produced. Nuclear fission is the process by which nuclear power plants generate energy (Section 11-12).

Nuclear fusion. In nuclear fusion, small nuclei fuse to make heavier nuclei. Nuclear fusion is the process by which the sun generates its energy (Section 11-12).

Exercises and Problems

Exercises and problems are arranged in matched pairs with the two members of a pair addressing the same concept(s). The answer to the odd-numbered member of a pair is given at the back of the book. Problems denoted with a ▲ involve concepts found not only in the section under consideration but also concepts found in one or more earlier sections of the chapter.

Notation for Nuclides (Section 11-1)

11-1 How many protons and neutrons are present in each of the following nuclides?
  a. $^{10}_{4}$Be   b. $^{23}_{11}$Na   c. silver-108   d. S-34

11-2 How many protons and neutrons are present in each of the following nuclides?
  a. $^{40}_{20}$Ca   b. $^{65}_{29}$Cu   c. gold-197   d. P-31

11-3 For each of the following pairings of nuclear notations indicate whether the two members of the pair denote the same nuclide?
  a. nitrogen-14 and $^{14}_{7}$N
  b. Al-27 and $^{28}_{13}$Al
  c. chlorine-35 and Cl-35
  d. O-18 and (18 protons + 18 neutrons)

11-4 For each of the following pairings of nuclear notations indicate whether the two members of the pair denote the same nuclide?
  a. magnesium-25 and $^{27}_{12}$Mg
  b. Si-29 and $^{29}_{14}$Si
  c. argon-40 and Ar-40
  d. Br-35 and (35 protons + 35 neutrons)

11-5 What physical manifestation indicates that an atom possesses an unstable nucleus?

11-6 What is the limit for nuclear stability in terms of number of nucleons present in a nucleus?

11-7 How do the neutron-to-proton ratios compare for stable nuclei of low atomic number and stable nuclei of high atomic number?

11-8 Indicate whether or not all isotopes would be radioactive for each of the following elements.
  a. $_{76}$Os   b. $_{86}$Rn   c. $_{96}$Cm   d. $_{104}$Sg

The Nature of Radioactive Emissions (Section 11-2)

11-9 Supply a complete symbol, with superscript and subscript, for each of the following types of radiation.
  a. Alpha particle   b. Beta particle   c. Gamma ray

11-10 Give the charge and mass (in amu) of each of the following types of radiation.
  a. Alpha particle   b. Beta particle   c. Gamma ray

11-11 State the composition of an alpha particle in terms of protons and neutrons.

11-12 What is the relationship between a beta particle and an electron?

Equations for Radioactive Decay (Section 11-3)

11-13 Write balanced nuclear equations for the alpha decay of each of the following nuclides.
  a. $^{200}_{84}$Po   b. Curium-240
  c. $^{244}_{96}$Cm   d. Uranium-238

11-14 Write balanced nuclear equations for the alpha decay of each of the following nuclides.
  a. $^{229}_{90}$Th   b. Bismuth-210
  c. $^{152}_{64}$Gd   d. Americium-243

11-15 Write balanced nuclear equations for the beta decay of each of the following nuclides.
  a. $^{10}_{4}$Be   b. Carbon-14
  c. $^{21}_{9}$F   d. Sodium-25

11-16 Write balanced nuclear equations for the beta decay of each of the following nuclides.
    a. $^{77}_{32}Ge$ b. Uranium-235
    c. $^{16}_{7}N$ d. Iron-60

11-17 What is the effect of alpha decay on the
    a. atomic number of the parent nuclide
    b. mass number of the parent nuclide

11-18 What is the effect of beta decay on the
    a. atomic number of the parent nuclide
    b. mass number of the parent nuclide

11-19 Classify each of the following decay reactions as alpha decay or beta decay.
    a. polonium-210 decays to lead-206
    b. thorium-225 decays to protactinium-225
    c. parent = Pt-190; daughter = Os-186
    d. parent = O-19; daughter = F-19

11-20 Classify each of the following decay reactions as alpha decay or beta decay.
    a. potassium-40 decays to calcium-40
    b. lead-204 decays to mercury-200
    c. parent = U-238; daughter = Th-234
    d. parent = Rh-104; daughter = Pd-104

11-21 Write a balanced nuclear equation for each of the reactions in Problem 11-19.

11-22 Write a balanced nuclear equation for each of the reactions in Problem 11-20.

11-23 Write nuclear equations for each of the following radioactive decay processes.
    a. Beta emission produces mercury-199 as a product.
    b. Palladium-109 undergoes beta emission.
    c. Alpha emission produces terbium-148 as a product.
    d. Fermium-249 undergoes alpha emission.

11-24 Write nuclear equations for each of the following radioactive decay processes.
    a. Beta emission produces thallium-206 as a product.
    b. Cadmium-120 undergoes beta emission.
    c. Alpha emission produces plutonium-241 as a product.
    d. Radium-226 undergoes alpha emission.

Rate of Radioactive Decay (Section 11-4)

11-25 A radionuclide has a half-life of 6.0 hr. What fraction of the atoms in a sample of this radionuclide will remain undecayed after the following times?
    a. 12 hr   b. 36 hr
    c. 3 half-lives   d. 6 half-lives

11-26 A radionuclide has a half-life of 5.0 min. What fraction of the atoms in a sample of this radionuclide will remain undecayed after the following times?
    a. 20 min   b. 30 min
    c. 3 half-lives   d. 8 half-lives

11-27 Determine the half-life of a radionuclide if after 5.4 days the fraction of undecayed nuclides present is
    a. 1/16   b. 1/64
    c. 1/256   d. 1/1024

11-28 Determine the half-life of a radionuclide if after 3.2 days the fraction of undecayed nuclides present is
    a. 1/8   b. 1/128
    c. 1/32   d. 1/512

11-29 Fill in the blanks in each line of the following table. The first line is already completed as an example.

	Time Elapsed	Half-Life	Fraction Undecayed	Fraction Decayed
	3.0 hr	1.0 hr	1/8	7/8
a.		2.0 hr	1/4	
b.		3.0 hr		3/4
c.	4.0 hr			15/16
d.	5.0 hr	5.0 hr		

11-30 Fill in the blanks in each line of the following table. The first line is already completed as an example.

	Time Elapsed	Half-Life	Fraction Undecayed	Fraction Decayed
	6.0 min	3.0 min	1/4	3/4
a.	2.0 min		1/4	
b.	8.0 min	2.0 min		
c.		2.0 min		7/8
d.	2.0 min			1/2

11-31 Iodine-125 has a half-life of 60 days. How long, in days, will it take for the radiation level of an iodine-125 sample to drop to
    a. one-fourth its original level
    b. 1/16 its original level

11-32 Fluorine-18 has a half-life of 110 minutes. How long, in minutes, will it take for the radiation level of a fluorine-18 sample to drop to
    a. one-eighth its original level
    b. 1/32 its original level

11-33 The half-life of Na-24 is 15.0 hours.
    a. How many grams of Na-24 in a 4.00 g sample of this nuclide will have decayed after 60.0 hours?
    b. How many hours are required to reduce the amount of Na-24 present in a 28.0 mg sample to 7.0 mg?

11-34 The half-life of Sr-90 is 28 years.
    a. How many grams of Sr-90 in a 8.00 g sample of this nuclide will have decayed after 84 years?
    b. How many hours are required to reduce the amount of Sr-90 present in a 80.0 mg sample to 10.0 mg?

11-35 Silicon-34 decays to phosphorus-34 through beta particle emission. Based on the following diagram, in which yellow spheres represent silicon-34 nuclides and red spheres represent phosphorus-34 nuclides, how many half-lives have elapsed for the sample?

11-36 Platinum-192 decays to osmium-188 through alpha particle emission. Based on the following diagram, in which yellow spheres represent platinum-192 nuclides and red spheres represent osmium-188 nuclides, how many half-lives have elapsed for the sample?

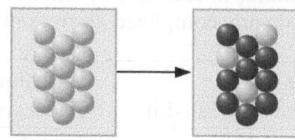

Bombardment Reactions (Section 11-5)

11-37 Approximately how many laboratory-produced radionuclides are known?

11-38 How does the number of laboratory-produced radionuclides compare with the number of naturally occurring nuclides?

11-39 What is the highest-atomic-numbered naturally occurring element?

11-40 What is the highest-atomic-numbered element for which nonradioactive isotopes exist?

11-41 Supply the missing nuclear symbol in each of the following equations for bombardment reactions.
a. $^{24}_{12}Mg + ? \rightarrow ^{27}_{14}Si + ^{1}_{0}n$
b. $^{27}_{13}Al + ^{2}_{1}H \rightarrow ? + ^{4}_{2}\alpha$
c. $^{9}_{4}Be + ? \rightarrow ^{12}_{6}C + ^{1}_{0}n$
d. $^{6}_{3}Li + ? \rightarrow ^{4}_{2}He + ^{3}_{2}He$

11-42 Supply the missing nuclear symbol in each of the following equations for bombardment reactions.
a. $? + ^{4}_{2}\alpha \rightarrow ^{250}_{99}Es + ^{3}_{1}H$
b. $^{14}_{7}N + ^{4}_{2}\alpha \rightarrow ? + ^{1}_{1}H$
c. $^{12}_{6}C + ^{2}_{1}H \rightarrow ^{13}_{7}N + ?$
d. $^{27}_{13}Al + ? \rightarrow ^{30}_{15}P + ^{1}_{0}n$

11-43 Write equations for the following nuclear bombardment processes.
a. Beryllium-9 is bombarded with an alpha particle, and a neutron is a product.
b. Sodium-23 is bombarded with hydrogen-2, and neon-21 is a product.
c. Bombardment of cadmium-113 with a small particle produces cadmium-114 and a gamma ray.
d. Bombardment of a nuclide with an alpha particle produces phosphorus-30 and a neutron.

11-44 Write equations for the following nuclear bombardment processes.
a. Nickel-58 is bombarded with a proton, and an alpha particle is a product.
b. Aluminum-27 is bombarded with an alpha particle, and a neutron is a product.
c. Bombardment of curium-246 with a small particle produces nobelium-254 and four neutrons.
d. Bombardment of a nuclide with an alpha particle produces curium-252 and one neutron.

11-45 Using Table 11-2 as your information source, determine how many of the transuranium elements have a half-life
a. greater than 1 year
b. less than 1 day

11-46 Using Table 11-2 as your information source, determine how many of the transuranium elements have a half-life
a. greater than 1000 years
b. less than 1 hour

Radioactive Decay Series (Section 11-6)

11-47 The uranium-235 decay series terminates with lead-207. Would you expect lead-207 to be a stable or an unstable nuclide? Explain your answer.

11-48 A textbook erroneously indicates that the uranium-235 decay series terminates with radon-222. Explain why such a situation cannot be.

11-49 A nucleus of Rn-222 decays by alpha emission, forming nucleus A. Nucleus A also decays by alpha emission to form nucleus B. What is the identity of nucleus B?

11-50 A nucleus of Po-214 decays by alpha emission, forming nucleus A. Nucleus A decays by beta emission to form nucleus B. What is the identity of nucleus B?

11-51 In the thorium-232 natural decay series, the thorium-232 initially undergoes alpha decay, the resulting daughter emits a beta particle, and the succeeding daughters emit a beta and an alpha particle in that order. Write four nuclear equations, one to represent each of the first four steps in the thorium-232 decay series.

11-52 In the uranium-235 natural decay series, the uranium-235 initially undergoes alpha decay, the resulting daughter emits a beta particle, and the succeeding daughters emit an alpha and a beta particle in that order. Write four nuclear equations, one to represent each of the first four steps in the uranium-235 decay series.

Detection of Radiation (Section 11-7)

11-53 Why do technicians who work around radiation usually wear film badges?

11-54 What is the principle upon which Geiger-counter operation is based?

Chemical Effects of Radiation (Section 11-8)

11-55 What is an ion pair?

11-56 What is a free radical?

11-57 Indicate whether each of the following species is a free radical.
a. H_2O^+
b. H_3O^+
c. OH
d. OH^-

11-58 Write a chemical equation that involves water as a reactant for the formation of the
a. water free radical
b. hydroxyl free radical

11-59 What is the fate of a radiation "particle" that is involved in an ion pair formation reaction?

11-60 What are two possible fates for a free radical produced from a molecule–radiation interaction?

Biochemical Effects of Radiation (Section 11-9)

11-61 Which of the naturally occurring radiation types (alpha, beta, and gamma) have the ability to "pass through"
a. a thick sheet of paper
b. 1 cm thick Al foil
c. 5 cm thick concrete
d. outer layers of human skin

11-62 Which of the naturally occurring radiation types (alpha, beta, and gamma) can have velocities that exceed
a. 0.2 the speed of light
b. 0.4 the speed of light
c. 0.6 the speed of light
d. 0.8 the speed of light

11-63 Contrast alpha and beta particles in terms of how far they can travel in air before their energy is dissipated.

11-64 Contrast alpha and beta particles in terms of how many ion pairs they can produce before their energy is dissipated.

11-65 What would be the expected effect of each of the following short-term, whole-body radiation exposures?
a. 10 rems
b. 150 rems

11-66 What would be the expected effect of each of the following short-term, whole-body radiation exposures?
a. 50 rems
b. 250 rems

Sources of Radiation Exposure (Section 11-10)

11-67 What is background radiation?

11-68 Contrast the radiation exposure that an average American receives from natural sources with the radiation exposure an average American receives from human-activity sources.

11-69 List the four major sources of low-level exposure to background radiation for an average American.

11-70 List major sources of low-level exposure to radiation generated from human activities for an average American.

Nuclear Medicine (Section 11-11)

11-71 Why are the radionuclides used for diagnostic procedures usually gamma emitters?

11-72 Why do the radionuclides used in diagnostic procedures nearly always have short half-lives?

11-73 Explain how each of the following radionuclides is used in diagnostic medicine.
a. Gallium-67
b. Potassium-42
c. Thallium-201
d. Barium-131

11-74 Explain how each of the following radionuclides is used in diagnostic medicine.
a. Iodine-123
b. Iodine-131
c. Sodium-24
d. Iron-59

11-75 How do the radionuclides used for therapeutic purposes differ from the radionuclides used for diagnostic purposes?

11-76 Contrast the different ways in which cobalt-60 and yttrium-90 are used in radiation therapy.

Nuclear Fission and Nuclear Fusion (Section 11-12)

11-77 Indicate whether each of the following characterizations is more closely related to nuclear fission or nuclear fusion processes.
a. A large nucleus splits into two intermediate-sized nuclei.
b. Hydrogen nuclei are important reactants.

11-78 Indicate whether each of the following characterizations is more closely related to nuclear fission or nuclear fusion.
a. Small nuclei combine to give a larger nucleus.
b. Uranium-235 is an important reactant.

11-79 Identify particle X in each of the following nuclear fission processes.
a. X undergoes fission to produce barium-143, rubidium-94, and three neutrons.
b. U-235 undergoes fission to produce barium-142, X, and three neutrons.

11-80 Identify particle X in each of the following nuclear fission processes.
a. X undergoes fission to produce cesium-143, rubidium-89, and two neutrons.
b. U-235 undergoes fission to produce rubidium-90, X, and two neutrons.

11-81 Identify particle X in each of the following nuclear fusion reactions.
a. Two helium-3 nuclei fuse to give two protons and particle X.
b. Lithium-7 and particle X fuse to give two alpha particles and a neutron.

11-82 Identify particle X in each of the following nuclear fusion reactions.
a. Hydrogen-3 and particle X fuse to give helium-4 and a neutron.
b. Two identical X particles fuse to give helium-4 and two protons.

11-83 Identify which of the following characteristics apply to the fission process, which to the fusion process, and which to both processes.
a. An extremely high temperature is required to start the process.
b. An example of the process occurs on the sun.
c. Transmutation of elements occurs.
d. Neutrons are needed to start the process.

11-84 Identify which of the following characteristics apply to the fission process, which to the fusion process, and which to both processes.
a. Large amounts of energy are released in the process.
b. Energy released in the process is called *nuclear energy.*
c. The process is now used to generate some electrical power in the United States.
d. A fourth state of matter called a *plasma* is encountered in studying this process.

11-85 Identify each of the following nuclear reactions as fission, fusion, or neither.

   a. $^3_2He + ^3_2He \rightarrow ^4_2He + 2^1_1H$

   b. $^{235}_{92}U + ^1_0n \rightarrow ^{144}_{55}Cs + ^{90}_{37}Rb + 2^1_0n$

   c. $^{209}_{83}Bi + ^4_2\alpha \rightarrow ^{210}_{85}At + 3^1_0n$

   d. $^{238}_{92}U \rightarrow ^{234}_{90}Th + ^4_2\alpha$

11-86 Identify each of the following nuclear reactions as fission, fusion, or neither.

   a. $^{239}_{92}U \rightarrow ^{239}_{93}Np + ^0_{-1}\beta$

   b. $^{230}_{90}Th + ^1_1p \rightarrow ^{223}_{87}Fr + 2^4_2\alpha$

   c. $^3_1H + ^2_1H \rightarrow ^4_2He + ^1_0n$

   d. $^{235}_{92}U + ^1_0n \rightarrow ^{139}_{54}Xe + ^{95}_{38}Sr + 2^1_0n$

Nuclear and Chemical Reactions Compared (Section 11-13)

11-87 Contrast the behavior of different isotopes of an element in nuclear and chemical reactions.

11-88 Contrast the energy changes that accompany nuclear and chemical reactions.

11-89 Contrast how factors such as temperature, pressure, and catalysts affect reaction rate for nuclear and chemical reactions.

11-90 Contrast how the state of chemical combination of an element affects reactivity for nuclear and chemical reactions.

12

Saturated Hydrocarbons

Bill Ross/Corbis

Crude oil (petroleum) constitutes the largest and most important natural source for saturated hydrocarbons, the simplest type of organic compound. Here is shown a pump and towers associated with obtaining crude oil from underground deposits.

This chapter is the first of six that deal with the subject of organic chemistry and organic compounds. Organic compounds are the chemical basis for life itself, as well as an important component of the current high standard of living enjoyed by people in many countries. Proteins, carbohydrates, enzymes, and hormones are organic molecules. Organic compounds also include natural gas, petroleum, coal, gasoline, and many synthetic materials such as dyes, plastics, and clothing fibers.

12-1 Organic and Inorganic Compounds

LEARNING FOCUS

Understand the historical and modern definitions for the terms *organic chemistry* and *inorganic chemistry*.

During the latter part of the eighteenth century and the early part of the nineteenth century, chemists began to categorize compounds into two types: organic and inorganic. Compounds obtained from living organisms were called *organic* compounds, and compounds obtained from mineral constituents of Earth were called *inorganic* compounds.

During this early period, chemists believed that a special "vital force" supplied by a living organism was necessary for the formation of an organic

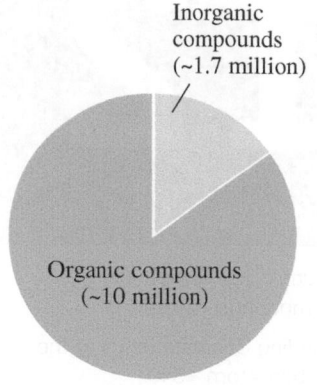

Inorganic compounds (~1.7 million)

Organic compounds (~10 million)

Figure 12-1 Sheer numbers is one reason why organic chemistry is a separate field of chemical study. Approximately 10 million organic compounds are known, compared to "just" 1.7 million inorganic compounds.

▶ *The prefixes* un-, dis-, *and* in- *are all used to convey the meaning "not" or "the opposite of." Thus the word* inorganic *is literally interpreted as* not organic. *A few other "in" prefix words where "in" means "not" are incorrect, invisible, inanimate, inadequate, and incapable.*

compound. This concept was proved incorrect in 1828 by the German chemist Friedrich Wöhler. Wöhler heated an aqueous solution of two inorganic compounds, ammonium chloride and silver cyanate, and obtained urea (a component of urine).

$$NH_4Cl + AgNCO \longrightarrow (NH_2)_2CO + AgCl$$
$$\text{Urea}$$

Soon other chemists had successfully synthesized organic compounds from inorganic starting materials. As a result, the vital-force theory was completely abandoned.

The terms *organic* and *inorganic* continue to be used in classifying compounds, but the definitions of these terms no longer reflect their historical origins. **Organic chemistry** *is the study of hydrocarbons (compounds of carbon and hydrogen) and their derivatives.* Nearly all compounds found in living organisms are still classified as organic compounds, as are many compounds that have been synthesized in the laboratory and have never been found in a living organism. **Inorganic chemistry** *is the study of all substances other than hydrocarbons and their derivatives.*

In essence, organic chemistry is the study of the compounds of one element (carbon), and inorganic chemistry is the study of the compounds of the other 117 elements. This unequal partitioning occurs because there are approximately 10 million organic compounds and only an estimated 1.7 million inorganic compounds (Figure 12-1). This is an approximately 6:1 ratio between organic and inorganic compounds. ◀

Section 12-1 Quick Quiz

1. Which of the following statements concerning *organic compounds* is correct?
   a. Organic compounds are found only in living organisms.
   b. Organic compounds always contain the element carbon.
   c. Organic compounds cannot be prepared in the laboratory.
   d. no correct response
2. Which of the following statements concerning the number of known organic and inorganic compounds is correct?
   a. Organic compounds greatly outnumber inorganic compounds.
   b. Inorganic compounds greatly outnumber organic compounds.
   c. Organic and inorganic compound numbers are about the same.
   d. no correct response

Answers: 1. b; 2. a

12-2 Bonding Characteristics of the Carbon Atom

LEARNING FOCUS

Describe the various ways carbon atoms can meet the requirement of forming four covalent bonds.

▶ *Some textbooks define organic chemistry as the study of carbon-containing compounds. Almost all carbon-containing compounds qualify as organic compounds. However, the oxides of carbon, carbonates, cyanides, and metallic carbides are classified as inorganic rather than organic compounds. Inorganic carbon compounds generally contain a single carbon atom and no hydrogen atoms (CO, CO_2, NaCN, Na_2CO_3, $MgCO_3$, and so on).*

Why does the element carbon form six times as many compounds as all the other elements combined? The answer is that carbon atoms have the ability to bond to each other in a wide variety of ways that involve long chains of carbon atoms or cyclic arrangements (rings) of carbon atoms. Sometimes both chains and rings of carbon atoms are present in the same molecule. ◀

The variety of covalent bonding "behaviors" possible for carbon atoms is related to carbon's electron configuration. Carbon is a member of Group IVA of the periodic table, so carbon atoms possess four valence electrons (Section 4-2). In compound formation, four additional valence electrons are needed to give carbon atoms an octet of valence electrons (the octet rule, Section 4-3). These additional electrons are obtained by electron sharing (covalent bond formation). The sharing of *four* valence electrons requires the formation of *four* covalent bonds.

Carbon can meet this four-bond requirement in three different ways:

1. *By bonding to four other atoms.* This situation requires the presence of four single bonds.

$$-\overset{|}{\underset{|}{C}}-$$

Four single bonds

2. *By bonding to three other atoms.* This situation requires the presence of two single bonds and one double bond.

$$-\overset{|}{C}=$$

Two single bonds and
one double bond

3. *By bonding to two other atoms.* This situation requires the presence of either two double bonds or a triple bond and a single bond.

$$=C=$$ $$-C\equiv$$

Two double bonds   One triple bond and
one single bond

Section 12-2 Quick Quiz

1. Which of the following statements about the covalent bonding capabilities of carbon atoms is *incorrect*?
   a. Single bond formation to another atom is possible.
   b. Double bond formation to another atom is possible.
   c. Triple bond formation to another atom is possible.
   d. no correct response
2. Which of the following "bonding behaviors" is *not* possible for a carbon atom?
   a. formation of four single bonds
   b. formation of two double bonds
   c. formation of two triple bonds
   d. no correct response

Answers: 1. d; 2. c

12-3 Hydrocarbons and Hydrocarbon Derivatives

LEARNING FOCUS

Define the terms *hydrocarbon* and *hydrocarbon derivative*; know the characteristic that differentiates *saturated hydrocarbons* from *unsaturated hydrocarbons*.

The field of organic chemistry encompasses the study of hydrocarbons and hydrocarbon derivatives (Section 12-1). A **hydrocarbon** *is a compound that contains only carbon atoms and hydrogen atoms.* Thousands of hydrocarbons are known. A **hydrocarbon derivative** *is a compound that contains carbon and hydrogen and one or more additional elements.* Additional elements commonly found in hydrocarbon derivatives include O, N, S, P, F, Cl, and Br. Millions of hydrocarbon derivatives are known.

Hydrocarbons may be divided into two large classes: saturated and unsaturated. A **saturated hydrocarbon** *is a hydrocarbon in which all carbon–carbon bonds are single bonds.* Saturated hydrocarbons are the simplest type of organic compound. An **unsaturated hydrocarbon** *is a hydrocarbon in which one or more carbon–carbon multiple bonds (double bonds, triple bonds, or both) are present.* In general, saturated and unsaturated hydrocarbons undergo distinctly different chemical reactions. ◄

Saturated hydrocarbons are the subject of this chapter. Unsaturated hydrocarbons are considered in the next chapter. Figure 12-2 summarizes the terminology presented in this section.

▶ *The term* saturated *has the general meaning that there is no more room for something. Its use with hydrocarbons comes from early studies in which chemists tried to add hydrogen atoms to various hydrocarbon molecules. Compounds to which no more hydrogen atoms could be added (because they already contained the maximum number) were called saturated, and those to which hydrogen could be added were called unsaturated.*

Figure 12-2 A summary of classification terms for organic compounds.

Two categories of saturated hydrocarbons exist, those with *acyclic* carbon atom arrangements and those with *cyclic* carbon atom arrangements. The term *acyclic* means "not cyclic." The following notations contrast simple acyclic and cyclic arrangements of six-carbon atoms.

Sections 12-4 through 12-11 of this chapter treat the subject of saturated hydrocarbons with *acyclic* carbon atom arrangements. ◄ A discussion of saturated hydrocarbons with *cyclic* carbon atom arrangements follows in Sections 12-12 through 12-14.

► *The prefix* a- *in* acyclic *means "not," so an* acyclic *hydrocarbon has an arrangement of carbon atoms within its structure that is not* cyclic.

Section 12-3 Quick Quiz

1. Which of the following characterizations is not possible for a *hydrocarbon derivative*?
   a. contains C and H
   b. contains C, H, and O
   c. contains C, H, and N
   d. no correct response
2. The distinction between a *saturated hydrocarbon* and an *unsaturated hydrocarbon* relates to
   a. flammability
   b. number of carbon atoms present
   c. types of carbon–carbon bonds present
   d. no correct response

Answers: 1. a; 2. c

12-4   Alkanes: Acyclic Saturated Hydrocarbons

LEARNING FOCUS

Know the general molecular formula for alkanes and the structural characteristic common to all alkanes.

An **alkane** *is a saturated hydrocarbon in which the carbon atom arrangement is acyclic.* Thus an alkane is a hydrocarbon that contains only carbon–carbon single bonds (saturated) and has no rings of carbon atoms (acyclic).

	Methane	Ethane	Propane
Dash-wedge-line structures			
Ball-and-stick models			
Space-filling models			

Figure 12-3 Three different three-dimensional ways of representing the structures of methane, ethane, and propane: dash-wedge-line structure, ball-and-stick model, and space-filling model.

The molecular formulas of all alkanes fit the general formula C_nH_{2n+2}, where n is the number of carbon atoms present. The number of hydrogen atoms present in an alkane is always twice the number of carbon atoms plus two more, as in C_4H_{10}, C_5H_{12}, and C_8H_{18}.

The three simplest alkanes are methane (CH_4), ethane (C_2H_6), and propane (C_3H_8). Three different methods for showing the three-dimensional structures of these simplest of all alkanes are given in Figure 12-3. They are dash-wedge-line structures, ball-and-stick models, and space-filling models. Note how each carbon atom in each of the models participates in four bonds (Section 12-2). Note also that the geometrical arrangement of atoms about each carbon atom is tetrahedral, an arrangement consistent with the principles of VSEPR theory (Section 5-8). The tetrahedral arrangement of the atoms bonded to alkane carbon atoms is fundamental to understanding the structural aspects of organic chemistry.

The natural environmental presence of methane, the simplest alkane, is considered in the focus on relevancy feature Chemical Connections 12-A—The Occurrence of Methane. The air we breathe contains a small amount of methane (2 parts per million by volume). The major component of natural gas used in residential home heating is methane.

Section 12-4 Quick Quiz

1. What is the general molecular formula for an alkane?
   a. C_nH_{2n}
   b. C_nH_{2n-2}
   c. C_nH_{2n+2}
   d. no correct response
2. How many hydrogen atoms are present in an alkane that contains seven atoms?
   a. 16
   b. 14
   c. 12
   d. no correct response

(continued)

3. The four hydrogen atoms bonded to the central carbon atom in methane, CH_4, lie at the corners of a
   a. rectangle
   b. square
   c. tetrahedron
   d. no correct response

Answers: 1. c; 2. a; 3. c

The Occurrence of Methane

Methane (CH_4), the simplest of all hydrocarbons, is a major component of the atmospheres of Jupiter, Saturn, Uranus, and Neptune but only a minor component of Earth's atmosphere (see the accompanying table). Earth's gravitational field, being weaker than that of the large outer planets, cannot retain enough hydrogen (H_2) in its atmosphere to permit the formation of large amounts of methane; H_2 molecules (the smallest and fastest-moving of all molecules) escape from it into outer space.

The small amount of methane present in Earth's atmosphere comes from terrestrial sources. The decomposition of animal and plant matter in an oxygen-deficient environment—swamps, marshes, bogs, and the sediments of lakes—produces methane. A common name for methane, marsh gas, refers to the production of methane in this manner.

Composition of Earth's Atmosphere
(in parts per million by volume)

Major Components		Minor Components	
nitrogen	780,800	argon	9340
oxygen	209,500	carbon dioxide	314
		neon	18
		helium	5
		methane	2
		krypton	1

Bacteria that live in termites and in the digestive tracts of plant-eating animals have the ability to produce methane from plant materials (cellulose). The methane output of a large cow (via belching and flatulence) can reach 20 liters per day. Livestock are the source of about 20% of methane emissions to the atmosphere each day.

Methane entering the atmosphere from terrestrial sources presents an environmental problem. Methane, like carbon dioxide, is a "greenhouse gas" that contributes to global warming. Methane is 15 to 30 times more efficient than carbon dioxide (the primary greenhouse gas—see Chemical Connections 9-A) in trapping re-radiated heat from Earth. Fortunately, atmospheric levels of methane (2.0 ppm by volume) are much lower than those of carbon dioxide (314 ppm by volume).

It should be noted that some greenhouse gas presence in the atmosphere is not only desirable but necessary. The average surface temperature of Earth is about 15°C. In the absence of "normal amounts" of greenhouse gases, Earth's average surface temperature would drop to about −18°C, which would not be a good situation for humans. Of concern are the ever increasing amounts of greenhouse gases entering the atmosphere as the result of human activities and the associated increase, still small, in Earth's average surface temperature.

Methane gas is also found associated with coal and petroleum deposits. Methane associated with coal mines is considered a hazard. If left to accumulate, it can form pockets where air is not present, and asphyxiation of miners can occur. When mixed with air in certain ratios, it can also present an explosion hazard. Methane associated with petroleum deposits is most often recovered, processed, and marketed as *natural gas*. The processed natural gas used in the heating of homes is 85% to 95% methane by volume. Because methane is odorless, an odorant (smelly compound) must be added to the processed natural gas used in home heating. Otherwise, natural gas leaks could not be detected.

Doug Martin / Science Source

Decomposition of plant and animal matter in marshes is a source of methane gas.

12-5 Structural Formulas

LEARNING FOCUS

Be able to write *expanded*, *condensed*, and *skeletal* structural formulas for simple alkanes.

The structures of alkanes, as well as other types of organic compounds, are generally represented in two dimensions rather than three (Figure 12-3) because of the difficulty in drawing the latter. These two-dimensional structural representations make no attempt to portray accurately the bond angles or molecular geometry of molecules. Their purpose is to convey information about which atoms in a molecule are bonded to which other atoms.

Two-dimensional structural representations for organic molecules are called structural formulas. A **structural formula** *is a two-dimensional structural representation that shows how the various atoms in a molecule are bonded to each other.* Structural formulas are of two types: expanded structural formulas and condensed structural formulas. An **expanded structural formula** *is a structural formula that shows all atoms in a molecule and all bonds connecting the atoms.* When written out, expanded structural formulas generally occupy a lot of space, and condensed structural formulas represent a shorthand method for conveying the same information. A **condensed structural formula** *is a structural formula that uses groupings of atoms, in which central atoms and the atoms connected to them are written as a group, to convey molecular structural information.* The expanded and condensed structural formulas for methane, ethane, and propane follow.

Expanded structural formula	H–C–H (with H above and below)	H–C–C–H (with H's)	H–C–C–C–H (with H's)
Condensed structural formula	CH_4	$CH_3–CH_3$	$CH_3–CH_2–CH_3$
	Methane	**Ethane**	**Propane**

The condensed structural formula for propane, $CH_3–CH_2–CH_3$, is interpreted in the following manner: The first carbon atom is bonded to three hydrogen atoms, and its fourth bond is to the middle carbon atom. The middle carbon atom, besides its bond to the first carbon atom, is also bonded to two hydrogen atoms and to the last carbon atom. The last carbon atom has bonds to three hydrogen atoms in addition to its bond to the middle carbon atom. As is always the case, each carbon atom has four bonds (Section 12-2). ◄

The condensed structural formulas of hydrocarbons in which a long chain of carbon atoms is present are often condensed even more. The formula

$$CH_3–CH_2–CH_2–CH_2–CH_2–CH_2–CH_2–CH_3$$

can be further abbreviated as

$$CH_3–(CH_2)_6–CH_3$$

where parentheses and a subscript are used to denote the number of —CH_2— groups in the chain.

It is important to note that expanded structural formulas show all bonds within a molecule and that condensed structural formulas show only certain bonds—the bonds between carbon atoms. Specifically, the bond line in the condensed structural formula

$$CH_3–CH_3$$

► *Structural formulas, whether expanded or condensed, do not show the geometry (shape) of the molecule. That information can be conveyed only by 3-D drawings or models such as those in Figure 12-3.*

denotes the bond between the first carbon atom and the second carbon atom; it is not a bond between hydrogen atoms and the second carbon atom.

In situations where the focus is solely on the arrangement of carbon atoms in an alkane, *skeletal structural formulas* that omit the hydrogen atoms are often used. A **skeletal structural formula** *is a structural formula that shows the arrangement and bonding of carbon atoms present in an organic molecule but does not show the hydrogen atoms attached to the carbon atoms.*

C—C—C—C—C   means the same as CH_3—CH_2—CH_2—CH_2—CH_3
Skeletal structural formula   Condensed structural formula

The skeletal structural formula still represents a unique alkane because we know that each carbon atom shown must have enough hydrogen atoms attached to it to give the carbon four bonds.

Section 12-5 Quick Quiz

1. The formula CH_3—CH_2—CH_2—CH_3 is an example of which of the following?
   a. expanded structural formula
   b. condensed structural formula
   c. skeletal structural formula
   d. no correct response
2. Which of the following is an incorrect structural representation for an alkane that contains a chain of five carbon atoms?
   a. C—C—C—C—C
   b. CH_3—CH_2—CH_2—CH_2—CH_3
   c. CH_3—$(CH_2)_4$—CH_3
   d. no correct response
3. The bond line in the structural formula CH_3—CH_3 denotes
   a. a carbon–hydrogen bond
   b. a carbon–carbon bond
   c. neither a carbon–hydrogen nor carbon–carbon bond
   d. no correct response

Answers: 1. b; 2. c; 3. b

12-6 Alkane Isomerism

LEARNING FOCUS

Be able to recognize *constitutional isomerism* as it relates to alkanes; be able to characterize an alkane as having a branched-chain structure or straight-chain structure.

The molecular formulas CH_4, C_2H_6, and C_3H_8 represent the alkanes methane, ethane, and propane, respectively. Next in the alkane molecular formula sequence (C_nH_{2n+2}) is C_4H_{10}, which would be expected to be the molecular formula of the four-carbon alkane. A new phenomenon arises, however, when an alkane has four or more carbon atoms. There is more than one structural formula that is consistent with the molecular formula. Consequently, more than one compound exists with that molecular formula. The topic of *isomerism* addresses this situation.

Isomers *are compounds that have the same molecular formula (that is, the same numbers and kinds of atoms) but that differ in the way the atoms are arranged.* Isomers, even though they have the same molecular formula, are always different compounds with different properties. ◄

There are two four-carbon alkane isomers, the compounds *butane* and *isobutane*. Both have the molecular formula C_4H_{10}.

CH_3—CH_2—CH_2—CH_3 CH_3—CH—CH_3
                                                                                    |
                                                                                  CH_3
                    Butane   Isobutane

▶ *The word* isomer *comes from the Greek* isos, *which means "the same," and* meros, *which means "parts." Isomers have the same parts put together in different ways.*

Butane and isobutane are different compounds with different properties. Butane has a density of $0.620\,g/ml$ at $-20°C$, a boiling point of $-1°C$, and a melting point of $-138°C$, whereas the corresponding values for isobutane are $0.605\,g/mL$, $-12°C$, and $-159°C$.

Contrasting the two C_4H_{10} isomers structurally, note that butane has a chain of four carbon atoms. It is an example of a continuous-chain alkane. A **continuous-chain alkane** *is an alkane in which all carbon atoms are connected in a continuous nonbranching chain.* The other C_4H_{10} isomer, isobutane, has a chain of three carbon atoms with the fourth carbon attached as a branch on the middle carbon of the three-carbon chain. It is an example of a branched-chain alkane. A **branched-chain alkane** *is an alkane in which one or more branches (of carbon atoms) are attached to a continuous chain of carbon atoms.*

There are three isomers for alkanes with five carbon atoms (C_5H_{12}):

Pentane	Isopentane	Neopentane

Figure 12-4 shows space-filling models for the three isomeric C_5 alkanes. Note how neopentane, the most branched isomer, has the most compact, most spherical three-dimensional shape. ◄

The number of possible alkane isomers increases dramatically with increasing numbers of carbon atoms in the alkane, as shown in Table 12-1. Such isomerism is one of the major reasons for the existence of so many organic compounds.

Several different types of isomerism exist. The alkane isomerism examples discussed in this section are examples of *constitutional isomerism.* **Constitutional isomers** *are isomers that differ in the connectivity of atoms, that is, in the order in which atoms are attached to each other within molecules.* In Section 12-14 of this chapter and in later chapters of the text, additional types of isomerism besides *constitutional* isomerism will be encountered. When carbohydrates, lipids, and proteins are considered (Chapters 18 to 20), it will be common to find that different isomers elucidate different responses within the human body. Often, when many isomers are possible with the same molecular formula, only one isomer will be physiologically active. ◄

► *The existence of isomers necessitates the use of structural formulas in organic chemistry. Isomers always have the same molecular formula and different structural formulas.*

► Constitutional isomers *are also frequently called* structural isomers. *The general characteristics of such isomers, independent of which name is used, are the same molecular formula and different structural formulas.*

Figure 12-4 Space-filling models for the three isomeric C_5H_{12} alkanes.

Pentane	Isopentane	Neopentane

a Boiling point = 36.1°C Density = 0.626 g/mL at 20 °C	b Boiling point = 27.8°C Density = 0.620 g/mL at 20 °C	c Boiling point = 9.5°C Density = 0.614 g/mL at 20 °C

Section 12-6 Quick Quiz

1. Isomers are compounds that have
   a. the same molecular formula but different structural formulas
   b. the same structural formula but different molecular formulas
   c. the same structural formula and the same molecular formula
   d. no correct response
2. One of the two four-carbon alkane constitutional isomers has the molecular formula C_4H_{10}. The molecular formula for the other isomer is
   a. C_4H_9
   b. C_4H_{10}
   c. C_4H_{11}
   d. no correct response

(continued)

▶ Table 12-1 **Number of Isomers Possible for Alkanes of Various Carbon Chain Lengths**

Molecular Formula	Possible Number of Isomers
CH_4	1
C_2H_6	1
C_3H_8	1
C_4H_{10}	2
C_5H_{12}	3
C_6H_{14}	5
C_7H_{16}	9
C_8H_{18}	18
C_9H_{20}	35
$C_{10}H_{22}$	75
$C_{15}H_{32}$	4347
$C_{20}H_{42}$	336,319
$C_{25}H_{52}$	36,797,588
$C_{30}H_{62}$	4,111,846,763

3. Constitutional isomers become possible in alkanes only when the number of carbon atoms present is
   a. three or more
   b. four or more
   c. five or more
   d. no correct response
4. How many of the three constitutional isomeric five-carbon alkanes are branched-chain alkanes?
   a. one
   b. two
   c. three
   d. no correct response

Answers: 1. a; 2. b; 3. b; 4. b

12-7 Conformations of Alkanes

LEARNING FOCUS
Be able to recognize structural formulas that represent different conformations of the same molecule.

Rotation about carbon–carbon single bonds is an important property of alkane molecules. Two groups of atoms in an alkane connected by a carbon–carbon single bond can rotate with respect to one another around that bond, much as a wheel rotates around an axle.

As a result of rotation around single bonds, alkane molecules (except for methane) can exist in infinite numbers of orientations, or conformations. A **conformation** *is the specific three-dimensional arrangement of atoms in an organic molecule at a given instant that results from rotations about carbon–carbon single bonds.*

The following skeletal formulas represent four different conformations for a continuous-chain six-carbon alkane molecule.

All four skeletal formulas represent the same molecule; that is, they are different conformations of the same molecule. In all four cases, a continuous chain of six carbon atoms is present. ◀ In all except the first case, the chain is "bent," but bends do not disrupt the continuity of the chain.

▶ *Learning to recognize several different versions (conformations) of a molecule as being "the same" is an important skill. Like friends, molecules can be recognized independent of whether they are sitting, reclining, or standing.*

Note that the structures

are not two conformations of the same alkane but, rather, represent two different alkanes. The first structure involves a continuous chain of six carbon atoms, and the second structure involves a continuous chain of five carbon atoms to which a branch is attached. There is no way that a continuous chain of six carbon atoms can be found in the second structure without "back-tracking," and "back-tracking" is not allowed.

EXAMPLE 12-1

Recognizing Different Conformations of a Molecule and Constitutional Isomers

Determine whether the members of each of the following pairs of structural formulas represent (1) different conformations of the same molecule, (2) different compounds that are constitutional isomers, or (3) different compounds that are not constitutional isomers.

a. $CH_3—CH_2—CH_2—CH_3$ and $\begin{array}{cc} CH_2—CH_2 \\ | \quad\quad | \\ CH_3 \quad CH_3 \end{array}$

b. $\begin{array}{c} CH_2—CH_2—CH_3 \\ | \\ CH_3 \end{array}$ and $\begin{array}{c} CH_2—CH_2—CH_2—CH_3 \\ | \\ CH_3 \end{array}$

c. $\begin{array}{c} CH_3—CH—CH_3 \\ | \\ CH_3 \end{array}$ and $\begin{array}{c} CH_3—CH_2—CH_2 \\ | \\ CH_3 \end{array}$

Solution

a. Both molecules have the molecular formula C_4H_{10}. The connectivity of carbon atoms is the same for both molecules: a continuous chain of four carbon atoms. For the second structural formula, the four-carbon-atom chain has two "bends" in it, which is fine because of the free rotation associated with single bonds in alkanes.

$$C—C—C—C \quad \xrightarrow{\quad} \quad \begin{array}{cc} C—C \\ | \quad | \\ \cdot C \quad C \downarrow \end{array}$$

With the same molecular formula and the same connectivity of atoms, these two structural formulas are different conformations of the same molecule.

b. The molecular formula of the first compound is C_4H_{10}, and that of the second compound is C_5H_{12}. Thus the two structural formulas represent different compounds that are not constitutional isomers. Constitutional isomers must have the same molecular formula.

c. Both molecules have the same molecular formula, C_4H_{10}. The connectivity of atoms is different. In the first case, a chain of three carbon atoms with a branch off the chain is present. In the second case, a continuous chain of four carbon atoms is present.

$$\overset{\displaystyle\cdot}{C}—C—C \quad \begin{array}{c} | \\ C \end{array} \qquad \overset{\displaystyle\cdot}{C}—C—C \begin{array}{c} | \\ C \downarrow \end{array}$$

These two structural formulas are those of constitutional isomers.

The condensed structural formulas for branched-chain alkanes can be further condensed to give linear (straight-line) condensed structural formulas. The linear condensed structural formula for the alkane

$$\begin{array}{ccccc} CH_3—CH—CH_2—CH—CH_3 \\ | \quad\quad\quad\quad | \\ CH_3 \quad\quad\quad CH_3 \end{array}$$

is

$$CH_3—CH—(CH_3)—CH_2—CH—(CH_3)—CH_3 \quad \text{or} \quad (CH_3)_2—CH—CH_2—CH—(CH_3)_2$$

Groups in parentheses in such formulas are understood to be attached to the carbon atom that *precedes* the group in the structural formula, unless the parenthesized group starts the formula. In that case, the group is attached to the carbon atom that *follows*. Writing structural formulas in this format is done primarily to reduce the vertical space that the structural formula takes.

Section 12-7 Quick Quiz

1. How many "branches" are present in the alkane with the structural formula

$$CH_2—CH_2—CH_2—CH_2$$
$$\quad|\qquad\qquad\qquad\quad|$$
$$CH_3\qquad\qquad\qquad CH_3$$

   a. 0
   b. 1
   c. 2
   d. no correct response

2. The structural formulas $CH_2—CH_2—CH_2—CH_3$ and $CH_2—CH_2—CH_2$ represent
   $$\qquad\qquad\qquad\qquad\qquad\qquad|\qquad\qquad\qquad\qquad\qquad|\qquad\quad|$$
   $$\qquad\qquad\qquad\qquad\qquad\qquad CH_3\qquad\qquad\qquad\qquad CH_3\quad CH_3$$

   a. two alkane constitutional isomers
   b. two conformations of the same alkane
   c. two branched-chain alkanes
   d. no correct response

Answers: 1. a; 2. b

12-8   IUPAC Nomenclature for Alkanes

LEARNING FOCUS

Given their structural formulas, name alkanes using IUPAC rules and vice versa.

When relatively few organic compounds were known, chemists arbitrarily named them using what today are called *common names*. These common names gave no information about the structures of the compounds they described. However, as more organic compounds became known, this nonsystematic approach to naming compounds became unwieldy.

Today, formal systematic rules exist for generating names for organic compounds. These rules, which were formulated and are updated periodically by the International Union of Pure and Applied Chemistry (IUPAC), are known as *IUPAC rules*. The advantage of the IUPAC naming system is that it assigns each compound a name that not only identifies it but also enables its structural formula to be drawn. ◄

In Section 12-6, the existence of both continuous-chain alkanes and branched-chain alkanes was noted, with the former being the simpler type of compound from a structural viewpoint. ▶ IUPAC names for the first 10 *continuous-chain* alkanes are given in Table 12-2. Note that all of these names end in *-ane*, the characteristic ending

▶ *IUPAC is pronounced "eye-you-pack."*

▶ *It is important to know the prefixes given in the second column of Table 12-2. This is the way to count from 1 to 10 in "organic chemistry language."*

▶ **Table 12-2   IUPAC Names for the First Ten Continuous-Chain Alkanes***

Molecular Formula	IUPAC Prefix	IUPAC Name	Condensed Structural Formula
CH_4	meth-	methane	CH_4
C_2H_6	eth-	ethane	$CH_3—CH_3$
C_3H_8	prop-	propane	$CH_3—CH_2—CH_3$
C_4H_{10}	but-	butane	$CH_3—CH_2—CH_2—CH_3$
C_5H_{12}	pent-	pentane	$CH_3—CH_2—CH_2—CH_2—CH_3$
C_6H_{14}	hex-	hexane	$CH_3—CH_2—CH_2—CH_2—CH_2—CH_3$
C_7H_{16}	hept-	heptane	$CH_3—CH_2—CH_2—CH_2—CH_2—CH_2—CH_3$
C_8H_{18}	oct-	octane	$CH_3—CH_2—CH_2—CH_2—CH_2—CH_2—CH_2—CH_3$
C_9H_{20}	non-	nonane	$CH_3—CH_2—CH_2—CH_2—CH_2—CH_2—CH_2—CH_2—CH_3$
$C_{10}H_{22}$	dec-	decane	$CH_3—CH_2—CH_2—CH_2—CH_2—CH_2—CH_2—CH_2—CH_2—CH_3$

*The IUPAC naming system also includes prefixes for naming continuous-chain alkanes that have more than 10 carbon atoms, but they will not be considered in this text.

for all alkane names. Note also that beginning with the five-carbon alkane, Greek numerical prefixes are used to denote the actual number of carbon atoms in the continuous chain. ◄

The key to naming *branched-chain* alkanes is knowing the name of the branch or branches that are attached to the main carbon chain. These branches are formally called substituents. A **substituent** *is an atom or group of atoms attached to a chain (or ring) of carbon atoms*. Note that *substituent* is a general term that applies to carbon-chain attachments in all organic molecules, not just alkanes.

For branched-chain alkanes, the substituents are specifically called *alkyl groups*. An **alkyl group** *is the group of atoms that would be obtained by removing a hydrogen atom from an alkane*.

The two most commonly encountered alkyl groups are the two simplest: the one-carbon and two-carbon alkyl groups. Their formulas and names are

$$\text{---CH}_3 \qquad \text{---CH}_2\text{---CH}_3$$
Methyl group   Ethyl group

In these formulas the "squiggle" on the left denotes the carbon chain to which the alkyl group is attached. Note that alkyl groups do not lead a stable, independent existence; that is, they are not molecules. They are always found attached to another entity (usually a carbon chain).

Alkyl groups are named by taking the stem of the name of the alkane that contains the same number of carbon atoms and adding the ending *-yl*. Table 12-3 gives the names for small continuous-chain alkyl groups. ◄

Formal IUPAC rules for naming branched-chain alkanes are as follows:

Rule 1: *Identify the longest continuous carbon chain (the parent chain), which may or may not be shown in a straight line, and name the chain.* ◄

The parent chain name is *pentane*, because it has five carbon atoms.

The parent chain name is *hexane*, because it has six carbon atoms.

► *Continuous-chain alkanes are also frequently called* straight-chain alkanes *and* normal-chain alkanes.

► *The ending -yl, as in methyl, ethyl, propyl, and butyl, appears in the names of all alkyl groups.*

► *An additional guideline for identifying the longest continuous carbon chain: If two different carbon chains in a molecule have the same largest number of carbon atoms, select as the parent chain the one with the larger number of substituents (alkyl groups) attached to the chain.*

▷ Table 12-3 **Names for the First Six Continuous-Chain Alkyl Groups**

Number of Carbons	Structural Formula	Stem of Alkane Name	Suffix	Alkyl Group Name
1	---CH_3	meth-	–yl	methyl
2	$\text{---CH}_2\text{---CH}_3$	eth-	–yl	ethyl
3	$\text{---CH}_2\text{---CH}_2\text{---CH}_3$	prop-	–yl	propyl
4	$\text{---CH}_2\text{---CH}_2\text{---CH}_2\text{---CH}_3$	but-	–yl	butyl
5	$\text{---CH}_2\text{---CH}_2\text{---CH}_2\text{---CH}_2\text{---CH}_3$	pent-	–yl	pentyl
6	$\text{---CH}_2\text{---CH}_2\text{---CH}_2\text{---CH}_2\text{---CH}_2\text{---CH}_3$	hex-	–yl	hexyl

▶ *Additional guidelines for numbering carbon-atom chains are:*

1. *If both ends of the chain have a substituent the same distance in, number from the end closest to the second-encountered substituent.*

2. *If there are substituents equidistant from each end of the chain and there is no third substituent to use as the "tie-breaker," begin numbering at the end nearest the substituent that has alphabetical priority—that is, the substituent whose name occurs first in the alphabet.*

Rule 2: *Number the carbon atoms in the parent chain from the end of the chain nearest a substituent (alkyl group).*

There are always two ways to number the chain (either from left to right or from right to left). This rule gives the first-encountered alkyl group the lowest possible number. ◀

Rule 3: *If only one alkyl group is present, name and locate it (by number), and prefix the number and name to that of the parent carbon chain.*

Note that the name is written as one word, with a hyphen between the number (location) and the name of the alkyl group.

Rule 4: *If two or more of the same kind of alkyl group are present in a molecule, indicate the number with a Greek numerical prefix (di-, tri-, tetra-, penta-, and so forth). In addition, a number specifying the location of each identical group must be included. These position numbers, separated by commas, precede the numerical prefix. Numbers are separated from words by hyphens.*

Note that the numerical prefix *di-* must always be accompanied by two numbers, *tri-* by three, and so on, even if the same number is used more than once, as in 3,3-dimethylpentane. ◀

▶ *There must be as many numbers as there are alkyl groups in the IUPAC name of a branched-chain alkane.*

Rule 5: *When two kinds of alkyl groups are present on the same carbon chain, number each group separately, and list the names of the alkyl groups in alphabetical order.*

$$\overset{5}{CH_3}-\overset{4}{CH_2}-\overset{3}{CH}-\overset{2}{CH}-\overset{1}{CH_3}$$

3-Ethyl-2-Methylpentane

$$\begin{array}{cc} CH_2 & CH_3 \\ | \\ CH_3 \end{array}$$

Note that ethyl is named first in accordance with the alphabetical rule.

$$\overset{1}{CH_3}-\overset{2}{CH_2}-\overset{3}{CH}-\overset{4}{CH}-\overset{5}{CH}-\overset{6}{CH_2}-\overset{7}{CH_2}-\overset{8}{CH_3}$$

3-Ethyl-4,5-dipropyloctane

Note that the prefix *di-* does not affect the alphabetical order; *ethyl* precedes *propyl.* ◄

Rule 6: *Follow IUPAC punctuation rules, which include the following: (1) Separate numbers from each other by commas. (2) Separate numbers from letters by hyphens. (3) Do not add a hyphen or a space between the last-named substituent and the name of the parent alkane that follows.* ◄

4-Ethyl-2,3-dimethyl-5-propylnonane

Hyphens separate numbers from words

No hyphen, no comma, no space

Comma separates two numbers

► *Numerical prefixes that designate numbers of alkyl groups, such as* di-, tri-, *and* tetra-, *are not considered when determining alphabetical priority for alkyl groups.*

► *A few smaller branched alkanes have common names— that is, non-IUPAC names—that still have widespread use. They make use of the prefixes* iso *and* neo, *as in isobutane, isopentane, and neohexane. These prefixes denote particular end-of-chain carbon atom arrangements.*

$$CH_3-CH-(CH_2)_n-CH_3$$
$$\overset{|}{\underset{}{CH_3}}$$

An isoalkane
(e.g., $n = 1$, Isopentane)

$$CH_3-\overset{\overset{CH_3}{|}}{\underset{\underset{CH_3}{|}}{C}}-(CH_2)_n-CH_3$$

A neoalkane
(e.g., $n = 1$, Neohexane)

EXAMPLE 12-2

Determining IUPAC Names for Branched-Chain Alkanes

Give the IUPAC name for each of the following branched-chain alkanes.

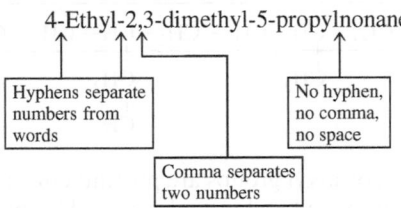

a. $CH_3-CH-CH-CH_3$

b. $CH_3-CH-CH_2-CH_2-CH-CH_2-CH-CH_3$

Solution

a. The longest carbon chain possesses five carbon atoms. Thus the parent-chain name is pentane.

$$CH_3-CH-CH-CH_3$$

This parent chain is numbered from right to left because an alkyl substituent is closer to the right end of the chain than to the left end.

$$CH_3-\overset{3}{CH}-\overset{2}{CH}-\overset{1}{CH_3}$$

There are two methyl group substituents (circled). One methyl group is located on carbon 2 and the other on carbon 3. The IUPAC name for the compound is 2,3-dimethylpentane.

(continued)

b. There are eight carbon atoms in the longest carbon chain, so the parent name is octane. There are three alkyl groups present (circled).

$$CH_3-CH-CH_2-CH_2-CH-CH_2-CH-CH_3$$

Selection of the numbering system to be used cannot be made based on the "first-encountered-alkyl-group rule" because an alkyl group is equidistant from each end of the chain. Thus the second-encountered alkyl group is used as the "tie-breaker." It is closer to the right end of the parent chain (carbon 4) than to the left end (carbon 5). Thus we use the right-to-left numbering system.

$$\overset{8}{C}H_3-\overset{7}{C}H-\overset{6}{C}H_2-\overset{5}{C}H_2-\overset{4}{C}H-\overset{3}{C}H_2-\overset{2}{C}H-\overset{1}{C}H_3$$

Two different kinds of alkyl groups are present: ethyl and methyl. Ethyl has alphabetical priority over methyl and precedes methyl in the IUPAC name. The IUPAC name is 4-ethyl-2,7-dimethyloctane.

Once the rules for naming alkanes are learned, it is relatively easy to reverse the procedure and translate the name of an alkane into a structural formula. Example 12-3 shows how this is done.

EXAMPLE 12-3

Generating the Structural Formula of an Alkane from Its IUPAC Name

Draw the condensed structural formula for 3-ethyl-2,3-dimethylpentane.

Solution

Step 1: The name of this compound ends in *pentane*, so the longest continuous chain has five carbon atoms. Draw this chain of five carbon atoms and number it.

$$\overset{1}{C}-\overset{2}{C}-\overset{3}{C}-\overset{4}{C}-\overset{5}{C}$$

Step 2: Complete the carbon skeleton by attaching alkyl groups as they are specified in the name. An ethyl group goes on carbon 3, and methyl groups are attached to carbons 2 and 3.

$$\overset{1}{C}-\overset{2}{C}-\overset{3}{C}-\overset{4}{C}-\overset{5}{C}$$

Step 3: Add hydrogen atoms to the carbon skeleton so that each carbon atom has four bonds.

$$\overset{1}{C}H_3-\overset{2}{C}H-\overset{3}{C}-\overset{4}{C}H_2-\overset{5}{C}H_3$$

The following example, which involves determining the structural formulas for and naming of alkane constitutional isomers, serves as a good review of the structural and naming concepts for alkanes considered so far in this chapter.

EXAMPLE 12-4

Determining Structural Formulas for and Naming Alkane Constitutional Isomers

Draw skeletal structural formulas for, and assign IUPAC names to, all C_6H_{14} alkane constitutional isomers.

Solution

Table 12-1 indicates that there are five constitutional isomers with the chemical formula C_6H_{14}. Part of the purpose of this example is to consider the "thinking pattern" needed to identify these five isomers. There are two concepts embedded in the thinking pattern.

1. Carbon chains of varying length are examined for isomerism possibilities, starting with the chain of maximum length and then examining increasingly shorter chain lengths.
2. Substituents are added to the various carbon chains, with the number of added carbons determined by the chain length. Various location possibilities for the substituents are examined.

Step 1: A C_6 carbon chain is the longest chain possible; it contains all available carbon atoms.

$$C—C—C—C—C—C$$

This is the molecule hexane, the first of the five constitutional isomers. No substituents are added to this chain, as that would increase the carbon count beyond six.

Step 2: Decreasing the carbon-chain length by one gives a C_5 chain.

$$C—C—C—C—C$$

A methyl group must be added to the chain to bring the carbon count back up to six.

Theoretically, there are five possible positions for the methyl group:

These five structures do not represent five new isomers. The first and last structures represent two alternate ways of drawing the molecule hexane, the first isomer. A methyl group (or any alkyl group) added to the end carbons of a carbon chain will always increase the chain length.

The second and third structures do represent new isomers:

2-methylpentane   3-methylpentane

The fourth of the five structures is not a new isomer. Numbering its carbon chain from the right end shows that it is 2-methylpentane rather than 4-methylpentane. Thus the second and fourth structures are two representations of the same molecule.

Step 3: Decreasing the chain length to four carbon atoms is the next consideration. Two carbon atoms must now be added as attachments. This can be done in two ways—dimethyl and ethyl.

Examining dimethyl possibilities first, eliminating structures that have methyl groups on terminal carbon atoms gives the following possibilities.

2,2-Dimethylbutane   2,3-Dimethylbutane

(continued)

The first and second structures are the same; both represent the molecule 2,2-dimethylbutane, a fourth isomer.

The third structure, 2,3-dimethylbutane, is different from the other two. It is the fifth isomer.

What about ethyl butanes?

Neither of these structures is a new isomer because both have a five-carbon chain. Both structures are actually depictions of 3-methylpentane, one of the isomers previously identified.

Step 4:   A chain length of three does not generate any new isomers. A trimethyl structure is impossible, as the middle carbon atom, the only carbon to which substituents can be attached, would have five bonds. An ethyl methyl structure extends the carbon chain length, as does a single three-carbon attachment.

Thus, there are five constitutional isomers: *hexane, 2-methylpentane, 3-methylpentane, 2,2-dimethylbutane, and 2,3-dimethylbutane.*

Section 12-8 Quick Quiz

1. The relationship between an alkyl group and its parent alkane is that the alkyl group possesses
   a. one more C atom
   b. one more H atom
   c. one less H atom
   d. no correct response
2. The name for the alkyl group CH_3—CH_2—CH_2— is
   a. propaneyl
   b. propyl
   c. alkylpropane
   d. no correct response
3. Which of the following statements about IUPAC nomenclature rules for alkanes is *incorrect*?
   a. The longest continuous chain of C atoms determines the parent chain name.
   b. Each alkyl group is located using a number that specifies its point of attachment.
   c. Carbon atoms in the main chain are numbered starting at the left end of the chain.
   d. no correct response
4. The IUPAC name for the alkane CH_3—$\overset{\overset{\displaystyle CH_3}{|}}{CH}$—$CH_2$—$CH_2$—$CH_3$ is
   a. methane pentane
   b. methylpentane
   c. 2-methylpentane
   d. no correct response
5. The IUPAC name for the alkane CH_3—CH_2—$\overset{\overset{\displaystyle CH_3}{|}}{CH}$—$\overset{\overset{\displaystyle CH_3}{|}}{CH}$—$CH_3$ is
   a. 2,3-methylpentane
   b. 3,4-methylpentane
   c. 3,4-dimethylpentane
   d. no correct response
6. Which of the following alkanes contains eight carbon atoms?
   a. 2,3-dimethylbutane
   b. 3-ethyl-2-methylpentane
   c. heptane
   d. no correct response

7. The number of alkyl groups and the number of substituents, respectively, in the alkane 4-ethyl-3,3-dimethyloctane are

  a. 2 and 3
  b. 3 and 2
  c. 3 and 3
  d. no correct response

Answers: 1. c; 2. b; 3. c; 4. c; 5. d; 6. b; 7. c

12-9 Line-Angle Structural Formulas for Alkanes

LEARNING FOCUS
Be able to draw line-angle structural formulas for alkanes.

Three two-dimensional methods for denoting alkane structures have been used in previous sections of this chapter. They are expanded structural formulas, condensed structural formulas, and skeletal structural formulas. An even more concise method for denoting molecular structure of alkanes (and other hydrocarbons and their derivatives) exists. This method, *line-angle structural formulas,* is particularly useful for molecules in which higher numbers of carbon atoms are present.

A **line-angle structural formula** *is a structural representation in which a line represents a carbon–carbon bond and a carbon atom is understood to be present at every point where two lines meet and at the ends of lines.* Ball-and-stick models and line-angle structural formulas for the alkanes propane, butane, and pentane are as follows:

Ball-and-stick model

Line-angle structural formula
Propane   Butane   Pentane

The zigzag (sawtooth) pattern used in line-angle structural formulas directly relates to the three-dimensional shape of the molecules that are represented.

In the line-angle structure for pentane note that there is a carbon atom at each end of the structure and three interior carbon atoms (at the points where two lines meet).

$$CH_3-CH_2-CH_2-CH_2-CH_3$$

The structures of branched-chain alkanes can also be designated using line-angle structural formulas. The five constitutional alkane isomers in which six carbon atoms are present (C_6H_{14}) have the following line-angle formulas:

Example 12-5 gives further insights concerning the use and interpretation of line-angle structural formulas.

Chemistry at a Glance—Structural Representations for Alkane Molecules—contrasts the line-angle structural formula notation for alkanes with all other structural formula notations for alkanes encountered so far in this chapter.

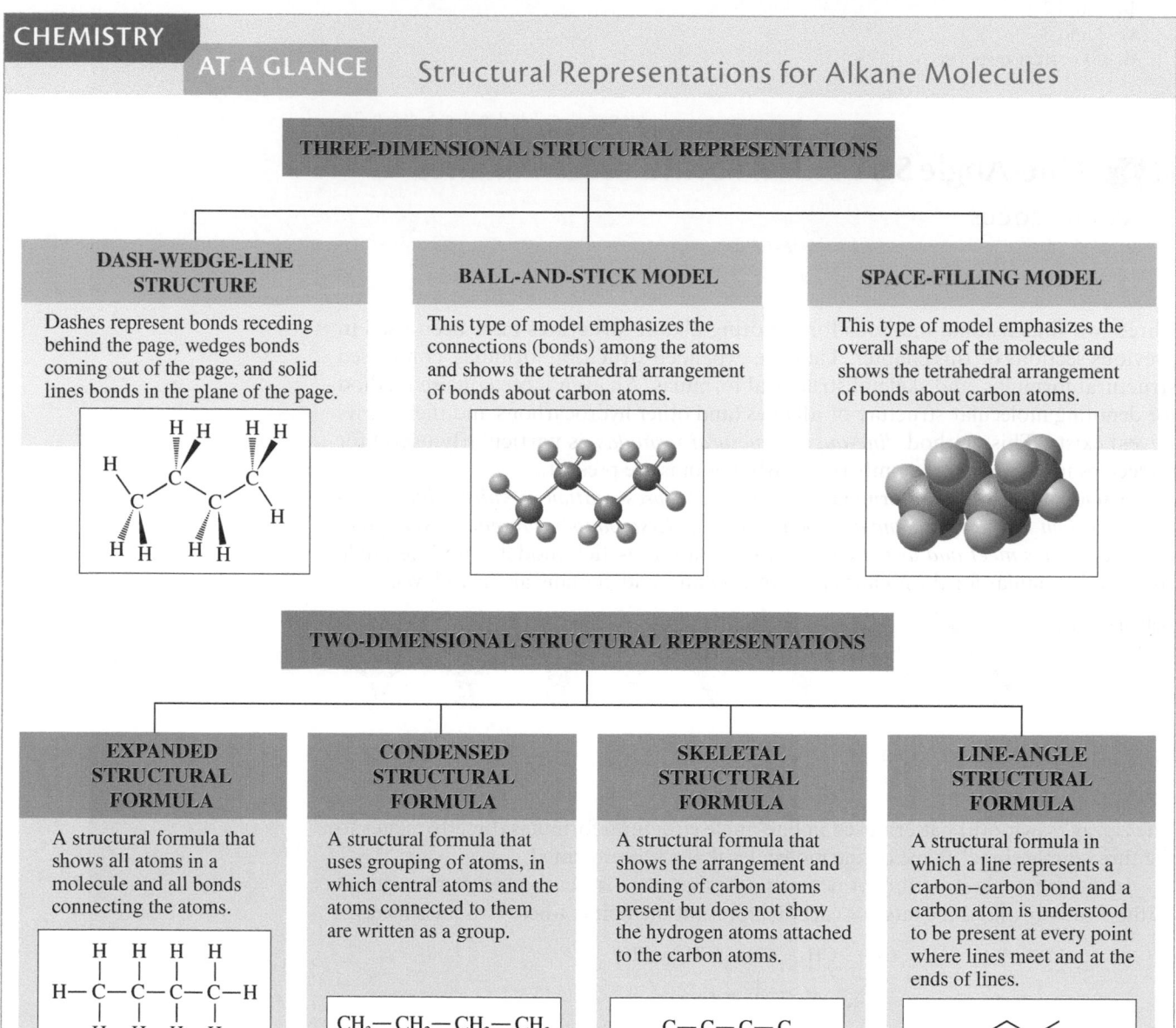

CHEMISTRY
AT A GLANCE Structural Representations for Alkane Molecules

THREE-DIMENSIONAL STRUCTURAL REPRESENTATIONS

DASH-WEDGE-LINE STRUCTURE

Dashes represent bonds receding behind the page, wedges bonds coming out of the page, and solid lines bonds in the plane of the page.

BALL-AND-STICK MODEL

This type of model emphasizes the connections (bonds) among the atoms and shows the tetrahedral arrangement of bonds about carbon atoms.

SPACE-FILLING MODEL

This type of model emphasizes the overall shape of the molecule and shows the tetrahedral arrangement of bonds about carbon atoms.

TWO-DIMENSIONAL STRUCTURAL REPRESENTATIONS

EXPANDED STRUCTURAL FORMULA

A structural formula that shows all atoms in a molecule and all bonds connecting the atoms.

CONDENSED STRUCTURAL FORMULA

A structural formula that uses grouping of atoms, in which central atoms and the atoms connected to them are written as a group.

$CH_3-CH_2-CH_2-CH_3$

SKELETAL STRUCTURAL FORMULA

A structural formula that shows the arrangement and bonding of carbon atoms present but does not show the hydrogen atoms attached to the carbon atoms.

$C-C-C-C$

LINE-ANGLE STRUCTURAL FORMULA

A structural formula in which a line represents a carbon–carbon bond and a carbon atom is understood to be present at every point where lines meet and at the ends of lines.

EXAMPLE 12-5

Generating Condensed Structural Formulas from Line-Angle Structural Formulas for Alkanes

For each of the following alkanes, determine the number of hydrogen atoms present on each carbon atom and then write the condensed structural formula for the alkane.

a.

b.

Solution

a. Each carbon atom in an alkane must be bonded to four atoms. Thus carbon atoms bonded to only one carbon atom have three hydrogen atoms attached;

those bonded to two other carbon atoms have two hydrogen atoms attached; those bonded to three other carbon atoms have only one atom attached; and those bonded to four other carbon atoms bear no hydrogen atoms. For this alkane, each carbon atom's hydrogen content is indicated by circled numbers as follows.

With this information on hydrogen content, the condensed structural formula is written as

$$CH_3-CH-CH_3$$
$$|$$
$$CH_3$$

b. Using the methods of part **a,** the hydrogen content of this alkane is

and the condensed structural formula becomes

$$CH_3-CH_2-CH-CH_2-CH-CH_2-CH_3$$
$$\qquad\quad |\qquad\qquad\quad |$$
$$\qquad\quad CH_2\qquad\qquad CH_3$$
$$\qquad\quad |$$
$$\qquad\quad CH_3$$

Section 12-9 Quick Quiz

1. How many carbon atoms are present in the alkane ⌇⌇⌇ ?
   a. 5
   b. 6
   c. 7
   d. no correct response
2. The line-angle structural formula for the alkane $CH_3-CH-CH_2-CH_3$ is
   $$\qquad\qquad\qquad\qquad\qquad\qquad\qquad\qquad |$$
   $$\qquad\qquad\qquad\qquad\qquad\qquad\qquad CH_3$$
   a.
   b.
   c.
   d. no correct response

Answers: 1. b; 2. b

12-10 Classification of Carbon Atoms

LEARNING FOCUS

Be able to classify the individual carbon atoms within an alkane structure as *primary, secondary, tertiary,* or *quaternary* carbon atoms.

▶ *The notations 1°, 2°, 3°, and 4° are often used as designations for the terms* primary, secondary, tertiary, *and* quaternary.
  1° carbon atom
  2° carbon atom
  3° carbon atom
  4° carbon atom

Each of the carbon atoms within a hydrocarbon structure can be classified as a *primary* (1°), *secondary* (2°), *tertiary* (3°), or *quaternary* (4°) carbon atom. ◀

A **primary carbon atom** *is a carbon atom in an organic molecule that is directly bonded to one other carbon atom.* Both carbon atoms in ethane are primary carbon atoms.

$$CH_3-CH_3$$
$$1° \quad 1°$$

A **secondary carbon atom** *is a carbon atom in an organic molecule that is directly bonded to two other carbon atoms.* A propane molecule contains a secondary carbon atom as well as two primary carbon atoms.

$$CH_3-CH_2-CH_3$$
$$1° \quad 2° \quad 1°$$

A **tertiary carbon atom** *is a carbon atom in an organic molecule that is directly bonded to three other carbon atoms.* The molecule 2-methylpropane contains a tertiary carbon atom.

$$CH_3$$
$$|$$
$$CH_3-CH-CH_3$$
$$3°$$

A **quaternary carbon atom** *is a carbon atom in an organic molecule that is directly bonded to four other carbon atoms.* The molecule 2,2-dimethylpropane contains a quaternary carbon atom.

$$CH_3$$
$$|$$
$$CH_3-C-CH_3$$
$$4° \quad | \quad CH_3$$

The alkane 2,2,3-trimethylpentane is the simplest alkane in which all four types of carbon atoms (1°, 2°, 3°, and 4°) are present.

$$CH_3 \quad CH_3$$
$$| \quad |$$
$$CH_3-CH_2-CH-C-CH_3$$
$$1° \quad 2° \quad 3° \quad | \quad 4°$$
$$CH_3$$

Section 12-10 Quick Quiz

1. A secondary carbon atom is directly bonded to how many other carbon atoms?
   a. 2
   b. 3
   c. 4
   d. no correct response
2. In which of the following alkanes are both 2° and 3° carbon atoms present?
   a. $CH_3-CH-CH_3$
              |
             CH_3
   b. $CH_3-CH_2-CH-CH_3$
                     |
                    CH_3
   c. $CH_3-CH-CH-CH_3$
             | |
            CH_3 CH_3
   d. no correct response

Answers: 1. a; 2. b

12-11 Branched-Chain Alkyl Groups

LEARNING FOCUS

Be able to recognize by structure and by name all of the three-carbon and four-carbon branched alkyl groups.

To this point in the chapter, all alkyl groups encountered in structures have been continuous-chain alkyl groups (Table 12-3), the simplest type of alkyl group. Just as there are continuous-chain and branched-chain alkanes, there are continuous-chain and branched-chain alkyl groups. There is one C_3 branched-chain alkyl group and three C_4 branched-chain alkyl groups. The names and structures of these four alkyl groups, the simplest of all branched-chain alkyl groups, are given in Figure 12-5.

For the two groups whose names contain the prefix *iso-*, the common structural feature is an end-of-chain arrangement that contains two methyl groups.

$$\overset{|}{C}H-CH_3$$
$$\underset{|}{\overset{|}{C}H_3}$$

For the *secondary*-butyl group, the point of attachment of the group to the main carbon chain involves a *secondary* carbon atom. For the *tertiary*-butyl group, the point of attachment of the group to the main carbon chain involves a *tertiary* carbon atom. The name secondary-butyl is often shortened to *sec*-butyl or simply *s*-butyl. Similarly, tertiary-butyl is often written as *tert*-butyl or *t*-butyl.

Two examples of alkanes containing branched-chain alkyl groups follow.

$$\overset{1}{C}H_3-\overset{2}{C}H_2-\overset{3}{C}H-\overset{4}{C}H_2-\overset{5}{C}H_2-\overset{6}{C}H-\overset{7}{C}H_2-\overset{8}{C}H_2-\overset{9}{C}H_3$$

3-Isopropyl-6-propylnonane

$$\overset{1}{C}H_3-\overset{2}{C}H_2-\overset{3}{C}H_2-\overset{4}{C}H-\overset{5}{C}H_2-\overset{6}{C}H_2-\overset{7}{C}H_2-\overset{8}{C}H_3$$

4-*tert*-Butyloctane

In IUPAC names, a hyphen always follows the designations *secondary* and *tertiary*, but no hyphen is used with the prefix *iso*.

secondary-butyl   tertiary-butyl   isobutyl

The hyphenated prefixes *sec-* and *tert-* are ignored when alphabetizing alkyl group names except when they are compared to each other. Thus, *tert*-butyl precedes isobutyl, and *sec*-butyl precedes *tert*-butyl. ◀

▶ *It is important to be able to recognize various conformations of branched-chain alkyl groups. For example, these structures all represent an isopropyl group:*

$$CH_3-CH-CH_3$$

$$CH_3-CH \qquad \overset{|}{C}H$$
$$\underset{|}{C}H_3 \qquad CH_3 \ CH_3$$

In each case, there is a chain of three carbon atoms with an attachment point (the long bond) involving the middle carbon atom of the chain.

Figure 12-5 The four most common branched-chain alkyl groups and their IUPAC names.

Long Chain of Carbon Atoms

| Isopropyl group | Isobutyl group | Secondary-butyl group | Tertiary-butyl group |

Complex Branched-Chain Alkyl Groups

"Simple" names, such as isobutyl and *tert*-butyl (Figure 12-5), do not exist for most branched-chain alkyl groups containing five or more carbon atoms. The IUPAC system provision for naming such larger groups involves naming them as if they were themselves compounds. The following rules are used.

Rule 1:   *The longest continuous carbon chain that begins at the point of attachment of the alkyl group becomes the base name.*

Rule 2:   *The base chain is numbered beginning at the point of attachment.*

$$\overset{\overset{\displaystyle 1}{CH_2}}{\underset{\underset{\displaystyle CH_3}{|}}{CH_3 - \overset{2}{C} - \overset{3}{CH_2} - \overset{4}{CH_3}}}$$

Rule 3:   *Substituents on the base chain are listed in alphabetical order, using numerical prefixes when necessary, and substituent locations are designated using numbers.*

(2,2-dimethylbutyl) group

Two additional examples of IUPAC nomenclature for complex branched-chain alkyl groups are

$$\overset{\overset{\displaystyle CH_3}{|}}{\underset{\underset{\displaystyle CH_3}{|}}{\overset{3}{CH_3} - \overset{2}{CH_2} - \overset{1}{C} -}}\Big\}$$ $$\overset{\overset{\displaystyle CH_3}{|}}{\underset{\underset{\displaystyle CH_3}{|}}{\overset{4}{CH_3} - \overset{3}{CH} - \overset{2}{CH_2} - \overset{1}{C} -}}\Big\}$$

(1,1-dimethylpropyl) group   (1,1,3-trimethylbutyl) group

The C_3 and C_4 branched-chain alkyl groups (Figure 12-5) can also be named using the preceding rules. Thus there are two names for these groups. An alternate name for the *tert*-butyl group is the 1,1-dimethylethyl group. ◄

▶ *A single compound or group can have several acceptable names, but no two compounds or groups can have the same name.*

$$\overset{\overset{\displaystyle CH_3}{|}}{\underset{\underset{\displaystyle CH_3}{|}}{\overset{2}{CH_3} - \overset{1}{C} -}}\Big\}$$

tert-butyl group
(1,1-dimethylethyl) group

Section 12-11 Quick Quiz

1. The number of different three-carbon and four-carbon alkyl groups are, respectively
   a. 2 and 3
   b. 2 and 4
   c. 3 and 3
   d. no correct response

2. Which of the following is *not* a representation for an isopropyl group?

  a. CH—CH₃   **b.** CH₃—CH—CH₃   **c.** CH₂—CH₂—CH₃   **d.** no correct response
     CH₃

3. Which of the following is a representation for a *sec*-butyl group?

  a. CH—CH₃   **b.** CH₂   **c.** CH₂   **d.** no correct response
     CH₂   CH—CH₃   CH₂
     CH₃   CH₃   CH₂—CH₃

Answers: 1. b; 2. c; 3. a

12-12 Cycloalkanes

LEARNING FOCUS

Know the general molecular formula for a cycloalkane; be able to represent a given cycloalkane using various types of structural formulas.

A **cycloalkane** *is a saturated hydrocarbon in which carbon atoms connected to one another in a cyclic (ring) arrangement are present.* The simplest cycloalkane is cyclopropane, which contains a cyclic arrangement of three carbon atoms. ◄ Figure 12-6 shows a three-dimensional model of cyclopropane's structure and those of the four-, five-, and six-carbon cycloalkanes.

▶ *It takes a minimum of three carbon atoms to form a cyclic arrangement of carbon atoms.*

Cyclopropane's three carbon atoms lie in a flat ring. In all other cycloalkane molecules, some puckering of the ring occurs; that is, the ring systems are nonplanar, as shown in Figure 12-6.

The general formula for cycloalkanes is C_nH_{2n}. Thus a given cycloalkane contains two fewer hydrogen atoms than an alkane with the same number of hydrogen atoms (C_nH_{2n+2}). ◄ Butane (C_4H_{10}) and cyclobutane (C_4H_8) are not isomers; isomers must have the same molecular formula (Section 12-6).

▶ *Cycloalkanes, unlike alkanes, have no end carbons. Hence, they always have two fewer hydrogen atoms than corresponding alkanes.*

Line-angle structural formulas are generally used to represent cycloalkane structures. The line-angle structural formula for cyclopropane is a triangle, that for cyclobutane a square, that for cyclopentane a pentagon, and that for cyclohexane a hexagon.

   Cyclopropane   Cyclobutane   Cyclopentane   Cyclohexane

In such structures, the intersection of two lines represents a CH_2 group. Three- and four-way intersections of lines are possible when substituents are present on a ring. A three-way intersection represents a CH group, and a four-way intersection is simply a carbon atom.

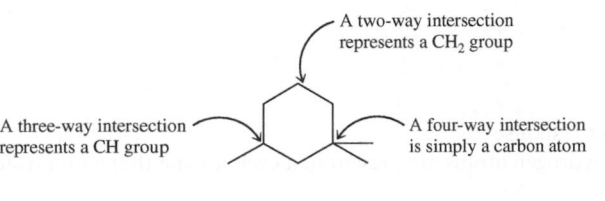

A two-way intersection represents a CH_2 group

A three-way intersection represents a CH group

A four-way intersection is simply a carbon atom

a Cyclopropane, C_3H_6

b Cyclobutane, C_4H_8

c Cyclopentane, C_5H_{10} **d** Cyclohexane, C_6H_{12}

Figure 12-6 Three-dimensional representations of the structures of simple cycloalkanes.

EXAMPLE 12-6

Generating Condensed Structural Formulas from Line-Angle Structural Formulas for Cycloalkanes

Generate the condensed structural formula for each of the following cycloalkanes.

a.

b.

Solution

a. First replace each angle and line terminus with a carbon atom, and then add hydrogens as necessary to give each carbon four bonds. The molecular formula of this compound is C_8H_{16}.

b. Similarly, we have

The observed C—C—C bond angles in cyclopropane are 60°, and those in cyclobutane are approximately 90°, values that are considerably smaller than the 109° angle associated with a tetrahedral arrangement of bonds about a carbon atom (Section 5-8). Consequently, cyclopropane and cyclobutane are relatively unstable compounds. Five- and six-membered cycloalkane structures are much more stable, and these structural entities are encountered in many organic molecules.

Section 12-12 Quick Quiz

1. When the molecular formulas for cyclic and noncyclic alkanes with the same number of carbon atoms are compared, it is always found that the cycloalkane has
   a. two more H atoms
   b. the same number of H atom
   c. two fewer H atoms
   d. no correct response
2. How many carbon atoms are present in the cycloalkane with the structural formula
   ?
   a. 4
   b. 5
   c. 6
   d. no correct response
3. How many hydrogen atoms are present in a cycloalkane that contains four carbon atoms?
   a. 8
   b. 10
   c. 12
   d. no correct response

Answers: 1. c; 2. b; 3. a

12-13 IUPAC Nomenclature for Cycloalkanes

LEARNING FOCUS

Given their structural formulas, assign IUPAC names to cycloalkanes, or vice versa.

IUPAC naming procedures for cycloalkanes are similar to those for alkanes. The ring portion of a cycloalkane molecule serves as the name base, and the prefix *cyclo-* is used to indicate the presence of the ring. ◀ Alkyl substituents are named in the same manner as in alkanes. Numbering conventions used in locating substituents on the ring include the following:

1. If there is just one ring substituent, it is not necessary to locate it by number.
2. When two ring substituents are present, the carbon atoms in the ring are numbered beginning with the substituent of higher alphabetical priority and proceeding in the direction (clockwise or counterclockwise) that gives the other substituent the lower number.
3. When three or more ring substituents are present, ring numbering begins at the substituent that leads to the lowest set of location numbers. When two or more equivalent numbering sets exist, alphabetical priority among substituents determines the set used. ◀

Example 12-7 illustrates the use of the ring-numbering guidelines.

▶ *Cycloalkanes of ring sizes ranging from 3 to over 30 are found in nature, and, in principle, there is no limit to ring size. Five-membered rings (cyclopentanes) and six-membered rings (cyclohexanes) are especially abundant in nature.*

▶ *When a ring system contains fewer carbon atoms than an alkyl group attached to it, the compound is named as an alkane rather than as a cycloalkane; the ring is named as a cycloalkyl group.*

$$CH_3 - CH - CH_2 - CH_2 - CH_2 - CH_3$$

2-cyclopentylhexane

EXAMPLE 12-7

Determining IUPAC Names for Cycloalkanes

Assign IUPAC names to each of the following cycloalkanes.

a.

b.

c.

Solution

a. This molecule is a cyclobutane (four-carbon ring) with a methyl substituent. The IUPAC name is simply methylcyclobutane. No number is needed to locate the methyl group because all four ring positions are equivalent.
b. This molecule is a cyclopentane with ethyl and methyl substituents. The numbers for the carbon atoms that bear the substituents are 1 and 2. On the basis of alphabetical priority, the number 1 is assigned to the carbon atom that bears the ethyl group. The IUPAC name for the compound is 1-ethyl-2-methylcyclopentane.
c. This molecule is a dimethylpropylcyclohexane. Two different 1,2,3 numbering systems exist for locating the substituents. On the basis of alphabetical priority, the numbering system that has carbon 1 bearing a methyl group is used; methyl has alphabetical priority over propyl. Thus the compound name is 1,2-dimethyl-3-propylcyclohexane.

Section 12-13 Quick Quiz

1. The IUPAC name for the cycloalkane [structure] is
   a. methylcyclopentane
   b. methylcyclohexane
   c. ethylcyclohexane
   d. no correct response
2. Which of the following cycloalkanes does not contain six carbon atoms ?
   a. methylcyclopentane
   b. propylcyclopropane
   c. ethylcyclohexane
   d. no correct response

(continued)

3. Which of the following is an *incorrect* IUPAC name for a cycloalkane?
   a. cyclopentane
   b. methylcyclobutane
   c. dimethylcyclopropane
   d. no correct response

Answers: 1. c; 2. c, 3. c

12-14 Isomerism in Cycloalkanes

LEARNING FOCUS
Be familiar with the concepts of constitutional isomerism and *cis–trans* isomerism as they relate to cycloalkanes.

Constitutional isomers are possible for cycloalkanes that contain four or more carbon atoms. For example, there are five cycloalkane constitutional isomers that have the formula C_5H_{10}: one based on a five-membered ring, one based on a four-membered ring, and three based on a three-membered ring. These isomers are

Cyclopentane   Methylcyclobutane   1,2-Dimethyl-cyclopropane   1,1-Dimethyl-cyclopropane   Ethylcyclopropane

A second type of isomerism, called *stereoisomerism,* is possible for some *substituted* cycloalkanes. Whereas constitutional isomerism results from differences in *connectivity,* stereoisomerism results from differences in *configuration.* **Stereoisomers** *are isomers that have the same molecular and structural formulas but different orientations of atoms in space.* Several forms of stereoisomerism exist. The form associated with cycloalkanes is called *cis–trans isomerism.* **Cis–trans** isomers *are isomers that have the same molecular and structural formulas but different orientations of atoms in space because of restricted rotation about bonds.*

In alkanes, there is free rotation about all carbon–carbon bonds (Section 12-7). In cycloalkanes, the ring structure restricts rotation for the carbon atoms in the ring. The consequence of this lack of rotation in a cycloalkane is the creation of "top" and "bottom" positions for the two attachments on each of the ring carbon atoms. This "top–bottom" situation leads to *cis–trans* isomerism in cycloalkanes in which each of two ring carbon atoms bears two different attachments. ◄

▶ Cis–trans isomers *have the same molecular formula and the same structural formula. The only difference between them is the orientation of atoms in space.* Constitutional isomers *have the same molecular formula but different structural formulas.*

Consider the following two structures for the molecule 1,2-dimethylcyclopentane.

Structure A   Structure B

In structure A, both methyl groups are above the plane of the ring (the "top" side). In structure B, one methyl group is above the plane of the ring (the "top" side) and the other below it (the "bottom" side). Structure A cannot be converted into structure B without breaking bonds. Hence structures A and B are isomers; there are two 1,2-dimethylcyclopentanes. The first isomer is called *cis*-1,2-dimethylcyclopentane and the second *trans*-1,2-dimethylcyclopentane. ◄

▶ The Latin cis *means "on the same side," and the Latin* trans *means "across from." Consider the use of the prefix* trans- *in the phrase "transatlantic voyage."*

cis-1,2-Dimethylcyclopentane
Boiling point = 99°C

trans-1,2-Dimethylcyclopentane
Boiling point = 92°C

Cis- is a prefix that means "on the same side." In *cis*-1,2-dimethylcyclopentane, the two methyl groups are on the same side of the ring. *Trans-* is a prefix that means "across from." In *trans*-1,2-dimethylcyclopentane, the two methyl groups are on opposite sides of the ring.

Cis–trans isomerism can occur in rings of all sizes. The presence of a substituent on each of two carbon atoms in the ring is the requirement for its occurrence. In biochemistry, it will be found that the human body often selectively distinguishes between the *cis* and *trans* isomers of a compound. One isomer will be active in the body and the other inactive. ◀

▶ Cis–trans *isomerism will also be encountered in the next chapter (Section 13-6), where the required restricted rotation barrier will be a carbon–carbon double bond rather than a ring of carbon atoms. Another type of stereoisomerism called enantiomerism (left- and right-handed forms of a molecule) will be considered in the discussion of carbohydrates in Chapter 18.*

EXAMPLE 12-8

Identifying and Naming Cycloalkane *Cis–Trans* Isomers

Determine whether *cis–trans* isomerism is possible for each of the following cycloalkanes. If so, then draw structural formulas for the *cis* and *trans* isomers.

a. Methylcyclohexane
b. 1,1-Dimethylcyclohexane
c. 1,3-Dimethylcyclobutane
d. 1-Ethyl-2-methylcyclobutane

Solution

a. *Cis–trans* isomerism is not possible because there are not two substituents on the ring.

b. *Cis–trans* isomerism is not possible. There are two substituents on the ring, but they are on the same carbon atom. Each of two different carbons must bear substituents.

c. *Cis–trans* isomerism does exist.

cis-1,3-Dimethylcyclobutane   *trans*-1,3-Dimethylcyclobutane

d. *Cis–trans* isomerism does exist.

cis-1-Ethyl-2-methylcyclobutane   *trans*-1-Ethyl-2-methylcyclobutane

Use of the terms *cis-* and *trans-* in designating stereoisomers in cycloalkanes is limited to substituted cycloalkanes in which the two substituted carbon atoms each have one hydrogen atom and one substituent other than hydrogen. ▶ The designations *cis-* and *trans-* become ambiguous in situations where either or both of the substituted carbons have two different substituents but no hydrogen atoms. Following is an example of such a situation in substituted cycloalkanes.

▶ *In cycloalkanes,* cis–trans *isomerism can also be denoted by using wedges and dotted lines. A heavy wedge-shaped bond to a ring structure indicates a bond* above *the plane of the ring, and a broken dotted line indicates a bond* below *the plane of the ring.*

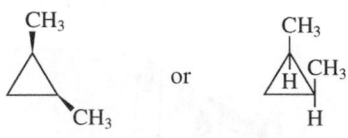

cis-1,2-Dimethylcyclopropane

The first structure is the *cis-* isomer if the focus is on H and the ethyl group; the second structure is the *cis-* isomer if the focus is on H and the methyl group. A different nomenclature system, called the *R,S* nomenclature system (which is not covered in this textbook), must be used to distinguish such isomerism.

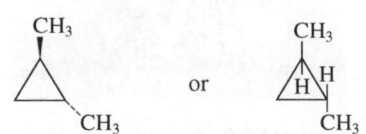

trans-1,2-Dimethylcyclopropane

Section 12-14 Quick Quiz

1. How many constitutional isomers are possible for a four-carbon cycloalkane?
   a. 2
   b. 3
   c. 4
   d. no correct response
2. For which of the following cycloalkanes is *cis–trans* isomerism possible?
   a. 1,1-dimethylcyclobutane
   b. 1-ethyl-1-methylcyclobutane
   c. 1-ethyl-2-methylcyclobutane
   d. no correct response
3. Which of the following cycloalkane structures has a *trans*-configuration for the alkyl groups?

   a.   b.

   c.   d. no correct response

Answers: 1. a; 2. c; 3. b

12-15 Sources of Alkanes and Cycloalkanes

LEARNING FOCUS
Be familiar with important natural sources for alkanes and cycloalkanes.

Alkanes and cycloalkanes are not "laboratory curiosities" but, rather, two families of extremely important naturally occurring compounds. Natural gas and petroleum (crude oil) constitute their largest and most important natural source. Deposits of these resources are usually associated with underground dome-shaped rock formations (Figure 12-7). When a hole is drilled into such a rock formation, it is possible to recover some of the trapped hydrocarbons—that is, the natural gas and/or petroleum (Figure 12-8). Note that petroleum and natural gas do not occur in Earth in the form of "liquid pools" but, rather, are dispersed throughout a porous rock formation. ◀

Unprocessed natural gas contains 50%–90% methane, 1%–10% ethane, and up to 8% higher-molecular-mass alkanes (predominantly propane and butanes). The higher alkanes found in crude natural gas are removed prior to release of the gas into the pipeline distribution systems. Because the removed alkanes can be liquefied by the use of moderate pressure, they are stored as liquids under pressure in steel cylinders and are marketed as bottled gas.

▶ *The word* petroleum *comes from the Latin* petra, *which means "rock," and* oleum, *which means "oil."*

Figure 12-8 An oil rig pumping oil from an underground rock formation.

Figure 12-7 A rock formation such as this is necessary for the accumulation of petroleum and natural gas.

Crude petroleum is a complex mixture of hydrocarbons (both cyclic and acyclic) that can be separated into useful fractions through refining. During refining, the physical separation of the crude into component fractions is accomplished by fractional distillation, a process that takes advantage of boiling-point differences between the components of the crude petroleum. Each fraction contains hydrocarbons within a specific boiling-point range. The gasoline fraction consists primarily of alkanes and cycloalkanes with 5 to 12 carbon atoms present. The fractions obtained from a typical fractionation process are shown in Figure 12-9.

Figure 12-9 The complex hydrocarbon mixture present in petroleum is separated into simpler mixtures by means of a fractionating column.

Section 12-15 Quick Quiz

1. Which of the following statements concerning alkanes and cycloalkanes is correct?
   a. Alkanes are naturally occurring compounds but cycloalkanes are not.
   b. Cycloalkanes are naturally occurring compounds but alkanes are not.
   c. Both alkanes and cycloalkanes are naturally occurring compounds.
   d. no correct response
2. Which of the following is *not* a mixture of cyclic and noncyclic alkanes?
   a. processed natural gas
   b. crude petroleum
   c. gasoline
   d. no correct response

Answers: 1. c; 2. a

12-16 Physical Properties of Alkanes and Cycloalkanes

LEARNING FOCUS
Be familiar with general physical properties of alkanes and cycloalkanes.

In this section, a number of generalizations about the physical properties of alkanes and cycloalkanes are considered.

1. *Alkanes and cycloalkanes are insoluble in water.* Water molecules are polar, and alkane and cycloalkane molecules are nonpolar. Molecules of unlike polarity

Figure 12-10 The insolubility of alkanes in water is used to advantage by many plants, which produce unbranched long-chain alkanes that serve as protective coatings on leaves and fruits. Such protective coatings minimize water loss for plants. Apples can be "polished" because of the long-chain alkane coating on their skin, which involves the unbranched alkanes $C_{27}H_{56}$ and $C_{29}H_{60}$. The leaf wax of cabbage and broccoli is mainly unbranched $C_{29}H_{60}$.

▶ *The variation of alkane and cycloalkane boiling point and melting point with carbon-chain length or ring size is used to advantage in gasoline production. Gasoline composition changes seasonally in locations that have very hot summers and very cold winters. "Summer" gasoline contains larger amounts of higher-boiling hydrocarbons so that it evaporates less readily. "Winter" gasoline contains larger amounts of lower-boiling hydrocarbons so that it vaporizes readily at low temperatures..*

have limited solubility in one another (Section 8-4). The water insolubility of alkanes makes them good preservatives for metals. They prevent water from reaching the metal surface and causing corrosion. They also have biological functions as protective coatings (Figure 12-10).

2. *Alkanes and cycloalkanes have densities lower than that of water.* Alkane and cycloalkane densities fall in the range 0.6 g/mL to 0.8 g/mL, compared with water's density of 1.0 g/mL. When alkanes and cycloalkanes are mixed with water, two layers form (because of insolubility), with the hydrocarbon layer on top (because of its lower density). This density difference between alkanes/cycloalkanes and water explains why oil spills in aqueous environments spread so quickly. The *floating* oil follows the movement of the water.

3. *The boiling points of continuous-chain alkanes and cycloalkanes increase with an increase in carbon–chain length or ring size.* For continuous-chain alkanes, the boiling point increases roughly 30°C for every carbon atom added to the chain. This trend, shown in Figure 12-11, is the result of increasing London force strength (Section 7-13). London forces become stronger as molecular surface area increases. Short, continuous-chain alkanes (1 to 4 carbon atoms) are gases at room temperature. Continuous-chain alkanes containing 5 to 17 carbon atoms are liquids, and alkanes that have carbon chains longer than this are solids at room temperature.

Branching on a carbon chain lowers the boiling point of an alkane. A comparison of the boiling points of unbranched alkanes and their 2-methyl-branched isomers is given in Figure 12-11. Branched alkanes are more compact, with smaller surface areas than their straight-chain isomers.

Cycloalkanes have higher boiling points than their noncyclic counterparts with the same number of carbon atoms (Figure 12-11). These differences are due in large part to cyclic systems having more rigid and more symmetrical structures. ◀

Cyclopropane and cyclobutane are gases at room temperature, and cyclopentane through cyclooctane are liquids at room temperature. Figure 12-12 is a physical-state summary for unbranched alkanes or unsubstituted cycloalkanes with 8 or fewer carbon atoms.

The alkanes and cycloalkanes whose boiling points are compared in Figure 12-11 constitute a *homologous series* of organic compounds. In a homologous series, the members differ structurally only in the number of —CH$_2$— groups present. Members exhibit gradually changing physical properties and usually have very similar chemical properties.

The existence of homologous series of organic compounds gives organization to organic chemistry in the same way that the periodic table gives organization

Figure 12-11 Trends in normal boiling points for continuous-chain alkanes, 2-methyl branched alkanes, and unsubstituted cycloalkanes as a function of the number of carbon atoms present. For a series of alkanes or cycloalkanes, melting point increases as carbon-chain length increases.

to the chemistry of the elements. Knowing something about a few members of a homologous series usually enables the properties of other members in the series to be deduced.

The physiological effects of alkanes on the human body depend heavily on alkane physical state (gas, liquid, or solid), which in turn depends heavily on carbon-chain length and degree of branching of the carbon chain. The focus on relevancy feature Chemical Connections 12-B—The Physiological Effects of Alkanes—discusses the physiological effects of alkanes. In general, liquid-state alkanes are skin "irritants" and solid-state alkanes "protect" the skin.

Unbranched Alkanes			
C_1	C_3	C_5	C_7
C_2	C_4	C_6	C_8

Unsubstituted Cycloalkanes			
✕	C_3	C_5	C_7
✕	C_4	C_6	C_8

☐ Gas ☐ Liquid

Figure 12-12 A physical-state summary for unbranched alkanes and unsubstituted cycloalkanes at room temperature and pressure.

Section 12-16 Quick Quiz

1. Which of the following is a general physical property of alkanes?
   a. not soluble in water
   b. more dense than water
   c. molecules are polar
   d. no correct response
2. Which of the following statements concerning alkane and cycloalkane boiling points is incorrect?
   a. Branching on a carbon chain lowers boiling point.
   b. Cycloalkanes have higher boiling points than their noncyclic counterparts.
   c. Unbranched alkane boiling points increase as carbon chain length increases.
   d. no correct response
3. Which of the following alkanes is a gas at room temperature?
   a. ethane
   b. pentane
   c. heptane
   d. no correct response

Answers: 1. a; 2. d; 3. a

12-17 Chemical Properties of Alkanes and Cycloalkanes

LEARNING FOCUS

Be able to predict the products for alkane and cycloalkane combustion and halogenation reactions.

Alkanes are the least reactive type of organic compound. They can be heated for long periods of time in strong acids and bases with no appreciable reaction. Strong oxidizing agents and reducing agents have little effect on alkanes. ◄

Alkanes are not absolutely unreactive. Two important reactions that they undergo are combustion, which is reaction with oxygen, and halogenation, which is reaction with halogens. Indeed, combustion is the most important chemical reaction for alkanes.

Combustion

A **combustion reaction** *is a chemical reaction between a substance and oxygen (usually from air) that proceeds with the evolution of heat and light (usually as a flame).* Alkanes readily undergo combustion when ignited. When sufficient oxygen is present to support total combustion, carbon dioxide and water are the products. ◄

$$CH_4 + 2O_2 \longrightarrow CO_2 + 2H_2O + \text{heat energy}$$
$$2C_6H_{14} + 19O_2 \longrightarrow 12CO_2 + 14H_2O + \text{heat energy}$$

The exothermic nature (Section 9-5) of alkane combustion reactions explains the extensive use of alkanes as fuels. Natural gas, used in home heating, is predominantly methane. Propane is used in home heating in rural areas and in gas barbecue units

▶ *The term* paraffins *is an older name for the alkane family of compounds. This name comes from the Latin* parum affinis, *which means "little activity." That is a good summary of the general chemical properties of alkanes.*

▶ *Atmospheric levels of carbon dioxide are increasing annually as a result of the extensive use of alkanes and cycloalkanes as energy sources. The link between combustion-generated carbon dioxide and the problem of global warming was previously considered in the feature box Chemical Connections 9-A—Combustion Reactions, Carbon Dioxide, and Global Warming.*

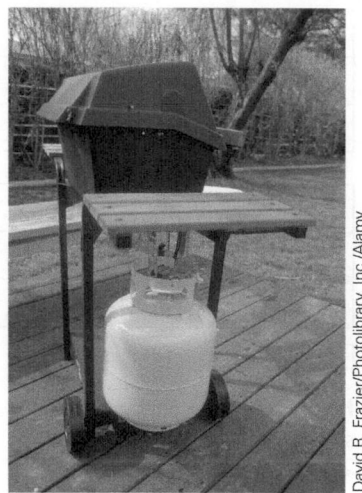

Figure 12-13 Propane fuel tank on a home barbecue unit.

(Figure 12-13). Butane fuels portable camping stoves. Gasoline is a complex mixture of many alkanes and other types of hydrocarbons.

Incomplete combustion can occur if insufficient oxygen is present during the combustion process. When this is the case, some carbon monoxide (CO) and/or elemental carbon are reaction products along with carbon dioxide (CO_2). In a chemical laboratory setting, incomplete combustion is often observed. The appearance of deposits of carbon black (soot) on the bottom of glassware is physical evidence that incomplete combustion is occurring. The problem is that the air-to-fuel ratio for the Bunsen burner is not correct. It is too rich; it contains too much fuel and not enough oxygen (air).

Halogenation

The halogens are the elements of Group VIIA of the periodic table: fluorine (F_2), chlorine (Cl_2), bromine (Br_2), and iodine (I_2) (Section 3-4). Since they have seven valence electrons (Section 4-2), halogen atoms need to share one electron with another atom in order to acquire an octet of electrons (Section 5-2). Normal bonding behavior for halogens is thus the formation of one single bond. Their bonding behavior is similar to that of hydrogen, which also forms only one single bond.

CHEMICAL CONNECTIONS 12-B

The Physiological Effects of Alkanes

The simplest alkanes (methane, ethane, propane, and butane) are gases at room temperature and pressure. Methane and ethane are difficult to liquefy, so they are usually handled as compressed gases. Propane and butane are easily liquefied at room temperature under a moderate pressure. They are stored in low-pressure cylinders in a liquefied form. These four gases are colorless, odorless, and nontoxic, and they have limited physiological effects. The danger in inhaling them lies in potential suffocation due to lack of oxygen. The major immediate danger associated with a natural gas leak is the potential formation of an explosive air–alkane mixture rather than the formation of a toxic air–alkane mixture.

The C_5 to C_8 alkanes, of which there are many isomeric forms, are free-flowing, nonpolar, volatile liquids. They are the primary constituents of gasoline. These compounds are not particularly toxic, but gasoline should not be swallowed because (1) some of the additives present are harmful and (2) liquid alkanes can damage lung tissue because of physical rather than chemical effects. Physical effects include the dissolving of lipid molecules of cell membranes (see Chapter 19), causing pneumonia-like symptoms. Liquid alkanes can also affect the skin for related reasons. These alkanes dissolve natural body oils, causing the skin to dry out. (This "drying out" effect is easily noticed when paint thinner, a mixture of hydrocarbons, is used to remove paint from the hands.)

In direct contrast to liquid alkanes, solid alkanes are used to protect the skin. Pharmaceutical-grade *petrolatum* and *mineral oil* (also called liquid petrolatum), obtained as products from petroleum distillation, have such a function. Petrolatum is a mixture of C_{25} to C_{30} alkanes, and mineral oil involves alkanes in the C_{18} to C_{24} range.

Petrolatum (Vaseline is a well-known brand name) is a semi-solid hydrocarbon mixture that is useful both as a skin softener and as a skin protector. Many moisturizing hand lotions and

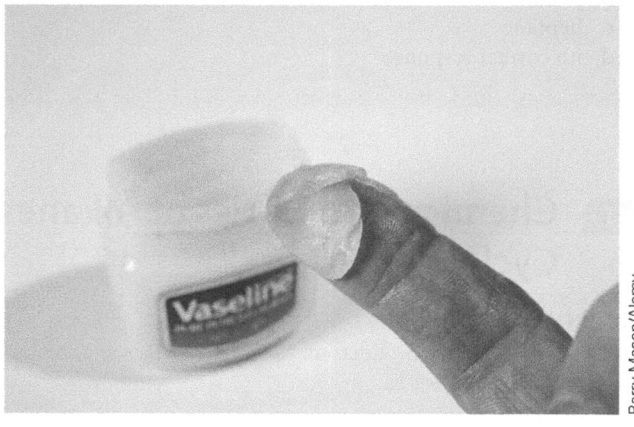

A semi-solid alkane mixture, such as Vaseline, is useful as a skin protector because neither water nor water solutions will penetrate a coating of it. Here, Vaseline is applied to a baby's bottom as a protection against diaper rash.

some medicated salves contain petrolatum. Neither water nor water solutions (for example, urine) will penetrate protective petrolatum coatings. This explains why petrolatum products protect a baby's bottom from diaper rash.

Mineral oil is often used to replace natural skin oils washed away by frequent bathing and swimming. Too much mineral oil, however, can be detrimental; it will dissolve nonpolar skin materials. Mineral oil has some use as a laxative; it effectively softens and lubricates hard stools. When taken by mouth, it passes through the gastrointestinal tract unchanged and is excreted chemically intact. Loss of fat-soluble vitamins (A, D, E, and K) can occur if mineral oil is consumed while these vitamins are in the digestive tract. Using a mineral-oil enema instead avoids this drawback.

A **halogenation reaction** *is a chemical reaction between a substance and a halogen in which one or more halogen atoms are incorporated into molecules of the substance.* Halogenation of an alkane produces a hydrocarbon derivative in which one or more halogen atoms have been substituted for hydrogen atoms. An example of an alkane halogenation reaction is

$$
\underset{\substack{\\ }}{\text{H}-\overset{\displaystyle H}{\underset{\displaystyle H}{\text{C}}}-\overset{\displaystyle H}{\underset{\displaystyle H}{\text{C}}}-\text{H}} + \boxed{\text{Br}_2} \xrightarrow[\text{light}]{\text{Heat or}} \text{H}-\overset{\displaystyle H}{\underset{\displaystyle H}{\text{C}}}-\overset{\displaystyle H}{\underset{\displaystyle H}{\text{C}}}-\boxed{\text{Br}} + \text{H}\boxed{\text{Br}}
$$

Alkane halogenation is an example of a substitution reaction, a type of reaction that occurs often in organic chemistry. **A substitution reaction** *is a chemical reaction in which part of a small reacting molecule replaces an atom or a group of atoms on a hydrocarbon or hydrocarbon derivative.* A diagrammatic representation of a substitution reaction is shown in Figure 12-14.

A *general* equation for the substitution of a single halogen atom for one of the hydrogen atoms of an alkane is

$$
\underset{\text{Alkane}}{\text{R}-\text{H}} + \underset{\text{Halogen}}{\boxed{\text{X}_2}} \xrightarrow[\text{light}]{\text{Heat or}} \underset{\substack{\text{Halogenated}\\\text{alkane}}}{\text{R}-\boxed{\text{X}}} + \underset{\substack{\text{Hydrogen}\\\text{halide}}}{\text{H}-\boxed{\text{X}}}
$$

Note the following features of this general equation:

1. The notation R—H is a general formula for an alkane. R— in this case represents an alkyl group. Addition of a hydrogen atom to an alkyl group produces the parent hydrocarbon of the alkyl group.
2. The notation R—X on the product side is the general formula for a halogenated alkane. X is the general symbol for a halogen atom.
3. Reaction conditions are noted by placing these conditions on the equation arrow that separates reactants from products. Halogenation of an alkane requires the presence of heat or light.

(The symbol R is used frequently in organic chemistry and will be encountered in numerous generalized formulas in subsequent chapters; it always represents a generalized organic group in a structural formula. An R group can be an alkyl group—methyl, ethyl, propyl, etc.—or any number of other organic groups. Consider the symbol R to represent the Rest of an organic molecule, which is not specifically indicated because it is not the focal point of the discussion occurring at that time.) ◀

In halogenation of an alkane, the alkane is said to undergo *fluorination, chlorination, bromination,* or *iodination,* depending on the identity of the halogen reactant. Chlorination and bromination are the two widely used alkane halogenation reactions. Fluorination reactions generally proceed too quickly to be useful, and iodination reactions go too slowly. ◀

▶ *Occasionally, it is useful to represent alkyl groups in a non-specific way. The symbol R is used for this purpose. Just as city is a generic term for Chicago, New York, or San Francisco, the symbol R is a generic designation for any alkyl group. The symbol R comes from the German word* radikal, *which means, in a chemical context, "molecular fragment."*

▶ *The standard bonding behavior for the halogens is formation of one covalent bond. Thus in organic compounds, a carbon atom forms four bonds, a hydrogen atom forms one bond, and a halogen atom forms one bond.*

Figure 12-14 In an alkane substitution reaction, an incoming atom or group of atoms (represented by the orange sphere) replaces a hydrogen atom in the alkane molecule.

Halogenation usually results in the formation of a mixture of products rather than a single product. More than one product results because more than one hydrogen atom on an alkane can be replaced with halogen atoms. To illustrate this concept, let us consider the chlorination of methane, the simplest alkane.

Methane and chlorine, when heated to a high temperature or in the presence of light, react as follows:

$$CH_4 + \boxed{Cl_2} \xrightarrow[\text{light}]{\text{Heat or}} CH_3\boxed{Cl} + HCl$$

The reaction does not stop at this stage, however, because the chlorinated methane product can react with additional chlorine to produce polychlorinated products.

$$CH_3Cl + \boxed{Cl_2} \xrightarrow[\text{light}]{\text{Heat or}} CH_2\boxed{Cl_2} + HCl$$

$$CH_2Cl_2 + \boxed{Cl_2} \xrightarrow[\text{light}]{\text{Heat or}} CHCl_3 + HCl$$

$$CHCl_3 + \boxed{Cl_2} \xrightarrow[\text{light}]{\text{Heat or}} CCl_4 + HCl$$

By controlling the reaction conditions and the ratio of chlorine to methane, it is possible to *favor* formation of one or another of the possible chlorinated methane products.

The chemical properties of cycloalkanes are similar to those of alkanes. Cycloalkanes readily undergo combustion, as well as chlorination and bromination. With unsubstituted cycloalkanes, monohalogenation produces a single product because all hydrogen atoms present in the cycloalkane are equivalent to one another.

Chemistry at a Glance—Properties of Alkanes and Cycloalkanes—summarizes the physical properties and chemical reactions of alkanes and cycloalkanes.

CHEMISTRY AT A GLANCE Properties of Alkanes and Cycloalkanes

1. The most important chemical use for alkanes involves their reaction with
   a. oxygen
   b. chlorine
   c. bromine
   d. no correct response
2. The chemical products formed when an alkane undergoes *complete* combustion are always
   a. C and H_2
   b. C and H_2O
   c. CO_2 and H_2O
   d. no correct response
3. Which of the following is not a product when an alkane molecule (R—H) reacts with a halogen molecule (X_2)?
   a. R—X
   b. H—X
   c. R_2—X_2
   d. no correct response
4. Which of the following statements concerning the chemical reactions of alkanes and cycloalkanes is correct?
   a. Alkanes undergo combustion reactions but cycloalkanes do not.
   b. Cycloalkanes undergo halogenation reactions but not combustion reactions.
   c. Halogenation of an alkane is an example of a substitution reaction.
   d. no correct response

Answers: 1. a; 2. c; 3. c; 4. c

12-18 Halogenated Alkanes and Cycloalkanes

LEARNING FOCUS

Given structural formulas, assign IUPAC names to halogenated alkane and halogenated cycloalkane molecules and vice versa; know common names and uses for selected halogenated methanes; know general physical properties for halogenated alkanes.

A **halogenated alkane** *is an alkane derivative in which one or more halogen atoms are present.* Similarly, a **halogenated cycloalkane** *is a cycloalkane derivative in which one or more halogen atoms are present.* Produced by halogenation reactions (Section 12-17), these two types of compounds represent the first class of hydrocarbon derivatives (Section 12-3) formally considered in this text.

Alkanes have the general molecular formula C_nH_{2n+2} (Section 12-4). Halogenated alkanes containing one halogen atom have the general molecular formula $C_nH_{2n+1}X$; a halogen atom has replaced a hydrogen atom. If two halogen atoms are present in a halogenated alkane, the general molecular formula is $C_nH_{2n}X_2$. Since cycloalkanes have the general molecular formula C_nH_{2n} (Section 12-12), a halogenated cycloalkane with one halogen atom present will have a general molecular formula of $C_nH_{2n-1}X$.

Nomenclature of Halogenated Alkanes

The IUPAC rules for naming halogenated alkanes are similar to those for naming branched alkanes, with the following modifications:

1. Halogen atoms, treated as substituents on a carbon chain, are called *fluoro-, chloro-, bromo-,* and *iodo-*.
2. When a carbon chain bears both a halogen and an alkyl substituent, the two substituents are considered of equal rank in determining the numbering system for the chain. The chain is numbered from the end closer to a substituent, whether it be a *halo* group or an alkyl group.
3. Alphabetical priority determines the order in which all substituents present are listed.

The following names are derived using these rule adjustments.

$$CH_3-CH-CH-CH_3$$
$$\quad\quad\; | \quad\;\; |$$
$$\quad\quad Cl \quad CH_3$$
2-Chloro-3-methylbutane

$$CH_3-CH-CH_2-CH_2$$
$$\quad\quad\; | \quad\quad\quad\; |$$
$$\quad\quad Br \quad\quad\quad Cl$$
3-Bromo-1-chlorobutane

1-Ethyl-2-fluorocyclohexane

Simple halogenated alkanes can also be named as *alkyl halides*. These common (non-IUPAC) names have two parts. The first part is the name of the hydrocarbon portion of the molecule (the alkyl group). The second part (as a separate word) identifies the halogen portion, which is named as if it were an ion (chloride, bromide, and so on), even though no ions are present (all bonds are covalent bonds). The following examples contrast the IUPAC names and the common names (in parentheses) of selected halogenated alkanes. ◀

$$CH_3-CH_2-Cl \quad\quad CH_3-CH_2-CH_2-Br \quad\quad CH_3-CH-CH_3$$
$$\quad\quad\quad\quad\quad\quad\quad\quad\quad\quad\quad\quad\quad\quad\quad\quad\quad\quad\quad\quad\quad\quad\quad | $$
$$\quad\quad\quad\quad\quad\quad\quad\quad\quad\quad\quad\quad\quad\quad\quad\quad\quad\quad\quad\quad\quad\quad\quad Cl$$

Chloroethane (ethyl chloride)   1-Bromopropane (propyl bromide)   2-Chloropropane (isopropyl chloride)

▶ *The contrast between IUPAC and common names for halogenated hydrocarbons is as follows:*

IUPAC (one word)

haloalkane

chloromethane

Common (two words)

alkyl halide

methyl chloride

Physical Properties of Halogenated Alkanes

Halogenated alkane boiling points are generally higher than those of the corresponding alkane. An important factor contributing to this effect is the polarity of carbon–halogen bonds, which results in increased dipole–dipole interactions.

Two general trends relative to boiling points and melting points of halogenated hydrocarbons containing a single halogen atom are:

1. Boiling points and melting points increase as the size of the alkyl group present increases. This is due to increasing intermolecular forces associated with increased molecular surface area (Section 7-13).
2. Boiling points and melting points increase as the size of the halogen atom increases from fluorine (F) to iodine (I).

Halogenated hydrocarbons do not have hydrogen-bonding capabilities since all hydrogen atoms are bonded to carbon atoms (Section 7-13). Thus water solubility is very limited regardless of molecular size.

Some halogenated alkanes have densities that are greater than that of water, a situation not common for organic compounds. Chloroalkanes containing two or more chlorine atoms, bromoalkanes, and iodoalkanes are generally more dense than water.

Chlorinated Methanes

Repeated chlorination of methane produces successively the compounds CH_3Cl, CH_2Cl_2, $CHCl_3$, and CCl_4. The generalized equation for this progression of chlorinated methane products is

$$CH_4 + xCl_2 \longrightarrow CH_{4-x}Cl_x + xHCl$$

A general property of these compounds is that of useful solvent. As solvents, they are relatively nonpolar, which makes them relatively immiscible with water.

Table 12-4 gives nomenclature (both IUPAC and common names) and specific uses (both past and present) for these compounds.

Chlorofluorocarbons

Chlorofluorocarbons (CFCs) have the general molecular formula CCl_xF_{4-x}. They are manufactured under the trade name Freon. Representative of such compounds are CCl_3F (trichlorofluoromethane, or Freon-11) and CCl_2F_2 (dichlorodifluoromethane, or Freon-12). For many years, Freons were the refrigerant gas of choice for both industrial and home refrigeration and air-conditioning, as well as automobile

▶ **Table 12-4 Properties and Uses of the Chlorinated Methanes**

Chemical Formula and Nomenclature	Physical Properties	Occurrence and Uses
CH_3Cl Chloromethane Methyl chloride	Colorless, extremely flammable gas with a mildly sweet odor	Present in volcanic gases; produced by algae and giant kelp; used as an industrial solvent; once used widely as a refrigerant; no longer found in consumer products because of toxicity concerns
CH_2Cl_2 Dichloromethane Methylene chloride	Colorless, volatile liquid with a mildly sweet odor	Chemical intermediate in production of silicone polymers; used as a paint stripper and degreaser; once used to decaffeinate coffee but has been replaced by liquid carbon dioxide due to concern about trace amounts of CH_2Cl_2 remaining in the coffee
$CHCl_3$ Trichloromethane Chloroform	Colorless, very dense sweet-smelling liquid	Used in manufacture of Teflon; good industrial solvent; was an early popular anesthetic but use discontinued because of toxicity effects
CCl_4 Tetrachloromethane Carbon tetrachloride Carbon tet	Colorless, nonflammable sweet-smelling liquid	Good solvent for fats, oils, and greases; once widely used in dry cleaning of clothing but has been replaced by tetrachloroethylene, which is more stable and less toxic

air-conditioning. Indeed, it is CFCs that made refrigeration units available, at reasonable cost, to the general household after World War II.

Use of Freons in refrigeration and air-conditioning has now been discontinued. It was not a toxicity problem that caused the change but, rather, an atmospheric environmental problem. After many years of use, it became apparent that Freons were adversely affecting the ozone layer present in the upper atmosphere. The focus on relevancy feature Chemical Connections 12-C—Chlorofluorocarbons and the Ozone Layer—gives details concerning the Freon–ozone layer problem and also discusses replacement compounds for Freons.

Section 12-18 Quick Quiz

1. What is the IUPAC name for the compound whose common name is propyl chloride?
   a. chloropropane
   b. 1-chloropropane
   c. 2-chloropropane
   d. no correct answer
2. What is the common name for the compound whose IUPAC name is 2-chloropropane?
   a. ethyl chloride
   b. propyl chloride
   c. isopropyl chloride
   d. no correct response
3. The halogenated methanes methylene chloride and chloroform have, respectively, the molecular formulas
   a. CH_3Cl and CH_2Cl_2
   b. CH_2Cl_2 and $CHCl_3$
   c. CH_3Cl and CCl_4
   d. no correct response
4. A Freon is a halogenated methane in which both
   a. F and Cl are present
   b. Cl and Br are present
   c. F and Br are present
   d. no correct response

Answers: 1. b; 2. c; 3. b; 4. a

CHEMICAL CONNECTIONS 12-C

Chlorofluorocarbons and the Ozone Layer

Chlorofluorocarbons (CFCs) are compounds composed of the elements chlorine, fluorine, and carbon. CFCs are synthetic compounds that have been developed primarily for use as refrigerants. The two most widely used of the CFCs are trichlorofluoromethane and dichlorodifluoromethane. Both of these compounds are marketed under the trade name Freon.

Trichlorofluoromethane
(Freon-11)

Dichlorodifluoromethane
(Freon-12)

Freon-11 and Freon-12 possess ideal properties for use as a refrigerant gas. Both are inert, nontoxic, and easily compressible. Prior to their development, ammonia was used in refrigeration. Ammonia is toxic, and leaks from ammonia-based refrigeration units have been fatal.

It is now known that CFCs contribute to a serious environmental problem: destruction of the stratospheric (high-altitude) ozone that is commonly called the ozone layer. Once released into the atmosphere, CFCs persist for long periods without reaction. Consequently, they slowly drift upward in the atmosphere, finally reaching the stratosphere.

It is in the stratosphere, the location of the "ozone layer," that environmental problems occur. At these high altitudes, the CFCs are exposed to ultraviolet light (from the sun), which activates them. The ultraviolet light breaks carbon–chlorine bonds within the CFCs, releasing chlorine atoms.

$$CCl_2F_2 + \text{ultraviolet light} \longrightarrow CClF_2 + Cl$$

The Cl atoms so produced (called atomic chlorine) are extremely reactive species. One of the molecules with which they react is ozone (O_3).

$$Cl + O_3 \longrightarrow ClO + O_2$$

A reaction such as this upsets the O_3–O_2 equilibrium in the stratosphere (Section 9-8).

The Montreal Protocol of 1987 (an international agreement on substances that deplete the ozone layer), and later amendments to this agreement, limit—and in some cases ban—future production and use of CFCs. The following graph shows the effects of the implementation of this agreement.

The most commonly used replacement compounds in refrigeration systems and as aerosol propellants for the phased-out CFCs are HFCs (hydrofluorocarbons), compounds that contain H and F (bonded to carbon atoms). The three most commonly used HFCs are

HFC-134a
1,1,1,2-tetrafluoroethane

HFC-152a
1,1-difluoroethane

HFC-23
trifluoromethane

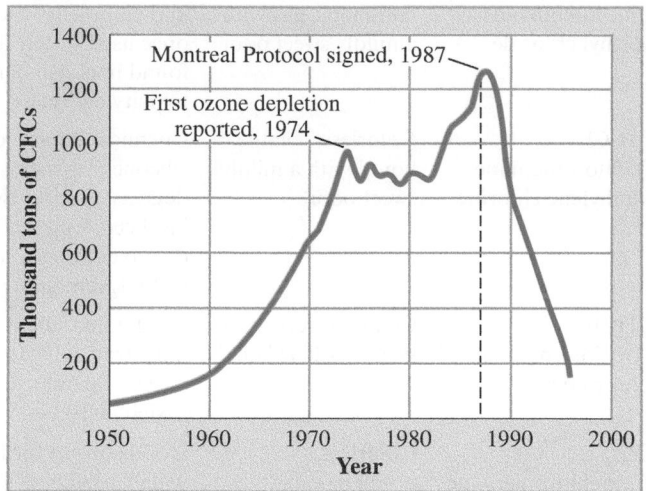

Worldwide Production of CFCs (1950–1996)

The presence of carbon–hydrogen bonds in these molecules makes them more reactive than CFCs, and they are generally destroyed at lower altitudes before they reach the stratosphere. Their refrigeration properties, although adequate, are not as good as those of the previously used CFCs.

HFCs, used heavily during the period 1990–2010, are now on the replacement (phase-out) list. They are now known to be potent greenhouse gases, and their concentrations in the lower atmosphere are increasing. HFC-134a, the most used of the HFCs, has a global warming potential that is 1340 times greater than that of an equivalent amount of carbon dioxide. HFC use in air-conditioning for new model cars is now restricted or banned in the European Union.

A new type of fluorinated hydrocarbon is being "hyped" as the "global replacement refrigerant." It is an HFO (hydrofluoroolefin). HFOs are unsaturated (a carbon–carbon double bond is present) rather than saturated hydrocarbon derivatives. The specific replacement compound coming to market is HFO-1234yf, a compound with the structure

HFO-1234yf
2,3,3,3-tetrafluoropropene

The IUPAC name for this compound is 2,3,3,3-tetrafluoropropene (Section 13-3). The global warming potential of this HFO is only slightly greater than that of carbon dioxide. HFO-1234yf use began in Europe with 2011 model-year cars and began in the United States with 2013 model-year cars.

Concepts to Remember

Carbon atom bonding characteristics. Carbon atoms in organic compounds must have four bonds (Section 12-2).

Types of hydrocarbons. Hydrocarbons, binary compounds of carbon and hydrogen, are of two types: saturated and unsaturated. In saturated hydrocarbons, all carbon–carbon bonds are single bonds. Unsaturated hydrocarbons have one or more carbon–carbon multiple bonds—double bonds, triple bonds, or both (Section 12-3).

Alkanes. Alkanes are saturated hydrocarbons in which the carbon atom arrangement is that of an unbranched or branched chain. The formulas of all alkanes can be represented by the general formula C_nH_{2n+2}, where n is the number of carbon atoms present (Section 12-4).

Structural formulas. Structural formulas are two-dimensional representations of the arrangement of the atoms in molecules. These formulas give complete information about the arrangement of the atoms in a molecule but not the spatial orientation of the atoms. Two types of structural formulas are commonly encountered: expanded and condensed (Section 12-5).

Isomers. Isomers are compounds that have the same molecular formula (that is, the same numbers and kinds of atoms), but that differ in the way the atoms are arranged (Section 12-6).

Constitutional isomers. Constitutional isomers are isomers that differ in the connectivity of atoms, that is, in the order in which atoms are attached to each other within molecules (Section 12-6).

Conformations. Conformations are differing orientations of the same molecule made possible by free rotation about single bonds in the molecule (Section 12-7).

Alkane nomenclature. The IUPAC name for an alkane is based on the longest continuous chain of carbon atoms in the molecule. A group of carbon atoms attached to the chain is an alkyl group. Both the position and the identity of the alkyl group are prefixed to the name of the longest carbon chain (Section 12-8).

Line-angle structural formulas. A line-angle structural formula is a structural representation in which a line represents a carbon–carbon bond and a carbon atom is understood to be present at every point where two lines meet and at the ends of the line. Line-angle structural formulas are the most concise method for representing the structure of a hydrocarbon or hydrocarbon derivative (Section 12-9).

Cycloalkanes. Cycloalkanes are saturated hydrocarbons in which at least one cyclic arrangement of carbon atoms is present. The formulas of all cycloalkanes can be represented by the general formula C_nH_{2n}, where n is the number of carbon atoms present (Section 12-12).

Cycloalkane nomenclature. The IUPAC name for a cycloalkane is obtained by placing the prefix *cyclo-* before the alkane name that corresponds to the number of carbon atoms in the ring. Alkyl groups attached to the ring are located by using a ring-numbering system (Section 12-13).

***Cis–trans* isomerism.** For certain disubstituted cycloalkanes, *cis–trans* isomers exist. *Cis–trans* isomers are compounds that have the same molecular and structural formulas but different arrangements of atoms in space because of restricted rotation about bonds (Section 12-14).

Natural sources of saturated hydrocarbons. Natural gas and petroleum are the largest and most important natural sources of both alkanes and cycloalkanes (Section 12-15).

Physical properties of saturated hydrocarbons. Saturated hydrocarbons are not soluble in water and have lower densities than water. Melting and boiling points increase with increasing carbon chain length or ring size (Section 12-16).

Chemical properties of saturated hydrocarbons. Two important reactions that saturated hydrocarbons undergo are combustion and halogenation. In combustion, saturated hydrocarbons burn in air to produce CO_2 and H_2O. Halogenation is a substitution reaction in which one or more hydrogen atoms of the hydrocarbon are replaced by halogen atoms (Section 12-17).

Halogenated alkanes. Halogenated alkanes are hydrocarbon derivatives in which one or more halogen atoms have replaced hydrogen atoms of the alkane (Section 12-18).

Halogenated alkane nomenclature. Halogenated alkanes are named by using the rules that apply to branched-chain alkanes, with halogen substituents being treated the same as alkyl groups (Section 12-18).

Exercises and Problems

Exercises and problems are arranged in matched pairs with the two members of a pair addressing the same concept(s). The answer to the odd-numbered member of a pair is given at the back of the book. Problems denoted with a ▲ involve concepts found not only in the section under consideration but also concepts found in one or more earlier sections of the chapter.

Organic and Inorganic Compounds (Section 12-1)

12-1 Indicate whether each of the following statements is true or false.
a. The number of organic compounds exceeds the number of inorganic compounds by a factor of about 2.
b. Chemists now believe that a special "vital force" is needed to form an organic compound.
c. Historically, the *org-* of the term *organic* was conceptually paired with the *org-* in the term *living organism.*
d. Most but not all compounds found in living organisms are organic compounds.

12-2 Indicate whether each of the following statements is true or false.
a. Approximately 10 million organic compounds have been characterized.
b. The number of known organic compounds and the number of known inorganic compounds are approximately the same.
c. In essence, organic chemistry is the study of the compounds of one element.
d. Numerous organic compounds are known that do not occur in living organisms.

12-3 Indicate whether each of the following compounds is an organic compound or an inorganic compound?
a. HNO_3 b. C_4H_{10} c. C_2H_6O d. CO_2

12-4 Indicate whether each of the following compounds is an organic compound or an inorganic compound?
a. H_2SO_4 b. Na_2CO_3 c. CH_5N d. C_6H_{12}

Bonding Characteristics of the Carbon Atom (Section 12-2)

12-5 Indicate whether each of the following situations meets or does not meet the "bonding requirement" for carbon atoms.
a. Two single bonds and a double bond
b. A single bond and two double bonds
c. Three single bonds and a triple bond
d. A double bond and a triple bond

12-6 Indicate whether each of the following situations meets or does not meet the "bonding requirement" for carbon atoms.
a. Four single bonds
b. Three single bonds and a double bond
c. Two double bonds and two single bonds
d. Two double bonds

Hydrocarbons and Hydrocarbon Derivatives (Section 12-3)

12-7 What is the difference between a *hydrocarbon* and a *hydrocarbon derivative*?

12-8 Contrast hydrocarbons and hydrocarbon derivatives in terms of number of compounds that are known.

12-9 What is the difference between a *saturated hydrocarbon* and an *unsaturated hydrocarbon*?

12-10 What structural feature is present in an unsaturated hydrocarbon that is not present in a saturated hydrocarbon?

12-11 Classify each of the following hydrocarbons as saturated or unsaturated.

12-12 Classify each of the following hydrocarbons as saturated or unsaturated.

a. $H—C\equiv C—H$ b.

General Formulas for Alkanes (Section 12-4)

12-13 Using the general formula for an alkane, derive the following for specific alkanes.
a. Number of hydrogen atoms present when 8 carbon atoms are present
b. Number of carbon atoms present when 10 hydrogen atoms are present
c. Number of carbon atoms present when 41 total atoms are present
d. Total number of covalent bonds present in the molecule when 7 carbon atoms are present

12-14 Using the general formula for an alkane, derive the following for specific alkanes.
a. Number of carbon atoms present when 14 hydrogen atoms are present
b. Number of hydrogen atoms present when 6 carbon atoms are present
c. Number of hydrogen atoms present when 32 total atoms are present
d. Total number of covalent bonds present in the molecule when 16 hydrogen atoms are present

Structural Formulas (Section 12-5)

12-15 Convert the following expanded structural formulas for alkanes into condensed structural formulas where all carbon–carbon bonds are explicitly shown.

12-16 Convert the following expanded structural formulas for alkanes into condensed structural formulas where all carbon–carbon bonds are explicitly shown.

12-17 Convert the expanded structural formulas in Problem 12-15 into condensed structural formulas where parentheses and a subscript are used to denote the number of CH_2 groups present.

12-18 Convert the expanded structural formulas in Problem 12-16 into condensed structural formulas where parentheses and a subscript are used to denote the number of CH_2 groups present.

12-19 Convert the expanded structural formulas in Problem 12-15 into skeletal structural formulas.

12-20 Convert the expanded structural formulas in Problem 12-16 into skeletal structural formulas.

12-21 Draw the indicated type of formula for the following alkanes.
a. The expanded structural formula for a continuous-chain alkane with the formula C_5H_{12}
b. The expanded structural formula for $CH_3—(CH_2)_6—CH_3$
c. The condensed structural formula using parentheses and a subscript to denote the number of CH_2 groups for the continuous-chain alkane $C_{10}H_{22}$
d. The molecular formula for the alkane $CH_3—(CH_2)_4—CH_3$

12-22 Draw the indicated type of formula for the following alkanes.
a. The expanded structural formula for a continuous-chain alkane with the molecular formula C_6H_{14}
b. The condensed structural formula using parentheses and a subscript to denote the number of CH_2 groups for the straight-chain alkane $C_{12}H_{26}$
c. The molecular formula for the alkane $CH_3—(CH_2)_6—CH_3$
d. The expanded structural formula for $CH_3—(CH_2)_3—CH_3$

12-23 Determine the following for the six-carbon alkane whose skeletal structural formula is

$$C-C-C-C-C-C$$

    a. How many hydrogen atoms are present?
    b. How many carbon–carbon bonds are present?
    c. How many CH_2 groups are present?
    d. How many total covalent bonds are present?

12-24 Determine the following for the five-carbon alkane whose skeletal structural formula is

$$C-C-C-C-C$$

    a. How many hydrogen atoms are present?
    b. How many carbon–hydrogen bonds are present?
    c. How many CH_3 groups are present?
    d. How many total covalent bonds are present?

12-25 What, if anything, is wrong with the following alkane condensed structural formulas?

    a. $CH_3-CH_2-\underset{\underset{CH_3}{|}}{CH}-CH_2$
    b. $CH_3-CH_2-\underset{\underset{CH_3}{|}}{CH_2}-CH_2-CH_3$

12-26 What, if anything, is wrong with the following alkane condensed structural formulas?

    a. $CH_3-CH_2-\underset{\underset{CH_2}{|}}{CH_2}-CH_3$
    b. $CH_2-CH_3-CH_2-CH_3$

Alkane Isomerism (Section 12-6)

12-27 Indicate whether each of the following would be expected to be the same or different for two alkane constitutional isomers.
    a. Number of hydrogen atoms present in a molecule
    b. Condensed structural formula
    c. Boiling point
    d. Melting point

12-28 Indicate whether each of the following would be expected to be the same or different for two alkane constitutional isomers.
    a. Number of carbon atoms present in a molecule
    b. Shape of molecule
    c. Density
    d. Molecular formula

12-29 Explain why two alkanes with the molecular formulas C_5H_{12} and C_6H_{12} could not be constitutional isomers.

12-30 Explain why two different straight-chain alkanes could not be constitutional isomers.

12-31 With the help of Table 12-1, indicate how many constitutional isomers exist for each of the following.
    a. Four-carbon alkanes   b. Six-carbon alkanes
    c. Eight-carbon alkanes   d. Ten-carbon alkanes

12-32 With the help of Table 12-1, indicate how many constitutional isomers exist for each of the following.
    a. Three-carbon alkanes   b. Five-carbon alkanes
    c. Seven-carbon alkanes   d. Nine-carbon alkanes

12-33 How many of the numerous eight-carbon alkane constitutional isomers are continuous-chain alkanes?

12-34 How many of the numerous seven-carbon alkane constitutional isomers are continuous-chain alkanes?

Conformations of Alkanes (Section 12-7)

12-35 For each of the following pairs of structures, determine whether they are
    1. Different conformations of the same molecule
    2. Different compounds that are constitutional isomers
    3. Different compounds that are not constitutional isomers

    a. $CH_3-CH_2-CH_2-\underset{\underset{CH_3}{|}}{CH}-CH_3$
    and $CH_3-\underset{\underset{CH_3}{|}}{CH}-CH_2-CH_3$

    b. $CH_3-CH_2-CH_2-CH_2-CH_3$
    and $CH_3-\underset{\underset{\underset{\underset{CH_3}{|}}{CH_2}}{|}}{CH}-CH_3$

    c. $CH_3-CH_2-\underset{\underset{CH_3}{|}}{CH_2}$ and $CH_3-\underset{\underset{CH_2-CH_3}{|}}{CH_2}$

    d. $CH_3-\underset{\underset{CH_3}{|}}{\overset{\overset{CH_3}{|}}{C}}-CH_3$ and $CH_3-\underset{\underset{CH_3}{|}}{CH}-CH_2-CH_3$

12-36 For each of the following pairs of structures, determine whether they are
    1. Different conformations of the same molecule
    2. Different compounds that are constitutional isomers
    3. Different compounds that are not constitutional isomers

    a. $CH_3-\underset{\underset{CH_2-CH_3}{|}}{CH}-CH_3$
    and $CH_3-\underset{\underset{CH_3}{|}}{CH}-CH_2-CH_3$

    b. $CH_3-\underset{\underset{CH_3}{|}}{CH}-CH_2-CH_3$
    and $CH_3-CH_2-\underset{\underset{CH_3}{|}}{CH}-CH_3$

    c. $CH_3-\underset{\underset{\underset{\underset{CH_3}{|}}{CH_2}}{|}}{CH}-CH_2-CH_3$
    and $CH_3-\underset{\underset{CH_3}{|}}{CH}-\underset{\underset{CH_3}{|}}{CH}-CH_3$

    d. $CH_3-CH_2-CH_2-CH_2-CH_2-CH_3$
    and $CH_3-\underset{\underset{CH_3}{|}}{\overset{\overset{CH_3}{|}}{C}}-CH_3$

12-37 Convert each of the following linear condensed structural formulas into "regular" condensed structural formulas.
    a. $CH_3-CH_2-CH-(CH_3)-CH_2-CH_3$
    b. $(CH_3)_2-CH-CH_2-CH-(CH_3)_2$
    c. $CH_3-CH-(CH_3)-CH_3$
    d. $CH_3-CH_2-CH-(CH_2-CH_3)-CH_2-CH_3$

12-38 Convert each of the following linear condensed structural formulas into "regular" condensed structural formulas.
a. $CH_3-CH-(CH_3)-CH_2-CH_3$
b. $CH_3-C-(CH_3)_2-CH_3$
c. $(CH_3)_2-CH-CH_3$
d. $CH_3-CH_2-CH-(CH_3)-CH-(CH_3)-CH_3$

12-39 Draw condensed structural formulas that do not contain any parentheses for each of the following compounds.
a. $CH_3-(CH_2)_3-CH_3$
b. $(CH_3)_2-CH-CH_2-CH_3$
c. $(CH_3)_3-C-CH_3$
d. $(CH_3)_2-(CH)_2-(CH_3)_2$

12-40 Draw condensed structural formulas that do not contain any parentheses for each of the following compounds.
a. $CH_3-(CH_2)_2-CH_3$
b. $(CH_3)_2-CH-CH_3$
c. $(CH_3)_3-C-CH_2-CH_3$
d. $(CH_3)_3-(C)_2-(CH_3)_3$

IUPAC Nomenclature for Alkanes (Section 12-8)

12-41 What is the name of the IUPAC prefix associated with each of the following numbers of carbon atoms?
a. two   b. four
c. six   d. eight

12-42 What is the name of the IUPAC prefix associated with each of the following numbers of carbon atoms?
a. one   b. three
c. seven   d. nine

12-43 What is the IUPAC name for each of the following alkyl groups?
a. $-CH_2-CH_3$
b. $-CH_2-CH_2-CH_2-CH_2-CH_3$

12-44 What is the IUPAC name for each of the following alkyl groups?
a. $-CH_2-CH_2-CH_3$
b. $-CH_2-CH_2-CH_2-CH_2-CH_2-CH_3$

12-45 What is the chemical formula for each of the following entities?
a. Ethane   b. Ethyl group
c. Pentane   d. Pentyl group

12-46 What is the chemical formula for each of the following entities?
a. Propane   b. Propyl group
c. Hexane   d. Hexyl group

12-47 The first step in naming an alkane is to identify the longest continuous chain of carbon atoms. For each of the following skeletal structural formulas, how many carbon atoms are present in the longest continuous chain?

a.
$$C-C-C-C-C-C-C$$
with C branch down, then C below

b.
$$C-C-C-C-C-C$$
with C branches

12-48 The first step in naming an alkane is to identify the longest continuous chain of carbon atoms. For each of the following skeletal structural formulas, how many carbon atoms are present in the longest continuous chain?

a.
$$C-C-C-C-C-C$$
with branches

b. $$C-C-C-C-C$$
with branches

c.
$$C-C-C-C$$
$$C-C-C-C$$

d. $$C-C-C-C-C-C-C$$
with branches

12-49 Give the IUPAC name for each of the following alkanes.
a. $CH_3-CH_2-CH-CH_2-CH_3$ with CH_3 branch
b. $CH_3-CH_2-CH_2-CH_2-CH-CH_3$ with CH_3 branch
c. $CH_2-CH_2-CH_2-CH-CH_3$ with CH_3 branches
d. $CH_3-CH_2-CH-CH_2-CH-CH_3$ with CH_3 branches

12-50 Give the IUPAC name for each of the following alkanes.
a. $CH_3-CH_2-CH-CH_2-CH_2-CH_3$ with CH_3 branch
b. $CH_3-CH_2-CH_2-CH-CH_3$ with CH_3 branch
c. $CH_2-CH_2-CH-CH_3$ with CH_3 branches
d. $CH_3-CH-CH_2-CH-CH_3$ with CH_3 branches

12-51 Give the IUPAC name for each of the following alkanes.

a. $CH_3-CH-CH_2-CH-CH-CH_3$
   with CH_3 below first CH, and CH_3 CH_3 below the CH—CH

b. $CH_3-\overset{\overset{\displaystyle CH_3}{|}}{\underset{\underset{\displaystyle CH_3}{|}}{C}}-CH_2-CH-CH_3$ with CH_3 below the CH

c. $CH_3-CH_2-\overset{\overset{\displaystyle CH_3}{|}}{\underset{\underset{\underset{\displaystyle CH_3}{|}}{CH_2}}{C}}-CH_2-CH_3$

d. $CH_3-CH_2-\overset{\overset{\displaystyle CH_3}{|}}{\underset{\underset{\underset{\displaystyle CH_3}{|}}{CH_2}}{C}}-CH_2-CH_2$ with CH_2 and CH_3 branches

12-52 Give the IUPAC name for each of the following alkanes.

a. $CH_3-CH_2-CH-CH-CH-CH_2-CH_3$ with CH_3, CH_2, CH_3 below and CH_3 at bottom

b. $CH_3-CH-CH_2-CH_2-\overset{\overset{\displaystyle CH_3}{|}}{\underset{\underset{\displaystyle CH_3}{|}}{C}}-CH_3$ with CH_3 below the CH

c. $CH_2-CH-CH_2-CH_2-CH_3$ with CH_3 CH_3 below

d. $CH_2-CH-CH-CH_2-CH_3$ with CH_3 CH_3 CH_3 below

12-53 Draw a condensed structural formula for each of the following alkanes.
a. 3,4-Dimethylhexane   b. 3-Ethyl-3-methylpentane
c. 3,5-Diethyloctane   d. 4-Propylnonane

12-54 Draw a condensed structural formula for each of the following alkanes.
a. 2,4-Dimethylhexane   b. 5-Propyldecane
c. 2,3,4-Trimethyloctane   d. 3-Ethyl-3-methylheptane

12-55 For each of the alkanes in Problem 12-53, determine (a) the number of alkyl groups present and (b) the number of substituents present.

12-56 For each of the alkanes in Problem 12-54, determine (a) the number of alkyl groups present and (b) the number of substituents present.

12-57 Explain why the name given for each of the following alkanes is not the correct IUPAC name. Then give the correct IUPAC name for the compound.
a. 2-Ethyl-2-methylpropane   b. 2,3,3-Trimethylbutane
c. 3-Methyl-4-ethylhexane   d. 2-Methyl-4-methylhexane

12-58 Explain why the name given for each of the following alkanes is not the correct IUPAC name. Then give the correct IUPAC name for the compound.
a. 2-Ethylpentane   b. 3,3,4-Trimethylpentane
c. 4-Ethyl-3-methylhexane   d. 3-Ethyl-4-ethylhexane

▲**12-59** Indicate whether or not the two alkanes in each of the following pairs of alkanes are constitutional isomers.
a. Butane and pentane
b. 2-Methylhexane and 3-methylhexane
c. Butane and 2-methylpropane
d. 2-Methylhexane and 3,3-dimethylpentane

▲**12-60** Indicate whether or not the two alkanes in each of the following pairs of alkanes are constitutional isomers.
a. Pentane and hexane
b. 2-Methylpentane and 3-methylpentane
c. Pentane and 2,2-dimethylpropane
d. 3,3-Dimethylpentane and 3,3-dimethylhexane

▲**12-61** How many of the 18 C_8 alkane constitutional isomers are named using the following base-chain names?
a. Octane   b. Heptane   c. Hexane   d. Pentane

▲**12-62** How many of the nine C_7 alkane constitutional isomers are named using the following base-chain names?
a. Heptane   b. Hexane   c. Pentane   d. Butane

Line-Angle Structural Formulas for Alkanes (Section 12-9)

12-63 Convert each of the following line-angle structural formulas to a skeletal structural formula.

12-64 Convert each of the following line-angle structural formulas to a skeletal structural formula.

12-65 Convert each of the following line-angle structural formulas to a condensed structural formula.

12-66 Convert each of the following line-angle structural formulas to a condensed structural formula.

12-67 Do the line-angle structural formulas in each of the following sets represent (1) the same compound, (2) constitutional isomers, or (3) different compounds that are not constitutional isomers?

a.

and

b.

and

12-68 Do the line-angle structural formulas in each of the following sets represent (1) the same compound, (2) constitutional isomers, or (3) different compounds that are not constitutional isomers?

a.

and

b.

and

▲**12-69** Convert each of the condensed structural formulas in Problem 12-51 to a line-angle structural formula.

▲**12-70** Convert each of the condensed structural formulas in Problem 12-52 to a line-angle structural formula.

▲**12-71** Assign an IUPAC name to each of the compounds in Problem 12-63.

▲**12-72** Assign an IUPAC name to each of the compounds in Problem 12-64.

▲**12-73** Determine the molecular formula for each of the compounds in Problem 12-65.

▲**12-74** Determine the molecular formula for each of the compounds in Problem 12-66.

Classification of Carbon Atoms (Section 12-10)

12-75 For each of the alkane structures in Problem 12-51, give the number of (a) primary, (b) secondary, (c) tertiary, and (d) quaternary carbon atoms present.

12-76 For each of the alkane structures in Problem 12-52, give the number of (a) primary, (b) secondary, (c) tertiary, and (d) quaternary carbon atoms present.

12-77 Indicate whether or not both 2° and 3° carbon atoms are present in each of the structures in Problem 12-67.

12-78 Indicate whether or not both 2° and 3° carbon atoms are present in each of the structures in Problem 12-68.

▲**12-79** Draw the condensed structural formula for an alkane with the molecular formula C_7H_{16} that contains
a. only 1° and 2° carbon atoms
b. both a 3° and 4° carbon atom

▲**12-80** Draw the condensed structural formula for an alkane with the molecular formula C_7H_{16} that contains
a. five 1° carbon atoms
b. two adjacent 3° carbon atoms

Branched-Chain Alkyl Groups (Section 12-11)

12-81 Give the name of the branched alkyl group attached to each of the following carbon chains, where the carbon chain is denoted by a horizontal line.

a.

$$CH-CH_3$$
$$\quad\quad CH_3$$

b.

$$CH_2$$
$$CH_3-CH-CH_3$$

c.

$$CH_3-CH-CH_3$$

d.

$$CH-CH_3$$
$$CH_2$$
$$CH_3$$

12-82 Give the name of the branched alkyl group attached to each of the following carbon chains, where the carbon chain is denoted by a horizontal line.

a.

$$CH_2$$
$$CH-CH_3$$
$$CH_3$$

b.

$$CH_3-C-CH_3$$
$$\quad\quad CH_3$$

c.

$$CH_3-CH_2-CH-CH_3$$

d.

$$CH$$
$$CH_3 \quad CH_3$$

12-83 Draw condensed structural formulas for the following branched alkanes.
a. 5-(*sec*-Butyl)decane
b. 4,4-Diisopropyloctane
c. 5-Isobutyl-2,3-dimethylnonane
d. 4-(1,1-Dimethylethyl)octane

12-84 Draw condensed structural formulas for the following branched alkanes.
a. 5-Isobutylnonane
b. 4,4-Di(*sec*-butyl)decane
c. 4-(*tert*-Butyl)-3,3-diethylheptane
d. 5-(2-Methylpropyl)nonane

12-85 To which carbon atoms in a hexane molecule can each of the following alkyl groups be attached without extending the longest carbon chain beyond six carbons?
a. Ethyl   b. Isopropyl
c. Isobutyl   d. *tert*-Butyl

12-86 To which carbon atoms in a heptane molecule can each of the following alkyl groups be attached without extending the longest carbon chain beyond seven carbons?
a. Ethyl   b. Isopropyl
c. *sec*-Butyl   d. *tert*-Butyl

12-87 Using IUPAC rules, name the following "complex" five-carbon branched alkyl groups.

a.

$$-CH_2-CH-CH_2-CH_3$$
$$\quad\quad CH_3$$

b.

$$\quad\quad\quad CH_3$$
$$-C-CH_2-CH_3$$
$$\quad\quad CH_3$$

12-88 Using IUPAC rules, name the following "complex" five-carbon branched alkyl groups.

a.

$$\quad\quad CH_3$$
$$-CH_2-CH-CH_3$$
$$\quad\quad CH_3$$

b.

$$\quad\quad\quad CH_3 \quad CH_3$$
$$-CH-CH-CH_3$$

12-89 Give an acceptable alternate name for each of the following branched-chain alkyl groups.
   a. Isopropyl group
   b. *tert*-Butyl group
   c. (1-Methylpropyl) group
   d. (2-Methylpropyl) group

12-90 Give an acceptable alternate name for each of the following branched-chain alkyl groups.
   a. *sec*-Butyl group
   b. Isobutyl group
   c. (1-Methylethyl) group
   d. (2,2-Dimethylethyl) group

▲**12-91** How many different alkyl groups exist that contain
   a. four carbon atoms   b. five carbon atoms

▲**12-92** How many different alkyl groups exist that contain
   a. three carbon atoms   b. six carbon atoms

Cycloalkanes (Section 12-12)

12-93 Using the general formula for a cycloalkane, derive the following for specific cycloalkanes.
   a. Number of hydrogen atoms present when 8 carbon atoms are present
   b. Number of carbon atoms present when 12 hydrogen atoms are present
   c. Number of carbon atoms present when a total of 15 atoms are present
   d. Number of covalent bonds present when 5 carbon atoms are present

12-94 Using the general formula for a cycloalkane, derive the following for specific cycloalkanes.
   a. Number of hydrogen atoms present when 4 carbon atoms are present
   b. Number of carbon atoms present when 6 hydrogen atoms are present
   c. Number of hydrogen atoms present when a total of 18 atoms are present
   d. Number of covalent bonds present when 8 hydrogen atoms are present

12-95 What is the molecular formula for each of the following cycloalkane molecules?

   a.   b.

   c.   d.

12-96 What is the molecular formula for each of the following cycloalkane molecules?

   a.   b.

   c.   d.

▲**12-97** How many alkyl groups are present in each of the structures in Problem 12-95?

▲**12-98** How many alkyl groups are present in each of the structures in Problem 12-96?

▲**12-99** How many secondary carbon atoms are present in each of the structures in Problem 12-95?

▲**12-100** How many secondary carbon atoms are present in each of the structures in Problem 12-96?

IUPAC Nomenclature for Cycloalkanes (Section 12-13)

12-101 Assign an IUPAC name to each of the following cycloalkanes.

   a.   b.

   c.   d.

12-102 Assign an IUPAC name to each of the following cycloalkanes.

   a.   b.

   c.   d.

12-103 What is wrong with each of the following attempts to name a cycloalkane using IUPAC rules?
   a. Dimethylcyclohexane
   b. 3,4-Dimethylcyclohexane
   c. 1-Ethylcyclobutane
   d. 2-Ethyl-1-methylcyclopentane

12-104 What is wrong with each of the following attempts to name a cycloalkane using IUPAC rules?
   a. Dimethylcyclopropane
   b. 1-Methylcyclohexane
   c. 2,4-Dimethylcyclobutane
   d. 1-Propyl-2-ethylcyclohexane

12-105 Draw line-angle structural formulas for the following cycloalkanes.
   a. Propylcyclobutane
   b. Isopropylcyclobutane
   c. 1,1-Dimethylcyclobutane
   d. (1-Methylethyl)cyclobutane

12-106 Draw line-angle structural formulas for the following cycloalkanes.
   a. Butylcyclopentane
   b. Isobutylcyclopentane
   c. 1,1-Dimethylcyclopentane
   d. (2-Methylpropyl)cyclopentane

▲**12-107** What is the molecular formula for each of the following hydrocarbons?
   a. 1,2-Dimethylcyclohexane
   b. 1,3-Dimethylcyclohexane
   c. 2,2-Dimethylhexane
   d. 2,3-Dimethylhexane

▲**12-108** What is the molecular formula for each of the following hydrocarbons?
a. 1,2-Dimethylcyclopentane
b. 1,3-Dimethylcyclopentane
c. 2,2-Dimethylpentane
d. 2,3-Dimethylpentane

▲**12-109** Classify each of the compounds in Problem 12-107 as a *saturated* hydrocarbon or an *unsaturated* hydrocarbon.

▲**12-110** Classify each of the compounds in Problem 12-108 as a *saturated* hydrocarbon or an *unsaturated* hydrocarbon.

Isomerism in Cycloalkanes (Section 12-14)

12-111 Determine the number of constitutional isomers that are possible for each of the following situations.
a. Four-carbon cycloalkanes
b. Five-carbon cycloalkanes where the ring has three carbon atoms
c. Six-carbon cycloalkanes where the ring has five carbon atoms
d. Seven-carbon cycloalkanes where the ring has five carbon atoms

12-112 Determine the number of constitutional isomers that are possible for each of the following situations.
a. Five-carbon cycloalkanes
b. Six-carbon cycloalkanes where the ring has four carbon atoms
c. Six-carbon cycloalkanes where the ring has three carbon atoms
d. Seven-carbon cycloalkanes where the ring has four carbon atoms

12-113 Determine whether *cis–trans* isomerism is possible for each of the following cycloalkanes. If it is, then draw structural formulas for the *cis* and *trans* isomers.
a. Isopropylcyclobutane
b. 1,2-Diethylcyclopropane
c. 1-Ethyl-1-propylcyclopentane
d. 1,3-Dimethylcyclohexane

12-114 Determine whether *cis–trans* isomerism is possible for each of the following cycloalkanes. If it is, then draw structural formulas for the *cis* and *trans* isomers.
a. *sec*-Butylcyclohexane
b. 1-Ethyl-3-methylcyclobutane
c. 1,1-Dimethylcyclohexane
d. 1,3-Dipropylcyclopentane

12-115 Classify as *cis*- or *trans*- the positioning of the alkyl groups in each of the following cycloalkanes.

a.   b.

c.   d.

12-116 Classify as *cis*- or *trans*- the positioning of the alkyl groups in each of the following cycloalkanes.

a.   b.

c.   d.

▲**12-117** Indicate whether the members of each of the following pairs of hydrocarbons are (1) constitutional isomers, (2) stereoisomers, or (3) not isomers.
a. Hexane and cyclohexane
b. Hexane and methylcyclopentane
c. Methylcyclobutane and methylcyclopentane
d. *cis*-1,2-Dimethylcyclobutane and *trans*-1,2-dimethylcyclobutane

▲**12-118** Indicate whether the members of each of the following pairs of hydrocarbons are (1) constitutional isomers, (2) stereoisomers, or (3) not isomers.
a. 2-Methylpentane and cyclopentane
b. 2-Methylpentane and 2-ethylpentane
c. Ethylcyclohexane and 1,2-dimethylcyclohexane
d. *cis*-1,3-Diethylcyclobutane and *trans*-1,3-diethylcyclobutane

Sources of Alkanes and Cycloalkanes (Section 12-15)

12-119 In terms of the types of hydrocarbons present, what is the composition of unprocessed natural gas?

12-120 In terms of the types of hydrocarbons present, what is the composition of the gasoline fraction obtained by processing crude petroleum?

12-121 What physical property of hydrocarbons is the basis for the fractional distillation process for separating hydrocarbons?

12-122 Describe the process by which crude petroleum is separated into simpler mixtures (fractions).

Physical Properties of Alkanes and Cycloalkanes (Section 12-16)

12-123 Which member in each of the following pairs of compounds has the higher boiling point?
a. Hexane and octane
b. Cyclobutane and cyclopentane
c. Pentane and 1-methylbutane
d. Pentane and cyclopentane

12-124 Which member in each of the following pairs of compounds has the higher boiling point?
a. Methane and ethane
b. Cyclohexane and hexane
c. Butane and methylpropane
d. Pentane and 2,2-dimethylpropane

12-125 With the help of Figures 12-11 and 12-12, determine in which of the following pairs of compounds both members of the pair have the same physical state (solid, liquid, or gas) at room temperature and pressure.
a. Ethane and hexane
b. Cyclopropane and butane
c. Octane and 3-methyloctane
d. Pentane and decane

12-126 With the help of Figures 12-11 and 12-12, determine in which of the following pairs of compounds both members of the pair have the same physical state (solid, liquid, or gas) at room temperature and pressure.
a. Methane and butane
b. Cyclobutane and cyclopentane

c. Hexane and 2,3-dimethylbutane
d. Pentane and octane

12-127 Answer the following questions about the unbranched alkane that contains six carbon atoms.
a. Is it a solid, liquid, or gas at room temperature?
b. Is it less dense or more dense than water?
c. Is it soluble or insoluble in water?
d. Is it flammable or nonflammable in air?

12-128 Answer the following questions about the unsubstituted cycloalkane that contains six carbon atoms.
a. Is it a solid, liquid, or gas at room temperature?
b. Is it less dense or more dense than water?
c. Is it soluble or insoluble in water?
d. Is it flammable or nonflammable in air?

Chemical Properties of Alkanes and Cycloalkanes (Section 12-17)

12-129 Write the formulas of the products from the complete combustion of each of the following alkanes or cycloalkanes.
a. C_3H_8 b. Butane
c. Cyclobutane   d. $CH_3-(CH_2)_{15}-CH_3$

12-130 Write the formulas of the products from the complete combustion of each of the following alkanes or cycloalkanes.
a. C_4H_{10} b. 2-Methylpentane
c. Cyclopentane   d. $CH_3-(CH_2)_7-CH_3$

12-131 Write molecular formulas for all the possible halogenated hydrocarbon products from the bromination of methane.

12-132 Write molecular formulas for all the possible halogenated hydrocarbon products from the fluorination of methane.

12-133 Write structural formulas for all the possible halogenated hydrocarbon products from the monochlorination of the following alkanes or cycloalkanes.
a. Ethane   b. Butane
c. 2-Methylpropane d. Cyclopentane

12-134 Write structural formulas for all the possible halogenated hydrocarbon products from the monobromination of the following alkanes or cycloalkanes.
a. Propane   b. Pentane
c. 2-Methylbutane   d. Cyclohexane

Halogenated Alkanes and Cycloalkanes (Section 12-18)

12-135 Assign an IUPAC name to each of the following halogenated hydrocarbons.

a. CH_3-I b. $CH_3-CH_2-CH_2-Cl$

c. $CH_3-CH-CH_2-CH_3$ d. ⬜—Cl
           |
           F

12-136 Assign an IUPAC name to each of the following halogenated hydrocarbons.

a. $CH_3-CH_2-CH_2-CH_2-Br$ b. $CH_3-CH-Cl$
                                                              |
                                                             CH_3

c. CH_3 d. ⬡—Br
             |
CH_3-C-CH_3
             |
             Cl

12-137 Name each of the compounds in Problem 12-135 as an alkyl halide.

12-138 Name each of the compounds in Problem 12-136 as an alkyl halide.

12-139 Draw structural formulas for the following halogenated hydrocarbons.
a. Trichloromethane
b. 1,2-Dichloro-1,1,2,2-tetrafluoroethane
c. Isopropyl bromide
d. *trans*-1-Bromo-3-chlorocyclopentane

12-140 Draw structural formulas for the following halogenated hydrocarbons.
a. Trifluorochloromethane
b. Pentafluoroethane
c. Isobutyl chloride
d. *cis*-1,2-Dichlorocyclohexane

12-141 Indicate whether each of the following molecular formulas is that for a halogenated alkane or that for a halogenated cycloalkane.
a. $C_4H_8Br_2$ b. $C_5H_9Cl_3$
c. $C_6H_{11}F$ d. $C_6H_{12}F_2$

12-142 Indicate whether each of the following molecular formulas is that for a halogenated alkane or that for a halogenated cycloalkane.
a. C_4H_7Cl b. $C_5H_{10}Cl_2$
c. $C_6H_{11}Br_3$ d. $C_6H_{10}F_2$

12-143 Which member of each of the following pairs of hydrocarbons and/or hydrocarbon derivatives would be expected to have the higher boiling point?
a. CH_3-Br or CH_3-I
b. CH_3-Cl or CH_3-CH_2-Cl
c. CH_3-Br or CH_3-CH_2-I
d. CH_4 or CH_3-Br

12-144 Which member of each of the following pairs of hydrocarbons and/or hydrocarbon derivatives would be expected to have the higher boiling point?
a. CH_3-CH_2-Br or CH_3-CH_2-Cl
b. CH_3-Cl or $CH_3-CH_2-CH_2-Cl$
c. CH_3-Cl or CH_3-CH_2-Br
d. CH_3-CH_3 or CH_3-CH_2-Cl

12-145 Indicate whether or not the following halogenated alkane chemical formulas are paired with a correct name.
a. CH_3Cl—Chloroform
b. CCl_4—Chloromethane
c. $CHCl_3$—Methylene chloride
d. CH_2Cl_2—Dichloromethane

12-146 Indicate whether or not the following halogenated alkane chemical formulas are paired with a correct name.
a. $CHCl_3$—Chloromethane
b. CH_2Cl_2—Carbon tet
c. CH_3Cl—Methylene chloride
d. CCl_4—Chloroform

12-147 Give the IUPAC names for the eight isomeric halogenated hydrocarbons that have the molecular formula $C_5H_{11}Cl$.

12-148 Give the IUPAC names for the nine isomeric halogenated hydrocarbons that have the molecular formula $C_4H_8Cl_2$.

Unsaturated Hydrocarbons

13

© stockfotoart/Shutterstock.com

The unsaturated hydrocarbon ethene is used to stimulate the ripening process in fruit that has been picked while still green, such as bananas.

Two general types of hydrocarbons exist: *saturated* and *unsaturated*. Saturated hydrocarbons, the topic of the previous chapter, include the alkane and cycloalkane families of hydrocarbons. All bonds in a saturated hydrocarbon are single covalent bonds. Unsaturated hydrocarbons, the topic of this chapter, contain at least one carbon–carbon double bond or carbon–carbon triple bond. There are three classes of unsaturated hydrocarbons, the *alkenes,* the *alkynes,* and the *aromatic hydrocarbons,* all of which are considered in this chapter.

13-1 Unsaturated Hydrocarbons

LEARNING FOCUS

Know the bonding characteristics that differentiate various classes of *unsaturated hydrocarbons* from each other; understand how and why the *functional group* concept is used in differentiating various classes of unsaturated hydrocarbons from each other.

An **unsaturated hydrocarbon** *is a hydrocarbon in which the carbon chain or ring contains at least one carbon–carbon double bond or carbon–carbon triple bond.* Such compounds have *physical* properties similar to those of saturated hydrocarbons. However, their *chemical* properties are much different. Unsaturated hydrocarbons are chemically more reactive than their saturated counterparts. The increased reactivity of unsaturated hydrocarbons is related to the presence of the carbon–carbon multiple bond(s) in such compounds. These multiple bonds serve as locations where chemical reactions can occur.

Whenever a specific portion of a molecule governs its chemical properties, that portion of the molecule is called a functional group. A **functional group** *is a structural feature in an organic molecule that is directly involved in most chemical reactions the molecule participates in.* Carbon–carbon double bonds and/or carbon–carbon triple bonds are the functional groups found in unsaturated hydrocarbons. ◄

The study of various functional groups and their respective reactions provides the organizational structure for organic chemistry. Each of the organic chemistry chapters that follow introduces new functional groups that characterize families of hydrocarbon derivatives.

Unsaturated hydrocarbons are subdivided into three types based on the functional group present: (1) *alkenes,* which contain one or more carbon–carbon double bonds, (2) *alkynes,* which contain one or more carbon–carbon triple bonds, and (3) *aromatic hydrocarbons,* which exhibit a special type of "delocalized" bonding that involves a six-membered carbon ring (to be discussed in Section 13-12).

Consideration of unsaturated hydrocarbons begins with a discussion of alkenes. Information about alkynes and aromatic hydrocarbons then follows.

► *Alkanes and cycloalkanes (Chapter 12) lack functional groups; as a result, they are relatively unreactive.*

Section 13-1 Quick Quiz

1. The common structural feature present in all *unsaturated* hydrocarbons is
   a. one or more carbon–carbon double bonds
   b. one or more carbon–carbon triple bonds
   c. one or more carbon–carbon multiple bonds
   d. no correct response
2. Which of the following is not a type of *unsaturated* hydrocarbon?
   a. alkane
   b. alkene
   c. alkyne
   d. no correct response
3. Which of the following statements about *unsaturated* hydrocarbon functional groups is correct?
   a. All unsaturated hydrocarbons contain the same functional group.
   b. Some, but not all, unsaturated hydrocarbons contain a functional group.
   c. All unsaturated hydrocarbon functional groups involve carbon–carbon multiple bonds.
   d. no correct response

Answers: 1. c; 2. a; 3. c

13-2 Characteristics of Alkenes and Cycloalkenes

LEARNING FOCUS

Define the terms *alkene* and *cycloalkene*; distinguish between alkene and cycloalkene molecules based on generalized molecular formula.

An **alkene** *is an acyclic unsaturated hydrocarbon that contains one or more carbon–carbon double bonds.* The alkene functional group is thus a C=C group. Note the close similarity between the family names *alkene* and *alkane* (Section 12-4); they differ only in their endings: *-ene* versus *-ane.* The *-ene* ending means a double bond is present. ◄

► *An older but still widely used name for alkenes is* olefins, *pronounced "oh-la-fins." The term* olefin *means "oil-forming." Many alkenes react with* Cl_2 *to form "oily" compounds.*

Figure 13-1 Three-dimensional representations of the structures of ethene and methane. In ethene, the atoms are in a planar (flat) rather than a tetrahedral arrangement. Bond angles are 120°.

Ethene—a planar molecule with bond angles of 120°

Methane—a tetrahedral molecule with bond angles of 109.5°

▶ *The general molecular formula for an alkene with one double bond, C_nH_{2n}, is the same as that for a cycloalkane (Section 12-12). Thus such alkenes and cycloalkanes with the same number of carbon atoms are isomeric with one another.*

The simplest type of alkene contains only one carbon–carbon double bond. Such compounds have the general molecular formula C_nH_{2n}. Thus alkenes with one double bond have two fewer hydrogen atoms than do alkanes (C_nH_{2n+2}). ◀

The two simplest alkenes are ethene (C_2H_4) and propene (C_3H_6).

$$CH_2{=}CH_2 \qquad CH_2{=}CH{-}CH_3$$
Ethene   Propene

Comparing the geometrical shape of ethene with that of methane (the simplest alkane) reveals a major difference. The arrangement of bonds about the carbon atom in methane is tetrahedral (Section 12-4), whereas the carbon atoms in ethene have a trigonal planar arrangement of bonds; that is, they have a flat, triangle-shaped arrangement (Figure 13-1). The two carbon atoms participating in a double bond and the four other atoms attached to these two carbon atoms always lie in a plane with a trigonal planar arrangement of atoms about each carbon atom of the double bond. Such an arrangement of atoms is consistent with the principles of VSEPR theory (Section 5-8).

Note that only carbon atoms that are directly participating in a carbon–carbon double bond have a trigonal planar arrangement for the atoms bonded to them. Thus, in the molecule

$$CH_2{=}CH{-}CH_3$$

the first and second carbon atoms have a trigonal planar bond arrangement but the last carbon atom has a tetrahedral bond arrangement as the latter is not involved in a double bond. The following structural diagram depicts this situation:

The bond arrangement geometry for two single bonds and a double bond is trigonal planar

The bond arrangement geometry for four single bonds is tetrahedral

A **cycloalkene** *is a cyclic unsaturated hydrocarbon that contains one or more carbon–carbon double bonds within the ring system.* Cycloalkenes in which there is only one double bond have the general molecular formula C_nH_{2n-2}. This general formula reflects the loss of four hydrogen atoms from that of an alkane (C_nH_{2n+2}). Note that two hydrogen atoms are lost because of the double bond and two because of the ring structure.

The simplest cycloalkene is the compound cyclopropene (C_3H_4), a three-membered carbon ring system containing one double bond.

Cyclopropene

Alkenes with more than one carbon–carbon double bond are relatively common. When two double bonds are present, the compounds are often called *dienes;* for three double bonds the designation *trienes* is used. Cycloalkenes that contain more than one double bond are possible but are not common.

Section 13-2 Quick Quiz

1. An alkene having only one carbon–carbon double bond will have the general formula
   a. C_nH_{2n+2}
   b. C_nH_{2n}
   c. C_nH_{2n-2}
   d. no correct response
2. A cycloalkene having only one carbon–carbon double bond will have the general formula
   a. C_nH_{2n+2}
   b. C_nH_{2n}
   c. C_nH_{2n-2}
   d. no correct response
3. Which of the following statements concerning alkenes and cycloalkenes is *incorrect*?
   a. The simplest possible alkene contains two carbon atoms.
   b. The simplest possible cycloalkene contains two carbon atoms.
   c. Alkenes and cycloalkenes contain the same functional group.
   d. no correct response
4. Which of the following statements concerning the alkene $CH_2{=}CH{-}CH_3$ is correct?
   a. All carbon atoms have a trigonal planar arrangement of bonds.
   b. All carbon atoms have a tetrahedral arrangement of bonds.
   c. Both trigonal planar and tetrahedral carbon atoms are present.
   d. no correct response

Answers: 1. b; 2. c; 3. b; 4. c

13-3 Nomenclature for Alkenes and Cycloalkenes

LEARNING FOCUS

Be able to name alkenes or cycloalkenes using IUPAC rules given their structural formula or vice versa; know common names for the simplest alkenes.

The IUPAC rules previously presented for naming alkanes and cycloalkanes (Sections 12-8 and 12-13) can be used, with some modification, to name alkenes and cycloalkenes. ◀

Rule 1. *Replace the alkane suffix -ane with the suffix -ene, which is used to indicate the presence of a carbon–carbon double bond.*

Rule 2. *Select as the parent carbon chain the longest continuous chain of carbon atoms that contains both carbon atoms of the double bond.* For example, select

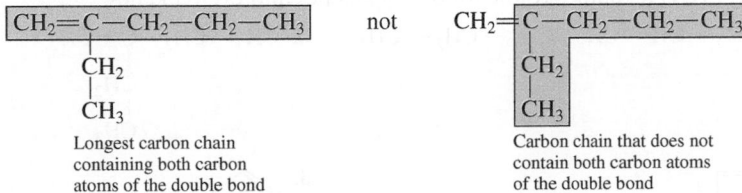

| Longest carbon chain containing both carbon atoms of the double bond | Carbon chain that does not contain both carbon atoms of the double bond |

Rule 3. *Number the parent carbon chain beginning at the end nearest the double bond.*

$$\overset{1}{C}H_3-\overset{2}{C}H{=}\overset{3}{C}H-\overset{4}{C}H_2-\overset{5}{C}H_3 \quad \text{not} \quad \overset{5}{C}H_3-\overset{4}{C}H{=}\overset{3}{C}H-\overset{2}{C}H_2-\overset{1}{C}H_3$$

If the double bond is equidistant from both ends of the parent chain, begin numbering from the end closer to a substituent. ◀

$$\overset{4}{C}H_3-\overset{3}{C}H{=}\overset{2}{C}H-\overset{1}{C}H_2 \quad \text{not} \quad \overset{1}{C}H_3-\overset{2}{C}H{=}\overset{3}{C}H-\overset{4}{C}H_2$$
$$\qquad\qquad\ \ \ \ | \qquad\qquad\qquad\qquad\qquad\qquad |$$
$$\qquad\qquad\ \ \ \ Cl \qquad\qquad\qquad\qquad\qquad\qquad Cl$$

▶ *IUPAC nomenclature rules are regularly revised. The most recent revisions occurred in 1979, 1993, and 2004. Issuance of an updated set of rules does not make earlier rule sets obsolete. Rather, with several sets of rules available and in use, there are often several acceptable ways to name a particular compound.*

▶ *Carbon–carbon double bonds take precedence over alkyl groups and halogen atoms in determining the direction in which the parent carbon chain is numbered.*

▶ *A number is not needed to specify double bond position in ethene and propene because there is only one way of positioning the double bond in these molecules.*

Rule 4.   *Give the position of the double bond in the chain as a single number, which is the lower-numbered carbon atom participating in the double bond. This number is placed immediately before the name of the parent carbon chain.* ◀

$$\overset{1}{C}H_3-\overset{2}{C}H=\overset{3}{C}H-\overset{4}{C}H_3 \qquad \overset{1}{C}H_2=\overset{2}{C}H-\overset{3}{C}H-\overset{4}{C}H_3$$
$$\underset{\quad\quad\quad\quad\quad\quad CH_3}{\qquad\qquad\qquad\qquad\;\;|}$$

2-Butene   3-Methyl-1-butene

▶ *In 1993, IUPAC rules were revised relative to the positioning of numbers used in names. Instead of placing the number immediately in front of the base name (2-pentene), IUPAC recommended that the number be placed immediately before the part of the name that the number serves as a locator for (pent-2-ene). In this textbook, the newer system will be used only when it helps clarify a name; otherwise the older system will be used. Two additional examples comparing the two systems are:*

2-methyl-1-butene (old)
2-methylbut-1-ene (new)

1,3-butadiene (old)
buta-1,3-diene (new)

Rule 5.   *Use the suffixes -diene, -triene, -tetrene, and so on when more than one double bond is present in the molecule. A separate number must be used to locate each double bond.* ◀

$$\overset{1}{C}H_2=\overset{2}{C}H-\overset{3}{C}H=\overset{4}{C}H_2 \qquad \overset{1}{C}H_2=\overset{2}{C}H-\overset{3}{C}H-\overset{4}{C}H=\overset{5}{C}H_2$$

1,3-Butadiene   3-Methyl-1,4-pentadiene

Rule 6.   *A number is not needed to locate the double bond in unsubstituted cycloalkenes with only one double bond because that bond is assumed to be between carbons 1 and 2.*

Rule 7.   *In substituted cycloalkenes with only one double bond, the double-bonded carbon atoms are numbered 1 and 2 in the direction (clockwise or counterclockwise) that gives the first-encountered substituent the lower number. Again, no number is used in the name to locate the double bond.*

Cyclohexene   4-Methylcyclohexene

Rule 8.   *In cycloalkenes with more than one double bond within the ring, assign one double bond the numbers 1 and 2 and the other double bonds the lowest numbers possible.*

1,4-Cyclohexadiene   5-Chloro-1,3-cyclohexadiene

EXAMPLE 13-1

Assigning IUPAC Names to Alkenes and Cycloalkenes

Assign IUPAC names to the following alkenes and cycloalkenes.

a. $CH_3-CH=CH-CH_2-CH_2-CH_3$ **b.** $CH_3-CH_2-\underset{\quad|}{C}=CH_2$
$$\underset{\quad\quad\;CH_2}{\qquad\qquad\qquad\qquad\qquad\qquad\qquad\quad\;|}$$
$$\underset{\quad\quad\;CH_3}{\qquad\qquad\qquad\qquad\qquad\qquad\qquad\quad\;|}$$

c.   **d.**

Solution

a. The carbon chain in this hexene is numbered from the end closest to the double bond.

$$\overset{1}{C}H_3-\overset{2}{C}H=\overset{3}{C}H-\overset{4}{C}H_2-\overset{5}{C}H_2-\overset{6}{C}H_3$$

The complete IUPAC name is 2-hexene.

b. The longest carbon chain containing *both* carbons of the double bond has four carbon atoms. Thus the base name is butene.

$$\boxed{CH_3-CH_2-\underset{\underset{\underset{CH_3}{|}}{\overset{|}{CH_2}}}{\overset{4\quad\quad 3\quad\quad 2\quad\quad 1}{C}}=CH_2}$$

The chain is numbered from the end closest to the double bond. The complete IUPAC name is 2-ethyl-1-butene.

c. This compound is a methylcyclobutene. The numbers 1 and 2 are assigned to the carbon atoms of the double bond, and the ring is numbered clockwise, which results in a carbon 3 location for the methyl group. (Counterclockwise numbering would have placed the methyl group on carbon 4.) The complete IUPAC name of the cycloalkene is 3-methylcyclobutene. The double bond is understood to involve carbons 1 and 2.

d. A ring system containing five carbon atoms, two double bonds, and a methyl substituent on the ring is called a methylcyclopentadiene. Two different numbering systems produce the same locations (carbons 1 and 3) for the double bonds.

The counterclockwise numbering system assigns the lower number to the methyl group. The complete IUPAC name of the compound is 2-methyl-1,3-cyclopentadiene.

Common Names (Non-IUPAC Names)

The simpler members of most families of organic compounds, including alkenes, have common names in addition to IUPAC names. In many cases, these common (non-IUPAC) names are used almost exclusively for the compounds. It would be nice if such common names did not exist, but they do. There is no choice but to know these names; fortunately, there are not many of them. ◀

    The two simplest alkenes, ethene and propene, have common names. They are ethylene and propylene, respectively.

▶ *Despite the universal acceptance and precision of the IUPAC nomenclature system, some alkenes (those of low molecular mass) are known almost exclusively by common names.*

$$\underset{\text{Ethylene}}{CH_2=CH_2} \quad\quad \underset{\text{Propylene}}{CH_2=CH-CH_3}$$

    Ethylene (ethene) is a very important industrial chemical. In terms of amount, its industrial production exceeds that of any other organic compound. Propylene (propene) is also industrially produced on a relatively large scale. The focus on relevancy feature Chemical Connections 13-A—Ethene: A Plant Hormone and High-Volume Industrial Chemical—gives further information about sources of and uses for ethylene.

Alkenes as Substituents

Just as there are *alkanes* and *alkyl groups* (Section 12-8), there are *alkenes* and *alkenyl groups*. An **alkenyl group** *is a noncyclic hydrocarbon substituent in which a carbon–carbon double bond is present.* The three most frequently encountered alkenyl groups are the one-, two-, and three-carbon entities, which may be named using IUPAC nomenclature (methylidene, ethenyl, and 2-propenyl) or common names (methylene, vinyl, and allyl).

$$\underset{\substack{\text{Methylene group}\\\text{(IUPAC name: methylidene group)}}}{CH_2=} \quad\quad \underset{\substack{\text{Vinyl group}\\\text{(IUPAC name: ethenyl group)}}}{CH_2=CH-} \quad\quad \underset{\substack{\text{Allyl group}\\\text{(IUPAC name: 2-propenyl group)}}}{CH_2=CH-CH_2-}$$

Ethene: A Plant Hormone and High-Volume Industrial Chemical

Ethene (ethylene), the simplest unsaturated hydrocarbon (C_2H_4), is a colorless, flammable gas with a slightly sweet odor. It occurs naturally in *small* amounts in plants, where it functions as a plant hormone. A few parts per million ethene (less than 10 parts per million) stimulates the fruit-ripening process.

The commercial fruit industry uses ethene's ripening property to advantage. Bananas, tomatoes, and some citrus fruits are picked green to prevent spoiling and bruising during transportation to markets. At their destinations, the fruits are exposed to small amounts of ethene gas, which stimulates the ripening process.

Despite having no large natural source, ethene is an exceedingly important industrial chemical. Indeed, industrial production of ethene exceeds that of every other organic compound. Petrochemicals (substances found in natural gas and petroleum) are the starting materials for ethene production.

In one process, ethane (from natural gas) is *dehydrogenated* at a high temperature to produce ethene.

$$CH_3-CH_3 \xrightarrow{750°C} CH_2{=}CH_2 + H_2$$

Ethane   Ethene

In another process, called *thermal cracking,* hydrocarbons from petroleum are heated to a high temperature in the absence of air (to prevent combustion), which causes the cleavage of carbon–carbon bonds. Ethene is one of the smaller molecules produced by this process.

Industrially produced ethene serves as a starting material for the production of many plastics and fibers. Almost one-half of ethene production is used in the production of the well-known plastic polyethylene (Section 13-10). Polyvinyl chloride (PVC) and polystyrene (Styrofoam) are two other important ethene-based materials. About one-sixth of ethene production is converted to ethylene glycol, the principal component of most brands of antifreeze for automobile radiators (Section 14-5).

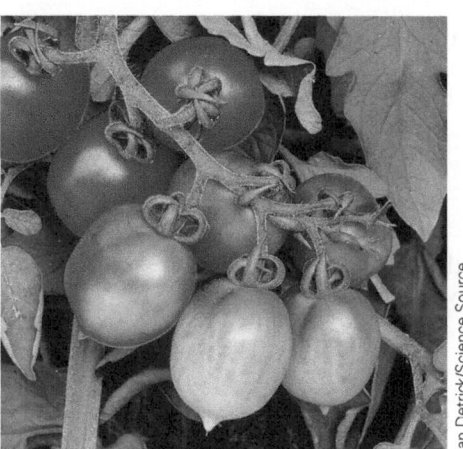

Alan Detrick/Science Source

Ethene is the hormone that causes tomatoes to ripen.

The use of these alkenyl group names in actual compound nomenclature is illustrated in the following examples.

$CH_2{=}\Diamond$	$CH_2{=}CH-Cl$	$CH_2{=}CH-CH_2-Br$
Methylene cyclopentane	Vinyl chloride	Allyl bromide
(IUPAC name: methylidenecyclopentane)	(IUPAC name: chloroethene)	(IUPAC name: 3-bromopropene)

Section 13-3 Quick Quiz

1. The correct IUPAC name for the compound $CH_2{=}CH-CH_2-CH_3$ is
   a. butene
   b. 1-butene
   c. 1,2-butene
   d. no correct response
2. The correct IUPAC name for the compound $CH_2{=}CH-CH{=}CH_2$ is
   a. 1,4-butene
   b. 1,3-butadiene
   c. 1,3-dibutene
   d. no correct response
3. The correct IUPAC name for the compound [structure] CH_3 is
   a. 1-methyl-2-cyclopentene
   b. 2-methyl-1-cyclopentene
   c. 3-methylcyclopentene
   d. no correct response

4. How many carbon atoms are present, respectively, in vinyl and allyl groups?
a. 1 and 2
b. 2 and 3
c. 3 and 2
d. no correct response

Answers: 1. b; 2. b; 3. c; 4.b

13-4 Line-Angle Structural Formulas for Alkenes

LEARNING FOCUS
Be able to draw and interpret line-angle structural formulas for alkenes and cycloalkenes.

Line-angle formulas for the three- to six-carbon acyclic 1-alkenes are as follows:

Propene   1-Butene   1-Pentene   1-Hexene

Representative line-angle structural formulas for substituent-bearing alkenes include

3,5-Dimethyl-1-hexene   2-Ethyl-3-methyl-1-pentene

Diene representations in terms of line-angle structural formulas include

1,4-Pentadiene   2-Methyl-1,3-butadiene

Section 13-4 Quick Quiz

1. What is the IUPAC name for the alkene ⟍⟋⟍⟍?
a. hexene
b. 3,4-hexene
c. 3-hexene
d. no correct response
2. What is the IUPAC name for the alkene ⟍⟍⟋⟍⟍?
a. 1,5-pentadiene
b. 1,5-hexadiene
c. 1,6-hexadiene
d. no correct response

Answers: 1. b; 2. b

13-5 Constitutional Isomerism in Alkenes

LEARNING FOCUS
Understand constitutional isomerism associated with alkene structures in terms of both positional and skeletal isomers.

Constitutional isomerism is possible for alkenes, just as it was for alkanes (Section 12-6). In general, there are more alkene isomers for a given number of carbon atoms than there are alkane isomers. This is because there is more than one location where a double bond can be placed in systems containing four or more carbon atoms. Figure 13-2 compares constitutional isomer possibilities for C_4 and C_5 alkanes and their counterpart alkenes with one double bond.

FOUR-CARBON ALKANES (TWO ISOMERS)	FOUR-CARBON ALKENES (THREE ISOMERS)	FIVE-CARBON ALKANES (THREE ISOMERS)	FIVE-CARBON ALKENES (FIVE ISOMERS)
$CH_3-CH_2-CH_2-CH_3$ **Butane**	$CH_2=CH-CH_2-CH_3$ **1-Butene**	$CH_3-CH_2-CH_2-CH_2-CH_3$ **Pentane**	$CH_2=CH-CH_2-CH_2-CH_3$ **1-Pentene**
$CH_3-\underset{\underset{CH_3}{\vert}}{CH}-CH_3$ **2-Methylpropane**	$CH_3-CH=CH-CH_3$ **2-Butene**	$CH_3-\underset{\underset{CH_3}{\vert}}{CH}-CH_2-CH_3$ **2-Methylbutane**	$CH_3-CH=CH-CH_2-CH_3$ **2-Pentene**
	$CH_2=\underset{\underset{CH_3}{\vert}}{C}-CH_3$ **2-Methylpropene**	$CH_3-\underset{\underset{CH_3}{\overset{\overset{CH_3}{\vert}}{\vert}}}{C}-CH_3$ **2,2-Dimethylpropane**	$CH_2=\underset{\underset{CH_3}{\vert}}{C}-CH_2-CH_3$ **2-Methyl-1-butene**
			$CH_3-\underset{\underset{CH_3}{\vert}}{C}=CH-CH_3$ **2-Methyl-2-butene**
			$CH_3-\underset{\underset{CH_3}{\vert}}{CH}-CH=CH_2$ **3-Methyl-1-butene**

Figure 13-2 A comparison of constitutional isomerism possibilities for four- and five-carbon alkane and alkene systems.

Two different constitutional isomer subtypes are found among the alkene isomers shown in Figure 13-2: *skeletal* isomers and *positional* isomers. **Skeletal isomers** *are constitutional isomers that have different carbon-atom arrangements and that contain identical functional groups if functional groups are present.* The Figure 13-2 C_4-alkenes

$$CH_2{=}CH{-}CH_2{-}CH_3 \quad \text{and} \quad CH_2{=}\underset{\underset{CH_3}{\vert}}{C}{-}CH_3$$

$$\text{1-Butene} \qquad\qquad\qquad \text{2-Methylpropene}$$

are skeletal isomers. The two compounds have different C_4 carbon-atom arrangements and contain the same functional group, a carbon–carbon double bond. All of the alkane isomers discussed in the previous chapter were skeletal isomers. This is the only type of constitutional isomerism possible for hydrocarbons that lack a functional group.

When functional groups are present in a hydrocarbon (or a hydrocarbon derivative) positional isomers become possible if there is more than one possible way for locating the functional groups present. ◀ **Positional isomers** *are constitutional isomers that have the same carbon-atom arrangement and that have differing locations for functional groups present.* Positional isomer sets found in Figure 13-2 are:

> ▶ *The carbon-atom arrangement must be the same in positional isomers and it must be different in skeletal isomers.*

1-butene and 2-butene

1-pentene and 2-pentene

2-methyl-1-butene, 3-methyl-1-butene, and 2-methyl-2-butene

EXAMPLE 13-2

Determining Structural Formulas for Alkene Constitutional Isomers

Draw condensed structural formulas for all alkene constitutional isomers that have the molecular formula C_5H_{10}.

Solution

The answers for this problem have already been considered. The structures of the five C_5H_{10} alkene constitutional isomers are given in Figure 13-2. The purpose of this example is to consider the "thinking pattern" used to obtain the given answers.

There are two concepts in the thinking pattern.

1. The different carbon skeletons (both unbranched and branched) that are possible using five carbon atoms are determined.
2. For each of the carbon skeletons determined, different positions for placement of the double bond are then considered.

Step 1: There are three possible arrangements for five carbon atoms:

$$C-C-C-C-C \qquad C-\overset{\overset{\displaystyle C}{|}}{C}-C-C \qquad C-\overset{\overset{\displaystyle C}{|}}{\underset{\underset{\displaystyle C}{|}}{C}}-C$$

(These arrangements are the constitutional isomers for a 5-carbon alk*ane,* the situation considered in Section 12-6 of the previous chapter.)

Step 2: For the first carbon skeleton (the unbranched chain), there are two possible locations for the double bond; that is, there are two positional isomers:

$$\underset{\text{1-Pentene}}{CH_2=CH-CH_2-CH_2-CH_3} \qquad \underset{\text{2-Pentene}}{CH_3-CH=CH-CH_2-CH_3}$$

Moving the double bond farther to the right than in the second structure does not produce new isomers but, rather, duplicates of the two given structures. A double bond between carbons 3 and 4 (numbering from the left side) is the same as having the double bond between carbons 2 and 3 (numbering from the right side).

For the second carbon skeleton, there are three positional isomers—that is, three different positions for the double bond:

$$\underset{\text{2-Methyl-1-butene}}{CH_2=\overset{\overset{\displaystyle CH_3}{|}}{C}-CH_2-CH_3} \qquad \underset{\text{2-Methyl-2-butene}}{CH_3-\overset{\overset{\displaystyle CH_3}{|}}{C}=CH-CH_3} \qquad \underset{\text{3-Methyl-1-butene}}{CH_3-\overset{\overset{\displaystyle CH_3}{|}}{CH}-CH=CH_2}$$

For the third carbon skeleton, alkene structures are not possible. Placing a double bond at any location within the structure creates a situation where the central carbon atom has five bonds. Thus there are five alkene constitutional isomers with the molecular formula C_5H_{10}.

Section 13-5 Quick Quiz

1. Positional constitutional isomers have
   a. the same carbon-atom arrangement
   b. the same hydrogen-atom arrangement
   c. both the same carbon-atom and hydrogen-atom arrangements
   d. no correct response
2. Skeletal constitutional isomers have
   a. the same carbon-atom arrangement
   b. the same hydrogen-atom arrangement
   c. both different carbon-atom and hydrogen-atom arrangements
   d. no correct response
3. Which of the following pairs of alkenes is an example of positional constitutional isomerism?
   a. 1-butene and 2-butene
   b. 1-pentene and 2-methyl-1-butene
   c. 2-methyl-1-butene and 3-methyl-1-butene
   d. no correct response

Answers: 1. a; 2. c; 3. a

13-6 *Cis–Trans* Isomerism in Alkenes

LEARNING FOCUS

Understand the concept of *cis–trans* isomerism and be able to recognize such in alkene molecules.

▶ *The double bond of alkenes, like the ring of cycloalkanes, imposes rotational restrictions.*

Cis–trans isomerism (Section 12-14) is possible for some alkenes. Such isomerism results from the structural rigidity associated with carbon–carbon double bonds. Unlike the situation in alkanes, where free rotation about carbon–carbon single bonds is possible (Section 12-7), no rotation about carbon–carbon double bonds (or carbon–carbon triple bonds) can occur. ◀

To determine whether an alkene has *cis* and *trans* isomers, draw the alkene structure in a manner that emphasizes the four attachments to the double-bonded carbon atoms.

$$\text{>C=C<}$$

If *each* of the two carbons of the double bond has two *different* groups attached to it, *cis* and *trans* isomers exist.

Two groups are different → CH_3 ... CH_2—CH_3 ← Two groups are different
$C=C$
→ H ... H ←

The simplest alkene for which *cis* and *trans* isomers exist is 2-butene.

$$CH_3\text{—}CH\text{=}CH\text{—}CH_3$$
2-Butene

CH_3 CH_3
$C=C$
H H
Structure A
(*cis*-2-Butene)

CH_3 H
$C=C$
H CH_3
Structure B
(*trans*-2-Butene)

▶ *If a linear (unbranched) alkene has the double bond in the 1- position cis–trans isomerism is not possible. Cis–trans isomers exist for all other double bond positions in a linear alkene other than 1-. Thus, cis–trans isomers exist for 2-hexene and 3-hexene but not 1-hexene.*

Recall from Section 12-14 that *cis* means "on the same side" and *trans* means "across from." Structure A is the *cis* isomer; both methyl groups are on the same side of the double bond. Structure B is the *trans* isomer; the methyl groups are on opposite sides of the double bond. The only way to convert structure A to structure B is to break the double bond. At room temperature, such bond breaking does not occur. Hence these two structures represent two different compounds (*cis–trans* isomers) that differ in boiling point, density, and so on. ◀ Figure 13-3 shows three-dimensional representations of the *cis* and *trans* isomers of 2-butene.

Figure 13-3 *Cis–trans* isomers: Different representations of the *cis* and *trans* isomers of 2-butene.

CH_3 CH_3
$C=C$
H H
cis-2-Butene
boiling point = 4°C
density = 0.62 g/mL
at 20°C

H CH_3
$C=C$
CH_3 H
trans-2-Butene
boiling point = 1°C
density = 0.60 g/mL
at 20°C

Cis–trans isomerism is not possible when one of the double-bonded carbons bears two identical groups. Thus neither 1-butene nor 2-methylpropene is capable of existing in *cis* and *trans* forms.

1-Butene

2-Methylpropene

When alkenes contain more than one double bond, *cis–trans* considerations are more complicated. Orientation about each double bond must be considered independently of that at other sites. For example, for the molecule 2,4-heptadiene (two double bonds) there are four different *cis–trans* isomers (*trans–trans, trans–cis, cis–trans,* and *cis–cis*). The structures of two of these isomers are

trans-trans-2,4-Heptadiene

trans-cis-2,4-Heptadiene

EXAMPLE 13-3

Determining Whether *Cis–Trans* Isomerism Is Possible in Substituted Alkenes

Determine whether each of the following substituted alkenes can exist in *cis–trans* isomeric forms.

a. 1-Bromo-1-chloroethene   **b.** 2-Bromo-3-chloro-2-butene

Solution

a. The condensed structural formula for this compound is

$$Br-C=CH_2$$
$$|$$
$$Cl$$

Redrawing this formula to emphasize the four attachments to the double-bonded carbon atoms gives

The carbon atom on the right has two identical attachments. Hence *cis–trans* isomerism is not possible.

b. The condensed structural formula for this compound is

$$CH_3-C=C-CH_3$$
$$\quad\;\; |\;\;\; |$$
$$\quad\;\; Br\; Cl$$

Redrawing this formula to emphasize the four attachments to the double-bonded carbon atoms gives

Because both carbon atoms of the double bond bear two different attachments, *cis–trans* isomers are possible.

cis-2-Bromo-3-chloro-2-butene

trans-2-Bromo-3-chloro-2-butene

CHEMICAL CONNECTIONS 13-B

Cis-Trans Isomerism and Vision

Cis–trans isomerism plays an important role in many biochemical processes, including the reception of light by the retina of the eye. Within the retina, microscopic structures called rods and cones contain a compound called *retinal*, which absorbs light. Retinal contains a carbon chain with five carbon–carbon double bonds, four in a *trans* configuration and one in a *cis* configuration. This arrangement of double bonds gives retinal a shape that fits the protein *opsin,* to which it is attached, as shown in the accompanying diagram.

When light strikes retinal, the *cis* double bond is converted to a *trans* double bond. The resulting *trans*-retinal no longer fits the protein opsin and is subsequently released. Accompanying this release is an electrical impulse, which is sent to the brain. Receipt of such impulses by the brain is what facilitates the vision process.

In order to trigger nerve impulses again, *trans*-retinal must be converted back to *cis*-retinal. This occurs in the membranes of the rods and cones, where enzymes change *trans*-retinal back into *cis*-retinal.

As noted previously (Section 12-14), *cis–trans* isomers are not constitutional isomers but, rather, stereoisomers. Each carbon atom in a pair of *cis–trans* isomers is bonded to the same atoms (groups); hence they cannot be constitutional isomers. The only difference, structurally, between the isomers is the orientation of the groups in space (stereoisomerism).

Cis–trans isomerism is an important part of many biochemical processes, including how the human eye responds to light. The focus on relevancy feature Chemical Connections 13-B—*Cis–Trans* Isomerism and Vision—gives information on the specific role of *cis* and *trans* isomers in the process of vision.

Section 13-6 Quick Quiz

1. *Cis–trans* isomerism occurs in which of the following situations?
   a. all alkenes
   b. some, but not all, alkenes
   c. only alkenes where two identical groups are attached to a double-bonded carbon
   d. no correct response
2. *Cis–trans* isomerism is possible for which of the following unbranched alkenes?
   a. $CH_2\!\!=\!\!CH\text{---}CH_2\text{---}CH_2\text{---}CH_3$
   b. $CH_3\text{---}CH\!\!=\!\!CH\text{---}CH_2\text{---}CH_3$
   c. $CH_3\text{---}CH\!\!=\!\!CH_2$
   d. no correct response
3. The alkene CH_3 CH_3 is in

   $$\underset{H}{\overset{CH_3}{\diagup}}C\!\!=\!\!C\underset{H}{\overset{CH_3}{\diagdown}}$$

   a. a *cis* configuration
   b. a *trans* configuration
   c. both a *cis* and a *trans* configuration
   d. no correct response

Answers: 1. b; 2. b; 3. a

13-7 Naturally Occurring Alkenes

LEARNING FOCUS

Understand the significance and characteristics of naturally occurring alkenes called *pheromones* and *terpenes*.

Alkenes are abundant in nature. Many important biological molecules are characterized by the presence of carbon–carbon double bonds within their structure. Two important types of naturally occurring substances to which alkenes contribute are pheromones and terpenes.

Pheromones

A **pheromone** *is a chemical substance secreted or excreted by insects (and some animals and plants) that triggers a response in other members of the same species.* Common types of pheromones include alarm pheromones, aggregation pheromones, territorial pheromones, trail pheromones, and sex pheromones. Several well-characterized pheromones have alkene structures; another common structural type is that of an ester (Section 16-12). The biological activity of alkene-type pheromones is usually highly dependent on whether the double bonds present are in a *cis* or a *trans* arrangement (Section 13-6).

The sex attractant of the female silkworm is a 16-carbon alkene derivative containing an —OH group. Two double bonds are present, *trans* at carbon 10 and *cis* at carbon 12.

$$CH_3-(CH_2)_2 \underset{H}{\overset{\text{(13)}}{\underset{}{C}}} = \underset{H}{\overset{\text{(12)}}{\underset{}{C}}} \underset{}{\overset{H \quad \text{(11)} \quad \text{(10)} \quad (CH_2)_8-CH_2-OH}{\underset{H}{C=C}}}$$

This compound is 10 billion times more effective in eliciting a response from the male silkworm than the 10-*cis*–12-*trans* isomer and 10 trillion times more effective than the isomer wherein both bonds are in a *trans* configuration.

Insect sex pheromones are useful in insect control. A small amount of synthetically produced sex pheromone is used to lure male insects of a single species into a trap (Figure 13-4). The trapped males are either killed or sterilized. Releasing sterilized males has proved effective in some situations. A sterile male can mate many times, preventing fertilization in many females, who usually mate only once. Sex attractant pheromones are now used to control the gypsy moth and the Mediterranean fruit fly.

Figure 13-4 The application of sex pheromones in insect control involves using a small amount of synthetically produced pheromone to lure a particular insect into a trap. This is accomplished without harming other "beneficial" insects.

© Steven Chadwick/Alamy

Terpenes

A **terpene** *is an organic compound whose carbon skeleton is composed of two or more 5-carbon isoprene structural units.* Isoprene (2-methyl-1,3-butadiene) is a five-carbon diene.

$$\overset{\text{CH}_3}{\underset{\overset{1}{CH_2}=\overset{2}{C}-\overset{3}{CH}=\overset{4}{CH_2}}{}}$$

2-Methyl-1,3-butadiene
(isoprene)

Terpenes are formed by joining the tail of one isoprene structural unit to the head of another unit.

$$\overset{\text{C}}{\underset{\text{tail } \searrow C-C-C-C \swarrow \text{ head}}{}}$$

Isoprene structural unit

The isopentyl structural unit (Section 12-8) of isoprene maintains its identity when isoprene units are joined together; however, the positioning of the double bonds often changes.

Figure 13-5 Selected terpenes containing two, three, and eight isoprene units. Dashed lines in the structures separate the individual isoprene units.

a Two isoprene units

Limonene
(from oil of lemon or orange)

α-Phellandrene
(eucalyptus)

Menthol
(mint)

Geraniol
(from roses and other flowers)

b Three isoprene units

Zingiberene
(from oil of ginger)

α-Farnesene
(from natural coating of apples)

β-Carotene
(present in carrots and other vegetables)

c Eight isoprene units

▶ *Why do plants produce isoprene and isoprene-based compounds? Studies indicate that isoprene "blanketed" about plant leaves protects them from damage induced from high summertime temperatures. The isoprene dissolves in leaf-cell membranes which increases thermal tolerance.*

Figure 13-6 The molecule β-carotene, whose structure is given in Figure 13-5, is responsible for the yellow-orange color of carrots, apricots, and yams.

Terpenes are among the most widely distributed compounds in the biological world, with more than 22,000 structures known. Such compounds are responsible for the odors of many trees and for many characteristic plant fragrances. ◀

The number of carbon atoms present in a terpene is always a multiple of the number 5 (10, 15, and so on). Parts (a) and (b) of Figure 13-5 give the structures of selected 10- and 15-carbon terpenes found in plants. Beta-carotene is a terpene whose structure has 40 carbon atoms present in 8 isoprene units (Figure 13-5c).

In the human body, dietary beta-carotene (obtained by eating yellow-colored vegetables) serves as a precursor for vitamin A (Figure 13-6); splitting of a beta-carotene molecule produces two vitamin A molecules (Section 21-13). In later chapters, additional isoprene-based molecules important in the functioning of the human body will be encountered. They include vitamin K (Section 21-13), coenzyme Q (Section 23-7), and cholesterol (Section 19-9).

Carotenoids, a group of yellow, red, and orange pigments found in plants, are terpenes in which eight isoprene units are present. The focus on relevancy feature Chemical Connections 13-C—Carotenoids: A Source of Color—gives further information about the presence of these compounds and their color in various fruits, vegetables, and the leaves of many plants.

CHEMICAL CONNECTIONS 13-C

Carotenoids: A Source of Color

Carotenoids are the most widely distributed of the substances that give color to our world; they occur in flowers, fruits, plants, insects, and animals. Structurally, carotenoids are terpenes (Section 13-7) in which a tail-to-tail linkage between two C_{20} units occurs. Carotenoids are of two major types: the hydrocarbon class (the *carotenes*) and the oxygenated hydrocarbon (alcohol) class (the *xanthophylls*).

The two most familiar carotenoids are both carotenes—β-carotene and lycopene. These compounds are easily isolated from carrots and ripe tomatoes, respectively.

β-Carotene

Lycopene

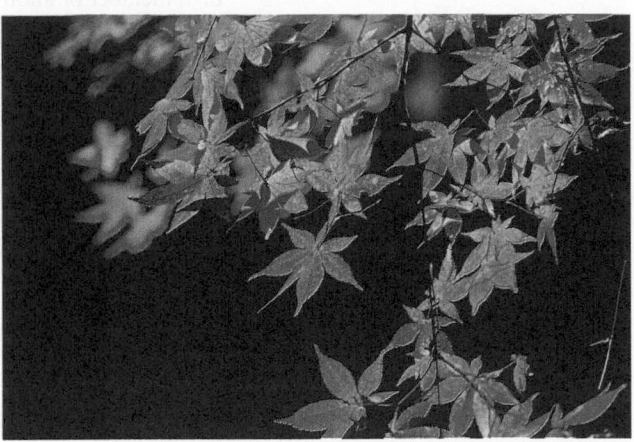

Carotenoids, molecules that contain eight isoprene units, are responsible for the yellow-orange color of autumn leaves.

Present in both of these carotene structures is a *conjugated* system of 11 double bonds. (Conjugated double bonds are double bonds separated from each other by one single bond.) Color is frequently caused by the presence of compounds that contain extended conjugated-double-bond systems. When *visible* light strikes these compounds, certain wavelengths of the visible light are absorbed by the electrons in the conjugated-bond system. The unabsorbed wavelengths of visible light are reflected and are perceived as color.

The molecule β-carotene is responsible for the yellow-orange color in carrots, apricots, and yams. The yellow-orange color of autumn leaves also comes from β-carotene. Leaves contain chlorophyll (green pigment) and β-carotene (yellow pigment) in a ratio of approximately 3 to 1. The yellow-orange β-carotene color is masked by the chlorophyll until autumn, when the chlorophyll molecules decompose as a result of lower temperatures and less sunlight and are not replaced.

The molecule lycopene is the red pigment in tomatoes and watermelon. Lycopene's structure differs from that of β-carotene in that the two rings in β-carotene have been opened. The ripening of a green tomato involves the gradual decomposition of chlorophyll with an associated unmasking of the red color of the lycopene present. A green pepper becomes red after ripening for the same reason.

Research studies indicate that lycopene has anticancer properties. One study comparing a group of men on a lycopene-rich diet with another group on a low-lycopene diet showed the incidence of prostate cancer was one-third lower in the lycopene-rich diet group.

Heat-processed tomatoes are a good source of dietary lycopene, with concentrated juice containing the highest levels of this substance. The lycopene in cooked tomatoes is absorbed more readily during digestion than is the lycopene in raw tomatoes. Recent studies indicate that red seedless watermelon contains as much lycopene as cooked tomatoes.

Carotenoids such as β-carotene and lycopene are synthesized only by plants. They can, however, reach animal tissues via feed and can be modified and deposited therein. The yellowish tint of animal fat comes from β-carotene present in animal diets. The chicken egg yolk is another example of color imparted by dietary carotenoids.

Xanthophylls are oxygen-containing carotenoids in which two —OH groups (the alcohol functional group—Section 14-2) have replaced hydrogen atoms. The two best-known xanthophylls are zeaxanthin (pronounced *zee-uh-zan-thin*) and lutein (pronounced *lue-teen*). Both have structures very similar to β-carotene.

R = H; β-Carotene (carrots)
R = OH; Zeaxanthin (yellow corn)

Structurally, zeaxanthin and lutein are isomeric, with lutein differing from zeaxanthin only in the placement of a double bond in one of the end rings.

Zeaxanthin

Lutein

The yellow color of corn involves zeaxanthin, and the red color of paprika relates to lutein's presence. At low concentrations these xanthophylls impart a yellow color, and at higher concentrations they impart an orange-red color. Zeaxanthin and lutein are also found in the retina of the eye, where they are believed to function as antioxidants, keeping the eyes safe from oxidative stress.

Section 13-7 Quick Quiz

1. A pheromone is a biologically active compound that can transmit a chemical message from the originating species to
   a. another member of the same species
   b. a member of another species
   c. either a member of the same species or a member of another species
   d. no correct response
2. The number of carbon atoms in a terpene is always a multiple of the number
   a. four
   b. five
   c. six
   d. no correct response
3. The carbon arrangement in an isoprene structural unit, the building block for terpenes, is
   a. $CH_3-CH_2-CH_2-CH_2-CH_3$

   b. $CH_3-CH-CH_2-CH_2-CH_3$
              |
             CH_3

   c. $CH_3-CH-CH_2-CH_3$
             |
           CH_3

   d. no correct response

Answers: 1. a; 2. b; 3. c

Unbranched 1-Alkenes			
✕	C_3	C_5	C_7
C_2	C_4	C_6	C_8

Unsubstituted Cycloalkenes			
✕	C_3*	C_5	C_7
✕	C_4*	C_6	C_8

☐ Gas ☐ Liquid

*Cyclopropene and cyclobutene are relatively unstable compounds, readily converting to other hydrocarbons because of the severe bond angle strain associated with a small ring containing a double bond.

Figure 13-7 A physical-state summary for unbranched 1-alkenes and unsubstituted cycloalkenes with one double bond at room temperature and pressure.

13-8 Physical Properties of Alkenes and Cycloalkenes

LEARNING FOCUS
List general physical properties for alkenes and cycloalkenes.

The general physical properties of alkenes and cycloalkenes include insolubility in water, solubility in nonpolar solvents, and densities lower than that of water. Thus they have physical properties similar to those of alkanes (Section 12-16). The melting point of an alkene is usually lower than that of the alkane with the same number of carbon atoms.

Alkenes with 2 to 4 carbon atoms are gases at room temperature. Unsubstituted alkenes with 5 to 17 carbon atoms and one double bond are liquids, and those with still more carbon atoms are solids. Figure 13-7 is a physical-state summary for unbranched 1-alkenes and unsubstituted cycloalkenes with 8 or fewer carbon atoms.

Section 13-8 Quick Quiz

1. Which of the following is a general physical property of alkenes and cycloalkenes?
   a. soluble in water
   b. soluble in nonpolar solvents
   c. higher density than water
   d. no correct response
2. Which of the following unbranched 1-alkenes would be a liquid at room temperature?
   a. ethene
   b. 1-butene
   c. 1-hexene
   d. no correct response

Answers: 1. b; 2. c

13-9 Preparation of Alkenes

LEARNING FOCUS

Be able to write a structural equation for the conversion of an alkane to an alkene via a dehydrogenation reaction.

Several laboratory methods exist for preparing alkenes from other organic compounds. Using special catalysts and appropriate temperatures an alkane can be converted to an alkene. In this reaction the alkane loses two hydrogen atoms in a process called *dehydrogenation*. A **dehydrogenation reaction** *is a chemical reaction in which a hydrogen atom is lost from each of two adjacent carbon atoms and a carbon–carbon double bond is formed.*

The structural equation for the formation of propene from propane via a dehydrogenation reaction is

Note that the two hydrogen atoms lost combine to form H_2.

The formation of an alkene from an alkane is usually a difficult process to carry out in that special catalysts and a high temperature, about 500°C, are required, with the high temperature being a distinct problem because many organic compounds are not stable at the high temperature required.

Easier methods exist for producing alkenes using other organic compound starting materials. One such method, the *dehydration* of an alcohol, is considered in the next chapter (Section 14-9). Note that this alcohol process involves *dehydration* (removal of water) rather than *dehydrogenation* (removal of hydrogen).

Section 13-9 Quick Quiz

1. When propane undergoes a dehydrogenation reaction the organic product is
   a. ethane
   b. butane
   c. propene
   d. no correct response
2. Which of the following statements about a dehydrogenation reaction is *incorrect*?
   a. The two H atoms lost come from the same carbon atom.
   b. The two H atoms lost come from adjacent carbon atoms.
   c. The two H atoms lost combine to form H_2.
   d. no correct response

Answers: 1. c; 2. a

13-10 Chemical Reactions of Alkenes

LEARNING FOCUS

Be able to write structural equations for both symmetrical and unsymmetrical addition reactions for alkenes; be able to use Markovnikov's rule, when needed, in writing such equations.

Alkenes, like alkanes, are very flammable. The combustion products, as with any hydrocarbon, are carbon dioxide and water.

$$C_2H_4 + 3O_2 \longrightarrow 2CO_2 + 2H_2O$$
Ethene

Pure alkenes are, however, too expensive to be used as fuel.

Figure 13-8 In an alkene addition reaction, the atoms provided by an incoming molecule are attached to the carbon atoms originally joined by a double bond. In the process, the double bond becomes a single bond.

Aside from combustion, nearly all other reactions of alkenes take place at the carbon–carbon double bond(s). These reactions are called *addition reactions* because a substance is *added* to the double bond. This behavior contrasts with that of alkanes, where the most common reaction type, aside from combustion, is *substitution* (Section 12-17). ◀

An **addition reaction** *is a chemical reaction in which atoms or groups of atoms are added to each carbon atom of a carbon–carbon multiple bond in a hydrocarbon or hydrocarbon derivative.* A general equation for an alkene addition reaction is

$$\diagdown\!C\!\!=\!\!C\diagup + \boxed{A\!-\!B} \longrightarrow -\underset{A}{\overset{|}{C}}\!\!=\!\!\underset{B}{\overset{|}{C}}-$$

In this reaction, the A part of the reactant A—B becomes attached to one carbon atom of the double bond, and the B part to the other carbon atom (Figure 13-8). As this occurs, the carbon–carbon double bond simultaneously becomes a carbon–carbon single bond.

Addition reactions can be classified as symmetrical or unsymmetrical. A **symmetrical addition reaction** *is an addition reaction in which identical atoms (or groups of atoms) are added to each carbon of a carbon–carbon multiple bond.* An **unsymmetrical addition reaction** *is an addition reaction in which different atoms (or groups of atoms) are added to the carbon atoms of a carbon–carbon multiple bond.*

Symmetrical Addition Reactions

The two most common examples of symmetrical addition reactions are hydrogenation and halogenation.

A **hydrogenation reaction** *is an addition reaction in which H_2 is incorporated into molecules of an organic compound.* In alkene hydrogenation, a hydrogen atom is added to each carbon atom of a double bond. This is accomplished by heating the alkene and H_2 in the presence of a catalyst (usually Ni or Pt).

$$\underset{\text{Propene}}{CH_2\!\!=\!\!CH\!-\!CH_3} + \boxed{H_2} \xrightarrow[\substack{150°C \\ 12-15\ atm \\ pressure}]{Ni\ or\ Pt} \underset{\text{Propane}}{CH_2\!-\!\overset{\overset{\displaystyle H}{|}}{\underset{\underset{\displaystyle H}{|}}{CH}}\!-\!CH_3}$$

The identity of the catalyst used in hydrogenation is specified by writing it above the arrow in the chemical equation for the hydrogenation. ◀ In general terms, hydrogenation of an alkene can be written as

$$\underset{\text{Alkene}}{\diagdown\!C\!\!=\!\!C\diagup} + \boxed{H_2} \xrightarrow[\substack{Heat, \\ pressure}]{Ni\ or\ Pt} \underset{\text{Alkane}}{-\overset{\overset{\displaystyle H}{|}}{C}\!-\!\overset{\overset{\displaystyle H}{|}}{C}-}$$

▶ *The following word associations are important to remember:*

*alkane—substitution reaction
alkene—addition reaction*

An analogy can be drawn to a basketball team. When a substitution is made, one player leaves the game as another enters. The number of players on the court remains at five per team. If addition were allowed during a basketball game, two players could enter the game and no one would leave; there would be seven players per team on the court rather than five.

▶ *Hydrogenation of an alkene requires a catalyst. No reaction occurs if the catalyst is not present.*

The hydrogenation of vegetable oils is a very important commercial process today. Vegetable oils from sources such as soybeans and cottonseeds are composed of long-chain organic molecules that contain several double bonds. When these oils are hydrogenated, they are converted to low-melting solids that are used in margarines and shortenings (see Section 19-6). ◀

Formation of an alkane from an alkene via hydrogenation is the "reverse reaction" of the formation of an alkene from an alkane via dehydrogenation (Section 13-9). This reverse reaction relationship can be diagrammed as follows:

▶ *The Chemical Connections feature "Trans Fatty Acids and Blood Cholesterol Levels" in Chapter 19 addresses health issues relative to consumption of partially hydrogenated products.*

The forward–reverse relationship between hydrogenation and dehydrogenation illustrates the fact that many organic reactions can go both forward and backward, depending on reaction conditions. Noting relationships such as this alkene–alkane one that involves gain/loss of hydrogen helps in keeping track of the numerous reactions that related compounds undergo.

A **halogenation reaction** *is an addition reaction in which two halogen atoms are incorporated into molecules of an organic compound.* In alkene halogenation, a halogen atom is added to each carbon atom of a double bond. Chlorination (Cl_2) and bromination (Br_2) are the two halogenation processes most commonly encountered. No catalyst is needed.

$$CH_3{-}CH{=}CH{-}CH_3 \ + \ Cl_2 \longrightarrow CH_3{-}\underset{\underset{Cl}{|}}{CH}{-}\underset{\underset{Cl}{|}}{CH}{-}CH_3$$

2-Butene · · · · · · · · · · · · 2,3-Dichlorobutane

In general terms, halogenation of an alkene can be written as

$$\underset{\text{Alkene}}{\diagup C{=}C\diagdown} \ + \ \underset{\text{Halogen}}{X_2} \longrightarrow \underset{\text{Dihalogenated alkane}}{-\overset{\overset{X}{|}}{C}{-}\overset{\overset{X}{|}}{C}-} \qquad (X = Cl, Br)$$

Bromination is often used to test for the presence of carbon–carbon double bonds in organic substances. Bromine in water or carbon tetrachloride is reddish-brown. The dibromo compound(s) formed from the symmetrical addition of bromine to an organic compound is (are) colorless. Thus the decolorization of a Br_2 solution indicates the presence of carbon–carbon double bonds (Figure 13-9).

 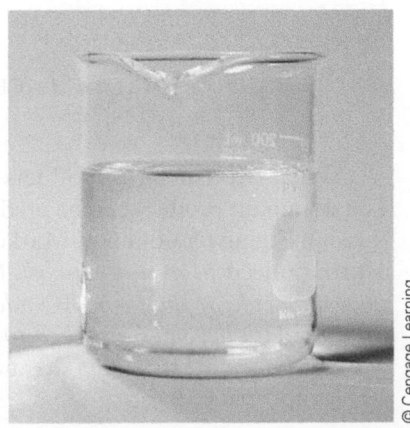

Figure 13-9 A bromine in water solution is reddish-brown (left). When a small amount of such a solution is added to an unsaturated hydrocarbon, the added solution is decolorized as the bromine adds to the hydrocarbon to form colorless dibromo compounds (right).

Figure 13-10 Vladimir Vasilevich Markovnikov (1837–1904). A professor of chemistry at several Russian universities, Markovnikov synthesized rings containing four carbon atoms and seven carbon atoms, thereby disproving the notion of the day that carbon could form only five- and six-membered rings.

▶ *The terms* hydration *and* hydration reaction *have different meanings. When a person hydrates oneself by drinking lots of water after excessive sweating they are simply replacing water that has been lost by evaporation. This process simply involves uptake of water; it does not involve a hydration reaction.*

▶ *The addition of water to carbon–carbon double bonds occurs in many biochemical reactions that take place in the human body—for example, in the citric acid cycle (Section 23-6) and in the oxidation of fatty acids (Section 25-4).*

▶ *Two catchy summaries of Markovnikov's rule are "hydrogen goes where hydrogen is" and "the rich get richer" (in terms of hydrogen).*

Unsymmetrical Addition Reactions

Two important types of unsymmetrical addition reactions are hydrohalogenation and hydration.

A **hydrohalogenation reaction** *is an addition reaction in which a hydrogen halide (HCl, HBr, or HI) is incorporated into molecules of an organic compound.* In alkene hydrohalogenation, one carbon atom of a double bond receives a halogen atom and the other carbon atom receives a hydrogen atom. Hydrohalogenation reactions require no catalyst. For *symmetrical* alkenes, such as ethene, only one product results from hydrohalogenation.

$$CH_2{=}CH_2 + H{-}Cl \longrightarrow \underset{\text{Chloroethane}}{\overset{\overset{\displaystyle H \quad Cl}{|\quad\;\;|}}{CH_2{-}CH_2}}$$

Ethene

A **hydration reaction** *is an addition reaction in which H_2O is incorporated into molecules of an organic compound.* In alkene hydration, one carbon atom of a double bond receives a hydrogen atom and the other carbon atom receives an —OH group. ◀ Alkene hydration requires a small amount of H_2SO_4 (sulfuric acid) as a catalyst. For *symmetrical* alkenes, only one product results from hydration.

$$CH_2{=}CH_2 + H{-}OH \xrightarrow{H_2SO_4} \underset{\text{An alcohol}}{\overset{\overset{\displaystyle H \quad OH}{|\quad\;\;|}}{CH_2{-}CH_2}}$$

Ethene

In this equation, the water (H_2O) is written as H—OH to emphasize how this molecule adds to the double bond. Note also that the product of this hydration reaction contains an —OH group. Hydrocarbon derivatives of this type are called *alcohols.* Such compounds are the subject of Chapter 14. ◀

When the alkene involved in a hydrohalogenation or hydration reaction is itself *unsymmetrical,* more than one product is possible. (An unsymmetrical alkene is one in which the two carbon atoms of the double bond are not equivalently substituted.) For example, the addition of HCl to propene (an unsymmetrical alkene) could produce either 1-chloropropane or 2-chloropropane, depending on whether the H from the HCl attaches itself to carbon 2 or carbon 1.

$$\overset{①\qquad②}{CH_2{=}CH{-}CH_3} + HCl \longrightarrow \underset{\text{1-Chloropropane}}{\overset{\overset{\displaystyle Cl \quad H}{|\quad\;\;|}}{CH_2{-}CH{-}CH_3}}$$

Propene

or

$$\overset{①\qquad②}{CH_2{=}CH{-}CH_3} + HCl \longrightarrow \underset{\text{2-Chloropropane}}{\overset{\overset{\displaystyle H \quad Cl}{|\quad\;\;|}}{CH_2{-}CH{-}CH_3}}$$

Propene

When two isomeric products are possible, one product usually predominates. The dominant product can be predicted by using Markovnikov's rule, named after the Russian chemist Vladimir V. Markovnikov (Figure 13-10). The surname Markovnikov is pronounced *Mar-cove-na-coff.* **Markovnikov's rule** *states that when an unsymmetrical molecule of the form* HQ *adds to an unsymmetrical alkene, the hydrogen atom from the* HQ *becomes attached to the unsaturated carbon atom that already has the most hydrogen atoms.* Thus the major product in our example involving propene is 2-chloropropane. ◀

EXAMPLE 13-4

Predicting Products in Alkene Addition Reactions Using Markovnikov's Rule

Using Markovnikov's rule, predict the predominant product in each of the following addition reactions.

a. $CH_3—CH_2—CH_2—CH=CH_2 + HBr \rightarrow$

b. $+ HCl \rightarrow$

c. $CH_3—CH=CH—CH_2—CH_3 + HBr \rightarrow$

Solution

a. The hydrogen atom will add to carbon 1 because carbon 1 already bears more hydrogen atoms than carbon 2. The predominant product of the addition will be 2-bromopentane.

$$CH_3—CH_2—CH_2—\overset{②}{CH}=\overset{①}{CH_2} + HBr \longrightarrow CH_3—CH_2—CH_2—\overset{Br}{\underset{|}{CH}}—\overset{H}{\underset{|}{CH_2}}$$

b. Carbon 1 of the double bond does not have any H atoms directly attached to it. Carbon 2 of the double bond has one H atom (H atoms are not shown in the structure but are implied) attached to it. The H atom from the HCl will add to carbon 2, giving 1-chloro-1-methylcyclopentane as the product.

c. Each carbon atom of the double bond in this molecule has one hydrogen atom. Thus Markovnikov's rule does not favor either carbon atom. The result is two isomeric products that are formed in almost equal quantities.

$$CH_3—\underset{\underset{Br}{|}}{CH}—CH_2—CH_2—CH_3 \qquad \text{and} \qquad CH_3—CH_2—\underset{\underset{Br}{|}}{CH}—CH_2—CH_3$$

2-Bromopentane   3-Bromopentane

In compounds that contain more than one carbon–carbon double bond, such as dienes and trienes, addition can occur at each of the double bonds. In the complete hydrogenation of a diene and in that of a triene, the amounts of hydrogen needed are twice as much and three times as much, respectively, as that needed for the hydrogenation of an alkene with one double bond.

$$CH_2=CH—CH_2—CH_2—CH_2—CH_3 + H_2 \xrightarrow{Ni} CH_3—(CH_2)_4—CH_3$$

$$CH_2=CH—CH=CH—CH_2—CH_3 + 2H_2 \xrightarrow{Ni} CH_3—(CH_2)_4—CH_3$$

$$CH_2=CH—CH=CH—CH=CH_2 + 3H_2 \xrightarrow{Ni} CH_3—(CH_2)_4—CH_3$$

EXAMPLE 13-5

Predicting Reactants and Products in Alkene Addition Reactions

Supply the structural formula of the missing substance in each of the following addition reactions.

a. $CH_3—CH_2—CH=CH_2 + H_2O \xrightarrow{H_2SO_4}$?

b.

c.

d. $CH_3—CH=CH—CH=CH_2 + 2H_2 \xrightarrow{Ni}$?

(continued)

Solution

a. This is a hydration reaction. Based on Markovnikov's rule, the H will become attached to carbon 1, which has more hydrogen atoms than carbon 2, and the —OH group will be attached to carbon 2.

$$\begin{array}{c} \text{OH} \\ | \\ \text{CH}_3\text{—CH}_2\text{—CH—CH}_3 \end{array}$$

b. The reactant alkene will have a double bond between the two carbon atoms that bromine atoms are attached to in the product.

c. The small reactant molecule that adds to the double bond is HBr. The added Br atom from the HBr is explicitly shown in the product's structural formula, but the added H atom is not shown.

d. Hydrogen will add at each of the double bonds. The product hydrocarbon is pentane.

$$\text{CH}_3\text{—CH}_2\text{—CH}_2\text{—CH}_2\text{—CH}_3$$

Section 13-10 Quick Quiz

1. Which of the following reactions is *not* a symmetrical addition reaction?
   a. propene + H₂
   b. propene + Br₂
   c. propene + HBr
   d. no correct response

2. Which of the following addition reactions would convert an alkene to an alkane?
   a. halogenation
   b. hydrohalogenation
   c. hydration
   d. no correct response

3. Hydrohalogenation of which of the following alkenes would produce two different halogenated hydrocarbons?
   a. $\text{CH}_2\text{=CH}_2$
   b. $\text{CH}_2\text{=CH—CH}_3$
   c. $\text{CH}_3\text{—CH=CH—CH}_3$
   d. no correct response

4. The reactant needed to convert 2-butene to 2,3-dichlorobutane is
   a. H₂
   b. HCl
   c. Cl₂
   d. no correct response

5. Based on Markovnikov's rule, the major product in the addition reaction involving $\text{CH}_2\text{=CH—CH}_3$ and HCl is

   a. $\begin{array}{c} \text{CH}_2\text{—CH}_2\text{—CH}_3 \\ | \\ \text{Cl} \end{array}$

   b. $\begin{array}{c} \text{CH}_3\text{—CH—CH}_3 \\ | \\ \text{Cl} \end{array}$

   c. $\begin{array}{c} \text{CH}_2\text{—CH—CH}_3 \\ | \quad\;\; | \\ \text{Cl} \quad \text{Cl} \end{array}$

   d. no correct response

Answers: 1. c; 2. d; 3. b; 4. c; 5. b

13-11 Polymerization of Alkenes: Addition Polymers

LEARNING FOCUS

Know what is meant by the term *addition polymer*; be familiar with common ethene-based and butadiene-based addition polymers; know what is meant by the term *copolymer*.

A **polymer** *is a large molecule formed by the repetitive bonding together of many smaller molecules.* The smaller repeating units of a polymer are called *monomers.* A **monomer** *is the small molecule that is the structural repeating unit in a polymer.* The process by which a polymer is made is called *polymerization.* ◀ A **polymerization reaction** *is a chemical reaction in which the repetitious combining of many small molecules (monomers) produces a very large molecule (the polymer).* With appropriate catalysts, simple alkenes and simple substituted alkenes readily undergo polymerization.

The type of polymer that alkenes and substituted alkenes form is an *addition polymer.* An **addition polymer** *is a polymer in which the monomers simply "add together" with no other products formed besides the polymer.* Addition polymerization is similar to the addition reactions described in Section 13-10 except that there is no reactant other than the alkene or substituted alkene. ◀

The simplest alkene addition polymer has ethylene (ethene) as the monomer. With appropriate catalysts, ethylene readily adds to itself to produce polyethylene. ◀

$$\cdots + \underset{\underset{\displaystyle H}{|}}{\overset{\overset{\displaystyle H}{|}}{C}}{=}\underset{\underset{\displaystyle H}{|}}{\overset{\overset{\displaystyle H}{|}}{C} + \underset{\underset{\displaystyle H}{|}}{\overset{\overset{\displaystyle H}{|}}{C}}{=}\underset{\underset{\displaystyle H}{|}}{\overset{\overset{\displaystyle H}{|}}{C}} + \underset{\underset{\displaystyle H}{|}}{\overset{\overset{\displaystyle H}{|}}{C}}{=}\underset{\underset{\displaystyle H}{|}}{\overset{\overset{\displaystyle H}{|}}{C}} + \cdots \xrightarrow{\text{Catalyst}} {\sim}\overset{}{C}{-}\overset{}{C}{-}\overset{}{C}{-}\overset{}{C}{-}\overset{}{C}{-}\overset{}{C}{\sim}$$

Polyethylene segment

An *exact* formula for a polymer such as polyethylene cannot be written because the length of the carbon chain varies from polymer molecule to polymer molecule. In recognition of this formula "inexactness," the notation used for denoting polymer formulas is independent of carbon-chain length. The formula of the simplest repeating unit (the monomer with the double bond changed to a single bond) is written in parentheses and then the subscript n is added after the parentheses, with n being understood to represent a very large number. The value of n often exceeds 100,000 and can sometimes exceed a million. Using this notation, the formula of polyethylene becomes

$$\left(\begin{array}{c} \overset{\displaystyle H}{\underset{\displaystyle H}{|}} \quad \overset{\displaystyle H}{\underset{\displaystyle H}{|}} \\ {-}C{-}C{-} \\ | \quad | \end{array}\right)_n$$

This notation clearly identifies the basic repeating unit found in the polymer.

Substituted-Ethene Addition Polymers

Many substituted alkenes undergo polymerization similar to that of ethene when they are treated with the proper catalyst. For a monosubstituted-ethene monomer, the general polymerization equation is

$$H_2C{=}\overset{\displaystyle Z}{\overset{|}{C}}H \xrightarrow{\text{Polymerization}} \left({-}CH_2{-}\overset{\displaystyle Z}{\overset{|}{C}}H{-}\right)_n$$

Variation in the substituent group Z can change polymer properties dramatically, as is shown by the entries in Table 13-1, a listing of monomers for the five ethene-based polymers *polyethylene, polypropylene, poly(vinyl chloride) (PVC), Teflon,* and *polystyrene,* along with several uses of each. Figure 13-11 depicts the preparation of polystyrene. Figure 13-12 contrasts the structures of polyethylene, polypropylene, and poly(vinyl chloride) as depicted in space-filling models.

▶ *The word* polymer *comes from the Greek* poly, *which means "many," and* meros, *which means "parts."*

▶ *Polymer types other than addition polymers will be considered in Sections 15-12 and 16-18.*

▶ *The ellipses (…) and tildes(~) in the structural equation have the meaning et cetera. The ellipses in the left portion of the equation indicate that the number of monomers present is greater than the three monomers shown. The tildes in the right portion of the equation indicate that the length of the polymeric structure extends in both directions for a greater number of additional units.*

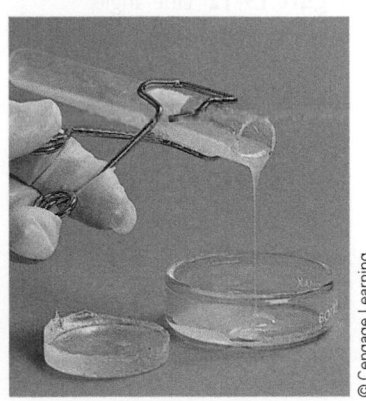

© Cengage Learning

Figure 13-11 Preparation of polystyrene. When styrene, $C_6H_5{-}CH{=}CH_2$, is heated with a catalyst (benzoyl peroxide), it yields a viscous liquid. After some time, this liquid sets to a hard plastic (sample shown at left).

▶ Table 13-1 **Some Common Polymers Obtained from Ethene-Based Monomers**

Polymer Formula and Name	Monomer Formula and Name	Uses of Polymer
polyethylene	ethylene	bottles, plastic bags, toys, electrical insulation
polypropylene	propylene	indoor–outdoor carpeting, bottles, molded parts (including heart valves)
poly(vinyl chloride) (PVC)	vinyl chloride	plastic wrap, bags for intravenous drugs, garden hose, plastic pipe, simulated leather (Naugahyde)
Teflon	tetrafluoroethylene	cooking utensil coverings, electrical insulation, component of artificial joints in body parts replacement
polystyrene	styrene	toys, Styrofoam packaging, cups, simulated wood furniture

Figure 13-12 Line-angle structural formulas and space-filling models of segments of the ethene-based polymers (a) polyethylene, (b) polypropylene, and (c) poly(vinyl chloride).

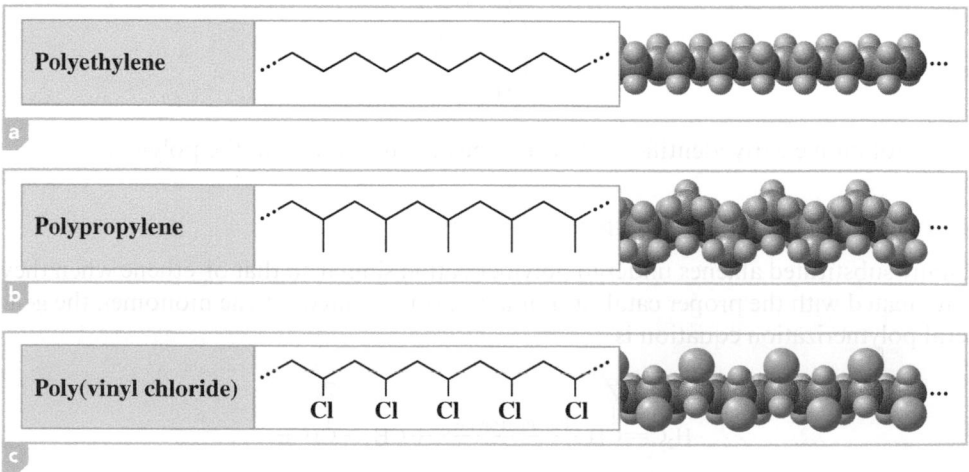

The properties of an ethene-based polymer depend not only on monomer identity but also on the average size (length) of polymer molecules and on the extent of polymer branching. For example, there are three major types of polyethylene: high-density polyethylene (HDPE), low-density polyethylene (LDPE), and linear low-density polyethylene (LLDPE). The major difference among these three materials is the degree of branching of the polymer chain. HDPE and LLDPE are composed of linear, unbranched carbon chains, whereas LDPE chains are branched. The strong and thick plastic bags from a shopping mall are made of LLDPE, the thin and flimsy grocery store plastic bags are made of HDPE, and the very wispy garment bags dry cleaners use are made of LDPE.

In general, HDPE materials are rigid or semi-rigid with uses such as threaded bottle caps, toys, bottles, and milk jugs, whereas LDPE materials are more flexible with uses such as plastic film and squeeze bottles (Figure 13-13). Objects made of HDPE hold their shape in boiling water, whereas objects made of LDPE become severely deformed at this temperature.

With their alkane-like structures, ethene-based addition polymers are very unreactive, as are alkanes. This unreactivity means that these polymers do not readily decompose when they are deposited into landfill sites.

Of the many hundreds of types of addition polymers in use, six account for approximately three-fourths by mass of polymer consumption. These six heavily used polymers are the focus of polymer recycling efforts. The six are assigned a numerical recycling code (the numbers 1 through 6) that relates to the ease of their recycling. The lower the recycling number, the easier it is to recycle the polymer. Table 13-2 lists the six most consumed addition polymers and their recycling codes.

After sorting by recycling code (see Figure 13-14), recycling involves shredding into small chips, removing components such as labels and adhesives, melting, and then remolding. Materials so recycled, because of possible residual contamination with adhesives and the like, are not reused in products that store food and drink. End uses include insulating wrap for new home construction (such as Tyvek) and fibers for carpets.

Figure 13-13 Examples of objects made of polyethylene. Polyethylene objects that are strong and rigid (bottles, toys, covering for wire) contain HDPE (high-density polyethylene). Polyethylene objects that are very flexible (plastic bags and packaging materials) most often contain LDPE (low-density polyethylene).

Butadiene-Based Addition Polymers

When dienes such as 1,3-butadiene are used as the monomers in addition polymerization reactions, the resulting polymers contain double bonds and are thus still unsaturated.

$$CH_2{=}CH{-}CH{=}CH_2 \xrightarrow{\text{Polymerization}} -(CH_2{-}CH{=}CH{-}CH_2)_n-$$

1,3-Butadiene   Polybutadiene

▶ Table 13-2 **Codes and Symbols Used in the Recycling of Ethene-Based Addition Polymers**

Code	Type	Name	Examples
PET	♳ (1)	Polyethylene terephthalate	soft drink bottles, peanut butter jars, vegetable oil bottles
HDPE	♴ (2)	High-density polyethylene	milk, water, and juice containers; squeezable ketchup and syrup bottles
PVC	♵ (3)	Polyvinyl chloride	shampoo bottles, plastic pipe, shower curtains
LDPE	♶ (4)	Low-density polyethylene	six-pack rings, shrink-wrap, sandwich bags, grocery bags
PP	♷ (5)	Polypropylene	margarine tubs, straws, diaper linings, toys
PS	♸ (6)	Polystyrene	egg cartons, disposable utensils, packing peanuts, foam cups
Other	♹ (7)	Multilayer plastics	various flexible items

Figure 13-14 Sorting of ethene-based polymers into various subtypes often occurs at recycling collection points.

In general, unsaturated polymers are much more flexible than the ethene-based saturated polymers listed in Table 13-1. Natural rubber is a flexible addition polymer whose repeating unit is isoprene (Section 13-7)—that is, 2-methyl-1,3-butadiene (see Figure 13-15).

$$CH_2{=}C{-}CH{=}CH_2 \xrightarrow{\text{Polymerization}} \left(CH_2{-}C{=}CH{-}CH_2\right)_n$$

CH₃	CH₃
Isoprene (2-methyl-1,3-butadiene)	Polyisoprene (natural rubber)

Addition Copolymers

Saran Wrap is a polymer in which two different monomers are present: chloroethene (vinyl chloride) and 1,1-dichloroethene.

Vinyl chloride   1,1-Dichloroethene   Saran Wrap

Such a polymer is an example of a *copolymer*. A **copolymer** *is a polymer in which two different monomers are present*. Another important copolymer is styrene–butadiene rubber, the leading synthetic rubber in use today. It contains the monomers 1,3-butadiene and styrene in a 3:1 ratio. It is a major ingredient in automobile tires.

  Chemistry at a Glance—Chemical Reactions of Alkenes—summarizes the reaction chemistry of alkenes presented in this and the previous section.

Figure 13-15 Natural rubber being harvested in Malaysia.

Section 13-11 Quick Quiz

1. The number of monomer units present in an addition polymer carbon chain varies but
   a. is between 5 and 10
   b. is less than 100
   c. can exceed 100,000
   d. no correct response
2. The description "only carbon and hydrogen are present" does not apply to which one of the following additional polymers?
   a. polyethylene
   b. polypropylene
   c. PVC
   d. no correct response

3. Which of the following substituted ethene-based addition polymers contains the element fluorine?
   a. PVC
   b. polystyrene
   c. Teflon
   d. no correct response
4. Which of the following addition polymers is produced from a diene monomer?
   a. synthetic rubber
   b. polyvinyl chloride
   c. Saran
   d. no correct response
5. Addition copolymers always contain
   a. two different monomers
   b. ethylene and one additional monomer
   c. C, H, and two additional elements
   d. no correct response

Answers: 1. c; 2. c; 3. c; 4. a; 5. a

CHEMISTRY AT A GLANCE — Chemical Reactions of Alkenes

ALKENE

COMBUSTION
- Products are CO_2 and H_2O
- Does not involve the process of addition

ADDITION

Addition of a small symmetrical molecule

Addition of a small unsymmetrical molecule

POLYMERIZATION
- Alkene molecules undergo an addition reaction with one another.
- Specific catalysts are needed.

H_2 Hydrogenation

$$H_2 + \, \overset{/}{\underset{\backslash}{C}} = \overset{\backslash}{\underset{/}{C}}$$

↓ Ni or Pt catalyst

$$-\overset{|}{\underset{H}{C}} - \overset{|}{\underset{H}{C}} -$$

Alkane

Br_2 or Cl_2 Halogenation

$$X_2 + \, \overset{/}{\underset{\backslash}{C}} = \overset{\backslash}{\underset{/}{C}}$$

↓

$$-\overset{|}{\underset{X}{C}} - \overset{|}{\underset{X}{C}} -$$

Dihaloalkane

HBr or HCl Hydrohalogenation

$$HX + \, \overset{/}{\underset{\backslash}{C}} = \overset{\backslash}{\underset{/}{C}}$$

↓

$$-\overset{|}{\underset{H}{C}} - \overset{|}{\underset{X}{C}} -$$

Monohaloalkane*

H_2O (H—OH) Hydration

$$H-OH + \, \overset{/}{\underset{\backslash}{C}} = \overset{\backslash}{\underset{/}{C}}$$

↓ H_2SO_4 catalyst

$$-\overset{|}{\underset{H}{C}} - \overset{|}{\underset{OH}{C}} -$$

Alcohol*

*Markovnikov's rule is needed to predict the product's exact structure if the alkene is unsymmetrical.

13-12 Alkynes

LEARNING FOCUS

Be familiar with the *alkyne* classification of unsaturated hydrocarbons in terms of generalized molecular formula, IUPAC nomenclature, isomerism possibilities, and general physical and chemical properties.

Alkynes are the second of the three classes of unsaturated hydrocarbons considered in this chapter; alkenes (previously considered) and aromatic hydrocarbons (yet to be considered) are the other two classes. An **alkyne** *is an acyclic unsaturated hydrocarbon*

Figure 13-16 Structural representations of ethyne (acetylene), the simplest alkyne. The molecule is linear—that is, the bond angles are 180°.

Ethyne—a linear molecule with bond angles of 180°

$$H—C\equiv C—H$$

that contains one or more carbon–carbon triple bonds. The alkyne functional group is, thus, a $C\equiv C$ group. As the family name *alkyne* indicates, the characteristic "ending" associated with a triple bond is *-yne.* ◄

The general formula for an alkyne with one triple bond is C_nH_{2n-2}. Thus the simplest member of this type of alkyne has the formula C_2H_2, and the next member, with $n = 3$, has the formula C_3H_4.

$$CH\equiv CH \qquad CH\equiv C—CH_3$$
Ethyne   Propyne

The presence of a carbon–carbon triple bond in a molecule always results in a linear arrangement for the two atoms attached to the carbons of the triple bond. Thus ethyne is a linear molecule (Figure 13-16).

The simplest alkyne, ethyne (C_2H_2), is the most important alkyne from an industrial standpoint. A colorless gas, it goes by the common name *acetylene* and is used in oxyacetylene torches, high-temperature torches used for cutting and welding materials. ◄

► *Very few biological molecules are known that contain a carbon–carbon triple bond.*

► *Cycloalkynes, molecules that contain a triple bond as part of a ring structure, are known, but they are not common. Because of the 180° angle associated with a triple bond, a ring system containing a triple bond has to be quite large. The smallest cycloalkyne that has been isolated is cyclooctyne.*

Nomenclature for Alkynes

The rules for naming alkynes are identical to those used to name alkenes (Section 13-3), except the ending *-yne* is used instead of *-ene.* Consider the following structures and their IUPAC names.

$$\overset{4}{CH_3}—\overset{3}{CH}—\overset{2}{C}\equiv \overset{1}{CH} \qquad \overset{1}{CH_3}—\overset{2}{CH_2}—\overset{3}{C}\equiv \overset{4}{C}—\overset{5}{CH_2}—\overset{6}{C}—\overset{7}{CH_3}$$

|CH_3| |CH_3|

3-Methyl-1-butyne   6,6-Dimethyl-3-heptyne

$$\overset{1}{CH}\equiv \overset{2}{C}—\overset{3}{CH_2}—\overset{4}{CH_2}—\overset{5}{CH_2}—\overset{6}{C}\equiv \overset{7}{CH}$$
1,6-Heptadiyne

Common names for simple alkynes are based on the name *acetylene,* as shown in the following examples. ◄

$$CH\equiv CH \qquad CH_3—C\equiv CH \qquad CH_3—C\equiv C—CH_3$$
Acetylene   Methylacetylene   Dimethylacetylene

Chemistry at a Glance—IUPAC Nomenclature for Alkanes, Alkenes, and Alkynes—summarizes IUPAC nomenclature procedures for alkanes, alkenes, and alkynes.

► *Early cars had carbide headlights that produced acetylene by the action of slowly dripping water on calcium carbide. This same type of lamp, which was also used by miners, is still often used by spelunkers (cave explorers).*

Isomerism and Alkynes

Because of the linearity (180° angles) about an alkyne's triple bond, *cis–trans* isomerism, such as that found in alkenes, is not possible for alkynes because there are no "up" and "down" positions. However, constitutional isomers are possible—both relative to the carbon chain (skeletal isomers) and to the position of the triple bond (positional isomers).

Skeletal isomers:

1-Pentyne   and   3-Methyl-1-butyne

Positional isomers:

1-Hexyne   and   3-Hexyne

CHEMISTRY AT A GLANCE — IUPAC Nomenclature for Alkanes, Alkenes, and Alkynes

IUPAC NOMENCLATURE SYSTEM

Each compound has a unique name that not only identifies it but also contains sufficient information for its structural formula to be drawn.

PARENT NAME
- Longest continuous chain of carbon atoms
- Largest ring of carbon atoms

PREFIXES
- Names of substituents (alkyl groups)
- Number of each type of substituent present (di-, tri-, etc.)

LOCANTS
- Numbers giving locations of substituent groups on the carbon chain or ring
- Numbers giving locations of carbon–carbon multiple bonds on the carbon chain or ring

SUFFIXES
- -ane for alkanes and cycloalkanes
- -ene for alkenes and cycloalkenes
- -yne for alkynes and cycloalkynes

3,3-dimethyl-1-heptyne

locants | numerical prefix | substituent prefix | locant | parent name | suffix

Physical and Chemical Properties of Alkynes

The physical properties of alkynes are similar to those of alkenes and alkanes. In general, alkynes are insoluble in water but soluble in organic solvents, have densities less than that of water, and have boiling points that increase with molecular mass. Low-molecular-mass alkynes are gases at room temperature. Figure 13-17 is a physical-state summary for unbranched 1-alkynes with eight or fewer carbon atoms.

The triple-bond functional group of alkynes behaves chemically quite similarly to the double-bond functional group of alkenes. Thus there are many parallels between alkene chemistry and alkyne chemistry. The same substances that add to double bonds (H_2, HCl, Cl_2, and so on) also add to triple bonds. However, two molecules of a specific reactant can add to a triple bond, as contrasted to the addition of one molecule of reactant to a double bond. In triple-bond addition, the first molecule converts the triple bond into a double bond, and the second molecule then converts the double bond into a single bond. For example, propyne reacts with H_2 to form propene first and then to form propane.

$$CH{\equiv}C-CH_3 \xrightarrow{H_2 \atop Ni} CH_2{=}CH-CH_3 \xrightarrow{H_2 \atop Ni} CH_3-CH_2-CH_3$$

An alkyne (propyne)   An alkene (propene)   An alkane (propane)

Alkynes, like alkenes and alkanes, are flammable; that is, they readily undergo combustion reactions. ◀

Section 13-12 Quick Quiz

1. The spatial arrangement of bonds for a C atom participating in a carbon–carbon triple bond is
   a. tetrahedral
   b. trigonal planar
   c. linear
   d. no correct response

(continued)

Unbranched 1-Alkynes		
✕	C_3	C_5	C_7
C_2	C_4	C_6	C_8

☐ Gas ☐ Liquid

Figure 13-17 A physical-state summary for unbranched 1-alkynes at room temperature and pressure.

▶ *Students often ask whether it is possible to have hydrocarbons in which both double and triple bonds are present. The answer is yes. Immediately, another question is asked. How are such compounds named? Such compounds are called* alkenynes. *An example is*

$$CH{\equiv}C-CH{=}CH_2$$
1-Buten-3-yne

A double bond has priority over a triple bond in numbering the chain when numbering systems are equivalent. Otherwise, the chain is numbered from the end closest to a multiple bond.

2. Which of the following is the correct IUPAC name for the compound $CH_3-C{\equiv}C-CH-CH_3$?
   a. 2-methyl-4-pentyne $|$
   b. 4-methyl-2-pentyne CH_3
   c. 2,4-methylpentyne
   d. no correct response
3. Which of the following alkynes goes by the common name acetylene?
   a. ethyne
   b. propyne
   c. 1-butyne
   d. no correct response
4. Which of the following types of isomerism is not possible for alkynes?
   a. positional
   b. skeletal
   c. *cis–trans*
   d. no correct response
5. Which of the following statements concerning alkyne properties is *incorrect*?
   a. Alkynes are generally insoluble in water.
   b. Alkynes do not undergo combustion reactions.
   c. Alkynes generally have densities less than that of water.
   d. no correct response

Answers: 1. c; 2. b; 3. a; 4. c; 5. b

13-13 Aromatic Hydrocarbons

LEARNING FOCUS

Be able to describe how the bonding in *aromatic* hydrocarbons differs from that in other *unsaturated* hydrocarbons.

Aromatic hydrocarbons are the third class of unsaturated hydrocarbons; the alkenes and alkynes (previously considered) are the other two classes. An **aromatic hydrocarbon** *is an unsaturated cyclic hydrocarbon that does not readily undergo addition reactions.* This reaction behavior, which is very different from that of alkenes and alkynes, explains the separate classification for aromatic hydrocarbons.

The fact that, even though they are unsaturated compounds, aromatic hydrocarbons do not readily undergo addition reactions suggests that the bonding present in this type of compound must differ significantly from that in alkenes and alkynes. Such is indeed the case.

A consideration of the bonding present in *benzene,* the simplest aromatic hydrocarbon, is the key to understanding the "special type" of bonding that is characteristic of an aromatic hydrocarbon and to specifying the identity of the aromatic hydrocarbon functional group. Benzene, a flat, symmetrical molecule with a molecular formula of C_6H_6 (Figure 13-18), has a structural formula that is often formalized as that of a cyclohexatriene—in other words, as a structural formula that involves a six-membered carbon ring in which three double bonds are present.

This structure is one of two equivalent structures that can be drawn for benzene that differ only in the locations of the double bonds (1,3,5 positions versus 2,4,6 positions):

Figure 13-18 Space-filling and ball-and-stick models for the structure of benzene.

Neither of these conventional structures, however, is totally correct. Experimental evidence indicates that all of the carbon–carbon bonds in benzene are equivalent (identical), and these preceding structures imply three bonds of one type (double bonds) and three bonds of a different type (single bonds).

The equivalent nature of the carbon–carbon bonds in benzene is addressed by considering the correct bonding structure for benzene to be an *average* of the two "triene" structures. Related to this "average"-structure situation is the concept that electrons associated with the ring double bonds are not held between specific carbon atoms; instead, they are free to move "around" the carbon ring. Thus the true structure for benzene, an intermediate between that represented by the two "triene" structures, is a situation in which all carbon–carbon bonds are equivalent; they are neither single nor double bonds but something in between. Placing a double-headed arrow between the conventional structures that are averaged to obtain the true structure is one way to denote the average structure.

An alternative notation for denoting the bonding in benzene—a notation that involves a single structure—is

In this "circle-in-the-ring" structure for benzene, the circle denotes the electrons associated with the double bonds that move "around" the ring. Each carbon atom in the ring can be considered to participate in three conventional (localized) bonds (two C—C bonds and one C—H bond) and in one *delocalized bond* (the circle) that involves all six carbon atoms. A **delocalized bond** *is a covalent bond in which electrons are shared among more than two atoms.* This delocalized bond is what causes benzene and its derivatives to be resistant to addition reactions, a property normally associated with unsaturation in a molecule.

The structure represented by the notation

is called an *aromatic ring system,* and it is the functional group present in aromatic compounds. An **aromatic ring system** *is a highly unsaturated carbon ring system in which both localized and delocalized bonds are present.*

Section 13-13 Quick Quiz

1. The molecular formula for benzene is
   a. C_5H_5
   b. C_6H_6
   c. C_6H_{12}
   d. no correct response
2. In the "circle-in-the-ring" structural notation for benzene, the circle denotes delocalized bonding in which
   a. all carbon atoms participate
   b. all hydrogen atoms participate
   c. all carbon atoms and all hydrogen atoms participate
   d. no correct response
3. The bonding in benzene differs from that of other types of unsaturated hydrocarbons in that each carbon atom participates in
   a. one single bond and one "delocalized" bond
   b. one single bond and three "delocalized" bonds
   c. three single bonds and one "delocalized" bond
   d. no correct response

Answers: 1. b; 2. a; 3. c

13-14 Nomenclature for Aromatic Hydrocarbons

LEARNING FOCUS

Given their structures, name aromatic hydrocarbons using IUPAC rules and common names when applicable, and vice versa.

Replacement of one or more of the hydrogen atoms on benzene with other groups produces benzene derivatives. Compounds with alkyl groups or halogen atoms attached to the benzene ring are commonly encountered. The naming of benzene derivatives with one substituent is considered first, then the naming of those with two substituents, and finally the naming of those with three or more substituents.

Benzene Derivatives with One Substituent

The IUPAC system of naming monosubstituted benzene derivatives uses the name of the substituent as a prefix to the name *benzene*. Examples of this type of nomenclature include

Fluorobenzene   Chlorobenzene   Isopropylbenzene   Ethylbenzene

A few monosubstituted benzenes have names wherein the substituent and the benzene ring taken together constitute a new parent name. Two important examples of such nomenclature with hydrocarbon substituents are

Toluene
(not methylbenzene)

Styrene
(not vinylbenzene)

Both of these compounds are industrially important chemicals.

Monosubstituted benzene structures are often drawn with the substituent at the "12 o'clock" position, as in the previous structures. However, because all the carbon atoms in benzene are equivalent, it does not matter at which carbon of the ring the substituted group is located. Each of the following formulas represents chlorobenzene.

▶ *The word* phenyl *comes from "phene," a European term used during the 1800s for benzene. The word is pronounced* fen-*nil.*

For monosubstituted benzene rings that have a group attached that is not easily named as a substituent, the benzene ring is often treated as a group attached to this substituent. In this reversed approach, the benzene ring attachment is called a *phenyl* group, and the compound is named according to the rules for naming alkanes, alkenes, and alkynes. ◀

▶ *The chemical formula for a phenyl group is* C_6H_5-. *This group contains one less hydrogen atom than its parent, benzene* (C_6H_6).

$$CH_2{=}CH{-}CH{-}CH_3$$

3-Phenyl-1-butene ◀

Benzene Derivatives with Two Substituents

When two substituents, either the same or different, are attached to a benzene ring, three isomeric structures are possible.

To distinguish among these three isomers, the positions of the substituents relative to one another must be specified. This can be done in either of two ways: by using numbers or by using nonnumerical prefixes.

When numbers are used, the three isomeric dichlorobenzenes have the first-listed set of names:

1,2-Dichlorobenzene   1,3-Dichlorobenzene   1,4-Dichlorobenzene
(*ortho*-dichlorobenzene)   (*meta*-dichlorobenzene)   (*para*-dichlorobenzene) ◀

The prefix system uses the prefixes *ortho-*, *meta-*, and *para-* (abbreviated *o-*, *m-*, and *p-*).

Ortho- means 1,2 disubstitution; the substituents are on adjacent carbon atoms.
Meta- means 1,3 disubstitution; the substituents are one carbon removed from each other.
Para- means 1,4 disubstitution; the substituents are two carbons removed from each other (on opposite sides of the ring).

When prefixes are used, the three isomeric dichlorobenzenes have the second-listed set of names above. ◀

When one of the two substituents in a disubstituted benzene imparts a special name to the compound (as, for example, toluene), the compound is named as a derivative of that parent molecule. The special substituent is assumed to be at ring position 1.

4-Bromotoluene   2-Ethyltoluene
(not 1-bromo-4-methylbenzene)   (not 1-ethyl-2-methylbenzene)

When neither substituent group imparts a special name, the substituents are cited in alphabetical order before the ending *-benzene*. The carbon of the benzene ring bearing the substituent with alphabetical priority becomes carbon 1.

1-Chloro-2-ethylbenzene   1-Bromo-3-chlorobenzene
(not 2-chloro-1-ethylbenzene)   (not 3-bromo-1-chlorobenzene)

▶ Cis–trans *isomerism is not possible for disubstituted benzenes. All 12 atoms of benzene are in the same plane—that is, benzene is a flat molecule. When a substituent group replaces an H atom, the atom that bonds the group to the ring is also in the plane of the ring.*

▶ *Learn the meaning of the prefixes* ortho-, meta-, *and* para-. *These prefixes are extensively used in naming disubstituted benzenes.*

The use of ortho-, meta-, *and* para- *in place of position numbers is reserved for disubstituted benzenes. The system is not used with cyclohexanes or other ring systems.*

A benzene ring bearing two methyl groups is a situation that generates a new special base name. Such compounds (there are three isomers) are not named as dimethylbenzenes or as methyltoluenes. They are called xylenes.

$$
\text{o-Xylene} \qquad \text{m-Xylene} \qquad \text{p-Xylene}
$$

The xylenes are good solvents for grease and oil and are used for cleaning microscope slides and optical lenses and for removing wax from skis. ◄

▶ *When parent names such as* toluene *and* xylene *are used, additional substituents present cannot be the same as those included in the parent name. If such is the case, name the compound as a substituted benzene. The compound*

$$
\text{CH}_3 \qquad \text{CH}_3
$$
$$
\text{CH}_3
$$

is named as a trimethylbenzene and not as a methylxylene or a dimethyltoluene.

Benzene Derivatives with Three or More Substituents

When more than two groups are present on the benzene ring, their positions are indicated with *numbers*. The ring is numbered in such a way as to obtain the lowest possible numbers for the carbon atoms that have substituents. If there is a choice of numbering systems (two systems give the same lowest set), then the group that comes first alphabetically is given the lower number.

$$
\text{1,2,4-Tribromobenzene} \qquad \text{1-Bromo-3,5-dichlorobenzene}
$$

EXAMPLE 13-6

Assigning IUPAC Names to Benzene Derivatives

Assign IUPAC names to the following benzene derivatives.

a.

b.

c. $\text{CH}_3-\overset{\text{Br}}{\underset{}{\text{CH}}}-\text{CH}-\text{CH}_3$

d.

Solution

a. No substituents that will change the parent name from benzene are present on the ring. Alphabetical priority dictates that the chloro group is on carbon 1 and the ethyl group on carbon 3. The compound is named 1-chloro-3-ethylbenzene (or *m*-chloroethylbenzene).

b. Again, no substituents that will change the parent name from benzene are present on the ring. Alphabetical priority among substituents dictates that the bromo group is on carbon 1, the chloro group on carbon 3, and the ethyl group on carbon 5. The compound is named 1-bromo-3-chloro-5-ethylbenzene.

c. This compound is named with the benzene ring treated as a substituent—that is, as a phenyl group. The compound is named 2-bromo-3-phenylbutane.

d. The methyl group present on the benzene ring changes the parent name from benzene to toluene. Carbon 1 bears the methyl group. Numbering clockwise, we obtain the name 2-chlorotoluene (Figure 13-19).

Figure 13-19 Space-filling model for the compound 2-chlorotoluene.

Section 13-14 Quick Quiz

1. The name *toluene* is assigned to the compound that has
   a. a methyl group attached to a benzene ring
   b. a vinyl group attached to a benzene ring
   c. two methyl groups attached to a benzene ring
   d. no correct response
2. In naming disubstituted benzenes, which of the following is a correct pairing of prefix and numbering systems used for locating substituents?
   a. *para-* and 1,2-
   b. *ortho-* and 1,4-
   c. *meta-* and 1,3-
   d. no correct response
3. Which of the following is a correct name for the compound ?
   a. 1-chloro-2-ethylbenzene
   b. 2-chloro-1-ethylbenzene
   c. 1-ethyl-2-chlorobenzene
   d. no correct response
4. The IUPAC name for the hydrocarbon CH₃— CH₂— CH₂— CH—CH₂—CH₃ is
   a. 3-benzylhexane
   b. 3-phenylhexane
   c. 3-hexylbenzene
   d. no correct response

Answers: 1. a; 2. c; 3. a; 4. b

13-15 Properties of and Sources for Aromatic Hydrocarbons

LEARNING FOCUS

Be familiar with the general physical and chemical properties and sources for aromatic hydrocarbons.

In general, aromatic hydrocarbons resemble other hydrocarbons in physical properties. They are insoluble in water, are good solvents for other nonpolar materials, and are less dense than water.

Benzene, monosubstituted benzenes, and many disubstituted benzenes are liquids at room temperature. Benzene itself is a colorless, flammable liquid that burns with a sooty flame because of incomplete combustion.

At one time, coal tar was the main source of aromatic hydrocarbons. Petroleum is now the primary source of such compounds. At high temperatures, with special catalysts, saturated hydrocarbons obtained from petroleum can be converted to aromatic hydrocarbons. The production of toluene from heptane is representative of such a conversion.

$$CH_3-CH_2-CH_2-CH_2-CH_2-CH_2-CH_3 \xrightarrow[\text{High temperature}]{\text{Catalyst}} \text{(toluene)} + 4H_2$$

Benzene was once widely used as an organic solvent. Such use has been discontinued because benzene's short- and long-term toxic effects are now recognized. Benzene inhalation can cause nausea and respiratory problems. ◀

Chemical Reactions of Aromatic Hydrocarbons

It was previously noted that aromatic hydrocarbons do not readily undergo the addition reactions characteristic of other unsaturated hydrocarbons. An addition reaction would require breaking up the delocalized bonding (Section 13-13) present in the ring system.

▶ *Two common situations in which a person can be exposed to low-level benzene vapors are*

1. *Inhaling gasoline vapors while refueling an automobile. Gasoline contains about 2% (v/v) benzene.*
2. *Being around a cigarette smoker. Benzene is a combustion product present in cigarette smoke. For smokers themselves, inhaled cigarette smoke is a serious benzene-exposure source.*

If benzene is so unresponsive to addition reactions, what reactions does it undergo? Benzene undergoes *substitution* reactions. Recall from Section 12-17 that substitution reactions are characterized by different atoms or groups of atoms replacing hydrogen atoms in a hydrocarbon molecule. Two important types of substitution reactions for benzene and other aromatic hydrocarbons are alkylation and halogenation.

1. *Alkylation:* An alkyl group (R—) from an alkyl chloride (R—Cl) substitutes for a hydrogen atom on the benzene ring. A catalyst, AlCl$_3$, is needed for alkylation. ◄

▶ *Alkylation, the reaction that attaches an alkyl group to an aromatic ring, is also known as a Friedel–Crafts reaction, named after Charles Friedel and James Mason Crafts, the French and American chemists responsible for its discovery in 1877.*

In general terms, the alkylation of benzene can be written as

Alkylation is the most important industrial reaction of benzene.

2. *Halogenation* (bromination or chlorination): A hydrogen atom on a benzene ring can be replaced by bromine or chlorine if benzene is treated with Br$_2$ or Cl$_2$ in the presence of a catalyst. The catalyst is usually FeBr$_3$ for bromination and FeCl$_3$ for chlorination.

Aromatic halogenation differs from alkane halogenation (Section 12-17) in that light is not required to initiate aromatic halogenation.

Section 13-15 Quick Quiz

1. At room temperature, benzene and most monosubstituted benzenes are
   a. gases
   b. liquids
   c. solids
   d. no correct response
2. The major starting material for the current production of aromatic hydrocarbons is
   a. natural gas
   b. coal tar
   c. petroleum
   d. no correct response
3. Which of the following statements concerning the chemical reactions of aromatic hydrocarbons is correct?
   a. They readily undergo addition reactions.
   b. They undergo substitution reactions rather than addition reactions.
   c. They do not undergo halogenation reactions.
   d. no correct response
4. With the catalyst AlCl$_3$ present, which reactant is needed to convert benzene to ethylbenzene?
   a. CH$_3$—CH$_3$
   b. CH$_3$—CH$_2$—Cl
   c. CH$_2$=CH$_2$
   d. no correct response

Answers: 1. b; 2. c; 3. b; 4. b

13-16 Fused-Ring Aromatic Hydrocarbons

LEARNING FOCUS

Understand the structural features associated with a *fused-ring* aromatic hydrocarbon.

Benzene and its substituted derivatives are not the only type of aromatic hydrocarbon that exists. Another large class of aromatic hydrocarbons is the fused-ring aromatic hydrocarbons. A **fused-ring aromatic hydrocarbon** *is an aromatic hydrocarbon whose structure contains two or more carbon rings fused together.* Two carbon rings that share a pair of carbon atoms are said to be *fused.*

The three simplest fused-ring aromatic compounds are naphthalene, anthracene, and phenanthrene. All three are solids at room temperature.

Naphthalene   Anthracene   Phenanthrene

A number of fused-ring aromatic hydrocarbons are known to be carcinogens—that is, to cause cancer. Three of the most potent carcinogens are

1,2-Benzanthracene   1,2,5,6-Dibenzanthracene   3,4-Benzpyrene

Very small amounts of these substances, when applied to the skin of mice, cause cancer.

Carcinogenic fused-ring aromatic hydrocarbons share some structural features. They all contain four or more fused rings, and they all have the same "angle" in the series of rings (the dark area in the structures shown).

CHEMISTRY AT A GLANCE Types of Unsaturated Hydrocarbons

Fused-ring aromatic hydrocarbons are often formed when hydrocarbon materials are heated to high temperatures. These resultant compounds are present in low concentrations in tobacco smoke, in automobile exhaust, and sometimes in burned (charred) food. The charred portions of a well-done steak cooked over charcoal are a likely source.

Angular, fused-ring hydrocarbon systems are believed to be partially responsible for the high incidence of lung and lip cancer among cigarette smokers because tobacco smoke contains 3,4-benzpyrene. The more a person smokes, the greater his or her risk of developing cancer.

It is now known that the high incidence of lung cancer in British chimney sweeps (documented over 200 years ago) was caused by fused-ring hydrocarbon compounds present in the chimney soot that the sweeps inhaled regularly.

Chemistry at a Glance—Types of Unsaturated Hydrocarbons—contrasts the three major types of unsaturated hydrocarbons—alkenes, alkynes, and aromatics—in terms of functional group present, suffix used in IUPAC nomenclature to denote the functional group, and the major type of chemical reaction the functional group undergoes.

Section 13-16 Quick Quiz

1. A fused-ring aromatic hydrocarbon always contains
   a. two or more carbon rings
   b. three or more carbon rings
   c. an even number of carbon rings
   d. no correct response
2. The number of carbon atoms in a structure involving two fused six-membered rings is
   a. 10
   b. 12
   c. 14
   d. no correct response

Answers: 1. a; 2. a

Concepts to Remember

Unsaturated hydrocarbons. An unsaturated hydrocarbon is a hydrocarbon that contains one or more carbon–carbon multiple bonds. Three main classes of unsaturated hydrocarbons exist: alkenes, alkynes, and aromatic hydrocarbons (Section 13-1).

Alkenes and cycloalkenes. An alkene is an acyclic unsaturated hydrocarbon in which one or more carbon–carbon double bonds are present. A cycloalkene is a cyclic unsaturated hydrocarbon that contains one or more carbon–carbon double bonds within the ring system (Section 13-2).

Alkene nomenclature. Alkenes and cycloalkenes are given IUPAC names using rules similar to those for alkanes and cycloalkanes, except that the ending -*ene* is used. Also, the double bond takes precedence both in selecting and in numbering the main chain or ring (Section 13-3).

Isomerism in alkenes. Two subtypes of constitutional isomers are possible for alkenes: skeletal isomers and positional isomers. Positional isomers differ in the location of the functional group (double bond) present (Section 13-5).

***Cis–trans* isomerism in alkenes.** *Cis–trans* isomerism is possible for some alkenes because there is restricted rotation about a carbon–carbon double bond (Section 13-6).

Physical properties of alkenes. Alkenes and alkanes have similar physical properties. They are nonpolar, insoluble in water, less dense than water, and soluble in nonpolar solvents (Section 13-8).

Addition reactions of alkenes. Numerous substances, including H_2, Cl_2, Br_2, HCl, HBr, and H_2O, add to an alkene carbon–carbon double bond. When both the alkene and the substance to be added

are unsymmetrical, the addition proceeds according to Markovnikov's rule: The carbon atom of the double bond that already has the greater number of H atoms gets one more (Section 13-10).

Addition polymers. Addition polymers are formed from alkene monomers that undergo repeated addition reactions with each other. Many familiar and widely used materials, such as fibers and plastics, are addition polymers (Section 13-11).

Alkynes and cycloalkynes. Alkynes and cycloalkynes are unsaturated hydrocarbons that contain one or more carbon–carbon triple bonds. They are named in the same way as alkenes and cycloalkenes, except that their parent names end in -*yne*. Like alkenes, alkynes undergo addition reactions. These occur in two steps, an alkene forming first and then an alkane (Section 13-12).

Aromatic hydrocarbons. Benzene, the simplest aromatic hydrocarbon, and other members of this family of compounds contain a six-membered ring with a cyclic, delocalized bond. This aromatic ring is often drawn as a hexagon containing a circle, which represents six electrons that move freely around the ring (Section 13-13).

Nomenclature of aromatic hydrocarbons. Monosubstituted benzene compounds are named by adding the substituent name to the word *benzene*. Positions of substituents in disubstituted benzenes are indicated by using a numbering system or the *ortho-* (1,2), *meta-* (1,3), and *para-* (1,4) prefix system (Section 13-14).

Chemical reactions of aromatic hydrocarbons. Aromatic hydrocarbons undergo substitution reactions rather than addition reactions. Important substitution reactions are alkylation and halogenation (Section 13-15).

Exercises and problems are arranged in matched pairs with the two members of a pair addressing the same concept(s). The answer to the odd-numbered member of a pair is given at the back of the book. Problems denoted with a ▲ involve concepts found not only in the section under consideration but also concepts found in one or more earlier sections of the chapter.

Unsaturated Hydrocarbons (Section 13-1)

13-1 Classify each of the following hydrocarbons as saturated or unsaturated.
a. $CH_3-CH_2-CH_3$
b. $CH_3-CH=CH_2$
c. $CH_3-C\equiv CH$
d. $CH_3-CH=CH-CH_3$

13-2 Classify each of the following hydrocarbons as saturated or unsaturated.
a. $CH_3-CH_2-CH=CH_2$
b. CH_3-CH_3
c. $CH_2=CH_2$
d. $CH\equiv C-CH_2-CH_3$

13-3 Classify each of the hydrocarbons in Problem 13-1 as an alkane, alkene, or alkyne.

13-4 Classify each of the hydrocarbons in Problem 13-2 as an alkane, alkene, or alkyne.

13-5 What is the functional group that is present in all alkenes?

13-6 What is the functional group that is present in all alkynes?

13-7 Characterize the physical properties of saturated and unsaturated hydrocarbons as being similar or dissimilar.

13-8 Characterize the chemical properties of saturated and unsaturated hydrocarbons as being similar or dissimilar.

Characteristics of Alkenes and Cycloalkenes (Section 13-2)

13-9 What is the molecular formula for each of the following hydrocarbons?
a. 4-carbon alkene with one double bond
b. 4-carbon alkene with two double bonds
c. 4-carbon cycloalkene with one double bond
d. 4-carbon cycloalkene with two double bonds

13-10 What is the molecular formula for each of the following hydrocarbons?
a. 5-carbon alkene with one double bond
b. 5-carbon alkene with two double bonds
c. 5-carbon cycloalkene with one double bond
d. 5-carbon cycloalkene with two double bonds

13-11 Indicate whether each of the following molecular formulas for noncyclic hydrocarbons is that for an alkene with one double bond, a diene, or a triene.
a. C_6H_{12}
b. C_5H_{10}
c. C_6H_{10}
d. C_5H_8

13-12 Indicate whether each of the following molecular formulas for hydrocarbons is that for an alkene with one double bond or a cycloalkene with one double bond?
a. C_4H_8
b. C_5H_8
c. C_6H_{10}
d. C_5H_{10}

13-13 What is wrong, if anything, with the following condensed structural formulas for alkenes?
a. $CH_3-CH=CH-CH_3$
b. $CH_2=CH-CH_2=CH_3$

13-14 What is wrong, if anything, with the following condensed structural formulas for alkenes?
a. $CH_2=CH_2=CH_2$
b. $CH_3-CH_2-CH_2-CH=CH$

13-15 What is the name of the spatial arrangement for bonds about a carbon atom that participates in one carbon–carbon double bond?

13-16 What are the bond angles associated with the spatial arrangement for bonds about a carbon atom that participates in one carbon–carbon double bond?

Nomenclature for Alkenes and Cycloalkenes (Section 13-3)

13-17 Assign an IUPAC name to each of the following unsaturated hydrocarbons.
a. $CH_3-CH=CH-CH_3$
b. $CH_3-\underset{\underset{CH_3}{|}}{C}=CH-\underset{\underset{CH_3}{|}}{CH}-CH_3$
c.
d.

13-18 Assign an IUPAC name to each of the following unsaturated hydrocarbons.
a. $CH_3-CH_2-CH=CH-CH_3$
b. $CH_3-CH_2-\underset{\underset{CH_3}{|}}{C}=CH-CH_3$
c.
d.

13-19 Draw a condensed structural formula for each of the following unsaturated hydrocarbons.
a. 3-Methyl-1-pentene
b. 3-Methylcyclopentene
c. 1,3-Butadiene
d. 3-Ethyl-1,4-pentadiene

13-20 Draw a condensed structural formula for each of the following unsaturated hydrocarbons.
    a. 4-Methyl-1-hexene
    b. 4-Methylcyclohexene
    c. 1,3-Pentadiene
    d. 2-Ethyl-1,4-pentadiene

13-21 The following names are *incorrect* by IUPAC rules. Determine the correct IUPAC name for each compound.
    a. 2-Ethyl-2-pentene
    b. 4,5-Dimethyl-4-hexene
    c. 3,5-Cyclopentadiene
    d. 1,2-Dimethyl-4-cyclohexene

13-22 The following names are *incorrect* by IUPAC rules. Determine the correct IUPAC name for each compound.
    a. 2-Methyl-4-pentene
    b. 3-Methyl-2,4-pentadiene
    c. 3-Methyl-3-cyclopentene
    d. 1,2-Dimethyl-3-cyclohexene

13-23 Draw a condensed structural formula for each of the following unsaturated hydrocarbons.
    a. Ethylene
    b. Methylenecyclobutane
    c. Vinyl bromide
    d. Allyl iodide

13-24 Draw a condensed structural formula for each of the following unsaturated hydrocarbons.
    a. Propylene
    b. Methylenecyclopentane
    c. Vinyl iodide
    d. Allyl chloride

▲**13-25** Classify each of the following compounds as *saturated* or *unsaturated*.
    a. Ethylcyclopentane
    b. Ethylcyclopentene
    c. 1,3-butadiene
    d. 2-methyl-2-pentene

▲**13-26** Classify each of the following compounds as *saturated* or *unsaturated*.
    a. 2-methylcyclopentene
    b. 1,3-cyclopentadiene
    c. 2,3-dimethylpentane
    d. 1-ethyl-2-methylcyclohexene

▲**13-27** How many hydrogen atoms are present in a molecule of each of the compounds in Problem 13-25?

▲**13-28** How many hydrogen atoms are present in a molecule of each of the compounds in Problem 13-26?

Line-Angle Structural Formulas for Alkenes (Section 13-4)

13-29 Draw a line-angle structural formula for each of the following unsaturated hydrocarbons.
    a. 1-Butene
    b. 2-Butene
    c. 1,3-Butadiene
    d. 3-Methyl-1-butene

13-30 Draw a line-angle structural formula for each of the following unsaturated hydrocarbons.
    a. 1-Pentene
    b. 2-Pentene
    c. 1,4-Pentadiene
    d. 4-Methyl-2-pentene

13-31 How many carbon atoms are present in each of the following unsaturated hydrocarbons?

13-32 How many carbon atoms are present in each of the following unsaturated hydrocarbons?

▲**13-33** What is the molecular formula for each of the compounds in Problem 13-31?

▲**13-34** What is the molecular formula for each of the compounds in Problem 13-32?

▲**13-35** What is the IUPAC name for each of the compounds in Problem 13-31?

▲**13-36** What is the IUPAC name for each of the compounds in Problem 13-32?

▲**13-37** What is the spatial arrangement for the chemical bonds that the left-most carbon atom in each of the structures in Problem 13-31 participates in?

▲**13-38** What is the spatial arrangement for the chemical bonds that the left-most carbon atom in each of the structures in Problem 13-32 participates in?

Constitutional Isomerism in Alkenes (Section 13-5)

13-39 For each of the following pairs of alkenes, indicate whether the members of each pair are *positional* constitutional isomers or *skeletal* constitutional isomers.
    a. 1-Hexene and 2-hexene
    b. 2-Methyl-1-pentene and 3-methyl-1-pentene
    c. 3-Hexene and 2-ethyl-1-butene
    d. 3-Methyl-2-pentene and 3-methyl-1-pentene

13-40 For each of the following pairs of alkenes, indicate whether the members of each pair are *positional* constitutional isomers or *skeletal* constitutional isomers.
    a. 2-Hexene and 3-hexene
    b. 4-Methyl-1-pentene and 4-methyl-2-pentene
    c. 2,3-Dimethyl-2-butene and 3,3-dimethyl-1-butene
    d. 2-Methyl-2-pentene and 2-methyl-1-pentene

13-41 How many constitutional isomers exist that fit each of the following specifications?
    a. Unbranched chain of five carbon atoms, one carbon–carbon double bond
    b. Unbranched chain of five carbon atoms, two carbon–carbon double bonds

c. Five carbon atoms, one methyl group, one carbon–carbon double bond

d. Five carbon atoms, two methyl groups, one carbon–carbon double bond

13-42 How many constitutional isomers exist that fit each of the following specifications?

a. Unbranched chain of six carbon atoms, one carbon–carbon double bond

b. Unbranched chain of six carbon atoms, two carbon–carbon double bonds

c. Six carbon atoms, one methyl group, one carbon–carbon double bond

d. Six carbon atoms, two methyl groups, one carbon–carbon double bond

13-43 Draw skeletal structural formulas and give the IUPAC names for the 13 possible alkene constitutional isomers with the formula C_6H_{12}. (Three of the constitutional isomers are hexenes, six are methylpentenes, three are dimethylbutenes, and one is an ethylbutene.)

13-44 Draw skeletal structural formulas and give the IUPAC names for the 16 possible alkadiene constitutional isomers with the formula C_6H_{10}. (Six of the constitutional isomers are hexadienes, eight are methylpentadienes, one is a dimethylbutadiene, and one is an ethylbutadiene.)

▲**13-45** Hydrocarbons with the formula C_4H_8 can be either alkenes or cycloalkanes. Draw skeletal structural formulas for the five possible constitutional isomers that fit this formula; three are alkenes and two are cycloalkanes.

▲**13-46** Hydrocarbons with the formula C_5H_{10} can be either alkenes or cycloalkanes. Draw skeletal structural formulas for the ten possible constitutional isomers that fit this formula; five are alkenes and five are cycloalkanes.

Cis–Trans Isomerism in Alkenes (Section 13-6)

13-47 For each molecule, indicate whether *cis–trans* isomers exist. If they do, draw the two isomers and label them as *cis* and *trans*.

a. $CH_2{=}CH{-}CH_3$ b. $CH_3{-}\underset{\underset{\textstyle CH_3}{|}}{C}{=}CH{-}CH_3$

c. 3-Hexene   d. 4-Methyl-2-pentene

13-48 For each molecule, indicate whether *cis–trans* isomers exist. If they do, draw the two isomers and label them as *cis* and *trans*.

a. $CH_3{-}CH_2{-}CH{=}CH_2$ b. $CH_3{-}CH_2{-}CH{=}\underset{\underset{\textstyle Cl}{|}}{CH}$

c. 2-Pentene   d. 1,2-Dichloroethene

13-49 Assign an IUPAC name to each of the following molecules. Include the prefix *cis-* or *trans-* when appropriate.

a.   b.

c.   d.

13-50 Assign an IUPAC name to each of the following molecules. Include the prefix *cis-* or *trans-* when appropriate.

a.   b.

c.   d.

13-51 Draw a structural formula for each of the following compounds.

a. *trans*-3-Methyl-3-hexene

b. *cis*-2-Pentene

c. *trans*-5-Methyl-2-heptene

d. *trans*-1,3-Pentadiene

13-52 Draw a structural formula for each of the following compounds.

a. *trans*-2-Hexene

b. *cis*-4-Methyl-2-pentene

c. *cis*-1-Chloro-1-pentene

d. *cis*-1,3-Pentadiene

▲**13-53** For each of the following molecules, indicate whether or not *cis–trans* isomerism is possible.

a. 2-Methyl-1-pentene

b. 1-Hexene

c. Methylcyclohexane

d. 1,2-Diethylcyclopentane

▲**13-54** For each of the following molecules, indicate whether or not *cis–trans* isomerism is possible.

a. 2-Pentene

b. 1-Chloro-2-pentene

c. Chlorocyclopentane

d. 1,2-Dichlorocyclopentane

Naturally Occurring Alkenes (Section 13-7)

13-55 What is a pheromone?

13-56 In alkene-type pheromones, biological activity is highly dependent on what structural feature associated with carbon–carbon double bonds?

13-57 What is the condensed structural formula for the molecule whose common name is isoprene?

13-58 What is the IUPAC name for the molecule whose common name is isoprene?

13-59 Why is the number of carbon atoms in a terpene always a multiple of the number 5?

13-60 How many isoprene units are present in

a. beta-carotene

b. vitamin A

Physical Properties of Alkenes and Cycloalkenes (Section 13-8)

13-61 Indicate whether each of the following statements about physical properties of 2-butene is true or false.

a. It is insoluble in water.

b. It is insoluble in nonpolar solvents.

c. It has a density less than that of water.

d. It has a melting point lower than that of butane.

13-62 Indicate whether each of the following statements about physical properties of propene is true or false.
   a. It is insoluble in water.
   b. It is insoluble in nonpolar solvents.
   c. It has a density less than that of water.
   d. It has a melting point lower than that of propane.

13-63 With the help of Figure 13-7, indicate whether each of the following alkenes would be expected to be a solid, liquid, or gas at room temperature and pressure.
   a. Ethane
   b. 1-Pentene
   c. Cyclobutane
   d. Cyclohexane

13-64 With the help of Figure 13-7, indicate whether each of the following alkenes would be expected to be a solid, liquid, or gas at room temperature and pressure.
   a. Propene
   b. 1-Hexene
   c. Cyclopentene
   d. Cycloheptene

Preparation of Alkenes (Section 13-9)

13-65 Describe what occurs during a *dehydrogenation* reaction.

13-66 What are the reaction conditions necessary to carry out an alkane dehydrogenation reaction?

13-67 What are the two products formed when ethane is subjected to dehydrogenation?

13-68 What are the two products formed when propane is subjected to dehydrogenation?

Chemical Reactions of Alkenes (Section 13-10)

13-69 Which of the following chemical reactions are addition reactions?
   a. $C_4H_8 + Cl_2 \rightarrow C_4H_8Cl_2$
   b. $C_6H_6 + Cl_2 \rightarrow C_6H_5Cl + HCl$
   c. $C_3H_6 + HCl \rightarrow C_3H_7Cl$
   d. $C_7H_{16} \rightarrow C_7H_8 + 4H_2$

13-70 Which of the following chemical reactions are addition reactions?
   a. $C_3H_6 + Cl_2 \rightarrow C_3H_6Cl_2$
   b. $C_8H_{10} \rightarrow C_8H_8 + H_2$
   c. $C_6H_6 + C_2H_5Cl \rightarrow C_8H_{10} + HCl$
   d. $C_4H_8 + HCl \rightarrow C_4H_9Cl$

13-71 Write a chemical equation showing reactants, products, and catalysts needed (if any) for the reaction of ethene with each of the following substances.
   a. Cl_2 b. HCl
   c. H_2 d. HBr

13-72 Write a chemical equation showing reactants, products, and catalysts needed (if any) for the reaction of ethene with each of the following substances.
   a. H_2O b. Br_2
   c. HI   d. I_2

13-73 Based on Markovnikov's rule, indicate whether hydration of each of the following alkenes produces one or two products.
   a. Propene
   b. 3-Hexene
   c. Cyclopropene
   d. Cyclopentene

13-74 Based on Markovnikov's rule, indicate whether hydration of each of the following alkenes produces one or two products.
   a. 2-Butene
   b. 2-Pentene
   c. Cyclobutene
   d. Cyclohexene

13-75 Write a chemical equation showing reactants, products, and catalysts needed (if any) for the reaction of propene with each of the reactants in Problem 13-71. Use Markovnikov's rule as needed.

13-76 Write a chemical equation showing reactants, products, and catalysts needed (if any) for the reaction of propene with each of the reactants in Problem 13-72. Use Markovnikov's rule as needed.

13-77 Supply the structural formula of the product in each of the following alkene addition reactions.
   a. $CH_3-CH=CH-CH_3 + Cl_2 \rightarrow$?
   b. $CH_3-CH_2-CH=CH_2 + HCl \rightarrow$?
   c.
   ⬠ $+ H_2 \xrightarrow[\text{catalyst}]{\text{Ni}}$?
   d.
   ☐ $+ H_2O \xrightarrow{H_2SO_4}$?

13-78 Supply the structural formula of the product in each of the following alkene addition reactions.
   a. $CH_3-CH_2-CH=CH_2 + Cl_2 \rightarrow$?
   b. $CH_3-CH-CH=CH_2 + HBr \rightarrow$?
           $|$
          CH_3
   c.
   ⬡ $+ H_2 \xrightarrow[\text{catalyst}]{\text{Ni}}$?
   d. $CH_3-CH=CH_2 + H_2O \xrightarrow{H_2SO_4}$?

13-79 What reactant would you use to prepare each of the following compounds from cyclohexene?
   a.   Br

   b.

   c.   Cl   d.   OH

13-80 What reactant would you use to prepare each of the following compounds from cyclopentene?

a.

b. OH

c. Cl, Cl

d. Br

13-81 How many molecules of H_2 gas will react with 1 molecule of each of the following unsaturated hydrocarbons?

a. $CH_3-CH=CH-CH=CH-CH_3$

b.

c. $CH=CH_2$

d. $CH_3-CH=C=C-CH=CH_2$
$\qquad\qquad\ \ \ |$
$\qquad\qquad\ \ CH_3$

13-82 How many molecules of H_2 gas will react with 1 molecule of each of the following unsaturated hydrocarbons?

a. $CH_3-CH=CH-CH_3$

b.

c. $CH=CH_2$

d. $CH_2=CH-C-CH=CH_2$
$\qquad\qquad\ \ \ ||$
$\qquad\qquad\ \ CH_2$

Polymerization of Alkenes: Addition Polymers (Section 13-11)

13-83 Draw the structural formula of the monomer(s) from which each of the following polymers was made.

a.

b.

c.

d.

13-84 Draw the structural formula of the monomer(s) from which each of the following polymers was made.

a.

b.

c.

d.

13-85 Draw the "start" (the first three repeating units) of the structural formula of the addition polymers made from the following monomers.
a. Ethylene
b. Vinyl chloride
c. 1,2-Dichloroethene
d. 1-Chloroethene

13-86 Draw the "start" (the first three repeating units) of the structural formula of the addition polymers made from the following monomers.
a. Propylene
b. 1,1,2,2-Tetrafluoroethene
c. 2-Methyl-1-propene
d. 1,2-Dichloroethylene

Alkynes (Section 13-12)

13-87 What is the general molecular formula for an alkyne in which two carbon–carbon triple bonds are present?

13-88 What is the general molecular formula for a cycloalkyne in which one carbon–carbon triple bond is present?

13-89 Assign an IUPAC name to each of the following unsaturated hydrocarbons.
a. $CH_3-CH_2-CH_2-CH_2-C\equiv CH$
b. $CH_3-C\equiv C-CH-CH_3$
$\qquad\qquad\qquad\ \ \ |$
$\qquad\qquad\qquad\ CH_3$
c. $\quad\quad\ CH_3$
$\qquad\qquad |$
$CH_3-C-C\equiv C-CH_2-CH_2-CH_3$
$\qquad\qquad |$
$\qquad\quad\ CH_3$
d.

13-90 Assign an IUPAC name to each of the following unsaturated hydrocarbons.

a. $CH_3-CH-C\equiv CH$
         |
         CH_3

b.

c. $CH_3-CH-C\equiv C-CH-CH_3$
         | |
         CH_3 CH_3

d. $CH_3-CH-CH_2-C$
         | ‖
         CH_2 CH
         |
         CH_3

13-91 Draw skeletal structural formulas and give the IUPAC names for the three possible alkyne isomers with the molecular formula C_5H_8.

13-92 Draw skeletal structural formulas and give the IUPAC names for the seven possible alkyne isomers with the molecular formula C_6H_{10}. (Three of the constitutional isomers are hexynes, three are pentynes, and one is a butyne.)

13-93 Why is *cis–trans* isomerism not possible for an alkyne?

13-94 What are the bond angles about the triple bond in an alkyne?

13-95 Contrast alkynes and alkenes in terms of general physical properties.

13-96 Contrast alkynes and alkenes in terms of general chemical properties.

13-97 Supply the condensed structural formula of the product in each of the following alkyne addition reactions.

a. $CH\equiv CH + 2H_2 \xrightarrow{Ni}$?

b. $CH_3-C\equiv CH + 2Br_2 \longrightarrow$?

c. $CH_3-C\equiv CH + 2HBr \longrightarrow$?

d. $CH\equiv CH + 1HCl \longrightarrow$?

13-98 Supply the condensed structural formula of the product in each of the following alkyne addition reactions.

a. $CH_3-C\equiv C-CH_3 + 2Br_2 \longrightarrow$?

b. $CH_3-C\equiv C-CH_3 + 2HBr \longrightarrow$?

c. $CH\equiv C-CH_2-CH_3 + 1H_2 \xrightarrow{Ni}$?

d. $CH\equiv C-CH_3 + 1HCl \longrightarrow$?

▲**13-99** Draw a condensed structural formula for each of the following hydrocarbons.

a. 5-Methyl-2-hexyne

b. 2-Methyl-2-butene

c. 1,6-Heptadiyne

d. 3-Penten-1-yne

▲**13-100** Draw a condensed structural formula for each of the following hydrocarbons.

a. 2-Butyne

b. 3,4-Dimethyl-2-pentene

c. 1,6-Heptadiene

d. 1-Buten-3-yne

▲**13-101** How many carbon atoms are present in a molecule of each of the following compounds?

a. Allyl chloride

b. Acetylene

c. Dimethylacetylene

d. 3-Cyclobutyl-1-hexyne

▲**13-102** How many carbon atoms are present in a molecule of each of the following compounds?

a. Vinyl bromide

b. Ethylene

c. Isopropylacetylene

d. 1-Cyclobutyl-3-hexene

Aromatic Hydrocarbons (Section 13-13)

13-103 Draw a structural representation for the functional group present in an aromatic hydrocarbon.

13-104 A circle (ring) within a hexagon is often used to represent an aromatic carbon ring. What does the circle represent?

13-105 What is the shortcoming of representing the bonding in a benzene ring using alternating single and double carbon–carbon bonds?

13-106 What is a *delocalized* bond?

Nomenclature for Aromatic Hydrocarbons (Section 13-14)

13-107 Assign an IUPAC name to each of the following disubstituted benzenes. Use numbers rather than prefixes to locate the substituents on the benzene ring.

a. Br / Br

b. F / Cl

c. Cl / F

d. CH_3 / Cl

13-108 Assign an IUPAC name to each of the following disubstituted benzenes. Use numbers rather than prefixes to locate the substituents on the benzene ring.

a. Br / F

b. $CH_2-CH_2-CH_3$ / CH_2-CH_3

c. CH_2-CH_3 / CH_2-CH_3

d. CH_3 / CH_3

13-109 Assign each of the compounds in Problem 13-107 an IUPAC name in which the substituents on the benzene ring are located using the *ortho-*, *meta-*, *para-* prefix system.

13-110 Assign each of the compounds in Problem 13-108 an IUPAC name in which the substituents on the benzene ring are located using the *ortho-*, *meta-*, *para-* prefix system.

13-111 Assign an IUPAC name to each of the following substituted benzenes.

a.

b.

c.

d.

13-112 Assign an IUPAC name to each of the following substituted benzenes.

a.

b. CH$_3$

c.

CH$_2$—CH$_2$—CH$_3$

d. Cl

13-113 Assign an IUPAC name to each of the following compounds in which the benzene ring is treated as a substituent.

a. CH$_3$—CH—CH$_2$—CH$_3$

b. CH$_3$—CH—CH=CH$_2$

c. CH$_3$—CH—CH$_2$—CH$_2$
           |
           CH$_3$

d. CH$_3$—CH—CH$_2$—CH—CH$_3$

13-114 Assign an IUPAC name to each of the following compounds in which the benzene ring is treated as a substituent.

a. CH$_3$—CH$_2$—CH—CH$_2$—CH$_3$

b. CH$_2$—CH$_2$—CH—CH$_3$

c. CH$_3$—CH—C≡CH

d. CH$_3$—CH—CH$_2$—CH—CH$_3$
           |
           CH$_3$

13-115 Write a structural formula for each of the following compounds.
  a. 1,3-Diethylbenzene   b. *o*-Xylene
  c. *p*-Ethyltoluene   d. Phenylbenzene

13-116 Write a structural formula for each of the following compounds.
  a. *o*-Ethylpropylbenzene   b. *m*-Xylene
  c. 2-Bromotoluene   d. 2-Phenylpropane

13-117 Eight isomeric substituted benzenes have the formula C$_9$H$_{12}$. What are the IUPAC names for these constitutional isomers?

13-118 How many constitutional isomers fit each of the following descriptions?
  a. bromochlorobenzenes
  b. trichlorobenzenes
  c. dibromodichlorobenzenes
  d. bromoanthracenes

▲**13-119** Which of the four compounds *cyclohexane, cyclohexene, 1,3-cyclohexadiene,* and *benzene* has each of the following characteristics? More than one compound may be correct in a given situation.
  a. contains a 6-membered carbon ring
  b. has the generalized formula C$_n$H$_{2n-2}$
  c. undergoes substitution reactions
  d. has delocalized bonding

▲**13-120** Which of the four compounds *cyclohexane, cyclohexene, 1,3-cyclohexadiene,* and *benzene* has each of the following characteristics? More than one compound may be correct in a given situation.
  a. contains the same number of carbon and hydrogen atoms
  b. has the generalized formula C$_n$H$_{2n-4}$
  c. undergoes addition reactions
  d. is an unsaturated hydrocarbon

Properties of and Sources for Aromatic Hydrocarbons (Section 13-15)

13-121 What is the physical state at room temperature for benzene, monosubstituted benzenes, and many disubstituted benzenes?

13-122 Indicate whether or not each of the following is a general physical property of aromatic hydrocarbons.
a. soluble in water
b. less dense than water
c. good solvent for nonpolar substances
d. all solids at room temperatures

13-123 What is currently the primary source for aromatic hydrocarbons?

13-124 What used to be the primary source for aromatic hydrocarbons?

13-125 For each of the following classes of compounds, indicate whether addition or substitution is the most characteristic reaction.
a. alkanes
b. dienes
c. alkylbenzenes
d. cycloalkenes

13-126 For each of the following classes of compounds, indicate whether addition or substitution is the most characteristic reaction.
a. alkynes
b. cycloalkanes
c. aromatic hydrocarbons
d. saturated hydrocarbons

13-127 Complete the following reaction equations by supplying the formula of the missing reactant or product.

a. benzene $+$? $\xrightarrow{\text{FeBr}_3}$ bromobenzene $+$ HBr

b. benzene $+$ $CH_3-CH-Cl$ (with CH_3 branch) $\xrightarrow{\text{AlCl}_3}$? $+$ HCl

c. benzene $+$? $\xrightarrow{\text{AlBr}_3}$ ethylbenzene (CH_2-CH_3) $+$ HBr

13-128 Complete the following reaction equations by supplying the formula of the missing reactant, product, or catalyst.

a. benzene $+$ Cl_2 $\xrightarrow{\text{FeCl}_3}$ chlorobenzene $+$?

b. benzene $+$? $\xrightarrow{\text{AlBr}_3}$ toluene (CH_3) $+$ HBr

c. benzene $+$ $CH_3-\underset{\underset{CH_3}{|}}{\overset{\overset{CH_3}{|}}{C}}-Br$ $\xrightarrow{\text{AlBr}_3}$? $+$ HBr

Fused-Ring Aromatic Hydrocarbons (Section 13-16)

13-129 What is the general characteristic associated with two carbon rings that are *fused* together?

13-130 What is the structural formula for naphthalene, the simplest fused-ring aromatic hydrocarbon?

Alcohols, Phenols, and Ethers

14

© Chamille White/Shutterstock.com

Two alcohols, 1-octanol and 3-octanol, contribute to the distinctive flavor of mushrooms.

This chapter is the first of three that consider hydrocarbon derivatives with *oxygen-containing functional groups*. Many biochemically important molecules contain carbon atoms bonded to oxygen atoms.

In this chapter, hydrocarbon derivatives whose functional groups contain one oxygen atom participating in two single bonds (alcohols, phenols, and ethers) are considered. Chapter 15 focuses on derivatives whose functional groups have one oxygen atom participating in a double bond (aldehydes and ketones), and Chapter 16 examines functional groups that contain two oxygen atoms, one participating in single bonds and the other in a double bond (carboxylic acids, esters, and other acid derivatives) are examined.

14-1 Bonding Characteristics of Oxygen Atoms in Organic Compounds

LEARNING FOCUS

Describe the normal bonding pattern for oxygen atoms in oxygen-containing organic compounds.

An understanding of the bonding characteristics of the oxygen atom is a prerequisite for the study of organic compounds with oxygen-containing functional groups. Normal bonding behavior for oxygen atoms in such functional groups is the formation of two covalent bonds. Oxygen is a member of Group VIA of the periodic table and thus possesses six valence electrons. To complete its octet by electron sharing, an oxygen atom can form either two single bonds or a double bond.

$$: \overset{|}{\underset{..}{O}} — \qquad : O =$$

Two single bonds   One double bond

Thus, in organic chemistry, carbon forms four bonds, hydrogen forms one bond, and oxygen forms two bonds.

$$—\overset{|}{\underset{|}{C}}— \qquad H— \qquad : \overset{|}{\underset{..}{O}} —$$

4 valence electrons,   1 valence electron,   6 valence electrons,
4 covalent bonds,   1 covalent bond,   2 covalent bonds,
no nonbonding   no nonbonding   2 nonbonding
electron pairs   electron pairs   electron pairs

Section 14-1 Quick Quiz

1. Which of the following is *not* a correct bonding pattern for oxygen atoms in organic compounds?
   a. formation of one double bond
   b. formation of one single bond
   c. formation of two single bonds
   d. no correct response
2. In organic compounds the number of bonds formed, respectively by carbon, hydrogen, and oxygen atoms is
   a. 4, 1, and 1
   b. 4, 2, and 2
   c. 4, 1, and 2
   d. no correct response

Answers: 1. b; 2. c

14-2 Structural Characteristics of Alcohols

LEARNING FOCUS
Know the generalized formula for and the functional group present in alcohols.

Alcohols are the first type of hydrocarbon derivative containing a single oxygen atom to be considered. They have the generalized formula

R—OH

An **alcohol** *is an organic compound in which an* —*OH group is bonded to a saturated carbon atom.* A *saturated* carbon atom is a carbon atom that is bonded to four other atoms.

$$\text{Saturated} \atop \text{carbon atom} \quad —\overset{|}{\underset{|}{C}}—\text{OH} \quad {\text{Alcohol} \atop \text{functional group}}$$

▶ *The hydroxyl group (*—*OH) should not be confused with the* hydroxide ion *(*OH⁻*) that was repeatedly encountered in the general chemistry chapters of this text. Alcohols are not* hydroxides. *Hydroxides are ionic compounds that contain the* OH⁻ *polyatomic ion (Section 4-10). Alcohols are not ionic compounds. In an alcohol, the* —*OH group, which is not an ion, is* covalently *bonded to a saturated carbon atom.*

The —OH group, the functional group that is characteristic of an alcohol, is called a *hydroxyl group.* ◀ A **hydroxyl group** *is the* —*OH functional group.*

Examples of condensed structural formulas for alcohols include

$$CH_3—OH \qquad CH_3—CH_2—OH \qquad CH_3—CH_2—CH_2—OH$$

Space-filling models for these three alcohols, the simplest alcohols possible that have unbranched carbon chains, are given in Figure 14-1.

Figure 14-1 Space-filling models for the three simplest unbranched-chain alcohols.

CH₃— OH
One-carbon alcohol

CH₃— CH₂— OH
Two-carbon alcohol

CH₃— CH₂— CH₂— OH
Three-carbon alcohol

Figure 14-1 Space-filling models for the three simplest unbranched-chain alcohols.

Alcohols may be viewed structurally as being alkyl derivatives of water in which a hydrogen atom has been replaced by an alkyl group.

$$H—\overset{..}{\underset{..}{O}}—H \qquad R—\overset{..}{\underset{..}{O}}—H$$
Water An alcohol

Figure 14-2 shows the similarity in oxygen bond angles for water and CH_3—OH, the simplest alcohol.

Alcohols may also be viewed structurally as hydroxyl derivatives of alkanes in which a hydrogen atom has been replaced by a hydroxyl group.

$$R—H \qquad R—OH$$
An alkane An alcohol

Alcohols in which the hydroxyl group is attached to a ring of carbon atoms (a cycloalkyl group) rather than a chain of carbon atoms (an alkyl group) also exist. Two such compounds are

~105°

Water (H–OH)

~109°

One-carbon alcohol (CH₃–OH)

Figure 14-2 A comparison of the molecular shapes of water and the one-carbon alcohol (the simplest alcohol). This simplest alcohol may be viewed structurally as an alkyl derivative of water.

Section 14-2 Quick Quiz

1. The alcohol functional group, —OH, is called the
   a. hydroxide group
   b. hydroxyl group
   c. hydroxide ion
   d. no correct response
2. The simplest alcohol possible contains how many hydrogen and oxygen atoms, respectively?
   a. 1 and 1
   b. 2 and 1
   c. 4 and 1
   d. no correct response
3. Which of the following statements concerning alcohols in *incorrect*?
   a. They may be viewed as alkyl or cycloalkyl derivatives of water.
   b. They may be viewed as hydroxyl derivatives of alkanes or cycloalkanes.
   c. The functional group is always attached to a *saturated* carbon atom.
   d. no correct response

Answers: 1. b; 2. c; 3. d

14-3 Nomenclature for Alcohols

LEARNING FOCUS

Given their structural formulas, be able to name alcohols using IUPAC rules or vice versa; know common names for alcohols with simple alkyl or cycloalkyl groups.

Common names exist for alcohols with simple (generally C_1 through C_4) alkyl groups. A common name is assigned using the following rules:

Rule 1: *Name all of the carbon atoms of the molecule as a single alkyl group.*

▶ *Line-angle structural formulas for selected simple alcohols:*

Propyl alcohol
(1-propanol)

Butyl alcohol
(1-butanol)

Isopropyl alcohol
(2-propanol)

Isobutyl alcohol
(2-methyl-1-propanol)

▶ *In the naming of alcohols with unsaturated carbon chains, two endings are needed: one for the double or triple bond and one for the hydroxyl group. The -ol suffix always comes last in the name; that is, unsaturated alcohols are named as* alkenols *or* alkynols.

$$\overset{3}{CH_2}=\overset{2}{CH}-\overset{1}{CH_2}-OH$$

2-Propen-1-ol
(common name: allyl alcohol)

▶ *The contrast between IUPAC and common names for alcohols is as follows:*

IUPAC (one word)

ethanol

Common (two words)

ethyl alcohol

Rule 2: *Add the word* alcohol, *separating the words with a space.*

$$CH_3-\boxed{OH} \qquad CH_3-CH_2-\boxed{OH} \qquad CH_3-CH_2-CH_2-\boxed{OH}$$
Methyl alcohol   Ethyl alcohol   Propyl alcohol

$$CH_3-CH-\boxed{OH}$$
$$\qquad | $$
$$\qquad CH_3$$
Isopropyl alcohol   Cyclobutyl alcohol

IUPAC rules for naming alcohols that contain a single hydroxyl group are:

Rule 1: *Name the longest carbon chain to which the hydroxyl group is attached. The chain name is obtained by dropping the final -e from the alkane name and adding the suffix -ol.*

Rule 2: *Number the chain starting at the end nearest the hydroxyl group, and use the appropriate number to indicate the position of the —OH group. (In numbering of the longest carbon chain, the hydroxyl group has precedence over ("outranks") double and triple bonds, as well as over alkyl, cycloalkyl, and halogen substituents.)* ◀

Rule 3: *Name and locate any other substituents present.*

Rule 4: *In alcohols where the —OH group is attached to a carbon atom in a ring, the ring is numbered beginning with the —OH group.* Numbering then proceeds in a clockwise or counterclockwise direction to give the next substituent the lower number. The number "1" (for the hydroxyl group) is omitted from the name since by definition the hydroxyl-bearing carbon is carbon 1.

Rule 5: *A hydroxyl group as a substituent in a molecule is called a* hydroxy group; *an -oxy rather than an -oxyl ending is used.*

Table 14-1 gives both IUPAC and common names for monohydroxy alcohols that contain four or fewer carbon atoms. ◀

▶ **Table 14-1 IUPAC and Common Names of Monohydroxy Alcohols That Contain up to Four Carbon Atoms** ◀

Formula	IUPAC Name	Common Name
One carbon atom (CH_3OH)		
CH_3-OH	methanol	methyl alcohol
Two carbon atoms (C_2H_5OH)		
CH_3-CH_2-OH	ethanol	ethyl alcohol
Three carbon atoms (C_3H_7OH); two constitutional isomers exist		
$CH_3-CH_2-CH_2-OH$	1-propanol	propyl alcohol
$CH_3-CH-OH$ $\quad\ \ \|$ $\quad\ \ CH_3$	2-propanol	isopropyl alcohol
Four carbon atoms (C_4H_9OH); four constitutional isomers exist		
$CH_3-CH_2-CH_2-CH_2-OH$	1-butanol	butyl alcohol
$CH_3-CH-CH_2-OH$ $\quad\ \ \|$ $\quad\ \ CH_3$	2-methyl-1-propanol	isobutyl alcohol
$CH_3-CH_2-CH-OH$ $\qquad\quad \|$ $\qquad\quad CH_3$	2-butanol	*sec*-butyl alcohol
$\quad\ \ CH_3$ $\quad\ \ \|$ CH_3-C-OH $\quad\ \ \|$ $\quad\ \ CH_3$	2-methyl-2-propanol	*tert*-butyl alcohol

EXAMPLE 14-1

Determining IUPAC Names for Alcohols

Name the following alcohols, utilizing IUPAC nomenclature rules.

a.
$$CH_3-CH_2-\underset{\underset{OH}{|}}{\overset{\overset{CH_3}{|}}{C}}-CH_2-CH_2-CH_3$$

b.
$$CH_3-CH_2-\underset{\underset{CH_2-OH}{|}}{CH}-CH_2-CH_3$$

c.

d.

Solution

a. The longest carbon chain that contains the alcohol functional group has six carbons. Changing the -*e* to -*ol*, hexane becomes *hexanol*. Numbering the chain from the end nearest the —OH group identifies carbon number 3 as the location of both the —OH group and a methyl group. The complete name is 3-methyl-3-hexanol.

$$\overset{1}{CH_3}-\overset{2}{CH_2}-\overset{3}{\underset{\underset{OH}{|}}{\overset{\overset{CH_3}{|}}{C}}}-\overset{4}{CH_2}-\overset{5}{CH_2}-\overset{6}{CH_3}$$

b. The longest carbon chain containing the —OH group has four carbon atoms. It is numbered from the end closest to the —OH group as follows:

$$CH_3-CH_2-\overset{2}{\underset{\underset{1\;CH_2-OH}{|}}{CH}}-\overset{3}{CH_2}-\overset{4}{CH_3}$$

The base name is 1-butanol. The complete name is 2-ethyl-1-butanol.

c. This alcohol is a cyclohexanol. The carbon to which the —OH group is attached is assigned the number 1. The complete name for this alcohol is 3,4-dimethylcyclohexanol. Note that the number 1 is not part of the name.

d. This alcohol is a dimethylheptanol. Numbering from right to left, the location of the hydroxyl group is 1, and locants for the methyl groups are 3 and 4. The complete IUPAC name is 3,4-dimethyl-1-heptanol.

Alcohols with More than One Hydroxyl Group

Polyhydroxy alcohols—alcohols that possess more than one hydroxyl group—can be named with only a slight modification of the preceding IUPAC rules. An alcohol in which two hydroxyl groups are present is named as a *diol*, one containing three hydroxyl groups is named as a *triol,* and so on. In these names for diols, triols, and so forth, the final -*e* of the parent alkane name is retained for pronunciation reasons.

$$CH_2 - CH_2$$
$$| \quad \quad |$$
$$OH \quad OH$$
1,2-Ethanediol

$$CH_3 - CH - CH_2$$
$$| \quad \quad |$$
$$OH \quad OH$$
1,2-Propanediol

$$CH_2 - CH - CH_2$$
$$| \quad \quad | \quad \quad |$$
$$OH \quad OH \quad OH$$
1,2,3-Propanetriol

The first two of the preceding compounds have the common names *ethylene glycol* and *propylene glycol*. These two alcohols are synthesized, respectively, from the alkenes ethylene and propylene (Section 13-3); hence the common names.

Section 14-3 Quick Quiz

1. What is the correct IUPAC name for the compound $CH_3 - CH_2 - CH - CH_3$?
   $\quad \quad \quad \quad \quad \quad \quad \quad \quad \quad \quad | $
   $\quad \quad \quad \quad \quad \quad \quad \quad \quad \quad OH$
   a. butanol
   b. 2-butanol
   c. 3-butanol
   d. no correct response
2. What is the correct common name for the compound [cyclobutane with OH] ?
   a. cyclobutyl alcohol
   b. hydroxy cyclobutane
   c. cyclobutanol
   d. no correct response
3. What is the correct IUPAC name for the compound $CH_3 - CH - CH_2 - CH_2 - CH_2$?
   $\quad \quad \quad \quad \quad \quad \quad \quad \quad \quad \quad \quad | \quad \quad \quad \quad \quad \quad \quad \quad \quad \quad |$
   $\quad \quad \quad \quad \quad \quad \quad \quad \quad \quad \quad \quad OH \quad \quad \quad \quad \quad \quad \quad \quad OH$
   a. pentyl dialcohol
   b. 1,4-dihydroxypentane
   c. 1,4-pentanediol
   d. no correct response
4. What is the correct IUPAC name for the compound [cyclohexane with OH and CH₃] ?
   a. 1-hydroxy-2-methylcyclohexane
   b. 1-methylcyclohexanol
   c. 2-methylcyclohexanol
   d. no correct response

Answers: 1. b; 2. a; 3. c; 4. c

14-4 Isomerism for Alcohols

LEARNING FOCUS
Be able to recognize and draw structural formulas for alcohol constitutional isomers.

Constitutional isomerism is possible for alcohols containing three or more carbon atoms. As with alkenes (Section 13-5), both *skeletal* isomers and *positional* isomers are possible. ◀ For monohydroxy saturated alcohols, there are two C_3 isomers, four C_4 isomers, and eight C_5 isomers. Structures for the C_3 and C_4 isomers are found in Table 14-1. The C_5 isomers are

▶ *Addition of a functional group greatly increases constitutional isomer possibilities. There are 75 alkane isomers with the formula $C_{10}H_{22}$ and 507 alcohol isomers with the formula $C_{10}H_{21}OH$.*

The three pentanols are positional isomers as are the four methylbutanols.

1. Which of following is a constitutional isomer of 2-pentanol?
   a. 2-hexanol
   b. 3-pentanol
   c. 2-methyl-2-pentanol
   d. no correct response
2. How many different methylpropanol molecules exist?
   a. 2
   b. 3
   c. 4
   d. no correct response
3. The number of constitutional isomers possible for C_3 and C_4 saturated alcohols, where no ring structure is present, is, respectively
   a. 2 and 2
   b. 2 and 3
   c. 2 and 4
   d. no correct response

Answers: 1. b; 2. a; 3. c

14-5 Important Commonly Encountered Alcohols

LEARNING FOCUS

Be familiar with the structures, properties, and uses of commonly encountered C_1, C_2, and C_3 alcohols.

In this section, the properties and uses of six commonly encountered alcohols are considered: methyl, ethyl, and isopropyl alcohols (all monohydroxy alcohols), ethylene glycol and propylene glycol (both diols), and glycerol (a triol).

Methyl Alcohol (Methanol)

Methyl alcohol, with one carbon atom and one —OH group, is the simplest alcohol. It is a colorless liquid that has excellent solvent properties, and it is the solvent of choice for many shellacs and varnishes.

Specially designed internal combustion engines can operate using methyl alcohol as a fuel. For 40 years, from 1965 to 2005, race cars at the Indianapolis Speedway were fueled with methyl alcohol (Figure 14-3). A major reason for the switch from gasoline to methyl alcohol relates to fires accompanying crashes. Methyl alcohol fires are easier to put out than gasoline fires because water mixes with and dilutes methyl alcohol. In 2006, a transition from methyl alcohol fuel use to ethyl alcohol race car fuel began, which is now complete. Reasons for the switch to ethyl alcohol are given in the discussion about ethyl alcohol later in this section.

Methyl alcohol is sometimes called *wood alcohol,* terminology that draws attention to an early method for its preparation—the heating of wood to a high temperature in the absence of air. Today, nearly all methyl alcohol is produced via the reaction between H_2 and CO.

$$CO + 2H_2 \xrightarrow[\text{300°C − 400°C, 200 atm}]{\text{ZnO—Cr}_2\text{O}_3} CH_3\text{—OH}$$

Drinking methyl alcohol is very dangerous. Within the human body, methyl alcohol is oxidized by the liver enzyme *alcohol dehydrogenase* to the toxic metabolites formaldehyde and formic acid. ◄

$$CH_3\text{—OH} \xrightarrow[\text{dehydrogenase}]{\text{Alcohol}} \underset{\text{Formaldehyde}}{H\text{—}\overset{\displaystyle O}{\overset{\|}{C}}\text{—}H} \xrightarrow[\text{oxidation}]{\text{Further}} \underset{\text{Formic acid}}{H\text{—}\overset{\displaystyle O}{\overset{\|}{C}}\text{—}OH}$$

Formaldehyde can cause blindness (temporary or permanent). Formic acid causes acidosis (see the Chemical Connections 10-D—Acidosis and Alkalosis). Ingesting as little as 1 oz (30 mL) of methyl alcohol can cause optic nerve damage.

Figure 14-3 Racing cars at the Indianapolis Speedway were fueled with methyl alcohol from 1965 to 2005.

Jonathan Ferrey/Getty Images

▶ *Methyl alcohol poisoning is treated with ethyl alcohol, which ties up the enzyme that oxidizes methyl alcohol to its toxic metabolites. Ethyl alcohol has 10 times the affinity for the alcohol dehydrogenase enzyme than methyl alcohol has. This situation is considered further in Section 21-7.*

Ethyl Alcohol (Ethanol)

Ethyl alcohol, the two-carbon monohydroxy alcohol, is the alcohol present in alcoholic beverages and is commonly referred to simply as alcohol or *drinking alcohol*. Like methyl alcohol, ethyl alcohol is oxidized in the human body by the liver enzyme *alcohol dehydrogenase*.

$$CH_3-CH_2-OH \xrightarrow[\text{dehydrogenase}]{\text{Alcohol}} CH_3-\overset{\overset{O}{\|}}{C}-H \xrightarrow[\text{oxidation}]{\text{Further}} CH_3-\overset{\overset{O}{\|}}{C}-OH$$

$$\text{Acetaldehyde} \qquad\qquad \text{Acetic acid}$$

Acetaldehyde, the first oxidation product, is largely responsible for the symptoms of hangover. The odors of both acetaldehyde and acetic acid are detected on the breath of someone who has consumed a large amount of alcohol. Ethyl alcohol oxidation products are less toxic than those of methyl alcohol.

Long-term excessive use of ethyl alcohol may cause undesirable effects such as cirrhosis of the liver, loss of memory, and strong physiological addiction. Links have also been established between certain birth defects and the ingestion of ethyl alcohol by women during pregnancy (fetal alcohol syndrome). ◀

Ethyl alcohol can be produced by yeast fermentation of sugars found in plant extracts (see Figure 14-4). The synthesis of ethyl alcohol in this manner, from grains such as corn, rice, and barley, is the reason why ethyl alcohol is often called *grain alcohol*.

> ▶ *Many people imagine ethanol to be relatively nontoxic and methanol to be extremely toxic. Actually, their toxicities differ by a factor of only 2. Typical fatal doses for adults are about 100 mL for methanol and about 200 mL for ethanol, although smaller doses of methanol may damage the optic nerve.*

> ▶ *The alcohol content of strong alcoholic beverages is often stated in terms of proof. Proof is twice the percentage of alcohol. This system dates back to the seventeenth century and is based on the fact that a 50% (v/v) alcohol–water mixture will burn. Its flammability was proof that a liquor had not been watered down.*

$$C_6H_{12}O_6 \xrightarrow[\text{Fermentation}]{\text{Yeast}} 2CH_3-CH_2-OH + 2CO_2$$

$$\underset{\text{(glucose)}}{\text{Sugar}} \qquad\qquad \text{Ethyl alcohol}$$

Fermentation is the process by which ethyl alcohol for alcoholic beverages is produced. The maximum concentration of ethyl alcohol obtainable by fermentation is about 18% (v/v) because yeast enzymes cannot function in stronger alcohol solutions. Alcoholic beverages with a higher concentration of alcohol than this are prepared by either distillation or fortification with alcohol obtained by the distillation of another fermentation product. ◀ Table 14-2 lists the alcohol content of common alcoholic beverages and of selected common household products and over-the-counter drug products.

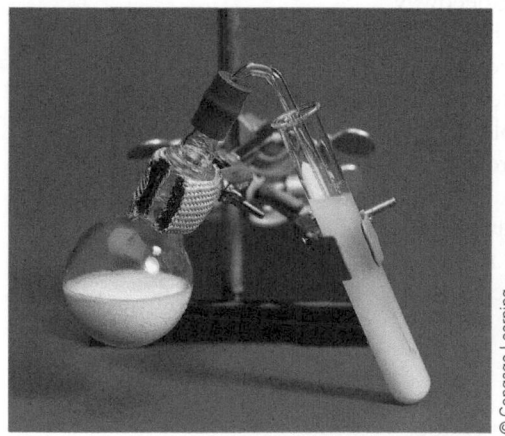

a A small amount of yeast has been added to the aqueous sugar solution in the flask. Yeast enzymes catalyze the decomposition of sugar to ethanol and carbon dioxide, CO_2. The CO_2 is bubbling through lime water, $Ca(OH)_2$, producing calcium carbonate, $CaCO_3$.

b More concentrated ethanol is produced from the solution in the flask by collecting the fraction that boils at about 78°C.

c Concentrated ethanol (50% v/v) burns when it is ignited.

Figure 14-4 An experimental setup for preparing ethyl alcohol by fermentation.

▷ Table 14-2 **Ethyl Alcohol Content (Volume Percent) of Common Alcoholic Beverages, Household Products, and Over-the-Counter Drugs**

Product Type	Product	Volume Percent Ethyl Alcohol
Alcoholic Beverages	beer	3.2–9
	wine (unfortified)	12
	brandy	40–45
	whiskey	45–55
	rum	45
Flavorings	vanilla extract	35
	almond extract	50
Cough and Cold Remedies	Pertussin Plus	25
	Nyquil	25
	Dristan	12
	Vicks 44	10
	Robitussin, DM	1.4
Mouthwashes	Listerine	25
	Scope	18
	Colgate 100	17
	Cepacol	14
	Lavoris	5

Denatured alcohol is ethyl alcohol that has been rendered unfit to drink by the addition of small amounts of toxic substances (denaturing agents). Almost all of the ethyl alcohol used for industrial purposes is denatured alcohol.

Most ethyl alcohol used in industry is prepared from ethene via a hydration reaction (Section 13-9).

$$CH_2=CH_2 + H_2O \xrightarrow{\text{Catalyst}} CH_3-CH_2-OH$$

The reaction produces a product that is 95% alcohol and 5% water. In applications where water does interfere with its use, the mixture is treated with a dehydrating agent to produce 100% ethyl alcohol. Such alcohol, with all traces of water removed, is called *absolute alcohol.*

The largest single end use for ethyl alcohol is that of a motor vehicle fuel. Gasoline blends containing up to 10% ethyl alcohol (E10) are approved for use in all gasoline-powered vehicles manufactured in the United States. In 2011 the Environmental Protection Agency (EPA) approved the use of gasoline blends containing 15% ethyl alcohol (E15) in gasoline-powered vehicles of model year 2006 or later. Blends with a greater alcohol content (up to E85) can be used in flexible-fuel vehicles that are sold as standard models by several automakers.

The ethyl alcohol fuel industry in the United States is based on the use of agricultural crops, predominantly corn. Sugars and starches present in the vegetation are fermented to produce the alcohol. Alcohol production in this manner supports local and regional economies while reducing the United States' reliance on imported petroleum. Blend use, particularly in cold weather with older and poorly maintained vehicles, also reduces carbon monoxide air pollution. On the downside, studies show that vehicle exhaust from *pure* ethanol use generates significantly greater amounts of compounds associated with smog production than does gasoline (1.7 versus 1.0 for gasoline on a relative scale). However, vehicle exhaust composition differences are minimal when *E10* fuel and gasoline are compared.

The previously mentioned switch from methyl alcohol to ethyl alcohol as a race car fuel was promoted and funded by a consortium of ethyl alcohol producers as a marketing effort to address public concerns that ethyl alcohol use in automobiles led to engine damage and poor performance. The transition from methyl to ethyl alcohol also boosts the fuel mileage of race cars. With the switch, the fuel-tank size of race cars has decreased, resulting in lower vehicle weight and decreased time required to refuel.

Isopropyl Alcohol (2-Propanol)

Isopropyl alcohol is one of two three-carbon monohydroxy alcohols; the other is propyl alcohol. A 70% isopropyl alcohol–30% water solution is marketed as *rubbing alcohol.* Isopropyl alcohol's rapid evaporation rate creates a dramatic cooling effect when it is applied to the skin, hence its use for alcohol rubs to combat high body temperature. ◄ It also finds use in cosmetics formulations such as aftershave lotion and hand lotions.

▶ *The "medicinal" odor associated with doctors' offices is usually that of isopropyl alcohol.*

Isopropyl alcohol has a bitter taste. Its toxicity is twice that of ethyl alcohol, but it causes few fatalities because it often induces vomiting and thus doesn't stay down long enough to be fatal. In the body, it is oxidized to acetone.

$$\underset{\text{Isopropyl alcohol}}{CH_3-\underset{\underset{OH}{|}}{CH}-CH_3} \xrightarrow[\text{dehydrogenase}]{\text{Alcohol}} \underset{\text{Acetone}}{CH_3-\underset{\overset{O}{\|}}{C}-CH_3}$$

Large amounts (about 150 mL) of ingested isopropyl alcohol can be fatal; death occurs from paralysis of the central nervous system.

Ethylene Glycol (1,2-Ethanediol) and Propylene Glycol (1,2-Propanediol)

▶ *Ethylene glycol and propylene glycol are synthesized from ethylene and propylene, respectively, hence their common names.*

Ethylene glycol and propylene glycol are the two simplest alcohols possessing two —OH groups. ◄ Besides being diols, they are also classified as glycols. A **glycol** *is a diol in which the two —OH groups are on adjacent carbon atoms.*

$$\underset{\text{Ethylene glycol}}{\underset{\boxed{OH}\ \ \boxed{OH}}{CH_2-CH_2}} \qquad \underset{\text{Propylene glycol}}{\underset{\boxed{OH}\ \ \boxed{OH}}{CH_3-CH-CH_2}}$$

Both of these glycols are colorless, odorless, high-boiling liquids that are completely miscible with water. Their major uses are as the main ingredient in automobile "year-round" antifreeze and airplane "de-icers" (Figure 14-5) and as a starting material for the manufacture of polyester fibers (Section 16-18). ◄

▶ *The ethylene glycol and propylene glycol used in antifreeze formulations are colorless and odorless; the color and odor of antifreezes come from additives for rust protection and the like.*

Ethylene glycol is extremely toxic when ingested. In the body, liver enzymes oxidize it to oxalic acid.

$$\underset{\text{Ethylene glycol}}{HO-CH_2-CH_2-OH} \xrightarrow[\text{enzymes}]{\text{Liver}} \underset{\text{Oxalic acid}}{HO-\underset{\overset{O}{\|}}{C}-\underset{\overset{O}{\|}}{C}-OH}$$

Oxalic acid, as a calcium salt, crystallizes in the kidneys, which leads to renal problems.

Figure 14-5 Ethylene glycol is the major ingredient in airplane "de-icers."

Propylene glycol, on the other hand, is essentially nontoxic and has been used as a solvent for drugs. Like ethylene glycol, it is oxidized by liver enzymes; however, pyruvic acid, its oxidation product, is a compound normally found in the human body, being an intermediate in carbohydrate metabolism (Chapter 24).

$$CH_3-CH-CH_2 \xrightarrow{\text{Liver enzymes}} CH_3-\overset{\overset{O}{\|}}{C}-\overset{\overset{O}{\|}}{C}-OH$$

$$\quad\quad\; \underset{OH}{|}\;\;\underset{OH}{|}$$

Propylene glycol   Pyruvic acid

Propylene glycol use as an antifreeze is increasing. Antifreeze brands marketed as "environmentally friendly" are usually propylene glycol formulations. Such antifreeze, however, costs more since propylene glycol production costs exceed those for ethylene glycol.

Accidental ethylene glycol poisoning is a problem that occurs much too frequently. Most often such poisonings occur when radiator fluid is changed and the spent fluid is not disposed of properly. Both cats and dogs as well as small children can be victims of such poisonings, which are often fatal.

Glycerol (1,2,3-Propanetriol)

Glycerol, which is often also called glycerin, is a clear, thick liquid that has the consistency of honey. Its molecular structure involves three —OH groups on three different carbon atoms.

$$CH_2-CH-CH_2$$
$$\;\underset{OH}{|}\;\;\;\underset{OH}{|}\;\;\;\underset{OH}{|}$$

Glycerol is normally present in the human body because it is a product of fat metabolism. It is present, in combined form, in all animal fats and vegetable oils (Section 19-4). In some arctic and northern species, glycerol functions as a "biological antifreeze" (Figure 14-6).

Because glycerol has a great affinity for water vapor (moisture), it is often added to pharmaceutical preparations such as skin lotions and soap. Florists sometimes use glycerol on cut flowers to help retain water and maintain freshness. Its lubricative properties also make it useful in shaving creams and in applications such as glycerol suppositories for rectal administration of medicines. It is used in candies and icings as a retardant for preventing sugar crystallization.

Figure 14-6 Glycerol is often called biological antifreeze. For survival in arctic and northern winters, many fish and insects, including the common housefly, produce large amounts of glycerol that dissolve in their blood, thereby lowering the freezing point of the blood.

James Cotier/The Image Bank/Getty Images

Section 14-5 Quick Quiz

1. Which of the following statements concerning commonly encountered alcohols is *incorrect*?
   a. Wood alcohol and methyl alcohol are two names for the same compound.
   b. Denatured alcohol is drinking alcohol rendered unfit to drink.
   c. Rubbing alcohol is a 70% aqueous solution of ethyl alcohol.
   d. no correct response
2. Which of the following pairs of alcohols have been used as racing car fuels?
   a. methanol and ethanol
   b. ethanol and 2-propanol
   c. ethanol and 1,2-ethanediol
   d. no correct response
3. In which of the following pairs of alcohols do both members of the pair contain two or more hydroxyl groups?
   a. ethanol and ethylene glycol
   b. ethylene glycol and glycerol
   c. isopropyl alcohol and propylene glycol
   d. no correct response
4. Which of the following is not a property of glycerol?
   a. thick liquid that has the consistency of honey
   b. is a good moisturizing agent
   c. its largest use is as automobile antifreeze
   d. no correct response

Answers: 1. c; 2. a; 3. b; 4. c

14-6 Physical Properties of Alcohols

LEARNING FOCUS

Know the general physical properties of alcohols and how hydrogen bonding influences such properties.

Alcohol molecules have both polar and nonpolar character. The hydroxyl groups present are polar, and the alkyl (R) group present is nonpolar.

The physical properties of an alcohol depend on whether the polar or the nonpolar portion of its structure "dominates." Factors that determine this include the *length* of the nonpolar carbon chain present and the *number* of polar hydroxyl groups present (Figure 14-7).

Boiling Points and Water Solubilities

Figure 14-8a shows that the boiling point for 1-alcohols, unbranched-chain alcohols with an —OH group on an end carbon, increases as the length of the carbon chain increases. This trend results from increasing London forces (Sections 7-13 and 12-16) with increasing carbon-chain length. Alcohols with more than one

Figure 14-7 Space-filling molecular models showing the nonpolar (green) and polar (pink) parts of methanol and 1-octanol.

$$CH_3 - OH$$
Nonpolar   Polar

$$CH_3CH_2CH_2CH_2CH_2CH_2CH_2CH_2 - OH$$
Nonpolar   Polar

a Methanol The polar hydroxyl functional group dominates the physical properties of methanol. The molecule is completely soluble in water (polar) but has limited solubility in hexane (nonpolar).

b 1-Octanol Conversely, the nonpolar portion of 1-octanol dominates its physical properties; it is infinitely soluble in hexane and has limited solubility in water.

Figure 14-8 (a) Boiling points and (b) solubilities in water of selected 1-alcohols.

a Boiling points.

b Solubilities in water of selected 1-alcohols.

hydroxyl group present have significantly higher boiling points (bp) than their monohydroxy counterparts.

$$CH_3-CH_2-CH_2$$
$$\underset{OH}{|}$$
bp = 97°C

$$CH_3-CH-CH_2$$
$$\underset{OH}{|}\ \underset{OH}{|}$$
bp = 188°C

$$CH_2-CH-CH_2$$
$$\underset{OH}{|}\ \underset{OH}{|}\ \underset{OH}{|}$$
bp = 290°C

This boiling-point trend is related to increased hydrogen bonding between alcohol molecules (to be discussed shortly). Figure 14-9 is a physical-state summary for unbranched 1-alcohols and unsubstituted cycloalcohols with eight or fewer carbon atoms.

Small monohydroxy alcohols are soluble in water in all proportions. As carbon-chain length increases beyond three carbons, solubility in water rapidly decreases (Figure 14-8b) because of the increasingly nonpolar character of the alcohol. Alcohols with two —OH groups present are more soluble in water than their counterparts with only one —OH group. Increased hydrogen bonding is responsible for this. Diols containing as many as seven carbon atoms show appreciable solubility in water.

Unbranched 1-Alcohols			
C$_1$	C$_3$	C$_5$	C$_7$
C$_2$	C$_4$	C$_6$	C$_8$

Unsubstituted Cycloalcohols			
✕	C$_3$	C$_5$	C$_7$
✕	C$_4$	C$_6$	C$_8$

☐ Liquid

Figure 14-9 A physical-state summary for unbranched 1-alcohols and unsubstituted cycloalcohols at room temperature and pressure.

Alcohols and Hydrogen Bonding

A comparison of the properties of alcohols with their alkane counterparts (Table 14-3) shows that

1. Alcohols have *higher* boiling points than alkanes of similar molecular mass.
2. Alcohols have much *higher* solubility in water than alkanes of similar molecular mass.

The differences in physical properties between alcohols and alkanes are related to hydrogen bonding. Because of their hydroxyl group(s), alcohols can participate in hydrogen bonding, whereas alkanes cannot. Hydrogen bonding between alcohol molecules (Figure 14-10) is similar to that which occurs between water molecules (Section 7-13).

Extra energy is needed to overcome alcohol–alcohol hydrogen bonds before alcohol molecules can enter the vapor phase. Hence alcohol boiling points are higher than those for the corresponding alkanes (where no hydrogen bonds are present).

Alcohol molecules can also hydrogen-bond to water molecules. As shown in Figure 14-11, a given alcohol molecule can hydrogen-bond to three different water molecules. The formation of such hydrogen bonds explains the solubility of small alcohol molecules in water. ◀ As the alcohol chain length increases, alcohols become more alkane-like (nonpolar) and solubility decreases.

▶ *In general, organic compounds that can form hydrogen bonds with water are more soluble in water than organic compounds that cannot form such hydrogen bonds.*

▶ **Table 14-3** **A Comparison of Selected Physical Properties of Alcohols with Alkane Counterparts of Similar Molecular Mass**

Type of Compound	Compound	Structure	Molecular Mass (amu)	Boiling Point (°C)	Solubility in Water
alkane	ethane	CH_3-CH_3	30	−89	slight solubility
alcohol	methanol	CH_3-OH	32	65	unlimited solubility
alkane	propane	$CH_3-CH_2-CH_3$	44	−42	slight solubility
alcohol	ethanol	CH_3-CH_2-OH	46	78	unlimited solubility
alkane	butane	$CH_3-CH_2-CH_2-CH_3$	58	−1	slight solubility
alcohol	1-propanol	$CH_3-CH_2-CH_2-OH$	60	97	unlimited solubility
alcohol	2-propanol	$CH_3-\underset{\underset{CH_3}{|}}{CH}-OH$	60	83	unlimited solubility

Figure 14-10 Alcohol boiling points are higher than those of the corresponding alkanes because of alcohol–alcohol hydrogen bonding.

Figure 14-11 Because of hydrogen bonding between alcohol molecules and water molecules, alcohols of small molecular mass have unlimited solubility in water.

Section 14-6 Quick Quiz

1. Which of the following statements concerning the physical properties of alcohols is *incorrect*?
   a. Alcohol solubility in water decreases as carbon-chain length increases.
   b. Alcohol solubility in water decreases as the number of hydroxyl groups present increases.
   c. Alcohol boiling points increase as carbon-chain length increases.
   d. no correct response
2. Alcohols have higher boiling points than alkanes of similar molecular mass because
   a. alcohols are ionic compounds and alkanes are covalent compounds
   b. alkane molecules are polar and alcohol molecules are nonpolar
   c. alcohol molecules can hydrogen–bond to each other whereas alkane molecules cannot
   d. no correct response
3. With how many water molecules can a given alcohol molecule hydrogen-bond?
   a. 2
   b. 3
   c. 4
   d. no correct response

Answers: 1. b; 2. c; 3. b

14-7 Preparation of Alcohols

LEARNING FOCUS
Describe two general methods by which alcohols can be prepared.

A general method for preparing alcohols—the hydration of alkenes—was discussed in the previous chapter (Section 13-9). Alkenes react with water (an unsymmetrical addition agent) in the presence of sulfuric acid (the catalyst) to form an alcohol. Markovnikov's rule is used to determine the predominant alcohol product.

$$\text{C=C} + \text{H—OH} \xrightarrow{\text{H}_2\text{SO}_4} -\overset{|}{\underset{|}{\text{C}}}-\overset{|}{\underset{|}{\text{C}}}-$$
$$\qquad\qquad\qquad\qquad\ \ \ \text{H} \ \ \text{OH}$$

Another method of synthesizing alcohols involves the addition of H_2 to a carbon–oxygen double bond (a carbonyl group, C=O). (The carbonyl group is a functional group that will be discussed in detail in Chapter 15.) A carbonyl group behaves very much like a carbon–carbon double bond when it reacts with H_2 under the proper conditions. ◀ As a result of H_2 addition, the oxygen of the carbonyl group is converted to an —OH group.

$$R—\overset{\overset{\displaystyle O}{\|}}{C}—H + H_2 \xrightarrow{\text{Catalyst}} R—\overset{\overset{\displaystyle OH}{|}}{\underset{\underset{\displaystyle H}{|}}{C}}—H$$

Aldehyde (Section 15-3)   Alcohol

$$R—\overset{\overset{\displaystyle O}{\|}}{C}—R' + H_2 \xrightarrow{\text{Catalyst}} R—\overset{\overset{\displaystyle OH}{|}}{\underset{\underset{\displaystyle H}{|}}{C}}—R'$$

Ketone (Section 15-3)   Alcohol

▶ *Alcohols are intermediate products in the metabolism of both carbohydrates (Chapter 24) and fats (Chapter 25). In these metabolic processes, both addition of water to a carbon–carbon double bond and addition of hydrogen to a carbon–oxygen double bond lead to the introduction of the alcohol functional group into a biomolecule.*

Section 14-7 Quick Quiz

1. A general method for preparing alcohols that involves alkenes is
   a. alkene hydration
   b. alkene combustion
   c. alkene hydrogenation
   d. no correct response
2. A general method for preparing alcohols that involves carbon–oxygen double bonds is addition of which of the following to the bond?
   a. H_2
   b. H_2O
   c. HCl
   d. no correct response

Answers: 1. a; 2. a

14-8 Classification of Alcohols

LEARNING FOCUS
Based on structural formula, be able to classify alcohols as primary, secondary, or tertiary.

Prior to considering chemical reactions of alcohols (Section 14-9), a classification system for alcohols that is often needed when predicting the products in a chemical reaction involving an alcohol needs to be in place.

Alcohols are classified as primary (1°), secondary (2°), or tertiary (3°) depending on the number of carbon atoms bonded to the carbon atom that bears the hydroxyl group. ◀ A **primary alcohol** *is an alcohol in which the hydroxyl-bearing carbon atom is bonded to only one other carbon atom.* A **secondary alcohol** *is an alcohol in which the hydroxyl-bearing carbon atom is bonded to two other carbon atoms.* A **tertiary alcohol** *is an alcohol in which the hydroxyl-bearing carbon atom is bonded to three other carbon atoms.* Chemical reactions of alcohols often depend on alcohol class (1°, 2°, or 3°). ◀

▶ *Pronounce 1° as "primary," 2° as "secondary," and 3° as "tertiary."*

▶ *Methyl alcohol, CH_3—OH, an alcohol in which the hydroxyl-bearing carbon atom is attached to three hydrogen atoms, does not fit any of the alcohol classification definitions. It is usually grouped with the primary alcohols because its reactions are similar to theirs.*

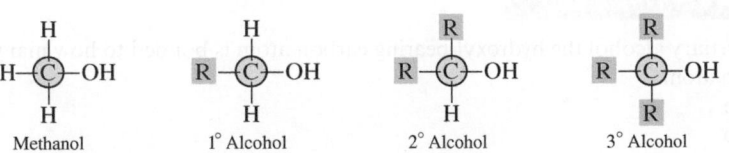

Methanol   1° Alcohol   2° Alcohol   3° Alcohol

Although all alcohols are able to participate in hydrogen bonding (Section 14-6), increasing the number of R groups around the carbon atom bearing the OH group decreases the extent of hydrogen bonding. This effect, called steric hindrance, becomes particularly important when the R groups are large. Thus, 1° alcohols are best able to hydrogen-bond and 3° alcohols are least able to hydrogen-bond.

For alcohols of similar molecular mass, 1° alcohols have higher boiling points than 2° alcohols, which in turn have higher boiling points than 3° alcohols, because of how steric hindrance affects hydrogen bonding. The following data for three C_4 alcohols illustrates this situation.

$$
\begin{array}{ccc}
\underset{\substack{\text{3° alcohol} \\ \text{b.p.} = 83°C}}{\overset{\overset{\displaystyle CH_3}{|}}{\underset{\underset{\displaystyle CH_3}{|}}{CH_3-C-OH}}} &
\underset{\substack{\text{2° alcohol} \\ \text{b.p.} = 98°C}}{\underset{\underset{\displaystyle CH_3}{|}}{CH_3-CH_2-CH-OH}} &
\underset{\substack{\text{1° alcohol} \\ \text{b.p.} = 118°C}}{CH_3-CH_2-CH_2-CH_2-OH}
\end{array}
$$

EXAMPLE 14-2

Classifying Alcohols as Primary, Secondary, or Tertiary Alcohols

Classify each of the following alcohols as a primary, secondary, or tertiary alcohol.

a. $CH_3-CH_2-CH_2-OH$

b. $CH_3-CH_2-\overset{\overset{\displaystyle CH_3}{|}}{\underset{\underset{\displaystyle CH_3}{|}}{C}}-OH$

c. $CH_3-\overset{\overset{\displaystyle CH_3}{|}}{CH}-\overset{\overset{\displaystyle CH_3}{|}}{CH}-\underset{\underset{\displaystyle OH}{|}}{CH}-CH_3$

d. (cyclohexane ring with OH)

Solution

a. This is a primary alcohol. The carbon atom to which the —OH group is attached is bonded to only one other carbon atom.
b. This is a tertiary alcohol. The carbon atom bearing the —OH group is bonded to three other carbon atoms.
c. This is a secondary alcohol. The hydroxyl-bearing carbon atom is bonded to two other carbon atoms.
d. This is a secondary alcohol. The ring carbon atom to which the —OH group is attached is bonded to two other ring carbon atoms.

Part d. of Example 14-2 illustrates that the 1°, 2°, and 3° classification system for alcohols applies not only to alcohols where the hydroxyl group is attached to an acyclic R group but also to alcohols where the R group is cyclic. All alcohols with cyclic R groups are either 2° or 3° alcohols; 1° alcohols with cyclic R groups are structurally not possible. A naturally occurring 2° alcohol with a cyclic R group whose name is familiar to most people is *menthol*. Many *mentholated* consumer products are available for use today. The focus on relevancy feature Chemical Connections 14-A—Menthol: A Useful Naturally Occurring Terpene Alcohol—gives information about this interesting secondary alcohol.

Section 14-8 Quick Quiz

1. In a tertiary alcohol the hydroxyl-bearing carbon atom is bonded to how many other carbon atoms?
   a. one
   b. two
   c. three
   d. no correct response

2. The alcohol CH_3—CH_2—CH_2—CH_2—OH is classified as a

a. 1° alcohol

b. 2° alcohol

c. 3° alcohol

d. no correct response

Answers: 1. c; 2. a

Menthol: A Useful Naturally Occurring Terpene Alcohol

Menthol is a naturally occurring terpene (Section 13-7) alcohol with a pleasant, minty odor. Its IUPAC name is 2-isopropyl-5-methylcyclohexanol.

In the pure state, menthol is a white crystalline solid with a melting point of 41°C to 43°C. Menthol occurs naturally in peppermint oil. As is the case with many natural products, the demand for menthol exceeds its supply from natural sources. Methods now exist for the synthetic production of menthol.

Topical application of menthol to the skin causes a refreshing, cooling sensation followed by a slight burning-and-prickling sensation. Its mode of action is that of a *differential* anesthetic. It stimulates the receptor cells in the skin that normally respond to cold to give a sensation of coolness that is unrelated to body temperature. (This cooling sensation is particularly noticeable in the respiratory tract when low concentrations of menthol are inhaled.) At the same time as cooling is perceived, menthol can depress the nerves for pain reception.

Menthol's mode of action is opposite that of capsaicin (Section 17-14), the natural product responsible for the "spiciness" of hot peppers. Capsaicin stimulates heat sensors without causing an actual change in body temperature.

Numerous products contain menthol.

- Throat sprays and lozenges containing menthol temporarily soothe inflamed mucous surfaces of the nose and throat. Lozenges contain 2−20 milligrams of menthol per wafer.

- Cough drops and cigarettes of the "mentholated" type use menthol for its counterirritant effect.
- Pre-electric shave preparations and aftershave lotions often contain menthol. A concentration of only 0.1% (m/v) gives ample cooling to allay the irritation of a "close" shave.
- Many dermatologic preparations contain menthol as an anti-pruritic (anti-itching agent).
- Chest-rub preparations containing menthol include BENGAY [7% (m/v)] and Mentholatum [6% (m/v)].
- Mint flavoring agents used in chewing gum and candies contain menthol as an ingredient. Several toothpastes and mouthwashes also contain menthol as a flavoring agent.

Many kinds of cough drops contain menthol as a counterirritant.

© Cengage Learning

14-9 Chemical Reactions of Alcohols

LEARNING FOCUS

Be aware of reaction conditions and products formed for each of the following alcohol reactions: combustion, dehydration, condensation, oxidation, and halogenation.

Of the many chemical reactions that alcohols undergo, five will be considered in this section: (1) combustion, (2) dehydration, (3) condensation, (4) oxidation, and (5) halogenation.

Figure 14-12 In alcohol dehydration, the components of water (H and OH) are removed from neighboring carbon atoms with the resultant introduction of a double bond into the molecule.

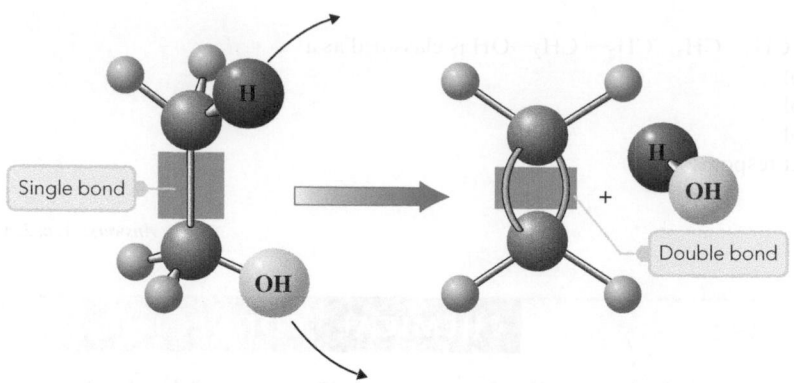

Combustion

As has been seen in the previous two chapters, hydrocarbons of all types undergo combustion in air to produce carbon dioxide and water. Alcohols are also flammable; as with hydrocarbons, the combustion products are carbon dioxide and water. Both methanol and ethanol, as well as alcohol–gasoline mixtures such as E10 and E85 (Section 14-5), are used as automotive fuels.

Dehydration

▶ *Excessive sweating and/or inadequate water intake can cause dehydration conditions in the human body. Such a dehydration situation (not enough water) involves a different use of the word dehydration than that involved with dehydration chemical reactions.*

▶ *Ease of alcohol dehydration depends on alcohol classification. Primary alcohols are the most difficult to dehydrate, requiring temperatures of around 180°C. Secondary alcohol dehydration occurs at lower temperatures, and tertiary alcohols dehydrate at temperatures slightly above room temperature.*

A **dehydration reaction** *is a chemical reaction in which water is formed from the removal of the components of water (H and OH) from a single reactant.* Dehydration of an alcohol produces an alkene. ◀ Reaction conditions for alcohol dehydration are a temperature of 180°C and the presence of sulfuric acid as a catalyst. ◀

A generalized structural equation for alcohol dehydration is

$$\underset{\text{An alcohol}}{\overset{\text{H} \quad \text{O}-\text{H}}{-\overset{|}{\underset{|}{\text{C}}}-\overset{|}{\underset{|}{\text{C}}}-}} \xrightarrow[180°C]{H_2SO_4} \underset{\text{An alkene}}{-\overset{|}{\text{C}}=\overset{|}{\text{C}}-} + \underset{\text{Water (}H_2O\text{)}}{\text{H}-\text{O}-\text{H}}$$

A specific example of alcohol dehydration, that involving 1-propanol, is

$$\underset{\text{1-propanol}}{CH_3-\underset{\text{H}}{\overset{|}{\text{CH}}}-\underset{\text{OH}}{\overset{|}{\text{CH}_2}}} \xrightarrow[180°C]{H_2SO_4} \underset{\text{Propene}}{CH_3-CH=CH_2} + H_2O$$

Alcohol dehydration is an example of an *elimination reaction* (Figure 14-12), as contrasted to a substitution reaction (Section 12-17) and an addition reaction (Section 13-9). An **elimination reaction** *is a reaction in which two groups or two atoms on neighboring carbon atoms are removed, or eliminated, from a molecule, leaving a multiple bond between the carbon atoms.*

$$-\overset{|}{\underset{\text{A}}{\text{C}}}-\overset{|}{\underset{\text{B}}{\text{C}}}- \longrightarrow \text{C}=\text{C} + \text{A}-\text{B}$$

What occurs in an elimination reaction is the reverse of what occurs in an addition reaction.

Dehydration of an alcohol can result in the production of more than one alkene product. This happens when there is more than one neighboring carbon atom from which hydrogen loss can occur. Dehydration of 2-butanol produces two alkenes.

$$\underset{\substack{\text{Removal} \\ \text{produces} \\ \text{1-butene}}}{CH_2-\underset{\text{H}}{}\underset{\text{2-Butanol}}{CH}-\underset{\text{OH}}{\overset{|}{\text{CH}}}-\underset{\substack{\text{Removal} \\ \text{produces} \\ \text{2-butene}}}{\underset{\text{H}}{\overset{|}{\text{CH}}}-CH_3}} \xrightarrow[180°C]{H_2SO_4}$$

$$\underset{\text{1-Butene}}{\overset{①}{C}H_2=\overset{②}{C}H-\underset{\text{H}}{\overset{③}{\overset{|}{C}H}}-\overset{④}{C}H_3} + \underset{\text{2-Butene}}{\overset{①}{C}H_2-\underset{\text{H}}{\overset{②}{\overset{|}{C}H}}=\overset{③}{C}H-\overset{④}{C}H_3} + H_2O$$

Although both products are formed, a large amount of one product is formed whereas only a small amount of the other product is formed. Prediction of which product is the major product and which is the minor product can be made using Zaitsev's rule, a rule that carries the name of the Russian chemist Alexander Zaitsev (pronounced "*zait-zeff* "). ◄ **Zaitsev's rule** states that *the major product in an alcohol dehydration reaction is the alkene that has the greatest number of alkyl groups attached to the carbon atoms of the double bond.* In the preceding reaction, 2-butene (with two alkyl groups) is favored over 1-butene (with one alkyl group). ◄

Two alkyl groups on double-bonded carbons: (CH₃)—CH=CH—(CH₃) 2-Butene

CH₂=CH—(CH₂—CH₃) 1-Butene One alkyl group on double-bonded carbons

▶ *Alexander Zaitsev (1841–1910), a nineteenth-century Russian chemist, studied at the University of Paris and then returned to his native Russia to become a professor of chemistry at the University of Kazan.*

▶ *An alternative way of expressing Zaitsev's rule is "Hydrogen atom loss, during alcohol dehydration to form an alkene, will occur preferentially from the carbon atom (adjacent to the hydroxyl-bearing carbon) that already has the fewest hydrogen atoms."*

Alcohols in which the hydroxyl-bearing carbon atom is a saturated carbon atom that is part of a ring structure can also be dehydrated. The following schematic equation shows the dehydration of 2-methylcyclohexanol, a situation where two different cycloalkene products are possible.

2-Methylcyclohexene

3-Methylcyclohexene

The major product, predicted using Zaitsev's rule, is 2-methylcyclohexene (three alkyl attachments) rather than 3-methylcyclohexene (two alkyl attachments).

A few alcohols cannot be dehydrated because the adjacent carbon atom to the hydroxyl-bearing carbon atom does not have any attached hydrogen atoms. An example of such an alcohol is

$$CH_3-\overset{\overset{\displaystyle CH_3}{|}}{\underset{\underset{\displaystyle CH_3}{|}}{C}}-CH_2-OH$$

Alkene formation via alcohol *dehydration* is the "reverse reaction" of the reaction for preparing an alcohol through *hydration* of an alkene (Section 13-9). This relationship can be diagrammed as follows:

Hydration

An alkene ⇄ An alcohol

Dehydration

This "reverse reaction" situation again illustrates the fact that many organic reactions can go both forward or backward, depending on reaction conditions. Noting relationships such as this helps in keeping track of the numerous reactions that hydrocarbon derivatives undergo. These two "reverse reactions" actually involve an equilibrium situation.

An alkene   An alcohol

Whether the forward reaction (alcohol formation) or the reverse reaction (alkene formation) is favored depends on experimental conditions. The favored direction for the reaction can be predicted using Le Châtelier's principle (Section 9-9).

1. The addition of water favors alcohol formation.
2. The removal of water favors alkene formation.

Experimental conditions for alcohol formation involve the use of a *dilute* sulfuric acid solution as a catalyst. *Concentrated* sulfuric acid (a dehydrating agent) as well as higher temperatures are used for alkene formation. ◀ Dilute acid solutions are mainly water; concentrated acid solutions have less water and heat also removes water.

▶ *Dehydration of alcohols to form carbon–carbon double bonds occurs in several metabolic pathways in living systems, such as the citric acid cycle (Section 23-6) and the β oxidation pathway (Section 25-4). In these biochemical dehydrations, enzymes serve as catalysts instead of acids, and the reaction temperature is 37°C instead of the elevated temperatures required in the laboratory.*

Condensation

Many hydrocarbon derivatives, including alcohols, participate in *condensation reactions*. In such reactions two small molecules are joined together to form a larger molecule and a molecule of water.

$$\text{small molecule} + \text{small molecule} \longrightarrow \text{larger molecule} + H_2O$$

A **condensation reaction** *is a chemical reaction in which two molecules combine to form a larger one and a molecule of water.* Condensation reactions involving alcohols, as well as many other molecular types, commonly occur in living organisms.

A condensation reaction can be visualized as occurring in two steps.

Step 1:   *A water molecule is formed from the removal of an H atom from one molecule and a hydroxyl group from another molecule, leaving behind two "organic fragments."*

Step 2:   *The two "organic fragments" are then joined together through formation of a new covalent bond.*

A common feature of condensation reactions and dehydration reactions (discussed earlier in this section) is the production of water from H and OH removal. Relative to water production, there are two important differences between these two reaction types.

1. In a condensation reaction the removed H and OH come from *different* molecules whereas in a *dehydration reaction* the removed H and OH come from the *same* molecule.
2. In a condensation reaction the H is removed from an O (or N) atom whereas in a dehydration reaction the H is removed from a C atom.

▶ *Ethers, like alcohols, constitute a many-membered important class of oxygen-containing hydrocarbon derivatives. An extended discussion of ethers, whose general properties are much different from those of alcohols, is found in Sections 14-15 through 14-19 of this chapter.*

Alcohols undergo both dehydration and condensation reactions. Alcohol dehydration produces an alkene. ◀ Alcohol condensation produces an ether, a type of compound to be discussed in detail later in this chapter. Ethers have the general structure

$$R\!-\!O\!-\!R$$

The structural equation for the formation of an ether from two molecules of the three-carbon alcohol 1-propanol is

$$CH_3\!-\!CH_2\!-\!CH_2\!-\!O\!-\!H + H\!-\!O\!-\!CH_2\!-\!CH_2\!-\!CH_3 \xrightarrow[140°C]{H_2SO_4}$$

$$CH_3\!-\!CH_2\!-\!CH_2\!-\!O\!-\!CH_2\!-\!CH_2\!-\!CH_3 + H_2O$$

What determines whether a dehydration or condensation reaction occurs when two alcohols react? A major consideration is temperature. At lower temperatures (140°C) ether formation is possible while at higher temperatures (180°C) alkene formation is likely. In practice, condensation reactions produce useful yields of ether only for 1° alcohols; even at lower temperatures, 2° and 3° alcohols usually undergo dehydration instead.

EXAMPLE 14-3

Predicting the Reactant in Alcohol Dehydration and Alcohol Condensation Reactions When Given the Product ◀

Identify the alcohol reactant needed to produce each of the following compounds as the *major product* of an alcohol dehydration or alcohol condensation reaction.

a. Alcohol $\xrightarrow[180°C]{H_2SO_4}$ $CH_3—CH=CH—CH_3$

b. Alcohol $\xrightarrow[180°C]{H_2SO_4}$ $CH_2=CH—CH—CH_3$
$\qquad\qquad\qquad\qquad\qquad\quad |$
$\qquad\qquad\qquad\qquad\qquad\; CH_3$

c. Alcohol $\xrightarrow[140°C]{H_2SO_4}$ $CH_3—CH—CH_2—O—CH_2—CH—CH_3$
$\qquad\qquad\qquad\qquad\quad\; |\qquad\qquad\qquad\qquad\;\; |$
$\qquad\qquad\qquad\qquad\; CH_3\qquad\qquad\qquad\quad\; CH_3$

▶ *The following is a summary of products obtained from alcohol dehydration/condensation reactions using H_2SO_4 as a catalyst.*

Primary alcohol $\overset{180°C}{\underset{140°C}{\rightleftarrows}}$ alkene / ether

Secondary alcohol $\overset{180°C}{\underset{140°C}{\rightleftarrows}}$ alkene / alkene

Tertiary alcohol $\overset{180°C}{\underset{140°C}{\rightleftarrows}}$ alkene / alkene

Solution

a. Both carbon atoms of the double bond are equivalent to each other. Add an H atom to one carbon atom of the double bond and an OH group to the other carbon atom of the double bond. It does not matter which goes where; you get the same molecule either way.

$$CH_3—CH—CH—CH_3 \quad \text{or} \quad CH_3—CH—CH—CH_3$$
$$\quad\;\; |\quad\; | \qquad\qquad\qquad\qquad\qquad | \quad\;\; |$$
$$\quad OH\;\; H \qquad\qquad\qquad\qquad\qquad H \quad OH$$

Looking at the alkene products obtained when this alcohol is dehydrated verifies that this is the correct alcohol. There are two possible dehydration products depending on which H atom is removed:

$$CH_2=CH—CH_2—CH_3 \quad \text{and} \quad CH_3—CH=CH—CH_3$$

Based on Zaitsev's rule, the second alkene is the dominant product as two alkyl groups are present compared to one in the other structure.

b. There are two possible parent alcohols: one with an —OH group on carbon 1 and the other with an —OH group on carbon 2.

$$CH_2—CH_2—CH—CH_3 \quad \text{or} \quad CH_3—CH—CH—CH_3$$
$$\;\; | \qquad\qquad\quad | \qquad\qquad\qquad\qquad\qquad | \quad\;\; |$$
$$OH \qquad\qquad CH_3 \qquad\qquad\qquad\qquad OH\;\; CH_3$$

Which of these two alcohols gives the desired dehydration product?
Only one product is possible from the dehydration of the first alcohol.

$$CH_2=CH—CH—CH_3$$
$$\qquad\qquad\;\; |$$
$$\qquad\qquad CH_3$$

This is the correct alkene.
Two products are possible for the dehydration of the second alcohol, depending on whether an H atom removed is to the left or right of the hydroxyl carbon atom.

$$CH_2=CH—CH—CH_3 \quad \text{or} \quad CH_3—CH=C—CH_3$$
$$\qquad\qquad\;\; | \qquad\qquad\qquad\qquad\qquad\qquad\qquad |$$
$$\qquad\qquad CH_3 \qquad\qquad\qquad\qquad\qquad\;\; CH_3$$

Based on Zaitsev's rule, the second alkene is the dominant product as more alkyl groups are attached to the double-bonded carbons. This is not the desired alkene product. Thus, the first alcohol considered is the parent alcohol.

c. This is a symmetrical ether. The primary alcohol from which the ether was formed via condensation will have the same alkyl group present as is in the ether. Thus the alcohol is

$$CH_3—CH—CH_2—OH$$
$$\qquad\;\; |$$
$$\qquad CH_3$$

Oxidation

Before discussing alcohol oxidation reactions, a new method for recognizing when oxidation and reduction have occurred in a chemical reaction will be considered.

The processes of oxidation and reduction were considered in Section 9-2 in the context of inorganic, rather than organic, reactions. Oxidation numbers were used to characterize oxidation–reduction processes. This same technique could be used in characterizing oxidation–reduction processes involving organic compounds, but it is not. Formal use of the oxidation number rules with organic compounds is usually cumbersome because of the many carbon and hydrogen atoms present; often, fractional oxidation numbers for carbon result.

A better approach for organic redox reactions is to use the following set of operational rules instead of oxidation numbers.

1. An *organic oxidation* is an oxidation that increases the number of C—O bonds and/or decreases the number of C—H bonds.
2. An *organic reduction* is a reduction that decreases the number of C—O bonds and/or increases the number of C—H bonds.

Note that these operational definitions for oxidation and reduction are "opposites." This is just as it should be; oxidation and reduction are "opposite" processes.

Some alcohols readily undergo oxidation with mild oxidizing agents; others are resistant to oxidation with these same oxidizing agents. Primary and secondary alcohols, but not tertiary alcohols, readily undergo oxidation in the presence of mild oxidizing agents to produce compounds that contain a carbon–oxygen double bond (aldehydes, ketones, and carboxylic acids). A number of different oxidizing agents can be used for the oxidation, including potassium permanganate ($KMnO_4$), potassium dichromate ($K_2Cr_2O_7$), and chromic acid (H_2CrO_4).

The net effect of the action of a mild oxidizing agent on a primary or secondary alcohol is the removal of two hydrogen atoms from the alcohol. One hydrogen comes from the —OH group, the other from the carbon atom to which the —OH group is attached. This H removal generates a carbon–oxygen double bond.

An alcohol   Compound containing
                  a carbon–oxygen
                  double bond

▶ *This chemical reaction is consistent with the operational definition given earlier in this section for an organic oxidation. A new C—O bond is formed and a C—H bond is broken.*

The two "removed" hydrogen atoms combine with oxygen supplied by the oxidizing agent to give H_2O. ◀

Primary and secondary alcohols, the two types of oxidizable alcohols, yield different products upon oxidation. A 1° alcohol produces an *aldehyde* that is often then further oxidized to a *carboxylic acid,* and a 2° alcohol produces a *ketone.*

$$\text{Primary alcohol} \xrightarrow[\text{ox. agent}]{\text{Mild}} \text{aldehyde} \xrightarrow[\text{ox. agent}]{\text{Mild}} \text{carboxylic acid}$$

$$\text{Secondary alcohol} \xrightarrow[\text{ox. agent}]{\text{Mild}} \text{ketone}$$

$$\text{Tertiary alcohol} \xrightarrow[\text{ox. agent}]{\text{Mild}} \text{no reaction}$$

The general reaction for the oxidation of a primary alcohol is

1° Alcohol   Aldehyde   Carboxylic acid

In this equation, the symbol [O] represents the mild oxidizing agent. The immediate product of the oxidation of a primary alcohol is an aldehyde. Because aldehydes themselves are readily oxidized by the same oxidizing agents that oxidize alcohols, aldehydes are further converted to carboxylic acids. A specific example of a primary alcohol oxidation reaction is

$$CH_3-\boxed{CH_2-OH} \xrightarrow{[O]} CH_3-\underset{\underset{\text{Ethanol}}{}}{\boxed{\overset{\overset{\text{O}}{\|}}{C}-H}} \xrightarrow{[O]} CH_3-\boxed{\overset{\overset{\text{O}}{\|}}{C}-OH}$$

This specific oxidation reaction—that of ethanol—is the basis for the "breathalyzer test" used by law enforcement officers to determine whether an automobile driver is "drunk" (Figure 14-13).

The general reaction for the oxidation of a secondary alcohol is

$$R-\underset{\underset{\boxed{H}}{|}}{\overset{\overset{\boxed{O-H}}{|}}{C}}-R \xrightarrow{[O]} R-\overset{\overset{\text{O}}{\|}}{C}-R + 2H$$

2° Alcohol   Ketone

As with primary alcohols, oxidation involves the removal of two hydrogen atoms. Unlike aldehydes, ketones are resistant to further oxidation. A specific example of the oxidation of a secondary alcohol is

$$CH_3-\underset{\boxed{OH}}{\overset{}{C}H}-CH_3 \xrightarrow{[O]} CH_3-\boxed{\overset{\overset{\text{O}}{\|}}{C}}-CH_3 + 2H$$

Tertiary alcohols do not undergo oxidation with mild oxidizing agents. This is because they do not have hydrogen on the —OH-bearing carbon atom.

$$R-\underset{\underset{\text{R}}{|}}{\overset{\overset{\text{OH}}{|}}{C}}-R \xrightarrow{[O]} \text{no reaction}$$

3° Alcohol

Damien Meyer/AFP/Getty Images

Figure 14-13 The oxidation of ethanol is the basis for the "breathalyzer test" that law enforcement officers use to determine whether an individual suspected of driving under the influence (DUI) has a blood alcohol level exceeding legal limits.

The DUI suspect is required to breathe into an apparatus containing a solution of potassium dichromate ($K_2Cr_2O_7$). The unmetabolized alcohol in the person's breath is oxidized by the dichromate ion ($Cr_2O_7^{2-}$), and the extent of the reaction gives a measure of the amount of alcohol present.

The dichromate ion is a yellow-orange color in solution. As oxidation of the alcohol proceeds, the dichromate ions are converted to Cr^{3+} ions, which have a green color in solution. The intensity of the green color that develops is measured and is proportional to the amount of ethanol in the suspect's breath, which in turn has been shown to be proportional to the person's blood alcohol level.

EXAMPLE 14-4

Predicting Products in Alcohol Oxidation Reactions

Draw the structural formula(s) for the product(s) formed by oxidation of the following alcohols with a mild oxidizing agent. If no reaction occurs, write "no reaction."

a. $CH_3-CH_2-CH_2-\underset{\overset{|}{\overset{OH}{|}}}{C}H-CH_3$ **b.** $CH_3-\underset{\underset{CH_3}{|}}{\overset{\overset{OH}{|}}{C}H}-CH_2-OH$

c. $CH_3-CH_2-\underset{\overset{|}{\overset{OH}{|}}}{C}H-CH_3$ **d.** [cyclohexane ring with OH and CH₃ on same carbon]

Solution

a. The oxidation product will be a ketone, as this is a 2° alcohol.

$$CH_3-CH_2-CH_2-\underset{\overset{|}{\overset{OH}{|}}}{C}H-CH_3 \longrightarrow CH_3-CH_2-CH_2-\overset{\overset{\text{O}}{\|}}{C}-CH_3$$

(continued)

b. A 1° alcohol undergoes oxidation first to an aldehyde and then to a carboxylic acid.

$$CH_3-\underset{\underset{CH_3}{|}}{CH}-CH_2-OH \longrightarrow CH_3-\underset{\underset{CH_3}{|}}{CH}-\overset{\overset{O}{||}}{C}-H \longrightarrow CH_3-\underset{\underset{CH_3}{|}}{CH}-\overset{\overset{O}{||}}{C}-OH$$

c. A ketone is the product from the oxidation of a 2° alcohol.

$$CH_3-CH_2-\underset{\underset{OH}{|}}{CH}-CH_3 \longrightarrow CH_3-CH_2-\overset{\overset{O}{||}}{C}-CH_3$$

d. This cyclic alcohol is a tertiary alcohol. The hydroxyl-bearing carbon atom is attached to two ring carbon atoms and a methyl group. Tertiary alcohols do not undergo oxidation with mild oxidizing agents. Therefore, "no reaction."

At the start of the discussion on oxidation of alcohols, the process of oxidation for organic molecules was defined as

1. an *increase* in the number of *carbon–oxygen* bonds present in a molecule, or
2. a *decrease* in the number of *carbon–hydrogen* bonds present in a molecule

Applying these rules to the oxidation of a 1° alcohol to an aldehyde gives the following results:

1 C—O bond

$$CH_3-CH_2\overset{\overset{OH}{\diagdown|}}{} \xrightarrow{\text{Oxidation}} CH_3-\overset{\overset{O}{\diagdown||}}{C}-H$$

1°Alcohol   Aldehyde

2 C—O bonds

The number of carbon–oxygen bonds increases, a characteristic of oxidation

5 C—H bonds

$$CH_3-CH_2\overset{\overset{OH}{\diagdown|}}{} \xrightarrow{\text{Oxidation}} CH_3-\overset{\overset{O}{||}}{C}-H$$

1° Alcohol   Aldehyde

4 C—H bonds

The number of carbon–hydrogen bonds decreases, a characteristic of oxidation

Halogenation

Alcohols undergo halogenation reactions in which a halogen atom is substituted for the hydroxyl group, producing an alkyl halide. Alkyl halide production in this manner is superior to alkyl halide production through halogenation of an alkane (Section 12-18) because mixtures of products are *not* obtained. A single product is produced in which the halogen atom is found only where the —OH group was originally located.

Several different halogen-containing reactants, including phosphorus trihalides (PX_3; X is Cl or Br), are useful in producing alkyl halides from alcohols.

$$3R-OH + PX_3 \xrightarrow{\text{heat}} 3R-X + H_3PO_3$$

Note that heating of the reactants is required.

Chemistry at a Glance—Summary of Chemical Reactions Involving Alcohols—summarizes the reaction chemistry of alcohols.

Section 14-9 Quick Quiz

1. The reaction conditions for an alcohol dehydration reaction are
  a. sulfuric acid catalyst, 180°C
  b. sulfuric acid catalyst, 0°C
  c. no catalyst needed, 180°C
  d. no correct response

2. Organic products obtained from alcohol dehydration reactions are
   a. alkenes
   b. aldehydes
   c. ethers
   d. no correct response
3. Organic products obtained from alcohol condensation reactions are
   a. alkenes
   b. aldehydes
   c. ethers
   d. no correct response
4. The organic product for the oxidation of a 2° alcohol is a(n)
   a. aldehyde
   b. ketone
   c. alkene
   d. no correct response
5. An organic oxidation process is a process that
   a. decreases the number of carbon–oxygen bonds present
   b. decreases the number of carbon–hydrogen bonds present
   c. increases the number of carbon–hydrogen bonds present
   d. no correct response
6. Zaitsev's rule is used in predicting the major product for some
   a. alcohol dehydration reactions
   b. primary alcohol oxidation reactions
   c. secondary alcohol oxidation reactions
   d. no correct response

Answers: 1. a; 2. a; 3. c; 4. b; 5. b; 6. a

CHEMISTRY AT A GLANCE Summary of Chemical Reactions Involving Alcohols

CHEMICAL REACTIONS OF ALCOHOLS

Combustion
■ O₂ (air) is required.
■ Heat and light are produced.

Alcohol ⟶ carbon dioxide + water

Halogenation
■ PCl₃ or PBr₃ are sources of halogen atoms.
■ Heat is required.

Alcohol ⟶ alkyl halide

Oxidation
■ KMnO₄ or K₂Cr₂O₇ are common oxidizing agents.

1° alcohol ⟶ aldehyde ⟶ carboxylic acid
2° alcohol ⟶ ketone
3° alcohol ⟶ no reaction

Dehydration
■ H₂SO₄ catalyst required
■ 180°C temperature

1° alcohol ⟶ alkene
2° alcohol ⟶ alkene
3° alcohol ⟶ alkene

Condensation
■ H₂SO₄ catalyst required
■ 140°C temperature

1° alcohol ⟶ ether

PREPARATION OF ALCOHOLS

Alkene Hydration
■ H₂SO₄ catalyst required
■ H₂O required

Alkene ⟶ alcohol

14-10 Structural Characteristics of Phenols

LEARNING FOCUS
Know the structural characteristic that distinguishes phenols from alcohols.

A **phenol** *is an organic compound in which an —OH group is attached to a carbon atom that is part of an aromatic carbon ring system.*

Aromatic ring system → OH ← Hydroxyl functional group

The general formula for phenols is Ar–OH, where Ar represents an *aryl group.* ◀
An **aryl group** *is an aromatic carbon ring system from which one hydrogen atom has been removed.*

> ▶ *The generic term* aryl group *(Ar) is the aromatic counterpart of the nonaromatic generic term* alkyl group *(R).*

> ▶ *A phenol is not considered to be an alcohol even though a hydroxyl group is present because the benzene ring significantly alters the reaction properties of the hydroxyl group.*

The reaction chemistry for phenols is sufficiently different from that for nonaromatic alcohols (Section 14-9) to justify discussing these compounds separately. Remember that phenols contain a "benzene ring" and that the chemistry of benzene is much different from that of other unsaturated hydrocarbons (Section 13-14). ◀

The following are examples of compounds classified as phenols.

Section 14-10 Quick Quiz

1. The structural characteristic for a phenol is a hydroxyl group attached to a(n)
   a. alkyl group
   b. cycloalkyl group
   c. benzene ring
   d. no correct response
2. The generalized formula for a phenol is
   a. R—OH
   b. Ar—OH
   c. R_2—OH
   d. no correct response

Answers: 1. c; 2. b

14-11 Nomenclature for Phenols

LEARNING FOCUS
Given structural formulas, be able to name phenols using IUPAC nomenclature or vice versa; know the common names for selected phenols.

Besides being the name for a family of compounds, *phenol* is also the IUPAC-approved name for the simplest member of the phenol family of compounds.

Phenol

A space-filling model for the compound *phenol* is shown in Figure 14-14. The name *phenol* is derived from a combination of the terms *phenyl* and alcoh*ol*.

The IUPAC rules for naming phenols are simply extensions of the rules used to name benzene derivatives with hydrocarbon or halogen substituents (Section 13-12). The parent name is phenol. Ring numbering always begins with the hydroxyl group and proceeds in the direction that gives the lower number to the next carbon atom bearing a substituent. The numerical position of the hydroxyl group is not specified in the name because it is 1 by definition.

Figure 14-14 A space-filling model for *phenol*, a compound that has an —OH group bonded directly to a benzene (aromatic) ring.

3-Chlorophenol
(or *meta*-Chlorophenol)

4-Ethyl-2-methylphenol

2,5-Dibromophenol

Methyl and hydroxy derivatives of phenol have IUPAC-accepted common names. Methylphenols are called cresols. The name *cresol* applies to all three isomeric methylphenols.

ortho-Cresol

meta-Cresol

para-Cresol

For hydroxyphenols, each of the three isomers has a different common name.

Catechol ◄

Resorcinol

Hydroquinone

▶ *Several neurotransmitters in the human body (Section 17-10), including norepinephrine, epinephrine (adrenaline), and dopamine, are catechol derivatives.*

Section 14-11 Quick Quiz

1. Which of the following is an *incorrect* statement concerning the structure of the compound phenol?
   a. A benzene ring is part of the structure.
   b. A hydroxyl group is part of the structure.
   c. A methyl group is part of the structure.
   d. no correct response
2. In IUPAC nomenclature for phenol derivatives, ring numbering always begins with the
   a. hydroxyl group and proceeds clockwise
   b. hydroxyl group and proceeds toward the closest additional substituent
   c. substituent of highest alphabetical priority
   d. no correct response
3. Methyl derivatives of phenol are called
   a. cresols
   b. hydroquinones
   c. catechols
   d. no correct response

Answers: 1. c; 2. b; 3. a

14-12 Physical and Chemical Properties of Phenols

LEARNING FOCUS

Be familiar with general physical and chemical properties of phenols.

Phenols are generally low-melting solids or oily liquids at room temperature. Most of them are only slightly soluble in water. Many phenols have antiseptic and disinfectant properties. The simplest phenol, phenol itself, is a colorless solid with a medicinal odor. Its melting point is 41°C, and it is more soluble in water than are most other phenols.

It has been previously noted that the chemical properties of phenols are significantly different from those of alcohols (Section 14-10). The similarities and differences between these two reaction chemistries are as follows:

1. Both alcohols and phenols are flammable.
2. Dehydration is a reaction of alcohols but not of phenols; phenols cannot be dehydrated.
3. Both 1° and 2° alcohols are oxidized by mild oxidizing agents. Tertiary (3°) alcohols do not react with the oxidizing agents that cause 1° and 2° alcohol oxidation. Phenols, although readily oxidized, do not undergo oxidation in the same way alcohols do because the hydroxyl-bearing carbon atom is (1) part of an aromatic ring system and (2) does not have any hydrogen atoms bonded to it. ◀
4. Both alcohols and phenols undergo halogenation in which the hydroxyl group is replaced by a halogen atom in a substitution reaction.

▶ *Oxidation of phenol produces the compound p-benzoquinone (common name quinone).*

Phenol   p-Benzoquinone

Acidity of Phenols

One of the most important properties of phenols is their acidity. Unlike alcohols, phenols are weak acids in solution. As acids, phenols have K_a values (Section 10-5) of about 10^{-10}. Such K_a values are lower than those of most weak inorganic acids (10^{-5} to 10^{-10}). The acid ionization reaction for phenol itself is

Phenol   Phenoxide ion

Note that the negative ion produced from the ionization is called the phenoxide ion. When phenol itself is reacted with sodium hydroxide (a base), the salt sodium phenoxide is produced.

Phenol   Sodium phenoxide

Section 14-12 Quick Quiz

1. Which of the following statements concerning properties of phenols is *incorrect*?
   a. They are generally low-melting solids or oily liquids.
   b. They do not undergo oxidation reactions.
   c. They are generally only slightly soluble in water.
   d. no correct response
2. Which of the following statements concerning the behavior of phenol in aqueous solution is correct?
   a. A small amount of phenoxide ion is produced.
   b. A large amount of phenoxide ion is produced.
   c. Phenol's behavior is that of a strong acid.
   d. no correct response

Answers: 1. b; 2. a

14-13 Occurrence of and Uses for Phenols

LEARNING FOCUS

Be familiar with the use of phenolic compounds as antioxidants, antibacterials, and flavoring agents.

Dilute (2%) solutions of phenol have long been used as antiseptics. Concentrated phenol solutions, however, can cause severe skin burns. Today, phenol has been largely replaced by more effective phenol derivatives such as 4-hexylresorcinol for antiseptic use. The compound 4-hexylresorcinol is an ingredient in many mouthwashes and throat lozenges.

4-Hexylresorcinol ◄

The phenol derivatives *o*-phenylphenol and 2-benzyl-4-chlorophenol are the active ingredients in Lysol, a disinfectant for walls, floors, and furniture in homes and hospitals. ◄

o-Phenylphenol   2-Benzyl-4-chlorophenol

▶ *The "parent" name for a benzene ring bearing two hydroxyl groups "meta" to each other is resorcinol (Section 14-12).*

▶ *An* antiseptic *is a substance that kills microorganisms on living tissue. A* disinfectant *is a substance that kills microorganisms on inanimate objects.*

A number of phenols possess antioxidant activity. An **antioxidant** *is a substance that protects other substances from being oxidized by being oxidized itself in preference to the other substances.* An antioxidant has a greater affinity for a particular oxidizing agent than do the substances the antioxidant is "protecting"; the antioxidant therefore reacts with the oxidizing agent first. ◄ Many foods sensitive to air are protected from oxidation through the use of phenolic antioxidants. Two commercial phenolic antioxidant food additives are BHA (butylated hydroxyanisole) and BHT (butylated hydroxytoluene) (Figure 14-15).

▶ *Within the human body, natural dietary antioxidants also offer protection against undesirable oxidizing agents. They include vitamin C (Section 21-12), β-carotene (Section 21-13), vitamin E (Section 21-14), and flavonoids (Section 23-11).*

BHA (2 isomers)

BHT

Figure 14-15 Many commercially baked goods contain the antioxidants BHA and BHT to help prevent spoilage.

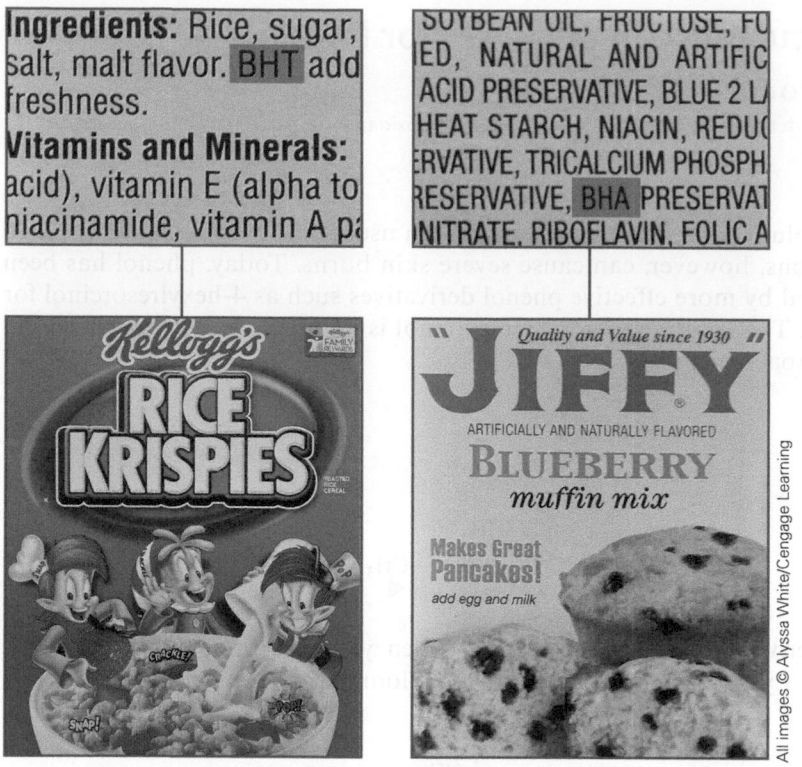

Ingredients: Rice, sugar, salt, malt flavor. BHT add freshness.

Vitamins and Minerals: acid), vitamin E (alpha to niacinamide, vitamin A p

SOYBEAN OIL, FRUCTOSE, FO ED, NATURAL AND ARTIFIC ACID PRESERVATIVE, BLUE 2 L HEAT STARCH, NIACIN, REDUC RVATIVE, TRICALCIUM PHOSPH RESERVATIVE, BHA PRESERVAT NITRATE, RIBOFLAVIN, FOLIC A

A naturally occurring phenolic antioxidant that is important in the functioning of the human body is vitamin E (Section 21-14).

Vitamin E

A number of phenols found in plants are used as flavoring agents and/or antibacterials. Included among these phenols are

Thymol

Eugenol

Isoeugenol

Vanillin

Thymol, obtained from the herb thyme, possesses both flavorant and antibacterial properties. It is used as an ingredient in several mouthwash formulations.

Eugenol is responsible for the flavor of cloves. Dentists traditionally used clove oil as an antiseptic because of eugenol's presence; they use it to a limited extent even today.

Isoeugenol, which differs in structure from eugenol only in the location of the double bond in the hydrocarbon side chain, is responsible for the odor associated with nutmeg (Figure 14-16).

Vanillin, which gives vanilla its flavor, is extracted from the dried seed pods of the vanilla orchid. Natural supplies of vanillin are inadequate to meet demand for this flavoring agent. Synthetic vanillin is produced by oxidation of eugenol. Vanillin is an unusual substance in that even though its odor can be perceived at extremely low concentrations, the strength of its odor does not increase greatly as its concentration is increased.

Certain phenols exert profound physiological effects. For example, the irritating constituents of poison ivy and poison oak are derivatives of catechol (Section 14-11). These skin irritants have 15-carbon alkyl side chains with varying degrees of unsaturation (zero to three double bonds).

Catechol

Poison ivy irritants

A diisopropyl phenol, propofol, has several medical uses. ◀

Polyphenols

A **polyphenol** *is a compound in which two or more phenol entities are present within the compound's structure.* One of the simplest types of polyphenols is that in which two phenol entities are connected via a short carbon chain.

Large numbers of naturally occurring polyphenols are found within the plant world, including those plants, fruits, and vegetables that are used by humans as a source of food. Generally these dietary polyphenols have more complicated structures than that of the preceding example and they exhibit antioxidant properties to varying degrees.

For a typical adult diet in the United States, daily ingestion of dietary polyphenols from plant sources is estimated to be in the range of 200 mg to 1000 mg (1 gram). This is a larger dietary intake than is the intake of the well-studied vitamin dietary antioxidants (β-carotene, vitamin C, and vitamin E), which is about 100 mg a day.

The role that polyphenol antioxidants play in human body chemistry is an area of active research. It is a challenging area of research in which the answers to the questions being posed do not come easily. Any given plant food contains dozens, even hundreds, of different antioxidant compounds, not all of which are polyphenols.

One of the most studied of the many polyphenol antioxidants is the compound resveratrol, a substance that is found in grapes and wines made from the grapes. It is commonly linked to a situation called the "French Paradox." The focus on relevancy feature Chemical Connections 14-B—Red Wine and Resveratrol—gives current research findings relative to resveratrol and the associated "French Paradox."

Figure 14-16 Nutmeg tree fruit. A phenolic compound, isoeugenol, is responsible for the odor associated with nutmeg.

▶ *A diisopropyl phenol, with the medical name* Propofol, *is a short-acting intravenous agent used for the induction of general anesthesia and for sedation in several current medical contexts.*

Propofol
(2,6-diisopropylphenol)

It is extensively used in medical contexts such as intensive care unit (ICU) sedation for intubated, mechanically ventilated adults and in procedures such as a colonoscopy. It provides no analgesia (pain relief).

Section 14-13 Quick Quiz

1. Which of the following is *not* an important use area for phenol derivatives?
   a. antiseptics
   b. antioxidants
   c. flavoring agents
   d. no correct response
2. An antioxidant is a compound that
   a. cannot be oxidized
   b. is readily oxidized
   c. cannot be used as a food additive
   d. no correct response
3. One of the most studied naturally occurring polyphenol antioxidants is the compound
   a. BHT
   b. resveratrol
   c. vanillin
   d. no correct response

Answers: 1. d; 2. b; 3. b

Red Wine and Resveratrol

The "French Paradox" is a name associated with a study indicating that people in France were less likely to die of heart attacks than people living in the United States, despite both groups having similar high levels of saturated fats in their diets. A proposed explanation for this "paradox" was the idea that regular moderate consumption of red wine with meals (a common French, but not American, tradition) provides some type of added protection from cardiovascular disease.

This idea that red wine consumption has cardiovascular health benefits has spawned numerous investigational studies concerning what compounds might be present in red wine that produce such benefits. From such studies, one particular compound whose presence in red wine was discovered in 1992 has garnered much attention. It is the compound resveratrol.

Resveratrol (pronounced "ress-ver-a-trole") is an antioxidant compound produced by some plants, including grapes, to protect themselves against environmental stresses such as fungal diseases and sun damage. It is a polyphenol derivative of the aromatic hydrocarbon stilbene.

Stilbene

Resveratrol

Because of the double bond present in the carbon chain connecting the two benzene (phenol) centers, *cis*- and *trans*- isomers exist for both stilbene and resveratrol. It is the *trans*- isomer of resveratrol that is produced in plants.

Resveratrol is found in grapes, grape juice, berries of the *vaccinum* species (which includes blueberries and cranberries), and peanuts. Grapes contain the highest levels of resveratrol, where it is concentrated in the skin of the grapes. Red wines contain more resveratrol than white wines because red wine is fermented with grape skins, allowing the wine to absorb the resveratrol, whereas white wine is fermented after the grape skins have been removed. On an ounce-for-ounce basis, peanuts have levels of resveratrol about half those in red wine. Blueberries and cranberries contain much smaller amounts of the substance.

trans-Resveratrol   *cis*-Resveratrol

Almost all research conducted to date on resveratrol has been done on animals and not humans. Research involving mice given resveratrol shows a positive correlation with reduced risk of inflammation and blood clotting, as well as a protective effect against obesity and diabetes. Of importance, the dose of resveratrol used in the mice studies would be equivalent to people consuming more than 100 bottles of wine a day. Resveratrol administration has also increased the life spans of yeast, worms, fruit flies, fish, and mice that were fed a high-calorie diet. Whether such effects would be observed in humans is not yet known.

Resveratrol supplements are now available in the United States. Their source varies from extracts of the plant kojo-kon to red wine extracts and red grape extracts. The effectiveness and safety of the supplements is not well established. It is known that throat lozenges are the most effective way of administering resveratrol to humans. About 70% of an orally given resveratrol dose is absorbed; however, oral bioavailability is low because the absorbed resveratrol is rapidly metabolized in the intestine and liver. The oral availability of resveratrol from wine has been found to be no higher than that from a pill.

Resveratrol concentration levels found in the human body as the result of moderate drinking of red wine do not appear to be sufficiently high to explain the observations associated with the "French Paradox."

14-14 Structural Characteristics of Ethers

LEARNING FOCUS

Characterize ethers in terms of general structural properties and functional group identity.

An **ether** *is an organic compound in which an oxygen atom is bonded to two carbon atoms by single bonds.* In an ether, the carbon atoms that are attached to the oxygen atom can be part of alkyl, cycloalkyl, or aryl groups. Examples of ethers include

CH_3-O-CH_3 CH_3-CH_2-O-⬠ CH_3-O-⬡

The two groups attached to the oxygen atom of an ether can be the same (first structure), but they need not be so (second and third structures).

All ethers contain a C—O—C unit, which is the ether functional group.

Ether functional group

$$\text{---}\overset{\frown}{C}\text{---}O\text{---}C\text{---}$$

Generalized formulas for ethers, which depend on the types of groups attached to the oxygen atom (alkyl or aryl), include R—O—R, R—O—R′ (where R′ is an alkyl group different from R), R—O—Ar, and Ar—O—Ar.

Structurally, an ether can be visualized as a derivative of water in which both hydrogen atoms have been replaced by hydrocarbon groups (Figure 14-17). Note that unlike alcohols and phenols, ethers do not possess a hydroxyl (—OH) group.

$$H\text{---}\overset{..}{\underset{..}{O}}\text{---}H \qquad R\text{---}\overset{..}{\underset{..}{O}}\text{---}R$$

Water   An ether

Water (H–O–H)

Two-carbon ether (CH₃–O–CH₃)

Figure 14-17 A comparison of the molecular shapes of water and the ether with two methyl groups (the simplest ether). The simplest ether may be viewed structurally as a dialkyl derivative of water.

Section 14-14 Quick Quiz

1. Structurally, ethers may be viewed as derivatives of water in which
   a. both hydrogen atoms have been replaced with hydrocarbon groups
   b. both hydrogen atoms have been replaced with hydroxyl groups
   c. one hydrogen has been replaced with a hydrocarbon group
   d. no correct response
2. The number of hydroxyl groups present in an ether is
   a. zero
   b. one
   c. two
   d. no correct response
3. Which of the following is the ether functional group?
   a. —O—O—C—
   b. —C—O—C—
   c. —C—O—H
   d. no correct response

Answers: 1. a; 2. a; 3. b

14-15 Nomenclature for Ethers

LEARNING FOCUS

Given their structural formulas, be able to name ethers using IUPAC rules or vice versa; be able to assign common names to ethers with simple alkyl groups.

Common names are almost always used for ethers whose alkyl groups contain four or fewer carbon atoms. There are two rules, one for unsymmetrical ethers (two different alkyl/aryl groups) and one for symmetrical ethers (two identical alkyl/aryl groups).

Rule 1: *For unsymmetrical ethers, name both hydrocarbon groups bonded to the oxygen atom in alphabetical order and add the word* ether, *separating the words with a space. Such ether names have three separate words within them.*

$$CH_3\text{---}O\text{---}CH_2\text{---}CH_3 \qquad CH_3\text{---}CH_2\text{---}O\text{---}\bigcirc$$

Ethyl methyl ether   Ethyl phenyl ether

Rule 2: *For symmetrical ethers, name the alkyl group, add the prefix* di-, *and then add the word* ether, *separating the words with a space. Such ether names have two separate words within them.* ◄

$$CH_3\text{---}O\text{---}CH_3 \qquad CH_3\text{---}CH_2\text{---}O\text{---}CH_2\text{---}CH_3$$

Dimethyl ether   Diethyl ether

► *Line-angle structural formulas for selected simple ethers:*

Ethyl methyl ether

Diethyl ether

Dipropyl ether

Ethers with more complex alkyl/aryl groups are named using the IUPAC system. In this system, ethers are named as substituted hydrocarbons. The smaller hydrocarbon attachment and the oxygen atom are called an *alkoxy group,* and this group is considered a substituent on the larger hydrocarbon group. An **alkoxy group** *is an —OR group, an alkyl group attached to an oxygen atom.* Simple alkoxy groups include the following:

$$CH_3—O— \qquad CH_3—CH_2—O— \qquad CH_3—CH_2—CH_2—O—$$
Methoxy group \qquad Ethoxy group \qquad Propoxy group

The general symbol for an alkoxy group is R—O— (or RO—).

The rules for naming an ether using the IUPAC system are

Rule 1: *Select the longest carbon chain and use its name as the base name.*

Rule 2: *Change the -yl ending of the other hydrocarbon group to -oxy to obtain the alkoxy group name;* methyl *becomes* methoxy, ethyl *becomes* ethoxy, *etc.*

Rule 3: *Place the alkoxy name, with a locator number, in front of the base chain name.* ◄

Two examples of IUPAC ether nomenclature, with the alkoxy groups present highlighted in each structure, are:

$$\boxed{CH_3—O}—CH_2—CH_2—CH_2—CH_3$$
1-Methoxybutane

$$CH_3—CH—CH_2—\boxed{O—CH_2—CH_3}$$
$$\qquad\quad |$$
$$\qquad\quad CH_3$$
1-Ethoxy-2-methylpropane

The simplest aromatic ether involves a methoxy group attached to a benzene ring. The IUPAC name for this ether is *methoxybenzene* and it has two frequently encountered common names, *anisole* and *methyl phenyl ether.*

Methoxybenzene
(anisole, methyl phenyl ether)

Common names for methoxybenzene derivatives using anisole as the base name are structured in a manner similar to that used for substituted phenols (Section 14-11); the carbon atom to which the methoxy group is attached is always carbon 1 and other attachments are located relative to it.

3-Ethylanisole

The IUPAC name for the preceding compound is *1-ethyl-3-methoxybenzene;* alphabetical priority is used in determining the ring numbering system. Anisole derivatives were encountered in Section 14-13 when considering antioxidant food additives: BHAs can be viewed as derivatives of either phenol or anisole. ◄

► *It is possible to have compounds that contain both ether and alcohol functional groups such as*

$$CH_3—CH—CH_2—CH_2—O—CH_3$$
$$\qquad |$$
$$\qquad OH$$
4-Methoxy-2-butanol

(The alcohol functional group has higher priority in IUPAC nomenclature, so the compound is named as an alcohol rather than as an ether.)

► *The compound responsible for the characteristic odor of anise and fennel is* anethole, *an allyl derivative of anisole.*

► *The contrast between IUPAC and common names for ethers is as follows:*

IUPAC (one word)
alkoxyalkane
2-methoxybutane
Common (three or two words)
alkyl alkyl ether
ethyl methyl ether
or
dialkyl ether
dipropyl ether

EXAMPLE 14-5

Determining IUPAC Names for Ethers ◄

Name the following ethers utilizing IUPAC nomenclature rules.

a. $CH_3—CH_2—O—CH_2—CH_2—CH_3$ \qquad **b.** $CH_3—O—CH—CH_2—CH_3$
$$\qquad\qquad\qquad\qquad\qquad\qquad\qquad\qquad\qquad\qquad |$$
$$\qquad\qquad\qquad\qquad\qquad\qquad\qquad\qquad\qquad\qquad CH_3$$

c. $CH_3—O—\bigcirc$ \qquad **d.** Ethyl methyl ether

Solution

a. The base name is propane. An ethoxy group is attached to carbon-1 of the propane chain.

$$CH_3—CH_2—O⌉CH_2—CH_2—CH_3⌋$$
$$\quad\quad\quad\quad\quad ① \quad\quad ② \quad\quad ③$$

The IUPAC name is 1-ethoxypropane.

b. The base name is butane, as the longest carbon chain contains four carbon atoms.

$$CH_3—O⌉CH—CH_2—CH_3⌋$$
$$\quad\quad\quad\quad ② \quad ③ \quad\quad ④$$
$$\quad\quad\quad\quad ① \; CH_3$$

The IUPAC name is 2-methoxybutane.

c. The base name is cyclohexane. The complete IUPAC name is methoxycyclohexane. No number is needed to locate the methoxy group since all ring carbon atoms are equivalent to each other.

d. The ether structure is $CH_3—CH_2—O—CH_3$, and the IUPAC name is methoxyethane.

Section 14-15 Quick Quiz

1. What is the IUPAC name for the ether whose common name is ethyl propyl ether?
   a. 1-ethoxypropane
   b. 2-ethoxypropane
   c. 1-propoxyethane
   d. no correct response
2. What is the common name for the ether whose IUPAC name is ethoxyethane?
   a. dimethyl ether
   b. methyl ethyl ether
   c. diethyl ether
   d. no correct response
3. What is the IUPAC name for the compound $CH_3—CH—CH_2—O—CH_2—CH_3$
   a. ethoxymethylpropane $\qquad\qquad\qquad\quad |$
   b. 1-ethoxy-2-methylpropane $\qquad\qquad\quad CH_3$
   c. ethyl isobutyl ether
   d. no correct response
4. Which of the following is an *incorrect* statement concerning the structure of the compound anisole?
   a. A benzene ring is part of the structure.
   b. A methyl group is part of the structure.
   c. A methoxy group is part of the structure.
   d. no correct response

Answers: 1. a; 2. c; 3. b; 4. b

14-16 Occurrence of and Uses for Ethers

LEARNING FOCUS

Be familiar with common uses for selected ethers.

The synthetic ether MTBE (methyl *tert*-butyl ether) was a widely used gasoline additive in the United States during the 1980s and 1990s.

$$\begin{array}{c} CH_3 \\ | \\ CH_3—O—C—CH_3 \\ | \\ CH_3 \end{array}$$

Methyl *tert*-butyl ether
(MTBE) ◄

▶ *Technically, the name methyl* tert-*butyl ether (MTBE) is incorrect because the convention for naming ethers dictates an alphabetical ordering of alkyl groups (*tert-*butyl methyl ether). However, the compound is called MTBE rather than TBME by those in the petroleum industry and by environmental scientists.*

As an additive, MTBE not only raised octane levels but also functioned as a clean-burning "oxygenate" in EPA-mandated reformulated gasolines used to improve air quality in areas that did not meet EPA air pollution criteria.

MTBE gasoline additive use in the United States has now been discontinued, with ethanol being the primary replacement. Discontinuance was the response to a growing environmental problem: contamination of water supplies by small amounts of MTBE from leaking gasoline tanks and from spills. MTBE in water supplies was not a health-and-safety issue but its presence did affect taste and odor in contaminated supplies. MTBE use as a gasoline additive still continues in many other parts of the world, including China.

Naturally occurring ethers are found throughout the plant world. Several such ethers have been previously mentioned: eugenol, isoeugenol, and vanillin (which are also phenols; Section 14-13) and allyl anisole (Section 14-15).

Use of ethers as anesthetics is a vital part of current medical practice. Ethers presently in use are halogenated, rather than nonhalogenated ethers. It has been found that introduction of halogen atoms into an ether reduces or eliminates its flammability. Many polyhalogenated ethers are nonflammable. The focus on relevancy feature Chemical Connections 14-C—Ethers as General Anesthetics—considers the use of ethers, from early nonhalogenated forms to current polyhalogenated forms, as anesthetics. Several ethers have antibacterial properties. ◀

▶ *Most hand sanitizers contain ethanol as the active ingredient (60%–85% by volume). The active antibacterial ingredient in "alcohol free" sanitizers is the complex ether* triclosan, *a molecule that contains aromatic, ether, and phenol functional groups.*

Triclosan

Section 14-16 Quick Quiz

1. During the period 1980–2000 the ether MTBE was used extensively as a(n)
   a. flavoring agent
   b. gasoline additive
   c. anesthetic
   d. no correct response
2. Introduction of halogen atoms into an ether
   a. decreases its flammability
   b. increases its flammability
   c. causes no change in its flammability
   d. no correct response

Answers: 1. b; 2. a

14-17 Isomerism for Ethers

LEARNING FOCUS

Be able to draw and recognize structural formulas for ether constitutional isomers; be familiar with the concept of *functional group* isomerism and how it relates to ethers and alcohols.

Ethers contain two carbon chains (two alkyl groups), unlike the one carbon chain found in alcohols. Constitutional isomerism possibilities in ethers depend on (1) the partitioning of carbon atoms between the two alkyl groups and (2) isomerism possibilities for the individual alkyl groups present. Only one C_2 ether (two methyl groups) exists and only one C_3 ether (an ethyl and a methyl group) exists. For C_4 ethers, isomerism arises not only from carbon-atom partitioning between the alkyl groups (C_1—C_3 and C_2—C_2) but also from isomerism within a C_3 group (propyl and isopropyl). There are three C_4 ether constitutional isomers.

$$CH_3-CH_2-O-CH_2-CH_3 \qquad CH_3-O-CH_2-CH_2-CH_3 \qquad CH_3-O-\underset{\underset{CH_3}{|}}{CH}-CH_3$$

Diethyl ether (C_2-C_2)

Methyl propyl ether (C_1-C_3)

Isopropyl methyl ether (C_1-C_3)

For C_5 ethers, carbon-partitioning possibilities are C_2—C_3 and C_1—C_4. For C_4 groups, there are four isomeric variations: butyl, isobutyl, *sec*-butyl, and *tert*-butyl (Section 12-11).

CHEMICAL CONNECTIONS 14-C

Ethers as General Anesthetics

For many people, the word *ether* evokes thoughts of hospital operating rooms and anesthesia. This response derives from the *former* large-scale use of diethyl ether as a general anesthetic. In 1846, the Boston dentist William Morton was the first to demonstrate publicly the use of diethyl ether as a surgical anesthetic.

In many ways, diethyl ether is an ideal general anesthetic. It is relatively easy to administer, it is readily made in pure form, and it causes excellent muscle relaxation. There is less danger of an overdose with diethyl ether than with almost any other anesthetic because there is a large gap between the effective level for anesthesia and the lethal dose.

Despite these ideal properties, diethyl ether is rarely used today because of two drawbacks: (1) It causes nausea and irritation of the respiratory passages and (2) it is a highly flammable substance, forming explosive mixtures with air, which can be set off by a spark.

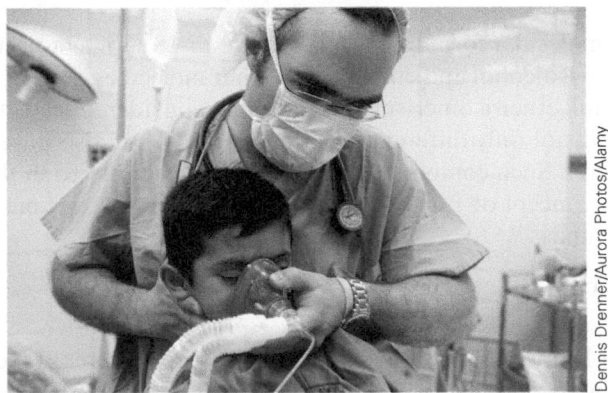

Preparing to administer an anesthetic to a child.

By the 1930s, non-ether anesthetics had been developed that solved the problems of nausea and irritation. They also, however, were extremely flammable compounds. The simple hydrocarbon cyclopropane was the most widely used of these newer compounds.

It was not until the late 1950s and early 1960s that non-flammable general anesthetics became available. Anesthetic nonflammability was achieved by incorporating halogen atoms into anesthetic molecules. Three of the most used of these "halogenated" anesthetics were enflurane, isoflurane, and halothane.

Enflurane and isoflurane, which are constitutional isomers, are hexahalogenated ethers.

Enflurane   Isoflurane

With these compounds, induction of anesthesia can be achieved in less than 10 minutes with an inhaled concentration of 3% in oxygen.

Halothane, which is potent at relatively low doses and whose effects wear off quickly, is a pentahalogenated alkane derivative rather than an ether.

Halothane

It is the only inhalation anesthetic that contains a bromine atom.

Phase-out of the use of the preceding three compounds began in the late 1980s and early 1990s. They have largely been replaced by a "second generation" of similar halogenated ethers with even better anesthetic properties. In general, these new compounds have more fluorine atoms and fewer chlorine atoms. Two of the most prominent of these second-generation anesthetic agents now in use are sevoflurane and desflurane.

Sevoflurane   Desflurane

Functional Group Isomerism

Ethers and alcohols with the same number of carbon atoms and the same degree of saturation have the same molecular formula. The simplest manifestation of this phenomenon involves dimethyl ether, the C_2 ether, and ethyl alcohol, the C_2 alcohol. Both have the molecular formula C_2H_6O.

$$CH_3{-}O{-}CH_3 \qquad CH_3{-}CH_2{-}OH$$
Dimethyl ether   Ethyl alcohol

Figure 14-18 Alcohols and ethers with the same number of carbon atoms and the same degree of saturation are functional group isomers, as is illustrated here for propyl alcohol and ethyl methyl ether.

Propyl alcohol (C_3H_8O)   **Ethyl methyl ether (C_3H_8O)**

▶ *Functional group isomerism is the third constitutional isomerism subtype to be considered. The other two subtypes—skeletal and positional—were encountered in Section 13-5.*

With the same molecular formula and different structural formulas, these two compounds are constitutional isomers. This type of constitutional isomerism is the subtype called *functional group isomerism* ◀. **Functional group isomers** *are constitutional isomers that contain different functional groups.* When three carbon atoms are present, the ether–alcohol functional group isomerism possibilities are

$$CH_3-CH_2-O-CH_3 \qquad CH_3-CH_2-CH_2-OH \qquad CH_3-CH-OH$$

Ethyl methyl ether   Propyl alcohol |
                                                               CH_3

Isopropyl alcohol

▶ *Later in this chapter (Section 14-21) and in each of the next two chapters, other pairs of functional groups for which functional group isomerism is possible will be encountered.*

All three compounds have the molecular formula C_3H_8O. Figure 14-18 shows molecular models for the isomeric propyl alcohol and ethyl methyl ether molecules. ◀

An extension of the alcohol–ether isomerism situation just considered leads to isomeric compounds containing not only different functional groups but also different numbers of functional groups. Such compounds were actually encountered in the previous chapter although the concept of functional group isomerism was not mentioned at that time. The compounds

$$CH_2=CH-CH_2-CH=CH_2 \qquad and \qquad CH_3-C\equiv C-CH_2-CH_3$$

1,4-pentadiene   2-pentyne

which both have the molecular formula C_5H_8, are isomers that involve different kinds of functional groups, double bond versus triple bond, and also different numbers of functional groups, two versus one.

An even simpler example of isomerism relating to functional groups involves the compounds

$$CH_2=CH-CH_2-CH_3 \qquad and \qquad \begin{array}{c} H_2C-CH_2 \\ | \quad\quad | \\ H_2C-CH_2 \end{array}$$

2-butene   cyclobutane

Both have the molecular formula C_4H_8. A functional group is present in the first compound, the double bond and the second compound lacks a functional group.

Section 14-17 Quick Quiz

1. How many C_4 isomeric ethers exist?
   a. two
   b. three
   c. four
   d. no correct response
2. How many isomeric ethers exist that contain C_2 and C_4 alkyl groups?
   a. three
   b. four
   c. five
   d. no correct response

3. Which of the following is a functional group isomer of ethyl methyl ether?
   a. dimethyl ether
   b. ethyl alcohol
   c. propyl alcohol
   d. no correct response

Answers: 1. b; 2. b; 3. c

14-18 Physical and Chemical Properties of Ethers

LEARNING FOCUS

Be familiar with general physical and chemical properties of ethers.

The boiling points of ethers are similar to those of alkanes of comparable molecular mass and are much lower than those of alcohols of comparable molecular mass.

Alkane $CH_3—CH_2—CH_2—CH_2—CH_3$ Mol. mass = 72 amu
   bp = 36°C

Ether $CH_3—CH_2—O—CH_2—CH_3$ Mol. mass = 74 amu
   bp = 35°C

Alcohol $CH_3—CH_2—CH_2—CH_2—OH$ Mol. mass = 74 amu
   bp = 117°C

The much higher boiling point of the alcohol results from hydrogen bonding between alcohol molecules. Ether molecules, like alkanes, cannot hydrogen-bond to one another. Ether oxygen atoms have no hydrogen atom attached directly to them. Figure 14-19 is a physical-state summary for unbranched alkyl alkyl ethers where the alkyl groups range in size from C_1 to C_4.

Ethers, in general, are more soluble in water than are alkanes of similar molecular mass because ether molecules are able to form hydrogen bonds with water (Figure 14-20).

Ethers have water solubilities similar to those of alcohols of the same molecular mass. For example, diethyl ether and butyl alcohol have the same solubility in water. Because ethers can also hydrogen-bond to alcohols, alcohols and ethers tend to be mutually soluble. Nonpolar substances tend to be more soluble in ethers than in alcohols because ethers have no hydrogen-bonding network that has to be broken up for solubility to occur.

Two chemical properties of ethers are especially important.

1. *Ethers are flammable.* Special care must be exercised in laboratories where ethers are used. Diethyl ether, whose boiling point of 35°C is only a few degrees above room temperature, is a particular flash-fire hazard.
2. *Ethers react slowly with oxygen from the air to form unstable hydroperoxides and peroxides.*

     $R—O—O—H$ $R—O—O—R$
     Hydroperoxide   Peroxide

Such compounds, when concentrated, represent an explosion hazard and must be removed before *stored* ethers are used.

Like alkanes, ethers are unreactive toward acids, bases, and oxidizing agents. Like alkanes, they do undergo combustion and halogenation reactions. ◄

The general chemical unreactivity of ethers, coupled with the fact that most organic compounds are ether soluble, makes ethers excellent solvents in which to carry out organic reactions. Their relatively low boiling points simplify their separation from the reaction products.

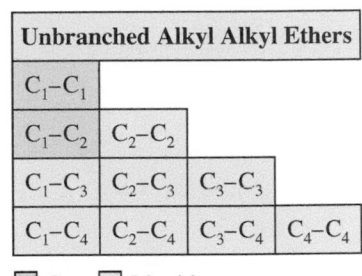

Unbranched Alkyl Alkyl Ethers			
C_1–C_1			
C_1–C_2	C_2–C_2		
C_1–C_3	C_2–C_3	C_3–C_3	
C_1–C_4	C_2–C_4	C_3–C_4	C_4–C_4

☐ Gas ☐ Liquid

Figure 14-19 A physical-state summary for unbranched alkyl alkyl ethers at room temperature and pressure.

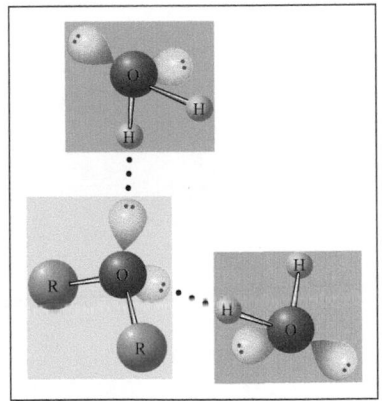

Figure 14-20 Although ether molecules cannot hydrogen-bond to one another, they can hydrogen-bond to water molecules. Such hydrogen bonding causes ethers to be more soluble in water than alkanes of similar molecular mass.

► *The term* ether *comes from the Latin* aether, *which means "to ignite." This name is given to these compounds because of their high vapor pressure at room temperature, which makes them very flammable.*

A chemical reaction for the preparation of ethers has been previously considered. In Section 14-9 it was noted that a condensation reaction involving a primary alcohol will produce an ether.

$$R_1\text{—OH} + R_2\text{—OH} \xrightarrow[\text{Heat}]{H^+} R_1\text{—O—}R_2 + H_2O$$

Alcohol   Alcohol   Ether   Water

Although additional methods exist for ether preparation, they will not be considered in this text.

14-19 Cyclic Ethers

LEARNING FOCUS
Know the structural characteristics associated with a cyclic ether.

Cyclic ethers contain ether functional groups as part of a ring system. Some examples of such cyclic ethers, along with their common names, follow.

Ethylene oxide   Tetrahydrofuran (THF)   Furan   Pyran

Ethylene oxide has few direct uses. Its importance is as a starting material for the production of ethylene glycol (Section 14-5), a major component of automobile antifreeze. THF is a particularly useful solvent in that it dissolves many organic compounds and yet is miscible with water. In the chapter on carbohydrate chemistry (Chapter 18), many cyclic structures that are polyhydroxy derivatives of the five-membered (furan) and six-membered (pyran) cyclic ether systems will be encountered. These carbohydrate derivatives are called *furanoses* and *pyranoses,* respectively (Section 18-10).

Cyclic ethers are examples of heterocyclic organic compounds, a compound type not previously encountered in this text. A **heterocyclic organic compound** *is a cyclic organic compound in which one or more of the carbon atoms in the ring have been replaced with atoms of other elements.* The heteroatom in cyclic ethers is oxygen.

Many cyclic ethers—compounds in which the ether functional group is part of a ring system—are known. ◀ In contrast, cyclic alcohols—compounds in which

▶ *Vitamin E, whose structure was given in Section 14-13, is both a phenol and a cyclic ether.*

the alcohol functional group is part of a ring system—do not exist. To incorporate an alcohol functional group into a ring system would require an oxygen atom with three bonds, and oxygen atoms in stable molecules form only two bonds.

The oxygen atom in this structure has three bonds, which is not possible.

Compounds such as

OH   OH

and

which do exist, are not cyclic alcohols in the sense in which the term is now being used because the alcohol functional group is attached to a ring system rather than being part of it.

▶ *The molecule THC (tetrahydrocannabinol), the primary physiologically active ingredient in marijuana, has a structure in which a cyclic ether ring system is present. THC's structure contains a fused three-ring system in which one ring is a cycloalkene, one ring is a phenol, and one ring is a cyclic ether.*

Tetrahydrocannabinol

Section 14-19 Quick Quiz

1. In a cyclic ether the ether functional group
   a. is an attachment to the ring system
   b. may or may not be part of the ring system
   c. must be part of the ring system
   d. no correct response
2. Which of the following characterizations for cyclic ethers is *incorrect*?
   a. They are always aromatic compounds.
   b. They are always heterocyclic compounds.
   c. They are always unsaturated compounds.
   d. no correct response

Answers: 1. c; 2. b

14-20 Thiols: Sulfur Analogs of Alcohols

LEARNING FOCUS

Be familiar with the structural characteristic and general properties of thiols.

Many organic compounds containing oxygen have sulfur analogs, in which a sulfur atom has replaced an oxygen atom. Sulfur is in the same group of the periodic table as oxygen, so the two elements have similar electron configurations (Section 3-8).

Thiols, the sulfur analogs of alcohols, contain —SH functional groups instead of —OH functional groups. The thiol functional group is called a *sulfhydryl group*. ◀ A **sulfhydryl group** *is the —SH functional group.* A **thiol** *is an organic compound in which a sulfhydryl group is bonded to a saturated carbon atom.* An older term used for thiols is *mercaptans.* Contrasting the general structures for alcohols and thiols, we have

▶ *Occasionally the term* thiol *is expanded to the term* thioalcohol. *In nomenclature, however, the* suffix *used is* thiol.

Hydroxyl group   Sulfhydryl group

R—OH   and   R—SH

An alcohol   A thiol

Nomenclature for Thiols

Thiols are named in the same way as alcohols in the IUPAC system, except that the suffix *-ol* becomes *-thiol.* The suffix *-thiol* indicates the substitution of a sulfur atom for an oxygen atom in a compound. ◀

CH₃—CH—CH₂—CH₃   CH₃—CH—CH₂—CH₃

OH   SH

2-Butanol   2-Butanethiol

▶ *The root* thio- *indicates that a sulfur atom has replaced an oxygen atom in a compound. It originates from the Greek* theion, *meaning "brimstone," which is an older name for the element sulfur.*

As in the case of diols and triols, the -*e* at the end of the alkane name is also retained for thiols.

Common names for thiols are based on use of the term *mercaptan,* the older name for thiols. The name of the alkyl group present (as a separate word) precedes the word *mercaptan.*

$$CH_3-CH_2-SH \qquad CH_3-\underset{\underset{\displaystyle CH_3}{|}}{CH}-SH$$

Ethyl mercaptan   Isopropyl mercaptan

EXAMPLE 14-6

Determining IUPAC and Common Names for Thiols

Convert each of the following common names for thiols to IUPAC names or vice versa.

a. Propyl mercaptan **b.** Isobutyl mercaptan
c. 1-Butanethiol **d.** 2-Propanethiol

Solution

a. The structural formula for propyl mercaptan is $CH_3-CH_2-CH_2-SH$. In the IUPAC system, the base name is propane; the complete name is 1-propanethiol.
b. The structural formula for isobutyl mercaptan is

$$CH_3-\underset{\underset{\displaystyle CH_3}{|}}{CH}-CH_2-SH$$

The longest carbon chain has three carbon atoms (propane), and both a methyl group and a sulfhydryl group are attached to the chain. The IUPAC name is 2-methyl-1-propanethiol.
c. The structure of this thiol is $CH_3-CH_2-CH_2-CH_2-SH$. The alkyl group is a butyl group, giving a common name of butyl mercaptan for this thiol.
d. The thiol structural formula is

$$CH_3-\underset{\underset{\displaystyle SH}{|}}{CH}-CH_3$$

The sulfhydryl group is attached to an isopropyl group; the common name is isopropyl mercaptan.

▶ *Even though thiols have a higher molecular mass than alcohols with the same number of carbon atoms, they have much lower boiling points because they do not exhibit hydrogen bonding as alcohols do.*

▶ *Not all thiols have unpleasant odors. A major contributor to the "pleasant" aroma of grapefruit is the thiol called thioterpineol.*

$$CH_3-\overset{\overset{\displaystyle SH}{|}}{\underset{\underset{\displaystyle CH_3}{|}}{C}}-CH_3$$

Thioterpineol

▶ *Bacteria in the mouth interact with saliva and leftover food to produce such compounds as hydrogen sulfide, methanethiol (a thiol), and dimethyl sulfide (a thioether). These compounds, which have odors detectable in air at concentrations of parts per billion, are responsible for "morning breath."*

Properties of Thiols

The physical properties of thiols and alcohols (—SH group versus —OH group) are distinctly different. The —SH functional group cannot form hydrogen bonds because of sulfur's lower electronegativity (compared to oxygen). ◀ Hence thiols have lower boiling points, higher volatility, and lower solubility in water than corresponding alcohols. Compared to corresponding alkanes, however, thiols are more soluble in water because the —SH group is slightly polar and thus attracted to polar water molecules. Thiol boiling points are higher than those of corresponding alkanes.

Thiols have strong odors that most often are characterized as being disagreeable. The threshold of detection of thiol odors is exceptionally low (in the 1–3 parts per billion range); hence thiols are easily detectable long before concentration levels reach the toxic range. ◀

Methanethiol (methyl mercaptan), with the formula CH_3-SH, is a colorless flammable gas, with an odor often described as that of rotten cabbage. It is the substance primarily responsible for "bad breath" ◀ and the smell of flatulence. Animals have the ability to produce methanethiol in their intestinal tract due to the action of bacteria on sulfur-containing proteins. Methanethiol production contributes to the odor associated with feedlots and barnyards.

In humans, methanethiol production is often a by-product of the metabolism of asparagus. When such metabolism occurs, a very strong odor is associated with urine in as few as 15 minutes after eating asparagus. This is not a universal problem because of genetic differences in how people metabolize sulfur-containing compounds. Studies show that a strong urine odor occurs in about 40% of the population; these individuals lack the ability to convert odiferous sulfur compounds present in asparagus to odor-free sulfate. ◄

Ethanethiol (ethyl mercaptan), with the formula $CH_3—CH_2—SH$, is a very low-boiling flammable liquid with an odor described as very strong green onions. When natural gas distributors began adding thiols to otherwise odorless natural gas (so that leaks could be detected), the original odorant was ethanethiol. Current natural gas odorants are usually mixtures of thiols and sulfides (Section 14-21) with *tert*-butylthiol as the major odiferous constituent. ◄

The scent of skunks (Figure 14-21) is due primarily to two thiols.

3-Methyl-1-butanethiol   *trans*-2-Butene-1-thiol

Thiols are easily oxidized but yield different products than their alcohol analogs. Thiols form *disulfides*. Each of two thiol groups loses a hydrogen atom, thus linking the two sulfur atoms together via a disulfide group, —S—S—.

$$R—SH + HS—R \xrightarrow{\text{Oxidation}} R—S—S—R + 2H$$
A disulfide

Reversal of this reaction, a reduction process, is also readily accomplished. Breaking of the disulfide bond regenerates two thiol molecules.

Oxidation

| Two thiols | | A disulfide |

Reduction

These two "opposite reactions" are of biological importance in the realm of protein chemistry. Disulfide bonds formed from the interaction of two —SH groups contribute in a major way to protein structure (Chapter 20).

▶ *Although hundreds of substances contribute to the aroma of freshly brewed coffee, the one most responsible for this characteristic odor is 2-(sulfhydrylmethyl)furan. Structurally, this compound is both a thiol and a cyclic ether.*

2-(Sulfhydrylmethyl)furan

▶ *A major contributor to the typical smell of the human armpit is a compound that contains both an alcohol and a thiol functional group.*

$$CH_2—CH_2—\overset{\overset{\displaystyle CH_3}{|}}{C}—CH_2—CH_2—CH_3$$
OH   SH

3-Methyl-3-sulfhydryl-1-hexanol

Figure 14-21 Thiols are responsible for the strong odor of "essence of skunk." Their odor is an effective defense mechanism.

Section 14-20 Quick Quiz

1. The functional group present in a thiol is the
   a. thioyl group
   b. sulfhydryl group
   c. sulfoxy group
   d. no correct response
2. Which of the following is *not* an alternate name for a thiol?
   a. thioalcohol
   b. sulfur alcohol
   c. mercaptan
   d. no correct response
3. The IUPAC name for the compound $CH_3—CH_2—CH_2—CH_2—SH$ is
   a. 4-thiolbutane
   b. 1-thiolbutane
   c. 1-butanethiol
   d. no correct response

(continued)

4. The common name for the compound $CH_3—CH_2—SH$ is
   a. ethyl thiol
   b. ethyl thioalcohol
   c. ethyl mercaptan
   d. no correct response
5. Oxidation of a thiol produces a
   a. thioether
   b. thioalcohol
   c. disulfide
   d. no correct response

Answers: 1. b; 2. b; 3. c; 4. c; 5. c

14-21 Thioethers: Sulfur Analogs of Ethers

LEARNING FOCUS

Be familiar with the structural characteristic and general properties of thioethers (sulfur analogs of ethers).

Sulfur analogs of ethers are known as thioethers (or sulfides). A **thioether** *is an organic compound in which a sulfur atom is bonded to two carbon atoms by single bonds.* The generalized formula for a thioether is R—S—R. Like thiols, thioethers have strong characteristic odors.

Thioethers are named in the same way as ethers, with *sulfide* used in place of *ether* in common names and *alkylthio* used in place of *alkoxy* in IUPAC names.

$$CH_3—S—CH_3$$
Dimethyl sulfide
(methylthiomethane)

Methyl phenyl sulfide
(methylthiobenzene)

4-(ethylthio)-2-Methyl-2-pentene

In general, thiols are more reactive than their alcohol counterparts, and thioethers are more reactive than their corresponding ethers. The larger size of a sulfur atom compared to an oxygen atom (Figure 14-22) results in a carbon–sulfur covalent bond that is weaker than a carbon–oxygen covalent bond. An added factor is that sulfur's electronegativity (2.5) is significantly lower than that of oxygen (3.5). Dimethyl sulfide is a gas at room temperature, and ethyl methyl sulfide is a liquid.

Thiols and thioethers are functional group isomers in the same manner that alcohols and ethers are functional group isomers (Section 14-17). For example, the thiol 1-propanethiol and the thioether methylthioethane both have the molecular formula C_3H_8S.

$$CH_3—CH_2—CH_2—SH \qquad CH_3—S—CH_2—CH_3$$
1-Propanethiol   Methylthioethane

Thioethers, like thiols, usually have strong odors. Dimethyl sulfide, $CH_3—S—CH_3$, the simplest thioether, is a water-soluble flammable liquid that has a cabbage-like smell described as pleasant (at low concentrations in air) and unpleasant (at higher concentrations in air).

Figure 14-22 A comparison involving space-filling models for dimethyl ether and dimethyl sulfide. A sulfur atom is much larger than an oxygen atom. This results in a carbon–sulfur bond being weaker than a carbon–oxygen bond.

Dimethyl ether

Dimethyl sulfide

CHEMICAL CONNECTIONS 14-D

Garlic and Onions: Odiferous Medicinal Plants

Garlic and onions, which botanically belong to the same plant genus, are vegetables known for the bad breath—and perspiration odors—associated with their consumption. These effects are caused by organic sulfur-containing compounds, produced when garlic and onions are cut, that reach the lungs and sweat glands via the bloodstream. The total sulfur content of garlic and onions amounts to about one percent of their dry weight.

Less well known about garlic and onions are the numerous studies showing that these same "bad breath" sulfur-containing compounds are health-promoting substances that have the capacity to prevent or at least ameliorate a host of ailments in humans and animals. The list of beneficial effects associated with garlic use is longer than that for any other medicinal plant. Only onions come close to having the same kind of efficacy. Garlic has been shown to function as an antibacterial, antiviral, antifungal, antiprotozal, and antiparasitic agent. In the area of heart and circulatory problems, garlic contains vasodilative compounds that improve blood fluidity and reduce platelet aggregation. The health-promoting role of onions has not been explored as thoroughly as that of garlic, but the studies undertaken so far seem to confirm that onions are second only to garlic in their "healing powers."

Whole garlic bulbs and whole onions that remain undisturbed and intact do not contain any strongly odiferous compounds and display virtually no physiological activity. The act of cutting or crushing these vegetables causes a cascade of reactions to occur in damaged plant cells. Exposure to oxygen in the air is an important facet of these reactions. More than one hundred sulfur-containing organic compounds are formed in garlic, and a similar number are probably produced in the less-studied onion. Many of the compounds so produced are common to both garlic and onions. The compounds associated with garlic ingestion that contribute to bad breath include allyl methyl sulfide, allyl methyl disulfide, diallyl sulfide, and diallyl disulfide. Their structures are given in the accompanying table.

Not all of the strongly odiferous compounds associated with garlic and onions elicit negative responses from the human olfactory system. For example, the smell of fried onions is considered a pleasant odor by most people. Compounds contributing to the "fried onion smell" include

methyl propyl disulfide, methyl propyl trisulfide, allyl propyl disulfide, and dipropyl trisulfide. Structures for these compounds are also given in the accompanying table.

In addition to physiologically active sulfur compounds, garlic and onions also contain a variety of other healthful ingredients. Among these are the B vitamins thiamine and riboflavin and vitamin C. Almost all of the trace elements are also present, including manganese, iron, phosphorus, selenium, and chromium. The actual amount of a given trace element depends on the soil in which the garlic or onion was grown.

Garlic Breath

CH_2=CH—CH_2—S—CH_3
Allyl methyl sulfide

CH_2=CH—CH_2—S—S—CH_3
Allyl methyl disulfide

CH_2=CH—CH_2—S—CH_2—CH=CH_2
Diallyl sulfide

CH_2=CH—CH_2—S—S—CH_2—CH=CH_2
Diallyl disulfide

Fried Onions

CH_3—S—S—CH_2—CH_2—CH_3
Methyl propyl disulfide

CH_3—S—S—S—CH_2—CH_2—CH_3
Methyl propyl trisulfide

CH_2=CH—CH_2—S—S—CH_2—CH_2—CH_3
Allyl propyl disulfide

CH_3—CH_2—CH_2—S—S—S—CH_2—CH_2—CH_3
Dipropyl trisulfide

Getty Images

Sulfides and disulfides contribute heavily to the odors of "garlic breath" and "fried onions." "Garlic breath" odorants are primarily sulfides, whereas the smell, usually considered pleasant, of fried onions is heavily influenced by the presence of disulfides. The focus on relevancy feature Chemical Connections 14-D—Garlic and Onions: Odiferous Medicinal Plants—further considers studies about garlic and onions, plants which belong to the same plant genus.

Chemistry at a Glance—Alcohols, Thiols, Ethers, and Thioethers—contrasts the four major types of compounds considered in this chapter—alcohols, thiols, ethers, and thioethers—in terms of structure, hydrogen-bonding characteristics, and nomenclature.

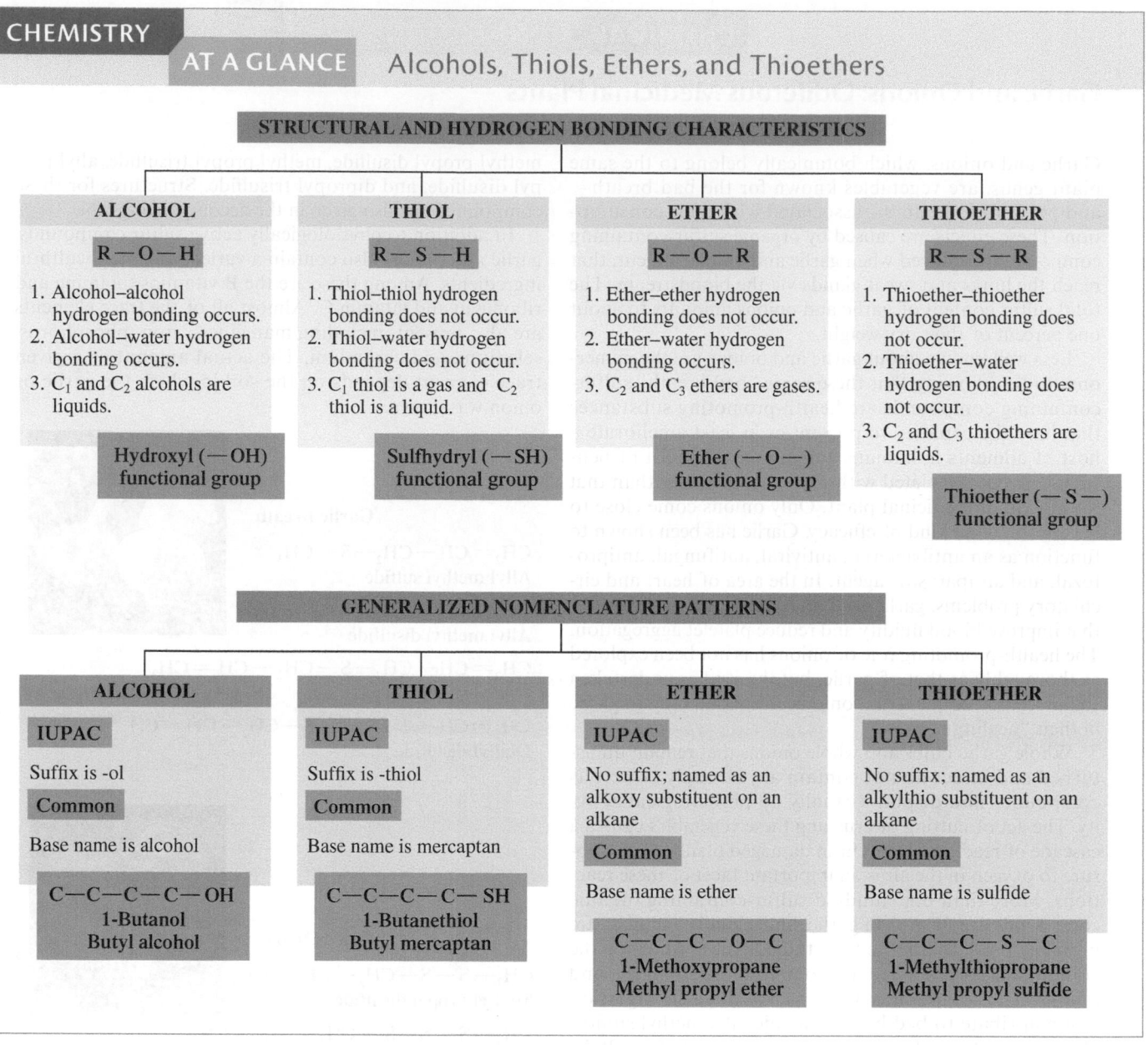

CHEMISTRY AT A GLANCE Alcohols, Thiols, Ethers, and Thioethers

STRUCTURAL AND HYDROGEN BONDING CHARACTERISTICS

ALCOHOL

R—O—H

1. Alcohol–alcohol hydrogen bonding occurs.
2. Alcohol–water hydrogen bonding occurs.
3. C_1 and C_2 alcohols are liquids.

Hydroxyl (—OH) functional group

THIOL

R—S—H

1. Thiol–thiol hydrogen bonding does not occur.
2. Thiol–water hydrogen bonding does not occur.
3. C_1 thiol is a gas and C_2 thiol is a liquid.

Sulfhydryl (—SH) functional group

ETHER

R—O—R

1. Ether–ether hydrogen bonding does not occur.
2. Ether–water hydrogen bonding occurs.
3. C_2 and C_3 ethers are gases.

Ether (—O—) functional group

THIOETHER

R—S—R

1. Thioether–thioether hydrogen bonding does not occur.
2. Thioether–water hydrogen bonding does not occur.
3. C_2 and C_3 thioethers are liquids.

Thioether (—S—) functional group

GENERALIZED NOMENCLATURE PATTERNS

ALCOHOL

IUPAC

Suffix is -ol

Common

Base name is alcohol

C—C—C—C—OH
1-Butanol
Butyl alcohol

THIOL

IUPAC

Suffix is -thiol

Common

Base name is mercaptan

C—C—C—C—SH
1-Butanethiol
Butyl mercaptan

ETHER

IUPAC

No suffix; named as an alkoxy substituent on an alkane

Common

Base name is ether

C—C—C—O—C
1-Methoxypropane
Methyl propyl ether

THIOETHER

IUPAC

No suffix; named as an alkylthio substituent on an alkane

Common

Base name is sulfide

C—C—C—S—C
1-Methylthiopropane
Methyl propyl sulfide

Section 14-21 Quick Quiz

1. Which of the following is the correct designation for a thioether?
   a. R—S—H
   b. R—S—R
   c. R—S—S—R
   d. no correct response
2. The IUPAC name for the compound CH_3—S—CH_3 is
   a. dimethyl thioether
   b. dimethyl sulfide
   c. methylthiomethane
   d. no correct response
3. In the thioether CH_3—S—CH_2—CH_2—CH_3, the CH_3—S— group present is called a
   a. methylthio group
   b. thiomethyl group
   c. thiomethoxy group
   d. no correct response

4. A common property for both thiols and thioethers is
 a. a strong odor
 b. ability to form strong hydrogen bonds
 c. very high boiling points
 d. no correct response
5. For which of the following pairs of compounds is functional group isomerism possible
 a. thioethers and ethers
 b. thioethers and alcohols
 c. thioethers and thiols
 d. no correct response

Answers: 1. b; 2. c; 3. a; 4. a; 5. c

Concepts to Remember

Alcohols. Alcohols are organic compounds that contain an —OH group attached to a saturated carbon atom. The general formula for an alcohol is R—OH, where R is an alkyl group (Section 14-2).

Nomenclature of alcohols. The IUPAC names of simple alcohols end in *-ol,* and their carbon chains are numbered to give precedence to the location of the —OH group. Alcohol common names contain the word *alcohol* preceded by the name of the alkyl group (Section 14-3).

Isomerism for alcohols. Constitutional isomerism is possible for alcohols containing three or more carbon atoms. Both skeletal and positional isomers are possible (Section 14-4).

Physical properties of alcohols. Alcohol molecules hydrogen-bond to each other and to water molecules. They thus have higher-than-normal boiling points, and the low-molecular-mass alcohols are soluble in water (Section 14-6).

Classification of alcohols. Alcohols are classified on the basis of the number of carbon atoms bonded to the carbon attached to the —OH group. In primary alcohols, the —OH group is bonded to a carbon atom bonded to only one other C atom. In secondary alcohols, the —OH-containing C atom is attached to two other C atoms. In tertiary alcohols, it is attached to three other C atoms (Section 14-8).

Alcohol Dehydration. Alcohols can be dehydrated to form alkenes. Reaction conditions involve sulfuric acid as a catalyst and a temperature of 180°C. At lower temperatures, 1° alcohols undergo condensation to form ethers; 2° and 3° alcohols still undergo dehydration to an alkene (Section 14-9).

Alcohol oxidation. Oxidation of primary alcohols first produces an aldehyde, which is then further oxidized to a carboxylic acid. Secondary alcohols are oxidized to ketones, and tertiary alcohols are resistant to oxidation (Section 14-9).

Phenols. Phenols have the general formula Ar—OH, where Ar represents an aryl group derived from an aromatic compound. Phenols are named as derivatives of the parent compound phenol, using the conventions for aromatic hydrocarbon nomenclature (Sections 14-10 and 14-11).

Properties of phenols. Phenols are generally low-melting solids; most are only slightly soluble in water. The chemical reactions of phenols are significantly different from those of alcohols, even though both types of compounds possess hydroxyl groups. Phenols are more resistant to oxidation and do not undergo dehydration. Phenols have acidic properties, whereas alcohols do not (Section 14-12).

Ethers. The general formula for an ether is R—O—R′, where R and R′ are alkyl, cycloalkyl, or aryl groups. In the IUPAC system, ethers are named as alkoxy derivatives of alkanes. Common names are obtained by giving the R group names in alphabetical order and adding the word *ether* (Sections 14-14 and 14-15).

Functional group isomerism. Ethers and alcohols with the same number of carbon atoms and the same degree of saturation have the same molecular formula and are thus isomers of each other. This type of constitutional isomerism is known as functional group isomerism (Section 14-17).

Properties of ethers. Ethers have lower boiling points than alcohols because ether molecules do not hydrogen-bond to each other. Ethers are slightly soluble in water because water forms hydrogen bonds with ethers (Section 14-18).

Thiols and disulfides. Thiols are the sulfur analogs of alcohols. They have the general formula R—SH. The —SH group is called the sulfhydryl group. Oxidation of thiols forms disulfides, which have the general formula R—S—S—R. The most distinctive physical property of thiols is their foul odor (Section 14-20).

Thioethers (sulfides). Thioethers (sulfides) are the sulfur analogs of ethers. They have the general formula R—S—R (Section 14-21).

Exercises and Problems

Exercises and problems are arranged in matched pairs with the two members of a pair addressing the same concept(s). The answer to the odd-numbered member of a pair is given at the back of the book. Problems denoted with a ▲ involve concepts found not only in the section under consideration but also concepts found in one or more earlier sections of the chapter.

Bonding Characteristics of Oxygen Atoms in Organic Compounds (Section 14-1)

14-1 In organic compounds, how many covalent bonds does each of the following types of atoms form?
 a. Oxygen
 b. Hydrogen
 c. Carbon
 d. A halogen

14-2 Indicate whether or not each of the following covalent bonding behaviors are possible for an oxygen atom in an organic compound.
　a. One single bond 　b. Two single bonds
　c. One double bond 　d. Two double bonds

Structural Characteristics of Alcohols (Section 14-2)

14-3 Contrast, in general terms, the structures of an alcohol and water.

14-4 Contrast, in general terms, the structures of an alcohol and an alkane.

14-5 What is the molecular formula for each of the following alcohols in which all carbon–carbon bonds are single bonds?
　a. three carbon atoms, one —OH group
　b. five carbon atoms, one —OH group

14-6 What is the molecular formula for each of the following alcohols in which all carbon–carbon bonds are single bonds?
　a. two carbon atoms, one —OH group
　b. four carbon atoms, one —OH group

Nomenclature for Alcohols (Section 14-3)

14-7 Assign an IUPAC name to each of the following alcohols.
　a.
$$CH_3—CH_2—CH_2—\overset{\overset{\displaystyle OH}{|}}{CH}—CH_3$$
　b.
$$CH_3—\overset{\overset{\displaystyle CH_3}{|}}{CH}—\overset{\overset{\displaystyle OH}{|}}{CH}—CH_3$$
　c. $CH_3—CH_2—CH_2—\overset{\overset{\displaystyle |}{CH}}{\underset{\underset{\displaystyle OH}{|}}{\underset{\displaystyle CH_2}{}}}—CH_2—CH_3$
　d. $CH_3—CH_2—\overset{\overset{\displaystyle |}{CH}}{\underset{\underset{\displaystyle CH_3}{|}}{}}—OH$

14-8 Assign an IUPAC name to each of the following alcohols.
　a. $CH_3—CH_2—\overset{\overset{\displaystyle |}{CH}}{\underset{\underset{\displaystyle OH}{|}}{}}—CH_2—CH_3$
　b. $CH_3—CH_2—\overset{\overset{\displaystyle OH}{|}}{CH}—\overset{\overset{\displaystyle CH_3}{|}}{CH}—CH_3$
　c. $CH_3—CH_2—\overset{\overset{\displaystyle |}{CH}}{\underset{\underset{\displaystyle CH_2—CH_2—CH_2—OH}{|}}{}}—CH_2—CH_2—CH_3$
　d.
$$CH_3—\overset{\overset{\displaystyle OH}{|}}{\underset{\underset{\displaystyle CH_3}{|}}{C}}—CH_2—CH_3$$

14-9 Assign an IUPAC name to each of the following alcohols.
　a. ... 　b. ...
　c. ... 　d. ...

14-10 Assign an IUPAC name to each of the following alcohols.
　a. ... 　b. ...
　c. ... 　d. ...

14-11 Write a condensed structural formula for each of the following alcohols.
　a. 2-Methyl-1-propanol b. 4-Methyl-2-pentanol
　c. 2-Phenyl-2-propanol d. 2-Methylcyclobutanol

14-12 Write a condensed structural formula for each of the following alcohols.
　a. 2-Methyl-2-heptanol b. 3-Ethyl-2-pentanol
　c. 3-Phenyl-1-butanol d. 3,5-Dimethylcyclohexanol

14-13 Write a condensed structural formula for, and assign an IUPAC name to, each of the following alcohols.
　a. Pentyl alcohol 　　b. Propyl alcohol
　c. Isobutyl alcohol 　d. *sec*-Butyl alcohol

14-14 Write a condensed structural formula for, and assign an IUPAC name to, each of the following alcohols.
　a. Butyl alcohol 　　b. Hexyl alcohol
　c. Isopropyl alcohol 　d. *tert*-Butyl alcohol

14-15 Assign an IUPAC name to each of the following polyhydroxy alcohols.
　a. $\underset{\underset{\displaystyle OH}{|}}{CH_2}—\underset{\underset{\displaystyle OH}{|}}{CH}—CH_2—CH_3$
　b. $\underset{\underset{\displaystyle OH}{|}}{CH_2}—CH_2—CH_2—CH_2—\underset{\underset{\displaystyle OH}{|}}{CH}—CH_3$
　c. $CH_3—CH_2—\underset{\underset{\displaystyle OH}{|}}{CH}—CH_2—\underset{\underset{\displaystyle OH}{|}}{CH}—CH_3$
　d. $\underset{\underset{\displaystyle OH}{|}}{CH_2}—\underset{\underset{\displaystyle OH}{|}}{CH}—\underset{\underset{\displaystyle CH_3}{|}}{CH}—CH_2—\underset{\underset{\displaystyle OH}{|}}{CH_2}$

14-16 Assign an IUPAC name to each of the following polyhydroxy alcohols.
　a. $\underset{\underset{\displaystyle OH}{|}}{CH_2}—\underset{\underset{\displaystyle CH_3}{|}}{CH}—\underset{\underset{\displaystyle OH}{|}}{CH}—CH_3$
　b. $\underset{\underset{\displaystyle OH}{|}}{CH_2}—\underset{\underset{\displaystyle OH}{|}}{CH}—\underset{\underset{\displaystyle CH_3}{|}}{CH}—OH$
　c. $CH_3—CH_2—\underset{\underset{\displaystyle OH}{|}}{CH}—\underset{\underset{\displaystyle OH}{|}}{CH}—CH_3$
　d. $\underset{\underset{\displaystyle OH}{|}}{CH_2}—\underset{\underset{\displaystyle OH}{|}}{CH}—\underset{\underset{\displaystyle OH}{|}}{CH}—CH_2—CH_3$

14-17 Write a condensed structural formula for each of the following *unsaturated* alcohols.
　a. 4-Penten-2-ol 　　b. 1-Pentyn-3-ol
　c. 3-Methyl-3-buten-2-ol d. 3-Buten-1-ol

14-18 Write a condensed structural formula for each of the following *unsaturated* alcohols.
　a. 1-Penten-3-ol 　　b. 3-Butyn-1-ol
　c. 2-Methyl-3-buten-1-ol d. 4-Penten-1-ol

14-19 Each of the following alcohols is named incorrectly. However, the names give correct structural formulas. Draw structural formulas for the compounds, and then write the correct IUPAC name for each alcohol.
  a. 2-Ethyl-1-propanol   b. 2,4-Butanediol
  c. 2-Methyl-3-butanol   d. 1,4-Cyclopentanediol

14-20 Each of the following alcohols is named incorrectly. However, the names give correct structural formulas. Draw structural formulas for the compounds, and then write the correct IUPAC name for each alcohol.
  a. 3-Ethyl-2-butanol
  b. 3,4-Pentanediol
  c. 3-Methyl-3-butanol
  d. 1,1-Dimethyl-1-butanol

Isomerism for Alcohols (Section 14-4)

14-21 Indicate whether each of the following compounds is or is not a constitutional isomer of 1-hexanol.

14-22 Indicate whether each of the following compounds is or is not a constitutional isomer of 2-pentanol.

14-23 How many alcohol constitutional isomers exist that fit each of the following descriptions?
  a. C_7 alcohols that are named as heptanols
  b. C_7 alcohols that are named as dimethylcyclopentanols
  c. Alcohols that have the molecular formula $C_5H_{12}O$
  d. Saturated alcohols that have the molecular formula C_4H_8O

14-24 How many alcohol constitutional isomers exist that fit each of the following descriptions?
  a. C_8 alcohols that are named as octanols
  b. C_8 alcohols that are named as dimethylcyclohexanols
  c. Alcohols that have the molecular formula $C_4H_{10}O$
  d. Saturated alcohols that have the molecular formula $C_5H_{10}O$

▲**14-25** For some alcohols, *cis-trans* isomerism (Sections 12-14, 13-6) is possible. Indicate whether each of the following alcohol structures denotes a *cis-* or *trans-* isomer.

▲**14-26** For some alcohols, *cis-trans* isomerism (Sections 12-14, 13-6) is possible. Indicate whether each of the following alcohol structures denotes a *cis-* or *trans-* isomer.

▲**14-27** Assign an IUPAC name to each of the alcohols in Problem 14-25.

▲**14-28** Assign an IUPAC name to each of the alcohols in Problem 14-26.

Important Commonly Encountered Alcohols (Section 14-5)

14-29 What does each of the following terms mean?
  a. Absolute alcohol   b. Grain alcohol
  c. Rubbing alcohol   d. Drinking alcohol

14-30 What does each of the following terms mean?
  a. Wood alcohol   b. Denatured alcohol
  c. 70-Proof alcohol   d. "Alcohol"

14-31 Give the IUPAC name of the alcohol that fits each of the following descriptions.
  a. Moistening agent in many cosmetics
  b. Major ingredient in "environmentally friendly" antifreeze formulations
  c. Industrially produced from CO and H_2
  d. Often produced via a fermentation process

14-32 Give the IUPAC name of the alcohol that fits each of the following descriptions.
  a. Major ingredient in most brands of antifreeze
  b. The alcohol present in alcoholic beverages
  c. Often applied to the skin because of its "cooling effects"
  d. Thick liquid that has the consistency of honey

14-33 From 1965 to 2005, methanol was the fuel of choice for Indianapolis Speedway race cars. What was a major reason for using methanol instead of gasoline, which was used previously?

14-34 Since 2007, Indianapolis Speedway race cars have used ethanol rather than methanol as a fuel. What was a major reason for this change?

Physical Properties of Alcohols (Section 14-6)

14-35 Explain why the boiling points of alcohols are much higher than those of alkanes with similar molecular masses.

14-36 Explain why the water solubilities of alcohols are much higher than those of alkanes with similar molecular masses.

14-37 Which member of each of the following pairs of compounds would you expect to have the higher boiling point?
  a. 1-Butanol and 1-heptanol
  b. Butane and 1-propanol
  c. Ethanol and 1,2-ethanediol

14-38 Which member of each of the following pairs of compounds would you expect to have the higher boiling point?
a. 1-Octanol and 1-pentanol
b. Pentane and 1-butanol
c. 1,3-Propanediol and 1-propanol

14-39 Which member of each of the following pairs of compounds would you expect to be more soluble in water?
a. Butane and 1-butanol
b. 1-Octanol and 1-pentanol
c. 1,2-Butanediol and 1-butanol

14-40 Which member of each of the following pairs of compounds would you expect to be more soluble in water?
a. 1-Pentanol and 1-butanol
b. 1-Propanol and 1-hexanol
c. 1,2,3-Propanetriol and 1-hexanol

14-41 Determine the maximum number of hydrogen bonds that can form between an ethanol molecule and
a. other ethanol molecules
b. water molecules
c. methanol molecules
d. 1-propanol molecules

14-42 Determine the maximum number of hydrogen bonds that can form between a methanol molecule and
a. other methanol molecules
b. water molecules
c. 1-propanol molecules
d. 2-propanol molecules

Preparation of Alcohols (Section 14-7)

14-43 Write the structure of the expected predominant organic product formed in each of the following reactions.

a. $CH_2\!=\!CH_2 + H_2O \xrightarrow{H_2SO_4}$

b.
$$CH_3\!-\!CH_2\!-\!\overset{\displaystyle O}{\overset{\|}{C}}\!-\!H + H_2 \xrightarrow{Catalyst}$$

c. $CH_3\!-\!CH_2\!-\!\underset{\underset{\displaystyle CH_3}{|}}{C}\!=\!CH_2 + H_2O \xrightarrow{H_2SO_4}$

d.
$$CH_3\!-\!CH_2\!-\!\overset{\displaystyle O}{\overset{\|}{C}}\!-\!CH_2\!-\!CH_3 + H_2 \xrightarrow{Catalyst}$$

14-44 Write the structure of the expected predominant organic product formed in each of the following reactions.

a. $CH_3\!-\!CH\!=\!CH\!-\!CH_3 + H_2O \xrightarrow{H_2SO_4}$

b.
$$CH_3\!-\!CH_2\!-\!\overset{\displaystyle O}{\overset{\|}{C}}\!-\!CH_3 + H_2 \xrightarrow{Catalyst}$$

c.
$$CH_3\!-\!\overset{\displaystyle O}{\overset{\|}{C}}\!-\!H + H_2 \xrightarrow{Catalyst}$$

d. $CH_3\!-\!\underset{\underset{\displaystyle CH_3}{|}}{CH}\!-\!CH\!=\!CH\!-\!CH_3 + H_2O \xrightarrow{H_2SO_4}$

Classification of Alcohols (Section 14-8)

14-45 Classify each of the alcohols in Problem 14-7 as a primary, secondary, or tertiary alcohol.

14-46 Classify each of the alcohols in Problem 14-8 as a primary, secondary, or tertiary alcohol.

14-47 Classify each of the following alcohols as a primary, secondary, or tertiary alcohol.

a.
b.
c.
d.

14-48 Classify each of the following alcohols as a primary, secondary, or tertiary alcohol.

a.
b.
c.
d.

▲**14-49** Classify each of the following alcohols as a primary, secondary, or tertiary alcohol.
a. 1-pentanol   b. 2-pentanol
c. 2-methyl-1-pentanol d. 2-methyl-2-pentanol

▲**14-50** Classify each of the following alcohols as a primary, secondary, or tertiary alcohol.
a. 1-butanol   b. 2-butanol
c. 2-methyl-1-butanol   d. 2-methyl-2-butanol

▲**14-51** Draw a structural formula for the simplest alcohol (fewest carbon atoms) that fits each of the following descriptions.
a. tertiary alcohol with an acyclic R group
b. secondary alcohol with a cyclic R group

▲**14-52** Draw a structural formula for the simplest alcohol (fewest carbon atoms) that fits each of the following descriptions.
a. secondary alcohol with an acyclic R group
b. tertiary alcohol with a cyclic R group

▲**14-53** How many alcohol constitutional isomers exist that have the chemical formula $C_5H_{12}O$ and that fit each of the following descriptions?
a. 1° alcohol
b. 2° alcohol
c. 3° alcohol
d. has a carbon ring as part of its structure

▲**14-54** How many alcohol constitutional isomers exist that have the chemical formula $C_4H_{10}O$ and that fit each of the following descriptions?
a. 1° alcohol
b. 2° alcohol
c. 3° alcohol
d. has a carbon ring as part of its structure

Chemical Reactions of Alcohols (Section 14-9)

14-55 Draw the structure of the predominant organic product formed in each of the following reactions involving alcohol molecules as the reactants.

a. $CH_3-CH-CH_3 \xrightarrow[180°C]{H_2SO_4}$
    |
    OH

b. $CH_3-CH_2-CH-CH_2-OH \xrightarrow[180°C]{H_2SO_4}$
                |
                CH_3

c. $CH_3-CH-OH \xrightarrow[140°C]{H_2SO_4}$
        |
        CH_3

d. $CH_3-CH_2-CH_2-OH \xrightarrow[140°C]{H_2SO_4}$

14-56 Draw the structure of the predominant organic product formed in each of the following reactions involving alcohol molecules as the reactants.

a. $CH_3-CH-CH_2-OH \xrightarrow[140°C]{H_2SO_4}$
        |
        CH_3

b. $CH_3-CH-CH_2-OH \xrightarrow[180°C]{H_2SO_4}$
        |
        CH_3

c. $CH_3-CH-CH_2-CH_3 \xrightarrow[180°C]{H_2SO_4}$
        |
        OH

d. $CH_3-CH-CH_2-CH_3 \xrightarrow[140°C]{H_2SO_4}$
        |
        OH

14-57 Draw the structure of the alcohol reactant needed to produce each of the given products under the reaction conditions specified. It is possible that more than one alcohol may qualify as the parent alcohol.

a. Alcohol $\xrightarrow[180°C]{H_2SO_4}$ $CH_2=CH-CH_2-CH_3$

b. Alcohol $\xrightarrow[180°C]{H_2SO_4}$ $CH_2=C-CH_3$
                                        |
                                        CH_3

c. Alcohol $\xrightarrow[140°C]{H_2SO_4}$ $CH_3-CH_2-O-CH_2-CH_3$

d. Alcohol $\xrightarrow[140°C]{H_2SO_4}$ $CH_3-CH_2-CH-O-CH-CH_2-CH_3$
                                        | |
                                        CH_3   CH_3

14-58 Draw the structure of the alcohol reactant needed to produce each of the given products under the reaction conditions specified. It is possible that more than one alcohol may qualify as the parent alcohol.

a. Alcohol $\xrightarrow[180°C]{H_2SO_4}$ $CH_3-CH=CH_2$

b. Alcohol $\xrightarrow[180°C]{H_2SO_4}$ $CH_3-CH=C-CH_3$
                                        |
                                        CH_3

c. Alcohol $\xrightarrow[140°C]{H_2SO_4}$ CH_3-O-CH_3

d. Alcohol $\xrightarrow[140°C]{H_2SO_4}$ $CH_3-CH-O-CH-CH_3$
                                        | |
                                        CH_3   CH_3

14-59 Draw the structures of all possible organic products that can form when the alcohol 3-methyl-3-hexanol is dehydrated.

14-60 Draw the structures of all possible organic products that can form when the alcohol 2,3-dimethyl-3-pentanol is dehydrated.

14-61 The alcohol 2,2-dimethyl-1-butanol cannot be dehydrated. Explain why.

14-62 The alcohol 2-ethyl-2-methyl-1-butanol cannot be dehydrated. Explain why.

14-63 Indicate whether an aldehyde or ketone is produced when each of the following alcohols is oxidized.

a. $CH_3-CH_2-CH_2-CH_2$
                        |
                        OH

b. $CH_3-CH-CH_2-CH_3$
        |
        OH

c. $CH_3-CH_2-CH-CH_2$
                | |
                CH_3 OH

d. $CH_3-CH-CH-CH_3$
        | |
        OH   CH_3

14-64 Indicate whether an aldehyde or ketone is produced when each of the following alcohols is oxidized.

a. $CH_3-CH_2-CH_2-CH_2-CH_2$
                              |
                              OH

b. $CH_3-CH-CH_2-CH_2-CH_3$
        |
        OH

c. $CH_3-CH_2-CH-CH_2-CH_2$
                | |
                CH_3   OH

d. $CH_3-CH-CH-CH_2-CH_3$
        | |
        OH CH_3

14-65 Draw the structure of the aldehyde or ketone produced when each of the alcohols in Problem 14-63 is oxidized.

14-66 Draw the structure of the aldehyde or ketone produced when each of the alcohols in Problem 14-64 is oxidized.

14-67 Draw the structure of the alcohol that could be used to prepare each of the following compounds in an oxidation reaction.

a.
$$CH_3-CH_2-\overset{\displaystyle O}{\overset{\displaystyle \|}{C}}-CH_3$$

b.
$$CH_3-CH_2-\overset{\displaystyle O}{\overset{\displaystyle \|}{C}}-OH$$

c.
$$CH_3-CH_2-\overset{\displaystyle O}{\overset{\displaystyle \|}{C}}-H$$

d.

14-68 Draw the structure of the alcohol that could be used to prepare each of the following compounds in an oxidation reaction.

a.
$$CH_3-CH-\overset{\displaystyle O}{\overset{\displaystyle \|}{C}}-H$$
        |
        CH_3

b.
$$CH_3-CH-\overset{\displaystyle O}{\overset{\displaystyle \|}{C}}-CH_3$$
        |
        CH_3

c.
$$CH_3-CH-CH_2-\overset{\displaystyle O}{\overset{\displaystyle \|}{C}}-OH$$
        |
        CH_3

d.

14-69 Draw the structure of the expected predominant organic product formed in each of the following reactions.

a. $CH_3-CH_2-CH_2-OH \xrightarrow[\text{heat}]{PCl_3}$

b. $\xrightarrow[\text{180°C}]{H_2SO_4}$

c. $CH_3-\underset{\underset{OH}{|}}{CH}-CH_2-CH_3 \xrightarrow{K_2Cr_2O_7}$

d. $CH_3-CH_2-OH \xrightarrow[\text{140°C}]{H_2SO_4}$

14-70 Draw the structure of the expected predominant organic product formed in each of the following reactions.

a. $\xrightarrow[\text{heat}]{PCl_3}$

b. $CH_2-CH_2-CH_2-CH_3 \xrightarrow[\text{140°C}]{H_2SO_4}$ with OH

c. $CH_3-CH_2-\underset{\underset{OH}{|}}{CH}-CH_2-CH_3 \xrightarrow{K_2Cr_2O_7}$

d. $CH_3-\underset{\underset{CH_3}{|}}{CH}-OH \xrightarrow[\text{180°C}]{H_2SO_4}$

▲**14-71** Three isomeric pentanols with unbranched carbon chains exist. Which of these isomers, upon dehydration at 180°C, yields only 1-pentene as a product?

▲**14-72** A mixture of methanol, 1-propanol, and H_2SO_4 (catalyst) is heated to 140°C. After reaction, the solution contains three different ethers. Draw a condensed structural formula for each of these ethers.

Structural Characteristics of Phenols (Section 14-10)

14-73 Indicate whether or not each of the following compounds is a phenol.

a. (cyclohexane with OH)   b. (cyclohexane with OH and CH₃)

c. (benzene with OH and CH₃)   d. (benzene with CH₂—OH)

14-74 Indicate whether or not each of the following compounds is a phenol.

a. (benzene with OH and CH₃)   b. (benzene with CH₂ and OH)

c. (benzene with CH₂—CH₂—OH)   d. (benzene with CH—CH₃ and OH)

Nomenclature for Phenols (Section 14-11)

14-75 Name the following phenols.

a. OH (benzene with CH₂—CH₃)   b. Cl, OH (benzene)

c. OH, CH₃ (benzene)   d. OH (benzene with OH at para)

14-76 Name the following phenols.

a. OH (benzene with CH₂—CH₂—CH₃)   b. OH, OH (benzene)

c. OH, CH₃ (benzene)   d. OH, Cl, CH—CH₃ with CH₃ (benzene)

14-77 Draw a structural formula for each of the following phenols.
a. 2-Ethylphenol   b. 2,4-Dibromophenol
c. *m*-Cresol   d. Resorcinol

14-78 Draw a structural formula for each of the following phenols.
a. 3-Bromophenol   b. *o*-Cresol
c. Catechol   d. 2,6-Dichlorophenol

Physical and Chemical Properties of Phenols (Section 14-12)

14-79 Characterize phenols in terms of their physical state at room temperature.

14-80 Characterize phenols in terms of their solubility in water.

14-81 What is the difference, if any, between phenols and alcohols in terms of the following?
a. Flammability
b. Ability to undergo halogenation reactions

14-82 What is the difference, if any, between phenols and alcohols in terms of the following?
a. Products formed when oxidized
b. Ability to undergo dehydration reactions

14-83 Phenols are weak acids. Write an equation for the acid ionization of the compound phenol.

14-84 How does the acidity of phenols compare with that of inorganic weak acids?

Occurrence of and Uses for Phenols (Section 14-13)

14-85 Phenolic compounds are frequently used as antiseptics and disinfectants. What is the difference between an antiseptic and a disinfectant?

14-86 Phenolic compounds are frequently used as antioxidants. What is an antioxidant?

14-87 Describe the structures of the phenolic antioxidants BHA and BHT in terms of groups attached to the phenolic ring system.

14-88 Identity the flavor/odor and uses associated with each of the following phenolic flavoring agents.
   a. Thymol
   b. Eugenol
   c. Isoeugenol
   d. Vanillin

Structural Characteristics of Ethers (Section 14-14)

14-89 Indicate whether each of the following structural notations denotes an ether.
   a. R—O—R
   b. R—O—H
   c. Ar—O—R
   d. Ar—O—Ar

14-90 What is the difference in meaning associated with each of the following pairs of notations?
   a. R—O—R and R—O—H
   b. Ar—O—R and Ar—O—Ar
   c. Ar—O—H and Ar—O—R
   d. R—O—R and Ar—O—Ar

▲**14-91** Classify each of the following compounds as an *ether*, an *alcohol*, or *neither an ether or alcohol*.

a. CH_3—O—CH_2
              |
             CH_3

b. CH_3—CH—OH
          |
         CH_3

c. CH_3—CH—CH_2—CH_3
          |
          OH

d. CH_3—CH_2
         |
         O—CH_3

▲**14-92** Classify each of the following compounds as an *ether*, an *alcohol*, or as *neither an ether or alcohol*.

a. CH_3—CH—CH_3
          |
          O
          |
   CH_3—CH—CH_3

b. HO—CH_2
         |
        CH_3

c. CH_3—CH—CH_2—CH_3
          |
          O—CH_2—CH_3

d. CH_3—CH—CH_2—CH_3
          |
   CH_3—CH—OH

▲**14-93** Draw or write the following for the simplest ether (fewest carbon atoms) in which both R groups present are identical.
   a. Expanded structural formula
   b. Condensed structural formula
   c. Skeletal structural formula
   d. Molecular formula

▲**14-94** Draw or write the following for the simplest ether (fewest carbon atoms) in which the R groups present are different alkyl groups.
   a. Expanded structural formula
   b. Condensed structural formula
   c. Skeletal structural formula
   d. Molecular formula

Nomenclature for Ethers (Section 14-15)

14-95 Assign an IUPAC name to each of the following ethers.
   a. CH_3—CH_2—CH_2—O—CH_2—CH_3
   b. CH_3—CH—CH_3
              |
              O—CH_3

   c. —O—CH_3

   d.

14-96 Assign an IUPAC name to each of the following ethers.
   a. CH_3—CH_2—O—CH_2—CH_3
   b. CH_3—CH—O—CH_3
              |
             CH_3
   c. CH_3—CH_2—CH—CH_3
                   |
                   O—CH_2—CH_3

   d. —O—CH_2—CH_3

14-97 Assign a common name to each of the ethers in Problem 14-95.

14-98 Assign a common name to each of the ethers in Problem 14-96.

14-99 Assign an IUPAC name to each of the following ethers.
   a.   b.
   c.   d.

14-100 Assign an IUPAC name to each of the following ethers.
   a.   b.
   c.   d.

14-101 Draw the structure of each of the following ethers.
   a. Isopropyl propyl ether   b. Ethyl phenyl ether
   c. 3-Methylanisole   d. Ethoxycyclobutane

14-102 Draw the structure of each of the following ethers.
   a. Butyl methyl ether   b. Anisole
   c. Phenyl propyl ether   d. 1,3-Dimethoxybenzene

▲**14-103** Assign an IUPAC name to each of the following compounds.
   a.   b.
   c.   d.

▲**14-104** Assign an IUPAC name to each of the following compounds.

a.   b. HO⌒⌒⌒

c. ⌒⌒O⌒⌒   d. (structure: benzene ring with O—CH₃ and OH)

Occurrence of and Uses for Ethers (Section 14-16)

14-105 What do the letters in the name MTBE stand for?

14-106 What is the structure of the gasoline additive MTBE?

14-107 Why has use of MTBE as a gasoline additive been discontinued in the United States?

14-108 What substance has replaced MTBE as a gasoline additive in the United States?

▲**14-109** Characterize the odor/flavor associated with each of the following naturally occurring ethers?
a. Eugenol   b. Isoeugenol
c. Vanillin   d. Allyl anisole

▲**14-110** Indicate whether or not a methoxy group is present in the structure of each of the compounds in Problem 14-109.

Isomerism for Ethers (Section 14-17)

14-111 Indicate whether each of the following ethers is or is not a constitutional isomer of ethyl propyl ether.

a.   b.

c.   d.

14-112 Indicate whether each of the following ethers is or is not a constitutional isomer of dipropyl ether.

a.   b.

c.   d.

14-113 Give common names for all ethers that are constitutional isomers of ethyl propyl ether.

14-114 Give common names for all ethers that are constitutional isomers of butyl methyl ether.

14-115 How many isomeric ethers exist when the R groups present in the ether are
a. C_1 and C_3 alkyl groups
b. C_2 and C_4 alkyl groups
c. C_3 and C_3 alkyl groups
d. C_3 and C_4 cycloalkyl groups

14-116 How many isomeric ethers exist when the R groups present in the ether are
a. C_2 and C_2 alkyl groups
b. C_2 and C_3 alkyl groups
c. C_4 and C_4 alkyl groups
d. C_4 and C_4 cycloalkyl groups

14-117 Draw condensed structural formulas for the following.
a. All ethers that are functional group isomers of 1-butanol
b. All alcohols that are functional group isomers of 2-methoxypropane

14-118 Draw condensed structural formulas for the following.
a. All ethers that are functional group isomers of 2-methyl-1-propanol
b. All alcohols that are functional group isomers of 1-ethoxyethane

▲**14-119** Draw condensed structural formulas for the eight isomeric alcohols and six isomeric ethers that have the molecular formula $C_5H_{12}O$.

▲**14-120** Draw condensed structural formulas for the four isomeric alcohols and three isomeric ethers that have the molecular formula $C_4H_{10}O$.

Physical and Chemical Properties of Ethers (Section 14-18)

14-121 Dimethyl ether and ethanol have the same molecular mass. Dimethyl ether is a gas at room temperature, and ethanol is a liquid at room temperature. Explain these observations.

14-122 Compare the solubility in water of ethers and alcohols that have similar molecular masses.

14-123 What are the two chemical hazards associated with ether use?

14-124 How do the chemical reactivities of ethers compare with those of
a. alkanes
b. alcohols

14-125 Explain why ether molecules cannot hydrogen-bond to each other.

14-126 How many hydrogen bonds can form between a single ether molecule and water molecules?

Cyclic Ethers (Section 14-19)

14-127 Classify each of the following molecular structures as that of a cyclic ether, a noncyclic ether, or a nonether.

a.   b.

c.   d.

14-128 Classify each of the following molecular structures as that of a cyclic ether, a noncyclic ether, or a nonether.

a.   b. (structure)

c.   d.

Thiols: Sulfur Analogs of Alcohols (Section 14-20)

14-129 Contrast the general structural formulas for a thiol and an alcohol.

14-130 What is the generalized structure for and name of the functional group present in a thiol?

14-131 Draw a condensed structural formula for each of the following thiols.
a. 1-Butanethiol
b. 3-Methyl-1-pentanethiol
c. Cyclopentanethiol
d. 1,2-Ethanedithiol

14-132 Draw a condensed structural formula for each of the following thiols.
a. 1-Propanethiol
b. 1,3-Pentanedithiol
c. 3-Methyl-3-pentanethiol
d. 2-Methylcyclopentanethiol

14-133 Assign a common name to each of the following thiols.
a. $CH_3—SH$
b. $CH_3—CH_2—CH_2—SH$
c. $CH_3—CH_2—CH—SH$
       |
       CH_3
d. $CH_3—CH—CH_2—SH$
       |
       CH_3

14-134 Assign a common name to each of the following thiols.
a. $CH_3—CH_2—SH$
b. $CH_3—CH—SH$
       |
       CH_3
c. $CH_3—CH_2—CH_2—CH_2—SH$
d. $CH_3—C—SH$ with CH_3 above and CH_3 below

14-135 Contrast the products that result from the oxidation of an alcohol and the oxidation of a thiol.

14-136 Write the formulas for the sulfur-containing organic products of the following reactions.
a. $2CH_3—CH_2—SH \xrightarrow[\text{agent}]{\text{Oxidizing}}$
b. $CH_3—CH_2—S—S—CH_2—CH_3 \xrightarrow[\text{agent}]{\text{Reducing}}$

14-137 For each of the following pairs of compounds, select the compound that has the higher solubility in water.
a. $CH_3—CH_2—CH_2—SH$ or $CH_3—CH_2—CH_2—OH$
b. $CH_3—CH_2—CH_2—SH$ or $CH_3—CH_2—CH_2—CH_3$

14-138 For each of the following pairs of compounds, select the compound that has the higher boiling point.
a. $CH_3—CH_2—CH_2—SH$ or $CH_3—CH_2—CH_2—OH$
b. $CH_3—CH_2—CH_2—SH$ or $CH_3—CH_2—CH_2—CH_3$

▲14-139 Assign an IUPAC name to each of the following compounds.
a. $CH_3—(CH_2)_4—SH$
b. $CH_3—(CH_2)_4—OH$
c. $CH_3—CH—CH—SH$
       | |
       CH_3 CH_3
d. $CH_3—CH—CH—OH$
       | |
       CH_3 CH_3

▲14-140 Assign an IUPAC name to each of the following compounds.
a. $CH_3—(CH_2)_3—CH—SH$
                  |
                  CH_3
b. $CH_3—(CH_2)_3—CH—OH$
                  |
                  CH_3
c. $CH_3—CH_2—CH—CH_2—OH$
              |
              CH_3
d. $CH_3—CH—CH_2—CH_2—SH$
       |
       CH_3

Thioethers: Sulfur Analogs of Ethers (Section 14-21)

14-141 Contrast the general structural formulas for a thioether and an ether.

14-142 What is the generalized structure for the functional group present in a thioether?

14-143 Assign both an IUPAC name and a common name to each of the following thioethers.
a. $CH_3—CH_2—S—CH_3$
b. $CH_3—CH—S—CH_3$
       |
       CH_3
c.
   $—S—CH_3$
d. $CH_2{=}CH—CH_2—S—CH_3$

14-144 Assign both an IUPAC name and a common name to each of the following thioethers.
a. $CH_3—CH_2—S—CH_2—CH_3$
b. $CH_3—CH—S—CH_2—CH_3$
       |
       CH_3
c.
   $—S—CH_3$
d. $CH_2{=}CH—CH_2—S—CH_2—CH_3$

▲14-145 Which of the terms *ether, alcohol, diol, thiol, thioether, thioalcohol, disulfide, sulfide,* and *peroxide* characterize(s) each of the following compounds? More than one term may apply in a given situation.
a. $CH_3—S—S—CH_3$
b. $CH_3—CH_2—O—O—CH_3$
c. $HO—CH_2—CH_2—OH$
d. $CH_3—O—CH_2—S—CH_3$

▲14-146 Which of the terms *ether, alcohol, diol, thiol, thioether, thioalcohol, disulfide, sulfide,* and *peroxide* characterize(s) each of the following compounds? More than one term may apply in a given situation.
a. $CH_3—S—CH_2—CH_3$
b. $HO—CH_2—CH_2—O—CH_3$
c. $HS—CH_2—CH_2—CH_2—OH$
d. $CH_3—O—CH_2—CH_2—SH$

Aldehydes and Ketones

15

Santokh Kochar/PhotoDisc/Getty Images

Benzaldehyde is the main flavor component in almonds. Aldehydes and ketones are responsible for the odor and taste of numerous nuts and spices.

This is the second of three chapters that consider hydrocarbon derivatives *that contain the element oxygen.* The hydrocarbon derivatives considered in the previous chapter, alcohols and ethers, have the common structural feature of carbon–oxygen *single* bonds. In this chapter, aldehydes and ketones, the simplest types of hydrocarbon derivatives that contain a carbon–oxygen *double* bond, are considered.

15-1 The Carbonyl Group

LEARNING FOCUS

Be able to describe the structural characteristics of a carbonyl group.

Both aldehydes and ketones contain a carbonyl functional group. A **carbonyl group** *is a carbon atom double-bonded to an oxygen atom.* The structural representation for a carbonyl group is

Carbonyl group

Carbon–oxygen and carbon–carbon double bonds differ in a major way. A carbon–oxygen double bond is *polar,* and a carbon–carbon double bond is *nonpolar.* The electronegativity (Section 5-9) of oxygen (3.5) is much greater than that of carbon (2.5). Hence the carbon–oxygen double bond is polarized, the oxygen atom acquiring a fractional negative charge (δ^-) and the carbon atom acquiring a fractional positive charge (δ^+) (Section 5-10). ◄

▶ *The difference in electronegativity between oxygen and carbon causes a carbon–oxygen double bond to be polar.*

$$\overset{\delta^+}{\text{C}}=\overset{\delta^-}{\text{O}} \quad \text{or} \quad \overset{+}{\text{C}}=\overset{\longrightarrow}{\text{O}}$$

Polar nature of carbon–oxygen double bond

The carbon atom in a carbonyl group has a trigonal planar arrangement of bonds about it. The bond angles between the three atoms attached to the carbonyl carbon atom are 120°, as would be predicted using VSEPR theory (Section 5-8).

120° $\left(\overset{\text{O}}{\underset{\text{C}}{\|}} \right)$ 120°   A trigonal planar structure

120°

15-2 Compounds Containing a Carbonyl Group

LEARNING FOCUS

Be able to characterize, on a structural basis, the five major classes of carbonyl-containing organic compounds.

The carbon atom of a carbonyl group must form two other bonds in addition to the carbon–oxygen double bond in order to have four bonds. The nature of these two additional bonds determines the type of carbonyl-containing compound it is. There are five major classes of carbonyl-containing hydrocarbon derivatives that are considered in this text. ◄

▶ *The word* carbonyl *is pronounced "carbon-EEL."*

1. **Aldehydes.** In an aldehyde, one of the two additional bonds that the carbonyl carbon atom forms must be to a hydrogen atom. The other may be to a hydrogen atom, an alkyl or cycloalkyl group, or an aromatic ring system.

Aldehyde functional group	Simplest aldehyde	Other examples of aldehydes

2. **Ketones.** In a ketone, both of the additional bonds of the carbonyl carbon atom must be to another carbon atom that is part of an alkyl, cycloalkyl, or aromatic group.

Ketone functional group	Simplest ketone	Other examples of ketones

3. **Carboxylic acids.** In a carboxylic acid, one of the two additional bonds of the carbonyl carbon atom must be to a hydroxyl group, and the other may be to a hydrogen atom, an alkyl or cycloalkyl group, or an aromatic ring system. The structural parameters for a carboxylic acid are the same as those for an aldehyde except that the mandatory hydroxyl group replaces the mandatory hydrogen atom of an aldehyde.

$$
\begin{array}{cccc}
\overset{\displaystyle O}{\underset{\displaystyle \parallel}{}} & \overset{\displaystyle O}{\underset{\displaystyle \parallel}{}} & \overset{\displaystyle O}{\underset{\displaystyle \parallel}{}} & \overset{\displaystyle O}{\underset{\displaystyle \parallel}{}} \\
-\text{C}-\text{OH} & \text{H}-\text{C}-\text{OH} & \text{CH}_3-\text{CH}_2-\text{C}-\text{OH} & \text{C}-\text{OH}
\end{array}
$$

| Carboxylic acid functional group | Simplest carboxylic acid | Other examples of carboxylic acids |

4. **Esters.** In an ester, one of the two additional bonds of the carbonyl carbon atom must be to an oxygen atom, which in turn is bonded to an alkyl, cycloalkyl, or aromatic group. The other bond may be to a hydrogen atom, alkyl or cycloalkyl group, or an aromatic ring system. The structural parameters for an ester differ from those for a carboxylic acid only in that an —OH group has become an —O—R or —O—Ar group.

$$
\begin{array}{cc}
\overset{\displaystyle O}{\underset{\displaystyle \parallel}{}} & \overset{\displaystyle O}{\underset{\displaystyle \parallel}{}} \\
-\text{C}-\text{O}-\text{C}- & \text{H}-\text{C}-\text{O}-\text{CH}_3
\end{array}
$$

| Ester functional group | Simplest ester |

$$
\begin{array}{cc}
\overset{\displaystyle O}{\underset{\displaystyle \parallel}{}} & \overset{\displaystyle O}{\underset{\displaystyle \parallel}{}} \\
\text{CH}_3-\text{C}-\text{O}-\text{CH}_2-\text{CH}_3 & \text{CH}_3-\text{C}-\text{O}-
\end{array}
$$

Other examples of esters

5. **Amides.** The previous four types of carbonyl compounds contain the elements carbon, hydrogen, and oxygen. Amides are different from these compounds in that the element nitrogen, in addition to carbon, hydrogen, and oxygen, is present. In an amide, an amino group (—NH$_2$) or substituted amino group replaces the —OH group of a carboxylic acid.

| Amide functional group | Simplest amide | Other examples of amides |

Aldehydes and ketones, the first two of the five major classes of carbonyl compounds, are the subject matter for the remainder of this chapter. They share the common structural feature of having *only hydrogen atoms or carbon atoms directly bonded to the carbonyl carbon atom.*

In Chapter 16, the third and fourth of the carbonyl classes, carboxylic acids and esters, are considered. The structural feature that links these two types of compounds together is that of having *an oxygen atom directly bonded to the carbonyl carbon atom.*

In Chapter 17, the fifth of the carbonyl classes, amides, is considered. In amides, *a nitrogen atom is directly bonded to the carbonyl carbon atom.* Thus, amides contain nitrogen, oxygen, carbon, and hydrogen.

Section 15-2 Quick Quiz

1. A hydrogen atom must be directly bonded to the carbonyl carbon atom in which of the following types of compounds?
   a. aldehydes
   b. ketones
   c. both aldehydes and ketones
   d. no correct response

2. Two carbon atoms must be directly bonded to the carbonyl carbon atom in which of the following types of compounds?
   a. aldehyde
   b. ketone
   c. both aldehydes and ketones
   d. no correct response
3. A nitrogen atom must be directly bonded to the carbonyl carbon atom in which of the following types of compounds?
   a. aldehyde
   b. carboxylic acid
   c. amide
   d. no correct response

Answers: 1. a; 2. b; 3. c

15-3 The Aldehyde and Ketone Functional Groups

LEARNING FOCUS

Know the structural features that distinguish aldehydes from ketones; know the structural notations used to denote aldehyde and ketone functional groups.

An **aldehyde** *is a carbonyl-containing organic compound in which the carbonyl carbon atom has at least one hydrogen atom directly attached to it.* The remaining group attached to the carbonyl carbon atom can be hydrogen, an alkyl group (R), a cycloalkyl group, or an aryl group (Ar). ▶ The aldehyde functional group is

Linear notations for an aldehyde functional group and for an aldehyde itself are —CHO and RCHO, respectively. Note that the ordering of the symbols H and O in these notations is HO, not OH (which denotes a hydroxyl group). The C in the notation RCHO is the carbonyl carbon atom. It is bonded to the R group (single bond), the H atom (single bond), and the O atom (double bond).

A **ketone** *is a carbonyl-containing organic compound in which the carbonyl carbon atom has two other carbon atoms directly attached to it.* The groups containing these bonded carbon atoms may be alkyl, cycloalkyl, or aryl. ◀

The ketone functional group is

The general condensed formula for a ketone is RCOR, in which the oxygen atom is understood to be double-bonded to the carbonyl carbon at the left of it in the formula. If both R groups of the ketone are the same, the notation R_2CO is often used.

An aldehyde functional group can be bonded to only one carbon atom because three of the four bonds from an aldehyde carbonyl carbon must go to oxygen and hydrogen. Thus an aldehyde functional group is always found at the end of a carbon chain. ◀ A ketone functional group, by contrast, is always found within a carbon chain, as it must be bonded to two other carbon atoms. ◀

Cyclic aldehydes are not possible. For an aldehyde carbonyl carbon atom to be part of a ring system, it would have to form two bonds to ring atoms, which would give it five bonds. Unlike aldehydes, ketones can form cyclic structures, such as

Six-membered ring, one ketone group

Six-membered ring, two ketone groups

Five-membered ring, one ketone group, two alkyl groups

Cyclic ketones are *not* heterocyclic ring systems as were cyclic ethers (Section 14-19).

▶ *The word* aldehyde *is pronounced "AL-da-hide."*

▶ *The word* ketone *is pronounced "KEY-tone."*

▶ *In an aldehyde, the carbonyl group is always located at the end of a hydrocarbon chain.*

$$CH_3-CH_2-CH_2-CH_2-\boxed{\overset{\overset{O}{\|}}{C}-H}$$

▶ *In a ketone, the carbonyl group is always at a nonterminal (interior) position on the hydrocarbon chain.*

$$CH_3-CH_2-CH_2-\boxed{\overset{\overset{O}{\|}}{C}}-CH_2-CH_3$$

Figure 15-1 Aldehydes and ketones are related to alcohols in the same manner that alkenes are related to alkanes; removal of two hydrogen atoms produces a double bond.

a Formation of a carbon–oxygen double bond

b Formation of a carbon–carbon double bond

Aldehydes and ketones are related to alcohols in the same manner that alkenes are related to alkanes. Removal of hydrogen atoms from each of two adjacent carbon atoms in an alkane produces an alkene. In a like manner, removal of a hydrogen atom from the —OH group of an alcohol and from the carbon atom to which the hydroxyl group is attached produces a carbonyl group (see Figure 15-1).

Section 15-3 Quick Quiz

1. In an aldehyde the carbonyl group
   a. is always located at the end of the carbon chain
   b. may be at the end of or in an interior position on the carbon chain
   c. is always located in an interior position on the carbon chain
   d. no correct response
2. In a ketone the carbonyl group
   a. is always located at the end of the carbon chain
   b. may be at the end of or in an interior position on the carbon chain
   c. is always located in an interior position on the carbon chain
   d. no correct response
3. Which of the following is a generalized linear structural designation for an aldehyde?
   a. RCOH
   b. RCHO
   c. RCOR
   d. no correct response

Answers: 1. a; 2. c; 3. b

15-4 Nomenclature for Aldehydes

LEARNING FOCUS

Given their structural formulas, be able to name aldehydes using IUPAC rules or vice versa; know the common names for the simpler aldehydes.

▶ *Line-angle structural formulas for the simpler unbranched-chain aldehydes:*

Methanal   Ethanal

Propanal   Butanal

▶ *The carbonyl carbon atom in an aldehyde cannot have any number but 1, so the number does not have to be included in the aldehyde's IUPAC name.*

In IUPAC nomenclature, aldehydes are named using the suffix *-al*. Note the closeness of this suffix to that used for naming alcohols, *-ol*. The two suffixes are often confused with each other. The suffix *-al* (pronounced like the man's name Al) denotes an aldehyde; the suffix *-ol* denotes an alcohol.

The IUPAC rules for naming aldehydes are as follows:

Rule 1: *Select as the parent carbon chain the longest chain that* includes *the carbon atom of the carbonyl group.*

Rule 2: *Name the parent chain by changing the* -e *ending of the corresponding alkane name to* -al. ◀

Rule 3: *Number the parent chain by assigning the number 1 to the carbonyl carbon atom of the aldehyde group. The number 1, however, does not become part of the name.* ◀

Rule 4: *Determine the identity and location of any substituents, and append this information to the front of the parent chain name.*

Rule 5: *When an aldehyde functional group is attached to a carbon ring, name the ring and add the suffix* -carbaldehyde.

EXAMPLE 15-1

Determining IUPAC Names for Aldehydes

Assign IUPAC names to the following aldehydes.

a.

$$CH_3-CH_2-CH_2-CH_2-\overset{\displaystyle O}{\overset{\displaystyle \|}{C}}-H$$

b.

c.

$$CH_3-CH_2-CH_2-\underset{\underset{\displaystyle CH_3}{\overset{\displaystyle |}{CH_2}}}{\overset{\displaystyle |}{CH}}-\overset{\displaystyle O}{\overset{\displaystyle \|}{C}}-H$$

d.

Solution

a. The parent chain name comes from pentane. Remove the *-e* ending and add the aldehyde suffix *-al*. The name becomes *pentanal*. The location of the carbonyl carbon atom need not be specified because this carbon atom is always number 1. The complete name is simply *pentanal*.

b. The parent chain name is *butanal*. To locate the methyl group, we number the carbon chain beginning with the carbonyl carbon atom. The complete name of the aldehyde is *3-methylbutanal*.

c. The longest chain containing the carbonyl atom is five carbons long, giving a parent chain name of *pentanal*. An ethyl group is present on carbon 2. Thus the complete name is *2-ethylpentanal*.

$$\overset{5}{C}H_3-\overset{4}{C}H_2-\overset{3}{C}H_2-\overset{2}{\underset{\underset{\displaystyle CH_3}{\overset{\displaystyle |}{CH_2}}}{C}H}-\overset{1}{\overset{\displaystyle O}{\overset{\displaystyle \|}{C}}}-H$$

d. In the IUPAC nomenclature system, when an aldehyde group is attached to a carbon ring (nonaromatic or aromatic) the ring name is given followed by the suffix *-carbaldehyde* (rule 5). The ring structure for this compound is benzene; hence, the IUPAC name for the compound is *benzenecarbaldehyde*. ◀

Small unbranched aldehydes have common names:

$$\underset{\text{Formaldehyde}}{H-\overset{\displaystyle O}{\overset{\displaystyle \|}{C}}-H} \qquad \underset{\text{Acetaldehyde}}{CH_3-\overset{\displaystyle O}{\overset{\displaystyle \|}{C}}-H}$$

$$\underset{\text{Propionaldehyde}}{CH_3-CH_2-\overset{\displaystyle O}{\overset{\displaystyle \|}{C}}-H} \qquad \underset{\text{Butyraldehyde}}{CH_3-CH_2-CH_2-\overset{\displaystyle O}{\overset{\displaystyle \|}{C}}-H}$$

Unlike the common names for alcohols and ethers, the common names for aldehydes are *one* word rather than two or three. ◀

These aldehyde common names illustrate a second method for counting from one to four in organic chemistry language: *form-, acet-, propion-,* and *butyr-*. (The first method for counting from one to four is *meth-, eth-, prop-,* and *but-,* as in methane, ethane, propane, and butane.) This new counting method will be used again in the next chapter (Section 16-3) when common names for carboxylic acids are encountered.

▶ *When a compound contains more than one type of functional group, the suffix for only one of them can be used as the ending of the name. The IUPAC rules establish priorities that specify which suffix is used. For the functional groups discussed up to this point in the text, the IUPAC priority system is*

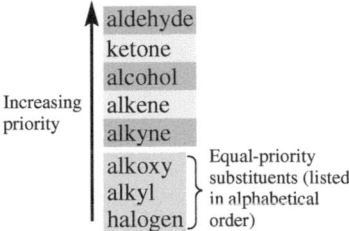

Increasing priority

aldehyde
ketone
alcohol
alkene
alkyne
alkoxy ⎫
alkyl ⎬ Equal-priority substituents (listed in alphabetical order)
halogen ⎭

aldehyde–ether

$$CH_3-O-CH_2-\overset{\displaystyle O}{\overset{\displaystyle \|}{C}}-H$$
2-Methoxyethanal

aldehyde–alkene

$$CH_2=CH-\overset{\displaystyle O}{\overset{\displaystyle \|}{C}}-H$$
2-Propenal

aldehyde–alcohol

$$HO-CH_2-CH_2-\overset{\displaystyle O}{\overset{\displaystyle \|}{C}}-H$$
3-Hydroxypropanal

▶ *The contrast between IUPAC names and common names for aldehydes is as follows:*

IUPAC (one word)

alkan*al*

pentanal
Common (one word)

(prefix) aldehyde*

butyraldehyde

**The common-name prefixes are related to natural sources for carboxylic acids with the same number of carbon atoms (Section 16-3).*

Figure 15-2 Space-filling model for benzaldehyde, the simplest aromatic aldehyde.

▶ *Aromatic aldehydes are not cyclic aldehydes (which do not exist). The carbonyl carbon atom in an aromatic aldehyde is not part of the ring system.*

In the common name system, aromatic aldehydes—compounds in which an aldehyde group is attached to a benzene ring—are named as derivatives of benzaldehyde, the parent compound (see Figure 15-2).

Benzaldehyde	3-Chloro-5-methylbenzaldehyde	4-Hydroxybenzaldehyde

The last of these compounds is named as a benzaldehyde rather than as a phenol because the aldehyde group has priority over the hydroxyl group. ◀

Section 15-4 Quick Quiz

1. The IUPAC name for the aldehyde $CH_3—CH_2—CH_2—\overset{\displaystyle O}{\overset{\|}{C}}—H$ is
   a. propyl aldehyde
   b. propanal
   c. butanal
   d. no correct response
2. The IUPAC name for the aldehyde $CH_3—\overset{\displaystyle CH_3}{\overset{|}{CH}}—CH_2—\overset{\displaystyle O}{\overset{\|}{C}}—H$ is
   a. isobutyl aldehyde
   b. methylpropanal
   c. 3-methylbutanal
   d. no correct response
3. For aldehyde common names, counting from 1 to 4 involves, respectively, the prefixes
   a. acet-, form-, propion-, butyr-
   b. acet-, propion-, butyr, form-
   c. form-, acet-, propion-, butyr-
   d. no correct response
4. The IUPAC for the aldehyde whose common name is formaldehyde is
   a. methanal
   b. ethanal
   c. propanal
   d. no correct response
5. The simplest aromatic aldehyde has the common name
   a. aldophenol
   b. benzaldehyde
   c. phenylaldehyde
   d. no correct response

Answers: 1. c; 2. c; 3. c; 4. a; 5. b

15-5 Nomenclature for Ketones

LEARNING FOCUS

Given their structural formulas, be able to name ketones using IUPAC rules or vice versa; know the common names for the simpler ketones.

Assigning IUPAC names to ketones is similar to naming aldehydes except that the ending -*one* is used instead of -*al*. The rules for IUPAC ketone nomenclature follow:

Rule 1: *Select as the parent carbon chain the longest carbon chain that* includes *the carbon atom of the carbonyl group.*

Rule 2: *Name the parent chain by changing the -e ending of the corresponding alkane name to -one. This ending, -one, is pronounced "own."*

Rule 3: *Number the carbon chain such that the carbonyl carbon atom receives the lowest possible number. The position of the carbonyl carbon atom is noted by placing a number immediately before the name of the parent chain.*

Rule 4: *Determine the identity and location of any substituents, and append this information to the front of the parent chain name.*

Rule 5: *Cyclic ketones are named by giving the name of the carbon ring and adding the suffix -one. Numbers and names for ring substituents are appended with the carbonyl carbon atom always being carbon 1. The "1" designating the carbonyl carbon atom location is not included in the name.* ◀

▶ *In IUPAC nomenclature, the ketone functional group has precedence over all groups discussed so far except the aldehyde group. When both aldehyde and ketone groups are present in the same molecule, the ketone group is named as a substituent (the* oxo- *group).*

$$CH_3-\overset{\displaystyle O}{\overset{\|}{C}}-CH_2-CH_2-\overset{\displaystyle O}{\overset{\|}{C}}-H$$

4-Oxopentanal

EXAMPLE 15-2

Determining IUPAC Names for Ketones

Assign IUPAC names to the following ketones:

a.

$$CH_3-\overset{\displaystyle O}{\overset{\|}{C}}-CH_2-CH_2-CH_3$$

b.

c.

d.

Solution

a. The parent chain name is *pentanone*. We number the chain from the end closest to the carbonyl carbon atom. Locating the carbonyl carbon at carbon 2 completes the name, *2-pentanone*.

b. The longest carbon chain of which the carbonyl carbon is a member is four carbons long. The parent chain name is *butanone*. There is one methyl group attached, and the numbering system is from right to left.

The complete name for the compound is *3-methyl-2-butanone.* ◀

c. The base name is *cyclohexanone*. The methyl group is bonded to carbon 2 because numbering begins at the carbonyl carbon. The name is *2-methylcyclohexanone*.

d. This ketone has the base name *1-pentanone*. The carbon chain contains five carbon atoms and is numbered in the direction that gives the carbonyl carbon atom the smaller number. A phenyl group (a benzene ring as an attachment) is attached to carbon 1. The IUPAC name is, thus, *1-phenyl-1-pentanone*.

▶ *Line-angle structural formulas for the simpler unbranched-chain 2-ketones:*

Propanone

Butanone

2-Pentanone

2-Hexanone

No locator number is needed in the names propanone *and* butanone *because there is only one possible location for the carbonyl group.*

The procedure for coining common names for ketones is the same as that used for ether common names (Section 14-16). They are constructed by giving, in alphabetical order, the names of the alkyl or aryl groups attached to the carbonyl functional group and then adding the word *ketone*. Unlike aldehyde common names, which are one word, those for ketones are two or three words.

$$CH_3-\overset{\displaystyle O}{\overset{\|}{C}}-CH_2-CH_3$$

Ethyl methyl ketone

$$CH_3-CH_2-\overset{\displaystyle O}{\overset{\|}{C}}-\bigcirc$$

Cyclohexyl ethyl ketone

$$CH_3-\underset{\underset{\displaystyle CH_3}{|}}{CH}-\overset{\displaystyle O}{\overset{\|}{C}}-CH_3$$

Isopropyl methyl ketone

Three ketones have additional common names besides those obtained with the preceding procedures. These three ketones are

Acetone
(dimethyl ketone)

Acetophenone
(methyl phenyl ketone)

Benzophenone
(diphenyl ketone)

▶ *The contrast between IUPAC names and common names for ketones is as follows:*

IUPAC (one word)

 alkanone

2-pentanone

Common (three or two words)

 alkyl alkyl ketone

ethyl methyl ketone

or

 dialkyl ketone

dipropyl ketone

Acetophenone is the simplest aromatic ketone. ◀

Section 15-5 Quick Quiz

1. The IUPAC name for the ketone $CH_3-CH_2-CH_2-\overset{\overset{O}{\|}}{C}-CH_3$ is
   a. pentaketone
   b. 4-pentanone
   c. 2-pentanone
   d. no correct response

2. The IUPAC name for the ketone $CH_3-\overset{\overset{CH_3}{|}}{CH}-\overset{\overset{O}{\|}}{C}-CH_2-CH_3$ is
   a. methylpentanone
   b. 2-methylpentanone
   c. 4-methylpentanone
   d. no correct response

3. What is the IUPAC name for the ketone whose common name is ethyl propyl ketone?
   a. 3-pentanone
   b. 3-hexanone
   c. 4-hexanone
   d. no correct response

4. Two additional acceptable names for *acetone* are
   a. propanone and dimethyl ketone
   b. ethanone and ethyl methyl ketone
   c. propanone and diethyl ketone
   d. no correct response

5. The simplest aromatic ketone has the common name
   a. benzone
   b. acetophenone
   c. benzophenone
   d. no correct response

Answers: 1. c; 2. d; 3. b; 4. a; 5. b

15-6 Isomerism for Aldehydes and Ketones

LEARNING FOCUS

Be familiar with isomerism possibilities for aldehydes and ketones.

Like the classes of organic compounds previously discussed (alkanes, alkenes, alkynes, alcohols, ethers, etc.), constitutional isomers exist for aldehydes and for ketones, and *between* aldehydes and ketones (functional group isomerism). The compounds butanal and 2-methylpropanal are examples of skeletal aldehyde isomers; the compounds 2-pentanone and 3-pentanone are examples of positional ketone isomers.

Aldehyde
skeletal isomers: $CH_3-CH_2-CH_2-\overset{\overset{O}{\|}}{C}-H$ and $CH_3-\overset{\overset{CH_3}{|}}{CH}-\overset{\overset{O}{\|}}{C}-H$

Ketone
positional isomers: $CH_3-\overset{\overset{O}{\|}}{C}-CH_2-CH_2-CH_3$ and $CH_3-CH_2-\overset{\overset{O}{\|}}{C}-CH_2-CH_3$

$$H-\overset{\overset{\displaystyle O}{\|}}{C}-CH_2-CH_3$$
C$_3$ aldehyde

$$CH_3-\overset{\overset{\displaystyle O}{\|}}{C}-CH_3$$
C$_3$ ketone

Figure 15-3 Aldehydes and ketones with the same number of carbon atoms and the same degree of saturation are functional group isomers, as is illustrated here for the three-carbon aldehyde (propanal) and the three-carbon ketone (propanone). Both have the molecular formula C$_3$H$_6$O.

Aldehydes and ketones with the same number of carbon atoms and the same degree of saturation are functional group isomers. Molecular models for the isomeric C$_3$ compounds propanal and propanone, which both have the molecular formula C$_3$H$_6$O, are shown in Figure 15-3. ◄

Section 15-6 Quick Quiz

1. How many different saturated six-carbon ketones exist that are named as hexanones?
   a. 2
   b. 3
   c. 4
   d. no correct response
2. Collectively, how many C$_5$ saturated unbranched-chain aldehydes and C$_5$ saturated unbranched-chain ketones exist?
   a. 1
   b. 2
   c. 3
   d. no correct response
3. The compound dimethyl ketone is a functional group isomer of
   a. ethanal
   b. propanal
   c. butanal
   d. no correct response

Answers: 1. a; 2. c; 3. b

► *This is the third time functional group isomerism has been encountered. Alcohols and ethers (Section 14-17) and thiols and thioethers (Section 14-21) also exhibit this type of isomerism.*

15-7 Selected Common Aldehydes and Ketones

LEARNING FOCUS
Be familiar with general properties of and uses for the common aldehydes and ketones.

The simplest aldehyde is the one-carbon aldehyde formaldehyde (methanal). The simplest ketone is the three-carbon ketone acetone (dimethyl ketone, propanone). One- and two-carbon ketones cannot exist. A minimum of three carbon atoms is required for a ketone: one carbon atom for the carbonyl group and one carbon atom for each of the groups attached to the carbonyl carbon atom. These two simple substances, formaldehyde and acetone, are two of the most well known and most used of all carbonyl-containing compounds.

Formaldehyde

At room temperature and pressure, formaldehyde is a colorless gas with a pungent irritating odor. ◄ Bubbling this gas through water produces *formalin,* an aqueous solution containing 37% formaldehyde by mass or 40% by volume. (This represents the solubility limit of formaldehyde gas in water.) Very little free formaldehyde gas is actually present in formalin; most of it reacts with water, producing methylene glycol.

$$H-\overset{\overset{\displaystyle O}{\|}}{C}-H + H-O-H \longrightarrow HO-CH_2-OH$$
Formaldehyde   Methylene glycol

► *The oxidation of methanol to formaldehyde has been previously mentioned (Section 14-5). Ingested methanol is oxidized in the human body to formaldehyde, and it is the formaldehyde that causes blindness.*

Figure 15-4 Formalin is used to preserve biological specimens. This coelacanth, a "prehistoric" fish, is preserved in formaldehyde.

▶ *Polymers made using both formaldehyde and phenol monomers, called phenolics, are the adhesives used in the production of plywood and particle board.*

Figure 15-5 The delightful odor of melted butter is largely due to butanedione, whose structure is given in Table 15-1.

Formalin is used for preserving biological specimens (Figure 15-4); anyone who has experience in a biology laboratory is familiar with the pungent odor of formalin. Formalin is also the most widely used preservative chemical in embalming fluids used by morticians. Its mode of action involves reaction with protein molecules in a manner that links the protein molecules together; the result is a "hardening" of the protein.

Formaldehyde is manufactured on a large scale by the oxidation of methanol.

$$CH_3{-}OH \xrightarrow[600°C\,-\,700°C]{\text{Ag catalyst}} H{-}\overset{\displaystyle O}{\overset{\|}{C}}{-}H + H_2$$

Its major use is in the manufacture of polymers. ◀

Acetone

Acetone, a colorless, volatile liquid with a pleasant, mildly "sweet" odor, is the ketone used in largest volume in industry. Acetone is an excellent solvent because it is miscible with both water and nonpolar solvents. Acetone is the main ingredient in gasoline treatments that are designed to solubilize water in the gas tank and allow it to pass through the engine in miscible form. Acetone can also be used to remove water from glassware in the laboratory. And it is a major component of some nail-polish removers.

Small amounts of acetone are produced in the human body in reactions related to obtaining energy from fats. Normally, such acetone is degraded to CO_2 and H_2O. Diabetic people produce larger amounts of acetone, not all of which can be degraded. The presence of acetone in urine is a sign of diabetes. In severe diabetes, the odor of acetone can be detected on the person's breath.

Flavorants and Odorants

Aldehydes and ketones occur widely in nature. Naturally occurring compounds of these types, with higher molecular masses, usually have pleasant odors and flavors and are often used for these properties in consumer products (perfumes, air fresheners, and the like). Table 15-1 gives the structures and uses for selected naturally occurring aldehydes and ketones. The unmistakable odor of melted butter is largely due to the four-carbon diketone butanedione (Figure 15-5).

▶ **Table 15-1 Selected Aldehydes and Ketones Whose Uses Are Based on Their Odor or Flavor**

Steroid Hormones

Many important steroid hormones (Section 19-12) are ketones, including testosterone, the hormone that controls the development of male sex characteristics; progesterone, the hormone secreted at the time of ovulation in females; and cortisone, a hormone from the adrenal glands. Synthetically produced cortisone is used as an anti-inflammatory medication. ◄

Testosterone

Progesterone

Cortisone

Sunscreens and Suntanning Agents

Many commercial sunscreen formulations have ketones as their active ingredients. Particularly common ingredients are aromatic ketones in which two non-fused benzene rings are present. Examples of such ingredients are avobenzone, oxybenzone, and dioxybenzone.

Avobenzone

Oxybenzone

Dioxybenzone

Ketones of this type absorb ultraviolet (UV) light, which enables sunbathers to control UV radiation dosage and thus avoid sunburn (caused by too much UV radiation) and yet develop a suntan (caused by a small amount of UV radiation). Many people believe that a suntan is desirable. Studies show, however, that sunbathing as well as suntans, especially when sunburn results, ages the skin prematurely and increases the risk of skin cancer.

An important compound in the "sunless" tanning industry is the acetone derivative dihydroxyacetone (DHA).

Dihydroxyacetone

DHA's mode of action is reaction with amino acids in skin protein, which produces different tones of coloration ranging from yellow to brown. The resulting pigments are called melanoidins. The coloration is similar to that produced by melanin, a pigment naturally present in the skin.

A "naturally produced" suntan, obtained through continual gradual exposure to sunlight, involves the previously mentioned compound melanin, which has a polymeric cyclic ketone structure. The focus on relevancy feature Chemical Connections 15-A—Melanin: A Hair and Skin Pigment—discusses the subject of "melanin pigmentation," a topic pertinent to both human skin and human hair.

▶ *An interesting synthetic ketone is Novec 1230, a gaseous fire-suppression agent. Structurally, it is the fully fluorinated analog of ethyl isopropyl ketone.*

This ketone is a colorless liquid at room temperature that has the feel of water. When placed on a fire, it vaporizes and smothers the fire in a manner similar to that of CO_2. It is a nonconductor of electricity and thus can be used on electrical fires and in other contexts, such as hospitals, museums, and computer equipment rooms, where water cannot be used.

CHEMICAL CONNECTIONS 15-A

Melanin: A Hair and Skin Pigment

Human hair, as well as human skin, is colored naturally by the pigment melanin—a polymeric substance involving many interconnected *cyclic ketone* units. The more melanin a person produces, which is genetically controlled, the darker is his or her hair and skin. The number of melanin-producing cells is essentially the same in dark-skinned and light-skinned people, but they are more active in dark-skinned people. The following is a representation of a portion of the structure of polymeric melanin pigment.

High-level exposure to ultraviolet radiation causes the skin to burn.

Hair pigmentation (hair color) results from biosynthesis of melanin within hair follicles. The melanin molecules so produced are incorporated into the growing hair shaft and distributed throughout the hair cortex. The melanin tends to accumulate within hair protein as granules. Hair, once it exits the scalp, is no longer alive and any damage to the melanin or the hair itself cannot be repaired by the body.

For most people, starting sometime in their thirties, the production of melanin in hair follicles begins to gradually decrease. Once a hair follicle stops producing melanin, the hair will be colorless but will appear white due to light scattering. A certain proportion of white hair in colored hair will make a head of hair appear gray.

Melanin molecules in the skin constitute a built-in defense system to protect the skin against UV radiation. The melanin molecules act as a protective barrier by absorbing and scattering the UV radiation. A dark-skinned person has more melanin molecules in the upper layers of the skin (and more protection against sunburn) than a light-skinned person.

Suntan and sunburn both involve melanin (as a skin pigment) and ultraviolet (UV) radiation. Sudden high-level exposure to UV radiation causes the skin to burn, and steady low-level exposure to UV radiation can cause tanning.

When melanin-producing cells deep in the skin are exposed to UV radiation, melanin production increases. The presence of this extra melanin in the skin gives the skin an appearance that is called a "tan." The larger the melanin molecules so produced, the deeper the tan. People who tan readily have skin that can produce a large amount of melanin.

When a person experiences a sunburn, the skin peels. When peeling occurs, any tan that has been built up (excess melanin) sloughs off with the dead skin. Thus the tanning process must begin anew.

Section 15-7 Quick Quiz

1. Which of the following statements concerning formaldehyde, the simplest aldehyde, is *incorrect*?
   a. It is a colorless gas with a pungent irritating odor.
   b. Its major industrial use is in the manufacture of polymers.
   c. As a 1% aqueous solution, it is used as an embalming fluid.
   d. no correct response
2. Which of the following statements concerning acetone, the simplest ketone, is *incorrect*?
   a. It is a colorless, volatile liquid.
   b. It has very limited solubility in water.
   c. It is a major component of some nail-polish removers.
   d. no correct response

Answers: 1. c; 2. b

15-8 Physical Properties of Aldehydes and Ketones

LEARNING FOCUS

Be familiar with general physical properties and hydrogen-bonding possibilities for aldehydes and ketones.

Unbranched 2-Ketones			
✕	C_3	C_5	C_7
✕	C_4	C_6	C_8

☐ Gas ☐ Liquid

The C_1 and C_2 aldehydes are gases at room temperature (Figure 15-6). The C_3 through C_{11} straight-chain saturated aldehydes are liquids, and the higher aldehydes are solids. The presence of alkyl groups tends to lower both boiling points and melting points, as does the presence of unsaturation in the carbon chain. Lower-molecular-mass ketones are colorless liquids at room temperature (Figure 15-6).

Figure 15-6 A physical-state summary for unbranched aldehydes and unbranched 2-ketones at room temperature and pressure.

The boiling points of aldehydes and ketones are intermediate between those of alcohols and alkanes of similar molecular mass. Aldehydes and ketones have higher boiling points than alkanes because of dipole–dipole attractions between molecules. Carbonyl group polarity (Section 15-1) makes possible these dipole–dipole interactions, which are weaker forces than hydrogen bonds (Section 7-13).

Dipole–dipole attraction

Aldehydes and ketones have lower boiling points than the corresponding alcohols because no hydrogen bonding occurs as it does with alcohols. The prerequisite for hydrogen bonding, a hydrogen atom attached to an oxygen (or nitrogen atom), is not present in aldehydes or ketones. Table 15-2 provides boiling-point information for selected aldehydes, alcohols, and alkanes. ◀

Aldehydes and ketones having fewer than six carbon atoms are soluble in both organic solvents and water. When six or more carbon atoms are present, such compounds are soluble in organic solvents but not in water. The water solubility of the smaller aldehydes and ketones results from water being able to hydrogen bond to the lone pairs of electrons on the carbonyl oxygen atom (Figure 15-7). Table 15-3 gives water solubility data for selected aldehydes and ketones.

Although low-molecular-mass aldehydes have pungent, penetrating, unpleasant odors, higher-molecular-mass aldehydes (above C_8) are more fragrant, especially benzaldehyde derivatives. Ketones generally have pleasant odors, and several are used in perfumes and air fresheners.

▶ *The ordering of boiling points for carbonyl compounds (aldehydes and ketones), alcohols, and alkanes of similar molecular mass is*

$$Alcohols > \frac{carbonyl}{compounds} > alkanes$$

▶ Table 15-2 **Boiling Points of Some Alkanes, Aldehydes, and Alcohols of Similar Molecular Mass**

Type of Compound	Compound	Structure	Molecular Mass	Boiling Point (°C)
alkane	ethane	CH_3—CH_3	30	−89
aldehyde	methanal	H—CHO	30	−21
alcohol	methanol	CH_3—OH	32	65
alkane	propane	CH_3—CH_2—CH_3	44	−42
aldehyde	ethanal	CH_3—CHO	44	20
alcohol	ethanol	CH_3—CH_2—OH	46	78
alkane	butane	CH_3—CH_2—CH_2—CH_3	58	−1
aldehyde	propanal	CH_3—CH_2—CHO	58	49
alcohol	1-propanol	CH_3—CH_3—CH_2—OH	60	97

Figure 15-7 Low-molecular-mass aldehydes and ketones are soluble in water because of hydrogen bonding.

a Aldehyde–Water Hydrogen Bonding   b Ketone–Water Hydrogen Bonding

▶ Table 15-3 **Water Solubility (g/100 g H₂O) for Various Aldehydes and Ketones**

Number of Carbon Atoms	Aldehyde	Water Solubility of Aldehyde	Ketone	Water Solubility of Ketone
1	methanal	infinite		
2	ethanal	infinite		
3	propanal	16	propanone	infinite
4	butanal	7	butanone	26
5	pentanal	4	2-pentanone	5
6	hexanal	1	2-hexanone	1.6
7	heptanal	0.1	2-heptanone	0.4
8	octanal	insoluble	2-octanone	insoluble

Section 15-8 Quick Quiz

1. Comparison of the boiling points of aldehydes and ketones with those of other compounds of similar molecular mass shows that they are
   a. lower than those of alcohols and alkanes
   b. higher than those of alcohols and alkanes
   c. higher than those of alkanes but lower than those of alcohols
   d. no correct response
2. For which of the following molecular combinations is hydrogen bonding possible?
   a. aldehyde–aldehyde
   b. ketone–ketone
   c. aldehyde–ketone
   d. no correct response

Answers: 1. c; 2. d

15-9 Preparation of Aldehydes and Ketones

LEARNING FOCUS
Be able to predict the aldehyde or ketone product obtained through alcohol oxidation.

Aldehydes and ketones can be produced by the oxidation of primary and secondary alcohols, respectively, using mild oxidizing agents such as $KMnO_4$ or $K_2Cr_2O_7$ (Section 14-9).

$$
\begin{array}{ccc}
\underset{\text{Primary alcohol}}{R-\overset{\displaystyle OH}{\underset{\displaystyle H}{C}}-H} & \xrightarrow{\text{Oxidation}} & \underset{\text{Aldehyde}}{R-\overset{\displaystyle O}{C}-H} \qquad \underset{\text{Secondary alcohol}}{R-\overset{\displaystyle OH}{\underset{\displaystyle H}{C}}-R'} \xrightarrow{\text{Oxidation}} \underset{\text{Ketone}}{R-\overset{\displaystyle O}{C}-R'}
\end{array}
$$

When this type of reaction is used for aldehyde preparation, reaction conditions must be sufficiently mild to avoid further oxidation of the aldehyde to a carboxylic acid (Section 14-9). Ketones do not undergo the further oxidation that aldehydes do.

In the oxidation of an alcohol to an aldehyde or a ketone, the alcohol molecule loses H atoms. Recall that a *decrease in the number of C—H bonds* in an organic molecule is one of the operational definitions for the process of *oxidation* (Section 14-9). ◄

▶ *The term* aldehyde *stems from* alcohol dehydrogenation, *indicating that aldehydes are related to alcohols by the loss of hydrogen.*

EXAMPLE 15-3

Predicting Products in Alcohol Oxidation Reactions

Draw the structure of the aldehyde or ketone formed from the oxidation of each of the following alcohols. Assume that reaction conditions are sufficiently mild that any aldehydes produced are not oxidized further.

a. $CH_3—CH_2—CH_2—OH$

b. $CH_3—\overset{\overset{\displaystyle |}{OH}}{CH}—CH_3$

c. —OH

d. $CH_3—\overset{\overset{\displaystyle CH_3}{|}}{\underset{\underset{\displaystyle CH_3}{|}}{C}}—OH$

Solution

a. This is a primary alcohol. It will give the aldehyde *propanal* as an oxidation product.

$$CH_3—CH_2—\overset{\overset{\displaystyle O}{\|}}{C}—H$$
Propanal

b. This is a secondary alcohol. Upon oxidation, secondary alcohols are converted to ketones.

$$CH_3—\overset{\overset{\displaystyle O}{\|}}{C}—CH_3$$
Propanone

c. This cyclic alcohol is a secondary alcohol; hence a ketone is the oxidation product.

Cyclohexanone

d. This is a tertiary alcohol. Tertiary alcohols do not undergo oxidation (Section 14-9).

Section 15-9 Quick Quiz

1. A general method for the preparation of aldehydes, using a mild oxidizing agent, is oxidation of which of the following?
   a. 1° alcohol
   b. 2° alcohol
   c. 3° alcohol
   d. no correct response
2. A general method for the preparation of ketones, using a mild oxidizing agent, is oxidation of which of the following?
   a. 1° alcohol
   b. 2° alcohol
   c. 3° alcohol
   d. no correct response

Answers: 1. a; 2. b

15-10 Oxidation and Reduction of Aldehydes and Ketones

LEARNING FOCUS

Describe the conditions necessary for and the products formed in reactions involving aldehyde oxidation and reduction and ketone oxidation and reduction.

Oxidation of Aldehydes and Ketones

Aldehydes readily undergo oxidation to carboxylic acids (Section 15-9), and ketones are resistant to oxidation.

$$\underset{\text{Aldehyde}}{R-\overset{\overset{\displaystyle O}{\|}}{C}-H} \xrightarrow{\text{[O]}} \underset{\text{Carboxylic acid}}{R-\overset{\overset{\displaystyle O}{\|}}{C}-OH} \qquad \underset{\text{Ketone}}{R-\overset{\overset{\displaystyle O}{\|}}{C}-R} \xrightarrow{\text{[O]}} \text{no reaction}$$

In aldehyde oxidation, the aldehyde gains an oxygen atom (supplied by the oxidizing agent). An *increase in the number of C—O bonds* is one of the operational definitions for the process of *oxidation* (Section 14-9).

Among the mild oxidizing agents that convert aldehydes into carboxylic acids is oxygen in air. Thus aldehydes must be protected from air. When an aldehyde is prepared from oxidation of a primary alcohol (Section 15-9), it is usually removed from the reaction mixture immediately to prevent it from being further oxidized to a carboxylic acid.

The oxidizing agent potassium dichromate ($K_2Cr_2O_7$) is often used for aldehyde oxidation reactions. This oxidizing agent was previously encountered in Section 14-7 as the agent used to oxidize primary and secondary alcohols.

Because both aldehydes and ketones contain carbonyl groups, we might expect similar oxidation reactions for the two types of compounds. Oxidation of an aldehyde involves breaking a carbon–hydrogen bond, and oxidation of a ketone involves breaking a carbon–carbon bond. The former is much easier to accomplish than the latter. For ketones to be oxidized, strenuous reaction conditions must be employed.

Several tests, based on the ease with which aldehydes are oxidized, have been developed for distinguishing between aldehydes and ketones, for detecting the presence of aldehyde groups in sugars (carbohydrates), and for measuring the amounts of sugars present in a solution. The most widely used of these tests are the Tollens test and Benedict's test.

The Tollens test, also called the silver mirror test, involves a solution that contains silver nitrate ($AgNO_3$) and ammonia (NH_3) in water. When Tollens solution is added to an aldehyde, Ag^+ ion (the oxidizing agent) is reduced to silver metal, which deposits on the inside of the test tube, forming a silver mirror. The appearance of this silver mirror (see Figure 15-8) is a positive test for the presence of the aldehyde group.

$$\underset{\text{Aldehyde}}{R-\overset{\overset{\displaystyle O}{\|}}{C}-H} + Ag^+ \xrightarrow[\text{heat}]{NH_3,\ H_2O} \underset{\text{Carboxylic acid}}{R-\overset{\overset{\displaystyle O}{\|}}{C}-OH} + \underset{\text{Silver metal}}{Ag}$$

The Ag^+ ion will not oxidize ketones. ◄

Benedict's test is similar to the Tollens test in that a metal ion is the oxidizing agent. With this test, Cu^{2+} ion is reduced to Cu^+ ion, which precipitates from solution as Cu_2O (a brick-red solid; see Figure 15-9).

$$\underset{\text{Aldehyde}}{R-\overset{\overset{\displaystyle O}{\|}}{C}-H} + Cu^{2+} \longrightarrow \underset{\text{Carboxylic acid}}{R-\overset{\overset{\displaystyle O}{\|}}{C}-OH} + \underset{\text{Brick-red solid}}{Cu_2O}$$

Benedict's solution is made by dissolving copper sulfate, sodium citrate, and sodium carbonate in water.

▶ *Reaction of Tollens solution with aldehydes represents a case of selective oxidation; this solution will oxidize the aldehyde group present in a molecule but not any other functional groups present. Thus, if a molecule contains both an aldehyde group and an alcohol group, the former is oxidized but not the latter.*

a An aqueous solution of ethanal is added to a solution of silver nitrate in aqueous ammonia and stirred.

b The solution darkens as ethanal is oxidized to ethanoic acid, and Ag^+ ion is reduced to silver.

c The inside of the beaker becomes coated with metallic silver.

Figure 15-8 A positive Tollens test for aldehydes involves the formation of a silver mirror.

Blood-glucose levels must be frequently measured when a person has diabetes. Glucose-monitoring systems now in use are based on aldehyde oxidation reactions. The focus on relevancy feature Chemical Connections 15-B—Diabetes, Aldehyde Oxidation, and Glucose Testing—further considers the topic of diabetes, aldehyde oxidation, and glucose testing.

Reduction of Aldehydes and Ketones

Aldehydes and ketones are easily reduced by hydrogen gas (H_2), in the presence of a catalyst (Ni, Pt, or Cu), to form alcohols. The reduction, via hydrogenation, of aldehydes produces primary alcohols, and the reduction of ketones yields secondary alcohols.

$$\text{Aldehyde} \xrightarrow{\text{Reduction}} \text{primary alcohol}$$

$$\text{Ketone} \xrightarrow{\text{Reduction}} \text{secondary alcohol}$$

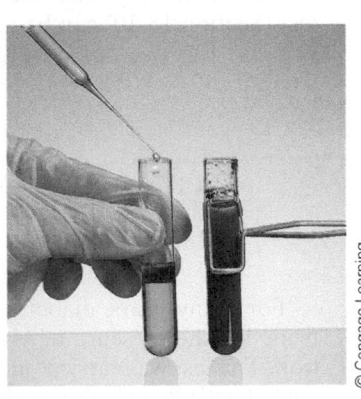

Figure 15-9 Benedict's solution, which is blue in color, turns brick-red when an aldehyde reacts with it.

Specific examples of such reactions follow.

Aldehyde reduction:
$$CH_3-\overset{\overset{\text{O}}{\|}}{C}-H + H_2 \xrightarrow{Ni} CH_3-\overset{\overset{\text{OH}}{|}}{\underset{\underset{\text{H}}{|}}{C}}-H$$

Ethanal   Ethanol

Ketone reduction:
$$CH_3-\overset{\overset{\text{O}}{\|}}{C}-CH_3 + H_2 \xrightarrow{Ni} CH_3-\overset{\overset{\text{OH}}{|}}{\underset{\underset{\text{H}}{|}}{C}}-CH_3$$

Propanone   2-Propanol

It is the addition of hydrogen atoms to the carbon–oxygen double bond that produces the alcohol in each of these reactions.

$$\overset{}{\underset{}{C}}=O + H_2 \xrightarrow{\text{Catalyst}} \overset{}{\underset{\underset{\text{H}}{|}}{C}}-\overset{}{\underset{\underset{\text{H}}{|}}{O}}$$

This hydrogenation process is very similar to the addition of hydrogen to the carbon–carbon double bond of an alkene to produce an alkane, which was encountered in Section 13-9.

$$\overset{}{\underset{}{C}}=\overset{}{\underset{}{C}} + H_2 \xrightarrow{\text{Catalyst}} \overset{}{\underset{\underset{\text{H}}{|}}{C}}-\overset{}{\underset{\underset{\text{H}}{|}}{C}}$$

CHEMICAL CONNECTIONS 15-B

Diabetes, Aldehyde Oxidation, and Glucose Testing

Diabetes mellitus is a disease that involves the hormone insulin, a substance necessary to control blood-sugar (glucose) levels. There are two forms of diabetes. In one form, the pancreas does not produce insulin at all. Patients with this condition require injections of insulin to control glucose levels. In the second form, the body cannot make proper use of insulin. Patients with this form of diabetes can often control glucose levels through their diet but may require medication. If the blood-sugar level of a diabetic becomes too high, serious kidney damage can result.

Normal urine does not contain glucose. When the kidneys become overloaded with glucose (the blood-glucose level is too high), glucose is excreted in the urine. Benedict's test (Section 15-10) can be used to detect glucose in urine because glucose has an aldehyde group present in its structure.

$$CH_2-CH-CH-CH-CH-\overset{\overset{\displaystyle O}{\|}}{C}-H$$
$$\quad|\quad\;\;|\quad\;\;|\quad\;\;|\quad\;\;|$$
$$OH\;\;\;OH\;\;\;OH\;\;\;OH\;\;\;OH$$

Glucose

For many years, diabetes monitoring involved testing urine for the presence of glucose with a Benedict's solution. The test was carried out using either plastic test strips coated with Benedict's solution or Clinitest tablets (a convenient solid form of Benedict's reagent). A few drops of urine were added to the plastic strip or tablet, and the degree of coloration was used to estimate the blood-glucose level. The solution turned greenish at a low glucose level, then yellow-orange, and finally a dark orange-red.

Today, use of Benedict's solution for urine glucose testing has been replaced largely by other chemical tests that provide better results. Blood-glucose testing has been found to detect rising glucose levels earlier than urine-glucose testing. Blood-glucose tests are now the preferred method for monitoring glucose levels.

Blood-glucose levels are now routinely monitored using electronic glucose meters. In the first generation of such meters, blood-glucose testing involved placing a drop of blood (from a finger prick) on a plastic strip containing a dye and an enzyme that would oxidize glucose's aldehyde group. A two-step reaction sequence then occurred. First, the enzyme caused glucose oxidation to a carboxylic acid, with hydrogen peroxide (H_2O_2) being another product of the reaction.

$$\underset{\substack{\text{Aldehyde}\\\text{(glucose)}}}{R-\overset{\overset{\displaystyle O}{\|}}{C}-H} + O_2 \xrightarrow{\text{Enzyme}} \underset{\text{Carboxylic acid}}{R-\overset{\overset{\displaystyle O}{\|}}{C}-OH} + \underset{\substack{\text{Hydrogen}\\\text{peroxide}}}{H_2O_2}$$

Then the H_2O_2 reacted with the dye to produce a colored product. The amount of color produced, measured by comparison with a color chart or by an electronic monitor, was proportional to the blood-glucose concentration.

Such glucose-monitoring systems have now been replaced by a second generation of meters that directly measure the amount of oxidizing agent that reacts with a known amount of blood. This value is electronically correlated with blood-glucose levels, and the concentration is displayed digitally.

Phanie/Science Source

In a blood-glucose test, a small drop of blood obtained from a finger prick is absorbed on a test strip present within the blood-glucose monitor. The results of the blood–strip interaction, which involves aldehyde oxidation, are processed electronically and displayed on an LCD readout.

Aldehyde reduction and ketone reduction to produce alcohols are the "opposite" of the oxidation of alcohols to produce aldehydes and ketones (Section 15-9). These "opposite" relationships can be diagrammed as follows:

As was noted in Section 14-9, "keeping track" of such relationships is an aid in remembering organic chemistry reaction schemes.

EXAMPLE 15-4

Predicting Product Identity in Aldehyde/Ketone Oxidation/Reduction Reactions

Draw the structure of the organic product formed when each of the following aldehydes and ketones are subjected to oxidation or reduction. If no reaction occurs, state that such is the case.

a. $CH_3-CH_2-\overset{\overset{\displaystyle O}{\|}}{C}-H \xrightarrow{K_2Cr_2O_7}$

b. $CH_3-CH_2-\overset{\overset{\displaystyle O}{\|}}{C}-H \xrightarrow[Ni]{H_2}$

c. $CH_3-CH_2-CH_2-\overset{\overset{\displaystyle O}{\|}}{C}-CH_3 \xrightarrow[\text{solution}]{\text{Benedict's}}$

d. $CH_3-CH_2-CH_2-\overset{\overset{\displaystyle O}{\|}}{C}-CH_3 \xrightarrow[Ni]{H_2}$

Solution

a. The reactant is an aldehyde, and the reaction conditions are those of oxidation; $K_2Cr_2O_7$ is an oxidizing agent. Aldehyde oxidation produces a carboxylic acid.

$$CH_3-CH_2-\overset{\overset{\displaystyle O}{\|}}{C}-H \longrightarrow CH_3-CH_2-\overset{\overset{\displaystyle O}{\|}}{C}-OH$$

b. The reactant is an aldehyde, and the reaction conditions are those of reduction; H_2 gas, with Ni present as a catalyst, is a reducing agent. Aldehyde reduction produces a primary alcohol.

$$CH_3-CH_2-\overset{\overset{\displaystyle O}{\|}}{C}-H \longrightarrow CH_3-CH_2-\overset{\overset{\displaystyle OH}{|}}{C}H_2$$

c. The reactant is a ketone, and the reaction conditions are those of oxidation; Benedict's solution is an oxidizing agent. Ketones cannot be oxidized by mild oxidizing agents; therefore, no reaction occurs.

d. The reactant is a ketone, and the reaction conditions are those of reduction; as in Part b, H_2 gas, with Ni present as a catalyst, is a reducing agent. Ketone reduction produces a secondary alcohol.

$$CH_3-CH_2-CH_2-\overset{\overset{\displaystyle O}{\|}}{C}-CH_3 \longrightarrow CH_3-CH_2-CH_2-\overset{\overset{\displaystyle OH}{|}}{C}H-CH_3$$

Section 15-10 Quick Quiz

1. Which of the following statements about the oxidation of aldehydes and ketones using mild oxidizing agents is correct?
   a. Both aldehydes and ketones are easily oxidized.
   b. Aldehydes, but not ketones, are easily oxidized.
   c. Ketones, but not aldehydes, are easily oxidized.
   d. no correct response
2. Aldehyde oxidation using a mild oxidizing agent produces a(n)
   a. alcohol
   b. carboxylic acid
   c. ketone
   d. no correct response
3. Which of the following oxidizing or reducing agents would convert a ketone to an alcohol?
   a. H_2, Ni catalyst
   b. Tollens' solution
   c. Benedict's solution
   d. no correct response

(continued)

4. Reduction of the compound $CH_3-CH_2-\overset{\overset{\displaystyle O}{\|}}{C}-H$ produces which of the following compounds?

   a. $CH_3-CH_2-CH_3$
   b. $CH_3-CH_2-CH_2-OH$
   c. $CH_3-\overset{\overset{\displaystyle O}{\|}}{C}-CH_3$
   d. no correct response

Answers: 1. b; 2. b; 3. a; 4. b

15-11 Reaction of Aldehydes and Ketones with Alcohols

LEARNING FOCUS

Know the structural features for *hemiacetals* and *acetals;* know how such compounds are prepared from alcohols and the reaction products when such compounds undergo hydrolysis.

Aldehydes and ketones react with alcohols to form hemiacetals and acetals. Reaction with *one* molecule of alcohol produces a hemiacetal, which is then converted to an acetal by reaction with a second alcohol molecule.

$$\text{Aldehyde or ketone + alcohol} \xrightarrow[\text{catalyst}]{\text{Acid}} \text{hemiacetal}$$

$$\text{Hemiacetal + alcohol} \xrightarrow[\text{catalyst}]{\text{Acid}} \text{acetal}$$

The Greek prefix *hemi-* means "half." When one alcohol molecule has reacted with the aldehyde or ketone, the compound is halfway to the final acetal. ◀

Further information about these two reactions follows.

▶ *Hemiacetal and acetal formation are very important biochemical reactions; they are crucial to understanding the chemistry of carbohydrates, which is considered in Chapter 18.*

Hemiacetal Formation

Hemiacetal formation is an addition reaction in which a molecule of alcohol adds to the carbonyl group of an aldehyde or ketone. The H portion of the alcohol adds to the carbonyl oxygen atom, and the R—O portion of the alcohol adds to the carbonyl carbon atom.

Formally defined, a **hemiacetal** *is an organic compound in which a carbon atom is bonded to both a hydroxyl group (—OH) and an alkoxy group (—OR).*

$$-\overset{\overset{\displaystyle OH}{|}}{\underset{|}{C}}-OR$$

The hemiacetal functional group has a direct relationship to the ether functional group. It can be visualized as an ether functional group to which an —OH group has been added. ◄

► *Hemiacetals contain an alcohol group (hydroxyl group) and an ether group (alkoxy group) on the same carbon atom.*

The ether
functional group

The hemiacetal
functional group

The carbon atom in the hemiacetal functional group that is bonded to two oxygen atoms is called the *hemiacetal carbon atom*.

hemiacetal
carbon atom

A reaction mixture containing a hemiacetal is always in equilibrium with the alcohol and carbonyl compound from which it was made, and the equilibrium lies to the carbonyl compound side of the reaction (Section 9-9).

Alcohol + aldehyde ⇌ hemiacetal

Alcohol + ketone ⇌ hemiacetal

This situation makes isolation of the hemiacetal difficult; in practice, it usually cannot be done.

An important exception to this difficulty with isolation is the case where the —OH and $\overset{\diagdown}{\diagup}$C=O functional groups that react to form the hemiacetal come from the *same* molecule. This produces a *cyclic* hemiacetal rather than a noncyclic one, and cyclic acetals are more stable than the noncyclic ones and can be isolated.

Illustrative of intramolecular hemiacetal formation is the reaction

Redrawing of
the structure
so the two ends of
the carbon chain
are close to
each other

Ring
closure

Cyclic hemiacetal

Cyclic hemiacetals are very important compounds in carbohydrate chemistry, the topic of Chapter 18. Glucose, the most common simple carbohydrate, exists primarily in the form of a cyclic hemiacetal (Section 18-10). This cyclic structure, which contains five —OH groups, is

Hemiacetal carbon atom

EXAMPLE 15-5

Recognizing Hemiacetal Structures

Indicate whether each of the following compounds is a hemiacetal.

a. $CH_3-CH-O-CH_3$
  |
  OH

b.
  OH
  |
  CH_3-C-CH_3
  |
  $O-CH_3$

c.
  CH_3
  |
  $CH_3-CH-CH-O-CH_3$
  |
  OH

d.

Solution

In each part, the focus will be on the presence or absence of an —OH group and an —OR group attached to the same carbon atom.

a. An —OH group and an —OR group are attached to the same carbon atom. The compound is a *hemiacetal*.
b. An —OH group and an —OR group are attached to the same carbon atom. The compound is a *hemiacetal*.
c. The —OH and —OR groups present in this molecule are attached to *different* carbon atoms. Therefore, the molecule is *not a hemiacetal*.
d. A ring carbon atom bonded to two oxygen atoms is present: one oxygen atom in an —OH substituent and the other oxygen atom bonded to the rest of the ring (the same as an R group). This is a *hemiacetal*.

Acetal Formation

▶ *This is the second encounter with condensation reactions. The first encounter involved alcohol dehydration (Section 14-9).*

If a small amount of acid catalyst is added to a hemiacetal reaction mixture, the hemiacetal reacts with a second alcohol molecule, in a condensation reaction, to form an acetal. ◀

$$R_1-\overset{\overset{\displaystyle OH}{|}}{\underset{\underset{\displaystyle H}{|}}{C}}-OR_2 + R_3-OH \overset{H^+}{\rightleftharpoons} R_1-\overset{\overset{\displaystyle OR_3}{|}}{\underset{\underset{\displaystyle H}{|}}{C}}-OR_2 + H-OH$$

A hemiacetal   An alcohol   An acetal

An **acetal** *is an organic compound in which a carbon atom is bonded to two alkoxy groups (—OR).*

$$-\overset{\overset{\displaystyle OR}{|}}{\underset{\underset{\displaystyle |}{}}{C}}-OR$$

▶ *Acetals have two alkoxy groups (—OR) attached to the same carbon atom.*

The relationship between the hemiacetal and acetal functional groups is shown in the following diagram. ◀

$$-\overset{|}{C}-O-\overset{|}{C}-O-H \qquad -\overset{|}{C}-O-\overset{|}{C}-O-\overset{|}{C}-$$

The hemiacetal   The acetal
functional group   functional group

A specific example of acetal formation from a hemiacetal is

$$CH_3-\overset{\overset{\displaystyle OH}{|}}{\underset{\underset{\displaystyle O-CH_3}{|}}{CH}} + CH_3-CH_2-OH \overset{H^+}{\rightleftharpoons} CH_3-\overset{\overset{\displaystyle O-CH_2-CH_3}{|}}{\underset{\underset{\displaystyle O-CH_3}{|}}{CH}} + H-OH$$

Figure 15-10 Molecular models for acetaldehyde and its hemiacetal and acetal formed by reaction with ethyl alcohol.

Note that acetal formation does not involve addition to a carbon–oxygen double bond as hemiacetal formation does; no double bond is present in either of the reactants involved in acetal formation. Acetal formation involves a substitution reaction; the —OR group of the alcohol replaces the —OH group on the hemiacetal.

Figure 15-10 shows molecular models for acetaldehyde (the two-carbon aldehyde) and the hemiacetal and acetal formed when this aldehyde reacts with ethyl alcohol. ◀

Acetal Hydrolysis

Acetals, unlike hemiacetals, are easily isolated from reaction mixtures. They are stable in basic solution but undergo *hydrolysis* in acidic solution. A **hydrolysis reaction** *is the chemical reaction of a compound with H_2O, in which the compound splits into two or more fragments as the elements of water (H— and —OH) are added to the compound.* The products of acetal hydrolysis are the aldehyde or ketone and alcohols that originally reacted to form the acetal. ◀

$$\begin{matrix} O-R_1 \\ | \\ -C-O-R_2 + H-OH \end{matrix} \underset{\text{catalyst}}{\overset{\text{Acid}}{\rightleftharpoons}} \begin{matrix} O \\ || \\ C \end{matrix} + R_1-OH + R_2-O-H$$

Acetal   Aldehyde or ketone

For example,

$$\begin{matrix} O-CH_2-CH_3 \\ | \\ CH_3-C-O-CH_3 \\ | \\ CH_3 \end{matrix} + H-OH \underset{\text{catalyst}}{\overset{\text{Acid}}{\rightleftharpoons}} \begin{matrix} O \\ || \\ CH_3-C-CH_3 \end{matrix} + CH_3-OH + CH_3-CH_2-OH$$

The carbonyl hydrolysis product is an aldehyde if the acetal carbon atom has a hydrogen atom attached directly to it, and it is a ketone if no hydrogen attachment is present. In the preceding example, the carbonyl product is a ketone because the two additional acetal carbon atom attachments are methyl groups.

▶ *An acetal is not an ether, even though both types of compounds have structures in which one or more alkoxy (—OR) groups are present.*

$$\begin{matrix} | \\ -C-OR \\ | \end{matrix} \qquad \begin{matrix} OR \\ | \\ -C-OR \\ | \end{matrix}$$
Ether   Acetal

An acetal has two alkoxy groups bonded to the same carbon atom, whereas an ether has one alkoxy group bonded to a carbon atom.

▶ *In Section 24-1, enzyme-catalyzed hydrolysis of acetals will be discussed as an important step in the digestion of carbohydrates.*

EXAMPLE 15-6

Predicting Products in Acetal Hydrolysis Reactions

Draw the structures of the aldehyde (or ketone) and the two alcohols produced when the following acetals undergo hydrolysis in acidic solution.

a.
$$\begin{matrix} O-CH_3 \\ | \\ CH_3-CH_2-CH \\ | \\ O-CH_2-CH_3 \end{matrix}$$

b.
$$\begin{matrix} CH_3 \\ | \\ CH_3-C-O-CH-CH_3 \\ | \qquad\quad | \\ O \qquad\quad CH_3 \\ | \\ CH_3-C-CH_3 \\ | \\ CH_3 \end{matrix}$$

(continued)

Solution

a. Each of the alkoxy (—OR) groups present will be converted into an alcohol during the hydrolysis. Because the acetal carbon atom has an H attachment, the remainder of the molecule becomes an aldehyde, with the carbon atom to which the alkoxy groups were attached becoming the carbonyl carbon atom.

b. Again, each of the alkoxy groups present will be converted into an alcohol during the hydrolysis. Because the acetal carbon atom lacks an H attachment, the remainder of the molecule becomes a ketone.

Nomenclature for Hemiacetals and Acetals

A "descriptive" type of common nomenclature that includes the terms *hemiacetal* and *acetal,* as well as the name of the carbonyl compound (aldehyde or ketone) produced in the hydrolysis of the hemiacetal or acetal, is commonly used in describing such compounds. Two examples of such nomenclature are

Methyl hemiacetal of propanal   Diethyl acetal of propanone

Chemistry at a Glance—Summary of Chemical Reactions Involving Aldehydes and Ketones—summarizes reactions that involve aldehydes and ketones.

Section 15-11 Quick Quiz

1. A hemiacetal is a compound in which
   a. a hydroxyl group and an alkoxy group are attached to the same carbon atom
   b. a hydroxyl group and an alkoxy group are attached to adjacent carbon atoms
   c. two alkoxy groups are attached to the same carbon atom
   d. no correct response
2. When an alcohol molecule adds across the carbon–oxygen double bond of a carbonyl group in an aldehyde or ketone the
   a. H atom from the alcohol bonds to the carbonyl carbon atom
   b. OH portion from the alcohol bonds to the carbonyl oxygen atom
   c. OR portion from the alcohol bonds to the carbonyl carbon atom
   d. no correct response
3. The structural difference between a hemiacetal and an acetal is the replacement of a hemiacetal
   a. —OH group with an —OR group
   b. H atom with an —OR group
   c. —OR group with an —OH group
   d. no correct response

4. To produce an acetal from a ketone, the ketone must react with which of the following?
   a. two identical alcohol molecules
   b. two different alcohol molecules
   c. two alcohol molecules, which may or may not be identical
   d. no correct response
5. Hydrolysis of an acetal in an acid solution would produce
   a. an aldehyde, a ketone, and two alcohol molecules
   b. an aldehyde or a ketone and one alcohol molecule
   c. an aldehyde or a ketone and two alcohol molecules
   d. no correct response

Answers: 1. a; 2. c; 3. a; 4. c; 5. c

CHEMISTRY AT A GLANCE

Summary of Chemical Reactions Involving Aldehydes and Ketones

CHEMICAL REACTIONS OF ALDEHYDES AND KETONES

Oxidation
- Common oxidizing agents include O_2(air), $K_2Cr_2O_7$, Tollens solution, and Benedict's solution.

  Aldehyde ⟶ carboxylic acid
  Ketone ⟶ no reaction

Hemiacetal and Acetal Formation
- Reaction with one alcohol molecule produces a hemiacetal.
- Reaction with two alcohol molecules produces an acetal.

  Aldehyde ⟶ hemiacetal ⟶ acetal
  Ketone ⟶ hemiacetal ⟶ acetal

Reduction
- H_2 gas is the reducing agent.
- Ni, Pt, or Cu is the catalyst.

  Aldehyde ⟶ 1° alcohol
  Ketone ⟶ 2° alcohol

PREPARATION OF ALDEHYDES AND KETONES

Alcohol Oxidation
- $KMnO_4$ and $K_2Cr_2O_7$ are common oxidizing agents.

  1° alcohol ⟶ aldehyde
  2° alcohol ⟶ ketone

15-12 Sulfur-Containing Carbonyl Groups

LEARNING FOCUS

Know the structural characteristics for sulfur-containing compounds known as *thiocarbonyls* and *sulfoxides.*

The introduction of sulfur into a carbonyl group produces two different classes of compounds, depending on whether the sulfur atom replaces the carbonyl oxygen atom or the carbonyl carbon atom.

Replacement of the carbonyl *oxygen* atom with sulfur produces *thiocarbonyl compounds*—thioaldehydes (thials) and thioketones (thiones)—the simplest of which are

$$\overset{\displaystyle S}{\underset{}{\underset{\displaystyle \parallel}{H-C-H}}} \qquad \overset{\displaystyle S}{\underset{}{\underset{\displaystyle \parallel}{CH_3-C-CH_3}}}$$

Thioformaldehyde (Methanethial) Thioacetone (Propanethione)

Thiocarbonyl compounds such as these are unstable and readily decompose.

Replacement of the carbonyl *carbon* atom with sulfur produces *sulfoxides,* compounds that are much more stable than thiocarbonyl compounds. The oxidation of a thioether (sulfide) [Section 14-21] constitutes the most common route to a sulfoxide.

$$R-S-R \xrightarrow{[O]} R-\overset{\overset{\textstyle O}{\|}}{S}-R$$

Thioether   Sulfoxide

A highly interesting sulfoxide is DMSO (dimethyl sulfoxide), a sulfur analog of acetone, the simplest ketone.

$$CH_3-\overset{\overset{\textstyle O}{\|}}{S}-CH_3 \qquad CH_3-\overset{\overset{\textstyle O}{\|}}{C}-CH_3$$

DMSO   Acetone

DMSO is an odorless liquid with unusual properties. Because of the presence of the polar sulfur–oxide bond, DMSO is miscible with water and also quite soluble in less polar organic solvents. When rubbed on the skin, DMSO has remarkable penetrating power and is quickly absorbed into the body, where it relieves pain and inflammation. For many years, it has been heralded as a "miracle drug" for arthritis, sprains, burns, herpes, infections, and high blood pressure. However, the FDA has for various reasons steadfastly refused to approve it for general medical use. For example, the FDA says that DMSO's powerful penetrating action could cause an insecticide on a gardener's skin to be accidentally carried into his or her bloodstream. Another complication is that DMSO is reduced in the body to dimethyl sulfide, a compound with a strong garlic-like odor that soon appears on the breath.

$$CH_3-\overset{\overset{\textstyle O}{\|}}{S}-CH_3 \xrightarrow{\text{Reduction}} CH_3-S-CH_3$$

The FDA has approved DMSO for use in treating certain bladder conditions and as a veterinary drug for topical use in nonbreeding dogs and horses. For example, DMSO is used as an anti-inflammatory rub for race horses.

Several aldehydes, ketones, and thioaldehydes have eye-irritant properties that often cause tear production in humans. An oxygenated derivative of the three-carbon thioaldehyde propanethial is the compound that induces tear production when onions are chopped or sliced. The focus on relevancy feature Chemical Connections 15-C—Lachrymatory Aldehydes and Ketones—presents information about this "onion compound," as well as about eye irritants associated with mace, tear gas, wood smoke, and barbecue smoke.

Section 15-12 Quick Quiz

1. Structurally, production of a thiocarbonyl compound involves replacement of
   a. the carbonyl carbon atom with sulfur
   b. the carbonyl oxygen atom with sulfur
   c. both the carbonyl carbon and oxygen atoms with sulfur
   d. no correct response
2. Structurally, production of a sulfoxide compound involves replacement of
   a. the carbonyl carbon atom with sulfur
   b. the carbonyl oxygen atom with sulfur
   c. both the carbonyl carbon and oxygen atoms with sulfur
   d. no correct response

Answers: 1. b; 2. a

CHEMICAL CONNECTIONS 15-C

Lachrymatory Aldehydes and Ketones

A lachrymator, pronounced "lack-ra-mater," is a compound that causes the production of tears. A number of aldehydes and ketones have lachrymatic properties.

Two lachrymal ketones are 2-chloroacetophenone and bromoacetone.

2-Chloroacetophenone
(2-chloro-1-phenylethanone)

Bromoacetone
(1-bromopropanone)

2-Chloroacetophenone is a component of the tear gas used by police and the military. It is also the active ingredient in mace canisters now marketed for use by individuals to protect themselves from attackers. The compound bromoacetone has been used as a chemical war gas.

Smoke contains compounds that cause the eyes to tear. A predominant lachrymator in wood smoke is formaldehyde, the one-carbon aldehyde. The smoke associated with an outdoor barbecue contains the unsaturated aldehyde *acrolein*.

$$CH_2{=}CH{-}\overset{\displaystyle O}{\overset{\|}{C}}{-}H$$

Acrolein
(propenal)

Acrolein is formed as fats that are present in meat break down when heated. (Besides being a lachrymator, acrolein is responsible for the "pleasant" odor associated with the process of barbecuing meat.)

The lachrymatory compound associated with onions is a derivative of thiopropionaldehyde.

$$CH_3{-}CH_2{-}\overset{\displaystyle S}{\overset{\|}{C}}{-}H$$

Thiopropionaldehyde
(propanethial)

$$CH_3{-}CH_2{-}\overset{\displaystyle S{=}O}{\overset{\|}{C}}{-}H$$

Thiopropionaldehyde-S-oxide
(propanethial-S-oxide)
[lachrymator in chopped onions]

Onions do not cause tear production until they are chopped or sliced. The onion cells damaged by these actions release the enzyme *allinase,* which converts an

The smoke generated from outdoor barbecuing contains the lachrymatory aldehyde *acrolein*.

odorless compound naturally present in onions to the lachrymatic compound.

Scientists are not sure why thiopropionaldehyde-S-oxide causes tear production, but it is known that it is an unstable molecule that is readily broken up by water into propanal, hydrogen sulfide, and sulfuric acid.

$$CH_3{-}CH_2{-}\overset{\displaystyle S{=}O}{\overset{\|}{C}}{-}H \xrightarrow{H_2O}$$

$$CH_3{-}CH_2{-}\overset{\displaystyle O}{\overset{\|}{C}}{-}H + H_2S + H_2SO_4$$

Sulfuric acid may be responsible for the eye irritation.

Many people can peel onions under water, or peel cold ones from the refrigerator, without crying. Water washes away the soluble lachrymator and also breaks it down chemically. If the onion is cold, the enzymatic reaction making the lachrymator is slower, so less is formed. Also the vapor pressure of the lachrymator is greatly reduced at the lower temperature, so its concentration in air is reduced.

Concepts to Remember

The carbonyl group. A carbonyl group consists of a carbon atom bonded to an oxygen atom through a double bond. Aldehydes and ketones are compounds that contain a carbonyl functional group. The carbonyl carbon in an aldehyde has at least one hydrogen attached to it, and the carbonyl carbon in a ketone has no hydrogens attached to it (Sections 15-1 through 15-3).

Nomenclature of aldehydes and ketones. The IUPAC names of aldehydes and ketones are based on the longest carbon chain that contains the carbonyl group. The chain numbering is done

from the end that results in the lowest number for the carbonyl group. The names of aldehydes end in *-al*, those of ketones in *-one* (Sections 15-4 and 15-5).

Isomerism for aldehydes and ketones. Constitutional isomerism is possible for aldehydes and for ketones when four or more carbon atoms are present. Aldehydes and ketones with the same number of carbon atoms and the same degree of saturation have the same molecular formula and thus are functional group isomers of each other (Section 15-6).

Physical properties of aldehydes and ketones. The boiling points of aldehydes and ketones are intermediate between those of alcohols and alkanes. The polarity of the carbonyl groups enables aldehyde and ketone molecules to interact with each other through dipole–dipole interactions. They cannot, however, hydrogen-bond to each other. Lower-molecular-mass aldehydes and ketones are soluble in water (Section 15-8).

Preparation of aldehydes and ketones. Oxidation of primary and secondary alcohols, using mild oxidizing agents, produces aldehydes and ketones, respectively (Section 15-9).

Oxidation and reduction of aldehydes and ketones. Aldehydes are easily oxidized to carboxylic acids; ketones do not readily undergo oxidation. Reduction of aldehydes and ketones produces primary and secondary alcohols, respectively (Section 15-10).

Hemiacetals and acetals. A characteristic reaction of aldehydes and ketones is the addition of an alcohol across the carbonyl double bond to produce hemiacetals. The reaction of a second alcohol molecule with a hemiacetal produces an acetal (Section 15-11).

Exercises and Problems

Exercises and problems are arranged in matched pairs with the two members of a pair addressing the same concept(s). The answer to the odd-numbered member of a pair is given at the back of the book. Problems denoted with a ▲ involve concepts found not only in the section under consideration but also concepts found in one or more earlier sections of the chapter.

The Carbonyl Group (Section 15-1)

15-1 Indicate whether or not each of the following three-carbon oxygen-containing compounds has a carbonyl group present in its structure.

a. $CH_3-CH_2-\overset{\displaystyle O}{\overset{\|}{C}}-H$

b. $CH_3-CH_2-CH_2-OH$

c. $CH_3-O-CH_2-CH_3$

d. $CH_3-\overset{\displaystyle O}{\overset{\|}{C}}-CH_3$

15-2 Indicate whether or not each of the following four-carbon oxygen-containing compounds has a carbonyl group present in its structure.

a. $CH_3-CH_2-O-CH_2-CH_3$

b. $CH_3-CH_2-\overset{\displaystyle O}{\overset{\|}{C}}-CH_3$

c. $CH_3-CH_2-CH_2-CH_2-OH$

d. $CH_3-CH_2-CH_2-\overset{\displaystyle O}{\overset{\|}{C}}-H$

15-3 In terms of polarity, how does a carbon–oxygen double bond differ from a carbon–carbon double bond?

15-4 In terms of polarity, which carbonyl group atom possesses a
a. partial positive charge   b. partial negative charge

15-5 What are the approximate bond angles between the atoms attached to the carbonyl carbon atom of a carbonyl group?

15-6 What is the geometrical arrangement for the atoms directly attached to the carbonyl carbon atom in a carbonyl compound?

Compounds Containing a Carbonyl Group (Section 15-2)

15-7 Indicate whether or not each of the following types of hydrocarbon derivatives must contain a carbonyl group.
a. aldehyde   b. ketone
c. amide   d. carboxylic acid

15-8 Indicate whether or not each of the following types of hydrocarbon derivatives must contain the element nitrogen.
a. aldehyde   b. ketone
c. ester   d. amide

15-9 Indicate whether or not each of the following types of hydrocarbon derivatives must contain a carbon–oxygen single bond.
a. aldehyde   b. ketone
c. ester   d. carboxylic acid

15-10 Indicate whether or not each of the following types of hydrocarbon derivatives must contain a oxygen–hydrogen single bond.
a. aldehyde
b. ketone
c. ester
d. carboxylic acid

The Aldehyde and Ketone Functional Groups (Section 15-3)

15-11 Classify each of the following structures as an aldehyde, a ketone, or neither.

a. $CH_3-CH_2-CH_2-\overset{\displaystyle O}{\overset{\|}{C}}-OH$

b. $CH_3-\overset{\displaystyle O}{\overset{\|}{C}}-CH_3$

c. $CH_3-O-CH_2-CH_3$

d. CH_3-CHO

15-12 Classify each of the following structures as an aldehyde, a ketone, or neither.

a. $CH_3-\overset{\displaystyle O}{\overset{\|}{C}}-CH_2-CH_3$

b. $CH_3-CH_2-CH_2-\overset{\displaystyle O}{\overset{\|}{C}}-O-CH_3$

c. $CH_3-CH_2-\underset{\underset{\displaystyle CH_3}{|}}{CH}-\overset{\displaystyle O}{\overset{\|}{C}}-H$

d. $CH_3-\underset{\underset{\displaystyle CH_3}{|}}{\overset{\overset{\displaystyle CH_3}{|}}{C}}-CH_2-CHO$

15-13 Draw condensed structural formulas for each of the following saturated straight-chain aldehydes or ketones or indicate that such a structure cannot exist.
a. C_1 aldehyde
b. C_2 ketone
c. C_3 aldehyde
d. C_4 ketone

15-14 Draw condensed structural formulas for each of the following saturated straight-chain aldehydes or ketones or indicate that such a structure cannot exist.
a. C_1 ketone
b. C_2 aldehyde
c. C_3 ketone
d. C_4 aldehyde

15-15 Classify each of the following structures as an aldehyde, a ketone, or neither.

a.

b.

c.

d.

15-16 Classify each of the following structures as an aldehyde, a ketone, or neither.

a.

b.

c.

d.

Nomenclature for Aldehydes (Section 15-4)

15-17 Assign an IUPAC name to each of the following aldehydes.

a.
$$CH_3-CH_2-\underset{\underset{CH_3}{|}}{CH}-\overset{\overset{O}{\|}}{C}-H$$

b.
$$CH_3-CH-CH_2-CH_2-\overset{\overset{O}{\|}}{C}-H$$
$$\underset{CH_2-CH_2-CH_3}{|}$$

c.

d. CH_3-CH_2-CHO

15-18 Assign an IUPAC name to each of the following aldehydes.

a.
$$CH_3-\underset{\underset{CH_3}{|}}{CH}-CH_2-CH_2-\overset{\overset{O}{\|}}{C}-H$$

b.
$$CH_3-CH_2-\underset{\underset{CH_2}{|}}{CH}-\overset{\overset{O}{\|}}{C}-H$$
$$\underset{CH_3}{|}$$

c.

d. $CH_3-CH_2-CH_2-CHO$

15-19 Assign an IUPAC name to each of the following aldehydes.

a.
b.
c.
d.

15-20 Assign an IUPAC name to each of the following aldehydes.

a.
b.
c.
d.

15-21 Draw a structural formula for each of the following aldehydes.
a. 3-Methylpentanal
b. 2-Ethylhexanal
c. 2,2-Dichloropropanal
d. 4-Hydroxy-2-methyloctanal

15-22 Draw a structural formula for each of the following aldehydes.
a. 2-Methylpentanal
b. 4-Ethylhexanal
c. 3,3-Dimethylhexanal
d. 2,3-Dibromopropanal

15-23 Each of the following aldehydes is named incorrectly. However, the names give correct structural formulas. What is the correct IUPAC name for each of these aldehydes?
a. 3-Methylpropanal
b. 2-Ethylpropanal
c. 3,4-Dimethylbutanal
d. Dimethylethanal

15-24 Each of the following aldehydes is named incorrectly. However, the names give correct structural formulas. What is the correct IUPAC name for each of these aldehydes?
a. 4-Ethylbutanal
b. 3-Ethylbutanal
c. 2-Ethyl-2-methylpropanal
d. Ethylmethylethanal

15-25 Draw a structural formula for each of the following aldehydes.
a. Formaldehyde
b. Propionaldehyde
c. 2-Chlorobenzaldehyde
d. 2,4-Dimethylbenzaldehyde

15-26 Draw a structural formula for each of the following aldehydes.
a. Acetaldehyde
b. Butyraldehyde
c. Dichloroacetaldehyde
d. 2-Methylbenzaldehyde

15-27 Assign a common name to each of the following aldehydes.

a.
$$CH_3-CH_2-\overset{\displaystyle O}{\overset{\|}{C}}-H$$

b. CH_3-CH_2-CHO

c.
$$Cl-\underset{\underset{Cl}{|}}{CH}-\overset{\displaystyle O}{\overset{\|}{C}}-H$$

d.
benzaldehyde with Cl substituent; $\overset{O}{\overset{\|}{C}}-H$

15-28 Assign a common name to each of the following aldehydes.

a.
$$CH_3-CH_2-CH_2-\overset{\displaystyle O}{\overset{\|}{C}}-H$$

b. $CH_3-CH_2-CH_2-CHO$

c.
$$Cl-\underset{\underset{Cl}{|}}{\overset{\overset{Cl}{|}}{C}}-\overset{\displaystyle O}{\overset{\|}{C}}-H$$

d.
benzaldehyde with Br substituent; $\overset{O}{\overset{\|}{C}}-H$

▲15-29 Name the functional group(s) present in each of the following compounds.
a. Propanal
b. Propenal
c. 2-Propanol
d. 3-Hydroxypropanal

▲15-30 Name the functional group(s) present in each of the following compounds.
a. Methanal
b. Methanol
c. 2-Butenal
d. 3-Methoxybutanal

Nomenclature for Ketones (Section 15-5)

15-31 Using IUPAC nomenclature, name each of the following ketones.

a.
$$CH_3-CH_2-\overset{\displaystyle O}{\overset{\|}{C}}-CH_3$$

b.
$$CH_3-\underset{\underset{CH_3}{|}}{CH}-\underset{\underset{CH_3}{|}}{CH}-\overset{\displaystyle O}{\overset{\|}{C}}-\underset{\underset{CH_3}{|}}{CH}-CH_3$$

c.
$$CH_3-\underset{\underset{CH_3}{|}}{CH}-CH_2-CH_2-\overset{\displaystyle O}{\overset{\|}{C}}-CH_2-CH_3$$

d.
$$CH_3-CH_2-\overset{\displaystyle O}{\overset{\|}{C}}-\underset{\underset{Cl}{|}}{CH}-Cl$$

15-32 Using IUPAC nomenclature, name each of the following ketones.

a.
$$CH_3-\overset{\displaystyle O}{\overset{\|}{C}}-CH_2-CH_2-CH_2-CH_3$$

b.
$$CH_3-CH_2-\overset{\displaystyle O}{\overset{\|}{C}}-CH_2-\underset{\underset{\underset{CH_3}{|}}{\underset{CH_2}{|}}}{CH}-CH_3$$

c.
$$CH_3-\underset{\underset{Cl}{|}}{CH}-\overset{\displaystyle O}{\overset{\|}{C}}-\underset{\underset{Br}{|}}{CH}-CH_3$$

d.
$$CH_3-\underset{\underset{Cl}{|}}{CH}-\overset{\displaystyle O}{\overset{\|}{C}}-CH_2-\underset{\underset{Cl}{|}}{CH_2}$$

15-33 Assign an IUPAC name to each of the following ketones.

a.

b.

c.

d.

15-34 Assign an IUPAC name to each of the following ketones.

a.

b.

c.

d.

15-35 Using IUPAC nomenclature, name each of the following ketones.

a.

b.

c.

d.

15-36 Using IUPAC nomenclature, name each of the following ketones.

a.

b.

c.

d.

15-37 Draw a structural formula for each of the following ketones.
a. 3-Methyl-2-pentanone   b. 3-Hexanone
c. Cyclobutanone   d. Chloropropanone

15-38 Draw a structural formula for each of the following ketones.
a. 2-Methyl-3-pentanone   b. 2-Pentanone
c. Bromopropanone   d. Cyclopentanone

15-39 Each of the following ketones is named incorrectly. However, the names give correct structural formulas. What is the correct IUPAC name for each of these ketones?
a. 3-Butanone   b. 2-Methyl-3-butanone
c. 3-Ethyl-2-butanone   d. 1,1-Dimethyl-2-butanone

15-40 Each of the following ketones is named incorrectly. However, the names give correct structural formulas. What is the correct IUPAC name for each of these ketones?
a. 4-Pentanone   b. 2-Methyl-4-pentanone
c. 2-Ethyl-3-butanone   d. 3,3-Diethyl-2-butanone

15-41 Draw a structural formula for each of the following ketones.
a. Isopropyl propyl ketone
b. Chloromethyl methyl ketone
c. Acetophenone
d. Methyl phenyl ketone

15-42 Draw a structural formula for each of the following ketones.
a. *tert*-Butyl methyl ketone
b. Dichloromethyl ethyl ketone
c. Benzophenone
d. Diphenyl ketone

▲**15-43** Name the functional group(s) present in each of the following compounds.
a. Propanone   b. Propanal
c. 4-Oxohexanal   d. 4-Octen-2-one

▲**15-44** Name the functional group(s) present in each of the following compounds.
a. Butanone   b. Butanal
c. 2-Butanol   d. 3-Oxobutanal

▲**15-45** Indicate whether each of the following compounds would be named as an alcohol, an aldehyde, or a ketone.

a.

b.

c.

d.

▲**15-46** Indicate whether each of the following compounds would be named as an alcohol, an aldehyde, or a ketone.

a.

b.

c.

d.

▲**15-47** What is the molecular formula for each of the following compounds?
a. 2-Butanol   b. Butanal
c. Butanone   d. Butanedial

▲**15-48** What is the molecular formula for each of the following compounds?
a. Propanal   b. Propanedial
c. Propanone   d. 2,4-Pentanedione

Isomerism for Aldehydes and Ketones (Section 15-6)

15-49 Give IUPAC names for all saturated unbranched-chain compounds that are named as the following.
a. Heptanals   b. Heptanones

15-50 Give IUPAC names for all saturated unbranched-chain compounds that are named as the following.
a. Hexanals   b. Hexanones

15-51 How many aldehydes and how many ketones exist with each of the following molecular formulas?
a. CH_2O b. C_3H_6O

15-52 How many aldehydes and how many ketones exist with each of the following molecular formulas?
a. C_2H_4O b. C_4H_8O

15-53 For which values of x is the ketone name x-methyl-3-hexanone a correct IUPAC name?

15-54 For which values of x is the ketone name x-methyl-3-pentanone a correct IUPAC name?

15-55 Draw skeletal structural formulas for the four aldehydes and three ketones that have the molecular formula $C_5H_{10}O$.

15-56 Draw skeletal structural formulas for the eight aldehydes and six ketones that have the molecular formula $C_6H_{12}O$.

Selected Common Aldehydes and Ketones (Section 15-7)

15-57 What is the difference between the substances formaldehyde and formalin?

15-58 What is the odor associated with, and what are the uses for, the substance formalin?

15-59 What are the general properties of and uses for the substance acetone?

15-60 What is the significance of the odor of acetone on the breath of a person?

15-61 How many aldehyde groups and how many ketone groups are present in each of the following molecules?
a. Vanillin
b. Carvone
c. Cortisone
d. Avobenzone

15-62 How many aldehyde groups and how many ketone groups are present in each of the following molecules?
a. Progesterone
b. 2-Heptanone
c. Dihydroxyacetone
d. Cinnamaldehyde

Physical Properties of Aldehydes and Ketones (Section 15-8)

15-63 Indicate whether each of the following compounds is a liquid or gas at room temperature (25°C).
a. Methanal
b. Butanal
c. Propanone
d. 2-Hexanone

15-64 Indicate whether each of the following compounds is a liquid or gas at room temperature (25°C).
a. Ethanal
b. Hexanal
c. Butanone
d. 2-Heptanone

15-65 Which member in each of the following pairs of molecules has the greater solubility in water?
a. Pentanal or Pentane
b. Pentanal or Heptanal

15-66 Which member in each of the following pairs of molecules has the greater solubility in water?
a. 2-Pentanone or Hexane
b. 2-Pentanone or 2-Octanone

15-67 Which member in each of the following pairs of molecules has the higher boiling point?
a. 2-Pentanone or 2-Pentanol
b. 2-Pentanone or 2-Methylpentane

15-68 Which member in each of the following pairs of molecules has the higher boiling point?
a. Butanal or 1-Butanol
b. Butanal or Pentane

15-69 How many hydrogen bonds can form between an ethanal molecule and
a. other ethanal molecules
b. water molecules

15-70 How many hydrogen bonds can form between an acetone molecule and
a. other acetone molecules
b. water molecules

Preparation of Aldehydes and Ketones (Section 15-9)

15-71 Draw the structure of the aldehyde or ketone formed from oxidation of each of the following alcohols. Assume that reaction conditions are sufficiently mild that any aldehydes produced are not oxidized further to carboxylic acids.
a. $CH_3-CH_2-CH_2-CH_2-CH_2-OH$
b. $CH_3-CH_2-CH-OH$ with CH_3 branch
c. $CH_3-C(CH_3)(CH_3)-CH_2-CH_2-OH$
d. CH_3-⬡$-OH$

15-72 Draw the structure of the aldehyde or ketone formed from oxidation of each of the following alcohols. Assume that reaction conditions are sufficiently mild that any aldehydes formed are not oxidized further to carboxylic acids.
a. $CH_3-CH_2-CH-CH_2-OH$ with CH_3 branch
b. $CH_3-CH-CH-OH$ with CH_3 and CH_3 branches
c. $CH_3-C(CH_3)(CH_3)-OH$
d. ⬡ with CH_2-CH_3 branch and $-OH$

15-73 Draw the structure of the alcohol needed to prepare each of the following aldehydes or ketones by alcohol oxidation.
a. Diethyl ketone
b. Phenylpropanone
c. Acetaldehyde
d. 2-Ethylhexanal

15-74 Draw the structure of the alcohol needed to prepare each of the following aldehydes or ketones by alcohol oxidation.
a. Propanal
b. Dipropyl ketone
c. 3-Phenyl-2-butanone
d. Cyclohexanone

Oxidation and Reduction of Aldehydes and Ketones (Section 15-10)

15-75 Draw the structural formula of the carboxylic acid formed when each of the following aldehydes is oxidized.
a. $CH_3-\overset{O}{\overset{\|}{C}}-H$
b. $CH_3-CH_2-\overset{CH_3}{\underset{\|}{CH}}-CH_2-\overset{O}{\overset{\|}{C}}-H$
c. $H-\overset{O}{\overset{\|}{C}}-H$
d. $CH_3-CH_2-\overset{Cl}{\underset{\|}{CH}}-\overset{Cl}{\underset{\|}{CH}}-CH_2-\overset{O}{\overset{\|}{C}}-H$

15-76 Draw the structural formula of the carboxylic acid formed when each of the following aldehydes is oxidized.

a. $CH_3-CH_2-CH_2-\overset{\overset{\displaystyle O}{\|}}{C}-H$

b. $CH_3-CH_2-CH_2-\overset{\overset{\displaystyle CH_3}{|}}{CH}-\overset{\overset{\displaystyle O}{\|}}{C}-H$

c. $CH_3-\overset{\overset{\displaystyle O}{\|}}{C}-H$

d. $CH_3-\overset{\overset{\displaystyle Cl}{|}}{CH}-CH_2-\overset{\overset{\displaystyle O}{\|}}{C}-H$

15-77 Draw the structural formula of the organic product or indicate that no reaction occurs for the following situations.
a. Butanal in the Tollens test
b. 2-Butanone in the Tollens test
c. 3-Methylpentanal in the Benedict's test
d. 3-Pentanone in the Benedict's test

15-78 Draw the structural formula of the organic product or indicate that no reaction occurs for the following situations.
a. Propanal in the Tollens test
b. 3-Pentanone in the Tollens test
c. Methylpropanal in the Benedict's test
d. Propanone in the Benedict's test

15-79 What is the chemical formula of the inorganic product formed, if any, in each of the reactions in Problem 15-77?

15-80 What is the chemical formula of the inorganic product formed, if any, in each of the reactions in Problem 15-78?

15-81 Which of the following compounds would react with Tollens solution?

a. $CH_3-CH_2-CH_2-\overset{\overset{\displaystyle O}{\|}}{C}-CH_3$

b. $CH_3-CH_2-CH_2-\overset{\overset{\displaystyle O}{\|}}{C}-H$

c. $CH_3-\overset{\overset{\displaystyle O}{\|}}{CH}-CH_2-\overset{\underset{\underset{\displaystyle OH}{|}}{}}{C}-H$

d. $CH_3-\overset{\underset{\underset{\displaystyle OH}{|}}{}}{CH}-\overset{\overset{\displaystyle O}{\|}}{C}-CH_3$

15-82 Which of the following compounds would react with Benedict's solution?

a. $CH_3-CH_2-\overset{\overset{\displaystyle O}{\|}}{C}-H$

b. $CH_3-\overset{\overset{\displaystyle O}{\|}}{C}-CH_3$

c. $CH_3-CH_2-\overset{\underset{\underset{\displaystyle OH}{|}}{}}{\overset{\overset{\displaystyle O}{\|}}{CH-C}}-CH_2-CH_3$

d. $CH_3-\overset{\underset{\underset{\displaystyle CH_3}{|}}{}}{CH}-\overset{\underset{\underset{\displaystyle CH_3}{|}}{}}{CH}-CH_2-\overset{\overset{\displaystyle O}{\|}}{C}-H$

15-83 Draw the structure of the alcohol produced when each of the following compounds is reduced using molecular H_2 and a Ni catalyst.

a. $CH_3-CH_2-CH_2-\overset{\overset{\displaystyle O}{\|}}{C}-H$

b. $CH_3-CH_2-\overset{\overset{\displaystyle O}{\|}}{C}-CH_2-CH_3$

c. $CH_3-\overset{\overset{\displaystyle CH_3}{|}}{CH}-CH_2-\overset{\overset{\displaystyle O}{\|}}{C}-H$

d. $CH_3-\overset{\overset{\displaystyle CH_3}{|}}{CH}-\overset{\overset{\displaystyle O}{\|}}{C}-CH_2-CH_2-CH_3$

15-84 Draw the structure of the alcohol produced when each of the following compounds is reduced using molecular H_2 and a Ni catalyst.

a. $CH_3-CH_2-CH_2-\overset{\overset{\displaystyle O}{\|}}{C}-CH_3$

b. $CH_3-CH_2-CH_2-CH_2-\overset{\overset{\displaystyle O}{\|}}{C}-H$

c. $CH_3-\overset{\underset{\underset{\displaystyle CH_3}{|}}{}}{\overset{\overset{\displaystyle CH_3}{|}}{C}}-CH_2-CH_2-\overset{\overset{\displaystyle O}{\|}}{C}-H$

d. $CH_3-CH_2-\overset{\overset{\displaystyle O}{\|}}{C}-CH_3$

▲**15-85** Which of the three compounds *pentanal, 2-pentanone,* and *2-pentanol* will react with each of the following oxidizing or reducing agents? There may be more than one correct answer in a given situation.
a. $K_2Cr_2O_7$ b. Tollens solution
c. Benedict's solution   d. H_2, Ni catalyst

▲**15-86** Which of the three compounds *hexanal, 2-butanone,* and *2-propanol* will react with each of the following oxidizing or reducing agents? There may be more than one correct answer in a given situation.
a. $K_2Cr_2O_7$ b. Tollens solution
c. Benedict's solution   d. H_2, Ni catalyst

▲**15-87** What is the IUPAC name of the aldehyde or ketone starting material needed to make each of the following compounds using an oxidation or reduction reaction?

a. CH_3-CH_2-OH b. $CH_3-\overset{\overset{\displaystyle OH}{|}}{CH}-CH_2-CH_3$

c. $CH_3-CH_2-\overset{\overset{\displaystyle O}{\|}}{C}-OH$

d.

▲**15-88** What is the IUPAC name of the aldehyde or ketone starting material needed to make each of the following compounds using an oxidation or reduction reaction?

a. $CH_3-CH_2-CH_2-OH$ b. $CH_3-\overset{\overset{\displaystyle OH}{|}}{CH}-CH_3$

c. $CH_3-\overset{\overset{\displaystyle O}{\|}}{C}-OH$

d.

Hemiacetal Formation (Section 15-11)

15-89 When an alcohol molecule (R—O—H) adds across a carbon–oxygen double bond, into what "fragments" is the alcohol split?

15-90 When an alcohol molecule (R—O—H) adds across a carbon–oxygen double bond, which part of the alcohol molecule adds to the carbonyl oxygen atom?

15-91 Indicate whether each of the following compounds is a hemiacetal.

a. $CH_3—CH_2—O—CH_3$

b.
$$CH_3—\overset{\overset{\displaystyle OH}{|}}{\underset{\underset{\displaystyle O—CH_3}{|}}{C}}—CH_3$$

c. (tetrahydrofuran ring with OH)

d. (tetrahydrofuran ring with O—CH$_3$)

15-92 Indicate whether each of the following compounds is a hemiacetal.

a.
$$CH_3—\overset{\overset{\displaystyle }{}}{\underset{\underset{\displaystyle OH}{|}}{CH}}—\overset{\overset{\displaystyle }{}}{\underset{\underset{\displaystyle OH}{|}}{CH}}—CH_3$$

b.
$$CH_3—CH_2—\overset{\overset{\displaystyle OH}{|}}{\underset{\underset{\displaystyle O—CH_3}{|}}{C}}—CH_3$$

c. (pyran ring with OH)

d. (cyclohexane ring with OH and O—CH$_3$)

15-93 Which carbon atom is the hemiacetal carbon atom in each of the following structures?

a. $C_1—\underset{\underset{\displaystyle OH}{|}}{C_2}—O—C_3$

b. (ring structure with O, OH, labeled C_5, C_1, C_4, C_2, C_3, C_6)

15-94 Which carbon atom is the hemiacetal carbon atom in each of the following structures?

a. $C_1—C_2—\underset{\underset{\displaystyle C_6}{|}}{C_3}—O—\underset{\underset{\displaystyle OH}{|}}{C_4}—C_5$

b. (ring structure with O, C_6, OH, labeled C_5, C_1, C_4, C_2, C_3)

15-95 Draw the structural formula of the hemiacetal formed from each of the following pairs of reactants.
a. Acetaldehyde and ethyl alcohol
b. 2-Pentanone and methanol
c. Butanal and ethanol
d. Acetone and isopropyl alcohol

15-96 Draw the structural formula of the hemiacetal formed from each of the following pairs of reactants.
a. Acetaldehyde and methanol
b. 2-Pentanone and ethyl alcohol
c. Butanal and isopropyl alcohol
d. Acetone and ethanol

15-97 Draw the structural formula of the missing compound in each of the following reactions.

a.
$$CH_3—(CH_2)_2—\overset{\overset{\displaystyle O}{\|}}{C}—H + CH_3—CH_2—OH \overset{H^+}{\rightleftharpoons} ?$$

b.
$$? + CH_3—OH \overset{H^+}{\rightleftharpoons} CH_3—CH_2—\overset{\overset{\displaystyle OH}{|}}{\underset{\underset{\displaystyle O—CH_3}{|}}{CH}}$$

c.
$$CH_3—CH_2—\overset{\overset{\displaystyle O}{\|}}{C}—CH_3 + CH_3—OH \overset{H^+}{\rightleftharpoons} ?$$

d. (cyclic structure with CH$_2$OH, O—H, HO, and C=O aldehyde)
$$\overset{H^+}{\rightarrow} ?$$

15-98 Draw the structural formula of the missing compound in each of the following reactions.

a.
$$CH_3—CH_2—\overset{\overset{\displaystyle O}{\|}}{C}—H + CH_3—OH \overset{H^+}{\rightleftharpoons} ?$$

b.
$$? + CH_3—CH_2—OH \overset{H^+}{\rightleftharpoons} CH_3—CH_2—\overset{\overset{\displaystyle OH}{|}}{\underset{\underset{\displaystyle O—CH_2—CH_3}{|}}{CH}}$$

c.
$$CH_3—CH_2—CH_2—\overset{\overset{\displaystyle O}{\|}}{C}—CH_3 + CH_3—CH_2—OH \overset{H^+}{\rightleftharpoons} ?$$

d. (cyclic structure with CH$_2$OH, O—H, HO, and C=O aldehyde)
$$\overset{H^+}{\rightleftharpoons} ?$$

Acetal Formation (Section 15-11)

15-99 Indicate whether each of the following compounds is an acetal.

a.
$$CH_3—CH_2—CH_2—\overset{\overset{\displaystyle O—CH_3}{|}}{\underset{\underset{\displaystyle O—CH_3}{|}}{CH}}$$

b.
$$CH_3—CH_2—CH_2—O—\overset{\overset{\displaystyle O—CH_3}{|}}{\underset{\underset{\displaystyle CH_3}{|}}{C}}—CH_3$$

c.
$$CH_3—CH_2—CH_2—O—\overset{\overset{\displaystyle CH_3}{|}}{\underset{\underset{\displaystyle CH_3}{|}}{C}}—OH$$

d.
$$CH_3—\overset{\overset{\displaystyle O—CH_2—CH_2—CH_3}{|}}{\underset{\underset{\displaystyle O—CH_2—CH_2—CH_3}{|}}{C}}—CH_2—CH_2—CH_3$$

15-100 Indicate whether each of the following compounds is an acetal.

a.
$$CH_3-CH_2-\underset{\underset{O-CH_3}{|}}{\overset{\overset{O-CH_2-CH_3}{|}}{CH}}$$

b.
$$CH_3-CH_2-O-\underset{\underset{CH_3}{|}}{\overset{\overset{O-CH_3}{|}}{C}}-CH_3$$

c.
$$CH_3-CH_2-CH_2-\underset{\underset{OH}{|}}{\overset{\overset{H}{|}}{C}}-O-CH_3$$

d.
$$CH_3-\underset{\underset{O-CH_3}{|}}{\overset{\overset{CH_3}{|}}{C}}-O-CH_3$$

15-101 Which carbon atom is the acetal carbon atom in each of the following structures?

a. $C_1-\underset{\underset{O-C_4}{|}}{C_2}-O-C_3$

b. structure with ring: O bridging C_5 and C_1, C_1 bearing $O-C_6$ and C_7; ring $C_5-C_4-C_3-C_2-C_1$

15-102 Which carbon atom is the acetal carbon atom in each of the following structures?

a. $C_1-C_2-\underset{\underset{C_6}{|}}{\overset{}{C_3}}-O-\underset{\underset{O-C_7}{|}}{C_1}-C_5$

b. structure with ring: O bridging C_5 and C_1, C_1 bearing $O-C_6$ and C_7; ring $C_5-C_4-C_3-C_2-C_7$

15-103 Draw the structural formula of the missing compound(s) in each of the following reactions.

a.
$$CH_3-\underset{\underset{CH_3}{|}}{\overset{\overset{O-CH_3}{|}}{C}}-OH + ? \xrightarrow{H^+} CH_3-\underset{\underset{CH_3}{|}}{\overset{\overset{O-CH_3}{|}}{C}}-O-CH_3 + H_2O$$

b.
$$? + CH_3-CH_2-OH \xrightarrow{H^+} CH_3-\underset{\underset{O-CH_2-CH_3}{|}}{\overset{\overset{H}{|}}{C}}-O-CH_3 + H_2O$$

c.
$$CH_3-CH_2-\underset{\underset{H}{|}}{\overset{\overset{OH}{|}}{C}}-O-CH_3 + CH_3-\underset{\underset{CH_3}{|}}{CH}-OH \xrightarrow{H^+}$$
$$? + H_2O$$

d.
$$\underset{\text{Hemiacetal}}{?} + \underset{\text{Alcohol}}{?} \xrightarrow{H^+} CH_3-\underset{\underset{O-CH_3}{|}}{CH}-O-CH_3 + H_2O$$

15-104 Draw the structural formula of the missing compound(s) in each of the following reactions.

a.
$$CH_3-CH_2-\underset{\underset{CH_3}{|}}{\overset{\overset{O-CH_3}{|}}{C}}-OH + ? \xrightarrow{H^+}$$
$$CH_3-CH_2-\underset{\underset{CH_3}{|}}{\overset{\overset{O-CH_3}{|}}{C}}-O-CH_3 + H_2O$$

b.
$$? + CH_3-CH_2-OH \xrightarrow{H^+}$$
$$CH_3-CH_2-\underset{\underset{O-CH_2-CH_3}{|}}{\overset{\overset{H}{|}}{C}}-O-CH_3 + H_2O$$

c.
$$CH_3-\underset{\underset{H}{|}}{\overset{\overset{OH}{|}}{C}}-O-CH_3 + CH_3-\underset{\underset{CH_3}{|}}{CH}-OH \xrightarrow{H^+}$$
$$? + H_2O$$

d.
$$\underset{\text{Hemiacetal}}{?} + \underset{\text{Alcohol}}{?} \xrightarrow{H^+}$$
$$CH_3-CH_2-\underset{\underset{O-CH_3}{|}}{CH}-O-CH_3 + H_2O$$

15-105 Draw the structural formulas of the aldehyde (or ketone) and the two alcohols produced when the following acetals undergo hydrolysis in acidic solution.

a.
$$CH_3-\underset{\underset{O-CH_3}{|}}{\overset{\overset{O-CH_3}{|}}{CH}}$$

b.
$$CH_3-\underset{\underset{O-CH_3}{|}}{\overset{\overset{O-CH_3}{|}}{C}}-CH_3$$

c.
$$CH_3-O-\underset{\underset{CH_2-CH_3}{|}}{\overset{\overset{CH_2-CH_3}{|}}{C}}-O-CH_2-CH_3$$

d.
$$CH_3-CH_2-CH_2-CH_2-\underset{\underset{H}{|}}{\overset{\overset{O-CH_3}{|}}{C}}-O-CH_3$$

15-106 Draw the structural formulas of the aldehyde (or ketone) and the two alcohols produced when the following acetals undergo hydrolysis in acidic solution.

a.
$$CH_3-CH_2-\underset{\underset{O-CH_3}{|}}{\overset{\overset{O-CH_3}{|}}{CH}}$$

b.
$$CH_3-CH_2-\underset{\underset{O-CH_3}{|}}{\overset{\overset{O-CH_3}{|}}{C}}-CH_3$$

c.
$$CH_3-CH_2-O-\underset{\underset{CH_3}{|}}{\overset{\overset{H}{|}}{C}}-O-CH_2-CH_3$$

d.
$$CH_3-CH_2-\underset{\underset{O-CH_2-CH_3}{|}}{\overset{\overset{O-CH_2-CH_3}{|}}{C}}-CH_2-CH_2-CH_3$$

15-107   Name each of the compounds in Problem 15-105 in the manner described in Section 15-11.

15-108   Name each of the compounds in Problem 15-106 in the manner described in Section 15-11.

▲**15-109**   What are the IUPAC names of the compounds formed when each of the following acetals or hemiacetals undergoes hydrolysis under acidic conditions?

$$\underset{\text{a.}}{}\quad CH_3-CH_2-\overset{\overset{\displaystyle OH}{|}}{CH}-O-CH_3$$

$$\underset{\text{b.}}{}\quad CH_3-CH_2-\overset{\overset{\displaystyle O-CH_3}{|}}{CH}-O-CH_3$$

$$\underset{\text{c.}}{}\quad CH_3-\overset{\overset{\displaystyle CH_3}{|}}{CH}-\overset{\overset{\displaystyle OH}{|}}{CH}-O-CH_3$$

$$\underset{\text{d.}}{}\quad CH_3-CH_2-\overset{\overset{\displaystyle O-CH_3}{|}}{CH}-O-CH_2-CH_3$$

▲**15-110**   What are the IUPAC names of the compounds formed when each of the following acetals or hemiacetals undergoes hydrolysis under acidic conditions?

$$\underset{\text{a.}}{}\quad CH_3-\overset{\overset{\displaystyle CH_3}{|}}{CH}-\overset{\overset{\displaystyle O-CH_3}{|}}{CH}-O-CH_2-CH_3$$

$$\underset{\text{b.}}{}\quad CH_3-\overset{\overset{\displaystyle O-CH_2-CH_3}{|}}{CH}-O-CH_3$$

$$\underset{\text{c.}}{}\quad CH_3-\overset{\overset{\displaystyle O-CH_3}{|}}{CH}-O-\overset{\overset{\displaystyle CH_3}{|}}{CH}-CH_3$$

$$\underset{\text{d.}}{}\quad CH_3-\overset{\overset{\displaystyle O-CH_3}{|}}{CH}-O-CH_2-CH_3$$

▲**15-111**   What is the condensed structural formula of the organic product when the compound pentanal is treated with each of the following reagents? If no reaction occurs, indicate that such is the case.
a. H_2, Ni catalyst
b. CH_3-CH_2-OH (1 to 1 reacting ratio), H^+ catalyst
c. CH_3-OH (2 to 1 reacting ratio), H^+ catalyst
d. $K_2Cr_2O_7$

▲**15-112**   What is the condensed structural formula of the organic product when the compound 3-pentanone is treated with each of the following reagents? If no reaction occurs, indicate that such is the case.
a. H_2, Ni catalyst
b. CH_3-OH (1 to 1 reacting ratio), H^+ catalyst
c. CH_3-CH_2-OH (2 to 1 reacting ratio), H^+ catalyst
d. $K_2Cr_2O_7$

▲**15-113**   Draw the condensed structural formula of a molecule with the formula $C_5H_{12}O_2$ that fits each of the following descriptions.
a. Hemiacetal of propanal
b. Hemiacetal of propanone
c. Acetal of propanal
d. Acetal of propanone

▲**15-114**   Draw the condensed structural formula of a molecule with the formula $C_6H_{14}O_2$ that fits each of the following descriptions.
a. Hemiacetal of butanol
b. Hemiacetal of butanone
c. Acetal of butanal
d. Acetal of butanone

Sulfur-Containing Carbonyl Groups (Section 15-12)

15-115   What type of compound is formed by replacement of the carbonyl oxygen atom with a sulfur atom?

15-116   What type of compound is formed by replacement of the carbonyl carbon atom with a sulfur atom?

15-117   Draw structural formulas for the following compounds.
a. Thioformaldehyde
b. Methanethial
c. Thioacetone
d. Propanethione

15-118   Dimethyl sulfoxide (DMSO) is a sulfur analog of acetone in which the sulfur has substituted for the carbonyl carbon atom.
a. Draw the structural formula for DMSO.
b. Describe the "unusual" solubility properties of DMSO.

Carboxylic Acids, Esters, and Other Acid Derivatives

16

© Valentyn Volkov/Shutterstock.com

Esters, a type of carboxylic acid derivative, are largely responsible for the flavors and fragrances of ripe fruits such as red raspberries.

In Chapter 15, the carbonyl group and two families of compounds—aldehydes and ketones—that contain this group were discussed. In this chapter, we discuss four more families of compounds in which the carbonyl group is present: carboxylic acids, esters, acid chlorides, and acid anhydrides.

16-1 Structure of Carboxylic Acids and Their Derivatives

LEARNING FOCUS

Know the structural characteristics associated with a *carboxyl group*, a *carboxylic acid*, and a *carboxylic acid derivative*; know the difference between a *carbonyl compound* and an *acyl compound*.

A **carboxylic acid** *is an organic compound whose functional group is the carboxyl group.* What is a carboxyl group? A **carboxyl group** *is a carbonyl group* ($C{=}O$) *that has a hydroxyl group* (—OH) *bonded to the carbonyl carbon atom.* A general structural representation for a carboxyl group is

Abbreviated linear designations for the carboxyl group are

$$—COOH \quad \text{and} \quad —CO_2H$$

Although a carboxyl group contains both a carbonyl group (C=O) and a hydroxyl group (—OH), the carboxyl group does not show characteristic behavior of either an alcohol or a carbonyl compound (aldehyde or ketone). Rather, it is a unique functional group with a set of characteristics different from those of its component parts. ◄

> ▶ The term carboxyl is a contraction of the words carbonyl and hydroxyl.

The simplest carboxylic acid has a hydrogen atom attached to the carboxyl group carbon atom.

$$\underset{\text{H}}{}—\overset{\overset{\text{O}}{\|}}{\text{C}}—\text{OH}$$

Structures for the next two simplest carboxylic acids, those with methyl and ethyl alkyl groups, are

$$CH_3—\overset{\overset{\text{O}}{\|}}{\text{C}}—OH \qquad CH_3—CH_2—\overset{\overset{\text{O}}{\|}}{\text{C}}—OH$$

The structure of the simplest aromatic carboxylic acid involves a benzene ring to which a carboxyl group is attached.

Cyclic carboxylic acids do not exist; having the carboxyl carbon atom as part of a ring system creates a situation where the carboxyl carbon atom would have five bonds. The nonexistence of cyclic carboxylic acids parallels the nonexistence of cyclic aldehydes (Section 15-3). ◄

> ▶ General formulas for carboxylic acids containing alkyl and aryl groups, respectively, are
>
> $$R—COOH \quad \text{and} \quad Ar—COOH$$

A **carboxylic acid derivative** *is an organic compound that can be synthesized from or converted into a carboxylic acid.* Four important families of carboxylic acid derivatives are esters, acid chlorides, acid anhydrides, and amides. The group attached to the carbonyl carbon atom distinguishes these derivative types from each other and also from carboxylic acids.

$$\underset{\text{Ester}}{R—\overset{\overset{\text{O}}{\|}}{\text{C}}—OR'} \qquad \underset{\text{Acid chloride}}{R—\overset{\overset{\text{O}}{\|}}{\text{C}}—Cl} \qquad \underset{\text{Acid anhydride}}{R—\overset{\overset{\text{O}}{\|}}{\text{C}}—O—\overset{\overset{\text{O}}{\|}}{\text{C}}—R} \qquad \underset{\text{Amide}}{R—\overset{\overset{\text{O}}{\|}}{\text{C}}—NH_2}$$

Carbonyl Compounds and Acyl Compounds

Generalized structures for carboxylic acids and carboxylic acid derivatives all have the form

$$R—\overset{\overset{\text{O}}{\|}}{\text{C}}—Z$$

Structurally, these compound types differ from each other only in the identity of the Z entity present, as shown in the preceding set of carboxylic acid derivative structures.

Carboxylic acids and their derivatives have a common structural component, which is called an *acyl group.*

An **acyl group** *is the* R—C— *portion of a molecule with the general formula* R—C—Z. The acyl group is the portion of such a molecule that remains if the Z entity is removed. The linear designation for an acyl group is RCO—. ◄

It is significant to note that aldehydes and ketones, the subject of the previous chapter, are also compounds that contain an acyl group.

Aldehyde   Ketone

$$
\underbrace{\text{R—C—H}}_{\text{acyl group}} \qquad \underbrace{\text{R—C—R}}_{\text{acyl group}}
$$

► *It is important to keep the terms* acyl group, carboxyl group, *and* carbonyl group *straight in the context of the structural characteristics of a carboxylic acid molecule. All three groups are considered to be present within such a molecule as shown in the following diagram.*

R—C—OH acyl group

R—C—OH → R—C—OH carboxyl group

R—C—OH carbonyl group

However, they are not carboxylic acid derivatives. Why is this so?

The chemical reactions that compounds containing an acyl group undergo are dependent on the nature of the bond between the carbonyl carbon atom of the acyl group and the "Z" group that is attached to it. Of particular concern is whether this bond is *nonpolar* or *polar*. On the basis of bond polarity, acyl-group-containing compounds are classified into two types: carbonyl compounds (nonpolar bond) and acyl compounds (polar bond).

R—C—Z   nonpolar bond   R—C—Z   polar bond

Carbonyl compound   Acyl compound

A **carbonyl compound** *contains an acyl group whose carbonyl carbon atom is bonded directly to a hydrogen atom or another carbon atom.* Carbon–carbon bonds and carbon–hydrogen bonds are nonpolar, as carbon and hydrogen electronegativities are almost the same (Section 5-9). Aldehydes and ketones are examples of carbonyl compounds.

R—C—H   nonpolar bond   R—C—R   nonpolar bond

Aldehyde   Ketone

An **acyl compound** *contains an acyl group whose carbonyl carbon atom is bonded directly to an oxygen, nitrogen, or halogen atom.* Such bonds (C—O, C—N, and C—halogen) are polar because O, N, and the halogens have electronegativities significantly greater than that of carbon (Section 5-9). Carboxylic acids and their derivatives (esters, acid chlorides, acid anhydrides, and amides) are examples of acyl compounds.

R—C—OH   polar bond   R—C—OR   polar bond   R—C—Cl   polar bond   R—C—O—C—R   polar bond   R—C—NH₂   polar bond

Carboxylic acid   Ester   Acid chloride   Acid anhydride   Amide

Structures, nomenclature, and chemical reactions for carbonyl compounds (aldehydes and ketones) were considered in the previous chapter. Structures, nomenclature, and chemical reactions for acyl compounds, except amides, are considered in this chapter. Amides are considered in the next chapter, which deals with nitrogen-containing hydrocarbon derivatives.

The reaction chemistry of acyl compounds is distinctly different from that of carbonyl compounds. For carbonyl compounds, reaction chemistry most often involves the carbon–oxygen double bond. For acyl compounds, as will be seen shortly, reaction chemistry most often involves the carbon–Z single bond, that is, the polar C—O, C—N, or C—halogen bond.

Section 16-1 Quick Quiz

1. The name of the functional group present in a carboxylic acid is
   a. carbonyl group
   b. carboxyl group
   c. carboxylate group
   d. no correct response

2. Which of the following statements involving structural characteristics of the functional group present in carboxylic acids is *incorrect*?
   a. A carbon–oxygen single bond is present.
   b. A carbon–oxygen double bond is present.
   c. A carbon–hydrogen single bond is present.
   d. no correct response

3. The common structural feature for carboxylic acids and also their derivatives is a (an)
   a. acyl group
   b. carbonyl group
   c. carboxyl group
   d. no correct response

4. Which of the following carboxylic acid derivatives is *not* an acyl compound?
$$\text{a. } CH_3-\overset{\displaystyle O}{\overset{\|}{C}}-OH$$
$$\text{b. } CH_3-\overset{\displaystyle O}{\overset{\|}{C}}-CH_3$$
$$\text{c. } CH_3-\overset{\displaystyle O}{\overset{\|}{C}}-NH_2$$
   d. no correct response

5. Which of the following carboxylic acid derivatives is *not* a carbonyl compound?
$$\text{a. } CH_3-\overset{\displaystyle O}{\overset{\|}{C}}-Cl$$
$$\text{b. } CH_3-\overset{\displaystyle O}{\overset{\|}{C}}-CH_3$$
$$\text{c. } CH_3-\overset{\displaystyle O}{\overset{\|}{C}}-H$$
   d. no correct response

Answers: 1. b; 2. c; 3. a; 4. b; 5. a

16-2   IUPAC Nomenclature for Carboxylic Acids

LEARNING FOCUS

Given their structural formulas, be able to name carboxylic acids (mono-, di-, and aromatic) using IUPAC rules or vice versa.

IUPAC rules for naming carboxylic acids resemble those for naming aldehydes (Section 15-4).

Monocarboxylic Acids

A **monocarboxylic acid** is a carboxylic acid in which one carboxyl group is present. IUPAC rules for naming such compounds are:

Rule 1:   *Select as the parent carbon chain the longest carbon chain that* includes *the carbon atom of the carboxyl group.*

Rule 2:   *Name the parent chain by changing the -e ending of the corresponding alkane to -oic acid. Note that there is a space between -oic and acid.*

▶ *A carboxyl group must occupy a terminal (end) position in a carbon chain because there can be only one other bond to it.*

Rule 3:   *Number the parent chain by assigning the number 1 to the carboxyl carbon atom, but omit this number from the name.* ◀

Figure 16-1 Space-filling models for the three simplest carboxylic acids: methanoic acid, ethanoic acid, and propanoic acid.

O
‖
H—C—OH
Methanoic acid

O
‖
CH₃—C—OH
Ethanoic acid

O
‖
CH₃—CH₂—C—OH
Propanoic acid

Rule 4: *Determine the identity and location of any substituents in the usual manner, and append this information to the front of the parent chain name.*

Rule 5: *If the carboxyl group is bonded to a carbon ring, name the ring and add the words* carboxylic acid. *The carbon bearing the carboxyl group is always carbon 1. Locate any other ring substituents in the usual manner.*

Space-filling models for the three simplest carboxylic acids—methanoic acid, ethanoic acid, and propanoic acid—are shown in Figure 16-1.

EXAMPLE 16-1

Determining IUPAC Names for Carboxylic Acids

Assign IUPAC names to the following carboxylic acids:

a.

O
‖
CH₃—CH₂—CH₂—CH₂—C—OH

b.

O
‖
‖
OH

c.

O
‖
CH₃—CH—CH—C—OH
|　　|
Br　CH₂
　　|
　　CH₃

d.

COOH

Solution

a. The parent chain name is based on pentane. Removing the *-e* ending from pentane and replacing it with the ending *-oic acid* gives *pentanoic acid*. The location of the carboxyl group need not be specified, because by definition the carboxyl carbon atom is always carbon 1.

b. The parent chain name is *butanoic acid*. To locate the methyl group substituent, we number the carbon chain beginning with the carboxyl carbon atom. The complete name of the acid is *3-methylbutanoic acid*. ◄

O
‖
4　3　2　1
OH

c. The longest carboxyl-carbon-containing chain has four carbon atoms. The parent chain name is thus *butanoic acid*. There are two substituents present, an ethyl group on carbon 2 and a bromo group on carbon 3. The complete name is *3-bromo-2-ethylbutanoic acid*.

O
‖
4　　3　　2　‖
CH₃—CH—CH—C—OH
　　|　　|
　　Br　CH₂
　　　　|
　　　　CH₃

d. The ring contains five carbon atoms; it is cyclopentane. The ring carbon atom to which the carboxyl group is attached becomes carbon 1. Note that the carboxyl group is denoted using "linear" notation. Ring carbon 2 has a methyl attachment. The acid's name is *2-methylcyclopentanecarboxylic acid*. ◄

► *Line-angle structural formulas for the simpler unbranched-chain carboxylic acids:*

O
‖
H　　OH
Methanoic acid

O
‖
OH
Ethanoic acid

O
‖
OH
Propanoic acid

O
‖
OH
Butanoic acid

► *The carboxyl functional group has the highest priority in the IUPAC naming system of all functional groups considered so far. When both a carboxyl group and a carbonyl group (aldehyde, ketone) are present in the same molecule, the prefix* oxo- *is used to denote the carbonyl group.*

O　　　　　O
‖　　　　　‖
H—C—CH₂—CH₂—C—OH
4-Oxobutanoic acid

Dicarboxylic Acids

A **dicarboxylic acid** *is a carboxylic acid that contains two carboxyl groups, one at each end of a carbon chain.* Saturated acids of this type are named by appending the suffix *-dioic acid* to the corresponding alkane name (the *-e* is retained to facilitate pronunciation). Both carboxyl carbon atoms must be part of the parent carbon chain, and the carboxyl locations need not be specified with numbers because they will always be at the two ends of the chain.

Pentanedioic acid

3-Methylpentanedioic acid

Aromatic Carboxylic Acids

The simplest aromatic carboxylic acid is called benzenecarboxylic acid (Figure 16-2).

Figure 16-2 Space-filling model for benzenecarboxylic acid, the simplest aromatic carboxylic acid.

Benzenecarboxylic acid

In substituted benzenecarboxylic acids, the ring carbon atom bearing the carboxyl group is always carbon 1.

4-Chlorobenzenecarboxylic acid
(*o*-chlorobenzenecarboxylic acid)

3,5-Dichlorobenzenecarboxylic acid

4. Which of the following compounds is *not* a monocarboxylic acid?
   a. hexanoic acid
   b. 2,3-dimethylhexanoic acid
   c. hexanedioic acid
   d. no correct response
5. The IUPAC name for the simplest aromatic carboxylic acid is
   a. benzoic acid
   b. phenolic acid
   c. cyclohexanoic acid
   d. no correct response

Answers: 1. a; 2. b; 3. c; 4. c; 5. d

16-3 Common Names for Carboxylic Acids

LEARNING FOCUS

Be familiar with the common names for the simplest monocarboxylic and dicarboxylic acids; know the Greek-letter system used for numbering carbon atoms in a carbon chain when common names are used.

The use of common names is more prevalent for carboxylic acids than for any other family of organic compounds. Because of their abundance in nature, carboxylic acids were among the earliest classes of organic compounds to be studied, and they acquired names before the advent of the IUPAC naming system. These common names are usually derived from a Latin or Greek word that is related to a source for the acid.

Monocarboxylic Acids

The common name of a monocarboxylic acid is formed by taking the Latin or Greek root name for the specific number of carbon atoms and appending the suffix *–ic acid*. Table 16-1 gives the parent root names and common names for the first six unbranched monocarboxylic acids. The historical basis for the Latin–Greek root name system is as follows.

   The stinging sensation associated with red ant bites is due in part to formic acid (Latin, *formica,* "ant"). Acetic acid gives vinegar its tartness (sour taste); vinegar contains small amounts of acetic acid (Latin, *acetum,* "sour"). Propionic acid is the smallest acid that can be obtained from fats (Greek, *protos,* "first," and *pion,* "fat"). Rancid butter contains butyric acid (Latin, *butyrum,* "butter"). Valeric acid, found in valerian root (an herb), has a strong odor (Latin, *valere,* "to be strong"). The skin secretions of goats contain caproic acid, which contributes to the odor associated with these animals (Latin, *caper,* "goats"). ◀

▶ *The common names of mono-carboxylic acids are the basis for aldehyde common names (Section 15-4).*

C_1: *formic acid and formaldehyde*
C_2: *acetic acid and acetaldehyde*
C_3: *propionic acid and propionaldehyde*
C_4: *butyric acid and butyraldehyde*

▶ Table 16-1 **Common Names for the First Six Unbranched Monocarboxylic Acids**

Length of Carbon Chain	Structural Formula	Latin or Greek Root	Common Name*
C_1 monoacid	H—COOH	form-	formic acid
C_2 monoacid	CH_3—COOH	acet-	acetic acid
C_3 monoacid	CH_3—CH_2—COOH	propion-	propionic acid
C_4 monoacid	CH_3—$(CH_2)_2$—COOH	butyr-	butyric acid
C_5 monoacid	CH_3—$(CH_2)_3$—COOH	valer-	valeric acid
C_6 monoacid	CH_3—$(CH_2)_4$—COOH	capro-	caproic acid

*The mnemonic "*Frogs are polite, being very courteous*" is helpful in remembering, in order, the first letters of the common names of these six simple saturated monocarboxylic acids.

AP Images/David Duprey

Figure 16-3 "Drug-sniffing" dogs used by narcotics agents can find hidden heroin by detecting the odor of acetic acid (vinegar odor). Acetic acid is a by-product of the final step in illicit heroin production, and trace amounts remain in the heroin.

▶ *There is a connection between acetic acid and sourdough bread. The yeast used in leavening the dough for this bread is a type that cannot metabolize the sugar maltose as most yeasts do. Consequently, bacteria that thrive on maltose become abundant in the dough. These bacteria produce acetic acid and lactic acid from the maltose, and the dough becomes* sour *(acidic); hence the name* sourdough *bread.*

▶ *Note that the common and IUPAC naming systems for carboxylic acids differ in three ways:*

1. *The base name for the carbon chain differs.*
2. *The suffix that ends the name differs, being -ic acid in the common system and -oic acid in the IUPAC system.*
3. *The carbon numbering system differs, involving Greek letters in the common system and Arabic numbers in the IUPAC system.*

Figure 16-4 A Greek-letter numbering system is used in common-name nomenclature for carboxylic acids.

Acetic acid is one of the most widely used of all carboxylic acids. Its primary use is as an *acidulant*—a substance that gives the proper acidic conditions for a chemical reaction. In the pure state, acetic acid is a colorless liquid with a sharp odor (Figure 16-3). Vinegar is a 4%–8% (v/v) acetic acid solution; its characteristic odor comes from the acetic acid present. Pure acetic acid is often called *glacial* acetic acid because it freezes on a moderately cold day (m.p. = 17°C), producing icy-looking crystals. ◀

When using common names for carboxylic acids, the positions (locations) of substituents are denoted by using letters of the Greek alphabet rather than numbers. The first four letters of the Greek alphabet are alpha (α), beta (β), gamma (γ), and delta (δ). The alpha-carbon atom is carbon 2, the beta-carbon atom is carbon 3, and so on.

$$\ldots\ldots \overset{}{C}-\overset{}{C}-\overset{}{C}-\overset{}{C}-\overset{\overset{\textstyle O}{\|}}{C}-OH$$

IUPAC: 5 4 3 2 1
Greek letter: δ γ β α

Figure 16-4 contrasts the different carbon-atom numbering systems in IUPAC and common-name nomenclature for carboxylic acids. ◀

Dicarboxylic Acids

Common names for the first six dicarboxylic acids are given in Table 16-2. Oxalic acid, the simplest dicarboxylic acid, is found in plants of the genus *Oxalis,* which includes rhubarb and spinach, and in cabbage (see Figure 16-5). This acid and its salts are poisonous in *high* concentrations. The amount of oxalic acid present in spinach, cabbage, and rhubarb is not harmful. Oxalic acid is used to remove rust, bleach straw and leather, and remove ink stains. Succinic and glutaric acids and their derivatives play important roles in biochemical reactions that occur in the human body (Section 23-6).

Aromatic Carboxylic Acids

The simplest aromatic carboxylic acid—a benzene ring with a carboxyl group attachment—has the common name *benzoic acid.* This common name is more frequently encountered than is the acid's IUPAC name (benzenecarboxylic acid). 2-Chlorobenzoic acid and 2,3-diethylbenzoic acid are examples of common names for substituted benzoic acids.

▶ Table 16-2 **Common Names for the First Six Unbranched Dicarboxylic Acids**

Length of Carbon Chain	Structural Formula	Latin or Greek Root	Common Name*
C_2 diacid	HOOC—COOH	oxal-	oxalic acid
C_3 diacid	HOOC—CH2—COOH	malon-	malonic acid
C_4 diacid	HOOC—$(CH_2)_2$—COOH	succin-	succinic acid
C_5 diacid	HOOC—$(CH_2)_3$—COOH	glutar-	glutaric acid
C_6 diacid	HOOC—$(CH_2)_4$—COOH	adip-	adipic acid
C_7 diacid	HOOC—$(CH_2)_5$—COOH	pimel-	pimelic acid

*The mnemonic "*Oh my, such good apple pie*" is helpful in remembering, in order, the first letters of the common names of these six simple dicarboxylic acids.

EXAMPLE 16-2

Generating the Structural Formulas of Carboxylic Acids from Their Common Names

Draw a structural formula for each of the following carboxylic acids given their common names. ◄

a. Caproic acid   **b.** Glutaric acid
c. α,β-Dimethylsuccinic acid   **d.** β-Chlorobutyric acid

Solution

a. Caproic acid is the six-carbon unsubstituted monocarboxylic acid. Its structural formula is

$$CH_3-CH_2-CH_2-CH_2-CH_2-\overset{\displaystyle O}{\overset{\|}{C}}-OH$$

b. Glutaric acid is the five-carbon unsubstituted dicarboxylic acid, with a carboxyl group at each end of the carbon chain.

$$HO-\overset{\displaystyle O}{\overset{\|}{C}}-CH_2-CH_2-CH_2-\overset{\displaystyle O}{\overset{\|}{C}}-OH$$

c. Succinic acid is the four-carbon unsubstituted dicarboxylic acid. Methyl groups are present on both the alpha- and beta-carbon atoms.

$$HO-\overset{\displaystyle O}{\overset{\|}{C}}-\overset{\alpha}{CH}-\overset{\beta}{CH}-\overset{\displaystyle O}{\overset{\|}{C}}-OH$$
$$\qquad\quad | \quad\ |$$
$$\qquad\quad CH_3 \ \ CH_3$$

d. Butyric acid is the four-carbon unsubstituted monocarboxylic acid. A chloro group is attached to the beta-carbon atom (carbon 3).

$$\overset{\gamma}{CH_3}-\overset{\beta}{CH}-\overset{\alpha}{CH_2}-\overset{\displaystyle O}{\overset{\|}{C}}-OH$$
$$\qquad\ | $$
$$\qquad\ Cl$$

Section 16-3 Quick Quiz

1. The common names for the C_2 mono- and dicarboxylic acids are, respectively,
   a. formic acid and oxalic acid
   b. acetic acid and formic acid
   c. acetic acid and oxalic acid
   d. no correct response
2. The common name for the C_4 unbranched dicarboxylic acid is
   a. malonic acid
   b. succinic acid
   c. glutaric acid
   d. no correct response
3. In which of the following pairs of carboxylic acids are both members of the pair monocarboxylic acids?
   a. propionic acid and malonic acid
   b. succinic acid and glutaric acid
   c. butyric acid and propionic acid
   d. no correct response

Answers: 1. c; 2. b; 3. c

▶ *The contrast between IUPAC names and common names for mono- and dicarboxylic acids is as follows:*

Monocarboxylic Acids
    IUPAC (two words)

    alkanoic acid

    Common (two words)

    (prefix)ic acid*

Dicarboxylic Acids
    IUPAC (two words)

    alkanedioic acid

    Common (two words)

    (prefix)ic acid*

*The common-name prefixes are related to natural sources for the acids.

Structure of oxalic acid

$$HO-\overset{\displaystyle O}{\overset{\|}{C}}-\overset{\displaystyle O}{\overset{\|}{C}}-OH$$

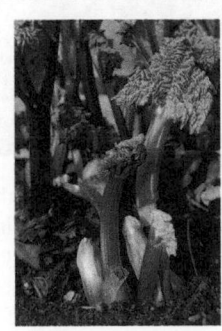

© Azure/Shutterstock.com

Figure 16-5 The C_2 dicarboxylic acid, (oxalic acid), contributes to the tart taste of rhubarb stalks.

16-4 Polyfunctional Carboxylic Acids

LEARNING FOCUS

Be familiar with the simplest members of each of the following classes of polyfunctional carboxylic acids: unsaturated acids, hydroxy acids, and keto acids.

A **polyfunctional carboxylic acid** *is a carboxylic acid that contains one or more additional functional groups besides one or more carboxyl groups.* Such acids occur naturally in many fruits, are important in the normal functioning of the human body (metabolism), and find use in over-the-counter skin-care products and in prescription drugs. Three commonly encountered types of polyfunctional carboxylic acids are *unsaturated* acids, *hydroxy* acids, and *keto* acids.

C—C=C—COOH   C—C—C—COOH   C—C—C—COOH
An unsaturated acid   A hydroxy acid   A keto acid

More information about these types of polyfunctional acids follows.

Unsaturated Acids

The simplest *unsaturated mono*carboxylic acid is propenoic acid (acrylic acid), a substance used in the manufacture of several polymeric materials. Two isomers exist for the simplest *unsaturated di*carboxylic acid, butenedioic acid. The two isomers have separate common names, fumaric acid (*trans*) and maleic acid (*cis*), a naming procedure seldom encountered.

CH_2=CH—COOH   Maleic acid (*cis* isomer)   Fumaric acid (*trans* isomer)

Acrylic acid

Some antihistamines (Section 17-10) are salts of maleic acid. The addition of small amounts of maleic acid to fats and oils prevents them from becoming rancid. Fumaric acid is a *metabolic acid.* Metabolic acids are intermediate compounds in the metabolic reactions (Section 23-4) that occur in the human body. ◀

The nonprescription pain relievers ibuprofen and naproxen are unsaturated carboxylic acids, with the unsaturation coming from the presence of an aromatic ring system within their structures. The focus on relevancy feature Chemical Connections 16-A—Nonprescription Pain Relievers Derived from Propanoic Acid—considers these compounds in further detail. They are two of the most used of the many "over-the-counter" medications now available.

Hydroxy Acids

Four of the simpler *hydroxy* acids are

CH_2—COOH CH_3—CH—COOH   HOOC—CH—CH_2—COOH   HOOC—CH—CH—COOH
   OH   OH   OH   OH   OH
Glycolic acid   Lactic acid   Malic acid   Tartaric acid

Malic and tartaric acids are derivatives of succinic acid, the four-carbon unsubstituted diacid (Section 16-3).

Hydroxy acids occur naturally in many foods. Glycolic acid is present in the juice from sugar cane and sugar beets. Lactic acid is present in sour milk, sauerkraut, and dill pickles. Both malic acid and tartaric acid occur naturally in fruits. The sharp taste of some apples (fruit of trees of the genus *Malus*) is due to malic acid. Tartaric acid is particularly abundant in grapes (Figure 16-6). It is also a component of tartar sauce and an acidic ingredient in many baking powders. Lactic and malic acids are also *metabolic acids* (Section 23-4). ◀

▶ *An unsaturated monocarboxylic acid with the structure*

CH_3—CH_2—CH_2—C=CH—COOH
                         |
                        CH_3
3-Methyl-2-hexenoic acid

has been found to be largely responsible for "body odor." It is produced by skin bacteria, particularly those found in armpits.

© Teri Virbickis/Shutterstock.com

Figure 16-6 Tartaric acid, the dihydroxy derivative of succinic acid, is particularly abundant in ripe grapes.

▶ *4-Hydroxybutanoic acid, which has the common name γ-hydroxybutyric acid (GHB), is an illegal recreational drug that depresses the central nervous system and causes intoxication. Its taste is masked when it is placed in alcoholic beverages; hence its illegal use as a "date rape" drug.*

Nonprescription Pain Relievers Derived from Propanoic Acid

Consumers are faced with a shelf full of choices when looking for an over-the-counter medicine to treat aches, pains, and fever. The vast majority of brands available, however, represent only four chemical formulations. Besides the long-available aspirin and acetaminophen, consumers can now purchase products that contain ibuprofen and naproxen.

Aspirin, acetaminophen, ibuprofen, and naproxen have antipyretic (fever-reducer) and mild analgesic (pain-reliever) properties. Aspirin, ibuprofen, and naproxen (but not acetaminophen) also have anti-inflammatory properties.

Ibuprofen and naproxen, the "newcomers" in the over-the-counter pain-reliever market, share a common structural feature. They are both derivatives of propanoic acid, the three-carbon monocarboxylic acid. Attached to the propanoic acid in both cases is an aromatic ring system with an attachment. In ibuprofen, the ring system is benzene and the ring attachment is an isobutyl group. In naproxen, the ring system is naphthalene (Section 13-16) with a methoxy attachment.

The active ingredients in Aleve and Advil are derivatives of propanoic acid.

Ibuprofen

Naproxen

Ibuprofen, marketed under the brand names Advil, Motrin-IB, and Nuprin, was cleared by the FDA in 1984 for nonprescription sales. Numerous studies have shown that nonprescription-strength ibuprofen relieves minor pain and fever as well as does aspirin or acetaminophen. Like aspirin, ibuprofen reduces inflammation. (Prescription-strength ibuprofen has extensive use as an anti-inflammatory agent for the treatment of rheumatoid arthritis.) There is evidence that ibuprofen is more effective than either aspirin or acetaminophen in reducing dental pain and menstrual pain. Both aspirin and ibuprofen can cause stomach bleeding in some people, although ibuprofen seems to cause fewer problems. Ibuprofen is more expensive than either aspirin or acetaminophen.

Naproxen, marketed under the brand names Aleve and Anaprox, was cleared by the FDA in 1994 for nonprescription use. The effects of naproxen last longer in the body (8–12 hr per dose) than the effects of ibuprofen (4–6 hr per dose) and of aspirin and acetaminophen (4 hr per dose). Naproxen is more likely to cause slight intestinal bleeding and stomach upset than is ibuprofen. It is also not recommended for use by children under 12.

Citric acid, perhaps the best known of all carboxylic acids, is a hydroxy acid with a structural feature not previously encountered. It is a hydroxy *tri*carboxylic acid. Besides there being acid groups at both ends of a carbon chain, a third acid group is present as a substituent on the chain. An acid group as a substituent is called a *carboxy* group. Thus citric acid is a hydroxycarboxy diacid.

$$\underset{\text{Citric acid}}{\text{HOOC}-\text{CH}_2-\overset{\overset{\displaystyle \text{OH}}{|}}{\underset{\underset{\displaystyle \text{COOH}}{|}}{\text{C}}}-\text{CH}_2-\text{COOH}}$$

Citric acid gives citrus fruits their "sharp" taste; lemon juice contains 4%–8% citric acid, and orange juice is about 1% citric acid. Citric acid is used widely in beverages and in foods. In jams, jellies, and preserves, it produces tartness and pH adjustment to optimize conditions for gelation. In fresh salads, citric acid prevents enzymatic browning reactions, and in frozen fruits it prevents deterioration of color and flavor. Addition of citric acid to seafood retards microbial growth by lowering pH. Citric acid is also a metabolic acid (Section 23-4).

▶ *The IUPAC name for citric acid is 2-hydroxypropane-1,2,3-tricarboxylic acid.*

A number of skin-care products contain hydroxy acids. The focus on relevancy feature Chemical Connections 16-B—Carboxylic Acids and Skin Care—considers such products, the advertising for which touts the presence of alpha-hydroxy acids as the active ingredients.

Keto Acids

Keto acids, as the designation implies, contain a carbonyl group within a carbon chain. Pyruvic acid, with three carbon atoms, is the simplest keto acid that can exist.

$$CH_3-\underset{\underset{\text{Pyruvic acid}}{}}{\overset{\overset{\displaystyle O}{\|}}{C}}-COOH$$

In the pure state, pyruvic acid is a liquid with an odor resembling that of vinegar (acetic acid; Section 16-3). Pyruvic acid is a metabolic acid (Section 23-4).

CHEMICAL CONNECTIONS 16-B

Carboxylic Acids and Skin Care

A number of carboxylic acids are used as "skin-care acids." Heavily advertised at present are cosmetic products that contain *alpha-hydroxy* acids, carboxylic acids in which a hydroxyl group is attached to the acid's alpha-carbon atom. Such cosmetic products address problems such as dryness, flaking, and itchiness of the skin and are highly promoted for removing wrinkles.

The alpha-hydroxy acids most commonly found in cosmetic products are glycolic acid and lactic acid, the two simplest alpha-hydroxy acids.

Alpha-carbon atom	Alpha-carbon atom
CH_2-COOH	$CH_3-CH-COOH$
$\|$	$\|$
OH	OH
Glycolic acid	Lactic acid

Both acids are naturally occurring substances. Glycolic acid occurs in sugar cane and sugar beets, and lactic acid occurs in sour milk.

The use of alpha-hydroxy acids in cosmetics is considered safe at acid concentrations of less than 10%; higher concentrations can cause skin irritation, burning, and stinging. (Lactic acid becomes a prescription drug at concentrations of 12% or more.) One drawback of the cosmetic use of alpha-hydroxy products is that such use can increase the skin's sensitivity to the ultraviolet light component of sunlight; it is this component that causes sunburn. Individuals who are using "alpha-hydroxys" should apply a sunscreen whenever they go outside for an extended period of time.

Alpha-hydroxy acids are often touted as substances that reverse the aging process of skin. Such is not the case. Instead, these acids simply react with outer-layer skin cells, causing them (and any blemishes they contain) to flake off. This exposes a new layer of skin cells that have not been subjected to sun exposure and which often temporarily have the appearance of "younger" skin.

Images © Alyssa White/Cengage Learning

Two skin-care products containing alpha-hydroxy acids.

Glycolic acid, at higher concentrations than that found in cosmetics, is used by dermatologists for the "spot" removal of *keratoses* (precancerous lesions and/or patches of darker, thickened skin).

Polyunsaturated carboxylic acids are used extensively in the treatment of severe acne. The prescription drugs Tretinoin and Accutane are such compounds.

Tretinoin (5 *trans*-double bonds)

Accutane (4 *trans*- and 1 *cis*-double bonds)

Section 16-4 Quick Quiz

1. Which of the following acids is a hydroxy acid?
   a. lactic acid
   b. pyruvic acid
   c. acrylic acid
   d. no correct response
2. Which of the following acids is a keto acid?
   a. lactic acid
   b. pyruvic acid
   c. acrylic acid
   d. no correct response
3. Which of the following structural statements about citric acid is incorrect?
   a. It is a hydroxy acid.
   b. It is a keto acid.
   c. It is a tricarboxylic acid.
   d. no correct response

Answers: 1. a; 2. b; 3. b

16-5 Physical Properties of Carboxylic Acids

LEARNING FOCUS:
Be familiar with general physical properties and hydrogen-bonding behavior for carboxylic acids.

Carboxylic acids are the most *polar* organic compounds we have discussed so far. Both the carbonyl part ($\diagdown$C=O) and the hydroxyl part (—OH) of the carboxyl functional group are polar. The result is very high melting and boiling points for carboxylic acids, the highest of any type of organic compound yet considered (Figure 16-7).

Unsubstituted saturated monocarboxylic acids containing up to nine carbon atoms are liquids that have strong, sharp odors (Figure 16-8). Acids with 10 or more carbon atoms in an unbranched chain are waxy solids that are odorless (because of low volatility). Aromatic carboxylic acids, as well as dicarboxylic acids, are also odorless solids.

The high boiling points of carboxylic acids indicate the presence of strong intermolecular attractive forces. A unique hydrogen-bonding arrangement, shown in Figure 16-9, contributes to these attractive forces. A given carboxylic acid molecule forms two hydrogen bonds to another carboxylic acid molecule, producing a "complex" known as a *dimer*. Because dimers have twice the mass of a single molecule, a higher temperature is needed to boil a carboxylic acid than would be needed for similarly sized aldehyde and alcohol molecules in which dimerization does not occur.

Carboxylic acids readily hydrogen-bond to water molecules. Such hydrogen bonding contributes to water solubility for short-chain carboxylic acids. The unsubstituted C_1 to C_4 monocarboxylic acids are completely miscible with water. Solubility then rapidly decreases with carbon number, as shown in Figure 16-10. Short-chain dicarboxylic acids are also water soluble. In general, aromatic acids are not water soluble.

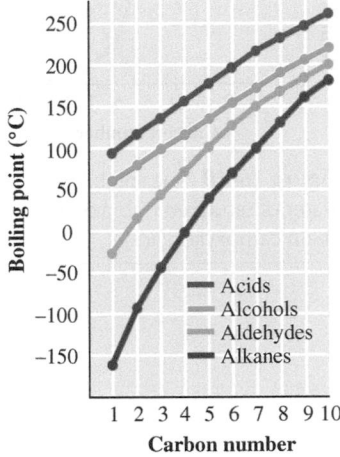

Figure 16-7 The boiling points of monocarboxylic acids compared to those of other types of compounds. All compounds in the comparison have unbranched carbon chains.

Unbranched Monocarboxylic Acids			
C_1	C_3	C_5	C_7
C_2	C_4	C_6	C_8

Unbranched Dicarboxylic Acids			
✕	C_3	C_5	C_7
C_2	C_4	C_6	C_8

☐ Liquid ☐ Solid

Figure 16-8 A physical-state summary for unbranched mono- and dicarboxylic acids at room temperature and pressure.

Figure 16-9 A given carboxylic acid molecule can form two hydrogen bonds to another carboxylic acid molecule, producing a "dimer," a complex with a mass twice that of a single molecule.

Figure 16-10 The solubility in water of saturated unbranched-chain carboxylic acids.

16-6 Preparation of Carboxylic Acids

LEARNING FOCUS

Be familiar with the process by which carboxylic acids are prepared via oxidation reactions.

Oxidation of primary alcohols or aldehydes, using an oxidizing agent such as CrO_3 or $K_2Cr_2O_7$, produces carboxylic acids, a process that was examined in Sections 14-9 and 15-10.

$$\text{Primary alcohol} \xrightarrow{[O]} \text{aldehyde} \xrightarrow{[O]} \text{carboxylic acid}$$

Recall, from Section 15-10, that although aldehydes are easily oxidized to carboxylic acids, ketones do not undergo a similar type reaction.

Aromatic acids can be prepared by oxidizing a carbon side chain (alkyl group) on a benzene derivative. In this process, all the carbon atoms of the alkyl group except the one attached to the ring are lost. The remaining carbon becomes part of a carboxyl group.

$$\underset{\text{C}_6\text{H}_5-}{CH_2-CH_2-CH_3} \xrightarrow[\text{H}_2\text{SO}_4]{\text{K}_2\text{Cr}_2\text{O}_7} \underset{\text{C}_6\text{H}_5-}{\overset{\overset{\displaystyle O}{\parallel}}{C}-OH} + 2CO_2 + 3H_2O$$

16-7 Acidity of Carboxylic Acids

LEARNING FOCUS

Understand the relationship between carboxylic acids and the carboxylate ions that they form in aqueous solution; know the structural characteristics of and naming rules for carboxylate ions.

Carboxylic acids, as the name implies, are *acidic*. When a carboxylic acid is placed in water, hydrogen ion transfer (proton transfer; Section 10-2) occurs to produce hydronium ion (the acidic species in water; Section 10-2) and carboxylate ion.

$$R\text{—COOH} + H_2O \longrightarrow \underset{\substack{\text{Hydronium} \\ \text{ion}}}{H_3O^+} + \underset{\substack{\text{Carboxylate} \\ \text{ion}}}{R\text{—COO}^-}$$

A **carboxylate ion** *is the negative ion produced when a carboxylic acid loses one or more acidic hydrogen atoms.*

Carboxylate ions formed from monocarboxylic acids always carry a $1-$ charge; only one acidic hydrogen atom is present in such molecules. Dicarboxylic acids, which possess two acidic hydrogen atoms (one in each carboxyl group), can produce carboxylate ions bearing a $2-$ charge.

Carboxylate ions are named by dropping the *-ic acid* ending from the name of the parent acid and replacing it with *-ate*.

$$\underset{\substack{\text{Acetic acid} \\ \text{(ethanoic acid)}}}{CH_3-\overset{\overset{O}{\|}}{C}-OH} + H_2O \longrightarrow H_3O^+ + \underset{\substack{\text{Acetate ion} \\ \text{(ethanoate ion)}}}{CH_3-\overset{\overset{O}{\|}}{C}-O^-}$$

$$\underset{\substack{\text{Oxalic acid} \\ \text{(ethanedioic acid)}}}{HO-\overset{\overset{O}{\|}}{C}-\overset{\overset{O}{\|}}{C}-OH} + 2H_2O \longrightarrow 2H_3O^+ + \underset{\substack{\text{Oxalate ion} \\ \text{(ethanedioate ion)}}}{{}^-O-\overset{\overset{O}{\|}}{C}-\overset{\overset{O}{\|}}{C}-O^-}$$

Carboxylic acids are weak acids (Section 10-4). The extent of proton transfer is usually less than 5%; that is, an equilibrium situation exists in which the equilibrium lies far to the left. ◀

$$R\text{—COOH} + H_2O \underset{\substack{\text{More than 95\%} \\ \text{of molecules in this form}}}{\overset{}{\rightleftharpoons}} H_3O^+ + \underset{\substack{\text{Less than 5\%} \\ \text{of molecules in this form}}}{R\text{—COO}^-}$$

▶ *At normal human body pH values (pH = 7.35 to 7.45), most carboxylic acids exist as carboxylate ions. Acetic acid is in the form of acetate ion, pyruvic acid is in the form of pyruvate ion, lactic acid is in the form of lactate ion, and so on.*

Table 16-3 gives K_a values and percent ionization values in 0.100 M solution (topics previously discussed in Section 10-5) and pK_a values (Section 10-10) for selected monocarboxylic acids.

▶ Table 16-3 **Acid Strength for Selected Monocarboxylic Acids**

Acid	K_a	Percent Ionization (0.100 M Solution)	pK_a
formic	1.8×10^{-4}	4.2%	3.75
acetic	1.8×10^{-5}	1.3%	4.75
propionic	1.3×10^{-5}	1.2%	4.89
butyric	1.5×10^{-5}	1.2%	4.82
valeric	1.5×10^{-5}	1.2%	4.82
caproic	1.4×10^{-5}	1.2%	4.85

1. Which of the following statements about acid strength for carboxylic acids is correct?
   a. All are weak acids.
   b. Some are weak acids and others are strong acids.
   c. All are strong acids.
   d. no correct response
2. Which of the following statements about carboxylate ions is correct?
   a. They may be positively or negatively charged.
   b. They contain fewer hydrogen atoms than their parent acid.
   c. They contain one more oxygen atom than their parent acid.
   d. no correct response
3. Carboxylate ions are named by dropping the *-ic acid* ending from the parent acid name and replacing it with the suffix
   a. -ate
   b. -one
   c. -ol
   d. no correct response

Answers: 1. a; 2. b; 3. a

16-8 Carboxylic Acid Salts

LEARNING FOCUS

Know the general reaction by which carboxylic acid salts are produced; know the structural characteristics, general uses, and naming rules for carboxylic acid salts.

▶ *Carboxylic acid salt formation involves an acid–base neutralization reaction (Section 10-7).*

In a manner similar to that of inorganic acids (Section 10-6), carboxylic acids react completely with strong bases to produce water and a carboxylic acid salt. ◀

$$CH_3-\overset{\overset{\displaystyle O}{\|}}{C}-OH + NaOH \longrightarrow CH_3-\overset{\overset{\displaystyle O}{\|}}{C}-O^- Na^+ + H_2O$$

Carboxylic acid   Strong base   Carboxylic   Water
                         acid salt

A **carboxylic acid salt** *is an ionic compound in which the negative ion is a carboxylate ion.*

Carboxylic acid salts are named similarly to other ionic compounds (Section 4-9): *The positive ion is named first, followed by a separate word giving the name of the negative ion.* The salt formed in the preceding reaction contains sodium ions and acetate ions (from acetic acid); hence the salt's name is sodium acetate.

EXAMPLE 16-3

Writing Equations for the Formation of Carboxylic Acid Salts

Using an acid–base neutralization reaction, write a chemical equation for the formation of each of the following carboxylic acid salts:

a. Sodium propionate   b. Potassium oxalate

Solution

a. This salt contains sodium ion (Na^+) and propionate ion, the three-carbon monocarboxylate ion.

$$CH_3-CH_2-\overset{\overset{\displaystyle O}{\|}}{C}-O^-Na^+$$

From a neutralization standpoint, the sodium ion's source is the base sodium hydroxide, NaOH, and the negative ion's source is the acid propanoic acid. The acid–base neutralization equation is

$$CH_3-CH_2-\overset{\overset{\displaystyle O}{\|}}{C}-OH + NaOH \longrightarrow CH_3-CH_2-\overset{\overset{\displaystyle O}{\|}}{C}-O^-Na^+ + H_2O$$

| Propionic acid | Sodium hydroxide | Sodium propionate | Water |

b. This salt contains potassium ions (K^+) whose source is the base potassium hydroxide, KOH. The salt also contains oxalate ions, whose source is the acid oxalic acid.

$$HO-\overset{\overset{\displaystyle O}{\|}}{C}-\overset{\overset{\displaystyle O}{\|}}{C}-OH + 2KOH \longrightarrow K^+{}^-O-\overset{\overset{\displaystyle O}{\|}}{C}-\overset{\overset{\displaystyle O}{\|}}{C}-O^-K^+ + 2H_2O$$

| Oxalic acid | Potassium hydroxide | Potassium oxalate | Water |

Note that two molecules of base are needed to react completely with one molecule of acid because the acid is a dicarboxylic acid.

Converting a carboxylic acid salt back to a carboxylic acid is very simple. React the salt with a solution of a strong acid such as hydrochloric acid (HCl) or sulfuric acid (H_2SO_4).

$$CH_3-\overset{\overset{\displaystyle O}{\|}}{C}-O^-\ Na^+ + HCl \longrightarrow CH_3-\overset{\overset{\displaystyle O}{\|}}{C}-OH + NaCl$$

| Sodium acetate | Hydrochloric acid | Acetic acid | Sodium chloride |

The interconversion reactions between carboxylic acid salts and their "parent" carboxylic acids are so easy to carry out that organic chemists consider these two types of compounds interchangeable.

Strong base

Carboxylic acid ⟶ Carboxylic acid salt

Strong acid

Uses for Carboxylic Acid Salts

The solubility of carboxylic acid salts in water is much greater than that of the carboxylic acids from which they are derived. Drugs and medicines that contain acid groups are usually marketed as the sodium or potassium salt of the acid. This greatly enhances the solubility of the medication, increasing the ease of its absorption by the body. ◀

Many *antimicrobials,* compounds used as food preservatives, are carboxylic acid salts. Particularly important are the salts of benzoic, sorbic, and propionic acids.

▶ *The solubility of benzoic acid in water at 25°C is 3.4 g/L. The solubility of sodium benzoate, the sodium salt of benzoic acid, in water at 25°C is 550 g/L.*

| Benzoic acid | Sorbic acid (2,4-hexadienoic acid) | Propionic acid |

$$CH_3-CH=CH-CH=CH-COOH \qquad CH_3-CH_2-COOH$$

Figure 16-11 Propionates, salts of propionic acid, extend the shelf life of bread by preventing the formation of mold.

The benzoate salts of sodium and potassium are effective against yeast and mold growth in beverages, jams and jellies, pie fillings, ketchup, and syrups. Concentrations of up to 0.1% (m/m) benzoate are found in such products.

Sodium benzoate   Potassium benzoate

Sodium and potassium sorbates inhibit mold and yeast growth in dairy products, dried fruits, sauerkraut, and some meat and fish products. Sorbate preservative concentrations range from 0.02% to 0.2% (m/m).

$$CH_3-CH=CH-CH=CH-\overset{\overset{\text{O}}{\|}}{C}-O^-\,Na^+$$
Sodium sorbate

$$CH_3-CH=CH-CH=CH-\overset{\overset{\text{O}}{\|}}{C}-O^-\,K^+$$
Potassium sorbate

Calcium and sodium propionates are used in baked products and also in cheese foods and spreads (Figure 16-11). Benzoates and sorbates cannot be used in yeast-leavened baked goods because they affect the activity of the yeast.

$$\left(CH_3-CH_2-\overset{\overset{\text{O}}{\|}}{C}-O^-\right)_2 Ca^{2+}\qquad CH_3-CH_2-\overset{\overset{\text{O}}{\|}}{C}-O^-\,Na^+$$
Calcium propionate   Sodium propionate

Carboxylate salts do not directly kill microorganisms present in food. Rather, they prevent further growth and proliferation of these organisms by increasing the pH of the foods in which they are used.

Section 16-8 Quick Quiz

1. Which of the following substances would react with a carboxylic acid to produce a carboxylic acid salt?
   a. a strong acid
   b. a strong base
   c. a soluble aldehyde
   d. no correct response
2. Carboxylic acid salts may be converted back to their "parent" carboxylic acids by reacting them with a
   a. strong base
   b. strong acid
   c. soluble aldehyde
   d. no correct response
3. Several carboxylic acid salts are used as
   a. food preservatives
   b. flavoring agents
   c. pheromones
   d. no correct response
4. The IUPAC name for the propanoic acid salt $CH_3-CH_2-\overset{\overset{\text{O}}{\|}}{C}-O^-Na^+$ is
   a. propyl sodiumate
   b. propanoic sodiumate
   c. sodium propanoate
   d. no correct response

Answers: 1. b; 2. b; 3. a; 4. c

16-9 Carboxylic Acid Decarboxylation Reaction

LEARNING FOCUS

Be able to draw the products formed when a carboxylic acid undergoes a decarboxylation reaction.

Carboxylic acids, in their carboxylate ion form, play key roles in many reactions that occur within the human body. In living organisms, the carboxyl functional group is not normally oxidized or reduced. There is, however, one reaction that it readily undergoes, that of decarboxylation. A **decarboxylation reaction** *is a chemical reaction in which a carboxylic acid is converted into smaller organic molecule and a molecule of carbon dioxide.* The general equation for a decarboxylation reaction is

$$\underset{\text{molecule}}{\widehat{\text{Rest of}}} - \overset{\overset{\displaystyle H}{|}}{\underset{\underset{\displaystyle H}{|}}{C}} - \overset{\overset{\displaystyle O}{\|}}{C} - O - H \longrightarrow \underset{\text{molecule}}{\widehat{\text{Rest of}}} - \overset{\overset{\displaystyle H}{|}}{\underset{\underset{\displaystyle H}{|}}{C}} - H + CO_2$$

Within the human body, decarboxylation most often involves polyfunctional carboxylic acids (Section 16-4) with an additional functional group located within two carbons of the carboxyl carbon atom rather than simple carboxylic acids. An example of decarboxylation of a polyfunctional carboxylic acid is

$$\underset{\text{Ketoacid}}{CH_3 - \overset{\overset{\displaystyle O}{\|}}{C} - CH_2 - \overset{\overset{\displaystyle O}{\|}}{C} - O - H} \longrightarrow \underset{\text{Ketone}}{CH_3 - \overset{\overset{\displaystyle O}{\|}}{C} - CH_3} + CO_2$$

Many additional details and additional examples of carboxylic acid decarboxylation reactions will be encountered in the biochemistry chapters of this text. A discussion of key carboxylate ions that participate in decarboxylation reactions is found in Section 23-4.

Section 16-9 Quick Quiz

1. The small inorganic molecule produced in a carboxylic acid decarboxylation reaction is
   a. H_2O
   b. O_2
   c. CO_2
   d. no correct response
2. The organic product produced when the molecule $CH_3 - CH_2 - \overset{\overset{\displaystyle O}{\|}}{C} - OH$ undergoes decarboxylation is
   a. $CH_3 - CH_2 - \overset{\overset{\displaystyle O}{\|}}{C} - H$
   b. $CH_3 - CH_2 - OH$
   c. $CH_3 - CH_3$
   d. no correct response

Answers: 1. c; 2. c

16-10 Structure of Esters

LEARNING FOCUS

Know the structural characteristics of the ester functional group and various ways used to denote this functional group.

An **ester** *is a carboxylic acid derivative in which the* —*OH portion of the carboxyl group has been replaced with an* —*OR group.*

$$\underset{\text{Carboxylic acid}}{R - \overset{\overset{\displaystyle O}{\|}}{C} - O - H} \qquad \underset{\text{Ester}}{R - \overset{\overset{\displaystyle O}{\|}}{C} - O - R}$$

The ester functional group is thus

$$\underset{\displaystyle -\overset{\displaystyle \text{O}}{\overset{\displaystyle \|}{\text{C}}}-\text{O}-\text{R}}{}$$

In linear form, the ester functional group can be represented as —COOR or —CO$_2$R.

The simplest ester, which has two carbon atoms, has a hydrogen atom attached to the ester functional group.

$$\text{H}-\overset{\displaystyle \text{O}}{\overset{\displaystyle \|}{\text{C}}}-\text{O}-\text{CH}_3$$

Note that the two carbon atoms present are not bonded to each other.

There are two three-carbon esters.

$$\text{H}-\overset{\displaystyle \text{O}}{\overset{\displaystyle \|}{\text{C}}}-\text{O}-\text{CH}_2-\text{CH}_3 \quad \text{and} \quad \text{CH}_3-\overset{\displaystyle \text{O}}{\overset{\displaystyle \|}{\text{C}}}-\text{O}-\text{CH}_3$$

The structure of the simplest aromatic ester is derived from the structure of benzoic acid, the simplest aromatic carboxylic acid.

$$\text{C}_6\text{H}_5-\overset{\displaystyle \text{O}}{\overset{\displaystyle \|}{\text{C}}}-\text{O}-\text{CH}_3$$

Note that the difference between a carboxylic acid and an ester is an "H versus R" relationship.

$$\underset{\text{Acid}}{\text{R}-\overset{\displaystyle \text{O}}{\overset{\displaystyle \|}{\text{C}}}-\text{O}-\text{H}} \quad \text{and} \quad \underset{\text{Ester}}{\text{R}-\overset{\displaystyle \text{O}}{\overset{\displaystyle \|}{\text{C}}}-\text{O}-\text{R}}$$

This "H versus R" relationship has been encountered several times before in our study of hydrocarbon derivatives. Chemistry at a Glance—Summary of the "H Versus R" Relationship for Pairs of Hydrocarbon Derivatives—summarizes the "H versus R" relationships that have been encountered so far.

Section 16-10 Quick Quiz

1. An ester is a carboxylic acid derivative in which the —OH portion of the carboxyl group has been replaced with which of the following?
   a. —OR group
   b. —O⁻Na⁺
   c. —R group
   d. no correct response
2. How many carbon atoms are present in the structure of the simplest possible ester?
   a. 2
   b. 3
   c. 4
   d. no correct response

Answers: 1. a; 2. a

16-11 Preparation of Esters

LEARNING FOCUS

Be able to predict the products of a condensation reaction between an alcohol and a carboxylic acid to form an ester.

CHEMISTRY AT A GLANCE

Summary of the "H Versus R" Relationship for Pairs of Hydrocarbon Derivatives

Esters are produced through *esterification*. An **esterification reaction** *is the condensation reaction of a carboxylic acid with an alcohol (or phenol) to produce an ester and water.* A strong acid catalyst (generally H_2SO_4) is needed for esterification. ◀

◀ *Esterification is a condensation reaction. This is the third time this type of reaction has been encountered. The first encounter involved the preparation of an ether (Section 14-9) and the second encounter involved the preparation of acetals (Section 15-11).*

In the esterification process, an —OH group is lost from the carboxylic acid, an —H atom is lost from the alcohol, and water is formed as a by-product. The net effect of this reaction is substitution of the —OR′ group of the alcohol for the —OH group of the acid.

A specific example of esterification is the reaction of acetic acid with methyl alcohol. ◀

◀ *Studies show that in ester formation, the hydroxyl group of the acid (not of the alcohol) becomes part of the water molecule.*

Esterification reactions are equilibrium processes, with the position of equilibrium (Section 9-8) usually favoring products only slightly. That is, at equilibrium, substantial amounts of both reactants and products are present. The amount of ester formed can be increased by using an excess of alcohol or by constantly removing one of the products. According to Le Châtelier's principle (Section 9-9), either of these techniques will shift the position of equilibrium to the right (the product side of the equation). This equilibrium problem explains the use of the "double-arrow notation" in all the esterification equations in this section.

It is often useful to think of the structure of an ester in terms of its "parent" alcohol and acid molecules; the ester has an acid part and an alcohol part.

In this context, it is easy to identify the acid and alcohol from which a given ester can be produced; just add an —OH group to the acid part of the ester and an —H atom to the alcohol part to generate the parent molecules.

Cyclic Esters (Lactones)

Hydroxy acids—compounds which contain both a hydroxyl and a carboxyl group (Section 16-4)—have the capacity to undergo intermolecular esterification to form cyclic esters. Such internal esterification easily takes place in situations where a five- or six-membered ring can be formed.

Note that cyclic esters, like cyclic ethers (Section 14-19), are *heterocyclic* organic compounds. The oxygen atom that remains after a molecule of water is formed becomes part of the ring structure.

Cyclic esters are formally called *lactones*. A **lactone** *is a cyclic ester.* The ring size in a lactone is indicated using a Greek letter. A lactone with a five-membered ring is a γ-lactone because the γ-carbon from the carbonyl carbon atom is bonded to the heteroatom (O) of the ring. Similarly, a six-membered lactone ring system is a δ-lactone because the δ-carbon is bonded to the heteroatom (O) of the ring system.

Chemical reactions that are expected to produce a hydroxy carboxylic acid often yield a lactone instead if a five- or six-membered ring can be formed.

Section 16-11 Quick Quiz

1. Esters are produced through a condensation reaction that involves a carboxylic acid and a(n)
   a. aldehyde
   b. alcohol
   c. ketone
   d. no correct response

2. The "parent" acid for the ester molecule $CH_3-CH_2-\overset{\overset{\displaystyle O}{\|}}{C}-O-CH_3$ is a(n)
   a. one-carbon acid
   b. two-carbon acid
   c. three-carbon acid
   d. no correct response
3. Which of the following is an incorrect characterization for a *lactone*?
   a. It is a heterocyclic compound.
   b. It is a cyclic ester.
   c. It is a cyclic ketone.
   d. no correct response

Answers: 1. b; 2. c; 3. c

$$CH_3-\overset{\overset{\displaystyle O}{\|}}{C}-O-CH_3$$
Methyl acetate

16-12 Nomenclature for Esters

LEARNING FOCUS

Given their structural formulas, be able to name esters using IUPAC rules or vice versa; be able to assign common names to simple esters.

$$CH_3-\overset{\overset{\displaystyle O}{\|}}{C}-O-CH_2-CH_3$$
Ethyl acetate

For naming purposes, an ester may be viewed structurally as containing an acyl group and an alkyl group.

acyl   alkyl
group group

Figure 16-12 Space-filling models for the methyl and ethyl esters of acetic acid.

This is the basis for the rules used in determining both common and IUPAC names for esters. The rules are as follows:

Rule 1: *The name for the alkyl part of the ester appears first and is followed by a separate word giving the name for the acyl part of the ester.*

Rule 2: *The name for the alkyl part of the ester is simply the name of the R group (alkyl, cycloalkyl, or aryl) present.*

Rule 3: *The name for the acyl part of the ester is obtained by dropping the -ic acid ending for the acid's name and adding the suffix -ate.*

Consider the ester derived from ethanoic acid (acetic acid) and methanol (methyl alcohol). Its name will be *methyl ethanoate* (IUPAC) or *methyl acetate* (common); see Figure 16-12. ◄

$$CH_3-\overset{\overset{\displaystyle O}{\|}}{C}-OH + HO-CH_3 \longrightarrow CH_3-\overset{\overset{\displaystyle O}{\|}}{C}-O-CH_3 + H_2O$$

IUPAC: Ethanoic acid   Methanol   Methyl ethanoate
Common: Acetic acid   Methyl alcohol Methyl acetate

Dicarboxylic acids can form diesters, with each of the carboxyl groups undergoing esterification. An example of such a molecule and how it is named is

IUPAC: Dimethyl butanedioate
Common: Dimethyl succinate

▶ *Salts and esters of carboxylic acids are named in the same way. The name of the positive ion (in the case of a salt) or the name of the organic group attached to the single-bonded oxygen of the carbonyl group (in the case of an ester) precedes the name of the acid. The -ic acid part of the name of the acid is converted to -ate.*

$$CH_3-CH_2-CH_2-\overset{\overset{\displaystyle O}{\|}}{C}-O^-\ Na^+$$

IUPAC: Sodium butanoate
Common: Sodium butyrate

$$CH_3-CH_2-CH_2-\overset{\overset{\displaystyle O}{\|}}{C}-O-CH_3$$

IUPAC: Methyl butanoate
Common: Methyl butyrate

▶ *The structural formulas of esters are usually written with the acyl group first (on the left) and the alkyl group last (on the right). When naming an ester, however, the situation is opposite. The alkyl group is named first, followed by the name of the acyl group.*

Further examples of ester nomenclature, for compounds in which substituents are present, are ◀

IUPAC: 2-Chloroethyl propanoate
Common: 2-Chloroethyl propionate

Ethyl 2-methylpropanoate
Ethyl α-methylpropionate

IUPAC: Methyl 3-oxobutanoate
Common: Methyl β-oxobutyrate

EXAMPLE 16-4

Determining IUPAC and Common Names for Esters

Assign both IUPAC and common names to the following esters:

a.
$$CH_3-CH_2-\overset{\overset{\displaystyle O}{\|}}{C}-O-CH_2-CH_3$$

b.

c.

Solution

a. The name *ethyl* characterizes the alkyl group in the molecule. The name of the acid is propanoic acid (IUPAC) or propionic acid (common). Deleting the *-ic acid* ending and adding *-ate* gives the name *ethyl propanoate* (IUPAC) or *ethyl propionate* (common).

b. The name of the alkyl group is methyl (from methanol or methyl alcohol). The name of the five-carbon acid is 3-methylbutanoic acid or β-methylbutyric acid. Hence the ester name is *methyl 3-methylbutanoate* (IUPAC) or *methyl β-methylbutyrate* (common). ◀

c. The name *propyl* characterizes the alkyl part of the molecule. The name of the acyl part of the molecule is derived from benzenecarboxylic acid (IUPAC name) or benzoic acid (common name). Hence, the ester names are *propyl benzenecarboxylate* and *propyl benzoate*. ◀

▶ *Line-angle structural formulas for the simpler unbranched-chain methyl esters:*

Methyl methanoate

Methyl ethanoate

Methyl propanoate

Methyl butanoate

▶ *The contrast between IUPAC names and common names for unbranched esters of carboxylic acids is as follows:*

IUPAC (two words)

methyl propanoate

Common (two words)

| alkyl (prefix)ate* |

methyl acetate

The common-name prefixes are related to natural sources for the "parent" carboxylic acids.

IUPAC names for lactones are generated by replacing the *-oic* ending of the parent hydroxycarboxylic acid name with *-olide* and identifying the hydroxyl-bearing carbon by number.

HO—CH₂—CH₂—CH₂—C—OH ⟶

4-Hydroxybutanoic acid   4-Butanolide

HO—CH₂—CH₂—CH₂—CH₂—C—OH ⟶

5-Hydroxypentanoic acid   5-Pentanolide

1. IUPAC ester nomenclature is very similar to that for
   a. carboxylic acids
   b. carboxylic acid salts
   c. ethers
   d. no correct response
2. The IUPAC name for the ester $CH_3-CH_2-\overset{\overset{\displaystyle O}{\|}}{C}-O-CH_3$ is
   a. ethyl methyl ester
   b. methyl propyl ester
   c. methyl propanoate
   d. no correct response
3. The IUPAC name for the ester formed when butanoic acid and ethanol react is
   a. ethyl butanoate
   b. butyl ethanoate
   c. butyl ethyl ester
   d. no correct response
4. The common name for the ester whose IUPAC name is methyl ethanoate is
   a. ethyl methyl ester
   b. methyl acetate
   c. ethyl acetate
   d. no correct response

Answers: 1. b; 2. c; 3. a; 4. b

16-13 Selected Common Esters

LEARNING FOCUS
Be familiar with several common uses for esters.

In this section, selected esters that function as flavoring agents, pheromones, and medications are considered.

Flavor/Fragrance Agents

Esters are largely responsible for the flavor and fragrance of fruits and flowers. Generally, a natural flavor or odor is caused by a mixture of esters, with one particular compound being dominant. The synthetic production of these "dominant" compounds is the basis for the flavoring agents used in ice cream, gelatins, soft drinks, and so on. Table 16-4 gives the structures of selected esters used as flavoring agents. What is surprising about the structures in Table 16-4 is how closely some of them resemble each other. For example, the apple and pineapple flavoring agents differ by one carbon atom (methyl versus ethyl); a five-carbon chain versus an eight-carbon chain makes the difference between banana and orange flavor.

Numerous lactones are common in plants. Two examples are 4-decanolide, a compound partially responsible for the taste and odor of ripe peaches, and coumarin (common name), the compound responsible for the pleasant odor of newly mown hay.

$CH_3-CH_2-CH_2-CH_2-CH_2-CH_2-$

4-Decanolide
(peach odor)

Coumarin
(newly mown hay odor)

Pheromones

A number of pheromones (Section 13-7) contain ester functional groups. The compound isoamyl acetate,

$CH_3-\overset{\overset{\displaystyle O}{\|}}{C}-O-CH_2-CH_2-\overset{\overset{\displaystyle CH_3}{|}}{CH}-CH_3$

▶ Table 16-4 **Selected Esters That Are Used as Flavoring Agents**

IUPAC Name	Structural Formula	Characteristic Flavor and Odor
isobutyl methanoate	$\overset{\displaystyle O}{\overset{\|}{H-C}}-O-CH_2-\overset{\overset{\displaystyle CH_3}{\|}}{CH}-CH_3$	raspberry
propyl ethanoate	$CH_3-\overset{\displaystyle O}{\overset{\|}{C}}-O-(CH_2)_2-CH_3$	pear
pentyl ethanoate	$CH_3-\overset{\displaystyle O}{\overset{\|}{C}}-O-(CH_2)_4-CH_3$	banana
octyl ethanoate	$CH_3-\overset{\displaystyle O}{\overset{\|}{C}}-O-(CH_2)_7-CH_3$	orange
pentyl propanoate	$CH_3-CH_2-\overset{\displaystyle O}{\overset{\|}{C}}-O-(CH_2)_4-CH_3$	apricot
methyl butanoate	$CH_3-(CH_2)_2-\overset{\displaystyle O}{\overset{\|}{C}}-O-CH_3$	apple
ethyl butanoate	$CH_3-(CH_2)_2-\overset{\displaystyle O}{\overset{\|}{C}}-O-CH_2-CH_3$	pineapple

is an alarm pheromone for the honey bee. The compound methyl *p*-hydroxybenzoate,

$$HO-\langle\bigcirc\rangle-\overset{\displaystyle O}{\overset{\|}{C}}-O-CH_3$$

is a sexual attractant for canine species. It is secreted by female dogs in heat and evokes attraction and sexual arousal in male dogs.

The compound nepetalactone, a lactone present in the catnip plant, is an attractant for cats of all types. It is not considered a pheromone, however, because different species are involved (Figure 16-13).

Medications

Numerous esters have medicinal value, including benzocaine (a local anesthetic), aspirin, and oil of wintergreen (a counterirritant). The structure of benzocaine is

$$H_2N-\langle\bigcirc\rangle-\overset{\displaystyle O}{\overset{\|}{C}}-O-CH_2-CH_3$$

Both aspirin and oil of wintergreen are esters of salicylic acid, an aromatic hydroxyacid.

$$\langle\bigcirc\rangle\overset{\overset{\displaystyle O}{\overset{\|}{C}-OH}}{\underset{OH}{}}$$

Salicylic acid

Because this acid has both an acid group and a hydroxyl group, it can form two different types of esters: one by reaction of its acid group with an alcohol, the other by reaction of its alcohol group with a carboxylic acid.

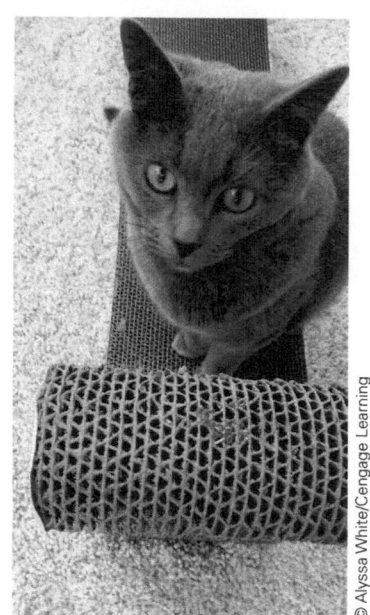

Figure 16-13 Cats of all types (from lions to house cats) are strongly attracted to the catnip plant. The attractant in the catnip plant is nepetalactone, a cyclic ester.

© Alyssa White/Cengage Learning

Nepetalactone

Reaction of acetic acid with the alcohol group of salicylic acid produces aspirin.

| Salicylic acid | Acetic acid | Aspirin |

Aspirin's mode of action in the human body is considered in the focus on relevancy feature Chemical Connections 16-C—Aspirin.

CHEMICAL CONNECTIONS 16-C

Aspirin

Aspirin, an ester of salicylic acid (Section 16-13), is a medication that has the ability to decrease pain (analgesic properties), to lower body temperature (antipyretic properties), and to reduce inflammation (anti-inflammatory properties). It is most frequently taken in tablet form, and the tablet usually contains 325 mg of aspirin held together with an inert starch binder. Aspirin's structure is:

After ingestion, aspirin undergoes hydrolysis to produce salicylic acid and acetic acid (see chemical equation below). Salicylic acid is the active ingredient of aspirin—the substance that has analgesic, antipyretic, and anti-inflammatory effects.

Salicylic acid is capable of irritating the lining of the stomach, inducing a small amount of bleeding. Breaking (or chewing) an aspirin tablet, rather than taking it whole, reduces the chance of bleeding by eliminating drug concentration on only one part of the stomach lining. Buffered aspirin products contain alkaline substances (such as aluminum glycinate or aluminum hydroxide) to neutralize the acidity of the aspirin when it contacts the stomach lining.

Aspirin—that is, salicylic acid—inhibits the synthesis of a class of hormones called prostaglandins (Section 19-13), molecules that cause pain, fever, and inflammation when present in the bloodstream in higher-than-normal levels. Salicylic acid's mode of action is irreversible inhibition (Section 21-7) of *cyclooxygenase,* an enzyme necessary for the production of prostaglandins.

Recent studies show that aspirin also increases the time it takes blood to coagulate (clot). For blood to coagulate, platelets must first be able to aggregate, and prostaglandins (which aspirin inhibits) appear to be necessary for platelet aggregation to occur. One study suggests that healthy men can cut their risk of heart attacks nearly in half by taking one baby aspirin per day (81 mg compared to the 325 mg in a regular tablet). Aspirin acts by making the blood less likely to clot. Heart attacks usually occur when clots form in the coronary arteries, cutting off blood supply to the heart.

Aspirin manufacturers indicate that "low dose" (81 mg) aspirin tablet use is rapidly increasing among adults in the United States. It is estimated that one-third of the adult population now regularly take "low-dose" aspirin for cardiovascular health reasons.

Low-dose aspirin tablets contain 81 mg of aspirin.

| Aspirin | | Salicylic acid | Acetic acid |

Reaction of methanol with the acid group of salicylic acid produces oil of wintergreen.

| Salicylic acid | Methanol | Oil of wintergreen |

Oil of wintergreen, also called methyl salicylate, is used in skin rubs and liniments to help decrease the pain of sore muscles. It is absorbed through the skin, where it is hydrolyzed to produce salicylic acid. Salicylic acid, as with aspirin, is the actual pain reliever.

The *macrolide antibiotics* are a family of large-ring lactones. Erythromycin, the best known member of this antibiotic family, has an antimicrobial spectrum similar to that of the penicillin drug family (Section 21-10) and is often used for people who have an allergy to penicillins. Structurally, this antibiotic contains a 14-membered lactone ring.

Erythromycin (R and R′ are carbohydrate units)

Erythromycin is a naturally occurring substance first isolated from a red-pigmented soil bacterium. The laboratory synthesis of this compound has now been achieved. Its chemical formula is $C_{37}H_{67}NO_{13}$.

Section 16-13 Quick Quiz

1. Small changes in the structures of esters can dramatically affect their use as
   a. flavoring agents
   b. coloring agents
   c. preservatives
   d. no correct response
2. Which of the following is an ester of salicylic acid?
   a. erythromycin
   b. benzocaine
   c. aspirin
   d. no correct response

Answers: 1. a; 2. c

16-14 Isomerism for Carboxylic Acids and Esters

LEARNING FOCUS

Be familiar with skeletal, positional, and functional group isomerism as it relates to carboxylic acids and esters.

As with the other families of organic compounds previously discussed, constitutional isomers based on different carbon skeletons and on different positions for the functional group are possible for carboxylic acids and esters as well as other types of carboxylic acid derivatives. The following two examples illustrate carboxylic acid skeletal isomerism and ester positional isomerism.

Carboxylic acid
skeletal isomers:

$$CH_3—CH_2—CH_2—CH_2—\overset{\overset{\displaystyle O}{\|}}{C}—OH \quad \text{and} \quad CH_3—CH_2—\overset{\overset{\displaystyle CH_3}{|}}{C}H—\overset{\overset{\displaystyle O}{\|}}{C}—OH$$

Pentanoic acid   2-Methylbutanoic acid

Ester positional
isomers:

$$CH_3—CH_2—\overset{\overset{\displaystyle O}{\|}}{C}—O—CH_3 \quad \text{and} \quad CH_3—\overset{\overset{\displaystyle O}{\|}}{C}—O—CH_2—CH_3$$

Methyl propanoate   Ethyl ethanoate

Carboxylic acids and esters with the same number of carbon atoms and the same degree of saturation are functional group isomers. The ester ethyl propanoate and the carboxylic acid pentanoic acid both have the molecular formula $C_5H_{10}O_2$ and are thus functional group isomers. ◀

Carboxylic acid–ester
functional group
isomers:

$$CH_3—CH_2—\overset{\overset{\displaystyle O}{\|}}{C}—O—CH_2—CH_3 \quad \text{and} \quad CH_3—CH_2—CH_2—CH_2—\overset{\overset{\displaystyle O}{\|}}{C}—OH$$

Ethyl propanoate   Pentanoic acid

▶ *Esters and carboxylic acid functional group isomerism represents the fourth time we have encountered this type of isomerism. Previous examples are alcohol–ether, thiol–thioether, and aldehyde–ketone isomers.*

Section 16-14 Quick Quiz

1. Esters can be functional group isomers with which of the following classes of compounds?
   a. ethers
   b. carboxylic acids
   c. ketones
   d. no correct response
2. Which of the following is *not* a positional isomer with ethyl ethanoate?
   a. methyl methanoate
   b. methyl propanoate
   c. propyl methanoate
   d. no correct response
3. Which of the following is a functional group isomer with pentanoic acid?
   a. ethyl propanoate
   b. ethyl pentanoate
   c. propyl butanoate
   d. no correct response

Answers: 1. b; 2. a; 3. a

16-15 Physical Properties of Esters

LEARNING FOCUS

Be familiar with the general physical properties of esters and know how hydrogen bonding influences these properties.

Ester molecules cannot form hydrogen bonds to each other because they do not have a hydrogen atom bonded to an oxygen atom. Consequently, the boiling points of esters are much lower than those of alcohols and carboxylic acids of comparable molecular mass. Esters are more like ethers in their physical properties. Table 16-5 gives boiling-point data for compounds of similar molecular mass that contain different functional groups.

Water molecules can hydrogen-bond to esters through the oxygen atoms present in the ester functional group (Figure 16-14). Because of such hydrogen bonding, low-molecular-mass esters are soluble in water. Solubility rapidly decreases with increasing

▶ Table 16-5 **Boiling Points of Compounds of Similar Molecular Mass That Contain Different Functional Groups**

Name	Functional-Group Class	Molecular Mass (amu)	Boiling Point (°C)
diethyl ether	ether	74	34
ethyl formate	ester	74	54
methyl acetate	ester	74	57
butanal	aldehyde	72	76
1-butanol	alcohol	74	118
propionic acid	acid	74	141

Figure 16-14 Low-molecular-mass esters are soluble in water because of ester–water hydrogen bonding.

Methyl Esters			
✕	C₃	C₅	C₇
C₂	C₄	C₆	C₈

Ethyl Esters			
✕	C₃	C₅	C₇
✕	C₄	C₆	C₈

☐ Liquid

Figure 16-15 A physical-state summary for methyl and ethyl esters of unbranched-chain carboxylic acids at room temperature and pressure.

carbon chain length; borderline solubility situations are reached when three to five carbon atoms are in a chain.

Low- and intermediate-molecular-mass esters are usually colorless liquids at room temperature (see Figure 16-15). Most have pleasant odors (Section 16-13).

Section 16-15 Quick Quiz

1. What is the physical state of all low-molecular-weight methyl and ethyl esters at room temperature?
   a. gases
   b. liquids
   c. some liquids and some solids
   d. no correct response
2. Theoretically, how many hydrogen bonds can an ester molecule form with water molecules?
   a. two
   b. three
   c. four
   d. no correct response
3. How many hydrogen bonds can an ester molecule form with other like ester molecules?
   a. zero
   b. two
   c. three
   d. no correct response

Answers: 1. b; 2. c; 3. a

16-16 Chemical Reactions of Esters

LEARNING FOCUS
Describe the conditions necessary for and the products formed during ester hydrolysis and ester saponification reactions.

The most important reaction of esters involves breaking the carbon–oxygen single bond that holds the "alcohol part" and the "acid part" of the ester together. This reaction process is called either ester hydrolysis or ester saponification, depending on reaction conditions.

Ester Hydrolysis

In ester hydrolysis, an ester reacts with water, producing the carboxylic acid and alcohol from which the ester was formed. ◄

► *This is the second time hydrolysis reactions have been encountered. The first encounter involved the hydrolysis of acetals (Section 15-11).*

$$
\underset{\text{Methyl acetate}}{R-\overset{\overset{\textstyle O}{\|}}{C}\!-\!O\!-\!R'} + \underset{\text{Water}}{\boxed{H-OH}} \xrightarrow{H^+} \underset{\text{Acetic acid}}{R-\overset{\overset{\textstyle O}{\|}}{C}\!-\!\boxed{OH}} + \underset{\text{Methyl alcohol}}{R'\!-\!O\!-\!\boxed{H}}
$$

$$
CH_3-\overset{\overset{\textstyle O}{\|}}{C}\!-\!O\!-\!CH_3 + \boxed{H-OH} \xrightarrow{H^+} CH_3-\overset{\overset{\textstyle O}{\|}}{C}\!-\!\boxed{OH} + CH_3\!-\!O\!-\!\boxed{H}
$$

Ester hydrolysis requires the presence of a strong-acid catalyst or enzymes. Ester hydrolysis is the reverse of esterification (Section 16-11), the formation of an ester from a carboxylic acid and an alcohol. ◄

► *In hydrolysis reactions the —OH group from a water molecule always bonds to a carbon atom and never to an oxygen (or nitrogen) atom. Oxygen–oxygen and oxygen–nitrogen bonds are not as stable as carbon–oxygen bonds.*

Ester Saponification

A **saponification reaction** *is the hydrolysis of an organic compound, under basic conditions, in which a carboxylic acid salt is one of the products.* Esters, amides (Section 17-17), and fats and oils (Section 19-6) all undergo saponification reactions.

In ester saponification, either NaOH or KOH is used as the base and the saponification products are an alcohol and a carboxylic acid salt. (Any carboxylic acid product formed is converted to its salt because of the basic reaction conditions.) ◄

► *In both ester hydrolysis and ester saponification, an alcohol is produced. Under acidic conditions (ester hydrolysis), the other product is a carboxylic acid. Under basic conditions (ester saponification), the other product is a carboxylic acid salt.*

$$
\underset{\text{An ester}}{R-\overset{\overset{\textstyle O}{\|}}{C}\!-\!O\!-\!R'} + \underset{\text{A strong base}}{\boxed{NaOH}} \xrightarrow{H_2O} \underset{\text{A carboxylate salt}}{R-\overset{\overset{\textstyle O}{\|}}{C}\!-\!O^-\,\boxed{Na^+}} + \underset{\text{An alcohol}}{R'\!-\!OH}
$$

A specific example of ester saponification is

$$
\underset{\text{Methyl benzoate}}{\text{C}_6H_5-\overset{\overset{\textstyle O}{\|}}{C}\!-\!O\!-\!CH_3} + \underset{\text{Sodium hydroxide}}{\boxed{NaOH}} \xrightarrow{H_2O} \underset{\text{Sodium benzoate}}{\text{C}_6H_5-\overset{\overset{\textstyle O}{\|}}{C}\!-\!O\,\boxed{Na}} + \underset{\text{Methyl alcohol}}{CH_3\!-\!OH}
$$

EXAMPLE 16-5

Structural Equations for Reactions That Involve Esters

Write structural equations for each of the following reactions:

a. Hydrolysis, with an acidic catalyst, of ethyl acetate
b. Saponification, with NaOH, of methyl formate
c. Esterification of propionic acid using isopropyl alcohol

Solution

a. Hydrolysis, under acidic conditions, cleaves an ester to produce its "parent" carboxylic acid and alcohol.

$$
\underset{\text{Ethyl acetate}}{CH_3-\overset{\overset{\textstyle O}{\|}}{C}\!-\!O\!-\!CH_2\!-\!CH_3} + H_2O \xrightarrow{H^+} \underset{\text{Acetic acid}}{CH_3-\overset{\overset{\textstyle O}{\|}}{C}\!-\!OH} + \underset{\text{Ethyl alcohol}}{CH_3\!-\!CH_2\!-\!OH}
$$

(continued)

b. Saponification cleaves an ester to produce its "parent" alcohol and the *salt* of its "parent" carboxylic acid.

$$
\underset{\text{Methyl formate}}{\overset{\displaystyle\overset{O}{\|}}{H-C}-O-CH_3} \;+\; \underset{\text{Sodium hydroxide}}{NaOH} \;\xrightarrow{\;H_2O\;}\; \underset{\text{Sodium formate}}{\overset{\displaystyle\overset{O}{\|}}{H-C}-O^-\,Na^+} \;+\; \underset{\text{Methyl alcohol}}{CH_3-OH}
$$

c. Esterification is the reaction in which a carboxylic acid and an alcohol react to produce an ester.

$$
\underset{\text{Propionic acid}}{CH_3-CH_2-\overset{\displaystyle\overset{O}{\|}}{C}-OH} \;+\; \underset{\text{Isopropyl alcohol}}{CH_3-\underset{\displaystyle CH_3}{\overset{|}{CH}}-OH} \;\xrightleftharpoons{\;H^+\;}\;
$$

$$
\underset{\text{Isopropyl propionate}}{CH_3-CH_2-\overset{\displaystyle\overset{O}{\|}}{C}-O-\underset{\displaystyle CH_3}{\overset{|}{CH}}-CH_3} \;+\; H_2O
$$

Chemistry at a Glance—Summary of Chemical Reactions Involving Carboxylic Acids and Esters—summarizes reactions that involve carboxylic acids and esters.

CHEMISTRY AT A GLANCE — Summary of Chemical Reactions Involving Carboxylic Acids and Esters

CHEMICAL REACTIONS OF CARBOXYLIC ACIDS

Ionization
- Occurs in aqueous solution

Acid → carboxylate ion + H_3O^+

Neutralization
- Reaction with a base (NaOH)

Acid → carboxylate salt + H_2O

Esterification
- Reaction with an alcohol
- Acid catalyst required

Acid → ester + H_2O

Decarboxylation
- A carbon dioxide molecule is produced

Acid → CO_2 + smaller organic molecule

HYDROLYSIS REACTIONS OF ESTERS

Acidic Hydrolysis
- Strong acid as catalyst

Ester → acid + alcohol

Basic Hydrolysis (Saponification)
- Strong base (NaOH or KOH)

Ester → carboxylate salt + alcohol

PREPARATION OF CARBOXYLIC ACIDS

Oxidation
- CrO_3 or $K_2Cr_2O_7$ as oxidizing agent

1° alcohol → aldehyde → acid
Aldehyde → acid

1. In ester hydrolysis under acidic conditions, the reaction products are a
   a. carboxylic acid and an alcohol
   b. carboxylic acid and a base
   c. carboxylic acid salt and water
   d. no correct response
2. In ester saponification, the reaction products are a
   a. carboxylic acid and an alcohol
   b. carboxylic acid salt and an alcohol
   c. carboxylic acid and a carboxylic acid salt
   d. no correct response
3. In ester hydrolysis the bond within the ester that is broken is the
   a. carbon–oxygen single bond
   b. carbon–oxygen double bond
   c. oxygen–hydrogen single bond
   d. no correct response

Answers: 1. a; 2. b; 3. a

16-17 Sulfur Analogs of Esters

LEARNING FOCUS
Know general structural characteristics for thioesters; be familiar with the generalized structure of the naturally occurring thioester called acetyl coenzyme A.

Just as alcohols react with carboxylic acids to produce esters, thiols (Section 14-20) react with carboxylic acids to produce thioesters. A **thioester** *is a sulfur-containing analog of an ester in which an* —SR *group has replaced the ester's* —OR *group.*

$$CH_3-\overset{\overset{\displaystyle O}{\|}}{C}-OH + CH_3-CH_2-S-H \longrightarrow CH_3-\overset{\overset{\displaystyle O}{\|}}{C}-S-CH_2-CH_3 + H_2O$$

A carboxylic acid   A thiol   A thioester

The thioester methyl thiobutanoate is used as an artificial flavoring agent. It generates the taste associated with strawberries.

$$CH_3-CH_2-CH_2-\overset{\overset{\displaystyle O}{\|}}{C}-S-CH_3$$

Methyl thiobutanoate
(methyl thiobutyrate)

Note, as seen in the IUPAC and common names of the preceding "strawberry" compound, that thioesters are named in a manner paralleling that for esters (Section 16-12) with the inclusion of the prefix *thio-* in the name. ◄

The most important naturally occurring thioester is acetyl coenzyme A, whose abbreviated structure is

$$CH_3-\overset{\overset{\displaystyle O}{\|}}{C}-S-CoA$$

Acetyl coenzyme A

Coenzyme A, the parent molecule for acetyl coenzyme A, is a large, complex *thiol* whose structure, for simplicity, is usually abbreviated as CoA—S—H. The formation of acetyl coenzyme A (acetyl CoA) from coenzyme A can be envisioned as a thioesterification reaction between acetic acid and coenzyme A.

$$CH_3-\overset{\overset{\displaystyle O}{\|}}{C}-OH + CoA-S-H \longrightarrow CH_3-\overset{\overset{\displaystyle O}{\|}}{C}-S-CoA + H_2O$$

Acetic acid   Coenzyme A   Acetyl coenzyme A
(a thiol)   (acetyl CoA)

▶ *The ester functional group is*

$$-\overset{\overset{\displaystyle O}{\|}}{C}-O-R$$

The thioester functional group is

$$-\overset{\overset{\displaystyle O}{\|}}{C}-S-R$$

Acetyl coenzyme A plays a central role in the metabolic cycles through which the body obtains energy to "run itself" (Section 23-6).

The complete structure of acetyl CoA is given in Section 23-3.

Section 16-17 Quick Quiz

1. Which of the following is the general structural formula for a thioester?

$$\text{a. } R-\overset{\overset{\displaystyle O}{\|}}{C}-S-H$$

$$\text{b. } R-\overset{\overset{\displaystyle O}{\|}}{C}-O-S-H$$

$$\text{c. } R-\overset{\overset{\displaystyle O}{\|}}{C}-S-R$$

d. no correct response

2. Acetyl coenzyme A, the most important naturally occurring thioester has the abbreviated structural formula

$$\text{a. } R-\overset{\overset{\displaystyle O}{\|}}{C}-S-CoA$$

$$\text{b. } CH_3-\overset{\overset{\displaystyle O}{\|}}{C}-S-CoA$$

$$\text{c. } CoA-\overset{\overset{\displaystyle O}{\|}}{C}-S-R$$

d. no correct response

Answers: 1. c; 2. b

16-18 Polyesters

LEARNING FOCUS

Characterize a polyester condensation polymer in terms of monomers used and products formed; discuss the formation of and uses for common polyesters.

A **condensation polymer** *is a polymer formed when difunctional monomers are linked together via condensation reactions with the production of by-product water molecules. Polyesters* are an important type of condensation polymer. A **polyester** *is a condensation polymer in which the monomers are joined through ester linkages.* Dicarboxylic acids and dialcohols are the monomers generally used in forming polyesters.

The best known of the many polyesters now marketed is *poly(ethylene terephthalate)*, which is also known by the acronym *PET.* The monomers used to produce PET are terephthalic acid (a diacid) and ethylene glycol (a dialcohol).

Terephthalic acid   Ethylene glycol

▶ *Condensation polymerization reactions produce two products: the polymer and a small molecule (usually H_2O). This contrasts with addition polymerization reactions (Section 13-9) in which the polymer is the only product.*

The reaction of one acid group of the diacid with one alcohol group of the dialcohol initially produces an ester molecule, with an acid group left over on one end and an alcohol group left over on the other end. ◀

Leftover acid group that can react further   Ester linkage   Leftover alcohol group that can react further

Figure 16-16 Space-filling model of a segment of the polyester condensation polymer known as poly(ethylene terephthalate), or PET.

This species can react further. The remaining acid group can react with an alcohol group from another monomer, and the remaining alcohol group can react with an acid group from another monomer. This process continues until an extremely long polymer molecule called a *polyester* is produced (Figure 16-16).

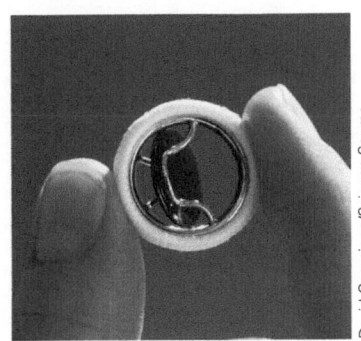

Figure 16-17 The polyester PET, as a fabric, is used in the construction of artificial heart valves.

About 50% of PET production goes into textile products, including clothing fibers, curtain and upholstery materials, and tire cord. The trade name for PET as a clothing fiber is *Dacron*. The other 50% of PET production goes into plastics applications. As a film-like material, it is called *Mylar*. Mylar products include the plastic backing for audio and video tapes and computer diskettes. Its chemical name PET is applied when this polyester is used in clear, flexible soft-drink bottles and as the wrapping material for frozen foods and boil-in-bag foods.

PET also has medical applications. Because it is physiologically inert, PET is used in the form of a mesh to replace diseased sections of arteries. It has also been used in artificial heart valves (Figure 16-17).

Plastic bottles made of PET cannot be reused because they cannot withstand the high temperatures needed to sterilize them for reuse. Also, such bottles cannot be used for any food items that must be packaged at high temperatures, such as jams and jellies. For these uses, the polyester PEN (polyethylene naphthalate), a polymer that can withstand higher temperatures, is available. The monomers for this polymer are ethylene glycol and one or more naphthalene dicarboxylic acids.

A variation of the diacid–dialcohol monomer formulation for polyesters involves using hydroxy acids as monomers. In this situation, both of the functional groups required are present in the same molecule.

A polymerization reaction in which lactic acid and glycolic acid (both hydroxy acids, Section 16-4) are monomers produces a biodegradable material (trade name *Lactomer*) that is used as surgical staples in several types of surgery. Traditional suture materials must be removed later on, after they have served their purpose. Lactomer staples start to dissolve (hydrolyze) after a period of several weeks. The hydrolysis products are the starting monomers, lactic acid and glycolic acid, both of which are readily metabolized within the human body. By the time the tissue has fully healed, the staples have fully degraded.

Another commercially available biodegradable polyester is PHBV, a substance that finds use in specialty packaging, orthopedic devices, and controlled drug-release formulations. Coating a drug formulation with PHBV, which degrades slowly over time, results in the drug being released slowly rather than all at once. The monomers for this polymer are 3-hydroxybutanoic acid (β-hydroxybutyrate) and 3-hydroxypentanoic acid (β-hydroxyvalerate). The properties of PHBV vary according to the reacting ratio for the two monomers. With more of the butanoic acid present, a stiffer polymer is produced, while more of the pentanoic acid imparts flexibility to the plastic. A nonconventional method for producing the polymer is used; the two monomers are produced by bacterial fermentation of mixtures containing acetic and propionic acids. The generalized formula for the polymer is written as

PHBV [poly(β-hydroxybutyrate-co-β-hydroxyvalerate)]

Section 16-18 Quick Quiz

1. Most commonly, the monomers for the formation of a polyester condensation polymer are
   a. a dicarboxylic acid and a monoalcohol
   b. a dicarboxylic acid and a dialcohol
   c. a monocarboxylic acid and a dialcohol
   d. no correct response
2. The monomers in a polyester are linked to each other via
   a. ether linkages
   b. ester linkages
   c. C—O—O—C linkages
   d. no correct response
3. Monomers for PET, the best-known polyester now marketed, are
   a. ethylene and benzoic acid
   b. ethylene glycol and terephthalic acid
   c. ethylene glycol and benzoic acid
   d. no correct response

Answers: 1. b; 2. b; 3. b

16-19 Acid Chlorides and Acid Anhydrides

LEARNING FOCUS
Be familiar with the following for *acid chlorides* and *acid anhydrides*: structural characteristics, preparation of, hydrolysis products of, and nomenclature.

Sections 16-10 through 16-18 have focused on the carboxylic acid derivatives called esters. This section considers acid chlorides and acid anhydrides, two of the other types of carboxylic acid derivatives mentioned in Section 16-1.

Acid Chlorides

An **acid chloride** *is a carboxylic acid derivative in which the —OH portion of the carboxyl group has been replaced with a —Cl atom.* Thus, acid chlorides have the general formula

$$R-\overset{\overset{\displaystyle O}{\|}}{C}-\boxed{Cl}$$

Acid chlorides are named in either of two ways:

Rule 1: *Replace the* -ic acid *ending of the common name of the parent carboxylic acid with* -yl chloride.

$$CH_3-CH_2-CH_2-CH_2-\overset{\overset{\displaystyle O}{\|}}{C}-Cl$$

Butyric acid becomes butyryl chloride.

Rule 2: *Replace the* -oic acid *ending of the IUPAC name of the parent carboxylic acid with* -oyl chloride.

$$CH_3-CH_2-\overset{\overset{\displaystyle CH_3}{|}}{CH}-CH_2-\overset{\overset{\displaystyle O}{\|}}{C}-Cl$$

3-Methylpentanoic acid becomes 3-methylpentanoyl chloride.

Preparation of an acid chloride from its parent carboxylic acid involves reacting the acid with one of several inorganic chlorides (PCl_3, PCl_5, or $SOCl_2$). The general reaction is

$$R-\overset{\overset{\displaystyle O}{\|}}{C}-OH \xrightarrow[\text{chloride}]{\text{Inorganic}} R-\overset{\overset{\displaystyle O}{\|}}{C}-Cl + \text{Inorganic products}$$

Acid chlorides react rapidly with water, in a hydrolysis reaction, to regenerate the parent carboxylic acid.

$$R-\overset{\overset{\displaystyle O}{\|}}{C}-\boxed{Cl} + H_2O \longrightarrow R-\overset{\overset{\displaystyle O}{\|}}{C}-\boxed{OH} + HCl$$

This reactivity with water means that acid chlorides cannot exist in biological systems.

Acid chlorides are useful starting materials for the synthesis of other carboxylic acid derivatives, particularly esters and amides. Synthesis of esters and amides using acid chlorides is a more efficient process than ester and amide synthesis using a carboxylic acid.

Acid Anhydrides

An **acid anhydride** *is a carboxylic acid derivative in which the —OH portion of the carboxyl group has been replaced with a* $-O-\overset{\overset{\displaystyle O}{\|}}{C}-R$ *group.* Thus, acid anhydrides have the general formula

$$R-\overset{\overset{\displaystyle O}{\|}}{C}-O-\overset{\overset{\displaystyle O}{\|}}{C}-R'$$

An acid anhydride's structure can be viewed as containing two carbonyl groups joined by a single oxygen atom or, alternatively, as two acyl groups joined by a single oxygen atom.

two carbonyl
groups

two acyl
groups

Symmetrical acid anhydrides (both R groups are the same) are named by replacing the *acid* ending of the parent carboxylic acid name with the word *anhydride*.

$$CH_3-\overset{\overset{\displaystyle O}{\|}}{C}-O-\overset{\overset{\displaystyle O}{\|}}{C}-CH_3$$

IUPAC name: Ethanoic anhydride
Common name: Acetic anhydride

Mixed acid anhydrides (different R groups present) are named by using the names of the individual parent carboxylic acids (in alphabetic order) followed by the word *anhydride*.

$$CH_3-CH_2-\overset{\overset{\displaystyle O}{\|}}{C}-O-\overset{\overset{\displaystyle O}{\|}}{C}-CH_3$$

IUPAC name: Ethanoic propanoic anhydride
Common name: Acetic propionic anhydride

In general, acid anhydrides cannot be formed by directly reacting the parent carboxylic acids together. Instead, an acid chloride is reacted with a carboxylate ion to produce the acid anhydride.

$$R-\overset{\overset{\displaystyle O}{\|}}{C}-Cl + R'-\overset{\overset{\displaystyle O}{\|}}{C}-O^- \longrightarrow R-\overset{\overset{\displaystyle O}{\|}}{C}-O-\overset{\overset{\displaystyle O}{\|}}{C}-R' + Cl^-$$

Acid   Carboxylate   Acid
chloride   ion   anhydride

Acid anhydrides are very reactive compounds, although generally not as reactive as the acid chlorides. Like acid chlorides, they cannot exist in biological systems, as they undergo hydrolysis to regenerate the parent carboxylic acids.

$$R-\overset{\overset{\displaystyle O}{\|}}{C}-O-\overset{\overset{\displaystyle O}{\|}}{C}-R' + H_2O \xrightarrow{\text{Heat}} R-\overset{\overset{\displaystyle O}{\|}}{C}-OH + R'-\overset{\overset{\displaystyle O}{\|}}{C}-OH$$

Acid   Acid   Acid
anhydride

Acyl Transfer Reactions

When compounds containing acyl groups (Section 16-1) react with an alcohol or phenol, the acyl group is transferred to the oxygen atom of the alcohol or phenol; an ester is the product.

$$R-\overset{\overset{\displaystyle O}{\|}}{C}-OH + R'-O-H \longrightarrow R-\overset{\overset{\displaystyle O}{\|}}{C}-O-R' + H_2O$$

Carboxylic acid   Ester

$$R-\overset{\overset{\displaystyle O}{\|}}{C}-Cl + R'-O-H \longrightarrow R-\overset{\overset{\displaystyle O}{\|}}{C}-O-R' + HCl$$

Acid chloride   Ester

$$R-\overset{\overset{\displaystyle O}{\|}}{C}-O-\overset{\overset{\displaystyle O}{\|}}{C}-R + R'-O-H \longrightarrow R-\overset{\overset{\displaystyle O}{\|}}{C}-O-R' + R-\overset{\overset{\displaystyle O}{\|}}{C}-OH$$

Acid anhydride   Ester

▶ *An acyl transfer reaction is also called an* acylation reaction.

Chemical reactions such as these are called *acyl transfer reactions*. ▶ An **acyl transfer reaction** *is a chemical reaction in which an acyl group is transferred from one molecule to another.* Acyl transfer reactions occur frequently in biochemical systems. The process of protein synthesis (Section 22-11) is dependent upon acyl transfer reactions, as are many metabolic reactions. Often in metabolic reactions the thioester acetyl coenzyme A serves as an acyl transfer agent (Section 23-6).

The acyl group present in carboxylic acids and carboxylic acid derivatives is named by replacing the *-ic acid* ending of the acid name with the suffix *-yl*.

Common names: *-ic acid* becomes *-yl*
IUPAC names: *-oic acid* becomes *-oyl*

Thus, the two- and three-carbonyl acyl groups are named as follows:

$$CH_3-\overset{\displaystyle O}{\overset{\|}{C}}- \qquad\qquad CH_3-CH_2-\overset{\displaystyle O}{\overset{\|}{C}}-$$

| IUPAC name: | Ethanoyl group (from ethanoic acid) | Propanoyl group (from propanoic acid) |
| Common name: | Acetyl group (from acetic acid) | Propionyl group (from propionic acid) |

Section 16-19 Quick Quiz

1. Preparation of an acid chloride from its parent carboxylic acid involves reacting the acid with
   a. Cl_2
   b. HCl
   c. one of several inorganic chlorides
   d. no correct response
2. Which of the following statements concerning acid chlorides is *incorrect*?
   a. They react rapidly with water to produce the parent carboxylic acid.
   b. They are very important compounds in biological systems.
   c. Butanoyl chloride is the IUPAC name for the chloride obtained from butanoic acid.
   d. no correct response
3. Hydrolysis of an acid anhydride produces
   a. two carboxylic acid molecules
   b. two alcohol molecules
   c. two ester molecules
   d. no correct response
4. Which of the following reactions would *not* be classified as an acyl transfer reaction?
   a. carboxylic acid + alcohol
   b. acid chloride + alcohol
   c. acid anhydride + alcohol
   d. no correct response

Answers: 1. c; 2. b; 3. a; 4. d

16-20 Esters and Anhydrides of Inorganic Acids

LEARNING FOCUS

Be able to recognize structural formulas for phosphoric acid, diphosphoric acid, and triphosphoric acid and for various esters of these three acids.

Inorganic acids such as sulfuric, phosphoric, and nitric acids react with alcohols to form esters in a manner similar to that for carboxylic acids and their derivatives.

$$HO-\overset{\overset{\displaystyle O}{\|}}{\underset{\underset{\displaystyle O}{\|}}{S}}-OH + CH_3-OH \longrightarrow HO-\overset{\overset{\displaystyle O}{\|}}{\underset{\underset{\displaystyle O}{\|}}{S}}-O-CH_3 + H_2O$$

Sulfuric acid (H_2SO_4)   Methyl ester of sulfuric acid

$$HO-\overset{\overset{\displaystyle O}{\|}}{\underset{\underset{\displaystyle OH}{|}}{P}}-OH + CH_3-OH \longrightarrow HO-\overset{\overset{\displaystyle O}{\|}}{\underset{\underset{\displaystyle OH}{|}}{P}}-O-CH_3 + H_2O$$

Phosphoric acid (H_3PO_4)   Methyl ester of phosphoric acid

$$N-\overset{\overset{\displaystyle O}{\|}}{\underset{\underset{\displaystyle O}{|}}{}}OH + CH_3-OH \longrightarrow N-\overset{\overset{\displaystyle O}{\|}}{\underset{\underset{\displaystyle O}{|}}{}}O-CH_3 + H_2O$$

Nitric acid (HNO_3)   Methyl ester of nitric acid

The substance nitroglycerin, which, somewhat surprisingly, is used both as an explosive and as a heart medication, is an inorganic ester formed from three molecules of nitric acid and one molecule of the glycerol, a triol. The focus on relevancy feature Chemical Connections 16-D—Nitroglycerin: An Inorganic Triester—gives structural as well as other information about this interesting inorganic ester.

The most important inorganic esters, from a biochemical standpoint, are those of phosphoric acid—that is, phosphate esters. A **phosphate ester** *is an organic compound formed by reaction of an alcohol with phosphoric acid.* Because phosphoric acid has three hydroxyl groups, it can form mono-, di-, and triesters by reaction with one, two, and three molecules of alcohol, respectively. ◄

▶ *Esters of inorganic acids undergo hydrolysis reactions in a manner similar to that for esters of carboxylic acids (Section 16-16).*

Phosphoric acid   Monoester (one —OR group)

Diester (two —OR groups)   Triester (three —OR groups)

Phosphoric Acid Anhydrides

Three biologically important phosphoric acids exist: phosphoric acid, diphosphoric acid, and triphosphoric acid. Phosphoric acid, the simplest of the three acids, undergoes a condensation reaction to produce diphosphoric acid.

Phosphoric acid   Phosphoric acid   Diphosphoric acid

Another condensation reaction, involving diphosphoric acid and phosphoric acid, produces triphosphoric acid.

Triphosphoric acid

All three phosphoric acids undergo esterification reactions with alcohols, producing species such as

Diphosphate monoester   Triphosphate monoester

Esters of these types will be encountered in Chapter 23 when the biochemical production of energy in the human body is considered. Adenosine diphosphate (ADP) and adenosine triphosphate (ATP) are important examples of such compounds.

Diphosphoric acid and triphosphoric acid are phosphoric acid anhydrides as well as acids. Note the structural similarities between a carboxylic acid anhydride and diphosphoric acid.

CHEMICAL CONNECTIONS 16-D

Nitroglycerin: An Inorganic Triester

The reaction of one molecule of glycerol (a triol) with three molecules of nitric acid produces the trinitrate ester called nitroglycerin; it is a component of dynamite.

$$CH_2\text{—}OH \qquad\qquad CH_2\text{—}O\text{—}NO_2$$
$$CH\text{—}OH \; + \; 3HO\text{—}NO_2 \longrightarrow CH\text{—}O\text{—}NO_2 \; + \; 3H_2O$$
$$CH_2\text{—}OH \qquad\qquad CH_2\text{—}O\text{—}NO_2$$

In the pure state, nitroglycerin is a shock-sensitive liquid that can decompose to produce large volumes of gases (N_2, CO_2, H_2O, and O_2). When used in dynamite, it is adsorbed on clay-like materials, giving products that will not explode without a formal ignition system.

Besides being a component of dynamite explosives, nitroglycerin has medicinal value. It is used in treating patients with angina pectoris—sharp chest pains caused by an insufficient supply of oxygen reaching heart muscle. Its effect on the human body is that of a vasodilator, a substance that increases blood flow by relaxing constricted muscles around blood vessels.

Nitroglycerin medication is available in several forms: (1) as a liquid diluted with alcohol to render it nonexplosive, (2) as a liquid adsorbed to a tablet for convenience of sublingual (under the tongue) administration, (3) in ointments for topical use, and (4) as "skin patches" that release the drug continuously through the skin over a 24-hr period. Nitroglycerin is rapidly absorbed through the skin, enters the bloodstream, and finds its way to heart muscle within seconds.

It is not nitroglycerin itself that relieves the heart muscle pain associated with angina, but, rather, a compound produced when the nitroglycerin is metabolized. That compound is the simple diatomic molecule NO (nitric oxide). Properties of nitric oxide were previously considered from an environmental perspective in Chemical Connections 5-A—Nitric Oxide: A Molecule Whose Bonding Does Not Follow "The Rules."

Nitroglycerin use for treatment of angina pain originated in the 1860s, more than 150 years ago. It came about from serendipitous observations. Factory workers involved in nitroglycerin production who suffered from angina pain noticed that their condition improved during the work week but then deteriorated on weekends. This regularly reported occurrence led physicians of the day to make the cause-effect connection that led to nitroglycerin use as a medication.

Alfred Nobel, who originally formulated what is now called dynamite, became a very rich man because of his discovery, amassing a fortune. It is his name and money that are associated with the prestigious Nobel Prizes awarded each year in the fall. In his later years, Alfred Nobel suffered from angina, and his doctor suggested that he use nitroglycerin to relieve the pain. He wrote to a friend, "Isn't it the irony of fate that I have been prescribed nitroglycerin? They call it Trinitrin so as not to scare the chemist and the public." He refused to take the medication. Further irony occurred in 1998 when the Nobel Prize in Physiology or Medicine was awarded to individuals involved in research on the body's generation of, as well as the biochemical effects of, NO in the human body.

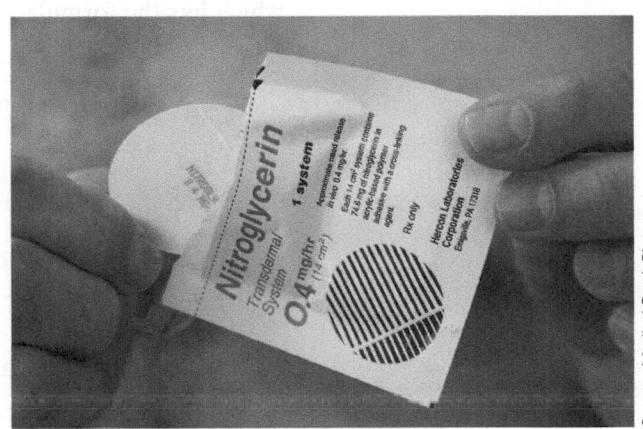

Nitroglycerin is used in treating chest pains related to angina pectoris.

Custom Medical Stock Photo

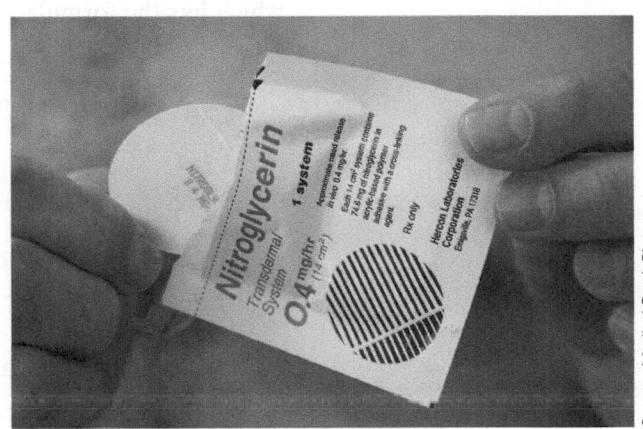

Carboxylic acid anhydride   Diphosphoric acid

Phosphoric acid anhydride systems play important roles in cellular processes through which biochemical energy is produced. The presence of phosphoric anhydride systems in biological settings contrasts markedly with carboxylic acid anhydride systems (Section 16-19), which are not found in biological settings because of their reactivity with water.

Ionic Forms of Phosphate Esters and Anhydrides

In the same manner that carboxylic acids are acidic (Section 16-7), phosphoric acid, diphosphoric acid, and triphosphoric acid are also acidic. The phosphoric acids are, however, always polyprotic acids rather than monoprotic acids. The hydrogen atom present in each of the —OH groups present possesses acidic properties. Such acidic hydrogen atoms are lost through ionization (Section 10-3) under appropriate conditions.

At the pH of body fluids (usually slightly alkaline), phosphoric acid esters and anhydrides (as well as the esters and anhydrides of other inorganic acids) lose their acidic hydrogen atoms and thus are converted to ionic species. The neutral and ionic forms of a phosphoric acid monoester are

$$
\underset{\text{Neutral form}}{\begin{array}{c} \text{O} \\ \| \\ \text{R—O—P—OH} \\ | \\ \text{OH} \end{array}}
\qquad
\underset{\text{Ionic form}}{\begin{array}{c} \text{O} \\ \| \\ \text{R—O—P—O}^- \\ | \\ \text{O}^- \end{array}}
$$

For a triphosphate monoester, the neutral and ionic forms are

$$
\underset{\text{Neutral form}}{\begin{array}{c} \text{O} \quad\; \text{O} \quad\; \text{O} \\ \| \quad\; \| \quad\; \| \\ \text{R—O—P—O—P—O—P—OH} \\ | \quad\;\; | \quad\;\; | \\ \text{OH} \;\; \text{OH} \;\; \text{OH} \end{array}}
\qquad
\underset{\text{Ionic form}}{\begin{array}{c} \text{O} \quad\; \text{O} \quad\; \text{O} \\ \| \quad\; \| \quad\; \| \\ \text{R—O—P—O—P—O—P—O}^- \\ | \quad\;\; | \quad\;\; | \\ \text{O}^- \;\; \text{O}^- \;\; \text{O}^- \end{array}}
$$

The terminal phosphate group in a phosphate-containing ester or anhydride, which has the formula PO_3^{2-}, is called a *phosphoryl group*. Note the location of the phosphoryl group in the following two structures.

A **phosphoryl group** *is a* $—PO_3^{2-}$ *group present in an organic molecule.*

Phosphorylation Reactions

A commonly encountered type of biochemical reaction is one that involves the transfer of a phosphoryl group from one organic molecule to another. This process is called *phosphorylation*. A **phosphorylation reaction** *is a chemical reaction in which a phosphoryl group is transferred from one molecule to another.* (Phosphorylation and acylation reactions are similar in that a group, phosphoryl or acyl, is transferred from one molecule to another.) The following structural equation typifies a phosphorylation reaction.

The preceding kind of phosphorylation reaction, the conversion of a triphosphate to a diphosphate, will be encountered repeatedly in the biochemical chapters that deal with metabolic reactions (Chapters 23–26).

1. The most important inorganic esters, from a biochemical standpoint, are those of
   a. nitric acid
   b. sulfuric acid
   c. phosphoric acid
   d. no correct response
2. How many oxygen atoms are present in a molecule of diphosphoric acid?
   a. three
   b. five
   c. seven
   d. no correct response
3. How many acidic hydrogen atoms are present in a monoester of phosphoric acid?
   a. one
   b. two
   c. three
   d. no correct response
4. The chemical formula for a phosphoryl group is
   a. PO_4^{3-}
   b. PO_4^{2-}
   c. PO_3^{2-}
   d. no correct response

Answers: 1. c; 2. c; 3. b; 4. c

Concepts to Remember

The carboxyl group. The functional group present in carboxylic acids is the carboxyl group. A carboxyl group is composed of a hydroxyl group bonded to a carbonyl carbon atom. It thus contains two oxygen atoms directly bonded to the same carbon atom (Section 16-1).

Carboxylic acid derivatives. Four important families of carboxylic acid derivatives are esters, acid chlorides, acid anhydrides, and amides. The group attached to the carbonyl carbon atom distinguishes these derivatives from each other and also from carboxylic acids (Section 16-1).

Nomenclature of carboxylic acids. The IUPAC name for a monocarboxylic acid is formed by replacing the final *-e* of the hydrocarbon parent name with *-oic acid*. As with previous IUPAC nomenclature, the longest carbon chain containing the functional group is identified, and it is numbered starting with the carboxyl carbon atom. Common-name usage is more prevalent for carboxylic acids than for any other type of organic compound (Sections 16-2 and 16-3).

Types of carboxylic acids. Carboxylic acids are classified by the number of carboxyl groups present (monocarboxylic, dicarboxylic, etc.), by the degree of saturation (saturated, unsaturated, aromatic), and by additional functional groups present (hydroxy, keto, etc.) (Sections 16-4 and 16-5).

Physical properties of carboxylic acids. Low-molecular-mass carboxylic acids are liquids at room temperature and have sharp or unpleasant odors. Long-chain acids are waxlike solids. The carboxyl group is polar and forms hydrogen bonds to other carboxyl groups or other molecules. Thus carboxylic acids have relatively high boiling points, and those with lower molecular masses are soluble in water (Section 16-5).

Preparation of carboxylic acids. Carboxylic acids are synthesized through oxidation of primary alcohols or aldehydes using strong oxidizing agents. Aromatic carboxylic acids can be prepared by oxidizing a carbon side chain on a benzene derivative using a strong oxidizing agent (Section 16-6).

Acidity of carboxylic acids. Soluble carboxylic acids behave as weak acids, donating protons to water molecules. The portion of the acid molecule left after proton loss is called a carboxylate ion (Section 16-7).

Carboxylic acid salts. Carboxylic acids are neutralized by bases to produce carboxylic acid salts. Such salts are usually more soluble in water than are the acids from which they were derived. Carboxylic acid salts are named by changing the *-ic* ending of the acid to *-ate* (Section 16-8).

Esters. Esters are formed by the reaction of an acid with an alcohol. In such reactions, the —OR group from the alcohol replaces the —OH group in the carboxylic acid. Esters are polar compounds, but they cannot form hydrogen bonds to each other. Therefore, their boiling points are lower than those of alcohols and acids of similar molecular mass (Sections 16-10 and 16-11).

Nomenclature of esters. An ester is named as an alkyl (from the name of the alcohol reactant) carboxylate (from the name of the acid reactant) (Section 16-12).

Chemical reactions of esters. Esters can be converted back to carboxylic acids and alcohols under either acidic or basic conditions. Under acidic conditions, the process is called hydrolysis, and the products are the acid and alcohol. Under basic conditions, the process is called saponification, and the products are the acid salt and alcohol (Section 16-16).

Thioesters. Thioesters are sulfur-containing analogs of esters in which an —SR group has replaced the —OR group (Section 16-17).

Polyesters. Polyesters are polymers in which the monomers (diacids and dialcohols) are joined through ester linkages (Section 16-18).

Acid chlorides and acid anhydrides. An acid chloride is a carboxylic acid derivative in which the —OH portion of the carboxyl group has been replaced with a —Cl atom. An acid anhydride involves two carboxylic acid molecules bonded together.

Both acid chlorides and acid anhydrides are very reactive molecules (Section 16-19).

Esters and anhydrides of inorganic acids. Alcohols can react with inorganic acids, such as nitric, sulfuric, and phosphoric

acids, to form esters. Phosphate esters are an important class of biochemical compounds. Anhydrides of phosphoric acid (diphosphoric acid and triphosphoric acid) and their esters are also important types of biochemical molecules (Section 16-20).

Exercises and Problems

Exercises and problems are arranged in matched pairs with the two members of a pair addressing the same concept(s). The answer to the odd-numbered member of a pair is given at the back of the book. Problems denoted with a ▲ involve concepts found not only in the section under consideration but also concepts found in one or more earlier sections of the chapter.

Structure of Carboxylic Acids and Their Derivatives (Section 16-1)

16-1   In which of the following compounds is a carboxyl group present?

a.
$$CH_3-CH_2-\overset{\overset{\displaystyle O}{\|}}{C}-OH$$

b.
$$CH_3-CH_2-CH_2-\overset{\overset{\displaystyle O}{\|}}{C}-O-CH_3$$

c.
$$CH_3-\overset{\overset{\displaystyle OH}{|}}{C}H-\overset{\overset{\displaystyle O}{\|}}{C}-CH_3$$

d. CH_3-CH_2-COOH

16-2   In which of the following compounds is a carboxyl group present?

a.
$$CH_3-CH_2-\overset{\overset{\displaystyle O}{\|}}{C}-O-CH_3$$

b.
$$CH_3-CH_2-\overset{\overset{\displaystyle O}{\|}}{C}-OH$$

c.
$$\overset{\overset{\displaystyle O}{\|}}{C}-H \text{ (on benzene ring)}$$

d. $CH_3-\overset{\overset{\displaystyle}{|}}{\underset{\underset{\displaystyle CH_3}{|}}{C}}H-CH_2-CH_2-CO_2H$

16-3   Indicate whether or not each of the compounds in Problem 16-1 is a carboxylic acid.

16-4   Indicate whether or not each of the compounds in Problem 16-2 is a carboxylic acid.

16-5   Write the general structural formula for each of the following types of carboxylic acid derivatives.
a. Ester   b. Acid chloride
c. Amide   d. Acid anhydride

16-6   Write the general structural formula for the functional group present in each of the following carboxylic acid derivatives.
a. Amide   b. Ester
c. Acid anhydride   d. Acid chloride

16-7   For each of the following types of compounds, all of which have the general formula $R-\overset{\overset{\displaystyle O}{\|}}{C}-Z$, indicate whether the "C—Z bond" is polar or nonpolar.

a. $R-\overset{\overset{\displaystyle O}{\|}}{C}-NH_2$ b. $R-\overset{\overset{\displaystyle O}{\|}}{C}-CH_3$

c. $R-\overset{\overset{\displaystyle O}{\|}}{C}-O-\overset{\overset{\displaystyle O}{\|}}{C}-CH_3$ d. $R-\overset{\overset{\displaystyle O}{\|}}{C}-O-CH_3$

16-8   For each of the following types of compounds, all of which have the general formula $R-\overset{\overset{\displaystyle O}{\|}}{C}-Z$, indicate whether the "C—Z bond" is polar or nonpolar.

a. $R-\overset{\overset{\displaystyle O}{\|}}{C}-OH$ b. $R-\overset{\overset{\displaystyle O}{\|}}{C}-H$

c. $R-\overset{\overset{\displaystyle O}{\|}}{C}-Cl$ d. $R-\overset{\overset{\displaystyle O}{\|}}{C}-O-CH_2-CH_3$

16-9   Classify each of the compounds in Problem 16-7 as a *carbonyl compound* or an *acyl compound*.

16-10   Classify each of the compounds in Problem 16-8 as a *carbonyl compound* or an *acyl compound*.

16-11   Which of the designations *carboxyl group present*, *carbonyl group present*, and *acyl group present* applies to each of the following types of compounds? More than one designation may be correct in a given situation, or only one or none of the designations may apply.
a. Amide   b. Carboxylic acid
c. Aldehyde   d. Ester

16-12   Which of the designations *carboxyl group present*, *carbonyl group present*, and *acyl group present* applies to each of the following types of compounds? More than one designation may be correct in a given situation, or only one or none of the designations may apply.
a. Acid chloride   b. Ketone
c. Acid anhydride   d. Ether

IUPAC Nomenclature for Carboxylic Acids (Section 16-2)

16-13   Give the IUPAC name for each of the following carboxylic acids.

a. $CH_3-CH_2-CH_2-\overset{\overset{\displaystyle O}{\|}}{C}-OH$ b. $CH_3-\overset{\overset{\displaystyle CH_3}{|}}{C}H-\overset{\overset{\displaystyle O}{\|}}{C}-OH$

c. $CH_3-CH_2-\overset{\overset{\displaystyle CH_3-CH_2}{|}}{C}H-\overset{\overset{\displaystyle O}{\|}}{C}-OH$ d. CH_3-CH_2-COOH

16-14 Give the IUPAC name for each of the following carboxylic acids.

a. $CH_3-CH_2-CH_2-CH_2-\overset{\overset{\displaystyle O}{\|}}{C}-OH$

b. $\underset{\underset{\displaystyle CH_3}{|}}{CH_2}-\underset{\underset{\displaystyle CH_3}{|}}{CH}-CH_2-\overset{\overset{\displaystyle O}{\|}}{C}-OH$

c. $CH_3-\underset{\underset{\displaystyle CH_3}{|}}{CH}-\underset{\underset{\displaystyle CH_3}{|}}{CH}-\overset{\overset{\displaystyle O}{\|}}{C}-OH$

d. $CH_3-CH_2-CH_2-COOH$

16-15 Assign an IUPAC name to each of the following carboxylic acids.

a.

b.

c.

d.

16-16 Assign an IUPAC name to each of the following carboxylic acids.

a.

b.

c.

d.

16-17 Draw a condensed structural formula that corresponds to each of the following carboxylic acids.
a. 2-Ethylbutanoic acid
b. 2,5-Dimethylhexanoic acid
c. Methylpropanoic acid
d. Dichloroethanoic acid

16-18 Draw a condensed structural formula that corresponds to each of the following carboxylic acids.
a. 3,3-Dimethylheptanoic acid
b. 4-Methylpentanoic acid
c. 3-Chloropropanoic acid
d. Trichloroethanoic acid

16-19 Give the IUPAC name for each of the following carboxylic acids.

a.

b.

c.

d.

16-20 Give the IUPAC name for each of the following carboxylic acids.

a.

b.

c.

d.

16-21 Draw a condensed structural formula that corresponds to each of the following carboxylic acids.
a. 2,2-Dimethylbutanoic acid
b. 2,2-Dimethylbutanedioic acid
c. 2,2-Dimethylcyclohexanecarboxylic acid
d. 2,4-Dichlorobenzenecarboxylic acid

16-22 Draw a condensed structural formula that corresponds to each of the following carboxylic acids.
a. 2,3-Dichlorohexanoic acid
b. 2,3-Dichlorohexanedioic acid
c. 2,3-Dichlorocyclopentanecarboxylic acid
d. 3,5-Dichlorobenzenecarboxylic acid

Common Names for Carboxylic Acids (Section 16-3)

16-23 What is the common name for each of the following unbranched carboxylic acids?
a. five-carbon monocarboxylic acid
b. two-carbon monocarboxylic acid
c. five-carbon dicarboxylic acid
d. two-carbon dicarboxylic acid

16-24 What is the common name for each of the following unbranched carboxylic acids?
a. four-carbon monocarboxylic acid
b. three-carbon monocarboxylic acid
c. four-carbon dicarboxylic acid
d. three-carbon dicarboxylic acid

16-25 How many carbon atoms are present in each of the following carboxylic acids?
a. Formic acid   b. Caproic acid
c. Succinic acid   d. Malonic acid

16-26 How many carbon atoms are present in each of the following carboxylic acids?
a. Acetic acid   b. Valeric acid
c. Oxalic acid   d. Adipic acid

16-27 Draw a condensed structural formula, using the notation $-\overset{\overset{\displaystyle O}{\|}}{C}-OH$ to denote a carboxyl group, for each of the carboxylic acids in Problem 16-23.

16-28 Draw a condensed structural formula, using the notation $-\overset{\overset{\displaystyle O}{\|}}{C}-OH$ to denote a carboxyl group, for each of the carboxylic acids in Problem 16-24.

16-29 Draw a condensed structural formula, using the notation —COOH to denote a carboxyl group, for each of the following carboxylic acids.
a. α-Chlorobutyric acid
b. β-Chlorobutyric acid
c. Chlorosuccinic acid
d. α,β-Dichlorosuccinic acid

16-30 Draw a condensed structural formula, using the notation —COOH to denote a carboxyl group, for each of the following carboxylic acids.
a. Chloroacetic acid
b. β-Chloropropionic acid
c. Chloromalonic acid
d. α,γ-Chloroglutaric acid

Polyfunctional Carboxylic Acids (Section 16-4)

16-31 Each of the following acids contains an additional type of functional group besides the carboxyl group. For each acid, specify the noncarboxyl functional group present.
a. Acrylic acid   b. Lactic acid
c. Maleic acid   d. Glycolic acid

16-32 Each of the following acids contains an additional type of functional group besides the carboxyl group. For each acid, specify the noncarboxyl functional group present.
a. Fumaric acid   b. Pyruvic acid
c. Malic acid   d. Tartaric acid

16-33 Give the IUPAC name for each of the acids in Problem 16-31.

16-34 Give the IUPAC name for each of the acids in Problem 16-32.

16-35 Draw a structural formula for each of the following acids.
a. 3-Oxopentanoic acid
b. 2-Hydroxybutanoic acid
c. *trans*-4-Hexenoic acid
d. α,β-Dihydroxyglutaric acid

16-36 Draw a structural formula for each of the following acids.
a. 3-Hydroxypentanoic acid
b. α,γ-Dihydroxyvaleric acid
c. 2-Oxobutanoic acid
d. *cis*-3-Heptenoic acid

▲**16-37** Classify each of the following carboxylic acids as (1) an unsaturated acid, (2) a hydroxy acid, (3) a keto acid, (4) a monocarboxylic acid, or (5) a dicarboxylic acid. More than one response may apply for a given acid.
a. Acrylic acid   b. Maleic acid
c. Succinic acid   d. Caproic acid

▲**16-38** Classify each of the following carboxylic acids as (1) an unsaturated acid, (2) a hydroxy acid, (3) a keto acid, (4) a monocarboxylic acid, or (5) a dicarboxylic acid. More than one response may apply for a given acid.
a. Lactic acid   b. Glutaric acid
c. Valeric acid   d. Pyruvic acid

Physical Properties of Carboxylic Acids (Section 16-5)

16-39 Indicate whether each of the following unbranched saturated carboxylic acids is a solid, liquid, or gas at room temperature.
a. C_4 monocarboxylic acid
b. C_4 dicarboxylic acid
c. C_5 monocarboxylic acid
d. C_6 dicarboxylic acid

16-40 Indicate whether each of the following unbranched saturated carboxylic acids is a solid, liquid, or gas at room temperature.
a. C_3 monocarboxylic acid
b. C_3 dicarboxylic acid
c. C_6 monocarboxylic acid
d. C_5 dicarboxylic acid

16-41 Determine the maximum number of hydrogen bonds that can form between an acetic acid molecule and
a. another acetic acid molecule
b. water molecules

16-42 Determine the maximum number of hydrogen bonds that can form between a butanoic acid molecule and
a. another butanoic acid molecule
b. water molecules

16-43 What is the physical state (solid, liquid, or gas) of each of the following carboxylic acids at room temperature?
a. Oxalic acid   b. Decanoic acid
c. Hexanoic acid   d. Benzoic acid

16-44 What is the physical state (solid, liquid, or gas) of each of the following carboxylic acids at room temperature?
a. Succinic acid   b. Octanoic acid
c. Pentanoic acid   d. *p*-Chlorobenzoic acid

Preparation of Carboxylic Acids (Section 16-6)

16-45 Draw a structural formula for the carboxylic acid expected to be formed when each of the following substances is oxidized using a strong oxidizing agent.
a. CH_3—CH_2—OH
b.
$$CH_3-\overset{\overset{\displaystyle O}{\|}}{C}-H$$
c.
$$CH_3-CH_2-\overset{\overset{\displaystyle CH_3}{|}}{CH}-CH_2-\overset{\overset{\displaystyle O}{\|}}{C}-H$$
d. CH_2—CH_3

16-46 Draw a structural formula for the carboxylic acid expected to be formed when each of the following substances is oxidized using a strong oxidizing agent.
a.
$$CH_3-CH_2-\overset{\overset{\displaystyle O}{\|}}{C}-H$$
b. CH_3—CH_2—CH_2—OH
c.
$$CH_3-\underset{\underset{\displaystyle CH_3}{|}}{CH}-\underset{\underset{\displaystyle CH_3}{|}}{CH}-\overset{\overset{\displaystyle O}{\|}}{C}-H$$
d. CH_3

Acidity of Carboxylic Acids (Section 16-7)

16-47 How many *acidic* hydrogen atoms are present in each of the following carboxylic acids?
a. Pentanoic acid
b. Citric acid
c. Succinic acid
d. Oxalic acid

16-48 How many *acidic* hydrogen atoms are present in each of the following carboxylic acids?
a. Acetic acid
b. Benzoic acid
c. Propanoic acid
d. Glutaric acid

16-49 What is the charge on the carboxylate ion formed when each of the acids in Problem 16-47 ionizes in water?

16-50 What is the charge on the carboxylate ion formed when each of the acids in Problem 16-48 ionizes in water?

16-51 What is the name of the carboxylate ion that forms when each of the acids in Problem 16-47 ionizes in water? (Use an IUPAC carboxylate name if the acid name is IUPAC; use a common name if the acid name is common.)

16-52 What is the name of the carboxylate ion that forms when each of the acids in Problem 16-48 ionizes in water? (Use an IUPAC carboxylate name if the acid name is IUPAC; use a common name if the acid name is common.)

16-53 Write a chemical equation for the formation of each of the following carboxylate ions, in aqueous solution, from its parent acid.
a. Acetate
b. Citrate
c. Ethanoate
d. 2-Methylbutanoate

16-54 Write a chemical equation for the formation of each of the following carboxylate ions, in aqueous solution, from its parent acid.
a. Butanoate
b. Succinate
c. Benzoate
d. α-Methylbutyrate

Carboxylic Acid Salts (Section 16-8)

16-55 Draw structural formulas for the following entities.
a. Propanoate ion
b. Sodium propanoate
c. Acetate ion
d. Sodium acetate

16-56 Draw structural formulas for the following entities.
a. Butanoate ion
b. Sodium butanoate
c. Formate ion
d. Sodium formate

16-57 Give the IUPAC name for each of the following carboxylic acid salts.

a. $CH_3-\overset{\overset{O}{\|}}{C}-O^- K^+$

b. $\left(CH_3-CH_2-\overset{\overset{O}{\|}}{C}-O^-\right)_2 Ca^{2+}$

c. $K^+{}^-O-\overset{\overset{O}{\|}}{C}-CH_2-CH_2-\overset{\overset{O}{\|}}{C}-O^- K^+$

d. $\diagup\diagdown\diagup\diagdown COO^- Na^+$

16-58 Give the IUPAC name for each of the following carboxylic acid salts.

a. $\left(H-\overset{\overset{O}{\|}}{C}-O^-\right)_2 Ca^{2+}$

b. $CH_3-CH_2-\overset{\overset{O}{\|}}{C}-O^- Na^+$

c. $\diagup\diagdown\diagup COO^- K^+$

d. (benzene ring)$-\overset{\overset{O}{\|}}{C}-O^- Na^+$

16-59 Give the common name for each of the carboxylic acid salts in Problem 16-57.

16-60 Give the common name for each of the carboxylic acid salts in Problem 16-58.

16-61 Write a chemical equation for the preparation of each of the salts in Problem 16-57 using an acid–base neutralization reaction.

16-62 Write a chemical equation for the preparation of each of the salts in Problem 16-58 using an acid–base neutralization reaction.

16-63 Write a chemical equation for the conversion of each of the following carboxylic acid salts to its parent carboxylic acid. Use hydrochloric acid (HCl) as the source of the needed hydronium ions.
a. Sodium butanoate
b. Potassium oxalate
c. Calcium malonate
d. Sodium benzoate

16-64 Write a chemical equation for the conversion of each of the following carboxylic acid salts to its parent carboxylic acid. Use hydrochloric acid (HCl) as the source of the needed hydronium ions.
a. Calcium propanoate
b. Sodium lactate
c. Magnesium succinate
d. Potassium benzoate

16-65 What is an antimicrobial?

16-66 Which three carboxylic acids have salts that are used extensively as food preservatives?

16-67 Which carboxylic acid has salts that are used to inhibit yeast and mold growth in the following?
a. Jams and jellies
b. Dairy products
c. Dried fruit
d. Cheese spreads

16-68 Which carboxylic acid has salts that are used to inhibit yeast and mold growth in the following?
a. Ketchup and syrup
b. Sauerkraut
c. Pie filling
d. Baked products

▲**16-69** Classify each of the following substances as (1) a salt of a monocarboxylic acid or (2) a salt of a dicarboxylic acid.
a. Sodium formate
b. Potassium pentanedioate
c. Calcium oxalate
d. Magnesium propanoate

▲**16-70** Classify each of the following substances as (1) a salt of a monocarboxylic acid or (2) a salt of a dicarboxylic acid.
a. Potassium ethanoate
b. Magnesium acetate
c. Sodium succinate
d. Calcium butanedioate

▲**16-71** How many ions are present in one formula unit of each of the compounds in Problem 16-69?

▲**16-72** How many ions are present in one formula unit of each of the compounds in Problem 16-70?

Carboxylic Acid Decarboxylation Reactions (Section 16-9)

16-73 What small inorganic molecule is always a product of a carboxylic acid decarboxylation reaction?

16-74 A prerequisite for a decarboxylation reaction is the presence of what functional group in the reacting organic molecule?

16-75 Draw the structures of the organic compounds formed when each of the following molecules is decarboxylated.

a. $CH_3-CH_2-CH_2-CH_2-\overset{\overset{\displaystyle O}{\|}}{C}-OH$

b. $CH_3-CH_2-\overset{\overset{\displaystyle O}{\|}}{C}-CH_2-\overset{\overset{\displaystyle O}{\|}}{C}-OH$

16-76 Draw the structures of the organic compounds formed when each of the following molecules is decarboxylated.

a. $CH_3-CH_2-\overset{\overset{\displaystyle O}{\|}}{C}-OH$ b. $CH_3-\overset{\overset{\displaystyle O}{\|}}{C}-\overset{\overset{\displaystyle O}{\|}}{C}-OH$

Structure of Esters (Section 16-10)

16-77 Characterize an ester functional group in terms of the following.
a. The number of oxygen atoms that are present
b. The minimum number of carbon atoms that must be present

16-78 Give two linear notations for designating the ester functional group.

16-79 Which of the following structures represent esters?

a.

$CH_3-CH_2-CH_2-\overset{\overset{\displaystyle O}{\|}}{C}-O-CH_3$

b.

$CH_3-O-\overset{\overset{\displaystyle O}{\|}}{C}-CH_3$

c.

$CH_3-O-CH_2-\overset{\overset{\displaystyle O}{\|}}{C}-CH_3$

d.

16-80 Which of the following structures represent esters?

a. $CH_3-\overset{\overset{\displaystyle CH_3}{|}}{CH}-\overset{\overset{\displaystyle O}{\|}}{C}-O-CH_3$

b. $CH_3-CH_2-O-\overset{\overset{\displaystyle O}{\|}}{C}-CH_2-CH_3$

c.

d.

▲**16-81** Classify each of the following substances as (1) an ester, (2) a carboxylic acid, or (3) a carboxylic acid salt.

a. $CH_3-\overset{\overset{\displaystyle O}{\|}}{C}-O-H$ b. $CH_3-\overset{\overset{\displaystyle O}{\|}}{C}-O-CH_3$

c. $CH_3-\overset{\overset{\displaystyle O}{\|}}{C}-O^-Na^+$ d. CH_3-COOH

▲**16-82** Classify each of the following substances as (1) an ester, (2) a carboxylic acid, or (3) a carboxylic acid salt.

a. $H-\overset{\overset{\displaystyle O}{\|}}{C}-O-CH_3$ b. $H-\overset{\overset{\displaystyle O}{\|}}{C}-O^-K^+$

c. $H-COOH$ d. $H-\overset{\overset{\displaystyle O}{\|}}{C}-O-H$

Preparation of Esters (Section 16-11)

16-83 Draw the structure of the ester produced from the condensation reaction between a $CH_3-CH_2-\overset{\overset{\displaystyle O}{\|}}{C}-OH$ molecule and each of the following molecules.
a. CH_3-CH_2-OH
b. CH_3-OH
c. $CH_3-\overset{\overset{\displaystyle CH_3}{|}}{CH}-CH_2-OH$
d. $CH_3-CH_2-\overset{\overset{\displaystyle OH}{|}}{CH}-CH_2-CH_3$

16-84 Draw the structure of the ester produced from the condensation reaction between a $CH_3-\overset{\overset{\displaystyle O}{\|}}{C}-OH$ molecule and each of the following molecules.
a. CH_3-CH_2-OH
b. CH_3-OH
c. $CH_3-\overset{\overset{\displaystyle CH_3}{|}}{CH}-CH_2-OH$
d. $CH_3-CH_2-\overset{\overset{\displaystyle OH}{|}}{CH}-CH_2-CH_3$

16-85 For each of the following esters, draw the structural formula of the "parent" acid and the "parent" alcohol.
a. $CH_3-CH_2-\overset{\overset{\displaystyle O}{\|}}{C}-O-CH_2-CH_3$

b. $CH_3-O-\overset{\overset{\displaystyle O}{\|}}{C}-CH_2-CH_2-CH_3$

c. $CH_3-\overset{\overset{\displaystyle O}{\|}}{C}-O-$⬡

d. ⬡$-\overset{\overset{\displaystyle O}{\|}}{C}-O-CH_3$

16-86 For each of the following esters, draw the structural formula of the "parent" acid and the "parent" alcohol.

a.

$$CH_3-\overset{\displaystyle O}{\overset{\displaystyle \|}{C}}-O-CH_2-CH_3$$

b.

$$CH_3-O-\overset{\displaystyle O}{\overset{\displaystyle \|}{C}}-CH_2-CH_3$$

c.

d.

$$CH_3-\overset{\displaystyle CH_3}{\overset{\displaystyle |}{CH}}-CH_2-\overset{\displaystyle O}{\overset{\displaystyle \|}{C}}-O-$$

16-87 What are lactones, and by what chemical reaction are they produced?

16-88 What is the difference between a γ-lactone and a δ-lactone?

Nomenclature for Esters (Section 16-12)

16-89 Assign an IUPAC name to each of the following esters.

a. $CH_3-CH_2-\overset{\displaystyle O}{\overset{\displaystyle \|}{C}}-O-CH_2-CH_3$

b. $CH_3-\overset{\displaystyle O}{\overset{\displaystyle \|}{C}}-O-CH_2-CH_2-CH_3$

c. $CH_3-CH_2-O-\overset{\displaystyle O}{\overset{\displaystyle \|}{C}}-CH_2-CH_3$

d. $H-\overset{\displaystyle O}{\overset{\displaystyle \|}{C}}-O-CH_2-CH_2-CH_2-CH_3$

16-90 Assign an IUPAC name to each of the following esters.

a. $CH_3-CH_2-CH_2-\overset{\displaystyle O}{\overset{\displaystyle \|}{C}}-O-CH_2-CH_3$

b. $CH_3-\overset{\displaystyle O}{\overset{\displaystyle \|}{C}}-O-CH_2-CH_2-CH_2-CH_3$

c. $CH_3-CH_2-O-\overset{\displaystyle O}{\overset{\displaystyle \|}{C}}-CH_2-CH_2-CH_3$

d. $H-\overset{\displaystyle O}{\overset{\displaystyle \|}{C}}-O-CH_2-CH_2-CH_3$

16-91 Assign common names to each of the esters in Problem 16-89.

16-92 Assign common names to each of the esters in Problem 16-90.

16-93 Assign an IUPAC name to each of the following esters.

a.

b.

c.

d.

16-94 Assign an IUPAC name to each of the following esters.

a.

b.

c.

d.

16-95 Draw a structural formula for each of the following esters.
a. Methyl formate
b. Ethyl phenylacetate
c. Isopropyl acetate
d. 2-Bromopropyl ethanoate

16-96 Draw a structural formula for each of the following esters.
a. Ethyl butyrate
b. Butyl ethanoate
c. 2-Methylpropyl formate
d. Ethyl α-methylpropionate

16-97 Assign IUPAC names to the esters that are produced from the reaction of the following carboxylic acids and alcohols.
a. Acetic acid and ethanol
b. Ethanoic acid and methanol
c. Butyric acid and ethyl alcohol
d. 2-Butanol and caproic acid

16-98 Assign IUPAC names to the esters that are produced from the reaction of the following carboxylic acids and alcohols.
a. Ethanoic acid and propyl alcohol
b. Acetic acid and 1-pentanol
c. Acetic acid and 2-pentanol
d. Ethanol and benzoic acid

▲**16-99** Classify each of the following compounds as (1) an ester, (2) a carboxylic acid, or (3) a carboxylic acid salt.
a. Methyl succinate
b. Sodium succinate
c. Methyl butanoate
d. Methyl 2-methylbutanoate

▲**16-100** Classify each of the following compounds as (1) an ester, (2) a carboxylic acid, or (3) a carboxylic acid salt.
a. Ethyl formate
b. Ethyl ethanoate
c. Potassium ethanoate
d. Potassium ethanedioate

▲**16-101** How many carbon atoms are present in a molecule of each of the compounds in Problem 16-99?

▲**16-102** How many carbon atoms are present in a molecule of each of the compounds in Problem 16-100?

Selected Common Esters (Section 16-13)

16-103 With the help of Table 16-4, identify the flavor or odor associated with each of the following esters.
a. Isobutyl methanoate
b. Pentyl ethanoate
c. Methyl butanoate

16-104 With the help of Table 16-4, identify the flavor or odor associated with each of the following esters.
a. Propyl ethanoate
b. Ethyl butanoate
c. Pentyl propanoate

16-105 Structurally contrast the ester flavoring agents that generate apple and pineapple flavors in terms of their "acid part" and "alcohol part."

16-106 Structurally contrast the ester flavoring agents that generate pear and banana flavors in terms of their "acid part" and "alcohol part."

16-107 How does the structure of aspirin differ from that of salicylic acid?

16-108 How does the structure of oil of wintergreen differ from that of salicylic acid?

▲**16-109** Why is the lactone nepetalactone, present in the catnip plant, not considered a pheromone for cats?

▲**16-110** What is the original source of the large-ring lactone antibiotic erythromycin?

Isomerism for Carboxylic Acids and Esters (Section 16-14)

16-111 Give IUPAC names for the four isomeric C_5 monocarboxylic acids with saturated carbon chains.

16-112 Give IUPAC names for the eight isomeric C_6 monocarboxylic acids with saturated carbon chains.

16-113 Give IUPAC names for the four isomeric methyl esters that contain six carbon atoms and saturated carbon chains.

16-114 Give IUPAC names for the two isomeric ethyl esters that contain six carbon atoms and saturated carbon chains.

16-115 How many esters exist that are isomeric with 2-methylbutanoic acid?

16-116 How many esters exist that are isomeric with 2-methylpropanoic acid?

16-117 Draw condensed structural formulas for all carboxylic acids and all esters that have the molecular formula $C_3H_6O_2$.

16-118 Draw condensed structural formulas for all carboxylic acids and all esters that have the molecular formula $C_4H_8O_2$.

▲**16-119** The general molecular formula for an alkane is C_nH_{2n+2}. What is the general molecular formula for an ester in which all carbon–carbon bonds are single bonds?

▲**16-120** How does the general molecular formula for an ester compare to that for a carboxylic acid, when all carbon–carbon bonds in both types of compounds are single bonds?

Physical Properties of Esters (Section 16-15)

16-121 What is the maximum number of hydrogen bonds that can form between a molecule of the ester

$$CH_3-\overset{\overset{\displaystyle O}{\|}}{C}-O-CH_3 \text{ and}$$

a. another like ester molecule
b. water molecules

16-122 What is the maximum number of hydrogen bonds that can form between a molecule of the ester

$$CH_3-\overset{\overset{\displaystyle O}{\|}}{C}-O-CH_2-CH_3 \text{ and}$$

a. another like ester molecule
b. water molecules

▲**16-123** With the help of Figure 16-15, determine the physical state at room temperature of each of the following esters.
a. Methyl ethanoate
b. Methyl propanoate
c. Ethyl ethanoate
d. Ethyl butanoate

▲**16-124** With the help of Figure 16-15, determine the physical state at room temperature of each of the following esters.
a. Methyl methanoate
b. Ethyl methanoate
c. Methyl pentanoate
d. Ethyl propanoate

Chemical Reactions of Esters (Section 16-16)

16-125 Write the structural formulas of the reaction products when each of the following esters is hydrolyzed under acidic conditions.

a. $CH_3-CH_2-\overset{\overset{\displaystyle O}{\|}}{C}-O-CH_3$

b. $CH_3-\overset{\overset{\displaystyle CH_3}{|}}{CH}-\overset{\overset{\displaystyle O}{\|}}{C}-O-CH_2-CH_2-CH_3$

c. $CH_3-CH_2-CH_2-\overset{\overset{\displaystyle O}{\|}}{C}-O-\bigcirc$

d. $\bigcirc-\overset{\overset{\displaystyle O}{\|}}{C}-O-CH_3$

16-126 Write the structural formulas of the reaction products when each of the following esters is hydrolyzed under acidic conditions.

a. $CH_3-CH_2-\overset{\overset{\displaystyle O}{\|}}{C}-O-CH_2-CH_3$

b. $CH_3-CH_2-\overset{\overset{\displaystyle CH_3}{|}}{CH}-\overset{\overset{\displaystyle O}{\|}}{C}-O-CH_2-CH_3$

c. $CH_3-CH_2-\overset{\overset{\displaystyle O}{\|}}{C}-O-\bigcirc$

d. $\bigcirc-\overset{\overset{\displaystyle O}{\|}}{C}-O-CH_2-CH_2-CH_3$

16-127 Write the structural formulas of the reaction products when each of the esters in Problem 16-125 is saponified using sodium hydroxide.

16-128 Write the structural formulas of the reaction products when each of the esters in Problem 16-126 is saponified using sodium hydroxide.

▲16-129 What are the IUPAC names of the products formed when each of the following esters is hydrolyzed under acidic conditions?
a. Methyl butanoate
b. Methyl ethanoate
c. Isopropyl propanoate
d. Isopropyl ethanoate

▲16-130 What are the IUPAC names of the products formed when each of the following esters is hydrolyzed under acidic conditions?
a. Ethyl pentanoate
b. Ethyl methanoate
c. Isopropyl pentanoate
d. Isopropyl methanoate

▲16-131 What are the IUPAC names of the products formed when each of the following esters is hydrolyzed under acidic conditions?

a.
b.
c.
d.

▲16-132 What are the IUPAC names of the products formed when each of the following esters is hydrolyzed under acidic conditions?

a.
b.
c.
d.

16-133 Draw structures of the reaction products in the following chemical reactions.

a. $CH_3-CH(CH_3)-C(=O)-O-CH_2-CH_3 + H_2O \xrightarrow{H^+}$

b. $CH_3-CH(CH_3)-C(=O)-O-CH_2-CH_3 + NaOH \xrightarrow{H_2O}$

c. $H-C(=O)-O-CH_2-CH_2-CH_2-CH_3 + H_2O \xrightarrow{H^+}$

d. $CH_3-C(=O)-O-CH_2-CH(CH_3)-CH(CH_3)-CH_3 + NaOH \xrightarrow{H_2O}$

16-134 Draw structures of the reaction products in the following chemical reactions.

a. $CH_3-CH(CH_3)-CH_2-C(=O)-O-CH_3 + H_2O \xrightarrow{H^+}$

b. $CH_3-CH(CH_3)-CH_2-C(=O)-O-CH_3 + NaOH \xrightarrow{H_2O}$

c. $CH_3-CH_2-C(=O)-O-(CH_2)_5-CH_3 + H_2O \xrightarrow{H^+}$

d. $CH_3-(CH_2)_5-C(=O)-O-CH_2-CH_3 + NaOH \xrightarrow{H_2O}$

Sulfur Analogs of Esters (Section 16-17)

16-135 Draw the structures of the thioesters formed as a result of each of the following reactions between carboxylic acids and thiols.

a. $CH_3-C(=O)-OH + CH_3-CH_2-SH \rightarrow$

b. $CH_3-(CH_2)_8-C(=O)-OH + CH_3-SH \rightarrow$

c. $C_6H_5-COOH + CH_3-CH(CH_3)-SH \rightarrow$

d. $H-C(=O)-OH + CH_3-CH_2-CH_2-SH \rightarrow$

16-136 Draw the structures of the thioesters formed as a result of each of the following reactions between carboxylic acids and thiols.

a. $CH_3-CH_2-C(=O)-OH + CH_3-CH_2-SH \rightarrow$
b. $CH_3-CH_2-CH_2-COOH + CH_3-SH \rightarrow$
c. $CH_3-C(=O)-OH + CH_3-CH_2-CH(CH_3)-SH \rightarrow$
d. $C_6H_5-COOH + C_6H_5-SH \rightarrow$

16-137 Draw the structural formula for each of the following thioesters.
a. Methyl thioethanoate
b. Methyl thioacetate
c. Ethyl thioformate
d. Ethyl thiomethanoate

16-138 Draw the structural formula for each of the following thioesters.
a. Methyl thiopropanoate
b. Methyl thiopropionate
c. Ethyl thioacetate
d. Ethyl thioethanoate

Polyesters (Section 16-18)

16-139 Write the structure (two repeating units) of the polyester polymer formed from oxalic acid and 1,3-propanediol.

16-140 Write the structure (two repeating units) of the polyester polymer formed from malonic acid and ethylene glycol.

16-141 Draw the structural formulas of the monomers needed to form the following polyester.

$$\left(\!O\!-\!(CH_2)_3\!-\!O\!-\!\overset{\displaystyle O}{\overset{\|}{C}}\!-\!(CH_2)_2\!-\!\overset{\displaystyle O}{\overset{\|}{C}}\!-\!O\!\right)_{\!n}$$

16-142 Draw the structural formulas of the monomers needed to form the following polyester.

$$\left(\!O\!-\!\overset{\displaystyle O}{\overset{\|}{C}}\!-\!(CH_2)_3\!-\!\overset{\displaystyle O}{\overset{\|}{C}}\!-\!O\!-\!(CH_2)_2\!-\!O\!\right)_{\!n}$$

16-143 What are the names of the monomers used to produce the polyester whose acronym is PET?

16-144 What are the names of the monomers used to produce the polyester whose acronym is PEN?

Acid Chlorides and Acid Anhydrides (Section 16-19)

16-145 Draw the condensed structural formula for each of the following compounds.
a. Propionyl chloride
b. 3-Methylbutanoyl chloride
c. Butyric anhydride
d. Butanoic ethanoic anhydride

16-146 Draw the condensed structural formula for each of the following compounds.
a. Acetyl chloride
b. 2-Methylbutanoyl chloride
c. Propionic anhydride
d. Ethanoic methanoic anhydride

16-147 Assign an IUPAC name to each of the following compounds.
a.
$$CH_3\!-\!\overset{\displaystyle O}{\overset{\|}{C}}\!-\!O\!-\!\overset{\displaystyle O}{\overset{\|}{C}}\!-\!CH_2\!-\!CH_3$$
b.
$$CH_3\!-\!CH_2\!-\!CH_2\!-\!CH_2\!-\!\overset{\displaystyle O}{\overset{\|}{C}}\!-\!Cl$$
c.
$$CH_3\!-\!\underset{\underset{\displaystyle CH_3}{|}}{CH}\!-\!\underset{\underset{\displaystyle CH_3}{|}}{CH}\!-\!\overset{\displaystyle O}{\overset{\|}{C}}\!-\!Cl$$
d.
$$CH_3\!-\!CH_2\!-\!\overset{\displaystyle O}{\overset{\|}{C}}\!-\!O\!-\!\overset{\displaystyle O}{\overset{\|}{C}}\!-\!H$$

16-148 Assign an IUPAC name to each of the following compounds.
a.
$$CH_3\!-\!CH_2\!-\!\overset{\displaystyle O}{\overset{\|}{C}}\!-\!O\!-\!\overset{\displaystyle O}{\overset{\|}{C}}\!-\!CH_2\!-\!CH_3$$
b.
$$CH_3\!-\!CH_2\!-\!\overset{\displaystyle O}{\overset{\|}{C}}\!-\!Cl$$
c.
$$CH_3\!-\!\underset{\underset{\displaystyle CH_3}{|}}{\overset{\overset{\displaystyle CH_3}{|}}{C}}\!-\!CH_2\!-\!\overset{\displaystyle O}{\overset{\|}{C}}\!-\!Cl$$
d.
$$CH_3\!-\!\overset{\displaystyle O}{\overset{\|}{C}}\!-\!O\!-\!\overset{\displaystyle O}{\overset{\|}{C}}\!-\!H$$

16-149 Draw a condensed structural formula for the organic product of the reaction of each of the following compounds with water.
a. Pentanoyl chloride
b. Pentanoic anhydride

16-150 Draw a condensed structural formula for the organic product of the reaction of each of the following compounds with water.
a. Butanoyl chloride
b. Butanoic anhydride

16-151 Draw the condensed structural formulas for the ester formed and the carboxylic acid formed when acetic anhydride reacts with the following alcohols.
a. Ethyl alcohol
b. 1-Butanol

16-152 Draw the condensed structural formulas for the ester formed and the carboxylic acid formed when ethanoic anhydride reacts with the following alcohols.
a. Propyl alcohol
b. 2-Butanol

16-153 What is the IUPAC name for the acyl group present in each of the following hydrocarbon derivatives?
a. Propanoic acid
b. Butanoic anhydride
c. Butanoyl chloride
d. Acetic acid

16-154 What is the IUPAC name for the acyl group present in each of the following hydrocarbon derivatives?
a. Butanoic acid
b. Propanoic anhydride
c. Propanoyl chloride
d. Formic acid

16-155 In general terms, what are the products obtained in an acyl transfer reaction involving an acid chloride and an alcohol?

16-156 In general terms, what are the products obtained in an acyl transfer reaction involving an acid anhydride and an alcohol?

Esters and Anhydrides of Inorganic Acids (Section 16-20)

16-157 Draw the structures of the esters formed by reacting the following substances.
a. 1 molecule methanol and 1 molecule phosphoric acid
b. 2 molecules methanol and 1 molecule phosphoric acid
c. 1 molecule methanol and 1 molecule nitric acid
d. 1 molecule ethylene glycol and 2 molecules nitric acid

16-158 Draw the structures of the esters formed by reacting the following substances.
a. 1 molecule ethanol and 1 molecule phosphoric acid
b. 2 molecules methanol and 1 molecule sulfuric acid
c. 1 molecule ethylene glycol and 1 molecule nitric acid
d. 1 molecule glycerol and 3 molecules nitric acid

16-159 Draw the generalized structure for each of the following.
a. neutral form for a monoester of phosphoric acid
b. ionic form for a monoester of phosphoric acid
c. neutral form for triphosphoric acid
d. ionic form for triphosphoric acid

16-160 Draw the generalized structure for each of the following.
a. neutral form for a diester of phosphoric acid
b. ionic form for a diester of phosphoric acid
c. neutral form for diphosphoric acid
d. ionic form for diphosphoric acid

16-161 What is a phosphoryl group?

16-162 What is a phosphorylation reaction?

16-163 Draw structural formulas (ionic form) for the organic products produced from a phosphorylation reaction that involves the methyl ester of diphosphoric acid and ethyl alcohol.

16-164 Draw structural formulas (ionic form) for the organic products produced from a phosphorylation reaction that involves the ethyl ester of diphosphoric acid and methyl alcohol.

Amines and Amides

17

© Royalty-Free/Cortis

Parachutist with a parachute made of the polyamide nylon.

The four most abundant elements in living organisms are carbon, hydrogen, oxygen, and nitrogen. In previous organic chemistry chapters, compounds containing the first three of these elements have been considered. Alkanes, alkenes, alkynes, and aromatic compounds are all carbon–hydrogen compounds. Carbon–hydrogen–oxygen compounds include alcohols, phenols, ethers, aldehydes, ketones, carboxylic acids, and esters. This chapter extends the discussion of organic compounds by focusing on those that contain the element nitrogen.

Two important types of organic nitrogen-containing compounds will be considered: *amines* and *amides*. Amines are carbon–hydrogen–nitrogen compounds, and amides contain oxygen in addition to these elements. Amines and amides occur widely in living organisms. Many of these naturally occurring compounds are very active physiologically. In addition, numerous drugs used for the treatment of mental illness, hay fever, heart problems, and other physical disorders are amines or amides.

17-1 Bonding Characteristics of Nitrogen Atoms in Organic Compounds

LEARNING FOCUS

Describe the normal bonding pattern for nitrogen atoms in nitrogen-containing organic functional groups.

An understanding of the bonding characteristics of the nitrogen atom is a prerequisite to the study of amines and amides. Nitrogen is a member of

Group VA of the periodic table; it has five valence electrons (Section 4-2) and forms three covalent bonds to complete its octet of electrons (Section 4-3). Thus, in organic chemistry, carbon forms four bonds (Section 12-2), nitrogen forms three bonds, and oxygen forms two bonds (Section 14-1).

$$-\overset{\displaystyle |}{\underset{\displaystyle |}{C}}- \qquad -\overset{\displaystyle |}{\underset{\displaystyle |}{\ddot{N}}}- \qquad :\overset{\displaystyle ..}{\underset{}{\ddot{O}}}-$$

4 valence electrons	5 valence electrons	6 valence electrons
4 covalent bonds	3 covalent bonds	2 covalent bonds
no nonbonding	1 nonbonding	2 nonbonding
electron pairs	electron pair	electron pairs

Section 17-1 Quick Quiz

1. The number of covalent bonds formed by nitrogen atoms in organic compounds is
   a. two
   b. three
   c. four
   d. no correct response
2. In organic compounds the number of bonds formed, respectively, by carbon, oxygen, and nitrogen atoms is
   a. 4, 3, and 2
   b. 4, 2, and 2
   c. 4, 2, and 3
   d. no correct response

Answers: 1.b; 2. c

17-2 Structure and Classification of Amines

LEARNING FOCUS
Know the characteristics of the amine functional group; know the generalized structural formulas for primary, secondary, and tertiary amines.

An **amine** *is an organic derivative of ammonia (NH₃) in which one or more alkyl, cycloalkyl, or aryl groups have replaced ammonia hydrogen atoms.* Amines are classified as primary (1°), secondary (2°), or tertiary (3°) on the basis of how many hydrocarbon groups have replaced ammonia hydrogen atoms (Figure 17-1). A **primary amine** *is an amine in which the nitrogen atom is bonded to one hydrocarbon group and two hydrogen atoms.* The generalized formula for a primary amine is RNH_2; one carbon–nitrogen bond is present. A **secondary amine** *is an amine in which the nitrogen atom is bonded to two hydrocarbon groups and one hydrogen atom.* The generalized formula for a secondary amine is R_2NH; two carbon–nitrogen bonds are present. A **tertiary amine** *is an amine in which the nitrogen atom is bonded to three hydrocarbon groups and no hydrogen atoms.* The generalized formula for a tertiary amine is R_3N; three carbon–nitrogen bonds are present. ◄

▶ *Amines bear the same relationship to ammonia that alcohols and ethers bear to water (Sections 14-2 and 14-15).*

Figure 17-1 Classification of amines is related to the number of R groups attached to the nitrogen atom.

AMMONIA	PRIMARY AMINE	SECONDARY AMINE	TERTIARY AMINE
$H-\ddot{N}-H$ $\overset{|}{H}$	$R-\ddot{N}-H$ $\overset{|}{H}$	$R-\ddot{N}-R'$ $\overset{|}{H}$	$R-\ddot{N}-R'$ $\overset{|}{R''}$
NH_3	CH_3-NH_2	$CH_3-NH-CH_3$	CH_3-N-CH_3 $\overset{|}{CH_3}$

The basis for the amine primary–secondary–tertiary classification system differs from that for alcohols (Section 14-8). ◄

1. For alcohols how many R groups are attached to a *carbon* atom, the hydroxyl-bearing carbon atom, is the determining factor.
2. For amines how many R groups are attached to the *nitrogen* atom is the determining factor.

tert-Butyl alcohol is a *tertiary* alcohol, whereas *tert*-butylamine is a *primary* amine.

Tertiary carbon atom → CH₃ — C — OH with CH₃ and CH₃

tert-Butyl alcohol
(a tertiary alcohol)

Tertiary carbon atom → CH₃ — C — NH₂ with CH₃ and CH₃, Primary nitrogen atom

tert-Butylamine
(a primary amine)

▶ *The word "amine" is pronounced "a-MEAN" (rhymes with "a bean").*

The functional group present in a primary amine, the —NH₂ group, is called an *amino* group. An **amino group** *is the —NH₂ functional group.* Secondary and tertiary amines possess substituted amino groups.

—NH₂

Amino group

—NH
  |
  R

Monosubstituted
amino group

—N—R'
  |
  R

Disubstituted
amino group

EXAMPLE 17-1

Classifying Amines as Primary, Secondary, or Tertiary

Classify each of the following amines as a primary, secondary, or tertiary amine.

a. CH₃—NH—⬡

b. CH₃—N—CH₃
       |
      CH₃

c. ⬡—N—⬡
       |
      CH₃

d. NH₂ (on a branched chain)

▶ *Line-angle structural formulas for selected primary, secondary, and tertiary amines.*

1° (chain) NH₂

1° (branched) NH₂

1° (branched) NH₂

2° NH

3° N

Solution

The number of carbon atoms directly bonded to the nitrogen atom determines the amine classification.

a. This is a secondary amine because the nitrogen is bonded to both a methyl group and a phenyl group.
b. This is a tertiary amine because the nitrogen atom is bonded to three methyl groups.
c. This is also a tertiary amine; the nitrogen atom is bonded to two phenyl groups and a methyl group.
d. This is a primary amine. The nitrogen atom is bonded to only one carbon atom, a carbon atom in the carbon chain. ◄

Cyclic amines exist. Such compounds, which are heterocyclic compounds (Section 14-19), are always either secondary or tertiary amines.

2° Cyclic amine   3° Cyclic amine

Numerous cyclic amine compounds are found in biochemical systems (Section 17-9). ◄

▶ *Cyclic amines are the fourth type of heterocyclic compound to be considered; cyclic ethers (Section 14-19), cyclic forms of hemiacetals and acetals (Section 15-11), and cyclic esters (Section 16-11) were previously discussed. In cyclic amines, the heteroatom is nitrogen; in the other heterocyclic compounds, oxygen is the heteroatom.*

17-3 Nomenclature for Amines

LEARNING FOCUS

Given their structural formulas, be able to name amines using IUPAC rules or vice versa; know the common name system for naming simple amines.

Both common and IUPAC names are extensively used for amines. In the common system of nomenclature, amines are named by listing the alkyl group or groups attached to the nitrogen atom in alphabetical order and adding the suffix *-amine;* all of this appears as one word. Prefixes such as *di-* and *tri-* are added when identical groups are bonded to the nitrogen atom. ◄

▶ *The common names of amines, like those of aldehydes, are written as a single word, which is different from the common names of alcohols (two words), ethers (two or three words), ketones (two or three words), acids (two words), and esters (two words).*

$$CH_3—CH_2—\boxed{NH_2} \qquad CH_3—\boxed{NH}—CH_3$$

Ethylamine   Dimethylamine   Cyclopentylethylmethylamine

The IUPAC rules for naming amines are similar to those for alcohols (Section 14-3). Alcohols are named as *alkanols* and amines are named as *alkanamines.* ◄ IUPAC rules for naming *primary* amines are as follows:

▶ *IUPAC nomenclature for primary amines is similar to that for alcohols, except that the suffix is -amine rather than -ol. An —NH_2 group, like an —OH group, has priority in numbering the parent carbon chain.*

Rule 1: *Select as the parent carbon chain the longest chain to which the nitrogen atom is attached.*

Rule 2: *Name the parent chain by changing the -e ending of the corresponding alkane name to -amine.*

Rule 3: *Number the parent chain from the end nearest the nitrogen atom.*

Rule 4: *The position of attachment of the nitrogen atom is indicated by a number in front of the parent chain name.*

Rule 5: *The identity and location of any substituents are appended to the front of the parent chain name.*

2-Butanamine   3-Methyl-1-butanamine

In diamines, the final -*e* of the carbon chain name is retained for ease of pronunciation. Thus the base name for a four-carbon chain bearing two amino groups is butan*e*diamine.

$$H_2N—CH_2—CH_2—CH_2—CH_2—NH_2$$
1,4-Butanediamine

Secondary and tertiary amines are named as *N*-substituted primary amines. The largest carbon group bonded to the nitrogen is used as the parent amine name. The names of the other groups attached to the nitrogen are appended to the front of the base name, and *N*- or *N,N*- prefixes are used to indicate that these groups are attached to the nitrogen atom rather than to the base carbon chain.

NH—CH₃
④ ③ ②| ①
CH₃—CH₂—CH—CH₃
N-Methyl-2-butanamine

CH₃
| ① ② ③
CH₃—N—CH₂—CH₂—CH₃
N,N-Dimethyl-1-propanamine

CH₃
| ① ② ③
CH₃—CH₂—N—CH₂—CH₂—CH₃
N-Ethyl-*N*-methyl-1-propanamine

CH₃ NH—CH₃
① ②| ③| ④ ⑤
CH₃—CH—CH—CH₂—CH₃
2,*N*-Dimethyl-3-pentanamine

In amines where additional functional groups are present, the amine group is treated as a substituent. ◀ As a substituent, an —NH₂ group is called an *amino* group.

NH₂   O
| ‖
CH₃—CH₂—CH—CH₂—C—OH
3-Aminopentanoic acid

NH₂   O
| ‖
CH₃—CH—CH₂—C—CH₃
4-Amino-2-pentanone

③ ② ①
CH₃—NH—CH₂—CH₂—CH₂—OH
3-(*N*-Methylamino)-1-propanol

The simplest aromatic amine, a benzene ring bearing an amino group, is called *aniline* (Figure 17-2). Other simple aromatic amines are named as derivatives of aniline, with the carbon atom bearing the amino group being carbon 1.

Aniline   *m*-Chloroaniline   2,3-Dichloroaniline

In secondary and tertiary aromatic amines, the additional group or groups attached to the nitrogen atom are located using a capital *N*-. ◀

N-Ethylaniline   *N,N*-Dimethylaniline   3,*N*-Dimethylaniline

▶ *In IUPAC nomenclature, the amino group has a priority just below that of an alcohol. The priority list for functional groups is*

carboxylic acid ↑
aldehyde   Increasing
ketone   priority
alcohol
amine

Figure 17-2 Space-filling model of aniline, the simplest aromatic amine. Aromatic amines, including aniline, are generally toxic; they are readily absorbed through the skin.

▶ *A benzene ring with both an amino group and a methyl group as substituents is called* toluidine. *This name is a combination of the names* toluene *and* aniline.

EXAMPLE 17-2

Determining IUPAC Names for Amines

Assign IUPAC names to each of the following amines.

a. CH₃—CH₂—NH—(CH₂)₄—CH₃

b.
Br—⟨benzene ring⟩—NH₂

c. H₂N—CH₂—CH₂—NH₂

d.

(continued)

▶ *The contrast between IUPAC names and common names for primary, secondary, and tertiary amines is as follows:*

Primary Amines

IUPAC (one word)

alkanamine

Common (one word)

alkylamine

Secondary Amines

IUPAC (one word)

N-alkylalkanamine

Common (one word)

alkylalkylamine

Tertiary Amines

IUPAC (one word)

N-alkyl-N-alkylalkanamine

Common (one word)

alkylalkylalkylamine

Solution

a. The longest carbon chain has five carbons. The name of the compound is N-*ethyl-1-pentanamine.*

b. This compound is named as a derivative of aniline: *4-bromoaniline* (or *p*-bromoaniline). The carbon in the ring to which the —NH_2 is attached is carbon 1.

c. Two —NH_2 groups are present in this molecule. The name is *1,2-ethanediamine.*

d. This is a tertiary amine in which the longest carbon chain has two carbons (ethane). The base name is thus *ethanamine.* Also two methyl groups are attached to the nitrogen atom. The name of the compound is N,N-*dimethylethanamine.* ◀

Section 17-3 Quick Quiz

1. What is the IUPAC name for the compound CH_3—CH_2—CH_2—CH_2—NH_2?
   a. butylamine
   b. aminobutane
   c. 1-butanamine
   d. no correct response

2. What is the IUPAC name for the compound CH_3—CH_2—$\overset{\displaystyle NH—CH_3}{\underset{|}{CH}}$—$CH_3$?
   a. methylaminobutane
   b. N-methylaminobutane
   c. N-methyl-2-butanamine
   d. no correct response

3. What is the IUPAC name for the compound ⬡—NH_2
   a. aminobenzene
   b. benzoamine
   c. aniline
   d. no correct response

4. What is the common name for the compound CH_3—NH—CH_3?
   a. dimethyl amine
   b. dimethylamine
   c. N,N-dimethylamine
   d. no correct response

Answers: 1. c; 2. c; 3. c; 4. b

17-4 ## Isomerism for Amines

LEARNING FOCUS

Be familiar with constitutional isomerism possibilities that exist for amines.

Constitutional isomerism in amines can arise from several causes. Different carbon atom arrangements produce skeletal isomers, as in

$$CH_3—CH_2—CH_2—CH_2—CH_2—NH_2 \quad \text{and} \quad CH_3—CH_2—\underset{\underset{CH_3}{|}}{CH}—CH_2—NH_2$$

1-Pentanamine   2-Methyl-1-butanamine

Different positioning of the nitrogen atom on a carbon chain produces positional isomers, illustrated in the following compounds.

$$\underset{\underset{NH_2}{|}}{CH_2}—CH_2—CH_2—CH_3 \quad \text{and} \quad CH_3—\underset{\underset{NH_2}{|}}{CH}—CH_2—CH_3$$

1-Butanamine   2-Butanamine

For secondary and tertiary amines, different partitioning of carbon atoms among the carbon chains present produces constitutional isomers. There are three C_4 secondary amines; carbon atom partitioning can be two ethyl groups, a propyl group and a methyl group, or an isopropyl group and a methyl group.

$$CH_3-CH_2-NH-CH_2-CH_3 \text{ and } CH_3-CH_2-CH_2-NH-CH_3 \text{ and } CH_3-\underset{\underset{CH_3}{|}}{CH}-NH-CH_3$$

N-Ethylethanamine   *N*-Methyl-1-propanamine   *N*-Methyl-2-propanamine

Section 17-4 Quick Quiz

1. In which of the following pairs of amines are the two members of the pair constitutional isomers?
   a. $CH_3-CH_2-CH_2-NH_2$ and $CH_3-CH_2-NH_2$
   b. $CH_3-\underset{\underset{NH_2}{|}}{CH}-CH_2-CH_3$ and $CH_3-CH_2-\underset{\underset{NH_2}{|}}{CH}-CH_3$
   c. $CH_3-CH_2-CH_2$ and $CH_3-\underset{\underset{NH_2}{|}}{CH}-CH_3$
   d. no correct response
2. In which of the following pairs of amines are the two members of the pair *not* constitutional isomers?
   a. $CH_3-NH-CH_2-CH_2-CH_3$ and $CH_3-CH_2-NH-CH_2-CH_3$
   b. $CH_3-NH-CH_2-CH_2-CH_3$ and $CH_3-CH_2-CH_2-CH_2-NH_2$
   c. $CH_3-CH_2-NH-CH_2-CH_3$ and $CH_3-CH_2-\underset{\underset{CH_3}{|}}{N}-CH_3$
   d. no correct response

Answers: 1. c; 2. d

17-5   Physical Properties of Amines

LEARNING FOCUS

Be familiar with general physical properties for amines and how hydrogen bonding relates to these properties.

The methylamines (mono-, di-, and tri-) and ethylamine are gases at room temperature and have ammonia-like odors. Most other amines are liquids (Figure 17-3), and many have odors resembling that of raw fish. A few amines, particularly diamines, have strong, disagreeable odors. The foul odor arising from dead fish and decaying flesh is due to amines released by the bacterial decomposition of protein. Two of these "odoriferous" compounds are the diamines putrescine and cadaverine.

$$H_2N-(CH_2)_4-NH_2 \qquad H_2N-(CH_2)_5-NH_2$$
Putrescine   Cadaverine
(1,4-butanediamine)   (1,5-pentanediamine)

The simpler amines are irritating to the skin, eyes, and mucous membranes and are toxic by ingestion. Aromatic amines are generally toxic. Many are readily absorbed through the skin and affect both the blood and the nervous system.

The boiling points of amines are intermediate between those of alkanes and alcohols of similar molecular mass. They are higher than alkane boiling points, because primary and secondary amines are capable of intermolecular hydrogen bonding, whereas alkane molecules lack such ability. Such amine intermolecular hydrogen bonding is depicted in Figure 17-4. Tertiary amines have boiling points that are much lower than primary and secondary amines of similar molecular mass; hydrogen bonding is not possible between tertiary amine molecules, as such amines have no hydrogen atoms directly bonded to the nitrogen atom.

Unbranched Primary Amines			
C_1	C_3	C_5	C_7
C_2	C_4	C_6	C_8

☐ Gas   ☐ Liquid

Figure 17-3 A physical-state summary for unbranched primary amines at room temperature and room pressure.

Figure 17-4 Hydrogen bonding interactions among amine molecules involve the hydrogen atoms and nitrogen atoms of amino groups.

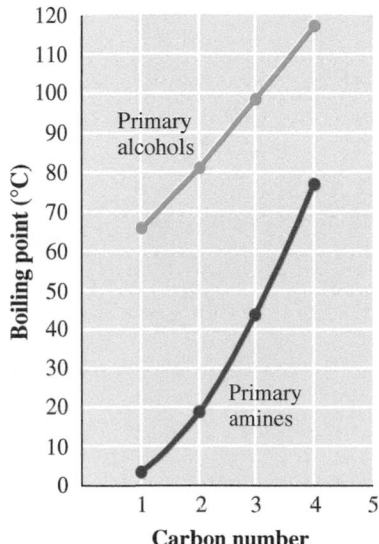

Figure 17-5 A comparison of boiling points of unbranched primary amines and unbranched primary alcohols.

Figure 17-6 Low-molecular-mass amines are soluble in water because of amine–water hydrogen bonding interactions.

The boiling points of amines are lower than those of corresponding alcohols (Figure 17-5), because N···H hydrogen bonds are weaker than O···H hydrogen bonds. [The difference in hydrogen-bond strength results from electronegativity differences; nitrogen is less electronegative than oxygen (Section 5-9).]

Amines with fewer than six carbon atoms are infinitely soluble in water. This solubility results from hydrogen bonding between the amines and water. Even tertiary amines are water soluble, because the amine nitrogen atom has a nonbonding electron pair that can form a hydrogen bond with a hydrogen atom of water (Figure 17-6).

Section 17-5 Quick Quiz

1. Most simple amines have odors that resemble that of
   a. garlic
   b. raw fish
   c. roses
   d. no correct response
2. The boiling points of amines are lower than those of alcohols of similar molecular mass because
   a. amine–amine hydrogen bonding is not possible
   b. amine–alcohol hydrogen bonding is not possible
   c. N···H hydrogen bonds are weaker than O···H hydrogen bonds
   d. no correct response
3. Which of the following types of hydrogen bonds are *not* possible?
   a. 1° amine–1° amine
   b. 2° amine–2° amine
   c. 3° amine–3° amine
   d. no correct response

Answers: 1. b; 2. c; 3. c

17-6 Basicity of Amines

LEARNING FOCUS

Understand why amines exhibit basic properties; be able to name the positive nitrogen-containing ions which result from the basic nature of amines.

Like the nitrogen atom in ammonia, an amine nitrogen atom possesses a lone pair of electrons.

$$H-\ddot{N}-H \quad R-\ddot{N}-H \quad R-\ddot{N}-R \quad R-\ddot{N}-R$$
$$\phantom{H-\ddot{N}-}H H H R$$
Ammonia   1° amine   2° amine   3° amine

This means that amines, like ammonia, are capable of exhibiting Brønsted–Lowry base behavior (Section 10-2); that is, they can function as proton acceptors. Paralleling the behavior of ammonia (Section 10-2), a basic solution is produced when an amine dissolves in water. A proton is transferred from a water molecule to the lone-pair site on the nitrogen atom. The following two equations show the similarities in the behaviors of ammonia and an amine in aqueous solution. ◄

$$\ddot{N}H_3 + HOH \rightleftharpoons NH_4^+ + OH^-$$
Ammonia   Ammonium   Hydroxide
         ion   ion

$$CH_3-\ddot{N}H_2 + HOH \rightleftharpoons CH_3-\overset{+}{N}H_3 + OH^-$$
Methylamine   Methylammonium   Hydroxide
             ion   ion

The result of the interaction of an amine with water is a basic solution containing substituted ammonium ions and hydroxide ions. ◄ A **substituted ammonium ion** *is an ammonium ion in which one or more alkyl, cycloalkyl, or aryl groups have been substituted for hydrogen atoms.*

Two important generalizations apply to substituted ammonium ions.

1. *Substituted ammonium ions are charged species rather than neutral molecules.*
2. *The nitrogen atom in an ammonium ion or a substituted ammonium ion participates in four bonds.* In a neutral compound, nitrogen atoms form only three bonds. Four bonds about a nitrogen atom are possible, however, when the species is a positive ion because the fourth bond is a coordinate covalent bond (Section 5-5). ◄

Naming the positive ion that results from the interaction of an amine with water is based on the following two rules:

Rule 1: *For alkylamines, the ending of the name of the amine is changed from* amine *to* ammonium ion.

$$CH_3-CH_2-NH_2 \xrightarrow{H_2O} CH_3-CH_2-\overset{+}{N}H_3 + OH^-$$
Ethylamine   Ethylammonium ion

$$CH_3-\underset{\underset{CH_3}{|}}{N}-CH_2-CH_3 \xrightarrow{H_2O} CH_3-\underset{\underset{CH_3}{|}}{\overset{+}{N}H}-CH_2-CH_3 + OH^-$$
Ethyldimethylamine   Ethyldimethylammonium ion

Rule 2: *For aromatic amines, the final -e in the name* aniline *is replaced by* -ium ion.

Aniline   Anilinium ion   N-methylanilinium ion

▶ *The lone pair of electrons present on an amine nitrogen atom is generally not shown when drawing structural formulas for amines. However, in acid–base considerations, the presence of this lone pair of electrons is of vital importance.*

▶ *Amines, like ammonia, have a pair of unshared electrons on the nitrogen atom present. These unshared electrons can accept a hydrogen ion from water. Thus both amines and ammonia produce basic aqueous solutions.*

▶ *Substituted ammonium ions always contain one more hydrogen atom than their "parent" amine. They also always carry a 1+ charge, whereas the "parent" amine is a neutral molecule.*

EXAMPLE 17-3

Determining Names for Substituted Ammonium and Substituted Anilinium Ions

Name the following substituted ammonium or substituted anilinium ions.

a. $CH_3-CH_2-\overset{+}{N}H_2-CH_2-CH_3$

b. $CH_3-\underset{\underset{CH_3}{|}}{CH}-CH_2-\overset{+}{N}H_3$

c. $CH_3-\underset{\underset{CH_3}{|}}{\overset{+}{N}H}-CH_3$

d. $CH_3-\overset{+}{N}H-CH_3$ (attached to benzene ring)

(continued)

Solution

a. The parent amine is diethylamine. Replacing the word *amine* in the parent name with *ammonium ion* generates the name of the ion, *diethylammonium ion.*

b. The parent amine is isobutylamine. The name of the ion is *isobutylammonium ion.*

c. The parent amine is trimethylamine. The name of the ion is *trimethylammonium ion.*

d. The parent name is *N,N*-dimethylaniline. Replacing the word *aniline* in the parent name with *anilinium ion* generates the name of the ion, *N,N-dimethylanilinium ion.*

Amines are stronger proton acceptors than oxygen-containing organic compounds such as alcohols and ethers; that is, they are stronger bases than these compounds. A 0.1 M aqueous solution of methylamine has a pH of 11.8, and a 0.1 M aqueous solution of aniline has a pH of 8.6. These solutions are sufficiently basic to turn red litmus paper blue (Section 10-1). Carboxylic acid salts (Section 16-8) are the only other type of organic compound sufficiently basic to turn red litmus paper blue. ◄

▶ *Amines are very weak bases when compared to strong inorganic bases like NaOH and KOH.*

Section 17-6 Quick Quiz

1. The basic properties of amines are related to
   a. the presence of a hydroxyl group on the nitrogen atom
   b. the presence of an unshared pair of electrons on the nitrogen atom
   c. the ability of the nitrogen atom to lose hydrogen atoms
   d. no correct response
2. Which of the following statements concerning substituted ammonium ions is *incorrect*?
   a. The nitrogen atom forms four bonds.
   b. The ion contains one less hydrogen atom than the "parent" amine.
   c. The ionic charge is 1+.
   d. no correct response
3. The IUPAC name for the ion $CH_3-CH_2-\overset{+}{N}H_3$ is
   a. ethylamine ion
   b. ethylammonium ion
   c. ethylanilium ion
   d. no correct response

Answers: 1. b; 2. b; 3. b

17-7 Reaction of Amines with Acids

LEARNING FOCUS

Be able to write chemical equations for the production of amine salts; be familiar with IUPAC nomenclature for amine salts.

The reaction of an acid with a base (neutralization) produces a salt (Section 10-7). Because amines are bases (Section 17-6), their reaction with an acid—either inorganic or carboxylic—produces a salt, an amine salt. In such a reaction, the proton (H^+) from the acid becomes bonded to the nitrogen atom of the amine by using the lone pair of electrons present on the nitrogen atom. In an amine–acid reaction, the amine always gains a hydrogen ion (proton acceptor), and the acid always loses a hydrogen ion (proton donor). ◄

▶ *An amine is neutral. When it accepts an H^+ from an acid, it becomes an ion with a 1+ charge (the charge coming from the hydrogen ion); a substituted ammonium ion is formed.*

$$CH_3-\overset{..}{N}H_2 + \overset{}{H}-Cl \longrightarrow CH_3-\overset{+}{N}H_3\ Cl^-$$

Amine   Acid   Amine salt

Aromatic amines react with acids in a similar manner.

An **amine salt** *is an ionic compound in which the positive ion is a mono-, di-, or trisubstituted ammonium ion* (RNH_3^+, $R_2NH_2^+$, *or* R_3NH^+) *and the negative ion comes from an acid.* Amine salts can be obtained in crystalline form (odorless, white crystals) by evaporating the water from the acidic solutions in which amine salts are prepared.

Amine salts are named using standard nomenclature procedures for ionic compounds (Section 4-9). The name of the positive ion, the substituted ammonium or anilinium ion, is given first and is followed by a separate word for the name of the negative ion.

$$CH_3-CH_2-\overset{+}{N}H_3\ Cl^- \qquad CH_3-\overset{+}{N}H_2-CH_3\ Br^-$$
Ethylammonium chloride   Dimethylammonium bromide

An older naming system for amine salts, still used in the pharmaceutical industry, treats amine salts as amine–acid complexes rather than as ionic compounds. In this system, the amine salt made from dimethylamine and hydrochloric acid is named and represented as

$$\underset{\substack{|\\CH_3}}{CH_3-NH}\cdot HCl \qquad \text{rather than as} \qquad \underset{\substack{|\\CH_3}}{CH_3-\overset{+}{N}H_2}\ Cl^-$$
Dimethylamine hydrochloride   Dimethylammonium chloride

Many medication labels refer to hydrochlorides or hydrogen sulfates (from sulfuric acid), indicating that the medications are in a water-soluble ionic (salt) form.

Many higher-molecular-mass amines are water insoluble; however, virtually all amine salts are water soluble. Thus amine salt formation, like carboxylic acid salt formation (Section 16-8), provides a means for converting water-insoluble compounds into water-soluble compounds. Many drugs that contain amine functional groups are administered to patients in the form of amine salts because of their increased solubility in water in this form. ◄

Many people unknowingly use acids to form amine salts when they put vinegar or lemon juice on fish. Such action converts amines in fish (often smelly compounds) to salts, which are odorless.

The process of forming amine salts with acids is an easily reversed process. Treating an amine salt with a strong base such as NaOH regenerates the "parent" amine.

$$CH_3-\overset{+}{N}H_3\ Cl^- + NaOH \longrightarrow CH_3-NH_2 + NaCl + H_2O$$
Amine salt   Base   Amine

The "opposite nature" of the processes of amine salt formation from an amine and the regeneration of the amine from its amine salt can be diagrammed as follows:

An amine gains a hydrogen ion to produce an amine salt when treated with an acid (a protonation reaction), and an amine salt loses a hydrogen ion to produce an amine when treated with a base (a deprotonation reaction).

▶ *Several physiologically active amines are dispensed to consumers in the form of amine salts. An example is phenylephrine hydrochloride, the decongestant present in Sudafed SE, Theraflu, and DayQuil. The structure of this amine salt is*

$$\text{HO}\underset{}{\overset{}{\bigcirc}}\begin{matrix}OH\\|\\CH\end{matrix}-CH_2-\overset{+}{N}H_2-CH_3\ Cl^-$$

EXAMPLE 17-4

Writing Chemical Equations for Reactions That Involve Amine Salts

Write the structures of the products that form when each of the following reactions involving amines or amine salts takes place.

a. $CH_3-NH-CH_3 + HCl \longrightarrow$

b.

     [benzene ring]—NH—CH₃   + H₂SO₄ ⟶

c. $CH_3-\overset{+}{N}H_2-CH_3\ Cl^- + NaOH \longrightarrow$

(continued)

Solution

a. The reactants are an amine and a strong acid. Their interaction produces an amine salt.

$$CH_3-NH-CH_3 + HCl \longrightarrow CH_3-\overset{+}{N}H_2-CH_3 \ Cl^-$$

Note that the H^+ ion from the acid always bonds to the amine nitrogen atom at the location where the lone pair of electrons is found.

b. Again, the reaction is that of an amine with a strong acid. A hydrogen ion is transferred from the acid to the amine.

$$\text{(ring)}-NH-CH_3 + H_2SO_4 \longrightarrow \text{(ring)}-\overset{+}{N}H_2-CH_3 \ HSO_4^-$$

c. The reactants are an amine salt and a strong base. Their interaction regenerates the "parent" amine.

$$CH_3-\overset{+}{N}H_2-CH_3 \ Cl^- + NaOH \longrightarrow CH_3-NH-CH_3 + NaCl + H_2O$$

▶ *The cocaine molecule is both an amine and an ester; one amine and two ester functional groups are present. As an illegal street drug, cocaine is consumed as a water-soluble amine salt and in a water-insoluble, free-base form (nonsalt form—freed of the base required to make the salt). Cocaine hydrochloride, the amine salt, is a white powder that is snorted or injected intravenously. Free-base cocaine is heated and its vapors are inhaled. Cocaine users and dealers call the water-insoluble form of the drug "crack." "Snow" and "coke" are street names for the water-soluble form of the drug.*

Cocaine
(an amine)

Cocaine hydrochloride
(an amine salt)

Because amines and their salts are so easily interconverted, the amine itself is often designated as the *free amine* or *free base* or as the *deprotonated form* of the amine, to distinguish it from the *protonated form* of the amine, which is present in the amine salt. ◀

$$CH_3-NH_2 \qquad\qquad CH_3-\overset{+}{N}H_3 \ Cl^-$$

Deprotonated form   Protonated form
(free amine or free base)

Whether an amine in solution exists in its deprotonated form or its protonated form is dependent on the pH of the solution. An aqueous solution of a simple amine has a pH of about 12 and at this pH the amine is almost entirely (99%) present in its deprotonated form. In biochemical solutions such as body fluids, which are buffered solutions with a pH near 7, amines exist predominantly in protonated form.

Section 17-7 Quick Quiz

1. The amine salt produced from the reaction of ethyl amine with HCl has the structural formula
   a. $CH_3-CH_2-\overset{+}{N}H_2 \ Cl^-$
   b. $CH_3-CH_2-\overset{+}{N}H_3 \ Cl^-$
   c. $NH_4^+ \ CH_3-CH_2-Cl^-$
   d. no correct response
2. Which of the following statements characterizes amine salt solubilities in water?
   a. more soluble than parent amine
   b. less soluble than the parent amine
   c. insoluble in water
   d. no correct response
3. The regeneration of an amine from its amine salt is
   a. easily accomplished by adding a strong base
   b. easily accomplished by adding a strong acid
   c. very difficult to accomplish
   d. no correct response

Answers: 1. b; 2. a; 3. a

17-8 Alkylation of Ammonia and Amines

LEARNING FOCUS

Be able to write chemical equations for the reaction of ammonia or amines with alkyl halides.

Several methods exist for preparing amines, one of which is *alkylation* in the presence of base. An **alkylation reaction** *is a chemical reaction in which an alkyl group is transferred from one molecule to another molecule.* In preparing amines, the alkylating agent is an alkyl halide (Section 12-18). General equations for the alkylation process, as it pertains to amines, are

$$\text{Ammonia} + \text{alkyl halide} \xrightarrow{\text{Base}} 1° \text{ amine}$$

$$1° \text{ Amine} + \text{alkyl halide} \xrightarrow{\text{Base}} 2° \text{ amine}$$

$$2° \text{ Amine} + \text{alkyl halide} \xrightarrow{\text{Base}} 3° \text{ amine}$$

$$3° \text{ Amine} + \text{alkyl halide} \xrightarrow{\text{Base}} \text{quaternary ammonium salt}$$

Alkylation under basic conditions is actually a two-step process. In the first step, using a primary amine preparation as an example, an amine salt is produced.

$$NH_3 + R\text{—}X \longrightarrow R\text{—}\overset{+}{N}H_3 \, X^-$$

The second step, which involves the base present (NaOH), converts the amine salt to free amine.

$$R\text{—}\overset{+}{N}H_3 \, X^- + NaOH \longrightarrow RNH_2 + NaX + H_2O$$

A specific example of the production of a primary amine from ammonia is the reaction of ethyl bromide with ammonia to produce ethylamine. The chemical equation (with both steps combined) is

$$\underset{\text{Ammonia}}{NH_3} + \underset{\text{Alkyl halide}}{CH_3\text{—}CH_2\text{—}Br} + \underset{\text{Base}}{NaOH} \longrightarrow \underset{\text{Primary amine}}{CH_3\text{—}CH_2\text{—}NH_2} + NaBr + H_2O$$

If the newly formed primary amine produced in an ammonia alkylation reaction is not quickly removed from the reaction mixture, the nitrogen atom of the amine may react with further alkyl halide molecules, giving, in succession, secondary and tertiary amines.

$$NH_3 \xrightarrow[\text{OH}^-]{RX} \underset{\substack{\text{Primary} \\ \text{amine}}}{RNH_2} \xrightarrow[\text{OH}^-]{RX} \underset{\substack{\text{Secondary} \\ \text{amine}}}{R_2NH} \xrightarrow[\text{OH}^-]{RX} \underset{\substack{\text{Tertiary} \\ \text{amine}}}{R_3N}$$

Examples of the production of a 2° amine and a 3° amine via alkylation are

$$\underset{\text{Primary amine}}{CH_3\text{—}CH_2\text{—}NH_2} + \underset{\text{Alkyl halide}}{CH_3\text{—}Br} + \underset{\text{Base}}{NaOH} \longrightarrow \underset{\text{Secondary amine}}{CH_3\text{—}CH_2\text{—}NH\text{—}CH_3} + NaBr + H_2O$$

$$\underset{\text{Secondary amine}}{CH_3\text{—}CH_2\text{—}NH\text{—}CH_3} + \underset{\text{Alkyl halide}}{CH_3\text{—}Br} + \underset{\text{Base}}{NaOH} \longrightarrow \underset{\substack{\text{Tertiary amine}}}{CH_3\text{—}CH_2\text{—}\underset{\underset{CH_3}{|}}{N}\text{—}CH_3} + NaBr + H_2O$$

Tertiary amines react with alkyl halides in the presence of a strong base to produce a quaternary ammonium salt. **A quaternary ammonium salt** *is an ammonium salt in which all four groups attached to the nitrogen atom of the ammonium ion are hydrocarbon groups.*

$$\underset{\underset{R}{|}}{R\text{—}N\text{—}R} + R\text{—}X \xrightarrow{\text{OH}^-} \underset{\underset{R}{|}}{R\text{—}\overset{\overset{R}{|}}{\underset{}{N^+}}\text{—}R} \, X^-$$

Figure 17-7 Space-filling models showing that the ammonium ion (NH_4^+) has a tetrahedral structure, as does the quaternary ammonium ion, in which four methyl groups are present [$(CH_3)_4N^+$].

Quaternary ammonium salts differ from amine salts in that the addition of a strong base does not convert quaternary ammonium salts back to their "parent" amines; there is no hydrogen atom on the nitrogen with which the OH^- can react. Quaternary ammonium salts are colorless, odorless, crystalline solids that have high melting points and are usually water soluble.

Quaternary ammonium salts are named in the same way as amine salts (Section 17-7), taking into account that four organic groups are attached to the nitrogen atom rather than a lesser number of groups. Figure 17-7 contrasts the structures of an ammonium ion and a tetramethyl ammonium ion.

Compounds that contain quaternary ammonium ions are important in biochemical systems. Choline and acetylcholine are two important quaternary ammonium ions present in the human body. Choline has important roles in both fat transport and growth regulation. Acetylcholine is involved in the transmission of nerve impulses.

$$CH_3-\overset{\overset{\displaystyle CH_3}{|}}{\underset{\underset{\displaystyle CH_3}{|}}{N^+}}-CH_2-CH_2-OH \qquad\qquad CH_3-\overset{\overset{\displaystyle CH_3}{|}}{\underset{\underset{\displaystyle CH_3}{|}}{N^+}}-CH_2-CH_2-O-\overset{\overset{\displaystyle O}{\|}}{C}-CH_3$$

Choline   Acetylcholine

Section 17-8 Quick Quiz

1. In an alkylation reaction what type of compound is the source of the alkyl group that is transferred from one molecule to another?
   a. branched alkane
   b. alkyl halide
   c. amine
   d. no correct response
2. Alkylation of a secondary amine, under basic conditions, will produce
   a. a tertiary amine
   b. a secondary amine
   c. an amine salt
   d. no correct response
3. Which of the following sets of reactants can be used to produce a quaternary ammonium salt?
   a. 1° amine and HCl
   b. 3° amine and alkyl halide
   c. amine salt and NaOH
   d. no correct response
4. How many R groups are attached to the N atom in a quaternary ammonium ion?
   a. two
   b. three
   c. four
   d. no correct response

Answers: 1. b; 2. a; 3. b; 4. c

17-9 Heterocyclic Amines

LEARNING FOCUS
Know the structural characteristics associated with unsubstituted heterocyclic amine systems.

A **heterocyclic amine** *is an organic compound in which nitrogen atoms of amine groups are part of either an aromatic or a nonaromatic ring system.* Heterocyclic amines are the most common type of heterocyclic organic compound (Section 14-19).

PYRROLIDINE	PYRROLE	IMIDAZOLE	INDOLE
PYRIDINE	PYRIMIDINE	QUINOLINE	PURINE

Figure 17-8 Structural formulas for selected heterocyclic amines that serve as "parent" molecules for more complex amine derivatives.

Figure 17-8 gives structures for a number of "key" unsubstituted heterocyclic amines. These compounds are the "parent" compounds for numerous derivatives that are important in medicinal, agricultural, food, and industrial chemistry, as well as in the functioning of the human body. ◀

Study of the heterocyclic amine structures in Figure 17-8 shows that (1) ring systems may be saturated, unsaturated, or aromatic, (2) more than one nitrogen atom may be present in a given ring, and (3) fused ring systems often occur.

The two most widely used central nervous system stimulants in the United States, caffeine and nicotine, have "core" structures based on ring systems found in Figure 17-8. Caffeine's structure is based on a purine ring system. Nicotine's structure contains one pyridine ring and one pyrrolidine ring.

▶ *Heterocyclic amines often have strong odors, some agreeable and others disagreeable. The "pleasant" aroma of many heat-treated foods is caused by heterocyclic amines formed during the heat treatment. The compounds responsible for the pervasive odors of popped popcorn and hot roasted peanuts are heterocyclic amines.*

Methyl-2-pyridyl ketone (odor of popcorn)

2-Methoxy-5-methylpyrazine (odor of peanuts)

Caffeine

Nicotine

The focus on relevancy feature Chemical Connections 17-A—Caffeine: The Most Widely Used Central Nervous System Stimulant—considers the biochemical effects and mode of action of caffeine in the human body, and the focus on relevancy feature Chemical Connections 17-B—Nicotine Addiction: A Widespread Example of Drug Dependence—details the biochemical effects of nicotine and the effect that pH change has on the action of this molecule.

A large cyclic structure built on four pyrrole rings (Figure 17-8), called a porphyrin, is important in the chemistry of living organisms. Porphyrins form metal ion complexes in which the metal ion is located in the middle of the large ring structure. *Heme,* an iron–porphyrin complex present in the hemoglobin found in blood, is responsible for oxygen transport in the human body.

Porphyrin ring

Heme, a component of hemoglobin

Caffeine: The Most Widely Used Central Nervous System Stimulant

Caffeine, which is naturally present in coffee beans and tea leaves and is added to many soft drinks, is both the most widely used and the most frequently used central nervous system (CNS) stimulant in human society. Its mild temporary stimulant effects are often described as an increased feeling of alertness and/or a decreased feeling of drowsiness.

Studies indicate that 82% of the adult U.S. population drink coffee and 52% drink tea. More than one-half of the coffee drinkers consume three or more cups daily. In the soft drink market, the use of caffeine has now spread beyond cola drinks to fruit-flavored drinks.

Caffeine belongs to a family of compounds called *xanthines*. Its formal chemical name is 1,3,7-trimethylxanthine, and its structure is

Caffeine
(1,3,7-trimethylxanthine)

Xanthine

Besides its CNS system effects, caffeine also increases basal metabolic rate, increases heart rate by stimulating heart muscles, promotes secretion of stomach acid, functions as a bronchial tube dilator, and increases urine production because of its diuretic properties. The overall effect that most individuals experience from caffeine consumption is interpreted as a "lift."

Used in small quantities, caffeine's effects are temporary; hence it must be consumed on a regular basis throughout the day. Its half-life in the body is 3.0–7.5 hours. Caffeine tolerance develops in regular users of the substance. Over time, larger amounts of caffeine are needed in order for an individual to achieve his or her "lift."

Caffeine is mildly addicting. Most people who ordinarily consume substantial amounts of caffeine-containing beverages or drugs experience withdrawal symptoms if caffeine is eliminated. Such symptoms may include headache and depression for a period of several days. As a result of caffeine dependence, many people need a cup of coffee before they feel good each morning.

In large quantities, caffeine has been shown to cause significant undesirable effects including anxiety, sleeplessness, headaches, and dehydration. The latter occurs because of caffeine's diuretic effects.

Several studies indicate that caffeine has an effect on the childbearing abilities of women. One study indicates a decreased rate of conception for women who consume more than three cups of coffee daily. Another study indicates that the consumption of this amount of caffeine increases the risk of miscarriage by 30% compared to women who do not drink coffee. Lactating mothers probably should limit

Caffeine is naturally present in coffee beans. Over 60 species of plants and trees cultivated by humans contain caffeine.

© VladislavGudovskiy/Shutterstock.com

their caffeine intake because it appears in breast milk, thus affecting newborn babies.

Current scientific thought holds that caffeine's mode of action in the body is exerted through a chemical substance called cyclic adenosine monophosphate (cyclic AMP). Caffeine inhibits an enzyme that ordinarily breaks down cyclic AMP to its inactive end product. The resulting increase in cyclic AMP leads to increased glucose production within cells and thus makes available more energy to allow higher rates of cellular activity.

Coffee is the major source of caffeine for most Americans. However, substantial amounts of caffeine may be consumed in energy drinks, soft drinks, tea, and numerous nonprescription medications including combination pain relievers (Anacin, Midol), cold remedies (Dristan), and antisleep agents (NO-DOZ, Vivarin).

The recommended daily limit of caffeine for a healthy adult is 400 mg, for a pregnant women 200 mg, and for a 10-year-old child 75 mg. The following table, which lists caffeine content of selected beverages, is useful in putting these daily limits in perspective.

Caffeine Content, in Milligrams, of Various Beverages
330 - Grande (16 oz) cup of Starbucks coffee
215 - 2-oz shot of 5-hour Energy drink
133 - 8-oz cup of brewed coffee
92 - 8-oz can of Monster Energy drink
90 - 20-oz bottle of Mountain Dew
83 - 8-oz can of Red Bull Energy drink
58 - 20-oz bottle of Coca-Cola
55 - 8-oz cup of brewed black tea
5 - 8-oz cup of coffee (decaf)

Nicotine Addiction: A Widespread Example of Drug Dependence

Next to caffeine, the heterocyclic amine nicotine is the most widely used central nervous system stimulant in our society. It is obtained primarily from the tobacco plant, where it constitutes 0.3% to 0.5% by dry mass of the plant. Biosynthesis of nicotine occurs in the roots of the plant and it then is translocated to the leaves, where it accumulates. In the pure state, in its free-base form, nicotine is an oily liquid that is miscible with water. It readily reacts with acids to form salts that are usually solids and water soluble, behavior associated with the amine nature of this substance (Section 17-7).

Structurally, nicotine contains both a pyrrolidine and a pyridine ring system (see Figure 17-8); these rings are connected through a carbon–carbon bond rather than fused. Two amine functional groups are present in a nicotine molecule.

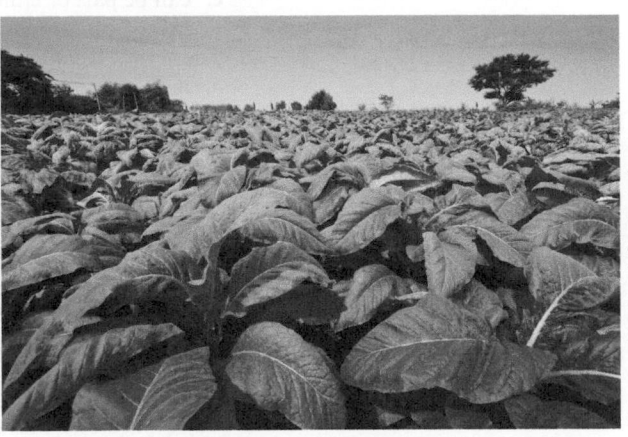

Nicotine is formed in the roots of tobacco plants and then translocates to the leaves, where it accumulates.

Nicotine

Cigarettes contain 8 to 20 milligrams of nicotine (depending on the brand), but only approximately 1 mg is actually absorbed by the body when a cigarette is smoked. This absorbed nicotine is responsible for the addictive process that develops with continued cigarette smoking. In its free-base form, nicotine will burn and its vapors will combust at 95°C in air. Thus, most of the nicotine is burned when a cigarette is smoked; however, enough is inhaled to provide the desired stimulatory effects.

Two biochemical effects of nicotine are

1. Nicotine acts on acetylcholine receptors, increasing their activity. This leads to an increased flow of adrenaline (Section 17-10), which in turn causes an increase in heart rate, blood pressure, and respiration rate, as well as higher blood-glucose levels.
2. Nicotine increases the release of the brain neurotransmitter dopamine (Section 17-10), which makes a person feel "good." Getting the dopamine boost is part of the addiction process.

Inhaled nicotine is rapidly distributed throughout the body. On average, it takes 7 seconds for nicotine to reach the brain once it is inhaled. The overall stimulatory effect of nicotine is, however, rather transient. After an initial response, depression follows. The half-life of nicotine in the body is between 1 and 2 hours.

Nicotine induces both physiological and psychological dependence. Withdrawal from nicotine is accompanied by headache, stomach pain, irritability, and insomnia. Full withdrawal can take six months or longer.

In large doses, nicotine is a potent poison. Nicotine poisoning causes vomiting, diarrhea, nausea, and abdominal pain. Death occurs from respiratory paralysis. The lethal dose of the drug is considered to be approximately 60 mg, a level that is never reached with cigarette smoking.

Nicotine can influence the action of prescription drugs that the smoker is taking concurrently. For example, propoxyphene (Darvon) can lose its painkilling effect in a smoker, and tranquilizers such as diazepam (Valium) exert a diminished effect on the central nervous system.

The carcinogenic effects associated with cigarette smoking are caused not by nicotine but by other substances present in tobacco smoke, including fused-ring aromatic hydrocarbons (Section 13-16).

There are actually three forms for a nicotine molecule, with the form adopted determined by the pH of the molecule's environment. At a low pH (less than 3.0) nicotine exists in a diprotonated form; at pH values between 3.0 and 8.0 it is monoprotonated; and at higher pH values it is in a nonprotonated (free-base) form (see Section 17-7).

Diprotonated form Monoprotonated form Nonprotonated form (free-base form)

Note that the protonation sites in the molecules are the nitrogen atoms of the amine functional groups (Section 17-7). The nonprotonated (free-base) form of nicotine is very volatile and evaporates (as well as combusts) at the temperatures associated with a burning cigarette.

Cigarette manufacturers purposely add ammonia to tobacco leaves to raise the pH and make the free-base form more available to the smoker. Such pH adjustment also occurs for smokeless tobacco products. Products of lower pH are marketed for new users, and higher pH products—which supply more nicotine to the user—are available for "experienced" users.

17-10 Selected Biochemically Important Amines

LEARNING FOCUS

Be familiar with common heterocyclic amines that have the following functions in the human body: (1) neurotransmitter, (2) central nervous system stimulant, and (3) decongestant.

Amines that contain no other functional groups than the amino group are often toxic substances and generally are not prevalent in biological systems. On the other hand, many amines that contain additional functional groups besides the amino group are physiologically active compounds that affect the functioning of the human body. Some are naturally present biosynthesized compounds, others are substances isolated from plants, and still others are laboratory-synthesized products that find use in both prescription and nonprescription drugs. In this section, amines that exert the following types of effects are considered: (1) neurotransmitters, (2) central nervous system stimulants, and (3) decongestants.

Two commonly encountered "core" structures for polyfunctional amines with physiological effects are the phenethylamine core and the tryptamine core. These two core structures, both of which are encountered in compounds discussed in this section are:

Phenethylamine core: [benzene ring]—CH_2—CH_2—NH_2

Tryptamine core: [indole ring]—CH_2—CH_2—NH_2

These two structures differ in the ring structure present [benzene versus indole (Figure 17-8)] and are similar in that an ethylamine group is attached to the ring structure.

Neurotransmitters

Neurotransmitters are substances present in the human body that assist in passing nerve impulses from one cell to another. Key neurotransmitters in the human body are acetylcholine (a quaternary ammonium salt, Section 17-8) and the amines dopamine, norepinephrine, and serotonin. ◀

▶ *The names of the amine neurotransmitters are pronounced DOPE-a-mean, nor-ep-in-NEFF-rin, and SER-oh-tone-in.*

Dopamine and norepinephrine are both phenethylamine derivatives whose biosynthesis depends on the presence of tyrosine, an amino acid (Section 20-2) present in proteins such as meats, nuts, and eggs.

HO—[benzene ring]—CH_2—CH($COOH$)—NH_2 ⟶ HO—[benzene ring with HO]—CH_2—CH_2—NH_2 ⟶ HO—[benzene ring with HO]—CH(OH)—CH_2—NH_2

Tyrosine   Dopamine   Norepinephrine

Note that the structures of dopamine and norepinephrine differ only by a hydroxy group; norepinephrine is a hydroxydopamine.

Dopamine is found in the brain. A deficiency of this neurotransmitter results in Parkinson's disease, a degenerative neurological disease. Administration of dopamine to a patient does not relieve the symptoms of this disease because dopamine in the blood cannot cross the blood–brain barrier. The drug L-dopa, which can pass through the blood–brain barrier, does give relief from Parkinson's disease. Inside brain cells, enzymes catalyze the conversion of L-dopa to dopamine.

L-Dopa $\longrightarrow$ Dopamine

Norepinephrine is also needed at appropriate levels by a properly functioning brain. Higher than normal levels of this neurotransmitter cause a person to feel elated; however, extremely high levels can cause manic behavior.

Besides functioning as a neurotransmitter, norepinephrine can also function as a central nervous system stimulant. Norepinephrine produced by the adrenal glands exhibits this stimulant function. The normal mode of action for adrenal norepinephrine is to constrict (narrow) blood vessels, which increases blood pressure, and also to increase blood-glucose levels. Administered as a drug, norepinephrine is used to treat life-threatening low blood pressure that occurs when a person goes into septic shock caused by severe infection. It is also often used during CPR (cardiopulmonary resuscitation) procedures by medical personnel. ◄ Normally, norepinephrine chemistry is, however, associated with maintaining normal body chemistry rather than treating emergency conditions.

Serotonin, naturally present in the brain, has a structure based on a tryptamine core rather than a phenethylamine core. It is involved in sleep, sensory perception, and the regulation of body temperature. Serotonin deficiency has been implicated in mental illness. Treatment of mental depression can involve the use of drugs that help maintain serotonin at normals levels by preventing its breakdown in the brain.

Biosynthesis of serotonin depends on the presence of tryptophan, an amino acid (Section 20-2) found in proteins. Turkey meat contains higher levels of tryptophan than most proteins; hence a Thanksgiving dinner is often followed by a case of drowsiness.

Tryptophan $\longrightarrow$ Serotonin

Recent research shows that serotonin also regulates lactation in women. Such serotonin is produced in the mammary glands rather than in the brain. At this location, it controls milk production and secretion. The concentration of serotonin builds up in mammary glands as they fill with milk. The increase in serotonin inhibits further milk synthesis and secretion by suppressing the expression of milk protein genes. After nursing, the cycle of milk and serotonin production begins again. ◄

Central Nervous System Stimulants

Epinephrine, also known as adrenaline, is the most well-known central nervous system stimulant found in the human body. It is produced by the adrenal glands from norepinephrine.

Norepinephrine $\longrightarrow$ Epinephrine (adrenaline)

► *Shock is a medical condition that can be caused by trauma, heatstroke, blood loss, an allergic reaction, severe infection, poisoning, and severe burns. The organs of a person in shock are not getting enough blood and/or oxygen, which, if left untreated, can lead to permanent organ damage or death.*

► *Fluoxetine (brand name: Prozac), the most widely prescribed drug for mental depression, inhibits the reuptake of serotonin, thus maintaining serotonin levels. Chemically, Prozac is a derivative of methyl propyl amine with three fluorine atoms present in the structure. The element fluorine is rarely encountered in biochemical molecules.*

$F_3C\text{---}\langle\rangle\text{---}O\text{---}CH\text{---}(CH_2)_2\text{---}NH\text{---}CH_3$

Note from these structures that epinephrine and norepinephrine differ in structure only in that the former has a methyl group substituent present on the nitrogen atom. ◄

Pain, excitement, and fear trigger the release of large amounts of epinephrine into the bloodstream. The effect is increased blood-glucose levels, which in turn increase blood pressure, rate and force of heart contraction, and muscular strength. These changes cause the body to function at a "higher" level. Epinephrine is often called the "fight or flight" hormone.

The use of epinephrine as a drug is often the immediate treatment for anaphylactic shock resulting from a severe allergic reaction to a bee sting, a drug, or even peanuts. People known to be susceptible to such allergic events often carry a dose of epinephrine for emergency use (Figure 17-9).

Amphetamine and methamphetamine, both of which have phenethylamine derivative structures, are powerful *synthetic* central nervous system stimulants. ◄

Amphetamine, under the trade name Adderall, is approved by the U.S. Food and Drug Administration (FDA) for treatment of ADHD (Attention Deficit Hyperactivity Disorder). It increases alertness, concentration, and overall cognitive performance while decreasing fatigue. Methamphetamine is also approved by the FDA for treatment of ADHD under the trade name Desoxyn.

Both amphetamine and methamphetamine have a high potential for abuse and addiction. In the illegal drug market, methamphetamine is colloquially referred to simply as "meth." Pharmacologically, the physiological reward system accompanying the use of these synthetic central nervous system stimulants results from increased levels of serotonin, dopamine, and norepinephrine in the brain. These stimulants were once approved as appetite suppressants to help with weight control, but such use is now strongly discouraged.

Figure 17-9 Individuals at known risk for anaphylactic shock caused by an allergen often carry with them at all times an epinephrine autoinjection pen.

Decongestants

Pseudoephedrine and phenylephrine are synthetic phenethylamine derivatives used as decongestants in several over-the-counter medications.

Pseudoephedrine is the decongestant present in the formulation marketed under the brand name *Sudafed.* Although still available for purchase without a prescription, Sudafed and other products containing this decongestant must now be kept behind the counter in a pharmacy so that their sale can be monitored. The reason for this recent change is that individuals within the illegal "meth" culture have discovered that pseudoephedrine can be easily converted to methamphetamine ("meth"). The structures of the two compounds differ only by a hydroxyl group.

On grocery-store shelves, *Sudafed PE* has now replaced *Sudafed.* This new reformulated Sudafed product contains the decongestant phenylephrine rather than pseudoephedrine. The addition of an —OH group (on the benzene ring) and the removal of a methyl group (from the carbon chain) is a sufficient structural change to prevent this compound from being converted to methamphetamine.

1. Which of the following physiologically active amines has a structure based on a tryptamine core?
   a. serotonin
   b. dopamine
   c. norepinephrine
   d. no correct response
2. Which of the following physiologically active amines functions as both a neurotransmitter and a central nervous system stimulant?
   a. serotonin
   b. dopamine
   c. norepinephrine
   d. no correct response
3. Which of the following physiologically active amines also goes by the name adrenaline
   a. epinephrine
   b. norepinephrine
   c. amphetamine
   d. no correct response
4. Structurally, norepinephrine and epinephrine differ by a
   a. methyl group
   b. hydroxyl group
   c. phenyl group
   d. no correct response

Answers: 1. a; 2. c; 3. a; 4. a

17-11 Alkaloids

LEARNING FOCUS

Know the meaning of the term alkaloid and be familiar with common alkaloids that are currently used in the medical field.

People in various parts of the world have known for centuries that physiological effects can be obtained by eating or chewing the leaves, roots, or bark of certain plants. More than 5000 different compounds that are physiologically active have been isolated from such plants. Nearly all of these compounds, which are collectively called alkaloids, contain amine functional groups. ◀ An **alkaloid** *is a nitrogen-containing organic compound extracted from plant material.*

Three well-known substances previously considered in this chapter are alkaloids, although they were not called such at the time they were discussed. They are nicotine (obtained from the tobacco plant), caffeine (obtained from coffee beans and tea leaves), and cocaine (obtained from the coca plant). The active ingredient in chocolate, a substance called theobromine, is also an alkaloid that comes from beans. Theobromine's source is the cocoa tree, and its structure is related to that of caffeine. Theobromine's properties are, however, very different from those of caffeine. The focus on relevancy feature Chemical Connections 17-C—Alkaloids Present in Chocolate—considers further the alkaloid content of chocolate products.

A number of alkaloids are currently used in medicine. Quinine, which occurs in cinchona bark, is used to treat malaria; it is a powerful antipyretic (fever-reducer). Atropine, which is isolated from the belladonna plant, is used to dilate the pupil of the eye in patients undergoing eye examinations (Figure 17-10). Atropine is also used

▶ *The name* alkaloid, *which means "like a base," reflects the fact that alkaloids react with acids. Such behavior is expected for substances with amine functional groups because amines are weak bases.*

Figure 17-10 Fruit of the belladonna plant; the alkaloid atropine is obtained from this plant.

CHEMICAL   CONNECTIONS 17-C

Alkaloids Present in Chocolate

Chocolate is a food preparation made from the beans (seeds) of the tropical cacao tree. Growth conditions for cacao trees require a warm, moist climate like that found near the equator. The majority of the world's supply of cacao beans comes from the west coast of Africa—Ivory Coast, Ghana, and Nigeria. (Because of a mistake in spelling, probably made by early English importers, cacao beans are known as cocoa beans in English-speaking countries.)

All chocolate products are manufactured from ground cocoa beans. The heat from the grinding process causes the cocoa bean mixture to melt, forming a free-flowing mixture called *chocolate liquor.* Baker's chocolate (unsweetened chocolate) is simply cooled, hardened chocolate liquor. Dark chocolate (semisweet chocolate) has small amounts of sugar added. Milk chocolate (sweetened chocolate) has larger amounts of sugar, as well as milk solids and vanilla flavoring, added.

Because of their plant origins, chocolate products contain alkaloids. The dominant alkaloid present is theobromine, with caffeine being present in a smaller amount. The name theobromine comes from the Greek term *theobroma* meaning "food of the Gods." The concentrations of these two alkaloids in cocoa beans varies depending on the origin of the beans. The following table gives the theobromine and caffeine content of several types of chocolate.

Theobromine and Caffeine Content of Various Types of Chocolate

Product	Theobromine %	Caffeine %	Theobromine/ Caffeine Ratio
baker's chocolate	1.386	0.164	8.45 to 1
dark chocolate	0.474	0.076	6.3 to 1
milk chocolate	0.197	0.022	9.0 to 1

The caffeine content of a typical chocolate bar is 30 mg and that of a slice of chocolate cake 20–30 mg. By contrast, a cup of coffee contains 100–150 mg of caffeine and a 12-ounce cola drink contains 33–52 mg.

Structurally, theobromine and caffeine differ only by a methyl group.

Theobromine
(3,7-dimethyxanthine)

Caffeine
(1,3,7-trimethylxanthine)

This close structural similarity does not, however, translate into close pharmacological properties. Theobromine's central nervous system stimulant effects are minimal compared to those of caffeine. A mild diuretic effect and relaxation of the smooth muscles of the bronchi in the lungs are effects of theobromine; caffeine has similar effects in these areas. Theobromine has been used as a pharmaceutical drug for its diuretic effect. Because of its ability to dilate blood vessels, theobromine also has been used to treat high blood pressure.

Research shows that pets, especially dogs, are sensitive to theobromine because the animals metabolize theobromine more slowly than humans. A chocolate bar, when ingested, is poisonous to dogs and can even be lethal. The same holds true for cats.

Occasionally, chocolate is touted as a "health" food because cocoa beans have relatively high levels of several kinds of antioxidant flavonoids (see Chemical Connections 23-D—Phytochemicals: Compounds with Color and Antioxidant Functions). Studies show that people with high blood levels of flavonoids are at lower risk of developing heart disease, asthma, and type 2 diabetes. Dark chocolate contains the most cocoa and thus the most flavonoids. As a "health" food, however, chocolate should be consumed only occasionally because the downside of consumption is the high number of calories associated with chocolate.

© Cengage Learning

Baker's chocolate (unsweetened chocolate), dark chocolate (semisweet chocolate), and milk chocolate (sweetened chocolate) differ in terms of the additives that are present.

as a preoperative drug to relax muscles and reduce the secretion of saliva in surgical patients.

Quinine

Atropine

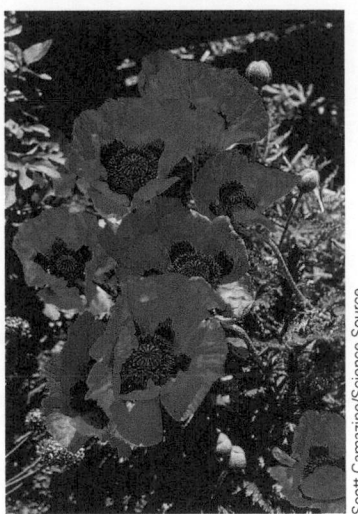

Figure 17-11 Oriental poppy plants, the source of several narcotic painkillers, including morphine.

Morphine, Codeine, and Heroin

An extremely important family of alkaloids is the narcotic painkillers, a class of drugs derived from the resin (opium) of the oriental poppy plant (see Figure 17-11). The most important drugs obtained from opium are morphine and codeine. ◄ Synthetic modification of morphine produces the illegal drug heroin.

These three compounds have similar chemical structures.

Morphine

Codeine

Heroin

▶ *Poppy seeds contain small amounts of morphine. Eating poppy-seed cake, bagels, or muffins can often introduce enough morphine into a person's body to produce a positive test in random drug screening procedures.*

Morphine is one of the most effective painkillers known; its painkilling properties are about a hundred times greater than those of aspirin. Morphine acts by blocking the process in the brain that interprets pain signals coming from the peripheral nervous system. The major drawback to the use of morphine is that it is addictive.

Codeine is a methylmorphine. Almost all codeine used in modern medicine is produced by methylating the more abundant morphine. Codeine is less potent than morphine, having a painkilling effect about one-sixth that of morphine. ◄

Heroin is a semi-synthetic compound, the diacetyl ester of morphine; it is produced from morphine. This chemical modification increases painkilling potency; heroin has more than three times the painkilling effect of morphine. Heroin's greater painkilling ability results from its molecular structure being less polar than that of morphine; hence it is more soluble in the body's fatty tissues. However, heroin is so addictive that it has no accepted medical use in the United States.

▶ *The demand for a painkiller as strong as morphine is very limited, and natural supply far exceeds demand. Demand for the much weaker codeine is, however, many times greater than its natural supply. Approximately 95% of the morphine obtained from legally grown poppy plants is converted to codeine, which is then converted to codeine derivatives, primarily hydrocodone and oxycodone.*

Hydrocodone, Oxycodone, and OxyContin

The most widely prescribed painkillers in the United States, at present, for the relief of moderate to heavy pain contain the *codeine derivatives* hydrocodone or oxycodone as an active ingredient. ◄ Usually a second painkilling agent is present in addition to the codeine derivative.

▶ *The total alkaloid content of a poppy plant is about 20% codeine and 70% morphine. Biosynthetically, a poppy plant first produces codeine, which is then modified to generate morphine. Plant biochemists recently discovered the gene needed for the poppy plant to convert codeine to morphine. Using genetic engineering procedures to modify poppy plants so that the expression of this gene was reduced, it was found that codeine levels increased from 20% to 65% of the total alkaloid content whereas morphine levels were reduced from 70% to 15% of the total alkaloid content. This discovery may eventually lead to better methods for obtaining the increased amounts of codeine needed for codeine derivative medications.*

Hydrocodone

Oxycodone

Lortab and Norco are examples of hydrocodone-containing formulations in which acetaminophen is the second painkilling agent present. The painkilling effect of this two-drug combination is actually greater than that of the sum of the individual effects. The presence of the acetaminophen also limits the potential for the unsafe addictive side effects associated with higher than prescribed doses of hydrocodone because of the liver-toxicity problem associated with higher doses of the accompanying acetaminophen.

Oxycodone-containing formulations include Percodan (an aspirin–oxycodone combination) and Percocet (an acetaminophen–oxycodone combination). The use of two-drug combinations for oxycodone is based on the same rationale as that for hydrocodone two-drug combinations.

OxyContin is a controlled-released formulation of pure oxycodone that provides 12 hours of pain relief. During the period 2005–2010 the name OxyContin became a household name because of many pharmacy robberies in which drug abusers demanded OxyContin. The stimulus for these robberies was the discovery by drug abusers that the controlled-released feature associated with OxyContin tablets could be destroyed by crushing, chewing, or dissolving the tablet, delivering the entire dose of oxycodone at once and a heroin-like high at the same time. To combat this serious situation, OxyContin's manufacturer, in 2010, reformulated the tablets in a form that made them nearly impossible to crush or dissolve. All OxyContin prescriptions are now filled using the reformulated OxyContin and the rash of pharmacy OxyContin robberies is no longer a major problem.

There are two driving forces for the preferred use of hydrocodone formulations over oxycodone formulations. The first is cost. Hydrocodone production requires a less-costly sequence of chemical reactions. The second is less potential for abuse of the drug. While the use of either codeine derivative can be habit-forming, and can lead to physical and psychological addiction, oxycodone effects are generally greater than those for hydrocodone at equivalent dosages. A driving force for the use of oxycodone formulations over hydrocodone formulations is that the onset of pain relief occurs faster for oxycodone.

Section 17-11 Quick Quiz

1. Which of the following is *not* an alkaloid?
   a. caffeine
   b. nicotine
   c. cocaine
   d. no correct response
2. Which of the following statements concerning narcotic painkillers is correct?
   a. Structurally, codeine is methylmorphine.
   b. Heroin is a substance naturally present in the oriental poppy plant.
   c. Codeine's painkilling effects are twice those of morphine.
   d. no correct response
3. The most widely prescribed painkillers in the United States, at present, are
   a. the codeine derivatives hydrocodone and oxycodone
   b. codeine and morphine
   c. codeine and hydrocodone
   d. no correct response

Answers: 1. d; 2. a; 3. a

17-12 **Structure and Classification of Amides**

LEARNING FOCUS

Know structural characteristics for the amide functional group; be able to classify amides into the categories primary, secondary, and tertiary.

An **amide** *is a carboxylic acid derivative in which the carboxyl —OH group has been replaced with an amino or a substituted amino group.* The amide functional group is thus

$$ -\overset{\overset{\displaystyle O}{\|}}{C}-NH_2 \quad \text{or} \quad -\overset{\overset{\displaystyle O}{\|}}{C}-NH-R \quad \text{or} \quad -\overset{\overset{\displaystyle O}{\|}}{\underset{\underset{\displaystyle R}{|}}{C}}-N-R $$

depending on the degree of substitution. ◄

Amides, like amines, can be classified as primary (1°), secondary (2°), or tertiary (3°), depending on how many hydrogen atoms are attached to the nitrogen atom.

▶ *The word "amide" is pronounced "a-MID" (rhymes with "a lid").*

$$ R-\overset{\overset{\displaystyle O}{\|}}{C}-NH_2 \qquad R-\overset{\overset{\displaystyle O}{\|}}{C}-NH-R' \qquad R-\overset{\overset{\displaystyle O}{\|}}{\underset{\underset{\displaystyle R''}{|}}{C}}-N-R' $$

Primary amide   Secondary amide   Tertiary amide

A **primary amide** *is an amide in which two hydrogen atoms are bonded to the amide nitrogen atom.* Such amides are also called *unsubstituted* amides. A **secondary amide** *is an amide in which an alkyl (or aryl) group and a hydrogen atom are bonded to the amide nitrogen atom.* Monosubstituted amide is another name for this type of amide. A **tertiary amide** *is an amide in which two alkyl (or aryl) groups and no hydrogen atoms are bonded to the amide nitrogen atom.* Such amides are *disubstituted* amides. ◄

Note that the difference between a 1° amide and a 2° amide is "H versus R" and that the difference between a 2° amide and a 3° amide is again "H versus R." These "H versus R" relationships are the same relationships that exist between 1° and 2° amines and 2° and 3° amines (Section 17-2), as is summarized in Figure 17-12.

▶ *Primary, secondary, and tertiary amides are also called unsubstituted, monosubstituted, and disubstituted amides, respectively.*

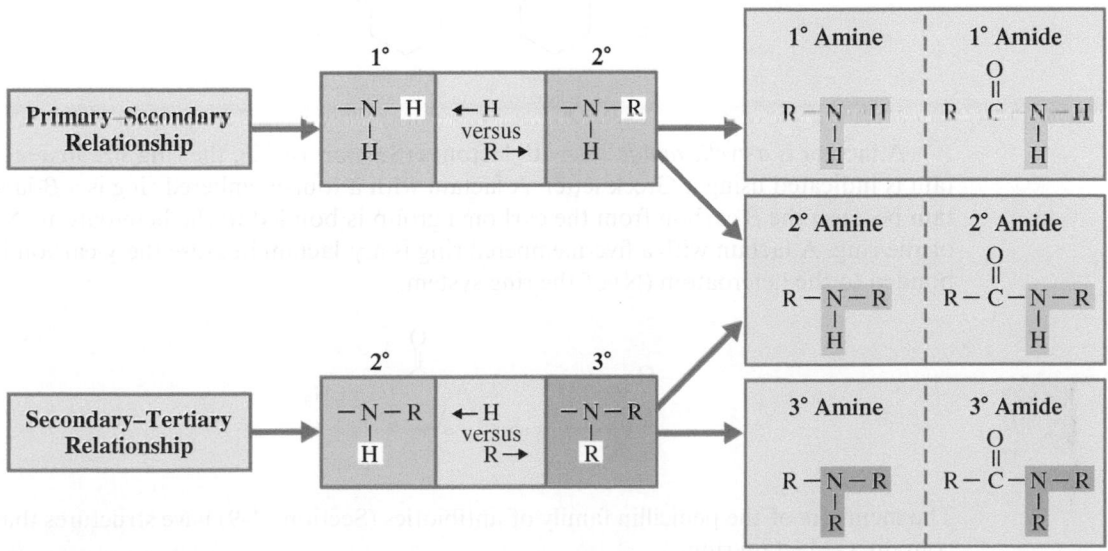

Figure 17-12 Primary, secondary, and tertiary amines and amides and the "H versus R" relationship.

The simplest amide has a hydrogen atom attached to an unsubstituted amide functional group.

$$H-\overset{\overset{\textstyle O}{\|}}{C}-NH_2$$

Next in complexity are amides in which a methyl group is present. There are two of them, one with the methyl group attached to the carbon atom and the other with the methyl group attached to the nitrogen atom.

$$CH_3-\overset{\overset{\textstyle O}{\|}}{C}-NH_2 \quad \text{and} \quad H-\overset{\overset{\textstyle O}{\|}}{C}-NH-CH_3$$

The first of these structures is a 1° amide, and the second structure is a 2° amide. ◄

The structure of the simplest aromatic amide involves a benzene ring to which an unsubstituted amide functional group is attached.

Cyclic amide structures are possible. Examples of such structures include

Cyclic amides are called *lactams,* a term that parallels the use of the term *lactones* for cyclic esters (Section 16-12).

A lactone   A lactam
(a cyclic ester)   (a cyclic amide)

A **lactam** *is a cyclic amide.* As with lactones (Section 16-12), the ring size in a lactam is indicated using a Greek letter. A lactam with a four-membered ring is a β-lactam because the β carbon from the carbonyl group is bonded to the heteroatom (N) of the ring. A lactam with a five-membered ring is a γ-lactam because the γ-carbon is bonded to the heteroatom (N) of the ring system.

β-Lactam γ-Lactam

The members of the penicillin family of antibiotics (Section 21-9) have structures that contain a β-lactam ring.

► *Line-angle structural formulas for selected primary, secondary, and tertiary amides:*

1. Which of the following is a complete listing of the elements present in the amide functional group?
   a. C, H, and N
   b. C, H, O, and N
   c. C, H, and O
   d. no correct response

2. The compound $CH_3-\overset{\overset{\displaystyle O}{\|}}{C}-NH-CH_3$ belongs to which of the following amide classifications?
   a. 1° amide
   b. 2° amide
   c. 3° amide
   d. no correct response

3. Secondary amides are also called
   a. unsubstituted amides
   b. monosubstituted amides
   c. disubstituted amides
   d. no correct response

4. Another designation for a cyclic amide is
   a. lactam
   b. lactone
   c. lactate
   d. no correct response

Answers: 1. b; 2. b; 3. b; 4. a

17-13 Nomenclature for Amides

LEARNING FOCUS

Given their structural formulas, be able to name amides using IUPAC rules or vice versa; be able to assign common names to simple amides.

For nomenclature purposes (both IUPAC and common), amides are considered to be derivatives of carboxylic acids. Hence their names are based on the name of the parent carboxylic acid. (A similar procedure was used for naming esters; Section 16-12.) The rules are as follows:

Rule 1: *The ending of the name of the carboxylic acid is changed from -ic acid (common) or -oic acid (IUPAC) to -amide. For example,* benzoic acid *becomes* benzamide.

Rule 2: *The names of groups attached to the nitrogen (2° and 3° amides) are appended to the front of the base name, using an N-prefix as a locator.*

Selected primary amide IUPAC names (with the common name in parentheses) are

Methanamide (formamide); Ethanamide (acetamide); Propanamide (propionamide); 3-Methylbutanamide (β-methylbutyramide); 2-Chloro-2-methylpropanamide (α-chloro-α-methylpropionamide)

O
‖
H—C—NH₂

**Methanamide
(a primary amide)**

O
‖
H—C—NH—CH₃

**N-Methyl methanamide
(a secondary amide)**

O
‖
H—C—N—CH₃
　　　|
　　　CH₃

**N,N-Dimethyl methanamide
(a tertiary amide)**

Figure 17-13 Space-filling models for the simplest primary, secondary, and tertiary amides.

▶ *The contrast between IUPAC names and common names for unbranched unsubstituted amides is as follows:*

IUPAC (one word)

‖alkanamide‖

ethanamide

Common (one word)

‖(prefix)amide*‖

acetamide

The common-name prefixes are related to natural sources for the acids.

Nomenclature for secondary and tertiary amides, amides with substituted amino groups, involves use of the prefix *N-*, a practice that was previously encountered with amine nomenclature (Section 17-3).

$$CH_3—CH_2—\overset{\overset{\displaystyle O}{\|}}{C}—NH—CH_3 \qquad CH_3—\overset{\overset{\displaystyle O}{\|}}{C}—\overset{\overset{\displaystyle CH_3}{|}}{N}—CH_3$$

N-Methylpropanamide　　　　　*N,N*-Dimethylethanamide
(*N*-methylpropionamide)　　　　(*N,N*-dimethylacetamide)

Molecular models for methanamide and its *N*-methyl and *N,N*-dimethyl derivatives (the simplest 1°, 2°, and 3° amides, respectively) are given in Figure 17-13.

The simplest aromatic amide, a benzene ring bearing an unsubstituted amide group, is called *benzamide*. Other aromatic amides are named as benzamide derivatives.

Benzamide　　　　2-Methylbenzamide　　　　*N*-Methylbenzamide

When an amide functional group is attached to a nonaromatic ring, the suffix *carboxamide* is used in the name.

3-Methylcyclopentanecarboxamide

EXAMPLE 17-5

Determining IUPAC and Common Names for Amides

Assign both common and IUPAC names to each of the following amides:

a.
$$CH_3—CH_2—CH_2—\overset{\overset{\displaystyle O}{\|}}{C}—NH_2$$

b.
$$CH_3—\overset{\overset{\displaystyle Br}{|}}{CH}—\overset{\overset{\displaystyle O}{\|}}{C}—NH—CH_3$$

c.

d.

Solution

a. The parent acid for this amide is butyric acid (common) or butanoic acid (IUPAC). The common name for this amide is *butyramide,* and the IUPAC name is *butanamide.* ◀

b. The common and IUPAC names of the acid are very similar; they are propionic acid and propanoic acid, respectively. The common name for this amide is *α-bromo-N-methylpropionamide,* and the IUPAC name is *2-bromo-N-methylpropanamide.* The prefix *N-* must be used with the methyl group to indicate that it is attached to the nitrogen atom.

c. The parent acid for this amide is benzenecarboxylic acid (IUPAC) or benzoic acid (common). The *carboxylic acid* ending is replaced with *carboxamide* and the *oic acid* ending is replaced with *amide,* giving the names N,N-*diphenylbenzenecarboxamide* (IUPAC) and N,N-*diphenylbenzamide* for this disubstituted amide.

d. The amide is derived from valeric acid (common name) or pentanoic acid (IUPAC name). The complete name must take into account the presence of the methyl group on the carbon chain. The amide's common name is *β-methylvaleramide* and its IUPAC name is *3-methylpentanamide.*

1. What is the IUPAC name for the compound CH_3—$\overset{\overset{\textstyle CH_3}{|}}{CH}$—$CH_2$—$\overset{\overset{\textstyle O}{\|}}{C}$—$NH_2$?
   a. isobutyl amide
   b. 2-methylbutanamide
   c. 3-methylbutanamide
   d. no correct response

2. What is the IUPAC name for the compound CH_3—CH_2—CH_2—$\overset{\overset{\textstyle O}{\|}}{C}$—$NH$—$CH_3$?
   a. methylpentamide
   b. 1-methylbutanamide
   c. N-methylbutanamide
   d. no correct response

3. What is the common name for the compound $\langle\!\!\!\bigcirc\!\!\!\rangle$—$\overset{\overset{\textstyle O}{\|}}{C}$—$NH_2$?
   a. benzamide
   b. phenylamide
   c. benzene amide
   d. no correct response

4. What is the IUPAC name for the amide whose common name is acetamide?
   a. methylamide
   b. ethylamide
   c. ethanamide
   d. no correct response

Answers: 1. c; 2. c; 3. a; 4. c

17-14 Selected Amides and Their Uses

LEARNING FOCUS

Be familiar with selected common amides and their uses.

The simplest naturally occurring amide is urea, a water-soluble white solid produced in the human body from carbon dioxide and ammonia through a complex series of metabolic reactions (Section 26-4).

$$CO_2 + 2NH_3 \longrightarrow (H_2N)_2CO + H_2O$$

Urea is a one-carbon diamide. Its molecular structure is

$$H_2N\!-\!\overset{\overset{\textstyle O}{\|}}{C}\!-\!NH_2$$

Urea formation is the human body's primary method for eliminating "waste" nitrogen. The kidneys remove urea from the blood and provide for its excretion in urine. With malfunctioning kidneys, urea concentrations in the body can build to toxic levels—a condition called *uremia*.

The complex amide melatonin is a hormone that is synthesized by the pineal gland and that regulates the sleep–wake cycle in humans. Melatonin levels within the body increase in evening hours and then decrease as morning approaches. High melatonin levels are associated with longer and more sound sleeping. The concentration of this hormone in the blood decreases with age; a six-year-old has a blood melatonin concentration more than five times that of an 80-year-old. This is one reason why young children have less trouble sleeping than senior citizens. As a prescription drug, melatonin is used to treat insomnia and jet lag. ◄

Structurally, melatonin is a polyfunctional amide; amine and ether groups are also present as well as unsaturation.

▶ *Synthetically produced melatonin is under investigation as a drug for treating jet lag. Jet lag is a condition caused by desynchronization of the biological clock. It is usually caused by drastically changing the sleep–wake cycle, as when crossing several time zones during an airline flight or when performing shift work. Symptoms of jet lag include fatigue, early awakening or inability to sleep, and headaches. Studies indicate that melatonin taken in the evening in a new time zone will usually reset a person's biological clock and almost totally alleviate (or prevent) the symptoms of jet lag.*

A number of synthetic amides exhibit physiological activity and are used as drugs in the human body. Foremost among them, in terms of use, is acetaminophen, which is the top-selling over-the-counter pain reliever. It, like melatonin, is a polyfunctional amide; a phenol group is also present.

$$CH_3-\overset{\overset{\displaystyle O}{\|}}{C}-NH-\!\!\!\left\langle\!\!\bigcirc\!\!\right\rangle\!\!-OH$$

N-(4-hydroxyphenyl)ethanamide

The focus on relevancy feature Chemical Connections 17-D—Acetaminophen: A Substituted Amide—considers the pharmacological chemistry of acetaminophen.

CHEMICAL CONNECTIONS 17-D

Acetaminophen: A Substituted Amide

Often called the aspirin substitute, acetaminophen (a-SEET-a-MIN-oh-phen) is the most widely used of all nonprescription pain relievers, accounting for over half of that market. Acetaminophen is a derivative of acetamide in which a hydroxyphenyl group has replaced one of the amide hydrogens.

$$CH_3-\overset{\overset{\displaystyle O}{\|}}{C}-NH_2 \qquad CH_3-\overset{\overset{\displaystyle O}{\|}}{C}-NH-\!\!\!\left\langle\!\!\bigcirc\!\!\right\rangle\!\!-OH$$

Acetamide   Acetaminophen

The pharmaceutical designation APAP for this compound comes from the common name *N*-acetyl-*p*-aminophenol for the compound.

Acetaminophen is the active ingredient in Tylenol, Datril, Tempra, Equate, and Anacin-3. Excedrin, which contains both acetaminophen and aspirin, is a combination pain reliever.

Because acetaminophen does not have a carboxyl functional group, as do aspirin, ibuprofen, and naproxen, it does not have irritating effects on the intestinal tract. Unlike the other three pain relievers, however, acetaminophen is not effective against inflammation and is of limited use for the aches and pains associated with arthritis. Also, acetaminophen, unlike aspirin, does not inhibit platelet aggregation and is therefore not useful for the prevention of blood clots.

Acetaminophen is available in a liquid form that is used extensively for small children and other patients who have difficulty taking solid tablets. The wide use of acetaminophen for children has a drawback; it is the drug most often involved in childhood poisonings.

In *large* doses, acetaminophen can cause liver and kidney damage. Such effects are not found when acetaminophen is taken as directed. For this reason, the maximum adult daily dosage of 4 g should not be exceeded (eight 500 mg tablets), and extra-strength formulations should be used with great caution. Analgesic abuse is a real potential with the heavily advertised extra-strength formulations.

Acetaminophen's mode of action in the body is similar to that of aspirin—inhibition of prostaglandin synthesis.

Currently under research development is an acetaminophen derivative that is touted as being safer and more versatile than its parent compound. It is an acetaminophen molecule to which a saccharin molecule (Section 18-13) has been attached.

$$\underset{\underset{\displaystyle O}{\|}}{\overset{\overset{\displaystyle HOOC}{}}{\left\langle\bigcirc\right\rangle}}\!\!-\!\!\overset{\overset{\displaystyle O}{\|}}{\underset{\underset{\displaystyle O}{\|}}{S}}\!\!-NH-CH_2-\overset{\overset{\displaystyle O}{\|}}{C}-NH-\!\!\!\left\langle\!\!\bigcirc\!\!\right\rangle\!\!-OH$$

This saccharin derivative is just as potent as acetaminophen at relieving pain but has better water solubility and decreased liver toxicity. It may also be able to diminish pain that arises from nervous system damage, something that acetaminophen does not do.

Over-the-counter pain relievers such as Tylenol and Equate contain acetaminophen as the active ingredient.

The active ingredient in most insect repellents currently available for purchase is the tertiary amide N,N-diethyl-m-toluamide, a substance better known by the acronym DEET. ◀

$$\underset{CH_3}{\overset{\overset{\displaystyle O}{\parallel}}{\underset{\quad}{}}} \quad C\!-\!N\!\begin{matrix} CH_2\!-\!CH_3 \\ CH_2\!-\!CH_3 \end{matrix}$$

It is a compound approved for direct application to skin and clothing.

DEET is an insect *repellent;* it does not kill insects but, rather, "repels" them. DEET's actual mode of action has been recently determined to involve inhibition of insect olfactory receptors; it affects insects' ability to detect various odors associated with human presence.

DEET is effective against ticks, fleas, and mosquitos (as well as other insects), thus offering protection against insect-borne diseases transmitted through insect bites, such as Lyme disease (ticks) and West Nile virus (mosquitos). ◀

▶ *The ortho- and para-isomers (Section 13-13) of N,N-diethyl-toluamide are less effective insect repellents than is the meta-isomer.*

Section 17-14 Quick Quiz

1. Urea, the simplest naturally occurring amide has the structure:

   a. $H\!-\!\overset{\overset{\displaystyle O}{\parallel}}{C}\!-\!NH_2$

   b. $CH_3\!-\!\overset{\overset{\displaystyle O}{\parallel}}{C}\!-\!NH_2$

   c. $H_2N\!-\!\overset{\overset{\displaystyle O}{\parallel}}{C}\!-\!NH_2$

   d. no correct response

2. The foremost synthetic amide, in terms of use, is
   a. melatonin
   b. acetaminophen
   c. DEET
   d. no correct response

3. Which of the following amides is an important hormone in the human body?
   a. melatonin
   b. DEET
   c. acetaminophen
   d. no correct response

Answers: 1. c; 2. b; 3. a

▶ *Acrylamide (2-propenamide), the simplest unsaturated amide, has the structure*

$$CH_2\!=\!CH\!-\!\overset{\overset{\displaystyle O}{\parallel}}{C}\!-\!NH_2$$

It is a neurotoxic agent and a possible human carcinogen.

Surprisingly, low concentrations of acrylamide have been found in potato chips, french fries, and other starchy foods prepared at high temperatures (greater than 120°C). Its possible source is the reaction between the amino acid asparagine (present in food proteins; Section 20-2) and carbohydrate sugars (Section 18-8) present in food.

Human risk studies are underway concerning acrylamide presence in fried and some baked foods. No traces of acrylamide have been found in uncooked or boiled foods.

17-15 Basicity of Amides

LEARNING FOCUS
Understand why amides do not exhibit basic behavior as do amines.

Both primary amines and primary amides have an —NH$_2$ group present in their structures. There is an important difference between these two —NH$_2$ groups. In an amine, the N atom is bonded to a carbon atom associated with a hydrocarbon group. In an amide, the N atom is bonded to the carbon atom of a carbonyl group. A carbonyl group is a polar entity, with the C atom possessing a partial positive charge and the O atom possessing a partial negative charge (Section 15-1).

$$R\!-\!\underset{\delta^+}{\overset{\overset{\displaystyle O^{\delta^-}}{\parallel}}{C}}\!-\!\overset{..}{N}\!-\!H \atop \underset{\displaystyle H}{|}$$

The partial positive charge on the carbonyl carbon atom is sufficient to exert an influence (attractive force) on the lone pair of electrons on the nitrogen atom, causing these electrons to be more tightly held by the nitrogen atom. The net result of this situation is that the nitrogen atom of the amide is prevented from acting as a Brønsted–Lowry base, that is, as a proton acceptor. Thus amides do not exhibit basic behavior as do amines, even though a lone pair of electrons is present on the amide N atom. This also means that the N atom of an amide does not readily serve as a hydrogen bonding site.

Section 17-15 Quick Quiz

1. Which of the following is a correct statement?
   a. Amides, but not amines, exhibit basic properties.
   b. Amines, but not amides, exhibit basic properties.
   c. Both amides and amines exhibit basic properties.
   d. no correct response
2. Which of the following directly influences the proton-acceptor behavior (basicity) of the nitrogen atom in a amide functional group?
   a. partial positive charge on the carbonyl carbon atom
   b. partial negative charge on the carbonyl carbon atom
   c. partial positive charge on the carbonyl oxygen atom
   d. no correct response

Answers: 1. b; 2. a

17-16 Physical Properties of Amides

LEARNING FOCUS

Be familiar with general physical properties of amides and how hydrogen bonding influences these properties.

Unbranched Primary Amides			
C_1	C_3	C_5	C_7
C_2	C_4	C_6	C_8

☐ Liquid ☐ Solid

Figure 17-14 A physical-state summary for unbranched primary amides at room temperature and pressure.

Methanamide and its *N*-methyl and *N,N*-dimethyl derivatives (the simplest 1°, 2°, and 3° amides, respectively), are all liquids at room temperature. All unbranched primary amides, except methanamide, are solids at room temperature (Figure 17-14), as are most other amides. In many cases, the amide melting point is even higher than that of the corresponding carboxylic acid. The high melting points result from the numerous intermolecular hydrogen-bonding possibilities that exist between amide H atoms and carbonyl O atoms. Figure 17-15 shows selected hydrogen-bonding interactions that are possible among several primary amide molecules.

Fewer hydrogen-bonding possibilities exist for 2° amides because the nitrogen atom now has only one hydrogen atom; hence lower melting points are the rule for

Figure 17-15 The high boiling points of amides are related to the numerous amide–amide hydrogen-bonding possibilities that exist.

such amides. Still lower melting points are observed for 3° amides because no hydrogen bonding is possible. The disubstituted *N,N*-dimethylacetamide has a melting point of −20°C, which is about 100°C lower than that of the unsubstituted acetamide.

Amides of low molecular mass, up to five or six carbon atoms, are soluble in water. Again, numerous hydrogen-bonding possibilities exist between water and the amide. Even disubstituted amides can participate in such hydrogen bonding.

$$
\begin{array}{c}
\downarrow \\
\ddot{O}\colon \leftarrow \\
\parallel \quad \ddot{} \\
R-C-N-H \leftarrow \\
\mid \\
H \\
\uparrow
\end{array}
$$

Arrows denote sites where hydrogen bonding to water can occur.

Section 17-16 Quick Quiz

1. At room temperature, most unbranched primary amides are
   a. gases
   b. liquids
   c. solids
   d. no correct response
2. In general, the boiling points of tertiary amides are
   a. lower than those of secondary amides
   b. higher than those of primary amides
   c. about the same as those of primary amides
   d. no correct response
3. Which of the following statements about amide–amide hydrogen bonding possibilities is correct?
   a. 1° amides can form more hydrogen bonds than 2° amides.
   b. 1° amides and 2° amides always form the same number of hydrogen bonds.
   c. 3° amides can form more hydrogen bonds than 1° amides.

Answers: 1. c; 2. a; 3. a

17-17 Preparation of Amides

LEARNING FOCUS
Be familiar with the identity of reactants and products in an amidification reaction.

Amides are the least reactive of the common carboxylic acid derivatives and they can be synthesized from an acid chloride, an acid anhydride, an ester, or the carboxylic acid itself.

The reaction of a carboxylic acid with ammonia or a 1° or 2° amine produces an amide, provided that the reaction is carried out at an elevated temperature (greater than 100°C) and a dehydrating agent is present.

$$\text{Ammonia} + \text{carboxylic acid} \xrightarrow{100°C} 1° \text{ amide}$$

$$1° \text{ Amine} + \text{carboxylic acid} \xrightarrow{100°C} 2° \text{ amide}$$

$$2° \text{ Amine} + \text{carboxylic acid} \xrightarrow{100°C} 3° \text{ amide}$$

If the preceding reactions are run at room temperature (25°C), no amide formation occurs; instead, an acid–base reaction occurs in which a carboxylic acid salt is produced. This acid–base reaction when a 1° amine is the reactant is

$$
\begin{array}{c}
\overset{\displaystyle O}{\underset{\displaystyle}{\parallel}} \qquad \overset{\displaystyle H}{\underset{\displaystyle}{\mid}} \\
R-C-OH + H-N-R \xrightarrow{25°C} \quad H-\overset{H}{\underset{H}{\overset{\mid}{\underset{\mid}{N^{+}}}}}-R \quad R-\overset{O}{\overset{\parallel}{C}}-O^{-}
\end{array}
$$

Acid   Primary   Carboxylate salt
           amine

General structural equations for 1°, 2°, and 3° amide production from carboxylic acids are

$$
\underset{\substack{\text{Carboxylic}\\\text{acid}}}{R-\overset{O}{\overset{\|}{C}}-OH} + \underset{\text{Ammonia}}{H-\overset{H}{\overset{|}{N}}-H} \xrightarrow{100°C} \underset{\text{Primary amide}}{R-\overset{O}{\overset{\|}{C}}-\overset{H}{\overset{|}{N}}-H} + H_2O
$$

$$
\underset{\substack{\text{Carboxylic}\\\text{acid}}}{R-\overset{O}{\overset{\|}{C}}-OH} + \underset{\substack{\text{Primary}\\\text{amine}}}{H-\overset{H}{\overset{|}{N}}-R} \xrightarrow{100°C} \underset{\text{Secondary amide}}{R-\overset{O}{\overset{\|}{C}}-\overset{H}{\overset{|}{N}}-R} + H_2O
$$

$$
\underset{\substack{\text{Carboxylic}\\\text{acid}}}{R-\overset{O}{\overset{\|}{C}}-OH} + \underset{\substack{\text{Secondary}\\\text{amine}}}{H-\overset{R}{\overset{|}{N}}-R} \xrightarrow{100°C} \underset{\text{Tertiary amide}}{R-\overset{O}{\overset{\|}{C}}-\overset{R}{\overset{|}{N}}-R} + H_2O
$$

> ▶ *This is the fifth time that condensation reactions have been encountered. Phosphoric acid anhydride formation (Section 16-20), esterification (Section 16-11), acetal formation (Section 15-11), and ether formation (Section 14-9) were the other four examples of condensation reactions.*

These reactions, which are all condensation reactions (Section 14-9), are more specifically called *amidification reactions.* ◀ An **amidification reaction** *is the reaction of a carboxylic acid with an amine (or ammonia) to produce an amide.* In amidification, an —OH group is lost from the carboxylic acid, a —H atom is lost from the ammonia or amine, and water is formed as a by-product.

Two specific amidification reactions, in which a 2° amide and a 3° amide are produced, respectively, are

$$
\underset{\text{Butanoic acid}}{CH_3-CH_2-CH_2-\overset{O}{\overset{\|}{C}}-OH} + \underset{\substack{\text{Methylamine}\\(1°\text{ amine})}}{H-\overset{H}{\overset{|}{N}}-CH_3} \xrightarrow{100°C} \underset{\substack{N\text{-Methylbutanamide}\\(\text{a } 2°\text{ amide})}}{CH_3-CH_2-CH_2-\overset{O}{\overset{\|}{C}}-\overset{H}{\overset{|}{N}}-CH_3} + H_2O
$$

$$
\underset{\text{Benzoic acid}}{\text{⌬}-\overset{O}{\overset{\|}{C}}-OH} + \underset{\substack{\text{Diethylamine}\\(2°\text{ amine})}}{H-\overset{H}{\overset{\underset{\displaystyle CH_2-CH_3}{|}}{N}}-CH_2-CH_3} \xrightarrow{100°C} \underset{\substack{N,N\text{-Diethylbenzamide}\\(\text{a } 3°\text{ amide})}}{\text{⌬}-\overset{O}{\overset{\|}{C}}-\overset{\underset{\displaystyle CH_2-CH_3}{|}}{N}-CH_2-CH_3} + H_2O
$$

> ▶ *The reaction of a carboxylic acid with ammonia or an amine to produce an amide is similar to the reaction of a carboxylic acid with an alcohol to produce an ester. In both cases, water is formed as a by-product as the —OH part of the carboxylic acid is replaced.*

Just as it is useful to think of the structure of an ester (Section 16-10) in terms of an "acid part" and an "alcohol part," it is useful to think of an amide in terms of an "acid part" and an "amine (or ammonia) part." ◀

Amide	Ester
$R-\overset{O}{\overset{\|}{C}}\,\|\,NH_2$	$R-\overset{O}{\overset{\|}{C}}\,\|\,O-R'$
Acid part / Amine or ammonia part	Acid part / Alcohol part

In this context, it is easy to identify the parent acid and amine from which a given amide can be produced; to generate the parent molecules, just add an —OH group to the acid part of the amide and an H atom to the amine part.

$$
\underset{\text{acid part}}{CH_3-CH_2-\overset{O}{\overset{\|}{C}}} \,\|\, \underset{\text{amine part}}{NH-CH_3}
$$

$$
\underset{\text{"Parent" acid}}{CH_3-CH_2-\overset{O}{\overset{\|}{C}}-(OH)} \qquad \underset{\text{"Parent" amine}}{(H)-\overset{\underset{\displaystyle |}{\displaystyle H}}{N}-CH_3}
$$

+OH   +H

EXAMPLE 17-6

Predicting Reactants Needed to Prepare Specific Amides

What carboxylic acid and amine (or ammonia) are needed to prepare each of the following amides?

a.

$$CH_3-\overset{\overset{\displaystyle O}{\|}}{C}-NH-CH_2-CH_3$$

b.

$$CH_3-CH_2-\overset{\overset{\displaystyle O}{\|}}{C}-NH_2$$

c.

$$CH_3-CH_2-\overset{\overset{\displaystyle O}{\|}}{C}-\overset{\overset{\displaystyle}{N}}{\underset{\underset{\displaystyle CH_3}{|}}{}}-CH_3$$

Solution

a. Viewing the molecule as having an acid part and an amine part, the following are obtained

Acid part   Amine part

Adding an —OH group to the acid part and a H atom to the amine part, the "parent" molecules are obtained, which are

$$CH_3-\overset{\overset{\displaystyle O}{\|}}{C}-OH \quad \text{and} \quad CH_3-CH_2-NH_2$$

b. Proceeding as in Part **a,** the "parent" acid and amine molecules are, respectively,

$$CH_3-CH_2-\overset{\overset{\displaystyle O}{\|}}{C}-OH \quad \text{and} \quad NH_3$$

c. Proceeding again as in Part **a,** the "parent" acid and amine molecules are, respectively,

$$CH_3-CH_2-\overset{\overset{\displaystyle O}{\|}}{C}-OH \quad \text{and} \quad CH_3-NH-CH_3$$

Section 17-17 Quick Quiz

1. The process of amidification involves a(n)
   a. addition reaction
   b. condensation reaction
   c. substitution reaction
   d. no correct response
2. Which of the following types of amides is produced when a carboxylic acid reacts with a primary amine under appropriate reaction conditions.
   a. 1° amide
   b. 2° amide
   c. 3° amide
   d. no correct response
3. The "parent" amine needed to produce the compound $CH_3-CH_2-\overset{\overset{\displaystyle O}{\|}}{C}-NH-CH_3$ using amidification is
   a. CH_3-NH_2
   b. $CH_3-CH_2-NH_2$
   c. $CH_3-CH_2-CH_2-NH_2$
   d. no correct response

Answers: 1. b; 2. b; 3. a

17-18 Hydrolysis of Amides

LEARNING FOCUS

Be familiar with the conditions necessary for and the products formed from amide hydrolysis reactions under both acidic and basic conditions.

▶ *The relative lack of reactivity of amides becomes very important in protein chemistry considerations (Chapter 20). Proteins are polymers in which the monomers are connected to each other via amide bonds (Section 20-7). Proteins are relatively stable in aqueous solution in the absence of acid or base; hence they can exert their various biochemical effects in aqueous solution without hydrolysis occurring.*

▶ *Amide hydrolysis under basic conditions is also called amide saponification, just as ester hydrolysis under basic conditions is called ester saponification (Section 16-16).*

Amides are the least reactive type of carboxylic acid derivative. They are relatively stable in aqueous solution but will undergo hydrolysis under strenuous conditions; the presence of an acid, base, or certain enzymes is required as a catalyst, and sustained heating is also often required. ◀ In such hydrolysis, the bond between the carbonyl carbon atom and the nitrogen is broken, and free acid and free amine are produced.

$$\underset{\text{Amide}}{R-\overset{\overset{\text{O}}{\|}}{C}-NH-R'} + H_2O \xrightarrow{\text{Heat}} \underset{\substack{\text{Carboxylic}\\\text{acid}}}{R-\overset{\overset{\text{O}}{\|}}{C}-OH} + \underset{\text{Amine}}{R'-NH_2}$$

Acidic or basic hydrolysis conditions have an effect on the products. *Acidic* conditions convert the product amine to an amine salt (Section 17-7). *Basic* conditions convert the product carboxylic acid to a carboxylic acid salt (Section 16-8). ◀

$$\underset{\text{Acidic hydrolysis of an amide}}{R-\overset{\overset{\text{O}}{\|}}{C}-NH-R'} + H_2O + \boxed{HCl} \xrightarrow{\text{Heat}} \underset{\text{Carboxylic acid}}{R-\overset{\overset{\text{O}}{\|}}{C}-OH} + \underset{\text{Amine salt}}{R'-\overset{+}{N}H_3\ Cl^-}$$

$$\underset{\text{Basic hydrolysis of an amide}}{R-\overset{\overset{\text{O}}{\|}}{C}-NH-R'} + \boxed{NaOH} \xrightarrow{\text{Heat}} \underset{\text{Carboxylic acid salt}}{R-\overset{\overset{\text{O}}{\|}}{C}-O^-\ Na^+} + \underset{\text{Amine}}{R'-NH_2}$$

EXAMPLE 17-7

Predicting the Products of Amide Hydrolysis Reactions

Draw structural formulas for the organic products of each of the following amide hydrolysis reactions. Be sure to take into account whether the hydrolysis occurs under neutral, acidic, or basic conditions.

a.
$$CH_3-CH_2-\overset{\overset{\text{O}}{\|}}{C}-NH-CH_3 + H_2O \xrightarrow{\text{Heat}}$$

b.
$$CH_3-CH_2-\overset{\overset{\text{O}}{\|}}{C}-NH-CH_2-CH_3 + H_2O \xrightarrow[\text{HCl}]{\text{Heat}}$$

c.
$$CH_3-\overset{\overset{\text{O}}{\|}}{C}-\underset{\underset{CH_3}{|}}{N}-CH_3 + H_2O \xrightarrow[\text{NaOH}]{\text{Heat}}$$

d.
$$CH_3-\underset{\underset{CH_3}{|}}{CH}-\overset{\overset{\text{O}}{\|}}{C}-NH_2 + H_2O \xrightarrow{\text{Heat}}$$

Solution

a. This reaction is hydrolysis under neutral conditions. The products will be the "parent" acid and amine for the amide. These "parents" are

$$CH_3-CH_2-\overset{\overset{\text{O}}{\|}}{C}-OH \qquad \text{and} \qquad CH_3-NH_2$$

b. This reaction is hydrolysis under acidic conditions. The acid is hydrochloric acid (HCl). The products will be the "parent" carboxylic acid and the chloride salt of the amine. The HCl converts the amine to its chloride salt.

$$CH_3—CH_2—\overset{\overset{\displaystyle O}{\|}}{C}—OH \quad \text{and} \quad CH_3—CH_2—\overset{+}{N}H_3 \; Cl^-$$

c. This reaction is hydrolysis under basic conditions. The base is sodium hydroxide (NaOH). The products will be the "parent" amine and the salt of the carboxylic acid. The NaOH converts the carboxylic acid to its sodium salt.

$$CH_3—\overset{\overset{\displaystyle O}{\|}}{C}—O^- \; Na^+ \quad \text{and} \quad CH_3—NH—CH_3$$

d. This reaction is hydrolysis under neutral conditions. The products will be the "parent" acid and amine of the amide. Because the amide is unsubstituted, the parent amine is actually ammonia.

$$CH_3—\underset{\underset{\displaystyle CH_3}{\|}}{CH}—\overset{\overset{\displaystyle O}{\|}}{C}—OH \quad \text{and} \quad NH_3$$

Chemistry at a Glance—Summary of Chemical Reactions Involving Amines and Amides—summarizes the reactions that involve amines and amides.

CHEMISTRY AT A GLANCE

Summary of Chemical Reactions Involving Amines and Amides

ALKYLATION OF AMINES

- Reaction with an alkyl halide
- Basic conditions (NaOH) required

Ammonia $\longrightarrow$ 1° amine
1° amine $\longrightarrow$ 2° amine
2° amine $\longrightarrow$ 3° amine
3° amine $\longrightarrow$ quaternary ammonium salt

AMIDIFICATION OF AMINES

- Reaction with a carboxylic acid
- Temperature of 100°C or greater
- Dehydrating agent

Ammonia $\longrightarrow$ 1° amide
1° amine $\longrightarrow$ 2° amide
2° amine $\longrightarrow$ 3° amide

REVERSIBLE AMINE SALT FORMATION

Acidic Conditions

- Reaction of amine with a strong acid
- Protonation of amine occurs.

Amine $\longrightarrow$ amine salt

Basic Conditions

- Reaction of amine salt with a strong base
- Deprotonation of amine salt occurs.

Amine salt $\longrightarrow$ amine

HYDROLYSIS OF AMIDES

- Heating is often required.

Acidic Hydrolysis

- Strong acid (HCl)

Amide $\longrightarrow$ acid + amine salt

Basic Hydrolysis (Saponification)

- Strong base (NaOH)

Amide $\longrightarrow$ acid salt + amine

Section 17-18 Quick Quiz

1. The organic products from the acidic hydrolysis of an amide are
   a. a carboxylic acid and an amine salt
   b. a carboxylic acid salt and an amine
   c. a carboxylic acid and an amine
   d. no correct response
2. The organic products from the basic hydrolysis of an amide are
   a. a carboxylic acid and an amine salt
   b. a carboxylic acid salt and an amine salt
   c. a carboxylic acid and an amine
   d. no correct response
3. In the hydrolysis of an amide which of the following bonds is broken?
   a. carbonyl carbon–nitrogen bond
   b. carbonyl carbon–carbonyl oxygen bond
   c. carbon–carbon bond
   d. no correct response

Answers: 1. a; 2. d; 3. a

17-19   Polyamides and Polyurethanes

LEARNING FOCUS

Be familiar with the general structural characteristics of polyamide and polyurethane polymers; be familiar with common naturally occurring and synthetically produced polyamides and polyurethanes.

Amide polymers—polyamides—are synthesized by combining diamines and dicarboxylic acids in a condensation polymerization reaction (Section 16-18). A **polyamide** *is a condensation polymer in which the monomers are joined through amide linkages.*

The most important synthetic polyamide is *nylon.* Nylon is used in clothing and hosiery, as well as in carpets, tire cord, rope, and parachutes. It also has nonfiber uses; for example, it is used in paint brushes, electrical parts, valves, and fasteners. It is a tough, strong, nontoxic, nonflammable material that is resistant to chemicals. Surgical suture is made of nylon because it is such a strong fiber.

There are actually many different types of nylon, most of which are based on diamine and diacid monomers. The most important nylon is nylon 66, which is made by using 1,6-hexanediamine and hexanedioic acid as monomers (Figure 17-16). ◄

▶ *The name* nylon 66 *comes from the fact that each of the monomers has six carbon atoms.*

1,6-Hexanediamine

Hexanedioic acid

The reaction of one acid group of the diacid with one amine group of the diamine initially produces an amide molecule; an acid group is left over on one end, and an amine group is left over on the other end.

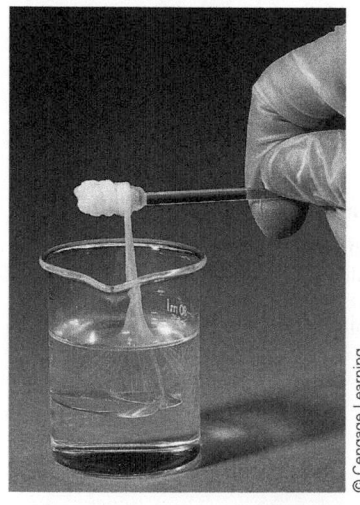

Figure 17-16 A white strand of a nylon polymer forms between the two layers of a solution containing a diacid (bottom layer) and a diamine (top layer).

© Cengage Learning

Figure 17-17 A regular hydrogen-bonding pattern among Kevlar polymer strands contributes to the great strength of this polymer.

This species then reacts further, and the process continues until a long polymeric molecule, nylon, has been produced.

A portion of the polyamide nylon 66

Additional stiffness and toughness are imparted to polyamides if aromatic rings are present in the polymer "backbone." The polyamide Kevlar is now used in place of steel in bullet-resistant vests. The polymeric repeating unit in Kevlar is

Kevlar

A uniform system of hydrogen bonds that holds polymer chains together accounts for the "amazing" strength of Kevlar (see Figure 17-17).

Nomex is a polyamide whose structure is a variation of that of Kevlar. With Nomex, the monomers are *meta* isomers rather than *para* isomers. Nomex is used in flame-resistant clothing for firefighters and race car drivers (Figure 17-18).

Silk and wool are examples of *naturally occurring* polyamide polymers. Silk and wool are proteins, and proteins are polyamide polymers. Because much of the human body is protein material, much of the human body is polyamide polymer. The monomers for proteins are amino acids, difunctional molecules containing both amino and carboxyl groups. Some representative structures for amino acids (Section 20-2), of which there are many, are:

$$H_2N-CH_2-COOH \qquad H_2N-\underset{\underset{CH_3}{|}}{CH}-COOH \qquad H_2N-\underset{\underset{\underset{CH_3}{|}}{CH-CH_3}}{\overset{|}{CH}}-COOH$$

A **urethane** *is a hydrocarbon derivative that contains a carbonyl group bonded to both an —OR group and an —NHR (or —NR$_2$) group.* Such compounds are prepared by reaction of an alcohol with an isocyanate (RN=C=O).

$$R-N=C=O + R'OH \longrightarrow$$

Isocyanate   Urethane

Figure 17-18 Firefighters with flame-resistant clothing containing Nomex.

Peter Skinner/Science Source

A **polyurethane** *is a polymer formed from the reaction of dialcohol and diisocyanate monomers.* With the monomers benzene diisocyanate and ethylene glycol, the polymerization reaction is

Benzene 1,3-diisocyanate + Ethylene glycol → A polyurethane

Structurally, polyurethanes have aspects of the structures of both polyesters and polyamides as shown in the following segment of a polyurethane structure.

Amide | Ester

Foam rubber in furniture upholstery, packaging materials, life preservers, elastic fibers, and many other products contain polyurethane polymers.

One of the best-known polyurethanes is Spandex, a strong yet flexible polymer used in both men's and women's athletic wear. It has also been used in support hosiery. On the molecular level, it has rigid regions (for strength) that are joined together by flexible segments.

Flexible portion

Rigid segment

Spandex
Trade name: Lycra

Section 17-19 Quick Quiz

1. Which of the following sets of monomers could be used to produce a polyamide?
   a. dicarboxylic acid and dialcohol
   b. dicarboxylic acid and diamine
   c. dialcohol and diamine
   d. no correct response
2. Which of the following sets of monomers could be used to produce a polyurethane?
   a. dicarboxylic acid and diurethane
   b. dialcohol and diurethane
   c. dialcohol and diisocyanate
   d. no correct response
3. Which of the following is *not* a polyamide?
   a. silk
   b. wool
   c. nylon
   d. no correct response
4. Which of the following is a polyurethane?
   a. Kevlar
   b. Nomax
   c. Spandex
   d. no correct response

Answers: 1. b; 2. c; 3. d; 4. c

Concepts to Remember

Structural characteristics of amines. Amines are derivatives of ammonia (NH_3) in which one or more hydrogen atoms have been replaced by an alkyl, a cycloalkyl, or an aryl group (Section 17-2).

Classification of amines. Amines are classified as primary, secondary, or tertiary, depending on the number of hydrocarbon groups (one, two, or three) directly attached to the nitrogen atom. The functional group present in a primary amine, the $—NH_2$ group, is called an *amino* group. Secondary and tertiary amines contain substituted amino groups (Section 17-2).

Nomenclature for amines. Common names for amines are formed by listing the hydrocarbon groups attached to the nitrogen atom in alphabetical order, followed by the suffix *-amine*. In the IUPAC system, the *-e* ending of the name of the longest carbon chain present is changed to *-amine,* and a number is used to locate the position of the amino group. Carbon-chain substituents are given numbers to designate their locations (Section 17-3).

Properties of amines. The methylamines and ethylamine are gases at room temperature; amines of higher molecular mass are usually liquids and smell like raw fish. Primary and secondary, but not tertiary, amines can participate in hydrogen bonding to other amine molecules (Section 17-5).

Basicity of amines. Amines are weak bases because of the ability of the unshared electron pair on the amine nitrogen atom to accept a proton in acidic solution (Section 17-6).

Amine salts. The reaction of a strong acid with an amine produces an amine salt. Such salts are more soluble in water than are the parent amines (Section 17-7).

Alkylation of ammonia and amines. Alkylation of ammonia, primary amines, secondary amines, and tertiary amines produces primary amines, secondary amines, tertiary amines, and quaternary ammonium salts, respectively (Section 17-8).

Heterocyclic amines. In a heterocyclic amine, the nitrogen atoms of amino groups present are part of either an aromatic or a nonaromatic ring system. Numerous heterocyclic amines are important biochemical compounds (Section 17-9).

Structural characteristics of amides. An amide is derived from a carboxylic acid by replacing the hydroxyl group with an amino or a substituted amino group (Section 17-12).

Classification of amides. Amides, like amines, can be classified as primary, secondary, or tertiary, depending on how many nonhydrogen atoms are attached to the nitrogen atom (Section 17-12).

Nomenclature for amides. The nomenclature for amides is derived from that for carboxylic acids by changing the *-oic acid* ending to *-amide*. Groups attached to the nitrogen atom of the amide are located using the prefix *N-* (Section 17-13).

Basicity of amides. Amides, unlike amines, do not exhibit basic properties. The nitrogen lone pair of electrons does not function as a proton acceptor because of the partial positive charge present on the nitrogen's neighboring carbonyl carbon atom (Section 17-15).

Physical properties of amides. Most unbranched amides are solids at room temperature and have correspondingly high boiling points because of strong hydrogen bonds between molecules (Section 17-16).

Preparation of amides. Reaction, at elevated temperature, of carboxylic acids with ammonia, primary amines, and secondary amines produces primary, secondary, and tertiary amides, respectively (Section 17-17).

Hydrolysis of amides. In amide hydrolysis, the bond between the carbonyl carbon atom and the nitrogen is broken, and free acid and free amine are produced. Acidic hydrolysis conditions convert the product amine to an amine salt. Basic hydrolysis conditions convert the product acid to an acid salt (Section 17-18).

Polyamides. Polyamides are condensation polymers with monomers joined together by amide linkages. The monomers for polyamides are diacids and diamines (Section 17-19).

Exercises and Problems

Exercises and problems are arranged in matched pairs with the two members of a pair addressing the same concept(s). The answer to the odd-numbered member of a pair is given at the back of the book. Problems denoted with a ▲ involve concepts found not only in the section under consideration but also concepts found in one or more earlier sections of the chapter.

Bonding Characteristics of Nitrogen Atoms in Organic Compounds (Section 17-1)

17-1 Contrast N, O, and C atoms in terms of the number of covalent bonds they usually form in organic compounds.

17-2 Contrast N, O, and C atoms in terms of the number of nonbonding electron pairs they normally possess when they are present in organic compounds.

Structure and Classification of Amines (Section 17-2)

17-3 How many R-groups are present in each of the following types of amines?
a. primary amine
b. secondary amine
c. tertiary amine

17-4 How many carbon–nitrogen bonds are present in each of the following types of amines?
a. primary amine
b. secondary amine
c. tertiary amine

17-5 How many N atoms are present in the functional group in each of the following types of amines?
a. 1° amine   b. 2° amine   c. 3° amine

17-6 How many nitrogen–hydrogen bonds are present in the functional group in each of the following types of amines?
a. 1° amine   b. 2° amine   c. 3° amine

17-7 Indicate whether or not each of the following compounds contains an *amine functional group*?
a. $CH_3—CH—CH_3$
           |
          NH_2

b. $CH_3—NH—CH_3$

c. O
             ‖
   $CH_3—CH_2—C—NH_2$

d. $CH_3—CH_2—N—CH_2—CH_3$
                 |
                CH_3

17-8 Indicate whether or not each of the following compounds contains an *amine functional group*?
a. CH_3—CH_2—CH_2—NH_2
b. CH_3—CH_2—N—CH_3
   |
   CH_3
c.
CH_3—NH—⟨ ⟩
d.
   CH_3—CH_2—CH_2—$\overset{\displaystyle O}{\overset{\|}{C}}$—$NH_2$

17-9 Indicate whether each of the compounds in Problem 17-7 contains (1) an amino group, (2) a monosubstituted amino group, (3) a disubstituted amino group, or (4) is not an amine.

17-10 Indicate whether each of the compounds in Problem 17-8 contains (1) an amino group, (2) a monosubstituted amino group, (3) a disubstituted amino group, or (4) is not an amine.

17-11 Classify each of the following amines as a primary, secondary, or tertiary amine.
a. CH_3—NH_2
b. CH_3—CH—CH_3
       |
       NH_2
c. CH_3—NH—CH_3
d. CH_3—CH_2—N—CH_2—CH—CH_3
             | |
             CH_3 CH_3

17-12 Classify each of the following amines as a primary, secondary, or tertiary amine.
a. CH_3—CH_2—CH—CH_2—CH_3
                |
                NH_2
b. CH_3
          |
   CH_3—C—CH_3
          |
          NH_2
c. CH_3—N—CH_3
          |
          CH_3
d. CH_3—CH—NH—CH—CH_2
          | |
          CH_3 CH_3

17-13 Classify each of the following amines as a primary, secondary, or tertiary amine.
a. [cyclopentane]—NH—CH_3 b. [pyrrolidine ring]—N—CH_3
c. [benzene ring]—N—CH_2—CH_3 d. [benzene ring]—CH_3—NH_2
              |
              CH_3

17-14 Classify each of the following amines as a primary, secondary, or tertiary amine.
a. [benzene ring]—NH_2, CH_3 b. [benzene ring]—NH—CH_3
c. [pyrrolidine ring with N—H]   d. [bicyclic ring with N—CH_3]

Nomenclature for Amines (Section 17-3)

17-15 Assign a common name to each of the following amines.
a. CH_3—NH—CH_2—CH_3
b. CH_3—CH_2—CH_2—NH_2
c. CH_3—CH_2—N—CH_2—CH_3
                |
                CH_3
d. CH_3—CH—NH—CH_3
          |
          CH_3

17-16 Assign a common name to each of the following amines.
a. CH_3—CH—CH_3
          |
          NH_2
b. H_2N—CH_2—CH_2—CH_2—CH_3
c. CH_3—CH_2—N—CH_2—CH_3
                |
                CH_2—CH_3
d. CH_3—CH_2—CH_2—NH—CH—CH_3
                            |
                            CH_3

17-17 Assign an IUPAC name to each of the following amines.
a. CH_3—CH_2—CH—CH_2—CH_3
                |
                NH_2
b. CH_3—CH—CH—CH_2—CH_3
          | |
          CH_3 NH_2
c. CH_3—CH_2—CH—CH_2—CH_3
                |
                NH—CH_3
d. CH_3—CH—CH—CH_3
          | |
          NH_2 NH_2

17-18 Assign an IUPAC name to each of the following amines.
a. CH_3—CH_2—CH_2—NH_2
b. CH_3—CH—NH_2
          |
          CH_3
c. CH_3—CH—CH—CH—CH_3
          | | |
          NH_2 CH_3 NH_2
d. CH_3—CH_2—CH_3—NH—CH_3

17-19 Assign an IUPAC name to each of the following amines.
a. [structure]—NH_2 b. [structure]—N
c. [structure]—NH—[structure]   d. [structure]—NH

17-20 Assign an IUPAC name to each of the following amines.
a. [structure]—NH_2 b. [structure]—NH_2
c. [structure]—NH—[structure]   d. [structure]—N—[structure]

17-21 Name each of the following aromatic amines as a derivative of aniline.

a. (benzene ring with —NH$_2$ and Br substituent)

b. (benzene ring with —NH—CH—CH$_3$, with CH$_3$ branch)

c. (benzene ring with —N—CH$_2$—CH$_3$, with CH$_3$ on N)

d. (two benzene rings attached to N, with CH$_3$ on N)

17-22 Name each of the following aromatic amines as a derivative of aniline.

a. Cl—(benzene ring)—NH$_2$

b. (benzene ring)—NH—CH$_2$—CH$_3$

c. CH$_3$—(benzene ring)—NH—CH$_3$

d. (benzene ring with NH$_2$, Br, and Cl substituents)

17-23 Draw a condensed structural formula for each of the following amines.
a. 2-Methyl-2-butanamine
b. 1,6-Hexanediamine
c. 2-Amino-3-pentanone
d. 2-Aminopropanoic acid

17-24 Draw a condensed structural formula for each of the following amines.
a. 2-Methyl-3-ethyl-1-hexanamine
b. 1,3-Pentanediamine
c. 3-Amino-2-pentanol
d. N,N-dimethyl-1-butanamine

▲**17-25** Classify each of the following compounds as a 1° amine, 2° amine, or 3° amine.
a. Ethylpropylamine
b. 2-Propanamine
c. N-Phenylaniline
d. 2-Cyclohexylethanamine

▲**17-26** Classify each of the following compounds as a 1° amine, 2° amine, or 3° amine.
a. Diisopropylamine
b. 3-Methylaniline
c. N,N-Dimethylmethanamine
d. N-Ethyl-2-methylcyclopentylamine

Isomerism for Amines (Section 17-4)

17-27 Indicate whether or not the two members of each of the following pairs of amines are constitutional isomers.
a. CH$_3$—CH$_2$—CH$_2$—CH$_2$—NH$_2$ and CH$_3$—CH$_2$—CH$_2$—NH$_2$

b. CH$_3$—CH$_2$—CH$_2$—NH—CH$_3$ and CH$_3$—CH$_2$—NH—CH$_2$—CH$_3$

c. CH$_3$—CH$_2$—CH$_2$—NH$_2$ and CH$_3$—CH—NH$_2$ (with CH$_3$ branch)

d. CH$_3$—CH$_2$—CH$_2$—CH$_2$—NH$_2$ and (cyclobutane)—NH$_2$

17-28 Indicate whether or not the two members of each of the following pairs of amines are constitutional isomers.
a. CH$_3$—CH$_2$—NH$_2$ and CH$_3$—CH$_2$—CH$_2$—NH$_2$

b. CH$_3$—CH$_2$—CH$_2$—NH—CH$_3$ and CH$_3$—NH—CH$_2$—CH$_2$—CH$_3$

c. CH$_3$—CH$_2$—CH$_2$—CH$_2$—NH$_2$ and CH$_3$—CH$_2$—NH—CH$_2$—CH$_3$

d. CH$_3$—CH$_2$—CH$_2$—CH$_2$—CH$_2$—NH$_2$ and (cyclopentane)—NH$_2$

17-29 How many saturated noncyclic amine constitutional isomers exist that have each of the following generalized formulations?
a. C$_4$—NH$_2$ b. C$_3$—NH—C$_2$
c. C$_3$—N—C$_2$ (with C$_2$ branch)   d. C$_3$—NH—C$_3$

17-30 How many saturated noncyclic amine constitutional isomers exist that have each of the following generalized formulations?
a. C$_3$—NH$_2$ b. C$_4$—NH—C$_2$
c. C$_3$—N—C$_3$ (with C$_2$ branch)   d. C$_4$—NH—C$_4$

▲**17-31** Assign IUPAC names to each of the eight isomeric primary amines that have the molecular formula C$_5$H$_{13}$N.

▲**17-32** Assign IUPAC names to each of the six isomeric secondary amines that have the molecular formula C$_5$H$_{13}$N.

Physical Properties of Amines (Section 17-5)

17-33 Indicate whether each of the following amines is a liquid or a gas at room temperature.
a. Butylamine   b. Dimethylamine
c. Ethylamine   d. Dibutylamine

17-34 Indicate whether each of the following amines is a liquid or a gas at room temperature.
a. Methylamine   b. Propylamine
c. Trimethylamine   d. Pentylamine

17-35 Determine the maximum number of hydrogen bonds that can form between a methylamine molecule and
a. other methylamine molecules
b. water molecules

17-36 Determine the maximum number of hydrogen bonds that can form between a dimethylamine molecule and
a. other dimethylamine molecules
b. water molecules

17-37   Although they have similar molecular masses (73 and 72 amu, respectively), the boiling point of butylamine is much higher (78°C) than that of pentane (36°C). Explain why.

17-38   Although they have similar molecular masses (73 and 74 amu, respectively), the boiling point of 1-butanamine is much lower (78°C) than that of 1-butanol (118°C). Explain why.

17-39   Which compound in each of the following pairs of amines would you expect to be more soluble in water? Justify each answer.
a. CH_3—CH_2—NH_2 and
      CH_3—CH_2—CH_2—CH_2—CH_2—NH_2
b. CH_3—CH_2—CH_2—NH_2 and
      H_2N—CH_2—CH_2—CH_2—NH_2

17-40   Which compound in each of the following pairs of amines would you expect to be more soluble in water? Justify each answer.
a. CH_3—CH_2—CH_2—NH_2 and
      CH_3—CH_2—CH_2—CH_2—NH_2
b. CH_3—CH_2—NH—CH_3 and CH_3—$\overset{\displaystyle |}{\underset{\displaystyle CH_3}{N}}$—$CH_3$

Basicity of Amines (Section 17-6)

17-41   Show the structures of the missing substance(s) in each of the following acid–base equilibria.
a. CH_3—CH_2—$NH_2 + H_2O \rightleftharpoons ? + OH^-$
b.

c. $? + H_2O \rightleftharpoons CH_3$—$\overset{\displaystyle |}{\underset{\displaystyle CH_3}{CH}}$—$\overset{+}{N}H_2$—$CH_3 + OH^-$

d.   Diethylamine + $H_2O \rightleftharpoons ? + ?$

17-42   Show the structures of the missing substance(s) in each of the following acid–base equilibria.
a. CH_3—CH_2—CH_2—$NH_2 + H_2O \rightleftharpoons$
      CH_3—CH_2—CH_2—$\overset{+}{N}H_3 + ?$
b.
      $? + H_2O \rightleftharpoons$ ⬡—CH_2—$\overset{+}{N}H_3 + OH^-$

c. CH_3—$\overset{\displaystyle |}{\underset{\displaystyle CH_3}{CH}}$—$CH_2$—$NH$—$CH_3 + H_2O \rightleftharpoons ? + OH^-$

d.   Trimethylamine + $H_2O \rightleftharpoons ? + ?$

17-43   Name each of the following substituted ammonium and substituted anilinium ions.
a. CH_3—$\overset{+}{N}H_2$—CH_3
b. CH_3—CH_2—$\overset{+}{\underset{\displaystyle CH_2—CH_3}{N}}H$—$CH_2$—$CH_3$

c. CH_3—CH_2—$\overset{+}{N}H$—CH_2—CH_3
      ⬡

d. CH_3
           $|$
      $\overset{+}{N}H_2$—CH—CH_3
      ⬡

17-44   Name each of the following substituted ammonium and substituted anilinium ions.
a. CH_3—$\overset{+}{N}H_3$
b. CH_3—CH_2—CH_2—$\overset{+}{N}H_2$—CH_3
c. $\overset{+}{N}H_2$—CH_2—CH_3
      ⬡

d. CH_3—CH_2—$\overset{+}{N}H$—CH_2—CH_2—CH_3
      ⬡

17-45   Draw a structural formula for the "parent" amine of each of the substituted ammonium and substituted anilinium ions in Problem 17-43.

17-46   Draw a structural formula for the "parent" amine of each of the substituted ammonium and substituted anilinium ions in Problem 17-44.

▲**17-47**   Draw skeletal structural formulas for the three isomeric disubstituted ammonium ions that have the chemical formula $C_4H_{12}N^+$.

▲**17-48**   Draw skeletal structural formulas for the three isomeric trisubstituted ammonium ions that have the chemical formula $C_5H_{14}N^+$.

Reaction of Amines with Acids (Section 17-7)

17-49   Draw the structure of the amine salt produced when each of the following amines reacts with HCl.

a. CH_3—CH_2—NH_2 b.   ⬠—NH_2

c. CH_3—$\overset{\displaystyle |}{\underset{\displaystyle CH_3}{CH}}$—$NH_2$ d. CH_3—CH_2—NH—CH_2—CH_3

17-50   Draw the structure of the amine salt produced when each of the following amines reacts with HCl.

a. CH_3—CH_2—CH_2—NH_2 b. CH_3—NH—CH_3

c. CH_3—$\overset{\displaystyle |}{\underset{\displaystyle CH_3}{CH}}$—$CH_2$—$NH_2$ d.   ⬠—NH—CH_2—CH_3

17-51   Draw the structure of the amine produced when each of the following amine salts reacts with NaOH.
a. CH_3—CH_2—$\overset{+}{N}H_3\ Cl^-$
b. CH_3—$\overset{+}{N}H_2$—CH_2—$CH_3\ Cl^-$

c. (cyclopentyl)$-\overset{+}{N}H_2-CH_3\ Cl^-$

d. $CH_3-\overset{CH_3}{\underset{|}{CH}}-\overset{+}{N}H_3\ Cl^-$

17-52 Draw the structure of the amine produced when each of the following amine salts reacts with NaOH.

a. $CH_3-CH_2-CH_2-\overset{+}{N}H_3\ Cl^-$

b. $CH_3-\overset{CH_3}{\underset{|}{CH}}-\overset{+}{N}H_2-CH_3\ Cl^-$

c. (cyclopentyl)$-\overset{+}{N}H_3\ Cl^-$

d. $CH_3-\overset{+}{N}H-\overset{|}{\underset{CH_3}{C}}H_3\ Cl^-$

17-53 Draw the structure of the missing substance or substances in each of the following reactions involving amines and amine salts.

a. $? + NaOH \longrightarrow CH_3-\overset{|}{\underset{CH_3}{N}}-CH_3 + NaBr + H_2O$

b. $CH_3-CH_2-NH-CH_3\ + ? \longrightarrow$
   $CH_3-CH_2-\overset{+}{N}H_2-CH_3\ Cl^-$

c. (phenyl)$-\overset{+}{\underset{CH_3}{N}}H-CH_3\ Br^- + NaOH \longrightarrow ? + ? + H_2O$

d. $? + HBr \longrightarrow CH_3-\overset{CH_3}{\underset{CH_3}{\overset{|}{C}}}-\overset{+}{N}H_3\ Br^-$

17-54 Draw the structure of the missing substance or substances in each of the following reactions involving amines and amine salts.

a. $CH_3-NH_2\ + ? \longrightarrow CH_3-\overset{+}{N}H_3\ Cl^-$

b. $? + HBr \longrightarrow CH_3-\overset{CH_3}{\underset{|}{CH}}-\overset{+}{N}H-\overset{|}{\underset{CH_3}{}}CH_3\ Br^-$

c. $? + NaOH \longrightarrow CH_3-NH-CH_3 + NaCl + H_2O$

d. (phenyl)$-\overset{+}{N}H_3\ Cl^- + NaOH \longrightarrow ? + NaCl + ?$

17-55 Name each of the following amine salts.

a. $CH_3-CH_2-CH_2-\overset{+}{N}H_3\ Cl^-$

b. $CH_3-CH_2-CH_2-\overset{+}{\underset{CH_3}{N}}H_2\ Cl^-$

c. $CH_3-CH_2-\overset{+}{\underset{CH_3}{N}}H-CH_3\ Br^-$

d. (phenyl)$-\overset{+}{\underset{CH_3}{N}}H-CH_3\ Br^-$

17-56 Name each of the following amine salts.

a. $CH_3-CH_2-\overset{+}{\underset{CH_3}{N}}H_2\ Cl^-$

b. $CH_3-CH_2-CH_2-CH_2-\overset{+}{N}H_3\ Cl^-$

c. $CH_3-\overset{+}{\underset{CH_3}{C}H}-NH-CH_3\ Br^-$ with $CH_3\ CH_3$ below

d. (phenyl)$-\overset{+}{\underset{CH_3}{N}}H_2\ Cl^-$

▲**17-57** What is the IUPAC name of the "parent" amine for each of the amine salts in Problem 17-55?

▲**17-58** What is the IUPAC name of the "parent" amine for each of the amine salts in Problem 17-56?

17-59 Which of the four terms *free amine, free base, deprotonated base,* and *protonated base* apply to each of the following amine species? More than one term may apply in a given situation.

a. $CH_3-CH_2-NH_2$

b. $CH_3-CH_2-CH_2-NH-CH_3$

c. $CH_3-\overset{+}{N}H_3$

d. $CH_3-CH_2-\overset{+}{N}H_2-CH_3$

17-60 Which of the four terms *free amine, free base, deprotonated base,* and *protonated base* apply to each of the following amine species? More than one term may apply in a given situation.

a. $CH_3-CH_2-CH_2-NH_2$

b. $CH_3-CH_2-CH_2-\overset{+}{N}H_2-CH_3$

c. $CH_3-NH-CH_2-CH_3$

d. $CH_3-CH_2-\overset{+}{N}H_3$

Alkylation of Ammonia and Amines (Section 17-8)

17-61 Indicate whether or not each of the following reactions is an alkylation reaction.

a. $NH_3 + CH_3-CH_2-CH_2-Cl + NaOH \longrightarrow$

b. $CH_3-Br + CH_3-\overset{|}{\underset{CH_3}{CH}}-NH-CH_3 + NaOH \longrightarrow$

c. $CH_3-CH_2-NH_2 + CH_3-CH_2-Cl + NaOH \longrightarrow$

d. $CH_3-\overset{CH_3}{\underset{CH_3}{\overset{|}{C}}}-Br + NH_3 + NaOH \longrightarrow$

17-62 Indicate whether or not each of the following reactions is an alkylation reaction.

a. $CH_3-\overset{|}{\underset{CH_3}{CH}}-Cl + NH_3 + NaOH \longrightarrow$

b. $CH_3-NH-CH_3 + CH_3-Br + NaOH \longrightarrow$

c. $CH_3-CH_2-CH_2-NH_2 + CH_3-CH_2-Br + NaOH \longrightarrow$

d. $CH_3-CH_2-\overset{|}{\underset{CH_3}{CH}}-Cl +$
   $CH_3-CH_2-NH-\overset{|}{\underset{CH_3}{CH}}-CH_3 + NaOH \longrightarrow$

17-63 Classify the organic product in each of the reactions in Problem 17-61 as (1) a 1° amine, (2) a 2° amine, (3) a 3° amine, or (4) a quaternary ammonium salt.

17-64 Classify the organic product in each of the reactions in Problem 17-62 as (1) a 1° amine, (2) a 2° amine, (3) a 3° amine, or (4) a quaternary ammonium salt.

17-65 For each of the reactions in Problem 17-61, draw the structure of the organic product and give the formulas of the two inorganic products produced.

17-66 For each of the reactions in Problem 17-62, draw the structure of the organic product and give the formulas of the two inorganic products produced.

17-67 List three different sets of alkyl chloride–secondary amine reactants that could be used to prepare the tertiary amine ethylmethylpropylamine.

17-68 List three different sets of alkyl chloride–secondary amine reactants that could be used to prepare the tertiary amine butylethylpropylamine.

17-69 Draw the structure of the amine or quaternary ammonium salt produced when each of the following pairs of compounds reacts in the presence of a strong base.
a. Trimethylamine and ethyl bromide
b. Diisopropylamine and methyl bromide
c. Ethylmethylpropylamine and methyl chloride
d. Ethylamine and ethyl chloride

17-70 Draw the structure of the amine or quaternary ammonium salt produced when each of the following pairs of compounds reacts in the presence of a strong base.
a. Dimethylamine and propyl bromide
b. Diethylmethylamine and isopropyl chloride
c. Methylpropylamine and ethyl chloride
d. Tripropylamine and propyl chloride

17-71 Classify each of the following salts as an amine salt or a quaternary ammonium salt.

a. $CH_3-\overset{+}{N}H-CH_3\ Br^-$
         |
        CH_3

b. CH_3
         |
   $CH_3-\overset{+}{N}-CH_3\ Cl^-$
         |
        CH_3

c. $CH_3-CH_2-\overset{+}{N}H_2-CH_3\ Br^-$

d. CH_3
              |
  $CH_3-CH_2-\overset{+}{N}-CH_2-CH_3\ Cl^-$
              |
             CH_3

17-72 Classify each of the following salts as an amine salt or a quaternary ammonium salt.

a. CH_3
          |
  $CH_3-\overset{+}{N}-CH_2-CH_3\ Cl^-$
          |
         CH_3

b.   H
          |
  $CH_3-\overset{+}{N}-CH_2-CH_3\ Cl^-$
          |
         CH_3

c.   H
          |
  $CH_3-\overset{+}{N}-CH_3\ Br^-$
          |
          H

d. CH_3
                           |
  $CH_3-CH_2-CH_2-\overset{+}{N}-CH_3\ Br^-$
                           |
                          CH_3

▲**17-73** Indicate whether or not each of the salts in Problem 17-71 can be converted back to its "parent" amine through reaction with a strong base.

▲**17-74** Indicate whether or not each of the salts in Problem 17-72 can be converted back to its "parent" amine through reaction with a strong base.

17-75 Name each of the salts in Problem 17-71.

17-76 Name each of the salts in Problem 17-72.

Heterocyclic Amines (Section 17-9)

17-77 Indicate whether or not each of the following compounds is a heterocyclic amine.

17-78 Indicate whether or not each of the following compounds is a heterocyclic amine.

17-79 With the help of Figure 17-8, indicate whether the ring system in each of the following heterocyclic amines is (1) saturated, (2) unsaturated, or (3) fused. More than one choice may be correct for a given heterocyclic amine.
a. Pyrrolidine   b. Imidazole
c. Pyridine   d. Quinoline

17-80 With the help of Figure 17-8, indicate whether the ring system in each of the following heterocyclic amines is (1) saturated, (2) unsaturated, or (3) fused. More than one choice may be correct for a given heterocyclic amine.
a. Pyrrole   b. Indole
c. Pyrimidine   d. Purine

17-81 What is the difference, if any, between a porphyrin ring and a heme unit in terms of the number of pyrrole rings present?

17-82 What is the difference, if any, between a porphyrin ring and a heme unit in terms of iron content?

Selected Biochemically Important Amines (Section 17-10)

17-83 Indicate whether each of the following statements about biochemically important amines is true or false.
a. Serotonin regulates lactation in women.
b. Structurally, dopamine and norepinephrine differ only by an —OH group.
c. L-Dopa and dopamine are two names for the same compound.
d. Prozac is a drug that helps maintain adrenaline levels in the brain.

17-84 Indicate whether each of the following statements about biochemically important amines is true or false.
a. Serotonin and dopamine both have structures based on a tryptamine core.
b. A deficiency of dopamine is associated with Parkinson's disease.
c. Structurally, norepinephrine and epinephrine differ only by a —CH$_3$ group.
d. Epinephrine and adrenaline are two names for the same compound.

17-85 Indicate whether each of the following amines has a phenethylamine structural core or a tryptamine structural core.
a. Dopamine   b. Epinephrine
c. Amphetamine   d. Serotonin

17-86 Indicate whether each of the following amines has a phenethylamine structural core or a tryptamine structural core.
a. Norephinephrine   b. Adrenaline
c. L-dopa   d. Methamphetamine

17-87 Indicate whether each of the following amines is (1) a decongestant, (2) a central nervous system stimulant, or (3) a neurotransmitter.
a. Dopamine   b. Methamphetamine
c. Pseudoephedrine   d. Desoxyn

17-88 Indicate whether each of the following amines is (1) a decongestant, (2) a central nervous system stimulant, or (3) a neurotransmitter.
a. Serotonin   b. Amphetamine
c. Phenylephrine   d. Adderall

Alkaloids (Section 17-11)

17-89 Indicate whether or not each of the following substances is an alkaloid.
a. Nicotine   b. Quinine
c. Morphine   d. Cocaine

17-90 Indicate whether or not each of the following substances is an alkaloid.
a. Caffeine   b. Theobromine
c. Atropine   d. Codeine

17-91 Indicate whether each of the following statements about particular alkaloids is true or false.
a. Medicinally, atropine is used to dilate the pupil of the eye.
b. Quinine is a powerful antipyretic.
c. Morphine is 100 times more powerful as a painkiller than codeine.
d. The opium of the oriental poppy plant contains both morphine and heroin.

17-92 Indicate whether each of the following statements about particular alkaloids is true or false.
a. Atropine's molecular structure contains two amine groups.
b. Quinine is used in the treatment of malaria.
c. The demand for morphine as a painkiller exceeds that for codeine.
d. Structurally, codeine is a methyl morphine.

17-93 Describe each of the following molecules, which have the same central core, in terms of functional groups attached to the common central core.
a. Codeine   b. Morphine
c. Hydrocodone   d. Oxycodone

17-94 Indicate whether each of the following prescription painkillers contains *oxycodone* or *hydrocodone*.
a. Lortab   b. Percocet
c. OxyContin   d. Percodan

Structure of and Classification of Amides (Section 17-12)

17-95 How many R-groups are present in each of the following types of amides?
a. primary amide
b. tertiary amide
c. monosubstituted amide

17-96 How many R-groups are present in each of the following types of amides?
a. unsubstituted amide
b. disubstituted amide
c. secondary amide

17-97 How many nitrogen atoms are present in the functional group in each of the following types of amides?
a. unsubstituted amide
b. disubstituted amide
c. secondary amide

17-98 How many nitrogen atoms are present in the functional group in each of the following types of amides?
a. primary amide
b. tertiary amide
c. monosubstituted amide

17-99 Indicate whether or not each of the following compounds contains an amide functional group.
a.
$$CH_3—CH_2—\overset{\overset{\displaystyle O}{\|}}{C}—NH_2$$
b.
c.
$$CH_3—\overset{\overset{\displaystyle O}{\|}}{C}—CH_2—CH_2—NH_2$$
d.

17-100 Indicate whether or not each of the following compounds contains an amide functional group.

a.

$$CH_3-\overset{\overset{\displaystyle O}{\|}}{C}-NH-CH_3$$

b.

$$CH_3-\overset{\overset{\displaystyle O}{\|}}{C}-\overset{\overset{\displaystyle CH_2-CH_3}{|}}{N}-CH_2-CH_2-CH_3$$

c.

$$H_2N-\overset{\overset{\displaystyle O}{\|}}{C}-CH_2-CH_3$$

d.

(ring structure with N—H and CH₃)

17-101 Classify each of the following amides as unsubstituted, monosubstituted, or disubstituted.

a.

$$CH_3-\overset{\overset{\displaystyle O}{\|}}{C}-NH-CH_3$$

b.

$$CH_3-\overset{\overset{\displaystyle O}{\|}}{C}-\overset{\overset{\displaystyle CH_3}{|}}{N}-CH_2-CH_3$$

c.

$$CH_3-\overset{\overset{\displaystyle O}{\|}}{C}-NH_2$$

d.

(ring structure with N—H)

17-102 Classify each of the following amides as unsubstituted, monosubstituted, or disubstituted.

a.

$$CH_3-\overset{\overset{\displaystyle O}{\|}}{C}-NH_2$$

b.

$$CH_3-CH_2-\overset{\overset{\displaystyle CH_3}{|}}{CH}-\overset{\overset{\displaystyle O}{\|}}{C}-NH-CH_3$$

c.

$$CH_3-\overset{\overset{\displaystyle O}{\|}}{C}-\overset{\overset{\displaystyle CH_3-CH-CH_3}{|}}{N}-CH_2-CH_2-CH_3$$

d.

(ring structure with N—CH₃)

17-103 Classify each of the amides in Problem 17-101 as a primary, secondary, or tertiary amide.

17-104 Classify each of the amides in Problem 17-102 as a primary, secondary, or tertiary amide.

▲**17-105** Classify each of the following compounds as (1) an amine, (2) an amide, or (3) both an amine and an amide.

a. (structure with NH₂) b. (structure with NH₂)

c. (ring structure with N—H) d. (ring structure with O, N, NH₂)

▲**17-106** Classify each of the following compounds as (1) an amine, (2) an amide, or (3) both an amine and an amide.

a. H_2N (structure with NH₂)   b. (structure with NH)

c. (ring structure with N—H and O) d. (ring structure with N, O, O, N—H)

Nomenclature for Amides (Section 17-13)

17-107 Assign an IUPAC name to each of the following amides.

a.

$$CH_3-\overset{\overset{\displaystyle O}{\|}}{C}-NH-CH_2-CH_3$$

b.

$$CH_3-CH_2-\overset{\overset{\displaystyle O}{\|}}{C}-\overset{\overset{\displaystyle CH_3}{|}}{N}-CH_3$$

c.

$$H_2N-\overset{\overset{\displaystyle O}{\|}}{C}-CH_2-CH_2-CH_3$$

d.

$$Cl-\overset{\overset{\displaystyle CH_3}{|}}{CH}-\overset{\overset{\displaystyle O}{\|}}{C}-NH_2$$

17-108 Assign an IUPAC name to each of the following amides.

a.

$$CH_3-CH_2-\overset{\overset{\displaystyle O}{\|}}{C}-NH-CH_2-CH_3$$

b.

$$CH_3-CH_2-CH_2-CH_2-\overset{\overset{\displaystyle O}{\|}}{C}-NH_2$$

c.

$$CH_3-CH_2-CH_2-\overset{\overset{\displaystyle O}{\|}}{C}-\overset{\overset{\displaystyle CH_3}{|}}{N}-CH_3$$

d.

$$CH_3-\overset{\overset{\displaystyle CH_3}{|}}{CH}-\overset{\overset{\displaystyle CH_3}{|}}{CH}-\overset{\overset{\displaystyle O}{\|}}{C}-NH-CH_3$$

17-109 Assign a common name to each of the amides in Problem 17-107.

17-110 Assign a common name to each of the amides in Problem 17-108.

17-111 Assign an IUPAC name to each of the following amides.

a. (structure with NH₂)

b. (structure with NH)

c. (structure with NH₂)

d. (structure with N)

17-112 Assign an IUPAC name to each of the following amides.

a.

b.

c.

d.

17-113 Write a structural formula for each of the following amides.
   a. *N*,*N*-Dimethylacetamide
   b. α-Methylbutyramide
   c. 3,*N*-Dimethylbutanamide
   d. Formamide

17-114 Write a structural formula for each of the following amides.
   a. *N*,*N*-Diethylpropanamide
   b. β-Methylbutyramide
   c. *N*-Methylbenzamide
   d. β,β,*N*-Trimethylbutyramide

▲**17-115** Assign IUPAC names to each of the following compounds.

a.

b.

c.

d.

▲**17-116** Assign IUPAC names to each of the following compounds.

a.

b.

c.

d.

Selected Amides and Their Uses (Section 17-14)

17-117 Indicate whether each of the following statements about the compound urea is true or false.
   a. Only one carbon atom is present in the structure of urea.
   b. In the pure state, urea is a yellow-colored liquid.
   c. Two of the starting materials for the biosynthetic production of urea are CO_2 and NH_3.

d. There are more nitrogen atoms than carbon atoms in the structure of urea.

17-118 Indicate whether each of the following statements about the compound melatonin is true or false.
   a. Melatonin concentrations in the body decrease with age.
   b. Low levels of melatonin are associated with a "good night's sleep."
   c. As a prescription drug, melatonin is used to treat "jet lag."
   d. There is an equal number of nitrogen atoms and carbon atoms in the structure of melatonin.

17-119 What is the mode of action for the insect repellent known as DEET?

17-120 What is the relationship between the acronym DEET and DEET's chemical name?

Basicity of Amides (Section 17-15)

17-121 What effect does a carbonyl group have on a nitrogen atom that is bonded directly to the carbonyl carbon atom?

17-122 Explain why the nitrogen atom in an amide functional group does not readily participate in hydrogen bonding.

17-123 Indicate whether or not each of the following substances exhibits basic behavior in aqueous solution.
   a. Propanamide
   b. 1-Propanamine

c.

$$CH_3-CH_2-\overset{\displaystyle O}{\overset{\|}{C}}-NH_2$$

d.

$$H_2N-CH_2-CH_2-\overset{\displaystyle O}{\overset{\|}{C}}-NH_2$$

17-124 Indicate whether or not each of the following substances exhibits basic behavior in aqueous solution.
   a. Methylethylamine
   b. Butanamide
   c. $H_2N-CH_2-CH_2-NH_2$

d.

$$H_2N-\overset{\displaystyle O}{\overset{\|}{C}}-CH_2-CH_2-\overset{\displaystyle O}{\overset{\|}{C}}-NH_2$$

Physical Properties of Amides (Section 17-16)

17-125 What is the physical state, at room temperature, of each of the following unbranched primary amides?
   a. methanamide   b. ethanamide
   c. butanamide   d. hexanamide

17-126 Would you expect *N*-ethylacetamide or *N*,*N*-diethyl-acetamide to have the higher boiling point? Explain.

17-127 Determine the maximum number of hydrogen bonds that can form between an acetamide molecule and
   a. other acetamide molecules
   b. water molecules

17-128 Determine the maximum number of hydrogen bonds that can form between a propanamide molecule and
   a. other propanamide molecules
   b. water molecules

Preparation of Amides (Section 17-17)

17-129 Indicate whether or not each of the following reactions is an amidification reaction.

a. $CH_3-\overset{O}{\underset{\|}{C}}-OH + NH_3 \xrightarrow{100°C}$

b. $CH_3-\overset{O}{\underset{\|}{C}}-OH + CH_3-NH_2 \xrightarrow{100°C}$

c. $CH_3-\overset{O}{\underset{\|}{C}}-OH + CH_3-NH-CH_3 \xrightarrow{100°C}$

d. $CH_3-\overset{O}{\underset{\|}{C}}-OH + CH_3-NH-CH_2-CH_3 \xrightarrow{100°C}$

17-130 Indicate whether or not each of the following reactions is an amidification reaction.

a. $CH_3-CH_2-\overset{O}{\underset{\|}{C}}-OH + NH_3 \xrightarrow{100°C}$

b. $CH_3-CH_2-\overset{O}{\underset{\|}{C}}-OH + CH_3-CH_2-NH_2 \xrightarrow{100°C}$

c. $CH_3-CH_2-\overset{O}{\underset{\|}{C}}-OH + CH_3-NH-CH_3 \xrightarrow{100°C}$

d. $CH_3-CH_2-\overset{O}{\underset{\|}{C}}-OH + CH_3-CH_2-NH-CH_3 \xrightarrow{100°C}$

17-131 For each of the reactions in Problem 17-129 indicate whether the organic product is (1) a 1° amide, (2) a 2° amide, (3) a 3° amide, or (4) not an amide.

17-132 For each of the reactions in Problem 17-130 indicate whether the organic product is (1) a 1° amide, (2) a 2° amide, (3) a 3° amide, or (4) not an amide.

17-133 What is the structure of the carboxylic acid needed to produce each of the following amides via an amidification reaction?

a. $CH_3-\overset{O}{\underset{\|}{C}}-NH_2$

b. $H-\overset{O}{\underset{\|}{C}}-NH-CH_3$

c. $CH_3-CH_2-\overset{O}{\underset{\|}{C}}-\overset{CH_3}{\underset{}{N}}-CH_3$

d. $CH_3-NH-\overset{O}{\underset{\|}{C}}-CH_2-CH_3$

17-134 What is the structure of the carboxylic acid needed to produce each of the following amides via an amidification reaction?

a. $H-\overset{O}{\underset{\|}{C}}-NH_2$

b. $CH_3-\overset{O}{\underset{\|}{C}}-NH-CH_3$

c. $CH_3-\overset{O}{\underset{\|}{C}}-\overset{CH_3}{\underset{}{N}}-CH_3$

d. $CH_3-CH_2-NH-\overset{O}{\underset{\|}{C}}-CH_2-CH_3$

17-135 What is the structure of the nitrogen-containing compound needed to produce each of the amides in Problem 17-133 via an amidification reaction?

17-136 What is the structure of the nitrogen-containing compound needed to produce each of the amides in Problem 17-134 via an amidification reaction?

17-137 Draw the structures of the missing substances in each of the following reactions involving amides.

a. $CH_3-CH_2-\overset{O}{\underset{\|}{C}}-OH + ? \xrightarrow{100°C}$
$CH_3-CH_2-\overset{O}{\underset{\|}{C}}-NH-CH_3 + H_2O$

b. $CH_3-\overset{CH_3}{\underset{CH_3}{C}}-\overset{O}{\underset{\|}{C}}-OH + CH_3-NH-CH_3 \xrightarrow{100°C}$ $? + H_2O$

c. $CH_3-\overset{O}{\underset{\|}{C}}-OH + ? \xrightarrow{100°C} CH_3-\overset{O}{\underset{\|}{C}}-NH_2 + H_2O$

d. $? + \bigcirc-NH_2 \xrightarrow{100°C}$
$\bigcirc-\overset{O}{\underset{\|}{C}}-NH-\bigcirc + H_2O$

17-138 Draw the structures of the missing substances in each of the following reactions involving amides.

a. $CH_3-CH_2-CH_2-\overset{O}{\underset{\|}{C}}-OH +$
$CH_3-CH_2-NH_2 \xrightarrow{100°C} ? + H_2O$

b. $? + NH_3 \xrightarrow{100°C} H-\overset{O}{\underset{\|}{C}}-NH_2 + H_2O$

c. $CH_3-\overset{CH_3}{\underset{}{CH}}-\overset{O}{\underset{\|}{C}}-OH + ? \xrightarrow{100°C}$
$CH_3-\overset{CH_3}{\underset{}{CH}}-\overset{O}{\underset{\|}{C}}-\overset{CH_3}{\underset{}{N}}-CH_3 + H_2O$

d. $? + CH_3-NH_2 \xrightarrow{100°C} \underset{CH_3}{\bigcirc}-\overset{O}{\underset{\|}{C}}-NH-CH_3$

Hydrolysis of Amides (Section 17-18)

17-139 Draw the structure of the carbonyl-containing compound produced when each of the following amides is hydrolyzed with HCl present (acidic conditions).

a. $CH_3-\overset{O}{\underset{\|}{C}}-NH_2$

b. $H-\overset{\overset{\displaystyle O}{\|}}{C}-NH-CH_3$

c. $CH_3-CH_2-\overset{\overset{\displaystyle O}{\|}}{C}-\overset{\overset{\displaystyle CH_3}{|}}{N}-CH_3$

d. $CH_3-NH-\overset{\overset{\displaystyle O}{\|}}{C}-CH_2-CH_3$

17-140 Draw the structure of the carbonyl-containing compound produced when each of the following amides is hydrolyzed with HCl present (acidic conditions).

a. $H-\overset{\overset{\displaystyle O}{\|}}{C}-NH_2$

b. $CH_3-\overset{\overset{\displaystyle O}{\|}}{C}-NH-CH_3$

c. $CH_3-\overset{\overset{\displaystyle O}{\|}}{C}-\overset{\overset{\displaystyle CH_3}{|}}{N}-CH_3$

d. $CH_3-CH_2-NH-\overset{\overset{\displaystyle O}{\|}}{C}-CH_2-CH_3$

17-141 Draw the structure of the carbonyl-containing compound produced when each of the amides in Problem 17-139 is hydrolyzed with NaOH present (basic conditions).

17-142 Draw the structure of the carbonyl-containing compound produced when each of the amides in Problem 17-140 is hydrolyzed with NaOH present (basic conditions).

17-143 Draw the structure of the nitrogen-containing compound produced when each of the amides in Problem 17-139 is hydrolyzed with HCl present (acidic conditions).

17-144 Draw the structure of the nitrogen-containing compound produced when each of the amides in Problem 17-140 is hydrolyzed with HCl present (acidic conditions).

17-145 Draw the structure of the nitrogen-containing compound produced when each of the amides in Problem 17-139 is hydrolyzed with NaOH present (basic conditions).

17-146 Draw the structure of the nitrogen-containing compound produced when each of the amides in Problem 17-140 is hydrolyzed with NaOH present (basic conditions).

17-147 Draw the structures of the organic products in each of the following hydrolysis reactions.

a. $CH_3-CH_2-CH_2-\overset{\overset{\displaystyle O}{\|}}{C}-NH-CH_3 + H_2O \xrightarrow{\text{Heat}}$

b. $CH_3-CH_2-CH_2-\overset{\overset{\displaystyle O}{\|}}{C}-NH-CH_3 + H_2O \xrightarrow[\text{HCl}]{\text{Heat}}$

c. $CH_3-CH_2-CH_2-\overset{\overset{\displaystyle O}{\|}}{C}-NH-CH_3 + H_2O \xrightarrow[\text{NaOH}]{\text{Heat}}$

d.

17-148 Draw the structures of the organic products in each of the following hydrolysis reactions.

a. $CH_3-CH_2-\overset{\overset{\displaystyle O}{\|}}{C}-NH-CH_2-CH_3 + H_2O \xrightarrow{\text{Heat}}$

b. $CH_3-CH_2-\overset{\overset{\displaystyle O}{\|}}{C}-NH-CH_2-CH_3 + H_2O \xrightarrow[\text{HCl}]{\text{Heat}}$

c. $CH_3-CH_2-\overset{\overset{\displaystyle O}{\|}}{C}-NH-CH_2-CH_3 + H_2O \xrightarrow[\text{NaOH}]{\text{Heat}}$

d.

Polyamides and Polyurethanes (Section 17-19)

17-149 List the general characteristics of the monomers needed to produce a polyamide.

17-150 Contrast the monomers needed to produce a polyamide with those needed to produce a polyester.

17-151 Draw a structural representation for the polyamide formed from the reaction of succinic acid and 1,4-butanediamine.

17-152 Draw a structural representation for the polyamide formed from the reaction of adipic acid and 1,2-ethanediamine.

17-153 Draw the generalized structural formula for a urethane.

17-154 What are the two types of monomers used to form a polyurethane polymer?

Carbohydrates

18

The naturally present sugars fructose, glucose, and sucrose all contribute to the sweetness of ripe peaches.

With this chapter, focus shifts from "organic chemistry" to "biochemistry." This chapter, and all remaining chapters in the textbook, deal with biochemical topics, that is, subjects associated with the chemistry of living systems. Only a few of the many facets of this vast subject can be considered. The approach for these considerations will be similar to that previously used for the organic subject matter. Initial chapters are devoted to each of the major classes of biochemical compounds (carbohydrates, lipids, proteins, and nucleic acids), followed by chapters addressing the metabolism of carbohydrates, lipids, and proteins. In this first "biochapter," the subject is carbohydrates.

The same functional groups found in organic compounds are also present in biochemical compounds. Usually, however, there is greater structural complexity associated with biochemical compounds as a result of polyfunctionality; several different functional groups are present. Often biochemical compounds interact with each other, within cells, to form larger structures. But the same chemical principles and chemical reactions associated with the various organic functional groups that were previously considered apply to these larger biochemical structures as well.

Biochemistry—An Overview

LEARNING FOCUS

Distinguish between *bioinorganic* and *bioorganic* substances; be able to list the major classes of bioorganic substances.

Biochemistry *is the study of the chemical substances found in living organisms and the chemical interactions of these substances with each other.* Biochemistry is a field in which new discoveries are made almost daily about how cells manufacture the molecules needed for life and how the chemical reactions by which life is maintained occur. The knowledge explosion that has occurred in the field of biochemistry during the last decades of the twentieth century and the beginning of the twenty-first is truly phenomenal.

A **biochemical substance** *is a chemical substance found within a living organism.* Biochemical substances are divided into two groups: bioinorganic substances and bioorganic substances. *Bioinorganic substances* include water and inorganic salts. *Bioorganic substances* include carbohydrates, lipids, proteins, and nucleic acids. Figure 18-1 gives an approximate mass composition for the human body in terms of types of biochemical substances present. ◄

Although the human body is usually thought of as containing mainly organic (biochemical) substances, such substances make up only about one-fourth of total body mass. The bioinorganic substance water constitutes more than two-thirds of the mass of the human body, and another 4%–5% of body mass comes from inorganic salts (Section 10-6).

▶ *As isolated compounds, bioinorganic and bioorganic substances have no life in and of themselves. Yet when these substances are gathered together in a cell, their chemical interactions are able to sustain life.*

Figure 18-1 Mass composition data for the human body in terms of major types of biochemical substances.

Section 18-1 Quick Quiz

1. In terms of mass percent, which of the following statements concerning human body composition is *correct*?
   a. Bioorganic substances are much more abundant than bioinorganic substances.
   b. Bioinorganic substances are much more abundant than bioorganic substances.
   c. Bioorganic substances are slightly more abundant than bioinorganic substances.
   d. no correct response
2. Which of the following is the most abundant type of bioorganic substance, by mass, in the human body?
   a. proteins
   b. carbohydrates
   c. nucleic acids
   d. no correct response

Answers: 1. b; 2. a

▶ *It is estimated that more than half of all organic carbon atoms are found in the carbohydrate materials of plants.*

▶ *Human uses for carbohydrates of the plant kingdom extend beyond food. Carbohydrates in the form of cotton and linen are used as clothing. Carbohydrates in the form of wood are used for shelter and heating and in making paper.*

Figure 18-2 Most of the matter in plants, except water, is carbohydrate material. Photosynthesis, the process by which carbohydrates are made, requires sunlight.

18-2   Occurrence and Functions of Carbohydrates

LEARNING FOCUS

Know the major sources of and the major functions for carbohydrates in the human body.

Carbohydrates are the most abundant class of bioorganic molecules on planet Earth. Although their abundance in the human body is relatively low (Section 18-1), carbohydrates constitute about 75% by mass of dry plant materials (Figure 18-2). ◀

Green (chlorophyll-containing) plants produce carbohydrates via *photosynthesis*. In this process, carbon dioxide from the air and water from the soil are the reactants, and sunlight absorbed by chlorophyll is the energy source.

$$CO_2 + H_2O + \text{solar energy} \xrightarrow[\text{Plant enzymes}]{\text{Chlorophyll}} \text{carbohydrates} + O_2$$

Plants have two main uses for the carbohydrates they produce. In the form of *cellulose*, carbohydrates serve as structural elements, and in the form of *starch*, they provide energy reserves for the plants.

Dietary intake of plant materials is the major carbohydrate source for humans and animals. The average human diet should ideally be about two-thirds carbohydrate by mass. ◀ Carbohydrates have the following functions in humans:

1. Carbohydrate oxidation provides energy.
2. Carbohydrate storage, in the form of glycogen, provides a short-term energy reserve.
3. Carbohydrates supply carbon atoms for the synthesis of other biochemical substances (proteins, lipids, and nucleic acids).
4. Carbohydrates form part of the structural framework of DNA and RNA molecules.
5. Carbohydrates linked to lipids (Chapter 19) are structural components of cell membranes.
6. Carbohydrates linked to proteins (Chapter 20) function in a variety of cell–cell and cell–molecule recognition processes.

Section 18-2 Quick Quiz

1. Which of the following statements concerning the abundance of carbohydrates is *incorrect*?
   a. They are the most abundant type of bioorganic molecule on planet Earth.
   b. They are the most abundant type of bioorganic molecule in the plant world.
   c. They are the most abundant type of bioorganic molecule in the human body.
   d. no correct response
2. Which of the following is *not* a function for carbohydrates in the human body?
   a. They serve as a source of energy.
   b. They are a structural component of DNA and RNA molecules.
   c. They are a structural component of cell membranes.
   d. no correct response

Answers: 1. c; 2. d

18-3   Classification of Carbohydrates

LEARNING FOCUS

Be able to differentiate among the carbohydrate classifications *monosaccharide*, *disaccharide*, *oligosaccharide*, and *polysaccharide*; be familiar with the functional groups present in carbohydrate molecules.

Most simple carbohydrates have empirical formulas that fit the general formula $C_nH_{2n}O_n$. An early observation by scientists that this general formula can also be written as $C_n(H_2O)_n$ is the basis for the term *carbohydrate*—that is, "hydrate of carbon."

It is now known that this hydrate viewpoint is not correct, but the term *carbohydrate* still persists. Today the term is used to refer to an entire family of compounds, only some of which have the formula $C_nH_{2n}O_n$.

A **carbohydrate** *is a polyhydroxy aldehyde, a polyhydroxy ketone, or a compound that yields polyhydroxy aldehydes or polyhydroxy ketones upon hydrolysis.* The carbohydrate glucose is a polyhydroxy aldehyde, and the carbohydrate fructose is a polyhydroxy ketone.

Glucose
(a polyhydroxy aldehyde)

Fructose
(a polyhydroxy ketone)

These two structures are representative of those of all simple carbohydrates. ◀ They all contain two or more alcohol functional groups (hydroxyl groups) as well as an aldehyde or ketone functional group. Note that the terms *polyhydroxy aldehyde* and *polyhydroxy ketone* each appear twice in the definition for a carbohydrate.

Another significant structural feature of simple carbohydrate molecules, including glucose and fructose, is the presence of a functional group on each of the carbon atoms present in the molecule.

Carbohydrates are classified on the basis of molecular size as monosaccharides, disaccharides, oligosaccharides, and polysaccharides.

A **monosaccharide** *is a carbohydrate that contains a single polyhydroxy aldehyde or polyhydroxy ketone unit.* Monosaccharides cannot be broken down into simpler units by hydrolysis reactions. Both glucose and fructose are monosaccharides. Naturally occurring monosaccharides have from three to seven carbon atoms; five- and six-carbon species are especially common. Pure monosaccharides are water-soluble, white, crystalline solids.

A **disaccharide** *is a carbohydrate that contains two monosaccharide units covalently bonded to each other.* Like monosaccharides, disaccharides are crystalline, water-soluble substances. Sucrose (table sugar) and lactose (milk sugar) are disaccharides. Hydrolysis of a disaccharide produces two monosaccharide units.

An **oligosaccharide** *is a carbohydrate that contains three to ten monosaccharide units covalently bonded to each other.* "Free" oligosaccharides are seldom encountered in biochemical systems. They are usually found associated with proteins and lipids in complex molecules that have both structural and regulatory functions. Complete hydrolysis of an oligosaccharide produces several monosaccharide molecules; a trisaccharide produces three monosaccharide units, a hexasaccharide produces six monosaccharide units, and so on. ◀

A **polysaccharide** *is a polymeric carbohydrate that contains many monosaccharide units covalently bonded to each other.* The number of monosaccharide units present in a polysaccharide varies from a few hundred units to over 50,000 units. Polysaccharides, like disaccharides and oligosaccharides, undergo hydrolysis under appropriate conditions to produce monosaccharides. ◀

Both cellulose and starch are naturally occurring polysaccharides that are very prevalent in the world of plants. The paper on which this book is printed is mainly cellulose, as is the cotton in clothing fabrics and the wood used in home construction. Starch is a component of many types of foods, including bread, pasta, potatoes, rice, corn, beans, and peas.

Figure 18-3 shows diagrammatically the relationships among the various classes of saccharides.

▶ *The term* monosaccharide *is pronounced "mon-oh-SACK-uh-ride."*

▶ *The* oligo *in the term* oligosaccharide *comes from the Greek* oligos, *which means "small" or "few." The term* oligosaccharide *is pronounced "OL-ee-go-SACK-uh-ride."*

▶ *Types of carbohydrates are related to each other through hydrolysis.*

Polysaccharides
↓ *Hydrolysis*
Oligosaccharides
↓ *Hydrolysis*
Disaccharides
↓ *Hydrolysis*
Monosaccharides

Figure 18-3 Monosaccharides can be bonded together to give disaccharides (two units), oligosaccharides (a few units), or polysaccharides (many units).

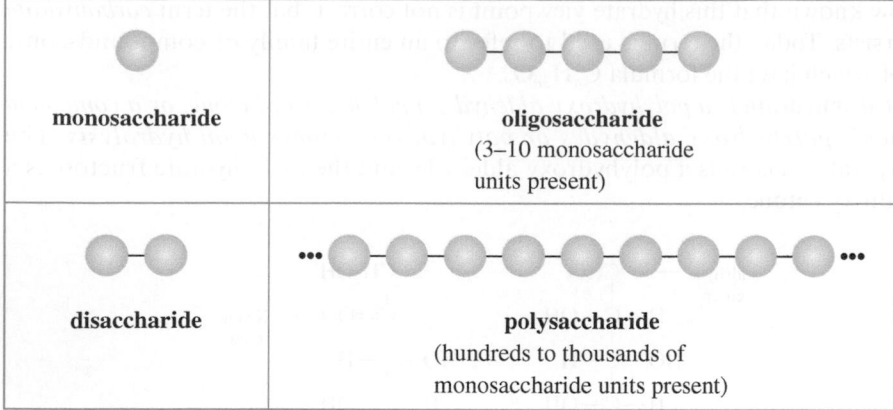

monosaccharide

oligosaccharide
(3–10 monosaccharide units present)

disaccharide

polysaccharide
(hundreds to thousands of monosaccharide units present)

Section 18-3 Quick Quiz

1. Which of the following functional groups is always present in a carbohydrate molecule?
   a. hydroxyl
   b. aldehyde
   c. ketone
   d. no correct response
2. Which of the following statements concerning monosaccharides is *incorrect*?
   a. They cannot be broken down into simpler units by hydrolysis.
   b. They are either polyhydroxy aldehydes or polyhydroxy ketones.
   c. They contain both an aldehyde and ketone functional group.
   d. no correct response
3. Which of the following is *not* a possible value for the number of monosaccharide units in an oligosaccharide?
   a. 5
   b. 8
   c. 12
   d. no correct response
4. The complete hydrolysis of a polysaccharide produces many
   a. oligosaccharides
   b. disaccharides
   c. monosaccharides
   d. no correct response

Answers: 1. a; 2. c; 3. c; 4. c

18-4 Chirality: Handedness in Molecules

LEARNING FOCUS

Be familiar with the concept of handedness as it applies to monosaccharides; be able to classify molecules as *chiral* or *achiral* and to identify *chiral centers* present in chiral molecules.

An important property of many molecules, including most carbohydrates, that has not been previously addressed in this text is the property of "handedness," which is a form of isomerism. Because of the importance of this property in carbohydrate chemistry considerations, details concerning it will now be presented, prior to discussing specifics about the various classes of carbohydrates. It will take several sections of text to formalize this "handedness concept" to the depth that is needed to understand carbohydrate chemistry.

Molecules that possess "handedness" exist in two forms: a "left-handed" form and a "right-handed" form. These two forms are related to each other in the same way that a pair of hands are related to each other. The relationship is that of *mirror images.* A left hand and a right hand are mirror images of each other, as shown in Figure 18-4. ◀

▶ *The property of handedness is not restricted to carbohydrates. It is a general phenomenon found in all classes of organic compounds.*

Left

Right

Mirror image of left hand
is in the back of the mirror

Figure 18-4 The mirror image of the right hand is the left hand. Conversely, the mirror image of the left hand is the right hand.

Mirror Images

The concept of *mirror images* is the key to understanding molecular handedness. All objects, including all molecules, have mirror images. **A mirror image** *is the reflection of an object in a mirror.* Objects can be divided into two classes on the basis of their mirror images: objects with *superimposable* mirror images and objects with *nonsuperimposable* mirror images. **Superimposable mirror images** *are images that coincide at all points when the images are laid upon each other.* A dinner plate with no design features has superimposable mirror images. **Nonsuperimposable mirror images** *are images where not all points coincide when the images are laid upon each other.* Human hands are nonsuperimposable mirror images, as Figure 18-5 shows; note in this figure that the two thumbs point in opposite directions and that the fingers do not align correctly. Like human hands, all objects with nonsuperimposable mirror images exist in "left-handed" and "right-handed" forms. ◀

Chirality

Some, but not all, molecules possess handedness. What determines whether or not a molecule possesses handedness? For organic and bioorganic compounds, the structural requirement for handedness is the presence of a carbon atom that has four *different* groups bonded to it in a tetrahedral orientation. The tetrahedral orientation requirement is met only if the bonds to the four different groups are all single bonds.

Any molecule that contains a carbon atom with four different groups bonded to it in a tetrahedral orientation possesses handedness. The handedness-generating carbon atom is called a *chiral center.* **A chiral center** *is an atom in a molecule that has four different groups bonded to it in a tetrahedral orientation.*

A molecule that contains a chiral center is said to be *chiral.* **A chiral molecule** *is a molecule whose mirror images are not superimposable.* Chiral molecules have handedness. ◀ **An achiral molecule** *is a molecule whose mirror images are superimposable.* Achiral molecules do not possess handedness.

The simplest example of a chiral organic molecule, that is, an organic molecule that has left-handed and right-handed forms, is a trisubstituted methane molecule such as bromochloroiodomethane.

Bromochloroiodomethane

Note the four different groups attached to the carbon atom: —H, —Br, —Cl, and —I. The fact that this molecule has left-hand and right-hand forms, that is handedness, can be demonstrated using molecular models, as shown in Figure 18-6a. As shown in this figure, the two forms are nonsuperimposable mirror images of each other, just as two hands are nonsuperimposable mirror images of each other.

© Cengage Learning

Figure 18-5 A person's left and right hands are not superimposable upon each other.

▶ *Every object has a mirror image. The question is, "Is the mirror image the same (superimposable) or different (nonsuperimposable)?"*

▶ *The term* chiral *(rhymes with* spiral*) comes from the Greek word* cheir, *which means "hand." Chiral objects are said to possess "handedness."*

Figure 18-6 Examples of simple molecules that are chiral.

a The mirror image forms of the molecule bromochloroiodomethane are nonsuperimposable.

b The mirror image forms of the molecule glyceraldehyde are nonsuperimposable.

The four different groups bonded to a chiral center need not be just single atoms as was the case in the previous example. In the following chiral-center-containing molecule, glyceraldehyde, three of the four bonded groups are polyatomic entities. ◀

▶ *Remember the meaning of the structural notations —CHO and —CH₂OH.*

$$\text{—CHO} \quad \text{means} \quad -\overset{\displaystyle O}{\underset{H}{\overset{\|}{C}}}-H$$

$$\text{—CH}_2\text{OH} \quad \text{means} \quad -\overset{\displaystyle H}{\underset{H}{C}}-OH$$

$$\begin{array}{c} CHO \\ | \\ H-C-OH \\ | \\ CH_2OH \end{array}$$
Glyceraldehyde

The four different groups attached to the carbon atom at the chiral center in this molecule are —H, —OH, —CHO, and —CH₂OH. The nonsuperimposability of the two mirror-image forms of glyceraldehyde is shown in Figure 18-6b.

Isopropyl alcohol (2-propanol) is not a chiral molecule. There are at least two identical groups attached to each of the three carbon atoms present, as is shown in the following analysis:

This carbon is not chiral, because the three groups shaded are identical.

This carbon is not chiral, because the two groups shaded are identical.

This carbon is not chiral, because the three groups shaded are identical.

$$H-\overset{H}{\underset{H}{C}}-\overset{OH}{\underset{H}{C}}-\overset{H}{\underset{H}{C}}-H$$

$$H-\overset{H}{\underset{H}{C}}-\overset{OH}{\underset{H}{C}}-\overset{H}{\underset{H}{C}}-H$$

$$H-\overset{H}{\underset{H}{C}}-\overset{OH}{\underset{H}{C}}-\overset{H}{\underset{H}{C}}-H$$

Chiral centers within molecules are often denoted by a small asterisk. Note the chiral centers in the following molecules.

$$CH_3-CH_2-\overset{H}{\underset{OH}{\overset{|}{*C}}}-CH_3 \qquad H-\overset{Cl}{\underset{I}{\overset{|}{*C}}}-CH_3 \qquad CH_3-CH_2-CH_2-\overset{CH_3}{\underset{H}{\overset{|}{*C}}}-CH_2-CH_3$$

2-Butanol   1-Chloro-1-iodoethane   3-Methylhexane

Guidelines for Identifying Chiral Centers

As has been noted in the preceding discussion, the master guideline for determining whether a carbon atom is a chiral center is: *A carbon atom must have four different groups attached to it in order for it to be a chiral center.*

Achiral molecule
(two "halves" of
ring are the same)

Chiral molecule
(two "halves" of
ring are different)

Achiral molecule
(two "halves" of
ring are the same)

Achiral molecule
(two "halves" of
ring are the same)

Figure 18-7 Examples of
both chiral and achiral cyclic
organic compounds. In achiral
cyclic compounds, the two
"halves" of the ring system are
equivalent to each other; in
chiral cyclic compounds, the two
"halves" of the ring system are not
equivalent.

The following additional guidelines are helpful in determining the presence or
lack of chiral centers in a molecule:

1. A carbon atom involved in a multiple bond (double or triple bond) cannot be
   a chiral center since it has fewer than four groups bonded to it. To have *four*
   groups present, all bonds about the chiral center must be single bonds.
2. The commonly encountered entities —CH_3 and —CH_2— in a structural
   formula never involve chiral centers because of the presence of two or more like
   hydrogen atoms.
3. Carbon atoms in a ring system, if not involved in multiple bonding, can be chiral
   centers. Such carbon atoms have four bonds—two to neighboring atoms in the
   ring and two to substituents on the ring. Chirality occurs when both (1) the two
   substituents are different and (2) the two "halves" of the ring emanating from
   the chiral center are different. This "difference in ring halves" concept is illustrated in Figure 18-7, where four different cyclic compounds are shown, one of
   which is chiral and three of which are achiral.

EXAMPLE 18-1

Identifying Chiral Centers in Molecules

Indicate whether the circled carbon atom in each of the following molecules is a chiral
center.

a. CH_3—ⒸH—CH_2—CH_3
              |
              Cl

b. CH_3—CH_2—Ⓒ—CH_3
                    ‖
                    O

c. CH_3—CH_2—ⒸH—OH
                  |
                  CH_2
                  |
                  CH_3

d.

Solution

a. This is a chiral center. The four different groups attached to the carbon atom
   are —CH_3, —Cl, —CH_2—CH_3, and —H.
b. No chiral center is present. The carbon atom is attached to only *three* groups
   because it is involved in a double bond.
c. No chiral center is present. Two of the groups attached to the carbon atom are
   identical.
d. The chirality rules for ring carbon atoms are the same as those for acyclic carbon
   atoms. A chiral center is present. Two of the groups are —H and —Br. The third
   group, obtained by proceeding clockwise around the ring, is —CH_2—CH_2—CH_2.
   The fourth group, obtained by proceeding counterclockwise around the ring, is
   —CH_2—CHBr—CH_2.

Organic molecules may contain more than one chiral center. For example, the following compound has two chiral centers.

$$
\begin{array}{ccc}
\text{CHO} & \text{CHO} & \text{CHO} \\
\text{H}-{}^*\text{C}-\text{OH} & \text{H}-{}^*\text{C}-\text{OH} & \text{H}-\text{C}-\text{OH} \\
\text{H}-\text{C}-\text{OH} & \text{H}-{}^*\text{C}-\text{OH} & \text{H}-{}^*\text{C}-\text{OH} \\
\text{CH}_2\text{OH} & \text{CH}_2\text{OH} & \text{CH}_2\text{OH}
\end{array}
$$

The Importance of Chirality

What is the importance of handedness, the topic now under discussion, in a biochemical setting such as the human body? In human-body chemistry it is found that right-handed and left-handed forms of a molecule usually elicit different responses and that our bodies can normally use only one of the two forms of a chiral compound. Sometimes both forms are biologically active, each form giving a different response; sometimes both elicit the same response, but one form's response is many times greater than that of the other; and sometimes only one of the two forms is biochemically active. For example, studies show that the body's response to the right-handed form of the hormone epinephrine (Section 17-10) is 20 times greater than its response to the left-handed form.

All proteins, most fats, and all common carbohydrates are chiral substances. Monosaccharides, the simplest type of carbohydrates, and the building block for more complex types of carbohydrates (Section 18-3), are almost always "right-handed" molecules. This is because plants, the main dietary sources for carbohydrates, produce only right-handed monosaccharides. Based on this observation, it is not correct to assume that "right-handed" is always dominant over "left-handed" in a biochemical setting. Interestingly, the building blocks for proteins, amino acids (Section 20-4), are always left-handed molecules.

The procedure for determining whether a given molecular structure represents a left-handed or right-handed molecule is considered in Section 18-6.

Section 18-4 Quick Quiz

1. Which of the following molecules possesses a chiral center?
   a. $\underset{\displaystyle\ \ \ |}{\text{CH}_2}{-}\text{CH}_2{-}\text{CH}_2{-}\text{CH}_2{-}\text{CH}_3$
      OH
   b. $\text{CH}_3{-}\underset{\displaystyle\ |}{\text{CH}}{-}\text{CH}_2{-}\text{CH}_2{-}\text{CH}_3$
      OH

   c. $\text{CH}_3{-}\text{CH}_2{-}\underset{\displaystyle\ \ |}{\text{CH}}{-}\text{CH}_2{-}\text{CH}_3$
      OH
   d. no correct response

2. Which of the following molecules is not an achiral molecule?
   a. $\underset{\displaystyle\ \ \ |}{\text{CH}_2}{-}\text{CH}_2{-}\text{CH}_2{-}\text{CH}_2{-}\text{CH}_3$
      OH
   b. $\text{CH}_3{-}\underset{\displaystyle\ |}{\text{CH}}{-}\text{CH}_2{-}\text{CH}_2{-}\text{CH}_3$
      OH

   c. $\text{CH}_3{-}\text{CH}_2{-}\underset{\displaystyle\ \ |}{\text{CH}}{-}\text{CH}_2{-}\text{CH}_3$
      OH
   d. no correct response

3. Which of the following molecules exists in left-handed and right-handed forms?
   a. $\underset{\displaystyle\ \ \ |}{\text{CH}_2}{-}\text{CH}_2{-}\text{CH}_2{-}\text{CH}_2{-}\text{CH}_3$
      OH
   b. $\text{CH}_3{-}\underset{\displaystyle\ |}{\text{CH}}{-}\text{CH}_2{-}\text{CH}_2{-}\text{CH}_3$
      OH

   c. $\text{CH}_3{-}\text{CH}_2{-}\underset{\displaystyle\ \ |}{\text{CH}}{-}\text{CH}_2{-}\text{CH}_3$
      OH
   d. no correct response

4. Which of the following molecules has a nonsuperimposable mirror image?

a. $CH_2-CH_2-CH_2-CH_2-CH_3$
    |
   OH

b. $CH_3-CH-CH_2-CH_2-CH_3$
       |
      OH

c. $CH_3-CH_2-CH-CH_2-CH_3$
          |
        OH

d. no correct response

Answers: 1. b; 2. b; 3. b; 4. b

18-5   Stereoisomerism: Enantiomers and Diastereomers

LEARNING FOCUS

Distinguish between the concepts of *stereoisomerism* and *constitutional isomerism*; distinguish between stereoisomers called *enantiomers* and those called *diastereomers*.

The left- and right-handed forms of a chiral molecule are isomers. They are not *constitutional isomers,* the type of isomerism that has been encountered repeatedly in the organic chemistry chapters of the text, but rather are *stereoisomers.* **Stereoisomers** *are isomers that have the same molecular and structural formulas but differ in the orientation of atoms in space.* By contrast, atoms are connected to each other in different ways in constitutional isomers (Section 12-6).

There are two major structural features that generate *stereoisomerism:* (1) the presence of a chiral center in a molecule and (2) the presence of "structural rigidity" in a molecule. Structural rigidity is caused by restricted rotation about chemical bonds. It is the basis for *cis–trans* isomerism, a phenomenon found in some substituted cycloalkanes (Section 12-14) and some alkenes (Section 13-5). Thus handedness is this text's second encounter with stereoisomerism. (The discussion of *cis–trans* isomerism did not mention that it is a form of stereoisomerism.)

Stereoisomers can be subdivided into two types: *enantiomers* and *diastereomers.* **Enantiomers** *are stereoisomers whose molecules are nonsuperimposable mirror images of each other.* Left- and right-handed forms of a molecule with a single chiral center are enantiomers. ◄

Diastereomers *are stereoisomers whose molecules are not mirror images of each other. Cis–trans* isomers (of both the alkene and the cycloalkane types) are diastereomers. ◄ Molecules that contain more than one chiral center can also exist in diastereomeric as well as enantiomeric forms, as will be shown in Section 18-6.

Figure 18-8 shows the "thinking pattern" involved in using the terms *stereoisomers, enantiomers,* and *diastereomers.*

▶ *The term* enantiomer *comes from the Greek* enantios, *which means "opposite." It is pronounced "en-AN-tee-o-mer."*

▶ *Some textbooks use the term* diastereoisomers *instead of* diastereomers. *The pronunciation for* diastereomer *is "dye-a-STEER-ee-o-mer."*

Figure 18-8 A summary of the "thought process" used in classifying molecules as enantiomers or diastereomers.

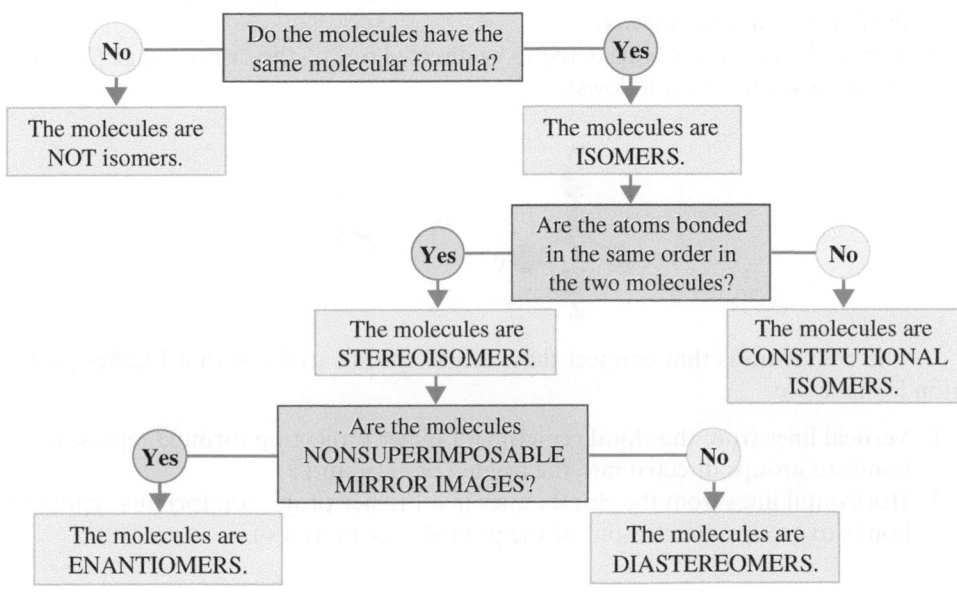

Section 18-5 Quick Quiz

1. The left-handed and right-handed forms of a chiral molecule are
   a. stereoisomers
   b. constitutional isomers
   c. both stereoisomers and constitutional isomers
   d. no correct response
2. The left-handed and right-handed forms of a chiral molecule are
   a. enantiomers
   b. diastereomers
   c. both enantiomers and diastereomers
   d. no correct response

Answers: 1. a; 2. a

18-6 Designating Handedness Using Fischer Projection Formulas

LEARNING FOCUS

Be familiar with the procedures for drawing Fischer projection formulas for monosaccharides; be able to recognize the D-form and L-form of a monosaccharide given its Fischer projection formula.

▶ *Fischer projection formulas carry the name of their originator, the German chemist Hermann Emil Fischer (see Figure 18-9).*

Drawing *three*-dimensional representations of chiral molecules to specify handedness can be both time consuming and awkward. Fischer projection formulas represent a method for giving molecular chirality specifications in *two* dimensions. A **Fischer projection formula** *is a two-dimensional structural notation for showing the spatial arrangement of groups about chiral centers in molecules.*

In a Fischer projection formula, a chiral center is represented as the intersection of vertical and horizontal lines. ◀ The atom at the chiral center, which is almost always carbon, is not explicitly shown.

The arrangement of the four groups attached to the atom at the chiral center is specified using conventions based on the following interpretation for a *printed* three-dimensional model of the tetrahedral bond orientations about the chiral center.

1. The central atom (the chiral center) is considered to be in the plane of the paper.
2. Two of the bonds are considered to be directed into the printed page (*w* and *z* in the illustration that follows).
3. Two of the bonds are considered to be directed out of the printed page (*x* and *y* in the illustration that follows).

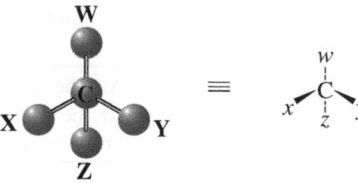

The conventions that connect these model specifications with a Fischer projection formula are

1. Vertical lines from the chiral center in a Fischer projection formula represent bonds to groups directed into the printed page (*w* and *z*).
2. Horizontal lines from the chiral center in a Fischer projection formula represent bonds to groups directed out of the printed page (*x* and *y*).

Figure 18-9 The German chemist Hermann Emil Fischer (1852–1919), the developer of the two-dimensional system for specifying chirality, was one of the early greats in organic chemistry. He made many fundamental discoveries about carbohydrates, proteins, and other natural products. In 1902 he was awarded the second Nobel Prize in Chemistry.

The Fischer projection formula thus becomes

Remaining discussion in this section involves drawing Fischer projection formulas to denote molecular chirality for specific molecules. All example molecules are monosaccharides, and the "directions" given are specific for monosaccharides. Recall from Section 18-3 that monosaccharides (the simplest type of carbohydrate) are polyhydroxy aldehydes or polyhydroxy ketones.

The simplest monosaccharide that has a chiral center is the three-carbon polyhydroxy aldehyde glyceraldehyde (2,3-dihydroxypropanal).

$$
\underset{\underset{\displaystyle OH}{|}}{CH_2}-\underset{\underset{\displaystyle OH}{|}}{{}^*CH}-\overset{\overset{\displaystyle O}{\parallel}}{C}-H
$$

There are two stereoisomers for this compound—a pair of enantiomers. The Fischer projection formulas for these two "mirror image" molecules are

$$
\begin{array}{ccc}
& CHO & & CHO \\
HO-\!\!\!-\!\!\!\!\mid\!\!\!-\!\!\!-H & \quad & H-\!\!\!-\!\!\!\!\mid\!\!\!-\!\!\!-OH \\
& CH_2OH & & CH_2OH \\
\text{L-Glyceraldehyde} & & \text{D-Glyceraldehyde}
\end{array}
$$

By convention, in a Fischer projection formula for a monosaccharide, the *carbon chain* is always positioned *vertically* with the carbonyl group (aldehyde or ketone) at or near the top. An aldehyde group is denoted using the notation CHO (Section 15-3).

For this particular molecule, the handedness (right-handed or left-handed) of the two enantiomers is specified by using the designations D and L. The enantiomer with the chiral center —OH group on the right in the Fischer projection formula is by definition the right-handed isomer (D-glyceraldehyde), and the enantiomer with the chiral center —OH group on the left in the Fischer projection formula is by definition the left-handed isomer (L-glyceraldehyde). ◄

The compound 2,3,4-trihydroxybutanal, a monosaccharide with four carbons and *two* chiral centers, has the structural formula

$$
\underset{\underset{\displaystyle OH}{|}}{CH_2}-\underset{\underset{\displaystyle OH}{|}}{{}^*CH}-\underset{\underset{\displaystyle OH}{|}}{{}^*CH}-\overset{\overset{\displaystyle O}{\parallel}}{C}-H
$$

There are four stereoisomers for this compound—two pairs of enantiomers. ◄ The Fischer projection formulas for these stereoisomers are

First enantiomeric pair   Second enantiomeric pair

► *The* D *and* L *designations for the handedness of the two members of an enantiomeric pair come from the Latin words* dextro, *which means "right," and* levo, *which means "left."*

► *To draw the mirror image of a Fischer projection structure, keep up-and-down and front-and-back aspects of the structure the same and reverse the left-and-right aspects.*

▶ *Any given molecular structure can have only one mirror image. Hence enantiomers always come in pairs; there can never be more than two.*

▶ *The highest numbered chiral center in a monosaccharide is always the chiral center that is farthest from the monosaccharide's carbonyl group.*

▶ *Diastereomers that have two chiral centers must have the same handedness (both left or both right) at one chiral center and opposite handedness (one left and one right) at the other chiral center.*

In the first enantiomeric pair, both chiral-center —OH groups are on the same side of the Fischer projection formula, and in the second enantiomeric pair, the chiral-center —OH groups are on opposite sides of the Fischer projection formula. ◀ These are the only —OH group arrangements possible.

The D,L system used to designate the handedness of glyceraldehyde enantiomers is extended to monosaccharides with more than one chiral center in the following manner. The carbon chain is numbered starting at the carbonyl group end of the molecule, and the highest-numbered chiral center is used to determine D or L configuration. ◀

CHO
H—2—OH
H—3—OH
4 CH₂OH
A
D isomer

CHO
HO—2—H
HO—3—H
4 CH₂OH
B
L isomer

CHO
HO—2—H
H—3—OH
4 CH₂OH
C
D isomer

CHO
H—2—OH
HO—3—H
4 CH₂OH
D
L isomer

The D,L nomenclature gives the configuration (handedness) only at the highest-numbered chiral center. The configuration at other chiral centers in a molecule is accounted for by assigning a different common name to each pair of D,L enantiomers. In the present example, compounds A and B (the first enantiomeric pair) are D-erythrose and L-erythrose; compounds C and D (the second enantiomeric pair) are D-threose and L-threose.

What is the relationship between compounds A and C in the present example? They are diastereomers (Section 18-5), stereoisomers that are not mirror images of each other. ◀ Other diastereomeric pairs in the present example are A and D, B and C, and B and D. The members of each of these four pairs are epimers. **Epimers** *are diastereomers whose molecules differ only in the configuration at one chiral center.*

EXAMPLE 18-2

Drawing Fischer Projection Formulas for Monosaccharides

Draw a Fischer projection formula for the enantiomer of each of the following monosaccharides.

a.
CHO
H——OH
H——OH
H——OH
CH₂OH

b.
CH₂OH
C=O
HO——H
H——OH
CH₂OH

Solution

Knowing the Fischer projection formula of one member of an enantiomeric pair, the other enantiomer's Fischer projection formula is drawn by reversing the substituents that are in *horizontal* positions *at each chiral center.*

a. Three chiral centers are present in this polyhydroxy aldehyde. Reversing the positions of the —H and —OH groups at each chiral center produces the Fischer projection formula of the other enantiomer.

CHO
H——OH
H——OH
H——OH
CH₂OH
The given enantiomer

⟶

CHO
HO——H
HO——H
HO——H
CH₂OH
The other enantiomer

b. This monosaccharide is a polyhydroxy ketone with two chiral centers. Reversing the positions of the —H and —OH groups at both chiral centers generates the Fischer projection formula of the other enantiomer.

$$
\begin{array}{ccc}
\text{CH}_2\text{OH} & & \text{CH}_2\text{OH} \\
| & & | \\
\text{C}=\text{O} & & \text{C}=\text{O} \\
\text{HO}\!-\!\!\!-\!\!\!\text{H} & \longrightarrow & \text{H}\!-\!\!\!-\!\!\!\text{OH} \\
\text{H}\!-\!\!\!-\!\!\!\text{OH} & & \text{HO}\!-\!\!\!-\!\!\!\text{H} \\
\text{CH}_2\text{OH} & & \text{CH}_2\text{OH}
\end{array}
$$

The given enantiomer   The other enantiomer

EXAMPLE 18-3

Classifying Monosaccharides as D or L Enantiomers

Classify each of the following monosaccharides as a D enantiomer or an L enantiomer.

a.
$$
\begin{array}{c}
{}^{1}\text{CHO} \\
\text{HO}\!-\!\!{}^{2}\!-\!\!\text{H} \\
\text{H}\!-\!\!{}^{3}\!-\!\!\text{OH} \\
\text{H}\!-\!\!{}^{4}\!-\!\!\text{OH} \\
{}^{5}\text{CH}_2\text{OH}
\end{array}
$$

b.
$$
\begin{array}{c}
{}^{1}\text{CH}_2\text{OH} \\
{}^{2}\text{C}=\text{O} \\
\text{H}\!-\!\!{}^{3}\!-\!\!\text{OH} \\
\text{HO}\!-\!\!{}^{4}\!-\!\!\text{H} \\
\text{HO}\!-\!\!{}^{5}\!-\!\!\text{H} \\
{}^{6}\text{CH}_2\text{OH}
\end{array}
$$

Solution

D or L configuration for a monosaccharide is determined by the highest-numbered chiral center, the one farthest from the carbonyl carbon atom.

a. The highest-numbered chiral center, which involves carbon 4, has the —OH group on the right. Thus this monosaccharide is a D enantiomer.

b. The highest-numbered chiral center, which involves carbon 5, has the —OH group on the left. Thus this monosaccharide is an L enantiomer.

EXAMPLE 18-4

Recognizing Enantiomers and Diastereomers

Characterize each of the following pairs of structures as enantiomers, diastereomers, or neither enantiomers nor diastereomers

a.
$$
\begin{array}{c}
\text{CHO} \\
\text{H}\!-\!\!-\!\!\text{OH} \\
\text{HO}\!-\!\!-\!\!\text{H} \\
\text{H}\!-\!\!-\!\!\text{OH} \\
\text{CH}_2\text{OH}
\end{array}
\quad\text{and}\quad
\begin{array}{c}
\text{CHO} \\
\text{H}\!-\!\!-\!\!\text{OH} \\
\text{H}\!-\!\!-\!\!\text{OH} \\
\text{HO}\!-\!\!-\!\!\text{H} \\
\text{CH}_2\text{OH}
\end{array}
$$

b.
$$
\begin{array}{c}
\text{CHO} \\
\text{H}\!-\!\!-\!\!\text{OH} \\
\text{HO}\!-\!\!-\!\!\text{H} \\
\text{H}\!-\!\!-\!\!\text{OH} \\
\text{CH}_2\text{OH}
\end{array}
\quad\text{and}\quad
\begin{array}{c}
\text{CHO} \\
\text{HO}\!-\!\!-\!\!\text{H} \\
\text{H}\!-\!\!-\!\!\text{OH} \\
\text{HO}\!-\!\!-\!\!\text{H} \\
\text{CH}_2\text{OH}
\end{array}
$$

c.
$$
\begin{array}{c}
\text{CHO} \\
\text{H}\!-\!\!-\!\!\text{OH} \\
\text{HO}\!-\!\!-\!\!\text{H} \\
\text{H}\!-\!\!-\!\!\text{OH} \\
\text{CH}_2\text{OH}
\end{array}
\quad\text{and}\quad
\begin{array}{c}
\text{CHO} \\
\text{H}\!-\!\text{C}\!-\!\text{H} \\
\text{H}\!-\!\!-\!\!\text{OH} \\
\text{HO}\!-\!\!-\!\!\text{H} \\
\text{CH}_2\text{OH}
\end{array}
$$

Solution

a. These two structures are *diastereomers*. All chiral centers have both an —H and —OH attachment. However, a mirror-image relationship between these two attachments is present at only two of the three chiral centers. At the third chiral center, carbon 2, the —H and —OH orientation is the same.

(continued)

b. These two structures represent *enantiomers*—a mirror-image substituent relationship exists between the two isomers at *each* chiral center.

c. These two structures are *neither enantiomers nor diastereomers.* The connectivity of atoms differs in the two structures at carbon 2. Stereoisomers (enantiomers and diastereomers) must have the same connectivity throughout both structures. (The two structures are not even constitutional isomers because the first structure contains one more oxygen atom than the second.)

▶ *The formula 2^n gives the maximum possible number of stereoisomers for a molecule with n chiral atoms. In a few cases, the actual number of stereoisomers is less than the maximum because of symmetry considerations that make some mirror images superimposable.*

In general, a compound that has *n* chiral centers may exist in a *maximum* of 2^n stereoisomeric forms. ◀ For example, when three chiral centers are present, at most eight stereoisomers ($2^3 = 8$) are possible (four pairs of enantiomers).

Chemistry at a Glance—Constitutional Isomers and Stereoisomers—summarizes information about the various types of isomers we have encountered so far in the text—the various subtypes of constitutional isomers and the various subtypes of stereoisomers.

Section 18-6 Quick Quiz

1. Which of the following Fischer projection formulas is that for an L-monosaccharide?

a.
```
       CHO
  HO ——|—— H
  HO ——|—— H
   H ——|—— OH
      CH₂OH
```

b.
```
       CHO
  HO ——|—— H
   H ——|—— OH
  HO ——|—— H
      CH₂OH
```

c.
```
       CHO
   H ——|—— OH
   H ——|—— OH
   H ——|—— OH
      CH₂OH
```

d. no correct response

2. Which of the following Fischer projection formulas is that for a monosaccharide that has two chiral centers?

a.
```
       CHO
   H ——|—— OH
  HO ——|—— H
  HO ——|—— H
      CH₂OH
```

b.
```
       CHO
  HO ——|—— H
  HO ——|—— H
  HO ——|—— H
      CH₂OH
```

c.
```
      CH₂OH
        |
       C=O
  HO ——|—— H
   H ——|—— OH
      CH₂OH
```

d. no correct response

3. In which pair of Fischer projection formulas are the two monosaccharides enantiomers?

a.
```
       CHO                  CHO
   H ——|—— OH          H ——|—— OH
  HO ——|—— H   and     H ——|—— OH
   H ——|—— OH          HO ——|—— H
      CH₂OH               CH₂OH
```

b.
```
      CH₂OH               CH₂OH
        |                   |
       C=O                 C=O
   H ——|—— OH   and    HO ——|—— H
   H ——|—— OH          HO ——|—— H
      CH₂OH               CH₂OH
```

c.
```
       CHO                  CHO
   H ——|—— OH          H —— C —— H
  HO ——|—— H   and     H ——|—— OH
   H ——|—— OH          HO ——|—— H
      CH₂OH               CH₂OH
```

d. no correct response

4. In which pair of Fischer projection formulas are the two monosaccharides diastereomers?

a.
```
       CHO                  CHO
   H ——|—— OH          H ——|—— OH
  HO ——|—— H   and     H ——|—— OH
   H ——|—— OH          HO ——|—— H
      CH₂OH               CH₂OH
```

b.
```
       CHO                  CHO
   H ——|—— OH          HO ——|—— H
  HO ——|—— H   and     H ——|—— OH
  HO ——|—— H           H ——|—— OH
      CH₂OH               CH₂OH
```

c.

```
      CHO              CHO
H ——— OH         H ——— C ——— H
HO ——— H   and   H ——— OH
H ——— OH          HO ——— H
     CH₂OH            CH₂OH
```

d. no correct response

Answers: 1. b; 2. c; 3. b; 4. a

CHEMISTRY AT A GLANCE Constitutional Isomers and Stereoisomers

CONSTITUTIONAL ISOMERS
Isomers in which the atoms have different connectivity

SKELETAL ISOMERS
Isomers with different carbon atom arrangements and different hydrogen atom arrangements

$CH_3 - CH_2 - CH_2 - CH_3$
Butane (C_4H_{10})

$CH_3 - CH - CH_3$
       $|$
     CH_3
2-Methylpropane (C_4H_{10})

POSITIONAL ISOMERS
Isomers that differ in the location of the functional group

$CH_2 = CH - CH_2 - CH_3$
1-Butene (C_4H_8)

$CH_3 - CH = CH - CH_3$
2-Butene (C_4H_8)

FUNCTIONAL GROUP ISOMERS
Isomers that contain different functional groups

$CH_3 - CH_2 - CH_2 - \overset{\overset{\displaystyle O}{\|}}{C} - H$
Butanal (aldehyde, C_4H_8O)

$CH_3 - CH_2 - \overset{\overset{\displaystyle O}{\|}}{C} - CH_3$
2-Butanone (ketone, C_4H_8O)

STEREOISOMERS
Isomers with atoms of the same connectivity that differ only in the orientation of the atoms in space

ENANTIOMERS
- Stereoisomers that are nonsuperimposable mirror images of each other
- Handedness (D and L forms) is determined by the configuration at the highest-numbered chiral center

D and L Enantiomers

```
 ¹CHO              CHO
H —²— OH       HO ——— H
H —³— OH       HO ——— H
 ⁴CH₂OH            CH₂OH
 D-Erythrose      L-Erythrose
```

DIASTEREOMERS
Stereoisomers that are not mirror images of each other

CIS–TRANS ISOMERS
Stereoisomerism that results from restricted rotation about chemical bonds
- Is sometimes possible when a ring is present
- Is sometimes possible when a double bond is present

cis-1,3-dimethylcyclopentane

trans-1,3-dimethylcyclopentane

cis-2-butene

trans-2-butene

MOST OTHER DIASTEREOMERS (two or more chiral centers)
Stereoisomerism that results from
- A mirror-image relationship at one (or more) chiral centers, and
- The same configuration at one (or more) chiral centers

Three chiral centers

```
      CHO              CHO
H ——— OH         HO ——— H
HO ——— H         H ——— OH
HO ——— H         HO ——— H
     CH₂OH            CH₂OH
  L-Arabinose       L-Xylose
```

a Ordinary (unpolarized) light

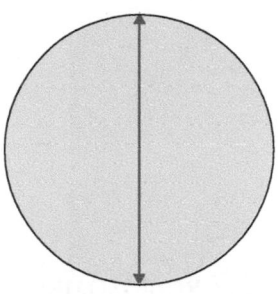

b Plane-polarized light

Figure 18-10 Vibrational characteristics of ordinary (unpolarized) light (a) and polarized light (b). The direction of travel of the light is toward the reader.

▶ *Achiral molecules are optically inactive. Chiral molecules are optically active.*

Figure 18-11 Schematic depiction of how a polarimeter works.

18-7 Properties of Enantiomers

LEARNING FOCUS

Contrast enantiomers in terms of their interactions with plane-polarized light and their interactions with other chiral substances.

Constitutional isomers differ in most chemical and physical properties. For example, constitutional isomers have different boiling points and melting points. Diastereomers also differ in most chemical and physical properties. They also have different boiling points and melting points. In contrast, nearly all the properties of a pair of enantiomers are the same; for example, they have identical boiling points and melting points. Enantiomers exhibit different properties in only two areas: (1) their interaction with plane-polarized light and (2) their interaction with other chiral substances.

Interaction of Enantiomers with Plane-Polarized Light

All light moves through space with a wave motion. Ordinary light waves—that is, unpolarized light waves—vibrate in *all* planes at right angles to their direction of travel. Plane-polarized light waves, by contrast, vibrate in *only one* plane at right angles to their direction of travel. Figure 18-10 contrasts the vibrational behavior of ordinary light with that of plane-polarized light.

Ordinary light can be converted to plane-polarized light by passing it through a *polarizer,* an instrument with lenses or filters containing special types of crystals. When plane-polarized light is passed through a solution containing a *single* enantiomer, the plane of the polarized light is rotated counterclockwise (to the left) or clockwise (to the right), depending on the enantiomer. The extent of rotation depends on the concentration of the enantiomer as well as on its identity. Furthermore, the two enantiomers of a pair rotate the plane-polarized light the same number of degrees, but in opposite directions. If a 0.50 M solution of one enantiomer rotates the light 30° to the right, then a 0.50 M solution of the other enantiomer rotates the light 30° to the left.

Instruments used to measure the degree of rotation of plane-polarized light by enantiomeric compounds are called *polarimeters.* The schematic diagram in Figure 18-11 shows the basis for these instruments.

Dextrorotatory and Levorotatory Compounds

Enantiomers are said to be optically active because of the way they interact with plane-polarized light. ◀ An **optically active compound** *is a compound that rotates the plane of polarized light.*

An enantiomer that rotates plane-polarized light in a clockwise direction (to the *right*) is said to be dextrorotatory (the Latin *dextro* means "right"). A **dextrorotatory compound**

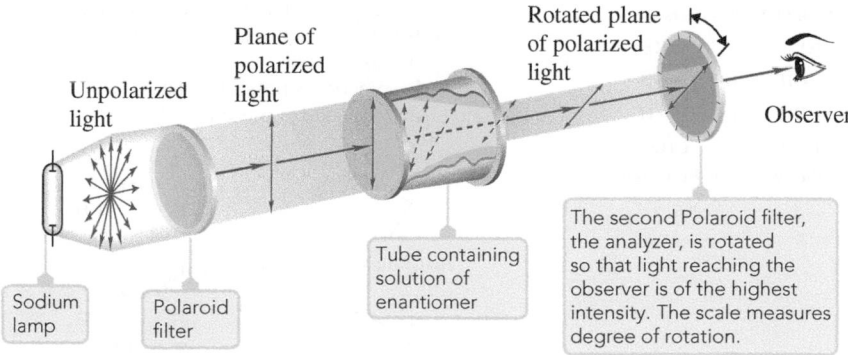

Unpolarized light

Plane of polarized light

Rotated plane of polarized light

Observer

Sodium lamp

Polaroid filter

Tube containing solution of enantiomer

The second Polaroid filter, the analyzer, is rotated so that light reaching the observer is of the highest intensity. The scale measures degree of rotation.

is a chiral compound that rotates the plane of polarized light in a clockwise direction. An enantiomer that rotates plane-polarized light in a counterclockwise direction (to the *left*) is said to be levorotatory (the Latin *levo* means "left"). A **levorotatory compound** *is a chiral compound that rotates the plane of polarized light in a counterclockwise direction.* If one member of an enantiomeric pair is dextrorotatory, then the other member must be levorotatory. ◄

A plus or minus sign inside parentheses is used to denote the direction of rotation of plane-polarized light by a chiral compound. The notation (+) means rotation to the right (clockwise), and (−) means rotation to the left (counterclockwise). Thus the dextrorotatory enantiomer of glucose is (+)-glucose. ◄

The handedness of enantiomers (D or L, Section 18-6) and the direction of rotation of plane-polarized light by enantiomers [(+) or (−)] are not connected entities. There is no way of knowing which way an enantiomer will rotate light until it is examined with a polarimeter. Not all D enantiomers rotate plane-polarized light in the same direction, nor do all L enantiomers rotate plane-polarized light in the same direction. Some D enantiomers are dextrorotatory; others are levorotatory. ◄

► *Because of their ability to rotate the plane of polarized light, enantiomers are sometimes referred to as* optical isomers.

► *In any pair of enantiomers, one, the (+)-enantiomer, always rotates the plane of polarized light to the right, and the other, the (−)-enantiomer, to the left.*

► *Both handedness and direction of rotation of plane-polarized light can be incorporated into the name of an enantiomer. For example, the notation* D-(+)-*mannose specifies that the right-handed isomer of the monosaccharide mannose rotates plane-polarized light in a clockwise direction (to the right).*

Interactions Between Chiral Compounds

A left-handed baseball player (chiral) and a right-handed baseball player (chiral) can use the same baseball bat (achiral) or wear the same baseball hat (achiral). However, left- and right-handed baseball players (chiral) cannot use the same baseball glove (chiral). This nonchemical example illustrates that the chirality of an object becomes important when the object interacts with another chiral object.

Applying this generalization to molecules, it is found that the two members of an enantiomeric pair have the same interaction with achiral molecules and different interactions with chiral molecules. Ramifications of this are

1. Enantiomers have identical boiling points, melting points, and densities because such properties depend on the strength of intermolecular forces (Section 7-13), and intermolecular force strength does not depend on chirality. Intermolecular force strength is the same for both forms of a chiral molecule because both forms have identical sets of functional groups.
2. A pair of enantiomers have the same solubility in an achiral solvent, such as ethanol, but differing solubilities in a chiral solvent, such as D-2-butanol.
3. The rate and extent of reaction of enantiomers with another reactant are the same if the reactant is achiral but differ if the reactant is chiral.
4. Receptor sites for molecules within the body have chirality associated with them. Thus enantiomers always generate different responses within the human body as they interact at such sites. Sometimes the responses are only slightly different, and at other times they are very different.

Two specific examples of differing chiral–chiral interactions involving enantiomers that occur within the human body are now considered. The first example involves taste perceptions. The distinctly different natural flavors "spearmint" and "caraway" are generated by molecules that are enantiomers interacting with chiral "taste receptors" (Figure 18-12).

The second example involves the body's response to the enantiomeric forms of the hormone epinephrine (adrenaline). The response of the body to the D isomer of the hormone is 20 times greater than its response to the L isomer of the hormone. Epinephrine binds to its cellular receptor site by means of a three-point contact, as is shown in Figure 18-13. D-Epinephrine makes a perfect three-point contact with the receptor surface, but the biochemically weaker L-epinephrine can make only a two-point contact. Because of the poorer fit, the binding of the L isomer is weaker, and less physiological response is observed.

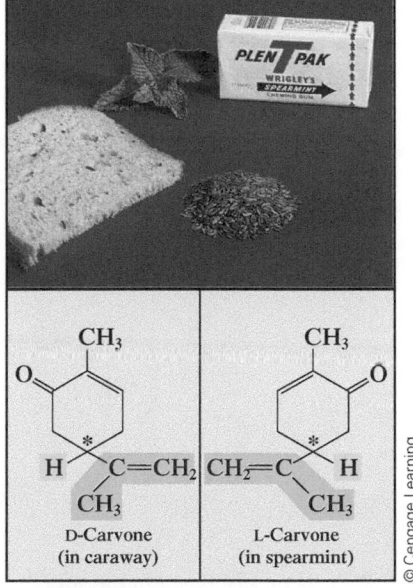

Figure 18-12 The distinctly different natural flavors of spearmint and caraway are caused by enantiomeric molecules. Spearmint leaves contain L-carvone, and caraway seeds contain D-carvone.

Figure 18-13 D-Epinephrine binds to the receptor at three points, whereas the biochemically weaker L-epinephrine binds at only two sites.

D-Epinephrine: three-point contact, positive response

L-Epinephrine: two-point contact, much smaller response

Section 18-7 Quick Quiz

1. If one member of an enantiomeric pair is a dextrorotatory compound then the other enantiomer
   a. must be a levorotatory compound
   b. must also be a dextrorotatory compound
   c. could be a levorotatory or a dextrorotatory compound
   d. no correct response
2. Which of the following properties would be the *same* for a pair of enantiomers?
   a. interaction with plane-polarized light
   b. solubility in a chiral solvent
   c. melting point
   d. no correct response

Answers: 1. a; 2. c

18-8 Classification of Monosaccharides

LEARNING FOCUS

Be able to classify monosaccharides by the number of carbon atoms present and by the type of carbonyl groups present.

With discussion about molecular chirality and its consequences (Sections 18-4 through 18-7) complete, additional details about carbohydrate chemistry will now be presented. The starting point for further carbohydrate considerations is monosaccharide classifications. It should be remembered that chirality is an underlying governing principle in all considerations.

Although there is no limit to the number of carbon atoms that can be present in a monosaccharide, only monosaccharides with three to seven carbon atoms are commonly found in nature. A three-carbon monosaccharide is called a *triose,* and those that contain four, five, and six carbon atoms are called *tetroses, pentoses,* and *hexoses,* respectively.

Monosaccharides are classified as *aldoses* or *ketoses* on the basis of what type of carbonyl group (Section 15-1) is present. An **aldose** *is a monosaccharide that contains an aldehyde functional group.* Aldoses are polyhydroxy aldehydes. A **ketose** *is a monosaccharide that contains a ketone functional group.* Ketoses are polyhydroxy ketones. ◀

Monosaccharides are often classified by both their number of carbon atoms and their functional group. A six-carbon monosaccharide with an aldehyde functional group is an *aldohexose*; a five-carbon monosaccharide with a ketone functional group is a *ketopentose*.

Monosaccharides are also often called sugars. Hexoses are six-carbon sugars, pentoses five-carbon sugars, and so on. The word *sugar* is associated with "sweetness," and most (but not all) monosaccharides have a sweet taste. ◀ The designation *sugar* is also applied to disaccharides, many of which also have a sweet taste. Thus **sugar** *is a general designation for either a monosaccharide or a disaccharide.*

▶ *Structurally, monosaccharides have a chain of three to seven carbon atoms, with a carbonyl carbon group at either the terminal carbon (C1) or the carbon adjacent to it (C2). If the carbonyl group involves C1, the monosaccharide is an aldose; if it involves C2, the monosaccharide is a ketose.*

▶ *The term* saccharide *comes from the Latin word for "sugar," which is* saccharum.

EXAMPLE 18-5

Classifying Monosaccharides on the Basis of Structural Characteristics

Classify each of the following monosaccharides according to both the number of carbon atoms and the type of carbonyl group present.

a.
```
        CHO
  HO ――― H
   H ――― OH
   H ――― OH
       CH₂OH
```

b.
```
       CH₂OH
        C=O
   H ――― OH
  HO ――― H
  HO ――― H
       CH₂OH
```

c.
```
        CHO
  HO ――― H
   H ――― OH
  HO ――― H
  HO ――― H
       CH₂OH
```

d.
```
       CH₂OH
        C=O
   H ――― OH
   H ――― OH
       CH₂OH
```

Solution

a. An aldehyde functional group is present as well as five carbon atoms. This monosaccharide is thus an *aldopentose*.
b. This monosaccharide contains a ketone group and six carbon atoms, so it is a *ketohexose*.
c. Six carbon atoms and an aldehyde group in a monosaccharide are characteristic of an *aldohexose*.
d. This monosaccharide is a *ketopentose*.

In terms of carbon atoms, trioses are the smallest monosaccharides that can exist. There are two such compounds, one an aldose (glyceraldehyde) and the other a ketose (dihydroxyacetone).

```
       CHO               CH₂OH
  H ――― OH                C=O
      CH₂OH              CH₂OH
  D-Glyceraldehyde   Dihydroxyacetone
```

These two triose structures serve as the reference points for consideration of the structures of aldoses and ketoses that contain more carbon atoms. ◀

The Fischer projection formulas of all D aldoses containing three, four, five, and six carbon atoms are given in Figure 18-14. Figure 18-14 starts with the triose glyceraldehyde at the top and proceeds downward through the tetroses, pentoses, and hexoses. The number of possible aldoses doubles each time an additional carbon atom is added because the new carbon atom is a chiral center. Glyceraldehyde has one chiral center, the tetroses two chiral centers, the pentoses three chiral centers, and the hexoses four chiral centers. ◀

In aldose structures such as those shown in Figure 18-14, the chiral center farthest from the aldehyde group determines the D or L designation for the aldose. The configurations about the other chiral centers present are accounted for by assigning a different common name to each set of D and L enantiomers. (Only the D isomer is shown in Figure 18-14; the L isomer is the mirror image of the structure shown.)

A major difference between glyceraldehyde and dihydroxyacetone is that the latter does not possess a chiral carbon atom. Thus D and L forms are not possible for dihydroxyacetone. This reduces by half (compared with aldoses) the number of

▶ *All monosaccharides have names that end in -ose except the trioses glyceraldehyde and dihydroxyacetone.*

▶ *Nearly all naturally occurring monosaccharides are D isomers. These D monosaccharides are important energy sources for the human body. L monosaccharides, which can be produced in the laboratory, cannot be used by the body as energy sources. Body enzymes are specific for D isomers.*

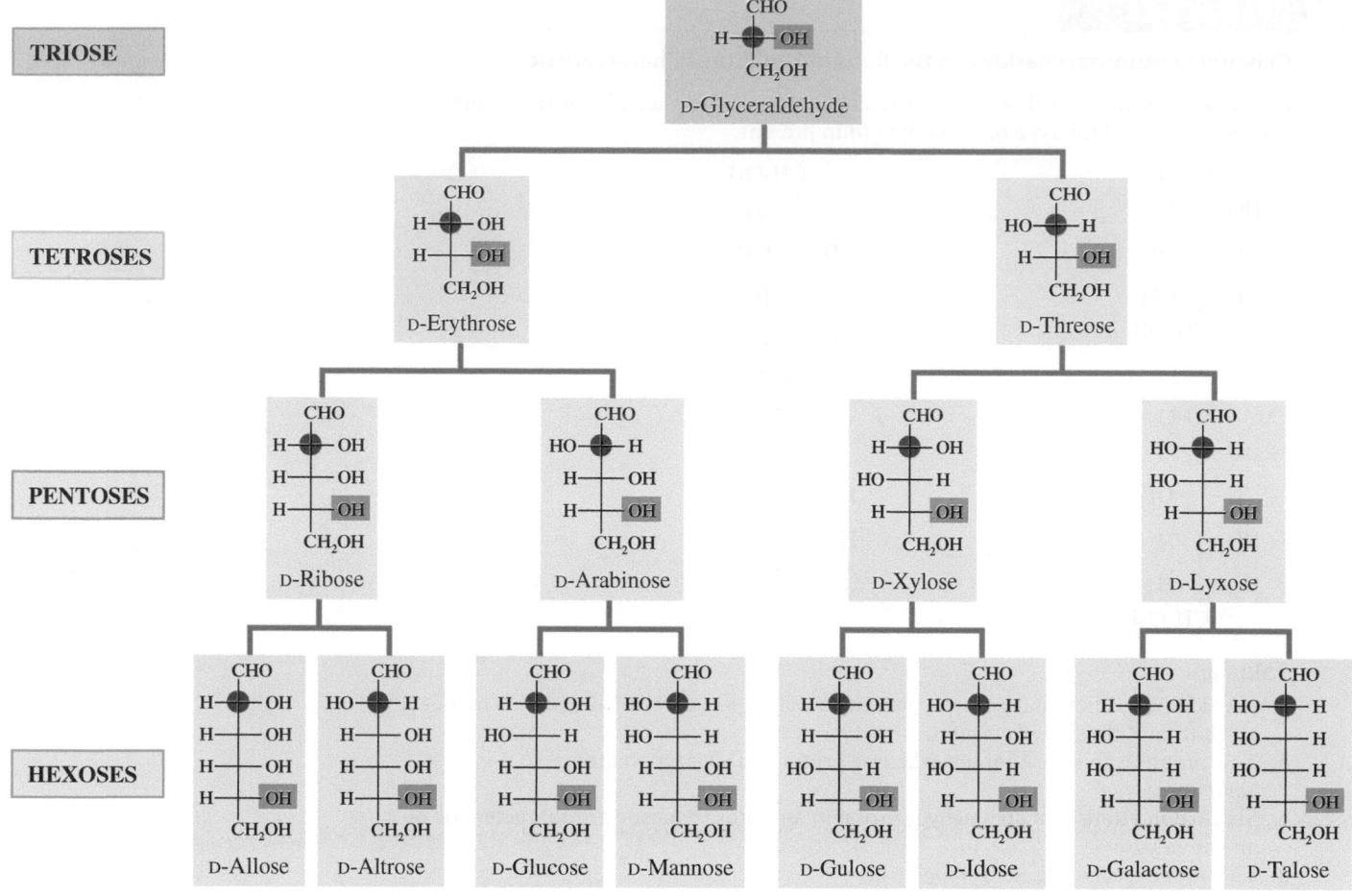

Figure 18-14 Fischer projection formulas and common names for D aldoses containing three, four, five, and six carbon atoms. The new chiral-center carbon atom added in going from triose to tetrose to pentose to hexose is marked in color. This new chiral center can have the hydroxyl group at the right or left in the Fischer projection formula, which doubles the number of stereoisomers. The hydroxyl group that specifies the D configuration is highlighted in dark pink.

stereoisomers possible for ketotetroses, ketopentoses, and ketohexoses. An aldohexose has four chiral carbon atoms, but a ketohexose has only three. Figure 18-15 gives the Fischer projection formulas and common names for the D forms of ketoses containing three, four, five, and six carbon atoms.

> ### Section 18-8 Quick Quiz
>
> 1. Which of the following statements about monosaccharides is *correct*?
>   a. Aldopentoses contain more carbon atoms than ketopentoses.
>   b. Ketopentoses contain more carbon atoms than aldopentoses.
>   c. Aldopentoses and ketopentoses contain the same number of carbon atoms.
>   d. no correct response
> 2. Which of the following statements about monosaccharides is *correct*?
>   a. Aldopentoses contain more chiral centers than ketopentoses.
>   b. Ketopentoses contain more chiral centers than aldopentoses.
>   c. Aldopentoses and ketopentoses contain the same number of chiral centers.
>   d. no correct response
> 3. The smallest monosaccharides that can exist are
>   a. trioses
>   b. tetroses
>   c. pentoses
>   d. no correct response
>
> *Answers:* 1. c; 2. a; 3. a

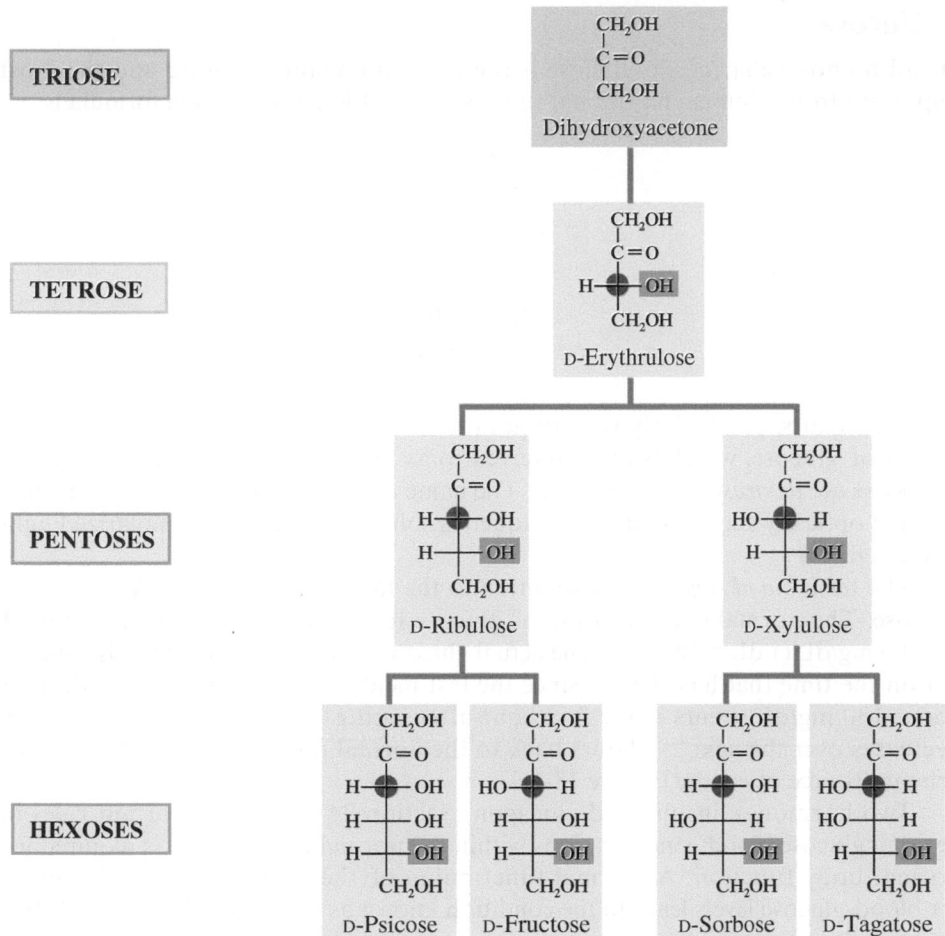

Figure 18-15 Fischer projection formulas and common names for D ketoses containing three, four, five, and six carbon atoms. The new chiral-center carbon atom added in going from triose to tetrose to pentose to hexose is marked in color. This new chiral center can have the hydroxyl group at the right or left in the Fischer projection formula, which doubles the number of stereoisomers. The hydroxyl group that specifies the D configuration is highlighted in dark pink.

TRIOSE

TETROSE

PENTOSES

HEXOSES

18-9 Biochemically Important Monosaccharides

LEARNING FOCUS

Be able to distinguish among, based on structural characteristics, the monosaccharides glyceraldehyde, dihydroxyacetone, glucose, galactose, fructose, and ribose.

Of the many monosaccharides, six that are particularly important in the functioning of the human body are the trioses D-glyceraldehyde and dihydroxyacetone and the D forms of glucose, galactose, fructose, and ribose. Glucose and galactose are aldohexoses, fructose is a ketohexose, and ribose is an aldopentose. All six of these monosaccharides are water-soluble, white, crystalline solids. ◀

▶ *It is often useful to have the structures of the six monosaccharides considered in this section memorized.*

D-Glyceraldehyde and Dihydroxyacetone

The simplest of the monosaccharides, these two trioses are important intermediates in the process of glycolysis (Section 24-2), a series of reactions whereby glucose is converted into two molecules of pyruvate. D-Glyceraldehyde is a chiral molecule, but dihydroxyacetone is not.

$$
\begin{array}{cc}
\text{CHO} & \text{CH}_2\text{OH} \\
\text{H}\!-\!\!-\!\text{OH} & \text{C}\!=\!\text{O} \\
\text{CH}_2\text{OH} & \text{CH}_2\text{OH} \\
\text{D-Glyceraldehyde} & \text{Dihydroxyacetone}
\end{array}
$$

D-Glucose

▶ *D-Glucose tastes sweet, is nutritious, and is an important component of the human diet. L-Glucose, on the other hand, is tasteless, and the body cannot use it.*

Of all monosaccharides, D-glucose is the most abundant in nature and the most important from a human nutritional standpoint. Its Fischer projection formula is

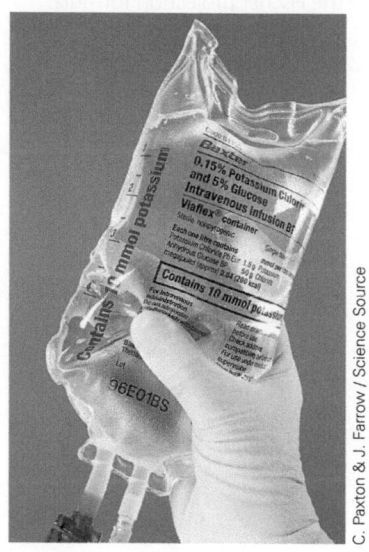

CHO
H——OH
HO——H
H——OH
H——OH
CH₂OH
D-Glucose

Ripe fruits, particularly ripe grapes (20%–30% glucose by mass), are a good source of glucose, which is often referred to as *grape sugar.* Two other names for D-glucose are *dextrose* and *blood sugar.* The name *dextrose* draws attention to the fact that the optically active D-glucose, in aqueous solution, rotates plane-polarized light to the right. ◀

The term *blood sugar* draws attention to the fact that blood contains dissolved glucose. The normal concentration of glucose in human blood is in the range of 70–100 mg/dL (1 dL = 100 mL). The actual glucose concentration in blood is dependent on the time that has elapsed since the last meal was eaten. A concentration of about 130 mg/dL occurs in the first hour after eating, and then the concentration decreases over the next 2–3 hours back to the normal range. Cells use glucose as a primary source of energy (Figure 18-16).

Two hormones, insulin and glucagon (Section 24-9), have important roles in keeping glucose blood concentrations within the normal range, which is required for normal body function. Abnormal functioning of the hormonal control process for blood-glucose levels leads to the condition known as diabetes (see Section 24-9).

Figure 18-16 A 5% (m/v) glucose solution is often used in hospitals as an intravenous source of nourishment for patients who cannot take food by mouth. The body can use it as an energy source without digesting it.

D-Galactose

A comparison of the Fischer projection formulas for D-galactose and D-glucose shows that these two compounds differ only in the configuration of the —OH group and —H group on carbon 4.

CHO   CHO
H——OH   H——OH
HO——H   HO——H
HO——H   H——OH
H——OH   H——OH
CH₂OH   CH₂OH
D-Galactose   D-Glucose

D-Galactose and D-glucose are epimers (diastereomers that differ only in the configuration at one chiral center; Section 18-6).

D-Galactose is seldom encountered as a free monosaccharide. It is, however, a component of numerous important biochemical substances. In the human body, galactose is synthesized from glucose in the mammary glands for use in lactose (milk sugar), a disaccharide consisting of a glucose unit and a galactose unit (Section 18-13). D-Galactose is sometimes called *brain sugar* because it is a component of glycoproteins (protein–carbohydrate compounds; Section 18-18) found in brain and nerve tissue. D-Galactose is also present in the chemical markers that distinguish various types of blood—A, B, AB, and O (see Chemical Connections 18-D—Blood Types and Oligosaccharides).

D-Fructose

D-Fructose is biochemically the most important ketohexose. It is also known as *levulose* and *fruit sugar*. Aqueous solutions of naturally occurring D-fructose rotate plane-polarized light to the left; hence the name *levulose*. The sweetest-tasting of all sugars, D-fructose is found in many fruits and is present in honey in equal amounts with glucose. It is sometimes used as a dietary sugar, not because it has fewer calories per gram than other sugars but because less is needed for the same amount of sweetness. Chemical Connections 18-B—Changing Sugar Patterns: Decreased Sucrose, Increased Fructose—provides additional information about fructose use as a sweetener in the form of high fructose corn syrup (HFCS).

From the third to the sixth carbon, the structure of D-fructose is identical to that of D-glucose. Differences at carbons 1 and 2 are related to the presence of a ketone group in fructose and of an aldehyde group in glucose.

D-Ribose

D-Glucose, D-galactose, and D-fructose are all hexoses. D-Ribose is a pentose. If carbon 3 and its accompanying —H and —OH groups were eliminated from the structure of D-glucose, the remaining structure would be that of D-ribose.

D-Ribose is a component of a variety of complex molecules, including ribonucleic acids (RNAs) and energy-rich compounds such as adenosine triphosphate (ATP). The compound 2-deoxy-D-ribose is also important in nucleic acid chemistry. This monosaccharide is a component of DNA molecules. The prefix *deoxy-* means "minus an oxygen"; the structures of ribose and 2-deoxyribose differ in that the latter compound lacks an oxygen atom at carbon 2.

Section 18-9 Quick Quiz

1. Which of the following is the Fischer projection formula for D-glucose?

   a.
   ```
        CHO
   H ——— OH
   H ——— OH
   H ——— OH
   HO ——— H
        CH₂OH
   ```

   b.
   ```
        CHO
   H ——— OH
   H ——— OH
   HO ——— H
   H ——— OH
        CH₂OH
   ```

   c.
   ```
        CHO
   H ——— OH
   HO ——— H
   H ——— OH
   HO ——— H
        CH₂OH
   ```

   d. no correct response

2. The structure of D-galactose differs from that of D-glucose at
   a. carbon 1 and carbon 2
   b. carbon 4
   c. carbon 5
   d. no correct response

3. The structure of D-fructose differs from that of D-glucose at
   a. carbon 1 and carbon 2
   b. carbon 4
   c. carbon 5
   d. no correct response

4. In which of the following pairs of monosaccharides do the members of the pair contain different numbers of carbon atoms?
   a. fructose and ribose
   b. glucose and galactose
   c. glyceraldehyde and dihydroxyacetone
   d. no correct response

5. In which of the following pairs of monosaccharides is one member of the pair an aldose and the other a ketose?
   a. ribose and galactose
   b. glucose and fructose
   c. dihydroxyacetone and fructose
   d. no correct response

Answers: 1. d; 2. b; 3. a; 4. a; 5. b

18-10   Cyclic Forms of Monosaccharides

LEARNING FOCUS

Be able to use Haworth projection formulas to denote the cyclic forms of monosaccharides.

So far in this chapter, the structures of monosaccharides have been depicted as open-chain polyhydroxy aldehydes or ketones. However, experimental evidence indicates that for monosaccharides containing five or more carbon atoms, such open-chain structures are actually in equilibrium with two cyclic structures, and the cyclic structures are the dominant forms at equilibrium. The cyclic forms of monosaccharides result from the ability of their carbonyl group to react intramolecularly with a hydroxyl group. Structurally, the resulting cyclic compounds are cyclic hemiacetals. ◄

▶ *Intramolecular cyclic hemiacetal formation was previously discussed in the chapter on aldehydes and ketones (Section 15-11). Recall that hemiacetals have both an —OH group and an —OR group attached to the same carbon atom. In the cyclic hemiacetals that monosaccharides form, it is the carbonyl carbon atom that bears the —OH and —OR groups.*

Cyclic Forms of D-Glucose

Further details about the cyclic forms of monosaccharides are obtained by considering in depth the formation of the cyclic forms of D-glucose. The platform for this in-depth consideration is Figure 18-17.

In Figure 18-17, structure 2 is a rearrangement of the projection formula for D-glucose in which the carbon atoms have locations similar to those found for carbon atoms in a six-membered ring. All hydroxyl groups drawn to the right in the original

Figure 18-17 The cyclic hemiacetal forms of D-glucose result from the intramolecular reaction between the carbonyl group and the hydroxyl group on carbon 5.

(1) Projection formula for D-glucose.

(2) All —OH groups to the right in the projection formula appear below the "ring," whereas —OH groups to the left appear above the "ring."

(3) Counterclockwise rotation of the groups attached to C5 gives this structure.

(4) The —OH group on C5 adds across the ⟩C=O.

(5) Two stereoisomers are possible,

(6) depending on how ring closure occurs.

α-D-Glucose

β-D-Glucose

Fischer projection formula appear below the ring. Those to the left in the Fischer projection formula appear above the ring.

Structure 3 in Figure 18-17 is obtained by rotating the groups attached to carbon 5 in a counterclockwise direction so that they are in the positions where it is easiest to visualize intramolecular hemiacetal formation. The intramolecular reaction occurs between the hydroxyl group on carbon 5 and the carbonyl group (carbon 1). The —OH group adds across the carbon–oxygen double bond, producing a heterocyclic ring that contains five carbon atoms and one oxygen atom.

Addition across the carbon–oxygen double bond with its accompanying ring formation produces a chiral center at carbon 1, so two stereoisomers are possible (see Figure 18-17, the two structures to the left of the "split" arrow). These two forms differ in the orientation of the —OH group on the hemiacetal carbon atom (carbon 1). In α-D-glucose, the —OH group is on the opposite side of the ring from the —CH₂OH group attached to carbon 5. In β-D-glucose, the —CH₂OH group on carbon 5 and the —OH group on carbon 1 are on the same side of the ring. ◀

In an aqueous solution of D-glucose, a dynamic equilibrium exists among the α, β, and open-chain forms, and there is continual interconversion among them. For example, a freshly mixed solution of pure α-D-glucose slowly converts to a mixture of both α- and β-D-glucose by an opening and a closing of the cyclic structure. When equilibrium is established, 63% of the molecules are β-D-glucose, 37% are α-D-glucose, and less than 0.01% are in the open-chain form.

▶ *Cyclization of glucose (hemiacetal formation) creates a new chiral center at carbon 1, and the presence of this new chiral center produces two stereoisomers, called α and β isomers.*

$$\text{α-D-Glucose} \rightleftarrows \text{Open-chain D-Glucose} \rightleftarrows \text{β-D-Glucose}$$
$$\text{(37\%)} \qquad\qquad \text{(less than 0.01\%)} \qquad\qquad \text{(63\%)}$$

The following structural diagram highlights the hemiacetal functional group that is present in cyclic forms of a monosaccharide.

The hemiacetal functional group

The location of the hemiacetal group in glucose

Special Terminology for Cyclic Monosaccharide Structures

Special terminology exists for the hemiacetal carbon atom present in a cyclic monosaccharide structure. This carbon atom is called the *anomeric carbon atom*. An **anomeric carbon atom** *is the hemiacetal carbon atom present in a cyclic monosaccharide structure.* It is the carbon atom that is bonded to an —OH group and to the oxygen atom in the heterocyclic ring.

Cyclic monosaccharide formation always produces two stereoisomers—an alpha form and a beta form. These two isomers are called *anomers*. **Anomers** *are cyclic monosaccharides that differ only in the positions of the substituents on the anomeric (hemiacetal) carbon atom.* The α-stereoisomer has the —OH group on the opposite side of the ring from the —CH$_2$OH group, and the β-stereoisomer has the —OH group on the same side of the ring as the —CH$_2$OH group.

Chirality considerations give further insights into the relationship between the alpha and beta forms of a cyclic monosaccharide. The anomeric carbon atom present in both structures is the carbonyl carbon atom in the open-chain form of glucose. This carbon atom, carbon 1, is achiral in the open-chain form but is chiral in the cyclic forms. Through cyclization, a new chiral center has been created, for which there will be two orientations for the —H and —OH groups attached to it; hence two stereoisomers exist (α-D-glucose and β-D-glucose).

It was previously noted in this section that in solution the two anomeric forms of a monosaccharide (alpha form and beta form) readily interconvert via the open-chain form. The alpha form can change into the beta form or vice versa. This interchange of OH-group and H-atom positions on the anomeric carbon atom is something that does not occur at other carbon atoms in the monosaccharide ring system. For example, the OH-group and H-atom that are bonded to carbon 4 of the ring cannot, in solution, interchange; hence glucose cannot change into galactose. Hydroxyl–hydrogen interchange is specific to the hemiacetal functional group which can break apart in solution to produce the open-chain form of the monosaccharide. Almost instantaneously the open-chain form returns to a cyclic form. Often, but not always, this reformation of the ring system results in interchange of the hydroxyl and hydrogen positions.

Cyclic Forms of Other Monosaccharides

Intramolecular cyclic hemiacetal formation and the equilibria among forms associated with it are not restricted to glucose. All aldoses with five or more carbon atoms establish similar equilibria, but with different percentages of the alpha, beta, and open-chain forms. Fructose and other ketoses with a sufficient number of carbon atoms also cyclize.

Galactose, like glucose, forms a six-membered ring, but both D-fructose and D-ribose form a five-membered ring.

α-D-Fructose   α-D-Ribose

D-Fructose cyclization involves carbon 2 (the keto group) and carbon 5, which results in two CH_2OH groups being outside the ring (carbons 1 and 6). D-Ribose cyclization involves carbon 1 (the aldehyde group) and carbon 4.

A cyclic monosaccharide containing a six-atom ring is called a *pyranose,* and one containing a five-atom ring is called a *furanose* because their ring structures resemble the ring structures in the cyclic ethers *pyran* and *furan* (Section 14-19), respectively.

Pyran   Furan

Such nomenclature leads to more specific names for the cyclic forms of monosaccharides—names that specify ring size. The more specific name for α-D-glucose is α-D-glucopyranose, and the more specific name for α-D-fructose is α-D-fructofuranose. The last part of each of these names specifies ring size.

EXAMPLE 18-6

Distinguishing Common Monosaccharides from Each Other on the Basis of Structural Characteristics

Which of the monosaccharides *glucose, fructose, galactose,* and *ribose* has each of the following structural characteristics? There may be more than one correct answer for a given characteristic.

a. It is a hexose.
b. It is an aldose.
c. Its cyclic form has a five-membered ring.
d. Its cyclic form exists in alpha and beta forms.

Solution

a. *Glucose, fructose,* and *galactose.* The only monosaccharide of the four listed that is not a hexose is ribose, which is a pentose.
b. *Glucose, galactose,* and *ribose.* The only monosaccharide of the four listed that is not an aldose is fructose, which is a ketose.
c. *Fructose* and *ribose.* Fructose is a ketohexose and when ketoses cyclize, the number of atoms in the ring is always one less than the number of carbon atoms in the open-chain form; the ring contains four carbon atoms and one oxygen atom and there are two carbon atoms outside the ring. Ribose is an aldopentose and when aldoses cyclize, the number of atoms in the ring is the same as the number of carbon atoms in the open-chain form; the ring contains four carbon atoms and one oxygen atom and there is one carbon atom outside the ring.
d. *Glucose, fructose, galactose,* and *ribose.* All monosaccharides have cyclic structures that have alpha and beta forms. As ring closure occurs, the random "twisting" of the two ends of the chain can produce two orientations for the —OH group on the hemiacetal carbon atom, giving rise to alpha and beta forms.

Section 18-10 Quick Quiz

1. How many different forms of a D-monosaccharide are present, at equilibrium, in an aqueous solution of the monosaccharide?
   a. one
   b. two
   c. three
   d. no correct response

2. Which of the following structures represents a β-monosaccharide?

   d. no correct response

3. Which carbon atom, by number, is the anomeric carbon atom in the structure
   a. carbon 2
   b. carbon 3
   c. carbon 4
   d. no correct response

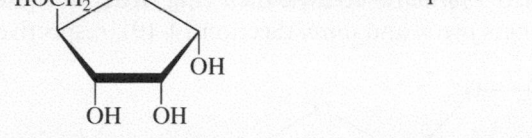

4. The cyclic forms of an aldohexose are based on a ring system containing
   a. 6 C atoms
   b. 5 C atoms and 1 O atom
   c. 4 C atoms and 2 O atoms
   d. no correct response

5. Which of the following types of monosaccharides have cyclic forms that involve a five-membered ring?
   a. aldopentoses and ketopentoses
   b. aldopentoses and ketohexoses
   c. aldohexoses and ketopentoses
   d. no correct response

Answers: 1. c; 2. b; 3. d; 4. b; 5. b

Figure 18-18 Walter Norman Haworth (1883–1950), the developer of Haworth projection formulas, was a British carbohydrate chemist. He helped determine the structures of the cyclic forms of glucose, was the first to synthesize vitamin C, and was a corecipient of the 1937 Nobel Prize in Chemistry.

18-11 Haworth Projection Formulas

LEARNING FOCUS

Be able to convert Fischer projection formulas to Haworth projection formulas.

The structural representations of the cyclic forms of monosaccharides found in the previous section are examples of Haworth projection formulas. A **Haworth projection formula** *is a two-dimensional structural notation that specifies the three-dimensional structure of a cyclic form of a monosaccharide.* Such projections carry the name of their originator, the British chemist Walter Norman Haworth (Figure 18-18).

In a Haworth projection, the hemiacetal ring system is viewed "edge on" with the oxygen ring atom at the upper right (six-membered ring) or at the top (five-membered ring).

The D or L form of a monosaccharide is determined by the position of the terminal –CH$_2$OH group on the highest-numbered ring carbon atom. In the D form, this group is positioned above the ring. In the L form, which is not usually encountered in biochemical systems, the terminal –CH$_2$OH group is positioned below the ring.

CH$_2$OH   Down = L
Up = D   O
O
CH$_2$OH

α or β configuration is determined by the position of the —OH group on carbon 1 relative to the –CH$_2$OH group that determines D or L series. In a β configuration, both of these groups point in the same direction; in an α configuration, the two groups point in opposite directions.

CH$_2$OH   CH$_2$OH   CH$_2$OH
O   OH   O   O
CH$_2$OH
HO
OH   OH   OH

β-D-Monosaccharide α-D-Monosaccharide β-L-Monosaccharide

In situations where α or β configuration does not matter, the —OH group on carbon 1 is placed in a horizontal position, and a wavy line is used as the bond that connects it to the ring.

CH$_2$OH
O
OH

D-Monosaccharide
(α/β not specified)

The specific identity of a monosaccharide is determined by the positioning of the other —OH groups in the Haworth projection formula. Any —OH group at a chiral center that is to the right in a Fischer projection formula points down in the Haworth projection formula. Any group to the left in a Fischer projection formula points up in the Haworth projection formula. The following is a matchup between Haworth projection formulas and a Fischer projection formula.

^{6}CH$_2$OH $_1$CHO ^{6}CH$_2$OH
^{5} O   HO—^{2}—H ^{5} O
OH
^{4} HO—^{3}—H ^{4}
OH   OH ^{1} =   =   OH   OH ^{1}
HO   OH   H—^{4}—OH   HO
$_3$ $_2$ H—^{5}—OH $_3$ $_2$
^{6}CH$_2$OH
α Form β Form

Comparison of this Fischer projection formula with those given in Figure 18-14 reveals that the monosaccharide is D-mannose. ◄

A similar matchup diagram for L-mannose shows that all up and down positions are inverted relative to the D-mannose diagram.

CHO
H—OH
HO   O   OH   H—OH   HO   O
CH$_2$OH   HO—H   CH$_2$OH
=   =   OH
HO—H
OH   OH   HO—H   OH   OH
CH$_2$OH
α-L-Mannose   L-Mannose β-L-Mannose

► *Common structural features for Haworth projection formulas for monosaccharides that are pentoses or hexoses are:*

1. *The structural core is a five- or six-membered ring.*
2. *The ring is heterocyclic containing one oxygen atom.*
3. *Carbon atoms not part of the ring are always attached to ring carbon atoms adjacent to the oxygen atom.*
4. *All except one of the carbon atoms carry a hydroxyl attachment.*

EXAMPLE 18-7

Changing a Fischer Projection Formula to a Haworth Projection Formula

Draw the Haworth projection formula for both anomers of D-talose, a monosaccharide whose Fischer projection formula is

$$
\begin{array}{c}
\text{CHO} \\
\text{HO}\!-\!\!-\!\!\text{H} \\
\text{HO}\!-\!\!-\!\!\text{H} \\
\text{HO}\!-\!\!-\!\!\text{H} \\
\text{H}\!-\!\!-\!\!\text{OH} \\
\text{CH}_2\text{OH}
\end{array}
$$

Solution

D-Talose is an aldohexose. An aldohexose cyclization produces a six-membered ring with one carbon atom (C6) outside the ring (Section 18-10).

Step 1:   Draw a planar hexagon ring with the oxygen atom in the upper right corner of the ring.

Step 2:   Add a —CH₂OH group to the first carbon to the left of the ring oxygen atom. This attachment is drawn up since the monosaccharide is D-talose rather than L-talose. For L-talose, the —CH₂OH group would have been drawn down.

Step 3:   Add to the anomeric carbon, the first carbon to the right of the ring oxygen atom, an —OH group that is drawn down for the α-anomer and drawn up for the β-anomer.

α-Anomer   β-Anomer

Step 4:   Add an —OH group to each of the remaining three carbons atoms (carbons 2–4). The —OH group is drawn down if it was to the right in the Fischer projection formula and drawn up if it was to the left in the Fischer projection formula.

α-D-Talose   β-D-Talose

Section 18-11 Quick Quiz

1. Any —OH group to the left of a chiral center in a Fischer projection formula points in which of the following directions in a Haworth projection formula?
   a. points to the right
   b. points up
   c. points down
   d. no correct response

2. Which of the following is the correct Haworth projection formula for a monosaccharide with the Fischer projection formula

$$
\begin{array}{c}
\text{CHO} \\
\text{HO}\!-\!\!-\!\!\text{H} \\
\text{H}\!-\!\!-\!\!\text{OH} \\
\text{HO}\!-\!\!-\!\!\text{H} \\
\text{H}\!-\!\!-\!\!\text{OH} \\
\text{CH}_2\text{OH}
\end{array}
$$

a. CH₂OH ... **b.** CH₂OH

c. CH₂OH ... **d.** no correct response

Answers: 1. b; 2. c

18-12 Reactions of Monosaccharides

LEARNING FOCUS

Be familiar with the characteristics of the following types of monosaccharide chemical reactions: oxidation, reduction, glycoside formation, phosphate ester formation, and amino sugar formation.

Five important reactions of monosaccharides are oxidation to acidic sugars, reduction to sugar alcohols, glycoside formation, phosphate ester formation, and amino sugar formation. In considering these reactions, glucose will be used as the monosaccharide reactant. Remember, however, that other aldoses, as well as ketoses, undergo similar reactions.

Oxidation to Produce Acidic Sugars

The redox chemistry of monosaccharides is closely linked to that of the alcohol and aldehyde functional groups. This latter redox chemistry, which was considered in Chapters 14 and 15, is summarized in the following diagram:

Monosaccharide oxidation can yield three different types of *acidic sugars*. The oxidizing agent used determines the product. ◀

Weak oxidizing agents, such as Tollens and Benedict's solutions (Section 15-10), oxidize the aldehyde end of an aldose to give an *aldonic acid.* Oxidation of the aldehyde end of glucose produces gluconic acid, and oxidation of the aldehyde end of galactose produces galactonic acid. ◀ The structures involved in the glucose reaction are

▶ *Glucose testing associated with diabetes (Chemical Connections 15-B—Diabetes, Aldehyde Oxidation, and Glucose Testing) involves oxidation of glucose to produce an acidic sugar.*

▶ *Vitamin C (Section 21-13) is a cyclic ester formed from a cyclization reaction involving L-gulonic acid, a six-carbon aldonic acid.*

$$
\begin{array}{c}
\text{COOH} \\
\text{HO}\!-\!\!-\!\!\text{H} \\
\text{HO}\!-\!\!-\!\!\text{H} \\
\text{H}\!-\!\!-\!\!\text{OH} \\
\text{HO}\!-\!\!-\!\!\text{H} \\
\text{CH}_2\text{OH}
\end{array}
$$

L-Gulonic acid

Because aldoses act as reducing agents in such reactions, they are called *reducing sugars*. With Tollens solution, glucose reduces Ag^+ ion to Ag, and with Benedict's solution, glucose reduces Cu^{2+} ion to Cu^+ ion (see Section 15-10). A **reducing sugar** *is a carbohydrate that gives a positive test with Tollens and Benedict's solutions.*

Under the basic conditions associated with Tollens and Benedict's solutions, ketoses are also reducing sugars. In this situation, the ketose undergoes a structural rearrangement that produces an aldose, and the aldose then reacts. Thus all monosaccharides, both aldoses and ketoses, are reducing sugars.

Strong oxidizing agents can oxidize both ends of a monosaccharide at the same time (the carbonyl group and the terminal primary alcohol group) to produce a dicarboxylic acid. Such polyhydroxy dicarboxylic acids are known as *aldaric acids*. For glucose, this oxidation produces glucaric acid.

D-Glucose → (Strong oxidizing agent) → D-Glucaric acid

Although it is difficult to do in the laboratory, in biochemical systems *enzymes* can oxidize the primary alcohol end of an aldose such as glucose, without oxidation of the aldehyde group, to produce an *alduronic acid*. For glucose, such an oxidation produces D-glucuronic acid. ◀

D-Glucose → (Enzymes) → D-Glucuronic acid

Reduction to Produce Sugar Alcohols

The carbonyl group present in a monosaccharide (either an aldose or a ketose) can be reduced to a hydroxyl group, using hydrogen as the reducing agent. For aldoses and ketoses, the product of the reduction is the corresponding polyhydroxy alcohols. Such polyhydroxy alcohols are called *sugar alcohols* or *alditols*. ◀ For example, the reduction of D-glucose gives D-glucitol.

D-Ribose   D-Ribitol

D-Glucose → (H_2 catalyst) → D-Glucitol

D-Glucitol is also known by the common name D-sorbitol. Hexahydroxy alcohols such as D-sorbitol have properties similar to those of the trihydroxy alcohol *glycerol* (Section 14-5). These alcohols are used as moisturizing agents in foods and cosmetics because of their affinity for water. D-Sorbitol is also used as a sweetening agent in chewing gum; bacteria that cause tooth decay cannot use polyalcohols as food sources, as they can glucose and many other monosaccharides. ◀

Glycoside Formation

In Section 15-11, hemiacetals were shown to react with alcohols in acid solution to produce acetals. Because the cyclic forms of monosaccharides are hemiacetals, they react with alcohols to form acetals, as is illustrated here for the reaction of β-D-glucose with methyl alcohol. ◀

▶ *Some people are particularly sensitive to D-sorbitol. They absorb it poorly and it thus passes undigested into the large intestine, where it is metabolized by bacteria. A by-product of such bacterial action is large amounts of intestinal gas, which can cause major discomfort.*

▶ *Remember, from Section 15-11, that acetals have two —OR groups attached to the same carbon atom.*

β-D-Glucose   Methyl-β-D-glucoside

The general name for monosaccharide acetals is *glycoside*. A **glycoside** *is an acetal formed from a cyclic monosaccharide by replacement of the hemiacetal carbon —OH group with an —OR group.* More specifically, a glycoside produced from glucose is called a glucoside, that from galactose is called a galactoside, and so on. Glycosides, like the hemiacetals from which they are formed, can exist in both α and β forms. Glycosides are named by listing the alkyl or aryl group attached to the oxygen, followed by the name of the monosaccharide involved, with the suffix *-ide* appended to it.

Methyl-α-D-glucoside   Methyl-β-D-glucoside

Phosphate Ester Formation

The hydroxyl groups of a monosaccharide can react with inorganic oxyacids to form inorganic esters (Section 16-20). Phosphate esters, formed from phosphoric acid and various monosaccharides, are commonly encountered in biochemical systems. For example, specific enzymes in the human body catalyze the esterification of the hemiacetal group (carbon 1) and the primary alcohol group (carbon 6) in glucose to produce the compounds glucose 1-phosphate and glucose 6-phosphate, respectively (Sections 24-2, 24-5, and 24-6).

α-D-Glucose 1-phosphate   α-D-Glucose 6-phosphate

These phosphate esters of glucose are stable in aqueous solution and play important roles in the metabolism of carbohydrates.

Amino Sugar Formation

If one of the hydroxyl groups of a monosaccharide is replaced with an amino group, an amino sugar is produced. In naturally occurring amino sugars, of which there are three common ones, the amino group replaces the carbon 2 hydroxyl group. The three common natural amino sugars are

D-Glucosamine   D-Galactosamine   D-Mannosamine

Amino sugars and their *N*-acetyl derivatives are important building blocks of polysaccharides found in chitin (Section 18-16) and hyaluronic acid (Section 18-17). The *N*-acetyl derivatives of D-glucosamine and D-galactosamine are present in the biochemical markers on red blood cells, which distinguish the various blood types. (See Chemical Connections 18-D—Blood Types and Oligosaccharides.) ◄

▶ *An acetyl group has the structure*

It can be considered to be derived from acetic acid by removal of the —OH portion of that structure.

Acetic acid

N-Acetyl-α-D-glucosamine   *N*-Acetyl-α-D-galactosamine

Chemistry at a Glance—"Sugar Terminology" Associated with Monosaccharides and Their Derivatives—summarizes the "sugar terminology" associated with the common types of monosaccharides and monosaccharide derivatives considered so far in this chapter.

Section 18-12 Quick Quiz

1. Which of the following types of acidic sugars produced by monosaccharide oxidation is *not* possible?
   a. Aldehyde end of monosaccharide is oxidized.
   b. Primary alcohol end of monosaccharide is oxidized.
   c. Both aldehyde and primary alcohol ends of monosaccharide are oxidized.
   d. no correct response
2. Sugar alcohols are obtained by
   a. oxidizing the aldehyde end of a monosaccharide
   b. reducing the aldehyde end of a monosaccharide
   c. oxidizing the primary alcohol end of a monosaccharide
   d. no correct response
3. In glycoside formation, the hemiacetal functional group of a cyclic monosaccharide is converted to an acetal group by reaction with a(n)
   a. alcohol
   b. carboxylic acid
   c. ester
   d. no correct response

CHEMISTRY AT A GLANCE — "Sugar Terminology" Associated with Monosaccharides and Their Derivatives

4. In phosphate ester formation, the phosphate group is usually found on carbon atoms
   a. 1 or 6
   b. 2 or 6
   c. 2 or 5
   d. no correct response
5. In common natural amino sugars, the amino group replaces the hydroxyl group on carbon
   a. 1
   b. 2
   c. 3
   d. no correct response

Answers: 1. d; 2. b; 3. a; 4. a; 5. b

18-13 Disaccharides

LEARNING FOCUS

For the disaccharides maltose, cellobiose, lactose, and sucrose be able to specify (1) the monosaccharide units present, (2) the type of glycosidic linkage present, and (3) whether or not the disaccharide is a reducing sugar.

A monosaccharide that has cyclic forms (hemiacetal forms) can react with an alcohol to form a glycoside (acetal), as noted in Section 18-12. This same type of reaction can be used to produce a *disaccharide*, a carbohydrate in which two monosaccharides are bonded together (Section 18-3). In disaccharide formation, one of the monosaccharide reactants functions as a hemiacetal, and the other functions as an alcohol.

$$\text{Monosaccharide} + \text{monosaccharide} \longrightarrow \text{disaccharide} + H_2O$$

$$\begin{pmatrix}\text{Functioning as a} \\ \text{hemiacetal}\end{pmatrix} \quad \begin{pmatrix}\text{Functioning as} \\ \text{an alcohol}\end{pmatrix} \qquad \text{(Glycoside)}$$

The bond that links the two monosaccharides of a disaccharide (glycoside) together is called a glycosidic linkage. A **glycosidic linkage** *is the bond between two monosaccharides resulting from the reaction between the hemiacetal carbon atom —OH group of one monosaccharide and an —OH group on the other monosaccharide.* It is always a carbon–oxygen–carbon bond in a disaccharide.

In Section 18-10, it was noted that a cyclic monosaccharide contains a hemiacetal (anomeric) carbon atom. Many disaccharides contain both a hemiacetal carbon atom and an acetal carbon atom, as is the case for the preceding disaccharide structure. Hemiacetal and acetal locations within disaccharides play an important role in the chemistry of these substances.

The remainder of this section deals with the specific structures and properties of four important disaccharides: maltose, cellobiose, lactose, and sucrose.

Maltose

Maltose, often called *malt sugar,* is produced whenever the polysaccharide starch (Section 18-15) breaks down, as happens in plants when seeds germinate and in human beings during starch digestion. It is a common ingredient in baby foods and is found in malted milk. Malt (germinated barley that has been baked and ground) contains maltose; hence the name *malt sugar.*

Structurally, maltose is made up of two D-glucose units, one of which must be α-D-glucose. The formation of maltose from two glucose molecules is as follows:

The glycosidic linkage between the two glucose units is called an $\alpha(1\rightarrow4)$ linkage. The two —OH groups that form the linkage are attached, respectively, to

Figure 18-19 The three forms of maltose present in aqueous solution.

carbon 1 of the first glucose unit (in an α configuration) and to carbon 4 of the second.

Maltose is a reducing sugar (Section 18-12) because the glucose unit on the right has a hemiacetal carbon atom (C-1). Thus this glucose unit can open and close; it is in equilibrium with its open-chain aldehyde form (Section 18-10). This means there are actually three forms of the maltose molecule: α-maltose, β-maltose, and the open-chain form. Structures for these three maltose forms are shown in Figure 18-19. In the solid state, the β form is dominant.

The most important chemical reaction of maltose is that of hydrolysis. Hydrolysis of D-maltose, whether in a laboratory flask or in a living organism, produces two molecules of D-glucose. An acidic environment or the enzyme *maltase* is needed for the hydrolysis to occur.

$$\text{D-Maltose} + \text{H}_2\text{O} \xrightarrow{\text{H}^+ \text{ or maltase}} 2 \text{ D-glucose}$$

Cellobiose

Cellobiose is produced as an intermediate in the hydrolysis of the polysaccharide cellulose (Section 18-16). Like maltose, cellobiose contains two D-glucose monosaccharide units. It differs from maltose in that one of the D-glucose units—the one functioning as a hemiacetal—must have a β configuration instead of the α configuration for maltose. This change in configuration results in a β(1 → 4) glycosidic linkage.

Like maltose, cellobiose is a reducing sugar, has three isomeric forms in aqueous solution, and upon hydrolysis produces two D-glucose molecules.

$$\text{D-Cellobiose} + \text{H}_2\text{O} \xrightarrow{\text{H}^+ \text{ or cellobiase}} 2 \text{ D-glucose}$$

Despite these similarities, maltose and cellobiose have different biochemical behaviors. These differences are related to the stereochemistry of their glycosidic linkages.

Maltase, the enzyme that breaks the glucose–glucose $\alpha(1 \rightarrow 4)$ linkage present in maltose, is found both in the human body and in yeast. Consequently, maltose is digested easily by humans and is readily fermented by yeast. Both the human body and yeast lack the enzyme cellobiase needed to break the glucose–glucose $\beta(1 \rightarrow 4)$ linkage of cellobiose. Thus cellobiose cannot be digested by humans or fermented by yeast. ◀

Lactose

In both maltose and cellobiose, the monosaccharide units present are identical—two glucose units in each case. However, the two monosaccharide units in a disaccharide need not be identical. *Lactose* is made up of a β-D-galactose unit and a D-glucose unit joined by a $\beta(1 \rightarrow 4)$ glycosidic linkage.

▶ *It is important to distinguish between the structural notation used for an $\alpha(1 \rightarrow 4)$ glycosidic linkage and that used for a $\beta(1 \rightarrow 4)$ glycosidic linkage.*

The glucose hemiacetal center is unaffected when galactose bonds to glucose in the formation of lactose, so lactose is a reducing sugar (the glucose ring can open to give an aldehyde).

▶ *The α form of lactose is sweeter to the taste and more soluble in water than the β form. The β form can be found in ice cream that has been stored for a long time; it crystallizes and gives the ice cream a gritty texture.*

Lactose is the major sugar found in milk. This accounts for its common name, *milk sugar.* Enzymes in mammalian mammary glands take glucose from the bloodstream and synthesize lactose in a four-step process. Epimerization (Section 18-6) of glucose yields galactose, and then the $\beta(1 \rightarrow 4)$ linkage forms between a galactose and a glucose unit. Lactose is an important ingredient in commercially produced infant formulas that are designed to simulate mother's milk. Souring of milk is caused by the conversion of lactose to lactic acid by bacteria in the milk. Pasteurization of milk is a quick-heating process that kills most of the bacteria and retards the souring process. ◀

▶ *The enzyme needed to break the $\beta(1 \rightarrow 4)$ linkage in lactose is different from the one needed to break the $\beta(1 \rightarrow 4)$ linkage in cellobiose. Because the two disaccharides have slightly different structures, different enzymes are required—lactase for lactose and cellobiase for cellobiose.*

Lactose can be hydrolyzed by acid or by the enzyme *lactase,* forming an equimolar mixture of galactose and glucose. ◀

$$\text{D-Lactose} + \text{H}_2\text{O} \xrightarrow{\text{H}^+ \text{ or lactase}} \text{D-galactose} + \text{D-glucose}$$

In the human body, the galactose so produced is then converted to glucose by other enzymes. The focus on relevancy feature Chemical Connections 18-A—Lactose Intolerance or Lactase Persistence—discusses the genetic condition *lactose intolerance,* an inability of the human digestive system to hydrolyze lactose.

Sucrose

Sucrose, common *table sugar,* is the most abundant of all disaccharides and occurs throughout the plant kingdom. It is produced commercially from the juice of sugar cane and sugar beets. Sugar cane contains up to 20% by mass sucrose, and sugar beets contain up to 17% by mass sucrose. Figure 18-20 shows a molecular model for sucrose.

The two monosaccharide units present in a D-sucrose molecule are α-D-glucose and β-D-fructose. The glycosidic linkage is not a $(1 \rightarrow 4)$ linkage, as was the case for maltose, cellobiose, and lactose. It is instead an α, $\beta(1 \rightarrow 2)$ glycosidic linkage.

Figure 18-20 Space-filling model of the disaccharide sucrose.

CHEMICAL CONNECTIONS 18-A

Lactose Intolerance or Lactase Persistence

Lactose is the principal carbohydrate in milk. Human mother's milk obtained by nursing infants contains 7%–8% lactose, almost double the 4%–5% lactose found in cow's milk.

For many people, the digestion and absorption of lactose are a problem. This problem, called *lactose intolerance,* is a condition in which people lack the enzyme *lactase,* which is needed to hydrolyze lactose to galactose and glucose.

$$\text{Lactose} + \text{H}_2\text{O} \xrightarrow{\text{Lactase}} \text{glucose} + \text{galactose}$$

Many adults cannot drink milk without discomfort because of inadequate amounts of the enzyme *lactase* within their body.

Deficiency of lactase can be caused by a genetic defect, by physiological decline with age, or by injuries to the mucosa lining the intestines. When lactose molecules remain in the intestine undigested, they attract water to themselves, causing fullness, discomfort, cramping, nausea, and diarrhea. Bacterial fermentation of the lactose further along the intestinal tract produces acid (lactic acid) and gas, adding to the discomfort.

The level of the enzyme lactase in humans varies with age. Most children have sufficient lactase during the early years of their life when milk is a much-needed source of calcium in their diet. In adulthood, the enzyme level decreases, and lactose intolerance develops. This explains the change in milk-drinking habits of many adults. Some researchers estimate that as many as one in three adult Americans exhibits a degree of lactose intolerance.

Note that the "normal" condition of lactose intolerance is not considered to be a food allergy situation. Food allergies arise when a person's immune system responds to an invading allergen. Lactose intolerance does not involve the body's immune system. Rather, it relates to an enzymatic condition—lack of the enzyme lactase.

The level of the enzyme lactase in humans varies widely among ethnic groups, indicating that the trait is genetically determined (inherited). The occurrence of lactose intolerance is lowest among Scandinavians and other northern Europeans and highest among native North Americans, Southeast Asians, Africans, and Greeks.

An alternate analysis of milk-drinking versus non-milk-drinking populations exists. Being able to drink milk is considered to be the "abnormal" situation, as less than 40% of the world's total adult population retain the ability to drink milk (digest lactose) after childhood. Thus more than 60% of adults (the majority) are non-milk-drinkers. The term *lactase persistence* is used to describe the condition where milk-drinking ability continues into adulthood.

The estimated prevalence of lactase persistence in various populations is as follows:

99% Sweden	81% U.S. (Iowa)
97% Denmark	12% Greece
95% Scotland	10% Japan
88% Germany	5% Native American

No other species but humans, as adults, can drink milk, and then only some of them. There are no milk-drinking adult animals; only baby animals drink milk.

For lactose-intolerant people, a lactose-free diet is difficult to pursue because lactose is an ingredient in many nondairy products including cereals, breads, breakfast drinks, instant potatoes, and salad dressings. In addition, lactose, as a filler, is added to some medications. It is estimated that 20% of prescription drugs and 5% of nonprescription medications contain lactose. The lactose content of selected foods is as follows:

1 dinner roll, 0.5 g
1 oz cheddar cheese, 1.0 g
1 cake donut, 1.2 g
1 oz chocolate candy, 2.3 g
1 c sherbet, 4.0 g
1 c low-fat yogurt, 10.0 g
1 c 1% milk, 11.0 g
1 c ice cream, 12.0 g

▶ *The glycosidic linkage in sucrose is very different from that in maltose, cellobiose, and lactose. The linkages in the latter three compounds can be characterized as "head-to-tail" linkages—that is, the front end (carbon 1) of one monosaccharide is linked to the back end (carbon 4) of the other monosaccharide. Sucrose has a "head-to-head" glycosidic linkage; the front ends of the two monosaccharides (carbon 1 for glucose and carbon 2 for fructose) are linked.*

The —OH group on carbon 2 of D-fructose (the hemiacetal carbon) reacts with the —OH group on carbon 1 of D-glucose (the hemiacetal carbon). ◀

Sucrose, unlike maltose, cellobiose, and lactose, is a *nonreducing sugar*. In sucrose, the hemiacetal center (anomeric carbon atom) of each monosaccharide is involved in the glycosidic linkage. The result is a molecule that contains two acetal centers. Sucrose, in the solid state and in solution, exists in only one form—there are no α and β isomers, and an open-chain form is not possible.

Sucrase, the enzyme needed to break the α, β(1 → 2) linkage in sucrose, is present in the human body. Hence sucrose is an easily digested substance. Sucrose hydrolysis (digestion) produces an equimolar mixture of glucose and fructose called *invert sugar* (see Figure 18-21).

$$\text{D-Sucrose} + \text{H}_2\text{O} \xrightarrow{\text{H}^+ \text{ or sucrase}} \underbrace{\text{D-glucose} + \text{D-fructose}}_{\text{Invert sugar}}$$

When sucrose is cooked with acid-containing foods such as fruits or berries, partial hydrolysis takes place, forming some invert sugar. Jams and jellies prepared in this manner are actually sweeter than the pure sucrose added to the original mixture because one-to-one mixtures of glucose and fructose taste sweeter than sucrose.

The focus on relevancy feature Chemical Connections 18-B—Changing Sugar Patterns: Decreased Sucrose, Increased Fructose—discusses the increasing trend of using fructose instead of sucrose as a sweetener in beverages and processed foods. A related item, sugar substitutes (artificial sweeteners), is the topic of the focus on relevancy feature Chemical Connections 18-C—Sugar Substitutes.

Figure 18-21 Honeybees and many other insects possess an enzyme called *invertase* that hydrolyzes sucrose to invert sugar. Thus honey is predominantly a mixture of D-glucose and D-fructose with some unhydrolyzed sucrose. The term *invert* sugar comes from the observation that the direction of rotation of plane-polarized light (Section 18-7) changes from positive (clockwise) to negative (counterclockwise) when sucrose is hydrolyzed to invert sugar. The rotation is +66° for sucrose. The net rotation for the invert sugar mixture of fructose (−92°) and glucose (+52°) is −40°.

©photofun/Shutterstock.com

CHEMICAL CONNECTIONS 18-B

Changing Sugar Patterns: Decreased Sucrose, Increased Fructose

Prior to 1970, the natural sweetener added to prepared foods and beverages consumed by humans was almost always the disaccharide sucrose (table sugar). Since that time, sucrose use has steadily declined with the monosaccharide fructose progressively displacing sucrose as a natural sweetener. Fructose use per capita per year is now almost equal to that of sucrose.

Fructose, the most abundant sugar in a variety of fruits and some vegetables, has a "sweetness factor" that is 73% greater than that of sucrose. (Chemical Connections 18-C—Sugar Substitutes—considers sweetness factors.) It is the presence of fructose that gives ripe fruit its "extra" sweetness.

The role that fructose use plays in (1) the formulation of fruit juice blends that are not 100% one juice and (2) the formulation of prepared foods and other types of soft drink beverages are considered in this Chemical Connection.

(1) The "base" juice for a fruit juice blend is almost always apple juice or pear juice or a mix of the two. To this is added a small amount of a stronger flavored juice such as blueberry or pomegranate juice. Why are apple juice and/or pear juice the "base juice?" Apples and pears are the two fruits with the highest fructose/glucose ratio and therefore the greatest sweetness. The fructose/glucose ratio is almost two times higher for these fruits than for most other fruits, as shown in the following graphical information.

Note from this graphical information that some fruits also contain significant amounts of sucrose itself, which when hydrolyzed produces a 1-to-1 mixture of fructose and glucose.

(2) Fructose is also used as a replacement for sucrose in many prepared foods and beverages other than fruit juice blends. Here, however, fruits are not the source for the fructose used. Rather, fructose in the form of high fructose corn syrup (HFCS), made from milled corn, is the fructose source.

The replacement of sucrose with HFCS is mainly an economically driven decision. It costs less to sweeten products with HFCS than with sucrose for three reasons.

1. Fructose (obtained from corn) is cheaper than sucrose (obtained from sugar beets and sugar cane) in the United States due to the relative abundance of corn, farm subsidies for corn, and sugar import tariffs.
2. HFCS is easier to blend and transport because it is a liquid.
3. HFCS usage leads to products with a much longer shelf life.

HFCS production involves milling corn to produce corn starch and then hydrolyzing the starch (a glucose polymer, Section 18-16) to glucose using the enzymes alpha-amylase and glucoamylase (Section 21-3). The glucose so produced is then treated with the enzyme glucose isomerase to produce a mixture of glucose and fructose. This latter enzymatic process produces a mixture whose composition is 42% fructose, 50% glucose, and 8% other sugars (HFCS-42). Concentration procedures are then used to produce a syrup that is 90% fructose (HFCS-90). HFCS-42 and HFCS-90 are then blended to produce HFCS-55, which is 55% fructose, 41% glucose, and 4% other sugars. HFCS-55 is the sweetener of preference in the soft drink industry. Its properties, including sweetness, are very similar to those of sucrose, which is 50% fructose and 50% glucose. HFCS-42 is commonly used as a sweetener in many processed foods, and HFCS-90 is often used in baked goods.

It is claimed by some health advocates that HFCS is more harmful to consumers than sucrose. Current research has not yet been able to give a definitive answer to this question. Metabolic studies involving the two substances show almost identical results for sucrose and HFCS. Such results should be expected as sucrose is 50% glucose and 50% fructose and HFCS has a ratio close to 1 for the two sugars. Claims that HFCS products contribute to an obesity problem probably relate to the fact that people who consume many sugary drinks have a higher caloric energy intake than those who do not use such drinks daily.

	Glucose per Serving*	%Fructose	%Glucose	%Sucrose	Fructose/Glucose Ratio**
Grapes	13.01 g	53%	46%	1%	1.1
Pear	10.34 g	64%	28%	8%	2.1
Watermelon	9.61 g	55%	26%	19%	1.8
Apple	8.14 g	57%	23%	20%	2.0
Blueberries	7.21 g	50%	49%	1%	1.0
Cherries	6.28 g	44%	55%	1%	0.82
Banana	5.72 g	40%	41%	19%	0.98
Strawberries	4.15 g	54%	44%	2%	1.2
Pineapple	3.18 g	22%	19%	59%	1.1
Orange	3.15 g	26%	23%	51%	1.1
Raspberries	2.89 g	53%	42%	5%	1.3
Peach	1.50 g	18%	24%	58%	0.92
Cantaloupe	1.29 g	24%	20%	56%	1.1

■ %Fructose ■ %Glucose ■ %Sucrose

* Serving size: 1 medium-sized fruit (apple, banana, orange, peach, pear); 1 cup (blueberries, cherries, grapes, pineapple, raspberries, strawberries); 1/8 melon (cantaloupe); 1/16 melon (watermelon)

** Fructose/glucose ratio: Calculated treating the sucrose present as one-half fructose and one-half glucose.

CHEMICAL   CONNECTIONS 18-C

Sugar Substitutes

Because of the high caloric value of sucrose, it is often difficult to satisfy a demanding "sweet tooth" with sucrose without adding pounds to the body frame or inches to the waistline. Sugar substitutes, which provide virtually no calories, are now used extensively as a solution to the "sucrose problem."

Two of the most widely used sugar substitutes are saccharin and aspartame whose structures are:

Saccharin

Aspartame

Saccharin is the oldest of the artificial sweeteners, having been in use for more than 100 years. Questions about its safety arose in 1977 after a study suggested that large doses of saccharin caused bladder tumors in rats. As a result, the FDA proposed banning saccharin, but public support for its use caused Congress to impose a moratorium on the ban. In 1991, on the basis of many further studies, the FDA withdrew its proposal to ban saccharin. Saccharin is 300 times sweeter than sucrose and relatively inexpensive to produce. Sweet'NLow and Sugar Twin are saccharin-based commercial products.

Aspartame (NutraSweet), approved by the FDA in 1981, is used in both the United States and Canada and accounts for three-fourths of current sugar-substitute use. It tastes like sucrose but is 180 times sweeter. It provides 4 kcal/g, as does sucrose, but because so little is used, its calorie contribution is negligible. Aspartame has quickly found its way into almost every diet food on the market today. Aspartame as well as saccharin are not heat-stable and therefore cannot be used in products that require cooking.

The safety of aspartame lies with its hydrolysis products: the amino acids aspartic acid and phenylalanine. These amino acids are identical to those obtained from digestion of proteins. The only danger aspartame poses is that it contains phenylalanine, an amino acid that can lead to mental retardation among young children suffering from PKU (phenylketonuria). Labels on all products containing aspartame warn phenylketonurics of this potential danger.

Sucralose, approved by the FDA in 1990, is a derivative of sucrose. It is synthesized from sucrose by substitution of three chlorine atoms for hydroxyl groups.

An advantage of sucralose use over that of aspartame is that sucralose is heat-stable and can therefore be used in cooked food. Aspartame loses its sweetness when heated. Sucralose is 600 times sweeter than sucrose and has a similar taste. It is calorie-free because it cannot be hydrolyzed as it passes through the digestive tract.

Sucralose

A newer sugar substitute working its way into the marketplace is neotame, approved by the FDA in 2002 as a general-purpose sweetener. Heat-stable, this sweetener can be used in a wide variety of products including baked goods, frostings, frozen desserts, puddings, and fruit juices. With a sweetness 7000 times greater than that of sucrose, the small amounts needed to sweeten products means its caloric impact is negligible. Economic savings also occur because of the small amounts required.

Structurally, neotame is an aspartame derivative. The same two amino acids are present as in aspartame. It differs structurally from aspartame in that a 3,3-dimethylbutyl group is attached to the terminal —NH$_2$ group of aspartame. This "bulky" attachment prevents the breakdown of neotame into its component amino acids, as occurs for aspartame. Hence individuals with PKU can use neotame without concern.

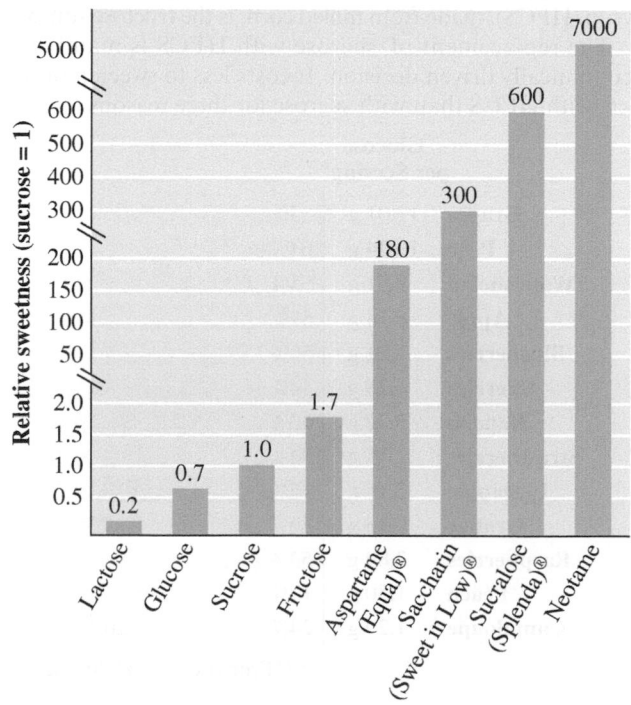

Sweetness of common sugars and sugar substitutes based on sucrose (table sugar) having an assigned value of 1.

Other Types of Glycosidic Linkages

Three of the four disaccharides considered in this section—maltose, cellobiose, and lactose—have (1→4) glycosidic linkages. The other disaccharide considered, sucrose, has a (1→2) glycosidic linkage. Other carbon atoms besides 1, 2, and 4 can also participate in glycosidic linkages. An additional common type of glycosidic linkage is one that involves carbons 1 and 6. Several disaccharides considered in later sections of this chapter have $\alpha(1\rightarrow6)$ glycosidic linkages. The following structure is that for two α-D-glucose molecules connected via an $\alpha(1\rightarrow6)$ glycosidic linkage.

This disaccharide is an entirely different compound than maltose or cellobiose, both of which involve two glucose molecules connected, respectively, via $\alpha(1 \rightarrow 4)$ and $\beta(1 \rightarrow 4)$ glycosidic linkages.

EXAMPLE 18-8

Distinguishing Common Disaccharides from Each Other on the Basis of Structural and Reaction Characteristics

Which of the disaccharides *maltose, cellobiose, lactose,* and *sucrose* has each of the following structural or reaction characteristics? There may be more than one correct answer for a given characteristic.

a. Both monosaccharide units present are glucose.
b. It is a reducing sugar.
c. It can exist in alpha and beta forms.
d. Its glycoside linkage is an $\alpha(1 \rightarrow 4)$ linkage.

Solution

a. *Maltose* and *cellobiose.* Both of these disaccharides contain two glucose units. They differ from each other in the type of glycosidic linkage present; maltose contains an $\alpha(1 \rightarrow 4)$ linkage and cellobiose contains a $\beta(1 \rightarrow 4)$ glycosidic linkage.

b. *Maltose, cellobiose,* and *lactose.* A reducing sugar has one "free" hemiacetal carbon atom. Such is the case any time two monosaccharides are bonded through a $(1 \rightarrow 4)$ glycosidic linkage. Sucrose is the only one of the four disaccharides that does not have a $(1 \rightarrow 4)$ glycosidic linkage; its glycosidic linkage is of the $(1 \rightarrow 2)$ variety.

c. *Maltose, cellobiose,* and *lactose.* A "free" hemiacetal carbon atom is a prerequisite for alpha and beta cyclic forms. Sucrose is the only one of the four disaccharides for which this is not the case. Reducing sugars (part **b**) and alpha/beta forms are based on the same structural feature.

d. *Maltose.* Maltose, cellobiose, and lactose all have $(1 \rightarrow 4)$ glycosidic linkages. However, only maltose has an $\alpha(1 \rightarrow 4)$ linkage; the other two disaccharides have $\beta(1 \rightarrow 4)$ linkages.

EXAMPLE 18-9

Drawing Structural Formulas for the Products from Disaccharide Hydrolysis

Draw the structural formulas for the products formed when the disaccharide lactose is hydrolyzed.

Solution

The glycosidic linkage that connects the two monosaccharide units present in a disaccharide structure is the "point of attack" during a hydrolysis reaction.

Cleavage of the glycosidic linkage releases the two monosaccharides. Water participates in the reaction by supplying an H atom to one monosaccharide (the one that retains the O atom of the glycosidic linkage) and supplying an —OH group entity to the other monosaccharide.

Section 18-13 Quick Quiz

1. Which of the following disaccharides contains glucose and fructose as structural units?
   a. sucrose
   b. lactose
   c. maltose
   d. no correct response
2. Which of the following disaccharides will produce only glucose upon hydrolysis?
   a. sucrose
   b. lactose
   c. maltose
   d. no correct response
3. In which of the following disaccharides is the bonding between monosaccharides units "head-to-head" rather than "head-to-tail"?
   a. lactose
   b. cellobiose
   c. maltose
   d. no correct response

4. In which of the following pairs of disaccharides do both members of the pair have the same type of glycosidic linkage?
   a. sucrose and lactose
   b. cellobiose and maltose
   c. lactose and cellobiose
   d. no correct response
5. Which of the following disaccharides is *not* a reducing sugar?
   a. maltose
   b. lactose
   c. sucrose
   d. no correct response
6. The terms *milk sugar* and *table sugar* apply, respectively, to the disaccharides
   a. lactose and maltose
   b. maltose and sucrose
   c. lactose and sucrose
   d. no correct response

Answers: 1. a; 2. c; 3. d; 4. c; 5. c; 6. c

18-14 Oligosaccharides

LEARNING FOCUS

Describe the structural features of and occurrence of the oligosaccharides raffinose and stachyose and the oligosaccharide-containing substance solanine.

Oligosaccharides are carbohydrates that contain three to ten monosaccharide units bonded to each other via glycosidic linkages (Section 18-3). Two naturally occurring oligosaccharides found in onions, cabbage, broccoli, brussel sprouts, whole wheat, and all types of beans are the trisaccharide raffinose and the tetrasaccharide stachyose. Raffinose's monosaccharide components are galactose, glucose, and fructose. Stachyose's structure differs from that of raffinose in that an additional galactose unit is present. Detailed structures for these two oligosaccharides are given in Figure 18-22. Note the presence in both structures of two different types of glycosidic linkages— $\alpha(1 \rightarrow 6)$ and $\alpha,\beta(1 \rightarrow 2)$ linkages.

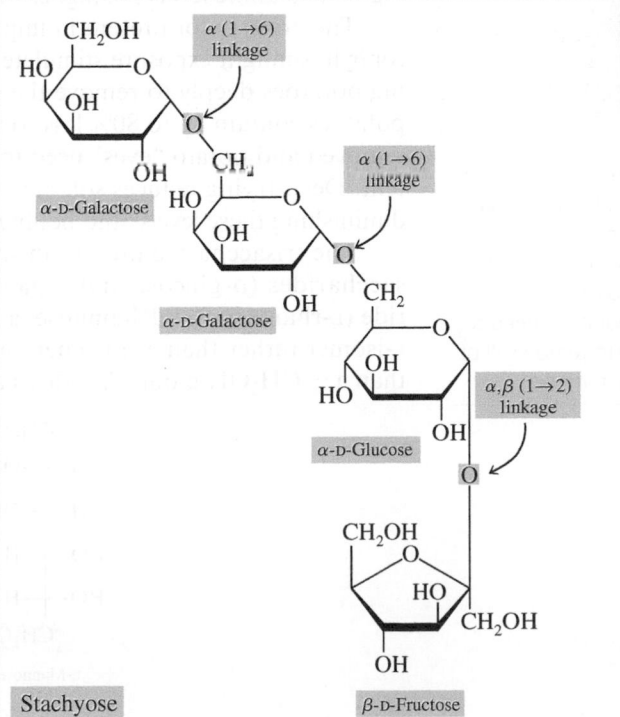

Figure 18-22 Structural formulas for the trisaccharide raffinose and the tetrasaccharide stachyose.

Figure 18-23 In humans, intestinal bacterial action on the undigestable raffinose and stachyose present in beans produces gaseous products that can cause discomfort and flatulence.

Humans lack the digestive enzymes necessary to metabolize either raffinose or stachyose. Hence these oligosaccharides, when ingested in food, pass undigested into the large intestine, where bacteria act upon them. This bacterial action usually produces discomfort and flatulence (gas). Taking a preparation such as Beano with a meal heavy in beans (Figure 18-23) can reduce the amount of flatulence produced. Beano and related products contain the enzyme (not found in humans) that facilitates the digestion of these oligosaccharides.

In biochemical systems, it is more common to encounter oligosaccharides as components of more complex molecules, rather than in the "free" state as is the case with raffinose and stachyose.

An important aspect of human body chemistry that involves an oligosaccharide attachment to more complex molecules is blood chemistry associated with blood type. The type of blood a person has (O, A, B, or AB) is determined by the type of oligosaccharide that is attached to the person's red blood cells. The focus on relevancy feature Chemical Connections 18-D—Blood Types and Oligosaccharides—gives further information about the oligosaccharides that determine blood type, as well as about the role that blood type plays in blood chemistry. Interestingly, one of the monosaccharides present in the oligosaccharides associated with blood type is a 6-deoxy-L-monosaccharide.

Solanine, a compound found in the potato plant, is another example of an oligosaccharide-containing "complex" molecule. The framework for solanine's structure is a large multi-ring amine system (an alkaloid; Section 17-11) to which a trisaccharide is attached. A major function of the trisaccharide entity, with its many hydroxy groups, is to impart solubility to the compound.

Many plants, including the potato plant, produce toxins as a defense against insects and predators. Solanine is the potato plant's toxin. The small amount of solanine present in properly stored potatoes is not dangerous and actually contributes to the flavor of potatoes. (When excessive amounts of solanine are present, potatoes taste bitter.)

Solanine amounts in potatoes increase when potatoes sprout and when they are exposed to sunlight. (Potato farmers store their product in the dark to minimize solanine production.) Improperly stored potatoes "green"; that is, a green color develops in their skin and the flesh just under the skin (Figure 18-24). Such greening is a warning that solanine levels are higher than normal, even approaching unhealthy levels.

Figure 18-24 The presence of an underlying green color in the skin of potatoes denotes the presence of chlorophyll (the green color), as well as the toxin solanine (which is unseen). Such potatoes need to be deeply peeled (to remove all of the green color) before use.

The green color present in improperly stored potatoes is not solanine, but chlorophyll; sunlight exposure stimulates both solanine and chlorophyll production. Peeling potatoes deeply to remove the green color also removes excess solanine; peeled potatoes contain up to 80% less solanine than unpeeled potatoes. Sprouts need to be removed and potato "eyes" need to be cut out; sprouts also have high solanine content. Deep-frying reduces solanine levels; microwaving is only somewhat effective in diminishing these levels; and boiling is ineffective in decreasing such levels.

The trisaccharide present in solanine's structure involves two common monosaccharides (D-glucose and D-galactose) and a rarely encountered monosaccharide (L-rhamnose). L-Rhamnose, an aldohexose, is unusual for two reasons: it is an L-isomer rather than a D-isomer and it contains a —CH$_3$ group on carbon 6 rather than a —CH$_2$OH group. Another name for L-rhamnose is 6-deoxy-L-mannose.

```
        CHO                   CHO
    H──────OH             H──────OH
    H──────OH             H──────OH
   HO──────H            HO──────H
   HO──────H            HO──────H
       CH₂OH                 CH₃
     L-Mannose            L-Rhamnose
                       (6-deoxy-L-mannose)
```

A complete structural representative for solanine is given in Figure 18-25.

CHEMICAL CONNECTIONS 18-D

Blood Types and Oligosaccharides

Human blood is classified into four types: A, B, AB, and O. If a blood transfusion is necessary and the patient's own blood is not available, the donor's blood must be matched to that of the patient. Blood of one type cannot be given to a recipient with blood of another type unless the two types are compatible. A transfusion of the wrong blood type can cause the blood cells to form clumps, a potentially fatal reaction. The following table shows compatibility relationships. People with type O blood are universal donors, and those with type AB blood are universal recipients.

Human Blood Group Compatibilities

	Recipient Blood Type			
Donor Blood Type	A	B	AB	O
A	+	−	+	−
B	−	+	+	−
AB	−	−	+	−
O	+	+	+	+

+ = compatible; − = incompatible

In the United States, sampling studies show that type O is the most common type of blood, with type A the second most common. There is a definite correlation between ethnicity and blood type, as shown in the following table.

Blood Types in the United States

	Caucasian	African	Hispanic	Asian
O	45%	51%	57%	40%
A	40%	26%	33%	27%
B	11%	19%	11%	26%
AB	4%	4%	2%	7%

Percentages may not add to 100 because of rounding.

The biochemical basis for the various types of blood involves oligosaccharide molecules that are attached to the plasma membrane of red blood cells. These oligosaccharide attachments, which are called biochemical markers, are of three different formulations: one is a tetrasaccharide and the other two are pentasaccharides.

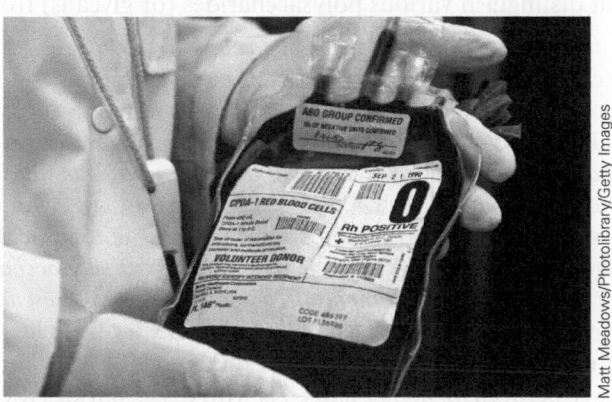

A unit of blood obtained from a blood bank.

Matt Meadows/Photolibrary/Getty Images

Four monosaccharides contribute to the makeup of the oligosaccharide "marking system." One is the simple monosaccharide D-galactose and the other three are monosaccharide derivatives. Two of these are N-acetyl amino derivatives (Section 18-12), those of D-glucose and D-galactose. The third is L-fucose (6-deoxy-L-galactose), an L-galactose derivative in which the oxygen atom at carbon 6 has been removed (converting the —CH_2OH group to a —CH_3 group). The L configuration of this derivative is unusual in that L-monosaccharides are seldom found in the human body.

α-D-Galactose

α-L-Fucose
(α-6-Deoxy-L-galactose)

α-N-Acetyl-D-glucosamine

α-N-Acetyl-D-galactosamine

The arrangement of these monosaccharides in the biochemical marker determines blood type.

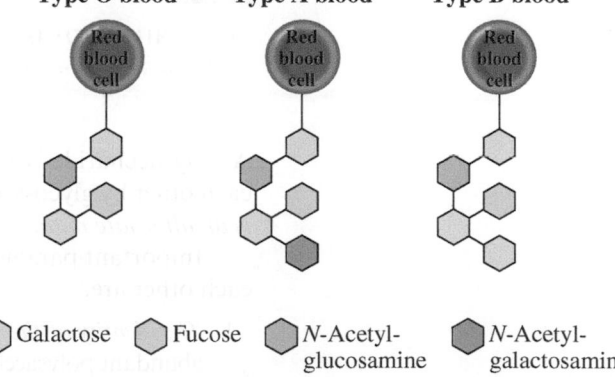

Type O blood **Type A blood** **Type B blood**

Galactose   Fucose   N-Acetyl-glucosamine   N-Acetyl-galactosamine

Note that all three of the oligosaccharide markers have a common four-monosaccharide sequence in their structure.

Galactose	N-acetylglucosamine	Galactose	Fucose

The absence or presence of a fifth monosaccharide (attached to the second galactose) determines blood type. Type O blood lacks a fifth monosaccharide unit. Type A blood has N-acetylgalactosamine as a fifth unit. Type B blood has galactose as a fifth unit. Type AB blood contains both type A and type B markers.

Figure 18-25 The structure of the potato toxin solanine has a large multi-ring alkaloid part and a smaller oligosaccharide part.

1. Which of the following is a naturally occurring trisaccharide that cannot be digested by humans?
   a. raffinose
   b. stachyose
   c. solanine
   d. no correct response
2. Which of the following is a toxin produced by potato plants?
   a. raffinose
   b. stachyose
   c. solanine
   d. no correct response

Answers: 1. a; 2. c

18-15 General Characteristics of Polysaccharides

LEARNING FOCUS

Know important general parameters that distinguish various polysaccharides from each other.

A polysaccharide is a polymer that contains many monosaccharide units bonded to each other by glycosidic linkages. Polysaccharides are often also called *glycans*. **Glycan** *is an alternate name for a polysaccharide.*

Important parameters that distinguish various polysaccharides (or glycans) from each other are:

1. *The identity of the monosaccharide repeating unit(s) in the polymer chain.* The more abundant polysaccharides in nature contain only one type of monosaccharide repeating unit. Such polysaccharides, including starch, glycogen, cellulose, and chitin, are examples of *homopolysaccharides*. A **homopolysaccharide** *is a polysaccharide in which only one type of monosaccharide monomer is present.* Polysaccharides whose structures contain two or more types of monosaccharide monomers, including hyaluronic acid and heparin, are called *heteropolysaccharides*. A **heteropolysaccharide** *is a polysaccharide in which more than one (usually two) type of monosaccharide monomer is present.*
2. *The length of the polymer chain.* Polysaccharide chain length can vary from less than a hundred monomer units to over 50,000 monomer units.
3. *The type of glycosidic linkage between monomer units.* As with disaccharides (Section 18-13), several different types of glycosidic linkages are encountered in polysaccharide structures.

a Unbranched-chain homopolysaccharide

b Branched-chain homopolysaccharide

c Unbranched-chain heteropolysaccharide

Figure 18-26 The polymer chain of a polysaccharide may be unbranched or branched. The monosaccharide monomers in the polymer chain may all be identical, or two or more kinds of monomers may be present.

4. *The degree of branching of the polymer chain.* The ability to form *branched-chain* structures distinguishes polysaccharides from the other two major types of biochemical polymers: proteins (Chapter 20) and nucleic acids (Chapter 22), which occur only as linear (unbranched) polymers.

Figure 18-26 summarizes diagrammatically general structural characteristics for homopolysaccharides and heteropolysaccharides. For the simplest type of heteropolysaccharide, one in which two different monosaccharides are present in an alternating pattern (Figure 18-26c), the repeating unit for the structure is taken to be the disaccharide that contains one unit each of the monosaccharides present. Heteropolysaccharides with a disaccharide repeating unit almost always have nonbranched structures.

Unlike monosaccharides and most disaccharides, polysaccharides are not sweet and do not test positive in Tollens and Benedict's solutions. They have limited water solubility because of their size. However, the —OH groups present can individually become hydrated by water molecules. The result is usually a thick colloidal suspension of the polysaccharide in water. Polysaccharides, such as flour and cornstarch, are often used as thickening agents in sauces, desserts, and gravy. ◄

Although there are many naturally occurring polysaccharides of biochemical importance, further polysaccharide discussion will be limited to six of them: starch, glycogen, cellulose, chitin, hyaluronic acid, and heparin. Starch and glycogen are examples of *storage polysaccharides* (Section 18-16); cellulose and chitin are *structural polysaccharides* (Section 18-17); and hyaluronic acid and heparin are *acidic polysaccharides* (Section 18-18).

▶ *When some vegetables, such as peas or corn, age too much (become overly mature), some of their sugars (mono- and disaccharides) are converted to polysaccharides (starch; Section 18-16). This conversion makes the vegetables taste less sweet.*

Section 18-15 Quick Quiz

1. Which of the following statements about polysaccharides is *incorrect*?
   a. Polysaccharides can have branched or unbranched structures.
   b. Polysaccharides can contain more than one type of monosaccharide.
   c. Polysaccharide chain length can never exceed one hundred units.
   d. no correct response
2. Which of the following statements about polysaccharides is *incorrect*?
   a. An alternate designation for a polysaccharide is glycan.
   b. Polysaccharides almost always have a sweet taste.
   c. Polysaccharides have limited solubility in water.
   d. no correct response

Answers: 1.c; 2. b

Storage Polysaccharides

LEARNING FOCUS

Describe the structural features of the storage polysaccharides starch and glycogen; contrast the biochemical functions of starch and glycogen.

A **storage polysaccharide** *is a polysaccharide that is a storage form for monosaccharides and is used as an energy source in cells.* In cells, monosaccharides are stored in the form of polysaccharides rather than as individual monosaccharides in order to lower the osmotic pressure within cells. Osmotic pressure depends on the number of *individual* molecules present (Section 8-9). Incorporating many monosaccharide molecules into a single polysaccharide molecule results in a dramatic reduction in molecular numbers. The most important storage polysaccharides are starch (in plant cells) and glycogen (in animal and human cells).

Starch

Starch is a homopolysaccharide containing only glucose monosaccharide units. It is the energy-storage polysaccharide in plants. If excess glucose enters a plant cell, it is converted to starch and stored for later use. When the cell cannot get enough glucose from outside the cell, it hydrolyzes starch to release glucose.

Two different polyglucose polysaccharides can be isolated from most starches: amylose and amylopectin. *Amylose,* an unbranched-chain glucose polymer, usually accounts for 15%–20% of the starch; *amylopectin,* a branched glucose polymer, accounts for the remaining 80%–85% of the starch.

In amylose's non-branched structure, the glucose units are connected by $\alpha(1 \rightarrow 4)$ glycosidic linkages.

▶ *Amylopectin is digested more rapidly than amylose. Digestive enzymes exert their effect primarily at the end (terminal) glucose units in a glucose chain. A branched-chain structure (amylopectin) has more "ends" than an unbranched-chain helical structure (amylose).*

Starch (amylose)

The number of glucose units present in an amylose chain depends on the source of the starch; 300–500 monomer units are usually present. The most stable configuration for the unbranched amylose chain is a helical arrangement (see Figure 18-27); this structure is formed from a twisting of the flexible glucose chain.

Amylopectin, the other polysaccharide in starch, has a high degree of branching in its polyglucose structure. A branch occurs about once every 25–30 glucose units. The branch points involve $\alpha(1 \rightarrow 6)$ linkages (Figure 18-28). Because of the branching, amylopectin has a larger average molecular mass than the linear amylose. Up to 100,000 glucose units may be present in an amylopectin polymer chain. ◀

All of the glycosidic linkages in starch (both amylose and amylopectin) are of the α type. In amylose, they are all $(1 \rightarrow 4)$; in amylopectin, both $(1 \rightarrow 4)$ and $(1 \rightarrow 6)$ linkages are present. Because both types of α linkages can be broken through hydrolysis within the human digestive tract (with the help of enzymes), starch has nutritional value for humans. The starches present in potatoes and cereal grains (wheat, rice, corn, etc.) account for approximately two-thirds of the world's food consumption.

Iodine is often used to test for the presence of starch in solution. Starch-containing solutions turn a dark blue-black when iodine is added (see Figure 18-29). As starch is broken down through acid or enzymatic hydrolysis to glucose monomers, the blue-black color disappears.

Figure 18-27 The most stable configuration for amylose, the unbranched form of starch, is a helical structure, with six glucose residues per turn.

Glycogen

Glycogen, like starch, is a polysaccharide containing only glucose units. It is the glucose storage polysaccharide in humans and animals. Its function is thus similar to

An $\alpha(1\rightarrow6)$ linkage is present in the amylopectin structure at each branch point.

a Molecular structure of amylopectin.

b An overview of the branching that occurs in the amylopectin structure. Each dot is a glucose unit

Figure 18-28 Two perspectives on the structure of the polysaccharide amylopectin.

Figure 18-29 Use of iodine to test for starch. Starch-containing solutions and foods turn dark blue-black when iodine is added.

▶ *The glucose polymers amylose, amylopectin, and glycogen compare as follows in molecular size and degree of branching.*

Amylose: Up to 1000 glucose units; no branching

Amylopectin: Up to 100,000 glucose units; branch points every 25–30 glucose units

Glycogen: over 50,000 glucose units; branch points every 8–12 glucose units

that of starch in plants, and it is sometimes referred to as *animal starch.* Liver cells and muscle cells are the storage sites for glycogen in humans.

Glycogen has a structure similar to that of amylopectin; all glycosidic linkages are of the α type, and both $(1 \rightarrow 4)$ and $(1 \rightarrow 6)$ linkages are present. Glycogen and amylopectin differ in the number of glucose units between branches and in the total number of glucose units present in a molecule. Glycogen is about three times more highly branched than amylopectin, and it is much larger, with up to 1,000,000 glucose units present. ◀

When excess glucose is present in the blood (normally from eating too much starch), the liver and muscle tissue convert the excess glucose to glycogen, which is then stored in these tissues. Whenever the glucose blood level drops (from exercise, fasting, or normal activities), some stored glycogen is hydrolyzed back to glucose. ◀ These two opposing processes, to be discussed in detail in Chapter 24, are called *glycogenesis* and *glycogenolysis,* the formation and decomposition of glycogen, respectively.

$$\text{Glucose} \underset{\text{Glycogenolysis}}{\overset{\text{Glycogenesis}}{\rightleftharpoons}} \text{glycogen}$$

Glycogen is an ideal storage form for glucose. The large size of these macromolecules prevents them from diffusing out of cells. Also, conversion of glucose

▶ *The amount of stored glycogen in the human body is relatively small. Muscle tissue is approximately 1% glycogen, liver tissue 2%–3%. However, this amount is sufficient to take care of normal-activity glucose demands for about 15 hours. During strenuous exercise, glycogen supplies can be exhausted rapidly. At this point, the body begins to oxidize fat as a source of energy.*

Many marathon runners eat large quantities of starchy foods the day before a race. This practice, called carbohydrate loading, *maximizes body glycogen reserves.*

to glycogen reduces osmotic pressure (Section 8-9). Cells would burst because of increased osmotic pressure if all of the glucose in glycogen were present in cells in free form. High concentrations of glycogen in a cell sometimes precipitate or crystallize into *glycogen granules*. These granules are discernible in photographs of cells under electron microscope magnification (Figure 18-30).

Section 18-16 Quick Quiz

1. Which of the following storage polysaccharides has an unbranched structure?
   a. amylose
   b. amylopectin
   c. glycogen
   d. no correct response
2. Which of the following storage polysaccharides is the storage form for glucose in the human body?
   a. amylose
   b. amylopectin
   c. glycogen
   d. no correct response
3. Which of the following storage polysaccharides is *not* a glucose polymer?
   a. amylose
   b. amylopectin
   c. glycogen
   d. no correct response
4. Which of the following statements about storage polysaccharides is *incorrect*?
   a. Glycogen has a more highly branched structure than amylopectin.
   b. If excess glucose enters a plant cell it is converted to starch.
   c. Amylose is the more abundant form of starch.
   d. no correct response

Answers: 1. a; 2. c; 3. d; 4. c

18-17 Structural Polysaccharides

LEARNING FOCUS

Describe the structure features of the structural polysaccharides *cellulose* and *chitin*; contrast the biochemical functions of *cellulose* and *chitin*.

A **structural polysaccharide** is *a polysaccharide that serves as a structural element in plant cell walls and animal exoskeletons.* Two of the most important structural polysaccharides are cellulose and chitin. Both are homopolysaccharides.

Cellulose

Cellulose, the structural component of plant cell walls, is the most abundant naturally occurring polysaccharide. The "woody" portions of plants—stems, stalks, and trunks—have particularly high concentrations of this fibrous, water-insoluble substance.

Like amylose, cellulose is an unbranched glucose polymer. The structural difference between cellulose and amylose, which gives them completely different properties, is that the glucose residues present in cellulose have a beta-configuration whereas the glucose residues in amylose have an alpha-configuration. The glycosidic linkages in cellulose are therefore $\beta(1 \rightarrow 4)$ linkages rather than $\alpha(1 \rightarrow 4)$ linkages.

This difference in glycosidic linkage type causes cellulose and amylose to have different molecular shapes. Amylose molecules tend to have spiral-like structures (see Figure 18-27) whereas cellulose molecules tend to have linear structures. The linear (straight-chain) cellulose molecules, when aligned side by side, become water-insoluble fibers because of inter-chain hydrogen bonding involving the numerous hydroxyl groups present.

Typically, cellulose chains contain about 5000 glucose units, which gives macromolecules with molecular masses of about 900,000 amu. Cotton is almost pure cellulose (95%), and wood is about 50% cellulose.

Even though it is a glucose polymer, cellulose is not a source of nutrition for human beings. Humans lack the enzymes capable of catalyzing the hydrolysis of $\beta(1 \rightarrow 4)$ linkages in cellulose. Even grazing animals lack the enzymes necessary for cellulose digestion. However, the intestinal tracts of animals such as horses, cows, and sheep contain bacteria that produce *cellulase,* an enzyme that can hydrolyze cellulose $\beta(1 \rightarrow 4)$ linkages and produce free glucose from cellulose. Thus grasses and other plant materials are a source of nutrition for grazing animals. The intestinal tracts of termites contain the same microorganisms, which enable termites to use wood as their source of food. Microorganisms in the soil can also metabolize cellulose, which makes possible the biodegradation of dead plants.

Despite its nondigestibility, cellulose is still an important component of a balanced diet. It serves as dietary fiber. Chemical Connections 18-E—Edible Fibers and Health—considers further details about the importance of dietary fiber in the human diet and some of the positive health benefits associated with fiber consumption.

Chemistry at a Glance—Types of Glycosidic Linkages for Common Glucose-Containing Di- and Polysaccharides—summarizes the types of glycosidic linkages present in commonly encountered glucose-containing di- and polysaccharides. Included in the summary is the $\beta(1 \rightarrow 4)$ linkage present in cellulose as well as in the disaccharides cellobiose and lactose (Section 18-13).

Chitin

Cellulose is the most abundant naturally occurring polysaccharide. Chitin is the second most abundant naturally occurring polysaccharide. ◀ Its function is to give rigidity to the exoskeletons of crabs, lobsters, shrimp, insects, and other arthropods (Figure 18-31). It also has been found in the cell walls of fungi.

Figure 18-31 Chitin, a linear $\beta(1 \rightarrow 4)$ polysaccharide, produces the rigidity in the exoskeletons of crabs and other arthropods.

▶ *The word* chitin *is pronounced "kye-ten"; it rhymes with* Titan.

Figure 18-32 The structures of cellulose (a) and chitin (b). In both substances, all glycosidic linkages are of the $\beta(1 \rightarrow 4)$ type.

Structurally, chitin is identical to cellulose, except the monosaccharide present is the glucose derivative *N*-acetyl-D-glucosamine (NAG) rather than D-glucose itself. The structure of NAG was previously encountered in Section 18-12 when amino sugar formation was discussed. Figure 18-32, which contrasts the structures of cellulose and chitin, also shows NAG's structure. All of the oligosaccharide markers that determine blood type (Chemical Connections 18-D—Blood Types and Oligosaccharides) contain an NAG monosaccharide unit.

The product of complete hydrolysis of chitin is D-glucosamine (Section 18-12). D-Glucosamine is marketed as a dietary supplement touted to help with joint problems. However, claims that D-glucosamine decreases joint inflammation and pain associated with osteoarthritis have yet to be substantiated.

Edible Fibers and Health

Edible fibers, that is, nondigestible carbohydrates, can be classified in two different ways. In the first classification system there are two types of edible fibers: functional fiber and dietary fiber. Distinguishing characteristics for these two types of fibers are as follows:

1. **Functional fiber** is nondigestible carbohydrate materials that have been produced commercially for use in fortifying foods or in fiber supplements. Most often they are carbohydrate materials extracted from foods. Examples of such fibers are psyllium and pectin.
2. **Dietary fiber** is nondigestible carbohydrate materials that are used intact as they occur naturally in foods. Many sources for such fiber exist including cellulose from plant materials (celery "strings," the outer layers of whole grain [bran], etc.), and the nondigestible starch components of dried beans (raffinose and stachyose; Section 18-14).

In the second classification system for edible fibers classification is based on how the fiber interacts with water. Edible fibers are either insoluble or soluble.

1. **Insoluble fiber** is nondigestible carbohydrate materials, that do not form viscous materials that is, materials that have a gel-like consistency in water. Also, in general, insoluble fibers are not readily fermented by bacteria in the human intestinal tract. The skin of fruits and vegetable are examples of insoluble fibers.
2. **Soluble fiber** is nondigestible carbohydrate materials that dissolve in water to produce thick liquids with a gel-like consistency. An example is pectin from fruit, which is used to thicken jellies. In general, bacteria in the human intestinal tract readily ferment soluble fibers, producing intestinal gas.

As shown in the following graph, most unrefined plant foods contain a mix of insoluble and soluble fibers. Note also that the fiber content of legumes is greater than that of most fruits and the proportion of insoluble fiber is generally greater for legumes than for fruits.

Many scientific studies have now validated the statement that health benefits are associated with dietary intake that is high in fiber. About 25–35 g of dietary fiber is a desirable intake. This is two to three times higher than the average dietary fiber intake of Americans. Included in the benefits of a high-fiber diet are the following:

1. **Digestive Tract Health:** Dietary fiber provides the digestive tract with "bulk" that helps move food through the intestinal tract and facilitate the excretion of solid waste. Cellulose readily absorbs water, leading to softer stools and frequent bowel action.
2. **Reduction in Heart Disease Risk:** Consuming 5 to 10 g of soluble fiber per day reduces blood cholesterol levels by 3%–5%. The cholesterol-lowering effect results from soluble fiber binding with cholesterol-containing compounds in bile thereby increasing their excretion. Without this binding effect, much of the cholesterol would be reabsorbed for reuse.
3. **Blood Glucose Control:** Soluble fiber in the digestive tract delays the transit of other materials through the digestive system thus slowing the rate of glucose production. The slower production rate for glucose is a positive factor in controlling glucose surges associated with type 2 diabetes.
4. **Weight Management:** High-fiber food may also play a role in weight control. It is known that foods high in fiber tend to be low in fat and added sugar. Obesity is not seen in parts of the world where people eat large amounts of fiber-rich foods.

One common misconception about fiber is that fresh fruits and vegetables contain more fiber than their canned counterparts. The fiber content is the same, aside from any peels or stems that are removed. Canned food may be softer but texture or crunchy bite is not a measure of fiber content. Water-soluble fiber may dissolve in the canning liquid but it is still present. In cooking fruits and vegetables, soluble fiber may dissolve in the cooking water.

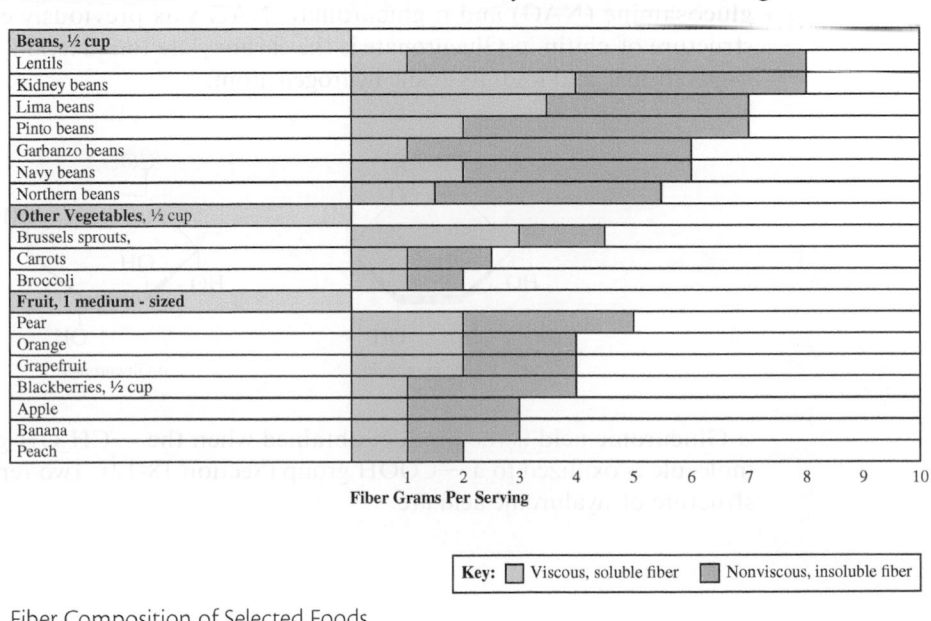

Fiber Composition of Selected Foods

Figure 18-33 Acidic polysaccharides associated with the connective tissue of joints give hurdlers such as these the flexibility needed to accomplish their task.

Jean Marc Barey/Vandystadt/Science Source

18-18 Acidic Polysaccharides

LEARNING FOCUS

Describe the structural features of the acidic polysaccharides *hyaluronic acid* and *heparin;* contrast the biochemical functions of hyaluronic acid and heparin.

An **acidic polysaccharide** *is a polysaccharide with a disaccharide repeating unit in which one of the disaccharide components is an amino sugar and one or both disaccharide components has a negative charge due to a sulfate group or a carboxyl group.* Unlike the polysaccharides discussed in the previous two sections, acidic polysaccharides are *heteropolysaccharides;* two different monosaccharides are present in an alternating pattern. Acidic polysaccharides are involved in a variety of cellular functions and tissues (Figure 18-33). Two of the most well-known acidic polysaccharides are hyaluronic acid and heparin, both of which have unbranched-chain structures.

Hyaluronic Acid

The structure of hyaluronic acid contains alternating residues of *N*-acetyl-β-D-glucosamine (NAG) and D-glucuronate. NAG was previously encountered in the structure of chitin. D-Glucuronate is the carboxylate ion (Section 16-7) formed when D-glucuronic acid loses its acidic hydrogen atom.

D-Glucuronic acid   D-Glucuronate

D-Glucuronic acid is the product obtained when the —CH_2OH group of a glucose molecule is oxidized to a —COOH group (Section 18-12). Two repeating units in the structure of hyaluronic acid are

In this structure, note the alternating pattern of glycosidic bond types, $\beta(1 \rightarrow 3)$ and $\beta(1 \rightarrow 4)$. There are approximately 50,000 disaccharide units per chain.

Highly viscous hyaluronic acid solutions serve as lubricants in the fluid of joints, and they are also associated with the jelly-like consistency of the vitreous humor of the eye. (The Greek word *hyalos* means "glass"; hyaluronic acid solutions have a glass-like appearance.)

Heparin

Heparin is a small highly sulfated polysaccharide with only 15–90 disaccharide residues per chain. The monosaccharides present in heparin's disaccharide repeating unit are a sulfate derivative of D-glucuronate (D-glucuronate-2-sulfate) and a doubly sulfated derivative of D-glucosamine (*N*-sulfo-D-glucosamine-6-sulfate). Both of these monosaccharide derivatives contain two negatively charged acidic groups.

Heparin is a blood anticoagulant. It is naturally present in mast cells and is released at the site of tissue injury. ◀ It prevents the formation of clots in the blood and retards the growth of existing clots within the blood. It does not, however, break down clots that have already formed.

Pharmaceutical-grade heparin is applied as an anticoagulant to the interior/exterior surface of external objects that come in contact with blood (test tubes, kidney dialysis machine surfaces, prosthetic implant materials) to prevent the blood from clotting. The source for pharmaceutical heparin is intestinal or lung tissue of slaughter-house animals (pigs and cows).

▶ *Mast cells are part of the body's immune system. They play an important role in wound healing and defense against pathogens. They are more abundant in tissues that commonly come into contact with the outside world (the skin, mucosa of the lungs, digestive tract, mouth, and nose) than in other tissues.*

Section 18-18 Quick Quiz

1. Which of the following statements about the polysaccharide hyaluronic acid is *incorrect*?
   a. The repeating unit present is a disaccharide.
   b. Two different types of glycosidic linkages are present.
   c. All monosaccharide units present are glucosamine derivatives.
   d. no correct response
2. Which of the following statements about the polysaccharide heparin is *incorrect*?
   a. It is a heteropolysaccharide.
   b. It is an acidic polysaccharide.
   c. It serves as a lubricant in the fluid of joints.
   d. no correct response

Answers: 1. c; 2. c

18-19 Dietary Considerations and Carbohydrates

LEARNING FOCUS

Contrast the dietary carbohydrate classifications *simple carbohydrate* and *complex carbohydrate;* contrast the terms *natural sugar* and *refined sugar.*

Foods high in carbohydrate content constitute over 50% of the diet of most people of the world—rice in Asia, corn in South America, cassava (a starchy root vegetable) in parts of Africa, the potato and wheat in North America, and so on. Current nutritional recommendations support such a situation; a balanced diet should ideally be about 60% carbohydrate.

Nutritionists usually subdivide dietary carbohydrates into the categories *simple* and *complex.* A **simple carbohydrate** *is a dietary monosaccharide or dietary disaccharide.* Simple carbohydrates are usually sweet to the taste and are commonly referred to as sugars (Section 18-8). A **complex carbohydrate** *is a dietary polysaccharide.* The main complex carbohydrates are starch and cellulose, substances not generally sweet to the taste.

Simple carbohydrates provide 20% of the energy in the U.S. diet. Half of this energy content comes from *natural sugars* and the other half from *refined sugars* added to foods. A **natural sugar** *is a sugar naturally present in whole foods.* Milk and fresh fruit are two important sources of natural sugars. A **refined sugar** *is a sugar that has been separated from its plant source.* Sugar beets and sugar cane are major sources of refined sugars. Despite claims to the contrary, refined sugars are chemically and structurally no different from the sugars naturally present in foods. The only difference is that the refined sugar is in a pure form, whereas natural sugars are part of mixtures of substances obtained from a plant source.

Refined sugars are often said to provide *empty calories* because they provide energy but few other nutrients. Natural sugars, on the other hand, are accompanied by nutrients. A tablespoon of sucrose (table sugar) provides 50 calories of energy just as a small orange does. The small orange, however, also supplies vitamin C, potassium, calcium, and fiber; table sugar provides no other nutrients.

The major dietary source for complex carbohydrates in the U.S. diet is grains, a source of both starch and fiber as well as of protein, vitamins, and minerals. The pulp of a potato provides starch, and the skin provides fiber. Vegetables such as broccoli and green beans are low in starch but high in fiber.

Section 18-19 Quick Quiz

1. Which of the following is *not* classified as a simple carbohydrate?
   a. the monosaccharide D-glucose
   b. the disaccharide D-sucrose
   c. the disaccharide D-lactose
   d. no correct response
2. The major dietary source for complex carbohydrates in the human diet is
   a. refined sugars
   b. natural sugars
   c. grains
   d. no correct response

Answers: 1. d; 2. c

18-20 Glycolipids and Glycoproteins: Cell Recognition

LEARNING FOCUS

Know the general structural characteristics for *glycolipids* and *glycoproteins;* be familiar with several roles that glycolipids and glycoproteins have in cell recognition processes.

Prior to 1960, the biochemistry of carbohydrates was thought to be rather simple. These compounds served (1) as energy sources for plants, humans, and animals and (2) as structural materials for plants and arthropods.

It is now known that mono-, di-, and oligosaccharides attached through glycosidic linkages to lipid molecules (Chapter 19) and protein molecules (Chapter 20) have a wide range of biochemical functions, including allowing cells to interact with invading bacteria and viruses and enabling cells of differing function to recognize each other. Such carbohydrate–lipid and carbohydrate–protein molecules are called, respectively, *glycolipids* and *glycoproteins*. A **glycolipid** *is a lipid molecule that has one or more carbohydrate (or carbohydrate derivative) units covalently bonded to it.* Similarly, a **glycoprotein** *is a protein molecule that has one or more carbohydrate (or carbohydrate derivative) units covalently bonded to it.*

Glycolipids called cerebrosides and gangliosides occur extensively in brain tissue (Section 19-8). Glycoproteins called immunoglobins are key components of the body's immune system response to invading foreign materials (Section 20-18). ◀

▶ *The prefix* glyco-, *used in the terms* glycolipid *and* glycoprotein, *is derived from the Greek word* glykys, *which means "sweet." Most monosaccharides and disaccharides have a sweet taste.*

In glycolipids and glycoproteins associated with cell membrane structure, the lipid or protein part of the glycolipid or glycoprotein is incorporated into the cell membrane structure and the carbohydrate (oligosaccharide) part functions as a marker on the outer cell membrane surface. Cell recognition generally involves the interaction between the carbohydrate marker of one cell and a protein or lipid that is part of the cell membrane of another cell.

In the human reproductive process, fertilization involves a binding interaction between oligosaccharide markers on the outer membrane surface of an ovulated egg and protein receptor sites on a sperm cell membrane. This binding process is followed by release of enzymes by the sperm cell which dissolve the egg cell membrane allowing for entry of the sperm cell and the ensuing egg–sperm fertilization process.

The cell recognition system associated with red blood cells, which is the basis for the various blood types, involves carbohydrate markers. This recognition system was previously discussed in Chemical Connections 18-D—Blood Types and Oligosaccharides.

Section 18-20 Quick Quiz

1. Which of the following types of compounds are glycoproteins?
   a. cerebrosides
   b. gangliosides
   c. immunoglobins
   d. no correct response
2. Which of the following is *not* a biochemical function for glycolipids and/or glycoproteins?
   a. interaction with invading bacteria
   b. participation in cell–cell recognition processes
   c. components of the body's immune system
   d. no correct response

Answers: 1. c; 2. d

Concepts to Remember

Biochemistry. Biochemistry is the study of the chemical substances found in living systems and the chemical interactions of these substances with each other (Section 18-1).

Carbohydrates. Carbohydrates are polyhydroxy aldehydes, polyhydroxy ketones, or compounds that yield such substances upon hydrolysis. Plants contain large quantities of carbohydrates produced via photosynthesis (Section 18-2).

Carbohydrate classification. Carbohydrates are classified into four groups: monosaccharides, disaccharides, oligosaccharides, and polysaccharides (Section 18-3).

Chirality and achirality. A chiral object is not identical to its mirror image. An achiral object is identical to its mirror image (Section 18-4).

Chiral center. A chiral center is an atom in a molecule that has four different groups tetrahedrally bonded to it. Molecules that contain a single chiral center exist in a left-handed and a right-handed form (Section 18-4).

Stereoisomerism. The atoms of stereoisomers are connected in the same way but are arranged differently in space. The major causes of stereoisomerism in molecules are structural rigidity and the presence of a chiral center (Section 18-5).

Enantiomers and diastereomers. Two types of stereoisomers exist: enantiomers and diastereomers. Enantiomers have structures that are nonsuperimposable mirror images of each other. Enantiomers have identical achiral properties but different chiral properties. Diastereomers have structures that are not mirror images of each other (Section 18-5).

Fischer projection formulas. Fischer projection formulas are two-dimensional structural formulas used to depict the three-dimensional shapes of molecules with chiral centers (Section 18-6).

Chirality of monosaccharides. Monosaccharides are classified as D or L stereoisomers on the basis of the configuration of the chiral center farthest from the carbonyl group (Section 18-6).

Optical activity. Chiral compounds are optically active—that is, they rotate the plane of polarized light. Enantiomers rotate the plane of polarized light in opposite directions. The prefix (+) indicates that the compound rotates the plane of polarized light in a clockwise direction, whereas compounds that rotate the plane of polarized light in a counterclockwise direction have the prefix (−) (Section 18-7).

Classification of monosaccharides. Monosaccharides are classified as aldoses or ketoses on the basis of the type of carbonyl group present. They are further classified as trioses, tetroses, pentoses, etc. on the basis of the number of carbon atoms present (Section 18-8).

Important monosaccharides. Important monosaccharides include glucose, galactose, fructose, and ribose. Glucose and galactose are aldohexoses, fructose is a ketohexose, and ribose is an aldopentose (Section 18-9).

Cyclic monosaccharides. Cyclic monosaccharides form through an intramolecular reaction between the carbonyl group and an alcohol group of an open-chain monosaccharide. These cyclic forms predominate in solution (Section 18-10).

Haworth projection formulas. Haworth projection formulas are two-dimensional structural representations used to depict the three-dimensional structure of a cyclic form of a monosaccharide (Section 18-11).

Reactions of monosaccharides. Five important reactions of monosaccharides are (1) oxidation to an acidic sugar, (2) reduction to a sugar alcohol, (3) glycoside formation, (4) phosphate ester formation, and (5) amino sugar formation (Section 18-12).

Disaccharides. Disaccharides are glycosides formed from the linkage of two monosaccharides. The most important disaccharides are maltose, cellobiose, lactose, and sucrose. Each of these has at least one glucose unit in its structure (Section 18-13).

Oligosaccharides. Oligosaccharides are carbohydrates that contain three to ten monosaccharide units covalently bonded to each other. Two important naturally occurring oligosaccharides are raffinose and stachyose (Section 18-14).

Polysaccharides. Polysaccharides are polymers in which monosaccharides are the monomers. In homopolysaccharides, only one type of monomer is present. Two or more monosaccharide monomers are present in heteropolysaccharides. Storage polysaccharides (starch, glycogen) are storage molecules for monosaccharides. Structural polysaccharides (cellulose, chitin) serve as structural elements in plant cell walls and animal exoskeletons (Sections 18-15 to 18-18).

Glycolipids and glycoproteins. Glycolipids and glycoproteins are molecules in which oligosaccharides are attached through glycosidic linkages to lipids and proteins, respectively. Such molecules often govern how cells of differing function interact with each other (Section 18-20).

Exercises and Problems

Exercises and problems are arranged in matched pairs with the two members of a pair addressing the same concept(s). The answer to the odd-numbered member of a pair is given at the back of the book. Problems denoted with a ▲ involve concepts found not only in the section under consideration but also concepts found in one or more earlier sections of the chapter.

Biochemistry—An Overview (Section 18-1)

18-1 Indicate whether each of the following statements concerning human body composition, in terms of mass percent, is true or false.
    a. Bioorganic substances are slightly more abundant than bioinorganic substances.
    b. Bioinorganic substances are much more abundant than bioorganic substances.

18-2 Indicate whether each of the following statements concerning human body composition, in terms of mass percent, is true or false.
    a. Bioorganic substances are much more abundant than bioinorganic substances.
    b. Bioinorganic substances are slightly less abundant than bioorganic substances.

18-3 With the help of Figure 18-1, indicate which member in the following pairs of types of biochemical

substances is more abundant, on a mass basis, in the human body.
    a. water and proteins
    b. carbohydrates and lipids
    c. nucleic acids and inorganic salts
    d. carbohydrates and proteins

18-4 With the help of Figure 18-1, indicate which member in the following pairs of types of biochemical substances is more abundant, on a mass basis, in the human body.
    a. inorganic salts and proteins
    b. proteins and nucleic acids
    c. lipids and water
    d. lipids and carbohydrates

Occurrence and Functions of Carbohydrates (Section 18-2)

18-5 Indicate whether each of the following statements concerning the occurrence and functions of carbohydrates is true or false.
    a. Carbohydrates are the most abundant class of bioorganic molecules on Earth.
    b. Dietary intake of plant materials is the major carbohydrate source for humans and animals.
    c. Plants use carbohydrates for structural elements but not as a source of energy.
    d. Part of the structural framework of DNA and RNA molecules involves carbohydrates.

18-6 Indicate whether each of the following statements concerning the occurrence and functions of carbohydrates is true or false.
   a. Carbohydrates linked to lipids are structural components of cell membranes.
   b. Carbohydrates cannot be stored in the human body.
   c. The reactants for carbohydrate production by plants are carbon dioxide and water.
   d. Human dietary intake should always be less than 50% carbohydrate by mass.

Classification of Carbohydrates (Section 18-3)

18-7 How many monosaccharide units are present in each of the following?
   a. trisaccharide   b. oligosaccharide.

18-8 How many monosaccharide units are present in each of the following?
   a. tetrasaccharide   b. polysaccharide

18-9 What is the carbohydrate classification for the product produced when each of the following undergoes complete hydrolysis?
   a. tetrasaccharide   b. polysaccharide

18-10 What is the carbohydrate classification for the product produced when each of the following undergoes complete hydrolysis?
   a. trisaccharide   b. oligosaccharide

18-11 Indicate whether each of the following statements about the structural characteristics of monosaccharides is true or false.
   a. Both an aldehyde group and a ketone group are always present.
   b. An aldehyde group and at least two hydroxyl groups must be present.

18-12 Indicate whether each of the following statements about the structural characteristics of monosaccharides is true or false.
   a. An aldehyde group or a ketone group, but not both, is always present.
   b. A hydroxyl group must be present on each carbon atom.

Chirality: Handedness in Molecules (Section 18-4)

18-13 Explain what the term *superimposable* means.

18-14 Explain what the term *nonsuperimposable* means.

18-15 Indicate whether the circled carbon atom in each of the following molecules is a chiral center.

   a. CH_3—ⓒH_2—OH   b. CH_3—ⓒH—OH
                                        |
                                       CH_3

   c. CH_3—ⓒH—OH   d. CH_3—CH_2—ⓒH—OH
             | |
             Cl CH_3

18-16 Indicate whether the circled carbon atom in each of the following molecules is a chiral center.

   a. CH_3—ⓒH_2—NH_2 b. CH_3—ⓒH—CH_3
                                          |
                                         NH_2

   c. CH_3—ⓒH—NH_2 d. CH_3—ⓒH—NH_2
             | |
            CH_3 Cl

18-17 Use asterisks to show the chiral center(s), if any, in the following structures.

   a. H Cl
       | |
    Cl—C—C—Br
       | |
       H Cl

   b. H Cl H
       | | |
    Br—C—C—C—Cl
       | | |
       H Br Br

   c.
                                    O
                                    ‖
    CH_2—CH—CH—CH—C—H
       | | | |
      OH   OH OH OH

   d. CH_2—CH—CH—CH—CH—CH_2
        | | | | | |
       OH   OH OH OH OH   OH

18-18 Use asterisks to show the chiral center(s), if any, in the following structures.

   a. Br Cl
       | |
    Cl—C—C—Cl
       | |
       Br Br

   b. H H H
       | | |
    Cl—C—C—C—Cl
       | | |
       Br OH Br

   c.
                                O
                                ‖
    CH_3—CH—CH—CH—C—H
          | | |
         OH OH OH

   d. CH_2—CH—CH—CH—CH_2
        | | | |
       OH   OH OH OH

18-19 How many chiral centers are present in each of the following molecular structures?

   a.   b.

   c.   d.

18-20 How many chiral centers are present in each of the following molecular structures?

   a.   b.

   c.   d.

18-21 Indicate whether or not each of the following molecules possesses a chiral center?
   a. CH_2—CH_2—CH_2—CH_3
        |
       OH
   b. CH_3—CH—CH_2—CH_3
             |
            OH
   c. CH_3—CH—CH—CH_3
             | |
            OH CH_3
   d. CH_3—CH_2—CH—CH_2—CH_3
                    |
                   OH

18-22 Indicate whether or not each of the following molecules possesses a chiral center?

a. $CH_2—CH_2—CH_3$
   |
   OH

b. $CH_3—CH—CH_3$
   |
   OH

c. $CH_3—CH—CH_2—CH_2—CH_3$
   |
   OH

d. $CH_2—CH—CH_2—CH_3$
   | |
   OH CH_3

18-23 Indicate whether or not each of the molecules in Problem 18-21 is an achiral molecule.

18-24 Indicate whether or not each of the molecules in Problem 18-22 is an achiral molecule.

18-25 Indicate whether or not each of the molecules in Problem 18-21 exists in left-handed and right-handed forms.

18-26 Indicate whether or not each of the molecules in Problem 18-22 exists in left-handed and right-handed forms.

18-27 Indicate whether or not each of the molecules in Problem 18-21 has a nonsuperimposable mirror image.

18-28 Indicate whether or not each of the molecules in Problem 18-22 has a nonsuperimposable mirror image.

Stereoisomerism: Enantiomers and Diastereomers (Section 18-5)

18-29 What is the difference between constitutional isomers and stereoisomers?

18-30 Both enantiomers and diastereomers are stereoisomers. How do they differ?

18-31 What are two major structural features that can generate stereoisomerism?

18-32 Explain why *cis–trans* isomers are diastereomers rather than enantiomers.

18-33 Indicate whether each of the following statements about *stereoisomers* is true or false.
   a. Stereoisomers always have the same molecular formula.
   b. Stereoisomers always have the same structural formula.
   c. Stereoisomers are always nonsuperimposable mirror images of each other.
   d. Stereoisomers always possess handedness.

18-34 Indicate whether each of the following statements about *enantiomers* is true or false.
   a. Enantiomers always have the same molecular formula.
   b. Enantiomers always have the same structural formula.
   c. Enantiomers are always nonsuperimposable mirror images of each other.
   d. Enantiomers always differ in handedness.

Designating Handedness Using Fischer Projection Formulas (Section 18-6)

18-35 Draw the Fischer projection formula for each of the following molecules.

a. H
   |
   Br—C—Cl
   |
   CH_3

b. CH_3
   |
   Br—C—Cl
   |
   H

c. CH_3
   |
   Br—C—H
   |
   Cl

d. CH_3
   |
   H—C—Br
   |
   Cl

18-36 Draw the Fischer projection formula for each of the following molecules.

a. Cl
   |
   HO—C—CH_3
   |
   H

b. OH
   |
   Cl—C—CH_3
   |
   H

c. CH_3
   |
   HO—C—Cl
   |
   H

d. CH_3
   |
   H—C—OH
   |
   Cl

18-37 Draw a Fischer projection formula for the enantiomer of each of the following monosaccharides.

a.
```
      CHO
  HO──┼──H
   H──┼──OH
   H──┼──OH
     CH2OH
```

b.
```
     CH2OH
      |
      C=O
   H──┼──OH
  HO──┼──H
   H──┼──OH
     CH2OH
```

c.
```
      CHO
   H──┼──OH
   H──┼──OH
   H──┼──OH
  HO──┼──H
     CH2OH
```

d.
```
      CHO
   H──┼──OH
  HO──┼──H
   H──┼──OH
  HO──┼──H
     CH2OH
```

18-38 Draw a Fischer projection formula for the enantiomer of each of the following monosaccharides.

a.
```
      CHO
  HO──┼──H
  HO──┼──H
  HO──┼──H
     CH2OH
```

b.
```
     CH2OH
      |
      C=O
  HO──┼──H
  HO──┼──H
     CH2OH
```

c.
```
      CHO
  HO──┼──H
  HO──┼──H
   H──┼──OH
   H──┼──OH
     CH2OH
```

d.
```
     CH2OH
      |
      C=O
   H──┼──OH
   H──┼──OH
  HO──┼──H
     CH2OH
```

18-39 Classify each of the molecules in Problem 18-37 as a D enantiomer or an L enantiomer.

18-40 Classify each of the molecules in Problem 18-38 as a D enantiomer or an L enantiomer.

18-41 Characterize the members of each of the following pairs of structures as (1) enantiomers, (2) diastereomers, or (3) neither enantiomers nor diastereomers.

a.
```
    CHO              CHO
 H——OH           H——OH
HO——H     and    H——OH
 H——OH           H——OH
   CH₂OH            CH₂OH
```

b.
```
    CHO              CHO
 H——OH           H——CH₃
HO——H     and   HO——H
   CH₂OH            CH₂OH
```

c.
```
    CHO              CHO
 H——OH          HO——H
HO——H     and    H——OH
 H——OH          HO——H
HO——H            H——OH
   CH₂OH            CH₂OH
```

d.
```
   CH₂OH            CH₂OH
   C=O              C=O
HO——H     and   HO——H
HO——H            H——OH
   CH₂OH            CH₂OH
```

18-42 Characterize the members of each of the following pairs of structures as (1) enantiomers, (2) diastereomers, or (3) neither enantiomers nor diastereomers.

a.
```
    CHO              CHO
 H——OH          HO——H
 H——OH     and  HO——H
HO——H            H——OH
   CH₂OH            CH₂OH
```

b.
```
    CHO              CHO
 H——OH           H——OH
 H——OH     and  HO——H
   CH₂OH            CH₂OH
```

c.
```
    CHO              CHO
 H——OH          HO——H
HO——H     and    H——OH
 H——OH           H——OH
 H——OH          HO——H
   CH₂OH            CH₂OH
```

d.
```
   CH₂OH            CH₂OH
   C=O      and    C=O
 H——OH           H——CH₃
 H——OH           H——OH
   CH₂OH            CH₂OH
```

18-43 Indicate whether or not each of the pairs of compounds in Problem 18-41 are epimers.

18-44 Indicate whether or not each of the pairs of compounds in Problem 18-42 are epimers.

▲**18-45** How many chiral centers are present in each of the compounds in Problem 18-41?

▲**18-46** How many chiral centers are present in each of the compounds in Problem 18-42?

Properties of Enantiomers (Section 18-7)

18-47 Indicate whether each of the following properties would be the same or different for the compounds D-glucose and L-glucose.
a. Solubility in an chiral solvent
b. Density
c. Freezing point
d. Reaction with ethanol

18-48 Indicate whether each of the following properties would be the same or different for the compounds D-glucose and L-glucose.
a. Melting point
b. Interaction with plane-polarized light
c. Solubility in an achiral solvent
d. Reaction with (+)-lactic acid

18-49 Indicate whether each of the following properties would be the same or different for the compounds (+)-lactic acid and (−)-lactic acid.
a. boiling point
b. optical activity
c. reaction with ethanol
d. reaction with (−)-2,3-butanediol

18-50 Indicate whether each of the following properties would be the same or different for the compounds (+)-glyceraldehyde and (−)-glyceraldehyde.
a. solubility in water
b. reaction with (+)-2,3-butanediol
c. rotation of plane-polarized light
d. reaction with methanol

Classification of Monosaccharides (Section 18-8)

18-51 Classify each of the following monosaccharides as an aldose or a ketose.

a.
```
       CHO
   H——C—OH
  HO——C—H
  HO——C—H
   H——C—OH
       CH₂OH
```

b.
```
       CH₂OH
       C=O
   H——C—OH
   H——C—OH
   H——C—OH
       CH₂OH
```

c.
```
   CH₂OH
   C=O
   CH₂OH
```

d.
```
       CH₂OH
       C=O
  HO——C—H
       CH₂OH
```

18-52 Classify each of the following monosaccharides as an aldose or a ketose.

a.
```
        CHO
        |
   HO—C—H
        |
   HO—C—H
        |
   HO—C—H
        |
    H—C—OH
        |
       CH₂OH
```

b.
```
       CH₂OH
        |
       C=O
        |
   HO—C—H
        |
   HO—C—H
        |
       CH₂OH
```

c.
```
        CHO
        |
   HO—C—H
        |
    H—C—OH
        |
       CH₂OH
```

d.
```
       CH₂OH
        |
       C=O
        |
   HO—C—H
        |
   HO—C—H
        |
    H—C—OH
        |
       CH₂OH
```

18-53 Classify each monosaccharide in Problem 18-51 by both its number of carbon atoms and its type of carbonyl group.

18-54 Classify each monosaccharide in Problem 18-52 by both its number of carbon atoms and its type of carbonyl group.

18-55 Using the information in Figures 18-14 and 18-15, assign a name to each of the monosaccharides in Problem 18-51.

18-56 Using the information in Figures 18-14 and 18-15, assign a name to each of the monosaccharides in Problem 18-52.

▲**18-57** How many chiral centers are present in the structure of each of the monosaccharides in Problem 18-51?

▲**18-58** How many chiral centers are present in the structure of each of the monosaccharides in Problem 18-52?

Biochemically Important Monosaccharides (Section 18-9)

18-59 Indicate at what carbon atom(s) the structures of each of the following pairs of monosaccharides differ.
a. D-Glucose and D-galactose
b. D-Glucose and D-fructose
c. D-Glyceraldehyde and dihydroxyacetone
d. D-Ribose and 2-deoxy-D-ribose

18-60 Indicate whether the members of each of the following pairs of monosaccharides have the same molecular formula.
a. D-Glucose and D-galactose
b. D-Glucose and D-fructose
c. D-Glyceraldehyde and dihydroxyacetone
d. D-Ribose and 2-deoxy-D-ribose

18-61 Indicate which of the terms *aldoses, ketoses, hexoses,* and *aldohexoses* apply to both members of each of the following pairs of monosaccharides. More than one term may apply in a given situation.
a. D-Glucose and D-galactose
b. D-Glucose and D-fructose
c. D-Galactose and D-fructose
d. D-Glyceraldehyde and D-ribose

18-62 Indicate which of the terms *aldoses, ketoses, trioses,* and *aldohexoses* apply to both members of each of the following pairs of monosaccharides. More than one term may apply in a given situation.
a. D-Glucose and D-ribose
b. D-Fructose and dihydroxyacetone
c. D-Glyceraldehyde and dihydroxyacetone
d. D-Galactose and D-ribose

18-63 Draw the Fischer projection formula for each of the following monosaccharides.
a. D-Glucose   b. D-Glyceraldehyde
c. D-Fructose   d. L-Galactose

18-64 Draw the Fischer projection formula for each of the following monosaccharides.
a. D-Galactose   b. D-Ribose
c. Dihydroxyacetone   d. L-Glucose

18-65 To which of the common monosaccharides does each of the following terms apply?
a. Levulose   b. Grape sugar   c. Brain sugar

18-66 To which of the common monosaccharides does each of the following terms apply?
a. Dextrose   b. Fruit sugar   c. Blood sugar

Cyclic Forms of Monosaccharides (Section 18-10)

18-67 Indicate whether each of the following types of monosaccharides, upon intramolecular cyclization, forms a six-membered ring, a five-membered ring, or a four-membered ring.
a. Aldohexose   b. Ketohexose
c. Aldopentose   d. Ketopentose

18-68 Identify the two carbon atoms, using numbers (C1, C2, C3, etc.), that bear the functional groups that interact during the intramolecular cyclization of each of the following types of monosaccharides.
a. Aldohexose   b. Aldopentose
c. Ketohexose   d. Ketopentose

18-69 How many carbon atoms end up outside the ring in the cyclization of the open-chain form of the following monosaccharides?
a. D-Glucose   b. D-Galactose
c. D-Fructose   d. D-Ribose

18-70 After cyclization of each of the monosaccharides in Problem 18-69, how many of the carbon atoms do not have a hydroxyl group directly attached to it?

18-71 One of the cyclic forms of D-glucose has the structure

```
         CH₂OH
         |————O
      ╱  |      ╲
   HO╱ OH │     ╲OH
      ╲         ╱
        ╲——————╱
          OH
```

a. How many anomeric carbon atoms are present in this structure?
b. How many hemiacetal carbon atoms are present in this structure?

18-72 One of the cyclic forms of D-galactose has the structure

a. How many anomeric carbon atoms are present in this structure?
b. How many hemiacetal carbon atoms are present in this structure?

18-73 Draw the structure for the anomer of the monosaccharide in Problem 18-71.

18-74 Draw the structure for the anomer of the monosaccharide in Problem 18-72.

18-75 Classify the monosaccharide structure in Problem 18-71 as an α-anomer or a β-anomer.

18-76 Classify the monosaccharide structure in Problem 18-72 as an α-anomer or a β-anomer.

18-77 The structure of D-glucose is sometimes written in an open-chain form and sometimes in a cyclic form. Explain why either form is acceptable.

18-78 When pure α-D-glucose is dissolved in water, both α-D-glucose and β-D-glucose are soon present. Explain why this is so.

Haworth Projection Formulas (Section 18-11)

18-79 Draw Haworth projection formulas for the α-anomer of monosaccharides with each of the following Fischer projection formulas.

a.
```
      CHO
   H—|—OH
   H—|—OH
  HO—|—H
   H—|—OH
     CH₂OH
```

b.
```
      CHO
   H—|—OH
  HO—|—H
   H—|—OH
     CH₂OH
```

18-80 Draw Haworth projection formulas for the β-anomer of monosaccharides with each of the following Fischer projection formulas.

a.
```
      CHO
  HO—|—H
  HO—|—H
  HO—|—H
   H—|—OH
     CH₂OH
```

b.
```
      CHO
   H—|—OH
   H—|—OH
   H—|—OH
     CH₂OH
```

18-81 Identify each of the following Haworth projection formulas as that of an α-D-monosaccharide or a β-D-monosaccharide.

a.

b.
(CH₂OH ... structure)

18-82 Identify each of the following Haworth projection formulas as an α-D-monosaccharide or a β-D-monosaccharide.

a.
```
   CH₂OH
      |—O
      |    OH
  HO—|—OH
      |
     OH
```

b.
```
   CH₂OH
      |—O
 HO—|
      |    OH
      |
   OH  OH
```

c.
```
   CH₂OH
      |—O
      |
  HO—|—OH
     OH  OH
```

d.
```
HOCH₂  O
   |      CH₂OH
  OH      OH
   |
  OH  OH
```

18-83 Draw the open-chain form for each of the monosaccharides in Problem 18-81.

18-84 Draw the open-chain form for each of the monosaccharides in Problem 18-82.

18-85 Assign a number (C1, C2, C3, etc.) to the left-most ring carbon atom in each of the structures in Problem 18-81.

18-86 Assign a number (C1, C2, C3, etc.) to the left-most ring carbon atom in each of the structures in Problem 18-82.

18-87 Assign a number (C1, C2, C3, etc.) to the anomeric carbon atom in each of the structures in Problem 18-81.

18-88 Assign a number (C1, C2, C3, etc.) to the anomeric carbon atom in each of the structures in Problem 18-82.

▲18-89 Classify each of the monosaccharides in Problem 18-81 as a triose, tetrose, pentose, or hexose.

▲18-90 Classify each of the monosaccharides in Problem 18-82 as a triose, tetrose, pentose, or hexose.

▲18-91 Using the information in Figures 18-14 and 18-15, assign a name to each of the monosaccharides in Problem 18-81.

▲18-92 Using the information in Figures 18-14 and 18-15, assign a name to each of the monosaccharides in Problem 18-82.

▲18-93 Draw the Haworth projection formula for each of the following monosaccharides.
a. α-D-Galactose   b. β-D-Galactose
c. α-L-Galactose   d. β-L-Galactose

▲18-94 Draw the Haworth projection formula for each of the following monosaccharides.
a. α-D-Mannose   b. β-D-Mannose
c. α-L-Mannose   d. β-L-Mannose

Reactions of Monosaccharides (Section 18-12)

18-95 Draw the Fischer projection formula for the galactose derivative formed when galactose undergoes each of the following changes.
a. The —CHO group is oxidized.
b. The —CH₂OH group is oxidized.
c. Both the —CHO group and —CH₂OH group are oxidized.
d. The —CHO group is reduced.

18-96 Draw the Fischer projection formula for the glucose derivative formed when glucose undergoes each of the following changes.
  a. The —CHO group is oxidized.
  b. Both the —CHO group and —CH₂OH group are oxidized.
  c. The —CHO group is reduced.
  d. The —CH₂OH group is oxidized.

18-97 Classify each of the galactose derivatives in Problem 18-95 as an acidic sugar or a sugar alcohol.

18-98 Classify each of the glucose derivatives in Problem 18-96 as an acidic sugar or a sugar alcohol.

18-99 Name each of the galactose derivatives in Problem 18-95.

18-100 Name each of the glucose derivatives in Problem 18-96.

18-101 Which of the following monosaccharides is a *reducing sugar*?
  a. D-Glucose   b. D-Galactose
  c. D-Fructose   d. D-Ribose

18-102 Which of the following monosaccharides will give a positive test with Benedict's solution?
  a. D-Glucose   b. D-Galactose
  c. D-Fructose   d. D-Ribose

18-103 Indicate whether each of the following structures is that of a glycoside.
  a.

  b.

  c.

  d.

18-104 Indicate whether each of the following structures is that of a glycoside.
  a.

18-105 For each structure in Problem 18-103, identify the configuration at the acetal carbon atom as α or β.

18-106 For each structure in Problem 18-104, identify the configuration at the acetal carbon atom as α or β.

18-107 Identify the alcohol needed to produce each of the compounds in Problem 18-103 by reaction of the alcohol with the appropriate monosaccharide.

18-108 Identify the alcohol needed to produce each of the compounds in Problem 18-104 by reaction of the alcohol with the appropriate monosaccharide.

▲**18-109** With the help of Figures 18-14 and 18-15, name each of the compounds in Problem 18-103.

▲**18-110** With the help of Figures 18-14 and 18-15, name each of the compounds in Problem 18-104.

18-111 Draw structures for the following compounds.
  a. α-D-Galactose 1-phosphate
  b. β-D-Galactose 1-phosphate

18-112 Draw structures for the following compounds.
  a. α-D-Galactose 6-phosphate
  b. β-D-Galactose 6-phosphate

▲**18-113** With the help of Figure 18-14, draw structures for the following compounds.
  a. α-D-Glucosamine
  b. N-acetyl-α-D-glucosamine

▲**18-114** With the help of Figure 18-14, draw structures for the following compounds.
  a. α-D-Allosamine
  b. N-acetyl-α-D-allosamine

Disaccharides (Section 18-13)

18-115 Indicate whether or not at least one glucose "monosaccharide building block" is present in each of the following disaccharides.
  a. Maltose   b. Cellobiose
  c. Lactose   d. Sucrose

18-116 Indicate whether or not at least one fructose "monosaccharide building block" is present in each of the following disaccharides.
  a. Maltose   b. Cellobiose
  c. Lactose   d. Sucrose

The following structures appear at the top right of the page:

  b.

  c. (HOCH₂ ... CH₂OH ... O—CH₂—CH₃ ... OH OH)
  d. (CH₂OH ... O—CH₃ ... OH OH ... HO)

18-117 Indicate whether or not an $\alpha(1 \rightarrow 4)$ glycosidic linkage is present in each of the following disaccharides.
    a. Maltose   b. Cellobiose
    c. Lactose   d. Sucrose

18-118 Indicate whether or not a $\beta(1 \rightarrow 4)$ glycosidic linkage is present in each of the following disaccharides.
    a. Maltose   b. Cellobiose
    c. Lactose   d. Sucrose

18-119 Indicate whether or not anomeric forms exist for each of the following disaccharides.
    a. Maltose   b. Cellobiose
    c. Lactose   d. Sucrose

18-120 Indicate how many forms exist for each of the following disaccharides in aqueous solution.
    a. Maltose   b. Cellobiose
    c. Lactose   d. Sucrose

18-121 Indicate whether or not each of the following disaccharides is a reducing sugar.
    a. Sucrose   b. Maltose
    c. Lactose   d. Cellobiose

18-122 Indicate whether or not each of the following disaccharides gives a positive Benedict's test.
    a. Maltose   b. Cellobiose
    c. Sucrose   d. Lactose

18-123 Indicate whether or not each of the following disaccharides contains (1) two acetal carbon atoms, (2) two hemiacetal carbon atoms, or (3) one acetal and one hemiacetal carbon atom.
    a.

    b.

    c.

    d.

18-124 Indicate whether or not each of the following disaccharides contains (1) two acetal carbon atoms, (2) two hemiacetal carbon atoms, or (3) one acetal and one hemiacetal carbon atom.
    a.

    b.

    c.
    d.

18-125 For each of the structures in Problem 18-123, specify whether the disaccharide is in an α configuration or a β configuration, or neither.

18-126 For each of the structures in Problem 18-124, specify whether the disaccharide is in an α configuration or a β configuration, or neither.

18-127 Identify each of the structures in Problem 18-123 as a reducing sugar or a nonreducing sugar.

18-128 Identify each of the structures in Problem 18-124 as a reducing sugar or a nonreducing sugar.

18-129 Draw the structures of the substances produced when each of the disaccharides in Problem 18-123 undergoes hydrolysis.

18-130 Draw the structures of the substances produced when each of the disaccharides in Problem 18-124 undergoes hydrolysis.

18-131 What type of glycosidic linkage [$\alpha(1 \rightarrow 4)$, etc.] is present in each of the disaccharides in Problem 18-123?

18-132 What type of glycosidic linkage [$\alpha(1 \rightarrow 4)$, etc.] is present in each of the disaccharides in Problem 18-124?

18-133 Draw the structure of the disaccharide sophorose, given that it contains an α-D-glucose unit, a β-D-glucose unit, and a β(1 → 2) glycosidic linkage.

18-134 Draw the structure of the disaccharide isomaltose, given that it contains an α-D-glucose unit, a β-D-glucose unit, and an α(1 → 6) glycosidic linkage.

▲**18-135** Indicate which of the terms *monosaccharide, disaccharide, reducing sugar, anomers, enantiomers,* and *aldohexose* applies to both members of each of the following pairs of substances. More than one term may apply to a given pair of substances.
  a. α-D-Glucose and β-D-glucose
  b. Sucrose and maltose
  c. D-Fructose and L-fructose
  d. Lactose and galactose

▲**18-136** Indicate which of the terms *monosaccharide, disaccharide, reducing sugar, anomers, enantiomers,* and *aldohexose* applies to both members of each of the following pairs of substances. More than one term may apply to a given pair of substances.
  a. α-D-Glucose and α-D-galactose
  b. Sucrose and cellobiose
  c. Glyceraldehyde and dihydroxyacetone
  d. D-Ribose and L-ribose

Oligosaccharides (Section 18-14)

18-137 Characterize the oligosaccharide raffinose in terms of
  a. total number of monosaccharide units present
  b. total number of different kinds of monosaccharide units present
  c. total number of glycosidic linkages present
  d. total number of different kinds of glycosidic linkages present

18-138 Characterize the oligosaccharide stachyose in terms of
  a. total number of monosaccharide units present
  b. total number of different kinds of monosaccharide units present
  c. total number of glycosidic linkages present
  d. total number of different kinds of glycosidic linkages present

▲**18-139** Indicate whether or not one or more galactose monosaccharide units is/are present in the structure of the following carbohydrates.
  a. Sucrose
  b. Ribose
  c. Stachyose
  d. Lactose

▲**18-140** Indicate whether or not one or more galactose monosaccharide units is/are present in the structure of the following carbohydrates.
  a. Cellobiose
  b. Fructose
  c. Raffinose
  d. Maltose

▲**18-141** Identify the type(s) of glycosidic linkage(s) [α(1 → 4), etc.] present in each of the following carbohydrates, or indicate that none are present.
  a. Maltose   b. Galactose
  c. Stachyose   d. Fructose

▲**18-142** Identify the type(s) of glycosidic linkage(s) [α(1 → 4), etc.] present in each of the following carbohydrates, or indicate that none are present.
  a. Sucrose
  b. Raffinose
  c. Cellobiose
  d. Lactose

General Characteristics of Polysaccharides (Section 18-15)

18-143 What is the difference, if any, between a polysaccharide and a glycan?

18-144 What is the difference, if any, between a homopolysaccharide and a heteropolysaccharide?

18-145 What is the range for the polymer chain length in a polysaccharide?

18-146 Contrast polysaccharides with mono- and disaccharides in terms of general property differences.

Storage Polysaccharides (Section 18-16)

18-147 Indicate whether or not each of the following is a correct characterization for the amylose form of starch.
  a. It is a homopolysaccharide.
  b. It contains two different types of monosaccharide molecules.
  c. It is a branched-chain glucose polymer.
  d. All glycosidic linkages present are α(1 → 4).

18-148 Indicate whether or not each of the following is a correct or incorrect characterization for the amylopectin form of starch.
  a. It is a homopolysaccharide.
  b. It contains two different types of monosaccharide molecules.
  c. It is a branched-chain glucose polymer.
  d. All glycosidic linkages present are α(1 → 4).

18-149 What is the difference, if any, between the amylopectin form of starch and glycogen in terms of the following?
  a. type of glycosidic linkages present
  b. type of monosaccharide monomers present
  c. degree of branching of the polymer chain
  d. number of monomer units present

18-150 Which of the characterizations *homopolysaccharide, heteropolysaccharide, straight-chain polysaccharide,* and *storage polysaccharide* applies to both members of each of the following pairs of substances? More than one characterization may apply in a given situation.
  a. Glycogen and starch
  b. Amylose and amylopectin
  c. Glycogen and amylose
  d. Starch and amylopectin

Structural Polysaccharides (Section 18-17)

18-151 Indicate whether or not each of the following is a correct characterization for cellulose.
  a. It is an unbranched glucose polymer.
  b. Its glycosidic linkages are of the same type as those in starch.
  c. It is a source of nutrition for humans.
  d. One of its biochemical functions is that of dietary fiber.

18-152 Indicate whether or not each of the following is a correct characterization for chitin.
a. It is an unbranched polymer.
b. Two different types of monomers are present.
c. Glycosidic linkages present are the same as those in cellulose.
d. The monomers present are glucose derivatives rather than glucose itself.

18-153 Indicate whether or not each of the following characterizations applies to (1) both cellulose and chitin, (2) to cellulose only, (3) to chitin only, or (4) to neither cellulose nor chitin.
a. Storage polysaccharide
b. Monomers are glucose units
c. Glycosidic linkages are all $\alpha(1 \rightarrow 4)$
d. An unbranched polymer

18-154 Indicate whether or not each of the following characterizations applies to (1) both cellulose and chitin, (2) to cellulose only, (3) to chitin only, or (4) to neither cellulose nor chitin.
a. Structural polysaccharide
b. Monomers are glucose derivatives
c. Glycosidic linkages are all $(1 \rightarrow 4)$
d. Homopolysaccharide

▲18-155 Match each of the following structural characteristics to the polysaccharides *amylopectin, amylose, glycogen, cellulose,* and *chitin.* A specific characteristic may apply to more than one of the polysaccharides.
a. $\alpha(1 \rightarrow 4)$ glycosidic linkages are present.
b. All of the glycosidic linkages present are of the same type.
c. The polymer chain is unbranched.
d. The monosaccharide repeating unit is not glucose.

▲18-156 Match each of the following structural characteristics to the polysaccharides *amylopectin, amylose, glycogen, cellulose,* and *chitin.* A specific characteristic may apply to more than one of the polysaccharides.
a. $\beta(1 \rightarrow 4)$ glycosidic linkages are present.
b. Two different kinds of glycosidic linkages are present.
c. The polymer chain is branched.
d. The monosaccharide repeating unit is a glucose derivative.

Acidic Polysaccharides (Section 18-18)

18-157 Indicate whether each of the following statements about the polysaccharide hyaluronic acid is true or false.
a. One of its monosaccharide building blocks is NAG.
b. One of its monosaccharide building blocks has a 2− charge.
c. Two types of glycosidic linkages are present.
d. One of its biochemical functions is as a lubricant for joints.

18-158 Indicate whether each of the following statements about the polysaccharide heparin is true or false.
a. Its biochemical function is to dissolve blood clots.
b. Both of its monosaccharide building blocks contain the element sulfur.
c. $\beta(1 \rightarrow 3)$ glycosidic linkages are present.
d. It has one of the longest chain lengths of any polysaccharide.

▲18-159 Which of the characterizations *homopolysaccharide, heteropolysaccharide, branched polysaccharide,* and *unbranched polysaccharide* applies to both members of each of the following pairs of carbohydrates? More than one characterization may apply in a given situation.
a. Starch and cellulose
b. Glycogen and amylopectin
c. Amylose and chitin
d. Heparin and hyaluronic acid

▲18-160 Which of the characterizations *homopolysaccharide, heteropolysaccharide, branched polysaccharide,* and *unbranched polysaccharide* applies to both members of each of the following pairs of carbohydrates? More than one characterization may apply in a given situation.
a. Glycogen and starch
b. Amylose and amylopectin
c. Chitin and hyaluronic acid
d. Heparin and cellulose

▲18-161 Indicate whether each of the following is a *storage polysaccharide,* a *structural polysaccharide,* an *acidic polysaccharide,* or a *non-polysaccharide.*
a. Amylose
b. Stachyose
c. Hyaluronic acid
d. Cellulose

▲18-162 Indicate whether each of the following is a *storage polysaccharide,* a *structural polysaccharide,* an *acidic polysaccharide,* or a *non-polysaccharide.*
a. Heparin
b. Chitin
c. Glycogen
d. Raffinose

▲18-163 Match the polysaccharides *amylopectin, amylose, cellulose, chitin, glycogen, heparin,* and *hyaluronic acid* to the following glycosidic linkage characterizations. More than one of the polysaccharides may be correct in a given situation.
a. All glycosidic linkages present are the same.
b. Some, but not all, glycosidic linkages are $\alpha(1 \rightarrow 4)$ linkages.
c. Both $\beta(1 \rightarrow 3)$ and $\beta(1 \rightarrow 4)$ glycosidic linkages are present.
d. All glycosidic linkages are $\alpha(1 \rightarrow 4)$ linkages.

▲18-164 Match the polysaccharides *amylopectin, amylose, cellulose, chitin, glycogen, heparin,* and *hyaluronic acid* to the following glycosidic linkage characterizations. More than one of the polysaccharides may be correct in a given situation.
a. Two different types of glycosidic linkages are present.
b. Some, but not all, glycosidic linkages are $\alpha(1 \rightarrow 6)$ linkages.
c. All glycosidic linkages are $(1 \rightarrow 4)$ linkages.
d. All glycosidic linkages are $\beta(1 \rightarrow 4)$ linkages.

Dietary Considerations and Carbohydrates (Section 18-19)

18-165 Indicate whether or not each of the following is classified as a *simple* carbohydrate.
a. Glucose   b. Sucrose
c. Starch   d. Cellulose

18-166   Indicate whether or not each of the following is classified as a *complex* carbohydrate.
 a. Fructose
 b. Lactose
 c. Amylose
 d. Amylopectin

18-167   In a dietary context, what is the difference between a *natural sugar* and a *refined sugar*?

18-168   Why are refined sugars said to contain *empty calories*?

Glycolipids and Glycoproteins (Section 18-20)

18-169   In terms of general structure, what is a glycolipid?

18-170   In terms of general structure, what is a glycoprotein?

18-171   Describe the general features of the cell recognition process in which glycoproteins participate.

18-172   Describe the general features of the cell recognition process in which glycolipids participate.

Lipids 19

Fats and oils are the most widely occurring types of lipids. Thick layers of fat help insulate polar bears against the effects of low temperatures.

There are four major classes of bioorganic substances: carbohydrates, lipids, proteins, and nucleic acids (Section 18-1). In the previous chapter the first of these classes, carbohydrates, was considered. Attention now turns to the second of the bioorganic classes, the compounds called lipids.

Lipids known as fats provide a major way of storing chemical energy and carbon atoms in the body. Fats also surround and insulate vital body organs, providing protection from mechanical shock and preventing excessive loss of heat energy. Phospholipids, glycolipids, and cholesterol (a lipid) are the basic components of cell membranes. Several cholesterol derivatives function as chemical messengers (hormones) within the body.

19-1 Structure and Classification of Lipids

LEARNING FOCUS

Be familiar with the solubility-based definition for a lipid; be able to classify lipids based on biochemical function and also based on saponification characteristics.

Unlike carbohydrates and most other classes of compounds, lipids do not have a common structural feature that serves as the basis for defining such compounds. Instead, their characterization is based on solubility characteristics. A **lipid** *is an organic compound found in living organisms that is insoluble (or only sparingly soluble) in water but soluble in nonpolar organic solvents.*

Figure 19-1 The structural formulas of these types of lipids illustrate the great structural diversity among lipids. The defining parameter for lipids is solubility rather than structure.

When a biochemical material (human, animal, or plant tissue) is homogenized in a blender and mixed with a nonpolar organic solvent, the substances that dissolve in the solvent are the lipids.

Figure 19-1 shows the structural diversity that is associated with lipid molecules. Some are esters, some are amides, and some are alcohols; some are acyclic, some are cyclic, and some are polycyclic. The common thread that ties all of the compounds of Figure 19-1 together is solubility rather than structure. All are insoluble in water.

Two common methods exist for subclassifying lipids into families for the purpose of study. One method uses the biochemical function of a lipid as the basis for classification, and the other method is based on whether or not a lipid can be broken down into smaller units through basic hydrolysis, that is, reaction with water under basic conditions. A hydrolysis reaction that occurs in basic solution is called a *saponification reaction* (Section 16-16).

Based on biochemical function, lipids are divided into five categories:

1. **Energy-storage lipids** (triacylglycerols)
2. **Membrane lipids** (phospholipids, sphingoglycolipids, and cholesterol)
3. **Emulsification lipids** (bile acids)
4. **Messenger lipids** (steroid hormones and eicosanoids)
5. **Protective-coating lipids** (biological waxes)

Based upon whether or not saponification occurs when a lipid is placed in basic aqueous solution, lipids are divided into two categories:

1. **Saponifiable lipids** (triacylglycerols, phospholipids, sphingoglycolipids, and biological waxes)
2. **Nonsaponifiable lipids** (cholesterol, steroid hormones, bile acids, and eicosanoids)

Saponifiable lipids are converted into two or more smaller molecules when hydrolysis occurs. Nonsaponifiable lipids cannot be broken up into smaller units since they do not react with water.

Some textbooks, including this one, use the first of these two classification systems (biochemical function) as the basis for lipid classification, whereas others use the second system (hydrolysis). The decision of which system to use is arbitrary; both systems have their merits. Because the saponification classification system is also widely used, the last section in this chapter reformats important chapter considerations in terms of the saponification classification system. This reformatting will serve as a useful review of the chapter's lipid considerations.

A parallel exists between carbohydrate chemistry of the last chapter and lipid chemistry. A fundamental premise of carbohydrate chemistry is the concept that monosaccharides are the basic structural unit, or building block, from which carbohydrate molecules are made. In a like manner, basic building blocks for lipid molecules exist. Because of the structural diversity found in lipid molecules, several different building blocks are needed. The most frequently encountered lipid building block is the structural unit called a *fatty acid*. Consideration of the structural characteristics and physical properties of fatty acids is the starting point for development of the subject of lipid chemistry. All energy-storage lipids, the most abundant type of lipid, contain fatty acid building blocks. Most membrane lipids, the second most abundant type of lipid, also contain this building block.

Section 19-1 Quick Quiz

1. A lipid is any substance of biochemical origin that is
   a. soluble in water but insoluble in nonpolar solvents
   b. insoluble in water but soluble in nonpolar solvents
   c. soluble in both water and nonpolar solvents
   d. no correct response
2. Which of the following is *not* a biochemical function classification for lipids?
   a. membrane lipid
   b. messenger lipid
   c. emulsification lipid
   d. no correct response
3. The saponifiable/nonsaponifiable classification system for lipids is based on
   a. lipid behavior in acidic solution
   b. lipid behavior in basic solution
   c. ability of lipids to react with alcohols
   d. no correct response

Answers: 1. b; 2. d; 3. b

19-2 Types of Fatty Acids

LEARNING FOCUS

Be familiar with the generalized definition for a fatty acid; be able to classify fatty acids in terms of structural characteristics of their carbon chains.

A **fatty acid** *is a naturally occurring monocarboxylic acid.* Because of the pathway by which they are biosynthesized (Section 25-7), fatty acids nearly always contain an even number of carbon atoms and have a carbon chain that is unbranched. In terms of carbon chain length, fatty acids are characterized as *long-chain fatty acids* (C_{12} to C_{26}), *medium-chain fatty acids* (C_8 and C_{10}), or *short-chain fatty acids* (C_4 and C_6). ◄ Fatty acids are rarely found free in nature but rather occur as part of the structure of more complex lipid molecules.

▶ *Fatty acids were first isolated from naturally occurring fats; hence the designation* fatty acids.

Saturated and Unsaturated Fatty Acids

The carbon chain of a fatty acid may or may not contain carbon–carbon double bonds. On the basis of this consideration, fatty acids are classified as saturated fatty acids (SFAs), monounsaturated fatty acids (MUFAs), or polyunsaturated fatty acids (PUFAs).

A **saturated fatty acid** *is a fatty acid with a carbon chain in which all carbon–carbon bonds are single bonds.* The structural formula for the 16-carbon SFA is

$$H-\overset{\displaystyle H}{\underset{\displaystyle H}{C}}-\overset{\displaystyle H}{\underset{\displaystyle H}{C}}-\overset{\displaystyle H}{\underset{\displaystyle H}{C}}-\overset{\displaystyle H}{\underset{\displaystyle H}{C}}-\overset{\displaystyle H}{\underset{\displaystyle H}{C}}-\overset{\displaystyle H}{\underset{\displaystyle H}{C}}-\overset{\displaystyle H}{\underset{\displaystyle H}{C}}-\overset{\displaystyle H}{\underset{\displaystyle H}{C}}-\overset{\displaystyle H}{\underset{\displaystyle H}{C}}-\overset{\displaystyle H}{\underset{\displaystyle H}{C}}-\overset{\displaystyle H}{\underset{\displaystyle H}{C}}-\overset{\displaystyle H}{\underset{\displaystyle H}{C}}-\overset{\displaystyle H}{\underset{\displaystyle H}{C}}-\overset{\displaystyle H}{\underset{\displaystyle H}{C}}-\overset{\displaystyle H}{\underset{\displaystyle H}{C}}-\overset{\displaystyle O}{\overset{\displaystyle \|}{C}}-OH$$

IUPAC name: hexadecanoic acid
Common name: palmitic acid

> ▶ *More than 500 different fatty acids have been isolated from the lipids of microorganisms, plants, animals, and humans. These fatty acids differ from one another in the length of their carbon chains, their degree of unsaturation (number of double bonds), and the positions of the double bonds in the chains.*

The structural formula for a fatty acid is usually written in a more condensed form than the preceding structural formula. ◀ Two alternative structural notations for palmitic acid are

$$CH_3-(CH_2)_{14}-\overset{\displaystyle O}{\overset{\displaystyle \|}{C}}-OH$$

and

(Line-angle structural formulas were first encountered in Section 12-9.)

A **monounsaturated fatty acid** *is a fatty acid with a carbon chain in which one carbon–carbon double bond is present.* In biochemically important MUFAs, the configuration about the double bond is nearly always *cis* (Section 13-5). ◀ Different ways of depicting the structure of a MUFA follow.

> ▶ *The fatty acids present in naturally occurring lipids almost always have the following three characteristics:*
>
> 1. *An unbranched carbon chain*
> 2. *An even number of carbon atoms in the carbon chain*
> 3. *Double bonds, when present in the carbon chain, in a* cis *configuration*

$$CH_3-(CH_2)_7-CH=CH-(CH_2)_7-\overset{\displaystyle O}{\overset{\displaystyle \|}{C}}-OH$$

IUPAC name: *cis*-9-octadecaenoic acid
Common name: oleic acid

The first of these structures correctly emphasizes that the presence of a *cis* double bond in the carbon chain puts a rigid 30° bend in the chain. Such a bend affects the physical properties of a fatty acid, as discussed in Section 19-3.

A **polyunsaturated fatty acid** *is a fatty acid with a carbon chain in which two or more carbon–carbon double bonds are present.* Up to six double bonds are found in biochemically important PUFAs.

Fatty acids are nearly always referred to using their common names. IUPAC names for fatty acids, although easily constructed, are usually quite long. These two types of names for an 18-carbon PUFA containing *cis* double bonds in the 9 and 12 positions are as follows:

IUPAC name: *cis,cis*-9,12-octadecadienoic acid
Common name: linoleic acid

Unsaturated Fatty Acids and Double-Bond Position

A numerically based shorthand system exists for specifying key structural parameters for fatty acids. In this system, two numbers separated by a colon are used to specify the number of carbon atoms and the number of carbon–carbon double bonds present. The notation 18:0 denotes a C_{18} fatty acid with no double bonds, whereas the notation 18:2 signifies a C_{18} fatty acid in which two double bonds are present.

To specify double-bond positioning within the carbon chain of an unsaturated fatty acid, the preceding notation is expanded by adding the Greek capital letter delta (Δ) followed by one or more superscript numbers. The notation $18:3(\Delta^{9,12,15})$ denotes a C_{18} PUFA with three double bonds at locations between carbons 9 and 10, 12 and 13, and 15 and 16.

MUFAs are usually Δ^9 acids, and the first two additional double bonds in PUFAs are generally at the Δ^{12} and Δ^{15} locations. [A notable exception to this generalization is the biochemically important arachidonic acid, a PUFA with the structural parameters $20:4(\Delta^{5,8,11,14})$.] Denoting double-bond locations using this "delta notation" always assumes a numbering system in which the carboxyl carbon atom is C1. ◀

Several different "families" of unsaturated fatty acids exist. These family relationships become apparent when double-bond position is specified relative to the methyl (noncarboxyl) end of the fatty acid carbon chain. Double-bond positioning determined in this manner is denoted by using the Greek lowercase letter omega (ω). An **omega-3 fatty acid** *is an unsaturated fatty acid with its endmost double bond three carbon atoms away from its methyl end.* An example of an omega-3 fatty acid is

An **omega-6 fatty acid** *is an unsaturated fatty acid with its endmost double bond six carbon atoms away from its methyl end.*

The following three acids all belong to the omega-6 fatty acid family.

The structural feature common to these omega-6 fatty acids is highlighted with color in the preceding structural formulas. All the members of an omega family of fatty acids have structures in which the same "methyl end" is present.

Table 19-1 gives the names and structures of the fatty acids most commonly encountered as building blocks in biochemically important lipid structures, as well as the "delta" and "omega" notations for the acids.

▶ *Different organisms differ in the overall structural characteristics of the fatty acids present.*

1. *Humans and animals have 5%–7% of fatty acids with 20 or 22 carbon atoms, while fish have 25%–30%.*
2. *Humans and animals have less than 1% of their fatty acids with 5–6 double bonds, while plants have 5%–6%, and fish 15%–30%.*

▶ Table 19-1 **Selected Fatty Acids of Biological Importance**

Structural Notation			Common Name	Structure
Saturated Fatty Acids				
12:0			lauric acid	
14:0			myristic acid	
16:0			palmitic acid	
18:0			stearic acid	
20:0			arachidic acid	
Monounsaturated Fatty Acids				
16:1	Δ^9	ω-7	palmitoleic acid	
18:1	Δ^9	ω-9	oleic acid	
Polyunsaturated Fatty Acids				
18:2	$\Delta^{9,12}$	ω-6	linoleic acid	
18:3	$\Delta^{9,12,15}$	ω-3	linolenic acid	
20:4	$\Delta^{5,8,11,14}$	ω-6	arachidonic acid	
20:5	$\Delta^{5,8,11,14,17}$	ω-3	EPA (eicosapentaenoic acid)	
22:6	$\Delta^{4,7,10,13,16,19}$	ω-3	DHA (docosahexaenoic acid)	

EXAMPLE 19-1

Classifying Fatty Acids on the Basis of Structural Characteristics

Classify the fatty acid with the following structural formula in the ways indicated.

a. What is the type designation (SFA, MUFA, or PUFA) for this fatty acid?
b. On the basis of carbon chain length and degree of unsaturation, what is the numerical shorthand designation for this fatty acid?
c. To which "omega" family of fatty acids does this fatty acid belong?
d. What is the "delta" designation for the carbon chain double-bond locations for this fatty acid?

Solution

a. Two carbon–carbon double bonds are present in this molecule, which makes it a *polyunsaturated fatty acid (PUFA)*.
b. Eighteen carbon atoms and two carbon–carbon double bonds are present. The shorthand numerical designation for this fatty acid is thus *18:2*.
c. Counting from the methyl end of the carbon chain, the first double bond encountered involves carbons 6 and 7. This fatty acid belongs to the *omega-6* family of fatty acids.
d. Counting from the carboxyl end of the carbon chain, with C1 being the carboxyl group, the double-bond locations are 9 and 12. This is a $\Delta^{9,12}$ *fatty acid*.

1. Which of the following statements concerning fatty acids is *correct*?
   a. They are naturally occurring dicarboxylic acids.
   b. They are rarely found in the free state in nature.
   c. They almost always contain an odd number of carbon atoms.
   d. no correct response
2. In which of the following pairs of fatty acids are both members of the pair polyunsaturated fatty acids?
   a. 18:0 acid and 18:1 acid
   b. 18:1 acid and 18:2 acid
   c. 18:2 acid and 18:3 acid
   d. no correct response
3. Which of the following fatty acids is an omega-6 fatty acid?
   a. $CH_3—(CH_2)_{18}—COOH$
   b. $CH_3—(CH_2)_7—CH=CH—(CH_2)_7—COOH$
   c. $CH_3—(CH_2)_4—CH=CH—(CH_2)_8—COOH$
   d. no correct response
4. The double bond present in a monounsaturated fatty acid almost always
   a. is in a *cis*-configuration
   b. involves the second carbon from the carboxyl end of the carbon chain
   c. involves the second carbon from the methyl end of the carbon chain
   d. no correct response

Answers: 1. b; 2. c; 3. c; 4. a

19-3 Physical Properties of Fatty Acids

LEARNING FOCUS

Understand the relationship between a fatty acid's structure and its melting point and its water solubility.

The physical properties of fatty acids, and of lipids that contain them, are largely determined by the length and degree of unsaturation of the fatty acid carbon chain.

Water solubility for fatty acids is a direct function of carbon chain length; solubility decreases as carbon chain length increases. Short-chain fatty acids have a slight solubility in water. Long-chain fatty acids are essentially insoluble in water. ◄ The slight solubility of short-chain fatty acids is related to the polarity of the carboxyl group present. In longer-chain fatty acids, the nonpolar nature of the hydrocarbon chain completely dominates solubility considerations.

Melting points for fatty acids are strongly influenced by both carbon chain length and degree of unsaturation (number of double bonds present). Figure 19-2 shows melting-point variation as a function of both of these variables. As carbon chain length increases, melting point increases. This trend is related to the greater surface area associated with a longer carbon chain and to the increased opportunities that this greater surface area affords for intermolecular attractions between fatty acid molecules.

A trend of particular significance is that saturated fatty acids have higher melting points than unsaturated fatty acids with the same number of carbon atoms. The greater the degree of unsaturation, the greater the reduction in melting points. Figure 19-2 shows this effect for the 18-carbon acids with zero, one, two, and three double bonds. Long-chain saturated fatty acids tend to be solids at room temperature, whereas long-chain unsaturated fatty acids tend to be liquids at room temperature.

The decreasing melting point associated with increasing degree of unsaturation in fatty acids is explained by decreased molecular attractions between carbon chains. The double bonds in unsaturated fatty acids, which generally have the *cis*

▶ *Fatty acids have low water solubilities, which decrease with increasing carbon chain length; at 30°C, lauric acid (12:0) has a water solubility of 0.063 g/L and stearic acid (18:0) a solubility of 0.0034 g/L. Contrast this with glucose's solubility in water at the same temperature, 1100 g/L.*

Figure 19-2 The melting point of a fatty acid depends on the length of the carbon chain and on the number of double bonds present in the carbon chain.

Figure 19-3 Space-filling models of four 18-carbon fatty acids, which differ in the number of double bonds present. Note how the presence of double bonds changes the shape of the molecule.

Stearic acid (18:0)

Oleic acid (18:1)

Linoleic acid (18:2)

Linolenic acid (18:3)

configuration, produce "bends" in the carbon chains of these molecules (Figure 19-3). These "bends" prevent unsaturated fatty acids from packing together as tightly as saturated fatty acids. The greater the number of double bonds, the less efficient the packing. As a result, unsaturated fatty acids always have fewer intermolecular attractions, and therefore lower melting points, than their saturated counterparts.

Section 19-3 Quick Quiz

1. In which of the following pairs of fatty acids does the first listed acid have a greater water solubility than the second listed acid?
   a. 18:0 acid and 14:0 acid
   b. 16:0 acid and 18:0 acid
   c. 20:0 acid and 16:0 acid
   d. no correct response

2. In which of the following pairs of fatty acids does the first listed acid have a lower melting point than the second listed acid?
   a. 16:0 acid and 16:1 acid
   b. 18:2 acid and 18:0 acid
   c. 18:2 acid and 18:3 acid
   d. no correct response

Answers: 1. b; 2. b

19-4 Energy-Storage Lipids: Triacylglycerols

LEARNING FOCUS

Be familiar with general structural representations for a triacylglycerol; distinguish between *simple* and *mixed* triacylglycerols and between fats and oils.

With the notable exception of nerve cells, human cells store small amounts of energy-providing materials for use when energy demand is high. The most widespread energy-storage material within cells is the carbohydrate glycogen (Section 18-15); it is present in small amounts in most cells.

Lipids known as triacylglycerols also function within the body as energy-storage materials. Rather than being widespread, triacylglycerols are concentrated primarily in special cells (adipocytes) that are nearly filled with the material. Adipose tissue containing these cells is found in various parts of the body: under the skin, in the abdominal cavity, in the mammary glands, and around various organs (Figure 19-4). Triacylglycerols are much more efficient at storing energy than is glycogen because large quantities of them can be packed into a very small volume. These energy-storage lipids are the most abundant type of lipid present in the human body.

In terms of functional groups present, triacylglycerols are triesters; three ester functional groups are present. Recall from Section 16-11 that an ester is a compound produced from the reaction of an alcohol with a carboxylic acid. The alcohol involved in triacylglycerol formation is always glycerol, a three-carbon alcohol with three hydroxyl groups.

Figure 19-4 An electron micrograph of adipocytes, the body's triacylglycerol-storing cells. Note the bulging spherical shape.

Steve Gschmeissner/Science Source

$$
\begin{array}{c}
CH_2\!-\!OH \\
| \\
CH\!-\!OH \\
| \\
CH_2\!-\!OH \\
\text{Glycerol}
\end{array}
$$

Fatty acids are the carboxylic acids involved in triacylglycerol formation. In the esterification reaction producing a triacylglycerol, a single molecule of glycerol reacts with three fatty acid molecules; each of the three hydroxyl groups present is esterified. Figure 19-5 shows the triple esterification reaction that occurs between glycerol and

Glycerol   Three fatty acids   Triester of glycerol   Three water molecules

Figure 19-5 Structure of the simple triacylglycerol produced from the triple esterification reaction between glycerol and three molecules of stearic acid (18:0 acid). Three molecules of water are a by-product of this reaction.

three molecules of stearic acid (18:0); note the production of three molecules of water as a by-product of the reaction.

Two general ways to represent the structure of a triacylglycerol are

The first representation, a block diagram, shows the four subunits (building blocks) present in the structure: glycerol and three fatty acids. ◀ The second representation, a general structural formula, shows the three ester linkages present in a triacylglycerol. Each of the fatty acids is attached to glycerol through an ester linkage.

Formally defined, a **triacylglycerol** *is a lipid formed by esterification of three fatty acids to a glycerol molecule.* Within the name *triacylglycerol* is the term *acyl*. An *acyl group,* previously defined and considered in Section 16-1, is the portion of a carboxylic acid that remains after the —OH group is removed from the carboxyl carbon atom. The structural representation for an acyl group is

$$\begin{array}{c} O \\ \parallel \\ R-C- \end{array}$$
An acyl group

Thus, as the name implies, triacylglycerol molecules contain three fatty acid residues (three acyl groups) attached to a glycerol residue. An older name that is still frequently used for a triacylglycerol is *triglyceride.*

The triacylglycerol produced from glycerol and three molecules of stearic acid (shown in Figure 19-5) is an example of a simple triacylglycerol. A **simple triacylglycerol** *is a triester formed from the esterification of glycerol with three identical fatty acid molecules.* If the reacting fatty acid molecules are not all identical, then the result is a mixed triacylglycerol. A **mixed triacylglycerol** *is a triester formed from the esterification of glycerol with more than one kind of fatty acid molecule.* Figure 19-6 shows the structure of a mixed triacylglycerol in which one fatty acid is saturated, another monounsaturated, and the third polyunsaturated. Naturally occurring *simple* triacylglycerols are rare. Most biochemically important triacylglycerols are *mixed* triacylglycerols. ◀

▶ *Triacylglycerols do not actually contain glycerol and three fatty acids, as the block diagram for a triacylglycerol implies. They actually contain a glycerol residue and three fatty acid residues. In the formation of the triacylglycerol, three molecules of water have been removed from the structural components of the triacylglycerol, leaving residues of the reacting molecules.*

▶ *Mixed triacylglycerol molecules, as well as those of most other types of lipids (yet to be discussed), are chiral (Section 18-4). The C2 carbon atom in the glycerol subunit of triacylglycerols is the chiral center present in these molecules. Thus, mixed triacylglycerol molecules like monosaccharides (Section 18-5) possess handedness, that is left-handed and right-handed forms (Section 18-4). Stereochemical considerations (Section 18-5) for mixed triacylglycerols and other types of lipid molecules are usually more complex than those for monosaccharides (Section 18-6) because of the greater complexity of their molecular structures and will not be further considered in this text.*

Figure 19-6 Structure of a mixed triacylglycerol in which three different fatty acid residues are present.

EXAMPLE 19-2

Drawing the Structural Formula of a Triacylglycerol

Draw the structural formula of the triacylglycerol produced from the reaction between glycerol and three molecules of myristic acid.

Solution

Table 19-1 shows that myristic acid is the 14:0 fatty acid. Draw the structure of glycerol and then place three molecules of myristic acid alongside the glycerol. The fatty acid placements should be such that their carboxyl groups are lined up alongside the hydroxyl groups of glycerol. Form an ester linkage between each carboxyl group and a glycerol hydroxyl group with the accompanying production of a water molecule.

| Glycerol | Fatty acids (14:0) | Triacylglycerol |

Fats and Oils

Fats are naturally occurring mixtures of triacylglycerol molecules in which many different kinds of triacylglycerol molecules are present. *Oils* are also naturally occurring mixtures of triacylglycerol molecules in which there are many different kinds of triacylglycerol molecules present. Given that both are triacylglycerol mixtures, what distinguishes a fat from an oil? The answer is physical state at room temperature. A **fat** *is a triacylglycerol mixture that is a solid or a semi-solid at room temperature (25°C).* Generally, fats are obtained from animal sources. An **oil** *is a triacylglycerol mixture that is a liquid at room temperature (25°C).* Generally, oils are obtained from plant sources. ◄ Because they are mixtures, no fat or oil can be represented by a single specific chemical formula. Many different fatty acids are present in the triacylglycerol molecules found in the mixture. The actual composition of a fat or oil varies even for the species from which it is obtained. Composition depends on both dietary and climatic factors. For example, fat obtained from corn-fed hogs has a different overall composition than fat obtained from peanut-fed hogs. Flaxseed grown in warm climates gives oil with a different composition from that obtained from flaxseed grown in colder climates.

> ▶ Petroleum oils *(Section 12-15)* *are structurally different from lipid oils. The former are mixtures of alkanes and cycloalkanes. The latter are mixtures of triesters of glycerol.*

Additional generalizations and comparisons between fats and oils follow.

1. Fats are composed largely of triacylglycerols in which saturated fatty acids predominate, although some unsaturated fatty acids are present. Such triacylglycerols can pack closely together because of the "linearity" of their fatty acid chains (Figure 19-7a), thus causing the higher melting points associated with fats. Oils contain triacylglycerols with larger amounts of mono- and polyunsaturated fatty acids than those in fats. Such triacylglycerols cannot pack as tightly together because of "bends" in their fatty acid chains (Figure 19-7b). The result is lower melting points. ◄

2. Fats are generally obtained from animals; hence the term *animal fat*. Although fats are solids at room temperature, the warmer body temperature of the living animal keeps the fat somewhat liquid (semi-solid) and thus allows for movement. Oils typically come from plants, although there are also fish oils. A fish would

> ▶ *Fats contain both saturated and unsaturated fatty acids. Oils also contain both saturated and unsaturated fatty acids. The difference between a fat and an oil lies in which type of fatty acid is more prevalent. In fats, saturated fatty acids are more prevalent; in oils, unsaturated fatty acids are more prevalent.*

Figure 19-7 Representative triacylglycerols from (a) a fat and (b) an oil.

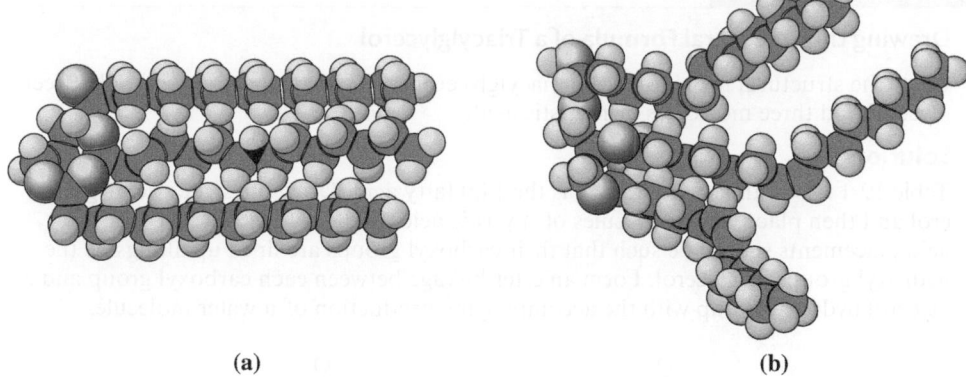

(a)   (b)

have some serious problems if its triacylglycerols "solidified" when it encountered cold water.

3. Pure fats and pure oils are colorless, odorless, and tasteless. The tastes, odors, and colors associated with dietary plant oils are caused by small amounts of other naturally occurring substances present in the plant that have been carried along during processing. The presence of these "other" compounds is usually considered desirable.

Figure 19-8 gives the percentages of saturated, monounsaturated, and polyunsaturated fatty acids found in common dietary oils and fats. In general, a higher degree of fatty acid unsaturation is associated with oils than with fats. A notable exception to this generalization is coconut oil, which is highly saturated. This oil is a liquid not because it contains many double bonds within the fatty acids but because it is rich in *shorter-chain* fatty acids, particularly lauric acid (12:0).

Figure 19-8 Percentages of saturated, monounsaturated, and polyunsaturated fatty acids in the triacylglycerols of various dietary fats and oils.

Dietary Oil or Fat	Saturated	Monounsaturated	Polyunsaturated
Canola oil	6%	58%	36%
Safflower oil	9%	13%	78%
Sunflower oil	11%	20%	69%
Avocado oil	12%	74%	14%
Corn oil	13%	25%	62%
Olive oil	14%	77%	9%
Soybean oil	15%	24%	61%
Peanut oil	18%	48%	34%
Cottonseed oil	27%	19%	54%
Pork fat	41%	47%	12%
Palm oil	51%	39%	10%
Beef fat	52%	44%	4%
Butterfat	66%	30%	4%
Coconut oil	92%	6%	2%

■ Saturated   ■ Monounsaturated   ■ Polyunsaturated

Section 19-4 Quick Quiz

1. How many structural "subunits" are present in the block diagram for a triacylglycerol?
   a. two
   b. three
   c. four
   d. no correct response

2. How many ester linkages are present in a triacylglycerol molecule?
   a. zero
   b. two
   c. four
   d. no correct response
3. How many different *simple* triglyceride molecules can be produced that include glycerol, stearic acid, and palmitic acid as part of their structure?
   a. zero
   b. one
   c. two
   d. no correct response
4. How many different *mixed* triglyceride molecules can be produced that include glycerol, stearic acid, and palmitic acid as part of their structure?
   a. two
   b. three
   c. four
   d. no correct response
5. Which of the following is a distinguishing characteristic between fats and oils?
   a. physical state at room temperature
   b. number of structural subunits present
   c. number of fatty acid residues present
   d. no correct response
6. Unsaturated fatty acid residues are structural components of
   a. both fats and oil
   b. fats but not oils
   c. oils but not fats
   d. no correct response

Answers: 1. c; 2. d; 3. a; 4. c; 5. a; 6. a

19-5 Dietary Considerations and Triacylglycerols

LEARNING FOCUS

Describe the response of the human body to dietary fats as a function of degree of unsaturation and unsaturation positioning in the carbon chain of fatty acid residues present in the dietary fat.

In recent years, considerable research has been carried out concerning the role of dietary factors as a cause of disease (obesity, diabetes, cancer, hypertension, and atherosclerosis). Numerous studies have shown that, *in general,* nations whose citizens have high dietary intakes of triacylglycerols (fats and oils) tend to have higher incidences of heart disease and certain types of cancers. This is the reason for concern that the typical American diet contains too much fat and the call for Americans to reduce their total dietary fat intake.

Contrary to the general trend, however, there are several areas of the world where high dietary fat intake does not translate into high risks for cardiovascular disease, obesity, and certain types of cancers. These exceptions, which include some Mediterranean countries and the Inuit people of Greenland, suggest that relationships between dietary triacylglycerol intake and risk factors for disease involve more than simply the *total amount* of triacylglycerols consumed. ◄

"Good Fats" Versus "Bad Fats"

In dietary discussions, the term *fat* is used as a substitute for the term *triacylglycerol.* Thus a dietary fat can be either a "fat" or an "oil." Ongoing studies indicate that both the *type of dietary fat* consumed and the *amount of dietary fat* consumed are important factors in determining human body responses to dietary fat. Current dietary fat recommendations are that people limit their total fat intake to 30% of total calories—with up to 15% coming from monounsaturated fat, up to 10% from polyunsaturated fat, and less than 10% from saturated fats.

▶ *A grain- and vegetable-rich diet that contains small amounts of extra-virgin olive oil (three to four teaspoons daily) has been found to help people with high blood pressure reduce the amount of blood pressure medication they require, on average, by 48%. Substitution of sunflower oil for the olive oil resulted in only a 4% reduction in medication dosage.*

The blood-pressure-reduction benefits of olive oil do not relate to the triacylglycerols present but rather come from other compounds naturally present, namely, from antioxidant polyphenols olive oil contains. These antioxidants help promote the relaxation of blood vessels.

▶ *When feeding, Burmese pythons can swallow prey as large as a small deer. After consumption of such a "large meal" the snake's accompanying dramatic increase in metabolic rate is also accompanied by a significant increase (up to 40%) in the mass of the snake's heart. Studies indicate that a specific mixture of fatty acids present in the snake's blood—involving 14:0, 16:0, and 16:1 fatty acids—is the signaling agent for heart growth. This same fatty acid mixture, when administered to a fasting Burmese python, also causes heart growth. Further studies show that the fatty acid mixture, when injected into the blood plasma of mice, causes heart growth in the mice. Research is now proposed to determine if there are applications for this discovery relative to human cardiac disease patients who have small heart chambers.*

The general significance of this research is that SFAs, which are usually considered to be "bad" for human health or simply as energy-producing substances for the heart, are now known to have important roles in cellular signaling in living organisms.

▶ *Freshly pressed extra-virgin olive oil contains a compound that has the same pharmacological activity as the over-the-counter pain reliever ibuprofen (Section 16-4). This finding suggests a possible explanation for some of the various health benefits attributed to a Mediterranean diet that typically is rich in olive oil. It is estimated that this olive oil compound, called oleocanthal, is present in a typical Mediterranean diet in an amount equivalent to about 10% of the ibuprofen dose recommended for headache relief.*

Oleocanthal

Figure 19-9 Fish that live in deep, cold water—mackerel, herring, tuna, and salmon—are better sources of omega-3 fatty acids than other fish.

These recommendations imply correctly that different types of dietary fat have different effects. In simplified terms, research studies indicate that saturated fats are "bad fat," monounsaturated fats are "good fat," and polyunsaturated fats can be both "good fat" and "bad fat." In the latter case, fatty acid omega classification (Section 19-2) becomes important, a situation addressed later in this section. Studies indicate that saturated fat can increase heart disease risk, that monounsaturated fat can decrease both heart disease and breast cancer risk, and that polyunsaturated fat can reduce heart disease risk but promote the risk of certain types of cancers. ◀

Referring to Figure 19-8, note the wide variance in the three general types of fatty acids (SFAs, MUFAs, and PUFAs) present in various kinds of dietary fats. Dietary fats high in "good" monounsaturated fatty acids include olive, avocado, and canola oils. ◀ Monounsaturated fatty acids help reduce the stickiness of blood platelets. This helps prevent the formation of blood clots and may also dissolve clots once they form.

Many people do not realize that most tree nuts and peanuts are good sources of MUFAs. The focus on relevancy feature Chemical Connections 19-A—The Fat Content of Tree Nuts and Peanuts—looks at recent research on the fat content of nuts.

Omega-3 and Omega-6 Fatty Acids

In the 1980s, researchers found that the Inuit people of Greenland exhibit a low incidence of heart disease despite having a diet very high in fat. This contrasts markedly with studies on the U.S. population, which show a correlation between a high-fat diet and a high incidence of heart disease. What accounts for the difference between the two peoples? The Inuit diet is high in omega-3 fatty acids (from fish), and the U.S. diet is high in omega-6 fatty acids (from plant oils). An American consumes about double the amount of omega-6 fatty acids and half the amount of omega-3 fatty acids that an Inuit consumes.

Several large studies now confirm that benefits can be derived from eating several servings of fish each week. The choice of fish is important, however. Not all fish are equal in omega-3 fatty acid content. Cold-water fish, also called fatty fish because of the extra amounts of fat they have for insulation against the cold, contain more omega-3 acids than leaner, warm-water fish. Fatty fish include albacore tuna, salmon, and mackerel (Figure 19-9). Leaner, warm-water fish, which include cod, catfish, halibut, sole, and snapper, do not appear to offer as great a positive effect on heart health as do their "fatter" counterparts. (Note that most of the fish used in fish and chips [e.g., cod, halibut] is on the low end of the omega-3 scale.) Table 19-2 gives the actual omega-3 fatty acid concentrations associated with various kinds of cold-water fish.

Recommendations that the U.S. population increase their consumption of cold-water fish has sparked a demand for omega-3 fish oil supplements. Wild salmon populations are the primary source for such oil. With plunging salmon populations due to overfishing, disease, and pollution, concern is rising about a lack of adequate

© Ugo Montaldo/Shutterstock.com

The Fat Content of Tree Nuts and Peanuts

People who bypass the nut tray at holiday parties usually believe a myth—that nuts are *unhealthful* high-fat foods. Indeed, nuts are high-fat food. However, the fat is "good fat" rather than "bad fat" (Section 19-5); that is, the fatty acids present are MUFAs and PUFAs rather than SFAs. In most cases, a handful of nuts is better for you than a cookie or bagel.

Numerous studies now indicate that eating nuts can have a strong protective effect against coronary heart disease. The most improvement comes from adding small amounts of nuts—an ounce (3–4 teaspoons)—to the diet five or more times a week. Raw, dry-roasted, or lightly salted varieties are best.

The recommendation of only one ounce of nuts per day relates to the high calorie content of nuts, which is 160 to 200 calories per ounce. The number of nuts and number of calories per ounce for common types of nuts is as follows:

Nuts	Calories
18 cashews	160
20 peanuts	160
47 pistachios	160
24 almonds	166
14 walnut halves	180
8 Brazil nuts	186
12 hazelnuts	188
15 pecan halves	190
12 macadamias	200

The amount of fat present in nuts ranges from 74% in the macadamia nut, 68% in pecans, and 63% in hazelnuts to around 50% in nuts such as the almond, cashew, peanut, and pistachio, as is shown in the table below.

The different fatty acid fractions (SFAs, MUFAs, and PUFAs) present in nuts also vary, but with definite trends. Unsaturated fatty acids always significantly dominate saturated fatty acids. The unsaturation/saturation ratio is highest for

The fat in nuts is "good fat"; the unsaturated/saturated fatty acid ratio is higher than that in most foods.

hazelnuts (11.9), pecans (10.9), walnuts (9.0), and almonds (9.0) and is lowest for cashews (3.9).

Their low amounts of saturated fatty acids are not the only reason why nuts help reduce the risk of coronary heart disease. Nuts also offer valuable antioxidant vitamins, minerals, and plant fiber protein. The protein content is highest (18%–26%) in the cashew, pistachio, almond, and peanut; here the amount of protein is about the same as in meat, fish, and cheese. The carbohydrate content of nuts is relatively low, less than 10% in most cases.

An unexpected discovery involving the anticancer drug Taxol and hazelnuts was made in the year 2000. The active chemical component in this drug, paclitaxel, was found in hazelnuts. It was the first report of this potent chemical being found in a plant other than in the bark of the Pacific yew tree, a slow-growing plant found in limited quantities in the Pacific Northwest. Although the amount of the chemical found in a hazelnut tree is about one-tenth that found in yew bark, the effort required to extract paclitaxel from these sources is comparable. Because hazelnut trees are more common, this finding could reduce the cost of the commercial drug and make it more readily available.

Fat and Fatty Acid Composition of Selected Nuts

	Total Fat (percentage of weight)	SFA	MUFA	PUFA	UFA/SFA Ratio
		(percentage of total fat)			
almonds	52	10	68	22	9.0
cashews	46	20	62	18	3.9
hazelnuts	63	8	82	10	11.9
macadamias	74	16	82	2	5.4
peanuts	49	15	51	34	5.7
pecans	68	8	66	26	10.9
pistachios	48	13	72	15	6.6
walnuts	62	10	24	66	9.0

▷ Table 19-2 **Omega-3 Fatty Acid Amounts Associated with Various Kinds of Cold-Water Fish**

Per 3.5-oz. Serving (raw)	Omega-3s (grams)*
mackerel	2.3
albacore tuna	2.1
herring, Atlantic	1.6
anchovy	1.5
salmon, wild king (Chinook)	1.4
salmon, wild sockeye (red)	1.2
tuna, bluefin	1.2
salmon, wild pink	1.0
salmon, wild Coho (silver)	0.8
oysters, Pacific	0.7
salmon, farm-raised Atlantic	0.6
swordfish	0.6
trout, rainbow	0.6

*Omega-3 content of fish can vary depending on harvest location and time of year.

fish oil supplies. Research is well advanced in getting "fish oil without any fish." Fish do not make the omega-3 fatty acids they have within themselves. Rather, they obtain these fatty acids from the algae that they feed on. Genetic engineering experiments (Section 22-14) are underway in which the genes that allow algae to synthesize omega-3 fatty acids are incorporated into plants. In the future, plants may become sources for omega-3 fatty acids.

Essential Fatty Acids

An **essential fatty acid** *is a fatty acid needed in the human body that must be obtained from dietary sources because it cannot be synthesized within the body, in adequate amounts, from other substances.* There are two essential fatty acids: *linoleic acid* and *linolenic acid.* Linoleic acid (18:2) is the primary member of the omega-6 acid family, and linolenic acid (18:3) is the primary member of the omega-3 acid family. Their structures are given in Table 19-1.

These two acids (1) are needed for proper membrane structure and (2) serve as starting materials for the production of several biochemically important longer-chain omega-6 and omega-3 acids. When these two acids are missing from the diet, the skin reddens and becomes irritated, infections and dehydration are likely to occur, and the liver may develop abnormalities. If the fatty acids are restored, then the conditions reverse themselves. Infants are especially in need of these acids for their growth. Human breast milk has a much higher percentage of the essential fatty acids than cow's milk.

Linoleic acid is the starting material for the biosynthesis of arachidonic acid.

$$\text{Linoleic acid (18:2)} \longrightarrow \text{arachidonic acid (20:4)}$$
Omega-6 fatty acids

Arachidonic acid is the major starting material for eicosanoids (Section 19-13), substances that help regulate blood pressure, clotting, and several other important body functions.

Linolenic acid is the starting material for the biosynthesis of two additional omega-3 fatty acids.

$$\text{Linolenic acid (18:3)} \longrightarrow \text{EPA (20:5)} \longrightarrow \text{DHA (22:6)}$$
Omega-3 fatty acids

EPA (eicosapentaenoic acid) and DHA (docosahexaenoic acid) are important constituents of the communication membranes of the brain and are necessary for normal brain development. EPA and DHA are also active in the retina of the eye. ◀

Table 19-3 gives pronunciation guidelines for the names of the two essential fatty acids and of the other acids mentioned that are biosynthesized from them.

▶ *In 2001, the FDA gave approval for manufacturers of baby formula to add the fatty acids DHA (docosahexaenoic acid) and AA (arachidonic acid) to infant formulas. Human breast milk naturally contains these acids, which are important in brain and vision development. Because not all mothers can breast-feed, health officials regulate the ingredients in infant formula so that formula-fed babies get the next best thing to mother's milk.*

▶ Table 19-3 **Biochemically Important Omega-3 and Omega-6 Fatty Acids**

Omega-3 Acids	Omega-6 Acids
linolenic acid (18:3) (lin-oh-LEN-ic)	linoleic acid (18:2) (lin-oh-LAY-ic)
eicosapentaenoic acid (20:5) (EYE-cossa-PENTA-ee-NO-ic)	arachidonic acid (20:4) (a-RACK-ih-DON-ic)
docosahexaenoic acid (20:6) (DOE-cossa-HEXA-ee-NO-ic)	

Fat Substitutes (Artificial Fats)

In response to consumer demand for low-fat, low-calorie foods, food scientists have developed several types of "artificial fats." Such substances replicate the taste, texture, and cooking properties of fats but are themselves not lipids. The focus on relevancy feature Chemical Connections 19-B—Fat Substitutes—considers further the topic of fat substitutes ("artificial fats").

Section 19-5 Quick Quiz

1. In terms of human body response to dietary fat, which of the following is considered to be "good fat"?
   a. saturated fats
   b. monounsaturated fats
   c. polyunsaturated fats
   d. no correct response
2. Current dietary recommendations for Americans, relative to omega-3 and omega-6 fatty acids, include a recommended increase in
   a. omega-3 fatty acid intake
   b. omega-6 fatty acid intake
   c. both omega-3 and omega-6 fatty acid intake
   d. no correct response
3. Linolenic acid and linoleic acid, the *essential* fatty acids, are, respectively,
   a. 16:1 and 18:1 fatty acids
   b. 18:1 and 18:2 fatty acids
   c. 18:2 and 18:3 fatty acids
   d. no correct response

Answers: 1. b; 2. a; 3. c

19-6 Chemical Reactions of Triacylglycerols

LEARNING FOCUS

Be familiar with four major types of chemical reactions that triacylglycerols undergo: hydrolysis, saponification, hydrogenation, and oxidation.

The chemical properties of triacylglycerols (fats and oils) are typical of esters and alkenes because these are the two functional groups present in triacylglycerols. Four important triacylglycerol reactions are hydrolysis, saponification, hydrogenation, and oxidation.

Hydrolysis

Hydrolysis of a triacylglycerol is the reverse of the esterification reaction by which it was formed (see Figure 19-5). Triacylglycerol hydrolysis, when carried out in a laboratory setting, requires the presence of an acid or a base. Under acidic conditions, the hydrolysis products are glycerol and fatty acids. Under basic conditions, the hydrolysis products are glycerols and fatty acid salts.

Fat Substitutes

Sugar substitutes (artificial sweeteners) have been an accepted part of the diet of most people for many years. New since the 1990s are fat substitutes—substances that create the sensations of "richness" of taste and "creaminess" of texture in food without the negative effects associated with dietary fats (heart disease and obesity). Today, in most grocery stores, sitting next to almost all high-fat foods on the shelf are lower-fat counterparts (see accompanying photo). In most cases, the lower-fat products contain fat substitutes.

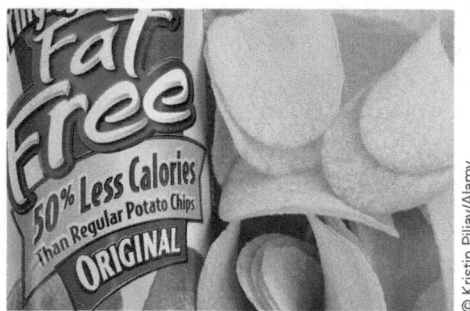

Foods that contain fat substitutes have less fat but not necessarily fewer calories.

Food scientists have been developing fat substitutes since the 1960s. Now available for consumer use are two types of fat substitutes: *calorie-reduced* fat substitutes and *calorie-free* substitutes. They differ in their chemical structures and therefore in how the body handles them.

Simplesse, the best-known calorie-reduced fat substitute, received FDA marketing approval in 1990. It is made from the protein of fresh egg whites and milk by a procedure called microparticulation. This procedure produces tiny, round protein particles so fine that the tongue perceives them as a fluid rather than as the solid they are. Their fineness creates a sensation of smoothness, richness, and creaminess on the tongue.

In the body, Simplesse is digested and absorbed, contributing to energy intake. But 1 g of Simplesse provides 1.3 cal, compared with the 9 cal provided by 1 g of fat. Simplesse is used only to replace fats in *formulated* foods such as salad dressings, cheeses, sour creams, and other dairy products. Simplesse is unsuitable for frying or baking because it turns rubbery or rigid (gels) when heated. Consequently, it is not available for home use.

Olestra, the best-known calorie-free fat substitute, received FDA marketing approval in 1996. It is produced by heating cottonseed and/or soybean oil with sucrose in the presence of methyl alcohol. Chemically, olestra has a structure somewhat similar to that of a triacylglycerol; sucrose takes the place of the glycerol molecule, and six to eight fatty acids are attached by ester linkages to it rather than the three fatty acids in a triacylglycerol.

Olestra.
R represents fatty acids.

Unlike triacylglycerols, however, olestra cannot be hydrolyzed by the body's digestive enzymes nor processed by colonic bacteria, and therefore passes through the digestive tract undigested.

Olestra looks, feels, and tastes like dietary fat and can substitute for fats and oils in foods such as shortenings, oils, margarines, snacks, ice creams, and other desserts. It has the same cooking properties as fats and oils.

In the digestive tract, Olestra interferes with the absorption of both dietary and body-produced cholesterol; thus it may lower total cholesterol levels. A problem with its use is that it also reduces the absorption of the fat-soluble vitamins A, D, E, and K. To avoid such depletion, Olestra is fortified with these vitamins. Another problem with Olestra use is that in some individuals it can cause gastrointestinal irritation and/or diarrhea. All products containing Olestra must carry the following label: "Olestra may cause abdominal cramping and loose stools. Olestra inhibits the absorption of some vitamins and other nutrients. Vitamins A, D, E, and K have been added."

The terminology used to describe products that contain fat substitutes can be confusing. Fat-free means less than 0.5 g of fat per serving. Low-fat means 3 g or less fat per 50 g serving. Reduced-fat or less-fat means at least 25% less fat per serving than the "regular" food. Calorie-free means less than 0.5 kilocalories per serving.

▶ *Naturally occurring mono- and diacylglycerols are seldom encountered. Synthetic mono- and diacylglycerols are used as emulsifiers in many food products. Emulsifiers prevent suspended particles in colloidal solutions (Section 8-7) from coalescing and settling. Emulsifiers are usually present in so-called fat-free cakes and other fat-free products.*

Within the human body, triacylglycerol hydrolysis occurs during the process of digestion. Such hydrolysis requires the help of enzymes (protein catalysts; Section 21-1) produced by the pancreas. These enzymes cause the triacylglycerol to be hydrolyzed in a stepwise fashion. First, one of the outer fatty acids is removed, producing a *diacylglycerol,* then the other outer one is removed, to produce a *monoacylglycerol.* In most cases, the monoacylglycerol is the end product of the initial digestion (enzymatic hydrolysis) of the triacylglycerol. Sometimes, enzymes remove all three fatty acids, leaving a free molecule of glycerol. ◀

Complete hydrolysis

Figure 19-10 Complete and partial hydrolysis of a triacylglycerol.

a Complete hydrolysis of a triacylglycerol produces glycerol and three fatty acid molecules.

Partial hydrolysis

b Partial hydrolysis (during digestion) of a triacylglycerol produces a monoacylglycerol and two fatty acid molecules.

In situations where all three fatty acids are removed, the hydrolysis process is referred to as *complete hydrolysis,* which is depicted in Figure 19-10a. If one or more of the fatty acid residues remains attached to the glycerol, the hydrolysis process is called *partial hydrolysis* (Figure 19-10b).

EXAMPLE 19-3

Writing a Structural Equation for the Acidic Hydrolysis of a Triacylglycerol

Write an equation for the acid-catalyzed hydrolysis of the following triacylglycerol:

$$
\begin{array}{c}
\quad\quad\quad\quad O \\
\quad\quad\quad\quad \| \\
CH_2-O-C\;\text{/\\/\\/\\/\\/} \\
| \\
\quad\quad\quad\quad O \\
\quad\quad\quad\quad \| \\
CH-O-C\;\text{/\\/\\/\\/} \\
| \\
\quad\quad\quad\quad O \\
\quad\quad\quad\quad \| \\
CH_2-O-C\;\text{/\\/\\/\\/}
\end{array}
$$

(continued)

Solution

Three water molecules are required for complete hydrolysis, one to interact with each of the ester linkages present in the triacylglycerol. Breaking of the three ester linkages produces four product molecules: glycerol and three fatty acids.

Saponification

Saponification (Section 16-16) is a hydrolysis reaction carried out in an alkaline (basic) solution. For fats and oils, the products of saponification are glycerol and fatty acid *salts*. ◀

The overall reaction of triacylglycerol saponification can be thought of as occurring in two steps. The first step is the hydrolysis of the ester linkages to produce glycerol and three fatty acid molecules:

Fat or oil + 3H$_2$O ⟶ 3 fatty acids + glycerol

The second step involves a reaction between the fatty acid molecules and the base (usually NaOH) in the alkaline solution. This is an acid–base reaction that produces water plus salts:

3 fatty acids + 3NaOH ⟶ 3 fatty acid salts + 3H$_2$O

Saponification of animal fat is the process by which soap was made in pioneer times. Soapmaking involved heating lard (fat) with lye (ashes of wood, an impure form of KOH). Today most soap is prepared by hydrolyzing fats and oils (animal fat and coconut oil) under high pressure and high temperature. Sodium carbonate is used as the base.

The cleansing action of soap is related to the structure of the carboxylate ions present in the fatty acid salts of soap and the fact that these ions readily participate in micelle formation. A **micelle** *is a spherical cluster of molecules in which the polar portions of the molecules are on the surface, and the nonpolar portions are located in the interior.* The focus on relevancy feature Chemical Connections 19-C—The Cleansing Action of Soap and Detergents—further discusses micelle formation as it relates to the cleansing action of soap.

Hydrogenation

Hydrogenation is a chemical reaction first encountered in Section 13-10. It involves hydrogen addition across carbon–carbon multiple bonds, which increases the degree of saturation as some multiple bonds are converted to single bonds. With this change, there is a corresponding increase in the melting point of the substance.

Hydrogenation involving just one carbon–carbon bond within a fatty acid residue of a triacylglycerol can be diagrammed as follows:

▶ *Recall from Section 16-8 the structural difference between a carboxylic acid and a carboxylic acid salt.*

The Cleansing Action of Soap and Detergents

Soaps are carboxylic acid salts (Section 16-8). They are thus ionic compounds, as are all salts. A representative structural formula for a carboxylic acid salt is

$$CH_3-CH_2-CH_2-CH_2-CH_2-CH_2-CH_2-CH_2-CH_2-CH_2-CH_2-CH_2-CH_2-CH_2-CH_2-CH_2-CH_2-\overset{\overset{\displaystyle O}{\|}}{C}-O^-Na^+$$

Detergents are also acid salts. They are, however, salts of sulfonic acids rather than carboxylic acids. Detergents were initially developed during World War II, a time when carboxylic acid supplies available for soapmaking were very limited. Sulfonic acids were used as substitutes for carboxylic acids. The general structures for a sulfonic acid and a carboxylic acid (for comparison purposes) are

$$\overset{\overset{\displaystyle O}{\|}}{\underset{\underset{\displaystyle O}{\|}}{R-S-OH}} \qquad \overset{\overset{\displaystyle O}{\|}}{R-C-OH}$$

Sulfonic acid   Carboxylic acid

Detergents are synthetic structural analogs of soaps, as the following representative structural formula for a detergent molecule shows.

$$CH_3-CH_2-CH_2-CH_2-CH_2-CH_2-CH_2-CH_2-CH_2-CH_2-CH_2-CH_2-CH_2-CH_2-CH_2-CH_2-CH_2-\overset{\overset{\displaystyle O}{\|}}{\underset{\underset{\displaystyle O}{\|}}{S}}-O^-Na^+$$

Structurally, both soaps and detergents contain a very small positive ion (usually Na^+ or K^+) and a negative ion that contains a very long carbon chain. The negative ion is the "active ingredient" in both soaps and detergents. In aqueous solution, salt dissociation occurs, which releases the salt's constituent ions. This allows the carboxylate ions (soaps) and sulfonate ions (detergents) present to exert their effects.

The cleansing action of soaps and detergents relates to the "dual polarity" that carboxylate and sulfonate ions possess. The long carbon chain present, which is called the "tail" of the ion, is nonpolar, whereas the small oxygen-containing group present, which is called the "head" of the ion, is polar.

Long carbon chain — oxygen-containing group
Nonpolar tail   Polar head

Nonpolar substances, such as fats, oils, and greases, are insoluble in water. Soap or detergent affects the solubility of such substances in water. The nonpolar "tail" of the soap or detergent molecule interacts with (dissolves in) the insoluble nonpolar substance, while the polar "head" of the soap or detergent molecule interacts with polar water molecules. The soap or detergent thus overcomes the nonpolar–polar solubility barrier.

Soaps and detergents solubilize oily and greasy materials in the following manner: The nonpolar portion of the carboxylate or sulfonate ion dissolves in the nonpolar oil or grease, and the polar portion maintains its solubility in the polar water.

The penetration of the oil or grease by the nonpolar end of the carboxylate or sulfonate ion is followed by the formation of micelles (see the accompanying diagram). The carboxyl or sulfonyl groups (micelle exterior) and water molecules are attracted to each other, causing the solubilizing of the micelle.

The micelles do not combine into larger drops because their surfaces are all negatively charged, and like charges repel each other. The water-soluble micelles are subsequently rinsed away, leaving a material devoid of oil and grease.

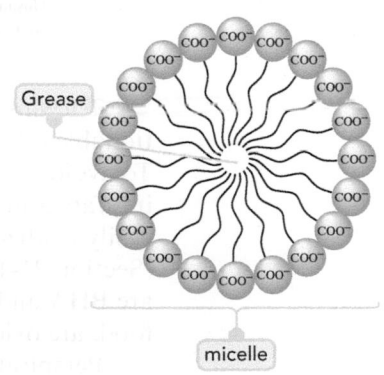

The structural equation for the complete hydrogenation of a triacylglycerol in which all three fatty acid residues are oleic acid (18:1) is shown in Figure 19-11.

Many food products are produced via partial hydrogenation. In partial hydrogenation, some, but not all, of the double bonds present are converted into single bonds. In this manner, liquids (usually plant oils) are converted into semi-solid materials.

Figure 19-11 Structural equation for the complete hydrogenation of a triacylglycerol with oleic acid (18:1) fatty acid residues.

Peanut butter is produced from peanut oil through partial hydrogenation. Solid cooking shortenings and stick margarine are produced from liquid plant oils through partial hydrogenation. Soft-spread margarines are also partial-hydrogenation products. Here, the extent of hydrogenation is carefully controlled to make the margarine soft at refrigerator temperatures (4°C). Concern has arisen about food products obtained from hydrogenation processes because the hydrogenation process itself converts some *cis* double bonds within fatty acid residues into *trans* double bonds, producing *trans* unsaturated fatty acids. The focus on relevancy feature Chemical Connections 19-D—*Trans* Fatty Acid Content of Foods—further explores the subject of *trans* fatty acids (TFAs) in food.

Oxidation

The carbon–carbon double bonds present in the fatty acid residues of a triacylglycerol are subject to oxidation with molecular oxygen (from air) as the oxidizing agent. Such oxidation breaks these bonds, producing both aldehyde and carboxylic acid products. ◄

▶ *Antioxidants are compounds that are easily oxidized. When added to foods, they are more easily oxidized than the food. Thus they prevent the food from being oxidized (see Section 14-14).*

The short-chain aldehydes and carboxylic acids so produced often have objectionable odors, and fats and oils containing them are said to have become *rancid*. To avoid this unwanted oxidation process, commercially prepared foods containing fats and oils nearly always contain *antioxidants*—substances that are more easily oxidized than the food. Two naturally occurring antioxidants are vitamin C (Section 21-12) and vitamin E (Section 21-13). Two synthetic oxidation inhibitors are BHA and BHT (Section 14-13). In the presence of air, antioxidants, rather than food, are oxidized.

Perspiration generated by strenuous exercise or by "hot and muggy" climatic conditions contains numerous triacylglycerols (oils). Rapid oxidation of these oils, promoted by microorganisms on the skin, generates the body odor that accompanies most "sweaty" people (Figure 19-12).

Trans Fatty Acid Content of Foods

All current dietary recommendations stress reducing saturated fat intake because of its association with elevated blood cholesterol levels. In accordance with such recommendations, many people have switched from butter to margarine and use partially hydrogenated vegetable oils rather than animal fat for cooking. Research now indicates that partially hydrogenated vegetable oil use in cooking, particularly in deep-frying, has negative health implications associated with it. Why is this so?

When the triacylglycerols in vegetable oils are subjected to partial hydrogenation (Section 19-6), two types of changes, rather than just one (as was previously thought), occur in the fatty acid residues present: (1) some of the *cis* double bonds present are converted to single bonds (the objective of the process) and (2) some of the remaining *cis* double bonds are converted to *trans* double bonds (an unanticipated result of the process). These latter *cis–trans* conversions affect the general shape of the fatty acid residues present in triacylglycerols, which in turn affects the biochemical behavior of the triacylglycerols. In the following diagram, note how conversion of a *cis,cis*-18:2 fatty acid to a *trans,trans*-18:2 fatty acid affects molecular shape. The *trans,trans*-18:2 fatty acid has a shape very much like that of an 18:0 saturated fatty acid (the last structure).

18:2 *(cis, cis)*

18:2 *(trans–trans)*

18:0

Studies show that fats containing fatty acids with *trans*-double bonds (commonly referred to as *trans* fats) affect blood cholesterol levels in a negative manner, similar, but not identical, to that of saturated fats. *Trans* fat raises bad (LDL) cholesterol (see Section 20-19), but it does not raise good (HDL) cholesterol (see Section 20-19). Saturated fat, on the other hand, raises both good and bad cholesterol. Thus, just as too much dietary saturated fat intake isn't healthy, too much dietary *trans* fat intake is also not healthy. Some trans fatty acids (TFAs) are naturally present in meat and dairy products. It is estimated that such TFAs constitute 15%–20% of dietary TFA intake. The remaining 80%–85% of TFAs dietary intake comes primarily from commercially produced foods prepared using partially hydrogenated cooking oils.

Major efforts are now in progress to draw attention to the presence of *trans* fats in food products and to reduce the use of partially hydrogenated vegetable oils, the major source of such fats. Since 2006, the U.S. Food and Drug Administration (FDA) has required that the *trans* fat content of a food be included in the nutrition facts panel found on all food products.

FDA regulations now require that trans fat content be listed as a separate item on nutrition facts labels.

A label of "zero grams *trans* fat per serving" on a product does not mean the product is absolutely *trans* fat free. FDA regulations allow *trans* fat levels of less than 0.5 gram per serving to be labeled as 0 grams per serving. Also, naturally occurring *trans* fats present are not required to be included in *trans* fat values.

Efforts to improve the fatty acid profile of foods by reducing their TFA content or by changing the relative amounts of various types of naturally occurring fatty acids present have occurred and are still occurring on numerous fronts including the following:

1. In deep-frying applications, traditional vegetable oils, such as olive, canola, corn, and soy oils, in their unprocessed form, are now used as replacements for the previously used partially hydrogenated vegetable oils that were high in *trans* fats. The switch to traditional vegetable oil use has occurred despite the drawback that these oils spoil more readily than do partially hydrogenated oils and thus have shorter useful lives.

2. In applications where a semi-soft fat is needed such as in margarine and baking, oils rich in unsaturated fatty acids are now *completely* hydrogenated rather than *partially* hydrogenated producing a completely saturated product which is *trans* fat free. This saturated product is then blended with unprocessed vegetable oil to produce a semi-soft fat.

3. Researchers, using genetic engineering techniques (Section 22-15), have inserted genes into soybean plants that block the formation of enzymes (Section 21-1) needed to convert monounsaturated fatty acids to polyunsaturated fatty acids, resulting the accumulation of desirable monounsaturated fatty acids at the expense of less desirable polyunsaturated acids. Such genetically modified soybeans produce oils that also have a lower saturated fatty acid content.

EXAMPLE 19-4

Determining the Products for Reactions That Triacylglycerols Undergo

Using words rather than structural formulas, characterize the products formed when the following triacylglycerol undergoes the reactions listed.

(18:0 fatty acid residue)

(18:1 fatty acid residue)

(18:2 fatty acid residue)

a. Complete hydrolysis
b. Complete saponification using NaOH
c. Complete hydrogenation

Solution

a. When a triacylglycerol undergoes complete hydrolysis, there are four organic products: glycerol and three fatty acids. For the given triacylglycerol, the products are *glycerol, an* 18:0 *fatty acid, an* 18:1 *fatty acid,* and *an* 18:2 *fatty acid.* Three molecules of water are also consumed.
b. When a triacylglycerol undergoes complete saponification, there are four organic products: glycerol and three fatty acid salts. For the given triacylglycerol, with NaOH as the base involved in the saponification, the products are *glycerol, the sodium salt of the* 18:0 *fatty acid, the sodium salt of the* 18:1 *fatty acid,* and *the sodium salt of the* 18:2 *fatty acid.*
c. Complete hydrogenation will change the given triacylglycerol into a *triacylglycerol in which all three fatty acid residues are* 18:0 *fatty acid residues.* That is, all of the fatty acid residues are completely saturated (there are no carbon–carbon double bonds).

The Chemistry at a Glance—Classification Schemes for Fatty Acid Residues Present in Triacylglycerols—contains a summary of the terminology used in characterizing the properties of the fatty acid residues that are part of the structure of triacylglycerols (fats and oils).

Figure 19-12 The oils (triacylglycerols) present in skin perspiration rapidly undergo oxidation. The oxidation products, short-chain aldehydes and short-chain carboxylic acids, often have strong odors.

Section 19-6 Quick Quiz

1. One molecule of a fat or oil, upon complete hydrolysis, produces how many product molecules?
   a. two
   b. three
   c. four
   d. no correct responses
2. Triacylglycerol hydrolysis associated with the human digestive process most often produces which of the following?
   a. a diacylglycerol
   b. a monoacylglycerol
   c. glycerol
   d. no correct response

CHEMISTRY AT A GLANCE   Classification Schemes for Fatty Acid Residues Present in Triacylglycerols

FATTY ACIDS
- Most contain an even number of carbon atoms.
- Carbon chain length is up to 24 carbon atoms.

Classification Based on Degree of Unsaturation

SATURATED	**MONOUNSATURATED**	**POLYUNSATURATED**
- No double bonds are present in the carbon chain. - Dietary effect is an increase in heart disease risk.	- One double bond is present in the carbon chain. - Dietary effect is a decrease in heart disease risk.	- Two or more double bonds are present in the carbon chain. - Dietary effect is "mixed"; there have been several conflicting studies relative to heart disease risk.

Classification Based on Configuration of Double Bond

CIS	***TRANS***
- Naturally occurring fatty acids generally contain *cis* double bonds.	- Hydrogenation converts some *cis* double bonds to *trans* double bonds. - *Trans* fatty acids have effects on blood chemistry similar to those of saturated fatty acids.

Classification Based on Location of Double Bond

OMEGA-3	**OMEGA-6**
- First double bond is three carbons away from the CH_3 end of the carbon chain. - Linolenic acid (18:3) is the primary member of this family.	- First double bond is six carbons away from the CH_3 end of the carbon chain. - Linoleic acid (18:2) is the primary member of this family.

3. Which of the following are the expected products when a fat undergoes saponification?
   a. glycerol and fatty acids
   b. glycerol and fatty acid salts
   c. fatty acids and fatty acid salts
   d. no correct response
4. Unwanted production of *trans* fats is associated with which of the following types of triacylglycerol reactions?
   a. saponification
   b. hydrogenation
   c. oxidation
   d. no correct response
5. The effect of *partial* hydrogenation of a fat or oil is which of the following?
   a. decrease in the degree of fatty acid unsaturation
   b. decrease in melting point of the fat or oil
   c. increase in the number of fatty acid residues present in a molecule
   d. no correct response
6. In the oxidation of fats and oils, which structural part of the molecule is attacked by the oxidizing agent?
   a. carbon–carbon double bonds
   b. carbon–carbon single bonds
   c. ester linkages
   d. no correct response

Answers: 1. c; 2. b; 3. b; 4. b; 5. a; 6. a

19-7 Membrane Lipids: Phospholipids

LEARNING FOCUS

Know the general structural characteristics for glycerophospholipids and sphingophospholipids; be able to relate phospholipid structures to the "head and two tails" model for such structures.

All cells are surrounded by a membrane that confines their contents. Up to 80% of the mass of a cell membrane can be lipid materials; the rest is primarily protein. It is membranes that give cells their individuality by separating them from their environment.

There are three common types of membrane lipids: phospholipids, sphingoglycolipids, and cholesterol. Phospholipids are considered in this section and the other two types of membrane lipids in the next two sections.

Phospholipids are the most abundant type of membrane lipid. A **phospholipid** *is a lipid that contains one or more fatty acids, a phosphate group, a platform molecule to which the fatty acid(s) and the phosphate group are attached, and an alcohol that is attached to the phosphate group.* The platform molecule on which a phospholipid is built may be the 3-carbon alcohol *glycerol* or a more complex C_{18} ▶ *An aminodialcohol contains two hydroxyl groups, —OH, and an amino group, —NH₂.* aminodialcohol called *sphingosine.* ◀ Glycerol-based phospholipids are called *glycerophospholipids,* and those based on sphingosine are called *sphingophospholipids.* The general block diagrams for a glycerophospholipid and a sphingophospholipid are as follows:

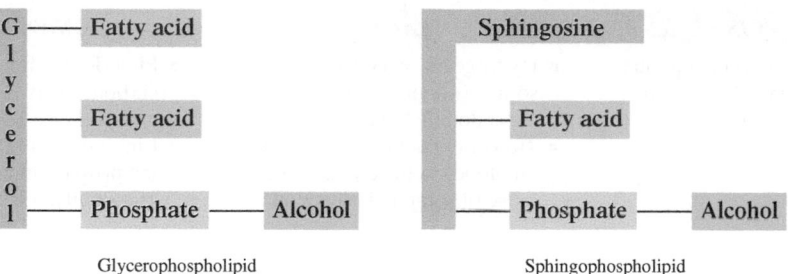

Glycerophospholipid   Sphingophospholipid

Glycerophospholipids

A **glycerophospholipid** *is a lipid that contains two fatty acids and a phosphate group esterified to a glycerol molecule and an alcohol esterified to the phosphate group.* All attachments (bonds) between groups in a glycerophospholipid are ester linkages, a situation similar to that in triacylglycerols (Section 19-4). However, glycerophospholipids have four ester linkages as contrasted to three ester linkages in triacylglycerols.

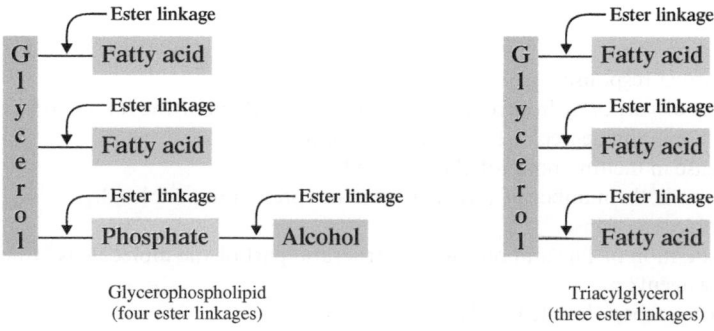

Glycerophospholipid
(four ester linkages)

Triacylglycerol
(three ester linkages)

Because of the ester linkages present, glycerophospholipids undergo hydrolysis and saponification reactions in a manner similar to that for triacylglycerols (Section 19-6). There are five reaction products, however, instead of the four for triacylglycerols.

Phosphoric acid is the parent source for the minus one charged phosphate group used in the formation of glycerophospholipids. The structures of these two entities are

$$
\begin{array}{cc}
\underset{\text{Phosphoric acid}}{HO-\overset{\displaystyle O}{\overset{\|}{P}}-OH} & \underset{\substack{\text{Minus one charged} \\ \text{phosphate group}}}{HO-\overset{\displaystyle O}{\overset{\|}{P}}-OH}
\\
OH & O^{-}
\end{array}
$$

Phosphoric acid structures were previously considered in Section 16-20 when esters of inorganic acids were considered.

The alcohol attached to the phosphate group in a glycophospholipid is usually one of three amino alcohols: choline, ethanolamine, or serine. The structures of these three amino alcohols, given in terms of the charged forms (Sections 17-8 and 20-4) that they adopt in neutral solution, are

$$
HO-CH_2-CH_2-\overset{+}{N}(CH_3)_3 \qquad HO-CH_2-CH_2-\overset{+}{N}H_3 \qquad HO-CH_2-\underset{\underset{COO^-}{|}}{CH}-\overset{+}{N}H_3
$$

Choline	Ethanolamine	Serine
(a quaternary ammonium ion)	(positive-ion form)	(two ionic groups present)

Glycerophospholipids containing these three amino alcohols are respectively known as phosphatidylcholines, phosphatidylethanolamines, and phosphatidylserines. The fatty acid, glycerol, and phosphate portions of a glycerophospholipid structure constitute a *phosphatidyl* group.

EXAMPLE 19-5

Drawing the Structural Formula for a Glycerophospholipid

Draw the structural formula for the glycerophospholipid that produces, upon hydrolysis, equimolar amounts of glycerol, phosphoric acid, and ethanolamine, and twice that molar amount of stearic acid, the 18:0 fatty acid.

Solution

The fact that the molar amount of stearic acid produced is twice that of the other products indicates that both fatty acid residues present in the glycerophospholipid are stearic acid residues.

To draw the structural formula for this lipid, arrange the component parts in the following manner. Draw on the left the structure of glycerol, the "backbone" of the structure. Then place alongside it the two stearic acid and one phosphoric acid molecules. The acid placements should be such that their acid groups are lined up alongside the hydroxyl groups of glycerol. Then place the ion form of ethanolamine alongside the phosphoric acid molecule.

$$
\begin{array}{ll}
CH_2-OH & HO-\overset{\displaystyle O}{\overset{\|}{C}}/\!/\!/\!/\!/\!/\!/\!/ \\[2ex]
CH-OH & HO-\overset{\displaystyle O}{\overset{\|}{C}}/\!/\!/\!/\!/\!/\!/\!/ \\[2ex]
CH_2-OH & HO-\underset{\underset{O^-}{|}}{\overset{\displaystyle O}{\overset{\|}{P}}}-OH \qquad HO-CH_2-CH_2-\overset{+}{N}H_3
\end{array}
$$

The five components of the overall structure are then bonded together via ester linkages. The product of the formation of each ester linkage is a molecule of water.

(continued)

The atoms involved in this water formation are highlighted in color in the structures at the left and the ester linkages formed are highlighted in color in the structure at the right.

$$CH_2-OH \quad HO-\overset{\overset{O}{\|}}{C} \diagdown\!\!\!\diagup\!\!\!\diagdown\!\!\!\diagup \qquad\qquad CH_2-O-\overset{\overset{O}{\|}}{C} \diagdown\!\!\!\diagup\!\!\!\diagdown\!\!\!\diagup$$

$$CH-OH \quad HO-\overset{\overset{O}{\|}}{C} \diagdown\!\!\!\diagup\!\!\!\diagdown\!\!\!\diagup \quad \Longrightarrow \quad 4H_2O \;+\; CH-O-\overset{\overset{O}{\|}}{C} \diagdown\!\!\!\diagup\!\!\!\diagdown\!\!\!\diagup$$

$$CH_2-OH \quad HO-\underset{\underset{O^-}{|}}{\overset{\overset{O}{\|}}{P}}-OH \quad HO-CH_2-CH_2-\overset{+}{N}H_3 \qquad CH_2-O-\underset{\underset{O^-}{|}}{\overset{\overset{O}{\|}}{P}}-O-CH_2-CH_2-\overset{+}{N}H_3$$

▶ *The amino alcohol in phosphatidylcholines (pronounced fahs-fuh-TIDE-ul-KOH-leens) is choline.*

Phosphatidylcholines are also known as *lecithins*. There are a number of different phosphatidylcholines because different fatty acids may be bonded to the glycerol portion of the phosphatidylcholine structure. ◀ In general, phosphatidylcholines are waxy solids that form colloidal suspensions in water. Egg yolks and soybeans are good dietary sources of these lipids. Within the body, phosphatidylcholines are prevalent in cell membranes.

Periodically, claims arise that phosphatidylcholine should be taken as a nutritive supplement; some even maintain it will improve memory. There is no evidence that these supplements are useful. The enzyme *lecithinase* in the intestine hydrolyzes most of the phosphatidylcholine taken orally before it passes into body fluids, so it does not reach body tissues. The phosphatidylcholine present in cell membranes is made by the liver; thus phosphatidylcholines are not essential nutrients.

The food industry uses phosphatidylcholines as emulsifiers to promote the mixing of otherwise immiscible materials. Mayonnaise, ice cream, and custards are some of the products they are found in.

Phosphatidylethanolamines and phosphatidylserines are also known as *cephalins*. These compounds are found in heart and liver tissue and in high concentrations in the brain. They are important in blood clotting. Much is yet to be learned about how these compounds function within the human body.

Although the general structural features of glycerophospholipids are similar in many respects to those of triacylglycerols, these two types of lipids have quite different biochemical functions. Triacylglycerols serve as storage molecules for metabolic fuel. Glycerophospholipids function almost exclusively as components of cell membranes (Section 19-10) and are not stored. A major structural difference between the two types of lipids, that of polarity, is related to their differing biochemical functions. Triacylglycerols are a nonpolar class of lipids, whereas glycerophospholipids are polar. In general, membrane lipids have polarity associated with their structures.

Further consideration of general glycerophospholipid structure reveals an additional structural characteristic of most membrane lipids. A phosphatidylcholine containing stearic and oleic acids will be used to illustrate this additional feature. The chemical structure of this molecule is shown in Figure 19-13a.

A molecular model for this compound, which gives the orientation of groups in space, is illustrated in Figure 19-13b. There are two important things to notice about this model: (1) There is a "head" part, the choline and phosphate and (2) there are two "tails," the two fatty acid carbon chains. The head part is polar. The two tails, the carbon chains, are nonpolar.

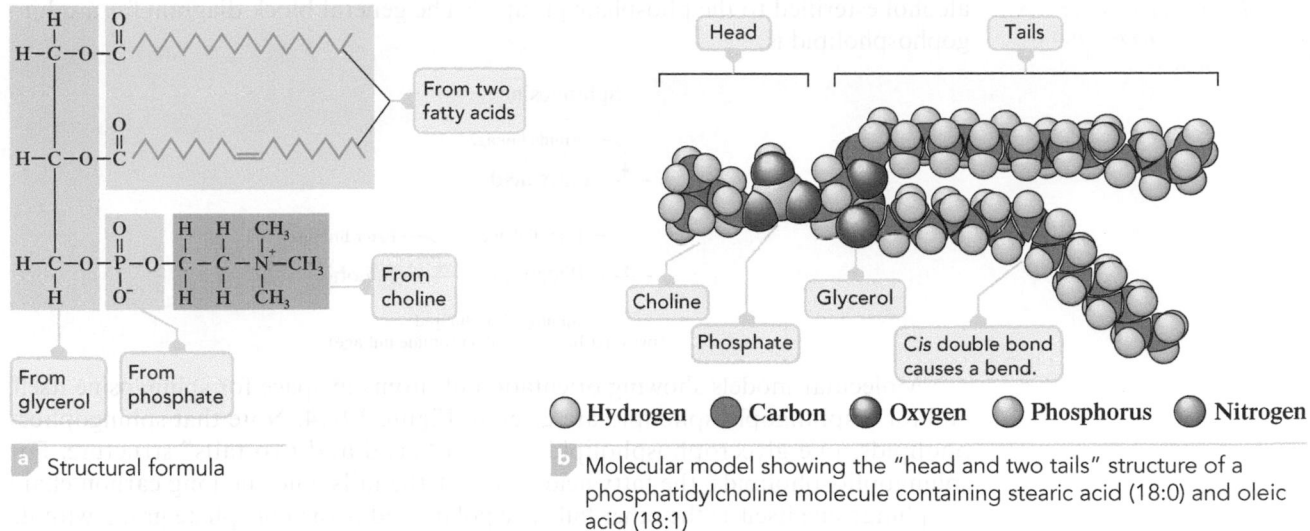

a Structural formula

b Molecular model showing the "head and two tails" structure of a phosphatidylcholine molecule containing stearic acid (18:0) and oleic acid (18:1)

Figure 19-13 Models showing the "head and two tails" arrangement of structural subunits in a phosphatidylcholine molecule.

All glycerophospholipids have structures similar to that shown in Figure 19-13. All have a "head" and two "tails." A simplified representation for this structure uses a circle to represent the polar head and two wavy lines to represent the nonpolar tails.

The polar head group of a glycerophospholipid is soluble in water. The nonpolar tail chains are insoluble in water but soluble in nonpolar substances. This dual polarity, which was previously encountered when soaps were discussed (see Chemical Connections 19-C—The Cleansing Action of Soap and Detergents), is a structural characteristic of most membrane lipids.

The structural portion of a glycerophospholipid that is compatible with water (soluble), the polar head in this case, is said to be *hydrophilic* (water-loving). A **hydrophilic group** *is the polar portion of a molecule that is attracted to water and is able to mix with it.* The structural portion of a glycerophospholipid that is not compatible with water (insoluble), the nonpolar tails in this case, is said to be *hydrophobic* (water-fearing). A **hydrophobic group** *is the nonpolar portion of a molecule that has little or no attraction for water and is unable to mix with it.*

Sphingophospholipids

Sphingophospholipids have structures based on the 18-carbon monounsaturated amino-dialcohol *sphingosine.* ◄ A **sphingophospholipid** *is a lipid that contains one fatty acid and one phosphate group attached to a sphingosine molecule and an alcohol attached to the phosphate group.*

The structure of sphingosine, the platform molecule for a sphingophospholipid, is

$$CH_3-(CH_2)_{12}-CH=CH-CH-CH-CH_2$$
$$\qquad\qquad\qquad\quad\; OH \quad NH_2 \quad OH$$

Sphingosine

All phospholipids derived from sphingosine have (1) the fatty acid attached to the sphingosine —NH$_2$ group via an *amide linkage,* (2) the phosphate group attached to the sphingosine terminal —OH group via an *ester linkage,* and (3) an additional

▶ *When sphingolipids were discovered over a century ago by the physician–chemist Johann Thudichum (1829–1901), their biochemical role seemed as enigmatic as the Sphinx, for which he named them.*

▶ *The double bond present in the sphingosine carbon chain is a* trans *double bond.*

alcohol esterified to the phosphate group. ◀ The general block diagram for a sphingophospholipid is

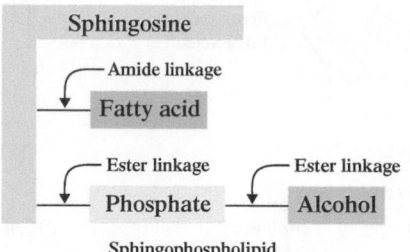

Sphingophospholipid
(two ester linkages and one amide linkage)

Molecular models showing orientation of atoms in space for sphingosine itself and for a sphingophospholipid are given in Figure 19-14. Note that sphingophospholipids, like glycerophospholipids, have a "head and two tails" structure. For sphingophospholipids, the fatty acid is one of the tails, and the long carbon chain of sphingosine itself is the other tail. The polar head is the phosphate group with its esterified alcohol. The two tails of a sphingophospholipid are hydrophobic and its head is hydrophilic, a parallel situation to that found in glycerophospholipids. ◀

▶ *In sphingophospholipids, the first three carbon atoms at the polar end of sphingosine are analogous to the three carbon atoms of glycerol in glycerophospholipids.*

Like glycerophospholipids, sphingophospholipid participate in hydrolysis and saponification reactions. Amide linkages behave much as ester linkages do in this type of reaction.

Sphingophospholipids in which the alcohol esterified to the phosphate group is *choline* are called *sphingomyelins*. Sphingomyelins are found in all cell membranes and are important structural components of the myelin sheath, the protective and insulating coating that surrounds nerves. The molecule depicted in Figure 19-14b is a sphingomyelin. The structural formula for a sphingomyelin in which stearic acid (18:0) is the fatty acid is

Sphingosine ⟶

$$HO-CH-CH=CH-(CH_2)_{12}-CH_3$$

$$CH-NH-\overset{\overset{\displaystyle O}{\|}}{C}-(CH_2)_{16}-CH_3$$

Stearic acid (18:0)

$$CH_2-O-\overset{\overset{\displaystyle O}{\|}}{\underset{\underset{\displaystyle O^-}{|}}{P}}-O-CH_2-CH_2-\overset{\overset{\displaystyle CH_3}{|}}{\underset{\underset{\displaystyle CH_3}{|}}{\overset{+}{N}}}-CH_3$$

Phosphate   Choline

Figure 19-14 Molecular models for (a) sphingosine and (b) a sphingophospholipid. The particular sphingophospholipid shown has choline as the alcohol esterified to the phosphate group. Note the "head and two tails" structure for the sphingophospholipid.

Sphingosine carbon chain

Fatty acid carbon chain

Polar head   Nonpolar tails

a Sphingosine   b A sphingophospholipid

Section 19-7 Quick Quiz

1. Based on biological function, phospholipids are classified as
   a. energy-storage lipids
   b. membrane lipids
   c. messenger lipids
   d. no correct response
2. Which of the following types of lipids contain both ester and amide linkages?
   a. triacylglycerols
   b. sphingophospholipids
   c. glycerophospholipids
   d. no correct response
3. Which of the following statements about the molecule sphingosine is *correct*?
   a. Two amino groups and one hydroxyl group are present.
   b. Two hydroxyl groups and one amino group are present.
   c. Two hydroxyl groups and two amino groups are present.
   d. no correct response
4. When the "head and two tails" structural model is applied to a glycerophospholipid, the two tails are
   a. both fatty acid residues
   b. a fatty acid residue and a phosphate group
   c. the phosphate group and the glycerol backbone
   d. no correct response
5. When the "head and two tails" structural model is applied to a sphingophospholipid, the two tails are
   a. the fatty acid residue and the phosphate group
   b. the fatty acid residue and part of the sphingosine molecule
   c. the phosphate group and part of the sphingosine molecule
   d. no correct response
6. In terms of the "head and two tails" model for phospholipids
   a. both tails are hydrophobic.
   b. both tails are hydrophilic.
   c. one tail is hydrophilic and the other hydrophobic.
   d. no correct response

Answers: 1. b; 2. b; 3. b; 4. a; 5. b; 6. a

19-8 Membrane Lipids: Sphingoglycolipids

LEARNING FOCUS

Recognize general structural characteristics for sphingoglycolipids and be familiar with the types of carbohydrate units present in such lipids.

The second of the three major types of membrane lipids is *sphingoglycolipids*. A **sphingoglycolipid** *is a lipid that contains both a fatty acid and a carbohydrate component attached to a sphingosine molecule.* A fatty acid is attached to the sphingosine through an amide linkage, and a monosaccharide or oligosaccharide (Section 18-3) is attached to the sphingosine at the terminal —OH carbon atom through a glycosidic linkage (Section 18-13). The generalized block diagram for a sphingoglycolipid is

Sphingoglycolipid
(one amide linkage and one or more
glycosidic linkages)

Like glycerophospholipids and sphingophospholipids (Section 19-7), sphingoglycolipids have a "head and two tails" structure. Sphingoglycolipids and sphingophospholipids have similar "tails," but their polar "heads" differ in the constituents present (mono- or oligosaccharide versus phosphate-alcohol).

Sphingoglycolipids undergo hydrolysis and saponification reactions; both the amide and the glycosidic linkages can be hydrolyzed.

The simplest sphingoglycolipids, which are called *cerebrosides,* contain a single monosaccharide unit—either glucose or galactose. As the name suggests, cerebrosides occur primarily in the brain (7% of dry mass). They are also present in the myelin sheath of nerves. The specific structure for a cerebroside in which stearic acid (18:0) is the fatty acid and galactose is the monosaccharide is

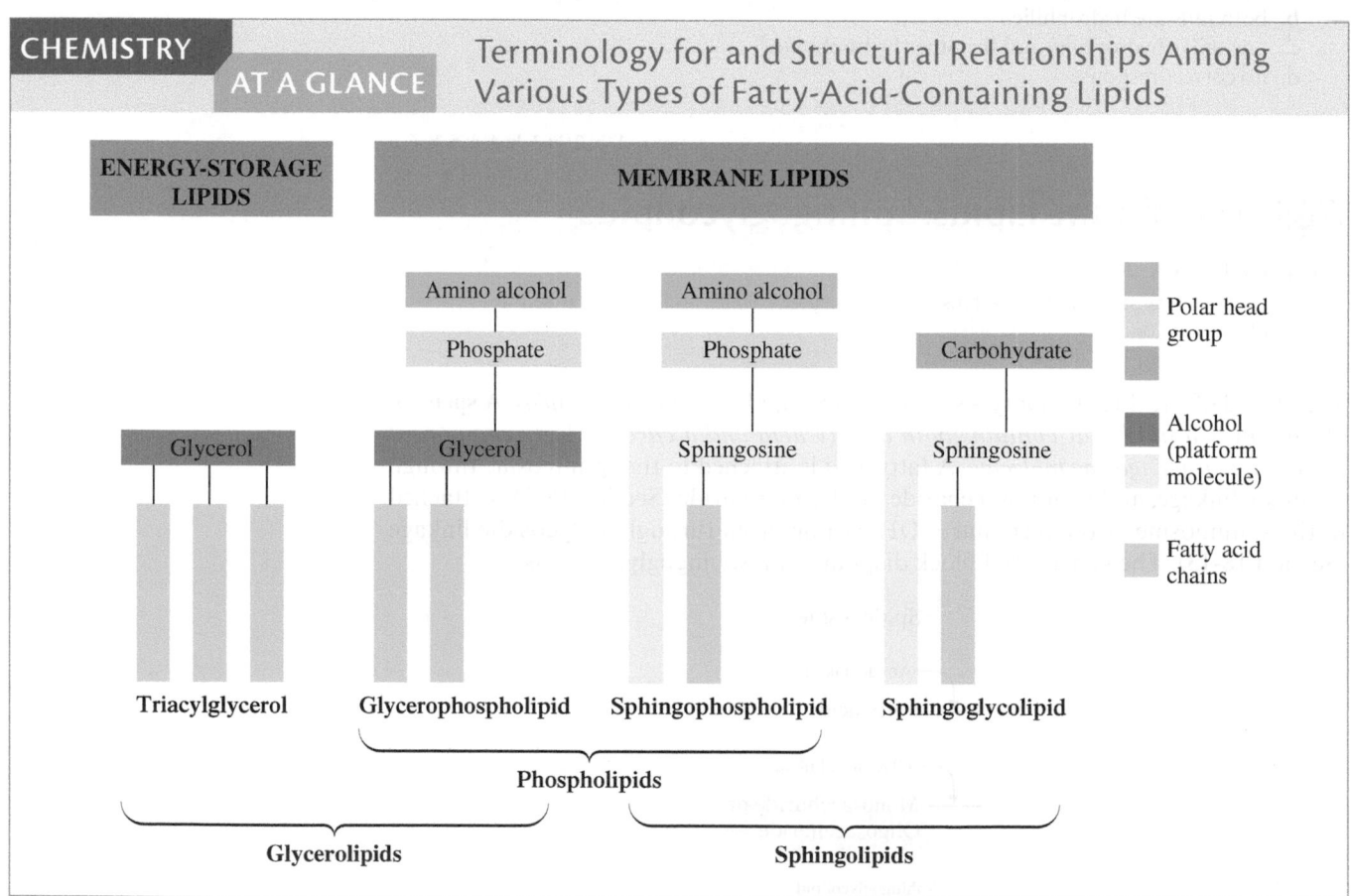

More complex sphingoglycolipids, called *gangliosides,* contain a branched chain of up to seven monosaccharide residues. These substances occur in the gray matter of the brain as well as in the myelin sheath.

CHEMISTRY AT A GLANCE

Terminology for and Structural Relationships Among Various Types of Fatty-Acid-Containing Lipids

ENERGY-STORAGE LIPIDS	MEMBRANE LIPIDS		

Amino alcohol — Phosphate — Glycerol

Amino alcohol — Phosphate — Sphingosine

Carbohydrate — Sphingosine

Triacylglycerol **Glycerophospholipid** **Sphingophospholipid** **Sphingoglycolipid**

Phospholipids

Glycerolipids   Sphingolipids

Polar head group

Alcohol (platform molecule)

Fatty acid chains

Chemistry at a Glance—Terminology for and Structural Relationships Among Various Types of Fatty-Acid-Containing Lipids—summarizes terminology and structural relationships among the types of lipids that have been considered up to this point. The common thread among all of the structures is the presence of at least one fatty acid residue.

19-9 Membrane Lipids: Cholesterol

LEARNING FOCUS

Be familiar with the structural characteristics for a steriod nucleus and for the molecule cholesterol; know the relationship between the lipoproteins HDL and LDL and the molecule cholesterol.

Cholesterol, the third of the three major types of membrane lipids, is a specific compound rather than a family of compounds like the phospholipids (Section 19-7) and sphingoglycolipids (Section 19-8). Cholesterol's structure differs markedly from that of other membrane lipids in that (1) there are no fatty acid residues present and (2) neither glycerol nor sphingosine is present as the platform molecule.

Cholesterol is a *steroid.* A **steroid** *is a lipid whose structure is based on a fused-ring system that involves three 6-membered rings and one 5-membered ring.* This steroid fused-ring system, which is called the *steroid nucleus,* has the following structure:

Steroid nucleus

Note that each of the rings of the steroid nucleus carries a letter designation and that a "consecutive" numbering system is used to denote individual carbon atoms.

Numerous steroids have been isolated from plants, animals, and human beings. Location of double bonds within the fused-ring system and the nature and location of substituents distinguish one steroid from another. Most steroids have an oxygen-containing functional group ($=O$ or $-OH$) at carbon 3 and some kind of side chain at carbon 17. Many also have a double bond from carbon 5 to either carbon 4 or carbon 6.

Cholesterol *is a C_{27} steroid molecule that is a component of cell membranes and a precursor for other steroid-based lipids.* It is the most abundant steroid in the human body. ◀ The *-ol* ending in the name cholester*ol* conveys the information that an alcohol functional group is present in this molecule; it is located on carbon 3 of the steroid nucleus. In addition, cholesterol has methyl group attachments at carbons 10 and 13, a carbon–carbon double bond between carbons 5 and 6, and an eight-carbon

▶ *Besides being an important molecule in and of itself, cholesterol serves as a precursor for several other important steroid molecules including bile acids (Section 19-11), steroid hormones (Section 19-12), and vitamin D (Section 21-13).*

Figure 19-15 Structural formula and molecular model for the cholesterol molecule.

branched side chain at carbon 17. Figure 19-15 gives both the structural formula and a molecular model for cholesterol. The molecular model shows the rather compact nature of the cholesterol molecule. The "head and two tails" arrangement found in other membrane lipids is not present. The lack of a *large* polar head group causes cholesterol to have limited water solubility. The —OH group on carbon 3 is considered the head of the molecule.

Within the human body, cholesterol is found in cell membranes (up to 25% by mass), in nerve tissue, in brain tissue (about 10% by dry mass), and in virtually all fluids. Every 100 mL of human blood plasma contains about 50 mg of free cholesterol and about 170 mg of cholesterol esterified with various fatty acids.

Although a portion of the body's cholesterol is obtained from dietary intake, most of it is biosynthesized by the liver and (to a lesser extent) the intestine. Typically, 800–1000 mg are biosynthesized each day. Ingested cholesterol decreases biosynthetic cholesterol production. However, the reduction is less than the amount ingested. Therefore, total body cholesterol levels increase with increased dietary intake of cholesterol.

Biosynthetic cholesterol is distributed to cells throughout the body for various uses via the bloodstream. Because cholesterol is only sparingly soluble in water (blood), a protein carrier system is used for its distribution. These cholesterol–protein combinations are called *lipoproteins.*

The lipoproteins that carry cholesterol *from the liver* to various tissues are called LDLs (low-density lipoproteins), and those that carry excess cholesterol from tissues *back to the liver* are called HDLs (high-density lipoproteins). If too much cholesterol is being transported by LDLs or too little by HDLs, the imbalance results in an increase in blood cholesterol levels. High blood cholesterol levels contribute to atherosclerosis, a form of cardiovascular disease characterized by the buildup of plaque along the inner walls of arteries. Plaque is a mound of lipid material mixed with smooth muscle cells and calcium. Much of the lipid material in plaque is cholesterol. Plaque deposits in the arteries that serve the heart reduce blood flow to the heart muscle and can lead to a heart attack. Figure 19-16 shows the occlusion that can occur in an artery as a result of plaque buildup.

The cholesterol associated with LDLs is often called "bad cholesterol" because it contributes to increased blood cholesterol levels, and the cholesterol associated with HDLs is often called "good cholesterol" because it contributes to reduced blood cholesterol levels. The focus on relevancy feature Chemical Connections 20-F— "Lipoproteins and Heart Disease Risk—considers this topic in further detail.

Much still needs to be learned concerning the actual role played by serum cholesterol in plaque buildup within arteries. Current knowledge suggests that it makes good sense to reduce the amount of cholesterol (as well as saturated fats) taken into the body through dietary intake. People who want to reduce dietary cholesterol intake should reduce the amount of animal products they eat (meat, dairy products, etc.)

Howard Sochurek/CORBIS

Figure 19-16 A severely occluded artery—the result of the buildup of cholesterol-containing plaque deposits.

▶ Table 19-4 **The Amount of Cholesterol Found in Various Foods**

Food	Cholesterol (mg)
liver (3 oz)	410
egg (1 large)	213
shrimp (3 oz)	166
pork chop (3 oz)	83
chicken (3 oz)	75
beef steak (3 oz)	70
fish fillet (3 oz)	54
whole milk (1 cup)	33
cheddar cheese (1 oz)	30
Swiss cheese (1 oz)	26
low-fat milk (1 cup)	22

and eat more fruit and vegetables. Plant foods contain negligible amounts of cholesterol; cholesterol is found primarily in foods of animal origin. Table 19-4 gives cholesterol amounts associated with selected foods.

Section 19-9 Quick Quiz

1. The "steroid nucleus" common to all steroid structures involves a fused-ring system that contains
   a. four 6-membered rings
   b. four 5-membered rings
   c. three 6-membered rings and one 5-membered ring
   d. no correct response
2. Which of the following types of membrane lipids has a steroid structure?
   a. cholesterol
   b. sphingoglycolipids
   c. sphingophospholipids
   d. no correct response
3. Which of the following statements concerning cholesterol is *correct*?
   a. An alcohol functional group is present in its structure.
   b. The lipoprotein HDL distributes cholesterol to various parts of the human body.
   c. The cholesterol associated with LDL is often called "good cholesterol."
   d. no correct response

Answers: 1. c; 2. a; 3. a

19-10 Cell Membranes

LEARNING FOCUS

Be able to describe cell membrane structure in terms of the structural arrangement called a lipid bilayer; be familiar with the three common transport mechanisms by which molecules can enter and leave cells through the cell membrane.

Prior to discussing additional types of lipid molecules—emulsification lipids (Section 19-11), messenger lipids (Sections 19-12 and 19-13), and protective-coating lipids (Section 19-14)—the discussion of membrane lipids will be extended to include how these types of lipids interact with each other to form cell membranes. ◀

Living cells contain an estimated 10,000 different kinds of molecules in an aqueous environment confined by a *cell membrane*. A **cell membrane** *is a lipid-based structure that separates a cell's aqueous-based interior from the aqueous environment*

▶ *Cell membranes are also commonly called* plasma membranes *because they separate the cytoplasm (aqueous contents) of a cell from its surroundings.*

▶ *The percentage of lipid and protein components in a cell membrane is related to the function of the cell. The lipid to protein ratio ranges from about 80% lipid / 20% protein by mass in the myelin sheath of nerve cells to the unique 20% lipid / 80% protein ratio for the inner mitochondrial membrane (Section 23-2). Red blood cell membranes contain approximately equal amounts of lipid and protein. A typical membrane also has a carbohydrate content that varies between 2% and 10% by mass.*

▶ *The glycerophospholipids and sphingoglycolipids found in a lipid bilayer are chiral molecules with the chiral center (Section 18-4) at carbon 2 of the glycerol or sphingosine components of the molecules. The stereoconfiguration of these chiral molecules is always "left-handed," that is, L isomers. The fact that they all have the same configuration enhances their ability to aggregate together in the lipid bilayer.*

surrounding the cell. Besides its "separation" function, a cell membrane also controls the movement of substances into and out of the cell. Up to 80% of the mass of a cell membrane is lipid material consisting primarily of the three types of membrane lipids previously discussed: phospholipids, glycolipids, and cholesterol. ◀

The keys to understanding the structural basis for a cell membrane are (1) the virtually insoluble nature of membrane lipids in water and (2) the "head and two tails" structure (Section 19-7) of phospholipids and sphingoglycolipids. When these lipids are placed in water, the polar heads of phospholipids and sphingoglycolipids favor contact with water (they are *hydrophilic;* Section 19-7, whereas their nonpolar tails interact with one another rather than with water (they are *hydrophobic;* Section 19-7). The result is a remarkable bit of molecular architecture called a *lipid bilayer.* A **lipid bilayer** *is a two-layer-thick structure of phospholipids and glycolipids in which the nonpolar tails of the lipids are in the middle of the structure and the polar heads are on the outside surfaces of the structure.* Such a bilayer is six-billionths to nine-billionths of a meter thick—that is, 6 to 9 nanometers thick. There are three distinct parts to the bilayer: the exterior polar "heads," the interior polar "heads," and the central nonpolar "tails," as shown in Figure 19-17.

Figure 19-18, which is based on space-filling models for phospholipids, gives a "close-up" view of the arrangement of lipid molecules in a section of a lipid bilayer. Note the "exterior" nature of the polar heads of these membrane lipids. ◀

Most lipid molecules in the bilayer contain at least one unsaturated fatty acid. The presence of such acids, with the kinks in their carbon chains (Section 19-3), prevents tight packing of fatty acid chains (Figure 19-19). The open packing imparts a flexible or fluid character to the membrane—a necessity because numerous types of biochemicals must pass into and out of a cell.

Cholesterol molecules are also components of cell membranes. They regulate membrane rigidity. Because of their compact shape (Section 19-9; Figure 19-15), cholesterol molecules fit between the fatty acid chains of the lipid bilayer (Figure 19-20), restricting movement of the fatty acid chains. Within the membrane, the cholesterol

Figure 19-17 Cross-section of a lipid bilayer. The circles represent the polar heads of the lipid components, and the wavy lines represent the nonpolar tails of the lipid components. The heads occupy "surface" positions, and the tails occupy "internal" positions.

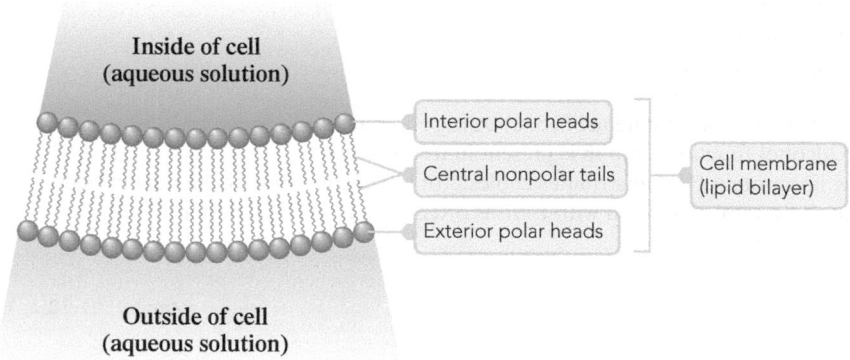

Figure 19-18 Space-filling model of a section of a lipid bilayer. The key to the structure is the "head and two tails" structure of the membrane lipids that constitute the bilayer.

molecule orientation is "head" (the hydroxyl group) to the exterior of the lipid bilayer and "tail" (the steroid ring system with attached alkyl groups) to the interior of the lipid bilayer.

Proteins are also components of lipid bilayers. The proteins are responsible for moving substances such as nutrients and electrolytes across the membrane, and they also act as receptors that bind hormones and neurotransmitters.

There are two general types of membrane proteins: *integral* and *peripheral*. An **integral membrane protein** *is a membrane protein that penetrates the cell membrane.* Some membrane proteins penetrate only partially through the lipid bilayer, whereas others go completely from one side to the other side of the lipid bilayer. A **peripheral membrane protein** *is a nonpenetrating membrane protein located on the surface of the cell membrane.* Figure 19-21 shows diagrammatically the relationship between membrane proteins and the overall structure of a cell membrane.

Cholesterol

Figure 19-20 Cholesterol molecules fit between fatty acid chains in a lipid bilayer.

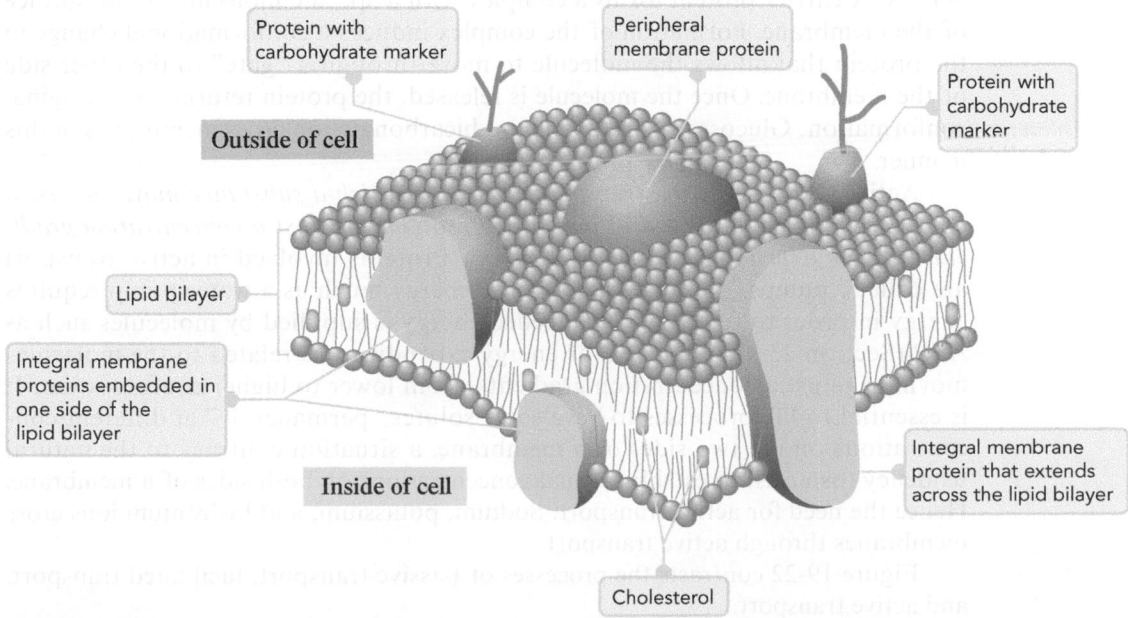

Protein with carbohydrate marker

Peripheral membrane protein

Protein with carbohydrate marker

Outside of cell

Lipid bilayer

Integral membrane proteins embedded in one side of the lipid bilayer

Inside of cell

Integral membrane protein that extends across the lipid bilayer

Cholesterol

Figure 19-21 Proteins are important structural components of cell membranes.

Small carbohydrate molecules, usually oligosaccharides, are also components of cell membranes. They are found on the outer side of the membrane and are covalently bonded to protein molecules or lipid molecules. The carbohydrate chains extend outward from the membrane into the surrounding aqueous environment. Such carbohydrate–protein and carbohydrate–lipid combinations are called, respectively, glycoproteins and glycolipids (Section 18-20). Functionally, the carbohydrate portions of these glycoproteins and glycolipids are *markers,* substances that play key roles in the process by which different cells recognize each other. The red-blood-cell marker system previously discussed in Chemical Connections 18-D—Blood Types and Oligosaccharides—involves glycoproteins.

Intermolecular forces (Section 7-13) rather than covalent bonds govern the interactions among the lipid and protein components of a lipid bilayer. Thus, the various lipids and proteins present are free to move about within the bilayer structure. Such movement, however, does not change the orientation of the various bilayer components present. For example, a protein surface that is orientated toward the exterior of the bilayer will always be found facing the exterior.

It is also important to note that the interior and exterior surfaces of a lipid bilayer do not have exactly the same lipid/protein composition; different mixtures of lipid and proteins are present.

Transport Across Cell Membranes

In order for cellular processes to be maintained, molecules of various types must be able to cross cell membranes. Three common transport mechanisms exist by which molecules can enter and leave cells. They are *passive* transport, *facilitated* transport, and *active* transport.

Passive transport *is the transport process in which a substance moves across a cell membrane by diffusion from a region of higher concentration to a region of lower concentration without the expenditure of any cellular energy.* Only a few types of molecules, including O_2, N_2, urea, and ethanol, can cross membranes in this manner. Passive transport is closely related to the process of osmosis (Section 8-9). ◄

Facilitated transport *is the transport process in which a substance moves across a cell membrane, with the aid of membrane proteins, from a region of higher concentration to a region of lower concentration without the expenditure of cellular energy.* The specific protein molecules involved in the process are called *carriers* or *transporters.* A carrier protein forms a complex with a specific molecule at one surface of the membrane. Formation of the complex induces a conformational change in the protein that allows the molecule to move through a "gate" to the other side of the membrane. Once the molecule is released, the protein returns to its original conformation. Glucose, chloride ion, and bicarbonate ion cross membranes in this manner.

Active transport *is the transport process in which a substance moves across a cell membrane, with the aid of membrane proteins, against a concentration gradient with the expenditure of cellular energy.* Proteins involved in active transport are called "pumps," because they require energy much as a water pump requires energy in order to function. The needed energy is supplied by molecules such as ATP (Section 23-3). The need for energy expenditure is related to the molecules moving against a concentration gradient—from lower to higher concentration. It is essential to life processes to have some solutes "permanently" at different concentrations on the two sides of a membrane, a situation contrary to the natural tendency (osmosis) to establish equal concentrations on both sides of a membrane. Hence the need for active transport. Sodium, potassium, and hydronium ions cross membranes through active transport.

Figure 19-22 contrasts the processes of passive transport, facilitated transport, and active transport.

► *Somewhat surprisingly, water, the solvent for the compounds and ions that cross cell membranes, cannot directly diffuse across cell membranes. Membrane proteins, however contain pores called aquapores, through which water molecules may freely pass.*

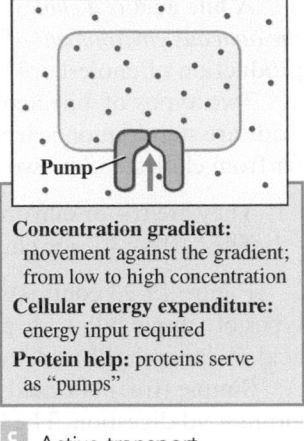

Concentration gradient: movement with the gradient; from high to low concentration	**Concentration gradient:** movement with the gradient; from high to low concentration	**Concentration gradient:** movement against the gradient; from low to high concentration
Cellular energy expenditure: none required	**Cellular energy expenditure:** none required	**Cellular energy expenditure:** energy input required
Protein help: none required	**Protein help:** proteins serve as "gates"	**Protein help:** proteins serve as "pumps"
a Passive transport	**b** Facilitated transport	**c** Active transport

Figure 19-22 Three processes by which substances can cross plasma membranes.

Section 19-10 Quick Quiz

1. Which of the following is a correct representation for the structure of a lipid bilayer?
   a. ▮ b. ▮ c. ▮ d. no correct response

2. The exterior surface positions in a lipid bilayer are occupied by
   a. hydrophilic entities
   b. hydrophobic entities
   c. nonpolar entities
   d. no correct response

3. Which of the following polarity-based descriptions is correct for the interior of a lipid bilayer?
   a. contains "polar heads"
   b. contains "nonpolar heads"
   c. contains "nonpolar tails"
   d. no correct response

4. The biochemical function for the cholesterol present in cell membranes is
   a. impart polarity to the interior membrane
   b. prevent other membrane components from reacting with each other
   c. regulate membrane fluidity
   d. no correct response

5. Which of the following membrane transport mechanisms requires both the aid of proteins and the expenditure of cellular energy?
   a. facilitated transport
   b. active transport
   c. passive transport
   d. no correct response

Answers: 1. c; 2. a; 3. c; 4. c; 5. b

19-11 Emulsification Lipids: Bile Acids

LEARNING FOCUS

Be familiar with the structural characteristics for bile acids and the biochemical function for such acids.

An **emulsifier** *is a substance that can disperse and stabilize water-insoluble substances as colloidal particles in an aqueous solution.* Cholesterol derivatives called *bile acids* function as emulsifying agents that facilitate the absorption of dietary lipids in the intestine. Their mode of action is much like that of soap during washing (see Chemical Connections 19-C—The Cleansing Action of Soap and Detergents).

A **bile acid** *is a cholesterol derivative that functions as a lipid-emulsifying agent in the aqueous environment of the digestive tract.* From one-third to one-half of the daily production of cholesterol by the liver is used to replenish bile acid stores.

Two types of bile acids exist: simple and complexed. Structurally, *simple* bile acids are steroid monocarboxylic acids, obtained by oxidation of cholesterol, that differ from cholesterol in two aspects:

1. They are tri- or dihydroxy cholesterol derivatives.
2. The carbon 17 side chain of cholesterol has been oxidized to a carboxylic acid.

Figure 19-23 contrasts the structure of cholesterol with that of the three major types of simple bile acids produced from biochemical oxidation of cholesterol: cholic acid, 7-deoxycholic acid, and 12-deoxycholic acid.

Simple (free) bile acids (Figure 19-23) are not the actual emulsifying agents that aid in lipid digestion. The free bile acids are converted to more complex bile acids by attachment of a small amino acid to the carbon 17 side chain carboxyl group via an amide linkage. The presence of this amino acid attachment increases both the polarity of the bile acid and its water solubility. The most common amino acid attachments that occur in complexed bile acids are glycine (an amino carboxylic acid) and taurine (an amino sulfonic acid) ◄

▶ *The average bile acid composition in normal human adult bile is 38% cholic acid derivatives, 34% 7-deoxycholic acid derivatives, and 28% 12-deoxycholic acid derivatives. Glycine-containing derivatives predominate over taurine-containing derivatives by a 3:1 to 4:1 ratio. Uncomplexed (free) bile acids are not present in bile.*

$$H_3\overset{+}{N}-CH_2-\overset{\overset{\displaystyle O}{\|}}{C}-O^-$$

Glycine

$$H_3\overset{+}{N}-CH_2-CH_2-\overset{\overset{\displaystyle O}{\|}}{\underset{\underset{\displaystyle O}{\|}}{S}}-O^-$$

Taurine

Figure 19-24 shows structures for the complexed bile acids glycocholic acid (glycine is the attachment) and taurocholic acid (taurine is the attachment). Complexed bile acids such as these have enhanced emulsifying ability stemming from one end of the molecule being strongly hydrophilic (the amino acid bearing carbon chain) and the rest of the molecule (the steroid nucleus with its small attachments) being largely hydrophobic. The "solubilizing" of lipids from bile acid action is similar to the action of soap in the washing process (Chemical Connections 19-C—The Cleansing Action of Soap and Detergents).

The medium through which bile acids are supplied to the small intestine is *bile.* **Bile** *is a fluid containing emulsifying agents that is secreted by the liver, stored in the gallbladder, and released into the small intestine during digestion.* Besides bile acids, bile also contains bile pigments (breakdown products of hemoglobin; Section 26-7), cholesterol itself, and electrolytes such as bicarbonate ion. The bile acids that are present increase the solubility of the cholesterol in the bile fluid.

Figure 19-23 Structural formulas for cholesterol, cholic acid, and two deoxycholic acids.

Cholesterol (C$_{27}$)

Cholic acid (C$_{24}$)

12-Deoxycholic acid (C$_{24}$)

7-Deoxycholic acid (C$_{24}$)

Figure 19-24 The structures of glycocholic acid and taurocholic acid.

Cholic acid

Taurine

Glycine

Taurocholic acid

Glycocholic acid

A number of factors, including increased secretion of cholesterol and a decrease in the size of the bile pool, can upset the balance between the cholesterol present in bile and the bile acid derivatives needed to maintain cholesterol's solubility in the bile. The result is the precipitation of crystallized cholesterol from the bile and the resulting formation of gallstones in the gallbladder. In Western countries, approximately 80% of gallstones are almost pure cholesterol (Figure 19-25).

Figure 19-25 A large percentage of gallstones, the causative agent for many "gallbladder attacks," are almost pure crystallized cholesterol that has precipitated from bile solution.

C. James Webb/Phototake

Section 19-11 Quick Quiz

1. Which of the following statements concerning bile acids is *incorrect*?
   a. They are cholesterol derivatives.
   b. They are emulsifying agents.
   c. They are insoluble in water.
   d. no correct response
2. Which of the following statements concerning structural characteristics of bile acids is *correct*?
   a. No hydroxyl groups are present.
   b. Fewer hydroxyl groups are present than in cholesterol.
   c. More hydroxyl groups are present than in cholesterol.
   d. no correct response

Answers: 1. c; 2. c

19-12 Messenger Lipids: Steroid Hormones

LEARNING FOCUS

Know the general structural characteristics for steroid hormones and the biochemical functions for the two major classes of steroid hormones.

Previously considered were lipids that function as energy-storage molecules (triacylglycerols; Section 19-4), as components of cell membranes (phospholipids, sphingoglycolipids, and cholesterol; Sections 19-7 through 19-9), and as emulsifying agents (bile acids; Section 19-11). An additional role played by lipids is that of "chemical messenger." *Steroid hormones* and *eicosanoids* are two large families of lipids that have messenger functions. In this section, steroid hormones, which are cholesterol derivatives, will be considered. In Section 19-13, eicosanoids, which are fatty acid derivatives, will be considered.

A **hormone** *is a biochemical substance, produced by a ductless gland, that has a messenger function.* Hormones serve as a means of communication *between* various tissues. Some hormones, though not all, are lipids.

A **steroid hormone** *is a hormone that is a cholesterol derivative.* There are two major classes of steroid hormones: (1) sex hormones, which control reproduction and secondary sex characteristics and (2) adrenocorticoid hormones, which regulate numerous biochemical processes in the body.

Sex Hormones

The sex hormones can be classified into three major subclasses:

1. Estrogens—the female sex hormones
2. Androgens—the male sex hormones
3. Progestins—the pregnancy hormones

Estrogens are synthesized in the ovaries and adrenal cortex (the outer part of the adrenal glands, which are located on the top of each kidney) and are responsible for the development of female secondary sex characteristics at the onset of puberty and for regulation of the menstrual cycle. They also stimulate the development of the mammary glands during pregnancy and induce estrus (heat) in animals. ◀

Androgens are synthesized in the testes and adrenal cortex and promote the development of male secondary sex characteristics. They also promote muscle growth.

Progestins are synthesized in the ovaries and the placenta and prepare the lining of the uterus for implantation of the fertilized ovum. They also suppress ovulation.

Figure 19-26a gives the structure of the primary hormone in each of the three subclasses of sex hormones. Other members of these hormone families are metabolized forms of the primary hormone.

Note in Figure 19-26a how similar the structures are for these principal hormones, and yet how different their functions are. The fact that seemingly minor changes in structure effect great changes in biofunction points out, again, the extreme specificity (Section 21-5) of the enzymes that control biochemical reactions.

Increased knowledge of the structures and functions of sex hormones has led to the development of a number of *synthetic* steroids whose actions often mimic those of the natural steroid hormones. The best known types of synthetic steroids are oral contraceptives and anabolic steroids.

▶ *Estrogens are a class of molecules rather than a single molecule. Statements like "the estrogen level is high" should be rephrased as "there is a high level of estrogens."*

Figure 19-26 Structures of selected sex hormones and synthetic compounds that have similar actions.

Estradiol
(the primary estrogen; responsible for secondary female characteristics)

Testosterone
(the primary androgen; responsible for secondary male characteristics)

Progesterone
(the primary progestin; prepares the uterus for pregnancy)

a Natural hormones

Norethynodrel
(a synthetic progestin)

RU-486
(mifepristone; a synthetic abortion drug)

Methandrostenolone
(a synthetic tissue-building steroid)

b Synthetic steroids

Oral contraceptives are used to suppress ovulation as a method of birth control. Generally, a mixture of a synthetic estrogen and a synthetic progestin is used. The synthetic estrogen regulates the menstrual cycle, and the synthetic progestin prevents ovulation, thus creating a false state of pregnancy. The structure of norethynodrel, a synthetic progestin, is given in Figure 19-26b. Compare its structure to that of progesterone (the real hormone); the structures are very similar.

Interestingly, the controversial "morning after" pill developed in France and known as RU-486, is also similar in structure to progesterone. RU-486 interferes with gestation of a fertilized egg and terminates a pregnancy within the first nine weeks of gestation more effectively and safely than surgical methods. The structure of RU-486 appears next to that of norethynodrel in Figure 19-26b. ◀

▶ *The C≡C functional group, which occurs in both norethynodrel and RU-486, is rarely found in biomolecules.*

Anabolic steroids include the illegal steroid drugs used by some athletes to build up muscle strength and enhance endurance. Such steroids are now known to have serious side effects in the user. The structure of one of the more commonly used anabolic steroids, methandrostenolone, is given in Figure 19-26b. Note the similarities between its structure and that of the naturally occurring testosterone. The focus on relevancy feature Chemical Connections 19-E—Anabolic Steroid Use in Competitive Sports—further explores the use, usually illegal, of anabolic steroids by athletes.

Adrenocorticoid Hormones

The second major group of steroid hormones consists of the adrenocorticoid hormones. Produced by the adrenal glands, at least 28 different hormones have been isolated.

There are two subclasses of adrenocorticoid hormones.

1. *Mineralocorticoids* control the balance of Na^+ and K^+ ions in cells and body fluids.
2. *Glucocorticoids* control glucose metabolism and counteract inflammation.

The major mineralocorticoid is aldosterone, and the major glucocorticoid is cortisol (hydrocortisone). Cortisol is the hormone synthesized in the largest amount by the adrenal glands. Cortisol and its synthetic ketone derivative cortisone exert powerful anti-inflammatory effects in the body. Both cortisone and prednisolone, a similar synthetic derivative, are used as prescription drugs to control inflammatory diseases such as rheumatoid arthritis. Figure 19-27 gives the structures of these adrenocorticoid hormones.

Aldosterone
(a mineralocorticoid)

Cortisol
(a glucocorticoid)

a Natural hormones

Cortisone
(an anti-inflammatory drug)

Prednisolone
(an anti-inflammatory drug)

b Synthetic steroids

Figure 19-27 Structures of selected adrenocorticoid hormones and related synthetic compounds.

Anabolic Steroid Use in Competitive Sports

The steroid hormone testosterone is the principal male sex hormone. It has masculinizing (androgenic) effects and muscle-building (anabolic) effects. Masculinizing effects of testosterone include the growth of facial and body hair, deepening of the voice, and maturation of the male sex organs. Testosterone's anabolic effects are responsible for the muscle development that boys experience at puberty.

Many synthetic derivatives of testosterone are now known. Some of these exert primarily androgenic effects, whereas others exert primarily anabolic effects. Androgenic steroids can be used to correct hormonal imbalances in the body. Anabolic steroids can be used to prevent the withering of muscle in persons recovering from major surgery or serious injuries.

Anabolic steroids have also been "discovered" by athletes, who have found that these compounds can be used to help build muscle mass and reduce the healing time for muscle injuries. Often the net result of anabolic hormone use by an athlete is enhanced athletic performance.

Anabolic steroid use by athletes in competitive sports is now referred to as "doping" and is banned by all major sporting organizations, including the International Olympic Committee (IOC), National Football League (NFL), National Basketball Association (NBA), and Major League Baseball (MLB). To enforce the ban on anabolic steroid use, athletes are subjected to random drug screening. In major events, such as the Olympics, testing is no longer random but mandatory for all competitors.

One major athletic event that has been plagued with doping in recent years is the Tour de France. This annual bicycle race, which is held in France and nearby countries, is one of the most physically grueling tests of endurance available to athletes (see accompanying photo). Lasting three weeks, the race covers 2200 miles, including major "mountain climbs." Numerous riders have been disqualified for testing positive for banned performance-enhancing drugs.

Major League Baseball is another sport that has encountered anabolic steroid problems. During the 1990s and the early part of the next decade, many players, including some of the League's most prominent ones, were involved in anabolic steroid use.

In response to the growing problem of illegal use of anabolic steroids, legislation was passed in the United States, which went into effect in 2005, that makes possession of a banned anabolic steroid a federal crime. Still, some athletes continue to use these substances illegally.

Two major reasons exist for prohibiting steroid use in athletes: (1) their use is considered a form of cheating because it confers an unfair advantage and (2) their "beneficial effects" are far outweighed by serious negative side effects.

Tour de France participants face one of the most physically grueling endurance tests in all of competitive athletics.

Regarding the latter of these two reasons, medical evidence now indicates that anabolic steroid use has many side effects that range from some that are physically unattractive, such as acne and breast development in men, to others that are life-threatening, such as heart attacks and liver problems. Most of these alarming effects are reversible if the abuser stops taking the drugs, but some are permanent.

The structures of synthetic anabolic steroids closely resemble that of the naturally occurring male sex hormone testosterone. Chemically, most anabolic steroids are testosterone derivatives. Testosterone can be viewed as the "template" structure from which many synthetic variations (analogs) have been "designed."

Two of the most publicized anabolic steroids that athletes have used illegally are "andro" and "THG." The structures of these two compounds, as well as that of testosterone for comparison purposes, are shown in the accompanying diagram.

"Andro," which is short for androstenedione, was the steroid used during the 1990s and early part of the following decade in Major League Baseball. It was initially developed for use as a dietary supplement. At the time of its use in MLB, it was a legal supplement that could be purchased over the counter. Now, its possession without a prescription is illegal.

THG, short for tetrahydrogestrinone, is a "designer" steroid. Its molecular structure was designed so that drug testing procedures of the time could not detect the drug. For several years, it went undetected in drug testing. In 2003, the illegal use of this drug was discovered only after a spent syringe was sent anonymously to a testing agency with the comment that the syringe might contain a new performance-enhancing drug. Once the drug was identified, tests were rapidly developed for its detection. Some Olympic sprinters have been disqualified for using THG.

Testosterone

"Andro"
Androstenedione

THG
Tetrahydrogestrinone

1. Which of the following statements concerning steroid hormones is *correct*?
   a. Some, but not all of them, are cholesterol derivatives.
   b. Some, but not all of them, are glucose derivatives.
   c. All of them are cholesterol derivatives.
   d. no correct response
2. Which of the following is a correct pairing of concepts?
   a. pregnancy hormones and estrogens
   b. female sex hormones and progestins
   c. male sex hormones and androgens
   d. no correct response
3. Which of the following substances is associated with Na^+/K^+ balance in the human body?
   a. aldosterone
   b. cortisol
   c. prednisolone
   d. no correct response

Answers: 1. c; 2. c; 3. a

19-13 Messenger Lipids: Eicosanoids

LEARNING FOCUS

Know the general structural features for eicosanoids, the three principal subclasses of eicosanoids, and the physiological effects associated with these types of compounds.

An **eicosanoid** *is an oxygenated C_{20}-fatty-acid derivative that functions as a messenger lipid.* The term *eicosanoid* is derived from the Greek word *eikos,* which means "twenty." The metabolic precursor for most eicosanoids is arachidonic acid, the 20:4 fatty acid.

Almost all cells, except red blood cells, produce eicosanoids. These substances, like hormones, have profound physiological effects at extremely low concentrations. ◄ Eicosanoids are hormone-like molecules rather than true hormones because they are not transported in the bloodstream to their site of action as true hormones are. Instead, they exert their effects in the tissues where they are synthesized. Eicosanoids usually have a very short "life," being broken down, often within seconds of their synthesis, to inactive residues (which are eliminated in urine). For this reason, they are difficult to study and monitor within cells.

► *Eicosanoids exert their effects at very low concentrations, sometimes less than one part in a billion (10^9).*

The physiological effects of eicosanoids include mediation of

1. The inflammatory response, a normal response to tissue damage
2. The production of pain and fever
3. The regulation of blood pressure
4. The induction of blood clotting
5. The control of reproductive functions, such as induction of labor
6. The regulation of the sleep/wake cycle

There are three principal types of eicosanoids: prostaglandins, thromboxanes, and leukotrienes.

Prostaglandins

A **prostaglandin** *is a messenger lipid that is a C_{20}-fatty-acid derivative that contains a cyclopentane ring and oxygen-containing functional groups.* Twenty-carbon fatty acids are converted into a prostaglandin structure when the eighth and twelfth

Figure 19-28 Relationship of the structures of various eicosanoids to their precursor, arachidonic acid. ◀

a Arachidonic acid

b Prostaglandin E$_2$

c Thromboxane B$_2$

d Leukotriene B$_4$

▶ *The capital letter–numerical subscript designations for individual eicosanoids is based on selected structural characteristics of the molecules. The numerical subscript indicates the number of carbon–carbon double bonds present. The letters denote subgroups of molecules. The prostaglandin E group, for example, has a carbonyl group on carbon 9.*

carbon atoms of the fatty acid become connected to form a five-membered ring (Figure 19-28b).

Prostaglandins are named after the prostate gland, which was first thought to be their only source. Today, more than 20 prostaglandins have been discovered in a variety of tissues in both males and females.

Within the human body, prostaglandins are involved in many regulatory functions, including raising body temperature, inhibiting the secretion of gastric juices, increasing the secretion of a protective mucus layer into the stomach, relaxing and contracting smooth muscle, directing water and electrolyte balance, intensifying pain, and enhancing inflammation responses. Aspirin reduces inflammation and fever because it inactivates enzymes needed for prostaglandin synthesis.

The focus on relevancy feature Chemical Connections 19-F—The Mode of Action for Anti-Inflammatory Drugs—considers further the relationship between prostaglandin synthesis and inflammation in terms of how anti-inflammatory drugs exert their effects in the human body.

Thromboxanes

A **thromboxane** *is a messenger lipid that is a C$_{20}$-fatty-acid derivative that contains a cyclic ether ring and oxygen-containing functional groups.* As with prostaglandins, the cyclic structure involves a bond between carbons 8 and 12 (Figure 19-28c). An important function of thromboxanes is to promote the formation of blood clots. Thromboxanes are produced by blood platelets and promote platelet aggregation. ◀

Leukotrienes

▶ *Naturally occurring fatty acids are normally found in the form of fatty acid residues in such molecules as triacylglycerols, phospholipids, and sphingolipids, substances previously considered in this chapter. In eicosanoids, the fatty acids are not esterified and carry out their biochemical roles in the form of the free acids, that is, free fatty acid derivatives.*

A **leukotriene** *is a messenger lipid that is a C$_{20}$-fatty-acid derivative that contains three conjugated double bonds and hydroxy groups.* Fatty acids and their derivatives do not normally contain *conjugated* double bonds (see Chemical Connections 13-C—Carotenoids: A Source of Color), as do leukotrienes (Figure 19-28d). Leukotrienes are found in leukocytes (white blood cells). Their source and the presence of the three conjugated double bonds account for their name. Various inflammatory and hypersensitivity (allergy) responses are associated with elevated levels of leukotrienes. The development of drugs that inhibit leukotriene synthesis has been an active area of research.

The Mode of Action for Anti-Inflammatory Drugs

Injury or damage to bodily tissue is associated with the process of inflammation. This inflammation response is mediated by prostaglandin molecules (Section 19-13). The mode of action for most anti-inflammatory drugs now in use involves decreasing prostaglandin synthesis within the body by inhibiting the action of one or more of the enzymes (biochemical catalysts; Chapter 21) needed for prostaglandin synthesis.

Prostaglandin molecules are derivatives of arachidonic acid, a 20:4 fatty acid (Section 19-13). Anti-inflammatory *steroid* drugs such as cortisone (Section 19-12) inhibit the action of the enzyme *phospholipase A_2*, the enzyme that facilitates the breakdown of complex arachidonic acid-containing lipids to produce free arachidonic acid. Inhibiting arachidonic acid release stops the prostaglandin synthesis process, which in turn prevents (or diminishes) inflammation.

Besides anti-inflammatory *steroid* drugs, many *nonsteroidal* anti-inflammatory drugs (NSAIDs) are also available for inflammation control. Aspirin (see Chemical Connections 16-C—Aspirin) is the oldest and best known NSAID. Ibuprofen (Advil) and naproxen (Aleve) (see Chemical Connections 16-A—Nonprescription Pain Relievers Derived from Propanoic Acid), which were initially prescription medications, are now commonly used over-the-counter anti-inflammatory drugs. The most often prescribed prescription NSAID is *diclofenac* (see accompanying photo), a compound whose chemical structure contains chlorine atoms.

Diclofenac, usually in the form of its sodium salt, is the most often prescribed prescription NSAID.

These substances are not only anti-inflammatories, but also have antipyretic (fever reducer) and mild analgesic (pain-reliever) properties. They prevent prostaglandin synthesis by inhibiting the enzyme needed for the ring closure reaction at carbons 8 and 12 in arachidonic acid, a necessary step in prostaglandin synthesis (Section 19-13). The enzyme that NSAIDs inhibit is called *cyclooxygenase*, an enzyme known by the acronym *COX*.

There are actually two forms of the COX enzyme: COX-1 and COX-2. COX-1 also produces prostaglandins that induce the production of a protective mucous coating for the stomach lining (a desirable situation). The COX-2 enzyme is responsible for the production of additional prostaglandin molecules involved in inflammatory diseases such as arthritis (an undesirable situation).

Aspirin, ibuprofen, naproxen, and diclofenac inhibit both COX-1 and COX-2 enzymes. Use of these NSAIDs thus decreases inflammation but also makes an individual more susceptible to stomach irritation and ulcer formation, as protective mucous secretions are decreased when COX-1 is inhibited.

A new generation of prescription anti-inflammatory agents, developed in the 1990s, is now in use. These drugs are COX-2 inhibitors but not COX-1 inhibitors. The best known of these COX-2 inhibitors are Vioxx and Celebrex, whose chemical structures are

Vioxx

Celebrex

In 2004, Vioxx was withdrawn from the market because of concerns relating to heart attacks and strokes. A study indicated that patients taking Vioxx were twice as likely to suffer a heart attack or stroke as a control group involved in the study who were taking a placebo. The actual risk was 3.5% in the Vioxx group, compared with 1.9% in the control group, according to the FDA. The difference became apparent after 18 months of Vioxx use. Celebrex has fewer side effects than Vioxx, so it is still available and is widely used as a prescription medication.

19-14 Protective-Coating Lipids: Biological Waxes

LEARNING FOCUS

Know the structural characteristics and important functions for biological waxes; be aware of the differences between biological waxes and mineral waxes.

A **biological wax** *is a lipid that is a monoester of a long-chain fatty acid and a long-chain alcohol.* Biological waxes are *monoesters,* unlike fats and oils (Section 19-4), which are *triesters.* The fatty acids found in biological waxes generally are saturated and contain from 14 to 36 carbon atoms. The alcohols found in biological waxes may be saturated or unsaturated and may contain from 16 to 30 carbon atoms.

The block diagram for a biological wax is

Long-chain fatty acid —— Long-chain alcohol

▶ *The term* wax *derives from the old English word* weax, *which means "the material of the honeycomb."*

with the fatty acid and alcohol linked through an ester linkage. ◀ An actual structural formula for a biological wax that bees secrete and use as a structural material is

$$CH_3-(CH_2)_{14}-\overset{\displaystyle O}{\overset{\displaystyle \|}{C}}-O-(CH_2)_{29}-CH_3$$

A component of beeswax

Note that the general structural formula for a biological wax is the same as that for a simple ester (Section 16-9).

$$R-\overset{\displaystyle O}{\overset{\displaystyle \|}{C}}-O-R'$$

However, for waxes, both R and R′ must be long carbon chains (usually 20–30 carbon atoms).

The water-insoluble, water-repellent properties of biological waxes result from the complete dominance of the nonpolar nature of the long hydrocarbon chains present (from the alcohol and the fatty acid) over the weakly polar nature of the ester functional group that links the two carbon chains together (Figure 19-29).

In living organisms, biological waxes have numerous functions, all of which are related directly or indirectly to their water-repellent properties. Both humans and animals possess skin glands that secrete biological waxes to protect hair and skin and

Stearic acid

Oleoyl alcohol

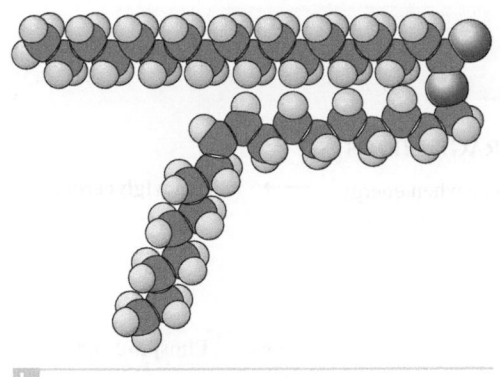

Figure 19-29 A biological wax has a structure with a small, weakly polar "head" and two long, nonpolar "tails." The polarity of the small "head" is not sufficient to impart any degree of water solubility to the molecule.

to keep it pliable and lubricated. With animal fur, waxes impart water repellency to the fur. Birds, particularly aquatic birds, rely on waxes secreted from preen glands to keep their feathers water-repellent. Such wax coatings also help minimize loss of body heat when the bird is in cold water. ◄ Many plants, particularly those that grow in arid regions, have leaves that are coated with a thin layer of biological waxes, which serve to prevent excessive evaporation of water and to protect against parasite attack (Figure 19-30). Similarly, insects with a high surface-area-to-volume ratio are often coated with a protective biological wax.

Biological waxes find use in the pharmaceutical, cosmetics, and "polishing" industries. Carnauba wax (obtained from a species of Brazilian palm tree) is a particularly hard wax whose uses involve high-gloss finishes: automobile wax, boat wax, floor wax, and shoe wax.

$$CH_3-(CH_2)_{28}-\overset{\overset{\displaystyle O}{\|}}{C}-O-(CH_2)_{31}-CH_3$$
A component of carnauba wax

Lanolin, a mixture of waxes obtained from sheep wool, is used as a base for skin creams and ointments intended to enhance retention of water (which softens the skin). ◄

Many synthetic materials are now available with properties that closely match—and even improve on—the properties of biological waxes. Such synthetic materials, which are generally polymers, have now replaced biological waxes in many cosmetics, ointments, and the like. The synthetic *carbowax,* for example, is a polyether.

Throughout this discussion, the term *biological wax,* rather than just *wax,* has been used. This is because the everyday meaning of the term *wax* is broader in scope than the chemical definition of the term *biological wax.* In general discussions, a **wax** *is a pliable, water-repelling substance used particularly in protecting surfaces and producing polished surfaces.* This broadened definition for waxes includes not only *biological waxes* but also *mineral waxes.* A **mineral wax** *is a mixture of long-chain alkanes obtained from the processing of petroleum.* (How mineral waxes are obtained from petroleum was considered in Section 12-15.) Mineral waxes, which are also called *paraffin waxes,* resist moisture and chemicals and have no odor or taste. They serve as a waterproof coating for such paper products as milk cartons and waxed paper. Most candles are made from mineral waxes. Some "wax products" are a blend of biological and mineral waxes. For example, beeswax is sometimes a component of candle wax. ◄

Chemistry at a Glance—Types of Lipids in Terms of How they Function—summarizes the function-based lipid classifications that have been considered in this chapter. Subclassifications within each function classification are also given in this summary.

▶ *When aquatic birds are caught in an oil spill, the oil dissolves the wax coating on their feathers. This causes the birds to lose their buoyancy (they cannot swim properly) and compromises their protection against the effects of cold water.*

© Kuttelvaserova Stuchelova/Shutterstock.com

Figure 19-30 Plant leaves often have a biological wax coating to prevent excessive loss of water.

▶ *Naturally occurring waxes are usually mixtures of several mono-esters rather than being a single monoester. This parallels the situation for fats and oils, which are mixtures of numerous triesters (triacylglycerols).*

▶ *Human ear wax, which acts as a protective barrier against infection by capturing airborne particles, is not a true biological wax—that is, it is not a mixture of simple esters. Human ear wax is a yellow waxy secretion that is a mixture of triacylglycerols, phospholipids, and esters of cholesterol. Its medical name is cerumen.*

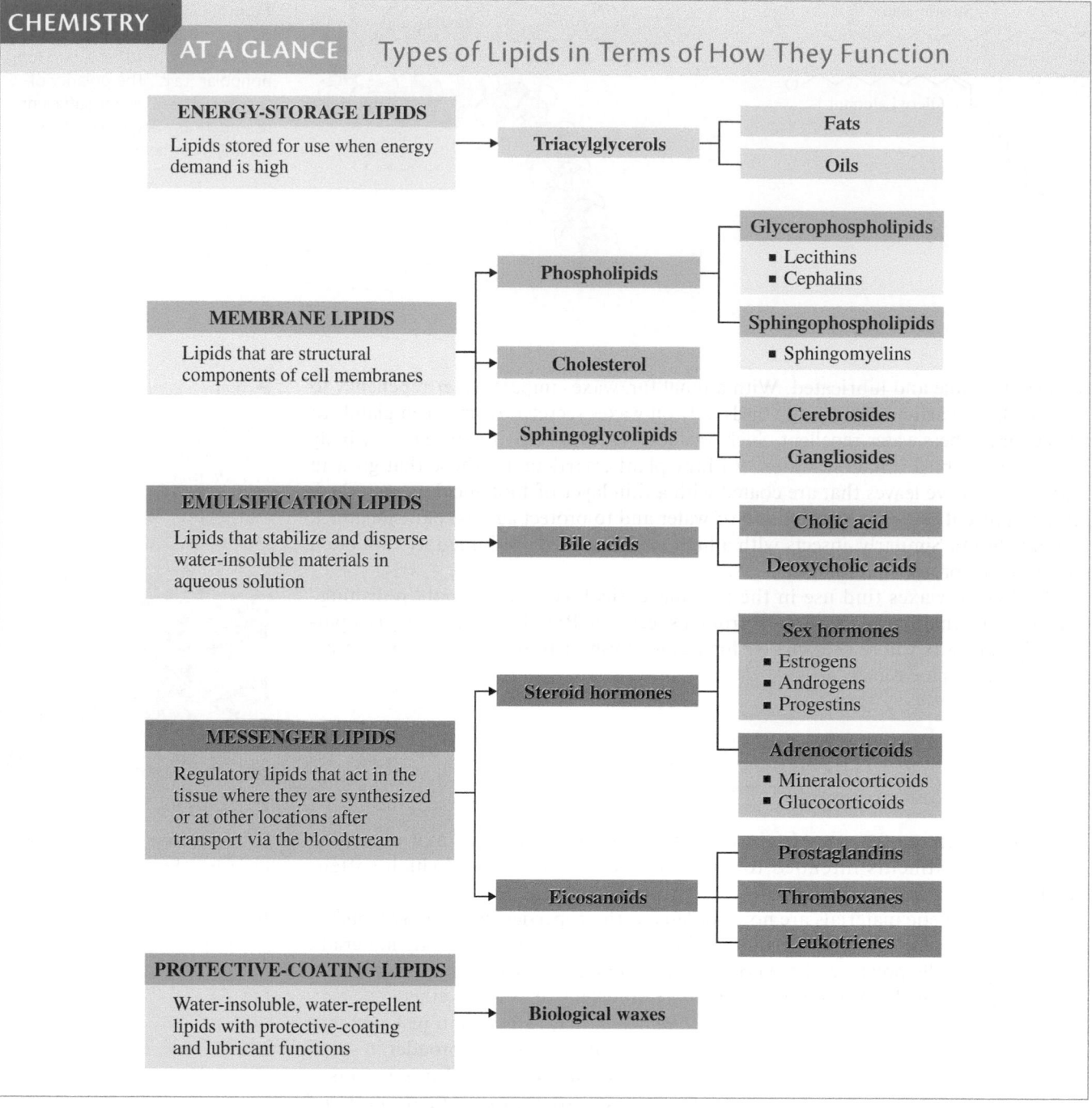

CHEMISTRY AT A GLANCE Types of Lipids in Terms of How They Function

ENERGY-STORAGE LIPIDS
Lipids stored for use when energy demand is high
→ Triacylglycerols
- Fats
- Oils

MEMBRANE LIPIDS
Lipids that are structural components of cell membranes
- Phospholipids
  - Glycerophospholipids
    - Lecithins
    - Cephalins
  - Sphingophospholipids
    - Sphingomyelins
- Cholesterol
- Sphingoglycolipids
  - Cerebrosides
  - Gangliosides

EMULSIFICATION LIPIDS
Lipids that stabilize and disperse water-insoluble materials in aqueous solution
→ Bile acids
- Cholic acid
- Deoxycholic acids

MESSENGER LIPIDS
Regulatory lipids that act in the tissue where they are synthesized or at other locations after transport via the bloodstream
- Steroid hormones
  - Sex hormones
    - Estrogens
    - Androgens
    - Progestins
  - Adrenocorticoids
    - Mineralocorticoids
    - Glucocorticoids
- Eicosanoids
  - Prostaglandins
  - Thromboxanes
  - Leukotrienes

PROTECTIVE-COATING LIPIDS
Water-insoluble, water-repellent lipids with protective-coating and lubricant functions
→ Biological waxes

Section 19-14 Quick Quiz

1. How many structural subunits are present in the "block diagram" for a biological wax?
   a. two
   b. three
   c. four
   d. no correct response
2. Which of the following functional groups in present in biological waxes?
   a. ester
   b. ether
   c. amide
   d. no correct response

3. The number of carbon chains present in the structures of biological waxes and mineral waxes are, respectively,
   a. 1 and 1
   b. 2 and 1
   c. 2 and 2
   d. no correct response

Answers: 1. a; 2. a; 3. b

19-15 Saponifiable and Nonsaponifiable Lipids

LEARNING FOCUS

Based on their names or on structural features present, be able to classify various lipids into the categories *saponifiable* and *nonsaponifiable.*

At the beginning of this chapter, in Section 19-1, the following items were noted:

1. Two commonly used classification systems for lipids exist: a system based on biochemical functions that lipids have and a system based on a particular reaction that lipids undergo, that of saponification.
2. The biochemical function classification system would be used as the basis for the chapter's organization.
3. The chemical reaction classification system would then be considered in the last section of the chapter, serving as a chapter summary.

The chemical reaction (saponification) classification system for lipids is very simple. There are only two categories of lipids in this system: saponifiable lipids and nonsaponifiable lipids. A saponification reaction, the basis for this classification system, is a hydrolysis reaction that is carried out in basic solution (Section 16-16). ◀

A **saponifiable lipid** *is a lipid that undergoes hydrolysis in basic solution to yield two or more smaller product molecules.* As a result of hydrolysis, a saponifiable lipid is broken up into smaller component parts. A **nonsaponifiable lipid** *does not undergo hydrolysis in basic solution.* Such lipids cannot be broken up into smaller component parts using hydrolysis.

There are five types of saponifiable lipids and four types of nonsaponifiable lipids. The saponifiable lipids are triacylglycerols, glycerophospholipids, sphingophospholipids, sphingoglycolipids, and waxes. The nonsaponifiable lipids are cholesterol, bile acids, steroid hormones, and eicosanoids (Figure 19-31).

What determines whether or not a lipid is saponifiable? It is the types of linkages (bonds) that hold its component parts (building blocks) together. Three types of linkages, all of which have been previously considered, can be hydrolyzed (broken) by reaction with water. These linkage types are (1) ester linkages, (2) amide linkages, and (3) glycosidic linkages. All three of these linkage types can be found in lipids.

▶ *This is the fourth time the concept of saponification has been encountered. Earlier encounters were ester saponification (Section 16-16), amide saponification (Section 17-18), and triacylglycerol saponification (Section 19-6 of this chapter).*

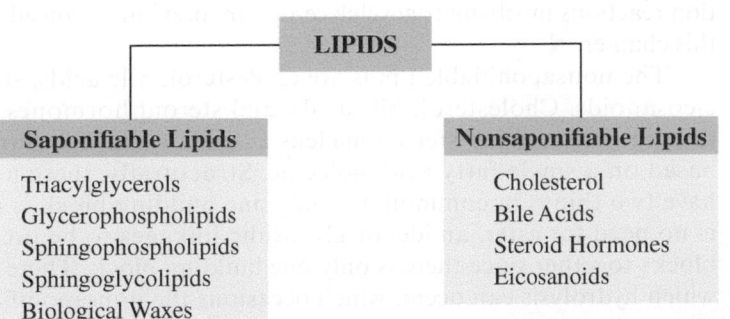

Figure 19-31 Classification of lipids into the categories *saponifiable* and *nonsaponifiable.*

Figure 19-32 Types of linkages present in the five kinds of saponifiable lipids.

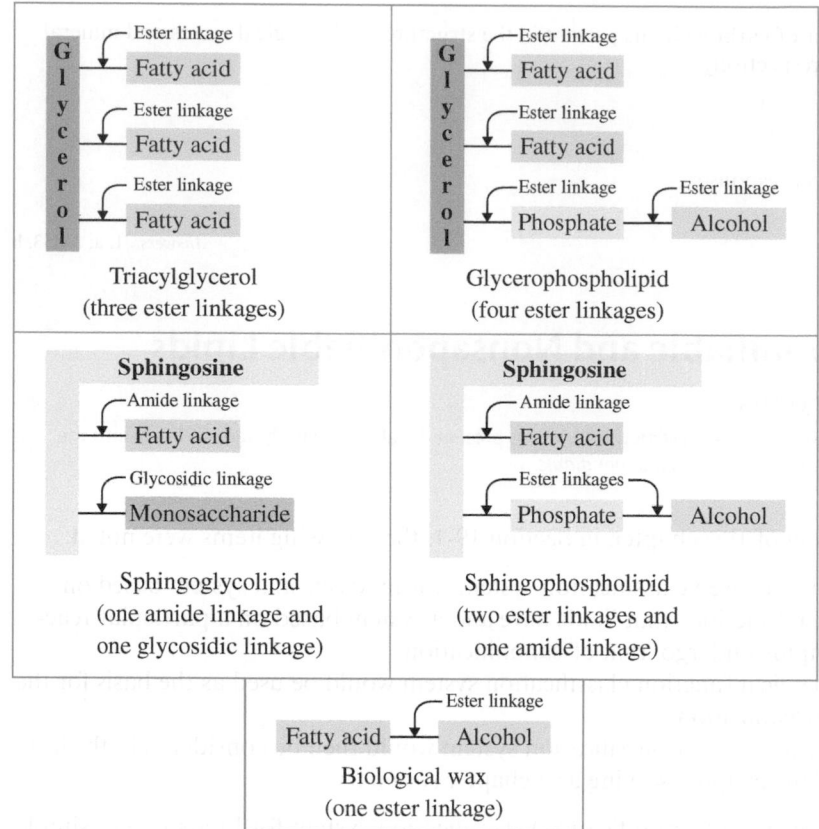

Saponifiable lipids always contain at least one of these three types of linkages. The linkage "makeup" for the five kinds of saponifiable lipids is as follows:

1. Triacylglycerols—three ester linkages
2. Glycerophospholipids—four ester linkages
3. Sphingophospholipids—one amide and two ester linkages
4. Sphingoglycolipids—one amide, one ester, and one glycosidic linkage
5. Biological waxes—one ester linkage

Figure 19-32 shows pictorially the location of the various linkages in these five types of lipids.

Using the block diagrams in Figure 19-32, it is easy to visualize the products that result from saponification of the various types of saponifiable lipids. The products are simply the "building blocks" from which each lipid can be considered to have been made. The ester, amide, and glycosidic linkages present are broken through reaction with water, which releases (frees up) the lipid's component parts. Any fatty acid molecules released will be converted to fatty acid salts because of the basic conditions associated with saponification (Sections 16-15 and 17-18). Hydrolysis and saponification reactions involving triacyclglycerol were previously considered in Section 19-6 of this chapter. ◀

The nonsaponifiable lipids are cholesterol, bile acids, steroid hormones, and eicosanoids. Cholesterol, bile acids, and steroid hormones have structures containing the four-ring steroid nucleus as a platform. Eicosanoids have structures based on a single fatty acid molecule. Structurally, these nonsaponifiable lipids have two things in common: (1) only one building block is present and (2) there is no need for ester, amide, or glycosidic linkages to be present to link building blocks together since there is only one building block. There is no site (linkage) at which hydrolysis can occur, which occasions the nonsaponifiable classification for these substances.

▶ *Hydrolysis reactions involving the ester, amide, and glycosidic linkages present in saponifiable lipids will be an important topic in Chapter 25, which considers the metabolic reactions that lipids undergo within the human body.*

Section 19-15 Quick Quiz

1. In which of the following pairs of lipid types are both members of the pair classified as saponifiable lipids?
   a. triacylglycerols and biological waxes
   b. glycerophospholipids and eicosanoids
   c. sphingophospholipids and bile acids
   d. no correct response
2. How many "building blocks" are present in the block diagram structure of a nonsaponifiable lipid?
   a. one
   b. two
   c. three
   d. no correct response
3. Which of the following statements concerning bond breaking that occurs under saponification conditions is *incorrect*?
   a. Ester linkages are broken.
   b. Amide linkages are broken.
   c. Glycosidic linkages are broken.
   d. no correct response

Answers: 1.a; 2. a; 3. d

Concepts to Remember

Lipids. Lipids are a structurally heterogeneous group of compounds of biochemical origin that are soluble in nonpolar organic solvents and insoluble in water. Lipids are divided into five major types on the basis of biochemical function: energy-storage lipids, membrane lipids, emulsification lipids, messenger lipids, and protective-coating lipids (Section 19-1).

Types of fatty acids. Fatty acids are monocarboxylic acids that contain long, unbranched carbon chains. The carbon chain may be saturated, monounsaturated, or polyunsaturated. Length of carbon chain, degree of unsaturation, and location of the unsaturation influence the properties of fatty acids. Omega-3 and omega-6 fatty acids are unsaturated fatty acids with the endmost double bond three and six carbons, respectively, away from the methyl end of the carbon chain (Section 19-2).

Triacylglycerols. Triacylglycerols are energy-storage lipids formed by esterification of three fatty acids to a glycerol molecule. Fats are triacylglycerol mixtures that are solids or semi-solids at room temperature; they contain a relatively high percentage of saturated fatty acid residues. Oils are triacylglycerol mixtures that are liquids at room temperature; they contain a relatively high percentage of unsaturated fatty acid residues (Section 19-4).

Phospholipids. Phospholipids are membrane lipids that contain one or more fatty acids, a phosphate group, a platform molecule to which the fatty acid(s) and phosphate group are attached, and an alcohol attached to the phosphate group. The platform molecule is either glycerol (glycerophospholipids) or sphingosine (sphingophospholipids). Phospholipids have a "head and two tails" structure. Lecithins, cephalins, and sphingomyelins are types of phospholipids (Section 19-7).

Sphingoglycolipids. Sphingoglycolipids are membrane lipids in which a fatty acid and a mono- or oligosaccharide are attached to the platform molecule sphingosine. Cerebrosides and gangliosides are types of sphingoglycolipids (Section 19-8).

Cholesterol. Cholesterol is a membrane lipid whose structure contains a steroid nucleus. It is the most abundant type of steroid. Besides its membrane functions, it also serves as a precursor for several other types of lipids (Section 19-9).

Lipid bilayer. A lipid bilayer is the fundamental structure associated with a cell membrane. It is a two-layer structure of lipid molecules (mostly phospholipids and glycolipids) in which the nonpolar tails of the lipids are in the interior and the polar heads are on the outside surfaces (Section 19-10).

Membrane transport mechanisms. The transport mechanisms by which molecules enter and leave cells include *passive* transport, *facilitated* transport, and *active* transport. Passive and facilitated transport follow a concentration gradient and do not involve cellular energy expenditure. Active transport involves movement against a concentration gradient and requires the expenditure of cellular energy (Section 19-10).

Bile acids. Bile acids are cholesterol derivatives that function as emulsification lipids. They cause dietary lipids to be soluble in the aqueous environment of the digestive tract. Cholic acid and deoxycholic acids are the major types of bile acids (Section 19-11).

Steroid hormones. Steroid hormones are cholesterol derivatives that function as messenger lipids. The two major types of steroid hormones are sex hormones and adrenocorticoid hormones (Section 19-12).

Eicosanoids. Eicosanoids are fatty acid derivatives that function as messenger lipids. The major classes of eicosanoids are prostaglandins, thromboxanes, and leukotrienes (Section 19-13).

Biological waxes. Biological waxes are protective-coating lipids formed through the esterification of a long-chain fatty acid to a long-chain alcohol (Section 19-14).

Saponifiable and nonsaponifiable lipids. Saponifiable lipids are lipids that undergo hydrolysis in basic solution to yield two or more smaller product molecules. Nonsaponifiable lipids are lipids that do not undergo hydrolysis in basic solution (Section 19-15).

Exercises and Problems

Exercises and problems are arranged in matched pairs with the two members of a pair addressing the same concept(s). The answer to the odd-numbered member of a pair is given at the back of the book. Problems denoted with a ▲ involve concepts found not only in the section under consideration but also concepts found in one or more earlier sections of the chapter.

Structure and Classification of Lipids (Section 19-1)

19-1 Indicate whether each of the following general statements about lipids is true or false.
 a. Lipids are compounds soluble in both polar and nonpolar solvents.
 b. Saponifiable lipid molecules are easily converted into two or more simpler molecules.

19-2 Indicate whether each of the following general statements about lipids is true or false.
 a. The concept that defines a lipid is related to solubility rather than structure.
 b. Nonsaponifiable lipid molecules undergo hydrolysis in basic aqueous solution.

19-3 Would you expect lipids to be soluble or insoluble in each of the following solvents?
 a. H_2O (polar)
 b. $CH_3-CH_2-O-CH_2-CH_3$ (nonpolar)
 c. CH_3-OH (polar)
 d. $CH_3-CH_2-CH_2-CH_2-CH_3$ (nonpolar)

19-4 Would you expect lipids to be soluble or insoluble in each of the following solvents?
 a. $CH_3-(CH_2)_7-CH_3$ (nonpolar)
 b. CH_3-Cl (polar)
 c. CCl_4 (nonpolar)
 d. CH_3-CH_2-OH (polar)

19-5 What is the biochemical function category for each of the following types of lipids?
 a. triacylglycerols   b. bile acids
 c. cholesterol   d. steroid hormones

19-6 What is the biochemical function category for each of the following types of lipids?
 a. sphingoglycolipids   b. eicosanoids
 c. biological waxes   d. phospholipids

Types of Fatty Acids (Section 19-2)

19-7 Classify each of the following fatty acids as long-chain, medium-chain, or short-chain.
 a. Myristic (14:0)   b. Caproic (6:0)
 c. Arachidic (20:0)   d. Capric (10:0)

19-8 Classify each of the following fatty acids as long-chain, medium-chain, or short-chain.
 a. Lauric (12:0)   b. Oleic (18:1)
 c. Butyric (4:0)   d. Stearic (18:0)

19-9 Classify each of the following fatty acids as saturated, monounsaturated, or polyunsaturated.
 a. Stearic (18:0)
 b. Linolenic (18:3)
 c. Docosahexaenoic (22:6)
 d. Oleic (18:1)

19-10 Classify each of the following fatty acids as saturated, monounsaturated, or polyunsaturated.
 a. Palmitic (16:0)   b. Linoleic (18:2)
 c. Arachidonic (20:4)   d. Palmitoleic (16:1)

19-11 What does the acronym MUFA stand for?

19-12 What does the acronym PUFA stand for?

19-13 Classify each of the following fatty acids as saturated, monounsaturated, or polyunsaturated.
 a. $CH_3-(CH_2)_{14}-COOH$

 b. $CH_3-(CH_2)_5-CH=CH-(CH_2)_7-COOH$

 c.

 d.

19-14 Classify each of the following fatty acids as saturated, monounsaturated, or polyunsaturated.
 a. $CH_3-(CH_2)_7-CH=CH-(CH_2)_7-COOH$

 b. $CH_3-(CH_2)_4-(CH=CH-CH_2)_2-(CH_2)_6-COOH$

 c.

 d.

19-15 Classify each of the fatty acids in Problem 19-13 using the omega classification system or indicate that the omega classification system does not apply to the fatty acid.

19-16 Classify each of the fatty acids in Problem 19-14 using the omega classification system or indicate that the omega classification system does not apply to the fatty acid.

19-17 Draw the condensed structural formula for the fatty acid whose numerical shorthand designation is 18:2 ($\Delta^{9,12}$).

19-18 Draw the condensed structural formula for the fatty acid whose numerical shorthand designation is 20:4 ($\Delta^{5,8,11,14}$).

19-19 Using the information given in Table 19-1, assign an IUPAC name to each of the following fatty acids.
 a. Myristic acid
 b. Palmitoleic acid

19-20 Using the information given in Table 19-1, assign an IUPAC name to each of the following fatty acids.
 a. Stearic acid
 b. Linolenic acid

Physical Properties of Fatty Acids (Section 19-3)

19-21 What is the relationship between carbon chain length and melting point for fatty acids?

19-22 What is the relationship between degree of unsaturation and melting point for fatty acids?

19-23 What structural change is associated with the introduction of a *cis*-double bond into a fatty acid molecule?

19-24 Why does the introduction of a *cis*-double bond into a fatty acid molecule lower its melting point?

19-25 In each of the following pairs of fatty acids, select the fatty acid that has the lower melting point.
a. 18:0 acid and 18:1 acid
b. 18:2 acid and 18:3 acid
c. 14:0 acid and 16:0 acid
d. 18:1 acid and 20:0 acid

19-26 In each of the following pairs of fatty acids, select the fatty acid that has the higher melting point.
a. 14:0 acid and 18:0 acid
b. 20:4 acid and 20:5 acid
c. 18:3 acid and 20:3 acid
d. 16:0 acid and 16:1 acid

Energy-Storage Lipids: Triacylglycerols (Section 19-4)

19-27 What are the four structural subunits that contribute to the structure of a triacylglycerol?

19-28 Draw the general block diagram for a triacylglycerol.

19-29 Determine the following for a triacylglycerol in which all fatty acid residues present come from saturated fatty acids.
a. the total number of functional groups present
b. the number of different kinds of functional groups present
c. the names for the functional groups present
d. the number of subunit linkages present

19-30 Determine the following for a triacylglycerol in which all fatty acid residues present come from monounsaturated fatty acids.
a. the total number of functional groups present
b. the number of different kinds of functional groups present
c. the names for the functional groups present
d. the number of subunit linkages present

19-31 Draw the condensed structural formula of a triacylglycerol formed from glycerol and three molecules of palmitic acid.

19-32 Draw the condensed structural formula of a triacylglycerol formed from glycerol and three molecules of stearic acid.

19-33 Draw block diagram structures for the four different triacylglycerols that can be produced from glycerol, stearic acid, and linolenic acid.

19-34 Draw block diagram structures for the three different triacylglycerols that can be produced from glycerol, palmitic acid, stearic acid, and linolenic acid.

19-35 Identify, by common name, fatty acids present in each of the following triacylglycerols.
a.

b.

19-36 Identify, by common name, fatty acids present in each of the following triacylglycerols.
a.

b.

19-37 A mixture of triacylglycerol molecules contains 67% SFAs, 28% MUFAs, and 5% PUFAs and has a melting point of 32°C.
a. Should this mixture be classified as a fat or an oil?
b. Explain the basis for the answer given in part a.

19-38 A mixture of triacylglycerol molecules contains 24% SFAs, 54% MUFAs, and 22% PUFAs and has a melting point of 5°C.
a. Should this mixture be classified as a fat or an oil?
b. Explain the basis for the answer given in part a.

▲19-39 For each of the triacylglycerol molecules in Problem 19-35, indicate how many of each of the following entities are present in the molecule. In certain cases, the answer may be zero.
a. Acyl groups
b. 18:2 fatty acid residues
c. SFA residues
d. Linolenic acid residues

▲19-40 For each of the triacylglycerol molecules in Problem 19-36, indicate how many of each of the following entities are present in the molecule. In certain cases, the answer may be zero.
a. Ester linkages
b. 18:1 fatty acid residues
c. PUFA residues
d. Stearic acid residues

Dietary Considerations and Triacylglycerols (Section 19-5)

19-41 In a dietary context, indicate whether each of the following pairings of concepts is correct.
a. "Saturated fat" and "good fat"
b. "Polyunsaturated fat" and "bad fat"

19-42 In a dietary context, indicate whether each of the following pairings of concepts is correct.
a. "Monounsaturated fat" and "good fat"
b. "Saturated fat" and "good and bad fat"

19-43 In a dietary context, which of the following pairings of concepts is correct?
a. "Cold-water fish" and "high in omega-3 fatty acids"
b. "Fatty fish" and "low in omega-3 fatty acids"

19-44 In a dietary context, which of the following pairings of concepts is correct?
a. "Warm-water fish" and "low in omega-3 fatty acids"
b. "Fish and chips" and "high in omega-3 fatty acids"

19-45 In a dietary context, classify each of the following fatty acids as an essential fatty acid or as a nonessential fatty acid.
  a. Lauric acid (12:0)
  b. Linoleic acid (18:2)
  c. Myristic acid (14:0)
  d. Palmitoleic acid (16:1)

19-46 In a dietary context, classify each of the following fatty acids as an essential fatty acid or as a nonessential fatty acid.
  a. Stearic acid (18:0)
  b. Linolenic acid (18:3)
  c. Oleic acid (18:1)
  d. Arachidic acid (20:0)

▲**19-47** For each of the triacylglycerol molecules in Problem 19-35, indicate how many of each of the following entities are present in the molecule. In certain cases, the answer may be zero.
  a. Omega-3 fatty acid residues
  b. Omega-6 fatty acid residues
  c. "Good" fatty acid residues
  d. Δ^9 fatty acid residues

▲**19-48** For each of the triacylglycerol molecules in Problem 19-36, indicate how many of each of the following entities are present in the molecule. In certain cases, the answer may be zero.
  a. Omega-3 fatty acid residues
  b. Omega-6 fatty acid residues
  c. "Bad" fatty acid residues
  d. $\Delta^{9,12}$ fatty acid residues

Chemical Reactions of Triacylglycerols (Section 19-6)

19-49 What are the general names for the products obtained when a triacylglycerol molecule participates in an acidic hydrolysis reaction in which
  a. three molecules of water participate
  b. two molecules of water participate
  c. one molecule of water participates

19-50 What additional products are formed when a triacylglycerol molecule is converted to each of the following in an acidic hydrolysis reaction.
  a. diacylglycerol
  b. monoacylglycerol
  c. glycerol

19-51 Classify each of the reaction situations in Problem 19-49 as involving *complete hydrolysis* or *partial hydrolysis*.

19-52 Classify each of the reaction situations in Problem 19-50 as involving *complete hydrolysis* or *partial hydrolysis*.

19-53 Draw condensed structural formulas for all products obtained from the complete hydrolysis of the following triacylglycerol under acidic conditions.

$$CH_2-O-\overset{\overset{\displaystyle O}{\|}}{C}-(CH_2)_{14}-CH_3$$
$$CH-O-\overset{\overset{\displaystyle O}{\|}}{C}-(CH_2)_{12}-CH_3$$
$$CH_2-O-\overset{\overset{\displaystyle O}{\|}}{C}-(CH_2)_7-CH=CH-(CH_2)_7-CH_3$$

19-54 Draw condensed structural formulas for all products obtained from the complete hydrolysis of the following triacylglycerol under acidic conditions.

$$CH_2-O-\overset{\overset{\displaystyle O}{\|}}{C}-(CH_2)_{16}-CH_3$$
$$CH-O-\overset{\overset{\displaystyle O}{\|}}{C}-(CH_2)_{12}-CH_3$$
$$CH_2-O-\overset{\overset{\displaystyle O}{\|}}{C}-(CH_2)_6-(CH_2-CH=CH)_3-CH_2-CH_3$$

19-55 Draw condensed structural formulas for all products you would obtain from the saponification with NaOH of the triacylglycerol in Problem 19-53.

19-56 Draw condensed structural formulas for all products you would obtain from the saponification with KOH of the triacylglycerol in Problem 19-54.

19-57 Why can only unsaturated triacylglycerols undergo hydrogenation?

19-58 A food package label lists an oil as "partially hydrogenated." What does this mean?

19-59 How many molecules of H_2 will react with one molecule of the following triacylglycerol?

$$CH_2-O-\overset{\overset{\displaystyle O}{\|}}{C}-(CH_2)_6-(CH_2-CH=CH)_2-(CH_2)_4-CH_3$$
$$CH-O-\overset{\overset{\displaystyle O}{\|}}{C}-(CH_2)_7-CH=CH-(CH_2)_7-CH_3$$
$$CH_2-O-\overset{\overset{\displaystyle O}{\|}}{C}-(CH_2)_6-(CH_2-CH=CH)_3-CH_2-CH_3$$

19-60 How many molecules of H_2 will react with one molecule of the following triacylglycerol?

$$CH_2-O-\overset{\overset{\displaystyle O}{\|}}{C}-(CH_2)_7-CH=CH-(CH_2)_7-CH_3$$
$$CH-O-\overset{\overset{\displaystyle O}{\|}}{C}-(CH_2)_{16}-CH_3$$
$$CH_2-O-\overset{\overset{\displaystyle O}{\|}}{C}-(CH_2)_6-(CH_2-CH=CH)_3-CH_2-CH_3$$

19-61 Draw block diagram structures for all possible products of the partial hydrogenation, with two molecules of H_2, of the following molecules.

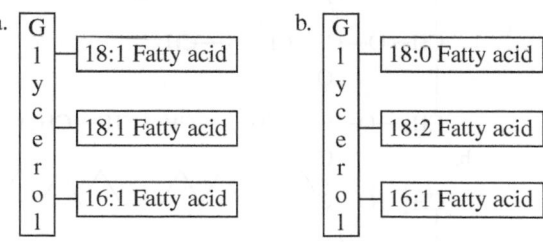

19-62 Draw block diagram structures for all possible products of the partial hydrogenation, with two molecules of H_2, of the following molecules.

a.
Glycerol	20:1 Fatty acid
	18:1 Fatty acid
	18:1 Fatty acid

b.
Glycerol	20:1 Fatty acid
	18:0 Fatty acid
	18:2 Fatty acid

19-63 Why do animal fats and vegetable oils become rancid when exposed to moist, warm air?

19-64 Why are the compounds BHA and BHT often added to foods that contain fats and oils?

19-65 Which of the terms *acidic hydrolysis, saponification, hydrogenation,* and *oxidation* apply to each of the following reaction changes? More than one term may apply in a given situation.
a. Carbon–carbon double bonds are broken.
b. Fatty acids are among the products.
c. *Cis* double bonds are converted to *trans* double bonds.
d. Water is a reactant.

19-66 Which of the terms *acidic hydrolysis, saponification, hydrogenation,* and *oxidation* apply to each of the following reaction changes? More than one term may apply in a given situation.
a. Carbon–oxygen single bonds are broken.
b. Glycerol is among the products.
c. Fatty acid salts are among the products.
d. Carbon–carbon double bonds are changed to carbon–carbon single bonds.

▲**19-67** How many *different* organic molecules are obtained when
a. a simple triacylglycerol undergoes complete acidic hydrolysis
b. a mixed triacylglycerol undergoes complete acidic hydrolysis
c. a simple triacylglycerol undergoes saponification
d. a mixed triacylglycerol undergoes saponification

▲**19-68** How many water molecules undergo reaction when
a. a simple triacylglycerol undergoes complete acidic hydrolysis
b. a mixed triacylglycerol undergoes complete acidic hydrolysis
c. a simple triacylglycerol undergoes saponification
d. a mixed triacylglycerol undergoes saponification

Membrane Lipids: Phospholipids (Section 19-7)

19-69 The following is a block diagram for a glycerophospholipid where the building blocks are labeled with letters and the linkages between building blocks are labeled with numbers.

a. Which building blocks are fatty acid residues?
b. Which building blocks are alcohol residues?
c. Which linkages are ester linkages?
d. Which linkages involve a phosphate residue?

19-70 Using the block diagram in Problem 19-69 for a glycerophospholipid where the building blocks are labeled with letters and the linkages between building blocks are labeled with numbers,
a. which building blocks are glycerol residues?
b. which building blocks are phosphate residues?
c. which linkages involve an alcohol residue?
d. which linkages involve both glycerol and fatty acid residues?

19-71 What structural subunits in the block diagram for a glycerophospholipid collectively constitute a phosphatidyl group?

19-72 What structural subunits in the block diagram for a glycerophospholipid are not part of its phosphatidyl group?

19-73 Indicate whether each of the following statements about the amino alcohol choline is true or false?
a. Two hydroxyl groups are present in its structure.
b. One nitrogen atom is present in its structure.
c. Five carbon atoms are present in its structure.
d. Glycerophospholipids in which it is present are called lecithins.

19-74 Indicate whether each of the following statements about the amino alcohol ethanolamine is true or false?
a. Two hydroxyl groups are present in its structure.
b. Two carbon atoms are present in its structure.
c. Two nitrogen atoms are present in its structure.
d. Glycerophospholipids in which it is present are called cephalins.

19-75 Based on the "head and two tails" model for the structure of a glycerophospholipid, classify each of the following structural units as being part of its "head" or being part of its "tails."
a. fatty acids
b. amino alcohol
c. phosphate group

19-76 Based on the "head and two tails" model for the structure of a glycerophospholipid, classify each of the following structural units as being strongly hydrophobic or strongly hydrophilic.
a. fatty acids
b. amino alcohol
c. phosphate group

Sphingophospholipids (Section 19-7)

19-77 Indicate whether each of the following descriptions concerning the molecule sphingosine is true or false.
a. Four functional groups are present.
b. The carbon chain is unsaturated.
c. It has a head-and-two-tails structure.
d. An amino functional group is present.

19-78 Indicate whether each of the following descriptions concerning the molecule sphingosine is true or false.
a. Carbons 1, 2, and 3 all bear the same kind of functional group.
b. Three different kinds of functional groups are present.
c. It is an unsaturated diaminoalcohol.
d. The carbon chain contains 20 carbon atoms.

19-79 The following is a block diagram for a sphingophospholipid where the building blocks are labeled with letters and the linkages between building blocks are labeled with numbers.

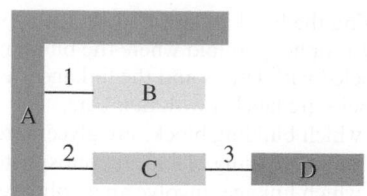

a. Which building blocks are fatty acid residues?
b. Which building blocks are phosphate residues?
c. Which linkages are amide linkages?
d. Which linkages involve a sphingosine residue?

19-80 Using the block diagram in Problem 19-79 for a sphingophospholipid where the building blocks are labeled with letters and the linkages between building blocks are labeled with numbers,
a. which building blocks are sphingosine residues?
b. which building blocks are alcohol residues?
c. which linkages are ester linkages?
d. which linkages involve a phosphate residue?

19-81 What is the name of the amino alcohol that is present in sphingophospholipids known as sphingomyelins?

19-82 Sphingomyelins are important components in the coating that surrounds what body component?

19-83 What portion or portions of the structure of a sphingophospholipid
a. constitute its head in the "head and two tails" model for its structure
b. have hydrophobic properties

19-84 What portion or portions of the structure of a sphingophospholipid
a. constitute its tails in the "head and two tails" model for its structure
b. have hydrophilic properties

▲**19-85** Which of the terms *triacylglycerol, glycerophospholipid,* and *sphingophospholipid* applies to each of the following characterizations? More than one term may apply in a given situation.
a. It contains four building blocks.
b. All linkages are ester linkages.
c. An alcohol building block is present.
d. It is an energy-storage lipid.

▲**19-86** Which of the terms *triacylglycerol, glycerophospholipid,* and *sphingophospholipid* applies to each of the following characterizations? More than one term may apply in a given situation.
a. It contains five building blocks.
b. It contains two kinds of linkages.
c. A phosphate building block is present.
d. It is a membrane lipid.

▲**19-87** Which of the terms *triacylglycerol, glycerophospholipid,* and *sphingophospholipid* applies to each of the following characterizations? More than one term may apply, or none of the terms may apply in a given situation.
a. Must contain ethanolamine
b. Phosphatidylcholine
c. Must contain an amide linkage
d. Nonsaponifiable

▲**19-88** Which of the terms *triacylglycerol, glycerophospholipid,* and *sphingophospholipid* applies to each of the following characterizations? More than one term may apply, or none of the terms may apply in a given situation.
a. Must contain choline
b. Lecithin
c. Must contain an ester linkage
d. Saponifiable

Membrane Lipids: Sphingoglycolipids (Section 19-8)

19-89 The following is a block diagram for a sphingoglycolipid where the building blocks are labeled with letters and the linkages between building blocks are labeled with numbers.

a. Which building blocks are fatty acid residues?
b. Which building blocks are carbohydrate residues?
c. Which linkages are amide linkages?
d. Which linkages could involve a monosaccharide?

19-90 Using the block diagram in Problem 19-89 for a sphingoglycolipid where the building blocks are labeled with letters and the linkages between building blocks are labeled with numbers,
a. which building blocks are sphingosine residues?
b. which building blocks are mono- or oligosaccharide residues?
c. which linkages are glycosidic linkages?
d. which linkages involve both sphingosine and fatty acid residues?

19-91 Indicate whether each of the following is a component of (1) a cerebroside but not a ganglioside, (2) a ganglioside but not a cerebroside, or (3) both a cerebroside and a ganglioside.
a. Monosaccharide   b. Oligosaccharide
c. Fatty acid   d. Sphingosine

19-92 A sphingoglycolipid has a "head and two tails" structure. Classify each of the following components of a sphingoglycolipid as being part of its "head" or part of its "tails."
a. Sphingosine   b. Fatty acid
c. Monosaccharide   d. Oligosaccharide

▲**19-93** Which of the terms *glycerophospholipid, sphingophospholipid,* and *sphingoglycolipid* applies to each of the following characterizations? More than one term may apply, or none of the terms may apply in a given situation.
a. Membrane lipid
b. Saponifiable lipid
c. Amide linkage present
d. Has a "head and two tails" structure

▲**19-94** Which of the terms *glycerophospholipid, sphingophospholipid,* and *sphingoglycolipid* applies to each of the following characterizations? More than one term may apply, or none of the terms may apply in a given situation.
a. Energy-storage lipid
b. Nonsaponifiable lipid
c. Glycosidic linkage present
d. Does not have a "head and two tails" structure

Membrane Lipids: Cholesterol (Section 19-9)

19-95 Indicate whether each of the following statements about a steroid nucleus is true or false.
 a. Rings A, B, and C are identical.
 b. Rings A and C are linked via a glycosidic linkage.
 c. Rings A and B share a common side.
 d. Twenty-seven carbon atoms are present in a steroid nucleus.

19-96 Indicate whether each of the following statements about a steroid nucleus is true or false.
 a. Rings B, C, and D are identical.
 b. Rings B and C are linked via an ester linkage.
 c. Ring B is fused to two other rings.
 d. Twenty carbon atoms are present in a steroid nucleus.

19-97 Give numerical answers to the following questions about the structure of a cholesterol molecule.
 a. How many six-membered rings are present?
 b. How many amide linkages are present?
 c. How many hydroxyl substituents are present?
 d. How many total functional groups are present?

19-98 Give numerical answers to the following questions about the structure of a cholesterol molecule.
 a. How many five-membered rings are present?
 b. How many ester linkages are present?
 c. How many methyl substituents are present?
 d. How many different kinds of functional groups are present?

19-99 Using the information in Table 19-4, rank a serving of the following four foods in order of increasing amount of cholesterol present: Swiss cheese, fish fillet, liver, chicken.

19-100 Using the information in Table 19-4, rank a serving of the following four foods in order of increasing amount of cholesterol present: egg, beef steak, cheddar cheese, whole milk.

19-101 In a dietary context, what is the difference between "good cholesterol" and "bad cholesterol"?

19-102 In a dietary context, how do HDL and LDL differ in function?

Cell Membranes (Section 19-10)

19-103 What is the general structural characteristic associated with the majority of lipids present in a lipid bilayer?

19-104 What constitutes the two outside surfaces of a lipid bilayer?

19-105 Indicate whether each of the following statements about a lipid bilayer is true or false.
 a. The outside surface positions in a lipid bilayer are occupied by hydrophobic entities.
 b. The interaction between the fluid *inside* a cell and the surface of a lipid bilayer is primarily an interaction between polar entities.
 c. The outside surface positions in a lipid bilayer are occupied by the nonpolar tails of phospholipids and glycolipids.
 d. The interactions between adjacent lipids in a lipid bilayer usually involve covalent bonding.

19-106 Indicate whether each of the following statements about a lipid bilayer is true or false.
 a. The outside surface positions in a lipid bilayer are occupied by the polar heads of phospholipids and glycolipids.
 b. The interaction between the fluid *outside* a cell and the surface of a lipid bilayer is primarily an interaction between nonpolar entities.
 c. The interactions between the tails of adjacent lipids in a lipid bilayer usually involve intermolecular forces.
 d. The outside surface positions in a lipid bilayer are occupied by alternating hydrophobic and hydrophilic entities.

19-107 What is the function of unsaturation in the hydrocarbon tails of membrane lipids?

19-108 What function does cholesterol serve when it is present in cell membranes?

19-109 What is an integral membrane protein?

19-110 What is a peripheral membrane protein?

19-111 What is the difference between *passive transport* and *facilitated transport*?

19-112 What is the difference between *facilitated transport* and *active transport*?

19-113 Match each of the following statements related to membrane transport processes to the appropriate term: *passive transport, facilitated transport, active transport*. More than one term may apply in a given situation.
 a. Movement across the membrane is against the concentration gradient.
 b. Proteins serve as "gates."
 c. Expenditure of cellular energy is required.
 d. Movement across the membrane is from a high to a low concentration.

19-114 Match each of the following statements related to membrane transport processes to the appropriate term: *passive transport, facilitated transport, active transport*. More than one term may apply in a given situation.
 a. Movement across the membrane is with the concentration gradient.
 b. Proteins serve as "pumps."
 c. Expenditure of cellular energy is not required.
 d. Movement across the membrane is from a low to a high concentration.

Emulsification Lipids: Bile Acids (Section 19-11)

19-115 What is an emulsifier?

19-116 The mode of action of an emulsification lipid is similar to that of what other type of substance?

19-117 Indicate whether each of the following statements concerning cholesterol and simple bile acids is true or false.
 a. Both cholesterol and cholic acid are C_{24} molecules.
 b. Both cholic acid and 7-deoxycholic acid are simple bile acids.
 c. Both 7-deoxycholic acid and 12-deoxycholic acid contain two hydroxyl groups.
 d. Both cholesterol and cholic acid contain a carboxyl group.

19-118   Indicate whether each of the following statements concerning cholesterol and simple bile acids is true or false.
a. Both cholic acid and 7-deoxycholic acid are C_{24} molecules.
b. Both 7-deoxycholic acid and 12-deoxycholic acid are simple bile acids.
c. Both cholic acid and 12-deoxycholic acid contain three hydroxyl groups.
d. Both cholesterol and cholic acid contain methyl group attachments.

19-119   Indicate whether each of the following statements concerning bile acids is true or false.
a. Both glycocholic acid and 7-deoxycholic acid are complexed bile acids.
b. Both glycocholic acid and taurocholic acid contain the element sulfur.
c. Both cholic acid and glycocholic and contain a side-chain amide linkage.
d. Both 12-deoxycholic acid and taurocholic acid contain a steroid nucleus.

19-120   Indicate whether each of the following statements concerning bile acids is true or false.
a. Both glycocholic acid and 7-deoxycholic acid are simple bile acids.
b. Both glycocholic acid and taurocholic acid contain the element nitrogen.
c. Both taurocholic acid and glycocholic acid contain an amino acid attachment.
d. Both 12-deoxycholic acid and taurocholic acid contain hydroxyl functional groups.

19-121   How many of each of the following structural features are present in a molecule of glycocholic acid?
a. number of attachments to the steroid nucleus
b. number of different functional groups present
c. total number of functional groups present
d. number of different elements present

19-122   How many of each of the following structural features are present in a molecule of taurocholic acid?
a. number of attachments to the steroid nucleus
b. number of different functional groups present
c. total number of functional groups present
d. number of different elements present

19-123   What part of the structure of a taurocholic acid molecule is strongly hydrophilic?

19-124   What part of the structure of a glycocholic acid molecule is largely hydrophobic?

19-125   What is the medium through which bile acids are supplied to the small intestine?

19-126   What is the chemical composition of bile?

19-127   At what location in the body are bile acids stored until needed?

19-128   What is the chemical composition of the majority of gallstones?

▲**19-129**   Classify each of the following as (1) an energy-storage lipid, (2) a membrane lipid, or (3) an emulsification lipid.
a. Taurocholic acid   b. Sphingoglycolipids
c. Triacylglycerols   d. Cholesterol

▲**19-130**   Classify each of the following as (1) an energy-storage lipid, (2) a membrane lipid, or (3) an emulsification lipid.
a. Oils
b. Glycocholic acid
c. Glycerophospholipids
d. Sphingophospholipids

Messenger Lipids: Steroid Hormones (Section 19-12)

19-131   Indicate whether each of the following statements about steroid hormones and their synthetic analogs is true or false.
a. Both estradiol and cortisol are cholesterol derivatives.
b. Both progesterone and testosterone are female sex hormones.
c. Both aldosterone and cortisone are adrenocorticoid hormones.
d. Both cortisol and aldosterone ae glucocorticoids.

19-132   Indicate whether each of the following statements about steroid hormones and their synthetic analogs is true or false.
a. Both estradiol and cortisol are mineralocorticoids.
b. Both progesterone and testosterone are male sex hormones.
c. Both aldosterone and cortisone are cholesterol derivatives.
d. Both cortisol and aldosterone are adrenocorticoid hormones.

19-133   Indicate whether each of the following is a naturally occurring steroid hormone or a synthetic analog of such.
a. aldosterone   b. cortisone
c. estradiol   d. norethynodrel

19-134   Indicate whether each of the following is a naturally occurring steroid hormone of a synthetic analog of such.
a. cortisol   b. prednisolone
c. progesterone   d. methandrostenolone

19-135   Indicate whether or not each of the following is an adrenal corticoid hormone or a sex hormone.
a. Aldosterone   b. Testosterone
c. Cortisol   d. Estradiol

19-136   Indicate whether or not each of the following is a natural steroid hormone or a synthetic steroid.
a. Cortisone   b. Progesterone
c. Prednisolone   d. Norethynodrel

19-137   What is the biochemical function for each of the steroids listed in Problem 19-135?

19-138   What is the biochemical function for each of the steroids listed in Problem 19-136?

▲**19-139**   Draw the structure of an anabolic steroid with the following structural characteristics: C1 and C2 are involved in a double bond, C3 is part of a carbonyl group, C4 and C5 are involved in a double bond, C10 and C13 have methyl group attachments, and C17 has both a hydroxyl group and a methyl group as substituents.

▲**19-140**   Draw the structure of an anabolic steroid with the following structural characteristics: C3 is part of a carbonyl group; carbon–carbon double bonds involve C4 and C5, C9 and C10, and C11 and C12; C13 has a methyl group attachment; and C17 has a hydroxyl group attachment.

Messenger Lipids: Eicosanoids (Section 19-13)

19-141 What is the major structural difference between a prostaglandin and its parent fatty acid?

19-142 What is the major structural difference between a leukotriene and its parent fatty acid?

19-143 What structural feature distinguishes a prostaglandin from a leukotriene?

19-144 What structural feature distinguishes a thromboxane from a leukotriene?

▲19-145 Classify each of the following types of lipids as (1) glycerol-based, (2) sphingosine-based, (3) steroid nucleus-based, or (4) fatty acid-based.
a. Bile acids
b. Oils
c. Prostaglandins
d. Thromboxanes

▲19-146 Classify each of the following types of lipids as (1) glycerol-based, (2) sphingosine-based, (3) steroid nucleus-based, or (4) fatty acid-based.
a. Fats
b. Cholesterol
c. Eicosanoids
d. Leukotrienes

▲19-147 Classify each of the following types of lipids as (1) an energy-storage lipid, (2) a membrane lipid, (3) an emulsification lipid, or (4) a messenger lipid.
a. Bile acids
b. Cholesterol
c. Eicosanoids
d. Sphingophospholipids

▲19-148 Classify each of the following types of lipids as (1) an energy-storage lipid, (2) a membrane lipid, (3) an emulsification lipid, or (4) a messenger lipid.
a. Triacylglycerols
b. Glycerophospholipids
c. Prostaglandins
d. Estrogens

Protective-Coating Lipids: Biological Waxes (Section 19-14)

19-149 Draw the general block diagram for a biological wax.

19-150 Draw the condensed structural formula of a wax formed from palmitic acid (Table 19-1) and cetyl alcohol, $CH_3—(CH_2)_{14}—CH_2—OH$.

▲19-151 What is the difference between a biological wax and a mineral wax?

▲19-152 Biological waxes have a "head and two tails" structure. Give the chemical identity of the head and of the two tails.

▲19-153 Which of the substance categories *biological wax, mineral wax, bile acid,* and *sphingophospholipid* has each of the following characteristics? More than one substance may have a given characteristic.
a. Structure is based on a steroid nucleus
b. A saponifiable lipid
c. Contains at least one fatty acid building block
d. Contains at least one amide linkage

▲19-154 Which of the substance categories *biological wax, mineral wax, bile acid,* and *sphingoglycolipid* has each of the following characteristics? More than one substance may have a given characteristic.
a. Contains at least one ester linkage
b. Contains at least one alcohol building block
c. Classified as a protective-coating lipid
d. Classified as an emulsification lipid

▲19-155 Indicate whether or not each of the following types of substances has a "head and two tails" structure.
a. Biological wax
b. Cholesterol
c. Sphingoglycolipid
d. Fat

▲19-156 Indicate whether or not each of the following types of substances has a "head and two tails" structure.
a. Mineral wax
b. Sphingosine
c. Sphingophospholipid
d. Oil

▲19-157 Indicate whether or not each of the following substances contains (1) an ester linkage, (2) an amide linkage, or (3) a glycosidic linkage. More than one characterization may apply, or none of the characterizations may apply.
a. Biological wax
b. Triacylglycerol
c. Bile acid
d. Sphingosine

▲19-158 Indicate whether or not each of the following substances contains (1) an ester linkage, (2) an amide linkage, or (3) a glycosidic linkage. More than one characterization may apply, or none of the characterizations may apply.
a. Mineral wax
b. Prostaglandin
c. Oil
d. Cholesterol

Saponifiable and Nonsaponifiable Lipids (Section 19-15)

19-159 Indicate whether or not both members of each of the following pairs of substances are saponifiable lipids.
a. Sphingoglycolipids and sphingophospholipids
b. Biological waxes and mineral waxes
c. Triacylglycerols and steroid hormones
d. Eicosanoids and cholesterol

19-160 Indicate whether or not both members of each of the following pairs of substances are saponifiable lipids.
a. Glycerophospholipids and triacylglycerols
b. Cholesterol and sphingoglycolipids
c. Mineral waxes and bile acids
d. Eicosanoids and biological waxes

19-161 How many saponifiable linkages are present in each of the following types of substances?
a. Cholesterol
b. Triacylglycerols
c. Bile acids
d. Biological waxes

19-162 How many saponifiable linkages are present in each of the following types of substances?
a. Eicosanoids
b. Sphingoglycolipids
c. Mineral waxes
d. Sphingophospholipids

Chapter 19 Appendix:

Section 4.7 Introduction to Hormonal Communication from Sherwood Human Physiology:
From Cells to Systems, 9th Edition

focus on the molecular and cellular features of hormonal action and compare the similarities and differences in how neurons and endocrine cells communicate with other cells in carrying out their regulatory actions.

4.7 Introduction to Hormonal Communication

Endocrinology is the study of homeostatic chemical adjustments and other activities accomplished by hormones, which are secreted into the blood by endocrine glands. Earlier we described the underlying molecular and cellular mechanisms of the nervous system—electrical signaling within neurons and chemical transmission of signals between neurons. We now

Hormones are classified chemically as hydrophilic or lipophilic.

Hormones fall into two chemical groups based on their solubility: *hydrophilic* and *lipophilic* hormones. Hormones can also be classified according to their chemical structure (namely, *peptides*, *amines*, and *steroids*) as follows (Table 4-5):

1. **Hydrophilic** ("water-loving") **hormones** are highly water soluble and have low lipid solubility. Most hydrophilic hormones are peptide or protein hormones consisting of specific amino acids arranged in a chain of varying length. The shorter chains are peptides, and the longer ones are proteins. For convenience, we refer to this entire category as **peptides**. Insulin from the pancreas is a peptide hormone. The **amines** are so called because they are amino acid derivatives. The amine hor-

TABLE 4-5 Chemical Classification of Hormones

Properties	Peptides	AMINES		Steroids
		Catecholamines and Indoleamines	Thyroid Hormone	
Solubility	Hydrophilic	Hydrophilic	Lipophilic	Lipophilic
Structure	Chains of specific amino acids	Tyrosine derivative (catecholamines) or tryptophan derivative (indoleamines)	Iodinated tyrosine derivative	Cholesterol derivative
Synthesis	In rough endoplasmic reticulum; packaged in Golgi complex	In cytosol	In colloid within thyroid gland (see p. 666)	Stepwise modification of cholesterol molecule in various intracellular compartments
Storage	Large amounts in secretory vesicles	In secretory vesicles	In colloid	Not stored; cholesterol precursor stored in lipid droplets
Secretion	Exocytosis of secretory vesicles	Exocytosis of secretory vesicles	Endocytosis of colloid	Simple diffusion
Transport in blood	As free hormone	Half bound to plasma proteins	Mostly bound to plasma proteins	Mostly bound to plasma proteins
Receptor site	Surface of target cell	Surface of target cell	Inside target cell	Inside target cell
Mechanism of action	Activation of second-messenger pathway to alter activity of preexisting proteins that produce the effect	Activation of second-messenger pathway to alter activity of preexisting proteins that produce the effect	Activation of specific genes to make new proteins that produce the effect	Activation of specific genes to make new proteins that produce the effect
Hormones of this type	Most hormones	Catecholamines: hormones from the adrenal medulla, dopamine from hypothalamus. Indoleamines: melatonin from pineal gland	Only hormones from the follicular cells of the thyroid gland	Hormones from the adrenal cortex and gonads and some placental hormones; vitamin D (a hormone) is steroidlike

mones include two types of hydrophilic hormones (catecholamines and indoleamines) and one type of lipophilic hormone (thyroid hormone). *Catecholamines* are derived from the amino acid tyrosine and are largely secreted by the adrenal medulla. The adrenal gland consists of an inner adrenal medulla surrounded by an outer adrenal cortex. (You will learn more about the location and structure of the endocrine glands and the functions of specific hormones in later chapters.) Epinephrine is the major catecholamine hormone. *Indoleamines* are derived from the amino acid tryptophan and are secreted by the pineal gland. Melatonin is the only indoleamine hormone. Some neurotransmitters are also amines, such as dopamine (a catecholamine) and serotonin (an indoleamine). Dopamine also acts as a neurohormone, and serotonin is the precursor for melatonin, serving as examples of the overlapping activities of the nervous and endocrine systems.

2. **Lipophilic** ("lipid-loving") **hormones** have high lipid solubility and are poorly soluble in water. Lipophilic hormones include thyroid hormone and the steroid hormones. *Thyroid hormone,* as its name implies, is secreted exclusively by the thyroid gland; it is an iodinated tyrosine derivative. Even though catecholamines and thyroid hormone are both derived from tyrosine, they behave differently because of their solubility properties. **Steroids** are neutral lipids derived from cholesterol. They include hormones secreted by the adrenal cortex, such as cortisol, and the sex hormones (testosterone in males and estrogen in females) secreted by the reproductive organs.

Minor differences in chemical structure among hormones within each category often result in profound differences in biological response. For example, in ❙Figure 4-24, note the subtle difference between the steroid hormone testosterone, the male sex hormone responsible for inducing the development of masculine characteristics, and the steroid hormone estradiol, a form of estrogen, which is the feminizing female sex hormone.

The mechanisms of synthesis, storage, and secretion of hormones vary according to their chemical differences.

The solubility properties of a hormone determine (1) how the hormone is synthesized, stored, and secreted by the endocrine cell; (2) how the hormone is transported in the blood; and (3) how the hormone exerts its effects at the target cell. We first consider the different ways in which hydrophilic and lipophilic hormones are processed at their site of origin, the endocrine cell, before comparing their means of transport and their mechanisms of action.

Processing of Hydrophilic Peptide Hormones Peptide hormones are synthesized and secreted by an endocrine cell via the same steps used for manufacturing any protein that is exported from a cell (see ❙Figure 2-3, p. 27). From the time peptide hormones are synthesized until they are secreted, they are always segregated from intracellular proteins within membrane-enclosed compartments. Here is a brief outline of these steps:

1. Large precursor proteins, or **preprohormones**, are synthesized by ribosomes on the rough endoplasmic reticulum (ER).

❙Figure 4-24 **Comparison of two steroid hormones: testosterone and estradiol.**

Testosterone, a masculinizing hormone

Estradiol, a feminizing hormone

They then migrate to the Golgi complex in membrane-enclosed transport vesicles that pinch off from the smooth ER.

2. During their journey through the ER and Golgi complex, the preprohormones are pruned to active hormones.

3. The Golgi complex packages the finished hormones into secretory vesicles that are pinched off and stored in the cytoplasm until an appropriate signal triggers their secretion.

4. On appropriate stimulation, the secretory vesicles fuse with the plasma membrane and release their contents to the outside by exocytosis. Such secretion usually does not go on continuously; it is triggered only by specific stimuli. The blood then picks up the secreted hormones for distribution.

Processing of Lipophilic Steroid Hormones All steroidogenic (steroid-producing) endocrine cells perform the following steps to produce and release their hormonal product:

1. Cholesterol is the precursor for all steroid hormones.

2. Synthesis of the various steroid hormones requires a series of enzymatic reactions that modify the basic cholesterol molecule—for example, by varying the type and position of side groups attached to the cholesterol framework. Each conversion from cholesterol to a specific steroid hormone requires the help of particular enzymes limited to certain steroidogenic organs. Thus, each steroidogenic organ can produce only the steroid hormone or hormones for which it has a complete set of appropriate enzymes. For example, a key enzyme necessary for producing cortisol is found only in the adrenal cortex, so no other steroidogenic organ can produce this hormone.

3. Unlike peptide hormones, steroid hormones are not stored. Once formed, the lipid-soluble steroid hormones immediately diffuse through the steroidogenic cell's lipid plasma membrane to enter the blood. Only the hormone precursor cholesterol is stored within steroidogenic cells. Accordingly, the rate of steroid hormone secretion is controlled entirely by the rate of hormone synthesis. In contrast, peptide hormone secretion is controlled primarily by regulating the release of presynthesized stored hormone.

4. Following their secretion into the blood, some steroid hormones (and thyroid hormone) undergo further interconversions within the blood or other organs, where they are changed into more potent or different hormones.

The adrenomedullary catecholamines and thyroid hormone have unique synthetic and secretory pathways that are described when we address each of these hormones specifically in the endocrine chapters (Chapters 18 and 19).

Hydrophilic hormones dissolve in the plasma; lipophilic hormones are transported by plasma proteins.

All hormones are carried by the blood, but they are not all transported in the same manner:

1. The hydrophilic peptide hormones simply dissolve in the blood.

2. Lipophilic steroids and thyroid hormone, which are poorly soluble in water, cannot dissolve to any extent in the watery blood. Instead, most lipophilic hormones circulate to their target cells reversibly bound to plasma proteins in the blood. Some plasma proteins carry only one type of hormone, whereas others, such as albumin, indiscriminately pick up any "hitchhiking" hormone.

Only the small, unbound, freely dissolved fraction of a lipophilic hormone is biologically active (that is, free to cross capillary walls and bind with target cell receptors to exert an effect). The bound form of steroid and thyroid hormones provides a large reserve of these lipophilic hormones that can be used to replenish the active free pool. To maintain normal endocrine function, the magnitude of the small, free, effective pool, rather than the total blood concentration of a particular lipophilic hormone, is monitored and adjusted.

3. Catecholamines are unusual in that only about 50% of these hydrophilic hormones circulate as free hormone; the other 50% are loosely bound to albumin. Because catecholamines are water soluble, the importance of this binding to plasma proteins is unclear.

Clinical Note The chemical properties of a hormone dictate not only how it is transported in the blood, but also the way in which it can be artificially introduced into the blood for therapeutic purposes. Because the digestive system does not secrete enzymes that can digest steroid and thyroid hormones, hormones such as the sex steroids contained in birth control pills can, when swallowed, be absorbed intact from the digestive tract into the blood. No other type of hormones can be taken orally (by mouth) because protein-digesting enzymes would attack and convert them into inactive fragments. Therefore, these hormones must be administered by non-oral routes; for example, insulin deficiency is treated with daily injections of insulin.

Next, we examine how the hydrophilic and lipophilic hormones vary in their mechanisms of action at their target cells.

Hormones generally produce their effect by altering intracellular proteins.

To induce their effect, hormones must bind with target cell receptors specific for them. Each interaction between a particular hormone and a target cell receptor produces a highly characteristic response that differs among hormones and among different target cells influenced by the same hormone. Both the location of the receptors within the target cell and the mechanism by which binding of the hormone with the receptors brings about a response vary, depending on the hormone's solubility characteristics.

Location of Receptors for Hydrophilic and Lipophilic Hormones Hormones can be grouped into two categories based on the location of their receptors:

1. The hydrophilic peptides and catecholamines, which are poorly soluble in lipid, cannot pass through the lipid membrane barriers of their target cells. Instead, they bind with specific receptors on the outer plasma membrane surface of the target cell.

2. The lipophilic steroids and thyroid hormone easily pass through the surface membrane to bind with specific receptors located inside the target cell.

General Means of Hydrophilic and Lipophilic Hormone Action Even though hormones cause a wide variety of responses, they ultimately influence their target cells by altering the cell's proteins in one of two major ways:

1. Surface-binding hydrophilic hormones function largely by activating second-messenger pathways within the target cell. This activation directly _alters the activity of preexisting intracellular proteins,_ usually enzymes, to produce the desired effect.

2. Lipophilic hormones function mainly by activating specific genes in the target cell to cause _formation of new intracellular proteins,_ which in turn produce the desired effect. The new proteins may be enzymatic or structural.

Let us examine the two major mechanisms of hormonal action (activation of second-messenger pathways and activation of genes) in more detail.

Hydrophilic hormones alter preexisting proteins via second-messenger systems.

Most hydrophilic hormones (peptides and catecholamines) bind to G-protein-coupled surface membrane receptors and produce their effects in their target cells by acting through a second-messenger pathway to alter the activity of preexisting proteins. There are two major second-messenger pathways: One uses **cyclic adenosine monophosphate (cyclic AMP, or cAMP)** as a second messenger, and the other uses Ca^{2+} in this role.

Both pathways use a G protein, which is found on the inner surface of the plasma membrane, as an intermediary between the receptor and the effector protein (see ❙ Figure 4-22). G proteins are so named because they are bound to guanine nucleotides—_guanosine triphosphate (GTP)_ when active or _guanosine diphosphate (GDP)_ when inactive. An inactive G protein consists of a complex of alpha (α), beta (β), and gamma (γ) subunits, with a GDP molecule bound to the α subunit. A number of different G proteins with varying α subunits have been identified. The different G proteins are activated in response to binding of various first messengers to surface receptors. When an appropriate extracellular messenger (a first messenger) binds with its receptor, the receptor attaches to the associated G pro-

I Figure 4-25 **Mechanism of action of hydrophilic hormones via activation of the cyclic AMP second-messenger pathway.**

FIGURE FOCUS: *Does active protein kinase A phosphorylate the same inactive designated proteins in all cells that use the cAMP second-messenger pathway?*

1. Binding of extracellular messenger to receptor activates a G protein, the α subunit of which shuttles to and activates adenylyl cyclase.

2. Adenylyl cyclase converts ATP to cAMP

3. cAMP activates protein kinase A.

4. Protein kinase A phosphorylates inactive designated protein, activating it.

5. Active designated protein brings about desired response.

KEY
P = Phosphate

tein, resulting in release of GDP from the G-protein complex. GTP then attaches to the α subunit, an action that activates the G protein. Once activated, the α subunit breaks away from the G-protein complex and moves along the inner surface of the plasma membrane until it reaches an effector protein, which is typically either an enzyme or an ion channel within the membrane. The a subunit links up with the effector protein and alters its activity. Researchers have identified more than 300 different receptors that convey instructions of extracellular messengers through the membrane to various effector proteins by means of G proteins. We next examine the cAMP pathway in more detail as an example of what happens after an effector protein is activated.

Cyclic AMP Second-Messenger Pathway

Cyclic AMP is the most widely used second messenger. In the following description of the cAMP pathway, the numbered steps correlate to the numbered steps in I Figure 4-25.When the appropriate extracellular messenger binds to its surface membrane receptor and activates the associated G protein, the G protein in turn activates the effector protein—in this case, the enzyme **adenylyl cyclase** (step **1**), which is located on the cytoplasmic side of the plasma membrane. Adenylyl cyclase converts intracellular ATP to cAMP by cleaving off two of the phosphates (step **2**). (This is the same ATP used as energy currency in the body.) Acting as the intracellular second messenger, cAMP triggers a preprogrammed series of chemical steps within the cell to bring about the response dictated by the first messenger. To begin, cAMP activates the intracellular enzyme, **protein kinase A (PKA)** (step **3**). Protein kinase A, in turn, phosphorylates a designated preexisting intracellular protein, such as an enzyme important in a particular metabolic pathway. Phosphorylation causes the protein to change its shape and function, thereby activating it (step **4**). This activated protein brings about the target cell's ultimate response to the first messenger (step **5**). For example, the activity of a particular enzymatic protein that regulates a specific metabolic event may be increased or decreased.

Note that in this signal transduction pathway the steps involving the extracellular first messenger, the receptor, the G-protein complex, and the effector protein occur *in the plasma membrane* and lead to activation of the second messenger. The extracellular messenger cannot enter the cell to "personally"

deliver its message to the proteins that carry out the desired response. Instead, it initiates membrane events that activate an intracellular second messenger, cAMP. The second messenger then triggers a chain reaction of biochemical events *inside the cell* that leads to the cellular response.

Different types of cells have different designated proteins available for phosphorylation and modification by PKA. Therefore, a *common second messenger such as cAMP can cause widely differing responses in different cells*, depending on what proteins are modified. Cyclic AMP can be thought of as an intracellular molecular "switch" that can "turn on" (or "turn off") different cell events, depending on the kinds of protein activity ultimately modified in the various target cells. The type of proteins altered by a second messenger depends on the unique specialization of a particular cell type. This can be likened to being able to either illuminate or cool a room depending on whether the wall switch you flip on is wired to a device specialized to shed light (a chandelier) or one specialized to create air movement (a ceiling fan). In the body, the variable responsiveness once the switch is turned on results from genetically programmed differences in the sets of proteins within different cells. For example, depending on its cellular location, activating the cAMP pathway can modify heart rate in the heart, stimulate the formation of female sex hormones in the ovaries, break down stored glucose in the liver, control water conservation during urine formation in the kidneys, create simple memory traces in the brain, or cause perception of a sweet taste by a taste bud.

After the response is completed, the α subunit cleaves off a phosphate, converting GTP to GDP, in essence shutting itself off, then rejoins the β and γ subunits to restore the inactive G-protein complex. Cyclic AMP and the other participating chemicals are inactivated so that the intracellular message is "erased" and the response can be terminated. For example, cAMP is quickly degraded by **phosphodiesterase**, a cytosolic enzyme that is continuously active. This action provides another highly effective means of turning off the response when it is no longer needed. Other complementary means of terminating the response are removal of the added phosphates from the designated proteins by protein phosphatase or removal of the first messenger.

Ca²⁺ Second-Messenger Pathway

Ca^{2+} **Second-Messenger Pathway** Some cells use Ca^{2+} instead of cAMP as a second messenger. In such cases, binding of the first messenger to the surface receptor eventually leads by means of G proteins to activation of the enzyme **phospholipase C**, an effector protein bound to the inner side of the membrane (step **1** in Figure 4-26). This enzyme breaks down **phosphatidylinositol bisphosphate** (abbreviated PIP_2), a component of the tails of the phospholipid molecules within the membrane itself. The products of PIP_2 breakdown are **diacylglycerol (DAG)** and **inositol trisphosphate (IP₃)** (step **2**). Lipid-soluble DAG remains in the lipid bilayer of the plasma membrane, but water-soluble IP_3 diffuses into the cytosol. IP_3 mobilizes intracellular Ca^{2+} stored in the endoplasmic reticulum to increase cytosolic Ca^{2+} by binding with IP_3-gated receptor-channels in the ER membrane (step **3a**). Ca^{2+} then takes on the role of second messenger, ultimately bringing about the response commanded by the first messenger. Many of the Ca^{2+}-dependent cellular events are triggered by activation of **calmodulin**, an intracellular Ca^{2+}-binding protein (step **4a**). The Ca^{2+}–calmodulin complex activates Ca^{2+}**–calmodulin dependent protein kinase (CaM kinase)** (or activates another kinase) (step **5a**). Activation of CaM kinase by the Ca^{2+}–calmodulin complex is similar to activation of PKA by cAMP. From here the patterns of the two pathways are similar. The activated CaM kinase phosphorylates the designated proteins (perhaps through multiple steps), thereby causing these proteins to change their shape and function (activating them) (step **6a**). The active designated proteins bring about the ultimate desired cellular response (step **7a**). For example, the Ca^{2+}–calmodulin pathway is the means by which chemical messengers can activate smooth muscle contraction.

Simultaneous to the IP_3 pathway, the other PIP_2 breakdown product, DAG, sets off another second-messenger pathway. (IP_3 and DAG themselves are sometimes considered to be second messengers.) DAG activates **protein kinase C (PKC)** (step **3b**), which phosphorylates designated proteins, different from those phosphorylated by calmodulin (step **4b**). The resultant change in shape and function of these proteins activates them. These active proteins produce another cellular response (step **5b**). Although currently the subject of considerable investigation, the DAG pathway is not yet understood as well as the other signaling pathways. IP_3 and DAG typically trigger complementary actions inside a target cell to accomplish a common goal because both of these products are formed at the same time in response to the same first messenger. For example, extracellular chemical messengers promote increased contractile activity of blood-vessel smooth muscle via the IP_3–intracellular Ca^{2+}–calmodulin pathway, and the DAG pathway enhances the sensitivity of the contractile apparatus to Ca^{2+}.

The IP_3 pathway is not the only means of increasing intracellular Ca^{2+}. Intracellular Ca^{2+} can be increased by entry from the ECF or by release from Ca^{2+} stores in the endoplasmic reticulum via means other than the IP_3 pathway. Ca^{2+} channels in both the surface membrane and in the ER may be opened by either electrical or chemical means. For example, Ca^{2+} entry on the opening of voltage-gated surface-membrane Ca^{2+} channels is responsible for exocytosis of neurotransmitter from the axon terminal. Alternatively, surface-membrane Ca^{2+} channels may be opened via activation of receptors that serve as channels themselves or via activation of GPCRs. In yet another pathway, the opening of surface-membrane Na^+ and K^+ channels by means of receptor-channels leads to electrical signals that open Ca^{2+} channels in the endoplasmic reticulum. The latter pathway is how neurotransmitter released from neuron terminals triggers skeletal muscle contraction. The resultant rise in intracellular Ca^{2+} turns on the contractile apparatus. The pathways get even more complex than this. Ca^{2+} entering from the ECF can serve as a second messenger to trigger an even larger release of Ca^{2+} from intracellular stores, as it does to bring about contraction in cardiac muscle. This all sounds confusing, but these examples are meant to illustrate the complexity of Ca^{2+} signaling, not to overwhelm. You will learn more about the details of these pathways when appropriate in later chapters.

Although the cAMP and Ca^{2+} pathways are the most prevalent second-messenger systems, they are not the only ones. For example, a few cells use **cyclic guanosine monophosphate (cyclic GMP)** as a second messenger in a system analogous to the cAMP system. In other cells, the second messenger is still unknown. Remember that activation of second messengers is a universal mechanism used by a variety of extracellular messengers in addition to hydrophilic hormones.

Amplification by a Second-Messenger Pathway

Amplification by a Second-Messenger Pathway Several remaining points about receptor activation and the ensuing events merit attention. First, considering the number of steps in a second-messenger relay chain, you might wonder why so many cell types use the same complex system to accomplish such a wide range of functions. The multiple steps of a second-messenger pathway are actually advantageous because the cascading (multiplying) effect of these pathways greatly amplifies the initial signal (Figure 4-27). *Amplification* means that the output of a system is much greater than the input. Using the cAMP pathway as an example, binding of one extracellular messenger molecule to a receptor activates a number of

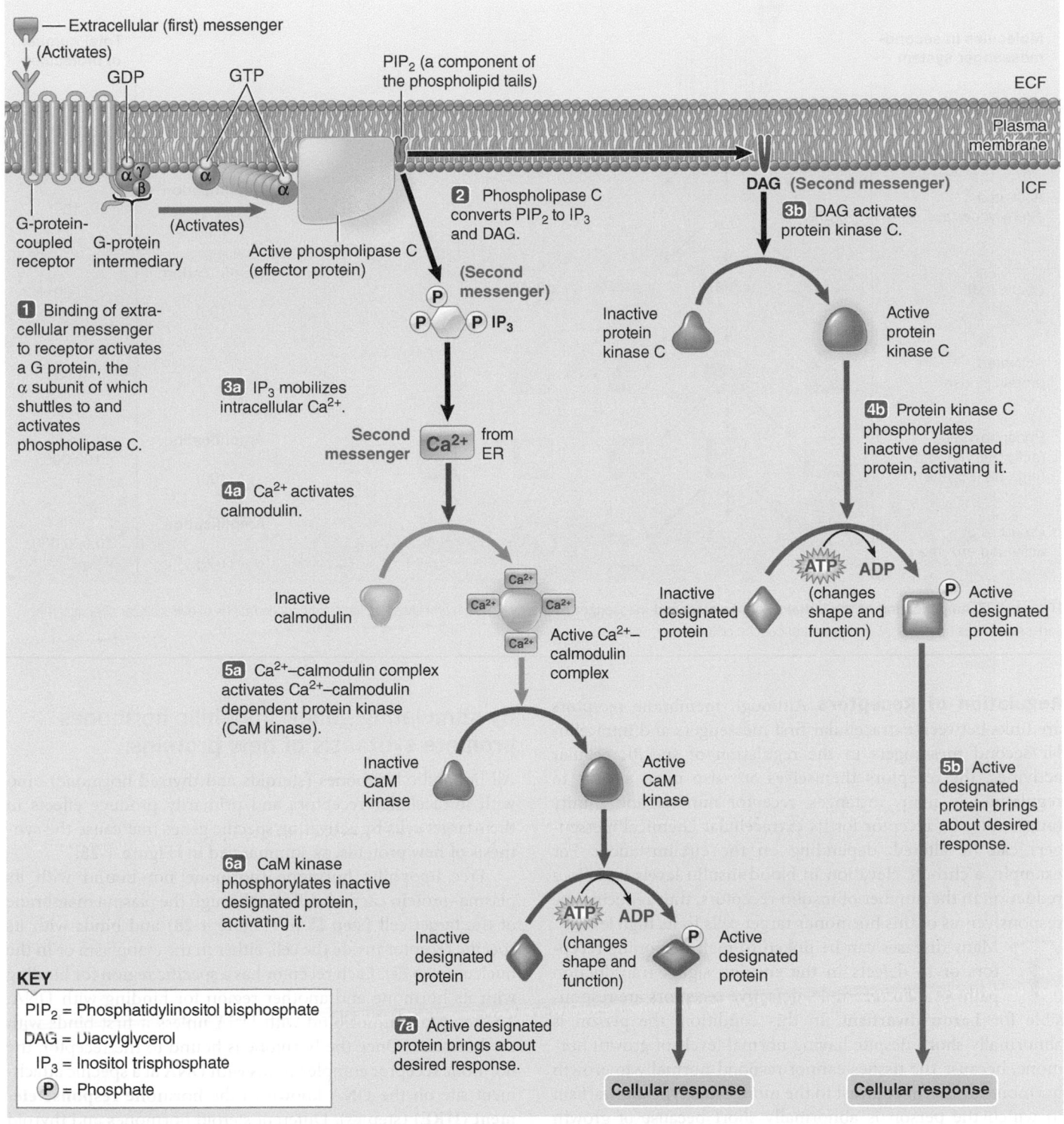

I Figure 4-26 **Mechanism of action of hydrophilic hormones via concurrent activation of the IP₃–Ca²⁺ second-messenger pathway and the DAG pathway.**

adenylyl cyclase molecules (let's arbitrarily say 10), each of which activates many (in our hypothetical example, let's say 100) cAMP molecules. Each cAMP molecule then acts on a single protein kinase A, which phosphorylates and thereby influences many (again, let's say 100) specific proteins, such as enzymes. Each enzyme, in turn, is responsible for producing many (perhaps 100) molecules of a particular product, such as

a secretory product. The result of this cascade, with one event triggering the next in sequence, is a tremendous amplification of the initial signal. In our hypothetical example, one extracellular messenger molecule has been responsible for inducing a yield of 10 million molecules of a secretory product. In this way, very low concentrations of hormones and other chemical messengers can trigger pronounced cell responses.

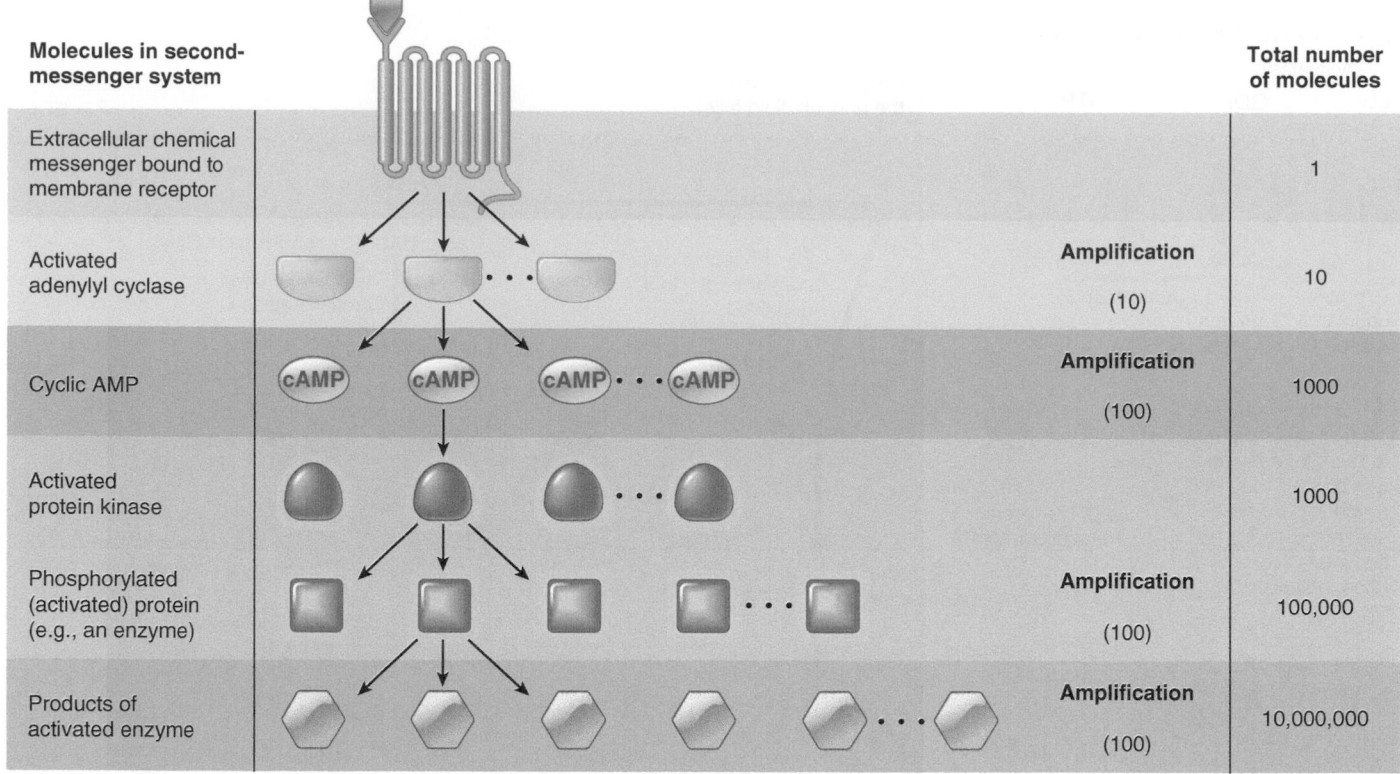

Molecules in second-messenger system		Total number of molecules
Extracellular chemical messenger bound to membrane receptor		1
Activated adenylyl cyclase	**Amplification** (10)	10
Cyclic AMP	**Amplification** (100)	1000
Activated protein kinase		1000
Phosphorylated (activated) protein (e.g., an enzyme)	**Amplification** (100)	100,000
Products of activated enzyme	**Amplification** (100)	10,000,000

❙Figure 4-27 **Amplification of the initial signal by a second-messenger pathway.** Through amplification, very low concentrations of extracellular chemical messengers, such as hormones, can trigger pronounced cellular responses.

Regulation of Receptors Although membrane receptors are links between extracellular first messengers and intracellular second messengers in the regulation of specific cellular activities, the receptors themselves are also often subject to regulation. In many instances, receptor number and affinity (attraction of a receptor for its extracellular chemical messenger) can be altered, depending on the circumstances. For example, a chronic elevation in blood insulin levels leads to a reduction in the number of insulin receptors, thus reducing the responsiveness of this hormone's target cells to its high levels.

Clinical Note Many diseases can be linked to malfunctioning receptors or to defects in the ensuing signal transduction pathways. For example, defective receptors are responsible for **Laron dwarfism**. In this condition, the person is abnormally short, despite having normal levels of growth hormone, because the tissues cannot respond normally to growth hormone. This is in contrast to the more usual type of dwarfism in which the person is abnormally short because of growth hormone deficiency. As another example, the toxins released by some infecting bacteria, such as those that cause cholera and whooping cough, keep second-messenger pathways "turned on" at a high level. **Cholera toxin** prevents the involved G protein from converting GTP to GDP, thus keeping the G protein in its active state. **Pertussis (whooping cough) toxin** blocks the inhibition of adenylyl cyclase, thereby keeping the ensuing second-messenger pathway continuously active.

Having examined the means by which hydrophilic hormones alter their target cells, we now focus on the mechanism of lipophilic hormone action.

By stimulating genes, lipophilic hormones promote synthesis of new proteins.

All lipophilic hormones (steroids and thyroid hormone) bind with intracellular receptors and primarily produce effects in their target cells by activating specific genes that cause the synthesis of new proteins, as summarized in ❙Figure 4-28.

Free lipophilic hormone (hormone not bound with its plasma–protein carrier) diffuses through the plasma membrane of the target cell (step ❶ in ❙Figure 4-28) and binds with its specific receptor inside the cell, either in the cytoplasm or in the nucleus (step ❷). Each receptor has a specific region for binding with its hormone and another region for binding with DNA. The receptor cannot bind with DNA unless it first binds with the hormone. Once the hormone is bound to the receptor, the hormone receptor complex binds with DNA at a specific attachment site on the DNA known as the **hormone response element (HRE)** (step ❸). Different steroid hormones and thyroid hormone, once bound with their respective receptors, attach at different HREs on DNA. For example, the estrogen receptor complex binds at DNA's *estrogen response element*.

Binding of the hormone receptor complex with DNA "turns on" or activates a specific gene within the target cell (step ❹). This gene contains a code for synthesizing a given protein. The code of the activated gene is transcribed into complementary messenger RNA (mRNA) (step ❺). The new mRNA leaves the nucleus and enters the cytoplasm (step ❻), where it binds to a ribosome, the "workbench" that mediates the assembly of new proteins (see pp. 23 and 25). Here, mRNA directs the synthesis

Mechanism of action of lipophilic hormones via activation of genes.
FIGURE FOCUS: *Which steps of this pathway by which lipophilic hormones bring about their effects occur in the cytoplasm and which take place in the nucleus?*

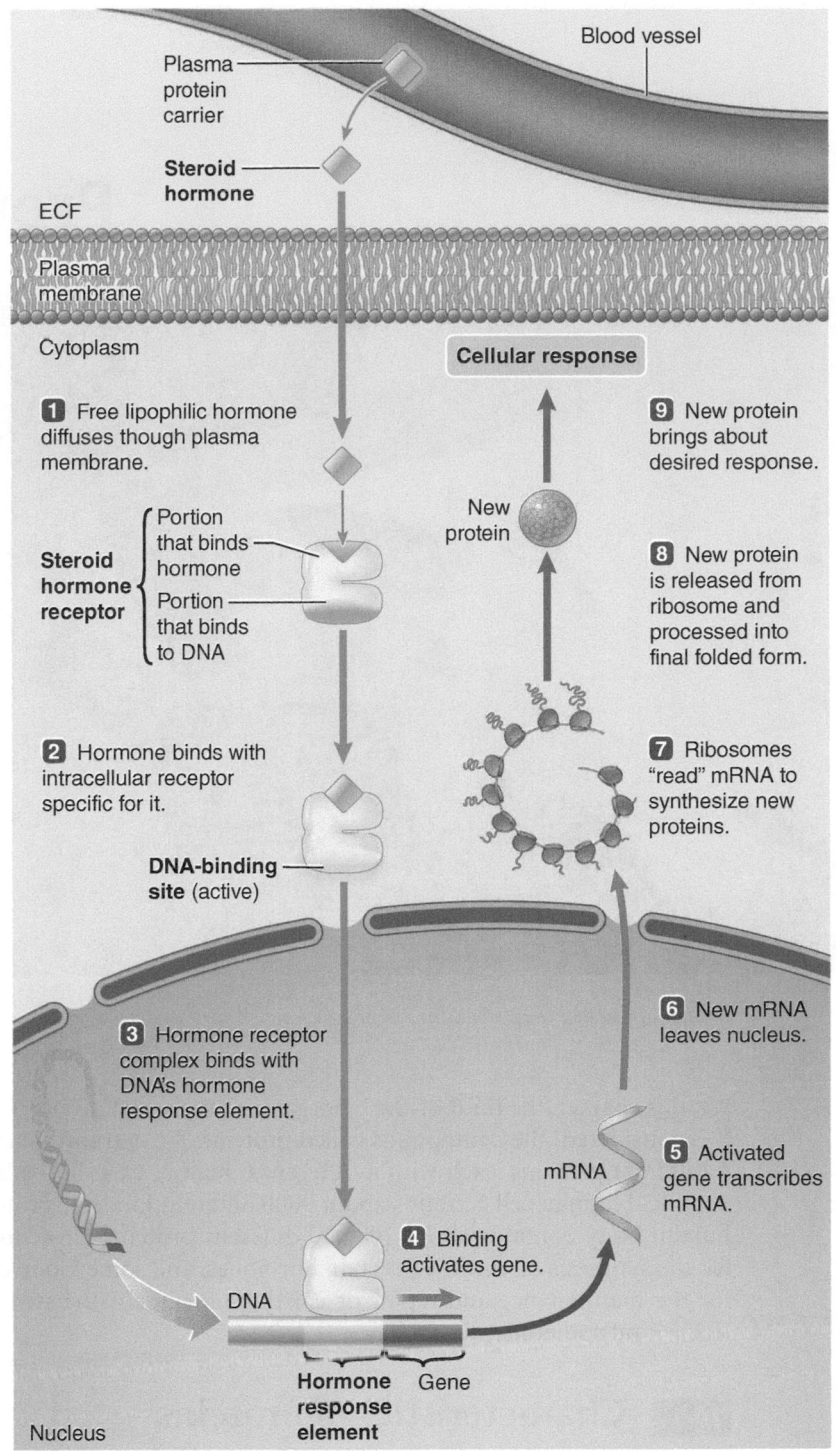

Cellular response

1 Free lipophilic hormone diffuses though plasma membrane.

Steroid hormone receptor { Portion that binds hormone / Portion that binds to DNA

2 Hormone binds with intracellular receptor specific for it.

DNA-binding site (active)

3 Hormone receptor complex binds with DNA's hormone response element.

4 Binding activates gene.

DNA

Hormone response element Gene

Nucleus

5 Activated gene transcribes mRNA.

mRNA

6 New mRNA leaves nucleus.

7 Ribosomes "read" mRNA to synthesize new proteins.

8 New protein is released from ribosome and processed into final folded form.

9 New protein brings about desired response.

New protein

Plasma protein carrier

Steroid hormone

ECF

Plasma membrane

Cytoplasm

Blood vessel

---

of the designated new proteins according to the DNA code in the activated genes (step **7**). The newly synthesized protein, either enzymatic or structural, is released from the ribosome (step **8**) and produces the target cell's ultimate response to the hormone (step **9**). Different genes are activated by different lipophilic hormones, resulting in different biological effects.

Even though most steroid actions are accomplished by hormonal binding with intracellular receptors that leads to gene activation, recent studies have unveiled another mechanism by which steroid hormones induce effects that occur too rapidly to be mediated by gene transcription. Some steroid hormones, most notably some of the sex hormones, bind with unique steroid receptors in the plasma membrane, in addition to binding with the traditional steroid receptors in the nucleus. This membrane binding leads to **nongenomic steroid receptor actions**—that is, actions accomplished by something other than altering gene activity, such as by inducing changes in ionic flux across the membrane or by altering activity of cellular enzymes.

Next, we compare the similarities and differences between neural and hormonal responses at the system level.

Check Your Understanding 4.7

1. Prepare a chart comparing the synthesis, storage, secretion, and transport in the blood of peptide hormones and steroid hormones.

2. Explain how a common second messenger such as cAMP can induce widely differing responses in different cells.

3. Describe the role of a hormone response element.

Proteins

20

jochem wijnands/Horizons WWP/Alamy

The fibrous protein α-keratin is the major structural element present in sheep's wool.

In this chapter, the third of the bioorganic classes of molecules (Section 18-1) is considered, the compounds called proteins. An extraordinary number of different proteins, each with a different function, exist in the human body. A typical human cell contains about 9000 different kinds of proteins, and the human body contains about 100,000 different proteins. Proteins are needed for the synthesis of enzymes, certain hormones, and some blood components; for the maintenance and repair of existing tissues; for the synthesis of new tissue; and sometimes for energy.

20-1 Characteristics of Proteins

LEARNING FOCUS

Characterize a protein in terms of the subunits present in its polymeric structure and in terms of the elements that are present.

Next to water, proteins are the most abundant substances in nearly all cells—they account for about 15% of a cell's overall mass (Section 18-1) and for almost half of a cell's dry mass. All proteins contain the elements carbon, hydrogen, oxygen, and nitrogen; most also contain sulfur. The presence of nitrogen in proteins sets them apart from carbohydrates and lipids, which most often do not contain nitrogen. The average nitrogen content of proteins is 15.4% by mass. Other elements, such as phosphorus and iron, are essential constituents of certain specialized proteins. Casein, the main protein of milk, contains phosphorus, an element very important in the diet of infants and children. Hemoglobin, the oxygen-transporting protein of blood, contains iron.

A **protein** *is a naturally occurring, unbranched polymer in which the monomer units are amino acids.* Thus the starting point for a discussion of proteins is an understanding of the structures and chemical properties of amino acids. ◄

> ▶ *The word* protein *comes from the Greek* proteios, *which means "of first importance." This reflects the key role that proteins play in life processes.*

Section 20-1 Quick Quiz

1. Which of the following sets of four elements are always present in a protein?
   a. C, H, O, S
   b. C, H, N, S
   c. C, H, O, N
   d. no correct response
2. Proteins are naturally occurring unbranched polymers in which the monomers are
   a. monocarboxylic acids
   b. dicarboxylic acids
   c. amino acids
   d. no correct response

Answers: 1. c; 2. c

20-2 Amino Acids: The Building Blocks for Proteins

LEARNING FOCUS

Be able to draw the generalized structure for an α-amino acid and be able to classify α-amino acids into four categories based on structures and polarity of their side chains.

An **amino acid** *is an organic compound that contains both an amino* (—NH$_2$) *group and a carboxyl* (—COOH) *group.* The amino acids found in proteins are always α-amino acids. An **α-amino acid** *is an amino acid in which the amino group and the carboxyl group are attached to the α-carbon atom.* The general structural formula for an α-amino acid is

The R group present in an α-amino acid is called the amino acid *side chain.* The nature of this side chain distinguishes α-amino acids from each other. Side chains vary in size, shape, charge, acidity, functional groups present, hydrogen-bonding ability, and chemical reactivity. ◄

More than 700 different naturally occurring amino acids are known, but only 20 of them, called standard amino acids, are normally present in proteins. A **standard amino acid** *is one of the 20 α-amino acids normally found in proteins.* The structures of the 20 standard amino acids are given in Table 20-1. Within Table 20-1, amino acids are grouped according to side-chain polarity. In this system, there are four categories: (1) nonpolar amino acids, (2) polar neutral amino acids, (3) polar acidic amino acids, and (4) polar basic amino acids. This classification system gives insights into how various types of amino acid side chains help determine the properties of proteins (Section 20-12).

A **nonpolar amino acid** *is an amino acid that contains one amino group, one carboxyl group, and a nonpolar side chain.* When incorporated into a protein, such amino acids are *hydrophobic* (Section 19-7); that is, they are not attracted to water molecules. They are generally found in the interior of proteins, where there is limited contact with water. There are nine nonpolar amino acids. Tryptophan is a borderline member of this group because water can weakly interact through hydrogen bonding with the NH ring location on tryptophan's side-chain ring structure. Thus, some textbooks list tryptophan as a polar neutral amino acid. ◄

> ▶ *The nature of the side chain (R group) distinguishes α-amino acids from each other, both physically and chemically.*

> ▶ *The nonpolar amino acid* proline *has a structural feature not found in any other standard amino acid. Its side chain, a propyl group, is bonded to both the α-carbon atom and the amino nitrogen atom, giving a cyclic side chain.*

Proline

▶ **Table 20-1** **The 20 Standard Amino Acids, Grouped According to Side-Chain Polarity**

Below each amino acid's structure are its name (with pronunciation), its three-letter abbreviation, and its one-letter abbreviation.

Nonpolar Amino Acids

Glycine (Gly, G)
GLY-seen

Alanine (Ala, A)
AL-ah-neen

Valine (Val, V)
VAY-leen

Leucine (Leu, L)
LOO-seen

Isoleucine (Ile, I)
eye-so-LOO-seen

Proline (Pro, P)
PRO-leen

Phenylalanine (Phe, F)
fen-il-AL-ah-neen

Methionine (Met, M)
me-THIGH-oh-neen

Tryptophan (Trp, W)
TRIP-toe-fane

Polar Neutral Amino Acids

Serine (Ser, S)
SEER-een

Cysteine (Cys, C)
SIS-teh-een

Threonine (Thr, T)
THREE-oh-neen

Asparagine (Asn, N)
ah-SPAR-ah-geen

Glutamine (Gln, Q)
GLU-tah-meen

Tyrosine (Tyr, Y)
(TIE-roe-seen)

Polar Acidic Amino Acids

Polar Basic Amino Acids

Aspartic acid (Asp, D)
ah-SPAR-tic acid

Glutamic acid (Glu, E)
glu-TAM-ic acid

Histidine (His, H)
HISS-tuh-deen

Lysine (Lys, K)
LYE-seen

Arginine (Arg, R)
ARG-ih-neen

The three types of polar amino acids have varying degrees of affinity for water. Within a protein, such amino acids are considered to be *hydrophilic* (Section 19-7).

A **polar neutral amino acid** *is an amino acid that contains one amino group, one carboxyl group, and a side chain that is polar but neutral.* In solution at physiological pH, the side chain of a polar neutral amino acid is neither acidic nor basic. There are six polar neutral amino acids. These amino acids are more soluble in water than the nonpolar amino acids as, in each case, the R group present can hydrogen-bond to water. ◄

A **polar acidic amino acid** *is an amino acid that contains one amino group and two carboxyl groups, the second carboxyl group being part of the side chain.* In solution at physiological pH, the side chain of a polar acidic amino acid bears a negative charge; the side-chain carboxyl group has lost its acidic hydrogen atom. There are two polar acidic amino acids: aspartic acid and glutamic acid.

A **polar basic amino acid** *is an amino acid that contains two amino groups and one carboxyl group, the second amino group being part of the side chain.* In solution at physiological pH, the side chain of a polar basic amino acid bears a positive charge; the nitrogen atom of the amino group has accepted a proton (basic behavior; Section 17-6). There are three polar basic amino acids: lysine, arginine, and histidine. ◄

The names of the standard amino acids are often abbreviated using three-letter codes. Except in four cases, these abbreviations are the first three letters of the amino acid's name. Also, a one-letter code for amino acid names exists that is particularly useful in computer applications that involve proteins. Both sets of abbreviations are used in specifying the amino acid makeup of protein. Both sets of abbreviations are given in Table 20-1.

All of the standard amino acids in Table 20-1 are necessary constituents of human proteins. Adequate amounts of 11 of the 20 standard amino acids can be synthesized from carbohydrates and lipids in the body if a source of nitrogen is also available. However, the adult human body cannot produce adequate amounts of the other nine standard amino acids. These amino acids, which are called *essential amino acids,* must be obtained from dietary protein.

► *The amino acids tryptophan (nonpolar side chain) and tyrosine (polar neutral side chain) were previously mentioned in Section 17-10. Serotonin is a tryptophan derivative and dopamine and norepinephrine are both tyrosine derivatives.*

► *A variety of functional groups are present in the side chains of the 20 standard amino acids: six have alkyl groups (Section 12-8), three have aromatic groups (Section 13-11), two have sulfur-containing groups (Section 14-20), two have hydroxyl (alcohol) groups (Section 14-2), three have amino groups (Section 17-2), two have carboxyl groups (Section 16-1), and two have amide groups (Section 17-12).*

Section 20-2 Quick Quiz

1. How many standard amino acids are there?
   a. 18
   b. 20
   c. 22
   d. no correct response
2. How do the various standard amino acids differ from each other?
   a. in the location of the amino group
   b. in the location of the carboxyl group
   c. in the identity of the R group (side chain)
   d. no correct response
3. The number of carboxyl groups and amino groups present, respectively, in a *nonpolar* amino acid is,
   a. 1 and 1
   b. 2 and 1
   c. 1 and 2
   d. no correct response
4. How many different subclassifications are there for polar amino acids?
   a. 2
   b. 3
   c. 4
   d. no correct response
5. Which of the following statements concerning elements present in standard amino acids is *correct*?
   a. Some, but not all of them, contain N.
   b. Some, but not all of them, contain O.
   c. Some, but not all of them, contain S.
   d. no correct response

Answers: 1. b; 2. c; 3. a; 4. b; 5. c

20-3 Essential Amino Acids

LEARNING FOCUS

Be familiar with the concepts of *essential amino acids, complete, incomplete, and complementary dietary proteins,* and *limiting amino acids.*

An **essential amino acid** *is a standard amino acid needed for protein synthesis that must be obtained from dietary sources because the human body cannot synthesize it in adequate amounts from other substances.* There are nine essential amino acids for adults, and a tenth one is needed for growth in children. Table 20-2 lists the essential amino acids. ◀

The human body can synthesize small amounts of some of the essential amino acids, but not enough to meet its needs, especially in the case of growing children.

A **complete dietary protein** *is a protein that contains all of the essential amino acids in the same relative amounts in which the body needs them.* A complete dietary protein may or may not contain all of the nonessential amino acids. Conversely, an **incomplete dietary protein** *is a protein that does not contain adequate amounts, relative to the body's needs, of one or more of the essential amino acids.* Associated with the term *incomplete dietary protein* is the term *limiting amino acid.* A **limiting amino acid** *is an essential amino acid that is missing, or present in inadequate amounts, in an incomplete dietary protein.*

Protein from animal sources is usually complete dietary protein. Casein from milk and proteins found in meat, fish, and eggs are complete dietary proteins. There is one common incomplete dietary protein that comes from animal sources. It is gelatin, a protein in which tryptophan is the limiting amino acid.

Protein from plant sources tends to be incomplete dietary protein. With plant proteins, three amino acids are often limiting: lysine (wheat, rice, oats, and corn), methionine (beans and peas), and tryptophan (corn and beans). Note that both corn and beans have two limiting amino acids. Soy is the only common plant protein that is a complete dietary protein.

Complementary dietary proteins *are two or more incomplete dietary proteins that, when combined, provide an adequate amount of all essential amino acids relative to the body's needs.* A mix of plant proteins generally provides high-quality (complete) protein. Rice by itself is an incomplete dietary protein, as is beans. A serving of rice and beans provides all of the essential amino acids by protein complementation (Figure 20-1).

Prior to the development of genetic engineering procedures (Section 22-14), the quality of a given plant's protein was something that could not be changed. Genetic modification techniques can improve a plant's protein by causing it to produce increased amounts of amino acids that it normally has in short supply. Such genetic modification, if fully implemented in the future, would be especially important in areas of the world that rely heavily on one incomplete protein food source (beans or corn or rice); a much higher quality protein would be available to the people for consumption.

▶ *Some infants born prematurely cannot make sufficient quantities of several of the nonessential amino acids and these amino acids become conditionally essential until the baby matures. In this situation the conditionally essential amino acids must be obtained through the diet. In most cases, human milk and infant formula contain sufficient amounts of these conditionally essential amino acids.*

▶ **Table 20-2 The Essential Amino Acids**

arginine*	methionine
histidine	phenylalanine
isoleucine	threonine
leucine	tryptophan
lysine	valine

*Arginine is required for growth in children but is not an essential amino acid for adults.

Figure 20-1 A serving of rice and beans, a common meal in many countries, involves complementary dietary proteins.

© iStockphoto.com/whitewish

Section 20-3 Quick Quiz

1. How many of the standard amino acids are classified as essential amino acids for adults?
   a. 7
   b. 9
   c. 15
   d. no correct response
2. Proteins from plant sources are
   a. always complete dietary protein
   b. frequently complete dietary protein
   c. seldom complete dietary protein
   d. no correct response

3. Incomplete dietary proteins contain inadequate amounts of
   a. one or more essential amino acids
   b. one or more nonessential amino acids
   c. at least one essential and one nonessential amino acid
   d. no correct response

Answers: 1. b; 2. c; 3. a

20-4 Chirality and Amino Acids

LEARNING FOCUS

Know the handedness pattern for standard amino acids and how handedness is designated using Fischer projection formulas for amino acids.

Four different groups are attached to the α-carbon atom in all of the standard amino acids except glycine, where the R group is a hydrogen atom.

$$H_2N-\underset{\underset{H}{|}}{\overset{\overset{R}{|}}{C}}-COOH$$

This means that the structures of 19 of the 20 standard amino acids possess a chiral center (Section 18-4) at this location, so enantiomeric forms (left- and right-handed forms; Section 18-5) exist for each of these amino acids. ◀

With few exceptions (in some bacteria), the amino acids found in nature and in proteins are L isomers. Thus, as is the case with monosaccharides (Section 18-8), nature favors one mirror-image form over the other. Interestingly, for amino acids the L isomer is the preferred form, whereas for monosaccharides the D isomer is preferred. ◀

The rules for drawing Fischer projection formulas (Section 18-6) for amino acid structures follow.

1. The —COOH group is put at the top of the projection formula, the R group at the bottom. This positions the carbon chain vertically.
2. The —NH$_2$ group is in a horizontal position. Positioning it on the left denotes the L isomer, and positioning it on the right denotes the D isomer.

Figure 20-2 shows molecular models that illustrate the use of these rules. ◀ Fischer projection formulas for both enantiomers of the amino acids alanine and serine are:

COOH	COOH	COOH	COOH
H$_2$N———H	H———NH$_2$	H$_2$N———H	H———NH$_2$
CH$_3$	CH$_3$	CH$_2$	CH$_2$
		OH	OH
L-Alanine	D-Alanine	L-Serine	D-Serine

▶ *Glycine, the simplest of the standard amino acids, is achiral. All of the other standard amino acids are chiral.*

▶ *Because only L amino acids are constituents of proteins, the enantiomer designation of L or D will be omitted in subsequent amino acid and protein discussions. It is understood that it is the L isomer that is always present.*

▶ *Two of the 19 chiral standard amino acids, isoleucine and threonine, possess two chiral centers (see Table 20-1). With two chiral centers present, four stereoisomers are possible for these amino acids. However, only one of the L isomers is found in proteins.*

Mirror

L-Amino acid   D-Amino acid

Figure 20-2 Designation of handedness in standard amino acid structures involves aligning the carbon chain vertically and looking at the position of the horizontally aligned —NH$_2$ group. The L form has the —NH$_2$ group on the left, and the D form has the —NH$_2$ group on the right.

1. Which of the following statements concerning the handedness of standard amino acids found in proteins is *correct*?
   a. All of them exhibit handedness.
   b. All except one of them exhibit handedness.
   c. All except two of them exhibit handedness.
   d. no correct response
2. Which of the following groups is positioned at the top of the Fischer projection formula for a standard amino acid?
   a. —COOH group
   b. —R group
   c. —NH₂ group
   d. no correct response
3. Which of the following statements concerning standard amino acids found in proteins that exhibit handedness is *correct*?
   a. Most are L-enantiomers but several are D-enantiomers.
   b. Most are D-enantiomers but several are L-enantiomers.
   c. All are D-enantiomers.
   d. no correct response

Answers: 1. b; 2. a; 3. d

20-5 Acid–Base Properties of Amino Acids

LEARNING FOCUS

Know the chemical basis for the zwitterion structure adopted by amino acids; know how zwitterion structure changes as a function of solution pH.

In pure form, amino acids are white crystalline solids with relatively high decomposition points. (Most amino acids decompose before they melt.) Also, most amino acids are *not* very soluble in water because of strong intermolecular forces within their crystal structures. Such properties are those often exhibited by compounds in which charged species are present. Studies of amino acids confirm that they are charged species both in the solid state and in solution. Why is this so?

Both an acidic group (—COOH) and a basic group (—NH₂) are present on the same carbon in an α-amino acid. ◀

▶ *In drawing amino acid structures, where handedness designation is not required, the placement of the four groups about the α-carbon atom is arbitrary. From this point on in the text, we will draw amino acid structures such that the —COOH group is on the right, the —NH₂ group is on the left, the R group points down, and the H atom points up. Drawing amino acids in this "arrangement" makes it easier to draw structures where amino acids are linked together to form longer amino acid chains.*

Section 16-8 indicated that in neutral solution, carboxyl groups have a tendency to lose protons (H⁺), producing a negatively charged species:

$$-COOH \longrightarrow -COO^- + H^+$$

Section 17-6 indicated that in neutral solution, amino groups have a tendency to accept protons (H⁺), producing a positively charged species:

$$-NH_2 + H^+ \longrightarrow -\overset{+}{N}H_3$$

Consistent with the behavior of these groups, in neutral solution, the —COOH group of an amino acid donates a proton to the —NH₂ of the same amino acid. We can characterize this behavior as an *internal* acid–base reaction. The net result is that in neutral solution, amino acid molecules have the structure

Such a molecule is known as a zwitterion, from the German term meaning "double ion." A **zwitterion** *is a molecule that has a positive charge on one atom and a negative charge on another atom, but which has no net charge.* Note that the net charge on a zwitterion is zero even though parts of the molecule carry charges. In solution and also in the solid state, α-amino acids exist as zwitterions. ◀

Zwitterion structure changes when the pH of a solution containing an amino acid is changed from neutral either to acidic (low pH) by adding an acid such as HCl or to basic (high pH) by adding a base such as NaOH. In an acidic solution, the zwitterion accepts a proton (H^+) to form a positively charged ion.

$$\overset{H}{\underset{R}{\overset{|}{\underset{|}{H_3\overset{+}{N}-C-}}}} \boxed{COO^-} + H_3O^+ \longrightarrow \overset{H}{\underset{R}{\overset{|}{\underset{|}{H_3\overset{+}{N}-C-}}}} \boxed{COOH} + H_2O$$

Zwitterion (no net charge)   Positively charged ion

In basic solution, the $-\overset{+}{N}H_3$ of the zwitterion loses a proton, and a negatively charged species is formed.

$$\overset{H}{\underset{R}{\overset{|}{\underset{|}{H_3\overset{+}{N}-C-COO^-}}}} + OH^- \longrightarrow \boxed{H_2N}-\overset{H}{\underset{R}{\overset{|}{\underset{|}{C}}}}-COO^- + H_2O$$

Zwitterion   Negatively charged ion
(no net charge)

Thus, in solution, three different amino acid forms can exist (zwitterion, negative ion, and positive ion). The three species are actually in equilibrium with each other, and the equilibrium shifts with pH change. ◀ The overall equilibrium process can be represented as follows:

$$\underset{\substack{\text{Acidic solution}\\(\text{low pH})}}{\overset{H}{\underset{R}{\overset{|}{\underset{|}{H_3\overset{+}{N}-C-COOH}}}}} \underset{H_3O^+}{\overset{OH^-}{\rightleftharpoons}} \underset{\substack{\text{Neutral solution}\\(\text{pH}=7.0)}}{\overset{H}{\underset{R}{\overset{|}{\underset{|}{H_3\overset{+}{N}-C-COO^-}}}}} \underset{H_3O^+}{\overset{OH^-}{\rightleftharpoons}} \underset{\substack{\text{Basic solution}\\(\text{high pH})}}{\overset{H}{\underset{R}{\overset{|}{\underset{|}{H_2N-C-COO^-}}}}}$$

In acidic solution, the positively charged species on the left predominates; nearly neutral solutions have the middle species (the zwitterion) as the dominant species; in basic solution, the negatively charged species on the right predominates. ◀

EXAMPLE 20-1

Determining Amino Acid Form in Solutions of Various pH

Draw the structural form of the amino acid alanine that predominates in solution at each of the following pH values. ◀

a. pH = 1.0   **b.** pH = 7.0   **c.** pH = 11.0

Solution

At low pH, both amino and carboxyl groups are protonated. At high pH, both groups have lost their protons. At neutral pH, the zwitterion is present.

a.
$$\overset{H}{\underset{CH_3}{\overset{|}{\underset{|}{H_3\overset{+}{N}-C-COOH}}}}$$
pH = 1.0
(net charge of +1)

b.
$$\overset{H}{\underset{CH_3}{\overset{|}{\underset{|}{H_3\overset{+}{N}-C-COO^-}}}}$$
pH = 7.0
(no net charge)

c.
$$\overset{H}{\underset{CH_3}{\overset{|}{\underset{|}{H_2N-C-COO^-}}}}$$
pH = 11.0
(net charge of −1)

▶ *Strong intermolecular forces between the positive and negative centers of zwitterions are the cause of the high melting points of amino acids.*

▶ *From this point on in the text, the structures of amino acids will be drawn in their zwitterion form unless information given about the pH of the solution indicates otherwise.*

▶ *The ability of amino acids to react with both H_3O^+ and OH^- ions means that amino acid solutions can function as buffers (Section 10-12). The same is true for proteins, which are amino acid polymers (Section 20-1). The buffering action of proteins present in blood is a major function of such proteins.*

▶ *Guidelines for amino acid form as a function of solution pH follow.*

Low pH: *All acid groups are protonated (—COOH). All amino groups are protonated (—$\overset{+}{N}H_3$).*

High pH: *All acid groups are deprotonated (—COO^-). All amino groups are deprotonated (—NH_2).*

Neutral pH: *All acid groups are deprotonated (—COO^-). All amino groups are protonated (—$\overset{+}{N}H_3$).*

The previous discussion assumed that the side chain (R group) of an amino acid remains unchanged in solution as the pH is varied. This is the case for neutral amino acids but not for acidic or basic ones. For these latter compounds, the side chain can also acquire a charge because it contains an amino or a carboxyl group that can, respectively, gain or lose a proton.

Because of the extra site that can be protonated or deprotonated, acidic and basic amino acids have four charged forms in solution. ◀ These four forms for aspartic acid, one of the acidic amino acids, are

▶ *The term* protonated *denotes gain of an H^+ ion, and the term* deprotonated *denotes loss of an H^+ ion.*

Low-pH form	Moderately-low-pH form	Intermediate-pH form	High-pH form
(+1 charge)	(no net charge) (zwitterion)	(−1 net charge)	(−2 net charge)

▶ *Side-chain carboxyl groups are weaker acids than α-carbon carboxyl groups.*

The existence of two low-pH forms for aspartic acid results from the two carboxyl groups being deprotonated at different pH values. ◀ For basic amino acids, two high-pH forms exist because deprotonation of the amino groups does not occur simultaneously. The side-chain amino group deprotonates before the α-amino group for histidine, but the opposite is true for lysine and arginine.

Isoelectric Points

An important pH value, relative to the various forms an amino acid can have in solution, is the pH at which it exists primarily in its zwitterion form, that is, its neutral form (no net charge). This pH value is known as the *isoelectric point* for the amino acid. An **isoelectric point** *is the pH at which an amino acid exists primarily in its zwitterion form.* At the isoelectric point, almost all amino acid molecules in a solution (more than 99%) are present in their zwitterion form.

Every amino acid has a different isoelectric point. Fifteen of the 20 amino acids, those with nonpolar or polar neutral side chains (Table 20-1), have isoelectric points in the range of 4.8–6.3. The three basic amino acids have higher isoelectric points, and the two acidic amino acids have lower ones. Table 20-3 lists the isoelectric points for the 20 standard amino acids.

▶ **Table 20-3 Isoelectric Points for the 20 Amino Acids Commonly Found in Proteins**

Name	Isoelectric Point
alanine	6.01
arginine	10.76
asparagine	5.41
aspartic acid	2.77
cysteine	5.07
glutamic acid	3.22
glutamine	5.65
glycine	5.97
histidine	7.59
isoleucine	6.02
leucine	5.98
lysine	9.74
methionine	5.74
phenylalanine	5.48
proline	6.48
serine	5.68
threonine	5.87
tryptophan	5.88
tyrosine	5.66
valine	5.97

Section 20-5 Quick Quiz

1. Which of the standard amino acids exist as zwitterions in the solid state?
   a. all of them
   b. only those that have nonpolar side chains
   c. only those that have polar side chains
   d. no correct response

2. Which of the following is the zwitterion ion structure for the amino acid alanine (R = —CH₃)?

3. Which of the following is the structural form for the amino acid alanine (R = —CH₃) in a solution that is highly acidic (low pH)?

Answers: 1. a; 2. b; 3. a

20-6 Cysteine: A Chemically Unique Amino Acid

LEARNING FOCUS

Be familiar with the unique ability of the amino acid *cysteine* to form disulfide covalent bonds.

Cysteine is the only standard amino acid (Table 20-1) that has a side chain that contains a sulfhydryl group (—SH group; Section 14-20). The presence of this sulfhydryl group imparts to cysteine a chemical property that is unique among the standard amino acids. Cysteine, in the presence of mild oxidizing agents, readily *dimerizes,* that is, reacts with another cysteine molecule to form a cystine molecule. (A *dimer* is a molecule that is made up of two like subunits.) In cystine, the two cysteine residues are linked via a covalent disulfide bond. ◄

▶ Cystine *contains two* cysteine *residues linked by a disulfide bond.*

The covalent disulfide bond of cystine is readily broken, using reducing agents, to regenerate two cysteine molecules. This oxidation–reduction behavior involving sulfhydryl groups and disulfide bonds was previously encountered in Section 14-20 when the reactions of thiols were considered.

$$-SH + HS- \xrightleftharpoons[\text{Reduction}]{\text{Oxidation}} -S-S- + 2H$$

As will be shown in Section 20-11, the formation of disulfide bonds between cysteine residues present in protein molecules has important consequences relative to protein structure and protein shape.

Section 20-6 Quick Quiz

1. Cysteine is unique among standard amino acids in that its R group contains a(n)
   a. sulfhydryl group
   b. chloro group
   c. ethyl group
   d. no correct response
2. Disulfide bond formation between two cysteine molecules results from the interaction of
   a. two —SH groups
   b. an —SH group and an —NH₂ group
   c. an —SH group and a —COOH group
   d. no correct response

Answers: 1. a; 2. a

20-7 Peptides

LEARNING FOCUS

Be familiar with the terminology *peptide, peptide bond,* and *amino acid residue;* be able to draw structural formulas for small peptides and to name them using IUPAC rules; know how the concept of isomerism relates to the sequence of amino acids in a peptide.

Under proper conditions, amino acids can bond together to produce an unbranched chain of amino acids. The length of the amino acid chain can vary from a few amino acids to many amino acids. Representative of such chains is the following five-amino-acid chain.

| Amino acid — Amino acid — Amino acid — Amino acid — Amino acid |

Such a chain of covalently linked amino acids is called a *peptide*. A **peptide** *is an unbranched chain of amino acids*. Peptides are further classified by the number of amino acids present in the chain. A compound containing two amino acids is specifically called a *dipeptide;* three amino acids joined together in a chain constitute a *tripeptide;* and so on. The name *oligopeptide* is loosely used to refer to peptides with 10 to 20 amino acid residues, and the name *polypeptide* is used to refer to longer peptides. A **polypeptide** *is a long unbranched chain of amino acids*.

Nature of the Peptide Bond

The bonds that link amino acids together in a peptide chain are called peptide bonds. There are four peptide bonds present in a pentapeptide.

The nature of the peptide bond becomes apparent by reconsidering a chemical reaction previously encountered. In Section 17-16, the reaction between a carboxylic acid and an amine to produce an amide was considered. The general equation for this reaction was

$$R-\overset{\overset{\displaystyle O}{\|}}{C}-OH \;+\; H-\overset{\overset{\displaystyle H}{|}}{N}-R \;\longrightarrow\; R-\overset{\overset{\displaystyle O}{\|}}{C}-\overset{\overset{\displaystyle H}{|}}{N}-R \;+\; H_2O$$

Acid   Amine   Amide

▶ *Amide bond formation is an example of a condensation reaction.*

Two amino acids can combine in a similar way—the carboxyl group of one amino acid interacts with the amino group of the other amino acid. The products are a molecule of water and a molecule containing the two amino acids linked by an amide bond. ◀

$$\overset{\overset{\displaystyle H}{|}}{\underset{\underset{\displaystyle R_1}{|}}{H_3\overset{+}{N}-C}}-COO^- \;+\; \overset{\overset{\displaystyle H}{|}}{\underset{\underset{\displaystyle R_2}{|}}{H_3\overset{+}{N}-C}}-COO^- \;\longrightarrow\; \overset{\overset{\displaystyle H}{|}}{\underset{\underset{\displaystyle R_1}{|}}{H_3\overset{+}{N}-C}}-\overset{\overset{\displaystyle O}{\|}}{C}-\overset{\overset{\displaystyle H}{|}}{N}-\overset{\overset{\displaystyle H}{|}}{\underset{\underset{\displaystyle R_2}{|}}{C}}-COO^- \;+\; H_2O$$

Amide bond

Removal of the elements of water from the reacting carboxyl and amino groups and the ensuing formation of the amide bond are better visualized when expanded structural formulas for the reacting groups are used.

$$-\overset{\overset{\displaystyle O}{\|}}{C}-O^- \;+\; H-\overset{\overset{\displaystyle H}{|}}{\underset{\underset{\displaystyle H}{|}}{\overset{+}{N}}} \;\longrightarrow\; -\overset{\overset{\displaystyle O}{\|}}{C}-\overset{\overset{\displaystyle H}{|}}{N}- \;+\; H_2O$$

Carboxyl   Amino   Amide
group   group   bond
$(-COO^-)$ $(H_3\overset{+}{N}-)$

In amino acid chemistry, amide bonds that link amino acids together are given the specific name of *peptide bond*. A **peptide bond** *is a covalent bond between the carboxyl group of one amino acid and the amino group of another amino acid*.

▶ *A peptide chain has* directionality *because its two ends are different. There is an N-terminal end and a C-terminal end. By convention, the direction of the peptide chain is always*

N-terminal end → C-terminal end

The N-terminal end is always on the left, and the C-terminal end is always on the right.

In all peptides, long or short, the amino acid at one end of the amino acid sequence has a free $H_3\overset{+}{N}$ group, and the amino acid at the other end of the sequence has a free COO^- group. The end with the free $H_3\overset{+}{N}$ group is called the *N-terminal end,* and the end with the free COO^- group is called the *C-terminal end*. By convention, the sequence of amino acids in a peptide is written with the N-terminal end amino acid on the left. ◀ The individual amino acids within a peptide chain are called *amino acid residues*. An **amino acid residue** *is the portion of an amino acid structure that remains, after the release of H_2O, when an amino acid participates in peptide bond formation as it becomes part of a peptide chain*.

The structural formula for a peptide may be written out in full, or the sequence of amino acids present may be indicated by using the standard three-letter amino acid abbreviations. The abbreviated formula for the tripeptide

which contains the amino acids glycine, alanine, and serine, is Gly–Ala–Ser. When we use this abbreviated notation, by convention, the amino acid at the N-terminal end of the peptide is always written on the left.

The repeating sequence of peptide bonds and α-carbon —CH groups in a peptide is referred to as the *backbone* of the peptide.

Backbone of peptide (in color)

The R group side chains are considered substituents on the backbone rather than part of the backbone.

Thus, structurally, a peptide has a regularly repeating part (the backbone) and a variable part (the sequence of R groups). It is the variable R group sequence that distinguishes one peptide from another.

EXAMPLE 20-2

Converting an Abbreviated Peptide Formula to a Structural Peptide Formula

Draw the structural formula for the tripeptide Ala–Gly–Val.

Solution

Step 1: The N-terminal end of the peptide involves alanine. Its structure is written first.

Step 2: The structure of glycine is written to the right of the alanine structure, and a peptide bond is formed between the two amino acids by removing the elements of H_2O and bonding the N of glycine to the carboxyl C of alanine.

(continued)

Step 3: To the right of the just-formed dipeptide, draw the structure of valine. Then repeat Step 2 to form the desired tripeptide.

$$\overset{+}{H_3}N-\overset{\overset{\displaystyle H}{|}}{\underset{\underset{\displaystyle CH_3}{|}}{C}}-\overset{\overset{\displaystyle O}{\parallel}}{C}-\overset{\overset{\displaystyle H}{|}}{\underset{\underset{\displaystyle H}{|}}{N}}-\overset{\overset{\displaystyle H}{|}}{C}-COO^- + \overset{+}{H_3}N-\overset{\overset{\displaystyle H}{|}}{\underset{\underset{\underset{\displaystyle CH_3}{|}}{CH-CH_3}}{C}}-COO^- \longrightarrow$$

$$\overset{+}{H_3}N-\overset{\overset{\displaystyle H}{|}}{\underset{\underset{\displaystyle CH_3}{|}}{C}}-\overset{\overset{\displaystyle O}{\parallel}}{C}-\overset{\overset{\displaystyle H}{|}}{\underset{\underset{\displaystyle H}{|}}{N}}-\overset{\overset{\displaystyle H}{|}}{C}-\overset{\overset{\displaystyle O}{\parallel}}{C}-\overset{\overset{\displaystyle H}{|}}{\underset{\underset{\displaystyle H}{|}}{N}}-\overset{\overset{\displaystyle H}{|}}{\underset{\underset{\underset{\displaystyle CH_3}{|}}{CH-CH_3}}{C}}-COO^- + H_2O$$

Peptide Nomenclature

Small peptides are named as derivatives of the C-terminal amino acid that is present. The IUPAC rules for doing this are:

Rule 1: *The C-terminal amino acid residue (located at the far right of the structure) keeps its full amino acid name.*

Rule 2: *All of the other amino acid residues have names that end in* -yl. *The* -yl *suffix replaces the* -ine *or* -ic acid *ending of the amino acid name, except for tryptophan (tryptophyl), cysteine (cysteinyl), glutamine (glutaminyl), and asparagine (asparaginyl).*

Rule 3: *The amino acid naming sequence begins at the N-terminal amino acid residue.*

EXAMPLE 20-3

Determining IUPAC Names for Small Peptides

Assign IUPAC names to each of the following small peptides.

a. Glu–Ser–Ala   **b.** Gly–Tyr–Leu–Val

Solution

a. The three amino acids present are glutamic acid, serine, and alanine. Alanine, the C-terminal residue (on the far right), keeps its full name. The other amino acid residues in the peptide receive "shortened" names that end in -*yl*. The -*yl* replaces the -*ine* or -*ic acid* ending of the amino acid name. Thus

> glutamic acid becomes glutamyl
> serine becomes seryl
> alanine remains alanine

The IUPAC name, which lists the amino acids in the sequence from N-terminal residue to C-terminal residue, becomes *glutamylserylalanine.*

b. The four amino acids present are glycine, tyrosine, leucine, and valine. Proceeding as in part **a,**

> glycine becomes glycyl
> tyrosine becomes tyrosyl
> leucine becomes leucyl
> valine remains valine

Combining these individual names gives the IUPAC name *glycyltyrosylleucylvaline.*

The complete name for a small peptide should actually include a handedness designation (L-designation; Section 20-4) before the name of each residue. For example, the dipeptide serylglycine (Ser–Gly) should actually be L-seryl–L-glycine (L-Ser–L-Gly). The L-handedness designation is, however, usually not included because it is understood that all amino acids present in a peptide, unless otherwise noted, are L enantiomers.

Isomeric Peptides

Peptides that contain the same amino acids but in different order are different molecules (constitutional isomers) with different properties. For example, two different dipeptides can be formed from one molecule of alanine and one molecule of glycine.

$$\overset{+}{H_3N}-\overset{\overset{\displaystyle H}{|}}{\underset{\underset{\displaystyle CH_3}{|}}{C}}-\overset{\overset{\displaystyle O}{\|}}{C}-\overset{\overset{\displaystyle H}{|}}{N}-\overset{\overset{\displaystyle H}{|}}{\underset{\underset{\displaystyle H}{|}}{C}}-COO^-$$

Ala–Gly

$$\overset{+}{H_3N}-\overset{\overset{\displaystyle H}{|}}{\underset{\underset{\displaystyle H}{|}}{C}}-\overset{\overset{\displaystyle O}{\|}}{C}-\overset{\overset{\displaystyle H}{|}}{N}-\overset{\overset{\displaystyle H}{|}}{\underset{\underset{\displaystyle CH_3}{|}}{C}}-COO^-$$

Gly–Ala

In the first dipeptide, the alanine is the N-terminal residue, and in the second molecule, it is the C-terminal residue. These two compounds are isomers with different chemical and physical properties. ◀

The number of isomeric peptides possible increases rapidly as the length of the peptide chain increases. Consider the tripeptide Ala–Ser–Cys as a second example. In addition to this sequence, five other arrangements of these three components are possible, each representing another isomeric tripeptide: Ala–Cys–Ser, Ser–Ala–Cys, Ser–Cys–Ala, Cys–Ala–Ser, and Cys–Ser–Ala. For a pentapeptide containing five different amino acids, 120 isomers are possible. ◀

▶ *Amino acid sequence in a peptide has biochemical importance. Isomeric peptides give different biochemical responses; that is, they have different biochemical specificities.*

▶ *For a peptide containing one each of* n *different kinds of amino acids, the number of constitutional isomers is given by* n! *(n factorial).*

$5! = 5 \times 4 \times 3 \times 2 \times 1 = 120$

Section 20-7 Quick Quiz

1. The joining together of two amino acids to form a dipeptide involves the chemical reaction between
   a. two amino groups
   b. two carboxyl groups
   c. an amino group and a carboxyl group
   d. no correct response
2. The number of peptide bonds present in a pentapeptide is
   a. four
   b. five
   c. six
   d. no correct response
3. Which of the following statements concerning the tripeptide Gly–Ala–Val is *correct*?
   a. The C-terminal amino acid residue is Gly
   b. The N-terminal amino acid residue in Val
   c. Another correct way of writing the formula is Val–Ala–Gly
   d. no correct response
4. What functional group is present in the bond formed when two amino acids are joined together to form a dipeptide?
   a. amide
   b. ester
   c. ether
   d. no correct response
5. How many isomeric tripeptides can be formed from two molecules of valine (Val) and one molecule of serine (Ser)?
   a. two
   b. three
   c. four
   d. no correct response

Answers: 1. c; 2. a; 3. d; 4. a; 5. b

20-8 Biochemically Important Small Peptides

LEARNING FOCUS

Know the names and characteristics of several biochemically important small peptides.

Many relatively small peptides have been shown to be biochemically active. Functions for them include hormonal action, neurotransmission, and antioxidant activity.

Small Peptide Hormones

The two best-known peptide hormones, both produced by the pituitary gland, are *oxytocin* and *vasopressin*. Each hormone is a nonapeptide (nine amino acid residues) with six of the residues held in the form of a loop by a disulfide bond formed from the interaction of two cysteine residues (Section 20-6). Structurally, these nonapeptides differ in the amino acid present in positions 3 and 8 of the peptide chain. In both structures, an amine group replaces the C-terminal single-bonded oxygen atom.

Oxytocin
Vasopressin

▶ Oxytocin *plays a role in stimulating the flow of milk in a nursing mother. The baby's suckling action sends nerve signals to the mother's brain, triggering the release of oxytocin, via the blood, to the mammary glands. The oxytocin causes muscle contraction in the mammary gland, forcing out milk. As suckling continues, more oxytocin is released and more milk is available for the baby.*

Oxytocin regulates uterine contractions and lactation. Vasopressin regulates the excretion of water by the kidneys; it also affects blood pressure. ◀ Another name for vasopressin is *antidiuretic hormone (ADH)*. This name relates to vasopressin's function in the kidneys, which is to decrease urine output in order to decrease water elimination from the body. Such action is necessary when the body becomes dehydrated. ◀

Small Peptide Neurotransmitters

Enkephalins are pentapeptide neurotransmitters produced by the brain itself that bind at receptor sites in the brain to reduce pain. The two best-known enkephalins are Met-enkephalin and Leu-enkephalin, whose structures differ only in the amino acid residue present at the C-terminal end (Section 20-6) of the peptide; this amino acid difference is incorporated into their names.

▶ *The action of another important peptide hormone, the octapeptide angiotensin, is considered in the next chapter (Section 21-10).*

Met-enkephalin: Tyr–Gly–Gly–Phe–Met
Leu-enkephalin: Tyr–Gly–Gly–Phe–Leu

The pain-reducing effects of enkephalin action play a role in the "high" reported by long-distance runners, in the competitive athlete's managing to finish the game despite being injured, and in the pain-relieving effects of acupuncture.

The action of the prescription painkillers morphine and codeine is based on their binding at the same receptor sites in the brain as the naturally occurring enkephalins. Enkephalin pain relief is short-term, whereas morphine-codeine pain relief lasts much longer. Enzymes present in the brain readily hydrolyze the peptide linkages in enkephalins; morphine and codeine do not have such linkages and are unaffected by the hydrolysis enzymes.

Small Peptide Antioxidants

The tripeptide *glutathione* (Glu–Cys–Gly) is present in significant concentrations in most cells and is of considerable physiological importance as a regulator of oxidation–reduction reactions. Specifically, glutathione functions as an antioxidant (Section 14-13), protecting cellular contents from oxidizing agents such as peroxides and superoxides (highly reactive forms of oxygen often generated within the cell in response to bacterial invasion) (Section 23-11). ◀

▶ *Other antioxidants previously considered are BHA and BHT (Section 14-13) and β-carotene (Section 13-7).*

The tripeptide structure of glutathione has an unusual feature. The amino acid Glu, an acidic amino acid, is bonded to Cys through the side-chain carboxyl group rather than through its α-carbon carboxyl group.

The side chains are circled in the above structure.

1. The two best-known peptide hormones present in the human body are
   a. oxytocin and vasopressin
   b. Met-enkephalin and Leu-enkephalin
   c. vasopressin and ADH
   d. no correct response
2. Which of the following peptides is an important antioxidant in the human body?
   a. ADH
   b. glutathione
   c. oxytocin
   d. no correct response

Answers: 1. a; 2. b

20-9 General Structural Characteristics of Proteins

LEARNING FOCUS

Distinguish between the terms *protein* and *polypeptide*, between the terms *monomeric protein* and *polymeric protein*, and between the terms *simple protein* and *conjugated protein*.

In Section 20-1, a protein was defined simply as a naturally occurring, unbranched polymer in which the monomer units are amino acids. ◀ A more specific protein definition is now in order. **A protein** *is a peptide in which at least 40 amino acid residues are present.* The defining line governing the use of the term *protein*—40 amino acid residues—is an arbitrary line. The terms *polypeptide* and *protein* are often used interchangeably; a protein is a relatively long polypeptide. The key point is that the term *protein* is reserved for peptides with a large number of amino acids; it is not correct to call a tripeptide a protein. More than 10,000 amino acid residues are present in several proteins; 400–500 amino acid residues are common in proteins; small proteins contain 40–100 amino acid residues.

More than one peptide chain may be present in a protein. On this basis, proteins are classified as *monomeric* or *multimeric*. **A monomeric protein** *is a protein in which only one peptide chain is present.* Large proteins, those with many amino acid residues, usually are multimeric. **A multimeric protein** *is a protein in which more than one peptide chain is present.* The peptide chains present in multimeric proteins are called *protein subunits.* The protein subunits within a multimeric protein may all be identical to each other or different kinds of subunits may be present. Proteins with up to 12 subunits are known. The small protein insulin, which functions as a hormone in the human body, is a multimeric protein with two protein subunits; one subunit contains 21 amino acid residues and the other 30 amino acid residues. The structure of insulin is considered in more detail in Section 20-12.

Proteins, on the basis of chemical composition, are classified as *simple* or *complex*. **A simple protein** *is a protein in which only amino acid residues are present.* More than one protein subunit may be present in a simple protein, but all subunits contain only amino acids. **A conjugated protein** *is a protein that has one or more non-amino-acid entities present in its structure in addition to one or more peptide chains.* The non-amino-acid components present in a conjugated protein, which may be organic or inorganic, are called *prosthetic groups.* **A prosthetic group** *is a non-amino-acid group present in a conjugated protein.*

Conjugated proteins may be further classified according to the nature of the prosthetic group(s) present. *Lipoproteins* contain lipid prosthetic groups, *glycoproteins* contain carbohydrate groups, *metalloproteins* contain specific metal ions, and so on (Table 20-4). Some proteins contain more than one type of prosthetic group. In general, prosthetic groups have important roles in the biochemical functions for conjugated proteins. Several examples of glycoproteins and lipoproteins are discussed in Sections 20-18 and 20-19, respectively.

▶ *Proteins are the second type of biochemical polymer encountered in this text; the other was polysaccharides (Section 18-14). Protein monomers are amino acids, whereas polysaccharide monomers are monosaccharides.*

▶ Table 20-4 **Types of Conjugated Proteins**

Class	Prosthetic Group	Specific Example	Function of Example
hemoproteins	heme unit	hemoglobin myoglobin	carrier of O_2 in blood oxygen binder in muscles
lipoproteins	lipid	low-density lipoprotein (LDL) high-density lipoprotein (HDL)	lipid carrier lipid carrier
glycoproteins	carbohydrate	gamma globulin mucin interferon	antibody lubricant in mucous secretions antiviral protection
phosphoproteins	phosphate group	glycogen phosphorylase	enzyme in glycogen phosphorylation
nucleoproteins	nucleic acid	ribosomes viruses	site for protein synthesis in cells self-replicating, infectious complex
metalloproteins	metal ion	iron–ferritin zinc–alcohol dehydrogenase	storage complex for iron enzyme in alcohol oxidation

In general, the three-dimensional structures of proteins, even those with just a single peptide chain, are more complex than those of carbohydrates and lipids—the biomolecules discussed in the two previous chapters. Describing and understanding this complexity in protein structure involves considering four levels of protein structure. These four protein structural levels, listed in order of increasing complexity, are *primary* structure, *secondary* structure, *tertiary* structure, and *quaternary* structure. They are the subject matter for the next four sections of this chapter.

Section 20-9 Quick Quiz

1. The term *protein* is generally reserved for describing polypeptides in which the number of amino acid residues present is
   a. 40 or greater
   b. 100 or greater
   c. 500 or greater
   d. no correct response
2. The presence of which of the following is a defining characteristic for a *multimeric* protein?
   a. at least 200 amino acid residues
   b. at least two polypeptide chains
   c. at least four polypeptide chains
   d. no correct response
3. Which of the following is *not* a distinguishing feature of a *conjugated* protein?
   a. presence of a prosthetic group
   b. presence of a non-amino-acid entity
   c. presence of one or more nonstandard amino acids
   d. no correct response

Answers: 1. a; 2. b; 3. c

20-10 Primary Structure of Proteins

LEARNING FOCUS

Understand what is meant by the term *primary protein structure* and how such structure is specified.

Primary protein structure *is the order in which amino acids are linked together in a protein.* Every protein has its own unique amino acid sequence. Primary protein structure always involves more than just the numbers and kinds of amino acids present; it also involves the *order of attachment* of the amino acids to each other through peptide bonds.

Insulin, the hormone that regulates blood-glucose levels, was the first protein for which primary structure was determined; the "sequencing" of its 51 amino acids was completed in 1953, after eight years of work by the British biochemist Frederick Sanger (Figure 20-3). Today, primary structures are known for many thousands of proteins, and the sequencing procedures involve automated methods that require relatively short periods of time (days). Figure 20-4 shows the primary structure of myoglobin, a protein involved in oxygen storage in muscles; it contains 153 amino acids assembled in the particular, definite order shown in this diagram.

The primary structure of a specific protein is always the same regardless of where the protein is found within an organism. The structures of certain proteins are even similar among different species of animals. For example, the primary structures of insulin in cows, pigs, sheep, and horses are very similar both to each other and to human insulin. Until recently, this similarity was particularly important for diabetics who required supplemental injections of insulin. The focus on relevancy feature Chemical Connections 20-A—"Substitutes" for Human Insulin—considers several old and new aspects of insulin chemistry.

Figure 20-3 The British biochemist Frederick Sanger (1918–2013) determined the primary structure of the protein hormone *insulin* in 1953. His work is a landmark in biochemistry because it showed for the first time that a protein has a precisely defined amino acid sequence. Sanger was awarded the Nobel Prize in chemistry in 1958 for this work. Later, in 1980, he was awarded a second Nobel Prize in chemistry, this time for work that involved the sequencing of units in nucleic acids (Chapter 22).

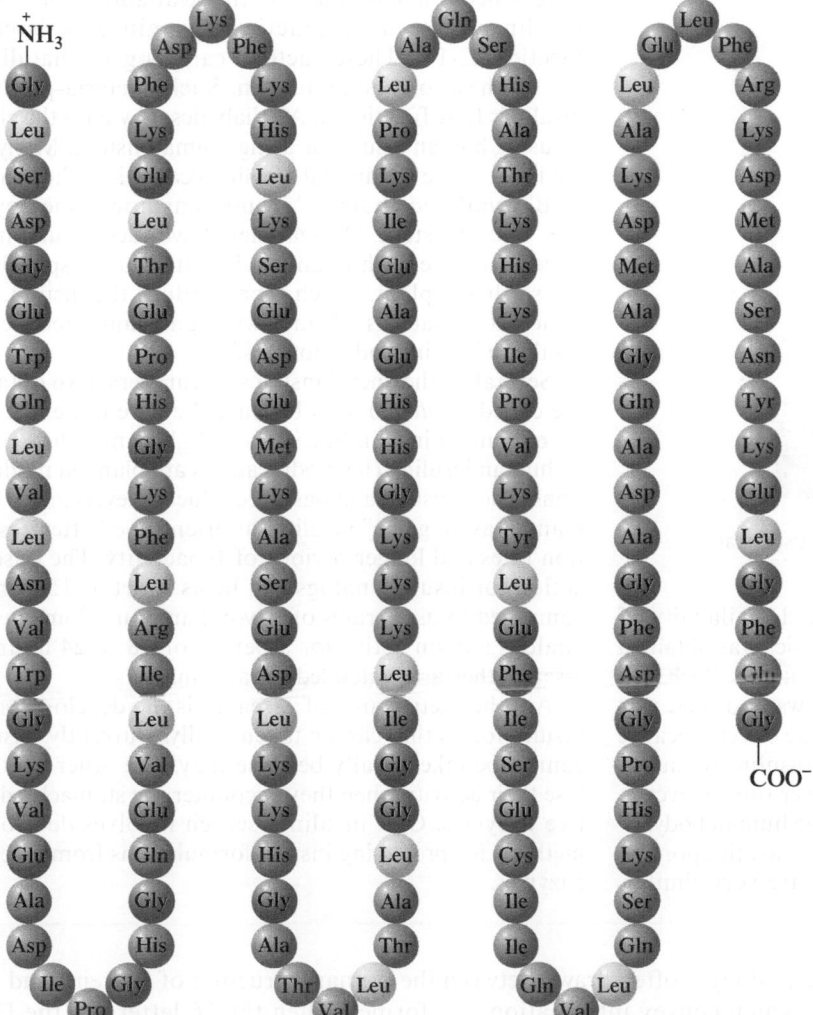

Figure 20-4 The primary structure of human myoglobin. This diagram gives only the sequence of the amino acids present and conveys no information about the actual three-dimensional shape of the protein. The "wavy" pattern for the 153 amino acid sequence was chosen to minimize the space used to present the needed information. The actual shape of the protein is determined by secondary and tertiary levels of protein structure, levels yet to be discussed.

"Substitutes" for Human Insulin

Insulin is a 51-amino-acid-containing protein hormone whose structure is given later in the chapter (Section 20-12). Its function within the human body primarily involves regulation of blood-glucose levels. It assists the entry of blood glucose into cells by interacting with receptors on cell membranes (Section 19-10). It also helps facilitate the conversion of glucose to the storage polysaccharide glycogen (Section 18-15) when blood-glucose levels become too high and facilitates the reverse process (conversion of glycogen back to glucose) when blood-glucose levels become too low.

Insufficient insulin production or an inability to use insulin produced (insulin resistance) results in the condition *diabetes mellitus*. Treatment of this condition often involves giving a person insulin via subcutaneous injection (see accompanying photo).

© Svanblar/Shutterstock.com

Currently, diabetics who require insulin must obtain it through injection rather than orally.

For many years, because of the limited availability of human insulin, most insulin used by diabetics was obtained from the pancreases of slaughter-house animals. Such animal insulin, obtained primarily from cows and pigs, was used by most diabetics without serious side effects because it is structurally very similar to human insulin. Immunological reactions gradually do increase over time, however, because the animal insulin is foreign to the human body.

In terms of primary structure, human insulin, porcine (pig) insulin, and bovine (cow) insulin are very similar.

Porcine and human insulin match at 50 of the 51 amino acid positions, and bovine and human insulin match at 48 of the 51 amino acid positions (see the table that follows and Figure 20-10).

Species	Chain A			Chain B
	#8	#9	#10	#30
human	Thr	Ser	Ile	Thr
pig (porcine)	Thr	Ser	Ile	Ala
cow (bovine)	Ala	Ser	Val	Ala

The dependency of diabetics on animal insulin is no longer necessary because of the availability of human insulin produced by genetically engineered bacteria (Section 22-14). These bacteria carry a gene that directs the synthesis of human insulin. Such bacteria-produced insulin is fully functional. All diabetics now have the choice of using human insulin or using animal insulin. Many still continue to use the animal insulin because it is cheaper.

Biosynthetic "human" insulin has now gone beyond the "bacteria stage." Researchers have successfully introduced the gene for human insulin into plants, specifically the safflower plant, which then produce the insulin. It is anticipated that this advance will significantly reduce biosynthetic insulin production costs.

Several of the "new" insulins researchers have obtained are called *insulin analogs* because they are not exact copies of human insulin but, rather, slightly modified copies of human insulin. The modifications are planned modifications. These insulin analogs affect glucose levels in the same manner as "regular" insulin but often have better absorption rates and longer periods of bioactivity. The onset of action for insulin analogs can be as short as 15 minutes compared to usual rates of beyond an hour. Some insulin analogs remain active for a period of 18 to 24 hours; in essence, they are "extended release" insulins.

Another active area of research is the development of insulin forms that can be taken orally. Currently, insulins cannot be taken orally because they, like other proteins, lose their activity when they encounter the stomach's digestive enzymes. Oral insulin research involves developing methods for protecting insulin formulations from digestive enzymes.

An analogy is often drawn between the primary structure of proteins and words. Words, which convey information, are formed when the 26 letters of the English alphabet are properly sequenced. Proteins are formed from proper sequences of the 20 standard amino acids. Just as the proper sequence of letters in a word is necessary for it to make sense, the proper sequence of amino acids is necessary to make biochemically active protein. Furthermore, the letters that form a word are written from left to right, as are amino acids in protein formulas. As any dictionary of the English language will document, a tremendous variety of words can be formed by different letter sequences. Imagine the number of amino acid sequences possible for a large protein. There are 1.55×10^{66} sequences possible for the 51 amino acids found in insulin! From these possibilities, the body reliably produces only *one,* illustrating the remarkable precision of life processes. From the simplest bacterium to the human brain cell, only those amino acid sequences needed by the cell are produced. The fascinating process of protein biosynthesis and the way in which genes in DNA direct this process will be discussed in Chapter 22. ◄

The various amino acids present in a protein, whose order is the primary structure of the protein, are linked to each other by peptide linkages. The peptide bonds are part of the "backbone" of the protein. The structural characteristics of a protein backbone are the same as those of a peptide backbone (Section 20-7); relative to backbone structure, a protein is simply an "extra long" peptide. A representative segment of a protein backbone is as follows:

► *In specifying the primary structure of a protein, the three-letter abbreviations for the amino acids are listed in sequential order starting with the amino acid that has a free amino group, that is starting at the N-terminal end (Section 20-7) of the peptide chain.*

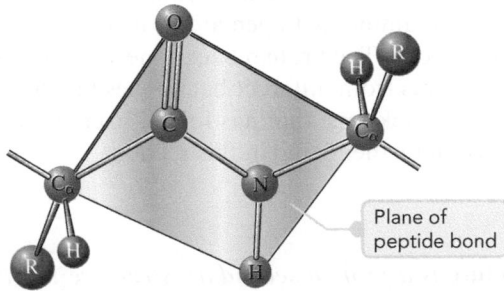

Segment of a protein backbone

Attached to the backbone, at the CH locations, are the various amino acid R groups.

The carbon and nitrogen atoms of a protein backbone are arranged in a "zigzag" manner. This zigzag pattern arises from the geometric characteristics of peptide bonds. Important points concerning peptide bond geometry are:

1. The peptide linkages are essentially planar. This means that for two amino acids linked through a peptide linkage, six atoms lie in the same plane: the α-carbon atom and the C=O group from the first amino acid and the N—H group and the α-carbon atom from the second amino acid.

Plane of peptide bond

2. The planar peptide linkage structure has considerable rigidity, which means that rotation of groups about the C—N bond is hindered, and *cis–trans* isomerism is possible about this bond. The *trans* isomer orientation is the preferred orientation, as shown in the preceding diagram. The O atom of the C=O group and the H atom of the N—H group are positioned *trans* to each other.

The net effect of "peptide bond planarity" is the zigzag arrangement, previously mentioned, of atoms within a protein backbone, which is shown in the following diagram.

Section 20-10 Quick Quiz

1. Specifying the primary structure of a protein involves specifying the
   a. number of peptide linkages present
   b. the number of amino acids present
   c. the sequence of the amino acids present
   d. no correct response

(continued)

2. When specifying the primary structure of a protein, the first amino acid listed is the one
  a. located at the N-terminal end of the peptide chain
  b. located at the C-terminal end of the peptide chain
  c. whose abbreviation has alphabetical priority
  d. no correct response
3. Two *different* proteins that contain the same number of each of the various standard amino acids
  a. is a structural impossibility
  b. must have the same primary structure
  c. cannot have the same primary structure
  d. no correct response

Answers: 1. c; 2. a; 3. c

20-11 Secondary Structure of Proteins

LEARNING FOCUS

Describe the role that hydrogen bonding plays in the secondary structure of a protein and be familiar with the two most common types of protein secondary structure.

N-terminal end C-terminal end

C-terminal end N-terminal end

Figure 20-5 The hydrogen bonding between the carbonyl oxygen atom of one peptide linkage and the amide hydrogen atom of another peptide linkage.

▶ *Proteins are chiral molecules because most of their amino acid building blocks are chiral. It is this protein chirality that causes an alpha-helix spiral (coil) to have a right-handed (clockwise) twist. If proteins contained D-amino acids rather than L-amino acids (Section 20-4), the spiral would twist in the opposite direction (counterclockwise). If proteins contained a mixture of D- and L- amino acids, it would not be possible to form a spiral.*

Secondary protein structure *is the arrangement in space adopted by the backbone portion of a protein.* The two most common types of secondary structure are the *alpha helix* (α helix) and the *beta pleated sheet* (β pleated sheet). The type of interaction responsible for both of these types of secondary structure is hydrogen bonding (Section 7-13) between a carbonyl oxygen atom of a peptide linkage and the hydrogen atom of an amino group of another peptide linkage farther along the protein backbone. Figure 20-5 shows the hydrogen-bonding possibilities that exist between carbonyl oxygen atoms and amino hydrogen atoms associated with different peptide linkages in a protein backbone. The protein backbone segments involved in hydrogen bonding can be two segments from different backbones (as shown in Figure 20-5) or two segments of the same backbone that has folded back upon itself. Both of these situations are considered in further detail in this section.

The Alpha Helix

An **alpha helix structure** *is a protein secondary structure in which a single protein chain adopts a shape that resembles a coiled spring (helix), with the coil configuration maintained by hydrogen bonds.* The hydrogen bonds are between $>$N—H and $>$C=O groups as is shown diagrammatically in Figure 20-6.

Further details about alpha helix secondary protein structure are:

1. The twist of the helix forms a right-handed, or clockwise, spiral. ◀
2. The hydrogen bonds between C=O and N—H entities are orientated parallel to the axis of the helix (Figure 20-6b).
3. A given hydrogen bond involves a C=O group of one amino acid and an N—H group of another amino acid located four amino acid residues further along the spiral (Figure 20-6b). This is because one turn of the spiral includes 3.6 amino acid residues.
4. All of the amino acid R groups extend outward from the spiral (Figure 20-6d). There is not enough room for the R groups within the spiral.

The Beta Pleated Sheet

A **beta pleated sheet structure** *is a protein secondary structure in which two fully extended protein chain segments in the same or different molecules are held together by hydrogen bonds.* Hydrogen bonds form between oxygen and hydrogen peptide linkage atoms that are either in different parts of a single chain that folds back on itself (intrachain bonds) or between atoms in different peptide chains in those proteins that

Figure 20-6 Four representations of the α helix protein secondary structure.

●	Carbon
●	Nitrogen
○	Hydrogen
●	Oxygen
●	Side group

a Arrangement of protein backbone with no detail shown.

b Backbone arrangement with hydrogen-bonding interactions shown.

c Backbone atomic detail shown, as well as hydrogen-bonding interactions.

d Top view of an α helix showing that amino acid side chains (R groups) point away from the long axis of the helix.

contain more than one chain (interchain bonds). ◄ In molecules where the β pleated sheet involves a single molecule, several U-turns in the protein chain arrangement are needed in order to form the structure.

▶ *The hydrogen bonding present in an α helix is intramolecular. In a β pleated sheet, the hydrogen bonding can be intermolecular (between two different chains) or intramolecular (a single chain folding back on itself).*

C-terminal end

N-terminal end

This "U-turn structure" is the most frequently encountered type of β pleated sheet structure.

Figure 20-7a shows a representation of the β pleated sheet structure that occurs when portions of two different peptide chains are aligned parallel to each other (interchain bonds). The term *pleated sheet* arises from the repeated zigzag pattern in the structure (Figure 20-7b). ◄

Further features of the β pleated sheet secondary protein structure are:

1. The hydrogen bonds between C=O and N—H entities lie in the plane of the sheet (Figure 20-7a).
2. The amino acid R groups are found above and below the plane of the sheet and within a given backbone segment alternating between the top and bottom positions (Figure 20-7b).

▶ *The β pleated sheet is found extensively in the protein of silk. Because such proteins are already fully extended, silk fibers cannot be stretched. When wool, which has an α helix structure, becomes wet, it stretches as hydrogen bonds of the helix are broken. The wool returns to its original shape as it dries. Wet stretched wool, dried under tension, maintains its stretched length because it has assumed a β pleated sheet configuration.*

Unstructured Segments

Very few proteins have entirely α helix or β pleated sheet structures. Instead, only certain portions of the molecules of most proteins are in these conformations. It is also possible to have both α helix and β pleated sheet structures within the same protein (see Figure 20-8). Helical structure and pleated sheet structure are found only in the portions of a protein where the amino acid R groups present are relatively small; large R groups tend to disrupt both of these types of secondary structure.

Carbon
Nitrogen
Hydrogen
Oxygen
R group

a A representation emphasizing the hydrogen bonds between protein chains.

b A representation emphasizing the pleats and the location of the R groups.

Figure 20-7 Two representations of the β pleated sheet protein structure.

Figure 20-8 The secondary structure of a single protein often shows areas of α helix and β pleated sheet configurations, as well as areas of "unstructure."

β Pleated sheet

α Helix

"Unstructured segment"

α Helix

The portions of a protein that have neither α helix nor β pleated sheet structure are called *unstructured segments*. This designation is somewhat of a misnomer because all molecules of a given protein exhibit *identical* unstructured segments. An **unstructured protein segment** *is a protein secondary structure that is neither an α helix nor a β pleated sheet.*

An active area of protein research involves learning more about the biochemical functions of the unstructured portions of proteins. A growing number of researchers now believe that some "unstructure" is essential to the functioning of many proteins. It confers flexibility to proteins, thereby allowing them to interact with several different substances, an important mechanism for rapid response to changing cellular conditions. Often unstructured regions of a protein have the flexibility to bind to several different protein partners, allowing the same amino acid sequence to multitask. The act of binding to another protein does bring added structure to the unstructured portion of the protein, but the added structure is lost when the binding interaction ceases.

20-12 Tertiary Structure of Proteins

LEARNING FOCUS

Distinguish *tertiary* protein structure from *secondary* protein structure in terms of the types of attractive forces that contribute to the structures.

Tertiary protein structure *is the overall three-dimensional shape of a protein that results from the interactions between amino acid side chains (R groups) that are widely separated from each other within a peptide chain.*

A good analogy for the relationships among the primary, secondary, and tertiary structures of a protein is that of a telephone cord (Figure 20-9). The primary structure is the long, straight cord. The coiling of the cord into a helical arrangement gives the secondary structure. The supercoiling arrangement the cord adopts after the receiver has been hung up a number of times is the tertiary structure.

Interactions Responsible for Tertiary Structure

Four types of stabilizing interactions contribute to the tertiary structure of a protein: (1) covalent disulfide bonds, (2) electrostatic attractions (salt bridges), (3) hydrogen bonds, and (4) hydrophobic attractions. All four of these interactions are interactions between amino acid R groups. This is a major distinction between tertiary-structure interactions and secondary structure interactions. Tertiary-structure interactions involve the R groups of amino acids; secondary-structure interactions involve the peptide linkages between amino acid residues.

Disulfide bonds, the strongest of the tertiary-structure interactions, result from the —SH groups of two cysteine residues reacting with each other to form a *covalent* disulfide bond (Section 20-6). ◀ This type of interaction is the only one of the

▶ *Cysteine is the only α-amino acid that contains a sulfhydryl group (—SH).*

Primary   Secondary   Tertiary
structure   structure   structure

Figure 20-9 A telephone cord has three levels of structure. These structural levels are a good analogy for the first three levels of protein structure.

Figure 20-10 Disulfide bonds involving cysteine residues can form in two different ways.

a Between two —SH groups on the same chain.

b Between two —SH groups on different chains.

Figure 20-11 Human insulin, a small two-chain protein, has both intrachain and interchain disulfide linkages as part of its tertiary structure.

four tertiary-structure interactions that involves a covalent bond. Disulfide bond formation may involve two cysteine units in the same peptide chain (an intramolecular disulfide bond; Figure 20-10a) or two cysteine units in different chains (an intermolecular disulfide bond; Figure 20-10b). Figure 20-11 gives the structure of the protein hormone insulin, a protein that has two peptide chains and a total of 51 amino acid residues; both inter- and intramolecular disulfide bonds are present in its structure.

Electrostatic interactions, also called *salt bridges,* always involve the interaction between an acidic side chain (R group) and a basic side chain (R group). The side chains of acidic and basic amino acids, at the appropriate pH, carry charges, with the acidic side chain being negatively charged and the basic side chain being positively charged. Such side chain charges occur when a —COOH group becomes a —COO⁻ group and when an —NH₂ group becomes an —NH₃⁺ group. The interaction that occurs between the two types of side chains is a positive–negative ion–ion attraction. Figure 20-12b shows an electrostatic interaction.

Hydrogen bonds can occur between amino acids with polar R groups. A variety of polar side chains can be involved, especially those that possess the following functional groups:

$$-OH \qquad -NH_2 \qquad \overset{\overset{\displaystyle O}{\|}}{-C}-OH \qquad \overset{\overset{\displaystyle O}{\|}}{-C}-NH_2$$

Hydrogen bonds are relatively weak and are easily disrupted by changes in pH and temperature. Figure 20-12c shows the hydrogen-bonding interaction between the R groups of glutamine and serine.

Hydrophobic interactions result when two nonpolar side chains are close to each other. In aqueous solution, many proteins have their polar R groups pointing outward,

Figure 20-12 The four types of stabilizing interactions between amino acid R groups that contribute to the tertiary structure of a protein.

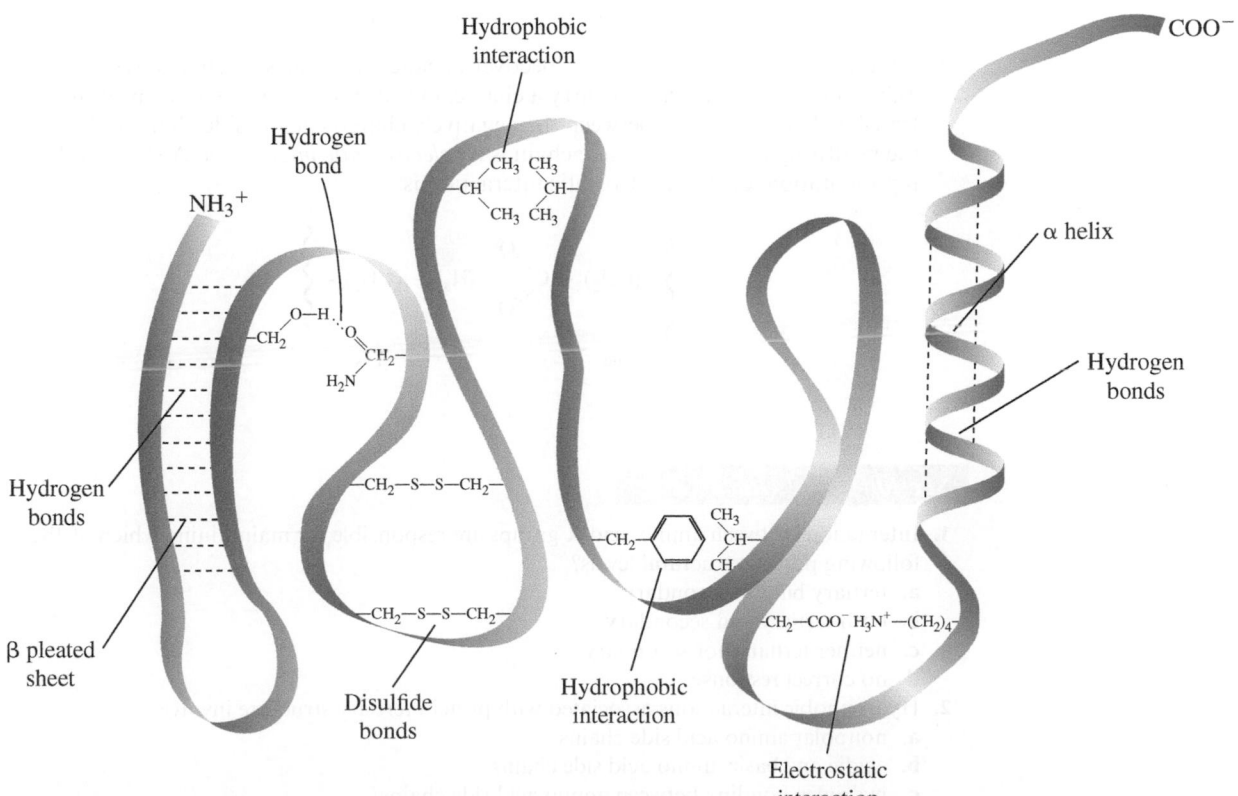

toward the aqueous solvent (which is also polar), and their nonpolar R groups pointing inward (away from the polar water molecules). The nonpolar R groups then interact with each other. The attractive forces are London forces (Section 7-13) resulting from the momentary uneven distribution of electrons within the side chains. Hydrophobic interactions are common between phenyl rings and alkyl side chains. Although hydrophobic interactions are weaker than hydrogen bonds or electrostatic interactions, they are a significant force in some proteins because there are so many of them; their cumulative effect can be greater in magnitude than the effects of hydrogen bonding. Figure 20-12d shows the hydrophobic interaction between the R groups of phenylalanine and leucine.

Figure 20-13 shows all four of the stabilizing interactions that contribute to tertiary protein structure in the context of a single peptide chain (a monomeric protein; Section 20-9).

In 1959, a protein tertiary structure was determined for the first time. The determination involved myoglobin, a conjugated protein (Section 20-9) whose function is

Figure 20-13 Disulfide bonds, electrostatic interactions, hydrogen bonds, and hydrophobic interactions are all stabilizing influences that contribute to the tertiary structure of a protein.

Figure 20-14 A schematic diagram showing the tertiary structure of the single-chain protein myoglobin.

oxygen storage in muscle tissue. Figure 20-14 shows myoglobin's tertiary structure. It involves a single peptide chain of 153 amino acids with numerous α helix segments within the chain. The structure also contains a prosthetic heme group, an iron-containing group with the ability to bind molecular oxygen.

A comparison of Figure 20-14 (myoglobin's tertiary structure) with Figure 20-4 (myoglobin's primary structure) shows how different the perspectives of primary and tertiary structure are for a protein.

Example 20-4 considers the mechanics involved in identifying and drawing structural representations for the various stabilizing interactions associated with protein tertiary structure.

EXAMPLE 20-4

Drawing Structural Representations for Amino Acid Side-Chain Interactions Associated with Protein Tertiary Structure

Identify the type of noncovalent interaction that occurs between the side chains of the following amino acids, and show the interaction using structural representations for the side chains.

a. Serine and asparagine
b. Glutamic acid and lysine

Solution

a. Both serine and asparagine are polar neutral amino acids (see Table 20-1). The side chains of such amino acids interact through *hydrogen bonding*. A structural representation for this hydrogen bonding interaction is:

$$\{-CH_2-O \quad \overset{H\cdots\ddot{O}}{\underset{H_2N}{}} C-CH_2-\}$$

Ser   Asn

b. Glutamic acid and lysine have, respectively, acidic and basic side chains (see Table 20-1). Such side chains carry a charge, in solution, as the result of proton transfer. The interaction between the negatively charged acidic side chain and the positively charged basic side chain is an *electrostatic interaction*. A structural representation for this electrostatic interaction is:

$$\{-(CH_2)_2-C\overset{O^-}{\underset{O}{}} \quad H_3\overset{+}{N}-(CH_2)_4-\}$$

Glu   Lys

Section 20-12 Quick Quiz

1. Interactions between amino acid R groups are responsible for maintaining which of the following protein structural levels?
   a. tertiary but not secondary
   b. both tertiary and secondary
   c. neither tertiary nor secondary
   d. no correct response
2. Hydrophobic interactions associated with protein tertiary structure involve
   a. nonpolar amino acid side chains
   b. acidic and basic amino acid side chains
   c. hydrogen bonding between amino acid side chains
   d. no correct response

3. R group interactions between which of the following pairs of amino acids produces a covalent bond?
   a. cysteine–cysteine
   b. proline–proline
   c. alanine–glycine
   d. no correct response

Answers: 1. a; 2. a; 3. a

Quaternary Structure of Proteins

LEARNING FOCUS
Know the necessary requirements for protein *quaternary* structure.

Quaternary structure is the highest level of protein organization. It is found only in multimeric proteins (Section 20-9). Such proteins have structures involving two or more peptide subunits that are independent of each other—that is, are not covalently bonded to each other. **Quaternary protein structure** *is the organization among the various peptide subunits in a multimeric protein.*

Most multimeric proteins contain an even number of subunits (two subunits = a dimer, four subunits = a tetramer, and so on). ◀ The subunits are held together by the same types of noncovalent interactions that contribute to tertiary structure (electrostatic interactions, hydrogen bonds, and hydrophobic interactions), with hydrophobic interactions being particularly important. Noncovalent interactions that contribute to quaternary structure, are, however, weaker and thus more easily disrupted. For example, only small changes in cellular conditions can cause a tetrameric protein to fall apart, dissociating into dimers or perhaps four separate subunits, with a resulting temporary loss of protein activity. As original cellular conditions are restored, the quaternary structure automatically re-forms, and normal protein function is restored.

An example of a protein with quaternary structure is hemoglobin, the oxygen-carrying protein in blood (Figure 20-15). It is a tetramer in which there are two identical α subunits and two identical β subunits. Each subunit enfolds a heme group, the site where oxygen binds to the protein.

Chemistry at a Glance—Protein Structure—reviews basic concepts about all four levels of protein structure.

▶ *It is significant that the different parts of a multimeric protein are called protein* subunits *rather than protein* chains. *Covalent bonding does not occur between protein subunits but can occur between protein chains.* (disulfide bonds).

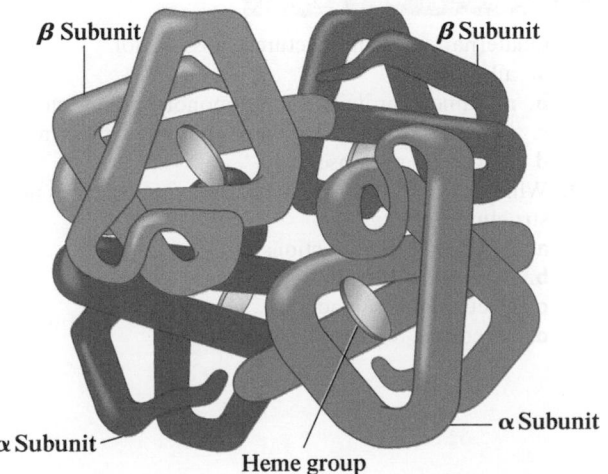

β Subunit   **β Subunit**

α Subunit   **α Subunit**
Heme group

Figure 20-15 A schematic diagram showing the tertiary and quaternary structure of the oxygen-carrying protein hemoglobin.

CHEMISTRY AT A GLANCE   Protein Structure

PRIMARY STRUCTURE
The sequence of amino acids present in a protein's peptide chain or chains

SECONDARY STRUCTURE
The regularly repeating ordered spatial arrangements of amino acids near each other in the protein chain, which result from hydrogen bonds between carbonyl oxygen atoms and amino hydrogen atoms

Alpha Helix
Hydrogen bonds between every fourth amino acid

Beta Pleated Sheet
Hydrogen bonds between two side-by-side chains, or a single chain that is folded back on itself

TERTIARY STRUCTURE
The overall three-dimensional shape that results from the attractive forces between amino acid side chains (R groups) that are not near each other in the protein chain

- Disulfide bonds
- Electrostatic interactions
- Hydrogen bonds
- Hydrophobic interactions

QUATERNARY STRUCTURE
The three-dimensional shape of a protein consisting of two or more independent peptide subunits, which results from noncovalent interactions between R groups

- Electrostatic interactions
- Hydrogen bonds
- Hydrophobic interactions

Section 20-13 Quick Quiz

1. Quaternary protein structure is possible for
   a. all proteins
   b. multimeric proteins but not monomeric proteins
   c. monomeric proteins but not multimeric proteins
   d. no correct response
2. Which of the following types of interactions does not contribute to quaternary protein structure stability?
   a. hydrophobic interactions
   b. hydrogen bonding
   c. electrostatic interactions
   d. no correct response

Answers: 1. b; 2. d

20-14 Protein Hydrolysis

LEARNING FOCUS

Know the conditions necessary for and the products produced when proteins are hydrolyzed.

When a protein or smaller peptide in a solution of strong acid or strong base is heated, the peptide bonds of the amino acid chain are hydrolyzed and free amino acids are produced. The hydrolysis reaction is the reverse of the formation reaction for a peptide bond. Amine and carboxylic acid functional groups are regenerated.

In *complete* protein hydrolysis all peptide bonds are broken freeing up all of the constituent amino acids; amino acids are the only products. Partial rather than complete hydrolysis of a protein is also possible. In *partial* protein hydrolysis some, but not all, of the peptide bonds are broken producing a product mixture that contains both free amino acids and small peptides.

The complete hydrolysis of the tripeptide Ala–Gly–Cys under acidic conditions produces one unit each of the amino acids alanine, glycine, and cysteine. The equation for the hydrolysis is

Note that the product amino acids in this reaction are written in positive-ion form because of the acidic reaction conditions.

Protein digestion (Section 26-1) is simply enzyme-catalyzed hydrolysis of ingested protein. ◀ The free amino acids produced from this process are absorbed through the intestinal wall into the bloodstream and transported to the liver. Here they become the raw materials for the synthesis of new protein. Also, the hydrolysis of cellular proteins to amino acids is an ongoing process, as the body resynthesizes needed molecules and tissue.

▶ *Medications that are proteins, such as insulin, must always be injected rather than taken by mouth. If taken by mouth they will be hydrolyzed in the aqueous acidic environment of the stomach.*

Section 20-14 Quick Quiz

1. The *complete* hydrolysis of a protein produces a mixture of
   a. polypeptides
   b. free amino acids
   c. both polypeptides and free amino acids
   d. no correct response
2. Which of the following statements concerning *complete* protein hydrolysis is *incorrect*?
   a. All peptide bonds are broken.
   b. Water is a reactant in the process.
   c. Tertiary and secondary protein structure, but not primary structure, is disrupted.
   d. no correct response

Answers: 1. b; 2. c

20-15 Protein Denaturation

LEARNING FOCUS

Know what occurs structurally when a protein is denatured; know the identity of common protein-denaturing agents.

Protein denaturation *is the partial or complete disorganization of a protein's characteristic three-dimensional shape as a result of disruption of its secondary, tertiary, and quaternary structural interactions.* Because the biochemical function of a protein depends on its three-dimensional shape, the result of denaturation is loss of biochemical activity. Protein denaturation does not affect the primary structure of a protein. ◀

▶ *A consequence of protein denaturation, the partial or complete loss of a protein's three-dimensional structure, is loss of biochemical activity for the protein.*

Figure 20-16 Protein denaturation involves loss of the protein's three-dimensional structure. Complete loss of such structure produces a "disordered" protein strand.

α Helix → Denaturation → "Disordered" protein strand

Figure 20-17 Heat denatures the protein in egg white, producing a white jellylike solid. The primary structure of the protein remains intact, but all higher levels of protein structure are disrupted.

▶ *If fresh pineapple is added to gelatin desserts, the gelatin will not gel. Fresh pineapple contains an enzyme that facilitates the hydrolysis of gelatin peptide linkages. Canned pineapple can be added to gelatin without preventing it from gelling. The heat used in processing the canned pineapple has denatured the hydrolysis enzymes.*

Figure 20-18 Storage room for cheese; during storage, cheese "matures" as bacteria and enzymes ferment the cheese, giving it a stronger flavor.

Although some proteins lose all of their three-dimensional structural characteristics upon denaturation (Figure 20-16), most proteins maintain some three-dimensional structure. Often, for limited denaturation changes, it is possible to find conditions under which the effects of denaturation can be reversed; this restoration process, in which the protein is "refolded," is called *renaturation*. However, for extensive denaturation changes, the process is usually irreversible.

Loss of water solubility is a frequent physical consequence of protein denaturation. The precipitation out of biochemical solution of denatured protein is called *coagulation*.

A most dramatic example of protein denaturation occurs when egg white (a concentrated solution of the protein albumin) is poured onto a hot surface. The clear albumin solution immediately changes into a white solid with a jellylike consistency (see Figure 20-17). A similar process occurs when hamburger juices encounter a hot surface. A brown jellylike solid forms.

When protein-containing foods are cooked, protein denaturation occurs. Such "cooked" protein is more easily digested because it is easier for digestive enzymes to "work on" denatured (unraveled) protein. Cooking foods also kills microorganisms through protein denaturation. For example, ham and bacon can harbor parasites that cause trichinosis. Cooking the ham or bacon denatures parasite protein. ◀

In surgery, heat is often used to seal small blood vessels. This process, which involves denaturation, is called *cauterization*. Small wounds can also be sealed by cauterization. Heat-induced denaturation is also used in sterilizing surgical instruments and in canning foods; bacteria are destroyed when the heat denatures their protein.

The body temperature of a patient with fever may rise to 102°F, 103°F, or even 104°F without serious consequences. A temperature above 106°F (41°C) is extremely dangerous, as the body's enzymes begin to be inactivated at this level. Enzymes, which function as catalysts for almost all body reactions, are protein. Inactivation of enzymes through denaturation can have lethal effects on body chemistry.

The effect of ultraviolet radiation from the sun, an ionizing radiation (Section 11-7), is similar to that of heat. Denatured skin proteins cause most of the problems associated with sunburn.

A curdy precipitate of casein, the principal protein in milk, is formed in the stomach when the hydrochloric acid of gastric juice denatures the casein. The curdling of milk that takes place when milk sours or cheese is made (Figure 20-18) results from the presence of lactic acid, a by-product of bacterial growth. Yogurt is prepared by growing lactic-acid-producing bacteria in skim milk. The coagulated denatured protein gives yogurt its semi-solid consistency.

Serious eye damage can result from eye tissue contact with acids or bases, when irreversibly denatured and coagulated protein causes a clouded cornea. This reaction is part of the basis for the rule that students wear protective eyewear in the chemistry laboratory.

Alcohols are an important type of denaturing agent. Denaturation of bacterial protein takes place when isopropyl or ethyl alcohol is used as a disinfectant—hence the common practice of swabbing the skin with alcohol before giving an injection. Interestingly, pure isopropyl or ethyl alcohol is less effective than the commonly used 70% alcohol solution. Pure alcohol quickly denatures and coagulates the bacterial surface, thereby forming an effective barrier to further penetration by the alcohol. The 70% solution denatures more slowly and allows complete penetration to be achieved before coagulation of the surface proteins takes place.

The chemical details associated with the process of giving someone a "hair permanent," which involves protein denaturation through the use of reducing agents, are considered in the focus on relevancy feature Chemical Connections 20-B—Denaturation and Human Hair.

CHEMICAL CONNECTIONS 20-B

Denaturation and Human Hair

The process used in waving hair—that is, in a hair permanent—involves reversible denaturation. Hair is protein in which many disulfide (—S—S—) linkages occur as part of its tertiary structure; 16%–18% of hair is the amino acid cysteine. It is these disulfide linkages that give hair protein its overall shape. When a permanent is administered, hair is first treated with a reducing agent (ammonium thioglycolate) that breaks the disulfide linkages in the hair, producing two sulfhydryl (—SH) groups:

Disulfide bridges $\xrightarrow[\text{agents}]{\text{Reducing}}$ sulfhydryl groups

The "reduced" hair, with disrupted tertiary structure, is then wound on curlers (see accompanying photo) to give it a new configuration.

Finally, the reduced and rearranged hair is treated with an oxidizing agent (potassium bromate) to form disulfide linkages at new locations within the hair:

Sulfhydryl groups $\xrightarrow[\text{agents}]{\text{Oxidizing}}$ re-formed disulfide bridges

The new shape and curl of the hair are maintained by the newly formed disulfide bonds and the resulting new tertiary structure accompanying their formation. Of course, as new hair grows in, the "permanent" process has to be repeated.

Winding hair on curlers and then treating it with an oxidizing agent, as part of receiving a hair permanent, is the stage in which disulfide linkages that had been previously broken are re-formed.

▶ Table 20-5 **Selected Physical and Chemical Denaturing Agents**

Denaturing Agent	Mode of Action
heat	disrupts hydrogen bonds by making molecules vibrate too violently; produces coagulation, as in the frying of an egg
microwave radiation	causes violent vibrations of molecules that disrupt hydrogen bonds
ultraviolet radiation	operates very similarly to the action of heat (e.g., sunburning)
violent whipping or shaking	causes molecules in globular shapes to extend to longer lengths, which then entangle (e.g., beating egg white into meringue)
detergent	affects R-group interactions
organic solvents (e.g., ethanol, 2-propanol, acetone)	interferes with R-group interactions because these solvents also can form hydrogen bonds; quickly denatures proteins in bacteria, killing them (e.g., the disinfectant action of 70% ethanol) ◀
strong acids and bases	disrupts hydrogen bonds and salt bridges; prolonged action leads to actual hydrolysis of peptide bonds
salts of heavy metals (e.g., salts of Hg^{2+}, Ag^+, Pb^{2+})	metal ions combine with —SH groups and form poisonous salts
reducing agents	reduces disulfide linkages to produce —SH groups

▶ *Disulfide bridges, which involve covalent bonds, impart considerable resistance to denaturation because they are much stronger than the noncovalent interactions otherwise present.*

Table 20-5 is a listing of selected physical and chemical agents that cause protein denaturation. The effectiveness of a given denaturing agent depends on the type of protein upon which it is acting.

Section 20-15 Quick Quiz

1. Which of the following levels of protein structure is *not* disrupted when protein denaturation occurs?
   a. primary structure
   b. secondary structure
   c. both primary and secondary structure
   d. no correct response
2. Which of the following does *not* involve protein denaturation?
   a. cooking of an egg
   b. cauterization of small blood vessels
   c. skin sunburn
   d. no correct response
3. Which of the following is not a denaturing agent for protein?
   a. heat
   b. microwave radiation
   c. strong acids
   d. no correct response

Answers: 1. a; 2. d; 3. d

20-16 Protein Classification Based on Shape

LEARNING FOCUS

Know the basis for the classification of proteins as *fibrous* or *globular;* know the structural characteristics and biochemical functions for the proteins α-keratin, collagen, hemoglobin, and myoglobin.

Based on molecular shape, which is determined primarily by tertiary and quaternary structural features, there are three main types of proteins: *fibrous, globular,* and *membrane.* A **fibrous protein** *is a protein whose molecules have an elongated shape with one*

▶ **Table 20-6 Some Common Fibrous and Globular Proteins**

Name	Occurrence and Function
Fibrous proteins (insoluble)	
keratins	found in wool, feathers, hooves, silk, and fingernails
collagens	found in tendons, bone, and other connective tissue
elastins	found in blood vessels and ligaments
myosins	found in muscle tissue
fibrin	found in blood clots
Globular proteins (soluble)	
insulin	regulatory hormone for controlling glucose metabolism
myoglobin	involved in oxygen storage in muscles
hemoglobin	involved in oxygen transport in blood
transferrin	involved in iron transport in blood
immunoglobulins	involved in immune system responses

dimension much longer than the others. Fibrous proteins tend to have simple, regular, linear structures. There is a tendency for such proteins to aggregate together to form macromolecular structures. A **globular protein** *is a protein whose molecules have peptide chains that are folded into spherical or globular shapes.* The folding in such proteins is such that most of the amino acids with hydrophobic side chains (nonpolar R groups) are in the interior of the molecule and most of the hydrophilic side chains (polar R groups) are on the outside of the molecule. ◀ Generally, globular proteins are water-soluble substances. A **membrane protein** *is a protein that is found associated with a membrane system of a cell.* Membrane protein structure is somewhat opposite that of globular proteins, with most of the hydrophobic amino acid side chains oriented outward. Thus, such proteins tend to be water insoluble and they usually have fewer hydrophobic amino acids than globular proteins.

Further discussion of proteins in this section is limited to fibrous and globular proteins, as membrane proteins were considered in the previous chapter in relation to cell membrane structure (Section 19-10).

Table 20-6 gives examples of selected fibrous and globular proteins. Comparison of fibrous and globular proteins in terms of general properties shows the following differences:

1. Fibrous proteins are generally water insoluble, whereas globular proteins dissolve in water. This enables globular proteins to travel through the blood and other body fluids to sites where their activity is needed.
2. Fibrous proteins usually have a single type of secondary structure, whereas globular proteins often contain several types of secondary structure. ◀
3. Fibrous proteins generally have structural functions that provide support and external protection, whereas globular proteins are involved in metabolic chemistry, performing functions such as catalysis, transport, and regulation.
4. The number of different kinds of globular protein far exceeds the number of different kinds of fibrous protein. However, because the most abundant proteins in the human body are fibrous proteins rather than globular proteins, the total mass of fibrous proteins present exceeds the total mass of globular proteins present.

The characteristics of two fibrous proteins (α-keratin and collagen) and two globular proteins (hemoglobin and myoglobin) as representatives of their types are now examined.

▶ *Globular proteins denature more readily than fibrous proteins because of weaker secondary and tertiary attractive forces.*

▶ *Natural silk (silkworm silk) and spider silk (spider webs) are made of fibroin, a fibrous protein that exists mainly in a beta pleated sheet form. The great strength and toughness of silk fibers, which exceed those of many synthetic fibers, is related to the close stacking of the beta sheets. A high percentage of the amino acid residues (primary structure) in silk are either glycine (R = H) or alanine (R = CH₃). It is the smallness of these two R groups that makes the close stacking possible.*

α-Keratin

The fibrous protein *α-keratin* is particularly abundant in nature, where it is found in protective coatings for organisms. It is the major protein constituent of hair, feathers (Figure 20-19), wool, fingernails and toenails, claws, scales, horns, turtle shells, quills, and hooves.

Figure 20-19 The tail feathers of a peacock contain the fibrous protein α-keratin.

Figure 20-20 The coiled-coil structure of the fibrous protein α-keratin.

a α Helix

b Coiled coil of two α helices

c Protofilament (pair of coiled coils)

d Microfilament (four coiled protofilaments)

Table 20-7 **The Collagen Content of Selected Body Tissues**

Tissue	Collagen (% dry mass)
Achilles tendon	86
aorta	12–24
bone (mineral-free)	88
cartilage	46–63
cornea	68
ligament	17
skin	72

▶ *Collagen, pronounced "KAHL-uh-jen," is the most abundant protein in the human body.*

The structure of a typical α-keratin, that of hair, is depicted in Figure 20-20. The individual molecules are almost wholly α helical (Figure 20-20a). Pairs of these helices twine about one another to produce a coiled coil (Figure 20-20b). In hair, two of the coiled coils then further twist together to form a protofilament (Figure 20-20c). Protofilaments then coil together in groups of four to form microfilaments (Figure 20-20d), which become the "core" unit in the structure of the α-keratin of hair. These microfilaments in turn coil at even higher levels. This coiling at higher and higher levels is what produces the strength associated with α-keratin-containing proteins. All levels of coiling organization are stabilized by attractive forces of the types previously considered in the discussion of generalized secondary and tertiary protein structure (Sections 20-11 and 20-12). Particularly important are *inter*coil disulfide bridges that form between cysteine residues.

Introduction of disulfide bridges within the several levels of coiling structure determines the "hardness" of an α-keratin. "Hard" keratins, such as those found in horns and nails, have considerably more disulfide bridges than their softer counterparts found in hair, wool, and feathers.

Collagen

Collagen, the most abundant of all proteins in humans (30% of total body protein), is a major structural material in tendons, ligaments, blood vessels, and skin; it is also the organic component of bones and teeth. ◀ Table 20-7 gives the collagen content of selected body tissues. The predominant structural feature within collagen molecules is a *triple helix* formed when three chains of amino acids wrap around each other to give a ropelike arrangement of polypeptide chains (see Figure 20-21).

The dominating presence of two amino acids, glycine and proline, are major driving forces for triple-helix formation. Approximately one-third of the amino acids present are glycine, the amino acid with the smallest R group (an H atom). Glycine's compact nature allows for close packing together of the protein chains. Another one-third of amino acids present are proline, the amino acid whose side chain is part of a cyclic system (Table 20-1). This side-chain structural feature prevents proline

Figure 20-21 A schematic diagram emphasizing how three helical polypeptide chains intertwine to form a triple helix. The chains are partially unwound and cut away to show their structure.

Polypeptide chains

Triple helical polypeptide chain

residues from easily fitting into the simpler common helical or sheetlike structures (Section 20-10).

$$-N-CH-C-N-CH-C-N-CH-C-$$

Portion of a collagen chain

Collagen molecules (triple helices) are very long, thin, and rigid. Many such molecules, lined up alongside each other, combine to make collagen fibrils. Cross-linking between helices gives the fibrils extra strength. The greater the number of cross-links, the more rigid the fibril is. The stiffening of skin and other tissues associated with aging is thought to result, at least in part, from an increasing amount of cross-linking between collagen molecules. The process of tanning, which converts animal hides to leather, involves increasing the degree of cross-linking.

Figure 20-22 shows an electron micrograph of collagen fibers.

Figure 20-22 Electron micrograph of collagen fibers.

Hemoglobin

The globular protein *hemoglobin* transports oxygen from the lungs to tissue. Its tertiary structure was shown in Figure 20-14. It is a tetramer (four peptide subunits) with each subunit also containing a *heme group,* the entity that binds oxygen. With four heme groups present, a hemoglobin molecule can transport four oxygen molecules at the same time.

The structure of a heme group is

Heme

It is the iron atom at the center of the heme molecule that actually interacts with the O_2. ◀

Myoglobin

The globular protein *myoglobin* functions as an oxygen-storage molecule in muscles. Its tertiary structure was shown in Figure 20-13. Myoglobin is a monomer, whereas hemoglobin is a tetramer. That is, myoglobin consists of a single peptide chain and a heme unit, and hemoglobin has four peptide subunits and four heme units. Thus only one O_2 molecule can be carried by a myoglobin molecule. The tertiary structure of the single peptide chain of myoglobin is almost identical to the tertiary structure of each of the subunits of hemoglobin.

Myoglobin has a higher affinity for oxygen than does hemoglobin. Thus the transfer of oxygen from hemoglobin to myoglobin occurs readily. Oxygen stored in myoglobin molecules serves as a reserve oxygen source for working muscles when their demand for oxygen exceeds that which can be supplied by hemoglobin. ◀

The focus on relevancy feature Chemical Connections 20-C—Protein Structure and the Color of Meat—considers how the amount of myoglobin present in animal muscle tissue is related to the color of the meats (chicken, turkey, fish, etc.) that humans eat.

▶ *The hemoglobin of a fetus is slightly different in structure from adult hemoglobin. Called* fetal hemoglobin, *this hemoglobin has a greater affinity for oxygen than the mother's hemoglobin. This ensures a steady flow of oxygen to the fetus. Shortly after birth, a baby's body ceases to produce fetal hemoglobin, and its production of "adult" hemoglobin begins.*

▶ *The function of hemoglobin is* oxygen *transfer, and the function of myoglobin is* oxygen *storage.*

CHEMICAL CONNECTIONS 20-C

Protein Structure and the Color of Meat

The meat that humans eat is composed primarily of muscle tissue. The major proteins present in such muscle tissue are *myosin* and *actin,* which lie in alternating layers and which slide past each other during muscle contraction. Contraction is temporarily maintained through interactions between these two types of proteins.

Structurally, myosin consists of a rodlike coil of two alpha helices (fibrous protein) with two globular protein heads. It is the "head portions" of myosin that interact with the actin.

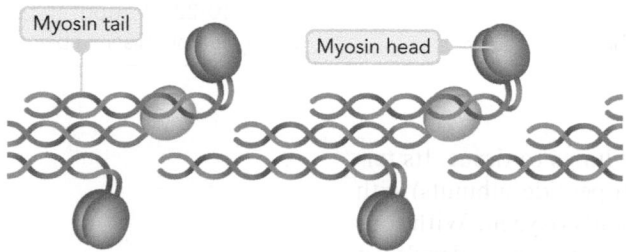

Structurally, actin has the appearance of two filaments spiraling about one another (see diagram below). Each circle in this structural diagram represents a monomeric unit of actin (called globular actin). The monomeric actin units associate to form a long polymer (called fibrous actin). Each identical monomeric actin unit is a globular protein containing many amino acid residues.

The chemical process associated with muscle contraction (interaction between myosin and actin) requires molecular oxygen. The oxygen-storage protein *myoglobin* (Section 20-16) is the oxygen source. The amount of myoglobin present in a muscle is determined by how the muscle is used. Heavily used muscles require larger amounts of myoglobin than infrequently used muscles require.

The amount of myoglobin present in muscle tissue is a major determiner of the color of the muscle tissue. Myoglobin molecules have a red color when oxygenated and a purple color when deoxygenated. Thus, heavily worked muscles have a darker color than infrequently used muscles

because myoglobin is colored in both its oxygenated and deoxygenated states.

The different colors of meat reflect the concentration of myoglobin in the muscle tissue. In turkeys and chickens, which walk around a lot but rarely fly, the leg meat is dark, the breast meat is white. On the other hand, game birds that do fly a lot have dark breast meat (see accompanying photo). In general, game animals (which use all of their muscles regularly) tend to have darker meat than domesticated animals.

Game birds (such as pheasants, wild geese, and wild ducks), which often fly, have darker breast meat than domestic birds (such as chickens and turkeys), which rarely fly. This difference is related to the amount of myoglobin present in muscle tissue.

All land animals and birds need to support their own weight. Fish, on the other hand, are supported by water as they swim, which reduces the need for myoglobin oxygen support. Hence fish tend to have lighter flesh. Fish that spend most of their time lying at the bottom of a body of water have the lightest (whitest) flesh of all. Salmon flesh contains additional pigments that give it its characteristic "orange-pink" color.

Meat, when cooked, turns brown as the result of changes in myoglobin structure caused by the heat; the iron atom in the heme unit of myoglobin (Section 20-16) becomes oxidized. When meat is heavily salted with preservatives (NaCl, $NaNO_2$, or the like), as in the preparation of ham, the myoglobin picks up nitrite ions, and its color changes to pink.

Section 20-16 Quick Quiz

1. Which of the following statements concerning fibrous and globular proteins is *correct*?
   a. Fibrous proteins, but not globular proteins, are generally water soluble.
   b. Globular proteins, but not fibrous proteins, are generally water soluble.
   c. Both fibrous and globular proteins are generally water soluble.
   d. no correct response
2. Which of the following proteins has a triple-helix structure?
   a. collagen
   b. α-keratin
   c. hemoglobin
   d. no correct response

3. Which of the following proteins is the major component of hair?
  a. collagen
  b. α-keratin
  c. myoglobin
  d. no correct response

4. In which of the following pairs of proteins are both members of the pair *fibrous* proteins?
  a. α-keratin and collagen
  b. collagen and hemoglobin
  c. hemoglobin and myoglobin
  d. no correct response

Answers: 1. b; 2. a; 3. b; 4. a

20-17 Protein Classification Based on Function

LEARNING FOCUS

Be able to classify proteins in terms of the functions that they exhibit in biochemical processes.

Proteins play crucial roles in almost all biochemical processes. The diversity of functions exhibited by proteins far exceeds that of other major types of biochemical molecules. The functional versatility of proteins stems from (1) their ability to bind small molecules specifically and strongly to themselves, (2) their ability to bind other proteins, often other like proteins, to form fiber-like structures, and (3) their ability to bind to, and often become integrated into, cell membranes.

The following list includes several major categories of proteins based on function. The order should not be taken as an indication of relative functional importance. The list should also be considered a selective list, with a number of functions not included because of space considerations.

1. **Catalytic proteins.** Proteins are probably best known for their role as catalysts. Proteins with the role of biochemical catalyst are called *enzymes*. An entire chapter in this text, Chapter 21, is devoted to this most important role for proteins. Enzymes participate in almost all of the metabolic reactions that occur in cells. The chemistry of human genetics, discussed in detail in Chapter 22, is very dependent on the presence of enzymes.

2. **Defense proteins.** These proteins, also called *immunoglobulins* or *antibodies* (Section 20-18), are central to the functioning of the body's immune system. They bind to foreign substances, such as bacteria and viruses, to help combat invasion of the body by foreign particles.

3. **Transport proteins.** These proteins bind to particular small biomolecules and transport them to other locations in the body and then release the small molecules as needed at the destination location. The most well-known example of a transport protein is *hemoglobin* (Section 20-13), which carries oxygen from the lungs to other organs and tissues. Another transport protein is *transferrin,* which carries iron from the liver to the bone marrow. *High-* and *low-density lipoproteins* (Section 20-18) are carriers of cholesterol in the bloodstream.

4. **Messenger proteins.** These proteins transmit signals to coordinate biochemical processes between different cells, tissues, and organs. A number of hormones (Section 19-12) that regulate body processes are messenger proteins, including *insulin* and *glucagon* (Section 24-9). *Human growth hormone* is another example of a messenger protein.

5. **Contractile proteins.** These proteins are necessary for all forms of movement. Muscles are composed of filament-like contractile proteins that, in response to nerve stimuli, undergo conformation changes that involve contraction and extension. *Actin* and *myosin* (Section 20-16) are examples of such proteins. Human reproduction depends on the movement of sperm. Sperm can "swim" because of long flagella made up of contractile proteins.

6. **Structural proteins.** These proteins confer stiffness and rigidity to otherwise fluid-like biochemical systems. *Collagen* (Section 20-16) is a component of cartilage, and *α-keratin* (Section 20-16) gives mechanical strength as well as protective covering to hair, fingernails, feathers, hooves, and some animal shells.

7. **Transmembrane proteins.** These proteins, which span a cell membrane (Section 19-10), help control the movement of small molecules and ions through the cell membrane. Many such proteins have channels through which molecules can enter and exit a cell. Such protein channels are very selective, often allowing passage of just one type of molecule or ion.

8. **Storage proteins.** These proteins bind (and store) small molecules for future use. During degradation of hemoglobin (Section 26-7) the iron atoms present are released and become part of *ferritin,* an iron-storage protein, which saves the iron for use in the biosynthesis of new hemoglobin molecules. *Myoglobin* (Section 20-16) is an oxygen-storage protein present in muscle; the oxygen so stored is a reserve oxygen source for working muscle.

9. **Regulatory proteins.** These proteins are often found "embedded" in the exterior surface of cell membranes. They act as sites at which messenger molecules, including messenger proteins such as insulin, can bind and thereby initiate the effect that the messenger "carries." Regulatory proteins are often the molecules that bind to enzymes (catalytic proteins), thereby turning them "on" and "off" and thus controlling enzymatic action (Section 21-8).

10. **Nutrient proteins.** These proteins are particularly important in the early stages of life, from embryo to infant. *Casein,* found in milk, and *ovalbumin,* found in egg white, are two examples of such proteins. The role of milk in nature is to nourish and provide immunological protection for mammalian young. Three-fourths of the protein in milk is casein. More than 50% of the protein in egg white is ovalbumin.

11. **Buffer proteins.** These proteins are part of the system by which the acid–base balance within body fluids is maintained. Within the blood, the protein *hemoglobin* has a buffering role in addition to being an oxygen carrier. Transmembrane proteins regulate the movement of ions in and out of cells, ensuring that ion concentrations are those needed for correct acidity/alkalinity.

12. **Fluid-balance proteins.** These proteins help maintain fluid balance between blood and surrounding tissue. Two well-known fluid-balance proteins, found in the capillary beds of the circulatory system, are *albumin* and *globulin.* When increased blood pressure generated by a pumping heart forces water and nutrients out of the capillaries, these proteins remain behind (since they are too big to cross cellular membranes). As their concentration increases (due to less fluid being present), osmotic pressure "forces" draw water back into the capillaries, which is necessary for fluid balance to be maintained.

Though not exhaustive, this list of protein functions is long. Its length draws attention to the diversity of functions for proteins within the human body, as well as to the diversity of protein types. ◄

▶ *In addition to the much "work" that proteins do in the human body, they also can be used to provide energy needed to "run" the human body in times of starvation or insufficient carbohydrate and lipid dietary intake. In this role proteins are broken down into their constituent amino acids which are then converted to glucose and several other energy-producing molecules, via processes to be discussed in Chapter 26.*

Section 20-17 Quick Quiz

1. Insulin and human growth hormone are examples of
   a. defense proteins
   b. messenger proteins
   c. buffer proteins
   d. no correct response
2. Myoglobin and transferrin are examples of
   a. transport proteins
   b. structural proteins
   c. storage proteins
   d. no correct response

3. Enzymes are examples of
   a. catalytic proteins
   b. contractile proteins
   c. regulatory proteins
   d. no correct response

Answers: 1. b; 2. c; 3. a

20-18 Glycoproteins

LEARNING FOCUS

Understand why collagen is classified as a glycoprotein; be familiar with the general structural characteristics of an immunoglobulin; know the relationship between the terms *antigen* and *antibody*.

A glycoprotein is a protein that contains carbohydrates or carbohydrate derivatives in addition to amino acids (Section 18-18). The carbohydrate content of glycoproteins is variable (from a few percent up to 85%), but it is fixed for any specific glycoprotein.

Glycoproteins include a number of very important substances; two of these, collagen and immunoglobulins, are considered in this section. Many of the proteins in cell membranes (lipid bilayers; see Section 19-10) are actually glycoproteins. The blood group markers of the ABO system (see Chemical Connections 18-D—Blood Types and Oligosaccharides) are also glycoproteins in which the carbohydrate content can reach 85%.

Collagen

The fibrous protein collagen, whose structure was first considered in Section 20-16, qualifies as a *glycoprotein* because carbohydrate units are present in its structure. This structural feature of collagen, not considered previously, involves the presence of the *nonstandard* amino acids 4-hydroxyproline (5%) and 5-hydroxylysine (1%)—derivatives of the standard amino acids proline and lysine (Table 20-1). ◄

▶ *Nonstandard amino acids consist of amino acid residues that have been chemically modified after their incorporation into a protein (as is the case with 4-hydroxyproline and 5-hydroxylysine) and amino acids that occur in living organisms but are not found in proteins.*

4-Hydroxyproline

5-Hydroxylysine

The presence of carbohydrate units (mostly glucose, galactose, and their disaccharides) attached by glycosidic linkages (Section 18-13) to collagen at its 5-hydroxylysine residues causes collagen to be classified as a *glycoprotein*. The function of the carbohydrate groups in collagen is related to cross-linking; they direct the assembly of collagen triple helices into more complex aggregations called *collagen fibrils*. ◄

When collagen is boiled in water, under basic conditions, it is converted to the water-soluble protein gelatin. This process involves both denaturation (Section 20-15) and hydrolysis (Section 20-14). Heat acts as a denaturant, causing rupture of the hydrogen bonds supporting collagen's triple-helix structure. Regions in the amino acid chains where proline and hydroxyproline concentrations are high are particularly susceptible to hydrolysis, which breaks up the polypeptide chains. Meats become more tender when cooked because of the conversion of some collagen to gelatin. Tougher cuts of meat (more cross-linking), such as stew meat, need longer cooking times.

▶ *A primary biochemical function of vitamin C involves the hydroxylation of proline and lysine during collagen formation. These hydroxylation processes require the enzymes proline hydroxylase and lysine hydroxylase. These enzymes can function only in the presence of vitamin C.*

Immunoglobulins

Immunoglobulins are among the most important and interesting of the soluble proteins in the human body. An **immunoglobulin** *is a glycoprotein produced by an organism as a protective response to the invasion of microorganisms or foreign molecules.* Different classes of immunoglobulins, identified by differing carbohydrate content and molecular mass, exist.

Immunoglobulins serve as *antibodies* to combat invasion of the body by *antigens.* An **antigen** *is a foreign substance, such as a bacterium or virus, that invades the human body.* An **antibody** *is a biochemical molecule that counteracts a specific antigen.* The immune system of the human body has the capability to produce immunoglobulins that respond to several million different antigens.

All types of immunoglobulin molecules have much the same basic structure, which includes the following features:

1. Four polypeptide chains are present: two identical heavy (H) chains and two identical light (L) chains.
2. The H chains, which usually contain 400–500 amino acid residues, are approximately twice as long as the L chains.
3. Both the H and L chains have constant and variable regions. The constant regions have the same amino acid sequence from immunoglobulin to immunoglobulin, and the variable regions have a different amino acid sequence in each immunoglobulin.
4. The carbohydrate content of various immunoglobulins varies from 1% to 12% by mass.
5. The secondary and tertiary structures are similar for all immunoglobulins. They involve a Y-shaped conformation (Figure 20-23) with disulfide linkages between H and L chains stabilizing the structure.

The interaction of an immunoglobulin molecule with an antigen occurs at the "tips" (upper-most part) of the Y structure. These tips are the variable-composition region of the immunoglobulin structure. It is here that the antigen binds specifically, and it is here that the amino acid sequence differs from one immunoglobulin to another.

Each immunoglobulin has two identical active sites and can thus bind to two molecules of the antigen it is "designed for." The action of many such immunoglobulins of a given type in concert with each other creates an *antigen–antibody complex* that precipitates from solution (Figure 20-24). Eventually, an invading antigen can be eliminated from the body through such precipitation. The bonding of an antigen to the variable region of an immunoglobulin occurs through hydrophobic interactions, dipole–dipole interactions, and hydrogen bonds rather than covalent bonds.

Figure 20-23 This schematic diagram shows the structure of an immunoglobulin. Two heavy (H) polypeptide chains and two light (L) polypeptide chains are cross-linked by disulfide bridges. The purple areas are the constant amino acid regions, and the areas shown in red are the variable amino acid regions of each chain. Carbohydrate molecules attached to the heavy chains aid in determining the destinations of immunoglobulins in the tissues.

Figure 20-24 In this immunoglobulin–antigen complex, note that more than one immunoglobulin molecule can attach itself to a given antigen. Also, any given immunoglobulin has only two sites where an antigen can bind.

Antigen

Immunoglobin molecule

CHEMICAL CONNECTIONS 20-D

Cyclosporine: An Antirejection Drug

The survival rate for patients undergoing human organ transplants such as heart, liver, or kidney replacements was relatively low until the mid-1980s when it dramatically increased, an increase that has since been maintained. Many patients who received transplanted organs 30 years ago are leading normal lives today (see accompanying photo). Increased transplant success is directly related to the development of new drugs to prevent transplant rejection by a patient's own immune system. The key new drug introduced in the 1980s, which remains a viable drug today, was the immunosuppressive agent (antirejection drug) cyclosporine. Cyclosporine is a compound that was initially isolated from a soil fungus; it is a fungal peptide.

Structurally, cyclosporine is a cyclic, 11-amino-acid-residue peptide (see accompanying structural diagram). The structure is simple, but yet complex.

$$\text{MeLeu—MeVal—N—C—C—Abu—MeGly—}$$

Cyclosporin

Structural characteristics of cyclosporine include:

1. Nine of the eleven amino acid residues present are those of standard amino acids with short hydrocarbon side chains—Gly, Ala, Val, and Leu. These are the simplest of the standard amino acids with respect to side chains.
2. The tenth amino acid residue present, shown as Abu in the structural diagram, also has a simple side chain; it is an ethyl group. The designation Abu for this nonstandard amino acid comes from the IUPAC name for the acid, which is 2-aminobutyric acid.
3. The eleventh amino acid residue present, which is the key to cyclosporine's pharmacological activity, had never been previously encountered in a natural product. Its side

chain is a 7-carbon branched, unsaturated, hydroxylated entity. This side chain is shown in detail in the structural diagram for cyclosporine.
4. Seven of the amino acid residues have their nitrogen atoms methylated; that is, a methyl group has replaced the nitrogen's hydrogen atom. Methylation is denoted in the structural diagram using the notation MeVal, MeLeu, etc.
5. An additional rarely encountered structural feature is present. One amino acid residue has a D-configuration rather than the normal L-configuration for amino acids. One of the Ala residues present is D-Ala. Interestingly, next to it in the structure is an L-Ala residue

The fat solubility of cyclosporine allows it to cross cell membranes readily and to be widely distributed in the body. It is administered either intravenously or orally. Because of its low water solubility, the drug is supplied in olive oil for oral administration. Cyclosporine has a narrow therapeutic index. When the blood concentration of cyclosporine is too low, inadequate immunosuppression occurs. On the other hand, a high cyclosporine concentration can lead to kidney problems.

Before the cyclosporine-era, available antirejection drugs weakened a patient's *entire* immune system, with the result that patients could not survive severe infections. Cyclosporine suppresses only part of the body's immune system (T-cells), the part associated with rejection of transplanted tissue. The bulk of the patient's immune system continues to function normally and remains able to fight general infections.

A donated organ (in ice) being carried to an operating room where a donor recipient awaits its arrival.

Individuals who receive organ transplants must be given drugs to suppress the production of immunoglobulins against foreign proteins in the new organ, thus preventing rejection of the organ. The major reason for the increasing importance of organ transplants is the successful development of drugs that can properly manipulate the body's immune system. The focus on relevancy feature Chemical Connections 20-D—Cyclosporine: An Antirejection Drug—gives information about cyclosporine, the best known "antirejection" drug. It has a very interesting origin, structure, and mode of action. It is the drug that made successful organ transplantation possible.

The importance of immunoglobulins is amply and tragically demonstrated by the effects of AIDS (acquired immunodeficiency syndrome). The AIDS virus upsets the body's normal production of immunoglobulins and leaves the body susceptible to what would otherwise not be debilitating and deadly infections.

Many reasons exist for a mother to breast-feed a newborn infant. One of the most important involves the transmission of immunoglobulins. During the first few days of lactation, immunoglobulins from the mother's blood are passed to the newborn via "milk," which gives the infant protection from the pathogens to which the mother has developed immunity. The focus on relevancy feature Chemical Connections 20-E—Colostrum: Immunoglobulins and Much More—considers further the protein chemistry associated with "mother's milk."

Section 20-18 Quick Quiz

1. Which of the following statements concerning the "glycoprotein nature" of collagen's structure is *correct*?
   a. Monosaccharide subunits have replaced some amino acid subunits.
   b. Monosaccharide subunits are attached to all amino acid residues.
   c. Monosaccharide subunits are attached to some derivatized amino acid residues.
   d. no correct response
2. Which of the following statements concerning basic immunoglobulin structure is *incorrect*?
   a. Four identical polypeptide chains are present.
   b. Two "heavy" and two "light" polypeptide chains are present.
   c. Two identical active sites are present.
   d. no correct response
3. Which of the following statements about antibodies is *correct*?
   a. They are foreign substances that invade the human body.
   b. They are substances that counteract the effects of antigens.
   c. They are substances that counteract the effects of immunoglobulins.
   d. no correct response

Answers: 1. c; 2. a; 3. b

20-19 Lipoproteins

LEARNING FOCUS

Be familiar with the four major classes of plasma lipoproteins in terms of biochemical function and density characteristics.

A **lipoprotein** *is a conjugated protein that contains lipids in addition to amino acids.* The major function of such proteins is to help suspend lipids and transport them through the bloodstream. Lipids, in general, are insoluble in blood (an aqueous medium) because of their nonpolar nature (Section 19-1).

A **plasma lipoprotein** *is a lipoprotein that is involved in the transport system for lipids in the bloodstream.* These proteins have a spherical structure that involves a central core of lipid material (triacylglycerols and cholesterol esters) surrounded by a

Colostrum: Immunoglobulins and Much More

Two types of milk are produced by a lactating mother as she feeds a newborn baby. They are:

1. **Colostrum:** During the first two to three days of lactation, a mother's breasts produce a *foremilk* called colostrum. This substance, secreted in low-volume amounts, is a thick yellow secretion that is rich in maternal antibodies (immunoglobulins) and carbohydrates and low in fat.
2. **Mature milk:** Within a week, mature milk has replaced colostrum production. Mature milk is much whiter in color than colostrum and has a watery appearance. It contains increased amounts of fat, carbohydrates, and calories, but less protein, particularly immunoglobulins. Some immunologically active substances are, however, still present. The high water content of mature milk is sufficient to meet an infant's hydration needs when he or she is exclusively breast-fed.

The composition of mature human milk and cow's milk differ significantly, as is shown in the accompanying table.

Comparison of Mature Human Milk and Cow's Milk (g/100 mL)

Nutrient	Human Milk	Cow's Milk
Total protein	1.1	3.1
Total fat	4.5	3.8
Total lactose	7.1	4.7

Lactose is the principal carbohydrate in milk (Section 18-13). Human milk obtained by a nursing infant (see accompanying photo) contains 7%–8% lactose, almost double the 4%–5% lactose found in cow's milk.

Human milk contains more lactose and fat, but less protein, than does cow's milk.

Many reasons exist for a mother to breast-feed a newborn. One of the most important is the immunoglobulins present in colostrum and, to a lesser extent, in mature milk. These immunoglobulins come from the mother's bloodstream and represent protection from those substances to which the mother has developed immunity. These substances in the mother's environment are precisely the entities the infant needs protection from. Infant formula is usually nutritionally equivalent to breast milk, but it is definitely not immunologically equivalent.

It is particularly important that the mother's immunological protection be transmitted to the infant's body during the first week of life. It is at this time, and no other time in life, that immunoglobulins and other whole proteins can pass unaltered through the infant's immature intestinal tract directly into the bloodstream.

A major antibody present in colostrum is secretory immunoglobulin A (IgA). IgA gives the infant protection in the locations where attack from germs is most likely to occur, namely, the mucous membranes in the throat, lungs, and intestines. Prior to birth, the baby received the benefit of immunoglobulin G (IgG) through the placenta. IgG is present in the baby's circulatory system. It is supplied to the baby via the placenta.

Newborns have *very small* digestive systems, and colostrum delivers its ingredients in a very concentrated low-volume form. Colostrum volumes obtained by breast-feeding are small—teaspoon amounts rather than several-ounce amounts. This is adequate for a newborn. The stomach capacity of a newborn is 0.20 oz.–0.25 oz. (one teaspoon = 0.16 oz) at day one, 0.75 oz.–1.0 oz. (one tablespoon = 0.50 oz) at day three, and 1.50 oz.–2.0 oz. (the volume of a ping-pong ball) at day seven. The small-volume amounts of colostrum produced are the right amounts needed for the infant's initial feedings.

Proteins other than those associated with immunological responses are also present in colostrum. Two of these additional proteins are *lactalbumin* and *lactoferrin*. These additional proteins are mostly synthesized within breast tissue, whereas immunoproteins come from the mother's bloodstream.

Lactalbumin is an easily digested protein that is less stressful on the infant's immature digestive system than are other proteins such as casein (the principal protein in cow's milk). Lactoferrin increases the rate of iron absorption by the infant. Due to its presence, more iron is absorbed from human milk than from infant formula or cow's milk even though human milk contains less iron. Lactoferrin also offers protection against bacteria and other pathogens by binding the iron, thus making it unavailable to these agents, which require it for growth.

Colostrum also helps the infant's developing digestive system in other ways. It has a mild laxative effect, which encourages the passing of the baby's first stool. It also reduces the permeability of the intestinal tract by giving it a protective coating that prevents foreign substances from penetrating it and entering the bloodstream.

In addition to the disaccharide lactose, breast milk contains specific oligosaccharides (Section 18-14) that an infant cannot digest. What is their role? Recent research indicates that they serve as "food" for a beneficial intestinal bacteria strain specific to humans known as *Bifidobacterium infantis* (*B. infantis*). With such "food" available, *B. infantis* is able to outcompete and prevent colonization of harmful bacteria such as *E. coli* strains.

Figure 20-25 A model for the structure of a plasma lipoprotein.

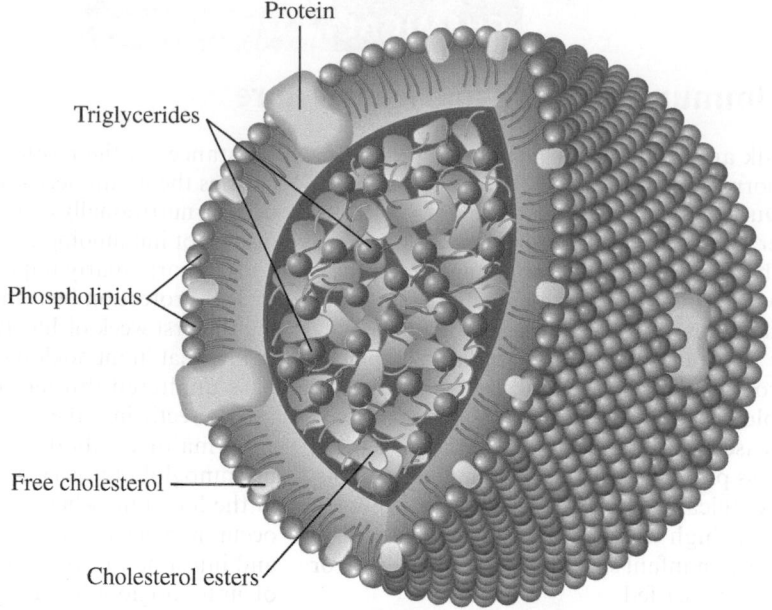

shell (membrane structure) of phospholipids, cholesterol, and proteins. In the blood, cholesterol exists primarily in the form of cholesterol esters formed from the esterification of cholesterol's hydroxyl group with a fatty acid.

A fatty acid ester of cholesterol

Figure 20-25 shows both the spherical nature of and individual components present in a plasma lipoprotein. The exterior surface of these spherical lipoproteins is polar; the polar heads of phospholipids face outward, as do the polar portions of cholesterol and membrane proteins. Nonpolar conditions prevail within these structures, with the predominant nonpolar molecules present being fatty acid esters of cholesterol. It is the polar exterior–nonpolar interior structural feature of plasma lipoproteins that makes them compatible with blood, which is an aqueous-based (polar) medium.

There are four major classes of plasma lipoproteins:

1. **Chylomicrons.** Their function is to transport dietary triacylglycerols from the intestine to the liver and to adipose tissue.
2. **Very-low-density lipoproteins (VLDLs).** Their function is to transport triacylglycerols synthesized in the liver to adipose tissue.
3. **Low-density lipoproteins (LDLs).** Their function is to transport cholesterol synthesized in the liver to cells throughout the body.
4. **High-density lipoproteins (HDLs).** Their function is to collect excess cholesterol from body tissues and transport it back to the liver for degradation to bile acids.

The density of a lipoprotein is related to the fractions of protein and lipid material present. The greater the amount of protein in the lipoprotein, the higher the density. Figure 20-26 characterizes the major plasma lipoprotein types in terms of density as well as lipid–protein composition.

The presence or absence of various types of lipoproteins in the blood have implications for the health of the heart and blood vessels. Lipoprotein levels in the blood are now used as an indicator of heart disease risk. The focus on relevancy feature Chemical Connections 20-F—Lipoproteins and Heart Disease Risk—gives information concerning the chemical interrelationships among the substances VLDL, LDL, HDL, and cholesterol in blood chemistry.

CHEMICAL CONNECTIONS 20-F

Lipoproteins and Heart Disease Risk

In the United States, heart disease is the number-one health problem for both men and women. There are many risk factors associated with heart disease, some of which are controllable and some of which are not. You can't change your age, race, or family history (genetics). But you can control (manage) factors such as your weight, whether or not you smoke, and your cholesterol level.

Relative to high cholesterol as a risk factor for heart disease, studies now indicate that focusing just on the numerical value of cholesterol present in the blood is an oversimplification of the problem. Consideration of the "form" in which the cholesterol is present is as important as the total amount. Much of the research concerning the "form" of cholesterol present relates to the lipoproteins LDL and HDL present in the blood.

Both LDLs and HDLs are involved in cholesterol transport (Section 20-19). LDLs carry approximately 80% of the cholesterol and HDLs the remainder. Of significance, LDLs and HDLs carry cholesterol for different purposes. LDLs carry cholesterol to cells for their use, whereas HDLs carry excess cholesterol away from cells to the liver for processing and excretion from the body.

Studies show that LDL levels correlate *directly* with heart disease, whereas HDL levels correlate *inversely* with heart disease risk. Thus HDL is sometimes referred to as "good" cholesterol (*H*DL = *H*ealthy) and LDL as "bad" cholesterol (*L*DL = *L*ess healthy).

The goal of dietary measures to slow the advance of atherosclerosis is to reduce LDL cholesterol levels. Reduction in the dietary intake of saturated fat appears to be a key action (Section 19-5).

High HDL levels are desirable because they give the body an efficient means of removing excess cholesterol. Low HDL levels can result in excess cholesterol depositing within the circulatory system.

In general, women have higher HDL levels than men—an average of 55 mg per 100 mL of blood serum versus 45 mg per 100 mL. This may explain in part why proportionately fewer women have heart attacks than men. Nonsmokers have uniformly higher HDL levels than smokers. Exercise on a regular basis tends to increase HDL levels. This discovery has increased the popularity of walking and running exercise (see accompanying photo). Genetics also plays a role in establishing HDL as well as other lipoprotein concentrations in the blood.

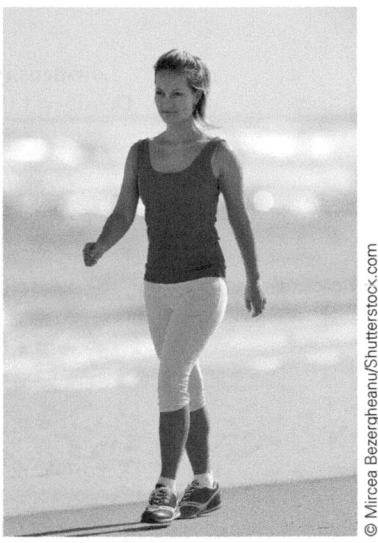

Moderate exercise done on a regular basis tends to increase HDL levels.

A person's *total* blood cholesterol level does not necessarily correlate with that individual's real risk for heart and blood vessel disease. A better measure is the *cholesterol ratio*, which is defined as

$$\text{Cholesterol ratio} = \frac{\text{total cholesterol}}{\text{HDL cholesterol}}$$

For example, if a person's total cholesterol is 200 and his or her HDL is 45, then the cholesterol ratio would be 4.4. According to the accompanying guidelines for interpreting cholesterol ratio values, this indicates an average risk for heart disease.

What Cholesterol Ratio Means

Ratio	Heart Disease Risk
6.0	high
5.0	above average
4.5	average
4.0	below average
3.0	low

Figure 20-26 Densities and relative amounts of proteins, phospholipids, cholesterol, and triacylglycerols present in the four major classes of plasma lipoproteins.

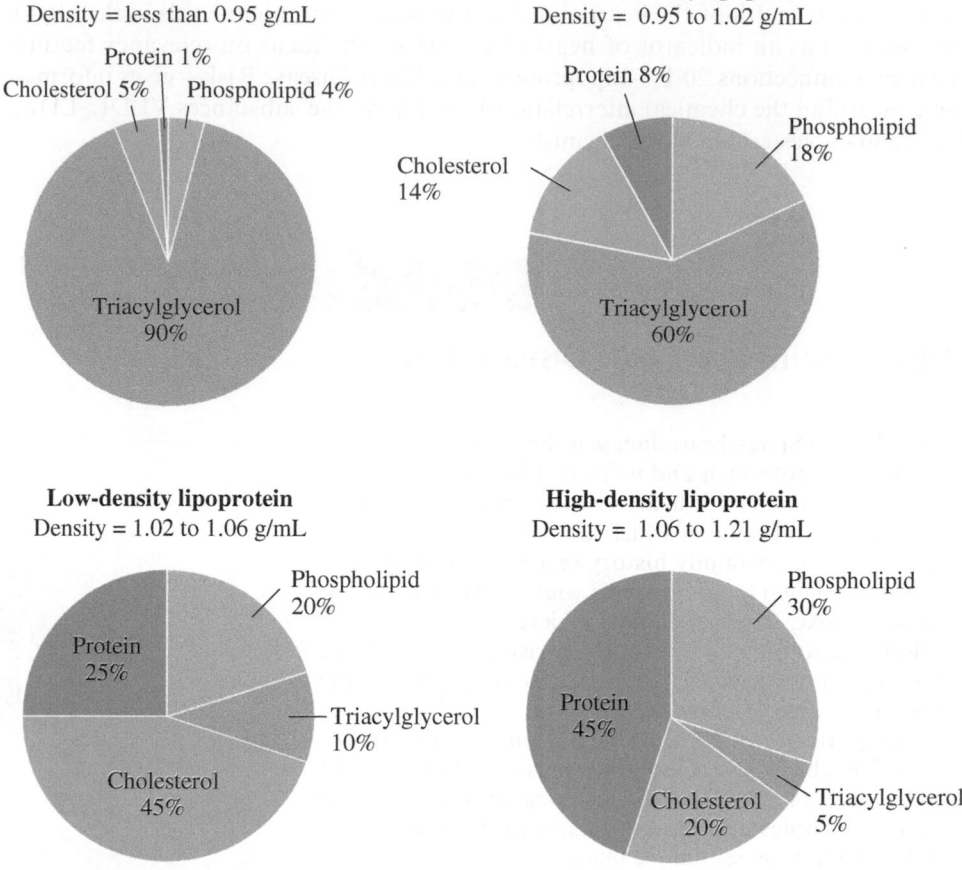

Chylomicron
Density = less than 0.95 g/mL

Protein 1%
Cholesterol 5%   Phospholipid 4%
Triacylglycerol 90%

Very-low-density lipoprotein
Density = 0.95 to 1.02 g/mL

Protein 8%
Phospholipid 18%
Cholesterol 14%
Triacylglycerol 60%

Low-density lipoprotein
Density = 1.02 to 1.06 g/mL

Phospholipid 20%
Protein 25%
Triacylglycerol 10%
Cholesterol 45%

High-density lipoprotein
Density = 1.06 to 1.21 g/mL

Phospholipid 30%
Protein 45%
Cholesterol 20%   Triacylglycerol 5%

Section 20-19 Quick Quiz

1. Which of the following statements about the structural characteristics of common plasma lipoproteins is *incorrect*?
   a. *Spherical* is the word used to describe their overall structure.
   b. They have a polar exterior–nonpolar interior arrangement of components.
   c. The predominant nonpolar molecules present are fatty acid esters of cholesterol.
   d. no correct response
2. Which of the following types of plasma lipoproteins transports cholesterol synthesized in the liver to cells through the human body?
   a. HDLs
   b. LDLs
   c. VLDLs
   d. no correct response
3. In which of the following pairs of plasma lipoprotein types does the first listed member of the pair have a greater cholesterol content, by mass, than the second listed member?
   a. LDL and HDL
   b. VLDL and LDL
   c. chylomicron and HDL
   d. no correct response

Answers: 1. d; 2. b; 3. a

Concepts to Remember

Protein. A protein is a polymer in which the monomer units are amino acids (Section 20-1).

α-Amino acid. An α-amino acid is an amino acid in which the amino group and the carboxyl group are both attached to the α-carbon atom (Section 20-2).

Standard amino acid. A standard amino acid is one of the 20 α-amino acids that are normally present in protein (Section 20-2).

Amino acid classifications. Amino acids are classified as nonpolar, polar neutral, polar basic, or polar acidic depending on the nature of the side chain (R group) present (Section 20-2).

Essential amino acid. A standard amino acid needed for protein synthesis that must be obtained from dietary sources because the human body cannot synthesize it in adequate amounts from other substances (Section 20-3).

Chirality of amino acids. Amino acids found in proteins are always left-handed (L isomer) (Section 20-4).

Zwitterion. A zwitterion is a molecule that has a positive charge on one atom and a negative charge on another atom. In neutral solution and in the solid state, amino acids exist as zwitterions. For amino acids in solution, the isoelectric point is the pH at which the amino acid exists primarily in its zwitterion form (Section 20-5).

Disulfide bond formation. The amino acid cysteine readily dimerizes; the —SH groups of two cysteine molecules interact to form a covalent disulfide bond (Section 20-6).

Peptide bond. A peptide bond is an amide bond involving the carboxyl group of one amino acid and the amino group of another amino acid. In a protein, the amino acids are linked to each other through peptide bonds (Section 20-7).

Biochemically important peptides. Numerous small peptides are biochemically active. Their functions include hormonal action, neurotransmission functions, and antioxidant activity (Section 20-8).

General characteristics of proteins. Proteins are peptides with at least 40 amino acid residues. A single peptide chain is present in a monomeric protein, and two or more peptide chains are present in a multimeric protein. A simple protein contains one or more peptide chains. A conjugated protein contains one or more additional chemical components, called prosthetic groups, in addition to peptide chains (Section 20-9).

Primary protein structure. The primary structure of a protein is the sequence of amino acids present in the peptide chain or chains of the protein (Section 20-10).

Secondary protein structure. The secondary structure of a protein is the arrangement in space of the backbone portion of the protein. The two major types of protein secondary structure are the α helix and the β pleated sheet (Section 20-11).

Tertiary protein structure. The tertiary structure of a protein is the overall three-dimensional shape that results from the attractive forces among amino acid side chains (R groups) (Section 20-12).

Quaternary protein structure. The quaternary structure of a protein involves the associations among the peptide chains present in a multimeric protein (Section 20-13).

Protein hydrolysis. Protein hydrolysis is a chemical reaction in which peptide bonds within a protein are broken through reaction with water. Complete hydrolysis produces free amino acids (Section 20-14).

Protein denaturation. Protein denaturation is the partial or complete disorganization of a protein's characteristic three-dimensional shape as a result of disruption of its secondary, tertiary, and quaternary structural interactions (Section 20-15).

Fibrous and globular proteins. Fibrous proteins are generally insoluble in water and have a long, thin, fibrous shape. α-Keratin and collagen are important fibrous proteins. Globular proteins are generally soluble in water and have a roughly spherical or globular overall shape. Hemoglobin and myoglobin are important globular proteins (Section 20-16).

Glycoproteins. Glycoproteins are conjugated proteins that contain carbohydrates or carbohydrate derivatives in addition to amino acids. Collagen and immunoglobulins are important glycoproteins (Section 20-18).

Lipoproteins. Lipoproteins are conjugated proteins that are composed of both lipids and amino acids. Lipoproteins are classified on the basis of their density (Section 20-19).

Exercises and Problems

Exercises and problems are arranged in matched pairs with the two members of a pair addressing the same concept(s). The answer to the odd-numbered member of a pair is given at the back of the book. Problems denoted with a ▲ involve concepts found not only in the section under consideration but also concepts found in one or more earlier sections of the chapter.

Characteristics of Proteins (Section 20-1)

20-1 What is the general name for the building blocks (monomers) from which a protein (polymer) is made?

20-2 What element is always present in proteins that is seldom present in carbohydrates and lipids?

20-3 What percent of a cell's overall mass is accounted for by proteins?

20-4 Approximately how many different proteins are present in a typical human cell?

Amino Acids: The Building Blocks for Protein (Section 20-2)

20-5 What is signified when an amino acid is designated as an α-amino acid?

20-6 What functional groups are present in all α-amino acids?

20-7 Indicate whether or not each of the following structural formulas is that of an α-amino acid.

a.
$$\text{H}_2\text{N}-\overset{\overset{\displaystyle \text{CH}_3}{|}}{\underset{\underset{\displaystyle \text{H}}{|}}{\text{C}}}-\text{COOH}$$

b.
$$\text{H}_2\text{N}-\text{CH}_2-\overset{\overset{\displaystyle \text{H}}{|}}{\underset{\underset{\displaystyle \text{H}}{|}}{\text{C}}}-\text{COOH}$$

20-8 Indicate whether or not each of the following structural formulas is that of an α-amino acid.

a.
$$\text{H}_2\text{N}-\text{CH}_2-\overset{\overset{\displaystyle \text{CH}_3}{|}}{\underset{\underset{\displaystyle \text{H}}{|}}{\text{C}}}-\text{COOH}$$

b.
$$\text{H}_2\text{N}-\overset{\overset{\displaystyle \text{H}}{|}}{\underset{\underset{\displaystyle \text{H}}{|}}{\text{C}}}-\text{COOH}$$

20-9 How many carbon atoms are present in the R group in each of the following standard amino acids?

a.
$$\text{H}_2\text{N}-\overset{\overset{\displaystyle \text{SH}}{|}\ \overset{\displaystyle \text{CH}_2}{|}}{\underset{\underset{\displaystyle \text{H}}{|}}{\text{C}}}-\text{COOH}$$

b.
$$\text{H}_2\text{N}-\overset{\overset{\displaystyle \text{NH}_2}{|}\ \overset{\displaystyle (\text{CH}_2)_4}{|}}{\underset{\underset{\displaystyle \text{H}}{|}}{\text{C}}}-\text{COOH}$$

c.
$$\text{H}_2\text{N}-\overset{\overset{\displaystyle \text{CH}_3}{|}\ \overset{\displaystyle \text{CH}-\text{CH}_3}{|}}{\underset{\underset{\displaystyle \text{H}}{|}}{\text{C}}}-\text{COOH}$$

d.
$$\text{H}_2\text{N}-\overset{\overset{\displaystyle \text{H}}{|}}{\underset{\underset{\displaystyle \text{H}}{|}}{\text{C}}}-\text{COOH}$$

20-10 How many carbon atoms are present in the R group in each of the following standard amino acids?

a.

$$
\begin{array}{c}
COOH \\
| \\
CH_2 \\
| \\
H_2N-C-COOH \\
| \\
H
\end{array}
$$

b.

$$
\begin{array}{c}
OH \\
| \\
CH_2 \\
| \\
H_2N-C-COOH \\
| \\
H
\end{array}
$$

c.

$$
\begin{array}{c}
CH_3 \\
| \\
CH-OH \\
| \\
H_2N-C-COOH \\
| \\
H
\end{array}
$$

d.

$$
\begin{array}{c}
CH_3 \\
| \\
CH_2 \\
| \\
CH-CH_3 \\
| \\
H_2N-C-COOH \\
| \\
H
\end{array}
$$

20-11 With the help of Table 20-1, determine the name and the three-letter abbreviation for the name for each of the standard amino acids in Problem 20-9.

20-12 With the help of Table 20-1, determine the name and three-letter abbreviation for the name for each of the standard amino acids in Problem 20-10.

20-13 With the help of Table 20-1, classify each of the standard amino acids in Problem 20-9 as nonpolar, polar neutral, polar acidic, or polar basic.

20-14 With the help of Table 20-1, classify each of the standard amino acids in Problem 20-10 as nonpolar, polar neutral, polar acidic, or polar basic.

20-15 With the help of Table 20-1, classify each of the standard amino acids in Problem 20-9 as hydrophobic or hydrophilic.

20-16 With the help of Table 20-1, classify each of the standard amino acids in Problem 20-10 as hydrophobic or hydrophilic.

20-17 With the help of Table 20-1, give the names of the standard amino acids that have side chains with each of the following characteristics.
a. contains only C and H
b. contains a carboxyl group
c. contains an amide group
d. contains the element oxygen

20-18 With the help of Table 20-1, give the names of the standard amino acids that have side chains with each of the following characteristics.
a. contains a hydroxyl group
b. contains the element sulfur
c. contains more than one N atom
d. does not contain the element carbon

20-19 Which standard amino acids have three-letter abbreviations that are not the first three letters of their names?

20-20 Which standard amino acids have one-letter abbreviations that are not the first letters of their names?

20-21 How many amino groups and how many carboxyl groups are present, respectively, in each of the following types of amino acids?
a. polar neutral
b. polar acidic

20-22 How many amino groups and how many carboxyl groups are present, respectively, in each of the following types of amino acids?
a. nonpolar
b. polar basic

20-23 In what way is the structure of the amino acid proline different from that of the other 19 standard amino acids?

20-24 Which two of the standard amino acids are constitutional isomers?

Essential Amino Acids (Section 20-3)

20-25 Indicate whether or not each of the following amino acids is classified as an *essential* amino acid.
a. Valine
b. Isoleucine
c. Trp
d. Pro

20-26 Indicate whether or not each of the following amino acids is classified as an *essential* amino acid.
a. Lysine
b. Glycine
c. Glu
d. Met

20-27 Indicate whether or not each of the following types of food is likely to be a *complete* protein.
a. Egg
b. Oats
c. Corn
d. Soy

20-28 Indicate whether or not each of the following types of food is likely to be a *complete* protein.
a. Pork
b. Wheat
c. Beans
d. Gelatin

20-29 Indicate whether or not each of the substances in Problem 20-27 would likely contain one or more *limiting* amino acids.

20-30 Indicate whether or not each of the substances in Problem 20-28 would likely contain one or more *limiting* amino acids.

20-31 Indicate whether or not the designation *complementary proteins* applies to each of the following pairs of dietary substances.
a. Soy and rice
b. Egg and milk
c. Beef and oats
d. Rice and corn

20-32 Indicate whether or not the designation *complementary proteins* applies to each of the following pairs of dietary substances.
a. Gelatin and wheat
b. Oats and corn
c. Salmon and trout
d. Beans and rice

20-33 Identify the *limiting* amino acid(s) present in each of the following protein sources. If none are present, indicate that such is the case.
a. Wheat
b. Beans
c. Soy
d. Peas

20-34 Identify the *limiting* amino acid(s) present in each of the following protein sources. If none are present, indicate that such is the case.
a. Oats
b. Rice
c. Corn
d. Gelatin

Chirality and Amino Acids (Section 20-4)

20-35 To which family of mirror-image isomers do nearly all naturally occurring amino acids belong?

20-36 In what way is the structure of glycine different from that of the other 19 common amino acids?

20-37 Draw Fischer projection formulas for the following amino acids.
a. L-Serine
b. D-Serine
c. D-Alanine
d. L-Leucine

20-38 Draw Fischer projection formulas for the following amino acids.
a. L-Cysteine
b. D-Cysteine
c. D-Alanine
d. L-Valine

▲**20-39** Answer the following questions about the amino acid whose Fischer projection formula is

$$\begin{array}{c} COOH \\ | \\ H\!-\!\!\!-\!\!\!-NH_2 \\ | \\ CH\!-\!CH_3 \\ | \\ CH_3 \end{array}$$

a. Is it a D-amino acid or an L-amino acid?
b. Is it a nonpolar or polar amino acid?
c. Is it an essential or nonessential amino acid?
d. Is it a standard or nonstandard amino acid?

▲**20-40** Answer the following questions about the amino acid whose Fischer projection formula is

$$\begin{array}{c} COOH \\ | \\ H_2N\!-\!\!\!-\!\!\!-H \\ | \\ CH_2 \\ | \\ SH \end{array}$$

a. Is it a D-amino acid or an L-amino acid?
b. Is it a nonpolar or polar amino acid?
c. Is it an essential or nonessential amino acid?
d. Is it a standard or nonstandard amino acid?

Acid–Base Properties of Amino Acids (Section 20-5)

20-41 At room temperature, amino acids are solids with relatively high decomposition points. Explain why.

20-42 At room temperature, most amino acids are not very soluble in water. Explain why.

20-43 Draw the zwitterion structure for each of the following amino acids.
a. Leucine
b. Isoleucine
c. Cysteine
d. Glycine

20-44 Draw the zwitterion structure for each of the following amino acids.
a. Serine
b. Methionine
c. Threonine
d. Phenylalanine

20-45 Draw the structure of serine at each of the following pH values.
a. 5.68
b. 1.0
c. 12.0
d. 3.0

20-46 Draw the structure of glycine at each of the following pH values.
a. 5.97
b. 13.0
c. 2.0
d. 11.0

20-47 Explain what is meant by the term *isoelectric point*.

20-48 Most amino acids have isoelectric points between 5.0 and 6.0, but the isoelectric point of lysine is 9.7. Explain why lysine has such a high value for its isoelectric point.

20-49 Glutamic acid exists in two low-pH forms instead of the usual one. Explain why.

20-50 Arginine exists in two high-pH forms instead of the usual one. Explain why.

20-51 In a low-pH aqueous solution, indicate whether each of the following amino acids has (1) a net positive charge of 2+, (2) a net positive charge of 1+, (3) a net charge of zero, (4) a net negative charge of 1−, or (5) a net negative charge of 2−.
a. Valine
b. Lysine
c. Aspartic acid
d. Serine

20-52 In a high-pH aqueous solution, indicate whether each of the following amino acids has (1) a net positive charge of 2+, (2) a net positive charge of 1+, (3) a net charge of zero, (4) a net negative charge of 1−, or (5) a net negative charge of 2−.
a. Arginine
b. Glutamic acid
c. Glutamine
d. Alanine

Cysteine: A Chemically Unique Amino Acid (Section 20-6)

20-53 When two cysteine molecules dimerize, what happens to the R groups present?

20-54 What chemical reaction involving the cysteine molecule produces a disulfide bond?

Peptides (Section 20-7)

20-55 What two functional groups are involved in the formation of a peptide bond?

20-56 Write a generalized structural representation for a peptide bond.

20-57 For the tripeptide Gly–Ala–Cys
a. What amino acid is located at the peptide's N-terminal end?
b. What amino acid is located at the peptide's C-terminal end?
c. How many peptide bonds are present?
d. How many amide linkages are present?

20-58 For the tripeptide Ser–Val–Met
a. What amino acid is located at the peptide's N-terminal end?
b. What amino acid is located at the peptide's C-terminal end?
c. How many peptide bonds are present?
d. How many amide linkages are present?

20-59 Draw a condensed structural representation for just the "backbone" portion of a tripeptide.

20-60 What are the two alternating structure units present in the "backbone" of a peptide?

20-61 Draw a complete condensed structural representation for the tripeptide Val–Ser–Cys.

20-62 Draw a complete condensed structural representation for the tripeptide Gly–Ala–Thr.

20-63 With the help of Table 20-1, identify the amino acids contained in each of the following tripeptides.

a.

$$H_3\overset{+}{N}-CH-\overset{O}{\overset{\|}{C}}-\overset{H}{\overset{|}{N}}-CH-\overset{O}{\overset{\|}{C}}-\overset{H}{\overset{|}{N}}-CH-COO^-$$

with side chains CH_2-OH on first carbon, CH_3 on second, and CH_2-SH on third.

b.

$$H_3\overset{+}{N}-CH-\overset{O}{\overset{\|}{C}}-\overset{H}{\overset{|}{N}}-CH-\overset{O}{\overset{\|}{C}}-\overset{H}{\overset{|}{N}}-CH-COO^-$$

with side chains CH_2-COO^- on first carbon, $CH-OH$ / CH_3 on second, and CH_2-C-NH_2 ($\overset{\|}{O}$) on third.

20-64 With the help of Table 20-1, identify the amino acids contained in each of the following tripeptides.

a.

$$H_3\overset{+}{N}-CH_2-\overset{O}{\overset{\|}{C}}-\overset{H}{\overset{|}{N}}-CH-\overset{O}{\overset{\|}{C}}-\overset{H}{\overset{|}{N}}-CH_2-COO^-$$

with side chain $CH-CH_3$ / CH_3 on the middle carbon.

b.

$$H_3\overset{+}{N}-CH-\overset{O}{\overset{\|}{C}}-\overset{H}{\overset{|}{N}}-CH-\overset{O}{\overset{\|}{C}}-\overset{H}{\overset{|}{N}}-CH-COO^-$$

with side chains CH_2-OH on first carbon, CH_2 / $CH-CH_3$ / CH_3 on second, and CH_2 / CH_2 / COO^- on third.

20-65 With the help of Table 20-1, assign an IUPAC name to each of the following small peptides.
   a. Ser–Cys b. Gly–Ala–Val
   c. Tyr–Asp–Gln d. Leu–Lys–Trp–Met

20-66 With the help of Table 20-1, assign an IUPAC name to each of the following small peptides.
   a. Cys–Ser b. Val–Ala–Gly
   c. Tyr–Gln–Asp d. Phe–Met–Tyr–Asn

20-67 Draw condensed structural formulas for the following peptides.
   a. glycylalanine
   b. cysteinylalanylglycine

20-68 Draw condensed structural formulas for the following peptides.
   a. threonylserine
   b. valylglycylcysteine

20-69 For the tripeptide Ala–Val–Gly which amino acid residues, if any,
   a. are hydrophilic
   b. are hydrophobic
   c. possess nonpolar R groups
   d. participate in two amide linkages

20-70 For the tripeptide Ser–Arg–Ile which amino acid residues
   a. are hydrophilic
   b. are hydrophobic
   c. possess polar neutral R groups
   d. participate in two amide linkages

▲**20-71** Consider the tripeptide tyrosylleucylisoleucine.
   a. Specify its structure using three-letter symbols for the amino acids.
   b. How many peptide bonds are present within the peptide?
   c. Which of the amino acid residues has the largest R group?
   d. Which of the amino acid residues, if any, has an acidic side chain?

▲**20-72** Consider the tripeptide leucylvalyltryptophan.
   a. Specify its structure using three-letter symbols for the amino acids.
   b. How many peptide bonds are present within the peptide?
   c. Which of the amino acid residues has the largest R group?
   d. Which of the amino acid residues, if any, has a basic side chain?

20-73 Explain why the notations Ser–Cys and Cys–Ser represent two different molecules rather than the same molecule.

20-74 Explain why the notations Ala–Gly–Val–Ala and Ala–Val–Gly–Ala represent two different molecules rather than the same molecule.

20-75 There are a total of six different amino acid sequences for a tripeptide containing one molecule each of serine, valine, and glycine. Using three-letter abbreviations for the amino acids, draw the six possible sequences of amino acids.

20-76 There are a total of six different amino acid sequences for a tetrapeptide containing two molecules each of serine and valine. Using three-letter abbreviations for the amino acids, draw the six possible sequences of amino acids.

Biochemically Important Small Peptides (Section 20-8)

20-77 Compare the structures of the protein hormones oxytocin and vasopressin in terms of
   a. what they have in common.
   b. how they differ.

20-78 Compare the protein hormones oxytocin and vasopressin in terms of their biochemical functions.

20-79 Compare the binding-site locations in the brain for enkephalins and the prescription painkillers morphine and codeine.

20-80 Compare the structures of the peptide neurotransmitters Met-enkephalin and Leu-enkephalin in terms of
   a. what they have in common.
   b. how they differ.

20-81 What is the unusual structural feature present in the molecule glutathione?

20-82 What is the major biochemical function of glutathione?

General Structural Characteristics of Proteins (Section 20-9)

20-83 What is the major difference between a monomeric protein and a multimeric protein?

20-84 What is the major difference between a simple protein and a conjugated protein?

20-85 Indicate whether each of the following statements about proteins is true or false.
a. Two or more peptide chains are always present in a multimeric protein.
b. A simple protein contains only one type of amino acid.
c. A conjugated protein can also be a monomeric protein.
d. The prosthetic group(s) present in a glycoprotein are carbohydrate groups.

20-86 Indicate whether each of the following statements about proteins is true or false.
a. Conjugated proteins always have only one peptide chain.
b. All peptide chains in a multimeric protein must be identical to each other.
c. A simple protein can also be a multimeric protein.
d. Both monomeric proteins and multimeric proteins can contain prosthetic groups.

Primary Structure of Proteins (Section 20-10)

20-87 What is meant by the *primary structure* of a protein?

20-88 Two proteins with the same amino acid composition do not have to have the same primary structure. Explain why.

20-89 How many different primary structures are possible for a four-amino-acid segment of a protein if the segment contains
a. two glycine units and two alanine units
b. two glycine units, one alanine unit, and one valine unit

20-90 How many different primary structures are possible for a four-amino-acid segment of a protein if the segment contains
a. three glycine units and one alanine unit
b. one glycine, one alanine, one valine, and one cysteine unit

20-91 How many different primary structures are possible for a four-amino-acid segment on a protein if there are
a. no restrictions on the amino acids that can be present
b. two each of two different amino acids present

20-92 How many different primary structures are possible for a four-amino-acid segment of a protein if
a. three of the amino acids present must be identical
b. the four amino acids must be different

▲**20-93** Draw a segment of the "backbone" of a protein that is long enough to attach three R groups (amino acid side chains).

▲**20-94** Draw a segment of the "backbone" of a protein that is long enough for three peptide linkages to be present.

Secondary Structure of Proteins (Section 20-11)

20-95 In an α helix secondary structure for a protein
a. describe the general shape of the protein backbone
b. describe the general locations for the amino acid R groups

20-96 In a β pleated sheet secondary structure for a protein
a. describe the general shape of the protein backbone
b. describe the general locations for the amino acid R groups

20-97 Indicate whether each of the following statements concerning secondary protein structure is true or false.
a. Hydrogen bonds present in an α helix structure involve two adjacent amino acids.
b. Both α helix and β pleated sheet structures can be present in the same protein.
c. In a β pleated sheet structure, the hydrogen bonding is always between different protein chains.
d. In an α helix, all of the amino acid R groups lie inside the helix.

20-98 Indicate whether each of the following statements concerning secondary protein structure is true or false.
a. In a β pleated sheet structure, the hydrogen bonds lie in the plane of the sheet.
b. The coil configuration in an α helix structure is maintained by covalent bonds.
c. In a β pleated sheet structure, the R groups are all oriented below the plane of the sheet.
d. Hydrogen bonds present in both the α helix structure and the β pleated sheet structure are always interactions between C=O and N—H groups.

20-99 What is meant by the statement that a portion of the secondary structure of a protein is "unstructured"?

20-100 Why is the phrase "unstructured segment of a protein" somewhat of a misnomer?

Tertiary Structure of Proteins (Section 20-12)

20-101 State the four types of attractive forces that give rise to tertiary protein structure.

20-102 What is the difference between the types of hydrogen bonding that occur in secondary and tertiary protein structure?

20-103 Give the type of amino acid R group that is involved in each of the following interactions that contribute to tertiary protein structure.
a. Hydrophobic interaction
b. Hydrogen bond
c. Disulfide bond
d. Electrostatic interaction

20-104 Classify each of the interactions listed in Problem 20-103 as a covalent bond or as a noncovalent interaction.

20-105 With the help of Table 20-1, specify the nature of each of the following tertiary-structure interactions, using the choices hydrophobic, electrostatic, hydrogen bond, and disulfide bond.
a. Phenylalanine and leucine
b. Arginine and glutamic acid
c. Two cysteines
d. Serine and tyrosine

20-106 With the help of Table 20-1, specify the nature of each of the following tertiary-structure interactions using the choices hydrophobic, electrostatic, hydrogen bond, and disulfide bond.
a. Lysine and aspartic acid
b. Threonine and tyrosine
c. Alanine and valine
d. Leucine and isoleucine

▲20-107 Indicate whether each of the following statements applies to *primary protein structure, secondary protein structure,* or *tertiary protein structure.* More than one type of structure may apply in a given situation.
  a. Salt bridges between amino acids with acidic and basic side chains are present.
  b. Hydrogen bonds are present.
  c. A segment of a protein chain folds back upon itself.
  d. The C-terminal amino acid in the protein chain is specified.

▲20-108 Indicate whether each of the following statements applies to *primary protein structure, secondary protein structure,* or *tertiary protein structure.* More than one type of structure may apply in a given situation.
  a. Peptide linkages are present in the protein chain.
  b. Disulfide bonds between cysteine amino acids are present.
  c. Hydrogen bonds between C=O and N—H groups are present.
  d. The sequential order of amino acids in a protein chain is given.

Quaternary Structure of Proteins (Section 20-13)

20-109 What is meant by the *quaternary structure* of a protein?

20-110 Not all proteins have quaternary structure. Explain why this is so.

20-111 Compare the types of noncovalent interactions that contribute to tertiary protein structure with those that contribute to quaternary protein structure.

20-112 Quaternary protein structure is more easily disrupted than tertiary protein structure. Explain why this is so.

Protein Hydrolysis (Section 20-14)

20-113 Identify all possible products when the tripeptide Ala–Ala–Val undergoes *complete* hydrolysis.

20-114 Identify all possible products when the tripeptide Ala–Val–Ala undergoes *complete* hydrolysis.

20-115 Identify all possible products when the tripeptide Ala–Ala–Val undergoes *partial* hydrolysis.

20-116 Identify all possible products when the tripeptide Ala–Val–Ala undergoes *partial* hydrolysis.

20-117 How many different di- and tripeptides could be present in a solution of partially hydrolyzed Ala–Gly–Ser–Tyr?

20-118 How many different di- and tripeptides could be present in a solution of partially hydrolyzed Ala–Gly–Ala–Gly?

20-119 Identify the primary structure of a hexapeptide containing six different amino acids if the following smaller peptides are among the partial-hydrolysis products:
Ala–Gly, His–Val–Arg, Ala–Gly–Met, and Gly–Met–His.

20-120 Identify the primary structure of a hexapeptide containing five different amino acids if the following smaller peptides are among the partial-hydrolysis products:
Gly–Cys, Ala–Ser, Ala–Gly, and Cys–Val–Ala.

▲20-121 Draw structural formulas for the products obtained when the tripeptide Ala–Gly–Ser undergoes complete hydrolysis under
  a. acidic conditions
  b. basic conditions

▲20-122 Draw structural formulas for the products obtained when the tripeptide Thr–Leu–Ile undergoes complete hydrolysis under
  a. acidic conditions   b. basic conditions

Protein Denaturation (Section 20-15)

20-123 Which structural levels of a protein are affected by denaturation?

20-124 Why is complete hydrolysis of a protein not also protein denaturation?

20-125 In what way is the protein in a cooked egg the same as that in a raw egg?

20-126 Why is "cooked" protein more easily digested than "uncooked" protein?

20-127 Indicate whether or not each of the following substances is a denaturing agent for protein.
  a. microwave radiation   b. detergent
  c. water   d. strong acid

20-128 Indicate whether or not each of the following substances is a denaturing agent for protein.
  a. heat   b. ultraviolet radiation
  c. ethanol   d. strong base

Protein Classification Based on Shape (Section 20-16)

20-129 Contrast fibrous and globular proteins in terms of
  a. solubility characteristics in water.
  b. general biochemical function.

20-130 Contrast fibrous and globular proteins in terms of
  a. general secondary structure.
  b. relative abundance within the human body.

20-131 Classify each of the following proteins as a globular protein or a fibrous protein.
  a. α-Keratin   b. Collagen
  c. Hemoglobin   d. Myoglobin

20-132 What is the major biochemical function of each of the following proteins?
  a. α-Keratin   b. Collagen
  c. Hemoglobin   d. Myoglobin

Protein Classification Based on Function (Section 20-17)

20-133 Using the list in Section 20-17, characterize each of the following proteins in terms of its function classification.
  a. Actin   b. Myoglobin
  c. Transferrin   d. Insulin

20-134 Using the list in Section 20-17, characterize each of the following proteins in terms of its function classification.
  a. Collagen   b. Hemoglobin
  c. Ferritin   d. Casein

20-135 What is the function classification for proteins known as enzymes?

20-136 What is the function classification for proteins known as immunoglobulins?

Glycoproteins (Section 20-18)

20-137 What two nonstandard amino acids are present in collagen?

20-138 Where are the carbohydrate units located in collagen?

20-139 What is the function of the carbohydrate groups present in collagen?

20-140 What is the role of vitamin C in the biosynthesis of collagen?

20-141 What is the difference between an antigen and an antibody?

20-142 What is an immunoglobulin?

20-143 Describe the structural features of a typical immunoglobulin molecule.

20-144 Describe the process by which blood immunoglobulins help protect the body from invading bacteria and viruses.

Lipoproteins (Section 20-19)

20-145 Describe the general overall structure of a plasma lipoprotein.

20-146 In what chemical form does cholesterol usually exist in the bloodstream?

20-147 What are the four major classes of plasma lipoproteins?

20-148 What do the designations VLDL, LDL, and HDL stand for?

20-149 What factor determines the density of a plasma lipoprotein?

20-150 As the lipid content of a plasma lipoprotein increases, does its density increase or decrease?

20-151 What is the biochemical function of the following?
a. Chylomicrons
b. Low-density lipoproteins

20-152 What is the biochemical function of the following?
a. Very-low-density lipoproteins
b. High-density lipoproteins

Enzymes and Vitamins

21

The microbial life present in hot springs and thermal vents possesses enzymes that are specially adapted to higher temperature conditions.

Two topics constitute the subject matter for this chapter: enzymes and vitamins. Most enzymes are specialized proteins that function as biochemical catalysts. Without enzymes, most chemical reactions in biochemical systems would occur too slowly to produce adequate amounts of the substances needed for cells to function properly. In some cases, needed reactions would not occur at all without the presence of enzymes.

Vitamins are dietary organic compounds required in very small quantities for normal cellular function. Many enzymes have vitamins as part of their structures, the presence of which is an absolute necessity for the enzymes to carry out their catalytic function. Hence the topic of vitamins is considered in conjunction with the topic of enzymes.

21-1 General Characteristics of Enzymes

LEARNING FOCUS

Know general characteristics for enzymes in terms of function and in terms of structure.

An **enzyme** *is a compound, usually a protein, that acts as a catalyst for a biochemical reaction.* Each cell in the human body contains thousands of different enzymes because almost every reaction in a cell requires its own specific enzyme. Enzymes cause cellular reactions to occur millions of times faster than corresponding uncatalyzed reactions. As catalysts (Section 9-6), enzymes are not consumed during the reaction but merely help the reaction occur more rapidly. ◄

The word *enzyme* comes from the Greek words *en,* which means "in," and *zyme,* which means "yeast." Long before their chemical nature was understood, yeast enzymes were used in the production of bread and alcoholic beverages. The action of yeast on sugars produces the carbon dioxide gas that causes bread to rise (Figure 21-1). Fermentation of sugars in fruit juices using the same yeast enzymes produces alcoholic beverages.

Most enzymes are globular proteins (Section 20-16). Some are simple proteins, consisting entirely of amino acid chains. Others are conjugated proteins, containing additional chemical components (Section 21-2). Until the 1980s, it was thought that *all* enzymes were proteins. A few enzymes are now known that are made of ribonucleic acids (RNA; Section 22-7) and that catalyze cellular reactions involving nucleic acids. In this chapter, only enzymes that are proteins are considered.

Enzymes undergo all the reactions of proteins, including *denaturation* (Section 20-15). Slight alterations in pH or temperature affect enzyme activity dramatically. Good cooks realize that overheating yeast kills the action of the yeast. A person suffering from a high fever (greater than 106°F) runs the risk of having cellular enzymes denatured. The biochemist must exercise extreme caution in handling enzymes to avoid the loss of their activity. Even vigorous shaking of an enzyme solution can destroy enzyme activity.

Enzymes differ from nonbiochemical (laboratory) catalysts not only in size, being much larger, but also in that their activity is usually regulated by other substances present in the cell in which they are found. Most laboratory catalysts need to be removed from a reaction mixture to stop their catalytic action; this is not so with enzymes. In some cases, if a certain chemical is needed in the cell, the enzyme responsible for its production is activated by other cellular components. When a sufficient quantity has been produced, the enzyme is then deactivated. In other situations, the cell may produce more or less enzyme as required. Because different enzymes are required for nearly all cellular reactions, certain necessary reactions can be accelerated or decelerated without affecting the rest of the cellular chemistry.

► *Enzymes, the most efficient catalysts known, increase the rates of biochemical reactions by factors of up to 10^{20} over uncatalyzed reactions. Nonenzymatic catalysts, on the other hand, typically enhance the rate of a reaction by factors of 10^2 to 10^4.*

Figure 21-1 Bread dough rises as the result of carbon dioxide production resulting from the action of yeast enzymes on sugars present in the dough.

Section 21-1 Quick Quiz

1. Which of the following statements concerning the nature of enzymes is *incorrect*?
   a. Most, but not all, enzymes are globular proteins.
   b. Some, but not all, enzymes are conjugated proteins.
   c. Most, but not all, enzymes are catalysts.
   d. no correct response
2. Which of the following comparisons involving enzymes and laboratory (nonbiochemical) catalysts is *correct*?
   a. Enzymes speed up reaction rates and laboratory catalysts slow down reaction rates.
   b. Enzymes are smaller in size than most laboratory catalysts.
   c. Enzymes activity, but not laboratory catalyst activity, is regulated by other substances.
   d. no correct response

Answers: 1. c; 2. c

21-2 Enzyme Structure

LEARNING FOCUS

Be familiar with the terminology used to classify enzymes based on their composition.

Enzymes can be divided into two general structural classes: simple enzymes and conjugated enzymes. A **simple enzyme** *is an enzyme composed only of protein (amino acid chains).* A **conjugated enzyme** *is an enzyme that has a nonprotein part in addition to a protein part.* By itself, neither the protein part nor the nonprotein portion of a conjugated enzyme has catalytic properties. An **apoenzyme** *is the protein part of a conjugated enzyme.* A **cofactor** *is the nonprotein part of a conjugated enzyme.* The term *holoenzyme* is often used to designate a biologically active combined apoenzyme–cofactor entity. A **holoenzyme** *is the biochemically active conjugated enzyme produced from an apoenzyme and a cofactor.*

$$\text{Apoenzyme} + \text{cofactor} = \text{holoenzyme}$$

Why do apoenzymes need cofactors? Cofactors provide additional chemically reactive functional groups besides those present in the amino acid side chains of apoenzymes.

Two broad categories of cofactors exist: simple metal ions and small organic molecules. Metal ion cofactors include Zn^{2+}, Mg^{2+}, Fe (Fe^{2+}, Fe^{3+}), and Cu (Cu^+, Cu^{2+}). All metal ions must be supplied to the human body through dietary mineral intake (Chemical Connections 3-A—Dietary Minerals and the Human Body). Almost any type of diet will provide adequate amounts of needed metallic cofactors because they are needed in very small (trace) amounts.

Small organic molecules, the second category of cofactors, as a group, are called *coenzymes.* A **coenzyme** *is a small organic molecule that serves as a cofactor in a conjugated enzyme.* Coenzymes are synthesized within the human body using building blocks obtained from other nutrients. Most often, one of these building blocks is a B vitamin or B vitamin derivative (Section 21-14). Vitamins must be obtained through dietary intake.

Many cofactors are *permanently* bonded, via covalent bonds, to the amino acid portion of an enzyme. Breaking of the covalent bonds deactivates the enzyme. Metal ions and many, but not all, coenzymes are permanently attached parts of enzymes. The coenzyme FAD, which has riboflavin (a B vitamin; Section 21-14) as part of its structure, is an example of a permanently attached coenzyme. The cofactor FAD has an important role in numerous biochemical redox reactions (see Section 23-7).

Permanent attachment is not an absolute requirement for a coenzyme to be an active part of an enzyme. Sometimes a coenzyme *temporarily* binds to the amino acid portion of an enzyme at the time it is needed and then it is released after the reaction has occurred. The coenzyme NAD^+ provides an example of such coenzyme behavior. The cofactor NAD^+, which has niacin (a B vitamin; Section 21-14) as part of its structure, is also an extremely important substance in biochemical redox reactions (see Section 23-7). The subject of temporary cofactor binding to an enzyme will be considered further in Section 21-14.

Section 21-2 Quick Quiz

1. Which of the following statements about a *conjugated* enzyme is *correct*?
   a. It contains only amino acids.
   b. It always contains a metal atom.
   c. It always contains a nonprotein part.
   d. no correct response
2. Which of the following statements about *cofactors* is *incorrect*?
   a. All conjugated enzymes contain cofactors.
   b. Metal ions can function as cofactors.
   c. Coenzyme is an alternate name for all cofactors.
   d. no correct response
3. Which of the following statements about the interaction of cofactors with apoenzymes is *correct*?
   a. They are always covalently bonded to the apoenzyme.
   b. They cannot be covalently bonded to the apoenzyme.
   c. They can, but do not have to be, covalently bonded to the apoenzyme.
   d. no correct response

Answers: 1. c; 2. c; 3. c

21-3 Nomenclature and Classification of Enzymes

LEARNING FOCUS

Know what a *substrate* is; understand important aspects of enzyme nomenclature; be familiar with the terminology used to classify enzymes based on the types of reactions they catalyze.

Enzymes are most commonly named by using a system that attempts to provide information about the *function* (rather than the structure) of the enzyme. The type of reaction catalyzed and the *substrate* identity are focal points for the nomenclature. A **substrate** *is the reactant in an enzyme-catalyzed reaction.* The substrate is the substance upon which the enzyme "acts."

Three important aspects of the enzyme-naming process are the following:

1. The suffix *-ase* identifies a substance as an enzyme. Thus ur*ease,* sucr*ase,* and lip*ase* are all enzyme designations. The suffix *-in* is still found in the names of some of the first enzymes studied, many of which are digestive enzymes. Such names include *trypsin, chymotrypsin,* and *pepsin.*
2. The type of reaction catalyzed by an enzyme is often noted with a prefix. An *oxidase* enzyme catalyzes an oxidation reaction, and a *hydrolase* enzyme catalyzes a hydrolysis reaction.
3. The identity of the substrate is often noted in addition to the type of reaction. Enzyme names of this type include *glucose oxidase, pyruvate carboxylase,* and *succinate dehydrogenase.* Infrequently, the substrate but not the reaction type is given, as in the names *urease* and *lactase.* In these names, the reaction involved is hydrolysis; *urease* catalyzes the hydrolysis of urea, *lactase* the hydrolysis of lactose.

EXAMPLE 21-1

Predicting Enzyme Function from an Enzyme's Name

Predict the function of the following enzymes:

a. Cellulase **b.** Sucrase
c. L-Amino acid oxidase **d.** Aspartate aminotransferase

Solution

a. Cellulase catalyzes the hydrolysis of cellulose.
b. Sucrase catalyzes the hydrolysis of the disaccharide sucrose.
c. L-Amino acid oxidase catalyzes the oxidation of L-amino acids.
d. Aspartate aminotransferase catalyzes the transfer of an amino group from aspartate to a different molecule.

Enzymes are grouped into six major classes on the basis of the types of reactions they catalyze.

1. An **oxidoreductase** *is an enzyme that catalyzes an oxidation–reduction reaction.* Because oxidation and reduction are not independent processes but linked processes that must occur together (Section 9-3), an oxidoreductase requires a coenzyme that is oxidized or reduced as the substrate is reduced or oxidized. *Lactate dehydrogenase* is an oxidoreductase that removes hydrogen atoms from a molecule. ◄

$$\underset{\substack{\text{Lactate}\\\text{Reduced}\\\text{substrate}}}{\overset{\text{COO}^-}{\underset{\text{CH}_3}{\text{HO}-\overset{|}{\underset{|}{\text{C}}}-\text{H}}}} + \underset{\substack{\text{Oxidized}\\\text{coenzyme}}}{\text{NAD}^+} \underset{\text{dehydrogenase}}{\overset{\text{Lactate}}{\rightleftharpoons}} \underset{\substack{\text{Pyruvate}\\\text{Oxidized}\\\text{product}}}{\overset{\text{COO}^-}{\underset{\text{CH}_3}{\text{C}=\text{O}}}} + \underset{\substack{\text{Reduced}\\\text{coenzyme}}}{\text{NADH}} + \text{H}^+$$

▶ *Recall from Section 14-9 that for organic redox reactions, the following two operational rules are used instead of oxidation numbers (Section 9-2) to characterize oxidation and reduction processes:*

1. *An organic oxidation reaction is an oxidation that increases the number of C—O bonds and/or decreases the number of C—H bonds.*
2. *An organic reduction reaction is a reduction that decreases the number of C—O bonds and/or increases the number of C—H bonds.*

2. A **transferase** *is an enzyme that catalyzes the transfer of a functional group from one molecule to another.* Two major subtypes of transferases are *transaminases* and *kinases.* A transaminase catalyzes the transfer of an amino group from one molecule to another. Kinases, which play a major role in metabolic energy-production reactions (see Section 24-2), catalyze the transfer of a phosphate group from adenosine triphosphate (ATP) to give adenosine diphosphate (ADP) and a phosphorylated product (a product containing an additional phosphate group).

Glucose + ATP $\xrightarrow{\text{Hexokinase}}$ ADP + Glucose 6-phosphate

Adenosine triphosphate	Adenosine diphosphate	
(3 phosphate groups present)	(2 phosphate groups present)	The symbol Ⓟ is a shorthand notation for a phosphate group.

3. A **hydrolase** *is an enzyme that catalyzes a hydrolysis reaction in which the addition of a water molecule to a bond causes the bond to break.* Hydrolysis reactions are central to the process of digestion. *Carbohydrases* effect the breaking of glycosidic bonds in oligo- and polysaccharides, *proteases* effect the breaking of peptide linkages in proteins, and *lipases* effect the breaking of ester linkages in triacylglycerols.

Maltose + H_2O $\xrightarrow{\text{Maltase}}$ Glucose + Glucose

4. A **lyase** *is an enzyme that catalyzes the addition of a group to a double bond or the removal of a group to form a double bond in a manner that does not involve hydrolysis or oxidation.* A *dehydratase* effects the removal of the components of water from a double bond and a *hydratase* effects the addition of the components of water to a double bond.

Fumarate + H_2O $\xrightarrow{\text{Fumarase}}$ L-Malate

5. An **isomerase** *is an enzyme that catalyzes the isomerization (rearrangement of atoms) of a substrate in a reaction, converting it into a molecule isomeric with itself.* There is only one reactant and one product in reactions where isomerases are operative.

3-Phosphoglycerate $\xrightleftharpoons{\text{Phosphoglyceromutase}}$ 2-Phosphoglycerate

6. A **ligase** *is an enzyme that catalyzes the bonding together of two molecules into one with the participation of ATP.* ATP involvement is required because such reactions are generally energetically unfavorable and they require the simultaneous input of energy obtained by a hydrolysis reaction in which ATP is converted to ADP (such energy release is considered in Section 23-3).

$$
CO_2 +
\begin{array}{c} COO^- \\ | \\ C=O \\ | \\ CH_3 \end{array}
\text{(Pyruvate)} + ATP \xrightarrow{\text{Pyruvate carboxylase}}
\begin{array}{c} COO^- \\ | \\ C=O \\ | \\ CH_2 \\ | \\ COO^- \end{array}
\text{(Oxaloacetate)} + ADP + \textcircled{P} + H^+
\text{ Phosphate}
$$

Within each of these six main classes of enzymes there are enzyme subclasses. Table 21-1 gives further information about enzyme subclass terminology, some of which was used in the preceding discussion of the main enzyme classes. For example, dehydratases and hydratases are subclass designations; both of these enzyme subtypes are lyases (Table 21-1).

▶ **Table 21-1 Main Classes and Subclasses of Enzymes**

Main Classes	Selected Subclasses	Type of Reaction Catalyzed
oxidoreductases	oxidases	oxidation of a substrate
	reductases	reduction of a substrate
	dehydrogenases	introduction of double bond (oxidation) by formal removal of two H atoms from a substrate, with one H being accepted by a coenzyme
transferases	transaminases	transfer of an amino group between substrates
	kinases	transfer of a phosphate group between substrates
hydrolases	lipases	hydrolysis of ester linkages in lipids
	proteases	hydrolysis of amide linkages in proteins ◀
	nucleases	hydrolysis of sugar–phosphate ester bonds in nucleic acids
	carbohydrases	hydrolysis of glycosidic bonds in carbohydrates
	phosphatases	hydrolysis of phosphate–ester bonds
lyases	dehydratases	removal of H_2O from a substrate
	decarboxylases	removal of CO_2 from a substrate
	deaminases	removal of NH_3 from a substrate
	hydratases	addition of H_2O to a substrate
isomerases	racemases	conversion of D isomer to L isomer, or vice versa
	mutases	transfer of a functional group from one position to another in the same molecule
ligases	synthetases	formation of a new bond between two substrates, with participation of ATP
	carboxylases	formation of a new bond between a substrate and CO_2, with participation of ATP

▶ *If fresh pineapple, kiwi, or papaya is added to a gelatin-dessert powder, such as Jello, the gelatin will not gel. Why is this so? These fruits contain a* protease *(Table 21-1) that catalyzes the hydrolysis of peptide (amide) linkages in proteins and gelatin is a protein. If canned pineapple is added to gelatin it will gel. The* protease *present is deactivated when the pineapple was cooked.*

EXAMPLE 21-2

Classifying Enzymes by the Type of Chemical Reaction They Catalyze

To what main enzyme class do the enzymes that catalyze the following chemical reactions belong?

a.

$$HO-\underset{\underset{\underset{COO^-}{|}}{\underset{CH_2}{|}}}{\overset{COO^-}{\underset{|}{C}}}-H \ + \ NAD^+ \ \longrightarrow \ \underset{\underset{\underset{COO^-}{|}}{\underset{CH_2}{|}}}{\overset{COO^-}{\underset{|}{C}}}=O \ + \ NADH \ + \ H^+$$

b.

$$\overset{+}{H_3}N-\underset{\underset{R_1}{|}}{CH}-\overset{O}{\overset{||}{C}}-\overset{H}{\overset{|}{N}}-\underset{\underset{R_2}{|}}{CH}-COO^- \ + \ H_2O \ \longrightarrow \ \overset{+}{H_3}N-\underset{\underset{R_1}{|}}{CH}-\overset{O}{\overset{||}{C}}-O^- \ + \ \overset{}{H_2}\overset{+}{N}-\underset{\underset{R_2}{|}}{CH}-COO^-$$

Solution

a. In this reaction, two H atoms are removed from the substrate and a carbon–oxygen double bond is formed. Loss of two hydrogen atoms by a molecule is an indication of oxidation. This is an oxidation–reduction reaction, and the enzyme needed to effect the change will be an *oxidoreductase*.

$$HO-\underset{\underset{\underset{\underset{Malate}{COO^-}}{|}}{\underset{CH_2}{|}}}{\overset{COO^-}{\underset{|}{C}}}-H \ + \ NAD^+ \ \longrightarrow \ \underset{\underset{\underset{\underset{Oxaloacetate}{COO^-}}{|}}{\underset{CH_2}{|}}}{\overset{COO^-}{\underset{|}{C}}}=O \ + \ NADH \ + \ H^+$$

b. In this reaction, the components of a molecule of H_2O are added to the substrate (a dipeptide) with the resulting breaking of the peptide bond to produce two amino acids. This is an example of a hydrolysis reaction. An enzyme that effects such a change is called a *hydrolase*.

$$\underset{Dipeptide}{\overset{+}{H_3}N-\underset{\underset{R_1}{|}}{CH}-\overset{O}{\overset{||}{C}}-\overset{H}{\overset{|}{N}}-\underset{\underset{R_2}{|}}{CH}-COO^-} \ + \ H_2O \ \longrightarrow \ \underset{Amino\ acid}{\overset{+}{H_3}N-\underset{\underset{R_1}{|}}{CH}-\overset{O}{\overset{||}{C}}-O^-} \ + \ \underset{Amino\ acid}{\overset{H}{\overset{|}{H_2}\overset{+}{N}}-\underset{\underset{R_2}{|}}{CH}-COO^-}$$

A commonly observed enzyme-influenced phenomenon that occurs outside the human body is the discoloration (browning) that occurs when freshly cut fruit (apples, pears, etc.) and vegetables (potatoes) are exposed to air for a short period of time. The enzyme involved, which is present in the food, is an oxidoreductase enzyme called *phenolase*. The focus on relevancy feature Chemical Connections 21-A—Enzymatic Browning: Discoloration of Fruits and Vegetables—gives further information about the effects of the action of *phenolase* on fruits and vegetables.

Section 21-3 Quick Quiz

1. Which of the following statements concerning an enzyme *substrate* is *incorrect*?
   a. It is the substance upon which the enzyme "acts."
   b. It is the reactant in an enzyme-catalyzed reaction.
   c. It is the product in an enzyme-catalyzed reaction.
   d. no correct response
2. Most enzyme names end with the suffix –*ase,* but a few names end in the suffix
   a. –ose
   b. –ine
   c. –in
   d. no correct response

3. Which of the following pairings of enzyme type and enzyme function is *incorrect*?
a. Lipase – hydrolysis of ester linkages in a lipid
b. Hydratase – addition of water to a substrate
c. Carboxylase – removal of carbon dioxide from a substrate
d. no correct response

4. Which of the following pairings of enzyme type and enzyme function is *incorrect*?
a. Kinase – transfer of a phosphate group between substrates
b. Mutase – introduction of a double bond within a molecule
c. Protease – hydrolysis of amide linkages in a protein
d. no correct response

Answers: 1. c; 2. c; 3. c; 4. b

CHEMICAL CONNECTIONS 21-A

Enzymatic Browning: Discoloration of Fruits and Vegetables

Everyone is familiar with the way fruits such as apples, pears, peaches, apricots, and bananas, and vegetables such as potatoes, quickly turn brown when their tissue is exposed to oxygen. Such oxygen exposure occurs when the food is sliced or bitten into or when it has sustained bruises, cuts, or other injury to the peel. This "browning reaction" is related to the work of an enzyme called phenolase (or polyphenoloxidase), a conjugated enzyme in which copper is present.

Phenolase is classified as an oxidoreductase. The substrates for phenolase are phenolic compounds present in the tissues of the fruits and vegetables. Phenolase hydroxylates phenol derivatives to catechol (Section 14-13) derivatives and then oxidizes the catechol derivatives to *o*-benzoquinone derivatives (see the chemical equations below for the structural relationships). The *o*-benzoquinone derivatives then enter into a number of other reactions, which produce the "unwanted" brown discolorations. *o*-Benzoquinone derivative formation is enzyme- and oxygen-dependent. Once the quinones have formed, the subsequent reactions occur spontaneously and no longer depend on the presence of phenolase or oxygen.

Enzymatic browning can be prevented or slowed in several ways. Immersing the "injured" food (for example, apple slices) in cold water slows the browning process. The lower temperature decreases enzyme activity, and the water limits the enzyme's access to oxygen. Refrigeration slows enzyme activity even more, and boiling temperatures destroy (denature) the enzyme. A long-used method for preventing browning involves lemon juice. Phenolase works very slowly in the acidic environment created by the lemon juice's presence. In addition, the vitamin C (ascorbic acid) present in lemon juice functions as an antioxidant. It is more easily oxidized than the phenolic-derived compounds, and its oxidation products are colorless.

At left, a freshly cut apple. Brownish oxidation products form in a few minutes (at right).

© Seqoya/Shutterstock.com

Genetic engineering (Section 22-15) is a new approach under study for preventing enzymatic browning. Granny Smith and golden delicious apples are now grown in a research setting in which the reaction for the production of phenolase, the enzyme necessary for enzymatic browning to occur, has been "turned off." Approval procedures for the marketing of such apples is near completion.

Interestingly, because the phenols which serve as substrates for phenolase function as antioxidants in apples, preventing their conversion to quinones actually improves the nutritional profile of apples; antioxidant concentrations are greater.

$$\underset{\text{Phenol derivatives}}{\text{OH}} \xrightarrow[\text{Phenolase}]{O_2} \underset{\text{Catechol derivatives}}{\text{OH, OH}} \xrightarrow[\text{Phenolase}]{O_2} \underset{\text{\textit{o}-Benzoquinone derivatives}}{\text{O, O}} \longrightarrow \begin{array}{l}\text{Brownish}\\\text{oxidation}\\\text{products}\end{array}$$

Figure 21-2 The active site of an enzyme is usually a crevicelike region formed as a result of the protein's secondary and tertiary structural characteristics.

Models of Enzyme Action

LEARNING FOCUS

Be familiar with the terms *enzyme active site* and *enzyme–substrate complex*; describe the *lock-and-key* model and the *induced-fit* model for enzyme action.

Explanations of *how* enzymes function as catalysts in biochemical systems are based on the concepts of an enzyme active site and enzyme–substrate complex formation.

Enzyme Active Site

Studies show that only a small portion of an enzyme molecule, called the active site, participates in the interaction with a substrate or substrates during a reaction. The **active site** *is the relatively small part of an enzyme's structure that is actually involved in catalysis.*

The active site in an enzyme is a three-dimensional entity formed by groups that come from different parts of the protein chain(s); these groups are brought together by the folding and bending (secondary and tertiary structure; Sections 20-11 and 20-12) of the protein. The active site is usually a "crevicelike" location in the enzyme (Figure 21-2).

Enzyme–Substrate Complex

Catalysts offer an alternative pathway with lower activation energy through which a reaction can occur (Section 9-6). In enzyme-controlled reactions, this alternative pathway involves the formation of an enzyme–substrate complex as an intermediate species in the reaction. An **enzyme–substrate complex** *is the intermediate reaction species that is formed when a substrate binds to the active site of an enzyme.* Within the enzyme–substrate complex, the substrate encounters more favorable reaction conditions than if it were free. The result is faster formation of product.

Lock-and-Key Model

To account for the highly specific way an enzyme recognizes a substrate and binds it to the active site, researchers have proposed several models. The simplest of these models is the lock-and-key model.

In the lock-and-key model, the active site in the enzyme has a fixed, rigid geometrical conformation. Only substrates with a complementary geometry can be accommodated at such a site, much as a lock accepts only certain keys. Figure 21-3 illustrates the lock-and-key concept of substrate–enzyme interaction. ◀

Induced-Fit Model

The lock-and-key model explains the action of numerous enzymes. It is, however, too restrictive for the action of many other enzymes. Experimental evidence indicates that many enzymes have flexibility in their shapes. They are not rigid and static; there is constant change in their shape. The induced-fit model is used for this type of situation.

The induced-fit model allows for small changes in the shape or geometry of the active site of an enzyme to accommodate a substrate. A good analogy is the changes

▶ *The lock-and-key model is more than just a "shape fit." In addition, there are weak binding forces (R group interactions) between parts.*

Figure 21-3 The lock-and-key model for enzyme activity. Only a substrate whose shape and chemical nature are complementary to those of the active site can interact with the enzyme.

Substrate

Products

Enzyme active site

Enzyme active site

Figure 21-4 The induced-fit model for enzyme activity. The enzyme active site, although not exactly complementary in shape to that of the substrate, is flexible enough that it can adapt to the shape of the substrate.

that occur in the shape of a glove when a hand is inserted into it. The induced fit is a result of the enzyme's flexibility; it adapts to accept the incoming substrate. This model, illustrated in Figure 21-4, is a more thorough explanation for the active-site properties of an enzyme because it includes the specificity of the lock-and-key model coupled with the flexibility of the enzyme protein.

The forces that draw the substrate into the active site are many of the same forces that maintain tertiary structure in the folding of peptide chains. Electrostatic interactions, hydrogen bonds, and hydrophobic interactions all help attract and bind substrate molecules. For example, a protonated (positively charged) amino group in a substrate could be attracted and held at the active site by a negatively charged aspartate or glutamate residue. Alternatively, cofactors such as positively charged metal ions often help bind substrate molecules. Figure 21-5 is a schematic representation of the amino acid R group interactions that bind a substrate to an enzyme active site.

Substrate

- R group interactions that bind the substrate to the enzyme active site
- R group interactions that maintain the three-dimensional structure of the enzyme
- Noninteracting R groups that help determine the solubility of the enzyme

Figure 21-5 A schematic diagram representing amino acid R group interactions that bind a substrate to an enzyme active site. The R group interactions that maintain the three-dimensional structure of the enzyme (secondary and tertiary structure) are also shown.

Section 21-4 Quick Quiz

1. An enzyme active site is the location in an enzyme where substrate molecules
   a. are produced
   b. are changed to catalysts
   c. react to form product
   d. no correct response
2. Which of the following statements concerning the lock-and-key model for enzyme activity is *incorrect*?
   a. The active site has a fixed, rigid geometry.
   b. The active site has a geometry complementary to that of substrate.
   c. The active site has a geometry identical to that of the substrate.
   d. no correct response
3. Which of the following enzyme properties is explained by the induced-fit model for enzyme activity?
   a. high specificity of an enzyme for a specific substrate
   b. ability of an enzyme to accommodate more than one kind of substrate
   c. susceptibility of enzymes to deactivation
   d. no correct response

Answers: 1. c; 2. c; 3. b

21-5 Enzyme Specificity

LEARNING FOCUS

Be able to categorize enzymes in terms of specificity characteristics.

Enzymes exhibit different levels of selectivity, or specificity, for substrates. **Enzyme specificity** *is the extent to which an enzyme's activity is restricted to a specific substrate, a specific group of substrates, a specific type of chemical bond, or a specific type of chemical reaction.* The degree of enzyme specificity is determined by the active site. Some active sites accommodate only one particular compound, whereas others can accommodate a "family" of closely related compounds. Types of enzyme specificity include:

1. *Absolute specificity*—the enzyme will catalyze only one reaction. This most restrictive of all specificities is not common. *Catalase* is an enzyme with absolute specificity. It catalyzes the conversion of hydrogen peroxide (H_2O_2) to O_2 and H_2O. Hydrogen peroxide is the only substrate it will accept.
2. *Group specificity*—the enzyme will act only on molecules that have a specific functional group, such as hydroxyl, amino, or phosphate groups. Carboxypeptidase is group specific; it cleaves amino acids, one at a time, from the carboxyl end of a peptide chain.
3. *Linkage specificity*—the enzyme will act on a particular type of chemical bond, irrespective of the rest of the molecular structure. Phosphatases hydrolyze phosphate–ester bonds in all types of phosphate esters. Linkage specificity is the most general of the common specificities.
4. *Stereochemical specificity*—the enzyme will act on a particular stereoisomer. Chirality is inherent in an enzyme active site because amino acids are chiral compounds. An L-amino acid oxidase will catalyze the oxidation of the L-form of an amino acid but not the D-form of the same amino acid.

Section 21-5 Quick Quiz

1. The specificity of an enzyme that catalyzes the oxidation of several different alcohols is termed
   a. absolute specificity
   b. stereochemical specificity
   c. group specificity
   d. no correct response
2. Linkage-specific enzymes will act on a particular type of
   a. chemical bond
   b. functional group
   c. stereoisomer (D- or L-)
   d. no correct response

Answers: 1. c; 2. a

21-6 Factors That Affect Enzyme Activity

LEARNING FOCUS

Know how temperature, pH, substrate concentration, and enzyme concentration affect enzyme activity.

Enzyme activity *is a measure of the rate at which an enzyme converts substrate to products in a biochemical reaction.* Factors that affect enzyme activity include temperature, pH, substrate concentration, and enzyme concentration.

Temperature

Temperature is a measure of the kinetic energy (energy of motion) of molecules. At higher temperatures molecules are moving faster and colliding more frequently. This concept applies to collisions between substrate molecules and enzymes. As the temperature of an enzymatically catalyzed reaction increases, so does the rate (velocity) of the reaction.

However, when the temperature increases beyond a certain point, the increased energy begins to cause disruptions in the tertiary structure of the enzyme; denaturation is occurring. Change in tertiary structure at the active site impedes catalytic action, and the enzyme activity quickly decreases as the temperature climbs past this point (Figure 21-6). The temperature that produces maximum activity for an enzyme is known as the optimum temperature for that enzyme. **Optimum temperature** *is the temperature at which an enzyme exhibits maximum activity.*

For human enzymes, the optimum temperature is around 37°C, normal body temperature. A person who has a fever where body core temperature exceeds 40°C can be in a life-threatening situation because such a temperature is sufficient to initiate enzyme denaturation. The loss of function of critical enzymes, particularly those of the central nervous system, can result in dysfunction sufficient to cause death.

The "destroying" effect of temperature on bacterial enzymes is used in a hospital setting to sterilize medical instruments and laundry. In high-temperature, high-pressure vessels called *autoclaves,* super-heated steam is used to produce a temperature sufficient to denature bacterial enzymes.

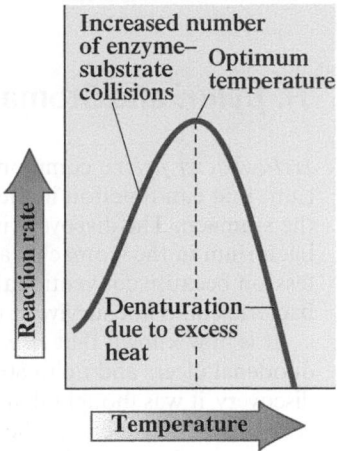

Figure 21-6 A graph showing the effect of temperature on the rate of an enzymatic reaction.

pH

The pH of an enzyme's environment can affect its activity. This is not surprising because the *charge* on acidic and basic amino acids (Section 20-2) located at the active site depends on pH. Small changes in pH (less than one unit) can result in enzyme denaturation (Section 20-16) and subsequent loss of catalytic activity.

Most enzymes exhibit maximum activity over a very narrow pH range. Only within this narrow pH range do the enzyme's amino acids exist in properly charged forms (Section 20-4). **Optimum pH** *is the pH at which an enzyme exhibits maximum activity.* Figure 21-7 shows the effect of pH on an enzyme's activity. Biochemical buffers help maintain the optimum pH for an enzyme.

Each enzyme has a characteristic optimum pH, which usually falls within the physiological pH range of 7.0–7.5. Notable exceptions to this generalization are the digestive enzymes pepsin and trypsin. Pepsin, which is active in the stomach, functions best at a pH of 2.0. On the other hand, trypsin, which operates in the small intestine, functions best at a pH of 8.0. The amino acid sequences present in pepsin and trypsin are those needed such that the R groups present can maintain protein tertiary structure (Section 20-11) at low (2.0) and high (8.0) pH values, respectively.

A variation from normal pH can also affect substrates, causing either protonation or deprotonation of groups on the substrate. The interaction between the altered substrate and the enzyme active site may be less efficient than normal—or even impossible.

The reason that pickles and other pickled foods do not readily undergo spoilage is due to the acidic conditions associated with their preparation. These acidic conditions significantly reduce the enzymatic activity of any microorganisms present.

An interesting bacterial adaptation to an acidic environment occurs within the human stomach. Bacteria are now known to be the cause of most stomach ulcers. How these ulcer-causing bacteria survive the highly acidic conditions of the human stomach is considered in the focus on relevancy feature Chemical Connections 21-B—*H. pylori* and Stomach Ulcers.

Figure 21-7 A graph showing the effect of pH on the rate of an enzymatic reaction.

CHEMICAL CONNECTIONS 21-B

H. pylori and Stomach Ulcers

Helicobacter pylori, commonly called *H. pylori,* is a bacterium that can function in the highly acidic environment of the stomach. The discovery in 1982 of the existence of this bacterium in the stomach was startling to the medical profession because conventional thought at the time was that bacteria could not survive at the stomach's pH of about 1.4.

It is now known that *H. pylori* causes more than 90% of duodenal ulcers and up to 80% of gastric ulcers. Before this discovery, it was thought that most ulcers were caused by excess stomach acid eating the stomach lining. Contributory causes were thought to be spicy food and stress. Conventional treatment involved acid-suppression or acid-neutralization medications. Now, treatment regimens involve antibiotics. The medical profession was slow to accept the concept of a bacterial cause for most ulcers, and it was not until the mid-1990s that antibiotic treatment became common.

How the enzymes present in the *H. pylori* bacterium can function in the acidic environment of the stomach (where they should be denatured) is now known. Present on the surface of the bacterium is the enzyme *urease,* an enzyme that converts urea to the basic substance ammonia. The ammonia then neutralizes acid present in its immediate vicinity; a protective barrier is thus created. The *urease* itself is protected from denaturation by its complex quaternary structure.

H. pylori causes ulcers by weakening the protective mucous coating of the stomach and duodenum, which allows acid to get through to the sensitive lining beneath. Both the acid and the bacteria irritate the lining and cause a sore—the ulcer. Ultimately the *H. pylori* themselves burrow into the lining to an acid-safe area within the lining.

Treatment for an *H. pylori* infection involves not only the administration of an antibiotic such as amoxicillin but also use of an acid production inhibitor such as omeprazole. The inhibitor blocks acid production from cells located just beneath the mucous coating of the stomach. With acid production temporarily stopped, stomach pH rises to a value around 4.0, permitting the antibiotic to survive long enough to exert its corrective effect. At normal stomach pH, around 1.5, the antibiotic would be rapidly deactivated.

Approximately two-thirds of the world's population is infected with *H. pylori.* In the United States 30% of the adult population is infected, with the infection most prevalent among older adults. About 20% of people under the age of 40 and half of those over 60 have it. Only one out of every six people infected with *H. pylori* ever suffer symptoms related to ulcers. Why *H. pylori* does not cause ulcers in every infected person is not known.

H. pylori bacteria are most likely spread from person to person through fecal–oral or oral–oral routes. Possible environmental sources include contaminated water sources. The infection is more common in crowded living conditions with poor sanitation. In countries with poor sanitation, 90% of the adult population can be infected.

H. pylori bacteria.

Figure 21-8 A graph showing the change in enzyme activity with a change in substrate concentration at constant temperature, pH, and enzyme concentration. Enzyme activity remains constant after a certain substrate concentration is reached.

Substrate Concentration

When the concentration of an enzyme is kept constant and the concentration of substrate is increased, the enzyme activity pattern shown in Figure 21-8 is obtained. This activity pattern is called a *saturation curve.* Enzyme activity increases up to a certain substrate concentration and thereafter remains constant.

What limits enzymatic activity to a certain maximum value? As substrate concentration increases, the point is eventually reached where enzyme capabilities are used to their maximum extent. The rate remains constant from this point on (Figure 21-8). Each substrate must occupy an enzyme active site for a finite amount of time, and the products must leave the site before the cycle can be repeated. When each enzyme molecule is working at full capacity, the incoming substrate molecules must "wait their turn" for an empty active site. At this point, the enzyme is said to be under saturation conditions.

The rate at which an enzyme accepts substrate molecules and releases product molecules at substrate saturation is given by its turnover number. An enzyme's **turnover number** is *the number of substrate molecules transformed per minute by one*

Table 21-2 **Turnover Numbers for Selected Enzymes**

Enzyme	Turnover Number (per minute)	Reaction Catalyzed
carbonic anhydrase	36,000,000	$CO_2 + H_2O \rightleftharpoons H_2CO_3$
catalase	5,600,000	$2H_2O_2 \rightleftharpoons 2H_2O + O_2$
cholinesterase	1,500,000	hydrolysis of acetylcholine
penicillinase	120,000	hydrolysis of penicillin
lactate dehydrogenase	60,000	conversion of pyruvate to lactate
DNA polymerase I	900	addition of nucleotides to DNA chains

molecule of enzyme under optimum conditions of temperature, pH, and saturation. Table 21-2 gives turnover numbers for selected enzymes. Some enzymes have a much faster mode of operation than others.

Enzyme Concentration

Because enzymes are not consumed in the reactions they catalyze, the cell usually keeps the number of enzymes low compared with the number of substrate molecules. This is efficient; the cell avoids paying the energy costs of synthesizing and maintaining a large work force of enzyme molecules. Thus, in general, the concentration of substrate in a reaction is much higher than that of the enzyme.

If the amount of substrate present is kept constant and the enzyme concentration is increased, the reaction rate increases because more substrate molecules can be accommodated in a given amount of time. A plot of enzyme activity versus enzyme concentration, at a constant substrate concentration that is high relative to enzyme concentration, is shown in Figure 21-9. The greater the enzyme concentration, the greater the reaction rate.

Chemistry at a Glance—Enzyme Activity—reviews what has been presented about enzyme activity.

Figure 21-9 A graph showing the change in reaction rate with a change in enzyme concentration for an enzymatic reaction. Temperature, pH, and substrate concentration are constant. The substrate concentration is high relative to enzyme concentration.

Determining How Enzyme Activity Is Affected by Various Changes

Describe the effect that each of the following changes would have on the rate of a biochemical reaction that involves the substrate urea and the liver enzyme urease.

a. Increasing the urea concentration
b. Increasing the urease concentration
c. Increasing the temperature from its optimum value to a value 10°C higher than this value
d. Decreasing the pH by one unit from its optimum value

Solution

a. The enzyme activity rate will *increase* until all of the enzyme molecules are engaged with urea substrate.
b. The enzyme activity rate will *increase* until all of the urea molecules are engaged with urease enzymes.
c. At temperatures higher than the optimum temperature, enzyme activity will *decrease* from that at the optimum temperature.
d. At pH values lower than the optimum pH value, enzyme activity will *decrease* from that at the optimum pH.

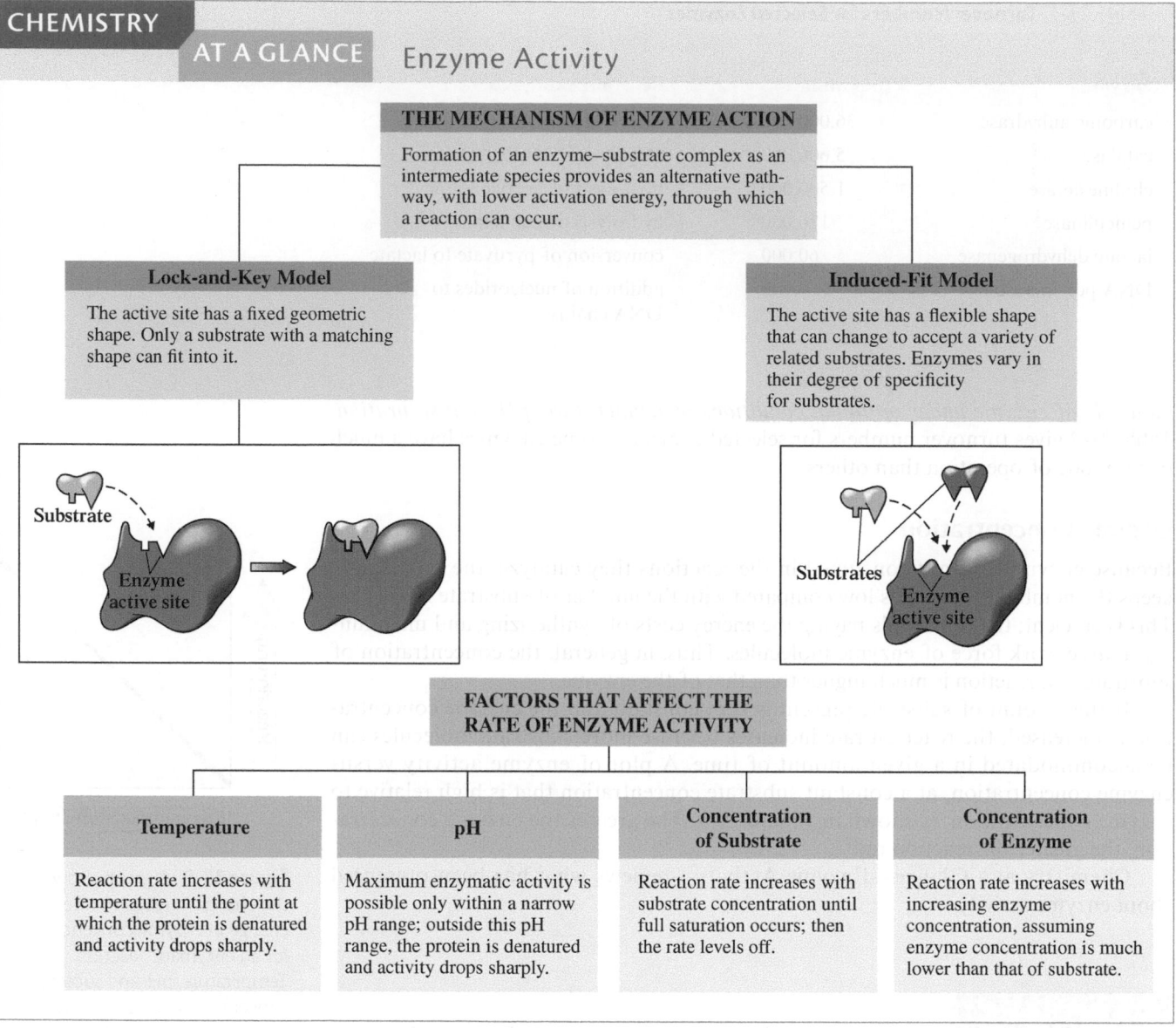

AT A GLANCE Enzyme Activity

THE MECHANISM OF ENZYME ACTION

Formation of an enzyme–substrate complex as an intermediate species provides an alternative pathway, with lower activation energy, through which a reaction can occur.

Lock-and-Key Model

The active site has a fixed geometric shape. Only a substrate with a matching shape can fit into it.

Substrate

Enzyme active site

Induced-Fit Model

The active site has a flexible shape that can change to accept a variety of related substrates. Enzymes vary in their degree of specificity for substrates.

Substrates

Enzyme active site

FACTORS THAT AFFECT THE RATE OF ENZYME ACTIVITY

Temperature	pH	Concentration of Substrate	Concentration of Enzyme
Reaction rate increases with temperature until the point at which the protein is denatured and activity drops sharply.	Maximum enzymatic activity is possible only within a narrow pH range; outside this pH range, the protein is denatured and activity drops sharply.	Reaction rate increases with substrate concentration until full saturation occurs; then the rate levels off.	Reaction rate increases with increasing enzyme concentration, assuming enzyme concentration is much lower than that of substrate.

Section 21-6 Quick Quiz

1. The number of substrate molecules converted to product per minute is a measure of
   a. enzyme activity
   b. enzyme concentration
   c. enzyme specificity
   d. no correct response
2. A plot of enzyme activity (*y*-axis) versus pH (*x*-axis) with other variables constant is a
   a. straight line with an upward slope
   b. line with an upward slope and a long flat top
   c. line with an upward slope followed by a downward slope
   d. no correct response
3. A plot of enzyme activity (*y*-axis) versus temperature (*x*-axis) with other variables constant is a
   a. straight line with an upward slope
   b. line with an upward slope and a long flat top
   c. line with an upward slope followed by a downward slope
   d. no correct response

Answers: 1. a; 2. c; 3. c

21-7 Extremozymes

LEARNING FOCUS

Be familiar with the concepts of *extremophiles* and *extremozymes*.

An **extremophile** *is a microorganism that thrives in extreme environments, environments in which humans and most other forms of life could not survive.* Extremophile environments include the hydrothermal areas of Yellowstone National Park (Figure 21-10) and hydrothermal vents on the ocean floor where temperatures and pressures can be extremely high. The ability of extremophiles to survive under such harsh conditions is related to the amino acid sequences present in the enzymes (proteins) of extremophiles. ◄ These sequences are stable under the extraordinary conditions present.

It was not until the 1970s that the existence of extremophiles was recognized. Research during the 1980s and 1990s resulted in the identification of numerous diverse types of extremophiles found in many different locations. Types identified include *acidophiles* (optimal growth at pH levels of 3.0 or below), *alkaliphiles* (optimal growth at pH levels of 9.0 or above), *halophiles* (high salinity, a salinity that exceeds 0.2 M NaCl needed for growth), *hyperthermophiles* (a temperature between 80°C and 121°C needed to thrive), *piezophiles* (a high hydrostatic pressure needed for growth), *xerophiles* (extremely dry conditions needed for growth), and *cryophiles* (a temperature of 15°C or lower needed for growth). ◄

The enzymes present in extremophiles are called *extremozymes*. An **extremozyme** *is a microbial enzyme active at conditions that would inactivate human enzymes as well as enzymes present in other types of higher organisms.*

The study of extremozymes is an area of high interest and active research for industrial chemists. Enzymes are heavily used in industrial processes, a context in which they offer advantages similar to those associated with enzyme function in biochemical reactions within living cells. Because industrial processes usually require higher temperatures and pressures than do physiological processes, extremozymes have characteristics that have been found to be useful. The enzymes present in some detergent formulations, which must function in hot water, are the result of research associated with high-temperature microbial enzymes. Similarly, cold-water-wash laundry detergents contain enzymes originally characterized in cold-environment microbial organisms.

The development of commercially useful enzymes using extremophile sources involves the following general approach:

1. Samples containing the extremophile are gathered from the extreme environment where it is found.
2. DNA material is extracted from the extremophile and processed.
3. Macroscopic amounts of the DNA are produced using the polymerase chain reaction (Section 22-15).
4. The macroscopic amount of DNA is analyzed to identify the genes present (Section 22-8) that are involved in extremozyme production.
5. Genetic engineering techniques (Section 22-14) are used to insert the extremozyme gene into bacteria, which then produce the extremozyme.
6. The process is then commercialized.

Commercially produced enzymes are used in the petroleum industry during oil-well drilling operations. A thick mixture of enzymes, guar gum, sand, and water is forced into the borehole as the drill works its way through rock. At the appropriate time, explosives are used to crack the rock and the enzyme-containing mixture enters the cracks produced. The enzymes present convert the gum mixture into a freely flowing liquid, through hydrolysis of the gum. The freely flowing liquid carries the oil and gas out of the rock. Because of the high temperature generated from the drilling operations and explosive use, the enzymes used must be stable at high temperatures; such enzymes must thus be extremozymes.

▶ *The term* extremophile *comes from the Latin* extremus *meaning "extreme" and the Greek* philia *meaning "love."*

▶ *The upper temperature limit for life now stands at 121°C as the result of the discovery, in 2004, of a new "heat-loving" microbe. The microbe was found in a water sample from a hydrothermal vent deep in the Northeast Pacific Ocean. Its method of respiration involves reduction of Fe(III) to Fe(II) to produce energy.*

Science Source/Photo Researchers

Figure 21-10 Extremophiles that live in the harsh environment of deep-ocean thermal vents possess enzymes that are adapted to such harsh conditions.

21-8 Enzyme Inhibition

LEARNING FOCUS

Distinguish among the enzyme inhibition modes called *reversible competitive inhibition, reversible noncompetitive inhibition,* and *irreversible inhibition.*

▶ *The treatment for methanol poisoning involves giving a patient intravenous ethanol (Section 14-5). This action is based on the principle of competitive enzyme inhibition. The same enzyme, alcohol dehydrogenase, detoxifies both methanol and ethanol. Ethanol has 10 times the affinity for the enzyme than methanol has. Keeping the enzyme busy with ethanol as the substrate gives the body time to excrete the methanol before it is oxidized to the potentially deadly formaldehyde (Section 14-5).*

The rates of enzyme-catalyzed reactions can be *decreased* by a group of substances called inhibitors. An **enzyme inhibitor** *is a substance that slows or stops the normal catalytic function of an enzyme by binding to it.* In this section, three modes by which inhibition takes place are considered: reversible competitive inhibition, reversible noncompetitive inhibition, and irreversible inhibition.

Reversible Competitive Inhibition

In Section 21-5 it was noted that enzymes are quite specific about the molecules they accept at their active sites. Molecular shape and charge distribution are key determining factors in whether an enzyme accepts a molecule. A **competitive enzyme inhibitor** *is a molecule that sufficiently resembles an enzyme substrate in shape and charge distribution that it can compete with the substrate for occupancy of the enzyme's active site.*

When a competitive inhibitor binds to an enzyme active site, the inhibitor remains unchanged (no reaction occurs), but its physical presence at the site prevents a normal substrate molecule from occupying the site. The result is a decrease in enzyme activity.

The formation of an enzyme–competitive inhibitor complex is a reversible process because it is maintained by weak interactions (hydrogen bonds, etc.). With time (a fraction of a second), the complex breaks up. The empty active site is then available for a new occupant. Substrate and inhibitor again compete for the empty active site. Thus the active site of an enzyme binds either inhibitor or normal substrate on a random basis. If inhibitor concentration is greater than substrate concentration, the inhibitor dominates the occupancy process. The reverse is also true. Competitive inhibition can be reduced by simply increasing the concentration of the substrate.

Figure 21-11 compares the binding of a normal substrate and that of a competitive inhibitor at an enzyme's active site. Note that the portions of these two molecules that bind to the active site have the same shape, but that the two molecules differ in *overall* shape. It is because of this overall difference in shape that the substrate reacts at the active site but the inhibitor does not.

Numerous drugs act by means of competitive inhibition. For example, antihistamines are competitive inhibitors of histidine decarboxylation, the enzymatic reaction that converts histidine to histamine. Histamine causes the usual allergy and cold symptoms: watery eyes and runny nose.

Figure 21-11 A comparison of an enzyme with a substrate at its active site (a) and an enzyme with a competitive inhibitor at its active site (b).

Figure 21-12 The difference between a reversible competitive inhibitor and a reversible noncompetitive inhibitor.

ⓐ An enzyme–substrate complex in absence of an inhibitor.

ⓑ A competitive inhibitor binds to the active site, which prevents the normal substrate from binding to the site.

ⓒ A noncompetitive inhibitor binds to a site other than the active site; the normal substrate still binds to the active site but the enzyme cannot catalyze the reaction due to the presence of the inhibitor.

Reversible Noncompetitive Inhibition

A **noncompetitive enzyme inhibitor** *is a molecule that decreases enzyme activity by binding to a site on an enzyme other than the active site.* The substrate can still occupy the active site, but the presence of the inhibitor causes a change in the structure of the enzyme sufficient to prevent the catalytic groups at the active site from properly effecting their catalyzing action. Figure 21-12 contrasts the processes of reversible competitive inhibition and reversible noncompetitive inhibition.

Unlike the situation in competitive inhibition, increasing the concentration of substrate does not completely overcome the inhibitory effect in this case. However, lowering the concentration of a noncompetitive inhibitor sufficiently does free up many enzymes, which then return to normal activity.

Examples of noncompetitive inhibitors include the heavy metal ions Pb^{2+}, Ag^+, and Hg^{2+}. The binding sites for these ions are sulfhydryl (—SH) groups located away from the active site. Metal sulfide linkages are formed, an effect that disrupts secondary and tertiary structure.

Irreversible Inhibition

An **irreversible enzyme inhibitor** *is a molecule that inactivates enzymes by forming a strong covalent bond to an amino acid side-chain group at the enzyme's active site.* In general, such inhibitors do *not* have structures similar to that of the enzyme's normal substrate. The inhibitor–active site bond is sufficiently strong that addition of excess substrate does not reverse the inhibition process. Thus the enzyme is permanently deactivated. The actions of chemical warfare agents (nerve gases) and organophosphate insecticides are based on irreversible inhibition.

Chemistry at a Glance—Enzyme Inhibition—summarizes what has been considered concerning enzyme inhibition.

EXAMPLE 21-4

Identifying the Type of Enzyme Inhibition from Inhibitor Characteristics

Identify the type of enzyme inhibition each of the following inhibitor characteristics is associated with.

a. An inhibitor that decreases enzyme activity by binding to a site on the enzyme other than the active site

b. An inhibitor that inactivates enzymes by forming a strong covalent bond at the enzyme active site

(continued)

Solution

a. Inhibitor binding at a location other than the active site is a characteristic of a *reversible noncompetitive inhibitor.*

b. Covalent bond formation at the active site, with amino acid residues located there, is a characteristic of an *irreversible inhibitor.*

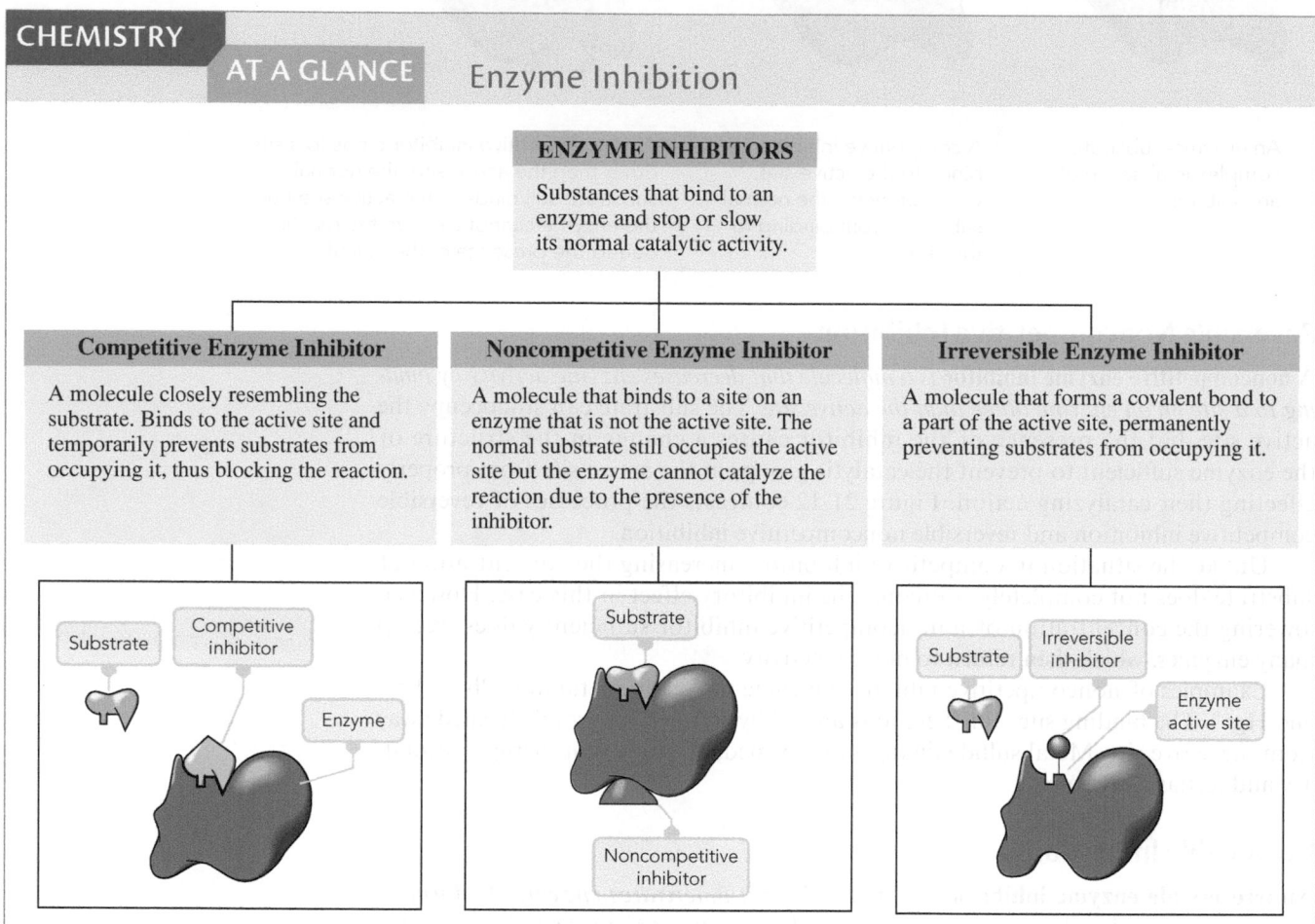

CHEMISTRY AT A GLANCE Enzyme Inhibition

ENZYME INHIBITORS

Substances that bind to an enzyme and stop or slow its normal catalytic activity.

Competitive Enzyme Inhibitor

A molecule closely resembling the substrate. Binds to the active site and temporarily prevents substrates from occupying it, thus blocking the reaction.

Noncompetitive Enzyme Inhibitor

A molecule that binds to a site on an enzyme that is not the active site. The normal substrate still occupies the active site but the enzyme cannot catalyze the reaction due to the presence of the inhibitor.

Irreversible Enzyme Inhibitor

A molecule that forms a covalent bond to a part of the active site, permanently preventing substrates from occupying it.

Section 21-8 Quick Quiz

1. Which of the following statements concerning a reversible competitive inhibitor is *incorrect*?
   a. resembles the substrate in shape
   b. binds at a site other than the active site
   c. its effect can be decreased by increasing the substrate concentration
   d. no correct response
2. Which of the following statements concerning an irreversible enzyme inhibitor is *incorrect*?
   a. forms a strong covalent bond to the active site
   b. permanently prevents normal substrate from entering the active site
   c. has a shape almost identical to that of normal substrate
   d. no correct response
3. Which of the following binds to an enzyme at a location other than the active site?
   a. irreversible inhibitor
   b. reversible competitive inhibitor
   c. reversible noncompetitive inhibitor
   d. no correct response

Answers: 1. b; 2. c; 3. c

21-9 Regulation of Enzyme Activity

LEARNING FOCUS

Understand common methods by which the activity of enzymes can be regulated; be familiar with the following concepts: allosteric enzyme, feedback control, zymogen, proteolytic enzyme, and covalent modification.

Regulation of enzyme activity within a cell is a necessity for many reasons. Illustrative of this need are the following two situations, both of which involve the concept of energy conservation.

1. A cell that continually produces large amounts of an enzyme for which substrate concentration is always very low is wasting energy. The production of the enzyme needs to be "turned off."
2. A product of an enzyme-catalyzed reaction that is present in plentiful (more than needed) amounts in a cell is a waste of energy if the enzyme continues to catalyze the reaction that produces the product. The enzyme needs to be "turned off."

Many mechanisms exist by which enzymes within a cell can be "turned on" and "turned off." In this section, three such mechanisms are considered: (1) feedback control associated with allosteric enzymes, (2) proteolytic enzymes and zymogens, and (3) covalent modification.

Allosteric Enzymes

Many, but not all, of the enzymes responsible for regulating cellular processes are *allosteric enzymes.* ◀ Characteristics of allosteric enzymes are as follows:

1. All allosteric enzymes have quaternary structure; that is, they are composed of two or more protein subunits.
2. All allosteric enzymes have two kinds of binding sites: those for substrate and those for regulators.
3. Active and regulatory binding sites are distinct from each other in both location and shape. In most cases the regulatory site is on one protein chain and the active site is on another.
4. Binding of a molecule at the regulatory site causes changes in the overall three-dimensional structure of the enzyme, including structural changes at the active site.

▶ *The term* allosteric *comes from the Greek* allo, *which means "other," and* stereos, *which means "site or space."*

Thus an **allosteric enzyme** *is an enzyme with two or more protein chains (quaternary structure) and two kinds of binding sites (substrate and regulator).*

Substances that bind at regulatory sites of allosteric enzymes are called *regulators.* The binding of a *positive regulator* increases enzyme activity; the shape of the active site is changed such that it can more readily accept substrate. The binding of a *negative regulator* (a noncompetitive inhibitor; Section 21-8) decreases enzyme activity; changes to the active site are such that substrate is less readily accepted. Figure 21-13 contrasts the different effects on an allosteric enzyme that positive and negative regulators produce. ◀

▶ *Some regulators of allosteric enzyme function are inhibitors (negative regulators), and some increase enzyme activity (positive regulators).*

Feedback Control

One of the mechanisms by which allosteric enzyme activity is regulated is feedback control. **Feedback control** *is a process in which activation or inhibition of the first reaction in a reaction sequence is controlled by a product of the reaction sequence.*

As illustrative of the feedback control mechanism, consider a biochemical process within a cell that occurs in several steps, each step catalyzed by a different enzyme. ◀

▶ *Most biochemical processes within cells take place in several steps rather than in a single step. A different enzyme is required for each step of the process.*

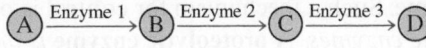

$$A \xrightarrow{\text{Enzyme 1}} B \xrightarrow{\text{Enzyme 2}} C \xrightarrow{\text{Enzyme 3}} D$$

The product of each step is the substrate for the next enzyme.

Figure 21-13 The differing effects of positive and negative regulators on an allosteric enzyme.

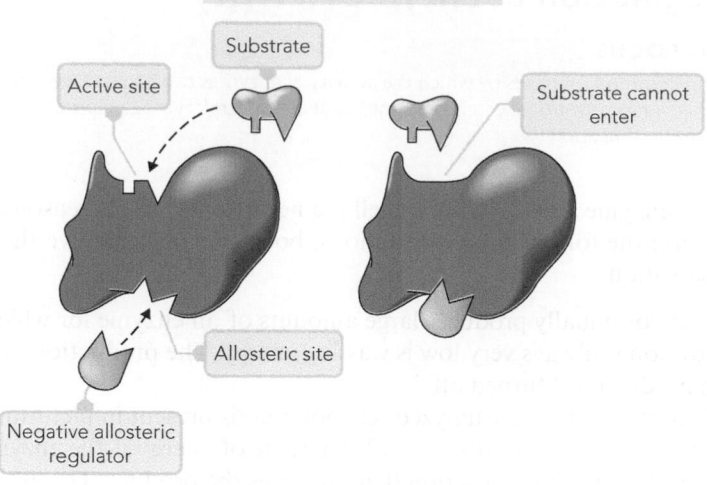

What will happen in this reaction series if the final product (D) is a negative regulator of the first enzyme (enzyme 1)? At low concentrations of D, the reaction sequence proceeds rapidly. At higher concentrations of D, the activity of enzyme 1 becomes inhibited (by feedback), and eventually the activity stops. At the stopping point, there is sufficient D present in the cell to meet its needs. Later, when the concentration of D decreases through use in other cell reactions, the activity of enzyme 1 increases and more D is produced. ◀

▶ *Feedback control is operative in devices that maintain a constant temperature, such as a furnace or an oven. If you set the control thermostat at 68°F, the furnace or oven produces heat until that temperature is reached, and then, through electronic feedback, the furnace or oven is shut off.*

Feedback control is not the only mechanism by which an allosteric enzyme can be regulated; it is just one of the more common ways. Regulators of a particular allosteric enzyme may be products of entirely different pathways of reaction within the cell, or they may even be compounds produced outside the cell (hormones). ◀

▶ *The general term* allosteric control *is often used to describe a process in which a regulatory molecule that binds at one site in an enzyme influences substrate binding at the active site in the enzyme.*

Proteolytic Enzymes and Zymogens

A second mechanism for regulating cellular enzyme activity is based on the production of enzymes in an inactive form. These inactive enzyme precursors are then "turned on" at the appropriate time. Such a mechanism for control is often encountered in the production of *proteolytic enzymes.* A **proteolytic enzyme** *is an enzyme that catalyzes*

Peptide fragment
to be removed

Activation

Zymogen
(inactive form of a
proteolytic enzyme)

Proteolytic enzyme
(an active enzyme)

Figure 21-14 Conversion of a zymogen (the inactive form of a proteolytic enzyme) to a proteolytic enzyme (the active form of the enzyme) often involves removal of a peptide chain segment from the zymogen structure.

the breaking of peptide bonds that maintain the primary structure of a protein. Because they would otherwise destroy the tissues that produce them, proteolytic enzymes are generated in an inactive form and then later, when they are needed, are converted to their active form. Most digestive and blood-clotting enzymes are proteolytic enzymes. The inactive forms of proteolytic enzymes are called *zymogens*. A **zymogen** *is the inactive precursor of a proteolytic enzyme.* (An alternative, but less often used, name for a zymogen is *proenzyme.*)

Activation of a zymogen requires an enzyme-controlled reaction that removes some part of the zymogen structure. Such modification changes the three-dimensional structure (secondary and tertiary structure) of the zymogen, which affects active site conformation. For example, the zymogen pepsinogen is converted to the active enzyme pepsin in the stomach, where it then functions as a digestive enzyme. Pepsin would digest the tissues of the stomach wall if it were prematurely generated in active form. Pepsinogen activation involves removal of a peptide fragment from its structure (Figure 21-14). ◄

▶ *The names of zymogens can be recognized by the suffix* -ogen *or the prefix* pre- *or* pro-.

Covalent Modification of Enzymes

A third mechanism for regulation of enzyme activity within a cell, called *covalent modification,* involves adding or removing a group from an enzyme through the forming or breaking of a covalent bond. **Covalent modification** *is a process in which enzyme activity is altered by covalently modifying the structure of the enzyme through attachment of a chemical group to or removal of a chemical group from a particular amino acid within the enzyme's structure.*

The most commonly encountered type of covalent modification involves the processes by which a phosphate group is added to or removed from an enzyme. The source of the added phosphate group is often an ATP molecule. The process of addition of the phosphate group to the enzyme is called *phosphorylation,* and the removal of the phosphate group from the enzyme is called *dephosphorylation.* This phosphorylation/dephosphorylation process is the off/on or on/off switch for the enzyme. For some enzymes, the active ("turned-on" form) is the phosphorylated version of the enzyme; however, for other enzymes, it is the dephosphorylated version that is active.

The preceding covalent modification processes are governed by other enzymes. *Protein kinases* effect the addition of phosphate groups, and *phosphatases* catalyze removal of the phosphate groups. Usually, the phosphate group is added to (or removed from) the R group of a serine, tyrosine, or threonine amino acid residue present in the protein (enzyme). The R groups of these three amino acids have a common structural feature, the presence of a free —OH group (see Table 21-1). The hydroxyl group is the site where phosphorylation or dephosphorylation occurs.

Glycogen phosphorylase, an enzyme involved in the breakdown of glycogen to glucose (Section 24-5), is activated by the addition of a phosphate group. *Glycogen synthase,* an enzyme involved in the synthesis of glycogen (Section 24-5), is deactivated by phosphorylation.

Section 21-9 Quick Quiz

1. Which of the following is an *incorrect* characterization for an allosteric enzyme?
   a. possesses quaternary structure
   b. substrate and regulator compete for the same binding site
   c. substrate and regulator occupy different binding sites
   d. no correct response
2. Enzyme activity regulation that involves a reaction sequence product inhibiting an enzyme in an earlier step in the reaction sequence is called
   a. negative regulator control
   b. feedback control
   c. covalent modification
   d. no correct response
3. Which of the following statements applies to a zymogen?
   a. inactive precursor of a proteolytic enzyme
   b. active form of a proteolytic enzyme
   c. substance that coverts an enzyme from an inactive form to an active form
   d. no correct response

Answers: 1. b; 2. b; 3. a

21-10 Prescription Drugs That Inhibit Enzyme Activity

LEARNING FOCUS
Be familiar with the mode of action for several enzyme-inhibiting prescription medications.

Several common types of prescription drugs have modes of action that involve enzyme inhibition. Included among them are ACE inhibitors, sulfa drugs, and penicillins. ACE inhibitors are used to treat high blood pressure conditions as well as several heart conditions. Sulfa drugs and penicillins are two well-known families of antibiotics. Discussion of how these three types of medications function in the human body, in terms of enzyme effects, is illustrative of how enzyme inhibition can be used in a positive manner in treating human disease.

ACE Inhibitors

The acronym ACE stands for *angiotensin-converting enzyme.* Angiotensin is an octapeptide hormone (Section 20-8) involved in blood pressure regulation. It increases blood pressure by narrowing blood vessels. Until needed, angiotensin is present in the body in an inactive form as the zymogen (Section 21-9) angiotensinogen, which is a decapeptide. ACE converts the inactive decapeptide zymogen to the active octapeptide form (angiotensin) by cleaving two amino acids from the zymogen structure.

Asp-Arg-Val-Tyr-Ile-His-Pro-Phe-His-Leu
(Angiotensinogen)

ACE

Asp-Arg-Val-Tyr-Ile-His-Pro-Phe + His-Leu
(Angiotensin)

ACE inhibitor medications block the action of ACE in converting angiotensinogen to angiotensin. The effect of this is a lower blood pressure than if the zymogen activation had occurred.

Representative of ACE inhibitors in use today is the compound lisinopril, a compound heavily prescribed for treatment of moderately elevated blood pressure conditions. Structurally, lisinopril is a 1-carboxy-3-phenylpropyl derivative of the dipeptide Lys-Pro.

Unlike most other ACE inhibitors, lisinopril is not metabolized (broken down) by liver enzymes; it is excreted unchanged in the urine. Interestingly, lisinopril, as well as several other ACE inhibitors, was first obtained from snake venom, the venom of the jararaca (a Brazilian pit viper).

Sulfa Drugs

The 1932 discovery of the antibacterial activity of the compound sulfanilamide by the German bacteriologist Gerhard Domagk (1895–1964) led to the characterization of a whole family of sulfanilamide derivatives collectively called sulfa drugs—the first "antibiotics" in the medical field.

An **antibiotic** *is a substance that kills bacteria or inhibits their growth.* Antibiotics exert their action selectively on bacteria and do not affect the normal metabolism of the host organism. Antibiotics usually inhibit specific enzymes essential to the life processes of the bacteria.

Sulfanilamide inhibits bacterial growth because it is structurally similar to PABA (*p*-aminobenzoic acid).

Many bacteria need PABA in order to produce an important coenzyme, folic acid. Sulfanilamide acts as a competitive inhibitor to enzymes in the biosynthetic pathway for converting PABA into folic acid in these bacteria. Folic acid deficiency retards growth of the bacteria and can eventually kill them.

Sulfa drugs selectively inhibit only bacteria metabolism and growth because humans absorb folic acid from their diet and thus do not use PABA for its synthesis. A few of the most common sulfa drugs and their structures are shown in Figure 21-15.

Penicillins

Penicillin, one of the most widely used antibiotics, was accidentally discovered by Alexander Fleming in 1928 while he was working with cultures of an infectious staphylococcus bacterium. A decade later, the scientists Howard Flory and Ernst Chain isolated penicillin in pure form and proved its effectiveness as an antibiotic.

Figure 21-15 Structures of selected sulfa drugs in use today as antibiotics.

General Structure of Sulfa Drugs	R Group Variations in Sulfa Drug Structures	
H_2N-⬡$-\overset{\overset{O}{\|\|}}{\underset{\overset{\|\|}{O}}{S}}-NH-R$	R = —H	Sulfanilamide
	R = $-\overset{\overset{O}{\|\|}}{C}-CH_3$	Sulfacetamide
	R = [isoxazole ring with CH₃ CH₃]	Sulfisoxazole
	R = [pyrimidine ring]	Sulfadiazine
	R = [pyrimidine ring with O—CH₃, O—CH₃]	Sulfadimethoxine

Increasing effectiveness against *E. coli* bacteria

Several naturally occurring penicillins have now been isolated, and numerous derivatives of these substances have been synthetically produced. All have structures containing a four-membered β-lactam ring (Section 17-12) fused with a five-membered thiazolidine ring (Figure 21-16). As with sulfa drugs, derivatives of the basic structure differ from each other in the identity of a particular R group.

Penicillins inhibit *transpeptidase,* an enzyme that catalyzes the formation of peptide cross-links between polysaccharide strands in bacterial cell walls. These cross-links strengthen cell walls. A strong cell wall is necessary to protect the bacterium from lysis (breaking open). By inhibiting transpeptidase, penicillin prevents the formation of a strong cell wall. Any osmotic or mechanical shock then causes lysis, killing the bacterium.

Penicillin's unique action depends on two aspects of enzyme deactivation that have been discussed before: structural similarity to the enzyme's natural substrate and irreversible inhibition. Penicillin is *highly specific* in binding to the active site of transpeptidase. In this sense, it acts as a very selective competitive inhibitor. However,

Figure 21-16 Structures of selected penicillins in use today as antibiotics.

General Structure of Penicillin	R Group Variations in Penicillin Structures	
β-lactam ring, Reactive amide bond, Thiazolidine ring [structure of penicillin core with $R-\overset{\overset{O}{\|\|}}{C}-NH$, S, CH₃, CH₃, N, O, COOH]	R = [benzene ring]—CH₂—	Penicillin G (benzyl penicillin)
	R = [benzene ring]—O—CH₂—	Penicillin V
	R = [benzene ring with O—CH₃, O—CH₃]	Methicillin
	R = [benzene ring]—CH—, NH₂	Ampicillin
	R = HO—[benzene ring]—CH—, NH₂	Amoxicillin
	R = [isoxazole ring with CH₃]	Oxacillin

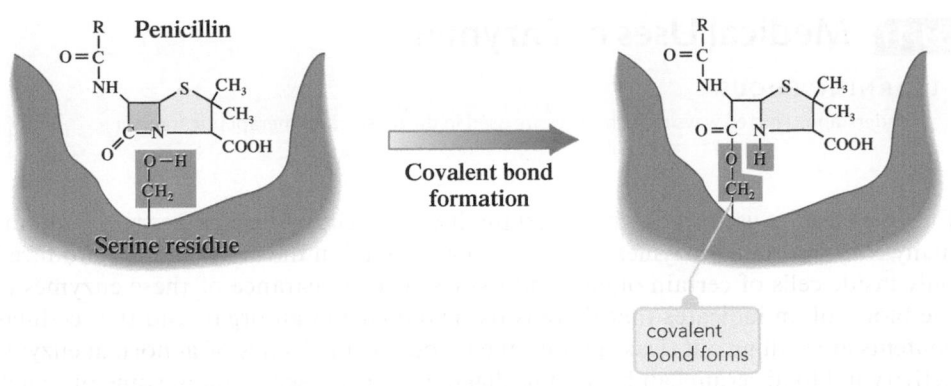

Figure 21-17 The selective binding of penicillin to the active site of transpeptidase. Subsequent irreversible inhibition through formation of a covalent bond to a serine residue permanently blocks the active site.

unlike a normal competitive inhibitor, once bound to the active site, the β-lactam ring opens as the highly reactive amide bond forms a covalent bond to a critical serine residue required for normal catalytic action. The result is an irreversibly inhibited transpeptidase enzyme (Figure 21-17).

Some bacteria produce the enzyme *penicillinase,* which protects them from penicillin. Penicillinase selectively binds penicillin and catalyzes the opening of the β-lactam ring before penicillin can form a covalent bond to the enzyme. Once the ring is opened, the penicillin is no longer capable of inactivating transpeptidase.

Certain semisynthetic penicillins such as methicillin and amoxicillin have been produced that are resistant to penicillinase activity and are thus clinically important.

Penicillin does not usually interfere with normal metabolism in humans because of its highly selective binding to bacterial transpeptidase. This selectivity makes penicillin an extremely useful antibiotic.

Food–Enzyme Interactions That Affect Prescription Medications

Liver enzymes known as *cytochrome P450s* are involved in the processes by which many prescription medications are metabolized in the body. It is now known that several foods and herbal remedies contain compounds that decrease (inhibit) the activity of these cytochrome P450 enzymes, thus decreasing the rate at which affected drugs are metabolized (deactivated and eliminated from the body). The net result of this slowing of enzyme action for affected drugs is that drug concentration in the bloodstream increases, sometimes to levels considered dangerous.

The most well-known and most studied of the known food–enzyme–drug interactions involves grapefruit and grapefruit juice, an interaction which is now called the "grapefruit effect." The focus on relevancy feature Chemical Connections 21-C—Enzymes, Prescription Medications and the "Grapefruit Effect"—explores the topic of how grapefruit and grapefruit juice affect numerous prescription medications.

Section 21-10 Quick Quiz

1. Inhibition of *angiotensin-converting enzyme* by the medication lisinopril is useful for
   a. treating moderately high blood pressure
   b. reducing inflammation
   c. treating bacterial infections
   d. no correct response
2. Inhibition of the enzyme *transpeptidase* is the mode of action for
   a. all antibiotics
   b. sulfa drugs
   c. penicillins
   d. no correct response

Answers: 1. a; 2. c

21-11 Medical Uses of Enzymes

LEARNING FOCUS

Understand selected ways that enzymes are used in diagnostic and therapeutic medicine.

Enzymes can be used to diagnose certain diseases. Although blood serum contains many enzymes, some enzymes are not normally found in the blood but are produced only inside cells of certain organs and tissues. The appearance of these enzymes in the blood often indicates that there is tissue damage in an organ and that cellular contents are spilling out (leaking) into the bloodstream. Assays of abnormal enzyme activity in blood serum can be used to diagnose many disease states, some of which are listed in Table 21-3.

Enzyme concentrations can be useful in obtaining information about a heart attack. The symptoms of a major heart attack are most often obvious and include irregular breathing and pain in the left chest that may radiate to the neck, left shoulder, and arm. Initial diagnosis of the heart attack is based on these and other physical symptoms, and treatment is initiated on this basis. Less serious heart attack situations, where all of the obvious symptoms may not be present, are harder to diagnose and blood enzyme information is very useful in such situations.

The blood levels of three enzymes are commonly assayed in heart attack situations: creatine phosphokinase (CPK), aspartate aminotransferase (AST), and lactate dehydrogenase (LDH). The levels of these three enzymes, which enter the bloodstream in increased amounts after heart muscle damage associated with a heart attack, show characteristic patterns of rising and falling after the heart attack as is shown in Figure 21-18. Analysis of such patterns of enzyme concentration changes leads to information on extent of heart muscle damage.

When clinical laboratories receive a blood sample for enzymatic analysis, they do not directly measure enzyme concentrations. Instead, they measure reaction rate for reactions that the enzymes catalyze. For example, the concentration of *lactate dehydrogenase (LDH)* in blood can be indirectly determined by adding pyruvic acid to the sample of blood and determining how fast the pyruvic acid is converted to lactic acid.

Table 21-3 Selected Blood Enzyme Assays Used in Diagnostic Medicine

Enzyme	Condition Indicated by Abnormal Level
lactate dehydrogenase (LDH)	heart disease, liver disease
creatine phosphokinase (CPK)	heart disease
aspartate aminotransferase (AST)	heart disease, liver disease, muscle damage
alanine aminotransferase (ALT)	heart disease, liver disease, muscle damage
gamma-glutamyl transpeptidase (GGTP)	heart disease, liver disease
alkaline phosphatase (ALP)	bone disease, liver disease

Figure 21-18 Blood levels of the enzymes CPK, AST, and LDH as a function of time after a heart attack has occurred.

CHEMICAL CONNECTIONS 21-C

Enzymes, Prescription Medications, and the "Grapefruit Effect"

Grapefruit and grapefruit juice are excellent sources of healthful compounds such as vitamin C and lycopene. The vitamin C content of half a grapefruit can be up to 80% of the recommended daily amount of this vitamin. The pink and red colors of grapefruit are due to the carotenoid lycopene (Section 13-7). Among the common dietary carotenoids, lycopene has one of the highest antioxidant activities (Section 14-14). Antioxidant activity is important in controlling oxygen free radicals, which are substances that can cause significant cellular damage.

Grapefruit and grapefruit juice also contain compounds that can slow down the metabolism of several common prescription medications by interacting with (inhibiting) the enzymes needed for their metabolism—liver enzymes called *cytochrome P450s*. This enzyme inhibition, known as the "grapefruit effect," leads to increased concentrations of the affected drugs in the bloodstream, which increases the risk of potentially serious side effects from the drugs.

Grapefruit and grapefruit juice contain several healthful compounds (vitamin C, lycopene, etc.), as well as a compound that, through enzyme interaction, can adversely affect the breakdown of prescription medications within the body.

More than 50 medications of diverse types are now known to be affected by the "grapefruit effect" including

1. Procardia, a high blood pressure medication
2. Lipitor, a high cholesterol medication
3. Cyclosporin, an immunosuppressant
4. Zoloft, an antidepressant
5. Cordarone, an antiarrhythmic heart medication

This grapefruit effect is significant enough that the United States Food and Drug Administration (FDA) now requires that all new medications be tested for problems arising from grapefruit interactions before the medication is approved for use. Drugs whose metabolism is affected by grapefruit and grapefruit juice must carry warnings in their patient information sheets.

The actual compounds responsible for the grapefruit effect have been identified. They are the compound bergamottin and one of its metabolites (a dihydroxyderivative of bergamottin). Both compounds have a fused three-ring structure containing ether and ester functional groups to which an unsaturated carbon chain is attached.

Bergamottin

6',7'-Dihydroxybergamottin

Bergamottin and its metabolite exert their effect by a process called *suicide inactivation:* The cytochrome P450 enzyme transforms them into highly reactive intermediates, which then react with (inhibit) the enzyme. The inhibiting interaction involves modification of a glutamine residue (an amino acid residue; Section 20-2) on the enzyme's surface; it is not the enzyme's active site that is affected.

Normally, the grapefruit effect is thought of as a negative interaction. There is, however, a potentially positive side to this effect. Several research studies underway are exploring the possibility of using bergamottin, its dihydroxy derivative, and synthetic analogs to increase the oral availability of drugs that would otherwise have limited use because they are metabolized too rapidly. In such a case, the dose required to achieve a required effective bloodstream concentration of the drug would be lowered, thus increasing the drug's usefulness.

There are also potential solutions in the offering for "grapefruit lovers" whose medications prevent them from consuming a desired food. Several research projects are underway whose goal is to remove bergamottin from grapefruit juice. One approach involves genetic engineering (Section 22-15) of grapefruit trees so that they produce fruit that does not contain bergamottin. Another approach seeks methods to remove bergamottin from grapefruit juice after the fact. This latter approach is a parallel idea to that which led to decaffeinated coffee; de-bergamottined grapefruit juice could someday be available for consumption.

Enzymes can also be used in the treatment of diseases. A recent advance in treating heart attacks is the use of tissue plasminogen activator (TPA), which activates the enzyme plasminogen. When so activated, this enzyme dissolves blood clots in the heart and often provides immediate relief.

Another medical use for enzymes is in clinical laboratory chemical analysis. For example, no simple direct test for the measurement of urea in the blood is available. However, if the urea in the blood is converted to ammonia via the enzyme *urease,* the ammonia produced, which is easily measured, becomes an indicator of urea. This *blood urea nitrogen (BUN) test* is a common clinical laboratory procedure. High urea levels in the blood indicate kidney malfunction.

Section 21-11 Quick Quiz

1. Measurement of blood levels for the enzymes LDH, CPK, and AST is useful in determining
   a. extent of heart muscle damage in heart attacks
   b. the location of blood clots
   c. urea levels in the blood
   d. no correct response
2. Use of the enzyme tissue plasminogen activator (TPA) is useful in
   a. assessing heart muscle damage in heart attacks
   b. dissolving blood clots
   c. determining kidney malfunction
   d. no correct response

Answers: 1. a; 2. b

21-12 General Characteristics of Vitamins

LEARNING FOCUS

Know the general definition for a vitamin and be familiar with general properties for water-soluble and fat-soluble vitamins.

This section and those that follow deal with vitamins. Vitamins are considered in conjunction with enzymes because many enzymes contain vitamins as part of their structure. Recall from Section 21-2 that conjugated enzymes have a protein part (apoenzyme) and a nonprotein part (cofactor). Vitamins, in many cases, are cofactors in conjugated enzymes.

A **vitamin** *is an organic compound, essential in small amounts for the proper functioning of the human body, that must be obtained from dietary sources because the body cannot synthesize it.*

Vitamins differ from the major classes of nutrients in foods (carbohydrates, lipids, and proteins) in the amount required; for vitamins, it is *micro*gram to *milli*gram quantities per day compared with 50–200 grams per day for the major food nutrients categories. To better understand the small amount of vitamins needed by the human body, consider the recommended daily allowance (RDA) of vitamin B_{12}, which is 2.0 μg per day for an adult. Just 1.0 g of this vitamin could theoretically supply the daily needs of 500,000 people.

A well-balanced diet usually meets all the body's vitamin requirements. However, supplemental vitamins are often required for women during pregnancy and for people recovering from certain illnesses. ◀

One of the most common myths associated with the nutritional aspects of vitamins is that vitamins from natural sources are superior to synthetic vitamins. In truth, synthetic vitamins, manufactured in the laboratory, are identical to the vitamins found in foods. The body cannot tell the difference and gets the same benefits from either source.

There are 13 known vitamins, and scientists believe that the discovery of additional vitamins is unlikely. Despite searches for new vitamins, it has been more than 70 years since the last of the known vitamins (folate) was discovered (see Table 21-4). Strong evidence that the vitamin family is complete comes from the fact that many people have

▶ *The spelling of the term* vitamin *was originally* vitamine, *a word derived from the Latin* vita, *meaning "life," and from the fact that these substances were all thought to contain the amine functional group. When this supposition was found to be false, the final* e *was dropped from* vitamine, *and the term* vitamin *came into use. Some vitamins contain amine functional groups, but others do not.*

Table 21-4 **The Discovery Dates of the 13 Known Vitamins. (Years can vary in different tabulations depending on the definition of "discovery.")**

Year of Discovery	Vitamin
1910	Thiamin
1913	Vitamin A
1920	Vitamin C
1920	Vitamin D
1920	Riboflavin
1922	Vitamin E
1926	Vitamin B_{12}
1929	Vitamin K
1931	Pantothenic acid
1931	Biotin
1934	Vitamin B_6
1936	Niacin
1941	Folate

lived for years being fed, intravenously, solutions containing the known vitamins and nutrients, and they have not developed any disease resulting from a nutritional deficiency.

Solubility characteristics divide the vitamins into two major classes: the water-soluble vitamins and the fat (lipid)-soluble vitamins. There are nine water-soluble vitamins and four fat-soluble vitamins. Table 21-5 lists the vitamins in each of these solubility categories. Water-soluble vitamins must be constantly replenished in the body because they are rapidly eliminated from the body in the urine. They are carried in the bloodstream, are needed in frequent, small doses, and are unlikely to be toxic except when taken in unusually large doses. The fat-soluble vitamins are found dissolved in lipid materials. They are, in general, carried in the blood by protein carriers, are stored in fat tissues, are needed in periodic doses, and are more likely to be toxic when consumed in excess of need.

An important difference exists, in terms of function, between water-soluble and fat-soluble vitamins. Water-soluble vitamins function as coenzymes for a number of important biochemical reactions in humans, animals, and microorganisms. Fat-soluble vitamins generally do not function as coenzymes in humans and animals and are rarely utilized in any manner by microorganisms. Other differences between the two categories of vitamins are summarized in Table 21-6. A few exceptions occur, but the differences shown in this table are generally valid.

Table 21-5 **The Water-Soluble and Fat-Soluble Vitamins**

Water-Soluble Vitamins	Fat-Soluble Vitamins
Vitamin C	Vitamin A
Thiamin	Vitamin D
Riboflavin	Vitamin E
Niacin	Vitamin K
Pantothenic acid	
Vitamin B_6	
Biotin	
Folate	
Vitamin B_{12}	

▶ **Table 21-6** **The General Properties of Water-Soluble Vitamins and Fat-Soluble Vitamins**

	Water-Soluble Vitamins (B vitamins and vitamin C)	Fat-Soluble Vitamins (vitamins A, D, E, and K)
absorption	directly into the blood	first enter into the lymph system
transport	travel without carriers	many require protein carriers
storage	circulate in the water-filled parts of the body	found in the cells associated with fat
excretion	kidneys remove excess in urine	tend to remain in fat-storage sites
toxicity	not likely to reach toxic levels when consumed from supplements	likely to reach toxic levels when consumed from supplements
dosage frequency	needed in frequent doses	needed in periodic doses
relationship to coenzymes	function as coenzymes	do not function as coenzymes

Section 21-12 Quick Quiz

1. The number of known vitamins is
   a. 10
   b. 13
   c. 15
   d. no correct answer
2. Which of the following statements concerning the known vitamins is *correct*?
   a. Some are inorganic compounds and others are organic compounds.
   b. Some, but not all, can be synthesized in the human body in adequate amounts.
   c. All are organic compounds that must be obtained from dietary intake of food.
   d. no correct response
3. Which of the following is a water-soluble vitamin?
   a. Vitamin A
   b. Vitamin C
   c. Vitamin D
   d. no correct response

Answers: 1. b; 2. c; 3. b

21-13 Water-Soluble Vitamins: Vitamin C

LEARNING FOCUS
Know the structural characteristics of and biochemical functions for vitamin C.

▶ *Vitamin C, the best known of all vitamins, was the first to be structurally characterized (1933), and the first to be synthesized in the laboratory (1933). Laboratory production of vitamin C, which exceeds 80 million pounds per year, is greater than the combined production of all the other vitamins. In addition to its use as a vitamin supplement, synthetic vitamin C is used as a food additive (preservative), a flour additive, and an animal feed additive.*

Vitamin C, which has the simplest structure of the 13 vitamins, exists in two active forms in the human body: an oxidized form and a reduced form.

L-Ascorbic acid (reduced) ⇌ (Oxidation / Reduction) L-Dehydroascorbic acid (oxidized) + 2H

This simple compound can be made from glucose derivatives by all plants and most animals. However, human beings, primates, fruit bats, and guinea pigs cannot biosynthesize the compound and, hence, must obtain it from dietary intake. ◀

Vitamin C's biosynthesis involves L-gulonic acid, an acid derivative of the monosaccharide L-gulose (see Figure 18-13). L-Gulonic acid is changed by the enzyme *lactonase* into a cyclic ester (lactone, Section 16-12); ring closure involves carbons 1 and 4. An *oxidase* then introduces a double bond into the ring, producing L-ascorbic acid. ◀

COOH
HO—H
HO—H
H—OH
HO—H
CH₂OH

L-Gulonic acid

→ Lactonase →

γ-L-Gulonolactone

→ Oxidase →

L-Ascorbic acid (reduced)

▶ *Why is vitamin C called ascorbic acid when there is no carboxyl group (acid group) present in its structure? Vitamin C is a cyclic ester in which the carbon 1 carboxyl group has reacted with a carbon 4 hydroxyl group, forming the ring structure.*

The four —OH groups present in vitamin C's reduced form are suggestive of its biosynthetic monosaccharide (*polyhydroxy* aldehyde) origins. Its chemical name, L-ascorbic acid, correctly indicates that vitamin C is a weak acid. Although no carboxyl group is present, the carbon 3 hydroxyl group hydrogen atom exhibits acidic behavior as a result of its attachment to an unsaturated carbon atom.

In human beings, an intake of 100 mg/day of vitamin C saturates all body tissues with the compound. After tissue saturation, all additional vitamin C is rapidly metabolized and excreted in the urine. The RDA for vitamin C varies from country to country. It is 30 mg/day in Great Britain, 60 mg/day in the United States and Canada, and 75 mg/day in Germany. A variety of fruits and vegetables have relatively high vitamin C content (see Figure 21-19).

Important biochemical functions for vitamin C in the human body include the following:

1. **Collagen Synthesis:** Vitamin C functions as a cosubstrate in the formation of the structural protein collagen (Section 20-16), which makes up much of the skin, ligaments, and tendons and also serves as the matrix on which bone and teeth are formed. Specifically, biosynthesis of the amino acids hydroxyproline and hydroxylysine (important in binding collagen fibers together) from proline and lysine requires the presence of both vitamin C and iron. Iron serves as a cofactor in the reaction, and vitamin C maintains iron in the oxidation state that allows it to function. In this role, vitamin C is functioning as a *specific* antioxidant.

2. **General Antioxidant:** Besides being a *specific* antioxidant, vitamin C has several *general* antioxidant (Section 14-14) functions for water-soluble substances in the blood and other body fluids. One way it acts as a general antioxidant is by "recharging" spent enzymes that contain metal atoms. For example, in iron-containing enzymes the iron present in the enzyme is changed from Fe^{2+} to Fe^{3+} as the enzyme acts on a substrate. For the enzyme to function again, the Fe^{3+} must be changed back to Fe^{2+}. Vitamin C has the ability to facilitate this change by donating electrons to the iron-containing enzyme, converting the Fe^{3+} back to Fe^{2+}. In this "recharging" of the enzyme, vitamin C, itself is "spent," being converted from its reduced form to its oxidized form. Several mechanisms exist for the recharging of the vitamin C, converting it back to its reduced form. Niacin, one of the B vitamins (Section 21-14) in the form of its coenzyme NADH, and glutathione (Section 20-8), in its reduced state, are two such substances that can regenerate spent vitamin C. ◀

   Vitamin C's antioxidant properties are also beneficial for several other vitamins. The active form of vitamin E is regenerated by vitamin C, and it also helps keep the active form of folate (a B vitamin) in its reduced state. Because of its antioxidant properties, vitamin C is often added to foods as a preservative.

3. **Synthesis of Neurotransmitters:** Synthesis of the neurotransmitters dopamine and norepinephrine (Section 17-10) from the amino acid tyrosine (Table 20-1) and the neurotransmitter serotonin (Section 17-10) from the amino acid tryptophan (Table 20-1) depend on the presence of vitamin C. Its function is the previously mentioned recharging of spent iron-containing enzymes.

© Chamille White/Shutterstock.com

Figure 21-19 Rows of cabbage plants. Although many people think citrus fruits (50 mg per 100 g) are the best source of vitamin C, peppers (128 mg per 100 g), cauliflower (70 mg per 100 g), strawberries (60 mg per 100 g), and spinach or cabbage (60 mg per 100 g) are all richer in vitamin C.

▶ *Other naturally occurring dietary antioxidants include glutathione (Section 20-8), vitamin E (Section 21-15), beta-carotene (Section 21-15), and flavonoids (Section 23-11).*

Section 21-13 Quick Quiz

1. Which of the following statements concerning vitamin C is *incorrect*?
   a. Its structure is the simplest of all vitamin structures.
   b. It exists in both an oxidized form and a reduced form.
   c. It has very limited solubility in water.
   d. no correct response
2. Which of the following statements about biosynthesis of vitamin C is *incorrect*?
   a. All plants can biosynthesize vitamin C.
   b. Some, but not all, animals as well as human beings can biosynthesize vitamin C.
   c. Human beings as well as a few animals cannot biosynthesize vitamin C.
   d. no correct response
3. In the "recharging" of a metal-containing enzyme by vitamin C, the charge on metal ions present is
   a. increased
   b. decreased
   c. neutralized
   d. no correct response

Answers: 1. c; 2. b; 3. b

21-14 Water-Soluble Vitamins: The B Vitamins

LEARNING FOCUS
Know general structural characteristics for and biochemical functions of the various B vitamins.

There are nine water-soluble vitamins (Table 21-5). One is called vitamin C (Section 21-13). The other eight are grouped together and are called B vitamins. This grouping is based on biochemical function. All of the B vitamins serve as *precursors for enzyme cofactors*. Vitamin C is not an enzyme cofactor precursor.

Nomenclature for B Vitamins

Perhaps the most confusing aspect of the chemistry of B vitamins is their nomenclature. Nomenclature in use today is a combination of three different nomenclature systems that have evolved over time. Early on in vitamin chemistry research, it was thought that only two vitamins existed—a fat-soluble one (designated as vitamin A) and a water-soluble one (designated as vitamin B). When further research showed that there were several fat-soluble vitamins and even more water-soluble vitamins, naming continued in an alphabetical manner (vitamin A, B, C, D, E, F, G, etc.). With the discovery of the similarity in function (coenzyme precursors) of the water-soluble vitamins (except vitamin C), the coenzyme vitamins were all renamed as numbered B vitamins (B_1, B_2, B_3, etc.). Later, the numbered B vitamin system was replaced with a system that gave common names to the B vitamins. ◀ The currently *preferred* names for the B vitamins (alternative names in parentheses) are

▶ *Pronunciation guidelines for the common names of the B vitamins:*

    THIGH-a-min
    RYE-boh-flay-vin
    NIGH-a-sin
    PAN-toe-THEN-ick acid
    PEER-a-DOX-all
    BYE-oat-in
    FOAL-ate
    CO-ball-a-min

1. Thiamin (vitamin B_1)
2. Riboflavin (vitamin B_2)
3. Niacin (nicotinic acid, nicotinamide, vitamin B_3)
4. Pantothenic acid (vitamin B_5)
5. Vitamin B_6 (pyridoxine, pyridoxal, pyridoxamine)
6. Biotin (vitamin B_7)
7. Folate (folic acid, vitamin B_9)
8. Vitamin B_{12} (cobalamin)

An additional nomenclatural complication, which shows up indirectly in the preceding listing, is that in early research several substances were mistakenly characterized as vitamins. Note that no vitamin B_4 or vitamin B_8 entry is found in the previous listing. The substance originally identified as vitamin B_4 was later found to be adenine, a DNA metabolite (Section 22-3), and vitamin B_8 was found to be adenylic acid, another DNA metabolite. Thus "vitamins" B_4 and B_8 dropped out of the system.

The following two examples illustrate the changing nature of B vitamin nomenclature:

1. Vitamin G became vitamin B_2, which became riboflavin.
2. Vitamin H became vitamin B_7, which became biotin.

Structural Characteristics of the B Vitamins

The structural form(s) in which B vitamins are found in food is (are) not the form(s) in which they are used in the human body. As mentioned previously, B vitamins serve as *precursors* for enzyme cofactors. The "active form" for vitamins in the body is their enzyme cofactor form, to which they are converted once they are obtained from food through digestion of the food. As structural aspects of the various B vitamins are now considered, emphasis is given to the chemical modifications that occur as the "free" vitamins are converted to enzyme cofactor form(s), that is, to their active forms in the human body.

Thiamin (Vitamin B_1)

The structures for the "free" and coenzyme form of thiamin are as follows:

Thiamin (vitamin B_1)   Thiamin pyrophosphate (TPP)

"Free" thiamin's structure consists of a central carbon atom to which is attached a six-membered heterocylic amine and a five-membered thiazole (sulfur-nitrogen) ring system. The name *thiamin* comes from "thio," which means "sulfur" and "amine" which refers to the numerous amine groups present.

The coenzyme form of thiamin is called thiamin pyrophosphate (TPP), a molecule in which a pyrophosphate group (two phosphates bonded to each other) has been attached to the side chain. The coenzyme TPP is needed in step 4 of the citric acid cycle (decarboxylation of an α-keto acid; Section 23-7) and also in the conversion of pyruvate to acetyl CoA (Section 24-3).

Riboflavin (Vitamin B_2)

Riboflavin's structure involves three fused six-membered rings (two of which contain nitrogen) with the monosaccharide ribose (Section 18-9) attached to the middle ring.

Riboflavin

Riboflavin was once called the "yellow vitamin" because of its color. Its name comes from its color (*flavin* means "yellow" in Latin) and its ribose component.

Two important riboflavin-based coenzymes exist: flavin adenine dinucleotide (FAD) and flavin mononucleotide (FMN). (Detailed structural information for FAD is given in Section 23-3 and for FMN in Section 23-7.) Both coenzymes are involved with oxidation–reduction reactions in which hydrogen atoms are transferred from one molecule to another.

Niacin (Vitamin B₃)

Niacin occurs in food in two different, but similar, forms: nicotinic acid and nicotinamide.

Nicotinic acid   Nicotinamide

Both forms convert to the same coenzymes, two of which will be encountered repeatedly in Chapters 23–26: nicotinamide adenine dinucleotide (NAD^+) and nicotinamide adenine dinucleotide phosphate ($NADP^+$). Detailed structural information for these two coenzymes is found, respectively, in Sections 23-3 and 24-8. Both coenzymes are involved with oxidation–reduction reactions in which hydrogen atoms are transferred from one molecule to another. ◄

The nicotinic acid form of niacin was first described in 1873, long before the concept of vitamins was known. It was prepared by oxidizing nicotine using nitric acid; hence the name nicotinic acid. When the biological significance of nicotinic acid was realized, the name niacin was coined to disassociate this vitamin from the name nicotine and to avoid the perception that niacin-rich foods contain nicotine or that cigarettes contain vitamins. The name *niacin* is derived in the following manner.

nicotinic acid + vitamin

Pantothenic Acid (Vitamin B₅)

The name pantothenic acid is based on the Greek word "pantothen," which means "from everywhere." This vitamin is found in almost every plant and animal tissue. The structure of pantothenic acid is

Pantothenic acid

This structure can be envisioned as an amide (Section 17-16) formed from the reaction of β-alanine (an amino acid; Section 20-2) and pantoic acid (2,4-dihydroxy-3,3-dimethylbutanoic acid), a carboxylic acid (Section 16-4).

Coenzyme A (CoA), one of the most used of all vitamin B coenzymes, contains pantothenic acid as part of its structure. Coenzyme A is required in the metabolism of carbohydrates, lipids, and proteins, where it is involved in the transfer of acetyl groups (Section 23-3) between molecules. Structural details for coenzyme A are given in Section 23-3. Another pantothenic-acid-containing coenzyme is acyl carrier protein (ACP), which may be regarded as a "giant coenzyme A molecule." ACP is important in the biosynthesis of fatty acids (Section 25-7).

► A major study, released in 2013, indicates that the long-standing commonly used practice of taking supplemental niacin as a means for lowering "bad" LDL cholesterol and increasing "good" HBL cholesterol (Section 20-19) does not have the intended benefit of improved cardiovascular health. Patients taking supplemental niacin showed no reduction in the rate of heart problems such as heart attacks and strokes when compared to those not taking additional niacin. Additionally, in some niacin users significant adverse side effects were observed, including higher risk of bleeding, infections, and new-onset type 2 diabetes.

Vitamin B$_6$ (Pyridoxine, Pyridoxal, and Pyridoxamine)

Vitamin B$_6$ is a collective term for three related compounds: pyridoxine (found in foods of plant origin) and pyridoxal and pyridoxamine (found in foods of animal origin). The coenzyme forms of these three compounds, which contain an added phosphate group, are related to each other in the same manner that the "free" forms are related to each other—alcohol functional group versus aldehyde functional group versus amine functional group. Structures for the vitamin B$_6$ "free" and "active" forms are as follows:

Vitamin B$_6$ coenzymes participate in reactions where amino groups are transferred between molecules. Such transfer occurs repeatedly when protein molecules are metabolized.

Biotin (Vitamin B$_7$)

Biotin is unique among the B vitamins in that it can be obtained both from dietary intake and also via biotin-producing bacteria (micro*biota*, hence the name *biotin*) present in the human large intestine. Structurally, biotin is a fused two-ring system with one ring containing sulfur and the other ring containing nitrogen. Attached to the sulfur-containing ring is a pentanoic acid residue.

"Free" biotin is biologically active. However, its principal active forms involve coenzymes formed when the carboxyl group of biotin's pentanoic acid forms an amide linkage with a residue of the amino acid lysine present at an enzyme's active site.

As a coenzyme, biotin participates in carboxylation reactions, reactions in which a carboxyl group is added to a molecule. For example, a biotin-containing enzyme is needed in the conversion of pyruvate to oxaloacetate (Section 26-5), a reaction that occurs as amino acids are broken down during protein metabolism.

Folate (Vitamin B₉)

Several forms of folate are found in foods. All of them have structures that consist of three parts: (1) a nitrogen-containing double-ring system (pteridine), (2) para-aminobenzoic acid (PABA), and (3) one or more residues of the amino acid glutamate. When only one glutamate residue is present, as is shown in the following structure, the folate is called *folic acid*.

Folic acid

In food, about 90% of the folate molecules have three or more glutamate residues present; such molecules are called *polyglutamates*. The green circles in the following structures denote glutamate residues.

Folic acid   a polyglutamate

The active coenzyme form of folate, which is known as tetrahydrofolate (THF), has only one glutamate, and four hydrogen atoms have been added to the double-ring nitrogen system.

Folic acid   Tetrahydrofolate (THF)

THF is needed in methylation reactions, reactions in which one or more methyl groups are transferred from one molecule to another.

The name *folate* comes from the Latin word "folium," which means "leaf." Dark green leafy vegetables are the best natural source for folate. Legislation that dates back to the 1940s requires that all grain products that cross state lines be enriched in thiamin, riboflavin, and niacin. Folate was added to the legislated enrichment list in 1996 when research showed that folate was essential in the prevention of certain birth defects.

Vitamin B₁₂ (Cobalamin)

The name *cobalamin* comes from the fact that an atom of the metal cobalt and numerous amine groups are present in the structure of vitamin B₁₂, which is by far the most complex of all vitamin structures. Vitamin B₁₂ is unique in that it is the only vitamin that contains a metal atom. As shown in the following two structures, "free" vitamin

B_{12} and coenzyme vitamin B_{12} differ only in one attachment to the cobalt atom; the free form is *cyano*cobalamin, and the coenzyme form is *methyl*cobalamin.

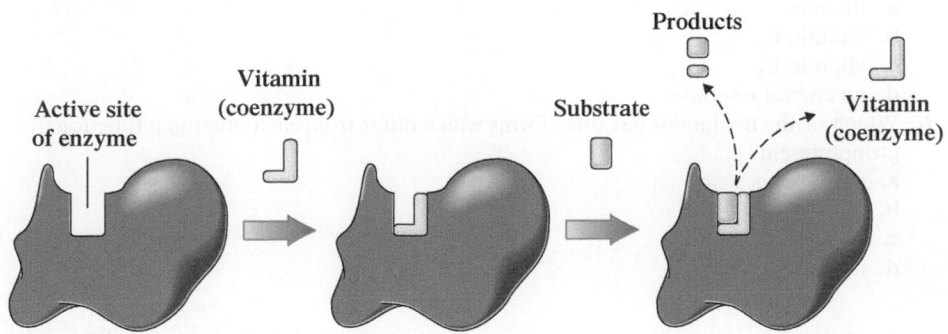

Cyanocobalamin   Methylcobalamin

Functionally, B_{12} coenzymes participate in the transfer of alkyl groups and hydrogen atoms from one molecule to another. One reaction that it is involved with is the production of succinyl CoA, an intermediate in the citric acid cycle (Section 23-7).

Vitamin B_{12} is also unique among vitamins in that only microorganisms can produce it; it cannot be made by plants, animals, birds, or humans. Grazing animals acquire vitamin B_{12} by ingesting some soil during the grazing process. Bacteria present in the multi-compartment stomachs of cows and sheep can also produce vitamin B_{12}. Humans must obtain vitamin B_{12} from foods of animal origin or from ready-to-eat breakfast cereals, many of which are now fortified with this vitamin.

B Vitamin Summary

Table 21-7 summarizes the B-vitamin coenzyme chemistry presented in this section. In general terms, vitamin B-containing coenzymes serve as *temporary* carriers of atoms or functional groups in redox and group transfer reactions associated with the metabolism of ingested food in order to obtain energy from the food. The details of metabolic reactions as they occur in the human body are the subject matter of Chapters 23–26.

In their function as coenzymes, B vitamins usually do not remain permanently bonded to the apoenzyme (Section 21-2) that they are associated with. This means that they can be repeatedly used by various enzymes. This reuse (recycling) diminishes the need for large amounts of the B vitamins in biochemical systems. Figure 21-20 shows diagrammatically how a vitamin is used and then released in an enzyme-catalyzed reaction.

Figure 21-20 Many enzymes require a vitamin-based coenzyme in order to be active. After the catalytic action, the vitamin is released and can be reused.

▶ Table 21-7 **Selected Important Coenzymes in Which B Vitamins Are Present**

B Vitamin	Coenzymes	Groups Transferred
thiamin	thiamin pyrophosphate (TPP)	carbon dioxide (carbonyl group)
riboflavin	flavin mononucleotide (FMN) flavin adenine dinucleotide (FAD)	hydrogen atoms
niacin	nicotinamide adenine dinucleotide (NAD^+) nicotinamide adenine dinucleotide phosphate ($NADP^+$)	hydrogen atoms
pantothenic acid	coenzyme A (CoA)	acyl groups
vitamin B_6	pyridoxal-5′-phosphate (PLP) pyridoxine-5′-phosphate (PNP) pyridoxamine-5′-phosphate (PMP)	amino groups
biotin	biotin	carbon dioxide (carboxyl group)
folate	tetrahydrofolate (THF)	one-carbon groups other than CO_2
vitamin B_{12}	methylcobalamin	methyl groups, hydrogen atoms

Section 21-14 Quick Quiz

1. Which of the following statements concerning the B vitamins is *correct*?
   a. They all have similar chemical structures.
   b. All except two of them are water soluble.
   c. All of them have preferred names that start with the letter B.
   d. no correct response
2. The major biochemical function for B vitamins within the human body is as
   a. antioxidants
   b. precursors for enzyme cofactors
   c. regulators for allosteric enzymes
   d. no correct response
3. Which of the B vitamins has a name that draws attention to the presence of sulfur and nitrogen in its molecular structure?
   a. pantothenic acid
   b. thiamine
   c. riboflavin
   d. no correct response
4. Which of the B vitamins has a name that draws attention to its production by intestinal bacteria?
   a. folate
   b. niacin
   c. biotin
   d. no correct response
5. The coenzyme form for which of the B vitamins contains a pyrophosphate group?
   a. thiamin
   b. vitamin B_6
   c. vitamin B_{12}
   d. no correct response
6. Which of the B vitamins has three forms which differ from each other in a functional group present?
   a. pantothenic acid
   b. niacin
   c. vitamin B_6
   d. no correct response

Answers: 1. d; 2. b; 3. b; 4. c; 5. a; 6. c

21-15 Fat-Soluble Vitamins

LEARNING FOCUS

Know general structural characteristics for and biochemical functions of the four fat-soluble vitamins (A, D, E, and K).

The four fat-soluble vitamins are designated using the letters A, D, E, and K. Many of the functions of the fat-soluble vitamins involve processes that occur in cell membranes. The structures of the fat-soluble vitamins are more hydrocarbon-like, with fewer functional groups than the water-soluble vitamins. Their structures as a whole are nonpolar, which enhances their solubility in cell membranes. ◀

Vitamin A

Normal dietary intake provides a person with both *preformed* and *precursor forms* of vitamin A. Preformed vitamin A forms are called *retinoids*. The retinoids include reti*nal*, retin*ol*, and retin*oic acid*. ◀

$R = CH_2OH$ (Retinol)
$R = CHO$ (Retinal)
$R = COOH$ (Retinoic acid)

Retinoids

Although all three forms of vitamin A are physiologically active, their activities are not equal. The biochemical activity of retinol exceeds that of the other two forms. The body can synthesize retinol from retinal in a reaction that is reversible; retinal can also be converted to retinoic acid in an irreversible reaction. Retinoic acid cannot be converted to either retinol or retinal. Double bonds in retinoids are most often in a *trans*-configuration although *cis*-configuration bonds can occur.

Foods derived from animals, including egg yolks and dairy products, provide vitamin A in the form of retinyl esters, compounds that are easily hydrolyzed to retinoids in the human intestine. Foods of plant origin provide carotenoids, which serve as precursor forms of vitamin A. (The subject of carotenoids as a source of color in plants was previously considered in Chemical Connections 13-C—Carotenoids: A Source of Color.) The major carotenoid with vitamin A activity is beta-carotene (β-carotene), which can be cleaved to yield two molecules of retinal, which can then be converted to retinol. ◀

Cleavage at this point can yield two molecules of vitamin A ◀

Beta-carotene, a precursor for vitamin A

Beta-carotene is the yellow to red-orange pigment present in carrots, squash, cantaloupe, apricots, and other yellow vegetables and fruits, as well as in leafy green vegetables (where the yellow pigment is masked by green chlorophyll). ◀

Vitamin A has four major functions in the body.

1. *Vision.* In the eye, vitamin A (as retinal) combines with the protein opsin to form the visual pigment rhodopsin (see Chemical Connections 13-B—*Cis-trans* Isomerism and Vision). Rhodopsin participates in the conversion of light energy into nerve impulses that are sent to the brain. Although vitamin A's involvement in the process of vision is its best-known function ("Eat your carrots and you'll see better"), only 0.1% of the body's vitamin A is found in the eyes.

▶ *Lipids are substances that are not soluble in water but are soluble in nonpolar substances such as fat (Section 19-1). Thus the four fat-soluble vitamins are a type of lipid. They could have been, but were not, discussed in Chapter 19.*

▶ *The functional groups that distinguish the three forms of vitamin A from each other—alcohol, aldehyde, and carboxyl acid—are the same three functional groups that distinguish the three forms of vitamin B_6 from each other (Section 21-14).*

▶ *The retinoids are terpenes (Section 13-7) in which four isoprene units are present. Beta-carotene has an eight-unit terpene structure.*

▶ *Beta-carotene cleavage does not always occur in a symmetrical fashion, in which case only one molecule of vitamin A is produced. Furthermore, not all beta-carotene undergoes cleavage to produce vitamin A. It is estimated that 6 mg of beta-carotene is needed to produce 1 mg of retinol. Unconverted beta-carotene serves as an antioxidant (see Section 13-7), a role independent of its conversion to vitamin A.*

▶ *Beta-carotene is a deep yellow (almost orange) compound. If a plant food is white or colorless, it possesses little or no vitamin A activity. Potatoes, pasta, and rice are foods in this category.*

2. *Regulating Cell Differentiation.* Cell differentiation is the process whereby immature cells change in structure and function to become specialized cells. For example, some immature bone marrow cells differentiate into white blood cells and others into red blood cells. In the cellular differentiation process, vitamin A (as retinoic acid) binds to protein receptors; these vitamin A–protein receptor complexes then bind to regulatory regions of DNA molecules.

3. *Maintenance of the Health of Epithelial Tissues.* Epithelial tissue covers outer body surfaces in addition to lining internal cavities and tubes. It includes skin and the linings of the mouth, stomach, lungs, vagina, and bladder. Lack of vitamin A (as retinoic acid) causes such surfaces to become drier and harder than normal. Vitamin A's role here is related to cellular differentiation involving mucus-secreting cells.

4. *Reproduction and Growth.* In men, vitamin A participates in sperm development. In women, normal fetal development during pregnancy requires vitamin A. In both cases, it is the retinoic acid form of vitamin A that is needed. Again vitamin A's role is related to cellular differentiation processes.

Vitamin D

Vitamin D, like vitamin A, exists in several forms, the most important of which are vitamin D_2 and vitamin D_3. Vitamin D_2 (ergocalciferol) is found in foods of plant origin and vitamin D_3 (cholecalciferol) is found in foods of animal origin. ◀ In addition vitamin D_3 can be made within the human body. When it is not important to distinguish between the two major forms of vitamin D, the term *calciferol* is used for vitamin D.

Structurally vitamins D_2 and D_3 are similar, differing only in the hydrocarbon side chain present in their structures.

▶ *The common names for Vitamin D_2 and Vitamin D_3 are pronounced as follows:*

er-go-cal-CIF-er-ol (Vitamin D_2)
cho-le-cal-CIF-er-ol (Vitamin D_3)

Vitamin D

Both the cholecalciferol and the ergocalciferol forms of vitamin D must undergo two further hydroxylation steps before the vitamin D becomes fully functional. The first step, which occurs in the liver, adds an —OH group to carbon 25, producing cal*cidiol*. The second step, which occurs in the kidneys, adds an —OH group to carbon 1, producing calci*triol*.

1,25-Dihydroxyvitamin D_3
(calcitriol)

Vitamin D_3 is produced in the skin of humans and animals by the action of sunlight (ultraviolet light) on its precursor molecule, the cholesterol derivative 7-dehydrocholesterol (a normal metabolite of cholesterol found in the skin) (Figure 21-21). ◀ Absorption of light energy induces breakage of the 9,10-carbon–carbon bond; a spontaneous isomerization (shifting of double bonds) then occurs.

7-Dehydrocholesterol → UV → Pre-vitamin D_3 → Spontaneous conversion → Vitamin D_3 (cholecalciferol)

▶ *Does tanning bed use result in increased vitamin D synthesis via the skin? The answer is yes and no. Some tanning bed machines emit the needed wavelengths of light needed for vitamin D synthesis while others do not. Relying of tanning beds for vitamin D is heavily discouraged because of the damage the radiation causes to the skin itself.*

Note the presence of the prefix "chole" (from cholesterol) in the name cholecalciferol, drawing attention to the parent molecule from which it is made. Note also that structurally vitamin D_3 is considered to be a steroid derivative rather than a steroid. One of the steroid nucleus's four rings (Section 19-9) has been broken. This structural change gives the molecule more conformational flexibility, allowing it to interact better with proteins to which it must bind.

Only a few foods, including liver, fatty fish (such as salmon), and egg yolks, are good natural sources of vitamin D. Such vitamin D is vitamin D_3. Foods fortified with vitamin D include milk and margarine. The rest of the body's vitamin D supplies are made within the body (skin) with the help of sunlight.

Recent studies indicate that many adults in the United States are vitamin D deficient. Fortification of foods with vitamin D and the taking of vitamin D supplements help with this situation. Many dairy products as well as breakfast cereals are fortified with vitamin D, although such is voluntary rather than required of manufacturers. ◀ Vitamin D supplements usually contain vitamin D_3. This form of vitamin D is less expensive to manufacture and is more potent than vitamin D_2 in terms of biochemical activity.

The principal function of vitamin D is to maintain normal blood levels of calcium ion and phosphate ion so that bones can absorb these ions. Vitamin D stimulates absorption of these ions from the gastrointestinal tract and aids in their retention by the kidneys. Vitamin D triggers the deposition of calcium salts into the organic matrix of bones by activating the biosynthesis of calcium-binding proteins. ◀

▶ *Vitamin D is quite stable and is not destroyed during food preparation, processing, or storage. However, in producing reduced-fat milk much of the vitamin D naturally present is removed. For this reason most brands of milk are fortified with vitamin D. Such fortification is optional and some "bargain-priced" milk brands are not fortified.*

▶ *The presence of the prefix "calci," in the names calciferol, ergocalciferol, cholecalciferol, calcidiol, and calcitriol draws attention to the element "calcium," the substance associated with vitamin D's major biochemical function in the human body.*

Vitamin E

There are four forms of vitamin E: alpha-, beta-, delta-, and gamma-tocopherol. These forms differ from each other structurally according to which substituents (—CH_3 or —H) are present at two positions on an aromatic ring.

Tocopherols

	R	R'
α	CH_3	CH_3
β	CH_3	H
γ	H	CH_3
δ	H	H

The tocopherol form with the greatest biochemical activity is alpha-tocopherol, the vitamin E form in which methyl groups are present at both the R and R' positions on the aromatic ring.

Melissa Grimes-Guy/Science Source

Figure 21-21 The quantity of vitamin D synthesized by exposure of the skin to sunlight (ultraviolet radiation) varies with latitude, the length of exposure time, and skin pigmentation. (Darker-skinned people synthesize less vitamin D because the pigmentation filters out ultraviolet light.)

> *The name* tocopherol *comes from the 1922 discovery that vitamin E–deficient rats could not reproduce. The Greek words* tokos *and* phero *mean, respectively "childbirth" and "to bear." It is pronounced "tuh-KOFF-er-ol."*

> *Vitamin E is unique among the vitamins in that antioxidant activity is its principal biochemical role.*

The four tocopherol forms of vitamin E are widespread in both plant and animal foods, being particularly abundant in vegetable oils, nuts, and seeds. ◄ The major dietary sources for vitamin E are vegetable oils and products made from them such as margarines and salad dressings. Some dark green vegetables, such as spinach and broccoli, are also good dietary sources. Vitamin E is easily destroyed by exposure to excessive heat (such as deep frying) and by oxidation. Fresh or lightly processed foods (minimal heat exposure) are thus the best sources for this vitamin. Storage of food in airtight containers is important for preventing oxidation.

The primary function of vitamin E in the body is as an antioxidant—a compound that protects other compounds from oxidation by being oxidized itself. ◄ Vitamin E is particularly important in preventing the oxidation of polyunsaturated fatty acids (Section 19-2) in membrane lipids. It also protects vitamin A from oxidation. Vitamin E's antioxidant action involves it giving up the hydrogen present on its —OH group to oxygen-containing free radicals. After vitamin E is "spent" as an antioxidant, reaction with vitamin C restores the hydrogen atom previously lost by the vitamin E.

A most important location in the human body where vitamin E exerts its antioxidant effect is the lungs, where exposure of cells to oxygen (and air pollutants) is greatest. Both red and white blood cells that pass through the lungs, as well as the cells of the lung tissue itself, benefit from vitamin E's protective effect.

Infants, particularly premature infants, do not have a lot of vitamin E, which is passed from the mother to the infant only in the last weeks of pregnancy. Often, premature infants require oxygen supplementation for the purpose of controlling respiratory distress. In such situations, vitamin E is administered to the infant along with oxygen to give antioxidant protection.

Vitamin E has also been found to be involved in the conversion of arachidonic acid (20:4) to prostaglandins (Section 19-13).

Vitamin K

Like the other fat-soluble vitamins, vitamin K has more than one form. Structurally, all forms involve a methylated napthoquinone structure to which a long side chain of carbon atoms is attached. The various forms differ structurally in the length and degree of unsaturation of the side chain.

Napthoquinone   Vitamin K

Vitamin K_1, also called phylloquinone, has a side chain that is predominantly saturated; only one carbon–carbon double bond is present. It is a substance found in plants. Vitamin K_2 has several forms, called menaquinones, with the various forms differing in the length of the side chain. Menaquinone side chains have several carbon–carbon double bonds, in contrast to the one carbon–carbon double bond present in phylloquinone. Vitamin K_2 is found in animals and humans and can be synthesized by bacteria, including those found in the human intestinal tract.

Vitamin K_1 (phylloquinone)   Vitamin K_2 (menaquinone)

Typically, about half of the human body's vitamin K is synthesized by intestinal bacteria and half comes from the diet. Menaquinones are the form of vitamin K found in vitamin K supplements. Only leafy green vegetables such as spinach and cabbage are particularly rich in vitamin K. Other vegetables such as peas and tomatoes, as well as animal tissues including liver, contain lesser amounts. ◀

Vitamin K is essential to the blood-clotting process. More than a dozen different proteins and the mineral calcium are involved in the formation of a blood clot. Vitamin K is essential for the formation of prothrombin and at least five other proteins involved in the regulation of blood clotting. Vitamin K is sometimes given to presurgical patients to ensure adequate prothrombin levels and to prevent hemorrhaging.

Vitamin K is also required for the biosynthesis of several other proteins found in the plasma, bone, and kidney.

▶ *The choice of the letter K to designate this vitamin comes from the Danish word* koagulation *("coagulation" or "clotting.")*

Section 21-15 Quick Quiz

1. The compound beta-carotene is closely associated with which of the following vitamins?
   a. vitamin A
   b. vitamin D
   c. vitamin E
   d. no correct response
2. Cholesterol is a precursor for synthesis of which of the following vitamins?
   a. vitamin D
   b. vitamin E
   c. vitamin K
   d. no correct response
3. The term *calciferol* is closely associated with which of the following vitamins?
   a. vitamin A
   b. vitamin D
   c. vitamin K
   d. no correct response
4. For which of the following vitamins is blood coagulation a primary biochemical function?
   a. vitamin D
   b. vitamin E
   c. vitamin K
   d. no correct response
5. Which of the following vitamins does *not* have more than one structural form?
   a. vitamin A
   b. vitamin D
   c. vitamin E
   d. no correct response

Answers: 1. a; 2. a; 3. b; 4. c; 5. d

Concepts to Remember

Enzymes. Enzymes are highly specialized protein molecules that act as biochemical catalysts. Enzymes have common names that provide information about their function rather than their structure. The suffix *-ase* is characteristic of most enzyme names (Section 21-1).

Enzyme structure. Simple enzymes are composed only of protein (amino acids). Conjugated enzymes have a nonprotein portion (cofactor) in addition to a protein portion (apoenzyme). Cofactors may be small organic molecules (coenzymes) or inorganic ions (Section 21-2).

Enzyme classification. There are six classes of enzymes based on function: oxidoreductases, transferases, hydrolases, lyases, isomerases, and ligases (Section 21-3).

Enzyme active site. An enzyme active site is the relatively small part of the enzyme that is actually involved in catalysis. It is where substrate binds to the enzyme (Section 21-4).

Lock-and-key model of enzyme activity. The active site in an enzyme has a fixed, rigid geometrical conformation. Only substrates with a complementary geometry can be accommodated at the active site (Section 21-4).

Induced-fit model of enzyme activity. The active site in an enzyme can undergo small changes in geometry in order to accommodate a series of related substrates (Section 21-4).

Enzyme activity. Enzyme activity is a measure of the rate at which an enzyme converts substrate to products. Four factors that affect enzyme activity are temperature, pH, substrate concentration, and enzyme concentration (Section 21-6).

Enzyme inhibition. An enzyme inhibitor slows or stops the normal catalytic function of an enzyme by binding to it. Three modes of inhibition are reversible competitive inhibition, reversible noncompetitive inhibition, and irreversible inhibition (Section 21-7).

Allosteric enzyme. An allosteric enzyme is an enzyme with two or more protein chains and two kinds of binding sites (for substrate and regulator) (Section 21-8).

Zymogen. A zymogen is an inactive precursor of a proteolytic enzyme; the zymogen is activated by a chemical reaction that removes part of its structure (Section 21-8).

Covalent modification. Covalent modification is a cellular process for regulation of enzyme activity in which the structure of an enzyme is modified through formation of, or breaking of, a covalent bond. The most commonly encountered type of covalent modification involves a phosphate group being added to, or removed from, an enzyme (Section 21-8).

Vitamins. A vitamin is an organic compound necessary in small amounts for the normal growth of humans and some animals.

Vitamins must be obtained from dietary sources because they cannot be synthesized in the body (Section 21-12).

Water-soluble vitamins. Vitamin C and the eight B vitamins are the water-soluble vitamins. Vitamin C is essential for the proper formation of bones and teeth and is also an important antioxidant. All eight B vitamins function as coenzymes (Sections 21-13 and 21-14).

Fat-soluble vitamins. The four fat-soluble vitamins are vitamins A, D, E, and K. The best-known function of vitamin A is its role in vision. Vitamin D is essential for the proper use of calcium and phosphorus to form bones and teeth. The primary function of vitamin E is as an antioxidant. Vitamin K is essential in the regulation of blood clotting (Section 21-15).

Exercises and Problems

Exercises and problems are arranged in matched pairs with the two members of a pair addressing the same concept(s). The answer to the odd-numbered member of a pair is given at the back of the book. Problems denoted with a ▲ involve concepts found not only in the section under consideration but also concepts found in one or more earlier sections of the chapter.

General Characteristics of Enzymes (Section 21-1)

21-1   What is the general role of enzymes in the human body?

21-2   Why does the body need so many different enzymes?

21-3   List two ways in which enzymes differ from inorganic laboratory catalysts.

21-4   Occasionally the "delicate" nature of enzymes is referred to. Explain why this adjective is appropriate.

Enzyme Structure (Section 21-2)

21-5   Indicate whether each of the following phrases describes a simple or a conjugated enzyme.
   a. An enzyme that has both a protein and a nonprotein portion
   b. An enzyme that requires Mg^{2+} ion for activity
   c. An enzyme in which only amino acids are present
   d. An enzyme in which a cofactor is present

21-6   Indicate whether each of the following phrases describes a simple or a conjugated enzyme.
   a. An enzyme that contains a carbohydrate portion
   b. An enzyme that contains only protein
   c. A holoenzyme
   d. An enzyme that has a vitamin as part of its structure

21-7   Explain why a metal ion can function as a cofactor but not as a coenzyme.

21-8   Explain why a small organic molecule can function as both a cofactor and a coenzyme.

21-9   Indicate whether each of the following statements about enzyme terminology is true or false.
   a. All conjugated enzymes contain a cofactor.
   b. An apoenzyme has both a protein and nonprotein part.
   c. Metal atoms cannot be present in a cofactor.
   d. An apoenzyme is present in all holoenzymes.

21-10   Indicate whether each of the following statements about enzyme terminology is true or false.
   a. Simple enzymes cannot contain cofactors.
   b. A holoenzyme has both a protein and nonprotein part.
   c. Metal atoms are present in all conjugated proteins.
   d. A cofactor is present in some, but not all, conjugated enzymes.

Nomenclature and Classification of Enzymes (Section 21-3)

21-11   Based on its name, indicate whether each of the following substances is an enzyme.
   a. sucrose
   b. lactase
   c. fructose oxidase
   d. creatine kinase

21-12   Based on its name, indicate whether each of the following substances is an enzyme.
   a. sucrase
   b. lactose
   c. xylulose reductase
   d. aspartate transaminase

21-13   Predict the function of each of the following enzymes.
   a. Pyruvate carboxylase
   b. Alcohol dehydrogenase
   c. L-Amino acid reductase
   d. Maltase

21-14   Predict the function of each of the following enzymes.
   a. Cytochrome oxidase
   b. *Cis–trans* isomerase
   c. Succinate dehydrogenase
   d. Lactase

21-15   What is the substrate for each of the enzymes listed in Problem 21-13?

21-16   What is the substrate for each of the enzymes listed in Problem 21-14?

21-17   Suggest a name for an enzyme that catalyzes each of the following reactions.
   a. Hydrolysis of sucrose
   b. Decarboxylation of pyruvate
   c. Isomerization of glucose
   d. Removal of hydrogen from lactate

21-18 Suggest a name for an enzyme that catalyzes each of the following reactions.
 a. Hydrolysis of lactose
 b. Oxidation of nitrite
 c. Decarboxylation of citrate
 d. Reduction of oxalate

21-19 Indicate whether each of the following pairings of enzyme classification terminology is correct.
 a. lipase and hydrolase
 b. mutase and isomerase
 c. kinase and ligase
 d. dehydratase and lyase

21-20 Indicate whether each of the following pairings of enzyme classification terminology is correct.
 a. protease and hydrolase
 b. racemase and isomerase
 c. phosphatase and ligase
 d. hydratase and lyase

21-21 To which of the six major classes of enzymes does the enzyme that catalyzes each of the following reactions belong?
 a. A *cis* double bond is converted to a *trans* double bond.
 b. An alcohol is dehydrated to form a compound with a double bond.
 c. An amino group is transferred from one substrate to another.
 d. An ester linkage is hydrolyzed.

21-22 To which of the six major classes of enzymes does the enzyme that catalyzes each of the following reactions belong?
 a. An L isomer is converted to a D isomer.
 b. A phosphate group is transferred from one substrate to another.
 c. An amide linkage is hydrolyzed.
 d. Hydrolysis of a carbohydrate to monosaccharides occurs.

21-23 Identify the enzyme needed in each of the following reactions as an isomerase, a decarboxylase, a dehydrogenase, a lipase, or a phosphatase.

 a. $CH_3-\overset{O}{\overset{\|}{C}}-COOH \rightarrow CH_3-\overset{O}{\overset{\|}{C}}-H + CO_2$

 b. $\begin{array}{l} CH_2-O-\overset{O}{\overset{\|}{C}}-R \\ | \\ CH-O-\overset{O}{\overset{\|}{C}}-R + 3H_2O \rightarrow \\ | \\ CH_2-O-\overset{O}{\overset{\|}{C}}-R \end{array} \begin{array}{l} CH_2-OH \\ | \\ CH-OH \ + 3R-COOH \\ | \\ CH_2-OH \end{array}$

 c. $\overset{+}{H_3N}-CH-COO^- + H_2O \rightarrow$
  $\quad\quad | $
  $\quad\quad CH_2$
  $\quad\quad | $
  $\quad\quad OPO_3^{2-}$

  $\overset{+}{H_3N}-CH-COO^- + HPO_4^{2-}$
  $\quad\quad | $
  $\quad\quad CH_2$
  $\quad\quad | $
  $\quad\quad OH$

 d. $\begin{array}{l} OH \\ | \\ CH_3-CH-COOH + NAD^+ \rightarrow \end{array}$

  $CH_3-\overset{O}{\overset{\|}{C}}-COOH + NADH + H^+$

21-24 Identify the enzyme needed in each of the following reactions as an isomerase, a decarboxylase, a dehydrogenase, a protease, or a phosphatase.

 a. $CH_3-\overset{O}{\overset{\|}{C}}-\overset{O}{\overset{\|}{C}}-OH \rightarrow CH_3-\overset{O}{\overset{\|}{C}}-H + CO_2$

 b. $\begin{array}{l} CHO \\ | \\ HC-OH \\ | \\ HO-CH \\ | \\ HC-OH \\ | \\ HO-CH \\ | \\ CH_2OPO_3^{2-} \end{array} \rightarrow \begin{array}{l} CH_2OH \\ | \\ C=O \\ | \\ HO-CH \\ | \\ HC-OH \\ | \\ HO-CH \\ | \\ CH_2OPO_3^{2-} \end{array}$

 c. $HO-\overset{O}{\overset{\|}{C}}-CH_2-CH_2-\overset{O}{\overset{\|}{C}}-OH \rightarrow$

  $HO-\overset{O}{\overset{\|}{C}}-CH=CH-\overset{O}{\overset{\|}{C}}-OH + 2H$

 d. $\overset{+}{H_3N}-CH-\overset{O}{\overset{\|}{C}}-NH-CH-COO^- + H_2O \rightarrow$
  $\quad\quad | \quad\quad\quad\quad\quad | $
  $\quad\quad CH_3 \quad\quad\quad\quad CH_3$

  $2\ \overset{+}{H_3N}-CH-COO^-$
  $\quad\quad\quad | $
  $\quad\quad\quad CH_3$

Models of Enzyme Action (Section 21-4)

21-25 Indicate whether each of the following statements about an enzyme *active site* is true or false.
 a. It is the location where substrate molecules are produced.
 b. It always has a fixed, rigid geometry.
 c. It always has a geometrical shape *exactly* complementary to that of substrate.
 d. It always accommodates several structurally related substrates.

21-26 Indicate whether each of the following statements about an enzyme *active site* is true or false.
 a. It is the location where substrate molecules are converted to product molecules.
 b. It always has a shape that has a degree of flexibility to it.
 c. It always has a geometrical shape identical to that of substrate.
 d. It always accommodates only one specific substrate.

21-27 Indicate whether each of the statements in Problem 21-25 applies to (1) the lock-and-key model for enzyme action, (2) the induced-fit model for enzyme action, (3) both models, or (4) neither model.

21-28 Indicate whether each of the statements in Problem 21-26 applies to (1) the lock-and-key model for enzyme action, (2) the induced-fit model for enzyme action, (3) both models, or (4) neither model.

21-29 What types of forces hold a substrate at an enzyme active site?

21-30 The forces that hold a substrate at an enzyme active site are not covalent bonds. Explain why not.

21-31 The following equation is a representation of an enzyme-catalyzed reaction.

$$E + S \rightleftharpoons ES \longrightarrow EP \longrightarrow E + P$$

a. What is the meaning of the notation "ES" in the equation?
b. What is the meaning of the notation "P" in the equation?

21-32 The following equation is a representation of an enzyme-catalyzed reaction.

$$E + S \rightleftharpoons ES \longrightarrow EP \longrightarrow E + P$$

a. What is the meaning of the notation "S" in the equation?
b. What is the meaning of the notation "EP" in the equation?

▲**21-33** Indicate whether each of the following statements concerning enzymes and their mode of action are true or false.
a. According to the lock-and-key model of enzyme action, the active site of an enzyme is flexible in shape.
b. In an enzyme-catalyzed reaction, the compound that undergoes a chemical change is called the substrate.
c. The nonprotein portion of a conjugated enzyme is the enzyme's active site.
d. Simple enzymes have inorganic cofactors, and conjugated enzymes have organic cofactors.

▲**21-34** Indicate whether each of the following statements concerning enzymes and their mode of action are true or false.
a. According to the induced-fit model of enzyme action, a substrate must be changed into a cofactor before a chemical reaction occurs.
b. The active site of an enzyme is the location within the enzyme where catalysis takes place.
c. The protein portion of a conjugated enzyme can accommodate several substrates at the same time.
d. Simple enzymes do not have active sites, whereas conjugated enzymes do have active sites.

Enzyme Specificity (Section 21-5)

21-35 Define the following terms dealing with enzyme specificity.
a. Absolute specificity
b. Linkage specificity

21-36 Define the following terms dealing with enzyme specificity.
a. Group specificity
b. Stereochemical specificity

21-37 Which enzyme in each of the following pairs would be more limited in its catalytic scope?
a. An enzyme that exhibits absolute specificity or an enzyme that exhibits group specificity
b. An enzyme that exhibits stereochemical specificity or an enzyme that exhibits linkage specificity

21-38 Which enzyme in each of the following pairs would be more limited in its catalytic scope?
a. An enzyme that exhibits linkage specificity or an enzyme that exhibits absolute specificity
b. An enzyme that exhibits group specificity or an enzyme that exhibits stereochemical specificity

▲**21-39** What type of specificity (absolute, group, linkage, or stereochemical) is associated with each of the following enzymes?
a. Sucrase
b. A lipase
c. A decarboxylase
d. L-glutamate oxidase

▲**21-40** What type of specificity (absolute, group, linkage, or stereochemical) is associated with each of the following enzymes?
a. A deaminase
b. A phosphatase
c. Maltase
d. L-Lactate dehydrogenase

Factors That Affect Enzyme Activity (Section 21-6)

21-41 The following graph shows the relationship between enzyme activity and both pH and temperature for two enzymes (A and B).

Based on this graphical information
a. What is the optimum pH for enzyme A?
b. What is the optimum temperature for enzyme B?
c. Which enzyme has the greater activity at a pH of 7.4?
d. Which enzyme has the greater activity at a temperature of 37.8°C?

21-42 Based on the graphical information in Problem 21-41 about enzymes A and B
a. What is the optimum pH for enzyme B?
b. What is the optimum temperature for enzyme A?
c. Which enzyme has the greater activity at a pH of 7.2?
d. Which enzyme has the greater activity at a temperature of 37.2°C?

21-43 Based on the graphical information in Problem 21-41 about enzymes A and B indicate whether the enzyme activity of enzyme A increases or decreases when the following changes in reaction conditions are made.
a. pH decreases from 7.2 to 7.0
b. pH increases from 7.2 to 7.4
c. temperature decreases from 36.8°C to 36.6°C
d. temperature increases from 36.8°C to 37.8°C

21-44 Based on the graphical information in Problem 21-41 about enzymes A and B indicate whether the enzyme activity of enzyme B increases or decreases when the following changes in reaction conditions are made.
a. pH decreases from 7.6 to 7.2
b. pH increases from 7.2 to 7.4
c. temperature decreases from 37.8°C to 37.6°C
d. temperature increases from 38.2°C to 38.4°C

21-45 Does the activity of a typical nondigestive human enzyme increase, decrease, or remain the same
a. as temperature is decreased from 35°C to 34°C
b. as pH is decreased from 7.1 to 6.8

21-46 Does the activity of a typical nondigestive human enzyme increase, decrease, or remain the same
a. as temperature is increased from 38°C to 40°C
b. as pH is increased from 6.8 to 7.0

21-47 Draw a graph that shows the effect of increasing substrate concentration on the rate of an enzyme-catalyzed reaction (at constant temperature, pH, and enzyme concentration).

21-48 Draw a graph that shows the effect of increasing enzyme concentration on the rate of an enzyme-catalyzed reaction (at constant temperature, pH, and substrate concentration).

21-49 In an enzyme-catalyzed reaction, all of the enzyme active sites are saturated by substrate molecules at a certain substrate concentration. What happens to the rate of the reaction when the substrate concentration is doubled?

21-50 What is an enzyme turnover number?

21-51 Describe the effect that each of the following changes would have on the rate of a biochemical reaction involving the substrate arginine and the enzyme arginase.
a. Decreasing the arginine concentration
b. Increasing the temperature from its optimum value to a value 10° higher
c. Increasing the arginase concentration
d. Decreasing the pH by one unit from its optimum value

21-52 Describe the effect that each of the following changes would have on the rate of a biochemical reaction involving the substrate hydrogen peroxide and the enzyme catalase.
a. Increasing the hydrogen peroxide concentration
b. Decreasing the temperature from its optimum value to a value 10° lower
c. Decreasing the catalase concentration
d. Increasing the pH by one unit from its optimum value

Extremozymes (Section 21-7)

21-53 What is an extremophile?

21-54 What are two common environmental settings where extremophiles are found?

21-55 Indicate whether each of the following pairings of extremophile subtype and environmental survival conditions is correct.
a. halophile and low salinity
b. hypothermophile and low temperatures
c. piezophile and high hydrostatic pressure
d. alkaliphile and low solution pH

21-56 Indicate whether each of the following pairings of extremophile subtype and environmental survival conditions is correct.
a. cryophile–high salinity
b. xerophile–dry conditions
c. acidophile–low pH
d. piezophile–low temperature

21-57 What type(s) of extremophiles are used in commercial laundry detergent formulations?

21-58 What type(s) of extremophiles are used in oil well drilling operations?

Enzyme Inhibition (Section 21-8)

21-59 In competitive inhibition, can both the inhibitor and the substrate bind to an enzyme at the same time? Explain your answer.

21-60 Compare the sites where competitive and noncompetitive inhibitors bind to enzymes.

21-61 Indicate whether each of the following statements concerning different types of enzyme inhibitors is true or false.
a. A reversible competitive inhibitor permanently blocks an enzyme's active site.
b. A reversible noncompetitive inhibitor temporarily blocks an enzyme's active site.
c. An irreversible inhibitor permanently occupies an enzyme's active site.
d. Pb^{2+} is an example of a reversible competitive inhibitor.

21-62 Indicate whether each of the following statements concerning different types of enzyme inhibitors is true or false.
a. A reversible competitive inhibitor temporarily blocks an enzyme's active site.
b. A reversible noncompetitive inhibitor permanently changes the shape of an enzyme's active site.
c. An irreversible inhibitor temporarily changes the shape of an enzyme's active site.
d. Insecticides are examples of reversible noncompetitive inhibitors.

21-63 Indicate whether each of the following statements describes a reversible competitive inhibitor, a reversible noncompetitive inhibitor, or an irreversible inhibitor. More than one answer may apply.
a. Both inhibitor and substrate bind at the active site on a random basis.
b. The inhibitor effect cannot be reversed by the addition of more substrate.
c. Inhibitor structure does not have to resemble substrate structure.
d. The inhibitor and substrate can bind to the enzyme simultaneously.

21-64 Indicate whether each of the following statements describes a reversible competitive inhibitor, a reversible noncompetitive inhibitor, or an irreversible inhibitor. More than one answer may apply.
a. It bonds covalently to the enzyme active site.
b. The inhibitor effect can be reversed by the addition of more substrate.
c. Inhibitor structure must be somewhat similar to that of the substrate.
d. The inhibitor and substrate cannot bind to the enzyme simultaneously.

Regulation of Enzyme Activity (Section 21-9)

21-65 Indicate whether each of the following statements about *allosteric enzymes* is true or false.
a. They always possess two or more protein subunits.
b. They have two distinct binding sites.
c. Regulators can increase but not decrease enzyme activity.
d. Regulator site and active site are usually located on different protein subunits.

21-66 Indicate whether each of the following statements about *allosteric enzymes* is true or false.
a. They always have quaternary protein structure.
b. They have two regulator sites and one active site.
c. Regulators can decrease but not increase enzyme activity.
d. Both substrate and regulator often bind at the same site.

21-67 Indicate whether each of the following pairings of concepts related to regulation of enzyme activity is a correct pairing.
a. zymogen production and regulation of proteolytic enzyme activity
b. feedback control and regulator is the initial reactant in a reaction sequence
c. covalent modification and phosphorylation
d. proteolytic enzyme activation and phosphatase enzyme

21-68 Indicate whether each of the following pairings of concepts related to regulation of enzyme activity is a correct pairing.
a. covalent modification and dephosphorylation
b. zymogen activation and removal of a peptide chain segment
c. feedback control and allosteric enzyme regulation
d. covalent modification and hormone regulator

21-69 What occurs during the covalent modification of an enzyme using a
a. phosphorylation reaction
b. phosphatase enzyme

21-70 What occurs during the covalent modification of an enzyme using a
a. dephosphorylation reaction
b. protein kinase enzyme

21-71 Is the phosphorylated version of an enzyme the "turned-on" or "turned-off" form of the enzyme?

21-72 Is the dephosphorylated version of an enzyme the "turned-on" or "turned-off" form of the enzyme?

▲**21-73** Explain the difference in meaning, if any, between the following pairs of "enzyme terms."
a. Apoenzyme and proenzyme
b. Simple enzyme and allosteric enzyme

▲**21-74** Explain the difference in meaning, if any, between the following pairs of "enzyme terms."
a. Coenzyme and zymogen
b. Extremozyme and proteolytic enzyme

Prescription Drugs That Inhibit Enzyme Activity (Section 21-10)

21-75 What is the relationship between the compounds angiotensinogen and angiotensin in terms of
a. general structure
b. biochemical activity

21-76 What is the relationship of angiotensin-converting enzyme (ACE) to the compounds
a. angiotensinogen
b. angiotensin

21-77 By what mechanism do sulfa drugs kill bacteria?

21-78 By what mechanism do penicillins kill bacteria?

Medical Uses of Enzymes (Section 21-11)

21-79 What does the acronym TPA stand for, and how is TPA used in therapeutic medicine?

21-80 What does the acronym BUN stand for, and how is this test used in clinical laboratory analysis?

21-81 What enzyme is denoted by each of the following acronyms?
a. LDH
b. AST

21-82 What enzyme is denoted by each of the following acronyms?
a. CPK
b. ALT

21-83 What is the medical diagnostic value associated with the presence of each of the following enzymes in the bloodstream?
a. CPK
b. ALT

21-84 What is the medical diagnostic value associated with the presence of each of the following enzymes in the bloodstream?
a. LDH
b. AST

General Characteristics of Vitamins (Section 21-12)

21-85 Indicate whether each of the following is a fat-soluble or a water-soluble vitamin.
a. Vitamin K
b. Vitamin B_{12}
c. Vitamin C
d. Thiamin

21-86 Indicate whether each of the following is a fat-soluble or a water-soluble vitamin.
a. Vitamin A
b. Vitamin B_6
c. Vitamin E
d. Riboflavin

21-87 Indicate whether each of the vitamins in Problem 21-85 would be likely or unlikely to be toxic when consumed in excess.

21-88 Indicate whether each of the vitamins in Problem 21-86 would be likely or unlikely to be toxic when consumed in excess.

21-89 Indicate whether each of the vitamins in Problem 21-85 would likely have a cofactor function in the human body.

21-90 Indicate whether each of the vitamins in Problem 21-86 would likely have a cofactor function in the human body.

Water-Soluble Vitamins: Vitamin C (Section 21-13)

21-91 What are the structural differences between the compounds ascorbic acid and dehydroascorbic acid?

21-92 What are the structural differences between the oxidized and reduced forms of vitamin C?

21-93 What is the biochemical relationship between vitamin C and the following substances?
a. Collagen
b. Vitamin E
c. Dopamine
d. Niacin (NADH)

21-94 What is the biochemical relationship between vitamin C and the following substances?
a. Fe^{3+} and Fe^{2+} ions
b. Serotonin
c. Folate
d. Glutathione

21-95 Vitamin C is biosynthesized in a two-step process. What is the reactant and product in each of these biosynthetic steps?

21-96 Two enzymes, lactonase and an oxidase, are involved in the biosynthesis of vitamin C. What is the substrate for each of these enzymes?

Water-Soluble Vitamins: The B Vitamins (Section 21-14)

21-97 What is the most characterized role of the B vitamins in the human body?

21-98 Only eight of the nine water-soluble vitamins are called B vitamins. What characteristic "separates" the ninth water-soluble vitamin from the other eight?

21-99 Indicate whether each of the following B vitamin names is the *preferred name* or an *alternative name* for the vitamin.
   a. Vitamin B_1
   b. Vitamin B_6
   c. Cobalamin
   d. Niacin

21-100 Indicate whether each of the following B vitamin names is the *preferred name* or an *alternative name* for the vitamin.
   a. Vitamin B_5
   b. Vitamin B_{12}
   c. Biotin
   d. Pyridoxal

21-101 Which of the B vitamins has a structure that fits each of the following characterizations? For a given characterization, more than one B vitamin may qualify.
   a. Contains the element sulfur
   b. Contains a fused two-ring component
   c. Exists in two or more different structural forms
   d. Contains a monosaccharide component

21-102 Which of the B vitamins has a structure that fits each of the following structural characterizations? For a given characterization, more than one B vitamin may qualify.
   a. Contains the element nitrogen
   b. Contains a fused three-ring component
   c. Exists in three or more different structural forms
   d. Contains an amino acid component

21-103 What is the difference structurally between the two forms of niacin?

21-104 What is the difference structurally between the three forms of vitamin B_6?

21-105 Name the B vitamin precursor for each of the following coenzymes.
   a. PLP
   b. TPP
   c. CoA
   d. NADP$^+$

21-106 Name the B vitamin precursor for each of the following coenzymes.
   a. NAD$^+$
   b. FMN
   c. FAD
   d. THF

21-107 The coenzyme forms of B vitamins are involved in the transfer of an atom or functional group from one molecule to another in metabolic reactions. Identify the atom or group transferred by coenzymes containing the following B vitamins.
   a. Thiamin
   b. Folate
   c. Pantothenic acid
   d. Vitamin B_{12}

21-108 The coenzyme forms of B vitamins are involved in the transfer of an atom or functional group from one molecule to another in metabolic reactions. Identify the atom or group transferred by coenzymes containing the following B vitamins.
   a. Niacin
   b. Biotin
   c. Riboflavin
   d. Vitamin B_6

Fat-Soluble Vitamins (Section 21-15)

21-109 Describe the structural differences among the three retinoid forms of vitamin A.

21-110 What is the relationship between the plant pigment beta-carotene and vitamin A?

21-111 What is *cell differentiation*, and how does vitamin A participate in this process?

21-112 List four major functions of vitamin A in the human body.

21-113 Indicate whether each of the following vitamin A conversions can occur in the human body.
   a. retinal to retinol
   b. retinoic acid to retinal

21-114 Indicate whether each of the following vitamin A conversions can occur in the human body.
   a. retinol to retinal
   b. retinal to retinoic acid

21-115 How do vitamin D_2 and vitamin D_3 differ in structure?

21-116 In terms of their source, how do vitamin D_2 and vitamin D_3 differ?

21-117 What is the principal function of vitamin D in the human body?

21-118 Why is vitamin D often called the "sunshine" vitamin?

21-119 For each of the following pairs of molecules indicate which member of the pair is encountered first in the biosynthetic pathway that produces active vitamin D_3 from cholesterol.
   a. 7-dehydrocholesterol or cholecalciferol
   b. calcidiol or calcitriol

21-120 For each of the following pairs of molecules indicate which member of the pair is encountered first in the biosynthetic pathway that produces active vitamin D_3 from cholesterol.
   a. 7-dehydrocholesterol or calcidiol
   b. cholecalciferol or calcitriol

21-121 Which structural form of vitamin E exhibits the greatest biochemical activity?

21-122 How do the various forms of vitamin E differ in structure?

21-123 What is the principal function of vitamin E in the human body?

21-124 Why is vitamin E often given to premature infants who are on oxygen therapy?

21-125 How do vitamin K_1 and vitamin K_2 differ in structure?

21-126 In terms of their source, how do vitamin K_1 and vitamin K_2 differ?

21-127 How are menaquinones, phylloquinones, and vitamin K related?

21-128 What is the principal function of vitamin K in the human body?

21-129 Indicate whether each of the following pairings of structure name and vitamin name is correct.
  a. retinal and vitamin E
  b. calciferol and vitamin D
  c. tocopherol and vitamin K
  d. napthoquinone and vitamin A

21-130 Indicate whether each of the following pairings of structure name and vitamin name is correct.
  a. calcitriol and vitamin A
  b. retinoic acid and vitamin D
  c. phylloquinone and vitamin E
  d. tocopherol and vitamin K

▲**21-131** Which vitamin or vitamins has (have) each of the following functions?
  a. Is a water-soluble antioxidant
  b. Is a fat-soluble antioxidant
  c. Is involved in the process of vision
  d. Is involved in the formation of collagen

▲**21-132** Which vitamin or vitamins has (have) each of the following functions?
  a. Is involved in prostaglandin synthesis
  b. Is a coenzyme precursor
  c. Is involved in calcium deposition in bone
  d. Is involved in cell differentiation

▲**21-133** Which of the 13 vitamins has a structure that fits each of the following characterizations? For a given characterization, more than one vitamin may qualify.
  a. Does not contain nitrogen
  b. Contains a metal atom
  c. Has a saturated or an unsaturated hydrocarbon chain component
  d. Contains one or more carboxyl (—COOH) functional groups

▲**21-134** Which of the 13 vitamins has a structure that fits each of the following characterizations? For a given characterization, more than one vitamin may qualify.
  a. Contains sulfur
  b. Does not have a cyclic component
  c. Contains one or more alcohol (—OH) functional groups
  d. Contains both fused and nonfused ring systems

Chapter 21 Appendix:

Page 719 from Stoker General, Organic, and Biological Chemistry, 5th Edition

CHEMICAL Connections   Heart Attacks and Enzyme Analysis

The symptoms of a heart attack—that is, a *myocardial infarction (MI)*—include irregular breathing and pain in the left chest that may radiate to the neck, left shoulder, and arm. An initial diagnosis of an MI is based on these and other physical symptoms, and treatment is initiated on this basis.

Physicians then use enzyme analysis to confirm the diagnosis and to monitor the course of treatment. The blood levels of three enzymes are commonly assayed in MI situations: creatine phosphokinase (CPK), aspartate transaminase (AST), and lactate dehydrogenase (LDH). The CPK level rises and falls relatively rapidly after a heart attack, reaching a maximum after about 30 hours at a level approximately six times normal. The AST level triples after about 40 hours. LDH, whose concentrations rise slowly, is used to monitor the later stages of the MI and to assess the extent of heart damage. The accompanying graph shows blood levels of these three enzymes as a function of time in an MI situation.

Further information about the seriousness of an MI is obtained by studying isoenzymes. **Isoenzymes** *are forms of the same enzyme with slightly different amino acid sequences.* The use of the prefix "iso" in the term *isoenzymes* implies that such enzymes catalyze the "same" reaction and not that they have isomeric structures. Lactate dehydrogenase is a mixture of five isoenzymes denoted LDH_1 to LDH_5. Creatine phosphokinase is a mixture of three isoenzymes denoted CK-MM, CK-MB, and CK-BB.

Consideration of further details about the LDH isoenzymes shows how isoenzymes give information about whether a heart attack has occurred or not. Note from the following table that heart tissue is particularly high in LDH_1 and that liver and skeletal muscle are particularly high in LDH_5.

When a heart attack occurs, some heart muscle cells are damaged (destroyed), and their enzymes "leak" into the bloodstream. This changes the ratios among the various LDHs present in blood, because heart muscle is particularly high in LDH_1. The accompanying graph of an LDH isoenzyme assay for a heart attack victim shows that the LDH_1/LDH_2 ratio, which is normally less than one in blood serum, is now greater than one.

Tissue	LDH_1	LDH_2	LDH_3	LDH_4	LDH_5
brain	23	34	30	10	3
heart	50	36	9	3	2
kidney	28	34	21	11	6
liver	4	6	17	16	57
lung	10	20	30	25	15
serum	28	41	19	7	5
skeletal muscle	5	5	10	22	58

The spelling of the term *vitamin* was originally *vitamine,* a word derived from the Latin *vita,* meaning "life," and from the fact that these substances were all thought to contain the *amine* functional group. When this supposition was found to be false, the final *e* was dropped from *vitamine,* and the term *vitamin* came into use. Some vitamins contain amine functional groups, but others do not.

Vitamins differ from the major classes of foods (carbohydrates, lipids, and proteins) in the amount required; for vitamins it is *micro*gram or *milli*gram quantities per day compared with 50–200 grams per day for the major food categories. To illustrate the small amount of vitamins needed by the human body, consider the recommended daily allowance (RDA) of vitamin B_{12}, which is 2.0 micrograms per day for an adult. Just 1.0 gram of this vitamin could theoretically supply the daily needs of 500,000 people.

A well-balanced diet usually meets all the body's vitamin requirements. However, supplemental vitamins are often required for women during pregnancy and for people recovering from certain illnesses.

One of the most common myths associated with the nutritional aspects of vitamins is that vitamins from natural sources are superior to synthetic vitamins. In truth, synthetic

Nucleic Acids

22

Dr. Yorgos Nikas/Phototake

Human egg and sperm.

A most remarkable property of living cells is their ability to produce exact replicas of themselves. Furthermore, cells contain all the instructions needed for making the complete organism of which they are a part. The molecules within a cell that are responsible for these amazing capabilities are nucleic acids.

The Swiss physiologist Friedrich Miescher (1844–1895) discovered nucleic acids in 1869 while studying the nuclei of white blood cells. The fact that they were initially found in cell nuclei and are acidic accounts for the name *nucleic acid*. Although it is now known that nucleic acids are found throughout a cell, not just in the nucleus, the name is still used for such materials.

22-1 Types of Nucleic Acids

LEARNING FOCUS

Distinguish between deoxyribonucleic acids and ribonucleic acids in terms of biochemical function and in terms of where they are found within a cell.

Two types of nucleic acids are found within cells of higher organisms: *deoxyribonucleic acid* (DNA) and *ribonucleic acid* (RNA). Nearly all the DNA is found within the cell nucleus. Its primary function is the storage

▶ *It was not until 1944, 75 years after the discovery of nucleic acids, that scientists obtained the first evidence that these molecules are responsible for the storage and transfer of genetic information.*

and transfer of genetic information. ◀ This information is used (indirectly) to control many functions of a living cell. In addition, DNA is passed from existing cells to new cells during cell division. RNA occurs in all parts of a cell. It functions primarily in synthesis of proteins, the molecules that carry out essential cellular functions. The structural distinctions between DNA and RNA molecules are considered in Section 22-4.

Section 22-1 Quick Quiz

1. Which of the following statements concerning deoxyribonucleic acids is *incorrect*?
   a. They are found in all parts of a cell.
   b. They are involved in the storage and transfer of genetic information.
   c. They are passed from existing cells to new cells during cell division.
   d. no correct response
2. Which of the following statements concerning ribonucleic acids is *correct*?
   a. They are found primarily within the nucleus of a cell.
   b. They are directly involved in the synthesis of proteins.
   c. They are passed from existing cells to new cells during cell division.
   d. no correct response

Answers: 1. a; 2. b

22-2 Nucleotides: Structural Building Blocks for Nucleic Acids

LEARNING FOCUS
Be familiar with the chemical composition of nucleotides, the structural building blocks for nucleic acids.

A **nucleic acid** *is an unbranched polymer containing monomer units called nucleotides.* A given nucleic acid molecule can contain in excess of one million nucleotide units. The starting point for a discussion of nucleic acids is, thus, an understanding of the chemical composition of nucleotides.

A **nucleotide** *is a three-subunit molecule in which a pentose sugar is bonded to both a phosphate group and a nitrogen-containing heterocyclic base.* With a three-subunit structure, nucleotides are more complex monomers than the monosaccharides of polysaccharides (Section 18-8) or the amino acids of proteins (Section 20-2). ◀ A block structural diagram for a nucleotide is

▶ *Proteins are polypeptides, many carbohydrates are polysaccharides, and nucleic acids are polynucleotides.*

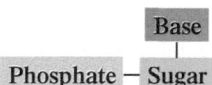

Pentose Sugars

The sugar unit of a nucleotide is either the pentose *ribose* or the pentose *2'-deoxyribose*.

▶ *The conventions for numbering the atoms in the pentose and nitrogen-containing base subunits of five nucleotides are important and will be used extensively in later sections of this chapter. The conventions are that*

1. *Pentose ring atoms are designated with* primed *numbers.*
2. *Nitrogen-containing base ring atoms are designated with* unprimed *numbers.*

Structurally, the only difference between these two sugars occurs at carbon 2'. The —OH group present on this carbon in ribose becomes an —H atom in 2'-deoxyribose. (The prefix *deoxy-* means "without oxygen.") ◀

RNA and DNA differ in the identity of the sugar unit in their nucleotides. In RNA, the sugar unit is *ribose*—hence the *R* in RNA. In DNA, the sugar unit is 2′-*de*oxyribose—hence the *D* in DNA.

Nitrogen-Containing Heterocyclic Bases

Five nitrogen-containing heterocyclic bases are nucleotide components. Three of them are derivatives of pyrimidine (Section 17-9), a monocyclic base with a six-membered ring, and two are derivatives of purine (Section 17-9), a bicyclic base with fused five- and six-membered rings. ◀

▶ *Pyrimidine and purine do not themselves occur naturally; numerous derivatives of these two compounds, however, are naturally occurring substances.*

Pyrimidine   Purine

Both of these heterocyclic compounds are bases because they contain amine functional groups and amine functional groups exhibit basic behavior (proton acceptors; Section 17-6).

The three pyrimidine derivatives found in nucleotides are thymine (T), cytosine (C), and uracil (U).

Thymine (T)   Cytosine (C)   Uracil (U)

Thymine is the 5-methyl-2,4-dioxo derivative, cytosine the 4-amino-2-oxo derivative, and uracil the 2,4-dioxo derivative of pyrimidine. ◀

▶ *A pyrimidine derivative that was encountered previously is the B vitamin thiamin (see Section 21-14).*

The two purine derivatives found in nucleotides are adenine (A) and guanine (G).

Adenine (A)   Guanine (G)

Adenine is the 6-amino derivative of purine, and guanine is the 2-amino-6-oxo purine derivative. A space-filling model for adenine is shown in Figure 22-1. ◀

▶ *Caffeine, the most widely used nonprescription central nervous system stimulant, is the 1,3,7-trimethyl-2,6-dioxo derivative of purine (Section 17-9).*

Adenine, guanine, and cytosine are found in both DNA and RNA. Uracil is found only in RNA, and thymine usually occurs only in DNA. Figure 22-2 summarizes the occurrences of nitrogen-containing heterocyclic bases in nucleic acids.

Phosphate

Phosphate, the third component of a nucleotide, is derived from phosphoric acid (H_3PO_4). Under cellular pH conditions, the phosphoric acid loses two of its hydrogen atoms to give a hydrogen phosphate ion (HPO_4^{2-}).

$$O{=}P{-}OH \rightleftharpoons O{=}P{-}OH + 2H^+$$

Phosphoric acid   Hydrogen phosphate ion

Figure 22-1 Space-filling model of the molecule adenine, a nitrogen-containing heterocyclic base present in both DNA and RNA.

Figure 22-2 Two purine bases and three pyrimidine bases are found in the nucleotides present in nucleic acids. ◀

▶ *To remember which two of the five nucleotide bases are the purine derivatives (fused rings), use the phrase "pure silver" and substitute the chemical symbol for silver, which is Ag.*

pure Ag
purine A and G

In both DNA and RNA

Purine

Adenine
A

Guanine
G

Pyrimidine

Thymine
T

Cytosine
C

Uracil
U

In DNA

In RNA

Section 22-2 Quick Quiz

1. Any given nucleotide in a nucleic acid contains
   a. two pentose sugars, one heterocyclic base, and one phosphate group
   b. one pentose sugar, two heterocyclic bases, and one phosphate group
   c. one pentose sugar, one heterocyclic base, and one phosphate group
   d. no correct response
2. How many different sugars and how many different heterocyclic bases are available, respectively, for incorporation into a nucleotide?
   a. 2 and 2
   b. 2 and 5
   c. 3 and 4
   d. no correct response
3. How many different heterocyclic bases that are purine derivatives are available for incorporation into a nucleotide?
   a. 2
   b. 3
   c. 4
   d. no correct response

Answers: 1. c; 2. b; 3. a

22-3 Nucleotide Formation

LEARNING FOCUS

Distinguish between the terms *nucleoside* and *nucleotide;* known names and abbreviations for the eight nucleotides that are found in nucleic acids.

The formation of a nucleotide from a sugar, a base, and a phosphate can be visualized as a two-step process.

1. First, the pentose sugar and nitrogen-containing base react to form a two-subunit entity called a *nucleoside* (not *nucleotide,* s versus t).
2. The nucleoside reacts with a phosphate group to form the three-subunit entity called a *nucleotide.* It is nucleotides that become the building blocks for nucleic acids. ◀

▶ *Nucleoside = Sugar + Base*
Nucleotide = Nucleoside + Phosphate

Nucleoside Formation

A **nucleoside** *is a two-subunit molecule in which a pentose sugar is bonded to a nitrogen-containing heterocyclic base.* The following structural equation is representative of nucleoside formation. ◄

► *Nucleosides are more soluble in water than free heterocyclic bases because of the hydrophilic nature of the pentose's —OH groups.*

Important characteristics of the nucleoside formation process of combining two molecules into one are:

1. The base is always attached to C1' of the sugar (the anomeric carbon atom [Section 18-10]), which is always in a β-configuration. For purine bases, attachment is through N9; for pyrimidine bases, N1 is involved. The bond connecting the sugar and base is a β-N-glycosidic linkage (Section 18-3).
2. A molecule of water is formed as the two molecules bond together; a condensation reaction occurs.

Eight nucleosides are associated with nucleic acid chemistry—four involve ribose (RNA nucleosides) and four involve deoxyribose (DNA nucleosides). The eight combinations are:

RNA Nucleosides	DNA Nucleosides
ribose–adenine	deoxyribose–adenine
ribose–cytosine	deoxyribose–cytosine
ribose–guanine	deoxyribose–guanine
ribose–uracil	deoxyribose–thymine

Nucleosides are named as derivatives of the base that they contain; the base's name is modified using a suffix.

1. For pyrimidine bases, the suffix -*idine* is used (cytidine, thymidine, uridine).
2. For purine bases, the suffix -*osine* is used (adenosine, guanosine).
3. The prefix *deoxy-* is used to indicate that the sugar present is deoxyribose. No prefix is used when the sugar present is ribose.

Using these rules, the nucleoside containing ribose and adenine is called *adenosine,* and the nucleoside containing deoxyribose and thymine is called *deoxythymidine.*

Nucleotide Formation

Nucleotides are nucleosides that have a phosphate group bonded to the pentose sugar present. The following structural equation is representative of the conversion of a nucleoside to a nucleotide.

▶ Table 22-1 **Information Concerning the Eight Nucleotides That Are Building Blocks for DNA and RNA**

Base	Abbreviation	Nucleoside	Nucleotide	Abbreviation
DNA				
Adenine	A	Deoxyadenosine	Deoxyadenosine 5'-monophosphate	dAMP
Guanine	G	Deoxyguanosine	Deoxyguanosine 5'-monophosphate	dGMP
Cytosine	C	Deoxycytidine	Deoxycytidine 5'-monophosphate	dCMP
Thymine	T	Deoxythymidine	Deoxythymidine 5'-monophosphate	dTMP
RNA				
Adenine	A	Adenosine	Adenosine 5'-monophosphate	AMP
Guanine	G	Guanosine	Guanosine 5'-monophosphate	GMP
Cytosine	C	Cytidine	Cytidine 5'-monophosphate	CMP
Uracil	U	Uridine	Uridine 5'-monophosphate	UMP

Important characteristics of the nucleotide formation process of adding a phosphate group to a nucleoside are the following:

1. The phosphate group is attached to the sugar at the C5' position through a phosphoester linkage.
2. As with nucleoside formation, a molecule of water is produced in nucleotide formation. Thus, overall, two molecules of water are produced in combining a sugar, base, and phosphate into a nucleotide.

Nucleotides are named by appending the term *5'-monophosphate* to the name of the nucleoside from which they are derived. Addition of a phosphate group to the nucleoside adenosine produces the nucleotide adenosine 5'-monophosphate.

Abbreviations for nucleotides exist, which are used in a manner similar to that for amino acids (Section 20-2). The abbreviations use the one-letter symbols for the base (*A, C, G, T,* and *U*), *MP* for monophosphate, and a lowercase *d* at the start of the abbreviation when deoxyribose is the sugar. The abbreviation for adenosine 5'-monophosphate is *AMP* and that for deoxyadenosine 5'-monophosphate is *dAMP*. Table 22-1 summarizes information presented in this section about nucleosides and nucleotides.

EXAMPLE 22-1

Identifying Components of a Nucleotide

For the nucleotide

a. What is the name of the pentose sugar present?
b. Is the heterocyclic base present a purine or a pyrimidine?
c. What is the name of the heterocyclic base present?
d. Would this nucleotide be found in DNA or RNA molecules?

Solution

a. The sugar has an —OH group on carbon 2′ and is therefore ribose; in deoxyribose, a hydrogen atom would have replaced this —OH group.

b. The base is a purine (two-ring base) rather than a pyrimidine (one-ring base).

c. The purine base with an amine ring attachment is adenine.

d. Nucleotides in which ribose is present are found in RNA molecules.

1. Which of the following is present in nucleotides but not in nucleosides?
   a. phosphate group
   b. heterocyclic base
   c. pentose sugar
   d. no correct response
2. Which of the following is an *incorrect* statement concerning the structural characteristics of a nucleotide?
   a. The phosphate subunit is bonded to the sugar subunit.
   b. The sugar subunit is bonded to the base subunit.
   c. The base subunit is bonded to the phosphate subunit.
   d. no correct response
3. How many of the eight nucleic acid nucleotides are found in DNA molecules?
   a. four
   b. five
   c. all of them
   d. no correct response
4. The nucleotide AMP is found in
   a. DNA molecules but not RNA molecules
   b. RNA molecules but not DNA molecules
   c. both DNA and RNA molecules
   d. no correct response

Answers: 1. a; 2. c; 3. a; 4. b

22-4 Primary Nucleic Acid Structure

LEARNING FOCUS

Know the common and differing structural characteristics of primary structure for DNA and RNA molecules.

Nucleic acids are polymers in which the repeating units, the monomers, are nucleotides (Section 22-2). The nucleotide units within a nucleic acid molecule are linked to each other through sugar–phosphate bonds. The resulting molecular structure (Figure 22-3) involves a chain of alternating sugar and phosphate groups with a base group protruding from the chain at regular intervals. ◀

In Section 22-1, the two general types of nucleic acids—ribonucleic acids and deoxyribonucleic acids—were mentioned, but their definitions were not given. Definitions are now in order. A **ribonucleic acid (RNA)** is *a nucleotide polymer in which each of the monomers contains ribose, a phosphate group, and one of the heterocyclic bases adenine, cytosine, guanine, or uracil.* Two changes to this definition generate the deoxyribonucleic acid definition; deoxyribose replaces ribose and thymine replaces uracil.

▶ *Nucleotides are related to nucleic acids in the same way that amino acids are related to proteins.*

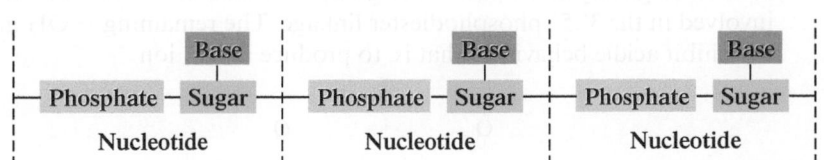

Figure 22-3 The general structure of a nucleic acid in terms of nucleotide subunits.

Figure 22-4 (a) The generalized backbone structure of a nucleic acid. (b) The specific backbone structure for a deoxyribonucleic acid (DNA). (c) The specific backbone structure for a ribonucleic acid (RNA).

Phosphate		Phosphate		Phosphate
Sugar		Deoxyribose		Ribose
Phosphate		Phosphate		Phosphate
Sugar		Deoxyribose		Ribose
Phosphate		Phosphate		Phosphate
Sugar		Deoxyribose		Ribose

a Nucleic Acid Backbone   **b** DNA Backbone   **c** RNA Backbone

A **deoxyribonucleic acid (DNA)** *is a nucleotide polymer in which each of the monomers contains deoxyribose, a phosphate group, and one of the heterocyclic bases adenine, cytosine, guanine, or thymine.*

The alternating sugar–phosphate chain in a nucleic acid structure is often called the *nucleic acid backbone.* This backbone is constant throughout the entire nucleic acid structure. For DNA molecules, the backbone consists of alternating phosphate and *deoxyribose* sugar units; for RNA molecules, the backbone consists of alternating phosphate and *ribose* sugar units. Figure 22-4 contrasts the generalized backbone structure for a nucleic acid with the specific backbone structures of DNAs and RNAs. ◀

The variable portion of nucleic acid structure is the sequence of bases attached to the sugar units of the backbone. The sequence of these base side chains distinguishes various DNAs from each other and various RNAs from each other. Only four types of bases are found in any given nucleic acid structure. This situation is much simpler than that for proteins, where 20 side-chain entities (amino acids) are available (Section 20-2). In both RNA and DNA, adenine, guanine, and cytosine are encountered as side-chain components; thymine is found mainly in DNA, and uracil is found only in RNA (Figure 22-2).

Primary nucleic acid structure *is the sequence in which nucleotides are linked together in a nucleic acid.* Because the sugar–phosphate backbone of a given nucleic acid does not vary, the primary structure of the nucleic acid depends only on the sequence of bases present. ◀ Further information about nucleic acid structure can be obtained by considering the detailed four-nucleotide segment of a DNA molecule shown in Figure 22-5.

The following list describes some important points about nucleic acid structure that are illustrated in Figure 22-5:

▶ *The backbone of a nucleic acid structure is always an alternating sequence of phosphate and sugar groups. The sugar is ribose in RNA and deoxyribose in DNA.*

▶ *Just as the order of amino acid side chains determines the primary structure of a protein (Section 20-10), the order of nucleotide bases determines the primary structure of a nucleic acid.*

▶ *For both nucleic acids and proteins, a distinction is made between the two ends of the polymer chain. For nucleic acids, there is a 5′ end and a 3′ end; for proteins, there is an N-terminal end and a C-terminal end (Section 20-7).*

1. Each nonterminal phosphate group of the sugar–phosphate backbone is bonded to two sugar molecules through a *3′,5′-phosphodiester linkage.* There is a phosphoester bond to the 5′ carbon of one sugar unit and a phosphoester bond to the 3′ carbon of the other sugar.
2. A nucleotide chain has *directionality.* One end of the nucleotide chain, the *5′ end,* normally carries a free phosphate group attached to the 5′ carbon atom. The other end of the nucleotide chain, the *3′ end,* normally has a free hydroxyl group attached to the 3′ carbon atom. By convention, the sequence of bases in a nucleic acid strand is read from the 5′ end to the 3′ end. ◀
3. Each nonterminal phosphate group in the backbone of a nucleic acid carries a 1− charge. The parent phosphoric acid molecule from which the phosphate was derived originally had three —OH groups (Section 22-2). Two of these become involved in the 3′,5′-phosphodiester linkage. The remaining —OH group is free to exhibit acidic behavior—that is, to produce an H^+ ion.

$$O=\overset{\overset{\displaystyle O}{|}}{\underset{\underset{\displaystyle OH}{|}}{P}}-O- \;\rightleftharpoons\; O=\overset{\overset{\displaystyle O}{|}}{\underset{\underset{\displaystyle O^-}{|}}{P}}-O- \;+\; H^+$$

Figure 22-5 A four-nucleotide-long segment of DNA. (The choice of bases was arbitrary.)

This behavior by the many phosphate groups in a nucleic acid backbone gives nucleic acids their acidic properties.

Specifying the primary structure for a nucleic acid is done by listing nucleotide base components (using their one-letter abbreviations) in sequential order starting with the base at the 5′ end of the nucleotide strand. The primary structure for the four-nucleotide DNA segment shown in Figure 22-5 is

$$5'\ T\text{–}G\text{–}C\text{–}A\ 3'$$

Three parallels between primary nucleic acid structure and primary protein structure (Section 20-10) are worth noting:

1. DNAs, RNAs, and proteins all have backbones that do not vary in structure (see Figure 22-6).

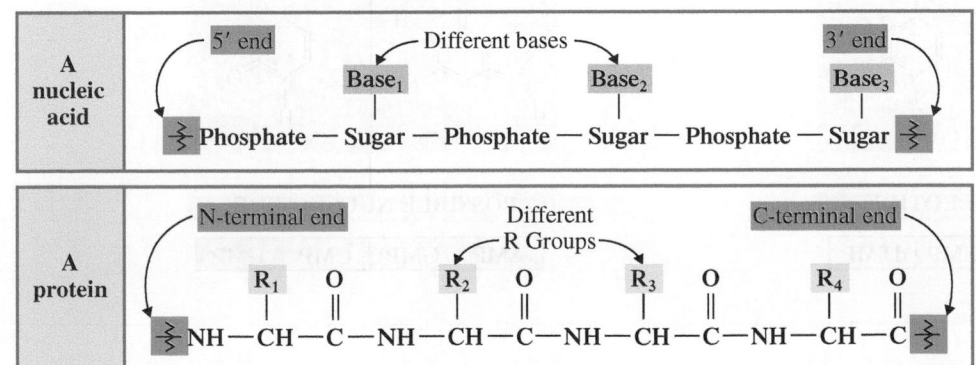

Figure 22-6 A comparison of the general primary structures of nucleic acids and proteins.

2. The sequence of attachments to the backbones (nitrogen bases in nucleic acids and amino acid R groups in proteins) distinguishes one DNA from another, one RNA from another, and one protein from another (Figure 22-6).

3. Both nucleic acid polymer chains and protein polymer chains have directionality; for nucleic acids, there is a 5′ end and a 3′ end, and for proteins, there is an N-terminal end and a C-terminal end.

Chemistry at a Glance—Nucleic Acid Structure—summarizes important concepts relative to the makeup of the nucleotide building blocks (monomers) present in polymeric DNA and RNA molecules.

CHEMISTRY AT A GLANCE — Nucleic Acid Structure

Section 22-4 Quick Quiz

1. The primary structure of a nucleic acid is determined by the sequence of
   a. pentoses present
   b. bases present
   c. phosphates present
   d. no correct response
2. The "backbone" of a nucleic acid molecule involves an alternating sequence of
   a. sugar and phosphate groups
   b. sugar and base groups
   c. phosphate and base groups
   d. no correct answer
3. In a segment of a nucleic acid each *nonterminal* phosphate group
   a. carries a 1– charge
   b. carries a 2– charge
   c. carries a 3– charge
   d. no correct response
4. In a segment of a nucleic acid a *terminal* phosphate group is found at
   a. the 3′ end of the segment
   b. the 5′ end of the segment
   c. both ends of the segment
   d. no correct response
5. The sequence of bases in a segment of nucleic acid
   a. is always read in the 5′-to-3′ direction
   b. is always read in the 3′-to-5′ direction
   c. can be read in either direction because directionality does not matter
   d. no correct response

Answers: 1. b; 2. a; 3. a; 4. b; 5. a

22-5 The DNA Double Helix

LEARNING FOCUS

Be familiar with the double-helix secondary structure feature associated with DNA molecules; be familiar with the concept of complementary base pairing and the rules associated with such pairing.

Like proteins, nucleic acids have secondary, or three-dimensional, structure as well as primary structure. The secondary structures of DNAs and RNAs differ, so they will be discussed separately.

The amounts of the bases A, T, G, and C present in DNA molecules were the key to determination of the general three-dimensional structure of DNA molecules. Base composition data for DNA molecules from many different organisms revealed a definite pattern of base occurrence. The amounts of A and T were always equal, and the amounts of C and G were always equal, as were the amounts of total purines and total pyrimidines.

The relative amounts of these base pairs in DNA vary depending on the life form from which the DNA is obtained. (Each animal or plant has a unique base composition.) However, the relationships

$$\%A = \%T \qquad \text{and} \qquad \%C = \%G$$

always hold true. For example, human DNA contains 30% adenine, 30% thymine, 20% guanine, and 20% cytosine.

In 1953, an explanation for the base composition patterns associated with DNA molecules was proposed by the American microbiologist James Watson and the English biophysicist Francis Crick. Their model, which has now been validated in numerous ways, involves a double-helix structure that accounts for the equality of bases present, as well as for other known DNA structural data.

Figure 22-7 Three views of the DNA double helix.

a A schematic drawing that emphasizes the hydrogen bonding between bases on the two chains.

b A space-filling model in which one DNA strand is blue and the other strand is orange. The bases are shown in lighter shades of blue and orange.

c A top view of the double helix.

The DNA double helix involves two polynucleotide strands coiled around each other in a manner somewhat like a spiral staircase. The sugar–phosphate backbones of the two polynucleotide strands can be thought of as being the outside banisters of the spiral staircase (Figure 22-7). The bases (side chains) of each backbone extend inward toward the bases of the other strand. The two strands are connected by *hydrogen bonds* (Section 7-13) between their bases. Additionally, the two strands of the double helix are *antiparallel*—that is, they run in opposite directions. One strand runs in the 5′-to-3′ direction, and the other is oriented in the 3′-to-5′ direction. ◄

Base Pairing

A physical restriction, the size of the interior of the DNA double helix, limits the base pairs that can hydrogen-bond to one another. Only pairs involving one small base (a pyrimidine) and one large base (a purine) correctly "fit" within the helix interior. There is not enough room for two large purine bases to fit opposite each other (they overlap), and two small pyrimidine bases are too far apart to hydrogen-bond to one another effectively. ◄ Of the four possible purine–pyrimidine combinations (A–T, A–C, G–T, and G–C), hydrogen-bonding possibilities are *most favorable* for the A–T and G–C pairings, and these two combinations are the *only two* that normally occur in DNA. Figure 22-8 shows the specific hydrogen-bonding interactions for the four possible purine–pyrimidine base-pairing combinations.

▶ *The* antiparallel *nature of the two polynucleotide chains in the DNA double helix means that there is a 5′ end and a 3′ end at both ends of the double helix.*

▶ *The α helix secondary structure of proteins (Section 20-11) involves* one *polypeptide chain; the double-helix secondary structure of DNA involves* two *polynucleotide chains. In the α helix of proteins, the R groups are on the* outside *of the helix; in the double helix of DNA, the bases are on the* inside *of the double helix.*

a Base-pairing combinations that do occur

Thymine–Adenine Base Pairing
(two hydrogen bonds form)

Cytosine–Guanine Base Pairing
(three hydrogen bonds form)

b Base-pairing combinations that do not occur

Thymine–Guanine Base Pairing
(only one hydrogen bond forms)

Cytosine–Adenine Base Pairing
(only one hydrogen bond forms)

| ● Carbon | ● Oxygen | 🝙 Lone pair | ••• Hydrogen bond |
| ● Nitrogen | ● Hydrogen | ═ Attachment to backbone | |

Figure 22-8 Hydrogen-bonding possibilities are more favorable when A–T and G–C base pairing occurs than when A–C and G–T base pairing occurs. (a) Two and three hydrogen bonds can form, respectively, between A–T and G–C base pairs. These combinations are present in DNA molecules. (b) Only one hydrogen bond can form between G–T and A–C base pairs. These combinations are not present in DNA molecules. ◄

▶ *A mnemonic device for recalling observed base-pairing combinations in DNA involves listing the base abbreviations in alphabetical order. Then the first and last bases pair, and so do the middle two bases.*

DNA: A C G T

Another way to remember these base-pairing combinations is to note that AT spells a word and that C and G look very much alike.

The pairing of A with T and that of G with C are said to be *complementary*. A and T are complementary bases, as are G and C. **Complementary bases** *are pairs of bases in a nucleic acid structure that hydrogen-bond to each other.* The fact that complementary base pairing occurs in DNA molecules explains, very simply, why the amounts of the bases A and T present are always equal, as are the amounts of G and C.

The two strands of DNA in a double helix are *not identical*—they are complementary. **Complementary DNA strands** *are strands of DNA in a double helix with base pairing such that each base is located opposite its complementary base.* Wherever G occurs in one strand, there is a C in the other strand; wherever T occurs in one strand, there is an A in the other strand. An important ramification of this complementary relationship is that knowing the base sequence of one strand of DNA enables prediction of the base sequence of the complementary strand. ◄

The base sequence of a single strand of a DNA molecule segment is always written in the direction from the 5′ end to the 3′ end of the segment.

5′ A–A–G–C–T–A–G–C–T–T–A–C–T 3′

If the end designations for a base sequence (5′ and 3′) are not specified for a sequence of bases, it is assumed that the sequence starts with the 5′ end base. In the base sequence

A–C–G–T–T–C

it is assumed that A is the 5′ end base. ◄

▶ *The two strands of DNA in a double helix are complementary. This means that if you know the order of bases in one strand, you can predict the order of bases in the other strand.*

▶ *The following two notations for a DNA base sequence have identical meaning.*

5′ A–C–G–T–T 3′
5′ ACGTT 3′

Bond lines between nucleotides do not have to be shown, and usually are not shown for longer polynucleotides.

EXAMPLE 22-2

Predicting Base Sequence in a Complementary DNA Strand

Predict the sequence of bases in the DNA strand that is complementary to the single DNA strand shown.

5′ C–G–A–A–T–C–C–T–A 3′

Solution

Because only A forms a complementary base pair with T, and only G with C, the complementary strand is as follows:

Given: 5′ C–G–A–A–T–C–C–T–A 3′

Complementary strand: 3′ G–C–T–T–A–G–G–A–T 5′

Note the reversal of the numbering of the ends of the complementary strand compared to the given strand. This is due to the antiparallel nature of the two strands in a DNA double helix.

When generating a complementary base sequence from a given 5′-to-3′ base sequence, as was done in Example 22-2, the complementary base sequence obtained runs in the 3′-to-5′ direction because of the antiparallel relationship that exists between paired base sequences. Such 3′-to-5′ base sequences are acceptable as long as the directionality of the sequence is specifically noted. When needed, a 3′-to-5′ base sequence can be converted to a 5′-to-3′ base sequence by simply reversing the order of the bases listed. The following two base sequence notations are entirely equivalent to each other.

3′ A–T–C–G 5′   and   5′ G–C–T–A 3′

Hydrogen Bonding Interactions

Hydrogen bonding between base pairs is an important factor in stabilizing the DNA double-helix structure. Although hydrogen bonds are relatively weak forces, each DNA molecule has so many base pairs that, collectively, these hydrogen bonds are a force of significant strength. In addition to hydrogen bonding, base-stacking interactions contribute to DNA double-helix stabilization.

Base-Stacking Interactions

The bases in a DNA double helix are positioned with the planes of their rings parallel (like a stack of coins). Stacking interactions involving a given base and the parallel bases directly above and below it also contribute to the stabilization of the DNA double helix. These stacking interactions are as important in their stabilization effects as is the hydrogen bonding associated with base pairing—sometimes even more important. ◄ Purine and pyrimidine bases are hydrophobic in nature, so their stacking interactions are those associated with hydrophobic molecules—mainly London forces (Section 7-13). The concept of hydrophobic interactions has been encountered twice previously. Hydrophobic interactions involving the nonpolar tails of membrane lipids contribute to the structural stability of cell membranes (Section 19-10), and hydrophobic interactions involving nonpolar R groups of amino acids contribute to protein tertiary structure stability (Section 20-12).

▶ *Both hydrogen bonding and base-stacking interactions contribute to secondary-structure stabilization in DNA molecules.*

Section 22-5 Quick Quiz

1. Which of the following statements concerning a DNA double-helix structure is *incorrect*?
   a. The two nucleotide strands present are identical.
   b. Hydrogen bonds help hold the two nucleotide strands together.
   c. Complementary base pairing occurs within the double helix.
   d. no correct response

2. Which of the following is the complementary base for C in DNA molecules?
   a. A
   b. G
   c. T
   d. no correct response
3. Fifteen percent of the bases in a certain DNA molecule are found to be T. What percent of the bases in the same molecule are G?
   a. 15%
   b. 35%
   c. 65%
   d. no correct response
4. Which of the following is the correct complementary DNA sequence for the DNA base sequence 5′ C–G–A–A–T 3′?
   a. 5′ T–A–A–G–C 3′
   b. 5′ G–C–T–T–A 3′
   c. 3′ G–C–T–T–A 5′
   d. no correct response

Answers: 1. a; 2. b; 3. b; 4. c

22-6 Replication of DNA Molecules

LEARNING FOCUS

Describe the various steps involved in the process of DNA replication; be familiar with terminology and enzymes associated with DNA replication.

DNA molecules are the carriers of genetic information within a cell; that is, they are the molecules of heredity. Each time a cell divides, an exact copy of the DNA of the parent cell is needed for the new daughter cell. The process by which new DNA molecules are generated is DNA replication. **DNA replication** *is the biochemical process by which DNA molecules produce exact duplicates of themselves.* The key concept in understanding DNA replication is the base pairing associated with the DNA double helix.

DNA Replication Overview

In DNA replication, the two strands of the DNA double helix are regarded as a pair of *templates,* or patterns. During replication, the strands separate. Each can then act as a template for the synthesis of a new, complementary strand. The result is two daughter DNA molecules with base sequences identical to those of the parent double helix. Details of this replication are as follows.

Under the influence of the enzyme *DNA helicase,* the DNA double helix unwinds, and the hydrogen bonds between complementary bases are broken. This unwinding process, as shown in Figure 22-9, is somewhat like opening a zipper. The point at which the DNA double helix is unwinding, which is constantly changing (moving), is called the *replication fork* (Figure 22-9).

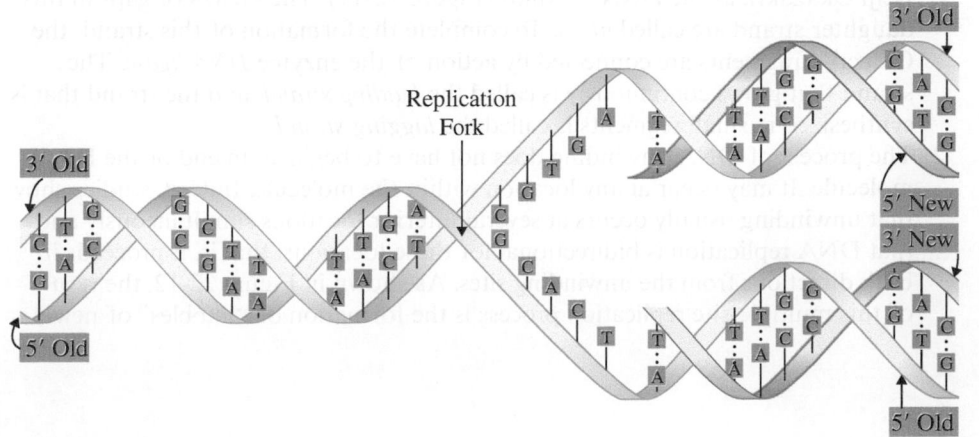

Figure 22-9 In DNA replication, the two strands of the DNA double helix unwind, with the separated strands serving as templates for the formation of new DNA strands. Free nucleotides pair with the complementary bases on the separated strands of DNA. This process ultimately results in the complete replication of the DNA molecule.

Figure 22-10 In DNA replication, two daughter DNA molecules are produced from one parent DNA molecule, with each daughter DNA molecule containing one parent DNA strand and one newly formed DNA strand.

PARENT STRAND

NEWLY FORMED STRAND

SEGMENT OF PARENT DNA

NEWLY FORMED STRAND

PARENT STRAND

SEGMENT OF DAUGHTER DNAs
(both of which are identical
and both of which contain
one parent strand and one
newly formed strand)

The bases of the separated strands are no longer connected by hydrogen bonds. They can pair with *free* individual nucleotides present in the cell's nucleus. As shown in Figure 22-9, the base pairing always involves C pairing with G and A pairing with T. The pairing process occurs one nucleotide at a time. After a free nucleotide has formed hydrogen bonds with a base of the old strand (the template), the enzyme *DNA polymerase* verifies that the base pairing is correct and then catalyzes the formation of a new phosphodiester linkage between the nucleotide and the growing strand (represented by the darker blue ribbons in Figure 22-9). The *DNA polymerase* then slides down the strand to the next unpaired base of the template, and the same process is repeated.

The net result of DNA replication is the production of two *daughter DNA molecules,* both of which are identical to the one *parent DNA molecule* from which they were formed. Figure 22-10 gives a "close-up" view of the relationships between parent DNA and the daughter DNA produced from it. Note that each daughter DNA molecule contains one strand from the parent DNA and one strand that is newly formed.

The Replication Process in Finer Detail

Though simple in principle, the DNA replication process has many intricacies.

1. The enzyme *DNA polymerase* can operate on a forming DNA daughter strand only in the 5′-to-3′ direction. Because the two strands of parent DNA run in opposite directions (one is 5′ to 3′ and the other 3′ to 5′; Section 22-4), only one strand can grow continuously in the 5′-to-3′ direction. The other strand must be formed in short segments, called *Okazaki fragments* (after their discoverer, Reiji Okazaki), as the DNA unwinds (Figure 22-11). The breaks or gaps in this daughter strand are called *nicks.* To complete the formation of this strand, the Okazaki fragments are connected by action of the enzyme *DNA ligase.* The strand that grows continuously is called the *leading strand,* and the strand that is synthesized in small segments is called the *lagging strand.*

2. The process of DNA unwinding does not have to begin at an end of the DNA molecule. It may occur at any location within the molecule. Indeed, studies show that unwinding usually occurs at several interior locations simultaneously and that DNA replication is bidirectional for these locations; that is, it proceeds in both directions from the unwinding sites. As shown in Figure 22-12, the result of this multiple-site replication process is the formation of "bubbles" of newly

Direction of movement of replication fork

Replication fork

3′

5′

Leading strand (grows continuously)

Okazaki fragments

Lagging strand (grows in segments)

Nick

3′

5′

5′

3′

5′

Figure 22-11 Because the enzyme *DNA polymerase* can act only in the 5′-to-3′ direction, one strand (top) grows continuously in the direction of the unwinding, and the other strand grows in segments in the opposite direction. The segments in this latter chain are then connected by a different enzyme, *DNA ligase*.

Origins of replication

Parent DNA

Early stage in replication

Later stage in replication

Daughter DNAs

Figure 22-12 DNA replication usually occurs at multiple sites within a molecule, and the replication is bidirectional from these sites.

synthesized DNA. The bubbles grow larger and eventually coalesce, giving rise to two complete daughter DNAs. Multiple-site replication enables large DNA molecules to be replicated rapidly.

Chemistry at a Glance—DNA Replication—summarizes the steps, as discussed in this section, that occur in the process of DNA replication.

Based on mode of action, several types of anticancer drugs exist. One large group of such drugs are the *antimetabolites,* drugs which are DNA-replication inhibitors. The focus on relevancy feature Chemical Connections 22-A—Antimetabolites: Anticancer Drugs That Inhibit DNA Synthesis—discusses several substances that find use as DNA-replication inhibitors.

Chromosomes

Once the DNA within a cell has been replicated, it interacts with specific proteins in the cell called *histones* to form structural units that provide the most stable arrangement for the long DNA molecules. These histone–DNA complexes are called *chromosomes.* **A chromosome** *is an individual DNA molecule bound to a group of proteins.* Typically, a chromosome is about 15% by mass DNA and 85% by mass protein. ◀

Cells from different kinds of organisms have different numbers of chromosomes. A normal human has 46 chromosomes per cell, a mosquito 6, a frog 26, a dog 78, and a turkey 82.

▶ *Chromosomes are nucleoproteins. They are a combination of nucleic acid (DNA) and various proteins.*

CHEMISTRY AT A GLANCE   DNA Replication

STEP 2

Free nucleotides pair with their complementary base on the template strands by means of hydrogen bonds.

STEP 3

DNA polymerase joins the newly attached nucleotides to create one continuous strand in the 5′-to-3′ direction.

STEP 1

The enzyme DNA helicase causes the two strands of DNA to unwind, producing two template strands.

3′ (old)

5′ (new)

5′ (old)

3′ (old)

3′ (new)

5′ (old)

STEP 4

The other strand is formed in short segments (Okazaki fragments) in the 3′-to-5′ direction. The segments are then joined together by DNA ligase.

Figure 22-13 Identical twins share identical physical characteristics because they received identical DNA from their parents.

Chromosomes occur in matched (*homologous*) pairs. The 46 chromosomes of a human cell constitute 23 homologous pairs. One member of each homologous pair is derived from a chromosome inherited from the father, and the other is a copy of one of the chromosomes inherited from the mother. Homologous chromosomes have similar, but not identical, DNA base sequences; both code for the same traits but for different forms of the trait (for example, blue eyes versus brown eyes). Offspring are like their parents, but they are different as well; part of their DNA came from one parent and part from the other parent. Occasionally, identical twins are born (Figure 22-13). Such twins have received identical DNA from their parents.

Antimetabolites: Anticancer Drugs That Inhibit DNA Synthesis

Cancer is a disease characterized by rapid uncontrolled cell division. Rapid cell division necessitates the synthesis of large amounts of DNA, as DNA must be present in each new cell produced. Numerous anticancer drugs are now available that block DNA synthesis and therefore decrease the rate at which new cancer cells are produced.

Antimetabolites are a class of anticancer drugs that interfere with DNA replication because their structures are similar to molecules required for normal DNA replication. The structural similarity is close enough that enzymes can be "tricked" into using the drug rather than the real substrate needed. This "trickery" shuts down DNA synthesis, which causes cells to die.

Four examples of commonly used antimetabolites and the molecules they "mimic" are as follows:

1. **6-Mercaptopurine (6-MP):** 6-MP structurally resembles adenine, one of the four nitrogen-containing bases present in all DNA molecules. Synthesis of adenine-containing nucleotides is inhibited when 6-MP is present; nonfunctional DNA results when 6-MP, rather than adenine, is incorporated into a nucleotide.

6-Mercaptopurine
(a modified adenine)

Adenine

2. **Thioguanine:** As was the case with 6-MP, the close structural resemblance between thioguanine and guanine leads to the incorporation of thioguanine, rather than guanine, into nucleotides. Nonfunctional DNA is the result.

Thioguanine
(a modified guanine)

Guanine

3. **5-Fluorouracil:** Uracil is a base found in RNA rather than DNA. However, the structure of 5-fluorouracil is close enough to that of thymine (which is methyluracil) that it can pass for thymine. It thus inhibits the synthesis of active thymine-containing nucleotides needed for DNA synthesis.

5-Fluorouracil
(a modified thymine)

Thymine

A cancer patient undergoing chemotherapy to inhibit DNA synthesis.

4. **Methotrexate:** The previous three antimetabolites were all close structural analogs of bases found in DNA nucleotides. Some antimetabolites are not base analogs. Methotrexate is one of these non-base analogs. It is a structural analog of folic acid (folate), which is one of the B vitamins (Section 21-14). A derivative of folic acid is needed in one of the early steps of nucleotide synthesis. Methotrexate inhibits the conversion of folic acid to this needed derivative, which shuts down DNA synthesis.

Methotrexate

Folic acid

Note that all four of these antimetabolites are synthetically produced molecules rather than naturally occurring ones. Many different synthetically modified purine and pyrimidine derivatives are now available for use in studies that involve DNA.

While some types of cancer respond very well to chemotherapy using antimetabolite drugs (leukemia is one such cancer), other types of cancer do not respond well to such treatment. Two other general types of anticancer drugs are available for use in these treatment situations. They are (1) DNA-damaging agents and (2) cell-division inhibitors. Cisplatin is a well-known DNA damaging agent, and the natural products vincristine (obtained from the periwinkle plant) and taxol (obtained from yew tree bark) are cell-division inhibitors.

Cells most affected by anticancer drugs are those undergoing rapid cell division (the cancer cells). However, normal cells are also affected, to a lesser extent, by these drugs. Eventually, the normal cells are affected to such a degree that use of the drugs must be discontinued, at least for a period of time.

Section 22-6 Quick Quiz

1. Replication of DNA produces two daughter molecules in which each daughter molecule contains
   a. a segment of both parent strands
   b. a segment of both newly synthesized strands
   c. one parent strand and one newly synthesized strand
   d. no correct response
2. In DNA replication the DNA double helix unwinds under the influence of
   a. DNA helicase
   b. DNA polymerase
   c. DNA ligase
   d. no correct response
3. In DNA replication the new strand that is synthesized in small segments is called
   a. the leading strand
   b. the lagging strand
   c. an Okazaki fragment
   d. no correct response
4. In DNA replication the unwinding of the DNA double helix
   a. begins at the 5' end and continues to the 3' end
   b. begins at the 3' end and continues to the 5' end
   c. occurs at many locations within the double helix
   d. no correct response
5. A chromosome is a protein–DNA complex that contains
   a. a single DNA molecule
   b. two interwined DNA molecules
   c. two structurally independent DNA molecules
   d. no correct response

Answers: 1. c; 2. a; 3. b; 4. c; 5. a

22-7 Overview of Protein Synthesis

LEARNING FOCUS

Be able to give an overview summary for protein synthesis.

In the previous section it was shown how the replication of DNA makes it possible for a new cell to contain the same genetic information as its parent cell. How the genetic information contained in a cell is expressed in cell operation will now be considered. This leads to the topic of protein synthesis. The synthesis of proteins (skin, hair, enzymes, hormones, and so on) is under the direction of DNA molecules. It is this role of DNA that establishes the similarities between parent and offspring that are regarded as hereditary characteristics.

The overall process of protein synthesis is divided into two phases. The first phase is called *transcription* and the second *translation*. The following diagram summarizes the relationship between transcription and translation.

Before discussing the details of transcription and translation, more information about RNA molecules is needed. They are involved in transcription, as the end products, and in translation, as the starting materials. Particularly important are the differences between RNA and DNA and among various types of RNA molecules.

Section 22-7 Quick Quiz

1. The first phase of protein synthesis is called
   a. replication
   b. transcription
   c. translation
   d. no correct response
2. The product of the first phase of protein synthesis is
   a. DNA molecules
   b. RNA molecules
   c. both DNA and RNA molecules
   d. no correct response

Answers: 1. b; 2. b

22-8 Ribonucleic Acids

LEARNING FOCUS

Be familiar with the major differences between DNA molecules and RNA molecules; be familiar with the characteristics of and functions for the five major types of RNA molecules.

Four major differences exist between RNA molecules and DNA molecules:

1. The sugar unit in the backbone of RNA is ribose; it is deoxyribose in DNA.
2. The base thymine found in DNA is replaced by uracil in RNA (Figure 22-2). In RNA, uracil, instead of thymine, pairs with (forms hydrogen bonds with) adenine. ◀
3. RNA is a single-stranded molecule; DNA is double-stranded (double helix). Thus RNA, unlike DNA, does not contain equal amounts of specific bases.
4. RNA molecules are much smaller than DNA molecules, ranging from 75 nucleotides to a few thousand nucleotides.

Note that the single-stranded nature of RNA does not prevent *portions* of an RNA molecule from folding back upon itself and forming double-helical regions. If the base sequences along two portions of an RNA strand are complementary, a structure with a hairpin loop results, as shown in Figure 22-14. The amount of double-helical structure present in an RNA varies with RNA type, but a value of 50% is not atypical.

▶ *The bases thymine (T) and uracil (U) have similar structures. Thymine is a methyluracil (Section 22-2). The hydrogen-bonding patterns (Figure 22-7) for the A–U base pair (RNA) and the A–T base pair (DNA) are identical.*

Types of RNA Molecules

RNA molecules found in human cells are categorized into five major types, distinguished by their function. These five RNA types are heterogeneous nuclear RNA (hnRNA), messenger RNA (mRNA), small nuclear RNA (snRNA), ribosomal RNA (rRNA), and transfer RNA (tRNA).

    Heterogeneous nuclear RNA (hnRNA) *is RNA formed directly by DNA transcription.* Post-transcription processing converts the heterogeneous nuclear RNA to messenger RNA. ◀

▶ *Heterogeneous nuclear RNA (hnRNA) also goes by the name* primary transcript RNA *(ptRNA).*

Figure 22-14 A hairpin loop is produced when single-stranded RNA doubles back on itself and complementary base pairing occurs.

Figure 22-15 An overview of types of RNA in terms of cellular locations where they are encountered and processes in which they are involved.

▶ *The most abundant type of RNA in a cell is ribosomal RNA (75%–80% by mass). Transfer RNA constitutes 10%–15% of cellular RNA; messenger RNA and its precursor, heterogeneous nuclear RNA, make up 5%–10% of RNA material in a cell.*

▶ *An additional role for RNA, besides its major involvement in protein synthesis, has been recently discovered by scientists. It also plays a part in the process of blood coagulation near a wound. RNA that is released from damaged cells associated with the wound helps to activate two enzymes needed for the blood coagulation process.*

▶ *A detailed look at cellular structure is found in Section 23-2.*

Messenger RNA (mRNA) *is RNA that carries instructions for protein synthesis (genetic information) to the sites for protein synthesis.* The molecular mass of messenger RNA varies with the length of the protein whose synthesis it will direct.

Small nuclear RNA (snRNA) *is RNA that facilitates the conversion of heterogeneous nuclear RNA to messenger RNA.* It contains from 100 to 200 nucleotides.

Ribosomal RNA (rRNA) *is RNA that combines with specific proteins to form ribosomes, the physical sites for protein synthesis.* Ribosomes have molecular masses on the order of 3 million amu. The rRNA present in ribosomes has no informational function. ◀

Transfer RNA (tRNA) *is RNA that delivers amino acids to the sites for protein synthesis.* Transfer RNAs are the smallest of the RNAs, possessing only 75–90 nucleotide units. ◀

At a nondetail level, a cell consists of a nucleus and an extranuclear region called the cytoplasm. The process of DNA transcription occurs in the nucleus, as does the processing of hnRNA to mRNA. (DNA replication [Section 22-5] also occurs in the nucleus.) The mRNA formed in the nucleus travels to the cytoplasm where translation (protein synthesis) occurs. Figure 22-15 summarizes the transcription and translation processes in terms of the types of RNA involved and the cellular locations where the processes occur. ◀

Section 22-8 Quick Quiz

1. RNA molecules differ from DNA molecules in that they
   a. are single stranded rather than double stranded
   b. contain five different bases rather than four
   c. contain a greater number of nucleotide units
   d. no correct response
2. The m in the designation mRNA stands for
   a. mega
   b. messenger
   c. monomeric
   d. no correct response
3. The t in the designation tRNA stands for
   a. tertiary
   b. translational
   c. transfer
   d. no correct response
4. Which of the following types of RNA is involved in the transcription phase of protein synthesis?
   a. rRNA
   b. tRNA
   c. hnRNA
   d. no correct response

Answers: 1. a; 2. b; 3. c; 4. c

22-9 Transcription: RNA Synthesis

LEARNING FOCUS

Be familiar with how DNA, genes, hnRNA, snRNA, and mRNA are involved in the process of transcription; distinguish between exons and introns and how the process of splicing relates to these entities.

Transcription *is the process by which DNA directs the synthesis of hnRNA/mRNA molecules that carry the coded information needed for protein synthesis.* Messenger RNA production via transcription is actually a "two-step" process in which an hnRNA molecule is initially produced and then is "edited" to yield the desired mRNA molecule. The mRNA molecule so produced then functions as the carrier of the information needed to direct protein synthesis.

Within a strand of a DNA molecule are instructions for the synthesis of numerous hnRNA/mRNA molecules. During transcription, a DNA molecule unwinds, under enzyme influence, at the particular location where the appropriate base sequence is found for the hnRNA/mRNA of concern, and the "exposed" base sequence is transcribed. A short segment of a DNA strand so transcribed, which contains instructions for the formation of a particular hnRNA/mRNA, is called a *gene*. A **gene** *is a segment of a DNA strand that contains the base sequence for the production of a specific hnRNA/mRNA molecule.*

In humans, most genes are composed of 1000–3500 nucleotide units. Hundreds of genes can exist along a DNA strand. Obtaining detailed information concerning the total number of genes and the total number of nucleotide base pairs present in human DNA was an area of intense research activity during the 1980s and 1990s. The central project in this research was the *Human Genome Project,* a decade-long internationally based project to determine the location and base sequence of each of the genes in the human *genome.* A **genome** *is all of the genetic material (the total DNA) contained in the chromosomes of an organism.*

Before the Human Genome Project began, current biochemical thought predicted the presence of about 100,000 genes in the human genome. Initial results of the Human Genome Project, announced in 2001, pared this number down to 30,000–40,000 genes and also indicated that the base pairs present in these genes constitute only a very small percentage (2%) of the 2.9 billion base pairs present in the chromosomes of the human genome. In 2004, based on reanalysis of Human Genome Project information, the human gene count was pared down further to 20,000–25,000 genes. (Later in this section, the significance and ramifications of this dramatic decrease in estimates of the human gene count are considered.) ◀

Steps in the Transcription Process

The mechanics of transcription are in many ways similar to those of DNA replication. Four steps are involved:

1. A *portion* of the DNA double helix unwinds, exposing a sequence of bases (a gene). The unwinding process is governed by the enzyme *RNA polymerase* rather than by *DNA helicase* (replication enzyme).
2. Free *ribo*nucleotides, one nucleotide at a time, align along *one* of the exposed strands of DNA bases, the *template* strand, forming new base pairs. In this process, U rather than T aligns with A in the base-pairing process. Only about 10 base pairs of the DNA template strand are exposed at a time. Because ribonucleotides rather than deoxyribonucleotides are involved in the base pairing, ribose, rather than deoxyribose, becomes incorporated into the new nucleic acid backbone. ◀
3. *RNA polymerase* is involved in the linkage of ribonucleotides, one by one, to the growing hnRNA molecule.
4. Transcription ends when the *RNA polymerase* enzyme encounters a sequence of bases that is "read" as a stop signal. The newly formed hnRNA molecule and the *RNA polymerase* enzyme are released, and the DNA then rewinds to re-form the original double helix.

▶ *The overall reaction of the scientific community to the results of the Human Genome Project is aptly summarized by the expression "There are things we didn't know that we didn't know."*

▶ *In DNA—RNA base pairing, the complementary base pairs are*

DNA RNA
A — U
G — C
C — G
T — A

RNA molecules contain the base U instead of the base T.

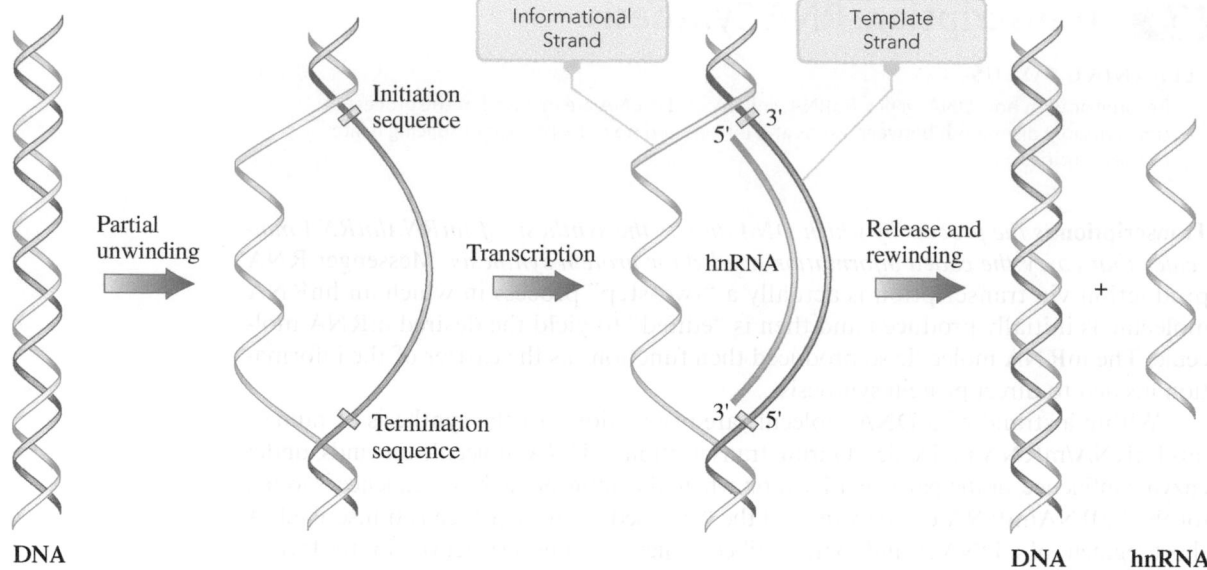

Figure 22-16 The transcription of DNA to form hnRNA involves an unwinding of a portion of the DNA double helix. Only one strand of the DNA is copied during transcription.

The strand of DNA used for hnRNA/mRNA synthesis is called the *template strand.* It is copied proceeding in the 3′-to-5′ direction. The other DNA strand (the non-template strand) is called the *informational strand.* The informational strand, although not involved in RNA synthesis, gives the base sequence present in the hnRNA strand being synthesized (with the exception of U replacing T).

Figure 22-16 shows the overall process of transcription of DNA to form hnRNA.

EXAMPLE 22-3

Base Pairing Associated with the Transcription Process

From the base sequence 5′ A–T–G–C–C–A 3′ in a DNA template strand, determine the base sequence in the hnRNA synthesized from the DNA template strand.

Solution

An RNA molecule cannot contain the base T. The base U is present instead. Therefore, U–A base pairing will occur instead of T–A base pairing. The other base-pairing combination, G–C, remains the same. The base sequence of the hnRNA strand is obtained using the following relationships:

DNA template strand: 5′ A–T–G–C–C–A 3′

┊ ┊ ┊ ┊ ┊ ┊   complementary base pairing

DNA informational strand: 3′ T–A–C–G–G–T 5′

T bases are replaced with U bases

hnRNA strand: 3′ U–A–C–G–G–U 5′

Note that the direction of the hnRNA strand is antiparallel to that of the DNA template. This will always be the case during transcription.

It is standard procedure, when writing and reading base sequences for nucleic acids (both DNAs and RNAs), always to specify base sequence in the 5′ → 3′ direction unless otherwise directed. Thus

3′ U–A–C–G–G–U 5′   becomes   5′ U–G–G–C–A–U 3′

Post-Transcription Processing: Formation of mRNA

The RNA produced from a gene through transcription is hnRNA, the precursor for mRNA. The conversion of hnRNA to mRNA involves *post-transcription processing* of the hnRNA. In this processing, certain portions of the hnRNA are deleted and the retained parts are then spliced together. This process leads to the concepts of *exons* and *introns.*

It is now known that not all bases in a gene convey genetic information. Instead, a gene is *segmented;* it has portions called *exons* that contain genetic information and portions called *introns* that do not convey genetic information.

An **exon** *is a gene segment that conveys (codes for) genetic information. Ex*ons are DNA segments that help *ex*press a genetic message. An **intron** *is a gene segment that does not convey (code for) genetic information. In*trons are DNA segments that *int*errupt a genetic message. A gene consists of alternating exon and intron segments (Figure 22-17).

Both the exons and the introns of a gene are transcribed during production of hnRNA. The hnRNA is then "edited," under enzyme direction, to remove the introns, and the remaining exons are joined together to form a shortened RNA strand that carries the genetic information of the transcribed gene. The removal of the introns and joining together of the exons takes place simultaneously in a single process. The "edited" RNA so produced is the messenger RNA (mRNA) that serves as a blueprint for protein assembly. Much is yet to be learned about introns and why they are present in genes; investigating their function is an active area of biochemical research.

Splicing *is the process of removing introns from an hnRNA molecule and joining the remaining exons together to form an mRNA molecule.* The splicing process involves snRNA molecules, the most recent of the RNA types to be discovered. This type of RNA is never found "free" in a cell. An snRNA molecule is always found complexed with proteins in particles called *small nuclear ribonucleoprotein particles,* which are usually called *snRNPs* (pronounced "snurps"). A **small nuclear ribonucleoprotein particle** *is a complex formed from an snRNA molecule and several proteins.* "Snurps" always further collect together into larger complexes called *spliceosomes.* A **spliceosome** *is a large assembly of snRNA molecules and proteins involved in the conversion of hnRNA molecules to mRNA molecules.*

Alternative Splicing

Prior to the announcement of the Human Genome Project's results, biochemistry had largely embraced the "one-protein-one-gene" concept. It was generally assumed that each type of protein had "its own" gene that carried the instructions for its synthesis. This is no longer plausible because the estimated number of different proteins present in the human body now significantly exceeds the estimated number of genes.

The concept of *alternative splicing* bridges the gap between the larger estimated number of proteins and the now-smaller estimated number of genes. **Alternative splicing** *is a process by which several different proteins that are variations of a basic structural motif can be produced from a single gene.* In alternative splicing, an hnRNA molecule with multiple exons present is spliced in several different ways. Figure 22-18 shows the four alternative splicing patterns that can occur when an hnRNA contains four exons, two of which are *alternative exons.* ◄

Spliceosome research lags behind that of most other biochemical frontiers because spliceosomes are difficult entities to study for two reasons. First, cells do not produce large amounts of these substances. They are scarce, making up less than 1% of the dry weight of a cell. This contrasts with the 25% of a cell's dry weight that is due to similarly sized ribosomes (the sites for protein synthesis; Section 22-12).

▶ *Humans have a huge proteome (an estimated 150,000 unique proteins) and a relatively small genome (20,000–25,000 unique genes). The "machinery" that bridges the genome–proteome "gap" is spliceosomes. It is spliceosomes that give humans their chemical complexity.*

Figure 22-17 Heterogeneous nuclear RNA contains both exons and introns. Messenger RNA is heterogeneous nuclear RNA from which the introns have been excised.

Figure 22-18 An hnRNA molecule containing four exons, two of which (B and C) are alternative exons, can be spliced in four different ways, producing four different proteins. Proteins can be produced with neither, either, or both of the alternative exons present.

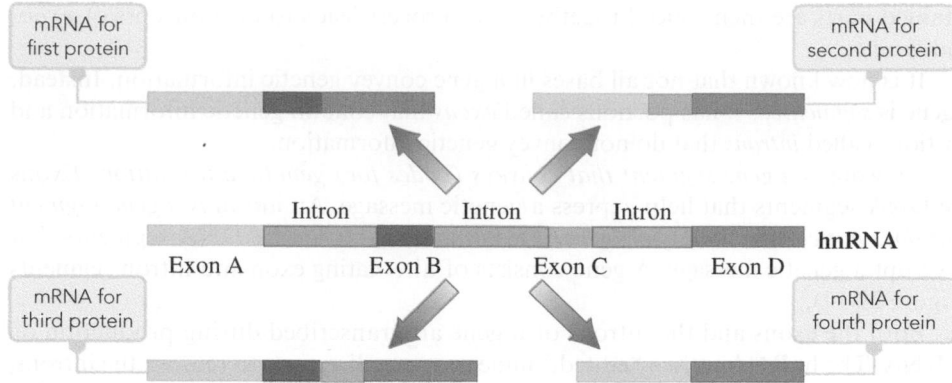

Second, bacteria, which are widely used in biochemical research, do not possess a spliceosome. Thus, research must always be carried out using multicellular organisms, which is a more difficult endeavor.

The Human Transcriptome

As biochemists were mapping the human genome, they anticipated that they were close to unlocking many secrets of the human body and that the results of the project would provide a list of human genes for which the function of each could be quickly investigated. The results of the project, however, only complicated the situation.

Results indicate that the total number of genes present in a genome is not as important in understanding human cell behavior as was previously thought, whereas mRNA transcripts obtained from the genes are *more* important in understanding human cell behavior than was previously thought. Because of alternative splicing, different cell types interpret the information encoded a DNA molecule differently and so produce a different number of mRNA molecules and ultimately a different number of proteins. For each cell type, the number of mRNA transcripts generated varies in response to complex signals within a cell and between cells.

Research now shows that the information-bearing sections of DNA within a gene can be spliced together an average of eight different ways. There could turn out to be around 150,000–200,000 relevant mRNA molecules as compared to 20,000–25,000 genes within the human genome. Collectively, the total number of mRNA molecules for an organism is known as its *transcriptome*. A **transcriptome** *is all of the mRNA molecules that can be generated from the genetic material in a genome.* A transcriptome differs from a genome in that it acknowledges the biochemical complexity created by splice variants obtained from hnRNA. Transcriptome research is now a developing biochemical frontier.

Additional Human Genome Project Considerations

It has been more than a decade since completion of the human genome project in 2003. A by-product of this project was a greatly increased interest in developing better technological methods for carrying out the experimental techniques associated with the project. Great technological advances have accompanied the project. Two examples of technological advances associated with the project are:

1. The time it takes to sequence a genome has fallen from 6–8 years in 1990, at the start of the project, to 2–3 days in 2013.
2. In 1990, the cost of sequencing the DNA in a genome was an estimated 1 billion dollars per genome. This cost had dropped to 10–50 million dollars per genome in 2003, at the end of the project, and in 2013 costs had fallen to 4–6 *thousand* dollars per genome.

A number of medical advances have also resulted from the project. Included among them are these:

1. In 2013, there were 4847 rare genetic diseases for which there was a *known* genetic basis, compared to 2264 in 2003 and 61 in 1990.
2. In 2003, 46 states tested for six genetic conditions in newborn babies using a dried blood spot from a heel prick. In 2013, all states tested for over 30 genetic conditions using a similar dried blood spot.

An additional surprising conclusion from the Human Genome Project, besides a much smaller than anticipated number of genes that encode for proteins, was the fact (mentioned earlier in this section) that only 2% of the base pairs in DNA molecules were accounted for in the base pairs present in mRNA, indicating that most of the base pairs in a DNA molecule are noncoding, with function not known at the conclusion of the project. These large DNA segments of unknown function were dubbed, at the time of their discovery, "junk" DNA for want of a better name.

Project ENCODE

Studies that have been carried out since the end of the Human Genome Project now reveal that at least 80% of the previously dubbed "junk" DNA (noncoding DNA sequences) is indeed functional, with functions that include interacting with regulatory proteins, switching biochemical processes on and off, and association with disease susceptibility. These new results come from a multiyear research project launched in 2003 for which preliminary results were announced in late 2012. This research project is called Project ENCODE. The acronym ENCODE comes from the phrase "<u>en</u>cyclopedia <u>of</u> <u>D</u>NA <u>e</u>lements." Involved in the project are hundreds of scientists across the United States, United Kingdom, Spain, Singapore, and Japan.

Project ENCODE results released in 2012 include the following functions for noncoding DNA regions:

1. It contains "docking sites" for proteins, which then switch genes "on" and "off."
2. It contains regions that can be used as transcription instructions for production of RNA molecules.
3. It contains "promoter sites" that control whether or not nearby genes are transcribed or not; it is estimated than more than 70,000 such sites exist.
4. It contains "enhancer sites" that affect the activity of genes, sometimes over great distances; it is estimated that more than 400,000 such sites exist.
5. It contains sites that can be associated with disease; disease-linked genetic changes appear to occur in noncoding regions of DNA.

Further studies are in progress concerning the remaining 20% of "junk DNA." It is anticipated that this DNA will also be found to have functional activity.

Clock Genes

An additional gene expression function for which much new information has been recently obtained is that of "regulatory control" of "biochemical clocks" found in almost all organisms—humans, animals, plants, and even bacteria. Although not specifically a part of the Human Genome Project or Project ENCODE, new information in this area has some very interesting aspects.

An example of new research findings concerning "timing" and biochemical reactions in the plant world is the knowledge that some plants increase production of chemical defense molecules in anticipation of sunrise, because most predator attacks (caterpillars) occur in early morning hours. For plants to make these defense molecules at other times of day would be a waste of plant energy resources.

"Biochemical clocks" are now known to exist in almost all cells in the human body, not just in the brain. The focus on relevancy feature Chemical Connections 22-B—The Circadian Clock and Clock Genes—discusses the fact that biological clocks related to gene expression occur in many parts of the human body.

The Circadian Clock and Clock Genes

The word *circadian* (pronounced sir-kaydee-en) describes a pattern repeated approximately every 24 hours. Human beings, as well as animals, plants, and even bacteria, have an internal biological clock that is circadian in nature and thus tracks time over a 24-hour interval.

The human circadian clock is genetically controlled and involves about 20 genes that are activated and deactivated (turned on and off) in a predictable and tightly orchestrated manner. Those who travel across multiple time zones in a short period of time are well aware that such timing mechanisms are present within the human body. Their situation becomes one in which their circadian clock and their wristwatch are set at different times and jet lag is the result. The body's clock has the ability to reset itself but such resetting can take several days.

Early research findings concerning the human circadian clock showed that there is a time-keeping control center in a portion of the brain called the suprachiasmatic nucleus (SCN). The SCN is a very small rice-grain-sized structure, located in the brain just above where the optic nerves cross. At this location, the SCN receives information about incoming light from the retina. The changing amount of light it receives correlates with the 24-hour light–darkness cycle that an individual experiences.

For many years, it was thought that the SCN was the sole place in the body where time was kept. It is now known that such is not the case. The SCN is now considered to be "a conductor of a symphony of clocks" found throughout the body. Every cell in the human body has time-keeping machinery within it that contribute to the body's time cycles that are directed by the SCN. Operation of these timing mechanisms involves genetic feedback loops.

Perhaps the best-known manifestation of the body's many clocks relates to the human sleep–wake cycle. The

SCN controls the production of melatonin, a hormone that makes a person sleepy. During periods of less light—at night—the SCN tells the brain to make more melatonin that facilitates sleep. Note the times of 7:30 and 21:00 on the accompanying clock diagram, which both relate to melatonin production.

Many biochemical cycles within the human body are controlled by circadian clock feedback. The daily rise and fall of human body temperature over a 24-hour period is an example of such control. Blood pressure also has a daily increase and decrease pattern that is clock-related (see accompanying clock diagram).

Another operation under circadian clock control is metabolism efficiency. Many metabolic processes have timing regulation. For example, when a person is sleeping, digestive enzymes are not needed in the stomach nor is chemical energy needed to promote muscle movement. Through timing mechanisms these processes are minimized at night and the body instead diverts energy resources to other important biochemical processes including increased immune system activity for upkeep and increased brain activity that relates to memory storage. Such efficiency methods occur in many individual cells because of the existence of circadian clocks within these cells.

Mechanisms based on circadian clock rhythm are now known to explain the long-known medical observation that heart attacks occur more frequently shortly after a person awakes from sleep than at other times of day. Circadian clock control decreases (during sleep) expression (production) of the protein KLF_{15}, which in turn controls the expression of an important component of a potassium ion channel required to keep hearts beating in a "regular" manner. Why this modulation of protein expression occurs is not known at present.

1. Which of the following statements concerning the *transcription* phase of protein synthesis is *correct*?
   a. A partial unwinding of the DNA double helix occurs.
   b. The DNA strand used to synthesize RNA is called the *informational* strand.
   c. mRNA molecules are converted to hnRNA molecules.
   d. no correct response
2. What is the complementary hnRNA base sequence produced from the DNA base sequence 5′ C–T–A–T–A–C 3′?
   a. 3′ C–A–T–A–T–C 5′
   b. 3′ G–A–T–A–T–G 5′
   c. 3′ G–A–U–A–U–G 5′
   d. no correct response
3. The location in a DNA strand carrying the information needed for synthesis of a specific hnRNA molecule is called a
   a. gene
   b. genome
   c. chromosome
   d. no correct response
4. Which of the following types of RNA contains introns and exons?
   a. hnRNA
   b. mRNA
   c. snRNA
   d. no correct response
5. Which of the following types of RNA is not part of the overall transcription process?
   a. hnRNA
   b. mRNA
   c. snRNA
   d. no correct response

Answers: 1. a; 2. c; 3. a; 4. a; 5. d

22-10 The Genetic Code

LEARNING FOCUS

Understand the relationship between codons and the genetic code; know important characteristics of the genetic code.

The nucleotide (base) sequence of an mRNA molecule is the informational part of such a molecule. This base sequence in a given mRNA determines the amino acid sequence for the protein synthesized under that mRNA's direction.

How can the base sequence of an mRNA molecule (which involves only *four* different bases—A, C, G, and U) encode enough information to direct proper sequencing of *20* amino acids in proteins? If each base encoded for a particular standard amino acid, then only four amino acids would be specified out of the 20 needed for protein synthesis, a clearly inadequate number. If two-base sequences were used to code amino acids, then there would be $4^2 = 16$ possible combinations, so 16 amino acids could be represented uniquely. This is still an inadequate number. If three-base sequences were used to code for amino acids, there would be $4^3 = 64$ possible combinations, which is more than enough combinations for uniquely specifying each of the 20 standard amino acids found in proteins.

Research has verified that sequences of three nucleotides in mRNA molecules specify the amino acids that go into synthesis of a protein. Such three-nucleotide sequences are called codons. A **codon** *is a three-nucleotide sequence in an mRNA molecule that codes for a specific amino acid.*

Which amino acid is specified by which codon? (There are 64 codons to choose from.) Researchers deciphered codon–amino acid relationships by adding different

▶ Table 22-2 **The Genetic Code**

The code is composed of 64 three-nucleotide sequences (codons), which can be read from the table. The left-hand column indicates the nucleotide base found in the first (5′) position of the codon. The nucleotide in the second (middle) position of the codon is given by the base listing at the top of the table. The right-hand column indicates the nucleotide found in the third (3′) position. Thus the codon ACG encodes for the amino acid Thr, and the codon GGG encodes for the amino acid Gly.

Second letter

First letter (5′ end)	U	C	A	G	Third letter (3′ end)
U	UUU UUC Phenylalanine Phe / UUA UUG Leucine Leu	UCU UCC UCA UCG Serine Ser	UAU UAC Tyrosine Tyr / UAA UAG Stop codon Stop codon	UGU UGC Cysteine Cys / UGA Stop codon UGG Tryptophan Trp	U C A G
C	CUU CUC CUA CUG Leucine Leu	CCU CCC CCA CCG Proline Pro	CAU CAC Histidine His / CAA CAG Glutamine Gln	CGU CGC CGA CGG Arginine Arg	U C A G
A	AUU AUC Isoleucine Ile / AUA Methionine Met / AUG Initiation codon	ACU ACC ACA ACG Threonine Thr	AAU AAC Asparagine Asn / AAA AAG Lysine Lys	AGU AGC Serine Ser / AGA AGG Arginine Arg	U C A G
G	GUU GUC GUA GUG Valine Val	GCU GCC GCA GCG Alanine Ala	GAU GAC Aspartic acid Asp / GAA GAG Glutamic acid Glu	GGU GGC GGA GGG Glycine Gly	U C A G

synthetic mRNA molecules (whose base sequences were known) to cell extracts and then determining the structure of any newly formed protein. After many such experiments, researchers finally matched all 64 possible codons with their functions in protein synthesis. It was found that 61 of the 64 codons formed by various combinations of the bases A, C, G, and U were related to specific amino acids; the other three combinations were termination codons ("stop" signals) for protein synthesis. Collectively, these relationships between three-nucleotide sequences in mRNA and amino acid identities are known as the genetic code. The **genetic code** *is the assignment of the 64 mRNA codons to specific amino acids (or stop signals)*. The determination of this code during the early 1960s is one of the most remarkable twentieth-century scientific achievements. A 1968 Nobel Prize in chemistry was awarded to Marshall Nirenberg and Har Gobind Khorana for their work in illuminating how mRNA encodes for proteins.

The genetic code is given in Table 22-2. Examination of this table indicates that the genetic code has several remarkable features:

1. *The genetic code is highly degenerate; that is, many amino acids are designated by more than one codon.* Three amino acids (Arg, Leu, and Ser) are represented by six codons. Two or more codons exist for all other amino acids except Met and Trp, which have only a single codon. Codons that specify the same amino acid are called *synonyms*. ◀

▶ *There is a rough correlation between the number of codons for a particular amino acid and that amino acid's frequency of occurrence in proteins. For example, the two amino acids that have a single codon, Met and Trp, are two of the least common amino acids in proteins.*

2. *There is a pattern to the arrangement of synonyms in the genetic code table.* All synonyms for an amino acid fall within a single box in Table 22-2, unless there are more than four synonyms, where two boxes are needed. The significance of the "single box" pattern is that with synonyms, the first two bases of the codon are the same—they differ only in the third base. For example, the four synonyms for the amino acid proline (Pro) are CCU, CCC, CCA, and CCG.

3. *The genetic code is almost universal.* Although Table 22-2 does not show this feature, studies of many organisms indicate that with minor exceptions, the code is the same in all of them. The same codon specifies the same amino acid whether the cell is a bacterial cell, a corn plant cell, or a human cell.

4. *An initiation codon exists.* The existence of "stop" codons (UAG, UAA, and UGA) suggests the existence of "start" codons. There is one initiation codon. Besides coding for the amino acid methionine, the codon AUG functions as an initiator of protein synthesis when it occurs as the first codon in an amino acid sequence.

EXAMPLE 22-4

Using the Genetic Code and mRNA Codons to Predict Amino Acid Sequences

Using the genetic code in Table 22-2, determine the sequence of amino acids encoded by the mRNA codon sequence

5′ GCC–AUG–GUA–AAA–UGC–GAC–CCA 3′

Solution

Matching the codons with the amino acids, using Table 22-2, yields

mRNA: 5′ GCC–AUG–GUA–AAA–UGC–GAC–CCA 3′

Peptide: Ala–Met–Val–Lys–Cys–Asp–Pro

EXAMPLE 22-5

Relating Exons and Introns to hnRNA and mRNA Structures

Sections A, C, and E of the following base sequence section of a DNA template strand are exons, and sections B and D are introns. ◄

DNA   5′ ATT – CGT – TGT – TTT – CCC – AGT – GCC 3′
         A   B   C   D   E

▶ *Introns and exons are actually never as short as those given in this simplified example.*

a. What is the structure of the hnRNA transcribed from this template?
b. What is the structure of the mRNA obtained by splicing the hnRNA?

Solution

a. The base sequence in the hnRNA will be complementary to that of the template DNA, except that U is used in the RNA instead of T. The hnRNA will have a directionality antiparallel to that of the DNA sequence.

hnRNA   3′ UAA – GCA – ACA – AAA – GGG – UCA – CGG 5′

Rewriting this base sequence so that it reads from the 5′ end to the 3′ end (which is standard notation) gives

hnRNA   5′ GGC – ACU – GGG – AAA – ACA – ACG – AAU 3′

Note that in reversing the directionality from 3′-to-5′ to 5′-to-3′, the sequence of bases in a codon is also reversed; for example, GAC becomes CAG.

b. In the splicing process, introns are removed and the exons combined to give the mRNA.

mRNA   5′ GGC – AAA – ACA – AAU 3′

EXAMPLE 22-6

Relating Protein Amino Acid Sequence to the Directionality of an mRNA Segment

The structure of an mRNA segment obtained from a DNA template strand is

mRNA   3′ AUU – CCG – UAC – GAC 5′

What polypeptide amino acid sequence will be synthesized using this mRNA?

Solution

The directionality of an mRNA segment obtained from template DNA is 3′-to-5′ because the two segments must be antiparallel to each other (Section 22-5). The codons in an mRNA must be read in the 5′-to-3′ direction to correctly use genetic code relationships to determine the sequence of amino acids in the peptide. Rewriting the given mRNA with reversed directionality (5′-to-3′ direction) gives

mRNA   5′ CAG – CAU – GCC – UUA 3′

Note that in reversing the directionality from 3′-to-5′ to 5′-to-3′, the sequence of bases in a codon is also reversed; for example, GAC becomes CAG.

Using the genetic code relationships between codon and amino acid (Table 22-2) shows that this mRNA codon sequence codes for the amino acid sequence

N-end   Gln—His—Ala—Leu   C-end

Codons written from the 5′-to-3′ end in an mRNA give amino acids that correspond to a peptide written from the N-terminal end to the C-terminal end.

Section 22-10 Quick Quiz

1. Which of the following statements concerning *codons* is *incorrect*?
   a. They are found within mRNA molecules.
   b. They specify base sequence in terms of four-nucleotide units.
   c. There are 64 of them.
   d. no correct response
2. The genetic code is a listing that gives relationships between codons and
   a. synonyms
   b. genes
   c. mRNAs
   d. no correct response
3. Which of the following statements concerning the functions for codons is *incorrect*?
   a. Each standard amino acid is designated by a single codon.
   b. Some standard amino acids are designated by more than one codon.
   c. Some codons have a "stop" function rather than an "amino acid" function.
   d. no correct response
4. Without reference to the genetic code, which of the following is *definitely* an incorrect codon–amino acid pairing?
   a. UUU–UUC and Phe–Phe
   b. ACU–AAU and Thr–Asn
   c. GCC–GCC and Ala–Gly
   d. no correct response

Answers: 1. b; 2. d; 3. a; 4. c

22-11 Anticodons and tRNA Molecules

LEARNING FOCUS

Be familiar with the relationships between (1) anticodons and tRNAs and (2) anticodons and codons.

The amino acids used in protein synthesis do not directly interact with the codons of an mRNA molecule. Instead, tRNA molecules function as intermediaries that deliver amino acids to the mRNA. At least one type of tRNA molecule exists for each of the 20 amino acids found in proteins.

Figure 22-19 A tRNA molecule. The amino acid attachment site is at the open end of the cloverleaf (the 3′ end), and the anticodon is located in the hairpin loop opposite the open end.

All tRNA molecules have the same general shape, and this shape is crucial to how they function. Figure 22-19a shows the general *two-dimensional* "cloverleaf" shape of a tRNA molecule, a shape produced by the molecule's folding and twisting into regions of parallel strands and regions of hairpin loops. (The actual three-dimensional shape of a tRNA molecule involves considerable additional twisting of the "cloverleaf" shape—Figure 22-19b.)

Two features of the tRNA structure are of particular importance:

1. The 3′ end of the open part of the cloverleaf structure is where an amino acid covalently bonds to the tRNA. The carboxyl group of the amino acid reacts with the 3′ OH group on the terminal nucleotide residue resulting in the formation of an aminoacyl ester. Each of the different tRNA molecules is specifically recognized by an *aminoacyl tRNA synthetase* enzyme. These enzymes also recognize the one kind of amino acid that "belongs" with the particular tRNA and facilitates its bonding to the tRNA (see Figure 22-20).
2. The loop *opposite* the open end of the cloverleaf, called the *anticodon loop,* consists of seven unpaired bases of which the middle three bases constitute the *anticodon.* This anticodon recognizes and base pairs with an mRNA codon that possesses a complementary three-base unit. An **anticodon** *is a three-nucleotide sequence on a tRNA molecule that is complementary to a codon on an mRNA molecule.*

Figure 22-20 An aminoacyl–tRNA synthetase has an active site for tRNA and a binding site for the particular amino acid that is to be attached to that tRNA.

Figure 22-21 The interaction between anticodon (tRNA) and codon (mRNA), which involves complementary base pairing, governs the proper placement of amino acids in a protein.

The interaction between the anticodon of the tRNA and the codon of the mRNA leads to the proper placement of an amino acid into a growing peptide chain during protein synthesis. This interaction, which involves complementary base pairing, is shown in Figure 22-21.

EXAMPLE 22-7

Determining Codon–Anticodon Relationships

A tRNA molecule has the anticodon 5′ AAG 3′. With which mRNA codon will this anticodon interact?

Solution

The interaction between a codon and an anticodon has directionality (antiparallel) considerations, that is,

$$3' \quad \text{Anticodon} \quad 5'$$
$$: : :$$
$$5' \quad \text{Codon} \quad 3'$$

The given anticodon, with reversed directionality, is

$$3' \quad \text{GAA} \quad 5'$$

and its codon interaction, which involves complementary base pairing, is

$$\text{Anticodon} \quad 3' \quad \text{GAA} \quad 5'$$
$$: : :$$
$$\text{Codon} \quad 5' \quad \text{CUU} \quad 3'$$

The codon is, thus, 5′ CUU 3′.

EXAMPLE 22-8

Determining Anticodon–tRNA Amino Acid Relationships

A tRNA molecule possesses the anticodon 5′ CGU 3′. Which amino acid will this tRNA molecule carry?

Solution

Codons, rather than anticodons, are involved in the genetic code relationships. The codon with which the anticodon 5′ CGU 3′ base pairs is 5′ ACG 3′. Remember, as shown in Example 22-6, that the codon–anticodon pairing involves the anticodon 3′ UGC 5′ (the anticodon written in the 3′-to-5′ direction).

$$\text{Anticodon} \quad 3' \quad \text{UGC} \quad 5'$$
$$: : :$$
$$\text{Codon} \quad 5' \quad \text{ACG} \quad 3'$$

The amino acid that the codon ACG codes for (see Table 22-2) is Thr (Threonine).

EXAMPLE 22-9

Determining Relationships Among DNA Base Sequences, mRNA Base Sequences, Codons, Anticodons, and Amino Acids

A DNA template strand is read as follows:

3′ ACG AAC CGA TAG GGA 5′

Determine each of the following using this base sequence.

a. The base sequence in the DNA informational strand
b. The codons present in the mRNA transcribed from the DNA template strand (assuming that no introns are present)

c. The tRNA anticodons that interact with the mRNA codons
d. The amino acids that the tRNA molecules carry
e. The structure of the peptide formed from the overall translation process

Solution

a. The DNA informational strand has bases complementary to those in the DNA template strand.

Template strand   3′ ACG AAC CGA TAG GGA 5′

Informational strand 5′ TGC TTG GCT ATC CCT 3′

b. The mRNA bases will be the same as those in the informational strand, except that U has replaced T. The codons are derived from the mRNA base sequence.

Informational strand 5′ TGC TTG GCT ATC CCT 3′

mRNA   5′ UGC UUG GCU AUC CCU 3′

Codons   5′ UGC UUG GCU AUC CCU 3′

c. The anticodon bases will be complementary bases of the codon bases.

Codons   5′ UGC UUG GCU AUC CCU 3′

Anticodons   3′ ACG AAC CGA UAG GGA 5′

Rewriting the anticodons in the 5′-to-3′ direction gives

Anticodons   5′ AGG GAU AGC CAA GCA 3′

d. The amino acids that the tRNAs carry are determined by codons rather than anticodons. The genetic code is used to make the connection between codons and amino acids.

Codons   5′ UGC UUG GCU AUC CCU 3′

Amino acids   Cys Leu Ala Ile Pro

e. The peptide structure parallels the amino acid sequence obtained from the codon sequence.

N-terminal end Cys–Leu–Ala–Ile–Pro C-terminal end

Section 22-11 Quick Quiz

1. Which of the following is an *incorrect* pairing of concepts?
   a. tRNA and "amino acid carrier"
   b. tRNA and "anticodon carrier"
   c. tRNA and "codon carrier"
   d. no correct response
2. Which of the following statements concerning the "cloverleaf" shape of tRNA molecules is *correct*?
   a. Four hairpin loops are present.
   b. Three hairpin loops and one open end are present.
   c. Two hairpin loops and two open ends are present.
   d. no correct response
3. A tRNA molecule with the anticodon 5′ AAG 3′ will interact with which of the following mRNA codons?
   a. 3′ AAG 5′
   b. 3′ UUC 5′
   c. 5′ UUC 3′
   d. no correct response

Answers: 1. c; 2. b; 3. b

22-12 Translation: Protein Synthesis

LEARNING FOCUS

Be familiar with how ribosomes, mRNA, rRNA, and tRNA are involved in the process of translation; be familiar with the five general steps of the translation part of protein synthesis.

Translation *is the process by which mRNA codons are deciphered and a particular protein molecule is synthesized.* The substances needed for the translation phase of protein synthesis are mRNA molecules, tRNA molecules, amino acids, ribosomes, and a number of different enzymes. A **ribosome** *is an rRNA–protein complex that serves as the site for the translation phase of protein synthesis.*

The number of ribosomes present in a cell for higher organisms varies from hundreds of thousands to even a few million. Recent research concerning ribosome structure suggests the following for such structures:

▶ *rRNA molecules provide the structural and functional foundation for ribosomes.*

1. They contain four rRNA molecules and about 80 proteins that are packed into two rRNA–protein subunits, one small subunit and one large subunit (Figure 22-22).
2. Each subunit contains approximately 65% rRNA and 35% protein by mass.
3. A ribosome's active site, the location where proteins are synthesized by one-at-a-time addition of amino acids to a growing peptide chain, is located in the large ribosomal subunit. ◀
4. The active site is mostly rRNA, with only one of the ribosome's many protein components being present.
5. Because rRNA is so predominant at the active site, the ribosome is thought to be an RNA enzyme (Section 21-1), that is, a *ribozyme*.
6. The mRNA involved in the translation phase of protein synthesis binds to the small subunit of the ribosome.

The rRNA and tRNA involved in the translation phase of protein synthesis are synthesized by transcription of DNA sequences just as is hnRNA/mRNA. However, unlike mRNA molecules, they do not have the characteristics (chemical composition) necessary for them to function as codon carriers.

There are five general steps to the translation process: (1) activation of tRNA, (2) initiation, (3) elongation, (4) termination, and (5) post-translation processing.

Activation of tRNA

There are two steps involved in tRNA activation. First, an amino acid interacts with an activator molecule (ATP; Section 23-3) to form a highly energetic complex. This complex then reacts with the appropriate tRNA molecule to produce an *activated tRNA molecule,* a tRNA molecule that has an amino acid covalently bonded to it at its 3′ end through an ester linkage.

Figure 22-22 Ribosomes, which contain both rRNA and protein, have structures that contain two subunits. One subunit is much larger than the other.

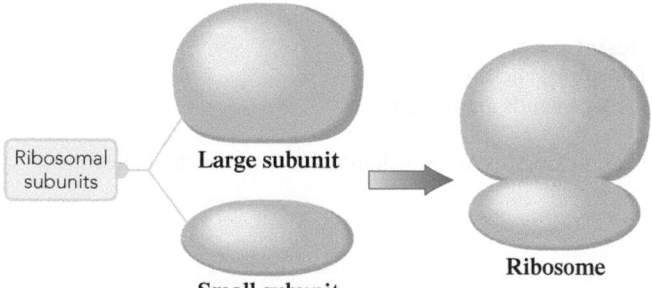

Ribosomal subunits

Large subunit

Small subunit

Ribosome

Initiation

The initiation of protein synthesis in human cells begins when mRNA attaches itself to the surface of a small ribosomal subunit such that its first codon, which is always the initiating codon AUG, occupies a site called the P site (peptidyl site) (Figure 22-23a). An activated tRNA molecule with an anticodon complementary to the codon AUG attaches itself, through complementary base pairing, to the AUG codon (Figure 22-23b). The resulting complex then interacts with a large ribosomal subunit to complete the formation of an initiation complex (Figure 22-23c). (Since the initiating codon AUG codes for the amino acid methionine, the first amino acid in a developing human protein chain will always be methionine.)

Elongation

Next to the P site in an mRNA–ribosome complex is a second binding site called the A site (aminoacyl site) (Figure 22-24a). At this second site the next mRNA codon is exposed, and a tRNA with the appropriate anticodon binds to it (Figure 22-24b). With amino acids in place at both the P and the A sites, the enzyme *peptidyl transferase* effects the linking of the P site amino acid to the A site amino acid to form a dipeptide. Such peptide bond formation leaves the tRNA at the P site empty and the tRNA at the A site bearing the dipeptide (Figure 22-24c).

The empty tRNA at the P site now leaves that site and is free to pick up another molecule of its specific amino acid. Simultaneously with the release of tRNA from the P site, the ribosome shifts along the mRNA. This shift puts the

Figure 22-23 Initiation of protein synthesis begins with the formation of an initiation complex.

a   The initiation tRNA carrying the amino acid Met binds at the P site.

b   A tRNA with amino acid 2 binds at the A site.

c   A peptide bond forms between amino acid 1 and amino acid 2 as amino acid 1 moves from the P site to the A site.

d   The first tRNA is released, the ribosome moves one codon to the right, translocating the dipeptide to the P site, and the tRNA with amino acid 3 occupies the A site.

e   Elongation continues as the dipeptide at the P site is bonded to the amino acid at the A site to form a tripeptide.

Figure 22-24 The process of translation that occurs during protein synthesis. The anticodons of tRNA molecules are paired with the codons of an mRNA molecule to bring the appropriate amino acids into sequence for protein formation.

▶ *In elongation, the polypeptide chain grows one amino acid at a time.*

▶ *The process of* translocation *occurs at approximately 50-millisecond intervals, that is, 20 times per second.*

newly formed dipeptide at the P site, and the third codon of mRNA is now available, at site A, to accept a tRNA molecule whose anticodon complements this codon (Figure 22-24d). ◀ The movement of a ribosome along an mRNA molecule is called *translocation*. **Translocation** *is the part of translation in which a ribosome moves down an mRNA molecule three base positions (one codon) so that a new codon can occupy the ribosomal A site.*

Now a repetitious process begins. The third codon, now at the A site, accepts an incoming tRNA with its accompanying amino acid; then the entire dipeptide at the P site is transferred and bonded to the A site amino acid to give a tripeptide (see Figure 22-24e). The empty tRNA at the P site is released, the ribosome shifts along the mRNA, and the process continues. ◀

The transfer of the growing peptide chain from the P site to the A site is an example of an *acyl transfer reaction*, a reaction type first introduced in Section 16-19. Figure 22-25 shows the structural detail for such transfer when Met is the amino acid at the P site and Gly is the amino acid at the A site.

Figure 22-25 The transfer of an amino acid (or growing peptide chain) from the ribosomal P site to the ribosomal A site during translation is an example of an acyl transfer reaction.

Termination

The polypeptide continues to grow by way of translocation until all necessary amino acids are in place and bonded to each other. Appearance in the mRNA codon sequence of one of the three stop codons (UAA, UAG, or UGA) terminates the process. No tRNA has an anticodon that can base pair with these stop codons. The polypeptide is then cleaved from the tRNA through hydrolysis.

Post-Translation Processing

Some modification of proteins usually occurs after translation. This *post-translation processing* gives the protein the final form it needs to be fully functional. Some of the aspects of post-translation processing are the following:

1. In most proteins, the methionine (Met) residue that initiated protein synthesis is removed by a specialized enzyme in a hydrolysis reaction. A second hydrolysis reaction releases the polypeptide chain from its tRNA carrier.
2. Some covalent modification of a protein can occur, such as the formation of disulfide bridges between cysteine residues (Section 20-6).
3. Completion of the folding of polypeptides into their active conformations occurs. Protein folding actually begins as the polypeptide chain is elongated on the ribosome. For proteins with quaternary structure (Section 20-13), the various components are assembled together. ◄

Recent research indicates that there may be a connection between synonymous codons within the genetic code (Section 22-10) and protein folding. It now appears that synonymous codons, even though they translate into the same amino acids during protein synthesis, have an effect on the way emerging proteins fold into their three-dimensional shapes (tertiary structure; Section 20-12) as they elongate and then leave a ribosome. This means that two stretches of mRNA that differ only in synonymous codons can produce proteins with identical amino acid sequences but different folding patterns. Two differently folded proteins would be expected to produce different biochemical responses within a cell when interacting with other substances; there is now some evidence that this is the case.

▶ *Research involving mice now links* mis*folding of protein molecules to neurological disorders. When mice were purposely injected with* misfolded *versions of certain proteins, they developed neurological symptoms similar to those associated with Alzheimer's and/or Parkinson's disease in humans. The researchers hope to find new drugs that can block disease progression by interfering with protein misfolding pathways.*

Efficiency of mRNA Utilization

Many ribosomes can move simultaneously along a single mRNA molecule (Figure 22-26). In this highly efficient arrangement, many identical protein chains can be synthesized almost at the same time from a single strand of mRNA. This multiple use of mRNA molecules reduces the amount of resources and energy that the cell expends to synthesize needed protein. Such complexes of several ribosomes and mRNA are called polyribosomes or polysomes. A **polyribosome** *is a complex of mRNA and several ribosomes.*

Chemistry at a Glance—Protein Synthesis: Transcription and Translation—summarizes the steps in protein synthesis.

The focus on relevancy feature Chemical Connections 22-C—Antibiotic Protein Synthesis Inhibitors—discusses how disruption of the protein synthesis process in bacteria, through use of antibiotics, is an effective method for killing undesirable bacteria present in the human body.

Figure 22-26 Several ribosomes can simultaneously proceed along a single strand of mRNA one after another. Such a complex of mRNA and ribosomes is called a polyribosome or polysome.

Section 22-12 Quick Quiz

1. Which of the following statements about ribosomes is correct?
   a. The number of ribosomes in a cell seldom exceeds 50.
   b. The active site of a ribosome contains mostly protein molecules.
   c. Structurally, ribosomes have two rRNA–protein subunits.
   d. no correct response
2. Which of the following events is *not* part of the translation phase of protein synthesis?
   a. mRNAs carry amino acids to the ribosome active site
   b. codon–anticodon interactions occur
   c. an mRNA attaches itself to the small subunit of a ribosome
   d. no correct response
3. The number of codon binding sites in an mRNA–ribosome complex that can be occupied at the same time by activated tRNA molecules is
   a. 2
   b. 3
   c. 4
   d. no correct response
4. A polyribosome is a complex that
   a. contains four ribosomal subunits instead of the usual two
   b. involves a ribosome and several mRNA molecules
   c. involves an mRNA molecule and several ribosomes
   d. no correct response
5. Which of the following is an activity that does not occur as part of post-translation processing?
   a. covalent modification through formation of disulfide bonds
   b. completion of folding of polypeptide chains
   c. elongation of a polypeptide chain
   d. no correct response

Answers: 1. c; 2. a; 3. a; 4. c; 5. c

CHEMISTRY AT A GLANCE — Protein Synthesis: Transcription and Translation

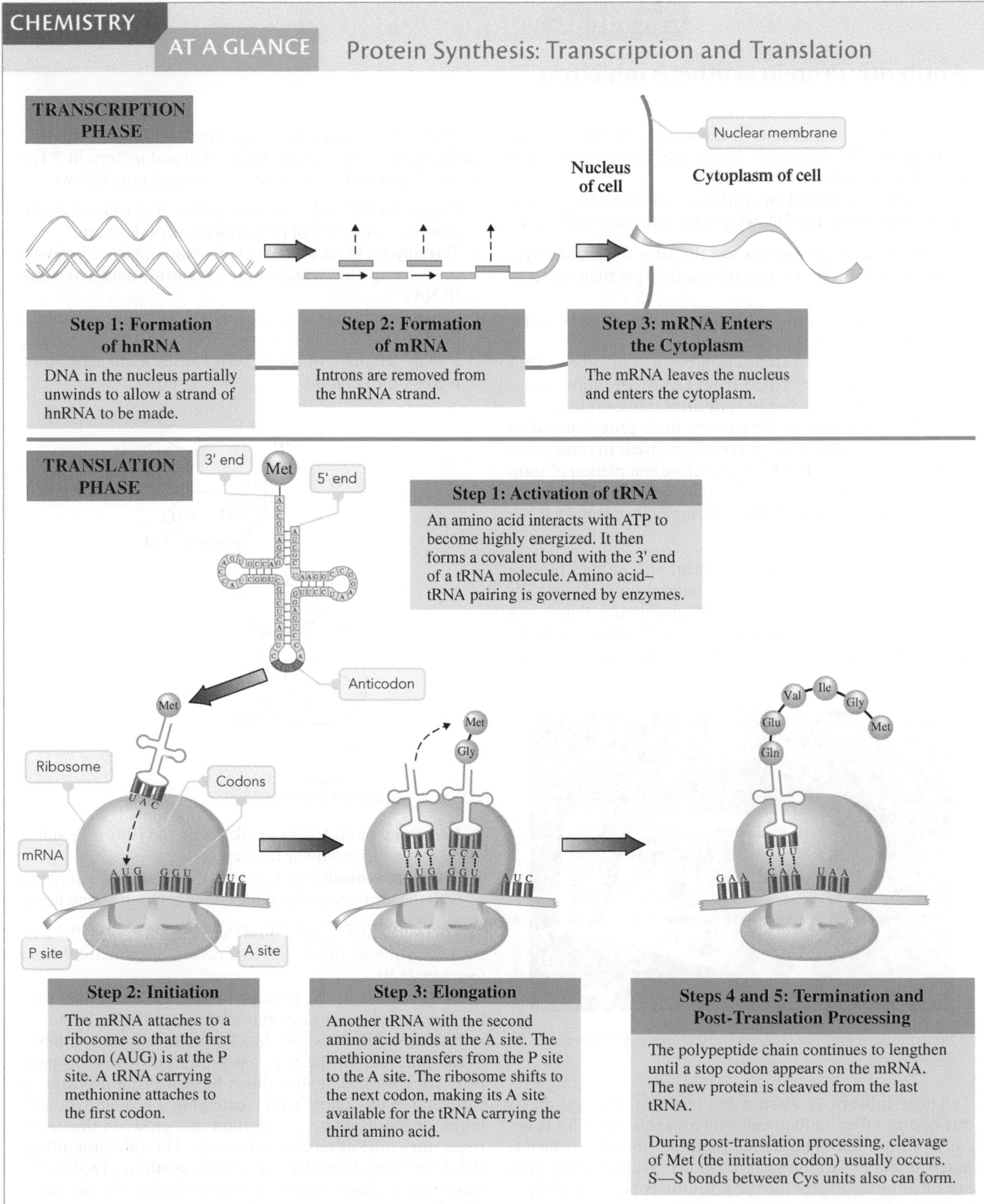

TRANSCRIPTION PHASE

Nuclear membrane

Nucleus of cell

Cytoplasm of cell

Step 1: Formation of hnRNA

DNA in the nucleus partially unwinds to allow a strand of hnRNA to be made.

Step 2: Formation of mRNA

Introns are removed from the hnRNA strand.

Step 3: mRNA Enters the Cytoplasm

The mRNA leaves the nucleus and enters the cytoplasm.

TRANSLATION PHASE

3' end   Met   5' end

Anticodon

Met

Ribosome   Codons

mRNA

P site   A site

Step 1: Activation of tRNA

An amino acid interacts with ATP to become highly energized. It then forms a covalent bond with the 3' end of a tRNA molecule. Amino acid–tRNA pairing is governed by enzymes.

Step 2: Initiation

The mRNA attaches to a ribosome so that the first codon (AUG) is at the P site. A tRNA carrying methionine attaches to the first codon.

Step 3: Elongation

Another tRNA with the second amino acid binds at the A site. The methionine transfers from the P site to the A site. The ribosome shifts to the next codon, making its A site available for the tRNA carrying the third amino acid.

Steps 4 and 5: Termination and Post-Translation Processing

The polypeptide chain continues to lengthen until a stop codon appears on the mRNA. The new protein is cleaved from the last tRNA.

During post-translation processing, cleavage of Met (the initiation codon) usually occurs. S—S bonds between Cys units also can form.

Antibiotic Protein Synthesis Inhibitors

Protein synthesis proceeds in the same general way in all forms of life. The synthesis details are, however, less complex for organisms such as bacteria.

Comparison of protein synthesis in bacteria with that in human cells shows the following similarities and differences:

1. In both cases, ribosomes are the sites for protein synthesis. Human ribosomes are much larger than bacterial ribosomes.
2. In bacteria, the initiator codon is N-formylmethionine. In human cells, it is methionine.
3. In bacteria, mRNA translation begins while the mRNA is still being transcribed from DNA. In human cells, mRNA translation begins only after transcription.
4. Bacteria/mRNAs undergo very little processing after being transcribed and are very short-lived. In some cases, degradation of mRNA begins before completion of transcription. In human cells, transcribed mRNA (hnRNA) undergoes considerable processing before mature RNA is formed.

The differences between bacterial and human protein synthesis are sufficient to make bacterial protein synthesis an ideal target for antibacterial chemotherapy, that is, use of antibiotics to kill bacteria. Many antibiotics now in use are bacterial protein synthesis inhibitors (see accompanying photo).

Erythromycin and similar drugs inhibit protein synthesis in bacteria.

These inhibitors disrupt bacterial protein synthesis but do not affect human cell protein synthesis. This is because the inhibitors target the bacterial ribosome, which is much smaller than human ribosomes. Human ribosomes are unsuitable targets for the antibiotics because of their larger size.

Many, but not all, of the protein synthesis inhibitor antibiotics now in use have names that end in "mycin." The mode of action of some of these inhibitors is as follows:

1. **Erythromycin:** binds to the larger bacterial ribosome subunit, blocking the exit of a growing peptide chain.
2. **Terramycin:** blocks the A-site location on the ribosome, preventing the attachment of amino-acid-carrying tRNAs.
3. **Streptomycin** (see accompanying structural diagram): binds to the smaller bacterial ribosome subunit causing a shape change, which in turn causes a misreading of mRNA information.

Streptomycin
(a trisaccharide derivative)

4. **Neomycin:** binds to the smaller bacterial ribosome subunit in a manner similar to streptomycin.
5. **Chloramphenicol:** binds to the ribosome and interferes with the formation of peptide bonds between amino acids.

The well-known penicillin family of antibiotics are not protein synthesis inhibitors but, rather, enzyme inhibitors (Section 21.9).

In a reversal of the process in which human intervention (drugs) disrupt bacterial protein synthesis, bacterial intervention (diseases) can block human protein synthesis. Several protein synthesis toxins produced by microorganisms are known that shut down human protein synthesis with fatal results. Diphtheria is caused by a protein synthesis inhibitor produced by a bacterium that grows in the upper respiratory tract of an infected person. This inhibitor affects the chain elongation phase of protein synthesis. Diphtheria was a major cause of death in children before the advent of effective immunization procedures.

22-13 Mutations

LEARNING FOCUS

Know the characteristics for both point and frameshift mutations; be familiar with common types of mutagens.

A **mutation** *is an error in base sequence in a gene that is reproduced during DNA replication.* Such errors alter the genetic information that is passed on during transcription. The altered information can cause changes in amino acid sequence during protein synthesis. Sometimes, such changes have a profound effect on an organism.

Two common types of mutations are (1) a point mutation and (2) a frameshift mutation. A **point mutation** *is a mutation in which one base in a DNA base sequence is replaced with another base.* Such a mutation is often also called a *substitution* mutation. Illustrative of this one-base change in a DNA sequence is the following:

Original DNA   T A G C A C
                                        C has replaced G
Point Mutated DNA   T A C C A C

The effect of a point mutation can vary from no effect to a change in primary protein structure to termination of protein synthesis, as is illustrated in Example 22-10.

EXAMPLE 22-10

Predicting the Effect of a Point Mutation

Predict the change that occurs in amino acid identity when each of the following point mutations occur on 3′-to-5′ DNA base segments.

a. GAG is point mutated to GAA.   **b.** AAA is point mutated to AAT.
c. ATA is point mutated to ATT.

Solution

The same analysis applies to each of the three parts of this example.

1. Determine the DNA informational strand base sequence that is complementary to the given DNA template strand base sequence.
2. Determine the mRNA base sequence using the informational strand base sequence. They will be the same except that the RNA base U has replaced the DNA base T.
3. Using the genetic code, determine the amino acid that is specified by the mRNA base sequence (codon).

a. Unmutated base sequence: GAG → CTC → CUC → Leu
                                                    template   informational   mRNA   amino
                                                    strand   strand   acid

      Mutated base sequence: GAA → CTT → CUU → Leu
                                                    template   informational   mRNA   amino
                                                    strand   strand   acid

This is a *silent* mutation. Amino acid identity is not affected, as both mRNA codons code for the same amino acid.

b. Unmutated base sequence: AAA → TTT → UUU → Phe
                                                    template   informational   mRNA   amino
                                                    strand   strand   acid

      Mutated base sequence: AAT → TTA → UUA → Leu
                                                    template   informational   mRNA   amino
                                                    strand   strand   acid

The point mutation has produced a codon that codes for a different amino acid.

(continued)

c. Unmutated base sequence: ATA → TAT → UAU → Tyr
template   informational   mRNA   amino
strand   strand   acid

Mutated base sequence: ATT → TAA → UAA → stop codon
template   informational   mRNA   amino
strand   strand   acid

The point mutation has produced a stop codon, resulting in termination of protein synthesis.

A **frameshift mutation** *is a mutation that inserts or deletes a base in a DNA molecule base sequence.* Such a change affects not only the base triplet located at the insertion or deletion point but also all triplets that follow in the sequence. This contrasts with a point mutation where only one triplet is affected. Figure 22-27 shows the effects that a frameshift mutation can have on an amino acid sequence in a protein.

A **mutagen** *is a substance or agent that causes a change in the structure of a gene.* Radiation and chemical agents are two important types of mutagens. Radiation, in the form of ultraviolet light, X-rays, radioactivity (Chapter 11), and cosmic rays, has the potential to be mutagenic. Ultraviolet light from the sun is the radiation that causes sunburn and can induce changes in the DNA of skin cells. Sustained exposure to ultraviolet light can lead to skin cancer problems.

Chemical agents can also have mutagenic effects. Nitrous acid (HNO_2) is a mutagen that causes deamination of heterocyclic nitrogen bases. For example, HNO_2 can convert cytosine to uracil.

Figure 22-27 Changes that occur in amino acid sequence resulting from a frameshift mutation that involves deletion of a base from a DNA sequence.

(a) Normal DNA and correct amino acid sequence

(b) Frameshift mutation involving removal of a base and the resulting change in amino acid sequence

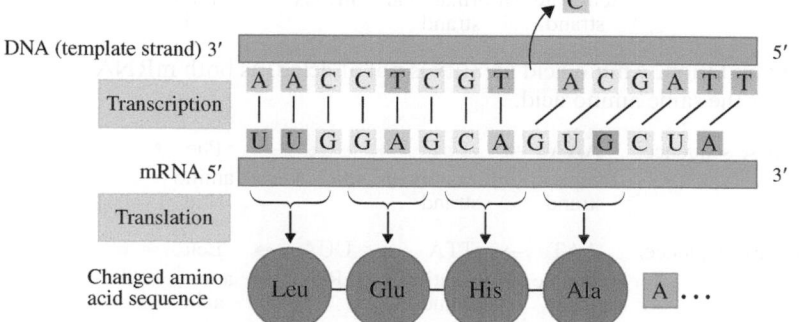

Cytosine   Uracil

Deamination of a cytosine that was part of an mRNA codon would change the codon; for example, CGG would become UGG.

A variety of chemicals—including nitrites, nitrates, and nitrosamines—can form nitrous acid in the body. The use of nitrates and nitrites as preservatives in foods such as bologna and hot dogs is a cause of concern because of their conversion to nitrous acid in the body and subsequent possible damage to DNA.

Fortunately, the body has *repair enzymes* that recognize and replace altered bases. Normally, the vast majority of altered DNA bases are repaired, and mutations are avoided. Occasionally, however, the damage is not repaired, and the mutation persists.

The focus of relevancy feature Chemical Connections 22-D—Erythropoietin (EPO): Red Blood Cells, Mutations, and Athletic Performance—discusses a situation where a mutation involving a protein hormone that regulates red blood cell production became an advantage for an individual.

Section 22-13 Quick Quiz

1. Which of the following describes the effect of a point mutation on amino acid identity in a protein?
   a. The identity of one amino acid must change.
   b. The identity of one amino acid may change.
   c. The identity of two amino acids must change.
   d. no correct response
2. Which of the following describes the effect of a frameshift mutation?
   a. All mRNA codons change.
   b. Some, but not all, mRNA codons change.
   c. There is no change in mRNA codons.
   d. no correct response
3. Which of the following statements applies to both point and frameshift mutations?
   a. A base is removed from a DNA template strand.
   b. A base is added to a DNA template strand.
   c. A base is substituted for another base in a DNA template strand.
   d. no correct response

Answers: 1. b; 2. b; 3. d

22-14 Nucleic Acids and Viruses

LEARNING FOCUS
Describe a common method by which a virus infects a cell; describe how a vaccine works.

Viruses are very small disease-causing agents that are considered the lowest order of life. Indeed, their structure is so simple that some scientists do not consider them truly alive because they are unable to reproduce in the absence of other organisms. Figure 22-28 shows an electron microscope image of an influenza virus.

A **virus** *is a small particle that contains DNA or RNA (but not both) surrounded by a coat of protein and that cannot reproduce without the aid of a host cell.* Viruses do not possess the nucleotides, enzymes, amino acids, and other molecules necessary to replicate their nucleic acid or to synthesize proteins. To reproduce, viruses must invade the cells of another organism and cause these host cells to carry out the reproduction of the virus. Such an invasion disrupts the normal operation of cells, causing diseases within the host organism. The only function of a virus is reproduction; viruses do not generate energy.

Figure 22-28 An electron microscope image of an influenza virus.

Erythropoietin (EPO): Red Blood Cells, Mutations, and Athletic Performance

Erythropoietin (pronounced ih-rith-roh-poi-eet-n) is a protein hormone produced by the kidney, and to a lesser extent by the liver, that promotes the development of red blood cells and initiates the synthesis of hemoglobin (Section 20-16), the molecule within red blood cells that transports oxygen. It is a glycoprotein (Section 20-18). Because of its somewhat difficult to pronounce name, erythropoietin is usually referred to using the shortened designation EPO.

The primary structure of EPO has been determined, and using this information and recombinant DNA technology (Section 22-15), synthetically produced EPO as well as several synthetic EPO analogs have been made. One of these synthetic analogs, epoetin alfa (Epo; lower case p and o), is one of the most widely used drugs created through recombinant DNA technology. Approved by the FDA in 1989, it is widely used in the treatment of certain types of anemia to increase red blood cell production. Most kidney dialysis patients now receive Epo.

EPO and red blood cells have some interesting connections to athletes and athletic performance. A major limiting factor in athletic performance is the oxygen-carrying capacity of blood. This capacity is directly related to the number of hemoglobin molecules present which in turn depends on the number of red blood cells present. EPO is a controlling factor for both hemoglobin and red-blood-cell count and thus has a direct relationship to athletic performance. Two situations relating to the connection between red blood cell levels and athletic performance are now considered.

The first situation involves cross-skiing events at the 1964 Winter Olympics held in Innsbruck, Austria. At these Olympic games, a Finnish cross-country skier named Eero Maentyranta won three gold medals. A major reason for his unusually strong performance was that his blood contained 25%–50% more hemoglobin than is found on average in blood. Thus, the oxygen-carrying capacity of his blood was much greater than that of his competitors. His enhanced oxygen-delivery system was not due, however, to use of illegal substances, as would be expected in today's athletic environment, but rather to a rare genetic defect (mutation), common in the Maentyranta family, that results in abnormally high levels of red blood cells. Thus, this skier's "oxygen advantage" was a natural advantage rather than an illegally obtained advantage.

Several years later, genetic studies carried out at the University of Helsinki determined that the Maentyranta family's genetic disorder involved a mutated protein responsible for red blood cell production. The mutated protein contained only 480 amino acids rather than the normal 550; a 70 amino acid segment was missing. It was then determined that the missing amino acid segment contained the "off

Kyodo/Newscom

switch" for red blood cell production. Hence, the elevated red blood cell level in persons with this protein mutation.

Despite the previously mentioned anemia-related health benefits associated with synthetic EPO production, there is also a downside to its production. Synthetic EPO was "discovered" by endurance athletes trying to gain an illegal advantage over their competitors. Obviously, enhanced oxygen carrying ability because of increased red blood cell production translates into enhanced muscle performance. EPO and its synthetic analogs are believed to have been widely used in certain sports in the 1990s, most notoriously in Tour de France cycling events, without detection. These synthetic compounds are metabolized quickly and are almost identical to the body's naturally produced EPO. Direct testing for EPO was not available until 2000. The 2002 Winter Olympics was the first event where samples testing positive for EPO were found.

EPO abuse by athletics is now known to be dangerous and several deaths have occurred because of its use. Water loss associated with extreme exertion coupled with EPO use produces a thickening of the blood that can reach dangerous levels. The thickened blood puts great strain on the heart. EPO and its analogs are now banned substances in athletic competitions. Back to the Finnish cross-country skier Eero Maentyranta. Because he had been born with an elevated red blood cell condition, his body had adapted to the condition, and it became an advantage, without negative effects, in athletic competitions. The serious disadvantages of EPO use by other athletics far outweigh any advantages obtained.

There is no known form of life that is not subject to attack by viruses. Viruses attack bacteria, plants, animals, and humans. Many human diseases are of viral origin. Among them are the common cold, mumps, measles, smallpox, rabies, influenza, infectious mononucleosis, hepatitis, and AIDS.

Viruses most often attach themselves to the outside of specific cells in a host organism. An enzyme within the protein overcoat of the virus catalyzes the breakdown of the cell membrane, opening a hole in the membrane. The virus then injects its DNA or RNA into the cell. Once inside, this nucleic acid material is mistaken by the host cell for its own, whereupon that cell begins to translate and/or transcribe the viral nucleic acid. When all the virus components have been synthesized by the host cell, they assemble automatically to form many new virus particles. Within 20 to 30 minutes after a single molecule of viral nucleic acid enters the host cell, hundreds of new virus particles have formed. So many are formed that they eventually burst the host cell and are free to infect other cells. ◄

If a virus contains DNA, the host cell replicates the viral DNA in a manner similar to the way it replicates its own DNA. The newly produced viral DNA then proceeds to make the proteins needed for the production of protein coats for additional viruses.

An RNA-containing virus is called a *retrovirus.* Once inside a host, such viruses first make viral DNA. This *reverse* synthesis is governed by the enzyme *reverse transcriptase.* The template is the viral RNA rather than DNA. The viral DNA so produced then produces additional viral DNA and the proteins necessary for the protein coats.

The AIDS (acquired immunodeficiency syndrome) virus is an example of a retrovirus. This virus has an affinity for a specific type of white blood cell called a *helper T cell,* which is an important part of the body's immune system. When helper T cells are unable to perform their normal functions as a result of such viral infection, the body becomes more susceptible to infection and disease.

A **vaccine** *is a preparation containing an inactive or weakened form of a virus or bacterium.* The antibodies produced by the body against these specially modified viruses or bacteria effectively act against the naturally occurring active forms as well. Thanks to vaccination programs, many diseases, such as polio and mumps (caused by RNA-containing viruses) and smallpox and yellow fever (caused by DNA-containing viruses), are now seldom encountered.

► *Viral infections are more difficult to treat than bacterial infections because viruses, unlike bacteria, replicate inside cells. It is difficult to design drugs that prevent the replication of the virus that do not also affect the normal activities of the host cells.*

Section 22-14 Quick Quiz

1. Which of the following statements about a virus is *correct*?
   a. Bacteria are not subject to attack by a virus.
   b. A virus contains both DNA and RNA.
   c. A virus cannot reproduce itself without aid of a host cell.
   d. no correct response
2. Which of the following pairings of concepts is an *incorrect* pairing?
   a. vaccine and inactive virus
   b. DNA-containing virus and retrovirus
   c. RNA-containing virus and viral DNA
   d. no correct response

Answers: 1. c; 2. b

22-15 Recombinant DNA and Genetic Engineering

LEARNING FOCUS

Be familiar with procedures by which recombinant DNA is produced; be able to give examples of important end products obtained using genetic engineering techniques.

Ever-increasing knowledge about DNA molecules and how they function under various chemical conditions has opened the door to an increasingly important field of technology known by several names, including *genetic engineering, genetic*

Figure 22-29 Percentage of major crops in the United States that were genetically engineered in 2000 and in 2013.

modification, bioengineering, and *biotechnology.* The term *genetic engineering* will be used in this text to refer to this developing field.

Genetic engineering *is the process whereby an organism is intentionally changed at the molecular (DNA) level so that it exhibits different traits.* The first organisms to be genetically engineered were bacteria in 1973 and mice in 1974. Insulin-producing bacteria were commercialized in 1982, and genetically modified food crops have been available since 1994. Genetically modified forms of foods and fibers now dominate several major crops in the United States, as is shown by the data in Figure 22-29. ◄

For the plant crops listed in Figure 22-29, the most common genetic modification involves introduction of a herbicide-tolerance trait. A gene is inserted that allows the crops to be sprayed with the weed killer glyphosate (also known as Roundup) without harm to the plants. These crops also frequently have an insect-resistant trait that is obtained from the presence of a gene obtained from the soil bacteria *Bacillus thuringiensis.* This gene's presence causes the plants to produce their own pesticide. Plantings of insect-resistant corn and cotton are common and research continues on tomato plants that carry this gene.

In 2011, the United States Department of Agriculture (USDA) gave approval for planting corn that is genetically modified to produce the enzyme *α-amylase,* an enzyme that rapidly breaks down starch into glucose (Section 18-6). For corn destined for ethanol production, the presence of this *amylase* improves the economics of the production process.

Two additional examples, still in the developmental stage, of the direction that genetic engineering can take are:

1. Genetically engineered tomato plants with a longer shelf life now exist. In this case, gene insertion is not needed. Instead, a gene naturally present in the tomato plant that is involved in the ripening process is "turned off" (deactivated). This slows, but does not completely stop, the ripening process, resulting in less over-ripening, softening, and overall deterioration.
2. A strawberry gene is introduced into a mustard plant variety that is very susceptible to attack by spider mites. The gene produces a chemical attractant for predator mites that eat the spidermites, thus solving a "mitey" problem.

Bacteria are now routinely used as "protein factories." These genetically engineered bacteria, which contain genes for human proteins, can produce large quantities of designated proteins because of their rapid reproduction rate. Human proteins in short supply that are produced in this manner include insulin (see Chemical Connections 20-A—Substitutes for Human Insulin), erythropoietin (see Chemical Connections 22-D—Erythropoietin (EPO): Red Blood Cells, Mutations, and Athletic Performance), and human growth hormone. Table 22-3 gives additional

▶ *Genetic engineering has been alluded to in several sections in previous chapters of the text, although no details were given about the process. Mentions of this subject are found in the following locations:*

Section 19-5 in the omega-3 fatty acid discussion

Section 19-6 in the trans-*fatty acid discussion*

Section 20-3 in the complete protein discussion

Section 20-10 in the insulin discussion

Section 21-8 in the extremozyme discussion

Section 21-11 in the "grapefruit effect" discussion

▶ Table 22-3 **Selected Human Proteins Produced Using Recombinant DNA Technology and Their Uses**

Protein	Treatment
insulin	diabetes
erythropoietin (EPO)	anemia
human growth hormone (HGH)	stimulate growth
interleukins	stimulate immune system
interferons	leukemia and other cancers
lung surfactant protein	respiratory distress
serum albumin	plasma supplement
tumor necrosis factor (TNF)	cancers
tissue plasminogen activator (TPA)	heart attacks
epidermal growth factor	healing of wounds and burns
fibroblast growth factor	ulcers

examples of human proteins used in therapeutic medicine that have become available through the use of genetic engineering technology.

Principles and Procedures of Genetic Engineering

Genetic engineering procedures involve a type of DNA called *recombinant DNA*. **Recombinant DNA** *is DNA that contains genetic material from two different organisms.* The notation rDNA is often used to designate recombinant DNA.

The bacterium *E. coli,* which is found in the intestinal tract of humans and animals, is the organism most often used in recombinant DNA experiments. Yeast cells are also used, with increasing frequency, in this research.

In addition to their chromosomal DNA, *E. coli* (and other bacteria) contain DNA in the form of small, circular, double-stranded molecules called *plasmids.* These plasmids, which carry only a few genes, replicate independently of the chromosome. Also, they are transferred relatively easily from one cell to another. Plasmids from *E. coli* are used in recombinant DNA work.

The procedure used to obtain *E. coli* cells that contain recombinant DNA involves the following steps (Figure 22-30):

Step 1: *Cell membrane dissolution.* E. coli *cells of a specific strain are placed in a solution that dissolves cell membranes, thus releasing the contents of the cells.*

Step 2: *Isolation of plasmid fraction. The released cell components are separated into fractions, one fraction being the plasmids. The isolated plasmid fraction is the material used in further steps.*

Step 3: *Cleavage of plasmid DNA. A special enzyme, called a* restriction enzyme, *is used to cleave the double-stranded DNA of a circular plasmid. The result is a linear (noncircular) DNA molecule.*

Step 4: *Gene removal from another organism. The same* restriction enzyme *is then used to remove a desired gene from a chromosome of another organism.*

Step 5: *Gene–plasmid splicing. The gene (from Step 4) and the opened plasmid (from Step 3) are mixed in the presence of the enzyme* DNA ligase, *which splices the two together. This splicing, which attaches one end of the gene to one end of the opened plasmid and attaches the other end of the gene to the other end of the plasmid, results in an altered circular plasmid (the recombinant DNA).*

Figure 22-30 Recombinant DNA is made by inserting a gene obtained from DNA of one organism into the DNA from another kind of organism.

Step 6:   ***Uptake of recombinant DNA.*** *The altered plasmids (recombinant DNA) are placed in a live* E. coli *culture, where they are taken up by the* E. coli *bacteria. The* E. coli *culture into which the plasmids are placed need not be identical to that from which the plasmids were originally obtained.*

Note in Step 3 that the conversion of a circular plasmid into a linear DNA molecule requires a restriction enzyme. A **restriction enzyme** *is an enzyme that recognizes specific base sequences in DNA and cleaves the DNA in a predictable manner at these sequences.* The discovery of restriction enzymes made genetic engineering possible.

Restriction enzymes occur naturally in numerous types of bacterial cells. Their function is to protect the bacteria from invasion by foreign DNA by catalyzing the cleavage of the invading DNA. The term *restriction* relates to such enzymes placing a "restriction" on the type of DNA allowed into the bacterial cells.

To understand how a restriction enzyme works, consider one that cleaves DNA between G and A bases in the 5′-to-3′ direction in the sequence G−A−A−T−T−C. This enzyme will cleave the double-helix structure of a DNA molecule in the manner shown in Figure 22-31.

Figure 22-31 Cleavage pattern resulting from the use of a restriction enzyme that cleaves DNA between G and A bases in the 5′-to-3′ direction in the sequence G—A—A—T—T—C. The double-helix structure is not cut straight across.

Figure 22-32 The "sticky ends" of the cut plasmid and the cut gene are complementary and combine to form recombinant DNA.

Note that the double helix is not cut straight across; the individual strands are cut at different points, giving a staircase cut. (Both cuts must be between G and A in the 5′-to-3′ direction.) This staircase cut leaves unpaired bases on each cut strand. These ends with unpaired bases are called "sticky ends" because they are ready to "stick to" (pair up with) a complementary section of DNA if they can find one.

If the same restriction enzyme used to cut a plasmid is also used to cut a gene from another DNA molecule, the sticky ends of the gene will be complementary to those of the plasmid. This enables the plasmid and gene to combine readily, forming a new, modified plasmid molecule. This modified plasmid molecule is called recombinant DNA. In addition to the newly spliced gene, the recombinant DNA plasmid contains all of the genes and characteristics of the original plasmid. Figure 22-32 shows diagrammatically the match between sticky ends that occurs when plasmid and gene combine.

Step 6 involves inserting the recombinant DNA (modified plasmids) back into *E. coli* cells. The process is called transformation. **Transformation** *is the process of incorporating recombinant DNA into a host cell.*

The transformed cells then reproduce, resulting in large numbers of identical cells called clones. **Clones** *are cells with identical DNA that have descended from a single cell.* Within a few hours, a single genetically altered bacterial cell can give rise to thousands of clones. Each clone has the capacity to synthesize the protein directed by the foreign gene it carries.

Researchers are not limited to selection of naturally occurring genes for transforming bacteria. Chemists have developed nonenzymatic methods of linking nucleotides together such that they can construct artificial genes of any sequence they desire. In fact, benchtop instruments are now available that can be programmed by a microprocessor to synthesize any DNA base sequence *automatically.* The operator merely enters a sequence of desired bases, starts the instrument, and returns later to obtain the product. Such flexibility in manufacturing DNA has opened many doors, accelerated the pace of recombinant DNA research, and redefined the term *designer genes*!

Section 22-15 Quick Quiz

1. The meaning for the lower case r in the designation rDNA is
   a. restriction
   b. recombinant
   c. retro
   d. no correct response

(continued)

2. Which of the following statements about rDNA is *correct*?
   a. It is naturally present in *E. coli* bacteria.
   b. It is naturally present in restriction enzymes.
   c. It contains genetic material from two different organisms.
   d. no correct response
3. The role of *E. coli* plasmids in obtaining rDNA is to
   a. create "sticky ends" on an extracted gene
   b. activate restriction enzymes
   c. serve as a host for a "foreign gene"
   d. no correct response
4. A restriction enzyme is an enzyme that
   a. prevents formation of rDNA
   b. produces a straight-across cut in a DNA double helix
   c. dissolves cell membranes
   d. no correct response
5. The process of inserting recombinant DNA into a host cell is called
   a. translocation
   b. transformation
   c. cloning
   d. no correct response

Answers: 1. b; 2. c; 3. c; 4. d; 5. b

22-16 The Polymerase Chain Reaction

LEARNING FOCUS
Be familiar with the nature of the *polymermase chain reaction* and what it accomplishes.

The **polymerase chain reaction (PCR)** *is a method for rapidly producing multiple copies of a DNA nucleotide sequence.* Billions of copies of a specific DNA sequence (gene) can be produced in a few hours via this reaction. The PCR is easy to carry out, requiring only a few chemicals, a container, and a source of heat. (In actuality, the PCR process is now completely automated.)

By means of the PCR process, DNA that is available only in very small quantities can be amplified to quantities large enough to analyze. The PCR process, devised in 1983, has become a valuable tool for diagnosing diseases and detecting pathogens in the body. It is now used in the prenatal diagnosis of a number of genetic disorders, including muscular dystrophy and cystic fibrosis, and in the identification of bacterial pathogens. It is also the definitive way to detect the AIDS virus.

The PCR process has also proved useful in certain types of forensic investigations. A DNA sample may be obtained from a single drop of blood or semen or a single strand of hair at a crime scene and amplified by the PCR process. A forensic chemist can then compare the amplified samples with DNA samples taken from suspects. Work with DNA in the forensic area is often referred to as *DNA fingerprinting.*

DNA polymerase, an enzyme present in all living organisms, is a key substance in the PCR process. It can attach additional nucleotides to a short starter nucleotide chain, called a *primer,* when the primer is bound to a complementary strand of DNA that functions as a template. The original DNA is heated to separate its strands, and then primers, DNA polymerase, and deoxyribonucleotides are added so that the *DNA polymerase* can replicate the original strand. The process is repeated until, in a short time, millions of copies of the original DNA have been made. ◄

Figure 22-33 shows diagrammatically, in very simplified terms, the basic steps in the PCR process.

▶ *PCR temperature conditions are higher than those in the human body. This is possible because the DNA polymerase used was isolated from an organism that lives in the "hot pots" of Yellowstone National Park at temperatures of 70°C–75°C.*

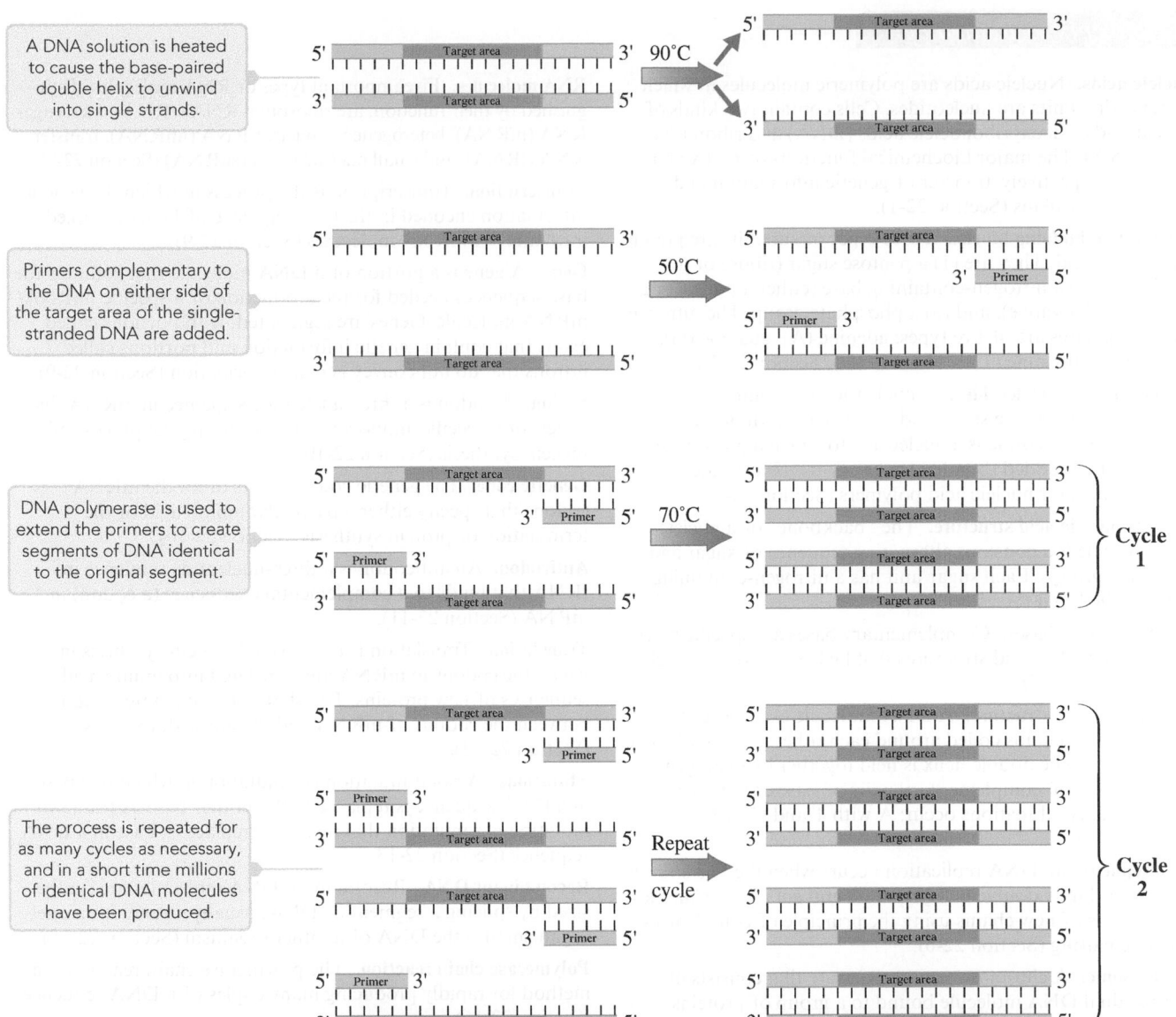

Figure 22-33 The basic steps, in simplified terms, of the polymerase chain reaction process. Each cycle of the polymerase chain reaction doubles the number of copies of the target DNA sequence. ◀

▶ *After* n *cycles of the PCR process, the amount of DNA will have increased* 2^n *times.*

2^{10} *is approximately 1000.*
2^{20} *is approximately 1,000,000.*

Twenty-five cycles of the PCR can be carried out in an hour in a process that is fully automated.

Section 22-16 Quick Quiz

1. The polymerase chain reaction is a method for rapidly
   a. producing multiple copies of a DNA base sequence
   b. producing multiple copies of an individual base present in a DNA sequence
   c. altering base sequence in a DNA segment
   d. no correct response
2. Each cycle of the polymerase chain reaction
   a. doubles the number of product molecules
   b. produces two new product molecules
   c. removes three nucleotides from a reactant DNA molecule
   d. no correct response

Answers: 1. a; 2. a

Concepts to Remember

Nucleic acids. Nucleic acids are polymeric molecules in which the repeating units are nucleotides. Cells contain two kinds of nucleic acids—deoxyribonucleic acids (DNA) and ribonucleic acids (RNA). The major biochemical functions of DNA and RNA are, respectively, transfer of genetic information and synthesis of proteins (Section 22-1).

Nucleic acid building blocks. Three types of subunits are present in a nucleic acid. They are (1) a pentose sugar (ribose or deoxyribose), (2) a nitrogen-containing base (either a purine or a pyrimidine derivative), and (3) a phosphate group. The nitrogen-containing bases are of five types: adenine (A), guanine (G), cytosine (C), thymine (T), and uracil (U) (Section 22-2).

Nucleosides and nucleotides. A nucleoside is a compound formed from a pentose sugar and a purine or pyrimidine base derivative. A nucleotide is a nucleoside to which a phosphate group has been added (bonded to the sugar). Nucleotides are the monomers for nucleic acid polymers (Section 22-3).

Primary nucleic acid structure. The "backbone" of a nucleic acid molecule is a constant alternating sequence of sugar and phosphate groups. Each sugar unit has a nitrogen-containing base attached to it (Section 22-4).

Complementary bases. Complementary bases are specific pairs of bases in nucleic acid structures that hydrogen-bond to each other (Section 22-5).

Secondary DNA structure. A DNA molecule exists as two polynucleotide chains coiled around each other in a double-helix arrangement. The double helix is held together by hydrogen bonding between complementary pairs of bases. Only two base-pairing combinations occur: A with T and C with G (Section 22-5).

DNA replication. DNA replication occurs when the two strands of a parent DNA double helix separate and act as templates for the synthesis of new chains using the principle of complementary base pairing (Section 22-6).

Chromosome. A chromosome is a structure that consists of an individual DNA molecule bound to a group of proteins (Section 22-6).

RNA molecules. Five important types of RNA molecules, distinguished by their function, are ribosomal RNA (rRNA), messenger RNA (mRNA), heterogeneous nuclear RNA (hnRNA), transfer RNA (tRNA), and small nuclear RNA (snRNA) (Section 22-8).

Transcription. Transcription is the process in which the genetic information encoded in the base sequence of DNA is copied into hnRNA/mRNA molecules (Section 22-9).

Gene. A gene is a portion of a DNA molecule that contains the base sequences needed for the production of a specific hnRNA/mRNA molecule. Genes are segmented, with portions called exons that contain genetic information and portions called introns that do not convey genetic information (Section 22-9).

Codon. A codon is a three-nucleotide sequence in mRNA that codes for a specific amino acid needed during the process of protein synthesis (Section 22-10).

Genetic code. The genetic code consists of all the mRNA codons that specify either a particular amino acid or the termination of protein synthesis (Section 22-10).

Anticodon. An anticodon is a three-nucleotide sequence in tRNA that binds to a complementary sequence (a codon) in mRNA (Section 22-11).

Translation. Translation is the stage of protein synthesis in which the codons in mRNA are translated into amino acid sequences of new proteins. Translation involves interactions between the codons of mRNA and the anticodons of tRNA (Section 22-12).

Mutations. A point mutation is a mutation in which one base in a DNA sequence is replaced with another base. A framework mutation is a mutation that inserts or replaces a base in a DNA sequence (Section 22-13).

Recombinant DNA. Recombinant DNA molecules are synthesized by splicing a segment of DNA, usually a gene, from one organism into the DNA of another organism (Section 22-15).

Polymerase chain reaction. The polymerase chain reaction is a method for rapidly producing many copies of a DNA sequence (Section 22-16).

Exercises and Problems

Exercises and problems are arranged in matched pairs with the two members of a pair addressing the same concept(s). The answer to the odd-numbered member of a pair is given at the back of the book. Problems denoted with a ▲ involve not only concepts found in the section under consideration but also concepts found in one or more earlier sections of the chapter.

Types of Nucleic Acids (Section 22-1)

22-1 Indicate whether each of the following statements concerning nucleic acids is true or false.
    a. All cells in higher organisms contain both DNA and RNA.
    b. Structurally, DNA, but not RNA, is an unbranched polymer.
    c. Involvement with protein synthesis is the primary function for RNA.
    d. DNA is found primarily in a cell's nucleus.

22-2 Indicate whether each of the following statements concerning nucleic acids is true or false.
    a. The monomer units in nucleic acids are amino acids.
    b. The primary function for DNA is storage and transfer of genetic information.
    c. RNA is found throughout a cell.
    d. RNA is passed from existing cells to new cells during cell division.

Nucleotide Building Blocks (Section 22-2)

22-3 Indicate whether each of the following pentoses is present in DNA molecules.
    a. Ribose
    b. 2-Deoxyribose

    c.
    d.

22-4 Indicate whether each of the pentoses in Problem 22-3 is present in RNA molecules.

22-5 With the help of Figure 22-2, identify each of the following nitrogen-containing bases as a purine derivative or a pyrimidine derivative.
  a. Cytosine
  b. Adenine
  c.
  d.

22-6 With the help of Figure 22-2, identify each of the following nitrogen-containing bases as a purine derivative or a pyrimidine derivative.
  a. Uracil
  b. Guanine
  c.
  d.

22-7 With the help of Figure 22-2, what is the one-letter abbreviation for the name of each of the bases in Problem 22-5?

22-8 With the help of Figure 22-2, what is the one-letter abbreviation for the name of each of the bases in Problem 22-6?

22-9 With the help of Figure 22-2, indicate whether each of the bases in Problem 22-5 is found in DNA only, RNA only, or both DNA and RNA.

22-10 With the help of Figure 22-2, indicate whether each of the bases in Problem 22-6 is found in DNA only, RNA only, or both DNA and RNA.

22-11 How many different choices are there for each of the following subunits in the specified type of nucleotide?
  a. Pentose sugar subunit in DNA nucleotides
  b. Nitrogen-containing base subunit in RNA nucleotides
  c. Phosphate subunit in DNA nucleotides

22-12 How many different choices are there for each of the following subunits in the specified type of nucleotide?
  a. Pentose sugar subunit in RNA nucleotides
  b. Nitrogen-containing base subunit in DNA nucleotides
  c. Phosphate subunit in RNA nucleotides

Nucleotide Formation (Section 22-3)

22-13 Indicate whether each of the following statements about nucleosides is true or false.
  a. All nucleosides contain ribose.
  b. Some, but not all, nucleosides contain a phosphate group.
  c. All nucleosides contain a nitrogen-containing base.
  d. The two subunits present in a nucleoside can be identical.

22-14 Indicate whether each of the following statements about nucleosides is true or false.
  a. Some, but not all, nucleosides contain deoxyribose.
  b. All nucleosides contain a phosphate group.
  c. Some, but not all, nucleosides contain a nitrogen-containing base.
  d. Both subunits in a nucleoside can be nitrogen-containing bases.

22-15 What is the name of the nucleoside that contains the following subunits?
  a. Ribose and adenine
  b. Uracil and ribose
  c. Deoxyribose and cytosine
  d. Thymine and deoxyribose

22-16 What is the name of the nucleoside that contains the following subunits?
  a. Ribose and guanine
  b. Cytosine and ribose
  c. Deoxyribose and adenine
  d. Uracil and deoxyribose

22-17 Indicate whether each of the following statements about nucleotides is true or false.
  a. All nucleotides contain ribose.
  b. Some, but not all, nucleotides contain a phosphate group.
  c. All nucleotides contain a purine base.
  d. Two of the three subunits in a nucleotide can be nitrogen-containing bases.

22-18 Indicate whether each of the following statements about nucleotides is true or false.
  a. Some, but not all, nucleotides contain deoxyribose.
  b. All nucleotides contain a pyrimidine base.
  c. All nucleotides contain a phosphate group.
  d. Two of the three subunits in a nucleotide can be pentose sugars.

22-19 Indicate whether each of the following is a DNA nucleotide or a RNA nucleotide.
  a. contains ribose, uracil, and phosphate
  b. contains deoxyribose, adenine, and phosphate
  c. dTMP
  d. CMP

22-20 Indicate whether each of the following is a DNA nucleotide or a RNA nucleotide.
  a. contains deoxyribose, guanine, and phosphate
  b. contains ribose, uracil, and phosphate
  c. dGMP
  d. AMP

22-21 Nucleotides containing ribose, thymine, and phosphate are not found in ribonucleic acids. Explain why this is the case.

22-22 Nucleotides containing deoxyribose, uracil, and phosphate are not found in deoxyribonucleic acids. Explain why this is the case.

22-23 What nitrogen-containing base and what sugar are present in each of the following nucleotides?
  a. AMP
  b. dGMP
  c. dTMP
  d. UMP

22-24 What nitrogen-containing base and what sugar are present in each of the following nucleotides?
    a. GMP   b. dAMP
    c. CMP   d. dCMP

22-25 What is the name of each of the nucleotides in Problem 22-23?

22-26 What is the name of each of the nucleotides in Problem 22-24?

22-27 Consider the following nucleotide.

    a. What is the name of the nucleotide?
    b. Would this nucleotide be found in both DNA and RNA, only in DNA, or only in RNA?
    c. What is the name for the type of bond that connects the phosphate and sugar subunits?
    d. What is the name for the type of bond that connects the sugar and base subunits?

22-28 Consider the following nucleotide.

    a. What is the name of the nucleotide?
    b. Would this nucleotide be found in both DNA and RNA, only in DNA, or only in RNA?
    c. What is the name for the type of bond that connects the phosphate and sugar subunits?
    d. What is the name for the type of bond that connects the sugar and base subunits?

▲**22-29** Indicate whether each of the following is (1) a nucleoside, (2) a nucleotide, or (3) neither a nucleoside nor a nucleotide.
    a. Adenosine
    b. Adenine
    c. dAMP
    d. Adenosine 5'-monophosphate

▲**22-30** Indicate whether each of the following is (1) a nucleoside, (2) a nucleotide, or (3) neither a nucleoside nor a nucleotide.
    a. Cytosine
    b. Cytidine
    c. CMP
    d. Deoxycytidine 5'-monophosphate

Primary Nucleic Acid Structure (Section 22-4)

22-31 For the trinucleotide 5' G–C–A 3'
    a. How many nucleotide subunits are present in its "backbone"?
    b. How many nucleotide "nonbackbone" subunits are present?
    c. How many phosphodiester linkages are present?
    d. What is the overall charge carried by the trinucleotide?

22-32 For the trinucleotide 5' U–C–G 3'
    a. How many nucleotide subunits are present in its "backbone"?
    b. How many nucleotide "nonbackbone" subunits are present?
    c. How many phosphodiester linkages are present?
    d. What is the overall charge carried by the trinucleotide?

22-33 Is the trinucleotide in Problem 22-31 found only in DNA, found only in RNA, or found in both DNA and RNA? Explain the basis for your answer.

22-34 Is the trinucleotide in Problem 22-32 found only in DNA, found only in RNA, or found in both DNA and RNA? Explain the basis for your answer.

22-35 In the lengthening of a polynucleotide chain, which type of nucleotide subunit would bond to the 3' end of the polynucleotide chain?

22-36 In the lengthening of a polynucleotide chain, which type of nucleotide subunit would bond to the 5' end of the polynucleotide chain?

22-37 Draw the structure of the RNA dinucleotide 5' U–G 3'.

22-38 Draw the structure of the DNA dinucleotide 5' T–A 3'.

22-39 For the trinucleotide 5' T-G-A 3'
    a. How many β-N-glycosidic linkages are present?
    b. How many phosphoester linkages are present?
    c. How many phosphodiester linkages are present?
    d. How many by-product water molecules are produced during the formation of the trinucleotide from three mononucleotides?

22-40 For the trinucleotide 5' U-C-G 3'
    a. How many β-N-glycosidic linkages are present?
    b. How many phosphoester linkages are present?
    c. How many phosphodiester linkages are present?
    d. How many by-product water molecules are produced during the formation of the trinucleotide from three mononucleotides?

The DNA Double Helix (Section 22.5)

22-41 Indicate whether each of the following statements about the double-helix secondary structure of DNA is true or false.
    a. The two polynucleotide strands are complementary rather than identical.
    b. Bases present extend outward from the double helix.
    c. Covalent bonding occurs between the two polynucleotide strands.
    d. The two polynucleotide strands run in the 5'-to-3' direction.

22-42 Indicate whether each of the following statements about the double-helix secondary structure of DNA is true or false.
a. Hydrogen bonding occurs between the two polynucleotide strands.
b. Bases present extend inward to the interior of the helix.
c. The two polynucleotide strands run in opposite directions: (5′ to 3′) and (3′ to 5′).
d. The two polynucleotide strands are identical.

22-43 Indicate whether each of the following are complementary base pairs in DNA molecules.
a. A–A   b. A–C
c. A–T   d. G–T

22-44 Indicate whether each of the following are complementary base pairs in DNA molecules.
a. C–A   b. C–C
c. C–G   d. G–A

22-45 The base content of a particular DNA molecule is 36% thymine. What is the percentage of each of the following bases in the molecule?
a. Adenine   b. Guanine
c. Cytosine

22-46 The base content of a particular DNA molecule is 24% guanine. What is the percentage of each of the following bases in the molecule?
a. Adenine   b. Cytosine
c. Thymine

22-47 What structural consideration prevents the bases A and G from forming a complementary base pair?

22-48 What structural consideration prevents the bases C and T from forming a complementary base pair?

22-49 The base composition for one of the strands of a DNA double helix is 19% A, 34% C, 28% G, and 19% T. What is the percent base composition for the other strand of the DNA double helix?

22-50 The base composition for one of the strands of a DNA double helix is 23% A, 31% C, 22% G, and 24% T. What is the percent base composition for the other strand of the DNA double helix?

22-51 Convert each of the following 3′-to-5′ DNA base sequences to 5′-to-3′ DNA base sequences.
a. 3′ ATCG 5′   b. 3′ AATA 5′
c. 3′ CACA 5′   d. 3′ CAAC 5′

22-52 Convert each of the following 3′-to-5′ DNA base sequences to 5′-to-3′ DNA base sequences.
a. 3′ CGTA 5′   b. 3′ CGCG 5′
c. 3′ ATTA 5′   d. 3′ CTAA 5′

22-53 Using the concept of complementary base pairing, write the complementary DNA strands, with their 5′ and 3′ ends labeled, for each of the following DNA base sequences.
a. 5′ ACGTAT 3′   b. 5′ TTACCG 3′
c. 3′ GCATAA 5′   d. AACTGG

22-54 Using the concept of complementary base pairing, write the complementary DNA strands, with their 5′ and 3′ ends labeled, for each of the following DNA base sequences.
a. 5′ CCGGTA 3′   b. 5′ CACAGA 3′
c. 3′ TTTAGA 5′   d. CATTAC

▲**22-55** For the DNA segment 5′ TTGCAC 3′ how many of each of the following are present?
a. nucleotides   b. purine bases
c. phosphate groups d. ribose subunits

▲**22-56** For the DNA segment 5′ TAGATG 3′ how many of each of the following are present?
a. nucleotides   b. purine bases
c. phosphate groups d. ribose subunits

Replication of DNA Molecules (Section 22-6)

22-57 What is the base sequence, specified in the 5′-to-3′ direction, for a segment of newly formed DNA if it was formed using the following template DNA segments?
a. 3′ AATGC 5′   b. 5′ AATGC 3′
c. 3′ GCAGC 5′   d. 5′ GCAGC 3′

22-58 What is the base sequence, specified in the 5′-to-3′ direction, for a segment of newly formed DNA if it was formed using the following template DNA segments?
a. 3′ GGCAA 5′   b. 5′ GTCCG 3′
c. 3′ ACGTA 5′   d. 5′ ACGTA 3′

22-59 In the replication of a DNA molecule, two daughter molecules, Q and R, are formed. The following base sequence is part of the newly formed strand in daughter molecule Q.

5′ ACTTAG 3′

Indicate the corresponding base sequence in
a. the newly formed strand in daughter molecule R.
b. the "parent" strand in daughter molecule Q.
c. the "parent" strand in daughter molecule R.

22-60 In the replication of a DNA molecule, two daughter molecules, S and T, are formed. The following base sequence is part of the "parent" strand in daughter molecule S.

5′ TTCAGAG 3′

Indicate the corresponding base sequence in
a. the newly formed strand in daughter molecule T.
b. the newly formed strand in daughter molecule S.
c. the "parent" strand in daughter molecule T.

22-61 How does the synthesis of a daughter DNA strand growing toward a replication fork differ from the synthesis of a daughter DNA strand growing away from a replication fork?

22-62 In the context of DNA replication, what is the difference between a "leading DNA strand" and a "lagging DNA strand"?

22-63 Indicate whether each of the following statements relating to aspects of DNA replication is true or false.
a. The lagging strand grows in the same direction as the replication fork moves.
b. Growth of the leading strand involves the production of Okazaki fragments.
c. Lagging strands always involve "daughter" DNA segments, and leading strands always involve "parent" DNA segments.
d. The enzyme *DNA ligase* effects the unwinding of a DNA double helix.

22-64 Indicate whether each of the following statements relating to aspects of DNA replication is true or false.
a. Leading strands always involve newly synthesized DNA, and lagging strands always involve template DNA.
b. The concept of "nicks" is associated with the growth of a lagging strand.
c. The leading strand involves template DNA.
d. The enzyme *DNA polymerase* effects the formation of new phosphodiester linkages.

22-65 Indicate whether each of the following statements relating to chromosomes is true or false.
a. Chromosomes contain proteins called histones.
b. Two identical DNA molecules are present in a chromosome.
c. Chromosomes occurs in matched pairs.
d. Most of the mass of a chromosome comes from the DNA present.

22-66 Indicate whether each of the following statements relating to chromosomes is true or false.
a. Chromosomes are DNA–protein complexes.
b. An alternate name for a chromosome is a histone.
c. Two nonidentical DNA molecules are present in a chromosome.
d. Cells of all higher organisms contain the same number of chromosomes.

▲**22-67** Suppose that 28% of the nucleotides in a DNA molecule are deoxythymidine 5′- monophosphate, and that during DNA replication the percentage amounts of *available* nucleotide bases are 22% A, 22% C, 28% G, and 28% T. Which base would be depleted first in the replication process?

▲**22-68** Suppose that 30% of the nucleotides in a DNA molecule are deoxyguanosine 5′- monophosphate, and that during DNA replication the percentage amounts of *available* nucleotide bases are 20% A, 20% C, 30% G, and 30% T. Which base would be depleted first in the replication process?

Overview of Protein Synthesis (Section 22-7)

22-69 Indicate whether each of the following statements relating to protein synthesis is true or false.
a. RNA is involved in both the transcription and translation phases of protein synthesis.
b. DNA is the starting material for protein synthesis.
c. The translation phase of protein synthesis converts RNA to DNA.
d. Transcription precedes translation in protein synthesis.

22-70 Indicate whether each of the following statements relating to protein synthesis is true or false.
a. The three phases of protein synthesis are transcription, translation, and transformation.
b. Translation precedes transcription in protein synthesis.
c. RNA is the starting material for protein synthesis.
d. The transcription phase of protein synthesis converts DNA to RNA.

RNA Molecules (Section 22-8)

22-71 Indicate whether each of the following statements involving differences between DNA and RNA molecules is true or false.
a. Base pairing occurs in DNA but not in RNA.
b. Both DNA and RNA are double-stranded molecules.
c. RNA molecules are much larger than DNA molecules.
d. The base T in DNA is replaced by the base A in RNA.

22-72 Indicate whether each of the following statements involving differences between DNA and RNA molecules is true or false.
a. DNA is a double-stranded molecule and RNA is a single-stranded molecule.
b. RNA and DNA molecules have about the same length.
c. Base pairing occurs in both DNA and RNA.
d. DNA and RNA have the same sugar unit present in their structural backbones.

22-73 Relative to various types of RNA, what does the small capital letter(s) stand for in each of the following designations?
a. tRNA   b. mRNA
c. rRNA   d. hnRNA

22-74 Relative to various types of RNA, what is the abbreviated designation for each of the following RNAs?
a. transfer RNA
b. small nuclear RNA
c. heterogeneous nuclear RNA
d. messenger RNA

22-75 Indicate whether the predominant cellular location where each of the following types of RNA carries out its biochemical functions is (1) the cell nucleus, (2) the cell cytoplasm, or (3) both the nucleus and cytoplasm.
a. mRNA
b. tRNA
c. ribosomal RNA
d. small nuclear RNA

22-76 Indicate whether the predominant cellular location where each of the following types of RNA carries out its biochemical functions is (1) the cell nucleus, (2) the cell cytoplasm, or (3) both the nucleus and cytoplasm.
a. rRNA
b. hnRNA
c. transfer RNA
d. messenger RNA

22-77 Indicate whether each of the following situations occurs within the nuclear or cytoplasmic regions of a cell.
a. DNA transcription
b. hnRNA is formed from DNA
c. tRNA is needed
d. snRNA is needed

22-78 Indicate whether each of the following processes occurs within the nuclear or cytoplasmic regions of a cell.
a. RNA translation
b. mRNA is formed
c. actual protein formation occurs
d. rRNA is needed

Transcription: RNA Synthesis (Section 22-9)

22-79 Indicate whether each of the following statements concerning the transcription phase of protein synthesis is true or false.
  a. DNA helicase causes a parting unwinding of a DNA helix.
  b. RNA ribonucleotides align themselves along the DNA's informational strand.
  c. RNA polymerase effects the linkage of ribonucleotides associated with the DNA template strand.
  d. The type of RNA molecule initially produced in transcription is mRNA.

22-80 Indicate whether each of the following statements concerning the transcription phase of protein synthesis is true or false.
  a. The enzymes DNA helicase and RNA polymerase are both needed in transcription.
  b. The DNA template strand is involved in converting hnRNA to mRNA.
  c. hnRNA base sequence is the same as that of the DNA informational strand.
  d. The type of RNA molecule initially produced in transcription is hnRNA.

22-81 What is the base sequence, given in the 5′-to-3′ direction, of the RNA initially synthesized from the following DNA template strand base sequences.
  a. 5′ ATAT 3′   b. 5′ ACCC 3′
  c. 5′ ATCG 3′   d. 5′ AAAA 3′

22-82 What is the base sequence, given in the 5′-to-3′ direction, of the RNA initially synthesized from the following DNA template strand base sequences.
  a. 5′ TAAT 3′   b. 5′ CGCG 3′
  c. 5′ TCAG 3′   d. 5′ TTTT 3′

22-83 For each of the following DNA template strands, determine (1) the base sequence of the DNA informational strand and (2) the base sequence of the hnRNA synthesized using the DNA template strand. Specify base sequences in the 5′-to-3′ direction.
  a. 3′ TACGGC 5′   b. 3′ CCATTA 5′
  c. 3′ ACATGG 5′   d. 3′ ACGTAC 5′

22-84 For each of the following DNA template strands, determine (1) the base sequence of the DNA informational strand and (2) the base sequence of the hnRNA synthesized using the DNA template strand. Specify base sequences in the 5′-to-3′ direction.
  a. 3′ TTCGTA 5′   b. 3′ CCGAAT 5′
  c. 3′ CATCAT 5′   d. 3′ TGCTGC 5′

22-85 What is the base sequence, specified in the 5′-to-3′ direction, for the DNA strand from which each of the following hnRNA base sequences was transcribed?
  a. 5′ CCUUAA 3′   b. 5′ ACGUAC 3′
  c. 5′ ACGACG 3′   d. 5′ UACCAU 3′

22-86 What is the base sequence, specified in the 5′-to-3′ direction, for the DNA strand from which each of the following hnRNA base sequences was transcribed?
  a. 5′ CUAGGC 3′   b. 5′ UACUGG 3′
  c. 5′ GACGAC 3′   d. 5′ UAAUAU 3′

22-87 What is the relationship between an exon and a gene?

22-88 What is the relationship between an intron and a gene?

22-89 What mRNA base sequence, specified in the 5′-to-3′ direction, would be obtained from the following portion of an hnRNA molecule?

| exon | intron | exon |
3′ UUAC–AACG–GCAU 5′

22-90 What mRNA base sequence, specified in the 5′-to-3′ direction, would be obtained from the following portion of an hnRNA molecule?

| exon | intron | exon |
3′ UCAG–UAGC–UUCA 5′

22-91 What mRNA base sequence, specified in the 5′-to-3′ direction, would be obtained from the following portion of a gene?

| exon | intron | exon |
5′ TCAG–TAGC–TTCA 3′

22-92 What mRNA base sequence, specified in the 5′-to-3′ direction, would be obtained from the following portion of a gene?

| exon | intron | exon |
5′ TTAC–AACG–GCAT 3′

22-93 In the process of splicing, which type of RNA
  a. undergoes the splicing?
  b. is present in the spliceosomes?

22-94 What is the difference between snRNA and snRNPs?

22-95 An hnRNA molecule contains three exons, with the middle one being an "alternative" exon. How many different mRNA molecules can be produced from this hnRNA molecule?

22-96 An hnRNA molecule contains three exons, with the middle one and one other being "alternative" exons. How many different mRNA molecules can be produced from this hnRNA molecule?

▲22-97 Indicate whether each of the following base-pairing situations (1) involves two DNA strands, (2) involves a DNA strand and an RNA strand, or (3) could involve either two DNA strands or a DNA strand and an RNA strand?
  a. A G T   b. A C T
     ⋮ ⋮ ⋮   ⋮ ⋮ ⋮
     U C A   T G A
  c. A G U   d. C G C
     ⋮ ⋮ ⋮   ⋮ ⋮ ⋮
     T C A   G C G

▲22-98 Indicate whether each of the following base-pairing situations (1) involves two DNA strands, (2) involves a DNA strand and an RNA strand, or (3) could involve either two DNA strands or a DNA strand and an RNA strand?
  a. A A T   b. A A T
     ⋮ ⋮ ⋮   ⋮ ⋮ ⋮
     T T A   U U A
  c. C G U   d. C C G
     ⋮ ⋮ ⋮   ⋮ ⋮ ⋮
     G C A   G G C

The Genetic Code (Section 22-10)

22-99 What is a codon?

22-100 On what type of RNA molecule are codons found?

22-101 Using the information in Table 22-2, determine what amino acid is coded for by each of the following codons.
   a. CUU   b. AAU
   c. AGU   d. GGG

22-102 Using the information in Table 22-2, determine what amino acid is coded for by each of the following codons.
   a. GUA   b. CCC
   c. CAC   d. CCA

22-103 Using the information in Table 22-2, determine the possible codons for each of the following amino acids?
   a. Tyrosine   b. Alanine
   c. Leu   d. Cys

22-104 Using the information in Table 22-2, determine the possible codons for each of the following amino acids?
   a. Valine   b. Serine
   c. Gly   d. Lys

22-105 Explain why the base sequence ATC could not be a codon.

22-106 Explain why the base sequence AGAC could not be a codon.

22-107 Predict the sequence of amino acids coded by the mRNA sequence

   5′ AUG–AAA–GAA–GAC–CUA 3′

22-108 Predict the sequence of amino acids coded by the mRNA sequence

   5′ GGA–GGC–ACA–UGG–GAA 3′

22-109 Predict the sequence of amino acids coded by the mRNA sequence

   3′ AUG–AAA–GAA–GAC–CUA 5′

22-110 Predict the sequence of amino acids coded by the mRNA sequence

   3′ GGA–GGC–ACA–UGG–GAA 5′

▲**22-111** Determine each of the following items using the hnRNA nucleotide sequence

| exon | intron | exon |
   5′ UCCG–CCAU–UAACA 3′

   a. The sequence of bases on the DNA template strand from which the hnRNA was synthesized
   b. The sequence of bases on the DNA informational strand associated with the DNA template strand.
   c. The sequence of bases in the mRNA produced from the hnRNA
   d. The sequence of amino acids in the peptide synthesized from the mRNA

▲**22-112** Determine each of the following items using the hnRNA nucleotide sequence

| exon | intron | exon |
   5′ AGGC–GGAU–UCACA 3′

   a. The sequence of bases on the DNA template strand from which the hnRNA was synthesized
   b. The sequence of bases on the DNA informational strand associated with the DNA template strand.
   c. The sequence of bases in the mRNA produced from the hnRNA
   d. The sequence of amino acids in the peptide synthesized from the mRNA

Anticodons and tRNA Molecules (Section 22-11)

22-113 Indicate whether each of the following statements about tRNA molecules and their structures is true or false.
   a. Four hairpin loops are always present in a tRNA molecule.
   b. The anticodon site involves the hairpin loop opposite the open end.
   c. The amino acid attachment site involves the tRNAs 5′ end.
   d. An amino acid hydrogen bonds to its attachments site.

22-114 Indicate whether each of the following statements about tRNA molecules and their structures is true or false.
   a. The amino acid attachment site involves a hairpin loop.
   b. An amino acid covalently bonds to its attachment site.
   c. Three hairpin loops are always present in a tRNA molecule.
   d. An anticodon is located at each hairpin loop site.

22-115 Indicate whether each of the following statements involving codons and anticodons is true or false.
   a. All codons involve three bases.
   b. Anticodons are found on rRNA molecules.
   c. The base U can be present in anticodons but not in codons.
   d. Interaction of a codon with an anticodon involves complementary base pairing.

22-116 Indicate whether each of the following statements involving codons and anticodons is true or false.
   a. All anticodons involve four bases.
   b. Codons are found on tRNA molecules.
   c. The base U can be present in codons but not in anticodons.
   d. Interaction of a codon with an anticodon involves hydrogen bonding.

22-117 What is the anticodon that would interact with each of the following codons?
   a. AGA   b. CGU
   c. UUU   d. CAA

22-118 What is the anticodon that would interact with each of the following codons?
   a. CCU   b. GUA
   c. AUC   d. GCA

22-119 Which amino acid will a tRNA molecule be carrying if its anticodon is the following?
   a. CCC   b. CAG
   c. UGC   d. GAG

22-120 Which amino acid will a tRNA molecule be carrying if its anticodon is the following?
   a. GGG   b. GAC
   c. AUA   d. CGA

22-121 Identify the amino acid associated with each of the following entities.
   a. 5′ ACG 3′ codon
   b. 3′ ACG 5′ codon
   c. 5′ ACG 3′ anticodon
   d. 3′ ACG 5′ anticodon

22-122 Identify the amino acid associated with each of the following entities.
   a. 5′ CCG 3′ codon
   b. 3′ CCG 5′ codon
   c. 5′ CCG 3′ anticodon
   d. 3′ CCG 5′ anticodon

▲22-123 The following is the base sequence of an exon portion of a template strand of a DNA molecule:

5′ TCCGCATTAACA 3′

a. What is the base sequence of the hnRNA strand synthesized from the DNA template strand?
b. What is the base sequence of the mRNA strand synthesized from the hnRNA strand?
c. What codons are present in the mRNA strand produced from the DNA template strand?
d. What tRNA molecule anticodons are needed to interact with the codons present in the mRNA strand produced from the template DNA strand?

▲22-124 The following is a base sequence for an exon portion of a template strand of a DNA molecule:

5′ TAACGCTTCACG 3′

a. What is the base sequence of the hnRNA strand synthesized from the DNA template strand?
b. What is the base sequence of the mRNA strand synthesized from the hnRNA strand?
c. What codons are present in the mRNA strand produced from the DNA template strand?
d. What tRNA molecule anticodons are needed to interact with the codons present in the mRNA strand produced from the template DNA strand?

Translation: Protein Synthesis (Section 22-12)

22-125 Indicate whether each of the following statements about ribosomes is true or false.
a. Ribosomes have two subunits that are approximately the same size.
b. The active site of a ribosome is predominantly RNA rather than protein.
c. The mRNA involved in protein synthesis binds to the small subunit of a ribosome.
d. A ribosome functions as an enzyme in protein synthesis.

22-126 Indicate whether each of the following statements about ribosomes is true or false.
a. The active site of a ribosome is located in its smaller subunit.
b. A ribosome is a tRNA–protein complex.
c. Ribosome subunits are approximately 75% protein and 25% RNA.
d. Human cells contain from 10 to 20 ribosomes.

22-127 Indicate whether each of the following statements concerning the translation phase of protein synthesis is true or false.
a. Elongation is the second step in the translation process.
b. The first amino acid in a developing polynucleotide chain is always Met.
c. The second site in an mRNA–ribosome complex is called the P site.
d. A polyribosome is a complex involving several mRNA molecules and a ribosome.

22-128 Indicate whether each of the following statements concerning the translation phase of protein synthesis is true or false.
a. Initiation is the first step in the translation process.
b. An amino acid must be activated before it can be attached to a tRNA molecule.
c. Incoming tRNA molecules always interact with the A site of an mRNA–ribosome complex.

d. The shifting of a ribosome three base positions further down an mRNA molecue is called transribation.

22-129 Write a possible mRNA base sequence that would lead to the production of the following pentapeptide. (There is more than one correct answer.)

Gly–Ala–Cys–Val–Tyr

22-130 Write a possible mRNA base sequence that would lead to the production of the following pentapeptide. (There is more than one correct answer.)

Lys–Met–Thr–His–Phe

22-131 Consider the translation of the following mRNA base sequence during protein synthesis.

5′ CAA CGA AAG 3′

a. What are the codons associated with this base sequence?
b. What tRNA anticodons are compatible with this base sequence?
c. What are the amino acids specified by this base sequence?

22-132 Consider the translation of the following mRNA base sequence during protein synthesis.

5′ CGC CGU UAC 3′

a. What are the codons associated with this base sequence?
b. What tRNA anticodons are compatible with this base sequence?
c. What are the amino acids specified by this base sequence?

▲22-133 Which of these RNA types—(1) mRNA, (2) hnRNA, (3) rRNA, or (4) tRNA—is most closely associated with each of the following terms or descriptions?
a. Codon   b. Intron
c. Amino acid carrier   d. Interacts with ribosomes

▲22-134 Which of these RNA types—(1) mRNA, (2) hnRNA, (3) rRNA, or (4) tRNA—is most closely associated with each of the following terms or descriptions?
a. Exon
b. Anticodon
c. Ribosome structural component
d. Interacts with spliceosomes

Mutations (Section 22-13)

22-135 Consider the following mRNA base sequence

5′ CUU CAG 3′

a. What dipeptide is coded for by this mRNA?
b. What dipeptide is formed if a point mutation converts CUU to CUC?
c. What dipeptide is formed if a point mutation converts CAG to AAG?
d. What dipeptide is formed if a point mutation converts CUU to CUC and CAG to AAG?

22-136 Consider the following mRNA base sequence

5′ ACC CAC 3′

a. What dipeptide is coded for by this mRNA?
b. What dipeptide is formed if a point mutation converts CAC to AAC?
c. What dipeptide is formed if a point mutation converts ACC to ACU?
d. What dipeptide is formed if a point mutation converts CAC to AAC and ACC to ACU?

▲22-137 Consider the following DNA base sequence

3′ TTA ATA 5′

a. What dipeptide is formed from the transcription and translation of this DNA segment?
b. What dipeptide is formed if a DNA point mutation converts ATA to ATG?
c. What dipeptide is formed if a DNA point mutation converts ATA to AGA?
d. What dipeptide is formed if a DNA point mutation converts TTA to TTT?

▲22-138 Consider the following DNA base sequence

3′ TAT CGG 5′

a. What dipeptide is formed from the transcription and translation of this DNA segment?
b. What dipeptide is formed if a DNA point mutation converts CGG to CGT?
c. What dipeptide is formed if a DNA point mutation converts CGG to AGG?
d. What dipeptide is formed if a DNA point mutation converts TAT to TTT?

22-139 The DNA template strand segment

3′ TTC AAA CCG TAC 5′

upon transcription and translation produces the amino acid sequence Lys-Phe-Gly-Met. What is the amino acid sequence produced if a frameshift mutation occurs in which the third A base in the original DNA sequence is removed?

22-140 The DNA template strand segment

3′ TTC AAA CCG TAC 5′

upon transcription and translation produces the amino acid sequence Lys–Phe–Gly–Met. What is the amino acid sequence produced if a frameshift mutation occurs in which a G base is inserted after the first C in the original DNA sequence?

Viruses and Vaccines (Section 22-14)

22-141 Indicate whether each of the following statements concerning viruses and vaccines is true or false.
a. No DNA is present in a virus.
b. A virus cannot reproduce itself without the help of a host cell.
c. Viruses that cause disease are called retroviruses.
d. Some, but not all, vaccines contain an active virus.

22-142 Indicate whether each of the following statements concerning viruses and vaccines is true or false.
a. All viruses contain both DNA and RNA.
b. Some, but not all, vaccines contain a virus in an inactive form.
c. A retrovirus contains RNA but not DNA.
d. All life-forms except bacteria are subject to attack by viruses.

Recombinant DNA and Genetic Engineering (Section 22-15)

22-143 How does recombinant DNA differ from normal DNA?

22-144 Give two reasons why bacterial cells are used for recombinant DNA procedures.

22-145 What role do plasmids play in recombinant DNA procedures?

22-146 Describe what occurs when a particular restriction enzyme operates on a segment of double-stranded DNA.

22-147 Describe what happens during transformation.

22-148 How are plasmids obtained from *E. coli* bacteria?

22-149 A particular restriction enzyme will cleave DNA between A and A in the sequence AAGCTT in the 5′-to-3′ direction. Draw a diagram showing the structural details of the "sticky ends" that result from cleavage of the following DNA segment.

22-150 A particular restriction enzyme will cleave DNA between A and A in the sequence AAGCTT in the 5′-to-3′ direction. Draw a diagram showing the structural details of the "sticky ends" that result from cleavage of the following DNA segment.

▲22-151 Which of the following processes—(1) transcription phase of protein synthesis, (2) translation phase of protein synthesis, (3) replication of DNA, and (4) formation of recombinant DNA—is associated with each of the events below?
a. Complete unwinding of a DNA molecule occurs.
b. Partial unwinding of a DNA molecule occurs.
c. An mRNA–ribosome complex is formed.
d. The process of transformation occurs.

▲22-152 Which of the following processes—(1) transcription phase of protein synthesis, (2) translation phase of protein synthesis, (3) replication of DNA, and (4) formation of recombinant DNA—is associated with each of the events below?
a. Amino acid–tRNA molecules are formed.
b. Anticodon–codon base pairing occurs.
c. Restriction enzymes are used.
d. Okazaki fragments are formed.

Polymerase Chain Reaction (Section 22-16)

22-153 Indicate whether each of the following statements concerning the polymerase chain reaction (PCR) is true or false.
a. The first step in the PCR process involves heating of a DNA solution.
b. The PCR process has applications in forensic investigations.
c. The PCR process requires that the target DNA sequence be bound to a primer.
d. After four cycles of the PCR process eight DNA molecules have been produced.

22-154 Indicate whether each of the following statements concerning the polymerase chain reaction (PCR) is true or false.
a. The enzyme DNA polymerase is needed in the first step of the PCR process.
b. A primer, a short starter nucleotide chain, is needed in the second step of the PCR process.
c. The PCR process has applications in detecting the AIDS virus.
d. Replication of DNA does not begin until the second cycle of the PCR process.

Chapter 22 Appendix:

Regulation of Gene Expression from Ingraham Introduction to Microbiology:
A Case-History Study Approach, 3rd Edition

REGULATION OF GENE EXPRESSION

Microbial cells use substrates and synthesize macromolecules just fast enough to meet their needs. Making them too fast would be wasteful. Making them too slowly would starve the cell of essential components. Either extreme would slow the rate of growth and make the microorganism less able to compete with other organisms in its environment. Cells can operate with such remarkable efficiency because their metabolism is precisely regulated.

Recall from Chapter 5 that metabolism is regulated in two ways: by changing the activity of certain enzymes (as discussed in Chapter 5) and by changing the rate of making proteins, including enzymes. This second type of regulation—which we'll discuss now—affects gene expression.

Regulation of gene expression increases a cell's metabolic efficiency in many ways. For example, some regulatory mechanisms allow the cell to make enzymes only when they are needed. On this basis enzymes are classified as follows:

- **Inducible enzymes** are made only when their substrates are present.
- **Repressible enzymes** are produced only when their product is needed.

- **Constitutive enzymes** are always produced because they are always needed.

The molecular mechanisms that cause enzymes to be induced or repressed are varied and complex, but they all fall into one or another of two broad classes. They either regulate transcription or they regulate translation. Let's look a little more closely at a few specific examples.

Regulation of Transcription

Most regulatory mechanisms act on transcription, usually by changing the activity of RNA polymerase. They do this by changing the frequency, rather than the rate, at which a particular gene is transcribed. When transcripts are made less frequently, less protein is made.

There are two principal mechanisms of regulating transcription: (1) by producing a regulatory protein that binds to DNA near the promoter of the gene that's being regulated and (2) by interrupting transcription after it has started. We'll examine examples of both mechanisms.

Regulatory Proteins That Bind to DNA. These proteins bind to specific regions of DNA, called **operators,** that are close to a gene's promoter (where RNA polymerase normally binds). Depending on what kind of protein is bound to the operator, transcription of the gene becomes more or less probable.

a

0.5 μm

b

FIGURE 6.10 Simultaneous transcription and translation. (a) This transmission electron micrograph shows a gene being transcribed from left to right. The arrow points to the DNA molecule at the midpoint of the gene. (b) This sketch interprets the micrograph. RNA polymerase molecules are not visible in micrograph; neither are the nascent protein molecules that would be attached to each ribosome. Because a ribosome attaches to the end of an mRNA molecule and moves toward the DNA, protein molecules would lengthen as the ribosome approaches the DNA.

LARGER FIELD

JANNINE ZEIG

In the late 1970s Jannine Zeig, a graduate student at the University of California, San Diego, was doing research on the bacterium *Salmonella typhimurium*. Specifically, she was trying to explain phase variation, periodic changes in the type of flagella made by *S. typhimurium* and many other bacterial pathogens.

Phase variation protects *S. typhimurium* from the host's immune system because by the time it is able to detect the kind of flagella that the invading *S. typhimurium* cells produce, some of them start to produce a second kind that the immune system cannot detect. Later some of these bacteria again start to produce the first

kind of flagella. Zeig knew that the change was not a mutation because it occurred too often. Mutations in any particular gene occur in about one out of a hundred million cells. Phase variation occurs in about one out of a thousand. After extensive experimentation, Zeig found that an enzyme caused a small piece of DNA (con-

taining a promoter) in the *S. typhimurium* chromosome to invert. In one position the DNA transcribes genes encoding one kind of flagella. In the other position the DNA causes the other type to be encoded. Zeig discovered a new basis for phase variation. It has since been found that gene switching occurs in many bacteria.

Most regulatory proteins that bind to DNA are allosteric proteins. Like all allosteric proteins, their activity changes depending on whether or not an effector is bound to them (Chapter 5). We'll consider the lactose **operon** (an operon is a set of genes that is regulated and transcribed together) as an example.

The Lactose Operon. The lactose (*lac*) operon encodes a set of inducible enzymes that confer the ability to use **lactose** (milk sugar) as a growth substrate. Both the enzymes needed to metabolize lactose are encoded by the lac operon (**Figure 6.11**). One of these enzymes, **galactoside permease,** brings the disaccharide, lactose, into the cell, and the other, **β-galactosidase,** splits it into its component monosaccharides (glucose and galactose). Galactoside permease is encoded by the *lacY* gene and β-galactosidase by the *lacZ* gene. In addition to these two genes, the *lac* operon contains a promoter-operator region and the *lacA* gene, which encodes **galactoside transacetylase,** an enzyme with unknown function.

The DNA-binding protein, called the *lac* **repressor,** which regulates expression of the *lac* operon, is encoded by a gene called *lacI,* which lies close to but outside the *lac* operon. It has its own promoter and is expressed constitutively.

In the absence of lactose, the *lac* repressor binds to the *lac* operator and prevents transcription of the *lac* operon. When lactose is present, a small amount of it is converted to an effector, called **allolactose,** which binds to the *lac* repressor, changing it so that it no longer binds to the *lac* operator. Thus only when lactose is present are the genes of the *lac* operon transcribed and expressed. The result is

the *lac* operon is expressed only when its products are needed—when lactose is available.

Note that the effector, allolactose, has a negative effect of the *lac* repressor: It prevents the *lac* repressor from binding to the operator. Note also that when the *lac* repressor binds to the operator, it too has a negative effect of transcription: It prevents transcription. Other effectors have positive effects on binding proteins, and other binding proteins have positive effects on transcription. This variability permits a huge variety of regulatory mechanisms. Almost all you can imagine actually exist.

Now we'll examine **attenuation,** an example of the second method of regulating transcription, namely, interrupting transcription after it has started.

Attenuation. Attenuation is a mechanism that regulates transcription without the participation of a DNA-binding protein. Instead, transcription of a partially completed mRNA molecule either stops or proceeds, depending on whether the gene product is needed.

Attenuation is usually used to regulate production of enzymes that participate in biosynthesis of an amino acid. When the intracellular concentration of the amino acid rises higher than the cell needs, attenuation decreases transcription. The consequence is less enzyme and eventually less amino acid. When the concentration of the amino acid falls to an inadequate level, transcription and enzyme synthesis begin again.

Let's look at a typical attenuation-regulated operon, the histidine operon of *Escherichia coli.* It encodes the enzymes needed to synthesize the amino acid histidine. This operon (**Figure 6.12**) begins with a gene that encodes a

FIGURE 6.11 Regulation of transcription through the *lac* operon. (a) The lactose operon has three genes, *lacZ*, *lacY*, and *lacA*, which are regulated by the nearby regulatory gene, *lacI*. (b) When lactose is absent, the *lac* repressor binds to the operator, stopping transcription. (c) But when lactose is present, some of it is converted to allolactose, which binds to the repressor. This changes the repressor so it can no longer bind to the operator. Then the genes are expressed.

leader protein. A leader protein is only a test protein. Its sole function is to determine whether the cell has an adequate supply of histidine. The leader protein is well suited to its job, because it contains seven histidine units in a row! As a result, its rate of translation is highly sensitive to intracellular concentrations of histidine. When the supply of histidine is adequate, translation of the leader protein occurs rapidly, so that the first translating ribosome is only slightly behind RNA polymerase. As a result, only a short stretch of free mRNA separates them. But this short stretch is highly active: It folds back on itself, creating an **attenuator loop** which displaces the RNA polymerase molecule ahead of it, stopping transcription and thereby stopping expression of the histidine operon.

When the supply of intracellular histidine falls, the situation changes. Then the leading ribosome slows or stops when it reaches the seven-histidine stretch, while RNA polymerase proceeds ahead, exposing an extended stretch of mRNA between them. This extended piece of free RNA folds back on itself, producing a new loop, an **antiterminator loop.** When the antiterminator loop forms, the attenuator loop can't. RNA polymerase is not displaced. It proceeds to transcribe the rest of the operon. Histidine enzymes are made.

Thus attenuation helps adjust the supply of histidine to the cell's need for it. When more histidine is needed, the cell makes more of the enzymes that synthesize it. When excess histidine is present, lesser amounts of these enzymes are made. Histidine also regulates the activity of one of these enzymes by end-product inhibition (Chapter 5). Together, attenuation and end-product inhibition set the intracellular concentration of histidine precisely at its optimal level. Attenuation spares the cell from making enzymes that are not needed.

Biochemical Energy Production

23

Juniors Bildarchiv GmbH/Alamy

The energy consumed by these scarlet ibises in flight is generated by numerous sequences of biochemical reactions that occur within their bodies.

This chapter is the first of four dealing with the chemical reactions that occur in a living organism. In this first chapter, those molecules that are repeatedly encountered in biological reactions are considered as well as those reactions that are common to the processing of carbohydrates, lipids, and proteins. The three following chapters consider the reactions associated uniquely with carbohydrate, lipid, and protein processing, respectively.

23-1 Metabolism

LEARNING FOCUS

Distinguish among the meanings for the terms *metabolism*, *catabolism*, and *anabolism*; know the difference between a *linear* and *cyclic* metabolic pathway.

Metabolism *is the sum total of all the biochemical reactions that take place in a living organism.* Human metabolism is quite remarkable. An average human adult whose weight remains the same for 40 years processes about 6 tons of solid food and 10,000 gallons of water, during which time the composition of the body is essentially constant. Just as gasoline is put into a car to make it go or a kitchen appliance is plugged in to make it run, the human body needs a source of energy to make it function. Even the simplest living cell is continually carrying on energy-demanding processes such as protein synthesis, DNA replication, RNA transcription, and membrane transport.

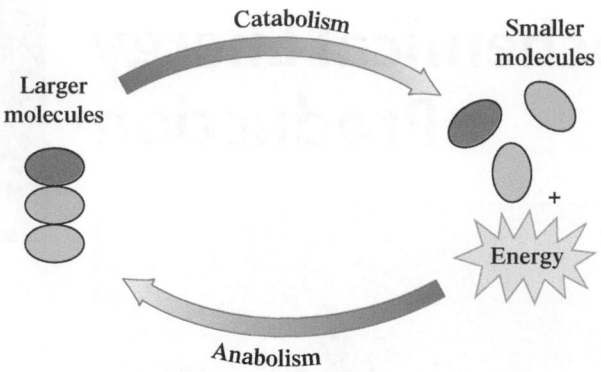

▶ Catabolism *is pronounced
ca-TAB-o-lism, and* anabolism
is pronounced an-ABB-o-lism.
Catabolic *is pronounced CAT-a-
bol-ic, and* anabolic *is pronounced
AN-a-bol-ic.*

Metabolic reactions fall into one of two subtypes: catabolism and anabolism.
Catabolism *is all metabolic reactions in which large biochemical molecules are broken down to smaller ones.* Catabolic reactions usually release energy. The reactions
involved in the oxidation of glucose are catabolic. **Anabolism** *is all metabolic reactions
in which small biochemical molecules are joined together to form larger ones.* Anabolic
reactions usually require energy in order to proceed. ◀ The synthesis of proteins
from amino acids is an anabolic process. Figure 23-1 contrasts catabolic and anabolic
processes.

The metabolic reactions that occur in a cell are usually organized into sequences
called *metabolic pathways.* A **metabolic pathway** *is a series of consecutive biochemical
reactions used to convert a starting material into an end product.* Such pathways may
be *linear,* in which a series of reactions generates a final product, or *cyclic,* in which a
series of reactions regenerates the first reactant.

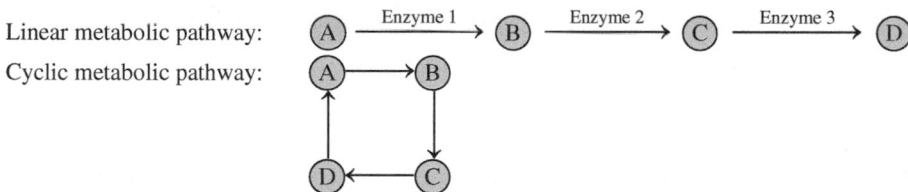

The major metabolic pathways for all life forms are similar. This enables scientists
to study metabolic reactions in simpler life forms and use the results to help understand the corresponding metabolic reactions in more complex organisms, including
humans.

EXAMPLE 23-1

Distinguishing Between Anabolic and Catabolic Processes

Classify each of the following chemical processes as anabolic or catabolic:

a. Synthesis of a polysaccharide from monosaccharides
b. Hydrolysis of a pentasaccharide to monosaccharides
c. Formation of a nucleotide from phosphate, nitrogenous base, and pentose sugar
d. Hydrolysis of a triacylglycerol to glycerol and fatty acids

Solution

a. *Anabolic.* A large molecule is formed from many small molecules.
b. *Catabolic.* Five monosaccharides are produced from a larger molecule.
c. *Anabolic.* Three subunits are combined to give a larger unit.
d. *Catabolic.* A four-subunit molecule is broken down into four smaller molecules.

1. Which of the following statements concerning metabolism and metabolic reactions is *correct*?
   a. Anabolism and metabolism are two terms with the same meaning.
   b. Some, but not all, metabolic reactions involve catabolism.
   c. Energy is a by-product of all metabolic reactions.
   d. no correct response
2. Which of the following statements concerning metabolic pathways is *incorrect*?
   a. Metabolic pathways always involve a series of consecutive reactions.
   b. All cyclic metabolic pathways regenerate the starting material for the pathway.
   c. All linear metabolic pathways generate a final product.
   d. no correct response

Answers: 1. b; 2. d

23-2 Metabolism and Cell Structure

LEARNING FOCUS

Be familiar with major structural components present within a cell and their functions; be familiar with detailed structural considerations for mitochondria.

Knowledge of the major structural features of a cell is a prerequisite to understanding *where* metabolic reactions take place.

Cells are of two types: prokaryotic and eukaryotic. *Prokaryotic cells* have no nucleus and are found only in bacteria. The DNA that governs the reproduction of prokaryotic cells is usually a single circular molecule found near the center of the cell in a region called the *nucleoid*. A **eukaryotic cell** *is a cell in which the DNA is found in a membrane-enclosed nucleus.* Cells of this type, which are found in all higher organisms, are about 1000 times larger than bacterial cells. ◄ The remainder of this section focuses on eukaryotic cells, the type present in humans. Figure 23-2 shows the general internal structure of a eukaryotic cell. Note the key components shown: the outer membrane, nucleus, cytosol, ribosomes, lysosomes, and mitochondria. ◄

▶ *The term* eukaryotic, *pronounced you-KAHR-ee-ah-tic, is from the Greek* eu, *meaning "true," and* karyon, *meaning "nucleus." The term* prokaryotic, *which contains the Greek* pro, *meaning "before," literally means "before the nucleus."*

▶ *Eukaryotic and prokaryotic cells differ in that the former contain a well-defined nucleus, set off from the rest of the cell by a membrane.*

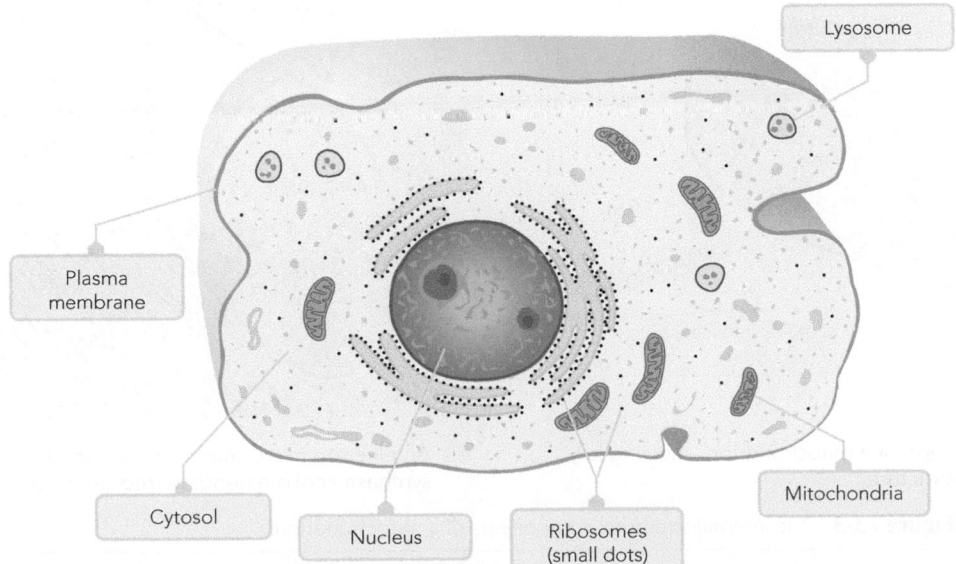

Figure 23-2 A schematic representation of a eukaryotic cell with selected internal components identified.

The **cytoplasm** *is the water-based material of a eukaryotic cell that lies between the nucleus and the outer membrane of the cell.* Within the cytoplasm are several kinds of small structures called *organelles.* An **organelle** *is a minute structure within the cytoplasm of a cell that carries out a specific cellular function.* The organelles are surrounded by the *cytosol.* The **cytosol** *is the water-based fluid part of the cytoplasm of a cell.*

Three important types of organelles are ribosomes, lysosomes, and mitochondria. Ribosomes were encountered in the last chapter; they are the sites where protein synthesis occurs (Section 22-12). A **lysosome** *is an organelle that contains hydrolytic enzymes needed for cellular rebuilding, repair, and degradation.* Some lysosome enzymes hydrolyze proteins to amino acids; others hydrolyze polysaccharides to monosaccharides. Bacteria and viruses "trapped" by the body's immune system (Section 20-18) are degraded and destroyed by enzymes from lysosomes. ◀

A **mitochondrion** *is an organelle that is responsible for the generation of most of the energy for a cell.* Much of the discussion of this chapter deals with the energy-producing chemical reactions that occur within mitochondria.

Mitochondria are sausage-shaped organelles containing both an *outer membrane* and a *multifolded inner membrane* (see Figure 23-3). The outer membrane, which is about 50% lipid and 50% protein, is freely permeable to small molecules. The inner membrane, which is about 20% lipid and 80% protein, is highly impermeable to most substances. The nonpermeable nature of the inner membrane divides a mitochondrion into two separate compartments—an interior region called the *matrix* and the region between the inner and outer membranes, called the *intermembrane space.* The folds of the inner membrane that protrude into the matrix are called *cristae.* ◀

The invention of high-resolution electron microscopes allowed researchers to see the interior structure of the mitochondrion more clearly and led to the discovery, in 1962, of small spherical knobs attached to the cristae called *ATP synthase complexes.* As their name implies, these relatively small knobs, which are located on the matrix side of the inner membrane, are responsible for ATP synthesis, and their association with the inner membrane is critically important for this task. More will be said about ATP in the next section.

▶ *A protective mechanism exists to prevent lysosome enzymes from destroying the cell in which they are found if they should be accidently released (via membrane rupture or leakage). The optimum pH (Section 21-6) for lysosome enzyme activity is 4.8. The cytoplasmic pH of 7.0–7.3 renders such enzymes inactive.*

▶ Mitochondria, *pronounced my-toe-KON-dree-ah, is plural. The singular form of the term is* mitochondrion. *The threadlike shape of the inner membrane of the mitochondria is responsible for this organelle's name;* mitos *is Greek for "thread," and* chondrion *is Greek for "granule."*

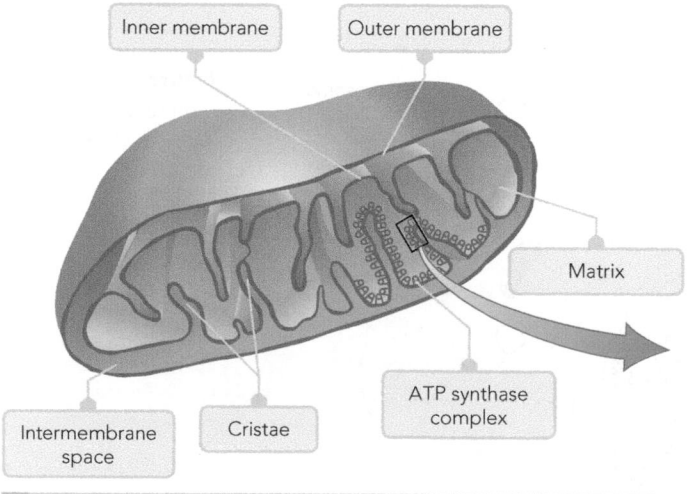

a A schematic representation of a mitochondrion, showing key features of its internal structure.

b An electron micrograph showing the ATP synthase knobs extending into the matrix.

Figure 23-3 The internal structural components of a mitochondrion.

EXAMPLE 23-2

Recognizing Structural Characteristics of a Mitochondrion

Identify each of the following structural features of a mitochondrion:

a. The more permeable of the two mitochondrial membranes
b. The mitochondrial membrane that has cristae
c. The mitochondrial membrane that determines the size of the matrix
d. The mitochondrial membrane that is interior to the intermembrane space

Solution

a. *Outer membrane.* The outer membrane is more permeable.
b. *Inner membrane.* Cristae are "folds" present on the inner membrane.
c. *Inner membrane.* The matrix is the center part of a mitochondrion and is surrounded by the inner membrane.
d. *Inner membrane.* The intermembrane space separates the outer membrane from the inner membrane.

Section 23-2 Quick Quiz

1. Which of the following is *not* found within the cytoplasm of a cell?
   a. mitochondria
   b. cellular nucleus
   c. cytosol
   d. no correct response
2. Which of the following is *not* an organelle?
   a. ribosome
   b. lysosome
   c. mitochondrion
   d. no correct response
3. The site for most energy-producing reactions in a cell is
   a. ribosome
   b. lysosome
   c. mitochondrion
   d. no correct response
4. Which of the following statements about mitochondrion structure is *correct*?
   a. The inner membrane separates the matrix from the intermembrane space.
   b. The inner membrane is more permeable than the outer membrane.
   c. The outer membrane has a highly folded structure.
   d. no correct response

Answers: 1. b; 2. d; 3. c; 4. a

23-3 Important Nucleotide-Containing Compounds in Metabolic Pathways

LEARNING FOCUS

Knowing structural subunit characteristics of and biochemical functions for the following compounds: ATP, ADP, AMP, FAD, FADH$_2$, NAD$^+$, NADH, and CoA–SH.

As a prelude to an overview presentation (Section 23-5) of the metabolic processes by which our food is converted to energy, several compounds that repeatedly function as key intermediates in these metabolic pathways will be considered. Knowing about these compounds will make it easier to understand the details of metabolic pathways. The compounds to be discussed all have *nucleotides* (Section 22-2) as part of their structures. ◄

▶ *Nucleotides, besides being the monomer units from which nucleic acids are made, are also present in several nonpolymeric molecules that are important in energy production in living things.*

Adenosine Phosphates (ATP, ADP, and AMP)

Several adenosine phosphates exist. Of importance in metabolism are adenosine *mono*phosphate (AMP), adenosine *di*phosphate (ADP), and adenosine *tri*phosphate (ATP). AMP is one of the nucleotides present in RNA molecules (Section 22-2). ADP and ATP differ structurally from AMP only in the number of phosphate groups present. Block structural diagrams for these three adenosine phosphates follow.

Figure 23-4 shows actual structural formulas for these three adenosine phosphates. Highlighted within the structural formulas are the bonds that the phosphate groups participate in. The phosphate–ribose bond is a *phosphoester bond,* and the phosphate–phosphate bonds are *phosphoanhydride bonds.* The word *anhydride* present in the term *phosphoanhydride* refers to the production of (loss of) a molecule of water when two phosphate groups bond to each other. A **phosphoanhydride bond** *is the chemical bond formed when two phosphate groups react with each other and a water molecule is produced.*

In Chapter 16 when inorganic phosphate esters were considered (Section 16-20), the term *phosphoryl group* was introduced. A phosphoryl group, which has the formula PO_3^{2-}, is the functional group derived from a phosphate ion when the latter becomes part of another molecule. As shown in Figure 23-4, ATP contains three phosphoryl groups, ADP two phosphoryl groups, and AMP one phosphoryl group.

ATP and ADP molecules readily undergo hydrolysis reactions in which phosphate groups (P_i, inorganic phosphate) are released.

$$ATP + H_2O \longrightarrow ADP + P_i + H^+ + energy$$
$$ADP + H_2O \longrightarrow AMP + P_i + H^+ + energy$$
$$ATP + 2H_2O \longrightarrow AMP + 2P_i + 2H^+ + energy$$

Figure 23-5 gives structural equations for the conversion of ATP to ADP and the conversion of ADP to AMP. Note from these structural equations that the chemical formula for a released phosphate group (P_i) is HPO_4^{2-} (the form in which phosphate ion exists in solution at physiological pH). Note also that an H^+ ion is a product of the hydrolysis; its source is the water molecule involved in the hydrolysis. The reacting water molecule is also the source of the OH unit present in P_i.

Figure 23-4 Structures of the various phosphate forms of adenosine.

Figure 23-5 Structural equations for the hydrolysis of ATP to ADP and the hydrolysis of ADP to AMP.

The preceding hydrolysis reactions are energy-producing reactions that are used to drive cellular processes that require energy input. The phosphoanhydride bonds in ATP and ADP are *very reactive* bonds that require less energy than normal to break. The presence of such reactive bonds, which are often called *strained bonds* (see Section 23-5), is the basis for the net energy production that accompanies hydrolysis. Greater-than-normal electron–electron repulsive forces at specific locations within a molecule are the cause for bond strain; in ATP and ADP, it is the highly electronegative oxygen atoms in the additional phosphate groups that cause the increased repulsive strain. ◀

A typical cellular reaction in which ATP functions as both a source of a phosphate group and a source of energy is the conversion of glucose to glucose 6-phosphate, a reaction that is the first step in the process of glycolysis (Section 24-2).

▶ *In metabolic pathways in which they are involved, the adenosine phosphates continually change back and forth among the various forms:*

$$ATP \rightleftharpoons ADP \rightleftharpoons AMP$$

The symbol Ⓟ is a shorthand notation for a PO_3^{2-} unit.

ATP is not the only nucleotide triphosphate present in cells, although it is the most prevalent. The other nitrogen-containing bases associated with nucleotides (Section 22-2) are also present in triphosphate form. Uridine triphosphate (UTP) is involved in carbohydrate metabolism, guanosine triphosphate (GTP) participates in protein and carbohydrate metabolism, and cytidine triphosphate (CTP) is involved in lipid metabolism.

The focus on relevancy feature Chemical Connections 23-A—Adenosine Phosphates and Muscle Relaxation/Contraction—provides an additional example of the use of energy obtained from ATP hydrolysis in the operation of the human body. This example involves muscle contraction and relaxation.

Flavin Adenine Dinucleotide (FAD, FADH₂)

Flavin adenine dinucleotide (FAD) is a coenzyme (Section 21-2) required in numerous metabolic redox reactions. Structurally, FAD can be visualized as containing either three subunits or six subunits. A block diagram of FAD from the three-subunit viewpoint is

The flavin and ribitol subunits in this structure together constitute the B vitamin riboflavin (Section 21-14). The coenzyme FAD is thus one of the biochemically active forms of riboflavin (Section 21-14); the activating factor is the ADP subunit.

CHEMICAL CONNECTIONS 23-A

Adenosine Phosphates and Muscle Relaxation/Contraction

Important structural compounds in muscle tissue are the filament proteins *myosin* and *actin*. These two types of muscle protein were previously considered in Chemical Connections 20-C—Protein Structure and the Color of Meat—relative to the color (dark versus light) of animal and fowl muscle tissue (meat) consumed as food. An additional aspect of the structural chemistry of muscle tissue, with its associated myosin and actin, is now considered, that of muscle contraction and relaxation.

A simplified diagram for a *relaxed* muscle, in terms of myosin (which are thick protein filaments) and actin (which are thin protein filaments) present is

In the process of muscle contraction the thin filaments (actin) slide inward between the thick filaments (myosin) producing a "contracted" structural arrangement for the filaments as shown in the following diagram.

Two key substances must be present for muscle contraction to occur. They are Ca^{2+} ions and ATP molecules. Low cellular Ca^{2+} concentration is associated with relaxed muscle and high Ca^{2+} concentration is associated with contracted muscle. An increase in Ca^{2+} concentration is the trigger for muscle contraction. Nerve impulses reaching muscle filament cells cause cell membrane Ca^{2+} ion channels to open with a resulting influx of Ca^{2+} ion in the muscle filament cell. The Ca^{2+} ion increase causes ATP molecules present in the cells to hydrolyze to ADP molecules, which provides the energy needed for muscle contraction—a myosin-actin interaction that pulls the actin molecules inward. The ATP hydrolysis equation is

$$ATP + H_2O \xrightarrow{Ca^{2+}} ADP + P_i + H^+ + energy$$

Contraction continues as long as both ATP and Ca^{2+} ion filament levels are high. Cessation of a nerve impulse causes the calcium channels within cellular membranes to close. Then ATP-provided energy is used to pump Ca^{2+} ions out of filament cells resulting in muscle relaxation. The process repeats itself when additional nerve impulses are generated.

The block diagram for FAD from the six-subunit viewpoint is

This block diagram shows the basis for the name *flavin adenine dinucleotide*. Ribitol is a reduced form of ribose; a —CH$_2$OH group is present in place of the —CHO group (Section 18-12).

$$
\begin{array}{cc}
\text{CHO} & \text{CH}_2\text{OH} \\
\text{H——OH} & \text{H——OH} \\
\text{H——OH} & \text{H——OH} \\
\text{H——OH} & \text{H——OH} \\
\text{CH}_2\text{OH} & \text{CH}_2\text{OH} \\
\text{D-Ribose} & \text{D-Ribitol}
\end{array}
$$

The complete structural formula of FAD is given in Figure 23-6a.

In examining what happens to coenzymes such as FAD when they participate in *redox* reactions, the definitions for oxidation and reduction used are those that relate to hydrogen atom change. These definitions, first given in Section 14-9, are:

1. Oxidation involves hydrogen atom loss.
2. Reduction involves hydrogen atom gain.

Also, in order to better keep track of changes that occur within a coenzyme as a result of oxidation or reduction, it is convenient to consider hydrogen atoms participating in redox reactions as being composed of a proton (H$^+$) and an electron (e$^-$). As a result of this consideration, when two hydrogens participate as reactants in a redox process, they are often shown in the structural equation for the process as $2H^+ + 2e^-$ rather than as 2H.

Flavin adenine dinucleotide has two forms—an oxidized form and a reduced form. The notation FAD denotes the oxidized form, the structure of which is given in Figure 23-6a. The reduced form, denoted by the notation FADH$_2$, contains two more H atoms than the oxidized form, which is consistent with the process of reduction involving hydrogen atom gain. The equation for this change is

$$
\underset{\substack{\text{oxidized} \\ \text{form}}}{\text{FAD}} + 2H^+ + 2e^- \longrightarrow \underset{\substack{\text{reduced} \\ \text{form}}}{\text{FADH}_2}
$$

Figure 23-6 Structural formulas of the molecules flavin adenine dinucleotide, FAD (a) and nicotinamide adenine dinucleotide, NAD$^+$ (b).

The active portion of flavin adenine dinucleotide in redox reactions is the flavin subunit of the molecule. It is this portion of the molecule that undergoes change (gains hydrogen atoms) when the oxidized form (FAD) is converted to the reduced form (FADH₂). ◄ The actual structural change that the flavin subunit undergoes upon reduction is as follows.

► *In metabolic pathways in which it is involved, flavin adenine dinucleotide continually changes back and forth between its oxidized form and its reduced form.*

$$2H^+ + 2e^- + \text{FAD} \rightleftharpoons \text{FADH}_2$$

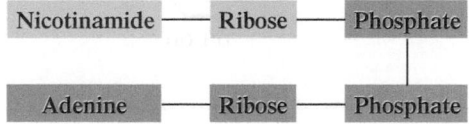

FAD
(oxidized form)

$+ 2H^+ + 2e^- \rightleftharpoons$
2 H atoms

FADH₂
(reduced form)

R = —— Ribitol —— ADP

A typical cellular reaction in which FAD serves as the oxidizing agent involves a —CH₂—CH₂— portion of a substrate being oxidized to produce a carbon–carbon double bond.

$$R-\underset{\underset{\text{H}}{|}}{\overset{\overset{\text{H}}{|}}{C}}-\underset{\underset{\text{H}}{|}}{\overset{\overset{\text{H}}{|}}{C}}-R + \text{FAD} \longrightarrow R-CH{=}CH-R + \text{FADH}_2$$

Saturated
(reduced)

Unsaturated
(oxidized)

The summary equation relating the oxidized and reduced forms of flavin adenine dinucleotide is usually written as

$$\underbrace{2H^+ + 2e^-}_{\text{2 H atoms}} + \text{FAD} \rightleftharpoons \text{FADH}_2$$

Nicotinamide Adenine Dinucleotide (NAD⁺, NADH)

Several parallels exist between the characteristics of nicotinamide adenine dinucleotide and those of FAD/FADH₂. Both have coenzyme functions in metabolic redox pathways, both have a B vitamin as a structural component, both can be represented structurally by using a three-subunit and six-subunit formulation, and both have an oxidized and a reduced form. The notation for the oxidized form of nicotinamide adenine dinucleotide is NAD⁺ and that for the reduced form is NADH. The B vitamin present in NAD⁺/NADH is nicotinamide (Section 21-14).

The three-subunit block diagram for the structure of NAD⁺ is

Nicotinamide —— Ribose —— ADP

The six-subunit block diagram, which emphasizes the dinucleotide nature of the coenzyme, as well as the origin of its name, is

Nicotinamide —— Ribose —— Phosphate
|
Adenine —— Ribose —— Phosphate

Examination of the detailed structure of NAD⁺ (Figure 23-6b) reveals the basis for its positive electrical charge. The + sign refers to the positive charge on the nitrogen atom in the nicotinamide component of the structure; this nitrogen atom has four bonds instead of the usual three (Section 17-6).

The active portion of NAD⁺ in metabolic redox reactions is the nicotinamide subunit of the molecule, the six-membered ring that contains the positively charged nitrogen atom. When this ring is reduced by reacting with two hydrogen atoms ($2H^+ + 2e^-$), the ring gains one H^+ ion and two electrons and one H^+ ion is left over (which enters cellular solution). In this way, NAD^+ is reduced to NADH. The equation for this change is

$$NAD^+ + 2H^+ + 2e^- \longrightarrow NADH + H^+$$

NAD$^+$
(oxidized form)

NADH
(reduced form)

R = —— Ribose —— ADP

Note that there is no positively charged nitrogen atom in NADH because of the second electron added. ◄

A typical cellular reaction in which NAD^+ serves as the oxidizing agent is the oxidation of a secondary alcohol to give a ketone.

In this reaction, one hydrogen atom of the alcohol substrate is directly transferred to NAD^+, whereas the other appears in solution as H^+ ion. Both electrons lost by the alcohol go to the nicotinamide ring in NADH. (Two electrons are required, rather than one, because of the original positive charge on NAD^+.) Thus the summary equation relating the oxidized and reduced forms of nicotinamide adenine dinucleotide is written as

$$\underbrace{2H^+ + 2e^-}_{\text{2 H atoms}} + NAD^+ \rightleftharpoons NADH + H^+$$

Coenzyme A (CoA–SH)

Another important coenzyme in metabolic pathways is coenzyme A (CoA), a derivative of the B vitamin pantothenic acid (Section 21-14). The three-subunit and six-subunit block diagrams for coenzyme A are

and

Note, in the three-subunit block diagram, that the ADP subunit present is phosphorylated. As shown in Figure 23-7, which gives the complete structural formula for coenzyme A, the phosphorylated version of ADP carries an extra phosphate group attached to carbon 3' of its ribose. ◄

The active portion of coenzyme A is the sulfhydryl group (—SH group; Section 14-20) in the ethanethiol subunit of the coenzyme. For this reason, the abbreviation CoA–SH is used for coenzyme A.

► In metabolic pathways, nicotinamide adenine dinucleotide continually changes back and forth between its oxidized form and its reduced form.

$$2H^+ + 2e^- + \boxed{NAD^+} \rightleftharpoons \boxed{NADH} + H^+$$

► Coenzyme A differs from the coenzymes $FAD/FADH_2$ and $NAD^+/NADH$ because it is not involved in oxidation/reduction processes. Its basic function is that of an acetyl group carrier. Coenzyme A is similar to $FAD/FADH_2$ and $NAD^+/NADH$ in that they are all vitamin B-based coenzymes. Coenzyme A contains the B vitamin pantothenic acid as one of its subunits.

Figure 23-7 Structural formula for coenzyme A (CoA–SH).

Think of the letter A in the name *coenzyme A* as reflecting a general metabolic function of this substance; it is the transfer of *acetyl* groups in metabolic pathways. An **acetyl group** *is the portion of an acetic acid molecule* (CH₃—COOH) *that remains after the —OH group is removed from the carboxyl carbon atom.* An acetyl group bonds to CoA–SH through a thioester bond (Section 16-16) to give acetyl CoA. ◄

▶ *In metabolic pathways, coenzyme A is continually changing back and forth between its CoA form and its acetyl CoA form.*

An acetyl group, which can be considered to be derived from acetic acid, has the structure

$$CH_3-\overset{\overset{\displaystyle O}{\|}}{C}- \qquad CH_3-\overset{\overset{\displaystyle O}{\|}}{C}-OH$$

Acetyl group   Acetic acid

Classification of Metabolic Intermediate Compounds

The metabolic intermediate compounds considered in this section can be classified into three groups based on function. The classifications are:

1. Intermediates for the storage of energy and transfer of phosphate groups
2. Intermediates for the transfer of electrons in metabolic redox reactions
3. Intermediates for the transfer of acetyl groups

Figure 23-8 shows the category assignment for the intermediates previously considered.

Figure 23-8 Classification of metabolic intermediate compounds in terms of function.

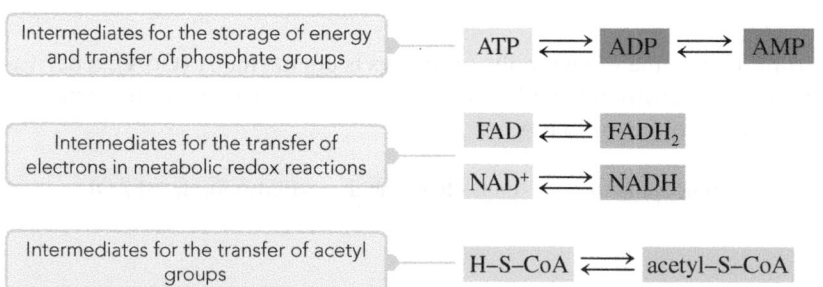

EXAMPLE 23-3

Recognizing Relationships Among Metabolic Intermediate Compounds

Give the abbreviated formula for the following metabolic intermediate compounds:

a. The intermediate produced when FAD is reduced
b. The intermediate produced when FADH₂ is oxidized
c. The intermediate produced when ATP loses two phosphoryl groups
d. The intermediate produced when acetyl–S–CoA transfers an acetyl group

Solution

a. In FAD reduction, two hydrogen ions and two electrons are acquired by the FAD to produce *FADH₂*.

b. In FADH₂ oxidation, two hydrogen ions and two electrons are released by the FADH₂ to produce *FAD*. FADH₂ oxidation and FAD reduction (Part **a**) are reverse processes.

c. Loss of one phosphoryl group by ATP as P_i produces ADP. Loss of two phosphoryl groups by ATP produces *AMP*.

d. Release of the acetyl group from acetyl CoA (acetyl–S–CoA) produces *coenzyme A (H–S–CoA)* itself.

Section 23-3 Quick Quiz

1. Which of the following statements concerning adenosine phosphates is incorrect?
   a. ATP, ADP, and AMP are all examples of adenosine phosphates.
   b. All adenosine phosphates contain the pentose sugar ribose.
   c. ATP contains five structural subunits, two of which are identical.
   d. no correct response
2. Which of the following compounds does *not* contain a "strained" phosphate bond?
   a. AMP
   b. ADP
   c. ATP
   d. no correct response
3. Which of the following statements concerning flavin adenine dinucleotides is incorrect?
   a. Both ribose and ribitol subunits are present.
   b. The notation FADH is used to denote its oxidized form.
   c. Both of its forms have coenzyme functions.
   d. no correct response
4. Which of the following statements concerning nicotinamide adenine dinucleotide is incorrect?
   a. One of the subunits present is a B vitamin.
   b. Two of the structural subunits present are ribose.
   c. The notation NADH is used to denote its oxidized form.
   d. no correct response
5. Which of the following statements concerning coenzyme A is incorrect?
   a. The B vitamin pantothenic acid is present as a subunit in its structure.
   b. The B vitamin present is the "active" subunit in the structure.
   c. Its main biochemical function is the transfer of acetyl groups.
   d. no correct response

Answers: 1. c; 2. a; 3. b; 4. c; 5. b

23-4 Important Carboxylate Ions in Metabolic Pathways

LEARNING FOCUS

Be familiar with the names and structures of five important polyfunctional carboxylate ions encountered in metabolic pathways.

In the previous section, it was noted that knowing about several nucleotide-containing compounds that function as key intermediates in metabolic pathways makes it easier to understand the yet-to-come details of metabolic processes. In a like manner, knowing about several structurally related polyfunctional carboxylate ions (Section 16-8) will facilitate a better understanding of the details of metabolic processes.

Five polyfunctional carboxylate ions serve as substrates for enzymes in the metabolic reactions to be considered later in this chapter. As shown in Figure 23-9, these five carboxylate ions have structures related to just two simple carboxylic acids—succinic acid (the four-carbon dicarboxylic acid) and glutaric acid (the five-carbon dicarboxylic acid). These two "parent acids" were previously considered in Section 16-3.

Figure 23-9   Structural formulas for polyfunctional carboxylate ions that serve as substrates for frequently encountered metabolic reactions.

The following structural relationships among these five carboxylate ions are of importance.

1. The three carboxylate ions derived from succinic acid all contain four carbon atoms, and all have a charge of 2−.
2. The positioning of the double bond in the fumarate ion is such that *cis–trans* isomerism is possible. It is the *trans* isomer that is involved in metabolic reactions.
3. The two carboxylate ions derived from glutaric acid differ in both the number of carbon atoms present and ion charge. The α-ketoglutarate ion is a five-carbon species that possesses a 2− charge. The citrate ion is a six-carbon species that possesses a 3− charge. These differences stem from the citrate ion having three carboxyl groups rather than the two present in α-ketoglutarate.

Section 23-4 Quick Quiz

1. Which of the following structural descriptions for metabolic carboxylate ions that are derivatives of succinic acid is incorrect?
   a. Malate contains a hydroxyl group and two carboxyl groups.
   b. Oxaloacetate contains a keto group and has a 2− charge.
   c. Fumarate contains a carbon–carbon double bond in a *cis* configuration.
   d. no correct response
2. Which of the following structural descriptions for metabolic carboxylate ions that are derivatives of glutaric acid is incorrect?
   a. Citrate contains a hydroxyl group and two carboxyl groups.
   b. Citrate has a 3− charge.
   c. α-Ketoglutarate contains five carbon atoms and a keto group.
   d. no correct response

Answers: 1. c; 2. a

23-5 High-Energy Phosphate Compounds

LEARNING FOCUS

Be familiar with the characteristics of compounds known as "high-energy" compounds.

In the previous two sections, it was noted that knowing about several key intermediate compounds in metabolic reactions makes it easier to understand the yet-to-come details of metabolic processes. In like manner, knowing about a particular type of bond present in certain phosphate-containing metabolic intermediates makes the details of metabolic processes easier to understand.

Several phosphate-containing compounds found in metabolic pathways are known as high-energy compounds. A **high-energy compound** *is a compound that has a greater free energy of hydrolysis than that of a typical compound.* High-energy compounds differ from other compounds in that they contain one or more *very reactive* bonds, often called *strained bonds.* The energy required to break these strained bonds during hydrolysis is less than that generally required to break a chemical bond. Consequently, the balance between the energy needed to break bonds in the reactants and that released by bond formation in the products is such that more than the typical amount of free energy is released during the hydrolysis reaction. ◀

Greater-than-normal electron–electron repulsive forces at specific locations within a molecule are the cause of bond strain. Highly electronegative atoms and/or highly charged atoms occurring together in a molecule cause increased repulsive forces and thus increase bond strain.

Further details concerning bond strain as it is related to phosphate-containing organic molecules involved in metabolic pathways are now considered. The parent molecule for phosphate groups is phosphoric acid, H_3PO_4, a weak triprotic inorganic acid (Section 10-4). This acid exists in aqueous solution in several forms, the dominant form at cellular pH being HPO_4^{2-} ion.

$$\overset{\displaystyle O}{\underset{\displaystyle O^-}{^-O-\overset{\|}{\underset{|}{P}}-OH}}$$

Diphosphate and triphosphate ions can also exist in cellular fluids.

$$\overset{\displaystyle O \quad\quad O}{\underset{\displaystyle O^- \quad O^-}{^-O-\overset{\|}{\underset{|}{P}}-O-\overset{\|}{\underset{|}{P}}-OH}} \quad\quad\quad \overset{\displaystyle O \quad\quad O \quad\quad O}{\underset{\displaystyle O^- \quad\; O^- \quad\; O^-}{^-O-\overset{\|}{\underset{|}{P}}-O-\overset{\|}{\underset{|}{P}}-O-\overset{\|}{\underset{|}{P}}-OH}}$$

Note the presence in these three phosphate structures of highly electronegative oxygen atoms, many of which bear negative charges. The factors that can produce bond strain are present when phosphates (mono-, di-, and tri-) are bonded to certain organic molecules. ◀

Table 23-1 gives the structures of commonly encountered phosphate-containing compounds, as well as a numerical parameter—the free energy of hydrolysis—that can be considered a measure of the extent of bond strain in the molecules. The more negative the free energy of hydrolysis, the greater the bond strain. A free-energy release greater than 6.0 kcal/mole is generally considered indicative of bond strain. In Table 23-1, strained bonds within the molecules are noted with a squiggle (~), a notation often employed to denote strained bonds. ◀

In Example 23-4 detailed consideration is given to key concepts related to how energy associated with ATP's two phosphate–phosphate bonds (strained bonds) becomes available for use in biochemical processes.

▶ *In a chemical reaction, the energy balance between bond breaking among reactants (energy input) and new bond formation among products (energy release) determines whether there is a net loss or a net gain of energy (Section 9-5).*

▶ *The designation* high-energy compound *does not mean that a compound is different from other compounds in terms of bonding. High-energy compounds obey the normal rules for chemical bonding. The only difference between such compounds and other compounds is the presence of one or more strained bonds. The breaking of such bonds requires lower-than-normal amounts of energy.*

▶ *In the definition for a high-energy compound, the term* free energy *rather than simply* energy *was used. Free energy is the amount of energy released by a chemical reaction that is actually available for further use at a given temperature and pressure. In reality, the energy released in a chemical reaction is divisible into two parts. One part, lost as heat, is not available for further use. The other part, the free energy, is available for further use; in cells, it can be used to "drive" reactions that require energy.*

▶ Table 23-1 **Free Energies of Hydrolysis of Common Phosphate-Containing Metabolic Compounds**

Type	Example	Free Energy of Hydrolysis (kcal/mole)
enol phosphates	phosphoenolpyruvate	−14.8
acyl phosphates	1,3-bisphosphoglycerate	−11.8
	acetyl phosphate	−11.3
guanidine phosphates	creatine phosphate	−10.3
	arginine phosphate	−9.1
triphosphates	ATP ⟶ AMP + PP$_i$*	−7.7
	ATP ⟶ ADP + P$_i$*	−7.5
diphosphates	PP$_i$ ⟶ 2P$_i$	−7.8
	ADP ⟶ AMP + P$_i$	−7.5
sugar phosphates	glucose 1-phosphate	−5.0
	fructose 6-phosphate	−3.8
	AMP ⟶ adenosine + P$_i$	−3.4
	glucose 6-phosphate	−3.3
	glycerol 3-phosphate	−2.2

▶ *The —PO$_3^{2-}$ group as part of a larger organic phosphate molecule is referred to as a phosphoryl group.*

*The notation P$_i$ is used as a general designation for any free monophosphate species present in cellular fluid. Free diphosphate ions are designated as PP$_i$ ("i" stands for *inorganic*).

EXAMPLE 23-4

Identifying the Weak Bond Broken and the Strong Bond Formed in the Conversion of ATP to ADP via Hydrolysis

The reaction equation for the hydrolysis of ATP to form ADP is

For this reaction:

a. Identify the bonds broken and the bonds formed that involve phosphate in this reaction.

b. Specify the relative strengths of the bonds broken and the bonds formed that involve phosphate in this reaction.

c. Indicate whether there is a net energy increase or decrease, relative to phosphate bonds, in this reaction.

Solution

The guiding principle for bond considerations in this problem is that bond breaking requires input of energy and bond formation releases energy. The weaker the bond the lower the input of energy needed to break it. For bond formation, the stronger the bond the greater the amount of energy released in its formation.

a. One phosphorus–oxygen bond is broken and one phosphorus–oxygen bond is formed as a free phosphate group is released as ATP is changed to ADP.

This phosphorus–oxygen bond must be broken to release a phosphate group.

The phosphorus–oxygen bond is newly formed with the –OH group coming from a water molecule.

b. The phosphorus–oxygen bond broken is a high-energy phosphate bond which is a weak bond which requires input of only a small amount of energy to break. The new phosphorus–oxygen bond formed is not a strained bond and therefore a stronger bond. Strong bond formation involves release of a relatively large amount of energy.

This is a weak (strained) bond that requires only a small amount of energy to break.

This newly formed bond is a strong (unstrained) bond that releases a larger amount of energy upon formation.

c. Since the energy released (bond formation) is greater than that absorbed (bond breaking), there is a net production of energy in the bond breaking/formation process involving phosphates. This contributes to the hydrolysis of ATP to produce ADP being an energy-producing reaction.

By contrast, the conversion of an ADP molecule to an ATP molecule through addition of a phosphate group is an energy-consuming reaction. The new phosphate–phosphate bond is a strained bond (weak bond) and only a small amount of energy is released upon its formation.

23-6   An Overview of Biochemical Energy Production

LEARNING FOCUS

Know the four general stages in biochemical energy production.

The energy needed to run the human body is obtained from ingested food through a multistep process that involves several different catabolic pathways. There are four general stages in the biochemical energy production process, and numerous reactions are associated with each stage.

▶ *The first stage of biochemical energy production, digestion, is not considered part of metabolism because it is extracellular. Metabolic processes are intracellular.*

Stage 1: The first stage, **digestion,** begins in the mouth (saliva contains starch-digesting enzymes), continues in the stomach (gastric juices), and is completed in the small intestine (the majority of digestive enzymes and bile salts). The end products of digestion—glucose and other monosaccharides from carbohydrates, amino acids from proteins, and fatty acids and glycerol from fats and oils—are small enough to pass across intestinal membranes and into the blood, with the aid of membrane transport systems (Section 19-10). Once in the blood, they are then distributed to the cells in various parts of the body. ◀

Stage 2: The second stage, **acetyl group formation,** involves numerous reactions, some of which occur in the cytosol of cells and some in cellular mitochondria. The small molecules from digestion are further oxidized during this stage. Primary products include two-carbon acetyl units (which become attached to coenzyme A to give acetyl CoA) and the reduced coenzyme NADH.

Stage 3: The third stage, the **citric acid cycle,** occurs inside mitochondria. Here acetyl groups are oxidized to produce CO_2 and energy. Some of the energy released by these reactions is lost as heat, and some is carried by the reduced coenzymes NADH and $FADH_2$ to the fourth stage. The CO_2 that is exhaled as part of the breathing process comes primarily from this stage.

Stage 4: The fourth stage, the **electron transport chain and oxidative phosphorylation,** also occurs inside mitochondria. NADH and $FADH_2$ supply the "fuel" (hydrogen ions and electrons) needed for the production of ATP molecules, the primary energy carriers in metabolic pathways. Molecular O_2, inhaled via breathing, is converted to H_2O in this stage.

The reactions in stages 3 and 4 are the same for all types of foods (carbohydrates, fats, proteins). These reactions constitute the common metabolic pathway. The **common metabolic pathway** *is the sum total of the biochemical reactions of the citric acid cycle, the electron transport chain, and oxidative phosphorylation.* The remainder of this chapter deals with the common metabolic pathway. The reactions of stages 1 and 2 of biochemical energy production differ for different types of foodstuffs. They are discussed in Chapters 24–26, which cover the metabolism of carbohydrates, fats (lipids), and proteins, respectively.

Chemistry at a Glance—Simplified Summary of the Four Stages of Biochemical Energy Production—summarizes the four general stages in the process of production of biochemical energy from ingested food. This diagram is a *very simplified* version of the "energy generation" process that occurs in the human body, as will become clear from the discussions presented in later sections of this chapter, which give further details of the process.

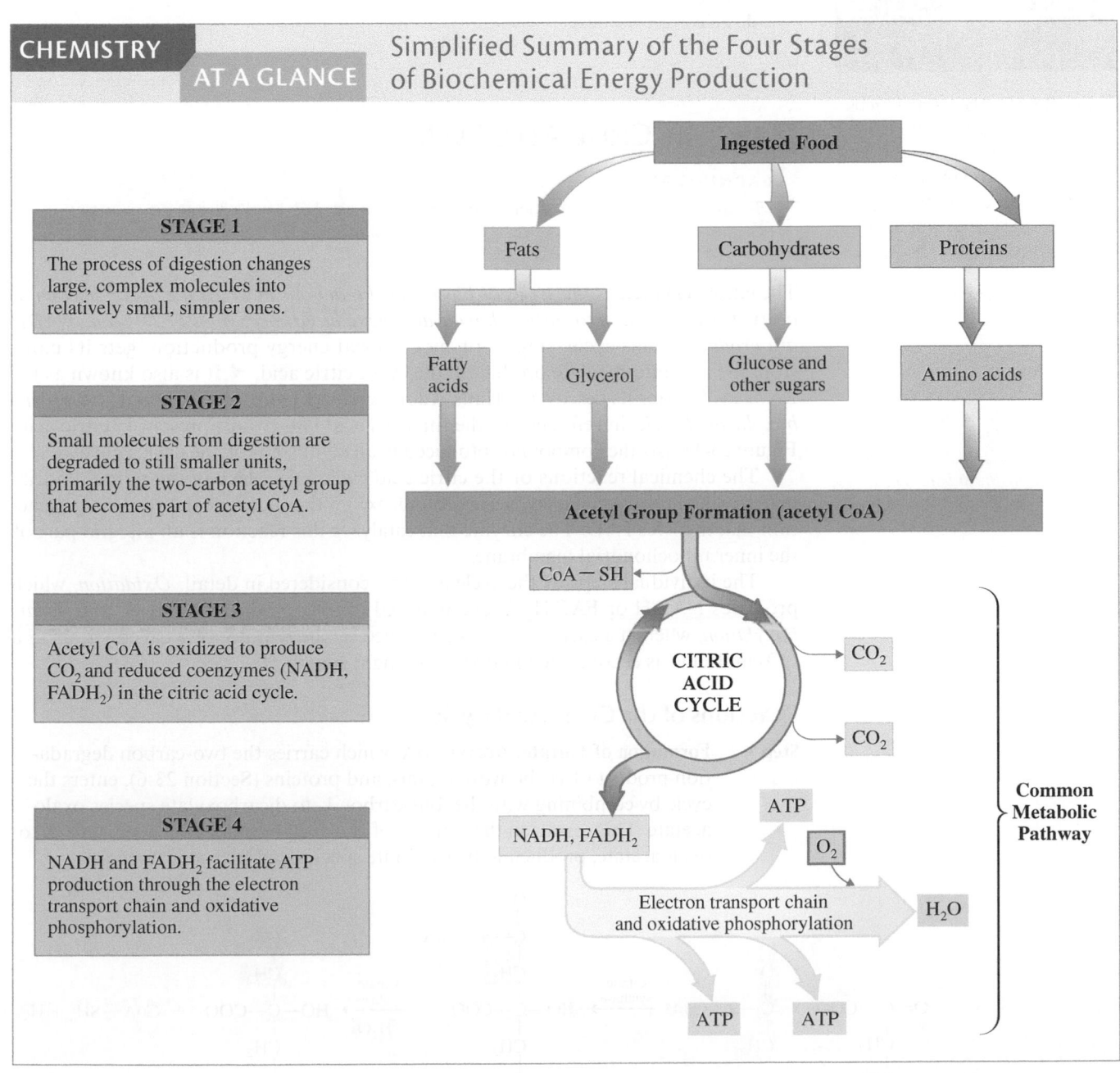

CHEMISTRY AT A GLANCE Simplified Summary of the Four Stages of Biochemical Energy Production

STAGE 1

The process of digestion changes large, complex molecules into relatively small, simpler ones.

STAGE 2

Small molecules from digestion are degraded to still smaller units, primarily the two-carbon acetyl group that becomes part of acetyl CoA.

STAGE 3

Acetyl CoA is oxidized to produce CO_2 and reduced coenzymes (NADH, $FADH_2$) in the citric acid cycle.

STAGE 4

NADH and $FADH_2$ facilitate ATP production through the electron transport chain and oxidative phosphorylation.

Ingested Food

Fats — Carbohydrates — Proteins

Fatty acids — Glycerol — Glucose and other sugars — Amino acids

Acetyl Group Formation (acetyl CoA)

CoA—SH

CITRIC ACID CYCLE → CO_2 → CO_2

NADH, $FADH_2$

ATP

O_2

Electron transport chain and oxidative phosphorylation → H_2O

ATP   ATP

Common Metabolic Pathway

1. Which of the following occurs in the second stage in the biochemical energy production process?
   a. electron transport chain
   b. citric acid cycle
   c. acetyl group formation
   d. no correct response
2. Which of the following stages in the biochemical energy production process immediately precedes the citric acid cycle?
   a. digestion
   b. acetyl group formation
   c. electron transport chain
   d. no correct response
3. Which of the following is part of the common metabolic pathway?
   a. citric acid cycle
   b. acetyl group formation
   c. digestion
   d. no correct response

Answers: 1. c; 2. b; 3. a

Figure 23-10 Hans Adolf Krebs (1900–1981), a German-born British biochemist, shared the 1953 Nobel Prize in medicine for establishing the relationships among the different compounds in the cycle that carries his name, the Krebs cycle.

▶ *At cellular pH, citric acid is actually present as citrate ion. Despite this, the name of the cycle is the citric acid cycle, which references the molecular, rather than ionic, form of the substance.*

23-7 The Citric Acid Cycle

LEARNING FOCUS

Be familiar with the eight reactions that constitute the citric acid cycle; describe the overall chemical transformation that occurs in one round of the citric acid cycle.

The **citric acid cycle** *is the series of biochemical reactions in which the acetyl portion of acetyl CoA is oxidized to carbon dioxide and the reduced coenzymes FADH$_2$ and NADH are produced.* This cycle, stage 3 of biochemical energy production, gets its name from the first intermediate product in the cycle, citric acid. ◀ It is also known as the *Krebs cycle,* after its discoverer Hans Adolf Krebs (Figure 23-10), and as the *tricarboxylic acid cycle,* in reference to the three carboxylate groups present in citric acid. Figure 23-11 lists the compounds produced in all eight steps of the citric acid cycle.

The chemical reactions of the citric acid cycle take place in the mitochondrial matrix where the needed enzymes are found, except the succinate dehydrogenase reaction that involves FAD. The enzyme that catalyzes this reaction is an integral part of the inner mitochondrial membrane.

The individual steps of the cycle are now considered in detail. *Oxidation,* which produces NADH or FADH$_2$, is encountered in four of the eight steps, and *decarboxylation,* wherein a carbon chain is shortened by the removal of a carbon atom as a CO$_2$ molecule, is encountered in two of the eight steps.

Reactions of the Citric Acid Cycle

Step 1: **Formation of Citrate.** Acetyl CoA, which carries the two-carbon degradation product of carbohydrates, fats, and proteins (Section 23-6), enters the cycle by combining with the four-carbon keto dicarboxylate species oxaloacetate. This results in the transfer of the acetyl group from coenzyme A to oxaloacetate, producing the C$_6$ citrate species and free coenzyme A.

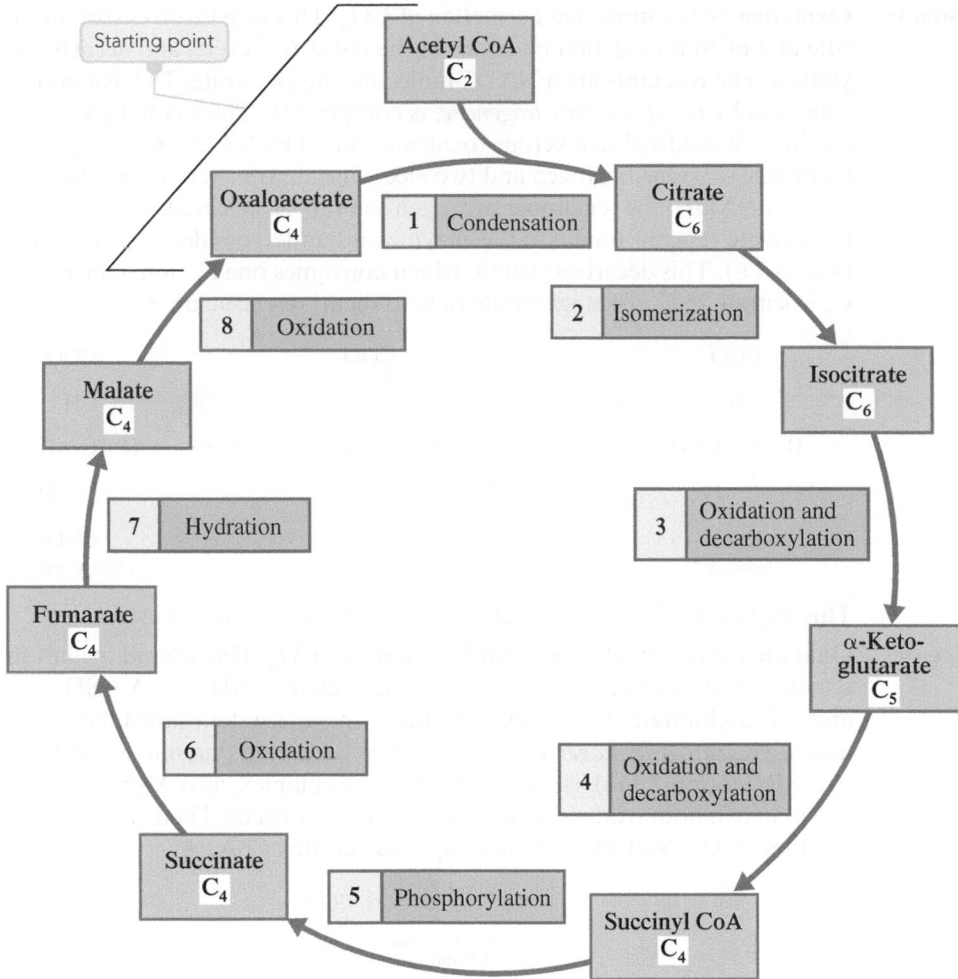

Figure 23-11 The citric acid cycle. Details of the numbered steps are given in the text.

There are two parts to the reaction: (1) the condensation of acetyl CoA and oxaloacetate to form citryl CoA, a process catalyzed by the enzyme *citrate synthase* ◄ and (2) hydrolysis of the thioester bond in citryl CoA to produce CoA—SH and citrate, also catalyzed by the enzyme *citrate synthase*. ◄

Step 2: **Formation of Isocitrate.** Citrate is converted to its less symmetrical isomer isocitrate in an isomerization process that involves a dehydration followed by a hydration, both catalyzed by the enzyme *aconitase*. The net result of these reactions is that the —OH group from citrate is moved to a different carbon atom.

▶ *The formation of citryl CoA involves addition of acetyl CoA to the carbon–oxygen double bond. A hydrogen atom of the acetyl* —CH_3 *group adds to the oxygen atom of the double bond, and the remainder of the acetyl CoA adds to the carbon atom of the double bond (Section 15-10).*

▶ *A synthase is an enzyme that makes a new covalent bond during a reaction without the direct involvement of an ATP molecule.*

$$
\begin{array}{ccccc}
\text{COO}^- & & \text{COO}^- & & \text{COO}^- \\
| & & | & & | \\
\text{CH}_2 & & \text{CH}_2 & & \text{CH}_2 \\
| & \xrightarrow[\text{Aconitase}]{\text{H}_2\text{O}} & | & \xrightarrow[\text{Aconitase}]{\text{H}_2\text{O}} & | \\
\text{HO}-\text{C}-\text{COO}^- & & \text{C}-\text{COO}^- & & \text{H}-\text{C}-\text{COO}^- \\
| & & \| & & | \\
\text{H}-\text{C}-\text{H} & & \text{C}-\text{H} & & \text{HO}-\text{C}-\text{H} \\
| & & | & & | \\
\text{COO}^- & & \text{COO}^- & & \text{COO}^- \\
\text{Citrate} & & \textit{cis}\text{-Aconitate} & & \text{Isocitrate} \blacktriangleleft
\end{array}
$$

▶ *All carboxylic acids found in the citric acid cycle exist as carboxylate ions (Section 16-7) at cellular pH.*

Citrate is an achiral compound (Section 18-4), and isocitrate is a chiral compound with two chiral centers (four stereoisomers possible). *Aconitase* produces only one of the four stereoisomers of isocitrate.

Citrate has a tertiary alcohol group and isocitrate has a secondary alcohol group. Tertiary alcohols are not readily oxidized; secondary alcohols are easier to oxidize (Section 14-9). The next step in the cycle involves oxidation.

Step 3: **Oxidation of Isocitrate and Formation of CO$_2$.** This step involves oxidation (the first of four oxidation reactions in the citric acid cycle) and decarboxylation. The reactants are a NAD$^+$ molecule and isocitrate. The reaction, catalyzed by *isocitrate dehydrogenase,* is complex: (1) The alcohol group in isocitrate is oxidized to a ketone (oxalosuccinate) by NAD$^+$, releasing two hydrogens. (2) One hydrogen and two electrons are transferred to NAD$^+$ to form NADH; the remaining hydrogen ion (H$^+$) is released. (3) The oxalosuccinate remains bound to the enzyme and undergoes decarboxylation (loses CO$_2$). This decarboxylation, which consumes one H$^+$ ion, converts C$_6$ isocitrate to C$_5$ α-ketoglutarate (a keto dicarboxylic acid). ◄

▶ *The key happenings in Step 3 are the following:*

1. *The hydroxyl group of isocitrate is oxidized to a ketone group.*
2. *NAD$^+$ is converted to its reduced form, NADH.*
3. *A carboxyl group from the original oxaloacetate is removed as CO$_2$.*

This step yields the first molecules of CO$_2$ and NADH in the cycle.

Step 4: **Oxidation of α-Ketoglutarate and Formation of CO$_2$.** This second oxidation reaction of the cycle involves one molecule each of NAD$^+$, CoA—SH, and α-ketoglutarate. The catalyst is a three-enzyme system called the *α-ketoglutarate dehydrogenase complex*. The B vitamin thiamin, in the form of TPP (Section 21-14), is part of the enzyme complex, as is Mg^{2+} ion. As in Step 3, both oxidation and decarboxylation occur. There are three products: CO$_2$, NADH, and the C$_4$ species succinyl CoA. ◄

▶ *The key happenings in Step 4 are the following:*

1. *A second NAD$^+$ is converted to its reduced form, NADH.*
2. *A second carboxyl group is removed as CO$_2$. The CO$_2$ molecules produced in Steps 3 and 4 of the citric acid cycle are the CO$_2$ molecules exhaled in the process of respiration.*
3. *Coenzyme A reacts with the decarboxylation product succinate to produce succinyl CoA, a compound with a high-energy thioester bond. This is the second involvement of a coenzyme A molecule in the cycle, the other instance occurring in Step 1.*

▶ *The enzyme needed in Step 1 is called a* synthase, *and the enzyme for Step 5 is called a* synthatase. *The difference between a* synthase *and a* synthatase *is that the latter uses energy from the breaking of a high-energy phosphate bond, whereas the former does not require such energy.*

Step 5: **Thioester Bond Cleavage in Succinyl CoA and Phosphorylation of GDP.** Two reactant molecules are involved in this step—a P$_i$ (HPO$_4^{2-}$) and a GDP (similar to ADP; Section 23-3). The entire reaction is catalyzed by the enzyme *succinyl-CoA synthetase*. ◄ For purposes of understanding the structural changes that occur, the reaction can be considered to occur in two steps. In the first step, succinyl CoA is converted to succinyl phosphate (a high-energy phosphate compound); CoA–SH is a product of this change. The phosphoryl group present in succinyl phosphate is then transferred to GDP; the products of this change are GTP and succinate.

Thinking of the two steps as occurring concurrently gives the following energy analysis: When broken, the high-energy thioester bond in succinyl

CoA releases energy, which is trapped by formation of GTP. The function of the GTP produced is similar to that of ATP, which is to store energy in the form of a high-energy phosphate bond (Section 23-5).

Steps 6 through 8 of the citric acid cycle involve a sequence of functional group changes that have been encountered several times in the organic sections of the text. The reaction sequence is

$$\text{Alkane} \xrightarrow[\text{(dehydrogenation)}]{\textcircled{6}\ \text{Oxidation}} \text{alkene} \xrightarrow{\textcircled{7}\ \text{Hydration}} \begin{array}{c}\text{secondary}\\\text{alcohol}\end{array} \xrightarrow[\text{(dehydrogenation)}]{\textcircled{8}\ \text{Oxidation}} \text{ketone}$$

Step 6: **Oxidation of Succinate.** This is the third oxidation reaction of the cycle. The enzyme involved is *succinate dehydrogenase*, and the oxidizing agent is FAD rather than NAD^+. Two hydrogen atoms are removed from the succinate to produce fumarate, a C_4 species with a *trans* double bond. ◄ FAD is reduced to $FADH_2$ in the process.

▶ *Fumarate, with its* trans *double bond, is an essential metabolic intermediate. Its isomer, with a* cis *double bond, is called maleate, and it is toxic and irritating to tissues. Succinate dehydrogenase produces only the* trans *isomer of this unsaturated diacid.*

Step 7: **Hydration of Fumarate.** The enzyme *fumarase* catalyzes the addition of water to the *trans* double bond of fumarate. The enzyme is stereospecific, so only the L isomer of the product malate is produced.

Step 8: **Oxidation of L-Malate to Regenerate Oxaloacetate.** In the fourth oxidation reaction of the cycle, a molecule of NAD^+ reacts with malate, picking up two hydrogen atoms with their associated energy to form $NADH + H^+$. ◄ The needed enzyme is *malate dehydrogenase*. The product of this reaction is regenerated oxaloacetate, which can combine with another molecule of acetyl CoA (Step 1), and the cycle can begin again. ◄

▶ *Step 8 is the second step of the cycle in which oxidation of a secondary alcohol occurs. Such an oxidation also occurred in Step 3.*

▶ *The product from Step 8 is the starting material for Step 1. Thus the cycle can repeat itself provided that an additional acetyl CoA is also available for reaction in Step 1.*

Summary of the Citric Acid Cycle

An overall summary equation for the citric acid cycle is obtained by adding together the individual reactions of the cycle:

$$\text{Acetyl CoA} + 3NAD^+ + FAD + GDP + HPO_4^{2-}(P_i) + 2H_2O \longrightarrow$$
$$2CO_2 + CoA\text{—}SH + 3NADH + 3H^+ + FADH_2 + GTP$$

Important features of the cycle include the following:

1. The "fuel" for the cycle is acetyl CoA, obtained from the breakdown of carbohydrates, fats, and proteins.
2. Four of the cycle reactions involve oxidation and reduction. The oxidizing agent is either NAD^+ (three times) or FAD (once). The operation of the cycle depends on the availability of these oxidizing agents.
3. In redox reactions, NAD^+ is the oxidizing agent when a carbon–oxygen double bond is formed; FAD is the oxidizing agent when a carbon–carbon double bond is formed.
4. The three NADH and one $FADH_2$ that are formed during the cycle carry electrons and H^+ to the electron transport chain (Section 23-8) through which ATP is synthesized.
5. Two carbon atoms enter the cycle as the acetyl unit of acetyl CoA, and two carbon atoms leave the cycle as two molecules of CO_2. The carbon atoms that enter and leave are not the same ones. The carbon atoms that leave during one turn of the cycle are carbon atoms that entered during the previous turn of the cycle.
6. Four B vitamins are necessary for the proper functioning of the cycle: riboflavin (in both FAD and the α-ketoglutarate dehydrogenase complex), nicotinamide (in NAD^+), pantothenic acid (in CoA—SH), and thiamin (in the α-ketoglutarate dehydrogenase complex).
7. One high-energy GTP molecule is produced by phosphorylation.

Chemistry at a Glance—Summary of the Reactions of the Citric Acid Cycle—gives a detailed diagrammatic summary of the reactions that occur in the citric acid cycle.

▶ *The eight B vitamins and their structures were discussed in Section 21-14.*

EXAMPLE 23-5

Recognizing the Reactants and Products of Various Steps in the Citric Acid Cycle

When one acetyl CoA is processed through the citric acid cycle, how many times does each of the following events occur?

a. A secondary alcohol group is oxidized to a ketone group.
b. An NADH molecule is produced.
c. A decarboxylation reaction occurs.
d. A C_6 molecule is produced.

Solution

a. *Two.* Both isocitrate (Step 3) and malate (Step 8) are secondary alcohols that are oxidized by NAD^+ to ketones.
b. *Three.* The product of the use of NAD^+ as an oxidizing agent is NADH. Oxidation using NAD^+ occurs in Steps 3, 4, and 8.
c. *Two.* In Step 3, isocitrate is decarboxylated, and in Step 4 α-ketoglutarate is decarboxylated. In each case, the product is a CO_2 molecule.
d. *Two.* Citrate and isocitrate are C_6 molecules. Citrate is produced in Step 1, and isocitrate is produced in Step 2.

Regulation of the Citric Acid Cycle

The rate at which the citric acid cycle operates is controlled by the body's need for energy (ATP). When the body's ATP supply is high, the ATP present inhibits the activity of citrate synthase, the enzyme in Step 1 of the cycle. When energy is being used at a high rate, a state of low ATP and high ADP concentrations, the ADP activates citrate synthase and the cycle speeds up. A similar control mechanism exists at Step 3, which involves isocitrate dehydrogenase; here NADH acts as an inhibitor and ADP as an activator.

CHEMISTRY AT A GLANCE Summary of the Reactions of the Citric Acid Cycle

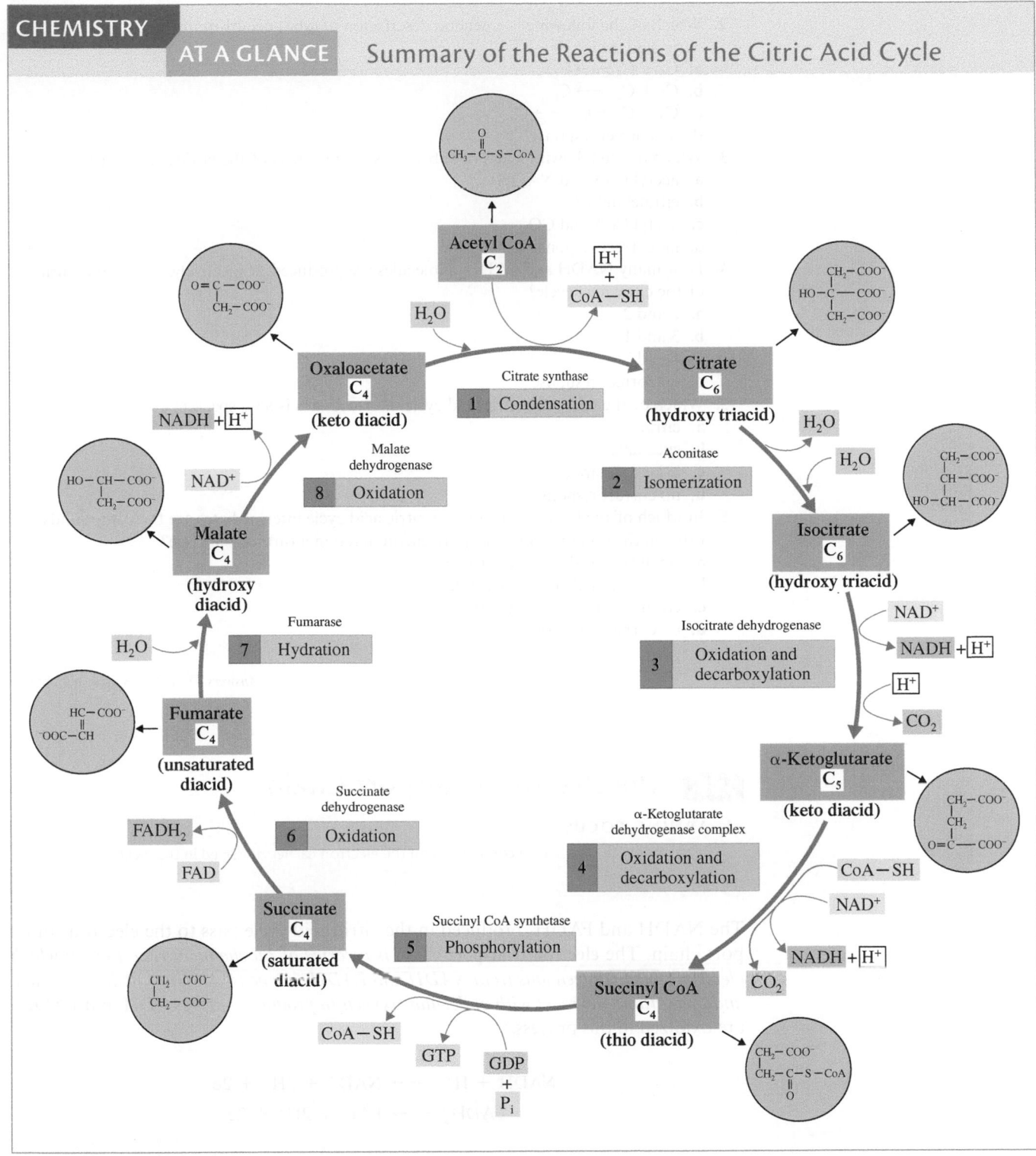

Section 23-7 Quick Quiz

1. The "fuel" for the citric acid cycle is
   a. acetyl CoA
   b. citrate
   c. carbon dioxide
   d. no correct response

(continued)

2. Which of the following is a general description of what occurs in the first step of the citric acid cycle?
   a. $C_3 + C_3 \longrightarrow C_6$
   b. $C_2 + C_4 \longrightarrow C_6$
   c. $C_2 + C_2 + C_2 \longrightarrow C_6$
   d. no correct response
3. Which of the following pairs of substances are products of the citric acid cycle?
   a. acetyl CoA and NADH
   b. citrate and CO_2
   c. acetyl CoA and CO_2
   d. no correct response
4. How many NADH and $FADH_2$ molecules are produced, respectively, during one turn of the citric acid cycle?
   a. 2 and 2
   b. 3 and 1
   c. 1 and 3
   d. no correct response
5. Which of the following citric acid cycle intermediates is a C_4 species?
   a. citrate
   b. succinate
   c. α-ketoglutarate
   d. no correct response
6. In which of the following listings of citric acid cycle intermediates are the compounds listed in the order in which they are encountered in a turn of the cycle?
   a. isocitrate, oxaloacetate, succinate
   b. succinate, malate, oxaloacetate
   c. citrate, oxaloacetate, fumarate
   d. no correct response

Answers: 1. a; 2. b; 3. d; 4. b; 5. b; 6. b

23-8 The Electron Transport Chain

LEARNING FOCUS

Be familiar with the enzyme complexes and the electron carriers involved in the electron transport chain.

The NADH and $FADH_2$ produced in the citric acid cycle pass to the electron transport chain. The **electron transport chain** *is a series of biochemical reactions in which electrons and hydrogen ions from NADH and $FADH_2$ are passed to intermediate carriers and then ultimately react with molecular oxygen to produce water.* NADH and $FADH_2$ are oxidized in this process.

$$NADH + H^+ \longrightarrow NAD^+ + 2H^+ + 2e^-$$
$$FADH_2 \longrightarrow FAD + 2H^+ + 2e^-$$

▶ *The oxygen involved in the water formation associated with the electron transport chain is the oxygen that is inhaled during the human breathing process. The* electron transport chain *is also sometimes called the* respiratory chain.

Water is formed when the electrons and hydrogen ions that originate from these reactions react with molecular oxygen. ◀

$$O_2 + 4e^- + 4H^+ \longrightarrow 2H_2O$$

The electrons that pass through the various steps of the electron transport chain (ETC) lose some energy with each transfer along the chain. Some of this "lost" energy is used to make ATP from ADP (oxidative phosphorylation), as is discussed in Section 23-9.

The enzymes and electron carriers needed for the ETC are located along the inner mitochondrial membrane. Within this membrane are four distinct protein complexes, each containing some of the molecules needed for the ETC process to occur. These four protein complexes, which are tightly bound to the membrane, are

Complex I: NADH–coenzyme Q reductase
Complex II: Succinate–coenzyme Q reductase
Complex III: Coenzyme Q–cytochrome c reductase
Complex IV: Cytochrome c oxidase

The electron carriers coenzyme Q and cytochrome c, which are not tightly associated with any of the four complexes, serve as mobile electron carriers that shuttle electrons between the various complexes.

The discussion of the individual reactions that occur in the ETC is divided into four parts, each part dealing with the reactions associated with one of the four protein complexes.

Complex I: NADH–Coenzyme Q Reductase

NADH, from the citric acid cycle, is the source for the electrons that are processed through complex I, the largest of the four protein complexes. Complex I contains more than 40 subunits, including the B-vitamin-containing flavin mononucleotide (FMN) and several iron–sulfur proteins (FeSP). The net result of electron movement through complex I is the transfer of electrons from NADH to coenzyme Q (CoQ), a result implied by the name of complex I: *NADH–coenzyme Q reductase*. The actual electron transfer process is not, however, a single-step direct transfer of electrons from NADH to CoQ; several intermediate carriers are involved.

The first electron transfer step that occurs in complex I involves the interaction of NADH with flavin mononucleotide (FMN). The NADH is oxidized to NAD^+ (which can again participate in the citric acid cycle) as it passes two hydrogen ions and two electrons to FMN, which is reduced to $FMNH_2$. ◄

$$NADH + H^+ \xrightarrow{\text{Oxidation}} NAD^+ + 2H^+ + 2e^-$$

$$2H^+ + 2e^- + FMN \xrightarrow{\text{Reduction}} FMNH_2$$

NADH supplies both electrons and one of the H^+ ions that are transferred; the other H^+ ion comes from the matrix solution. The actual changes that occur within the structure of FMN as it accepts the two electrons and two H^+ ions are shown in Figure 23-12a.

► Both FMN and $FMNH_2$ contain a flavin subunit. Previously encountered flavin-containing molecules are FAD, $FADH_2$, and the B vitamin riboflavin. FMN differs from FAD in not having an adenine nucleotide. Both FMN and FAD are synthesized within the body from riboflavin.

a The oxidized form (FMN) and reduced form ($FMNH_2$) of the electron carrier flavin mononucleotide.

b The oxidized form (CoQ) and reduced form ($CoQH_2$) of the electron carrier coenzyme Q.

Figure 23-12 Structural characteristics of the electron carriers flavin mononucleotide and coenzyme Q.

Figure 23-13 Electron movement through complex I is initiated by the electron carrier NADH/H$^+$. In several steps, the electrons are passed to CoQ.

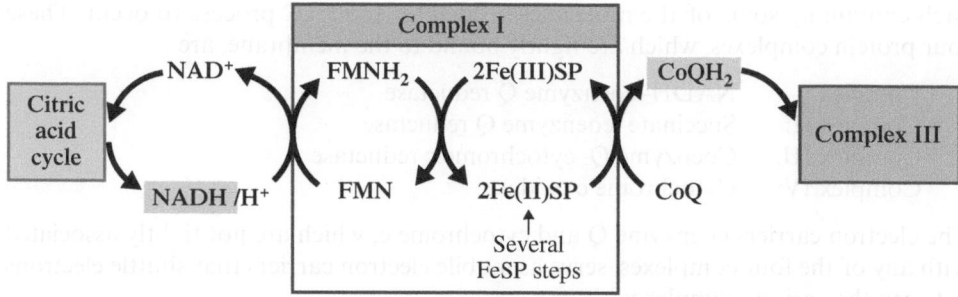

The next steps involve transfer of electrons from the reduced FMNH$_2$ through a series of iron/sulfur proteins (FeSPs). The iron present in these FeSPs is Fe^{3+}, which is reduced to Fe^{2+}. The two H atoms of FMNH$_2$ are released to solution as two H$^+$ ions. Two FeSP molecules are needed to accommodate the two electrons released by FMNH$_2$ because an Fe^{3+}/Fe^{2+} reduction involves only one electron.

$$FMNH_2 \xrightarrow{\text{Oxidation}} FMN + 2H^+ + \boxed{2e^-}$$

$$\boxed{2e^-} + 2Fe(III)SP \xrightarrow{\text{Reduction}} 2Fe(II)SP$$

In the final complex I reaction, Fe(II)SP is reconverted into Fe(III)SP as each of two Fe(II)SP units passes an electron to CoQ, changing it from its oxidized form (CoQ) to its reduced form (CoQH$_2$).

$$2Fe(II)SP \xrightarrow{\text{Oxidation}} 2Fe(III)SP + \boxed{2e^-}$$

$$\boxed{2e^-} + 2H^+ + CoQ \xrightarrow{\text{Reduction}} CoQH_2$$

Coenzyme Q, in both its oxidized and reduced forms, is lipid soluble and can move laterally within the mitochondrial membrane. Its function is to shuttle its newly acquired electrons to complex III, where it becomes the initial substrate for reactions at this complex.

The Q in the designation coenzyme Q comes from the name quinone. Structurally, coenzyme Q is a quinone derivative. ◄ In its most common form, coenzyme Q has a long carbon chain containing 10 isoprene units (Section 13-7) attached to its quinone unit. The actual changes that occur within the structure of CoQ as it accepts the two electrons and the two H$^+$ ions involve the quinone part of its structure, as is shown in Figure 23-12b. The two H$^+$ ions that CoQ picks up in forming CoQH$_2$ come from solution.

Figure 23-13 summarizes diagrammatically the electron transfer events associated with complex I of the electron transport chain.

Complex II: Succinate–Coenzyme Q Reductase

Complex II, which is much smaller than complex I, contains only four subunits, including two FeSPs. This complex is used to process the FADH$_2$ that is generated in the citric acid cycle when succinate is converted to fumarate. (Thus the use of the term *succinate* in the name of complex II.)

CoQ is associated with the operations in complex II in a manner similar to its actions in complex I. It is the final recipient of the electrons from FADH$_2$, with iron–sulfur proteins serving as intermediaries. Figure 23-14 summarizes diagrammatically the electron transfer events associated with complex II of the electron transport chain.

► *Quinone is the common name for the cyclic ketone (Section 15-3) with the structure*

The IUPAC name for this compound is p-benzoquinone. Quinone derivatives were previously encountered in Chemical Connections 21-A— Enzymatic Browning: Discoloration of Fruits and Vegetables.

Figure 23-14 Electron movement through complex II is initiated by the electron carrier FADH$_2$. In several steps, the electrons are passed to CoQ.

Figure 23-15 An overview of electron movement through complexes I and II. CoQH₂ is the common recipient for the electrons passed through these two complexes.

Thus complexes I and II produce a common product, the reduced form of coenzyme Q (CoQH₂). As was the case with complex I, the reduced CoQH₂ shuttles electrons to complex III. ◄

▶ *All H⁺ ions required for the reactions of NADH, CoQ, and O₂ in the ETC come from the matrix side of the inner mitochondrial membrane.*

$$FADH_2 \xrightarrow{\text{Oxidation}} FAD + 2H^+ + 2e^-$$

$$2e^- + 2Fe(III)SP \xrightarrow{\text{Reduction}} 2Fe(II)SP$$

$$2Fe(II)SP \xrightarrow{\text{Oxidation}} 2Fe(III)SP + 2e^-$$

$$2e^- + 2H^+ + CoQ \xrightarrow{\text{Reduction}} CoQH_2$$

Note the general pattern that is developing for electron carriers present in the electron transport chain. They are reduced (accept electrons) in one step and then are regenerated (oxidized; lose electrons) in the next step so that they can again participate in electron transport chain reactions. ◄

Figure 23-15 shows the common delivery point for the electrons passed through complexes I and II. From both of these complexes, the electrons are carried by CoQH₂ to complex III.

▶ *A feature that all steps in the ETC share is that as each electron carrier passes electrons along the chain, it becomes reoxidized and thus able to accept more electrons.*

Complex III: Coenzyme Q–Cytochrome c Reductase

Complex III contains 11 different subunits. Electron carriers present include several iron–sulfur proteins as well as several cytochromes. A **cytochrome** *is a heme-containing protein in which reversible oxidation and reduction of an iron atom occur.* Heme, a compound also present in hemoglobin and myoglobin (Section 20-16), has the structure

Heme-containing proteins function similarly to FeSP; iron changes back and forth between the +3 and +2 oxidation states. ◄

Various cytochromes, abbreviated cyt a, cyt b, cyt c, and so on, differ from each other in (1) their protein constituents, (2) the manner in which the heme is bound to the protein, and (3) attachments to the heme ring. Again, because the Fe^{3+}/Fe^{2+} system involves only a one-electron change, two cytochrome molecules are needed to move two electrons along the chain.

▶ *In cytochromes, the heme present is bound to protein in such a way as to prevent the heme from combining with oxygen as it does when it is present in hemoglobin.*

Iron/sulfur protein (FeSP) is a nonheme iron protein. Most proteins of this type contain sulfur, as is the case with FeSP. Often the iron is bound to the sulfur atom in the amino acid cysteine.

The initial substrate for complex III is $CoQH_2$ molecules carrying the electrons that have been processed through complex I (from NADH) and also those processed through complex II (from $FADH_2$). The electron transfer process proceeds from $CoQH_2$ to an FeSP, then to cyt b, then to another FeSP, then to cyt c_1, and finally to cyt c. Cyt c can move laterally in the intermembrane space; it delivers its electrons to complex IV. Cyt c is the only one of the cytochromes that is water soluble.

The initial oxidation–reduction reaction at complex III is between $CoQH_2$ and an iron–sulfur protein (FeSP).

$$CoQH_2 \xrightarrow{\text{Oxidation}} CoQ + 2e^- + 2H^+$$

$$2e^- + 2Fe(III)SP \xrightarrow{\text{Reduction}} 2Fe(II)SP$$

The H^+ ions produced from the oxidation of $CoQH_2$ go into cellular solution. All further redox reactions at complex III involve only electrons, which are conveyed further down the enzyme complex chain. Figure 23-16 shows diagrammatically the electron transfer steps associated with complex III.

Complex IV: Cytochrome c Oxidase

Complex IV contains 13 subunits, including two cytochromes. The electron movement flows from cyt c (carrying electrons from complex III) to cyt a to cyt a_3. In the final step of electron transfer, the electrons from cyt a_3 and hydrogen ions from cellular solution combine with oxygen (O_2) to form water.

$$O_2 + 4H^+ + 4e^- \longrightarrow 2H_2O$$

It is estimated that 95% of the oxygen used by cells serves as the final electron acceptor for the ETC.

The two cytochromes present in cytochrome c oxidase (a and a_3) differ from previously encountered cytochromes in that each has a copper atom associated with it in addition to its iron center. The copper atom sites participate in the electron transfer process as do the iron atom sites, with the copper atoms going back and forth between the reduced Cu^+ state and the oxidized Cu^{2+} state. Figure 23-17 shows the electron transfer sequence through these copper and iron sites.

The presence of copper in the enzyme complex cytochrome c oxidase is not a unique copper situation. Copper functions as a cofactor in enzymes involved in

Figure 23-17 The electron transfer pathway through complex IV (cytochrome c oxidase). Electrons pass through both copper and iron centers and in the last step interact with molecular O_2. Reduction of one O_2 molecule requires the passage of four electrons through complex IV, one at a time.

Summary of the Flow of Electrons Through the
Four Complexes of the Electron Transport Chain

Both hydrogen and electrons from NADH and FADH$_2$ participate in the reactions involving enzyme complexes I and II. Following the formation of CoQH$_2$, hydrogen ions no longer directly participate in enzyme complex reactions; that is, they are not passed further down the enzyme complex chain. Instead, they become part of the cellular solution, where they participate in several reactions including the process by which ATP is synthesized (Section 23-9).

a variety of processes. Copper is a cofactor for the well-known enzyme *superoxide dismutase* (Section 23-12), which converts superoxide free radical (O$_2^-$) to the less harmful hydrogen peroxide (H$_2$O$_2$). Copper is also required for synthesis of the neurotransmitter norepinephrine (Section 17-10) and the connective tissue protein collagen (Section 20-16).

Chemistry at a Glance—Summary of the Flow of Electrons Through the Four Complexes of the Electron Transport Chain—is a schematic diagram summarizing the flow of electrons through the four complexes of the electron transport chain.

EXAMPLE 23-6

Recognizing Relationships Among Electron Carriers and Enzyme Complexes in the Electron Transport Chain

With which of the four complexes in the electron transport chain is each of the following events associated? (There may be more than one correct answer in a given situation.)

a. Iron–sulfur proteins (FeSPs) are needed as reactants.
b. The mobile electron carrier CoQ serves as a "shuttle molecule."
c. Molecular O$_2$ is needed as a reactant.
d. FAD is a product.

Solution

a. *Complexes I, II, and III.* Iron–sulfur proteins accept electrons from NADH (complex I), FADH$_2$ (complex II), and CoQH$_2$ (complex III).
b. *Complexes I, II, and III.* CoQH$_2$ functions as a shuttle molecule between complex I and complex III and also between complex II and complex III.
c. *Complex IV.* The final electron acceptor in the ETC is molecular O$_2$. It combines with electrons and H$^+$ ions to produce H$_2$O.
d. *Complex II.* FADH$_2$ is converted to FAD at complex II.

Section 23-8 Quick Quiz

1. Which of the following is a "fuel" for the electron transport chain?
   a. acetyl CoA
   b. carbon dioxide
   c. NADH
   d. no correct response
2. Which of the following is a mobile electron carrier in the electron transport chain?
   a. $CoQH_2$
   b. FeSP
   c. cyt a
   d. no correct response
3. What is the substrate that initially interacts with protein complex II in the electron transport chain
   a. NADH
   b. $FADH_2$
   c. CoQ
   d. no correct response
4. The number of fixed enzyme sites in the electron transport chain is
   a. three
   b. four
   c. five
   d. no correct response
5. In which of the following listings of electron carriers in the electron transport chain are the carriers listed in the order in which they are first encountered?
   a. FeSP, CoQ, cyt b
   b. FMN, cyt c, CoQ
   c. CoQ, FMN, cyt a
   d. no correct response
6. In which step in the electron transport chain does O_2 participate?
   a. second step
   b. next to last step
   c. last step
   d. no correct response

Answers: 1. c; 2. a; 3. b; 4. b; 5. a; 6. c

23-9 Oxidative Phosphorylation

LEARNING FOCUS

Be familiar with the relationships among oxidative phosphorylation, ATP synthesis, and the electron transport chain.

Oxidative phosphorylation *is the biochemical process by which ATP is synthesized from ADP as a result of the transfer of electrons and hydrogen ions from NADH or* $FADH_2$ *to* O_2 *through the electron carriers involved in the electron transport chain.* Oxidative phosphorylation is conceptually simple but mechanistically complex. Determining the details of oxidative phosphorylation has been—and still is—one of the most challenging research areas in biochemistry. ◄

One concept central to the oxidative phosphorylation process is that of *coupled* reactions. **Coupled reactions** *are pairs of biochemical reactions that occur concurrently in which energy released by one reaction is used in the other reaction.* Oxidative phosphorylation and the oxidation reactions of the electron transport chain are coupled systems.

The interdependence (coupling) of ATP synthesis with the reactions of the ETC is related to the movement of protons (H^+ ions) across the inner mitochondrial membrane. Three of the four protein complexes involved in the ETC chain (I, III, and IV) have a second function besides electron transfer down the chain. They also serve as "proton pumps," transferring protons from the matrix side of the inner mitochondrial membrane to the intermembrane space (Figure 23-18).

▶ Oxidative phosphorylation *is not the only process by which ATP is produced in cells. A second process,* substrate phosphorylation *(Section 24-2), can also be an ATP source. However, the amount of ATP produced by this second process is much less than that produced by oxidative phosphorylation.*

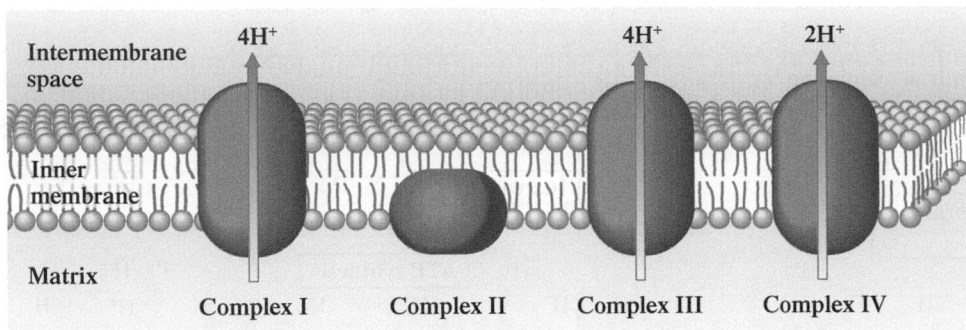

Figure 23-18 A second function for protein complexes I, III, and IV involved in the electron transport chain is that of proton pump. The proton transfer shown is per every two electrons that pass through the ETC.

Some of the H^+ ions crossing the inner mitochondrial membrane come from the reduced electron carriers, and some come from the matrix; the details of how the H^+ ions cross the inner mitochondrial membrane are not fully understood.

For every two electrons passed through the ETC, four protons cross the inner mitochondrial membrane through complex I, four through complex III, and two more through complex IV. This proton flow causes a buildup of H^+ ions (protons) in the intermembrane space; this high concentration of protons becomes the basis for ATP synthesis. ◄

The relationship between number of protons crossing the mitochondrial inner membrane into the intermembrane space and the electron carriers NADH and $FADH_2$ entering the electron transport chain is as follows:

1. The oxidation of an NADH molecule results in 10 H^+ ions crossing the membrane.
2. The oxidation of an $FADH_2$ molecule results in 6 H^+ ions crossing the membrane.

The difference in proton pumping results for the two oxidations stems from $FADH_2$ initially interacting with complex II, thus bypassing complex I which is a proton-pumping station.

The "proton flow" explanation for ATP–ETC coupling is formally called chemiosmotic coupling. **Chemiosmotic coupling** *is an explanation for the coupling of ATP synthesis with electron transport chain reactions that requires a proton gradient across the inner mitochondrial membrane.* The main concepts in this explanation for coupling follow.

1. The result of the pumping of protons from the mitochondrial matrix across the inner mitochondrial membrane is a higher concentration of protons in the intermembrane space than in the matrix (Figure 23-19). This concentration difference constitutes an *electrochemical (proton) gradient.* A chemical gradient exists whenever a substance has a higher concentration in one region than in another. Because the proton has an electrical charge (H^+ ion), an electrical gradient also exists. Potential energy (Section 7-2) is always associated with an electrochemical gradient. ◄
2. A spontaneous flow of protons from the region of high concentration to the region of low concentration occurs because of the electrochemical gradient. This proton flow is not through the membrane itself (it is not permeable to H^+ ions) but rather through enzyme complexes called *ATP synthases* located on the inner mitochondrial membrane (Section 23-2). This proton flow through the ATP synthases "powers" the synthesis of ATP. ATP synthases are thus the *coupling factors* that link the processes of oxidative phosphorylation and the electron transport chain.
3. ATP synthase has two subunits, the F_0 and F_1 subunits, as is shown on the middle right side of Figure 23–19. The F_0 part of the synthase is the channel for proton flow, whereas the formation of ATP takes place in the F_1 subunit. As protons return to the mitochondrial matrix through the F_0 subunit, the potential energy associated with the electrochemical gradient is released and used in the F_1 subunit for the synthesis of ATP.

$$H^+ + ADP + P_i \xrightarrow{\text{ATP synthase}} ATP + H_2O$$

▶ *The difference in H^+ ion concentration between the two sides of the inner mitochondrial membrane causes a pH difference of about 1.4 units. A pH difference of 1.4 units means that the intermembrane space, the more acidic region, has 25 times more protons than the matrix.*

▶ *Some of the energy released at each of the protein complexes I, III, and IV is consumed in the movement of H^+ ions across the inner membrane from the matrix into the intermembrane space. Movement of ions from a region of lower concentration (the matrix) to one of higher concentration (the intermembrane space) requires the expenditure of energy because it opposes the natural tendency, as exhibited in the process of osmosis (Section 8-10), to equalize concentrations.*

Figure 23-19 Formation of ATP accompanies the flow of protons from the intermembrane space back into the mitochondrial matrix. The proton flow results from an electrochemical gradient across the inner mitochondrial membrane.

4. The ATP produced through oxidative phosphorylation must be moved from the matrix back to the intermembrane space before it can be used in metabolic reactions. This is accomplished through a transport protein embedded in the inner mitochondrial membrane. This transport process involves movement of molecules in both directions through the protein. For each ATP molecule transferred from the matrix to the intermembrane space an ADP, a P_i, and an H^+ ion move in the opposite direction.

Thus the process of making an ATP molecule available for cellular use consumes four H^+ ions. Three H^+ ions must pass through ATP synthase into the matrix in order to make an ATP molecule and one H^+ passes accompanies the passing of ADP into the matrix as ATP leaves via the transport protein. This movement of molecules through the transport protein is shown diagrammatically on the extreme right side of Figure 23-19.

Chemistry at a Glance—Summary of the Common Metabolic Pathway—brings together into one diagram the three processes that constitute the common metabolic pathway: the citric acid cycle, the electron transport chain, and oxidative phosphorylation. These three processes operate together. Discussing them separately, as we have done, is a matter of convenience only.

As indicated previously in this section, the coupling of reactions is central to the process of oxidative phosphorylation. Interestingly, the body naturally produces a protein (thermogenin) that functions as an *uncoupling agent* that allows the electron transport chain to proceed without ATP production. The focus on relevancy feature Chemical Connections 23-B—Brown Fat, Newborn Babies, and Hibernating Animals—addresses the topic of *when* and *why* the uncoupling agent thermogenin is needed by the human body.

The enzymes involved in the operation of the ETC can be inhibited by other substances just as other enzymes can. The gas hydrogen cyanide (HCN) exerts its deadly effect by inhibiting the ETC enzyme cytochrome c oxidase. The focus on relevancy feature Chemical Connections 23-C—Cyanide Poisoning—explores further the topic of the biochemical effects of cyanide ion and hydrogen cyanide on the human body.

Summary of the Common Metabolic Pathway

CHEMICAL CONNECTIONS 23-B

Brown Fat, Newborn Babies, and Hibernating Animals

Ordinarily, metabolic processes generate enough heat to maintain normal body temperature. In certain cases, however, including newborn infants and hibernating animals, normal metabolism is not sufficient to meet the body's heat requirements. In these cases, a supplemental method of heat generation, which involves *brown fat tissue,* occurs.

Brown fat tissue, as the name implies, is darker in color than ordinary fat tissue, which is white. Brown fat is specialized for heat production. It contains many more blood vessels and mitochondria than white fat. (The increased number of mitochondria gives brown fat its color.)

Another difference between the two types of fat is that the mitochondria in brown fat cells contain a protein called *thermogenin,* which functions as an *uncoupling agent.* This protein "uncouples" the ATP production associated with the electron transport chain. The ETC reactions still take place, but the energy that would ordinarily be used for ATP synthesis is simply released as heat.

Brown fat tissue is of major importance for newborn infants. Newborns are immediately faced with a temperature regulation problem. They leave an environment of constant 37°C temperature and enter a much colder environment (25°C). A supply of *active* brown fat, present at birth, helps the baby adapt to the cooler environment.

Very limited amounts of brown fat are present in most adults. However, stores of brown fat increase in adults who are regularly exposed to cold environs. Thus the production of brown fat is one of the body's mechanisms for adaptation to cold.

Thermogenin, the uncoupling agent in brown fat, is a protein bound to the inner mitochondrial membrane.

Hibernating bears rely on brown fat tissue to help meet their bodies' heat requirements.

When activated, it functions as a proton channel through the inner membrane. The proton gradient produced by the electron transport chain is dissipated through this "new" proton channel, and less ATP synthesis occurs because the normal proton channel, ATP synthase, has been bypassed. The energy of the proton gradient, no longer useful for ATP synthesis, is released as heat.

In 2013, a new hormone, whose production is exercise-induced, was discovered by researchers. This hormone, called irisin by its discoverers, is likely responsible for some of the positive health effects that come from exercise, including weight loss and lower risk for type 2 diabetes. In effect, the hormone confers the "heat-release" properties of brown fat cells on white fat cells. Additional investigational studies on the hormone are in progress.

Cyanide Poisoning

Inhalation of hydrogen cyanide gas (HCN) or ingestion of solid potassium cyanide (KCN) rapidly inhibits the electron transport chain in all tissues, making cyanide one of the most potent and rapidly acting poisons known. The attack point for the cyanide ion (CN^-) is cytochrome c oxidase, the last of the four protein complexes in the electron transport chain. Cyanide inactivates this complex by bonding itself to the Fe^{3+} in the complex's heme portions. As a result, Fe^{3+} is unable to transfer electrons to oxygen, blocking the cell's use of oxygen. Death results from tissue asphyxiation, particularly of the central nervous system. Cyanide also binds to the heme group in hemoglobin, blocking oxygen transport in the bloodstream.

One treatment for cyanide poisoning is to administer various nitrites, NO_2^-, which oxidize the iron atoms of hemoglobin to Fe^{3+}. This form of hemoglobin helps draw CN^- back into the bloodstream, where it can be converted to thiocyanate (SCN^-) by thiosulfate ($S_2O_3^{2-}$), which is administered along with the nitrite (see the accompanying figure).

A number of plants (cassava, sugar cane, white clover) and fruits (almonds, peach and apricot pits, apple seeds) are natural sources of HCN. Compounds known as cyanoglycosides of which the best known is *amygdalin*, are the HCN source. Amygdalin's molecular structure is

Amygdalin

The disaccharide part of amygdalin's structure involves two D-glucose units joined via a $\beta(1\rightarrow6)$ linkage (Section 18-13).

Amygdalin is naturally present in the pits of apricots, peaches, and plums (see accompanying photo). Enzymatic hydrolysis of amygdalin, as well as other cyanoglycosides, produces HCN as one of the hydrolysis products.

Amygdalin, produced primarily in Mexico and sold under the name *laetrile,* was once heavily promoted as a substance useful in treating cancer. Studies have now established that laetrile has little or no effect in treating cancer. The HCN produced when ingested laetrile is hydrolyzed affects all cells rather than selectively targeting cancer cells; the side effects produced closely resemble those associated with chronic HCN exposure: headache, vomiting, and in some cases coma and death.

The United States Federal Drug Administration (FDA) now seeks jail sentences for vendors who sell laetrile within the United States for cancer treatment. In scientific literature, the use of laetrile as an anticancer agent has been described as the most sophisticated and most remunerative example of medical quackery in medical history.

Apricot pits are the most common source of amygdalin.

1. How many of the four enzyme complexes in the electron transport chain function as proton pumps in oxidative phosphorylation?
   a. 2
   b. 3
   c. all 4
   d. no correct response
2. The entering of one NADH molecule into the electron transport chain effects the transfer of how many protons across the inner mitochondrial membrane?
   a. 6
   b. 8
   c. 10
   d. no correct response
3. Which of the following statements concerning "proton flow" during ATP synthesis is incorrect?
   a. The proton gradient is dissipated as protons flow out of the matrix.
   b. The proton gradient is dissipated as protons flow into the matrix.
   c. Proton flow through ATP synthase occurs.
   d. no correct response

Answers: 1. b; 2. c; 3. a

23-10 ATP Production for the Common Metabolic Pathway

LEARNING FOCUS

Be familiar with the amounts of ATP produced in each of the various parts of the common metabolic pathway per entering acetyl CoA molecule.

For each mole of NADH oxidized in the ETC, 2.5 moles of ATP are formed. $FADH_2$, which does not enter the ETC at its start, produces only 1.5 moles of ATP per mole of $FADH_2$ oxidized. $FADH_2$'s entrance point into the chain, complex II, is beyond the first "proton-pumping" site, complex I. Hence fewer ATP molecules are produced from $FADH_2$ than from NADH. ◄

The energy yield, in terms of ATP production, can now be totaled for the common metabolic pathway (Section 23-6). Every acetyl CoA entering the citric acid cycle (CAC) produces three NADH, one $FADH_2$, and one GTP (which is equivalent in energy to ATP; Section 23-6). Thus 10 molecules of ATP are produced for each acetyl CoA catabolized.

$$
\begin{array}{rcl}
3\ \text{NADH} & \longrightarrow & 7.5\ \text{ATP} \\
1\ \text{FADH}_2 & \longrightarrow & 1.5\ \text{ATP} \\
1\ \text{GTP} & \longrightarrow & \underline{1\quad \text{ATP}} \\
& & 10\quad \text{ATP}
\end{array}
$$

The preceding numbers need to be interpreted as mole amounts rather than molecule amounts. The body cannot make 1.5 molecules of ATP, since half molecules of ATP do not exist. The body can, however, make 1.5 moles of ATP. Ten moles of ATP are produced as the result of one mole of acetyl CoA entering the common metabolic pathway.

Figure 23-20 relates the preceding 10 ATP production figures to individual steps in the citric acid cycle in which NADH, $FADH_2$, and GTP are produced.

ATP molecules in cells have a high turnover rate. Normally, a given ATP molecule in a cell does not last more than a minute before it is converted to ADP. The concentration of ATP in a cell varies from 0.5 to 2.5 milligrams per milliliter of cellular fluid. ◄

▶ *Biochemistry textbooks published before the mid-1990s make the following statements:*

1 NADH produces 3 ATP in the ETC.

1 FADH₂ produces 2 ATP in the ETC.

As more has been learned about the electron transport chain and oxidative phosphorylation, these numbers have had to be reduced. The overall conversion process is more complex than was originally thought, and not as much ATP is produced.

▶ *Without oxygen, the biochemical systems of the human body quickly shut down and death occurs. Why? Without oxygen as the final electron acceptor in the ETC, the ETC chain shuts down and ATP production stops. Without ATP to power life's processes (Chapters 24–26), these processes stop.*

Figure 23-20 Citric acid cycle origins for the ATP produced through operation of the electron transfer chain and oxidative phosphorylation per one acetyl CoA entering the citric acid cycle.

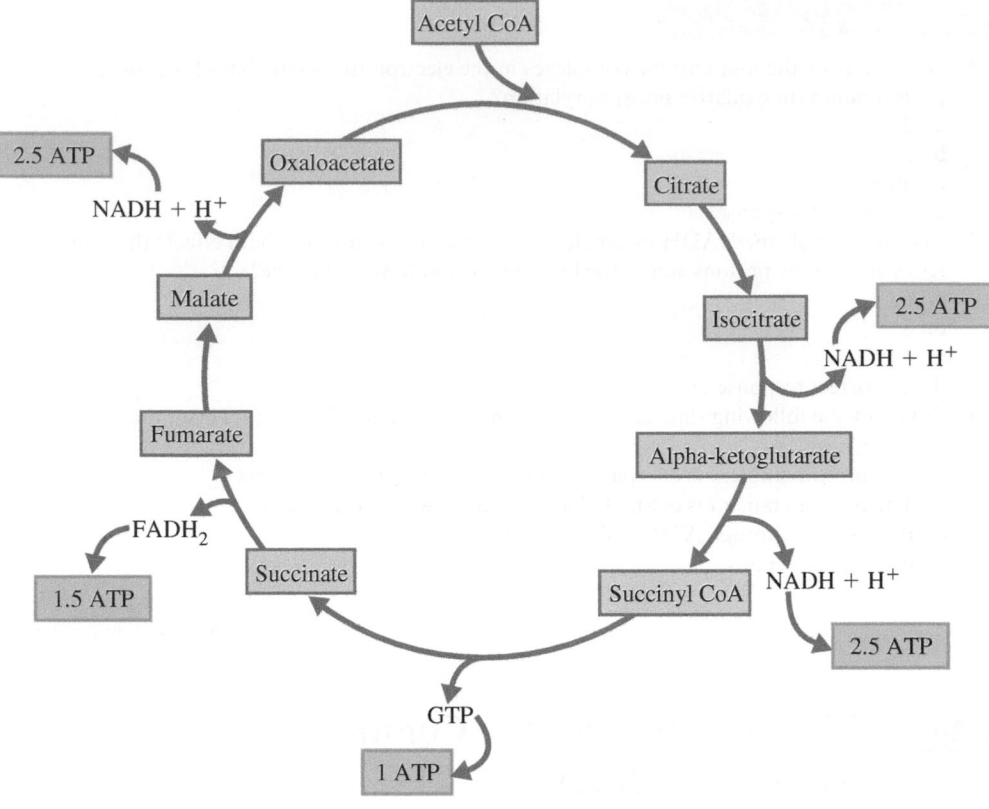

23-11 Non-ETC Oxygen-Consuming Reactions

LEARNING FOCUS

Be familiar with non-electron-transfer-chain uses for O_2 supplied by respiration.

The electron transport chain/oxidative phosphorylation phase of metabolism consumes more than 90% of the oxygen taken into the human body via respiration. What happens to the remainder of the inspired O_2?

As a normal part of metabolic chemistry, significant amounts of this remaining O_2 are converted into several highly reactive oxygen species (ROS). Among these ROSs are hydrogen peroxide (H_2O_2), superoxide ion (O_2^-), and hydroxyl radical (OH). The latter two of these substances are free radicals, substances that contain an unpaired electron (Section 11-7). Reactive oxygen species have beneficial functions within the body, but they can also cause problems if they are not eliminated when they are no longer needed.

White blood cells have a significant concentration of superoxide free radicals. Here, these free radicals aid in the destruction of invading bacteria and viruses. Their formation reaction is

$$2O_2 + NADPH \longrightarrow 2O_2^- + NADP^+ + H^+$$

(NADPH is a phosphorylated version of the coenzyme NADH; see Section 24-8.)

Superoxide ion that is not needed is eliminated from cells in a two-step process governed by the enzymes *superoxide dismutase* and *catalase,* two of the most rapidly working enzymes known (see Table 21-2). In the first step, superoxide ion is converted to hydrogen peroxide, which is then, in the second step, converted to H_2O. ◄

$$2O_2^- + 2H^+ \xrightarrow{\text{superoxide}\atop\text{dismutase}} H_2O_2 + O_2$$

$$2H_2O_2 \xrightarrow{\text{catalase}} 2H_2O + O_2$$

Immediate destruction of the hydrogen peroxide produced in the first of these two steps is critical, because if it persisted, then unwanted production of hydroxyl radical would occur via hydrogen peroxide's reaction with superoxide ion.

$$H_2O_2 + O_2^- + H^+ \longrightarrow H_2O + O_2 + OH$$

Hydroxyl radicals quickly react with other substances by taking an electron from them. Such action usually causes bond breaking. Lipids in cell membranes are particularly vulnerable to such attack by hydroxyl radicals.

It is estimated that 5% of the ROSs escape destruction through normal channels (superoxide dimutase and catalase). Operating within a cell is a backup system— a network of antioxidants—to deal with this problem. Participating in this antioxidant network are glutathione (Section 20-8), vitamin C (Section 21-13), and beta-carotene and vitamin E (Section 21-15), as well as numerous compounds, known as *phytochemicals*, obtained from plants through dietary intake. A **phytochemical** *is a nonnutrient compound found in plant-derived foods that has a positive effect on human health.* The focus on relevancy feature Chemical Connections 23-D—Phytochemicals: Compounds with Color and Antioxidant Functions—gives further information about selected phytochemicals that have antioxidant functions in the human body. ◄ The vitamin antioxidants as well as phytochemical antioxidants prevent oxidative damage by reacting with harmful ROS oxidizing agents before they can react with other biologically important substances. ◄

Reactive oxygen species can also be formed in the body as the result of external influences such as polluted air, cigarette smoke, and radiation exposure (including solar radiation). Vitamin C is particularly effective against such free-radical damage.

▶ *Commercially, hydrogen peroxide (H_2O_2) is used as a bleaching agent. In the human body, H_2O_2 is the indirect cause of dark hair turning gray and then often white as a person ages. This natural bleaching effect is caused by the presence of excess H_2O_2 within cells. The H_2O_2 buildup occurs because of a decline in the production of the enzyme* catalase, *the enzyme that converts H_2O_2 to H_2O. The H_2O_2 oxidizes amino acid residues (methioine) in proteins associated with hair pigment production, limiting their ability to function properly; hence hair with less pigmentation results.*

▶ *The suffix* phyto *as used in the term* phyto*chemical means "plant."*

▶ *Antioxidant molecules provide electrons to convert free radicals and other ROSs into less-reactive substances.*

Phytochemicals: Compounds with Color and Antioxidant Functions

Compounds identified as *phytochemicals* (Section 23-11) besides having positive functions in the human body, obviously have important roles to play in plants themselves. In plants they can provide protection against insect predators, against infections (bacterial, viral, and fungal), and against tissue damage associated with oxidation processes. Some phytochemicals are known to have plant hormone functions. Plant pigmentation (color) is also a major phytochemical function.

The following listing gives selected color-active phytochemicals in specific foods.

Phytochemical	Color	Food Source
Lycopene (lye-koh-peen)	Red	Tomatoes
Allicin (all-is-sin)	White	Garlic
Lutein (loo-teen)	Yellow-green	Spinach
Flavonoids (flay-von-oids)	Yellow	Citrus fruits
Anthocyanins (an-tho-sigh-ah-nins)	Blue/purple	Blueberries, grapes
Beta-carotene (bay-tah-kare-oh-teen)	Orange	Carrots

Sometimes the green chlorophyll present in plants obscures phytochemical color. Dark green leafy vegetables usually contain yellow and orange pigments.

Numerous studies indicate that diets high in fruits and vegetables are associated with a healthy lifestyle. One reason for this is the many phytochemicals that fruits and vegetables contain. Each fruit and vegetable is a unique package of phytochemicals, so consuming a wide variety of fruits and vegetables provides the body with the broadest spectrum of benefits. In this situation, many phytochemicals are consumed in *small* amounts. This approach is much safer than taking supplemental doses of particular phytochemicals; in larger doses some phytochemicals are toxic.

The major function in the human body for the majority of phytochemicals is that of an antioxidant (Section 14-13; Section 23-11). A major family of antioxidant phytochemicals are the *flavonoids,* of which more than 4000 individual compounds are known. All flavonoids are antioxidants, but some are stronger antioxidants than others, depending on molecular structure. About 50 flavonoids are present in foods and beverages obtained from plants (tea leaves, grapes, oranges, and so on).

The core *flavonoid* structure is

Apples are the fruit that contains the greatest amount of the antioxidant quercetin; the skin (peel) contains the majority of the quercetin.

© BestPhotoPlus/Shutterstock.com

The most widespread flavonoid in food is *quercetin* (queer-sah-tin).

It is predominant in fruits, vegetables, and the leaves of various vegetables. In fruits, apples contain the highest amounts of quercetin, the majority of it being found in the outer tissues (skin, peel). A small peeled apple contains about 5.7 mg of the antioxidant vitamin C. But the same amount of apple *with the skin* contains flavonoids and other phytochemicals that have the effect of 1500 mg of vitamin C. Onions are also major dietary sources of quercetin.

In addition to their antioxidant benefits, flavonoids may also help fight bacterial infections. Recent studies indicate that flavonoids can stop the growth of some strains of drug-resistant bacteria.

23-12 B Vitamins and the Common Metabolic Pathway

Structurally modified B vitamins function as coenzymes in metabolic pathways (Section 21-14). Now that the reactions of the common metabolic pathway have been considered, it is useful to formalize, in a summary fashion, B-vitamin involvement in the citric acid cycle and the electron transport chain. As is shown in Figure 23-21, four vitamins have involvement in these metabolic reactions.

1. Niacin—as NAD^+ and NADH
2. Riboflavin—as FAD, $FADH_2$, and FMN
3. Thiamin—as TPP
4. Pantothenic acid—as CoA

Without these B vitamins, the human body would be unable to utilize carbohydrates, fats, and proteins as sources of energy. Additionally, the fuel for the citric acid cycle, acetyl CoA, would be unavailable since it contains a B vitamin (pantothenic acid).

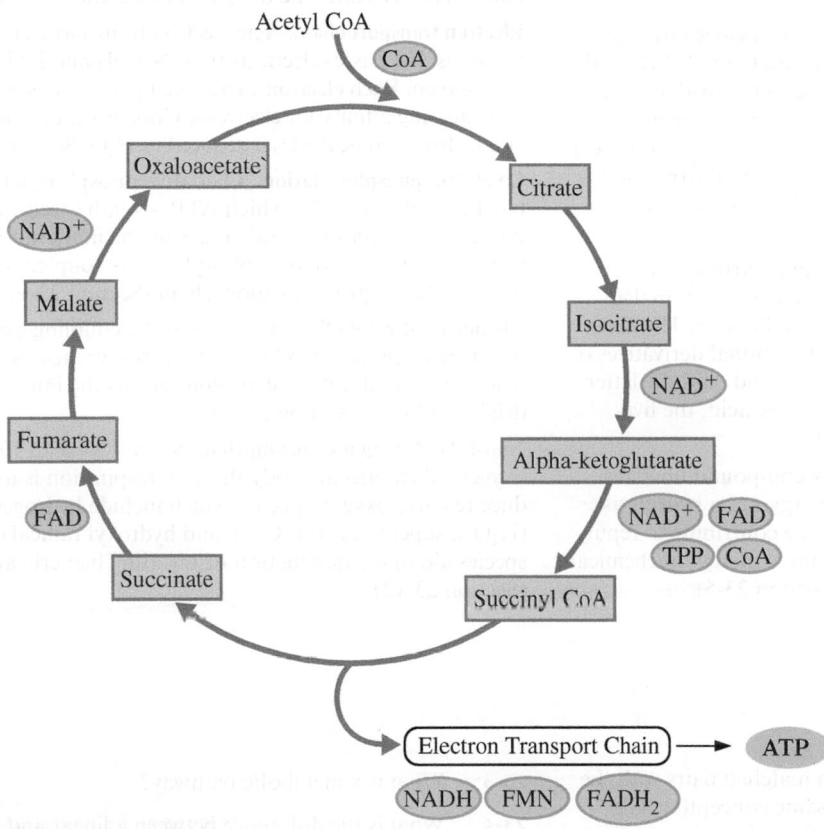

Figure 23-21 B-vitamin participation in chemical reactions associated with the common metabolic pathway.

Section 23-12 Quick Quiz

1. How many different B vitamins participate in the common metabolic pathway in the form of coenzymes?
   a. 4
   b. 6
   c. 7
   d. no correct response

(continued)

2. Which of the following is *not* a B-vitamin-containing coenzyme that is needed in the common metabolic pathway?
   a. FAD
   b. NAD⁺
   c. TPP
   d. no correct response

Answers: 1. a; 2. d

Concepts to Remember

Metabolism. Metabolism is the sum total of all the biochemical reactions that take place in a living organism. Metabolism consists of catabolism and anabolism. Catabolic biochemical reactions involve the breakdown of large molecules into smaller fragments. Anabolic biochemical reactions synthesize large molecules from smaller ones (Section 23-1).

Mitochondria. Mitochondria are membrane-enclosed subcellular structures that are the site of energy production in the form of ATP molecules. Enzymes for both the citric acid cycle and the electron transport chain are housed in the mitochondria (Section 23-2).

Metabolic coenzymes. Three important coenzymes involved in metabolic reactions are NAD⁺, FAD, and CoA. NAD⁺ and FAD are oxidizing agents that participate in the oxidation reactions of the citric acid cycle. They transport hydrogen atoms and electrons from the citric acid cycle to the electron transport chain. CoA interacts with acetyl groups produced from food degradation to form acetyl CoA. Acetyl CoA is the "fuel" for the citric acid cycle (Section 23-3).

Metabolic carboxylate ions. Five important carboxylate ions involved as substrates in metabolic reactions are malate, oxaloacetate, fumarate, α-ketoglutarate, and citrate. The first three of these carboxylate ions are polyfunctional derivatives of succinic acid, the four-carbon dicarboxylic acid, and the latter two are polyfunctional derivatives of glutaric acid, the five-carbon dicarboxylic acid (Section 23-4).

High-energy compounds. A high-energy compound liberates a larger-than-normal amount of free energy upon hydrolysis because structural features in the molecule contribute to repulsive strain in one or more bonds. Most high-energy biochemical molecules contain phosphate groups (Section 23-5).

Common metabolic pathway. The common metabolic pathway includes the reactions of the citric acid cycle and those of the electron transport chain and oxidative phosphorylation. The degradation products from all types of foods (carbohydrates, fats, and proteins) participate in the reactions of the common metabolic pathway (Section 23-6).

Citric acid cycle. The citric acid cycle is a cyclic series of eight reactions that oxidize the acetyl portion of acetyl CoA, resulting in the production of two molecules of CO_2. The complete oxidation of one acetyl group produces three molecules of NADH, one of $FADH_2$, and one of GTP besides the CO_2 (Section 23-7).

Electron transport chain. The electron transport chain is a series of reactions that passes electrons from NADH and $FADH_2$ to molecular oxygen. Each electron carrier that participates in the chain has an increasing affinity for electrons. Upon accepting the electrons and hydrogen ions, the O_2 is reduced to H_2O (Section 23-8).

Oxidative phosphorylation. Oxidative phosphorylation is the biochemical process by which ATP is synthesized from ADP as the result of a proton gradient across the inner mitochondrial membrane. Oxidative phosphorylation is coupled to the reactions of the electron transport chain (Section 23-9).

Chemiosmotic coupling. Chemiosmotic coupling explains how the energy needed for ATP synthesis is obtained. Synthesis takes place because of a flow of protons across the inner mitochondrial membrane (Section 23-10).

Non-ETC Oxygen Consumption. Some, less than 10%, of the oxygen taken into the body through respiration is used to produce reactive oxygen species, which include hydrogen peroxide (H_2O_2), superoxide ion (O_2^-), and hydroxyl radical (OH). Such species aid in the destruction of invading bacteria and viruses (Section 23-12).

Exercises and Problems

Exercises and problems are arranged in matched pairs with the two members of a pair addressing the same concept(s). The answer to the odd-numbered member of a pair is given at the back of the book. Problems denoted with a ▲ involve concepts found not only in the section under consideration but also concepts found in one or more earlier sections of the chapter.

Metabolism (Section 23-1)

23-1   Classify anabolism and catabolism as synthetic or degradative processes.

23-2   Classify anabolism and catabolism as energy-producing or energy-consuming processes.

23-3   What is a metabolic pathway?

23-4   What is the difference between a linear and a cyclic metabolic pathway?

23-5   Classify each of the following processes as anabolic or catabolic.
   a. Synthesis of a protein from amino acids
   b. Formation of a triacylglycerol from glycerol and fatty acids
   c. Hydrolysis of a polysaccharide to produce monosaccharides
   d. Formation of a polynucleotide from nucleotides

23-6 Classify each of the following processes as anabolic or catabolic.
   a. Synthesis of a nucleotide from a nucleoside and phosphate
   b. Degradation of a protein to individual amino acids
   c. Formation of a disaccharide from two monosaccharides
   d. Hydrolysis of a trisaccharide to form three monosaccharides

Metabolism and Cell Structure (Section 23-2)

23-7 List several differences between prokaryotic cells and eukaryotic cells.

23-8 What kinds of organisms have prokaryotic cells and what kinds have eukaryotic cells?

23-9 Indicate whether each of the following statements concerning the components present in a eukaryotic cell is true or false.
   a. Ribosomes are organelles.
   b. Lysosomes are found in the cytoplasm of a cell.
   c. The terms cytoplasm and cytosol have the same meaning.
   d. Generation of cellular energy occurs within mitochondria.

23-10 Indicate whether each of the following statements concerning the components present in a eukaryotic cell is true or false.
   a. The cytosol is a component of the cytoplasm.
   b. Mitochondria are sites where protein synthesis occurs.
   c. Ribosomes are found in the nucleus of a cell.
   d. Lysosomes are organelles.

23-11 Indicate whether each of the following statements about mitochondrion structural characteristics is true or false.
   a. The mitochondrion inner membrane is highly permeable to small molecules.
   b. Mitochondria have a sausage-like shape.
   c. Cristae are small folds on the inner membrane.
   d. The inner most area of a mitochondrion is called the matrix.

23-12 Indicate whether each of the following statements about mitochondrion structural characteristics is true or false.
   a. The outer membrane of a mitochondrion is more permeable than the inner membrane.
   b. The outer membrane has a highly folded structure.
   c. Cristae are attachments on the inner mitochondrial membrane.
   d. The matrix is the area between the inner and outer mitochondrial membranes.

Important Nucleotide-Containing Compounds in Metabolic Pathways (Section 23-3)

23-13 What does each letter in ATP stand for?

23-14 What does each letter in ADP stand for?

23-15 Specify, by name and by number present, the structural subunits present in an ATP molecule.

23-16 Specify, by name and by number present, the structural subunits present in an ADP molecule.

23-17 How many of each of the following are present in an ADP molecule?
   a. Phosphoanhydride bonds
   b. Phosphoester bonds

23-18 How many of each of the following are present in an ATP molecule?
   a. Phosphoanhydride bonds
   b. Phosphoester bonds

23-19 What is the structural difference between the members of each of the following pairs of molecules?
   a. ATP and AMP
   b. ADP and GDP

23-20 What is the structural difference between the members of each of the following pairs of molecules?
   a. ADP and AMP
   b. ATP and CTP

23-21 What does the designation P_i stand for?

23-22 What is the chemical formula for a P_i entity?

23-23 Write a generalized chemical equation, containing acronyms, for the hydrolysis of ATP to ADP.

23-24 Write a generalized chemical equation, containing acronyms, for the hydrolysis of ATP to AMP.

23-25 What does each letter in FAD stand for?

23-26 What does each letter in NAD^+ stand for?

23-27 Draw each of the following types of block diagrams for FAD.
   a. Three-subunit diagram
   b. Six-subunit diagram

23-28 Draw each of the following types of block diagrams for NAD^+.
   a. Three-subunit diagram
   b. Six-subunit diagram

23-29 What is the name of the B vitamin present in each of the following molecules?
   a. NAD^+
   b. $FADH_2$.

23-30 What is the name of the B vitamin present in each of the following molecules?
   a. FAD
   b. NADH

23-31 Indicate whether the B vitamin portion of each of the following molecules is the "active" subunit of the molecule in redox reactions.
   a. FAD
   b. NADH

23-32 Indicate whether the B vitamin portion of each of the following molecules is the "active" subunit of the molecule in redox reactions.
   a. NAD^+
   b. $FADH_2$

23-33 Indicate whether each of the following notations denotes the oxidized or reduced form of the molecule.
   a. FAD
   b. $FADH_2$

23-34 Indicate whether each of the following notations denotes the oxidized or reduced form of the molecule.
a. NADH
b. NAD^+

23-35 What identical structural subunits do the following pairs of molecules have in common?
a. NAD^+ and NADH
b. NAD^+ and $FADH_2$

23-36 What identical structural subunits do the following pairs of molecules have in common?
a. FAD and $FADH_2$
b. FAD and NADH

23-37 Draw the three-subunit block diagram for CoA.

23-38 Draw the six-subunit block diagram for CoA.

23-39 Which of the subunits in the six-subunit block diagram for CoA
a. involves a B vitamin
b. is the "active" subunit in chemical reactions

23-40 Which of the subunits in the three-subunit block diagram for CoA
a. involves a B vitamin
b. is the "active" subunit in chemical reactions

23-41 Indicate whether the biochemical function of each of the following molecules involves transfer of (1) phosphate groups, (2) electrons, or (3) acetyl groups.
a. ATP
b. $FADH_2$
c. NAD^+
d. CoA–SH

23-42 Indicate whether the biochemical function of each of the following molecules involves transfer of (1) phosphate groups, (2) electrons, or (3) acetyl groups.
a. ADP
b. NADH
c. FAD
d. Coenzyme A

23-43 Classify each of the following molecules as (1) an oxidizing agent, (2) a reducing agent, or (3) neither an oxidizing agent nor a reducing agent.
a. $FADH_2$
b. ADP
c. Coenzyme A
d. NAD^+

23-44 Classify each of the following molecules as (1) an oxidizing agent, (2) a reducing agent, or (3) neither an oxidizing agent nor a reducing agent.
a. NADH   b. ATP
c. FAD   d. CoA–SH

23-45 Which of the substances ATP, CoA–SH, FAD, and NAD^+ contains the following subunits within their structure? More than one substance may apply in a given situation.
a. Contains two ribose subunits
b. Contains two phosphate subunits
c. Contains one adenine subunit
d. Contains four different kinds of subunits

23-46 Which of the substances ATP, CoA–SH, FAD, and NAD^+ contains the following subunits within their structure? More than one substance may apply in a given situation.
a. Contains one ribose subunit
b. Contains one phosphorylated ribose subunit
c. Contains both a ribitol and a ribose subunit
d. Contains five different kinds of subunits

Important Carboxylate Ions in Metabolic Pathways (Section 23-4)

23-47 Draw structural formulas for each of the following substances.
a. Oxaloacetic acid   b. Oxaloacetate ion
c. Citric acid   d. Citrate ion

23-48 Draw structural formulas for each of the following substances.
a. Fumaric acid
b. Fumarate ion
c. Malic acid
d. Malate ion

23-49 Which of the substances *malate, oxaloacetate, fumarate, α-ketoglutarate,* and *citrate* have each of the following characteristics? More than one substance may apply in a given situation.
a. Contains four carbon atoms
b. Contains a keto functional group
c. Has a charge of 2−
d. Is a succinic acid derivative

23-50 Which of the substances *malate, oxaloacetate, fumarate, α-ketoglutarate,* and *citrate* have each of the following characteristics? More than one substance may apply in a given situation.
a. Contains six carbon atoms
b. Contains a hydroxyl functional group
c. Has a charge of 3−
d. Is a glutaric acid derivative

High-Energy Phosphate Compounds (Section 23-5)

23-51 What is a high-energy compound?

23-52 What factors contribute to a strained bond in high-energy phosphate compounds?

23-53 What does the designation P_i denote?

23-54 What does the designation PP_i denote?

23-55 With the help of Table 23-1, determine which compound in each of the following pairs of phosphate-containing compounds releases more free energy upon hydrolysis.
a. ATP and phosphoenolpyruvate
b. Creatine phosphate and ADP
c. Glucose 1-phosphate and 1,3-bisphosphoglycerate
d. AMP and glycerol 3-phosphate

23-56 With the help of Table 23-1, determine which compound in each of the following pairs of phosphate-containing compounds releases more free energy upon hydrolysis.
a. ATP and creatine phosphate
b. Glucose 1-phosphate and glucose 6-phosphate
c. ADP and AMP
d. Phosphoenolpyruvate and PP_i

23-57 In the conversion of ADP to AMP and P_i via hydrolysis
a. how many phosphorus–oxygen bonds are broken
b. how many new phosphorus–oxygen bonds are formed

23-58 In the conversion of ATP to AMP and 2 P_i via hydrolysis
a. how many phosphorus–oxygen bonds are broken
b. how many new phosphorus–oxygen bonds are formed

An Overview of Biochemical energy Production (Section 23-6)

23-59 List, by name, the four general stages of the process by which biochemical energy is obtained from food.

23-60 Which, by name, of the four general stages of the process by which biochemical energy is obtained from food are part of the common metabolic pathway.

The Citric Acid Cycle (Section 23-7)

23-61 What are two other names for the citric acid cycle?

23-62 What is the basis for the name *citric acid cycle*?

23-63 What two compounds are needed to start a turn of the citric acid cycle?

23-64 What is the "fuel" for the citric acid cycle?

23-65 At what location in a mitochondrion does seven out of the eight reactions of the citric acid cycle take place?

23-66 One of the eight reactions of the citric acid cycle takes place at a mitochondrion location different from where the other seven occur. What is the location for this one reaction?

23-67 In the citric acid cycle what is the general type of reaction in which
a. Malate is involved as a reactant
b. Malate is involved as a product
c. Isocitrate is involved as a reactant
d. Isocitrate is involved as a product

23-68 In the citric acid cycle what is the general type of reaction in which
a. Fumarate is involved as a reactant
b. Fumarate is involved as a product
c. Oxaloacetate is involved as a reactant
d. Oxaloacetate is involved as a product

23-69 Consider the reactions that occur during *one turn* of the citric acid cycle in answering each of the following questions.
a. How many CO_2 molecules are formed?
b. How many molecules of $FADH_2$ are formed?
c. How many times is a secondary alcohol oxidized?
d. How many times does water add to a carbon–carbon double bond?

23-70 Consider the reactions that occur during *one turn* of the citric acid cycle in answering each of the following questions.
a. How many molecules of NADH are formed?
b. How many GTP molecules are formed?
c. How many decarboxylation reactions occur?
d. How many oxidation–reduction reactions occur?

23-71 There are eight steps in the citric acid cycle. List those steps, by number, that involve
a. Oxidation.
b. Isomerization.
c. Hydration.

23-72 There are eight steps in the citric acid cycle. List those steps, by number, that involve
a. Oxidation and decarboxylation.
b. Phosphorylation.
c. Condensation.

23-73 There are four C_4 dicarboxylic acid species in the citric acid cycle. What are their names and structures?

23-74 There are two keto carboxylic acid species in the citric acid cycle. What are their names and structures?

23-75 Characterize, in terms of number of carbon atoms present, each of the following citric acid cycle changes as (1) a C_6 to C_6 change, (2) a C_6 to C_5 change, (3) a C_5 to C_4 change, or (4) a C_4 to C_4 change.
a. Citrate to isocitrate
b. Succinate to fumarate
c. Malate to oxaloacetate
d. Isocitrate to α-ketoglutarate

23-76 Characterize, in terms of number of carbon atoms present, each of the following citric acid cycle changes as (1) a C_4 to C_4 change, (2) a C_4 to C_6 change, (3) a C_5 to C_4 change, or (4) a C_6 to C_5 change.
a. Oxaloacetate to citrate
b. α-Ketoglutarate to succinyl CoA
c. Fumarate to malate
d. Succinyl CoA to succinate

23-77 Identify the oxidized coenzyme (NAD^+ or FAD) that participates in each of the following citric acid cycle reactions.
a. Isocitrate $\longrightarrow$ α-ketoglutarate
b. Succinate $\longrightarrow$ fumarate

23-78 Identify the oxidized coenzyme (NAD^+ or FAD) that participates in each of the following citric acid cycle reactions.
a. Malate $\longrightarrow$ oxaloacetate
b. α-Ketoglutarate $\longrightarrow$ succinyl CoA

23-79 List the two citric acid cycle intermediates involved in the reaction governed by each of the following enzymes. List the reactant first.
a. Isocitrate dehydrogenase
b. Fumarase
c. Malate dehydrogenase
d. Aconitase

23-80 List the two citric acid cycle intermediates involved in the reaction governed by each of the following enzymes. List the reactant first.
a. α-Ketoglutarate dehydrogenase
b. Succinate dehydrogenase
c. Citrate synthase
d. Succinyl CoA synthetase

The Electron Transport Chain (Section 23-8)

23-81   What two substances provide the electrons needed for operation of the electron transport chain?

23-82   What change occurs relative to electron energy as electrons pass through the electron transport chain?

23-83   What substance is the final electron acceptor in the electron transport chain?

23-84   What substance is the final product in the electron transport chain?

23-85   Indicate whether the electron carriers in each of the following listings are in the order in which they are first encountered in the electron transport chain.
   a. FeSP, CoQ, cyt b
   b. FMN, cyt c, CoQ
   c. CoQ, FMN, cyt a
   d. $FADH_2$, NADH, FeSP

23-86   Indicate whether the electron carriers in each of the following listings are in the order in which they are first encountered in the electron transport chain.
   a. FeSP, CoQ, FMN
   b. Cyt b, cyt c, cyt a
   c. NADH, $FADH_2$, cyt c
   d. FMN, FeSP, CoQ

23-87   Indicate whether each of the following electron carriers is in its oxidized form or its reduced form.
   a. Fe(III)SP
   b. Cyt b (Fe^{3+})
   c. NADH
   d. FAD

23-88   Indicate whether each of the following electron carriers is in its oxidized form or its reduced form.
   a. $FMNH_2$
   b. Fe(II)SP
   c. Cyt c_1 (Fe^{2+})
   d. NAD^+

23-89   Indicate whether each of the following changes represents oxidation or reduction.
   a. $CoQH_2 \longrightarrow CoQ$
   b. $NAD^+ \longrightarrow NADH$
   c. Cyt c (Fe^{2+}) $\longrightarrow$ cyt c (Fe^{3+})
   d. Cyt b (Fe^{3+}) $\longrightarrow$ cyt b (Fe^{2+})

23-90   Indicate whether each of the following changes represents oxidation or reduction.
   a. $FADH_2 \longrightarrow FAD$
   b. $FMN \longrightarrow FMNH_2$
   c. Fe(III)SP $\longrightarrow$ Fe(II)SP
   d. Cyt c_1 (Fe^{3+}) $\longrightarrow$ cyt c_1 (Fe^{2+})

23-91   With which of the protein complexes (I, II, III, and IV) of the ETC is each of the following electron carriers associated? More than one answer may apply in a given situation.
   a. NADH
   b. CoQ
   c. Cyt b
   d. Cyt a

23-92   With which of the protein complexes (I, II, III, and IV) of the ETC is each of the following electron carriers associated? More than one answer may apply in a given situation.
   a. $FADH_2$
   b. FeSP
   c. Cyt c
   d. Cyt c_1

23-93   Which electron carrier shuttles electrons between protein complexes I and III?

23-94   Which electron carrier shuttles electrons between protein complexes II and III?

23-95   How many electrons does the electron carrier between complexes II and III carry per "trip"?

23-96   How many electrons does the electron carrier between complexes III and IV carry per "trip"?

23-97   Fill in the missing substances in the following electron transport chain reaction sequences.

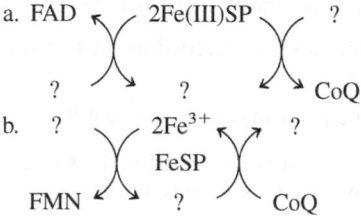

23-98   Fill in the missing substances in the following electron transport chain reaction sequences.

▲**23-99**   Classify each of the following substances as (1) a reactant in the CAC, (2) a reactant in the ETC, or (3) a reactant in both the CAC and the ETC.
   a. NADH
   b. O_2
   c. Fumarate
   d. Cytochrome a

▲**23-100**   Classify each of the following substances as (1) a product in the CAC, (2) a product in the ETC, or (3) a product in both the CAC and the ETC.
   a. FAD
   b. CO_2
   c. Malate
   d. $FMNH_2$

▲**23-101**   Put the following substances in the correct order in which they are first encountered in the common metabolic pathway: succinate, FeSP, CO_2, $FADH_2$.

▲**23-102**   Put the following substances in the correct order in which they are first encountered in the common metabolic pathway: $CoQH_2$, GTP, O_2, isocitrate.

▲23-103 Indicate whether each of the following substances undergoes (1) oxidation but not reduction, (2) reduction but not oxidation, (3) both oxidation and reduction, or (4) neither oxidation nor reduction in the common metabolic pathway.
a. Oxaloacetate
b. NAD^+
c. $FADH_2$
d. FeSP

▲23-104 Indicate whether each of the following substances undergoes (1) oxidation but not reduction, (2) reduction but not oxidation, (3) both oxidation and reduction, or (4) neither oxidation nor reduction in the common metabolic pathway.
a. Malate
b. NADH
c. FAD
d. Cyt b

Oxidative Phosphorylation (Section 23-9)

23-105 What is oxidative phosphorylation?

23-106 What are coupled reactions?

23-107 At what two locations in a mitochondrion are the protons found that are involved in the proton gradient that is present?

23-108 At what mitochondrion location does H^+ ion buildup occur as the result of proton pumping?

23-109 How many protons cross the inner mitochondrial membrane when an NADH molecule is oxidized?

23-110 How many protons cross the inner mitochondrial membrane when an $FADH_2$ molecule is oxidized?

23-111 How many protons cross the inner mitochondrial membrane at the following enzyme complex locations when two electrons from an NADH molecule are passed through the electron transport chain.
a. Complex I
b. Complex II
c. Complex III
d. Complex IV

23-112 How many protons cross the inner mitochondrial membrane at the following enzyme complex locations when two electrons from an $FADH_2$ molecule are passed through the electron transport chain.
a. Complex I
b. Complex II
c. Complex III
d. Complex IV

23-113 What is the name of the enzyme that catalyzes ATP production during oxidative phosphorylation?

23-114 What is the location of the enzyme that uses stored energy in a proton gradient to drive the reaction that produces ATP?

23-115 In oxidative phosphorylation, what is oxidized and what is phosphorylated?

23-116 In oxidative phosphorylation, what are the identities of the
a. three reactants
b. two products

23-117 What process must occur before an ATP molecule produced in oxidative phosphorylation becomes available for cellular use?

23-118 How many H^+ ions are consumed in the process of making a newly produced ATP molecule available for cellular use?

ATP Production for the Common Metabolic Pathway (Section 23-10)

23-119 How many ATP molecules are formed for
a. each NADH molecule that enters the ETC?
b. each $FADH_2$ molecule that enters the ETC?

23-120 NADH and $FADH_2$ molecules do not yield the same number of ATP molecules. Explain why.

23-121 In which step(s) of the CAC are ATP-precursor-molecules generated that are equivalent to
a. 2.5 units of ATP
b. 1.5 units of ATP
c. 1.0 unit of ATP

23-122 In which step(s) of the CAC are ATP-precursor-molecules generated that
a. enter the ETC at enzyme complex I
b. enter the ETC at enzyme complex II
c. do not enter the ETC

23-123 How many moles of ATP become available for cellular use if 4 moles of NADH and 3 moles of $FADH_2$ are oxidized within a mitochondrion?

23-124 How many moles of ATP become available for cellular use if 3 moles of NADH and 4 moles of $FADH_2$ are oxidized within a mitochondrion?

Non-ETC Oxygen-Consuming Reactions (Section 23-11)

23-125 What does the designation ROS stand for?

23-126 Give the chemical formula for each of the following.
a. Superoxide ion   b. Hydroxyl radical

23-127 Give the chemical equation for the reaction by which
a. superoxide ion is generated within cells.
b. superoxide ion is converted to hydrogen peroxide within cells.

23-128 Give the chemical equation for the reaction by which
a. hydrogen peroxide is converted to desirable products within cells.
b. hydrogen peroxide is converted to an undesirable product within cells.

B Vitamins and the Common Metabolic Pathway (Section 23-12)

23-129 Indicate whether or not each of the following B vitamins is needed for the proper functioning of the CAC.
a. Thiamin   b. Biotin
c. Niacin   d. Vitamin B_6

23-130 Indicate whether or not each of the following B vitamins is needed for the proper functioning of the CAC.
   a. Riboflavin
   b. Pantothenic acid
   c. Folate
   d. Vitamin B_{12}

23-131 Indicate whether or not each of the following B vitamins is needed for the proper functioning of the ETC.
   a. Thiamin
   b. Riboflavin
   c. Folate
   d. Vitamin B_{12}

23-132 Indicate whether or not each of the following B vitamins is needed for the proper functioning of the ETC.
   a. Niacin
   b. Biotin
   c. Pantothenic acid
   d. Vitamin B_6

Carbohydrate Metabolism

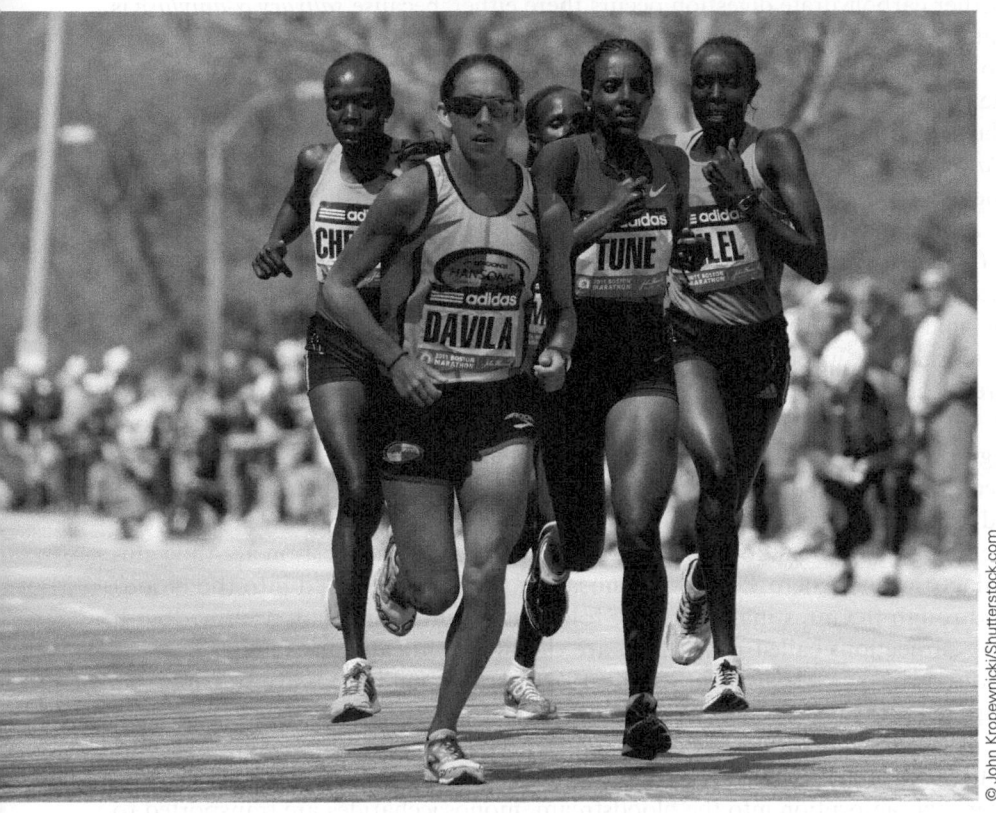

Carbohydrates are a major energy source for human beings.

© John Kropewnicki/Shutterstock.com

In this chapter the relationship between carbohydrate metabolism and energy production in cells is explored. The molecule glucose is the focal point of carbohydrate metabolism. Commonly called blood sugar, glucose is supplied to the body via the circulatory system and, after being absorbed by a cell, can be either oxidized to yield energy or stored as glycogen for future use. When sufficient oxygen is present, glucose is totally oxidized to CO_2 and H_2O. However, in the absence of oxygen, glucose is only partially oxidized to lactic acid. Besides supplying energy needs, glucose and other six-carbon sugars can be converted into a variety of different sugars (C_3, C_4, C_5, and C_7) needed for biosynthesis. Some of the oxidative steps in carbohydrate metabolism also produce NADH and NADPH, sources of reductive power in cells.

24-1 Digestion and Absorption of Carbohydrates

LEARNING FOCUS

Be familiar with the steps in the carbohydrate digestion process in terms of the sites where they occur and the products at each of the sites.

Digestion *is the biochemical process by which food molecules, through hydrolysis, are broken down into simpler chemical units that can be used by cells for their metabolic needs.* Digestion is the first stage in the processing of food products.

The digestion of carbohydrates begins in the mouth, where the enzyme *salivary α-amylase* catalyzes the hydrolysis of α-glycosidic linkages (Section 18-13) in starch from plants and glycogen from meats to produce smaller polysaccharides and the disaccharide maltose. ◀

► *Salivary α-amylase is a constituent of saliva, the fluid secreted by the salivary glands. Saliva is 99% water plus small amounts of several inorganic ions and organic molecules. Saliva secretion can be triggered by the taste, smell, sight, and even thought of food. Average saliva output is about 1.5 L per day.*

Only a small amount of carbohydrate digestion occurs in the mouth because food is swallowed so quickly. Although the food mass remains longer in the stomach, very little further carbohydrate digestion occurs there either, because *salivary α-amylase* is inactivated by the acidic environment of the stomach, and the stomach's own secretions do not contain any carbohydrate-digesting enzymes.

The primary site for carbohydrate digestion is within the small intestine, where α-amylase, this time secreted by the pancreas, again begins to function. *Pancreatic α-amylase* breaks down polysaccharide chains into shorter and shorter segments until the disaccharide maltose (two glucose units; Section 18-13) is the dominant species. At this stage, the carbohydrate mixture present is a disaccharide mixture of lactose (originally present as such), sucrose (originally present as such), and maltose (obtained from polysaccharide breakdown).

The final step in carbohydrate digestion occurs on the outer membranes of intestinal mucosal cells, where the enzymes that convert disaccharides to monosaccharides are located. The important disaccharidase enzymes are *maltase, sucrase,* and *lactase.* These enzymes convert, respectively, maltose to two glucose units, sucrose to one glucose and one fructose unit, and lactose to one glucose and one galactose unit (Section 18-13). (The disaccharides sucrose and lactose present in food are not digested until they reach this point.)

The three major breakdown products from carbohydrate digestion are thus glucose, galactose, and fructose. These monosaccharides are absorbed into the bloodstream through the intestinal wall. The folds of the intestinal wall are lined with fingerlike projections called *villi,* which are rich in blood capillaries (Figure 24-1). Absorption is by *active transport* (Section 19-10), which, unlike passive transport, is an energy-requiring process. In this case, ATP is needed. Protein carriers mediate the passage of the monosaccharides through cell membranes. Figure 24-2 summarizes the different phases in the digestive process for carbohydrates.

After their absorption into the bloodstream, monosaccharides are transported to the liver, where fructose and galactose are rapidly converted into compounds that are metabolized by the same pathway as glucose. Thus the central focus of carbohydrate metabolism is the pathway by which glucose is further processed, a pathway called *glycolysis* (Section 24-2)—a series of ten reactions, each of which involves a different enzyme.

Figure 24-1 A section of the small intestine, showing its folds and the villi that cover the inner surface of the folds. Villi greatly increase the inner intestinal surface area.

Villi

Folds of inner intestinal wall

Figure 24-2 Summary of carbohydrate digestion in the human body.

EXAMPLE 24-1

Determining the Sites Where Various Aspects of Carbohydrate Digestion Occur

Based on the information in Figure 24-2, determine the location within the human body where each of the following aspects of carbohydrate digestion occurs:

a. The enzyme sucrase is active.
b. Hydrolysis reactions converting polysaccharides to disaccharides occur.
c. First site where breaking of glycosidic linkages occurs.
d. The monosaccharides glucose, fructose, and galactose are produced.

Solution

a. *Intestinal mucosal cells* are the sites where hydrolysis of disaccharides, effected by the enzymes maltase, sucrase, and lactase, occurs.
b. The *small intestine* is the location where pancreatic digestive enzymes convert polysaccharides to disaccharides.
c. Digestion of carbohydrates begins in the *mouth,* where salivary enzymes convert some polysaccharides to smaller polysaccharides through breakage of glycosidic linkages.
d. *Intestinal mucosal cells* are the sites where disaccharides, through hydrolysis, are converted to the monosaccharides glucose, fructose, and galactose.

Section 24-1 Quick Quiz

1. The primary site within the human body where carbohydrate digestion occurs is the
   a. mouth
   b. stomach
   c. small intestine
   d. no correct response
2. What is the first site within the human body where breaking of polysaccharide glycosidic bonds occurs?
   a. mouth
   b. stomach
   c. small intestine
   d. no correct response

(continued)

3. What effect does gastric juice in the stomach have on dietary polysaccharides?
   a. converts polysaccharides to disaccharides
   b. converts polysaccharides to monosaccharides
   c. has no effect on polysaccharides
   d. no correct response
4. The enzymes that convert disaccharides to monosaccharides are associated with
   a. intestinal villi
   b. intestinal mucosal cells
   c. the pancreas
   d. no correct response
5. Which of the following substances is needed for monosaccharides to enter the bloodstream?
   a. ATP
   b. α-amylase
   c. sucrase
   d. no correct response

Answers: 1. c; 2. a; 3. c; 4. b; 5. a

24-2 Glycolysis

LEARNING FOCUS

Be familiar with the details of both the six-carbon stage and the three-carbon stage of glycolysis in terms of reactants and products in the various steps of each stage.

Glycolysis *is the metabolic pathway by which glucose (a C_6 molecule) is converted into two molecules of pyruvate (a C_3 molecule), chemical energy in the form of ATP is produced, and NADH-reduced coenzymes are produced.* It is a linear rather than cyclic pathway (see Section 23-1) that functions in almost all cells. ◀

The conversion of glucose to pyruvate is an oxidation process in which no molecular oxygen is utilized. ◀ The oxidizing agent is the coenzyme NAD$^+$. Metabolic pathways in which molecular oxygen is not a participant are called *anaerobic* pathways. Pathways that require molecular oxygen are called *aerobic* pathways. Glycolysis is an anaerobic pathway. ◀

Glycolysis is a ten-step process (compared to the eight steps of the citric acid cycle; Section 23-7) in which every step is enzyme-catalyzed. Figure 24-3 gives an overview of glycolysis. There are two stages in the overall process, a *six-carbon stage* (Steps 1–3) and a *three-carbon stage* (Steps 4–10). All of the enzymes needed for glycolysis are present in the cell cytosol (Section 23-2), which is where glycolysis takes place. Details of the individual steps within the glycolysis pathway are now considered. ◀

▶ *The term* glycolysis, *pronounced "gligh-KOLL-ih-sis," comes from the Greek* glyco, *meaning "sweet," and* lysis, *meaning "breakdown."*

▶ Pyruvate, *pronounced "PIE-roo-vate," is the carboxylate ion (Section 16-7) produced when pyruvic acid (a three-carbon keto acid) loses its acidic hydrogen atom.*

$$
\begin{array}{ccc}
\text{CH}_3 & & \text{CH}_3 \\
| & & | \\
\text{C}=\text{O} & \longrightarrow & \text{C}=\text{O} \quad +\text{H}^+ \\
| & & | \\
\text{COOH} & & \text{COO}^- \\
\text{Pyruvic acid} & & \text{Pyruvate ion}
\end{array}
$$

▶ Anaerobic *is pronounced "AN-air-ROE-bic."* Aerobic *is pronounced "air-ROE-bic."*

▶ *Glycolysis is also called the* Embden–Meyerhof pathway *after the German chemists Gustav Embden (1874–1933) and Otto Meyerhof (1884–1951), who discovered many of the details of the pathway in the early 1930s.*

Six-Carbon Stage of Glycolysis (Steps 1–3)

The six-carbon stage of glycolysis is an *energy-consuming stage.* The energy release associated with the conversion of two ATP molecules to two ADP molecules is used to transform monosaccharides into monosaccharide phosphates. The intermediates of the six-carbon stage of glycolysis are all either *glucose* or *fructose* derivatives in which phosphate groups are present.

Step 1:   **Phosphorylation Using ATP:** *Formation of Glucose 6-Phosphate.* Glycolysis begins with the phosphorylation of glucose to yield glucose 6-phosphate, a glucose molecule with a phosphate group attached to the hydroxyl oxygen on carbon 6 (the carbon atom outside the ring). The phosphate group comes from an ATP molecule. *Hexokinase,* an enzyme that requires Mg^{2+} ion for its activity, catalyzes the reaction.

Figure 24-3 An overview of glycolysis.

Glucose

Glucose 6-phosphate

The symbol (P) is a shorthand notation for a PO_3^{2-} unit.

▶ *A kinase is an enzyme that catalyzes the transfer of a phosphoryl group (PO_3^{2-}) from ATP (or some other high-energy phosphate compound) to a substrate (Section 21-3).*

▶ *Step 1 of glycolysis is the first of two steps in which an ATP molecule is converted to an ADP with the energy released used to effect a phosphorylation. The other ATP-phosphorylation reaction occurs in Step 3.*

This reaction requires energy, which is provided by the breakdown of an ATP molecule. ◀ This energy expenditure will be recouped later in the glycolysis pathway. Phosphorylation of glucose provides a way of "trapping" glucose within a cell. Cell membranes have protein transporters for glucose but not for glucose 6-phosphate. Phosphorylation of glucose changes it from a neutral molecule to a negatively charged substance; charge severely limits the ability of phosphorylated molecules to cross cell membranes.

Step 2: **Isomerization:** *Formation of Fructose 6-Phosphate.* Glucose 6-phosphate is isomerized to fructose 6-phosphate by *phosphoglucoisomerase.*

Glucose 6-phosphate

Fructose 6-phosphate

The net result of this change is that carbon 1 of glucose is no longer part of the ring structure. [Glucose, an aldose, forms a six-membered ring, and fructose, a ketose, forms a five-membered ring (Section 18-10); both sugars, however, contain six carbon atoms.]

Step 3: **Phosphorylation Using ATP:** *Formation of Fructose 1,6-Bisphosphate.* This step, like Step 1, is a phosphorylation reaction and therefore requires the expenditure of energy. ATP is the source of the phosphate and the energy. ◀ The enzyme involved, *phosphofructokinase,* is another enzyme that requires Mg^{2+} ion for its activity. The fructose molecule now contains two phosphate groups. ◀

▶ *Step 3 of glycolysis commits the original glucose molecule to the glycolysis pathway. Glucose 6-phosphate (Step 1) and fructose 6-phosphate (Step 2) can enter other metabolic pathways, but fructose 1,6-bisphosphate can enter only glycolysis.*

▶ *The term bisphosphate is used instead of diphosphate to indicate the two phosphates are on different carbon atoms in fructose and not connected to each other.*

Fructose 6-phosphate

Fructose 1,6-bisphosphate

Three-Carbon Stage of Glycolysis (Steps 4–10)

The three-carbon stage of glycolysis is an *energy-generating stage* rather than an energy-consuming stage. All of the intermediates in this stage are C_3-phosphates, two of which are high-energy phosphate species (Section 23-5). Loss of a phosphate from these high-energy species effects the conversion of ADP molecules to ATP molecules. ◀

▶ *The three-carbon stage of glycolysis is often called the* payoff stage *of glycolysis since ATP is produced rather than consumed; the latter was the situation in the six-carbon stage of glycolysis.*

The C_3 intermediates in this stage of glycolysis are all phosphorylated derivatives of *dihydroxyacetone, glyceraldehyde, glycerate,* or *pyruvate,* which in turn are derivatives of either glycerol or acetone. Figure 24-4 shows the structural relationships among these molecules.

Step 4: **Cleavage:** *Formation of Two Triose Phosphates.* In this step, the reacting C_6 bisphosphate is split into two C_3 monophosphate species. Because fructose

Figure 24-4 Structural relationships among glycerol and acetone and the C_3 intermediates in the process of glycolysis.

1,6-bisphosphate, the molecule being split, is unsymmetrical, the two trioses produced are not identical. One product is dihydroxyacetone phosphate, and the other is glyceraldehyde 3-phosphate. *Aldolase* is the enzyme that catalyzes this reaction. ◄ A better understanding of the structural relationships between reactant and products is obtained if the fructose 1,6-bisphosphate is written in its open-chain form (Section 18-10) rather than in its cyclic form.

▶ *Recall, from Section 18-9, that the aldotriose glyceraldehyde and the ketotriose dihydroxyacetone are the two simplest monosaccharides. The Step 4 products are phosphorylated versions of these two trioses.*

Step 5: **Isomerization:** *Formation of Glyceraldehyde 3-Phosphate.* Only one of the two trioses produced in Step 4, glyceraldehyde 3-phosphate, is a glycolysis intermediate. Dihydroxyacetone phosphate, the other triose, can, however, be readily converted into glyceraldehyde 3-phosphate. Dihydroxyacetone phosphate (a ketose) and glyceraldehyde 3-phosphate (an aldose) are isomers, and the isomerization process from ketose to aldose is catalyzed by the enzyme *triosephosphate isomerase.*

$$
\begin{array}{ccc}
\text{CH}_2\text{O}-\text{P} & & \text{CH}_2\text{O}-\text{P} \\
\text{O}=\text{C} & \xrightarrow{\text{Triosephosphate}} & \text{HO}-\text{C}-\text{H} \\
\text{HO}-\text{C}-\text{H} & \underset{\text{isomerase}}{\rightleftharpoons} & \text{C} \\
\text{H} & & \text{O} \quad \text{H} \\
\end{array}
$$

Dihydroxyacetone phosphate   Glyceraldehyde 3-phosphate

Step 6:   Oxidation and Phosphorylation Using P$_i$: *Formation of 1,3-Bisphosphoglycerate.* In a reaction catalyzed by *glyceraldehyde 3-phosphate dehydrogenase*, a phosphate group is added to glyceraldehyde 3-phosphate to produce 1,3-bisphosphoglycerate. The hydrogen of the aldehyde group becomes part of NADH. ◄

▶ *Keep in mind that from Step 6 onward, two molecules of each of the C$_3$ compounds take part in every reaction for each original C$_6$ glucose molecule.*

$$
\begin{array}{c}
\text{O} \quad \text{H} \\
\text{C} \\
\text{H}-\text{C}-\text{OH} \\
\text{CH}_2\text{O}-\text{P}
\end{array}
+ \text{NAD}^+ + \text{P}_i
\xrightarrow[\text{dehydrogenase}]{\text{Glyceraldehyde 3-phosphate}}
\begin{array}{c}
\text{O} \quad \text{O}{\sim}\text{P} \\
\text{C} \\
\text{H}-\text{C}-\text{OH} \\
\text{CH}_2\text{O}-\text{P}
\end{array}
+ \text{NADH} + \text{H}^+
$$

Glyceraldehyde 3-phosphate   1,3-Bisphosphoglycerate

The newly added phosphate group in 1,3-bisphosphoglycerate is a high-energy phosphate group (Section 23-5). A high-energy phosphate group is produced when a phosphate group is attached to a carbon atom that is also participating in a carbon–carbon or carbon–oxygen double bond. ◄

▶ *Step 6 is the first of two glycolysis steps in which a high-energy phosphate compound, that is, an "energy-rich" compound, is formed. The other high-energy phosphate compound is formed in Step 9. In the step that follows each of these two situations, energy from the high-energy phosphate compound is used to convert ADP to ATP.*

Note that a molecule of the reduced coenzyme NADH is a product of this reaction and also that the source of the added phosphate is inorganic phosphate (P$_i$) rather than ATP.

The heading for this Step 6 reaction reads "oxidation and phosphorylation." That both processes occur is more easily understood if the reaction is considered to occur in two steps. In the first step, the aldehyde is oxidized to an acid (carboxylate ion) by NAD$^+$.

$$
\begin{array}{c}
\text{O} \quad \text{H} \\
\text{C} \\
\text{H}-\text{C}-\text{OH} \\
\text{CH}_2\text{O}-\text{P}
\end{array}
+ \text{NAD}^+ + \text{H}_2\text{O}
\xrightarrow{\text{oxidation}}
\begin{array}{c}
\text{O} \quad \text{O}^- \\
\text{C} \\
\text{H}-\text{C}-\text{OH} \\
\text{CH}_2\text{O}-\text{P}
\end{array}
+ \text{NADH} + 2\text{H}^+
$$

Glyceraldehyde 3-phosphate   3-Phosphoglycerate

In the second step, carboxylate ion and phosphate (P$_i$) are joined together to form the bisphosphate product.

$$
\begin{array}{c}
\text{O} \quad \text{O}^- \\
\text{C} \\
\text{H}-\text{C}-\text{OH} \\
\text{CH}_2\text{O}-\text{P}
\end{array}
+ \text{H}^+ + \text{P}_i
\xrightarrow{\text{phosphorylation}}
\begin{array}{c}
\text{O} \quad \text{O}{\sim}\text{P} \\
\text{C} \\
\text{H}-\text{C}-\text{OH} \\
\text{CH}_2\text{O}-\text{P}
\end{array}
+ \text{H}_2\text{O}
$$

3-Phosphoglycerate   1,3-Bisphosphoglycerate

The newly formed oxygen-phosphate bond is not an ester linkage since an ester linkage requires an acid and an alcohol (Section 16-11). Two acids are reacting here, phosphoglycerate (glyceric acid) and phosphate (phosphoric acid), and the bond formed is a mixed anhydride bond (Section 16-19) between two acids. This anhydride bond is the high-energy bond.

Step 7: **Phosphorylation of ADP:** *Formation of 3-Phosphoglycerate.* In this step, the diphosphate species just formed is converted back to a monophosphate species. This is an ATP-producing step in which the C1 phosphate group of 1,3-bisphosphoglycerate (the high-energy phosphate) is transferred to an ADP molecule to form the ATP. The enzyme involved is *phosphoglycerokinase.*

Remember that two ATP molecules are produced for each original glucose molecule because both C$_3$ molecules produced from the glucose react.

ATP production in this step involves substrate-level phosphorylation. **Substrate-level phosphorylation** *is the biochemical process whereby ATP is produced from ADP by hydrolysis of a high-energy compound (the substrate).* Production of ATP in this manner differs from the ATP formation considered in the last chapter (oxidative phosphorylation; Section 23-9) where a proton gradient is required for the process to occur. ◄

Substrate-level phosphorylation also differs from the phosphorylation that occurs in Step 6 of glycolysis. There the source of the phosphate is a free phosphate (P$_i$) and the reaction is linked to electron transfer (oxidation) involving NAD$^+$.

Step 8: **Isomerization:** *Formation of 2-Phosphoglycerate.* In this isomerization step, the phosphate group of 3-phosphoglycerate is moved from carbon 3 to carbon 2. The enzyme *phosphoglyceromutase* catalyzes the exchange of the phosphate group between the two carbons. ◄

Diagram: 3-Phosphoglycerate converted via Phosphoglyceromutase to 2-Phosphoglycerate

Step 9: **Dehydration:** *Formation of Phosphoenolpyruvate.* This is an alcohol dehydration reaction that introduces a carbon–carbon double bond into the molecule. The presence of the enzyme *enolase,* another Mg^{2+}-requiring enzyme, is required. The result is another compound containing a high-energy phosphate group; the phosphate group is attached to a carbon atom that is involved in a carbon–carbon double bond. ◄

Diagram: 2-Phosphoglycerate converted via Enolase to Phosphoenolpyruvate + HOH ◄

► *Step 7 is the first of two steps in which ATP is formed from ADP. This process, called* substrate-level phosphorylation, *always involves a high-energy phosphate compound. This same process also occurs in Step 10.*

► *A* mutase *is an enzyme that effects the shift of a functional group from one position to another within a molecule (Section 21-2).*

► *Step 9 is the second of two glycolytic steps in which a high-energy phosphate compound, that is, "energy-rich" compound, is formed; the other step was Step 6. In the next step, energy from the high-energy phosphate compound will be used to convert ADP and ATP.*

► *An* enol *(from* ene + ol *), as in phospho*enol*pyruvate, is a compound in which an —OH group is attached to a carbon atom involved in a carbon–carbon double bond. Note that in phosphoenolpyruvate, the —OH group has been phosphorylated.*

▶ *Step 10 is the second of two steps in which ATP is formed from ADP. This same process also occurred in Step 7.*

Step 10:   **Phosphorylation of ADP:** *Formation of Pyruvate.* In this step, substrate-level phosphorylation again occurs. Phosphoenolpyruvate transfers its high-energy phosphate group to an ADP molecule to produce ATP and pyruvate. ◀

Phosphoenolpyruvate ◀   Pyruvate

▶ *Phosphoenolpyruvate is pronounced "foss-foe-ee-nawl-pie-roo-vate."*

The enzyme involved, *pyruvate kinase,* requires both Mg^{2+} and K^+ ions for its activity. Again, because two C_3 molecules are reacting, two ATP molecules are produced.

ATP molecules are involved in Steps 1, 3, 7, and 10 of glycolysis. Considering these steps collectively shows that there is a net gain of two ATP molecules for every glucose molecule converted into two pyruvates (Table 24-1). Though useful, this is a small amount of ATP compared to that generated in oxidative phosphorylation (Section 23-9).

The net overall equation for the process of glycolysis is

$$\text{Glucose} + 2NAD^+ + 2ADP + 2P_i \longrightarrow$$
$$2 \text{ pyruvate} + 2NADH + 2ATP + 2H^+ + 2H_2O$$

▶ **Table 24-1   ATP Production and Consumption During Glycolysis**

Step	Reaction	ATP Change per Glucose
1	Glucose → glucose 6-phosphate	−1
3	Fructose 6-phosphate → fructose 1,6-bisphosphate	−1
7	2(1,3-Bisphosphoglycerate → 3-phosphoglycerate)	+2
10	2(Phosphoenolpyruvate → pyruvate)	+2
		Net +2

EXAMPLE 24-2

Recognizing Structural Characteristics of Glycolysis Intermediates

Specify the number of carbon atoms present and the number of phosphate groups present in each of the following glycolysis intermediates:

a. Glucose 6-phosphate
b. Fructose 1,6-bisphosphate
c. Glyceraldehyde 3-phosphate
d. 3-Phosphoglycerate

Solution

a. Glucose is a hexose. Glucose 6-phosphate is a C_6 *molecule* that carries *one phosphate group,* attached to carbon 6.
b. Fructose is also a hexose. Fructose 1,6-bisphosphate is a C_6 *molecule* that carries *two phosphate groups,* one attached to carbon 1 and the other attached to carbon 6.
c. Glyceraldehyde 3-phosphate is a C_3 *molecule* with *one phosphate group,* attached to carbon 3.
d. 3-Phosphoglycerate, like glyceraldehyde, is a C_3 *molecule.* It has *one phosphate group,* attached to carbon 3.

EXAMPLE 24-3

Recognizing Reaction Types and Events That Occur in the Various Steps of Glycolysis

Indicate at what step in the glycolysis pathway each of the following events occurs:

a. First phosphorylation of ADP occurs.
b. First "energy-rich" compound is produced.
c. Second "energy-rich" compound undergoes reaction.
d. First isomerization reaction occurs.

Solution

a. Phosphorylation of ADP produces ATP with the added phosphate coming from a glycolysis intermediate. This process occurs for the first time in *Step 7*, where 1,3-bisphosphoglycerate is converted to 3-phosphoglycerate. It occurs a second time in *Step 10*.
b. In carbohydrate metabolism, an "energy-rich" compound is a high-energy phosphate. Two such compounds are produced during glycolysis, the first in *Step 6* and the second in *Step 9*. The *Step 6* compound is 1,3-bisphosphoglycerate.
c. The second "energy-rich" compound is phosphoenolpyruvate, which is produced in *Step 9* and undergoes reaction in *Step 10*.
d. There are three isomerization reactions in glycolysis. They occur in *Steps 2, 5, and 8*. In the first occurrence, *Step 2*, glucose 6-phosphate is converted to fructose 6-phosphate. Glucose and fructose are isomeric hexose (Section 18-8) molecules.

EXAMPLE 24-4

Relating Enzyme Names and Functions to Steps in the Process of Glycolysis

Relate the names and functions of the following glycolytic enzymes to steps in the process of glycolysis:

a. Phosphofructokinase
b. Phosphoglyceromutase
c. Triosephosphate isomerase
d. Enolase

Solution

a. A kinase is an enzyme that is involved with phosphate group transfer. The phosphofructo portion of the enzyme name refers to a fructose phosphate. Transfer of a phosphate group to a fructose phosphate occurs in *Step 3*. Fructose 6-phosphate is converted to fructose 1,6-bisphosphate.
b. A mutase is an enzyme that shifts the position of a functional group within a molecule. Such a functional group shift occurs in *Step 8*, where 3-phosphoglycerate is isomerized to 2-phosphoglycerate. The phosphoglycerol portion of the enzyme name indicates that a glycerate phosphate is the substrate for the enzyme.
c. A triosephosphate isomerase effects the isomerization of a triose. Such a process occurs in *Step 5*, where dihydroxyacetone phosphate (a ketone) is converted to glyceraldehyde 3-phosphate (an aldehyde). Ketones and aldehydes with the same number of carbon atoms are often isomers.
d. The only enol species in glycolysis is the compound phosphoenolpyruvate produced in *Step 9* through a dehydration reaction that introduces a carbon–carbon double bond in the molecule. An enolase effects such a change.

Entry of Galactose and Fructose into Glycolysis

The breakdown products from carbohydrate digestion are glucose, galactose, and fructose (Section 24-1). Both galactose and fructose are converted, in the liver, to intermediates that enter into the glycolysis pathway.

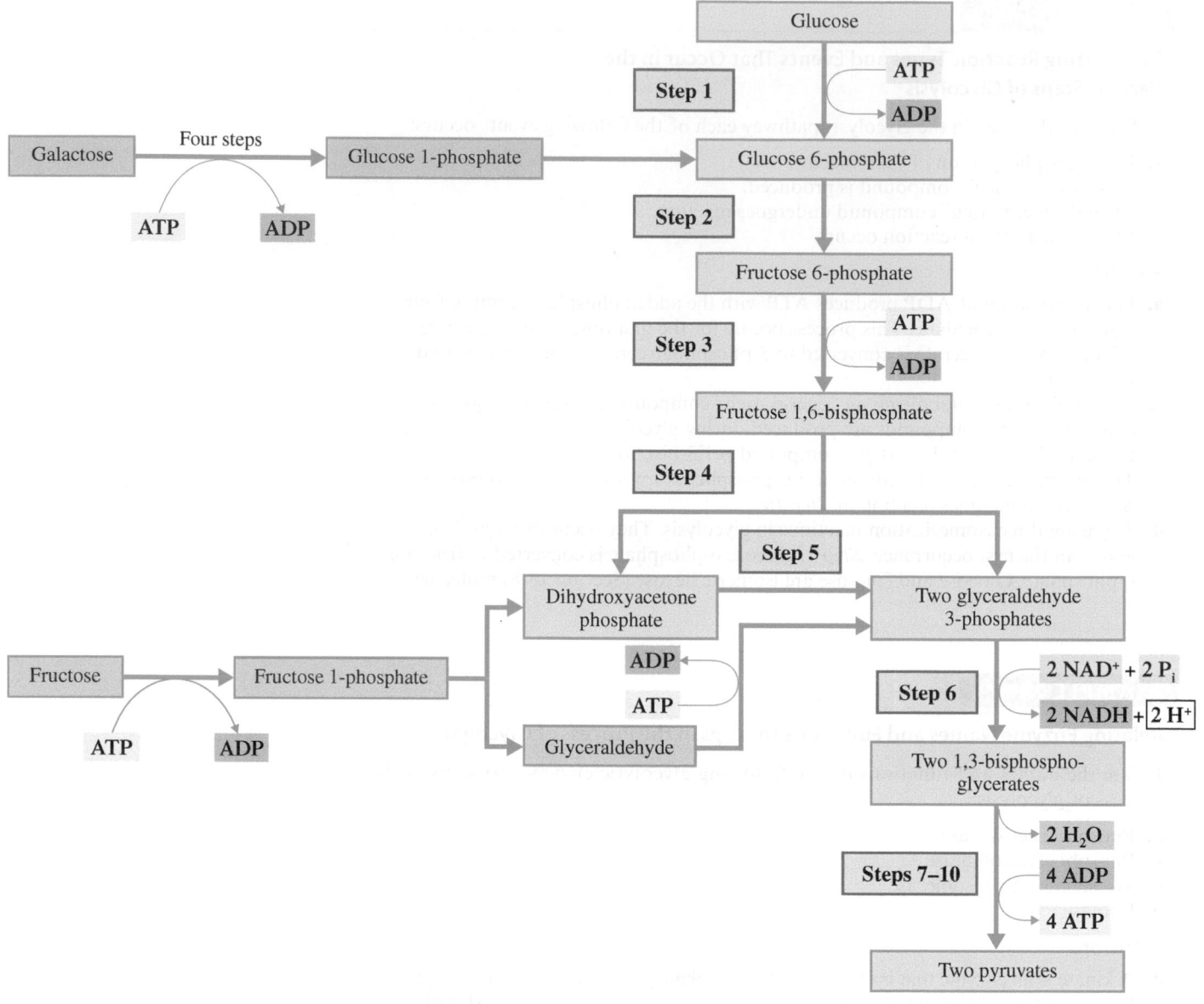

Figure 24-5 Entry points for fructose and galactose into the glycolysis pathway.

The entry of galactose into the glycolytic pathway begins with its conversion to glucose 1-phosphate (a four-step sequence), which is then converted to glucose 6-phosphate, a glycolysis intermediate (Figure 24-5).

The entry of fructose into the glycolytic pathway involves phosphorylation by ATP to produce fructose 1-phosphate, which is then split into two trioses—glyceraldehyde and dihydroxyacetone phosphate. Dihydroxyacetone phosphate enters glycolysis directly; glyceraldehyde must be phosphorylated by ATP to glyceraldehyde 3-phosphate before it enters the pathway (Figure 24-5).

Regulation of Glycolysis

Glycolysis, like all metabolic pathways, must have control mechanisms associated with it. In glycolysis, the control points are Steps 1, 3, and 10 (see Figure 24-3).

Step 1, the conversion of glucose to glucose 6-phosphate, involves the enzyme *hexokinase*. This particular enzyme is inhibited by glucose 6-phosphate, the substance produced by its action (feedback inhibition; Section 21-9).

At Step 3, where fructose 6-phosphate is converted to fructose 1,6-bisphosphate by the enzyme *phosphofructokinase,* high concentrations of ATP and citrate inhibit enzyme activity. A high ATP concentration, which is characteristic of a state of low energy consumption, thus stops glycolysis at the fructose 6-phosphate stage. This stoppage also causes increases in glucose 6-phosphate stores because glucose 6-phosphate is in equilibrium with fructose 6-phosphate.

The third control point involves the last step of glycolysis, the conversion of phosphoenolpyruvate to pyruvate. *Pyruvate kinase,* the enzyme needed at this point, is inhibited by high ATP concentrations. Both pyruvate kinase (Step 10) and phosphofructokinase (Step 3) are allosteric enzymes (Section 21-8).

Section 24-2 Quick Quiz

1. Which of the following statements concerning glycolysis is *correct*?
   a. The pathway for the process is a cyclic pathway.
   b. It occurs in the mitochondrial matrix.
   c. Molecular O_2 is not needed for the process to occur.
   d. no correct response
2. The overall process of glycolysis converts a C_6 molecule into
   a. two C_3 molecules
   b. three C_2 molecules
   c. a different C_6 molecule
   d. no correct response
3. What are the total number of steps in the C_6 and C_3 stages of glycolysis, respectively?
   a. 5 and 5
   b. 4 and 6
   c. 3 and 7
   d. no correct response
4. The first two intermediates in the process of glycolysis are, respectively
   a. glucose 6-phosphate and glucose 1-phosphate
   b. glucose 1-phosphate and fructose 6-phosphate
   c. glucose 6-phosphate and fructose 6-phosphate
   d. no correct response
5. Pyruvate, the end product of glycolysis, is a
   a. three-carbon keto acid
   b. three-carbon hydroxy acid
   c. two-carbon keto acid
   d. no correct response
6. When one glucose molecule is processed through the glycolysis pathway, relative to ATP production/consumption, there is a
   a. net loss of two ATP
   b. net gain of two ATP
   c. net gain of four ATP
   d. no correct response
7. In what two steps of glycolysis is ATP converted to ADP?
   a. Steps 1 and 2
   b. Steps 1 and 3
   c. Steps 7 and 10
   d. no correct response

Answers: 1. c; 2. a; 3. b; 4. c; 5. a; 6. b; 7. b

24-3 Fates of Pyruvate

LEARNING FOCUS

Be familiar with the common fates for pyruvate molecules produced by glycolysis.

The production of pyruvate from glucose (glycolysis) occurs in a similar manner in most cells. In contrast, the fate of the pyruvate so produced varies with cellular conditions and the nature of the organism. Three common fates for pyruvate, all of importance, exist.

Figure 24-6 The three common fates of pyruvate generated by glycolysis.

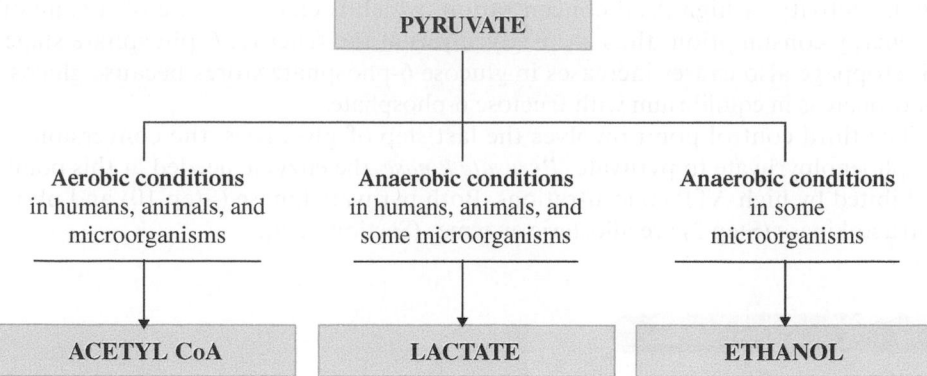

They are conversion to acetyl CoA, conversion to lactate, and conversion to ethanol. As is shown in Figure 24-6, acetyl CoA formation requires aerobic (oxygen-rich) conditions, lactate and ethanol formation occur under anaerobic (oxygen-deficient) conditions, and ethanol formation is limited to some microorganisms. ◄

A key concept in considering these fates of pyruvate is the need for a continuous supply of NAD^+ for glycolysis. As glucose is oxidized to pyruvate in glycolysis, NAD^+ is reduced to NADH.

$$\text{Glucose} + 2NAD^+ \xrightarrow[\quad 2ADP + 2P_i \qquad 2ATP \quad]{} 2 \text{ pyruvate} + 2NADH + 2H^+$$

It is significant that each of the three pathways for processing pyruvate, which will now be discussed, have a provision for regenerating NAD^+ from NADH so that glycolysis can continue.

Oxidation to Acetyl CoA

Under *aerobic* (oxygen-rich) conditions, pyruvate is oxidized to acetyl CoA. Pyruvate formed in the cytosol through glycolysis crosses the two mitochondrial membranes and enters the mitochondrial matrix, where the oxidation takes place. ◄ The overall reaction, in simplified terms, is

$$\underset{\text{Pyruvate}}{CH_3-\overset{\overset{\textstyle O}{\|}}{C}-COO^-} + CoA-SH + NAD^+ \xrightarrow[\text{complex}]{\overset{\text{Pyruvate}}{\text{dehydrogenase}}} \underset{\text{Acetyl CoA}}{CH_3-\overset{\overset{\textstyle O}{\|}}{C}-S-CoA} + NADH + CO_2$$

This reaction, which involves both oxidation and decarboxylation (CO_2 is produced), is far more complex than the simple stoichiometry of the equation suggests. The enzyme complex involved contains three different enzymes, each with numerous subunits. The overall reaction process involves four separate steps and requires NAD^+, CoA–SH, FAD, and two other coenzymes (lipoic acid and thiamin pyrophosphate, the latter derived from the B vitamin thiamin).

Most acetyl CoA molecules produced from pyruvate enter the citric acid cycle. Citric acid cycle operations change more NAD^+ to its reduced form, NADH. The NADH from glycolysis, from the conversion of pyruvate to acetyl CoA, and from the citric acid cycle enters the electron transport chain directly (Section 23-8) or indirectly (Section 24-4). In the ETC, electrons from NADH are transferred to O_2, and the NADH is changed back to NAD^+. The NAD^+ needed for glycolysis, pyruvate–acetyl CoA conversion, and the citric acid cycle is regenerated. ◄

The net overall reaction for processing one glucose molecule to two molecules of acetyl CoA is

$$\text{Glucose} + 2ADP + 2P_i + 4NAD^+ + 2CoA-SH \longrightarrow$$
$$2 \text{ acetyl CoA} + 2CO_2 + 2ATP + 4NADH + 4H^+ + 2H_2O$$

Margin notes:

▶ *An additional fate for pyruvate is conversion to oxaloacetate. This fate for pyruvate, which occurs during the process called gluconeogenesis, is discussed in Section 24-6.*

▶ *Pyruvate, the end product of glycolysis, can leave the cytosol, cross the two mitochondrial membranes, and enter the mitochondrial matrix. None of the glycolysis intermediates can do this. The glycolysis intermediates are all phosphorylated substances; pyruvate is not phosphorylated.*

▶ *Not all acetyl CoA produced from pyruvate enters the citric acid cycle. Particularly when high levels of acetyl CoA are produced (from excess ingestion of dietary carbohydrates), some acetyl CoA is used as the starting material for the production of the fatty acids needed for fat (triacylglycerol) formation (Section 25-7).*

Fermentation Processes

When the body becomes oxygen deficient (anaerobic conditions), such as during strenuous exercise, the electron transport chain process slows down because its last step is dependent on oxygen. The result of this "slowing down" is a buildup in NADH concentration (it is not being consumed as fast) and a decreased amount of available NAD^+ (it is not being produced as fast). Decreased NAD^+ concentration then negatively affects the rate of glycolysis. An alternative method for conversion of NADH to NAD^+—a method that does not require oxygen—is needed if glycolysis is to continue, it being the only available source of *new* ATP under these conditions.

Fermentation processes solve this problem. **Fermentation** *is a biochemical process by which NADH is oxidized to NAD^+ without the need for oxygen.* Two fermentation processes—lactate fermentation and ethanol fermentation—are now considered. Both types of fermentation occur within cellular cytosol rather than within a mitochondria.

Lactate Fermentation

Lactate fermentation *is the enzymatic anaerobic reduction of pyruvate to lactate.* The equation for lactate formation from pyruvate is

$$CH_3-\underset{\underset{\text{Pyruvate}}{}}{\overset{\overset{O}{\|}}{C}}-COO^- + \boxed{NADH} + \boxed{H^+} \xrightarrow[\text{dehydrogenase}]{\text{Lactate}} CH_3-\underset{\underset{\text{Lactate}}{}}{\overset{\overset{OH}{|}}{C}H}-COO^- + \boxed{NAD^+}$$

The sole purpose of this process is the conversion of NADH to NAD^+. The lactate so formed is converted back to pyruvate when aerobic conditions are again established in a cell (Section 24-6).

The chemical structure of lactate closely resembles that of pyruvate and also glycerate. Lactate, pyruvate, and glycerate are all derivatives of propionic acid, the three-carbon saturated monocarboxylic acid, as is shown in Figure 24-7.

As mentioned previously, the purpose of lactate formation is to replenish NAD^+ supplies; such supplies are needed for Step 6 of glycolysis. This "recycling" of NAD^+ is shown diagrammatically in Figure 24-8.

Working muscles often produce lactate. If strenuous work (or exercise) continues for too long, lactate buildup contributes to muscle soreness, muscle cramping, and fatigue. The focus on relevancy feature Chemical Connections 24-A—Lactate Accumulation—explores further the topic of lactate accumulation in muscles. ◀

The net equation for glycolysis (Section 24-2) is

$$\text{Glucose} + \boxed{2NAD^+} + \boxed{2ADP} + 2P_i \longrightarrow 2\text{ pyruvate} + \boxed{2NADH} + \boxed{2ATP} + 2H^+ + 2H_2O$$

▶ *An interesting phenomena relating to lactate production involves freshwater turtles and their survival for several months underneath frozen lakes during wintertime. Under such conditions they have adapted to surviving without oxygen. Studies show that their brain activity is very minimal and their hearts beat only once in a 10-minute period. The biochemistry associated with this situation involves lactate fermentation. Key metabolic reactions that do occur within the turtle involve use of a small amount of glycogen; fat stores cannot be used because fat metabolism requires the use of oxygen. The glycogen is converted to glucose (glycogenolysis; no oxygen required; Section 24-5) and the glucose is converted to pyruvate (glycolysis; no oxygen required) and then lactate fermentation (no oxygen required) occurs. An undesirable decrease in blood pH that usually occurs with lactate accumulation is mitigated by buffering action (Section 10-12) involving release of minerals deposited in the turtle's shell; some lactate is also deposited into the shell. Chemistry associated with a turtle's shell is thus the key to the turtle's survival underneath the ice.*

Figure 24-7 Structural relationships among the carboxylate ions lactate, glycerate, and pyruvate.

Figure 24-8 Anaerobic lactate formation allows for "recycling" of NAD⁺, providing the NAD⁺ needed for Step 6 of glycolysis.

The net equation for conversion of pyruvate to lactate is

$$\text{Pyruvate} + \text{NADH} + \text{H}^+ \longrightarrow \text{lactate} + \text{NAD}^+$$

Adding these two equations together, and taking into account that one glucose produces two pyruvates and therefore two lactates, yields the following equation for the overall conversion of glucose to lactate. ◄

$$\text{Glucose} + \text{2ADP} + 2\text{P}_i \longrightarrow 2 \text{ lactate} + \text{2ATP} + 2\text{H}_2\text{O}$$

There is a net gain of two ATP for the conversion of glucose to two lactates.

Note that NADH and NAD⁺ do not appear in this equation, even though the process cannot proceed without them. The NADH generated during glycolysis (Step 6) is consumed in the conversion of pyruvate to lactate. Thus there is no net oxidation–reduction in the conversion of glucose to lactate.

► *Red blood cells have no mitochondria and therefore always process pyruvate to lactate.*

Ethanol Fermentation

Under anaerobic conditions, several simple organisms, including yeast, possess the ability to regenerate NAD⁺ through ethanol, rather than lactate, production. Such a process is called ethanol fermentation. **Ethanol fermentation** *is the enzymatic anaerobic conversion of pyruvate to ethanol and carbon dioxide.* Ethanol fermentation involving yeast causes bread and related products to rise as a result of CO_2 bubbles being released during baking. ◄ Beer, wine, and other alcoholic drinks are produced by ethanol fermentation of the sugars in grain and fruit products.

► *With bread and other related products obtained using yeast, the ethanol produced by fermentation evaporates during baking.*

The first step in conversion of pyruvate to ethanol is a decarboxylation reaction to produce acetaldehyde.

$$\underset{\text{Pyruvate}}{\text{CH}_3\text{—}\overset{\overset{\text{O}}{\|}}{\text{C}}\text{—COO}^-} + \text{H}^+ \xrightarrow[\text{decarboxylase}]{\text{Pyruvate}} \underset{\text{Acetaldehyde}}{\text{CH}_3\text{—}\overset{\overset{\text{O}}{\|}}{\text{C}}\text{—H}} + \text{CO}_2$$

The second step involves acetaldehyde reduction to produce ethanol.

$$\underset{\text{Acetaldehyde}}{\text{CH}_3\text{—}\overset{\overset{\text{O}}{\|}}{\text{C}}\text{—H}} + \text{NAD H} + \text{H}^+ \xrightarrow[\text{dehydrogenase}]{\text{Alcohol}} \underset{\text{Ethanol}}{\text{CH}_3\text{—}\overset{\overset{\text{O H}}{|}}{\underset{\overset{|}{\text{H}}}{\text{C}}}\text{—H}} + \text{NAD}^+$$

Lactate Accumulation

During strenuous exercise, conditions in muscle cells change from aerobic to anaerobic as the oxygen supply becomes inadequate to meet demand. Such conditions cause pyruvate to be converted to lactate rather than acetyl CoA. (Lactate production can also be high at the start of strenuous exercise before the delivery of oxygen is stepped up via an increased respiration rate.)

The resulting lactate begins to accumulate in the cytosol of cells where it is produced. Some lactate diffuses out of the cells into the blood, where it contributes to a slight decrease in blood pH. This lower pH triggers fast breathing, which helps supply more oxygen to the cells.

Lactate accumulation and pH change are the cause of muscle pain and cramping during prolonged, strenuous exercise. As a result of such cramping, muscles may be stiff and sore the next day. Regular, hard exercise increases the efficiency with which oxygen is delivered to the body. Thus athletes can function longer than nonathletes under aerobic conditions without lactate production.

Recent research indicates that pH change in muscle cells (H^+ accumulation) may be as important as lactate accumulation as a cause of muscle pain. Hydrogen ions are produced when NAD^+ is reduced to NADH when glucose (as well as fats) is used by the body as a source of energy.

$$NAD^+ + 2H^+ + 2e^- \longrightarrow NADH + H^+$$

Lactate production consumes hydrogen ions as the reverse of the preceding reaction occurs. During strenuous exercise, lactate production (H^+ ion consumption) may not be fast enough to keep up with H^+ ion production.

Lactate accumulation can also occur in heart muscle if it experiences decreased oxygen supply (from artery blockage). The heart muscle experiences cramps and stops beating (cardiac arrest). Massage of heart muscle often reduces such cramps, just as it does for skeletal muscle, and it is sometimes possible to start the heart beating again by using such a technique. The pain associated with a heart attack is related to lactate and H^+ accumulation.

Hunters are usually aware that meat from game animals that have been run to exhaustion usually tastes sour; lactate accumulation is the reason for this problem.

Lactate formation is also relevant to a practice that short-distance sprinters often use just prior to a race, the practice of hyperventilation. Rapid breathing (hyperventilation) raises slightly the pH of blood. The CO_2 loss associated with the rapid breathing causes carbonic acid (H_2CO_3) present in the blood to dissociate in CO_2 and H_2O to replace the lost CO_2.

$$H_2CO_3 \rightleftharpoons CO_2 + H_2O$$

A decreased amount of carbonic acid causes blood pH to rise, which makes the blood slightly more basic. A few seconds before the start of the race, sprinters decrease the amount of CO_2 in their lungs through hyperventilation, making their blood a little bit more basic. This slight increase in basicity means the runner can absorb slightly more lactic acid before the blood pH drops to the point where cramping becomes a problem. Having such an advantage for only a few seconds in a short race can be helpful.

In diagnostic medicine, lactate levels in blood can often be used to determine the severity of a patient's condition. Higher than normal lactate levels are a sign of impaired oxygen delivery to tissue. Conditions that can cause higher lactate levels include lung disease and congestive heart failure.

Premature infants with underdeveloped lungs are often given increased amounts of oxygen to minimize lactate accumulation. They are also often given bicarbonate (HCO_3^-) solution to counteract the acidity change in the blood that accompanies lactate buildup.

Strenuous muscular activity can result in lactate accumulation.

© Pitsanu Kraichana/Shutterstock.com

The overall equation for the conversion of pyruvate to ethanol (the sum of the two steps) is

$$\text{Pyruvate} + 2H^+ + \boxed{\text{NADH}} \xrightarrow{\text{Two steps}} \text{Ethanol} + \boxed{NAD^+} + CO_2$$

An overall reaction for the production of ethanol from glucose is obtained by combining the reaction for the conversion of pyruvate with the net reaction for glycolysis (Section 24-2).

Figure 24-9 All three of the common fates of pyruvate from glycolysis provide for the regeneration of NAD$^+$ from NADH.

$$\text{Glucose} + \boxed{2\text{ADP}} + 2\text{P}_i \longrightarrow 2\text{ ethanol} + 2\text{CO}_2 + \boxed{2\text{ATP}} + 2\text{H}_2\text{O}$$

Again note that NADH and NAD$^+$ do not appear in the final equation; they are both generated and consumed.

Figure 24-9 summarizes the relationship between the fates of pyruvate and the regeneration of NAD$^+$ from NADH.

EXAMPLE 24-5

Identifying Characteristics of the Three Common Pathways by Which Pyruvate Is Converted to Other Products

Which of the three common metabolic pathways for pyruvate is compatible with each of the following characterizations concerning the reactions that pyruvate undergoes?

a. CO$_2$ is not a product for this pathway.
b. A C$_3$ molecule is a product for this pathway.
c. NAD$^+$ is needed as an oxidizing agent for this pathway.
d. A C$_2$ molecule is a product under anaerobic reaction conditions for this pathway.

Solution

a. CO$_2$ is a product for both acetyl CoA formation and ethanol fermentation. In both of these processes, the C$_3$ pyruvate is converted to a C$_2$ species and CO$_2$. No CO$_2$ production occurs during *lactate fermentation*, as C$_3$ pyruvate is converted to C$_3$ lactate.
b. The only pathway that produces a C$_3$ molecule is *lactate fermentation*. In the other two pathways, a C$_2$ molecule and CO$_2$ are produced.
c. NAD$^+$, as an oxidizing agent, is needed in pathways that function under aerobic conditions. NADH, as a reducing agent, is needed in pathways that function under anaerobic conditions. The only pathway that involves aerobic conditions is *acetyl CoA formation*.
d. *Alcohol fermentation,* an anaerobic process, produces ethanol, a C$_2$ molecule. The other anaerobic process, lactate fermentation, produces the C$_3$ molecule lactate.

Section 24-3 Quick Quiz

1. In the human body, under oxygen-rich and oxygen-poor conditions, respectively, pyruvate is converted to
   a. lactate and ethanol
   b. lactate and acetyl CoA
   c. acetyl CoA and lactate
   d. no correct response
2. In which of the following conversions is CO$_2$ produced?
   a. lactate to pyruvate
   b. pyruvate to acetyl CoA
   c. pyruvate to lactate
   d. no correct response

3. The major purpose of lactate fermentation is the production of
   a. acetyl CoA
   b. O_2
   c. NAD^+
   d. no correct response
4. Which of the following processes involves the conversion of a C_3 molecule to another C_3 molecule?
   a. lactate fermentation
   b. ethanol fermentation
   c. pyruvate oxidation to acetyl CoA
   d. no correct response
5. Accumulation of which of the following substances in muscle cells is the cause of stiffness and soreness after vigorous exercise?
   a. pyruvate
   b. lactate
   c. acetyl CoA
   d. no correct response

Answers: 1. c; 2. b; 3. c; 4. a; 5. b

24-4 ATP Production from the Complete Oxidation of Glucose

LEARNING FOCUS
Be able to calculate an ATP production value for the complete oxidation of a glucose molecule.

Using assembled energy production figures for glycolysis, oxidation of pyruvate to acetyl CoA, the citric acid cycle, and the electron transport chain—with one added piece of information—gives the ATP yield for the *complete* oxidation of one molecule of glucose.

The new piece of information involves the NADH produced during Step 6 of glycolysis. This NADH, produced in the cytosol, cannot *directly* participate in the electron transport chain because mitochondria are impermeable to NADH (and NAD^+). A transport system shuttles the electrons from NADH, but not NADH itself, across the outer membrane. This shuttle involves dihydroxyacetone phosphate (a glycolysis intermediate) and glycerol 3-phosphate.

The first step in the shuttle is the cytosolic reduction of dihydroxyacetone phosphate by NADH to produce glycerol 3-phosphate and NAD^+ (Figure 24-10). Glycerol 3-phosphate then crosses the outer mitochondrial membrane, where it is reoxidized to dihydroxyacetone phosphate. The oxidizing agent is FAD rather than NAD^+. The regenerated dihydroxyacetone phosphate diffuses out of the mitochondrion and returns to the cytosol for participation in another "turn" of the shuttle. The $FADH_2$ coproduced in the mitochondrial reaction can participate in the electron transport chain reactions. The net reaction of this shuttle process is

$$\underset{\text{(cytosolic)}}{\text{NADH}} + H^+ + \underset{\text{(mitochondrial)}}{\text{FAD}} \longrightarrow \underset{\text{(cytosolic)}}{\text{NAD}^+} + \underset{\text{(mitochondrial)}}{\text{FADH}_2}$$

The consequence of this reaction is that only 1.5 rather than 2.5 molecules of ATP are formed for each cytosolic NADH, because $FADH_2$ yields one less ATP than does NADH in the electron transport chain. ◀

Table 24-2 shows ATP production for the complete oxidation of a molecule of glucose. The final number is 30 ATP, 26 of which come from the oxidative phosphorylation associated with the electron transport chain. This total of 30 ATP for complete oxidation contrasts markedly with a total of 2 ATP for oxidation of glucose to lactate and 2 ATP for oxidation of glucose to ethanol. Neither of these latter processes involves the citric acid cycle or the electron transport chain. Thus the aerobic

▶ *The continual interconversion back and forth between ATP and ADP in the human body is a highly efficient recycling system for these molecules. Without such recycling body operation would not be possible because synthetic requirements for newly formed ATP could not be met. The mathematics of ATP production, without recycling, is an impossible situation.*

It has been estimated, through calculation, that an average adult human body (70 kg mass) consumes approximately 65 kg (yes, kilograms) of ATP per day, which is a mass almost equal to that of body mass. Yet, there is only about 50 g (yes, grams) of ATP/ADP present in the body at any given time. For these numbers to be compatible with each other, each ATP molecule in the body must be recycled about 1300 times per day to meet body energy requirements.

$$ATP \rightarrow ADP$$
$$\uparrow \qquad \downarrow$$
$$ADP \leftarrow ATP$$

Figure 24-10 The dihydroxy-acetone phosphate–glycerol 3-phosphate shuttle.

> **Table 24-2** **Production of ATP from the Complete Oxidation of One Glucose Molecule in a Skeletal Muscle Cell**

Reaction	Comments	Yield of ATP
Glycolysis		
glucose → glucose 6-phosphate	consumes 1 ATP	−1
fructose 6-phosphate → fructose 1,6-bisphosphate	consumes 1 ATP	−1
2(glyceraldehyde 3-phosphate → 1,3-bisphosphoglycerate)	each produces 1 cytosolic NADH	—
2(1,3-bisphosphoglycerate → 3-phosphoglycerate)	each produces 1 ATP	+2
2(phosphoenolpyruvate → pyruvate)	each produces 1 ATP	+2
Oxidation of Pyruvate		
2(pyruvate → acetyl CoA + CO_2)	each produces 1 NADH	—
Citric Acid Cycle		
2(isocitrate → α-ketoglutarate + CO_2)	each produces 1 NADH	—
2(α-ketoglutarate → succinyl CoA + CO_2)	each produces 1 NADH	—
2(succinyl CoA → succinate)	each produces 1 GTP	+2
2(succinate → fumarate)	each produces 1 $FADH_2$	—
2(malate → oxaloacetate)	each produces 1 NADH	—
Electron Transport Chain and Oxidative Phosphorylation		
2 cytosolic NADH formed in glycolysis	each produces 1.5 ATP	+3
2 NADH formed in the oxidation of pyruvate	each produces 2.5 ATP	+5
2 $FADH_2$ formed in the citric acid cycle	each produces 1.5 ATP	+3
6 NADH formed in the citric acid cycle	each produces 2.5 ATP	+15
Net Production of ATP		+30

oxidation of glucose is 15 times more efficient in the production of ATP than the anaerobic lactate and ethanol processes.

The production of 30 ATP molecules per glucose (Table 24-2) is for those cells where the dihydroxyacetone phosphate–glycerol 3-phosphate shuttle operates (skeletal muscle and nerve cells). In certain other cells, particularly heart and liver cells, a more complex shuttle system called the malate–aspartate shuttle functions. In this shuttle, 2.5 ATP molecules result from 1 cytosolic NADH, which changes the total ATP production to 32 molecules per glucose.

The net overall reaction for the *complete* metabolism (oxidation) of a glucose molecule is the simple equation

$$\text{Glucose} + 6O_2 + 30ADP + 30P_i \longrightarrow 6CO_2 + 6H_2O + 30\ ATP$$

Note that substances such as NADH, NAD^+, and $FADH_2$ are not part of this equation. Why? They cancel out—that is, they are consumed in one step (reactant) and regenerated in another step (product). Note also what the net equation does not acknowledge: the many dozens of reactions that are needed to generate the 30 molecules of ATP.

Section 24-4 Quick Quiz

1. For the complete oxidation of a glucose molecule, the majority of the ATP produced comes from which of the following phases in the oxidation process?
   a. glycolysis
   b. citric acid cycle
   c. electron transport chain
   d. no correct response
2. The net yield of ATP for the complete oxidation of one molecule of glucose is
   a. 12 ATP
   b. 24 ATP
   c. 30 ATP
   d. no correct response
3. The net yield of ATP per glucose molecule in the process of glycolysis is
   a. 12 ATP
   b. 14 ATP
   c. 18 ATP
   d. no correct response

Answers: 1. c; 2. c; 3. d

24-5 Glycogen Synthesis and Degradation

LEARNING FOCUS

Be familiar with how the processes of glycogenesis and glycogenolysis relate to the molecule glycogen; be familiar with the intermediate compounds associated with these two processes.

Glycogen, a branched polymeric form of glucose (Section 18-15), is the storage form of carbohydrates in humans and animals. It is found primarily in muscle and liver tissue. In muscles, it is the source of glucose needed for glycolysis. In the liver, it is the source of glucose needed to maintain normal glucose levels in the blood.

Glycogenesis

Glycogenesis *is the metabolic pathway by which glycogen is synthesized from glucose 6-phosphate.* Glycogenesis involves three reactions (steps).

Step 1:   **Isomerization**: *Formation of Glucose 1-phosphate.* The starting material for this step is not glucose itself but, rather, glucose 6-phosphate (available from the first step of glycolysis). The enzyme *phosphoglucomutase* effects the change from a 6-phosphate to a 1-phosphate.

Glucose 6-phosphate   Glucose 1-phosphate

Step 2: **Activation:** *Formation of UDP-glucose.* Glucose 1-phosphate from Step 1 must be activated before it can be added to a growing glycogen chain. The activator is the high-energy compound UTP (uridine triphosphate). A UMP is transferred to glucose 1-phosphate, and the resulting PP$_i$ is hydrolyzed to 2P$_i$.

Glucose 1-phosphate

Uridine triphosphate (UTP)

▶ *UDP-glucose is the activated carrier of glucose in glycogen synthesis (glycogenesis).*

Uridine diphosphate glucose (UDP-glucose) ◀

Step 3: **Linkage to Chain:** *Glucose Transfer to a Glycogen Chain.* The glucose unit of UDP-glucose is then attached to the end of a glycogen chain.

$$\text{UDP-glucose} + (\text{glucose})_n \xrightarrow[\substack{\text{Glycogen} \\ \text{chain}}]{\substack{\text{Glycogen} \\ \text{synthase}}} (\text{glucose})_{n+1} + \text{UDP}$$

Glycogen with an additional glucose unit

In a subsequent reaction, the UDP produced in Step 3 is converted back to UTP, which can then react with another glucose 1-phosphate (Step 2). The conversion reaction requires ATP.

$$\text{UDP} + \text{ATP} \longrightarrow \text{UTP} + \text{ADP}$$

Adding a single glucose unit to a growing glycogen chain requires the investment of two ATP molecules: one in the formation of glucose 6-phosphate and one in the regeneration of UTP.

Glycogenolysis

Glycogenolysis *is the metabolic pathway by which glucose 6-phosphate is produced from glycogen.* This process is not simply the reverse of glycogen synthesis (glycogenesis) because it does not require UTP or UDP molecules. Glycogenolysis is a two-step process rather than a three-step process.

▶ *The chain cleavage reaction that occurs in Step 1 that releases a glucose residue is called* phosphorolysis *by analogy with the process of* hydrolysis, *which also involves breaking a molecule into two parts. Here, it is P$_i$ rather than H$_2$O that participates in the bond breaking. A phosphoryl group is added to the released glucose residue.*

A phosphorylase, *the type of enzyme needed in step 1, is an enzyme that catalyzes the cleavage of a bond by P$_i$ (in contrast to a hydrolase, which effects bond cleavage by water).*

Step 1: *Phosphorolysis: Formation of Glucose-1-phosphate.* The enzyme glycogen phosphorylase effects the removal of an end glucose unit from a glycogen molecule as glucose 1-phosphate. ◀

$$(\text{Glucose})_n + \text{P}_i \xrightarrow[\text{Glycogen}]{\substack{\text{Glycogen} \\ \text{Phosphorylase}}} (\text{glucose})_{n-1} + \text{glucose 1-phosphate}$$

Glycogen with one fewer glucose unit

Step 2:   ***Isomerization::*** *Formation of Glucose 6-phosphate.* The enzyme phosphogluco-mutase catalyzes the isomerization process whereby the phosphate group of glucose 1-phosphate is moved to the carbon 6 position.

$$\text{Glucose 1-phosphate} \xrightleftharpoons{\text{Phosphogluco-mutase}} \text{glucose 6-phosphate}$$

This process is the reverse of the first step of glycogenesis.

Neither ATP nor any of the other nucleotide triphosphates is needed in the reactions of glycogenolysis.

In muscle and brain cells, an immediate need for energy is the stimulus that initiates glycogenolysis. The glucose 6-phosphate that is produced directly enters the glycolysis pathway at Step 2 (Figure 24-3), and its multistep conversion to pyruvate begins. A low level of glucose is the stimulus that initiates glycogenolysis in liver cells. Here, the glucose 6-phosphate produced must be converted to free glucose before it can enter the bloodstream, as glucose 6-phosphate cannot cross cell membranes (Section 24-2). This change is effected by the enzyme *glucose 6-phosphatase,* an enzyme found in liver cells but not in muscle cells or brain cells. ◄

$$\text{Glucose 6-phosphate} + H_2O \xrightarrow{\substack{\text{Glucose} \\ \text{6-phosphatase}}} \text{glucose} + P_i$$

▶ *A phosphatase is an enzyme that effects the removal of a phosphate group (P_i) from a molecule, such as converting glucose 6-phosphate to glucose, with H_2O as the attacking species.*

Because muscle and brain cells lack glucose 6-phosphatase, they cannot form free glucose from glucose 6-phosphate. Thus muscle and brain cells can use glucose 6-phosphate from glycogen for energy production only. The liver, however, with this enzyme present, has the capacity to use glucose 6-phosphate obtained from glycogen to supply additional glucose to the blood.

Figure 24-11 contrasts the "opposite" processes of glycogenesis and glycogenolysis. Both processes involve the glycolysis intermediate glucose 1-phosphate. UDP-glucose is unique to glycogenesis. ◄

▶ *The fact that glycogen synthesis (glycogenesis) and glycogen degradation (glycogenolysis) are not totally reverse processes has significance. In fact, it is almost always the case in biochemistry that "opposite" biosynthetic and degradative pathways differ in some steps. This allows for separate control of the pathways.*

When glycogen rather than free glucose is the starting material for glycolysis, the net gain in ATP is three molecules rather than two for each glucose processed. Glucose from glycogen enters glycolysis at Step 2, as glucose 6-phosphate, and thus bypasses ATP-consuming Step 1. Thus glycogen is a more effective energy source than is free glucose. Remember, however, that it costs the equivalent of two ATP to incorporate a glucose molecule into glycogen (glycogenesis).

Figure 24-11 The processes of glycogenesis and glycogenolysis contrasted. The intermediate UDP-glucose is part of glycogenesis but not of glycogenolysis.

Section 24-5 Quick Quiz

1. The process by which glucose is converted to glycogen is called
   a. glycolysis
   b. glycogenesis
   c. glycogenolysis
   d. no correct response
2. The intermediate glucose 1-phosphate is encountered in
   a. glycogenesis but not glycogenolysis
   b. glycogenolysis but not glycogenesis
   c. both glycogenesis and glycogenolysis
   d. no correct response
3. Adding a glucose unit to a growing glycogen chain
   a. requires the investment of the equivalent of 2 ATP molecules
   b. results in the production of 1 ATP molecule
   c. does not involve triphosphate molecules
   d. no correct response

Answers: 1. b; 2. c; 3. a

24-6 Gluconeogenesis

LEARNING FOCUS

Be familiar with the process of gluconeogenesis in terms of how it differs from glycolysis; know what is encompassed by the Cori cycle.

Gluconeogenesis *is the metabolic pathway by which glucose is synthesized from noncarbohydrate materials.* The noncarbohydrate starting materials for gluconeogenesis are pyruvate, lactate (from hard-working muscles and from red blood cells), glycerol (from triacylglycerol hydrolysis), and certain amino acids (from dietary protein hydrolysis or from muscle protein during starvation). ◀ About 90% of gluconeogenesis takes place in the liver. Hence gluconeogenesis helps to maintain normal blood-glucose levels in times of inadequate dietary carbohydrate intake (such as between meals).

Pyruvate is considered to be the entering (initial) substrate for the gluconeogenesis pathway. Thus, gluconeogenesis (the conversion of pyruvate to glucose) is the reverse of glycolysis (the conversion of glucose to pyruvate). The two pathways are not, however, "exact opposites." Twelve compounds are involved in gluconeogenesis and only 11 in glycolysis. Why the difference? The last step of glycolysis is the conversion of the high-energy compound phosphoenolpyruvate to pyruvate. The reverse of this process, which is the beginning of gluconeogenesis, cannot be accomplished in a single step because of the large energy difference between the two compounds and the slow rate of the reaction. Instead, a two-step process by way of oxaloacetate is required to effect the change, and this adds an extra compound to the gluconeogenesis pathway (Figure 24-12). Both an ATP molecule and a GTP molecule are needed to drive this two-step process.

▶ *Transamination/deamination of amino acids (Section 26.3) produces molecules which can enter gluconeogenesis either directly (as pyruvate or oxaloacetate) or indirectly via citric acid cycle intermediates that are converted to oxaloacetate (Section 23-7).*

Lactate is converted to pyruvate via the Cori cycle (to be discussed later in this text section) and enters gluconeogenesis in the latter form.

Glycerol, the "backbone" of fats and oils, is converted to dihydroxyacetone phosphate (Section 25-3), which is a gluconeogenesis intermediate.

Figure 24-12 The "opposite" processes of gluconeogenesis (pyruvate to glucose) and glycolysis (glucose to pyruvate) are not exact opposites. The reversal of the last step of glycolysis requires two steps in gluconeogenesis. Therefore, gluconeogenesis has 11 steps, whereas glycolysis has only 10 steps.

$$
\begin{array}{c}
\text{COO}^- \\
| \\
\text{C}=\text{O} \\
| \\
\text{CH}_3 \\
\text{Pyruvate}
\end{array}
+ \text{CO}_2 + \text{ATP} + \text{H}_2\text{O}
\xrightarrow[\text{Biotin}]{\text{Pyruvate}\atop\text{carboxylase}}
\begin{array}{c}
\text{COO}^- \\
| \\
\text{C}=\text{O} \\
| \\
\text{CH}_2 \\
| \\
\text{COO}^- \\
\text{Oxaloacetate}
\end{array}
+ \text{ADP} + \text{P}_i
$$

$$
\begin{array}{c}
\text{COO}^- \\
| \\
\text{C}=\text{O} \\
| \\
\text{CH}_2 \\
| \\
\text{COO}^- \\
\text{Oxaloacetate}
\end{array}
+ \text{GTP}
\xrightarrow{\text{Phosphoenolpyruvate}\atop\text{carboxykinase}}
\begin{array}{c}
\overset{\displaystyle O \quad O^-}{\underset{\displaystyle C}{\diagdown\diagup}} \\
| \\
\text{C}-\text{O}-\text{P} \\
\| \\
\text{CH}_2 \\
\text{Phosphoenolpyruvate}
\end{array}
+ \text{CO}_2 + \text{GDP}
$$

The oxaloacetate intermediate in this two-step process provides a connection to the citric acid cycle. In the first step of this cycle, oxaloacetate combines with acetyl CoA. If energy rather than glucose is needed, then oxaloacetate can go directly into the citric acid cycle.

As is shown in Figure 24-13, there are three other locations where gluconeogenesis and glycolysis differ in terms of enzymes identity and/or ATP requirements. ◀

▶ *When carbohydrate intake is high (glucose is plentiful), little use of the gluconeogenesis metabolic pathway occurs. On the other hand, gluconeogenesis becomes an important pathway for a person on a low carbohydrate diet (glucose is available in only limited amounts). Through gluconeogenesis, fat and even proteins can be converted to glucose.*

Figure 24-13 The pathway for gluconeogenesis is similar, but not identical, to the pathway for glycolysis.

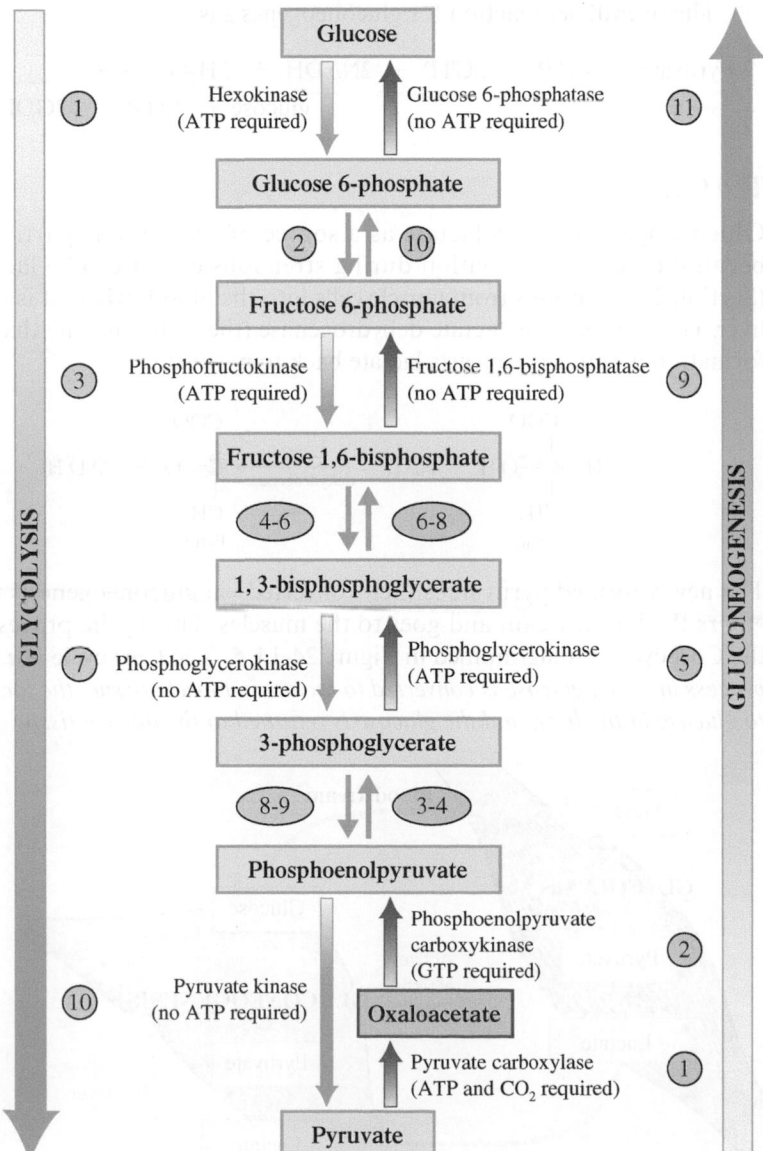

In Steps 9 and 11 of gluconeogenesis (Steps 1 and 3 of glycolysis) the reactant–product combinations match between pathways but different enzymes are needed and ATP is required in glycolysis but not in gluconeogenesis. The new enzymes for gluconeogenesis are *fructose 1,6-bisphosphatase* and *glucose 6-phosphatase*. In Step 5 of gluconeogenesis (Step 7 of glycolysis) the same enzyme is operative in both directions; however, ATP is required in gluconeogenesis but not in glycolysis.

From another viewpoint, during glycolysis ATP production occurs in Steps 7 and 10. The reverse of these two steps in gluconeogenesis, Step 5 and Steps 1 and 2, are the steps where ATP is needed.

In terms of total ATP consumption, note that six nucleotide triphosphate molecules (4 ATP, 2 GTP) are hydrolyzed in synthesizing glucose from pyruvate in gluconeogenesis whereas there is a net production of 2 ATP in glycolysis (Section 24-2). This is consistent with glycolysis being a catabolic process (energy-generating) and gluconeogenesis being a anabolic process (energy is needed for it to occur). ◄

▶ *Glycolysis has a net production of 2 ATP (Section 24-2). Gluconeogenesis has a net expenditure of 4 ATP and 2 GTP, which is equivalent to the expenditure of 6 ATP.*

Gluconeogenesis, because of its ATP-consuming nature, occurs only under specific conditions, which include:

1. Replenishing depleted liver glycogen stores.
2. Converting lactate, produced by strenuous exercise, back to glucose.
3. Maintaining blood glucose level when glycogen stores have been depleted.

The overall net reaction for gluconeogenesis is

$$2 \text{ Pyruvate} + \boxed{4\text{ATP}} + \boxed{2\text{GTP}} + \boxed{2\text{NADH}} + 2\text{H}_2\text{O} \longrightarrow$$
$$\text{glucose} + \boxed{4\text{ADP}} + \boxed{2\text{GDP}} + 6\text{P}_i + \boxed{2\text{NAD}^+}$$

The Cori Cycle

Gluconeogenesis using lactate as a source of pyruvate is particularly important because of lactate formation during strenuous exercise. The lactate so produced (Section 24-3) diffuses from muscle cells into the blood, where it is transported to the liver. Here the enzyme lactate dehydrogenase (the same enzyme that catalyzes lactate formation in muscle) converts lactate back to pyruvate.

▶ *The Cori cycle is named in honor of Gerty Radnitz Cori (1896–1957) and Carl Cori (1896–1984), the husband-and-wife team who discovered it. They were awarded a Nobel Prize in 1947, the third husband-and-wife team to be so recognized. Marie and Pierre Curie were the first, Irene and Frederic Joliot-Curie the second.*

$$\underset{\text{Lactate}}{\overset{\displaystyle \text{COO}^-}{\underset{\displaystyle \text{CH}_3}{\text{H}-\text{C}-\text{OH}}}} + \text{NAD}^+ \xrightarrow[\text{dehydrogenase}]{\text{Lactate}} \underset{\text{Pyruvate}}{\overset{\displaystyle \text{COO}^-}{\underset{\displaystyle \text{CH}_3}{\text{C}=\text{O}}}} + \boxed{\text{NADH}} + \boxed{\text{H}^+}$$

The newly formed pyruvate is then converted via gluconeogenesis to glucose, which enters the bloodstream and goes to the muscles. This cyclic process, which is called the Cori cycle, is diagrammed in Figure 24-14 ◄. The **Cori cycle** *is a cyclic biochemical process in which glucose is converted to lactate in muscle tissue, the lactate is reconverted to glucose in the liver, and the glucose is returned to the muscle tissue.*

Figure 24-14 The Cori cycle. Lactate, formed from glucose under anaerobic conditions in muscle cells, is transferred to the liver, where it is reconverted to glucose, which is then transferred back to the muscle cells.

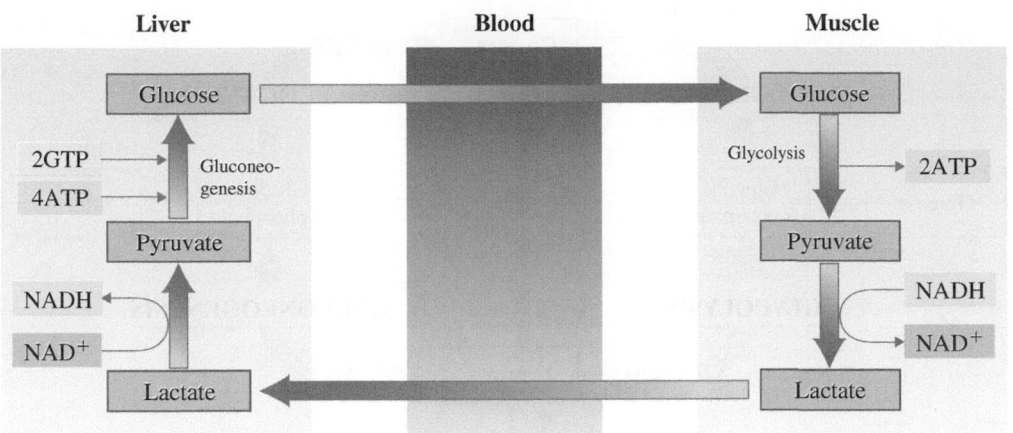

Figure 24-15 Nucleotide triphosphate change (gain or loss) associated with the two parts of the Cori cycle.

A net loss of nucleotide triphosphates (ATP, GTP) accompanies Cori cycle operation. As is shown in Figure 24-15, in the muscle, there is a net gain of 2 ATP in the glycolytic part of the cycle. However, in the liver, there is a net loss of 6 triphosphates (4 ATP and 2 GTP) in the portion of the cycle involving gluconeogenesis. Overall, a net loss of 4 nucleotide triphosphates occurs.

Section 24-6 Quick Quiz

1. When gluconeogenesis and glycolysis are compared in terms of reaction steps
   a. gluconeogenesis has one more step
   b. glycolysis has one more step
   c. both processes have the same number of steps
   d. no correct response
2. Which of the following intermediates is involved in gluconeogenesis but *not* in glycolysis?
   a. glucose 1-phosphate
   b. pyruvate
   c. oxaloacetate
   d. no correct response
3. In the process of gluconeogenesis, which of the following is a reactant in the first step?
   a. CO_2
   b. O_2
   c. acetyl CoA
   d. no correct response
4. Which of the following statements about ATP equivalents in gluconeogenesis is *correct*?
   a. 4 ATP equivalents are expended.
   b. 6 ATP equivalents are expended.
   c. 4 ATP equivalents are produced.
   d. no correct response
5. Which of the following substances are participants in the reactions encompassed by the Cori cycle?
   a. pyruvate and acetyl CoA
   b. pyruvate and lactate
   c. pyruvate, lactate, and acetyl CoA
   d. no correct response

Answers: 1. a; 2. c; 3. a; 4. b; 5. b

24-7 Terminology for Glucose Metabolic Pathways

LEARNING FOCUS

Distinguish from each other the terms *glycolysis, glycogenesis, glycogenolysis,* and *gluconeogenesis.*

In the preceding three sections, the processes of glycolysis, glycogenesis, glycogenolysis, and gluconeogenesis were considered. Because of their like-sounding names, keeping the terminology for these four processes "straight" is often a problem.

Figure 24-16 The relationships among four common metabolic pathways that involve glucose.

Figure 24-16 shows the relationships among these processes. Note that the glycogen degradation pathways (left side of Figure 24-16) have names ending in -*lysis*, which means "breakdown." The pathways associated with glycogen synthesis (right side of Figure 24-16) have names ending in -*genesis,* which means "making."

EXAMPLE 24-6

Recognizing Characteristics of Glycolysis, Glycogenesis, Glycogenolysis, and Gluconeogenesis

Identify each of the following as a characteristic of one or more of the following processes: glycolysis, glycogenesis, glycogenolysis, and gluconeogenesis.

a. Glucose 6-phosphate is the initial reactant.
b. Glucose is the final product.
c. Glucose 6-phosphate is produced in the first step.
d. UTP is involved in this process.

Solution

a. *Glycogenesis.* In this three-step process, glucose 6-phosphate units are added to a growing glycogen molecule.
b. *Gluconeogenesis.* This 11-step process converts pyruvate into glucose.
c. *Glycolysis.* The first step of glycolysis is the production of glucose 6-phosphate from glucose. The glucose 6-phosphate produced can then be further processed in the glycolysis pathway or processed to glycogen using the glycogenesis pathway.
d. *Glycogenesis.* The second step of glycogenesis is the conversion of glucose 1-phosphate to UDP-glucose.

Section 24-7 Quick Quiz

1. Which of the following statements concerning metabolic processes that involve glucose is *correct*?
   a. Pyruvate is the initial reactant in glycogenolysis.
   b. Glycogen is the final product in glycogenesis.
   c. Glucose is the final product in glycolysis.
   d. no correct response
2. Which of the following pairs of processes are the reverse of each other in terms of initial reactant and final product?
   a. glycolysis and gluconeogenesis
   b. glycogenesis and gluconeogenesis
   c. glycolysis and glycogenolysis
   d. no correct response

Answers: 1. b; 2. a

24-8 The Pentose Phosphate Pathway

LEARNING FOCUS

Be familiar with the *pentose phosphate pathway* in terms of the major products obtained via the pathway.

Glycolysis is not the only pathway by which glucose may be degraded. Depending on the type of cell, various amounts of glucose are degraded by the pentose phosphate pathway, a pathway whose main focus is *not* subsequent ATP production as is the case for glycolysis. Major functions of this alternative pathway are (1) synthesis of the coenzyme NADPH needed in lipid biosynthesis (Section 25-7) and (2) production of ribose 5-phosphate, a pentose derivative needed for the synthesis of nucleic acids and many coenzymes. The **pentose phosphate pathway** *is the metabolic pathway by which glucose 6-phosphate is used to produce NADPH, ribose 5-phosphate (a pentose phosphate), and numerous other sugar phosphates.* The operation of the pentose phosphate pathway is significant in cells that produce lipids: fatty tissue, the liver, mammary glands, and the adrenal cortex (an active producer of steroid lipids).

NADPH, the coenzyme produced in the pentose phosphate pathway, is the reduced form of NADP$^+$ (nicotinamide adenine dinucleotide phosphate). Structurally, NADP$^+$/NADPH is a phosphorylated version of NAD$^+$/NADH (Figure 24-17).

The nonphosphorylated and phosphorylated versions of this coenzyme have significantly different functions. The nonphosphorylated version is involved, mainly in its oxidized form (NAD$^+$), in the reactions of the common metabolic pathway (Section 23-6). The phosphorylated version is involved, mainly in its reduced form (NADPH), in biosynthetic reactions of lipids and nucleic acids.

There are two stages within the pentose phosphate pathway—an oxidative stage and a nonoxidative stage. The oxidative stage, which occurs first, involves three steps through which glucose 6-phosphate is converted to ribulose 5-phosphate and CO$_2$.

Figure 24-17 The structure of NADPH. The phosphate group shown in color is the structural feature that distinguishes NADPH from NADH.

The net equation for the oxidative stage of the pentose phosphate pathway is

Glucose 6-phosphate + 2NADP$^+$ + H$_2$O $\longrightarrow$
ribulose 5-phosphate + CO$_2$ + 2NADPH + 2H$^+$

Note the production of two NADPH molecules per glucose 6-phosphate processed during this stage.

In the first step of the nonoxidative stage of the pentose phosphate pathway, ribulose 5-phosphate (a ketose) is isomerized to ribose 5-phosphate (an aldose).

The pentose ribose is a component of ATP, GTP, UTP, CoA, NAD$^+$/NADH, FAD/FADH$_2$, and RNA. Further steps in the nonoxidative stage contain provision for the conversion of ribose 5-phosphate to numerous other sugar phosphates.

Ultimately, glyceraldehyde 3-phosphate and fructose 6-phosphate (both glycolysis intermediates) are formed. The overall net reaction for the pentose phosphate pathway is

$$3\,\text{Glucose 6-phosphate} + 6\text{NADP}^+ + 3\text{H}_2\text{O} \longrightarrow$$
$$2\,\text{fructose 6-phosphate} + 3\text{CO}_2 + \text{glyceraldehyde 3-phosphate} + 6\text{NADPH} + 6\text{H}^+$$

The pentose phosphate pathway, with its many intermediates, helps meet cellular needs in numerous ways:

1. When ATP demand is high, the pathway continues to its end products, which enter glycolysis.
2. When NADPH demand is high, intermediates are recycled to glucose 6-phosphate (the start of the pathway), and further NADPH is produced. ◀
3. When ribose 5-phosphate demand is high, for nucleic acid and coenzyme production, most of the nonoxidative stage is nonfunctional, leaving ribose 5-phosphate as a major product.

Chemistry at a Glance—Glucose Metabolism—shows how the pentose phosphate pathway is related to the other major pathways of glucose metabolism that have been considered.

▶ *Glutathione (Section 20-8) is the main antioxidant used by the body to keep hemoglobin in its reduced form. NADPH is needed for the regeneration of depleted glutathione. An insufficient supply of NADPH, and the ensuing lack of regeneration of glutathione, leads to the destruction of hemoglobin-containing red blood cells; severe anemia can result.*

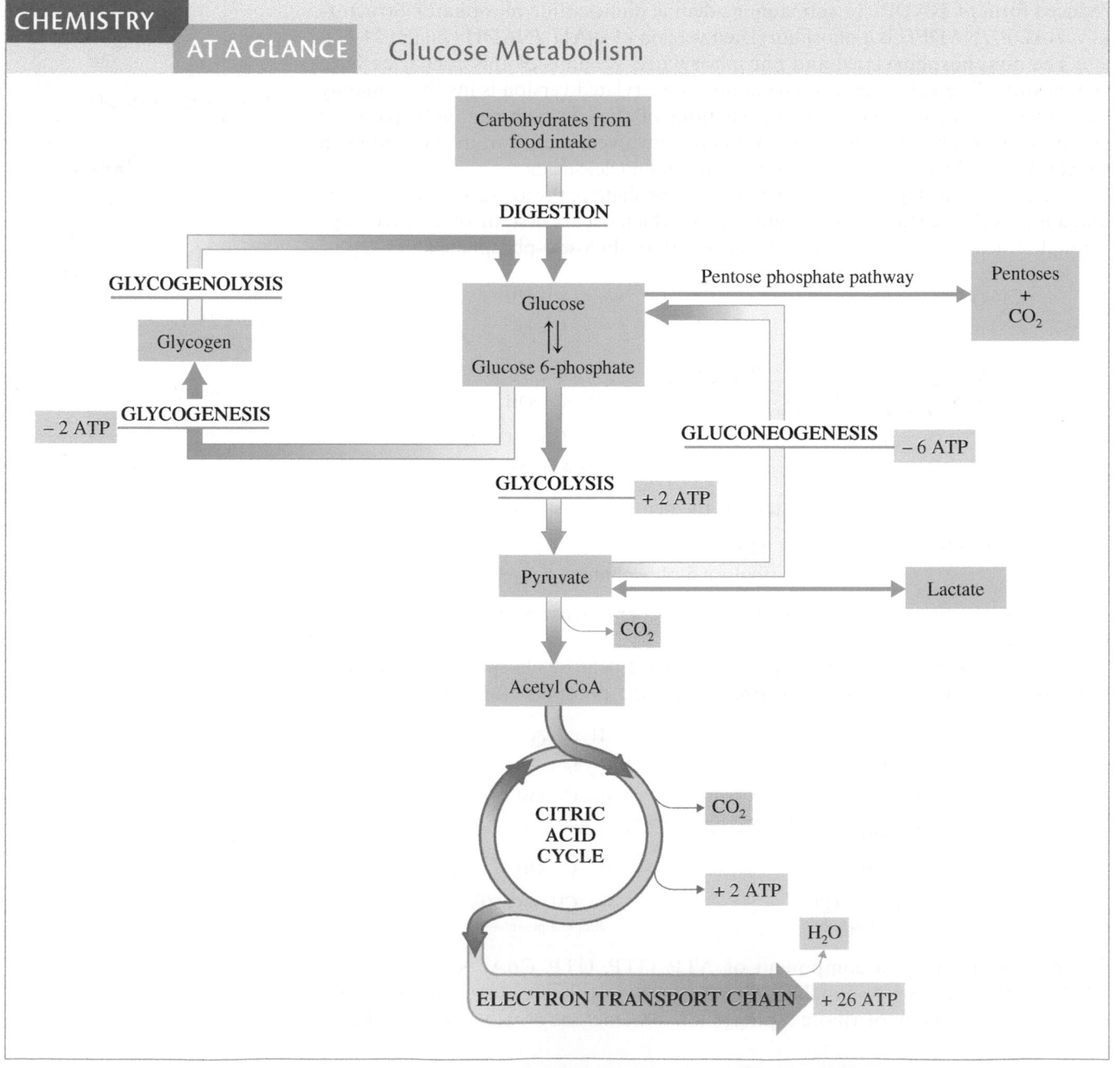

CHEMISTRY AT A GLANCE Glucose Metabolism

1. A major purpose of the first stage of the pentose phosphate pathway is the production of
   a. $NADP^+$
   b. NADPH
   c. NADH
   d. no correct response
2. A major purpose of the second stage of the pentose phosphate pathway is the production of
   a. ribulose 5-phosphate
   b. ribose 5-phosphate
   c. glucose 6-phosphate
   d. no correct response
3. The pentose phosphate pathway when run to its completion produces
   a. glycogen
   b. two glycolysis intermediates
   c. lactate
   d. no correct response

Answers: 1. b; 2. b; 3. b

24-9 Hormonal Control of Carbohydrate Metabolism

LEARNING FOCUS

Discuss how the hormones *insulin, glucagon,* and *epinephrine* relate to carbohydrate metabolism.

A second major method for regulating carbohydrate metabolism, besides enzyme inhibition by metabolites (Section 24-2), is hormonal control. Among others, three hormones—insulin, glucagon, and epinephrine—affect carbohydrate metabolism.

Insulin

Insulin, a 51-amino-acid protein hormone whose structure was considered in Section 20-12, is produced by the beta cells of the pancreas. Insulin promotes the uptake and utilization of glucose by cells. Thus its function is to lower blood-glucose levels. It is also involved in lipid metabolism.

The release of insulin is triggered by *high* blood-glucose levels. The mechanism for insulin action involves insulin binding to protein receptors on the outer surfaces of cells, which facilitates entry of glucose into the cells. Insulin also produces an increase in the rates of glycogenesis, glycolysis, and fatty acid synthesis.

Insulin is at the core of the metabolic disorder known as diabetes; either the body does not produce enough insulin or body cells do not respond properly to the insulin that is produced. The focus on relevancy feature Chemical Connections 24-B—Diabetes Mellitus—examines further the diabetic condition that afflicts an ever-increasing portion of the human population.

Glucagon

Glucagon is a polypeptide hormone (29 amino acids) produced in the pancreas by alpha cells. It is released when blood-glucose levels are *low.* Its principal function is to increase blood-glucose concentrations by speeding up the conversion of glycogen to glucose (glycogenolysis) and gluconeogenesis in the liver. Thus glucagon's effects are opposite those of insulin.

Epinephrine

Epinephrine (Section 17-10), also called adrenaline, is released by the adrenal glands in response to anger, fear, or excitement. Its function is similar to that of glucagon—stimulation of glycogenolysis, the release of glucose from glycogen. Its primary target is muscle cells, where energy is needed for quick action. It also functions in lipid metabolism.

CHEMICAL CONNECTIONS 24-B

Diabetes Mellitus

Diabetes mellitus, which is usually simply referred to as *diabetes,* is a metabolic disorder characterized by elevated levels of glucose in the blood. Classic symptoms associated with an uncontrolled diabetic condition are frequent urination, increased thirst, and increased hunger. These symptoms are the basis for the name *diabetes mellitus,* which originates from the Greek words "diabetes," meaning "siphon," and "mellitus," meaning "sweet." In the second century A.D., the Greek physician Aretaeus the Cappadocian named this condition; he observed that some people had a condition in which the body acts like a siphon—taking water in at one end and discharging it at the other—and that the urine produced was sweet to the taste. The name *diabetes mellitus* can roughly be translated as "sweet urine."

As of 2010, it is estimated that 26 million Americans (about 1 in 12) are diabetic. Diagnosis of diabetes is based on measurement of fasting blood-glucose levels. A fasting blood-glucose level greater than 126 mg/dL is considered a positive test, and a level less than 100 mg/dL is considered a negative test. Readings between 100 mg/dL and 126 mg/dL indicate a prediabetic condition; the blood-glucose level is higher than it should be but not high enough to be classified as diabetic. Prediabetic conditions are found in 15% of Americans.

There are two major forms of diabetes mellitus: type 1 (insulin-dependent) and type 2 (non-insulin-dependent).

Type 1 diabetes is the result of inadequate insulin production by the beta cells of the pancreas. Control of this condition involves insulin injections and special dietary programs. A risk associated with the insulin injections is that too much insulin can produce severe hypoglycemia (insulin shock); blackout or a coma can result. Treatment involves a quick infusion of glucose. Diabetics often carry candy bars (quick glucose sources) for use if they feel any of the symptoms that signal the onset of insulin shock.

Type 2 diabetes results from insulin resistance, a condition in which cells fail to use insulin properly. Bodily insulin production may be normal, but the cells do not respond to it normally. Treatment involves use of medications that decrease glucose production and/or increase insulin levels, as well as a carefully regulated diet to decrease obesity if the latter is a problem. More efficient use of undamaged insulin receptors occurs at increased insulin levels.

About 10% of all cases of diabetes are type 1. The more common non-insulin-dependent type 2 diabetes occurs in the other 90% of cases. The effects of both types of diabetes are the same—inadequate glucose uptake by cells. The result is blood-glucose levels much higher than normal (hyperglycemia). With an inadequate glucose intake, cells must resort to other procedures for energy production, procedures that involve the breakdown of fats and protein.

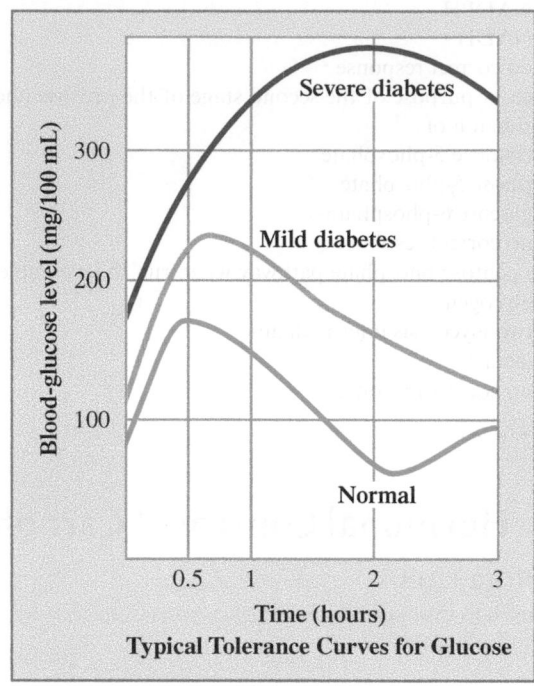

Typical Tolerance Curves for Glucose

The above graph contrasts blood-glucose levels for diabetic and nondiabetic individuals in the context of a two-hour oral glucose-tolerance test. A person must fast for eight hours prior to testing. A blood sample is taken at the beginning of the test, a 50-g glucose beverage is consumed, and a second blood sample is taken two hours later.

Most people with diabetes take oral medication rather than insulin, and the proportion who do so is increasing. Oral medication use rose from 60% in 1997 to 77% in 2007. One of the most used oral anti-diabetic drugs is the compound metformin. Structurally, metformin is a noncyclic organic compound that contains more nitrogen atoms (five) than carbon atoms (four).

Metformin does not increase how much insulin the pancreas makes; instead it acts on the liver, decreasing the amount of glucose it produces. An average person with type 2 diabetes has a gluconeogenesis rate that is three times the normal rate. Metformin slows down the production of glucose via gluconeogenesis (Section 24-6).

Epinephrine acts by binding to a receptor site on the outside of the cell membrane, stimulating the enzyme *adenyl cyclase* to begin production of a *second messenger,* cyclic AMP (cAMP) from ATP. The cAMP is released in the cell interior, where, in a series of reactions, it activates *glycogen phosphorylase,* the enzyme that

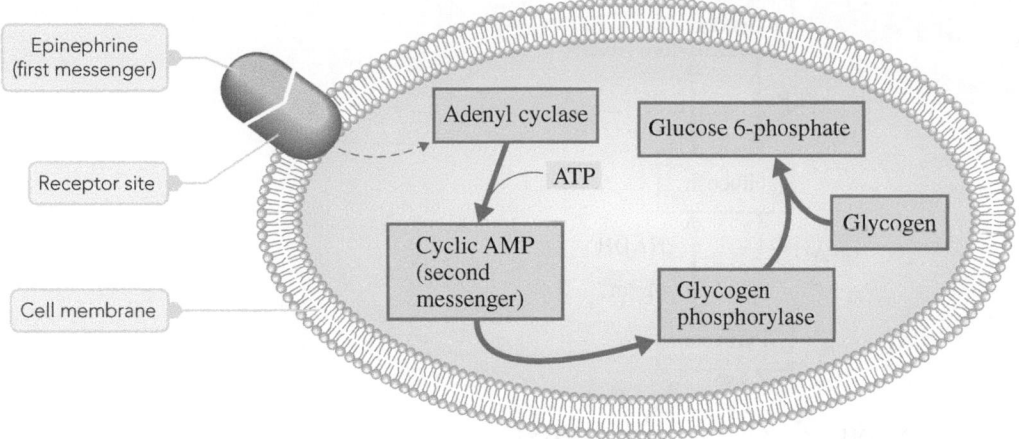

Figure 24-18 The series of events by which the hormone epinephrine stimulates glucose production.

initiates glycogenolysis. The glucose 6-phosphate that is produced from the glycogen breakdown provides a source of quick energy. Figure 24-18 shows the series of events initiated by the release of the hormone epinephrine. Cyclic AMP also inhibits glycogenesis, thus preventing glycogen production at the same time.

Section 24-9 Quick Quiz

1. Which of the following hormones promotes the uptake and use of glucose by cells?
   a. insulin
   b. glucagon
   c. epinephrine
   d. no correct response
2. Which of the following pairs of hormones increases blood-glucose levels?
   a. insulin and glucagon
   b. glucagon and epinephrine
   c. insulin and epinephrine
   d. no correct response

Answers: 1. a; 2. b

24-10 B Vitamins and Carbohydrate Metabolism

LEARNING FOCUS

Be familiar with the involvement that B vitamins have in carbohydrate metabolism.

The major function of B vitamins is that of coenzymes in metabolic reactions (Section 21-14). Now that the reactions involved in carbohydrate metabolism have been considered, it is informative to consider, in summary fashion, B vitamin involvement in the processes of glycolysis, gluconeogenesis, glycogenesis, glycogenolysis, and conversion of pyruvate to acetyl CoA and lactate. As is shown in Figure 24-19, six of the eight B vitamins are involved in carbohydrate metabolism.

Four of the six B vitamins involved in carbohydrate metabolism are the same four that are involved in the common metabolic pathway (see Figure 22-20). These four vitamins are niacin (as NAD^+, NADH), riboflavin (as FAD), thiamin (as TPP), and pantothenic acid (as CoA).

The two newly involved B vitamins are biotin and vitamin B_6:

1. Biotin involvement occurs in the enzyme pyruvate carboxylate, the enzyme needed to convert pyruvate to oxaloacetate (the new first step in gluconeogenesis).
2. Vitamin B_6 in the form of PLP is involved in glycogenolysis (Section 21-14).

Figure 24-19 B-vitamin participation in chemical reactions associated with carbohydrate metabolism.

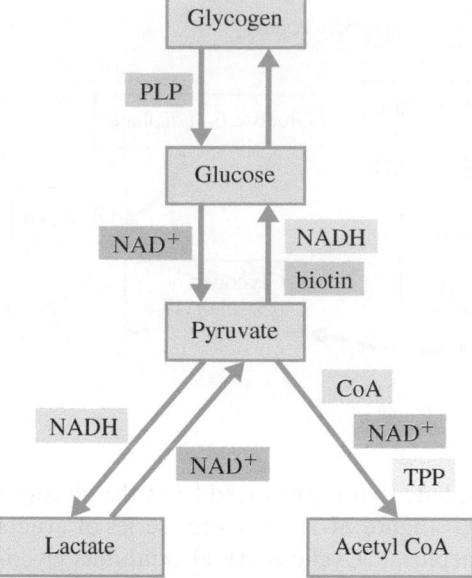

Concepts to Remember

Glycolysis. Glycolysis, a series of 10 reactions that occur in the cytosol, is a process in which one glucose molecule is converted into two molecules of pyruvate. A net gain of two molecules of ATP and two molecules of NADH results from the metabolizing of glucose to pyruvate (Section 24-2).

Fates of pyruvate. With respect to energy-yielding metabolism, the pyruvate produced by glycolysis can be converted to acetyl CoA under aerobic conditions or to lactate under anaerobic conditions. Some microorganisms convert pyruvate to ethanol, an anaerobic process (Section 24-3).

Glycogenesis. Glycogenesis is the process whereby excess glucose 6-phosphate is converted into glycogen. The glycogen is stored in the liver and in muscle tissue (Section 24-5).

Glycogenolysis. Glycogenolysis is the breakdown of glycogen into glucose 6-phosphate. This process occurs when muscles need energy and when the liver is restoring a low blood-sugar level to normal (Section 24-5).

Gluconeogenesis. Gluconeogenesis is the formation of glucose from pyruvate, lactate, and certain other substances. This process takes place in the liver when glycogen supplies are being depleted and when carbohydrate intake is low (Section 24-6).

Cori cycle. The Cori cycle is the cyclic process involving the transport of lactate from muscle tissue to the liver, the resynthesis of glucose by gluconeogenesis, and the return of glucose to muscle tissue (Section 24-6).

Pentose phosphate pathway. The pentose phosphate pathway metabolizes glucose to produce ribose (a pentose), NADPH, and other sugars needed for biosynthesis (Section 24-8).

Carbohydrate metabolism and hormones. Insulin decreases blood-glucose levels by promoting the uptake of glucose by cells. Glucagon increases blood-glucose levels by promoting the conversion of glycogen to glucose. Epinephrine stimulates the release of glucose from glycogen in muscle cells (Section 24-9).

Exercises and Problems

Exercises and problems are arranged in matched pairs with the two members of a pair addressing the same concept(s). The answer to the odd-numbered member of a pair is given at the back of the book. Problems denoted with a ▲ involve concepts found not only in the section under consideration but also concepts found in one or more earlier sections of the chapter.

Digestion and Absorption of Carbohydrates (Section 24-1)

24-1 Where does carbohydrate digestion begin in the body, and what is the name of the enzyme involved in this initial digestive process?

24-2 Very little digestion of carbohydrates occurs in the stomach. Why?

24-3 What is the primary site for carbohydrate digestion, and what organ produces the enzymes that are active at this location?

24-4 Where does the final step in carbohydrate digestion take place, and in what form are carbohydrates as they enter this final step?

24-5 Where does the digestion of sucrose begin, and what is the reaction that occurs?

24-6 Where does the digestion of lactose begin, and what is the reaction that occurs?

24-7 Identify the three major monosaccharides produced by digestion of carbohydrates.

24-8 The various stages of carbohydrate digestion all involve the same general type of reaction. What is this reaction type?

Glycolysis (Section 24-2)

24-9 Indicate whether each of the following glycolysis intermediates is a C_6 molecule or a C_3 molecule.
a. Fructose 6-phosphate
b. Phosphoenolpyruvate
c. 3-Phosphoglycerate
d. Dihydroxyacetone phosphate

24-10 Indicate whether each of the following glycolysis intermediates is a C_6 molecule or a C_3 molecule.
a. 2-Phosphoglycerate
b. 1,3-Bisphosphoglycerate
c. Glucose 6-phosphate
d. Fructose 1,6-bisphosphate

24-11 How many phosphate groups are present in each of the molecules in Problem 24-9?

24-12 How many phosphate groups are present in each of the molecules in Problem 24-10?

24-13 At which step in glycolysis is each of the molecules in Problem 24-9 encountered as a reactant?

24-14 At which step in glycolysis is each of the molecules in Problem 24-10 encountered as a reactant?

24-15 Characterize each of the following steps in glycolysis relative to the type of reaction that occurs (oxidation, phosphorylation, isomerization, etc.).
a. Step 1   b. Step 3
c. Step 5   d. Step 7

24-16 Characterize each of the following steps in glycolysis relative to the type of reaction that occurs (oxidation, phosphorylation, isomerization, etc.).
a. Step 2   b. Step 4
c. Step 6   d. Step 8

24-17 Of the 10 steps in glycolysis, how many of them
a. produce ATP
b. involve phosphorylation
c. involve NAD^+ as a reactant
d. involve a compound with a high-energy bond as a reactant

24-18 Of the 10 steps in glycolysis, how many of them
a. consume ATP
b. involve oxidation
c. involve NADH as a reactant
d. involve a compound with a high-energy bond as a product

24-19 Replace the question mark in each of the following word equations with the name of a substance.

a. Glucose + ATP $\xrightarrow{\text{Hexokinase}}$? + ADP

b. ? $\xrightarrow{\text{Enolase}}$ phosphoenolpyruvate + water

c. 3-Phosphoglycerate $\xrightarrow{?}$ 2-phosphoglycerate

d. 1,3-Bisphosphoglycerate + ? $\xrightarrow{\text{Phosphoglycero-}\atop\text{kinase}}$
3-phosphoglycerate + ATP

24-20 Replace the question mark in each of the following word equations with the name of a substance.

a. Glucose 6-phosphate $\xrightarrow{\text{Phosphogluco-}\atop\text{isomerase}}$?

b. ? $\xrightarrow{\text{Aldolase}}$ dihydroxyacetone phosphate + glyceraldehyde 3-phosphate

c. Phosphoenolpyruvate + ? $\xrightarrow{\text{Pyruvate}\atop\text{kinase}}$
pyruvate + ATP

d. Dihydroxyacetone phosphate $\xrightarrow{?}$
glyceraldehyde 3-phosphate

24-21 In which step of glycolysis does each of the following occur?
a. Second substrate-level phosphorylation reaction
b. First ATP-consuming reaction
c. Third isomerization reaction
d. Use of NAD^+ as an oxidizing agent

24-22 In which step of glycolysis does each of the following occur?
a. First energy-producing reaction
b. First ATP-producing reaction
c. A dehydration reaction
d. First isomerization reaction

24-23 Galactose enters the glycolysis metabolic pathway in the form of which glycolysis intermediate?

24-24 Fructose enters the glycolysis metabolic pathway in the form of which glycolysis intermediates?

24-25 How does net ATP production from the processing of one fructose molecule and one glucose molecule through the glycolysis metabolic pathway compare to each other?

24-26 How does net ATP production from the processing of one galactose molecule and one glucose molecule through the glycolysis metabolic pathway compare to each other?

24-27 Why is the first step in glycolysis important in retaining glucose inside a cell?

24-28 Why is Step 3 of glycolysis called the "commitment step"?

24-29 At what location within a cell does glycolysis occur?

24-30 Are the locations within a cell where glycolysis and the citric acid cycle (Section 23-7) occur the same? Explain.

▲**24-31** Indicate whether each of the following molecules or reaction types is associated with (1) carbohydrate digestion or (2) the glycolysis metabolic pathway.
a. Hexokinase
b. Lactase
c. Hydrolysis
d. Dehydration

▲**24-32** Indicate whether each of the following molecules is associated with (1) carbohydrate digestion or (2) the glycolysis metabolic pathway.
a. α-Amylase
b. Aldolase
c. Fructose
d. Fructose 6-phosphate

Fates of Pyruvate (Section 24-3)

24-33 Under what cellular conditions is pyruvate converted to acetyl CoA in the human body?

24-34 Under what cellular conditions is pyruvate converted to lactate in the human body?

24-35 What coenzyme(s) are needed to convert pyruvate to lactate in the human body?

24-36 What coenzyme(s) are needed to convert pyruvate to acetyl CoA in the human body?

24-37 At what location within a cell is pyruvate converted to acetyl CoA in the human body?

24-38 At what location within a cell is pyruvate converted to lactate in the human body?

24-39 What is the chemical purpose for lactate fermentation?

24-40 Name two methods by which NAD^+ supplies needed for Step 6 of glycolysis can be replenished.

24-41 In ethanol fermentation a C_3 pyruvate molecule is converted to a C_2 ethanol molecule. What is the fate of the third pyruvate carbon atom.

24-42 In pyruvate oxidation a C_3 pyruvate molecule is converted to a C_2 acetyl group. What is the fate of the third pyruvate carbon atom.

24-43 What is the overall reaction equation for the conversion of pyruvate to acetyl CoA?

24-44 What is the overall reaction equation for the conversion of pyruvate to lactate?

24-45 With which of the possible fates of pyruvate—acetyl CoA, lactate, and ethanol—is each of the following reaction characterizations associated? More than one answer (fate) may apply in a given situation.
a. CO_2 is produced.
b. NADH is a reactant.
c. NAD^+ is a reactant.
d. The end product is a C_3 molecule.

24-46 With which of the possible fates of pyruvate—acetyl CoA, lactate, and ethanol—is each of the following reaction characterizations associated? More than one answer (fate) may apply in a given situation.
a. Acetaldehyde is an intermediate.
b. NADH is a product.
c. NAD^+ is a product.
d. The end product is a C_2 molecule.

▲**24-47** Indicate whether each of the following compounds is associated with (1) glycolysis, (2) pyruvate oxidation, (3) lactate fermentation, or (4) ethanol fermentation. There may be more than one correct response in a given situation.
a. CO_2
b. Acetyl CoA
c. ATP
d. NADH

▲**24-48** Indicate whether each of the following compounds is associated with (1) glycolysis, (2) pyruvate oxidation, (3) lactate fermentation, or (4) ethanol fermentation. There may be more than one correct response in a given situation.
a. Pyruvate
b. CoA
c. ADP
d. NAD^+

ATP Production from the Complete Oxidation of Glucose (Section 24-4)

24-49 What is the relationship between cytosolic NADH and the dihydroxyacetone phosphate–glycerol 3-phosphate shuttle system?

24-50 In the dihydroxyacetone phosphate–glycerol 3-phosphate shuttle system, what molecule crosses the outer mitochondrial membrane in the
a. cytosol to intermembrane space direction
b. intermembrane space to cytosol direction

24-51 What is the "cargo" for glycerol 3-phosphate in the dihydroxyacetone phosphate–glycerol 3-phosphate shuttle system?

24-52 What is the source of the "cargo" for glycerol 3-phosphate in the dihydroxyacetone phosphate–glycerol 3-phosphate shuttle system?

24-53 Contrast, in terms of ATP production, the oxidation of glucose to CO_2 and H_2O with the oxidation of glucose to pyruvate.

24-54 Contrast, in terms of ATP production, the oxidation of glucose to CO_2 and H_2O with the oxidation of glucose to ethanol.

24-55 How many of the 30 ATP molecules produced from the complete oxidation of 1 glucose molecule are produced during
  a. glycolysis
  b. the oxidation of pyruvate

24-56 How many of the 30 ATP molecules produced from the complete oxidation of 1 glucose molecule are produced during
  a. the citric acid cycle
  b. the electron transport chain and oxidative phosphorylation

Glycogen Synthesis and Degradation (Section 24-5)

24-57 What is the initial reactant or reactants in the process called
  a. glycogenesis
  b. glycogenolysis

24-58 What is the final product or products in the process called
  a. glycogenesis
  b. glycogenolysis

24-59 Indicate whether each of the following substances is involved in (1) glycogenesis but not glycogenolysis, (2) glycogenolysis but not glycogenesis, (3) both glycogenesis and glycogenolysis, or (4) neither glycogenesis nor glycogenolysis.
  a. Glucose 6-phosphate
  b. UDP
  c. Glycogen
  d. P_i

24-60 Indicate whether each of the following substances is involved in (1) glycogenesis but not glycogenolysis, (2) glycogenolysis but not glycogenesis, (3) both glycogenesis and glycogenolysis, or (4) neither glycogenesis nor glycogenolysis.
  a. Glucose 1-phosphate
  b. UDP-glucose
  c. UTP
  d. PP_i

24-61 Indicate whether each of the following statements concerning glycogenesis is true or false.
  a. Glucose 1-phosphate is an intermediate in the process.
  b. An isomerization reaction changes glucose 1-phosphate to glucose 6-phosphate.
  c. A UTP molecule is used to activate a glucose 6-phosphate molecule.
  d. The equivalent of two ATP molecules are produced.

24-62 Indicate whether each of the following statements concerning glycogenolysis is true or false.
  a. Glucose 1-phosphate is an intermediate in the process.
  b. An isomerization reaction changes glucose 6-phosphate to glucose 1-phosphate.
  c. An ATP molecule is used to activate a glucose 1-phosphate molecule.
  d. The equivalent of two ATP molecules are consumed.

24-63 Characterize each of the following steps in glycogenolysis in terms of the type of reaction that occurs (oxidation, hydration, etc.).
  a. Step 1
  b. Step 2

24-64 Characterize each of the following steps in glycogenesis in terms of the type of reaction that occurs (oxidation, hydration, etc.).
  a. Step 1
  b. Step 2
  c. Step 3

24-65 What is the difference between the processing of glucose 6-phosphate in liver cells and that in muscle cells?

24-66 The liver, but not the brain or muscle cells, has the capacity to supply free glucose to the blood. Explain.

24-67 In what form does glycogen enter the glycolysis pathway?

24-68 Explain why one more ATP is produced when glucose is obtained from glycogen than when it is obtained directly from the blood.

▲**24-69** Indicate whether each of the following compounds is associated with (1) glycolysis, (2) glycogenesis, or (3) glycogenolysis. There may be more than one correct response in a given situation.
  a. Glucose 6-phosphate
  b. UTP
  c. Phosphoglucomutase
  d. Pyruvate

▲**24-70** Indicate whether each of the following compounds is associated with (1) glycolysis, (2) glycogenesis, or (3) glycogenolysis. There may be more than one correct response in a given situation.
  a. Glucose 1-phosphate
  b. Glucose
  c. Phosphoglucoisomerase
  d. UDP-glucose

Gluconeogenesis (Section 24-6)

24-71 What are the starting reactants for the process of gluconeogenesis?

24-72 What is the end product for the process of gluconeogenesis?

24-73 Contrast the reactants in the first three steps of gluconeogenesis with the products in the last three steps on glycolysis.

24-74 Contrast the products in the last three steps of gluconeogenesis with the reactants in the first three steps on glycolysis.

24-75 In how many steps of gluconeogenesis and glycolysis, respectively, are
a. triphosphate nucleotides produced
b. triphosphate nucleotides consumed

24-76 In the processes of gluconeogenesis and glycolysis, how many "common" steps are there in which
a. the reactant/products are the reverse of each other and the same enzyme is used
b. the reactant/products are the reverse of each other and different enzymes are used

24-77 In which step in gluconeogenesis is
a. a C_3 molecule converted to a C_4 molecule
b. CO_2 a product

24-78 In which step in gluconeogenesis is
a. a C_4 molecule converted to a C_3 molecule
b. CO_2 a reactant

24-79 Indicate whether each of the following statements relating to the Cori cycle is true or false.
a. Lactate is converted to pyruvate in the liver.
b. Lactate travels from the liver to skeletal muscle via the bloodstream.
c. Lactate is produced in the liver.
d. Both lactate and pyruvate are present in the liver.

24-80 Indicate whether each of the following statements relating to the Cori cycle is true or false.
a. Pyruvate is converted to lactate in skeletal muscle.
b. Glucose from the liver travels to skeletal muscle as part of the cycle.
c. Pyruvate is converted to lactate in the liver.
d. Both lactate and pyruvate are present in skeletal muscle.

24-81 Write an equation for the conversion of lactate to pyruvate in the Cori cycle in which the structures of lactate and pyruvate are shown.

24-82 Write an equation for the conversion of pyruvate to lactate in the Cori cycle in which the structures of pyruvate and lactate are shown.

▲**24-83** Indicate whether each of the following enzymes is involved in (1) glycolysis but not gluconeogenesis, (2) gluconeogenesis but not glycolysis, or (3) both glycolysis and gluconeogenesis.
a. Hexokinase
b. Phosphofructokinase
c. Pyruvate carboxylase
d. Phosphoglyceromutase

▲**24-84** Indicate whether each of the following enzymes is involved in (1) glycolysis but not gluconeogenesis, (2) gluconeogenesis but not glycolysis, or (3) both glycolysis and gluconeogenesis.
a. Glucose 6-phosphatase
b. Fructose 1,6-bisphosphatase

c. Pyruvate kinase
d. Phosphoglucoisomerase

▲**24-85** Indicate whether each of the following compounds is involved in (1) glycolysis but not gluconeogenesis, (2) gluconeogenesis but not glycolysis, or (3) both glycolysis and gluconeogenesis.
a. 2-Phosphoglycerate
b. Phosphoenolpyruvate
c. Fructose 1,6-bisphosphate
d. Glucose 6-phosphate

▲**24-86** Indicate whether each of the following compounds is involved in (1) glycolysis but not gluconeogenesis, (2) gluconeogenesis but not glycolysis, or (3) both glycolysis and gluconeogenesis.
a. 3-Phosphoglycerate
b. Oxaloacetate
c. Fructose 6-phosphate
d. Dihydroxyacetone phosphate

▲**24-87** How many different "C_3 molecules" are involved in
a. the Cori cycle
b. gluconeogenesis
c. glycolysis
d. lactate fermentation

▲**24-88** How many different "C_6 molecules" are involved in
a. the Cori cycle
b. gluconeogenesis
c. glycolysis
d. ethanol fermentation

Terminology for Glucose Metabolic Pathways (Section 24-7)

24-89 Indicate whether each of the following statements concerning terminology for glucose metabolic pathways is true or false.
a. Pyruvate is the initial reactant for glycolysis.
b. Lactate is the initial reactant for gluconeogenesis.
c. Glycogen is the initial reactant for glycogenolysis.
d. Glucose 6-phosphate is the initial reactant for glycogenesis.

24-90 Indicate whether each of the following statements concerning terminology for glucose metabolic pathways is true or false.
a. Pyruvate is the final product for glycolysis.
b. Lactate is the final product for gluconeogenesis.
c. Glycogen is the final product for glycogenolysis.
d. Glucose 6-phosphate is the final product for glycogenesis.

▲**24-91** Indicate in which of the four processes *glycolysis, glycogenesis, glycogenolysis,* and *gluconeogenesis* each of the following compounds is encountered. There may be more than one correct answer for a given compound.
a. Glucose 6-phosphate
b. Dihydroxyacetone phosphate
c. Oxaloacetate
d. UDP-glucose

▲24-92 Indicate in which of the four processes *glycolysis, glycogenesis, glycogenolysis,* and *gluconeogenesis* each of the following compounds is encountered. There may be more than one correct answer for a given compound.
a. Glucose 1-phosphate
b. Glycogen
c. Pyruvate
d. Fructose 6-phosphate

▲24-93 Indicate in which of the four processes *glycolysis, glycogenesis, glycogenolysis,* and *gluconeogenesis* each of the following situations is encountered. There may be more than one correct answer for each.
a. NAD^+ is consumed.
b. ATP is produced.
c. UDP is involved.
d. ADP is consumed.

▲24-94 Indicate in which of the four processes *glycolysis, glycogenesis, glycogenolysis,* and *gluconeogenesis* each of the following situations is encountered. There may be more than one correct answer for each.
a. NADH is consumed.
b. ATP is consumed.
c. CO_2 is involved.
d. H_2O is a product.

▲24-95 What is the net gain or net loss in triphosphates (ATP, UTP, etc.) in each of the following metabolic processes?
a. Gluconeogenesis
b. Glycogenesis
c. Glycogen glucose unit to pyruvate
d. Cori cycle

▲24-96 What is the net gain or net loss in triphosphates (ATP, UTP, etc.) in each of the following metabolic processes?
a. Glycolysis
b. Glycogenolysis
c. Glycogen glucose unit to glucose
d. Glycogen glucose unit to lactate

The Pentose Phosphate Pathway (Section 24-8)

24-97 Indicate whether each of the following statements relating to the pentose phosphate pathway (PPP) is true or false.
a. Phosphorylated versions of NAD^+/NADH are encountered in the PPP.
b. The initial reactant for the PPP is a pentose.
c. The oxidative stage of the PPP precedes the nonoxidative stage of the PPP.
d. CO_2 is a product of the first stage of the PPP.

24-98 Indicate whether each of the following statements relating to the pentose phosphate pathway (PPP) is true or false.
a. The initial reactant for the PPP is ribose.
b. The final products of the PPP include two glycolysis intermediates.
c. Ribose 5-phosphate is a product of the first stage of the PPP.
d. In the first step of the second stage of the PPP ribulose 5-phosphate is converted to ribose 5-phosphate.

24-99 How many phosphate groups are present in the structures of the following coenzymes?
a. NAD^+
b. $NADP^+$

24-100 How many phosphate groups are present in the structures of the following coenzymes?
a. NADH
b. NADPH

24-101 Write a general equation for the oxidative stage of the pentose phosphate pathway.

24-102 Write a general equation for the entire pentose phosphate pathway.

24-103 What compound contains the carbon atom lost from glucose (a hexose) in its conversion to ribose (a pentose)?

24-104 How many molecules of NADPH are produced per glucose 6-phosphate in the pentose phosphate pathway?

▲24-105 Indicate whether each of the following compounds is involved in (1) the pentose phosphate pathway, (2) the Cori cycle, (3) glycolysis, or (4) lactate fermentation. More than one response may be correct in a given situation.
a. Lactate
b. NAD^+
c. Glucose 6-phosphate
d. Ribose 5-phosphate

▲24-106 Indicate whether each of the following compounds is involved in (1) the pentose phosphate pathway, (2) the Cori cycle, (3) glycolysis, or (4) lactate fermentation. More than one response may be correct in a given situation.
a. Pyruvate
b. $NADP^+$
c. Glucose
d. Fructose 6-phosphate

Hormonal Control of Carbohydrate Metabolism (Section 24-9)

24-107 What effect does insulin have on glycogen metabolism?

24-108 What effect does insulin have on blood-glucose levels?

24-109 What effect does glucagon have on blood-glucose levels?

24-110 What effect does glucagon have on glycogen metabolism?

24-111 What organ is the source of insulin?

24-112 What organ is the source of glucagon?

24-113 The hormone epinephrine generates a "second messenger." Explain.

24-114 What is the relationship between cAMP and the hormone epinephrine?

24-115 Compare the target tissues for glucagon and epinephrine.

24-116 Compare the biological functions of glucagon and epinephrine.

B Vitamins and Carbohydrate Metabolism (Section 24-10)

24-117 For the B vitamins below, indicate which of the following processes each vitamin is involved in as a cofactor: (1) glycolysis, (2) gluconeogenesis, (3) lactate fermentation, or (4) glycogenolysis. For a given vitamin, there may be more than one correct response, or only one or none of the responses may apply.

    a. Thiamin   b. Riboflavin

    c. Pantothenic acid   d. Vitamin B_6

24-118 For the B vitamins below, indicate which of the following processes each vitamin is involved in as a cofactor: (1) glycolysis, (2) gluconeogenesis, (3) lactate fermentation, or (4) glycogenolysis. For a given vitamin, there may be more than one correct response, or only one or none of the responses may apply.

    a. Niacin

    b. Biotin

    c. Folate

    d. Vitamin B_{12}

Lipid Metabolism

25

© David Steele/Shutterstock.com

The fat stored in a camel's hump serves not only as a source of energy but also as a source of water. Water is one of the products of fat (triacylglycerol) metabolism.

C ertain classes of lipids play an extremely important role in cellular metabolism because they represent an energy-rich "fuel" that can be stored in large amounts in adipose (fat) tissue. Between one-third and one-half of the calories present in the diet of the average U.S. resident are supplied by lipids. Furthermore, excess energy derived from carbohydrates and proteins beyond normal daily needs is stored in lipid molecules (in adipose tissue), to be mobilized later and used when needed.

25-1 Digestion and Absorption of Lipids

LEARNING FOCUS

Be familiar with the steps in the triacylglycerol digestion process in terms of the sites where they occur and the products produced at each of the sites.

Because 98% of total *dietary* lipids are triacylglycerols (fats and oils; Section 19-4), this chapter focuses on triacylglycerol metabolism. Like all lipids, triacylglycerols (TAGs) are insoluble in water. Hence water-based salivary enzymes in the mouth have little effect on them. ◄ The *major* change that TAGs undergo in the stomach is physical rather than chemical. The churning action of the stomach breaks up triacylglycerol materials into small globules, or droplets, which float as a layer above the other components of swallowed food. The resulting material is called *chyme*. **Chyme** *is a thick*

▶ *The saliva of infants contains a lipase that can hydrolyze TAGs, so digestion begins in the mouth for nursing infants. Because mother's milk is already a lipid-in-water emulsion, emulsification by stomach churning is a much less important factor in an infant's processing of fat. Mother's milk also contains a lipase that supplements the action of the salivary lipases the infant itself produces. After weaning, infants cease to produce salivary lipases.*

semi-liquid material made up of small triacylglycerol globules, other partially digested food, and gastric secretions (hydrochloric acid and several enzymes).

High-fat foods remain in the stomach longer than low-fat foods. The conversion of high-fat materials into chyme takes longer than the breakup of low-fat materials. This is why a high-fat meal causes a person to feel "full" for a longer period of time. ◄

Lipid digestion also begins in the stomach. Under the action of *gastric lipase* enzymes, hydrolysis of TAGs occurs. Normally, about 10% of TAGs undergo hydrolysis in the stomach, but regular consumption of a high-fat diet can induce the production of higher levels of gastric lipases.

The arrival of chyme from the stomach triggers in the small intestine, through the action of the hormone *cholecystokinin,* the release of bile stored in the gallbladder. The bile (Section 19-11), which contains no enzymes, acts as an emulsifier (Section 19-11). Colloid particle formation (Section 8-8) through bile emulsification "solubilizes" the triacylglycerol globules, and digestion of the TAGs resumes. The major enzymes involved at this point are the *pancreatic lipases,* which hydrolyze ester linkages between the glycerol and fatty acid units of the TAGs. *Complete* hydrolysis does not usually occur; only two of the three fatty acid units are liberated, producing a monoacylglycerol and two free fatty acids. Occasionally, enzymes remove all three fatty acid units, leaving a free glycerol molecule.

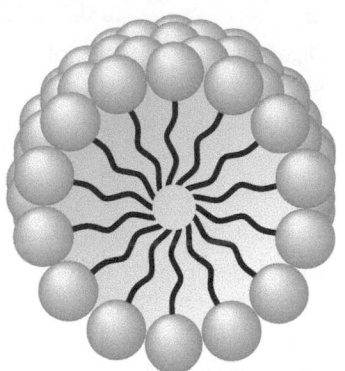

Figure 25-1 In a fatty acid micelle, the hydrophobic chains of the fatty acids and monoacylglycerols are in the interior of the micelle.

► *Chyme is pronounced "kyme" (rhymes with* dime*).*

► *When freed of the triacylglycerol molecules they "transport" during digestion, bile acids are mostly recycled. Small amounts are excreted.*

► *Chylomicron is pronounced "kye-lo-MY-cron."*

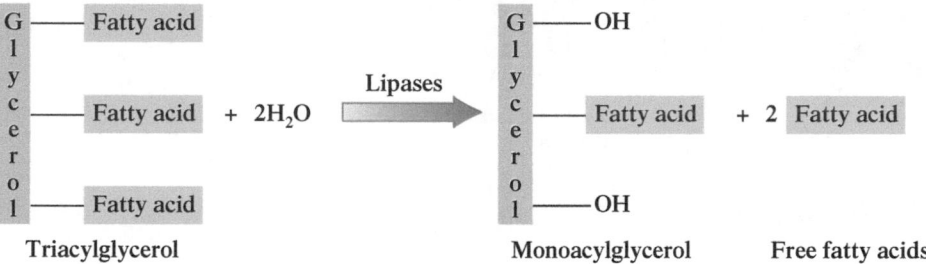

With the help of bile, the free fatty acids and monoacylglycerols produced from hydrolysis are combined into tiny spherical droplets called micelles (Section 19-6). A **fatty acid micelle** *is a micelle in which fatty acids and/or monoacylglycerols and some bile are present.* Fatty acid micelles are very small compared to the original triacylglycerol globules, which contain thousands of triacylglycerol molecules. Figure 25-1 shows a cross-section of the three-dimensional structure of a fatty acid micelle. ◄

Micelles, containing free fatty acid and monoacylglycerol components, are small enough to be readily absorbed through the membranes of intestinal cells. Within the intestinal cells, a "repackaging" occurs in which the free fatty acids and monoacylglycerols are reassembled into triacylglycerols. The newly formed triacylglycerols are then combined with membrane lipids (phospholipids and cholesterol) and water-soluble proteins to produce a type of lipoprotein (Section 20-19) called a *chylomicron* (Figure 25-2). A **chylomicron** *is a lipoprotein that transports triacylglycerols from intestinal cells, via the lymphatic system, to the bloodstream.* Triacylglycerols constitute 95% of the core lipids present in a chylomicron. ◄

Chylomicrons are too large to pass through capillary walls directly into the bloodstream. Consequently, delivery of the chylomicrons to the bloodstream is accomplished through the body's lymphatic system. Chylomicrons enter the lymphatic system through tiny lymphatic vessels in the intestinal lining. They enter the bloodstream through the thoracic duct (a large lymphatic vessel just below the collarbone), where the fluid of the lymphatic system flows into a vein, joining the bloodstream.

Once the chylomicrons reach the bloodstream, the TAGs they carry are again hydrolyzed to produce glycerol and free fatty acids. TAG release from chylomicrons and their ensuing hydrolysis are mediated by *lipoprotein lipases.* These enzymes are located on the lining of blood vessels in muscle and other tissues that use fatty acids

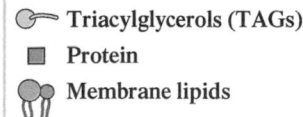

⌐ Triacylglycerols (TAGs)
☐ Protein
Membrane lipids

Figure 25-2 A three-dimensional model of a chylomicron, a type of lipoprotein. Chylomicrons are the form in which TAGs are delivered to the bloodstream via the lymphatic system.

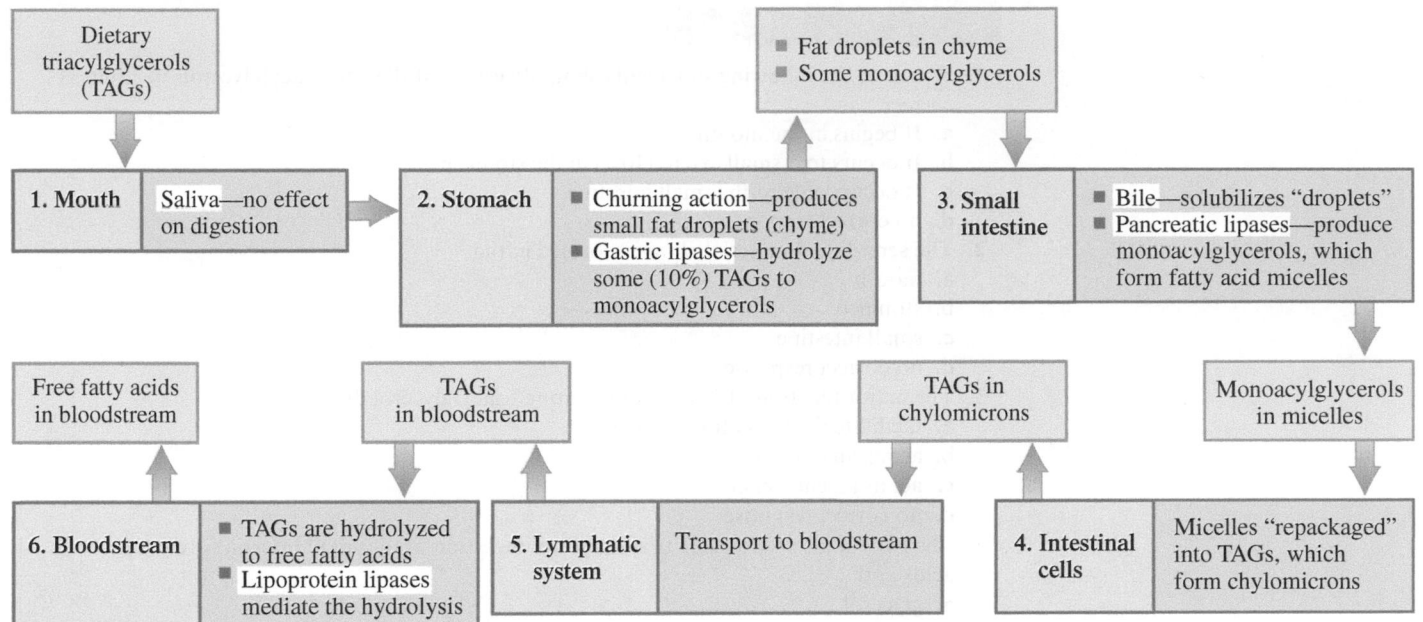

Figure 25-3 A summary of the events that must occur before triacylglycerols (TAGs) can reach the bloodstream through the digestive process.

for fuel and fat synthesis. The fatty acid and glycerol hydrolysis products from TAG hydrolysis are absorbed by the cells of the body and are either broken down to acetyl CoA for energy or stored as lipids (they are again repackaged as TAGs). Figure 25-3 summarizes the events that must occur before triacylglycerols can reach the bloodstream through the digestive process.

Soon after a meal heavily laden with TAGs is ingested, the chylomicron content of both blood and lymph increases dramatically. Chylomicron concentrations usually begin to rise within 2 hr after a meal, reach a peak in 4–6 hr, and then drop rather rapidly to a normal level as chylomicrons move into adipose cells (Section 25-2) or into the liver.

EXAMPLE 25-1

Determining the Sites Where Various Aspects of Lipid Digestion Occur

Based on the information in Figure 25-3, determine the location within the human body where each of the following aspects of lipid digestion occurs.

a. Interaction with bile occurs.
b. Monoacylglycerols are produced.
c. Chyme is produced.
d. Gastric lipases are active.

Solution

a. The *small intestine* is the location where bile released from the gallbladder interacts with the fat droplets present in chyme. The bile functions as an emulsifying agent.
b. Pancreatic lipases present in the *small intestine* convert triacylglycerols to monoacylglycerols.
c. The churning action of the *stomach* breaks triacylglycerol materials into small droplets that float on top of other ingested food materials; the resulting mixture is called chyme.
d. Gastric lipases present in the *stomach* begin the triacylglycerol hydrolysis process; about 10% of triacylglycerols undergo hydrolysis in the stomach.

1. Which of the following statements about digestion of dietary triacylglycerols in adults is *correct*?
   a. It begins in the mouth.
   b. It occurs to a small extent (10%) in the stomach.
   c. It occurs only in the small intestine.
   d. no correct response
2. The semi-liquid material *chyme* is formed in the
   a. mouth
   b. stomach
   c. small intestine
   d. no correct response
3. The major function of bile released during triacylglycerol digestion is to
   a. facilitate the formation of chyme
   b. act as an enzyme
   c. act as an emulsifier
   d. no correct response
4. The two major products of triacylglycerol digestion in the small intestine are fatty acids and
   a. glycerol
   b. monoacylglycerols
   c. acetyl CoA
   d. no correct response
5. Lipoproteins that transport triacylglycerols from intestinal cells to the bloodstream are called
   a. chylomicrons
   b. fatty acid micelles
   c. chymes
   d. no correct response

Answers: 1. b; 2. b; 3. c; 4. b; 5. a

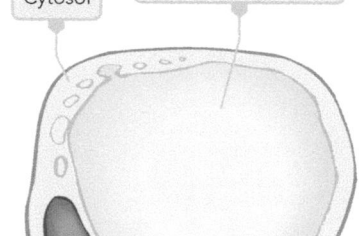

Cytosol

Large central globule of triacylglycerols

Cell nucleus

Figure 25-4 Structural characteristics of an adipose cell.

▶ *Adipose tissue is the only tissue in which* free *TAGs occur in appreciable amounts. In other types of cells and in the bloodstream, TAGs are part of lipoprotein particles.*

25-2 Triacylglycerol Storage and Mobilization

LEARNING FOCUS

Be familiar with the concept of *triacylglycerol mobilization* and the nature of the storage sites from which the triacylglycerols are mobilized.

Most cells in the body have limited capability for storage of TAGs. However, this activity is the major function of specialized cells called adipocytes, found in adipose tissue. An **adipocyte** *is a triacylglycerol-storing cell.* **Adipose tissue** *is tissue that contains large numbers of adipocyte cells.*

Adipose tissue is located primarily directly beneath the skin (subcutaneous), particularly in the abdominal region, and in areas around vital organs. Besides its function as a storage location for the chemical energy inherent in TAGs, subcutaneous adipose tissue serves as an insulator against excessive heat loss to the environment and provides organs with protection against physical shock. ◀

Adipose cells are among the largest cells in the body. They differ from other cells in that most of the cytoplasm has been replaced with a large triacylglycerol droplet (Figure 25-4). This droplet accounts for nearly the entire volume of the cell. As newly formed TAGs are imported into an adipose cell, they form small droplets at the periphery of the cell that later merge with the large central droplet.

Use of the TAGs stored in adipose tissue for energy production is triggered by several hormones, including epinephrine and glucagon. Hormonal interaction with adipose cell membrane receptors stimulates production of cAMP from ATP inside the adipose cell. In a series of enzymatic reactions, the cAMP activates *hormone-sensitive lipase (HSL)* through phosphorylation. HSL is the lipase needed for triacylglycerol

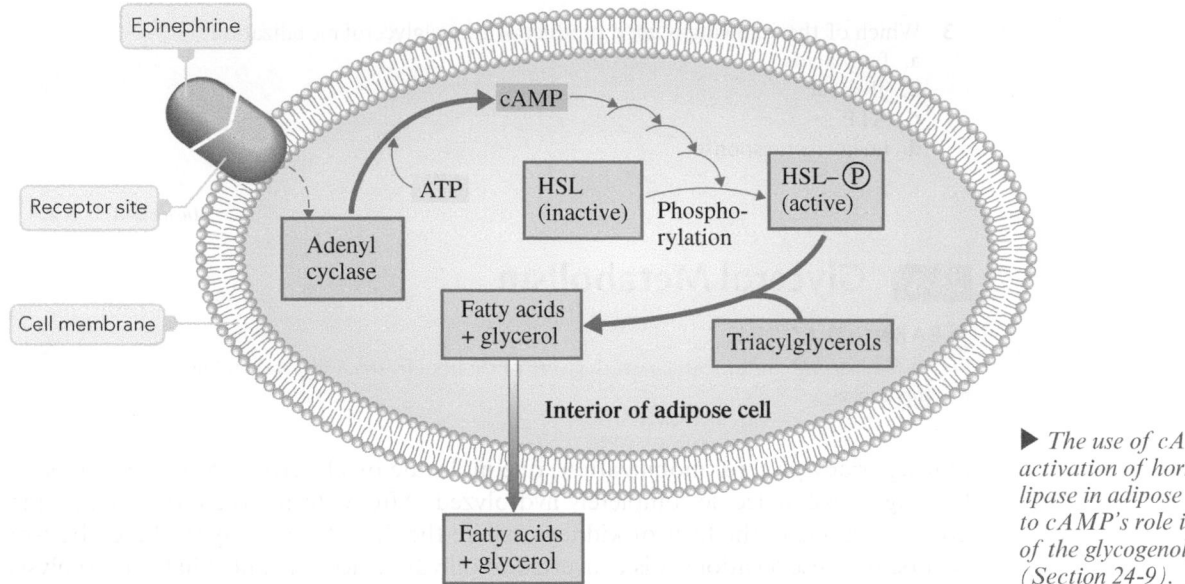

Figure 25-5 Hydrolysis of stored triacylglycerols in adipose tissue is triggered by hormones that stimulate cAMP production within adipose cells.

▶ *The use of cAMP in the activation of hormone-sensitive lipase in adipose cells is similar to cAMP's role in the activation of the glycogenolysis process (Section 24-9).*

hydrolysis, a prerequisite for fatty acids to enter the bloodstream from an adipose cell. This cAMP activation process is illustrated in Figure 25-5.

The overall process of tapping the body's triacylglycerol energy reserves (adipose tissue) for energy is called triacylglycerol mobilization. **Triacylglycerol mobilization** *is the hydrolysis of triacylglycerols stored in adipose tissue, followed by release into the bloodstream of the fatty acids and glycerol so produced.* Triacylglycerol mobilization is an ongoing process. On the average, about 10% of the TAGs in adipose tissue are replaced daily by new triacylglycerol molecules. ◀

Triacylglycerol energy reserves (fat reserves) are the human body's major source of stored energy. Energy reserves associated with protein, glycogen, and glucose are small to very small when compared to fat reserves. ◀ Table 25-1 shows relative amounts of stored energy associated with the various types of energy reserves present in the human body.

▶ *Dietary TAGs deposited in adipose tissue have undergone hydrolysis two times (to form free fatty acids and/or monoacylglycerols) and are repackaged twice (to re-form TAGs) in reaching that state. They undergo hydrolysis for a third time when triacylglycerol mobilization occurs.*

▶ *Triacylglycerol reserves would enable the average person to survive starvation for about 30 days, given sufficient water. Glycogen reserves (stored glucose) would be depleted within 1 day.*

▶ Table 25-1 **Stored Energy Reserves of Various Types for a 150-lb (70-kg) Person**

Type of Energy Reserve	Amount of Stored Energy (kcal)	Percent of Total Stored Energy
triacylglycerol	135,000	84.3
protein	24,000	15
glycogen	720	0.45
blood glucose	80	0.05

Section 25-2 Quick Quiz

1. Hormone-sensitive lipase needed for triacylglycerol mobilization is activated by
   a. epinephrine
   b. cAMP
   c. adipocytes
   d. no correct response
2. In triacylglycerol mobilization, triacylglycerol molecules undergo
   a. hydrolysis
   b. oxidation
   c. phosphorylation
   d. no correct response

(continued)

3. Which of the following is *not* a product of triacylglycerol mobilization?
   a. fatty acids
   b. glycerol
   c. ATP
   d. no correct response

Answers: 1. b; 2. a; 3. c

25-3 Glycerol Metabolism

LEARNING FOCUS

Be familiar with the process by which glycerol produced by triacylglycerol mobilization is metabolized.

During triacylglycerol mobilization, one molecule of glycerol is produced for each triacylglycerol molecule completely hydrolyzed. After entering the bloodstream, the glycerol travels to the liver or kidneys, where the first stage of glycerol metabolism occurs. At these locations it is converted to dihydroxyacetone phosphate, a glycolysis (Section 24-2)/gluconeogenesis (Section 24-6) intermediate. The dihydroxyacetone phosphate can be converted to pyruvate, then acetyl CoA, and finally carbon dioxide, or it can be used to form glucose. Dihydroxyacetone phosphate formation from glycerol represents the first of several situations that will be encountered where lipid and carbohydrate metabolism are connected.

The conversion of glycerol to dihydroxyacetone phosphate is a two-step ATP-consuming process.

The first step involves phosphorylation of a primary hydroxyl group of the glycerol. In the second step, glycerol's secondary alcohol group (C2) is oxidized to a ketone.

The following equation represents the overall reaction for the metabolism of glycerol.

Glycerol + ATP + NAD⁺ ⟶ Dihydroxyacetone phosphate + ADP + NADH + H⁺

Section 25-3 Quick Quiz

1. The first stage of glycerol metabolism is a two-step process in which glycerol is converted to
   a. glycerol 3-phosphate
   b. dihydroxyacetone phosphate
   c. pyruvate
   d. no correct response
2. What is the intermediate compound in the two-step first stage of glycerol metabolism?
   a. glycerol 2-phosphate
   b. glycerol 3-phosphate
   c. dihydroxyacetone phosphate
   d. no correct response
3. After the first stage of glycerol metabolism, the remaining stages are the same as
   a. glucose pathways
   b. glycogen pathways
   c. fatty acid pathways
   d. no correct response

Answers: 1. b; 2. b; 3. a

25-4 Oxidation of Fatty Acids

LEARNING FOCUS

Be familiar with the four-step β-oxidation pathway by which fatty acids are converted to acetyl CoA; know the cellular location where the chemical reactions of the β-oxidation pathway occur.

There are three parts to the process by which fatty acids are broken down to obtain energy. ◄

1. The fatty acid must be *activated* by bonding to coenzyme A.
2. The fatty acid must be *transported* into the mitochondrial matrix by a shuttle mechanism.
3. The fatty acid must be repeatedly *oxidized,* cycling through a series of four reactions, to produce acetyl CoA, FADH$_2$, and NADH.

▶ The stored TAGs in adipose tissue supply approximately 60% of the body's energy needs when the body is in a resting state.

Fatty Acid Activation

The outer mitochondrial membrane is the site of fatty acid *activation,* the first stage of fatty acid oxidation. Here the fatty acid is converted to a high-energy derivative of coenzyme A. Reactants are the fatty acid, coenzyme A, and a molecule of ATP.

$$\underset{\text{Free fatty acid}}{R-\overset{\overset{\textstyle O}{\|}}{C}-O^-} + \underset{}{HS-CoA} \xrightarrow[\quad ATP \quad AMP + 2P_i \quad]{\overset{\text{Acyl CoA}}{\text{synthetase}}} \underset{\text{Acyl CoA}}{R-\overset{\overset{\textstyle O}{\|}}{C}-S-CoA}$$

This reaction requires the expenditure of two high-energy phosphate bonds from a single ATP molecule; the ATP is converted to AMP rather than ADP, and the resulting pyrophosphate (PP$_i$) is hydrolyzed to 2P$_i$.

The activated fatty acid–CoA molecule is called *acyl* CoA. The difference between the designations *acyl* CoA and *acetyl* CoA is that *acyl* refers to a random-length fatty acid carbon chain that is covalently bonded to coenzyme A, whereas *acetyl* refers to a two-carbon chain covalently bonded to coenzyme A. ◄

$$\underset{\substack{\text{Acyl CoA} \\ \text{R = carbon chain of any length}}}{R-\overset{\overset{\textstyle O}{\|}}{C}-S-CoA} \qquad \underset{\substack{\text{Acetyl CoA} \\ \text{R = CH}_3 \text{ group}}}{CH_3-\overset{\overset{\textstyle O}{\|}}{C}-S-CoA}$$

▶ Recall, from Section 16-1, that acyl is a generic term for

which is the species formed when the carboxyl —OH is removed from a carboxylic acid. The R group can involve a carbon chain of any length.

Fatty Acid Transport

Acyl CoA is too large to pass through the inner mitochondrial membrane to the mitochondrial matrix, where the enzymes needed for fatty acid oxidation are located. A shuttle mechanism involving the molecule carnitine effects the entry of acyl CoA into the matrix (Figure 25-6). The acyl group is transferred to a carnitine molecule, which carries it through the membrane. The acyl group is then transferred from the carnitine back to a CoA molecule.

Reactions of the β-Oxidation Pathway

In the mitochondrial matrix, a sequence of four reactions *repeatedly* cleaves two carbon units from the carboxyl end of the acyl CoA molecule. This repetitive four-reaction sequence is called the *β-oxidation pathway* because the second carbon from the carboxyl end of the chain, the beta carbon, is the carbon atom that is oxidized. The **β-oxidation pathway** *is a repetitive series of four biochemical reactions that degrade acyl CoA to acetyl CoA by removing two carbon atoms at a time, with FADH$_2$ and NADH also being produced.* Each repetition of the four-reaction sequence generates an acetyl CoA molecule and an acyl CoA molecule that has two fewer carbon atoms.

Figure 25-6 Fatty acids are transported across the inner mitochondrial membrane in the form of acyl carnitine.

For a *saturated* fatty acid, the β-oxidation pathway involves the following functional group changes at the β carbon and the following reaction types.

$$\textbf{Alkane} \xrightarrow[\text{(oxidation)}]{\text{①} \atop \text{Dehydrogenation}} \textbf{alkene} \xrightarrow[]{\text{②} \atop \text{Hydration}} \genfrac{}{}{0pt}{}{\textbf{secondary}}{\textbf{alcohol}} \xrightarrow[\text{(oxidation)}]{\text{③} \atop \text{Dehydrogenation}} \textbf{ketone} \xrightarrow[\text{(chain cleavage)}]{\text{④} \atop \text{Thiolysis}}$$

Details about Steps 1–4 of the β-oxidation pathway follow. ◄

▶ *The reaction sequence dehydrogenation–hydration–dehydrogenation in the β-oxidation pathway has a parallel in Steps 6–8 of the citric acid cycle (Section 23-7), where succinate is dehydrogenated to fumarate, which is hydrated to malate, which is dehydrogenated to oxaloacetate.*

Step 1: **First dehydrogenation.** Hydrogen atoms are removed from the α and β carbons, creating a double bond between these two carbon atoms. FAD is the oxidizing agent, and an $FADH_2$ molecule is a product.

The enzyme involved is stereospecific in that only *trans* double bonds are produced.

Step 2: **Hydration.** A molecule of water is added across the *trans* double bond, producing a secondary alcohol at the β-carbon position. Again, the enzyme involved is stereospecific in that only the L-hydroxy isomer is produced from the *trans* double bond.

The enzyme involved in this hydration will also hydrate a *cis* double bond, but the product then is the D isomer. D Isomer formation is of importance when considering how unsaturated fatty acids are oxidized, a topic discussed later in this section.

▶ *The loss of hydrogen atoms (oxidation) occurs in both Steps 1 and 3. The oxidizing agents differ because the type of double bond formed differs. The body uses FAD as the oxidizing agent when C=C double bond formation occurs and uses NAD^+ as the oxidizing agent when C=O double bond formation occurs.*

Step 3: **Second dehydrogenation.** Removal of two hydrogen atoms converts the β-hydroxy group to a keto group, with NAD^+ serving as the oxidizing agent. The required enzyme exhibits absolute stereospecificity for the L isomer. ◄

L-β-Hydroxyacyl CoA → β-Ketoacyl CoA (β-Hydroxyacyl CoA dehydrogenase; NAD⁺ → NADH + H⁺)

It is now apparent why the name for this series of reactions is the β-oxidation pathway. The β-carbon atom has been oxidized from a —CH_2— group to a ketone group.

Step 4: **Thiolysis.** The fatty acid carbon chain is broken between the α and β carbons by reaction with a coenzyme A molecule. The result is an acetyl CoA molecule and a new acyl CoA molecule that is shorter by two carbon atoms than its predecessor. ◄

▶ *The chain cleavage reaction that occurs in Step 4 is called* thiolysis *by analogy with the process of* hydrolysis, *which also involves breaking a molecule into two parts. It is the thiol group of coenzyme A that undergoes reaction.*

The new acyl CoA molecule (now shorter by two carbons) is *recycled* through the same set of four reactions again. This yields another acetyl CoA, a two-carbon-shorter new acyl CoA, $FADH_2$, and NADH. Recycling occurs again and again, until the entire fatty acid is converted to acetyl CoA. Thus the fatty acid carbon chain is sequentially degraded, two carbons at a time. ◄

Figure 25-7 summarizes the reactions of the β-oxidation pathway for stearic acid (18:0) as the starting fatty acid.

The fatty acids normally found in dietary triacylglycerols contain an *even* number of carbon atoms. Thus the number of acetyl CoA molecules produced in the β-oxidation pathway is equal to half the number of carbon atoms in the fatty acid. The number of *repetitions* of the β-oxidation pathway that are needed to produce the acetyl CoA is always one less than the number of acetyl CoA molecules produced because the last repetition produces two acetyl CoA molecules as a C_4 unit splits into two C_2 units.

▶ *This sequence of reactions is called the β-oxidation* pathway *rather than the β-oxidation* cycle *because a different product results from each repetition.*

$$C_{18} \text{ fatty acid} \longrightarrow 9 \text{ acetyl CoA (8 repetitive sequences)}$$
$$C_{14} \text{ fatty acid} \longrightarrow 7 \text{ acetyl CoA (6 repetitive sequences)}$$

EXAMPLE 25-2

Recognizing Reaction Types and Events That Occur in the β-Oxidation Pathway

Indicate at what step in the β-oxidation pathway each of the following events occurs.

a. A carbon–carbon single bond is converted to a carbon–carbon double bond.
b. NAD^+ is reduced to NADH.
c. A hydration reaction occurs.
d. An acetyl CoA molecule is produced.

Solution

a. *Step 1.* A dehydrogenation reaction involving removal of two hydrogen atoms changes the carbon–carbon single bond to a carbon–carbon double bond.
b. *Step 3.* This step is the second of two dehydrogenation (oxidation) reactions that occur. The oxidizing agent for this oxidation is NAD^+, which is converted to NADH. Note that the oxidizing agent for the first dehydrogenation reaction (Step 1) is not NAD^+ but rather FAD.
c. *Step 2.* A molecule of water is added to the carbon–carbon double bond, producing a secondary alcohol at the β-carbon position.
d. *Step 4.* Breakage of the bond between the α- and β-carbon atoms produces an acetyl CoA molecule and an acyl CoA molecule whose carbon chain is two atoms shorter than at the start of the pathway.

Figure 25-7 Reactions of the β-oxidation pathway for an 18:0 fatty acid (stearic acid).

Relating Characteristics of the β-Oxidation Pathway to Types of Reactions That Occur

Match each of the following characteristics of the β-oxidation pathway to the terms (1) first dehydrogenation, (2) hydration, (3) second dehydrogenation, and (4) thiolysis.

a. The enzyme needed is thiolase.
b. The enzyme needed is acyl CoA dehydrogenase.

c. The substance *trans*-enoyl CoA is a product.

d. The substance β-ketoacyl CoA is a reactant.

Solution

a. *Thiolysis* (Step 4). The prefix *thio* in the enzyme name *thiolase* indicates a reaction that involves an SH functional group. When coenzyme A reacts with the acyl group produced by chain cleavage to form acyl CoA, a new C—S bond is formed.

b. *First dehydrogenation* (Step 1). This dehydrogenation step, as well as the second one, involves the removal of two hydrogen atoms, with the resulting creation of a double bond. A dehydrogenase enzyme effects such a change.

c. *First dehydrogenation* (Step 1). *trans*-Enoyl CoA is produced in Step 1 and becomes the reactant for Step 2.

d. *Thiolysis* (Step 4). β-Ketoacyl CoA is produced in Step 3 and becomes the reactant for Step 4.

Unsaturated Fatty Acids

Unsaturated fatty acids are common components of dietary triacylglycerols. Their oxidation through the β-oxidation pathway requires two additional enzymes besides those needed for oxidation of saturated fatty acids. These two—an epimerase that can change a D configuration to an L configuration and a *cis–trans* isomerase—are needed for two reasons. First, the double bonds in naturally occurring unsaturated fatty acids are nearly always *cis* double bonds, which yield on hydration a D-hydroxy product rather than the L-hydroxy product needed for Step 3 of the pathway. The epimerase enzyme effects a configuration change from the D form to the L form.

D-β-Hydroxyacyl CoA → (Epimerase) → L-β-Hydroxyacyl CoA

Second, the double bonds in naturally occurring unsaturated fatty acids often occupy odd-numbered positions (Section 19-2). The hydratase in Step 2 of the pathway can effect hydration of only an even-numbered double bond. The *cis–trans* isomerase produces a *trans*-(2,3) double bond from a *cis*-(3,4) double bond.

cis-(3,4) → (cis–trans Isomerase) → *trans* (2,3)

The Step 2 hydratase can then work on the *trans*-(2,3) double bond in the normal fashion.

1. In the oxidation of fatty acids, what two molecules are needed to initially activate a fatty acid molecule?
   a. acetyl CoA and ATP
   b. CoA and acyl CoA
   c. CoA and ATP
   d. no correct response

2. In the oxidation of fatty acids, what molecule shuttles activated fatty acid molecules across the inner mitochondrial membrane?
   a. citrate
   b. carnitine
   c. CoA
   d. no correct response

(*continued*)

3. The correct sequence for the four reactions of the β-oxidation pathway in terms of the "functional group acted upon" is
   a. alkene, alkane, ketone, 2° alcohol
   b. alkane, alkene, 2° alcohol, ketone
   c. ketone, 2° alcohol, alkene, alkane
   d. no correct response
4. The correct sequence for the four reactions of the β-oxidation pathway in terms of the "type of reaction occurring" is
   a. dehydrogenation, dehydrogenation, hydration, thiolysis
   b. dehydrogenation, hydration, dehydrogenation, thiolysis
   c. hydration, dehydrogenation, thiolysis, dehydrogenation
   d. no correct response
5. How many turns of the β-oxidation pathway are needed to "process" a C_{16} *saturated* fatty acid?
   a. 7
   b. 8
   c. 16
   d. no correct response
6. How many turns of the β-oxidation pathway are needed to "process" a C_{16} *unsaturated* fatty acid?
   a. 7
   b. 8
   c. 16
   d. no correct response

Answers: 1. c; 2. b; 3. b; 4. b; 5. a; 6. a

25-5 ATP Production from Fatty Acid Oxidation

LEARNING FOCUS

Be able to calculate net ATP production for the oxidation of a given fatty acid; be able to compare in terms of ATP production, fatty acid oxidation, and glucose oxidation.

How does the total energy output from fatty acid oxidation compare to that of glucose oxidation? Calculation of ATP production for the oxidation of a specific fatty acid molecule, stearic acid (18:0), and comparison of the result with that from glucose are now considered.

Figure 25-7 shows that for each four-reaction sequence except the last one, one $FADH_2$ molecule, one NADH molecule, and one acetyl CoA molecule are produced. In the final four-reaction sequence, two acetyl CoA molecules are produced in addition to the $FADH_2$ and NADH molecules.

Eight repetitions of the β-oxidation pathway are required for the oxidation of stearic acid, an 18-carbon acid. These eight repetitions of the pathway produce nine acetyl CoA molecules, eight $FADH_2$ molecules, and eight NADH molecules. Further processing of these products through the common metabolic pathway (citric acid cycle, electron transport chain, and oxidative phosphorylation) leads to ATP production as follows:

$$9 \text{ acetyl CoA} \times \frac{10 \text{ ATP}}{1 \text{ acetyl CoA}} = 90 \text{ ATP}$$

$$8 \text{ FADH}_2 \times \frac{1.5 \text{ ATP}}{1 \text{ FADH}_2} = 12 \text{ ATP}$$

$$8 \text{ NADH} \times \frac{2.5 \text{ ATP}}{1 \text{ NADH}} = \underline{20 \text{ ATP}}$$
$$122 \text{ ATP}$$

The conversion factors used in this calculation were first presented in Section 23-10.

This *gross* production of 122 ATP must be decreased by the ATP needed to activate the fatty acid before it enters the β-oxidation pathway. The activation consumes two high-energy phosphate bonds of an ATP molecule. For accounting purposes, this is equivalent to hydrolyzing 2 ATP molecules to ADP. Thus the *net* ATP production from oxidation of stearic acid is 120 ATP (122 minus 2). ◄

► *The oxidation of an unsaturated fatty acid generates fewer ATP molecules than the oxidation of a saturated fatty acid with the same number of carbon atoms. Step 1 of the β-oxidation pathway, a dehydrogenation reaction that produces a double bond and an FADH₂ molecule, is not needed since the carbon chain already contains a double bond. One fewer FADH₂ molecule is produced for each double bond already present in the hydrocarbon chain.*

EXAMPLE 25-4

Calculating Net ATP Production from the Complete Oxidation of a Fatty Acid

What is the net ATP production for the complete oxidation of lauric acid, the C_{12} saturated fatty acid, to CO_2 and H_2O?

Solution

The total ATP production for oxidation of a fatty acid is the sum of the ATP produced from the metabolic products $FADH_2$, NADH, and acetyl CoA. In obtaining the *net* ATP production, it must be remembered that the activation of a fatty acid molecule prior to its oxidation requires ATP consumption equivalent to two ATP molecules (Section 25-4).

Oxidation of a C_{12} fatty acid requires five passages through the four-reaction sequence of the β-oxidation pathway. These five repetitions produce a total of six acetyl CoA, five $FADH_2$, and five NADH. The number of acetyl CoA produced is always equal to the number of carbon atoms present in the fatty acid divided by 2, which is $12/2 = 6$ in this case. The number of $FADH_2$ and NADH produced will always be one less than the number of acetyl CoA produced.

Further processing of these metabolic products through the citric acid cycle, electron transport chain, and oxidative phosphorylation leads to ATP production as follows:

Fatty acid activation: −2 ATP

Acetyl CoA production:

$$6 \text{ acetyl CoA} \times \frac{10 \text{ ATP}}{1 \text{ acetyl CoA}}$$ +60 ATP

FADH₂ production:

$$5 \text{ FADH}_2 \times \frac{1.5 \text{ ATP}}{1 \text{ FADH}_2}$$ +7.5 ATP

NADH production:

$$5 \text{ FADH} \times \frac{2.5 \text{ ATP}}{1 \text{ NADH}}$$ +12.5 ATP

Net ATP production: +78 ATP

The ATP equivalents for acetyl CoA, $FADH_2$, and NADH used in this calculation were first presented in Section 23-10.

The comparison between complete fatty acid oxidation and complete glucose oxidation (Section 24-4) shows that a C_{18} stearic acid molecule produces four times as much ATP as a glucose molecule.

1 glucose ⟶   30 ATP

1 stearic acid ⟶ 120 ATP

Taking into account the fact that glucose has only 6 carbon atoms and stearic acid has 18 carbon atoms still shows more ATP production from the fatty acid.

3 glucose (18 C) ⟶   90 ATP

1 stearic acid (18 C) ⟶ 120 ATP

Thus, on the basis of equal numbers of carbon atoms, lipids are 33% more efficient than carbohydrates as energy-storage systems.

On an equal-mass basis, fatty acids produce 2.5 times as much energy per gram as carbohydrates (glucose); this is shown by the following calculation involving 1.00 g of stearic acid and 1.00 g of glucose. ◀

$$1.00 \text{ g stearic acid} \times \left(\frac{1 \text{ mole stearic acid}}{284 \text{ g stearic acid}} \right) \times \left(\frac{120 \text{ moles ATP}}{1 \text{ mole stearic acid}} \right) = 0.423 \text{ mole ATP}$$

$$1.00 \text{ g glucose} \times \left(\frac{1 \text{ mole glucose}}{180 \text{ g glucose}} \right) \times \left(\frac{30 \text{ moles ATP}}{1 \text{ mole glucose}} \right) = 0.167 \text{ mole ATP}$$

The fact that fatty acids (stearic acid) yield 2.5 times as much energy per gram as carbohydrates (glucose) means that, in terms of calories consumed, the former "do 2.5 times as much damage" to a person on a diet. On the other hand, fatty acids are much better energy-storing molecules than is glucose; they can store more than twice as much energy per gram than glucose.

In dietary considerations, nutritionists say that 1 g of carbohydrate equals 4 kcal and that 1 g of fat equals 9 kcal. We now know the basis for these numbers. The value of 9 kcal for fat takes into account the fact that not all fatty acids present in fat contain 18 carbon atoms (the basis for the preceding calculations) and also the fact that fats contain glycerol, which produces ATP when degraded. ◀

Is the preferred fuel for "running" the human body fatty acids, which yield 2.5 times as much energy per gram as glucose, or is it glucose? In a normally functioning human body, certain organs use both fuels, others prefer glucose, and still others prefer fatty acids. Some generalizations about "fuel" use are

1. Skeletal muscle uses glucose (from glycogen) when in an active state. In a resting state, it uses fatty acids.
2. Cardiac muscle depends first on fatty acids and secondarily on ketone bodies (Section 25-6), glucose, and lactate.
3. The liver uses fatty acids as the preferred fuel.
4. Brain function is maintained by glucose and ketone bodies (Section 25-6). Fatty acids cannot cross the blood–brain barrier and thus are unavailable.

The focus on relevancy feature Chemical Connections 25-A—High-Intensity Versus Low-Intensity Workouts—contrasts how fuel use (carbohydrate versus fatty acid) changes within the human body over time during an exercise workout and also contrasts the fuel use mix associated with high- and low-intensity workouts.

Section 25-5 Quick Quiz

1. How many acetyl CoA molecules are produced when a C_{18} fatty acid is completely processed through the β-oxidation pathway?
   a. 8
   b. 9
   c. 18
   d. no correct response
2. How many $FADH_2$ and NADH molecules are produced, respectively, during one turn of the fatty acid β-oxidation pathway?
   a. 1 and 1
   b. 1 and 2
   c. 2 and 1
   d. no correct response
3. Net ATP production during a β-oxidation process is always 2 less than gross ATP production because ATP is consumed in fatty acid
   a. activation
   b. transport
   c. both activation and transport
   d. no correct response

Answers: 1. b; 2. a; 3. a

CHEMICAL CONNECTIONS 25-A

High-Intensity Versus Low-Intensity Workouts

In a resting state, the human body burns more fat than carbohydrate. The fuel consumed is about one-third carbohydrate and two-thirds fat.

Information about fuel consumption ratios is obtainable from respiratory gas measurements, specifically from the respiratory exchange ratio (RER). The RER is the ratio of carbon dioxide to oxygen inhaled divided by the ratio of carbon dioxide to oxygen exhaled. For 100% fat burning, the RER would be 0.7; for 100% carbohydrate burning, the RER would be 1.0.

When a person at rest begins exercising, his or her body suddenly needs energy at a greater rate—more fuel and more oxygen are needed. It takes 0.7 L of oxygen to burn 1 g of carbohydrate and 1.0 L of oxygen to burn 1 g of fat. At the onset of exercise, the body is immediately short of oxygen. Also, there is a time delay in triacylglycerol mobilization. Triacylglycerols have to be broken down to fatty acids, which have to be attached to protein carriers before

they can be carried in the bloodstream to working muscles. At their destination, they must be released from the carriers and then undergo energy-producing reactions. By contrast, glycogen is already present in muscle cells, and it can release glucose 6-phosphate as an instant fuel.

Consequently, the initial stages of exercise are fueled primarily by glucose—it requires less oxygen and can even be burned anaerobically (to lactate). During the first few minutes of exercise, up to 80% of the fuel used comes from glycogen.

With time, increased breathing rates increase oxygen supplies to muscles, and triacylglycerol use increases. Continued activity for three-quarters of an hour achieves a 50–50 balance of triacylglycerol and glucose use. Beyond an hour, triacylglycerol use may be as high as 80%.

Suppose a person is exercising at a moderate rate and decides to speed up. Immediately, body fuel and oxygen needs are increased. The response is increased use of glycogen supplies.

The accompanying table compares exercise on a stationary cycle at 45% and 70% of maximum oxygen uptake sufficient to burn 300 calories.

Adam Sylvester/Science Source

The initial stages of exercise are fueled primarily by glucose; in later stages, triacylglycerols become the primary fuel.

	Low-Intensity Exercise	High-Intensity Exercise
percent of maximum oxygen uptake	45	70
time required to burn 300 calories	48 min	30 min
calories obtained from fat	133 cal	65 cal
percent of calories from fat	44	22
rate of fat burning	2.8 cal/min	2.1 cal/min

25-6 Ketone Bodies and Ketogenesis

LEARNING FOCUS

Know the identity and structural characteristics of the three *ketone bodies*; be familiar with the individual steps in the process of *ketogenesis*.

Ordinarily, when there is adequate balance between lipid and carbohydrate metabolism, most of the acetyl CoA produced from the β-oxidation pathway is further processed through the citric acid cycle. The first step of the citric acid cycle (Section 23-7) involves the reaction between oxaloacetate and acetyl CoA. Sufficient oxaloacetate must be present for the acetyl CoA to react with. Oxaloacetate concentration depends on pyruvate produced from glycolysis (Section 24-2); pyruvate can be converted to oxaloacetate by *pyruvate carboxylase* (Section 24-6).

Certain body conditions upset the lipid–carbohydrate balance required for acetyl CoA generated by fatty acids to be processed by the citric acid cycle. These conditions include (1) dietary intake high in fat and low in carbohydrates, (2) diabetic conditions in which the body cannot adequately process glucose even though it is present, and (3) *prolonged* fasting conditions, including starvation, where glycogen supplies are exhausted. Under these conditions, the problem of inadequate oxaloacetate supplies arises, which is compounded by the body using oxaloacetate that is present to produce glucose through gluconeogenesis (Section 24-6).

What happens when acetyl CoA supplies are too high for all the acetyl CoA present to be processed through the citric acid cycle? The excess acetyl CoA is diverted to the formation of ketone bodies. ◀ A **ketone body** *is one of three substances (acetoacetate, β-hydroxybutyrate, and acetone) produced from acetyl CoA when an excess of acetyl CoA from fatty acid degradation accumulates because of triacylglycerol–carbohydrate metabolic imbalances.* The structural formulas for the three ketone bodies, two of which are C_4 molecules and the other a C_3 molecule, are

▶ *Ketone bodies are produced when the amount of acetyl CoA is excessive compared with the amount of oxaloacetate available to react with it (Step 1 of the citric acid cycle).*

Chemically, these three structures are closely related. The relationships are most easily seen if the focus starts with the molecule acetoacetate.

1. Reduction of the ketone group present in acetoacetate to a secondary alcohol produces β-hydroxybutyrate. Such a reduction process was initially considered in Section 15-10.

Structurally, there is no ketone functional group present in β-hydroxybutyrate. Despite it not being a ketone, it is still called a ketone body because of its structural relationship to acetoacetate.

2. Decarboxylation of acetoacetate produces acetone.

For a number of years, ketone bodies were thought of as degradation products that had little physiological significance. It is now known that ketone bodies can serve as sources of energy for various tissues and are very important energy sources in heart muscle and the renal cortex. Even the brain, which requires glucose, can adapt to obtain a portion of its energy from ketone bodies in dieting situations that involve a properly constructed low-carbohydrate diet.

EXAMPLE 25-5

Recognizing Structural Characteristics of Ketone Bodies

For each of the following structural characterizations for ketone bodies, identify the ketone body to which it applies. There may be more than one correct answer for a given characterization.

a. It is a C_4 molecule.
b. It is a ketoacid.
c. It can be produced by reduction of acetoacetate.
d. Its structure contains a ketone functional group.

Solution

a. *Acetoacetate* and β-*hydroxybutyrate*. Acetoacetate is a C_4 ketoacid, and β-hydroxybutyrate is a C_4 hydroxyacid.
b. *Acetoacetate*. Both acetoacetate and β-hydroxybutyrate are acids; the first is a ketoacid, and the second is a hydroxyacid.
c. β-*Hydroxybutyrate*. Reduction of the ketone functional group in acetoacetate to a secondary alcohol group produces the molecule β-hydroxybutyrate.
d. *Acetoacetate* and *acetone*. Acetoacetate is a ketoacid, and acetone is a simple ketone.

Ketogenesis

Ketogenesis *is the metabolic pathway by which ketone bodies are synthesized from acetyl CoA.* Items to consider about this process prior to looking at the actual steps in this four-step process are

1. The primary site for the process is liver mitochondria.
2. The first ketone body to be produced in ketogenesis is acetoacetate.
3. Some of the acetoacetate produced is next converted to β-hydroxybutyrate, the second ketone body.
4. The acetoacetate and β-hydroxybutyrate synthesized by ketogenesis in the liver are released to the bloodstream where acetone, the third ketone body, is produced.
5. Acetoacetate is somewhat unstable and can spontaneously or enzymatically lose its carboxyl group to form acetone. Thus the ketone body acetone is not actually a product of the metabolic pathway ketogenesis.
6. The ketone body acetone present in the bloodstream is a volatile substance that is mainly excreted by exhalation. Its sweet odor is detectable in the breath of a diabetic.
7. The amount of acetone present is usually small compared to the concentrations of the other two ketone bodies.

The actual reaction steps in the process of ketogenesis involve condensation, a second condensation, chain cleavage, and hydrogenation in that order.

Step 1: **First condensation.** Two acetyl CoA molecules combine to produce acetoacetyl CoA, a reversal of the last step of the β-oxidation pathway (Section 25-4) via a condensation reaction.

Step 2: **Second condensation.** Acetoacetyl CoA reacts with a third acetyl CoA and water to produce 3-hydroxy-3-methylglutaryl CoA (HMG-CoA) and CoA–SH.

$$CH_3-\overset{\overset{\displaystyle O}{\|}}{C}-CH_2-\overset{\overset{\displaystyle O}{\|}}{C}-S-CoA \ + \ CH_3-\overset{\overset{\displaystyle O}{\|}}{C}-S-CoA \ + \ H_2O \ \xrightarrow[\text{synthase}]{\text{HMG-CoA}}$$

Acetoacetyl CoA · · · · · · · · · · · · · Acetyl CoA

$$\overset{-}{O}-\overset{\overset{\displaystyle O}{\|}}{C}-CH_2-\overset{\overset{\displaystyle OH}{|}}{\underset{\underset{\displaystyle CH_3}{|}}{C}}-CH_2-\overset{\overset{\displaystyle O}{\|}}{C}-S-CoA \ + \ CoA-SH \ + \ H^+$$

HMG-CoA

Step 3: **Chain cleavage.** HMG-CoA is cleaved to acetyl CoA and acetoacetate.

$$\overset{-}{O}-\overset{\overset{\displaystyle O}{\|}}{C}-CH_2-\overset{\overset{\displaystyle OH}{|}}{\underset{\underset{\displaystyle CH_3}{|}}{C}}-CH_2-\overset{\overset{\displaystyle O}{\|}}{C}-S-CoA \ \xrightarrow[\text{lyase}]{\text{HMG-CoA}}$$

HMG-CoA

$$\overset{-}{O}OC-CH_2-\overset{\overset{\displaystyle O}{\|}}{C}-CH_3 \ + \ CH_3-\overset{\overset{\displaystyle O}{\|}}{C}-S-CoA$$

Acetoacetate · · · · · · · · · · Acetyl CoA

Step 4: **Hydrogenation.** Acetoacetate is reduced to β-hydroxybutyrate. The reducing agent is NADH.

$$\overset{-}{O}OC-CH_2-\overset{\overset{\displaystyle O}{\|}}{C}-CH_3 \ \xrightarrow[\text{NADH/H}^+ \quad \text{NAD}^+]{\substack{\beta\text{-Hydroxybutyrate} \\ \text{dehydrogenase}}} \ \overset{-}{O}OC-CH_2-\overset{\overset{\displaystyle OH}{|}}{CH}-CH_3$$

Acetoacetate · β-Hydroxybutyrate

The four chemical reactions associated with ketogenesis are summarized diagrammatically in Figure 25-8.

Figure 25-8 Ketogenesis involves the production of ketone bodies from acetyl CoA.

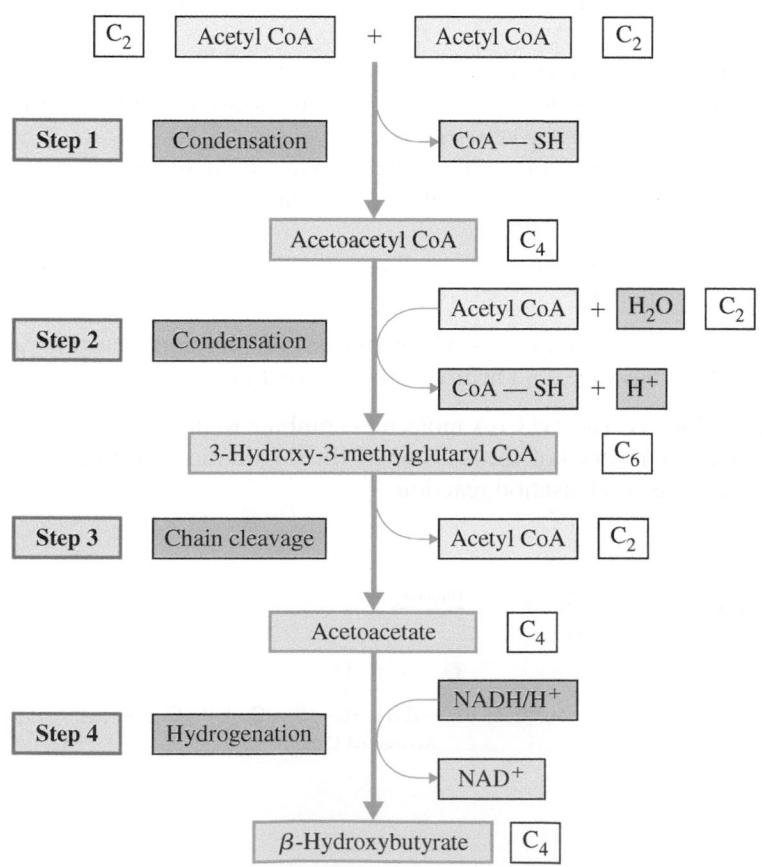

Energy Production from Acetoacetate

The principal site for ketone body production is liver mitochondria. However, ketone bodies cannot be used there for energy generation as the liver lacks the enzymes necessary to generate (recover) acetyl CoA from these substances. Hence, the ketone bodies are transported to other organs where the enzymes needed for their use are present. Unlike fatty acids, ketone bodies are water soluble and do not need a protein transport system.

The recovery of acetyl CoA from ketone bodies occurs primarily via acetoacetate. The ketone bodies β-hydroxybutyrate and acetoacetate are connected by a reversible reaction. Using a different enzyme than used in ketogenesis, β-hydroxybutyrate can be converted back to acetoacetate when cellular energy needs require it.

For acetoacetate to be used as a fuel—in heart muscle, for example—it must first be activated. Acetoacetate is activated by transfer of a CoA group from succinyl CoA (a citric acid cycle intermediate). The resulting acetoacetyl CoA is then cleaved to give two acetyl CoA molecules that can enter the citric acid cycle (see Figure 25-9). In effect, acetoacetate is a water-soluble, transportable form of acetyl units. ◀

▶ *Heart muscle and the renal cortex use acetoacetate in preference to glucose. The brain adapts to the utilization of acetoacetate with starvation or diabetes. Seventy-five percent of the fuel needs of the brain are obtained from acetoacetate during prolonged starvation.*

Ketosis

Under normal metabolic conditions (an appropriate glucose–fatty acid balance), the concentration of ketone bodies in the blood is very low—about 1 mg/100 mL. Abnormal metabolic conditions, such as those mentioned at the start of this section, produce elevated blood ketone levels, levels 50–100 times greater than normal. Excess accumulation of ketone bodies in blood (20 mg/100 mL) is called *ketonemia*. At a level of 70 mg/100 mL, the renal threshold is exceeded and ketone bodies are excreted in the urine, a condition called *ketonuria*. **Ketosis** *is the body condition in which high levels of ketone bodies are present in both the blood and urine.* Both ketonemia and ketonuria are contributors to the condition called ketosis. Ketosis is often detectable by the smell of acetone on a person's breath; acetone is very volatile and is excreted through the lungs.

For the vast majority of persons following a low-carbohydrate diet, the effects of ketosis appear to be harmless or nearly so. The symptoms of the *mild* ketosis that occurs as the result of such dieting include headache, dry mouth, and sometimes acetone-smelling breath. Typically, the same is true for fasting situations; only mild ketosis effects are observed.

Figure 25-9 The pathway for utilization of acetoacetate as a fuel. The required succinyl CoA comes from the citric acid cycle.

A serious to extremely serious ketosis problem called *ketoacidosis* can develop in persons with uncontrolled Type 1 diabetes. Two of the three ketone bodies—acetoacetate and β-hydroxybutyrate—are acids; a carboxyl group is present in their structure. At elevated levels, the presence of these two ketone bodies can cause a significant decrease in blood pH. This change in blood acidity, if left untreated, leads to heavy breathing (acidic blood carries less oxygen) and increased urine output that can lead to dehydration. Ultimately the condition of ketoacidosis can cause coma and death.

Ketoacidosis is also called *metabolic acidosis* to distinguish it from *respiratory acidosis* (Section 10-12), which is not linked to ketone bodies.

Section 25-6 Quick Quiz

1. Which of the following is *not* a ketone body?
   a. acetoacetate
   b. β-hydroxybutyrate
   c. acetone
   d. no correct response
2. How many of the ketone bodies are C_4 molecules?
   a. 1
   b. 2
   c. 3
   d. no correct response
3. How many acetyl CoA molecules are used as reactants in the process of ketogenesis?
   a. 1
   b. 2
   c. 3
   d. no correct response
4. The correct sequence for the four reactions of ketogenesis in terms of the "type of reaction occurring" is
   a. condensation, condensation, hydrogenation, cleavage
   b. condensation, cleavage, condensation, hydrogenation
   c. condensation, condensation, cleavage, hydrogenation
   d. no correct response
5. The characterization $C_4 + C_2 \longrightarrow C_6$ applies to which step in the process of ketogenesis?
   a. Step 1
   b. Step 2
   c. Step 3
   d. no correct response
6. How many units of acetyl CoA are produced when an acetoacetyl CoA undergoes cleavage using a thiolase?
   a. 1
   b. 2
   c. 3
   d. no correct response

Answers: 1. d; 2. b; 3. c; 4. c; 5. b; 6. b

25-7 Biosynthesis of Fatty Acids: Lipogenesis

LEARNING FOCUS

Be familiar with the steps in the lipogenesis pathway by which fatty acids are synthesized from acetyl CoA.

Lipogenesis *is the metabolic pathway by which fatty acids are synthesized from acetyl CoA.* As was the case for the opposing processes of glycolysis and gluconeogenesis, lipogenesis is not simply a reversal of the steps for degradation of fatty acids (the β-oxidation pathway). Before looking at the details of fatty acid synthesis, some differences between the synthesis and degradation of fatty acids are considered.

1. Lipogenesis occurs in the cell cytosol, whereas degradation of fatty acids occurs in the mitochondrial matrix. Because they have different reaction sites, these two opposing processes can occur at the same time when necessary.
2. Different enzymes are involved in the two processes. Lipogenesis enzymes are collected into a multienzyme complex called *fatty acid synthase*. This enzyme complex ties the reaction steps of lipogenesis closely together. The enzymes involved in fatty acid degradation are not physically associated, so the reaction steps are independent.
3. Intermediates of the two processes are covalently bonded to different carriers. The carrier for fatty acid degradation intermediates is CoA. Lipogenesis intermediates are bonded to ACP (acyl carrier protein).
4. Fatty acid synthesis is dependent on the reducing agent NADPH. Fatty acid degradation is dependent on the oxidizing agents FAD and NAD^+.
5. Fatty acids are built up two carbons at a time during synthesis and are broken down two carbons at a time during degradation. The source of the two carbon units differs between the two processes. In lipogenesis, acetyl CoA is used to form malonyl ACP, which becomes the carrier of the two carbon units. CoA derivatives are involved in all steps of fatty acid degradation.

In general, fatty acid biosynthesis (lipogenesis) occurs any time dietary intake provides more nutrients than are needed for energy requirements. The primary lipogenesis sites are the liver, adipose tissue, and mammary glands. The mammary glands show increased synthetic activity during periods of lactation.

The Citrate–Malate Shuttle System

Acetyl CoA is the starting material for lipogenesis. Because acetyl CoA is generated in mitochondria and lipogenesis occurs in the cytosol, the acetyl CoA must first be transported to the cytosol. It exits the mitochondria through a transport system that involves citrate ion.

The outer mitochondrial matrix is freely permeable to acetyl CoA, as well as many other substances such as citrate, malate, and pyruvate. The inner mitochondrial membrane, however, is not permeable to acetyl CoA. An indirect shuttle system involving citrate solves this problem.

This shuttle system, which is diagrammed in Figure 25-10, functions as follows. Mitochondrial acetyl CoA reacts with oxaloacetate (the first step of the citric acid cycle; Section 23-6) to produce citrate, which is then transported through the inner mitochondrial membrane by a citrate transporter (a membrane protein structure). Once in the cytosol, the citrate undergoes the reverse reaction to its formation to regenerate the acetyl CoA and oxaloacetate, with ATP involved in the process. The acetyl CoA so generated becomes the "fuel" for lipogenesis; the oxaloacetate so generated reacts further to produce malate, in an NADH-dependent change. The malate reenters the mitochondrial matrix through a malate transporter and is then converted to oxaloacetate, which can then react with another acetyl CoA molecule to form citrate and the shuttle process repeats itself. Additional particulars about the shuttle system are found in Figure 25-10.

Compared to the carnitine shuttle system for long-chain fatty acid groups (acyl groups; Figure 25-6), the citrate–malate shuttle system is more complex. However, the intermediates in the shuttle have been encountered before, in the citric acid cycle. ◀

ACP Complex Formation

Studies show that all intermediates in fatty acid biosynthesis (lipogenesis) are bound to acyl carrier proteins (ACP–SH) rather than coenzyme A (CoA–SH). This applies even to the C_2 acetyl group. An acyl carrier protein can be regarded as a "giant coenzyme A molecule." Involved in the ACP structure are the 2-ethanethiol and

▶ *The reaction sequence malate-to-oxaloacetate-to-citrate is also part of the citric acid cycle. This reaction sequence constitutes the last and first steps of the cycle (Section 23-7). Malate-to-oxaloacetate is the last step of the cycle, and oxaloacetate-to-citrate the first step of the cycle.*

Figure 25-10 The citrate–malate shuttle system for transferring acetyl CoA from a mitochondrion to the cytosol.

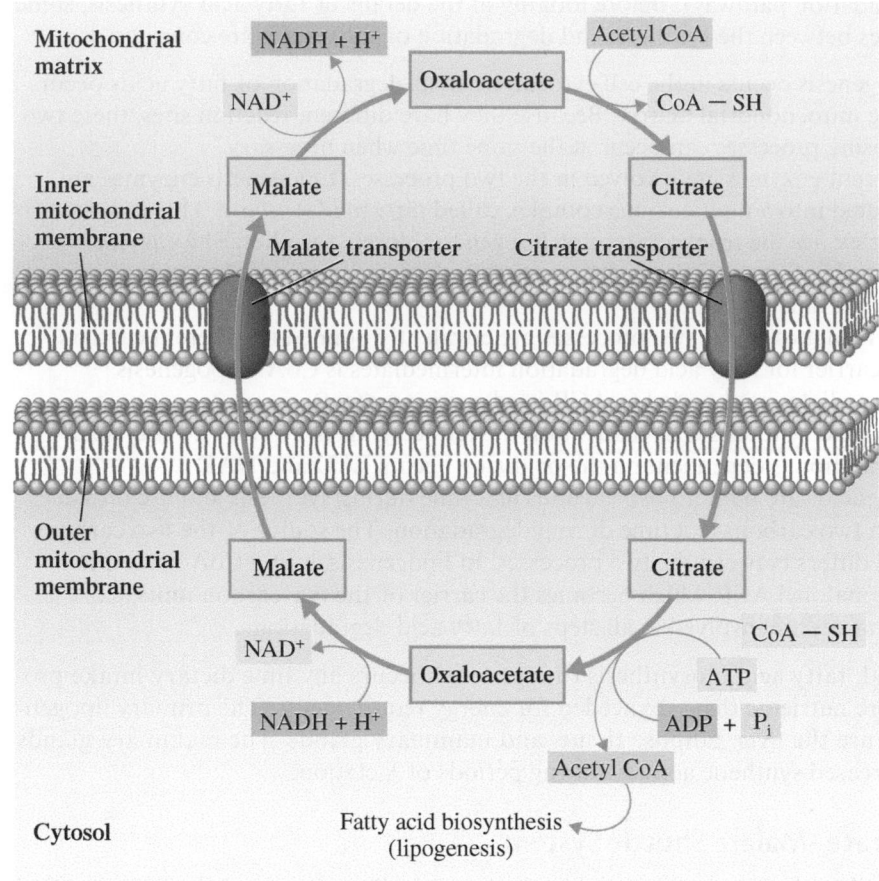

pantothenic acid components present in CoA–SH (Section 23-3), which are attached to a polypeptide chain containing 77 amino acid residues.

Two simple ACP complexes are needed to start the lipogenesis process. They are acetyl ACP, a C_2–ACP, and malonyl ACP, a C_3–ACP. Additional malonyl ACP molecules are needed as the lipogenesis process proceeds. ◄

▶ *The parent compound for the malonyl group is malonic acid, the C_3 dicarboxylic acid*

Cytosolic acetyl CoA is the starting material for the production of both of these simple ACP complexes. Acetyl ACP is produced by the direct reaction of acetyl CoA with an ACP molecule.

$$\underset{\text{Acetyl CoA}}{CH_3-\overset{O}{\overset{\|}{C}}-S-CoA} + \underset{\text{ACP}}{ACP-S-H} \xrightarrow{\text{Acetyl transferase}} \underset{\text{Acetyl ACP}}{CH_3-\overset{O}{\overset{\|}{C}}-S-ACP} + \underset{\text{CoA}}{CoA-S-H}$$

The reaction to produce malonyl ACP requires two steps. The first step is a carboxylation reaction with ATP involvement. ◄

▶ *The conversion of acetyl CoA to malonyl CoA is an activation step. Malonyl CoA is the activated form of acetyl CoA. It is malonyl ACP rather than acetyl ACP that is the two-carbon donor in each cycle of the chain elongation phase of lipogenesis.*

$$\underset{\text{Acetyl CoA}}{CH_3-\overset{O}{\overset{\|}{C}}-S-CoA} + CO_2 \xrightarrow[\underset{ATP \quad ADP + P_i}{}]{\text{Acetyl CoA carboxylase}} \underset{\text{Malonyl CoA}}{{}^-O-\overset{O}{\overset{\|}{C}}-CH_2-\overset{O}{\overset{\|}{C}}-S-CoA-A} + H^+$$

This reaction occurs only when cellular ATP levels are high. It is catalyzed by *acetyl CoA carboxylase complex*, which requires both Mg^{2+} ion and the B vitamin biotin for its activity. The malonyl CoA so produced then reacts with ACP to produce malonyl ACP.

$$\underset{\text{Malonyl CoA}}{{}^-O-\overset{O}{\overset{\|}{C}}-CH_2-\overset{O}{\overset{\|}{C}}-S-CoA} + \underset{\text{ACP}}{ACP-S-H} \xrightarrow{\text{Malonyl transferase}} \underset{\text{Malonyl ACP}}{{}^-O-\overset{O}{\overset{\|}{C}}-CH_2-\overset{O}{\overset{\|}{C}}-S-ACP} + \underset{\text{CoA}}{CoA-S-H}$$

Figure 25-11 In the first "turn" of the fatty acid biosynthetic pathway, acetyl ACP is converted to butyryl ACP. In the next cycle (not shown), the butyryl ACP reacts with another malonyl ACP to produce a 6-carbon acid. Continued cycles produce acids with 8-, 10-, 12-, 14-, and 16-carbon atoms.

Chain Elongation

Four reactions that occur in a cyclic pattern within the multienzyme *fatty acid synthase complex* constitute the chain elongation process used for fatty acid synthesis. The reactions of the *first* turn of the cycle, in general terms, are shown in Figure 25-11. Specific details about this series of reactions follow.

Step 1: **Condensation.** Acetyl ACP and malonyl ACP condense together to form acetoacetyl ACP.

$$H^+ + \underset{\text{Acetyl ACP}}{CH_3-\overset{\overset{O}{\|}}{C}-S-ACP} + \underset{\text{Malonyl ACP}}{O-\overset{\overset{O}{\|}}{C}-CH_2-\overset{\overset{O}{\|}}{C}-S-ACP} \longrightarrow \underset{\text{Acetoacetyl ACP}}{CH_3-\overset{\overset{O}{\|}}{C}-CH_2-\overset{\overset{O}{\|}}{C}-S-ACP} + CO_2 + ACP-SH$$

Note that a C_2 species (acetyl) and a C_3 species (malonyl) react to produce a C_4 species (acetoacetyl) rather than a C_5 species. One carbon atom leaves the reaction in the form of a CO_2 molecule.

Steps 2 through 4 involve a sequence of functional group changes that have been encountered twice before—in fatty acid degradation (Section 25-4) and in the citric acid cycle (Section 23-7). This time, however, the changes occur in the reverse sequence to that previously encountered. ◀ The functional group changes are

▶ *Steps 2, 3, and 4 of fatty acid biosynthesis accomplish the reverse of Steps 3, 2, and 1 of the β-oxidation pathway.*

$$\textbf{Ketone} \xrightarrow[\text{(Reduction)}]{\overset{②}{\text{Hydrogenation}}} \textbf{secondary alcohol} \xrightarrow{\overset{③}{\text{Dehydration}}} \textbf{alkene} \xrightarrow[\text{(Reduction)}]{\overset{④}{\text{Hydrogenation}}} \textbf{alkane}$$

Step 2: **First hydrogenation.** The keto group of the acetoacetyl complex, which involves the β-carbon atom, is reduced to the corresponding alcohol by NADPH.

$$\underset{\text{Acetoacetyl ACP}}{CH_3-\overset{\overset{O}{\|}}{C}-CH_2-\overset{\overset{O}{\|}}{C}-S-ACP} \xrightarrow[\underset{\text{NADPH/H}^+ \quad \text{NADP}^+}{}]{} \underset{\beta\text{-Hydroxybutyryl ACP}}{CH_3-\overset{\overset{OH}{|}}{CH}-CH_2-\overset{\overset{O}{\|}}{C}-S-ACP}$$

Step 3: **Dehydration.** The alcohol produced in Step 2 is dehydrated to introduce a double bond into the molecule (between the α and β carbons).

$$\underset{\text{β-Hydroxybutyryl ACP}}{CH_3-\underset{\underset{OH}{|}}{CH}-CH_2-\overset{\overset{O}{\|}}{C}-S-ACP} \xrightarrow[H_2O]{} \underset{\text{Crotonyl ACP}}{CH_3-\overset{trans}{CH}=CH-\overset{\overset{O}{\|}}{C}-S-ACP}$$

Step 4: **Second hydrogenation.** The double bond introduced in Step 3 is converted to a single bond through hydrogenation. As in Step 2, NADPH is the reducing agent. ◀

$$\underset{\text{Crotonyl ACP}}{CH_3-\overset{trans}{CH}=CH-\overset{\overset{O}{\|}}{C}-S-ACP} \xrightarrow[\underset{NADPH/H^+ \quad NADP^+}{}]{} \underset{\text{Butyryl ACP}}{CH_3-CH_2-CH_2-\overset{\overset{O}{\|}}{C}-S-ACP}$$

▶ *The hydrogenation reactions in Steps 2 and 4 of the fatty acid chain elongation process are reduction reactions, with NADPH serving as the reducing agent.*

▶ *Among enzymes, the multienzyme complex fatty acid synthase is considered to be a "monster" or "gargantuan" enzyme in terms of size. Recent research relating to a fungal fatty acid synthase indicates that the enzyme has two reaction chambers with three full sets of active sites, so six fatty acids can be synthesized simultaneously. ACP shuttles intermediates around the reaction chamber, and the fatty acid chain length increases by two carbons with each cycle.*

Further cycles of the preceding four-step process convert the four-carbon acyl group to a six-carbon acyl group, then to an eight-carbon acyl group, and so on (Figure 25-12). Elongation of the acyl group chain through this procedure, which is tied to the fatty acid synthase complex, stops upon formation of the C_{16} acyl group (palmitic acid). Different enzyme systems and different cellular locations are required for elongation of the chain beyond C_{16} and for introduction of double bonds into the acyl group (unsaturated fatty acids). ◀

A relatively large input of energy is needed to biosynthesize a fatty acid molecule, as can be seen from the data in Table 25-2, which gives a net summary of the reactants and products involved in the synthesis of one molecule of palmitic acid, the 16:0 fatty acid.

Figure 25-12 The sequence of cycles needed to produce a C_{16} fatty acid from acetyl ACP.

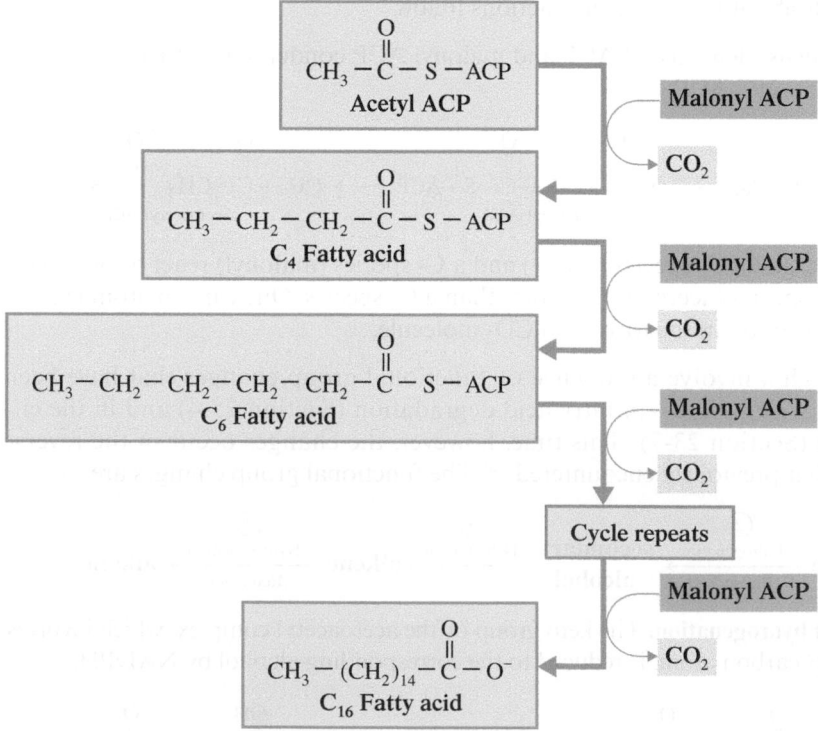

EXAMPLE 25-6

Characterizing Intermediates as to When They Are Produced in the Lipogenesis Process

In which step (of Steps 1 through 4) and in which cycle (first or second turn) of fatty acid biosynthesis (lipogenesis) is each of the following compounds encountered as a product?

a.

$$CH_3-CH_2-CH_2-\overset{\overset{\displaystyle OH}{|}}{CH}-CH_2-\overset{\overset{\displaystyle O}{\|}}{C}-S-ACP$$

b.

$$CH_3-CH=CH-\overset{\overset{\displaystyle O}{\|}}{C}-S-ACP$$

c.

$$CH_3-\overset{\overset{\displaystyle O}{\|}}{C}-CH_2-\overset{\overset{\displaystyle O}{\|}}{C}-S-ACP$$

d.

$$CH_3-CH_2-CH_2-CH_2-CH_2-\overset{\overset{\displaystyle O}{\|}}{C}-S-ACP$$

Solution

All intermediates produced during the first turn of the cycle will have a C_4 carbon chain, those produced during the second turn a C_6 carbon chain, those during the third turn a C_8 carbon chain, and so on.

Determination of which step in a turn is involved is based on the functional group present in the carbon chain. Step 1 produces a keto acid chain, Step 2 a hydroxy acid chain, Step 3 an unsaturated acid chain, and Step 4 a saturated acid chain.

a. The characterization for this molecule's carbon chain is C_6 hydroxyacid. The hydroxyacid designation indicates *Step 2*, and the C_6 chain length indicates *second turn*.

b. The carbon chain is a C_4 unsaturated acid; this indicates *Step 3* and *first turn*.

c. The carbon chain is a C_4 keto acid; this indicates *Step 1* and *first turn*.

d. The carbon chain is a C_6 saturated acid; this indicates *Step 4* and *second turn*.

Unsaturated Fatty Acid Biosynthesis

Production of unsaturated fatty acids (insertion of double bonds) requires molecular oxygen (O_2). In an oxidation step, hydrogen is removed and combined with the O_2 to form water.

In humans and animals, enzymes can introduce double bonds only between C4 and C5 and between C9 and C10. Thus the important unsaturated fatty acids linoleic (C_{18} with C9 and C12 double bonds) and linolenic (C_{18} with C9, C12, and C15 double bonds) cannot be biosynthesized. They must be obtained from the diet. (Plants have the enzymes necessary to synthesize these acids.) Acids such as linoleic and linolenic, which cannot be synthesized by the body but are necessary for its proper functioning, are called *essential fatty acids* (Section 19-2).

Lipogenesis can be used to convert glucose to fatty acids via acetyl CoA. The reverse process, conversion of fatty acids to glucose, is not possible within the human body.

Table 25-2 Reactants and Products in the Biosynthesis of One Molecule of Palmitic Acid, the 16:0 Fatty Acid

Reactants	Products
8 acetyl CoA	1 palmitate
7 ATP	8 CoA
14 NADPH	7 ADP
6 H$^+$	7 P$_i$
	14 NADP$^+$
	6 H$_2$O

Fatty acids can be broken down to acetyl CoA, but there is no enzyme present for the conversion of acetyl CoA to pyruvate or oxaloacetate, starting materials for gluconeogenesis (Section 24-6). Plants and some bacteria do possess the needed enzymes and thus can convert fatty acids to carbohydrates.

Section 25-7 Quick Quiz

1. The process of lipogenesis occurs in the
   a. mitochondrial matrix
   b. cell nucleus
   c. cell cytosol
   d. no correct response
2. The notation ACP stands for
   a. acyl carnitine protein
   b. acyl carrier protein
   c. acetyl carrier protein
   d. no correct response
3. Which of the following is the *correct* characterization for the first step in the first turn of the chain elongation phase of lipogenesis?
   a. $C_2 + C_2 \longrightarrow C_4$
   b. $C_2 + C_3 \longrightarrow C_5$
   c. $C_2 + C_3 \longrightarrow C_4 + C_1$
   d. no correct response
4. Steps 2 through 4 of the chain elongation phase of lipogenesis involve, respectively, which of the following reaction sequences?
   a. dehydrogenation, dehydration, dehydrogenation
   b. hydrogenation, hydration, hydrogenation
   c. hydrogenation, dehydration, hydrogenation
   d. no correct response
5. The reducing agent needed in the process of lipogenesis is
   a. NADPH
   b. NADH
   c. $FADH_2$
   d. no correct response
6. The carrier of the "two carbon units" used to biosynthesize a fatty acid is
   a. acetyl CoA
   b. acetyl ACP
   c. malonyl ACP
   d. no correct response

Answers: 1. c; 2. b; 3. c; 4. c; 5. a; 6. c

25-8 Relationships Between Lipogenesis and Citric Acid Cycle Intermediates

LEARNING FOCUS

Know the structural relationships that exist between C_4-ACP lipogenesis intermediates and C_4 citric acid intermediates.

The intermediates in the last four steps of the citric acid cycle are all C_4 molecules (Section 23-7). In the first cycle of the four repetitive reactions in lipogenesis, all of the carbon chains attached to ACP are C_4 chains. Several relationships exist between these two sets of C_4 entities.

The last four intermediates of the citric acid cycle bear the following relationship to each other.

Saturated C_4 diacid → unsaturated C_4 diacid → hydroxy C_4 diacid → keto C_4 diacid

The intermediate C_4 carbon chains of lipogenesis bear the following relationship to each other.

Figure 25-13 Structural relationships between C_4 citric acid cycle intermediates and C_4 lipogenesis intermediates. C_4 citric acid cycle intermediates are diacid derivatives, and C_4 lipogenesis intermediates are monoacid derivatives. The same derivative types are present in both series of intermediates.

Keto C_4 monoacid → hydroxy C_4 monoacid → unsaturated C_4 monoacid

→ saturated C_4 monoacid

Note two important contrasts in these compound sequences:

1. The citric acid intermediates involve C_4 *di*acids, and the lipogenesis intermediates involve C_4 *mono*acids.
2. The order in which the various acid derivative types are encountered in lipogenesis is the reverse of the order in which they are encountered in the citric acid cycle.

Figure 25-13 contrasts the structures of the various C_4 diacid intermediates from the citric acid cycle with the various C_4 monoacid intermediates encountered in lipogenesis.

Section 25-8 Quick Quiz

1. Which of the following statements concerning the intermediates in lipogenesis and the citric acid cycle is *incorrect*?
   a. Lipogenesis intermediates are C_4 derivatives of a monocarboxylic acid.
   b. Citric acid cycle intermediates are C_4 derivatives of a dicarboxylic acid.
   c. Intermediates in both processes are derivatives of C_3 carboxylic acids.
   d. no correct response
2. The ketoacid intermediates in lipogenesis and the citric acid cycle are, respectively,
   a. acetoacetate and oxaloacetate
   b. acetoacetate and malate
   c. crotonate and fumarate
   d. no correct response

Answers: 1. c; 2. a

25-9 Fate of Fatty-Acid-Generated Acetyl CoA

LEARNING FOCUS

Be familiar with several common pathways by which fatty-acid-generated acetyl CoA is consumed.

What happens to the acetyl CoA obtained from fatty acid oxidation? Several different options are available for its use. These options include the following:

1. The acetyl CoA can be further processed through the common metabolic pathway (CAC, ETC, and oxidative phosphorylation) to obtain ATP. Section 25-5 considered how much ATP is obtained from the oxidation of selected fatty acids.

2. The acetyl CoA can undergo conversion to ketone bodies (Section 25-6). Such ketone bodies can be reconverted, when needed, back to acetyl CoA, which can then be processed for ATP production.

3. The acetyl CoA can be stored in the body in the form of triacylglycerols (Section 19-4) by reconverting via lipogenesis the acetyl CoA to fatty acids (Section 25-7) that are then converted to triacylglycerols. ◄

4. The acetyl CoA can be used as the starting material for the production of lipids other than fatty acids that the body needs. A specific example of such "other lipid" production is the biosynthesis of cholesterol. As was previously discussed (Section 19-9), cholesterol is a necessary component of cell membranes. It is also the precursor for bile salts, sex hormones, and adrenal hormones (Sections 19-11 and 19–12).

   The biosynthesis of cholesterol, a C_{27} molecule, occurs primarily in the liver. Biosynthesis of cholesterol consumes 18 molecules of acetyl CoA and involves at least 27 separate enzymatic steps. An overview of cholesterol biosynthesis, which shows key intermediate compounds, is given in Figure 25-14.

   The rate-determining step in the formation of cholesterol occurs early in its biosynthesis. It involves the formation of the C_6 intermediate mevalonate; in a multistep sequence, three acetyl CoA molecules are condensed together to produce this C_6 species. Extensive research has been carried out concerning this "slow step," with the goal being prevention of its occurrence as a means of decreasing the body's internal production of cholesterol in order to decrease blood cholesterol levels. The focus on relevancy feature Chemical Connections 25-B—Statins: Drugs That Lower Plasma Levels of Cholesterol—discusses the success obtained in achieving this goal.

5. It is also important to note what *cannot* happen to the acetyl CoA obtained from fatty acid oxidation. In humans and animals, it *cannot* be used for the *net* synthesis of glucose.

   Pyruvate or oxaloacetate is the needed starting material for glucose production via gluconeogenesis (Section 24-6). Humans and animals do not possess the enzymes needed to convert acetyl CoA to pyruvate. (By contrast, plants do contain the two additional enzymes needed.) Pyruvate can be converted to acetyl CoA (Section 24-3) in a reaction sequence that is *irreversible*. Acetyl CoA cannot be converted to pyruvate.

   In Step 1 of gluconeogenesis, pyruvate is converted to oxaloacetate (Section 24-6). Oxaloacetate is also produced in the last reaction of the citric acid cycle. However, use of such oxaloacetate in glucose production cannot lead to a *net* increase in glucose. In each round of the citric acid cycle, two carbon atoms enter the cycle (as acetyl CoA) and two carbon atoms leave the cycle (as CO_2). Thus there is no gain in carbon atoms in a turn of the cycle. The oxaloacetate produced in the last step of the cycle is not newly formed oxaloacetate but, rather, regenerated oxaloacetate; in Step 1 of the citric acid cycle oxaloacetate is consumed, and in Step 8 it is regenerated. Thus no net increase in oxaloacetate production occurs during the citric acid cycle because there is no net increase in carbon atoms processed; as a result, no net increase in glucose production can occur using oxaloacetate.

▶ *Fatty acids, once synthesized, do not react directly with glycerol to form triacylglycerol molecules. Glycerol must first be activated. The energy for this activation is supplied by an ATP molecule, and glycerol 1-phosphate is the activation product.*

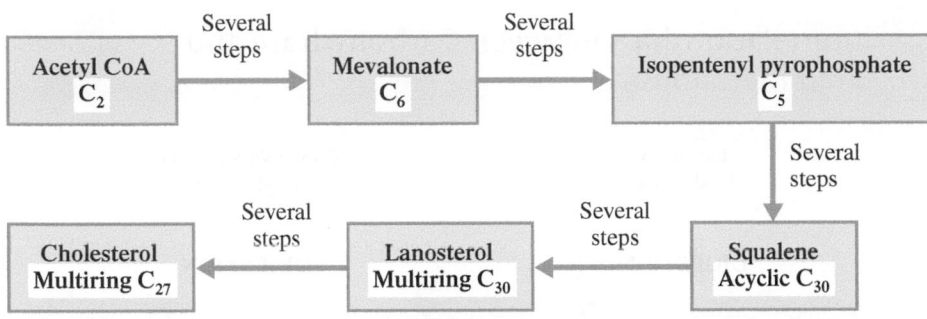

Figure 25-14 An overview of the biosynthetic pathway for cholesterol synthesis.

CHEMICAL CONNECTIONS 25-B

Statins: Drugs That Lower Plasma Levels of Cholesterol

More than half of all deaths in the United States are directly or indirectly related to heart disease, in particular to atherosclerosis. Atherosclerosis results from the buildup of plaque (fatty deposits) on the inner walls of arteries. Cholesterol, obtained from low-density lipoproteins (LDLs) that circulate in blood plasma, is also a major component of plaque.

Because most of the cholesterol in the human body is synthesized in the liver, from acetyl CoA, much research has focused on finding ways to inhibit its biosynthesis. The rate-determining step in cholesterol biosynthesis involves the conversion of 3-hydroxy-3-methylglutaryl CoA (HMG-CoA) to mevalonate, a process catalyzed by the enzyme HMG-CoA reductase.

3-Hydroxy-3-methylglutaryl-CoA (HMG-CoA)

Mevalonate

In 1976, as the result of screening more than 8000 strains of microorganisms, a compound now called *mevastatin*—a potent inhibitor of HMG-CoA reductase—was isolated from culture broths of a fungus. Soon thereafter, a second, more active compound called *lovastatin* was isolated.

$R_1 = R_2 = H$, mevastatin
$R_1 = H, R_2 = CH_3$, lovastatin (Mevacor)
$R_1 = R_2 = CH_3$, simvastatin (Zocor)

These "statins" are very effective in lowering plasma concentrations of LDL by functioning as competitive inhibitors of HMG-CoA reductase.

After years of testing, the statins are now available as prescription drugs for lowering blood cholesterol levels.

Clinical studies indicate that use of these drugs lowers the incidence of heart disease in individuals with mildly elevated blood cholesterol levels. A later-generation statin with a ring structure distinctly different from that of earlier statins—atorvastatin (Lipitor)—became the most prescribed medication in the United States starting in the year 2000. Note the structural resemblance between part of the structure of Lipitor and that of mevalonate.

Mevalonate

Atorvastatin (Lipitor)

Recent research studies have unexpectedly shown that the cholesterol-lowering statins have two added benefits.

Laboratory studies with animals indicate that statins prompt growth of cells to build new bone, replacing bone that has been leached away by osteoporosis ("brittle-bone disease"). A retrospective study of osteoporosis patients who also took statins shows evidence that their bones became more dense than did bones of osteoporosis patients who did not take the drugs.

Statins have also been shown to function as anti-inflammatory agents that counteract the effects of a common virus, cytomegalovirus, which is now believed to contribute to the development of coronary heart disease. Researchers believe that by age 65, more than 70% of all people have been exposed to this virus. The virus, along with other infecting agents in blood, may actually trigger the inflammation mechanism for heart disease.

CHEMISTRY AT A GLANCE — Interrelationships Between Carbohydrate and Lipid Metabolism

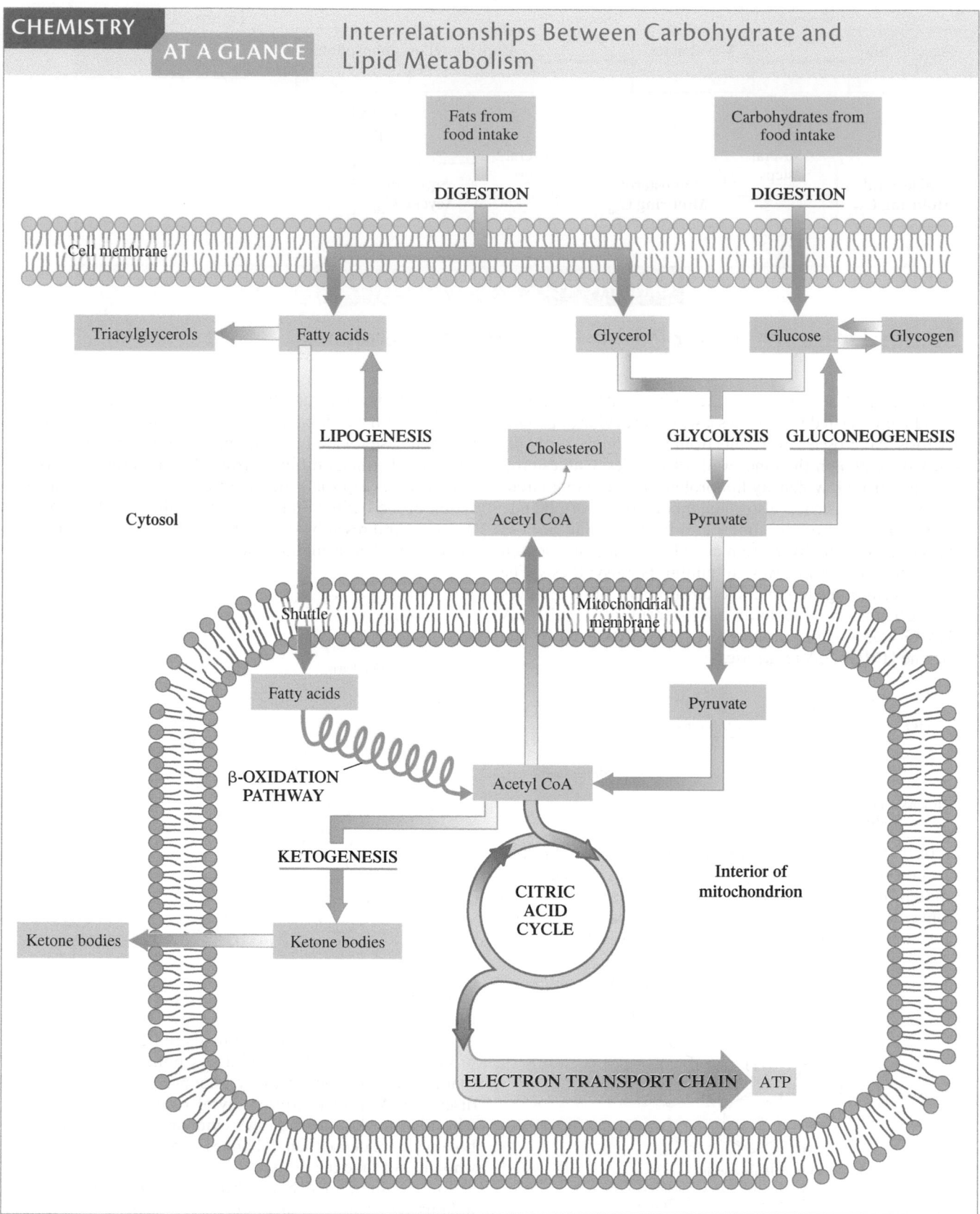

1. Which of the following fates for fatty acid–generated acetyl CoA is *not* possible?
   a. It can be processed through the common metabolic pathway.
   b. It can be used to biosynthesize fatty acids.
   c. It can be used to form ketone bodies.
   d. no correct response
2. Which of the following is a *correct* statement about the biosynthetic pathway for cholesterol synthesis?
   a. All intermediates are C_5 species.
   b. All intermediates are C_6 species.
   c. It is a multistep process.
3. How many molecules of acetyl CoA are consumed in the production of a cholesterol molecule?
   a. 7
   b. 18
   c. 27
   d. no correct response
4. Acetyl CoA *cannot* be converted to which of the following molecules?
   a. pyruvate
   b. malonyl CoA
   c. acetoacetyl CoA
   d. no correct response

Answers: 1. d; 2. c; 3. b; 4. a

25-10 Relationships Between Lipid and Carbohydrate Metabolism

LEARNING FOCUS

Be familiar with key interrelationships between lipid metabolism and carbohydrate metabolism.

Acetyl CoA is the primary link between lipid and carbohydrate metabolism. As shown in the Chemistry at a Glance feature—Interrelationships Between Carbohydrate and Lipid Metabolism—acetyl CoA is the degradation product for glucose, glycerol, and fatty acids, and it is also the starting material for the biosynthesis of fatty acids, cholesterol, and ketone bodies.

This Chemistry at a Glance summary diagram also depicts *where* within a cell the reactions associated with carbohydrate and lipid metabolism occur. As shown in the diagram, for both types of metabolism some of the reactions occur within the mitochondrion and others occur within the cytosol.

1. Which of the following substances cannot be converted to pyruvate?
   a. fatty acids
   b. glycerol
   c. glucose
   d. no correct response
2. Which of the following processes could *not* be used as a source of acetyl CoA needed for ketone body formation?
   a. glycolysis
   b. β-oxidation pathway
   c. lipogenesis
   d. no correct response
3. Which of the following processes occurs within the cytosol of a cell?
   a. ketogenesis
   b. β-oxidation pathway
   c. electron transport chain
   d. no correct response

Answers: 1. a; 2. c; 3. d

25-11 B Vitamins and Lipid Metabolism

LEARNING FOCUS

Be familiar with the involvement that B vitamins have in lipid metabolism.

The final section in each of the last two chapters includes a summary diagram showing how B vitamins, as coenzymes, participate in the metabolic reactions discussed in the chapter. This pattern continues in this chapter.

Collectively, for the processes of β-oxidation, ketogenesis, and lipogenesis, as is shown in Figure 25-15, four of the eight B vitamins are needed. These are niacin (as NAD$^+$, NADH, and NADPH), riboflavin (as FAD), pantothenic acid (as CoA, acetyl CoA, and ACP), and biotin.

Figure 25-15 B vitamin participation, as coenzymes, in chemical reactions associated with lipid metabolism.

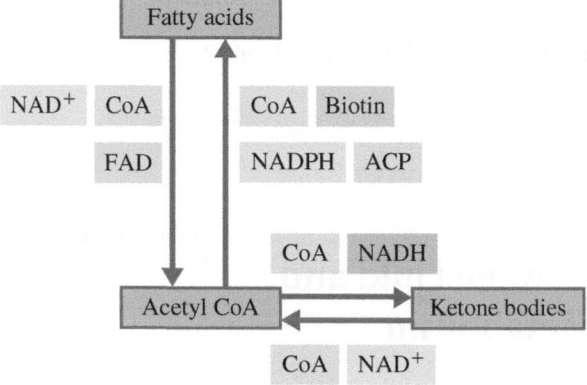

Section 25-11 Quick Quiz

1. How many different B vitamins participate in the reactions involved in lipid metabolism?
   a. 4
   b. 5
   c. 6
   d. no correct response
2. Which of the following B-vitamin-containing coenzymes is needed in the reactions associated with the conversion of acetyl CoA to ketone bodies?
   a. NAD$^+$
   b. NADPH
   c. ACP
   d. no correct response
3. Which of the following B-vitamin-containing coenzymes is needed in the reactions associated with the conversion of fatty acids to acetyl CoA?
   a. NADP
   b. FAD
   c. biotin
   d. no correct response

Answers: 1. a; 2. a; 3. b

Concepts to Remember

Triacylglycerol digestion and absorption. Triacylglycerols are digested (hydrolyzed) in the intestine and then reassembled after passage into the intestinal wall. Chylomicrons transport the reassembled triacylglycerols from intestinal cells to the bloodstream (Section 25-1).

Triacylglycerol storage and mobilization. Triacylglycerols are stored as fat droplets in adipose tissue. When they are needed for energy, enzyme-controlled hydrolysis reactions liberate the fatty acids, which then enter the bloodstream and travel to tissues where they are utilized (Section 25-2).

Glycerol metabolism. Glycerol is first phosphorylated and then oxidized to dihydroxyacetone phosphate, a glycolysis pathway intermediate. Through glycolysis and the common metabolic pathway, the glycerol can be converted to CO_2 and H_2O (Section 25-3).

Fatty acid degradation. Fatty acid degradation is accomplished through the β-oxidation pathway. The degradation process involves removal of carbon atoms, two at a time, from the carboxyl end of the fatty acid. There are four repeating reactions that accompany the removal of each two-carbon unit. A turn of the cycle also produces one molecule each of acetyl CoA, NADH, and FADH$_2$ (Section 25-4).

Ketone bodies. Acetoacetate, β-hydroxybutyrate, and acetone are known as ketone bodies. Synthesis occurs mainly in the liver from acetyl CoA as a result of excessive fatty acid degradation. During starvation and in unchecked diabetes, the level of ketone bodies in the blood becomes very high (Section 25-6).

Fatty acid biosynthesis. Fatty acid biosynthesis, lipogenesis, occurs through the addition of two-carbon units to a growing acyl chain. The added two-carbon units come from malonyl CoA. A multienzyme complex, an acyl carrier protein (ACP), and NADPH are important parts of the biosynthetic process (Section 25-7).

Biosynthesis of cholesterol. Cholesterol is biosynthesized from acetyl CoA in a multistep series of reactions. Eighteen molecules of acetyl CoA are consumed in the process. Cholesterol is the precursor for the various classes of steroid hormones (Section 25-9).

Exercises and Problems

Exercises and problems are arranged in matched pairs with the two members of a pair addressing the same concept(s). The answer to the odd-numbered member of a pair is given at the back of the book. Problems denoted with a ▲ involve concepts found not only in the section under consideration but also in one or more earlier sections of the chapter.

Digestion and Absorption of Lipids (Section 25-1)

25-1 Indicate whether each of the following aspects of triacylglycerol digestion is associated with the (1) mouth, (2) stomach, (3) small intestine, (4) intestinal cells, or (5) bloodstream.
a. Chyme is produced.
b. Gastric lipases are active.
c. Initial production of monoacylglycerols occurs.
d. Fatty acid micelles are formed.

25-2 Indicate whether each of the following aspects of triacylglycerol digestion is associated with the (1) mouth, (2) stomach, (3) small intestine, (4) intestinal cells, or (5) bloodstream
a. Chylomicrons are formed.
b. Pancreatic lipases are active.
c. Stored bile is released.
d. Lipoprotein lipases are active.

25-3 Indicate whether each of the following pairings of terms/concepts is correct.
a. Chyme and semi-thick liquid mixture
b. Bile and mixture of several enzymes
c. Bloodstream and lipoprotein lipases
d. Chylomicron and lipoprotein

25-4 Indicate whether each of the following pairings of terms/concepts is correct.
a. Bile and solubilizing agent
b. Chylomicron and monoacylglycerol formation
c. Cholecystokinin and bile release
d. Chyme and partially digested food

25-5 Indicate whether each of the following statements relating to triacylglycerol (TAG) digestion is true or false.
a. Saliva has no effect on TAGs.
b. Gastric lipases present in the stomach trigger the release of bile.
c. Churning action in the stomach causes TAG hydrolysis.
d. High-fat foods remain in the stomach longer than low-fat foods.

25-6 Indicate whether each of the following statements relating to triacylglycerol (TAG) digestion is true or false.
a. About 50% of TAGs undergo complete hydrolysis in the stomach.
b. Cholecystokinin is the chemical name for bile.
c. Most TAGs usually enter the small intestine in the form of monoacylglycerols.
d. Chyme produced in the stomach settles to the bottom of the stomach.

25-7 What is a fatty acid micelle?

25-8 What is a chylomicron?

25-9 What are the products of the *complete* hydrolysis of a triacylglycerol?

25-10 What are the major products of the *incomplete* hydrolysis of a triacylglycerol?

25-11 At what location are free fatty acids and monoacylglycerols "repackaged" into triacylglycerols for the *first* time?

25-12 At what location are free fatty acids and monoacylglycerols "repackaged" into triacylglycerols for the *second* time?

Triacylglycerol Storage and Mobilization (Section 25-2)

25-13 What is the distinctive structural feature of *adipocytes*?

25-14 What is the major metabolic function of adipose tissue?

25-15 What is triacylglycerol mobilization?

25-16 What situation signals the need for mobilization of triacylglycerols from adipose tissue?

25-17 What role does cAMP play in triacylglycerol mobilization?

25-18 Triacylglycerols in adipose tissue do not enter the bloodstream as triacylglycerols. Explain.

Glycerol Metabolism (Section 25-3)

25-19 In which step of glycerol metabolism does each of the following events occur?
a. ATP is consumed.
b. A phosphorylation reaction occurs.
c. Dihydroxyacetone phosphate is produced.
d. Glycerol kinase is active.

25-20 In which step of glycerol metabolism does each of the following events occur?
  a. The oxidizing agent NAD^+ is needed.
  b. ADP is produced.
  c. Glycerol 3-phosphate is a reactant.
  d. A secondary alcohol group is oxidized.

25-21 How does the structure of glycerol 3-phosphate differ from the structure of glycerol?

25-22 How does the structure of dihydroxyacetone phosphate differ from the structure of glycerol 3-phosphate?

Oxidation of Fatty Acids (Section 25-4)

25-23 Indicate whether each of the following statements concerning the fatty acid activation process that occurs prior to β oxidation is true or false.
  a. CoA–SH is a reactant.
  b. A molecule of ADP is produced.
  c. The site for the process is the outer mitochondrial membrane.
  d. Two ATP molecules are consumed.

25-24 Indicate whether each of the following statements concerning the fatty acid activation process that occurs prior to β oxidation is true or false.
  a. Acetyl CoA is a product.
  b. A phosphorylation enzyme is needed.
  c. A molecule of AMP is produced.
  d. The activation product is acyl CoA.

25-25 Indicate whether each of the following aspects of the carnitine shuttle system associated with the process of β oxidation occurs in the mitochondrial matrix or in the mitochondrial intermembrane space.
  a. Acyl CoA is a reactant.
  b. Carnitine enters the inner mitochondrial membrane.
  c. Carnitine is converted to acyl carnitine.
  d. Free CoA is a reactant.

25-26 Indicate whether each of the following aspects of the carnitine shuttle system associated with the process of β oxidation occurs in the mitochondrial matrix or in the mitochondrial intermembrane space.
  a. Acyl CoA is a product.
  b. Acyl carnitine enters the inner mitochondrial membrane.
  c. Acyl carnitine is converted to carnitine.
  d. Coenzyme A is a product.

25-27 Identify the oxidizing agent needed in Step 1 of a turn of the β-oxidation pathway.

25-28 Identify the oxidizing agent needed in Step 3 of a turn of the β-oxidation pathway.

25-29 What functional group change occurs in each of the following steps of a turn of the β-oxidation pathway?
  a. Step 1
  b. Step 2
  c. Step 3

25-30 What type of reaction occurs in each of the following steps in a turn of the β-oxidation pathway?
  a. Step 1   b. Step 2
  c. Step 3   d. Step 4

25-31 What is the configuration of the unsaturated enoyl CoA formed by dehydrogenation during a turn of the β-oxidation pathway?

25-32 What is the configuration of the β-hydroxyacyl CoA formed by hydration during a turn of the β-oxidation pathway?

25-33 Draw structural formulas for the following compounds, all of which are associated with the fatty acid β-oxidation pathway.
  a. C_6 acyl CoA
  b. C_4 hydroxyacyl CoA
  c. C_8 enoyl CoA
  d. C_{10} ketoacyl CoA

25-34 Draw structural formulas for the following compounds, all of which are associated with the fatty acid β-oxidation pathway.
  a. C_4 acyl CoA   b. C_8 hydroxyacyl CoA
  c. C_{10} enoyl CoA   d. C_6 ketoacyl CoA

25-35 What type of compound—acyl CoA, enoyl CoA, hydroxyacyl CoA, or ketoacyl CoA—is involved in each of the following aspects of one "turn" of the β-oxidation pathway?
  a. Reactant in Step 1   b. Product in Step 2
  c. Product in Step 3   d. Reactant in Step 4

25-36 What type of compound—acyl CoA, enoyl CoA, hydroxyacyl CoA, or ketoacyl CoA—is involved in each of the following aspects of one "turn" of the β-oxidation pathway?
  a. Product in Step 1   b. Reactant in Step 2
  c. Reactant in Step 3   d. Product in Step 4

25-37 In the context of fatty acid oxidation to acetyl CoA, indicate whether each of the following substances is involved in (1) fatty acid activation, (2) fatty acid transport, or (3) β-oxidation pathway. More than one choice may be correct in a given situation.
  a. AMP   b. FAD
  c. Acyl CoA   d. H_2O

25-38 In the context of fatty acid oxidation to acetyl CoA, indicate whether each of the following substances is involved in (1) fatty acid activation, (2) fatty acid transport, or (3) β-oxidation pathway. More than one choice may be correct in a given situation.
  a. Acyl carnitine   b. Enoyl CoA
  c. CoA   d. NAD^+

25-39 In which step (of Steps 1 through 4) and in which turn (second or third) of the β-oxidation pathway is each of the following compounds encountered as a reactant if the fatty acid to be degraded is decanoic acid?

  a.
  $$CH_3-(CH_2)_4-\overset{\overset{\displaystyle OH}{|}}{CH}-CH_2-\overset{\overset{\displaystyle O}{||}}{C}-S-CoA$$

  b.
  $$CH_3-(CH_2)_2-CH=CH-\overset{\overset{\displaystyle O}{||}}{C}-S-CoA$$

  c.
  $$CH_3-(CH_2)_2-\overset{\overset{\displaystyle O}{||}}{C}-CH_2-\overset{\overset{\displaystyle O}{||}}{C}-S-CoA$$

  d.
  $$CH_3-(CH_2)_6-\overset{\overset{\displaystyle O}{||}}{C}-S-CoA$$

25-40 In which step (of Steps 1 through 4) and in which turn (second or third) of the β-oxidation pathway is each of the following compounds encountered as a reactant if the fatty acid to be degraded is decanoic acid?

a.

$$CH_3-(CH_2)_4-\overset{\overset{\displaystyle O}{||}}{C}-CH_2-\overset{\overset{\displaystyle O}{||}}{C}-S-CoA$$

b.

$$CH_3-(CH_2)_4-\overset{\overset{\displaystyle O}{||}}{C}-S-CoA$$

c.

$$CH_3-(CH_2)_4-CH{=}CH-\overset{\overset{\displaystyle O}{||}}{C}-S-CoA$$

d.

$$CH_3-(CH_2)_2-\overset{\overset{\displaystyle OH}{|}}{C}H-CH_2-\overset{\overset{\displaystyle O}{||}}{C}-S-CoA$$

25-41 Which compound(s) in Problem 25-39 undergo(es) a dehydrogenation reaction during a turn of the β-oxidation pathway?

25-42 Which compound(s) in Problem 25-40 undergo(es) a thiolysis reaction during a turn of the β-oxidation pathway?

25-43 How many turns of the β-oxidation pathway would be needed to degrade each of the following fatty acids to acetyl CoA?
a. 16:0 fatty acid
b. 12:0 fatty acid

25-44 How many turns of the β-oxidation pathway would be needed to degrade each of the following fatty acids to acetyl CoA?
a. 20:0 fatty acid
b. 10:0 fatty acid

25-45 The degradation of *cis*-3-hexenoic acid, a 6:1 acid, requires one more step than the degradation of hexanoic acid, a 6:0 acid. Describe the nature of the extra step.

25-46 The degradation of *cis*-4-hexenoic acid, a 6:1 acid, requires one more step than the degradation of hexanoic acid, a 6:0 acid. Describe the nature of this extra step.

▲**25-47** Indicate whether each of the following substances is involved in (1) glycerol metabolism to dihydroxyacetone phosphate, (2) fatty acid metabolism to acetyl CoA, or (3) both glycerol metabolism and fatty acid metabolism. More than one choice may be correct in a given situation.
a. NAD^+
b. ADP
c. Kinase
d. Ketoacyl CoA

▲**25-48** Indicate whether each of the following substances is involved in (1) glycerol metabolism to dihydroxyacetone phosphate, (2) fatty acid metabolism to acetyl CoA, or (3) both glycerol metabolism and fatty acid metabolism. More than one choice may be correct in a given situation.
a. Dehydrogenase
b. AMP
c. Acyl CoA
d. Glycerol 3-phosphate

ATP Production from Fatty Acid Oxidation (Section 25-5)

25-49 Identify the major fuel for skeletal muscle in
a. an active state.   b. a resting state.

25-50 Explain why fatty acids cannot serve as fuel for the brain.

25-51 Consider the conversion of a C_{10} saturated acid entirely to acetyl CoA.
a. How many turns of the β-oxidation pathway are required?
b. What is the yield of acetyl CoA?
c. What is the yield of NADH?
d. What is the yield of $FADH_2$?

25-52 Consider the conversion of a C_{14} saturated acid entirely to acetyl CoA.
a. How many turns of the β-oxidation pathway are required?
b. What is the yield of acetyl CoA?
c. What is the yield of NADH?
d. What is the yield of $FADH_2$?

25-53 How many ATP molecules ultimately result from further processing through the common metabolic pathway of the products from the *first* turn of the β-oxidation pathway?

25-54 How many ATP molecules ultimately result from further processing through the common metabolic pathway of the products from the *second* turn of the β-oxidation pathway?

25-55 What is the net ATP production for the complete oxidation to CO_2 and H_2O of the fatty acid in Problem 25-51?

25-56 What is the net ATP production for the complete oxidation to CO_2 and H_2O of the fatty acid in Problem 25-52?

25-57 Which yield more $FADH_2$, saturated or unsaturated fatty acids? Explain.

25-58 Which yield more NADH, saturated or unsaturated fatty acids? Explain.

25-59 Compare the energy released when 1 g of carbohydrate and 1 g of lipid are completely degraded in the body.

25-60 Compare the net ATP produced from 1 molecule of glucose and 1 molecule of hexanoic acid when they are completely degraded in the body

Ketone Bodies and Ketogenesis (Section 25-6)

25-61 What three body conditions are conducive to ketone body formation?

25-62 Why does a deficiency of carbohydrates in the diet lead to ketone body formation?

25-63 What is the relationship between oxaloacetate concentration and ketone body formation?

25-64 What is the relationship between pyruvate concentration and ketone body formation?

25-65 Draw the structures of the three compounds classified as ketone bodies.

25-66 Two of the three ketone bodies can be formed from the third one. Write equations for the formation of these two compounds.

25-67 Identify the ketone body (or bodies) to which each of the following statements applies.
    a. Its structure contains a ketone functional group.
    b. Its structure contains a hydroxyl functional group.
    c. It is produced in Step 3 of ketogenesis.
    d. It is produced from the decomposition of acetoacetate.

25-68 Identify the ketone body (or bodies) to which each of the following statements applies.
    a. Its structure contains two methyl groups.
    b. Its structure contains a carboxyl functional group.
    c. It is produced in Step 4 of ketogenesis.
    d. It is produced from the reduction of acetoacetate.

25-69 In which step of ketogenesis is each of the following changes effected?
    a. $C_2 + C_2 \longrightarrow C_4$
    b. $C_4 \longrightarrow C_4$
    c. $C_6 \longrightarrow C_4 + C_2$
    d. $C_4 + C_2 \longrightarrow C_6$

25-70 In the context of ketogenesis, classify each of the reactions in Problem 25-69 as (1) a condensation, (2) a chain cleavage, (3) a hydrogenation, or (4) an oxidation.

25-71 In the context of ketogenesis, indicate whether each of the following molecules is a C_2, C_4, C_6, or C_8 species.
    a. Acetoacetyl CoA
    b. 3-Hydroxy-3-methylglutaryl CoA
    c. Acetoacetate
    d. β-Hydroxybutyrate

25-72 In the context of ketogenesis reaction steps, indicate whether each of the molecules in Problem 25-71 is (1) a reactant but not a product, (2) a product but not a reactant, or (3) a reactant in one step and a product in another step.

25-73 Before acetoacetate can be used as a "fuel," it must first be activated. What are the names of the reactants and products in the activation reaction?

25-74 What are the names of the reactants and products in the reaction by which "usable fuel" is produced from the activated form of acetoacetate?

25-75 What is ketosis?

25-76 Severe ketosis situations produce acidosis. Explain.

▲**25-77** In the context of lipid metabolism, indicate whether each of the following compounds is associated with (1) the β-oxidation pathway, (2) ketogenesis, or (3) both the β-oxidation pathway and ketogenesis.
    a. Acyl CoA
    b. Enoyl CoA
    c. Acetyl CoA
    d. β-Hydroxybutyrate

▲**25-78** In the context of lipid metabolism, indicate whether each of the following compounds is associated with (1) the β-oxidation pathway, (2) ketogenesis, or (3) both the β-oxidation pathway and ketogenesis.
    a. Ketoacyl CoA
    b. Acetoacetyl CoA
    c. Acetoacetate
    d. Hydroxyacyl CoA

▲**25-79** Indicate whether each of the following is a characteristic of (1) the β-oxidation pathway but not ketogenesis, (2) ketogenesis but not the β-oxidation pathway, (3) both the β-oxidation pathway and ketogenesis, or (4) neither the β-oxidation pathway nor ketogenesis.
    a. Two different condensation reactions occur.
    b. The process has four distinct steps.
    c. Thiolysis occurs.
    d. A hydrogenation reaction occurs.

▲**25-80** Indicate whether each of the following is a characteristic of (1) the β-oxidation pathway but not ketogenesis, (2) ketogenesis but not the β-oxidation pathway, (3) both the β-oxidation pathway and ketogenesis, or (4) neither the β-oxidation pathway nor ketogenesis.
    a. Two different dehydrogenation reactions occur.
    b. A molecule is broken into two parts.
    c. A hydrolysis reaction occurs.
    d. A hydration reaction occurs.

Biosynthesis of Fatty Acids: Lipogenesis (Section 25-7)

25-81 Indicate whether each of the following statements contrasting the processes of lipogenesis and the β-oxidation pathway is true or false.
    a. Both processes occur in the cell cytosol.
    b. Both processes use the same enzymes.
    c. Both processes use CoA as a carrier molecule.
    d. Both processes use the same oxidizing agents.

25-82 Indicate whether each of the following statements contrasting the processes of lipogenesis and the β-oxidation pathway is true or false.
    a. Both processes occur in the mitochondrial matrix.
    b. Both processes use ACP as a carrier molecule.
    c. Both processes use the same reducing agents.
    d. Both processes involve the same functional group change sequence.

25-83 Indicate whether each of the following statements about the molecules CoA and ACP is true or false.
    a. CoA, but not ACP, contains a 2-ethanethiol structural subunit.
    b. ACP, but not CoA, contains a pantothenic acid structural subunit.
    c. Both CoA and ACP have an –SH functional group.
    d. CoA is a much larger molecule than ACP.

25-84 Indicate whether each of the following statements about the molecules CoA and ACP is true or false.
    a. Both CoA and ACP contain a 2-ethanethiol structural subunit.
    b. CoA, but not ACP, contains a pantothenic acid structural subunit.
    c. ACP is a much larger molecule than CoA.
    d. ACP, but not CoA, has an –SH functional group.

25-85 Indicate whether each of the following aspects of the citrate–malate shuttle system associated with the process of lipogenesis occurs in the mitochondrial matrix or in the cytosol.
    a. Citrate is produced from oxaloacetate and acetyl CoA.
    b. ATP is converted to ADP.
    c. Acetyl CoA and oxaloacetate are produced from citrate.
    d. NADH is used as a reducing agent.

More than one answer may be correct in a given situation.
a. The process has four distinct reaction steps.
b. Two different hydrogenation reactions occur.
c. Two different dehydrogenation reactions occur.
d. A thiolysis reaction occurs.

▲25-100 Indicate whether each of the following is a characteristic of (1) the β-oxidation pathway, (2) ketogenesis, or (3) the chain elongation phase of lipogenesis. More than one answer may be correct in a given situation.
a. Acetyl CoA is a reactant.
b. Acyl CoA is a reactant.
c. Two different condensation reactions occur.
d. A dehydration reaction occurs.

▲25-101 Indicate whether each of the following is a characteristic of (1) the β-oxidation pathway, (2) ketogenesis, or (3) lipogenesis. More than one answer may be correct in a given situation.
a. The carnitine shuttle system is used.
b. Malonyl ACP is a reactant.
c. CO_2 is a product.
d. Molecular O_2 is sometimes needed.

▲25-102 Indicate whether each of the following is a characteristic of (1) the β-oxidation pathway, (2) ketogenesis, or (3) lipogenesis. More than one answer may be correct in a given situation.
a. The citrate shuttle system is used.
b. Acetyl ACP is a reactant.
c. H_2O is a product.
d. H_2O is a reactant.

▲25-103 In which of the processes (1) glycerol metabolism to dihydroxyacetone phosphate, (2) β-oxidation pathway, (3) ketogenesis, and (4) lipogenesis is each of the following molecules encountered? There may be more than one correct response in a given situation.
a. Enoyl CoA
b. FAD
c. β–Hydroxybutyrate
d. Glycerol 3-phosphate

▲25-104 In which of the processes (1) glycerol metabolism to dihydroxyacetone phosphate, (2) β-oxidation pathway, (3) ketogenesis, and (4) lipogenesis is each of the following molecules encountered? There may be more than one correct response in a given situation.
a. HMG-CoA
b. NADPH
c. Malonyl ACP
d. Acetoacetyl CoA

Relationships Between Lipogenesis and Citric Acid Cycle Intermediates (Section 25-8)

25-105 What is the citric acid cycle diacid intermediate counterpart for each of the following lipogenesis C_4—ACP monoacid intermediates?
a. Butyrate
b. Acetoacetate
c. β-Hydroxybutyrate
d. Crotonate

25-106 What is the lipogenesis C_4—ACP monoacid intermediate counterpart for each of the following citric acid cycle C_4 diacid intermediates?
a. Succinate
b. Malate
c. Oxaloacetate
d. Fumarate

25-107 Identify each of the following C_4 species as a (1) hydroxy acid, (2) keto acid, (3) saturated acid, or (4) unsaturated acid.
a. Crotonate
b. Oxaloacetate
c. Acetoacetate
d. Malate

25-108 Identify each of the following C_4 species as a monocarboxylic acid or dicarboxylic acid.
a. Succinate
b. Butyrate
c. β-Hydroxybutyrate
d. Fumarate

Fate of Fatty-Acid-Generated Acetyl CoA (Section 25-9)

25-109 Indicate whether or not each of the following substances can be produced from acetyl CoA using the choices (1) can be produced in a one-step process, (2) can be produced in a multistep process, or (3) cannot be produced from acetyl CoA.
a. Cholesterol
b. Acetoacetyl CoA
c. Malonyl CoA
d. Pyruvate

25-110 Indicate whether or not each of the following substances can be produced from acetyl CoA using the choices (1) can be produced in a one-step process, (2) can be produced in a multistep process, or (3) cannot be produced from acetyl CoA.
a. HMG-CoA
b. Acetyl ACP
c. Mevalonate
d. Acetoacetate

Relationships Between Lipid and Carbohydrate Metabolism (Section 25-10)

25-111 Indicate whether each of the following metabolic processes occurs within mitochondria of a cell or in a cell's cytosol.
a. Ketogenesis
b. Glycolysis
c. Citric acid cycle
d. β-Oxidation pathway

25-112 Indicate whether each of the following metabolic processes occurs within mitochondria of a cell or in a cell's cytosol.
a. Electron transport chain
b. Lipogenesis
c. Glycerol metabolism
d. Gluconeogenesis

B Vitamins and Lipid Metabolism (Section 25-11)

25-113 Indicate whether each of the following B vitamins is involved (as a cofactor) in (1) β-oxidation pathway, (2) ketogenesis, (3) lipogenesis, or (4) conversion of ketone bodies to acetyl CoA. There may be more than one correct response or no correct response for a particular B vitamin.
a. Niacin
b. Thiamin
c. Pantothenic acid
d. Folate

25-114 Indicate whether each of the following B vitamins is involved (as a cofactor) in (1) β-oxidation pathway, (2) ketogenesis, (3) lipogenesis, or (4) conversion of ketone bodies to acetyl CoA. There may be more than one correct response or no correct response for a particular B vitamin.
a. Biotin
b. Vitamin B_6
c. Vitamin B_{12}
d. Riboflavin

Protein Metabolism

26

blickwinkel/McPHOTO/BIO/blickwinkel/Alamy

Fish, such as the Atlantic salmon, and other aquatic species process (eliminate) the nitrogen from protein in a manner different from that which occurs in human beings.

From an energy production standpoint, proteins supply only a small portion of the body's needs. With a normal diet, carbohydrates and fats supply 90% of the body's energy, and only 10% comes from proteins. However, despite its minor role in energy production, protein metabolism plays an important role in maintaining good health. The amino acids obtained from proteins are needed for both protein synthesis and synthesis of other nitrogen-containing compounds in the cell. In this chapter, protein digestion, the oxidative degradation of amino acids, and amino acid biosynthesis are examined.

26-1 Protein Digestion and Absorption

LEARNING FOCUS

Be familiar with the steps in the protein digestion process in terms of the sites where they occur and the products produced at each of the sites.

Protein digestion begins in the stomach rather than in the mouth because saliva contains no enzymes that affect proteins. Both protein denaturation (Section 20-15) and protein hydrolysis (Section 20-14) occur in the stomach. The partially digested protein (large polypeptides) passes from the stomach into the small intestine, where digestion is completed (Figure 26-1).

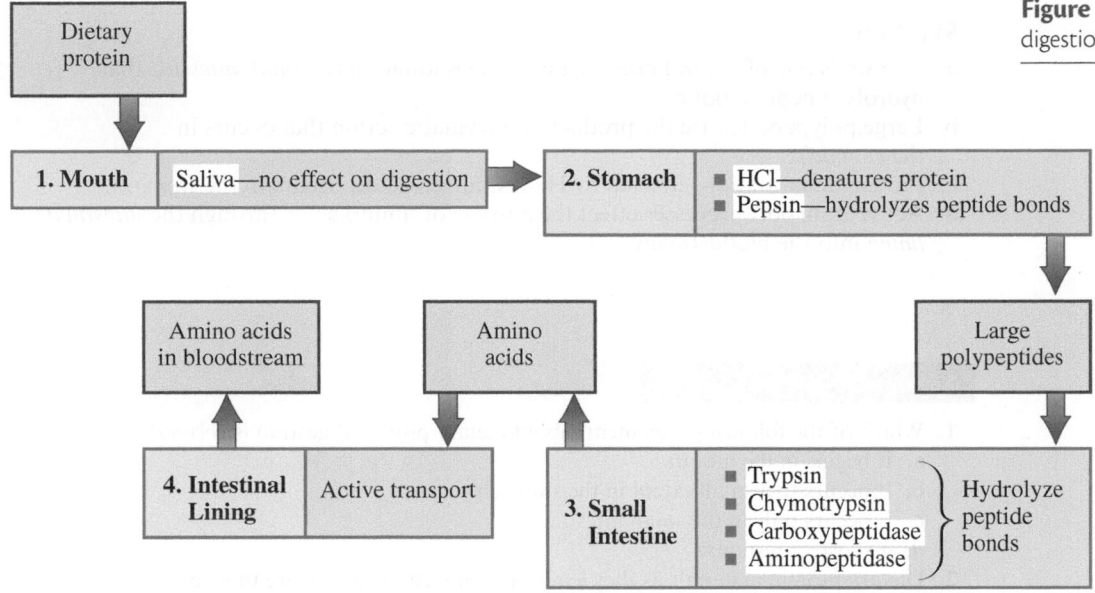

Figure 26-1 Summary of protein digestion in the human body.

Dietary protein entering the stomach effects the release of the hormone *gastrin* by stomach mucosa cells. Gastrin's presence causes both hydrochloric acid and pepsinogen secretion. Hydrochloric acid has three major functions within the stomach: (1) its antiseptic properties kill most bacteria, (2) its denaturing action (Section 20-15) "unwinds" globular proteins, making peptide bonds more accessible to digestive enzymes, and (3) its acidity leads to the activation of pepsinogen, which is the inactive form of the digestive enzyme *pepsin*; because of the hydrochloric acid present, gastric juice has a pH between 1.5 and 2.0. Pepsin effects the hydrolysis of approximately 10% of peptide bonds present in proteins, producing a variety of polypeptides. ◄

Passage, in small batches, of the stomach's acidic protein contents into the small intestine stimulates production of the hormone *secretin*, which in turn stimulates pancreatic production of bicarbonate ion, HCO_3^-, whose function is neutralization of gastric hydrochloric acid. With such neutralization, the partially digested protein mix becomes slightly basic, with a pH value between 7.0 and 8.0. This basic environment allows for the production of the pancreatic digestive enzymes *trypsin, chymotrypsin, and carboxypeptidase*, all of which attack peptide bonds. *Aminopeptidase*, secreted by intestinal mucosal cells, also attacks peptide bonds. Pepsin, trypsin, chymotrypsin, carboxypeptidase, and aminopeptidase are all examples of *proteolytic* enzymes (Section 21-9). Enzymes of this type are produced in inactive forms called *zymogens* that are activated at their site of action (Section 21-9).

The net result of protein digestion is the release of the protein's constituent amino acids. Absorption of these "free" amino acids through the intestinal wall requires active transport with the expenditure of energy (Section 19-10). Different transport systems exist for the various kinds of amino acids. After passing through the intestinal wall, the free amino acids enter the bloodstream, which distributes them throughout the body. ◄

▶ *A very small number of people are unable to synthesize enough gastric hydrochloric acid, and these individuals must ingest capsules of dilute hydrochloric acid with every meal.*

▶ *The passage of polypeptide chains and small proteins across the intestinal wall is uncommon in adults. In infants, however, such transport allows the passage of antibodies (proteins) in colostral milk from a mother to a nursing infant to build up immunologic protection in the infant.*

EXAMPLE 26-1

Determining the Sites Where Various Aspects of Protein Digestion Occur

Based on the information in Figure 26-1, determine the location within the human body where each of the following aspects of protein digestion occurs:

a. The enzyme trypsin is active.
b. Large polypeptides are produced.
c. Protein is denatured by HCl.
d. Active transport moves amino acids into the bloodstream.

(continued)

Solution

a. Trypsin is one of several proteolytic enzymes found in the *small intestine* that hydrolyze peptide bonds.

b. Large polypeptides are the product of enzymatic action that occurs in the *stomach*.

c. Protein denaturation, effected by HCl (stomach acid), occurs in the *stomach*.

d. Active transport processes effect the passage of amino acids through the *intestinal lining* into the bloodstream.

Section 26-1 Quick Quiz

1. Which of the following statements about dietary protein digestion is *correct*?
   a. It begins in the mouth.
   b. It occurs to a small extent in the stomach.
   c. It occurs only in the small intestine.
   d. no correct response

2. Dietary protein materials as they leave the stomach are a mixture that contains
   a. approximately 50% free amino acids
   b. approximately 90% free amino acids
   c. predominately polypeptides
   d. no correct response

3. The inactive form of pepsin is converted to its active form
   a. in the small intestine
   b. by hydrochloric acid
   c. by gastrin
   d. no correct response

4. Which of the following is *not* a proteolytic enzyme?
   a. trypsin
   b. aminopeptidase
   c. secretin
   d. no correct response

Answers: 1. b; 2. c; 3. b; 4. c

26-2 Amino Acid Utilization

LEARNING FOCUS

Be able to list four major ways in which amino acids from the body's amino acid pool are used; be familiar with the concepts of *protein turnover* and *nitrogen balance*.

▶ *The amino acid pool is not a specific location within the body where free amino acids "congregate." Rather, these free amino acids are present throughout the body, accumulating in the blood and within cells where they are available when needed for further use, which in most instances is for protein synthesis.*

▶ *The rate of protein turnover varies from a few minutes to several hours. Proteins with short turnover rates include many enzymes and regulatory hormones. In a healthy adult, about 2% of the body's protein is broken down and resynthesized every day.*

Amino acids produced from the digestion of proteins enter the amino acid pool of the body. The **amino acid pool** *is the total supply of free amino acids available for use in the human body.* Dietary protein is one of three sources that contributes amino acids to the amino acid pool. The other two sources are *protein turnover* and *biosynthesis* of amino acids in the liver. ◀

Within the human body, proteins are continually being degraded (hydrolyzed) to amino acids and resynthesized. Disease, injury, and "wear and tear" are all causes of degradation. The degradation–resynthesis process is called protein turnover. ◀ **Protein turnover** *is the repetitive process in which proteins are degraded and resynthesized within the human body.*

Biosynthesis of amino acids by the liver also supplies the amino acid pool with amino acids. However, only the *nonessential* amino acids (Sections 20-3 and 26-6) can be produced in this manner.

In a healthy adult, the amount of nitrogen taken into the body each day (dietary proteins) equals the amount of nitrogen excreted from the body. Such a person is said to be in a state of nitrogen balance. **Nitrogen balance** *is the state that results when the amount of nitrogen taken into the human body as protein equals the amount of nitrogen excreted from the body in waste materials.*

Two types of nitrogen imbalance can occur. When protein degradation exceeds protein synthesis, the amount of nitrogen in the urine exceeds the amount of nitrogen ingested (dietary protein). This condition of *negative nitrogen balance* accompanies a state of "tissue wasting," because more tissue proteins are being catabolized than are being replaced by protein synthesis. Protein-poor diets, starvation, and wasting illnesses produce a negative nitrogen balance.

A *positive nitrogen balance* (nitrogen intake exceeds nitrogen output) indicates that the rate of protein anabolism (synthesis) exceeds that of protein catabolism. This state indicates that large amounts of tissue are being synthesized, such as during growth, pregnancy, and convalescence from an emaciating illness.

Although the overall nitrogen balance in the body often varies, the relative concentrations of amino acids within the amino acid pool remain essentially constant. ◄ No specialized storage forms for amino acids exist in the body, as is the case for glucose (glycogen) and fatty acids (triacylglycerols). Therefore, the body needs a relatively constant source of amino acids to maintain normal metabolism. During negative nitrogen balance, the body must resort to degradation of proteins that were synthesized for other functions.

The amino acids from the body's amino acid pool are used in four different ways.

► *There are approximately 100 grams of free amino acids present in the amino acid pool. Glutamine is the most abundant, followed closely by alanine, glycine, and valine. The essential amino acids constitute approximately 10 grams of the pool.*

1. *Protein synthesis.* It is estimated that about 75% of the free amino acids in a healthy, well-nourished adult go into protein synthesis. Proteins are continually needed to replace old tissue (protein turnover) and also to build new tissue (growth). The subject of protein synthesis was considered in Section 22-12.

2. *Synthesis of nonprotein nitrogen-containing compounds.* Amino acids are regularly withdrawn from the amino acid pool for the synthesis of nonprotein nitrogen-containing compounds. Such molecules include the purines and pyrimidines of nucleic acids (A, C, G, T, and U; Section 22-2), the heme of hemoglobin (Section 26-7), the choline and ethanolamine of phosphoglycerides (Section 19-7), hormones such as adrenaline (Section 17-10), and neurotransmitters such as norepinephrine, dopamine, and serotonin (Section 17-10). The neurotransmitter serotonin is synthesized from the amino acid tryptophan, and the neurotransmitters norepinephrine and dopamine are synthesized from the amino acid tyrosine. Figure 26-2 shows the close structural resemblance between these two amino acids and the neurotransmitters synthesized from them.

3. *Synthesis of nonessential amino acids.* When required, the body draws on the amino acid pool for raw materials for the production of *nonessential* amino acids that are in short supply. The "roadblock" preventing the synthesis of the *essential* amino acids is not lack of nitrogen but lack of a correct carbon skeleton upon which enzymes can work. ◄ In general, the essential amino acids contain carbon chains or aromatic rings not present in other amino acids or the intermediates of carbohydrate or lipid metabolism. Table 26-1 lists the essential amino acids and the nonessential amino acids with the precursors needed to form the latter.

► *Higher plants and certain microorganisms are capable of synthesizing all the protein amino acids from carbon dioxide, water, and inorganic salts.*

4. *Production of energy.* Amino acids in excess of those needed for biosynthetic processes cannot be stored in the body nor directly excreted. Those in excess are used as energy sources, being degraded to substances that can be processed through the common metabolic pathway. The degradation process is complex because each of the 20 standard amino acids has a different degradation pathway.

Figure 26-2 Structural relationships between the neurotransmitters serotonin, norepinephrine, and dopamine and their amino acid precursors.

Table 26-1 **Essential and Nonessential Amino Acids**

Nutritionally Essential Amino Acids	Nutritionally Nonessential Amino Acids	
	Amino Acid	Precursor
arginine*	alanine	pyruvate
histidine	asparagine	aspartate
isoleucine	aspartic acid	oxaloacetate
leucine	cysteine	serine
lysine	glutamic acid	α-ketoglutarate
methionine	glutamine	glutamate
phenylalanine	glycine	serine
threonine	proline	glutamate
tryptophan	serine	3-phosphoglycerate
valine	tyrosine	phenylalanine

*Arginine is essential in the diets of children, but not adults.

In all the degradation pathways, the amino nitrogen atom is removed and ultimately is excreted from the body as urea. The remaining carbon skeleton is then converted to pyruvate, acetyl CoA, or a citric acid cycle intermediate, depending on its makeup, with the resulting energy production or energy storage. Figure 26-3 shows the various pathways available for the further use of amino acid catabolism products. Subsequent sections of this chapter give further details about these processes.

Figure 26-3 Possible fates for amino acid degradation products.

Section 26-2 Quick Quiz

1. The dominant use for the amino acids of the amino acid pool is the synthesis of
   a. proteins
   b. nonprotein nitrogen compounds
   c. nonessential amino acids
   d. no correct response
2. The most abundant amino acid in the amino acid pool is
   a. alanine
   b. aspartate
   c. glutamate
   d. no correct response
3. Which of the following conditions would produce a negative nitrogen balance within the human body?
   a. pregnancy
   b. starvation
   c. growth spurt in a child
   d. no correct response

Answers: 1. a; 2. c; 3. b

26-3 Transamination and Oxidative Deamination

LEARNING FOCUS

Be familiar with the processes of *transamination* and *oxidative deamination* in terms of the reactants and products that are involved.

Energy generation using amino acids as fuel differs from the previously considered energy generation processes involving carbohydrates and fats in a major way. Amino acids, unlike carbohydrates and fats, contain nitrogen, and the human body cannot oxidize nitrogen-containing compounds. Before amino acids can be used as energy sources, the nitrogen atoms in their structures must be removed. Then the "carbon skeleton" that remains can be processed for energy.

Thus, there are two stages to obtaining energy through the degradation of amino acids: (1) the removal of the α-amino group and (2) the degradation of the remaining carbon skeleton. In this section and the next, what happens to the amino group is considered; in Section 26-5, the fate of the carbon skeleton is considered.

Two different types of biochemical reactions are needed for the removal of amino groups from amino acids. They are *transamination reactions* and *oxidative deamination reactions*, both of which are considered in this section.

Transamination Reactions

A **transamination reaction** *is a biochemical reaction that involves the interchange of the amino group of an* α-*amino acid with the keto group of an* α-*keto acid*. This definition specifies the identity of the two reactants in a transamination reaction: an amino acid and a keto acid. It also specifies what happens during the reaction; amino and keto groups are interchanged between reactants. This interchange results in a *new* amino acid and a *new* keto acid being produced, as is shown in the following generalized structural equation for a transamination reaction.

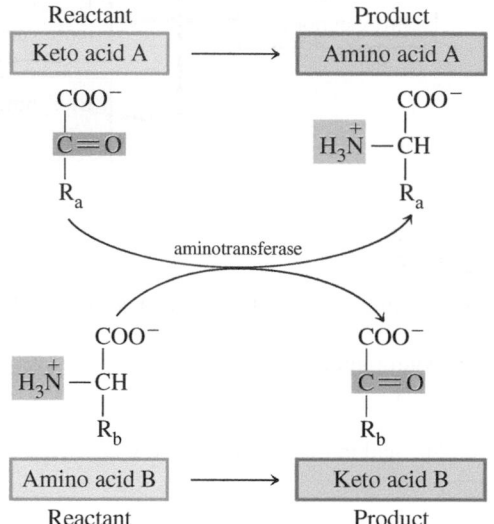

The needed enzyme for a transamination reaction is an *aminotransferase*. Its action effects the transfer of the amino group from one carbon skeleton to another. There is no loss or gain of amino groups in transamination. Amino group transfer is all that occurs; hence the name *transamination* (transfer of an amino group) for this type of reaction.

What is the purpose for the amino group/keto group exchange that occurs during transamination? Obviously there is one; otherwise the reaction would not be needed. The following considerations show transamination's purpose.

Many different amino acids, obtained from protein digestion, are encountered as reactants in transamination. Such is not the case for keto acids. Only two, rather than many, keto acids are commonly encountered as reactants in transamination. These two keto acids are α-ketoglutarate and oxaloacetate, both of which have previously been encountered as intermediates in the citric acid cycle (Section 23-7). The significance of having only two keto acid reactants is that this limits amino acid products to only two. With many amino acid reactants and only two amino acid products, the purpose of transamination becomes apparent. Its purpose is to collect the amino groups from many different amino acids into just two amino acids, thus simplifying greatly the process of amino acid metabolism. Only two amino acids then need to be processed further with their nitrogen atoms ultimately being eliminated from the body in urea (Section 26-4).

Figure 26-4 shows the structures of the two "transamination keto acids" and the amino acids produced from them, which are glutamate and aspartate. Note that the one keto/amino acid pair involves succinic acid (C_4 diacid) derivatives and the other keto/amino acid pair involves glutaric acid (C_5 diacid) derivatives.

Although a transamination reaction appears to involve the simple transfer of an $-\overset{+}{N}H_3$ group between two molecules, the reaction involves several steps and

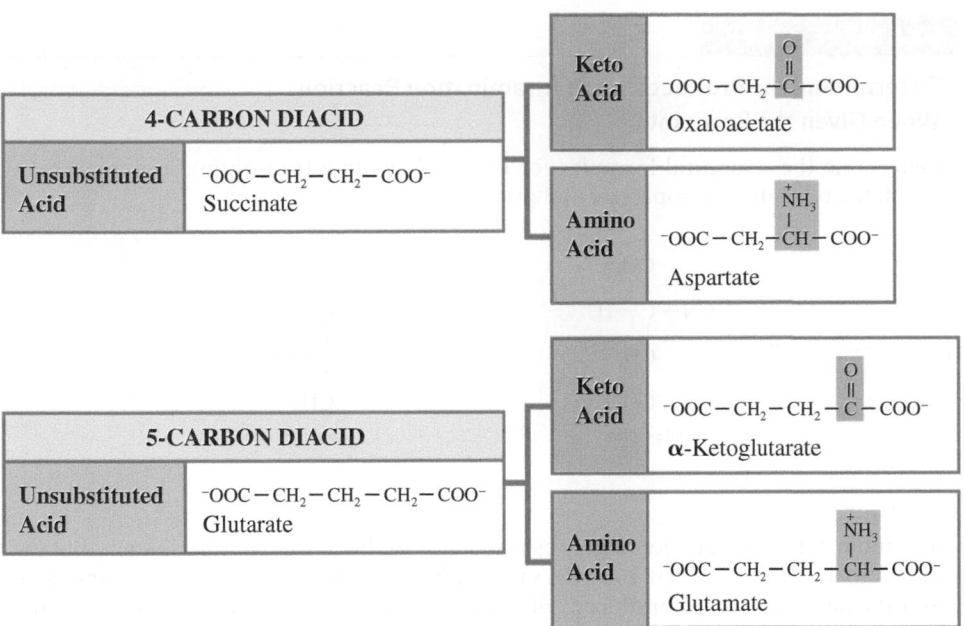

Figure 26-4 Key keto/amino acid pairs encountered in transamination reactions.

requires the presence of pyridoxal phosphate, a coenzyme produced from pyridoxine (vitamin B$_6$).

HOCH$_2$ — Pyridoxine (vitamin B$_6$) P—OCH$_2$ — Pyridoxal phosphate (coenzyme)

This coenzyme is an integral part of the transamination process. The amino group of the amino acid is transferred first to the coenzyme and then from the coenzyme to the α-keto acid. Figure 26-5 shows the role of this coenzyme in the transamination process, where alanine is the amino acid and α-ketoglutarate is the α-keto acid. ◀

▶ *Transamination reactions are reversible and can easily go in either direction, depending on the reactant concentrations. This reversibility is the basis for regulation of amino acid concentrations in the body.*

Figure 26-5 The role of pyridoxal phosphate in the process of transamination.

EXAMPLE 26-2

Determining the Products in a Transamination Reaction When Given the Reactants

Determine the structural formulas for the products in a transamination reaction in which the reactants are aspartate and pyruvate.

$$
\begin{array}{c}
\text{COO}^- \\
| \\
\text{H}_3\overset{+}{\text{N}}-\text{C}-\text{H} \\
| \\
\text{CH}_2 \\
| \\
\text{COO}^-
\end{array}
\qquad\qquad
\begin{array}{c}
\text{COO}^- \\
| \\
\text{C}=\text{O} \\
| \\
\text{CH}_3
\end{array}
$$

Aspartate (amino acid)   Pyruvate (keto acid)

Solution

The interchange of functional groups associated with transamination is such that the new keto acid produced will have the same carbon skeleton as the reacting amino acid, and the new amino acid produced will have the same carbon skeleton as the reacting keto acid.

For aspartate, the reacting amino acid, the functional group change produces the following keto acid, which has the same carbon skeleton as the aspartate.

$$
\begin{array}{c}
\text{COO}^- \\
| \\
\text{H}_3\overset{+}{\text{N}}-\text{C}-\text{H} \\
| \\
\text{CH}_2 \\
| \\
\text{COO}^-
\end{array}
\longrightarrow
\begin{array}{c}
\text{COO}^- \\
| \\
\text{C}=\text{O} \\
| \\
\text{CH}_2 \\
| \\
\text{COO}^-
\end{array}
$$

Reacting amino acid   Product keto acid

For pyruvate, the reacting keto acid, the functional group change produces the following amino acid, which has the same carbon skeleton as pyruvate.

$$
\begin{array}{c}
\text{COO}^- \\
| \\
\text{C}=\text{O} \\
| \\
\text{CH}_3
\end{array}
\longrightarrow
\begin{array}{c}
\text{COO}^- \\
| \\
\text{H}_3\overset{+}{\text{N}}-\text{C}-\text{H} \\
| \\
\text{CH}_3
\end{array}
$$

Reacting keto acid   Product amino acid

Glutamate Production via Transamination

The most important transamination reaction in protein metabolism, in terms of frequency of occurrence, is the one in which the keto acid α-ketoglutarate is the amino group acceptor. Glutamate is the amino acid produced when α-ketoglutarate accepts the amino group.

$$^{-}OOC-\overset{\overset{\displaystyle O}{\|}}{C}-CH_2-CH_2-COO^{-} \qquad ^{-}OOC-\overset{\overset{\displaystyle +}{\underset{|}{NH_3}}}{CH}-CH_2-CH_2-COO^{-}$$

$$\text{α-Ketoglutarate} \qquad\qquad \text{Glutamate}$$

PLP

aminotransferase

$$^{-}OOC-\overset{\overset{\displaystyle +}{\underset{|}{NH_3}}}{CH}-R \qquad\qquad ^{-}OOC-\overset{\overset{\displaystyle O}{\|}}{C}-R$$

$$\text{α-Amino acid} \qquad\qquad \text{α-Keto acid}$$

There are at least 50 aminotransferases associated with transamination reactions. They differ in which amino acid substrates they accept. ◄ Aminotransferases are highly specific relative to which keto acid substrates they accept. Most aminotransferases accept only α-ketoglutarate and to a lesser extent oxaloacetate. Thus glutamate (from α-ketoglutarate) and aspartate (from oxaloacetate) are the two amino acids produced in transamination reactions. ◄

Further Processing of Glutamate

There are two pathways for further processing of the many glutamate molecules produced via transamination. One pathway is a second transamination reaction that produces the amino acid aspartate, and the other pathway involves production of ammonium ion (NH_4^+) via *oxidative deamination*. Both the ammonium ion and the aspartate, which now become the "amino group carriers," are participants in the urea cycle (Section 26-4) through which, as the name implies, urea is produced. ◄ Further details concerning these two pathways—a second transamination reaction and oxidative deamination—are as follows.

Aspartate Production via Transamination

Transamination in which glutamate is the reacting amino acid and oxaloacetate is the reacting keto acid produces aspartate as the new amino acid.

$$^{-}OOC-\overset{\overset{\displaystyle O}{\|}}{C}-CH_2-COO^{-} \qquad ^{-}OOC-\overset{\overset{\displaystyle +}{\underset{|}{NH_3}}}{CH}-CH_2-COO^{-}$$

$$\text{Oxaloacetate} \qquad\qquad \text{Aspartate}$$

PLP

aminotransferase

$$^{-}OOC-\overset{\overset{\displaystyle +}{\underset{|}{NH_3}}}{CH}-CH_2-CH_2-COO^{-} \qquad ^{-}OOC-\overset{\overset{\displaystyle O}{\|}}{C}-CH_2-CH_2-COO^{-}$$

$$\text{Glutamate} \qquad\qquad \text{α-Ketoglutarate}$$

Note that the second product in this reaction is α-ketoglutarate. The "regenerated" α-ketoglutarate becomes available for re-participation in the transamination reactions whereby glutamate was initially produced. Note also that aspartate is now a carrier of nitrogen atoms that are to be eliminated from the body as urea.

Ammonium Ion Production via Oxidative Deamination

Not all glutamates undergo transamination to produce aspartate. A significant number instead undergo *oxidative deamination*. An **oxidative deamination reaction** *is a*

▶ *The concentration of aminotransferases in blood is used to diagnose liver and heart disorders. Liver damage releases alanine aminotransferase (ALT) into the blood. Aspartate aminotransferase (AST) is abundant in heart muscle, and increased blood levels of this enzyme indicate that heart muscle damage (myocardial infarction) has occurred.*

▶ *Various aminotransferases are differentiated from each other, name-wise, by including as part of the name the amino group donor that participates in the transamination. Aspartate aminotransferase is involved in the transfer of an amino group from the amino acid aspartate, and alanine aminotransferase transfers an amino group from the amino acid alanine.*

▶ *Both pathways for the further processing of glutamate— transamination and oxidative deamination—produce the keto acid α-ketoglutarate as one of the products. The N-containing product differs, being aspartate in the first case and ammonium ion in the second case.*

biochemical reaction in which an α-amino acid is converted into an α-keto acid with release of an ammonium ion. Oxidative deamination occurs primarily in liver and kidney mitochondria.

Oxidative deamination of glutamate requires the enzyme *glutamate dehydrogenase*. This enzyme is unusual in that it is the only known enzyme that can function with either NADP⁺ or NAD⁺ as a coenzyme. With NAD⁺ as the coenzyme, the reaction is:

$$^-OOC-CH_2-CH_2-\overset{\overset{+}{N}H_3}{\underset{\text{Glutamate}}{CH}}-COO^- + \boxed{NAD^+} + H_2O \xrightarrow[\text{dehydrogenase}]{\text{Glutamate}}$$

$$\boxed{NH_4^+} + {}^-OOC-CH_2-CH_2-\overset{O}{\overset{\|}{C}}-\underset{\alpha\text{-Ketoglutarate}}{COO^-} + \boxed{NADH} + H^+$$

Note that α-ketoglutarate is a product of this process. It can be reused in the first series of transamination reactions. The NADH and H⁺ formed can participate in the electron transport chain and oxidative phosphorylation to produce ATP molecules (Sections 23-8 and 23-9). ◄

The net equation for combined action of an aminotransferase (transamination) and glutamate dehydrogenase (oxidative deamination) is:

$$\alpha\text{-Amino acid} + NAD^+ + H_2O \longrightarrow \alpha\text{-keto acid} + NH_4^+ + NADH + H^+$$

The NH₄⁺ so produced, a toxic substance if left to accumulate in the body, is then converted to urea in the urea cycle (Section 26-4). ◄

▶ *Of the 20 different amino acids (Section 20-2) obtained from protein digestion, 12 of them participate in transamination reactions. The other eight undergo more complex degradation processes through which NH₄⁺ ion is produced. Since a combined transamination–oxidative deamination sequence also produces NH₄⁺ ions, the generalization that the nitrogen present in all amino acids is converted to NH₄⁺ ions is valid.*

▶ *The toxicity of ammonium ion is related to the oxidative deamination reaction by which it is formed, the conversion of glutamate to α-ketoglutarate. This reaction, which is an equilibrium situation, is shifted to the glutamate side by increased ammonium ion levels. This shift decreases α-ketoglutarate levels significantly, which affects the citric acid cycle, of which α-ketoglutarate is an intermediate. Cellular ATP production drops, and the lack of ATP causes central nervous system problems.*

EXAMPLE 26-3

Distinguishing Between Characteristics of Transamination and Oxidative Deamination

Indicate whether each of the following reaction characteristics is associated with the process of *transamination* or with the process of *oxidative deamination*:

a. The enzyme glutamate dehydrogenase is active.
b. The coenzyme pyridoxal phosphate is needed.
c. An amino acid is converted into a keto acid with release of ammonium ion.
d. One of the reactants is an amino acid, and one of the products is an amino acid.

Solution

a. *Oxidative deamination.* The substrate for oxidative deamination is glutamate, and the process is an oxidation reaction (removal of H atoms) with NAD⁺ serving as the oxidizing agent.
b. *Transamination.* The coenzyme pyridoxal phosphate, a derivative of vitamin B₆, is an intermediate in the amino group transfer process.
c. *Oxidative deamination.* Ammonium ion production is a characteristic of oxidative deamination; no ammonium ion is produced during transamination.
d. *Transamination.* In transamination, there are two reactants (an amino acid and a keto acid) and two products (a new amino acid and a new keto acid).

Section 26-3 Quick Quiz

1. The reactants in a transamination reaction are
   a. a keto acid and an amino acid
   b. two amino acids
   c. a keto acid and ammonia
   d. no correct response

2. The products in a transamination reaction are
   a. a keto acid and an amino acid
   b. two keto acids
   c. an amino acid and ammonia
   d. no correct response
3. The net effect of transamination is to collect the amino groups from a variety of amino acids into two compounds, which are
   a. an amino acid and a keto acid
   b. both amino acids
   c. both keto acids
   d. no correct response
4. The nitrogen-containing product of an oxidative deamination reaction is
   a. an amino acid
   b. ammonium ion
   c. urea
   d. no correct response
5. A derivative of pyridoxine (vitamin B_6) is required as a coenzyme in
   a. transamination
   b. oxidative deamination
   c. both transamination and oxidative deamination
   d. no correct response
6. Most aminotransferases are specific for the keto acid
   a. α-ketoglutarate
   b. oxaloacetate
   c. pyruvate
   d. no correct response

Answers: 1. a; 2. a; 3. b; 4. b; 5. a; 6. a

26-4 The Urea Cycle

LEARNING FOCUS
Be familiar with the four steps in the urea cycle and how the fuel for the urea cycle is obtained.

From a nitrogen standpoint, the net effect of transamination and deamination reactions (Section 26-3) is production of ammonium ions and aspartate molecules. Both of these nitrogen-carrying entities are processed further in the urea cycle. Ammonium ions enter the cycle indirectly, being first incorporated into another molecule (carbamoyl phosphate) that then enters the cycle's first step. Aspartate molecules enter the cycle directly in the cycle's second step.

The **urea cycle** *is a cyclic biochemical pathway in which urea is produced, for excretion, using ammonium ions and aspartate molecules as nitrogen sources.* The urea, produced in the liver, is transported in the blood to the kidneys and eliminated from the body in urine.

In the pure state, urea is a white solid with a melting point of 133°C. Its structure is

$$\underset{\displaystyle H_2N-\overset{\displaystyle \overset{O}{\|}}{C}-NH_2}{}$$

Urea is very soluble in water (1 g per 1 mL), is odorless and colorless, and has a salty taste. (Urea does not contribute to the odor or color of urine.) With normal metabolism, an adult excretes about 30 g of urea daily in urine, although the exact amount varies with the protein content of the diet.

Three amino acids are involved as intermediates in the operation of the urea cycle. These acids are arginine, ornithine, and citrulline, the latter two of which are nonstandard amino acids—that is, amino acids not found in protein. Structurally, all three of these amino acids have the same carbon chain.

Arginine
(standard amino acid)

Ornithine
(nonstandard amino acid)

Citrulline
(nonstandard amino acid)

▶ *Arginine is the most nitrogen-rich of the standard amino acids. It contains four nitrogen atoms.*

Carbamoyl Phosphate

Ammonia, one of the two "nitrogen-carrying molecules" associated with urea cycle operation, does not enter the cycle directly. Rather, it is converted to carbamoyl phosphate that serves as one of two "fuel" molecules for the cycle; the other "fuel" is aspartate. The reactants for carbamoyl phosphate formation are ammonium ion (from oxidative deamination; Section 26-3), carbon dioxide (from the citric acid cycle), water, and two ATP molecules. The formation equation for carbamoyl phosphate is

▶ *The functional group attached to the phosphate in carbamoyl phosphate is the simple amide functional group*

$$NH_4^+ + CO_2 + H_2O + \boxed{2ATP} \longrightarrow H_2N-\overset{O}{\overset{\|}{C}}-O\sim\overset{O}{\underset{O^-}{\overset{\|}{P}}}-O^- + \boxed{2ADP} + P_i + 3H^+$$

Carbamoyl phosphate ◀

Note that two ATP molecules are expended in the formation of one carbamoyl phosphate molecule and that carbamoyl phosphate contains a high-energy phosphate bond. The carbamoyl phosphate formation reaction, like the reactions of the citric acid cycle, takes place in the mitochondrial matrix. ◀

▶ *The term* carbamoyl *is a prefix that denotes an amide group.*

Steps of the Urea Cycle

Figure 26-6 shows the four-step urea cycle in outline form. Note that the urea cycle occurs partially in the mitochondria and partially in the cytosol and that ornithine and citrulline must be transported across the inner mitochondrial membrane. The individual steps of the urea cycle will now be considered in detail.

▶ *Ornithine has a role similar to that of oxaloacetate in the citric acid cycle (Section 23-6), accepting an entering group at the start of each turn of the cycle.*
The standard amino acid lysine and ornithine, both basic amino acids, have closely related structures.

Step 1: **Carbamoyl group transfer.** Carbamoyl phosphate, "fuel," upon entering the urea cycle, transfers its carbamoyl group to ornithine to form citrulline, with release of P_i in a reaction catalyzed by *ornithine transcarbamoylase*. ◀

Lysine

Ornithine

Lysine has one more CH₂ group than does ornithine.

Ornithine

Carbamoyl phosphate

Citrulline

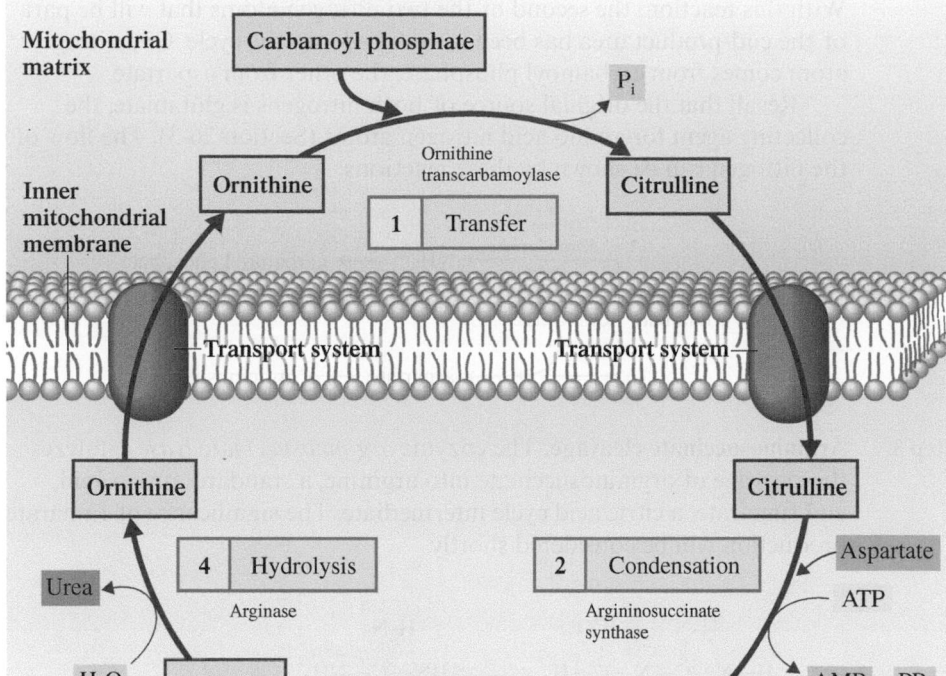

Figure 26-6 The four-step urea cycle in which carbamoyl phosphate is converted to urea.

The breaking of the high-energy phosphate bond in carbamoyl phosphate drives the transfer process. With the carbamoyl transfer, the first of the two nitrogen atoms and the carbon atom needed for the formation of urea have been introduced into the cycle.

Step 2: **Citrulline–aspartate condensation.** In contrast to Step 1, which occurred in the mitochondrial matrix, Steps 2, 3, and 4 of the cycle occur in the cytosol. Citrulline, from Step 1, is transported into the cytosol where a condensation reaction between it and aspartate occurs. Aspartate is the second molecule of "fuel" entering the cycle, having been previously generated from glutamate by transamination (Section 26-3). The condensation, which produces argininosuccinate, is catalyzed by *argininosuccinate synthetase;* the reaction is driven by the expenditure of ATP.

▶ *In argininosuccinate formation, an oxygen atom is "lost"; the reactants contain seven oxygen atoms and the product only six oxygen atoms. Adding a water molecule to the product side of the equation achieves oxygen–hydrogen balance. This is, however, an oversimplification. The reaction is actually a two-step process involving a citrullyl–AMP intermediate. When the AMP is released, the "lost" oxygen atom becomes part of the AMP structure.*

With this reaction, the second of the two nitrogen atoms that will be part of the end-product urea has been introduced into the cycle. One nitrogen atom comes from carbamoyl phosphate, the other from aspartate.

Recall that the original source of both nitrogens is glutamate, the collecting agent for amino acid nitrogen atoms (Section 26-3). The flow of the nitrogen can be shown by these reactions:

$$\text{Glutamate} \left\{ \begin{array}{l} \xrightarrow[\text{dehydrogenase}]{\text{Glutamate}} NH_4^+ \longrightarrow \text{carbamoyl phosphate} \\[2ex] \text{Oxaloacetate} \\ \xrightarrow[\text{Aminotransferase}]{} \text{aspartate} \longrightarrow \text{argininosuccinate} \end{array} \right.$$

Step 3: **Argininosuccinate cleavage.** The enzyme *argininosuccinate lyase* catalyzes the cleavage of argininosuccinate into arginine, a standard amino acid, and fumarate, a citric acid cycle intermediate. The significance of fumarate production will be considered shortly.

Argininosuccinate   Arginine   Fumarate

Step 4: **Urea from arginine hydrolysis.** Hydrolysis of arginine produces urea and regenerates ornithine, one of the cycle's starting materials. The enzyme involved is *arginase.*

Arginine   Urea   Ornithine

The oxygen atom present in the urea comes from the water involved in the hydrolysis. The ornithine is transported back into the mitochondria, where it becomes available to participate in the urea cycle again.

Figure 26-7 analyzes the urea cycle in terms of the nitrogen content of the various compounds that participate in it. N_2 ornithine condenses with entering N_1 carbamoyl phosphate "fuel" to produce N_3 citrulline. N_3 citrulline then interacts with entering N_1 aspartate "fuel" to produce N_4 argininosuccinate. N_4 argininosuccinate is changed into N_4 arginine in a cleavage reaction in which the second product (fumarate) does not contain nitrogen. N_4 arginine undergoes hydrolysis to produce N_2 urea and regenerate N_2 ornithine.

▶ *Humans and most terrestrial animals excrete excess nitrogen as urea. Urea is not, however, the only biochemical means for disposing of excess nitrogen. Aquatic species (bacteria and fish) release ammonia directly into the surrounding water. Birds, terrestrial reptiles, and many insects secrete nitrogen as uric acid; it is the familiar white solid in bird droppings. The structure of uric acid, a compound with a purine ring system (Section 17-9), is*

Uric acid

EXAMPLE 26-4

Relating Urea Cycle Intermediates to Events That Occur in the Urea Cycle

For each of the following urea cycle events, identify the urea cycle intermediate that is involved. The urea cycle intermediates are ornithine, citrulline, argininosuccinate, and arginine.

a. Intermediate participates in a condensation reaction.
b. Intermediate is produced at the same time that urea is formed.
c. Intermediate must be transported from the mitochondrial matrix to the cytosol.
d. Intermediate is the product in Step 3 of the urea cycle.

Solution

a. *Citrulline*. The reaction between citrulline and aspartate in Step 2 of the urea cycle is a condensation reaction.
b. *Ornithine*. In Step 4 of the urea cycle, arginine undergoes hydrolysis to produce ornithine and urea.
c. *Citrulline*. Citrulline is formed in the mitochondrial matrix, transported across the inner mitochondrial membrane, and reacts with aspartate in the cytosol.
d. *Arginine*. In Step 3 of the urea cycle, in a cleavage reaction, the large molecule argininosuccinate is split into two pieces—arginine and fumarate molecules.

Urea Cycle Net Reaction

The net reaction for urea formation, in which all of the urea cycle intermediates cancel out of the equation, is:

$$NH_4^+ + CO_2 + 3ATP + 2H_2O + aspartate \longrightarrow$$
$$urea + 2ADP + AMP + PP_i + 2P_i + fumarate$$

Carbamoyl phosphate is not shown as a reactant in this net equation; precursor molecules needed for its formation (NH_4^+, CO_2, ATP, and H_2O) have been substituted for it.

The equivalent of a total of four ATP molecules is expended in the production of one urea molecule. Two ATP molecules are consumed in the production of carbamoyl phosphate, and the equivalent of two ATP molecules is consumed in Step 2 of the urea cycle, where an ATP is hydrolyzed to AMP and PP_i and the PP_i is then further hydrolyzed to two P_i.

Urea formed via the urea cycle is excreted in urine. Urea is one of several molecules eliminated from the body through urine. The focus on relevancy feature Chemical Connections 26-A—The Chemical Composition of Urine—considers some of the additional compounds found in urine.

The Chemical Composition of Urine

Urine is a dilute aqueous solution containing many solutes whose concentrations are dependent on the diet and state of health of the individual. On average, about 4 g of solutes are present in a 100-g urine sample; thus urine is an approximately 4%-by-mass aqueous solution of materials eliminated from the body.

The solutes present in urine are of two general types: organic compounds and inorganic ions. Generally, the organic compounds are more abundant because of the dominance of urea, as shown in the following composition data.

Major Constituents of Urine (for a 1400-mL specimen obtained over a 24-hour period)

Organic Constituents		Inorganic Constituents	
urea	25.0 g	chloride (Cl^-)	6.3 g
creatinine	1.5 g	sodium (Na^+)	3.0 g
amino acids	0.8 g	potassium (K^+)	1.7 g
uric acid	0.7 g	sulfate (SO_4^{2-})	1.4 g
		dihydrogen phosphate ($H_2PO_4^-$)	1.2 g
		ammonium (NH_4^+)	0.8 g
		calcium (Ca^{2+})	0.2 g
		magnesium (Mg^{2+})	0.2 g

Urea, the solute present in the greatest quantity in urine, is odorless and colorless in solution (Section 26-4). (The pale yellow color of urine is due to small amounts of urobilin and related compounds, as discussed in Section 26-7.) Urea is the principal nitrogen-containing end product of protein metabolism.

The amount of urea in urine is significantly affected by dietary intake. Large high-protein-content meals (see accompanying photo) often provide protein amounts in excess of the body's needs, and the excess protein cannot be stored. Processing of the nitrogen content of the excess protein load increases the urea concentration in urine.

Creatinine (not to be confused with creatine, to be discussed shortly) is the second-most abundant organic product in urea. The structure of this nitrogen-containing compound is:

Urea concentrations in urine increase after ingestion of large amounts of dietary protein as the nitrogen content of excess protein is metabolized to urea.

Creatinine and creatine are related molecules. Creatinine is produced from the metabolism (degradation) of creatine. Approximately 2% of the body's creatine is converted to creatinine each day.

Creatine, in the form of creatine phosphate, is a high-energy phosphate (Section 23-5) compound naturally present in skeletal muscle. Its function is to supply phosphate groups to ADP (produced from spent ATP due to muscle activity) to regenerate ATP for further use:

$$\text{Creatine phosphate} + \text{ADP} \rightleftharpoons \text{Creatine} + \text{ATP}$$

The most abundant inorganic constituent of urine is chloride ion. Its primary source is dietary table salt (NaCl). Correspondingly, the second most abundant ion present is sodium ion, the positive ion in table salt. The sulfate ion present in urine comes primarily from the metabolism of sulfur-containing amino acids. Ammonium ions come primarily from the hydrolysis of urea.

Urine is normally slightly acidic, having an average pH value of 6.6. However, the pH range is wide—from 4.5 to 8.0. Fruits and vegetables in the diet tend to raise urine pH, and high-protein foods tend to lower urine pH.

A normal adult excretes 1000–1500 mL of urine daily. Actual urine volume depends on liquid intake and weather. During hot weather, urine volume decreases as a result of increased water loss through perspiration.

Chemistry at a Glance—Metabolic Reactions That Involve Nitrogen-Containing Compounds—combines the reactions of Section 26-3 (transamination and oxidative deamination) and those of the urea cycle (Section 26-4) into a single diagram, which serves as a useful summary of important reactions associated with the nitrogen portion of protein metabolism.

CHEMISTRY AT A GLANCE

Metabolic Reactions That Involve Nitrogen-Containing Compounds

Transamination ⟶ Glutamate ⟵ Transamination

20 amino acids — Glutamate — Aspartate

Glutamate → Oxidative deamination → NH_4^+ ion

NH_4^+ ion + CO_2, H_2O, ATP → Carbamoyl phosphate

Urea Cycle

Carbamoyl phosphate → Citrulline → (Aspartate) → Argininosuccinate → Arginine → Urea + Ornithine → (back to Carbamoyl phosphate)

Linkage Between the Urea and Citric Acid Cycles

The net equation for urea formation shows fumarate, a citric acid cycle intermediate, as a product. This fumarate enters the citric acid cycle, where it is converted to malate and then to oxaloacetate, which can then be converted to aspartate through transamination. The aspartate then re-enters the urea cycle at Step 2 (Figure 26-8).

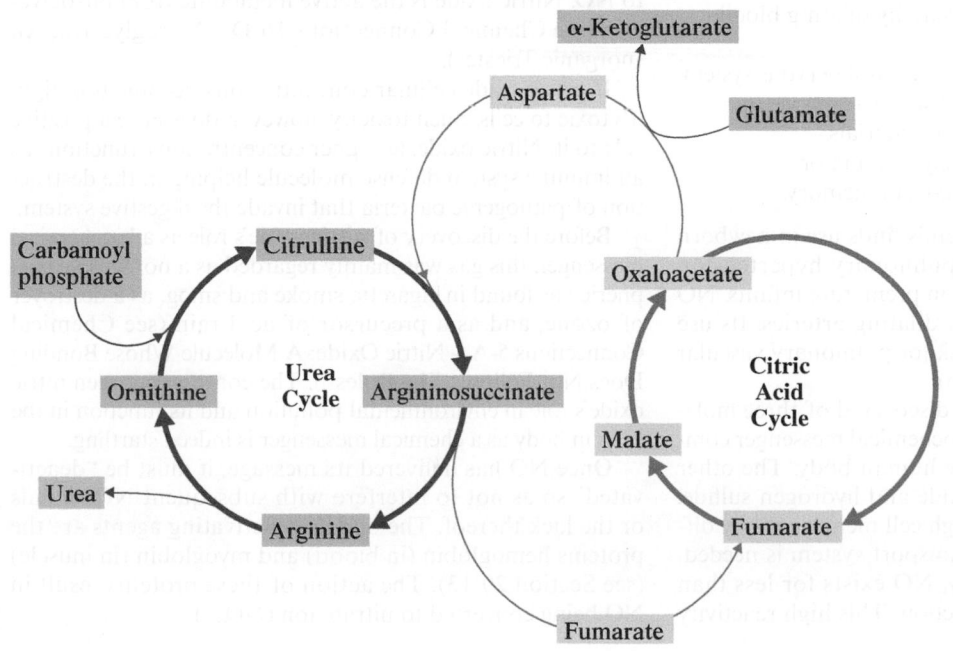

Figure 26-8 Fumarate from the urea cycle enters the citric acid cycle, and aspartate produced from oxaloacetate of the citric acid cycle enters the urea cycle.

Besides undergoing transamination, the oxaloacetate produced from fumarate of the urea cycle can be (1) converted to glucose via gluconeogenesis, (2) condensed with acetyl CoA to form citrate, or (3) converted to pyruvate.

Urea Cycle Intermediates and NO Production

In the mid-1980s, it was discovered that two of the urea cycle intermediates, arginine and citrulline, are involved in an important biochemical reaction that is completely independent of the urea cycle. This newly discovered biochemical role is participation in the production of the biochemical messenger molecule nitric oxide, NO. The focus on relevancy feature Chemical Connections 26-B—Arginine, Citrulline, and the Chemical Messenger Nitric Oxide—explores this discovery further.

CHEMICAL CONNECTIONS 26-B

Arginine, Citrulline, and the Chemical Messenger Nitric Oxide

A somewhat startling biochemical discovery made during the mid-1980s was the existence within the human body of a *gaseous* chemical messenger, the simple diatomic molecule nitric oxide (NO). Its production involves two of the amino acid intermediates of the urea cycle—arginine and citrulline. Arginine reacts with oxygen to produce citrulline, H_2O, and NO. The reaction requires NADPH and the enzyme *nitric oxide synthase* (NOS).

Premature infants often have respiratory problems associated with underdeveloped lungs. NO at low concentrations is useful in treating this problem.

Even though this reaction involves urea cycle intermediates, it is completely independent of the urea cycle.

Nitric oxide affects many kinds of cells and has particularly striking effects in the following areas:

1. NO helps maintain blood pressure by dilating blood vessels.
2. NO is a chemical messenger in the central nervous system.
3. NO is involved in the immune system's response to invasion by foreign organisms or materials.
4. NO is found in the brain and may be a major biochemical component of long-term memory.

At low levels NO in NO/O_2 blends finds use in newborn intensive care units in treating pulmonary hypertension (high blood pressure in the lungs) in premature infants. NO action reduces blood pressure by dilating arteries. Its use can save the life of an infant at risk for pulmonary vascular diseases (see accompanying photo).

Nitric oxide was the first to be discovered of three molecules now known to function as biochemical messenger compounds *in the gaseous state* in the human body. The other two molecules are carbon monoxide and hydrogen sulfide. Nitric oxide can easily pass through cell membranes by diffusion. No specific receptor or transport system is needed. Because of its extreme reactivity, NO exists for less than 10 seconds before undergoing reaction. This high reactivity

prevents it from getting more than 1 millimeter from its site of synthesis.

The action of nitroglycerin, when it is used as a heart medication (for angina pectoris), is now known to be related to NO. Nitric oxide is the active metabolite from nitroglycerin (see Chemical Connections 16-D—Nitroglycerin: An Inorganic Triester).

If nitric oxide cellular concentrations become too high, it's toxic to cells. Such toxicity, however, does have a positive side to it. Nitric oxide, at higher concentrations, functions as an immune system defense molecule helping in the destruction of pathogenic bacteria that invade the digestive system.

Before the discovery of nitric oxide's role as a biochemical messenger, this gas was mainly regarded as a noxious atmospheric gas found in cigarette smoke and smog, as a destroyer of ozone, and as a precursor of acid rain (see Chemical Connections 5-A—Nitric Oxide: A Molecule Whose Bonding Does Not Follow "The Rules"). The contrast between nitric oxide's role in environmental pollution and its function in the human body as a chemical messenger is indeed startling.

Once NO has delivered its message, it must be "deactivated" so as not to interfere with subsequent NO signals or the lack thereof. The body's deactivating agents are the proteins hemoglobin (in blood) and myoglobin (in muscle) (see Section 20-13). The action of these proteins result in NO being converted to nitrate ion (NO_3^-).

1. Which of the following statements concerning the compound *urea* is *incorrect*?
   a. Two $-NH_2$ groups are present in its structure.
   b. It is a white solid in its pure state.
   c. It gives urine its yellow color.
   d. no correct response
2. Which of the following is *not* a reactant in the formation of carbamoyl phosphate?
   a. carbon dioxide
   b. water
   c. ammonium ion
   d. no correct response
3. The two "fuels" for the urea cycle are
   a. carbamoyl phosphate and acetyl CoA
   b. carbamoyl phosphate and aspartate
   c. citrulline and arginine
   d. no correct response
4. Which of the following is the correct "nitrogen characterization" for the first step in the urea cycle?
   a. $N_1 + N_2 \longrightarrow N_3$
   b. $N_2 + N_2 \longrightarrow N_4$
   c. $N_2 + N_2 \longrightarrow N_3 + N_1$
   d. no correct response
5. The two nitrogen atoms in a urea molecule have as their biosynthetic source
   a. two ammonium ions
   b. two aspartate ion
   c. an ammonium ion and an aspartate ion
   d. no correct response
6. In the urea cycle, the urea-producing step involves the reaction of water with
   a. aspartate
   b. arginine
   c. argininosuccinate
   d. no correct response

Answers: 1. c; 2. d; 3. b; 4. a; 5. c; 6. b

26-5 Amino Acid Carbon Skeletons

LEARNING FOCUS

Be familiar with the products that result from amino acid "carbon skeleton" degradation; understand what is meant by the terms *glucogenic amino acid* and *ketogenic amino acid*.

The removal of the amino group of an amino acid by transamination/oxidative deamination (Section 26-3) produces an α-keto acid that contains the carbon skeleton from the amino acid. Because each of the 20 amino acids has a different carbon skeleton, each amino acid has a different degradation pathway for its carbon skeleton. For alanine and serine, the degradation requires a single step. For most carbon arrangements, however, multistep sequences are required. The details of the various degradation pathways are not considered in this text. Of importance, however, are the products obtained from the various degradations. The 20 degradation pathways do not produce 20 different products. Rather, the pathways converge in a manner that results in just seven metabolic products (intermediates), all of which have been encountered in previously discussed metabolic pathways. ◄ Four of the seven degradation products are citric acid cycle intermediates: α-ketoglutarate, succinyl CoA, fumarate, and oxaloacetate. The other three products are pyruvate, acetyl CoA, and acetoacetyl CoA. Figure 26-9 relates these seven degradation products to the amino acids from which they are obtained. Some amino acids appear in more than one box in Figure 26-9. This means that either there is more than one pathway for degradation or that some of the carbon atoms of the skeleton emerge as one product and others as another product.

▶ *The 20 standard amino acids are degraded by 20 different pathways that converge to produce just 7 products (metabolic products).*

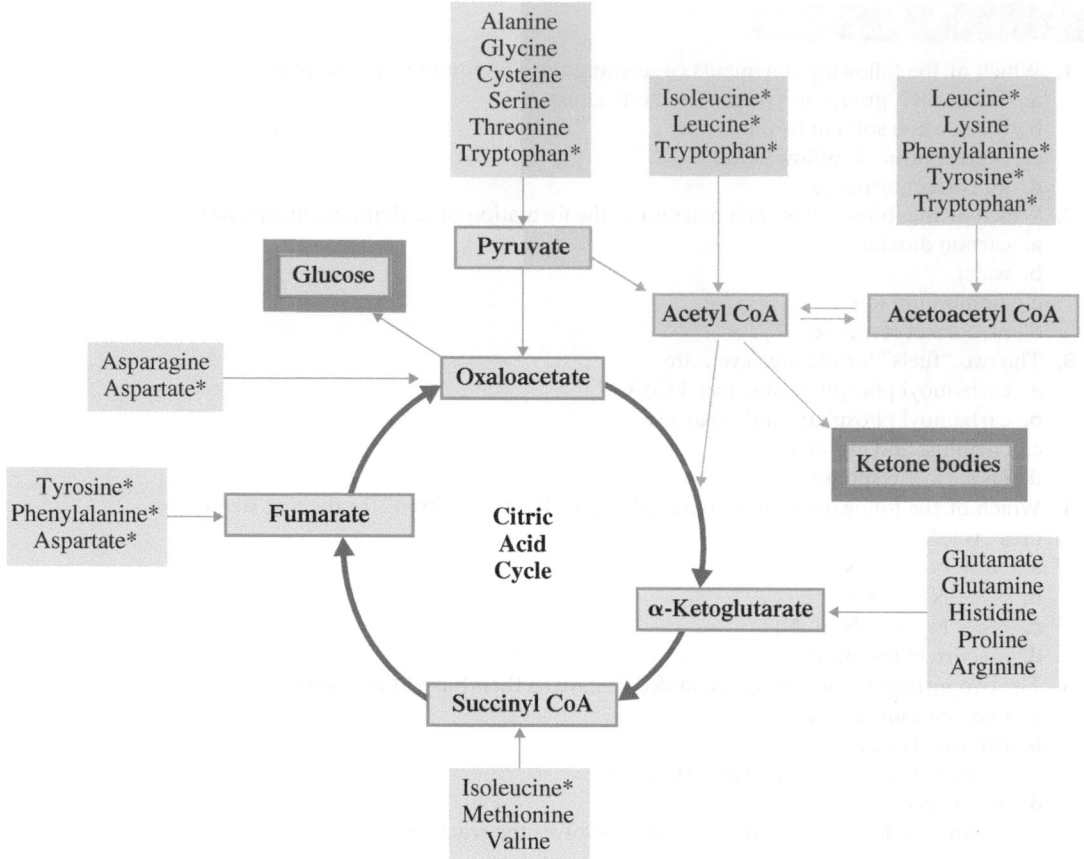

Figure 26-9 Fates of the carbon skeletons of amino acids. Glucogenic amino acids are shaded blue, and ketogenic amino acids are shaded green. Some amino acids (marked with an asterisk) have more than one degradation pathway and are thus present more than once in the diagram.

▶ *Only amino acids that can replenish, either directly or indirectly, oxaloacetate supplies are glucogenic, that is, can be used to produce glucose through gluconeogenesis.*

▶ *Degradation of amino acids in which an aromatic group is present in the side chain, such as phenylalanine and tryptophan, is not as straightforward as that of other amino acids. Molecular oxygen (O_2) is required in several steps of the degradation process. However, the degradation products are still common intermediates, as is the case for other amino acids.*

Amino acids that are degraded to citric acid cycle intermediates can serve as glucose precursors and are called glucogenic. ◀ A **glucogenic amino acid** *is an amino acid that has a carbon-containing degradation product that can be used to produce glucose via gluconeogenesis.*

Amino acids that are degraded to acetyl CoA or acetoacetyl CoA can contribute to the formation of fatty acids or ketone bodies and are called ketogenic. A **ketogenic amino acid** *is an amino acid that has a carbon-containing degradation product that can be used to produce ketone bodies.* Even though acetyl CoA can enter the citric acid cycle, there can be no *net* production of glucose from it. Acetyl groups are C_2 species, and such species only maintain the carbon count in the cycle because two CO_2 molecules exit the cycle (Section 23-6). Thus amino acids that are degraded to acetyl CoA (or acetoacetyl CoA) are not glucogenic.

Amino acids that are degraded to pyruvate can be either glucogenic or ketogenic. Pyruvate can be metabolized to either oxaloacetate (glucogenic) or acetyl CoA (ketogenic).

Only two amino acids are purely ketogenic: leucine and lysine. Nine amino acids are both glucogenic and ketogenic: those degraded to pyruvate (see Figure 26-9), as well as tyrosine, phenylalanine, and isoleucine (which have two degradation products). The remaining nine amino acids are purely glucogenic. ◀

The existence of glucogenicity and ketogenicity for amino acids points out that ATP production (common metabolic pathway) is not the only fate for amino acid degradation products. They can also be converted to glucose, ketone bodies, or fatty acids (via acetyl CoA).

1. Which of the following statements concerning the degradation of standard amino acid "carbon skeletons" is *correct*?
   a. Each type of carbon skeleton is degraded to a different product.
   b. All carbon skeletons are degraded to the same product.
   c. Each type of carbon skeleton is degraded by a different metabolic pathway.
   d. no correct response
2. How many standard amino acid carbon skeleton degradation products are citric acid cycle intermediates?
   a. 3
   b. 4
   c. 6
   d. no correct response
3. Which of the following statements concerning the genicity of standard amino acid degradation products is *incorrect*?
   a. Some, but not all, standard amino acids are ketogenic.
   b. Some, but not all, standard amino acids are glucogenic.
   c. All amino acids are both ketogenic and glucogenic.
   d. no correct response
4. Which of the following pairings of standard amino acid carbon skeleton degradation product and amino acid genicity is correct?
   a. citric acid cycle intermediate and ketogenic
   b. acetyl CoA and glucogenic
   c. pyruvate and both ketogenic and glucogenic
   d. no correct response

Answers: 1. c; 2. b; 3. c; 4. c

26-6 Amino Acid Biosynthesis

LEARNING FOCUS

Understand the difference between essential and nonessential amino acids in terms of their biosynthetic pathways.

The classification of amino acids as essential or nonessential for humans (Section 20-3) roughly parallels the number of steps in their biosynthetic pathways and the energy required for their synthesis. Nonessential amino acids require fewer reaction steps in their biosynthetic pathways than essential amino acids, judging on the basis of observations on their synthesis in microorganisms, as is shown in Table 26-2. Most bacteria and plants can synthesize all the amino acids by pathways not present in humans. Plants, consumed as food, are the major source of the essential amino acids in humans and animals. ◀

▶ *There is considerable variation in biosynthetic pathways for amino acids among different species. By contrast, the basic pathways of carbohydrate and lipid metabolism are almost universal.*

▶ Table 26-2 **Number of Reaction Steps Required for the Synthesis of Nonessential and Essential Amino Acids**

Nonessential Amino Acids		Essential Amino Acids	
Name	Reaction Steps	Name	Reaction Steps
Alanine	1	Threonine	6
Aspartic acid	1	Valine	9
Glutamic acid	1	Isoleucine	13
Asparagine	2	Leucine	14
Glutamine	2	Lysine	14
Serine	5	Methionine	17
Glycine	6	Arginine **	24
Proline	6	Histidine	27
Cysteine	7	Phenylalanine	29
Tyrosine*	30	Tryptophan	33

*Tyrosine is classified as nonessential only because it can be readily formed from essential phenylalanine in one step.
**Arginine is essential in the diets of children, but not adults.

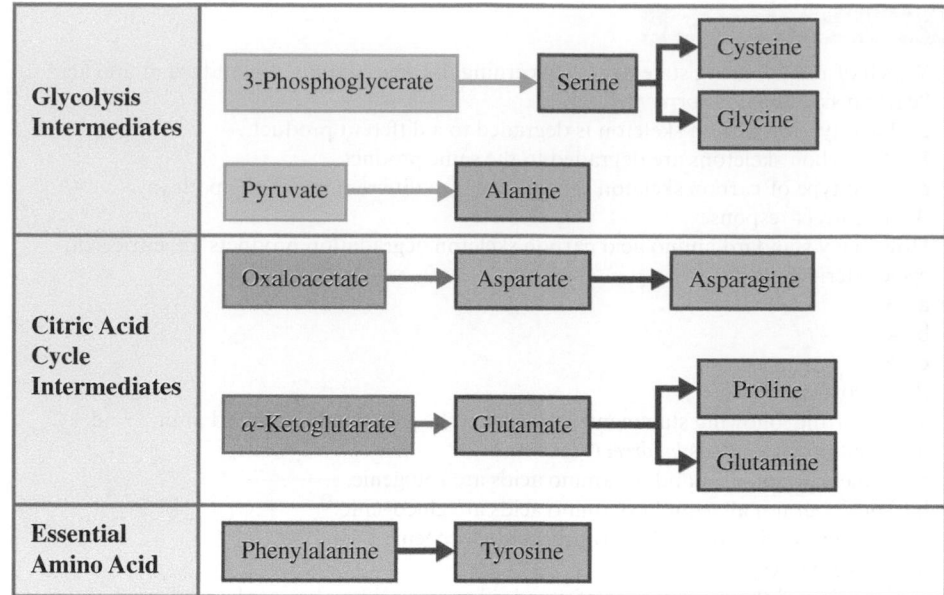

The starting materials for the biosynthesis of the 10 nonessential amino acids are the glycolysis intermediates 3-phosphoglycerate and pyruvate, the citric acid cycle intermediates oxaloacetate and α-ketoglutarate, and the amino acid phenylalanine. (Figure 26-10).

Three of the nonessential amino acids—alanine, aspartate, and glutamate—are biosynthesized by transamination (Section 26-3) of the appropriate α-keto acid starting material.

▶ *PKU is characterized
by elevated blood levels of
phenylalanine and phenylpyruvate. The physical consequence
of PKU is damage to developing
brain cells. In children up to six
years old, PKU leads to retarded
mental development. The major
defense against PKU is mandatory screening of newborns to
identify the one in every 20,000
who is afflicted and then restricting those children's dietary phenylalanine intake to that needed for
protein synthesis until they are six
years old. After that age, brain
cells are not so susceptible to the
toxic effect of phenylpyruvate.*

$$CH_3-\overset{\overset{\displaystyle O}{\|}}{C}-COO^- \xrightarrow{\text{Transamination}} CH_3-\overset{\overset{\displaystyle \overset{+}{NH_3}}{|}}{CH}-COO^-$$

Pyruvate   →   Alanine

$$^-OOC-CH_2-\overset{\overset{\displaystyle O}{\|}}{C}-COO^- \xrightarrow{\text{Transamination}} {}^-OOC-CH_2-\overset{\overset{\displaystyle \overset{+}{NH_3}}{|}}{CH}-COO^-$$

Oxaloacetate   →   Aspartate

$$^-OOC-CH_2-CH_2-\overset{\overset{\displaystyle O}{\|}}{C}-COO^- \xrightarrow{\text{Transamination}} {}^-OOC-CH_2-CH_2-\overset{\overset{\displaystyle \overset{+}{NH_3}}{|}}{CH}-COO^-$$

α-Ketoglutarate   →   Glutamate

The nonessential amino acid tyrosine is obtained from the essential amino acid phenylalanine in a one-step oxidation that involves molecular O_2, NADPH, and the enzyme *phenylalanine hydroxylase*. Lack of this enzyme causes the metabolic disease phenylketonuria (PKU). ◀

Section 26-6 Quick Quiz

1. The classification of an amino acid as essential or nonessential for humans can be related to the
   a. number of steps in its biosynthetic pathway
   b. number of carbon atoms in its side chain
   c. degree of polarity of its side chain
   d. no correct response

2. How many of the standard amino acids are biosynthesized in adequate amounts in an adult human body?
   a. 5
   b. 9
   c. 10
   d. no correct response
3. The *simplest* pathways for amino acid biosynthesis in the human body involve
   a. transamination reactions
   b. oxidative deamination reactions
   c. a reversal of urea cycle reactions
   d. no correct response

Answers: 1. a; 2. c; 3. a

26-7 Hemoglobin Catabolism

LEARNING FOCUS
Be familiar with the reaction steps in the degradation of the heme part of a hemoglobin molecule.

Red blood cells are highly specialized cells whose primary function is to deliver oxygen to, and remove carbon dioxide from, body tissues. Mature red blood cells have no nucleus or DNA. Instead, they are filled with the red pigment hemoglobin. Red blood cell formation occurs in the bone marrow, and about 200 billion new red blood cells are formed daily. The life span of a red blood cell is about four months.

The oxygen-carrying ability of red blood cells is due to the protein hemoglobin present in such cells (Figure 26-11). Hemoglobin is a conjugated protein (Section 20-9); the protein portion is called *globin*, and the prosthetic group (nonprotein portion) is *heme*. Heme contains four pyrrole groups (Section 17-9) joined together with an iron atom in the center.

Figure 26-11 A molecular model of the protein hemoglobin.

Pyrrole

Heme

It is the iron atom in heme that interacts with O_2, forming a reversible complex with it. This complexation increases the amount of O_2 that the blood can carry by a factor of 80 over that which simply "dissolves" in the blood.

Old red blood cells are broken down in the spleen (primary site) and liver (secondary site). Part of this process is degradation of hemoglobin. The globin protein is hydrolyzed to amino acids, which become part of the amino acid pool (Section 26-2).

▶ *The tetrapyrrole heme ring is the only component of hemoglobin that is not reused by the body.*

The iron atom of heme becomes part of *ferritin*, an iron-storage protein, which saves the iron for use in the biosynthesis of new hemoglobin molecules. The tetrapyrrole carbon arrangement of heme is degraded to *bile pigments* that are eliminated in feces and to a lesser extent in urine. ◀

Degradation of heme begins with a ring-opening reaction in which a single carbon atom is removed. The product is called *biliverdin*.

Heme

Biliverdin

This reaction has several important characteristics. (1) Molecular oxygen, O_2, is required as a reactant. (2) Ring opening releases the iron atom to be incorporated into ferritin. (3) The product containing the excised carbon atom is *carbon monoxide* (a substance toxic to the human body). The carbon monoxide so produced reacts with functioning hemoglobin, forming a CO–hemoglobin complex; this decreases the oxygen-carrying ability of the blood. CO–hemoglobin complexes are very stable; CO release to the lungs is a slow process. ◀

▶ *The level of carbon monoxide produced in the first step of hemoglobin degradation is sufficient to complex 1% of the oxygen-binding sites of the blood's hemoglobin.*

An alternative rendering of the structure of biliverdin is:

Biliverdin

M = —CH₃ (methyl)
V = —CH=CH₂ (vinyl)
P = —CH₂—CH₂—COO⁻ (propionate)

This structure employs a notation, common in heme chemistry, in which letters are used to denote attachments to the pyrrole rings; such notation easily distinguishes the attachments. The structure's linear arrangement of pyrrole rings also saves space compared to the heme-like representation of the rings. However, the linear structure incorrectly implies that the arrangement of the pyrrole rings that results from the ring opening is linear (straight-line); rather, the pyrrole rings actually have a heme-like arrangement.

In the second step of heme degradation, biliverdin is converted to bilirubin. This change involves reduction of the central methylene bridge of biliverdin. ◀

Biliverdin

NADPH + H⁺

NADP⁺

Bilirubin

▶ In 2002, it was discovered that bilirubin has antioxidant properties. It protects against peroxyl radicals (Section 23-11) by being oxidized back to biliverdin. Its antioxidant properties are significantly better than those of glutathione (Section 20-8), the molecule believed for 80 years to be the most important cellular antioxidant.

Bilirubin is found only in low concentrations in cells but in higher concentrations in blood. This new research suggests that bilirubin is probably the major antioxidant protector for cell membranes, while glutathione protects components inside cells.

The change from heme to biliverdin to bilirubin usually occurs in the spleen. The bilirubin is then transported by serum albumin to the liver, where it is rendered more water soluble by the attachment of sugar residues to its propionate side chains (P side chains). The solubilizing sugar is *glucuronate* (glucose with a —COO⁻ group on C6 instead of a —CH₂OH group; Section 18-12).

COO⁻

COO⁻

HO

OH

OH

OH

OH

OH

Bilirubin

Bilirubin diglucuronide

The solubilized bilirubin is excreted from the liver in bile, which flows into the small intestine. Here the bilirubin diglucuronide is changed, in a multistep process, to either stercobilin for excretion in feces or urobilin for excretion in urine. Intestinal bacteria are primarily responsible for the changes that produce stercobilin and urobilin. ◀

The first part of the names biliverdin *and* bilirubin *and the last part of the names* stercobilin *and* urobilin *all come from the Latin* bilis, *which means* "bile." *As for the other parts of the names:*

1. *Latin* virdis *means "green";* biliverdin = *"green bile."*
2. *Latin* rubin *means "red";* bilirubin = *"red bile."*
3. *Latin* urina *means "urine";* urobilin = *"urine bile."*
4. *Latin* sterco *means "dung";* stercobilin = *"dung bile."*

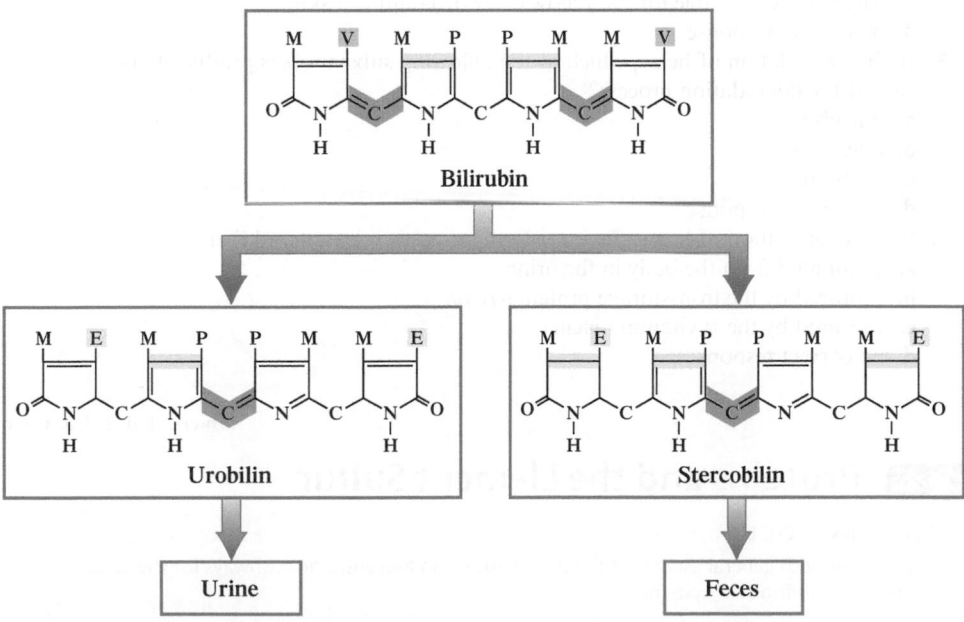

Figure 26-12 Stercobilin and urobilin have structures closely resembling that of bilirubin. Changes include reduction of vinyl (V) groups to ethyl (E) groups and reduction of —CH₂— and ═CH— bridges.

Bile Pigments

The tetrapyrrole degradation products obtained from heme are known as bile *pigments* because they are secreted with the bile (Section 19-11), and most of them are highly colored. A **bile pigment** *is a colored tetrapyrrole degradation product present in bile.* Biliverdin and bilirubin are, respectively, green and reddish-orange in color. Stercobilin has a brownish hue and is the compound that gives feces their characteristic color. Urobilin is the pigment that gives urine its characteristic yellow color. Normally, the body excretes 1–2 mg of bile pigments in urine daily and 250–350 mg of bile pigments in feces daily.

When the body is functioning properly, the degradation of heme in the spleen to bilirubin and the removal of bilirubin from the blood by the liver balance each other. *Jaundice* is the condition that occurs when this balance is upset such that bilirubin concentrations in the blood become higher than normal. ◄ The skin and the white of the eyes acquire a yellowish tint because of the excess bilirubin in the blood. Jaundice can occur as a result of liver diseases, such as infectious hepatitis and cirrhosis, that decrease the liver's ability to process bilirubin; from spleen malfunction, in which heme is degraded more rapidly than it can be absorbed by the liver; and from gallbladder malfunction, usually from an obstruction of the bile duct. ◄

The local coloration associated with a deep bruise is also related to the pigmentation associated with heme, biliverdin, and bilirubin. The changing color of the bruise as it heals reflects the dominant degradation product present as the tissue repairs itself.

▶ *The word* jaundice *comes from the French* jaune, *which means "yellow."*

▶ *A mild form of jaundice is common among premature infants because of underdeveloped liver function. Treatment involves the use of white or ultraviolet light, which breaks the bilirubin down to simpler compounds that are more easily excreted.*

Section 26-7 Quick Quiz

1. Which of the following statements concerning the first step of the degradation of the heme portion of hemoglobin is *incorrect*?
   a. molecular O_2 is needed as a reactant
   b. carbon monoxide is a product
   c. ring opening with release of an iron atom occurs
   d. no correct response
2. Which of the following statements concerning the bile pigments produced from the degradation of the heme portion of hemoglobin is *incorrect*?
   a. They are responsible for the yellow color of urine.
   b. They are responsible for the brown color of feces.
   c. They are responsible for the yellow color of jaundiced skin.
   d. no correct response
3. In the degradation of heme, which of the following substances is produced in the second step of the degradation process?
   a. bilirubin
   b. biliverdin
   c. urobilin
   d. no correct response
4. In the degradation of heme, the iron atom present is released and then
   a. eliminated from the body in the urine
   b. captured by the iron-storage protein *ferritin*
   c. captured by the B vitamin niacin
   d. no correct response

Answers: 1. d; 2. d; 3. a; 4. b

26-8 Proteins and the Element Sulfur

LEARNING FOCUS

Be familiar with general aspects of the degradation and biosynthetic pathways for the sulfur-containing amino acid cysteine.

All of the standard amino acids (Section 20-2) found in proteins contain the elements carbon, hydrogen, oxygen, and nitrogen. Much of the discussion in preceding sections of this chapter has focused on the element nitrogen and the need for it to be removed from amino acid molecules prior to their further processing for energy generation. In this section, focus shifts from the element nitrogen to the element sulfur. Two of the twenty standard amino acids—cysteine and methionine—have a sulfur atom in their side chain.

$$
\begin{array}{cc}
& CH_3 \\
& | \\
& S \\
& | \\
SH & CH_2 \\
| & | \\
CH_2 & CH_2 \\
| & | \\
H_3\overset{+}{N}-CH-COO^- & H_3\overset{+}{N}-CH-COO^- \\
\text{Cysteine} & \text{Methionine}
\end{array}
$$

The biochemistry associated with the element sulfur in the synthesis and degradation of sulfur-containing amino acids is now considered. The focus will be on cysteine rather than methionine as the former is the simpler of the two molecules. The key sulfur-containing compound in the discussion will be the simple inorganic molecule hydrogen sulfide, H_2S, and the simple inorganic ions sulfate, SO_4^{2-}, an sulfite, SO_3^{2-}.

Biodegradation of Cysteine

Pyruvate is the degradation product for the carbon skeleton of cysteine (Section 26-5; Figure 26-9). This degradation is a simple two-step process. First, a transamination reaction occurs and then release of the sulfhydryl group ($-SH$) is effected with H_2S as the sulfur-containing product.

The H_2S derived from cysteine degradation has been found to be a powerful gaseous signaling agent in the human body with involvement in the regulation of blood flow and blood pressure. This function for H_2S will be considered in more detail later in this section.

Biosynthesis of Cysteine

The precursor for cysteine biosynthesis is the amino acid serine (see Figure 26-10). The transition from serine (whose synthesis requires numerous steps) to cysteine is a two-step process. First, the serine must be activated using an acetyl CoA molecule and then sulfhydrylation occurs with H_2S as the source of the sulfhydryl group.

What is the source for the H_2S needed for synthesis of new cysteine? Studies involving microorganisms and plants indicate that *sulfate assimilation* is one process by which H_2S can be produced. Sulfate ion (SO_4^{2-}), the starting material for sulfate assimilation, is the common inorganic form for combined sulfur in nature and is routinely present in drinking water. The sulfur present in sulfate is in an oxidized state

Figure 26-13 The conversion of sulfate ion (SO_4^{2-}) to sulfide ion (S^{2-}) via sulfate assimilation.

Step 1

SO_4^{2-} + ATP $\xrightarrow{PP_i}$ [structure]

Sulfate

Adenosine 5'-phosphosulfate (APS)

Step 2

APS + ATP $\xrightarrow{ADP}$ [structure]

3'-Phosphoadenosine 5'-phosphosulfate (PAPS)

Step 3

PAPS $\xrightarrow{NADPH \quad NADP^+ + H^+}$ SO_3^{2-} + [structure]

Sulfite

3'-Phosphoadenosine 5'-phosphate

$\longrightarrow$ AMP + P_i

Step 4

$3\,NADPH + 3\,H^+ + SO_3^{2-} \longrightarrow S^{2-} + 3\,NADPH^+ + 3\,H_2O$

Sulfide

and hydrogen sulfide contains sulfur in a reduced state. Thus, sulfate assimilation is an oxidation–reduction process. Important intermediates in the conversion of sulfate to hydrogen sulfide are shown in Figure 26-13. These intermediates are ATP derivatives that are seldom encountered in other metabolic processes.

The first intermediate formed comes from the direct interaction of SO_4^{2-} with an ATP molecule producing a sulfate–AMP complex (APS) whose structure is shown in Figure 26-13a. This APS complex reacts with another ATP producing an ADP molecule and a new complex (PAPS) that contains the released phosphate group (Figure 26-13b). Sulfite ion (SO_3^{2-}) is then released from the PAPS with NADPH being the reducing agent (Figure 26-13c). The other product, ADP, then undergoes change to AMP and P_i. Further reduction of SO_3^{2-} using NADPH produces the S^{2-} ion (Figure 26-13d). The species

S^{2-}, HS^-, and H_2S are interconvertible species in solution, being members of two conjugate acid/base pairs (HS^-/S^{2-} and H_2S/HS^-) (see Section 10-2).

$$S^{2-} \xrightleftharpoons[-H^+]{+H^+} HS^- \xrightleftharpoons[-H^+]{+H^+} H_2S$$

Hydrogen Sulfide as a Biochemical Signaling Agent

Besides being a sulfur source for biosynthesis of the sulfur-containing amino acids cysteine and methionine, H_2S has several biochemical signaling functions whose discovery is of relatively recent origin. Important discoveries relative to the actions of H_2S in the human body include:

1. H_2S acts as a smooth muscle relaxant and vasodilator and thus has a role in the regulation of vascular blood flow and blood pressure. Its role here is a cardioprotective role.
2. H_2S is active in the brain. In Alzheimer's disease, the brain's hydrogen sulfide concentrations are lower than normal.
3. H_2S is involved in type I diabetes considerations. In type I diabetes, pancreatic beta cells produce an excess of H_2S, leading to beta cell death and reduced insulin production.

Many of hydrogen sulfide's functions as a gaseous signaling agent parallel those of nitric oxide, the gaseous signaling agent discussed earlier in this chapter (see Chemical Connections 26-B—Arginine, Citrulline, and the Chemical Messenger Nitric Oxide). The mechanisms by which these two molecules exert their effects are, however, different. For example, nitric oxide relaxes blood vessels through enzyme activation, whereas hydrogen sulfide exerts its effect through activation of cell membrane potassium channels. Recent studies suggest that there is an interdependency to these actions, with NO involved in the relaxation of large blood vessels and H_2S acting primarily on small blood vessels.

The process for elimination of H_2S from the body has some reverse parallels to the way it enters the body. For elimination, it is first converted to sulfite (SO_3^{2-}) which is then further oxidized to sulfate (SO_4^{2-}) ion, which is then excreted in the urine. Up to 90% of the sulfur content of urine is in the form of sulfate.

Section 26-8 Quick Quiz

1. In degradation of the sulfur-containing amino acid cysteine, the sulfur is released in the form of
   a. hydrogen sulfide
   b. sulfate ion
   c. sulfur dioxide
   d. no correct response
2. The process of sulfate assimilation converts SO_4^{2-} to
   a. H_2S
   b. S^{2-}
   c. SO_2
   d. no correct response
3. In the first step of the sulfate assimilation process, which of the following is a reactant?
   a. acetyl CoA
   b. ATP
   c. cysteine
   d. no correct response
4. A nonmetabolic function for hydrogen sulfide is that of a
   a. denaturing agent
   b. gaseous signaling agent
   c. emulsifying agent
   d. no correct response

Answers: 1. a; 2. a; 3. b; 4. b

26-9   Interrelationships Among Metabolic Pathways

LEARNING FOCUS

Be familiar with general aspects of the interdependencies that exist among carbohydrate, lipid, and protein metabolic pathways; be familiar with the human body's general response to the conditions of feasting, fasting, and starvation.

In this chapter and the previous two chapters, metabolic pathways of carbohydrates, lipids, and proteins have been considered. These pathways are not independent of each other but, rather, are integrally linked, as shown in Chemistry at a Glance—Interrelationships Among Carbohydrate, Lipid, and Protein Metabolism. The numerous connections among pathways mean that a change in one pathway can affect many other pathways.

A good illustration of the interrelationships among pathways emerges from comparing the processes of eating (feasting), not eating for a short period (fasting), and not eating for a prolonged period (starvation). Figure 26-14 shows how the body responds to each of these situations.

CHEMISTRY AT A GLANCE   Interrelationships Among Carbohydrate, Lipid, and Protein Metabolism

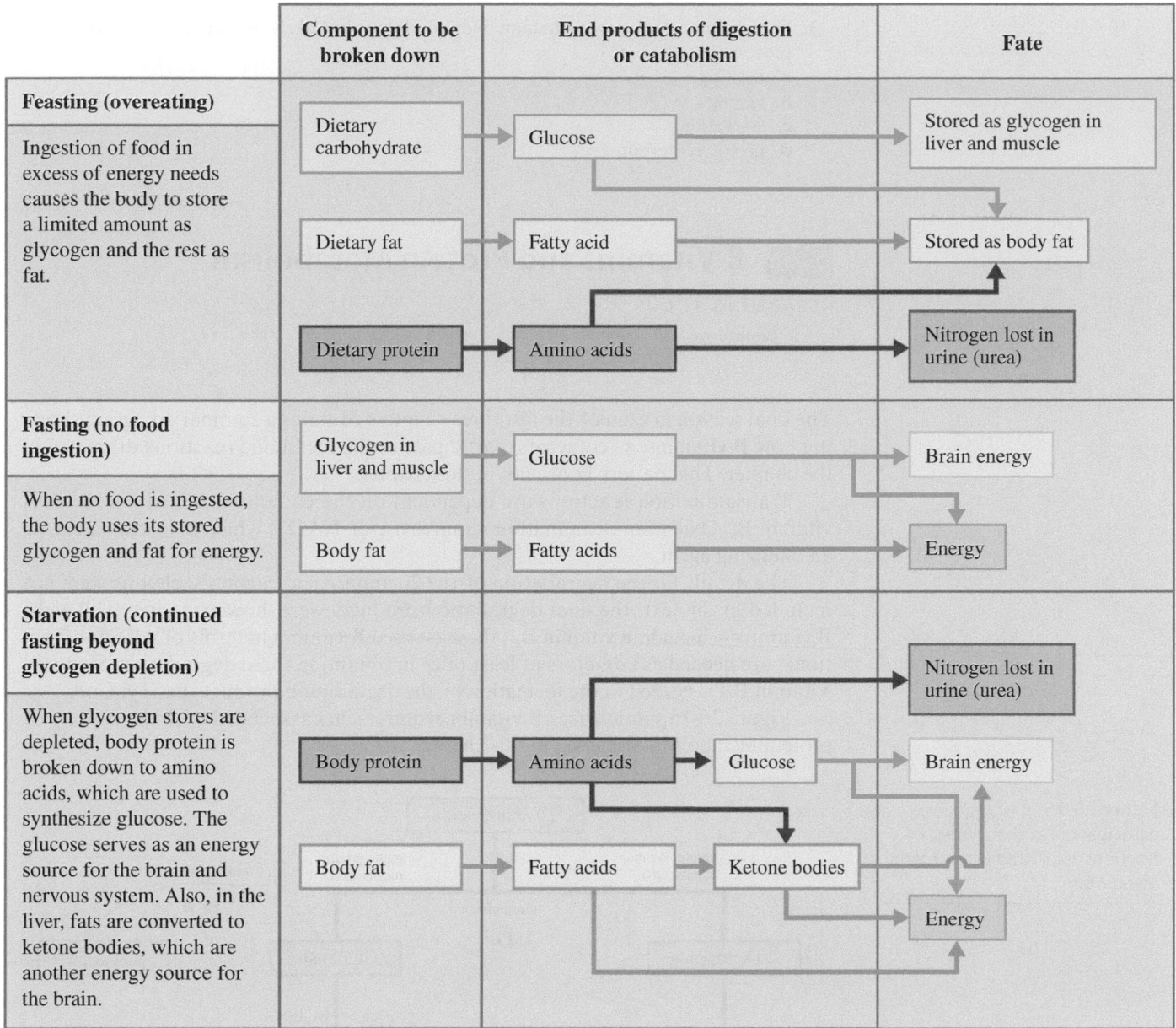

Figure 26-14 The human body's response to feasting, to fasting, and to starvation.

1. Fumarate produced during urea cycle operation is processed further via
   a. the citric acid cycle
   b. glycolysis
   c. β-oxidation pathway
   d. no correct response
2. Oxaloacetate produced during citric acid cycle operation can enter the urea cycle in the form of
   a. fumarate
   b. aspartate
   c. ammonium ion
   d. no correct response

(continued)

3. For which of the following human body conditions is it likely for amino acids to be processed to glucose?
   a. feasting
   b. fasting
   c. starvation
   d. no correct response

Answers: 1. a; 2. b; 3. c

26-10 B Vitamins and Protein Metabolism

LEARNING FOCUS

Be familiar with the involvement that B vitamins have in protein metabolism.

The final section in each of the last three chapters contains a summary diagram showing how B vitamins, as cofactors, participate in the metabolic reactions discussed in the chapter. That pattern continues in this chapter.

Transamination reactions are dependent on the cofactor PLP, which involves vitamin B_6. Oxidation deamination requires use of NAD^+, which involves niacin, as an oxidizing agent.

The details for the degradation of the 20 amino acid carbon skeletons were not included in the text; the final degradation products were, however, given. All eight B vitamins—including vitamin B_{12}, the least used B vitamin in terms of cofactor function—are needed as cofactors at least once in obtaining these degradation products. Vitamin B_{12} is needed in the formation of the degradation product succinyl CoA.

Figure 26-15 summarizes B vitamin requirements associated with the aspects of protein metabolism discussed in this chapter.

Figure 26-15 B vitamin participation, as coenzymes, in reactions associated with protein metabolism.

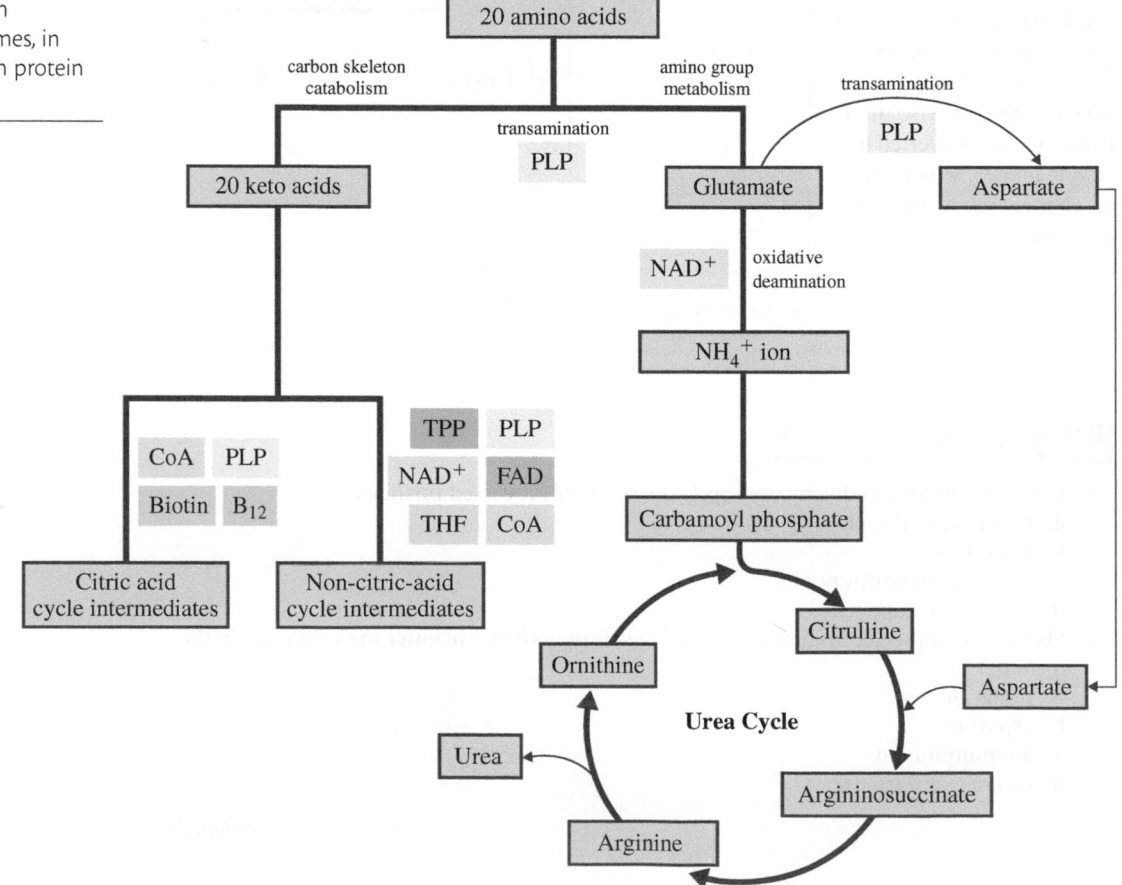

1. Transamination reactions require the cofactor PLP which involves the B vitamin
   a. folate
   b. riboflavin
   c. vitamin B_6
   d. no correct response
2. Oxidative deamination reactions require the oxidizing agent NAD^+ which involves the B vitamin
   a. biotin
   b. thiamin
   c. vitamin B_{12}
   d. no correct response
3. How many of the B vitamins are needed in the degradation pathways for the carbon skeletons of the 20 standard amino acids?
   a. 4
   b. 6
   c. all of them
   d. no correct response

Answers: 1. c; 2. d; 3. c

Concepts to Remember

Protein digestion and absorption. Digestion of proteins involves the hydrolysis of the peptide bonds that link amino acids to each other. This process begins in the stomach and is completed in the small intestine. The amino acids released by digestion are absorbed through the intestinal wall into the bloodstream (Section 26-1).

Amino acid pool. The amino acid pool within cells consists of varying amounts of each of the 20 standard amino acids found in proteins (Section 26-2).

Amino acid utilization. Amino acids from the amino acid pool are used for protein synthesis, synthesis of nonprotein nitrogen compounds, synthesis of nonessential amino acids, and energy production (Section 26-2).

Transamination. A transamination reaction is an enzyme-catalyzed transfer of an amino group from an α-amino acid to an α-keto acid. Transamination is a step in obtaining energy from amino acids (Section 26-3).

Oxidative deamination. An oxidative deamination reaction is a reaction in which an α-amino acid is converted into an α-keto acid, accompanied by the release of a free ammonium ion. Oxidative deamination is a step in obtaining energy from amino acids (Section 26-3).

Urea cycle. The urea cycle is the metabolic pathway that converts ammonium ions and aspartate into urea. This cycle processes the ammonium ions in the form of carbamoyl phosphate, a compound formed from CO_2, NH_4^+, ATP, and H_2O (Section 26-4).

Amino acid carbon skeletons. Amino acid carbon skeletons (keto acids) are classified as glucogenic or ketogenic on the basis of their catabolic pathways. Glucogenic amino acids are degraded to intermediates of the citric acid cycle and can be used for glucose synthesis. Ketogenic amino acids are degraded into acetoacetyl CoA or acetyl CoA and can be used to make ketone bodies (Section 26-5).

Amino acid biosynthesis. Amino acid biosynthesis is the process in which the body synthesizes amino acids from intermediates of the glycolysis pathway and the citric acid cycle. Ten amino acids can be synthesized by the body. The other 10 amino acids, called essential amino acids, must be obtained from the diet (Section 26-6).

Hemoglobin catabolism. Hemoglobin from red blood cells undergoes a stepwise degradation to biliverdin, to bilirubin, and then to bile pigments that are excreted from the body (Section 26-7).

Exercises and Problems

Exercises and problems are arranged in matched pairs with the two members of a pair addressing the same concept(s). The answer to the odd-numbered member of a pair is given at the back of the book. Problems denoted with a ▲ involve concepts found not only in the section under consideration but also in one or more earlier sections of the chapter.

Protein Digestion and Absorption (Section 26-1)

26-1 Indicate whether each of the following aspects of protein digestion is associated with the (1) mouth, (2) stomach, (3) small intestine, or (4) intestinal lining.

a. Protein is denatured
b. Trypsin is active
c. Breaking of peptide bonds is completed
d. Hydrochloric acid is secreted

26-2 Indicate whether each of the following aspects of protein digestion is associated with the (1) mouth, (2) stomach, (3) small intestine, or (4) intestinal lining.

a. Breaking of peptide bonds begins
b. Pepsin is active
c. Active transport of amino acids occurs
d. Aminopeptidase is active

26-3 Indicate whether each of the following pairings of terms/concepts is correct.
  a. Secretin/hydrochloric acid secretion
  b. Hydrochloric acid/pepsinogen activation
  c. Bicarbonate ion/proteolytic enzyme
  d. Aminopeptidase/pancreatic digestive enzyme

26-4 Indicate whether each of the following pairings of terms/concepts is correct.
  a. Small intestine/slightly acidic pH
  b. Trypsin/free amino acids
  c. Bicarbonate ion/acid neutralization
  d. Gastrin/digestive enzyme

26-5 Indicate whether each of the following statements relating to protein digestion is true or false.
  a. Pepsinogen is the active form of the zymogen pepsin.
  b. Approximately 50% of protein digestion occurs in the stomach.
  c. Hydrochloric acid present in the stomach kills most bacteria.
  d. Secretin is a hormone that stimulates the production of pancreatic digestive enzymes.

26-6 Indicate whether each of the following statements relating to protein digestion is true or false.
  a. Gastrin is a hormone released by stomach mucosa cells.
  b. Approximately 90% of protein digestion occurs in the small intestine.
  c. Hydrochloric acid functions as a denaturing agent in the stomach.
  d. Pancreatic digestive enzymes include carboxypeptidase and aminopeptidase.

26-7 Contrast the partially digested protein mixture in the stomach with its counterpart in the small intestine in terms of mixture pH.

26-8 Contrast the partially digested protein mixture in the stomach with its counterpart in the small intestine in terms of digestive enzymes present.

26-9 In the context of protein digestion, indicate whether each of the following substances is associated with the *stomach* or the *small intestine*.
  a. Gastrin
  b. Trypsin
  c. HCl
  d. Carboxypeptidase

26-10 In the context of protein digestion, indicate whether each of the following substances is associated with the *stomach* or the *small intestine*.
  a. Aminopeptidase
  b. Pepsin
  c. HCO_3^-
  d. Secretin

26-11 Indicate whether each of the substances in Problem 26-9 is (1) a hormone, (2) a digestive enzyme, or (3) neither a hormone nor a digestive enzyme.

26-12 Indicate whether each of the substances in Problem 26-10 is (1) a hormone, (2) a digestive enzyme, or (3) neither a hormone nor a digestive enzyme.

Amino Acid Utilization (Section 26-2)

26-13 Indicate whether each of the following statements relating to the body's amino acid pool is true or false.
  a. Protein turnover contributes amino acids to the pool.
  b. The location for the pool is the liver.
  c. Synthesis of new protein requires withdrawal of amino acids from the pool.
  d. The pool contains all of the nonessential amino acids but none of the essential ones.

26-14 Indicate whether each of the following statements relating to the body's amino acid pool is true or false.
  a. The pool is a mix of all 20 standard amino acids.
  b. The main use for the pool's amino acids is protein synthesis.
  c. Dietary protein is the sole source of amino acids for the pool.
  d. Only essential amino acids can be withdrawn from the pool.

26-15 Indicate whether each of the following situations produces (1) a positive nitrogen balance or (2) a negative nitrogen balance within the human body.
  a. Protein degradation exceeds protein synthesis
  b. Pregnancy
  c. Convalescence from an emaciating illness
  d. Protein-poor diet

26-16 Indicate whether each of the following situations produces (1) a positive nitrogen balance or (2) a negative nitrogen balance within the human body.
  a. Protein synthesis exceeds protein degradation
  b. Growth "spurt"
  c. Degradation of protein for energy production
  d. Wasting illness

26-17 What are the three major sources of amino acids for the amino acid pool?

26-18 What are the four major uses for amino acids present in the amino acid pool?

26-19 With the help of Table 26-1, classify each of the following amino acids as an essential amino acid or a nonessential amino acid.
  a. Lysine
  b. Cysteine
  c. Serine
  d. Tryptophan

26-20 With the help of Table 26-1, classify each of the following amino acids as an essential amino acid or a nonessential amino acid.
  a. Proline
  b. Glycine
  c. Valine
  d. Methionine

26-21 Indicate whether each of the amino acids in Problem 26-19 can or cannot be synthesized in the body in amounts adequate to meet the body's needs.

26-22 Indicate whether each of the amino acids in Problem 26-20 can or cannot be synthesized in the body in amounts adequate to meet the body's needs.

Transamination and Oxidative Deamination (Section 26-3)

26-23 In general terms, what two types of compounds are the reactants in a transamination reaction?

26-24 In general terms, what two types of compounds are the products in a transamination reaction?

26-25 Indicate whether each of the following compounds is a keto acid.
a. Glutamate
b. Oxaloacetate
c. Aspartate
d. Glutarate

26-26 Indicate whether each of the following compounds is an amino acid.
a. Glutamate
b. Oxaloacetate
c. α-Ketoglutarate
d. Succinate

26-27 Indicate whether each of the compounds in Problem 26-25 is a C_5 species.

26-28 Indicate whether each of the compounds in Problem 26-26 is a C_4 species.

26-29 Write structural equations for the transamination reactions that involve the following pairs of reactants. Use Table 20-1 as the source for any needed amino acid structural information.
a. Serine and oxaloacetate
b. Alanine and oxaloacetate
c. Glycine and α-ketoglutarate
d. Threonine and α-ketoglutarate

26-30 Write structural equations for the transamination reactions that involve the following pairs of reactants. Use Table 20-1 as the source for any needed amino acid structural information.
a. Threonine and oxaloacetate
b. Glycine and oxaloacetate
c. Alanine and α-ketoglutarate
d. Serine and α-ketoglutarate

26-31 For each of the following pairs of compounds, indicate whether the first listed compound can be converted to the second listed compound via a transamination reaction.
a. Oxaloacetate to aspartate
b. Aspartate to oxaloacetate
c. Aspartate to glutamate
d. Oxaloacetate to α-ketoglutarate

26-32 For each of the following pairs of compounds, indicate whether the first listed compound can be converted to the second listed compound via a transamination reaction.
a. Glutamate to α-ketoglutarate
b. α-Ketoglutarate to glutamate
c. Glutamate to aspartate
d. α-Ketoglutarate to oxaloacetate

26-33 For each of the following pairs of compounds, indicate whether the paired compounds could function as the two reactants in a transamination reaction.
a. Oxaloacetate and α-ketoglutarate
b. Glutamate and oxaloacetate
c. Glutarate and glutamate
d. Oxaloacetate and succinate

26-34 For each of the following pairs of compounds, indicate whether the paired compounds could function as the two reactants in a transamination reaction.
a. Glutamate and aspartate
b. Aspartate and α-ketoglutarate
c. Succinate and α-ketoglutarate
d. Glutarate and aspartate

26-35 What are the two α-keto acids that are most often reactants in transamination reactions?

26-36 What are the two α-keto acids that are most often substrates for aminotransferases?

26-37 What is the overall purpose for the transamination phase of protein catabolism?

26-38 What distinction does glutamate have in the transamination phase of protein catabolism?

26-39 What is the function of pyridoxal phosphate in transamination processes?

26-40 Which one of the B vitamins is important in the process of transamination?

26-41 In the further processing of glutamate via oxidative deamination:
a. what are the other two reactants?
b. what are the four products?
c. what type of enzyme is needed?
d. what product becomes the "nitrogen carrier" for further reactions?

26-42 In the further processing of glutamate via a glutamate–oxaloacetate transamination:
a. what are the two reactants?
b. what are the two products?
c. what type of enzyme is needed?
d. what product becomes the "nitrogen carrier" for further reactions?

26-43 Draw the structure of the α-keto acid produced from the oxidative deamination of each of the following amino acids.
a. Glutamate
b. Cysteine
c. Alanine
d. Phenylalanine

26-44 Draw the structure of the α-keto acid produced from the oxidative deamination of each of the following amino acids.
a. Glycine
b. Leucine
c. Aspartate
d. Tyrosine

26-45 Characterize each of the following as a possible reactant, product, or enzyme involved in (1) transamination, (2) oxidative deamination, or (3) both transamination and oxidative deamination.
a. α-Ketoglutarate
b. Glutamate
c. Glutamate dehydrogenase
d. NH_4^+

26-46 Characterize each of the following as a possible reactant, product, or enzyme involved in (1) transamination, (2) oxidative deamination, or (3) both transamination and oxidative deamination.
a. Oxaloacetate
b. Aspartate
c. Glutamate aminotransferase
d. H_2O

The Urea Cycle (Section 26-4)

26-47 What are the two "nitrogen-containing entities" that are processed further in the urea cycle?

26-48 What are the two "fuels" for the urea cycle?

26-49 Which of the two urea cycle fuels enters the cycle directly and which enters the cycle indirectly?

26-50 Which of the two urea cycle fuels was produced via transamination/oxidative deamination and which was produced via several transamination reactions?

26-51 What is the desired end product of urea cycle operation?

26-52 What happens to the desired end product of urea cycle operation after it is produced?

26-53 What is the chemical structure of the desired end product of urea cycle operation?

26-54 What are selected physical properties of the desired end product of urea cycle operation when it is in the pure state?

26-55 What is a carbamoyl group?

26-56 What is the chemical structure of carbamoyl phosphate?

26-57 What are the chemical reactants needed to produce the compound carbamoyl phosphate?

26-58 What chemical products besides carbamoyl phosphate are produced at the same time it is produced?

26-59 What are the names of the two *standard* amino acids that participate in the urea cycle?

26-60 What are the names of the two *nonstandard* amino acids that participate in the urea cycle?

26-61 Characterize each of the following "urea cycle compounds" in terms of its nitrogen content (N_0, N_1, N_2, N_3, or N_4).
   a. Ornithine
   b. Citrulline
   c. Aspartate
   d. Argininosuccinate

26-62 Characterize each of the following "urea cycle compounds" in terms of its nitrogen content (N_0, N_1, N_2, N_3, or N_4).
   a. Carbamoyl phosphate
   b. Ammonium ion
   c. Fumarate
   d. Urea

26-63 In each of the following pairs of compounds associated with the urea cycle, specify which one is encountered first in the cycle.
   a. Citrulline and arginine
   b. Ornithine and aspartate
   c. Argininosuccinate and fumarate
   d. Carbamoyl phosphate and citrulline

26-64 In each of the following pairs of compounds associated with the urea cycle, specify which one is encountered first in the cycle.
   a. Carbamoyl phosphate and fumarate
   b. Argininosuccinate and arginine
   c. Ornithine and aspartate
   d. Citrulline and ATP

26-65 In which step of the urea cycle does each of the following events occur?
   a. Aspartate enters the cycle.
   b. A condensation reaction occurs.
   c. Ornithine is a product.
   d. The reaction $N_4 \longrightarrow N_2 + N_2$ occurs.

26-66 In which step of the urea cycle does each of the following events occur?
   a. Citrulline is a product.
   b. Carbamoyl phosphate enters the cycle.
   c. A hydrolysis reaction occurs.
   d. The reaction $N_3 + N_1 \longrightarrow N_4$ occurs.

26-67 Which step(s) of the urea cycle occur in the mitochondrial matrix?

26-68 Which step(s) of the urea cycle occur in the cell cytosol?

26-69 How much energy, in terms of ATP consumption, is expended in the formation of a molecule of urea from ammonium ion and oxaloacetate?

26-70 In which steps, if any, of the urea cycle is
   a. ATP consumed   b. ATP produced

26-71 What is the fate of the fumarate formed in the urea cycle?

26-72 Explain how the urea cycle is linked to the citric acid cycle.

▲**26-73** Indicate whether each of the following compounds is associated with (1) transamination, (2) oxidative deamination, or (3) the urea cycle. More than one response may be correct in a given situation.
   a. Oxaloacetate   b. Arginine
   c. H_2O d. ATP

▲**26-74** Indicate whether each of the following compounds is associated with (1) transamination, (2) oxidative deamination, or (3) the urea cycle. More than one response may be correct in a given situation.
   a. Ornithine   b. NH_4^+
   c. NAD^+ d. Aspartate

▲**26-75** Classify each of the following nitrogen-containing entities as an N_1, N_2, N_3, or N_4 species.
   a. Carbamoyl phosphate
   b. Glutamate
   c. Urea
   d. Citrulline

▲**26-76** Classify each of the following nitrogen-containing entities as an N_1, N_2, N_3, or N_4 species.
   a. Ornithine   b. Ammonium ion
   c. Aspartate   d. Arginine

Amino Acid Carbon Skeletons (Section 26-5)

26-77 What are the four possible degradation products of the carbon skeletons of amino acids that are citric acid cycle intermediates?

26-78 What are the three possible degradation products of the carbon skeletons of amino acids that are not citric acid cycle intermediates?

26-79 With the help of Figure 26-9, write the name of the compound (or compounds) to which each of the following amino acid carbon skeletons is metabolized.
   a. Leucine   b. Isoleucine
   c. Aspartate   d. Arginine

26-80 With the help of Figure 26-9, write the name of the compound (or compounds) to which each of the following amino acid carbon skeletons is metabolized.
a. Serine
b. Tyrosine
c. Tryptophan
d. Histidine

26-81 With the help of Figure 26-9, classify each of the amino acids in Problem 26-79 as (1) ketogenic, (2) glucogenic, or (3) both ketogenic and glucogenic.

26-82 With the help of Figure 26-9, classify each of the amino acids in Problem 26-80 as (1) ketogenic, (2) glucogenic, or (3) both ketogenic and glucogenic.

26-83 What degradation characteristics do all purely glucogenic amino acids share?

26-84 What degradation characteristics do all purely ketogenic amino acids share?

Amino Acid Biosynthesis (Section 26-6)

26-85 What are the five starting materials for the biosynthesis of the 10 nonessential amino acids?

26-86 What is a major difference between the biosynthetic pathways for the essential and the nonessential amino acids?

26-87 What is the starting material for the biosynthesis of each of the following nonessential amino acids?
a. Alanine
b. Serine
c. Cysteine
d. Proline

26-88 What is the starting material for the biosynthesis of each of the following nonessential amino acids?
a. Glutamate
b. Aspartate
c. Glycine
d. Glutamine

26-89 Which four nonessential amino acids can be biosynthesized using glycolysis intermediates?

26-90 Which five nonessential amino acids can be biosynthesized using citric acid cycle intermediates?

Hemoglobin Catabolism (Section 26-7)

26-91 What happens to the globin produced from the breakdown of hemoglobin?

26-92 What happens to the iron (Fe^{2+}) produced from the breakdown of hemoglobin?

26-93 What are the structural differences between heme and biliverdin?

26-94 What are the structural differences between biliverdin and bilirubin?

26-95 Arrange the following substances in the order in which they are encountered during the catabolism of heme: bilirubin, urobilin, biliverdin, and bilirubin diglucuronide.

26-96 Carbon monoxide is a by-product of the degradation of heme. At what point in the degradation process is it formed, and what happens to it once it is formed?

26-97 Which bile pigment is responsible for the yellow color of urine?

26-98 Which bile pigment is responsible for the brownish-red color of feces?

26-99 What chemical condition is responsible for jaundice?

26-100 What physical conditions cause jaundice?

26-101 Which of the heme degradation products (1) bilirubin, (2) biliverdin, (3) stercobilin, and (4) urobilin is associated with each of the following heme degradation characterizations?
a. CO is produced at the same time as this substance.
b. This substance is associated with the condition called jaundice.
c. Molecular O_2 is a reactant in the production of this substance.
d. This bile pigment has a brownish color.

26-102 Which of the heme degradation products (1) bilirubin, (2) biliverdin, (3) stercobilin, and (4) urobilin is associated with each of the following heme degradation characterizations?
a. "Ring-opening" occurs in the production of this substance.
b. A carbon–carbon double bond is changed to a carbon–carbon single bond in the production of this substance.
c. This substance is rendered more water soluble by use of a glucose derivative.
d. This bile pigment has a yellowish color.

▲**26-103** In which of the processes (1) urea cycle, (2) heme degradation, and (3) oxidative deamination would each of the following molecules be encountered?
a. Citrulline
b. Glutamate
c. Bilirubin
d. Ammonium ion

▲**26-104** In which of the processes (1) urea cycle, (2) heme degradation, and (3) oxidative deamination would each of the following molecules be encountered?
a. Carbon monoxide
b. Stercobilin
c. Biliverdin
d. Ornithine

Proteins and the Element Sulfur (Section 26-8)

26-105 Indicate whether each of the following statements concerning sulfur-containing amino acids is true or false.
a. Four of the 20 standard amino acids contain sulfur.
b. The first step in the degradation of the amino acid cysteine is a transamination reaction.
c. Pyruvate is the sulfur-containing product from the degradation of the amino acid cysteine.
d. ATP is the activating agent in the first step of the conversion of serine to cysteine.

26-106 Indicate whether each of the following statements concerning sulfur-containing amino acids is true or false.
a. Cysteine and serine are standard amino acids that contain the element sulfur.
b. The molecule H_2S is released in the first step of the degradation of the amino acid cysteine.
c. The first step in the synthesis of cysteine from serine is an activation step.
d. In the synthesis of cysteine from serine it is an H_2S molecule that supplies the sulfur.

26-107 In the process called *sulfate assimilation* what is/are the
a. two reactants in the first step of the process?
b. sulfur-containing reactant in the second step of the process?
c. nonsulfur-containing product in the third step of the process?
d. sulfur-containing product in the fourth step of the process?

26-108 In the process called *sulfate assimilation* what is/are the
   a. sulfur-containing product in the first step of the process?
   b. nonsulfur-containing reactant in the second step of the process?
   c. sulfur-containing product in the third step of the process?
   d. reactants in the fourth step of the process?

Interrelationships Among Metabolic Pathways (Section 26-9)

26-109 What molecule is the connecting link from the urea cycle to the citric acid cycle?

26-110 What two molecules are involved in the connecting link from the citric acid cycle to the urea cycle?

26-111 Briefly explain how the carbon atoms from amino acids can end up in ketone bodies.

26-112 Briefly explain how the carbon atoms from amino acids can end up in glucose.

26-113 How are the amino acids from protein "processed" when they are present in amounts that exceed the body's needs?

26-114 How are the amino acids from protein "processed" when an individual is in a state of starvation?

B Vitamins and Protein Metabolism (Section 26-10)

26-115 Indicate whether each of the following B vitamins is involved as a cofactor in the processes of (1) transamination, (2) oxidative deamination, (3) urea cycle, (4) carbon skeleton degradation to CAC intermediates, or (5) carbon skeleton degradation to non-CAC intermediates. For a given vitamin, more than one response may be correct.
   a. Niacin
   b. Folate
   c. Biotin
   d. Vitamin B_6

26-116 Indicate whether each of the following B vitamins is involved as a cofactor in the processes of (1) transamination, (2) oxidative deamination, (3) urea cycle, (4) carbon skeleton degradation to CAC intermediates, or (5) carbon skeleton degradation to non-CAC intermediates. For a given vitamin, more than one response may be correct.
   a. Riboflavin
   b. Thiamin
   c. Pantothenic acid
   d. Vitamin B_{12}

Answers to Selected Exercises

Chapter 1 **1.1** has mass, occupies space **1.3** (a) matter (b) matter (c) energy (d) matter **1.5** (a) indefinite shape versus definite shape (b) indefinite volume versus definite volume **1.7** (a) does not, yes (b) does, no (c) does, yes (d) does, yes **1.9** (a) physical property (b) chemical property (c) chemical property (d) physical property **1.11** (a) chemical (b) physical (c) chemical (d) physical **1.13** (a) chemical property (b) chemical property (c) physical property (d) physical property **1.15** (a) physical (b) physical (c) chemical (d) physical **1.17** (a) physical (b) physical (c) chemical (d) physical **1.19** (a) physical (b) physical (c) chemical (d) physical **1.21** (a) chemical change (b) chemical property (c) physical change (d) physical property **1.23** (a) false (b) true (c) false (d) true **1.25** (a) heterogeneous mixture (b) homogeneous mixture (c) pure substance (d) heterogeneous mixture **1.27** (a) homogeneous mixture, one phase (b) heterogeneous mixture, two phases (c) heterogeneous mixture, three phases (d) heterogeneous mixture, two phases **1.29** (a) compound (b) compound (c) classification not possible (d) classification not possible **1.31** (a) A, classification not possible; B, classification not possible; C, compound (b) D, compound; E, classification not possible; F, classification not possible; G, classification not possible **1.33** (a) true (b) false (c) false (d) false **1.35** first box: mixture, second box: compound **1.37** (a) compound (b) mixture (c) element (d) mixture **1.39** (a) homogeneous mixture (b) heterogeneous mixture (c) heterogeneous mixture (d) compound **1.41** (a) true (b) true (c) false (d) true **1.43** (a) true (b) false (c) false (d) false **1.45** (a) true (b) true (c) false (d) true **1.47** (a) more abundant (b) less abundant (c) less abundant (d) more abundant **1.49** (a) nitrogen (b) nickel (c) lead (d) tin **1.51** (a) Al (b) Ne (c) H (d) U **1.53** (a) Na, S (b) Mg, Mn (c) Ca, Cd (d) As, Ar **1.55** (a) no (b) yes (c) yes (d) no **1.57** (a) heteroatomic molecules (b) heteroatomic molecules (c) homoatomic molecules (d) heteroatomic molecules **1.59** (a) triatomic molecules (b) triatomic molecules (c) diatomic molecules (d) diatomic molecules **1.61** (a) compound (b) compound (c) element (d) compound **1.63** (a) could be an element or compound (b) must be an element (c) must be a compound (d) must be an element **1.65** (a) true (b) false; Triatomic molecules must contain at least one kind of atom. (c) true (d) false; Both homoatomic and heteroatomic molecules may contain three or more atoms. **1.67** (a) diagram I (b) diagram III (c) diagram II (d) diagrams I and IV **1.69** (a) element (b) mixture (c) mixture (d) mixture **1.71** (a) changes 3 and 4 (b) change 1 **1.73** (a) H_2O (b) CO_2 (c) O_2 (d) CO **1.75** (a) chemical formula of a compound, 6 atoms (b) chemical formula of a compound, 5 atoms (c) chemical symbol of an element, 1 atom (d) chemical formula of a compound, 2 atoms **1.77** (a) $C_{12}H_{22}O_{11}$ (b) $C_8H_{10}O_4N_2$ **1.79** XZ_4, X_2Z_3, X_3Z_2, X_4Z **1.81** (a) HCN (b) H_2SO_4 **1.83** (a) same, both 4 (b) more, 6 and 5 (c) same, both 5 (d) fewer, 13 and 15 **1.85** (a) $1 + 2 + x = 6; x = 3$ (b) $2 + 3 + 3x = 17; x = 4$ (c) $1 + x + x = 5; x = 2$ (d) $x + 2x + x = 8; x = 2$ **1.87** (a) 2 (N_2, NH_3) (b) 4 (N, H, C, Cl) (c) 110; 5(2 + 6 + 4 + 5 + 5) (d) 56; 4(4 + 3 + 4 + 3)

Chapter 2 **2.1** It is easier to use because it is decimal based. **2.3** (a) giga-, 10^9 (b) n, 10^{-9} (c) mega-, M (d) micro-, 10^{-6} **2.5** (a) kilogram, mass (b) length, Mm (c) nanogram, mass (d) volume, mL **2.7** (a) nanogram, milligram, centigram (b) kilometer, megameter, gigameter (c) picoliter, microliter, deciliter (d) microgram, milligram, kilogram **2.9** (a) centimeter (b) kilogram (c) liter (d) decimeter **2.11** 60 minutes is a defined (exact) number and 60 feet is a measured (inexact) number. **2.13** (a) exact (b) exact (c) inexact (d) exact **2.15** (a) inexact (b) exact (c) exact (d) inexact **2.17** (a) the 4 (b) the zero (c) the 4 (d) the 4 **2.19** (a) ±1 (b) ±0.1 (c) ±0.001 (d) ±0.00001 **2.21** (a) 0.1°C (b) 0.01 mL (c) 1 mL (d) 0.1 mm **2.23** (a) 0.1 (b) 0.1 **2.25** (a) 2.70 cm (b) 27 cm **2.27** (a) 4 (b) 1 or 4 (c) 2 (d) 3 **2.29** (a) 3 (b) 3 (c) 4 (d) 1 **2.31** (a) 5 (b) 3 (c) 3 (d) 5 **2.33** (a) same (b) different (c) same (d) same **2.35** (a) yes (b) no (c) no (d) yes **2.37** (a) 4, the 1, ±1 (b) 2, the 1, ±0.01 (c) 2, the 2, ±100 (d) 3, the last 5, ±10 **2.39** (a) 40,000–60,000 (b) 49,000–51,000 (c) 49,900–50,100 (d) 49,990–50,010 **2.41** (a) 0.3508 (b) 13.4 (c) 22 (d) 0.0303 **2.43** (a) 3570 (b) 323,000 (c) 18.0 (d) 2,350,000 **2.45** (a) 1.883, 1.9 (b) 24,230, 24,000 (c) 0.5118, 0.51 (d) 7.450, 7.5 **2.47** (a) 2 (b) 2 (c) 2 (d) 2 **2.49** (a) 0.0080 (b) 0.0143 (c) 14 (d) 0.182 (e) 1.1 (f) 5720 **2.51** (a) 162 (b) 9.3 (c) 1261 (d) 20.0 **2.53** (a) 0.0001 (b) 0.01 (c) 0.1 (d) 1 **2.55** (a) negative (b) positive (c) negative (d) positive **2.57** (a) 2 (b) 5 (c) 1 (d) 1 **2.59** (a) 3 (b) 3 (c) 3 (d) 4 **2.61** (a) 1.207×10^2 (b) 3.4×10^{-3} (c) 2.3100×10^2 (d) 2.31×10^4 **2.63** (a) 234 (b) 234.00 (c) 0.00234 (d) 0.0023400 **2.65** (a) 5.50×10^{12} (b) 1.5×10^4 (c) 2.0×10^{-7} (d) 1.2×10^6 **2.67** (a) 10^2 (b) 10^4 (c) 10^4 (d) 10^{-4} **2.69** (a) 3.00×10^{-3} (b) 9.4×10^5 (c) 2.35×10^1 (d) 4.50000×10^8 **2.71** (a) 1 day/24 hours, 24 hours/1 day (b) 10 decades/1 century, 1 century/10 decades (c) 3 feet/1 yard, 1 yard/3 feet (d) 4 quarts/1 gallon, 1 gallon/ 4 quarts **2.73** (a) 1 kL/10^3 L, 10^3 L/1 kL (b) 1 mg/10^{-3} g, 10^{-3} g/1 mg (c) 10^{-2} m/1 cm, 1 cm/10^{-2} m (d) 1 μsec/10^{-6} sec, 10^{-6} sec/1 μsec **2.75** (a) exact (b) inexact (c) exact (d) exact **2.77** (a) 1.6×10^2 m (b) 2.4×10^{-8} m (c) 3 m (d) 3.0×10^5 m **2.79** 2.5 L **2.81** 3.41 lb **2.83** 0.0066 gal **2.85** 183 lb, 6.30 ft **2.87** (a) 2 (b) 3 (c) 5 (d) 6 **2.89** (a) 2 (b) 3 (c) 4 (d) 4 **2.91** 13.55 g/cm³ **2.93** 25.3 mL **2.95** 243 g **2.97** (a) float (b) sink **2.99** (a) 5.0×10^{-1} (b) 5.00×10^{-1} (c) 5.0000×10^{-1} (d) 5.000×10^{-1} **2.101** (a) 130 mL (b) 81 mL (c) 98,800 mL (d) 5.51 mL **2.103** 274°C **2.105** −38.0°F **2.107** −10°C

Chapter 3 **3.1** (a) electron (b) neutron (c) proton (d) proton **3.3** (a) false (b) false (c) false (d) true **3.5** (a) 7p, 8n, 7e (b) 20p, 20n, 20e (c) 11p, 12n, 11e (d) 35p, 44n, 35e **3.7** (a) 50p, 68n, 50e (b) 78p, 117n, 78e (c) 31p, 41n, 31e (d) 12p, 14n, 12e **3.9** (a) 5 (b) 7 (c) 13 (d) 20 **3.11** (a) 11 (b) 15 (c) 27 (d) 48 **3.13** (a) 11 (b) 16 (c) 27 (d) 48 **3.15** (a) 10 (b) 14 (c) 26 (d) 40 **3.17** (a) +5 (b) +7 (c) +13 (d) +20 **3.19** (a) $^{232}_{94}$Pu, 94, 94 (b) 16, 32, 16, 16 (c) $^{56}_{26}$Fe, 26, 30 (d) $^{40}_{20}$Ca, 20, 20 **3.21** (a) 22 (b) 14 (c) 25 (d) 11 **3.23** (a) 34 (b) 23 (c) 23 (d) +11 **3.25** (a) same number of nucleons (b) same number of subatomic particles (c) same number of

protons (d) same number of neutrons   **3.27** $^{12}_6$C, $^{13}_6$C, $^{14}_6$C
3.29 (a) not the same (b) same (c) not the same (d) same
3.31 (a) 6.95 amu (b) 24.31 amu   **3.33** (a) false (b) false (c) true
(d) true   **3.35** (a) not isotopes (b) not isotopes (c) isotopes
3.37 (a) false (b) false (c) true (d) true   **3.39** (a) same (b) different
(c) same (d) different   **3.41** (a) $^{54}_{24}$Cr (b) $^{50}_{24}$Cr (c) $^{54}_{24}$Cr (d) $^{65}_{24}$Cr
3.43 (a) period 2, group IIA (b) period 3, group VA (c) period 4 ,
group IA (d) period 5, group VIIA   **3.45** (a) 6 (b) 28.09 amu (c) 39
(d) 9.01 amu   **3.47** (a) K and Rb (b) P and As (c) F and I (d) Na
and Cs   **3.49** (a) F (b) Be (c) Li (d) Ne   **3.51** (a) 3 (b) 4 (c) 4 (d) 4
3.53 (a) blue element (b) yellow element (c) yellow element (d) green
element   **3.55** (a) $^{12}_4$Be (b) $^{132}_{54}$Xe (c) $^{16}_8$O (d) $^{40}_{20}$Ca   **3.57** (a) no
(b) no (c) yes (d) yes   **3.59** (a) S (b) P (c) I (d) Cl   **3.61** (a) metal
(b) nonmetal (c) metal (d) nonmetal   **3.63** (a) metal (b) nonmetal
(c) poor conductor of electricity (d) good conductor of heat
3.65 (a) Be, Al (b) Be, Al, Ag, Au (c) N, Be, Ar, Al, Ag, Au
(d) Ag, Au   **3.67** (a) 2 (b) 4 (c) 3 (d) 5   **3.69** (a) 2 (b) 2 (c) 10 (d) 6
3.71 (a) 2 (b) 2 (c) 2 (d) 2   **3.73** (a) 1 (b) 1 (c) 5 (d) 3   **3.75** (a) true
(b) true (c) false (d) true   **3.77** (a) $1s^2 2s^2 2p^2$ (b) $1s^2 2s^2 2p^6 3s^1$
(c) $1s^2 2s^2 2p^6 3s^2 3p^4$ (d) $1s^2 2s^2 2p^6 3s^2 3p^6$ **3.79** (a) oxygen (b) neon
(c) aluminum (d) calcium   **3.81** (a) $1s^2 2s^2 2p^6 3s^2 3p^5$ (b) $1s^2 2s^2 2p^6 3s^2$
$3p^6 4s^2 3d^{10} 4p^6 5s^2 4d^7$ (c) $1s^2 2s^2 2p^6 3s^2 3p^6 4s^2$ (d) $1s^2 2s^2 2p^6 3s^2 3p^6 4s^2 3d^1$
3.83

(a) ⇅ ⇅ | ↑ ↑ ○

(b) ⇅ ⇅ | ⇅ ⇅ ⇅ | ⇅

(c) ⇅ ⇅ | ⇅ ⇅ ⇅ | ⇅ | ↑ ↑ ↑

(d) ⇅ ⇅ | ⇅ ⇅ ⇅ | ⇅ | ⇅ ⇅ ⇅ | ⇅ | ⇅ ↑ ↑ ↑

3.85 (a) 2 (b) 0 (c) 3 (d) 3   **3.87** the same—$1s^2 2s^2 2p^4$
3.89 (a) $1s^2 2s^2 2p^1$ (b) $1s^2 2s^2 2p^6 3s^2 3p^1$ (c) $1s^2 2s^2$ (d) $1s^2 2s^2 2p^6 3s^2$ and
$1s^2 2s^2 2p^6 3s^2 3p^6$ **3.91** (a) no (b) yes (c) no (d) yes   **3.93** (a) s area
(b) d area (c) p area (d) d area   **3.95** (a) p^1 (b) d^3 (c) s^2 (d) p^6
3.97 (a) s area (b) d area (c) p^4 element (d) s^2 element   **3.99** (a) representative element (b) noble gas (c) transition element (d) inner
transition element   **3.101** (a) 4 (b) 1 (c) 2 (d) 6   **3.103** (a) noble
gas (b) representative element (c) transition element (d) representative element

Chapter 4   **4.1** The mechanism for ionic bond formation is
electron transfer and that for covalent bond formation is electron
sharing.   **4.3** (a) 2 (b) 2 (c) 3 (d) 4   **4.5** (a) VA, 5e (b) IA, 1e
(c) VIA, 6e (d) IA, 1e   **4.7** (a) $1s^2 2s^2 2p^2$ (b) $1s^2 2s^2 2p^5$ (c) $1s^2 2s^2 2p^6 3s^2$
(d) $1s^2 2s^2 2p^6 3s^2 3p^3$ **4.9** (a) more (b) same (c) more (d) fewer
4.11 (a) one (b) one (c) one (d) two   **4.13** (a) ·P: ·S: ·Cl:
(b) Na· K· Rb·   **4.15** (a) Li (b) F (c) Be (d) N   **4.17** (a) Be·
(b) Mg· (c) ·S: (d) ·Ge·   **4.19** They are the most unreactive of
all elements.   **4.21** They lose, gain, or share electrons in such a way
that they achieve a noble-gas electron configuration.   **4.23** (a) O^{2-}
(b) Mg^{2+} (c) F$^-$ (d) Al^{3+} **4.25** (a) Ca^{2+} (b) O^{2-} (c) N^{3-} (d) Be^{2+}
4.27 (a) N^{3-}, 7p (b) 12p, 10e, 2e lost (c) F$^-$, 10e (d) Li$^+$, 1e lost
4.29 (a) Be^{2+}, 4 (b) I, I$^-$ (c) Al, 13 (d) S, 18, 16   **4.31** (a) Mg
(b) Ca (c) P (d) F   **4.33** (a) Be^{2+} (b) O^{2-} (c) B^{3+} (d) C^{4-}
4.35 (a) [:P:]$^{3-}$ (b) [:N:]$^{3-}$ (c) [:C:]$^{4-}$ (d) [:F:]$^-$ **4.37** (a) 2+
(b) 3− (c) 1+ (d) 1−   **4.39** (a) 2 lost (b) 1 gained (c) 2 lost (d) 2
gained   **4.41** (a) Ne (b) Ar (c) Ar (d) Ar   **4.43** (a) Ne (b) Ar (c) Ar
(d) Ar   **4.45** (a) yes (b) yes (c) no (d) yes   **4.47** (a) 4 (b) 4 (c) 1 (d) 1
4.49 (a) $1s^2 2s^2 2p^6 3s^2 3p^1$ (b) $1s^2 2s^2 2p^6$ **4.51** (a) 8 (b) 8 (c) 8 (d) 2

4.53 (a) Be ⤳ O: (b) Mg ⤳ S:

    K ⤳   ⤳ F:
(c) K ⤳ N: (d) Ca ⤳
    K ⤳   ⤳ F:

4.55 (a) 2 extra electrons, 2− charge (b) 1 extra electron, 1− charge
(c) 3 extra electrons, 3− charge (d) 2 extra electrons, 2− charge
4.57 (a) Na$_2$S (b) CaI$_2$ (c) Li$_3$N (d) AlBr$_3$ **4.59** (a) CaF$_2$, CaO,
Ca$_3$N$_2$, Ca$_2$C (b) AlF$_3$, Al$_2$O$_3$, AlN, Al$_4$C$_3$ (c) AgF, Ag$_2$O, Ag$_3$N,
Ag$_4$C (d) ZnF$_2$, ZnO, Zn$_3$N$_2$, Zn$_2$C   **4.61** (a) BeCl$_2$ (b) BaI$_2$
(c) Na$_2$O (d) AlN   **4.63** (a) K$^+$ (b) Ca^{2+} (c) Mg^{2+} (d) Al^{3+}
4.65 (a) XZ$_2$ (b) X$_2$Z (c) XZ (d) ZX   **4.67** (a) LiCl (b) MgF$_2$
(c) CaS (d) K$_3$N   **4.69** (a) VIA (b) ·X: (c) 6e (d) CaX
4.71 K, 1e (b) S, 2e (c) K$^+$ (d) S^{2-} **4.73** an extended array of
alternating positive and negative ions   **4.75** smallest whole-number
repeating ratio of ions present   **4.77** ions of opposite charge must
be present (a metal and a nonmetal)   **4.79** Al$_2$O$_3$ and K$_2$S
4.81 (a) potassium iodide (b) beryllium oxide (c) aluminum fluoride
(d) sodium phosphide   **4.83** (a) +1 (b) +2 (c) +4 (d) +2
4.85 (a) gold(I) oxide (b) nickel(II) oxide (c) tin(IV) oxide (d) tin(II)
oxide   **4.87** it must include a Roman numeral, copper(II) oxide
4.89 (a) gold(I) chloride (b) potassium chloride (c) silver chloride
(d) copper(II) chloride   **4.91** (a) lead(II) oxide, lead(IV) oxide
(b) magnesium chloride, iron(II) chloride (c) sodium oxide, magnesium oxide (d) copper(I) sulfide, copper(II) sulfide   **4.93** (a) KBr
(b) Ag$_2$O (c) BeF$_2$ (d) Ba$_3$P$_2$ **4.95** (a) CoS (b) Co$_2$S$_3$ (c) SnI$_4$
(d) Pb$_3$N$_2$ **4.97** (a) magnesium nitride (b) Mg$_3$N$_2$ (c) 5 ions (d) 6e
4.99 (a) NaCl, sodium chloride (b) K$_2$Se, potassium selenide
(c) BeF$_2$, beryllium fluoride (d) AlN, aluminum nitride
4.101 (a) −2 (b) −1 (c) −3 (d) −2   **4.103** (a) 1 (b) none (c) 1
(d) none   **4.105** (a) hydrogen carbonate ion (b) dihydrogen phosphate ion (c) hydronium ion (d) ammonium ion   **4.107** (a) NaOH
(b) Fe(HSO$_4$)$_3$ (c) Ba(NO$_3$)$_2$ (d) Al$_2$(CO$_3$)$_3$ **4.109** (a) Al(CN)$_3$,
Al(NO$_3$)$_3$, Al(HCO$_3$)$_3$, Al$_2$(SO$_4$)$_3$ (b) AgCN, AgNO$_3$, AgHCO$_3$,
Ag$_2$SO$_4$ (c) Ca(CN)$_2$, Ca(NO$_3$)$_2$, Ca(HCO$_3$)$_2$, CaSO$_4$ (d) NH$_4$CN,
NH$_4$NO$_3$, NH$_4$HCO$_3$, (NH$_4$)$_2$SO$_4$ **4.111** (a) two (b) two (c) five
(d) two   **4.113** (a) magnesium carbonate (b) zinc sulfate (c) beryllium nitrate (d) silver phosphate   **4.115** (a) iron(II) hydroxide
(b) copper(II) carbonate (c) gold(I) cyanide (d) manganese(II) phosphate   **4.117** (a) KHCO$_3$ (b) Au$_2$(SO$_4$)$_3$ (c) AgNO$_3$ (d) Cu$_3$(PO$_4$)$_2$
4.119 (a) Na$_2$S (b) Na$_2$SO$_4$ (c) Na$_2$CO$_3$ (d) NaHCO$_3$
4.121 (a) aluminum carbonate (b) Al$_2$(CO$_3$)$_3$ (c) three (d) two
4.123 (a) Ba^{2+}, Br$^-$, barium bromide (b) Zn(NO$_3$)$_2$, zinc nitrate
(c) Fe^{3+}, CO$_3^{2-}$, Fe$_2$(CO$_3$)$_3$ (d) Pb^{4+}, O^{2-}, lead(IV) oxide

Chapter 5   **5.1** ionic: metal and nonmetal; covalent: two or more
nonmetals   **5.3** ionic: extended array of alternating positive and
negative ions; covalent: molecules   **5.5** (a) yes (b) yes (c) yes (d) no
5.7 (a) :Cl:Cl: (b) H:Cl: (c) :Br:Cl: (d) :Cl:F:
5.9 (a) 8 (b) 4 (c) 0 (d) 6   **5.11** (a) H$_2$S (b) CBr$_4$ (c) OF$_2$ (d) NCl$_3$
5.13 (a) one triple bond (b) three single bonds (c) one double and
two single bonds (d) one double and four single bonds
5.15
(a) :N≡N: (b) H—C=C—H (c) H—C—H (d) H—Ö—Ö—H
                    | | ||
                    H   H   :O:

5.17 (a) normal (b) normal (c) not normal (d) normal   **5.19** (a) N
(b) C (c) N (d) C   **5.21** (a) 5 (b) 4 (c) 5 (d) 4   **5.23** Oxygen forms
three bonds instead of the normal two.   **5.25** (a) nitrogen–oxygen
(b) none present (c) oxygen–chlorine (d) two (oxygen–bromine)
5.27 (a) 32 (b) 20 (c) 8 (d) 20   **5.29** (a) 32 (b) 20 (c) 8 (d) 20
5.31

          :Br:
           |
(a) :Br—C—Br: (b) :F—S—F: (c) H—P—H (d) :F—Ö—F:
           | |
          :Br: H
           ··

5.33

                                                          H
(a) H:C::C::C:H (b) :F:N::N:F: (c) H:C:C:::N:
      H   H   H   H

(d)
$$H:\overset{\overset{\displaystyle H}{..}}{\underset{\underset{\displaystyle H}{..}}{C}}:C:::C:H$$
5.35 (a) 14 (b) 20 (c) 14 (d) 8

5.37

(a) $\left[:\overset{..}{\underset{..}{O}}:H\right]^-$ (b) $\left[H:\overset{\overset{\displaystyle H}{}}{\underset{\underset{\displaystyle H}{}}{Be}}:H\right]^{2-}$ (c) $\left[:\overset{..}{\underset{..}{Cl}}:\overset{\overset{\displaystyle :\overset{..}{\underset{..}{Cl}}:}{}}{\underset{\underset{\displaystyle :\overset{..}{\underset{..}{Cl}}:}{}}{Al}}:\overset{..}{\underset{..}{Cl}}:\right]^-$ (d) $\left[:\overset{..}{\underset{..}{O}}:N:\overset{..}{\underset{..}{O}}:\right]^-$ with $:\overset{..}{\underset{..}{O}}:$

5.39 (a) $Na^+[:C:::N:]^-$ (b) $3[K]^+\left[:\overset{\overset{\displaystyle :\overset{..}{O}:}{}}{\underset{\underset{\displaystyle :\overset{..}{\underset{..}{O}}:}{}}{\underset{..}{O}}}:P:\overset{..}{\underset{..}{O}}:\right]^{3-}$

5.41 (a) $:\overset{..}{O}-\overset{\overset{\displaystyle :\overset{..}{\underset{..}{O}}:}{}}{S}=\overset{..}{O}:$ (b) $\left[:\overset{..}{O}-\overset{\overset{\displaystyle :\overset{..}{\underset{..}{O}}:}{}}{\underset{..}{S}}-\overset{..}{\underset{..}{O}}:\right]^{2-}$

5.43 (a) same (both single) (b) different (double and single) (c) same (both triple) (d) same (both single) **5.45** (a) tetrahedral (b) angular (c) trigonal planar **5.47** (a) linear (b) angular (c) tetrahedral (d) linear **5.49** (a) angular (b) angular (c) angular (d) linear **5.51** (a) trigonal pyramidal (b) trigonal planar (c) tetrahedral (d) tetrahedral **5.53** (a) trigonal planar about each carbon atom (b) tetrahedral about carbon atom and angular about oxygen atom **5.55** (a) trigonal pyramidal (b) tetrahedral (c) angular (d) angular **5.57** (a) tetrahedral, tetrahedral (b) tetrahedral, angular (c) trigonal planar, angular (d) trigonal planar, trigonal planar **5.59** (a) true (b) false (c) false (d) false **5.61** (a) Na, Mg, Al, P (b) I, Br, Cl, F (c) Al, P, S, O (d) Ca, Mg, C, O **5.63** (a) N, O, Cl, F, Br (b) Na, K, Rb, (c) F, O, Cl, N (d) 0.5 units **5.65** (a) $\overset{\delta+}{B}-\overset{\delta-}{N}$ (b) $\overset{\delta+}{N}-\overset{\delta-}{C}$ (c) $\overset{\delta-}{S}-\overset{\delta+}{O}$ (d) $\overset{\delta-}{F}-\overset{\delta+}{O}$ **5.67** (a) H—Br, H—Cl, H—O (b) O—F, P—O, Al—O (c) Br—Br, H—Cl, B—N (d) P—N, S—O, Br—F **5.69** (a) polar covalent (b) ionic (c) nonpolar covalent (d) ionic **5.71** (a) polar covalent (b) polar covalent (c) nonpolar covalent (d) nonpolar covalent **5.73** (a) Se, Se, nonpolar covalent (b) O, O, polar covalent (c) Br, Br, polar covalent (d) F, F, polar covalent **5.75** (a) BA, CA, DB, DA (b) BA, CA, DB, DA **5.77** (a) nonpolar (b) polar (c) polar (d) polar **5.79** (a) nonpolar (b) polar (c) polar (d) polar **5.81** (a) polar (b) polar (c) nonpolar (d) polar **5.83** (a) Polarity cannot be determined. (b) polar

5.85 (a) BrI (b) SO_2 (c) NH_3 (d) CH_3Cl **5.87** $H-\overset{\overset{\displaystyle H}{|}}{\underset{\underset{\displaystyle H}{|}}{C}}-H$

$H-\overset{\overset{\displaystyle H}{|}}{\underset{\underset{\displaystyle H}{|}}{C}}\quad\overset{..}{\underset{..}{F}}: \qquad H-\overset{\overset{\displaystyle H}{|}}{\underset{\underset{\displaystyle :\overset{..}{\underset{..}{F}}:}{|}}{C}}-\overset{..}{\underset{..}{F}}: \qquad :\overset{..}{\underset{..}{F}}-\overset{\overset{\displaystyle H}{|}}{\underset{\underset{\displaystyle :\overset{..}{\underset{..}{F}}:}{|}}{C}}-\overset{..}{\underset{..}{F}}: \qquad :\overset{..}{\underset{..}{F}}-\overset{\overset{\displaystyle :\overset{..}{\underset{..}{F}}:}{|}}{\underset{\underset{\displaystyle :\overset{..}{\underset{..}{F}}:}{|}}{C}}-\overset{..}{\underset{..}{F}}:$

(b) All are tetrahedral. (c) nonpolar, polar, polar, polar, nonpolar **5.89** (a) no (b) no (c) yes (d) yes **5.91** (a) dinitrogen tetrafluoride (b) carbon tetrachloride (c) oxygen difluoride (d) carbon monoxide **5.93** (a) one (b) zero (c) zero (d) two **5.95** (a) hydrogen peroxide (b) nitric oxide (c) methane (d) ammonia **5.97** (a) diagram I (b) diagram II (c) diagram IV (d) diagram III **5.99** (a) ICl (b) N_2O_2 (c) NCl_3 (d) HBr **5.101** (a) H_2O_2 (b) CH_4 (c) NH_3 (d) NO **5.103** the less electronegative element is named first **5.105** It is an ionic compound (sodium carbonate). **5.107** (a) N_2O_3, KCl, HF, CO_2 (b) N_2O_3 (c) none of them (d) KCl, HF, CH_4

Chapter 6 **6.1** (a) 342.34 amu (b) 100.23 amu (c) 183.20 amu (d) 132.17 amu **6.3** $y=8$ **6.5** (a) 6.02×10^{23} apples (b) 6.02×10^{23} elephants (c) 6.02×10^{23} Zn atoms (d) 6.02×10^{23} CO_2 molecules **6.7** (a) 3.01×10^{23} atoms (b) 3.01×10^{23} atoms (c) 3.01×10^{23} molecules (d) 3.01×10^{23} molecules **6.9** (a) 0.200 mole (b) Avogadro's number (c) 1.50 moles (d) 6.50×10^{23} atoms **6.11** (a) 40.08 g

(b) 107.9 g (c) 30.01 g (d) 63.02 g **6.13** (a) 24.0 g (b) 84.0 g (c) 95.0 g (d) 190. g **6.15** (a) 0.179 mole (b) 0.114 mole (c) 0.0937 mole (d) 0.0210 mole **6.17** 44.01 amu **6.19** 20.0 amu **6.21** (a) 6.00 moles (b) 14.00 moles (c) 2.00 moles (d) 4.00 moles **6.23** (a) 12.00 moles (b) 22.00 moles (c) 8.00 moles (d) 10.00 moles

6.25 (a) $\dfrac{2\text{ moles H}}{1\text{ mole }H_2SO_4}$ $\dfrac{1\text{ mole }H_2SO_4}{2\text{ mole H}}$ $\dfrac{1\text{ mole S}}{1\text{ mole }H_2SO_4}$ $\dfrac{1\text{ mole }H_2SO_4}{1\text{ mole S}}$ $\dfrac{4\text{ mole O}}{1\text{ mole }H_2SO_4}$ $\dfrac{1\text{ mole }H_2SO_4}{4\text{ moles O}}$

(b) $\dfrac{1\text{ mole P}}{1\text{ mole }POCl_3}$ $\dfrac{1\text{ mole }POCl_3}{1\text{ mole P}}$ $\dfrac{1\text{ mole O}}{1\text{ mole }POCl_3}$ $\dfrac{1\text{ mole }POCl_3}{1\text{ mole O}}$ $\dfrac{3\text{ mole Cl}}{1\text{ mole }POCl_3}$ $\dfrac{1\text{ mole }POCl_3}{3\text{ moles Cl}}$

6.27 (a) $\dfrac{3\text{ moles H}}{1\text{ mole }H_3PO_4}$ (b) $\dfrac{4\text{ moles O}}{1\text{ mole }H_3PO_4}$ (c) $\dfrac{8\text{ moles atoms}}{1\text{ mole }H_3PO_4}$ (d) $\dfrac{4\text{ moles O}}{1\text{ mole P}}$

6.29 (a) 1.34×10^{24} atoms (b) 3.01×10^{23} atoms (c) 2.32×10^{23} atoms (d) 1.01×10^{23} atoms **6.31** (a) 63.6 g (b) 31.8 g (c) 5.88×10^{-20} g (d) 1.06×10^{-22} g **6.33** (a) 2.50 moles (b) 0.227 mole (c) 6.6×10^{-14} mole (d) 6.6×10^{-14} mole **6.35** (a) 6.14×10^{22} atoms S (b) 1.50×10^{23} atoms S (c) 3.61×10^{23} atoms S (d) 2.41×10^{24} atoms S **6.37** (a) 32.1 g S (b) 6.39×10^{-22} g S (c) 64.1 g S (d) 1150 g S **6.39** (a) 1.00 mole S_8 (b) 28.00 g Al (c) 30.09 g Mg (d) 6.02×10^{23} atoms He **6.41** H_2O_2 **6.43** (a) balanced (b) balanced (c) not balanced (d) balanced **6.45** (a) 8 atoms (b) 24 atoms (c) 24 atoms (d) 42 atoms **6.47** (a) 2 and 2 (b) 4 and 4 (c) 26 and 26 (d) 12 and 12 **6.49** (a) $2Na + 2H_2O \rightarrow 2NaOH + H_2$ (b) $2Na + ZnSO_4 \rightarrow Na_2SO_4 + Zn$ (c) $2NaBr + Cl_2 \rightarrow 2NaCl + Br_2$ (d) $2ZnS + 3O_2 \rightarrow 2ZnO + 2SO_2$ **6.51** (a) $CH_4 + 2O_2 \rightarrow CO_2 + 2H_2O$ (b) $2C_6H_6 + 15O_2 \rightarrow 12CO_2 + 6H_2O$ (c) $C_4H_8O_2 + 5O_2 \rightarrow 4CO_2 + 4H_2O$ (d) $C_5H_{10}O + 7O_2 \rightarrow 5CO_2 + 5H_2O$ **6.53** C_4H_6 **6.55** (a) $A_2 + 3B_2 \rightarrow 2AB_3$ (b) $A_2 + B_2 \rightarrow 2AB$ **6.57** diagram III

6.59 $\dfrac{2\text{ moles }NH_3}{3\text{ moles }H_2}$ $\dfrac{3\text{ moles }H_2}{2\text{ moles }NH_3}$ $\dfrac{2\text{ moles }NH_3}{1\text{ mole }N_2}$ $\dfrac{1\text{ mole }N_2}{2\text{ moles }NH_3}$ $\dfrac{3\text{ moles }H_2}{1\text{ mole }N_2}$ $\dfrac{1\text{ mole }N_2}{3\text{ moles }H_2}$

6.61 (a) $\dfrac{3\text{ moles }H_2S}{2\text{ moles }SbCl_3}$ (b) $\dfrac{6\text{ moles }HCl}{1\text{ mole }Sb_2S_3}$ (c) $\dfrac{6\text{ moles }HCl}{3\text{ moles }H_2S}$ (d) $\dfrac{2\text{ moles }SbCl_3}{1\text{ mole }Sb_2S_3}$

6.63 (a) 0.714 mole (b) 5.00 moles (c) 5.00 moles (d) 10.0 moles **6.65** 84 product molecules **6.67** 8 water molecules **6.69** (a) CO_2 and H_2O (b) 6.0 moles CO_2 and 12 moles H_2O **6.71** 30.0 moles **6.73** 5.09 g O_2 **6.75** 14.3 g O_2 **6.77** 5.63 g H_2O **6.79** 43.4 g Be **6.81** 99.50% **6.83** (a) 11.2 g (b) 9.75 g (c) 87.1% **6.85** 82.0%

Chapter 7 **7.1** (a) true (b) true (c) false (d) false **7.3** (a) potential energy (b) magnitude increases as temperature increases (c) cause order within the system (d) electrostatic attractions **7.5** (a) liquid state (b) solid state (c) gaseous state (d) solid state **7.7** (a) liquid, solid (b) solid (c) gas (d) gas **7.9** (a) amount (b) volume (c) pressure (d) temperature **7.11** (a) 0.730 atm (b) 2.18 atm (c) 0.888 atm (d) 0.0989 atm **7.13** (a) 3 (b) 3 (c) 3 (d) 3 **7.15** (a) 0.892 atm (b) 0.895 atm (c) 0.908 atm (d) 0.921 atm **7.17** 7.2 atm **7.19** 2.71 L **7.21** (a) 2.00 atm (b) 6.00 L (c) 1.00 L (d) 8.00 atm **7.23** diagram II **7.25** 3.64 L **7.27** 144°C **7.29** (a) 0.974 L (b) 207°C (c) 127°C (d) 2.54 L **7.31** diagram II

7.33 (a) $P_1 = \dfrac{P_2V_2T_1}{V_1T_2}$ (b) $V_2 = \dfrac{P_1V_1T_2}{P_2T_1}$

7.35 (a) 5.90 L (b) 2.11 atm (c) -171°C (d) 3.70×10^3 mL

7.37 diagram II **7.39** (a) 0.871 atm (b) 0.915 atm
7.41 (a) Boyle's, Charles's, and combined gas laws (b) Boyle's
law **7.43** Charles's law **7.45** (a) 32.8 atm (b) 10.9 L (c) 0.459
mole (d) −214°C **7.47** −209°C **7.49** 1.12 L **7.51** (a) 4.11 L
(b) 3.16 atm (c) −98°C (d) 16,300 mL **7.53** (a) 4.6 atm (b) 29 atm
(c) 0.14 atm (d) 0.90 atm **7.55** 62.37 L-torr/mole-K **7.57** 0.42 atm
7.59 98 mm Hg **7.61** (a) 2.4 atm (b) 2.4 atm (c) 1.2 atm
7.63 (a) All are 1.00 atm. (b) All are 1.00 atm. (c) He = 1.50 atm,
Ne = 1.00 atm, Ar = 0.50 atm (d) He = 0.50 atm, Ne = 1.00 atm,
Ar = 1.50 atm **7.65** (a) no (b) no (c) yes (d) yes **7.67** (a) no (b) no
(c) no (d) yes **7.69** (a) no (b) no (c) no (d) no **7.71** 24.7 L
7.73 amount of liquid decreases; temperature of liquid decreases
7.75 rate increases **7.77** B has weaker intermolecular attraction
forces between molecules than A. **7.79** (a) true (b) true **7.81** the
higher the temperature, the higher the vapor pressure **7.83** volatile **7.85** (a) true (b) true (c) false (d) false **7.87** the higher the
external pressure, the higher the boiling point **7.89** (a) boils
(b) does not boil **7.91** (a) false (b) false (c) true (d) false
7.93 Boiling point increases as intermolecular force strength
increases. **7.95** (a) London forces (b) London forces, hydrogen
bonding (c) London forces, dipole–dipole interactions
(d) London forces **7.97** (a) London forces (b) hydrogen
bonding (c) dipole–dipole interactions (d) London forces
7.99 (a) no (b) yes (c) yes (d) no **7.101** four (see Figure 7.21)

7.103 —Ö: ··· H—Ö: and —H ··· :Ö—H **7.105** (a) Br_2
         | |
         H   H

(b) H_2O (c) CO (d) HF

Chapter 8 **8.1** (a) true (b) true (c) true (d) false **8.3** (a) solute:
sodium chloride; solvent: water (b) solute: sucrose; solvent: water
(c) solute: water; solvent: ethyl alcohol (d) solute: ethyl alcohol; solvent: methyl alcohol **8.5** (a) first solution (b) first solution (c) first
solution (d) second solution **8.7** (a) supersaturated (b) saturated
(c) saturated (d) unsaturated **8.9** (a) unsaturated (b) concentrated
8.11 saturated solution **8.13** (a) hydrated ion (b) hydrated ion
(c) oxygen atom (d) hydrogen atom **8.15** (a) decrease (b) increase
(c) increase (d) increase **8.17** (a) slightly soluble (b) very soluble
(c) slightly soluble (d) slightly soluble **8.19** (a) ethanol (b) carbon
tetrachloride (c) ethanol (d) ethanol **8.21** (a) soluble with exceptions (b) soluble (c) insoluble with exceptions (d) insoluble with
exceptions **8.23** (a) soluble (b) soluble (c) insoluble (d) soluble
8.25 (a) soluble (b) insoluble (c) soluble (d) soluble **8.27** (a) yes
(b) yes (c) yes (d) yes **8.29** insoluble **8.31** (a) diagram IV
(b) diagrams I and III **8.33** (a) 7.10% (m/m) (b) 6.19% (m/m)
(c) 9.06% (m/m) (d) 0.27% (m/m) **8.35** (a) 20.0% (m/m) (b) 1.39%
(m/m) (c) 3.42% (m/m) (d) 20.6% (m/m) **8.37** (a) 3.62 g (b) 14.5 g
(c) 68.8 g (d) 124 g **8.39** 0.6400 g **8.41** (a) 0.55 mg/100 mL
(b) 0.00055 g/100 mL (c) 0.0055 g/L (d) 0.00055% (m/v)
8.43 (a) 4.21% (v/v) (b) 4.60% (v/v) **8.45** 18% (v/v)
8.47 (a) 2.0% (m/v) (b) 15% (m/v) **8.49** 0.500 g **8.51** 3.75 g
8.53 (a) 0.966 M (b) 0.980 M (c) 0.567 M (d) 0.940 M
8.55 (a) 0.405 mole (b) 0.0800 mole (c) 0.525 mole (d) 0.0156 mole
8.57 (a) 40.0 g (b) 160. g (c) 2.00 g (d) 7.35 g **8.59** (a) 7.06 L
(b) 9.52 L (c) 10.7 L (d) 14.2 L **8.61** 2.50 M **8.63** (a) 37.5% (m/v)
(b) 2.23 M **8.65** (a) 0.183 M (b) 0.0733 M (c) 0.0120 M
(d) 0.00275 M **8.67** (a) 1450 mL (b) 18.0 mL (c) 85,600 mL
(d) 7.5 mL **8.69** (a) 3.0 M (b) 3.0 M (c) 4.5 M (d) 1.5 M
8.71 diagram II **8.73** 1.04 M **8.75** (a) 1.17% (m/v) (b) 1.17%
(v/v) (c) 1.17% (m/m) (d) 1.17 M **8.77** (a) suspension (b) suspension (c) true solution and colloidal dispersion (d) true solution
8.79 (a) false (b) false (c) false (d) true **8.81** The presence of solute molecules decreases the ability of solvent molecules to escape.
8.83 It is a more concentrated solution and thus has a lower vapor
pressure. **8.85** diagram III **8.87** (a) 101.53°C (b) 101.53°C

(c) 103.06°C (d) 106.12°C **8.89** (a) −5.58°C (b) −5.58°C
(c) −11.16°C (d) −22.32°C **8.91** (a) 1.0 M NaCl (b) 1.0 M
Na_2SO_4 (c) 2.0 M KBr (d) 1.0 M Na_2SO_4 **8.93** (a) −7.4°C
(b) −3.7°C (c) −1.9°C (d) −0.93°C **8.95** (a) same as (b) greater
than (c) less than (d) greater than **8.97** 2 to 1 **8.99** (a) 4.0 OsM
(b) 6.0 OsM (c) 8.0 OsM (d) 6.0 OsM **8.101** (a) hypotonic
(b) isotonic (c) hypotonic (d) hypertonic **8.103** (a) swell (b) remain
the same size (c) swell (d) shrink **8.105** (a) hemolyze (b) remain
unaffected (c) hemolyze (d) crenate **8.107** (a) isotonic (b) hypertonic (c) isotonic (d) hypertonic **8.109** (a) remain the same size
(b) shrink (c) remain the same size (d) shrink **8.111** (a) remain
unaffected (b) crenate (c) remain unaffected (d) crenate
8.113 (a) decrease (b) increase (c) not change (d) decrease
8.115 (a) 1.0 M glucose (b) 1.0 M NaCl (c) 1.0 M glucose
(d) 1.0 M NaCl **8.117** (a) NaCl (b) NaBr

Chapter 9 **9.1** (a) X + YZ ⟶ Y + XZ (b) X + Y ⟶ XY
9.3 (a) displacement (b) decomposition (c) exchange
(d) combination **9.5** (a) CO_2, H_2O (b) CO_2, H_2O (c) CO_2, H_2O
(d) CO_2, H_2O **9.7** (a) yes (b) yes (c) yes (d) no **9.9** (a) combination, displacement, combustion (b) decomposition, displacement
(c) combination, decomposition, displacement, exchange, combustion
(d) combination, decomposition, displacement, exchange, combustion **9.11** (a) 0 (b) 0 (c) −2 (d) +6 **9.13** (a) +3 (b) −2 (c) +5
(d) +5 **9.15** (a) +1 (b) +5 (c) +7 (d) −1 **9.17** (a) +4 (Si), −1 (F)
(b) +1 (H), +6 (S), −2 (O) (c) +1 (Na), +5 (P), −2 (O) (d) +6 (Cr),
−2 (O) **9.19** (a) redox (b) nonredox (c) redox (d) redox
9.21 (a) redox (b) redox (c) redox (d) can't classify **9.23** (a) redox
displacement (b) redox combustion (c) redox decomposition
(d) nonredox exchange **9.25** (a) oxidation (b) oxidation
(c) reduction (d) oxidation **9.27** (a) H_2 oxidized, N_2 reduced
(b) KI oxidized, Cl_2 reduced (c) Fe oxidized, Sb_2O_3 reduced
(d) H_2SO_3 oxidized, HNO_3 reduced **9.29** (a) N_2 oxidizing agent,
H_2 reducing agent (b) Cl_2 oxidizing agent, KI reducing agent
(c) Sb_2O_3 oxidizing agent, Fe reducing agent (d) HNO_3 oxidizing
agent, H_2SO_3 reducing agent **9.31** (a) gain (b) loss (c) loss
(d) gain **9.33** (a) incorrect (b) correct (c) incorrect (d) incorrect
9.35 molecular collisions, activation energy, and collision
orientation **9.37** total kinetic energy of colliding reactants;
collision orientation **9.39** (a) exothermic (b) endothermic
(c) endothermic (d) exothermic **9.41** (a) product (b) reactant
(c) reactant (d) product **9.43** (a) exothermic (b) released
9.45

9.47 (a) As temperature increases, so does the number of
collisions per second. (b) A catalyst lowers the activation energy.
9.49 The concentration of O_2 has increased from 21% to 100%.
9.51 (a) increase (b) decrease (c) increase (d) decrease
9.53 (a) increase (b) increase (c) increase (d) increase
9.55

9.57 (a) 1 (b) 3 (c) 4 (d) 3 **9.59** rate of forward reaction = rate of
reverse reaction **9.61** Conversion of reactants to products and
conversion of products to reactants occur simultaneously.
9.63 (a) $N_2(g) + O_2(g) \longrightarrow 2NO(g)$ (b) $2NO(g) \longrightarrow N_2(g) + O_2(g)$

9.65

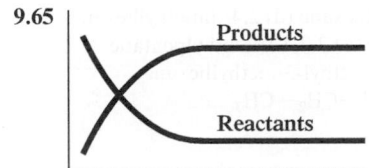

Products

Reactants

9.67 Yes, the concentrations of molecules in diagrams III and IV are the same. **9.69** Diagrams II and IV; diagram III cannot be produced from the original mixture.

9.71 (a) $\dfrac{[Z]^2}{[X]^2[Y]^3}$ (b) $\dfrac{[Z]^2}{[X]^2}$ (c) $[Z]^2$ (d) $\dfrac{1}{[X]^2[Y]^3}$

9.73 (a) $\dfrac{[NO]^2[Cl_2]}{[NOCl]^2}$ (b) $\dfrac{[NO]^4[H_2O]^6}{[NH_3]^4[O_2]^5}$

(c) $\dfrac{1}{[Cl_2]}$ (d) $\dfrac{[NaNO_3]}{[AgNO_3][NaCl]}$

9.75 4.8×10^{-5} **9.77** (a) more products than reactants (b) essentially all reactants (c) significant amounts of both reactants and products (d) significant amounts of both reactants and products **9.79** $4\,NH_3(g) + 3\,O_2\,(g) \rightleftharpoons 2\,N_2(g) + 6\,H_2O(g)$ **9.81** diagram IV **9.83** diagram IV **9.85** (a) no (b) no (c) yes (d) no **9.87** (a) decrease (b) decrease (c) increase (d) decrease **9.89** (a) left (b) left (c) left (d) left **9.91** (a) left (b) no effect (c) right (d) no effect **9.93** endothermic reaction **9.95** (a) yes (b) yes (c) no (d) yes **9.97** (a) no (b) no (c) no (d) yes

Chapter 10 **10.1** (a) H^+ (b) OH^- **10.3** (a) Arrhenius acid (b) Arrhenius base **10.5** (a) $HI \xrightarrow{H_2O} H^+ + I^-$ (b) $HClO \xrightarrow{H_2O}$ $H^+ + ClO^-$ (c) $LiOH \xrightarrow{H_2O} Li^+ + OH^-$ (d) $CsOH \xrightarrow{H_2O} Cs^+ +$ OH^- **10.7** (a) acid (b) base (c) acid (d) base **10.9** (a) $HOCl +$ $H_2O \longrightarrow H_3O^+ + OCl^-$ (b) $NH_3 + H_2O \longrightarrow NH_4^+ + OH^-$ (c) $H_2PO_4^- + H_2O \longrightarrow H_3O^+ + HPO_4^{2-}$ (d) $CO_3^{2-} + H_2O \longrightarrow$ $HCO_3^- + OH^-$ **10.11** (a) yes (b) yes (c) no (d) yes **10.13** (a) HSO_3^- (b) HCN (c) $C_2O_4^{2-}$ (d) $H_2PO_4^-$ **10.15** $HC_2H_3O_2/C_2H_3O_2^-$ and H_3O^+/H_2O **10.17** (a) $HCO_3^- + H_2O \longrightarrow H_2CO_3 + OH^-$ (b) $HCO_3^- + H_2O \longrightarrow H_3O^+ + CO_3^{2-}$ **10.19** (a) monoprotic (b) monoprotic (c) triprotic (d) triprotic **10.21** (a) 1, 0 (b) 1, 5 (c) 3, 5 (d) 3, 0 **10.23** (a) $H_2CO_3 + H_2O \longrightarrow H_3O^+ + HCO_3^-$; $HCO_3^- + H_2O \longrightarrow H_3O^+ + CO_3^{2-}$ (b) $H_2C_3H_2O_4 + H_2O \longrightarrow$ $H_3O^+ + HC_3H_2O_4^-$; $HC_3H_2O_4^- + H_2O \longrightarrow H_3O^+ + C_3H_2O_4^{2-}$ **10.25** To show that it is a monoprotic acid **10.27** Monoprotic; only one H atom is involved in a polar bond. **10.29** (a) strong (b) weak (c) weak (d) weak **10.31** (a) stronger (b) weaker (c) weaker (d) weaker **10.33** (a) yes (b) yes (c) yes (d) no **10.35** 0.10 M in both H_3O^+ and Cl^- ions and zero in HCl **10.37** acid in diagram IV **10.39** (a) weak, triprotic (b) weak, triprotic (c) strong, monoprotic (d) weak, monoprotic

10.41 (a) $K_a = \dfrac{[H^+][F^-]}{[HF]}$ (b) $K_a = \dfrac{[H^+][C_2H_3O_2^-]}{[HC_2H_2O_2]}$

10.43 (a) $K_b = \dfrac{[NH_4^+][OH^-]}{[NH_3]}$ (b) $K_b = \dfrac{[C_6H_5NH_3^+][OH^-]}{[C_6H_5NH_2]}$

10.45 (a) H_3PO_4 (b) HF (c) H_2CO_3 (d) HNO_2 **10.47** 4.9×10^{-5} **10.49** (a) Y (b) Z (c) Y (d) Y **10.51** (a) acid (b) salt (c) salt (d) base **10.53** (a) yes (b) no (c) no (d) yes **10.55** (a) $Ba(NO_3)_2 \xrightarrow{H_2O}$ $Ba^{2+} + 2NO_3^-$ (b) $Na_2SO_4 \xrightarrow{H_2O} 2Na^+ + SO_4^{2-}$ (c) $CaBr_2 \xrightarrow{H_2O}$ $Ca^{2+} + 2Br^-$ (d) $K_2CO_3 \xrightarrow{H_2O} 2K^+ + CO_3^{2-}$ **10.57** (a) no (b) yes (c) yes (d) no **10.59** (a) 1 to 1 (b) 1 to 2 (c) 1 to 1 (d) 2 to 1 **10.61** $HCl + NaOH \rightarrow NaCl + H_2O$ (b) $HNO_3 + KOH \rightarrow KNO_3 +$ H_2O (c) $H_2SO_4 + 2LiOH \rightarrow Li_2SO_4 + 2H_2O$ (d) $2H_3PO_4 +$ $3Ba(OH)_2 \rightarrow Ba_3(PO_4)_2 + 6H_2O$ **10.63** (a) $H_2SO_4 + 2LiOH \rightarrow$ $Li_2SO_4 + 2H_2O$ (b) $HCl + NaOH \rightarrow NaCl + H_2O$ (c) $HNO_3 +$ $KOH \rightarrow KNO_3 + H_2O$ (d) $2H_3PO_4 + 3Ba(OH)_2 \rightarrow Ba_3(PO_4)_2 + 6H_2O$

10.65 (a) $2.9\ 10^{-12}$ M (b) 2.1×10^{-9} M (c) 9.1×10^{-7} M (d) 1.1×10^{-5} M **10.67** (a) basic (b) basic (c) acidic (d) acidic **10.69** (a) 1.8×10^{-13} M (b) 1.1×10^{-10} M (c) 4.3×10^{-8} M (d) 1.5×10^{-3} M **10.71** (a) acidic (b) acidic (c) acidic (d) basic **10.73** (a) 3.0×10^{-12}, basic (b) 1.5×10^{-7}, basic (c) 1.4×10^{-7}, acidic (d) 2.12×10^{-10}, acidic **10.75** (a) 5.000 (b) 8.000 (c) 5.323 (d) 7.052 **10.77** (a) 10.000 (b) 4.000 (c) 11.045 (d) 7.782 **10.79** (a) 1.0×10^{-5} M (b) 1.0×10^{-7} M (c) 3.5×10^{-4} M (d) 7.1×10^{-8} M **10.81** (a) 7.4×10^{-4} M (b) 5.6×10^{-4} M (c) 3.2×10^{-4} M (d) 1.8×10^{-4} M **10.83** (a) acidic (b) basic (c) basic (d) acidic **10.85** (a) 1.4×10^{-5}, 9.14, basic (b) 5.0×10^{-6}, 2.0×10^{-9}, acidic (c) 1.4×10^{-5}, 4.85, acidic (d) 5.8×10^{-9}, 1.7×10^{-6}, basic **10.87** (a) 3 (b) 4 (c) 4, 1, 2, 3 (d) 4, 1, 2, 3 **10.89** (a) higher (b) lower (c) lower (d) higher **10.91** (a) 3.35 (b) 6.37 (c) 7.21 (d) 1.82 **10.93** acid B **10.95** 1.9×10^{-9} **10.97** (a) strong acid–strong base salt (b) weak acid–strong base salt (c) strong acid–weak base salt (d) strong acid–strong base salt **10.99** (a) none (b) $C_2H_3O_2^-$ (c) NH_4^+ (d) none **10.101** (a) neutral (b) basic (c) acidic (d) neutral **10.103** CN^- ion hydrolyzes to a greater extent than the NH_4^+ ion. **10.105** HCl, HCN, NaCl, NaCN **10.107** (a) no (b) yes (c) no (d) yes **10.109** (a) HCN and CN^- (b) H_3PO_4 and $H_2PO_4^-$ (c) H_2CO_3 and HCO_3^- (d) HCO_3^- and CO_3^{2-} **10.111** (a) $F^- + H_3O^+ \rightarrow HF + H_2O$ (b) $H_2CO_3 + OH^- \rightarrow$ $HCO_3^- + H_2O$ (c) $CO_3^{2-} + H_3O^+ \rightarrow HCO_3^- + H_2O$ (d) $H_3PO_4 +$ $OH^- \rightarrow H_2PO_4^- + H_2O$ **10.113** HNO_2 increases and NO_2^- decreases. **10.115** (a) 8.1 (b) 8.3 **10.117** all four diagrams **10.119** (a) HCN/CN^- (b) HNO_2/NO_2^- **10.121** (a) HPO_4^{2-} (b) Cl^- (c) HPO_4^{2-}, CO_3^{2-} (d) HPO_4^{2-}, CO_3^{2-}, H_2SO_3 **10.123** 7.06 **10.125** 5.17 **10.127** (a) weak (b) strong (c) strong (d) strong **10.129** (a) both (b) molecules (c) ions (d) both **10.131** (a) 2 (b) 3 (c) 3 (d) 2 **10.133** (a) $NaCl \rightarrow Na^+ + Cl^-$ (b) $Mg(NO_3)_2 \rightarrow Mg^{2+} + 2NO_3^-$ (c) $K_2S \rightarrow 2K^+ + S^{2-}$ (d) $NH_4CN \rightarrow NH_4^+ + CN^-$ **10.135** diagram 3 **10.137** (a) 1 Eq (b) 1 Eq (c) 2 Eq (d) 1 Eq **10.139** (a) 2 Eq (b) 3 Eq (c) 4 Eq (d) 14 Eq **10.141** (a) 0.048 Eq (b) 0.024 mole **10.143** 6.0 mEq/L **10.145** (a) yes (b) no (c) yes (d) yes **10.147** 15 mEq **10.149** (a) 0.0500 M (b) 0.800 M (c) 0.950 M (d) 0.120 M

Chapter 11 **11.1** (a) 4, 6 (b) 11, 12 (c) 47, 61 (d) 16, 18 **11.3** (a) yes (b) no (c) yes (d) no **11.5** the spontaneous emission of radiation from the nucleus of the atom **11.7** approximately 1-to-1 ratio for low-atomic-numbered stable nuclei and 3-to-2 ratio for higher-atomic-numbered stable nuclei **11.9** (a) $^4_2\alpha$ (b) $^0_{-1}\beta$ (c) $^0_0\gamma$ **11.11** 2 protons and 2 neutrons **11.13** (a) $^{200}_{84}Po \rightarrow ^4_2\alpha + ^{196}_{82}Pb$ (b) $^{240}_{96}Cm \rightarrow ^4_2\alpha + ^{236}_{94}Pu$ (c) $^{244}_{96}Cm \rightarrow ^4_2\alpha + ^{240}_{94}Pu$ (d) $^{238}_{92}U \rightarrow ^4_2\alpha + ^{234}_{90}Th$ **11.15** (a) $^{10}_4Be \rightarrow ^0_{-1}\beta + ^{10}_5B$ (b) $^{14}_6C \rightarrow ^0_{-1}\beta + ^{14}_7N$ (c) $^{21}_9F \rightarrow ^0_{-1}\beta + ^{21}_{10}Ne$ (d) $^{25}_{11}Na \rightarrow ^0_{-1}\beta + ^{25}_{12}Mg$ **11.17** (a) decrease by 2 (b) decrease by 4 **11.19** (a) alpha (b) beta (c) alpha (d) beta **11.21** (a) $^{210}_{84}Po \rightarrow ^{206}_{82}Pb + ^4_2\alpha$ (b) $^{225}_{90}Th \rightarrow ^{225}_{91}Pa + ^0_{-1}\beta$ (c) $^{190}_{78}Pt \rightarrow ^{186}_{76}Os + ^4_2\alpha$ (d) $^{19}_8O \rightarrow ^{19}_9F + ^0_{-1}\beta$ **11.23** (a) $^{199}_{79}Au \rightarrow ^{199}_{80}Hg + ^0_{-1}\beta$ (b) $^{109}_{46}Pd \rightarrow ^{109}_{47}Ag + ^0_{-1}\beta$ (c) $^{152}_{67}Ho \rightarrow ^{148}_{65}Tb + ^4_2\alpha$ (d) $^{249}_{100}Fm \rightarrow ^{245}_{98}Cm + ^4_2\alpha$ **11.25** (a) ¼ (b) $^1/_{64}$ (c) $^1/_8$ (d) $^1/_{64}$ **11.27** (a) 1.4 days (b) 0.90 day (c) 0.68 day (d) 0.54 day **11.29** (a) 4.0 hr, $^3/_4$ (b) 6.0 hr, ¼ (c) 1.0 hr, $^1/_{16}$ (d) ½, ½ **11.31** (a) 120 days (b) 240 days **11.33** (a) 3.75 g (b) 30.0 hours **11.35** three half-lives **11.37** 2000 **11.39** 92 **11.41** (a) $^4_2\alpha$ (b) $^{25}_{12}Mg$ (c) $^4_2\alpha$ (d) ^1_1p **11.43** (a) $^9_4Be + ^4_2\alpha \rightarrow ^{12}_6C + ^1_0n$ (b) $^{23}_{11}Na + ^2_1H \rightarrow ^{21}_{10}Ne + ^4_2\alpha$ (c) $^{113}_{48}Cd + ^1_0n \rightarrow ^{114}_{48}Cd + ^0_0\gamma$ (d) $^{27}_{13}Al + ^4_2\alpha \rightarrow ^{30}_{15}P + ^1_0n$ **11.45** (a) 7 (b) 17 **11.47** Termination of a decay series requires a stable nuclide. **11.49** lead-214 **11.51** $^{232}_{90}Th \rightarrow ^4_2\alpha + ^{228}_{88}Ra$, $^{228}_{88}Ra \rightarrow ^0_{-1}\beta + ^{228}_{89}Ac$, $^{228}_{89}Ac \rightarrow ^0_{-1}\beta + ^{228}_{90}Th$, $^{228}_{90}Th \rightarrow ^4_2\alpha + ^{224}_{88}Ra$ **11.53** The films record the extent of their exposure to radiation. **11.55** the electron and positive ion that are produced during an ionizing interaction between a molecule (or atom) and radiation **11.57** (a) yes (b) no (c) yes (d) no **11.59** It continues on, interacting with other atoms and forming more ion pairs. **11.61** (a) beta, gamma (b) gamma (c) gamma (d) gamma **11.63** 6 cm versus 1000 cm **11.65** (a) no detectable effects (b) nausea, fatigue, lowered blood cell count **11.67** naturally occurring ionizing radiation **11.69** radon seepage, cosmic radiation, rocks and minerals, food and drink **11.71** so radiation can be detected externally **11.73** (a) locate sites of infection (b) determination of intercellular spaces in fluids (c) assessment of blood flow in heart muscle (d) detection of bone tumors **11.75** They are usually α or β emitters. **11.77** (a) fission (b) fusion **11.79** (a) neptunium-239 (b) krypton-91 **11.81** (a) $^4_2\alpha$ (b) $^2_1$H **11.83** (a) fusion (b) fusion (c) both (d) fission **11.85** (a) fusion (b) fission (c) neither (d) neither **11.87** Different isotopes of an element have the same chemical properties but different nuclear properties. **11.89** Temperature, pressure, and catalysts affect chemical reaction rates but do not affect nuclear reaction rates.

Chapter 12 **12.1** (a) false (b) false (c) true (d) true
12.3 (a) inorganic (b) organic (c) organic (d) inorganic
12.5 (a) meets (b) does not meet (c) does not meet (d) does not meet
12.7 Hydrocarbons contain C and H, and hydrocarbon derivatives contain at least one additional element besides C and H.
12.9 All bonds are single bonds in a saturated hydrocarbon, and at least one carbon–carbon multiple bond is present in an unsaturated hydrocarbon. **12.11** (a) saturated (b) unsaturated (c) unsaturated (d) unsaturated **12.13** (a) 18 (b) 4 (c) 13 (d) 22
12.15 (a) CH_3—CH_2—CH_2—CH_3 (b) CH_3—CH_2—CH_2—CH_2—CH_2—CH_2—CH_3 **12.17** (a) CH_3—$(CH_2)_2$—CH_3 (b) CH_3—$(CH_2)_5$—CH_3
12.19 (a) C—C—C—C (b) C—C—C—C—C—C—C
12.21 (a)

```
      H   H   H   H   H
      |   |   |   |   |
  H—C—C—C—C—C—H
      |   |   |   |   |
      H   H   H   H   H
```

(b)

```
      H  H  H  H  H  H  H  H
      |  |  |  |  |  |  |  |
  H—C—C—C—C—C—C—C—C—H
      |  |  |  |  |  |  |  |
      H  H  H  H  H  H  H  H
```

(c) CH_3—$(CH_2)_8$—CH_3 (d) C_6H_{14} **12.23** (a) 14 (b) 5 (c) 4 (d) 19
12.25 (a) The last carbon in the carbon chain should have three hydrogen atoms. (b) The third carbon in the carbon chain should have only one hydrogen atom. **12.27** (a) the same (b) different (c) different (d) different **12.29** Constitutional isomers must have the same molecular formula. **12.31** (a) 2 (b) 5 (c) 18 (d) 75 **12.33** one **12.35** (a) different compounds that are not constitutional isomers (b) different compounds that are constitutional isomers (c) different conformations of the same molecule (d) different compounds that are constitutional isomers
12.37

(a) CH_3—CH_2—CH—CH_2—CH_3
                |
               CH_3

(b) CH_3—CH—CH_2—CH—CH_3
        | |
       CH_3 CH_3

(c) CH_3—CH—CH_3
        |
     CH_3

(d) CH_3—CH_2—CH—CH_2—CH_3
               |
             CH_2
             |
             CH_3

12.39 (a) CH_3—CH_2—CH_2—CH_2—CH_3
                  CH_3
                  |
(c) CH_3—C—CH_3
       |
    CH_3

(b) CH_3—CH—CH_2—CH_3
         |
       CH_3

(d) CH_3—CH—CH—CH_3
        | |
      CH_3 CH_3

12.41 (a) eth– (b) but– (c) hex– (d) oct– **12.43** (a) ethyl (b) pentyl **12.45** (a) C_2H_6 (b) C_2H_5 (c) C_5H_{12} (d) C_5H_{11} **12.47** (a) seven-carbon chain (b) eight-carbon chain (c) eight-carbon chain (d) seven-carbon chain **12.49** (a) 3-methylpentane

(b) 2-methylhexane (c) 2-methylhexane (d) 2,4-dimethylhexane
12.51 (a) 2,3,5-trimethylhexane (b) 2,2,4-trimethylpentane (c) 3-ethyl-3-methylpentane (d) 3-ethyl-3-methylhexane
12.53 (a) CH_3—CH_2—CH—CH—CH_2—CH_3
                    | |
                 CH_3 CH_3

(b)
              CH_3
              |
CH_3—CH_2—C—CH_2—CH_3
              |
              CH_2
              |
              CH_3

(c) CH_3—CH_2—CH—CH_2—CH—CH_2—CH_2—CH_3
                | |
              CH_2 CH_2
              | |
              CH_3 CH_3

(d) CH_3—CH_2—CH_2—CH—CH_2—CH_2—CH_2—CH_2—CH_3
                     |
                 CH_2
                 |
                 CH_2
                 |
                 CH_3

12.55 (a) 2, 2 (b) 2, 2 (c) 2, 2 (d) 1, 1 **12.57** (a) not based on longest carbon chain; 2,2-dimethylbutane (b) carbon chain numbered from wrong end; 2,2,3-trimethylbutane (c) carbon chain numbered from wrong end and alkyl groups not listed alphabetically; 3-ethyl-4-methylhexane (d) like alkyl groups listed separately; 2,4-dimethylhexane **12.59** (a) no (b) yes (c) yes (d) yes **12.61** (a) 1 (b) 3 (c) 7 (d) 6
12.63 (a) C—C—C—C—C—C—C—C
                 |
                 C

(b) C—C—C—C—C—C
        | |
       C   C

(c) C—C—C—C—C
        |
       C

(d) C—C—C—C—C—C—C—C
    | |
   C   C—C
             |
            C

12.65 (a) CH_3—CH—CH—CH—CH_3
           | | |
        CH_3 CH_3 CH_3

(b) CH_3—CH—CH—CH_2—CH_3
          | |
       CH_3 CH_2
             |
            CH_3

(c) CH_3—CH_2—CH—CH—CH_2—CH_2—CH_3
                | |
              CH_3 CH_2
                   CH_3

(d) CH_3—CH—CH_2—CH_2—CH—CH_2—CH_2—CH_3
        | |
      CH_3 CH_2
                    CH_3

12.67 (a) constitutional isomers (b) same compound
12.69 (a)   (b)
  (c)   (d)

12.71 (a) 2-methyloctane (b) 2,3-dimethylhexane (c) 3-methylpentane (d) 5-isopropyl-2-methyloctane **12.73** (a) C_8H_{18} (b) C_9H_{20} (c) $C_{10}H_{22}$ (d) $C_{11}H_{24}$ **12.75** (a) 5, 1, 3, 0 (b) 5, 1, 1, 1 (c) 4, 3, 0, 1 (d) 4, 4, 0, 1 **12.77** (a) first structure, yes; second structure, no (b) first structure, yes; second structure, yes
12.79 (a) CH_3—CH_2—CH_2—CH_2—CH_2—CH_2—CH_3

(b)
$$CH_3-\underset{\underset{CH_3}{|}}{\overset{\overset{CH_3}{|}}{C}}-\underset{\underset{CH_3}{|}}{CH}-CH_3$$

12.81 (a) isopropyl (b) isobutyl (c) isopropyl (d) *sec*-butyl
12.83
(a) CH_3—CH_2—CH_2—CH_2—CH—CH_2—CH_2—CH_2—CH_2—CH_3
with branch below the CH: CH—CH_3 / CH_2 / CH_3

(b) CH_3—CH_2—CH_2—C—CH_2—CH_2—CH_2—CH_3
with above: CH_3 / CH—CH_3; below: CH—CH_3 / CH_3

(c) CH_3—CH—CH—CH_2—CH—CH_2—CH_2—CH_2—CH_3
with CH_3 CH_3 below first two, and below the middle CH: CH_2 / CH—CH_3 / CH_3

(d) CH_3—CH_2—CH_2—CH—CH_2—CH_2—CH_2—CH_3
with below: CH_3—C—CH_3 / CH_3

12.85 (a) 3 or 4 (b) 3 or 4 (c) none of them (d) 3 or 4
12.87 (a) (2-methylbutyl) group (b) (1,1-dimethylpropyl) group **12.89** (a) (1-methylethyl) group (b) (1,1-dimethylethyl) group (c) *sec*-butyl group (d) isobutyl group **12.91** (a) 4 (b) 8 **12.93** (a) 16 (b) 6 (c) 5 (d) 15 **12.95** (a) C_4H_8 (b) C_8H_{16} (c) C_9H_{18} (d) C_8H_{16} **12.97** (a) 0 (b) 2 (c) 1 (d) 3 **12.99** (a) 4 (b) 5 (c) 5 (d) 2 **12.101** (a) cyclopentane (b) ethylcyclopentane (c) 1,2-dimethylcyclopentane (d) 1-isopropyl-2,4-dimethylcyclopentane **12.103** (a) must locate methyl groups with numbers (b) wrong numbering system for ring (c) no number needed (d) wrong numbering system for ring

12.105 (a) (b) (c) (d)
12.107 (a) C_8H_{16} (b) C_8H_{16} (c) C_8H_{18} (d) C_8H_{18} **12.109** (a) saturated (b) saturated (c) saturated (d) saturated **12.111** (a) two (cyclobutane, methylcyclopropane) (b) three: dimethyl (1,1; 1,2); ethyl (c) one (methyl) (d) four: dimethyl (1,1; 1,2; 1,3); ethyl
12.113 (a) not possible
(b) CH_3—CH_2△CH_2—CH_3 CH_3—CH_2△H
H H   H CH_2—CH_3
cis   *trans*
(c) not possible   (d)
cis   *trans*
12.115 (a) *cis*- (b) *trans*- (c) *trans*- (d) *cis*- **12.117** (a) not isomers (b) not isomers (c) not isomers (d) stereoisomers

12.119 50%–90% methane, 1%–10% ethane, up to 8% propane and butanes **12.121** boiling point **12.123** (a) octane (b) cyclopentane (c) pentane (d) cyclopentane **12.125** (a) different states (b) same state (c) same state (d) same state **12.127** (a) liquid (b) less dense (c) insoluble (d) flammable **12.129** (a) CO_2 and H_2O (b) CO_2 and H_2O (c) CO_2 and H_2O (d) CO_2 and H_2O **12.131** CH_3Br, CH_2Br_2, $CHBr_3$, CBr_4
12.133 (a) CH_3—CH_2
Cl

(b) CH_2—CH_2—CH_2—CH_3 CH_3—CH—CH_2—CH_3
Cl   Cl

(c) CH_2—CH—CH_3 CH_3—C(Cl)(CH_3)—CH_3 (d) cyclopentane with Cl
Cl   CH_3

12.135 (a) iodomethane (b) 1-chloropropane (c) 2-fluorobutane (d) chlorocyclobutane **12.137** (a) methyl iodide (b) propyl chloride (c) sec-butyl fluoride (d) cyclobutyl chloride
12.139 (a)
$$H-\underset{\underset{Cl}{|}}{\overset{\overset{Cl}{|}}{C}}-Cl$$
(b)
$$F-\underset{\underset{Cl}{|}}{\overset{\overset{F}{|}}{C}}-\underset{\underset{Cl}{|}}{\overset{\overset{F}{|}}{C}}-F$$
(c) CH_3—CH—Br / CH_3 (d) cyclopentane with Br and Cl, H, H
12.141 (a) alkane (b) alkane (c) cycloalkane (d) alkane
12.143 (a) CH_3—I (b) CH_3—CH_2—Cl (c) CH_3—CH_2—I (d) CH_3—Br **12.145** (a) incorrect (b) incorrect (c) incorrect (d) correct **12.147** 1-chloropentane, 2-chloropentane, 3-chloropentane, 1-chloro-2-methylbutane, 2-chloro-2-methylbutane, 2-chloro-3-methylbutane, 1-chloro-3-methylbutane, 1-chloro-2,2-dimethylpropane

Chapter 13 **13.1** (a) saturated (b) unsaturated (c) unsaturated (d) unsaturated **13.3** (a) alkane (b) alkene (c) alkyne (d) alkene **13.5** carbon–carbon double bond **13.7** similar **13.9** (a) C_4H_8 (b) C_4H_6 (c) C_4H_6 (d) C_4H_4 **13.11** (a) alkene with one double bond (b) alkene with one double bond (c) diene (d) diene **13.13** (a) nothing wrong (b) 3rd and 4th carbons have one too many hydrogen atoms **13.15** trigonal planar **13.17** (a) 2-butene (b) 2,4-dimethyl-2-pentene (c) 3-methylcyclohexene (d) 1,3-cyclopentadiene
13.19 (a) CH_2=CH—CH—CH_2—CH_3
CH_3

(b)   (c) CH_2=CH—CH=CH_2

(d) CH_2=CH—CH—CH=CH_2
CH_2 / CH_3

13.21 (a) 3-methyl-3-hexene (b) 2,3-dimethyl-2-hexene (c) 1,3-cyclopentadiene (d) 4,5-dimethylcyclohexene
13.23 (a) CH_2=CH_2 (b) (c) CH_2=CH—Br

(d) CH_2=CH—CH_2—I
13.25 (a) saturated (b) unsaturated (c) unsaturated (d) unsaturated
13.27 (a) 14 (b) 12 (c) 6 (d) 12

13.29 (a) [structure] (b) [structure]

(c) [structure] (d) [structure]

13.31 (a) 8 (b) 8 (c) 8 (d)10   **13.33** (a) C_8H_{16} (b) C_8H_{16} (c) C_8H_{14} (d) $C_{10}H_{18}$ **13.35** (a) 3-octene (b) 3-octene (c) 1,3-octadiene (d) 3,7-dimethyl-1,5-octadiene   **13.37** (a) tetrahedral (b) tetrahedral (c) trigonal planar (d) tetrahedral   **13.39** (a) positional (b) skeletal (c) skeletal (d) positional   **13.41** (a) 2 (b) 4 (c) 3 (d) zero

13.43

C=C—C—C—C—C   C—C=C—C—C—C
　　1-Hexene　　　　　　　2-Hexene

C—C—C=C—C—C　C=C—C—C—C　C=C—C—C—C
　　　3-Hexene　　　　　　　　|　　　　　　　　|
　　　　　　　　　　　　　　　 C　　　　　　　 C
　　　　　　　　　2-Methyl-1-pentene　3-Methyl-1-pentene

C=C—C—C—C　C—C=C—C—C　C—C=C—C—C
　　　　 |　　　　　　　 |　　　　　　　 |
　　　　 C　　　　　　　 C　　　　　　　 C
4-Methyl-1-pentene　2-Methyl-2-pentene　3-Methyl-2-pentene

C—C=C—C—C　C=C—C—C　　　　　C
　　　 |　　　　 |　 |　　　　　　　|
　　　 C　　　　 C　 C　　　　C=C—C—C
4-Methyl-2-pentene　2,3-Dimethyl-1-butene　　|
　　　　　　　　　　　　　　　　　　　　　C
　　　　　　　　　　　　　　　3,3-Dimethyl-1-butene

C—C=C—C　　　C=C—C—C
　 |　 |　　　　　　 |
　 C　 C　　　　　　 C
2,3-Dimethyl-2-butene　　|
　　　　　　　　　　　　 C
　　　　　　　　　2-Ethyl-1-butene

13.45 C=C—C—C　C—C=C—C　C=C—C　□　△
　　　　　　　　　　　　　　　　|
　　　　　　　　　　　　　　　 C

13.47 (a) no (b) no

(c) [cis and trans structures]
　　cis　　　　　　　trans

(d) [cis and trans structures]
　　cis　　　　　　　trans

13.49 (a) cis-2-pentene (b) trans-1-bromo-2-iodoethene (c) tetrafluoroethene (d) 2-methyl-2-butene

13.51 (a) [structure]

(b) [structure]

(c) [structure]

(d) CH_2=CH [structure]

13.53 (a) no (b) no (c) no (d) yes   **13.55** A chemical substance produced by a species which triggers a response in other members of the same species.

13.57 CH_2=C—CH=CH_2
　　　　　　|
　　　　　 CH_3

13.59 Its structure is formed from C_5 isoprene units.
13.61 (a) true (b) false (c) true (d) true   **13.63** (a) gas (b) liquid (c) gas (d) liquid   **13.65** An H atom is lost from each of two adjacent C atoms and a carbon–carbon double bond is formed.   **13.67** ethene and H_2 **13.69** (a) yes (b) no (c) yes (d) no

13.71 (a) CH_2=CH_2 + Cl_2 ⟶ CH_2—CH_2
　　　　　　　　　　　　　　　　　　 |　　 |
　　　　　　　　　　　　　　　　　 Cl　 Cl

(b) CH_2=CH_2 + HCl ⟶ CH_3—CH_2
　　　　　　　　　　　　　　　　　　　　 |
　　　　　　　　　　　　　　　　　　　　 Cl

(c) CH_2=CH_2 + H_2 $\xrightarrow{Ni}$ CH_3—CH_3

(d) CH_2=CH_2 + HBr ⟶ CH_3—CH_2
　　　　　　　　　　　　　　　　　　　　 |
　　　　　　　　　　　　　　　　　　　　 Br

13.73 (a) two products (b) one product (c) one product (d) one product

13.75 (a) CH_2=CH—CH_3 + Cl_2 ⟶ CH_2—CH—CH_3
　　　　　　　　　　　　　　　　　　　　　 |　　 |
　　　　　　　　　　　　　　　　　　　　　 Cl　 Cl

(b) CH_2=CH—CH_3 + HCl ⟶ CH_3—CH—CH_3
　　　　　　　　　　　　　　　　　　　　　　 |
　　　　　　　　　　　　　　　　　　　　　　 Cl

(c) CH_2=CH—CH_3 + H_2 $\xrightarrow{Ni}$ CH_3—CH_2—CH_3

(d) CH_2=CH—CH_3 + HBr ⟶ CH_3—CH—CH_3
　　　　　　　　　　　　　　　　　　　　　　 |
　　　　　　　　　　　　　　　　　　　　　　 Br

13.77 (a) CH_3—CH—CH—CH_3
　　　　　　　　 |　　 |
　　　　　　　　 Cl　 Cl

(b) CH_3—CH_2—CH—CH_3 (c) [structure] (d) HO [structure]
　　　　　　　　　　　 |
　　　　　　　　　　　 Cl

13.79 (a) Br_2 (b) H_2+Ni catalyst (c) HCl (d) H_2O+H_2SO_4 catalyst
13.81 (a) 2 (b) 2 (c) 2 (d) 3   **13.83** (a) CF_2=CF_2
(b) CH_2=C—CH=CH_2 (c) CH_2=CH (d) CH_2=CH
　　　　　 |　　　　　　　　　　 |
　　　　 Cl　　　　　　　　　 Cl　　　 [benzene ring]

13.85 (a) —CH_2—CH_2—CH_2—CH_2—CH_2—CH_2—

(b) —CH_2—CH—CH_2—CH—CH_2—CH—
　　　　　　 |　　　　 |　　　　 |
　　　　　　 Cl　　　 Cl　　　 Cl

(c) —CH—CH—CH—CH—CH—CH—
　　　 |　 |　 |　 |　 |　 |
　　　 Cl　Cl　Cl　Cl　Cl　Cl

(d) —CH_2—CH—CH_2—CH—CH_2—CH—
　　　　　　 |　　　　 |　　　　 |
　　　　　　 Cl　　　 Cl　　　 Cl

13.87 (a) C_nH_{2n-6} **13.89** (a) 1-hexyne (b) 4-methyl-2-pentyne (c) 2,2-dimethyl-3-heptyne (d) 1-butyne
13.91 C≡C—C—C—C (1-pentyne)

C—C≡C—C—C (2-pentyne)

C≡C—C—C (3-methyl-1-butyne)
　　　 |
　　　 C

13.93 because of the linearity (180° angles) about an alkyne's carbon–carbon triple bond   **13.95** Their physical properties are very similar.

13.97 (a) CH$_3$—CH$_3$ (b)

CH$_3$—C—CH with Br Br on top and Br Br on bottom

(c) CH$_3$—C—CH$_3$ with Br on top and Br on bottom

(d) CH$_2$=CH—Cl

13.99 (a) CH$_3$—C≡C—CH$_2$—CH—CH$_3$ with CH$_3$ branch

(b) CH$_3$—C=CH—CH$_3$ with CH$_3$ branch

(c) CH≡C—CH$_2$—CH$_2$—CH$_2$—C≡CH

(d) CH≡C—CH=CH—CH$_3$

13.101 (a) 3 (b) 2 (c) 4 (d) 10 **13.103** (benzene ring)

13.105 Implies that there are two types of carbon–carbon bonds present which is not the case. **13.107** (a) 1,3-dibromobenzene (b) 1-chloro-2-fluorobenzene (c) 1-chloro-4-fluorobenzene (d) 3-chlorotoluene **13.109** (a) *m*-dibromobenzene (b) *o*-chlorofluorobenzene (c) *p*-chlorofluorobenzene (d) *m*-chlorotoluene **13.111** (a) 2,4-dibromo-1-chlorobenzene (b) 3-bromo-5-chlorotoluene (c) 1-bromo-3-chloro-2-fluorobenzene (d) 1,4-dibromo-2,5-dichlorobenzene **13.113** (a) 2-phenylbutane (b) 3-phenyl-1-butene (c) 3-methyl-1-phenylbutane (d) 2,4-diphenylpentane

13.115 (a) (structure: benzene ring with CH$_2$—CH$_3$ and CH$_2$—CH$_3$) (b) (structure: benzene ring with CH$_3$ and CH$_3$)

(c) (structure: benzene ring with CH$_3$ and CH$_2$—CH$_3$) (d) (biphenyl structure)

13.117 1,2,3-trimethylbenzene, 1,2,4-trimethylbenzene, 1,3,5-trimethylbenzene, 2-ethyltoluene, 3-ethyltoluene, 4-ethyltoluene, propylbenzene, isopropylbenzene **13.119** (a) all four (b) cyclohexene (c) cyclohexane, benzene (d) benzene **13.121** liquid state **13.123** petroleum **13.125** (a) substitution (b) addition (c) substitution (d) addition

13.127 (a) Br$_2$ (b) (benzene ring with CH—CH$_3$) (c) CH$_3$—CH$_2$—Br

13.129 carbon atoms are shared between rings

Chapter 14
14.1 (a) 2 (b) 1 (c) 4 (d) 1 **14.3** R—O—H versus H—O—H **14.5** (a) C$_3$H$_8$O (b) C$_5$H$_{12}$O **14.7** (a) 2-pentanol (b) 3-methyl-2-butanol (c) 2-ethyl-1-pentanol (d) 2-butanol **14.9** (a) 2-hexanol (b) 3-methyl-1-butanol (c) 3-methyl-1-pentanol (d) 4-heptanol

14.11 (a) CH$_2$—CH—CH$_3$ with OH and CH$_3$ (b) CH$_3$—CH—CH$_2$—CH—CH$_3$ with OH and CH$_3$

(c) OH with CH$_3$—C—CH$_3$ and benzene ring (d) (cyclobutane with OH and CH$_3$)

14.13 (a) CH$_2$—CH$_2$—CH$_2$—CH$_2$—CH$_3$ with OH
1-Pentanol

(b) CH$_2$—CH$_2$—CH$_3$ with OH
1-Propanol

(c) CH$_3$—CH—CH$_2$—OH with CH$_3$
2-Methyl-1-Propanol

(d) CH$_3$—CH$_2$—CH—OH with CH$_3$
2-Butanol

14.15 (a) 1,2-butanediol (b) 1,5-hexanediol (c) 2,4-hexanediol (d) 3-methyl-1,2,5-pentanetriol
14.17 (a) CH$_3$—CH—CH$_2$—CH=CH$_2$ with OH

(b) CH≡C—CH—CH$_2$—CH$_3$ with OH (c) CH$_3$—CH—C=CH$_2$ with OH CH$_3$

(d) CH$_2$—CH$_2$—CH=CH$_2$ with OH

14.19 (a) CH$_2$—CH—CH$_3$ with OH, CH$_2$, CH$_3$
2-Methyl-1-butanol

(b) CH$_3$—CH—CH$_2$—CH$_2$ with OH and OH
1,3-Butanediol

(c) CH$_3$—CH—CH—CH$_3$ with CH$_3$ OH
3-Methyl-2-butanol

(d) (cyclopentane with OH and HO)
1,3-Cyclopentanediol

14.21 (a) no (b) yes (c) yes (d) yes **14.23** (a) 4 (b) 8 (c) 8 (d) 4 **14.25** (a) *trans* (b) *cis* (c) *cis* (d) *trans* **14.27** (a) *trans*-2-buten-1-ol (b) *cis*-3-penten-1-ol (c) *cis*-2-methylcyclohexanol (d) *trans*-3-chlorocyclohexanol **14.29** (a) ethanol with all traces of H$_2$O removed (b) ethanol (c) 70% solution of isopropyl alcohol (d) ethanol **14.31** (a) 1,2,3-propanetriol (b) 1,2-propanediol (c) methanol (d) ethanol **14.33** Methanol fires, but not gasoline fires, can be put out using water. **14.35** Alcohol molecules can hydrogen-bond to each other; alkane molecules cannot. **14.37** (a) 1-heptanol (b) 1-propanol (c) 1,2-ethanediol **14.39** (a) 1-butanol (b) 1-pentanol (c) 1,2-butanediol **14.41** (a) 3 (b) 3 (c) 3 (d) 3 **14.43** (a) CH$_2$—CH$_3$ with OH (b) CH$_3$—CH$_2$—CH$_2$ with OH

(c) OH with CH$_3$—CH$_2$—C—CH$_3$ and CH$_3$ (d) CH$_3$—CH$_2$—CH—CH$_2$—CH$_3$ with OH

14.45 (a) 2° (b) 2° (c) 1° (d) 2° **14.47** (a) 2° (b) 2° (c) 3° (d) 1° **14.49** (a) 1° (b) 2° (c) 1° (d) 3°

14.51 (a) C—C—OH with C on top and C on bottom (b) (cyclopropane)—OH

14.53 (a) 4 (b) 3 (c) 1 (d) 0
14.55 (a) CH$_2$=CH—CH$_3$ (b) CH$_3$—CH$_2$—C=CH$_2$ with CH$_3$

(c) CH$_3$—CH=CH$_2$

(d) CH$_3$—CH$_2$—CH$_2$—O—CH$_2$—CH$_2$—CH$_3$

14.57

(a) $CH_2-CH_2-CH_2-CH_3$ (b) $CH_2-CH-CH_3$ or $CH_3-\underset{\underset{CH_3}{|}}{\overset{\overset{OH}{|}}{C}}-CH_3$
   $\overset{|}{OH}$ $\underset{OH}{|}\;\;\underset{CH_3}{|}$

(c) CH_3-CH_2-OH (d) $CH_3-CH_2-\underset{\underset{CH_3}{|}}{CH}-OH$

14.59 $CH_3-CH=\underset{\underset{CH_3}{|}}{C}-CH_2-CH_2-CH_3$,

$CH_3-CH_2-\underset{\underset{CH_3}{|}}{C}=CH-CH_2-CH_3$,

$CH_3-CH_2-\underset{\underset{CH_2}{|\!|}}{C}-CH_2-CH_2-CH_3$

14.61 The carbon to which the hydroxyl-bearing carbon is attached has no hydrogen atoms.   **14.63** (a) aldehyde (b) ketone (c) aldehyde (d) ketone

14.65 (a) $CH_3-CH_2-CH_2-\overset{\overset{O}{|\!|}}{C}-H$ (b) $CH_3-\overset{\overset{O}{|\!|}}{C}-CH_2-CH_3$

(c) $CH_3-CH_2-\underset{\underset{CH_3}{|}}{CH}-\overset{\overset{O}{|\!|}}{C}-H$ (d) $CH_3-\overset{\overset{O}{|\!|}}{C}-\underset{\underset{CH_3}{|}}{CH}-CH_3$

14.67 (a) $CH_3-CH_2-\underset{\underset{OH}{|}}{CH}-CH_3$ (b) $CH_3-CH_2-\underset{\underset{OH}{|}}{CH_2}$

(c) $CH_3-CH_2-\underset{\underset{OH}{|}}{CH_2}$ (d) cyclopentyl-CH_2-OH

14.69 (a) $CH_3-CH_2-CH_2-Cl$ (b) cyclopentene-CH_3

(c) $CH_3-\overset{\overset{O}{|\!|}}{C}-CH_2-CH_3$ (d) $CH_3-CH_2-O-CH_2-CH_3$

14.71 1-pentanol   **14.73** (a) no (b) no (c) yes (d) no
14.75 (a) 3-ethylphenol (b) 2-chlorophenol (c) o-cresol (d) hydroquinone
14.77 (a) OH, CH_2-CH_3 (b) OH, Br, Br (c) OH, CH_3 (d) OH, OH

14.79 low-melting solids or oily liquids   **14.81** (a) both are flammable (b) both undergo halogenation
14.83 phenol-OH $+ H_2O \rightleftharpoons$ phenol-$O^- + H_3O^+$

14.85 An antiseptic kills microorganisms on living tissue; a disinfectant kills microorganisms on inanimate objects.   **14.87** BHA has methoxy and *tert*-butyl groups; BHT has a methyl group and two *tert*-butyl groups.—   **14.89** (a) yes (b) no (c) yes (d) yes
14.91 (a) ether (b) alcohol (c) alcohol (d) ether

14.93 (a) $H-\underset{\underset{H}{|}}{\overset{\overset{H}{|}}{C}}-O-\underset{\underset{H}{|}}{\overset{\overset{H}{|}}{C}}-H$ (b) CH_3-O-CH_3

(c) $C-O-C$ (d) C_2H_6O **14.95** (a) 1-ethoxypropane
(b) 2-methoxypropane (c) methoxybenzene (d) cyclohexoxycyclohexane   **14.97** (a) ethyl propyl ether (b) isopropyl methyl ether
(c) methyl phenyl ether (d) dicyclohexyl ether
14.99 (a) 1-methoxypentane (b) 1-ethoxy-2-methylpropane
(c) 2-ethoxybutane (d) 2-methoxybutane
14.101

(a) $CH_3-\underset{\underset{CH_3}{|}}{CH}-O-CH_2-CH_2-CH_3$ (b) CH_3-CH_2-O-phenyl

(c) $O-CH_3$ benzene with CH_3 (d) cyclobutyl $O-CH_2-CH_3$

14.103 (a) ethoxyethane (b) 2-methoxy-2-methylpropane (c) methoxymethanol (d) 2-methylanisole   **14.105** methyl *tert*-butyl ether
14.107 spillage has been found in water supplies   **14.109** (a) cloves
(b) nutmeg (c) vanilla (d) anise and fennel   **14.111** (a) no (b) no
(c) yes (d) no   **14.113** butyl methyl ether, *sec*-butyl methyl ether,
isobutyl methyl ether, *tert*-butyl methyl ether, ethyl isopropyl ether
14.115 (a) 2 (b) 4 (c) 3 (d) 3
14.117 (a) $CH_3-O-CH_2-CH_2-CH_3$, $CH_3-O-\underset{\underset{CH_3}{|}}{CH}-CH_3$

$CH_3-CH_2-O-CH_2-CH_3$

(b) $CH_3-CH_2-CH_2-CH_2-OH$, $CH_3-CH_2-\underset{\underset{CH_3}{|}}{CH}-OH$,

$CH_3-\underset{\underset{CH_3}{|}}{CH}-CH_2-OH$, $CH_3-\underset{\underset{CH_3}{|}}{\overset{\overset{CH_3}{|}}{C}}-OH$

14.119
$\underset{\underset{OH}{|}}{CH_2}-CH_2-CH_2-CH_2-CH_3$ $CH_3-\underset{\underset{OH}{|}}{\overset{\overset{CH_3}{|}}{C}}-CH_2-CH_3$

$\underset{\underset{OH}{|}}{CH_2}-\underset{\underset{CH_3}{|}}{CH}-CH_2-CH_3$ $CH_3-\underset{\underset{OH}{|}}{CH}-CH_2-CH_2-CH_3$

$\underset{\underset{OH}{|}}{CH_2}-CH_2-\underset{\underset{CH_3}{|}}{CH}-CH_3$ $CH_3-\underset{\underset{CH_3}{|}}{\overset{\overset{CH_3}{|}}{C}}-\underset{\underset{OH}{|}}{CH_2}$

$CH_3-CH_2-\underset{\underset{OH}{|}}{CH}-CH_2-CH_3$ $CH_3-\underset{\underset{OH}{|}}{CH}-\underset{\underset{CH_3}{|}}{CH}-CH_3$

$CH_3-CH_2-CH_2-CH_2-O-CH_3$ $CH_3-\underset{\underset{CH_3}{|}}{CH}-CH_2-O-CH_3$

$CH_3-CH_2-\underset{\underset{CH_3}{|}}{CH}-O-CH_3$ $CH_3-\underset{\underset{CH_3}{|}}{\overset{\overset{CH_3}{|}}{C}}-O-CH_3$

$CH_3-CH_2-CH_2-O-CH_2-CH_3$ $CH_3-\underset{\underset{CH_3}{|}}{CH}-O-CH_2-CH_3$

14.121 Dimethyl ether molecules cannot hydrogen-bond to each other; ethanol molecules can.   **14.123** flammability and peroxide formation   **14.125** No oxygen–hydrogen bonds are present.
14.127 (a) noncyclic ether (b) noncyclic ether (c) cyclic ether

(d) nonether **14.129** R—S—H versus R—O—H
14.131
(a) CH₃—CH₂—CH₂—CH₂   (b) CH₃—CH₂—CH—CH₂—CH₂
                        SH   CH₃   SH

(c) [cyclopentane]—SH   (d) CH₂—CH₂
                            SH   SH

14.133 (a) methyl mercaptan (b) propyl mercaptan (c) *sec*-butyl mercaptan (d) isobutyl mercaptan   **14.135** Alcohol oxidation produces aldehydes and ketones; thioalcohol oxidation produces disulfides.
14.137 (a) CH₃—CH₂—CH₂—OH   (b) CH₃—CH₂—CH₂—SH
14.139 (a) 1-pentanethiol (b) 1-pentanol (c) 3-methyl-2-butanethiol (d) 3-methyl-2-butanol   **14.141** R—S—R versus R—O—R
14.143 (a) methylthioethane; ethyl methyl sulfide (b) 2-methylthiopropane; isopropyl methyl sulfide (c) methylthiocyclohexane; cyclohexyl methyl sulfide (d) 3-(methylthio)-1-propene; allyl methyl sulfide
14.145 (a) disulfide (b) peroxide (c) diol (d) ether, thioether, sulfide

Chapter 15 **15.1** (a) yes (b) no (c) no (d) yes   **15.3** carbon–oxygen double bond is polar; carbon–carbon double bond is nonpolar
15.5 120°   **15.7** (a) yes (b) yes (c) yes (d) yes   **15.9** (a) no (b) no (c) yes (d) yes   **15.11** (a) neither (b) ketone (c) neither (d) aldehyde
15.13
(a) H—C—H (b) cannot exist   [O double bond on C]
(c) CH₃—CH₂—C—H (d) CH₃—C—CH₂—CH₃   [O double bonds]
15.15 (a) aldehyde (b) neither (c) ketone (d) ketone
15.17 (a) 2-methylbutanal (b) 4-methylheptanal (c) 3-phenylpropanal (d) propanal   **15.19** (a) pentanal (b) 3-methylbutanal (c) 3-methylpentanal (d) 2-ethyl-3-methylpentanal

15.21 (a)
                        CH₃   O
CH₃—CH₂—CH—CH₂—C—H

(b)
                                        O
CH₃—CH₂—CH₂—CH₂—CH—C—H
                            CH₂
                            CH₃

(c)
            Cl O
CH₃—C—C—H
            Cl

(d)
                                    OH   CH₃ O
CH₃—CH₂—CH₂—CH₂—CH—CH₂—CH—C—H

15.23 (a) butanal (b) 2-methylbutanal (c) 3-methylpentanal (d) 2-methypropanal
15.25 (a) O (b) O
H—C—H   CH₃—CH₂—C—H

(c) O   (d) O
[benzene C—H with Cl]   [benzene C—H with CH₃ CH₃]

15.27 (a) propionaldehyde (b) propionaldehyde (c) dichloroacetaldehyde (d) *o*-chlorobenzaldehyde   **15.29** (a) aldehyde (b) alkene, aldehyde (c) alcohol (d) alcohol, aldehyde   **15.31** (a) 2-butanone (b) 2,4,5-trimethyl-3-hexanone (c) 6-methyl-3-heptanone

(d) 1,1-dichloro-2-butanone   **15.33** (a) 2-hexanone (b) 5-methyl-3-hexanone (c) 2-pentanone (d) 4-ethyl-3-methyl-2-hexanone
15.35 (a) cyclohexanone (b) 3-methylcyclohexanone (c) 2-methylcyclohexanone (d) 3-chlorocyclopentanone
15.37
(a)   O   CH₃   (b)   O
CH₃—C—CH—CH₂—CH₃   CH₃—CH₂—C—CH₂—CH₂—CH₃
(c) O   (d) Cl   O
[cyclobutanone]   CH₂—C—CH₃

15.39 (a) 2-butanone (b) 3-methyl-2-butanone (c) 3-methyl-2-pentanone (d) 2-methyl-3-pentanone
15.41 (a)   CH₃ O   (b) Cl   O
CH₃—CH—C—CH₂—CH₂—CH₃   CH₂—C—CH₃
(c) O   (d)   O
CH₃—C—[benzene]   CH₃—C—[benzene]

15.43 (a) ketone (b) aldehyde (c) ketone, aldehyde (d) alkene, ketone
15.45 (a) ketone (b) aldehyde (c) aldehyde (d) aldehyde
15.47 (a) $C_4H_{10}O$ (b) C_4H_8O (c) C_4H_8O (d) $C_4H_6O_2$ **15.49** (a) heptanal (b) 2-heptanone, 3-heptanone, 4-heptanone   **15.51** (a) 1 aldehyde, no ketones (b) 1 aldehyde, 1 ketone   **15.53** $x = 2, 4, 5$
15.55
            O   O   O
C—C—C—C—C—H, C—C—C—C—H, C—C—C—C—H,
                                C   C

  C O   O   O   O
C—C—C—H, C—C—C—C—C, C—C—C—C, C—C—C—C—C
  C   C

15.57 formaldehyde is an irritating gas at room temperature; formalin is an aqueous solution containing 37% formaldehyde by mass
15.59 a colorless, volatile liquid that is miscible with both water and nonpolar solvents; its main use is as a solvent   **15.61** (a) 1, 0 (b) 0, 1 (c) 0, 3 (d) 0, 2   **15.63** (a) gas (b) liquid (c) liquid (d) liquid
15.65 (a) pentanal (b) pentanal   **15.67** (a) 2-pentanol (b) 2-pentanone   **15.69** (a) zero (b) two
15.71
(a)   O   (b)   O
CH₃—CH₂—CH₂—CH₂—C—H   CH₃—CH₂—C—CH₃
(c)   CH₃   O   (d)
CH₃—C—CH₂—C—H   [cyclohexanone CH₂ ... O]
        CH₃

15.73
(a) CH₃—CH₂—CH—CH₂—CH₃ (b) [benzene]—CH₂—CH—CH₃
                    OH   OH

(c) CH₃—CH₂—OH   (d) CH₃—CH₂—CH₂—CH₂—CH—CH₂
                                            CH₃—CH₂ OH

15.75
        O   CH₃   O   O
(a) CH₃—C—OH (b) CH₃—CH₂—CH—CH₂—C—OH (c) H—C—OH

        Cl   Cl   O
(d) CH₃—CH₂—CH—CH—CH₂—C—OH

15.77

(a) CH₃—CH₂—CH₂—C(=O)—OH (b) no reaction occurs

(c) CH₃—CH₂—CH(CH₃)—CH₂—C(=O)—OH (b) no reaction occurs

15.79 (a) Ag (b) no reaction occurs (c) Cu₂O (d) no reaction occurs
15.81 (a) no (b) yes (c) yes (d) no
15.83

(a) CH₃—CH₂—CH₂—CH₂(OH) (b) CH₃—CH₂—CH(OH)—CH₂—CH₃

(c) CH₃—CH(CH₃)—CH₂—CH₂(OH) (d) CH₃—CH(CH₃)—CH(OH)—CH₂—CH₂—CH₃

15.85 (a) pentanal, 2-pentanol (b) pentanal (c) pentanal (d) pentanal, 2-pentanone **15.87** (a) ethanal (b) butanone (c) propanal (d) benzaldehyde **15.89** R—O— and H— **15.91** (a) no (b) yes (c) yes (d) no **15.93** (a) C₂ (b) C₁

15.95
(a) CH₃—CH(OH)—O—CH₂—CH₃ (b) CH₃—C(OH)(O—CH₃)—CH₂—CH₂—CH₃

(c) CH₃—CH₂—CH₂—CH(OH)(O—CH₂—CH₃)

(d) CH₃—C(OH)(O—CH(CH₃)—CH₃)—CH₃

15.97
(a) CH₃—CH₂—CH₂—CH(OH)(O—CH₂—CH₃)

(b) CH₃—CH₂—C(=O)—H

(c) CH₃—CH₂—C(OH)(O—CH₃)—CH₃

(d) CH₂OH (pyranose ring with —OH, —OH, —O— and —OH)

15.99 (a) yes (b) yes (c) no (d) yes **15.101** (a) C₂ (b) C₁
15.103
(a) CH₃—OH (b) CH₃—CH(OH)—O—CH₃

(c) CH₃—CH₂—CH(O—CH(CH₃)—CH₃)—O—CH₃ (d) CH₃—CH(OH)—O—CH₃, CH₃—OH

15.105
(a) CH₃—C(=O)—H, 2 CH₃—OH (b) CH₃—C(=O)—CH₃, 2 CH₃—OH

(c) CH₃—CH₂—C(=O)—CH₂—CH₃, CH₃—OH, CH₃—CH₂—OH

(d) CH₃—CH₂—CH₂—CH₂—C(=O)—H, 2 CH₃—OH

15.107 (a) dimethyl acetal of ethanal (b) dimethyl acetal of propanone (c) ethyl methyl acetal of 3-pentanone (d) dimethyl acetal of pentanal **15.109** (a) methanol, propanal (b) methanol, propanal (c) methanol, 2-methylpropanal (d) methanol, ethanol, propanal
15.111 (a) CH₃—CH₂—CH₂—CH₂—CH₂—OH

(b) CH₃—CH₂—CH₂—CH₂—CH—O—CH₂—CH₃

(c) CH₃—CH₂—CH₂—CH₂—CH(O—CH₃)—O—CH₃

(d) CH₃—CH₂—CH₂—CH₂—C(=O)—OH

15.113
(a) CH₃—CH₂—CH—O—CH₂—CH₃ (with OH) (b) CH₃—C(OH)(CH₃)—O—CH₂—CH₃

(c) CH₃—CH₂—CH(O—CH₃)—O—CH₃ (d) CH₃—C(O—CH₃)₃

15.115 thiocarbonyl compound

15.117 (a) H—C(=S)—H (b) H—C(=S)—H

(c) CH₃—C(=S)—CH₃ (d) CH₃—C(=S)—CH₃

Chapter 16 **16.1** (a) yes (b) no (c) no (d) yes **16.3** (a) yes (b) no (c) no (d) yes

16.5 (a) R—C(=O)—O—R (b) R—C(=O)—Cl (c) R—C(=O)—NH₂

(d) R—C(=O)—O—C(=O)—R

16.7 (a) polar (b) nonpolar (c) polar (d) polar **16.9** (a) acyl (b) carbonyl (c) acyl (d) acyl **16.11** (a) carbonyl, acyl (b) carboxyl, carbonyl, acyl (c) carbonyl, acyl (d) carbonyl, acyl **16.13** (a) butanoic acid (b) 2-methylpropanoic acid (c) 2-ethylbutanoic acid (d) propanoic acid **16.15** (a) pentanoic acid (b) 3-methylbutanoic acid (c) 2-methylbutanoic acid (d) 4-methylhexanoic acid
16.17 (a) CH₃—CH₂—CH(CH₂CH₃)—C(=O)—OH

(b) CH₃—CH(CH₃)—CH₂—CH₂—CH(CH₃)—C(=O)—OH

(c) CH₃—CH(CH₃)—C(=O)—OH (d) Cl—CH(Cl)—C(=O)—OH

16.19 (a) propanedioic acid (b) 3-methylpentanedioic acid (c) 2-chlorobenzoic acid (d) 2-chlorocyclopentanecarboxylic acid
16.21
(a) CH₃—CH₂—C(CH₃)₂—C(=O)—OH

(b) HO—C(=O)—C(CH₃)₂—CH₂—C(=O)—OH

(c) HO—C(=O)—C(CH₃)(CH₃)—CH₂—CH₂—C(=O)—OH

(d) cyclohexane with COOH and two methyl groups

16.23 (a) valeric acid (b) acetic acid (c) glutaric acid (d) oxalic acid
16.25 (a) 1 (b) 6 (c) 4 (d) 3

16.27 (a) CH₃—(CH₂)₃—C(=O)—OH (b) CH₃—C(=O)—OH

(c) $\underset{\text{HO}}{}-\overset{\overset{\text{O}}{\|}}{\text{C}}-(CH_2)_3-\overset{\overset{\text{O}}{\|}}{\text{C}}-\text{OH}$ (d) $\text{HO}-\overset{\overset{\text{O}}{\|}}{\text{C}}-\overset{\overset{\text{O}}{\|}}{\text{C}}-\text{OH}$

16.29 (a) $CH_3-CH_2-\underset{\underset{\text{Cl}}{|}}{\text{CH}}-\text{COOH}$ (b) $CH_3-\underset{\underset{\text{Cl}}{|}}{\text{CH}}-CH_2-\text{COOH}$

(c) $\text{HOOC}-\underset{\underset{\text{Cl}}{|}}{\text{CH}}-CH_2-\text{COOH}$ (d) $\text{HOOC}-\underset{\underset{\text{Cl}}{|}}{\text{CH}}-\underset{\underset{\text{Cl}}{|}}{\text{CH}}-\text{COOH}$

16.31 (a) carbon–carbon double bond (b) hydroxyl group
(c) carbon–carbon double bond (d) hydroxyl group
16.33 (a) propenoic acid (b) 2-hydroxypropanoic acid
(c) *cis*-butenedioic acid (d) 2-hydroxyethanoic acid
16.35 (a) $CH_3-CH_2-\overset{\overset{\text{O}}{\|}}{\text{C}}-CH_2-\overset{\overset{\text{O}}{\|}}{\text{C}}-\text{OH}$

(b) $CH_3-CH_2-\underset{\underset{\text{OH}}{|}}{\text{CH}}-\overset{\overset{\text{O}}{\|}}{\text{C}}-\text{OH}$

(c) $\underset{CH_3}{}\underset{\diagdown}{}\text{CH}{=}\text{CH}\underset{\diagdown}{}CH_2-CH_2-\overset{\overset{\text{O}}{\|}}{\text{C}}-\text{OH}$

(d) $\text{HO}-\overset{\overset{\text{O}}{\|}}{\text{C}}-\underset{\underset{\text{OH}}{|}}{\text{CH}}-\underset{\underset{\text{OH}}{|}}{\text{CH}}-CH_2-\overset{\overset{\text{O}}{\|}}{\text{C}}-\text{OH}$

16.37 (a) unsaturated, monocarboxylic (b) unsaturated, dicarboxylic (c) dicarboxylic (d) monocarboxylic **16.39** (a) liquid (b) solid (c) liquid (d) solid **16.41** (a) 2 (b) 5 **16.43** (a) solid (b) solid (c) liquid (d) solid
16.45 (a) $CH_3-\overset{\overset{\text{O}}{\|}}{\text{C}}-\text{OH}$ (b) $CH_3-\overset{\overset{\text{O}}{\|}}{\text{C}}-\text{OH}$

(c) $CH_3-CH_2-\underset{\underset{\text{CH}_3}{|}}{\text{CH}}-CH_2-\overset{\overset{\text{O}}{\|}}{\text{C}}-\text{OH}$ (d) $\underset{\bigcirc}{}\overset{\overset{\text{O}}{\|}}{\text{C}}-\text{OH}$

16.47 (a) 1 (b) 3 (c) 2 (d) 2 **16.49** (a) –1 (b) –3 (c) –2 (d) –2
16.51 (a) pentanoate ion (b) citrate ion (c) succinate ion (d) oxalate ion
16.53
(a) $CH_3-\overset{\overset{\text{O}}{\|}}{\text{C}}-\text{OH} + H_2O \rightarrow H_3O^+ + CH_3-\overset{\overset{\text{O}}{\|}}{\text{C}}-\text{O}^-$

(b) $\text{HO}-\overset{\overset{\text{O}}{\|}}{\text{C}}-CH_2-\underset{\underset{\underset{\text{O}}{\|}}{\overset{}{\text{C}}-\text{OH}}}{\overset{\overset{\text{OH}}{|}}{\text{C}}}-CH_2-\overset{\overset{\text{O}}{\|}}{\text{C}}-\text{OH} + 3H_2O \rightarrow$

$3H_3O^+ + {}^-\text{O}-\overset{\overset{\text{O}}{\|}}{\text{C}}-CH_2-\underset{\underset{\underset{\text{O}}{\|}}{\overset{}{\text{C}}-\text{O}^-}}{\overset{\overset{\text{OH}}{|}}{\text{C}}}-CH_2-\overset{\overset{\text{O}}{\|}}{\text{C}}-\text{O}^-$

(c) $CH_3-\overset{\overset{\text{O}}{\|}}{\text{C}}-\text{OH} + H_2O \rightarrow H_3O^+ + CH_3-\overset{\overset{\text{O}}{\|}}{\text{C}}-\text{O}^-$

(d) $CH_3-CH_2-\underset{\underset{\text{CH}_3}{|}}{\text{CH}}-\overset{\overset{\text{O}}{\|}}{\text{C}}-\text{OH} + H_2O \rightarrow$

$H_3O^+ + CH_3-CH_2-\underset{\underset{\text{CH}_3}{|}}{\text{CH}}-\overset{\overset{\text{O}}{\|}}{\text{C}}-\text{O}^-$

16.55 (a) $CH_3-CH_2-\overset{\overset{\text{O}}{\|}}{\text{C}}-\text{O}^-$ (b) $CH_3-CH_2-\overset{\overset{\text{O}}{\|}}{\text{C}}-\text{O}^-\text{Na}^+$

(c) $CH_3-\overset{\overset{\text{O}}{\|}}{\text{C}}-\text{O}^-$ (d) $CH_3-\overset{\overset{\text{O}}{\|}}{\text{C}}-\text{O}^-\text{Na}^+$

16.57 (a) potassium ethanoate (b) calcium propanoate (c) potassium butanedioate (d) sodium pentanoate **16.59** (a) potassium acetate
(b) calcium propionate (c) potassium succinate (d) sodium valerate
16.61
(a) $CH_3-\overset{\overset{\text{O}}{\|}}{\text{C}}-\text{OH} + KOH \rightarrow CH_3-\overset{\overset{\text{O}}{\|}}{\text{C}}-\text{O}^-\,K^+ + H_2O$

(b) $2\,CH_3-CH_2-\overset{\overset{\text{O}}{\|}}{\text{C}}-\text{OH} + Ca(OH)_2 \rightarrow$

$\left(CH_3-CH_2-\overset{\overset{\text{O}}{\|}}{\text{C}}-\text{O}^-\right)_2 Ca^{2+} + 2H_2O$

(c) $\text{HO}-\overset{\overset{\text{O}}{\|}}{\text{C}}-CH_2-CH_2-\overset{\overset{\text{O}}{\|}}{\text{C}}-\text{OH} + 2KOH \rightarrow$

$K^+\,{}^-\text{O}-\overset{\overset{\text{O}}{\|}}{\text{C}}-CH_2-CH_2-\overset{\overset{\text{O}}{\|}}{\text{C}}-\text{O}^-\,K^+ + 2H_2O$

(d) $CH_3-CH_2-CH_2-CH_2-\overset{\overset{\text{O}}{\|}}{\text{C}}-\text{OH} + NaOH \rightarrow$

$CH_3-CH_2-CH_2-CH_2-\overset{\overset{\text{O}}{\|}}{\text{C}}-\text{O}^-\,Na^+ + H_2O$

16.63
(a) $CH_3-CH_2-CH_2-\overset{\overset{\text{O}}{\|}}{\text{C}}-\text{O}^-\,Na^+ + HCl \rightarrow$

$CH_3-CH_2-CH_2-\overset{\overset{\text{O}}{\|}}{\text{C}}-\text{OH} + NaCl$

(b) $K^+\,{}^-\text{O}-\overset{\overset{\text{O}}{\|}}{\text{C}}-\overset{\overset{\text{O}}{\|}}{\text{C}}-\text{O}^-\,K^+ + 2HCl \rightarrow$

$\text{HO}-\overset{\overset{\text{O}}{\|}}{\text{C}}-\overset{\overset{\text{O}}{\|}}{\text{C}}-\text{OH} + 2KCl$

(c) $\left({}^-\text{O}-\overset{\overset{\text{O}}{\|}}{\text{C}}-CH_2-\overset{\overset{\text{O}}{\|}}{\text{C}}-\text{O}^-\right)_2 Ca^{2+} + 2HCl \rightarrow$

$\text{HO}-\overset{\overset{\text{O}}{\|}}{\text{C}}-CH_2-\overset{\overset{\text{O}}{\|}}{\text{C}}-\text{OH} + CaCl_2$

(d) $\underset{\bigcirc}{}\overset{\overset{\text{O}}{\|}}{\text{C}}-\text{O}^-\,Na^+ + HCl \rightarrow \underset{\bigcirc}{}\overset{\overset{\text{O}}{\|}}{\text{C}}-\text{OH} + NaCl$

16.65 a compound used as a food preservative **16.67** (a) benzoic acid (b) sorbic acid (c) sorbic acid (d) propionic acid
16.69 (a) monocarboxylic acid salt (b) dicarboxylic acid salt
(c) dicarboxylic acid salt (d) monocarboxylic acid salt
16.71 (a) two (b) three (c) two (d) three **16.73** CO_2

16.75 (a) $CH_3-CH_2-CH_2-CH_3$ (b) $CH_3-CH_2-\overset{\overset{\text{O}}{\|}}{\text{C}}-CH_3$
16.77 (a) two oxygen atoms (b) two carbon atoms **16.79** (a) yes
(b) yes (c) no (d) yes **16.81** (a) carboxylic acid (b) ester
(c) carboxylic acid salt (d) carboxylic acid
16.83

(a) $CH_3-CH_2-\overset{\overset{\text{O}}{\|}}{\text{C}}-\text{O}-CH_2-CH_3$ (b) $CH_3-CH_2-\overset{\overset{\text{O}}{\|}}{\text{C}}-\text{O}-CH_3$

(c) $CH_3-CH_2-\overset{\overset{\displaystyle O}{\|}}{C}-O-CH_2-\overset{\overset{\displaystyle CH_3}{|}}{CH}-CH_3$

(d) $CH_3-CH_2-\overset{\overset{\displaystyle O}{\|}}{C}-O-\overset{\overset{\displaystyle CH_2-CH_3}{|}}{CH}-CH_2-CH_3$

16.85

(a) $CH_3-CH_2-\overset{\overset{\displaystyle O}{\|}}{C}-OH;\ CH_3-CH_2-OH$

(b) $CH_3-CH_2-CH_2-\overset{\overset{\displaystyle O}{\|}}{C}-OH;\ CH_3-OH$

(c) $CH_3-\overset{\overset{\displaystyle O}{\|}}{C}-OH;$ (benzene ring)—OH

(d) (benzene ring)—$\overset{\overset{\displaystyle O}{\|}}{C}-OH;\ CH_3-OH$

16.87 a cyclic ester; intermolecular esterification of a hydroxyacid

16.89 (a) ethyl propanoate (b) propyl ethanoate (c) ethyl propanoate (d) butyl methanoate **16.91** (a) ethyl propionate (b) propyl acetate (c) ethyl propionate (d) butyl formate **16.93** (a) ethyl butanoate (b) propyl pentanoate (c) methyl 3-methylpentanoate (d) ethyl propanoate

16.95

(a) $H-\overset{\overset{\displaystyle O}{\|}}{C}-O-CH_3$

(b) (benzene ring)—$CH_2-\overset{\overset{\displaystyle O}{\|}}{C}-O-CH_2-CH_3$

(c) $CH_3-\overset{\overset{\displaystyle O}{\|}}{C}-O-\overset{\overset{\displaystyle CH_3}{|}}{CH}-CH_3$

(d) $CH_3-\overset{\overset{\displaystyle O}{\|}}{C}-O-CH_2-\overset{\overset{\displaystyle Br}{|}}{CH}-CH_3$

16.97 (a) ethyl ethanoate (b) methyl ethanoate (c) ethyl butanoate (d) 1-methylpropyl hexanoate **16.99** (a) ester (b) carboxylic acid salt (c) ester (d) ester **16.101** (a) five (b) four (c) five (d) six **16.103** (a) raspberry (b) banana (c) apple **16.105** acid part is the same; alcohol part is methyl (apple) versus ethyl (pineapple) **16.107** the —OH group of salicylic acid has been esterified (methyl ester) in aspirin **16.109** Different species are involved (plant and animal). **16.111** pentanoic acid, 2-methylbutanoic acid, 3-methylbutanoic acid, 2,2-dimethylpropanoic acid **16.113** methyl pentanoate, methyl 2-methylbutanoate, methyl 3-methylbutanoate methyl 2,2-dimethylpropanoate **16.115** nine (methyl butanoate, methyl 2-methylpropanoate, ethyl propanoate, propyl ethanoate, isopropyl ethanoate, butyl methanoate, *sec*-butyl methanoate, isobutyl methanoate, *tert*-butyl methanoate)

16.117

$CH_3-CH_2-\overset{\overset{\displaystyle O}{\|}}{C}-OH,\ CH_3-\overset{\overset{\displaystyle O}{\|}}{C}-O-CH_3,\ H-\overset{\overset{\displaystyle O}{\|}}{C}-O-CH_2-CH_3$

16.119 $C_nH_{2n}O_2$ **16.121** (a) zero (b) four **16.123** (a) liquid (b) liquid (c) liquid (d) liquid

16.125

(a) $CH_3-CH_2-\overset{\overset{\displaystyle O}{\|}}{C}-OH,\ CH_3-OH$

(b) $CH_3-\overset{\overset{\displaystyle CH_3}{|}}{CH}-\overset{\overset{\displaystyle O}{\|}}{C}-OH,\ CH_3-CH_2-CH_2-OH$

(c) $CH_3-CH_2-CH_2-\overset{\overset{\displaystyle O}{\|}}{C}-OH,$ (benzene ring)—OH

(d) (benzene ring)—$\overset{\overset{\displaystyle O}{\|}}{C}-OH,\ CH_3-OH$

16.127

(a) $CH_3-CH_2-\overset{\overset{\displaystyle O}{\|}}{C}-O^-Na^+,\ CH_3-OH$

(b) $CH_3-\overset{\overset{\displaystyle CH_3}{|}}{CH}-\overset{\overset{\displaystyle O}{\|}}{C}-O^-Na^+,\ CH_3-CH_2-CH_2-OH$

(c) $CH_3-CH_2-CH_2-\overset{\overset{\displaystyle O}{\|}}{C}-O^-Na^+,$ (benzene ring)—OH

(d) (benzene ring)—$\overset{\overset{\displaystyle O}{\|}}{C}-O^-Na^+,\ CH_3-OH$

16.129 (a) methanol, butanoic acid (b) methanol, ethanoic acid (c) 2-propanol, propanoic acid (d) 2-propanol, ethanoic acid **16.131** (a) ethanol, butanoic acid (b) 1-propanol, pentanoic acid (c) methanol, 3-methylpentanoic acid (d) ethanol, propanoic acid

16.133

(a) $CH_3-\overset{\overset{\displaystyle CH_3}{|}}{CH}-\overset{\overset{\displaystyle O}{\|}}{C}-OH;\ CH_3-CH_2-OH$

(b) $CH_3-\overset{\overset{\displaystyle CH_3}{|}}{CH}-\overset{\overset{\displaystyle O}{\|}}{C}-O^-\ Na^+;\ CH_3-CH_2-OH$

(c) $H-\overset{\overset{\displaystyle O}{\|}}{C}-OH;\ CH_3-CH_2-CH_2-CH_2-OH$

(d) $CH_3-\overset{\overset{\displaystyle O}{\|}}{C}-O^-\ Na^+;\ CH_3-\overset{\overset{\displaystyle CH_3}{|}}{CH}-\overset{\overset{\displaystyle CH_3}{|}}{CH}-CH_2-OH$

16.135

(a) $CH_3-\overset{\overset{\displaystyle O}{\|}}{C}-S-CH_2-CH_3$

(b) $CH_3-(CH_2)_8-\overset{\overset{\displaystyle O}{\|}}{C}-S-CH_3$

(c) (benzene ring)—$\overset{\overset{\displaystyle O}{\|}}{C}-S-\overset{\overset{\displaystyle CH_3}{|}}{CH}-CH_3$

(d) $H-\overset{\overset{\displaystyle O}{\|}}{C}-S-CH_2-CH_2-CH_3$

16.137

(a) $CH_3-\overset{\overset{\displaystyle O}{\|}}{C}-S-CH_3$ (b) same as part a.

(c) $H-\overset{\overset{\displaystyle O}{\|}}{C}-S-CH_2-CH_3$ (d) same as part c.

16.139 $-\overset{\overset{\displaystyle O}{\|}}{C}-\overset{\overset{\displaystyle O}{\|}}{C}-O-(CH_2)_3-O-\overset{\overset{\displaystyle O}{\|}}{C}-\overset{\overset{\displaystyle O}{\|}}{C}-O-(CH_2)_3-O-$

16.141 $HO-\overset{\overset{\displaystyle O}{\|}}{C}-CH_2-CH_2-\overset{\overset{\displaystyle O}{\|}}{C}-OH;\ HO-CH_2-CH_2-CH_2-OH$

16.143 ethylene glycol and terephthalic acid

16.145

(a) $CH_3-CH_2-\overset{\overset{\displaystyle O}{\|}}{C}-Cl$ (b) $CH_3-\overset{\overset{\displaystyle CH_3}{|}}{CH}-CH_2-\overset{\overset{\displaystyle O}{\|}}{C}-Cl$

(c) $CH_3-CH_2-CH_2-\overset{\overset{\displaystyle O}{\|}}{C}-O-\overset{\overset{\displaystyle O}{\|}}{C}-CH_2-CH_2-CH_3$

(d) $CH_3-CH_2-CH_2-\overset{\overset{\displaystyle O}{\|}}{C}-O-\overset{\overset{\displaystyle O}{\|}}{C}-CH_3$

16.147 (a) ethanoic propanoic anhydride (b) pentanoyl chloride (c) 2,3-dimethylbutanoyl chloride (d) methanoic propanoic anhydride

16.149 (a)

$$CH_3-CH_2-CH_2-CH_2-\overset{\overset{\displaystyle O}{\|}}{C}-OH$$

(b) $CH_3-CH_2-CH_2-CH_2-\overset{\overset{\displaystyle O}{\|}}{C}-OH$

16.151 (a)

$$CH_3-\overset{\overset{\displaystyle O}{\|}}{C}-OH, \quad CH_3-\overset{\overset{\displaystyle O}{\|}}{C}-O-CH_2-CH_3$$

(b)

$$CH_3-\overset{\overset{\displaystyle O}{\|}}{C}-OH, \quad CH_3-\overset{\overset{\displaystyle O}{\|}}{C}-O-CH_2-CH_2-CH_2-CH_3$$

16.153 (a) propanoyl group (b) butanoyl group (c) butanoyl group (d) ethanoyl group   **16.155** an ester and HCl

16.157

(a) $HO-\overset{\overset{\displaystyle O}{\|}}{\underset{\underset{\displaystyle OH}{|}}{P}}-O-CH_3$

(b) $HO-\overset{\overset{\displaystyle O}{\|}}{\underset{\underset{\displaystyle O-CH_3}{|}}{P}}-O-CH_3$

(c) $O=N-O-CH_3$

(d) $O=N-O-CH_2-CH_2-O-N=O$

16.159 (a) $R-O-\overset{\overset{\displaystyle O}{\|}}{\underset{\underset{\displaystyle OH}{|}}{P}}-OH$

(b) $R-O-\overset{\overset{\displaystyle O}{\|}}{\underset{\underset{\displaystyle O^-}{|}}{P}}-O^-$

(c) $HO-\overset{\overset{\displaystyle O}{\|}}{\underset{\underset{\displaystyle OH}{|}}{P}}-O-\overset{\overset{\displaystyle O}{\|}}{\underset{\underset{\displaystyle OH}{|}}{P}}-O-\overset{\overset{\displaystyle O}{\|}}{\underset{\underset{\displaystyle OH}{|}}{P}}-OH$

(d) $^-O-\overset{\overset{\displaystyle O}{\|}}{\underset{\underset{\displaystyle O^-}{|}}{P}}-O-\overset{\overset{\displaystyle O}{\|}}{\underset{\underset{\displaystyle O^-}{|}}{P}}-O-\overset{\overset{\displaystyle O}{\|}}{\underset{\underset{\displaystyle O^-}{|}}{P}}-O^-$

16.161 $-PO_3^{2-}$ group

16.163

$$CH_3-O-\overset{\overset{\displaystyle O}{\|}}{\underset{\underset{\displaystyle O^-}{|}}{P}}-O^-, \quad CH_3-CH_2-O-\overset{\overset{\displaystyle O}{\|}}{\underset{\underset{\displaystyle O^-}{|}}{P}}-O^-$$

Chapter 17   **17.1** 3 (N), 2 (O), and 4 (C)   **17.3** (a) one (b) two (c) three   **17.5** (a) one (b) one (c) one   **17.7** (a) yes (b) yes (c) no (d) yes   **17.9** (a) amino group (b) monosubstituted amino group (c) not an amine (d) disubstituted amino group   **17.11** (a) 1° (b) 1° (c) 2° (d) 3°   **17.13** (a) 2° (b) 3° (c) 3° (d) 1°   **17.15** (a) ethylmethylamine (b) propylamine (c) diethylmethylamine (d) isopropylmethylamine   **17.17** (a) 3-pentanamine (b) 2-methyl-3-pentanamine (c) N-methyl-3-pentanamine (d) 2,3-butanediamine   **17.19** (a) 1-propanamine (b) N-ethyl-N-methylethanamine (c) N-methyl-1-propanamine (d) N-methyl-2-butanamine   **17.21** (a) 2-bromoaniline (b) N-isopropylaniline (c) N-ethyl-N-methylaniline (d) N-methyl-N-phenylaniline

17.23 (a)

$$CH_3-\overset{\overset{\displaystyle NH_2}{|}}{\underset{\underset{\displaystyle CH_3}{|}}{C}}-CH_2-CH_3$$

(b) $H_2N-CH_2-CH_2-CH_2-CH_2-CH_2-CH_2-NH_2$

(c)

$$CH_3-\overset{\overset{\displaystyle NH_2}{|}}{CH}-\overset{\overset{\displaystyle O}{\|}}{C}-CH_2-CH_3$$

(d)

$$CH_3-\overset{\underset{\underset{\displaystyle NH_2}{|}}{}}{CH}-\overset{\overset{\displaystyle O}{\|}}{C}-OH$$

17.25 (a) 2° amine (b) 1° amine (c) 2° amine (d) 1° amine   **17.27** (a) no (b) yes (c) yes (d) no   **17.29** (a) four (b) two (c) two (d) three   **17.31** 1-pentamine, 2-pentamine, 3-pentamine, 2-methyl-1-butanamine, 3-methyl-1-butanamine, 2-methyl-2-butanamine, 3-methyl-2-butanamine, 2,2-dimethyl-1-propanamine   **17.33** (a) liquid (b) gas (c) gas (d) liquid   **17.35** (a) 3 (b) 3   **17.37** Hydrogen bonding is possible for the amine.   **17.39** (a) $CH_3-CH_2-NH_2$; it has fewer carbon atoms. (b) $H_2N-CH_2-CH_2-CH_2-NH_2$; it has two amino groups rather than one.

17.41 (a) $CH_3-CH_2-\overset{+}{N}H_3$ (b) OH^-
(c) $CH_3-\overset{\overset{}{}}{\underset{\underset{\displaystyle CH_3}{|}}{CH}}-NH-CH_3$
(d) $CH_3-CH_2-\overset{+}{N}H_2-CH_2-CH_3$; OH^-

17.43 (a) dimethylammonium ion (b) triethylammonium ion (c) N,N-diethylanilinium ion (d) N-isopropylanilinium ion

17.45 (a) $CH_3-NH-CH_3$

(b) $CH_3-CH_2-\overset{\underset{\underset{\displaystyle CH_2-CH_3}{|}}{}}{N}-CH_2-CH_3$

(c) $CH_3-CH_2-\overset{\overset{}{}}{\underset{\underset{\displaystyle \bigcirc}{|}}{N}}-CH_2-CH_3$

(d) $\underset{\bigcirc}{NH}-\overset{\underset{\underset{\displaystyle CH_3}{}}{}}{CH}-CH_3$

17.47

$$C-C-C-\overset{+}{N}H_2-C, \quad C-\overset{}{C}-\overset{+}{N}H_2-C, \quad C-C-\overset{+}{N}H_2-\underset{\underset{\displaystyle C}{|}}{C}-C$$

17.49

(a) $CH_3-CH_2-\overset{+}{N}H_3\ Cl^-$ (b) $\underset{\bigcirc}{}-\overset{+}{N}H_3\ Cl^-$ (c) $CH_3-\overset{\overset{\displaystyle CH_3}{|}}{CH}-\overset{+}{N}H_3\ Cl^-$

(d) $CH_3-CH_2-\overset{+}{N}H_2-CH_2-CH_3\ Cl^-$

17.51 (a) $CH_3-CH_2-NH_2$ (b) $CH_3-NH-CH_2-CH_3$

(c) $\underset{\bigcirc}{}-NH-CH_3$ (d) $CH_3-\overset{\overset{\displaystyle CH_3}{|}}{CH}-NH_2$

17.53 (a) $CH_3-\overset{+}{\underset{\underset{\displaystyle CH_3}{|}}{N}}H-CH_3\ Cl^-$ (b) HCl

(c) $\underset{\bigcirc}{}-\overset{\underset{\underset{\displaystyle CH_3}{|}}{}}{N}-CH_3$, NaBr (d) $CH_3-\overset{\overset{\displaystyle CH_3}{|}}{\underset{\underset{\displaystyle CH_3}{|}}{C}}-NH_2$

17.55 (a) propylammonium chloride (b) methylpropylammonium chloride (c) ethyldimethylammonium bromide (d) N,N-dimethylanilinium bromide   **17.57** (a) 1-propanamine (b) N-methyl-1-propanamine (c) N,N-dimethylethanamine (d) N,N-dimethylphenylamine   **17.59** (a) free amine, free base, deprotonated base (b) free amine, free base, deprotonated base (c) protonated base (d) protonated base   **17.61** (a) yes (b) yes (c) yes (d) yes   **17.63** (a) 1° amine (b) 3° amine (c) 2° amine (d) 1° amine

17.65 (a) $CH_3—CH_2—CH_2—NH_2$, NaCl, H_2O

(b) $CH_3—\underset{\underset{CH_3}{|}}{\overset{\overset{CH_3}{|}}{CH}}—N—CH_3$, NaBr, H_2O

(c) $CH_3—CH_2—NH—CH_2—CH_3$, NaCl, H_2O

(d) $CH_3—\underset{\underset{CH_3}{|}}{\overset{\overset{CH_3}{|}}{C}}—NH_2$, NaBr, H_2O

17.67 ethylmethylamine and propyl chloride, ethylpropylamine and methyl chloride, methylpropylamine and ethyl chloride

17.69 (a)
$CH_3—\underset{\underset{CH_3}{|}}{\overset{\overset{CH_3}{|}}{N^+}}—CH_2—CH_3$ Br^-

(b)
$CH_3—\underset{\underset{CH_3}{|}}{CH}—\overset{\overset{CH_3}{|}}{N}—CH—CH_3$ with CH_3

(c)
$CH_3—CH_2—\underset{\underset{CH_3}{|}}{\overset{\overset{CH_3}{|}}{N^+}}—CH_2—CH_2—CH_3$ Cl^-

(d) $CH_3—CH_2—NH—CH_2—CH_3$

17.71 (a) amine salt (b) quaternary ammonium salt (c) amine salt (d) quaternary ammonium salt **17.73** (a) yes (b) no (c) yes (d) no **17.75** (a) trimethylammonium bromide (b) tetramethylammonium chloride (c) ethylmethylammonium bromide (d) diethyldimethylammonium chloride **17.77** (a) yes (b) yes (c) no (d) yes **17.79** (a) saturated (b) unsaturated (c) unsaturated (d) unsaturated, fused **17.81** no difference **17.83** (a) true (b) true (c) false (d) false **17.85** (a) phenethylamine (b) phenethylamine (c) phenethylamine (d) tryptamine **17.87** (a) neurotransmitter (b) central nervous system stimulant (c) decongestant (d) central nervous system stimulant **17.89** (a) yes (b) yes (c) yes (d) yes **17.91** (a) true (b) true (c) false (d) false **17.93** (a) hydroxy, methoxy (b) two hydroxy (c) methoxy, keto (d) methoxy, hydroxy **17.95** (a) one (b) three (c) two **17.97** (a) one (b) one (c) one **17.99** (a) yes (b) yes (c) no (d) yes **17.101** (a) monosubstituted (b) disubstituted (c) unsubstituted (d) monosubstituted **17.103** (a) secondary amide (b) tertiary amide (c) primary amide (d) secondary amide **17.105** (a) amide (b) amine (c) amine (d) amine and amide **17.107** (a) N-ethylethanamide (b) N,N-dimethylpropanamide (c) butanamide (d) 2-chloropropanamide **17.109** (a) N-ethylacetamide (b) N,N-dimethyl-propionamide (c) butyramide (d) α-chloropropionamide **17.111** (a) propanamide (b) N-methylpropanamide (c) 3,5-dimethylhexanamide (d) N,N-dimethylbutanamide

17.113 (a)
$CH_3—\overset{\overset{O}{||}}{C}—\underset{\underset{CH_3}{|}}{N}—CH_3$

(b)
$CH_3—CH_2—\underset{\underset{CH_3}{|}}{CH}—\overset{\overset{O}{||}}{C}—NH_2$

(c)
$CH_3—\underset{\underset{CH_3}{|}}{CH}—CH_2—\overset{\overset{O}{||}}{C}—NH—CH_3$

(d)
$H—\overset{\overset{O}{||}}{C}—NH_2$

17.115 (a) hexanamide (b) 1-hexanamine (c) 5-aminopentanamide (d) 2,5-dimethyl-1,6-hexanediamine **17.117** (a) true (b) false (c) true (d) true **17.119** inhibition of insect olfactory receptors **17.121** draws N lone pair of electrons closer to the N atom **17.123** (a) no, an amide (b) yes, an amine (c) no, an amide (d) yes, an amine **17.125** (a) liquid (b) solid (c) solid (d) solid **17.127** (a) 4 (b) 4 **17.129** (a) yes (b) yes (c) yes (d) yes **17.131** (a) 1° amide (b) 2° amide (c) 3° amide (d) 3° amide

17.133 (a) $CH_3—\overset{\overset{O}{||}}{C}—OH$ (b) $H—\overset{\overset{O}{||}}{C}—OH$

(c) $CH_3—CH_2—\overset{\overset{O}{||}}{C}—OH$ (d) $CH_3—CH_2—\overset{\overset{O}{||}}{C}—OH$

17.135 (a) NH_3 (b) $CH_3—NH_2$ (c) $CH_3—NH—CH_3$ (d) $CH_3—NH_2$

17.137 (a) $CH_3—NH_2$ (b)
$CH_3—\underset{\underset{CH_3}{|}}{\overset{\overset{CH_3}{|}}{C}}—\overset{\overset{O}{||}}{C}—\underset{\underset{CH_3}{|}}{N}—CH_3$
(c) NH_3

(d)
benzene ring$—\overset{\overset{O}{||}}{C}—OH$

17.139 (a) $CH_3—\overset{\overset{O}{||}}{C}—OH$ (b) $H—\overset{\overset{O}{||}}{C}—OH$

(c) $CH_3—CH_2—\overset{\overset{O}{||}}{C}—OH$ (d) $CH_3—CH_2—\overset{\overset{O}{||}}{C}—OH$

17.141 (a) $CH_3—\overset{\overset{O}{||}}{C}—O^-Na^+$ (b) $H—\overset{\overset{O}{||}}{C}—O^-Na^+$

(c) $CH_3—CH_2—\overset{\overset{O}{||}}{C}—O^-Na^+$ (d) $CH_3—CH_2—\overset{\overset{O}{||}}{C}—O^-Na^+$

17.143 (a) $NH_4^+\ Cl^-$ (b) $CH_3—\overset{+}{N}H_3\ Cl^-$

(c) $CH_3—\overset{+}{N}H_2—CH_3\ Cl^-$ (d) $CH_3—\overset{+}{N}H_3\ Cl^-$

17.145 (a) NH_3 (b) $CH_3—NH_2$ (c) $CH_3—NH—CH_3$ (d) $CH_3—NH_2$

17.147 (a)
$CH_3—CH_2—CH_2—\overset{\overset{O}{||}}{C}—OH$, $CH_3—NH_2$

(b)
$CH_3—CH_2—CH_2—\overset{\overset{O}{||}}{C}—OH$, $CH_3—\overset{+}{N}H_3\ Cl^-$

(c)
$CH_3—CH_2—CH_2—\overset{\overset{O}{||}}{C}—O^-\ Na^+$, $CH_3—NH_2$

(d)
benzene ring$—\overset{\overset{O}{||}}{C}—OH$, benzene ring$—NH—CH_3$

17.149 diacid and diamine

17.151
$$\left(—\overset{\overset{O}{||}}{C}—CH_2—CH_2—\overset{\overset{O}{||}}{C}—\underset{\underset{H}{|}}{N}—CH_2—CH_2—CH_2—CH_2—\overset{\overset{H}{|}}{N}—\right)_n$$

17.153
$$R—\underset{\underset{H}{|}}{N}—\overset{\overset{O}{||}}{C}—O—R$$

Chapter 18 **18.1** (a) false (b) true **18.3** (a) water (b) lipids (c) inorganic salts (d) proteins **18.5** (a) true (b) true (c) false (d) true **18.7** (a) three (b) three to ten **18.9** (a) monosaccharide (b) monosaccharide **18.11** (a) false (b) false **18.13** Superimposable objects have parts that coincide exactly at all points when the objects are laid upon each other. **18.15** (a) no (b) no (c) yes (d) yes **18.17** (a) no chiral center (b)
$CH_2—\overset{*}{C}—\overset{*}{CH}$ with Cl, Cl on top and Br, Br, Br below

(c)
$CH_2—\overset{*}{CH}—\overset{*}{CH}—\overset{*}{CH}—\overset{\overset{O}{||}}{C}—H$ with OH, OH, OH, OH below

(d) $CH_2—\overset{*}{CH}—\overset{*}{CH}—\overset{*}{CH}—\overset{*}{CH}—CH_2$ with OH, OH, OH, OH, OH, OH below

18.19 (a) zero (b) two (c) zero (d) zero **18.21** (a) no (b) yes (c) yes (d) no **18.23** (a) yes (b) no (c) no (d) yes **18.25** (a) no (b) yes (c) yes (d) no **18.27** (a) no (b) yes (c) yes (d) no **18.29** Constitutional isomers have a different connectivity of atoms. Stereoisomers have the same connectivity of atoms with different arrangements of the atoms in space. **18.31** the presence of a chiral center and the presence of "structural rigidity" **18.33** (a) true (b) true (c) false (d) false
18.35

18.39 (a) D enantiomer (b) D enantiomer (c) L enantiomer (d) L enantiomer **18.41** (a) diastereomers (b) neither enantiomers nor diastereomers (c) enantiomers (d) diastereomers **18.43** (a) yes (b) no (c) no (d) yes **18.45** (a) 3, 3 (b) 2, 2 (c) 4, 4 (d) 2, 2 **18.47** (a) different (b) same (c) same (d) same **18.49** (a) same (b) different (c) same (d) different **18.51** (a) aldose (b) ketose (c) ketose (d) ketose **18.53** (a) aldohexose (b) ketohexose (c) ketotriose (d) ketotetrose **18.55** (a) D-galactose (b) D-psicose (c) dihydroxyacetone (d) L-erythrulose **18.57** (a) 4 (b) 3 (c) 0 (d) 1 **18.59** (a) carbon 4 (b) carbons 1 and 2 (c) carbons 1 and 2 (d) carbon 2 **18.61** (a) aldoses, hexoses, aldohexoses (b) hexoses (c) hexoses (d) aldoses

18.63

18.65 (a) D-fructose (b) D-glucose (c) D-galactose **18.67** (a) 6 (b) 5 (c) 5 (d) 4 **18.69** (a) 1 (b) 1 (c) 2 (d) 1 **18.71** (a) 1 (b) 1
18.73

18.75 α-anomer **18.77** The cyclic and noncyclic forms interconvert; an equilibrium exists between the forms.

18.79 (a) (b)

18.81 (a) α-D-monosaccharide (b) α-D-monosaccharide (c) β-D-monosaccharide (d) α-D-monosaccharide
18.83 (a) (b) (c) (d)

18.85 (a) C-4 (b) C-4 (c) C-4 (d) C-5 **18.87** (a) C-1 (b) C-1 (c) C-1 (d) C-2 **18.89** (a) hexose (b) hexose (c) hexose (d) hexose **18.91** (a) α-D-glucose (b) α-D-galactose (c) β-D-mannose (d) α-D-sorbose
18.93 (a) (b) (c) (d)

18.95
(a) (b) (c) (d)

18.97 (a) acidic sugar (b) acidic sugar (c) acidic sugar (d) sugar alcohol **18.99** (a) galactonic acid (b) galacturonic acid (c) galactaric acid (d) galactitol **18.101** (a) reducing sugar (b) reducing sugar (c) reducing sugar (d) reducing sugar **18.103** (a) yes (b) yes (c) yes (d) yes **18.105** (a) alpha (b) beta (c) alpha (d) beta **18.107** (a) methyl alcohol (b) ethyl alcohol (c) ethyl alcohol (d) methyl alcohol **18.109** (a) methyl-α-D-alloside (b) ethyl-β-D-altroside (c) ethyl-α-D-fructoside (d) methyl-β-D-glucoside
18.111
(a) (b)

18.113 (a)

CH₂OH / OH / OH NH₂ (structures)

(b)

CH₂OH / OH / OH NH / C=O / CH₃ (structures)

18.115 (a) yes (b) yes (c) yes (d) yes **18.117** (a) yes (b) no (c) no (d) no **18.119** (a) yes (b) yes (c) yes (d) no **18.121** (a) no (b) yes (c) yes (d) yes **18.123** (a) one acetal and one hemiacetal (b) one acetal and one hemiacetal (c) one acetal and one hemiacetal (d) one acetal and one hemiacetal **18.125** (a) alpha (b) beta (c) alpha (d) beta **18.127** (a) reducing sugar (b) reducing sugar (c) reducing sugar (d) reducing sugar

18.129 (a)

(structures with CH₂OH, OH groups)

(b)

(structures)

(c)

(structures)

(d)

(structures)

18.131 (a) α(1→6) (b) β(1→4) (c) α(1→4) (d) α(1→4)

18.133

CH₂OH / OH / OH / OH / CH₂OH / O / OH / OH / OH (structure)

18.135 (a) monosaccharide, reducing sugar, anomers, aldohexose (b) disaccharide (c) monosaccharide, reducing sugar, enantiomers (d) reducing sugar **18.137** (a) 3 (b) 3 (c) 2 (d) 2 **18.139** (a) no (b) no (c) yes (d) yes **18.141** (a) α(1 → 4) (b) none (c) α(1 → 6), α,β(1 → 2) (d) none **18.143** They are two names for the same thing. **18.145** less than 100 monomer units up to a million monomer units

18.147 (a) correct (b) incorrect (c) incorrect (d) correct **18.149** (a) no difference (b) no difference (c) glycogen has more branching (d) glycogen has more units **18.151** (a) correct (b) incorrect (c) incorrect (d) correct **18.153** (a) to neither (b) to cellulose only (c) to neither (d) to both **18.155** (a) amylopectin, amylose, glycogen (b) amylose, cellulose, chitin (c) amylose, cellulose, chitin (d) chitin **18.157** (a) true (b) false (c) true (d) true **18.159** (a) homopolysaccharide (b) homopolysaccharide, branched polysaccharide (c) homopolysaccharide, unbranched polysaccharide (d) heteropolysaccharide, unbranched polysaccharide **18.161** (a) storage (b) non (c) acidic (d) structural **18.163** (a) amylose, cellulose, chitin, heparin (b) amylopectin, glycogen (c) hyaluronic acid (d) amylose, heparin **18.165** (a) yes (b) yes (c) no (d) no **18.167** A refined sugar has been separated from its plant source whereas a natural sugar has not. **18.169** a lipid molecule that has a carbohydrate molecule covalently bonded to it **18.171** interaction between the carbohydrate unit of one cell and a protein imbedded in the cell membrane of another cell

Chapter 19 **19.1** (a) false (b) true **19.3** (a) insoluble (b) soluble (c) insoluble (d) soluble **19.5** (a) energy storage (b) emulsification (c) membrane (d) messenger **19.7** (a) long-chain (b) short-chain (c) long-chain (d) medium-chain **19.9** (a) saturated (b) polyunsaturated (c) polyunsaturated (d) monounsaturated **19.11** monounsaturated fatty acid **19.13** (a) saturated (b) monounsaturated (c) monounsaturated (d) polyunsaturated **19.15** (a) does not apply (b) omega-7 (c) omega-9 (d) omega-6 **19.17** CH₃—(CH₂)₄—CH═ CH—CH₂—CH═CH—(CH₂)₇—COOH **19.19** (a) tetradecanoic acid (b) *cis*-9-hexadecenoic acid **19.21** as carbon chain length increases melting point increases **19.23** a bend in the carbon chain **19.25** (a) 18:1 acid (b) 18:3 acid (c) 14:0 acid (d) 18:1 acid **19.27** a glycerol molecule and three fatty acid molecules **19.29** (a) 3 (b) 1 (c) ester (d) 3

19.31

19.33

S L
L S
L L

S S
S L
L S

19.35 (a) palmitic, myristic, oleic (b) oleic, palmitic, palmitoleic **19.37** (a) fat (b) substance is a solid at room temperature **19.39** (a) 3, 0, 2, 0 (b) 3, 0, 1, 0 **19.41** (a) not correct (b) not correct **19.43** (a) correct (b) not correct **19.45** (a) nonessential fatty acid (b) essential fatty acid (c) nonessential fatty acid (d) nonessential fatty acid **19.47** (a) 0, 0, 1, 1 (b) 0, 0, 2, 3 **19.49** (a) glycerol, 3 fatty acids (b) monoacylglycerol, 2 fatty acids (c) diacylglycerol, fatty acid **19.51** (a) complete hydrolysis (b) partial hydrolysis (c) partial hydrolysis

19.53 CH₂—CH—CH₂
             | | |
             OH OH OH

CH₃—(CH₂)₁₂—COOH

CH₃—(CH₂)₁₄—COOH

CH₃—(CH₂)₇—CH═CH—(CH₂)₇—COOH

19.55

CH₂—CH—CH₂
| | |
OH OH OH

CH_3—$(CH_2)_{12}$—COO^- Na^+

CH_3—$(CH_2)_{14}$—COO^- Na^+

CH_3—$(CH_2)_7$—CH═CH—$(CH_2)_7$—COO^- Na^+

19.57 Carbon–carbon double bond(s) must be present. **19.59** six
19.61 (a)

—18:0		—18:0		—18:1
—18:0		—18:1		—18:0
—16:1		—16:0		—16:0

(b)

—18:0		—18:0		—18:0
—18:1A		—18:1B		—18:0
—16:0		—16:0		—16:1

There are two possibilities for converting the 18:2 acid to 18:1 acid depending on which double bond is hydrogenated (denoted as 18:1A and 18:1B). **19.63** Rancidity results from hydrolysis of ester linkages and oxidation of carbon–carbon double bonds. **19.65** (a) hydrogenation (b) hydrolysis, oxidation (c) hydrogenation (d) hydrolysis, saponification **19.67** (a) two (b) three or four (c) two (d) three or four **19.69** (a) B, C (b) E (c) 1, 2, 3, 4 (d) 3, 4 **19.71** fatty acid, glycerol, and phosphate subunits **19.73** (a) false (b) true (c) true (d) true **19.75** (a) tails (b) head (c) head **19.77** (a) true (b) true (c) false (d) true **19.79** (a) B (b) C (c) 1 (d) 1, 2 **19.81** choline **19.83** (a) phosphate and amino alcohol (b) fatty acid and carbon chain of sphingosine **19.85** (a) triacylglycerol, sphingophospholipid (b) triacylglycerol, glycerophospholipid (c) glycerophospholipid, sphingophospholipid (d) triacylglycerol **19.87** (a) none apply (b) glycerophospholipid (c) sphingophospholipid (d) none apply **19.89** (a) B (b) C (c) 1 (d) 2 **19.91** (a) (1) (b) (2) (c) (3) (d) (3) **19.93** (a) glycerophospholipid, sphingophospholipid, sphingoglycolipid (b) glycerophospholipid, sphingophospholipid, sphingoglycolipid (c) sphingophospholipid, sphingoglycolipid (d) glycerophospholipid, sphingophospholipid, sphingoglycolipid **19.95** (a) true (b) false (c) true (d) false **19.97** (a) 3 (b) 0 (c) 1 (d) 2 **19.99** Swiss cheese, fish fillet, chicken, liver **19.101** "Good cholesterol" is that present in HDLs, and "bad cholesterol" is that present in LDLs. **19.103** head and two tail structure **19.105** (a) false (b) true (c) false (d) false **19.107** creates "open" areas in the bilayer **19.109** a membrane protein that penetrates the interior of the lipid bilayer (cell membrane) **19.111** Protein help is required in facilitated transport but not in passive transport. **19.113** (a) active transport (b) facilitated transport (c) active transport (d) passive transport and facilitated transport **19.115** A substance that can disperse and stabilize water-insoluble substances as colloidal particles in an aqueous solution. **19.117** (a) false (b) true (c) true (d) false **19.119** (a) false (b) false (c) false (d) true **19.121** (a) 6 (b) 3 (c) 5 (d) 4 **19.123** amino-acid-bearing carbon chain **19.125** bile fluid **19.127** gall bladder **19.129** (a) emulsification lipid (b) membrane lipid (c) energy-storage lipid (d) membrane lipid **19.131** (a) true (b) false (c) false (d) false **19.133** (a) natural (b) synthetic (c) natural (d) synthetic **19.135** (a) adrenocorticoid hormone (b) sex hormone (c) adrenocorticoid hormone (d) sex hormone **19.137** (a) control Na^+/K^+ ion balance in cells and body fluids (b) responsible for secondary male characteristics (c) controls glucose metabolism and is an anti-inflammatory agent (d) responsible for secondary female characteristics
19.139

19.141 Prostaglandins have a bond between carbons 8 and 12 that creates a cyclopentane ring structural feature. **19.143** a prostaglandin is similar to a leukotriene but has a cyclopentane ring formed by a bond between C8 and C12 **19.145** (a) steroid nucleus-based (b) glycerol-based (c) fatty acid-based (d) fatty-acid based **19.147** (a) emulsification lipid (b) membrane lipid (c) messenger lipid (d) membrane lipid **19.149** long-chain alcohol – long-chain fatty acid
19.151 mixture of esters involving a long-chain fatty acid and a long-chain alcohol versus a long-chain alkane mixture **19.153** (a) bile acid (b) biological wax, sphingophospholipid (c) biological wax, sphingophospholipid (d) sphingophospholipid **19.155** (a) yes (b) no (c) yes (d) yes **19.157** (a) ester linkage (b) ester linkage (c) none apply (d) none apply **19.159** (a) yes (b) no (c) no (d) no **19.161** (a) 0 (b) 3 (c) 0 (d) 1

Chapter 20 **20.1** amino acids **20.3** 15% by mass **20.5** Both the amino group and the carboxyl group are attached to the α-carbon atom **20.7** (a) yes (b) no **20.9** (a) 1 (b) 4 (c) 3 (d) 0 **20.11** (a) cysteine, Cys (b) lysine, Lys (c) valine, Val (d) glycine, Gly **20.13** (a) polar neutral (b) polar basic (c) nonpolar (d) nonpolar **20.15** (a) hydrophilic (b) hydrophilic (c) hydrophobic (d) hydrophobic **20.17** (a) alanine, valine, leucine, isoleucine, proline, phenylalanine (b) aspartic acid, glutamic acid (c) asparagines, glutamine (d) serine, threonine, asparagine, glutamine, tyrosine, aspartic acid, glutamic acid **20.19** isoleucine, tryptophan, asparagine, glutamine **20.21** (a) l, l (b) 1, 2 **20.23** The side chain covalently bonds to the amino acid's amino group, producing a cyclic structure. **20.25** (a) yes (b) yes (c) yes (d) no **20.27** (a) yes (b) no (c) no (d) yes **20.29** (a) no (b) yes (c) yes (d) no **20.31** (a) no (b) no (c) no (d) no **20.33** (a) lysine (b) methionine, tryptophan (c) none (d) methionine **20.35** L family
20.37 (a)   COOH (b)   COOH

H_2N——H   H——NH_2

     CH_2 CH_2

     OH   OH

(c)   COOH (d)   COOH

H——NH_2 H_2N——H

   CH_3 CH_2

             CH—CH_3

             CH_3

20.39 (a) D- (b) nonpolar (c) essential (d) standard **20.41** They exist as zwitterions.
20.43 (a)   H (b)   H

H_3N^+——COO^- H_3N^+——COO^-

    CH_2 CH—CH_3

    CH—CH_3 CH_2

    CH_3 CH_3

(c)   H (d)   H

H_3N^+——COO^- H_3N^+——COO^-

    CH_2 H

    SH

20.45 (a)

$$H_3\overset{+}{N}-\overset{\overset{\displaystyle H}{|}}{\underset{\underset{\displaystyle OH}{|}}{\underset{\displaystyle CH_2}{|}}}-COO^-$$

(b)

$$H_3\overset{+}{N}-\overset{\overset{\displaystyle H}{|}}{\underset{\underset{\displaystyle OH}{|}}{\underset{\displaystyle CH_2}{|}}}-COOH$$

(c)

$$H_2N-\overset{\overset{\displaystyle H}{|}}{\underset{\underset{\displaystyle OH}{|}}{\underset{\displaystyle CH_2}{|}}}-COO^-$$

(d)

$$H_3\overset{+}{N}-\overset{\overset{\displaystyle H}{|}}{\underset{\underset{\displaystyle OH}{|}}{\underset{\displaystyle CH_2}{|}}}-COOH$$

20.47 the pH at which zwitterion concentration in a solution is maximized **20.49** Two —COOH groups are present, which deprotonate at different pH values. **20.51** (a) +1 (b) +2 (c) +1 (d) +1 **20.53** They react with each other to produce a covalent disulfide bond. **20.55** —COOH and —NH$_2$ **20.57** (a) Gly (b) Cys (c) 2 (d) 2

20.59

$$-NH-\overset{\displaystyle H}{\underset{\underset{\displaystyle R}{|}}{\overset{|}{C}}}-\overset{\overset{\displaystyle O}{\|}}{C}-NH-\overset{\overset{\displaystyle H}{|}}{\underset{\underset{\displaystyle R}{|}}{C}}-\overset{\overset{\displaystyle O}{\|}}{C}-NH-\overset{\overset{\displaystyle H}{|}}{\underset{\underset{\displaystyle R}{|}}{C}}-\overset{\overset{\displaystyle O}{\|}}{C}-$$

20.61

$$H_3\overset{+}{N}-\overset{\overset{\displaystyle H}{}}{\underset{\underset{\underset{\displaystyle CH_3}{|}}{\displaystyle CH-CH_3}}{|}}-\overset{\overset{\displaystyle O}{\|}}{C}-NH-\overset{\underset{\underset{\displaystyle OH}{|}}{\displaystyle CH_2}}{\underset{}{}}-\overset{\overset{\displaystyle O}{\|}}{C}-NH-\overset{\underset{\underset{\displaystyle SH}{|}}{\displaystyle CH_2}}{\underset{}{}}-COO^-$$

20.63 (a) Ser–Ala–Cys (b) Asp–Thr–Asn **20.65** (a) serylcysteine (b) glycylalanylvaline (c) tyrosylaspartylglutamine (d) leucyllysyltryptophylmethionine

20.67 (a)

$$H_3\overset{+}{N}-\overset{\overset{\displaystyle H}{|}}{\underset{\underset{}{}}{C}}-\overset{\overset{\displaystyle O}{\|}}{C}-NH-\overset{\underset{\underset{\displaystyle CH_3}{|}}{}}{C}-COO^-$$

(b)

$$H_3\overset{+}{N}-\overset{\underset{\underset{\displaystyle SH}{|}}{\displaystyle CH_2}}{C}-\overset{\overset{\displaystyle O}{\|}}{C}-NH-\overset{\underset{\underset{\displaystyle CH_3}{|}}{}}{C}-\overset{\overset{\displaystyle O}{\|}}{C}-NH-\overset{\underset{\underset{\displaystyle H}{|}}{}}{C}-COO^-$$

20.69 (a) none (b) Ala, Val, Gly (c) Ala, Val, Gly (d) Val **20.71** (a) Tyr-Leu-Ile (b) two (c) Tyr (d) none **20.73** Ser is the N-terminal end of Ser–Cys and Cys is the N-terminal end of Cys–Ser. **20.75** Ser–Val–Gly, Val–Ser–Gly, Gly–Ser–Val, Ser–Gly–Val, Val–Gly–Ser, Gly–Val–Ser **20.77** (a) Both are nonapeptides with six of the residues held in the form of a loop by a disulfide bond. (b) They differ in the identity of the amino acid present at two positions in the nonapeptide. **20.79** They bind at the same sites. **20.81** Glu is bonded to Cys through the side-chain carboxyl group rather than through the α-carbon carboxyl group. **20.83** Monomeric proteins contain a single peptide chain and multimeric proteins have two or more peptide chains. **20.85** (a) true (b) false (c) true (d) true **20.87** the order in which the amino acids are bonded to each other **20.89** (a) 6 (b) 12 **20.91** (a) 160,000; (20 × 20 × 20 × 20) (b) 2,280; 6(20 × 1 × 19 × 1)

20.93

$$-\overset{\displaystyle }{\underset{\underset{}{|}}{C}}H-\overset{\overset{\displaystyle O}{\|}}{C}-NH-\overset{\underset{}{|}}{C}H-\overset{\overset{\displaystyle O}{\|}}{C}-NH-\overset{\underset{}{|}}{C}H-$$

20.95 (a) a helix (coiled spring) (b) extend outward from the coil **20.97** (a) false (b) true (c) false (d) false **20.99** an arrangement other than α helix or β pleated sheet **20.101** disulfide bonds, electrostatic interactions, hydrogen bonds, and hydrophobic interactions **20.103** (a) nonpolar (b) polar neutral R groups (c) —SH groups

(d) acidic and basic R groups **20.105** (a) hydrophobic (b) electrostatic (c) disulfide bond (d) hydrogen bonding **20.107** (a) tertiary (b) secondary, tertiary (c) secondary (d) primary **20.109** the organization among the various peptide chains in a multimeric protein **20.111** They are the same. **20.113** Ala and Val **20.115** Ala, Val, Ala–Ala, and Ala–Val **20.117** five: Ala–Gly–Ser, Gly–Ser–Tyr, Ala–Gly, Gly–Ser, Ser–Tyr **20.119** Ala–Gly–Met–His–Val–Arg **20.121**

(a)

$$H_3\overset{+}{N}-\overset{\underset{\underset{\displaystyle CH_3}{|}}{}}{C}H-COOH, \quad H_3\overset{+}{N}-\overset{\underset{\underset{\displaystyle H}{|}}{}}{C}H-COOH, \quad H_3\overset{+}{N}-\overset{\underset{\underset{\underset{\displaystyle OH}{|}}{\displaystyle CH_2}}{|}}{C}H-COOH$$

(b)

$$H_2N-\overset{\underset{\underset{\displaystyle CH_3}{|}}{}}{C}H-COO^-, \quad H_2N-\overset{\underset{\underset{\displaystyle H}{|}}{}}{C}H-COO^-, \quad H_2N-\overset{\underset{\underset{\underset{\displaystyle OH}{|}}{\displaystyle CH_2}}{|}}{C}H-COO^-$$

20.123 secondary, tertiary, and quaternary **20.125** same primary structure **20.127** (a) yes (b) yes (c) no (d) yes **20.129** (a) fibrous: generally water-insoluble; globular: generally water-soluble (b) fibrous: support and external protection; globular: involvement in metabolic reactions **20.131** (a) fibrous (b) fibrous (c) globular (d) globular **20.133** (a) contractile protein (b) storage protein (c) transport protein (d) messenger protein **20.135** catalytic protein **20.137** 4-hydroxyproline and 5-hydroxylysine **20.139** They are involved with cross-linking. **20.141** An antigen is a substance foreign to the human body, and an antibody is a substance that defends against an invading antigen. **20.143** four polypeptide chains that have constant and variable amino acid regions; two chains are longer than the other two; 1%–12% carbohydrates present; long and short chains are connected through disulfide linkages **20.145** a spherical structure with an inner core of lipid material surrounded by a shell of phospholipids, cholesterol, and proteins **20.147** chylomicrons, very-low-density lipoproteins, low-density lipoproteins, and high-density lipoproteins **20.149** the lipid/protein mass ratio **20.151** (a) transport dietary triacylglycerols from the intestine to various locations (b) transport cholesterol from the liver to cells throughout the body

Chapter 21 **21.1** catalyst **21.3** larger molecular size, activity regulated by other substances **21.5** (a) conjugated (b) conjugated (c) simple (d) conjugated **21.7** A cofactor can be inorganic or organic. A coenzyme must be organic. **21.9** (a) true (b) false (c) true (d) true **21.11** (a) no (a) yes (c) yes (d) yes **21.13** (a) add a carboxylate group to pyruvate (b) remove H$_2$ from an alcohol (c) reduce an L-amino acid (d) hydrolyze maltose **21.15** (a) pyruvate (b) an alcohol (c) an L-amino acid (d) maltose **21.17** (a) sucrase (or sucrose hydrolase) (b) pyruvate decarboxylase (c) glucose isomerase (d) lactate dehydrogenase **21.19** (a) yes (b) yes (c) no (d) yes **21.21** (a) isomerase (b) lyase (c) transferase (d) hydrolase **21.23** (a) decarboxylase (b) lipase (c) phosphatase (d) dehydrogenase **21.25** (a) false (b) false (c) false (d) false **21.27** (a) neither (b) lock-and-key (c) lock-and-key (d) induced-fit **21.29** interactions with amino acid R groups **21.31** (a) enzyme–substrate complex (b) product of enzyme reaction **21.33** (a) false (b) true (c) false (d) false **21.35** (a) accepts only one substrate (b) accepts substrate with a particular type of bond **21.37** (a) absolute (b) stereochemical **21.39** (a) absolute (b) linkage (c) group (d) stereochemical **21.41** (a) 7.0 (b) 38°C (c) B (d) B **21.43** (a) increases (b) decreases (c) decreases (d) decreases **21.45** (a) decreases (b) decreases **21.47**

21.49 nothing; the rate remains constant   **21.51** (a) decreased rate (b) decreased rate (c) increased rate (d) decreased rate   **21.53** a microorganism that thrives in extreme environments   **21.55** (a) no (b) no (c) yes (d) no   **21.57** those that can withstand a hot-water environment and/or cold-water environment   **21.59** no; only one molecule may occupy the active site at a given time   **21.61** (a) false (b) false (c) true (d) false   **21.63** (a) reversible competitive (b) reversible noncompetitive, irreversible (c) reversible noncompetitive, irreversible (d) reversible noncompetitive   **21.65** (a) true (b) true (c) false (d) true   **21.67** (a) yes (b) no (c) yes (d) no   **21.69** (a) a phosphate group is added (b) a phosphate group is removed   **21.71** it can be either   **21.73** (a) apoenzyme: protein portion of a conjugated enzyme; proenzyme: inactive precursor of an enzyme (b) simple enzyme: contains only protein; allosteric enzyme: contains two or more protein chains and two binding sites   **21.75** (a) decapeptide versus octapeptide (b) inactive form versus active form   **21.77** competitive inhibition of the conversion of PABA to folic acid   **21.79** tissue plasminogen activator, which activates an enzyme that dissolves blood clots   **21.81** (a) lactate dehydrogenase (b) aspartate transaminase   **21.83** (a) indicator of possible heart disease (b) indicator of possible heart disease, liver disease, and muscle damage   **21.85** (a) fat-soluble (b) water-soluble (c) water-soluble (d) water-soluble   **21.87** (a) likely (b) unlikely (c) unlikely (d) unlikely   **21.89** (a) no (b) yes (c) no (d) yes   **21.91** two hydroxyl groups versus two ketone groups; ring double bond versus ring single bond   **21.93** (a) cosubstrate in collagen formation (b) reactivates spent vitamin E (c) reactivates enzymes needed for dopamine synthesis (d) it is reactivated by niacin   **21.95** L-gulonic acid and γ-L-gulonolactone; γ-L-gulonolactone and L-ascorbic acid   **21.97** precursor for enzyme cofactors   **21.99** (a) alternative (b) preferred (c) alternative (d) preferred   **21.101** (a) thiamin, biotin (b) folate, biotin (c) niacin, vitamin B_6, folate (d) riboflavin   **21.103** carboxyl substituent versus amide constituent   **21.105** (a) vitamin B_6 (b) thiamin (c) pantothenic acid (d) niacin   **21.107** (a) carbon dioxide (b) one-carbon group other than CO_2 (c) acyl (d) methyl, hydrogen   **21.109** alcohol, aldehyde, acid   **21.111** Cell differentiation is the process whereby immature cells change in structure and function to become specialized cells. Vitamin A binds to protein receptors in the process.   **21.113** (a) yes (b) no   **21.115** They differ only in the identity of the side chain present.   **21.117** to maintain normal blood levels of calcium and phosphate ion so that bones can absorb these minerals   **21.119** (a) 7-dehydrocholesterol (b) calcidiol   **21.121** alpha form   **21.123** antioxidant effect   **21.125** in the length and degree of unsaturation of the side chain present   **21.127** phylloquinone is an alternate name for vitamin K_1 and menaquinones is an alternate name for the various forms of vitamin K_2 **21.129** (a) no (b) yes (c) no (d) no   **21.131** (a) vitamin C (b) vitamin E (c) vitamin A (d) vitamin C   **21.133** (a) vitamins A, D, E, and K (b) vitamin B_{12} (c) vitamins A, D, E, and K (d) niacin, pantothenic acid, folate, biotin

Chapter 22   **22.1** (a) true (b) false (c) true (d) true   **22.3** (a) no (b) yes (c) yes (d) no   **22.5** (a) pyrimidine (b) purine (c) purine (d) pyrimidine   **22.7** (a) C (b) A (c) G (d) U   **22.9** (a) both (b) both (c) both (d) RNA   **22.11** (a) one (b) four (c) one   **22.13** (a) false (b) false (c) true (d) false   **22.15** (a) adenosine (b) uridine (c) deoxycytidine (d) deoxythymidine   **22.17** (a) false (b) false (c) false (d) false   **22.19** (a) RNA nucleotide (b) DNA nucleotide (c) DNA nucleotide (d) RNA nucleotide   **22.21** The base T is not found in RNA (ribose) nucleotides.   **22.23** (a) adenine, ribose (b) guanine, deoxyribose (c) thymine, deoxyribose (d) uracil, ribose   **22.25** (a) adenosine 5′-monophosphate (b) deoxyguanosine 5′-monophosphate (c) deoxythymidine 5′-monophosphate (d) uridine 5′-monophosphate   **22.27** (a) deoxythymidine 5′-monophosphate

(b) DNA only (c) phosphoester bond (d) β-N-glycosidic bond   **22.29** (a) nucleoside (b) neither nucleoside nor nucleotide (c) nucleotide (d) nucleotide   **22.31** (a) 6 (b) 3 (c) 2 (d) -4 **22.33** G, C, and A are bases found in both DNA and RNA   **22.35** phosphate subunit   **22.37**

22.39 (a) three (b) one (c) two (d) two   **22.41** (a) true (b) false (c) false (d) false   **22.43** (a) no (b) no (c) yes (d) no   **22.45** (a) 36% (b) 14% (c) 14%   **22.47** two double-ring bases are too large to fit in the helix interior   **22.49** the same (19% A, 34% C, 28% G, and 19% T)   **22.51** (a) 5′ GCTA 3′ (b) 5′ ATAA 3′ (c) 5′ ACAC 3′ (d) 5′ CAAC 3′   **22.53** (a) 3′ TGCATA 5′ (b) 3′ AATGGC 5′ (c) 5′ CGTATT 3′ (d) 3′ TTGACC 5′   **22.55** (a) six (b) two (c) six (d) zero   **22.57** (a) 5′ TTACG 3′ (b) 5′ GCATT 3′ (c) 5′ CGTCG 3′ (d) 5′ GCTGC 3′   **22.59** (a) 3′ TGAATC 5′ (b) 3′ TGAATC 5′ (c) 5′ ACTTAG 3′   **22.61** strand growing toward fork is synthesized continuously; strand growing away from fork is synthesized in segments   **22.63** (a) false (b) false (c) false (d) false   **22.65** (a) true (b) false (c) true (d) false   **22.67** A   **22.69** (a) true (b) true (c) false (d) true   **22.71** (a) false (b) false (c) false (d) false   **22.73** (a) transfer (b) messenger (c) ribosomal (d) heterogeneous nuclear   **22.75** (a) nucleus and cytoplasm (b) cytoplasm (c) cytoplasm (d) nucleus   **22.77** (a) nuclear region (b) nuclear region (c) cytoplasmic region (d) nuclear region   **22.79** (a) true (b) false (c) true (d) false   **22.81** (a) 5′ AUAU 3′ (b) 5′ GGGC 3′ (c) 5′ CGAU 3′ (d) 5′ UUUU 3′   **22.83** (a) 5′ ATGCCG 3′ and 5′ AUGCCG 3′ (b) 5′ GGTAAT 3′ and 5′ GGUAAU 3′ (c) 5′ TGTACC 3′ and 5′ UGUACC 3′ (d) 5′ TGCATG 3′ and 5′ UGCAUG 3′   **22.85** (a) 5′ TTAAGG 3′ (b) 5′ GTACGT 3′ (c) 5′ CGTCGT 3′ (d) ATGGTA 3′   **22.87** Exons convey genetic information whereas introns do not.   **22.89** 5′ UACGCAUU 3′   **22.91** 5′ UGAACUGA 3′   **22.93** (a) hnRNA (b) snRNA   **22.95** two (exons 1, 2, 3; exons 1,3)   **22.97** (a) DNA–RNA (b) DNA–DNA (c) DNA–RNA (d) DNA–DNA or DNA–RNA   **22.99** A three-nucleotide sequence in mRNA that codes for a specific amino acid   **22.101** (a) Leu (b) Asn (c) Ser (d) Gly   **22.103** (a) UAA, UAC (b) GCU, GCC, GCA, GCG (c) UUA, UUG, CUU, CUC, CUA, CUG (d) UGU, UGC   **22.105** The base T cannot be present in a codon.   **22.107** Met–Lys–Glu–Asp–Leu   **22.109** Ile–Gln–Lys–Lys–Val   **22.111** (a) 3′ AGGC-GGTA-ATTGT 5′ (b) 5′ TCCG-CCAT-TAACA 3′ (c) 5′ UCCG-UAACA 3′ (d) Ser-Val-Thr   **22.113** (a) false (b) true (c) false (d) false   **22.115** (a) true (b) false (c) false (d) true   **22.117** anticodons written in the 3′-to-5′ direction: (a) UCU (b) ACG (c) AAA (d) UUG   **22.119** (a) Gly (b) Leu (c) Ala (d) Leu   **22.121** (a) Thr (b) Ala (c) Arg (d) Cys   **22.123** (a) 3′ AGGCGUAAUUGU 5′ (b) 3′ AGGCGUAAUUGU 5′ (c) UGU UAA UGC GGA (d) ACA AUU ACG CCU   **22.125** (a) false (b) true (c) true (d) true   **22.127** (a) false (b) true (c) false (d) false   **22.129** Gly: GGU, GGC, GGA or GGG; Ala: GCU, GCC, GCA or GCG; Cys: UGU or UGC; Val: GUU, GUC, GUA or GUG; Tyr: UAU or UAC

22.131 (a) CAA CGA AAG (b) GUU GCU UUC (c) Gln-Arg-Lys
22.133 (a) mRNA (b) hnRNA (c) tRNA (d) mRNA
22.135 (a) Leu–Gln (b) Leu–Gln (c) Leu–Lys (d) Leu–Lys
22.137 (a) Asn–Tyr (b) Asn–Tyr (c) Asn–Ser (d) Lys–Tyr
22.139 Lys–Leu–Ala–(two bases) **22.141** (a) false (b) true (c) false
(d) false **22.143** contains a "foreign" gene **22.145** host for a
"foreign" gene **22.147** Recombinant DNA is incorporated into a
host cell.
22.149 5′

C C A   A G C T T G
                             A C

G G T T C G A
3′   5′

22.151 (a) replication (b) transcription (c) translation (d) recombinant DNA **22.153** (a) true (b) true (c) false (d) false

Chapter 23

23.1 anabolism—synthetic; catabolism—degradative
23.3 a series of consecutive biochemical reactions **23.5** (a) anabolic
(a) anabolic (c) catabolic (a) anabolic **23.7** Prokaryotic cells have
no nucleus, and the DNA is usually a single circular molecule.
Eukaryotic cells have their DNA in a membrane-enclosed nucleus.
23.9 (a) true (b) true (c) false (d) true **23.11** (a) false (b) true (c) true
(d) true **23.13** adenosine triphosphate **23.15** adenine (1), ribose (1),
phosphate (3) **23.17** (a) one (b) one **23.19** (a) three phosphate
groups versus one phosphate group (b) adenine versus guanine
23.21 inorganic phosphate **23.23** ATP + H_2O → ADP + P_i +
H^+ + energy **23.25** flavin adenine dinucleotide

23.27 (a) | flavin |—| ribitol |—| ADP |

(b) | nicotinamide |—| ribose |—| phosphate |

| adenine |—| ribose |—| phosphate |

23.29 (a) nicotinamide (b) riboflavin
23.31 (a) yes (b) yes **23.33** (a) oxidized (b) reduced **23.35** (a) two
riboses, two phosphates, adenine (b) two phosphates, ribose, adenine
23.37 | 2-aminoethanethiol |—| pantothenic acid |—| phosphorylated ADP |
23.39 (a) pantothenic acid (b) 2-aminoethanethiol
23.41 (a) phosphate groups (b) electrons (c) electrons (d) acetyl
groups **23.43** (a) reducing agent (b) neither (c) neither (d) oxidizing
agent **23.45** (a) NAD^+ (b) CoA–SH, FAD, NAD^+ (c) all four
(d) CoA–SH, FAD, NAD^+

23.47 (a) HOOC—C(=O)—CH_2—COOH

(b) ^-OOC—C(=O)—CH_2—COO^-

(c) HOOC—CH_2—C(OH)(COOH)—CH_2—COOH

(d) ^-OOC—CH_2—C(OH)(COO$^-$)—CH_2—COO^-

23.49 (a) malate, oxaloacetate, fumarate (b) oxaloacetate, α-ketoglutarate (c) malate, oxaloacetate, fumarate, α-ketoglutarate (d) malate,
oxaloacetate, fumarate **23.51** a compound with a greater free
energy of hydrolysis than is typical for a compound **23.53** free
monophosphate species **23.55** (a) phosphoenolpyruvate (b) creatine
phosphate (c) 1,3-bisphosphoglycerate (d) AMP **23.57** (a) one
(b) one **23.59** digestion, acetyl group formation, citric acid
cycle, electron transport chain and oxidative phosphorylation
23.61 tricarboxylic acid cycle, Krebs cycle **23.63** oxaloacetate and
acetyl CoA **23.65** matrix **23.67** (a) oxidation (b) hydration

(c) oxidation/decarboxylation (d) isomerization **23.69** (a) 2 (b) 1
(c) 2 (Steps 3, 8) (d) 2 (Steps 2, 7) **23.71** (a) Steps 3, 4, 6, 8 (b) Step 2
(c) Step 7
23.73 succinate (^-OOC—CH_2—CH_2—COO^-);
fumarate (^-OOC—CH=CH—COO^-);
malate [^-OOC—CH_2—CH(OH)—COO^-];
oxaloacetate [^-OOC—CH_2—C(=O)—COO^-]
23.75 (a) C_6 to C_6 (b) C_4 to C_4 (c) C_4 to C_4 (d) C_6 to C_5
23.77 (a) NAD^+ (b) FAD **23.79** (a) isocitrate, α-ketoglutarate
(b) fumarate, malate (c) malate, oxaloacetate (d) citrate, isocitrate
23.81 NADH and $FADH_2$ **23.83** O_2 **23.85** (a) yes (b) no (c) no
(d) no **23.87** (a) oxidized (b) oxidized (c) reduced (d) oxidized
23.89 (a) oxidation (b) reduction (c) oxidation (d) reduction
23.91 (a) I (b) I, II, III (c) III (d) IV **23.93** $CoQH_2$ **23.95** two
23.97 (a) $FADH_2$, 2 Fe(II)SP, $CoQH_2$ (b) $FMNH_2$, 2 Fe^{2+}, $CoQH_2$
23.99 (a) ETC (b) ETC (c) CAC (d) ETC **23.101** CO_2, succinate,
$FADH_2$, FeSP **23.103** (a) neither (b) reduced (c) oxidized (d) both
23.105 ATP synthesis from ADP and P_i using energy from the electron
transport chain **23.107** matrix and intermembrane space
23.109 10 protons **23.111** (a) four (b) zero (c) four (d) two
23.113 ATP synthase **23.115** Coenzymes are oxidized; ADP is
phosphorylated. **23.117** must be moved from matrix back into the
intermembrane space **23.119** (a) 2.5 molecules ATP (b) 1.5 molecules
ATP **23.121** (a) 3,4, and 8 (b) 6 (c) 5 **23.123** 14.5 moles ATP
23.125 reactive oxygen species
23.127 (a) $2O_2$ + NADPH ⟶ $2O_2^-$ + $NADP^+$ + H^+

(b) $2O_2^-$ + $2H^+$ ⟶ H_2O_2 + O_2

23.129 (a) yes (b) no (c) yes (d) no **23.131** (a) no (b) yes (c) no (d) no

Chapter 24

24.1 mouth, salivary α-amylase **24.3** small
intestine, pancreas **24.5** outer membranes of intestinal mucosal
cells, sucrose hydrolysis **24.7** glucose, galactose, fructose
24.9 (a) C_6 (b) C_3 (c) C_3 (d) C_3 **24.11** (a) 1 (b) 1 (c) 1 (d) 1
24.13 (a) step 3 (b) step 10 (c) step 8 (d) step 5 **24.15** (a) phosphorylation using ATP (b) phosphorylation using ATP (c) isomerization (d) phosphorylation of ADP **24.17** (a) two (b) five (c) one
(d) two **24.19** (a) glucose 6-phosphate (b) 2-phosphoglycerate
(c) phosphoglyceromutase (d) ADP **24.21** (a) Step 10 (b) Step 1
(c) Step 8 (d) Step 6 **24.23** glucose 6-phosphate **24.25** they are
the same **24.27** glucose 6-phosphate has no membrane transporter
24.29 cytosol **24.31** (a) glycolysis (b) digestion (c) digestion
(d) glycolysis **24.33** aerobic conditions **24.35** NADH
24.37 mitochondrial matrix **24.39** oxidation of NADH to
NAD^+ **24.41** CO_2 molecule formed **24.43** pyruvate +
CoA–SH + NAD^+ → acetyl CoA + NADH + CO_2 **24.45** (a) acetyl
CoA, ethanol (b) lactate, ethanol (c) acetyl CoA (d) lactate
24.47 (a) pyruvate oxidation, ethanol fermentation (b) pyruvate
oxidation (c) glycolysis (d) all four **24.49** electrons from NADH,
but not NADH itself, are shuttled into mitochondria **24.51** electrons
24.53 30 ATP versus 2 ATP **24.55** (a) 2 (b) 0 **24.57** (a) glucose
6-phosphate (b) glycogen **24.59** (a) both processes (b) glycogenesis
but not glycogenolysis (c) both processes (d) both processes
24.61 (a) true (b) false (c) false (d) false **24.63** (a) phosphorolysis
(b) isomerization **24.65** Glucose 6-phosphate is converted to
glucose in liver cells and used as is in muscle cells. **24.67** as glucose
6-phosphate **24.69** (a) all three (b) glycogenesis (c) glycogenesis
(d) glycolysis **24.71** pyruvate, CO_2, ATP **24.73** gluconeogenesis:
pyruvate, oxaloacetate, phosphoenolpyruvate; glycolysis:
2-phosphoglycerate, phosphoenolpyruvate, pyruvate
24.75 (a) 0 and 2 (b) 3 and 2 **24.77** (a) step 1 (b) step 2
24.79 (a) true (b) false (c) false (d) true

24.81
$$\underset{\overset{|}{CH_3}}{\overset{\overset{COO^-}{|}}{H-C-OH}} + NAD^+ \longrightarrow \underset{\overset{|}{CH_3}}{\overset{\overset{COO^-}{|}}{C=O}} + NADH + H^+$$

24.83 (a) glycolysis but not gluconeogenesis (b) glycolysis but not gluconeogenesis (c) gluconeogenesis but not glycolysis (d) both glycolysis and gluconeogenesis **24.85** (a) both glycolysis and gluconeogenesis (b) both glycolysis and gluconeogenesis (c) both glycolysis and gluconeogenesis (d) both glycolysis and gluconeogenesis **24.87** (a) eight (b) seven (c) seven (d) two
24.89 (a) false (b) false (c) true (d) true **24.91** (a) all four processes (b) glycolysis and gluconeogenesis (c) gluconeogenesis (d) glycogenesis
24.93 (a) glycolysis (b) glycolysis (c) glycogenesis (d) glycolysis
24.95 (a) loss of six (b) loss of two (c) gain of three (d) loss of four
24.97 (a) true (b) false (c) true (d) true **24.99** (a) two (b) three
24.101 Glucose 6-phospate + 2 $NADP^+$ + H_2O → ribulose 5-phosphate + CO_2 + 2 NADPH + $2H^+$ **24.103** CO_2
24.105 (a) Cori cycle, lactate fermentation (b) Cori cycle, lactate fermentation, glycolysis (c) pentose phosphate pathway, Cori cycle, glycolysis (d) pentose phosphate pathway **24.107** increases rate of glycogen synthesis **24.109** increases blood glucose levels
24.111 pancreas **24.113** Epinephrine attaches to cell membrane and stimulates the production of cAMP, which activates glycogen phosphorylase. **24.115** glucagon (liver cells) and epinephrine (muscle cells) **24.117** (a) none (b) none (c) none (d) glycogenolysis

Chapter 25 **25.1** (a) stomach (b) stomach (c) stomach (d) small intestine **25.3** (a) true (b) false (c) true (d) true **25.5** (a) true (b) false (c) false (d) true **25.7** a spherical droplet containing fatty acids/monoacylglycerols and bile **25.9** 3 fatty acids and glycerol
25.11 intestinal cells **25.13** They have a large storage capacity for triacylglycerols. **25.15** hydrolysis of triacylglycerols in adipose tissue; entry of hydrolysis products into bloodstream **25.17** activates hormone-sensitive lipase **25.19** (a) Step 1 (b) Step 1 (c) Step 2 (d) Step 1 **25.21** carbon 3 has an O–Ⓟ group rather than an OH group **25.23** (a) true (b) false (c) true (d) false **25.25** (a) intermembrane space (b) matrix (c) intermembrane space (d) matrix
25.27 FAD **25.29** (a) alkane to alkene (b) alkene to 2° alcohol (c) 2° alcohol to ketone **25.31** *trans* isomer

25.33 (a) $CH_3-(CH_2)_4-\overset{\overset{O}{\|}}{C}-S-CoA$

(b) $CH_3-\underset{\overset{|}{}}{\overset{\overset{OH}{|}}{CH}}-CH_2-\overset{\overset{O}{\|}}{C}-S-CoA$

(c) $CH_3-(CH_2)_4-CH=CH-\overset{\overset{O}{\|}}{C}-S-CoA$

(d) $CH_3-(CH_2)_6-\overset{\overset{O}{\|}}{C}-CH_2-\overset{\overset{O}{\|}}{C}-S-CoA$

25.35 (a) acyl CoA (b) hydroxyacyl CoA (c) ketoacyl CoA (d) ketoacyl CoA **25.37** (a) activation (b) oxidation (c) all three (d) oxidation **25.39** (a) Step 3, turn 2 (b) Step 2, turn 3 (c) Step 4, turn 3 (d) Step 1, turn 2 **25.41** compounds a and d
25.43 (a) 7 turns (b) 5 turns **25.45** A *cis–trans* isomerase converts a *cis* bond to a *trans* bond **25.47** (a) both (b) glycerol metabolism (c) glycerol metabolism (d) fatty acid metabolism **25.49** (a) glucose (b) fatty acids **25.51** (a) 4 turns (b) 5 acetyl CoA (c) 4 NADH (d) 4 $FADH_2$ **25.53** 14 ATP **25.55** 64 ATP **25.57** unsaturated fatty acid produces less $FADH_2$ **25.59** 4 kcal versus 9 kcal
25.61 (1) dietary intakes high in fat and low in carbohydrates, (2) inadequate processing of glucose present, and (3) prolonged fasting
25.63 Ketone body formation occurs when oxaloacetate concentrations are low.

25.65 $CH_3-\overset{\overset{O}{\|}}{C}-CH_2-\overset{\overset{O}{\|}}{C}-O^-$ $\underset{\overset{|}{}}{\overset{\overset{OH}{|}}{CH_3-CH}}-CH_2-\overset{\overset{O}{\|}}{C}-O^-$

$CH_3-\overset{\overset{O}{\|}}{C}-CH_3$

25.67 (a) acetoacetate, acetone (b) β-hydroxybutyrate
(c) acetoacetate (d) acetone **25.69** (a) step 1 (b) step 4 (c) step 3
(d) step 2 **25.71** (a) C_4 (b) C_6 (c) C_4 (d) C_4 **25.73** acetoacetate and succinyl CoA are reactants; acetoacetyl CoA and succinate are products **25.75** accumulation of ketone bodies in blood and urine
25.77 (a) β-oxidation (b) β-oxidation (c) both (d) ketogenesis
25.79 (a) ketogenesis only (b) both (c) β-oxidation only (d) ketogenesis
25.81 (a) false (b) false (c) false (d) false **25.83** (a) false (b) false
(c) true (d) false **25.85** (a) matrix (b) cytosol (c) cytosol (d) cytosol
25.87 (a) malonyl CoA (b) acetyl ACP (c) malonyl CoA (d) acetyl ACP **25.89** (a) Step 2 (b) Step 3 (c) Step 1 (d) Step 4
25.91 (a) acetoacetyl ACP (b) crotonyl ACP (c) crotonyl ACP
(d) acetoacetyl ACP **25.93** (a) condensation (b) hydrogenation
(c) dehydration (d) hydrogenation **25.95** needed to convert saturated fatty acids to unsaturated fatty acids **25.97** (a) 6 turns
(b) 6 malonyl ACP (c) 6 ATP bonds (d) 12 NADPH
25.99 (a) all three (b) lipogenesis (c) β-oxidation (d) β-oxidation
25.101 (a) β-oxidation (b) lipogenesis (c) lipogenesis (d) lipogenesis
25.103 (a) β-oxidation (b) β-oxidation (c) ketogenesis (d) glycerol metabolism **25.105** (a) succinate (b) oxaloacetate (c) malate
(d) fumarate **25.107** (a) unsaturated acid (b) ketoacid (c) ketoacid
(d) hydroxyacid **25.109** (a) produced in multi-step process
(b) produced in one step (c) produced in one step (d) cannot be produced **25.111** (a) mitochondria (b) cytosol (c) mitochondria
(d) mitochondria **25.113** (a) all four (b) no correct response
(c) all four (d) no correct response

Chapter 26 **26.1** (a) stomach (b) small intestine (c) small intestine (d) stomach **26.3** (a) no (b) yes (c) no (d) yes **26.5** (a) false
(b) false (c) true (d) false **26.7** very acidic versus slightly basic **26.9** (a) stomach (b) small intestine (c) stomach (d) small intestine **26.11** (a) hormone (b) digestive enzyme (c) neither
(d) digestive enzyme **26.13** (a) true (b) false (c) true (d) false
26.15 (a) negative (b) positive (c) positive (d) negative
26.17 dietary protein, protein turnover, and biosynthesis of amino acids **26.19** (a) essential (b) nonessential (c) nonessential (d) essential
26.21 (a) cannot (b) can (c) can (d) cannot **26.23** amino acid and keto acid **26.25** (a) no (b) yes (c) no (d) no **26.27** (a) yes (b) no
(c) no (d) yes
26.29

(a) $HO-CH_2-\underset{\overset{|}{NH_3}}{CH}-COO^- + {}^-OOC-CH_2-\overset{\overset{O}{\|}}{C}-COO^- \longrightarrow$

$HO-CH_2-\overset{\overset{O}{\|}}{C}-COO^- + {}^-OOC-CH_2-\underset{\overset{|}{NH_3}}{\overset{\overset{+}{}}{CH}}-COO^-$

(b) $CH_3-\underset{\overset{|}{NH_3}}{\overset{\overset{+}{}}{CH}}-COO^- + {}^-OOC-CH_2-\overset{\overset{O}{\|}}{C}-COO^- \longrightarrow$

$CH_3-\overset{\overset{O}{\|}}{C}-COO^- + {}^-OOC-CH_2-\underset{\overset{|}{NH_3}}{\overset{\overset{+}{}}{CH}}-COO^-$

(c) $H-\underset{\overset{|}{NH_3}}{\overset{\overset{+}{}}{CH}}-COO^- + {}^-OOC-CH_2-CH_2-\overset{\overset{O}{\|}}{C}-COO^- \longrightarrow$

$H-\overset{\overset{O}{\|}}{C}-COO^- + {}^-OOC-CH_2-CH_2-\underset{\overset{|}{NH_3}}{\overset{\overset{+}{}}{CH}}-COO^-$

(d)

$$CH_3-\underset{\underset{CH_3}{|}}{\overset{\overset{+}{N}H_3}{\overset{|}{C}H}}-CH-COO^- + {}^-OOC-CH_2-CH_2-\overset{O}{\overset{||}{C}}-COO^- \longrightarrow$$

$$CH_3-\underset{\underset{CH_3}{|}}{CH}-\overset{O}{\overset{||}{C}}-COO^- + {}^-OOC-CH_2-CH_2-\overset{\overset{+}{N}H_3}{\overset{|}{C}H}-COO^-$$

26.31 (a) yes (b) yes (c) no (d) no   **26.33** (a) no (b) yes (c) no (d) no
26.35 pyruvate, α-ketoglutarate   **26.37** to collect amino groups from many amino acids into one amino acid   **26.39** coenzyme that participates in the amino group transfer   **26.41** (a) NAD$^+$, H$_2$O (b) α-ketoglutarate, NH$_4^+$, NADH, H$^+$ (c) dehydrogenase (d) NH$_4^+$
26.43 (a)

$$^-OOC-CH_2-CH_2-\overset{O}{\overset{||}{C}}-COO^-$$

(b)

$$HS-CH_2-\overset{O}{\overset{||}{C}}-COO^-$$

(c)

$$CH_3-\overset{O}{\overset{||}{C}}-COO^-$$

(d)

$$\langle \text{benzene ring} \rangle-CH_2-\overset{O}{\overset{||}{C}}-COO^-$$

26.45 (a) both (b) both (c) oxidative deamination (d) oxidative deamination   **26.47** aspartate and NH$_4^+$ **26.49** asparate directly and NH$_4^+$ indirectly   **26.51** urea

$$H_2N-\overset{O}{\overset{||}{C}}-NH_2$$

26.53 $H_2N-\overset{O}{\overset{||}{C}}-NH_2$

26.55 the amide functional group, $-\overset{O}{\overset{||}{C}}-NH_2$

26.57 NH$_4^+$, CO$_2$, H$_2$O, ATP   **26.59** aspartate and arginine
26.61 (a) N$_2$ (b) N$_3$ (c) N$_1$ (d) N$_4$ **26.63** (a) citrulline (b) ornithine (c) argininosuccinate (d) carbamoyl phosphate   **26.65** (a) step 2 (b) step 2 (c) step 4 (d) step 4   **26.67** step 1   **26.69** equivalent of 4 ATP   **26.71** goes to the citric acid cycle where it is converted to oxaloacetate, which is then converted to aspartate   **26.73** (a) transamination (b) urea cycle (c) oxidative deamination, urea cycle (d) urea cycle   **26.75** (a) N$_1$ (b) N$_1$ (c) N$_2$ (d) N$_3$
26.77 α-ketoglutarate, succinyl CoA, fumarate, oxaloacetate
26.79 (a) acetoacetyl CoA and acetyl CoA (b) succinyl CoA and acetyl CoA (c) fumarate and oxaloacetate (d) α-ketoglutarate
26.81 (a) ketogenic (b) both (c) glucogenic (d) glucogenic
26.83 Degradation products can be used to make glucose.
26.85 pyruvate, α-ketoglutarate, 3-phosphoglycerate, oxaloacetate, and phenylalanine   **26.87** (a) pyruvate (b) 3-phosphoglycerate (c) 3-phosphoglycerate (d) α-ketoglutarate   **26.89** serine, cysteine, glycine, and alanine   **26.91** hydrolyzed to amino acids   **26.93** In biliverdin the heme ring has been opened and one carbon atom has been lost (as CO).   **26.95** biliverdin, bilirubin, bilirubin diglucuronide, urobilin   **26.97** urobilin   **26.99** excess bilirubin
26.101 (a) biliverdin (b) bilirubin (c) biliverdin (d) stercobilin
26.103 (a) urea cycle (b) oxidative deamination (c) heme degradation (d) oxidative deamination   **26.105** (a) false (b) true (c) false (d) false   **26.107** (a) SO$_4^{2-}$ and ATP (b) APS (c) 3'-phosphoadenosine 5'-phosphate (d) S^{2-} **26.109** fumarate   **26.111** Amino acid carbon skeletons are degraded to acetyl CoA or acetoacetyl CoA; ketogenesis converts these degradation products to ketone bodies.
26.113 converted to body fat stores   **26.115** (a) oxidative deamination, non-CAC intermediates (b) non-CAC intermediates (c) CAC intermediates (d) transamination, CAC intermediates, non-CAC intermediates

Index/Glossary

Absolute alcohol, 427
Absolute specificity, enzymes and, 752
Accutane, 506
ACE, *see Angiotension-converting enzyme*
Acetal An organic compound in which a carbon atom is bonded to two alkoxy groups (—OR), 408
  formation of, from cyclic monosaccharides, 613
  hydrolysis of, 489–490
  nomenclature for, 490
  preparation of, from hemiacetals, 488–489
Acetaminophen
  pharmacology of, 568
  structure of, 568
Acetoacetate
  ketogenesis and, 934
  ketone body formation and, 932
  utilization of, as energy source, 935
Acetoacetyl ACP, lipogenesis and, 939
Acetoacetyl CoA
  amino acid degradation product, 970
  ketogenesis and, 933–934
Acetone
  derivatives of, glycolysis and, 889
  ketone body formation and, 932
  properties of, 476
Acetyl ACP
  formation of, lipogenesis and, 938
  structure of, 938
Acetyl CoA
  amino acid degradation product, 970
  citric acid cycle and, 860–861
  fatty-acid generated, possible fates of, 944
  ketogenesis and, 933
  production of, beta oxidation pathway, 925–926
  pyruvate oxidation and, 896
  thioester structure of, 527–528
Acetyl coenzyme A, *see acetyl CoA*
Acetyl group The portion of an acetic acid molecule (CH₃—COOH) that remains after the —OH group is removed from the carboxyl carbon atom, 852
  coenzyme A as carrier of, 852
Achiral molecule A molecule whose mirror images are superimposable, 585
Acid
  acidic and nonacidic hydrogen atoms within, 272
  aldaric, 612
  aldonic, 611
  alduronic, 612
  Arrhenius, 265–266
  Brønsted-Lowry, 267–271
  carboxylic, 495–498
  chemical formula notation for, 272
  diprotic, 272
  fatty, 643–648
  monoprotic, 271

  neutralization of, 277–278
  polyprotic, 272
  strength of, 273
  strong, 273
  summary diagram concerning, 287
  triprotic, 272
  weak, 273
Acid anhydride A carboxylic acid derivative in which the —OH portion of the carboxyl group has been replaced with a
  $$-O-\overset{O}{\overset{\|}{C}}-R \text{ group, } 531$$
  general formula for, 531
  hydrolysis of, 532
  nomenclature for, 532
  phosphoric acid, 534–535
  preparation of, 532
Acid-base indicator A compound that exhibits different colors in a solution depending on the pH of its solution, 303
  need for in titrations, 303–304
Acid-base neutralization reaction A chemical reaction between an acid and a hydroxide base in which a salt and water are the products, 277
  balancing equations for, 278
  examples of, 277–278
Acid-base titration A neutralization reaction in which a measured volume of an acid or a base of known concentration is completely reacted with a measured volume of a base or an acid of unknown concentration, 303
  indicator use in, 303–304
  use of data from, in calculations, 304
Acid chloride A carboxylic acid derivative in which the —OH portion of the carboxyl group has been replaced with a —Cl atom, 531
  general formula for, 531
  hydrolysis of, 531
  nomenclature for, 531
  preparation of, 531
Acid inhibitor, 278
Acid ionization constant (K_a) An equilibrium constant for the reaction of a weak acid with water, 274
  calculating value of, 275
  listing of, selected acids, 275
  mathematical expression for, 274
Acid rain
  effects of, 286
  formation of, 286
  pH values for, 286
Acidic hydrogen atom A hydrogen atom in an acid molecule that can be transferred to a base in an acid-base reaction, 272
  polyprotic acids and, 272
Acidic polysaccharide A polysaccharide with a disaccharide repeating unit in which

  one of the disaccharide components is an amino sugar and in which one or both disaccharide components has a negative charge due to a sulfate group or a carboxyl group, 636
  heparin, 637
  hyaluronic acid, 636–637
Acidic solution An aqueous solution in which the concentration of H_3O^+ ion is higher than that of OH^- ion; an aqueous solution whose pH is less than 7.0, 281, 285
  hydronium ion concentration and, 281–282
  pH value and, 285
  pK_a of, 288
  summary diagram concerning, 287
Acidophile, characteristics of, 757
Acidosis
  blood pH values and, 296
  buffer systems and, 296
  metabolic, 296, 936
  respiratory, 296, 936
ACP complex, *see acyl carrier protein complex*
Acrolein, 493
Acrylamide, 569
Acrylic acid, 504
Actin
  muscle tissue and, 848
  structural characteristics of, 730–731
Activation energy The minimum combined kinetic energy that colliding reactant particles must possess in order for their collision to result in a chemical reaction, 246
  energy diagrams and, 248
Active site The relatively small part of an enzyme's structure that is actually involved in catalysis, 750
  function of, in enzyme, 750
Active transport The transport process in which a substance moves across a cell membrane, with the aid of membrane proteins, against a concentration gradient with the expenditure of cellular energy, 678
  process of, characteristics for, 678–679
Actual yield The amount of product actually obtained from a chemical reaction, 170
  use of, calculations and, 170–171
Acyl-carnitine
  shuttle system participant, 923–924
Acyl carrier protein complex, formation of, lipogenesis and, 938
Acyl CoA, beta oxidation pathway and, 924, 926
Acyl compound A compound that contains an acyl group whose carbonyl carbon atom is bonded directly to an oxygen, a nitrogen, or a halogen atom, 497
  examples of, 497
  reactions of, 497

Common Functional Group

Name of Class	Structural Feature
Alkane	$-\underset{\vert}{\overset{\vert}{C}}-$
Alkene	$\mathrm{C}=\mathrm{C}$
Alkyne	$-\mathrm{C}\equiv\mathrm{C}-$
Aromatic hydrocarbon	(benzene ring) or (benzene ring)
Alcohol	$-\underset{\vert}{\overset{\vert}{C}}-\mathrm{OH}$
Phenol	(benzene ring)—OH
Ether	$-\underset{\vert}{\overset{\vert}{C}}-\mathrm{O}-\underset{\vert}{\overset{\vert}{C}}-$
Thiol	$-\underset{\vert}{\overset{\vert}{C}}-\mathrm{SH}$
Aldehyde	$-\overset{\overset{\displaystyle O}{\|}}{C}-\mathrm{H}\ (-\mathrm{CHO})$
Ketone	$-\underset{\vert}{\overset{\vert}{C}}-\overset{\overset{\displaystyle O}{\|}}{C}-\underset{\vert}{\overset{\vert}{C}}-$
Carboxylic acid	$-\overset{\overset{\displaystyle O}{\|}}{C}-\mathrm{OH}\ (-\mathrm{COOH}\ \text{or}\ -\mathrm{CO_2H})$
Ester	$-\overset{\overset{\displaystyle O}{\|}}{C}-\mathrm{O}-\underset{\vert}{\overset{\vert}{C}}-\ (-\mathrm{COOR}\ \text{or}\ -\mathrm{CO_2R})$
Amine	$-\underset{\vert}{\overset{\vert}{C}}-\mathrm{NH_2}$
Amide	$-\overset{\overset{\displaystyle O}{\|}}{C}-\mathrm{NH_2}$